Frommer's®

Europe

12th Edition

WILEY

John Wiley & Sons, Inc.

Published by:

JOHN WILEY & SONS, INC.

Copyright © 2013 John Wiley & Sons Ltd, The Atrium, Southern Gate, Chichester, West Sussex PO19 8SQ, UK

Telephone (+44) 1243 779777

Email (for orders and customer service enquiries): cs-books@wiley.co.uk. Visit our Home Page on www.wiley.com

Publisher: Kelly Regan

Project Manager: Daniel Mersey

Editors: Fiona Quinn, Jill Emeny

Project Editors: Hannah Clement, Lindsay Conner

Cartography: Roberta Stockwell

Photo Editors: Cherie Cincilla, Richard H. Fox, Jill Emeny

Front cover photo: Belltower campanile from Brunelleschis Dome (Duomo), Florence, Tuscany, Italy © Peter Barritt / Alamy Images

Back Cover photo: Algarve scenic, Lagos, Portugal © Parasola.net / Alamy Images

For information on our other products and services or to obtain technical support, please contact our Customer Care Department within the U.S. at 877/762-2974, outside the U.S. at 317/572-3993 or fax 317/572-4002.

British Library Cataloguing in Publication Data

A catalogue record for this book is available from the British Library

ISBN 978-1-118-36907-4 (pbk)

ISBN 978-1-118-48630-6 (ebk)

ISBN 978-1-118-48631-3 (ebk)

ISBN 978-1-118-54555-3 (ebk)

Typeset by Wiley Indianapolis Composition Services

Printed and bound in the United States of America

5 4 3 2 1

CONTENTS

LIST OF MAPS

ABOUT THE AUTHORS

Donald Strachan is a Frommer's writer and author of recent guidebooks to Florence, Tuscany, England and Great Britain. He is also a contributor for Frommer's *London 2013* guidebook, as well as a regular writer for the Sunday Telegraph on consumer travel technologies and the Web. Donald wrote the Planning chapter, is co-author of the Florence, and Tuscany & Umbria sections of the Italy chapter and contributed to the England chapter.

Dardis McNamee is currently editor in chief of the English-language monthly *The Vienna Review*. In her long career in journalism, she has been correspondent for, among others, *The New York Times* and *Conde Nast Traveler* in New York, and for the *Wall Street Journal Europe* and *Die Zeit* in Vienna, the city where she has lived for 15 years. Dardis is the author of the Austria chapter.

George McDonald is a freelance journalist and travel writer who has written extensively about both the Netherlands and Belgium for magazines and guidebooks, including several Frommer's titles. He is the author of The Netherlands and Belgium chapters.

Mark Baker is a long-time American expat who lives in Prague. He's one of the original editors of *The Prague Post* and was for years a correspondent and editor for Radio Free Europe/Radio Liberty, based in Prague. He is now a freelance editor and reporter. Mark is the author of The Czech Republic chapter.

Christian Martinez was born in Spain but grew up in Copenhagen where he majored in Anthropology and Spanish. He's been a long-time editor and staff writer at Politiken Travel Books, a Danish publishing house, and is the author of guidebooks on Madrid, Peru, Bolivia, and Brazil. He's now a freelance writer and reporter and has published articles in all major Danish newspapers and magazines. Christian is the author of the Denmark chapter.

Joe Fullman has lived in London for just over 40 years and has worked as a travel writer for more than a decade. He has written for most of the major guidebook publishers and is author of guides to London, England, among others. He contributed to the London section of the England chapter. **Sian Meades** has lived in southeast London for a decade and has spent most of that time hunting for the perfect boutiques. Sian contributed to the shopping section of London in the England chapter. **John Power** is a London-based DJ, club promoter and writer with nearly 2 decades experience traversing the pubs, clubs, and nightlife of the capital. He contributed to London nightlife in the England chapter.

Lily Heise has been living in Paris for over 10 years, having refused to go back to Canada after studying art first in Italy and then in France. In addition to contributing to *Frommer's Paris* and *France*, she reports on Paris cultural news for local and international online and print publications. She lives in Montmartre and spends her free time exploring off-beat Paris and traveling around Europe. **Joseph Alexiou** works as a freelance journalist and has contributed to *France For Dummies* and *Europe For Dummies*. His work has appeared in the

New York Press, the *New York Observer*, *Newsday*, and *Paper* magazine. He lives in Brooklyn. **Sophie Nellis** came to Paris for a summer adventure in 2007. Four years later, she is still here. She currently lives in Belleville and divides her time among writing, teaching, translating, and leading walking tours of Paris. **Kate van den Boogert** is founding editor of the popular Paris blog gogoparis.com, an insider's guide to fashion, food, arts, gigs, and gossip in the French capital. Kate moved to Paris from Melbourne in 2000. **Tristan Rutherford** moved to Nice and began a career in freelance travel journalism in 2002. He writes travel features for *Financial Times* and London's *Sunday Times Travel Magazine* among others, and lectures in Travel and Journalism at Central Saint Martin's in London.

Caroline Sieg has been a travel writer for many years and has contributed on Germany chapters for three Lonely Planet guidebooks (*Western Europe 9*, *Central Europe 8*, *Europe on a Shoestring 6*); as well as *Frommer's Germany* and a number of other titles: *Frommer's San Diego*; *Frommer's Dream Vacations*; and features for Frommers.com. Caroline wrote the Germany chapter.

Peter Kerasiotis, a native Athenian, currently lives in New York City, where he works as a web developer and editor. He is the author of Athens, in the Greece chapter. **Sherry Marker's** love of Greece began when she majored in Classical Greek at Harvard. She attended American School of Classical Studies in Athens and studied ancient history at the University of California at Berkeley. Sherry is the author of The Northern Peloponnese & Delphi, and The Cyclades in the Greece chapter.

Dr. Ryan James was born and raised in Long Branch, New Jersey. He earned his doctorate in education from the University of San Francisco, and has taught English at ELTE University in Budapest since 2002. He and his partner own BudaBaB, a bed and breakfast on the Pest side of Budapest. Ryan wrote the Hungary chapter.

Christi Daugherty is an expat American living in London. A former journalist, she's the author of several travel books including *Frommer's Ireland*. Christi and her husband, **Jack Jewers**, wrote the Ireland chapter.

Eleonora Baldwin is an American born-Italian raised, global citizen. As a food and travel writer, and wanderlust addict living in Rome, she divides her time between guiding foodie adventures, writing food stories and columns, traveling, and designing custom culinary vacations in Italy. She is the author/editor of four blogs in which she writes about Italian lifestyle, reviews restaurants, provides useful tools for parents traveling with kids in Rome, and captures the Eternal City's essence in her photography. Eleonora contributed to the Italy chapter. **John Moretti**, a freelance writer based in Italy, has written for *The International Herald Tribune*, *The Independent on Sunday*, *Italy Daily*, The Associated Press, and www.ft.com (Financial Times online). He is the author of *Living Abroad in Italy*, co-editor of *Rome in Detail*, and a contributor to Time Out's Milan and Naples city guides. John contributed to the Italy chapter.

Stephen Keeling is a journalist and writer who lives in New York but returns to his native England several times a year. He has authored or co-authored several books on European destinations including *Frommer's Tuscany, Umbria & Florence With Your Family* and *Frommer's Italy*. He is co-author of the Florence, and Tuscany & Umbria sections of the Italy chapter, and contributed to the England chapter.

Roger Norum, an award-winning writer and photographer, studied Norwegian literature at the University of Tromsø before reading a PhD in Social Anthropology at the University of Oxford. He currently makes London his home, from where he covers travel and food for a range of publications. Roger wrote the Norway chapter.

Darwin & Danforth are a team of veteran travel writers who have authored dozens of Frommer's titles over the years. Porter is a film critic and noted biographer of Hollywood celebrities. Prince was employed by the Paris bureau of the *New York Times*, and is today the president of BloodMoonProductions.com. They authored the Switzerland and Portugal chapters.

Lesley Anne Rose is a travel and script writer who has lived in and explored Scotland for many years. She has written guidebooks, articles, and travel columns for various publishers and organizations on worldwide destinations, including Malta, Florida, and Canada, and her U.K. specialisms are the Lake District and Scotland. Lesley Anne is the author of the Scotland chapter.

Patricia Harris and **David Lyon** have journeyed the world for American, British, Swiss, and Asian publishers to write about food, culture, art, and design. Wherever their assignments take them, they are drawn back to Spain for the flamenco nightlife, the Moorish architecture of Andalucía, the world-weary and lust-ridden saints of Zurbarán, and the phantasmagoric visions of El Greco. They make their online home at HungryTravelers.com. Together, they are the authors of the Spain chapter.

Mary Anne Evans is one of the leading travel writers on London and Britain, particularly on restaurants. She is an experienced guidebook writer and has been an editor for many years. She has recently written *Frommer's Day by Day Stockholm*. Mary Anne wrote the Sweden chapter and contributed to London hotels and restaurants in the England chapter.

HOW TO CONTACT US

In researching this book, we discovered many wonderful places—hotels, restaurants, shops, and more. We're sure you'll find others. Please tell us about them, so we can share the information with your fellow travelers in upcoming editions. If you were disappointed with a recommendation, we'd love to know that, too. Please write to:

Frommer's Europe, 12th Edition
John Wiley & Sons, Inc. • 111 River St. • Hoboken, NJ 07030-5774
frommersfeedback@wiley.com

ADVISORY & DISCLAIMER

Travel information can change quickly and unexpectedly, and we strongly advise you to confirm important details locally before traveling, including information on visas, health and safety, traffic and transport, accommodation, shopping and eating out. We also encourage you to stay alert while traveling and to remain aware of your surroundings. Avoid civil disturbances, and keep a close eye on cameras, purses, wallets and other valuables.

While we have endeavored to ensure that the information contained within this guide is accurate and up-to-date at the time of publication, we make no representations or warranties with respect to the accuracy or completeness of the contents of this work and specifically disclaim all warranties, including without limitation warranties of fitness for a particular purpose. We accept no responsibility or liability for any inaccuracy or errors or omissions, or for any inconvenience, loss, damage, costs or expenses of any nature whatsoever incurred or suffered by anyone as a result of any advice or information contained in this guide.

The inclusion of a company, organization or Website in this guide as a service provider and/or potential source of further information does not mean that we endorse them or the information they provide. Be aware that information provided through some Websites may be unreliable and can change without notice. Neither the publisher or author shall be liable for any damages arising herefrom.

FROMMER'S STAR RATINGS, ICONS & ABBREVIATIONS

Every hotel, restaurant, and attraction listing in this guide has been ranked for quality, value, service, amenities, and special features using a **star-rating system.** In country, state, and regional guides, we also rate towns and regions to help you narrow down your choices and budget your time accordingly. Hotels and restaurants are rated on a scale of zero (recommended) to three stars (exceptional). Attractions, shopping, nightlife, towns, and regions are rated according to the following scale: zero stars (recommended), one star (highly recommended), two stars (very highly recommended), and three stars (must-see).

In addition to the star-rating system, we also use **seven feature icons** that point you to the great deals, in-the-know advice, and unique experiences that separate travelers from tourists. Throughout the book, look for:

🎁   **special finds**—those places only insiders know about

💬   **fun facts**—details that make travelers more informed and their trips more fun

☺   **kids**—best bets for kids and advice for the whole family

📷   **special moments**—those experiences that memories are made of

✋   **overrated**—places or experiences not worth your time or money

✐   **insider tips**—great ways to save time and money

🏷   **great values**—where to get the best deals

The following abbreviations are used for credit cards:

AE	American Express	DISC	Discover	V	Visa
DC	Diners Club	MC	MasterCard		

TRAVEL RESOURCES AT FROMMERS.COM

Frommer's travel resources don't end with this guide. Frommer's website, **www.frommers.com**, has travel information on more than 4,000 destinations. We update features regularly, giving you access to the most current trip-planning information and the best airfare, lodging, and car-rental bargains. You can also listen to podcasts, connect with other Frommers.com members through our active-reader forums, share your travel photos, read blogs from guidebook editors and fellow travelers, and much more.

PLANNING YOUR TRIP TO EUROPE

by Donald Strachan

Alittle planning goes a long way, especially when you are traveling to and through a continent with several different languages, transport systems, airlines, festivals, and sights to see. This chapter provides a variety of invaluable aids, including information on how to get there from the U.S. and Canada, the U.K., and Australia or New Zealand; the most efficient and budget-friendly ways of getting around; tips on where to stay; and quick, on-the-ground resources for savvy travel around Europe.

GETTING THERE

By Plane

Pretty much every major world airline offers competitive fares to a variety of European cities. Price wars break out regularly, deals come on- and offstream, and tariffs can change overnight. The key factor determining what you'll pay is **season:** Tickets tend to be cheaper if you fly off season. **High season** on most routes is usually from June to mid-September and around Christmas and New Year—the most expensive and most crowded time to travel. **Shoulder season** is from April to May and mid-September to October. **Low season**—usually with the cheapest fares and regular aggressive offers—is from November to mid-December and January to March. You can sometimes save money by flying midweek, too, or at least spending a Saturday night in your destination.

Begin thinking about flying plans at least 6 months ahead of time. Consider exchange rate movements: Fares may be calculated in U.S. dollars, British pounds, or euros, depending on the airline. The key window for finding a **deal** is usually between 3 months and 4 weeks ahead of your departure for long-haul flights. (Short-haul deals tend to go live a little further ahead of time, between 6 and 2 months before departure.) The glory days of generous **frequent-flyer programs** and bucketloads of free miles are no more, but it's still worth checking for offers, upgrades, and rewards from airlines and alliances (and also hotel chains). The forum **Flyertalk.com** is a handy resource for this.

Europe

Remember that the cheapest way between two points may not always be a straight line. Flying into a major European hub such as London, Frankfurt, or Paris might be cheaper than flying direct to your final destination. If you're heading to the U.K., consider entering via Dublin, Ireland, to save on Air Passenger Duty (APD, the British flight tax). Run searches through the regular online agents such as Expedia, as well as metasearch engines like **Kayak.com**, **Skyscanner.net**, and **Momondo. com**. For complex journeys, with multiple departures, a specialist flight agent such as **RoundtheWorldFlights.com** or **AirTreks.com** will likely save you money. And don't forget the travel agent around the corner from your home. He or she may have been digging out cheap fares to Europe for decades.

MAJOR NORTH AMERICAN AIRLINES   North American carriers with frequent service and flights to Europe include **Air Canada** (www.aircanada.ca; ℂ 888/ 247-2262 in the U.S. and Canada), **American Airlines** (www.aa.com; ℂ 800/433-7300 in the U.S. and Canada), **Delta Airlines** (www.delta.com; ℂ 800/241-4141 in the U.S. and Canada), **United Airlines** (www.united.com; ℂ 800/864-8331 in the U.S. and Canada), and **US Airways** (www.usairways.com; ℂ 800/428-4322 in the U.S. and Canada).

EUROPEAN AIRLINES   Not only will the major carriers of European countries offer the greatest number of direct flights from the United States (and can easily book you through to cities beyond the major hubs), but because their entire market outside Europe is to fly you to (or via) their home country, they sometimes run more competitive deals than other global carriers—sometimes, via codeshare agreements, for the same flights. Major national and country-affiliated European airlines include the following:

- **Austria: Austrian Airlines** (www.austrian.com; ℂ 800/843-0002 in the U.S. and Canada; ℂ 0870/124-2625 in the U.K.).
- **Belgium: Brussels Airlines** (www.brusselsairlines.com; ℂ 516/296-9500 in the U.S.; ℂ 514/789-2230 in Canada; ℂ 0905/6095-609 in the U.K.).
- **Czech Republic: CSA Czech Airlines** (www.czechairlines.com; ℂ +420-239/ 007112; ℂ 02/8248-0000 in Australia).
- **France: Air France** (www.airfrance.com; ℂ 800/237-2747 in the U.S.; ℂ 800/667-2747 in Canada; ℂ 0871/6633-777 in the U.K.).
- **Germany: Lufthansa** (www.lufthansa.com; ℂ 800/645-3880 in the U.S.; ℂ 800/563-5954 in Canada; ℂ 0871/945-9747 in the U.K.; ℂ 1300-655-727 in Australia; ℂ 0800/945-220 in New Zealand) and **Air Berlin** (www.airberlin. com; ℂ 866/266-5588 in the U.S. and Canada; ℂ 0871/5000-737 in the U.K.).
- **Greece: Olympic Air** (www.olympicair.com).
- **Ireland: Aer Lingus** (www.aerlingus.com; ℂ 800/IRISH-AIR [474-7424] in the U.S. and Canada; ℂ 0871/718-2020 in the U.K.).
- **Italy: Alitalia** (www.alitalia.com; ℂ 800/223-5730 in the U.S. and Canada; ℂ 0871/424-1424 in the U.K.).
- **The Netherlands: KLM** (www.klm.com; ℂ 800/618-0104 in the U.S. and Canada; ℂ 0871/231-0000 in the U.K.).
- **Portugal: TAP Portugal** (www.flytap.com; ℂ 800/221-7370 in the U.S. and Canada; ℂ 0845/601-0932 in the U.K.).

Don't Stow It—Ship It

Though pricey, it's sometimes worth-while for North Americans heading to Europe to travel luggage-free. Special-ists in door-to-door luggage delivery include **Virtual Bellhop** (www.virtual bellhop.com; ℂ **877/235-5467** in the U.S. and Canada) and **Luggage Express** (www.myluggageexpress.com; ℂ **866/744-7224** in the U.S. and Canada).

○ **Scandinavia (Denmark, Norway, Sweden): SAS Scandinavian Airlines** (www. flysas.com; ℂ **800/221-2350** in the U.S. and Canada; ℂ **0871/226-7760** in the U.K.; ℂ **1300/727-707** in Australia).

○ **Spain: Iberia** (www.iberia.com; ℂ **800/772-4642** in the U.S. and Canada; ℂ **0870/609-0500** in the U.K.).

○ **Switzerland: Swiss** (www.swiss.com; ℂ **877/359-7947** in the U.S. and Canada; ℂ **0845/601-0956** in the U.K.).

○ **United Kingdom: British Airways** (www.britishairways.com; ℂ **800/247-9297** in the U.S. and Canada; ℂ **0844/493-0787** in the U.K.; ℂ **1300/767-177** in Aus-tralia) and **Virgin Atlantic** (www.virgin-atlantic.com; ℂ **800/862-8621** in the U.S. and Canada; ℂ **0844/209-7777** in the U.K.; ℂ **1300/727-340** in Australia).

By Train from the United Kingdom

High-speed rail services connect London's **St. Pancras International Station** with Paris and Brussels, via the **Channel Tunnel.** You can now reach Brussels in under 2 hours, and Paris in 2¼ hours. There are also direct trains to other halts in France: Lille and Disneyland Paris, all year, and seasonal direct trains to Avignon, Provence, and the French Alps, terminating at Bourg St. Maurice (the so-called "Snow Train"). The London terminus boasts Europe's longest champagne bar, all the Wi-Fi you'll ever need, plus dozens of stores—and saw a new luxury hotel open in 2011, the **St. Pancras Renaissance London** (p. 238). In the U.K., make reservations for the train by calling **Eurostar** on ℂ **08432/186-186;** in North America, book online at **www.eurostar.com**, or contact **Rail Europe** (www.raileurope.com; ℂ **800/622-8600** in the U.S. or **800/361-7245** in Canada). There are several more European city connections available via Eurostar through-ticketing. For Cologne (4¼ hr. from London), Germany, or Amsterdam (4¼ hr.), in the Netherlands, change in Brussels. You'll need to change in Paris for Dijon (4¾ hr.), in Burgundy, France, or Geneva (6½ hr.), Switzerland, for example.

By Ferry to/from the United Kingdom or Ireland

A number of ferry companies link England's southern coast with the Channel ports of northern **France** and **Spain. Brittany Ferries** (www.brittanyferries.com; ℂ **0871/244-0744**) sails to five destinations in France: From Portsmouth, sailings reach St.-Malo, Cherbourg, and Caen. From Poole, you can ferry to Cherbourg, and from Plymouth sailings go to Roscoff. The same company connects southern England directly with the north coast of Spain; sailings to Santander or Bilbao take around 24 hours. **P&O Ferries** (www.poferries.com; ℂ **0871/664-2121,** or **+44-1304/863-000** from outside the U.K.) operates car and passenger ferries between Dover and

Calais, France (the most popular route across the Channel, with 25–46 sailings per day; 1¼ hr.), and overnight between Hull, in northern England, and Zeebrugge, Belgium, or Rotterdam, the Netherlands. **DFDS Seaways** (www.dfdsseaways.co.uk; ✆ **0871/574-7235,** or **+44-20/8127-8303** from outside the U.K.) connects Dover with Calais, as well as Dover and Dunkerque, France; Newcastle, in northern England, overnight with Amsterdam; and Harwich, east of London, with Esbjerg, in Denmark, also overnight. **LD Lines** (www.ldlines.co.uk; ✆ **0844/576-8836** in the U.K.) specializes in linking England and France, connecting Dover with Calais, Newhaven with Dieppe, and Portsmouth with Le Havre.

The quickest sea route to **Ireland** is from the western coast of Wales. From Holyhead, in the northwest of Anglesey, **Stena Line** (www.stenaline.co.uk; ✆ **0844/770-7070**) and **Irish Ferries** (www.irishferries.com; ✆ **08717/300-400**) both offer services to Dublin. There are also ferries to Rosslare, County Wexford, further south in Ireland: from Fishguard, southwest Wales, operated by Stena Line; and from nearby Pembroke, operated by Irish Ferries. Stena Line also connects Liverpool with Belfast, Northern Ireland. You can sail between Liverpool and Dublin with P&O Ferries. To reach **France** from Ireland (or vice versa), there's no need to go via England: Irish Ferries connects Rosslare with Cherbourg and Roscoff.

Ferry route search and booking site **Aferry.co.uk** is invaluable for any traveler planning to use ferries anywhere in Europe. Many car-rental companies won't let you rent a car in Britain and take it to the Continent, so always check ahead if you're considering that option.

By Tunnel from the United Kingdom

The quickest way for drivers to cross the English Channel is via a car-transporting train that connects Folkestone, southern England, and Calais via the **Channel Tunnel.** Prices tend to be higher than for the ferry (see above), but crossing time is only around 35 minutes. Book online at **www.eurotunnel.com** or call ✆ **08443/353-535** from the U.K.

By Bus from the United Kingdom

Although travel by long-distance coach is slower and less comfortable than travel by train, if you're on a tight budget you could opt for one of **Eurolines**'s (www.eurolines.com; ✆ **0871/781-8178**) regular departures from London's Victoria Coach Station to destinations across Europe. Direct connections from London that don't require a change of bus include Paris (9½ hr.), Vienna (23 hr.), and Amsterdam (12½ hr.). If you are very quick off the mark, you may be able to get a super-budget ("from £1") **Megabus** (www.megabus.com; ✆ **0871/266-3333,** or **+44-141/332-9644** from outside the U.K.) fare between London and Paris, Amsterdam, Brussels, or Boulogne, France.

GETTING AROUND
By Train

In Europe, the shortest—and often cheapest—distance between two points is usually lined with rail tracks. Compared to the United States, for example, European trains are often less expensive, far more advanced in many ways, and certainly more extensive. While not rivaling modern Asian rail networks, such as Japan's, the European rail system still ranks as one of the best in the world: Not always integrated, and with occasional ticketing frustrations that vary from country to country, but a fine way to travel nonetheless.

Modern **high-speed trains** (traveling up to around 180 mph) make the rails faster than the plane for short journeys; airlines have gone into rapid decline on routes such as London–Brussels, Barcelona–Madrid, and Milan–Rome that have efficient high-speed links. **Overnight trains** get you where you're going without wasting valuable daylight hours—and you save money on lodging to boot.

SOME IMPORTANT TRAIN NOTES

Many European high-speed trains require you to pay a **supplement** in addition to the regular ticket fare. It's included when you buy tickets, but not usually in any prepaid rail pass, so check at the ticket window before boarding; otherwise, the conductor will sell you the supplement on the train—along with a fine. **Seat reservations** (from 10€ up) are required on some high-speed runs, too. You can usually reserve a seat within a few hours of departure, but be on the safe side and book your seat a few days in advance for any key connections you're building into an itinerary. You need to reserve any sleeping couchette or sleeping berth too.

With some exceptions, there's usually no need to buy individual train tickets or make seat reservations many months before you leave home. However, it's always wise to reserve a seat on the **Eurostar,** as England's **bank holidays** (long weekends with holiday Mondays) book the train solid with Londoners taking a short vacation to Paris or Brussels. Tickets go on sale 120 days before departure, and you'll usually bag the best prices if you book early and avoid Fridays and Sundays. The overnight **Thello** train (www.thello.com; Paris to Milan, Rome, and Venice) is another service worth reserving well ahead of time. You won't save any money, because tariffs are fixed, but as there's only one service each way per day, booking early will help with itinerary planning.

The difference between **first class** and **second class** on European trains is often minor—a matter of 1 or 2 inches of extra padding and maybe a bit more elbowroom. However, upgrades can sometimes be fairly cheap (for first-class seats booked in advance on weekends in the U.K., for example). There's sometimes a complimentary snack thrown in, along with free Wi-Fi. So, our general advice is: Upgrade if it doesn't cost very much to do so, but don't break the bank. Overnight trains can provide more for your upgrade, in terms of space and privacy, but you'll pay for the privilege.

European **train stations** are usually as clean and efficient as the trains, if a bit chaotic at times. In stations you'll find departures boards showing the track number and timetables for regularly scheduled runs (departures are sometimes on a yellow poster, too). Many stations also have tourist offices, banks with ATMs, and newsstands where you can buy phone cards, bus and metro tickets, maps, and local English-language event magazines. Some have shopping malls and hotels, or even public showers.

You can get more details about train travel in Europe by contacting **Rail Europe** (www.raileurope.com; also 📞 08448/484-064 in the U.K.). Other excellent agents worth consulting for planning assistance and advance ticket or pass sales include **International Rail** (www.internationalrail.com; 📞 **0871/231-0790** in the U.K.) and **TrainsEurope** (www.trainseurope.co.uk; 📞 **0871/700-7722** in the U.K.). Note that schedules are confirmed and tickets released between 60 and 90 days from travel dates. If you plan to travel a great deal on the European railroads, it's worth buying an up-to-date copy of the **_Thomas Cook European Rail Timetable._** It's

Countries Honoring Eurail Passes

At the time of writing there were 23: Austria, Belgium, Bulgaria, Croatia, Czech Republic, Denmark, Finland, France, Germany, Greece, Hungary, Ireland, Italy, Luxembourg, Netherlands, Norway, Portugal, Romania, Slovakia, Slovenia, Spain, Sweden, Switzerland.

available online at **www.thomascookpublishing.com/railguides**, as well as via the usual retailers. The most valuable bookmark for planning complex European rail journeys is **The Man in Seat Sixty-One** (www.seat61.com).

RAIL PASSES

The greatest value in European travel has traditionally been the **rail pass,** a single ticket allowing you unlimited travel (or travel on a certain number of days) within a set time period. If you plan on going all over Europe by train, buying a rail pass will end up being less expensive than buying individual tickets. Plus, a rail pass gives you the freedom to hop on a train whenever you feel like it, and there's no waiting in ticket lines. For more focused trips, look into single-country or regional passes. If you're only planning a few point-to-point journeys plus the odd local excursion, individual tickets will be the cheapest way to go.

PASSES AVAILABLE IF YOU LIVE OUTSIDE EUROPE The granddaddy of passes is the **Eurail Global Pass,** covering some 23 countries (most of western Europe except Britain, alongside chunks of eastern Europe).

It's best to buy these passes before you leave home. You can get them from most travel agents, but the biggest supplier is **Rail Europe** (www.raileurope.com), which also sells most national passes via its comprehensive website.

The most popular pass is the **Eurail Global Pass,** which offers unlimited first-class travel for adults 26 and older. Options are US$768 for 15 days, US$990 for 21 days, US$1,219 for 1 month, US$1,720 for 2 months, or US$2,121 for 3 months. Substantial reductions are granted on the **First Class Saver Pass** for two or more people traveling together or for **Second Class Youth Travel** for those 25 and younger. Children, ages 4 to 11, on their first day of travel, receive a 50% discount on the first-class adult fare, and those 3 and under travel free.

You can also consider a **Eurail Select Pass,** allowing travel in three, four, or five bordering European countries connected by train or ferry. With this pass, you can customize your own trip, traveling by train from 5 to 15 days within a 2-month period.

A **Eurail Regional Pass** is for those who want to see only a small part of Europe in a short time frame. Several different combination regional passes are offered, granting train travel on various numbers of days within periods up to 2 months. Such a pass, for example, might grant you unlimited travel in both France and Switzerland (Eurail France–Switzerland Pass), or a Scandinavia Pass granting travel in four countries. Most European countries, including Austria and Italy, also participate in the **Eurail One Country Pass.** This pass grants unlimited train travel from 3 to 10 days within a 1- or 2-month period in a single participating European country of your choice. Eight days of travel in Austria, within a 1-month period, costs US$381

TRAIN TRIP tips

To make your train travels as pleasant as possible, remember a few general rules:

o **Hold on to your train ticket** after it's been marked or punched by the conductor. Some European rail networks require that you present your ticket when you leave the station platform at your destination.

o While you sleep—or even nap—**be sure your valuables are in a safe place.** You might temporarily attach a small bell to each bag to warn you if someone attempts to take it. If you've left bags on a rack in the front or back of the car, consider securing them with a small bicycle chain and lock to deter thieves, who consider trains happy hunting grounds.

o Few European trains have drinking fountains, and the dining car may be closed just when you're at your thirstiest, so **take along a bottle of mineral water.** As you'll soon discover, the experienced rail traveler comes loaded with hampers of food and drink and munches away throughout the trip—buying food onboard can be very expensive.

o If you want to leave bags in a train station locker, **don't let anyone help you store them in it.** An old trick among thieves is feigned helpfulness, and then pocketing the key to your locker while passing you the key to an empty one.

first-class, US$268 second-class. In Italy, 10 days' rail travel within a 2-month window costs US$503 first-class, US$409 second-class.

You have to study these passes carefully to see which one would be ideal for you. You can check online or call for the latest prices and offerings, which are always subject to changes. Many countries also offer rail passes with add-ons of a few days' car rental, but be sure to cross check the value against standalone deals.

If you plan on traveling in Great Britain, then **BritRail** (www.britrail.com; © **866/938-RAIL** in the U.S. and Canada), which specializes in rail passes for use in Great Britain, is your best bet.

PASSES FOR U.K. RESIDENTS VISITING CONTINENTAL EUROPE   A vast array of rail passes are available in the United Kingdom for travel around Europe. The most popular ticket is the **InterRail Global Pass,** which is offered for persons who have lived in a participating country in Europe at least 6 months. It offers unlimited travel in up to 30 European countries within 5 days, 10 days, 15 days, 22 days, or 1 month and is valid on all normal trains; the card is valid on high-speed trains such as TGV and overnight trains if you pay a supplement ranging between £5.50 and £46 per journey. The price of the pass depends on the trip duration and whether you want your validity to run continuously or for a set number of days in a fixed period. A typical fare for 5 days of travel within 10 days is 316€ in first class, 240€ in second class, and 158€ for a youth fare. **One-Country Passes** are also available. Passes are not valid in your country of residence.

For help in determining the best option for your trip and to buy tickets, contact a reliable reseller such as **Rail Europe** (www.raileurope.co.uk; © **08448/484-064**) or **International Rail** (www.internationalrail.com; © **0871/231-0790**).

THE RULES OF THE ROAD: driving IN EUROPE

- First, know that European drivers tend to be more **aggressive** than their counterparts from other parts of the world.

- **Drive on the right** except in England, Scotland, and Ireland, where you drive on the left. And *do not drive* in the left lane on a four-lane highway; it is only for passing.

- If someone comes up from behind and flashes his lights at you, it's a signal for you to slow down and drive more on the shoulder so that he can pass you more easily (two-lane roads here sometimes become three cars wide).

- Except for the German Autobahn, most highways do indeed have **speed limits** of around 100 to 130kmph (62–81 mph).

- Remember that, outside the U.K., everything's measured in **kilometers** (distance and speed limits). For a rough conversion, 1km = 0.6 miles.

- Be aware that fuel is *very* expensive, so you should **rent the smallest, most fuel-efficient car** you think you can manage. Prices at the pumps are quoted in liters (1 US gallon = 3.78 liters).

- Never leave anything of value in a car overnight, and don't leave anything visible when you leave the car (this goes double in London, triple in Naples).

By Car

Most rental companies offer their best prices to customers who **reserve in advance** from their home country. Weekly rentals are almost always less expensive than day rentals. Three or more people traveling together can often get around cheaper by car than by train, depending on the distances traveled and the size and efficiency of the engine—compared to most other parts of the world, fuel is very expensive almost everywhere in Europe. You should also factor in **road tolls** that many countries charge.

When you reserve a car, be sure to ask if the price includes: all taxes including value-added tax (VAT); breakdown assistance; unlimited mileage; personal accident or liability insurance (PAI); collision-damage waiver (CDW); theft waiver; and any other insurance options. If not, ask what these extras cost, because they can make a big dent in your bottom line. The CDW and other insurance might be covered by your credit card if you use the card to pay for the rental; check with your card issuer to be sure.

If your credit card doesn't cover the CDW, consider Car Rental Collision Coverage from **Travel Guard** (www.travelguard.com; ℭ **800/826-1300** in the U.S. and Canada), which will insure you for around US$7 to US$9 per day. In the U.K., **Insurance 4 Car Hire** (www.insurance4carhire.com; ℭ **0844/892-1770**) offers similar cover. An annual policy covering unlimited car rental for a maximum of 31 consecutive days on any one trip costs £49.

The main international companies all have rental points across Europe: **Avis** (www.avis.com; ℭ **800/331-1212** in the U.S. and Canada), **Budget** (www.budget.com; ℭ **800/472-3325** in the U.S. and Canada), **Dollar** (www.dollar.com; ℭ **800/800-4000** in the U.S. and Canada), **Hertz** (www.hertz.com; ℭ **800/654-3131** in the U.S. and Canada), and **National** (www.nationalcar.com; ℭ **877/222-9058** in the U.S. and Canada). U.S.-based companies specializing in European rentals include **Auto Europe** (www.autoeurope.com; ℂ **888/223-5555** in the U.S. and Canada), **Europe by Car** (www.europebycar.com; ℂ **800/223-1516** in the U.S. and Canada), and **Kemwel** (www.kemwel.com; ℂ **877/820-0668** in the U.S. and Canada). It's also worth checking prices offered by U.K.-based rental agents such as **Holiday Autos** (www.holidayautos.co.uk; ℂ **0871/472-5229** in the U.K.). Europe by Car, Kemwel, and **Renault USA** (www.renaultusa.com; ℂ **888/532-1221** in the U.S. and Canada) also offer a competitive alternative to renting for longer than 15 days: **short-term leases** in which you technically buy a fresh-from-the-factory car and then sell it back when you return it. All insurance is included, from liability and theft to personal injury and CDW, with no deductible. And unlike at many rental agencies, who won't rent to anyone 24 and under, the minimum age for a lease is 18. You should also always check your quote against quotes from general travel search sites like **Kayak.com**, as well as car-rental search specialists such as **RhinoCarHire.com** and **CarHireSearch.co.uk**.

For visitors coming from North America, the **AAA** supplies good maps to its members. **Michelin maps** (www.viamichelin.co.uk) are made with the tourist in mind, and are widely available in shops and fuel stations across Europe. There's also a handy route planner online. Be aware that, if you are planning to navigate using your cellphone, data costs for roaming can be very expensive. **Nokia smartphones** come with mapping preinstalled on the handset, and generally work 100% offline.

By Plane

Although trains remain the greenest and easiest way to get around in Europe, air transport networks have also improved drastically in the past decade. Intense competition—and the mushrooming of low-cost airlines serving destinations that even few Europeans had heard of 15 years ago—has forced airfares into the bargain basement. Routes such as London–Paris, Milan–Rome, and London–Brussels have also come under sustained competitive pressure from high-speed trains. While the political climate in Europe's higher echelons very much favors the environmental credentials of trains over planes, for journeys longer than a few hundred miles, you'll likely find flying to be the cheapest option.

The predictable airline news in Europe is the continued dominance of the **no-frills airline,** originally modeled on American upstarts like Southwest. By keeping their overhead down through electronic ticketing, forgoing meal service, charging for every "extra," and flying only point-to-point, often from less popular airports, these airlines are able to offer very low fares. This means now you can save lots of time (and usually, money) over transcontinental train hauls, especially from, say, London to Venice or from Paris to Greece and Spain, or eastern Europe. You should still compare low-cost carrier flights against the mainstream airlines (see "European Airlines," earlier in this chapter); many budget airline fares have extra fees such as luggage or credit-card charges buried in their small print. Lower airfares are also sometimes available throughout Europe on **charter flights** rather than regularly scheduled ones. Look in local newspapers to find out about these kinds of late deals. Consolidators cluster in cities like London and Athens.

Flying across Europe on regularly scheduled airlines can destroy a budget and be super expensive. Whenever possible, book your total flight on one ticket before leaving. For example, if you're flying from New York to Rome, but also plan to visit Palermo and Paris, have the total trip written up on one ticket. Don't arrive in Rome and

FLYING WITH EUROPE'S budget AIRLINES

Europe's skies are awash with budget, low-cost, and no-frills airlines. The names can change, because these small airlines are sometimes at the mercy of a fickle market. They can fail or merge with a bigger airline or smaller competitor. Still, as quickly as one disappears, another takes off, perhaps even another two. You should note that some popular flight search engines do not compare fares from budget airlines: You should either check websites individually, or consult a specialist low-cost website such as **www.whichbudget.com**.

At the time of writing, the following airlines were among the established European no-frills players, offering a selection of useful routes for visitors to Europe:

Air One (www.flyairone.com; ✆ **894-444** in Italy) has hubs in Milan, Pisa, and Venice with a good domestic Italian network, as well as key links with the likes of London, Prague, and Athens.

Blu-Express (www.blu-express.com; ✆ **06/9895-6666** in Italy) has a routemap focused on Italian domestic and Mediterranean island destinations, served mostly from Rome.

easyJet (www.easyjet.com) connects airports across Britain with much of Europe, including Switzerland.

FlyBe (www.flybe.com) serves more of Britain's regional airports than any other airline, joining them particularly well with France and Germany.

Germanwings (www.germanwings.com; ✆ **0906/294-1918**) serves over 90 destinations from hubs in Germany, Switzerland, Italy, and London.

Niki (www.flyniki.com) has a wide network centered on Austria, linking it with destinations in central and eastern Europe, Spain, Italy, and the United Kingdom.

Norwegian (www.norwegian.com; ✆ **020/8099-7254** in the U.K.) offers cheap flights from across Europe to cities in Scandinavia including Oslo, Stockholm, and Copenhagen.

Ryanair (www.ryanair.com; ✆ **0871/246-0000** in the U.K., **1520/444-004** in Ireland) is Europe's busiest point-to-point airline, with hubs in the United Kingdom, Germany, Ireland, and Italy, among others.

SmartWings (www.smartwings.com; ✆ **900/166-565** in the Czech Republic) offers flights to Prague from cities across southern Europe, as well as from Paris.

Transavia (www.transavia.com) has hubs in France and the Netherlands, and routes focused on southern Europe.

Vueling (www.vueling.com) is Spain's leading low-cost carrier, with all the country's major cities well served from around Europe.

Wizz Air (www.wizzair.com; ✆ **0906/959-0002** in the U.K., or **1550/475-970** in Ireland) has the best range of destinations in eastern Europe, including Budapest and Prague.

book separate legs of the journey, which costs far more when it's done piecemeal. See "Getting There: By Plane," earlier in this chapter, for advice.

By Bus

Bus transportation is readily available throughout Europe; it is often less expensive than train travel and covers a more extensive area, but is slower and can be much less comfortable. European buses, like the trains, outshine their American counterparts, but they're perhaps best used only to pick up where the extensive train network leaves off. One major long-haul bus company serves almost all the countries of western,

FROMMERS.COM: THE COMPLETE travel RESOURCE

Planning a trip or just returned? Head to **Frommers.com**, voted Best Travel Site by *PC Magazine*. We think you'll find our site indispensable before, during, and after your travels—with expert advice and tips; independent reviews of hotels, restaurants, attractions, and preferred shopping and nightlife venues; vacation giveaways; and an online booking tool. We publish the complete contents of more than 135 travel guides in our **Destinations** section, covering more than 4,000 places worldwide. Each weekday, we publish original articles that report on **Deals and News** via our free **Frommers. com Newsletters.** What's more, **Arthur**

Frommer himself blogs 5 days a week, with strong opinions about the state of travel in the modern world. We're betting you'll find our **Events** listings an invaluable resource; it's an up-to-the-minute roster of what's happening in cities everywhere—including concerts, festivals, lectures, and more. We've also added weekly **podcasts, interactive maps,** and hundreds of new images across the site. Finally, don't forget to visit our **Message Boards,** where you can join in conversations with thousands of fellow Frommer's travelers and post your trip report once you return.

northern, and eastern Europe (no service to Greece): **Eurolines** (www.eurolines. com; ✆ **0871/781-8178** in the U.K., **055/357-059** in Italy, **069/7903-501** in Germany). The staff at Eurolines can check schedules, make reservations, and quote prices for travel between cities Europewide.

WHEN TO GO

Europe has a continental climate with distinct seasons, but there are great variations in temperature from one part to another. Northern Norway is plunged into arctic darkness in winter, but in sunny Sicily the climate is usually temperate—although snow can fall even on the Greek islands in winter, and winter nights are cold (or at least, cool) pretty much anywhere. Europe is north of most of the United States, but along the Mediterranean are weather patterns more along the lines of the U.S. southern states. In general, however, seasonal changes are less extreme than in most of the United States. In Southern Hemisphere terms, Seville, in southern Spain, is at 37° N, about the same distance from the Equator as Auckland, New Zealand (36° S).

The **high season** almost everywhere lasts from mid-May to mid-September, with the most tourists hitting the Continent between mid-June and late August. In general, this is the most expensive time to travel, except in Austria and Switzerland, where prices are a little higher in winter during the ski season. Because Scandinavian city hotels depend mostly on business clients instead of tourists, you can often find lower prices in the fleeting summer, when business clients vacation and a smaller number of tourists take over.

You'll find smaller crowds, relatively fair weather, and often lower prices at hotels in the **shoulder seasons,** from Easter to mid-May and mid-September to October. **Off season** (except at ski resorts in the Alps, Dolomites, Tyrol, Pyrenees, and elsewhere) is from November to Easter, with the exception of the Christmas period. Much of Europe, Italy especially, takes August off, and August 15 to August 30 is vacation time for many locals, so expect the cities to be devoid of natives but the beaches and lakes packed.

Weather

BRITAIN & IRELAND It rains a lot in Britain and Ireland, especially in the west of both countries, but winters are rainier than summers, and in fact London receives less annual rainfall than Rome or Sydney. The sunniest period in the British Isles is usually from June to mid-September. Average summer daytime temperatures are from the low 60s Fahrenheit (mid-teens Celsius) to the mid-60s (upper teens Celsius), with daily highs in summer hovering around the low 70s (low 20s Celsius). Average temperatures drop to the 40s (single digits Celsius) on winter nights, with many nights dropping below freezing inland. Ireland, whose shores are bathed by the Gulf Stream, has a slightly milder winter climate, but is wetter in summer. The Scottish Lowlands have a climate similar to England's, but the Highlands are much colder, with storms and snow in winter.

CENTRAL EUROPE In **Vienna** and along the **Danube Valley** the climate is moderate. Summer daytime temperatures average in the low 70s Fahrenheit (low 20s Celsius), falling at night to the low 50s (low teens Celsius). Winter temperatures are usually in the 30s Fahrenheit (between −1 and +4°C) and 40s (4–9°C) during the day. In Budapest, temperatures can often reach 80°F (27°C) in August and dip to 30°F (−1°C) in January. Winter is damp and chilly, spring is mild, and May and June are often wet. The best weather is in the late summer through October. In **Prague** and **Bohemia,** summer months have an average temperature around 65°F (18°C), with daytime highs in the mid-70s (low 20s Celsius), but are generally the rainiest, while January and February are usually sunny and clear, with temperatures around freezing.

FRANCE & GERMANY The weather in Paris is approximately the same as in the U.S. mid-Atlantic states, but as in most of Europe, there's usually less extreme variation. In summer, the temperature doesn't linger for long above the mid-70s Fahrenheit (mid-20s Celsius). Winters tend to be mild, in the 40s Fahrenheit (4–9°C). It's warmer along the Riviera year-round, and wetter than elsewhere on the western, Atlantic coast. Germany's climate ranges from moderate summers and chilly, damp winters in the north to warm summers and very cold, sunny winters in the alpine south. Away from the coasts, however, both France and Germany can experience sustained periods of summer heat or winter cold, too.

NORTHERN EUROPE In the **Netherlands**, the weather is rarely extreme at any time of year. Summer temperatures average around 67°F (19°C) and the winter average is about 40°F (4°C). The climate is rainy, with the driest months April and May—from mid-April to mid-May, the tulip fields burst into color. The climate of **northern Germany** is very similar, as is **Belgium's** climate: moderate, varying from daytime highs of 73°F (23°C) in July and August to an average of 40°F (4°C) in December and January. It can rain at almost any time, but the weather is at its finest in July and August.

SCANDINAVIA Above the Arctic Circle, summer temperatures hover around the mid-50s Fahrenheit (low teens Celsius), dropping to around 14°F (−10°C) during the dark winters. In the south, summer temperatures hit highs of around 70°F (21°C), dropping to the 20s Fahrenheit (below 0 Celsius) in winter. Fjords and even the ocean are often warm enough for summer swimming, but rain is frequent. The sun shines 24 hours in midsummer above the Arctic Circle; winter brings semipermanent twilight. Denmark's climate is relatively mild by comparison. It has moderate summer temperatures and winters that can be damp and foggy, with average daytime high temperatures around the mid-30s Fahrenheit (single digits Celsius).

SOUTHERN EUROPE Summers are hot in **Italy, Spain,** and **Greece,** with daytime temperatures around the high 80s Fahrenheit (low 30s Celsius) or even higher in some parts of Spain. Along the Italian coast, winter temperatures are usually mild; and except in the mountains, Italian winter temperatures rarely drop below freezing for long. The area around Madrid is dry and arid, and much colder than you'd expect in the winter (average daily lows of 32°F/0°C). Summers in Spain are coolest along the Atlantic coast, with mild temperatures year-round on the coast of Galicia, much hotter along the Mediterranean Costa del Sol. Seaside Portugal is rainy in the winter, but has average temperatures of 50°F to 75°F (10°C–24°C) year-round. In Greece there's sunshine all year, and winters are usually mild on the islands, with temperatures around 50°F to 54°F (10°C–12°C). Hot summer temperatures are often fanned by cool breezes. The best seasons to visit Greece are from mid-April to June, when the wildflowers bloom, and from mid-September to late October, after the high-season tourists have gone home.

SWITZERLAND & THE ALPS The alpine climate is shared by Bavaria in **southern Germany,** the **Austrian Tyrol,** and the **Italian Dolomites**—winters are cold and bright, and spring comes late, with snow falls well into April. Summers are mild and sunny, with delightfully fresh air, though the alpine regions can experience dramatic changes in weather any time of year. Summer storms aren't uncommon.

Europe Calendar of Events

For an exhaustive list of events beyond those listed here, check http://events.frommers.com, where you'll find a searchable, up-to-the-minute roster of what's happening in cities all over the world.

JANUARY

Epiphany celebrations, Italy, nationwide. All cities, towns, and villages in Italy stage Roman Catholic Epiphany observances, which celebrate the visit of the Magi to the infant Jesus. One of the most extensive celebrations is the Festa Nazionale della Befana in Urbania, Le Marche. www.labefana.com. January 6.

FEBRUARY

Carnevale, Venice, Italy. At this riotous time, theatrical presentations and masked balls take place throughout Venice and on the islands in the lagoon. The balls are by invitation only (except the Doge's Ball), but the street events and fireworks are open to everyone. www.carnevale.venezia.it. The week before Ash Wednesday, the beginning of Lent.

February Basler Fasnacht, Basel, Switzerland. Switzerland's "wildest of carnivals,"

with a parade of "cliques" (clubs and associations). Visit www.fasnacht.ch for more information. First Monday after Ash Wednesday.

MARCH

Holmenkollen Ski Festival, Oslo, Norway. This is one of Europe's largest ski festivals, with World Cup Nordic skiing and biathlons and international ski-jumping competitions, all held at Holmenkollen Ski Jump on the outskirts of Oslo. To participate or request more information, www.holmenkollenworldcup.no. Early March.

St. Patrick's Day Festival, Dublin, Ireland. This massive 4-day fest is open, free, and accessible to all. Street theater, carnival acts, music, fireworks, and more culminate in Ireland's grandest parade. Go to www.stpatricksfestival.ie or call ℂ **01/676-3205,** March 16 to March 19.

Budapest Spring Festival, Budapest, Hungary. For 2 weeks, performances of everything from opera to ballet, from classical music to drama, are held in all the major halls and theaters of Budapest. Simultaneously, temporary exhibitions open in many of Budapest's museums. Tickets are available from www.festivalcity.hu or by calling ☎ **36/1-486-3311.** Mid- to late March.

APRIL

Semana Santa (Holy Week), Seville, Spain. Although many of the country's smaller towns stage similar celebrations, the festivities in Seville are by far the most elaborate. From Palm Sunday to Easter Sunday, processions with hooded penitents move to the piercing wail of the *saeta*, a love song to the Virgin or Christ. Contact the **Seville Tourism Office** for details (www.visitasevilla.es; ☎ **955-471-232**). Ten days before Easter Sunday.

Holy Week observances, Italy, nationwide. Processions and age-old ceremonies—some from pagan days, some from the Middle Ages—are staged. The most notable procession is led by the pope, passing the Colosseum and the Roman Forum up to Palatine Hill; a torch-lit parade caps the observance. Sicily's observances are also noteworthy. Beginning 4 days before Easter Sunday; sometimes at the end of March but often in April.

Pasqua (Easter Sunday), Rome, Italy. In an event broadcast around the world, the pope gives his blessing from the balcony of St. Peter's. Easter Sunday.

Feria de Abril de Sevilla (Seville April Fair), Seville, Spain. This is the most celebrated week of revelry in all of Spain, with all-night flamenco dancing, entertainment booths, bullfights, flower-decked coaches, and dancing in the streets. Reserve your hotel early. Contact the **Seville Tourism Office** for details (www.visitasevilla.es; ☎ **955-471-232**). Second week after Easter.

MAY

Brighton Festival, Brighton, England. The country's largest arts festival features some 400 cultural events. Go to www.brightonfestival.org or call ☎ **01273/709-709.** Most of May.

Prague Spring International Music Festival, Prague, Czech Republic. This world-famous, 3-week series of classical music and dance performances brings some of the globe's best talent to Prague. For details, book online at www.festival.cz, call ☎ **420/226539-623,** or stop in at the central box office. Mid-May to early June.

Festival International du Film (Cannes Film Festival), Cannes, France. Movie madness transforms this city into a media circus. Reserve early and make a deposit. Admission to the competition itself is by invitation only; however, many screenings are made available to the public and play round-the-clock. Contact the **Festival de Cannes Association Francaise du Festival International du Film,** 3 rue Amélie, 75007 Paris (www.festival-cannes.com; ☎ **01-53-59-61-00**). Mid-May.

Wiener Festwochenkonzerte (International Music Festival, Vienna), Austria. This traditional highlight of Vienna's concert calendar features top-class international orchestras, conductors, and classical greats. Book via the **Wiener Musikverein** (www.musikverein.at; ☎ **01/505-8190**). See also www.festwochen.at. Early May through first 3 weeks of June.

Fiesta de San Isidro, Madrid, Spain. Madrileños run wild with a 5-day celebration honoring their city's patron saint. Food fairs, street parades, parties, dances, bullfights, flamenco, and other events mark the occasion. Expect crowds and traffic. For details, see www.esmadrid.com/sanisidro or call ☎ **091/588-1636.** Mid-May.

Maggio Musicale Fiorentino (Florentine Musical May), Florence, Italy. Italy's oldest and most prestigious music festival emphasizes music from the 14th to the 20th centuries, but also presents ballet and opera in the city's grandest venues. See www.maggiofiorentino.com. Tickets are available in Italy through **Viva Ticket** (www.vivaticket.it; ☎ **899/666-805** in Italy). Late April to early June.

Festspillene i Bergen (Bergen International Festival), Bergen, Norway. This world-class music event features artists from

Norway and around the world. Many styles of music are presented, but classical music—especially the work of Grieg—is emphasized. This is one of the largest annual musical events in Scandinavia. Contact the **Bergen International Festival** (www.fib.no/en; ✆ **55-21-06-30**); buy tickets online through www.billetservice.no or through the **Grieghallen Ticket Office** on ✆ **55-21-61-50.** Mid-May to early June.

Bath International Music Festival, Bath, England. One of Europe's most prestigious international festivals of music and the arts features as many as 1,000 performers at various venues over 12 days. Contact **Bath Festivals** (www.bathmusicfest.org.uk; ✆ **01225/ 462-231**) or call the box office on ✆ **01225/ 463-362.** Late May to early June.

JUNE

Hellenic Festival (Athens and Epidaurus Festivals), Greece. Greece's flagship cultural festivals are now organized under the umbrella of one "Hellenic Festival." The Athens Festival traditionally features superb productions of ancient drama, opera, modern dance, ballet, and more in the Odeon of Herodes Atticus, on the southwest side of the Acropolis, and recently at other venues around the city. The Epidaurus Festival presents classic Greek drama in two amphitheaters. Go to www.greekfestival.gr/en or call ✆ **210/928-2900.** Tickets are sold online and via the box office on ✆ **210/327-2000** and can be collected in person. June to early October.

Festival di Spoleto, Spoleto, Italy. Dating from 1958, this festival was the artistic creation of maestro and world-class composer Gian Carlo Menotti, who died in 2007. International performers convene for 3 weeks of dance, drama, opera, concerts, and art exhibits in this Umbrian hill town. The main focus is music composed from 1300 to 1799. For tickets and details, check www.festivaldispoleto.com or call ✆ **0743/ 221689.** Late June to mid-July.

Roskilde Festival, Roskilde, Denmark. Northern Europe's biggest rock and indie festival has been going strong for more than 40 years, now bringing about 90,000 revelers each year to the central Zealand town. Besides major bands on multiple stages, scheduled activities include theater and film presentations. Check www.roskilde-festival.dk or call ✆ **46-36-66-13.** Late June to early July.

JULY

Il Palio, Siena, Italy. Palio fever grips this Tuscan hill town for a wild and exciting horse race with roots in the Middle Ages. Pageantry, costumes, and the celebrations of the victorious *contrada* (sort of a neighborhood social club) mark the spectacle. It's a "no-rules" event: Even a horse without a rider can win the race. Contact the **Siena Tourist Office** on ✆ **0577/280551** for information, or see www.terresiena.it and www.paliodisiena.net. July 2 and August 16.

Tour de France, France. Europe's most hotly contested bicycle race pits crews of wind-tunnel-tested athletes along an itinerary that spans the entire country, detours deep into the Massif Central, and ranges across the Alps and Pyrenees. The race is decided at a finish line drawn across the Champs-Elysées. See www.letour.fr. Month of July.

Karlovy Vary International Film Festival, Karlovy Vary, Czech Republic. This annual 10-day event predates Communism and is almost in the same program-quality league as Cannes and Venice, but without the star-drawing power of those more glitzy stops. For more information, check www.kviff.com/ en. You can purchase tickets individually or buy a pass for the whole festival. Early to mid-July.

Montreux International Jazz Festival, Montreux, Switzerland. More than jazz, this festival features everything from reggae bands to African tribal chanters to soul singers. Monster dance fests also break out nightly. The 2½-week festival concludes with a 12-hour marathon of world music. For program and ticketing information, check www.montreuxjazz.com or call ✆ **021/966-4444.** Early July.

Bastille Day, France, nationwide. Celebrating the French Revolution, the nation's festivities reach their peak in Paris with street fairs, pageants, fireworks, and feasts. In Paris, the day begins with a parade down the Champs-Elysées and ends with fireworks at Montmartre. July 14.

Stockholm–Gotland Offshore Race, Sandhamn and Stockholm, Sweden. The biggest and most exciting open-water Scandinavian sailing race starts in Stockholm and finishes at Sandhamn in the Stockholm archipelago. About 450 boats, mainly from Nordic countries, take part. See www.ksss.se and www.visitstockholm.com for information. Two days in June or July.

The Proms, London, England. A night at The Proms—the annual Henry Wood promenade concerts at the Royal Albert Hall—attracts classical music aficionados from around the world. Staged almost daily (except for a few Sundays), these traditional concerts were launched in 1895 and are the principal summer engagements for the BBC Symphony Orchestra. Cheering and clapping, Union Jacks on parade, banners, and balloons—it's great summer fun. See www.bbc.co.uk/proms for information and book via the Royal Albert Hall box office (www.royalalberthall.com). Mid-July to mid-September.

Salzburger Festspiele (Salzburg Festival), Salzburg, Austria. Since the 1920s, this has been one of the premier cultural events in Austria, sparkling with opera, chamber music, plays, concerts, appearances by world-class artists, and many other cultural presentations. Always count on stagings of Mozart operas. For tickets, check www.salzburgerfestspiele.at several months in advance, or call ✆ **0662/8045-500** for the box office. Late July to early September.

Richard Wagner Festival, Bayreuth Festspielhaus, Germany. One of Europe's iconic opera events, this festival takes place in the composer's Festspielhaus in Bayreuth, the capital of upper Franconia. **Note:** Opera tickets often must be booked for many years before an application is successful. Send your application annually to the **Bayreuther Festspiele,** Kartenbüro, Postfach 10 02 62, 95402 Bayreuth (www.

bayreuther-festspiele.de; ✆ **0921/78-780**). Late July to late August.

Festival d'Avignon, Avignon, France. This world-class festival has a reputation for exposing new talent to critical acclaim. The focus is usually on avant-garde works in theater, dance, and music. Much of the music is presented within the medieval courtyard of the Pope's Palace. Make hotel reservations early. For information and tickets, go to www.festival-avignon.com or call ✆ **04-90-14-14-14.** Last 3 weeks of July.

AUGUST

Edinburgh International Festival, Edinburgh, Scotland. Scotland's best-known festival is held for 3 weeks. An "arts bonanza," it draws major talent from around the world, with more than a thousand shows presented and a million tickets sold. Book, jazz, and film festivals are also staged around this time. Contact the **Edinburgh International Festival** (www.eif.co.uk; ✆ **0131/473-2000**). Three weeks in August.

Festas da Senhora da Agonia, Viana do Castelo, north of Porto, Portugal. The most spectacular festival in northern Portugal honors "Our Lady of Suffering." A replica of the Virgin is carried through the streets over carpets of flowers. Float-filled parades mark the 3-day event as a time of revelry. A blaze of fireworks ends the festival. See www.vianafestas.com or call ✆ **0258/809-394** for exact dates, which vary from year to year. Mid-August.

St. Stephen's Day, Hungary. This is Hungary's national day. The country's patron saint is celebrated with cultural events and a dramatic display of fireworks over the Danube. Hungarians also ceremoniously welcome the first new bread from the crop of July wheat. August 20.

SEPTEMBER

Highland Games & Gathering, Braemar, Scotland. The Queen and members of the royal family often show up for this annual event, with its massed bands, piping and dancing competitions, and performances of great strength by a tribe of gigantic men playing Highland sports. For tickets and information, see www.braemargathering.

org or call ℡ **01339/741-098.** First Saturday in September.

Oktoberfest, Munich, Germany. Germany's most famous festival happens mainly in September, not October. Millions show up, and hotels are packed. Most activities are at Theresienwiese, where local breweries sponsor gigantic tents that can hold up to 6,000 beer drinkers. Always reserve hotel rooms well in advance. Contact the **Munich Tourist Office** (www.muenchen.de; ℡ **089/233-96-500**) or see www.oktoberfest.de. Mid-September to the first Sunday in October.

OCTOBER

Autumn Festival, Lugano, Switzerland. A parade and other festivities mark harvest time for the region's bounty of foodstuffs and (especially) wine. Little girls throw flowers from blossom-covered floats, and oxen pull festooned wagons in a colorful procession. For information contact the **Lugano Tourist Office** (www.lugano-tourism.ch; ℡ **091/913-32-32**). Three days in early October.

NOVEMBER

All Saints' Day, Spain, nationwide. This public holiday is reverently celebrated, as relatives and friends lay flowers on the graves of the dead. November 1.

DECEMBER

La Scala Opera Season, Teatro alla Scala, Milan, Italy. At the most famous opera house of them all, the season opens on December 7, the feast day of Milan's patron St. Ambrose, and runs into July, plus September to mid-November. Even though opening-night tickets are close to impossible to get, it's worth a try. See www.teatro allascala.org or call the telephone booking line on ℡ **02/86-07-75.** Early December to mid-July.

Nobel Peace Prize Ceremony, Oslo, Norway. This major event on the Oslo calendar attracts world attention. It's held at Oslo City Hall on the anniversary of Alfred Nobel's death, and attendance is by invitation only. For details, see www.nobelprize.org. December 10.

TIPS ON WHERE TO STAY

Traditional European hotels tend to be **simpler** than North American ones, and rooms are on average significantly **smaller.** Hoteliers tend to emphasize character and friendliness over amenities. For example, even in the cheapest American chain motel, free cable is as standard as indoor plumbing. In Europe, however, some independent hotels below the moderate level don't even have in-room TVs. But then, you're probably not over here to watch *The X-Factor*.

Make **reservations** as far in advance as possible, even in the quieter months from November to April. Travel to most places in Europe peaks between May and October, and during that period, it's hard to come by a moderate or inexpensive hotel room. In a trendy spot such as Cornwall in England, Tuscany, or the Dordogne, France, it's nigh impossible to find an excellent hotel room, apartment, or cottage to rent at short notice in the summer. And many smaller, boutique hotels can fill up year-round, especially at weekends and in popular city-break or weekend bolthole destinations.

You'll find hotels and other accommodations inside every conceivable kind of building, from 21st-century concrete cubes to medieval coaching inns. In older hotels, guest rooms can be smaller than you might expect (if you base your expectation on a modern U.S. Radisson, for example), and each room is usually different, sometimes quirkily so. But this is part of the charm. Some rooms may only have a shower, not a bathtub, so if you feel you can't survive without a tub, make that clear when booking.

Most European countries rate hotels by **stars,** ranging from five stars (luxe) to one star (modest). A four- or five-star hotel offers first-class accommodations, a three-star hotel is usually moderately priced, and a one- or two-star hotel is inexpensively priced. Governments grant stars based on rigid criteria, evaluating such amenities as elevators, private bathrooms, pools, and air-conditioning. The hotel with the most stars is not necessarily the most elegant or charming. For example, a five-star hotel might be an ugly, modern building, whereas a one-star hotel might be a town house but with no elevator, bar, or restaurant. Plenty of fashionable boutique accommodations have no stars at all. Unless otherwise noted, all hotel rooms in this book have **private en suite bathrooms.** Hotels in every European country are well represented on the mainstream booking websites such as **Hotels.com** and **Booking. com**.

You probably don't want to stay in a chain hotel, but for car-tourers, **Ibis** (www. ibishotel.com) are reliable, clean, well-equipped, and good-value overnight motel-style stops close to many major highways. There are over 700 in Europe, about half of them in France. In fact, Ibis's parent **Accor** group (www.accorhotels.com) has hotel offerings at just about every level of comfort in several European countries— brands include Mercure, Sofitel, and Novotel. **B&B Hotels** (www.hotel-bb.com) are cheaper, simpler, and also concentrated close to major routes in France. **Louvre Hotels** (www.louvrehotels.com) has a number of affordable brands, including Campanile. **Logis de France** (www.logishotels.com) is a marketing group, not a chain. Properties tend to be more characterful than the chains, but also more variable. If you're winding your way around the French backroads, their website is worth investigating. Reliable, mid-range brands and chains like **Best Western** (www.best western.com) and **Holiday Inn** (www.holidayinn.com) are here too. **Radisson Blu** (www.radissonblu.com) has a strong presence in Europe's cities. However, you'll find our favorite hotels by consulting the individual chapters in this book.

A **villa** or **rental property** can be great for getting up-close to a European destination, if you're lingering in one spot for more than a couple of nights. **Untours** (www. untours.com; ✆ 888/868-6871 in the U.S. and Canada) provides apartment, farmhouse, or cottage stays of 2 weeks or more in many destinations for a reasonable price. **HomeAway.com** is the largest rental property broker on the planet, and offers properties of every kind all over Europe. **Holidaylettings.co.uk** and **Homelidays** (www.homelidays.co.uk) both have vast rental property portfolios, including villas with private or shared outdoor pools. The simplicity of a French *gîte* (self-catering holiday home) is another to consider in this category, especially for cost-conscious visitors: Check **www.gites-de-france.com**. In Great Britain, search cottage rental agents such as **English Country Cottages** (www.english-country-cottages.co.uk) and **Cottages 4 You** (www.cottages4you.co.uk). In Spain, **Rustical Travel** (www. rusticaltravel.com) has an excellent portfolio in Andalusia and across the North. **Ionian & Aegean Island Holidays** (www.ionianislandholidays.com) rents villas on several Greek islands.

HomeLink International (www.homelink.org; ✆ 800/638-3841 in the U.S. or ✆ 01962/886882 in the U.K.), which costs $119/£115 for a year's membership, is the oldest, largest, and best home-exchange holiday group in the world. An alternative is **Intervac International** (www.intervac-homeexchange.com; ✆ 800/756-HOME [4663] in the U.S., ✆ 0845/260-5776 in the U.K.), which costs $100 annually. Both have members spread around Europe.

Many European cities are also well represented in online peer-to-peer accommodation networks, including international giants like **AirBnB.com**; **9flats.com** is another peer-to-peer site worth checking out for U.K. and German accommodations in particular. **OneFineStay.com** has a small, but special portfolio of apartments in London, serviced in a hotel style.

Agritourism is increasingly popular for visitors to rural areas looking to "get away from it all." Most places in this category offer rooms or small apartments on a working agricultural property—which could be anything from an olive oil farm to a wine estate. Many make and sell their own produce (salami, conserves, wine, and the like) to guests. Accommodations aren't always rough and ready: Plenty of Italian *agriturismi*, for example, offer amenities, luxury, and outdoor swimming pools. **Farm Stay UK** (www.farmstay.co.uk; ✆ 024/7669-6909), set up in part by the Royal Agricultural Society of England, and still owned by a consortium of farmers, features more than 1,200 rural retreats including farms, B&Bs, and campsites in Britain. The best Italian *agriturismo* websites are **www.terranostra.it** and **ww.agriturismo.it**. One U.S.-based agency worth contacting is **Italy Farm Holidays** (www.italyfarmholidays.com). In Spain, you'll find rural properties *(casas rurales)* at excellent prices listed at such sites as **www.iberiarural.es** and **www.toprural.com**.

There are still more off-the-wall options for truly "alternative" European accommodations. One of our favorites is **Monastery Stays** (www.monasterystays.com), which represents hundreds of religious institutions in Italy. Rooms range from basic to spacious and comfortable, and staying in a monastery or convent provides an experience you're unlikely to forget. Only married couples or blood relatives can share the same room.

ORGANIZED TOURS

Activity Tours

CYCLING

Cycling tours are a great way to see Europe at your own pace. In cycling-mad countries such as Italy and France, you'll be getting the same view as many locals do—from the saddle. Some of the best are conducted by the **CTC (Cyclists' Tourist Club) Cycling Holidays** (www.cyclingholidays.org). **Hindriks European Bicycle Tours** (www.hindrikstours.com) leads 10-day bicycle tours throughout Europe. **ExperiencePlus** (www.experienceplus.com; ✆ 800/685-4565 or 970/484-8489 in the U.S. and Canada) runs bike tours in France, Spain, Italy, the Czech Republic, and elsewhere. **Ciclismo Classico** (www.ciclismoclassico.com; ✆ 800/866-7314 or 781/646-3377 in the U.S. and Canada) is an excellent outfit running tours of Italy, Norway, Portugal, and elsewhere in Europe. Florence-based **I Bike Italy** (www.ibikeitaly.com; ✆ +39-055/012-3994) offers guided single-day rides around the city and into the Chianti winelands.

HIKING & WALKING

Wilderness Travel (www.wildernesstravel.com; ✆ 800/368-2794 or 510/558-2488 in the U.S. and Canada) specializes in walking tours, treks, and inn-to-inn hiking tours of almost 20 European countries, as well as less strenuous walking tours. **Sherpa Expeditions** (www.sherpaexpeditions.com; ✆ 020/8577-2717 in the U.K.) offers both self-guided and group treks through off-the-beaten-track regions. Two somewhat upscale walking-tour companies are **Butterfield & Robinson** (www.butterfield.com; ✆ 866/551-9090 in the U.S. and Canada) and **Country Walkers** (www.countrywalkers.com; ✆ 800/464-9255 in the U.S. and Canada, or 1300/663-206 in Australia). **Macs Adventure** (www.macsadventure.com; ✆ 866/355-1037 in the U.S. and Canada, *℡* **0141/530-8866** in the U.K.) has an impressive portfolio of serviced active holidays, including walking Scotland's Highlands or Italy's Amalfi Coast. **Exodus** (www.exodus.co.uk; *℡* **0845/863-9600** in the U.K.) has walks and hikes for all ability levels all over Europe, from Croatia's Dalmatian coast to the frozen Scandinavian north.

Most European countries have associations geared toward aiding hikers and walkers. In Britain, it's the **Ramblers** (www.ramblers.org.uk; *℡* **020/7339-8500** in the U.K.). In Italy, contact the **Club Alpino Italiano** (www.cai.it; *℡* **02/205-7231** in Italy). For Austria, try the **Österreichischer Alpenverein (Austrian Alpine Club)** (www.alpenverein.at or www.facebook.com/alpenverein; *℡* **0512/59547** in Austria). In Norway, it's **Den Norske Turistforening (Norwegian Trekking Association)** (www.turistforeningen.no/english; *℡* **4000-1868** in Norway).

HORSEBACK RIDING

One of the best companies is **Equitour** (www.ridingtours.com; *℡* **800/545-0019** or **307/455-3363** in the U.S. and Canada), which offers 5- to 7-day rides through many of Europe's most beautiful areas, such as the Scottish Highlands, the Greek island of Crete, and France's Loire Valley. **FlorenceTown** (www.florencetown.com; *℡* **055/012-3994** in Italy) runs easy 1-day rides around the Chianti region of Tuscany.

EDUCATIONAL TRAVEL

The best (and one of the most expensive) of the escorted group tour companies is **Group IST (International Specialty Travel;** www.groupist.com; *℡* **212/594-8787** in the U.S. and Canada), whose offerings are first class all the way and accompanied by a certified expert in whatever field the trip focuses on. If you missed out on study abroad in college, the brainy **Smithsonian Journeys** (www.smithsonianjourneys.org; *℡* **855/330-1542** in the U.S. and Canada) may be just the ticket, albeit a pricey one. Study leaders are often world-renowned experts in their field. Journeys are carefully crafted and go to some of the most compelling places in Europe, avoiding tourist traps.

Andante Travels (www.barebonestours.co.uk; *℡* **01722/713-800** in the U.K.) specialists lead guided tours of the most exciting archaeological areas in the world, including Sicilian temples, the ruins of Pompeii, Provence in France, and Ireland's megalithic sites. Butterflies of the Dolomites, Norway's Arctic wilderness, and other flora and fauna throughout Europe are the focus of trips from **Naturetrek** (www.naturetrek.co.uk; *℡* **01962/733-051** in the U.K.), whose naturalists lead walks through some of the continent's most spectacular scenery. A clearinghouse for information on Europe-based language schools is **Lingua Service Worldwide** (www.linguaserviceworldwide.com; *℡* **800/394-LEARN [394-5327]** or **203/938-7406** in the U.S. and Canada).

COOKING SCHOOLS

If you're staying in **agritourism** accommodations (see "Tips on Where to Stay," above) anywhere in Europe, inquire about cookery courses. Many offer half- and full-day tuition in traditional methods and dishes for very reasonable rates. From May to October, the **International Cooking School of Italian Food and Wine** (www.internationalcookingschool.com) offers courses in Bologna, the "gastronomic capital of Italy," Piedmont (Italy's truffle capital), and Tuscany. Chef Judy Francini of **Divina Cucina** (www.divinacucina.com) leads students through Florence's central market to buy the ingredients to prepare a meal, and also spices up the menu with wine tastings, cooking tours of Chianti, Apulia, and Sicily, and visits to makers of balsamic vinegar and other Italian specialties. **Le Cordon Bleu** (www.cordonbleu.edu; ✆ 01/53-68-22-50 in France) was established in 1895 as a means of spreading the tenets of French cuisine to the world at large. It offers many programs outside its flagship Paris school.

Escorted General-Interest Tours

Escorted tours are structured group tours, with a group leader. The price usually includes everything from airfare to hotels, meals, tours, admission costs, and local transportation.

The two largest tour operators conducting escorted tours of Europe are various brands under the umbrella of **Globus/Cosmos** (www.globusandcosmos.com; ✆ 877/245-6287 in the U.S. and Canada, or ✆ 020/8464-3444 in the U.K.) and **Trafalgar** (www.trafalgartours.com; ✆ 0148/175-4799 in the U.K.). Both companies have first-class tours that vary in prices. The differences are mainly in hotel location and the number of activities. There's little difference in the companies' services, so choose your tour based on the itinerary and preferred date of departure. Brochures are available at travel agencies, and there's plenty of itinerary information and ideas online.

Despite the fact that escorted tours require upfront deposits and predetermine hotels, restaurants, and itineraries, many people derive security and peace of mind from the structure they offer. Escorted tours—whether they're navigated by bus, motorcoach, train, boat, or all of the above—let travelers sit back and enjoy the trip without having to drive or worry about details. They take you to the maximum number of sights in the minimum amount of time with the least amount of hassle. They're particularly convenient for people with limited mobility and they can be a great way for solo travelers to make new friends.

On the downside, you'll have little opportunity for serendipitous interactions with locals. The tours can be jampacked with activities, leaving little room for individual sightseeing, whim, or adventure—plus they often focus on the heavily touristed sites.

Packages for Independent Travelers

Package tours are simply a way to buy the airfare, accommodations, and other elements of your trip (such as car rentals, airport transfers, and sometimes even activities) at the same time and often at discounted prices.

All major airlines flying from North America to Europe sell vacation packages, including **American Airlines Vacations** (www.aavacations.com; ✆ 800/321-2121 in the U.S. and Canada), **Delta Vacations** (www.deltavacations.com; ✆ 800/800-1504 in the U.S. and Canada), and **United Vacations** (www.unitedvacations.com; ✆ 888/854-3899 in the U.S. and Canada). Several big **online travel agencies**—Expedia, Travelocity, Orbitz, and Lastminute.com—also do a brisk business in packages for visitors flying from just about anywhere to pretty much anywhere else. Pretty much every European short-haul airline these days—including British Airways, Ryanair, and others—offers flight plus hotel plus car rental deals. Keep an eye on their websites.

A leading North American packager offering European trips is **EuroVacations** (www.eurovacations.com; ✆ 877/471-3876 in the U.S. and Canada), featuring highlights of such countries as England, France, Germany, Italy, and Spain, but also

ONE-STOP tour SHOPPING

An excellent overall resource is **Shaw-Guides** (www.shawguides.com), an online resource to language vacations, cooking schools, art and photography workshops, and much more. **Tourdust** (www.tourdust.com) is an independent online agency with a handpicked portfolio of cultural and adventure trips in 13 European countries, always offered by locally based operators. Wine tasting, cycling, photography, and *agriturismo* vacations are all offered. A good overall introduction to several European cities is a tour with **City Sightseeing**, the bus-tour company that allows 24 hours' worth of transport to major sights around a city, allowing you to hop on and off the bus as you wish. The canned, multilingual commentary is not going to enlighten you greatly, but rolling through a strange city is a delight. The best approach is to stay aboard once for the whole route, then redo the circuit making the stops that interest you. Check out routes and prices for the city you are visiting at **www.city-sightseeing.com**. Also check online tour agents such as the excellent **Context** (www.contexttravel.com), **Viator.com**, and **Isango!** (www.isango.com).

dealing in eastern Europe. More great deals are offered by **Sherman's Travel** (www.shermanstravel.com), which features bargains on airfare and hotel deals. You can reach the outfit via e-mail at info@shermanstravel.com. For all kinds of packages with a sustainable or eco-friendly ethos, check the listings at **Responsible Travel** (www.responsibletravel.com or www.responsiblevacation.com).

Deals on packages come and go, and the latest are often listed in the travel section of your local weekend newspaper. North Americans should check ads in the national travel magazines such as *Budget Travel, Travel + Leisure, National Geographic Traveler,* and *Condé Nast Traveler*. Brits may find suitable packages advertised in the likes of *National Geographic Traveller, Wanderlust,* or *Sunday Times Travel Magazine*.

[FastFACTS] EUROPE

Car Rental   See "Getting Around by Car," earlier in this chapter.

Cellphones   The three letters that define much of the world's wireless capabilities are **GSM** (Global System for Mobiles), a satellite network that makes for easy cross-border cellphone use throughout most of the planet, including all of Europe. If you own an unlocked GSM phone, pack it in your hand luggage and buy a contract-free **SIM-only tariff** when you arrive. The SIM card will cost very little, but you will need to load it up with credit to make calls. A few familiar names (Vodafone, t-Mobile, and Orange among them) have local network operators in a number of European countries; some operators appear in just one. Tariffs change constantly in response to the market and by country, but in general expect call charges of around .15€ per minute (or the equivalent), .10€ for a text message, and a deal on data that might include 200MB in a week for under 5€. There are phone and SIM-card retailers on practically every high street in every country, and pretty much whichever operator you go with, you will make substantial savings over roaming with your home SIM.

There are other options if you're visiting from overseas but don't own an unlocked GSM phone. For a short visit, **renting** a phone may be a good idea, and we suggest renting the handset before you leave home. North Americans can rent from **InTouch USA** (www.intouchusa.us; ✆ **800/872-7626** or **703/222-7161**) or **BrightRoam** (www.bright roam.com; ✆ **888/622-3393**). However, handset prices have fallen to a level where you can often buy a basic local **pay-as-you-go (PAYG) phone** for less than one week's hand-set rental. Prices at many European cellphone retailers start from under US$50 for a cheap model, and you can often find an entry-level Android smartphone for around US$100. Buy one, use it while you're here, and recycle it on the way home. Unfortunately, per-minute charges for international calls to your home country can be high, so if you plan to do a lot of calling home, use a VoIP service such as **Skype** (www.skype.com) in conjunction with a Web connection. See "Internet & Wi-Fi," below.

Customs   Individual countries usually have their own customs regulations (see the individual chapters in this book). However, members of the European Union (E.U.) share many guidelines for arrivals. **Non-E.U. nationals aged 17 and over** can bring in 4 liters of wine and 16 liters of beer plus either 1 liter of alcohol more than 22% ("spirits") or 2 liters of "fortified" wine at less than 22%. Visitors may also bring in other goods, including per-fume, gifts, and souvenirs, totaling 430€ in value. (Customs officials tend to be lenient about these general merchandise regulations, realizing the limits are unrealistically low.) Tobacco regulations vary by country, although an import limit of 200 cigarettes and 50 cigars is typical. For **arrivals from within the E.U.,** there are no limits as long as goods are for your own personal use, or are gifts. You can find details on customs and excise rules for anyone entering the E.U. at **www.ec.europa.eu/taxation_customs/common/travellers**.

For specifics on what you can take home and the corresponding fees, U.S. citizens should download the free pamphlet *Know Before You Go* at **www.cbp.gov**. Alternatively, contact the **U.S. Customs & Border Protection (CBP),** 1300 Pennsylvania Ave. N.W., Washington, DC 20229 (✆ **877/CBP-5511**), and request the pamphlet. For a clear sum-mary of their own rules, Canadians should consult the booklet *I Declare,* issued by the **Canada Border Services Agency** (www.cbsa-asfc.gc.ca; ✆ **800/461-9999** in Canada, or **204/983-3500**). Australians need to read *Guide for Travellers: Know Before You Go.* For more information, call the **Australian Customs Service** at ✆ **1300/363-263,** or download the leaflet from **www.customs.gov.au/webdata/resources/files/GuideForTravellers.pdf**. For New Zealanders, most questions are answered under "Coming into NZ" at **www.customs.govt.nz**. For more information, contact the **New Zealand Customs Service** (✆ **0800/428-786,** or **09/927-8036**).

Electricity   Not all European electrical systems are the same. Most of continental Europe uses the 220-volt system (two round prongs). However, British electricity operates at 240 volts AC (50 cycles), and almost all overseas plugs don't fit British three-hole wall outlets. Always bring suitable transformers and/or adapters, such as world multiplugs—if you plug some American appliances directly into an electrical outlet without a transformer, for example, you'll destroy your appliance and possibly start a fire. Portable electronic devices such as iPods and cellphones, however, recharge without problems via USB or using a multiplug. Many long-distance European trains have plugs, for the charging of lap-tops and cellphones.

Emergencies   See individual chapters for local police, fire, and ambulance numbers. Dialing ✆ **112** will summon the emergency services wherever you are in the E.U.

Family Travel   Europe, especially southern Europe, is a very welcoming place to travel with children. To locate accommodations, restaurants, and attractions that are particularly kid-friendly, look for the "Kids" icon throughout this guide.

Insurance   For information on traveler's insurance, trip cancelation insurance, and medi-cal insurance while traveling, please visit **www.frommers.com/planning**.

Internet & Wi-Fi   The availability of the Internet across Europe is in a constant state of development. How you access it depends on whether you've brought your own computer or smartphone, or if you're searching for a public terminal. Many hotels have computers for guest use, although pricing can vary from gratis to extortionate. To find a local Internet cafe, start by checking **www.cybercaptive.com**; it's not especially up-to-date, but is worth a try nevertheless. Although such places have suffered due to the spread of smartphones and free Wi-Fi (see below), they do tend to be prevalent close to popular tourist spots, especially ones frequented by backpackers. Aside from cybercafes, most **hostels** have Internet access, and **public libraries** in some countries allow nonresidents to use terminals.

If you have your own computer or smartphone, **Wi-Fi** makes access much easier. Always check before using your hotel's network—some charge exorbitant rates, and free or cheap Wi-Fi isn't hard to find elsewhere, in urban locations at least. Ask locally, or Google "free Wi-Fi + [town]" before you arrive. To locate free Wi-Fi hotspots, it's also worth using the hotspot locator at **www.jiwire.com**. It's worth asking the local tourist office, too. They will likely be able to point you toward local providers where you can surf for free, or for the price of a cup of coffee at most. See individual chapters for tourist information office details. Many **long-distance trains,** especially on high-speed networks, have onboard Wi-Fi.

Legal Aid   If you're visiting from overseas, contact your consulate or embassy (see individual chapters). They can advise you of your rights and will usually provide a list of local attorneys (for which you'll have to pay if services are used), but they cannot interfere on your behalf in a local legal process. For questions about American citizens who are arrested abroad, including ways of getting money to them, telephone the **Citizens Emergency Center** of the Office of Special Consular Services in Washington, D.C. (© **202/647-5225**).

Medical Requirements   Unless you're arriving from an area known to be suffering from an epidemic (particularly cholera or yellow fever), inoculations or vaccinations are not required for entry into Europe.

Money & Costs   Frommer's lists exact prices in the local currency. The currency conversions provided were correct at press time. However, rates fluctuate, so before departing consult a currency exchange website such as **www.oanda.com/currency/converter** to check up-to-the-minute rates.

THE VALUE OF THE EURO VS. OTHER POPULAR CURRENCIES

Euro€	Aus$	Can$	NZ$	UK£	US$
€1	A$1.28	C$1.30	NZ$1.65	£.80	$1.29

ATMs are everywhere in Europe—depending on the country, you'll find them at banks, some fuel stations, highway rest stops, supermarkets, post offices, or all of the above. The **Cirrus** (www.mastercard.com) and **PLUS** (www.visa.com) networks span the globe; look at the back of your bank card to see which network you're on, and then check online for ATM locations at your destination if you want to be ultra-organized. Be sure you know your personal identification number (PIN) and daily withdrawal limit before you depart. Note that European machines use **4-digit PINs,** so if your bank issues a 6-digit number, contact them before you leave home. Credit cards are accepted just about everywhere, save street markets, small independent retailers, street-food vendors, and occasional small or family-owned businesses. However, North American visitors should note that American Express is accepted far less widely than at home, and Diners only at the very highest of highflying establishments. To be sure of your credit line, bring a Visa or MasterCard as well.

Some countries, especially Britain, have been very aggressive in the fight against credit card fraud. As a result, many places are moving away from the magnetic strip credit card to the new system of **Chip and PIN** ("smartcards" with chips embedded in them). Most retailers ask for your 4-digit PIN to be entered into a keypad near the cash register. In restaurants, a server might bring a hand-held device to your table to authorize payment. If you're visiting from a country where Chip and PIN is less prevalent (such as the U.S.), it's possible that some retailers will be reluctant to accept your swipe cards. Be prepared to argue your case: Swipe cards are still valid and the same machines that read the smartcard chips can also read your magnetic strip. However, do carry some cash with you too, just in case.

For help with currency conversions, tip calculations, and more, download Frommer's convenient Travel Tools app for your mobile device. Go to **www.frommers.com/go/ mobile** and click on the Travel Tools icon.

Packing   For helpful information on packing for your trip, download our convenient Travel Tools app for your mobile device. Go to **www.frommers.com/go/mobile** and click on the Travel Tools icon. See also "When to Go," earlier in this chapter.

Passports & Visas   To travel throughout Europe, all U.S. and British citizens, Canadians, Australians, and New Zealanders must have a passport valid through their length of stay. No visa is required. The immigration officer may also want to see proof of your intention to return to your point of origin (usually a round-trip ticket) and of visible means of support while you're in Europe. If you're planning to fly from the United States or Canada to Europe and then on to a country that requires a visa (India, for example), you should secure that visa before you depart.

Passport Offices:

○ **Australia**   Australian Passport Information Service (www.passports.gov.au or ℂ **131-232**).

○ **Canada**   Passport Canada, Foreign Affairs and International Trade Canada, Gatineau, QC K1A 0G3 (www.ppt.gc.ca; ℂ **800/567-6868**).

○ **New Zealand**   Passport Office, Department of Internal Affairs, Level 3, 109 Featherston Street, P.O. Box 1568, Wellington 6140 (www.passports.govt.nz; ℂ **0800/22-50-50** in New Zealand or 04/463-9360).

○ **United Kingdom**   Visit your nearest passport office, major post office, or travel agency or contact the **Identity and Passport Service** (www.ips.gov.uk; ℂ **0300/222-0000**).

○ **United States**   To find your regional passport office, check the U.S. State Department website (http://travel.state.gov/passport) or call the **National Passport Information Center** (ℂ **877/487-2778**) for automated information.

Taxes   All European countries charge a **value-added tax (VAT)** of between 8% (in Switzerland) and 27% (in Hungary) on goods and services, with most hovering on the high side of 20%. Unlike a U.S. sales tax, it is already included in any store price you see quoted. Rates vary from country to country (as does the name—it's called IVA in Italy and Spain, TVA in France, and so on), though in E.U. countries the minimum rate is 15% for most goods. Usually, some items in each country (books, food, and children's clothes in the U.K., for example) are exempt.

Citizens of non-E.U. countries can, as they leave the country, get back most of the tax on purchases (not services) if they spend above a designated amount (usually £50) in a single store. Regulations vary from country to country, so inquire at the tourist office when you arrive to find out the procedure; ask what percentage of the tax is refunded, and whether the refund is given to you at the airport or mailed to you later. Look for a TAX-FREE SHOPPING FOR TOURISTS sign posted in participating stores. Always ask the storekeeper for the necessary forms, and keep the purchases in their original packages if you want them to be valid for a VAT refund. Save your receipts and VAT forms from each E.U. country to process all of them at your final exit point from the E.U. (allow an extra 30 min. or so at an airport to process forms).

To avoid VAT refund hassles, when leaving an E.U. country for the last leg of your trip, take your goods, receipts, and passport to have the form stamped by Customs. Then take all your documentation to the VAT Refund counter you'll find at hundreds of airports and border crossings. Your money is refunded on the spot. For more information, contact **Global Blue** (www.global-blue.com).

Time　Britain, Ireland, and Portugal are 5 hours ahead of New York City (U.S. Eastern Standard Time); Greece is 7 hours ahead of New York. The rest of the countries in this book observe CET (Central European Time), and are 6 hours ahead of New York. For instance, when it's noon in New York, it's 5pm in London and Lisbon; 6pm in Paris, Copenhagen, and Budapest; and 7pm in Athens. London is 10 hours behind Sydney; Paris and other CET cities are 9 hours behind; and Athens is 8 hours. European countries all observe daylight saving time, but the time change doesn't usually occur on the same day as in North America or the Southern Hemisphere countries. There's plenty of extra guidance at **www.timeanddate.com**.

For help with time translations, and more, download our convenient Travel Tools app for your mobile device. Go to **www.frommers.com/go/mobile** and click on the Travel Tools icon.

Tipping　The cultural ins-and-outs of tipping vary widely across Europe. And indeed, the whole concept of tipping isn't without controversy: Some Europeans, for example, resent a "tipping culture being imported" from North America and elsewhere—the practice, where it exists, is nowhere near as ingrained as it is in the U.S. There are, however, a few instances when a tip is appreciated, no matter where you are.　In grand hotels, tip **bellhops** around 1€ per bag and tip the **chamber staff,** too, if you like—though it's not expected in most establishments. In family-run hotels, it's not always considered polite to leave anything at all. Tip the **doorman** or **concierge** of a grand hotel only if he or she has provided you with some specific service (for example, obtaining difficult-to-get theater tickets). If you come across **valet parking,** tip the attendant 1€ when your car arrives.

In restaurants, tip **service staff** 10% of the check if you feel the service has warranted it, though again this is by no means standard practice among locals in most European countries. Be sure to check if a **service charge** has already been applied; if it has, there's no need to leave more. **Bar staff** expect nothing, unless you're in a very high-toned nightspot, when you should round up and add a euro or two. **Cab drivers** may expect a euro or two on top of the fare, especially if they have helped with your luggage—though luggage fees often apply anyway, so don't feel obliged. **Hairdressers** and **barbers** also appreciate an extra euro or so for a job well done.

For help with tip calculations, currency conversions, and more, download our convenient Travel Tools app for your mobile device. Go to **www.frommers.com/go/mobile** and click on the Travel Tools icon. For further guidance on tipping, see the individual chapters later in this book.

VAT　See "Taxes," earlier in this section.

Visitor Information　Start with the **European tourist offices** in your own country; for a complete list, see below. If you aren't sure which countries you want to visit, have a glance at **www.visiteurope.com**.

Austrian Tourist Office
www.austria.info
In the U.S.　☏ 212/944-6880
In Canada　☏ 416/967-3381
In the U.K.　☏ 0845/101-1818
In Australia　☏ 02-9299-3621

Belgian Tourist Office

www.visitbelgium.com or www.belgiumtheplaceto.be

In the U.S.   220 E. 42nd St., Ste. 3402, New York, NY 10017 (✆ 212/758-8130)

In Canada   43 rue de Buade, Bureau 525, Quebec Ville, Quebec G1R 4A2 (✆ 418/692-4939)

In the U.K.   217 Marsh Wall, London E14 9FJ (✆ 020/7537-1132)

Visit Britain

www.visitbritain.com, www.facebook.com/LoveUK, www.enjoyengland.com, www.visit wales.com, or www.visitscotland.com

Czech Tourism

www.czechtourism.com

In the U.S.   1109 Madison Ave., New York, NY 10028 (✆ 212/288-0830)

In the U.K.   13 Harley St., London W1G 9QG (✆ 020/7631-0427)

French Government Tourist Office

www.franceguide.com

In the U.S.   E-mail info.us@franceguide.com

In Canada   Maison de la France/French Government Tourist Office, 1800 av. McGill College, Ste. 1010, Montreal, QC H3A 3J6 (✆ 514/288-2026)

In the U.K.   Maison de la France/French Government Tourist Office, 300 High Holborn, London WC1V 7JH (✆ 09068/244-123)

In Australia   French Tourist Bureau, Level 13, 25 Bligh St., Sydney, NSW 2000 (✆ 02/ 9231-5244)

German National Tourist Office

www.germany.travel or www.facebook.com/GermanyTravelDestination

In the U.S.   122 E. 42nd St., Suite 2000, New York, NY 10168-0072 (✆ 212/661-7200)

In the U.K.   65 Curzon St., London W1J 8PE (✆ 020/7317-0905)

Greek National Tourist Organization

www.visitgreece.gr

In the U.S. & Canada   305 E. 47th St., New York, NY 10017 (✆ 212/421-5777)

In the U.K.   4 Conduit St., London W1S 2DJ (✆ 020/7495-9300)

In Australia   37–49 Pitt St., Sydney, NSW 2000 (✆ 02/9241-1663)

Hungarian National Tourist Office

www.gotohungary.com or www.gotohungary.co.uk

In the U.S. & Canada   450 Seventh Ave., Ste. 2601, New York, NY 10123 (✆ 212/695-1221)

In the U.K.   46 Eaton Place, London SW1X 8AL (✆ +361/438-8080)

Irish Tourist Board

www.discoverireland.com

In the U.S.   ✆ 800/SHAMROCK

In the U.K.   ✆ 0800/313-4000

In Australia   36 Carrington St., Level 5, Sydney, NSW 2000 (✆ 02/9964-6900)

ENIT – Italian Government Tourist Board

www.enit.it or www.italiantourism.com

In the U.S.   630 Fifth Ave., Ste. 1565, New York, NY 10111 (✆ 212/245-5618); 500 N. Michigan Ave., Ste. 506, Chicago, IL 60611 (✆ 312/644-0996); 12400 Wilshire Blvd., Ste. 550, Los Angeles, CA 90025 (✆ 310/820-1898)

In Canada   110 Yonge St. E., Ste. 503, Toronto, ON M5C 1T4 (✆ 416/925-4882)

In the U.K.   1 Princes St., London W1B 2AY (✆ 020/7399-3562)

Monaco Government Tourist & Convention Office

www.visitmonaco.com

In the U.S.   565 Fifth Ave., 23rd Floor, New York, NY 10017 ((✆ 212/286-3330)

In the U.K.   7 Upper Grosvenor St., London W1K 2LX ((✆ 020/7491-4264)

Netherlands Board of Tourism & Conventions

www.holland.com or www.facebook.com/visitholland

In the U.S.   215 Park Avenue South, Suite 2005, New York, NY 10003 ((✆ 212/370-7360)

In the U.K.   Imperial House, 6th Floor, 15–19 Kingsway, London WC2B 6UN ((✆ 020/7539-7950)

Visit Portugal

www.visitportugal.com or www.facebook.com/visitportugal

In the U.S.   590 Fifth Ave., 3rd Floor, New York, NY 10036 ((✆ 646/723-0200)

In Canada   60 Bloor St. W., Ste. 1005, Toronto, ON M4W 3B8 ((✆ 416/921-7376)

In the U.K.   11 Belgrave Sq., London SW1X 8PP ((✆ 0845/355-1212)

Scandinavian Tourism (Denmark, Finland, Iceland, Norway & Sweden)

www.goscandinavia.com, www.visitdenmark.com, www.visitnorway.com, or www.visitsweden.com

In the U.S. & Canada   E-mail info@goscandinavia.com or call ((✆ 212/885-9700

In the U.K.   Visit Denmark, 55 Sloane St., London SW1X 9SY (no phone); Innovation Norway, Charles House, 5 Lower Regent St., London SW1Y 4LR ((✆ 020/7389-8800); Visit Sweden ((✆ 020/7108-6168)

Tourist Office of Spain

www.spain.info

In the U.S.   60 E. 42nd St., Ste. 5300, New York, NY 10165 ((✆ 212/265-8822); 845 N. Michigan Ave., Ste. 915E, Chicago, IL 60611 ((✆ 312/642-1992); 8383 Wilshire Blvd., Ste. 960, Los Angeles, CA 90211 ((✆ 323/658-7188); 1395 Brickell Ave., Ste. 1130, Miami, FL 33131 ((✆ 305/358-1992)

In Canada   2 Bloor St. W., 34th Floor, Toronto, ON M4W 3E2 ((✆ 416/961-3131)

In the U.K.   64 North Row, London W1K 7DE ((✆ 020/7317-2011)

Switzerland Tourism

www.myswitzerland.com

In the U.S.   Swiss Center, 608 Fifth Ave., New York, NY 10020 ((✆ 011800/100-200-29)

In Canada   48 University Ave., Ste. 1500, Toronto, ON M9G 1V2 ((✆ 800/794-7795)

In the U.K.   30 Bedford St., London WC2E 9ED ((✆ 00800/100-200-29)

Wi-Fi   See "Internet & Wi-Fi," earlier in this section.

AUSTRIA

by Dardis McNamee

Today, the "Alpine Republic" of Austria is again the heart of Europe, as it was in the heyday of the Austro-Hungarian Empire, and its capital, Vienna, a crossroads of talent and ideas from across the region. With stunning landscapes, legendary hospitality, and world-class culture, a visitor shares the unparalleled quality of life, which few Austrians willingly leave behind.

The country offers plenty to do, from exploring historic castles and palaces to skiing on some of the world's finest alpine slopes.

VIENNA ★★★

"Vienna stays Vienna," says a famous old tavern song, and despite the agonies of the last century's wars and political upheaval, this lovely city nurtures a sense of leisure and the good life that sets it apart. The Viennese work hard and then hurry home—or out—to enjoy it.

Thus Vienna is a cultivated and cosmopolitan city, with a wealth of cafes, culture, parks, pastries, waltzes, and wine. Over the last four decades, with renewed prosperity, it has emerged from a cocoon of sorts and morphed into a vibrant modern metropolis in which the new complements the old. Imperial palaces, opera houses, concert halls, and museums mingle with a modern world of cutting-edge technology, art, and design. And as for dining, Vienna is a gourmet paradise.

So having lived through war, siege, victory, defeat, the death of an empire, and the birth of a republic, foreign occupation, independence, and the new internationalism of the European Union, the Viennese *Gemütlichkeit* (civility and comfort), has endured.

Essentials

GETTING THERE

BY PLANE **Vienna International Airport** (www.viennaairport.at; **VIE;** ✆ **01/7007-22233**) is about 19km (12 miles) southeast of the city center. There's a regular speed-train service (the City Airport Train or CAT) between the airport and the **Wien Mitte** station, next to the Vienna Hilton, where you can easily connect with subway and tramlines. Trains run every 30 minutes from 6:05am to 11:35pm. The trip takes 16 minutes and costs 9€ per person. There's also a bus service between the airport and other destinations: Schwedenplatz, Westbahnhof, the UN Complex, and Südtirolerplatz, leaving every 30 minutes to an hour. Fares are 8€.

The local train service, Schnellbahn (S-Bahn), also runs from the airport to Wien Nord and Wien Mitte rail stations. Trains go every half hour from 5am to 11:40pm and leave from the station below the airport. Trip time is 25 to 30 minutes, and the fare is 4€. This ticket can also be used for further travel by public transportation within Vienna.

The official **Vienna Tourist Information Office** in the arrival hall of the airport is open daily 7am to 10pm and there is free Wi-Fi throughout the airport.

BY TRAIN   Vienna has two main rail stations, which offer frequent connections to all Austrian cities and towns and from all major European cities. For train and station information, call ✆ **05/1717** from anywhere in Austria.

The **Hauptbahnhof (Main Station)** is Vienna's sparkling new transportation hub, on the site of the former Südbahnhof (South Station). The construction work is not expected to be fully completed until 2015, although trains will stop here from early 2013. Connections, train schedules, and orientation will depend on the phase of construction, but never fear: the ÖBB agents are typically good at helping you get your bearings. A short walk away is the Südtirolerplatz stop on the U1 underground line (also known as the U-Bahn).

The newly revamped **Westbahnhof (West Station),** Mariahilferstrasse 132, serves trains arriving from western Austria, France, Germany, Switzerland, and some eastern European countries like Hungary. It continues to have links to major Austrian cities such as Salzburg, Innsbruck, and Linz. Trains arrive on the second level of the two-level station. For reservations, rail information, and pass validation, head for the ÖBB office, open daily 5:20am to 10:45pm. The Westbahnhof also has a money exchange office and Western Union, which is open daily from 8am to 9pm. There are lockers for luggage. Westbahnhof connects with local trains, the U3 and U6 lines, and several tram and bus routes.

Vienna has rail links to all the major cities of Europe. From Paris (Gare de l'Est), a train at around 8am gets in around 9pm; from Munich, a train at around 9am gets in around 2pm; from Zurich, a train at around 9pm gets in around 7am.

Rail travel in Austria is superb, with fast, clean trains taking you just about anywhere in the country and through some incredibly scenic regions.

Train passengers using the **tunnel** under the English Channel can go from London to Paris in just 3 hours on Eurostar, then on to Vienna (see above). The Eurotunnel Shuttle accommodates passenger cars, charter buses, taxis, and motorcycles and covers the 50km (31-mile) journey in just 35 minutes. This train runs from Folkestone, England, to Calais, France. Service is year-round, 24 hours a day.

EURAILPASS   If you plan to travel extensively in Europe, the **Eurail Global Pass** might be a good bet. It's valid for first-class rail travel in 20 European countries. With one ticket, you travel whenever and wherever you please; more than 100,000 rail miles are at your disposal. Eurailpass holders are also entitled to substantial discounts on certain buses and ferries. Travel agents in all towns and railway agents in such major cities as New York, Montréal, and Los Angeles sell all of these tickets. For information on Eurailpasses and other European train data, call **RailEurope** at ✆ **877/272-RAIL,** or visit it on the Web at www.eurail.com.

For European travelers there are the three rail passes designed for unlimited train travel within a designated region during a predetermined number of days. These passes are sold in most European countries and can be used only by European residents.

An **InterRail Global Pass** (www.interrail.net) allows unlimited travel through Europe, except Albania. An **InterRail Global Youth Pass** is also sold and is available only in second class. A youth is defined as those from age 12 up to and including 25. For information, contact any larger train station in Europe or the Austrian ÖBB (www.oebb.at; ℰ **01/930-000**).

BY CAR If you're already on the Continent, you might want to drive to Vienna; however, arrangements should be made in advance with your car rental company.

The Eurotunnel running under the English Channel takes 35 minutes. Passengers drive aboard the train, the Eurotunnel Shuttle, at Folkestone in England, and vehicles are transported to Calais, France. Your continuing journey to Vienna can also be partly covered by train. Prices are reasonable (but vary), and the system is easy to use.

Vienna can be reached from all directions on major highways called *Autobahnen* or by secondary highways. The main artery from the west is Autobahn A-1, coming in from Munich (466km/291 miles), Salzburg (334km/207 miles), and Linz (186km/115 miles). Autobahn A-2 runs from the south from Graz and Klagenfurt (both in Austria). Autobahn A-4 comes in from the east, connecting with route E-58, which runs to Bratislava and Prague. Autobahn A-22 takes traffic from the northwest, and Route E-10 brings you to the cities and towns of southeastern Austria and Hungary.

Unless otherwise marked, the speed limit on *Autobahnen* is 130km/h (81 mph); figure on 80 to 100km/h (50–62 mph) because of traffic, weather, and road conditions.

When you arrive, park your car or find a garage, because in Vienna driving and parking is no fun at all. (See "Getting around By Car" and "Parking" below.)

BY BOAT To arrive in Vienna with flair, take advantage of the many cruise lines that navigate the Danube. One of the most accessible carriers is **DDSG, The *Donaudampfschiffartsgesellschaft,*** one of the longest words in the German language, or **Blue Danube Shipping Company,** Donaureisen, c/o Österreichisches Verkehrsbüro, Friedrichstrasse 7, 1010 Vienna (www.ddsg-blue-danube.at; ℰ **01/58880**).

Vienna

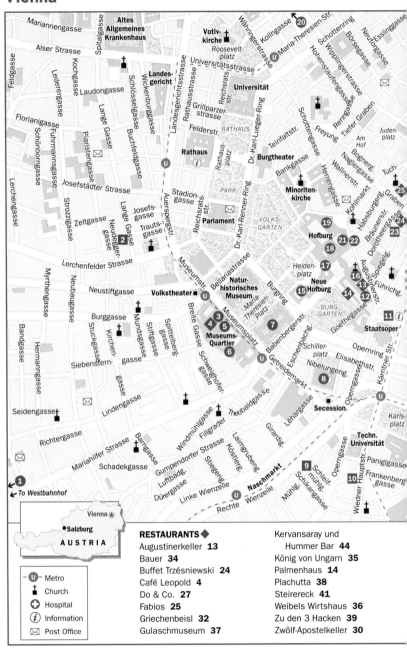

RESTAURANTS ◆

Augustinerkeller **13**
Bauer **34**
Buffet Trzésniewski **24**
Café Leopold **4**
Do & Co. **27**
Fabios **25**
Griechenbeisl **32**
Gulaschmuseum **37**

Kervansaray und
  Hummer Bar **44**
König von Ungarn **35**
Palmenhaus **14**
Plachutta **38**
Steirereck **41**
Weibels Wirtshaus **36**
Zu den 3 Hacken **39**
Zwölf-Apostelkeller **30**

- **U** – Metro
- ♱ Church
- ✚ Hospital
- (i) Information
- ✉ Post Office

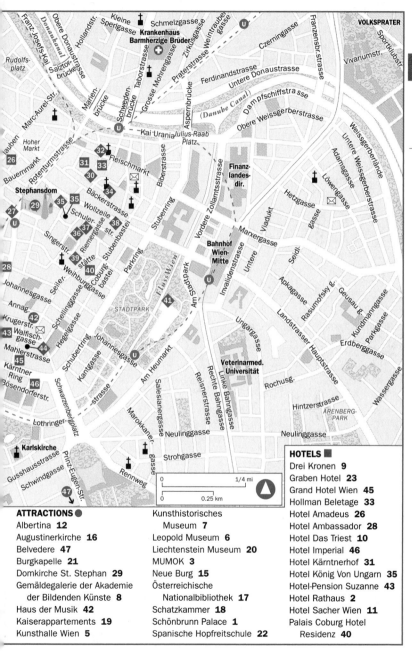

HOTELS ■
Drei Kronen **9**
Graben Hotel **23**
Grand Hotel Wien **45**
Hollman Beletage **33**
Hotel Amadeus **26**
Hotel Ambassador **28**
Hotel Das Triest **10**
Hotel Imperial **46**
Hotel Kärntnerhof **31**
Hotel König Von Ungarn **35**
Hotel-Pension Suzanne **43**
Hotel Rathaus **2**
Hotel Sacher Wien **11**
Palais Coburg Hotel
   Residenz **40**

ATTRACTIONS ●
Albertina **12**
Augustinerkirche **16**
Belvedere **47**
Burgkapelle **21**
Domkirche St. Stephan **29**
Gemäldegalerie der Akademie
   der Bildenden Künste **8**
Haus der Musik **42**
Kaiserappartements **19**
Kunsthalle Wien **5**
Kunsthistorisches
   Museum **7**
Leopold Museum **6**
Liechtenstein Museum **20**
MUMOK **3**
Neue Burg **15**
Österreichische
   Nationalbibliothek **17**
Schatzkammer **18**
Schönbrunn Palace **1**
Spanische Hopfreitschule **22**

They offer 1- and 2-day trips to Vienna from as far away as Passau, Germany, from Bratislava, Budapest, and beyond, depending on the season. Extended trips can be arranged, and cruises are priced to meet every budget.

BY BUS   **Eurolines,** part of National Express Coach Lines (www.nationalexpress.com; © 0871/781-8181), operates two express buses per week between London's Victoria Coach Station and Vienna. The trip takes about 29 hours and makes 45-minute rest stops en route about every 4 hours. Buses depart from London at 8:15am every Friday and Sunday, and are equipped with reclining seats, toilets, and reading lights. The one-way fare is 52€ to 72€; a round-trip ticket costs 80€ to 104€.

VISITOR INFORMATION   **Tourist Office**   The official **Vienna Tourist Information Office (Wien Tourismus),** Albertinaplatz 7 (www.wien.info; © 01/24555), is open daily from 9am to 7pm, for all tickets, and room reservations.

Websites   Besides **Wien Tourist Information** (www.wien.info), go to the **Austrian National Tourist Office** (www.austria.info/us) for current information on cultural sites and events.

CITY LAYOUT   Vienna has evolved into one of the largest metropolises of central Europe, with a surface area covering 415 sq. km (160 sq. miles). It's divided into 23 districts (*Bezirke*), each identified by a numeral and a neighborhood name.

The size and shape of the **1st District,** known as the **Innere Stadt (Inner City),** roughly corresponds to the original borders of medieval Vienna. Other than St. Stephan's Cathedral, very few Gothic or medieval buildings remain—many were reconstructed in the baroque or neoclassical style, whereas others are modern replacements of those bombed during World War II. As Austria's commercial and cultural nerve center, the central district contains dozens of streets devoted exclusively to pedestrian traffic. The most famous is **Kärntnerstrasse,** which passes the Vienna State Opera House as it heads south toward the province of Carinthia (Kärnten).

The Ringstrasse is a circular boulevard about 4km (2½ miles) long whose construction between 1859 and 1888 was one of the most ambitious (and controversial) examples of urban restoration in the history of central Europe. The boulevard surrounds the Inner City. Confusingly, the name of this boulevard changes as it encircles

---

NATIVE behavior

Get accustomed to hearing *"Grüss Gott"* ("God bless you") when Austrians greet you and *"Auf Wiedersehen"* or *"Tschüss"* when they leave. These greetings are practiced by everybody from your hotel manager to waiters and store clerks.

Austria is perhaps the most formal of the countries reviewed in this guide. It is local custom, for example, to dress up for a night at the opera, theater, or ballet. Jeans and baseball jackets won't get you thrown out, but you will be out of place. And yes, men will still give a slight

bow and "kuss die Hand" when introduced to a lady. Prepare to shake hands on both meeting and parting, and to be kissed on both cheeks by friends. The Austrians are keen on titles, so you'll hear *Herr Doktor* or *Frau Professor.*

If you've never hung out in a coffeehouse, make one your second living room while you're here. The Viennese can sit for hour after hour over a single cup of coffee, reading magazines and newspapers or simply watching the world go by.

THE VIENNA card

The **Vienna Card** is the best ticket when using public transportation within the city limits. It's extremely flexible and functional for tourists because it allows unlimited travel, plus various discounts at city museums, restaurants, and shops. You can buy a Vienna Card for 19.90€ at tourist information or public transport offices of Wiener Linien, and some hotels, or order one over the phone with a credit card (✆ **01/7984-400148**).

You can also buy tickets that will save you money if you plan to ride a lot on the city's transport system. A ticket valid for unlimited rides during any 24-hour period costs 6.70€; an equivalent ticket valid for any 72-hour period goes for 14.50€.

These tickets are also available at *Tabac-Trafiken,* vending machines in underground stations, the airport's arrival hall (next to baggage claim), the *Reichsbrücke* (DDSG landing pier), and the *Österreichisches Verkehrsbüro* (travel agencies) of the two main train stations.

the Inner City. Names that apply to it carry the suffix *-ring:* for example, Opernring, Schottenring, Burgring, Universitätsring (formerly Dr.-Karl-Lueger-Ring), Stubenring, Parkring, Schubertring, and Kärntner Ring.

Surrounding the Ringstrasse and the Inner City, in a more or less clockwise direction, are the inner suburban districts (2–9), which contain many hotels and restaurants popular for their close proximity to the city center. The outer districts (10–23) form another concentric ring of suburbs, comprising a variety of neighborhoods from industrial parks to rural villages.

Northeast of the Inner City, beyond the Danube Canal, is the **2nd District,** home to the Prater, the famous amusement park. East of the center, in the **3rd District,** you'll find the art treasures and baroque setting of the Belvedere Palace. West of the center is Schönbrunn Palace, located in the **13th District.**

GETTING AROUND   Whether you want to visit the Inner City's historic buildings or the outlying Vienna Woods, the *Wiener Linien* (Vienna Transit Authority) can take you there. This vast network of U-Bahns (subway), streetcars, and buses is safe, clean, and easy to use. Pick up a map that outlines their routes and those of the local trains (Schnellbahn, or S-Bahn).

For directions or information on tickets and passes visit one of the five **Vienna Public Transport Information Centers (***Informationdienst der Wiener Verkehrsbetriebe***)** at Opernpassage (an underground passageway next to the Wiener Staatsoper), Karlsplatz, Stephansplatz (near the cathedral), Westbahnhof, and Praterstern. These are open Monday to Friday 6:30am to 6:30pm. For information, call ✆ **01/790-9100.**

Vienna maintains a uniform fare that applies to all forms of public transport. A ticket for the bus, subway, or tram costs 2€ if you buy it in advance at one of the automated machines in U-Bahn stations, or at a *Tabac-Trafik* (a store or kiosk selling tobacco products and newspapers), a strip-card of 4 for 8€, or 2.20€ if you buy it onboard. Once a ticket has been stamped (validated) by machine or railway attendant, it's valid for one trip in one direction, anywhere in the city, including transfers.

BY U-BAHN (SUBWAY)   The U-Bahn is a fast way to get across town or reach the suburbs. It consists of five lines labeled **U1, U2, U3, U4,** and **U6** (there is no U5).

Karlsplatz, in the heart of the Inner City, is the most important underground station for visitors: the U4, U2, and U1 converge there. The U2 traces part of the Ring and then continues across the Danube, the U4 goes to Schönbrunn, and the U1 can take you from Stephansplatz to the Prater. The U3 also stops in Stephansplatz and connects to Westbahnhof. During the week the underground runs from 5am to shortly after midnight and on Friday and Saturday it runs all day and night.

BY TRAM   Riding the trams (*Strassenbahnen*) is not only a practical way to get around but also a great way to see the city. Tram stops are well marked. Each line bears a number or letter. Lines include the 18 (Hauptbahnhof to Westbahnhof), D (from Nussdorf hedging around part of the Ring before veering off to Hauptbahnhof), and 1 and 2 (each do a half circle of the Ring and continue into outer districts). The 1 takes you past the University and Rathaus on the north side of the Ring and the 2 takes you past the Stadtpark. Both leave the Ring at the opera and at Schwedenplatz. There is also a yellow Ring Tram that circles the Ring and costs 6€ for adults and 4€ for children. The 38 tram also takes you from Schottentor to the vineyards in Grinzing.

BY BUS   Buses with hybrid engines traverse Vienna in all directions. They are clean, comfortable, and operate daily, including at night. Tickets can be purchased from the driver on boarding. Night buses leave every 10 to 30 minutes from Schwedenplatz, fanning out across the city. It's usually not necessary to change lines more than once.

BY TAXI   Taxis are easy to find within the city, but be warned that fares can quickly add up. Taxi stands are marked by signs, or you can call ✆ **01/31300, 01/60160, 01/713-7196,** or **01/40100.** The basic fare is 2.50€, plus 1.20€ per kilometer. There are extra charges of 1€ for luggage. For night rides after 11pm, and for trips on Sunday and holidays, there is a surcharge of 2.50€. There is an additional charge of 2€ if you ordered the car by phone. The fare for trips between Vienna and the airport is 33€. The fare for trips outside the city should be agreed upon with the driver in advance, and a 10% tip is normal.

BY BIKE   Vienna has more than 1,000km (620 miles) of marked bicycle paths within the city limits. In the summer, many Viennese leave their cars in the garage and ride bikes. You can take bicycles on specially marked U-Bahn cars for free, but only from Monday to Friday, 9am to 3pm and 6:30pm to midnight, during which time you'll pay half the full ticket price to transport a bike. At weekends in July and August, bicycles are carried free from 9am to midnight.

There is a cheap way to cycle in Vienna, which is to use a **Citybike** (www.city bikewien.at). The kiosks are all over the city and the bikes can be rented with a Visa or Maestro card from which 1 euro is taken. After registering you can ride your city bike for free for the first hour of every rental and then simply return it to any other kiosk. The second hour costs 1€, the third 2€, and every further hour 4€. For a more comfortable or high-tech bike try rental stores around the Prater and along the banks of the Danube Canal, which is a much-loved bike route for most Viennese. One of the best of the many places for bike rentals is **Pedal Power,** Ausstellungsstrasse 3 (www.pedalpower.at; ✆ **01/729-7234**), which is open from March to October from 8am to 7pm. The Vienna Tourist Board can also supply a list of rental shops and more information about bike paths. Bike rentals begin at about 27€ per day.

BY CAR   When in Austria use a car only for excursions outside Vienna's city limits; don't try to drive around the city. Parking is a problem; the city is a maze of one-way streets; and the public transportation is too good to endure the hassle of driving. If you do venture out by car, information on road conditions is available in English (and French) on the radio station FM4 (103.8) and also 7 days a week from 6am to 8pm from the **Österreichischer Automobil, Motorrad- und Touringclub (ÖAMTC)**, Schubertring 1–3, A-1010 Vienna (☏ **01/711-990**). This auto club also maintains a 24-hour emergency road service number (☏ **120** or **0810/120-120**).

Major car-rental companies include **Avis**, Laaer Berg Strasse 43 (☏ **01/587-6241**); **Budget Rent-a-Car**, Laaer Berg Strasse 43 (☏ **01/601-870**); and **Hertz**, Kärntner Ring 17 (☏ **01/512-8677**).

[FastFACTS] VIENNA

Business Hours   Banks are open Monday to Friday from 8am to 3pm, and 5pm on Thursday; closed 12:30 to 1:30pm. **Government Offices** are generally open Monday to Friday from 8 or 9am to noon, 2pm or 3pm. **Other Offices** are open from 8 or 9am to 6pm, often closed noon or 12:30 for an hour. Regular **shopping** hours are Mon to Friday 9 or 10am to 6pm, sometimes later at Christmas; and Saturday 9am to 5pm. Some stores are open Sunday noon to 5pm.

Cellphones (Mobile Phones)   The Austrian cellphone network is state of the art: you even have reception in the U-Bahn. You'll need a SIM card—a small chip that gives you a local phone number in a regional network. If your cellphone is locked to your home provider, you can use an Austrian card from that provider, or get it unlocked at certain stores. Unfortunately, per-minute charges can be high in western Europe. Make sure you find out before your trip.

Driving & Traffic Regulations   In general, Austria's traffic regulations are consistent with those of other countries where you *drive on the right*. In Vienna, the speed limit is 50kmph (31 mph). Out of town, in areas like the Wienerwald, the limit is 130kmph (81 mph) on motorways and 100kmph (62 mph) on all other roads. Honking car horns is forbidden everywhere in the city, and there is no "right on red."

Embassies & Consulates   The main building of the Embassy of the **United States** is at Boltzmanngasse 16, 1090 (http://austria. usembassy.gov; ☏ **01/313-390**). However, the **U.S. Consulate** is at Parkring 12, 1010 (☏ **01/512-5835**). Lost passports, tourist emergencies, and other matters are handled by the consular section. Both are open Mon–Fri 8 to 11:30am. Emergency services 8:30am to 5pm.

The Embassy of **Canada,** Laurenzerberg 2 (☏ **01/531-383-000**), is open Mon–Fri 8:30am to 12:30pm and 1:30 to 3:30pm.

The Embassy of the **United Kingdom,** Jauresgasse 12, 1030 (http://uk inaustria.fco.gov.uk; ☏ **01/716-130**), is open Mon–Fri 9am to 1pm and 2 to 5pm.

The Embassy of **Australia,** Mattiellistrasse 2–4 (☏ **01/506-740**), is open Mon–Fri 8:30am to 4:30pm.

The nearest Embassy of **New Zealand** is located in Berlin, Germany, Friedrichstrasse 60 (☏ **030/206-210**), and is open Mon–Fri 9am to noon, however there is a consulate in Vienna at Salesianergasse 15/3, hours vary (☏ **01/318-8505**).

The Embassy of **Ireland,** Rotenturmstrasse 16–18 (☏ **01/715-4246**), is open Mon–Fri 8:30 to 11am and 1 to 4pm.

Emergencies   Call ☏ **122** to report a fire, ☏ **133** for the police, or ☏ **144** for an ambulance.

Holidays   Bank holidays in Austria are: January 1, January 6 (Epiphany), Easter Monday, May 1, Ascension Day, Whit Monday, Corpus Christi Day, August 15, October

26 (Nationalfeiertag), November 1, December 8, and December 25 and 26. Check locally when you arrive in Austria. Some of these holidays fall on different days each year.

Hospitals Two hospitals with an emergency service are the **Allgemeines Krankenhaus Wien,** Währinger Gürtel 18–20, 1090, 1020 (www.akhwien.at; ✆ **01/404-000;** U-Bahn: U6 Michaelbeuern/Allgemeines Krankenhaus); and the **Krankenhaus der Barmherzigen Brüder,** Johannes von Gott Platz 1 (www.barmherzigebrueder.at; ✆ **01/2112-11100;** U-Bahn: Nestroyplatz, Tram: 2 Karmeliterplatz). The **Barmherzigen Brüder** (Merciful Brothers) is run by a Catholic order and will accept all emergency cases without insurance at no charge.

Internet Access Many traditional coffeehouses now offer Wi-Fi: Some appealing choices include **Café Central,** Herrengasse 14 (www.palaisevents.at/cafecentral; ✆ **01/5333-76324**), open Mon–Sat 7:30am to 10pm, Sun and holidays 10am to 10pm; **Café Sperl,** Gumpendorferstrasse 11 (www.cafesperl.at; ✆ **01/586-4158**), open Mon–Sat 7am to 11pm, Sun 11am to 8pm; **Café Stein,** Währingerstrasse 6–8 (www.cafe-stein.com; ✆ **01/3197-2419**), open Mon–Sat 7am to 1am, Sun 9am to 1am.

Language Austrians speak German, but English is taught in schools from the early grades and almost anyone providing tourist services will be reasonably fluent. Cab drivers, store clerks, and waiters are another story, however.

Mail Post offices (*das Postamt, die Post*) in Vienna are easy to spot with the yellow signs of "Post" or "PSK." The postal system in Austria is, for the most part, efficient and speedy. You can buy stamps at a post office or from the hundreds of news and tobacco kiosks, designated locally as *Tabac-Trafik*. Mailboxes are painted yellow. Newer ones usually have the golden trumpet of the Austrian Postal Service. At the **Central Post Office** (Fleischmarkt 19; ✆ **0577/677-1010**) you can post letters and packages all weekend: Mon–Fri 7am–10pm, Sat, Sun 9am–10pm. All over the city branches are open Mon–Fri 8am–6pm.

Pharmacies Called *Apotheke*, they're open Mon–Fri 8am to noon and 2 to 6pm and Sat 8am to noon. Each *Apotheke* posts in its window a list of locations that take turns staying open at night and on Sunday.

Safety Austria has a low crime rate; the streets are safe at night and violent crime is rare. However, visitors can become targets of pickpockets who operate where tourists gather.

Smoking A smoking ban came into effect throughout Austria on January 1, 2009. Still, this being Austria, the ban has many exceptions. Bars and restaurants are allowed to divide the space. And bars and restaurants under 60 sq. m (645 sq. ft.) can decide to be either smoking or nonsmoking. In general, Vienna is one of the last smoking havens in Europe, so don't be surprised that most bars and clubs are smoker-friendly.

Telephone The **country code** for Austria is **43.** Dial **00 43** from the U.K. and continental Europe, and **011 43** from the U.S. The **city code** for Vienna is **1;** use this code when you're calling from outside Austria. If you're within Austria, use **01** before the local number.

Tipping A service charge of 10% to 15% is often included on hotel bills, but it's a good policy to leave 2€ per day for your hotel maid. Railroad station, airport, and hotel porters get 1.50€ per piece of luggage, plus a 1€ tip. When paying restaurant bills, Austrians usually round up by approximately 10% and to the nearest euro.

Toilets Public toilets (*Toiletten* (twa-*lett*-en)) or "WC" (*vay tsay*) in Vienna (not "restrooms") are marked *Herren* (men) or *Damen* (women) and kept clean by a person who sits at the entrance. He or she has a saucer in which you're supposed to deposit your donation, usually 1€.

Water Tap water in Vienna, piped in from mountain springs, is not only safe to drink, it also tastes good and is automatically served with coffee and red wine. Many people also drink bottled mineral water, generally called *Mineralwasser*.

Exploring Vienna

The Inner City (Innere Stadt) is the tangle of streets from which Vienna grew in the Middle Ages. Much of your exploration will be confined to this area, encircled by the boulevards of "The Ring" and the Danube Canal. The main street of the Inner City is **Kärntnerstrasse,** most of which is a pedestrian mall. The heart of Vienna is **Stephansplatz,** the square on which St. Stephan's Cathedral sits.

THE HOFBURG PALACE COMPLEX ★★★

Once the winter palace of the Habsburgs, the vast and impressive **Hofburg** sits in the heart of Vienna. To reach it (you can hardly miss it), head up Kohlmarkt to Michaelerplatz 1, Burgring, where you'll stumble across two enormous fountains embellished with statuary. You can also take the U-Bahn to Stephansplatz, Herrengasse, or Mariahilferstrasse, or trams no. 1, 2, D, or J to Burgring.

This complex of imperial edifices, the first of which was constructed in 1279, grew with the empire; and today the palace is virtually a city within a city. The earliest parts surround the **Swiss Court,** a courtyard named for the Swiss mercenaries who performed guard duty here. The Hofburg's styles, which are not always harmonious, result from each emperor's opting to add to or take away some of the work done by his predecessors. Called simply *die Burg,* or "the Palace," by the Viennese, the Hofburg withstood three major sieges and a great fire. Of its more than 2,600 rooms, some two dozen are open to the public.

Albertina ★ ART MUSEUM   This Hofburg museum, named for a son-in-law of Maria Theresa, houses one of the world's great art collections, spanning 6 centuries. The museum underwent an extensive renovation at the beginning of the century that restored the magnificent statuary, fountain, and facade and opened three major exhibition spaces that have put the Albertina on the map as one of the most exciting museums in Europe. Its permanent collection includes Dürer's *Hare* and *Clasped Hands,* which the Albertina has owned for centuries, as well as some 60,000 drawings and one million prints; the best known include Ruben's studies of children. In addition, the museum owns masterpieces by Schiele, Cézanne, Klimt, Kokoschka, Picasso, and Rauschenberg. The collection was badly threatened in 2008 in the unprecedented flooding that submerged towns all along the Danube, when its high-security depot, thought to be waterproof, began leaking. Some 950,000 works, including Dürer's *Rabbit,* were evacuated until the damage could be repaired and the site dried out. The Albertina is also considered one of the most beautiful classical palaces in the world, its state apartments among the most admired examples of classical architecture.

Albertinaplatz 1. www.albertina.at. ℂ **01/534-830.** Admission 9.50€ adults, 8€ seniors, 7€ students, free for under-19s. Thurs–Tues 10am–6pm; Wed 10am–9pm.

Augustinerkirche (Church of the Augustinians) ★ CHURCH   This 14th-century church was built within the Hofburg complex to serve as the parish church for the imperial court. In the latter part of the 18th century, it was stripped of its baroque embellishments and returned to its original Gothic appearance. Enter the **Chapel of St. George,** dating from 1337, from the right aisle. The **Tomb of Maria Christina ★**, the favorite daughter of Maria Theresa, is housed in the main nave near the rear entrance; but there's no body in it. (The princess was actually buried in the Imperial Crypt, described later in this section.) This richly ornamented empty tomb is one of Canova's masterpieces. A small room in the **Loreto Chapel** is filled with urns containing the hearts of the imperial Habsburg family. The urns are visible through a window in an iron door. The Chapel of St. George and the Loreto Chapel are open to the public by prearranged guided tour.

The Augustinerkirche was also where Maria Theresa married her beloved François of Lorraine in 1736, with whom she had 16 children. Other royal weddings included Marie Antoinette to Louis XVI of France in 1770, Marie-Louise of Austria to Louis Napoleon in 1810 (by proxy—he didn't show up), and Franz Joseph to Elisabeth of Bavaria in 1854.

The best time to visit the church is on Sunday at 11am, when a high Mass features the works of Mozart, Haydn, Schubert, Gounod, Kodaly, or Faure, with full choir and orchestra.

Augustinerstrasse 3. ✆ **01/533-7099.** Free admission. Daily 6:30am–6pm. U-Bahn: Stephansplatz.

Burgkapelle PERFORMING ARTS VENUE   Construction of this Gothic chapel began in 1447 during the reign of Emperor Frederick III, but it was later massively renovated. Today, the Burgkapelle hosts the **Hofburgkapelle ★★**, an ensemble of the Vienna Boys' Choir and members of the Vienna State Opera chorus and orchestra, which performs works by classical and modern composers. Send a written application to reserve seats at least 8 weeks in advance. Write to **Verwaltung der Hofmusikkapelle,** Hofburg, A-1010 Vienna. If you failed to reserve in advance, you might be lucky enough to secure tickets from a block sold at the Burgkapelle box office every Friday from 11am to 1pm or 3 to 5pm.

Hofburg (entrance on Schweizerhof). ✆ **01/533-9927.** Mass: Seats and concerts 5€–29€; standing room free. Masses (performances) held only Jan–June and mid-Sept to Dec, Sun and holidays 9:15am. Concerts held May–June and Sept–Oct Fri 4pm.

Kaiserappartements (Imperial Apartments) ★★ HISTORIC HOME These were the imperial family residence of Franz Joseph and Elisabeth and their children, reached through the rotunda of Michaelerplatz. Here you can see not only their reception, dining, and living rooms, but also their bedrooms and private studies, the nursery, and even bathrooms. In the reception rooms, wall panels are filled with huge oil paintings of life at court; the more private rooms, however, are covered with deep red moiré, which, while beautiful, also helped insulate against the cold. The court tableware and silver is of breathtaking opulence, reflecting the pomp of a court whose lands included two-thirds of all Europe. You'll see the narrow "iron bed" of Franz Joseph, who claimed he slept like his own soldiers, and the exercise equipment the empress used to stay fit. A separate "Sissi Museum" has six rooms devoted to the life and complex personality of this tragic empress.

The remaining imperial quarters, once occupied by the Empress Maria Theresa, are now used by the president of Austria and are not open to the public. However, the **Imperial Silver and Porcelain Collection** from the Habsburg household of the 18th and 19th centuries, also on view downstairs, provides a window into the court etiquette of Maria Theresa's time.

Michaelerplatz 1 (inside the Ring, about a 7-min. walk from Stephansplatz; entrance via the Kaisertor in the Inneren Burghof). www.hofburg-wien.at. ✆ **01/533-7570.** Admission 9.90€ adults, 8.90€ students and seniors, 5.90€ children 6–18, free for children 5 and under. Open daily, Sept–Jun 9am–5.30pm, Jul–Aug 9am–6pm. U-Bahn: U1 or U3 to Stephansplatz. Tram: 1, 2 (to Burgring).

Neue Burg MUSEUM   The most recent addition to the Hofburg complex is the Neue Hofburg. Construction was started in 1881 and continued through 1913. The palace was the residence of Archduke Franz Ferdinand, the nephew and heir

In 1498, the emperor Maximilian I decreed that 12 boys should be included among the official court musicians. Over the next 500 years, this group evolved into the world-renowned Vienna Boys' Choir (*Wiener Sängerknaben*). Today made up of three choirs, the boys perform in Vienna at various venues, including the Staatsoper, the Volksoper, and Schönbrunn Palace. The choir also performs at Sunday and Christmas Masses with the Hofmusikkapelle (Court Musicians) at the Burgkapelle (see above review for details). The choir's boarding school is at Augartenpalais, Obere Augartenstrasse. For more information on where they are performing and how to get tickets, go to the choir's website (**www.wsk.at**).

apparent of Franz Joseph, whose assassination at Sarajevo by Serbian nationalists set off the chain of events that led to World War I.

The arms and armor collection, said to be second only to the Metropolitan Museum in New York, is in the **Hofjagd und Rüstkammer ★★**. On display are crossbows, swords, helmets, pistols, and other armor, mostly of Habsburg emperors and princes, some disarmingly small. Some of the items, such as scimitars, were captured from the Turks as they fled their unsuccessful siege.

The **Sammlung alter Musikinstrumente ★** is devoted to old instruments, mainly from the 17th and 18th centuries, but some as early as the 16th century. Some of the pianos and harpsichords were played by Brahms, Schubert, Mahler, Beethoven, and Austrian emperors several of whom, like Joseph II, were also devoted musicians.

In the **Ephesos-Museum (Museum of Ephesian Sculpture),** with an entrance behind the Prince Eugene monument, you'll see high-quality finds from Ephesus in Turkey and the Greek island of Samothrace. Here the prize is the **Parthian monument,** the most important relief frieze from Roman times ever found in Asia Minor. It was erected to celebrate Rome's victory in the Parthian wars (A.D. 161–65).

Visit the **Museum für Völkerkunde (Museum of Ethnology)** for no other reason than to see the only original Aztec feather headdress in the world. Also on display are Benin bronzes, Cook's collections of Polynesian art, and Indonesian, African, Eskimo, and pre-Columbian exhibits.

1 Heldenplatz. www.khm.at. ℂ **01/525-240.** Admission 12€ adults, 9€ students and seniors, under-19s free. Sammlung alter Musikinstrumente and Ephesos-Museum: Wed–Sun 10am–6pm. Museum für Völkerkunde: Wed–Mon 10am–6pm. Admission 8€ adults, 6€ students and seniors, under-19s free.

Österreichische Nationalbibliothek (Austrian National Library)

LIBRARY   The royal library of the Habsburgs dates from the 14th century; and the library building, developed on the premises of the court from 1723 on, is still expanding to the Neue Hofburg. The **Great Hall ★★** of the present-day library was ordered by Karl VI and designed by those masters of the baroque, the Fischer von Erlachs, father and son. The complete collection of Prince Eugene of Savoy includes manuscripts, rare autographs, globes, maps, and more. This is among the finest libraries in the world.

Josefsplatz 1. www.onb.ac.at. © **01/53410.** Admission 7€ adults, 4.50€ students and seniors, 12€ family (2 adults and children under 19). Tues–Wed, Fri–Sun 10am–6pm, Thurs 10am–9pm.

Schatzkammer (Imperial Treasury) ★★★ MUSEUM   Combining the Imperial Profane and the Sacerdotal Treasuries, this is the greatest treasury in the world. One part displays the crown jewels and an assortment of imperial riches; the other exhibits ecclesiastical treasures. You'll see the imperial crown, dating from 962, studded with emeralds, sapphires, diamonds, and rubies, as well as a later one worn by the Habsburg rulers from 1804 to the fall of the empire. You'll also see the saber of Charlemagne and the holy lance, as well as the Burgundian Treasure seized in the 15th century, rich investments, oil paintings, gems, and robes.

Hofburg, Schweizerhof. © **01/525-240.** Admission 12€ adults, free for students and children 18 and under. Wed–Mon 10am–6pm.

Spanische Hopfreitschule (Spanish Riding School) ★ SPORTS VENUE The Spanish Riding School is in the crystal-chandeliered white ballroom in an 18th-century building of the Hofburg complex. These are the world's most famous, classically styled equine performers. Reservations for performances must be made in advance, as early as possible. Order your tickets for the Sunday and Wednesday shows by writing to **Spanische Reitschule,** Hofburg, A-1010 Vienna (fax 01/533-903-240), through a travel agency in Vienna (tickets for Saturday shows can be ordered only through a travel agency), or online at the website listed below. Tickets for training sessions with no advance reservations can be purchased at the entrance.

Michaelerplatz 1, Hofburg. www.srs.at. © **01/533-9032.** Regular performances 38€–130€ seats, 20€–25€ standing room; children 2 and under not admitted to performances. Morning exercise with music 12€ adults, 9€ seniors, 6€ children 7 and over, free for children 6 and under. Training session with music and guided tour 19€ adults, 16€ seniors, 12€ children 7 and over, free for children 6 and under. Regular shows Mar–June and Sept–mid-Dec, most Sun at 11am and some Fri at 6pm. Classical dressage with music performances Apr–June and Sept, most Sun at 11am. Training sessions vary, but are held Tues–Sat 10–11am. Call ahead for open dates. U-Bahn: Stephansplatz.

THE MUSEUMSQUARTIER COMPLEX ★★★

Opened in 2001, the giant modern art complex of the **MuseumsQuartier** (www. mqw.at; U-Bahn: MuseumsQuartier) has tipped the city's cultural center of gravity away from Habsburgian pomp into the new millennium.

Kunsthalle Wien ★ ART MUSEUM   This is a showcase for cutting-edge contemporary and classic modern art. You'll find works by everyone from Picasso, Joán Miró, and Jackson Pollock to Paul Klee, Andy Warhol, and Yoko Ono. From expressionism to cubism, exhibits reveal the major movements in contemporary art since the mid-20th century. Exploring the five floors takes 1 to 2 hours, depending on what interests you.

Museumsplatz 1. www.kunsthallewien.at. © **01/521-8933.** Admission 11.50€ adults, 4.60€ students, 2€ children aged 10–18, children under 10 free. Mon–Wed and Fri–Sun 10am–7pm; Thurs 10am–9pm.

Leopold Museum ★★ ART MUSEUM   This extensive collection of Austrian art includes the world's largest treasure-trove of the works of Egon Schiele (1890–1918), who now takes his place alongside van Gogh and Modigliani in the ranks of great doomed artists, dying before he was 28 years old. The selection at the Leopold includes more than 2,500 drawings and watercolors and 330 oil canvases. Other Austrian modernist masters on display include Oskar Kokoschka, the great Gustav Klimt, Anton Romaki, and Richard Gerstl. Major statements in Arts and Crafts from the late 19th and 20th centuries include works by Josef Hoffmann, Kolo Moser, Adolf Loos, and Franz Hagenauer.

Museumsplatz 1. www.leopoldmuseum.org. *©* **01/525-700.** Admission 10€ adults, 7.50€ seniors, 6.50€ students and children 8 and over. Mon–Wed and Fri–Sun 10am–6pm; Thurs 10am–9pm.

MUMOK (Museum of Modern Art Ludwig Foundation) ★ ART MUSEUM
One of the most outstanding collections of contemporary art in central Europe, the MUMOK exhibits American pop art, mixed with continental movements such as hyperrealism of the 1960s and 1970s. There are five levels, three above ground, two below.

Museumsplatz 1. www.mumok.at. *©* **01/525-000.** 9€ adults, 7.20€ seniors. Free admission for those under 19 and students up to 27. Mon–Wed and Fri–Sun 10am–6pm; Thurs 10am–9pm.

OTHER ATTRACTIONS IN THE INNER DISTRICTS

Belvedere ★★ PALACE/ART MUSEUM Southeast of Karlsplatz, the **Öster-reichische Galerie Belvedere** sits on a slope above Vienna. The approach to the palace is memorable—through a long garden with a huge circular pond that reflects the sky and the looming palace buildings. Designed by Johann Lukas von Hildebrandt, the last major Austrian baroque architect, the Belvedere was built as a summer home for Prince Eugene of Savoy. It consists of two palatial buildings made up of a series of interlocking cubes. Two great, flowing staircases dominate the interior. The **Gold Salon** in Lower Belvedere is one of the most beautiful rooms in the palace. A regal French-style garden lies between the two buildings.

Unteres Belvedere (**Lower Belvedere**), Rennweg 6A, was constructed from 1714 to 1716. **Oberes Belvedere (Upper Belvedere)** was started in 1721 and completed in 1723. Anton Bruckner, the composer, lived in one of the buildings until his death in 1896. The palace was the residence of Archduke Franz Ferdinand, whose assassination sparked World War I. In May 1955, the Allied powers signed the peace treaty recognizing Austria as a sovereign state in Upper Belvedere. The treaty is on display in a large salon decorated in red marble.

Lower Belvedere houses the **Barockmuseum (Museum of Baroque Art).** Displayed here are the original sculptures from the Neuer Markt fountain (replaced now by copies), the work of Georg Raphael Donner, who died in 1741. During his life, Donner dominated the development of Austrian sculpture. The fountain's four figures represent the major tributaries of the Danube. Works by Franz Anton Maulbertsch, an 18th-century painter, are also exhibited here. Maulbertsch, strongly influenced by Tiepolo, was the greatest and most original Austrian painter of his day. He was best known for his iridescent colors and flowing brushwork.

Domkirche St. Stephan (St. Stephan's Cathedral) ★★★ CATHEDRAL
The cathedral was founded in the 12th century in what was the town's center. Stephansdom was virtually destroyed in a 1258 fire, and in the early 14th century the ruins of the Romanesque basilica gave way to a Gothic building. It suffered terribly in the Turkish siege of 1683 and from the Russian bombardments of 1945. Reopened in 1948, the cathedral is today one of the greatest Gothic structures in Europe, rich in woodcarvings, altars, sculptures, and paintings. The chief treasure of the cathedral is the carved, wooden **Wiener Neustadt altarpiece** ★★ that dates from 1447. The steeple, rising some 135m (443 ft.), has come to symbolize the very spirit of Vienna. You can climb the 343-step South Tower, which dominates the Viennese skyline and offers a view of the Vienna Woods. Called Alter Steffl (Old Steve), the tower with its needle-like spire was built between 1350 and 1433. The North Tower (Nordturm),

reached by elevator, was never finished, but was crowned in the Renaissance style in 1579. From here you get a panoramic sweep of the city and the Danube.

Stephansplatz 3. www.stephanskirche.at. ✆ **01/5155-23526.** Cathedral: free admission; tour of catacombs 4.50€ adults, 1.50€ children 14 and under. Guided tour of cathedral: 4.50€ adults, 1.50€ children 14 and under. North Tower: 4.50€ adults, 1.50€ children 14 and under. South Tower: 4.50€ adults, 2.50€ students, 1.50€ children 14 and under. Evening tours June–Sept, including tour of the roof, 10€ adults, 4€ children 14 and under. Cathedral daily 6am–10pm except times of service. Tour of catacombs Mon–Sat 10, 11, and 11:30am, 12:30, 1:30, 2, 2:30, 3:30, 4, and 4:30pm; Sun 2, 2:30, 3, 3:30, 4, and 4:30pm. Guided tour of cathedral Mon–Sat 9am and 1pm; Sun 3pm. Special evening tour Sat 7pm (June–Sept). North Tower Oct–Mar daily 8am–5pm; Apr–Sept daily 6am–10pm. South Tower daily 6am–10pm. U-Bahn: Stephansplatz. Bus: 1A, 2A, or 3A.

Gemäldegalerie der Akademie der Bildenden Künste (Painting Gallery of the Academy of Fine Arts) ★ ART MUSEUM

This gallery is home to the *Last Judgment* ★★ triptych by Hieronymus Bosch. In this masterpiece, the artist conjured up all the demons of hell for a terrifying view of the suffering and sins that humankind must endure. You'll also be able to view many Dutch and Flemish paintings, some from as far back as the 15th century, although the academy is noted for its 17th-century art. The gallery boasts works by Van Dyck, Rembrandt, and a host of others. There are several works by Lucas Cranach the Elder, the most outstanding being his *Lucretia* from 1532. Some say it's as enigmatic as *Mona Lisa*. Rubens is represented here by more than a dozen oil sketches. You can see Rembrandt's *Portrait of a Woman* and Guardi's scenes from 18th-century Venice.

Schillerplatz 3. www.akademiegalerie.at. ✆ **01/5881-62222.** Admission 8€ adults, 5€ students and seniors, under-19s free. Tues–Sun 10am–6pm. U-Bahn: Karlsplatz.

Haus der Musik ★ MUSEUM

This full-scale museum devoted to music is both hands-on and high-tech. Wandering the building's halls and niches, you encounter reminders of the great composers who have lived in Vienna—not only Mozart, but also Beethoven, Schubert, Brahms, and others. In the rooms, you can listen to your favorite renditions of their works or explore memorabilia. You can even take to the podium and conduct the Vienna Philharmonic that responds to your baton. A memorial, "Exodus," pays tribute to the Viennese musicians driven into exile or murdered by the Nazis. At the Musicantino Restaurant on the top floor, enjoy a panoramic view of the city and some good food. There's also a coffeehouse near the entrance.

Seilerstätte 30. www.hdm.at. ✆ **01/5134-850.** Admission 10€ adults, 8.50€ students and seniors, 5.50€ children aged 3–12, free for children under 3. Open daily 10am–10pm. U-Bahn: Karlsplatz.

Kunsthistorisches Museum (Museum of Art History) ★★★ ART MUSEUM

Across from the Hofburg, this huge building houses the fabulous art collections gathered by the Habsburgs. A highlight is the display of ancient Egyptian and Greek art. The museum also has works by many of the greatest European masters, such as Velázquez, Titian, Brueghel the Elder, Van Dyck, Ruben, Rembrandt, and Dürer.

Maria-Theresien-Platz, Burgring 5. www.khm.at. ✆ **01/5252-44025.** Admission 12€ adults, free for ages 19 and under. Tues, Wed, Fri–Sun 10am–6pm; Thurs 10am–9pm. U-Bahn: Mariahilferstrasse. Tram: 1, 2, or D.

Liechtenstein Museum ★★★ ART MUSEUM

The Liechtenstein's princely collections are on display in a renovated family palace in the 9th District for the first time. Frans Hals and Van Dyck, Raphael, Rubens, and Rembrandt, as well as Austrian greats like Friedrich Amerling and Waldmüller, are displayed in the neoclassical Garden Palace, some 1,700 works in all. Of spectacular beauty is the splendid

Hercules Hall ★, the largest secular baroque room in Vienna. Frescoes were painted between 1704 and 1708 by Andrea Pozzo. There are two restaurants, both with gardens.

Liechtenstein Garden Palace, Fürstengasse 1. www.liechtensteinmuseum.at. © **01/3195-7670.** Admission 10€ adults, 5€ students and seniors, under-19s free. Fri–Tues 10am–5pm. U-Bahn: Rossauer Lände. Tram: D to Bauernfeldplatz.

Attractions outside the Inner City

Schönbrunn Palace ★★★ PALACE   The 1,441-room Schönbrunn Palace was designed for the Habsburgs by those masters of the baroque, the von Erlachs. It was built between 1696 and 1712 at the request of Emperor Leopold I for his son Joseph I. Leopold envisioned a palace whose grandeur would surpass that of Versailles. However, Austria's treasury was drained by the cost of wars, and the original plans were never carried out.

Today Schönbrunn looks much as the Empress Maria Theresa conceived it, with delicate rococo touches designed for her by Austrian Nikolaus Pacassi. During her 40-year reign, the palace was the scene of great ceremonial balls, lavish banquets, and fabulous receptions. At the age of 6, Mozart performed in the Hall of Mirrors, and the empress held secret meetings with her chancellor, Prince Kaunitz, in the round Chinese Room. The last of the Habsburg rulers, Karl I, renounced his participation in affairs of state here on November 11, 1918—not quite an abdication, but tantamount to one. Allied bombs damaged the palace during World War II, but restoration has covered the scars.

The **Gloriette ★★**, a marble summerhouse topped by a stone canopy with an imperial eagle, embellishes the palace's **Imperial Gardens ★**. The so-called Roman Ruins (a collection of marble statues and fountains) date from the late 18th century, when it was fashionable to simulate the ravaged grandeur of Rome, and were designed by Adria van Steckhoven. It is open to visitors until sunset daily.

The **State Apartments ★★★** are the most stunning display in the palace. Much of the interior ornamentation is in the rococo style, with red, white, and 23½-karat gold predominating. Of the 40 open rooms, the **Room of Millions,** with Indian and Persian miniatures, is particularly fascinating. English-language guided tours start every half-hour beginning at 9:30am. You should tip the guide 1€.

Also in the grounds is the lovely baroque **Schlosstheater (Palace Theater; © 01/876-4272),** which stages summer performances. The **Wagenburg ★ (Carriage Museum © 01/877-3244)** shows imperial coaches from four centuries.

The **Schloss Schönbrunn Experience** is a 60- to 90-minute children's tour led by English-speaking guides through rooms with hands-on displays.

Admission includes a tour (the Grand Tour) of 40 state rooms with audio guide.

Schönbrunner Schlossstrasse. www.schoenbrunn.at. © **01/8111-3239.** Admission 9.50€ adults, 8.50€ students and seniors, 6.50€ children 6–18, free for children under 6; Wagenburg 6€ adults, 4€ seniors and students, under-19s free. Nov–March daily 10am–4pm, Apr–Oct daily 9am–6pm. Schloss Schönbrunn Experience 4.90€ children (3–18). Apr–June and Sept–Oct daily 8:30am–5pm; July–Aug daily 8:30am–6pm; Nov–Mar daily 8:30am–4:30pm. U-Bahn: Schönbrunn.

ORGANIZED TOURS

Wiener Rundfahrten (Vienna Sightseeing Tours), Starhemberggasse 25 (www.viennasightseeingtours.com; © 01/7124-6830), offers the best tours, including a 1-day motor-coach excursion to Budapest costing 99€ per person. The historical city tour costs 36€ for adults and is free for children 12 and under. It's ideal for visitors who are pressed for time and yet want to be shown the major (and most frequently photographed) monuments of Vienna. Tours leave the Staatsoper daily at 9:45 and 10:30am and 2:45pm. The tour lasts 3½ hours (U-Bahn: Karlsplatz).

Vienna Woods–Mayerling, another popular excursion, leaves from the Staatsoper and takes you to the towns of Perchtoldsdorf and Mödling, and to the Abbey of Heiligenkreuz, a center of Christian culture since medieval times. The approximately 4-hour tour also takes you for a short walk through Baden, the spa that was once a favorite summer resort of the aristocracy. Tours cost 43€ for adults and 15€ for children aged 10 to 16.

Information and booking for these tours can be obtained either through Vienna Sightseeing Tours (see above) or through its affiliate, **Elite Tours,** Operngasse 4 (www.elitetours.at; ✆ **01/513-2225**).

Where to Eat
VERY EXPENSIVE

Fabios ★★ INTERNATIONAL/MEDITERRANEAN This is the trendiest and most sought-after restaurant in Vienna, with considerable jockeying among the city's glitterati. The creation of the talented Fabio Giacobello, this space is bigger inside than you might think from the street. The menu might include warm octopus served on a bed of cold gazpacho cream sauce, and roasted rack of lamb with marinated tomatoes served with deep-fried polenta *gnocchetti*. The wine bar is also a top nightlife option. Enough drama unfolds around its rectangular surface to keep a few tabloid writers busy, and someone famous in media and politics always seems to be popping up for air and a drink or two.

Tuchlauben 6. www.fabios.at. ✆ **01/532-2222.** Reservations recommended. Main courses 29€–35€. AE, MC, V. Mon–Sat 10am–1am. U-Bahn: Stephansplatz.

Kervansaray und Hummer Bar ★★ SEAFOOD Here you'll sense the historic link between the Habsburgs and the 19th-century Ottoman Empire. In the restaurant, polite waiters announce a changing array of daily specials and serve tempting salads from an *hors d'oeuvre* table. Upstairs, guests enjoy the bounties of the sea at the Lobster Bar. A meal often begins with a champagne cocktail, followed by a lobster and salmon caviar cocktail. The menu also includes filet mignon with Roquefort sauce, but it is mostly seafood, including grilled filet of sole with fresh asparagus, Norwegian salmon with a horseradish-and-champagne sauce, and, of course, lobster. There's lots of shellfish, but be prepared to pay for your indulgence.

Mahlerstrasse 9. www.hummerbar.at. ✆ **01/512-8843.** Reservations recommended. Main courses 25€–50€. AE, DC, MC, V. Restaurant Mon–Sat noon–midnight. U-Bahn: Karlsplatz. Tram: 1 or 2. Bus: 3A.

Steirereck ★★★ VIENNESE/AUSTRIAN/INTERNATIONAL *Steirereck* means "corner of Styria," which is exactly what Heinz and Margarethe Reitbauer have created in the rustic decor of this intimate restaurant, serving both traditional Viennese dishes and "New Austrian" selections. You might begin with a caviar-semolina dumpling, roasted turbot with fennel (served as an appetizer), or the most elegant and expensive item of all, goose liver Steirereck. The restaurant is popular with aftertheater diners; the large wine cellar holds some 35,000 bottles. In addition to the fabled restaurant, there is also Ess. Bar, plus a Light-Restaurant for gourmet-level food during the day, and Meierei, specializing in dairy products, with 150 kinds of cheese.

Steirereck im Stadtpark. http://steirereck.at. ✆ **01/713-3168.** Reservations required. Main courses 24€–44€; 5-course fixed-price dinner 95€. AE, DC, MC, V. Steirereck-Restaurant Mon–Fri from 7pm; Light-Restaurant Mon–Fri 11am–5pm; Meierei Mon–Fri 2pm–midnight; Ess. Bar 5pm–midnight. Closed holidays. U-Bahn: Stadtpark.

EXPENSIVE

Bauer ★★ AUSTRIAN/CONTINENTAL   It's upscale, it's *gemütlich* (warm and welcoming), and it's on the shortlist of restaurants that concierges at some of Vienna's best hotels recommend to guests. You'll find it on a narrow street a few blocks northeast of the cathedral, beneath 500-year-old ceiling vaults, now painted a dark shade of pink, that evoke a venue that's more folksy and rustic than this sophisticated restaurant really is. Expect glamorous food. The finest examples include carpaccio of beef with mustard sauce; sweetbreads with vanilla sauce and braised chicory; and stuffed squid with lemon sauce and pepper cream sauce.

Sonnenfelsgasse 17. ✆ **01/512-9871.** Reservations recommended. Main courses 26€–32€; set menu 62€ 4 courses. AE, DC, MC, V. Mon 6–11pm, Tues–Fri noon–2pm and 6–11pm. Closed Sat and Sun, 1 week at Easter, and mid-July to mid-Aug. U-Bahn: Schwedenplatz, or Stubentor.

Do & Co. ★ INTERNATIONAL   On the seventh floor of a radically angular hypermodern building (the also-recommended hotel), across from St. Stephan's, this restaurant is in demand. It's difficult to overstate its fame within the complicated but steely hierarchy of fine and/or stylish Viennese dining. If you didn't reserve, or your table isn't ready, consider a pre-dinner cocktail at the stylish Onyx Bar on the building's sixth floor, then climb a circular staircase to the seventh-floor dining room. Here, *if you've reserved,* you'll be presented with a slightly claustrophobic table and a confusingly diverse set of menu items. Dishes are divided into categories that include "Tastes of the World" (Tataki of Atlantic tuna, or sushi), "Catch of the Day" (potpourri of scallops), "Beef & Co." (French breast of duck with green beans and creamy kumquat polenta), "Kebab, Wok & Curries" (dishes inspired by Asia, especially Thailand), and "Austrian Classics" (deep-fried monkfish with potato salad).

In the Haas Haus, Stephansplatz 12. www.doco.com. ✆ **01/535-3939.** Reservations required. Main courses 18€–26€. AE, DC, MC, V. Daily noon–3pm and 6–11:45pm. U-Bahn: Stephansplatz.

König von Ungarn (King of Hungary) ★ VIENNESE/INTERNATIONAL   This beautifully decorated restaurant is inside the famous hotel of the same name. The well-prepared food is traditional—not at all experimental. You dine under a vaulted ceiling in an atmosphere of crystal, chandeliers, antiques, and marble columns. If you're in doubt about what to order, try the Tafelspitz. Other seasonal choices include a ragout of seafood with fresh mushrooms, tournedos of beef with a mustard-and-horseradish sauce, and appetizers such as scampi in caviar sauce. The service is superb.

Schulerstrasse 10. www.kvu.at. ✆ **01/515-840.** Reservations recommended. Main courses 13€–20€; set menus 29€–40€. AE, DC, MC, V. Daily 6–10:30pm. U-Bahn: Stephansplatz. Bus: 1A.

Plachutta ★ VIENNESE   Few restaurants have built such a fetish around one dish as Plachutta has done with *Tafelspitz,* offering 10 variations of the boiled beef dish, which was adored by Emperor Franz Josef throughout his prolonged reign. The differences between the versions are a function of the cut of beef you request. We recommend *Schulterscherzel* (shoulder of beef) and *Beinfleisch* (shank of beef), but if you're in doubt, the waiters are knowledgeable about one of the most oft-debated subjects in Viennese cuisine. Hash brown potatoes, chives, and an appealing mixture of horseradish and chopped apples accompany each order. Other Viennese staples such as goulash soup, calf's liver, and braised pork with cabbage are also available.

Wollzeile 38. www.plachutta.at. © **01/512-1577.** Reservations recommended. Main courses 18€–26€. DC, MC, V. Daily 11:30am–midnight. U-Bahn: Stubentor.

Weibels Wirtshaus ★ 🛏 AUSTRIAN   Don't be fooled by the unpretentious feel to this place, which at first glance might look like a simple tavern. Food is considerably above what the *Wirtshaus* (tavern) appellation implies, and the clientele is a lot more upscale than the usual wurst-with-potatoes-and-beer crowd. There are only about 40 seats within this paneled restaurant, in a building some 400 years old. In good weather, there are further seats in the garden. The wine list includes more than 250 varieties of Austrian wine, and the menu items like pumpkin-seed soup, sliced breast of duck with lentils, well-prepared schnitzels of veal and chicken, and a superb saddle of lamb with polenta and spinach.

Kumpfgasse 2. www.weibel.at. © **01/512-3986.** Reservations recommended. Main courses 14€–19€; set menu 36€. AE, MC, V. Daily 11:30am–midnight. U-Bahn: Stephansplatz.

MODERATE

Griechenbeisl ★ AUSTRIAN   Astonishingly, after 500 years, the Griechenbeisl established in 1450, is still one of the city's leading restaurants. There's a maze of dining areas on three different floors, with low-vaulted ceilings, smoky paneling, and wrought-iron chandeliers. The walls of the "inner sanctum" have signatures of former patrons like Mozart, Beethoven, and Mark Twain. The beer is chilled, and the food is hearty and ample. Menu items include fried breaded chicken with cucumber-potato salad; and roast pikeperch with almonds. Liveried waiters scurry around with large trays of food and there's live accordion and zither music.

Fleischmarkt 11. www.griechenbeisl.at. © **01/533-1941.** Reservations required. Main courses 16€–23€. AE, DC, MC, V. Daily 11am–1am (last order 11:30pm). Tram: N, 1, 2, or 21.

INEXPENSIVE

Augustinerkeller AUSTRIAN   Since 1857, the Augustinerkeller has served wine, beer, and food from the basement of one of the grand Hofburg palaces. It attracts a lively and diverse crowd that gets more boisterous as the *schrammel* is played late into the night. The vaulted brick room, with worn pine-board floors and wooden banquettes, is an inviting place to grab a drink and a simple meal. Be aware that this long and narrow dining room is usually as packed with people as it is with character. An upstairs room is quieter and less crowded. The ground-floor lobby lists prices of vintage local wines by the glass and you can sample from hundreds near the service counter. Otherwise, the kitchen serves simple food, including roast chicken, schnitzel, and *Tafelspitz.*

Augustinerstrasse 1. © **01/533-1026.** Main courses 9€–17€. AE, DC, MC, V. Daily 10am–midnight. U-Bahn: Stephansplatz.

Buffet Trzésniewski ★ SANDWICHES   Everyone in Vienna, from the most hurried office worker to the most elite hostess, knows about this spot. Franz Kafka lived next door and used to come here for sandwiches and beer. It's unlike any buffet you've seen, with six or seven cramped tables and a rapidly moving line of people, all jostling for space next to the glass counters. Indicate to the waitress the kind of sandwich you want (if you can't read German, just point). The delicious finger sandwiches

COFFEEHOUSES & cafes

The windows of the **Café Demel,** Kohlmarkt 14 (www.demel.at; ℭ **01/5351-7170;** U-Bahn: Stephansplatz or Herrengasse), are filled with spun-sugar and marzipan tributes to literature or local history. Inside is a baroque Viennese landmark with black marble tables and crystal chandeliers covered with white milk-glass globes. Dozens of pastries such as cream-filled horns (Gugelhupfs) are on offer. Open daily 10am to 7pm.

Café Dommayer, Auhofstrasse 2 (www.oberlaa-wien.at; ℭ **01/877-5460;** U-Bahn: Schönbrunn), boasts a reputation for courtliness that dates from 1787. In 1844, Johann Strauss, Jr., made his musical debut here, and beginning in 1924, the site became known as the place in Vienna for tea dancing. On Saturdays from 2 to 4pm, a pianist and violinist perform, and on the first Saturday of every month, a chamber orchestra plays mostly Strauss. It's open daily 7am to 10pm.

One of the Ring's great cafes, **Café Landtmann,** Dr.-Karl-Lueger-Ring 4 (www.landtmann.at; ℭ **01/2410-0100;** tram: 1, 2, or D), dates from the 1880s. Overlooking the Burgtheater and the Rathaus, it has traditionally drawn a mix of politicians, journalists, and actors, and was Freud's favorite. The cafe is open daily 7:30am to midnight (meals are served 11am–11:30pm).

Café Central ★, Herrengasse 14 (ℭ **01/533-3764;** U-Bahn: Herrengasse), stands in the middle of Vienna across from the Hofburg and the Spanish Riding School. This grand cafe offers a glimpse into 19th-century Viennese life—it was once the haunt of Austria's literati. Even Lenin is said to have edited Pravda at a corner table. It is open Mon–Sat from 7:30am to 10pm, Sun 10am to 10pm.

At **Café Sperl,** Gumpendorferstrasse 11 (www.cafesperl.at; ℭ **01/586-4158;** U-Bahn: Karlsplatz), the wondrous Gilded Age decor made the setting for scenes in films like A Dangerous Method and Before Sunrise. Well-prepared platters include salads, toast, baked noodles with ham and mushrooms, steaks, and Wiener Schnitzel. The staff are unusually friendly and there are fine old billiard tables and dartboards. Open Mon–Sat 7am to 11pm and Sun 11am to 8pm (closed Sun July–Aug).

Café Tirolerhof, Fürichgasse 8 (ℭ **01/5127833;** U-Bahn: Stephansplatz or Karlsplatz), has been under the same management for decades. One coffee special is the Maria Theresia, a large cup of mocha with apricot liqueur and topped with whipped cream. Open Mon–Sat 7:30am to 10pm.

Café Phil, Gumpendorferstrasse 10–12 (www.phil.info; ℭ **01/581-0489;** U-Bahn: MuseumsQuartier), appears to be a live-in reading room for university students and stage people. With a mix of worn easy chairs, upholstered benches, and booths in and around several rooms of books, as well as public readings, and the required assortment of newspapers, the place can be habit-forming. Open Tues–Sun, 9am to 1am.

come in 18 different combinations of cream cheese, egg, onion, salami, herring, tomatoes, lobster, and more. You can also order small glasses of fruit juice, beer, or wine with your snack. If you do order a drink, the cashier will give you a rubber token, which you'll present to the person at the far end of the counter.

Dorotheergasse 1. ℭ**01/512-3291.** Reservations not accepted. Sandwiches .90€. No credit cards. Mon–Fri 8:30am–7:30pm; Sat 9am–5pm. U-Bahn: Stephansplatz.

Café Leopold ★ 🏚 INTERNATIONAL Set one floor above street level in the Leopold Museum, and open long after the museum is closed for the night, it has the same pale pink sandstone as the museum and huge windows accenting the touches of Jugendstil. During the day, it's a conventional cafe and restaurant, serving a post-modern blend of central European and Asian food, including roasted shoulder of veal with Mediterranean vegetables, Thai curries, Vietnamese spring rolls, and arugula-studded risottos. Several nights a week, top DJs crank out dance tunes until late.

In the Leopold Museum, Museumsplatz 1. www.cafe-leopold.at. ✆ **01/523-6732.** Main courses 5.90€–11€. AE, DC, MC, V. Sun–Wed 10am–2am; Fri–Sat 10am–4pm. U-Bahn: Volkstheater or MuseumsQuartier.

Gulaschmuseum ★ ☺ AUSTRIAN/HUNGARIAN If you thought that goulash was available in only one form, think again. This restaurant celebrates at least 15 varieties, each an authentic survivor of the culinary traditions of Hungary, and each redolent with the taste of the national spice, paprika. Variations of the dish are made with roast beef, veal, pork, or even fried chicken livers, and for vegetarians, there are versions with potato, beans, or mushrooms. An excellent starter is the Magyar national crepe, *hortobágy palatschinken,* stuffed with minced beef and paprika cream sauce.

Schulerstrasse 20. www.gulasch.at. ✆ **01/512-1017.** Reservations recommended. Main courses 8€–16€. MC, V. Mon–Fri 9am–midnight; Sat–Sun 10am–midnight. U-Bahn: Wollzeile or Stephansplatz.

Palmenhaus AUSTRIAN The Jugendstil glass canopy of this greenhouse is among the most beautiful in Austria. Overlooking the formal terraces of the Burggarten, it was built between 1901 and 1904 by the Habsburgs' court architect, Friedrich Ohmann, joining the Albertina and the National Library. Today, it contains a chic cafe with an appealingly informal atmosphere. There's a sophisticated menu that changes monthly and might include fresh Austrian goat's cheese with stewed peppers; young herring with sour cream, horseradish, and deep-fried beignets stuffed with apples and cabbage. But no one will mind if you drop in for just a drink or coffee, along with one of the seductive pastries displayed near the entrance.

In the Burggarten. www.palmenhaus.at. ✆ **01/533-1033.** Reservations recommended for dinner. Main courses 14€–25€; pastries 3.50€–7.80€. AE, DC, MC, V. Mon–Thurs 10am–12pm, Fri–Sat 10am–1am, Sun 10am–11pm. U-Bahn: Opera.

Zu den 3 Hacken (At the Three Axes) ★ AUSTRIAN Small and charming, this 350-year-old paneled restaurant is believed to be the oldest *Gasthaus* (guesthouse) in Vienna. In 1827, Franz Schubert had a regular table. Today, the establishment has a pleasing summer *Shanigarten* of green-painted lattices and potted ivy for outside tables. Expect a traditional menu of *Tafelspitz,* beef goulash, mixed grills piled high with chops and sausages, and desserts like *Palatschinken* (crepes) with chocolate-hazelnut sauce. The Czech and Austrian beer from a keg tastes especially good.

Singerstrasse 28. www.vinum-wien.at. ✆ **01/512-5895.** Reservations recommended. Main courses 7.50€–18€. AE, DC, MC, V. Mon–Sat 11am–11pm. U-Bahn: Stephansplatz.

Zwölf-Apostelkeller VIENNESE For those seeking a taste of Old Vienna, this is the place, with sections dating back to 1561. Rows of wooden tables stand under vaulted ceilings, with lighting partially provided by streetlights set into the masonry floor. Students love the low prices and proximity to the center. In addition to beer and wine, you can get hearty Austrian fare, including Hungarian goulash soup, meat dumplings, and a *Schlachtplatte,* a selection of hot black pudding, liverwurst, pork, and pork sausage with a hot bacon and cabbage salad.

Sonnenfelsgasse 3. www.zwoelf-apostelkeller.at. ✆ **01/512-6777.** Main courses 6.50€–12€. AE, DC, MC, V. Daily 11am–midnight. Closed July. U-Bahn: Stephansplatz. Tram: 1, 2, 21, D, or N. Bus: 1A.

Shopping

While *Trachten* (traditional dress) and handicrafts are part of a long-established tradition, save time to browse in the many antiques stores and art galleries, and shops selling unique design pieces.

In general there are two main shopping areas. One is the Inner City (1st District). Here you'll find **Kärntnerstrasse,** between the State Opera and Stock-im-Eisen-Platz (U-Bahn: Karlsplatz or Stephansplatz); the **Graben,** between Stock-im-Eisen-Platz and Kohlmarkt (U-Bahn: Stephansplatz); **Kohlmarkt,** between the Graben and Michaelerplatz (U-Bahn: Herrengasse); and **Rotenturmstrasse,** between Stephansplatz and Schwedenplatz (U-Bahn: Stephansplatz or Schwedenplatz). The side streets off the Graben, especially Dorotheergasse, are lots of fun to browse through, with their high concentration of antiques stores.

In addition, there's the more mainstream stretch on **Mariahilferstrasse,** between MuseumsQuartier and Westbahnhof, one of the longest (and often busiest) shopping streets in Europe (U-Bahn: MuseumsQuartier, Neubaugasse, Zieglergasse, or Westbahnhof). Off this boulevard there are many hidden treasures, such as the so-called Furniture Mile on Siebensterngasse, or between Mariahilferstrasse and the Naschmarkt, where you'll find Gumpendorferstrasse with fine boutiques, good restaurants, and stylish hairdressers at every turn.

Every district has an open-air market. The **Naschmarkt** is a vast international fine foods market with a lively scene every day. To visit, head south of the opera district (U-Bahn: Karlsplatz or Kettenbrückengasse).

Elegant department stores line the pedestrian streets, which are wonderful to browse in on colder days. On Kärntnerstrasse it is the **Steffl,** a glass tower from which an elevator sticks out into the street. On Mariahilferstrasse, the place to find everything under one roof is **Gerngross,** the renovated, century-old shopping palace. Shops are normally open Mon–Fri from 9am to 6pm, and Sat from 9am to 1pm. On Thursdays many shops stay open longer, generally until 7pm. Small shops usually close between noon and 2pm for lunch. Shops in the rail stations are open daily from 7am to 11pm, offering groceries, stationery, books, and flowers.

Entertainment & Nightlife

For a guide to events in and around the city (in English), ask for **The Vienna Review** at any *Tabac-Trafik* or newsstand, and some bookstores. The best official source of information is the **Wien Monatsprogramm,** partially in English and distributed free at tourist information offices and at many hotel reception desks.

THE PERFORMING ARTS

OPERA & CLASSICAL MUSIC Opera is sacred in Vienna: when World War II was over, the city's top priority was the restoration of the heavily damaged **Wiener Staatsoper** (Opernring 2; www.staatsoper.at; ✆ **01/5144-42960;** U-Bahn: Karlsplatz). With musicians from Vienna Philharmonic Orchestra in the pit, and the leading opera stars of the world on stage, combined with the generous budgets of a government-supported house, the results are legendary. In their day, Richard Strauss and

Gustav Mahler were artistic directors. The Vienna State Opera stages more than 60 productions a year, including ballet and, with 1,700 seats and 560 standing-room places, performs for about 10,000 concert-goers a week. Daily performances run from September 1 until the end of June; with a little planning, tickets are to be had for almost any performance, although many sell out. Tickets are priced between 10€ and 220€. Tours 6.50€ per person.

Count yourself fortunate if you get to hear a concert at **Musikverein,** Bösendorferstrasse 12 (www.staatsoper.at; ℂ **01/505-8190** for the box office; U-Bahn: Karlsplatz). The Golden Hall is regarded as one of the four acoustically best concert halls in the world. Some 600 concerts per season (Sept–June) are presented here, of which only two dozen are played by the Vienna Philharmonic, sold out long in advance. Standing room is available at almost any performance, but you must be ready to queue up hours before the show. Tickets for standing room are 6€ to 7€; 10€ to 80€ for seats. The box office is open Mon–Fri 9am to 8pm, Sat from 9am to 1pm.

Vienna is the home of four major symphony orchestras, including the world-acclaimed Vienna Philharmonic and the Vienna Symphony, the ÖRF Symphony Orchestra and the Niederösterreichische Tonkünstler. The orchestras sometimes perform at the **Konzerthaus,** Lothringerstrasse 20 (www.konzerthaus.at; ℂ **01/2420-0100;** U-Bahn: Stadtpark), a major concert hall with three auditoriums, and also the venue for chamber music and other programs.

THEATER Vienna's English Theatre, Josefsgasse 12 (www.englishtheatre.at; ℂ **01/4021-2600;** U-Bahn: Rathaus), established in 1963, offers a mix of comedy and drama, classics and premieres, that in recent years have included Yazmina Reza's *Art,* winner of the Prix Molière, and the Austrian premiere of *Old Wicked Songs.* The box office is open Mon–Fri 10am to 7:30pm. Tickets range in price from 20€ to 38€.

The **Burgtheater (National Theater),** Dr.-Karl-Lueger-Ring 2 (www.burgtheater.at; ℂ **01/5144-4140;** tram: 1, 2, or D to Burgtheater), produces classical and modern plays in German, and is universally accepted as the leading stage in the German-speaking world. Among its permanent company today are Oscar winners Klaus Maria Brandauer (*Mephisto, Out of Africa*) and Christoph Waltz (*Inglourious Basterds),* and Sonke Workmann (*Pope Joan).* Tickets cost from 5€ to 48€ for seats, and 1.50€ for standing room.

Since opening on June 13, 1801, **Theater an der Wien,** Linke Wienzeile 6 (www.theateranderwien.at; ℂ **01/588-300;** U-Bahn: Karlsplatz), has been a leading venue for highly acclaimed productions of lesser-known opera and music theater. Tickets cost from 30€ to 140€.

The **Volksoper,** Währingerstrasse 78 (www.volksoper.at; ℂ **01/5144-43670;** U-Bahn: Volksoper), presents lavish productions of traditional Viennese operettas, light opera, as well as 18th-, 19th-, and 20th-century operas (*The Magic Flute, Tosca, La Boheme,* etc.), classical musicals (*My Fair Lady),* and ballet, some 300 performances from September 1 until the end of June. Tickets go on sale at the Volksoper only 1 hour before performances, priced 7€ to 150€ for seats, 2.50€ to 4€ for standing room.

Home to the Wiener Symphoniker, **Wiener Konzerthaus,** Lothringerstrasse 20 (www.konzerthaus.at; ℂ **01/242-002;** U-Bahn: Stadtpark), is the venue for a wide range of musical events, including orchestral concerts, chamber music recitals, and choral concerts. The box office is open Mon–Fri 9am to 7:45pm; and Sat 9am to 1pm. In August, Mon–Fri 9am to 1pm. Ticket prices depend on the event.

NIGHTCLUBS, CABARETS & BARS

The **Loos American Bar** ★, Kärntnerdurchgang 10 (www.loosbar.at; ✆ **01/512-3283;** U-Bahn: Stephansplatz), is one of the most unusual and interesting bars in Vienna; this very dark, and almost mythical bar was designed by the famed architect, Adolf Loos, in 1908. Originally the drinking room of a private men's club, today, it welcomes an international crowd of hip singles from Vienna's arts-and-media scene. No food is served, but the mixologist's specials include six kinds of martinis, plus five kinds of Manhattans, each 10€. Beer starts at 2.60€. It's open daily, from noon to 4am.

The most famous jazz pub in Austria, **Jazzland,** Franz-Josefs-Kai 29 (✆ **01/533-2575;** U-Bahn: Schwedenplatz), is noted for the quality of its U.S. and central European performers. It's in a deep, 200-year-old cellar, of the type the Viennese used to store staples during the city's many sieges. Amid exposed brick walls and dim lighting, you can order drinks or dinner. The place is open Mon–Sat from 7pm to 1am. Music begins at 9pm, and three sets are performed.

Anyone who thought drinking wine in Vienna meant accordion players and dirndl-clad servers has a surprise in store. **Weinquartier,** Hanuschgasse 3 (www.weinquartier.at; ✆ **01/513-4319;** U-Bahn: Karlsplatz), is Vienna's embassy for the *Weinviertel* (Austria's wine region). Subdued lighting, chic waiters, and slightly kitschy B/W glossies of the vineyards whose wares you're sampling somehow suit the location between the opera and the Albertina.

THE LGBT SCENE

In addition to the permanent gay bars, cafes, and restaurants there are also a number of notable gay club events. The most prominent and popular of these is Heaven, every Saturday at the **Camera Club,** Neubaugasse 2 (www.camera-club.at; ✆ **01/5233-23063;** Cover 10€; U-Bahn: Neubaugasse). This is the hottest party in town and many hetero men and women love it because this scene just knows how to party.

Alfi's Goldener Spiegel, Linke Wienzeile 46 (✆ **01/586-6608;** U-Bahn: Kettenbruckengasse), the most enduring gay restaurant in Vienna, is also its most popular gay bar, attracting mostly male clients to its position near Vienna's Naschmarkt. You don't need to come here to dine to enjoy the bar, where almost any gay male from abroad drops in for a look-see. The place is very cruisy, and the bar is open Wed–Mon 7pm to 2am.

The **Frauencafé,** Langegasse 11 (✆ **01/406-3754;** U-Bahn: Lerchenfelderstrasse), is exactly what its name implies: a politically conscious cafe for women, lesbian or otherwise. Established in 1977 in a century-old building, it's filled with magazines, newspapers, modern paintings, and a clientele of Austrian and international women. Next door is a feminist bookstore loosely affiliated with the cafe. Open Tues–Sat 6:30pm to 2am. Glasses of wine begin at 2.50€.

Where to Stay
VERY EXPENSIVE

Grand Hotel Wien ★★   Some of the most discerning hotel guests in Europe, from visiting soloists to diplomats, prefer this deluxe hotel to the more traditional and famous Imperial or Bristol. Just along from the Staatsoper, the spacious soundproof rooms and suites have all the modern luxuries, such as heated floors, coffeemakers, and phones in marble bathrooms. The more expensive rooms have more elaborate furnishings and decoration, including ornamental plaster features. The main dining room has Austrian and international dishes, and there's also a Japanese restaurant that serves the town's best sushi brunch on Sunday.

Kärntner Ring 9, 1010 Vienna. www.grandhotelwien.com. ✆ **01/515-800.** Fax 01/515-1310. 205 units. 211€–299€ double; from 1,000€ suite. AE, DC, MC, V. Parking 28€. U-Bahn: Karlsplatz. **Amenities:** 3 restaurants; 2 bars; exercise room; room service; babysitting; boutiques; rooms for those w/limited mobility. *In room:* A/C, TV, minibar, hair dryer, Wi-Fi (free).

Hotel Ambassador ★   Until it became a hotel in 1866, the Ambassador was a wheat and flour warehouse, a far cry from its status today as one of Vienna's most refined contemporary hotels. Modern and stylish, it has the advantage of a great location, between the Vienna State Opera and St. Stephan's Cathedral, on the Neuer Markt square facing the Donner Fountain. Mark Twain stayed here, as has a host of diplomats and celebrities, including Theodore Roosevelt. Bedrooms are furnished with Biedermeier and Art Nouveau period pieces. The quieter rooms overlook Neuer Markt. The restaurant, **Léhar,** serves high-quality Austrian and international cuisine.

Kärntnerstrasse 22, A-1010 Vienna. www.ambassador.at. ✆ **01/961-610.** Fax 01/513-2999. 86 units. 220€–404€ double; 700€ junior suite. AE, DC, MC, V. Parking 30€. U-Bahn: Stephansplatz. **Amenities:** Restaurant; bar; room service. *In room:* A/C, TV, minibar, hair dryer, Wi-Fi (1 hr. 8€, 3 hr. 15€, 24 hr. 18€).

Hotel Imperial ★★★   Listed by Relais et Chateaux as among the world's most beautiful hostelries, this hotel of princes has been the host of Austria's visitors of state since it was reclaimed from Russian forces in 1955. Here, in the former home of the Prince of Württemberg, you are afforded the essence of royalty in every velvet brocade curtain and cherry-wood cabinet, and your butler serves a hand-ironed newspaper with morning coffee. It also has a cocktail bar, where Thomas at the Bösendorfer plays everything from Hungarian polkas to Cole Porter. Some of the most desirable rooms are on the fourth and fifth floors, on a more human scale than the overwhelming "state" suites. If this superb 5-star hotel has a weakness, it is the fitness rooms and (despite the lovely sauna) the lack of a spa.

Kärntner Ring 16, 1015 Vienna. www.luxurycollection.com/imperial. ✆ **800/325-3589** in the U.S., or 01/501-100. Fax 01/5011-0410. 138 units. 700€ double; from 1,000€ suite. AE, DC, MC, V. Parking 32€. U-Bahn: Karlsplatz. **Amenities:** 2 restaurants; bar; health club; sauna; room service; babysitting; rooms for those w/limited mobility. *In room:* A/C, TV, minibar, hair dryer, Wi-Fi (1 hr. 9€, 24 hr. 19€).

Hotel Sacher Wien ★★★   The fame of this hotel could just as well be due to the luxurious brocade drapes and attentive service, but for most people, it's all about chocolate cake. The Café Sacher Wien, where the world-famous delicacy with its apricot middle and shiny near-black chocolate top was invented, is still going strong, but there's also an enchanting hotel attached, at the heart of Viennese life since 1876. Recently renovated, this hotel opposite the Staatsoper couldn't be more central, with silk wallpaper, 19th-century oils, and Biedermeier furniture. Nine suites have adjoining 23 sq. m (250 sq. ft.) terraces with stunning views. The Spa offers "hot chocolate treatments" following the Sachers' sweet tradition. Along with the Confiserie and Café, there's the Anna Sacher Restaurant, the Blaue Bar, and the sexy Rote Bar, with its charming winter garden.

Philharmonikerstrasse 4, 1010 Vienna. www.sacher.com. ✆ **01/514-560.** Fax 01/5125-6810. 152 units. 299€–464€ double; from 650€ junior suite; from 720€ executive suite. AE, DC, MC, V. Parking 32€. U-Bahn: Karlsplatz. Tram: 1, 2, 62, 65, D, or J. Bus: 4A. **Amenities:** 2 restaurants; 2 bars; cafe; spa; babysitting; room service; confiserie. *In room:* A/C, TV, minibar, hair dryer, Wi-Fi (1 hr. 6€, 24 hr. 36€).

Palais Coburg Hotel Residenz ★★ Built in 1846 by August von Sachsen-Coburg-Saalfeld (whose family managed to sire the House of Windsor and most of the monarchs of western Europe) as the dynasty's Vienna residence, this magnificent, sprawling palace, wrecked by the occupying Russian army, was recently rebuilt over 6 years, and all traces of the mundane have been banished. The smaller and less expensive suites are contemporary, design-conscious, and very comfortable. The more expensive are high-end posh, with pale satin upholstery and valuable antiques. All this grandeur is the personal property of an (individual) Austrian investor, whose stated ambition involves the on-site compilation of the largest and most comprehensive wine collection in Europe. A full-service spa is reserved for residents.

Coburgbastei 4, 1010 Vienna. www.palais-coburg.com. ✆ **01/518-180.** Fax 01/518-181. 35 suites. 560€–1,900€ suites. Rates include breakfast. Parking 40€. AE, DC, MC, V. **Amenities:** 2 restaurants; indoor pool; health club; spa; room service. *In room:* A/C, TV, full kitchen w/bar, Wi-Fi (free).

EXPENSIVE

Hotel Das Triest ★★ 🏆 Sir Terence Conran, the famous English restaurant owner and designer, created the interior for this contemporary hotel which is frequented by artists and musicians. It is in the heart of Vienna, a 5-minute walk from St. Stephan's Cathedral. The building was originally a stable for stagecoach horses travelling between Vienna and Trieste—hence its name, "City of Trieste." Its old cross-vaulted rooms, which give the structure a distinctive flair, have been transformed into lounges and suites. Bedrooms are midsize to spacious, tastefully furnished, and comfortable.

Wiedner Hauptstrasse 12, 1040 Vienna. www.dastriest.at. ✆ **01/589-180.** Fax 01/5891818. 73 units. 273€ double; 338€–556€ suite. Rates include buffet breakfast. AE, DC, MC, V. Parking 25€. U-Bahn: Stephansplatz. **Amenities:** Restaurant; bar; exercise room; sauna; room service; babysitting; solarium. *In room:* A/C, TV, minibar, hair dryer, Wi-Fi (free).

Hotel König Von Ungarn ★ On a narrow street near St. Stephan's, this hotel occupies a dormered building dating back to the early 17th century and is Vienna's oldest continuously operated hotel. Once a pied-à-terre for Hungarian noble families, Mozart reportedly resided here in 1791 and wrote music in the upstairs apartment. A mirrored solarium/bar area has a glass-roofed atrium with a tree growing in it. Tall windows overlook the Old Town, and Venetian mirrors adorn the walls. Everywhere, this lovely hotel is a masterpiece of low-key luxury, tradition, and modern convenience. Guest rooms are modern, with Biedermeier accents and traditional furnishings, two with balconies. Some rooms lack an outside window.

Schulerstrasse 10, 1010 Vienna. www.kvu.at. ✆ **01/515-840.** Fax 01/515-848. 33 units. 215€ double; 295€–345€ apt. Rates include breakfast. AE, DC, MC, V. U-Bahn: Stephansplatz. **Amenities:** Restaurant; bar; room service; babysitting. *In room:* A/C, TV, minibar, hair dryer, Wi-Fi (free).

MODERATE

Graben Hotel Over several centuries, the former "Zum Goldenen Jägerhorn" has attracted Bohemian writers and artists. The poet Franz Grillparzer was a regular guest; and during the dark days of World War II, it was a gathering place for writers like Franz Kafka, Max Brod, and Peter Altenberg. The hotel stands on a narrow street off the Kärntnerstrasse, in the very heart of the city. Guests gather around the stone fireplace in winter and look at fascinating memorabilia, including original postcards left by Altenberg. The small but high-ceilinged rooms feel spacious. The furniture is simple with *Jugendstil* touches but will feel spartan to someone looking for luxury. Sunlight streams into the front rooms, with those in the rear darker and very quiet.

Dorotheergasse 3, 1010 Vienna. www.kremslehnerhotels.at. ℰ **01/5121-5310.** Fax 01/5121-53120. 41 units. 160€–195€ double. Rates include buffet breakfast. AE, DC, MC, V. Parking 27€. U-Bahn: Karlsplatz. **Amenities:** Restaurant; lounge; babysitting; room service. *In room:* TV, minibar, hair dryer, Wi-Fi (30 min. 3€, 24 hr. 12€).

Hollman Beletage ★★ 🏨 This discovery, above Schwedenplatz in the heart of town, has beautifully designed rooms in a stylish "Wien modern" style. The waterfall showers and beautiful baths, plus the spa area, will pamper after long, eventful days. The in-house cinema shows three films a day all relating to Vienna, including Graham Greene's *The Third Man.* This lovely boutique hotel is small, with a sophisticated, uncluttered elegance. Make sure you book ahead, as it only has 24 rooms.

Köhlnerhofgasse 6. www.hollmann-beletage.at. ℰ **01/961-1960.** Fax: 01-513-9698. 24 units. 140€–250€ double. Rates include breakfast. AE, DC, MC, V. U-Bahn: Stephansplatz. **Amenities:** Restaurant; exercise room; spa; garden; cinema. *In room:* TV, minibar, hair dryer, Wi-Fi (free).

Hotel Amadeus Cozy and convenient, this boxlike hotel is only 2 minutes from Stephansdom, within walking distance of practically everything. It is on the site of a once-legendary tavern (Zum roten Igel), a haunt of Johannes Brahms and Franz Schubert. Behind a dull 1960s facade, the bedrooms and public rooms are pleasant, furnished in a comfortable, modern style, many with views of the cathedral. However, street noise can be an issue. Still, this is a good value-for-money option.

Wildpretmarkt 5, 1010 Vienna. www.hotel-amadeus.at. ℰ **01/533-8738.** Fax 01/533-8738-3838. 30 units. 178€–203€ double. Rates include buffet breakfast. AE, DC, MC, V. U-Bahn: Stephansplatz. **Amenities:** Lounge; babysitting; rooms for those w/limited mobility. *In room:* A/C, TV, minibar, hair dryer, Wi-Fi (free).

Hotel Rathaus ★★ This is a hotel for vinophiles, dedicated to wine and wine-growers. There are even "wine cosmetics" in the bedrooms, and the Fleischhacker family organizes wine tastings for their guests and 1-day excursions to nearby wine regions. The modern bedrooms are spread across four floors in a restored town house.

Lange Gasse 13, A-1080 Vienna. www.hotel-rathaus-wien.at. ℰ **01/400-1122.** Fax 01/400-1122-88. 39 units. 160€–210€ double; 398€ suite. AE, MC, V. Parking 15€. U-Bahn: Herrengasse. **Amenities:** Lounge; room service. *In room:* TV, minibar, hair dryer, Internet (free).

INEXPENSIVE

Drei Kronen 🍴 The "3 crowns" in the German name (Austria, Hungary, and Bohemia from the old Austro-Hungarian Empire) are displayed on top of the building. The hotel enjoys one of Vienna's best locations, right next to the Naschmarkt. Built in 1894, the five-floor Jugendstil hotel designed by celebrated architect Ignaz Drapala has comfortable rooms although they are small, some not big enough for full-size beds.

Schleifmuehlgasse 25, 1040 Vienna. www.hotel3kronen.at. ℰ **01/587-3289.** Fax 01/587-3289-11. 41 units. 75€ double; 85€ triple. AE, DC, MC, V. Parking 15€. U-Bahn: Karlsplatz. **Amenities:** Lounge; babysitting. *In room:* TV, Wi-Fi (free).

Hotel Kärntnerhof ★ ☺ Only a 4-minute walk from the cathedral, the recently renovated Kärntnerhof is a comfortable and friendly option. The decor of the public rooms is tastefully arranged around Oriental rugs, well-upholstered chairs and couches with cabriole legs, and an occasional 19th-century portrait. The midsize to spacious rooms often feature the original parquet floors and striped or patterned wallpaper set off by curtains. Many of the guest rooms are large enough to handle an extra bed, making this good for families. The owner is also helpful, directing guests to nearby services and Vienna landmarks.

Grashofgasse 4, 1011 Vienna. www.karntnerhof.com. ℭ **01/512-1923.** Fax 01/513-2228-33. 44 units. 110€–175€ double; 180€–280€ suite. Rates include buffet breakfast. AE, DC, MC, V. Parking 17€. U-Bahn: Stephansplatz. **Amenities:** Lounge; room service; laundry/dry cleaning service. *In room:* TV, Wi-Fi (free).

Hotel-Pension Suzanne ★ ☺ Just along from the opera house, this is a real discovery. Once you get past its postwar facade, the interior warms considerably; it is brightly decorated in comfortable, Viennese turn-of-the-20th-century style with antique beds, plush chairs, and the original molded ceilings. Rooms are a reasonable size and well maintained, facing either the busy street or a courtyard. There are family-sized rooms, and some bedrooms are like small apartments, with kitchenettes.

Walfischgasse 4. www.pension-suzanne.at. ℭ **01/513-2507.** Fax 01/513-2500. 26 units. 100€–112€ double; 135€–145€ triple. Rates include buffet breakfast. AE, DC, MC, V. U-Bahn: Karlsplatz. **Amenities:** Lounge; breakfast-only room service; babysitting; Wi-Fi at reception (free). *In room:* TV, hair dryer.

SALZBURG ★★★

A baroque city on the banks of the Salzach River, set against a mountain backdrop, Salzburg is the beautiful capital of the State of Salzburg. The city and the river were named after its early residents who earned their living in the salt mines. In this "heart of the heart of Europe," Mozart was born in 1756, and the composer's association with the city beefs up tourism.

The **Old Town** lies on the left bank of the river, where a monastery was founded in 700. From that start, Salzburg grew in power and prestige, becoming an archbishopric in 798. In the heyday of the prince-archbishops, the city became known as the "German Rome." Responsible for much of its architectural grandeur are those masters of the baroque, Fischer von Erlach and Lukas von Hildebrandt.

The City of Mozart, "Silent Night," and *The Sound of Music*—Salzburg lives essentially off its rich past. It is a front-ranking cultural mecca for classical music year-round. The city is the setting for the Salzburg Festival, a world-renowned annual event that attracts music lovers, especially Mozart fans, from all over the globe. Salzburg's natural setting among alpine peaks on both banks of the Salzach River gives it the backdrop perpetuating its romantic image.

As one of Europe's greatest tourist capitals, most of Salzburg's day-to-day life revolves around promoting its music and other connections. Although *The Sound of Music* was filmed in 1964, this Julie Andrews blockbuster has become a cult attraction and is definitely alive and well in Salzburg. Ironically, Austria was the only country in the world where the musical failed when it first opened. It played for only a single week in Vienna, closing after audiences dwindled.

Salzburg is only a short distance from the Austrian–German frontier, so it's convenient for exploring many of the attractions of Bavaria. Situated on the northern slopes of the Alps, the city lies at the intersection of traditional European trade routes and is well served by air, Autobahn, and rail.

Essentials
GETTING THERE
BY PLANE   The **Salzburg Airport–W.A. Mozart,** Innsbrucker Bundesstrasse 95 (www.salzburg-airport.com; ℭ **0662/8580-7911**), lies 3km (1¾ miles) southwest of

the city center. It has regularly scheduled air service to all Austrian airports, as well as to Frankfurt, Berlin, Düsseldorf, Hamburg, London, and Vienna.

Bus no. 2 runs between the airport and Salzburg's main rail station, while no. 8 goes to Hanuschplatz and the **Altstadt (Old Town).** Departures are frequent, and the 20-minute trip costs 2€ one-way for adults, 1€ for children. By taxi it's only about 15 minutes, but you'll pay at least 13€ to 15€.

BY TRAIN   Salzburg's main rail station, the **Salzburg Hauptbahnhof,** Südtirolerplatz (*✆* **05/1717**), is on the major rail lines of Europe, with frequent arrivals from all the main cities of Austria and from European cities such as Zurich, Munich, Budapest, and Zagreb. Between 8:22am and 12:44am the next day, two trains per hour arrive from Vienna (trip time: 3½ hr.); standard one-way fare is 48€. There are 16 daily trains from Innsbruck (2 hr.); standard one-way fare is 38€. Trains also arrive roughly every hour from Munich (90 min.–2 hr.), with a one-way ticket costing 34€.

The new private company **Westbahn** (www.westbahn.at; *✆* **01/899-00**) offers service between Salzburg and Vienna's Westbahnhof station at rates lower than ÖBB's. However, their trains run only every one to two hours. Tickets can be purchased onboard at no extra charge. Standard fare between Vienna and Salzburg is 24€.

The Salzburg rail station is undergoing reconstruction that is slated to last until 2014. Many of the amenities have been transferred to temporary constructions on the Südtirolerplatz in front of the construction site. Follow temporary yellow signs to navigate through the site to the square. There's a **Reisezentrum** with train information, open Monday to Saturday 5:30am to 9:10pm, as well as luggage-storage lockers. There's a small tourist information office in the InfoBox on the square, open daily 8:15am to 7:30pm.

From the train station, buses depart to various parts of the city, including the Altstadt. Or you can walk to the Altstadt in about 20 minutes. Taxis are also available. The rail station has a currency exchange and storage lockers.

BY BUS   A part of the Westbahn group mentioned above, **Westbus** (www.westbus.at; *✆* **01/361-1112**) offers bus service from Salzburg to Villach, as well as connections from Vienna to Bratislava, Budapest, and Prague. Standard one-way fare from Villach costs 11€, and from Klagenfurt 19€.

BY CAR   Salzburg is 334km (208 miles) west of Vienna and 152km (94 miles) east of Munich. It's reached from all directions by good roads, including Autobahn A8 from the west (Munich), A1 from the east (Vienna), and A10 from the south. Route 20 comes into Salzburg from points north on the German side of the Salzach, and Route 158 cuts through the picturesque lake district to the southeast.

VISITOR INFORMATION   In addition to the branch at the rail station, the larger **Salzburg Tourist Information Office** is located in the heart of the city's historic core, at Mozartplatz 5 (www.salzburg.info; *✆* **0662/889-870**). The Mozartplatz office is open from October through May, Monday to Saturday 9am to 6pm; and, from June through September, daily 9am to 7pm.

CITY LAYOUT   Most of what visitors come to see lies on the left bank of the Salzach River in the **Altstadt (Old Town),** although the more modern right bank with the train station offers a few old streets and shops leading up to the river. If you're driving, you must leave your car in the right bank and enter the Old Town on foot, as most of it is for pedestrians only.

The heart of the inner city is **Residenzplatz,** which has the largest and finest baroque fountain this side of the Alps. On the western side of the square stands the

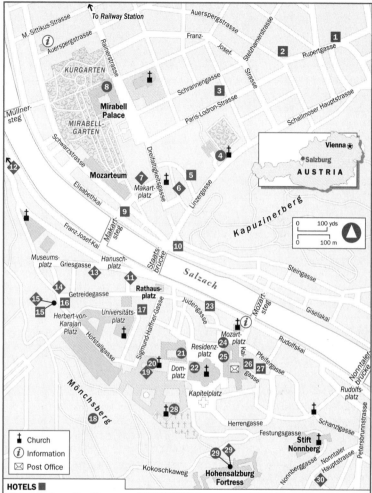

The Salzburg Card

The **Salzburg Card** not only lets you use unlimited public transportation, but it also acts as an admission ticket to the city's most important cultural sights, like Mozart's birthplace, the Hohensalzburg Fortress, the Residenz gallery, the world-famous water fountain gardens at Hellbrunn, and more. Cards are valid for 24, 48, and 72 hours and cost 22€, 30€, and 35€, respectively, except from May through October, when the prices rise to 25€, 34€, and 40€. Children up to 15 years of age receive a 50% discount. You can purchase the pass from Salzburg travel agencies, hotels, tobacco shops *(Trafik)*, and municipal offices.

Residenz, palace of the prince-archbishops, and on the southern side of the square is the **Salzburg Cathedral** (or Dom). To the west of the Dom lies **Domplatz,** linked by archways dating from 1658. Squares to the north and south appear totally enclosed. On the southern side of Max-Reinhardt-Platz and Hofstallgasse, edging toward **Mönchsberg,** stands the **Festspielhaus (Festival Theater),** built on the foundations of the 17th-century court stables.

GETTING AROUND

BY BUS/TRAM The city buses and trams provide quick, comfortable service through the city center from the Nonntal parking lot (located just next to the old city center) to Sigsmundsplatz, the city-center parking lot. The one-ride fare is 2€ adults, 1€ children 6 to 15; those 5 and under travel free. Note that buses stop running at 11pm.

BY TAXI You'll find taxi stands scattered at key points all over the city center and in the suburbs. The **Salzburg Funktaxi–Vereinigung** (radio taxis) office is at Rainerstrasse 27 (www.taxi.at; ✆ **0662/8111** to order a taxi in advance). Fares start at 3.70€.

BY CAR Driving a car in Salzburg is definitely *not* recommended. In most places it's impossible, since the monumental landmark center is for pedestrians only. If you're driving into Salzburg, leave your car on the left bank of the Salzach River. You'll find convenient underground parking lots like the one at Mönchsberg, from which it's an easy walk to the center and Domplatz. Try **Avis** (✆ **0662/877-278**) or **Hertz** (✆ **0662/876-674**), both at Ferdinand-Porsche-Strasse 7 and open Monday to Friday 8:30am to 6pm and Saturday 8am to 1pm.

BY HORSE-DRAWN CARRIAGE Hire one of 14 horse-drawn carriages (called a *Fiaker* in German) from Residenzplatz for a unique tour of the town (www.salzburg.info; ✆ **0662/889-870**). Four people usually pay 40€ for 20 to 25 minutes, and 80€ for 50 minutes. You can try your bartering skills if you like.

BY BICYCLE City officials have developed a network of bicycle paths, which are indicated on city maps. May through September, you can rent bicycles at **Topbike,** at the Staatsbrücke (www.topbike.at; ✆ **0627/24656**), daily from 9am to 7pm. Rentals cost about 15€ per day, with a 20% discount for Salzburg Card holders.

[FastFACTS] SALZBURG

Business Hours Most shops and stores are open Monday to Friday 9am to 6pm and Saturday usually 9am to noon. Some of the smaller shops shut down at noon for a lunch break. Salzburg observes *langer Samstag*, which means that most stores stay open until 5pm on selected Saturdays. Banks are open Monday to Friday 8am to noon and 2 to 4:30pm.

Currency Exchange You can exchange money at the Hauptbahnhof on Südtirolerplatz daily 7am to 10pm, and at the airport daily 9am to 4pm.

Dentists For an English-speaking dentist, call **Zahnarztkammer,** Faberstrasse 2 (© **0662/873-466**).

Doctors If you suddenly fall ill, your best source of information for finding a doctor is the reception desk of your hotel. If you want a comprehensive list of doctors and their respective specialties, which you can acquire in Salzburg or even before your arrival, contact **Ärztekammer für Salzburg,** Bergstrasse 14, A-5020 Salzburg (www.aeksbg.at; © **0662/871-327**). If your troubles flare up over a weekend, the **Medical**

Emergency Center of the Austrian Red Cross maintains a hot line and English-language website (www.roteskreuz.at; © **141**), which you can use to describe your problem. A staff member there will either ask you to visit their headquarters at Karl Renner Strasse 7, or send a medical expert to wherever you're staying. This service is available from 5pm on Friday to 8am on Monday, and on public holidays.

Embassies & Consulates The **Consulate of Great Britain,** Alter Markt 4 (© **0662/848-133**), is open in winter Monday to Friday 9am to noon, and in summer 8am to 11am. **U.S. citizens** must contact consulates in Vienna or Munich.

Emergencies Call © **133** for police, © **122** to report a fire, and © **144** for an ambulance. The hearing-impaired can send a text message to © **0800/133-133.**

Internet Access The most convenient cafe with Internet capability is **Cybar,** Mozartplatz 5 (© **0662/843-696**), across from the tourist office. It's open daily 9am to 10pm and charges 2€ for 10 min. of Internet access.

Pharmacies Larger pharmacies, especially those in the city center, tend to remain open without a break Monday to Friday 8am to 6pm and Saturday 8am to noon. For night service, and service on Saturday afternoon and Sunday, pharmacies display a sign giving the address of the nearest pharmacy that has agreed to remain open over the weekend or throughout the night. A pharmacy that's particularly convenient to Salzburg's commercial center is **Elisabeth-Apotheke,** Elisabethstrasse 1 (© **0662/871-484**), north of Rainerstrasse toward the train station.

Post Office The main post office is at Residenzplatz 9 (© **0662/844-1210;** bus: 5 or 6). The post office at the main railway station is open Monday to Friday 8am to 8:30pm, Saturday 8am to 2pm, and Sunday 1pm and 6pm.

Telephone The **country code** for Austria is **43.** The **city code** for Salzburg is **662;** use this code when you're calling from outside Austria. If you're within Austria, use **0662.**

Exploring Salzburg

Much of the Old Town, or *Altstadt,* lies between the ridge known as the **Mönchsberg,** which rises to a height of 500m (1,640 ft.), and the Salzach River streaming down from the Alps. Its right bank also retains a smaller, well-preserved medieval district with baroque highlights like the **Mirabell Gardens** that merit a look. The main street of the Altstadt is **Getreidegasse,** a narrow thoroughfare lined with five- and six-story burghers' buildings. Most of the houses along the street date from the 17th and 18th centuries. Mozart was born at no. 9 (see below). Many of the houses display lace-like wrought-iron signs over carved windows.

You might begin your explorations at **Mozartplatz,** with its outdoor cafes. From here you can walk to the even more expansive **Residenzplatz,** where torchlight dancing is staged every year, along with outdoor performances.

ALTSTADT—THE LEFT BANK

Dom (Salzburg Cathedral) ★ CATHEDRAL/MUSEUM   Located where Res- idenzplatz flows into Domplatz (where you'll see a 1771 statue of the Virgin), this cathedral is world-renowned for its 4,000-pipe organ. The original building from A.D. 774 was superseded by a late-Romanesque structure erected from 1181 to 1200. When this edifice was destroyed by fire in 1598, Prince-Archbishop Wolf Dietrich commissioned construction of a new cathedral, but his overthrow prevented the completion of this project. His successor, Archbishop Markus Sittikus Count Hohen- ems, commissioned the Italian architect Santino Solari to build the present cathedral, which was consecrated in 1628 by Archbishop Paris Count Lodron.

Hailed by some critics as the most perfect Renaissance building in the Germanic countries, the cathedral has a marble facade and twin symmetrical towers. The inte- rior has a rich baroque style with elaborate frescoes, the most important of which, along with the altarpieces, were designed by Mascagni of Florence. In the cathedral, you can see the Romanesque font at which Mozart was baptized. The dome was damaged during World War II but was restored by 1959. In the crypt, traces of the old Romanesque cathedral that once stood on this spot have been unearthed.

The treasure of the cathedral, and the "arts and wonders" the archbishops col- lected in the 17th century, are displayed in the **Dom Museum** (℗ **0662/8047- 1860**), entered through the cathedral.

South side of Residenzplatz. www.salzburger-dom.at. ℗ **0662/844-189.** Free admission to cathe- dral; museum 6€ adults, 2€ children. Cathedral: May–Sept 8am–7pm; Mar–Apr, Oct, Dec 8am– 6pm; Jan–Feb, Nov 8am–5pm. Opens all year on Sundays at 1pm. Museum: Mon–Sat 10am–5pm, Sun 11am–6pm. Closed Nov–Apr. Bus: 3, 5, 6, 7, 8, or 10.

Glockenspiel (Carillon) HISTORIC SITE   Following a 2-year renovation, the celebrated Glockenspiel with its 35 bells can once again be visited. You can hear this 18th-century carillon at 7am, 11am, and 6pm from the square, or cover your ears and see them up close on a guided tour.

Mozartplatz 1. www.salzburgmuseum.at. ℗ **0662/8042-2784.** Guided tour 3€ adults, 2€ children. Guided tours given end Mar–end Oct, Thurs 5:30pm, Fri 10:30am. Bus: 3, 5, 6, 7, or 10.

Hohensalzburg Fortress ★★ ☺ CASTLE/MUSEUM   The stronghold of the ruling prince-archbishops before they moved "downtown" to the Residenz, this for- tress towers 122m (400 ft.) above the Salzach River on a rocky dolomite ledge. The massive fortress crowns the Festungsberg and literally dominates Salzburg. To get here, you can hike up one of the paths or lanes leading to the fortress, or you can walk from Kapitelplatz by way of Festungsgasse or from the Mönchsberg via the Scharten- tor. You can also take the funicular from Festungsgasse (℗ **0662/842-682**) at the station behind the cathedral. Museum tickets include admission and the funicular ride. Call the museum or the Festungsgasse number to check availability.

This is the largest completely preserved castle left in central Europe. Functions of defense and state were combined in this fortress for 6 centuries. The elegant state apartments, once the dwellings of the prince-archbishops and their courts, are on display. Note the coffered ceilings and intricate ironwork, and check out the early 16th-century porcelain stove in the Golden Room.

The **Burgmuseum** is distinguished mainly by its collection of medieval art. Plans and prints tracing the growth of Salzburg are on display, as are instruments of torture and many Gothic artifacts. The **Salzburger Stier** (Salzburg Bull), an open-air barrel organ built in 1502, plays melodies by Mozart and his friend Haydn in daily concerts following the glockenspiel chimes. The **Rainermuseum** has arms and armor exhibits. The beautiful late-Gothic St. George's Chapel, dating from 1501, has marble *bas-reliefs* of the Apostles.

Visit Hohensalzburg just for the view from the terrace. From the Reck watchtower, you get a panoramic sweep of the Alps. The Kuenberg bastion has a fine view of Salzburg's domes and towers.

Mönchsberg 34. www.salzburg-burgen.at. ⓒ **0662/8424-3011.** Admission (combination Fortress Card includes funicular, museums, fortress, and multimedia show) 11€ adults, 6.30€ children 6–14, free for children 5 and under, 26€ family ticket. Ticket without the funicular 7.80€ adults, 4.40€ children 6–14, 17.70€ family ticket. Fortress and museums daily Oct–Apr 9:30am–5pm; May–Sept 9am–7pm.

Mönchsberg ★★ NATURAL ATTRACTION
This heavily forested ridge extends for some 2km (1¼ miles) above the Altstadt and has fortifications dating from the 15th century. A panoramic view of Salzburg is possible from Mönchsberg Terrace just in front of the Grand Café Winkler.

West of the Hohensalzburg Fortress. Elevator at Gstättengasse 13. ⓒ **0662/8884-9750.** A round-trip fare is 3.20€ adults, 1.60€ children 6–14, free for children 5 and under. The elevators leave daily 8am–7pm, Jul and Aug until 9pm. Bus: 1, 4, or 8.

Petersfriedhof (St. Peter's Cemetery) ★★ CEMETERY
St. Peter's Cemetery lies at the stone wall that merges into the bottom of the rock called the Mönchsberg. Many of the aristocratic families of Salzburg lie buried here alongside many other noted people, including Nannerl Mozart, sister of Wolfgang Amadeus (also an exceptionally gifted musician, 4 years older than her brother). You can also see the Romanesque Chapel of the Holy Cross and St. Margaret's Chapel, dating from the 15th century. The cemetery and its chapels are rich in blue-blooded history; monuments to a way of life long vanished. You can also take a self-guided tour through the early Christian catacombs in the rock above the church cemetery.

St.-Peter-Bezirk. ⓒ **0662/844-5780.** Free admission to cemetery. Catacombs 1€ adults, .60€ children 6–15. Cemetery open daily 6:30am–7pm. Catacombs open May–Sept Tues–Sun 10:30am–5pm; Oct–Apr Wed–Thurs 10:30am–3:30pm, Fri–Sun 10:30am–4pm. Bus: 1, 4, 7, 8, or 10.

Residenz zu Salzburg/Residenzgalerie Salzburg ★★ PALACE
This opulent palace, just north of Domplatz in the pedestrian zone, was the seat of the Salzburg prince-archbishops after they no longer needed the protection of the gloomy Hohensalzburg Fortress of Mönchsberg. The Residenz dates from 1120, but work on its series of palaces, which comprised the ecclesiastical complex of the ruling church princes, began in the late 1500s and continued until about 1796. The 17th-century **Residenz fountain** is one of the largest and most impressive baroque fountains north of the Alps. More than a dozen state rooms, each richly decorated, are open to the public via guided tour. On the second floor you can visit the **Residenzgalerie**

IN MOZART'S footsteps

Wolfgang Amadeus Mozart was born in Salzburg on January 27, 1756, son of an obsessive, stage-door father, Leopold Mozart, whose control he eventually fled. "Wolfi" was a child prodigy, writing music at the age of 4, before he could even shape the letters of the alphabet. By the age of 6, he was performing at the Palace of Schönbrunn in Vienna before assembled royalty and aristocrats.

But the public at home bored him: In Salzburg, audiences were wooden, he complained, no more responsive than "tables and chairs." He often struggled to make ends meet. In spite of the success of *The Magic Flute* in 1791, his career ended in obscurity; he died penniless and was buried in a pauper's grave, the St. Marx cemetery in Vienna.

Today, though, Salzburg lives off the reputation of a young musician they barely paid heed to in his lifetime. Mozart's image is everywhere. In the heart of town on the left bank, **Mozartplatz** bears his name, with a statue of the composer erected in 1842, the first recognition of his birth he'd received in the town since his death. A music

academy is named after him, and, of course, his music dominates the Salzburg Festival.

Also on this side of the Salzach, you can visit **Mozart Geburtshaus (Birthplace)** ★, Getreidegasse 9 (www.mozarteum.at; (ℂ) **0662/844-313**). He lived here until he was 17—that is, when he was in Salzburg at all and wasn't touring such cities as Prague, Milan, or Vienna. There are three floors of exhibition rooms, which include the Mozart family apartment. The main treasures are the valuable paintings (such as the well-known Joseph Lange oil painting *Mozart and the Piano*, left unfinished) and the original instruments: the violin Mozart used as a child, his concert violin, and his viola, fortepiano, and clavichord.

On the right bank, you can also visit the restored **Mozart Wohnhaus (Residence)** ★, Makartplatz 8 (www.mozarteum.at; (ℂ) **0662/8742-2740**), where the composer lived from 1773 to 1780. Damaged in World War II air raids, the house reopened in 1996, honoring the year of Mozart's 240th birthday. In 1773, the Mozart family vacated the

Salzburg ((ℂ) **0662/840-451,** ext. 24), an art gallery containing European paintings from the 16th century to the 19th century.

Residenzplatz 1. www.salzburg-burgen.at. (ℂ) **0662/8042-2690.** Combined ticket to state rooms and gallery 9€ adults, 7€ seniors and students, 3€ children 6–14, 20.50€ family. Daily 10am–5pm. Bus: 3, 5, 6, 8, or 10.

Salzburg Museum MUSEUM This award-winning museum is housed in the New Residence complex, which actually dates from the 1600s, when it was Prince-Archbishop Wolf-Dietrich's "overflow palace." The main part of the complex is a series of state reception rooms that marked the beginning of the Renaissance in Salzburg.

There are exhibits here that were once housed in the Museum Carolino Augusteum; rare archaeological treasures, including Hallstatt Age relics, plus fragments of ruins from the town's Roman occupation. A Celtic bronze flagon is one of the chief treasures. The museum is also noted for its collection of Old Masters, with a rich trove of Gothic panel paintings and many works from the Romantic period.

Mozartplatz 1. www.salzburgmuseum.at. (ℂ) **0662/6208-08700.** Admission 7€ adults, 6€ seniors, 4€ ages 16 to 26, 3€ children 6–15, free for children 5 and under, 14€ family. Tues–Sun 9am–5pm. Bus: 5 or 6.

cramped quarters of Mozart's birthplace for this haunt on Makartplatz. In the rooms of these former apartments, a museum documents the history of the house, life, and work of Wolfgang Amadeus Mozart. There's a mechanized audio tour in six languages with musical samples.

Both the Geburtshaus and Wohnhaus are open September to June daily 9am to 5:30pm and July and August daily 9am to 8pm (you must enter 30 min. before closing). A combination ticket to both costs 12€ adults, 10€ seniors and students, 4.50€ children aged 15 to 18, 3.50€ children aged 6 to 14 (free for children under 6), and 25.50€ families. Otherwise, a ticket to either costs 7€, 6€, 3€, 2.50€, and 16.50€ respectively.

Aficionados will want to stop by the International Mozarteum Foundation's **Mozart Audio & Film Museum,** Makartplatz 8 (© **0662/883-454**). Here is a collection of 11,000 audio and 1,000 video titles of Mozart. There are also sections devoted to the work of contemporary Austrian composers, available at eight video and 10 audio stations, and there's

a large-scale screen for groups. The museum, which is free, is open Monday, Tuesday, and Friday 9am to 1pm and Wednesday and Thursday 1 to 5pm.

The 1914 Jugendstil **Mozarteum,** at Schwarzstrasse 26 (© **0662/889-4030**), can be visited by appointment and is well worth it. Today, it's the College of Music and the Performing Arts. Most lovely is the library—a *Bibliotheca Mozartiana*—on the second floor, with approximately 12,000 titles devoted to Mozart. It's open Monday to Friday from 9am to noon and 2 to 5pm.

The Mozarteum's wing at Schwarzstrasse 28 houses the large concert hall, where up to 800 guests enjoy concerts held throughout the year. The smaller one, next door, is the Viennese Hall, for 200. The highlight is the celebratory festival *Mozartwoche*, which commemorates Mozart's birthday (Jan 27) with 10 days of concerts and operas. In the garden is the **Magic Flute House,** the little wood structure in which Mozart composed *The Magic Flute* in 1791, shipped to Salzburg from the Naschmarkt in Vienna.

Stiftskirche St. Peter ★★ CHURCH   Founded in A.D. 696 by St. Rupert, whose tomb is here, this is the church of St. Peter's Abbey and Benedictine Monastery. Once a Romanesque basilica with three aisles, it was completely overhauled in the 17th and 18th centuries in elegant baroque style. The west door dates from 1240. The church is richly adorned with art treasures, including some altar paintings by Kremser Schmidt. The Salzburg Madonna, in the left chancel, is from the early 15th century.

St.-Peter-Bezirk. © **0662/844-5780.** Free admission. Apr–Oct 8am–9pm; Nov–Mar 8am–7pm. Bus: 3, 5, 6, 8, or 10.

ALTSTADT—THE RIGHT BANK

Friedhof St. Sebastian CEMETERY   Prince-Archbishop Wolf Dietrich commissioned this charming cemetery in 1595 to be laid out like an Italian *campo santo*. Mozart fans will find the tombs of the composer's wife and his father, Leopold. In the middle of the cemetery is St. Gabriel's Chapel, containing the mausoleum of Dietrich. Paracelsus, the Renaissance doctor and philosopher who died in 1541, is also entombed here.

Linzer Gasse 41. © **0662/875-208.** Free admission. Daily 9am–7pm (until dusk in winter). Bus: 1, 3, 4, 5, or 6.

Schloss Mirabell & Gardens (Mirabell Palace & Gardens) ★ PALACE/
GARDENS   This palace and its gardens were originally built as a luxurious private
residence called Altenau. Prince-Archbishop Wolf Dietrich had it constructed in
1606 for his mistress and the mother of his children, Salome Alt. Unfortunately, not
much remains of the original grand structure. Johann Lukas von Hildebrandt rebuilt
the Schloss in the first quarter of the 18th century, and it was modified after a great
fire in 1818. The ceremonial marble Barockstiege-Engelsstiege (angel staircase), with
sculptured cherubs, carved by Raphael Donner in 1726, leads to the Marmorsaal, a
marble-and-gold hall used for private concerts and weddings.

The gardens were laid out by baroque wizard Fischer von Erlach on the right bank
of the river off Makartplatz, and are studded with statuary and reflecting pools, making them a virtual open-air museum. Be sure to visit the bastion for its fantastic
marble baroque dwarfs and other figures, located by the Pegasus Fountains in the
lavish garden west of Schloss Mirabell. You'll also find a natural theater. In summer,
free brass band concerts are held Wednesday at 8:30pm and Sunday at 10:30am.
From the gardens, you have an excellent view of the Hohensalzburg Fortress.

Rainerstrasse. © **0662/80720.** Free admission. Palace: Mon, Wed, Thurs 8am–4pm; Tues, Fri
1–4pm. Staircase: daily 8am–6pm. Gardens: Daily 6am–8pm. Bus: 1, 2, 3, 4, 5, or 6.

ORGANIZED TOURS

The best-organized tours are offered by **Salzburg Panorama Tours,** Mirabellplatz
(www.panoramatours.at; © **0662/883-2110**), which is the Gray Line company for
Salzburg.

The original **"Sound of Music Tour"** combines the Salzburg city tour with an
excursion to the Lake District and other places where the 1965 film with Julie
Andrews was shot. The English-speaking guide shows you not only the highlights
from the film but also historical and architectural landmarks in Salzburg and parts of
the Salzkammergut countryside. The 4-hour tour departs daily at 9:30am and 2pm
and costs 37€ for adults, 18€ for children aged 4 to 12.

Where to Eat
ON THE LEFT BANK (ALTSTADT)
Very Expensive
Goldener Hirsch ★★★ AUSTRIAN/VIENNESE   Fans of this place are willing
to travel long distances just to enjoy the authentic ambiance of this renovated inn,
established in 1407. Don't be fooled by the relatively simple decor, a kind of well-
scrubbed and decent simplicity that's emulated by dozens of other restaurants in resorts
throughout Austria. The venue is chic, top-notch, impeccable, charming, and richly
sought after during peak season. The food is so tasty and beautifully served that the
kitchen ranks among the top three in Salzburg. Specialties include saddle of farm-raised
venison with red cabbage, king prawns in an okra-curry ragout served with perfumed
Thai rice, and tenderloin of beef and veal on morel cream sauce with cream potatoes.
In season, expect a dish devoted to game, such as venison or roast duckling.

Getreidegasse 37. © **0662/80840.** Reservations required. Main courses 20€–28€. Set lunch 29€ 3
courses; set dinner 34€ 3 courses. AE, MC, V. Daily noon–2:30pm and 6:30–9:30pm. Bus: 1, 4, 8, or 10.

Expensive
Purzelbaum ★ AUSTRIAN/FRENCH   Located in a residential neighborhood
not often frequented by tourists, this sophisticated bistro is near a duck pond at the
bottom of a steep incline leading up to Salzburg Castle. A cramped corner of the bar

CAFE society

At the **Café-Konditorei Fürst,** Brodgasse 13 (www.original-mozartkugel.com; ℂ **0662/843-759**), *Mozart-Kugeln* (traditional marzipan-pistachio chocolate-dipped cookies) are sold. The owner invented this sweet in 1890 but forgot to patent the recipe. The treat is often duplicated, but here you can sample it from the authentic and original recipe. Norbert Fürst, a descendant of the original founder, still makes these fine chocolates with a recipe handed down to him by his great-grandfather. In addition to the *Mozart-Kugeln*, there's a wide range of other chocolates and truffle specialties. Open Monday to Saturday 8am to 8pm, Sunday 9am to 8pm, and until 9pm in summer.

Established in 1705, **Café Tomaselli** ★, Alter Markt 9 (www.

tomaselli.at; ℂ **0662/844-488;** bus: 2 or 5), opens onto one of the most charming cobblestone squares of the Altstadt. Aside from the chairs placed outdoors during summer, you'll find a room with a high ceiling and many tables (it's a great place to sit and talk), and another more formal room to the right of the entrance that houses oil portraits of well-known 19th-century Salzburgers and attracts a haute bourgeois crowd. Choose from 40 different kinds of cakes or other menu items, including omelets, wursts, ice cream, and a wide range of drinks. Of course, the pastries and ice cream are all homemade. The cafe is open Monday to Saturday 7am to 9pm; until 12am during the Festspiele.

is reserved for visitors who want to drop in for only a drink. Most guests, however, reserve a table in one of the trio of rooms containing an Art Nouveau ceiling and marble buffets from an antique bistro in France. Menu items change according to the whim of the chef and include well-prepared dishes such as turbot-and-olive casserole, a selection of wild game (in season), Styrian mountain lamb in white-wine sauce with beans and polenta, and the house specialty, scampi *Gröstl*, composed of fresh shrimp with sliced potatoes baked with herbs in a casserole. During the Salzburg Festival, the restaurant is also open on Sunday and Monday midday.

Zugallistrasse 7. www.purzelbaum.at. ℂ **0662/848-843.** Reservations required. Main courses 19€–26€. Set menu 46€ 4 courses. AE, DC, MC, V. Mon 6–11pm; Tues–Sat noon–2pm and 6–11pm. Bus: 5, 20, or 25.

Moderate
Carpe Diem Finest Fingerfood ★★ 🖆 INTERNATIONAL   This establishment is one of the snazziest in town. Owned by Dietrich Mateschitz, creator of Red Bull, and launched by star chef Jörg Wörther, the two-story lounge and cafe offers a new culinary concept: fine cuisine packed into waffle shells or cones. The chef's intricate inventions come neatly tucked in a crisp shell, at times with contrasting temperatures. Some of the dishes from the revolving menu include steak filet in mushroom cream with a dumpling, cream of avocado with carrots tempura, and, finally, turbot with fennel, chorizo ravioli, and paprika sauce. The breakfast, lunch, and dinner menus differ in selection, and the patio area teems with activity.

Getreidegasse 50. www.finestfingerfood.com. ℂ **0662/848-800.** Reservations required. Breakfast 10€–16€. Cones 4.80€–10.50€ depending on the filling. Set menus 17.50€ 3 courses; 23.50€ 4 courses; 28.50€ 5 courses; 33.50€ 6 courses; 38.50€ 7 courses. AE, DC, MC, V. Daily 8:30am–midnight. Bus: 1, 4, or 8.

Krimpelstätter SALZBURGER/AUSTRIAN   This restaurant is an enduring favorite, dating from 1548. It was originally designed and constructed as an inn, with chiseled stone columns that support the vaulted ceilings and heavy timbers. Both the informal room marked GASTZIMMER and a trio of cozy antique dining rooms serve the same menu, tasty and high-quality Land Salzburg regional cuisine featuring wild game dishes. Start with the cream of goose soup or else homemade chamois sausage. Traditional main courses include roast pork with dumplings, and white sausage *Gröstl* with mustard and sauerkraut. Spinach dumplings are topped with a cheese sauce, and marinated beef stew comes with noodles in butter. Wash it all down with an Augustiner beer.

Müllner Hauptstrasse 31. www.krimpelstaetter.at. ✆ **0662/432-274.** Reservations recommended. Main courses 8€–16€. No credit cards. Mon–Sat 11am–midnight. Bus: 7 or 10.

Restaurant s'Herzl ★★ 🍴 AUSTRIAN/VIENNESE   With an entrance on the landmark Karajanplatz, s'Herzl sits next door and is connected to the glamorous Goldener Hirsch. Good value attracts visitors and locals alike to its pair of cozy rooms, one paneled and timbered. Waitresses in dirndls serve appetizing entrees, which are likely to include roast pork with dumplings, various grills, game stew (in season), and, for the heartiest eaters, a farmer's plate of boiled pork, roast pork, grilled sausages, dumplings, and sauerkraut.

Karajanplatz 7. www.goldenerhirsch.com/herzl. ✆ **0662/808-4889.** Reservations recommended. Main courses 7€–24€. Set menu 13€–20€. AE, DC, MC, V. Daily 11:30am–10pm. Bus: 1, 4, or 8.

Sternbräu AUSTRIAN   The entrance to this establishment is through an arched cobblestone passageway leading off a street in the Old Town. The place seems big enough to have fed half the Austro-Hungarian army, with a series of eight rooms in varying degrees of formality—a rustic fantasy combining masonry columns with hand-hewn beams and wood paneling. You can also eat in the chestnut tree-shaded beer garden, which is usually packed on summer nights, or under the weathered arcades of an inner courtyard. Drinks are served in the restaurant's bar, Grünstern. Daily specials include typically Austrian dishes such as Wiener and chicken schnitzels, trout, cold marinated herring, Hungarian goulash, and hearty regional soups.

Griesgasse 23. www.sternbraeu.at. ✆ **0662/842-140.** Reservations not accepted. Main courses 6€–17€. AE, MC, V. Daily 9am–11pm. Bus: 1, 4, 7, or 8.

Stiftskeller St. Peter (Peterskeller) ★ AUSTRIAN/VIENNESE   Legend has it that Mephistopheles met with Faust in this tavern, which isn't that far-fetched, considering it was established by Benedictine monks in A.D. 803. In fact, it's the oldest restaurant in Europe and is housed in the abbey of the church that supposedly brought Christianity to Austria. Aside from a collection of baroque banquet rooms, there's an inner courtyard with rock-cut vaults, a handful of dignified wood-paneled rooms, and a brick-vaulted cellar. In addition to wine from the abbey's own vineyards, the tavern serves good home-style Austrian cooking, including roast pork in gravy with sauerkraut and bread dumplings, and loin of lamb with asparagus. Vegetarian dishes, such as semolina dumplings on noodles in a parsley sauce, are also featured. They are especially known here for their desserts. Try the apple strudel or sweet curd strudel with vanilla sauce or ice cream, and most definitely the famed *Salzburger Nockerln*.

St.-Peter-Bezirk 1/4. www.stpeter-stiftskeller.at. ✆ **0662/841-2680.** Reservations recommended. Main courses 12€–25€. Set menus 16€–45€. AE, DC, MC, V. Mon–Sun 11:30am–midnight. Bus: 1, 4, or 10.

Zum Eulenspiegel ★ AUSTRIAN/VIENNESE   Housed in a white-and-peach building opposite Mozart's birthplace, Zum Eulenspiegel sits at one end of a quiet cobblestone square in the Old Town. Inside, guests have a choice of five rooms on three different levels, all rustically but elegantly decorated, including a small bar area for pre-dinner drinks. Traditional Austrian cuisine is meticulously adhered to here. The menu features such classic dishes as *Tafelspitz*, Wiener schnitzel, spinach dumplings stuffed with ewe cheese in a tomato sauce and topped with parmesan, filet of pork with warm cabbage salad and bacon, and, for dessert, nutty *Mozart Knödel* with fruit topping.

Hagenauerplatz 2. www.zum-eulenspiegel.at. ℂ **0662/843-180.** Reservations required. Main courses 13€–23€. AE, MC, V. Mon–Sat 11am–2pm and 6–10:30pm. Bus: 1, 4, 7, 8, or 10.

Inexpensive

Festungsrestaurant ★ ☺ SALZBURG/AUSTRIAN   The venue of this well-known restaurant is modern, warmly decorated, and airy, perched atop the former stronghold of the prince-archbishops of Salzburg, on a huge rocky spur about 122m (400 ft.) above the Old Town and the Salzach River. From its windows, you'll have a sweeping view over the city and the surrounding countryside. The kitchen offers fish, well-prepared beef, pork, lamb, and such old-fashioned and traditional dishes as *Salzburger bauernschmaus* (a bubbling stewpot of veal, pork, sausage, and dumplings), *Salzburger Schnitzel, Salzburger Gröstl* (a form of beef hash with potatoes and onions), and *käse Spätzle* (*spätzle* with cheese). There's also wild game dishes served in season. The Fürstenzimmer offers occasional concerts, often Mozart. For ticket information, call ℂ **0662/825-858.**

Hohensalzburg, Mönchsberg 34. www.festungsrestaurant.at. ℂ **0662/841-780.** Reservations required July–Aug. Main courses 10€–21€. AE, DC, MC, V. Mar–Jan 7 daily 10am–9pm. Funicular from the Old Town.

ON THE RIGHT BANK
Expensive

Polo Lounge (in the Bristol Hotel) CONTINENTAL   This is the dining counterpart of the upscale restaurant within Salzburg's other top-notch hotel, the Goldener Hirsch. In this case, the venue is a stately, baronial-looking area outfitted in tones of pale orange and accented with large-scale oil paintings. Menus feature freshwater crab salad with mango, tuna carpaccio with horseradish cream sauce, goose-liver parfait with apple chutney, grilled filet of beef with pinot noir sauce, roast loin of lamb with a pumpkin-flavored risotto, or perhaps grilled loin of veal with morel-flavored cream sauce. And for dessert, consider the warm chocolate mousse served with hot and sour cherries. Immediately adjacent to the restaurant is a club-style bar.

In the Hotel Bristol, Makartplatz 4. www.bristol-salzburg.at. ℂ **0662/873-5577.** Reservations recommended. Main courses 18€–32€. AE, DC, MC, V. Mon–Sat noon–2pm and 6–10pm. Bus: 1, 3, 4, 5, or 6.

Inexpensive

Zum Fidelen Affen AUSTRIAN   Set on the eastern edge of the river near the Staatsbrücke, this is an animated and jovial pub offering simple, inexpensive, and mostly regional cuisine. A house specialty is a gratin of green (spinach-flavored) noodles in tomato sauce with fresh parmesan and salad. Also popular are Wiener schnitzels, ham goulash with dumplings, and the filling Monkey Steak: grilled pork with *Rösti* potatoes, mushrooms, bacon, tomatoes, and cheese. Dessert might be a cheese dumpling or one of several kinds of pastries. True to the establishment's name, translated as "The Merry Monkey," its interior depicts painted and sculpted simians cavorting across the walls.

Priesterhausgasse 8. ⓒ **0662/877-361.** Main courses 10€–17€. DC, MC, V. Mon–Sat 5pm–midnight. Bus: 1, 3, 4, 5, or 6.

Shopping

Getreidegasse is a main shopping thoroughfare in Salzburg, but you'll also find some intriguing little shops on **Residenzplatz.**

Opened in 1871, **Gertraud Lackner,** Badergasse 2 (www.woodart.at; ⓒ **0662/842-385**; bus: 3, 5, or 6), offers both antique and modern country wood furniture. Among the new items are chests, chessboards, angels, cupboards, crèches, candlesticks, and especially chairs. **Musikhaus Pühringer,** Getreidegasse 13 (ⓒ **0662/843-267**; bus: 1, 2, 29, or 49), established in 1910, sells all kinds of classical musical instruments, especially those popular in central Europe, as well as a large selection of electronic instruments (including synthesizers and amplifiers). You'll find classical and folk music CDs and tapes, plus many classical recordings, especially those by Mozart.

Salzburger Heimatwerk, Am Residenzplatz 9 (ⓒ **0662/844-110**; bus: 3, 5, 6, 7, 8, or 10), is one of the best places in town to buy local Austrian handicrafts and original regional clothing.

Wiener Porzellanmanufaktur Augarten Gesellschaft, Alter Markt 11 (www.augarten.at; ⓒ **0662/840-714**; bus: 3, 5, 6, 8, or 10) is the premier shop in Salzburg for Austrian porcelain, specializing in Augarten. Such patterns as Viennese Rose and Maria Theresia are still very popular, but its most famous item is the black-and-white coffee set created by architect/designer Josef Hoffmann.

Entertainment & Nightlife
THE PERFORMING ARTS

It's said there's a musical event—often a Mozart concert—staged virtually every night in Salzburg. Visit the **Salzburg tourist office,** Auerspergstrasse 6 (ⓒ **0662/889-870**), for a free copy of *Offizieller Wochenspiegel,* a monthly pamphlet listing all major and many minor local cultural events.

The major ticket agency affiliated with the city of Salzburg is located adjacent to Salzburg's main tourist office, at Mozartplatz 5. The **Salzburger Ticket Office** (ⓒ **0662/840-310**) is open Monday to Friday 9am to 6pm (to 7pm in midsummer) and Saturday 9am to noon.

If you don't want to pay a ticket agent's commission, you can go directly to the box office of a theater or concert hall. However, many of the best seats may have already been sold, especially those at the Salzburg Festival.

The rich collection of concerts that combine every summer to form the Salzburg Festival's program is presented in several concert halls scattered throughout Salzburg. The largest is the **Festspielhaus,** Hofstallgasse 1 (ⓒ **0662/8045**; bus: 1, 5, or 6). Within the Festspielhaus complex you'll find the **Felsenreitschule,** an outdoor auditorium with a makeshift roof. Originally built in 1800 as a riding rink, it's famous as the site where scenes from *The Sound of Music* were filmed. Tickets cost from 15€ to 360€, with the more expensive representing the higher cost for the best seats at the Salzburg Festival; average but good seats run 35€ to 105€. Instead of going directly to the Festspielhaus, you can purchase tickets in advance at the box office at

Getting Tickets to the Salzburg Festival

One of the premier music attractions of Europe, the Salzburg Festival celebrates its 93rd season in 2013. Details on the festival are available by contacting **Salzburg Festival,** Hofstallgasse 1, A-5010 Salzburg, Austria (www. salzburgerfestspiele.at; ✆ **0662/804-5500**).

Waagplatz 1A (✆ **0662/845-346**), close to the tourist office, Monday to Friday 8am to 6pm.

The **Mozarteum** (see box "In Mozart's Footsteps", p. 66) at Schwarzstrasse 26 and Mirabellplatz 1 (✆ **0662/873-154;** bus: 1, 2, 3, 5, or 6) also offers large orchestra concerts, as well as organ recitals and chamber-music evenings. It's also a music school, and you can ask about free events staged by the students. The box office is in Mozart's Wohnhaus, Theatergasse 2, open Monday to Friday 9am to 5pm and Saturday 9am to noon with some exceptions. Performances are usually at 11am or 7:30pm. Tickets cost 8€ to 220€.

Besides the venues above, you can attend a concert in dramatic surroundings in the Fürstenzimmer (Prince's Chamber) of the **Hohensalzburg Fortress.** You're likely to hear heavy doses of Mozart and, to a lesser degree, works by Schubert, Brahms, and Beethoven. From mid-May to mid-October, performances are generally held at 9am or 8:30pm every night of the week. The rest of the year, they're presented most (but not all) nights, with occasional week-long breaks, usually at 7:30pm. The box office for the events is at Adlgasser Weg 22 (www.salzburghighlights.at; ✆ **0662/825-858**). To reach the fortress, take the funicular from Festungsgasse.

BEER GARDENS

Regardless of the season, you'll have one of your most enjoyable and authentic evenings in Salzburg at **Augustiner Bräustübl,** Augustinergasse 4 (www.augustinerbier. at; ✆ **0662/431-2460;** bus: 7 or 10). This Bierstube and Biergarten has been dispensing oceans of beer since it was established in 1622. Depending on the weather, the city's beer-drinking fraternity gathers either within the cavernous interior, where three separate rooms each hold up to 400 people, or in the chestnut-shaded courtyard. You'll find about a dozen kiosks, where you can buy takeout portions of wursts, sandwiches, and pretzels. Farther on, choose a thick stoneware mug from the racks and carry it to the beer tap, paying the cashier as you go. A full liter begins at 6€; a half liter costs 4€ depending on the type of beer. The open hours are Monday to Friday 3 to 11pm and Saturday and Sunday 2:30 to 11pm.

Immediately below the Hohensalzburg Fortress and established in the early 1800s is the **Restaurant StieglKeller,** Festungsgasse 10 (www.taste-gassner.com; ✆ **0662/842-681;** bus: 2, 3, 5, 6, 8, or 10), part of which is carved into the rocks of Mönchsberg. To get here, you'll have to negotiate a steep cobblestone street that drops off on one side to reveal a panoramic view of Salzburg. The cavernous interior is open only in summer, when you can join hundreds of others in drinking beer and eating sausages, schnitzels, and other Bierkeller food.

The **Sternbräu,** Getreidegasse 34, in the heart of historic Salzburg has a Biergarten atmosphere and serves traditional Austrian cuisine. The Sternbräu is also home to the **Sound of Salzburg Dinner Show** (www.soundofsalzburgshow.com;

© **0662/826-617**), featuring the music of Mozart, traditional Salzburg folk music, and, of course, songs from *The Sound of Music*. The show takes place from May 15 to October 15, daily at 7:30pm. A three-course meal, including your choice of chicken and noodles or roast pork, and the show cost 48€. If you want to skip the meal, you can arrive at 8:15pm to see the show for 33€.

2 Where to Stay

ON THE LEFT BANK (ALTSTADT)
Very Expensive

Altstadt Radisson Blu ★★   This is not your typical Radisson property—in fact, its style and charm are a rather radical departure for the chain. Dating from 1377, this is a luxuriously and elegantly converted Altstadt inn. The old and new are blended in perfect harmony here, with the historic facade concealing top-rate comforts and luxuries. The cozy, antiques-filled lobby sets the tone, while a flower-lined, sky-lit atrium adds cheer even on the darkest of days. Stone arches from the medieval structure still remain. Rooms vary greatly in size but have a certain charm and sparkle, with some of the city's best beds, complemented by elegant bathrooms equipped with tub/shower combinations.

Rudolfskai 28/Judengasse 15, A-5020 Salzburg. www.austria-trend.at. © **0662/848-571.** Fax 0662/848-571-6. 62 units. 310€–345€ double; 650€ suite. Rates include buffet breakfast. AE, DC, MC, V. Parking 26€. Bus: 3, 5, 6, 7, 8, or 10. **Amenities:** Restaurant; bar; babysitting; nonsmoking rooms. *In room:* TV, minibar, hair dryer, Wi-Fi (free).

Goldener Hirsch ★★★   Goldener Hirsch wins the award for the finest hotel in Salzburg; this establishment is so steeped in legend and history that any Austrian will instantly recognize its name. The hotel is built on a small scale, yet it absolutely exudes aristocratic elegance, which is enhanced by the superb staff. Sitting in an enviable position in the Old Town, a few doors from Mozart's birthplace, it's composed of three medieval town houses joined together in a labyrinth of rustic hallways and staircases. A fourth, called "The Coppersmith's House," is across the street and has 17 charming and elegant rooms.

Getreidegasse 37, A-5020 Salzburg. www.goldenerhirsch.com. © **800/325-3589** in the U.S. and Canada, or **0662/80840.** Fax 0662/843-349. 69 units. 180€–535€ double; from 1,080€ suite. Higher rates at festival time (the 1st week of Apr and mid-July to Aug). AE, DC, MC, V. You can double-park in front of the Getreidegasse entrance or at the Karajanplatz entrance, and a staff member will take your vehicle to the hotel's garage for 28€. Bus: 1, 4, 8, or 10. **Amenities:** 2 restaurants; bar; room service; nonsmoking rooms. *In room:* A/C, TV, minibar, hair dryer, safe, Wi-Fi (free).

Moderate

Altstadthotel Weisse Taube   Constructed in 1365 the Weisse Taube, or White Dove, has been known as such since 1904, and is now run by the friendly Wollner family. Rooms are, for the most part, renovated and comfortably streamlined, with traditional furnishings, and frequently renewed beds. The hotel is in the pedestrian area of the Old Town a few steps from Mozartplatz, but you can drive up to it to unload baggage.

Kaigasse 9, A-5020 Salzburg. www.weissetaube.at. © **0662/842-404.** Fax 0662/841-783. 31 units. 98€–152€ double. Rates include breakfast. AE, MC, V. Parking 9€–15€. Garage 9€. Bus: 3, 5, 6, 7, 8, or 10. **Amenities:** Bar; lounge. *In room:* TV, minibar, hair dryer, Wi-Fi (1€ for code, then free).

Altstadthotel Wolf ✦   Ideally located near Mozartplatz, this place dates from 1429. A stucco exterior with big shutters hides the rustic and inviting interior that is decorated with a few baroque touches and often sunny rooms. Many new bathrooms have been installed, making this a more inviting choice than ever. The rooms are a bit cramped, as are the shower-only bathrooms. Still, this pension represents very good value for high-priced Salzburg. Since the hotel is usually full, reservations are imperative.

Kaigasse 7, A-5020 Salzburg. www.hotelwolf.com. © **0662/843-4530.** Fax 0662/842-4234. 15 units. 110€–214€ double; 188€–248€ junior suite. Rates include buffet breakfast. V. No parking. Bus: 3, 5, 6, 7, 8, or 10. **Amenities:** Babysitting. *In room:* TV, Internet (free).

Hotel Blaue Gans   The Blue Goose lies in the historic core of Salzburg, near the underground garages of the Mönchsberg, a few doors away from hotels that charge almost twice as much. Although the building is almost 700 years old, a 2002 renovation transformed the establishment into an art hotel. Each room has modern furniture and generous space, and those opening onto the courtyard are quieter than those facing the street; no. 332 and 336 are probably the biggest. You'll register in an understated lobby, one that's so discreetly tucked away that it might be hard to identify.

Getreidegasse 41–43, A-5020 Salzburg. www.blauegans.at. © **0662/842-4910.** Fax 0662/842-4919. 38 units. 132€–220€ double; 245€–339€ junior suite. Rates include buffet breakfast. AE, DC, MC, V. Parking 10€. Bus: 1, 4, or 8. **Amenities:** Restaurant; bar; babysitting. *In room:* TV, minibar, hair dryer, safe, Wi-Fi (free).

Hotel Elefant   Near the Old Town Rathaus, in a quiet alley off Getreidegasse, is this well-established, family-run hotel with the Best Western stamp of approval. It, too, is in one of Salzburg's most ancient buildings, more than 700 years old. The well-furnished and high-ceilinged rooms have small bathrooms and redesigned interiors with radiant color schemes. The vaulted Bürgerstüberl restaurant serves up Austrian and international cuisine.

Sigmund-Haffner-Gasse 4, A-5020 Salzburg. www.elefant.at. © **800/780-7234** in the U.S. and Canada, or **0662/843-3970.** Fax 0662/8401-0928. 31 units. 102€–200€ double. Rates include buffet breakfast. AE, DC, MC, V. Nearby parking 10€. Bus: 1, 4, 8, or 10. **Amenities:** 2 restaurants; bar; room service; babysitting; nonsmoking rooms. *In room:* TV, minibar, hair dryer, safe, Wi-Fi (free).

ON THE RIGHT BANK
Expensive
Sacher Salzburg Österreichischer Hof ★★★   Built originally as the Hotel d'Autriche in 1866, this popular hotel was soon attracting guests from all over the world. It has survived the ravages of war, always keeping up with the times through renovations and expansions. Inside are big windows with panoramic views of the Old Town. The cheerful and comfortable rooms are well furnished, with excellent beds. Try to reserve a room overlooking the river. A host of drinking and dining facilities is available, including a cozy bar with piano music in the evening; the **Roter Salon,** an elegant dining room facing the river; the **Zirbelzimmer,** an award-winning restaurant; the **Salzachgrill,** offering everything from a snack to a steak, with a riverside terrace; the **Café Sacher,** a traditional Austrian cafe, also with a riverside terrace; and a pastry shop that sells the famous Sachertorte.

Schwarzstrasse 5–7, A-5020 Salzburg. www.sacher.com. © **800/745-8883** in the U.S. and Canada, or 0662/88977. Fax 0662/8897-7551. 113 units. 225€–391€ double; suites from 471€. AE, DC, MC, V. Parking 25€. Bus: 1, 3, 5, or 6. **Amenities:** 3 restaurants; 2 bars; cafe; lounge; health club; sauna; steam room; room service; babysitting; rooms for those w/limited mobility. *In room:* A/C, TV, minibar, hair dryer, Wi-Fi (free).

Hotel Stein ★★   This stunning, revitalized Bauhaus hotel lies directly on the water with a panoramic view of the historic Old Town of Salzburg. The Stein, which had grown stodgy, was refitted with a contemporary look from its animal prints to its flatscreen TVs, and the rooftop cafe has accurately been called divine. The bedrooms, ranging from beautifully furnished doubles to luxurious suites, are well appointed, with state-of-the-art private marble bathrooms. Suites have leather bedspreads, leather upholstery, and zebra-skin patterns on other in-room fabrics; other rooms are outfitted in either a Mozart motif (that is, vaguely rococo patterns) or the Stein design (conservatively modern) style. After a restful night's sleep, you're served a breakfast buffet on the terrace overlooking the city.

Giselakai 3–5, A-5020 Salzburg. www.hotelstein.at. ⓒ **0662/874-3460.** Fax 0662/874-3469. 54 units. 175€–230€ double; 245€–290€ junior suite; 265€–310€ suite. Rates include breakfast. AE, DC, MC, V. Parking: 19€. Bus: 1, 3, 4, 5, 6, 7, 8, or 10. **Amenities:** Cafe bar; room service; babysitting; laundry service; dry cleaning. In room: TV, hair dryer, safe, Wi-Fi (free).

Moderate

Altstadthotel Wolf-Dietrich ★ ☺   Two 19th-century town houses were joined together to make this select little hotel. The smallish rooms are comfortably furnished and appealing, with excellent beds. The "Wiener Kaffeehaus" pays successful homage to the large extravagant coffeehouses built in the former century in Vienna, Budapest, and Prague. Alpine carvings and graceful pine detailing adorn one of the two restaurants. Decorating the indoor swimming pool are mirrors and unusual murals of Neptune chasing a sea nymph.

Wolf-Dietrich-Strasse 7, A-5020 Salzburg. www.salzburg-hotel.at. ⓒ **0662/871-275.** Fax 0662/871-2759. 27 units. 100€–230€ double; 155€–277€ suite. Children under 12 stay free in parent's room. Rates include buffet breakfast. AE, DC, MC, V. Parking 15€. Bus: 2 or 4. **Amenities:** Restaurant; bar; cafe; indoor heated pool; spa; room service; babysitting; solarium. In room: TV, minibar, hair dryer, Wi-Fi (free).

Hotel & Villa Auersperg ★   A traditional family-run hotel near the right bank of the Salzach, this hotel lies only a 5-minute walk from the Altstadt. With its own sunny gardens, it consists of two buildings: a main structure and a smaller villa. The inviting rooms are warm, large, and cozy, with big windows, and well-equipped bathrooms, moderate in size. A 2009 renovation added a touch of sleek modernity to its old-fashioned charm. The library bar is not only convivial and informal, but also one of our favorite spots for drinking and conversation in Salzburg. On the top floor, you'll find a roof terrace offering views of Salzburg.

Auerspergstrasse 61, A-5020 Salzburg. www.auersperg.at. ⓒ **0662/889-440.** Fax 0662/889-4455. 55 units. 155€–195€ double; 225€–295€ suite. Rates include buffet breakfast. AE, DC, MC, V. Free parking. Bus: 2 from the train station. **Amenities:** Bar; exercise room; sauna; steam room; laundry service; dry cleaning. In room: TV, minibar, hair dryer, safe, Wi-Fi (free).

Hotel Trumer Stube   Originally built in 1869 as a private home, this flower-bedecked town house is tucked in a side street of the Old Town, well buffered from the bustle of Linzergasse, but only a 6-minute stroll from Mirabell Gardens and the Mozart Wohnhaus. Ideal for couples and families, it's managed by the friendly Marianne Hirschbichler, who speaks English and is happy to give sightseeing tips, and make restaurant and guided-tour reservations. An elevator provides access to comfortable rooms in a country style that are elegant in their simplicity, accentuated with Asian or small-town baroque touches, and equipped with spotless bathrooms.

Bergstrasse 6, A-5020 Salzburg. www.trumer-stube.at. ℂ **0662/874-776** or **0662/875-168.** Fax 0662/874-326. 22 units. 96€–135€ double; 154€ triple. Served breakfast available. AE, DC, MC, V. Parking 11€. Bus: 1, 3, 5, or 6 to Makartplatz. **Amenities:** Lounge. *In room:* TV, Wi-Fi (free).

Inexpensive

Berglandhotel ★ ▮ This guesthouse sits within a quiet residential neighborhood, a 15-minute walk from the train station and only a 10-minute walk from the Altstadt (rental bikes are available). It is managed by the friendly English-speaking Peter Kuhn, who has decorated the *Pension* with his own artwork, oversees breakfast, and is on hand most evenings to converse with guests in the lounge bar. An outdoor terrace is also available for relaxing. There's a green *Kachelofen* (tiled stove), and decor that might remind you of a ski lodge high in the Alps.

Rupertsgasse 15, A-5020 Salzburg. www.berglandhotel.at. ℂ **0662/872-318.** Fax 0662/872-3188. 18 units. 80€–139€ double; 120€–170€ suite. Rates include buffet breakfast. AE, DC, MC, V. Free parking. Closed Dec 20–Jan 31. Bus: 4. **Amenities:** Lounge bar. *In room:* TV, hair dryer, Wi-Fi (free).

INNSBRUCK ★ & TYROL

Ice and mountains, dark forests and alpine meadows full of spring wildflowers, summer holidays and winter sports—that's Tyrol. Those intrepid tourists, the British, discovered its vacation delights and made it a fashionable destination in the last century. Tyrol (*Tirol* in German) is now the most frequented winter playground in Austria, and in summer, the extensive network of mountain paths lures visitors.

Skiers flock here in winter for a ski season that runs from mid-December to the end of March. Many prefer its ski slopes to those of Switzerland. It's been a long time since the eyes of the world focused on Innsbruck at the Winter Olympics in 1964 and 1976, but the legacy lives on in the ski conditions and facilities on some of the world's choicest slopes.

Innsbruck

Innsbruck has a particularly lovely medieval town center, and town planners have protected this historic Altstadt. Visitors can take countless excursions in the environs; at Innsbruck's doorstep lie some of the most beautiful drives in Europe. Just take your pick: Head in any direction, up any valley, and you'll be treated to mountains and alpine beauty.

ESSENTIALS
Getting There

BY PLANE   Innsbruck's airport, **Flughafen Innsbruck-Kranebitten,** Fürstenweg 180 (www.innsbruck-airport.com; ℂ **0512/225-250**), is 3km (1¾ miles) west of the city. It offers regularly scheduled air service from the major airports of Austria and Europe's major cities.

BY TRAIN   Innsbruck is connected with all parts of Europe by international railway links. Trains arrive at the main railway station, the **Hauptbahnhof,** Südtiroler Platz (ℂ **05/1717** for all rail information). There are at least eight daily trains from Munich (trip time: 2 hr.) and 18 daily trains from Salzburg (2 hr.).

BY CAR   If you're **driving** down from Salzburg in the northeast, take Autobahn A8 west through Germany, then Autobahn A93 south back into Austria, where it becomes the A12 and heads southwest to Innsbruck. From Italy in the south, you can take the Brenner toll motorway.

VISITOR INFORMATION   The **tourist office,** Burggraben 3 (www.innsbruck. info; ✆ **0512/59850**), is open daily 9am to 6pm.

CITY LAYOUT   This historic city is divided by the Inn River into left- and right-bank districts. Two major bridges cross the Inn, the **Universitätsssbrücke** and the **Alte Innsbrücke (Old Inn Bridge).** Many of the attractions, including the Hofkirche and the Goldenes Dachl, are on the right bank. If you arrive at the Haupt-bahnhof, take Salurner Strasse and Brixner Strasse to Maria-Theresien-Strasse, which will put you into the very heart of Innsbruck.

The **Altstadt** is bounded on the north by the Inn River and on the south by Burg-graben and Marktgraben. The main street of this historic district is **Herzog-Fried-rich-Strasse,** which becomes **Maria-Theresien-Strasse,** the axis of the postmedieval new part of town. The Altstadt becomes a pedestrian zone after 10:30am (wear good shoes on the cobblestone streets).

GETTING AROUND   A network of 3 **tram** and 25 **bus lines** covers all of Inns-bruck and its close environs, and buses and trams use the same tickets. Single tickets in the central area cost 1.80€ (1.90€ from the driver), and a booklet of four tickets goes for 6€. The tram is called either *Strassenbahn* or *Trambahn.* On the left bank of the Inn River, the main tram and bus arteries are Museumstrasse and Mariahilfer-strasse. On the right bank, trams and buses aren't routed into the pedestrian zone but to their main stop in Marktgraben. For information about various routes, call the **Innsbrucker Verkehrsbetriebe** (www.ivb.at; ✆ **0512/53070**). Most tickets can be purchased at the Innsbruck tourist office, tobacco shops, and automated vending machines. A *Tageskarte* **(day pass),** costing 4.30€ for 24 hours, is available only from the tourist information office, tobacco shops, and cafes. It allows you to ride on all trains and buses. If you plan to move about the Innsbruck area extensively, ask about the **Innsbruck Card,** which offers unlimited transportation and other advan-tages. A 24-hour pass sells for 31€, a 48-hour pass for 39€, and a 72-hour pass for 45€.

Austria Postal Service buses (one of two different bus networks maintained by the Austrian government) leave from the Autobushof (Central Bus Station), adjacent to the Hauptbahnhof on Sterzinger Strasse. Here buses head for all parts of Tyrol. The station is open Monday to Friday 7:30am to 6pm and Saturday 7am to 1pm. For information about bus schedules, call ✆ **0512/500-5307.**

Taxi stands are scattered at strategic points throughout the city, or you can call a radio car (✆ **0512/5311** or **1718**). For a nostalgic ride, you can hire a horse-drawn carriage *(Fiaker)* from a spot adjacent to the **Tiroler Landestheater,** Rennweg.

If neither the tram nor the carriage option appeals to you, consider renting a **bike** at the Hauptbahnhof. Rentals cost 22€ per day or 18€ for 5 hours. You can return these bikes to any rail station in Austria if you don't plan to return to Innsbruck. Rent-als are available April to early November only. For more information, call **Sport Neuner** (www.bike-innsbruck-tirol.at; ✆ **0512/561-501**).

Although you can make a better deal renting a car before you leave North America, it's possible to rent cars in Innsbruck. You might try **Avis,** Salurner Strasse 15 (✆ **0512/571-754**); or **Hertz,** Südtirolerplatz 1 (✆ **0512/580-901**), across from the Hauptbahnhof. Although paperwork and billing errors are harder to resolve whenever you rent from a non-U.S.-based car-rental outfit, you might also check the rates at a local car outfitter, **Ajax,** Amrasserstrasse 6 (✆ **0512/583-232**).

Innsbruck

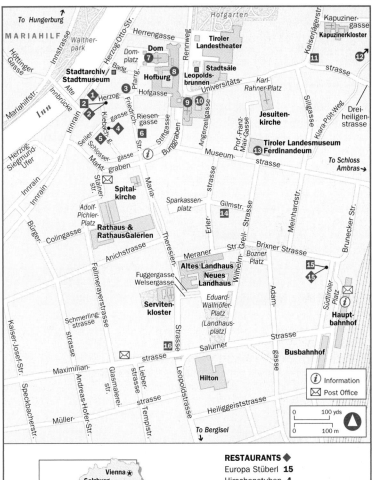

RESTAURANTS ◆
Europa Stüberl **15**
Hirschenstuben **4**
Restaurant Goldener Adler **2**
Restaurant Ottoburg **1**
Weisses Rössl **5**

ATTRACTIONS ●
Dom zu St. Jakob **7**
Goldenes Dachl & Maximilianeum **3**
Hofburg **8**
Hofkirche **9**
Swarovski Kristallwelten **12**
Tiroler Landesmuseen Ferdinandeum **13**
Tiroler Volkskunst-Museum **10**

HOTELS ■
Gasthof-Hotel Weisses Kreuz **6**
Goldene Krone **16**
Grand Hotel Europa **15**
Hotel Central **14**
Hotel Goldener Adler **2**
Romantik Hotel-Restaurant
  Schwarzer Adler **11**

[FastFACTS] INNSBRUCK

Currency Exchange   Banks are usually open Monday to Thursday 7:45am to 12:30pm and 2:30 to 4pm, and Friday 7:45am to 3pm. There are also exchange facilities at Innsbruck's tourist office (see above). The automated currency exchange facilities at the Hauptbahnhof are available 24 hours a day.

Dentists & Doctors   Check with the tourist office for a list of private English-speaking dentists and doctors; or contact the **University Clinic,** Anichstrasse 35 (✆ **0512/504**).

Emergencies   Call ✆ **133** for the police, ✆ **122** for a fire, or ✆ **144** for an ambulance.

Internet Access   You can check e-mail or access the Internet free with your own laptop at the **Picasso Internet Café,** Maria-Theresien-Strasse 16 (✆ **0512/584-848;** tram: 3). It's open Monday to Saturday from 6:30am to 1am.

Pharmacies   In the heart of Innsbruck, **St.-Anna Apotheke,** Maria-Theresien-Strasse 4 (www.apotheke-innsbruck.at; ✆ **0512/585-847**), is open Monday to Saturday 8am to 6pm. The pharmacy posts addresses of other pharmacies open on weekends or at night.

Post Office   The **Hauptpostamt (Central Post Office),** Innrain 15 (✆ **0512/5000**), is open Monday to Friday from 7am to 8pm, Saturday 9am to 3pm, and Sunday 10am to 6pm. The post office at the **Hauptbahnhof,** Bruneckstrasse 1–3 (✆ **0512/5000**), is open Monday to Friday 8am to 6pm, and 9am to noon on Saturday.

Telephone   The **country code** for Austria is **43.** The **city code** for Innsbruck is **512;** use this code when you're calling from outside Austria. If you're within Austria, use **0512.**

EXPLORING INNSBRUCK

The Altstadt and the surrounding alpine countryside are Innsbruck's main attractions. Often it's fascinating just to watch the passersby, who are occasionally attired in Tyrolean regional dress.

Maria-Theresien-Strasse, which cuts through the heart of the city from north to south, is the main street and a good place to begin exploring the city. Many 17th- and 18th-century houses line this wide street. On the south end of the street, there's a **Triumphpforte (Triumphal Arch),** modeled after those in Rome. Maria Theresa ordered it built in 1765 to honor her son's marriage and to commemorate the death of her beloved husband, Emperor Franz I. From this arch southward the street is called **Leopoldstrasse.**

Going north from the arch along Maria-Theresien-Strasse, you'll see **Annasäule (St. Anna's Column)** in front of the 19th-century Rathaus (town hall). The column was erected in 1706 to celebrate the withdrawal in 1703 of invading Bavarian armies during the War of the Spanish Succession. Not far north of the Annasäule, the wide street narrows and becomes **Herzog-Friedrich-Strasse,** running through the heart of the medieval quarter. This street is arcaded and flanked by a number of well-maintained burghers' houses with their jumble of turrets and gables; look for the multitude of dormer windows and oriels.

Dom zu St. Jakob (Cathedral of St. James) CATHEDRAL   Designed and rebuilt from 1717 to 1724 by Johann Jakob Herkommer, the Dom has a lavishly embellished baroque interior. A chief treasure is Lucas Cranach the Elder's *Maria Hilf (St. Mary of Succor).*

Domplatz 6. ✆ **0512/583-902.** Free admission. Winter daily 6:30am–6pm; summer daily 7am–7pm. Closed Fri noon–3pm. Tram: 1 or 3.

Goldenes Dachl (Golden Roof) & Maximilianeum ★ ARCHITECTURE/ MUSEUM "The Golden Roof," Innsbruck's greatest tourist attraction and its most characteristic landmark, is a three-story balcony on a house in the Altstadt; the late-Gothic oriels are capped with 2,657 gold-plated tiles. It was constructed for Emperor Maximilian I in the beginning of the 16th century to serve as a royal box where he could sit in luxury and enjoy tournaments in the square below.

A small museum, the **Maximilianeum,** is on the second floor of the municipal building attached to the Goldenes Dachl. Inside are exhibits celebrating the life and accomplishments of the Innsbruck-based Habsburg emperor, Maximilian I, who bridged the gap between the Middle Ages and the German Renaissance.

Herzog-Friedrich-Strasse 15. www.innsbruck.gv.at/goldenesdachl. ℂ **0512/5360-1441.** Admission to the Maximilianeum 4€ adults; 2€ seniors, students, and children 17 and under. No charge for views of the Goldenes Dachl, and no restrictions as to when it can be viewed. Maximilianeum May–Sept daily 10am–5pm; Oct–Apr Tues–Sun 10am–5pm; closed Nov. Tram: 1 or 3.

Hofburg ★ PALACE The 15th-century imperial palace of Emperor Maximilian I, flanked by a set of domed towers, was rebuilt in the baroque style (with rococo detailing) during the 18th century on orders of Maria Theresa. It's a fine example of baroque secular architecture, with four wings and a two-story *Riesensaal* (Giant's Hall), painted in white and gold and filled with portraits of the Habsburgs. Also of compelling interest are the State Rooms, the chapel, and a scattering of private apartments. You can wander at will through the rooms, but if you want to participate in a guided tour, management conducts two a day, at 11am and 2pm, in a multilingual format that includes English. Each tour lasts 30 to 45 minutes and costs 3€.

Rennweg 1. www.hofburg-innsbruck.at. ℂ **0512/5871-8612.** Admission 8€ adults, 6€ seniors and students 19–27, 18 and under free. Daily 9am–5pm. Open Wed Mar–Aug until 7pm. Tram: 1 or 3.

Hofkirche MONUMENT The most important treasure in the Hofkirche is the cenotaph of Maximilian I, a great example of German Renaissance style. It has 28 bronze 16th-century statues of Maximilian's real and legendary ancestors surrounding the kneeling emperor.

Universitätsstrasse 2. www.hofkirche.at. ℂ **0512/584-302.** Admission 8€ adults, 2€ students, 4€ seniors, free for children 5 and under. Mon–Sat 9am–5pm. Tram: 1 or 3.

Swarovski Kristallwelten (Crystal Worlds) ★★★ ☺ MUSEUM Designed by the Viennese multimedia artist Andrew Heller, this attraction some 15km (9⅓ miles) from Innsbruck is dedicated to the vision of Daniel Swarovski, founder of the world's leading producer of full crystal.

After entering the giant head with its glittering eyes and waterfall, you'll immediately see a long wall of crystal with 12 tons of the finest cut stones in the world. In other chambers you can wander into the "Planet of the Crystals," with a 3-D light show. Crystalline works of art on display were designed by everybody from Andy Warhol to Salvador Dalí. In the Crystal Dome you get an idea of what it's like being inside a giant crystal, and in the Crystal Theater a fairy tale world of color, mystery, and graceful movement unfolds. You can easily spend 2 hours here.

Kristallweltenstrasse 1. http://kristallwelten.swarovski.com. ℂ **05224/51080.** Admission 11€, free for children 14 and under. Daily 8am–6:30pm (last entrance 5:30pm). Take the Wattens motorway exit (A12) and follow signs to Kristallwelten, or take the shuttle bus from the Hauptbahnhof that leaves at 9am, 11am, 1pm, and 3pm.

Tiroler Landesmuseen Ferdinandeum (Ferdinandeum Tyrol Museum) ★

ART MUSEUM   This celebrated gallery of Flemish and Dutch masters also traces the development of popular art in Tyrol, with highlights from the Gothic period. You'll see the original bas-reliefs used in designing the Goldenes Dachl.

Museumstrasse 15. www.tiroler-landesmuseum.at. © **0512/5948-9510.** Admission 8€ adults, 4€ students, 4€ children 6 and under. June–Sept daily 10am–6pm; Oct–May Tues–Sat 10am–5pm, Sun 10am–1pm. Tram: 1 or 3.

Tiroler Volkskunst-Museum (Tyrol Museum of Folk Art) ★★ ART

MUSEUM   This popular art museum is in the Neues Stift (New Abbey) adjoining the Hofkirche on its eastern side. It contains one of the largest and most impressive collections of Tyrolean artifacts, ranging from handicrafts, furniture, Christmas cribs, and national costumes to religious and secular popular art. You'll also find a collection of models of typical Tyrolean houses.

Universitätsstrasse 2. www.tiroler-volkskunstmuseum.at. © **0512/5948-9510.** Admission 8€ adults, 4€ seniors, 4€ children 6 and under. Mon–Sat 9am–5pm; Sun 10am–5pm. Tram: 1 or 3.

OUTDOOR ACTIVITIES

Five sunny, snow-covered, avalanche-free **ski areas** around the Tyrol are served by five cableways, 44 chairlifts, and ski hoists. The area is also known for bobsled and toboggan runs and ice-skating rinks.

In summer you can play tennis at a number of courts, and golf on either a nine- or an 18-hole course; or you can go horseback riding, mountaineering, gliding, swimming, hiking, or shooting.

The **Hofgarten,** a public park containing lakes and many shade trees, lies north of Rennweg. Concerts are often presented in the garden during the summer.

WHERE TO EAT
Expensive

Europa Stüberl ★★ AUSTRIAN/INTERNATIONAL   This distinguished restaurant, with a delightful Tyrolean ambience, is in a hotel that's the finest address in Innsbruck. The chef succeeds beautifully in fashioning creative takes on traditional regional cooking. Diners can choose from both warm and cold appetizers, ranging from iced angler fish with Chinese tree morels to a small ragout of crayfish in a spicy biscuit with kohlrabi. Some dishes are served only for two people, such as Bresse guinea hen roasted and presented with a herb sauce. Fresh Tyrolean trout almost always appears on the menu, or you may prefer one of the many meat dishes, including red deer ragout and saddle of venison.

In the Grand Hotel Europa, Brixnerstrasse 6. © **0512/5931.** Reservations required. Main courses 13€–33€. Set menus 58€ 5 courses, 74€ 7 courses. AE, DC, MC, V. Daily noon–2pm and 6:30–10pm. Tram: 4. Bus: D, E, or S.

Restaurant Goldener Adler ★ AUSTRIAN/TYROLEAN/INTERNATIONAL
Richly Teutonic and steeped in the decorative traditions of alpine Tyrol, this beautifully decorated restaurant has a deeply entrenched reputation and a loyal following among local residents. The menu includes good, hearty fare inspired by cold-weather outdoor life—the chefs aren't into delicate subtleties. Examples of the cuisine are Tyrolean bacon served with horseradish and farmer's bread; cream of cheese soup with croutons; and Tyroler *Zopfebraten,* a flavorful age-old specialty consisting of strips of veal steak served with herb-enriched cream sauce and spinach dumplings. A well-regarded specialty is a platter known as *Adler Tres.* It contains spinach

dumplings, stuffed noodles, and cheese dumplings, all flavorfully tied together with a brown butter sauce and a gratin of mountain cheese.

Herzog-Friedrich-Strasse 6. © **0512/571-111.** Reservations recommended. Main courses 15€–27€. Set menus 18€–50€. AE, DC, MC, V. Daily 11:30am–10:30pm. Tram: 1 or 3.

Moderate
Hirschenstuben INTERNATIONAL   Beneath a vaulted ceiling in a house built in 1631, this well-established restaurant is charming and welcoming. By its own admission, the establishment is at its best in spring, autumn, and winter, as it lacks a garden or an outdoor terrace for alfresco summer dining. Menu items include steaming platters of pasta, fish soup, trout meunière, sliced veal in cream sauce Zurich-style, beef stroganoff, pepper steak, stewed deer with vegetables, and filet of flounder with parsley and potatoes.

Kiebachgasse 5. © **0512/582-979.** Reservations recommended. Main courses 9€–22€. DC, MC, V. Mon–Sat 6–11pm; Tues–Sat noon–2pm and 6–11pm. Tram: 1 or 3.

Restaurant Ottoburg ★ AUSTRIAN/INTERNATIONAL   This historic restaurant, established around 1745, occupies a 13th-century building that some historians say is the oldest in Innsbruck. Inside, four intimate and atmospheric dining rooms—with a decor that is best described as "19th-century neo-Gothic"—lie scattered over two different floors. Hearty dishes include venison stew, "grandmother's mixed grill," and fried trout. In summer, a beer garden operates in the rear, open April to October, Tuesday to Sunday from 11am to midnight.

Herzog-Friedrich-Strasse 1. www.ottoburg.at. © **0512/584-338.** Reservations recommended. Main courses 10€–25€. AE, DC, MC, V. Tues–Sun 11am–2:30pm and 6pm–midnight. Closed 3 weeks in Jan and 2 weeks in late May and early June. Tram: 1 or 3.

Inexpensive
Weisses Rössl ★ AUSTRIAN/TYROLEAN   You'll enter this time-honored place through a stone archway set on one of the Old Town's most famous streets. At the end of a flight of stairs, marked with a very old crucifix, you'll find a trio of dining rooms with red-tiled floors and a history of welcoming guests since 1590. The menu has simple "down-home" cooking, listing such dishes as a Tyroler *Gröstl* (a kind of hash composed of sautéed onions, sliced beef, alpine herbs, and potatoes cooked and served in a frying pan), *Saftgoulash* with polenta, several kinds of schnitzels, and a grilled platter *(Alt Insprugg)* for two diners.

Kiebachgasse 8. www.roessl.at. © **0512/583-057.** Reservations recommended. Main courses 8€–20€. Set lunch 8€–12€ 3 courses; set dinner 18€–23€ 3 courses. AE, DC, MC, V. Daily 9am–3pm and 5pm–midnight. Closed Nov. Tram: 1 or 3.

SHOPPING
You'll find a large selection of Tyrolean specialties and all sorts of skiing and mountain-climbing equipment for sale in Innsbruck. Stroll around **Maria-Theresien-Strasse, Herzog-Friedrich-Strasse,** and **Museumstrasse,** ducking in and making discoveries of your own. Here are some suggestions.

    Zillertaler Trachtenwelt, Brixner Strasse 4 (www.trachtenwelt.com; © **0512/580-911**), is devoted to regional Tyrolean dress, most of which is made in Austria. There's a full array for men, women, and children. **Tiroler Heimatwerk,** Meraner Strasse 2 (http://tiroler.heimatwerk.at; © **0512/582-320**), is one of the best stores in Innsbruck for handcrafted sculpture and pewter, carved chests, furniture, and lace.

Do-it-yourselfers can buy regionally inspired fabrics and dress patterns, and whip up a dirndl.

ENTERTAINMENT & NIGHTLIFE

THE PERFORMING ARTS   The major venue for the performing arts is the 150-year-old **Landestheater,** Rennweg 2 (www.landestheater.at; ✆ **0512/52074**). The box office is open daily from 9:30am to 7pm, and performances usually begin at 7:30 or 8pm. Ticket prices are 4€ to 49€ for most operas or operettas, 5€ to 56€ for theater seats. It's also the showcase for musicals and light operetta. For tickets, call ✆ **0512/520-744**. Concerts are presented in the Hofgarten in summer.

BARS, CLUBS & FOLK MUSIC   One of Innsbruck's most whimsical discos is **Blue Chip,** Wilhelm-Greil-Strasse 17 (www.chip-ibk.com; ✆ **0512/890-158**), situated in a modern building in the center of town. The busy dance floor attracts a clientele in the 25-to-40 age range, and music includes an appealing mixture of funk and soul. Entrance is free, and hours are Tuesday to Saturday from 11pm to 4am. One flight up in the same building is **Jimmy's Bar** (www.jimmys.at; ✆ **0512/570-473**). There's no dance floor and no live music, but it's something of an Innsbruck cliché that you should begin your evening at Jimmy's with a drink or two before proceeding downstairs to Blue Chip. Jimmy's is open Tuesday to Saturday 7pm to 2am.

If you're looking for the biggest and the best in Innsbruck, head for the **Hofgartencafé,** Rennweg 6 (www.der-hofgarten.at; ✆ **0512/588-871**), where a lively crowd of young people, mostly in their 20s and 30s, grace the largest beer garden in town. With three massive outdoor bars and a modern indoor decor, this hot spot is the place to be seen. You'll find live music here during the summer. It's open Tuesday to Sunday 11am to 3am.

Young people hang out at **Treibhaus,** Angerzellgasse 8 (www.treibhaus.at; ✆ **0512/572-000**), a combination cafe, bar, and social club. Within its battered walls, you can attend a changing roster of art exhibitions, cabaret shows, and protest rallies, Monday to Saturday 10am to 1am, with live music presented at erratic intervals. Cover for live performances is 10€ to 25€.

Limerick Bill's Irish Pub, Maria-Theresia-Strasse 9 (✆ **0512/582-0111**), is dark and cavelike because of its location in a building without windows, a short walk north of Old Town. It's a genuine Irish pub for Celtic wannabes, and the cellar attracts a dancing crowd on Friday and Saturday nights, especially between December and March, when there's live music from 9pm to midnight. It's open daily from 3:30pm to 2am.

Fischerhausel Bar, Herrengasse 8 (✆ **0512/583-535**), is a rustic second-floor restaurant and street-level bar open Monday to Saturday from 10am to 2am, Sunday from 6pm to 2am. In the Tyrolean style, it's a good, friendly joint for quaffing schnapps or suds. In warm weather, drinkers move out to the garden in back.

WHERE TO STAY

Expensive

Grand Hotel Europa ★★   The town's finest and most elegant hotel stands opposite the rail station, inviting you inside its formal lobby. The spacious rooms and suites are handsomely furnished, with all the modern conveniences and Tyrolean or Biedermeier-style decorations. Each tasteful unit offers a well-equipped bathroom. The restaurant, **Europa Stüberl** (above), is the finest in Tyrol.

Südtirolerplatz 2, A-6020 Innsbruck. www.grandhoteleuropa.at. ✆ **0512/5931.** Fax 0512/587-800. 122 units. 149€–372€ double; 369€–584€ suite. Rates include breakfast. AE, DC, MC, V. Parking 15€.

Amenities: Restaurant; bar; sauna; room service; babysitting. *In room:* A/C, TV, hair dryer, Wi-Fi (free).

Romantik Hotel-Restaurant Schwarzer Adler ★★   This is it for those who like authentic Austrian charm. The hotel's owners, the Ultsch family, have furnished the charming interior with hand-painted regional furniture, antiques, and lots of homey clutter, making for an inviting ambiance. The midsize rooms are virtually one of a kind, each with its special character. Beds are exceedingly comfortable, with some of the thickest mattresses in town and well-stuffed duvets. We prefer the older accommodations, which are more spacious and have more Tyrolean character.

Kaiserjägerstrasse 2, A-6020 Innsbruck. www.deradler.com. ℰ **0512/587-109.** Fax 0512/561-697. 39 units. 78€–114€ double; 124€–134€ suite. Rates include breakfast. AE, DC, MC, V. Parking 10€. Tram: 1 or 3. **Amenities:** Restaurant; bar; spa; room service. *In room:* A/C, TV, minibar, hair dryer, Internet (free).

Moderate

Hotel Central   One of the most unusual hotels in Innsbruck, Hotel Central was originally built in the 1860s, but from its very modern exterior you might not realize it. The comfortable rooms have an Art Deco design that evokes an almost Japanese simplicity. Most rooms are quite spacious with excellent beds. Bathrooms are small, with shower units. In total contrast to the simplicity of the rest of the hotel, the grand Viennese cafe has marble columns, sculpted ceilings, and large gilt-and-crystal chandeliers.

Gilmstrasse 5, A-6020 Innsbruck. www.central.co.at. ℰ **0512/5920.** Fax 0512/580-310. 85 units. 125€–170€ double. Rates include breakfast. AE, DC, MC, V. Parking 12€. Tram: 1 or 3. **Amenities:** Restaurant; bar; exercise room; sauna; room service. *In room:* TV, minibar, hair dryer, Internet (4€ per hour).

Hotel Goldener Adler ★★   Even the phone booth near the reception desk of this 600-year-old family-run hotel is outfitted in antique style. Famous guests have included Goethe, Mozart, and the violinist Paganini, who cut his name into the win-dowpane of his room. Rooms are handsomely furnished, and vary in size and decor. Some have decorative Tyrolean architectural features such as beamed ceilings. Others are furnished in a more modern style. This is now a Best Western-affiliated property.

Herzog-Friedrich-Strasse 6, A-6020 Innsbruck. www.goldeneradler.com. ℰ **0512/571-111** or **800/780-7234** in the U.S. and Canada. Fax 0512/584-409. 31 units. 119€–210€ double; from 250€ suite. Rates include breakfast. AE, DC, MC, V. Parking 11€. Tram: 1 or 3. **Amenities:** Restaurant; bar; room service; babysitting. *In room:* TV, minibar, hair dryer, Wi-Fi (free).

Inexpensive

Gasthof-Hotel Weisses Kreuz ★ 🍴   This atmospheric inn, located in the center of Innsbruck, has not changed much since 13-year-old Wolfgang Mozart and his father, Leopold, stayed here in 1769. Rooms are cozy and atmospheric, either small or medium size, with comfortable furnishings. Double rooms have private bathrooms with neatly kept shower units. Hallway bathrooms for single rooms are adequate and well maintained.

Herzog-Friedrich-Strasse 31, A-6020 Innsbruck. www.weisseskreuz.at. ℰ **0512/594-790.** Fax 0512/594-7990. 40 units, 31 with bathroom. 75€ double without bathroom; 112€–135€ double with bathroom. Rates include breakfast. AE, MC, V. Parking 12€. Tram: 3. **Amenities:** Restaurant; bar; room service; Wi-Fi (free). *In room:* TV.

Goldene Krone ✦   Near the Triumphal Arch on Innsbruck's main street, this baroque house is one of the city's best budget bets. All rooms are modern, comfortable, well maintained, and, for the most part, spacious with plenty of light. The duvet-covered beds are comfortable, and bathrooms are small but spotless, with shower stalls. The hotel offers a Viennese-inspired coffeehouse/restaurant, the **Art Gallery-Café.**

Maria-Theresien-Strasse 46, A-6020 Innsbruck. www.goldene-krone.at. ℭ **0512/586-160.** Fax 0512/580-1896. 36 units. 79€–199€ double; 120€ suite. Rates include breakfast. AE, MC, V. Parking 10€. Tram: 1. Bus: A, H, K, or N. **Amenities:** Restaurant; bar; cafe. *In room:* TV.

St. Anton am Arlberg ★★★

A modern resort has grown out of this old village on the Arlberg Pass, 99km (62 miles) west of Innsbruck. At St. Anton (1,288m/4,226 ft.), Hannes Schneider developed modern skiing techniques and began teaching tourists how to ski in 1907. Before his death in 1955, Schneider saw his ski school rated as the world's finest. Today, St. Anton am Arlberg is popular over the winter months with wealthy and occasionally royal visitors—a more conservative segment of the rich and famous than you'll see at other posh ski resorts.

There's so much emphasis on skiing here that few seem to talk of the summertime attractions. In warm weather, St. Anton is tranquil and bucolic, surrounded by meadowland. A riot of wildflowers blooming in the fields announces the beginning of spring.

ESSENTIALS
Getting There
BY TRAIN   St. Anton has good rail connections to eastern and western Austria, and is an express stop on the main lines crossing the Arlberg Pass between Innsbruck and Bregenz. About one train per hour arrives in St. Anton from each direction. Trip time from Innsbruck is 75 to 85 minutes; from Bregenz, around 85 minutes. For rail information, call ℭ **05/1717.**

BY CAR   Motorists should take Route 171 west from Innsbruck.

VISITOR INFORMATION   The **tourist office** at Dorfstrasse 8 (www.stanton amarlberg.com; ℭ **05446/22690**) is open Monday to Friday 8am to noon and 1 to 5pm.

HITTING THE SLOPES IN ST. ANTON
The snow in this area is perfect for skiers, and the total lack of trees on the slopes makes the situation ideal. The ski fields of St. Anton stretch over some 16 sq. km (6¼ sq. miles). Beginners stick to the slopes down below, and more experienced skiers head to the runs from the peaks of **Galzig** (2,092m/6,864 ft.) and **Valluga** (2,812m/9,226 ft.), both reached by cableway.

Other major ski areas include the **Gampen/Kapall,** an advanced–intermediate network of slopes, whose lifts start just behind St. Anton's railway station; and the **Rendl,** a relatively new labyrinth of runs to the south of St. Anton that offers many novice and intermediate slopes.

You'll find many other cold-weather pursuits in St. Anton, including ski jumping, mountain tours, curling, skating, tobogganing, and sleigh rides, plus après-ski relaxing.

WHERE TO STAY & EAT
If you're not able to secure a reservation at Raffl-Stube (see below), don't despair. You can get classic Austrian dishes at the historic **Hotel Alte Post Restaurant,** A-6580

St. Anton am Arlberg (www.hotel-alte-post.at; © **05446/25530**); and at the first-rate **Hotel Kertess Restaurant,** A-6580 St. Anton am Arlberg (© **05446/2005**), located high on a slope in the suburb of Oberdorf.

Hotel Schwarzer Adler ★★   Owned and operated by the Tschol family since 1885, this beautiful building in the center of St. Anton was constructed as an inn in 1570. The interior is rustic yet elegant, with blazing fireplaces, painted Tyrolean baroque armoires, and Oriental rugs. There are handsomely furnished and well-equipped guest rooms in the main hotel, plus 13 slightly less well-furnished (but less expensive) rooms in the annex across the street. For superb international cuisine, head to the hotel's **Restaurant.**

A-6580 St. Anton am Arlberg. www.schwarzeradler.com. © **05446/22440.** Fax 05446/22440-62. 72 units. Winter 190€–422€ double; summer 150€–170€ double. Rates include half board. MC, V. Closed May–June and Sept–Nov. **Amenities:** Restaurant; bar; exercise room; sauna; room service; babysitting. *In room:* TV, hair dryer, Internet (free).

Raffl-Stube ★ AUSTRIAN   This place contains only eight tables, and in the peak of the season, reservations are imperative. Overflow diners are offered a seat in a spacious but less special dining room across the hall. Quality ingredients are always used, and the kitchen prepares such tempting specialties as roast goose liver with salad, cream of parsley soup with sautéed quail eggs, filet of salmon with wild rice, and roast filet of pork, along with the ever-popular fondue bourguignon.

In the Hotel St. Antoner Hof, St. Anton am Arlberg. www.antonerhof.at. © **05446/2910.** Reservations required. Main courses 17€–42€. AE, DC, MC, V. Daily 11:30am–2pm and 7–9:30pm. Closed May–Nov.

The Kitzbühel Alps ★★★

Hard-core skiers and the rich and famous are attracted to this ski region. The Kitzbühel Alps are covered with such a dense network of lifts that they now form the largest skiing complex in the country, with a series of superlative runs. The action centers on the town of Kitzbühel, but there are many satellite resorts that are much less expensive, including St. Johann in Tyrol. Kitzbühel is, in a sense, a neighbor of Munich, which lies 130km (81 miles) to the northeast: Most visitors to the Kitzbühel Alps use Munich's international airport.

ESSENTIALS
Arriving
BY TRAIN   Two and three **trains** per hour (many express) arrive in Kitzbühel from Innsbruck (trip time: 60 min.) and Salzburg (2½ hr.), respectively.

BY BUS   The most useful of these bus lines runs every 30 to 60 minutes between Kitzbühel and St. Johann in Tyrol (25 min.). In addition, about half a dozen buses travel every day from Salzburg's main railway station to Kitzbühel (2¼ hr.). For regional bus information, call © **05356/62715.**

BY CAR   Kitzbühel is 449km (279 miles) west of Vienna and 100km (62 miles) east of Innsbruck. If you're driving from Innsbruck, take Autobahn A12 east to the junction with Route 312 heading to Ellmau. After bypassing Ellmau, continue east to the junction with Route 342, which you take south to Kitzbühel.

VISITOR INFORMATION   The **tourist office,** Hinterstadt 18 (www.kitzbuehel. com; © **05356/66660**), is open Monday to Friday 8:30am to 6pm.

EXPLORING KITZBÜHEL

The town has two main streets, both pedestrian walkways: **Vorderstadt** and **Hinterstadt.** Along these streets Kitzbühel has preserved its traditional architectural style. You'll see three-story stone houses with oriels and scrollwork around the doors and windows, heavy overhanging eaves, and Gothic gables.

The **Pfarrkirche (Parish Church)** was built from 1435 to 1506 and renovated in the baroque style during the 18th century. The lower part of the **Liebfrauenkirche (Church of Our Lady)** dates from the 13th century, the upper part from 1570. Between these two churches stands the **Ölbergkapelle (Ölberg Chapel)** with a 1450 "lantern of the dead" and frescoes from the latter part of the 16th century.

In the **Heimatmuseum,** Hinterstadt 34 (© **05356/64588**), you'll see artifacts from prehistoric European mining eras and the north alpine Bronze Age, a wintersports section with trophies of Kitzbüheler skiing greats, and exhibits detailing the town's history. The museum is open year-round Monday through Saturday from 10am to 1pm. Admission is 6.50€ adults, 3€ persons 17 and under.

SKIING & OTHER OUTDOOR ACTIVITIES

SKIING In winter the emphasis in Kitzbühel, 702m (2,300 ft.) above sea level, is on skiing, and facilities are offered for everyone from novices to experts. The ski season starts just before Christmas and lasts until late March. With more than 62 lifts, gondolas (cable cars), and mountain railroads on five different mountains, Kitzbühel has two main ski areas, the **Hahnenkamm** (renovated in 1995) and the **Kitzbüheler Horn ★★**. Cable cars (Hahnenkammbahn) are within easy walking distance, even for those in ski boots.

The linking of the lift systems on the Hahnenkamm has created the celebrated **Kitzbühel Ski Circus,** which makes it possible to ski downhill for more than 80km (50 miles), with runs that suit every stage of proficiency. Numerous championship ski events are held here. The toughest, fastest downhill course in the world, a stretch of the Hahnenkamm especially designed for maximum speed called Die Streif, is both feared and respected among skiers.

OTHER WINTER ACTIVITIES There's also curling, ski-bobbing, ski jumping, ice-skating, tobogganing, hiking on cleared trails, and hang gliding, as well as indoor activities such as tennis, bowling, and swimming. The children's ski school, **Schischule Rote Teufel,** Museumkeller, Hinterstadt (www.rote-teufel.at; © **05356/625-00**), provides training for the very young skier. And don't forget the après-ski, with bars, nightclubs, and dance clubs rocking from teatime to the early hours.

SUMMER ACTIVITIES Kitzbühel has summer pastimes, too, such as walking tours, visits to the **Wild Life Park at Aurach** (about 3km/1¼ miles from Kitzbühel), tennis, horseback riding, golf, squash, brass-band concerts in the town center, cycling, and swimming. For the last, there's an indoor swimming pool, but we recommend going to the **Schwarzsee (Black Lake).** This *See,* about a 15-minute walk northwest of the center of town, is an alpine lake with a peat bottom that keeps the water relatively murky. Covering an area of 6.4 hectares (16 acres), it's the site of beaches and **Seiwald Bootsverleih,** Schwarzsee (© **05356/62381**), an outfit that rents rowboats and electric-driven boats for fishing trips or for just sunbathing on the water.

One of the region's most exotic collections of alpine flora is clustered into the jagged and rocky confines of the **Alpine Flower Garden Kitzbühel,** where various species of gentian, gorse, heather, and lichens are found on the sunny slopes of the Kitzbüheler Horn. Set at a height of around 1,830m (6,000 ft.) above sea level, the garden is open from late May to early September, daily 8:30am to 5:30pm, and is most impressive in June, July, and August. Admission is free. Many visitors see the garden by taking the Seilbahn Kitzbüheler cable car to its uppermost station and then descending on foot via the garden's labyrinth of footpaths to the gondola's middle station. The **Seilbahn Kitzbüheler cable car** (www.bergbahn-kitzbuehel.at; ✆ 05356/6951), 25€ round-trip, departs from Kitzbühel at half-hour intervals daily throughout the summer and winter. In spring and autumn, it operates Saturday 9am to 5pm, and Sunday 10am to noon only.

WHERE TO STAY & EAT

Hotel Bruggerhof ★ 📷   About 1.6km (1 mile) west of the town center, near the Schwarzsee, is this countryside chalet with a sun terrace. Originally built as a farm-house in the 1920s, it later gained local fame as a restaurant. Rooms are comfortable and cozy and decorated in an alpine style. All have a well-lived-in look, although housekeeping is attentive. Bathrooms can be a bit cramped.

Reitherstrasse 24, A-6370 Kitzbühel. www.bruggerhof-camping.at. ✆ **05356/62806.** Fax 05356/ 644-7930. 28 units. Winter 160€–265€ double; summer 120€–190€ double. Rates include half board. AE, DC, MC, V. Free parking. Closed Apr and Oct 15–Dec 15. **Amenities:** Restaurant; bar; exercise room; Jacuzzi; sauna; room service; babysitting; Wi-Fi (free). *In room:* TV, minibar, hair dryer.

Hotel Zur Tenne ★   This hotel combines Tyrolean congeniality with urban style and panache, and the staff shows genuine concern for its clientele. The hotel was created in the 1950s by joining a trio of 700-year-old houses. Rooms are as glamorous as anything in Kitzbühel: wood trim, comfortable beds, eiderdowns, and copies of Tyrolean antiques. Many have working fireplaces and canopied beds for a romantic touch. In addition to intimate lounges, niches, and nooks, the hotel sports the most luxurious health complex in town, complete with a tropical fountain, two hot tubs, and a hot-and-cold foot bath.

Vorderstadt 8–10, A-6370 Kitzbühel. www.hotelzurtenne.com. ✆ **05356/644-440.** Fax 05356/648-0356. 51 units. 154€–409€ double; 239€–492€ junior suite; 324€–749€ suite. Rates include breakfast. Half board 38€ per person. AE, DC, MC, V. Free parking outdoors; 14€ in covered garage nearby. **Amenities:** 3 restaurants; bar; exercise room; 2 Jacuzzis; sauna; room service; babysitting; Internet (free). *In room:* TV, minibar, hair dryer.

The Dining Rooms in the Schloss Lebenberg ★ AUSTRIAN/INTERNA-TIONAL   Although the Schloss Lebenberg hotel offers comfortable rooms, we actually prefer it for its well-managed restaurant and its sense of history. Originally built in 1548, it was transformed in 1885 into Kitzbühel's first family-run hotel. Always-reliable specialties include cream of tomato soup with gin, Tyrolean-style calves' liver, Wiener schnitzel, roulade of beef, and many desserts.

Lebenbergstrasse 17. www.schloss-lebenberg.at. ✆ **05356/69010.** Reservations required. Main courses 14€–32€. AE, DC, MC, V. Daily 7–10am and 6:45–9pm.

Restaurant Goldener Greif ★★ TYROLEAN   The setting is cozy and warm, and the cuisine is some of the resort's best. The dining room features vaulted ceilings, intricate paneling, and, in some cases, views out over the base of some of Kitzbühel's busy cable cars. Menu items are savory and designed to satisfy appetites heightened by the bracing alpine climate. You might order veal steak with fresh vegetables, pepper steak Madagascar, or venison. Many kinds of grilled steaks are regularly featured. A "Vienna pot" is one of the chef's specials, and fresh Tyrolean trout is offered daily.

Hinterstadt 24. www.hotel-goldener-greif.at. ✆ **05356/64311.** Reservations recommended. Main courses 10€–30€. Set menus 20€–35€. AE, DC, MC, V. June to mid-Oct daily 10am–2pm and 7–10pm; mid-Dec to mid-Apr daily 6–10pm. Closed mid-Apr to late May and mid-Oct to mid-Dec.

BELGIUM

by George McDonald

M odest little Belgium has never been known to boast of its charms, yet its variety of languages, cultures, history, and cuisines would do credit to a country many times its size. Belgium's diversity stems from its location at a cultural crossroads. The boundary between Europe's Germanic north and Latin south cuts clear across the nation's middle, leaving Belgium divided into two major ethnic regions: Dutch-speaking Flanders and French-speaking Wallonia.

International attention generally focuses on Brussels as the "capital of Europe," and the city has upped its cultural game to meet the expectations that go along with this label. Yet another Belgium waits in the wings, a place of Gothic cathedrals, medieval castles, cobblestone streets, and tranquil canals. In a country you can drive clear across in little more than 2 hours, the timeless beauty of Bruges, Ghent, and Antwerp is accessible even to the most hurried visitor.

BRUSSELS ★★★

As the headquarters city of the European Union, Brussels both symbolizes the continent's vision of unity and is a bastion of officialdom, a breeding ground for the regulations that govern and often exasperate the rest of Europe. The armies of well-heeled Eurocrats, lobbying, and the media, have created a cosmopolitan, business-driven city, but one must not forget that this was once the city that inspired surrealism and Art Nouveau, and still worships comic strips, prides itself on handmade lace and chocolate, and serves each one of its craft beers in its own unique glass.

The city's original spirit survives in traditional bars, bistros, and restaurants. Whether elegantly Art Nouveau or eccentrically festooned with posters, curios, and knick-knacks, such centuries-old establishments provide a warm, convivial ambience that is peculiarly Belgian.

Essentials
GETTING THERE
BY PLANE   Modern, efficient **Brussels Airport** (www.brusselsairport. be; ℂ **0900/70000** in Belgium, or **02/753-77-53** from abroad), 11km (6¾ miles) northeast of the city center, is Belgium's principal airport and handles virtually all of the country's international flights.

Brussels Airport Express trains connect the airport's below-ground station with Brussels's three major rail stations (see below) up to four times an hour, daily from 5:30am to 11:30pm; a one-way ride is 7.20€

first-class and 5.40€ second-class; the ride to Bruxelles-Central is 15–20 minutes (other city stops are just minutes away).

The **Airport Line bus** no. 12 (Mon–Fri express) or 21 departs from the airport about every half-hour to the European District in the city; the fare is 3.50€ for a one-way ticket purchased before boarding the bus, and 6€ for one purchased onboard. **De Lijn bus** no. 471 (express) or 272 departs from the airport hourly to Bruxelles-Nord rail station; the fare is 2€ for a one-way ticket purchased before boarding the bus, and 3€ for one purchased onboard.

A **taxi** from the airport to the city center is around 45€; be sure to use only licensed cabs from the stand outside the terminal.

BY TRAIN High-speed trains—Eurostar from London; Thalys from Paris, Amsterdam, and Cologne; TGV from France (not Paris); and ICE from Frankfurt—zip into town from all points of the compass, and arrive at Bruxelles-Midi, south of the city center. Other international trains arrive at Bruxelles-Midi, as well as at Bruxelles-Central, downtown, a few blocks from the Grand-Place, and Gare du Nord, north of the city center. For train information, visit www.b-rail.be or call ☏ **02/528-28-28.**

All three stations have currency exchange offices, luggage storage, cafes, and stores, with Gare du Midi being outfitted the best in all these services. Both Bruxelles-Midi and Bruxelles-Nord have a bus station and stops for tram (streetcar) lines; Bruxelles-Central has an adjacent Métro (subway) station and multiple bus stops outside. All three have taxi stands outside.

BY BUS Eurolines (www.eurolines.com; ☏ **02/274-13-50**) buses from London, Paris, Amsterdam, and other European cities arrive at the bus station below Bruxelles-Nord rail station.

BY CAR Major expressways to Brussels are E19 south from Amsterdam (2 hr. 20 min.) and north from Paris (3 hr. 20 min.), and E40 east from Bruges (1 hr. 15 min.) and west from Cologne (2 hr. 15 min.). Avoid if possible driving the "hell on wheels" R0 Brussels ring road. After you arrive in the center of Brussels, do yourself a favor and leave the car at a parking garage.

VISITOR INFORMATION

TOURIST OFFICES The most central office of **VISITBRUSSELS** (www.visit brussels.be; ☏ **02/513-89-40;** fax 02/513-83-20), the city's tourist information organization, is in the Hôtel de Ville (Town Hall), on the Grand-Place (Métro: Gare Centrale; daily 9am–6pm). Other offices are at rue Royale 2, close to the Royal Palace (tram: 92 or 94; Mon–Fri 9am–6pm, Sat–Sun and holidays 10am–6pm); and at rue Wiertz 43, in the European District (bus: 22 or 54; daily 10am–6pm). There's an information desk in the main hall at Bruxelles-Midi rail station (Métro: Gare du Midi; daily 9am–6pm). All offices are closed January 1 and December 25.

A good starting point for exploring Brussels and the Wallonia and Flanders regions of Belgium on the Web is at the official tourist-office websites **www.visitbrussels. be, www.visitbelgium.com, www.opt.be,** and **www.visitflanders.com**. A useful website for hotel research, where you can compare prices and see pictures of the rooms, is **www.hotels-belgium.com**. For dining-out pointers, go to **www.resto.be**.

CITY LAYOUT Brussels is divided into 19 districts known as *communes,* although most of the city's premier sightseeing is experienced in the central commune. Brussels is flat in its center and western reaches, where the Senne River now flows underground. To the east, a range of low hills rises to the upper city, which is crowned by

the Royal Palace and has some of the city's most affluent residential and prestigious business and shopping districts. The **Grand-Place** stands at the heart of Brussels and is both a starting point and reference point for most visitors.

Pick up a copy of *Brussels Guide & Map* from a city tourist office. You'll get a fairly detailed street map of the inner city marked with principal tourist attractions. If you need a comprehensive street map, purchase the *Géocart Bruxelles et Périphérie* at most news vendors and bookstores. The city is bilingual, French and Dutch: Bruxelles in French and Brussel in Dutch, and street names and places are in both languages. Grand-Place is Grote Markt in Dutch; Théâtre Royal de la Monnaie is Koninklijke Munttheater. To keep things simple, I use only the French names in this chapter.

Neighborhoods in Brief

The Lower Town (Bas de la Ville) The core area of the Old Town, has at its heart the Grand-Place and its environs. Two of the most traveled lanes nearby are restaurant-lined rue des Bouchers and Petite rue des Bouchers, part of an area known as the Ilot Sacré (Sacred Isle). Brussels's busiest shopping street, pedestrianized rue Neuve, starts from place de la Monnaie and runs north for several blocks. Central Brussels also includes the Marché-aux-Poissons (Fish Market) district.

The Upper Town (Haut de la Ville This area lies east of and uphill from the Grand-Place, along rue Royale and rue de la Régence. Here is the city's second grand square, place du Grand Sablon, and nearby

Brussels

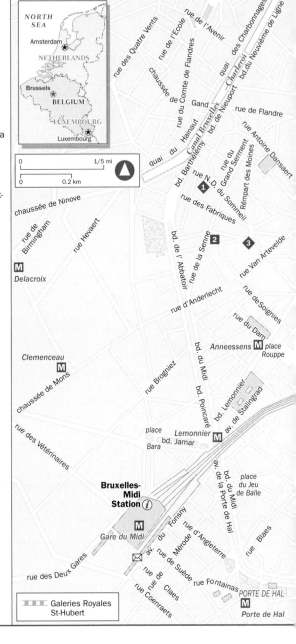

† Church
ⓘ Information
⊠ Post Office
— Railway
Ⓜ Metro Station

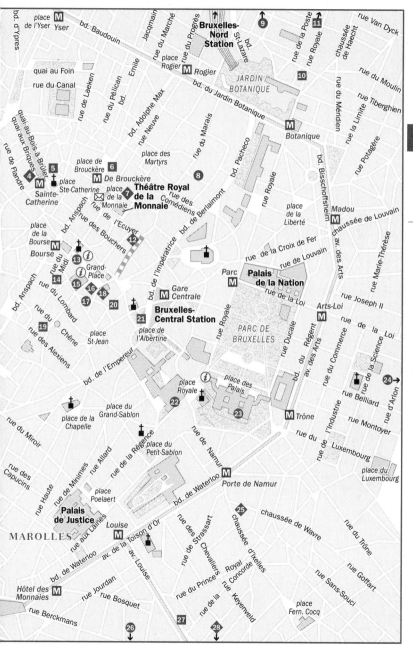

the Royal Museums of Fine Arts, and the Royal Palace. If you head southwest and cross the broad boulevard de Waterloo, where you find the most exclusive designer stores, you come to place Louise. This area adjoins the slowly gentrifying Marolles district, noted for its cozy cafes, drinking-man's bars, and inexpensive restaurants.

Avenue Louise From place Louise, Brussels's most fashionable thoroughfare runs south all the way to a large wooded park, the Bois de la Cambre, and beyond, the leafy Forêt de Soignes. On either side of avenue Louise are the classy districts of Ixelles and Uccle, good places for restaurants, bars, cafes, and shopping, both chic and inexpensive.

European District Here, around place Schuman, the European Commission, Parliament, and Council of Ministers buildings jostle for space in a warren of offices populated by civil servants, journalists, and lobbyists. The area is home to a wealth of restaurants and cafes that cater to Euroappetites. Cinquantenaire, a park crisscrossed with tree-lined avenues, extends from just east of the European District to the Porte de Tervuren, and is bisected east to west by avenue John F. Kennedy. At the park's eastern end are the monumental Palais du Cinquantenaire and the Arc du Cinquantenaire.

Bruparck Inside this recreation complex in the north of the city, you'll find the Mini-Europe theme park; the 26-screen Kinepolis multiplex movie theater; a made-to-order village with stores, cafes, and restaurants; and the Océade water recreation center. Beside it is the Atomium, Brussels Planetarium, the Roi Baudoin Soccer Stadium, and the Parc des Expositions congress center.

GETTING AROUND

BY MÉTRO, TRAM & BUS Public transportation begins at around 6am and the regular service ends around midnight. After that, there is limited service by night buses. The Métro (subway) network is good for getting to major destinations around and on the edge of town. Métro stations are indicated by signs showing a large white M on a blue background. Trams (streetcars) and buses are colored silver and bronze; stop them by extending your arm as they approach. Stops are marked with red-and-white signs. Though not as fast as the Métro, trams are generally faster than buses and are a great way to get around, because you can view the cityscape while you ride. Tram lines 92 and 94 cover a bunch of key city sights along rue Royale, rue de la Régence, and as far as avenue Louise.

Free pocket maps of the public transportation network are available from the tourist office, and from the main Métro stations of the city's transit authority, **STIB** (www.stib.be; ✆ **070/23-20-00**). Maps of the network are posted at all Métro stations and on many bus and tram shelters.

A one-ride card costs 2.50€ when purchased from tram and bus drivers, and 2€ when purchased before boarding. It is 7.50€ for a 5-ride card, 13€ for a 10-ride card, and 6€ for a 1-day card. The 5-ride, 10-ride, and 1-day cards cannot be purchased onboard STIB trams or buses, but from sales points and ticket machines. Whatever card you go for, if you plan to use it on Métro trains you must purchase it before boarding.

You validate your card by inserting it into the orange electronic machines that stand inside buses and trams and at the access to Métro platforms. Though the card must be revalidated each time you board, you are allowed multiple transfers within a 1-hour period of the initial validation, so you can hop on and off Métro trains, trams, and buses during that time and only one journey will be canceled by the electronic scanner. If more than one person is traveling on one ticket, the ticket must be validated each time for each traveler. Up to four children age 5 and under per paying adult ride free.

In addition, STIB has an electronic stored-value card, the **MOBIB,** available from KIOSK and BOOTIK sales points at some rail and Métro stations. It is more complicated to purchase and use this card compared with those detailed above, and for short-stay visitors it may not be worth the extra hassle. Still, you'll get a saving of around 10% over the price of ordinary cards purchased from sales points and ticket machines. In addition, MOBIB Discover Brussels cards are available, at 6€ for 24 hr., 10€ for 48 hr., and 13€ for 72 hr.

BY TAXI   The fare starts at 2.40€ from 6am to 10pm, and at 4.40€ between 10pm and 6am, increasing by 1.66€ a kilometer inside the city (tariff 1), and 2.70€ a kilometer outside (tariff 2). Make sure the meter is set to the correct tariff. Taxis cannot be hailed on the street, but there are stands at prominent locations around town. Call **Taxis Bleus** (✆ 02/268-00-00) or **Taxis Verts** (✆ 02/349-49-49).

BY CAR   Driving in central Brussels is best avoided. In some cases (not always), traffic from the right has the right of way, even if it is coming from a minor street onto a more important one. This can cause havoc at multistreet intersections, particularly since many Belgian drivers will relinquish their *priorité à droite* under no known circumstances, cost what it might. If you must drive, rental cars are available from **Hertz** (www.hertz.be; ✆ **800/654-3001** in the U.S., or **02/717-32-01** in Belgium); **Avis** (www.avis.be; ✆ **800/331-1212** in the U.S., or **070/22-30-01** in Belgium); **Budget** (www.budget.be; ✆ **800/472-3325** in the U.S., or **02/712-08-40** in Belgium); and **Europcar** (www.europcar.be; ✆ **02/522-95-37**). All of these firms have city offices and desks at the airport. Rates begin at around 60€ a day for a small car with unlimited mileage.

BY FOOT   There's no better way to explore the historic core of the town than walking, especially around Grand-Place. You'll also enjoy strolling uptown around place du Grand Sablon. Beyond these areas, you'll want to use public transportation. Don't expect cars to stop for you just because you're crossing at a black-and-white "pedestrian crossing."

[FastFACTS] BRUSSELS

ATMs/Banks   **Banks** are open Monday to Friday from 9am to 1pm and 2 to 4:30 or 5pm. You'll find many **ATMs** around town, identified by BANCONTACT and MISTER CASH signs. A centrally located bank with ATMs is the branch of **BNP Paribas Fortis,** rue de la Colline 12 (✆ **02/547-12-11;** Métro: Gare Centrale).

Business Hours   Most **stores** are open Monday to Saturday from 9 or 10am to 6 or 7pm; some stay open on Friday to 8 or 9pm.

Currency   Belgium's currency is the **euro** (€). At press time, 1€ equals US$1.30.

Dentists   For urgent dental care, call **Service de Garde Dentaire** (✆ **02/426-10-26**).

Doctors & Hospitals   For doctors, call **Médi-Garde** at ✆ **02/479-18-18** or **SOS Médecins** at ✆ **02/513-02-02,** and ask for an English-speaking doctor.

Should you need hospital care, the **Cliniques Universitaires St-Luc,** av. Hippocrate 10 (✆ **02/764-11-11;** Métro: Alma), has an emergency department.

Embassies & Consulates   The embassy of the **United States** is at bd. du Régent 25–27 (www.usembassy.be; ✆ **02/811-40-00** embassy; ✆ **02/811-43-00** consular section; Métro: Arts-Loi). The embassy of **Canada** is at av. de Tervueren 2 (www.ambassade-canada.be; ℂ **02/741-06-11;** Métro: Mérode). The embassy of the **United Kingdom** is at av. d'Auderghem 10 (http://ukinbelgium.fco.gov.uk/en; ℂ **02/287-62-11;** Métro: Schuman); the consulate general is around the corner at av. des Nerviens 9–31 (ℂ **02/287-62-11;** bus: 22 or 27). The embassy of **Ireland** is at chaussée d'Etterbeek 180 (www.embassyofireland.be; ℂ **02/282-34-00;** bus: 59). The Embassy of **Australia** is at rue Guimard 6–8 (www.belgium.embassy.gov.au; ℂ **02/286-05-00;** Métro: Arts-Loi). The embassy of **New Zealand** is at av. des Nerviens 9–31 (www.nzembassy.com/belgium; ℂ **02/512-10-40;** bus: 22 or 27).

Emergencies For police assistance, call ℂ **101.** For an ambulance or the fire department, call ℂ **100.**

Internet Access A large number of hotels, hostels, bars, fast-food restaurants, coffeehouses, and cafes have Wi-Fi hotspots.

Mail & Postage The office of **bpost** at Centre Monnaie, place de la Monnaie (ℂ **022/01-23-45;** Métro: De Brouckère), is open Monday to Friday from 8am to 6pm, and

Saturday from 10:30am to 4:30pm. Depending on the speed of delivery you select, postage for a postcard or an ordinary letter up to 50 grams (1¾ oz.) to the U.K., Ireland, and other European countries is 1.09€ or .99€; to the U.S., Canada, Australia, New Zealand, and the rest of the world, it's 1.29€ or 1.19€.

Newspapers & Magazines English-language newspapers and magazines are available from **Waterstone's,** bd. Adolphe Max 71–75 (www.waterstones.com; ℂ **02/219-27-08;** Métro: Rogier). Newsstands at Brussels Airport and the Bruxelles-Central, Bruxelles-Midi, and Bruxelles-Nord rail stations stock many international publications. For English-speaking visitors, the most useful publication is the magazine *The Bulletin,* published every 2 weeks and filled with local news, articles, shopping, and information on cultural events.

Pharmacies For both prescription and nonprescription medicines, go to a pharmacy (*pharmacie* in French; *apotheek* in Dutch). Regular pharmacy hours are Monday to Saturday from 9am to 6pm (some close

earlier on Sat). Try the centrally located **Grande Pharmacie de Brouckère,** Passage du Nord 10–12 (ℂ **02/218-05-07;** Métro: De Brouckère). All pharmacies post locations of nearby all-night and Sunday pharmacies on the door.

Safety Brussels is generally safe so far as the threat of violent crime goes, but there's a risk of bag snatching, pick-pocketing, and robbery in deserted places at night and in Métro station foot tunnels. There's no need to overestimate the risk, only to take sensible precautions, particularly in obvious circumstances such as on crowded Métro trains and when taking cash from an ATM at night.

Telephone Belgium's **country code** is **32.** Brussels's **city code** is **2;** use the **32-2** code when calling from the United States or any other country outside Belgium. In Belgium, use the **area code 02.** You need to dial the **02** area code both from inside Brussels and from elsewhere in Belgium. You can purchase SIM cards from any mobile phone store. Prices start out at 5€ (or maybe even free), plus the amount of credit you choose to purchase.

Exploring Brussels

Brussels has such a wide variety of things to see and do. There are more than 75 museums dedicated to just about every special interest under the sun (from cartoons to cars), in addition to impressive public buildings and leafy parks. History is just around every corner. Fortunately, numerous sidewalk cafes offer respite for weary feet, and there's good public transportation to those attractions beyond walking distance of the compact, heart-shaped city center.

THE GRAND-PLACE ★★★

Ornamental gables, medieval banners, gilded facades, sunlight flashing off gold-fili-greed rooftop sculptures, a general impression of harmony and timelessness… there's a lot to take in all at once when you first enter the historic **Grand-Place** (Métro: Gare Centrale). The city's central square has always been the very heart of Brussels. Characterized by French playwright Jean Cocteau as "a splendid stage," it's the city's theater of life.

The Grand-Place has been the center of the city's commercial life and public celebrations since the 12th century. Most of it was destroyed in 1695 by the army of France's Louis XIV and then rebuilt over the next few years. Each building preserves its baroque splendor. Important guilds owned most of these buildings, and each competed to outdo the others with highly ornate facades of gold leaf and statuary. The illuminated square is even more beautiful at night than during the day.

Top honors go to the Gothic **Hôtel de Ville** and the neo-Gothic **Maison du Roi.** You'll also want to admire no. 9, **Le Cygne,** former headquarters of the butchers' guild. ; no. 10, **L'Arbre d'Or,** headquarters of the brewers' guild and location of the Brewing Museum; and nos. 13 to 19, an ensemble of seven mansions known as the **Maison des Ducs de Brabant,** adorned with busts of 19 dukes.

Hôtel de Ville ★★ ARCHITECTURE   The facade of the dazzling Town Hall, from 1402, shows off Gothic intricacy at its best, complete with dozens of arched windows and sculptures. A 66m (217-ft.) tower sprouts from the middle, yet it's not placed directly in the center. You can visit the interior on 40-minute tours, which start in a room full of paintings of the past foreign rulers of Brussels, who have included the Spanish, Austrians, French, and Dutch. The spectacular Gothic Hall, surrounded by mirrors, is open for visits when the city's aldermen are not in session. In other chambers are 16th- to 18th-century tapestries.

Grand-Place. ℂ **02/548-04-47.** Admission (guided tours only) 5€ adults, 3€ seniors and students, free for children 5 and under. Guided tours in English: Wed 3pm, Sun 10am and 2pm; tours at other times in French and Dutch. Closed Jan 1, May 1, Nov 1 and 11, and Dec 25. Métro: Gare Centrale.

Musée de la Ville de Bruxelles (Museum of the City of Brussels) ★

MUSEUM   Housed in the 19th-century neo-Gothic Maison du Roi (King's House)—though no royal sovereign ever lived here—the museum displays a collection associated with the art and history of Brussels. You can admire detailed tapestries from the 16th and 17th centuries, and porcelain, silver, and stone statuary. After climbing a beautiful wooden staircase, you can trace the history of Brussels in old maps, prints, photos, and models. Among the most fascinating exhibits are old paintings and scaled reconstructions of the historic city center, particularly those showing the riverside ambience along the now-vanished River Senne. On an upper floor are around 800 costumes that have been donated to *Manneken-Pis* (see "A Cool Little Guy" box below), including an Elvis costume.

Grand-Place. www.brusselsmuseums.be. ℂ **02/279-43-50.** Admission 4€ adults; 3€ seniors and students; 1.50€ travelers with limited mobility and children 6–15; free for children 5 and under, and for children 17 and under Sat–Sun. Tues–Sun 10am–5pm (to 8pm Thurs). Closed Jan 1, May 1, Nov 1 and 11, and Dec 25. Métro: Gare Centrale.

THE LOWER TOWN

Centre Belge de la Bande-Dessinée (Belgian Comic-Strip Center) ★ ☺

MUSEUM   As you'll soon find out, Belgians are crazy for cartoons. The unique

A COOL little GUY

Two blocks south of the Grand-Place, at the intersection of rue de l'Etuve and rue du Chêne, is the **Manneken-Pis ★** (Métro: Bourse). A small bronze statue of a urinating child, Brussels's favorite character, gleefully does what a little boy's gotta do, generally ogled by a throng of admirers. Children especially enjoy his bravura performance.

No one knows when this child first came into being, but he dates from quite a few centuries ago; as far back as the 8th century, according to one legend. Thieves have made off with the tyke several times in history. One criminal who stole and shattered the statue in 1817 was sentenced to a life of hard labor. The pieces were used to recast another version and that "original" was removed for safekeeping.

King Louis XV of France began the tradition of presenting colorful costumes to "Little Julian," which he wears on special occasions, to make amends for Frenchmen having kidnapped the statue in 1747. The 800-piece wardrobe is housed in the Musée de la Ville de Bruxelles on the Grand-Place (see above).

"CéBéBéDé" focuses on Belgium's own popular cartoon characters, like *Lucky Luke, Thorgal,* and, of course, *Tintin,* complete with red-and-white-checkered moon rocket, yet it doesn't neglect the likes of *Superman, Batman,* and the *Green Lantern.* The building, the Maisons des Waucquez, designed by Art Nouveau architect Victor Horta, is an attraction in itself.

Rue des Sables 20 (off bd. de Berlaimont). www.comicscenter.net. ✆ **02/219-19-80.** Admission 8€ adults, 6€ seniors, 3€ students and children 12–18, free for children 11 and under. Tues–Sun 10am–6pm. Closed Jan 1 and Dec 25. Métro: Gare Centrale.

Musée du Costume et de la Dentelle MUSEUM   Honoring a once-vital industry that now operates in a reduced but still notable fashion, this museum shows off particularly fine costumes and lace from 1599 to the present, and mounts frequently-changing exhibits.

Rue de la Violette 12 (off Grand-Place). www.brusselsmuseums.be. ✆ **02/213-44-50.** Admission 4€ adults; 3€ seniors and students; 1.50€ travelers with limited mobility and children 6–15; free for children 5 and under, and for children 17 and under Sat–Sun. Tues–Sun 10am–5pm. Closed Jan 1, May 1, Nov 1 and 11, and Dec 25. Métro: Gare Centrale.

THE UPPER TOWN

The most attractive park in town, the **Parc de Bruxelles ★★** (Métro: Parc), extending in front of the Palais Royal, has been restored as close as possible to its 18th-century appearance. Once the property of the Dukes of Brabant, the park has geometrically divided paths running through it that form the outline of Masonic symbols. Its many benches make it a fine place to stop for a picnic. The refurbished 1840s bandstand hosts regular summer concerts.

At the meeting point of rue de la Régence and rue Royale (streets on which stand many of the city's premier attractions), **place Royale ★** (tram: 92, 93, or 94) is graced by an equestrian statue of Duke Godefroid de Bouillon, leader of the First Crusade. Also on place Royale is the neoclassical St-Jacques-sur-Coudenberg Church.

Musées Royaux des Beaux-Arts de Belgique (Royal Museums of Fine Arts of Belgium) ★★★ ART MUSEUM   In a vast museum of several buildings,

Passport to Brussels

One of the best discounts is the **Brussels Card** (www.brusselscard.be), available from Visit Brussels tourist offices, and from hotels, museums, and offices of the STIB city transit authority. Valid for 24, 48, or 72 hours, for 24€, 34€, and 40€ respectively, the card affords free use of public transportation; free and discounted admission to around 30 of the city's museums and attractions; and discounts at some restaurants and other venues, and on some guided tours.

this complex combines the **Musée d'Art Ancien** and the **Musée d'Art Moderne** under one roof, connected by a passage. The collection displays mostly Belgian works, from the 14th century to the 20th century. Included in the historical collection are Hans Memling's portraits from the late 15th century, which are marked by sharp lifelike details; works by Hieronymus Bosch; and Lucas Cranach's *Adam and Eve.* Be sure to see the works of Pieter Brueghel, including his *Adoration of the Magi,* and his unusual *Fall of the Rebel Angels,* featuring grotesque faces and beasts. Later artists represented include Rubens, Van Dyck, Frans Hals, and Rembrandt.

Next door, in a circular building connected to the main entrance, the modern art museum's eight floors are all below street level. The overwhelming collection includes works by van Gogh, Matisse, Dalí, Ernst, Chagall, Miró, and local heroes Magritte, Delvaux, de Braekeleer, and Permeke.

Rue de la Régence 3 (at place Royale). www.fine-arts-museum.be. ℂ **02/508-32-11.** Admission 8€ adults, 5€ seniors and students, free for children 17 and under, free for everyone 1st Wed afternoon of the month (except during special exhibits). Tues–Sun 10am–5pm. Closed Jan 1, May 1, Nov 1 and 11, and Dec 25. Métro: Parc.

Palais Royal (Royal Palace) PALACE   The King's Palace, which overlooks the Parc de Bruxelles, was begun in 1820 and had a grandiose Louis XVI-style facelift in 1904. The older side wings date from the 18th century and are flanked by two pavilions, one of which sheltered numerous notables during the 1800s. Today the palace is used for state receptions. It contains the offices of King Albert II, though he and Queen Paola do not live there, but at the suburban Royal Palace in Laeken.

Place des Palais. www.monarchie.be. ℂ **02/551-20-20.** Free admission. From 3rd week of July to late Sept (exact dates announced yearly), Tues–Sun 10:30am–4:30pm. Métro: Parc.

THE SABLON DISTRICT

Considered classier than the Grand-Place by the locals, though busy traffic diminishes your enjoyment of its cafe-terraces, **place du Grand Sablon ★★** (tram: 92, 93, or 94) is lined with gabled mansions. There are many antiques stores and private art galleries, with pricey merchandise on display. On Saturday and Sunday an excellent antiques market sets up its stalls in front of the **Eglise Notre-Dame du Sablon.** Across rue de la Régence, the Grand Sablon's little cousin, **place du Petit Sablon ★**, has a small garden with a fountain and pool at its center. This magical little retreat from the city bustle is surrounded by wrought-iron railings, atop which stand 48 small statues of medieval guildsmen.

PARC DU CINQUANTENAIRE

Designed to celebrate the half centenary of Belgium's 1830 independence, the Cinquantenaire Park was a work in progress from the 1870s until well into the 20th century. Extensive gardens have at their heart a triumphal arch topped by a bronze four-horse chariot sculpture, representing *Brabant Raising the National Flag,* flanked by several fine museums.

Autoworld ☺ MUSEUM   Even if you're not a car enthusiast, you'll likely find this display of 500 historic cars set in the hangar-like Palais Mondial fascinating. The collection starts with early motorized tricycles from 1899 and moves on to a 1911 Model T Ford, a 1924 Renault, a 1938 Cadillac that was the official White House car for FDR and Truman, a 1956 Cadillac used by Kennedy during his June 1963 visit to Berlin, and more.

Parc du Cinquantenaire 11. www.autoworld.be. ℂ **02/736-41-65.** Admission 9€ adults; 6€ students, seniors, and disabled visitors; 4.50€ children 6–12; free for children 5 and under. Apr–Sept daily 10am–6pm; Oct–Mar daily 10am–5pm. Closed Jan 1 and Dec 25. Métro: Mérode.

Musée du Cinquantenaire ★ MUSEUM   This vast museum shows off an eclectic collection of antiques, decorative arts (tapestries, porcelain, silver, and sculptures), and archaeology. Highlights include an Assyrian relief from the 9th century B.C., a Greek vase from the 6th century B.C., a tabletop model of imperial Rome in the 4th century A.D., the A.D. 1145 reliquary of Pope Alexander, some exceptional tapestries, and colossal statues from Easter Island.

Parc du Cinquantenaire 10. www.kmkg-mrah.be. ℂ **02/741-72-11.** Admission 4€ adults; 1.50€ seniors, students, and children 13–17; free for children 12 and under; free for everyone 1st Wed afternoon of the month (except during special exhibits) from 1pm. Tues–Fri 9:30am–5pm; Sat–Sun and holidays 10am–5pm. Closed Jan 1, May 1, Nov 1 and 11, and Dec 25. Métro: Mérode.

AROUND AVENUE LOUISE

The large public park called the **Bois de la Cambre** ★ begins at the top of avenue Louise in the southern section of Brussels (tram: 23, 90, 93, or 94). It gets busy on sunny weekends. Its centerpiece is a small lake with an island that can be reached via an electrically operated pontoon. *Note:* Some busy roads run through the park, so be careful with children at these points.

Continuing south from the Bois, the **Forêt de Soignes** is no longer a park with playing areas and regularly mown grass, but a forest stretching almost to Waterloo; an ideal place for getting away from it all, and particularly alluring in the fall, when the colors are dazzling.

Musée Horta 🏠 HISTORIC HOME   Brussels owes much of its rich Art Nouveau heritage to Victor Horta (1861–1947), a resident architect who led the development of the style. His home and studio in St-Gilles, restored to their original condition, showcase his use of flowing, sinuous shapes and colors, in both interior decoration and architecture.

Rue Américaine 25 (off chaussée de Charleroi). www.hortamuseum.be. ℂ **02/543-04-90.** Admission 7€ adults, 3.50€ seniors and students, 2.50€ children 5–18, free for children 4 and under. Tues–Sun 2–5:30pm. Closed national holidays. Tram: 81, 82, 91, or 92.

BRUPARCK ★★

Built on the site of the 1958 Brussels World Fair, this park (Métro: Heysel) is home to the **Atomium** and **Mini-Europe** (see below); the **Village,** a collection of restaurants and cafes; **Océade,** an indoor/outdoor watersports pavilion with water slides, pools, and saunas; a **planetarium;** and **Kinepolis,** a 26-screen movie multiplex. Ask about combination tickets if you plan to visit more than one Bruparck attraction.

Atomium ★ ☺ ICON   As the Eiffel Tower is the symbol of Paris, the Atomium is the symbol of Brussels, and, like Paris's landmark, it was built for a world fair, this one held in the Belgian city in 1958. Rising 102m (335 ft.) like a giant plaything of the gods, fallen to earth, the Atomium is an iron crystal magnified 165 billion times. Its metal-clad spheres, representing individual atoms, are connected by enclosed escalators and elevators. It's the topmost atom that attracts most people: a restaurant/observation deck that provides a sweeping panorama of the metropolitan area.

Sq. De l'Atomium (at bd. du Centenaire), Heysel. www.atomium.be. ✆ **02/475-47-75.** Admission 11€ adults; 8€ students, seniors, and children 12–18; 6€ children 6–11; free for children 5 and under, and for disabled visitors. Daily 10am–6pm. Métro: Heysel.

Mini-Europe ★★ ☺ PARK/GARDEN   Because Brussels is the "capital of Europe," it's fitting that the city is home to a miniature rendering of all the continent's most notable architectural sights. Even a few natural wonders and technological developments are represented. Built on a scale of $^1/_{25}$ of the originals, Big Ben, the Leaning Tower of Pisa, the Seville bullring, the Channel Tunnel, the Brandenburg Gate, and more exhibit remarkable detail. Although children like Mini-Europe the best, adults certainly find it fun.

Bruparck, Heysel. www.minieurope.com. ✆ **02/478-05-50.** Admission 14€ adults, 10€ children 11 and under, free for children under 1.2m (4 ft.) accompanied by parent. Mid-Mar to June and Sept daily 9:30am–6pm; July–Aug daily 9:30am–8pm (except Aug Sat–Sun 9:30am–midnight); Oct–Dec and 1st week Jan 10am–6pm. Closed rest of Jan to mid-Mar. Métro: Heysel.

TERVUREN

Musée Royal de l'Afrique Centrale (Royal Museum for Central Africa) ★★ MUSEUM   Originally founded to celebrate Belgium's colonial empire in the Belgian Congo (now the Democratic Republic of the Congo), this museum has moved beyond imperialism to feature exhibits on ethnography and environment, mostly in Africa, but also in Asia and South America. The beautiful grounds of this impressive museum are as much a draw as the exhibits inside. The collection includes animal dioramas, African sculpture, and other artwork, and even some of the colonial-era guns and artillery pieces that no doubt helped make Belgium's claim to its African colonies more persuasive. A modern perspective is added by environmental displays that explain desertification, the loss of rainforests, and the destruction of habitats.

Leuvensesteenweg 13, Tervuren (a suburban Flemish district just east of Brussels). www.africa museum.be. ✆ **02/769-52-11.** Admission 4€ adults, 3€ seniors, 1.50€ students and children 13–15, free for children 12 and under. Tues–Fri 10am–5pm; Sat–Sun 10am–6pm. Closed Jan 1, May 1, and Dec 25. Tram: 44 from Montgomery Métro station to Tervuren terminus.

ORGANIZED TOURS

A guided bus tour which lasts 2 hr. 45 min. is available from **Brussels City Tours,** rue du Marché aux Herbes 82 (www.brussels-city-tours.com; ✆ **02/513-77-44**). Tours are 26€ for adults; 23€ for students, seniors, and children aged 13 to 18; 13€ for children aged 6 to 12; and free for children 5 and under. You can book tours at most hotels, and arrangements can be made for hotel pickup.

From June 15 to September 15, **Le Bus Bavard,** rue des Thuyas 12 (www.bus bavard.be; ✆ **02/673-18-35**), operates a daily 3-hour "chatterbus" tour at 10am from the Galeries Royales St-Hubert (Métro: Gare Centrale), a mall next to rue du

Marché aux Herbes 90, a few steps off the Grand-Place. A walking tour covers the historic city center, followed by a bus ride through areas the average visitor never sees. You hear about life in Brussels and get a real feel for the city. Most tours cost in the region of 8€. You don't need a reservation for this fascinating experience—just be there by 10am.

ARAU, bd. Adolphe Max 55 (www.arau.org; ✆ **02/219-33-45;** Métro: De Brouckère), organizes tours that help you discover not only Brussels's countless treasures but also problems the city faces. It runs 3-hour themed coach tours: "Grand-Place and Its Surroundings," "Brussels 1900—Art Nouveau," "Brussels 1930—Art Deco," "Surprising Parks and Squares," and "Alternative Brussels." You are advised to book ahead. Tours by bus are 17€ for adults, and 13€ for seniors and those 25 and under; tours by foot are 10€; in both cases, children 11 and under are free. Tours take place on Saturday mornings from March to November; private group tours can be arranged year-round.

Where to Eat

The Brussels restaurant scene covers the entire city, but one or two culinary pockets exist that you should know about. It has been said that you haven't truly visited this city unless you've dined at least once along **rue des Bouchers** or its offshoot, **Petite rue des Bouchers,** near the Grand-Place. Both streets are lined with an extraordinary array of eateries. Reservations are not usually necessary; if you cannot be seated at one, you simply stroll on to the next one.

Then there's the cluster of fine restaurants at the **Marché aux Poissons (Fish Market)**—or Vismet in the local dialect—around place Ste-Catherine. This is where fishermen once unloaded their daily catches from a now-covered canal. Seafood, as you'd expect, is the specialty.

AROUND THE GRAND-PLACE

De l'Ogenblik ★★ FRENCH/BELGIAN   In the elegant surrounds of the Galeries Royales St-Hubert, this restaurant supplies good taste in a Parisian bistro-style setting, popular with off-duty actors and audiences from the nearby Gallery theater. It often gets busy, but the ambience in the split-level, wood-and-brass-outfitted dining room, with a sand-strewn floor, is convivial, though a little too tightly packed when it's full. The garlicky meat and seafood dishes are worth sampling, but expect to pay a smidgen more for atmosphere than might be strictly justified by results on the plate.

Galerie des Princes 1 (in the Galeries Royales St-Hubert). www.ogenblik.be. ✆ **02/511-61-51.** Reservations recommended. Main courses 23€–32€; *plat du jour* (lunch only) 11€. AE, DC, MC, V. Mon–Thurs noon–2:30pm and 7pm–midnight; Fri–Sat noon–2:30pm and 7pm–12:30am. Métro: Gare Centrale.

La Maison du Cygne ★ CLASSIC FRENCH   This grande dame of Brussels's internationally recognized restaurants overlooks the Grand-Place from the former guild house of the butchers' guild, where a certain Karl Marx and Friedrich Engels cooked up *The Communist Manifesto.* The service is as elegant as the polished walnut walls and bronze wall sconces, and the menu features haute cuisine Belgian and French classics. Due to its popular location, the restaurant is usually crowded at lunchtime.

Grand-Place 9 (entrance at rue Charles Buls 2). www.lamaisonducygne.be. ✆ **02/511-82-44.** Reservations recommended. Main courses 36€–45€; lunch menu 40€; fixed-price menu 65€. AE, DC, MC, V. Mon–Fri noon–2pm and 7pm–midnight; Sat 7pm–midnight. Métro: Gare Centrale.

A few restaurants (not reviewed here) in this colorful district just off the Grand-Place take advantage of tourists. If you don't want to get fleeced, be sure to ask the price of everything *before* you order it. Most visitors leave the Ilot Sacré with no more serious complaint than an expanded waistline, but a little caution is in order.

't Kelderke ★★ ✦ TRADITIONAL BELGIAN   The Little Cellar is one of the Grand-Place's most delightful surprises but the entrance is not immediately obvious—it's hidden beneath an ornate guild house. A stairway leads down to a crowded, lively restaurant in a 17th-century brick-vaulted room, decked out with long wooden tables. The menu features Belgian favorites like *stoemp*, served with a pork chop; Flemish beef stew; rabbit in beer; and Zeeland mussels in season, all served from an open kitchen.

Grand-Place 15. www.restaurant-het-kelderke.be. ✆ **02/513-73-44.** Main courses 11€–27€; *plat du jour* 11€. AE, DC, MC, V. Daily noon–2am. Métro: Gare Centrale.

THE LOWER CITY

Belga Queen ★ CONTEMPORARY BELGIAN   Set in a Belle Epoque building that once housed the plush 19th-century Hôtel de la Poste, the brasserie fills its vast space with a cool clientele. You'll tuck into food of character that runs from Ostend shrimp, through Namurois snail soup and tender Charolais beef sirloin, to roasted Mechelen cuckoo. In addition to a restaurant, the Belga Queen contains an oyster bar, a beer bar, and a club and cigar lounge.

Rue du Fossée aux Loups 32 (at rue Neuve). www.belgaqueen.be. ✆ **02/217-21-87.** Reservations recommended on weekends. Main courses 20€–45€; lunch menu 16€; fixed-price menus 30€–45€. AE, DC, MC, V. Daily noon–2:30pm and 7–11pm. Métro: De Brouckère.

François ★★ SEAFOOD   A bright and cheerful ambience complements fine cuisine at this restaurant in a 19th-century town house that has housed fishmongers since 1922, a tradition which is taken very seriously. Superb is the best word to describe seafood specialties, like the *sole ostendaise* (North Sea sole cooked in butter) and the bouillabaisse, and their signature lobster dishes, mussels, and Zeeland oysters. The menu includes a few meat choices. In fine weather, you can dine on a sidewalk terrace across the street on the old Fish Market square. If you're seated indoors, try to get a table with a view on the square.

Quai aux Briques 2 (at the Marché aux Poissons). www.restaurantfrancois.be. ✆ **02/511-60-89.** Reservations recommended. Main courses 23€–58€; fixed-price lunch menu 27€; fixed-price menu 42€. AE, DC, MC, V. Tues–Sat noon–2:30pm and 7–11:30pm. Métro: Ste-Catherine.

In 't Spinnekopke ★ 🍴 TRADITIONAL BELGIAN   This restaurant, translated as "In the Spider's Web," occupies a coach inn from 1762, just far enough off the beaten track downtown to be frequented mainly by those in the know. You dine in a tilting, tiled-floor building, at plain tables, and more likely than not squeezed into a tight space. This is one of Brussels's most traditional restaurants, so much so that the menu lists its hardy regional standbys in the old Bruxellois dialect. *Stoemp mi sossisse* is stew with sausage, and *toung ave mei* is sole. The bar stocks a large selection of Belgian beers.

Place du Jardin aux Fleurs 1 (off rue Van Artevelde). www.spinnekopke.be. © **02/511-86-95.** Reservations recommended. Main courses 18€–30€. AE, DC, MC, V. Mon–Fri noon–3pm and 6–11pm; Sat 6pm–midnight. Métro: Bourse.

La Manufacture ★ FRENCH/INTERNATIONAL   This was formerly the factory of chic leather-goods maker Delvaux, and even in its former industrial incarnation, style was a primary concern—though the neighborhood is unprepossessing. Fully refurbished, with parquet floors, polished wood, leather banquettes, and stone tables set amid iron pillars, it produces trendy world cuisine with a French foundation for a mostly youthful public. It might at first seem disconcerting to find dim sum, sushi, Moroccan couscous, Lyon sausage, and Belgian waterzooi on the same menu, but don't worry—it works.

Rue Notre-Dame du Sommeil 12–20 (off place du Jardin aux Fleurs). www.lamanufacture.be. © **02/502-25-25.** Reservations recommended. Main courses 14€–27€; *menu du jour* (lunch only) 17€; fixed-price menus 35€–50€. AE, DC, MC, V. Mon–Fri noon–2pm and 6–11pm; Sat 6pm–midnight. Métro: Bourse.

AROUND AVENUE LOUISE

Au Vieux Bruxelles ★ BELGIAN/SEAFOOD   This convivial, brasserie-style restaurant from 1882 specializes in mussels, which it serves in a wide variety of ways. Indeed it's a kind of temple to the Belgian obsession with mussels. In Belgium, the personality of this humble but tasty sea creature is a staple of conversation as much as of diet, and people assess the quality of each year's crop with the same critical eye that other countries reserve for fine wines. Should you not wish to dine on mussels, you can opt for one of the great steaks on offer, like *steak au poivre flambé* (flamed pepper steak).

Rue St-Boniface 35 (close to Porte Namur). www.auvieuxbruxelles.com. © **02/503-31-11.** Reservations not accepted. Main courses 11€–21€; mussel plates 18€–20€. AE, MC, V. Mon–Thurs 6:30–11:30pm; Fri–Sat 6:30pm–midnight; Sun noon–2:30pm and 6:30–11:30pm. Métro: Porte de Namur.

La Mirabelle 🍴 TRADITIONAL BELGIAN   Due to its "democratic" prices, convivial atmosphere, and consistently good food, this brasserie-restaurant in Ixelles is popular both with students from the nearby Université Libre de Bruxelles and with Bruxellois in general. Plainly decorated, with wooden tables crowded together, it looks more like a bar than a restaurant and often has a boisterous pub-style atmosphere to match. The *steak-frites* (steak with French fries), a Belgian staple, is particularly good here. The garden terrace is a great setting for alfresco dining in summer.

Chaussée de Boondael 459 (at av. Arnaud Fraiteur). www.mirabelle.be. © **02/649-51-73.** Main courses 13€–25€; *plat du jour* 9.20€. MC, V. Daily noon–3pm and 6pm–1:30am. Bus: 71, 72, or 95 to Cimetière d'Ixelles.

La Quincaillerie ★★ MODERN FRENCH/OYSTER BAR   In the Ixelles district, where fine restaurants are as common as streetlights, this spot stands out, even though it may be a little too aware of its own modish good looks and is a shade pricey. The setting is a traditional former hardware store from 1903, with a giant rail-station clock, wood paneling, and masses of wooden drawers, designed by students of Art Nouveau master Victor Horta. It's busy but the waiting staff here is always friendly. Seafood dishes predominate on the menu.

Rue du Page 45 (at rue Américaine). www.quincaillerie.be. © **02/533-98-33.** Reservations recommended. Main courses 17€–46€; lunch menu 14€. AE, DC, MC, V. Mon–Sat noon–2:30pm and 7pm–midnight; Sun 7pm–midnight. Tram: 81 to Trinité.

Shopping

Don't look for many bargains. As a general rule, Upper Town around avenue Louise and Porte de Namur is more expensive than Lower Town around rue Neuve. You can enjoy a stroll along modern shopping promenades, the busiest of which is the pedestrians-only rue Neuve, starting at place de la Monnaie and running north to place Rogier: It's home to boutiques, big department stores, general clothing shops, and several malls.

Some of the trendiest boutiques are on rue Antoine Dansaert, across from the Bourse. An interesting street for window-shopping, rue des Eperonniers, near the Grand-Place, hosts many small stores selling antiques, toys, old books, and clothing.

The **Galeries Royales St-Hubert** (Métro: Gare Centrale) is an airy arcade hosting expensive boutiques, cafes with outdoor terraces, and buskers playing classical music. Opened in 1847, architect Pierre Cluysenaer's Italian neo-Renaissance gallery has a touch of class and is well worth a stroll through, even if you have no intention of shopping. The elegant gallery is near the Grand-Place, between rue du Marché aux Herbes and rue de l'Ecuyer, and is split by rue des Bouchers.

In a former guild house, **Maison Antoine ★**, Grand-Place 26 (℃ **02/512-48-59**; Métro: Gare Centrale), is one of the best places in town to buy lace. The quality is superb, the service is friendly, and the prices aren't unreasonable.

Dandoy ★, rue au Beurre 31 (www.biscuiteriedandoy.be; ℃ **02/511-03-26**; Métro: Bourse), is where cookie and cake fans can try traditional Belgian specialties like spicy *speculoos* (traditional Belgian cookies made with brown sugar and cinnamon and baked in wooden molds) and *pain à la grecque* (caramelized, sugary, flaky pastries).

If you have a sweet tooth, you'll feel you're in heaven when you see Brussels's famous chocolate stores, filled with sumptuous soft-centered pralines, from around 12€ a kilogram (2¼ lb.). You find some of the best confections at **Mary Chocolatier ★★**, rue Royale 73 (www.marychoc.com; ℃ **02/217-45-00**; Métro: Parc); **Neuhaus,** Galerie de la Reine 25–27 (www.neuhaus.be; ℃ **02/512-63-59**; Métro: Gare Centrale); **Wittamer,** place du Grand Sablon 12 (www.wittamer.com; ℃ **02/512-37-42**; tram: 92, 93, or 94); and **Léonidas,** bd. Anspach 46 (www. leonidas.com; ℃ **02/218-03-63**; Métro: Bourse).

For kids, pick up some *Tintin* mementos from **Boutique de Tintin,** rue de la Colline 13 (℃ **02/514-51-52**; Métro: Gare Centrale). **Waterstone's,** bd. Adolphe Max 71–75 (www.waterstones.com; ℃ **02/219-27-08**; Métro: Rogier), has English-language books, newspapers, and magazines.

MARKETS

The city's favorite *marché aux puces* (flea market) is the **Vieux Marché (Old Market;** Métro: Porte de Hal), on place du Jeu de Balle, a large cobblestone square in the Marolles district, open daily from 7am to 2pm. Every Sunday from 7am to 2pm, hundreds of merchants assemble their wares in a **street market** outside Gare du Midi (Métro: Gare du Midi). It has many excellent food bargains, making it a perfect place to gather provisions for a few days. Hold on to your wallet, though: The market attracts pickpockets.

Entertainment & Nightlife

A listing of what's happening on the cultural scene is in the bi-weekly English-language magazine *The Bulletin.*

PERFORMING ARTS

An opera house in the grand style, the **Théâtre Royal de la Monnaie ★★**, place de la Monnaie (www.lamonnaie.be; ✆ 070/23-39-39; Métro: De Brouckère), is home to the Opéra Royal de la Monnaie, which has been called the best in the French-speaking world, and to the Orchestre Symphonique de la Monnaie. The box office is open Tuesday to Saturday from 11am to 6pm. Tickets 10€ to 170€.

The **BOZAR,** rue Ravenstein 23 (www.bozar.be; ✆ 02/507-82-00; Métro: Gare Centrale)—formerly the Palais des Beaux-Arts—is home to the Belgian National Orchestra. The box office is open Monday to Saturday from 11am to 6pm, with tickets costing 10€ to 80€. The **Cirque Royal,** rue de l'Enseignement 81 (www.botanique.be; ✆ 02/218-37-32; Métro: Parc), formerly a real circus, now hosts music, opera, and ballet. The box office is open Tuesday to Saturday from 11am to 6pm, with tickets for 10€ to 75€.

BARS

The city's many watering holes run the gamut from Art Nouveau palaces to plain and convivial. You should linger a few hours in one, preferably savoring one of the incredible beers for which Belgium is famous. It's always satisfying to sit at a sidewalk cafe on the Grand-Place and drink in the beauty of the floodlit golden buildings ringing the square. Drinks on a Grand-Place terrace are more expensive than those in ordinary cafes, but once you've ordered one you can nurse it for hours, or until the waiter's patience wears out and he grabs the glass from you, empty or not.

The city's oldest cafe, in a 1690 building, **Le Roy d'Espagne,** Grand-Place 1 (✆ 02/513-08-07; Métro: Gare Centrale), accommodates patrons in several areas. In addition to the outdoor tables, you can drink within the 17th-century Flemish interior—a masterpiece of wooden architecture, with a wooden walkway, timber beams, and a fireplace covered by a black metal hood. The top-floor view of the Grand-Place is spectacular. It's open daily from 10am to 1am.

Although its name means "Sudden Death," you'll likely survive **A la Mort Subite,** rue Montagne aux Herbes Potagères 7 (✆ 02/513-13-18; Métro: Gare Centrale), a 1911 cafe with stained-glass mirrors, old photographs, paintings, and prints. A good option for an afternoon coffee or an evening beer, it's open daily from 10am to 1am. A block from the Grand-Place, in a 1642 house, **A l'Imaige de Nostre-Dame,** rue du Marché aux Herbes 6–8 (✆ 02/219-42-49; Métro: Gare Centrale), attracts a mixed crowd enjoying reasonably priced beer amid wooden ceiling beams and old wooden tables. It's open daily from noon to midnight.

In a 17th-century building, **La Fleur en Papier Doré,** rue des Alexiens 53, off place de la Chapelle (✆ 02/511-16-59; Métro: Bourse), calls itself a "temple of surrealism" because Magritte used to relax here. Despite the old-fashioned decor, the cafe attracts a wide assortment of arty types. On Friday and Saturday from 9 or 10pm, an accordion player pumps out some tunes, and there are occasional poetry readings upstairs. The cafe is open daily from 11am to 11pm.

LIVE-MUSIC & DANCE CLUBS

Top dance clubs include **You ★,** rue Duquesnoy 18 (www.leyou.be; ✆ 02/639-14-00; Métro: Gare Centrale); **Fuse,** rue Blaes 208 (www.fuse.be; ✆ 02/511-97-89; bus: 20 or 48), for techno; and **Duke's Night Club,** rue de l'Homme Chrétien 2 (www.dukes.be; ✆ 02/639-14-00; Métro: Gare Centrale), fashionable for older hoofers.

Belgian Brews Pack a Punch

Brussels is well known for its *lambic* beers, which use naturally occurring yeast for fermentation; they are often flavored with fruit, and come in bottles with champagne-type corks. Unlike any other beer, they're more akin to a sweet sparkling wine. *Gueuze,* a blend of young and aged lambic beers, is one of the least sweet. If you prefer something sweeter, try raspberry-flavored *framboise* or cherry-flavored *kriek. Faro* is a low-alcohol beer, sometimes sweetened or lightly spiced. The rich, dark Trappist ales are brewed by monks from Chimay, Orval, Rochefort, Sint-Benedictus, Westmalle, and Westvleteren monasteries.

Jazz is a popular but ever-changing scene. **L'Archiduc,** rue Antoine Dansaert 6 (www.archiduc.net; ✆ 02/512-06-52; Métro: Bourse), puts on jazz concerts on Saturday and Sunday. **Le Sounds,** rue de la Tulipe 28 (www.soundsjazzclub.be; ✆ 02/512-92-50; bus: 54 or 71), has daily jazz concerts, and a workshop on Mondays at 7:30pm. For those who like their licks a tad restrained, there's a jazz brunch at the **Airport Sheraton Hotel,** facing the terminal building (www.sheratonbrussels airport.com; ✆ 02/725-10-00; train: Brussels Airport), every Sunday from noon to 3pm.

The city's main venue for big rock concerts (along with spectacles like *Holiday on Ice* and *Lord of the Dance*) is **Forest National,** av. du Globe 36 (www.forestnational. be; ✆ 070/25-20-20; tram: 32, 82, or 97). Not-quite-so-big acts are likely to find a stage at **Cirque Royal,** rue de l'Enseignement 81 (www.cirque-royal.org; ✆ 02/218-20-15; Métro: Parc).

THE LGBT SCENE

Rue des Riches-Claires and **rue du Marché au Charbon** host gay and lesbian bars. **Macho 2,** rue du Marché au Charbon 108 (✆ 02/512-45-87; Métro: Bourse), a block from rue des Riches-Claires, has a gay men's sauna, pool, steam room, and cafe. **Le Fuse** and **You** (see above) have gay nights.

For more information about LGBT life in Brussels, stop by the gay and lesbian community center, **Tels Quels,** rue du Marché au Charbon 81 (www.telsquels.be; ✆ 02/512-45-87; Métro: Bourse), open Saturday to Thursday 5pm to 2am, Friday 5pm to 4am.

Where to Stay

If you arrive in Brussels without a reservation, you should stop by one of the **Brussels International Tourism & Congress** tourist offices or information desks (see "Visitor Information," earlier in this chapter). The staff in these offices can make same-day reservations, if you go in person, for a small fee (deducted by the hotel from its rate).

The most popular Brussels districts in which to stay are the center of town, broadly defined as the extended zone around the **Grand-Place,** and in the upper-town district around place Stéphanie, boulevard de Waterloo, and **avenue Louise.** Other concentrations of hotels can be found around the **Marché aux Poissons (Fish Market),** and the **Bruxelles-Nord** and **Bruxelles-Midi** train stations (in the case of Bruxelles-Nord, avoid the less pleasant north side of the station). **European**

District hotels are convenient for visiting Eurocrats, politicians, lobbyists, and media types, but not necessarily a good choice for "real people."

AROUND THE GRAND-PLACE

Amigo ★★ In Brussels slang, an *amigo* is a prison, and indeed a prison once stood here. But any resemblance to the former accommodations is purely nominal, as this Rocco Forte hotel is among the city's finest lodgings. Its Spanish Renaissance architecture, stately corridors, and flagstone lobby are right at home in this ancient neighborhood. The rooms are spacious and traditionally elegant, but with touches of modern Belgian design to brighten things up—and motifs from the classic comic *Tintin* in the bathrooms to add an element of whimsy. Ask for a room with a view of the Town Hall's Gothic spire.

Rue de l'Amigo 1–3 (off Grand-Place), 1000 Bruxelles. www.hotelamigo.com. (C) **02/547-47-47** or **888/667-9477** in the U.S. and Canada. Fax 02/513-52-77. 173 units. 660€–790€ double; from 1,010€ suite. AE, DC, MC, V. Valet parking 30€. Métro: Bourse. **Amenities:** Restaurant; bar; lounge; exercise room; concierge; room service; babysitting; executive rooms. *In room:* A/C, TV, minibar, hair dryer, Wi-Fi (20€/24 hr.).

La Vieille Lanterne A tiny place with two rooms on each floor and no elevator, the family-owned hotel is diagonally across a narrow street from the *Manneken-Pis*. It can be hard to spot, as you enter through the side door of a trinket store selling hundreds of *Manneken-Pis* replicas. You should feel quite at ease in rooms that are plainly furnished but bright and clean, with old-style leaded windows, and with small bathrooms with marble counters and tiled walls. Breakfast is served in your room. It's advisable to reserve well ahead.

Rue des Grands Carmes 29 (facing *Manneken-Pis*), 1000 Bruxelles. www.lavieillelanterne.be. (C) **02/512-74-94.** Fax 02/512-13-97. 6 units. 86€–95€ double with continental breakfast. AE, DC, MC, V. Limited street parking. Métro: Bourse. *In room:* TV, Wi-Fi (free).

Le Dixseptième ★★ 🗝 This graceful 17th-century house, once the official residence of the Spanish ambassador, stands close to the Grand-Place in a neighborhood of restored dwellings. Guest rooms have wood paneling and marble chimneys, and are as big as the suites in many hotels; some have balconies, and most overlook a tranquil courtyard patio. All are in 18th-century style and are named after Belgian painters from Brueghel to Magritte. Both the bar and the lounge are decorated with carved wooden medallions and 18th-century paintings.

Rue de la Madeleine 25 (off place de l'Albertine), 1000 Bruxelles. www.ledixseptieme.be. (C) **02/517-17-17.** Fax 02/502-64-24. 24 units. 200€ double; 200€–430€ suite. Rates include buffet breakfast. AE, DC, MC, V. Very limited street parking. Métro: Gare Centrale. **Amenities:** Bar; lounge. *In room:* A/C, TV, minibar, hair dryer, Wi-Fi (free).

Mozart ★ Go up a flight from the busy, cheap-eats street level, and guess which famous composer's music wafts through the lobby? Salmon-colored walls and old paintings create a warm, intimate ambience that's carried over into the guest rooms. Furnishings are in Louis XV style, and exposed beams lend each room a cozy originality. Several are duplexes with a sitting room underneath the loft bedroom. Top-floor rooms offer guests impressive views.

Rue du Marché aux Fromages 23 (close to the Grand-Place), 1000 Bruxelles. www.hotel-mozart.be. (C) **02/502-66-61.** Fax 02/502-77-58. 50 units. 120€–250€ double. AE, DC, MC, V. No parking. Métro: Gare Centrale. **Amenities:** Lounge. *In room:* TV, hair dryer.

THE LOWER CITY

George V   This agreeable hotel is tucked away on a corner of the city center that has been emerging as a trendy shopping-and-eating area in recent years. Situated in a renovated town house from 1859 within walking distance of the Grand-Place, the George has rooms that are basic but clean with new furnishings.

Rue 't Kint 23 (off place du Jardin aux Fleurs), 1000 Bruxelles. www.hotelgeorge5.be. ✆ **02/513-50-93.** Fax 02/513-44-93. 17 units. 60€–90€ double. Rates include continental breakfast. AE, MC, V. Limited street parking. Métro: Bourse. **Amenities:** Bar; room service. *In room:* TV, minibar, hair dryer, Wi-Fi (9€/stay).

Métropole ★★★   Even if you're not staying here, the hotel is well worth a visit. An ornate, marble-and-gilt interior distinguishes this late-19th-century hotel several blocks from the Grand-Place. Soaring ceilings, potted palms, and lavishly decorated public rooms add to the Belle Epoque allure. Spacious rooms have classic furnishings and some modern luxuries.

Place de Brouckère 31 (close to Centre Monnaie), 1000 Bruxelles. www.metropolehotel.com. ✆ **02/217-23-00.** Fax 02/218-02-20. 305 units. 275€–450€ double; from 650€ suite. AE, DC, MC, V. Valet parking 25€. Métro: De Brouckère. **Amenities:** Restaurant; lounge; concierge; exercise room; room service; babysitting. *In room:* TV, minibar, hair dryer, Wi-Fi (free).

Welcome ★★   The name of this gem of a hotel, overlooking the Fish Market, couldn't be more accurate, thanks to the untiring efforts of the husband-and-wife proprietors. You can think of it as a country *auberge* (inn) right in the heart of town. Rooms are furnished and styled on individual, unrelated themes, such as Provence, Africa, and Laura Ashley, all to a high standard.

Quai au Bois à Brûler 23 (at the Marché aux Poissons), 1000 Bruxelles. www.hotelwelcome.com. ✆ **02/219-95-46.** Fax 02/217-18-87. 17 units. 100€–155€ double; 170€–210€ suite. Rates include buffet breakfast. AE, DC, MC, V. Parking 13€. Métro: Ste-Catherine. **Amenities:** Lounge; room service. *In room:* A/C (some units), TV, minibar, hair dryer, Wi-Fi (free).

THE UPPER CITY

Albert ★ 🦶   A modern hotel next to the bronze-domed 19th-century Eglise Royale Ste-Marie, and close to an enclave of the most authentic Turkish restaurants in town. Rooms are clean and bright, with a touch of design flair and tiled bathrooms. There are also five large studio apartments in the Résidence Albert next door, all with refrigerators. Although the hotel is on the outer edge of the city center, trams from a nearby stop take you straight to the Royal Palace, Royal Museums of Fine Arts, and Sablon antiques district.

Rue Royale-Ste-Marie 27–29 (off place de la Reine), 1030 Bruxelles. www.hotelalbert.be. ✆ **02/217-93-91.** Fax 02/219-20-17. 19 units. 70€–75€ double; 75€–90€ studio apartment. Rates include continental breakfast. MC, V. Free parking. Tram: 25, 92, or 94. **Amenities:** Bar. *In room:* TV, hair dryer, Wi-Fi (free).

Bloom! ★★   This lodging is worthy of note for having made such an innovative job of reinventing a space that once housed the grand but staid Royal Crown Hotel. Each of the guest rooms sports a fresco on the theme of flowers created by young European artists. Edgy artworks these aren't, but they contribute to an air of New Age calm that infuses the hotel's bright and vibrantly colored interiors, and help to counter a location on a busy street. The guest rooms are spacious, none more so than the XXL and loft rooms.

Rue Royale 250 (adjacent to Le Botanique), 1210 Bruxelles. www.hotelbloom.com. ✆ **02/220-66-11.** Fax 02/217-84-44. 305 units. 75€–220€ double. AE, DC, MC, V. Parking 22€. Métro: Botanique.

Amenities: Restaurant/lounge; exercise room; room service. *In room:* A/C, TV, minibar, hair dryer, MP3 docking station, Wi-Fi (free, up to 60MB/day).

AROUND AVENUE LOUISE

Thon Hotel Bristol Stephanie ★★   From its lobby fittings to furnishings in the kitchenette suites, every feature of this sleek Norwegian-owned hotel, set on one of the city's toniest shopping streets, is streamlined, functional, and representative of the best in Nordic design. Some rooms have four-poster beds and "anti-allergy" hardwood floors; all are quite large, and furnished to a high level of modern style and comfort (though the standard rooms could use a little more drawer space).

Av. Louise 91–93, 1050 Bruxelles. www.thonhotels.com. ℂ **02/543-33-11.** Fax 02/538-03-07. 142 units. 240€–320€ double; from 500€ suite. AE, DC, MC, V. Parking 25€. Métro: Louise. **Amenities:** Restaurant; bar; lounge; exercise room; Jacuzzi; sauna; concierge; room service; babysitting. *In room:* A/C, TV, minibar, hair dryer, Wi-Fi (18€/24 hr.).

A Side Trip to Waterloo ★

Europe's Gettysburg, the battle that ended Napoleon's empire, was fought on rolling farmland near **Waterloo,** just south of Brussels. On June 18, 1815, 72,000 British, Dutch, Belgian, and German troops, aided before the day's end by around 40,000 Prussians, defeated the mighty Napoleon Bonaparte and his 76,000 French, leaving 40,000 dead and wounded on the field. Napoleon survived, but his attempt to rebuild his empire was crushed; he was exiled to the island of St. Helena, where he died 6 years later.

GETTING THERE

From Brussels, the TEC bus W departs twice hourly from Bruxelles-Midi rail station (Métro: Gare du Midi) to the battlefield visitor center, south of Waterloo. The 18km (11-mile) ride takes 55 minutes and costs 4.25€. By **car** from Brussels, take the ring road (R0) to exit 27 for Waterloo, and N5 south to the battlefield.

EXPLORING WATERLOO

The battlefield remains much as it was on that fateful day. Before touring it, you can study the 360-degree **Panoramic Mural** and view an audiovisual presentation of the battle, at the **Centre du Visiteur,** route du Lion 252–254, Braine l'Alleud (www. waterloo1815.be; ℂ **02/385-19-12**). To survey the battlefield, climb the nearby **Butte du Lion (Lion Mound),** a conical hill surmounted by a bronze lion. Across the road from the visitor center is the **Musée des Cires (Waxworks Museum),** where Napoleon, Wellington, Blücher, and other key participants appear as rather tatty wax figures.

These four sites are open daily April to October from 9:30am to 6:30pm and November to March from 10am to 5pm; closed January 1 and December 25. Admission to the visitor center is free. Admission to its audiovisual presentation and the on-site attractions is 8.70€ for adults, 6.50€ for seniors and students, 5.50€ for children aged 7 to 17, and free for children 6 and under.

BRUGES ★★★

Walking around the almost perfectly preserved city of Bruges is like taking a step back in time. From its 13th-century origins as a cloth-manufacturing town to its current incarnation as a tourism mecca, Bruges (its name is Brugge in Dutch) seems to have changed little. As in a fairy tale, swans glide down the winding canals and the stone

Bruges

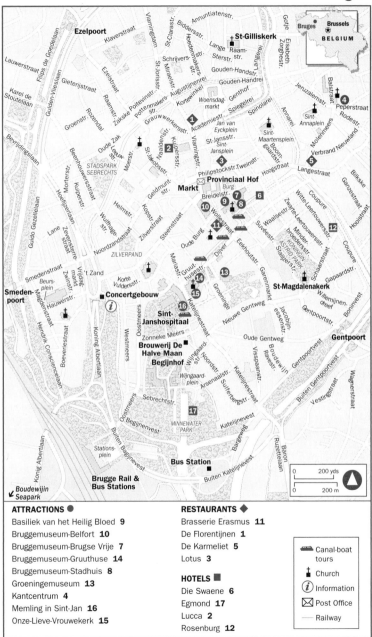

ATTRACTIONS ●
Basiliek van het Heilig Bloed **9**
Bruggemuseum-Belfort **10**
Bruggemuseum-Brugse Vrije **7**
Bruggemuseum-Gruuthuse **14**
Bruggemuseum-Stadhuis **8**
Groeningemuseum **13**
Kantcentrum **4**
Memling in Sint-Jan **16**
Onze-Lieve-Vrouwekerk **15**

RESTAURANTS ◆
Brasserie Erasmus **11**
De Florentijnen **1**
De Karmeliet **5**
Lotus **3**

HOTELS ■
Die Swaene **6**
Egmond **17**
Lucca **2**
Rosenburg **12**

Canal-boat tours
‡ Church
ⓘ Information
✉ Post Office
— Railway

houses look like they're made of gingerbread. Even though glass-fronted stores have taken over the street-level floors of ancient buildings, and tour boats spend most of the day chugging along the canals, Bruges has made the transition from medieval to modern with remarkable grace. The town seems revitalized rather than crushed by the tremendous influx of tourists.

Essentials

GETTING THERE

BY TRAIN　Bruges is a 1-hour train ride from Brussels. Trains depart every hour; a one-way ticket is 21€ first-class, 14€ second-class. The city has good rail connections to Ghent, Antwerp, and the North Sea ferry ports of Oostende (Ostend) and Zeebrugge. For train schedule and fare information, visit www.b-rail.be or call © 02/528-28-28. Bruges station is on Stationsplein, 1.5km (1 mile) by foot from the center of town; to get there by bus, take any **De Lijn** (www.delijn.be; © 070/220-200) bus for CENTRUM from outside the rail station and get out at the Markt.

BY BUS　**Eurolines** (www.eurolines.com; © 02/274-13-50) buses from Brussels, London, Paris, Amsterdam, and other cities arrive at the bus station adjoining Bruges rail station.

BY CAR　If you're driving from Brussels or Ghent, take A10/E40. Drop off your car at a parking lot or garage (see "Getting Around," below). The network of one-way streets in the city center makes driving a trial.

VISITOR INFORMATION

TOURIST OFFICE　The tourist information office, **Toerisme Brugge,** Concertgebouw, 't Zand 34, 8000 Brugge (www.brugge.be; © 050/44-46-46), is open daily from 10am to 6pm. A separate office at the rail station is open Monday to Friday from 10am to 5pm, and Saturday and Sunday from 10am to 2pm. Ask for the complimentary annual *events@brugge* brochure and monthly *Exit* newsletter, both of them excellent directories of current goings-on.

CITY LAYOUT　Narrow streets fan out from two central squares, the **Markt** and the **Burg.** A network of canals threads its way to every section of the small city, and the city center is almost encircled by a canal that opens at its southern end to become a swan-filled lake, the **Minnewater,** bordered by the Begijnhof and a fine park.

GETTING AROUND

ON FOOT　Walking is by far the best way to see Bruges, since much of the city center is traffic-free (but wear good walking shoes, as those charming cobblestones can be hard going).

BY BICYCLE　Biking is a terrific way to get around town. You can rent a bike from the rail station for 10€ a day, plus a deposit. Some hotels and stores rent bikes, for 8€ to 10€ a day.

BY BUS　**De Lijn** city buses (www.delijn.be; © 070/22-02-00) depart from the bus station outside the rail station, and from the big square called 't Zand, west of the Markt. Several bus routes pass through the Markt.

BY TAXI　There's a taxi stand outside the rail station (© 050/38-46-60), and another at the Markt (© 050/33-44-44).

BY CAR　Movement by car through the city center is tightly restricted. Leave your car in your hotel's parking garage, if it has one. You can use one of the large,

A Card for Bruges

Should you plan to do a lot of sight-seeing in Bruges, consider purchasing a **Brugge City Card** (www.bruggecitycard. be). This will give you free admission to many city museums and attractions, a canal boat tour or bus tour, a 60% reduction on the price of a 3-day public transportation pass, and more. The cards cost 35€ for 48 hours and 40€ for 72 hours; and 32€ and 35€, respectively, for those aged 25 and under. In addition to purchasing online, you can buy one at locations around the city, including the Concertgebouw on 't Zand (see later in this chapter) and the rail station (see above).

prominently signposted underground parking garages around the city center—these get expensive for long stays—or the inexpensive parking lot at the rail station, from where you can take a bus or walk into the heart of the city.

Exploring Bruges

THE MARKT ★★

Begin at this historic market square, where a **sculpture group** in the middle depicts two Flemish heroes, butcher Jan Breydel and weaver Pieter de Coninck. They led a bloody 1302 uprising against pro-French merchants and nobles who dominated the city, and then went on to an against-all-odds victory over French knights later the same year at the Battle of the Golden Spurs. The large neo-Gothic **Provinciaal Hof,** which was constructed in 1887, houses the government of West Flanders province.

Bruggemuseum-Belfort (Belfry) ★★ MUSEUM   The 13th-to-16th-century belfry's octagonal tower soars 84m (276 ft.) and has a magnificent 47-bell carillon. If you have enough energy, climb the 366 steps to the summit for a panoramic view of the old town—you can pause for breath at the second-floor Treasury, where the town seal and charters were kept behind multiple wrought-iron grilles. In centuries past, much of the city's cloth trade and other commerce was conducted in the vast **Hallen (Market Halls),** below the Belfry.

Markt. © **050/44-87-43.** Admission 8€ adults, 6€ seniors and ages 12–25, free for children 11 and under. Daily 9:30am–5pm. Closed Jan 1, Ascension Day afternoon, and Dec 25. Bus: All buses to Markt.

THE BURG ★★★

An array of beautiful buildings, which adds up to a trip through the history of Bruges architecture, stands on this beautiful square just steps away from the Markt. During the 9th century, Count Baldwin "Iron Arm" of Flanders built a castle here at a then-tiny riverside settlement that would grow into Bruges.

Basiliek van het Heilig Bloed (Basilica of the Holy Blood) ★ RELI-GIOUS SITE   Since 1150, this basilica next to the Town Hall has been the reposi-tory of a fragment of cloth stained with what's said to be Christ's holy blood, brought to Bruges after the Second Crusade by the count of Flanders. You enter through the original Romanesque St. Basil's Chapel. The relic is housed upstairs, in the basilica museum next door to the later, richly decorated Gothic Relic Chapel. It's kept inside a rock-crystal vial that's stored in a magnificent gold-and-silver reliquary, and is exposed frequently for the faithful to kiss. Every Ascension Day, in the Procession of the Holy Blood, the relic is carried through the streets, accompanied by costumed residents acting out biblical scenes.

Burg 10. www.holyblood.org. ℂ **050/33-67-92.** Basilica free admission; museum 2€ adults, 1.50€ students, free for children 12 and under. Apr–Sept daily 9:30am–noon and 2–5pm; Oct–Mar Thurs–Tues 10am–noon and 2–5pm, Wed 10am–noon. Closed Jan 1, Nov 1, and Dec 25. Bus: All buses to Markt.

Bruggemuseum-Brugse Vrije (Liberty of Bruges) PALACE   This palace dates mostly from 1722 to 1727, when it replaced a 16th-century building as the seat of the Liberty of Bruges—the Liberty being the district around Bruges in the early Middle Ages. Inside, at no. 11A, is the **Renaissancezaal (Renaissance Hall)** ★, the Liberty's council chamber, which has been restored to its original 16th-century condition. The hall has a superb black-marble fireplace decorated with an alabaster frieze and topped by an oak chimney piece carved with statues of Emperor Charles V, who visited Bruges in 1515, and his grandparents: Emperor Maximilian of Austria, Duchess Mary of Burgundy, King Ferdinand II of Aragon, and Queen Isabella I of Castile.

Burg 11. ℂ **050/44-87-43.** Courtyard free admission; Renaissance Hall (includes admission to Town Hall's Gothic Room; see below) 4€ adults, 3€ seniors and ages 12–25, free for children 11 and under. Daily 9:30am–12:30pm and 1:30–5pm. Closed Jan 1, Ascension Day afternoon, and Dec 25. Bus: All buses to Markt.

Bruggemuseum-Stadhuis (Town Hall) ★ ARCHITECTURE   This beautiful Gothic building, from the late 1300s, is Belgium's oldest. Don't miss the upstairs **Gotische Zaal (Gothic Room)** ★★, with an ornate, oak-carved vaulted ceiling and murals depicting biblical scenes and highlights of the town's history. The statues in the niches on the Town Hall facade are 1980s replacements for the originals, which had been painted by Jan van Eyck and were destroyed by the French in the 1790s.

Burg 12. ℂ **050/44-87-43.** Admission (includes admission to Renaissance Hall in the Liberty of Bruges; see above) 4€ adults, 3€ seniors and ages 12–25, free for children 11 and under. Daily 9:30am–5pm. Closed Jan 1, Ascension Day afternoon, and Dec 25. Bus: All buses to Markt.

SOUTH OF THE MARKT

One of the most tranquil spots in Bruges is the **Begijnhof** ★★, Wijngaardstraat (bus: 1). *Begijnen* were religious women, similar to nuns, who accepted vows of chastity and obedience but drew the line at poverty. Today, the *begijns* are no more, and the Begijnhof is occupied by Benedictine nuns who try to keep the *begijn* traditions alive. Little whitewashed houses surrounding a lawn with trees make a marvelous place of escape. The Begijnhof is permanently open, and admission is free.

Bruggemuseum-Gruuthuse (Gruuthuse Museum) MUSEUM   In a courtyard next to the Groeninge Museum is the ornate mansion where Flemish nobleman Lodewijk van Gruuthuse lived in the 1400s. It contains thousands of antiques and antiquities, including paintings, sculptures, tapestries, lace, weapons, glassware, and richly carved furniture.

Dijver 17 (in a courtyard next to the Groeningemuseum). ℂ **050/44-87-43.** Admission 8€ adults, 6€ seniors and ages 12–25, free for visitors 11 and under. Tues–Sun 9:30am–5pm (also Easter Monday, Pentecost Monday). Closed Jan 1, Ascension Day afternoon, and Dec 25. Bus: 1.

Groeningemuseum ★★★ ART MUSEUM   This is one of Belgium's leading traditional museums of fine arts, with a collection that covers Low Countries painting from the 15th century to the 20th century. The Flemish Primitives Gallery has 30 works—which seem far from primitive—by such painters as Jan van Eyck (portrait of his wife, Margareta van Eyck), Rogier van der Weyden, Hieronymus Bosch (*The Last Judgment*), and Hans Memling. Works by Magritte and Delvaux are also on display.

Dijver 12. ℂ **050/44-87-43.** Admission (combined ticket with neighboring Arentshuis) 8€ adults, 6€ seniors, 1€ visitors 12–25, free for children 11 and under. Tues–Sun 9:30am–5pm (also Easter Monday, Pentecost Monday). Closed Jan 1, Ascension Day afternoon, and Dec 25. Bus: 1 or 11.

Memling in Sint-Jan ★ ART MUSEUM The former Sint-Janshospitaal (Hospital of St. John), where the earliest wards date from the 13th century, houses a magnificent collection of paintings by the German-born artist Hans Memling (ca. 1440–94), who moved to Bruges in 1465. You can view masterpieces like his triptych altarpiece of St. John the Baptist and St. John the Evangelist, which consists of the paintings *The Mystic Marriage of St. Catherine*, the *Shrine of St. Ursula*, and the *Virgin with Child and Apple*. A 17th-century apothecary in the cloisters near the hospital entrance is furnished as it was when the building's main function was to care for the sick.

Mariastraat (across from Onze-Lieve-Vrouwekerk). ℂ **050/44-87-43.** Admission 8€ adults, 6€ seniors, 1€ ages 12–25, free for visitors 11 and under. Tues–Sun 9:30am–5pm (also Easter Monday, Pentecost Monday). Closed Jan 1, Ascension Day afternoon, and Dec 25. Bus: 1.

Onze-Lieve-Vrouwekerk (Church of Our Lady) ★★ CHURCH It took 2 centuries (13th–15th) to build the magnificent Church of Our Lady, and its soaring spire, 122m (400 ft.) high, is visible from a wide area around Bruges. Among its many art treasures are a marvelous marble ***Madonna and Child*** ★★★ by Michelangelo (one of his few works outside Italy); the *Crucifixion*, a painting by Anthony Van Dyck; and inside the church sanctuary the impressive side-by-side bronze **tomb sculptures** ★ of Charles the Bold of Burgundy (d. 1477) and his daughter Mary of Burgundy (d. 1482).

Onze-Lieve-Vrouwekerkhof Zuid (at Mariastraat). ℂ **050/44-87-43.** Admission 6€ adults, 5€ seniors and ages 12–25, free for children 11 and under. Mon–Sat 9:30am–5pm, Sun 1:30–5pm. Bus: 1.

EAST OF THE MARKT

Kantcentrum (Lace Center) CULTURAL INSTITUTION Bruges lace is famous the world over, and there's no lack of stores to tempt you with the opportunity to take some home. The Lace Center, in the 15th-century Jerusalem Almshouse founded by the Adornes family of Genoese merchants, is where the ancient art of lace making is passed on to the next generation. In the afternoon, you get a first-hand look at craftspeople making items for future sale in the town's lace stores.

Peperstraat 3A (at Jeruzalemstraat). www.kantcentrum.eu. ℂ **050/33-00-72.** Admission 3€ adults; 2€ seniors, students, and children 7–12; free for children 6 and under. Mon–Sat 10am–5pm. Closed holidays. Bus: 6 or 16 to Langestraat.

ORGANIZED TOURS

Be sure to take a **boat trip** ★★★ on the canals, on board one of the open-top tour boats that cruise year-round from five departure points around the city center (see Bruges map). The boats operate March to November, daily from 10am to 6pm. A half-hour cruise is 7.60€ for adults, 3.40€ for children aged 4 to 11 accompanied by an adult, and free for children 3 and under.

Another lovely way to tour Bruges is by **horse-drawn carriage** (www.hippo.be; ℂ **050/34-54-01**). From March to November, carriages are stationed on the Markt; a 30-minute ride is 39€ for a carriage, which holds up to five people.

Minibus tours by **City Tour Brugge** (www.citytour.be; ☏ **050/35-50-24**) last 50 minutes and depart hourly every day from the Markt. The first tour departs at 10am; the last tour departs at 8pm July to September, at 7pm April to June, at 6pm October, at 5pm March, and at 4pm November to February. Fares are 15€ for adults, 8.50€ for children aged 6 to 11, free for children 5 and under, and 30€ for a family of two adults and two children.

In July and August, join a daily guided **walking tour** (Sat–Sun only in other months), at 3pm from the tourist office for 9€, and free for children 11 and under.

You can ride through Bruges, and get out of town into the West Flanders countryside, on a bicycling tour with **QuasiMundo Bike Tours Brugge** (www. quasimundo.eu; ☏ **050/33-07-75**). Call ahead to book; meeting and departure point is the Burg. Tours cost 25€ for adults, 25€ for students, and free for children 7 and under.

Where to Eat

Brasserie Erasmus ★ FLEMISH   Small but popular, this is a great stop after viewing the cathedral and nearby museums. It serves a large variety of Flemish dishes, all prepared with beer. Try the typically Flemish soup-like stew dish *waterzooi*, which is served with fish here, as it's supposed to be, although they also make it with chicken instead, a style that has become the norm elsewhere. If that doesn't grab you, how about *lapin à la bière* (rabbit in a beer sauce)? More than 200 different brands of Belgian beer are available (for drinking), 16 of them on tap.

In the Hotel Erasmus, Wollestraat 35 (off the Markt). www.hotelerasmus.com. ☏ **050/33-57-81.** Main courses 15€–25€; fixed-price menus 35€–43€. MC, V. Tues–Sun noon–4pm (summer also Mon) and 6–11pm. Bus: All buses to Markt.

De Florentijnen ★ CONTINENTAL   Were they to be cloned and returned to their Bruges pied à terre, it's a fair bet that those Renaissance-era Florentine merchants wouldn't recognize their gabled old lodging house. It now houses this sophisticated restaurant, a dazzlingly white confection in which shades could be a useful accessory. The menu is more than a little showy, with items like a dollop of caviar starter that costs more than twice the most expensive main course, and Barents Sea king crabs. Still, most dishes live up to both their billing and their tab.

Academiestraat 1 (at Vlamingstraat). www.deflorentijnen.be. ☏ **050/67-75-33.** Main courses 34€–63€; fixed-price menus: lunch 24€, dinner 39€–65€. AE, DC, MC, V. Tues–Sat noon–2pm and 7–9:30pm, Sun 7–9:30pm. Bus: 3 or 13.

De Karmeliet ★★★ BELGIAN/FRENCH   In 1996, chef Geert Van Hecke became the first Flemish chef to be awarded three Michelin stars. He has described his award-winning menu as "international cuisine made with local products" that aims to merge French quality with Flemish quantity. Menu items might include lamb shoulder with locally sourced vegetables, or seabass with a hazelnut, pistachio, and Parmesan crust. The result is outstanding, and the decor in the 1833 town house is as elegant as the cuisine deserves.

Langestraat 19 (off Hoogstraat). www.dekarmeliet.be. ☏ **050/33-82-59.** Reservations required. Main courses 70€–110€; fixed-price menus 85€–200€. AE, DC, MC, V. Tues–Sat noon–2pm and 7–9:30pm; Sun 7–9:30pm (except June–Sept). Bus: 6 or 16.

Lotus ★ VEGETARIAN   Vegetarians craving an alternative to omelet, frites, or waffles in this meat-loving city should head to Lotus. There are just two menu options—but you can choose from small, medium, or large servings—each with a hearty assortment of imaginatively prepared vegetables, served in a tranquil but cheery Scandinavian-style dining room.

Wapenmakersstraat 5 (off the Burg). www.lotus-brugge.be. © **050/33-10-78.** Fixed-price lunch menus 9€–12€. No credit cards. Mon–Sat 11:30am–2pm. Bus: All buses to Markt.

Shopping

No one comes here for stylish shopping—for that you need Brussels or Antwerp. What Bruges is famous for is **lace.** Most of it is machine made, but there's still plenty of genuine, high-quality (if expensive) handmade lace to be found. The most famous lace styles are *bloemenwerk, rozenkant,* and *toversesteek.* Foodies may want to seek out Oud-Brugge **cheese,** locally made chocolate, or pick from a massive selection of Belgian **beers** such as Straffe Hendrik, Brugs Tarwebier, and Brugge Tripel.

Upmarket stores and boutiques can be found on the streets around the Markt and 't Zand squares, among them Geldmuntstraat, Noordzandstraat, Steenstraat, Zuidzandstraat, and Vlamingstraat. There are souvenir, lace, chocolate and small specialty stores everywhere.

Entertainment & Nightlife
THE PERFORMING ARTS

Classical music, opera, and ballet are performed at the ultramodern **Concertgebouw,** 't Zand 34 (www.concertgebouw.be; © **050/47-69-99**). A medieval spectacle, set in Burgundian-era Bruges, can be experienced at **Celebrations Entertainment,** Vlamingstraat 86 (www.celebrations-entertainment.be; © **050/34-75-72**). Situated in a former Jesuit church, you can pile into a period banquet while enjoying the performance. Open April to October, Friday and Saturday from 7:30 to 10:30pm; and November to March, Saturday from 7:30 to 10:30pm. Tickets are 45€ to 76€ for adults, 50% of the adult price for children aged 11 to 14, 13€ for children aged 6 to 10, and free for children 5 and under.

BARS & CLUBS

A lively and cozy atmosphere can be found at **Cambrinus,** Philipstockstraat 19 (www.cambrinus.eu; © **050/33 23 28**), a bar which serves more than 400 different beers. For a raucous dancing-on-the-tables kind of night, head to **Café de Vuurmolen,** Kraanplein 5 (www.vuurmolen.com; © **050/33-00-79**), a few blocks north of the Markt; it's open nightly 10pm until the wee hours. **Ma Rica Rokk,** 't Zand 7–8 (www.maricarokk.be; © **050/33-83-58**), attracts a young and (for a medieval town like Bruges) trendy crowd to its DJ evenings.

Where to Stay

Die Swaene ★★★   This small hotel on the beautiful city-center Groenerei canal has been called one of the most romantic in Europe, thanks in part to the care lavished on it by the Hessels family. The comfortable rooms are elegantly and individually furnished, and the lounge, from 1779, was once the guild hall of the tailors. You might be expected to lodge in an annex across the canal, where the rooms are luxurious enough but not so convenient—you have to recross the canal to take advantage of the main building's amenities, for instance. The in-house **Pergola Kaffee** restaurant has deservedly earned great reviews from guests and food critics alike.

Steenhouwersdijk 1 (across the canal from the Burg), 8000 Brugge. www.dieswaene.be. © **050/34-27-98.** Fax 050/33-66-74. 30 units. 125€–245€ double; 320€–450€ suite. AE, DC, MC, V. Parking 15€.

Bus: 1 or 6. **Amenities:** Restaurant; bar; lounge; heated indoor pool; exercise room; sauna; room service; babysitting; Wi-Fi in lobby (free). *In room:* A/C (some rooms), TV, minibar, hair dryer.

Egmond ★★ In a rambling mansion next to Minnewater Park, the Egmond has just eight rooms, but the lucky few who stay here will find ample space, plenty of family ambience, abundant local color, and lots of peace and tranquility. All guest rooms are furnished in an individual style with views of the garden and Minnewater Park. Every afternoon, free coffee and tea are served in the new garden terrace or in the lounge, which has an 18th-century fireplace. At the "honesty bar" you can help yourself to a drink and leave the payment.

Minnewater 15 (at Minnewater Park), 8000 Brugge. www.egmond.be. ✆ **050/34-14-45.** Fax 050/34-29-40. 8 units. 98€–140€ double. Rates include buffet breakfast. MC, V. Parking 10€. Bus: 1 or 11. *In room:* TV, hair dryer, Wi-Fi (free).

Lucca ✍ This mansion right in the heart of romantic Bruges was built in the 14th century by a wealthy merchant from Lucca, Italy. The high ceilings and wide halls convey a sense of luxury—not that this is entirely backed up in reality, though the guest rooms are in reasonable condition and sport pine furnishings. Units with bathrooms also have TVs. Breakfast is served in a cozy medieval cellar decorated with antiques.

Naaldenstraat 30 (off Sint-Jakobsstraat), 8000 Brugge. www.hotellucca.be. ✆ **050/34-20-67.** Fax 050/33-34-64. 19 units, 14 with bathroom. 53€ double without bathroom; 78€–98€ double with bathroom. Rates include buffet breakfast. AE, DC, MC, V. Limited street parking. Bus: 3 or 13. *In room:* TV (some units).

Rosenburg ★ This ultramodern brick hotel is set alongside a lovely canal, a short walk west from the center of Bruges. The hotel is an artful marriage of old Bruges style and modern amenities and fittings. Its spacious guest rooms are restfully decorated in warm colors and furnished with bamboo and rattan beds. Most have a view of the canal at Coupure.

Coupure 30 (close to Gentpoort), 8000 Brugge. www.rosenburg.be. ✆ **050/34-01-94.** Fax 050/34-35-39. 27 units. 100€–170€ double; 200€–350€ suite. AE, DC, MC, V. Limited street parking. Bus: 6, 16. **Amenities:** Bar; lounge; room service. *In room:* TV, minibar, hair dryer.

GHENT ★★

Much less a "chocolate box" location than Bruges although still attractive, Ghent (it is written *Gent* in Dutch, and you may see it as *Gand* in French) has been spruced up in recent years and has never looked so good. This historic seat of the powerful counts of Flanders, at the confluence of the Scheldt and Leie rivers, has plenty of cobblestone streets, meandering canals, and antique Flemish architecture.

Essentials

GETTING THERE Ghent is a 35-minute **train** ride from Brussels. Trains depart every 20 minutes or so; tickets cost 13€ first-class, 8.50€ second-class. For schedule and fare information, visit www.b-rail.be, or call ✆ **02/528-28-28.** The city's main rail station, Gent-Sint-Pieters, is 1.5km (1 mile) south of the city center, on Maria Hendrikaplein. To get quickly and easily to the heart of town, take tram no. 1 from the first platform under the bridge to your left as you exit the station, and get out at Korenmarkt.

By **car,** take A10/E40 from both Brussels and Bruges.

Ghent

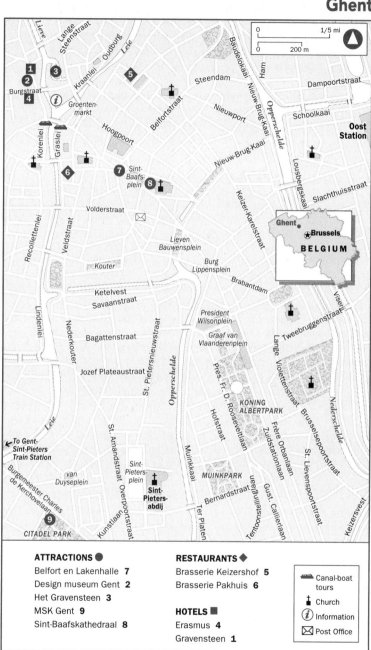

ATTRACTIONS ●
Belfort en Lakenhalle **7**
Design museum Gent **2**
Het Gravensteen **3**
MSK Gent **9**
Sint-Baafskathedraal **8**

RESTAURANTS ◆
Brasserie Keizershof **5**
Brasserie Pakhuis **6**

HOTELS ■
Erasmus **4**
Gravensteen **1**

🚢 Canal-boat
  tours
✝ Church
ⓘ Information
✉ Post Office

VISITOR INFORMATION   The tourist information office, **Dienst Toerisme Gent,** in the Oude Vismijn (Old Fish Market), Sint-Veerleplein 5, 9000 Gent (www. visitgent.be; ☎ **09/266-56-60**), is open mid-March to mid-October daily from 9:30am to 6:30pm, and mid-October to mid-March daily from 9:30am to 4:30pm.

GETTING AROUND   Ghent has a public transportation network of **trams, buses,** and a single **trolleybus** line, operated by **De Lijn** (www.delijn.be; ☎ **070/22-02-00**). Many lines converge at central Korenmarkt and at Gent-Sint-Pieters rail station in the south of the city. Walking is the best way to view the heart of town and experience its combination of history and modernity at a human pace. Beyond the city center, use public transportation. For a **taxi,** call **V-Tax** (☎ **09/222-22-22**).

Exploring Ghent
CITY CENTER

A row of gabled **guild houses** ★ built along **Graslei** between the 1200s and 1600s, when the waterway was Ghent's harbor, forms an ensemble of colored facades reflected on the Leie River. To view them as a whole, cross the bridge over the Leie to **Korenlei,** and stroll along the bank. These buildings were once the headquarters of the craftsmen, tradespeople, and merchants who formed the city's commercial core.

In the **Vrijdagmarkt,** a statue of Jacob Van Arteveld pays tribute to a rebel hero of the 1300s. This large, lively square hosts a street market every Friday.

The mixed Renaissance and Gothic style of the **Stadhuis (Town Hall),** Botermarkt 1, reflects a construction period that ran from 1518 until the 18th century. In an upstairs chamber called the **Pacificatiezaal** was signed the 1567 Pacification of Ghent, by which the Low Countries repudiated Spanish rule and declared religious freedom. The building can be visited only by guided tour from the tourist office (see above).

Belfort en Lakenhalle (Belfry and Cloth Hall) ★★ ARCHITECTURE
These form a glorious medieval ensemble. From the 14th-century Belfry, great bells have rung out Ghent's civic pride down through the centuries, and a 54-bell carillon does so today. You can get high in the belfry with a guide and the aid of an elevator. The Cloth Hall of 1425 was the gathering place of medieval wool and cloth merchants.

Emile Braunplein. www.belfortgent.be. ☎ **09/233-39-54.** Admission 5€ adults, 3.75€ seniors and ages 19–26, free for children 18 and under. Daily 10am–6pm. Free guided tours of Belfry daily 3:30pm. Closed Jan 1 and Dec 25–26. Tram: 1 or 4 to Sint-Baafsplein.

Design Museum Gent ★ MUSEUM
Something of a split personality, this worthwhile museum is housed in the Hotel de Coninck, an elegant baroque mansion dating from 1755 that's been joined by an ultramodern extension at the rear. Its collection ranges through a series of period rooms furnished and decorated in 18th- and 19th-century style, in the old place, and modern design in the new. Tapestries and a collection of Chinese porcelain are among the stellar items in the former setting. The new wing is strong on Art Nouveau—from Belgian masters of the genre Victor Horta, Henry van de Velde, and Paul Hankar, among others—and Art Deco design.

Jan Breydelstraat 5 (off Korenlei). http://design.museum.gent.be. ☎ **09/267-99-99.** Admission 5€ adults, 3.75€ seniors, 1€ ages 6–25, free for children 5 and under. Tues–Sun 10am–6pm. Closed Jan 1 and Dec 25–26 and 31. Tram: 1 or 4 to Gravensteen.

Het Gravensteen (Castle of the Counts) ★ CASTLE Formidable and forbidding, the castle was designed by the counts of Flanders to send a clear message to rebellion-inclined Gentenaars. Surrounded by the waters of the Leie River, the castle begun by Count Philip of Alsace in 1180 has walls 2m (6½ ft.) thick, and battlements and turrets. If these failed to intimidate the populace, the counts could always turn to a well-equipped torture chamber; some of its accoutrements are on display in a small museum.

Sint-Veerleplein. ☏ **09/225-93-06.** Admission 8€ adults, 6€ seniors and ages 19–26, free for visitors 18 and under. Apr–Sept daily 9am–6pm; Oct–Mar daily 9am–5pm. Closed Jan 1 and Dec 24–25 and 31. Tram: 1 or 4 to Gravensteen.

Sint-Baafskathedraal (St. Bavo's Cathedral) ★★★ CATHEDRAL The 14th-century cathedral's plain Gothic exterior belies a splendid baroque interior and some priceless art. A 24-panel altarpiece, *The Adoration of the Mystic Lamb*, completed by Jan van Eyck in 1432, is St. Bavo's showpiece. Other treasures include Rubens's *The Conversion of St. Bavo* (1624), in the Rubens Chapel off the semicircular ambulatory behind the high altar.

Sint-Baafsplein. www.sintbaafskathedraal.be. ☏ **09/269-20-45.** Cathedral free admission; *Mystic Lamb* chapel and crypt 4€ adults (includes audio guide in English), 1.50€ children 8–12, free for children 7 and under. Cathedral Apr–Oct Mon–Sat 8:30am–6pm, Sun 1–6pm; Nov–Mar Mon–Sat 8:30am–5pm, Sun 1–5pm; chapel and crypt Apr–Oct Mon–Sat 9:30am–5pm, Sun 1–5pm; Nov–Mar Mon–Sat 10:30am–4pm, Sun 1–4pm. Closed Jan 1 and church holiday mornings. Tram: 1 or 4 to Sint-Baafsplein.

SOUTH OF THE CITY CENTER

MSK Gent ★ ART MUSEUM In a park close to Sint-Pieters rail station, the Museum voor Schone Kunsten (Museum of Fine Arts) is home to old and new masterpieces, including works by Van der Weyden, Brueghel, Rubens, Van Dyck, and Bosch, along with moderns like James Ensor and Constant Permeke.

Fernand Scribedreef 1, Citadelpark. www.mskgent.be. ☏ **09/240-07-00.** Admission 5€ adults, 3.75€ seniors, 1€ ages 19–26, free for ages 18 and under. Tues–Sun 10am–6pm. Closed Jan 1 and Dec 25–26 and 31. Bus: 34, 35, 36, 55, 57, 58, 65, 70, 71, 72, 73, 74, 76, or 77 to Heuvelpoort.

ORGANIZED TOURS

A **boat trip** ★ on the canals with **Rederij Dewaele** (www.debootjesvangent.be; ☏ **09/229-17-16**) is a good way to view the city's highlights. Tour boats sail from Graslei and Korenlei April to October, daily from 10am to 6pm; November to March, on weekends from 11am to 4pm. Forty-minute cruises cost 6.50€ for adults, 6€ for seniors and disabled, 3.50€ for children aged 3 to 12, and free for children 2 and under. Longer tours are available.

May to November, you can join a daily guided **walking tour** at 2:30pm (Apr, weekends only) from the tourist office for 8€, and free for children 11 and under. Easter to October, tours by **horse-drawn carriage** (www.koetsenvangent.be; ☏ **0475/82-16-20**) depart from Sint-Baafsplein daily from 10am to 6pm. A half-hour ride is 30€ for a four- or five-seat carriage.

Entertainment & Nightlife

You should have a memorable evening in any one of Ghent's many atmospheric taverns. At **Dulle Griet** ★, Vrijdagmarkt 50 (☏ **09/224-24-55**), also known as Bier Academie, you'll be asked to deposit one of your shoes before being given a potent Kwak beer in a too-collectible glass with a wood frame that allows the glass to stand up. **Het Waterhuis aan de Bierkant,** Groentenmarkt 9 (www.waterhuisaande bierkant.be; ✆ **09/225-06-80**), has more than 100 different Belgian beers, including locally made Stopken. A couple of doors along, **'t Dreupelkot,** Groentenmarkt 12 (www.dreupelkot.be; ✆ **09/224-21-20**), specializes in deadly little glasses of *jenever* (a stiff spirit similar to gin). Across the tram lines, the tiny **'t Galgenhuisje,** Groentenmarkt 5 (✆ **09/233-42-51**), is popular with students.

Opera is performed at the 19th-century **Vlaamse Opera ★★**, Schouwburgstraat 3 (www.vlaamseopera.be; ✆ **070/22-02-02; tram: 1**).

Where to Stay & Eat

Brasserie Keizershof ★★ BELGIAN/CONTINENTAL   Convivial and trendy, this place on the garish market square has an attractively informal ambience. Behind its narrow, 17th-century baroque facade, even a capacity crowd of 150 diners can seem sparsely dispersed at the plain wood tables on multiple floors around a central stairwell. The decor beneath the timber ceiling beams is spare, tastefully tattered, and speckled with paintings by local artists. Service for office workers doing lunch is fast but not furious; in the evenings you're expected to linger. In summer, you can dine alfresco in a courtyard at the rear.

Vrijdagmarkt 47. www.keizershof.net. ✆ **09/223-44-46.** Main courses 10€–25€. MC, V. Tues–Sat noon–2:30pm and 6–11pm. Tram: 1 or 4 to Geldmunt.

Brasserie Pakhuis ★ FLEMISH/CONTINENTAL   In a town where the Middle Ages are big, this brasserie is almost modern and certainly hip. In fact, Pakhuis (which means "warehouse" in Dutch) may be a little too conscious of its own sense of style. The oyster and seafood platters are notable, and you won't go wrong with meat-based offerings like baked ham in a mustard sauce, or Flemish favorites like *waterzooi* and *garnaalkroketten* (shrimp croquettes).

Schuurkenstraat 4 (off Veldstraat). www.pakhuis.be. ✆ **09/223-55-55.** Main courses 11€–23€; fixed-price menus: lunch 14€; dinner 27€–43€. AE, DC, MC, V. Mon–Thurs 11:30am–1am; Fri–Sat 11:30am–2am (full meals at lunch and dinner only). Tram: 1 or 4 to Korenmarkt.

Erasmus ★   Each room is different in this converted 16th-century house, and all are plush, furnished with antiques and knick-knacks. Rooms have high oak-beam ceilings, and bathrooms are modern. Some rooms have leaded-glass windows, some overlook a carefully manicured inner garden, and some have elaborate marble fireplaces. Breakfast is served in an impressive room that would have pleased the counts of Flanders.

Poel 25 (off Sint-Michielsstraat), 9000 Gent. www.erasmushotel.be. ✆ **09/224-21-95.** Fax 09/233-42-41. 11 units. 99€–150€ double. Rates include buffet breakfast. AE, MC, V. Limited street parking. Bus: 3 (trolleybus), 17, 18, 38, and 39 to Poel. **Amenities:** Bar. *In room:* TV, minibar, hair dryer.

Gravensteen ★★   You enter this lovely mansion, built in 1865 as the home of a Ghent textile baron, through the old carriageway (made up of ornamented pillars and an impressive wall niche occupied by a marble statue), which sets the tone for what you find inside. The elegant, high-ceilinged parlor is a sophisticated blend of pastels, gracious modern furnishings, and antiques, with a small bar tucked into one corner. The rooms are attractive and comfortably furnished.

Jan Breydelstraat 35 (close to the Castle of the Counts), 9000 Gent. www.gravensteen.be. ✆ **09/225-11-50.** Fax 09/225-18-50. 49 units. 99€–210€ double. AE, DC, MC, V. Parking 10€. Tram: 1 or 4 to Gravensteen. **Amenities:** Bar; lounge; exercise room; sauna. *In room:* A/C (some units), TV, minibar, hair dryer, Wi-Fi (free).

ANTWERP ★

Antwerp's reputation as a harbor and diamond trade center is well deserved, but that's far from being all there is to say about this lively, sophisticated city. It boasts monuments from the medieval, Renaissance, and baroque periods, and a vibrant nightlife and cultural scene.

Essentials

GETTING THERE   Antwerp is a 35-minute **train** ride from Brussels. Trains depart every 20 minutes or so; tickets cost 13€ first-class, 8.50€ second-class. For schedule and fare information, visit www.b-rail.be, or call ℂ **02/528-28-28.** The city's main rail station, **Antwerpen Centraal,** is 4km (2½ miles) south of the city center, on Maria Hendrikaplein.

By **car,** major roads connecting to Antwerp's R1 Ring Expressway (beltway) are A1/ E19 from Brussels via Mechelen and from Amsterdam; A12 from Brussels via Laeken; A14/E17 from Ghent; and N49 from Knokke, Bruges, and Zeebrugge.

VISITOR INFORMATION   The tourist information office, **Toerisme Antwerpen,** Grote Markt 13, 2000 Antwerpen (www.antwerpen.be; ℂ **03/232-01-03;** tram: 2, 3, 4, 8, or 15), is open Monday to Saturday from 9am to 5:45pm, Sunday and holidays from 9am to 4:45pm (closed Jan 1 and Dec 25). An **Info Desk** at Centraal Station is open the same hours as the main tourist office.

GETTING AROUND   Besides walking, using the tram is the best way to get around. The most useful trams for tourists are lines 2, 3, 5, and 15, which run between Centraal Station and Groenplaats, near the cathedral; and lines 10 and 11, which run past the Grote Markt. Public transportation information is available from a kiosk inside Centraal Station and from **De Lijn** (www.delijn.be; ℂ **070/22-02-00**). The people to call for a taxi are **Antwerp Tax** (www.antwerp-tax.be; ℂ **03/238-38-38**).

Exploring Antwerp

CITY CENTER

Onze-Lieve-Vrouwekathedraal (Cathedral of Our Lady) ★★ CHURCH
A masterpiece of the Brabant-Gothic architectural style, this towering edifice is the largest church in the Low Countries. There are seven aisles and 125 pillars in the cathedral, but of the original design's five towers, only one was completed. This is the tallest church spire in the Low Countries, 123m (404 ft.) high, and the idea that the designers could have planned to construct five such behemoths is a graphic indication of the wealth and power of Antwerp at that time. Begun in 1352 and completed by around 1520, it stands on the site of a 10th-century chapel dedicated to the Virgin that later grew to be a church in the Romanesque style. Its interior embellishment is a mix of baroque and neoclassical. Today the cathedral houses four Rubens altarpieces.

Groenplaats 21 (at Handschoenmarkt). www.dekathedraal.be. ℂ **03/213-99-51.** Admission 5€ adults, 3€ seniors and students, free for children 11 and under. Mon–Fri 10am–5pm; Sat 10am–3pm; Sun and religious holidays 1–4pm. Closed to tourist visits during services. Tram: 2, 3, 5, or 15 to Groenplaats.

Rubenshuis (Rubens House) ★ HISTORIC HOME
Touch Antwerp's cultural heart at the house where Antwerp's most illustrious son, the artist Peter Paul Rubens (1577–1640), lived and worked. Examples of Rubens's works, and others by Master painters who were his contemporaries, are sprinkled throughout. The superb,

The Diamond Trade

Antwerp is the world's leading market for cut diamonds and second only to London as an outlet for raw and industrial diamonds. The trade, with its diamond cutters and polishers, workshops, brokers, and merchants, is centered on the city's **Diamantkwartier (Diamond Quarter)**, a surprisingly down-at-heel-looking area, only steps away from Centraal Station. It is supervised by the Antwerp World Diamond Center, and is mostly though not exclusively run by members of the city's Hasidic Jewish community.

A good place to get close to the city's diamond trade is the **Diamantmuseum**

(Diamond Museum), Koningin Astridplein 19–23 (www.provant.be; ℰ **03/202-48-90**; Metro: Diamant or Astrid). Exhibits trace the history, geology, mining, and cutting of diamonds. Diamond-cutting and polishing demonstrations are on Saturday afternoon from 1:30 to 4:30pm. The museum is open Thursday to Tuesday (and Wed when national holiday) from 10am to 5:30pm (closed Jan 1–2 and Dec 25–26). Admission is 6€ for adults, 4€ for seniors and those aged 12 to 25, and free for children 11 and under.

restored ornamental garden is well worth a stroll around, and a pleasant place to take a breather in fine weather.

Wapper 9–11 (off Meir). www.rubenshuis.be. ℰ **03/201-15-55.** Admission 6€ adults; 4€ ages 19–26; free for seniors, visitors with disabilities and companion, and children 18 and under; free admission for all last Wed of month. Tues–Sun (also Easter Monday, Pentecost Monday) 10am–5pm. Closed Jan 1–2, May 1, Ascension Day, Nov 1–2, and Dec 25–26. Tram: 2, 3, 5, or 15 to Meir.

THE GROTE MARKT

A lively 16th-century square lined with sidewalk cafes and restaurants, the Grote Markt, though not quite as dramatic as Brussels's Grand-Place, is no less the focus of the city's everyday life. The fountain in the middle recalls the city's founding legend.

Stadhuis (City Hall) ARCHITECTURE   The Renaissance City Hall (1561–65), designed by Cornelius Floris de Vriendt, is an outstanding example of the Flemish mannerism that replaced the formerly supreme Gothic style. It was burned during the city's sack by Spanish troops in 1576, an episode the city still recalls with a shiver as the "Spanish Fury," and then rebuilt as you see it now. Look for the frescoes by Hendrik Leys, a 19th-century Antwerp painter; murals; and, in the burgomaster's chamber, an impressive 16th-century fireplace.

Grote Markt. ℰ **03/221-13-33.** Free guided tours. Mon–Wed and Fri–Sat 2pm and 3pm (council business permitting). Tram: 10 or 11 to Sint-Katelijne.

ANTWERP'S PORT

The city's prime location just above the point where the river meets the tidal Westerschelde (Western Scheldt) Estuary made it an important port as far back as the 2nd century B.C. Antwerp was a trading station of the powerful medieval Hanseatic League, but unlike Bruges, did not have the status of a full-fledged *Kontor*, with its own separate district and mercantile installations. In the early days, ships moored along the city's own wharves, where the Steen (see below) stands; nowadays the port has moved 13km (8 miles) downstream to huge excavated docks that jam up against

Antwerp

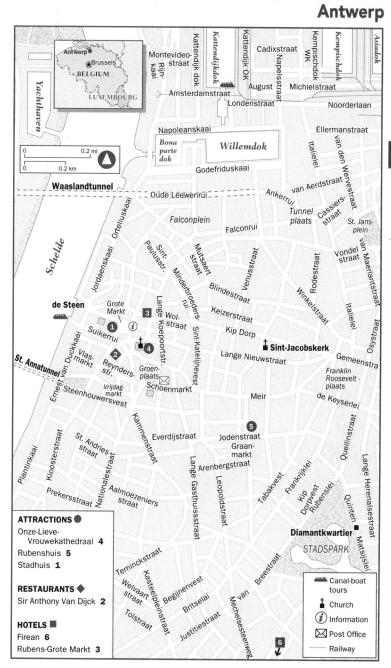

Antwerp
Brussels
BELGIUM

LUXEMBOURG

Yachthaven

0   0.2 mi
0   0.2 km

Montevideo-straat
Kattendijk dok
Kattendijkdok
Kattendijk OK
Cadixstraat
Kempischdok WK
Kempischdok
Asiadok
Rijn-kaai
Amsterdamstraat
Napelsstraat
August   Michielstraat
Londenstraat
Noorderlaan

Napoleanskaai
Ellermanstraat
Bona parte dok
Willemdok
van den Wervestraat
Italielei
Godefriduskaai
van Aerdstraat
Waaslandtunnel
Oude Leeuwenrui
Ankerrui
Tunnel plaats
Cassiers straat
St. Jans-plein
Falconplein
Falconrui
Vondel straat
van Maerlantstraat
Schelde
Jordaenskaai
Orteliuskaai
Sint-Paulusstr.
Mutsaert straat
Minderbroeders-rui
Venusstraat
Blindestraat
Rodestraat
Winkelstraat
Italielei

de Steen   Grote Markt
3 Lange Wol-straat
Koepoortstr.
Keizerstraat
Kip Dorp
Sint-Jacobskerk
Suikerrui
1
i
Kammenstr.
4
Sint-Katelijnevest
Lange Nieuwstraat
Gemeenstra
Vlas-markt
Reynders-str.
Groen-plaats
Franklin Roosevelt-plaats
St. Annatunnel
Ernest van Dijckkaai
Steenhouwersvest
Vrijdag-markt
Schoenmarkt
Meir
de Keyserlei

5
Everdijstraat
Jodenstraat
Graan-markt
Frankrijklei
Quellinstraat
Lange Herenalsestraat

Plantinkaai
St. Andries straat
Nationalestraat
Lange Gasthuisstraat
Arenbergstraat
Leopoldstraat
Tabakvest
Kip Dorpvest
Rubenslei
Quinten Matsislei

Kloosterstraat
Prekersstraat
Aalmoezeniers straat

Diamantkwartier
STADSPARK

Terninckstraat
Kasteelpleinstraat
Begijnenvest
Britselei
Breestraat

Welvaart straat
Tolstraat
Justitiestraat
Mechelsesteenweg
van

6

ATTRACTIONS ●
Onze-Lieve-
    Vrouwekathedraal **4**
Rubenshuis **5**
Stadhuis **1**

RESTAURANTS ◆
Sir Anthony Van Dijck **2**

HOTELS ■
Firean **6**
Rubens-Grote Markt **3**

Canal-boat tours
✝ Church
ⓘ Information
✉ Post Office
---- Railway

the Dutch border. Antwerp is Europe's second biggest port (after Rotterdam) for goods handled, and the third biggest (after Rotterdam and Hamburg) for containers. The port is well worth a visit, if only to appreciate its vast size.

On the waterfront in the center of town, Antwerp's oldest building, **De Steen (The Castle),** Steenplein 1, is a glowering 13th-century fortress on the banks of the Scheldt, just along the street from the Grote Markt.

ORGANIZED TOURS

From July to September, a daily guided walking tour of the center city, in English (and French), departs at 2pm from the tourist office; the cost is 8€ per person if purchased at departure, and 6€ if purchased ahead of time.

Try to take a cruise around Antwerp's awesome harbor. Departures are from the Scheldt waterfront next to the Steen. **Rederij Flandria** (www.flandria.nu; ✆ 03/231-31-00) runs a 2½-hour harbor cruise for 15€ for adults; 13€ for seniors, students, and people with disabilities; 12€ for school students; and free for children under school age. A 50-minute excursion on the river is less interesting but still worthwhile, with half-hourly departures during summer months, and costs half the price of the harbor tour.

Shopping

Expensive, upmarket stores, boutiques, and department stores abound in De Keyserlei and the Meir. For haute couture, go to Leopoldstraat; for lace, the streets surrounding the cathedral; for books, Hoogstraat; and for antiques, Minderbroedersrui. For diamonds, visit the glittering jewelry and gold stores of the **Diamantkwartier (Diamond Quarter),** around Centraal Station. At **Diamondland,** Appelmansstraat 33A (www.diamondland.be; ✆ 03/229-29-90; Metro: Centraal Station).

Antwerp's famed street markets are fun and good bargain-hunting territory. If you're in town on a Saturday from April to September, shop for a steal at the **Antiques Market,** Lijnwaadmarkt (tram: 10 or 11), Saturdays from Easter to October, from 10am to 6pm. The outstanding **Bird Market** is a general market that features live animals, plants, textiles, and foodstuffs; it takes place Sunday mornings on Oude Vaartplaats (tram: 12 or 14), off Frankrijklei. At the **street market** on Wednesday and Friday morning on Vrijdagmarkt (tram: 2, 3, 5, or 15), facing the Plantin-Moretus Museum, household goods and secondhand furniture are put on public auction.

Entertainment & Nightlife

Antwerp is as lively after dark as it is busy during the day. The main entertainment zones are Grote Markt and Groenplaats, which both contain concentrations of bars, cafes, and theaters; High Town (Hoogstraat, Pelgrimstraat, Pieter Potstraat, and vicinity) for jazz clubs and bistros; Stadswaag for jazz and punk; and the Centraal Station area for discos, nightclubs, and gay bars.

THE PERFORMING ARTS

Top of the line for theater and classical music is the **Stadsschouwburg,** Theaterplein 1 (www.stadsschouwburgantwerpen.be; ✆ 0900/69-900; tram: 12 or 24). Contemporary music and dance is performed at **deSingel,** Desguinlei 25 (www.desingel.be; ✆ 03/248-28-28; tram: 2).

BARS

No city watering hole has a better outlook than **Den Engel** ★, Grote Markt 3 (www.cafedenengel.be; ℰ **03/233-12-52;** tram: 10 or 11), an old-style cafe dating from 1579 on the main square, where a round glass called a *bolleke* (little ball) of Antwerp's very own yeasty, copper-toned De Koninck beer becomes a work of liquid art. Get into the abbey habit at **De Groote Witte Arend,** Reyndersstraat 18 (www.degroote wittearend.be; ℰ **03/233-50-33;** tram: 2, 3, 5, or 15), a cafe in a 17th-century former monastery, where customers are serenaded by classical music. Go underground to **De Pelgrom,** Pelgrimsstraat 15 (ℰ **03/234-08-09;** tram: 2, 3, 5, or 15), in a candlelit, brick-arched cellar, and get convivial at long wood benches. A huge selection of beers, including virtually every Belgian brand, is displayed behind glass and served at candlelit tables in **Kulminator,** Vleminckveld 32 (ℰ **03/232-45-38;** tram: 7 or 8).

Where to Stay & Eat

Firean ★ 🏨   In a superb, restored Art Deco mansion from 1929, replete with delicate enamel work and Tiffany glass, this family-owned hotel is a bit off the beaten track south of the center. The deco elements are offset, and given added warmth, by a wealth of Persian rugs, antiques, and chandeliers. Each of the individually styled rooms is a cozy delight of pastel tones, tasteful furnishings, armchairs or sofas, and comfortable beds. Breakfast is served in the garden in fine weather.

Karel Oomsstraat 6 (at Koning Albertpark), 2018 Antwerpen. www.hotelfirean.com. ℰ **03/237-02-60.** Fax 03/238-11-68. 15 units. 150€–157€ double; 212€ suite. AE, DC, MC, V. Parking 14€. Tram: 2 or 6 to Provinciehuis. **Amenities:** Restaurant; bar. *In room:* A/C, TV, minibar, hair dryer, Wi-Fi (free).

Rubens-Grote Markt ★★   Only steps away from the Grote Markt, this comfortable hotel with an attentive staff combines the classical elegance of a 16th-century mansion with plush, modern furnishings. The spacious rooms are individually decorated in a style that's a modern take on old-fashioned coziness, and from some of them you can see the cathedral steeple. Shady rooms are perked up with bright, tropical colors and sunny rooms have more muted, pastel tones.

Oude Beurs 29 (1 block north of the Grote Markt), 2000 Antwerpen. www.hotelrubensantwerp.be. ℰ **03/222-48-48.** Fax 03/225-19-40. 36 units. 150€–230€ double; 250€–445€ suite. Rates include buffet breakfast. AE, DC, MC, V. Parking 16€. Tram: 10 or 11 to Melkmarkt. **Amenities:** Bar; room service. *In room:* A/C, TV, minibar, hair dryer, Wi-Fi (12€/24 hr.).

Sir Anthony Van Dijck ★★ BELGIAN/CLASSIC FRENCH   A location amid the delightful 16th-century Vlaeykensgang courtyard's jumble of cafes, restaurants, and antique apartments all but guarantees a pleasant atmosphere here. Owner and chef Marc Paesbrugghe's relaxed brasserie/restaurant has an elegantly minimalist setting flooded with natural light from the old-world courtyard. It doubles as a contemporary art gallery but retains a commitment to good food.

Oude Koornmarkt 16 (inside Vlaeykensgang). www.siranthonyvandijck.be. ℰ **03/231-61-70.** Main courses 34€–35€; fixed-price menus: lunch 37€; gastronomic menu 47€. AE, DC, MC, V. Mon–Sat noon–1:30pm and 6:30–9:30pm. Tram: 2, 3, 5, or 15 to Groenplaats.

THE CZECH REPUBLIC

by Mark Baker

The Czech Republic, comprising the ancient kingdoms of Bohemia, Moravia, and Silesia, is the westernmost of the former Soviet satellite countries and the best place to explore what used to be the other side of the iron curtain. In May 2004, nearly 15 years after 1989's bloodless "Velvet Revolution" over Communism and over a decade after the peaceful split with the Slovak part of the former Czechoslovakia, the Czechs topped the list of new states admitted to the European Union.

4

If you have time to visit only one eastern European city, it should be Prague—widely regarded as one of the most beautiful cities in Europe, if not the world. The quirky and compact heart of Bohemia is a jumble of architecture. Gothic bestrides baroque, Renaissance adjoins cubist, with a splash of socialist realism and postmodern kitsch thrown in for good measure. On the hills and plains fronting the River Vltava you will glimpse the triumphs and tragedies of the past 10 centuries spiked with the peculiarity of the post-Communist reconstruction.

But Prague isn't the Czech Republic's only draw. Visitors are flocking to west Bohemia's world-renowned spas, which have been restored to their Victorian-era splendor, and to its many historic castles.

PRAGUE

Prague continues to climb up the list of Europe's (and the world's) most visited cities, attracting around 4 million foreign tourists annually. For visitors, Prague's growing popularity can be a double-edged sword. The sheer number of people, particularly over the Easter holidays and in midsummer, puts a noticeable strain on the city's infrastructure, resulting in crowded tram and metro cars, clogged streets, and overburdened restaurants and hotels. On a more personal level, the crowds detract—at least a little—from the city's ineffable mystery and charm. Alas, those days when one could boast of "discovering" this central European gem are probably over for good.

But the changes have by no means all been for the bad. Over the past decade, visitors have pumped literally billions of dollars into the local economy, funding major, long-overdue renovations of historical sights like Prague Castle, Charles Bridge, and Old Town Square. Tourism income has fueled the emergence of some of Europe's most beautiful hotels and

The Czech Republic

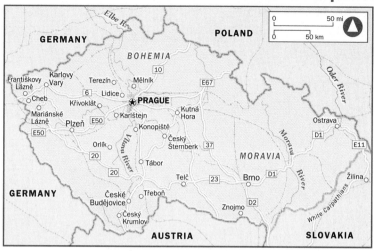

pensions, many occupying renovated Renaissance and baroque town houses that had been derelict for decades before.

Similarly, the restaurant scene is more vibrant than ever, thanks at least partly to visitors, who have pushed Praguers to try foods and cuisines that range far beyond traditional pork, sauerkraut, and dumplings. Tourists have also fueled the city's growing number of concerts, cultural events, and music clubs. It's no exaggeration to say they've played a big part in transforming the annual Prague spring music festival into one of the world's great celebrations of classical music.

Maybe the best effect of the city's growing international popularity is simply energy. Without its thousands of visitors every day, Prague would be quainter for sure, but far quieter—a beauty, but still a backwater. Try to keep that in mind as you're standing in the middle of Old Town Square on a hot sunny day surrounded by hundreds of fellow travelers all taking part in what feels like a global street party. Prague has always been at the geographic heart of Europe, and now it's at its spiritual heart as well.

Essentials

GETTING THERE

BY PLANE Prague Airport (code PRG; www.prg.aero; ℭ **220-113-314**) is the main international air gateway to the Czech Republic. The airport lies in the suburb of Ruzyně, about 18km (12 miles) northwest of the center. The airport has two main passenger terminals: 1 and 2. Terminal 1 handles destinations outside the European Union's common border area (known in E.U.-speak as the *Schengen Zone*), including overseas flights to and from the U.S. as well as flights from Ireland and the U.K. Terminal 2 handles what are considered to be internal flights within the European Union (inside the Schengen Zone), including flights to and from France, Germany, Italy, and Switzerland.

Prague

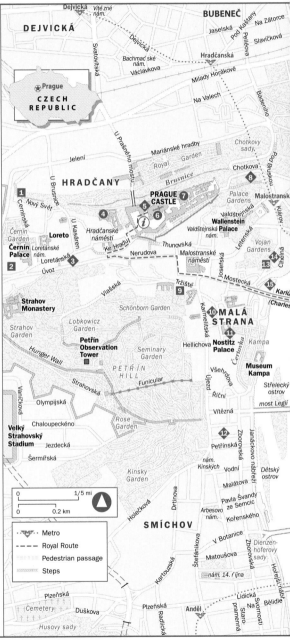

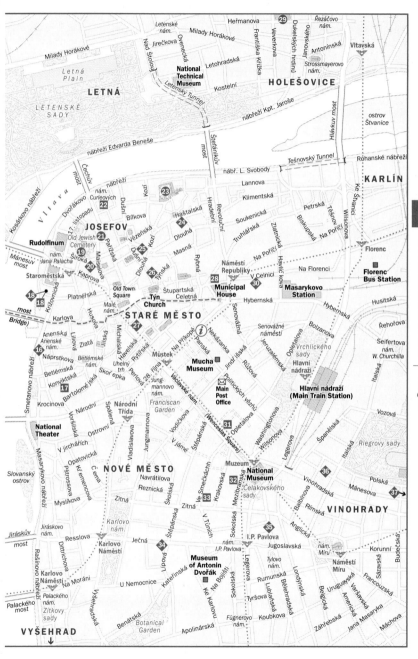

Prague is well served by the major European and international carriers, including several budget airlines. The Czech national carrier, **CSA** (www.csa.cz) operates regular direct service to New York's JFK airport, as well as, in high summer season, to Atlanta. **Delta Airlines** (www.delta.com) also offers regular direct service between Prague and both New York JFK and Atlanta (summer only).

To get to Prague from the airport, taxis are the quickest but most expensive option. The most reliable of the lot is **AAA Radiotaxi** (www.aaa-taxi.cz; ✆ **222-333-222**). Look for yellow AAA cabs lined up outside both main terminals: 1 and 2. Fares with AAA average about 600Kč to the center. The trip normally takes about 25 minutes, but the drive can run as long as an hour during peak times.

If you're staying in the immediate center of town, a cheaper alternative is to take a minibus operated by **CEDAZ** (www.cedaz.cz; ✆ **221-111-111**). Minibuses depart from both terminals every 30 minutes from 7:30am to 7pm and drop you at V celnici street in central Prague (near Náměstí Republiky) for 120Kč per person, including one piece of luggage. Use the V celnici stop for the return trip to the airport as well. Schedules are similar in both directions. The CEDAZ minibus can also take you to the Dejvická metro station (on Line A) for onward travel on the metro, for 90Kč per person.

The most affordable option is public transportation. City bus no. 119 stops at both terminals and runs regularly from the airport to the Dejvická metro station (on Line A), from where the center is just three metro stops away. Bus no. 100 runs south from the airport to the area of Zličín and connects to metro Line B. Travel on both requires a 32Kč ticket purchased from yellow ticketing machines at the bus stop (note that the machines only accept change). Buy two tickets if you're carrying large luggage. A special **Airport Express** (designated "AE" on buses) runs to and from Prague's main train station and costs 50Kč per person each way. Buy tickets directly from the driver. This is convenient if you are connecting directly to an international train.

BY CAR Prague is easily accessible by major highway from points around Europe. The main four-lane highways leading into and out of the city include the D1 expressway, which runs south and east from Prague and links the city to Brno (2 hr.), Bratislava (3 hr.), and with onward connections to Kraków, Poland (8 hr.) and Budapest, Hungary (6 hr.). The D5 motorway runs southwest from Prague to the Czech city of Plzeň (Pilsen; 1 hr.) and onward to Nürnberg, Germany (3 hr.), with connections to Italy and points in southern and western Europe. The D8 runs north out of Prague to Dresden, Germany (2 hr.), and eventually to Berlin (5 hr.) and points north. Road connections to Vienna, alas, are not what they should be. The trip takes about 5 hours by car, with most of the way along a crowded two-lane highway.

BY TRAIN Prague lies on major European rail lines, with good connections to Dresden (2 hr.) and Berlin (5 hr.) to the north, and Brno (2–3 hr.), Vienna (4–5 hr.), Bratislava (3 hr.), Budapest (7 hr.), and Kraków (8 hr.) to the east. A new high-speed rail service, the Pendolino, has been introduced on the Prague–Vienna run, shortening the travel time on some trains to as little as 4 hours. More high-speed rail links are on the drawing board.

Prague has two international train stations, so make sure to ask which station your train is using when you buy your ticket. Most international trains arrive at the main station, **Hlavní nádraží** (Wilsonova 8, Prague 1; www.cd.cz; ✆ **840-112-113**; metro stop: Hlavní nádraží, Line C). Many trains to and from Berlin, Vienna, and Budapest, however, often stop at the northern suburban station, **Nádraží Holešovice**

(Vrbenského ul., Prague 7; www.cd.cz; ✆ **840-112-113;** metro stop: Nádraží Holešovice, Line C). Train information is available at the telephone numbers indicated or on the Web at http://jizdnirady.idnes.cz.

Of the two main stations, Hlavní nádraží is more central and better equipped. It has undergone a massive facelift in the past few years and these days is bustling with useful shops, bank ATMs, currency exchanges, restaurants (including a Burger King), and a left-luggage office. From the train platform, you'll walk down a flight of stairs and through a tunnel before arriving in the ground-level main hall, which contains ticket windows, a useful **Prague Information Service** office that sells city maps and dispenses information, and restrooms. Also useful is the **ČD center** (www.cd.cz; ✆ **840-112-113**) run by the Czech Railways. It provides domestic and international train information as well as currency exchange and accommodations services. It is open daily 7 to 11am, 11:30am to 2pm, and 2:30 to 5:45pm. Visa and MasterCard are accepted.

After you leave the modern terminal hall, a 10-minute walk to the left puts you at the top of Wenceslas Square and 20 minutes by foot from Old Town Square. Metro Line C connects the station easily to the other two subway lines and the rest of the city. Metro trains depart from the lower level, and tickets are available from one of several newsstands in the station's main lobby. Taxi drivers line up outside the station and are plentiful throughout the day and night but are not recommended.

Prague has two smaller train stations. **Masaryk Station,** Hybernská ul., Prague 1 (✆ **840-112-113**), is primarily for commuters traveling to nearby Bohemian cities. Situated about 10 minutes by foot from the main train station, Masaryk is near Staré Město, just a stone's throw from náměstí Republiky metro station. **Smíchov Station,** Nádražní ul. at Rozkošného, Prague 5 (✆ **840-112-113**), is the terminus for commuter trains from western and southern Bohemia, though it's a convenient station for getting to popular day-trip destinations like Karlštejn and Plzeň. The station has a 24-hour baggage check and is serviced by metro Line B.

BY BUS The **Central Bus Station–Florenc,** Křižíkova 4–6, Prague 8 (www. florenc.cz; ✆ **900-144-444** for timetable info), is a few blocks north of the main train station. Most local and long-distance buses arrive here. The adjacent Florenc metro station is on both Line B (yellow) and Line C (red). Florenc station is relatively small and doesn't have many visitor services. There are even smaller bus depots at **Želivského** (metro Line A), **Smíchovské nádraží** (metro Line B), and **Nádraží Holešovice** (metro Line C).

VISITOR INFORMATION

TOURIST OFFICES The official tourist information service for the Czech Republic is the **Czech Tourist Authority,** known as CzechTourism (www.czechtourism. com). They have offices in several countries abroad and can help make basic travel arrangements and answer questions.

Once in Prague, the main tourist information center is the **Prague Information Service (Prague Welcome)** (www.praguewelcome.cz; ✆ **221-714-444**), with offices at the Old Town Hall on Old Town Square, several other points around the city, and at the main train station and airport. **Prague Welcome** hands out maps, organizes tours, and can help book rooms.

WEBSITES Helpful websites include **www.mapy.cz**, an online map and journey planner that covers Prague and the entire Czech Republic. Simply type in an address and a map shows you exactly where it is. For the ins and outs of Prague's public transportation system, including maps and info on tickets and travel passes, go to **www.dpp.cz/en/**.

The site **www.idos.cz** provides an online timetable for trains and buses, including international destinations. Type in the city (using the Czech spellings, such as "Praha" for Prague, but note diacritical marks are not required) and you'll get a complete listing of train and bus connections. The main website for the National Gallery in Prague, including practical information, admissions fees, and opening times for many of the city's major museums, is **www.ngprague.cz**.

CITY LAYOUT

The **River Vltava** bisects Prague and provides the best line of orientation; you can use **Charles Bridge** as your central point. From the bridge, turn toward **Prague Castle,** the massive complex on the hill with the cathedral thrusting out. Now you're facing west.

Up on the hill is the Castle District known as **Hradčany.** Running up the hill between the bridge and the castle is the district known as **Malá Strana** (literally the "Small Side," but known as Lesser Town in English). Turn around, and behind you on the right (east) bank is **Staré Město (Old Town),** and farther to the south and east **Nové Město (New Town).** The highlands even farther east used to be the royal vineyards, **Vinohrady,** now a popular neighborhood for expatriates with a growing array of accommodations and restaurants.

On the left bank coming off Charles Bridge is **Mostecká Street,** and at the end of it sits the cozy square under the castle hill, **Malostranské náměstí.** On the hill outside the main castle gate is the motorcade-worn **Hradčanské náměstí,** on the city side of which you'll find a spectacular view of spires and red roofs below.

On the east side of Charles Bridge, the tourist-packed route through Old Town is **Karlova Street.** Like Karlova, almost any other route in Old Town will eventually lead you to **Staroměstské náměstí (Old Town Square),** the breathtaking heart of Staré Město. A black monument to Jan Hus, the martyred Czech Protestant leader, dominates the square. The tree-lined boulevard to the right behind Hus is **Pařížská (Parisian Blvd.),** with boutiques and restaurants; it forms the edge of the Jewish Quarter. Over Hus's left shoulder is **Dlouhá Street,** and in front of him to his left is the kitschy shopping zone on **Celetná.** Across the square to Hus's right, past the clock tower of Old Town Hall (Staroměstská radnice), is **Železná Street,** which leads to Mozart's Prague venue, the Estates' Theater. Farther to Hus's right is the narrow alley **Melantrichova,** which winds southeast to **Václavské náměstí (Wenceslas Square),** site of pro-democracy demonstrations in 1968 and 1989.

Neighborhoods in Brief

Hradčany (Castle District) The Castle District dominates the hilltop above Malá Strana. Here you'll find not only the fortress that remains the presidential palace and national seat of power, but also the seat of religious authority in the country, St. Vitus Cathedral, as well as the Loreto Church, Strahov Monastery, and the European masters branch of the National Gallery. You can take a scenic walk down the hill via Nerudova or through the lush Petřín Hill gardens.

Malá Strana (Lesser Town) Prague's storybook Lesser Town was founded in 1257 by Germanic merchants who set up shop at the base of the castle. Nestled between the bastion and the Vltava River, Malá Strana is laced with narrow, winding lanes boasting palaces, and red-roofed town houses. The parliament and government and several embassies reside in palaces here. Kampa Park, on the riverbank just south of Charles Bridge, forms the southeastern edge of

Lesser Town. Nerudova is the steep, shop-lined alley leading from the Lesser Town Square (Malostranské nám.) to the castle. Alternate castle routes for the strong of heart are the New Castle Stairs (Nové zámecké schody), 1 block north of Neru-dova, and the Old Castle Stairs (Staré zámecké schody), just northwest from the Malostranská metro station. Tram no. 22 will take you up the hill toward the castle if you don't want to make the heart-pounding hike.

Staré Město (Old Town) Staré Město was chartered in 1234, as Prague became an important stop on trade routes. Its meander-ing streets, radiating from Old Town Square (Staroměstské nám.), are still a big visitor draw. Old Town is compact, bordered by the Vltava on the north and west and Revoluční and Národní streets on the east and south. You can wander safely without having to worry about straying into danger. Once here, stick to the cobblestone streets and don't cross any bridges, any streets contain-ing tram tracks, or any rivers, and you'll know that you're still in Old Town. You'll stumble across beautiful Gothic, Renaissance, and baroque architecture and find some wonder-ful restaurants, shops, bars, cafes, and pubs.

Josefov Prague's Jewish ghetto, entirely within Staré Město, was surrounded by a wall before almost being completely destroyed to make way for more modern 19th-century apartment buildings. The Old-New Synagogue is in the geographical cen-ter of Josefov, and the surrounding streets are wonderful for strolling. Prague is one of Europe's great historic Jewish cities, and exploring this remarkable area will make it clear why. For details, see "Walking Tour 4: Josefov (Jewish Quarter)," in Chapter 7

Nové Město (New Town) Draped like a crescent around Staré Město, Nové Město is where you'll find Václavské Náměstí (Wenc-eslas Square), the National Theater, and the central business district. When it was founded by Charles IV in 1348, Nové Město was Europe's largest wholly planned munici-pal development, and the street layout has remained largely unchanged from those times. It's hard to believe now, but Nové Město was once as majestic as Old Town (Staré Město), but many of the ancient struc-tures were razed in the late 19th century to make way for more modern buildings. There are just a handful of tourist attractions here, but the neighborhood is filled with good hotels and restaurants.

Outlying Areas The four core neighbor-hoods are surrounded on all sides by attrac-tive, mostly residential neighborhoods, with fewer attractions for visitors but plenty of hotels, restaurants, clubs, and pubs. **Vinohrady,** to the east of Nové Město, is filled with graceful town houses and leafy streets and is the neighborhood of choice for the city's upwardly mobile. There's a big beer garden here (Riegrovy sady) that's a fun destination on a warm summer night, plus many of the city's best dining spots. **Žižkov,** just north of Vinohrady, has a long tradition of being a hard-drinking, working-class neighborhood. Nevertheless, lower rents here have drawn an arty, alternative crowd in recent years. Žižkov is home to Pálac Akrop-olis, still the best venue in town for live rock and alternative music. **Dejvice, Letná,** and **Holešovice,** across the river and north of Staré Město, are mostly residential areas. Dejvice, with its pre-World War II mansions, is home to many embassies. Letná has a great park and a lovely beer garden in its own right. Holešovice is home to the city's best modern art collection at the Veletržní Palác and has some great nightlife spots. **Smíchov,** south of Malá Strana, is a formerly poor section of town that has found a new lease of life in the form of trendy hotels, shopping centers, and office parks. There are still lots of down-home pubs here, as everywhere in Prague.

GETTING AROUND

ON FOOT Prepare to do plenty of walking. Most of the center of the city is closed to vehicles, including taxis, meaning you'll have to walk pretty much everywhere.

Distances are relatively close, but always wear comfortable shoes since many of the streets are paved (if that's the right word) with cobblestones.

BY PUBLIC TRANSPORT   Prague's highly efficient public transportation network of metros (subways), trams, and buses (www.dpp.cz; ✆ **296-191-817**) is one of the few sound Communist-era legacies. In central Prague, metro stations abound. Trams and buses offer a cheap sightseeing experience but also require a strong stomach for jostling with fellow passengers in close quarters.

For single-use **tickets,** there are two choices. The first is a short-term ticket, which costs 24Kč, or 12Kč for 6- to 15-year-olds (children 5 and under ride free) and seniors (70 and over). This allows unlimited travel on metros, trams, and buses for a period of 30 minutes from the time the ticket is validated. A long-term ticket costs 32Kč, 16Kč for 10- to 15-year-olds and seniors, and allows unlimited travel on public transit for up to 90 minutes after validation. The cheaper ticket is usually sufficient for most trips within the center.

You can also buy a **1-day pass** for 110Kč, children 6–15 and seniors pay 55Kč, which is good for unlimited travel on metros, buses, and trams for 24 hours from when the ticket is validated. A similar **3-day pass** costs 310Kč, with no discounts for children or seniors.

You can buy tickets from yellow coin-operated machines in metro stations or at most newsstands marked TABÁK or TRAFIKA. The machines have English instructions but are a little clunky to operate. First push the button for the ticket you want (either 24Kč or 32Kč) and then insert the money in the slot. Validate your ticket in the little stamping machine before you descend the escalator in the metro or as you enter the tram or bus. Hold on to your validated ticket throughout your ride—you'll need to show it if a ticket collector (be sure to check for his or her badge) asks you. If you're caught without a valid ticket, you'll be asked, and not so kindly, to pay a fine on the spot while all the locals look on, shaking their heads in disgust. The fine is 700Kč if paid on the spot and 950Kč if paid later.

Metro trains operate daily from 5am to midnight and run every 2 to 10 minutes depending on the time of day. The three lines are identified by both letter and color: A (green), B (yellow), and C (red). The most convenient central stations are Muzeum, on both the A and C lines at the top of Václavské náměstí (Wenceslas Square); Můstek, on both the A and B lines at the foot of Václavské náměstí; Staroměstská on the A line, for Old Town Square and the Charles Bridge; and Malostranská, on the A line, serving Malá Strana and the Castle District. Refer to the transit map on the inside back cover for details.

The city's 24 **tram** lines run practically everywhere, and there's always another tram with the same number traveling back. You never have to hail trams; they make every stop. The most popular tram, no. 22 (aka the "tourist tram" or the "pickpocket express") runs past top sights like the National Theater and Prague Castle. Regular bus and tram service stops at midnight, after which selected routes run reduced night schedules, usually only once per hour. Schedules are posted at stops. If you miss a night connection, expect a long wait for the next.

Buses tend to be used only outside the older districts of Prague and have three-digit numbers. Both the buses and tram lines begin their morning runs around 4:30am.

BY FUNICULAR   The funicular (cog railway) makes the scenic run up and down Petřín Hill every 10 minutes (15 min. in winter season) daily from 9am to 11:30pm with an intermediate stop at the Nebozízek restaurant halfway up the hill, which overlooks the city. It requires the 26Kč ticket or any of the same transport passes as other modes of public transport and departs from a small house in the park near the Újezd tram stop (tram: 12, 20, or 22) in Malá Strana.

BY CAR   Driving in Prague isn't worth the money or effort. The roads are crowded and the high number of one-way streets can be incredibly frustrating. Parking in the center is often restricted and available only to residents with prepaid parking stickers. The only time you *might* want a car is if you have only a few days and plan to explore other parts of the Czech Republic.

If you want to rent a car, try **Europcar,** Elišky Krásnohorské 9, Prague 1 (www. europcar.cz; ℰ **224-811-290**). There's also **Hertz,** Karlovo nám. 15, Prague 2 (www.hertz.cz; ℰ **225-345-031**). **Budget** is at Prague Airport (www.budget.cz; ℰ **220-560-443**) and at the main train stations Hlavní nádraží, Wilsonova 8, Prague 1 (ℰ **222-319-595**).

Local car-rental companies sometimes offer lower rates than the big international firms. Compare **CS Czechocar,** Kongresové centrum (Congress Center at Vyšehrad metro stop on the C line), Prague 4 (www.czechocar.cz; ℰ **261-222-079** or 261-222-143), or at Prague Airport, Prague 6 (ℰ **220-113-454**); or try **SeccoCar,** Přístavní 39, Prague 7 (www.seccocar.cz; ℰ **220-802-361**).

Car rates can be negotiable. Try to obtain the best possible deal with the rental company by asking about discounts. Special deals are often offered for keeping the car for an extended period, for unlimited mileage (or at least getting some miles thrown in free), or for a bigger car at a lower price. It also usually helps to book over the Internet as far in advance as possible.

[FastFACTS] PRAGUE

Area Codes There are no area or city codes in the Czech Republic. Each telephone number is a unique nine-digit number, usually written xxx-xxx-xxx. Numbers that begin with a "6" or "7" indicate a cellphone.

Business Hours Normal business and banking hours run from 9am to 5pm Monday to Friday. Stores in central Prague are typically open weekdays from 9am to 7pm and on Saturday from 9am to at least 1pm; larger stores and shopping centers are likely to be open on Sundays and holidays as well. Museums are almost always closed on

Mondays. Tourist attractions may have shorter hours or shut down altogether during the winter (Nov–Apr).

Currency The Czech currency is the **koruna (crown).** It is usually noted as "Kč" in shops or "CZK" in banks. At press time US$1 = 18Kč.

Currency Exchange Banks and ATMs generally offer the best rates and lowest commissions. Changing money is not a problem in the Czech Republic. If you're arriving at Prague Airport, skip the currency-exchange booths in the arrivals hall and instead use the ATMs

that are lined up just as you enter the main airport hall from Customs clearance.

Whatever you do, resist the temptation to use one of the private currency-exchange offices that line Václavské náměstí and other areas with heavy tourist concentrations. These outfits seldom pay the rates they advertise on the outside and the commissions (and hidden commissions) can be prohibitive, especially on relatively small amounts of money.

You will find ATMs on practically every street corner in central Prague. Komerční banka has three convenient Prague 1 locations with ATMs that accept Visa, MasterCard, and American Express: Na Příkopě 33, Spálená 51, and Václavské nám. 42 (www.kb.cz; ✆ **800-111-055,** central switchboard for all branches). The exchange offices are open Monday to Friday from 8am to 5pm, but the ATMs are accessible 24 hours.

Doctors, Dentists & Hospitals For emergency medical treatment, go to Nemocnice Na Homolce (Hospital Na Homolce) at Roentgenova 2, Prague 5, Smíchov (www.homolka.cz; ✆ **257-271-111**). If you need nonurgent medical attention, practitioners in many fields can be found at the Canadian Medical Care center at Veleslavínská 1, Prague 6, Dejvice (www.cmcpraha.cz; ✆ **235-360-133**). For dental service, call American Dental Associates at V Celnici 4, Prague 1, Nové Město (www.americandental.cz; ✆ **221-181-121**), open 9am to 7pm Monday to Friday.

Embassies & Consulates All foreign embassies are located in the capital, Prague. The embassy of the **United States** is located at Tržiště 15, Prague 1, Malá Strana (http://prague.usembassy.gov; ✆ **257-022-000**). The embassy of **Canada** is at Muchova 6, Prague 6, Dejvice (www.canada.cz; ✆ **272-101-800**). The embassy of the **United Kingdom** is at Thunovská 14, Prague 1, Malá Strana

(www.britain.cz; ✆ **257-402-111**). The local consular office of **Australia** is at Klimentská 10, Prague 1, Nové Město (✆ **296-578-350**).

Emergencies Dial the following numbers in an emergency: ✆ **112** (general emergency, equivalent to U.S. 911); ✆ **155** (ambulance); ✆ **158** (police); ✆ **150** (fire); and ✆ **1230** or **1240** (emergency road service).

Internet & Wi-Fi
Prague and the Czech Republic are well-wired. Nearly every hotel above a basic pension will have some form of Internet access. Around town, many bars and cafes offer free Wi-Fi for customers (usually password-protected). The only drawback is that Wi-Fi tends to be spotty, and networks seem to be down about as often as they are up.

Mail & Postage Postcards and light letters sent within the E.U. cost 18Kč. Those going outside the E.U. (to the U.S., Canada, and Australia) cost 21Kč, though rates vary by weight and letters should always be weighed at the post office to ensure proper postage. Mail service is reliable and unless you're sending something very important or fragile, there's usually no need to use a trackable service like FedEx or DHL. Letters to destinations within Europe take 3 to 5 days, and to the U.S. 7 to 10 days. Most post offices are open Monday through Friday from 8am to 7pm. The main post office (Hlavní

pošta), at Jindřišská 14, Prague 1 (✆ **221-131-111**), is open 24 hours. You can receive mail, marked "Poste Restante" and addressed to you, in care of this post office.

Police Dial the European Emergency Number ✆ **112** from any phone in an emergency. For Czech police dial ✆ **158.**

Safety In Prague's center you'll feel generally safer than in most big cities, but always take commonsense precautions. Be aware of your immediate surroundings. Don't walk alone at night around Wenceslas Square—one of the main areas for prostitution and where a lot of unexplainable loitering takes place. All visitors should be watchful of pickpockets in heavily touristed areas, especially on Charles Bridge, in Old Town Square, and in front of the main train station.

Smoking As of 2010, all restaurants, bars, and cafes must post their smoking policies at the door. A yellow triangle with the words *kouření povoleno* indicates the establishment has a separate smoking section, while a red circle with a line through the middle means no smoking allowed. Note that it's illegal to smoke outdoors near bus and tram stops. This rule is rarely enforced, but the fine, 1,000Kč, is steep.

Taxes All goods and services in the Czech Republic are levied a value-added tax (VAT, or *DPH* in Czech), ranging from 10% to 20%

depending on the item. This tax is normally included in the price.

Telephones The country code for the Czech Republic is 420. To dial the Czech Republic from abroad, dial your country's international access code (for example, 011 in the United States) plus 420 and then the unique nine-digit local number. Once you arrive, to dial any number anywhere in the Czech Republic, simply dial the unique nine-digit number. There are no area or city codes in the Czech Republic.

To make a direct international call from the Czech Republic, dial 00 plus the country code of the country you are calling and then the area code and number. The country code for the U.S. and Canada is 1; Great Britain, 44; and Australia, 61.

For directory inquiries regarding phone numbers within the Czech Republic, dial ✆ **1180.** For information about services and rates abroad, call ✆ **1181.**

Tipping In hotels, tip **bellhops** 20Kč per bag (more if you have a lot of luggage), and though it's not expected, it's a nice gesture to leave the **chamber staff** 20Kč per night (depending on the level of service). Tip the **doorman** or **concierge** only if he or she has provided a specific service (for example, calling a cab for you or obtaining difficult-to-get theater tickets).

In restaurants, bars, and nightclubs, tip **service staff or bartenders** 10% of the check to reward good service. On smaller tabs it's easiest just to round up to the next highest multiple of 10. For example, if the bill comes to 72Kč, hand the waiter 80Kč and tell him to keep the change.

Tip **cab drivers** 5% to 10% of the fare (provided they haven't already overcharged you).

Toilets Acceptably clean public pay toilets are scattered around tourist areas and can be found in every metro station. Expect to pay 5Kč to 10Kč for the privilege.

Exploring Prague

Prague's most intriguing aspects are its architecture and atmosphere, best enjoyed while slowly wandering through the city's heart. So, with that in mind, your itinerary should be a loose one. If you have the time and energy, go to Charles Bridge at sunrise and then at sunset to view the grand architecture of Prague Castle and the Old Town skyline. You'll see two completely different cities.

PRAŽSKÝ HRAD (PRAGUE CASTLE) & KARLŮV MOST (CHARLES BRIDGE)

Dating from the 14th century, **Charles Bridge (Karlův most)** ★★★, Prague's most celebrated statue-studded structure, links Staré Město and Malá Strana. For most of its 600 years, the 510m-long (1,673-ft.) span has been a pedestrian promenade, though for centuries walkers had to share the concourse with horse-drawn vehicles and trolleys. These days, the bridge is filled to brimming with tourists, souvenir hawkers, portraitists, and the occasional busking musician in what feels like a 24/7 Mardi Gras celebration.

The best times to stroll across the bridge are early morning and around sunset, when the crowds have thinned and the shadows are more mysterious.

Pražský Hrad (Prague Castle) ★★★ ◙ CASTLE   This huge hilltop complex on Hradčanské náměstí encompasses dozens of houses, towers, churches, courtyards, and monuments. A visit to the castle can easily take an entire day, depending on how thoroughly you explore it. Still, you can see the top sights—St. Vitus Cathedral, the Royal Palace, St. George's Basilica, the Powder Tower, and Golden Lane—in the space of a morning or an afternoon.

Chrám sv. Víta (St. Vitus Cathedral), named for a wealthy 4th-century Sicilian martyr, isn't just the dominant part of the castle, it's the most important section historically. Built over various phases, beginning in A.D. 926 as the court church of the Přemyslid princes, the cathedral has long been the center of Prague's religious and political life. Of the massive Gothic cathedral's 21 chapels, the **Svatováclavská kaple (St. Wenceslas Chapel)** ★★ is one of Prague's few must-see indoor sights. Midway toward the high altar on the right, it's encrusted with hundreds of pieces of jasper and amethyst and decorated with paintings from the 14th to the 16th centuries. The chapel sits atop the gravesite of Bohemia's patron saint, St. Wenceslas.

For more than 700 years, beginning in the 9th century, Bohemian kings and princes resided in the **Starý královský palác (Old Royal Palace)** ★★, located in the third courtyard of the castle grounds. Vaulted **Vladislavský sál (Vladislav Hall),** the interior's centerpiece, hosted coronations and is still used for special occasions of state such as inaugurations of presidents.

Bazilika sv. Jiří (St. George's Basilica) ★, adjacent to the Old Royal Palace, is Prague's oldest Romanesque structure, dating from the 10th century. Inside the sparse and eerie basilica you will find relics of the castle's history along with a genealogy of those who have passed through it.

St. George's Convent (Klášter sv. Jiří na Pražském hradě) ★, just to the left of the basilica entrance, no longer serves a religious function and houses a fascinating collection of 19th-century Czech paintings.

Zlatá ulička (Golden Lane) and Daliborka Tower is a picturesque street of tiny 16th-century houses built into the castle fortifications. Once home to castle sharpshooters, the lane got a fresh makeover in 2011 to restore its 17th-century appearance. In 1917, Franz Kafka is said to have lived briefly at no. 22; however, the debate continues as to whether Kafka actually took up residence or just worked in a small office there.

The **Prašná věž (Powder Tower, aka Mihulka)** forms part of the northern bastion of the castle complex just off the Golden Lane. Originally a gunpowder storehouse and a cannon tower, it was turned into a laboratory for the 17th-century alchemists serving the court of Emperor Rudolf II.

Hradčanské náměstí, Hradčany, Prague 1. www.hrad.cz. (C) **224-372-423.** Grounds free. Combination ticket for permanent exhibition, St. George's Basilica, Powder Tower, Golden Lane, Daliborka Tower, the Prague Castle Picture Gallery, without guide, 350Kč adults, 175Kč students; short tour (Royal Palace, St. George's Basilica, Golden Lane, and Daliborka Tower) 250Kč adults, 125Kč students. Tickets valid 2 days. Daily 9am–6pm (to 4pm Nov–Mar). Metro: Malostranská, then tram no. 22 or 23, up the hill 2 stops.

THE JEWISH MUSEUM

The **Jewish Museum in Prague** (www.jewishmuseum.cz; (C) **221-711-511**) doesn't refer to one building, but rather the organization that manages the main sites of the former Jewish quarter. These include the **Old Jewish Cemetery,** the **Pinkas Synagogue,** the **Klaus Synagogue,** the **Maisel Synagogue,** the **Ceremonial Hall,** and the **Spanish Synagogue.** Each synagogue features a different exhibition on various aspects of Jewish customs and history. It's not possible to visit the sites individually; instead, you have to purchase a combined-entry ticket that allows access to all the main buildings. You'll find ticket counters selling the tickets inside the synagogues and at ticket windows around the quarter. Admission is 300Kč for adults, 200Kč for students, and free for children 5 and under. The museum's sites are open from April to October Sunday to Friday 9am to 6pm, and November to March Sunday to Friday 9am to 4:30pm. Note that the museum is closed on Saturdays and Jewish holidays. Another synagogue, the **Old-New Synagogue** (see below), is considered separate from the Jewish Museum's main holdings and requires an additional admission ticket.

Staronová synagóga (Old-New Synagogue) ★ SYNAGOGUE   First called the New Synagogue to distinguish it from an even older one that no longer exists, the Old-New Synagogue, built around 1270, is Europe's oldest remaining Jewish house of worship. The faithful have prayed here continuously for more than 700 years, carrying on even after a massive 1389 pogrom in Josefov that killed more than 3,000 Jews. Its use as a house of worship was interrupted only between 1941 and 1945 because of the Nazi occupation. The synagogue is also one of Prague's great Gothic buildings, built with vaulted ceilings and retrofitted with Renaissance-era columns. It is not part of the Jewish Museum and requires a separate admission ticket.

Červená 2. www.synagogue.cz. ② **224-800-812.** Admission 200Kč adults, 140Kč students (if part of the package for Jewish Museum, 490Kč adults, 330Kč students), free for children 5 and under. Jan–Mar Sun–Thurs 9:30am–4:30pm, Fri 9am–2pm; Apr–Oct Sun–Fri 9:30am–6pm; Nov–Dec Sun–Thurs 9:30am–5pm, Fri 9am–2pm. Closed Sat and Jewish holidays. Metro: Line A to Staroměstská.

Starý židovský hřbitov (Old Jewish Cemetery) ★★ CEMETERY   One block from the Old-New Synagogue, this is one of Europe's oldest Jewish burial grounds, dating from the mid-15th century. Because the local government of the time didn't allow Jews to bury their dead elsewhere, graves were dug deep enough to hold 12 bodies vertically, with each tombstone placed in front of the last. The result is one of the world's most crowded cemeteries: a 1-block area filled with tens of thousands of graves. Among those buried here are the celebrated Rabbi Loew (Löw; 1520–1609), who created the legend of Golem (a giant clay "monster" to protect Prague's Jews); and banker Markus Mordechai Maisel (1528–1601), then the richest man in Prague and protector of the city's Jewish community during the reign of Rudolf II.

U Starého hřbitova; the entrance is from Široká 3. www.jewishmuseum.cz. ② **221-711-511.** Admission (combined entry to all of the Jewish Museum sites) 300Kč adults, 200Kč students, free for children 5 and under. Apr–Oct Sun–Fri 9am–6pm; Nov–Mar Sun–Fri 9am–4:30pm. Closed Sat and Jewish holidays. Metro: Line A to Staroměstská.

THE NATIONAL GALLERY SITES

The national collection of fine art is grouped for display in a series of venues known collectively as the **Národní Galerie (National Gallery).** Remember that this term refers to several locations, not just one gallery.

The National Gallery's holdings are eclectic and range from classic European masters at the **Šternberský palác** across from the main gate to Prague Castle to modern Czech and European works from the 20th and 21st centuries at the **Veletržní palác** in the neighborhood of Holešovice in Prague 7. Other important museums include a collection of 19th-century Czech art at **St. George's Convent** in the Prague Castle complex and the extensive holdings of medieval and Gothic art at **St. Agnes Convent** near the river in Old Town.

The key Prague sites within the national gallery system are listed below.

Klášter sv. Anežky České (St. Agnes Convent) ★★ ART MUSEUM   A complex of early Gothic buildings and churches dating from the 13th century, the convent, tucked in a quiet corner of Staré Město, began exhibiting much of the National Gallery's collection of medieval art in 2000. Once home to the Order of the Poor Clares, it was established in 1234 by St. Agnes of Bohemia, sister of Wenceslas I. The Blessed Agnes became St. Agnes when Pope John Paul II paid his first visit to Prague in 1990 for her canonization. The most famous among the unique collection of Czech Gothic panel paintings are those by the Master of the Hohenfurth Altarpiece and the Master Theodoricus. The convent is at the end of Anežka, off Haštalské náměstí.

U Milosrdných 17, Prague 1. www.ngprague.cz. © **224-810-628.** Admission 150Kč adults, 80Kč children. Tues–Sun 10am–6pm. Metro: Line A to Staroměstská.

Klášter sv. Jiří na Pražském hradě (St. George's Convent at Prague Castle) ★ ART MUSEUM The former convent at St. George's houses a fascinating collection of 19th-century Czech painting and sculpture that is especially strong on landscapes and pieces from the Czech national revival period. The collection shows the progression of the Czech lands from a largely agrarian province at the start of the century to a highly developed cultural and industrial space by the end.

Jiřské nám. 33. www.ngprague.cz. © **257-531-644.** Admission 150Kč adults, 80Kč students, free for children 5 and under. Daily 10am–6pm. Metro: Line A to Malostranská plus tram 22.

Šternberský palác (Sternberg Palace) ★★ ART MUSEUM The jewel in the National Gallery crown, the gallery at Sternberg Palace, adjacent to the main gate of Prague Castle, displays a wide menu of European art throughout the ages. It features 5 centuries of everything from Orthodox icons to Renaissance oils by Dutch masters. Pieces by Rembrandt, El Greco, Goya, and van Dyck are mixed among numerous pieces from Austrian imperial court painters. Exhibits rotate throughout the seasons.

Hradčanské nám. 15, Prague 1. www.ngprague.cz. © **233-090-570.** Admission 150Kč adults, 80Kč students, free for children 5 and under. Tues–Sun 10am–6pm. Metro: Line A to Malostranská plus tram no. 22.

Veletržní palác (Museum of 20th- and 21st-Century Art) ★★ ART MUSEUM This 1928 Functionalist (Bauhaus-style) palace, built for trade fairs, was remodeled and reopened in 1995 to hold the bulk of the National Gallery's collection of 20th- and 21st-century works by Czech and other European artists. The highlights on three floors of exhibition space include paintings by Klimt, Munch, Schiele, and Picasso, among other modern European masters, as well as a riveting display of Czech constructivist and surrealist works from the 1920s and 1930s. The first floor features temporary exhibits from traveling shows. There's also a good gift shop.

Veletržní at Dukelských hrdinů 47, Prague 7. www.ngprague.cz. © **224-301-122.** Admission 250Kč adults, 120Kč students, free for children 5 and under. Tues–Sun 10am–6pm. Metro: Line C to Vltavská. Tram: 12, 14, or 17 to Strossmayerovo nám.

HISTORIC SQUARES

The most celebrated square in the city, **Staroměstské Náměstí (Old Town Square)** ★★★, is surrounded by baroque buildings and packed with colorful craftspeople, cafes, and entertainers. In ancient days, the site was a major crossroads on central European merchant routes. In its center stands a memorial to Jan Hus, the 15th-century martyr who crusaded against Prague's German-dominated religious and political establishment. It was unveiled in 1915, on the 500th anniversary of Hus's execution. Its most compelling features are the dark asymmetry and fluidity of the figures. Take metro Line A to Staroměstská.

One of the city's most historic squares, **Václavské Náměstí (Wenceslas Square)** ★★, was formerly the horse market (Koňský trh). The once muddy swath between the buildings played host to the country's equine auctioneers. The top of the square, where the National Museum now stands, was the outer wall of the New Town fortifications, bordering the Royal Vineyards. Unfortunately, the city's busiest highway now cuts the museum off from the rest of the square it dominates. Trolleys streamed up and down the square until the early 1980s. Today the 1km-long (⅔-mile) boulevard is lined with cinemas, shops, hotels, restaurants, and casinos.

The square was given its present name in 1848. The giant equestrian statue of St. Wenceslas on horseback surrounded by four other saints has become a popular platform for speakers. Actually, the square has thrice been the site of riots and revolutions—in 1848, 1968, and 1989. Take metro Line A or B to Můstek.

OUTDOOR ACTIVITES

A favorite getaway is **Vyšehrad Park** ★ above the Vltava south of the city center. This 1,000-year-old citadel encloses a peaceful set of gardens, playgrounds, footpaths, and the national cemetery next to the twin-towered Church of Sts. Peter and Paul, reconstructed from 1885 to 1887. The park provides a fantastic wide-angle view of the whole city. Take metro Line C to Vyšehrad or tram no. 3 or 16 to Výtoň. The park is open at all times.

The **Královská zahrada (Royal Garden)** ★ at Prague Castle, Prague 1, once the site of the sovereigns' vineyards, was founded in 1534. Dotted with lemon trees and surrounded by 16th-, 17th-, and 18th-century buildings, the park is consciously and conservatively laid out with abundant shrubbery and fountains. Entered from U Prašného mostu street, north of the castle complex, it's open daily from 10am to 6pm in the summer season.

The castle's **Zahrada na Valech (Garden on the Ramparts)** ★ is on the cityside hill below the castle. Beyond beautifully groomed lawns and sparse shrubbery is a tranquil low-angle view of the castle above and the city below. Enter the garden from the south side of the castle complex, below Hradčanské náměstí. The garden is open daily from 10am to 6pm in the summer season.

Looming over Malá Strana, adjacent to Prague Castle, lush green **Petřínské sady (Petřín Hill)** is easily recognizable by the miniature replica of the Eiffel Tower that tops it. Gardens and orchards bloom in spring and summer. Throughout the myriad monuments and churches are a mirror maze and an observatory. The Hunger Wall, a decaying 6m-high (20-ft.) stone wall that runs up through Petřín to the grounds of Prague Castle, was commissioned by Charles IV in the 1360s as a medieval welfare project designed to provide jobs for Prague's starving poor. Take tram no. 12, 20, or 22 to Újezd and ride the funicular or start climbing.

Part of the excitement of **Valdštejnská zahrada (Waldstein [Wallenstein] Gardens)** ★ at Letenská, Prague 1 (ⓒ **257-072-759**), is its location, behind a 9m (30-ft.) wall on the back streets of Malá Strana. Inside, elegant gravel paths dotted with classical bronze statues and gurgling fountains fan out in every direction. Laid out in the 17th century, the baroque park was the garden of Gen. Albrecht Waldstein (or Wallenstein; 1581–1634), commander of the Roman Catholic armies during the Thirty Years' War. These gardens are the backyards of Waldstein's Palace—Prague's largest—which replaced 23 houses, three gardens, and the municipal brick kiln. It's now home to the Czech Senate. The gardens are open March to October, daily from 10am to 6pm.

Where to Eat

Prague still has a long way to go before people travel here just for the food, but the quality and variety of restaurants have improved tremendously in the past decade. Today, thanks to a massive influx of tourist dollars as well as rising incomes of ordinary Czechs, Prague now supports many very good restaurants, with traditional Czech places supplemented by French, Italian, Japanese, Chinese, and Indian restaurants.

The most recent craze is for locally sourced and organic foods, all to the benefit of the dining public.

HRADČANY

A Divadlo Pokračuje ★ 📷 CZECH/INTERNATIONAL   This is a cute coffee-shop and pancake house that's recommendable chiefly for its great terrace overlooking the valley, location close to the castle, and exceedingly reasonable prices for sweet and savory pancakes that are both delicious and filling. The main drawback is the slow service, but scout out a seat on the terrace, settle in, and enjoy the afternoon.

Loretánská 13, Prague 1. www.adivadlopokracuje.com. ℂ **733-483-900.** Reservations not necessary. Main courses 80Kč–150Kč. No credit cards. Daily 10am–10pm. Tram: 22 one stop beyond Prague Castle.

Vikárka ★ ☺ CZECH   Decent places to eat in Hradčany are rare. Not only does this restored Romanesque and Gothic cellar restaurant within the castle walls offer good Czech and international dishes at decent prices, but you also get to eat amid more than 600 years of history. The staff gets into the mood with period costumes, but this is no tourist trap. For a real Czech treat, try the pork knee baked in dark beer served in the traditional style with slices of brown bread, horseradish, and mustard.

Vikářská 39, inside the Prague Castle complex, Prague 1. http://vikarka.cz. ℂ **233-311-962.** Main courses 180Kč–250Kč. AE, DC, MC, V. Daily 11am–9pm. Tram: 22 to Prague Castle.

Villa Richter ★ CONTINENTAL/CZECH   A relatively recent entry into Prague's top echelon is this luxury restaurant in a hilltop vineyard just as you exit the Prague Castle complex on the eastern end. There are actually three restaurants here, including a relatively inexpensive option that serves burgers and has wine tastings for 45Kč a glass, but the big culinary draw is the "Piano Nobile," a gourmet restaurant offering the best of Czech and international cooking and a wine vault with some 2,000 bottles. In winter, dress up for the fancy dining room; in summer, it's more relaxed, with dining on the terrace overlooking Malá Strana to your right and the Old Town across the river.

Staré zámecké schody 6, Prague 1. www.villarichter.cz. ℂ **257-219-079.** Reservations recommended. Main courses 610Kč–690Kč; five-course tasting menu 1,690 Kč. AE, DC, MC, V. Daily 11am–1am. Metro: Malostranská plus a walk up the stairs.

MALÁ STRANA (LESSER TOWN)
Very Expensive
Kampa Park ★ CONTINENTAL   This restaurant is worth the considerable splurge, but only if you can snag one of the highly coveted riverside tables. If you can't, move on and try for the terrace at Hergetova Cihelna (see below). For years, Kampa Park was considered Prague's premier restaurant and lured its fair share of visiting celebs (check out the photos on the wall). These days, there's lots more competition, but the setting on the Vltava is still arguably the best in town. The menu, with items like seared monkfish and roast saddle of lamb, looks relatively tame, but the quality of the food is excellent.

Na Kampě 8b, Prague 1. www.kampagroup.com. ℂ **296-826-112.** Reservations recommended. Main courses 495Kč–895Kč. AE, DC, MC, V. Daily 11:30am–1am. Metro: Malostranská.

Expensive
Hergetova Cihelna ★ INTERNATIONAL/CZECH   The main draw here is the riverside terrace with an unparalleled view of the Charles Bridge—plus the very good food (from the same people who run the more expensive Kampa Park; see above). The building, dating from the 18th century, once served as a brick factory (*cihelna*)

before it was renovated into this stylish modern restaurant around a decade ago. The first dining concept here was burgers and pizza, which the owners quickly ditched for more expensive items like rib-eye steaks with maple-glazed carrots (525Kč). Still, it's possible to eat cheaply if you stick to the Czech specialties and pasta dishes.

Cihelná 2b, Prague 1. www.kampagroup.com. ℂ **296-826-103.** Reservations recommended. Main courses 215Kč–695Kč. AE, MC, V. Daily 11:30am–1am. Metro: Malostranská.

Ichnusa Botega & Bistro ★★ ITALIAN   This small, family-owned Sardinian restaurant is a real treat. There's no menu, no staff, and practically no tables to speak of (which makes reserving in advance a necessity). Instead, it's like you're welcomed into the kitchen of a talented Italian friend. The chef doubles as the waiter and there are only usually a couple of entrees available. Start with a family platter of appetizers, including Italian sausages, vegetables, and cheeses, and then dip into an exquisitely prepared main dish that could be anything from linguini pasta to calamari to tripe. Rest assured, it's all good.

Plaská 5, Prague 5. ℂ **605-525-748.** Reservations essential. Antipasto platter 200Kč, main courses 195Kč–300Kč. AE, DC, MC, V. Daily 7pm–10pm. Tram: 6, 9, 12, 20, 22, stop Újezd.

U modré kachničky ★ CZECH   The "Blue Duckling," on a narrow Malá Strana street, comes close to refining standard Czech dishes into true Bohemian haute cuisine. The menu is loaded with an array of wild game and quirky spins on Czech village favorites. Starters include lightly spiced venison pâté and duck liver on toast. You can choose from six duck main courses. Finally, the ubiquitous *palačinky* crepes are thin and tender and filled with fruit, nuts, and chocolate. There is an even more popular sister to the first "kachnička," at Michalská 16, Prague 1 (ℂ **224-213-418**), with a similar menu and prices.

Nebovidská 6, Prague 1. www.umodrekachnicky.cz. ℂ **257-320-308.** Reservations recommended for lunch, required for dinner. Main courses 290Kč–690Kč. AE, MC, V. Daily noon–4pm and 6:30pm–midnight. Metro: Malostranská.

Moderate
Café de Paris ★ CAFE/FRENCH/CONTINENTAL   This delightful French bistro perched on pretty Maltézské náměstí is a perfect addition to a beautiful part of Prague. The menu is tiny with just a few items, though there are daily specials marked on the board outside. The specialty is grilled steak, entrecote, served with salad, homemade fries, and a secret sauce known as "Café de Paris" sauce. The service is informal but attentive and the wine list is extensive and good value. An ideal spot for a long lunch or unfussy but good dinner.

Maltézské nám. 4, Prague 1. www.cafedeparis.cz. ℂ **603-160-718.** Reservations recommended. Main courses 250Kč–350Kč. AE, MC, V. Daily noon–midnight. Metro: Malostranská plus tram no. 12, 20, or 22 to Malostranské nám.

STARÉ MĚSTO (OLD TOWN)
Very Expensive
Allegro ★★ ITALIAN/INTERNATIONAL   The house restaurant of the Four Seasons Hotel has been at the forefront of Prague dining since opening its doors a few years ago. It was the first recipient of a Michelin star in central Europe and has now grabbed the prize 2 years running. The cooking mixes northern Italian influences with international trends and even a few local influences. Dinners can be prohibitively expensive for anyone not traveling on the company's dime, though the daily

prix-fixe lunch specials, 750Kč for two courses and 950Kč for three courses, help bring the food within reach of mere mortals.

Veleslavínova 2a, Prague 1. www.fourseasons.com. ✆ **221-427-000.** Reservations recommended. Main courses 750Kč–1,250Kč. AE, DC, MC, V. Daily 11:30am–5pm and 5:30–10:30pm; Sun brunch 11:30am–3pm. Metro: Staroměstská.

Bellevue ★★ INTERNATIONAL   With its excellent views of Prague Castle, the Bellevue is a perennial top choice. The ambitious owners have put all their energy into the intelligent menu: beef, nouvelle sauces, well-dressed fish and duck, delicate pastas, and artistic desserts. For a tamer but extraordinary treat, try the roasted veal cheek with potato purée. Desserts feature a vanilla-bean crème brûlée. Reserve in advance to snag a coveted table with a castle view.

Smetanovo nábřeží 18, Prague 1. www.bellevuerestaurant.cz. ✆ **222-221-443.** Reservations recommended. Set meals from 990Kč (2-course) to 1,390Kč (5-course), excluding wine. AE, DC, MC, V. Daily noon–3pm and 5:30–11pm; Sun brunch 11am–3pm. Metro: Staroměstská.

La Degustation ★★★ CONTINENTAL/CZECH   Without a doubt, this is one of the city's best dining spots. It is housed in an Old Town corner building and has a minimalist interior. Two different prix-fixe, seven-course menus are served, as diners are invited to sample a wide array of food and wine. The Bohême Bourgeois menu finds inspiration in old Czech cookbooks and raises by miles the level of Czech cuisine usually served in restaurants here. The *Chef's Menu* adds more exotic items such as Kobe beef. Each dish is accompanied by an excellent selection of wines served by experienced sommeliers.

Haštalská 18, Prague 1. www.ladegustation.cz. ✆ **222-311-234.** Reservations recommended. Fixed-price menu 2,250Kč–2,750Kč, fixed-price wines 1,390Kč–1,890Kč. AE, MC, V. Mon–Sat 6pm–midnight; Tues–Thurs noon–2:30pm. Metro: Staroměstská.

Expensive

King Solomon Restaurant ★ KOSHER   Under the supervision of the Orthodox Council of Kashrut, the King Solomon has brought to Prague a truly kosher restaurant, across from the Pinkas Synagogue. The restaurant's dozen booths are camped under an industrial-looking atrium. During dining hours, which strictly adhere to the Sabbath, you can choose from a variety of fresh vegetable and meat dishes following kosher dietary rules. The broad menu ranges from vegetable béchamel to stuffed roast quail. Selections of Israeli, American, and Moravian kosher wine include the restaurant's pride: a Frankovka red from the Baron Aaron Günsberger Moravian cellars.

Široká 8, Prague 1. www.kosher.cz. ✆ **224-818-752.** Reservations recommended. Main courses 250Kč–1,600Kč. AE, MC, V. Sun–Thurs noon–11pm; Fri dinner and Sat lunch by arrangement only. Metro: Staroměstská.

Moderate

Kogo ★ ITALIAN   This modern, upscale trattoria has for years been a local favorite for brokers and bankers who work nearby. Tucked away on a side street just opposite the Havel Market, Kogo manages to combine the warmth and boisterousness of a family restaurant with a high culinary standard in its pastas, meaty entrees, and desserts. Try the fresh, zesty mussels in white wine and garlic (*cozze al vino bianco e aglio*) or the tangy grilled salmon. The wine list is extensive, and the tiramisu is light and sweet without being soggy.

Kogo has a second, even more popular, location in the atrium of the Slovanský Dům shopping center at Na Příkopě 22 (✆ **221-451-259**). The prices are higher here but the location makes it a logical choice for a meal before or after taking in a movie at the multiplex cinema.

Havelská 27, Prague 1. www.kogo.cz. ⓒ **224-214-543.** Reservations recommended. Main courses 210Kč–480Kč. AE, MC, V. Daily 9am–midnight. Metro: Můstek.

Inexpensive

Maitrea ★ VEGETARIAN Wildly popular vegetarian restaurant with a loyal local following that comes for the traditional couscous and rice dishes as well as concoctions like "meatless" chicken and sushi. The main dining rooms are refined and relatively formal for a vegetarian place, making this a great option for a big meatless night out. Týnská ulička is a little hard to find. From Old Town Square, head east on Dlouhá, making a right at the first small lane, opposite Dušní Street.

Týnská ulička 6, Prague 1. www.restaurace-maitrea.cz. ⓒ **222-316-265.** Reservations recommended. Main courses 120Kč–240Kč. AE, DC, MC, V. Mon–Fri 11:30am–11:30pm; Sat–Sun noon–11:30pm. Metro: Staroměstská.

Pizzeria Rugantino ★★ ☺ PIZZA Pizzeria Rugantino serves generous salads and the best selection of individual pizzas in Prague. Wood-fired stoves and handmade dough result in a crisp and delicate crust. The pizza "calabrese," with hot chili peppers and spicy pepperoni, is as close as you'll find to American-style pepperoni pizza in this part of Europe. A more spacious Rugantino II is located at Klimentská 40, Prague 1 (ⓒ **224-815-192;** metro: Florenc or Náměstí Republiky), with a children's corner and plasma TV. The constant buzz, nonsmoking area, heavy childproof wooden tables, and lots of baby chairs make this a family favorite.

Dušní 4, Prague 1. www.rugantino.cz. ⓒ **222-318-172.** Individual pizzas 120Kč–220Kč. AE, MC, V. Mon–Sat 11am–11pm; Sun noon–11pm. Metro: Staroměstská.

NOVÉ MĚSTO (NEW TOWN)

Corso ★ CZECH/INTERNATIONAL This cozy cafe, just off Náměstí Republiky, is an ideal choice for lunch or a light dinner, particularly in nice weather when you can dine on the small terrace out front. The lunch menu is built around a daily special, usually something Czech, and supplemented by a regular menu of very good salads, pastas, and light meat entrees. During the evenings, it's just the normal menu. The Caesar salad (168Kč) is authentic and may just be the best in Prague. Good coffees and cakes and a reliable and free Wi-Fi connection.

V Celnici 4, Prague 1. www.corsocafe.cz. ⓒ **224-281-137.** Reservations recommended. Main courses: lunch specials 100Kč, dinner 120Kč–200Kč. AE, DC, MC, V. Daily 11am–11pm. Metro: Náměstí Republiky.

Pivovarský dům ★★ CZECH Good Czech beer is not only made by the big brewers. This very popular microbrewery produces its own excellent lager as well as harder-to-find varieties like dark beer and wheat beer. The "Brewery House" also dabbles in borderline-blasphemous (but still pretty good) concoctions such as coffee-, cherry-, and banana-flavored beer. Sharing the spotlight with the beer is excellent traditional Czech food including pork, dumplings, rabbit, goulash, and schnitzel, served in an upscale pub-like setting. The dining areas are all nonsmoking. You'll need reservations to walk in the door—it's that popular.

Lípová 15 (corner of Ječná), Prague 2. www.gastroinfo.cz/pivodum. ⓒ **296-216-666.** Reservations recommended. Main courses 135Kč–275Kč. AE, MC, V. Daily 11am–11:30pm. Metro: I. P. Pavlova plus tram no. 4, 6, 10, or 22, one stop to Štěpánská.

VINOHRADY

Aromi ★★ ITALIAN Definitely worth the splurge and trip out to residential Vinohrady for easily the best Italian cooking and possibly the best seafood in Prague. The swank interior manages to be both fancy and inviting at the same time, lending any meal the feeling of an occasion. The waiting staff is professional yet surprisingly unpretentious for a restaurant of this caliber. My favorite is the homemade ravioli stuffed with potatoes and seabass, but everything is delicious. Sticking to the pastas can keep the bill manageable. The daily lunch special is a steal at around 200Kč per person.

Mánesova 78, Prague 2. www.aromi.cz. ℂ **222-713-222.** Reservations recommended. Pastas and main courses 345Kč–600Kč. AE, MC, V. Daily noon–11pm. Metro: Jiřího z Poděbrad or Muzeum plus tram no. 11.

Masala ★★ INDIAN This Indian mom-and-pop place is just what the doctor ordered if you have a taste for a well-made curry. Be sure to reserve, especially on a Friday or Saturday night, as there's only a handful of tables and they fill up quickly. The engaging staff will ask you how much spice you want—go for broke, since even "very spicy" would only qualify as "medium" in the U.S. or England, let alone back home in India. All the classics are offered, including crispy naan bread and flavored yogurt drinks to start.

Mánesova 13, Prague 2 (behind the National Museum). www.masala.cz. ℂ **222-251-601.** Reservations recommended. Main courses 175Kč–395Kč. AE, MC, V. Mon–Fri 11:30am–10:30pm; Sat–Sun 12:30–10:30pm. Metro: Muzeum.

Radost FX VEGETARIAN Radost has been coasting for years on a menu that was considered daring when it was introduced in 1993, but it's still one of the few—and best—vegetarian options in Prague. The veggie burger served on a grain bun is well seasoned and substantial, and the soups, like lentil and onion, are light and full of flavor. Sautéed vegetable dishes, tofu, and huge Greek salads round out the health-conscious menu. The hipster interior draws a stylish clientele, but the offhand waiting staff lends an impression they are a little too cool to work hard. The bill already includes an obligatory 10% tip, so no need to leave any extra money on the table.

Bělehradská 120, Prague 2. www.radostfx.cz. ℂ **603-181-500.** Main courses 80Kč–285Kč. AE, MC, V. Daily 11:30am–5am. Metro: I. P. Pavlova.

Shopping

Prague has become a fun shopping destination in recent years, spurred by rising wages and the influx of visitors with euros and dollars to spend. This is especially true for women's (and to a lesser extent men's) fashion. If your taste runs to the high-end, look no further than the Old Town's Pařížská Street, where a half-mile stroll takes you past luxury boutiques like Cartier and Prada, though these shops tend to have smaller inventory (and even higher price tags) than their brethren in Paris or New York. Slightly less-expensive but still top-quality Czech fashion designers have opened up shops throughout the Old Town, and Na Příkopě and Václavské Náměstí (Wenceslas Sq.) are lined with trendy, mid-market European clothing retailers like Zara and Mango.

For those looking to take a little bit of the Czech Republic home with them, popular souvenirs include Bohemian crystal and glass, garnet jewelry, hand-crafted wooden toys and puppets, old books and maps, and, naturally, distinctly Czech liquid refreshments like Moravian wine, beer, and Becherovka. The best advice is simply to walk around and poke your nose in wherever it looks interesting. Throughout the city center, you'll find quaint, obscure shops, some without phones or advertising.

Entertainment & Nightlife

For many Czechs, the best way to spend an evening is at the neighborhood pub, enjoying the good beer and some boisterous conversation. These types of evenings are always open to visitors, of course, though the language may occasionally be an issue (at least at the start of the night before the beer kicks in).

If raucous beer nights are not your thing, Prague offers plenty of other diversions. The contemporary music scene is alive and kicking, and clubs all across town offer live acts or DJs playing rock, indie, techno, hip-hop, or whatever is popular at the moment. Prague has also developed into a popular stop for visiting international acts, both large and small.

Jazz, too, has enjoyed a long tradition in the Czech lands from the early decades of the 20th century when American jazzmen were played on gramophones on imported vinyl. You'll find no fewer than five decent jazz clubs in the city center and the quality of the playing is high.

Czechs are avid theatergoers and Prague for decades has enjoyed a vibrant drama scene (though with nearly all of the output in Czech, much of this sadly is inaccessible to visitors). Occasionally the National Theater will subtitle in English important works aimed at international audiences, and theaters like Švandovo divadlo in Smíchov and Divadlo Archa in Nové Město sometimes stage English and American productions in their original language.

Opera is more accessible and Prague has at least two premier venues: the State Opera at the top of Wenceslas Square (Václavské nám.) and the National Theater. The former's repertoire is made up largely of Italian classics, while the latter frequently holds performances of works by national composers like Bedřich Smetana and Leoš Janáček. Both theaters are good value and tickets are often available at short notice, though the quality will vary from show to show.

Prague's longest-running entertainment tradition, of course, is classical music. Serious music lovers are best advised to take in a performance of the **Czech Philharmonic** at the Rudolfinum in Staré Město or the **Prague Symphony Orchestra** at the Obecní dům, near Náměstí Republiky. Another option is to see one of the many **chamber concerts** offered at churches and palaces around town. These can be very good, though ticket prices are often higher than for the Philharmonic and the quality may not be nearly as good.

If you're getting tired just reading about all these entertainment possibilities, there's always the option of a good dinner followed by a quiet stroll over the Charles Bridge and through Malá Strana over ancient cobblestones and lit by mellow gas lamps.

TICKETS

An easy way to get tickets once you're in Prague is to visit one of the local ticket agency offices and buy the tickets in person. The man or woman behind the counter is likely to have a good idea of the biggest events happening on that day or in the coming days and provide good advice. Pay in cash or with a credit card. **Ticketpro** has several offices around town, including at **Prague Information Services** (www.pis.cz; ✆ **221-714-444**) offices at the Old Town Hall and at Rytířská 31. Ticketpro also sells tickets at Václavské nám. 38, Prague 1 (✆ **296-329-999**), and through the helpful **Prague Tourist Center,** near the Můstek metro stop at Rytířská 12, Prague 1 (✆ **296-333-333**), open daily from 9am to 8pm. **Bohemia Ticket** has offices at Na Příkopě 16, Prague 1 (www.bohemiaticket.cz; ✆ **224-215-031**), and is open Monday to Friday from 10am to 7pm, Saturday from 10am to 5pm, and Sunday from 10am to 3pm.

PERFORMING ARTS

Although there's plenty of music year-round, the city's orchestras all come to life during the international **Prague Spring Festival,** an annual 3-week series of classical music events that runs from mid-May to early June; the events began as a rallying point for Czech culture in the aftermath of World War II. The main performances are held at the Art Nouveau **Smetana Hall** at the **Municipal House,** though concerts are held at other venues around town. Tickets for festival concerts range from 400Kč to more than 3,000Kč and are available in advance through Ticketpro or in person at Hellichova 18, Prague 1 (www.festival.cz; ℂ **257-310-414**).

The Czech Philharmonic Orchestra performs at the **Rudolfinum,** Alšovo nábřeží 12, Prague 1 (www.ceskafilharmonie.cz; ℂ **227-059-227**). It's the traditional voice of the country's national pride, often playing works by Dvořak and Smetana. The Philharmonic's main rival, the **Prague Symphony Orchestra,** known locally by the initials **"FOK,"** has positioned itself as a fresher alternative, with a frequently livelier and more daring repertoire, and many more modern composers on the roster. The FOK performs regularly at the **Smetana Hall** of the **Municipal House** (Náměstí Republiky 5, Prague 1. www.fok.cz; ℂ **222-002-336**), and this is where you'll find the company's box office and scheduling information.

Lavishly constructed in the late-Renaissance style of northern Italy, the gold-crowned **Národní divadlo (National Theater),** Národní 2, Prague 1 (www.narodni-divadlo.cz; ℂ **224-901-448**), overlooking the Vltava River, is one of Prague's most recognizable landmarks. Completed in 1881, the theater was built to nurture the Czech National Revival—a grass-roots movement to replace the dominant German culture with that of native Czechs. Today, classic productions are staged here.

BARS, CLUBS & LIVE MUSIC

AghaRTA Jazz Centrum ★★ Upscale by Czech standards, the AghaRTA regularly features some of the best music in town, from standard acoustic trios and quartets to Dixieland, funk, and fusion. Bands usually begin at 9pm, but try to come much earlier to snag one of the few places to sit. Open daily from 7pm to midnight. Železná 16, Prague 1. www.agharta.cz. ℂ 222-211-275. Cover 250Kč. Metro: Můstek.

Cross Club ★★ The reigning king of Prague's alternative, indie, and clubbing scene, Cross Club fuses a funky industrial-age interior—pipes and wires hanging from the ceiling (and lots more)—with DJ-led trance and electronic dance music. Draws a mix of university students, backpackers, and anyone else looking for something that feels a little more authentic than some of the clubs downtown. The location in the nether reaches of Holešovice, Prague 7, keeps the tourists away, though in fact it's only a few minutes' walk from the Nádraží Holešovice metro stop (Line C), meaning you can be there from the top of Wenceslas Square in under 20 minutes. Plynární 23, Prague 7. www.crossclub.cz. ℂ 775-541-430. Admission 100Kč. Metro: Nádraží Holešovice.

Iron Curtain (Propaganda Club) ★ This fun, English-friendly pub and club in the center of the Old Town occupies a huge Gothic cellar festooned with all kinds of Communist era bric-a-brac (posters of Lenin and the like). There's live music some nights and always a good crowd on hand. Also serves decent bar food. Open daily 6pm to 4am. Michalska 12, Prague 1. www.propagandapub.cz. ℂ 242-480-728. Metro: Mustek.

Klub Lávka This classic late-night meat-market dance club has been around since shortly after the Velvet Revolution. It's actually a lot of fun if you're in the mood for it, and the crowd is a good mix of Czechs and visitors. The setting couldn't be lovelier, on a jetty that extends into the river just south of the Charles Bridge, with castle views to die for. For hard-core partiers, the good news is that Klub Lávka is open late, and the music goes on until 5am. Novotného lávka 1, Prague 1. www.lavka.cz. ℂ 221-082-299. Cover 150Kč. Metro: Staroměstská.

Lucerna Music Bar ★ Big and a bit dingy, this Prague landmark in the belly of the downtown palace built by Václav Havel's father provides the best lineup of Czech garage bands, ex-underground acts, and an occasional reggae or blues gig. The drinks are still cheap for the city center. The crowd is mostly local and the biggest draws are the wildly popular '80s- and '90s-themed dance nights on Fridays and Saturdays. Open daily from 8pm to 3am, with live music usually beginning at 9pm. Vodičkova 36, Prague 1. www.musicbar.cz. ℂ 224-217-108. Cover 100Kč–200Kč. Metro: Můstek.

Malostranská Beseda ★★ One of the city's leading venues for Czech rock and folk acts, particularly groups and singers from the '80s and '90s. In addition to a music club, there's an art gallery and theater, plus a busy pub, cafe, and restaurant.. The box office is open Monday to Saturday from 5 to 10pm, Sunday 3 to 8pm. Malostranské nám. 21, Prague 1. www.malostranska-beseda.cz. ℂ 257-409-123 (box office). Metro: Malostranská.

Mecca For those who don't mind trekking into the depths of Prague 7 to be with some of the trendiest people in town, make your way to Mecca. You don't have to pray to the east to get in, but you'd better be one of the beautiful people, dressed well enough to get by the bouncers at the usually packed entrance. This converted warehouse in northeast Prague has been one of the most popular discos in town for several years now and shows no signs of letting up. Open Wednesday to Saturday 11am to 5am. U Průhonu 3, Prague 7. www.mecca.cz. ℂ 283-870-522. Cover 190Kč–290Kč, women enter free on Wed. Metro: Vltavská, then tram 1.

Palác Akropolis ★★★ This reconverted cinema in Žižkov is Prague's premier venue for club-level live rock and world music acts. Brings in a surprisingly good roster of bands, including in recent years the Flaming Lips, the Strokes, Jon Spencer Blues Explosion, N.O.H.A., and many more. The main concert hall, the old screening room, is makeshift and still feels kind of edgy after all these years. The back room doubles as a bar and a DJ room, with dancing going on into the wee hours long after the concert's over. Kubelíkova 27, Prague 3. www.palacakropolis.cz. ℂ 296-330-911. Cover 100Kč–250Kč, depending on the show. Metro: Jiřího z Poděbrad.

Radost FX This was one of the first big dance clubs to open up after the Velvet Revolution and, surprisingly, it's still here and still going strong. The ground-floor vegetarian restaurant and cafe are mainstays of the neighborhood dining scene (p. 150), and the trendy downstairs club draws a mixed straight and gay crowd for themed dance nights. Open daily from 10pm to 5am. Bělehradská 120, Prague 2. www. radostfx.cz. ℂ 224-254-776. Cover 150Kč–250Kč. Metro: I. P. Pavlova.

Reduta Jazz Club ★ Reduta has been around since the 1950s and still has a kind of welcoming retro feel, as if Charlie Parker or Miles Davis himself might walk in at some point during the night. The club brings in basically the same mix of performers that the other clubs do, and standards here most nights are pretty high. The music usually starts around 9:30pm. Open daily from 9pm to midnight. Národní 20, Prague 1. www.redutajazzclub.cz. ℂ 224-933-487. Cover 150Kč. Metro: Národní třída.

Roxy ★★ Another dance club and live music venue in a reconverted theater, Roxy pushes the boundaries of bizarre in its dark, stark dance hall down Dlouhá Street, near Old Town Square. Acid jazz, funk, techno, salsa, and reggae are among the tunes on the playlist. The list of acts, including the Hives, Asian Dub Foundation, and

Franz Ferdinand, among others, is legendary. Bands usually hit the stage early because of noise restrictions, but the party goes on until the wee hours. Dlouhá 33, Prague 1. www.roxy.cz. ✆ 224-826-296. Cover 100Kč–250Kč. Metro: Staroměstská.

PUBS

Good pub brews and conversations are Prague's preferred late-evening entertainment. Unlike British, Irish, or German beer halls, a true Czech pub ignores accoutrements like cushy chairs and warm wooden paneling, and cuts straight to the chase—beer. While some Czech pubs do serve a hearty plate of food alongside the suds, it's the *pivo,* uncommonly cheap at usually less than 40Kč a pint, that keeps people sitting for hours.

Foreign-theme pubs are popping up all over Prague, offering tastes ranging from Irish to Mexican. Still, it feels a bit like trying to sell Indian tea in China. Below are listed the best of the Czech brew stops.

Kolkovna ★   Hard-core pub aficionados will claim this is not a true pub, since it's relatively free of smoke, has clean restrooms, and serves excellent food, including both Czech classics and international dishes. On the other hand, no one will argue with the beer: Pilsner Urquell served from huge tanks brought in directly from the brewery to ensure freshness. It's a great spot to relax after a stroll through Old Town. Open daily from 11am to midnight. V kolkovně 8, Prague 1. www.kolkovna.cz. ✆ 224-819-701. Metro: Staroměstská.

Prague Beer Museum ★★   Unlike what you might think from the name, this is not a "museum," it's a pub. What makes it stand out, though, is that it eschews the typical pub practice of selling one or two beers from a supporting brewery. Instead, the mission here is to bring in hard-to-find smaller regional and microbrews. Leaf through the menu and name your poison. Open daily from 11am to 1am. Dlouhá 46, Prague 1. www.praguebeermuseum.com. ✆ 732-330-912. Metro: Staroměstská.

U medvídků (At the Little Bears) ★   This 5-century-old pub off Národní třída was the first in town to serve the original Budweiser, Budvar, on tap. It now serves its own microbrews, including some incredibly strong beers it calls "X-Beers." It also serves typical Czech pub food, including *cmunda,* potato pancakes topped with sauerkraut and cured meat. It's smoky inside, but still easier to breathe here than at most local pubs. Open daily from 11:30am to 11pm. Na Perštýně 7, Prague 1. www.umedvidku.cz. ✆ 224-211-916. Metro: Národní třída.

THE LGBT SCENE

The residential district of Vinohrady (Prague 2) has evolved into Prague's de facto gay district. While it's certainly no match for San Francisco's Castro or New York's West Village, the area does sport a number of clubs, cafes, and discos that are gay or gay-friendly.

Klub Termix   This small basement in Vinohrady is one of the city's most popular gay discos and can get impossibly crowded on weekend evenings. Enter by ringing the buzzer and the doorman will let you in, but be sure to get there early in order to ensure entry. Open Monday to Saturday 8pm to 5am. Třebízského 4a, Prague 2. www.club-termix.cz. ✆ 222-710-462. Metro: Muzeum, then tram 11 two stops.

Saints Bar ★★   This relaxed bar on a quiet Vinohrady street is the place to go if big, loud discos are not your thing and you're more interested in kicking back and enjoying some friendly conversation. Open daily from 7pm to 4am. Polská 32, Prague 2. ✆ 222-250-326. Metro: Jiřího z Poděbrad.

Where to Stay

Prague's hotels are spread out all over the four central districts of Hradčany, Malá Strana, Staré Město, and Nové Město, plus outlying areas like Vinohrady, Smíchov, and Dejvice. Each of these areas offers advantages and disadvantages. In general, the highest demand and highest prices are for properties in Malá Strana and Staré Město. They offer the closest proximity to the main sites and the possibility of a castle or river view out your window. Nové Město, the city's commercial heart, is also a popular lodging choice. A hotel here will probably offer the same walk-to proximity to the major sights, but may lack some of the innate charm of Malá Strana or Staré Město. The leafy inner suburb of Vinohrady has increasingly evolved into an alternative lodging locale. This is an upscale and highly desirable area, but requires a metro or tram ride to get to the center. For other outlying districts, look at the map carefully before booking your room. Try to get as close to a metro or tramline as possible, or you'll spend too much time trying to figure out your transit routes and not enough time enjoying the sights.

HRADČANY

Hotel Savoy ★   One of Prague's finest hotels, the Savoy occupies a quiet spot behind the Foreign Ministry and Černín Palace, and is just a few blocks from the castle. The guest rooms are richly decorated and boast every amenity as well as spacious marble bathrooms. The beds are huge, which contrasts with the customary central European style of two twin beds shoved together. The pleasant staff provides an attention to detail that's a cut above that at most hotels in Prague. The Hradčany restaurant is excellent.

Keplerova 6, Prague 1. www.savoyhotel.cz. ✆ **224-302-430.** Fax 224-302-128. 61 units. From 4,500Kč double; from 8,000Kč suite. Rates include breakfast. AE, DC, MC, V. Tram: 22 to Pohořelec. Parking. **Amenities:** Restaurant; bar; exercise room; health club & spa; sauna; room service; whirlpool; Wi-Fi (free in lobby). *In room:* A/C, TV, minibar, hair dryer, DVD player, Internet.

Romantik Hotel U raka ★   Hidden among the stucco houses and cobblestone streets of a pristine medieval neighborhood below Prague Castle is this pleasant surprise. The Romantik Hotel U raka (At the Crayfish) has been lovingly reconstructed as an old-world farmhouse. The rustic rooms have heavy wooden furniture, open-beamed ceilings, and stone walls. The owners are relaxed but attentive. Prague Castle is a 10-minute walk away, and you can catch a tram into the city center by walking up ancient steps at the side of the hotel. Make reservations well in advance.

Černínská 10, Prague 1. www.romantikhotel-uraka.cz. ✆ **220-511-100.** Fax 233-358-041. 6 units (5 with shower only). From 3,500Kč double; from 7,000Kč suite. Rates include breakfast. AE, MC, V. Tram: 22 to stop Pohořelec. **Amenities:** Restaurant. *In room:* A/C, TV, minibar, hair dryer.

MALÁ STRANA (LESSER TOWN)

Hotel Aria ★   This music-themed hotel occupies a luxuriously reconstructed town house in the heart of Malá Strana, just around the corner from the St. Nicholas Cathedral. Each of its four floors is tastefully decorated to evoke a different genre of music, famous composer, or musician. The rooms and bathrooms vary in their size and layout, and all are kept to the same exceptionally high standard. There is an impressive library of CDs, DVDs, and books about music off the lobby, and a full-time resident musicologist is available to help you choose a concert in the city.

Tržiště 9, Prague 1. www.aria.cz. ✆ **225-334-111.** Fax 225-334-666. 52 units. From 5,800Kč double; 9,500Kč suite. Rates include breakfast. AE, MC, V. Metro: Malostranská and then tram 12, 20, or 22 to Malostranské nám. **Amenities:** Restaurant; bar; exercise room; room service; free airport transfers (for suite stays); Wi-Fi. *In room:* A/C, minibar, hair dryer, CD/DVD player, MP3 docking station, Internet.

Hotel U páva ★ The "Peacock" is a fine B&B in Malá Strana, a stone's throw from Charles Bridge. This family-run hotel has the intimacy of a farmhouse and offers room service from its decent kitchen. Original wooden ceilings, antique chairs, and comfortable beds accent the reasonably spacious rooms. The best rooms on the top floor facing the front have a fantastic low-angle view of Prague Castle. The fully tiled bathrooms of adequate size have tub/shower combinations.

U Lužického semináře 32, Prague 1. www.romantichotels.cz. ✆ **257-533-360.** Fax 257-530-919. 27 units (tub/shower combo). From 3,000Kč double, from 4,500Kč suite. Rates include breakfast. AE, MC, V. Metro: Malostranská. **Amenities:** Restaurant; cafe; bar; health club & spa; room service; babysitting. *In room:* TV, minibar, hair dryer, Wi-Fi (free).

STARÉ MĚSTO (OLD TOWN) & JOSEFOV
Very Expensive
Four Seasons Hotel ★★★ Located in an imposing position on the banks of the Vltava River right next to Charles Bridge, the Four Seasons provides an elegant base for exploring Old Town and has a wonderful panoramic view of Prague Castle across the river. The property actually melds three historic buildings from the city's most important architectural periods—baroque, Renaissance, and Art Nouveau. The most impressive wing, the 17th-century baroque villa, houses the Presidential Suite as well as some smaller (but still nicely appointed) executive suites and guest rooms. The best have sweeping views and sunken marble tubs. The Art Nouveau wing is less expensive but the street-side views are less impressive. All rooms are fitted with fine solid-wood furniture: some with antique pieces, others with more modern avant-garde accents. The house restaurant, Allegro (p. 147), is a Michelin star winner.

Veleslavínova 2a, Prague 1. www.fourseasons.com. ✆ **221-427-000.** Fax 221-426-000. 161 units. From 9,000Kč double; from 20,000Kč suite. AE, DC, MC, V. Metro: Staroměstská. Parking. **Amenities:** Restaurant; bar; exercise room; health club & spa; room service; executive-level rooms. *In room:* A/C, TV, minibar, hair dryer, CD, DVD player, Wi-Fi (free).

Expensive
Hotel InterContinental Prague The upper suites of this hotel have hosted luminaries including former U.S. secretary of state Madeleine Albright, and legend has it global terrorist Carlos the Jackal. The 1970s facade is unappealing, but the interior has been updated with modern rooms, a glittering fitness center, and an atrium restaurant. The standard guest rooms aren't very large but are comfortable, with decent but not exceptional upholstered furniture, computer ports, and marble bathrooms.

Pařížská 30, Prague 1. www.icprague.com. ✆ **296-631-111.** Fax 224-811-216. 364 units. From 4,161Kč double; from 7,605Kč suite. Rates include buffet breakfast. AE, DC, MC, V. Metro: Staroměstská. Parking. **Amenities:** 2 restaurants; cafe; indoor pool; exercise room; health club & spa; room service; executive-level rooms. *In room:* TV, minibar, hair dryer, Internet.

Hotel Josef ★★ The Josef is the hippest of Prague's hip hotels. British-based Czech architect Eva Jiřičná brings a new study on the interior use of glass to her native land with its own long history of the glazier's craft. Every piece of space breathes with life and light, breaking the stuffy mold of most high-end hotels. Superior rooms are so bold as to offer transparent bath nooks, shower stalls, and washrooms with a full view of grooming activities for your partner to absorb in the main sleeping chamber.

Rybná 20, Prague 1. www.hoteljosef.com. ☏ **221-700-111.** Fax 221-700-999. 109 units. From 3,400Kč double. AE, DC, MC, V. Metro: Nám. Republiky. Parking. **Amenities:** Restaurant; bar; exercise room; health club; room service; babysitting. *In room:* A/C, TV, minibar, hair dryer, DVD, CD player, Wi-Fi (free).

Moderate

Hotel Cloister Inn ★★ ✦ Between Old Town Square and the National Theater, this property has been renovated into a good-value, midrange hotel. The original rooms of this unique spot were developed from holding cells used by the Communist secret police, the StB; the cells themselves were converted from a convent. It sounds ominous, but the Cloister Inn rooms are actually very inviting. A new proprietor has taken over management from the secret police and has refurbished and expanded the hotel with smart colors and comfortable Nordic furniture. The rooms offer enough space, beds with firm mattresses, and reasonably sized bathrooms with showers only.

Konviktská 14, Prague 1. www.cloister-inn.cz. ☏ **224-211-020.** Fax 224-210-800. 73 units (showers only). From 2,400Kč double. Rates include breakfast. AE, DC, MC, V. Metro: Národní třída. *In room:* A/C (some), TV, minibar, hair dryer, Wi-Fi (free).

NOVÉ MĚSTO (NEW TOWN)

Andante ✦ This best-value choice near Wenceslas Square is tucked away on a dark side street, about two blocks off the top of the square. Despite the unappealing neighborhood, this is the most comfortable property at this price. With modern beds and good firm mattresses, as well as high-grade Scandinavian furniture and colorful decorations, the rooms are extremely comfortable. They offer plenty of space and white, well-kept bathrooms with tub/shower combinations, some with shower only.

Ve Smečkách 4, Prague 1. www.andante.cz. ☏ **222-210-021.** Fax 222-210-591. 32 units (some with shower only, some with tub only). From 2,400Kč double; 3,600Kč suite. Rates include breakfast. AE, MC, V. Metro: Muzeum. **Amenities:** Restaurant; room service. *In room:* TV, minibar, hair dryer, Internet.

Hotel Jalta ★ The Jalta is arguably the nicest hotel directly on the square. It was reconstructed a few years ago, giving the lobby, public areas, and rooms a much-needed makeover. The decor ranges from stripped-down midcentury modern, in keeping with the hotel's 1950s facade, to more colorful contemporary. The rooms facing the square have balconies, allowing a broad view of the busy square and a chance to imagine the scene on those historic, revolutionary nights from 1989.

Václavské nám. 45, Prague 1. www.hoteljalta.com. ☏ **222-822-111.** Fax 222-822-833. 94 units. From 4,500Kč double; 5,500Kč suite. Rates include breakfast. AE, DC, MC, V. Metro: Muzeum. **Amenities:** 2 restaurants; exercise room; concierge; room service. *In room:* A/C, TV, minibar, hair dryer, Wi-Fi (free).

Pension Museum ★ ✦ This is yet another example of a successful renovation of a 19th-century building in the very center of the city. Located just across from the National Museum, the Pension offers clean and comfortable rooms with modern furniture. Do not be put off by the busy road in front, however. There are actually only two rooms facing it, and their new double-glazed windows block the noise very well. The private cozy courtyard garden serves as an oasis for relaxation, which is otherwise hard to find around Václavské náměstí, the city's liveliest shopping area.

Mezibranská 15, Prague 1. www.pension-museum.cz. ☏ **296-325-186.** Fax 296-325-188. 12 units with bathroom (shower only). From 2,200Kč double; 2,700Kč suite. Rates include breakfast. AE, MC, V. Metro: Muzeum. **Amenities:** Atrium garden; Internet. *In room:* A/C, TV, fridge, hair dryer.

Side Trips from Prague
KARLŠTEJN CASTLE
29km (18 miles) SW of Prague

By far the most popular destination in the Czech Republic after Prague, **Karlštejn Castle ★★** is an easy day trip for those interested in getting out of the city. Charles IV built this medieval castle from 1348 to 1357 to safeguard the crown jewels of the Holy Roman Empire. Although the castle had been changed over the years, with such additions as late Gothic staircases and bridges, renovators have removed these additions, restoring the castle to its original medieval state.

As you approach, little can prepare you for your first view: A spectacular Disney-like castle perched on a hill, surrounded by lush forests and vineyards. In its early days, the king's jewels housed within enhanced the castle's importance and reputation. Vandalism having forced several of its finest rooms to close, these days the castle is most spectacular from the outside. Unfortunately, many of the more interesting restored rooms are kept off-limits and open only for special guests.

ESSENTIALS
GETTING THERE   Trains leave regularly from either Prague's main station (at the Hlavní nádraží metro stop on Line C) or from Smíchovské nádraží, metro Line B, and take about 40 minutes to reach Karlštejn. The one-way, second-class fare is 50Kč. It's a short, relaxing trip along the Berounka River. On the way, you pass through Řevnice, Martina Navrátilová's birthplace. Keep your eyes open for your first glimpse of the majestic castle. Once you arrive at Karlštejn train station, it's a 20- to 30-minute hike up the road to the castle. While you're at the station, mark down the return times for trains to Prague to better plan your trip back.

You can also **drive** along one of two routes, both of which take 30 minutes. Here's the more scenic one: Leave Prague from the southwest along Hwy. 4 in the direction of Strakonice and take the Karlštejn cutoff, following the signs (and traffic!). The second, much less scenic route follows the main highway leading out of Prague from the west as if you were going to Plzeň. About 20 minutes down the road is the well-marked cutoff for Karlštejn. (You can tell you have missed the cutoff if you get to the town of Beroun. If that happens, take any exit and head back the other way; the signs to Karlštejn are also marked heading toward Prague.)

VISITOR INFORMATION   The ticket/castle information booth (© **311-681-370**) can help you, as can any of the restaurants or stores. The castle website at www. hradkarlstejn.cz is easy to navigate and has lots of useful information on the castle's history as well as tours and opening hours. You can also book tour tickets online.

EXPLORING THE CASTLE
Since Karlštejn's beauty lies more in its facade and environs than in the castle itself, the 20- to 30-minute walk up the hill is, along with the view, one of the main features that makes the trip spectacular. It's an excursion well worth making if you can't get farther out of Prague to see some of the other castles. Seeing hordes of visitors coming, locals have discovered the value of fixing up the facades of their homes and opening small businesses (even if they have gone a little overboard on the number of outlets selling crystal). Restaurants have improved tremendously. When you finally do reach the top, take some time to look out over the town and down the Well Tower.

To see the interior of the castle, you can choose from one of two tours. The 50-minute **Tour 1** will take you through the **Imperial Palace, Hall of Knights,**

Chapel of St. Nicholas, Royal Bedroom, and **Audience Hall. Tour 2,** which lasts 70 minutes, offers a look at the **Holy Rood Chapel,** famous for the more than 2,000 precious and semi-precious inlaid gems adorning its walls; the **Chapel of St. Catherine,** Charles IV's own private oratory; the **Church of Our Lady;** and the **library.** Note that you need to make a reservation to visit the Holy Rood Chapel on Tour 2 (www.hradkarlstejn.cz; 𝄐 **274-008-154;** fax 274-008-152). You can buy tickets and make reservations online.

The shorter Tour 1 costs 270Kč adults, 180Kč students, 20Kč children 5 and under. Tour 2 with the Holy Rood Chapel costs 300Kč adults, 200Kč students, free for children 5 and under. The castle is open Tuesday to Sunday: May, June, and September 9am to noon and 12:30 to 5pm; July and August 9am to noon and 12:30 to 6pm; April and October 9am to noon and 1 to 4pm; November, December, and March 9am to noon and 1 to 3pm; closed January and February.

TEREZÍN (THERESIENSTADT)
48km (30 miles) NW of Prague

Noticing that northwest Bohemia was susceptible to Prussian attacks, Joseph II, the son of Austrian Empress Maria Theresa, decided to build **Terezín ★★** to ward off further offensives. Two fortresses were built, but the Prussian army bypassed the area during the last Austro-Prussian conflict and in 1866 attacked Prague anyway. That spelled the end of Terezín's fortress charter, which was repealed in 1888. More than 50 years later, the fortifications were just what occupying Nazi forces needed.

When people around the world talk of Nazi atrocities during World War II, the name Terezín (*Theresienstadt* in German) rarely comes up. At the so-called Paradise Ghetto, there were no gas chambers, no mass machine-gun executions, and no medical testing rooms. Terezín wasn't used to exterminate the Jews, Gypsies, homosexuals, and political prisoners it held. Rather, the occupying Nazi forces used it as a transit camp. About 140,000 people passed through Terezín's gates; more than half ended up at the death camps of Auschwitz and Treblinka.

Instead, Terezín will live in infamy for the cruel trick that SS chief Heinrich Himmler played on the world within its walls. On June 23, 1944, three foreign observers—two from the Red Cross—came to Terezín to find out if the rumors of Nazi atrocities were true. They left with the impression that all was well, duped by a well-planned "beautification" of the camp. The Germans carefully choreographed every detail of the visit. The observers saw children studying at staged schools that didn't exist, and store shelves, which had been specially set up, stocked with goods. So that the observers wouldn't think the camp was overcrowded, the Nazis transported some 7,500 of the camp's sick and elderly prisoners to Auschwitz. Children even ran up to an SS commandant just as the observers passed; the commandant handed the children cans of sardines to shouts of "What? Sardines again?" The trick worked so well that the Nazis made a film of the camp, *A Town Presented to the Jews from the Führer,* while it was still "self-governing."

Russian forces liberated Terezín on May 10, 1945, several days after Berlin had fallen to the Allies. Today, the camp stands as a memorial to the dead and a monument to human depravity.

ESSENTIALS
GETTING THERE   If you're **driving,** Terezín lies just off the D-8 motorway that leads north out of Prague in the direction of Dresden and Berlin. Watch for the turn-off signs. It's a 45-minute drive. There's a large public parking lot just outside the

Large Fortress area (40Kč per car), but it's a long walk to the entrance to the Ghetto Museum. With a car, it's easy to combine a trip here with Mělník (see above), which lies pretty much in the same direction.

Several **buses** leave daily during the week from the small bus station above the **Nádraží Holešovice metro stop** (Line C, red). On weekends, this slows down to just a few, so best to plan accordingly. The ride takes about an hour and costs 80Kč.

VISITOR INFORMATION The Museum of the Ghetto has a gift shop that stocks maps and reading material in several languages. Before heading out, you can read up on the area at the well-organized website www.pamatnik-terezin.cz.

ORGANIZED TOURS Nearly all the major touring companies offer a guided tour of Terezín (see "Organized Day Tours," above). **Wittmann Tours,** Novotného lávka 5, Prague 1 (www.wittmann-tours.com; ✆ **222-252-472**), specializes in Jewish heritage trips and has dedicated tours both to Terezín and combined trips to Terezín and Lidice (see below).

SEEING THE CAMP

Terezín is a little hard to grasp at first. There are two main areas: The **Large Fortress** is essentially the town itself, the rectilinear streets laid out according to the best 18th-century military technology. Here was where the majority of ghetto residents lived during the Nazi occupation and the drab houses look remarkably little changed from how they must have looked then. Start your exploration here at the **Museum of the Ghetto** *(Muzeum Ghetta),* which is headquartered in what was once the ghetto's school. The exhibits here chronicle the rise of Nazism and daily life in the camp. Another focal point in the Large Fortress is the **Magdeburg Barracks,** which was formally the seat of the Jewish Council. Today, the barracks holds a replica of a ghetto dormitory to give a feel of how the people lived.

A 10-minute walk from the Large Fortress over the Ohře River brings you to the second main site, the **Small Fortress,** a smaller, more heavily fortified area that the Nazis used as a prison and torture zone for political prisoners. As you enter the main gate, the sign above, ARBEIT MACHT FREI (Work Sets One Free), sets a gloomy tone. You are free to walk through the prison barracks, execution grounds, workshops, and isolation cells. In front of the fortress's main entrance is the **National Cemetery (Národní hřbitov),** where the bodies exhumed from the mass graves were buried.

A combined admission allows entry to the Museum of the Ghetto, Magdeburg Barracks, and Small Fortress, and costs 200Kč for adults and 150Kč for children. Alternatively, you can buy separate admissions to the Ghetto Museum and Small Fortress for 160Kč adults and 130Kč children. The museum complex is open daily: November to March from 9am to 5:30pm and April to October from 9am to 6pm. For more information or reservations for guided tours, call ✆ **416-782-225** (www.pamatnik-terezin.cz).

WEST BOHEMIA & THE SPAS

Of the two regions that make up the Czech Republic, the better known is the westernmost one, Bohemia. It is the land that gave Europe its favorite catchall term for free spirit: "Bohemian."

Home to the country's spa towns, Western Bohemia is one of the few places where a full-blown tourist infrastructure was already in place by the time of the Velvet Revolution in 1989. Its main towns—**Karlovy Vary (Carlsbad), Mariánské Lázně**

(Marienbad), and **Plzeň**—offer a wide array of accommodations, restaurants, and services to meet every visitor's needs and means.

A relatively inexpensive network of trains and buses covers the region, allowing travel between towns and to and from Prague with a minimum of fuss. Regular trains and buses link Prague to the main industrial city in the region, Plzeň, while buses ply the route to Karlovy Vary hourly from Prague's Florenc bus station. Western Bohemia is generally rougher terrain, so only serious bikers should consider seeing the area on two wheels.

Karlovy Vary (Carlsbad) ★

The discovery of Karlovy Vary (Carlsbad) by Charles IV reads like a 14th-century episode of the old hit TV show *The Beverly Hillbillies.* According to local lore, the king was out huntin' for some food when up from the ground came a-bubblin' *water* (though discovered by his dogs and not an errant gunshot). Knowing a good thing when he saw it, Charles immediately set to work building a small castle in the area, naming the town that evolved around it Karlovy Vary, which translates as "Charles's Boiling Place." The first spa buildings were built in 1522, and before long, notables like Albrecht of Wallenstein, Peter the Great, and later Bach, Beethoven, Freud, and even Karl Marx all came to Karlovy Vary for a holiday retreat.

After World War II, Eastern Bloc travelers (following in the footsteps of Marx, no doubt) discovered the town, and Karlovy Vary became a destination for the proletariat. On doctors' orders, most workers would enjoy regular stays of 2 or 3 weeks, letting the mineral waters ranging from 110°F (43°C) to 162°F (72°C) from the town's 12 springs heal their tired and broken bodies. Even now, a large number of spa guests are here on doctors' orders and many of the "resorts" you see, in fact, are upscale hospitals.

Most of the 40-plus years of Communist neglect have been erased as a barrage of renovations continues to restore the spa's former glory. Gone is the statue of Russian cosmonaut Yuri Gagarin. Gone are almost all the fading, crumbling building facades that used to line both sides of the river. In their places stand restored buildings, cherubs, caryatids, and more.

Today, some 150,000 people, both traditional clientele and newer patrons, travel to the spa resort every year to sip, bathe, and frolic, though most enjoy the "13th spring" (actually a hearty herb-and-mineral liqueur called Becherovka) as much as— if not more than—the 12 nonalcoholic versions. Czechs will tell you that all have medical benefits. In a historical irony, the Russians have rediscovered Karlovy Vary in droves, so don't be surprised to hear Russian on the streets much more frequently than English, German, or Czech.

ESSENTIALS

GETTING THERE   Karlovy Vary is one of those destinations that it makes much more sense to take the bus than the **train** from Prague. The train travels a comically circuitous route and can take longer than 4 hours. The train is a more feasible option if you happen to be arriving from Mariánské Lázně or Cheb. Trains from Cheb, for example, depart hourly during the day and take around an hour. The fare is 72Kč second-class.

Note that Karlovy Vary has two train stations. Trains from Prague and most other points arrive at Horní nádraží (upper station), while trains from Mariánské Lázně and a few other small towns (as well as all buses) arrive at Dolní nádraží (lower station). This latter station has better services and houses a branch of the local tourist information office. Horní nádraží is connected to the main spa area and town center by bus no. 12 or 13. Dolní nádraží is a 10-minute walk from the spa area or take local bus no. 4.

Traveling to Karlovy Vary by **bus** from Prague is much more convenient. Frequent express buses travel from Prague's Florenc bus station in around 2 hours at a cost of about 150Kč. One of the best bus lines offering the trip is **Student Agency** (www. studentagency.cz; ℂ **841-101-101**), which runs hourly buses to Karlovy Vary from Florenc bus station, and even shows a film during the trip. For information on train and bus timetables, go to www.jizdnirady.cz.

The nearly 2-hour **drive** from Prague to Karlovy Vary can be very busy and dangerous due to undisciplined Czech drivers. If you're going by car, take Hwy. E48 from the western end of Prague and follow it straight through to Karlovy Vary. This two-lane highway widens in a few spots to let cars pass slow-moving vehicles on hills. The spa area is closed to private vehicles, so you'll have to leave the car in one of several parking lots surrounding the area or use paid street parking (40Kč/hr.).

VISITOR INFORMATION   Confusingly, Karlovy Vary is one of those towns that changes the location of its tourist information office, the **Infocentrum města Karlovy Vary** (www.karlovyvary.cz), every couple of years or so. Currently, the city has three tourist offices, with branches at the Hotel Thermal, I. P. Pavlova 11 (ℂ **355-321-171**), the Vřídelní Kolonáda along the main spa promenade (ℂ **773-291-243**), and the Dolní nádraží bus and train station, Západní ul. 2a (ℂ **353-232-838**). All of the offices are open Monday to Friday from 9am to 5pm and Saturday and Sunday from 10am to 5pm, including an hour break for lunch. These offices can be real life savers and can hand out maps, advise on rooms, and help you plan a day of sightseeing or a spa treatment.

EXPLORING KARLOVY VARY

The town's slow pace and pedestrian promenades, lined with turn-of-the-20th-century Art Nouveau buildings, turn strolling into an art form. Night-time walks take on an even more mystical feel as the sewers, the river, and the many major cracks in the roads emit steam from the hot springs running underneath.

Avoid Karlovy Vary's "New Town," which happens to be conveniently left off most tourist maps. Its only real attractions are a McDonald's and a couple of ATMs (which you can also find in the historic center).

If you're traveling here by train or bus, a good place to start your exploration is the **Hotel Thermal,** I. P. Pavlova 11 (ℂ **359-001-111**), at the northern end of the Old Town's center. Built in the 1970s, it exemplifies how obtrusive Communist architecture could be. Nestled between the town's eastern hills and the Ohře River, the glass, steel, and concrete Thermal sticks out like a sore thumb amid the rest of the town's 19th-century architecture. Nonetheless, you'll find three important places at the Thermal: the only centrally located outdoor public pool; an upper terrace boasting a truly spectacular view of the town; and Karlovy Vary's largest theater, which holds many of the film festival's premier events. Take it all in. But since the Hotel Thermal is not that pleasing to the eye, it's best to keep walking so you won't remember too much of it.

As you enter the heart of the town on the river's west side, you'll see the ornate white wrought-iron gazebo named **Sadová Kolonáda** adorning the beautifully manicured park, **Dvořákovy Sady.** Continue to follow the river, and about 100m (328 ft.) later you'll encounter the **Mlýnská Kolonáda ★**. This long, covered walkway houses

West Bohemia & the Spas

THE CZECH REPUBLIC

several Karlovy Vary springs, which you can sample free 24 hours a day. Each spring has a plaque beside it describing its mineral elements and temperature. Bring your own cup or buy one just about anywhere (see the box "Spa Cures & Treatments," below) to sip the waters, since most are too hot to drink from with your hands. When you hit the river bend, you'll see the majestic **Church of St. Mary Magdalene** perched atop a hill, overlooking the **Vřídlo,** the hottest spring. Built in 1736, the church is the work of Kilián Ignác Dientzenhofer, who also created two of Prague's more notable churches—both named St. Nicholas.

Housing Vřídlo, which blasts water some 15m (49 ft.) into the air, is the glass building where a statue of Soviet cosmonaut Yuri Gagarin once stood. (Gagarin's statue has since made a safe landing at the Karlovy Vary Airport, where it greets the waves of Russian visitors who flood the town.) Now called the **Vřídelní Kolonáda ★**, the structure, built in 1974, houses several hot springs that you can sample for free daily from 6am to 7pm. There are also public restrooms, open daily 6am to 6pm and costing 10Kč.

Heading away from the Vřídelní Kolonáda are Stará and Nová Louka streets, which line either side of the river. Along **Stará (Old) Louka** are several fine cafes and glass and crystal shops. **Nová (New) Louka** is lined with many hotels and the historic town's main theater, built in 1886, which houses paintings by notable artists like Klimt and has just finished a major renovation project that has restored the theater to its original splendor.

Both streets lead eventually to the **Grandhotel Pupp ★**, Mírové nám. 2 (**© 353-109-111**). The Pupp's main entrance and building underwent extensive renovations several years ago that more or less erased the effects of 40 years of state ownership under Communism (under the former regime, the hotel's name was actually "Moskva-Pupp," just to remind everyone who was actually calling the shots). Regardless of Capitalism or Communism, the Pupp remains what it always was: the grande dame of hotels in central Europe. Once catering to nobility from all over Europe, the Pupp still houses one of the town's finest restaurants, the Grand (see below), while its grounds are a favorite with the hiking crowd.

If you still have the energy, atop the hill behind the Pupp stands the **Diana Lookout Tower ★** (**© 353-222-872**). Footpaths lead to the tower through the forests and eventually spit you out at the base of the tower, as if to say, "Ha, the trip is only half over." The five-story climb up the tower tests your stamina, but the view of the town is more than worth it. For those who aren't up to the climb up the hill, a cable car runs up the hill every 15 minutes June to September daily from 9:15am to 6:45pm; February, March, November, and December 9:15am to 4:45pm; April, May, and October 9:15am to 5:45pm; for 40Kč one-way, 70Kč round-trip.

And if you have some time left at the end of your stay, visit the **Jan Becher Museum,** T. G. Masaryka 57 (www.becherovka.cz; **© 359-578-142**), to find out about the history of the town's secret: the formula for Becherovka. This herbal liquor is a sought-after souvenir, and you will get to taste it here. The museum is open daily 9am to 5pm; admission is 100Kč adults, 50Kč students.

WHERE TO EAT

Embassy Restaurant ★★ CZECH/CONTINENTAL Located within the Embassy Hotel, this is one of the oldest and best restaurants in town. It offers an intimate dining room with historic interior. If you visit in winter, get a table next to the original hearth. In summer, sit on the bridge outside the front door. Here you'll find many traditional Czech dishes with slight twists that make them interesting. The grilled loin of pork covered with a light, creamy green-pepper sauce makes a nice change from the regular roast pork served by most Czech restaurants.

Nová Louka 21. © **353-221-161.** Reservations recommended. Main courses 220Kč–600Kč. AE, MC, V. Daily 11am–11pm.

Grand Restaurant CONTINENTAL   It's no surprise that the Grandhotel Pupp has the nicest dining room in town: an elegant space with tall ceilings, huge mirrors, and glistening chandeliers. A large menu features equally large portions of salmon, chicken, veal, pork, turkey, and beef in a variety of heavy and heavier sauces. Even the mouthwatering trout with mushrooms is smothered in butter sauce.

In the Grandhotel Pupp, Mírové nám. 2. © **353-109-646.** Reservations recommended. Main courses 290Kč–750Kč. AE, MC, V. Daily noon–3pm and 6–11pm.

Hospoda U Švejka CZECH   This addition to the pub scene plays on the tried-and-true touristy *Good Soldier Švejk* theme. Luckily, the tourist trap goes no further and, once inside, you find a refreshingly nonsmoky though thoroughly Czech atmosphere. Locals and tourists alike rub elbows while throwing back some fine lager for 69Kč per half liter, and standard pub favorites such as goulash and beef tenderloin in cream sauce.

Stará Louka 10. © **353-232-276.** Main courses 159Kč–319Kč. AE, MC, V. Daily 11am–10pm.

Promenáda ★ CZECH/CONTINENTAL   This cozy, intimate spot may not be as elegant as the Grand Restaurant, but the cooking is more adventurous. Across from the Vřídelní Kolonáda, the Promenáda offers a wide menu with generous portions. The daily menu usually includes well-prepared wild game, but the mixed grill for two and the chateaubriand, both flambéed at the table, are the chef's best dishes. An order of crêpes suzette, big enough to satisfy two, tops off a wonderful meal.

Tržiště 31. © **353-225-648.** Reservations recommended. Main courses 290Kč–750Kč. AE, MC, V. Daily noon–11pm.

SHOPPING

Crystal and porcelain are Karlovy Vary's other claims to fame. Dozens of shops throughout town sell everything from plates to chandeliers.

Ludvík Moser founded his first glassware shop in 1857 and became one of this country's foremost names in glass. You can visit and take a 30-minute tour of the **Moser Factory,** kapitána Jaroše 19 (www.moser-glass.com; © **353-416-112;** bus no. 1 or 22 from the bus stop Tržnice), just west of the town center. Its glass museum is open daily 9am to 5pm, and tours run daily 9am to 3pm. There's also a **Moser Store,** on Tržiště 7 (© **353-235-303**), right in the heart of New Town; it's open daily from 10am to 7pm (Sat–Sun until 6pm). Dozens of other smaller shops also sell the famed glass and are as easy to find in the Old Town as spring water.

If you're looking for something a little cheaper, try a box of *Oplatky,* thin round wafer cookies on sale throughout the spa area. The fillings range from vanilla to chocolate to nut and occasionally coffee—just don't try to wash them down with a mug of spa water!

WHERE TO STAY

Private rooms used to be the best places to stay in Karlovy Vary with regard to quality and price. But this is changing as more and more hotels renovate and raise standards—as well as prices. Private accommodations can still provide better value, but

West Bohemia & the Spas

THE CZECH REPUBLIC

SPA CURES & treatments IN KARLOVY VARY

Most visitors to Karlovy Vary come for a spa treatment, a therapy that lasts 1 to 3 weeks. After consulting with a spa physician, you're given a specific regimen of activities that may include mineral baths, massages, waxings, mud-packs, electrotherapy, and pure oxygen inhalation. After spending the morning at a spa or sanatorium, you're usually directed to walk the paths of the town's surrounding forest.

The common denominator of all the cures is an ample daily dose of hot mineral water, which bubbles up from 12 springs. This water definitely has a distinct odor and taste. You'll see people chugging it down, but it doesn't necessarily taste very good. Some thermal springs actually taste and smell like rotten eggs. You may want to take a small sip at first. Do keep in mind that the waters are used to treat internal disorders, so the minerals may cleanse the body thoroughly—in other words, they can cause diarrhea.

You'll also notice that almost everyone in town seems to be carrying "the cup." This funny-looking cup is basically a mug with a built-in straw running through the handle. Young and old alike parade around with their mugs, filling and refilling them at each thermal water tap. You can buy these mugs everywhere for as little as 80Kč or as much as 300Kč; they make a quirky souvenir. *But be warned:* None of the mugs can make the warmer hot springs taste any better.

The minimum spa treatment lasts 1 week and must be arranged in advance. A spa treatment package traditionally includes room, full board, and complete therapy regimen; the cost varies from about 900Kč to 2,500Kč per person per day, depending on season and facilities. Rates are highest from May to September and lowest from November to February. Nearly all of the hotels in town will provide spa and health treatments, so ask when you book your room. Most will happily arrange a treatment if they don't provide them directly.

If you're coming for just a day or two, you can experience the waters on an "outpatient" basis. The largest therapeutic complex in town (and in the Czech Republic) is the **Alžbětiny Lázně-Lázně V,** Smetanovy sady 1145/1 (www.spa5.cz; © **353-304-211**). On its menu are more than 60 kinds of treatments, including water cures, massages, a hot-air bath, a steam bath, a whirlpool, and a pearl bath, as well as use of their swimming pool. You can choose packages of different procedures that run from 430Kč for an anti-cellulite beer bath to 1,200Kč for a hot stone massage. It's open Monday to Friday 8am to 3pm for spa treatments; the pool is open Monday to Friday 9am to noon and 1 to 9pm, Saturday 9am to 9pm, and Sunday 9am to 6pm.

The Castle Spa (Zámecké Lázně), Zámecký vrch 1 (http://carlsbad-plaza. com; © **353-225-502**), is a relatively new (and fancy) spa and wellness house located in a reconstructed site at the foot of the Castle Tower (Zámecká věž) in the old city center. You can make reservations over the website and see a menu of treatments, including both those that require a medical exam and those that don't. The latter include massages, and various baths and aroma treatments.

they take a little extra work. If you want to arrange a room, try the **Infocentrum** (see above). Expect to pay about 1,500Kč for a double.

Some of the town's major spa hotels accommodate only those who are paying for complete treatment, unless for some reason their occupancy rates are particularly low. The hotels listed below accept guests for stays of any length.

Parking is a problem for nearly all of the hotels, aside from the bigger properties like the Grandhotel Pupp, which have their own paid parking lots. You're best advised to leave your car in one of the paid lots just outside the immediate spa area and walk (or take a taxi) to your hotel.

Grandhotel Pupp ★　　The Pupp, built in 1701, is one of Europe's oldest grand hotels. Its public areas boast the expected splendor and charm, as do the renovated guest rooms. The best ones tend to be those facing the town center and are located on the upper floors; these have good views and sturdy wooden furniture. Some rooms have amenities such as air-conditioning, television, minibar, and safe, though not all do. The Grand has as grand a dining room as you'll find, with food to match (see p. 164). The hotel also has a stylish casino (open midnight–4am). The rack rates are high, but check the website for occasional deals.

Mírové nám. 2, 360 91, Karlovy Vary. www.pupp.cz. ✆ **353-109-111.** Fax 353-226-032. 111 units. 6,000Kč double deluxe; from 9,000Kč suite. Rates include breakfast. AE, DC, MC, V. Valet parking. **Amenities:** 4 restaurants; bar; cafe; pool (indoor); golf course; tennis courts; health club; room service; casino. *In room:* TV, minibar, hair dryer, Wi-Fi.

Hotel Dvořák ★　　As part of the Vienna International hotel chain, the Dvořák has improved immensely over the past several years, especially in terms of service. This hotel is within sight of the Pupp, but it's less expensive. The Pupp may have the history and elegance, but the Dvořák has the facilities. The rooms are spacious, with elegant decor and medium-size bathrooms with lots of marble. The staff is very attentive. Business travelers will appreciate the hotel's business facilities.

Nová Louka 11, 360 21 Karlovy Vary. www.hotel-dvorak.cz. ✆ **353-102-111.** Fax 353-102-119. 126 units. 3,375Kč double. AE, DC, MC, V. Parking. **Amenities:** Restaurant; pool (indoor); exercise room; sauna. *In room:* TV, minibar, hair dryer, Wi-Fi.

Hotel Embassy ★　　On the riverbank across from the Pupp, the Embassy has well-appointed rooms, many with an early-20th-century motif. Set in a historic house, the rooms are medium size with medium-size bathrooms. The staff here really helps make this hotel worthy of consideration, as does the proximity to the pub, which serves some of the best goulash and beer in the city.

Nová Louka 21, 360 01 Karlovy Vary. www.embassy.cz. ✆ **353-221-161.** Fax 353-223-146. 20 units. 3,130Kč double; 3,990Kč suite. AE, MC, V. **Amenities:** Restaurant; bar; exercise room. *In room:* TV, minibar, Wi-Fi.

Hotel Palacký ✦　　This is one of the better deals in town. The hotel is ideally situated on the west side of the river so it gets sun almost all day. The rooms, with their mostly bare walls and low beds, seem huge, especially the ones with a river view. The staff can seem more like furniture than people who help guests, but that's a small price to pay for the relatively good value.

Stará Louka 40, 360 01 Karlovy Vary. www.hotelpalacky.cz. ✆ **353-222-544.** Fax 353-223-561. 20 units. 2,250Kč–2,730Kč double. AE, MC, V. **Amenities:** Restaurant. *In room:* TV, fridge, hair dryer.

České Budějovice

This fortress town was born in 1265, when Otakar II decided that the intersection of the Vltava and Malše rivers would be the site of a bastion to protect the approaches to southern Bohemia. Although Otakar was killed at the Battle of the Moravian Field in 1278 and the town was subsequently ravaged by the rival Vítkovic family, the construction of České Budějovice continued, eventually taking the shape originally envisaged.

Today, České Budějovice, the hometown of the original Budweiser-brand beer, is now more a bastion for the beer drinker than a protector of Bohemia. But its slow pace, relaxed atmosphere, and interesting architecture make it a worthy stop, especially as a base for exploring southern Bohemia or for those heading on to Austria.

ESSENTIALS

GETTING THERE If you're **driving,** leave Prague to the south via the main D1 expressway and take the cutoff for Hwy. E55, which runs straight to České Budějovice. The trip takes about 1½ hours.

Daily express **trains** from Prague make the trip to České Budějovice in about 2½ hours. The fare is 320Kč first-class or 213Kč second-class. Several express **buses** run from Prague's Roztyly station (on the metro's C line) each day and take 3 hours; tickets cost about 160Kč. Buy tickets from the bus driver.

VISITOR INFORMATION Tourist Infocentrum, náměstí Přemysla Otakara II. 1-2 (www.c-budejovice.cz; ✆ 386-801-413), just next to the historic town hall, provides maps and guidebooks and can help find lodgings. It is open Monday to Friday 8:30am to 6pm, Saturday until 5pm, and Sunday 10am to 4pm. In winter it is open Monday and Wednesday 9am to 5pm; Tuesday, Thursday, Friday 9am to 4pm; and Saturday 9am to 1pm. Don't be fooled by the "Infocentrum" at náměstí Přemysla Otakara II. 21. Though it looks like a full-fledged tourist information office, in reality it's a souvenir shop looking to sell maps to unsuspecting tourists.

EXPLORING ČESKÉ BUDĚJOVICE

You can comfortably see České Budějovice in a day. At its center is one of central Europe's largest squares, the cobblestone **náměstí Přemysla Otakara II**—it may actually be too large, as many of the buildings tend to get lost in all the open space. The square contains the ornate **Fountain of Sampson,** an 18th-century water well that was once the town's principal water supply, plus a mishmash of baroque and Renaissance buildings. On the southwest corner is the **Town Hall,** an elegant baroque structure built by Martinelli between 1727 and 1730. On top of the Town Hall, the larger-than-life statues by Dietrich represent the civic virtues: justice, bravery, wisdom, and diligence.

One block north of the square is the **Černá věž (Black Tower),** which you can see from almost every point in the city. Consequently, it's worth the climb to the top to get a bird's-eye view in all directions. The most famous symbol of České Budějovice, this 70m-tall (236-ft.) 16th-century tower was built as a belfry for the adjacent **St. Nicholas Church.** This 13th-century church, one of the town's most important sights, was a bastion of Roman Catholicism during the 15th-century Hussite rebellion. You shouldn't miss the church's flamboyant, white-and-cream, 17th-century baroque interior.

The tower is open Tuesday to Sunday (daily Apr–Oct) from 10am to 6pm; admission is 30Kč for adults and 20Kč for children and seniors. The church is open daily from 9am to 6pm.

TOURING A BEER SHRINE

On the town's northern edge sits a shrine to those who pray to the gods of the amber nectar. This is where **Budějovický Budvar,** Karolíny Světlé 4 (✆ 387-705-111), the original brewer of Budweiser beer, has its one and only factory. Established in 1895, Budvar draws on more than 700 years of the area's brewing tradition to produce one of the world's best beers.

One trolley bus—no. 2—stops by the brewery; this is how the brewery ensures that its workers and visitors reach the plant safely each day. You can also hop in a cab from the town square for about 150Kč.

The brewery offers 1-hour guided tours in Czech, English, and German at 2pm from Monday to Friday in season (Apr–Oct) and Tuesday to Friday at 2pm during the rest of the year. Normally, it's okay just to show up, but to be sure call ahead to the **Budvar Visitors' Center** at the brewery (http://budweiser-budvar.cz; ✆ **387-705-341**) to reserve a place. Tours cost 100Kč per person.

Once you're inside the brewery, the smell may cause flashbacks to some of the wilder frat parties you've attended. This is a traditional brew, and not much has changed at the brewery over the past hundred years or so. The room where everything moves along conveyer belts and goes from dirty old bottles to boxed cartons is fascinating.

WHERE TO STAY & EAT

Grandhotel Zvon　Traditionally regarded as České Budějovice's finest hotel. These days, most of the clients are businessmen traveling on expenses—hence room rates that are a notch above the competition. Rooms are divided into executive, business, and standard, with executive rooms boasting views out over the square and air-conditioning, among other amenities. There are several bars and restaurants on the premises and the location, right on the square, is ideal.

Náměstí Přemysla Otakara II. 28, 370 01 České Budějovice. www.hotel-zvon.cz. ✆ **381-601-601.** Fax 381-601-605. 75 units. 2,600Kč standard double, 3,400Kč business double, 4,400Kč executive double. AE, DC, MC, V. **Amenities:** Restaurant; bar; cafe. *In room:* TV, minibar, Wi-Fi.

Hotel Malý Pivovar (Small Brewery) ★　Around the corner from the Zvon, this renovated 16th-century microbrewery combines the charms of a B&B with the amenities of a modern hotel. The kind of management found here is a rarity in the Czech tourism industry: They work hard to help out. The rooms are bright and cheery, with antique-style wooden furniture and exposed wooden ceiling beams providing a farmhouse feeling in the center of town. It's definitely worth consideration if being directly on the square isn't a priority.

Ulice Karla IV. 8–10, 370 01 České Budějovice. www.malypivovar.cz. ✆ **386-360-471.** Fax 386-360-474. 29 units. 2,760Kč double; 3,200Kč suite. Rates include breakfast. AE, DC, MC, V. **Amenities:** Restaurant; bar. *In room:* TV, minibar, Wi-Fi.

Kavárna Placidus ★　CAFE　Every town should have a coffeeshop like Placidus, with its serving counter crammed with homemade pastries, cookies, and cakes, as well as sandwiches and ice cream. There are several booths to have a seat and enjoy a coffee with your cake. Placidus opens early in the morning, which can be a lifesaver if you're staying at a place that doesn't serve breakfast as part of the deal or you turn up in town before anything is open.

Na Mlýnské Stoce 11. ✆ **777-312-093.** Main courses 60Kč–120Kč. No credit cards. Mon–Sat 7:30am–9pm.

Masné Krámy ★★　CZECH　České Budějovice's fabled watering hole, named after the town's former meat market, just northwest of náměstí Přemysla Otakara II, serves up tasty Czech tavern food. It's wildly popular, so advance booking is essential if you want to eat. If you're just there for the beer, it's almost always possible to find a seat near the bar.

Krajinská 29. www.masne-kramy.cz. ✆ **387-201-301.** Main courses 120Kč–270Kč. AE, MC, V. Mon–Thurs 10:30am–11pm; Fri–Sat 10:30am–midnight; Sun 10:30am–9pm.

Český Krumlov ★★★

If you have time on your visit to the Czech Republic for only one excursion, seriously consider making it **Český Krumlov.** One of Bohemia's prettiest towns, Krumlov is a living gallery of elegant Renaissance-era buildings housing charming cafes, pubs, restaurants, shops, and galleries. In 1992, UNESCO named Český Krumlov a World Heritage Site for its historical importance and physical beauty.

Bustling since medieval times, the town, after centuries of embellishment, is exquisitely beautiful. In 1302, the Rožmberk family inherited the castle and moved in, using it as their main residence for nearly 300 years. You'll feel that time has stopped as you look from the Lazebnický Bridge and see the waters of the Vltava below snaking past the castle's gray stone. At night, by the castle lights, the view becomes even more dramatic.

Few dared change the appearance of Český Krumlov over the years, not even the Schwarzenbergs, who had a flair for opulence. At the turn of the 19th century, several facades of houses in the town's outer section were built, as were inner courtyards. Thankfully, economic stagnation in the area under Communism meant little money for "development," so no glass-and-steel edifices (the Hotel Thermal in Karlovy Vary comes to mind) jut out to spoil the architectural beauty. Instead, a medieval sense reigns supreme, now augmented by the many festivals and renovations that keep the town's spirit alive.

ESSENTIALS

GETTING THERE   From České Budějovice, it's about a 30-minute **drive** to Krumlov, depending on traffic. Take Hwy. 3 from the south of České Budějovice and turn onto Hwy. 159. The roads are clearly marked, with several signs directing traffic to the town. From Prague, it's a 3-hour drive down Hwy. 3 through Tábor. Once you reach Krumlov, bear in mind that driving in the center is strictly prohibited and if caught you face a stiff fine. Instead, stow your car in one of several numbered, pay parking lots around the city (5Kč/hr.). The best one in our opinion is **parking lot no. 2,** which takes you just to the gates of the Eggenberg brewery and about a 10-minute walk from the main square.

The only way to reach Český Krumlov **by train** from Prague is via České Budějovice, a slow ride that deposits you at a station relatively far from the town center (trip time: 3 hr., 50 min.). Several trains leave daily from Prague's Hlavní nádraží; the fare is 250Kč. If you are already in České Budějovice and you want to make a trip to Krumlov, several trains connect these two cities throughout the day. The trip takes about an hour and costs 50Kč. For timetables, go to www.jizdnirady.cz.

The nearly 3-hour **bus** ride from Prague sometimes involves a transfer in České Budějovice. The fare is 180Kč, and the bus station in Český Krumlov is a 10-minute walk from the town's main square.

VISITOR INFORMATION   Right on the main square, the **Information Centrum,** náměstí Svornosti 2, 381 01 Český Krumlov (www.ckrumlov.info; ✆ **380-704-622;** fax 380-704-619), provides a complete array of services, including booking accommodations, reserving tickets for events, and arranging travel back to Prague or onward to destinations such as Vienna, Salzburg, and Linz in Austria. There are also terminals here where you can check e-mail (5Kč for 5 min.). It's open daily June through September from 9am to 7pm; in April, May, and October from 9am to 6pm; and from November to March from 9am to 5pm.

Be warned that the municipal hall is in the same building, and it's crowded with weddings on weekends. If someone holds out a hat, throw some change into it, take a traditional shot of liquor from them, and say *"Blahopřeji!"* ("Congratulations!") to everyone in the room.

EXPLORING ČESKÝ KRUMLOV

Bring a good pair of walking shoes and be prepared to wear them out. Český Krumlov's hills and alleyways cry out for hours of exploration, but if you push the pace you can see everything in 1 day. Few cars, thank goodness, are allowed in the historic town, and the cobblestones keep most other vehicles at bay. The town is split into two parts—the **Inner Town** and **Latrán,** which houses the castle. They're best tackled separately, so you won't have to crisscross the bridges several times.

Begin your walk at the **Okresní Muzeum (Regional Museum; ✆ 380-711-674)** at the top of Horní ulice 152. Once a Jesuit seminary, the three-story museum now contains artifacts and displays relating to Český Krumlov's 1,000-year history. The highlight of this mass of folk art, clothing, furniture, and statues is a giant model of the town that offers a bird's-eye view of the buildings. Admission is 60Kč. The museum is open May to September, daily 10am to 5pm (until 6pm July–Aug); in October to December and March to April, it's open Tuesday to Friday 9am to 4pm, and Saturday and Sunday 1 to 4pm. Just to the left of the museum entrance is a small park with arguably the town's most dramatic photo backdrop (which really says something in a place as photogenic as Český Krumlov).

Across the street from the museum is the **Hotel Růže (Rose),** Horní 154 (www.hotelruze.cz; ✆ 380-772-100), which was once a Jesuit student house. Built in the late 16th century, the hotel and the prelature next to it show the development of architecture—Gothic, Renaissance, and rococo influences are all present. If you're not staying at the hotel, don't be afraid to walk around and even ask questions at the reception desk.

Continue down the street to the impressive late-Gothic **St. Vitus Cathedral.** The church is open daily from 9am to 5pm.

As you continue down the street, you'll come to **náměstí Svornosti.** Few buildings here show any character, making the main square of such an impressive town a little disappointing. The **Radnice (Town Hall),** at náměstí Svornosti 1, is one of the few exceptions. Open daily from 9am to 6pm, its Gothic arcades and Renaissance vault inside are exceptionally beautiful. From the square, streets fan out in all directions. Take some time to wander through them.

When you get closer to the river, you still can see the high-water marks on some of the quirky bank-side houses, which were devastated by the floods of 2002. Most of the places have taken the opportunity to make a fresh start after massive reconstruction. **Krumlovský Mlýn (The Krumlov Mill),** Široká 80 (www.krumlovsky mlyn.cz; ✆ 736-634-460), is a combination restaurant, gallery, antiques shop, and exhibition space. For an additional treat, stroll through the exhibition of historical motorcycles. Open daily 10am to 10pm.

One of Český Krumlov's most famous residents was Austrian-born artist Egon Schiele. He was a bit of an eccentric who on more than one occasion raised the ire of the town's residents (many found his use of young women as nude models distressing), and his stay was cut short when the locals' patience ran out. But the town readopted the artist in 1993, setting up the **Egon Schiele Art Centrum ★★** in Inner Town, Široká 70–72, 381 01, Český Krumlov (www.schieleartcentrum.cz;

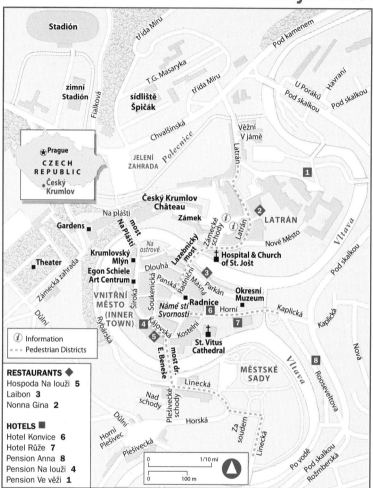

Stadión

třída Míru

zimní Stadión

Fialková

T.G. Masaryka

sídliště Špičák

třída Míru

Chvalšinská

Pod kamenem

U Poráků

Havraní

Pod skalkou

Pod skalkou

Věžní
V jámě

Prague
CZECH REPUBLIC
Český Krumlov

JELENÍ ZAHRADA

Polečnice

Latrán

1

Na plášti

Český Krumlov Château

Zámek

Zámecké schody

2 **LATRÁN**

Latrán

Nové Město

Vltava

Gardens

Na Plášti

most Na Plášti

Na ostrově

Lazebnický most

Theater

Zámecká zahrada

Krumlovský Mlýn

Egon Schiele Art Centrum

Dlouhá

Soukenická

Panská

Radniční

Masná

Parkán

Horní

✝ **Hospital & Church of St. Jošt**

3

Okresní Muzeum

Pod skalkou

Kaplická

Kaplická

VNITŘNÍ MĚSTO (INNER TOWN)

Široká

Náměstí Svornosti

Radnice

6

4

Kájovská

5

Kostelní

Rybářská

Důlní

most dr. E. Beneše

✝ **St. Vitus Cathedral**

7

Nová

Vltava

Roosveltova

(i) **Information**
▪ ▪ ▪ **Pedestrian Districts**

MĚSTSKÉ SADY

8

RESTAURANTS ◆
Hospoda Na louži **5**
Laibon **3**
Nonna Gina **2**

Linecká

Nad schody

Plešivecké schody

Horská

Za soudem

Linecká

HOTELS ▪
Hotel Konvice **6**
Hotel Růže **7**
Pension Anna **8**
Pension Na louži **4**
Pension Ve věži **1**

Důlní

Horní Plešivec

Plešivecká

Po vodě

Pod skalkou

Rožmberská

0   1/10 mi
0   100 m

4

THE CZECH REPUBLIC | West Bohemia & the Spas

(✆ **380-704-011**). It documents his life and work, housing a permanent selection of his paintings as well as exhibitions of other 20th-century artists. Admission is 120Kč; hours are daily from 10am to 6pm.

After you've seen the museum, stop in at the excellent coffeehouse next door, the **Egon Schiele Café**, Široká 71, 381 01, Český Krumlov (www.egonschielecafe.com; ✆ **725-511-219**), which specializes in "Fairtrade" coffees, exotic tea drinks, and homemade pastries. Open daily 10am to 7pm.

EXPLORING THE CHÂTEAU

Reputedly the second-largest castle in Bohemia (after Prague Castle), **Český Krum-lov Château** ★★ was constructed in the 13th century as part of a private estate.

Throughout the ages, it has been passed on to a variety of private owners, including the Rožmberk family, Bohemia's largest landholders, and the Schwarzenbergs, the Bohemian equivalent of the Hilton family. Perched high atop a rocky hill, the château is open only from April to October, exclusively by guided tours.

Follow the path for the long climb up to the **castle.** Greeting you is a round 12th-century **Castle Tower**—painstakingly renovated, with its Renaissance balcony. You'll pass over the moat, now occupied by two brown bears. Next is the **Dolní Hrad (Lower Castle)** and then the **Horní Hrad (Upper Castle).**

There are several options for seeing the sights, but be forewarned that prices have crept up in recent years, and a full viewing of the castle (including the three main guided tours) can be an expensive proposition. Family discounts (for up to three accompanying children) can help take the sting out of the prices. One budget option is to simply stroll the grounds (which are free to enter) and climb the Castle Tower (50Kč) for sweeping views out over the town and surrounding countryside. The castle grounds are also open at night, when the views down on the town are even more dramatic and the crowds thin out to a trickle.

The cash desk (*pokladna*) to book one of the three main tours is situated in the main courtyard after you've crossed the moat. Tour 1 begins in the rococo **Chapel of St. George,** and continues through the portrait-packed **Renaissance Rooms,** and the **Schwarzenberg Baroque Suite,** outfitted with ornate furnishings that include Flemish wall tapestries, European paintings, and also the extravagant 17th-century **Golden Carriage.** Tour 2 includes the **Schwarzenberg portrait gallery** as well as their 19th-century suite. Tour 3 presents the Castle's fascinating **Baroque Theater,** though at 380Kč a ticket (including English commentary), sadly, this is priced more for real theater aficionados than the general public. Tours last about 1 hour and depart frequently. Most are in Czech or German, however. If you want an English-language tour, arrange it ahead of time (www.castle.ckrumlov.cz; ⓒ **380-704-711**). The tours in English cost 250Kč adults, 160Kč students, 600Kč family (Tour 1); 240Kč adults, 140Kč students, 500Kč family (Tour 2); 380Kč adults, 220Kč students, and 780Kč family (Tour 3). The tickets are sold separately. The castle hours are from Tuesday to Sunday: June to August 8:45am to 5pm; April, May, September, and October 8:45am to 4pm. The last entrance is 1 hour before closing.

Once past the main castle building, you can see one of the more stunning views of Český Krumlov from **Most Na Plášti,** a walkway that doubles as a belvedere to the Inner Town. Even farther up the hill lie the castle's riding school and gardens.

WHERE TO EAT

Hospoda Na louži CZECH   The large wooden tables encourage you to get to know your neighbors at this Inner Town pub, located in a 15th-century house. The atmosphere is fun and the food above average. If no table is available, stand and have a drink; tables turn over pretty quickly, and the staff is accommodating. In summer, the terrace seats only six, so dash over if a seat empties. Be sure to save space for homemade fruit dumplings for dessert.

Kájovská 66. 📞 **380-711-280.** Main courses about 120Kč. No credit cards. Mon–Sat 10am–11pm; Sun 10am–10pm.

Laibon ★ VEGETARIAN   The best vegetarian option in town fuses eastern and local influences. The menu features things like couscous and spiced lentils alongside entrees like traditional bryndzové halušky (sheep's-milk cheese and gnocchi), but here without the usual bacon drippings on top.

Parkán 105. 📞 **728-676-654.** Main courses about 120Kč. No credit cards. Mon–Sat 10am–11pm; Sun 10am–10pm.

Nonna Gina ★★ ITALIAN/PIZZA   Hands down the best pizza in Český Krumlov and arguably the best in all of Southern Bohemia. The Italian owners have gone out of their way to recreate an authentic Italian dining experience at prices that represent excellent value for money. Our favorite is pizza "parmigiano-funghi," fresh mushrooms with shavings of parmesan cheese on top. There's also a full range of pastas and Italian wines.

Klášterní 52. 📞 **380-717-187.** Pizzas about 140Kč. No credit cards. Daily 11am–11pm.

WHERE TO STAY

There are tons of hotels in Český Krumlov and you'll rarely have a problem getting a room, but summer weekends and festival periods can still get tight, so it's always best to book in advance. In addition to the hotels, hundreds of property owners have opened up pensions, and the best of these can rival the hotels for comfort and location—at around half the price. Look for PENSION or ZIMMER FREI signs outside houses. Two of the best streets for seeking out pensions are tiny Parkán lane in the center and Rooseveltova, which extends out beyond Horní ul., to the south and east of the main square. For a comprehensive list of area hotels and help with bookings, call or write to the Information Centrum listed above in "Visitor Information."

Hotel Konvice ★★   The Konvice wins perennial—justifiable—rave reviews for coziness, cleanliness, and location, just a block from the main square. The large suite, room no. 11, has two separate bedrooms and a castle view from the terrace, and is excellent value for money for families. There's a very good restaurant on the premises. Book well in advance as this place gets booked up in peak season.

Horní ul. 144. 381 01 Český Krumlov. www.boehmerwaldhotels.de. 📞 **380-711-611.** Fax 380-711-327. 10 units. 1,800Kč double; 3,500Kč suite with castle view. Rates include breakfast. AE, MC, V. **Amenities:** Restaurant. *In room:* TV, minibar, hair dryer, Wi-Fi.

Hotel Růže (Rose Hotel)   Once a Jesuit seminary, this stunning Italian Renaissance building has been converted into a well-appointed hotel. Comfortable in a big-city kind of way, it's packed with amenities and is one of the top places to stay in Český Krumlov (though prices have risen considerably in recent years and it's not clear it's still really worth this much money). For families or large groups, the larger suites (while still *very* expensive for what you get) have eight beds and at least provide better value.

Horní 154, 381 01 Český Krumlov. www.hotelruze.cz. 📞 **380-772-100.** Fax 380-713-146. 70 units. 5,300Kč double; 6,900Kč suite. Rates include breakfast. AE, MC, V. **Amenities:** Restaurant; bar; pool (indoor); health club & spa; room service. *In room:* TV, minibar, hair dryer, Wi-Fi.

Pension Anna ★ ☺ Along "pension alley," this is a comfortable and rustic place. What makes the pension a favorite are the friendly management and homey feeling you get as you walk up to your room. Forget hotels—this is the kind of place where you can relax. The suites, with four beds and a living room, are great for families and groups. Good homemade breakfast and onsite parking available.

Rooseveltova 41, 381 01 Český Krumlov. www.pensionanna-ck.cz. ℂ/fax 380-711-692. 8 units. 1,250Kč double; 1,550Kč suite. Rates include breakfast. No credit cards. **Amenities:** Bar. *In room:* TV.

Pension Na louži ★ Smack-dab in the heart of the Inner Town, the small Na louži, decorated with early-20th-century wooden furniture, is a charming change from many of the bigger, bland rooms found in nearby hotels. The only drawback is that the beds (maybe the people for whom the rooms were named were all short) can be a little on the short side.

Kájovská 66, 381 01 Český Krumlov. www.nalouzi.cz. ℂ/fax **380-711-280.** 7 units. 1,350Kč double; 2,200Kč triple; 2,400Kč suite. No credit cards. **Amenities:** Restaurant; bar.

Pension Ve věži (In the Tower) ★ 🎁 A private pension in a renovated medieval tower just a 5-minute walk from the castle, Ve Věži is one of the most magnificent places to stay in town. It's not the accommodations themselves that are so grand; none has a bathroom and all are decorated sparsely. What's wonderful is the ancient ambience. Reservations are recommended.

Pivovarská 28, 381 01 Český Krumlov. www.pensionvevezi.cz. ℂ **721-523-030.** 4 units (all with shared bathroom). 1,300Kč double. Rates include breakfast. No credit cards.

DENMARK

by Christian Martinez

I n this chapter, we focus on Copenhagen, Denmark's capital, adding a few tantalizing day trips. Copenhagen got its name from
the word københavn, meaning "merchants' harbor." This city
grew in size and importance because of its position on the Øresund
between Denmark and Sweden, guarding the entrance to the Baltic. From
its humble beginnings in the 12th century, Copenhagen has become the
largest city in Scandinavia, home to 1.7 million people. It retains a historical skyline, lots of green patches, a vibrant music and art scene—and an
infinite number of bike lanes.

If you'd like to tie in a visit to Copenhagen with the château country of
Sweden, it's as easy as crossing a bridge: In 2000, Denmark was linked to
Sweden by the 16km (10-mile) Øresund Bridge. The two cities of Copenhagen and Malmö, Sweden, are the hubs of the Øresund Region, northern Europe's largest domestic market, larger than Stockholm and equal in
size to Berlin, Hamburg, and Amsterdam. The bridge is the longest combined rail-and-road bridge in the world.

5

COPENHAGEN

Copenhagen is a city with much charm, as reflected in its canals, narrow
streets, and old houses. Its most famous resident was the writer Hans
Christian Andersen, whose memory still lives on here. Another of Copenhagen's world-renowned inhabitants was Søren Kierkegaard, who used to
take long morning strolls in the city, planning his next essay; his completed writings eventually earned him the title "father of existentialism."

But few modern Copenhageners are reading Kierkegaard today, and
neither are they as melancholy as Hamlet. Most of them are out having
too much fun. Copenhagen epitomizes the Nordic *joie de vivre,* and the
city is filled with a lively atmosphere, good times (none better than at the
Tivoli Gardens), the occasional sex show, countless outdoor cafes, and
all-night dance clubs. Of course, if you come in winter, the fierce realities
of living above the 55th parallel set in. That's when Copenhageners retreat
inside trendy cafes, cocktail bars, jazz clubs, and beer taverns.

Modern Copenhagen still retains some of the characteristics of a village. If you forget the suburbs, you can cover most of the central belt on
foot, which makes it a great tourist spot. It's almost as if the city were
designed for pedestrians, as reflected by its Strøget (strolling street),
Europe's longest and oldest walking street.

Essentials

GETTING THERE

BY PLANE **SAS** (www.flysas.com; ℂ **800/221-2350**) and **United Airlines** (www.united.com; ℂ **800-864-8331**) are the major carriers to Copenhagen. **Finnair** (www.finnair.com; ℂ **800/950-5000**) offers flights through Helsinki from New York and Miami. **Icelandair** (www.icelandair.com; ℂ **800/223-5500**) has service through Reykjavik from several North American cities.

You arrive at **Kastrup Airport** (www.cph.dk; ℂ **45/3231-3231**), 10km (7½ miles) from the center of Copenhagen. Air-rail trains link the airport with Copenhagen's Central Railway Station, in the center of the hotel zone, and the whole journey takes a mere 11 minutes and costs 36DKK. The Air Rail Terminal is underneath the airport's arrivals at Terminal 3 and departure halls, just a short escalator ride from the gates. You can also take the Metro to Kongens Nytorv in the heart of the old city center. This takes just 13 minutes and costs 36DKK. The Metro also departs from Terminal 3, but unlike the train, the Metro does not have a stop at the Central Railroad Station. Furthermore, there's an SAS bus to the city terminal; the fare is 36DKK. A taxi to the city center costs around 200DKK. Yet another option is a local bus, no. 250S, which leaves from the international arrivals terminal every 15 or 20 minutes for Town Hall Square in central Copenhagen and costs 36DKK.

BY TRAIN Trains from the continent arrive at Københavns **Hovedbanegård (Central Railroad Station),** in the very center of Copenhagen, near the Tivoli and the Rådhuspladsen. For **rail information,** call ℂ **70-13-14-15.** The station operates a luggage-checking service, but room bookings are available only at the tourist office (see "Visitor Information," below). You can also exchange money at the **Forex** branch on-site (near exit facing Tivoli), ℂ **33-11-22-20,** open daily from 8am to 9pm.

From the Central Railroad Station, you can connect with **S-tog,** the commuter rail link to the suburbs, with departures from platforms in the terminus itself. To find out which train you should board to reach your destination, inquire at the information desk near tracks 9 and 12.

BY CAR If you're driving from Germany, a car-ferry will take you from Travemünde to Gedser in southern Denmark. From Gedser, get on E-55 north, an express highway that will deliver you to the southern outskirts of Copenhagen. If you're coming from Sweden and crossing at Helsingborg, you'll land on the Danish side at Helsingør. Take express highway E-55 south to the northern outskirts of Copenhagen. If you're coming from Malmö, Sweden, you can cross on the Øresund Bridge; a single trip over the toll bridge costs 310DKK.

VISITOR INFORMATION

TOURIST OFFICE **Copenhagen Visitor Center,** Vesterbrogade 4A-DK-1620 (www.visitcopenhagen.dk; ℂ **70-22-24-42**), is open September to April, Monday to Friday 9am to 4pm, Saturday 9am to 2pm; May and June, Monday to Saturday 9am to 8pm, Sunday 10am to 2pm; July and August, Monday to Saturday 9am to 8pm, Sunday 10am to 6pm.

CITY LAYOUT

The heart of **Old Copenhagen** is a maze of pedestrian streets, formed by Nørreport Station to the north, Town Hall Square (Rådhuspladsen) to the west, Kongens Nytorv to the east, and the Inderhavnen (Inner Harbor) to the south. One continuous route,

Denmark

Strøget, the world's longest pedestrian street, goes east from Town Hall Square to Kongens Nytorv and is made up of five streets: Frederiksberggade, Nygade, Vimmelskaftet, Amagertorv, and Østergade. Strøget is lined with shops, bars, restaurants, and sidewalk cafes in summer. **Gråbrødretorv,** a beautiful cobbled square just north of Strøget, is a popular hang-out.

Fiolstræde (Violet St.), a dignified street with antique shops and book shops, cuts through the university (Latin Quarter). If you turn into Rosengaarden at the top of Fiolstræde, you'll come to **Kultorvet (Coal Sq.)** just before you reach Nørreport Station. Here you join the third main pedestrian street, **Købmagergade (Butcher St.),** which winds around and finally meets Strøget on Amagertorv.

At the end of Strøget you approach **Kongens Nytorv (King's Sq.),** the site of the Royal Theater and Magasin, the largest department store. This will put you at the beginning of **Nyhavn,** the former seamen's quarter that has been gentrified into an upmarket area of expensive restaurants, apartments, cafes, and boutiques. The government of Denmark is centered on the small island of **Slotsholmen,** connected to the center by eight bridges. Several museums, notably Christiansborg Castle, are found here.

The center of Copenhagen is **Rådhuspladsen (Town Hall Sq.).** From here it's a short walk to the Tivoli Gardens, and to the Central Railroad Station, the main

Copenhagen

5

DENMARK | Copenhagen

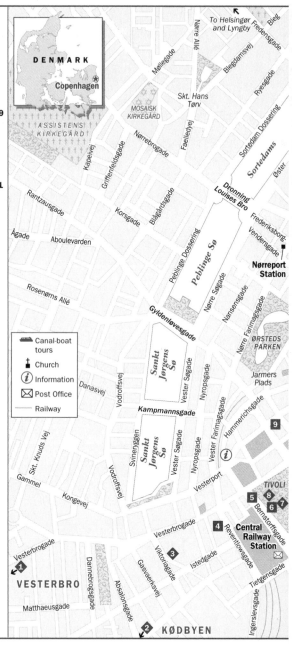

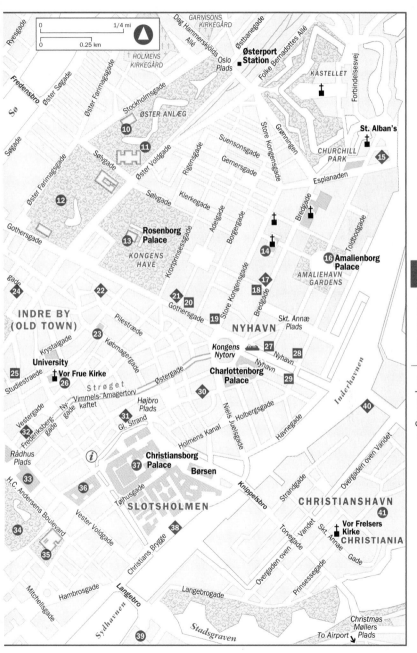

railroad and subway terminus. The wide boulevard, **Vesterbrogade,** passes by Tivoli until it reaches the Central Railroad Station. Another major thoroughfare, **H. C. Andersens Boulevard,** is named after Denmark's most famous writer and runs along Rådhuspladsen and the Tivoli Gardens. It passes by the Glyptotek Museum and leads straight to the Copenhagen Harbor Baths.

Outside the old city center are the **inner bridge areas,** developed after the medieval city walls were torn down in 1854. They are **Østerbro** , **Vesterbro**, **Nørrebro**, **Amagerbro** and **Islands Brygge**. **Vesterbro** and **Nørrebro** offer a great selection of restaurants, cafes, and shops. **Kødbyen,** the former meat-packing district and an increasingly popular scene for gourmet lovers and party-goers, is in Vesterbro and within easy walking distance from the Central Railroad Station.

Copenhagen lies in the northeastern part of the island of Zealand. In spite of Copenhagen, most of North Zealand is rather rural and enjoys many associations with Danish royalty. It is, in fact, the site of Helsingør (*Elsinore,* Hamlet's castle) and many seashores, lakes, fishing villages, and woodlands.

GETTING AROUND

A joint zone-fare system includes Copenhagen Transport buses and State Railway and S-tog trains in Copenhagen and North Zealand, plus some private rail routes within a 40km (25-mile) radius of the capital, enabling you to transfer from train to bus and vice versa with the same ticket.

A *grundbillet* (basic ticket) for both buses and trains costs 24DKK and covers two zones (see maps of train stations and bus stops to determine how many zones you'll be traveling in). You can also buy a **klippekort** (a punch card worth 10 rides). For most inner-city commutes a two-zone klippekort is sufficient; it costs 145DKK. (**Note:** To and from the city center to the airport is three zones). Children 15 and under ride for half fare; those 11 and under travel free on local trains if accompanied by an adult. A child with a children's pass is allowed to bring another child age 11 and under along for free. Furthermore, an adult is allowed to bring along two children aged 11 and under for free. You can purchase a ticket allowing 24-hour bus and train travel through nearly half of Zealand for 130DKK; children 15 and under 40DKK. The pass is also available as a 72-hour ticket, costing 190DKK for adults and 95DKK for children 15 and under.

Eurailpasses and Nordturist Pass tickets are accepted on local trains.

BY BUS   Copenhagen's well-maintained buses are the least expensive method of getting around. Most buses leave from Rådhuspladsen. A basic ticket costing 24DKK

Traveling for Less

The **Copenhagen Card** entitles you to free and unlimited travel by bus and rail throughout the metropolitan area (including North Zealand), 25% to 50% discounts on crossings to and from Sweden, and free admission to more than 70 sights and museums. The card is available for 1, 3, or 5 days. The 24-hour card costs 249DKK adults, 119DKK children between 10 and 15 years old; the 72-hour card, 479DKK adults, 239DKK children; the 120-hour card 699DKK adults, 349DKK children. For more information, contact the Copenhagen Tourist Information Center (see above) or www.visitcopenhagen.com.

allows 1 hour of travel and unlimited transfers within two zones. For information, call ☎ **36-13-14-15.**

BY S-TOG (SUBWAY)   The S-tog connects heartland Copenhagen with its suburbs. Use of the tickets is the same as on buses (above). You can transfer from a bus line to an S-train on the same ticket. Eurailpass holders generally ride free. For more information, call ☎ **70-13-14-15** anytime.

BY METRO   Copenhagen's Metro consists of two lines, M1 and M2. Two additional lines are scheduled to complete the City Circle Line by 2018. Operating round-the-clock daily, the Metro runs as far west as Vanløse and as far south as Vestamager. Nørreport is the transfer station to the S-tog system, the commuter rail link to the suburbs. Metro trains run every 2 minutes during rush hours and every 15 minutes at night. Fares are integrated into the existing zone system (see "By Bus," above). For information, check www.m.dk or call ☎ **70-15-16-15** (Mon–Fri 8am–4pm).

BY CAR   Copenhagen is an easy city to drive in compared to other European capitals. There are three parking zones in the city, divided into red, green, and blue sections. They cover the city center and the inner bridge areas, known as "brokvarterer" in Danish. They are Østerbro, Vesterbro, Nørrebro, Amagerbro and Islands Brygge. The closer you get to the city center, the more expensive it gets. In the parking zones, you have to pay for your parking from Monday 8am to Saturday 5pm. Parking is free between the two intervals. Cheapest is the blue zone (10DKK per hour), next is the green zone (17DKK per hour), and last is the red zone (29DKK per hour). In all three zones, prices are 10DKK per hour between 6pm and 11pm and 3DKK per hour between 11pm and 8am. There are also big car parks to choose from. Signs at the major roads lead into major multistorey car parks in Copenhagen. Costs tend to be about 35DKK to 40DKK per hour or 425DKK per 24 hours. One of the most central parking lots is P-huset Gammel Mønt, Gammel Mønt 1–3 (☎ **41-99-75-00**), open Monday through Saturday 6am to 9pm.

BY TAXI   Watch for the FRI (free) sign or green light to hail a taxi. Be sure the taxis are metered. **4x35** (☎ **35-35-35-35**) operates one of the most central taxi companies. *Note:* Tips are included in the meter price: 24DKK at the drop of the flag and 13.80DKK per kilometer thereafter, Monday to Friday from 7am to 4pm. From 4pm to 7am, the fare is 14.80DKK. On Friday, Saturday, and Sunday between 11pm and 7am, the cost is 17.40DKK per kilometer. Basic drop-of-the-flag costs 40DKK Friday to Sunday between 11pm and 7am. Booking via an operator Monday to Friday costs 37DKK, Friday to Sunday between 11pm and 7am this service costs 50DKK. Many drivers speak English.

BY BICYCLE   To reduce pollution from cars, and because it's a fast, easy, and cheap means of transportation, Copenhageners ride bicycles. For 75DKK to 200DKK (plus a 300DKK to 500DKK deposit depending on the model of your choosing), you can rent a bike for a full day at **Københavns Cyklebørs,** Gothersgade 157 (www.cykelborsen.dk; ☎ **33-14-07-17**). Hours are Monday to Friday 8:30am–5:30pm, Saturday 10am–1:30pm, and Sunday by appointment.

[FastFACTS] COPENHAGEN

Business Hours Most **banks** are open from Monday to Friday 10am to 4pm (Thurs to 6pm). **Stores** are generally open Monday to Thursday 9am to 6pm, Friday 9am to 7 or 8pm, and Saturday 9am to 3pm; most are closed Sunday.

Currency The Danish currency is the **krone (crown)**, or DKK, made up of 100 øre.

Currency Exchange Banks are generally your best bet to exchange currency. When banks are closed, you can exchange money at **Forex** (☎ 33-11-22-20; S-tog: Central Station) in the Central Railroad Station, open daily from 8am to 9pm.

Dentists & Doctors For emergency dental treatment, go to **Tandlægevagten,** Oslo Plads 14 (☎ 35-38-02-51), near Østerport Station and the U.S. Embassy. It's open Monday to Friday 8 to 9:30pm and Saturday, Sunday, and holidays 10am to noon and 8–9.30pm. Payment in cash. To reach a doctor, dial ☎ **1813,** a 24-hour emergency number. The doctor's fee is payable in cash. Virtually every doctor speaks English.

Embassies All embassies are in Copenhagen. The embassy of the **United States** is at Dag Hammärskjölds Allé 24, DK-2100 København 0 (denmark. usembassy.gov; ☎ **33-41-71-00**). Other embassies are the **United Kingdom,** Kastelsvej 36–40, DK-2100 København (ukindenmark.fco.gov.uk; ☎ **35-44-52-00**); **Canada,** Kristen Berniskowsgade 1, DK-1105 København (denmark.gc.ca; ☎ **33-48-32-00**); **Australia,** Dampfærgevej 26, DK-2100 København (www. denmark.embassy.gov.au; ☎ **70-26-36-76**); and

Ireland, Østbanegade 21, DK-2100 København (www. embassyofireland.dk; ☎ **35-47-32-00**).

Emergencies Dial ☎ **112** for the fire department, the police, or an ambulance, or to report a sea or air accident.

Internet Access Cafes and hotels with Wi-Fi can be found throughout the city. Just outside Copenhagen Central Station is **TeleStation** Mobilecommunications, Banegårdspladsen 1, 1. Floor (☎ **33-93-00-02**). Copenhagen Airport also offers free Wi-Fi.

Pharmacies An *apotek* open 24 hours a day in central Copenhagen is **Steno Apotek,** Vesterbrogade 6C (☎ **33-14-82-66;** bus: 6).

Post Office For information about the Copenhagen post office, call ☎ **80-20-70-30.** The post office at the Central Railroad Station (Københavns Hovedbanegård) is open Monday to Friday 8am to 9pm, Saturday and Sunday 10am to 4pm.

Taxes If you are resident outside the E.U., you are entitled to a refund of the Danish VAT ("moms" in Danish) on goods you have purchased in Denmark. It is a condition that the goods are transported to a location outside the E.U. before the end of the third month after the month of delivery. You must take the goods with you on departure, or send them to a country outside the E.U. The purchase price

must be more than 300DKK, including VAT, for you to be entitled to a refund. Ask for a tax-free form in the shop. If you carry goods in your personal luggage on leaving the E.U., you must contact the last customs authority in the E.U. country from which you departed. If you have bought the goods in a shop in Denmark, but then sent the goods yourself, e.g. by post, rail, or carrier, you must make sure you get an import certificate from the customs authority in your own country. If you have a tax-free form from the shop, you can receive your refund at Copenhagen's Airport when you depart from the E.U. If you go by land or sea, or if you send the goods, you can mail your custom-stamped receipt and tax-free form to Customer Services and claim your refund. Learn more on www.global-blue.com.

Telephone The country code for Denmark is **45.** It should precede any call made to Denmark from another country.

Danish phones are fully automatic. Dial the eight-digit number; there are no city area codes. At public telephone booths, don't insert any coins until your party answers. Use two 50-øre coins or a 1-krone or 5-krone coin only. You can make more than one call on the same payment if your time hasn't run out. Remember that calling direct from your hotel room can be expensive. Emergency calls are free.

DENMARK | Fast Facts: Copenhagen

Tipping Tips are seldom expected. Service is built into the system, and hotels, restaurants, and even taxis include a 15% service charge in their rates. Because of the service charge, plus the 25% *moms*, you'll probably have to pay an additional 40% for some services. However, it is normal to leave a 10% tip in restaurants (mainly in the evening) if the service has been good.

Exploring Copenhagen
NEAR RÅDHUSPLADSEN (TOWN HALL SQUARE)

Ny Carlsberg Glyptotek ★★★ 🎒 MUSEUM   The Glyptotek, behind the Tivoli, is one of Scandinavia's most important art museums. Founded by 19th-century art collector Carl Jacobsen, the museum holds modern art and antiquities. The modern section has both French and Danish works, mainly from the 19th century; sculpture, including works by Rodin; and works of the Impressionists and related artists, including van Gogh's *Landscape from St-Rémy*. Antiquities include Egyptian, Greek, Roman, and Etruscan artifacts. The Egyptian collection is outstanding; the prize is a prehistoric rendering of a hippopotamus. In 1996, the Ny Glyptotek added a French Masters' wing, where an extensive collection of masterpieces can be viewed. Among the museum's many charms is a lush palm court and cafe, the so-called winter garden, with mosaic floors, palms, and a fountain under a copper and wrought iron dome.

Dantes Plads 7. ⓒ **33-41-81-41.** www.glyptoteket.dk. Admission 75DKK adults, free for children 17 and under, free for all Sun. Tues–Sun 11am–5pm. Bus: 1, 2, 5, 6, 8, or 10.

Rådhus (Town Hall) and World Clock ★ HISTORIC SITE/MUSEUM   Built in 1905, the Town Hall has impressive statues of H. C. Andersen and Niels Bohr, the Nobel prize-winning physicist. Jens Olsen's famous **World Clock** is open for viewing Monday to Friday 11am to 2pm and Saturday at noon. The clockwork is so exact that the variation over 300 years is 0.4 second. Climb the tower for an impressive view.

Rådhuspladsen. ⓒ **33-66-25-82.** Free admission; tour 30DKK. World clock 10DKK adults, 5DKK children; tower 20DKK per person. Mon–Fri 8am-5pm, Sat 9.30am–1pm (limited access). Rådhus tour Mon–Fri 10am and 1pm (in Danish), 3pm (in English), Sat 10 (in Danish) and 11am (in English). World clock Mon–Fri 11 am and 2pm, Sat noon. Bus: 1, 6, or 8.

Tivoli Gardens ★★★ ☺ ICON/AMUSEMENT PARK/PARK/GARDEN   Since it opened in 1843, this 8-hectare (20-acre) garden and amusement park in the center of Copenhagen has been a resounding success, with its thousands of flowers, a merry-go-round of tiny Viking ships, games (pinball arcades, slot machines, shooting galleries), and a Ferris wheel of hot-air balloons and cabin seats. There's even a playground, no wait, this *is* one big playground for kids and adults alike. Whether you're looking for a romantic evening in fairytale surroundings or a fun day out with the family, Tivoli somehow manages to do the trick. At night more than 100,000 specially made soft-glow light bulbs and at least a million regular bulbs are turned on. Cheesy, perhaps, but quite charming nevertheless.

An Arabian-style fantasy palace houses a boutique hotel and several restaurants. Tivoli has more than two dozen eateries, from a lakeside inn to a beer garden.

A parade of the red-uniformed Tivoli Boys' Guard takes place on weekends at 5:30 and 7:30pm, and their regimental band gives concerts on Sundays at 3pm on the open-air stage. The oldest building at Tivoli, the Chinese-style **Pantomime Theater,** with its peacock curtain, stages pantomimes in the evening.

Vesterbrogade 3. www.tivoli.dk. ⓒ **33-15-10-01.** Admission 95DKK, children under 8 free; multi-ride ticket 199DKK. Mid-Apr to mid-Sept Sun–Thurs 11am–10pm (11pm July to mid-Aug), Fri

5

DENMARK

Copenhagen

11am–12.30am, Sat 11am–midnight. Closed mid-Sept to mid-Apr. Any buses heading to City Hall Square or Central Station.

NEAR NYHAVN

Amalienborg Palace ★★ PALACE These four 18th-century French-inspired rococo mansions have been home to the Danish royal family since 1794, when the original royal palace burned. Visitors flock here to witness the **changing of the guard** at noon when the royal family is in residence. A swallowtail flag at mast signifies that the queen is in Copenhagen. The Royal Life Guard in black bearskin busbies leaves Rosenborg Castle at 11:30am and marches to Amalienborg. After the event, the guard, still accompanied by the band, returns to Rosenborg Castle.

In 1994, some of the official and private rooms in Amalienborg were opened to the public for the first time. The rooms, reconstructed to reflect the period 1863 to 1947, belonged to members of the reigning royal family, the Glücksborgs, who ascended the throne in 1863. The highlight is the period devoted to the long reign (1863–1906) of King Christian IX and Queen Louise.

Christian VIII's Palace. www.amalienborgmuseet.dk. ℂ **33-12-21-86.** Admission 65DKK adults, 40DKK students, 45DKK seniors, free for children 17 and under. Sep–Apr Tues–Sun 11am–4pm; May–Oct daily 7am–4pm; Sept daily 11am–4pm. Closed Dec 14–25. Bus: 1, 6, 9, or 10.

Frederikskirke ★ CHURCH This 2-centuries-old church, with its green copper dome—one of the largest in the world—is a short walk from Amalienborg Palace. After an unsuccessful start during the neoclassical revival of the 1750s in Denmark, the church was finally completed in Roman baroque style in 1894. In many ways, it's more impressive than Copenhagen's cathedral. Don't miss the view from the dome.

Frederiksgade 4. ℂ **33-15-01-44.** Free admission to church; dome 25DKK adults, 10DKK children. Church Mon–Tues and Thurs 10am–5pm; Wed 10am–6pm; Fri–Sun noon–5pm. Dome June–Aug daily 1–3pm; Sept–May Sat–Sun 1–3pm. Bus: 1, 6, or 9.

NEAR KONGENS HAVE (KING'S GARDEN)

Botanisk Have (Botanical Gardens) ★ GARDEN/PARK   Planted from 1871 to 1874, the Botanical Gardens, across from Rosenborg Castle, are on a lake that was once part of the city's defensive moat. Special features include cactus and palm houses, and an alpine garden containing mountain plants from all over the world.

Gothersgade 140. (✆ **35-32-22-40.** Free admission. May–Sept daily 8:30am–6pm; Oct–Apr Tues–Sun 8:30am–4pm. S-tog: Nørreport. Bus: 5A, 14, 40, 42, or 43.

Den Hirschsprungske Samling (The Hirschsprung Collection) ★ MUSEUM   This collection of 19th- and early-20th-century Danish art is in Ostre Anlæg, a park in the city center. Tobacco merchant Heinrich Hirschsprung (1836–1908) founded the collection, and it has been growing ever since. The emphasis is on the Danish golden age, with such artists as Eckersberg, Købke, and Lundbye, and on the Skagen painters, P. S. Krøyer, and Anna and Michael Ancher.

Stockholmsgade 20. www.hirschsprung.dk. (✆ **35-42-03-36.** Admission 75DKK adults, 65DKK seniors and students, free for children 17 and under. Tues–Sun 11am–5pm. Bus: 6A, 14, 40, 42, 43, 150S, 184, or 185.

Rosenborg Castle ★★★ CASTLE   This red-brick Renaissance-style castle houses everything from narwhal-tusk and ivory coronation chairs to Frederik VII's baby shoes—all from the Danish royal family. Its biggest draws are the dazzling crown jewels and regalia in the basement Treasury, where a lavishly decorated coronation saddle from 1596 is also shown. Try to see the Knights Hall (room no. 21), with its coronation seat, three silver lions, and relics from the 1700s. Room no. 3 was used by founding father Christian IV, who died in this bedroom decorated with Asian lacquer art and a stucco ceiling.

Øster Voldgade 4A. www.dkks.dk. (✆ **33-15-32-86.** Admission 80DKK adults, 50DKK students and seniors, free for children 17 and under. Palace and treasury (royal jewels) Jan–Mar Tues–Sun 11am–4pm; Apr daily 11am–4pm; May 10am–4pm, June–Aug daily 10am–5pm, Sep–Oct daily 10am–4pm; Nov–Dec 18 Tues–Sun 11am–4pm. S-tog: Nørreport. Bus: 5, 10, 14, 16, 31, 42, 43, 184, or 185. Metro: Nørreport.

Statens Museum for Kunst (Royal Museum of Fine Arts) ★★ ART MUSEUM   This well-stocked museum, one of the best in Scandinavia, houses painting and sculpture from the 13th century to the present. There are Dutch golden-age landscapes and marine paintings by Rubens, plus portraits by Frans Hals and Rembrandt. Eckersberg, Købke, and Hansen represent the Danish golden age. The French 20th-century art collection includes 20 works by Matisse. In the Royal Print Room are 300,000 drawings, prints, lithographs, and other works by such artists as Dürer, Rembrandt, Matisse, and Picasso. There's also a concert hall, a Children's Art Museum, and a glass wing designed for temporary exhibits.

Sølvgade 48–50. www.smk.dk. (✆ **33-74-84-94.** Admission 95DKK adults, 75DKK seniors, 65DKK students, free for children 17 and under. Separate admission for special exhibitions. Tues–Sun 10am–5pm (until 8pm Wed). Bus: 6A, 14, 40, 42, 43, 150S, 184, or 185.

INDRE BY (INNER HARBOUR/OLD TOWN)

Rundetårn (Round Tower) ★ ☺ HISTORIC SITE/OBSERVATION POINT   This 17th-century public observatory, attached to a church, is visited by thousands who come to climb the spiral ramp (no steps) for a panoramic view of Copenhagen. The tower is one of the crowning architectural achievements of the Christian IV era. Peter the Great, in Denmark on a state visit, once galloped up the ramp on horseback.

The Tower is located on Købmagergade, one of the city's oldest and most popular shopping streets.

Købmagergade 52A. www.rundetaarn.dk. © **33-73-03-73.** Admission 25DKK adults, 5DKK children 5–15. May 21–Sept 20 daily 10am–8pm, Sept 21–May 20 daily 10am–5pm. Bus: 5, 7E,14, 16, or 42. Metro: Nørreport.

Vor Frue Kirke (Copenhagen Cathedral) CATHEDRAL This Greek Revival-style church features Bertel Thorvaldsen's white marble neoclassical works, including *Christ and the Apostles.* The funeral of H. C. Andersen took place here in 1875, and that of Søren Kierkegaard in 1855. The interior is a thing of stunning, austere beauty. To boot, the surrounding square, Vor Frue Plads, harbors the Copenhagen University (founded 1479) and is easily one of the most well-preserved and beautiful squares in the Old Town.

Nørregade 8. © **33-14-21-28.** Free admission. Mon–Fri 9am–5pm; Sat 8:30am–5pm; Sun noon–4:30pm. Bus: 5.

SLOTSHOLMEN

Christiansborg Palace ★ HISTORIC SITE This granite-and-copper palace on the Slotsholmen—a small island that has been the center of political power in Denmark for more than 800 years—houses the Danish parliament, the Supreme Court, the prime minister's offices, and the Royal Reception Rooms. A guide will lead you through richly decorated rooms, including the Throne Room, banqueting hall, and Queen's Library. Before entering, you'll be asked to put on soft overshoes to protect the floors. Under the palace, visit the well-preserved ruins of the 1167 castle of Bishop Absalon, founder of Copenhagen.

Christiansborg Slotsplads. www.ses.dk. © **33-92-64-92.** Royal Reception Rooms 80DKK adults, 70DKK seniors and students, 40DKK children 7–14. Castle ruins 40DKK adults, 30DKK seniors and students, 20DKK children 7–14. Reception rooms guided tours May–Sept daily at 11am (Danish) and 3pm (English); Oct–Apr Tues–Sun at 3pm. Parliament English-language tours—call for appointment (© **33-37-32-21;** Mon–Fri 9am–4pm). Ruins May–Sept daily 10am–4pm; Oct–Apr Tues–Sun 10am–4pm.

Nationalmuseet (National Museum) ★★ ☺ MUSEUM A gigantic repository of archaeological and anthropological artifacts, this museum features objects from prehistory, the Middle Ages, and the Renaissance in Denmark, including Viking stones, helmets, and fragments of battle gear. Especially interesting are the "lur" horn, a Bronze Age musical instrument among the oldest in Europe, and the world-famous Sun Chariot, an elegant Bronze Age piece of pagan art. The **Royal Collection of**

  Native Behavior

If you want to be taken for a real Copenhagener, rent a bike and pedal your way around the city, up and down its streets and along its canals. It's estimated that half the population does the same. After all that exercise, do as the Danes do and order your fill of smørrebrød for lunch. Sold all over the city, these are open-faced sandwiches on which Danes are known to pile almost anything edible. Our favorite is a mound of baby shrimp, although roast beef topped with pickle is another tasty offering. And to top off the native experience, order a chaser, an *aquavit* (also called snaps in Denmark) with your lunch, though less reliable stomachs may opt instead for a Carlsberg or Tuborg beer only.

Coins and Medals contains various pieces from antiquity. There are also outstanding Egyptian and classical exhibits.

Ny Vestergade 10. www.natmus.dk. ✆ **33-13-44-11.** Free admission. Tues–Sun 10am–5pm. Closed Dec 24, 25, and 31. Bus: 1, 5, 6, 8, or 10.

OUTDOOR ACTIVITIES

Christiania (Freetown Christiania) ★★★ ICON/PARK/GARDEN   Ready for something truly different? Head out to the world-famous freetown of Christiania, founded in 1971 by a group of hippies who developed their own set of rules, independent of the Danish government. Its cannabis trade, taking place in the centrally located "Pusher Street," was tolerated by authorities until 2004. However, negotiations with Parliament have led to measures for normalizing the legal status of the community. Today Christiania offers a mix of creatively built houses, workshops, galleries, music venues, and cheap eateries. For your own safety, visitors are advised not to photograph in Christiania, especially not in the area in and around Pusher Street.

Bådsmandsstræde 43. DK-1407. www.rundvisergruppen.dk. ✆ **32-95-65-07.** Free admission. Christiania English-language tours (call for appointment) 250DKK for individuals or small groups up to 7 persons. Bus: 66. Metro: Christianshavn.

Havnebadet Islands Brygge (Harbour Bath) ★★ 👕 ☺ SPORTS VENUE/ PARK/GARDEN   If you fancy a swim in the center of the city in the summer, follow the natives and take a nose dive in the harbor at Islands Brygge (it's perfectly safe, Copenhagen municipality operates weekly water tests and there's a life guard). You'll meet families, skateboarders, basket ball players, and swimmers alike. There are diving towers and five pools, two of which are specifically for children. The lawn in front of the pools is usually busy until late with people cooking on BBQs, enjoying a beer, or listening to music.

Islands Brygge 7. ✆ **23-71-31-89.** Free admission. Daily 7am–7pm, 1 June to 31 Aug. Bus: 5A, 12, or 33.

ORGANIZED TOURS

Canal Tours Copenhagen, Mindeankeret Nyhavn (www.cex.dk; ✆ **32-96-30-00;** Metro: Kongens Nytorv), offers a great way to experience the city in a 1-hour Grand City Tour that covers the major scenic highlights like *The Little Mermaid,* Rosenborg Castle, and Amalienborg Palace. Tours depart daily (up to six departures per hour) from 9.30am–8pm (summer), 9.30–5pm (spring/autumn), and 9.30am–3pm (winter). They cost 70DKK for adults and 40DKK for children aged 6–11; children under 5 free. The Hop on/Hop off is a 24-hour audio-guided tour by launch and bus that departs from Town Hall Square. As soon as the ticket is validated you can freely decide when and where you want to go within the 24 hours. Tours cost 175DKK adults and 85DKK children 6–11, children under 5 free. Departures 31 March to 30 September.

   Shakespeare buffs will be interested in an afternoon excursion to the castles of North Zealand. The 7-hour English-language tour explores the area north of Copenhagen, including a visit to Kronborg (Hamlet's Castle); a brief trip to Fredensborg, the queen's residence; and a stopover at Frederiksborg Castle and the National Historical Museum. The cost is 395DKK for adults, 195DKK for children. For more information about these tours, contact **Sightseeing DK** (www.sightseeing.dk; ✆ 32-66-00-00).

   Licensed Danish tour guides conduct 2-hour guided walking tours of the city Monday to Saturday at 10:30am, between May and September. For information, contact **Copenhagen Walking Tours** (www.copenhagen-walkingtours.dk;

© **40-81-12-17**). All tours are private and must be pre-booked. Minimum price is 1300DKK for a group (1–13 persons).

Where to Eat

In recent years Copenhagen has earned a reputation as *food capital* of Scandinavia. The 2012 edition of the Michelin Guide awarded the city's restaurants 14 stars, reaffirming Copenhagen's position as a culinary hot-spot. Furthermore, many new and more affordable places have sprung up. In Copenhagen, food matters.

The national institution, the smørrebrød (open-faced sandwich), means "bread and butter," but the Danes stack this sandwich as if it were the Leaning Tower of Pisa—then they throw in a slice of curled cucumber and bits of parsley or perhaps sliced peaches or a mushroom for added color. **Note:** Depending on the restaurant and its serving sizes, most people will eat 2–4 smørrebrød each. The price stated in listings description (after review copy) is the price of one smørrebrød.

NEAR KONGENS NYTORV & NYHAVN
Very Expensive
NOMA ★★★ NEW NORDIC   Believe the hype. Noma stands for "Nordisk Mad" (Nordic Food) and has changed diners' perceptions of what Scandinavian cuisine is all about. Head chef René Redzepi has engineered creative menus that in the past have comprised everything from live shrimp, halibut in a foamy wasabi-flavored cream sauce, radishes planted in soil, fish doughnuts, and Norwegian crab and ashed leek. Guests have even been equipped with hunting knives in order to properly deal with a portion of summer deer. Positioned within a beautifully restored stone-sided warehouse in Christianshavn, Noma imports fish and shellfish three times a week from Greenland, Iceland, and the Faroe Islands. Getting a table is tricky. Noma opens up for reservations once every month (for 4 months later) and tables are booked within minutes. It may prove easier if you book for lunch instead of dinner. If there are no tables available, you can sign up for a waiting list.

Strandgade 93. www.noma.dk. © **32-96-32-97.** Reservations required. Fixed-price lunch/dinner (18–20 small dishes) 1500DKK. AE, DC, MC, V. Tues–Sat noon–4pm, 7pm–12.30am. Bus: 2 or 8.

AOC ★★★ NEW NORDIC   This 1-star Michelin restaurant has caused quite a stir among Copenhagen foodies ever since head chef Ronny Emborg launched his so-called "Sensory Evenings." Emborg, a former El Bulli apprentice, aims at surprising dinner guests with food that involves all the senses. Located in the vaulted cellar of an attractive Copenhagen town house, AOC offers an all-inclusive experience of either 7 or 10 courses, but guests can also choose from an a la carte menu. Popular dishes include poached Danish oyster with new green peas, pods, and cabbage turnip or the pork brisket grilled with radishes, potatoes, and ramsons. Award-winning sommelier Christian Aarø makes sure you get the wines to enhance the experience.

Dronningens Tværgade 2, DK-1302. www.restaurantaoc.dk. © **33-11-11-45.** Reservations required. Fixed-price menus 1875–2175DKK (7 courses), 2375–2675DKK (10 courses). DC, MC, V. Tues–Sat 6pm–1am. Bus: 15, 26, or 1A. Metro: Kongens Nytorv.

Expensive
Kong Hans Kælder ★★★ MODERN DANISH/INTERNATIONAL   Housed in the oldest building in the city that's still in commercial use, this vaulted Gothic cellar may be the best restaurant in Denmark. On "the oldest corner of Copenhagen," the restaurant has been carefully restored and is now a Relais Gourmand. A typical three-course dinner would include smoked salmon, breast of duck with *bigarade* (sour

orange) sauce, and plum ice cream with Armagnac. One signature dish is sautéed lobster with Jerusalem artichokes in a soy-ginger butter. These dishes can be served as either a starter or a main course.

Vingårdsstræde 6, DK-1070. www.konghans.dk. © **33-11-68-68.** Reservations required. Main courses 450DKK–470DKK; fixed-price menu 1,150DKK. AE, DC, MC, V. Mon–Sat 6–10pm. Bus: 11A. Metro: Kongens Nytorv.

Moderate

Bistro Pastis ★ FRENCH   For a taste of Paris, stop by this busy bistro. Okay, the waiters might be Scandinavian, but the chefs are very French and so is the menu, which covers classics such as onion soup, Salade Niçoise, escargot, moules frites, bouillabaisse, rabbit, and steak. As in any bistro, tables are placed close to each other, making eavesdropping and elbow rubbing a part of the culinary experience.

Gothersgade 52, DK-1123. www.bistro-pastis.dk. © **33-93-44-11.** Main courses 145DKK–245DKK. AE, DC, MC, V. Mon–Fri 11.30am–3pm, 5.30pm–10.30pm; Sat 11.30–3.30pm, 5.30pm–10.30pm. Bus: 5A, 11A, or 350S. Metro: Kongens Nytorv.

Café Lumskebugten ★★ 🍴 DANISH   This restaurant is a well-managed bastion of Danish charm, with an unpretentious elegance. Now-legendary matriarch Karen Marguerita Krog established it in 1854 as a rowdy tavern for sailors. A tastefully gentrified version of the original beef hash is still served. Two white dining rooms are decorated with antique ships' models and oil paintings. The food and service are excellent, even more so after renowned Danish chef Erwin Lauterbach gave the place a makeover in 2011. Specialties include tartar of salmon with herbs, Danish fish cakes with mustard sauce and minced beetroot, and sugar-marinated salmon with mustard-cream sauce.

Esplanaden 21, DK-1263. www.lumskebugten.dk. © **33-15-60-29.** Reservations recommended. Main courses 125DKK–300DKK. Set lunch 425DKK 3 courses. Set dinner 395DKK 3 courses, 575DKK 5 courses. AE, DC, MC, V. Mon–Tues 11.30am–3pm; Wed–Sat 11.30–3pm, 5.30pm–10pm. Bus: 1A or 15.

Inexpensive

Cocks & Cows AMERICAN   A regular burger joint with not so regular burgers. Cocks & Cows is a busy place, which is just another way of saying you'll probably have to wait for your order. However, most believe it is well worth the wait. If you're starving, dig into "The Governator," a double beef, double bacon, double cheddar colossus with onion rings and BBQ-sauce. The place also offers cocktails such as Old Fashioned, Mango Daiquiris, or a Blood and Sand, a treat from the 1930s with scotch, vermouth, cherry, and sweet orange juice.

Gammel Strand 44, DK-1202. www.cocksandcows.dk. © **69-69-60-00.** Main courses 78DKK–118DKK. AE, DC, MC, V. Mon–Thurs 11am–midnight; Fri–Sun 11am–2am; kitchen hours daily 11am–10.30pm. Bus 1A, 14, or 26.

NEAR RÅDHUSPLADSEN & TIVOLI

Nimb Louise ★★ DANISH   A former "Chef of the Year," Allan Poulsen is in charge of this newcomer gourmet restaurant in the Nimb complex at Tivoli (in front of the Central Railroad Station). Nimb also houses a wine bar, a bakery, a brasserie, and even a gourmet hotdog-stand. In contrast to other high-end eateries around town Nimb Louise abstains from fixed menus and offers an a la carte menu with favorites such as black lobster and white asparagus with ramsons, rowanberries, and mushrooms. Not to mention the advent of that utmost Danish classic, *frikadeller* (meatballs), and a selection of Danish cheeses.

Bernstorffsgade 5, DK-1577. www.nimblouise.dk. ℂ **88-70-00-20.** Main courses 245DKK–595DKK. AE, DC, MC, V. Mon–Fri noon–4pm and 6pm–midnight; Sat 6pm–midnight. Bus: 2A, 5A, 10, or 250S.

Schawarma Grill House ★★ 🏛 LEBANESE   Grab a kebab and go—or take a seat upstairs and watch people go by on "Strøget," while you negotiate a delicious bite of barbecued, marinated lamb, lettuce, tomatoes, onions, and a good helping of chili (if you dare) in a toasted pita bread. This eatery prides itself on being the first ever Shawarma house in Scandinavia, dating back to 1980. Nothing fancy, just plain and simple good food. Former Prime Minister Anders Fogh Rasmussen (current Secretary General of NATO) is a fan.

Frederiksberggade 36, DK-1459. www.shawarmagrillhouse.dk. ℂ **33-12-63-23.** Main courses 35DKK–75DKK. AE, DC, MC, V. Sun–Wed 11am–2am, Thurs 11am–3am, Fri–Sat 11am–6am. Bus: 1, 6, or 8 (or any bus headed for Town Hall Square).

Søren K ★ MODERN/EUROPEAN   Named after Denmark's most celebrated philosopher, this is an artfully minimalist dining room that's on the ground floor of the latest addition to the Royal Library. Menu items change frequently but might include carpaccio of veal, foie gras, oyster soup, and main courses such as veal chops served with lobster sauce and a half-lobster, and venison roasted with nuts and seasonal berries and a marinade of green tomatoes. The restaurant virtually never cooks with butter, cream, or high-cholesterol cheeses, making a meal here a healthier option than most.

On the ground floor of the Royal Library's Black Diamond Wing, 1 Søren Kierkegaards Plads, DK-1221. www.soerenk.dk. ℂ **33-47-49-49.** Reservations recommended. Main courses 75DKK–195DKK lunch, 235DKK–275DKK dinner; 5-course fixed-price dinner 490DKK. AE, DC, MC, V. Mon–Sat noon–4pm, 5.30–10pm. Bus: 1, 2, 5, 6, or 8.

NEAR ROSENBORG SLOT

Schønnemann ★★★ 🏛 DANISH   Located in a basement at Hauser Plads, this little gem can be hard to find. A cozy, dated, yet elegant place packed densely with tables and customers, this traditional Danish lunch restaurant makes some of the city's best smørrebrød (open sandwiches). A quintessential Danish food, smørrebrød was mostly ignored by chefs and foodies until recent years. Schønnemann has been a front runner in the restoration of the specialty. The pickled herring is especially good, but so is the smoked halibut or other classics such as *Pariserbøf,* minced beef on a slice of butter toasted bread. Schønnemann is also famous for its schnapps and there are 59 of them to choose from. Got room for dessert? Try a portion of *rabarberkage,* a compote of rhubarb with whipped cream.

Hauser Plads 16, DK-1127. www.restaurantschonnemann.dk. ℂ **33-12-07-85.** Reservations essential. Smørrebrød 65DKK–168DKK; set lunch 338DKK 3 courses. AE, DC, MC, V. Mon–Sat 11.30am–5pm. Bus: 5A or 6A. Metro: Nørreport Station.

Torvehallerne ★★ 🏛 INTERNATIONAL   A brand new culinary hot spot in the city center, Torvehallerne is a covered market, coolly designed in that minimalist Scandinavian style. In fact, you'd be excused if you thought the sleek pavilions housed modern art. The marketplace is located in Israels Plads, a public square just off Nørreport Station, one of the busiest intersections in the city. It caters to a broad variety of connoisseurs looking for anything from fresh fish, organic sausage, orchids in bloom, gourmet coffee, and other must-haves. Try **Palæo** (Hall 1, www.palaeo.dk) for food inspired by the so-called Stone Age diet, consisting mainly of low carb food, or grab a delicious coffee at **The Coffee Collective** (Hall 2, www.coffeecollective.dk).

Frederiksborggade 21, DK-1360. www.torvehallernekbh.dk. ℂ **70-10-60-70.** AE, DC, MC, V. Tues–Thurs 10am–7pm; Fri 10am–8pm; Sat 10am–6pm; Sun 11am–5pm. Metro: Nørreport Station.

AT GRÅBRØDRETORV

The charming Gråbrødre Square in the center of Copenhagen is a favorite hang-out spot for locals, especially in summer, when restaurants spill outdoors. In spite of the many eateries around, most locals will settle for a snack or a drink here, as the food in many places is not the best, and often grossly overpriced. A good bet however is the modest **Sporvejen** (www.sporvejen.dk; © **33-13-31-01;** open Mon–Sat 11am–10pm; Sun noon–10pm), designed as an old tram, which serves up lean burgers, chicken, omelets, and salads. Main courses are priced between 50DKK and 70DKK. In summer it offers outside seating with a great view to the lively plaza with its huge, old sycamore tree.

IN VESTERBRO
Expensive

Kadeau DANISH   This small-scale favorite is known to locals as one of the most ambitious, yet unpretentious, gourmet eateries in town. In fact, readers of Danish daily *Politiken* voted it as "Best Restaurant in Town" in 2012. Kadeau specializes in the cuisine of Bornholm, a Danish island in the Baltic between Sweden and Poland. What makes Kadeau different from the rest is not just their focus on regional food; it's the playfulness—and the low-key atmosphere. The menu features grilled brill fish and cockles with cabbage and black salsify, all made from Bornholm-sourced produce. The impressive wine card consists mainly of ecological wines.

Vesterbrogade 135, DK-1620. www.kadeau.dk. © **33-25-22-23.** 3-course fixed-price 450 DKK; 5 courses 600DKK and 6 courses including champagne, wines, and coffee 1,500DKK. AE, DC, MC, V. Tues–Sat 6pm–midnight. Bus: 3A or 6A.

Moderate

Copenhagen Food Consulting Company ("Cofoco") ★★ DANISH/FRENCH   In the trendy Vesterbro area, this haven of haute cuisine is in a minimalist Danish style and offers one of the best-value fixed-price menus in town. Each day brings something new and market-fresh to the menu. The cuisine is based on fresh seafood and local farm products from the Danish countryside, which are skillfully handled by well-trained Danish and continental chefs. You're likely to revel in such dishes as cod with apple and mint or duck cooked in yogurt with beets and horseradish. Their soups are among the best in town.

Abel Cathrines gade 7. www.cofoco.dk. © **33-31-70-55.** Reservations required. All main courses 85DKK (set menu with 4 courses 295DKK). AE, DC, MC, V. Mon–Sun 5:30pm–midnight. Bus: 6A.

Madsvinet DANISH/INTERNATIONAL   Located in an old butcher's shop just off Enghave Plads, a busy square in Vesterbro, this small restaurant mainly caters to carnivores. The owners have left the original tiles in place, making it a rather rustic experience, although it's what's on the plate that really matters here. Favorites include lobster with smoked chili, mayo and greens, smoke-baked hake with Jerusalem artichoke and ramson, as well as braised veal entrecote with beetroot and spinach. The pricing is as simple as the decor: The first dish is 150DKK and every additional dish costs 90DKK. The name, Madsvinet, refers to a glutton in Danish, or, quite literally, "a food pig." We don't care. We salute thee with an oink.

Enghavevej 58. www.madsvinet.dk. © **31-32-39-35.** Main courses 150DKK; 5-course tasting menu 400DKK. AE, DC, MC, V. Wed–Sat 6pm–midnight. Bus: 1A or 10.

Inexpensive

Dyrehaven ★★ 🍴 DANISH   There's a distinct retro look to this place with its vintage furniture and orange lamps, not to mention a considerable selection of antlers hanging on the walls. Lunch favorites include eggs Benedict and *Kartoffelmad* (potatoes, home-made mayo, fried onions, radish, and chives served on delicious rye bread). For dinner the kitchen serves specialties such as grated goat's cheese with mixed green salad, lentil soup with ground-elder pesto and garfish fried in rye flour with knob celery, mustard compote, pickled red onions, and chives. Dyrehaven is a popular hang-out for trendy locals and tends to be noisy. In summer there's outdoor seating on wooden benches.

Sdr. Boulevard 72, DK-1720. www.dyrehavenkbh.dk. No phone. Main courses 55DKK–75DKK lunch; 82DKK–135DKK dinner. Mon–Wed 9am–midnight; Thurs–Fri 9am–2am, Sat 10am–2am, Sun 10am–midnight. Bus: 10A.

IN KØDBYEN(VESTERBRO)

Fiskebaren ★★ SEAFOOD   In the increasingly trendy meat-packing district known as Kødbyen, just a short walk from the Central Station, this seafood restaurant stands out as a real treat. Testament to the freshness of the ingredients is the menu which varies from day to day, depending on the catch, and naturally reflects the changing seasons. With a cool industrial-style interior and a sleek bar, it attracts a fashionable crowd of locals. We particularly like the huge oysters from Limfjorden in Northern Denmark as a starter and the lightly smoked Pollack with fried Gotlandic potatoes and raw remoulade. Whether you love scallops, shrimps, mussels, or a variety of fresh fish from the North Sea, you'll find it here. Excellent wine selection and knowledgeable staff.

Flæsketorvet 100, DK-1711. www.fiskebaren.dk. *C* **32-15-56-56.** Reservations required. Main courses 195DKK–245DKK. AE, DC, MC, V. Tues–Fri 5.30pm–midnight; Sat 3.30pm–midnight; Sun 11am–3pm. Bus: 1A or 10.

IN TIVOLI

Food prices inside Tivoli are about 30% higher than elsewhere. Try skipping dessert at a restaurant and picking up a less expensive treat at one of the many stands. Take bus no. 1, 6, 8, 16, 29, 30, 32, or 33 to reach the park and either of the following restaurants. *Note:* Restaurants in Tivoli are open only May to mid-September.

Brdr. Price ★★ DANISH/FRENCH   The Price brothers—Adam and James—are considered by most Danes as something of a national institution after appearing in a series of popular food shows on TV. Their buoyant good spirits and knack for finer cooking attracts a hungry clientele to this restaurant focusing on classic Danish dishes such as smørrebrød and other homegrown specialties including lightly salted beef brisket with horseradish and tartlet with seafood fricassee. The decor takes it cue from Commedia dell'Arte and the pantomime tradition associated with Tivoli.

Tivoli, Vesterbrogade 3, DK-1630. www.tivoli.brdr-price.dk. *C* **38-41-51-51.** Reservations recommended. Smørrebrød 65DKK–95DKK, lunch. Main courses 185DKK–265DKK dinner. AE, DC, MC, V. Mon–Sun 12am–10pm. Mid-Apr to mid Sept daily noon–10pm. Bus: Any buses heading to City Hall Square or Central Station.

Shopping

Illums Bolighus, Amagertorv 10 (www.illumsbolighus.dk; *C* **33-14-19-41;** Mon–Fri 10am–7pm, Sun 10am–6pm), a store comprising four floors of mainly Scandinavian designer furniture, textiles, and art objects. Next door is **Royal Copenhagen,** Amagertorv 6 (www.royalcopenhagen.com; *C* **33-13-71-81;** bus: 1, 2, 6, 8, 28, 29, or 41 for the retail outlet, 1 or 15 for the factory), which was founded in 1775. Royal Copenhagen's trademark, three wavy blue lines, has come to symbolize quality in porcelain throughout the world.

In the Royal Copenhagen retail center, legendary **Georg Jensen,** Amagertorv 6 (www.georgjensen.com; *✆* **33-11-40-80;** bus: 1, 6, 8, 9, or 10), is known for its fine silver and watches. For the connoisseur, there's no better address—this is the largest and best collection of Jensen holloware in Europe. Jewelry in traditional and modern design is also featured. One department specializes in seconds produced by various porcelain and glassware manufacturers.

The elegant **Magasin,** Kongens Nytorv 13 (http://shop.magasin.dk; *✆* **33-11-44-33;** bus: 1, 6, 9, or 10), is the biggest department store in Scandinavia. It offers an assortment of Danish designer fashion, glass and porcelain, and souvenirs. Goods are shipped abroad tax-free.

For a more local shopping experience take a 5-minute walk north of Kongens Nytorv to Kronprinsessegade and Pilestræde, both narrow streets are teeming with boutiques offering Scandinavian fashion. **Bruuns Bazaar,** Kronprinsessegade 9 (www.bruunsbazaar.dk; *✆* **33-32-19-69**), specializes in well-cut and understated clothing for men and women. Open Mon–Thurs 10am–6pm, Fri 10–7pm, Sat 10–4pm.

Entertainment & Nightlife

In Copenhagen, a good night means a late night. On warm weekends hundreds of rowdy revelers crowd Strøget until sunrise, and jazz clubs, traditional beer houses, and wine cellars are routinely packed. Those in the know head for trendy Vesterbro and the increasingly popular former meat-packing district, Kødbyen. Here, a variety of low-key eateries and artsy bars and nightclubs keep most people partying until the early hours. The city has a more serious cultural side as well, exemplified by excellent theaters, operas, and ballets. On summer evenings outdoor concerts, even tango sessions, and other activities are held in Fælled Park; inquire about dates and times at the Copenhagen tourist office (*✆* **70-22-24-42**).

THE PERFORMING ARTS

Opened by Queen Margrethe, this $441-million 1,700-seat **Copenhagen Opera House ★★★**, Ekuipagemesteruej 10 (*✆* **33-69-69-33**), is the luxurious home of the Royal Danish Opera. In addition to international artists, the opera house also showcases the works of Danish composers such as Carl Nielsen and Poul Ruders. You can dine at the on-site **Restauranten** before curtain time (a five-course menu costs 275DKK) or there is an **Opera Café,** serving sandwiches, salads, and light Danish specialties. The season runs from mid-August to the beginning of June. During performance season, tours of the building are offered daily on a frequently changing schedule, which usually requires a phone call as a means of hammering out the schedule. Tickets are 100DKK each. The box office (www.kglteater.dk; *✆* **33-69-69-69**) is open Monday to Saturday from noon to 6pm.

On the other side of the harbor is the new **Royal Danish Playhouse,** Sankt Annæ Plads 36 (www.kglteater.dk; *✆* **33-69-39-31;** open Mon–Sat 10am–11pm)—a long, slim, deep-brown brick building, twinkling its eye at the Opera House across the water. It's dominated by a glass-encased top story with backstage facilities for the actors.

Det Kongelige Teater (Royal Theater), Kongens Nytorv (www.kglteater.dk; *✆* **33-69-69-69;** bus: 1, 6, 9, or 10), dates from 1748 and is a venue for cultural events. Because the arts are state-subsidized in Denmark, ticket prices are comparatively low and it's recommended you make reservations in advance. The season runs from August to May. Tickets are 90DKK to 895DKK, half price for seniors 65 and over and for those 17 and under. For those between 18 and 25, half-price tickets are available with prior online registration at the Royal Theater's website. The central box office, August Bournonvilles Passage 1 (just off Kongens Nytorv), is open Monday to Saturday 2 to 6pm; phone hours are Monday to Saturday 10am to 4pm.

Koncerthuset, Emil Holms Kanal 20 (www.dr.dk/koncerthuset; ℭ **35-20-30-40;** bus: 33, 35, 77, or 78. Metro: Amager Strand), provides the best modern acoustic and visual setting for concertgoers. This new Copenhagen landmark was designed by Jean Nouvel with a monumental, yet airy, blue frontage. Events range widely from small-scale jazz concerts in the foyer, chamber music, choral, rock, and pop concerts in the three smaller concert halls and symphony concerts, guest appearances, and large-scale rhythmic concerts in the large concert hall.

LIVE MUSIC CLUBS

VEGA, Enghavevej 40 (www.vega.dk; ℭ **33-25-70-11;** bus: 10), hosts some of the best live concerts in Copenhagen from electronica and techno to soul, funk, pop, indie, and rock (see website for coming venues). **Ideal Bar** on the corner of Enghavevej and Rejsbygade is a part of VEGA and a popular place for 20- and 30-somethings to catch DJ sessions, concerts, and the occasional cocktail. Open hours are Thurs 8pm–2am, Fri–Sat 11pm–5am.

Copenhagen JazzHouse, Niels Hemmingsensgade 10 (www.jazzhouse.dk; ℭ **33-15-47-00;** S-tog: Nørreport), plays host to more non-Danish jazz artists than just about any other jazz bar in town. After a thorough restoration, it reopened in the summer of 2012 with a new concert hall and bar. Live music begins Mon–Sun 8pm and usually finishes reasonably early. Extra jazz sessions begin at midnight Fri–Sat. Cover is 40DKK to 300DKK.

Mojo Blues Bar, Løngangsstræde 21C (ℭ **33-11-64-53;** bus: 2, 8, or 30), is a candlelit drinking spot that offers blues music, mostly performed by Scandinavian groups. It's open daily from 8pm to 5am.

BARS & CLUBS

Ruby Cocktail Bar, Nybrogade 10 (www.rby.dk; ℭ **33-93-12-03;** bus: 1A, 14, 15, or 26), is a warm, snug living room to settle into for the night. The dimly lit rooms have rugs on the floor, flickering candles, and Chesterfield sofas. Open Mon–Sat 4pm–2am and Sun 6pm–midnight.

Frequented by celebrities and royalty, the **Library Bar,** in the Profil Copenhagen Plaza Hotel, Bernstorffsgade 4 (ℭ **33-14-92-62;** bus: 6), was rated by the late Malcolm Forbes as one of the top five bars in the world. In a setting of antique books and works of art, you can order everything from a cappuccino to a cocktail. It's open daily 4pm to midnight.

Malbeck Vinoteria, Birkegade 2 (www.malbeck.dk; ℭ **32-21-52-15;** bus: 5A or 350S), is an Argentinean wine bar playing an eclectic mix of old tango tunes and hiphop. Great selection of wines (also by the glass) and tapas. Open Sun–Thurs 11.30am–midnight, Fri–Sat 11.30am–1am.

Nyhavn 17, Nyhavn 17 (ℭ **33-12-54-19;** bus: 1, 6, 27, or 29; Metro: Kongens Nytorv), is the last of the honky-tonks that used to make up the former sailors' quarter. In summer you can sit outside. In the evening there's free entertainment from a solo guitarist or guitar duet. The cafe is open Sunday to Thursday 10am to 2am and Friday and Saturday 10am until 3am. A local favorite since World War I, **Bo-Bi Bar,** Klareboderne 14 (ℭ **33-12-55-43;** bus: 11A or 350S), is a smoky tavern with red velvet walls and a dimly lit safe haven for an eclectic, slightly bohemian crowd of mainly writers, journalists, students, and the odd politician. Open daily 10am–2am.

In the trendy western neighborhood of Vesterbro, **Mikeller,** Viktoriagade 8 (www. mikkeller.dk; ✆ **33-31-04-15;** bus: 10), offers some of the best gourmet beer in town in a minimalist cellar that attracts young bearded hipsters and businessmen alike. Choose from more than 20 different beers that are bound to rock your boat. Open Sun–Wed 3pm–midnight; Thurs–Fri 2pm–2am.

Where to Stay

NEAR KONGENS NYTORV & NYHAVN

Very Expensive

Nimb Hotel ★★★ This boutique hotel has only a dozen or so rooms, but its devotees hail it as one of the best places to stay in all of Copenhagen. This small Moorish-style palace with a striking Venetian facade fills its rooms with antiques, and all rooms overlook the Tivoli except no. 14 (2800DKK), which faces the rail station. Each room is individually designed, with fireplaces, four-poster beds, and spacious bathrooms. One of the bars here, a former ballroom, has chandeliers, a grand piano, and a blazing fireplace. Even if you don't stay here, consider a meal in one of its first-class restaurants. There's a deli, even a dairy (the hotel churns its own butter and cream). There's also a gourmet sausage stand adjacent to the Tivoli.

Bernstorffsgade 5, DK-1577. www.nimb.dk. ✆ **88-70-00-00.** Fax 88-70-00-99. 14 units. 2,800DKK–4,900DKK double; 6,900DKK junior suite; 9,000DKK suite no. 11. AE, DC, MC, V. Parking nearby 350DKK. Bus: 1 or 16. **Amenities:** 2 restaurants; 2 bars; access to health club; room service; baby-sitting. *In room:* A/C, TV/DVD, minibar, hair dryer, Wi-Fi (free).

Expensive

Phoenix Copenhagen ★★ More than any other hotel, this top-of-the-line lodging poses a challenge to the discreet grandeur of the nearby D'Angleterre. Opened in 1991, the Phoenix was a royal guesthouse, originally built in 1780 to accommodate the aristocratic courtiers of Amalienborg Palace. The spacious rooms are tastefully elegant and decorated with discreet Louis XVI reproductions. The large beds sport fine linens, and the bathrooms are state of the art. The very best units also have faxes, bathrobes, and phones in the bathrooms.

Bredgade 37, DK-1260 København. www.phoenixcopenhagen.com. ✆ **33-95-95-00.** Fax 33-33-98-33. 213 units. 1,000DKK–2,500DKK double; 3,500DKK–4985DKK junior suite; 6,300DKK–8585DKK suite. AE, DC, MC, V. Parking 250DKK. Bus: 1A, 15, or 26. **Amenities:** Restaurant; bar; room service; babysitting. *In room:* A/C, TV, minibar, hair dryer, Wi-Fi (free).

71 Nyhavn ★★ On the corner between Copenhagen harbor and Nyhavn Canal, this hotel is housed in a restored old warehouse from 1804, and was thoroughly renovated in 1997. The rooms have a nautical decor, with exposed brick, dark woods, and crisscrossing timbers. Bathrooms are rather small; most have a stall shower. The best rooms are equipped with bathrobes and faxes. Most of the rooms have a harbor and canal view.

Nyhavn 71, DK-1051 København. www.71nyhavnhotel.com. ✆ **33-43-62-00.** Fax 33-43-62-01. 150 units. 1,800DKK–2,450DKK double; 3,950DKK junior suite; 6,950DKK suite. AE, DC, MC, V. Parking 195DKK. Bus: 1A, 11A, 15, 26, or 350-S. Metro: Kongens Nytorv. **Amenities:** Restaurant; bar; room service; babysitting. *In room:* A/C (in some), TV, minibar, hair dryer, Wi-Fi (free).

Moderate

Christian IV This small, cozy hotel enjoys one of the most desirable locations in Copenhagen. Dating from 1958, the hotel takes its name from Christian IV, who constructed Rosenborg Castle lying adjacent to the hotel. The hotel provides a "bridge" linking King's Garden, the castle, and the more modern structures in the neighborhood. Enjoying a lot of repeat business, it offers contemporary, modern Danish decor, along with immaculate bathrooms, most with a bath tub and shower.

Dronningens Tværgade 45, DK-1302 København. www.hotelchristianiv.dk. ⓒ **33-32-10-44.** Fax 33-32-07-06. 42 units. 1,120DKK–1,220DKK double. Rates include breakfast. MC, V. Parking 195DKK. Bus: 1A, 15, or 26. **Amenities:** Breakfast room; bar; access to nearby health club. *In room:* TV, Wi-Fi (free).

Copenhagen Strand ★ One of the city's most modern hotels, opened in 2000, lies within a pair of former brick-and-timber factories. The savvy architects retained as many of the old-fashioned details as they could. The medium-size rooms are filled with comfortable, contemporary-looking furnishings. The hotel is rated three stars by the Danish government, but frankly, all that it lacks for elevation into four-star status is a full-fledged restaurant.

Havnegade 37, DK-1058. www.copenhagenstrand.dk. ⓒ **33-48-99-00.** Fax 33-48-99-01. 174 units. 890DKK–2,300DKK double; 1,290DKK–3,900DKK suite. AE, DC, MC, V. Parking 250DKK. Metro: Kongens Nytorv. **Amenities:** Bar; room service; babysitting. *In room:* TV, minibar, hair dryer, Internet (free).

Inexpensive

Sømandshjemmet Bethel ★★ Within easy access of the central Kongens Nytorv and with a beautiful view of the Nyhavn Canal, this old "seaman's home" (literally what "Sømandshjem" means) offers great value for money in an otherwise expensive area. Clean, simple, comfortable rooms (all with private bath and toilet). Friendly staff.

Nyhavn 22, DK-1051. www.hotel-bethel.dk. ⓒ **33-13-03-70.** 645DKK single, 845DKK–1045DKK double (with the possibility of adding two additional beds). All rates include breakfast. Metro: Kongens Nytorv. *In room:* TV, Internet (free).

NEAR RÅDHUSPLADSEN & TIVOLI

Absalon Hotel ★ ✦ Since 1938 the Nedergaard family has been welcoming guests to its hotel, which has grown and expanded over the years in the neighborhood near the rail station. Today the hotel comprises a government-rated three-star hotel with private bathrooms, and a one-star annex without private bathrooms, the two facilities sharing the same entrance and reception. You can stay here in comparative luxury or on a budget, depending on your choice of accommodation. Most bedrooms are medium in size or even somewhat cramped, but all are comfortably furnished and well maintained. If you are not on a budget, opt for one of the large and elegantly furnished top-floor rooms, decorated in a classical English or French Louis XIV style.

Helgolandsgade 15, DK-1653 København. www.absalon-hotel.dk. ⓒ **33-24-22-11.** Fax 33-24-34-11. 186 units. Absalon Hotel (with private bathroom) 895DKK–1,245DKK double; annex (without private bathroom) 550DKK–875DKK double. Rates include breakfast. MC, V. Parking 260DKK. Closed Dec 19–Jan 2. Bus: 1A, 6A, or 10. **Amenities:** Lounge. *In room:* TV, fridge (in some), hair dryer (in some), Wi-Fi (free).

Ascot Hotel ★ ✦ On a side street, 180m (591 ft.) from the Tivoli and a 2-minute walk from Town Hall Square, sits one of Copenhagen's best small hotels. The Ascot was built in 1902 and enlarged and modernized in 2007. The furniture is tasteful and very comfortable, and a few of the units are rented as apartments. The finest rooms open onto the street, though the accommodations in the rear benefit from more natural light.

Studiestræde 61, DK-1554 København. www.ascot-hotel.dk. ⓒ **33-12-60-00.** Fax 33-14-60-40. 190 units. 1,000DKK–2,000DKK double; 1,390DKK–2,790DKK apt. AE, DC, MC, V. Parking 175DKK. Bus:

2A, 5A, 6A, 12, 14, 15, 26, 30, 40, 66, 68, or 250S. Metro: Nørreport. **Amenities:** Bar; exercise room; room service; babysitting. *In room:* TV, kitchenette (in some), hair dryer, Wi-Fi (free).

Hotel Alexandra ★ 🎁 This conveniently located address is a designer hotel with period furniture from Danish modern masters Arne Jacobsen and Ole Wanscher, and avant-garde lighting by Paul Henningsen. Each room is uniquely decorated, and 13 units are "special design rooms." The rooms are further enhanced by Danish artworks. Guests meet fellow guests in the hotel's restaurant, **Lê Lê Street Kitchen,** specializing in delicious Vietnamese dishes.

H. C. Andersens Blvd. 8, D-1553 København. www.hotelalexandra.dk. 🕐 **33-74-44-44.** Fax 33-74-44-88. 61 units. 1,745DKK–2,545DKK double. Rates include continental breakfast. AE, DC, MC, V. S-tog: Copenhagen Central Station or Vesterport Station. **Amenities:** Restaurant; bar; room service. *In room:* TV, hair dryer, Wi-Fi (free).

Profil Copenhagen Plaza ★ This successful overhaul of an older hotel near the rail station combines first-class comfort and antique furnishings. Opposite the Tivoli Gardens, the hotel was commissioned by King Frederik VIII in 1913 and has entertained its share of celebrities and royalty. Rooms vary greatly in size and have an English country house style—but with all the modern amenities. The antiques, double-glazed windows, and views from many rooms make this a good choice. Bathrooms are generous in size. The **Library Bar** is one of Copenhagen's most charming.

Bernstorffsgade 4, DK-1577 København. www.profilhotels.dk. 🕐 **33-14-92-62.** Fax 33-93-93-62. 93 units. 1,095DKK–2,300DKK double; from 4,500DKK–6000DK suite. AE, DC, MC, V. Parking 235DKK. Bus: 2A, 5A, 6A, 26, 150S, or 250S. **Amenities:** Restaurant; bar; exercise room; room service; babysitting. *In room:* A/C, TV, minibar, hair dryer, Wi-Fi (free).

DAY TRIPS FROM COPENHAGEN

Dragør ★★

Visit the past in this old seafaring town on the island of Amager, 5km (3 miles) south of Copenhagen's Kastrup Airport. It's filled with cobblestoned streets and well-preserved, half-timbered, 18th-century cottages with steep red-tile or thatch roofs, many of them under the protection of the National Trust.

Dragør (pronounced Drah-wer) was a busy port on the herring-rich Baltic Sea in the early Middle Ages, but when fishing fell off, it became just another sleepy waterfront village. After 1520, Amager Island and its villages—Dragør and Store Magleby—were inhabited by the Dutch, who brought their own customs, Low-German language, and agricultural expertise, especially their love of bulb flowers. Do as Copenhageners on a sunny day: Equip yourself with an ice-cream and take a stroll around town or find a nice spot in one of the restaurants by the waterfront. The old **Café Espersen** (www.cafe-espersen.dk; 🕐 **32-94-07-70;** Færgevej 1–3; bus: 5A in conjunction with 350S), housed in the former ticket office of the Dragør–Linhamn ferry, offers front-row seats to the life on the harbor and an excellent view of Øresund.

Louisiana ★★★

If you only go to one museum in Denmark, go to the **Louisiana Museum of Modern Art ★★★** Gl. Strandvej 13 (www.louisiana.dk; 🕐 **49-19-07-19**). Established in 1958, it is beautifully set in a 19th-century mansion on the Danish Riviera, surrounded by a sculpture park opening directly onto the Øresund. Paintings and sculptures by modern masters, such as Giacometti and Henry Moore, can be viewed here. The museum's name came from the estate's first owner, Alexander Brun, who had three wives, each named Louise. There's an excellent cafe where you can enjoy the daily specials while taking in the ocean view from an Arne Jacobsen chair. Most visitors will find themselves drooling over the downstairs gift store with designer goods, posters, etc. Admission is 95DKK adults, 85DKK students and seniors, free for those 18 and under. It's open Tues–Fri 10am to 10pm, Sat–Sun 11am to 8pm.

GETTING THERE **Humlebæk,** the nearest town to Louisiana, may be reached by train from Copenhagen (København–Helsingør). Two trains an hour leave from the main station in Copenhagen (trip time: 40 min.). Once you're at Humlebæk, follow signs to the museum, a 15-minute walk.

Helsingør (Elsinore) ★

Helsingør is visited chiefly for "Hamlet's Castle." Aside from its literary associations, the town has a certain charm: a quiet market square, medieval lanes, and old half-timbered and brick buildings, remains of its once-prosperous shipping industry. The **Tourist Office,** Havnepladsen 3 (www.visitnordsjaelland.com; ℰ **49-21-13-33**), is open September to June 19, Monday to Friday from 10am to 4pm and Saturday from 10am to 1pm; June 20 to August 31, Monday to Thursday 10am to 5pm, Friday 10am to 6pm, and Saturday 10am to 3pm.

There's no evidence Shakespeare ever saw this sandstone-and-copper Dutch Renaissance-style castle, full of intriguing secret passages and casemates, but he made **Kronborg Slot ★★★**, Kronborg (www.ses.dk; ℰ **49-21-30-78**), famous in *Hamlet.* According to 12th-century historian Saxo Grammaticus, though, if Hamlet had really existed, he would have lived centuries before Kronborg was erected (1574–85). Over the years, some famous productions of *Hamlet* have been staged here, the castle's bleak atmosphere providing a good foil to the drama.

During its history, the castle has been looted, bombarded, gutted by fire, and used as a barracks (1785–1922). The starkly furnished **Great Hall** is the largest in northern Europe. The church, with its original oak furnishings, and the royal chambers are also worth exploring. Admission prices vary depending on the type of ticket. Full admission to the castle, dance hall, and other rooms is 95DKK for adults, 75DKK for children aged 15 to 17, and 30DKK for children aged 6 to 14. Open May daily 11am to 4pm; June to August daily 10am to 5.30pm; September to October daily 11am to 4pm; November to March Tues–Sun 11am to 4pm. The castle is 1km (⅔ mile) from the rail station.

GETTING THERE Once you reach Helsingør, 40km (25 miles) north of Copenhagen, you'll be deposited in the center of town and can cover all the major attractions on foot. There are frequent trains from Copenhagen, taking about 1 hour. A one-way ticket from Copenhagen Central Station (Hovedbanegården) is 108DKK.

ENGLAND

by Donald Strachan, Joe Fullman, Mary Anne Evans,
Sian Meades, John Power, Stephen Keeling

London never seems to get tired. It's the greatest quality of this city with two millennia of history, that it stays forever young and energetic. Britain's capital is home to the great art collections of the National Gallery, architectural icons like Westminster Abbey, and a rich royal heritage, but it also spawns underground design and musical innovation. It is a city of independent villages—Chelsea or Greenwich has little in common with Shoreditch or Soho—and a conurbation of grand parks as well as great buildings.

LONDON

Samuel Johnson said, "When a man is tired of London, he is tired of life; for there's in London all that life can afford." We'll survey a segment of that life: ancient monuments, literary shrines, museums, walking tours, Parliament debates, royal castles, palaces, cathedrals, and parks.

Essentials

GETTING THERE

BY PLANE London's flagship airport for arrivals from across the globe is **London Heathrow** (LHR; www.heathrowairport.com), 17 miles west of the center and boasting five hectic, bustling terminals (named, imaginatively, Terminals 1 to 5, although Terminal 2 is closed until 2014). This is the U.K. hub of most major airlines, including British Airways, Virgin Atlantic, Qantas, and the North American carriers. **London Gatwick** (LGW; www.gatwickairport.com) is the city's second major airport, with two terminals (North and South), 31 miles south of central London in the Sussex countryside.

Increasingly, however, passengers are arriving at London's smaller airports—particularly since the proliferation of budget airlines, which now dominate short-haul domestic and international routes. **London Stansted** (STN; www.stanstedairport.com), 37 miles northeast of the center, is the gateway to short-haul destinations in the U.K., continental Europe, and parts of the Middle East. It's also a hub for Ryanair. **London Luton** (LTN; www.london-luton.co.uk) anchors a similarly diverse short-haul network, and lies 34 miles northwest of the center. Ryanair and easyJet are regular visitors. **London City** (LCY; www.londoncityairport.com), the only commercial airport actually in London itself, is frequented mainly by business travelers from nearby Docklands and the City, but does have some key intercity links with regular direct flights to New York, Edinburgh, Florence, and Madrid. British Airways and Cityjet are its two major airlines. **London Southend** (SEN; www.southendairport.com), 40 miles east of the center, became a secondary base for easyJet short-haul services in 2012.

BY TRAIN Precisely which of London's many mainline stations you arrive at depends on where you started your journey. **Paddington station** serves Heathrow Airport and destinations west of London—including Oxford, Reading, Bristol, and South Wales. **Marylebone station** is used mostly by commuters, but also serves Warwick. **Euston station** serves North Wales and major cities in northwest England, including Liverpool and Manchester; trains also depart from here to the Lake District and Glasgow, Scotland, via the West Coast Mainline. **King's Cross station** is the endpoint of the East Coast Mainline—trains arrive here from York, Newcastle, and Edinburgh. **Liverpool Street station** is the City's main commuter hub, but also links London with Stansted Airport, Cambridge, and Norwich. The City's other mainline stations—Cannon Street, Moorgate, Blackfriars, and Fenchurch Street—are also heavily used by commuters from the neighboring counties of Hertfordshire, Essex, Kent, Surrey, and Sussex, as is **Charing Cross station,** close to Trafalgar Square. **Waterloo station** serves the southwest of England: Trains from Devon, Dorset, and Hampshire terminate here, as do Salisbury services. **Victoria station** serves Gatwick Airport, as well as cities and towns across southern England, including Brighton. South of the River Thames, **London Bridge station** is another busy commuter hub, and also serves Brighton and Gatwick Airport. Each of London's mainline stations is connected to the city's vast bus and Tube networks (see below), and each has phones, sandwich bars, fast-food joints, luggage storage areas, and somewhere to ask for transport information.

Missing from the list above is **St. Pancras station,** the London hub for high-speed Eurostar services to Paris and Brussels, as well as some domestic services to the East Midlands and South Yorkshire. Restored and reopened in 2007, it connects England with Belgium and France through the multibillion-pound **Channel Tunnel.**

BY CAR To anyone thinking of arriving in the capital by car, our most important piece of advice would be: "Don't." Roads in and around the city are clogged with traffic, and the M25 highway that rings the city is prone to major traffic jams at any time of day—but especially between 7:30 and 9am, or 4 and 7pm on weekdays, and on Sundays from mid-afternoon until late in the evening. On top of that, and despite the complaints and grumbles of Londoners, the public transportation system is pretty efficient.

VISITOR INFORMATION

TOURIST OFFICES The official **Visit London** online home is the excellent **www.visitlondon.com**. You can download PDF brochures and maps, or have them mailed to a U.K. or U.S. address, or ask any question about the city by filling out the online contact form at **www.visitlondon.com/contact-us**.

Once in the city, the **Britain and London Visitor Centre,** 1 Lower Regent Street, London SW1 4XT (© **08701/566-366;** Tube: Piccadilly Circus), can help you with almost anything, from the superficial to the most serious queries. Located just downhill from Piccadilly Circus, it deals with procuring accommodations in all price categories through an on-site travel agency, and you can also book bus or train tickets throughout the U.K. It's open year-round Monday 9:30am to 6pm, Tuesday to Friday 9am to 6pm, and Saturday and Sunday 9am to 4pm. Between April and

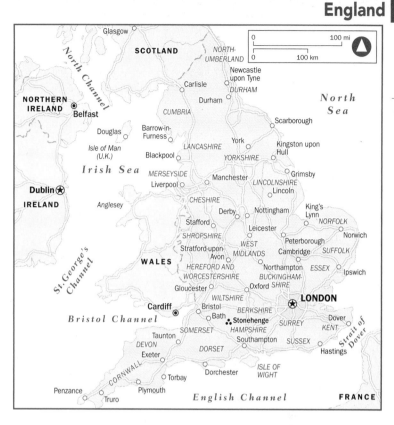

September, weekday closing is a half-hour later. There are further central information points at: **King's Cross St. Pancras,** LUL Western Ticket Hall, Euston Rd. (Mon–Sat 7:15am–9:15pm, Sun 8:15am–8:15pm); **Holborn station,** Kingsway (Mon–Fri 8am–6pm); **Victoria rail station,** opposite Platform 8 (Mon–Sat 7:15am–9:15pm, Sun 8:15am–8:15pm); **Piccadilly Circus Underground station** (daily 9:15am–7pm); **Liverpool Street Underground station** (Mon–Sat 7:15am–9:15pm, Sun 8:15am–8:15pm); **Euston rail station,** opposite Platform 8 (Mon–Fri 7:15am–9:15pm, Sat 8:15am–6:15pm, Sun 8:15am–6:15pm); **Greenwich,** 2 Cutty Sark Gardens (© **0870/608-2000;** daily 10am–5pm).

The Square Mile (see below) has its own visitor information center, the **City of London Tourist Information Centre,** St. Paul's Churchyard (© **020/7332-1456**). Opening hours are Monday to Saturday 9:30am to 5:30pm, Sunday 10am to 4pm.

CITY LAYOUT

For our purposes, London begins at Chelsea, on the north bank of the Thames, and stretches north through Kensington to Hampstead, and then east and south to Tower Bridge. Within this area, you'll find all the hotels and restaurants and nearly all the sights that are usually of interest to visitors.

The logical, though not geographical, center of this area is Trafalgar Square. Stand here facing the steps of the imposing National Gallery; you're looking northwest. That's the direction of Piccadilly Circus—the real core of tourist London—and the maze of streets that makes up Soho. Farther north runs Oxford Street, London's gift to moderately priced shopping, and still farther northwest lie Regent's Park and the zoo.

At your back (south from Trafalgar Sq.) runs Whitehall, which houses or skirts nearly every British government building, including the official residence of the prime minister at 10 Downing St. A bit farther south stand the Houses of Parliament and Westminster Abbey. Flowing southwest from Trafalgar Square is the table-smooth Mall, flanked by parks and mansions and leading to Buckingham Palace, the queen's residence. Farther along in the same direction lie Belgravia and Knightsbridge, the city's plushest residential areas; and south of them are chic Chelsea and King's Road (an upscale boulevard for shopping).

Due west from Trafalgar Square stretches the superb and high-priced shopping area bordered by Regent Street and Piccadilly. Farther west lie the equally elegant shops and even more elegant homes of Mayfair. Then comes Park Lane, with its deluxe hotels. Beyond is Hyde Park, the biggest park in central London and one of the largest in the world.

Charing Cross Road runs north from Trafalgar Square, past Leicester Square, and intersects with Shaftesbury Avenue. This is London's theatreland. A bit farther along, Charing Cross Road turns into a browser's paradise, lined with shops selling new and secondhand books. At last, it funnels into St. Giles Circus. Beyond is Bloomsbury, site of the University of London, the British Museum, and erstwhile stamping ground of the famed "Bloomsbury group," led by Virginia Woolf. Northeast from Trafalgar Square lies Covent Garden, known for its Royal Opera House; today it's a major shopping, restaurant, and cafe district.

Follow The Strand eastward from Trafalgar Square and you'll come to Fleet Street. From the 19th century through most of the 20th century, this area was the most concentrated newspaper district in the world. Temple Bar stands where The Strand becomes Fleet Street, and only here do you enter the actual City of London, or "the City." Its focal point and shrine is the Bank of England on Threadneedle Street, with the Stock Exchange next door and the Royal Exchange across the street. In the midst of all the hustle and bustle rises St. Paul's Cathedral, Sir Christopher Wren's monument to beauty and tranquility. At the far eastern fringe of the City looms the Tower of London, shrouded in legend, blood, and history and permanently besieged by battalions of visitors.

GETTING AROUND

The first London word that any visitor needs to learn is "Oyster." The **Oyster Card** is a plastic smartcard that is your gateway to pretty much every form of London public transport. You can still pay to use all these services with cash, but an Oyster offers big savings on just about every journey. The pay-as-you-go card costs £5 for adults from any Tube or major rail station—a charge that's refundable if you return the card after use. As well as these discounts, your daily bill for using an Oyster is capped at the price of an equivalent 1-Day Travelcard (see below), so there's no longer any need to calculate in advance whether to buy a discounted multi-trip travel ticket. Basically, if you're staying more than a day or so, and plan to use London's public transport network, then investing in an Oyster is a no-brainer. It saves you time and money.

To use an Oyster, simply touch it against the yellow card-reader that guards the entry/exit gates at Tube and rail stations. The gates will open. You should always swipe your Oyster card as you leave the station, even if the gate is open, otherwise you will get charged maximum fare next time you use your card because you haven't "completed" your previous journey. On the bus you'll find the reader next to the driver. If you're caught traveling without having swiped your Oyster, you're liable for an on-the-spot fine.

You can order an Oyster in advance, preloaded with as much credit as you like, from **www.tfl.gov.uk/oyster**. Postage to the U.K. is free, but worldwide delivery costs £4.25. It's cheaper for overseas residents to wait and purchase from the first Tube station they enter—activation is immediate. To top up your balance, use cash or a credit card at any Oyster machine, which you'll find inside most London rail stations, at any of a network of around 4,000 newsagents citywide (see http://ticketstop locator.tfl.gov.uk), or online if you register your card in advance.

THE TUBE & DOCKLANDS LIGHT RAILWAY   The **"Tube"** is the quickest and easiest way to move around the capital. All Tube stations are marked with a red circle and blue crossbar. There are 10 extensive lines, plus the short Waterloo & City line linking Waterloo and Bank, all of which are conveniently color-coded and clearly mapped on the walls of every Tube station. The Tube generally operates Monday to Saturday 5am to 12:30am, Sunday 7:30am to 11:30pm. The above-ground extension of the Tube that links the City with points around the East End and Docklands, including London City Airport, is known as the **Docklands Light Railway,** or "DLR." This metro rail system is essentially integrated with the Tube.

Tickets for the Tube operate on a system of nine fare zones. The fare zones radiate in concentric rings from the central Zone 1, which is where most visitors spend the majority of their time. Zone 1 covers the area from Liverpool Street in the east to Notting Hill in the west, and from Waterloo in the south to Baker Street, Euston, and King's Cross in the north. Tube maps should be available at any Tube station. You can also download one before your trip from the excellent Transport for London (TfL) website, at **www.tfl.gov.uk/assets/downloads/standard-tube-map.pdf**, or download one of the many London Tube apps from your smartphone's app store. A 24-hour information service is also available at ✆ **0843/222-1234.** The best planning tool is the TfL Journey Planner, online at **www.tfl.gov.uk/journeyplanner**.

If you don't have an Oyster (see above), you can get your ticket at a vending machine or a ticket window. But note the prices: The cash fare for travel across up to three zones is £4.30, rising to £5.30 to travel across six zones. A journey from anywhere in zones 1 or 2 to anywhere else in zones 1 or 2 using Oyster pay-as-you-go costs £2 outside peak hours, £2.70 before 9:30am. Oyster will get you across all six zones for £2.90 after 9:30am. On all ticketed journeys, you can transfer as many times as you like as long as you stay on the Tube or DLR network.

THE BUS NETWORK   London's buses can be a delightful way to navigate the city. Not only are they regular, efficient, and—late nights aside—comfortable, but also cheap compared to the Tube system. Buses also allow you to see where you're going—no need for an open-topped bus tour when you can ride the upper deck of an old-fashioned heritage **Routemaster** from Knightsbridge to Trafalgar Square on route no. 9, or Regent Street to St. Paul's and the Tower on the no. 15. Other excellent "sightseeing" routes include the no. 8 (from Oxford Circus to the Bank of

England) and the no. 11 (from Victoria, past Parliament, and through Trafalgar Square to Bank).

Unfortunately, the bewildering array of services and routes deters many visitors—and even some locals. There are online route maps and downloadable area maps available at **www.tfl.gov.uk/tfl/gettingaround/maps/buses**. If you have Web access, you could also try **Busmapper.co.uk**: Simply click your start and end points on an embedded Google Map and the site will suggest the best routes and tip you off about forthcoming departures. It's also available as an iPhone and Android app. **When's My Bus** (http://whensmybus.tumblr.com) is a handy service for Twitter users: Tweet your bus number and location to @whensmybus and it tweets back the next departure.

Unlike on the Tube, fares do not vary according to distance traveled—but if you transfer buses, you must pay again. A single journey from anywhere to anywhere costs £2.30 with cash, £1.35 with an Oyster Card. You can travel on buses all day with an Oyster for £4.20.

Buses generally run from 5am to just after midnight. Some run 24 hours, but other popular routes are served by **night buses,** running once every half-hour or so during the night, and with service numbers prefixed by an "N." For **open-top bus tours** of the city, see "Bus Tours," p. 221.

THE OVERGROUND & OTHER RAIL SERVICES   The remarkable improvements in London's surface rail network have been the big transport story of recent years. Especially useful for visitors to north and southeast London is the **London Overground** (marked in orange on most transport maps). The Overground connects Kew in southwest London with Highbury in North London, Stratford in East London adjacent to the 2012 Olympic Park, as well as Whitechapel and Wapping in the East End, and then points south of the river to Crystal Palace and beyond. The new, air-conditioned carriages and upgraded track ensure an efficient, comfortable ride. Oyster Cards are valid on Overground services. See **www.tfl.gov.uk/overground** for more. Oyster Cards are also valid on the remainder of London's surface rail network—encompassing a vast web of commuter and local services.

TRAVELCARDS   For the **1-Day Off-Peak Travelcard,** valid for travel anywhere within zones 1 and 2 after 9:30am, the cost is £7 for adults or £3.20 for children aged 5 to 15. **One-Week Travelcards** cost adults £29.20 for travel in zones 1 and 2. For more Travelcard prices, visit **www.tfl.gov.uk/tickets**.

BY TAXI   London "black cab" taxi drivers must pass a series of tests known as "the Knowledge," and cabbies generally know every London street within 6 miles of Charing Cross. You can pick up a taxi either by heading for a cab rank—stations, marquees of West End hotels and department stores, and major attractions all have them—or by hailing one in the street. The taxi is available if the yellow taxi sign on its roof is lit. Cabs are among the best designed in the world, and seat up to 5 passengers. Standard vehicles are wheelchair friendly.

Black-taxi meters start at £2.20, with increments of £2 or more per mile thereafter, based on distance and elapsed time. Surcharges are imposed after 8pm and on weekends and public holidays. Expect a mile-long journey to average around £6 to £8, a 2-mile journey around £8 to £13, and so on. There's no need to tip, although you may like to round the fare upward if you receive friendly service. To book, phone **One-Number Taxi** on © **0871/871-8710.** There's a £2 booking fee.

Minicabs are also plentiful, and are useful when regular taxis are scarce, as is often the case in the suburbs or late at night. These cabs are often meterless, so do discuss the fare in advance. If you text CAB to ℂ **60835,** TfL's Cabwise service will text you back with the telephone number of the nearest two licensed minicab offices. Premium minicab operator **Addison Lee** also has taxi booking apps for smartphone platforms including iPhone, Android, and Blackberry; see **www.addisonlee.com/ discover/mobile. Kabbee** (www.kabbee.com) is an Android and iPhone app that compares minicab prices and lets you book from your handset.

BY BOAT   Once London's watery highway, the River Thames is these days more suited to a sightseeing trip than an A-to-B journey. However, it is used by some Docklands commuters, and that commuter service is as fun a way as any to get to the maritime sights of Greenwich (p. 215). **Thames Clippers** (www.thamesclippers.com) runs a year-round fleet of catamarans between the London Eye Pier and North Greenwich Pier, stopping at Embankment Pier, Bankside Pier, Tower Millennium Pier, Canary Wharf Pier, and Greenwich Pier, among others. Services run every 20 to 30 minutes for most of the day; journey time from Embankment to Greenwich is 35 minutes. An adult single costs £5.50, £5 with an Oyster Card, £3.70 if you hold a valid Travelcard, and £2.80 for children aged 5 to 15. A **River Roamer,** allowing unlimited travel between 9am and 9pm—or all day at weekends—costs £12.60, £8.40 for Travelcard holders, and £6.30 for children. A Family River Roamer costs £26.50. Buy online, on board, or at any of the piers. There's also a separate **Tate-to-Tate** service that connects Tate Modern, in Bankside, with Tate Britain, in Pimlico. Tickets cost £5, and boats depart at least hourly, between 10am and 5pm.

For trips upriver to Hampton Court and Kew, see "River Cruises on the Thames," p. 220.

BY BICYCLE   The **Barclays Cycle Hire scheme** (www.tfl.gov.uk/barclayscycle-hire) was launched in 2010. Anyone can rent a so-called "Boris Bike"—jocularly named after mayor at the time, Boris Johnson—from any of the hundreds of docking stations dotted around the center from Bow and Hackney to Olympia, and Regent's Park to the Oval. There's no need to return the bike to the same docking station you collected it from, making the scheme ideal for short-range, spontaneous tourism. Charges are made up of a fixed access fee—£1 per day or £5 per week—and a usage fee—it's free to rent a bike for 30 minutes, £1 for an hour, £6 for 2 hours. Buy access with a credit or debit card at the docking station or join online. Bikes are suited to anyone aged 14 or over.

You should always ride London's roads with extreme care. For more on cycling in London, see **www.tfl.gov.uk/cycling**.

[FastFACTS] LONDON

Area Codes   The country telephone code for Great Britain is **44.** The area code for London is **020.** The full telephone number is then usually eight digits long. As a general rule, businesses and homes in central London have numbers beginning with a **7;** those from further out begin with an **8.** For more info, see "Telephones," later in this section.

Business Hours   With many exceptions, business hours are Monday to Friday 9am to 5pm. In general, retail stores are open Monday to Saturday 9am to 6pm, Sunday 11am to 5pm (sometimes noon to 6pm). Thursday is often late-night opening for central retailers; until 8pm or later isn't unusual.

Doctors If you need a nonemergency doctor, your hotel can recommend one, or you can contact your embassy or consulate. Failing that, try the G.P. (General Practitioner) finder at **www.nhsdirect.nhs.uk**. North American members of the **International Association for Medical Assistance to Travelers (IAMAT;** www.iamat.org; ℂ **716/754-4883,** or **416/652-0137** in Canada) can consult that organization for lists of local approved doctors. **Note:** U.S. and Canadian visitors who become ill while they're in London are eligible only for free *emergency* care. For other treatment, including follow-up care, you'll pay.

Embassies & Consulates The **U.S. Embassy** is at 24 Grosvenor Sq., London W1A 1AE (http://london.usembassy.gov; ℂ **020/7499-9000;** Tube: Bond St.). Standard hours are Monday to Friday 8:30am to 5:30pm. However, for passport and visa services relating to U.S. citizens, contact the **Passport and Citizenship Unit,** 55–56 Upper Brook St., London W1A 2LQ (phone number as above, but the preferred method is e-mail: londonpassports@state.gov). Most nonemergency

inquiries require an appointment.

The **High Commission of Canada,** Canada House, 1 Trafalgar Sq., London SW1Y 5BJ (www.canadainternational.gc.ca/united_kingdom-royaume_uni/index.aspx; ℂ **020/7258-6600;** Tube: Charing Cross), handles passport and consular services for Canadians. Hours are Monday to Friday 9:30am to 1pm.

The **Australian High Commission** is at Australia House, Strand, London WC2B 4LA (www.uk.embassy.gov.au; ℂ **020/7887-5776;** Tube: Covent Garden or Temple). Hours are Monday to Friday 9am to 5pm.

The **New Zealand High Commission** is at New Zealand House, 80 Haymarket (at Pall Mall), London SW1Y 4TQ (www.nzembassy.com/uk; ℂ **020/7930-8422;** Tube: Charing Cross or Piccadilly Circus). Hours are Monday to Friday 9am to 5pm.

The **Irish Embassy** is at 17 Grosvenor Place, London SW1X 7HR (www.embassyofireland.co.uk; ℂ **020/7235-2171;** Tube: Hyde Park Corner). Hours are Monday to Friday 9:30am to 5pm.

Emergencies In any medical emergency, call ℂ **999,** or 112 immediately.

Hospitals There are 24-hour, walk-in Accident & Emergency departments at the following central hospitals: **University College London Hospital,** 235 Euston Rd., London NW1 2BU (www.uclh.nhs.uk;

ℂ **020/3456-7890;** Tube: Warren St.); **St. Thomas's Hospital,** Westminster Bridge Rd. (entrance on Lambeth Palace Rd.), London SE1 7EH (www.guysandstthomas.nhs.uk; ℂ **020/7188-7188;** Tube: Westminster or Waterloo). The **NHS Choices** website (www.nhs.uk) has a search facility that enables you to locate your nearest Accident & Emergency department wherever you are in the U.K. In a medical emergency, you should dial ℂ **999.** Note that emergency care is free for all visitors, irrespective of country of origin.

Internet & Wi-Fi To find a local Internet cafe, start by checking **www.cybercaptive.com**. They tend to be prevalent close to centers of cheap, backpacker-focused accommodations, such as Victoria, Paddington, and Earl's Court.

If you have your own computer or smartphone, **Wi-Fi** makes access much easier. Always check before using your hotel's network—many charge exorbitant rates, and free or cheap Wi-Fi isn't hard to find elsewhere. There's an erratically updated list and map of free hotspots at **http://londonist.com/2007/05/free_wifi_in_lo.php**—many are in coffeeshops where you'll be expected to buy something small, but you won't raise an eyebrow if you walk into either of the city's two Apple Stores to log on (235 Regent St., near

Oxford Circus; and 1–7 The Piazza, Covent Garden). That map has also morphed into the **Free Wifi London** iPhone app, available for £1.619/$1.99 from the iTunes Store. Chains like J. D. Wetherspoon (pubs), Starbucks, and McDonalds are other safe bets, as are many museum cafes. **Work-Snug** (www.worksnug.com) is another great—and free—multiplatform mobile app that helps you locate a Wi-Fi-equipped mobile work-space in the city. To locate more free Wi-Fi, it's also worth using the hotspot locator at **www.jiwire.com**.

Savvy smartphone users from overseas may even find it cheaper and practical to switch off 3G altogether and call using freely available Wi-Fi in combination with a **Skype** (www.skype.com) account and mobile app.

Mail & Post Office An airmail letter to anywhere outside Europe costs 76p for up to 10g ($\frac{1}{3}$ oz.) and generally takes 5 to 7 working days to arrive; postcards also require a 76p stamp. Within the E.U., letters or postcards under 20g ($\frac{2}{3}$ oz.) cost 68p. Within the U.K.,

First Class mail ought to arrive the following working day; Second Class mail takes around 3 days. The main post office is at 24–28 William IV St., WC2 (**(© 020/ 7484-9307;** Tube: Charing Cross). Hours for stamps and postal services are Monday to Friday 8:30am to 6:30pm and Saturday 9am to 5:30pm. Other post office branches are open Monday to Friday 9am to 5:30pm and Saturday 9am to 12:30pm. Many post office branches are closed for an hour at lunch.

Police In an emergency, dial (© **999** (no coins are needed).

Taxes All prices in the U.K. must be quoted inclusive of taxes. Since 2011 the national value-added tax (**VAT**) has stood at 20%. This is included in all hotel and restaurant bills, and in the price of most items you purchase.

If you are permanently resident outside the E.U., VAT on goods can be refunded if you shop at stores that participate in the **Retail Export Scheme**— look for the window sticker or ask the staff. See p. 27 for details. Information

about the scheme is also posted online.

Telephone For **directory assistance** for London, dial (© **118212** for a full range of services; for the rest of Britain, dial (© **118118.** See also "Area Code," above.

Tipping For cab drivers, add about 10% to 15% to the fare on the meter. However, if the driver loads or unloads your luggage, add something extra.

In hotels, porters receive 75p per bag, even if you have only one small suitcase. Hall porters are tipped only for special services. Maids receive £1 per day. In top-ranking hotels, the concierge will often submit a separate bill showing charges for newspapers and other items; if he or she has been particularly helpful, tip extra.

In both restaurants and nightclubs, a 15% service charge is added to the bill. To that, add another 3% to 5%, depending on the service. Tipping in pubs isn't common.

Tour guides expect £2, though it's not mandatory. Theatre ushers don't expect tips.

Exploring London

London isn't a city to visit hurriedly. It is so vast, so stocked with treasures, that it would take a lifetime to explore it thoroughly. But even a quick visit will give you a chance to see what's creating the hottest buzz in shopping and nightlife as well as the city's time-tested treasures.

British Museum ★★★ ☺ MUSEUM The "BM" was born in the age of Enlightenment and Empire, the progeny of two great British desires—the desire for knowledge and the desire for other people's possessions. In the 18th and 19th centuries, the British upper classes traveled the globe, uncovering the artifacts of distant civilizations, packing them in crates, and shipping them home. Their acquisitions formed

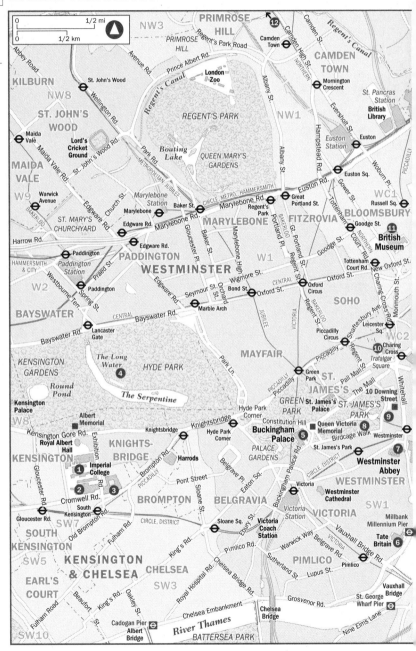

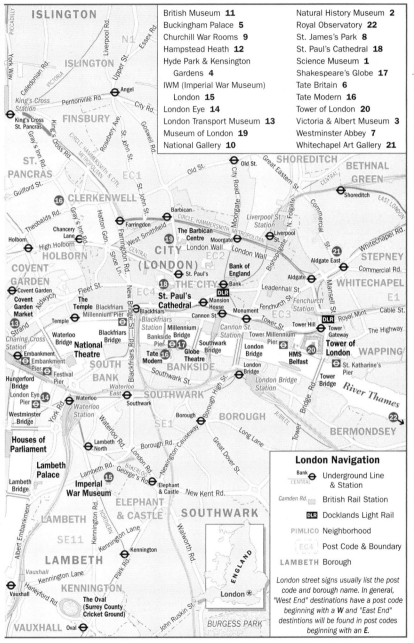

British Museum **11**
Buckingham Palace **5**
Churchill War Rooms **9**
Hampstead Heath **12**
Hyde Park & Kensington
   Gardens **4**
IWM (Imperial War Museum)
   London **15**
London Eye **14**
London Transport Museum **13**
Museum of London **19**
National Gallery **10**

Natural History Museum **2**
Royal Observatory **22**
St. James's Park **8**
St. Paul's Cathedral **18**
Science Museum **1**
Shakespeare's Globe **17**
Tate Britain **6**
Tate Modern **16**
Tower of London **20**
Victoria & Albert Museum **3**
Westminster Abbey **7**
Whitechapel Art Gallery **21**

London Navigation

Bank ⊖
CENTRAL   Underground Line
          & Station

Camden Rd.   British Rail Station

DLR   Docklands Light Rail

PIMLICO   Neighborhood

EC4   Post Code & Boundary

LAMBETH   Borough

*London street signs usually list the post
code and borough name. In general,
"West End" destinations have a post code
beginning with a W and "East End"
destinations will be found in post codes
beginning with an E.*

the basis of the museum's collection, which has since been built into one of the world's largest and finest.

The collection is arranged along roughly geographical lines, so you could order your tour accordingly, taking in the **Rosetta Stone** from Egypt (the object that finally enabled scholars to decipher hieroglyphics), the **Elgin (or Parthenon) Marbles** from Ancient Greece, or the treasures of a 7th-century Saxon ship burial from **Sutton Hoo,** in Suffolk. But there's so much more—Babylonian astronomical instruments, giant heads from Easter Island, totem poles from Canada, mummies from Egyptian tombs, Chinese sculptures, Indian texts, Roman statues, African art . . . the list goes on. In fact, the museum has more objects in storage than it ever does on display.

And if that wasn't enough, the BM hosts a succession of blockbuster temporary exhibitions, which are often staged in the **Reading Room,** the former home of the British Library. It lies at the center of the **Great Court,** the building's central courtyard, which is topped by a giant glass roof designed by Foster and Partners, and boasts various cafes and picnic areas.

Of course you could always take the easy option, and let someone else decide what you should see. Free half-hour "Eye Opener Tours" to different sections of the museum are given every 15 to 30 minutes from 11am to 3:45pm.

Great Russell St., WC1. www.britishmuseum.org. ☎ **020/7323-8299.** Free admission. Sat–Thurs 10am–5:30pm; Fri 10am–8:30pm. Tube: Holborn, Tottenham Court Rd., Goodge St., or Russell Sq.

Buckingham Palace ★ ☺ 🖐 PALACE   The first house to stand on the site of what is now the principal London home of the monarch was built by the Duke of Buckingham in 1702. It was acquired by George II in 1761 and expanded and renovated throughout the 19th century, first by the flamboyant John Nash for George IV, and later by the more dour Edward Blore (dubbed "Blore the Bore") for Victoria. A new facade—including the famous balcony from which the royal family waves to the masses on major royal occasions—was added in 1913.

Although the exterior is rather boxy and uninspiring, the interior has more going on. For 8 weeks in August and September, while the royals are elsewhere, you can look for yourself. Tours visit a small selection of the palace's 600-plus rooms, including the Grand Staircase, the Throne Room, the Picture Gallery (which displays masterpieces by Van Dyck, Rembrandt, Rubens, and others), and the lavish State Rooms, where the Queen entertains heads of government with grand formal banquets. You can also take a walk along a 3-mile path through 40 acres of landscaped gardens.

Outside of the summer months, the only parts of the palace open to the public are the **Queen's Gallery** and the **Royal Mews.**

Buckingham Palace is also the setting for a daily dose of public pageantry, **Changing of the Guard.** Pretty much every guidebook says the same thing about the ceremony—it's terribly British and a bit dull, and who are we to buck the trend? The needlessly elaborate ceremony for changing the 40 men guarding Buckingham Palace with another contingent from Wellington Barracks only exists for the benefit of visitors these days. It's actually interesting for about 5 minutes—with bearskin-wearing, red-coated soldiers, music from the marching band, shouted orders, complicated marching patterns. The trouble is the whole thing lasts for around 40 minutes—and if you want a decent vantage point, you'll need to turn up at least 1 hour early.

📎 The Guard Doesn't Change Every Day

The ceremony begins at 11:30am sharp every day between May and July, and on alternate days for the rest of the year—in theory, anyway. However, it's often canceled in bad weather, which shows just what an unnecessary ceremony it is. If it looks like it's going to rain, it's probably best to head somewhere else instead.

A much more accessible piece of pageantry can be seen at nearby **Horse Guards Parade** in Whitehall.

At end of The Mall. www.royalcollection.org.uk. ℂ **020/7766-7300.** Palace tours £18 adults, £16.50 seniors and students, £10.25 children 5–16, £47 family ticket, free for ages 4 and under. Changing of the Guard free. Aug 1–Sept 25 (dates can vary), and additional dates may be added. Daily 9:45am–6pm. Changing of the Guard daily May–July at 11:30am and alternating days for the rest of the year. Tube: St. James's Park, Green Park, or Victoria.

Churchill War Rooms ★★ HISTORIC SITE   These cramped subterranean rooms were the nerve center of the British war effort during the final years of World War II, where Winston Churchill and his advisors planned what they hoped would be an Allied victory. In August 1945, with the conflict finally won, the rooms were abandoned exactly as they were, creating a time capsule of the moment of victory.

You can see the **Map Room** and its huge wall maps; the Atlantic map is a mass of pinholes (each hole represents at least one convoy). Next door is Churchill's bedroom-cum-office, which has a bed and a desk with the two BBC microphones on it via which he tried to rally the nation. Other rooms include Churchill's kitchen and dining room, and the Transatlantic Telephone Room that is little more than a broom closet housing the scrambler phone with which Churchill conferred with U.S. President Roosevelt.

Also in the war rooms is the **Churchill Museum,** the world's first major museum dedicated to the life of Sir Winston Churchill.

Clive Steps, at end of King Charles St., SW1. www.iwm.org.uk/visits/churchill-war-rooms. ℂ **020/7930-6961.** Admission £16 adults, £13 seniors and students, free for children 15 and under. Daily 9:30am–6pm (last admission 5pm). Tube: Westminster or St. James's Park.

Hampstead Heath ★★★ ☺ PARK/GARDEN   This 320-hectare (791-acre) expanse of high heath is made up of formal parkland, woodland, heath, meadowland, and ponds. One of the few places in the big city that feels properly wild, it's a fantastic place to lose yourself on a rambling wander. On a clear day, you can see St. Paul's Cathedral, the Houses of Parliament, and even the hills of Kent from the prime viewing spot atop Parliament Hill, 98m (322 ft.) up. For years Londoners have come here to sun-worship, fly kites, fish the ponds, swim, picnic, jog, or just laze about.

Much of the northern end is taken up by the manicured grounds of **Kenwood House,** a great spot for a picnic, where concerts are staged on summer evenings. Along its eastern end are ponds set aside for bathing (there's a ladies' pool, a men's pool, and a mixed pool), sailing model boats, and as a bird sanctuary—the heath is one of London's best **birdwatching** locations.

South of the heath is the leafy, well-to-do **Hampstead Village,** a longtime favorite haunt of writers, artists, architects, musicians, and scientists. Keats, D. H. Lawrence,

Shelley, Robert Louis Stevenson, and Kingsley Amis all lived here. The village's Regency and Georgian houses offer a quirky mix of historic pubs, toy shops, and chic boutiques, especially along **Flask Walk.**

Hampstead, NW3. www.cityoflondon.gov.uk. (*C*) **020/7482-7073.** Free admission. Open 24 hours. Tube: Hampstead/Train: Hampstead Heath or Gospel Oak.

Hyde Park ★★★ & Kensington Gardens ★★ ☺ PARK/GARDEN   Once a favorite deer-hunting ground of Henry VIII, Hyde Park is central London's largest park. With the adjoining Kensington Gardens it forms a single giant open space, made up of 246 hectares (608 acres) of velvety lawns interspersed with ponds, flowerbeds, trees, meadows, playgrounds, and more. The two parks are divided by a 17-hectare (42-acre) lake known as the **Serpentine.** Paddleboats and rowboats can be rented from the **boathouse** (open Easter–Oct) on the north side ((*C*) **020/7262-1330**), costing £10 per hour for adults, £5 per hour for children. Part of the Serpentine has also been set aside for use as a **lido** ((*C*) **020/7706-3422**), where you can swim, provided you don't mind the often "challenging" water temperature. It costs £4 for adults, £3 for children.

Near the Serpentine bridge is the **Princess Diana Memorial Fountain,** the somewhat (perhaps appropriately) troubled monument to the late princess. When first opened in 2004, its slippery granite surfaces proved unsuited for something intended as a swimming and paddling venue, leading to its almost instant closure. It has since reopened with additional safety features.

At the northeastern tip of Hyde Park, near Marble Arch, is **Speakers' Corner,** where people have the right to speak (and more often shout) about any subject that takes their fancy. In the past you might have heard Karl Marx, Lenin, or George Orwell trying to convert the masses; today's speakers tend to be less well known, if no less fervent, and heckling is all part of the fun.

Blending with Hyde Park to the west of the Serpentine, and bordering the grounds of Kensington Palace (see below), are the well-manicured **Kensington Gardens.** They contain numerous attractions including the **Serpentine Gallery,** a famous statue of **Peter Pan** erected by J. M. Barrie himself (secretly, in the middle of the night), and the **Diana, Princess of Wales Memorial Playground,** a pirate-themed fun area that has proved a more successful tribute to the late Princess of Wales than Hyde Park's fountain. At the park's southern edge is the **Albert Memorial,** a gloriously over-the-top, gilded monument erected by Queen Victoria in honor of her late husband.

Hyde Park, W2. www.royalparks.org.uk/Hyde-Park.aspx. (*C*) **030/0061-2100.** Free admission. Hyde Park open daily 5am–midnight. Kensington Gardens open daily 6am–dusk. Tube: Hyde Park Corner, Marble Arch, or Lancaster Gate.

IWM (Imperial War Museum) London ★★★ ☺ MUSEUM   From 1814 to 1930, this deceptively elegant, domed building was the Bethlehem Royal Hospital, an old-style "madhouse," where the "patients" formed part of a Victorian freak show—visitors could pay a penny to go and stare at the lunatics. (The hospital's name since entered the language as "Bedlam," a slang expression for chaos and confusion.) Thankfully, civilization has moved on in its treatment of the mentally ill, although as this warfare museum shows, nations are still as capable of cruelty and organized madness as they ever were.

The great, gung-ho 38-cm (15-in.) naval guns parked outside the entrance give an indication of what you can expect in the main hall. This is the boys' toys section with a whole fleet of tanks, planes, and missiles on display (including a Battle of Britain Spitfire, a V2 rocket, and a German one-man submarine), and plenty of interactivity for the kids, with cockpits to climb into and touchscreen terminals to explore.

After the initial bombast, however, comes a selection of thoughtful, sobering exhibits, focusing on the human cost of war. These include galleries exploring life during World Wars I and II—both on the battlefield and at home—a new gallery celebrating exploits of supreme valor, "Extraordinary Heroes," and the "Secret War" exhibition which looks at the use of duplicity, subterfuge, and spying in wartime.

On the upper floors, things become more thoughtful still. The third floor provides an intense account of the Holocaust, examining the first attempt to apply modern industrial techniques to the destruction of people. And, just to remind you that this is not an evil that has been permanently consigned to history, the "Crimes against Humanity" exhibition explores modern genocides. Its central exhibit is a harrowing 30-minute film. These two galleries are not recommended for children 13 and under.

Lambeth Rd., SE1. www.iwm.org.uk/visits/iwm-london. ℭ **020/7416-5320.** Free admission. Daily 10am–6pm. Tube: Lambeth North or Elephant and Castle.

London Eye ★★ ☺ OBSERVATION WHEEL The largest observation wheel in Europe, the London Eye has become, in the decade since it opened, a potent icon of the capital, as clearly identified with London as the Eiffel Tower is with Paris. And indeed, it performs much the same function—giving people the chance to observe the city from above. Passengers are carried in 32 glass-sided "pods," each representing one of the 32 boroughs of London (which lucky travelers get Croydon?), that make a complete revolution every half-hour. Along the way you'll see bird's-eye views of some of London's most famous landmarks, including the Houses of Parliament, Buckingham Palace, the B.T. Tower, St. Paul's, the "Gherkin," and of course, the River Thames itself. "Night flights," when you can gaze at the twinkling lights of the city, are available in winter. Ticket prices are 10% cheaper if booked online.

Millennium Jubilee Gardens, SE1. www.londoneye.com. ℭ **0871/781-3000.** Admission £18.60 adults, £15 seniors and students, £9.50 children 4–15. Times vary, but the Eye is open daily from 10am, usually till 9pm in summer (9:30pm in July–Aug) and till 8:30pm in winter. Tube: Waterloo or Westminster.

 London's Best "Bird's-Eye" Views

The **London Eye** (above) is the most obvious of the attractions offering a "bird's-eye" view of the capital, but it's by no means the only vantage point. For centuries, **St. Paul's Cathedral** (p. 217) has been letting Londoners willing to climb its 500 plus steps gaze out over their city, spread out below them like a great 3-D map. Worthy, albeit slightly less elevated, panoramas are also offered from the top of **Westminster Abbey** (p. 220), the **National Portrait Gallery** restaurant, and the **Oxo**

Tower—this last one is particularly recommended, because it's free.

At the time of writing, these were set to be joined by some new views on the block, including a 60m (200-ft.) **Cable Car** over the Thames between the ExCel Centre and the O2 Arena, the 115m (377-ft.) **ArcelorMittal Orbit Tower** at Olympic Park, and—towering over them all—the 310m (1,017-ft.) **Shard,** western Europe's tallest building. Its 72nd-floor observation deck will be London's highest public space.

London Transport Museum ★★ ☺ MUSEUM   Arranged more or less chronologically, this museum, housed in the swish glass-and-iron confines of Covent Garden's former flower market, traces the history of the capital's transport network from the days of steam and horse power to the green technologies of today. There are some wonderful old contraptions on display, including a reconstruction of an 1829 horse-drawn omnibus, a steam locomotive that ran along the world's first underground railway, and London's first trolleybus.

In addition to all the impressive hardware, the museum has displays on the often-overlooked aesthetics of public transport, particularly the signs, posters, and logos that together provided London Transport with such a clear graphic sensibility in the early 20th century.

There's lots of great stuff for kids here, too, including a hands-on section where they can climb aboard miniature buses, trams, trains, and tubes, and trails to pick up at the front desk. ***Insider tip:*** The £13.50 entrance fee entitles you to unlimited visits over a 12-month period—hang on to your ticket.

Covent Garden Piazza, WC2. www.ltmuseum.co.uk. ⓒ **020/7379-6344.** Admission £13.50 adults, £10 seniors and students, free for children 15 and under. Sat–Thurs 10am–6pm; Fri 11am–6pm (last admission 5:15pm). Tube: Covent Garden.

Museum of London ★★ ☺ MUSEUM   Although the location is rather grim, in the center of an unappealing roundabout in London's Barbican district, this museum is an absolute joy, particularly since a recent revamp gives visitors a real sense of the drama of London's story unfolding. Exhibits are arranged so that you can begin and end your chronological stroll through 250,000 years at the main entrance to the museum. Upstairs you'll find sections devoted to "London before London" (with flint arrow heads and Bronze Age weapons); Roman London (mosaics, statues, and scale models of the city); Medieval London (Viking battleaxes and knights' armor); and War, Plague, and Fire (models of Shakespeare's Rose Theatre, the Great Fire, and Cromwell's death mask). The recently revamped downstairs galleries bring the story up to date with displays on the "Expanding City: 1666–1850" (including a recreated 18th-century prison and a 240-year-old printing press); "People's City: 1850s–1940s" (walk a replica Victorian street); and "World City: 1950s–Today" (explore an interactive model of the Thames), as well as perhaps the museum's most eye-catching exhibit, the **Lord Mayor's Coach,** a gilt-and-scarlet fairytale carriage built in 1757.

London Wall, EC2. www.museumoflondon.org.uk. ⓒ **020/7001-9844.** Free admission. Daily 10am–6pm. Tube: St. Paul's or Barbican.

National Gallery ★★★ ☺ ART MUSEUM   The National's collection of more than 2,300 paintings provides a comprehensive overview of the development of Western art from the mid-1200s to 1900, rivaling any of Europe's great art galleries, such as the Louvre, the Prado, or the Uffizi. It's certainly more impressive than the original collection, founded by the British Government in 1824, which had just 38 works.

The layout is chronological. Passing through the sturdy neoclassical facade on Trafalgar Square, you turn left to find the gallery's oldest works, housed, by way of contrast, in its newest section, the 1990s-built **Sainsbury Wing.** It covers the period from 1250 to 1500, including paintings by such Renaissance and pre-Renaissance greats as Giotto, Piero della Francesca, Botticelli, Leonardo da Vinci, and Van Eyck (including his famed *Arnolfini Portrait*).

The chronology then moves on to the West Wing, covering 1500 to 1600 and filled with European Old Masters, such as Titian, Raphael, El Greco, and Hans Holbein.

Next in line is the North Wing (1600–1700), where highlights include a Rembrandt self-portrait and works by Caravaggio and Velázquez, with things culminating in the East Wing (1700–1900), with a celebrated selection of Impressionist and Post-Impressionist paintings, including various water lilies by Monet, Van Gogh's *Sunflowers,* and Renoir's *Les Parapluies* (The Umbrellas)—some of the most popular (not to say most valuable) paintings in the collection.

If you can't decide where to begin, try joining a free 1-hour taster tour of the collection given every day at 11:30am and 2:30pm. Children's trails are available for £1 from the front desk (or can be downloaded for free in advance from the website).

Trafalgar Sq., WC2. www.nationalgallery.org.uk. 📞 **020/7747-2885.** Free admission; fee charged for temporary exhibitions. Sat–Thurs 10am–6pm; Fri 10am–9pm. Tube: Charing Cross or Leicester Sq.

Natural History Museum ★★★ ☺ MUSEUM   It seems fitting that one of London's great museums should be housed in such a grand building, a soaring Romanesque structure that provides a suitably reverent setting for what is often described as a "cathedral of nature." The museum's remit is to cover the great diversity of life on Earth, although that coverage is by no means uniform. One group of life forms gets a lot more attention lavished on it than any others, much to the delight of visiting 8-year-olds—**dinosaurs.** As you arrive, your first vision will be the giant cast of a diplodocus looming down above you. If you want to see more of these great prehistoric beasts—but with added rubbery skin and jerky movements—then turn left where you'll find a hall filled with fossils and finds, as well as displays of animatronic dinosaurs permanently surrounded by wide-eyed children.

The dinosaurs form part of the Blue Zone, one of the four color-coded sections that make up the museum. This zone is primarily concerned with animals, both past and present, and has plenty of other showstoppers, including a 40m (90-ft.) model of a blue whale hanging from the ceiling, a saber-tooth tiger skeleton, and an adult-size model of a fetus.

The Green Zone's galleries focus on the environment, evolution, and ecology. Highlights include giant models of insects (in the Creepy Crawlies gallery), and a collection of precious stones in the museum's new section, the **Vault.**

The Earth's interior processes are explored in the Red Zone, where you can try and stay upright on an earthquake simulator, and see plastercasts of victims preserved in ash by the volcanic eruption at Pompeii.

The final zone, the Orange Zone, is the museum's latest pride and joy, comprising the eight-story glass-and-steel **Darwin Centre,** the most significant addition to the museum since it opened in 1881. Constructed in 2008 for the 150th anniversary of Darwin's *Origin of the Species,* the center is primarily a research institute, but also boasts hi-tech attractions for the public. The museum offers resources for younger visitors, including free discovery guides, explorer backpacks, and family workshops.

Cromwell Rd., SW7. www.nhm.ac.uk. 📞 **020/7942-5000.** Free admission. Daily 10am–5:50pm. Tube: South Kensington.

Royal Observatory ★ ☺ HISTORIC SITE   The home of **Greenwich Mean Time,** the Observatory was designed by Sir Christopher Wren in the early 18th century and boasts the country's largest refracting telescope, as well as displays on timekeeping, a *camera obscura,* and (the only part of the site that's free to visit) an interactive astronomy exhibition. The highlight, however, is the **Planetarium** (the only one in the country), where effects-laden star shows are projected onto its ceiling.

Outside, overlooking Greenwich's serene park, you can enjoy one of London's most popular photo opportunities, standing across the **Prime Meridian,** the line of 0° longitude marked in the courtyard, with one foot in the Earth's eastern hemisphere and one foot in the western. At lunch you can set your watch precisely by watching the red **"time ball"** atop the roof, which has dropped at exactly 1pm since 1833, to enable passing shipmasters to set their chronometers accurately.

Blackheath Ave., SE10. www.nmm.ac.uk/places/royal-observatory. ℂ **020/8858-4422.** Admission to Observatory £7 adults, £5 seniors and students, free for children aged 15 and under; Planetarium £6.50 adults, £4.50 children, £17.50 family. Daily 10am–5pm. Train: Greenwich/DLR: Cutty Sark.

Science Museum ★★★ ☺ MUSEUM   Founded in the 1850s in the wake of—and largely with left-over contraptions from—the Great Exhibition, the "Museum of Patents," as it was originally known, has grown to become the country's pre-eminent museum of science. It's also one of the capital's great interactive experiences, filled with buttons to press, levers to pull, and experiments to absorb you. There's plenty of impressive hardware on display, beginning, just after the entrance, in the **Energy Hall,** where you can meet the great clunking behemoths of the Industrial Revolution, including steam locomotives and giant beam engines. Beyond, the **Making the Modern World** exhibition celebrates 150 of the most significant icons of industrial progress from the past 250 years, including Charles Babbage's "Difference Engine," the first automatic calculator, Watson and Crick's model of the structure of DNA, and the Apollo 10 command module. On the same floor is the **Legend of Apollo 4-D Cinema,** offering viewers a computer-simulated round-trip to the moon, complete with stirring music and a portentous voiceover.

And that's just the start of the museum. Elsewhere you'll find galleries dedicated to medicine, telecommunications, computers, and flight—the last now with state-of-the-art flight simulators—as well as the ever-popular **Launchpad,** where there are more than 50 hands-on experiments for kids to try, as well as an IMAX cinema showing spectacular nature and space-related reels on a giant screen.

Exhibition Rd., SW7. www.sciencemuseum.org.uk. ℂ **0870/870-4868.** Free admission. Daily 10am–6pm. Closed Dec 24–26. Tube: South Kensington.

Shakespeare's Globe ★ HISTORIC SITE/THEATRE   This is a recent recreation of one of the most significant public theatres ever built, Shakespeare's Globe, where the Bard premiered many of his most famous plays. The new Globe isn't an exact replica: It seats 1,500 patrons, not the 3,000 who regularly squeezed in during the early 1600s, and this thatched roof has been specially treated with a fire retardant—just as well, as a shot from a stage cannon fired during a performance of *Henry VIII* provided the ultimate finale, setting the roof alight and burning the original theatre to the ground.

Insider tip: Guided tours of the facility are offered throughout the day in the theatre's winter off-season. From May to September, however, Globe tours are only available in the morning. In the afternoon, when matinee performances are taking place, alternative (and cheaper) tours to the scanty remains of the **Rose Theatre,** the Globe's precursor (which was torn down in the early 17th century), are offered instead.

See p. 234 for details on attending a play here.

21 New Globe Walk, SE1. www.shakespearesglobe.com. ℂ **020/7902-1400.** Admission and Globe Tour/Rose Tour £13.50/10 adults, £12/9 seniors, £11/8.50 students, £8/7 children 5–15, free for children 4 and under, £35/29 family ticket. Oct–Apr daily 10am–5pm; May–Sept daily 9am–noon and 12:30–5pm. Tube: Mansion House or London Bridge.

St. James's Park ★★ ☺ PARK/GARDEN   With its scenic central pond, tended flowerbeds, and picnic-friendly lawns, it's difficult to believe that this Royal Park was once a swamp near a leper colony. Today it's as elegant a green space as London can muster, and one of the best places in the center of town to watch wildfowl. Its pond is home to more than 20 species, including ducks, geese, and even four pelicans—the descendants of a pair presented to Charles II by a Russian ambassador in 1662—which are all fed daily between 2:30 and 3:30pm.

The Mall, SW1. www.royalparks.org.uk/parks/st_james_park. ✆**030/0061-2350.** Free admission. Open 24 hr. Tube: St. James's Park.

St. Paul's Cathedral ★★★ ☺ CATHEDRAL   London's skyline has changed dramatically during the past three centuries. Buildings have come and gone, architectural styles have waxed and waned, but throughout there has been one constant—the great plump dome of St. Paul's Cathedral gazing beatifically down upon the city. Despite the best intentions of the Luftwaffe and modern skyscraper designers, Sir Christopher Wren's masterpiece is still the defining landmark of the skyline.

The interior is a neck-craningly large space. Dotted around at ground level are tombs and memorials to various British heroes, including the Duke of Wellington, Lawrence of Arabia, and in the South Quire Aisle, an effigy of John Donne, one of the country's most celebrated poets and a former dean of St. Paul's. It's one of the few items to have survived from the previous, medieval cathedral, which was destroyed by the Great Fire in 1666; you can still see scorch marks on its base.

The cathedral offers some of the capital's best views, although you'll have to earn them by undertaking a 500-plus-step climb up to the **Golden Gallery.** Here you can enjoy giddying 360° panoramas of the capital, as well as perhaps equally stomach-tightening views down to the floor 111m (364 ft.) below.

Down in the crypt is a bumper crop of memorials, including those of Alexander Fleming, Admiral Lord Nelson, William Blake, and Wren himself—the epitaph on his simple tombstone reads: "Reader, if you seek a monument, look around you."

St. Paul's Churchyard, EC4. www.stpauls.co.uk. ✆**020/7246-8350.** Cathedral and galleries £14.50 adults, £13.50 seniors and students, £5.50 children 6–18, £34.50 family ticket, free for children 5 and under. Cathedral (excluding galleries) Mon–Sat 8:30am–4pm; galleries Mon–Sat 9:30am–4pm. No sightseeing Sun (services only). Tube: St. Paul's.

Tate Britain ★★★ ART MUSEUM   Fronting the Thames near Vauxhall Bridge, the Tate looks like a smaller and more graceful relation of the British Museum. Within is the country's finest collection of domestic art, dating from the 16th century to the present, with most of the country's leading artists represented, including such notables as Gainsborough, Reynolds, Stubbs, and Constable; William Hogarth, and the incomparable William Blake; as well as such modern greats as Stanley Spencer, Francis Bacon, and David Hockney. The collection of works by J. M. W. Turner is the Tate's largest by a single artist, spread over seven rooms. Turner himself willed most of his paintings and watercolors to the nation.

And, just to show the young ones that it can still swing with the best of them, Tate Britain is also the host each autumn of the annual **Turner Prize,** the media-baiting, controversy-seeking competition for the best contemporary British art.

Free tours of parts of the collection are offered Monday to Friday (at 11am, noon, 2pm, and 3pm) and on Saturdays and Sundays at noon and 3pm, and the first Friday of each month sees the "Late at Tate" event, which involves extended opening hours ('til 10pm) and free events, such as talks, film screenings, or live music.

If you want to make an art-filled day of it, the **Tate-to-Tate boat service** departs from just out front to **Tate Modern** all day (see p. 205).

Millbank, SW1. www.tate.org.uk/britain. ✆ **020/7887-8888.** Free admission; special exhibitions incur a charge of £5–£15. Daily 10am–6pm (last admission 5:15pm). Tube: Pimlico.

Tate Modern ★★★ ART MUSEUM   Welcoming more than four million visitors a year, Tate Modern is the world's most popular modern art gallery (the free admission helps), and one of the capital's best attractions. From the day it opened in 2000, it has received almost as many plaudits for its setting as for its contents. It's housed in a converted 1940's brick power station, the brooding industrial functionalism of the architecture providing a fitting canopy for the challenging art within. Through the main entrance you enter a vast space, the **Turbine Hall,** where a succession of giant temporary exhibitions are staged—the bigger and more ambitious, the better.

The permanent collection encompasses a great body of modern art dating from 1900 to the present. Spread over several levels, it covers all the big hitters, including Matisse, Rothko, Pollock, Picasso, Dalí, Duchamp, and Warhol, and is arranged according to themes and movements—surrealism, minimalism, cubism, expressionism, and so on. Further explanation—always useful where modern art is concerned—is provided by the free 45-minute guided tours of the collection given daily at 11am, noon, 2pm, and 3pm. Tate Modern stays open late on Friday and Saturday, when events, such as concerts and talks, are often held.

Such has been Tate Modern's success that a new extension has been built, which should be complete by the time this guide hits the shelves. Taking the form of an asymmetrical pyramid, it uses the same type of bricks as the original building, making it look as if the power station has simply sprouted a new, angular growth. It will contain new art spaces, some occupying the massive underground oil tanks that once powered the station's turbines.

Bankside, SE1. www.tate.org.uk/modern. ✆ **020/7887-8888.** Free admission. Sun–Thurs 10am–6pm; Fri–Sat 10am–10pm. Tube: Southwark or London Bridge.

Tower of London ★★★ ☺ CASTLE   The Tower is actually a compound of structures built at various times for varying purposes. The oldest part is the **White Tower,** begun by William the Conqueror in 1078 to keep London's native Saxon population in check. Later rulers added towers, walls, and fortified gates, until the buildings became like a small town within a city. Although it began life as a stronghold against rebellion, the tower's main role eventually became less about keeping people out, than making sure whoever was inside couldn't escape. It became the favored prison and execution site for anyone who displeased the monarch. Notable prisoners served their last meals here include the "princes in the tower," Lady Jane Grey (who reigned as queen for just 9 days before being toppled by Mary I in 1553), and Anne Boleyn, one of several unfortunates who thought that marrying that most unforgiving of monarchs, Henry VIII, was a good idea. A plaque on Tower Green marks the spot where they met their grisly ends.

Displays on some of the Tower's captives can be seen in the **Bloody Tower,** including a reconstruction of the study of Sir Walter Raleigh, the great Elizabethan adventurer who is generally credited with having introduced tobacco smoking to England. A favorite of Elizabeth I, he was executed by James I, a fervent anti-smoker, having spent 13 years as a prisoner here.

In addition to being a prison, the Tower has also been used as a royal palace, a mint, and an armory. Today, however, it's perhaps best known as the keeper of the

Crown Jewels, the main ceremonial regalia of the British monarch, which—when not being used—are displayed in the tower's **Jewel House.** It's probably best to tackle this soon after your arrival, as the lines seem to build exponentially over the course of the day. You hop aboard a travelator for a slow glide past some of the Queen's top trinkets, including the Imperial State Crown (as modeled each year at the State Opening of Parliament), which looks like a child's fantasy of a piece of royal headwear, set with no fewer than 3,000 jewels, including the fourth-largest diamond in the world.

After the jewels, the tower's next most popular draw is probably the **Royal Armory** located in the White Tower, where you can see various fearsome-looking weapons, including swords, halberds, and morning stars, as well as bespoke suits of armor made for kings. The complex also boasts the only surviving medieval palace in Britain, dating back to the 1200s. It stands in the riverside wall above **Traitors' Gate,** through which prisoners were brought to the Tower. Within are reconstructed bedrooms, a throne room, and chapel.

Be sure to take advantage of the free hour-long tours offered by the iconic guards, the Yeoman Warders—more commonly known as **Beefeaters.** They'll regale you with tales of royal intrigue, and introduce you to the Tower's current most famous residents, the six ravens who live on Tower Gardens. According to legend, if the ravens ever leave the Tower, the monarchy will fall—the birds' wings are kept clipped, just to make sure. The tours take place every half-hour from 9:30am until 3:30pm in summer (2:30pm in winter) and leave from the Middle Tower near the entrance.

Tower Hill, EC3. www.hrp.org.uk/TowerOfLondon. *©***0844/482-7777.** Admission £20 adults, £17 students and seniors, £10.45 children 5–15, £55 family ticket, free for children 4 and under. Mar–Oct Tues–Sat 9am–5:30pm, Sun–Mon 10am–5:30pm; Nov–Feb Tues–Sat 9am–4:30pm, Sun–Mon 10am–4:30pm. Tube: Tower Hill/DLR: Tower Gateway.

Victoria & Albert Museum ★★★ ☺ MUSEUM The V&A (as it's usually known) could justly claim to be the world's greatest collection of applied arts, comprising seven floors and 150 galleries, in which are displayed, at a rough estimate, around four million items of decorative art from across the world and throughout the ages—sculptures, jewelry, textiles, clothes, paintings, ceramics, furniture, architecture, and more. Many of the collections are among the finest of their type. The V&A has the largest collection of Renaissance sculptures outside Italy, the greatest collection of Indian art outside India (in the Nehru Gallery), and the country's most comprehensive collection of antique dresses (in the Fashion Gallery). The Photography Gallery can draw on some 500,000 individual images, the recently added William & Judith Bolling Gallery holds one of the world's largest (and most glittering) collections of European jewelry, while the British Galleries can offer perhaps the greatest diversity of British design available anywhere, with all the great names of the past 400 years represented, including Chippendale, Charles Rennie Mackintosh, and William Morris.

To help you plot your path, your first stop should be the front desk where you can pick up leaflets, floor plans, and themed family trails. If you'd rather somebody else made the decisions for you, free guided tours leave from the grand entrance daily, hourly between 10:30am and 3:30pm. Art-based drop-in events are laid on for families on weekends.

Cromwell Rd., SW7. www.vam.ac.uk. *©***020/7942-2000.** Free admission. Temporary exhibitions often £12.50. Sun–Thurs 10am–5:45pm; Fri 10am–10pm. Tube: South Kensington.

Westminster Abbey ★★★ CHURCH   The Abbey is not just one of the finest examples of ecclesiastical architecture in Europe, it's also the shrine of the nation where monarchs are anointed before their god and memorials to the nation's greatest figures fill every corner. From the outside, it's a magnificently earnest-looking structure, its two great square towers and pointed arches the very epitome of medieval Gothic, while the inside is a cluttered mass of symbols and statuary. The building was begun in 1245 under the reign of Henry II and finally completed in the early 16th century. This replaced an earlier structure commissioned in 1045 by Edward the Confessor (which itself had replaced a 7th-century original) and was consecrated in 1065, just in time to host Edward's funeral and (following a brief tussle in Hastings) the coronation of William the Conqueror. It has been, with a couple of exceptions, the setting for every coronation since, and it was here on April 29, 2011, that Prince William married Kate Middleton.

More or less at the center of the Abbey stands the shrine of Edward the Confessor, while scattered around are the tombs of various other royals, including Henry V, Elizabeth I, and Richard III—all rather overshadowed by the Renaissance tomb of Henry VII. Nearby is the surprisingly shabby **Coronation Chair,** on which almost every monarch since Edward II, including the current one, has sat during their coronation.

In **Poet's Corner** you'll find a great assortment of memorials to the country's greatest men (and a few women) of letters, clustered around the grave of Geoffrey Chaucer, who was buried here in 1400. These include a statue of Shakespeare, his arm resting on a pile of books, Jacob Epstein's bust of William Blake, as well as tributes to Jane Austen, Coleridge, John Milton, Dylan Thomas, and D. H. Lawrence.

Statesmen and men of science—Disraeli, Newton, Charles Darwin—are also interred in the Abbey or honored by monuments. Near to the west door is the 1965 memorial to Sir Winston Churchill and the tomb of the **Unknown Warrior,** commemorating the British dead of World War I.

Broad Sanctuary, SW1. www.westminster-abbey.org. ℂ **020/7222-5152.** Admission £16 adults, £13 students and seniors, £6 children 11–18, £32 family ticket, free for children 10 and under. Mon–Tues and Thurs–Fri 9:30am–4:30pm (last admission 3.30pm); Wed 9:30am–7pm (last admission 6pm); Sat 9:30am–2:30pm (last admission 1.30pm). Tube: Westminster or St. James's Park.

Whitechapel Art Gallery ★★ ART MUSEUM   In 2009 East London's premier art museum reopened following the most significant revamp since its foundation in 1901. Throughout its history the gallery has often played a leading role in the development of artistic movements. In the 1930s, it hosted Britain's first showing of Picasso's *Guernica,* as part of an exhibition protesting the Spanish Civil War. It then shocked postwar audiences by introducing them to Jackson Pollock's abstracts, and championed Pop Art in the 1960s. Expect further revelations in the future. It also offers regular free talks, as well as cheap film screenings and concerts.

77–82 Whitechapel Rd., E1. www.whitechapelgallery.org. ℂ **020/7522-7888.** Free admission. Tues–Sun 11am–6pm. Tube: Aldgate East.

ORGANIZED TOURS
RIVER CRUISES ON THE THAMES   A trip on the river gives you an entirely different angle on London. You'll see how the city grew along and around the Thames, and how many of its landmarks turn toward the water. The Thames was London's first highway.

A perfectly fine option for downriver trips from Embankment Pier to the London Eye, Bankside, the Tower of London, Canary Wharf, and/or Greenwich are the regular, fast water-borne commuter services operated by **Thames Clippers ★**. One-day, unlimited travel roamer passes are available. For details, see p. 205.

BUS TOURS   For the bewildered first-timer, the quickest way to bring London into focus is probably to take a bus tour—but it isn't cheap. The **Original London Sightseeing Tour** passes by many of the major sights in a couple of hours or so, depending on traffic. The tour—that uses a traditional double-decker bus with live commentary by a guide—costs £26 for adults, £13 for children aged 5 to 15, free for those 4 and younger. A family ticket costs £91 and includes up to 3 children. The ticket, valid for 48 hours, allows you to hop on or off the bus at any point on any of three different circuits around the city. Your ticket also entitles you to a free riverboat ride and a choice of free 90-minute walking tours.

Tickets can be purchased on the bus or at any of the five start-points—Marble Arch, Trafalgar Square, Woburn Place, Piccadilly Circus, or Grosvenor Gardens—and from the **Original London Visitor Centre,** 17–19 Cockspur St., Trafalgar Square, SW1 (© **020/7389-5040;** Tube: Charing Cross). For information or phone purchases, call © **020/8877-1722.** It's also possible to book online at **www.the originaltour.com**.

WALKING TOURS   **London Walks ★** (www.walks.com; © **020/7624-3978**) is the oldest established walking-tour company in London—and still offers the best range of guided walks, departing every day of the week from points around town. Their hallmarks are variety, value, reasonably sized groups (generally under 30), and—above all—superb guides. The renowned crime historian Donald Rumbelow leads the daily **Jack the Ripper walk** (www.jacktheripperwalk.com) on Sundays, and occasional Mondays, Tuesdays, and Fridays; gather outside Tower Hill station before 7:30pm. Other notable themed walks include "Shakespeare's and Dickens' London," "The Beatles Magical Mystery Tour," Harry Potter movie locations, and "Hidden London." Several walks run every day, and all cost £8 for adults, £6 for students and seniors; children 14 and younger go free. Check the website for a schedule, or consult the London walks leaflet that you'll find in almost every information center and hotel in London; no reservations are needed and walks last around 2 hours.

Where to Eat

THE WEST END
Very Expensive
L'Atelier de Joël Robuchon ★★★ FRENCH   The London Atelier of Robuchon (the chef with 26 Michelin stars and restaurants around the world) is based on his concept of an informal restaurant. There are three areas: La Cuisine, which is the most conventional; the Le Salon bar; and the moody red-and-black "Atelier." For the most dramatic effect, eat at Atelier's counter. Here you can watch the theatre of the chefs producing tapas-style dishes—small bombshells of taste as in beef and foie gras mini-burger; pig's trotter on parmesan toast; and the signature egg cocotte with wild mushroom cream, all wildly inventive and beautifully presented. The a la carte menu follows the conventional three-course approach, using superb ingredients. Given the skill and the prices, the set lunches are a wonderful, relatively inexpensive way to sample some of London's best cooking.

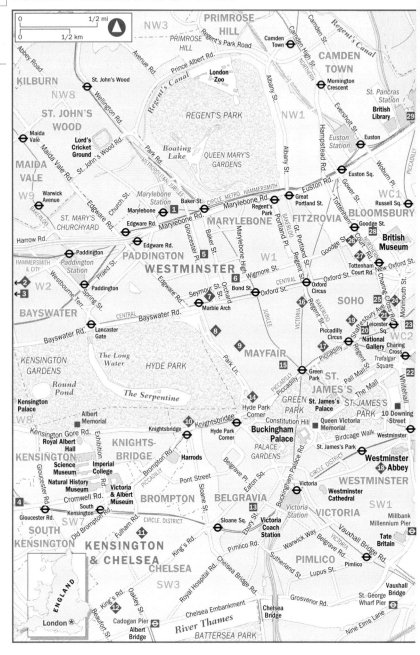

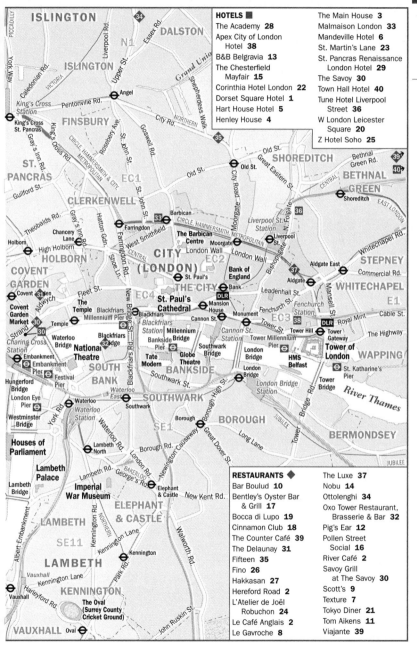

HOTELS ■

The Academy **28**
Apex City of London
  Hotel **38**
B&B Belgravia **13**
The Chesterfield
  Mayfair **15**
Corinthia Hotel London **22**
Dorset Square Hotel **1**
Hart House Hotel **5**
Henley House **4**

The Main House **3**
Malmaison London **33**
Mandeville Hotel **6**
St. Martin's Lane **23**
St. Pancras Renaissance
  London Hotel **29**
The Savoy **30**
Town Hall Hotel **40**
Tune Hotel Liverpool
  Street **36**
W London Leicester
  Square **20**
Z Hotel Soho **25**

RESTAURANTS ◆

Bar Boulud **10**
Bentley's Oyster Bar
  & Grill **17**
Bocca di Lupo **19**
Cinnamon Club **18**
The Counter Café **39**
The Delaunay **31**
Fifteen **35**
Fino **26**
Hakkasan **27**
Hereford Road **2**
L'Atelier de Joël
  Robuchon **24**
Le Café Anglais **2**
Le Gavroche **8**

The Luxe **37**
Nobu **14**
Ottolenghi **34**
Oxo Tower Restaurant,
  Brasserie & Bar **32**
Pig's Ear **12**
Pollen Street
  Social **16**
River Café **2**
Savoy Grill
  at The Savoy **30**
Scott's **9**
Texture **7**
Tokyo Diner **21**
Tom Aikens **11**
Viajante **39**

13–15 West St., WC2. www.joel-robuchon.com. ✆ **020/7010-8600.** Reservations essential. Main courses £19–£38; small tasting dishes £11–£19; Menu Découverte 8 courses £125; Vegetarian Découverte 8 courses £80; lunch and pretheatre 2-course menu £28, 3 courses £32, 4 courses £40. AE, MC, V. Daily noon–2:30pm and 5:30–10:30pm. Tube: Leicester Sq.

Le Gavroche ★★★ FRENCH   There may be new kids on the block, new cuisines, and new young chefs, but Le Gavroche remains the number-one choice in London for classical French cuisine from Roux, Jr., son of the chef who founded the restaurant in 1966. The famous cheese soufflé is still there, alongside lobster mousse with caviar and a champagne butter sauce. From the main courses: grilled scallops with carrots and salad and tarragon mustard sauce or roast veal with creamed morel mushroom sauce and mashed potatoes; and desserts including apricot and Cointreau soufflé. It's beautifully presented and served with style by faultless staff. The wine list is a masterclass in top French wines, and is kind to the purse on lesser-known varieties. It all takes place in a comfortable, conventional basement dining room which may be too old-fashioned for some, but with its Picassos on the walls, perfectly sets the scene for a classic meal.

43 Upper Brook St., W1. www.le-gavroche.co.uk. ✆ **020/7408-0881.** Reservations required as far in advance as possible. Main courses £26.90–£54.80; set lunch £52; *Le Menu Exceptionnel* (whole table) £100. AE, MC, V. Mon–Fri noon–2pm; Mon–Sat 6:30–11pm. Tube: Marble Arch.

Expensive

Bentley's Oyster Bar & Grill ★★ SEAFOOD/TRADITIONAL BRITISH
Bentley's is a London institution that opened in 1916 and went through various ups and downs, before being rescued by the highly talented and charming Irish chef, Richard Corrigan. Under his expert guidance, Bentley's (according to its many fans) now serves the best fish in London. The **Oyster Bar,** vaguely Arts and Crafts in feel, is a great place for watching the guys shucking oysters behind the bar and dining off the likes of dressed crab, smoked salmon, or smoked eel. In the more formal upstairs **Grill,** divided into the Grill Room and the Rib Room, the menu includes stalwarts such as the rich Bentley's fish soup, but it's worth being more adventurous and trying something like the pan-seared scallops with sardines, horseradish, and lemon pickled grapes. It's all conducted in a genuinely friendly atmosphere, though high-ish prices put off some people.

11–15 Swallow St., W1. www.bentleysoysterbarandgrill.co.uk. ✆ **020/7734-4756.** Oyster Bar: Main courses £11–£24. Grill: Main courses £21.50–£32. AE, MC, V. Oyster Bar: Mon–Sat 7:30–10:30am, noon–midnight; Sun noon–9:30pm. Restaurant: Mon–Fri noon–3pm and 5:30–10:30pm; Sat, Sun 7–10am, noon–2:30pm and 5:30–11pm. Tube: Piccadilly Circus.

Hakkasan ★ CHINESE/CANTONESE   Opened by the restaurateur Alan Yau (who has done so much to transform London's dining scene), this sexy, moody, subtly lit basement venue serves top-notch modern Cantonese cuisine. During the day, the dim sum is among the best in London—delicate, exquisitely fresh, and beautifully cooked. In the evening top-end ingredients are cooked with subtle skill. Sweet-and-sour Duke of Berkshire pork with pomegranate takes the concept to new heights; stir-fry ostrich comes in yellow bean sauce. From the seafood section, the Chilean seabass with Szechuan pepper, sweet basil, and spring onion is perfectly treated, the sauce complementing, not overpowering the fish. Even desserts, often the poor relation in Chinese restaurants, are superb. The wine list is a lesson in matching food and wine; ask the knowledgeable waiting staff for advice.

8 Hanway Place, W1. www.hakkasan.com. © 020/7927-7000. Reservations recommended. Main courses £9.80–£28.80. AE, MC, V. Mon–Fri noon–3pm; Sat–Sun noon–4pm; Sun–Wed 6–11pm; Thurs–Sat 6–11.45pm. Tube: Tottenham Court Rd. Also at 17 Bruton St., W1 (© 020/7907-1888).

Nobu ★★ JAPANESE   Upstairs in the Metropolitan Hotel, London's original Nobu is still a celebrity haunt—despite the departure of some of the fickle fashion crowd to the louder, flashier **Nobu Berkeley,** where the bar is packed nightly with high spenders. Founded by actor Robert De Niro, restaurateur Drew Nieporent, and chef Nobu Matsuhisa, the original Nobu remains a destination restaurant, its enduring popularity a testament to the skillful cooking of chef Mark Edwards. And it has had a much-needed facelift. All the fireworks are here: stunning appetizers of unusual combinations such as lobster ceviche, shrimp with caviar; new-style sweet shrimp sashimi; plus classic Japanese dishes that Nobu Matsuhisa has famously combined with Peruvian influences. Favorites including black cod with miso are as popular as when Nobu opened in 1997. There's also a small 10-seater sushi bar. For a cheaper option, order the £33 lunch of six dishes with salad, rice, and miso soup.

Inside Metropolitan Hotel, 19 Old Park Lane, W1. www.noburestaurants.com. © 020/7447-4747. Reservations required 1 month in advance. Main courses £5–£33.50; sushi and sashimi £3–£10 per piece; fixed-price lunch £33. AE, DC, MC, V. Mon–Fri noon–2:15pm; Mon–Thurs 6–10:15pm; Sat–Sun 12:30–2:30pm; Fri-Sat 6–11pm; Sun 6–9:30pm. Tube: Hyde Park Corner. Also at 15 Berkeley St., © 020/7290-9222.

Savoy Grill at The Savoy ★★★ TRADITIONAL BRITISH   The Savoy Grill is an integral part of the discreet luxury of the Savoy Hotel. Run by Gordon Ramsay, it is everything it should be. The Art Deco-inspired interior is a real gem, with sparkling chandeliers, walls that gleam a deep amber, and black-and-white photographs of past stars including Bogart and Bacall. The menu balances the classics with a lighter modern touch: Cornish crab mayonnaise with apple salad, wild celery, and wafer-thin Melba toast; lobster bisque with brandy butter. Mains of steamed steak and onion pudding; or roast duck breast with foie gras make choosing difficult. At lunch traditionalists opt for the daily trolley that glides around the room. There are desserts such as Eton mess, or rice pudding with poached cherries. This is a return to past glories.

In the Savoy Hotel, Strand, WC2. www.gordonramsay.com. © 020/7592-1600. Reservations required. Main courses £17–£38. Set price lunch menu £26; pretheatre menu 2 courses £20, 3 courses £26. AE, DC, MC, V. Mon–Sat noon–3pm and 5:30–11pm; Sun noon–4pm and 6–10:30pm. Tube: Charing Cross.

Scott's ★★ SEAFOOD   Scott's is glamorous and glitzy, a seafood restaurant that is on every celebrity's speed dial. Opened as an oyster warehouse in 1851 by a young fishmonger, John Scott, the restaurant moved to Mayfair in 1968. The dining room is drop-dead gorgeous, oak-paneled with art on the walls and a show-stopping crustacean display in the central bar. Meat eaters are taken care of, as are vegetarians and vegans, but fish is the raison d'être; it seems perverse to ignore the freshest of oysters, caviar that starts at £80, octopus carpaccio, smoked haddock with colcannon, or a simple, perfectly cooked seabass. The owners have opened the **Mount Street Deli ★**, 100 Mount St., W1 (www.themountstreetdeli.co.uk; © 020/7499-6843), opposite, a perfect place for breakfast, a light lunch, or afternoon tea.

20 Mount St., W1. www.scotts-restaurant.com. © 020/7495-7309. Reservations required. Main courses £17.50–£42. AE, DC, MC, V. Mon–Sat noon–10:30pm; Sun noon–10pm. Tube: Green Park or Bond St.

Moderate

Bocca di Lupo ★★ ITALIAN   This hugely popular smart restaurant has an open kitchen, tiled floors, wooden tables, and large paintings of food on the walls. The only downside of its popularity is that it's busy, cramped, and noisy—and you must book in advance. Chef Jacob Kenedy has toured Italy in his search for genuine regional dishes, and the result is a glorious trot around the country. If you want the full tour, go for the small plates and share as many as possible, perhaps tortellini of prosciutto and mortadella with cream and nutmeg from Emilia; and the Venetian fried squid, prawns, and blood orange. More substantial dishes include roast suckling pig and chestnuts, and Ligurian sea bream baked in salt. The all-Italian wine list offers a good selection by the carafe or the glass.

12 Archer St., W1. www.boccadilupo.com. © **020/7734-2223.** Main courses £7–£26.50. AE, MC, V. Mon–Sat 12:30–3pm and 5:30–11pm; Sun 12:45–3:45pm and 5–9pm. Tube: Piccadilly Circus.

The Delaunay ★★★ 🦞 CONTEMPORARY EUROPEAN   Ace restaurateurs, Jeremy King and Chris Corbin, have done it again. In The Delaunay, which opened in early 2012, they've reproduced their fantastically popular and successful The Wolseley. A sophisticated David Collins design has brought dark wood, lots of brass fittings, and dark green banquettes, perfectly evoking the grand European cafes of the past. It's open all day, starting with a breakfast of muesli or the full English. The a la carte menu takes in trad Brit dishes like sardines on toast, sandwiches, kedgeree, moules frites, steaks, and Schnitzels, all very reasonably priced. There's afternoon tea, brunch, in fact pretty much everything you could wish for. The addition of the chic Counter with its own entrance, operating as both cafe and takeaway, is just another plus to this great addition to London's dining scene.

55 Aldwych, WC2. www.thedelaunay.com. © **020/7499-8558.** Main courses £9–£21.75. AE, DC, MC, V. Mon–Fri 7am–midnight, Sat 8am–midnight, Sun 11am–11pm. Tube: Temple or Covent Garden.

Fino ★ SPANISH/TAPAS   Started by Sam and Eddie Hart, whose parents own the smart country house hotel Hambleton Hall in Rutland Water, Fino introduced London to traditional tapas with a modern twist. The smart basement venue with comfortable banquettes and substantial wooden tables buzzes with well-dressed Brits and knowledgeable Spaniards ordering dishes that emphasize first-rate ingredients cooked with skill. Try clams with sherry and ham, or squid wrapped with pancetta in ink sauce from *"la plancha;"* or some of the best Spanish cold meats like lomo or chorizo you'll get outside the Iberian peninsula. The brothers have expanded from their first success to open the smaller, but equally popular, **Barrafina,** 54 Frith St., W1 (www.barrafina.co.uk; © **020/7440-1463;** Tube: Tottenham Court Rd.).

33 Charlotte St., W1. www.finorestaurant.com. © **020/7813-8010.** Tapas £1.50–£21.50 AE, MC, V. Mon–Fri noon–2:30pm and 6–10:30pm; Sat 6–10:30pm. Tube: Goodge St. or Tottenham Court Rd.

Pollen Street Social ★★ MODERN BRITISH   Jason Atherton made his name working for Gordon Ramsay, then left to open this amazingly successful restaurant. Casual diners make for the lounge bar and a menu of tapas dishes. Small plates are also on the main restaurant menu, so you can share starters then order a regular main. Scallop ceviche, cucumber, and radish with a soy dressing and apple; Cornish crab with pear and a sweet and sour cauliflower and frozen peanut powder; or cauliflower and squid will not take the edge off your appetite. So move on to pork belly with apple, curly kale, mulled blackberries, and cob nut paste; or halibut with paella and sprouting broccoli. It's sophisticated cooking in a relaxed, casual venue.

TEATIME

Formal afternoon tea in London is a relaxing, civilized affair. Elegantly served on delicate china, there are dainty finger sandwiches, fresh-baked scones served with jam and clotted cream, and an array of small cakes and pastries. An attentive waiter is ready to refill your pot of tea. At many places, you can gild the lily with a glass of champagne. It makes a great alternative to pretheatre dining.

Afternoon tea, a British institution since the 18th century, was traditionally taken around 4pm, although today it's an all-afternoon affair in the top London spots. High tea, originally a working-class alternative to dinner, is a grander affair and available in some venues.

Ritz Palm Court ★★★ remains the top place for afternoon tea in London—and the hardest to get into without reserving way in advance. It's a spectacular stage setting, complete with marble steps and columns, a baroque fountain, and little gilded chairs. Nibble on a smoked salmon sandwich and egg mayonnaise roll and then pig out on the chocolate cake. But you're really here to feel like a duchess. Inside Ritz Hotel, 150 Piccadilly, W1. www.theritzlondon.com. ✆ **020/7493-8181.** Reservations required at least 8 weeks in advance. Jeans and sneakers not accepted. Jacket and tie required for men. Afternoon tea £42–£53, with champagne £64. AE, DC, MC, V. Five seatings daily at 11:30am, 1:30, 3:30, 5:30, and 7:30pm. Tube: Green Park.

8 Pollen St., W1. www.pollenstreetsocial.com. ✆ **020/7290-7600.** Main courses £22.50–£25. AE, MC, V. Mon–Sat noon–12:45pm and 6–10.45pm. Tube: Oxford Circus.

Texture ★★ NORDIC Scandinavian and Nordic restaurants may be relatively rare in London, but they're making an impact. And so with Texture, where Agnar Sverrisson is cooking up a cool storm. The decor is pared down, smart wood, and high ceilings with bright artwork on the walls. Fireworks come in the cooking where classic dishes are given an Icelandic touch, using light flavors rather than traditional French cream sauces. Asian influences appear as well. Try Cornish brill with lemon grass quinoa, barley, and cauliflower touches, or three cuts of lamb with swede. The wine list is one of London's best, with some of the world's top and unusual wines.

34 Portman St., W1. www.texture-restaurant.co.uk. ✆ **020/7224-0028.** Reservations required. Main courses £27.50–£34.50. Set lunch menus 2 courses £19, 3 courses £24, 7-course tasting menu £76. AE, MC, V. Tues–Sat noon–2:30pm and 6:30–11pm. Tube: Marble Arch.

Inexpensive

Tokyo Diner 🍴 JAPANESE This three-storied Japanese interloper into prime Chinatown territory is cheap and friendly, refuses tips, has lasted 20 years, and is open every day of the year from noon to midnight; no wonder it's so popular. Donburi rice dishes pull in students and the impecunious to fill up on beef and onion braised in sweet Japanese sauce with ginger. Others go for their popular bento box set meals: £14.80 gets you a chicken teriyaki box, in which chicken flambéed in teriyaki sauce is served with rice, vegetables, and pickles. Sushi and soup noodles complete the picture.

2 Newport Place, WC2. www.tokyodiner.com. ✆ **020/7287-8777.** Main courses £6.60–£19.50. Bento box set meals £14.80–£19.90. MC, V. Daily noon–midnight. Tube: Leicester Sq.

WEST LONDON

Expensive

River Café ★★ ITALIAN   This is one of London's iconic restaurants, an attractive space with an open-plan kitchen and private dining room in a sleek, blue-and-white, canteen-style space. The restaurant continues to attract those after the best rustic Italian cooking in London, despite the tragic death in 2010 of co-founder Rose Gray. Ruth Rogers, whose world-famous architect husband Richard co-designed the restaurant, produces authentic home-style cooking. Ingredients are flown in from Italy and France; the seafood and fish arrive daily from Britain's shores. All this comes at a price, but it's one the clientele is happy to pay. This is self-assured, knowledgeable cooking where Parma prosciutto is perfectly paired with bruschetta of broad beans, mint, and Pecorino cheese; and a Tuscan bread soup comes full of robust flavors. For the habitués, the wood-fired oven has produced new classics such as herb-stuffed pigeon roasted on bruschetta in Chianti with peas and prosciutto.

Thames Wharf, Rainville Rd., W6. www.rivercafe.co.uk. ℂ **020/7386-4200.** Reservations required. Main courses £13–£38. Set lunch 2 courses £25, 3 courses £31, 4 courses £39. AE, DC, MC, V. Mon–Thurs 12:30–2:15pm and 7–9pm; Fri 12:30–2:15pm and 7–9:15pm; Sat 12:30–2:30pm and 7–9:15pm; Sun noon–3pm. Tube: Hammersmith.

Moderate

Hereford Road ★★ MODERN BRITISH   Once a butcher's shop, this is now a restaurant in the St. John mode of British no-fuss, no-fancy cooking. Chef Tom Pemberton's time at St. John Bread & Wine shows in a menu that takes in potted crab as well as grilled ox heart and roast quail with that most British (but underused) meddler jelly for starters, and moves on to mains of pot-roast duck leg and fennel, or deviled lamb's kidneys and mash. The regulars of Notting Hill have taken this offal-heavy restaurant to their heart.

13 Hereford Rd., W2. www.herefordroad.org. ℂ **020/7727-1144.** Reservations recommended. Main courses £10–£14; set lunch, 2 courses Mon–Fri £13, 3 courses £15.50. AE, MC, V. Mon–Sat noon–3pm and 6–10:30pm; Sun noon–4pm and 6–10pm. Tube: Bayswater.

Le Café Anglais ★★ ☺ MODERN BRITISH   This is a grand brasserie in feel with huge windows, high ceilings, and banquette seating, located in Whiteleys shopping center. There's also a glamorous all-day cafe and oyster bar, ideal for those seeking an elegant light snack between buying posh frocks. Chef/restaurateur Rowley Leigh started Notting Hill's landmark restaurant, Kensington Place, becoming one of the founding fathers of contemporary British cookery in the process. He has since become a national figure via his food column for the *Financial Times.* There are plenty of his classics on the menu, such as Parmesan custard and anchovy toast for a starter and any of the excellent game dishes. With its wide choice of dishes, set menus, children's meals and parties, and friendly welcome, Le Café Anglais works hard to create a neighborhood atmosphere and succeeds; this is a restaurant that pleases everyone.

8 Porchester Gardens, W2. www.lecafeanglais.co.uk. ℂ **020/7221-1415.** Reservations required. Main courses £12.50–£30; set lunch Mon–Fri 2 courses £18.50, 3 courses £22.50; Sun lunch 2 courses £25, 3 courses £30. AE, MC, V. Daily noon–3:30pm; Mon–Thurs 6:30–10:30pm; Fri–Sat 6:30–11pm; Sun 6:30–10pm. Tube: Bayswater or Queensway.

SOUTHWEST LONDON

Very Expensive

Tom Aikens ★★★ FRENCH   The refurbishment of Tom Aikens' eponymous restaurant has produced a more informal space with bare wooden tables, mismatched china, and concrete walls etched with food-related quotes. And the punters seem to like it. What hasn't changed is his remarkable style: a modern interpretation of haute French cuisine, produced with confidence and skill, though with fewer gourmet flourishes than before. Lobster comes with pickled cucumber and yogurt granita; Kentish lamb with sheep's-milk cheese, anchovy, and confit garlic. The cooking shows harmony and cohesion, as exemplified by turbot with crisp chicken skin, cress, and sorrel. The end result is supremely satisfying, and it is beautifully presented.

43 Elystan St., SW3. www.tomaikens.co.uk. © **020/7584-2003.** Reservations required. Set lunch 2 courses £24, 3 courses £29; a la carte menus 2 courses £40, 3 courses £55; tasting menu 6 courses £55, 8 courses £75 (whole table). AE, DC, MC, V. Mon–Fri noon–2:30pm; Mon–Sat 6:45–11pm. Tube: South Kensington.

Expensive

Cinnamon Club ★★ INDIAN   This former Victorian library is a gorgeous, stately building with wooden paneling, high ceilings, and a book-lined gallery. It's a suitably grand setting for the many MPs (Members of Parliament) who seem to regard it as their club. And it's a suitably theatrical setting for the exciting modern Indian cooking from executive chef Vivek Singh. European ingredients, Indian spicing, classical cooking techniques, and Western-style presentation make for a heady mix. Such a balancing act could be disastrous in less skilled hands, but here it produces some of the most innovative Indian cooking. Try carpaccio of cured salmon; tandoor salmon with green pea relish; baked prawns with special spices and tomato lemon sauce; tandoori partridge breast with pickling spices. Go conventional at breakfast with a perfect, light kedgeree—the dish of fish, rice, eggs, parsley, and cream brought back from the Raj by British colonials.

Old Westminster Library, 30–32 Great Smith St., SW1. www.cinnamonclub.com. © **020/7222-2555.** Main courses £14–£25; set meal pre- and posttheatre 2 courses £22, 3 courses £24; tasting menu £75. AE, DC, MC, V. Mon–Fri 7:30–9:30am, noon–2:45pm, and 6–10:30pm; Sat noon–2:45pm and 6–10:30pm. Tube: St. James's Park or Westminster. Also at Cinnamon Kitchen, 9 Devonshire Sq., EC2 (© **020/7626-5000**).

Moderate

Bar Boulud ★★ FRENCH   French-born, U.S.-raised, superstar chef Daniel Boulud opened the doors of his first London venture to universal approval in 2009. It's in the Mandarin Oriental, but with its own entrance, and has an attractive decor of red banquette seating, an open kitchen, and a real buzz. You won't encounter the Michelin three-star cuisine of his New York restaurant, but hearty, rustic cooking. A charcuterie counter rightly takes pride of place—Daniel Boulud was born in Lyon. Feast on classic French bistro fare such as a *petit aioli* of seafood and vegetables with a perfect garlic mayonnaise; a coq au vin that had us rushing home to dig out the French recipe books; homemade sausages; and for dessert, a rich dark chocolate and raspberry gateau. The wine list is built around the chef's favorite Burgundy and Rhône wines. Prices are very reasonable for this part of London and level of glamour.

In the Mandarin Oriental Hyde Park, 66 Knightsbridge, SW1. www.barboulud.com. © **020/7201-3899.** Reservations recommended. Main courses £9–£27.50; 3-course fixed price £23. AE, MC, V. Daily noon–3pm and 5–11pm (10:30pm on Sun). Tube: Knightsbridge.

Pig's Ear ★ 🍴 MODERN BRITISH/GASTROPUB   The packed bar serves excellent traditional beers, and dishes such as risotto or roast guinea fowl in the back dining room. The Blue Room serves meals that are more sophisticated: smoked salmon mousse; a good charcuterie plate for starters; slow-cooked pork belly with horseradish mash, carrots, and parsnip crisps as a typical main. It's a posh gastropub, befitting its posh location in Chelsea, but it's friendly and casual and you're always made to feel welcome.

35 Old Church St., SW3. www.thepigsear.info. ☏**020/7352-2908.** Reservations required in restaurant. Main courses £13.75–£25. AE, DC, MC, V. Mon–Fri 12:30–3pm and 6–10pm; Sat 12:30–10:30pm; Sun 12:30–9pm. Tube: Sloane Sq.

THE SOUTH BANK
Expensive
Oxo Tower Restaurant, Brasserie & Bar ★★ INTERNATIONAL   The Oxo Tower is one of London's top dining spots—literally, as it's on the eighth floor of Oxo Tower Wharf. Stunning views up and down river make the terrace one of summer's most sought-after venues. Both the Brasserie and the Restaurant share the same chic, 1930's-liner decor, and the same contemporary ethos in the cooking. The **Brasserie** is more casual, offering all the current modish mixes of tastes, spices, and inspirations such as chargrilled, Moroccan-spiced quail followed by teriyaki salmon with soba noodle salad. Dishes on the **Restaurant** menu use more luxury ingredients: langoustines; foie gras; seabass with crab, samphire, truffle beurre blanc, and fennel salad; and wild game in season. It's all seasonally led, with carefully sourced British ingredients to the fore. The refurbished **bar** with its excellent food has become one of London's most desirable meeting places.

22 Barge House St., SE1. www.harveynichols.com/restaurants. ☏**020/7803-3888.** Reservations recommended. Main courses £21.50–£35; 3 courses £35. AE, DC, MC, V. Mon–Fri noon–2:30pm and 6–11pm; Sat noon–2:30pm and 5:30–11pm; Sun noon–3pm and 6:30–10pm. Tube: Blackfriars or Waterloo.

THE CITY & EAST LONDON
Very Expensive
Viajante ★★ CONTEMPORARY EUROPEAN   When he was performing culinary miracles at various East London venues, Portuguese-born Nuno Mendes was the darling of diners desperately seeking the next big thing. Now he's resurfaced inside the **Town Hall Hotel** (p. 240). In a restaurant with a kitchen so open it feels like you're in somebody's living room, this El Bulli-trained chef serves dishes that will either knock your socks off or leave you scratching your head. From the first *amuse bouche* that is sublime—through dishes that pair braised octopus with potatoes, chorizo, and eggs; slow-cooked pig neck with savoy cabbage, fried capers, and grated egg—the surprises keep coming. This is supremely skillful, playful, flawlessly executed cooking. Now that El Bulli has closed, this is your best bet for an adventure. The Corner Room is a cheaper option and has a no-bookings policy.

Inside Town Hall Hotel, Patriot Sq., E2. www.viajante.co.uk. ☏ **020/7871-0461.** Reservations required. Lunch menus 3 courses £28, 6 courses £65, 9 courses £80. Dinner 6 courses £65, 9 courses £80, 12 courses £90. AE, MC, V. Mon–Thurs noon–2pm and 6–9:30pm; Fri–Sun 6–9:30pm. Tube: Bethnal Green.

Moderate
Fifteen ★★ ITALIAN   Jamie Oliver, bestselling cookbook author, TV personality, and international restaurateur of note, opened Fifteen in 2002 with the laudable aim of training disadvantaged young people as chefs. Today the redbrick Victorian building has been smartened up, but the kitchen is still a training ground. The downstairs restaurant serves a daily changing Italian menu, using impeccably sourced

ingredients from Britain and Italy. Start with a simple mozzarella with tomatoes and basil, or perhaps a satisfying ravioli of veal ragu. Mains of Sicilian fisherman's stew, or lamb with fennel, olives, pine nuts, and gremolata show how well the kitchen can perform. The street-level **Trattoria** is more casual, with an a la carte menu. Weekend brunch here is a pleasant, relaxed meal to linger over.

15 Westland Place, N1. www.fifteen.net. ✆ **0871/330-1515.** Reservations required. Restaurant: main courses £11.50–£29; breakfast £2–£11; set lunch Mon–Fri 2 courses £26, 3 courses £30, 4 courses £35. Trattoria: main courses £9–£18.50. AE, MC, V. Mon–Sat 7:30–10:45am and noon–3pm; Sun 8am–11am, noon–3pm and 6–10pm. Tube: Old St.

The Luxe ★ CONTEMPORARY EUROPEAN   John Torode has expanded from his original venture, Smiths of Smithfield, into the refurbished Spitalfields Market, where restaurants sit cheek-by-jowl in the modernized Victorian structure. Torode's four-storey Luxe offers a multi-purpose restaurant experience. The cafe buzzes all day, and is a favorite place of ours for breakfast. There's a basement music and cocktail bar, and upstairs is a dining room, complete with open kitchen, exposed brick walls, and silk wallpaper recalling the area's Huguenot silk-weaving heritage. Start with gravadlax with caper berry, shallot, and parsley salad, and then move on to slow roast belly of pork with mash and green sauce. For dessert go the blueberry cheesecake with lemon curd or chocolate pudding route.

109 Commercial St., E1. www.theluxe.co.uk. ✆ **020/7101-1751.** Main courses £13.75–£28.50. AE, MC, V. Restaurant Mon–Fri noon–3pm; Sun noon–4pm; Mon–Sat 6–9:30pm. Cafe-bar Mon–Sat 9am–11:30pm; Sun 9:30am–10pm. Tube: Liverpool St.

Inexpensive
The Counter Café ★ 🎁 TRADITIONAL BRITISH/TAPAS   The two-storied Stour Space is home to various artists' studios and the Counter Café. Offering views over the Regent's Canal to the Olympic Stadium, it has a shabby chic industrial decor, long tables and chairs as well as a sofa, fun atmosphere, and good food. Not surprisingly, it's extremely popular. Start the day with a great breakfast or brunch, or go for a pie at lunch. On Thursday to Sunday evenings, it becomes a bar serving tapas.

4a Roach Rd., E3. www.thecountercafe.co.uk. ✆ **07834/275-920.** Main courses £3.50–£8. AE, MC, V. Mon–Wed 7:30am–5pm; Thurs–Fri 7am–11pm; Sat 9am–11pm; Sun 9am–5pm. Overground: Hackney Wick.

NORTH LONDON
Inexpensive
Ottolenghi ★★ INTERNATIONAL   The cool, sleek, white interior of this traiteur-cum-cafe has become the meeting place for the chattering classes of Islington. There are currently four Ottolenghi outlets in London, and a new more expensive restaurant, **Nopi** (21–22 Warwick Street, W1; ✆ **020/7494-9584**). But the Islington branch is the flagship, with seating at long tables and a kitchen that produces some of the best Mediterranean-influenced food in town. It's open all day for healthy and hearty lunches of superb salads; snacks from the mounds of meringues, tarts, and cakes; and dinners such as seabass with baba ganoush, pomegranate, and shallots. Devotees buy the owner Yotam Ottolenghi's cookbooks (he's also a food columnist on the *Guardian* newspaper). If you visit just one cafe in London, make it this one.

287 Upper St., N1. www.ottolenghi.co.uk. ✆ **020/7288-1454.** Reservations recommended at dinner. Main courses £8–£12. AE, MC, V. Mon–Sat 8am–11pm; Sun 9am–7pm. Tube: Angel or Highbury & Islington. Other locations throughout London.

Shopping

THE TOP SHOPPING STREETS & NEIGHBORHOODS

THE WEST END   Oxford Street is undeniably the West End's main shopping attraction. Start at Marble Arch—the westernmost end—for designer department store **Selfridges.** As you walk the length of the famous street toward Tottenham Court Road, you'll notice that the quality of shops goes downhill, especially east of Oxford Circus. **Topshop** remains an Oxford Street must-visit (the branch here is the largest clothes shop in Europe). You're certainly very brave to attempt Oxford Street at the weekend; weekday mornings are best for your sanity.

Oxford Street is also a great starting point for hitting the more interesting shopping areas, such as affluent **Marylebone.** It's impossible not to fall in love with the quaintness of Marylebone's High Street. The street's chocolate shops and interiors brands ooze luxury.

Regent Street shopping is more toward the high end of "high street," typified by the affordable luxury of chain shops like **Mango** and **French Connection.** Head south from Oxford Circus for the world-famous **Liberty** department store. You're now at the top of **Carnaby Street,** although it's not quite the '60s-style mecca it once was.

Parallel to Regent Street, the **Bond Street** area connects **Piccadilly** with Oxford Street, and is synonymous with the luxury rag trade. It's not just one street, but a whole area, mainly comprising New Bond Street and Old Bond Street. It's the flagship location for the best designers—you'll find Prada and Gucci here, and **Tiffany** is quite at home nestled among designer jewelry shops. A slew of international hotshots, from Chanel to Versace, have digs nearby. Make sure you stop off at **Dover Street Market**—not a market at all, but actually a designer shop housing all sorts of fashionable folk under one roof.

Burlington Arcade (www.burlington-arcade.co.uk; Tube: Piccadilly Circus), a glass-roofed Regency passage leading off Piccadilly, looks like a period exhibition, and is lined with mahogany-fronted intriguing shops and boutiques. Lit by wrought-iron lamps and decorated with clusters of ferns and flowers, its small, upscale stores specialize in fashion, gold jewelry, Irish linen, and cashmere.

The West End theatre district borders two more shopping areas: **Soho** (Tube: Tottenham Court Rd. or Leicester Sq.), where the sex shops are slowly morphing into cutting-edge designer boutiques and **Covent Garden,** a shopping masterpiece stocked with fashion, food, books, and everything else.

Just off trendy **Neal Street** and **Seven Dials, Neal's Yard** is a stunning splash of color on rainy days if you're looking to buy foodstuffs from **Neal's Yard Dairy.** **Monmouth Street** is somewhat of a local secret: Many shops here serve as outlets for British designers, selling both used and new clothing. In addition, stores specialize in everything from musical instruments from the Far East to palm readings. Make sure, too, to take in **Charing Cross Road** and get your nose into one of the many bookstores.

SOUTHWEST LONDON   The home of **Harrods, Knightsbridge** is probably the second most famous London retail district (Oxford St. just edges it out). **Sloane Street** is traditionally regarded as a designer area, but these days it's more "upscale high street," and nowhere near as luxurious as **Bond Street** (see above).

Walk southwest on **Brompton Road**—toward the V&A Museum (p. 219)—and you'll find **Cheval Place,** lined with designer resale shops, and **Beauchamp Place** (pronounced *Bee*-cham). It's high end, but with a hint of irony. Expect to see little lapdogs poking their heads out of handbags.

You'll also be near **King's Road** (Tube: Sloane Square); another beacon of '60s cool, this is now a haven for designer clothes and home designs. About a third of King's Road is devoted to independent fashion shops, another third houses design-trade showrooms and stores for household wares: Scandinavian designs are prominent.

Finally, don't forget all those museums in nearby **South Kensington.** They have fantastic and exclusive gift shops. If you're looking for jewelry and housewares, the **V&A** (p. 219) and the **Design Museum** are must-visits. The **Science Museum** (p. 216) shop is perfect for inquisitive kids. Make sure to view the collections, too. The big names don't charge for entry, and have some world-class exhibits.

WEST LONDON   If you're heading west, the first place you should find yourself in is **Notting Hill.** Of course, one of the main draws for shopping in West London is **Portobello Market.** Every Sunday, the whole of Portobello Road turns into a sea of antiques, cool clothing (and even cooler shoppers), and maybe even a celebrity or three.

Some of the best boutiques in London are also here. The independent shopping scene thrives; this is an area where people want to be unique, but still look expensive and groomed. Expect one-off boutiques housing designer labels you've never heard of, quirky homewares, and plenty of retro record shops. Stick to Portobello for the antiques, but head to **Westbourne Grove** and **Ledbury Road** for the boutiques.

THE CITY & EAST LONDON   The financial district itself doesn't really offer much in the way of shopping—especially at the weekend, when everything tends to be shut. However, the **One New Change** shopping center (www.onenewchange. com; Tube: St. Paul's) is attracting a rich crowd for its luxury goods. It's opposite the eastern end of St. Paul's Cathedral. You'll also find a handful of tailors in the area, and there are high-end brands in the nearby **Royal Exchange** (www.theroyalexchange. com; Tube: Bank). However, unless you're often suited up for work, it's really not a shopping destination by itself.

Continue your adventure farther east on **Commercial Street** (Tube: Liverpool St./Train: Shoreditch High St.). Around here is where you'll find the best vintage shops in the city. They're on almost every corner and side-street, and new ones seem to appear every day, alongside pop-up stores just here for the weekend. Make sure you hit **Absolute Vintage** and the smaller **Blondie** around the corner, on the way to the antiques market in **Spitalfields.**

A short stroll north, **Columbia Road** (see below) is more than just a flower market; in many ways, the main attractions are the artist studios that line the street. Head up every single one of those staircases you see. If the door is open, you're allowed in. Once you're done with the studios and shops—**Ryan Town** sells fabulous paper-cuts—everything at the flower market will be going cheap come 3pm. **Westfield Stratford City** (www.westfield.com/stratfordcity; Tube: Stratford) brought mass mainstream shopping to East London in the form of this giant mall right next to London's 2012 Olympic Park.

Entertainment & Nightlife

Weekly publications such as *Time Out* carry full entertainment listings, including information on restaurants, nightclubs, and bars. You'll also find listings in all the daily newspapers, and the *Guide* distributed every Saturday inside the *Guardian* newspaper is an invaluable source of up-to-date information.

THE PERFORMING ARTS

To see specific shows, especially hits, purchase your tickets in advance. Ticket prices vary greatly depending on the seat and venue—from £25 to £85 is typical. Occasionally gallery seats (the cheapest) are sold only on the day of the performance, so you'll have to head to the box office early in the day and return an hour before the performance to line up, because they're not reserved seats.

Founded in 2000, **London Theatre Direct** (www.londontheatredirect.com; ✆ **0845/505-8500**) represents a majority of the major theatres in the city and tickets for all productions can be purchased in advance, either over the phone or via their website. Alternatively try the **Society of London Theatre** (www.officiallondon theatre.co.uk; ✆ **020/7557-6700**), whose ticket booth (**"tkts"**) on the southwest corner of Leicester Square is open Monday to Saturday 10am to 7pm and Sunday 11am to 4pm. You can purchase all tickets here, although the booth specializes in half-price sales for shows that are undersold. These tickets must be purchased in person—not over the phone. A £2 service fee is charged. For phone orders, you should call **Ticketmaster** (www.ticketmaster.co.uk; ✆ **0870/060-2340**).

THEATRE   One of the world's finest theatre companies, the **Royal Shakespeare Company ★★★**, performs at various theatres throughout London. Check its website at www.rsc.org.uk/whats-on/london/ for current shows and venues, or call ✆ **0844/800-1110** Monday to Saturday 9am to 8pm. The theatre troupe performs in London during the winter months, naturally specializing in the plays of the Bard. In summer, it tours England and abroad.

Occupying a prime site on the South Bank of the River Thames is one of the world's greatest stage companies, the **National Theatre,** South Bank, SE1 (www. nationaltheatre.org.uk; ✆ **020/7452-3000;** Tube: Waterloo, Embankment, or Charing Cross). The National Theatre houses three theatres. Tickets range from £10 to £50.

At the replica of **Shakespeare's Globe Theatre,** New Globe Walk, Bankside, SE1 (www.shakespeares-globe.org; ✆ **020/7902-1400** for box office; Tube: Mansion House or Blackfriars), productions vary in style and setting; not all are performed in Elizabethan costume. In keeping with the historic setting, no lighting is focused just on the stage, but floodlighting is used during evening performances to replicate daylight in the theatre—Elizabethan performances took place in the afternoon. From May to September, the company holds performances Tuesday to Saturday at 2 and 7pm. There is a limited winter schedule. In any season, the schedule may be affected by weather because this is an outdoor theatre. Tickets are £5 for groundlings (patrons who stand in the uncovered area around the stage), £15 to £35 for gallery seats.

CLASSICAL MUSIC, OPERA & DANCE   The Royal Ballet and the Royal Opera perform at the **Royal Opera House,** Bow Street, Covent Garden, WC2 (www.royal opera.org; ✆ **020/7304-4000;** Tube: Covent Garden). Performances of the Royal Opera are usually sung in the original language, but supertitles are projected. The Royal Ballet, which ranks with top companies such as the Kirov and the Paris Opera Ballet, performs a repertory with a tilt toward the classics, including works by its earlier choreographer-directors Sir Frederick Ashton and Sir Kenneth MacMillan. Tickets are £9 to £200.

Royal Albert Hall, Kensington Gore, SW7 2AP (www.royalalberthall.com; ℂ 020/7589-8212; Tube: South Kensington), is the annual setting for the BBC Henry Wood Promenade Concerts, known as "the Proms," an annual series that lasts for 8 weeks between mid-July and mid-September. The Proms, incorporating a medley of rousing, mostly British orchestral music, have been a British tradition since 1895. Although most of the audience occupies reserved seats, true aficionados usually opt for standing room in the orchestra pit, with close-up views of the musicians on stage. Newly commissioned works are often premièred here. Tickets range from £5 to £150, depending on the event.

Across Waterloo Bridge rises the **Royal Festival Hall,** part of the Southbank Centre, SE1 (www.southbankcentre.co.uk; ℂ **0871/663-2500,** box office; Tube: Waterloo or Embankment). Here are three of the most comfortable and acoustically perfect concert halls in the world: Royal Festival Hall, Queen Elizabeth Hall, and the Purcell Room. Together they host more than 1,200 concerts per year. Tickets are £8 to £80.

Sadler's Wells Theatre, Rosebery Avenue, EC1 (www.sadlerswells.com; ℂ **0844/412-4300;** Tube: Northern Line to Angel), is London's premier venue for dance and opera. It occupies the site of a series of theatres, the first built in 1683. In the early 1990s, the turn-of-the-20th-century theatre was mostly demolished, and construction began on an innovative new design completed at the end of 1998, which can change its interior shape, size, and mood for almost any performance. The theatre offers classical ballet, modern dance of all degrees of "avant-garde-ness," and children's theatrical productions, including a Christmas ballet. Performances are usually at 7:30pm. The box office is open Monday to Saturday from 9am to 8:30pm. Tickets range from £10 to £70.

THE CLUB & MUSIC SCENE

JAZZ & BLUES   Inquire about jazz in London, and people immediately think of **Ronnie Scott's Jazz Club,** 47 Frith St., W1 (www.ronniescotts.co.uk; ℂ **020/7439-0747;** Tube: Leicester Sq. or Piccadilly Circus), the European vanguard for modern jazz. Only the best English and American combos, often fronted by top-notch vocalists, are booked here. In the main room, you can watch the show from the bar or sit at a table, at which you can order dinner. The downstairs bar is more intimate; among the regulars at your elbow may be some of the world's most talented musicians. The club is open Monday to Saturday 6pm to 3am, Sunday 6pm to midnight. Reservations are recommended. Tickets run from £10 to £50, depending on the event.

DANCE CLUBS   It shares a Tube station with Ministry of Sound, but in every other respect **Corsica Studios** ★★★, 5 Elephant Rd., SE17 (www.corsicastudios. com; ℂ **020/7703-4760;** Tube: Elephant & Castle), is a world away from its internationally famous neighbor. Housed under the railway arches behind the Coronet, it harks back to the days before clubbing became corporate and safe. Corsica Studios provides a haven for those seeking underground sounds. For this reason, it's regularly voted among the U.K.'s best small clubs.

For much of London's clubbing cognoscenti, this 200-capacity basement in Shoreditch is simply the best this city has to offer—and it's easy to see why. With probably the sharpest sound system in town and a crowd who know their music, **Plastic People** ★★, 149 Curtain Rd., EC2 (www.plasticpeople.co.uk; ℂ **020/7739-6471;** Tube: Old St./Overground: Shoreditch High St.), manages to attract DJs more

Dropping into the local pub for a pint of real ale or bitter is the best way to soak up the character of the different villages that make up London. You'll hear the accents and slang and see firsthand how far removed upper-crust Kensington is from blue-collar Wapping. Catch the local gossip or football talk and, of course, enjoy some of the finest ales, stouts, ciders, and malt whiskeys in the world.

Central London is awash with wonderful historic pubs as rich and varied as the city itself. Wedged between Covent Garden and Trafalgar Square, the **Harp,** 47 Chandos Place, WC2 (www.harpcovent garden.com; ✆ **020/7836-0291;** Tube: Leicester Sq. or Charing Cross), is a much-loved traditional pub offering an authentic experience, the winner of several awards over the years. Break up the shopping trip with a leisurely pint or two from their interesting range of ales and lagers.

Pubs attached to train stations are often fairly dispiriting affairs, functional spaces for transient drinkers. **The Euston Tap,** West Lodge, 190 Euston Rd., NW1 (www.eustontap.com; ✆ **020/7387-2890;** Tube: Euston), throws all that on its head. Occupying a small but curiously grand lodge in front of the station it attracts not just those temporarily marooned by London's woeful transport network but discerning ale drinkers from across the city. An ever-changing list of rare lagers and ales ensures that there's always something new on the menu and a reason to visit again and again.

The Holly Bush ★★, 22 Holly Mount, NW3 (www.hollybushpub.com; ✆ **020/ 7435-2892;** Tube: Hampstead), is the real thing: authentic Edwardian gas lamps, open fires, private booths, and a tap selection of Fuller's London Pride, Adnams, and Harveys. Hidden away in a quiet area of Hampstead, the Holly Bush provides a warm welcome to those who find it. After a hard day's shopping or walking on Hampstead Heath, settle into one of its snugs and revive yourself with a quality pint and traditional pub food from its well-regarded kitchen.

used to playing to parties numbered in the thousands. For dubstep, techno, or house, few other venues can compare to a night at Plastic People.

THE BAR SCENE

Mark's Bar ★★   Attached to noted restaurant **Hix,** this dark and stylish bar offers up a slice of Manhattan deep in the heart of Soho. Its imaginative drinks menu, devised by Nick Strangeway, is packed full of historical curiosities that "hark back to another era before the Temperance Movement had reared its ugly head." Leave your mojitos at the door and instead try something a little different, such as the 19th-century inspired "Punch à la Regent." 66–70 Brewer St., W1. www.hixsoho.co.uk. ✆ **020/ 7292-3518.** Tube: Piccadilly Circus.

Nightjar ★★   Hidden away just a stone's throw from Old Street roundabout is subterranean cocktail speakeasy, The Nightjar. It might not be much to look at from the outside but once you've found the place, you can settle into a dark corner and treat yourself to one (or several) of the drinks from their impressive menu of elegant and inventively presented cocktails. 129 City Road, EC1V. www.barnightjar.com. ✆ **020/7253-4101.** Tube: Old Street.

Worship Street Whistling Shop ★★ 📷   Just as the likes of Heston Blumenthal have revolutionized the British dining experience, combining both ultra-modern cooking techniques with a rediscovery of past menus, we're increasingly seeing a more experimental and inventive approach to the science of mixology. If you're looking to slake your thirst with something beyond a mojito then definitely add The Worship Street Whistling Shop to your checklist. Recreating long-forgotten drinks and applying new techniques to create libations never possible before, the alchemists behind the bar create liquid gold every time. 63 Worship St., EC2A. www.whistlingshop.com. ℰ **020/7247-0015.** Tube: Old Street.

THE LGBT SCENE

Many of the better clubs are located in the north and south of the city.

Dalston Superstore ★★ Cafe by day, disco bar by night, this Superstore is a welcome addition to trendy Dalston, providing a space for gays, lesbians, and their straight friends to party away from the mainstream scene. It's packed most nights with a friendly, arty, and open-minded crowd, and the music is much the same as at any cutting-edge bar in this part of town, with disco, electro, and underground house. 117 Kingsland High St., E8. www.dalstonsuperstore.com. ℰ **020/7254-2273.** No cover. Overground: Dalston Kingsland or Dalston Junction.

Royal Vauxhall Tavern ★ The Royal Vauxhall Tavern was here long before Vauxhall became London's gay village, but even back in the late 1890s it was home to some of London's most colorful cabaret. London's oldest surviving gay venue, the Royal Vauxhall is a much-loved institution and an essential stop-off before hitting one of the local clubs. It's open 7 nights a week and you're likely to find all manner of fun inside from camp burlesque and cabaret to bingo, comedy, and plain old-fashioned discos. 372 Kennington Lane, SE11. www.theroyalvauxhalltavern.co.uk. ℰ **020/7820-1222.** Admission £5–£15. Tube: Vauxhall.

Where to Stay
VERY EXPENSIVE

Corinthia Hotel London ★★★ 📷 Opened in April 2011 as the Corinthia Hotels' flagship property, the triangular-shaped building has retained the huge spaces, marble columns, and ceilings of its sumptuous past as the Metropole Hotel. Bringing it right up-to-date is the commissioned artwork and eye-catching lighting, like the Baccarat chandelier that dominates the central Lobby Lounge—a great meeting place, which serves a lovely afternoon tea. Bedrooms are amongst the largest in London, decorated in natural colors; each has a media hub and a Nespresso machine; bathrooms have wall-mounted TV screens. The restaurants are equally grand: Northall serves British traditional dishes while Massimo is the inspiration of Italian chef Massimo Riccioli. Recall the 1930's Jazz age in the Bassoon bar. The flagship **Espa Life** on four floors is now London's most glamorous and spacious spa.

Whitehall Place, London SW1A 2BD. www.corinthia.com. ℰ **020/7930 8181.** Toll-free USA **1-877-842-6269.** Fax 020/7321 3001. 294 units. £339–£680 plus VAT double. AE, DC, MC, V. Tube: Embankment. **Amenities:** 2 restaurants; 2 bars; 24-hr. gym; spa; concierge; room service. *In room:* A/C, TV/DVD, minibar, hair dryer, media hub, Wi-Fi (free).

St. Martin's Lane ★★★ "Eccentric and irreverent, with a sense of humor," is how Ian Schrager described his cutting-edge Covent Garden hotel, which he transformed from a 1960's office building into a chic enclave. This was the first hotel that Schrager designed outside the U.S. and the mix of hip design and sense of cool has been imported across the pond. Whimsical touches abound, for example, a string of daisies replaces "do not disturb" signs. Rooms are all white, but you can use the full-spectrum lighting to make them any color. Floor-to-ceiling windows in every room offer panoramic views of London.

45 St. Martin's Lane, London WC2N 4HX. www.stmartinslane.com. ℰ**020/7300-5500** or **800/697-1791** in the U.S. and Canada. Fax 020/7300-5501. 204 units. £229–£330 double. AE, DC, MC, V. Tube: Covent Garden or Leicester Sq. **Amenities:** Restaurant; 2 bars; exercise room; concierge; room service; babysitting. *In room:* A/C, TV/DVD, minibar, hair dryer, movie library, Wi-Fi (£15/day).

St. Pancras Renaissance London Hotel   This hotel has been lovingly restored into an opulent reinterpretation of the golden age of railway hotels. Gilbert Scott's iconic Gothic hotel above St. Pancras station stood unused for 76 years and narrowly escaped being torn down. The centerpiece is the sweeping double staircase that whisks you from the ornate vault of the lobby (more like a medieval church than a hotel) into luxuriously wide corridors and a maze of grand halls and intimate lounges. The attention to detail is so extraordinary—every surface gleams with Gothic ornamentation and period wallpaper—that the modern rooms, though large and perfectly serviceable, are a bit of a let-down. But this is as much hotel as spectacle; a place to sip martinis in style, to explore at leisure, and to plan that European adventure.

Euston Rd., London NW1 2AR. www.stpancrasrenaissance.com. ℰ **020/7841-3540.** 245 units. £306–£834 double. AE, MC, V. Valet parking £50/day. Tube: King's Cross St. Pancras. **Amenities:** Restaurant; bar; pool; gym; spa; concierge; room service. *In room:* A/C, TV/DVD, minibar, CD player, Wi-Fi (£15/day).

The Savoy ★★   After a 3-year, £200 million restoration, the Savoy has settled into its role of providing glitzy, high-octane business. Updating such an iconic hotel—at various times home to Coco Chanel, Humphrey Bogart, Marlene Dietrich, Oscar Wilde, and Churchill's war cabinet—was tricky but it's lost none of its turn-of-the-century appeal with rich fabrics and acres of gold leaf on display, and a very subtle updating to draw the 21st-century *belle monde* back to their spiritual home. No two rooms are the same, despite their mix of Art Deco and Edwardian palettes. If you can, take one of the Edwardian rooms near the rear—the combination of Thames views and a real fireplace is London at its finest. The Savoy Grill (p. 225) is as grand as ever.

Strand, London WC2R 0EU. www.fairmont.com/savoy. ℰ**020/7836-4343.** Fax 020/7420-6040. 268 units. £350–£775 double. AE, DC, MC, V. Tube: Embankment or Charing Cross. **Amenities:** 3 restaurants, including Savoy Grill (p. 225); 2 bars; exercise room; concierge; room service; babysitting. *In room:* A/C, TV/DVD, minibar, hair dryer, movie library, CD player, Wi-Fi (£10/day).

W London Leicester Square ★★   W London is so deliberately chic it sharply divides opinion: You either love it or hate it. You enter the hotel past an enormous W into a large space with nothing but doormen. Take the lift to the first floor to an impressive, lofty reception with low-key check-in desks. There are buzzing public spaces, a serious gym, Screening Room, popular bar, and a pan-Asian two-story restaurant with an additional street entrance. Rooms are minimal and chic, with long windows and a second outer decorated glass wall to give privacy. Color schemes are mainly white and gray, with splashes of red, and gold bed coverings. It is undeniably fashionable in every way (rooms are classified in terms like "Wonderful," "Cool Corner," "Wow Suite," etc.); if you're a traditionalist after cozy comfort, this is not for you.

10 Wardour St, London W1D 6QF. www.wlondon.co.uk. ℰ**020/758-1000;** fax 020-7758-1001. 192 units. From £335 double. AE, DC, MC, V. Tube: Oxford Circus or Piccadilly Circus. **Amenities:** Restaurant; 2 bars; exercise room; concierge; room service; Wi-Fi (free in public areas). *In room:* A/C, TV, minibar, hair dryer, MP3 docking station, Wi-Fi (£16/24 hr.).

EXPENSIVE

The Academy ★ With a pretty, private garden out back, this row of converted Georgian houses offers a sense of sanctuary just yards from the bustle of Bloomsbury and Oxford Street. The original architectural details—glass panels, colonnades, and intricate plasterwork on the facade—contribute to the classic air (this is the area where Virginia Woolf and the other members of the literary Bloomsbury Set would wander). Rooms mix a smart Georgian ambience with 21st-century touches such as MP3 docking stations—those at the rear are at a premium because of their garden views; they're also quieter, even allowing for the double-glazing of the front rooms. *Note:* There are no elevators in this four-floor hotel.

21 Gower St., London WC1E 6HG. www.theetoncollection.co.uk/academy. ✆ **020/7631-4115.** Fax 020/7636-3442. 49 units. £120–£395 double. AE, DC, MC, V. Tube: Tottenham Court Rd., Goodge St., or Russell Sq. **Amenities:** Bar; room service. *In room:* A/C, TV, minibar, hair dryer, MP3 docking station, Wi-Fi (free).

The Chesterfield Mayfair ★★ Only in super-expensive Mayfair could the Chesterfield be considered a bargain, but it serves up that ritzy grand hotel feeling at a better price than the Connaught or the Dorchester. The hotel, once home to the Earl of Chesterfield, still sports venerable features, including richly decorated public rooms featuring woods, antiques, fabrics, and marble. The secluded Library Lounge is a great place to relax, and the glassed-in conservatory is a good spot for tea. The guest rooms are dramatically decorated and make excellent use of space, including generous closets.

35 Charles St., London W1J 5EB. www.chesterfieldmayfair.com. ✆ **020/7491-2622** or **877/955-1515** in the U.S. and Canada. Fax 020/7491-4793. 107 units. £160–£375 double. AE, DC, MC, V. Tube: Green Park. **Amenities:** 1 restaurant; bar; use of nearby health club; concierge; room service; babysitting. *In room:* A/C, TV/DVD, minibar (in suites only or on request), hair dryer, Wi-Fi (free).

Dorset Square Hotel ★★ Just steps from Regent's Park, this is one of London's best and most stylish "house hotels"—it even overlooks Thomas Lord's (the man who set up London's first private cricket club) first pitch. It was the first property of the Kemps (the Soho Hotel), who sold it, then reacquired it, and have just reopened after a refurbishment. Expect all the usual style, from a drawing room with open fireplace to swathes of glorious fabrics and one-off and bespoke objects gathered from around the world. Bedrooms follow the same individual style and are beautifully equipped.

39–40 Dorset Sq., London NW1 6QN. www.firmdalehotels.com. ✆ **020/7723-7874.** Fax 020/724-3328. 38 units. £190–£380 double. AE, DC, MC, V. Parking £35/day, free on weekends. Tube: Baker St. or Marylebone. **Amenities:** Restaurant; bar; concierge, room service. *In room:* A/C, TV, minibar, hair dryer, MP3 docking station, Wi-Fi (£20/day).

Malmaison London This Victorian mansion block—once a nursing home—overlooks a leafy cobbled square and is the London showcase for the boutique hotel chain known for clever contemporary designs, state-of-the-art facilities, and, as always, a little brasserie serving French classics. On the southern rim of once-workaday, now trendy, Clerkenwell, Malmaison is decorated in dark teak wood; has tall, glowing floor lamps; tasteful fabrics in neutral shades; and a portrait and bust in the lobby of Napoleon and Josephine, who spent many a "wanton night" at the original Château Malmaison outside Paris. The dark-wood guest rooms are individually designed and larger than average for central London.

18–21 Charterhouse Sq., London EC1M 6AH. www.malmaison.com/hotels/london. ✆ **020/7012-3700.** Fax 020/7012-3702. 97 units. £225–£295 double. AE, MC, V. Tube: Barbican or Farringdon. **Amenities:** Restaurant; bar; concierge; room service. *In room:* A/C, TV/DVD, minibar, CD player, CD library, Wi-Fi (free/30 min., and then £10/day).

Mandeville Hotel ★★　The jewel in the crown of Marylebone Village—one of London's best-kept secrets and a charming warren of independent shops, neighborhood restaurants, and busy bars—is the refurbished Mandeville. This once-staid property is now a hot address. One of London's leading decorators, Stephen Ryan, was brought in to restyle the lobby, restaurant, and bar. Bedrooms too have had a makeover and are thankfully free of the chintz of some Marylebone hotels—rich autumnal tones and masculine furnishings are the order of the day here.

Mandeville Place, London W1U 2BE. www.mandeville.co.uk. ✆ **020/7935-5599.** Fax 020/7935-9588. 142 units. £127–£339 double. AE, DC, MC, V. Tube: Bond St. **Amenities:** Restaurant; bar; exercise room; concierge; room service. *In room:* A/C, TV, minibar (in some), hair dryer, Wi-Fi (£13/day).

Town Hall Hotel ★★　There were sharp intakes of breath when this grand hotel opened in 2010 on an ordinary Bethnal Green side-street: An imposing design hotel, with one of the hippest young chefs doing the food, this far east? The gamble paid off, and London's East End finally has the luxury accommodation it needed. The former Bethnal Green Town Hall has been converted into a palace of design and taste. Rooms are somber and clean-lined with beautiful mid-century design pieces. The Viajante restaurant (p. 230) is the hottest ticket in town, but you can get a taste of the chef's superb cooking at the more casual, walk-in, no-reservations Corner Room restaurant. The bar has a great creative staff and the smart pool and spa are a rare treat for East London.

8 Patriot Sq., London E2 9NF. www.townhallhotel.com. ✆ **020/7871-0460.** Fax 020/7160-5214. 98 units. £162–£192 double. AE, DC, MC, V. Tube: Bethnal Green. **Amenities:** 2 restaurants; bar; indoor pool; exercise room; spa. *In room:* A/C, TV/DVD, hair dryer, Wi-Fi (free).

MODERATE

Apex City of London Hotel　This modern hotel stands next to St. Olave's church with views over the peaceful garden on one side. Mainly a business hotel (so emptier at weekends), its relaxed feel, informal restaurant, and colorful public lounges make it friendlier than many of its neighbors. Bedrooms are smart with pretty cushions and curtains softening the blocks of color; tea- and coffee-making facilities and free mineral water plus nibbles are thoughtful touches. Bathrooms have walk-in power showers and Elemis toiletries. Good inexpensive bar snacks and drinks, and the restaurant, with its modern British cooking, is also very sensibly priced, with a fixed-price dinner menu from £15.95. A well-equipped gym will help work off the calories.

No. 1 Seething Ln., London EC3N 4AX. www.apexhotels.co.uk. ✆ **020/7977-9500.** Fax 020/7702-2217. 179 units. £99–£340 double. AE, DC, MC, V. Tube: Tower Hill. **Amenities:** Restaurant; bar; concierge; room service. *In room:* A/C, TV, DVD (in most rooms), minibar, hair dryer, MP3 docking station, Wi-Fi (free).

B&B Belgravia ★　In its first year of operation (2005), this elegant town house won a Gold Award as "the best B&B in London." Design, service, quality, and comfort paid off. The prices are reasonable, the atmosphere in this massively renovated building is stylish, and the location is grand: Just a 5-minute walk from Victoria station. The good-size bedrooms are luxuriously furnished. There is also a DVD library, and tea and coffee are served 24 hours a day. Late risers may want to avoid Room 1—it's above the breakfast room and isn't the quietest. Unusually for London, pets are welcome.

64–66 Ebury St., London SW1W 9QD. www.bb-belgravia.com. © **020/7259-8570.** Fax 020/7259-8591. 17 units. £135-£145 double; £165–£175 family room. Rates include English breakfast. AE, MC, V. Tube: Victoria. **Amenities:** Breakfast room. *In room:* TV, Wi-Fi (free).

Hart House Hotel ★ ☺ Hart House, run by the Bowden family for 44 years, is a long-standing favorite of Frommers' readers. In the heart of the West End, this well-preserved Georgian mansion lies within walking distance of West End shopping and dining. The rooms—done in a combination of furnishings, ranging from antique to modern—are spick-and-span, each one with its own character. Favorites include no. 7, a triple with a big bathroom and shower; no. 3 is large, sleeps four and is at the back. For singles, no. 11 is a brightly lit aerie. Hart House has long been known as a good, safe place for traveling families, with many triple rooms and special interconnecting family units.

51 Gloucester Place, London W1U 8JF. www.harthouse.co.uk. © **020/7935-2288.** Fax 020/7935-8516. 15 units. £145–£185 double; £150–£225 triple. Rates include English breakfast. MC, V. Tube: Marble Arch or Baker St. *In room:* TV, hair dryer, Wi-Fi (£5/stay).

The Main House ★★ ✦ The term home-from-home is bandied around all too frequently, but the Main House deserves the tag. Each guest gets a high-ceilinged floor of this Notting Hill town house to themselves, decorated in rare style from on-the-doorstep Portobello Road market—expect gilded mirrors, watercolors of elegantly dressed 1930s women, and similar antiques. Some extra little touches make this place unique: Early morning tea or coffee in the room; a wonderfully cheap deal on chauffeur service; cellphones to keep your call costs down; helpful maps, books, films, and umbrellas to borrow; and gleaming wood floors swathed in animal skins (reflecting owner Caroline Main's time as an explorer).

6 Colville Rd., London W11 2BP. www.themainhouse.co.uk. © **020/7221-9691.** 4 suites. £120–£150 suite. MC, V. Parking £2.50/hr. Tube: Notting Hill Gate. **Amenities:** Access to health club & spa; bikes; room service; Internet (free). *In room:* TV, hair dryer.

INEXPENSIVE

Henley House ★★ ✦ This B&B stands out from the pack around Earl's Court—and it's better value than most. The redbrick Victorian row house is on a communal fenced-in garden entered by borrowing a key from the reception desk. The decor is bright and contemporary; a typical room has warmly patterned wallpaper, chintz fabrics, and solid-brass lighting fixtures. The friendly staff members are happy to take bewildered newcomers under their wing, so this is an ideal place for London first-timers.

30 Barkston Gardens, London SW5 0EN. www.henleyhousehotel.com. © **020/7370-4111.** Fax 020/7370-0026. 21 units. £75–£159 double. Rates include continental breakfast. AE, DC, MC, V. Tube: Earl's Court. *In room:* TV, hair dryer, Wi-Fi (free).

Tune Hotel Liverpool Street ✦ Tune's appeal lies in its location in the middle of trendy Spitalfields, simple but spotlessly clean rooms (some without windows, so check when you book), power shower in the pod bathrooms, and straightforward pricing policy. You pay for the room, then add on items like towels, use of TV, hairdryer, safe, etc. It feels a little like a hostel, but a very friendly one. There's a coffee machine and snacks and a large garden. There's also the **Tune Hotel Westminster** at 118–120 Westminster Bridge Road, SE1 7RW (✆ **020/7633 9317;** Tube: Waterloo), and more planned to open in 2013.

13-15 Folgate St., London E1 6BX. www.tunehotels.com/uk. ✆ **020/7456-0400.** Fax 020/7456-0409. 183 units. £35–£95 double. AE, MC, V. Tube: Old St. **Amenities:** Garden. *In room:* A/C, TV (£3/24 hr., £10/unlimited), hairdryer (£1), Wi-Fi (£1.50/1 hr., £3/24 hr., £10/unlimited).

Z Hotel Soho ★ 🏨 The team behind Z Hotels produces five-star quality at three-star prices, challenging the cheap chains. What is sacrificed is space: Rooms are small, your suitcase goes under the bed and clothes hang on hooks on the walls. But you do get stylish decor, triple-glazed windows, good bathrooms with frosted glass walls and top toiletries, goose feather pillows, best quality bed linen, a chic wood and marble decor, and a 42-inch TV with Sky, bang in the middle of Soho. The only criticism concerns the hard mattresses. Created from 12 derelict town houses over five floors, you reach your room via an elevator and an open-air corridor of wooden walls that gives a real Scandinavian feel. State-of-the-art Wi-Fi, a 24-hour cafe, rapid check-in and check-out, and a Lanson champagne bar complete the package. Plans include 15 new hotels in and around London.

17 Moor St, London W1D 5AP. www.thezhotels.com. ✆ **020/3551-3700.** 85 units. £102. AE, MC, V. Tube: Oxford Circus or Tottenham Court Rd. **Amenities:** 2 bars; cafe. *In room:* A/C, TV/DVD, hair dryer, MP3 charger, Wi-Fi (free).

Day Trips from London

Hampton Court Palace ★★★ ☺ PALACE The 16th-century palace of Cardinal Wolsey can teach us a lesson: Don't try to outdo your boss, particularly if he happens to be Henry VIII. The rich cardinal did just that, and he eventually lost his fortune, power, and prestige, and ended up giving his lavish palace to the Tudor monarch. Henry's additions include an Astronomical Clock above the Clock Court (still showing the phases of the moon, the position of the sun, and signs of the Zodiac to this day), the aptly named Great Hall with its hammerbeam roof (in Henry VIII's Private Apartments), a Tiltyard (where jousting competitions were held), and a "real tennis" court.

Although the palace enjoyed prestige in Elizabethan days, it owes much of its present look to William and Mary—or rather, to Sir Christopher Wren. You can parade through their apartments today, filled with porcelain, furniture, paintings, and tapestries. Also, be sure to inspect the **Chapel Royal** (Wolsey wouldn't recognize it), **Henry VIII's Kitchens** where great Tudor feasts are regularly prepared, and the **Base Court** where the latest addition to this composite palace can be found in the form of a replica Wine Fountain built on the foundations of an original discovered in 2008.

The 24-hectare (59-acre) **gardens**—including Tudor and Elizabethan Knot Gardens—are open daily year-round. The most popular section is the serpentine shrubbery **Maze,** also the work of Wren, and accounting for countless lost children every year. A garden **cafe** and restaurant are located in the Tiltyard.

Plenty of family entertainments are laid on throughout the year, and free children's activity trails and audio guides, for both adults and children, are available from the information center.

Insider's tip: Tickets are considerably cheaper if bought online. Below are the walk-up prices.

East Molesey, Surrey. www.hrp.org.uk/HamptonCourtPalace. © **0844/482-7777.** Palace admission £15.95 adults, £13.20 students and seniors, £8 children 5–15, £43.45 family ticket, free for children 4 and under; gardens admission £5.30 adults, £4.60 students and seniors, free for children without palace ticket during summer. Maze: £3.85 adults, £2.75 children 5–15, free for children 4 and under. Cloisters, courtyards, state apartments, great kitchen, cellars, and Hampton Court exhibition Mar–Oct daily 10am–6pm; Nov–Feb daily 10am–4:30pm. Gardens year-round daily 7am–dusk (no later than 9pm). Rail: Hampton Court (30 min. from Waterloo).

Windsor Castle ★★★ William the Conqueror first ordered a castle built on this location, and, since his day, it has been a fateful spot for English sovereigns: King John cooled his heels at Windsor while waiting to put his signature on the Magna Carta at nearby Runnymede; Charles I was imprisoned here before losing his head; Queen Bess did some renovations; Victoria mourned her beloved Albert, who died at the castle in 1861; the royal family rode out much of World War II behind its sheltering walls; and when Queen Elizabeth II is in residence, the Royal Standard flies. With 1,000 rooms, Windsor is the world's largest inhabited castle.

The apartments display many works of art, armor, three Verrio ceilings, and several 17th-century Gibbons carvings. Several works by Rubens adorn the King's Drawing Room. In the relatively small King's Dressing Room is a Dürer, along with Rembrandt's portrait of his mother and Van Dyck's triple portrait of Charles I. Of the apartments, the grand reception room, with its Gobelin tapestries, is the most spectacular.

Queen Mary's Dolls' House is a palace in perfect miniature. The Dolls' House was given to Queen Mary in 1923. It was a gift of members of the royal family, including the king, along with contributions made by some 1,500 tradesmen, artists, and authors.

St. George's Chapel is a gem of the Perpendicular style; this chapel shares the distinction with Westminster Abbey of being a pantheon of English monarchs (Victoria is a notable exception). The present St. George's was founded in the late 15th century by Edward IV on the site of the original Chapel of the Order of the Garter (Edward III, 1348).

It is recommended that you take a free guided tour of the castle grounds, including the Jubilee Gardens. Guides are very well informed and recapture the rich historical background of the castle.

Windsor Castle lies 34km (21 miles) west of London; you can reach it in 50 minutes by train from Paddington Station. Castle Hill. www.royalcollection.org.uk. © **01753/83118.** Admission £17 adults, £15.50 students and seniors, £10.20 children 16 and under, free 4 and under, £44.75 family of 5 (2 adults and 3 children 16 and under). Daily Mar–Oct 9:45am–5:15pm; Nov–Feb 9:45am–4:15pm. Last admission 3pm. Closed for periods in Apr, June, and Dec, when the royal family is in residence.

OXFORD ★★

54 miles NW of London

The city of Oxford, dominated by Britain's oldest university, is a bastion of English tradition, history, and eccentricity. Here students still get selected to join the archaic Bullingdon Club, rowing competitions attract a larger audience than soccer, and students still take exams dressed in black gowns (seriously). The creator of detective *Inspector Morse*, Colin Dexter, lives in town, and where else would you film the Harry Potter series? Oxford certainly retains a special sort of magic.

The hallowed halls and gardens of ancient colleges such as Magdalen and Christ Church are architectural gems, but not museums—students live and work here year-round. The High Street (often referred to as The High) hasn't changed much since Oscar Wilde walked along it and the water meadows and spires that inspired architect Sir Christopher Wren and writers as diverse as John Donne, C.S. Lewis, Iris Murdoch, and J.R.R. Tolkien are still here.

ESSENTIALS

GETTING THERE **Trains** from London's Paddington station reach Oxford in around 1 hour (direct trains run every 30 minutes). A cheap round-trip ticket costs £22.50 (off-peak).

If you're **driving,** take the M40 west from London and follow the signs. **Parking** is a nightmare in Oxford; however, there are five large **park-and-ride** lots (www. parkandride.net). Buses run every 8 to 10 minutes until 11:30pm Monday to Saturday and between 11am and 5pm on Sundays. Off-peak tickets cost £2.20 per adult for a round-trip ticket.

VISITOR INFORMATION The **Oxford Tourist Information Centre** is at 15–16 Broad St. (www.visitoxfordandoxfordshire.com; ✆ **01865/252200**). Hours are Monday to Saturday 9:30am to 5pm, Sunday 10am to 4pm.

EXPLORING OXFORD AND ITS COLLEGES

Most first-time visitors to Oxford have trouble working out exactly where the university is. Indeed, the quickest way to sound like a dumb tourist in Oxford is to ask "Where's the university?" This is because Oxford University is in fact made up of 39 autonomous, self-governing colleges sprinkled throughout the center of town; there's no campus as such and no central university building. Touring every college would be a formidable task, so it's best to focus on just a handful of the most intriguing and famous ones (described below). Note that most of the free colleges are only open in the afternoon.

For a bird's-eye view of the city and colleges, climb the 99 steps up the 23m (74-ft.) Gothic **Carfax Tower** ★ (www.citysightseeingoxford.com; ✆ **01865/790522**) in the center of town. This structure is distinguished by its clock and figures that strike on the quarter-hour. Open daily from 10am to 5:30pm (4:30pm in October), admission costs £2.20 for adults, £1.10 for children 15 and under.

The Ashmolean ★★ This oft-overlooked history museum contains some real gems, not least the Alfred Jewel, a rare Anglo-Saxon gold ornament dating from the late 9th century adorned with the words "Alfred ordered me made" (in Saxon). There are also some high-quality paintings from the Italian Renaissance (Raphael and Michelangelo among them), a large Ancient Egypt section, and some rare Asian ceramics and sculptures. The rooftop restaurant, the Ashmolean Dining Room, is a great place for a bite after a visit.

Beaumont St. at St. Giles. www.ashmolean.org. ✆ **01865/278002.** Free admission. Tues–Sun 10am–6pm. Closed Dec 24–26.

Bodleian Library ★★ This famed library was established in 1602, initially funded by Sir Thomas Bodley, and today is a complex of several buildings in the heart of Oxford. Over the years, it has expanded from the Old Library on Catte Street and now includes the iconic **Radcliffe Camera** next door. The Bodleian is home to an astonishing 50,000 manuscripts and more than 11 million books (including a rare Gutenberg Bible).

Catte St. www.bodleian.ox.ac.uk. © **01865/277182.** Admission £1 Divinity School only; £6.50 (standard tour) or £4.50 for mini-tour (30 min.); £13 (extended tour). Mon–Fri 9am–5pm; Sat 9am–4:30pm; Sun 11am–5pm. Closed Dec 24–Jan 3. Call to confirm specific tour times.

Christy Church ★★ Nothing quite matches the beauty and grandeur of Christ Church, one of the most prestigious and the largest of Oxford colleges. Christ Church has a well-deserved reputation for exclusivity, wealth, and power: It has produced 13 British prime ministers, including William Gladstone, with other alumni including John Locke, John Wesley, William Penn, W. H. Auden, and Lewis Carroll.

The college chapel, which dates from the 12th century, also serves as **Oxford Cathedral;** and bowler-hatted "custodians" still patrol the pristine lawns. It boasts the most distinctive main entrance in Oxford, Sir Christopher Wren's **Tom Tower,** completed in 1682. The tower houses Great Tom, an 8,165kg (18,000lb) bell, which rings at 9:05pm nightly with 101 peals. Walk through the gate and you'll immediately face the largest quadrangle of any college in Oxford ("Tom Quad"). The two main highlights inside the college are the 16th-century Great Hall, where there are some portraits by Gainsborough and Reynolds, and the cathedral with its delicate vaulting dating from the 15th century. Many scenes from the *Harry Potter* films were shot here.

St. Aldate's. www.chch.ox.ac.uk. © **01865/276150.** Admission £8 adults, £6.50 students, children 5–17 and seniors, free 4 and under. Mon–Sat 9am–5pm; Sun 2–5pm. Last admission 4:30pm. Closed Christmas Day.

Magdalen College ★★ Pronounced *Maud*-lin, Magdalen is the most beautiful college in Oxford, thanks to its bucolic location on the banks of the River Cherwell and some dazzling Gothic architecture, notably the elegant Magdalen Tower. There's even a deer park in the grounds and tranquil Addison's Walk, a picturesque footpath along the river. Towering over the tranquil Botanic Garden opposite (the oldest in Britain), Magdalen Tower is the tallest building in Oxford (44m/144 ft.), completed in 1509 and where the choristers sing in Latin at dawn on May Day. You can also visit the 15th-century chapel, where the same choir sings Evensong Tuesday to Sunday at 6pm.

It's another influential college whose alumni range from Thomas Wolsey to Oscar Wilde; prominent ex-students in the current Conservative Party include William Hague and George Osborne.

High St. www.magd.ox.ac.uk. © **01865/276000.** Admission £4.50 adults, £3.50 seniors, students, and children. Jul–Sep daily noon–7pm; Oct–Jun daily 1–6pm or dusk (whichever is the earlier). Closed Dec 21–31.

 Punting the River Cherwell

Punting on the River Cherwell is an essential if slightly eccentric Oxford pastime. At the **Cherwell Boathouse,** Bardwell Rd. (www.cherwellboathouse.co.uk; © **01865/515978**), you can rent a punt (a flat-bottomed boat maneuvered by a long pole and a small oar) for £14 (weekdays) to £17 (weekends) per hour, plus a £70 to £80 deposit. **Magdalen Bridge Boathouse,** the Old Horse Ford, High St. (www.oxfordpunting.co.uk; © **01865/202643**), charges £16 (weekdays) to £20 (weekends) per hour. Punts are available from mid-March to mid-October, daily from 10am until dusk.

Merton College ★   Founded in 1264, Merton College is among the three oldest colleges at the University and is the most academically successful college of the last 20 years. Merton's alumni list is eclectic and includes T. S. Eliot, J. R. R. Tolkien, unlikely Rhodes Scholar Kris Kristofferson, and even Naruhito, Crown Prince of Japan. The college is especially noted for its library, built between 1371 and 1379, and said to be the oldest college library in England. One of the library's treasures is an astrolabe (an astronomical instrument used for measuring the altitude of the sun and stars) thought to have belonged to Chaucer.

14 Merton St. www.merton.ox.ac.uk. (C) **01865/276310.** Admission £2. Mon–Fri 2–5pm; Sat–Sun 10am–5pm. Closed for 1 week at Easter and Christmas.

Museum of Natural History & Pitt Rivers Museum ★ ☺   These two enlightening museums lie a short walk northeast of the center, well off the beaten path for most tourists but a worthwhile diversion. The Museum of Natural History houses the University's extensive collections of zoological, entomological, and geological specimens; everything from stuffed crocodiles and a giant open-jaw of a Sperm Whale, to the tsetse fly collected by the explorer David Livingstone. The Pitt Rivers Museum was founded in 1884 and displays more than half a million archeological and ethnographic objects from all over the world. Highlights include a precious Tahitian mourner's costume collected by Captain Cook in 1773–74, ghostly Japanese Noh masks, and thick Inuit fur coats.

Parks Rd. and S Parks Rd. Oxford University Museum of Natural History: www.oum.ox.ac.uk. (C) **01865/272950.** Free admission. Daily 10am–5pm. Pitt Rivers Museum: www.prm.ox.ac.uk. (C) **01865/270927.** Free admission. Mon noon–4:30pm; Tues–Sun 10am–4:30pm.

New College   New College is another must-see, primarily for its exceptional architecture and spacious grounds; it's also a favorite *Harry Potter* location. The college was founded in 1379 by William of Wykeham, bishop of Winchester, but the real masterpiece here is the chapel, with its handsome interior, stained glass (some designed by Joshua Reynolds), Jacob Epstein's remarkable modern sculpture of Lazarus, and a fine El Greco painting of St. James. Don't miss the beautiful garden outside the college, where you can stroll among the remains of the old city wall.

Holywell St., at New College Lane. www.new.ox.ac.uk. (C) **01865/279500.** Admission £3 March–Oct; free during Winter.

Sheldonian Theatre   This ravishing piece of Palladian architecture stands next door to the Bodleian, completed in 1668 to a design by Sir Christopher Wren. As well as admiring the immaculate interior and ceiling frescoes, you can climb up to the cupola and enjoy fine views over Oxford.

Broad St. www.ox.ac.uk/sheldonian. (C) **01865/277299.** Admission £2.50. Mar–Oct Mon–Sat 10am–12:30pm & 2–4:30pm; Nov–Feb Mon–Sat 10am–12:30pm & 2–3:30pm. Closed when in use.

ORGANIZED TOURS   For an easy orientation, take a 1-hour, open-top bus tour with **City Sightseeing Oxford** (www.citysightseeingoxford.com; (C) **01865/790522**). Tours start from the railway station. Buses leave daily at 9:30am and then every 10 to 15 minutes. The last bus departs at 4pm November to February, at 5pm March and October, and at 6pm April to September. The cost is £13 for adults, £11 for students, £10 for seniors, and £6 for children 5 to 14 years; a family ticket for two adults and three children is £33. Tickets can be purchased from the driver. They are valid for 24 hours and 48-hour tickets are available at a discount.

WHERE TO EAT

An Oxford landmark on the River Cherwell, the suitably expensive **Cherwell Boathouse Restaurant ★**, Bardwell Rd. (www.cherwellboathouse.co.uk; ℂ **01865/ 552746**), takes advantage of the freshest vegetables, fish, and meat. Try the pork belly with a foie gras terrine or confit of duck in a port sauce, but save room for traditional English puddings.

For more moderately priced English dining, you'll find the delightful **Gee's Restaurant ★**, 61 Banbury Rd. (www.gees-restaurant.co.uk; ℂ **01865/553540**), in a spacious Victorian glass conservatory dating from 1898 serving classic British dishes. It's worth staying for the live jazz every Sunday evening (8–9:45pm), even if you're just having drinks.

To cater to the student budget, there are plenty of inexpensive cafes in Oxford. **Brown's ★★** at the Covered Market, Market St. (ℂ **01865/243436**), is a traditional "greasy spoon" British cafe serving sausage sandwiches, fish and chips, hearty fry-ups, apple pie and custard, and mugs of tea. For dessert, **George & Davis,** 55 Little Clarendon St. (www.gdcafe.com; ℂ **01865/516652**), is Oxford's ice-cream headquarters, a brightly painted cafe serving indulgent flavors such as super chocolate and golden secret (honeycomb and chocolate in a cream base), topped with gummy bears, nuts, or chocolate sprinkles. For something a little healthier, **Vaults & Garden Café ★** (www.vaultsandgarden.com; ℂ **01865/279112**) is set in the gorgeous 14th-century hall on the grounds of the University Church of St. Mary the Virgin and serves tasty soups (try the leek and potato), made with organic vegetables from nearby Worton Organic Garden, as well as salads, vegetable stir fry, and organic beef lasagna.

SHOPPING

Golden Cross, an arcade of first-class shops and boutiques, lies between Cornmarket Street and the Covered Market. Parts of the colorful gallery date from the 12th century; many buildings remain from the medieval era, along with some 15th- and 17th-century structures.

Alice's Shop, 83 St. Aldate's (www.aliceinwonderlandshop.co.uk; ℂ **01865/ 723793**), is where Alice Liddell, thought to have been the model for *Alice in Wonderland,* used to buy her barley sugar sweets when Lewis Carroll was a professor of mathematics at Christ Church. Today, you'll find commemorative pencils, chess sets, bookmarks, and, in rare cases, original editions of some of Carroll's works.

The **Bodleian Library Shop,** Old School's Quadrangle, Radcliffe Sq., Broad St. (www.shop.bodley.ox.ac.uk; ℂ **01865/277091**), specializes in Oxford souvenirs, from books and paperweights to Oxford banners and coffee mugs. **Castell & Son (The Varsity Shop),** 13 Broad St. (www.varsityshop.co.uk; ℂ **01865/244000**), is the best outlet in Oxford for clothing emblazoned with the Oxford logo or heraldic symbol.

The best bookshop in Oxford is venerable **Blackwell** at 48–51 Broad St. (bookshop.blackwell.co.uk; ℂ **01865/333536**).

ENTERTAINMENT & NIGHTLIFE
The Pub Scene

Pubs in Oxford have a fittingly rich heritage, and you'll be drinking in the same oak-paneled rooms once frequented by Samuel Johnson, Lawrence of Arabia, Graham Greene, Bill Clinton, and Margaret Thatcher. The city does have a life beyond the

CALLING ON CHURCHILL AT blenheim PALACE

The extravagantly baroque **Blenheim Palace,** Brighton Rd., Woodstock (www.blenheimpalace.com; ℂ **08700/602080**), is England's answer to Versailles. Blenheim is still the home of the Dukes of Marlborough, descendants of the first duke John Churchill, victor of the Battle of Blenheim (1704), a crushing defeat of Britain's archenemy Louis XIV. Blenheim was built for him as a gift from Queen Anne in the 1720s. The family, virtually bankrupt, hung on to the palace thanks to the brutally commercial marriage of Charles, 9th Duke of Marlborough (1871–1934) to Consuelo Vanderbilt, heiress to the wealthy American railroad dynasty. Blenheim was also the birthplace of the 9th duke's first cousin, Sir Winston Churchill. The room in which he was born in 1874 is included in the palace tour, as is the Churchill exhibition: four rooms of letters, books, photographs, and other relics.

The palace was designed by Sir John Vanbrugh, who was also the architect of Castle Howard; the landscaping was created by Capability Brown. The interior is loaded with riches: antiques, porcelain, oil paintings, tapestries, and chinoiserie. The present owner is the 11th Duke of Marlborough (b. 1926), whom you may see wandering around. The duke had a small cameo in Kenneth Branagh's movie *Hamlet* (1996), which was filmed at Blenheim.

Insider tip: **Marlborough Maze,** 540m (1,800 ft.) from the palace, is the largest symbolic hedge maze on earth, with a herb and lavender garden, a butterfly house, and inflatable castles for children. Also, be sure to look for the castle's gift shops, tucked away in an old palace dairy. Here you can purchase a wide range of souvenirs, handicrafts, and even locally made preserves.

Admission is £20 adults (parks and gardens £11.50), £15.50 students and seniors (parks and gardens £8.50), £11 children 5–15 (parks and gardens £6), and £52 family ticket (parks and gardens £30); free for children 4 and under. The park and house are open daily 10:30am to 5:30pm with last admission at 4:45pm (the house is closed mid-Dec to mid-Feb).

University too: Radiohead played their first gig at Oxford's **Jericho Tavern** in 1986, an alternative venue that still hosts live bands.

Known as the "Bird and Baby," the **Eagle and Child,** 49 Saint Giles St. (ℂ **01865/302925**), was frequented in the 1930s and '40s by the "Inklings," a writers' group that included the likes of C. S. Lewis and J. R. R. Tolkien. In fact, *The Chronicles of Narnia* and *The Hobbit* were first read aloud here. In contrast, the **Head of the River,** Abingdon Rd. at Folly Bridge, near the Westgate Centre Mall (ℂ **01865/721600**), is a lively place offering traditional ales, along with good sturdy bar food. In summer, guests can sit by the river and rent a punt or a boat with an engine. The tiny **White Horse ★**, 52 Broad St. (www.whitehorseoxford.co.uk; ℂ **01865/204801**), squeezed between Blackwell's bookshops, is one of Oxford's oldest pubs, dating from the 16th century.

The **Bear Inn ★**, 6 Alfred St. (ℂ **01865/728164**), is an Oxford landmark, built in the 13th century. Around the lounge bar you'll see the remains of thousands of ties, which have been labeled with their owners' names. Even older than the Bear is the **Turf Tavern ★★**, 7 Bath Place, off Holywell St. (www.theturftavern.co.uk;

$\mathcal{C}$ **01865/243235**), on a very narrow passageway near the Bodleian Library, reached via St. Helen's Passage. Thomas Hardy used the place as the setting for *Jude the Obscure*, and it was "the local" of Bill Clinton during his student days at Oxford.

Most Oxford pubs open from around 11am to midnight.

WHERE TO STAY
Expensive

Macdonald Randolph Hotel ★ Open since 1864, the venerable Randolph is an Oxford landmark with elegant guest rooms furnished in a conservative English style. Fans of Inspector Morse should check out the Morse Bar (the fictional Morse often asserted that "they serve a decent pint" at the Randolph, and author Colin Dexter set several of the detective stories here), while the lounges, though modernized, are cavernous enough for dozens of separate and intimate conversational groupings. Some rooms are quite large; others are a bit cramped, and overall the hotel is a little overpriced: You are paying primarily for the location and the rich history.

Beaumont St., Oxford OX1 2LN. www.macdonaldhotels.co.uk/Randolph. $\mathcal{C}$**0844/879-9132.** Fax: 01865/791678. 151 units. £230–£280 double; £528–£607 suite. AE, DC, MC, V. Limited parking £27 or public parking £30 for 24 hr. **Amenities:** Restaurant; 2 bars; spa; concierge; room service; babysitting. *In room:* TV, hair dryer, CD player, Wi-Fi (£9.99 per day).

Malmaison Oxford Castle ★★ 🛎 This place was formerly for inmates detained at Her Majesty's pleasure, and many aspects of prison life, including barred windows, have been retained. Guest rooms, in a converted Victorian building, are actually remodeled "cells" that flank two sides of a large central atrium, a space that rises three stories and is crisscrossed by narrow walkways. The former inmates never had it so good—great beds, mood lighting, power showers, satellite TV, and serious wines. In spite of its origins, this is a stylish and comfortable place to stay.

3 Oxford Castle, Oxford OXI 1AY. www.malmaison.com. $\mathcal{C}$ **01865/268400.** 94 units. £185–£245 double; £275–£345 suite. AE, DC, MC, V. Parking (pre-booking required) £20. **Amenities:** Restaurant; bar; exercise room; room service. *In room:* TV/DVD, minibar, CD player, Wi-Fi (free).

Old Bank Hotel ★★ The first hotel created in the center of Oxford in 135 years, the Old Bank opened in 1999 and immediately surpassed the traditional favorite, the Randolph (see above), in both style and amenities. Located on Oxford's main street and surrounded by some of its oldest colleges and sights, the building dates back to the 18th century and was indeed once a bank. The hotel currently features a collection of 20th-century British art handpicked by the owners. Bedrooms are comfortably and elegantly appointed, many opening onto views. A combination of velvet and shantung silk-trimmed linen bedcovers gives the guest rooms added style.

92–94 High St., Oxford OX1 4BN. www.oldbank-hotel.co.uk. $\mathcal{C}$**01865/799599.** Fax 01865/799598. 42 units. £230–£350 double. AE, DC, MC, V. Free parking. Bus: 7. **Amenities:** Restaurant; bar; room service; babysitting. *In room:* A/C, TV, hair dryer, CD player, Internet (free).

Old Parsonage Hotel ★★ This extensively renovated hotel, near St. Giles Church and Keble College, looks like an extension of one of the ancient colleges. Originally a 13th-century hospital, it was restored in the 1660s. In 1991, it was completely renovated and made into a first-rate hotel. This intimate old property is filled with hidden charms, such as tiny gardens in the courtyard and on the roof terrace. In this tranquil area of Oxford, you'll feel like you're living at one of the colleges yourself. The rooms are individually designed but not large; each opens onto the private gardens.

1 Banbury Rd., Oxford OX2 6NN. www.oldparsonage-hotel.co.uk. ℭ **01865/310210.** Fax 01865/311262. 30 units. £131–£152 double. AE, DC, MC, V. Free parking. **Amenities:** Restaurant; bar; room service. *In room:* A/C, TV, hair dryer, Internet (free).

Moderate

Burlington House ★★ ⚑   This top choice on the edge of town makes up for the slightly inconvenient location with fabulous service, bargain prices, and immaculate, boutique-like rooms. Inside, old fittings and fireplaces blend with modern beds and flat-screen TVs; the power showers are especially welcome. Breakfasts are another highlight, with high-quality continental and hot items to try (marmalade omelet anyone?). The hotel sits on Banbury Road near a bus stop with frequent buses into the center (10- or 20-min. walk), and there are plenty of bars and restaurants nearby, too.

374 Banbury Rd., Oxford OX2 7PP. www.burlington-hotel-oxford.co.uk. ℭ **01865/513513.** 12 units. £86–£160 double. AE, DC, MC, V. Rates include English breakfast. Free parking (weekends only). Bus: 2 or 7. **Amenities:** Lounge; dining room. *In room:* A/C, TV, hair dryer, Wi-Fi (free).

Inexpensive

Tilbury Lodge ★★ 🎁   This unassuming red-brick home on the outskirts holds one of Oxford's secret gems, a B&B with fresh, modern decor, new bathrooms, and spacious rooms. It's the extras that make this special: Bathrobes, foot-massage machines, and a bevy of sweet treats baked by the affable owners, Stefan and Melanie. Expect homemade fudge, cookies, tea and coffee, and warm scones on arrival. The breakfasts are hard to beat, a wonderful spread of fresh fruits, yogurts, homemade breads, muffins, and tasty cooked plates. The city center is just 10 minutes by bus (the bus stop is on the corner).

5 Tilbury Lane, Oxford OX2 9NB. www.tilburylodge.com. ℭ **01865/862138.** 9 units. £88–£110 double. Rates include English breakfast. MC, V. Free parking. Bus: 4C, S1. **Amenities:** Conservatory lounge. *In room:* TV, hair dryer, CD player, Wi-Fi (free). From Oxford, take the A420 then Westway to Botley, turn right onto Eynsham Rd. (B4044) and look for Tilbury Lane (first right). Closed Dec–Jan.

STRATFORD-UPON-AVON ★★

91 miles NW of London; 40 miles NW of Oxford; 8 miles S of Warwick

The birthplace of **William Shakespeare,** England's greatest playwright, Stratford commemorates the Bard with a spread of beautifully maintained historic sites from the Tudor period. The other major draw for visitors is the **Royal Shakespeare Theatre,** where Britain's foremost actors perform during a long season that lasts from April to November.

Shakespeare was born here in 1564, and though he spent most of his career in London, this otherwise plain-looking town has been cashing in on the connection ever since. Crowds, bus tours, and unashamed tourism now dominate the center, but visiting the sights themselves, and especially taking in a play or two, transports you right back to the 16th century.

ESSENTIALS

GETTING THERE   Trains from London Marylebone to Stratford-upon-Avon take about 2¼ hours, with one-way tickets ranging from £15 to £46. Trains link Stratford with Birmingham Snow Hill station (55 min.) every hour, for £6.80, and less frequently, with Warwick (25 min.) for £5.

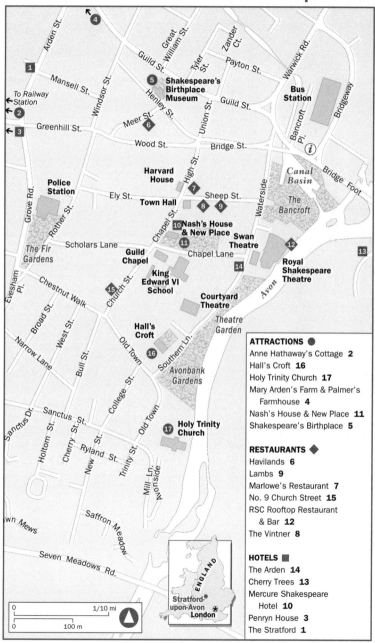

ATTRACTIONS ●
Anne Hathaway's Cottage **2**
Hall's Croft **16**
Holy Trinity Church **17**
Mary Arden's Farm & Palmer's
    Farmhouse **4**
Nash's House & New Place **11**
Shakespeare's Birthplace **5**

RESTAURANTS ◆
Havilands **6**
Lambs **9**
Marlowe's Restaurant **7**
No. 9 Church Street **15**
RSC Rooftop Restaurant
    & Bar **12**
The Vintner **8**

HOTELS ■
The Arden **14**
Cherry Trees **13**
Mercure Shakespeare
    Hotel **10**
Penryn House **3**
The Stratford **1**

If you're **driving** from London, take the M40 to junction 15 and continue to Stratford-upon-Avon on the A46/A439.

VISITOR INFORMATION The **Tourist Information Centre,** Bridgefoot, on the A3400 (www.discover-stratford.com; ✆ **01789/264293**), provides any details you may wish to know about the Shakespeare houses and properties; it will also assist in booking rooms (see "Where to Stay," below). The center is open daily 10am to 5pm (10am–4pm Nov–Feb).

EXPLORING STRATFORD

Most of Stratford's historic attractions are administrated by the **Shakespeare Birthplace Trust** (www.shakespeare.org.uk; ✆ **01789/204016**). One combination ticket (£21 for adults, £19 for seniors and students, and £13.50 for children 5–15 and 16–17 in full-time education) lets you visit the five most important sights, described below. You can also buy a family ticket, £55.50 for two adults and three children—a good deal. Buy the ticket at your first stop at any one of the Trust properties. Free admission for children 4 and under.

Anne Hathaway's Cottage ★ HISTORIC HOME   The childhood home of Anne Hathaway, Shakespeare's long-suffering wife, is the Trust property most evocative of the Tudor period—a gorgeous thatched wattle-and-daub cottage going back to the 1480s, located in the hamlet of Shottery, 1 mile from the center of Stratford. The Hathaways were yeoman sheep farmers, and their descendants lived in this cottage until 1911. Many original furnishings, including various kitchen utensils and the courting settle (the bench on which Shakespeare is said to have wooed Anne), are preserved inside the house. Will was only 18 when he married Anne Hathaway in 1582 (she was 8 years older), and a special exhibit chronicles the marriage.

Cottage Lane, Shottery (take the City Sightseeing bus, p. 254, from Bridge St., or walk via a marked pathway from Evesham Place in Stratford across the meadow to Shottery). www.shakespeare.org. uk. ✆ **01789/292100.** Admission £8.50 adults, £7.50 seniors and students, £5 children 5–15 and 16–17 in full-time education, £22 family ticket. Combination tickets available (see above). Apr–Oct daily 9am–5pm; Nov–Mar 10am–4pm. Closed Dec 25–26.

Hall's Croft HISTORIC HOME   Hall's Croft is an outstanding Tudor house with a walled garden, furnished in the style of a middle-class home of the time. It was here that Shakespeare's eldest daughter Susanna probably lived with her husband, Dr. John Hall, who was widely respected and built up a large medical practice in the area. Fascinating exhibits illustrate the theory and practice of medicine in Dr. Hall's time.

Old Town St. (near Holy Trinity Church). www.shakespeare.org.uk. ✆ **01789/292107.** Admission includes Shakespeare's Birthplace and Nash's House & New Place; £13.50 adults, £12.50 seniors and students, £9 children 5–15 and 16–17 in full-time education, £36 family ticket. Apr–Oct daily 10am–5pm; Nov–Mar 11am–4pm. Closed Dec 25–26.

Holy Trinity Church (Shakespeare's Tomb) CHURCH   In a bucolic setting near the River Avon is the Norman parish church where Shakespeare is buried ("and curst be he who moves my bones"). The Parish Register records his baptism in 1564 and burial in 1616; copies of the original documents are on display. Shakespeare's tomb lies in the chancel. Alongside his grave are those of his widow, Anne, and other members of his family. Nearby on the north wall is a bust of Shakespeare that was erected approximately 7 years after his death.

Old Town St. (walk 4 min. past the Royal Shakespeare Theatre, with the river on your left). www. stratford-upon-avon.org. ✆ **01789/290128.** Free admission to church; Shakespeare's tomb £2 adults, £1 students. Apr–Sept Mon–Sat 8:30am–6pm, Sun 12:30–5pm; Mar and Oct Mon–Sat 9am–5pm, Sun 12:30–5pm; Nov–Feb Mon–Sat 9am–4pm, Sun 12:30–5pm. Closed to visitors Good Friday, Christmas Day, Boxing Day (St. Stephen's Day), and New Year's Day.

Mary Arden's Farm & Palmer's Farmhouse ★ FARM   The childhood home of Mary Shakespeare, née Mary Arden (1537–1608), the mother of Will Shakespeare, still operates as a working farm in Wilmcote, 3 miles from Stratford. Visitors can tour the property and see firsthand how a farming household functioned in the 1570s—cows to be milked, bread to be baked, and vegetables cultivated in an authentic 16th-century manner. In the barns, stable, cowshed, and farmyard is an extensive collection of farming implements illustrating life and work in the local countryside from Shakespeare's time to the present. Until 2000 the Arden's red-brick farmhouse was known as Glebe Farm—the far more romantic, timber-framed house next door was thought to be the Arden home. Thanks to research by local historian Dr. Nat Alcock, Glebe Farm was properly renamed, and what was known for years as "Mary Arden's House" was dubbed Palmer's Farmhouse.

Station Rd., Wilmcote (take the A3400 toward Birmingham for 3½ miles). www.shakespeare.org.uk. ✆ **01789/293455.** Admission £9.50 adults, £8.50 students and seniors, £6.50 children 5–15 and 16–17 in full-time education, £25.50 family ticket. Combination tickets available (see above). Apr–Oct daily 10am–5pm. Closed Nov–Mar.

Nash's House & New Place HISTORIC HOME   Shakespeare retired to New Place in 1610 (a prosperous man by the standards of his day) and died here 6 years later. Regrettably, the house was torn down, so only the garden remains. A mulberry tree planted by the Bard was so popular with latter-day visitors to Stratford that the garden's owner chopped it down. It is said that the mulberry tree that grows here today was planted from a cutting of the original tree. You enter the gardens through Nash's House, which contains 17th-century period rooms and an exhibition illustrating the history of Stratford. Thomas Nash married Elizabeth Hall, a granddaughter of the poet.

Chapel St. www.shakespeare.org.uk. ✆ **01789/292325.** Admission includes Shakespeare's Birthplace and Hall's Croft; £13.50 adults, £12.50 seniors and students, £9 children 5–15 and 16–17 in full-time education, £36 family ticket. Nov–Mar daily 11am–4pm; Apr–Oct daily 10am–5pm. Closed Dec 25–26.

Shakespeare's Birthplace ★★ MUSEUM   The son of a glover and whittawer (leather worker), Will Shakespeare was born in this half-timbered structure in 1564. Bought by public donors in 1847, it has been preserved as a national shrine ever since and is filled with Shakespeare memorabilia. You can visit the living room, the bedroom where Shakespeare was probably born, a fully equipped kitchen of the period (look for the "babyminder"), and a Shakespeare museum, illustrating his life and times.

Built next door to commemorate the 400th anniversary of the Bard's birth, the modern **Shakespeare Centre** serves both as the administrative headquarters of the Birthplace Trust and as a library and study center. An extension houses the **Birthplace Visitor Centre.**

Henley St. www.shakespeare.org.uk. ✆ **01789/204016.** Admission includes entry to Hall's Croft and Nash's House & New Place; £13.50 adults, £12.50 seniors and students, £9 children 5–15 and 16–17 in full-time education, £36 family ticket. Nov–Mar daily 10am–4pm; Apr–May and Sept–Oct daily 10am–5pm; June–Aug daily 9am–6pm. Closed Dec 23–26.

ORGANIZED TOURS   City Sightseeing (www.citysightseeing-stratford.com; ✆ 01789/412680) runs 1-hour guided bus tours, taking in the town's five Shakespeare properties, on a constant loop. The most logical starting point is the sidewalk in front of the Pen & Parchment Pub, at the bottom of Bridge Street. Tour tickets are valid all day, so you can hop on and off the buses as many times as you want. The tours cost £11.75 for adults, £9.75 for seniors and students, and £6 for children 5 to 15 (children 4 and under ride free). A family ticket goes for £25.50. April to September buses depart daily every 15 minutes from 9:30am to 6pm; October to March buses run Monday to Friday 10am to 3pm every hour, and Saturday and Sunday 9:30am to 3:30pm every 30 minutes.

WHERE TO EAT
Moderate

Lambs ★ CONTEMPORARY ENGLISH   Near the Royal Shakespeare Theatre, this stylish cafe/bistro is housed in a building dating from 1547. It's ideal for a light meal or pretheatre dinner. The menu changes monthly, but expect finely executed English classics such as slow-roasted lamb shank with creamed potato and glazed carrots, as well as more exotic creations such as Goan-style fish curry (salmon, halibut, prawn, and mussels). It's hard to beat the addictive sticky toffee pudding for dessert.

12 Sheep St. www.lambsrestaurant.co.uk. ✆ **01789/292554.** Reservations required for dinner Fri–Sat. Main courses £10.25–£18.75. MC, V. Mon and Tues 5–9pm; Wed–Sat noon–2pm and 5–9pm; Sun noon–2pm and 6–9pm.

Marlowe's Restaurant CONTEMPORARY ENGLISH   The place to come for olde Elizabethan atmosphere—the large bar, with a fireplace blazing with logs in winter, opens onto a splendid oak-paneled room, and in summer there is a spacious courtyard for alfresco dining. The food is also pretty good; start with seared scallops or chicken livers flambéed in masala cream, and continue with one of the chargrilled steaks or homemade pie of the day. Drunken duck has been a long-time specialty here: It's marinated in gin, red wine, and juniper berries before being roasted in the oven.

18 High St. www.marlowes.biz. ✆ **01789/204999.** Reservations recommended. Main courses £7.95–£20.15. AE, MC, V. Mon–Thurs noon–2:15pm and 5:30–10pm; Fri noon–2:15pm and 5:30–10:30pm; Sat noon–2:15pm and 5:30–11pm; Sun noon–2:15pm.

No 9 Church Street ★★ CONTEMPORARY ENGLISH   This is one of Stratford's finest and most stylish restaurants, with a creative seasonal menu by talented chefs Wayne Thomson and Dan Robinson. Starters might include piquant delights such as Warwickshire rarebit, marinated mushrooms, artichokes, and crispy pancetta, with main courses such as winter squash and black truffle ravioli, prime cuts of venison, and Cornish ling (fish) with seared scallops. Leave room for the Bramley apple and sultana tipsy cake with cinnamon palmiers.

9 Church St. www.no9churchst.com. ✆ **01789/415522.** Reservations recommended. Main courses £11–£18. MC, V. Tues–Sat noon–2:30pm, 5–9:30pm; Sun noon–3:30pm.

RSC Rooftop Restaurant & Bar ENGLISH/CONTINENTAL   This restaurant enjoys the best location in town—it's wrapped around the top of the Royal Shakespeare Theatre itself—with floor-to-ceiling windows providing an unobstructed view of the swans on the Avon. Consider the cafe a venue for lunch, pre-show dining,

A VISIT TO WARWICK castle

Perched on a rocky cliff above the River Avon, the magnificent 14th-century **Warwick Castle ★★★** (www.warwick-castle.co.uk; ℂ **0870/442-2000**) looms over Warwick like a giant fist. It's the definitive medieval castle, with chunky towers, crenellated battlements, and a moat surrounded by gardens, lawns, and woodland where peacocks roam freely. You'll need the best part of a day to do it justice.

Although it has roots in the Anglo-Saxon period, the Beauchamp family, which controlled the medieval earldom of Warwick during its most illustrious period, is responsible for the appearance of the castle today; much of the external structure remains unchanged from the mid-14th century. When the castle was granted to Sir Fulke Greville by James I in 1604, he spent £20,000 (an enormous sum in those days) converting the existing castle buildings into a luxurious mansion. The Grevilles have held the Earl of Warwick title since 1759, but sold the castle to Tussaud's in 1978. As a result, the ornate interiors have been embellished with exhibitions and waxwork displays to create a vivid picture of the castle's turbulent past and its important role in the history of England. The new **Merlin: The Dragon Tower** attraction (inspired by the hit BBC drama), and trips to the ghoulish **Castle Dungeon** (unsuitable for young children) cost extra.

Warwick Castle is open daily from 10am to 5pm. Closed December 25. Admission is £21.60 adults, £15.60 children 4–11, £16.80 seniors, £69 family ticket, free for children 3 and under; with castle dungeon £28.20 adults, £22.80 children 4–11, £24 seniors, £97.20 family ticket; with dungeon and Merlin: The Dragon Tower £30.60 adults, £25.80 children 4–11, £27 seniors, £107.40 family ticket; 15% discount for tickets purchased online.

Trains run every 2 hours between Stratford-upon-Avon and Warwick (25–30 min.). A one-way ticket costs around £5. Hourly trains run to Warwick from Birmingham Snow Hill station (30 min.) for £6.80. **Stagecoach** bus no. 16 departs Stratford-upon-Avon every hour during the day. The trip takes roughly half an hour. Go to **www.stagecoachbus.com** for schedules.

Take the A46 if you're driving from Stratford-upon-Avon.

---

or a supper of freshly prepared and simply cooked modern English food. Main courses might include John Dory with braised gem, cauliflower, and oyster fritter, or lip-smacking roast lamb with potatoes, olives, and beans.

Royal Shakespeare Theatre, Waterside. www.rsc.org.uk. ℂ **01789/403449.** Reservations recommended. Main courses £13.95–£19.95; fixed-price menu (before 6.15pm) £11.50 for 1 course, £15.50 for 2 courses, or £18.50 for 3 courses. AE, MC, V. Mon–Sat 11:30am–11pm; Sun noon–6pm.

The Vintner ENGLISH/CONTINENTAL   In a timber-framed structure little altered since its construction in the late 15th century, the Vintner may very well be the place where William Shakespeare went to purchase his wine. The Vintner is both a cafe/bar and a restaurant owned by the same family for 5 centuries; its location makes it ideal for a pretheatre lunch or supper. Good-tasting main courses include salmon fishcakes with wilted spinach and sorrel sauce, and well-priced steaks. For dessert, try that British favorite, sticky toffee pudding with vanilla ice cream.

4–5 Sheep St. www.the-vintner.co.uk. ℂ **01789/297259.** Reservations not necessary. Main courses £11.25–£22.50. DC, MC, V. Mon–Sat 9:30am–10pm; Sun 9:30am–9pm.

Inexpensive

Havilands ENGLISH TEA/CAFE This well-respected caterer opened a charming tearoom and take-out in 2009, serving fresh, locally sourced food. Grab a stilton and grape sandwich; turkey, cranberry, and stuffing quiche; or spicy teacake, and relax on the sunny terrace. They also serve high-quality pies, soups, and salads.

4–5 Meer St. www.havilandscatering.com. ℂ **01789/415477.** Cakes from £1.35, sandwiches from £2.25. MC, V. Mon–Sat 9am–5pm; Sun 10:30am–5pm.

SHOPPING

The **Shakespeare Bookshop,** 39 Henley St. (www.shakespeare.org.uk; ℂ **01789/292176;** Wed–Sat 9:30am–5:30pm, Sun noon–5pm), across from the Shakespeare Birthplace Centre, is the region's premier source for books on the Bard and his works, from picture books for junior-high students to weighty tomes geared to those pursuing a Ph.D. in literature.

NIGHTLIFE & ENTERTAINMENT
Pubs

Despite the millions of tourists passing through, Stratford is essentially a small town where nightlife revolves around the RSC Theatre and local pubs. Everyone who visits Stratford grabs at least one drink at the **Dirty Duck** ★★ (www.dirtyduck-pub-stratford-upon-avon.co.uk; ℂ **01789/297312;** restaurant daily noon–10pm, bar daily 11am–11pm), close to the RSC Theatre on Waterside. This creaky old watering hole has been a popular hangout for Stratford players since the 18th century, its walls lined with autographed photos of its many famous patrons.

The Royal Shakespeare Theatre

In Shakespeare's day, Stratford didn't have a theatre—all the Bard's plays were performed in London. The current red-brick **Royal Shakespeare Theatre** (www. rsc.org.uk; ℂ **01789/403444**) was completed in 1932 on the banks of the Avon, and reopened in 2010 after an ambitious renovation. It remains a major showcase for the acclaimed **Royal Shakespeare Company (RSC),** with a season that runs from April to November and typically features five Shakespearean plays. The RSC also stages productions in the smaller **Swan Theatre,** an intimate 430-seat space next to the Royal Shakespeare Theatre.

For **ticket reservations** book online or call ℂ **0844/8001110.** A small number of tickets is always held for sale on the day of a performance, but it may be too late to get a good seat if you wait until you arrive in Stratford. The box office is open Monday to Saturday 9am to 8pm, although it closes at 6pm on days when there are no performances. Seats range in price from £14 to £58.

Even if you're not seeing a performance, you can take a guided **Theatre Tour,** which lasts an hour and runs every 2 hours from 9:15am (Mon–Sat) and from 10:15am (Sun and bank holidays). Tickets cost £6.50 for adults and £3 for children 17 and under. Advance booking is recommended.

You can also take an elevator up the newly constructed 36m (118-ft.) **Tower** (daily 10am–5pm) for a unique bird's-eye view of the town. Tickets cost £2.50 for adults and £1.25 for children 17 and under.

Part of the Greene King stable, the **Garrick Inn ★**, at 25 High St. (www.garrick-inn-stratford-upon-avon.co.uk; ℂ **01789/292186;** daily 11am–11pm), is the oldest pub in Stratford, a handsome black-and-white timbered structure that dates back to the 14th century.

Stratford's oldest structure (not its oldest pub) is reputed to be the **White Swan** on Rother Street (www.fullershotels.com; ℂ **01789/297022;** daily noon–11pm). Dating back to 1450, it's a plush hotel today, but the pub section is an atmospheric place for a drink, with cushioned leather armchairs, oak paneling, and fireplaces.

WHERE TO STAY
Very Expensive
The Arden ★★★   Stratford's best hotel and the most convenient for the RSC Theatre reopened in 2010 after a comprehensive refurbishment. All the rooms have been decked out in an elegant, contemporary English style with the latest amenities, some with views of the river; the main difference between the Deluxe, Superior, and Classic rooms is size. The excellent location and on-site dining choices–the **Waterside Brasserie** and **Champagne Bar**–means you won't need to stray far from the hotel.

Waterside, Stratford-upon-Avon, Warwickshire CV37 6BA. www.theardenhotelstratford.com. ℂ **01789/298682.** Fax 01789/206989. 45 units. £99–£235. Basic package rates include English breakfast. AE, MC, V. Free parking. **Amenities:** 3 restaurants; 2 bars; room service. *In room:* TV/DVD, hair dryer, Wi-Fi (free).

Moderate
Cherry Trees ★★ 🛏️   This small B&B has a fabulous location, a short walk across the bridge to the RSC Theatre and the center of Stratford. The Garden Room features a king-size four-poster, there's a modern leather king-size bed in the Terrace Room (both have large conservatories and access to the garden), and the gorgeous Tiffany Suite offers a king-size bed and separate sitting room. Whichever room you choose, you'll be welcomed with tea and scones on arrival, get a huge cooked breakfast, and have access to a well-stocked fridge and selection of teas.

Swans Nest Lane, Stratford-upon-Avon, Warwickshire CV37 7LS. www.cherrytrees-stratford.co.uk. ℂ **01789/292989.** 3 units. £105–£125 double. Rates include breakfast. MC, V. Free parking. *In room:* TV, hair dryer, Wi-Fi (free).

Mercure Shakespeare Hotel ★   Filled with historical associations, the original core of this hotel dates from the 1400s. Quieter and plusher than the Falcon it is equaled in the center of Stratford only by the Arden (see above). Bedrooms are named in honor of noteworthy actors, Shakespeare plays, or Shakespearean characters. The oldest are capped with hewn timbers, and all have modern comforts. Even the newer accommodations are at least 40 to 50 years old, and have rose-and-thistle patterns carved into many of their exposed timbers.

Chapel St., Stratford-upon-Avon, Warwickshire CV37 6ER. www.mercure.com. ℂ **01789/294997.** Fax 01789/415411. 74 units. £56–£96 double. Children 12 and under stay free in parent's room. AE, DC, MC, V. Breakfast £15.50. Parking £10. **Amenities:** Restaurant; bar; room service, Wi-Fi (free, in public areas, for 1hr.). *In room:* A/C, TV, minibar (in some), hair dryer, Wi-Fi (first hour free, then £9/24hr.).

The Stratford ★   This is definitely not one of the historic inns of Stratford-upon-Avon, but a plush, modern hotel with up-to-date conveniences. A member of the QHotels group, its location is only a short walk from the banks of the River Avon. The bedrooms are spaciously and elegantly appointed, some with four-poster beds and

Tudor style, but others are more geared to commercial travelers seeking streamlined conveniences—not romance. Deftly prepared market-fresh dishes change with the seasons in the on-site **Quills Restaurant.**

Arden St., Stratford-upon-Avon, Warwickshire CV37 6QQ. www.qhotels.co.uk. ℂ/Fax **01789/271000.** 102 units. £112.50–£175 double. AE, DC, MC, V. Parking £5. **Amenities:** Restaurant; bar; small exercise room; room service; Wi-Fi (free, in public areas). *In room:* TV, hair dryer, Internet (free).

Inexpensive

Penryn House ★ ♦   The location is convenient and the price is right at this B&B, where hosts Anne and Robert Dawkes are among the most welcoming in town. They justifiably take special pride in their breakfasts, right down to their superb "Harvest of Arden" English apple juice. Free-range Worcestershire eggs are served along with fresh seasonal fruit and locally produced bacon and sausage. They even prepare a vegetarian breakfast if requested. The bedrooms are a bit small, but well-furnished and comfortable. The location is close to the train station, Anne Hathaway's Cottage, and the heart of town.

126 Alcester Rd., Stratford-upon-Avon, Warwickshire CV37 9DP. www.penrynguesthouse.co.uk. ℂ **01789/293718.** Fax 01789/266077. 7 units. £60–£70 double. Rates include English breakfast. MC, V. Free parking. *In room:* TV, hair dryer, Wi-Fi (free).

SALISBURY, STONEHENGE & BATH

Many visitors with very limited time head for the West Country, where they explore its two major attractions: Stonehenge—the most important prehistoric monument in Britain, and Bath—England's most elegant city, famed for its architecture and its hot springs. If you have the time, you may also want to visit Salisbury Cathedral and the other prehistoric sites in the area, at Avebury and Old Sarum.

Salisbury ★★ & Stonehenge ★★

90 miles SW of London

Long before you enter the city, the spire of Salisbury Cathedral comes into view—just as John Constable and J. M. W. Turner captured it on canvas. The 123m (404-ft.) pinnacle of the Early English Gothic cathedral is the tallest in England, but is just one among many historical points of interest in this thriving county town.

Salisbury, once known as "New Sarum," lies in the valley of South Wiltshire's River Avon. Filled with Tudor inns and tearooms, it is also an excellent base for visitors keen to explore nearby Stonehenge. The old market town also has a lively arts scene, and is an interesting destination on its own. If you choose to linger for a day or two, you find an added bonus: Salisbury's pub-to-citizen ratio is among the highest in England.

ESSENTIALS

GETTING THERE   **Trains** for Salisbury depart half-hourly from Waterloo Station in London; the trip takes under 1½ hours. A return ticket costs from £34.80. For more information, check **www.nationalrail.co.uk**.

If you're **driving** from London, head west on the M3 and then the M27 to junction 2, continuing the rest of the way on the A36.

VISITOR INFORMATION   Salisbury's friendly **Tourist Information Centre** is on Fish Row (www.visitsalisbury.com; ✆ **01722/334956**). It's open Monday to Saturday 10am to 5pm March to October (closes at 4pm Nov–Feb). For information on the wider South Wiltshire area, you should also consult **www.visitwiltshire.co.uk**.

EXPLORING SALISBURY

Head to the cathedral and **The Close,** some say the most beautiful of its kind, where you'll find the slightly haphazard collection at the **Salisbury & South Wiltshire Museum ★**, King's House, 65 The Close (www.salisburymuseum.org.uk; ✆ **01722/332151**). The "History of Salisbury" gallery houses a small collection of Turner's Salisbury watercolors. The museum is open Monday to Saturday 10am to 5pm, and between June and September also Sunday noon to 5pm. Admission costs £6 for adults, £2 for children aged 5 to 15, free for children 4 and under.

Salisbury Cathedral ★★★   You'll find no better example of the Early English Gothic architectural style than Salisbury Cathedral. Construction of this magnificent building began as early as 1220 and took only 38 years to complete. (Many of Europe's grandest cathedrals took up to 300 years to build.) As a result, Salisbury Cathedral is one of the most homogenous and harmonious of all the great cathedrals.

The cathedral's 13th-century octagonal Chapter House possesses one of the four surviving original texts of Magna Carta—one of the founding documents of democracy and justice, signed by King John in 1215.

The 123m (404-ft.) spire is the tallest in Britain, and was one of the tallest structures in the world when completed in 1315. In its day, this was seriously advanced technology. Amazingly, the spire was not part of the original design, and the name of the master mason is lost to history. In 1668, Sir Christopher Wren expressed alarm at the tilt of the spire, but no further shift has since been measured. You can now explore the heights on a 1½-hour **Tower Tour ★★** costing £8.50 for adults, £6.50 for children and seniors, £25 for a family of five (this fee includes your cathedral donation). Between April and September, there are five tours a day Monday to Saturday (hourly from 11:15am), and two on Sunday (1 and 2:30pm). From October to March, there are usually one or two daily, depending on weather, but no tour on Sunday. Children must be aged 5 or over, and everyone will need a head for heights.

The Close. www.salisburycathedral.org.uk. ✆ **01722/555156.** Suggested donation £5.50 adults, £4.50 students and seniors, £3 children 5–17, £13 family. Daily 7:15am–6:15pm; Chapter House closes 4:30pm (5:30pm Apr–Oct) and all morning Sun.

EXPLORING STONEHENGE & SOUTH WILTSHIRE

Old Sarum ★   Believed to have been an Iron Age fortification, Old Sarum was used again by the Saxons and flourished as a walled town into the Middle Ages. The Normans built a cathedral and a castle here; parts of this old cathedral were taken down to build the city of "New Sarum," later known as Salisbury, leaving behind the dramatically sited remains you see today. In the early 19th century, Old Sarum was one of the English Parliament's most notorious "Rotten Boroughs," constituencies that were allowed to send a Member of Parliament to Westminster despite having few—in Old Sarum's case, no—residents. The Rotten Boroughs were finally disbanded in 1832.

2 miles north of Salisbury off A345 Castle Rd. www.english-heritage.org.uk/oldsarum. ✆ **01722/335398.** Admission £3.70 adults, £3.30 seniors, £2.20 children 5–15. Daily Apr–June and

Sept 10am–5pm; July–Aug 9am–6pm; Mar and Oct 10am–4pm; Nov–Jan 11am–3pm; Feb 11am–4pm. Bus: 5, 6, 7, 8, or 9, every 30 min. during the day, from Salisbury bus station.

Stonehenge ★★ 📷 This iconic circle of lintels and megalithic pillars is perhaps the most important prehistoric monument in Britain. The concentric rings of standing stones represent an amazing feat of late Neolithic engineering because many of the boulders were moved many miles to this site: From Pembrokeshire in southwest Wales, and the local Marlborough Downs. If you're a romantic, come see the ruins in the early glow of dawn or else when shadows fall at sunset. The light is most dramatic at these times, the shadows longer, and the effect is often far more mesmerizing than in the glaring light of midday. The mystical experience is marred only slightly by an ugly (but necessary) perimeter fence. Your admission ticket gets you inside the fence, but no longer all the way up to the stones.

The widely held view of 18th- and 19th-century Romantics, who believed Stonehenge was the work of the Druids, is without foundation. The boulders, many weighing several tonnes, are believed to have predated the arrival in Britain of the Celtic culture. Controversy surrounds the prehistoric site—in truth, its purpose remains a mystery. The first of the giant stones were erected around 2500 B.C.

Insider's tip: From the road, if you don't mind the noise from traffic, you can get a good view of Stonehenge without paying the admission charge for a close-up encounter. Alternatively, climb **Amesbury Hill,** clearly visible 1½ miles up the A303. From here, you'll get a free panoramic view.

At the junction of A303 and A344. www.english-heritage.org.uk/stonehenge. ℂ **08703/331181.** Admission £7.50 adults, £6.80 students and seniors, £4.50 children 5–15, £17.30 family ticket. Daily. June–Aug 9am–7pm; Mar 16–May and Sept–Oct 15 9:30am–6pm; Oct 16–Mar 15 9:30am–4pm. If you're driving, head north on Castle Rd. from the center of Salisbury on to the A345 to Amesbury, and then the A303 to Exeter. You'll see signs for Stonehenge, leading you up the A344 to the right. It's 2 miles west of Amesbury.

ORGANIZED TOURS You can easily see Salisbury on foot, either on your own or by taking a guided daytime or evening walk run by **Salisbury City Guides** (www.salisburycityguides.co.uk; ℂ **07873/212941**). Tickets are £4 for adults and £2 for children.

The hop-on, hop-off **Stonehenge Tour** bus (www.thestonehengetour.info; ℂ **01983/827005**) picks up several times an hour (on the hour from 10am to 2pm in winter) from Salisbury railway and bus stations, passing via Salisbury Cathedral (additional cost), Old Sarum (see above) all the way to the stones, taking 35 minutes each way. A round-trip ticket costs £11 for adults, £5 for children; including entrance to Stonehenge and Old Sarum, prices are £18 adults, £15 students, and £9 children.

WHERE TO EAT

Salisbury has plenty of characterful pubs, where a lunch of typical British pub grub fare awaits. **The Haunch of Venison** (see p. 261) serves up roasts and grills to hungry visitors.

For British bistro classics with some refined, French-influenced cooking in a redbrick building on Salisbury's marketplace, try **Charter 1227 ★**, 6–7 Ox Row, Market Sq. (www.charter1227.co.uk; ℂ **01722/333118**). Expect pan-roasted filet of beef with potato terrine and a horseradish velouté, or fish and double-cooked chunky chips, followed by sticky toffee "pud" with butterscotch sauce. Closed Sunday and Monday.

Or try out one of Britain's new breed of 21st-century Indian restaurants: **Anokaa ★**, 60 Fisherton St., Salisbury (www.anokaa.com; ✆ **01722/414142**). This relaxed and colorful dining room serves up contemporary cuisine from a variety of Indian regions. *Anokaa* means "different," and when you taste the chicken lababdar, flavored with coconut, ginger, and sweet chili, or the tandoori seared lamb rack, you'll understand why. At lunchtime it's a limited buffet service only, but at £8.95 it offers excellent value.

SHOPPING

Many shops in Salisbury are set in beautiful medieval timber-framed buildings. As you wander through the colorful **Charter market** (Tues and Sat) held in **Market Square** since 1361, or walk the ancient streets, you'll find everything from touristy gift shops to unique specialty stores.

Locals gravitate to the **Old George Mall Shopping Centre,** 23B High St. (www.oldgeorgemall.co.uk; ✆ **01722/333500**), a short walk from the cathedral and with more than 40 individual shops and high-street stores.

Another place of note, situated within a 14th-century building with hammered beams and original windows, is **Watsons,** 8–9 Queen St. (www.watsonsofsalisbury.co.uk; ✆ **01722/32031**). This elegant store carries paperweights, bone china from Wedgwood, Royal Doulton, and Aynsley, and Dartington glassware.

ENTERTAINMENT & NIGHTLIFE
The Pub Scene

Hopback is the local brewer to look out for, and the best of Salisbury's many pubs usually have at least one of their fine beers on tap. Standing just outside the center, **Deacons ★**, 118 Fisherton St. (✆ **01722/504723**), has a local reputation for keeping and serving ale the way it should be. The tiny, characterful bar is worth the short walk. Even in a city full of ancient, half-timbered inns, there's nowhere quite like the **Haunch of Venison ★**, 1 Minster St. (www.haunchofvenison.uk.com; ✆ **01722/411313**). The haphazard interior layout and wood-paneled rooms of this former chophouse ooze medieval charm—and are reputedly haunted.

WHERE TO STAY

Legacy Rose & Crown Hotel ★   This half-timbered 13th-century inn stands with its feet almost in the River Avon, in a tranquil location that's an easy 10-minute walk over a stone bridge to the center of Salisbury. The hotel has both new and old wings: Room nos. 1 through 5 have original beamed ceilings and antique decor, but look out over a (generally quiet) road. Newer units are bigger with less character, but they have a view over the water meadows to Salisbury Cathedral. Take your pick.

Harnham Rd., Salisbury SP2 8JQ. www.legacy-hotels.co.uk. ✆ **0844/4119046.** Fax 0844/4119047. 29 units. £95–£160 double. Rates include breakfast. Free parking. AE, DC, MC, V. Take the A3094 1½ miles south from the center. **Amenities:** Restaurant; 2 bars; room service. *In room:* TV, hair dryer; Wi-Fi (free).

Peartree Serviced Apartments ★ 🛏   Opened in 2010, these modern apartments inside a whitewashed former station hotel offer the convenience of kitchen facilities on top of all the basic hotel amenities. Units are well designed, simply decorated, and come in a range of sizes from compact studios to 2-bedroom apartments suited to families, or even adults traveling together—both bedrooms are en suite. It's worth the extra £15 or so to upgrade to a more spacious executive unit. The apartments overlook a busy road, but soundproofing is excellent.

Mill Rd., Salisbury SP2 7RT. www.peartreeapartments.co.uk. ✆**01722/322055.** Fax 01722/327677.
11 units. £85–£150 apartment. Free parking. AE, MC, V. *In apartment:* TV, kitchen, hair dryer, MP3
docking station (on request), Wi-Fi (free), no phone.

St. Ann's House ★★ 🍴   This refined town-house B&B is a delightful mix of the
contemporary and the traditional: A typical room might see fresh colors partnering a
restored walnut armoire and antique writing desk. Mattresses are luxurious, linens of
the highest quality, and a spritz of lavender water on your pillow sends you gently off
to sleep. No unit is large, in keeping with the original Georgian floorplan, so spend
an extra £5 to upgrade to a bigger Premium Room. Breakfast is an event, indulging
the food passions of the owner, a former chef. Expect a daily fresh *frittata* or *asheray,*
a Turkish dish made with fruits, nuts, and cinnamon.

32–34 St. Ann's St., Salisbury SP1 2DP. www.stannshouse.co.uk. ✆**01722/335657.** 8 units. £64–
£89 double. Rates include breakfast. AE, MC, V. *In room:* TV, hair dryer, Wi-Fi (free), no phone.

Bath ★★★

115 miles W of London; 13 miles SE of Bristol

Strolling along Bath's sweeping Royal Crescent with its wide pavements and grand
Georgian terraced homes, you immediately feel part of a Jane Austen novel. Tourism
has been the main industry in Bath for more than 2,000 years: From Roman times to
the present-day tourism, which began in the 18th century when Queen Anne came
to "take the waters" in 1702. Imagine the fantastic balls and parties held in the Pump
Rooms and Assembly Rooms, overseen by the dandy Richard "Beau" Nash, and then
take a nose into the grand homes along the Royal Crescent, designed to fit their social
status.

ESSENTIALS

GETTING THERE   **Trains** leave London's Paddington station bound for Bath once
every half-hour during the day; the trip takes about 1½ hours: **National Rail** (www.
nationalrail.co.uk; ✆ **0845/748-4950**).

   National Express (www.nationalexpress.com; ✆ **0871/781-8178**) buses leave
London's Victoria coach station every 90 minutes during the day. The trip takes
3½ hours.

   If you're **driving,** head west on the M4 to Junction 18. Parking in Bath is expensive, and many roads are blocked off during busy times for buses, and so park at the
Lansdown Park & Ride, 3 miles south of Junction 18. Open Monday to Saturday
6:15am to 8:30pm (pay on the bus).

VISITOR INFORMATION   The **Bath Tourist Information Centre** is at Abbey
Chambers, Abbey Church Yard (www.visitbath.co.uk; ✆ **09067/112000** toll call,
50p per minute; from overseas call +**44/844/847525**). It's open Monday to Saturday
9:30am to 5:30pm and Sunday 10am to 4pm. Closed December 25 and January 1.

EXPLORING BATH

Begin your tour of Georgian Bath at **Queen Square** and discover some of the
famous streets laid out by John Wood the Elder (1704–54). Walk up to the
Circus ★★★, three Palladian crescents arranged in a circle, with 524 different
carved emblems above the doors. His son, the younger John Wood designed the
Royal Crescent ★★★, an elegant half-moon row of town houses. Also take a look
at the shop-lined **Pulteney Bridge ★**, designed by Robert Adam, and often compared to the Ponte Vecchio of Florence.

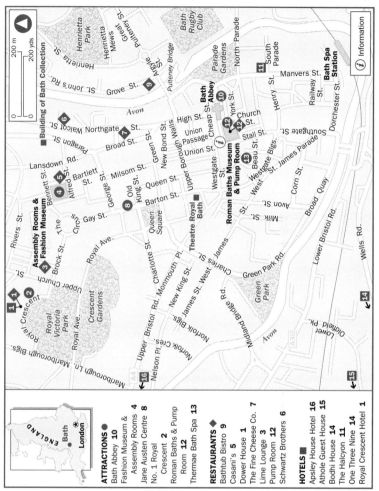

ATTRACTIONS ●
Bath Abbey **10**
Fashion Museum & Assembly Rooms **4**
Jane Austen Centre **8**
No. 1 Royal Crescent **2**
Roman Baths & Pump Room **12**
Thermae Bath Spa **13**

RESTAURANTS ◆
Bathtub Bistro **9**
Casani's **5**
Dower House **1**
The Fine Cheese Co. **7**
Lime Lounge **3**
Pump Room **12**
Schwartz Brothers **6**

HOTELS ■
Apsley House Hotel **16**
Athole Guest House **15**
Bodhi House **14**
The Halcyon **11**
One Three Nine **14**
Royal Crescent Hotel **1**

Bath Abbey ★★ Completed in 1611, Bath Abbey is the last of the great medieval churches of England, and known as the "lantern of the west" for its many ornate windows. Beau Nash—honored by a simple monument totally out of keeping with his flamboyant character—is buried in the nave. For a bird's-eye view of the city take the **Abbey Tower Tour** (45–50 min.), climbing 212 steps.

Orange Grove. www.bathabbey.org. ℂ **01225/422462.** Suggested donation £3 adults, free for children 15 and under. Abbey: Apr–Oct Mon–Sat 9am–6pm; Nov–Mar Mon–Sat 9am–4:30pm; year-round Sun 1–2:30pm (Apr–Oct also 4:30–5:30pm). Abbey Tower Tour: £6 adults, £3 children 5–14 (under-5s not allowed). Apr–Oct Mon–Sat 10am–4pm on the hour; Nov–Mar 11am, noon, and 2pm.

Fashion Museum & Assembly Rooms ★ The grand **Assembly Rooms,** designed by the younger John Wood and completed in 1771, once played host to dances, recitals, and tea parties. Damaged in World War II, the elegant rooms have been gloriously restored and look much as they did when Jane Austen and Thomas Gainsborough attended society events here. Housed in the same building, the **Fashion Museum** offers audio tours through the history of fashion from the 16th century to the present day. Exhibits change every 6 months. There's also a special "Corsets and Crinolines" display where enthusiastic visitors can try on reproduction period garments.

Bennett St. www.fashionmuseum.co.uk. ☎ **01225/477789.** Admission (includes audio tour) £7.50 adults, £6.75 students and seniors, £5.50 children 6–16, £21 family ticket, free for children 5 and under. Admission to Assembly Rooms only £2, children under 17 free. Nov–Feb daily 10:30am–4pm; Mar–Oct daily 10:30am–5pm. Closed Dec 25–26.

Jane Austen Centre This small homage to Britain's favorite 19th-century writer occupies a graceful Georgian town house on the street where Miss Austen once lived (at no. 25). Exhibits and a video convey a sense of what life was like when Austen lived here between 1801 and 1806. Ladies can also learn the esoteric skill of using a fan to attract an admirer. The tearoom is worth a visit (see "Taking Tea in Bath," p. 265).

40 Gay St. www.janeausten.co.uk. ☎ **01225/443000.** Daily 9:45am–5:30pm Apr–Oct. 11am–4:30pm Nov–Mar. Allow at least 45 min. Admission £7.45 adults, £5.95 students and over-65s, £4.25 children 6 to 15, £19.50 family.

No. 1 Royal Crescent This small but edifying museum provides a sense of life at Bath's most sought-after address. The Georgian interior has been redecorated and furnished in late 18th-century style, replete with period furniture and authentic flowery wallpaper.

1 Royal Crescent. www.bath-preservation-trust.org.uk. ☎ **01225/428126.** Admission £6.50 adults, £5 students and seniors, £2.50 children 5–16, family ticket £13. Mid-Feb–Oct Tues–Sun 10:30am–5pm, Nov–mid-Dec Tues–Sun 10:30am–4pm (last admission 30 min. before closing).

Roman Baths ★★★ **& Pump Room** ★ Blending Roman ingenuity and Georgian style, the best-preserved thermo-mineral Roman baths in the world have been cleaned, and the steaming (35°C/95°F hot-spring water) Great Bath now looks more like the Roman original. Audio guides, displays, and costumed actors interpret the site as you wander past the Sacred Spring, remains of a Roman Temple, plunge pools, and the Great Bath itself. To take in everything allow at least 2 hours. After wandering the baths, visit the 18th-century **Pump Room,** overlooking the hot springs, and try a glass of the water—although be warned that it's not exactly tasty. It has been fashionable since the 18th century to take coffee, lunch, and afternoon tea here.

Bath Abbey Church Yard, Stall St. www.romanbaths.co.uk. ☎ **01225/477785.** Admission £12.25 adults (saver ticket with Fashion Museum £15.75), £10.75 seniors, £78 children 6–16, £35 family ticket. Daily 9am–10pm Jul–Aug; 9am–5pm Sep–Oct; 9:30am–5:30pm Nov–Feb; 9am–6pm Mar–Jun. Last admission 1 hr. before closing. Closed Dec 25–26.

Thermae Bath Spa ★★ The waters at the old Roman Baths are unfit for bathing, so if you want to sample the city's celebrated hot springs make for this plush, modern spa. From the outdoor pool in the New Royal Bath complex you can watch the sun setting over Bath's rooftops while you soak.

Hot Bath St. www.thermaebathspa.com. ☎ **0844/888-0844.** Admission New Royal Bath £26 for 2 hr., £36 for 4 hr. (16 and under not permitted). New Royal Bath daily 9am–10pm; Spa Visitor Centre Apr–Oct Mon–Sat 10am–5pm, Sun 10am–4pm. Closed Dec 24–25 & Dec 31–Jan 7.

Made popular by the Georgians and popularized by Jane Austen, Bath is the ideal place to indulge in that quintessentially English tradition of afternoon tea, served with jam, clotted cream, and scones. Try the **Pump Room ★★** at the Roman Baths (p. 264), which serves "Bath buns" (sweet buns sprinkled with sugar), or **Sally Lunn's ★** at 4 North Parade Passage (www.sallylunns.co.uk; *①* **01225/461634**). The latter's building itself is one of the oldest in Bath, dating from 1482, and shows little hint of any changes with its crooked, creaking floors and low ceilings. For £6.18 to £11.88, you can sample a range of fabulous Sally Lunn cream teas, which include toasted and buttered Sally Lunn buns served with strawberry jam and clotted cream. The **Regency Tea Rooms ★** at the Jane Austen Centre (p. 264) offers "Tea with Mr Darcy" sets for £11.50 to £20.50 for two, and basic cream tea sets from £5.50. For a more luxurious afternoon tea, head to **The Royal Crescent Hotel** at 16 Royal Crescent (www.royalcrescent.co.uk; *①* **01225/823333**) between 3 and 5pm for sandwiches, quiche, cakes, Bath buns, and champagne for £32.50 per person. Booking is essential.

ORGANIZED TOURS The Mayor's office provides professionally guided free 2-hour **Walking Tours of Bath** daily (Sun–Fri 10:30am and 2pm; Sat 10:30am. May–Sept also Tues and Fri 7pm). Meet outside the Abbey Churchyard entrance to the Pump Room.

WHERE TO EAT

Dining in Bath is as fine as the architecture. If you're looking for exceptional cuisine in a wonderful setting, Bath is not short on locations, from the best of the West Country's fine dining at the **Dower House ★★★** in the Royal Crescent Hotel, 16 Royal Crescent (www.royalcrescent.co.uk; *①* **01225/823333**), to the chandelier-lit **Pump Room** (see above) overlooking the Roman Baths.

For authentic French food, visit **Casani's,** 4 Saville Row (www.casanis.co.uk; *①* **01225/780055**; reservations required), where simple but stylish dishes are mostly inspired by Provence.

Less expensive, the fashionable **Bathtub Bistro ★,** 2 Grove St. (www.thebathtub bistro.co.uk; *①* **01225/460593;** closed Sun pm), features home-style British cooking with hearty plates for lunch such as ham hock, and split pea and mint stew. The day-time menu at **Lime Lounge ★★,** 11 Margarets Buildings (www.limelounge bath.co.uk; *①* **01225/421251**), features home-made soups and cakes, salads, burgers, and sandwiches. Hot chocolate fans are also in for a treat. In the evenings there are riffs on old Brit classics; think "posh" fish and chips, or pork with creamed apple and a cider and stilton sauce.

For food on the go, head to **The Fine Cheese Co. ★,** 29 & 31 Walcot St. (www.finecheese.co.uk; *①* **01225/483407**), for sandwiches made with cheese from artisan cheesemongers. If you prefer a chargrilled garlic mayoburger or an irresistible Danish blue cheeseburger, stop at gourmet burger bar **Schwartz Brothers,** 102 Walcot St. (www.schwartzbros.co.uk; *①* **01225/463613**).

SHOPPING

Bath is crammed with markets, antiques centers, specialist food stores, and fashion boutiques. Prices, however, are comparable to London. Arriving by train, you'll

Bristol, the West Country's largest city (pop. 441,000), is a medieval port that has reinvented itself as a dynamic cultural center in the last few decades, home not just to a reinvigorated downtown but a host of pop icons, from 1990s "trip-hop" bands such as Tricky, Massive Attack, and Portishead, to irreverent graffiti artist Banksy and the risqué teenage UK TV series *Skins*.

Linked to the Severn Estuary by 7 miles of the navigable River Avon, Bristol has long been rich in seafaring traditions. In 1497, Venetian John Cabot sailed from Bristol and was the first European to "discover" North America (at Newfoundland) since the Vikings. The city's most celebrated sights were built by **Isambard Kingdom Brunel** in the Victorian era: the Clifton Suspension Bridge and the SS *Great Britain*.

Bristol's pride and joy, the **SS *Great Britain* ★★★**, Great Western Dockyard, Gas Ferry Rd. (off Cumberland Rd.) (www.ssgreatbritain.org; ✆ **0117/926-0680**), was the world's first iron steamship when it was launched here in 1843. Two years later it crossed the Atlantic in 14 days—a record at the time. Damaged in a ferocious storm off Cape Horn in 1886, it served out its days as a floating warehouse in the Falkland Islands, and was abandoned in the 1930s. Thanks to a remarkable salvage project in 1970 and subsequent restoration, you can now appreciate the skill and vision of designer Isambard Kingdom Brunel. The revolutionary dry dock takes you below the water line into a climate-controlled chamber where the awe-inspiring outer hull is preserved, while the adjacent Dockyard Museum provides detailed background and history on the ship. Finally, you get to explore the ship itself, magnificently restored to evoke the 1850s—even smells (coal fires, cooking food) are recreated, and free audio guides add context to the first-class and steerage quarters, the engine room, and the bowels of the ship.

When it's in port, a replica of John Cabot's ship, **The Matthew** (check www.matthew.co.uk for cruise times; ✆ **0117/927-6868**) is usually moored just outside the Great Britain site. You can usually look around for free during office hours (11am–5pm; donation suggested).

Admission to both costs £12.50 adults, £9.95 seniors, £6.25 children 5–16, £33.50 family ticket (which includes unlimited entry for 1 yr). It's open daily 10am to 5:30pm April to October and until 4:30pm November to March. Last admission 1 hr. before closing. You can catch bus no. 500 from Bristol Temple Meads and the city centre.

Often overshadowed by Bath, its elegant neighbor, Bristol is nevertheless studded with handsome Georgian relics. **Queen's Square** is Bristol at its most refined, a wide, leafy space completed in 1727 and sporting an equestrian statue of William III in the center. **Georgian House,** Great George St. (✆ **0117/921-1362;** May–Oct Wed–Sun 10:30am–4pm, July–Aug open Tues also; free), was built in 1790 for John Pinney, a wealthy slave plantation owner and sugar merchant. It has been restored to its 18th-century appearance, providing an insight into life for the upper and lower classes at the time. The humble **New Room,** 36 The

encounter a new shopping center, **SouthGate** (www.southgatebath.com; ✆ **01225/469061**), with plenty of high-street stores.

Head to **Milsom Street** for fashion and the department store **Jolly's** (www.houseoffraser.co.uk; ✆ **0844/8003704**), or wander the boutiques along the **Corridor** and **North and South Passages,** and arty, independent stores in **Walcot Street.** Here

Horsefair (www.newroombristol.org.uk; ☎ 0117/926-4740; Mon–Sat 10am–4pm; free), dates from 1739, when it was built as the base of John and Charles Wesley, founders of Methodism—as such, it's considered the oldest Methodist chapel in the world. Today you can view the chapel as it was in the 18th century, wander the gallery and visit the enlightening museum on the top floor, which highlights the lives of the Wesley brothers and early Methodism with portraits, rare mementos (such as a lock of John's hair), and personal effects. The **Red Lodge Museum** on Park Row (☎ 0117/921-1360; May–Oct Wed–Sun 10:30am–4pm; free), was added to in Georgian times, but actually dates back to 1580, with rooms restored in both Georgian and Tudor styles.

Exploring central Bristol is relatively easy on foot, with the rough-and-ready 19th-century docks now the heart of the modern city, converted into hotels, enticing restaurants, shops, and art centers. The Floating Harbour—a watery ribbon that shadows the River Avon—rounds the old city with most sights within walking distance of Centre Promenade and the visitor center, or close to a Bristol Ferry stop.

Soak up Bristol's seafaring roots by jumping on board a **Bristol Ferry Boat Company** ★★ ferry (www.bristolferry.com; ☎ 0117/927-3416). Boats run throughout the day along the River Avon, enabling you to hop on and hop off for £1.90 per trip or £4.90 for a circular tour of the entire route. For a more exhilarating view of the city, take to the skies with **Bailey Balloons** ★★ (www.baileyballoons.co.uk; ☎ 01275/375300), which runs a variety of thrilling "flights" from just £90.

Two miles west of central Bristol lies the leafy Georgian neighborhood of Clifton, best known for the graceful **Clifton Suspension Bridge,** spanning the precipitous Avon Gorge. The architect, Isambard Kingdom Brunel, died 5 years before its final completion in 1864. Today you can walk across the soaring structure (free; cars £0.50) to the small visitor center (daily 10am–5pm; free) on the other side, which contains a display area and DVD explaining the history of the bridge. **Clifton Village** itself is worth exploring, a gorgeous collection of Georgian homes and streets dating back to the 18th century; wander along the Mall or Clifton Down Road for the best of the shops and restaurants.

Officially, it's a secret, although the now world-famous graffiti artist, **Banksy,** is certainly a Bristol native. You can see plenty of his iconic work around the city: His Frogmore Street "Love Triangle" (a man hangs from an open window to escape his lover's husband) adorns the side of a sexual health clinic (get the best views from the small bridge on Park Street), while "Mild Mild West" (riot police versus a teddy bear) is located on Stokes Croft, next to the Canteen Bristol. Banksy also stenciled the Grim Reaper on the side of the Thekla, a boat moored in the harbor (best viewed from the opposite bank). See also www.banksy.co.uk.

The **train** ride from Bath to Bristol Temple Meads takes 12 minutes (£6.80).

you'll find a Saturday flea market and **The Fine Cheese Co.** (see p. 265), which sells a vast array of artisan British cheeses.

The **Bartlett Street Antiques Centre,** 5 Bartlett St. (Mon–Tues, Thurs–Sat 9:30am–5pm, Wed 8am–5pm; ☎ 01225/466689), encompasses 60 stands displaying furniture, silver, antique jewelry, paintings, toys, and military items.

ENTERTAINMENT & NIGHTLIFE

As befits one of Britain's oldest cities, there are plenty of characterful pubs in Bath and nightlife tends to revolve around them—for nightclubs, Bristol is better.

Look out for beers by **Abbey Ales,** Bath's only microbrewery. You'll find them among nine cask ales served at the **Bell,** 103 Walcot St. (www.walcotstreet.com; ✆ **01225/460426**), with live music on Monday and Wednesday nights and Sunday. Vegetarians and students love the **Porter,** 15 George St. (www.theporter.co.uk; ✆ **01225/424104**), a grungier option specializing in vegetarian food, live music, open mic nights, ambient DJs, and comedy. Next door is **Moles** (www.moles.co.uk; ✆ **01225/404445**), Bath's popular dance club and live music venue.

WHERE TO STAY
Very Expensive
Royal Crescent Hotel ★   Rates at this venerable hotel reflect the stunning location, in the center of the famed Royal Crescent. Guest rooms, including the Jane Austen Suite (a converted coach house), are luxuriously furnished with four-poster beds and marble tubs. Generally quite spacious, the bedrooms are also decked out with thick wool carpeting, silk wall coverings, and antiques. Each room is individually designed and offers such comforts as bottled mineral water and fruit plates.

16 Royal Crescent, Bath, Somerset BA1 2LS. www.royalcrescent.co.uk. ✆ **01225/823333.** Fax 01225/339401. 45 units. £199–£445 double; £449–£935 suite. Rates include English breakfast. AE, DC, MC, V. Free parking. **Amenities:** Restaurant (Dower House, p. 265); bar; indoor heated pool; exercise room; sauna; room service; babysitting. *In room:* TV/DVD, minibar (in some), hair dryer, Wi-Fi (free).

Expensive
Apsley House Hotel ★★   This charming hotel, only about a mile west of the center of Bath, is one of the best deals in the city. The house dates from 1830 and was built for the Duke of Wellington (you can stay in his room). Style and comfort are the keynotes here, and all the relatively spacious bedrooms are invitingly appointed with plush beds (some four-posters), country-house chintzes, antiques, and oil paintings.

141 Newbridge Hill, Bath, Somerset BA1 3PT. www.apsley-house.co.uk. ✆ **01225/336966.** Fax 01225/425462. 12 units. £70–£185 double. Rates include English breakfast. AE, MC, V. Free parking. Take the A4 to Upper Bristol Rd., fork right at the traffic signals into Newbridge Hill, and turn left at Apsley Rd. **Amenities:** Bar; room service; Wi-Fi (free). *In room:* TV, hair dryer; Wi-Fi (free).

Moderate
Athole Guest House ★★ 🖋   Spacious, luxurious rooms, and friendly owners make this one of the best deals in the city. The key is value for money; rooms cost less than £100 most of the year, yet you get the amenities associated with a four-star hotel, as well as free transfers from the train station (taxis to the center are around £5). The house is Victorian, but the rooms are bright and contemporary. And the breakfasts are magical; from full English (with everything) to kippers, Welsh rarebit, and pancakes.

33 Upper Oldfield Park, Bath, Somerset BA2 3JX. www.atholehouse.co.uk. ✆ **01225/320000.** 4 units. £60–£130 double. Rates include English breakfast. 2-night minimum stay Sat–Sun. AE, MC, V. Free parking. **Amenities:** Free transfer from/to the railway or bus station. *In room:* A/C, TV, fridge, hair dryer, Wi-Fi (free).

The Halcyon ★   This is a true boutique hotel amid all the Georgian chintz, with a crisp contemporary theme. The property is a 1743 Georgian town house, but the compact rooms feature large, springy beds, bright colors (yellow, scarlet, or mauve), big plasma TVs, and Philippe Starck fittings in the bathroom. Fun extras in the rooms include jars filled with colored candy and gummy bears (though you have to pay for these). Rooms on the first floor are biggest, and the ones at the front have the best views.

2/3 South Parade, Bath, Somerset BA2 4AA. www.thehalcyon.com. ⓒ **01225/444100.** Fax: 01225/331200. 21 units. £99–£125 double. Breakfast extra £6.99. AE, MC, V. Public parking nearby £12. **Amenities:** Bar. *In room:* A/C, TV, Wi-Fi (free).

One Three Nine 🔥 This is another inviting alternative to Bath's numerous Georgian-theme hotels, a stylish contemporary B&B with nary an antique in sight. The house is a Victorian residence from the 1870s, but rooms feature modern English design, power showers, flat-screen TVs, and Molton Brown products. It's on the southern side of the city, on the A367 road to Exeter, just a 10-minute walk from the center of Bath, with minibuses passing by frequently.

139 Wells Rd., Bath, Somerset BA2 3AL. www.139bath.co.uk. ⓒ **01225/314769.** Fax 01225/443079. 8 units. £59–£185 double. Rates include English breakfast. 2-night minimum stay Sat–Sun. AE, MC, V. Free parking. *In room:* A/C, TV/DVD, CD player, hair dryer, Wi-Fi (free).

Inexpensive

Bodhi House ★ Stylish, modern B&B just outside the center (but within walking distance), hosted by the friendly and knowledgeable Taylor family (they'll usually give you a lift into town). Rooms come with comfy beds, flat-screen TVs, and tea- and coffee-making facilities (room 1 has the best views of Bath). Eco-friendly touches include hot water provided by solar power (rainwater is harvested and used wherever possible), rooms cleaned without the use of harsh chemicals, and breakfasts containing mostly locally sourced and organic produce.

31A Englishcombe Lane, Bath, Somerset BA2 2EE. www.bodhihouse.co.uk. ⓒ **01225/461990.** 3 units. £70–£98 double; £70–140 family room. Rates include English breakfast. AE, DC, MC, V. Free parking. Bus: 17. *In room:* TV, DVD, hair dryer; Wi-Fi (free).

FRANCE

by Lily Heise, Joseph Alexiou, Sophie Nellis, Kate van den Boogert, Tristan Rutherford

7

Although France is slightly smaller than the state of Texas, no other country has such a diversity of sights and scenery in such a compact area. A visitor can travel to Paris, one of the world's great cities; drive among the Loire Valley's green hills; or head south to sunny Provence and the French Riviera. Discover the attractions (and transport, lodging, and dining offerings) in each of these regions in this chapter.

PARIS ★★★

The City of Light always lives up to its reputation as one of the world's most romantic cities. Ernest Hemingway referred to the splendors of Paris as a "moveable feast" and wrote, "There is never any ending to Paris, and the memory of each person who has lived in it differs from that of any other."

Here you can stroll along the Seine and the broad tree-lined boulevards; browse the chic shops and relax over coffee or wine at a cafe; visit the museums, monuments, and cathedrals; and savor the cuisine.

Essentials

GETTING THERE

BY PLANE Paris has two international airports: Aéroport Roissy–Charles de Gaulle, 22km (14 miles) northeast and Aéroport d'Orly, 13km (8 miles) south of the city. A shuttle (19€) makes the 50- to 75-minute journey between the two airports about every 30 minutes.

At **Aéroport Roissy–Charles de Gaulle** (✆ 01-48-62-12-12, or 39-50 in France), foreign carriers use Aérogare 1, while Air France uses Aérogare 2. From Aérogare 1, you take a moving walkway to the passport checkpoint and the Customs area. A *navette* (shuttle bus) links the two terminals.

Fast **RER** trains (Réseau Express Régional) depart the airport and **Roissy rail station** every 10 minutes between 5am and midnight for Métro stations including Gare du Nord, Châtelet, Luxembourg, Port-Royal, and Denfert-Rochereau. A typical fare from Roissy to any point in central Paris is 8.20€ per person (5.60€ children 4–10). Travel time from the airport to central Paris is around 35 to 40 minutes.

You can also take an **Air France shuttle bus** (www.cars-airfrance. com; ✆ 08-92-35-08-20 or 01-48-64-14-24) to central Paris for 15€ one-way. It stops at the Palais des Congrès (Port Maillot) and continues to place Charles-de-Gaulle–Etoile, where subway lines can carry you to

France

any point in Paris. That ride, depending on traffic, takes 45 to 55 minutes. The shuttle departs about every 20 minutes between 5:40am and 11pm.

The **Roissybus** (www.ratp.fr; ☏ 01-58-76-16-16), operated by the RATP, departs from the airport daily 6am to 11:45pm and costs 8.60€ for the 45- to 50-minute ride. Departures are about every 15 minutes, and the bus leaves you near the corner of rue Scribe and place de l'Opéra in the heart of Paris.

A **taxi** from Charles-de-Gaulle into the city will cost about 47€ to 60€; from 8pm to 7am, the fare is 40% higher. Long orderly lines for taxis form outside each of the airport's terminals.

Aéroport d'Orly (☏ 01-49-75-52-52, or **39-50** in France) has two terminals—Orly Sud (south) for international flights and Orly Ouest (west) for domestic flights. A free shuttle bus connects them in 3 minutes.

Air France buses leave from Exit E of Orly Sud and from Exit F of Orly Ouest every 12 minutes between 6am and 11:30pm for Gare des Invalides; the fare is 9€ one-way, 14€ round-trip. Returning to the airport (about 30 min.), buses leave both the Montparnasse and the Invalides terminal for Orly Sud or Orly Ouest every 15 minutes.

The Paris Airport Shuttle

The **Paris Airport Shuttle** (www.paris-shuttle.com; ☎ **01-53-39-18-18;** fax 01-53-39-13-13) is the best option. It charges 25€ for one person or 19€ per person for two or more going to and from Charles de Gaulle or Orly. Service is daily 6am to 11pm. Both shuttles accept American Express, Visa, and MasterCard, with 1-day advance reservations required.

Another way to get to central Paris is to take the RER from points throughout central Paris to the station at Pont-de-Rungis/Aéroport d'Orly for a per-person one-way fare of 6€, and from here, take the free shuttle bus that departs every 15 minutes from Pont-de-Rungis to both of Orly's terminals. Combined travel time is about 45 to 55 minutes.

A **taxi** from Orly to central Paris costs about 30€ to 50€, more at night. Don't take a meterless taxi from Orly; it's much safer (and usually cheaper) to hire one of the metered cabs, which are under the scrutiny of a police officer.

BY TRAIN   Paris has six major stations: **Gare d'Austerlitz,** 55 quai d'Austerlitz, 13e (serving the southwest, with trains to and from the Loire Valley, Bordeaux, the Pyrénées, and Spain); **Gare de l'Est,** place du 11-Novembre-1918, 10e (serving the east, with trains to and from Strasbourg, Reims, and beyond, to Zurich and Austria); **Gare de Lyon,** 20 bd. Diderot, 12e (serving the southeast, with trains to and from the Côte d'Azur [Nice, Cannes, St-Tropez], Provence, and beyond, to Geneva and Italy); **Gare Montparnasse,** 17 bd. Vaugirard, 15e (serving the west, with trains to and from Brittany); **Gare du Nord,** 18 rue de Dunkerque, 15e (serving the north, with trains to and from London, Holland, Denmark, and northern Germany); and **Gare St-Lazare,** 13 rue d'Amsterdam, 8e (serving the northwest, with trains to and from Normandy). Buses operate between the stations, and each station has a Métro stop. For train information and to make reservations, call ☎ **08-92-35-35-35,** or **36-35** in France, between 8am and 8pm daily. From Paris, one-way rail passage to Tours costs 30€ to 51€; one-way to Strasbourg costs 55€ or 80€, depending on the routing.

Warning: The stations and surrounding areas are usually seedy and frequented by pickpockets, hustlers, hookers, and addicts. Be alert, especially at night.

BY BUS   Most buses arrive at the **Eurolines France** station, 28 av. du Général-de-Gaulle, Bagnolet (www.eurolines.fr; ☎ **08-92-89-90-91;** Métro: Gallieni).

BY CAR   Driving in Paris is *not* recommended. Parking is difficult and traffic dense. If you drive, remember that Paris is encircled by a ring road, the *périphérique.* Always obtain detailed directions to your destination, including the name of the exit on the *périphérique* (exits aren't numbered). Avoid rush hours.

The major highways into Paris are A1 from the north; A13 from Rouen, Normandy, and other points northwest; A10 from Spain and the southwest; A6 and A7 from the French Alps, the Riviera, and Italy; and A4 from eastern France.

VISITOR INFORMATION

The **Paris Convention and Visitors Bureau** (www.paris-info.com; ☎ **08-92-68-30-00;** .35€ per minute) has offices throughout the city, with the main headquarters at 25–27 rue des Pyramides, 1er (Métro: Pyramides). It's open Monday through Saturday 10am to 7pm (June–Oct from 9am), Sunday and holidays from 11am to

7pm. Less comprehensive branch offices include Clémenceau Welcome Center, corner of Avenue des Champs-Elysées and Avenue Marigny (8e; Métro: Champs-Elysées), open April 6 to October 20 daily 9am to 7pm. **Espace Tourisme Ile-de-France,** in the Carrousel du Louvre, 99 rue de Rivoli, 1er (Métro: Palais-Royal–Louvre), open daily 10am to 6pm; in the **Gare de Lyon,** 20 bd. Diderot, Paris 12e (Métro: Gare de Lyon), open Monday through Saturday 8am to 6pm; in the **Gare du Nord,** 18 rue de Dunkerque, 10e (Métro: Gare du Nord), open daily 8am to 6pm; and in **Montmartre,** 21 place du Tertre, 18e (Métro: Abbesses or Lamarck-Caulaincourt), open daily 10am to 7pm. You can walk in at any branch to make a hotel reservation; the service charge is free. The offices are extremely busy year-round, especially in midsummer, so be prepared to wait in line.

CITY LAYOUT

Paris is surprisingly compact. Occupying 2,723 sq. km (1,051 sq. miles), its urban area is home to more than 11 million people. The river Seine divides Paris into the **Rive Droite (Right Bank)** to the north and the **Rive Gauche (Left Bank)** to the south. These designations make sense when you stand on a bridge and face downstream (west)—to your right is the north bank, to your left the south. A total of 32 bridges link the Right Bank and the Left Bank. Some provide access to the two islands at the heart of the city: **Ile de la Cité,** the city's birthplace and site of Notre-Dame; and **Ile St-Louis,** a moat-guarded oasis of 17th-century mansions.

The "main street" on the Right Bank is **Avenue des Champs-Elysées,** beginning at the Arc de Triomphe and running to place de la Concorde. Avenue des Champs-Elysées and 11 other avenues radiate like the arms of an asterisk from the Arc de Triomphe, giving it its original name, place de l'Etoile (*étoile* means "star"). It was renamed place Charles-de-Gaulle following the general's death; today, it's often referred to as **place Charles-de-Gaulle–Etoile** or Etoile.

If you're staying more than 2 or 3 days, purchase an inexpensive pocket-size book called *Paris par arrondissement,* available at newsstands and bookshops; prices start at 6.50€. This guide has a Métro map, a foldout map of the city, and maps of each arrondissement, with all streets listed and keyed.

NEIGHBORHOODS IN BRIEF

The heart of medieval Paris was the **Ile de la Cité** and the areas immediately surrounding it. As Paris grew, it absorbed many of the once-distant villages, and today each of these *arrondissements* (districts) retains a distinct character. They're numbered 1 to 20 starting at the center and progressing in a clockwise spiral. The key to finding any address in Paris is to look for the arrondissement number, rendered as a number followed by "er" or "e" (1er, 2e, and so on). If the address is written out more formally, you can tell what arrondissement it's in by looking at the postal code. For example, the address may be written with the street name, and then "75014 Paris." The last two digits, "14," indicate that the address is in the 14th arrondissement, Montparnasse.

On the Right Bank, the **1er** is home to the Louvre, Place Vendôme, Rues de Rivoli and St-Honoré, Palais Royal, and Comédie-Française—an area filled with grand institutions and grand stores. At the center of the **2e,** the city's financial center, is the Bourse (Stock Exchange). Most of the **3e** and the **4e** is referred to as the Marais, the old Jewish quarter that in the 17th century was home to the aristocracy. Today it's a trendy area of boutiques and restored mansions as well as the center of Paris's gay and lesbian community. On the Left Bank, the **5e** is known as the Latin Quarter, home to the Sorbonne and associated with the intellectual life that thrived in the 1920s and

1930s. Today it is Paris's intellectual soul, featuring bookstores, schools, churches, jazz clubs, student dives, Roman ruins, and boutiques. The **6e,** known as St-Germain-des-Prés, stretches from the Seine to Boulevard du Montparnasse. It is associated with the 1920s and 1930s and known as a center for art and antiques; it boasts the Palais and Jardin du Luxembourg. The **7e,** containing both the Eiffel Tower and Hôtel des Invalides, is a residential district for the well-heeled.

Back on the Right Bank, the **8e** epitomizes monumental Paris, with the triumphal Avenue des Champs-Elysées, the Elysées Palace, and the fashion houses along Avenue Montaigne and the Rue du Faubourg St-Honoré. The **18e** is home to Sacré-Coeur and Montmartre and all that the name conjures of the bohemian life painted most notably by Toulouse-Lautrec. The **14e** incorporates most of Montparnasse, including its cemetery. The **20e** is where the city's famous lie buried in Père-Lachaise and is home to Muslims and members of Paris's Sephardic Jewish community, many of whom fled Algeria or Tunisia. Beyond the arrondissements stretch the vast *banlieue,* or suburbs, of Greater Paris, where the majority of Parisians live.

GETTING AROUND

Paris is a city for strollers, whose greatest joy is rambling through unexpected alleys and squares. Given a choice of conveyance, try to make it on your own two feet whenever possible.

BY MÉTRO (SUBWAY) The Métro (www.ratp.fr; ☎ **32-46** in France, or **08-92-69-32-46** from abroad) is the most efficient and fastest way to get around Paris. All lines are numbered, and the final destination of each line is clearly marked on subway maps, in the system's underground passageways, and on the train cars. The Métro runs daily from 5:30am to 1:15am (last departure at 2am on Sat). It's reasonably safe at any hour, but beware of pickpockets.

Most stations display a map of the Métro at the entrance. To locate your correct train on a map, find your destination, follow the line to the end of its route, and note the name of the final stop, which is that line's direction. In the station, follow the signs for your direction in the passageways until you see the label on a train. Many larger stations have maps with push-button indicators that light up your route when you press the button for your destination.

Transfer stations are *correspondances,* and some require long walks; Châtelet is the most difficult—but most trips require only one transfer. When transferring, follow the orange CORRESPONDANCE signs to the proper platform. Don't follow a SORTIE (exit) sign, or you'll have to pay again to get back on the train.

On the urban lines, one ticket for 1.60€ lets you travel to any point. On the Sceaux, Boissy-St-Léger, and St-Germain-en-Laye lines to the suburbs, fares are based on distance. A *carnet* is the best buy—10 tickets for about 12€.

At the turnstile entrances to the station, insert your ticket and pass through. At some exits, tickets are also checked, so hold onto yours. There are occasional ticket checks on trains and platforms and in passageways too.

BY RER TRAINS A suburban train system, RER (Réseau Express Regional), passes through the heart of Paris, traveling faster than the Métro and running daily from 5:30am to 1am. This system works like the Métro and requires the same tickets. The major stops within central Paris, linking the RER to the Métro, are Nation, Gare de Lyon, Charles de Gaulle–Etoile, Gare-Etoile, and Gare du Nord, as well as Châtelet-Les-Halles. All of these stops are on the Right Bank. On the Left Bank, RER stops include Denfert-Rochereau and St-Michel. The five RER lines are

DISCOUNT transit PASSES

The **Paris-Visite pass** (☎ **32-46**) is valid for 1, 2, 3, or 5 days on public transport, including the Métro, buses, the funicular ride to Montmartre, and RER trains. For access to zones 1 to 3, which includes central Paris and its nearby suburbs, its cost ranges from 8.80€ for 1 day to 28.30€ for 5 days. Get it at RATP (Régie Autonome des Transports Parisiens) offices, the tourist office, and Métro stations.

marked A through E. Different branches are labeled by a number, the C5 Line serving Versailles–Rive Gauche, for example. Electric signboards next to each track outline all the possible stops along the way. Make sure that the little square next to your intended stop is lit.

BY BUS   Buses are much slower than the Métro. The majority run Monday through Saturday from 6:30am to 9:30pm (a few operate until 12:30am, and 10 operate during early-morning hours). Service is limited on Sundays and holidays. Bus and Métro fares are the same; you can use the same tickets on both. Most bus rides require one ticket, but some destinations require two (never more than two within the city limits).

At certain stops, signs list destinations and bus numbers serving that point. Destinations are usually listed north to south and east to west. Most stops are also posted on the sides of the buses. During rush hours, you may have to take a ticket from a dispensing machine, indicating your position in the line at the stop.

If you intend to use the buses a lot, pick up an RATP bus map at the office on Place de la Madeleine, 8e, or at the tourist offices at RATP headquarters, 54 quai de La Rapée, 12e. For detailed recorded information (in English) on bus and Métro routes, call ☎ **32-46,** open Monday to Friday 7am to 9pm.

The RATP also operates the **Balabus,** big-windowed orange-and-white motorcoaches that run only during limited hours: Sunday and national holidays from noon to 8:30pm, from April 15 to the end of September. Itineraries run in both directions between Gare de Lyon and the Grande Arche de La Défense, encompassing some of the city's most beautiful vistas. It's a great deal—three Métro tickets, for 1.60€ each, will carry you the entire route. You'll recognize the bus and the route it follows by the BB symbol emblazoned on each bus's side and on signs posted beside the route it follows.

BY TAXI   It's virtually impossible to get a taxi at rush hour, so don't even try. Taxi drivers are organized into a lobby that limits their number to 15,000.

Watch out for common rip-offs: Always check the meter to make sure you're not paying the previous passenger's fare; beware of cabs without meters, which often wait outside nightclubs for tipsy patrons; and settle the tab in advance.

You can hail regular cabs on the street when their signs read LIBRE. Taxis are easier to find at the many stands near Métro stations. The flag drops at 5.50€, and from 10am to 5pm, you pay .90€ per kilometer. From 5pm to 10am, you pay 1.15€ per kilometer. On airport trips, you're not required to pay for the driver's empty return ride.

You're allowed several pieces of luggage free if they're transported inside and are less than 5kg (11 lb.). Heavier suitcases carried in the trunk cost 1€ to 1.50€ apiece. Tip 12% to 15%—the latter usually elicits a *merci.* For radio cabs, call **Les Taxis Bleus** (☎ **08-25-16-10-10**) or **Taxi G7** (☎ **01-47-39-47-39**)—but note that you'll be charged from the point where the taxi begins the drive to pick you up.

BY BOAT The **Batobus** (www.batobus.com; ☎ 08-25-05-01-01) is a 150-passenger ferry with big windows. The boats operate along the Seine, stopping at such points of interest as the **Eiffel Tower, Musée d'Orsay,** the **Louvre, Notre-Dame,** and the **Hôtel de Ville.** The Batobus does not provide recorded commentary. The only fare option available is a day pass valid for either 1, 2, or 5 days, each allowing as many entrances and exits as you want. A 1-day pass costs 12€ for adults, 6€ for children 15 and under; a 2-day pass costs 16€ for adults, 8€ for children 15 and under; a 5-day pass costs 19€ for adults, 9€ for children 15 and under. Boats operate daily (closed most of Jan) every 15 to 30 minutes, starting between 10 and 10:30am and ending between 4:30 and 10:30pm, depending on the season of the year.

[Fast FACTS] PARIS

ATMs/Banks Most banks in Paris are open Monday through Friday from 9am to 4:30pm and you will find an ATM on nearly every street corner.

Currency France fell under the **euro** (€) umbrella in 2002.

Currency Exchange American Express can fill most banking needs. For the best exchange rate, visit banks, post offices, or foreign-exchange offices, not shops and hotels. Currency exchanges are also at Paris airports and train stations and along most of the major boulevards. They charge a small commission.

Some exchange places charge favorable rates to lure you into their stores. For example, **Paris Vision,** 214 rue de Rivoli, 1er (☎ 01-42-60-30-01; Métro: Tuileries), maintains a mini-bank in the back of a travel agency, open daily 6:30am to 9pm. Its rates are a fraction less favorable than those offered for large blocks of money as listed by the Paris stock exchange.

Doctors Some large hotels have a doctor on staff. You can also try the **American Hospital,** 63 bd. Victor-Hugo, in the suburb of Neuilly-sur-Seine (☎ 01-46-41-25-25; www.american-hospital.org; Métro: Pont-de-Levallois or Pont-de-Neuilly; bus: 82), which operates a 24-hour emergency service. The bilingual staff accepts Blue Cross and other American insurance plans.

Drugstores After hours, have your concierge contact the Commissariat de Police for the nearest 24-hour pharmacy. French law requires one pharmacy in any given neighborhood to stay open 24 hours. You'll find the address posted on the doors or windows of all other drugstores. One of the most central all-nighters is **Pharmacie Les Champs "Derhy,"** 84 av. des Champs-Elysées, 8e (☎ 01-45-62-02-41; Métro: George V).

Embassies & Consulates If you have a passport, immigration, legal, or

other problem, contact your consulate. Call *before* you go—they often keep odd hours and observe both French and home-country holidays. The Embassy of the **United States,** 2 av. Gabriel, 8e (http://france.usembassy.gov; ☎ 01-43-12-22-22; Métro: Concorde), is open Monday to Friday 9am to 6pm. The Embassy of **Canada,** 35 av. Montaigne, 8e (www.canadainternational.gc.ca/france/index.aspx; ☎ 01-44-43-29-00; Métro: Franklin-D-Roosevelt or Alma-Marceau), is open Monday to Friday 9am to noon and 2 to 5pm. The Embassy of the **United Kingdom,** 35 rue du Faubourg St-Honoré, 8e (http://ukinfrance.fco.gov.uk/en; ☎ 01-44-51-31-00; Métro: Concorde or Madeleine), is open Monday to Friday 9:30am to 1pm and 2:30 to 5pm. The Embassy of **Ireland,** 4 rue Rude, 16e (www.embassyofireland.fr; ☎ 01-44-17-67-00; Métro: Etoile), is open Monday to Friday 9:30am to 1pm and 2:30 to 5:30pm. The Embassy of **Australia,**

4 rue Jean-Rey, 15e (www. france.embassy.gov.au; ℂ **01-40-59-33-00;** Métro: Bir Hakeim), is open Monday to Friday 9:15am to noon and 2:30 to 4:30pm. The Embassy of **New Zealand,** 7 ter rue Léonard-de-Vinci, 16e (www.nzembassy. com/france; ℂ **01-45-01-43-43;** Métro: Victor Hugo), is open Monday to Friday 9am to 1pm and 2:30 to 6pm. The Embassy of **South Africa,** 59 quai d'Orsay, 7e (www.afriquesud.net; ℂ **01-53-59-23-23;** Métro: Invalides), is open Monday to Friday 9am to noon.

Emergencies   For the police, call ℂ **17;** to report a fire, call ℂ **18.** For an ambulance, call ℂ **15** or 01-45-67-50-50.

Police   In an emergency, call ℂ **17.** For nonemergency situations, the principal *préfecture* is at 9 bd. du Palais, 4e (ℂ **01-53-73-53-73;** Métro: Cité).

Post Offices   Most post offices (PTT) in Paris are open Monday through Friday from 8am to 7pm and every Saturday from 8am to noon. One of the biggest and most central is the main post office for the 1er arrondissement, at 52 rue du Louvre (ℂ **01-40-28-76-00;** Métro: Musée du Louvre). It maintains the hours noted above for services that include sale of postal money orders, mail collection and distribution, and expedition of faxes. For buying stamps and accepting packages, it's open on a

limited basis 24 hours a day. If you find it inconvenient to go to the post office just to buy stamps, they're sold at the reception desks of many hotels and at cafes designated with red TABAC signs.

Safety   Beware of child pickpockets, who prey on visitors around sites such as the Louvre, Eiffel Tower, Notre-Dame, and Montmartre, and who like to pick pockets in the Métro, often blocking the entrances and exits to the escalator. Women should hang on to their purses.

Taxes   As a member of the European Union (E.U.), France routinely imposes a value-added tax (VAT in English; TVA in French) on many goods and services. The standard VAT is 19.6% on merchandise, including clothing, appliances, liquor, leather goods, shoes, furs, jewelry, perfumes, cameras, and even caviar. Refunds are made for the tax on certain goods and merchandise, but not on services. The minimum purchase is 184€ at one time for nationals or residents of countries outside the E.U.

Telephones   The country code for France is **33.** All phone numbers in France have 10 digits, including the **area code** (or regional prefix). For example, the phone number for the Paris police, **01-53-73-53-73,** contains the area code for Paris and the Ile de France **(01).** To make a **long-distance call**

within France, dial the 10-digit number. **When calling from outside France,** dial the international prefix for your country (**011** for the U.S. and Canada), the country code for France, and then the last nine digits of the number, dropping the 0 (zero) from the regional prefix.

Public phones are found everywhere in France. The most widely accepted method of payment is the *télécarte,* a prepaid calling card available at kiosks, post offices, and Métro stations. Sold in two versions, they cost 11€ and 16€ for 50 and 120 units, respectively. A local call costs one unit, or 6 to 18 minutes of conversation, depending on the rate at the time you make the call. Avoid making calls from your hotel, which may double or triple the charges.

Tipping   The law requires all bills to say *service compris,* which means the total includes the tip. But French diners often leave some small change as an additional tip, especially if service has been exceptional.

Some general guidelines: For hotel staff, tip 1.05€ to 1.50€ for every item of baggage the porter carries on arrival and departure, and 1.50€ for the maid. Tip taxi drivers 10% to 15% of the amount on the meter. For guides for group visits to museums and monuments, 1.50€ is a reasonable tip.

Paris Attractions

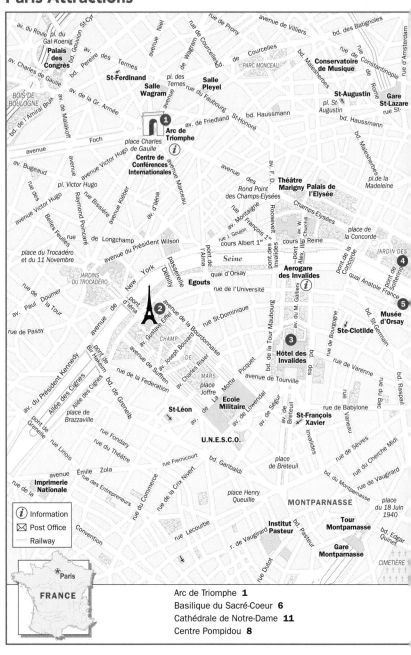

Arc de Triomphe **1**
Basilique du Sacré-Coeur **6**
Cathédrale de Notre-Dame **11**
Centre Pompidou **8**

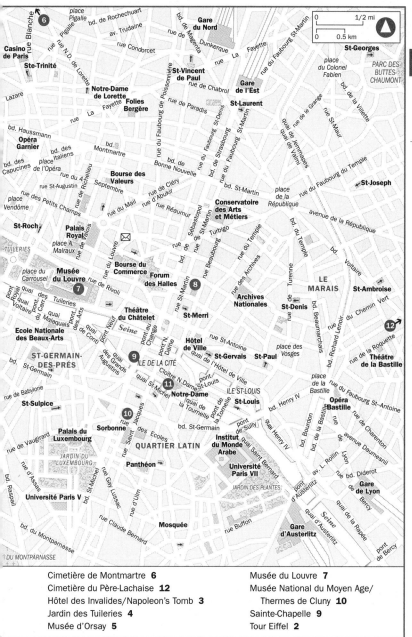

Cimetière de Montmartre **6**
Cimetière du Père-Lachaise **12**
Hôtel des Invalides/Napoleon's Tomb **3**
Jardin des Tuileries **4**
Musée d'Orsay **5**

Musée du Louvre **7**
Musée National du Moyen Age/
   Thermes de Cluny **10**
Sainte-Chapelle **9**
Tour Eiffel **2**

Exploring Paris

The best way to discover Paris is **on foot.** Walk along the Avenue des Champs-Elysées, tour the quays of the Seine, wander the Ile de la Cité and Ile St-Louis, browse the shops and stalls, and stroll the squares and parks. A walk at dawn can be enthralling as you see the city come to life: Merchants wash shop fronts, cafes begin serving coffee and croissants, and vegetable and fruit vendors start setting up their stalls and arranging their produce.

RIGHT BANK
Les Halles, Louvre & Palais Royal (1e & 2e)

Crowned by the Louvre, this central area that flanks the Seine packs in a high density of important museums, centered on the magnificent former royal palace and its expansive Jardin des Tuileries. Although the Louvre is top of most visitors' to-do lists, don't forget that there are also some wonderful smaller museums close by, and great shopping, too.

Centre Pompidou ★★★ ☺ MUSEUM   When it first opened in the 1970s, the Centre Pompidou was hailed as "the most avant-garde building in the world," and today it still continues to pack in the art-loving crowds. Conceived by former French president Georges Pompidou and designed by architects Renzo Piano and Richard Rogers, this building originally opened in 1977, and it underwent a major renovation in 2000, which expanded and improved the space. The building's exterior is very bold: brightly painted pipes and ducts crisscross its transparent facade (green for water, red for heat, blue for air, and yellow for electricity), and an outdoor escalator flanks the building, freeing up interior space for exhibitions.

The Centre Pompidou encompasses four separate attractions. The **Musée National d'Art Moderne (National Museum of Modern Art)** displays a large collection of 20th-century art. With some 40,000 works, this is the big draw, although it can show only about 850 works at one time. If you want to view some real charmers, see Alexander Calder's 1926 *Josephine Baker,* one of his earlier versions of the mobile, an art form he invented. Marcel Duchamp's *Valise* is a collection of miniature reproductions of his fabled dada sculptures and drawings; they're displayed in a carrying case. Every time we visit we have to see Salvador Dalí's *Portrait of Lenin Dancing on Piano Keys.*

Place Georges-Pompidou, 4e. www.centrepompidou.fr. ✆ **01-44-78-12-33.** Admission 11€–13€ adults, 9€–10€ students, free for children 17 and under; admission varies depending on exhibits. Wed–Mon 11am–10pm. Métro: Rambuteau, Hôtel de Ville, or Châtelet–Les Halles.

Jardin des Tuileries ★★ ☺ GARDEN   The spectacular statue-studded Jardin des Tuileries, bordering place de la Concorde, is as much a part of Paris as the Seine. Le Nôtre, Louis XIV's gardener and planner of the Versailles grounds, designed the gardens. Some of the gardens' most distinctive statues are the 18 enormous bronzes by Maillol, installed within the Jardin du Carrousel, a subdivision of the Jardin des Tuileries, between 1964 and 1965, under the direction of Culture Minister André Malraux.

About 400 years before that, Catherine de Médici ordered a palace built here, the **Palais des Tuileries;** other occupants have included Louis XVI (after he left Versailles) and Napoleon. Twice attacked by Parisians, it was burned to the ground in 1871 and never rebuilt. The gardens, however, remain. In orderly French manner, the trees are arranged according to designs, and even the paths are arrow-straight. Bubbling fountains break the sense of order and formality.

Each summer, over the months of July and August, the parks hosts a traditional **funfair** (www.feteforaine-jardindestuileries.com) alongside the Rue de Rivoli—be sure to take a Ferris Wheel ride for excellent views.

Rue de Rivoli, 1er. © **01-40-20-90-43.** Free admission. Daily Apr–May 7am–9pm; June–Aug 7am–11pm; Sept 7am–9pm; Oct–Mar 7:30am–7:30pm. Métro: Tuileries or Concorde.

Musée du Louvre ★★★ MUSEUM   The Louvre is the world's largest palace and museum, and it houses one of the greatest art collections ever. To enter, pass through I. M. Pei's controversial 21m (69-ft.) **glass pyramid ★**—a startling though effective contrast of the ultramodern against the palace's classical lines. Commissioned by the late president François Mitterrand and completed in 1989, it allows sunlight to shine on an underground reception area with a complex of shops and restaurants.

People on one of those "Paris-in-a-day" tours try to break track records to get a glimpse of the Louvre's two most famous ladies: the beguiling *Mona Lisa* and the armless *Venus de Milo* ★★★. The herd then dashes on a 5-minute stampede in pursuit of *Winged Victory* ★★★, the headless statue discovered at Samothrace and dating from about 200 B.C. In defiance of the assembly line theory of art, we head instead for David's *Coronation of Napoleon,* showing Napoleon poised with the crown aloft as Joséphine kneels before him, just across from his *Portrait of Madame Récamier* ★, depicting Napoleon's opponent at age 23; she reclines on her sofa agelessly in the style of classical antiquity.

Pressed for time? Take a **guided tour** (in English), which lasts about 90 minutes. The short tour, which is your only option if you visit on Monday, covers the "highlights of the highlights." Tours start under the pyramid at the station marked ACCUEIL DES GROUPES. If you would rather do your own tour, you can also borrow a Nintendo 3DS audio guide (5€ adults; 3€ children) with 3D capability.

The collections are divided into eight departments: Asian antiquities; Egyptian antiquities; Greek, Etruscan, and Roman antiquities; Islamic art; sculpture; paintings; prints and drawings; and objets d'art. The **Grande Galerie,** a 180m (591-ft.) hall opening onto the Seine, is dedicated to mostly Italian paintings from the 1400s to the 1700s, including works by Raphael and Leonardo da Vinci.

The **Richelieu wing ★★★** houses northern European and French paintings, along with decorative arts, sculpture, Oriental antiquities (including a rich collection of both Islamic and Far Eastern Art), and the Napoleon III salons. One of its galleries displays 21 works that Rubens painted in a space of only 2 years for Marie de Médici's Palais de Luxembourg. The masterpieces here include Dürer's *Self-Portrait,* van Dyck's *Portrait of Charles I of England,* and Holbein the Younger's *Portrait of Erasmus of Rotterdam.*

34–36 quai du Louvre, 1er. Main entrance in the glass pyramid, Cour Napoléon. www.louvre.fr. © **01-40-20-53-17, 01-40-20-50-50** for operator, or **08-92-68-46-94** for advance credit card sales. Admission 10€, children 17 and under free, free to all 1st Sun of every month. Sat–Mon and Thurs 9am–6pm; Wed and Fri 9am–9:45pm. English-language tours (1½-hr. Mon and Wed–Sun) 9€, 6€ children 12 and younger with museum ticket. Métro: Palais-Royal–Musée du Louvre.

Le Marais, Ile St-Louis & Ile de la Cité (3e & 4e)

This historic neighborhood, home to royalty and aristocracy in the 17th and 18th centuries, preserves exceptional architecture—some of it dating back to the Renaissance. Its narrow, winding streets are from another age. While it features some blockbuster attractions, including the **Hôtel de Ville** and the **Centre Pompidou,** the Marais is notable for its density of charming smaller museums, where you hopefully won't be fighting through crowds. The two islands in the Seine, Ile St-Louis and Ile de la Cité, set the stage for some impressive medieval monuments, the **Cathédrale de Notre-Dame,** the **Conciergerie,** and the glorious **Sainte-Chapelle.**

Cathédrale de Notre-Dame ★★ CATHEDRAL   Notre-Dame is the heart of Paris and even of the country itself: Distances from the city to all parts of France are calculated from a spot at the far end of place du Parvis, in front of the cathedral, where a circular bronze plaque marks **Kilomètre Zéro.**

For 6 centuries, it has stood as a Gothic masterpiece of the Middle Ages. Though many disagree, we feel Notre-Dame is more interesting outside than in, and you'll want to walk all around it to fully appreciate this "vast symphony of stone." Better yet, cross over the Pont au Double to the Left Bank and view it from the quai.

The houses of old Paris used to crowd in on Notre-Dame, but during his redesign of the city, Baron Haussmann ordered them torn down to show the cathedral to its best advantage from the parvis. This is the best vantage for seeing the three sculpted 13th-century portals (the Virgin, the Last Judgment, and St. Anne).

The central Portal of the Last Judgment is in three levels: The first shows Vices and Virtues; the second, Christ and his Apostles; and the third, Christ in triumph after the Resurrection. On the right is the Portal of St. Anne, depicting such scenes as the Virgin enthroned with Child. Over the central portal is a remarkable **rose window,** 9m (30 ft.) in diameter, forming a showcase for a statue of the Virgin and Child. Equally interesting is the Cloister Portal (around on the left), with its 13th-century Virgin, a unique survivor of many that originally adorned the facade. (Unfortunately, the Child she's holding is decapitated.)

If possible, view the interior at sunset. Of the three giant medallions that warm the austere cathedral, the north rose window in the transept, from the mid-13th century, is best. The interior is typical Gothic, with slender, graceful columns. The carved-stone choir screen from the early 14th century depicts biblical scenes. Near the altar stands the 14th-century Virgin and Child. Behind glass in the treasury is a display of vestments and gold objects, including crowns. Notre-Dame is especially proud of its relic of the True Cross and the Crown of Thorns.

To visit the gargoyles immortalized by Victor Hugo (where Quasimodo lurked), you have to scale steps leading to the twin square towers, rising to a height of 68m (223 ft.). Once here, you can inspect those devils (some sticking out their tongues), hobgoblins, and birds of prey.

Approached through a garden behind Notre-Dame is the **Memorial des Martyrs Français de la Déportation** (© 01-46-33-87-56), jutting out on the tip of the Ile de la Cité. This memorial honors the French martyrs of World War II, who were deported to camps such as Auschwitz and Buchenwald. In blood red are these words (in French): FORGIVE, BUT DON'T FORGET. The memorial is open June to September daily from 10am to noon and from 2 to 7pm, and off-season daily from 10am to noon and 2 to 5pm; admission is free.

6 place du Parvis Notre-Dame, 4e. www.notredamedeparis.fr. © **01-53-10-07-02.** Admission free to cathedral. Towers 8.50€ adults, 5€ seniors and ages 13–25, free for children 12 and under. Treasury 3€ adults, 2.20€ seniors, 1.60€ ages 13–25, free for children 12 and under. Cathedral year-round daily 8am–6:45pm (Sat–Sun 7:15pm). Towers and crypt daily 10am–6pm (until 11pm Sat–Sun June–Aug). Museum Wed and Sat–Sun 2–5pm. Treasury Mon–Fri 9:30am–6pm; Sat 9:30am–6:30pm; Sun 1:30–6:30pm. Métro: Cité or St-Michel. RER: St-Michel.

Sainte-Chapelle ★★★ CHURCH Countless writers have called this tiny chapel a jewel box, yet that hardly suffices. Go when the sun is shining, and you'll need no one else's words to describe the remarkable effects of natural light on Sainte-Chapelle. You approach the church through the Cour de la Sainte-Chapelle of the Palais de Justice.

Begun in 1246, the bi-level chapel was built to house relics of the True Cross, including the Crown of Thorns acquired by St. Louis (the Crusader King, Louis IX) from the emperor of Constantinople.

You enter through the *chapelle basse* (**lower chapel**), used by the palace servants; it's supported by flying buttresses and ornamented with fleur-de-lis designs. The king and his courtiers used the *chapelle haute* (**upper chapel**), one of the greatest achievements of Gothic art; you reach it by ascending a narrow spiral staircase. On a bright day, the 15 stained-glass windows seem to glow with Chartres blue and wine-colored reds. The walls consist almost entirely of the glass, 612 sq. m (6,588 sq. ft.) of it, which had to be removed for safekeeping during the revolution and again during both world wars. In the windows' Old and New Testament designs are embodied the hopes and dreams (and pretensions) of the kings who ordered their construction. The 1,134 scenes depict the Christian story from the Garden of Eden through the Apocalypse; you read them from bottom to top and from left to right. The great **rose window** depicts the Apocalypse.

Sainte-Chapelle stages **concerts** from March to November, daily at 7 and 8:30pm; tickets cost 19€ to 25€. Call ☏ **01-44-07-12-38** from 11am to 6pm daily for details.

Palais de Justice, 4 bd. du Palais, 4e. www.monum.fr. ☏ **01-53-40-60-80.** 8.50€ adults, 5.50€ ages 18–25, free children 17 and under. Mar–Oct daily 9:30am–6pm; Nov–Feb daily 9am–5pm. Métro: Cité, St-Michel, or Châtelet–Les Halles. RER: St-Michel.

Champs-Elysées & Western Paris (8e, 16e & 17e)

Money and power dominate this neighborhood and its emblematic avenue, the Champs-Elysées. There is also a wealth of exceptional museums here from **Musée d'art Moderne,** a testament to Paris's Modernist glory days, to the **Palais de Tokyo,** a pioneering contemporary art space.

Arc de Triomphe ★★ MONUMENT At the western end of the Champs-Elysées, the Arc de Triomphe is the largest triumphal arch in the world, about 49m (161 ft.) high and 44m (144 ft.) wide. Don't cross the square to reach it! With a dozen streets radiating from the "Star," the traffic circle is vehicular roulette. It's the busiest traffic hub in Paris. Instead, take the underground passage.

Commissioned by Napoleon in 1806 to commemorate his Grande Armée's victories, the arch wasn't completed until 1836, under Louis-Philippe. Four years later, Napoleon's remains—brought from his grave on St. Helena—passed under the arch en route to his tomb at the Hôtel des Invalides. Since then it has become the focal point for state funerals. It's also the site of the Tomb of the Unknown Soldier, where an eternal flame burns.

Of the sculptures decorating the monument, the best known is Rude's *Marseillaise,* also called *The Departure of the Volunteers.* J. P. Cortot's *Triumph of Napoleon in 1810,* along with the *Resistance of 1814* and *Peace of 1815,* both by Etex, also adorn the facade. The arch is engraved with the names of hundreds of generals who commanded troops in Napoleonic victories.

You can take an elevator or climb the stairway to the top, where there's an exhibition hall with lithographs and photos depicting the arch throughout its history. From the observation deck, you have a panoramic view of the Champs-Elysées as well as the Louvre, Eiffel Tower, and Sacré-Coeur.

Place Charles de Gaulle–Etoile, 8e. www.monum.fr. ℂ **01-55-37-73-77.** Admission 9.50€ adults, 6€ for those 18–24, free children 17 and under. Apr–Sept daily 10am–11pm; Oct–Mar daily 10am–10:30pm. Métro: Charles-de-Gaulle–Etoile. Bus: 22, 30, 31, 52, 73, or 92.

Pigalle & Montmartre (18e)

Perched on the city's highest point, the **Sacré-Coeur** basilica may be the area's only significant monument, but Montmartre's cobblestone streets and unique, villagelike architecture are an attraction in themselves. The harmless red light district of neighboring Pigalle can't be reduced to a single attraction either, but it is an exciting area to explore.

Before its discovery, Montmartre was a sleepy farming community, with windmills dotting the landscape. Those who find the trek up to Paris's highest elevations too much of a climb may prefer to ride **Le Petit Train de Montmartre,** which passes all the major landmarks; it seats 55 passengers and offers English commentary. Board at place Blanche (near the Moulin Rouge); the fare is 6€ adults, 3.50€ children 4 to 10, free for children 3 and under. Trains run daily 10am to 6pm, until midnight in July and August. For information, contact **Promotrain,** 131 rue de Clignancourt, 18e (ℂ **01-42-62-24-00**).

The simplest way to reach Montmartre is to take the Métro to Anvers and then walk up Rue du Steinkerque to the **funicular,** which runs to the precincts of Sacré-Coeur every day 6:15am to 12:45am. The fare is one Métro ticket. Except for Sacré-Coeur (see below), Montmartre has only minor attractions; it's the historic architecture and the atmosphere that are compelling.

Basilique du Sacré-Coeur ★★ ☺ CHURCH   Montmartre's crowning achievement is Sacré-Coeur, with its gleaming white domes and campanile (bell tower), though from outside on the steps its **view of Paris** ★★★ takes precedence over the basilica itself. On a clear day, the vista from the dome can extend for 56km (35 miles). You can also walk around the inner dome of the church, peering down like a pigeon (a few of which will likely be there to keep you company).

After France's defeat by the Prussians in 1870, the basilica was planned as an offering to cure the country's misfortunes; rich and poor alike contributed. Construction began in 1873, but the church wasn't consecrated until 1919. The interior is decorated with mosaics, the most striking of which are the ceiling depiction of Christ and the mural of the Passion at the back of the altar. The crypt contains what some believe is a piece of the sacred heart of Christ—hence the church's name.

Place St-Pierre, 18e. www.sacre-coeur-montmartre.com. ℂ **01-53-41-89-00.** Free admission to basilica, joint ticket to dome and crypt: adults 8€, children 4–16 5€ or dome only 6€/4€, crypt only 3€/2€. Basilica daily 6am–11pm; dome and crypt daily 9am–6pm. Métro: Abbesses; take elevator to surface and follow signs to funicular.

Cimetière de Montmartre ★ CEMETERY   Novelist Alexandre Dumas and Russian dancer Vaslav Nijinsky are just a few of the famous composers, writers, and artists interred here. The remains of the great Stendhal are here, as are Hector Berlioz, Heinrich Heine, Edgar Degas, Jacques Offenbach, and even François Truffaut. We like to pay our respects at the tomb of Alphonsine Plessis, the courtesan on whom Dumas based his Marguerite Gautier in *La Dame aux Camélias.*

20 av. Rachel (west of the Butte Montmartre and north of bd. de Clichy), 18e. ℰ **01-53-42-36-30.**
Free admission. Mon–Fri 8am–6pm; Sat 8:30am–6pm; Sun 9am–6pm. Métro: La Fourche.

Belleville, Canal St-Martin & Northeast Paris (10e, 19e & 20e)

Perhaps the greatest attraction in this area is the picturesque **Canal St-Martin** itself. Beyond that is **La Villette,** which encompasses Paris's biggest park, Parc de la Villette. It is also an exceptional 21st-century cultural compound including museums, concert halls, circus tents, and exhibition spaces that host a great year-round program. The lure of this former industrial zone is its outdoor attractions: In addition to La Villette, the renowned **Père-Lachaise cemetery** and the wonderful **Buttes Chaumont park** are also located in this area. Note that the area around the Belleville Métro station is also home to one of the city's bustling Chinatowns.

Cimetière du Père-Lachaise ★★★ ☺ CEMETERY   When it comes to name-dropping, this cemetery knows no peer; it has been called the "grandest address in Paris." Everybody from Sarah Bernhardt to Oscar Wilde (his tomb is by Epstein) is buried here. So are Balzac, Delacroix, and Bizet, as well as Chopin and Molière. Rock star Jim Morrison's tombstone usually draws the most visitors—and causes the most disruption. If you search hard enough, you can find the tombs of Abélard and Héloïse, the ill-fated lovers of the 12th century.

16 rue de Repos, 20e. www.pere-lachaise.com. ℰ **01-55-25-82-10.** Free admission. Mon–Fri 8am–6pm; Sat–Sun 8:30am–6pm (closes at 5pm Nov to early Mar). Métro: Père-Lachaise or Philippe Auguste.

LEFT BANK
Latin Quarter (5e & 13e)

This leafy neighborhood is defined by the medieval university at its heart: the Sorbonne. In fact, it gets its name from the Latin the students spoke in their classes there up until 1793. The Roman occupation, from 52 B.C. until A.D. 486, remains visible too; the Rue Saint-Jacques and **Boulevard Saint-Michel** (*Boul'-Mich*) mark the former Roman cardo, and you can explore Roman ruins at the Cluny Museum.

Musée National du Moyen Age/Thermes de Cluny (Musée de Cluny) ★★ MUSEUM   This museum has two draws: the world's finest collection of art from the Middle Ages, including jewelry and tapestries; and the well-preserved manor house, built atop Roman baths, that holds the collection. The Cluny was the mansion of a 15th-century abbot. By 1515, it was the home of Mary Tudor, the widow of Louis XII and daughter of Henry VII of England and Elizabeth of York. Seized during the Revolution, it was rented in 1833 to Alexandre du Sommerard, who adorned it with medieval works of art. After his death in 1842, the government bought the building and the collection.

Most people come to see the **Unicorn Tapestries** ★★★, the world's most outstanding tapestries. They were discovered a century ago in the Château de Boussac in Auvergne. Five of the six tapestries seem to deal with the senses (one depicts a unicorn looking into a mirror held by a maiden). The sixth shows a woman under an elaborate tent, her pet dog resting on an embroidered cushion beside her. The lovable unicorn and its friendly companion, a lion, hold back the flaps. The red-and-green background forms a rich carpet of spring flowers, fruit-laden trees, birds, rabbits, donkeys, dogs, goats, lambs, and monkeys.

Downstairs are the ruins of the Roman baths, dating from around A.D. 200. You can wander through a display of Gallic and Roman sculptures and an interesting marble bathtub engraved with lions.

Insider tip: The garden represents a return to the Middle Ages. It was inspired by the luxuriant detail of the museum's most fabled treasure, the 15th-century tapestry of *The Lady of the Unicorn.* It's small but richly planted.

6 pl. Paul Painlevé, 5e. www.musee-moyenage.fr. © **01-53-73-78-00.** Admission 8€ adults, free 25 and under. Add .50€ for access to the temporary exhibitions. Wed–Mon 9:15am–5:45pm. Closed Tues. Métro: Miromesnil or St-Philippe-du-Roule.

Eiffel Tower & Nearby (7e)

From place du Trocadéro, you can stand between the two curved wings of the Palais de Chaillot and gaze out on a panoramic view. At your feet are the Jardins du Trocadéro, centered by fountains. Directly in front, Pont d'Iéna spans the Seine, leading to the **Eiffel Tower.** Beyond, stretching as far as your eye can see, is the **Champ-de-Mars,** once a military parade ground and now a garden with arches, grottoes, and cascades. After admiring and climbing the elegant structure, stroll west along the river to the **Musée d'Orsay.**

Hôtel des Invalides/Napoleon's Tomb ★★ HISTORIC BUILDING The glory of the French military lives on in the Musée de l'Armée. Louis XIV decided to build the "hotel" to house soldiers with disabilities. It wasn't entirely a benevolent gesture, because the veterans had been injured, crippled, or blinded while fighting Louis's battles. Included in the collections (begun in 1794) are Viking swords, Burgundian basinets, 14th-century blunderbusses, Balkan khanjars, American Browning machine guns, war pitchforks, salamander-engraved Renaissance serpentines, musketoons, and grenadiers. There are suits of armor worn by kings and dignitaries, including the famous "armor suit of the lion" that was made for François I. The displays of swords are among the world's finest.

Crossing the Cour d'Honneur (Court of Honor), you'll come to **Eglise du Dôme,** designed by Hardouin-Mansart for Louis XIV. He began work on the church in 1677, though he died before its completion. In the Napoleon Chapel is the hearse used at the emperor's funeral on May 9, 1821.

To accommodate the Tomb of Napoleon—made of red porphyry, with a green granite base—architect Visconti had to redesign the high altar. First buried at St. Helena, Napoleon's remains were returned to Paris in 1840.

Place des Invalides, 7e. www.invalides.org. © **01-44-42-37-72.** Admission to Musée de l'Armée, Napoleon's Tomb, and Musée des Plans-Reliefs 9€ adults, 7€ students, free for children 17 and under. Oct 1–Mar 31 Mon–Sat 10am–5pm, Sun 10am–5:30pm; Apr 1–Sept 30 Mon, Wed–Sat 10am–6pm, Sun 10am–6:30pm, Tues 10am–9pm; June–Aug daily 10am–7pm. Closed Jan 1, May 1, Nov 1, and Dec 25. Métro: Latour-Maubourg, Varenne, Invalides, or St-Francois-Xavier.

Musée d'Orsay ★★★ MUSEUM Architects created one of the world's great museums from an old rail station, the neoclassical Gare d'Orsay, across the Seine from the Louvre. Don't skip the Louvre, of course, but come here even if you have to miss all the other art museums in town. It contains an important collection devoted to the pivotal years from 1848 to 1914 and is a repository of works by the Impressionists, symbolists, pointillists, realists, and late Romantics. Artists represented include van Gogh, Manet, Monet, Degas, and Renoir. It houses thousands of sculptures and paintings across 80 galleries, plus Belle Epoque furniture, photographs, objets d'art, architectural models, and a cinema.

One of Renoir's most joyous paintings is here: *Moulin de la Galette* (1876). Another celebrated work is by the American James McNeill Whistler—*Arrangement in Gray and Black: Portrait of the Painter's Mother.* The most famous piece in the museum is

Manet's 1863 *Déjeuner sur l'herbe* (Picnic on the Grass), which created a scandal when it was first exhibited; it depicts a nude woman picnicking with two fully clothed men in a forest. Two years later, his *Olympia*, lounging on her bed wearing nothing but a flower in her hair and high-heeled shoes, met with the same response.

1 rue de Bellechasse or 62 rue de Lille, 7e. www.musee-orsay.fr. © **01-40-49-48-14.** Admission 9€ adults, 6.50€ ages 18–24, free ages 17 and under. Joint ticket to this museum and the Musée de l'Orangerie 13€. Tues–Wed and Fri–Sun 9:30am–6pm; Thurs 9:30am–9:45pm. Closed Jan 1 and Dec 25. Métro: Solférino. RER: Musée d'Orsay.

Tour Eiffel ★★★ ☺ MONUMENT   This may be the single-most-recognizable structure in the world—it's the symbol of Paris. Weighing 7,000 tons but exerting about the same pressure on the ground as a person sitting in a chair, the tower was not meant to be permanent. Gustave-Alexandre Eiffel, the engineer whose fame rested mainly on his iron bridges, built it for the Universal Exhibition of 1889. (He also designed the framework for the Statue of Liberty.)

The tower, including its 17m (56-ft.) TV antenna, is 317m (1,040 ft.) tall. On a clear day you can see it from 64km (40 miles) away. Its open-framework construction ushered in the almost-unlimited possibilities of steel construction, paving the way for skyscrapers.

You can visit the tower in three stages: Taking the elevator to the first landing, you'll have a view over the rooftops of Paris. A cinema, museum, restaurants, and bar are open year-round. The second landing provides a panoramic look at the city (on this level is Le Jules Verne restaurant, a great place for lunch or dinner). The third landing offers the best view, allowing you to identify monuments and buildings.

To get to **Le Jules Verne** (www.lejulesverne-paris.com; © **01-45-55-61-44**), the Ducasse-owned fine dining restaurant on the second platform, take the private south foundation elevator. You can enjoy an aperitif in the piano bar and then take a seat at one of the dining room's tables, all of which provide an inspiring view. The menu changes seasonally, offering fish and meat dishes that range from filet of turbot with seaweed and buttered sea urchins to veal chops with truffled vegetables. Reservations are recommended and a fixed-price luncheon menu goes for 85€, set dinners for 200€.

You can ice-skate inside the Eiffel Tower, doing figure eights while taking in views of the rooftops of Paris. Skating takes place on an observation deck 57m (187 ft.) above ground. The rectangular rink is a bit larger than an average tennis court, holding 80 skaters at once. Admission to the rink and skate rentals is free once you pay the initial entry fee below. The rink is open for 6 weeks during December and January.

Insider tip: The least expensive way to visit the tower is to walk up the first two floors for 4€ adults or 3.10€ ages 25 and under. With this route, you also bypass the long lines for the elevator.

Champ de Mars, 7e. www.tour-eiffel.fr. © **01-44-11-23-23.** Admission to 2nd landing 8.20€ adults, 6.60€ ages 12–24, 4.10€ ages 4–11; admission to 3rd landing 13€ adults, 12€ ages 12–24, 9.30€ ages 4–11; admission for stairs to 2nd floor 4.70€ adults, 3.70€ ages 12–24, 3.20€ ages 4–11. Free admission for children 3 and under. Sept–May daily 9:30am–11:45pm; June–Aug daily 9am–12:45am. Sept–June stairs open only to 6:30pm. Métro: Trocadéro, Ecole Militaire, or Bir Hakeim. RER: Champ de Mars–Tour Eiffel.

ORGANIZED TOURS

BY BUS   Cityrama, 149 rue St-Honoré, 1er (www.pariscityrama.com; © **01-44-55-61-00;** Métro: Louvre-Rivoli), offers a 1½-hour ride through the city on a double-decker bus with enough windows for Versailles. While you don't go inside any attractions, you get a look at the outside of Notre-Dame and the Eiffel Tower, among other sites, and a good feel for the city. Earphones provide commentary in 16 languages. Tours depart daily at 10am, 11:30am, 1pm, and 2:30pm, and cost 22€ adults and 10€ children. A morning tour with interior visits to the Louvre costs 44€. Half-day tours to Versailles are 64€, or 63€ to Chartres. A joint ticket that includes Versailles and Chartres costs 110€. A tour of the nighttime illuminations leaves daily at 10pm in summer, 7pm in winter, and costs 30€; it tends to be tame and touristy.

The **RATP** (www.ratp.fr; ✆ **08-92-68-77-14**), which runs regular public transportation, also offers tours on the **Balabus,** a fleet of orange-and-white big-windowed motorcoaches. For information, see "Getting Around," earlier in this chapter.

BY BOAT Bateaux-Mouche (www.bateaux-mouches.fr; ✆ **01-42-25-96-10;** Métro: Alma-Marceau) cruises depart from the Right Bank of the Seine, adjacent to Pont de l'Alma, and last about 75 minutes. Tours leave daily at 20-minute intervals from 10:15am to 11pm between April and September. Between October and March, there are at least five departures daily between 11am and 9pm, with a schedule that changes according to demand and the weather. Fares are 10€ for adults and 5€ for children 4 to 13. Dinner cruises depart daily at 8:30pm, last 2 hours, and cost 95€ to 135€. On dinner cruises, jackets and ties are required for men. There are also lunch cruises Saturday and Sunday departing at 1pm, costing 50€ for adults, 25€ for kids 11 and under.

Batobus (www.batobus.com; ✆ **08-25-05-01-01**) operates 150-passenger ferries with big windows. See "Getting Around," earlier in this chapter, for information.

Where to Eat

Although Paris has long been home to high-end gourmet restaurants, a growing number of affordable, high-end bistros serving gourmet food have entered Paris's culinary scene. For more than a decade now, chefs who have trained under three-star chefs have been leaving these "palace" restaurants to open more reasonably priced neo-bistros, where you can get a three-course meal for about 30€ to 40€. Combining classic technique with an emphasis on fresh, seasonal ingredients, this new generation of chefs is revitalizing the culinary scene.

One important challenge remains, even at the informal bistro level: Getting in. Paris restaurants tend to be small in size, and they rarely offer multiple seatings during a lunch or dinner service. The result is a smaller number of available seats, and these are often reserved in advance. Reservations are a very good idea at most of the restaurants we recommend, but you needn't worry about booking weeks in advance. The majority will have space if you call the same day or a few days in advance. Ask your hotel concierge to help if you can't manage the telephone, but don't shy away from this step if food is an important part of your Paris visit. The quality of what you can "stumble in" and find, versus what you can experience when you reserve, is radically different.

LES HALLES, LOUVRE & PALAIS ROYAL (1ER & 2E)
Very Expensive
Le Grand Véfour TRADITIONAL FRENCH   Tucked inside the Palais Royal and boasting one of the most beautiful restaurant interiors in Paris, Le Grand Véfour remains a history-infused citadel of classic French cuisine. This restaurant has been around since the reign of Louis XV. Napoleon, Danton, Hugo, Colette, and Cocteau dined here—as the brass plaques on the tables testify—and it's still a gastronomic experience. Guy Martin, chef for the past decade, continues to serve the restaurant's

signature dishes like Prince Ranier III pigeon and truffled oxtail parmentier alongside new dishes that feature more contemporary flavors like yuzu and tonka bean. Other specialties are noisettes of lamb with star anise, Breton lobster with fennel, and cabbage sorbet in dark-chocolate sauce. The desserts are always grand, such as the *gourmandises au chocolat* (medley of chocolate), served with chocolate sorbet.

17 rue de Beaujolais, 1er. www.grand-vefour.com. ✆ **01-42-96-56-27.** Reservations required far in advance. Main courses 75€–125€; fixed-price lunch 96€; fixed-price dinner 282€. AE, DC, MC, V. Mon–Fri 12:30–1:45pm and 8–9:30pm. Closed Aug 2–30. Métro: Louvre–Palais-Royal or Pyramides.

Expensive
Passage 53 ★★ MODERN FRENCH   After a stint at L'Astrance (p. 291), chef Shinichi Sato joined forces with famous butcher Hugo Desnoyer to open this petite restaurant inside the city's oldest covered passage. His cuisine has been so successful that it earned the restaurant two Michelin stars in 2011. Start with a splash of Champagne Jacquesson before diving into a tasting menu that might begin with pink cubes of raw veal topped with a bracing and briny raw oyster. Up next, you might be served some pristine fish or a *civet* (a type of stew) of wild hare served with chocolate sauce. Flavors are bold and clear, and the technical skill on display is impressive. End the meal with a delicious tart with the thinnest-possible pastry crust.

53 passage des Panoramas, 2e. www.passage53.com. ✆ **01-42-33-04-35.** Reservations recommended. Fixed-price lunch 60€; fixed-price dinner 110€. MC, V. Tues–Sat noon–2:30pm and 7–10pm. Métro: Grands Boulevards.

Moderate
Le Fumoir ★★ CONTEMPORARY FRENCH   With views onto the Louvre's eastern edge, this chic colonial-style restaurant, with a zinc bar and leather chesterfield armchairs, is a plum spot for escaping the tourists. Cocktails and coffee are served throughout the day, and at mealtimes inventive, affordable dishes are served to swarms of those in the know. The menu might include a starter of beef marinated in port wine, turnips, and salmon roe (an unsual combination, but it works); followed by pan-roasted cod with citrus and rosemary crust; and for dessert, blood-orange ricepudding. The 24€ Sunday brunch menu is popular too: fruit juice, hot drinks, pancakes, poached eggs, and smoked ham or a juicy French steak with fries are on offer—and of course, there are those chesterfields for slumping into.

6 rue de l'Amiral Coligny, 1e. http://lefumoir.com. ✆ **01-42-92-00-24.** Reservations recommended. Main courses 20€–25€; 3-course fixed-price menu 35€. AE, DC, MC, V. Daily 11am–2am. Métro: Louvre–Rivoli.

Inexpensive
Le Garde Robe FRENCH/WINE BAR   In a quaint side-street off rue de Rivoli in Châtelet, Le Garde Robe is a tiny wine bar with exposed stone walls and wine bottles lining the walls. Fans of French wine come for the large selection of organic and biodynamic wines, which you can buy to take away; or if you decide to stay (which you will) corkage is 7€ extra. A laidback, suited crowd usually rolls up to the bar after work for a glass of red or white, accompanied by a *petit chèvre au pesto* (creamy goat's cheese with pesto) or the excellent *croque robe* (a house take on traditional French *croque monsieur,* with cheese, ham, and salad). For extra comfort (the bar stools can be awkward), reserve one of the tables in the back, then relax and enjoy the buzzy atmosphere.

41 rue de l'Arbre Sec, 1er. ✆ **01-49-26-90-60.** Reservations recommended. Main courses 10€–16€; MC, V. Mon–Sat 7:30–11pm; Métro: Louvre Rivoli or Châtelet.

RIGHT BANK: LE MARAIS, ILE ST LOUIS & ILE DE LA CITÉ (3E & 4E)

Inexpensive

Breizh Café ★ 🌶 CRÊPERIE/CAFÉ This popular spot in the Marais serves crepes like you've never had them before. Run by a Breton–Japanese couple, this warm and modern wood-paneled space that is decorated with funky Japanese art has friendly service and quality food. Start with oysters or go straight to a savory buckwheat *galette,* which is crisp and nutty and filled with high-quality organic ingredients, such as farm-fresh eggs, Bordier butter, and seasonal produce. Sip on one of the artisan ciders, and save room for a sweet crepe, drizzled with chocolate or salted butter caramel. Reservations highly recommended.

109 rue Vieille du Temple, 3e. www.breizhcafe.com. ⓒ **01-42-72-13-77.** Reservations recommended. Main courses 5.50€–11€. MC, V. Wed–Sat noon–11pm; Sun noon–10pm. Métro: Filles du Calvaire.

Le Potager du Marais ★ VEGETARIAN Arguably the best vegetarian restaurant in Paris, vegetarians flock to this place for its range of delicious organic offerings. Dishes are so tasty, even meat eaters won't complain. Many items are gluten-free. Your veggie meal might start with mushroom pâté, followed by tofu and pumpkin parmentier (pumpkin baked with mashed potato) seasoned with herbs and lentils, and finished with homemade apple compote. Just be prepared to get friendly with your neighbors: the restaurant is so narrow that the tables are packed in like sardines along just one wall.

22 rue Rambuteau, 3e. www.lepotagerdumarais.com. ⓒ **01-42-74-24-66.** Entrees 9€–16€. MC, V. Daily noon–2pm and 7–10:30pm. Métro: Rambuteau.

RIGHT BANK: CHAMPS ELYSÉES & WESTERN PARIS (8E, 16E & 17E)

Very Expensive

Pierre Gagnaire ★★★ MODERN FRENCH Of all the three-star chefs working in Paris today, Gagnaire is by far the most playful and experimental. He spent years collaborating with molecular gastronomy pioneer Hervé This to create boundary-pushing dishes with unusual textures and forms. The menu changes regularly, but recent meals have featured lobster hidden under brightly colored blankets of vegetable gel, and raw clams on a bed of sweet and sour pumpkin. One tip if you plan to order a la carte: each *plat* is actually made up of four to five small dishes, so ordering both a starter and a main dish may yield more food than you could possibly eat. Perhaps it's not a bad thing that the desserts here are not as strong as you'll find at other three-star restaurants.

6 rue Balzac, 8e. www.pierre-gagnaire.com. ⓒ **01-58-36-12-50.** Fax 01-58-36-12-51. Reservations required. Main courses 65€–165€; fixed-price lunch 105€; fixed-price dinner 265€. AE, DC, MC, V. Mon–Fri noon–1:30pm; Sun–Fri 7:30–10pm. Métro: George V.

Restaurant Plaza Athénée (Alain Ducasse) ★★ TRADITIONAL FRENCH This three-star restaurant bears the name of internationally renowned chef Alain Ducasse and serves as the flagship of his restaurant empire. The globe-trotting chef is rarely here himself, but he has left his kitchen in the capable hands of Christophe Saintagne. A special emphasis is placed on "rare and precious ingredients"—the chef whips up flavorful and very expensive combinations of caviar, lobster, crayfish, and truffles (both black and white). Dishes may include sea scallops with salsify and black truffles, duck liver "pot au feu," or sole meunière with Belgian endives. The wine list is superb, with selections deriving from the best vintages of France, Germany, Switzerland, Spain, California, and Italy. The dining room, designed by Patrick Jouin and featuring a jaw-dropping "deconstructed" chandelier, is among the most beautiful in Paris.

In the Hôtel Plaza Athénée, 25 av. Montaigne, 8e. www.alain-ducasse.com. ✆ **01-53-67-65-00.** Fax 01-53-67-65-12. Reservations required 4–6 weeks in advance. Main courses 90€–180€; fixed-price menu 260€–360€. AE, DC, MC, V. Thurs–Fri 12:45–2:15pm; Mon–Fri 7:45–10:15pm. Closed mid-July to Aug 25 and 10 days in late Dec. Métro: Alma-Marceau.

Expensive

L'Astrance ★★★ MODERN FRENCH   This small and charming spot is owned by two former employees (some say "disciples") of megachef Alain Passard, scion of L'Arpège; Christophe Rohat supervises the dining room, while Pascal Barbot is a true culinary force in the kitchen. The menu changes seasonally, but might include an unusual form of "ravioli," wherein thin slices of avocado encase a filling of seasoned crabmeat, all of it accompanied by salted almonds and a splash of almond oil. Other delights to the palate include turbot flavored with lemon and ginger, or sautéed pigeon with potatoes au gratin. The signature dish is a galette of thinly sliced raw mushrooms and verjus-marinated foie gras with hazelnut oil and lemon confit.

4 rue Beethoven, 16e. ✆ **01-40-50-84-40.** Reservations required at least one month in advance. Main courses 24€–80€; fixed-price lunch 70€–120€; fixed-price dinner 125€–290€. AE, DC, MC, V. Tues–Fri 12:15–1:30pm and 8:15–9pm. Closed Aug. Métro: Passy.

Moderate

Le Hide ★ 🏛 TRADITIONAL FRENCH   This bistro near the Eiffel Tower takes its name from chef Hide Kobayashi, who describes his food as French bistro cooking. The cuisine is certainly French, but a few of the recipes hint at his Japanese origins. Kobayashi perfected his craft in the kitchens of some of the world's greatest chefs, including Joël Robuchon. The menu changes regularly, and main courses, like fricassee of rabbit flavored with mustard or sweetbreads in cream with truffles, all carry the same price tag. In a neighborhood full of expensive and unmemorable restaurants, Le Hide is one of the best options for well-executed French bistro cuisine at an affordable price.

10 rue du General Lanrezac, 17e. www.lehide.fr. ✆ **01-45-74-15-81.** Reservations required. Main courses 16€; fixed-price menu 23€–30€. MC, V. Mon–Fri noon–3pm and Mon–Sat 7–10:30pm. Métro: Charles-de-Gaulle–Etoile.

RIGHT BANK: 9TH, 10TH & 12TH ARRONDISSEMENTS

Moderate

Le Pantruche ★ 🏛 TRADITIONAL FRENCH/BISTRO   From the moment it opened in early 2011, this modern bistro not far from Pigalle impressed critics with its friendly atmosphere, affordable prices, and better-than-average bistro fare. Dishes include a rich celery root soup, tender glazed beef cheeks, oyster tartare, and a classic Grand Marnier soufflé. Although it's dressed like a humble neighborhood joint, Franck Baranger's cooking puts Le Pantruche in another league altogether.

3 rue Victor Massé, 9e. http://lepantruche.com. ✆ **01-48-78-55-60.** Reservations recommended. Fixed-price dinner 32€; fixed-price lunch 17€. Mon–Fri noon–2:30pm and 7:15–10:30pm. Métro: Pigalle.

Inexpensive

Chartier ★ TRADITIONAL FRENCH/BRASSERIE   Opened in 1896, this unpretentious *fin-de-siècle* restaurant is now an official historic monument featuring a whimsical mural with trees, a flowering staircase, and an early depiction of an air-plane (it was painted in 1929 by an artist who traded his work for food). The menu follows brasserie-style traditions, including items you might not dare to eat—beef tartare, chitterling sausages, tongue of beef with spicy sauce—as well as some classic temptations, like duck confit. The waiter will steer you through such dishes as *choucroute* (sauerkraut), *pavé* (a thick slice of rump steak), and at least five kinds of fish. High gastronomy this isn't, but you can't beat Chartier for a cheerful night on the cheap. Arrive as early as possible to avoid the queues.

7 rue du Faubourg Montmartre, 9e. www.restaurant-chartier.com. ℂ **01-47-70-86-29.** Main courses 9€–12€. AE, DC, MC, V. Daily 11:30am–10pm. Métro: Grands-Boulevards.

LEFT BANK: LATIN QUARTER (5E & 13E)
Moderate

Bouillon Racine ★ BISTRO/BRASSERIE   This jewel-box dining room is the best example of baroque Art Nouveau in Paris—a magnificent affair of swirling iron and woodwork, with twinkling stained glass, mirrors, and tiles. The excellent brasserie fare might include carpaccio of beef with basil, lemon, and Parmesan; scallop risotto; or chicken blanquette. If you've got a sweet tooth, the crème-brûlée flavored with maple syrup is delicious. The two-course lunch menu offered Monday to Friday is a steal at just 15€.

3 rue Racine, 6e. www.bouillon-racine.com.ℂ **01-44-32-15-60.** Mains 15€–23€; fixed-price dinner 30€ and 41€; fixed-price lunch 15€. MC, V. Daily noon–11pm. Métro: Odéon.

Le Pré Verre ★ 🍴 MODERN FRENCH/ASIAN FUSION   Around the corner from the Sorbonne in the heart of the Latin Quarter sits a refreshing restaurant where you can get seriously good food at an affordable price. The Delacourcelle brothers are firmly based in the French tradition but many of their chosen flavorings are inspired by Asia (they've got a second Pré Verre in Tokyo). In a welcoming, relaxed, and convivial atmosphere, tables are placed so close together that you're literally dining and rubbing elbows with your neighbors. For starters, dig into a well-flavored terrine—like the one made with layers of foie gras and mashed potatoes—or oysters marinated with ginger and poppy seeds or scallops with cinnamon. Main courses might include suckling pig with aromatic spices and crisp-cooked cabbage, or roasted codfish.

8 rue Thenard, 5e. www.lepreverre.com.ℂ **01-43-54-59-47.** Reservations required. Main courses 18€; fixed-price lunch 13€–29€; fixed-price dinner 39€. MC, V. Tues–Sat noon–2pm and 7:30–10:30pm. Closed Aug. Métro: Maubert-Mutualité.

LEFT BANK: ST-GERMAIN-DES-PRÈS & LUXEMBOURG (6E)
Expensive

Le Comptoir du Relais ★★ TRADITIONAL FRENCH/BISTRO   Le Comptoir is the domain of Yves Camdeborde, the pioneering chef who kicked off the bistronomy movement, serving high-caliber food in a casual bistro setting, when he left a three-star kitchen to open his own bistro at the edge of the city. He sold La Régalade (which remains good) years ago to open this "counter," serving guests of the attached hotel and foodies who book dinner months and months in advance. Lunch is an easier table to score because reservations are not accepted—just line up before the doors open at noon and you're likely to get a table. All this fuss can be attributed to Camdeborde's well-executed bistro cuisine that reflects his southwestern roots and is made from high-quality ingredients. The menu changes regularly—it's comfort food with a touch of luxury, and it will spoil you for all subsequent bistros.

9 carrefour de l'Odéon, 6e. www.hotel-paris-relais-saint-germain.com.ℂ **01-44-27-07-97.** Reservations required several weeks in advance. Main courses weekends 27€–35€; fixed-price dinner weeknights 50€. MC, V. Daily noon–2am. Métro: Odéon.

Inexpensive

La Crémerie Restaurant Polidor ☺ TRADITIONAL FRENCH/BISTRO
Crémerie Polidor is the most traditional (and heavily touristed) bistro in the Odéon area, serving *cuisine familiale*. Its name dates from the early 1900s, when it specialized in frosted cream desserts, but the restaurant can trace its history from 1845. The Crémerie was André Gide's favorite, and Joyce, Hemingway, Valéry, Artaud, and Kerouac also dined here. Peer beyond the lace curtains and brass hat racks to see drawers where, in olden days, regular customers used to lock up their cloth napkins. Try the day's soup followed by kidneys in Madeira sauce, *boeuf bourguignon* (beef braised in red wine), *confit de canard* (leg of duck), or *blanquette de veau* (veal ragout in cream sauce). For dessert, order a chocolate, raspberry, or lemon tart.

39 rue Monsieur-le-Prince, 6e. www.polidor.com. ✆ **01-43-26-95-34.** Main courses 12€–20€; fixed-price menu 22€–32€. No credit cards. Daily noon–2:30pm; Mon–Sat 7pm–12:30am; Sun 7–11pm. Métro: Odéon.

LEFT BANK: EIFFEL TOWER & NEARBY (7E)
Expensive

L'Atelier Saint-Germain de Joël Robuchon ★★ MODERN FRENCH
World-renowned Chef Joël Robuchon came out of a short-lived retirement in 2003 in order to open this ground-breaking culinary workshop on the left bank. He recently added the words "Saint-Germain" when he opened a second Atelier near the Arc de Triomphe. This original location remains packed with gastronomes who want to eat well without the fuss implied by a three-star restaurant. Sitting informally upon high stools at a U-shaped bar, you can order the tasting menu or a series of sharable small plates including sea bream carpaccio, caviar with smoked eel and horseradish, grilled marrow bones, and the famous Robuchon mashed potatoes. Reservations are accepted for the extremely early and late seatings only (at 11:30am and 2pm for lunch, and 6:30pm for dinner); these spots are booked well in advance. Otherwise, it's first come, first served.

5 rue Montalembert, 7e. www.joel-robuchon.net. ✆ **01-42-22-56-56.** Reservations required. Main courses 28€–75€; dinner tasting menu 150€. AE, MC, V. Daily 11:30am–3:30pm, 6:30pm–midnight. Métro: Rue du Bac.

Restaurant Auguste ★★ TRADITIONAL FRENCH/SEAFOOD Right by the Assemblée Nationale (the seat of French government along with the Senat), chef Gael Orieux's red and white contemporary eatery is coveted by politians—a handy clientele for this young chef, whose love of the sea has led him to represent "Mr Good Fish," a European association dedicated to protecting the oceans. Serving some of the best seafood in town, Orieux's meals might include red mullet with Thai condiments; scallops with creamy risotto; and oysters in horseradish mousse. But there are also meat dishes, with fabulous preparations like celtic duck with caramelized citrus fruits, and *ris de veau* (veal sweetbreads) with oyster mushrooms and apricots. For dessert, delicacies like pistachio soufflé finish everything off perfectly.

54 rue de Bourgogne, 7e. www.restaurantauguste.fr. ✆ **01-45-51-61-09.** Reservations required. Main courses 30€–48€; fixed-price lunch 35€; fixed-price dinner 80€. MC, V. Daily noon–2:30pm and 7–10:30pm. Métro: Assemblée Nationale.

LEFT BANK: MONTPARNASSE & SOUTHERN PARIS (13E, 14E & 15E)
Expensive

Le Casse Noix ★ ⓘ TRADITIONAL FRENCH/BISTRO After cooking for six years at La Régalade (p. 292), Chef Pierre-Olivier Lenormand opened his own

THE top CAFES

Whatever your pleasure—reading, meeting a lover, writing your memoirs, nibbling a hard-boiled egg, or drinking yourself into oblivion—you can do it at a French cafe.

Jean-Paul Sartre came to **Café de Flore,** 172 bd. St-Germain, 6e (www.cafe-de-flore.com; ✆ **01-45-48-55-26;** Métro: St-Germain-des-Prés), where it's said he wrote his trilogy *Les Chemins de la Liberté (The Roads to Freedom)*. The cafe is still going strong, though celebrities have moved on. Open daily from 7:30am to 1:30am.

Next door, the legendary **Deux Magots,** 6 place St-Germain-des-Prés, 6e (www.lesdeuxmagots.fr; ✆ **01-45-48-55-25;** Métro: St-Germain-des-Prés), is still the hangout for sophisticated residents and a tourist favorite in summer. Inside are two Asian statues that give the cafe its name. It's open daily from 7:30am to 1am.

In the Marais, **La Belle Hortense,** 31 rue Vieille du Temple, 4e (✆ **01-48-04-71-60;** Métro: Hôtel de Ville or St-Paul), is the most literary cafe in a legendary literary neighborhood. It offers an erudite and accessible staff; an inventory of French literary classics as well as modern tomes about art, psychoanalysis, history, and culture; and two high-ceilinged, 19th-century rooms little changed since the days of Baudelaire and Balzac. The zinc-covered bar serves wine for 3€ to 9€ a glass. Open daily as a cafe and bookstore from 5pm to 2am.

To fans of French history, **Le Procope,** 13 rue de l'Ancienne-Comédie, 6e (www.procope.com; ✆ **01-40-46-79-00;** Métro: Odéon), is the holy grail of Parisian cafes. Opened in 1686, it has nine salons and dining rooms, each of whose 300-year-old walls have been carefully preserved and painted a deep red, and are available for languorous afternoon coffee breaks or old-fashioned meals. Especially charming is the ground-floor room outfitted like an antique library. It's open from 11:30am to 1am daily.

Amélie was a quirky low-budget film that was set in Montmartre. In the film, Amélie worked as a waitress at the **Café des Deux Moulins,** 15 rue Lepic, 18e (✆ **01-42-54-90-50;** Métro: Blanche). The musty atmosphere, with its 1950s decor, mustard-colored ceiling, and lace curtains, has been preserved—even the wall lamps and unisex toilet. It's open daily from 7am to 2am.

bistro—a place that serves high-caliber food in a casual setting—in 2010. The decor is nostalgic and the traditional French cooking is sincere and generous. Dishes like smoked chestnut soup, Iberian pork belly with choucroute of turnips, and the classic *petit salé aux lentilles* (lentils with smoky ham) are followed by crowd-pleasing desserts such as *île flottante* ("floating island," a meringue floating on custard). The wine list includes a good selection by the glass as well as many moderately priced bottles. This is a good option if you're looking for an affordable, traditional bistro that's not yet overrun with tourists.

56 rue de la Fédération, 15e. www.le-cassenoix.fr. ✆ **01-45-66-09-01.** Reservations recommended. Fixed-price dinner 32€; fixed-price lunch 25€. Mon–Fri noon–2:30pm and 7:30–10:30pm. Métro: Dupleix.

Shopping

Shopping is the local pastime. The City of Light is one of the rare places in the world where shopping surrounds you on almost every street. The windows, stores, and people (and even their dogs) brim with energy, creativity, and a sense of expression. You don't have to buy anything, just peer in the *vitrines* (display windows), absorb cutting-edge ideas, witness new trends, and take home an education in style.

Shops are usually open Monday to Saturday from 9:30 or 10am to 8pm, but hours vary, and Paris doesn't run at full throttle on Monday morning. Small shops sometimes take a 2-hour lunch break and may not open until after lunch on Monday. While most stores open at 10am, some open at 9:30am or even 11am. Thursday is the best day for late-night shopping, with stores open until 9 or 10pm.

THE BEST BUYS

Perfumes and **cosmetics,** including such famous brands as Guerlain, Chanel, Schiaparelli, and Jean Patou, are almost always cheaper in Paris than in the United States. Paris is also a good place to buy Lalique and Baccarat **crystal.** They're expensive but still priced below international market value.

From Chanel to Yves Saint Laurent, Nina Ricci to Sonia Rykiel, the city overflows with **fashion** boutiques, ranging from haute couture to the truly outlandish. Accessories, such as those by Louis Vuitton and Céline, are among the finest in the world.

Lingerie is another great French export. All the top lingerie designers are represented in boutiques as well as in the major department stores, Galeries Lafayette and Le Printemps.

Chocolate lovers will find much to tempt them in Paris. **Christian Constant,** 37 rue d'Assas, 6e (www.christianconstant.com; ✆ **01-53-63-15-15;** Métro: St-Placide), produces some of Paris's most sinfully delicious chocolates.

SHOPPING BY AREA

1ER & 8E These two *quartiers* adjoin each other and form the heart of Paris's best Right Bank shopping neighborhood. This area includes the famed **Rue du Faubourg St-Honoré,** with the big designer houses, and **Avenue des Champs-Elysées,** where the mass-market and teen scenes are hot. At one end of the 1er is the **Palais Royal**—one of the city's best-kept shopping secrets, where an arcade of boutiques flanks the garden of the former palace.

On the other side of town, at the end of the 8e, is **Avenue Montaigne,** two blocks of the fanciest shops in the world, where you float from one big name to another.

2E Behind the Palais Royal lies the **Garment District (Sentier)** and a few upscale shopping secrets such as **Place des Victoires.** This area also holds a few *passages,* such as **Galerie Vivienne** on Rue Vivienne, alleys filled with tiny stores.

3E & 4E The difference between these two arrondissements gets fuzzy, especially around **Place des Vosges,** center stage of the Marais. Even so, they offer several dramatically different shopping experiences.

On the surface, the shopping includes the real-people stretch of **Rue de Rivoli** (which becomes **Rue St-Antoine**). **BHV** (Bazar de l'Hôtel de Ville), which opened in 1856, is the major department store in this area; it has seven floors and lies adjacent to Paris's City Hall at 52–64 rue de Rivoli (www.bhv.fr; ✆ **01-42-74-90-00**). Many shoppers will also be looking for La Samaritaine, 19 rue de la Monnaie, once the most famous department store in France. It occupied four noteworthy buildings erected between 1870 and 1927. These buildings have been sold and are undergoing renovation to be completed in 2012. The new owner has not made his intentions clear about the future of this Parisian landmark.

Hidden in the **Marais** is a medieval warren of tiny, twisting streets chockablock with cutting-edge designers and up-to-the-minute fashions and trends. Start by walking around place des Vosges to see galleries, designer shops, and fabulous finds.

Finally, the 4e is also home of **La Bastille,** an up-and-coming area for artists and galleries where you'll find the newest entry on the retail scene, the **Viaduc des Arts** (which stretches into the 12e).

6E & 7E   Whereas the 6e is one of the most famous shopping districts in Paris—it's the soul of the Left Bank—much of the good stuff is hidden in the zone that becomes the wealthy residential 7e. **Rue du Bac,** stretching from the 6e to the 7e in a few blocks, stands for all that wealth and glamour can buy. The street is jammed with art galleries, home-decor stores, and gourmet food shops.

9E   To add to the fun of shopping the Right Bank, the 9e sneaks in behind the 1er, so if you choose not to walk toward the Champs-Elysées and the 8e, you can head to the big department stores in a row along **Boulevard Haussmann** in the 9e. Here you'll find the two big French icons, **Au Printemps** and **Galeries Lafayette.**

Entertainment & Nightlife
THE PERFORMING ARTS

Announcements of shows, concerts, and operas are on kiosks all over town. You can find listings in *Pariscope,* a weekly entertainment guide, and in the English-language *Boulevard,* a bimonthly magazine.

There are many ticket agencies in Paris, mostly near the Right Bank hotels. *Avoid them if possible.* You can buy the cheapest tickets at the theater box office. Tip the usher who shows you to your seat in a theater or movie house.

Several agencies sell tickets for cultural events and plays at discounts of up to 50%. One is the **Kiosque Théâtre,** 15 place de la Madeleine, 8e (www.kiosquetheatre. com; ✆ **01-42-65-35-64;** Métro: Madeleine), offering day-of-performance tickets for about half price (average price is 20€). Tickets for evening performances and matinees are sold Tuesday to Saturday 12:30 to 8pm, Sunday 12:30 to 4pm.

For easy access to tickets for festivals, concerts, and the theater, try one of two locations of the **FNAC** electronics-store chain: 136 rue de Rennes, 6e (✆ **08-25-02-00-02;** Métro: St. Placide); and 1–7 rue Pierre-Lescot, in the Forum des Halles, 1er (✆ **08-25-02-00-20;** Métro: Châtelet–Les Halles).

Even those with only a modest understanding of French can delight in a sparkling production of Molière at the **Comédie-Française,** 2 rue de Richelieu, 1er (www. comedie-francaise.fr; ✆ **08-25-10-16-80;** Métro: Palais-Royal–Musée du Louvre), established to keep the classics alive and to promote important contemporary authors. The box office is open daily from 11am to 6pm; the hall is dark from July 21 to September 5. The Left Bank annex is the **Comédie-Française-Théâtre du Vieux-Colombier,** 21 rue du Vieux-Colombier, 4e (✆ **01-44-39-87-00;** Métro: Sèvres-Babylone or Saint-Sulpice). Although its repertoire can vary, it's known for presenting some of the most serious French dramas in town.

The controversial building known as the **Opéra Bastille ★★★**, place de la Bastille, 120 rue de Lyon (www.operadeparis.fr; ✆ **08-92-89-90-90** or **01-40-01-17-89;** Métro: Bastille), was inaugurated in July 1989 (for the Revolution's bicentennial), and on March 17, 1990, the curtain rose on Hector Berlioz's *Les Troyens.* Since its much-publicized opening, the opera house has presented works such as Mozart's *Marriage of Figaro* and Tchaikovsky's *Queen of Spades.* The main hall is the largest

French opera house, with 2,700 seats, but music critics have lambasted the acoustics. The building contains two additional concert halls, including an intimate room seating 250, usually used for chamber music. Both traditional opera performances and symphony concerts are presented here. Call to find out about occasional free concerts on French holidays.

Opéra Garnier ★★★, place de l'Opéra, 9e (www.operadeparis.fr; ℂ **08-92-89-90-90;** Métro: Opéra), is the premier stage for dance and opera. Because of competition from the Opéra Bastille, the original opera has made great efforts to present more up-to-date works, including choreography by Jerome Robbins, Twyla Tharp, and George Balanchine. The architect Charles Garnier designed this rococo wonder in the heyday of the empire. The facade is adorned with marble and sculpture, including *The Dance* by Carpeaux. Restoration has returned the Garnier to its former glory: Its boxes and walls are lined with flowing red and blue damask, the ceiling (painted by Marc Chagall) has been cleaned, and air-conditioning has been added. The box office is open Monday to Saturday 10:30am to 6:30pm.

At the city's northeastern edge in what used to be a run-down neighborhood, **Cité de la Musique ★★★**, 221 av. Jean-Jaurès, 19e (www.cite-musique.fr; ℂ **01-44-84-45-00,** or **01-44-84-44-84** for tickets and information; Métro: Porte-de-Pantin), has been widely applauded. The $120-million stone-and-glass structure, designed by Christian de Portzamparc, incorporates a network of concert halls, a library and research center, and a museum. The complex stages a variety of concerts, ranging from Renaissance to 20th-century programs.

New York has its Carnegie Hall, but for years Paris lacked a permanent home for its orchestra. That is, until 2006, when the restored **Salle Pleyel ★★★**, 252 rue du Faubourg-St-Honoré, 8e (www.sallepleyel.fr; ℂ **01-42-56-13-13;** Métro: Miromesnil), opened once again. Built in 1927 by the piano-making firm of the same name, Pleyel was the world's first concert hall designed exclusively for a symphony orchestra. Ravel, Debussy, and Stravinsky performed their masterpieces here, only to see the hall devastated by fire less than 9 months after its opening. The original sound quality was never recovered because of an economic downturn. In 1998, real-estate developer Hubert Martigny purchased the concert hall, restoring the Art Deco spirit of the original and also refining the acoustics it once knew. Nearly 500 seats were removed to make those that remained more comfortable. The Orchestre Philharmonique de Radio France and the Orchestre de Paris now have a home worthy of their reputations, and the London Symphony Orchestra makes Pleyel its venue in Paris. Tickets range from 10€ to 145€, and seniors and young people 26 and under can arrive an hour before a concert and fill any available seat for just 10€. Reservations are made by phone Monday to Saturday 11am to 7pm.

CABARETS

The **Folies-Bergère,** 32 rue Richer, 9e (www.foliesbergere.com; ℂ **01-44-79-98-60** or **08-92-68-16-50;** Métro: Grands Boulevards or Cadet), has been an institution since 1869. Josephine Baker, the African–American singer who danced in a banana skirt and threw bananas into the audience, became "the toast of Paris" here. According to legend, the first GI to reach Paris at the 1944 Liberation asked for directions to the club. Don't expect the naughty and slyly permissive, skin-and-glitter revue that used to be the trademark of this place. In 1993, that all ended with a radical restoration of the theater and a reopening under new management. Today, it's a conventional 1,600-seat theater devoted to a frequently changing roster of big-stage performances in French, many of which are adaptations of Broadway blockbusters. Shows are usually given Tuesday to Saturday at 9pm and Sunday at 3pm. Tickets cost 25€ to 84€.

The **Moulin Rouge,** 82 boulevard de Clichy, Place Blanche, 18e (www.moulin rouge.fr; ✆ **01-53-09-82-82;** Métro: Blanche), is a camp classic. The establishment that Toulouse-Lautrec immortalized is still here, but the artist would probably have a hard time recognizing it. Try to get a table; the view is much better on the main floor than from the bar. What's the theme? Strip routines and the saucy sexiness of *la Belle Epoque.* Handsome men and girls, girls, girls, virtually all topless, keep the place going. Revues begin nightly at 9 and 11pm. Cover including a 7pm dinner and show costs 175€ to 200€.

LIVE MUSIC & DANCING

JAZZ The great jazz revival that long ago swept America is still going strong here, with Dixieland or Chicago rhythms pounding out in dozens of jazz cellars, mostly called *caveaux.* Most clubs are on the Left Bank near the Seine, between rue Bonaparte and rue St-Jacques.

It's hard to say which is more intriguing at **Caveau des Oubliettes ★**, 52 rue Galande, 5e (www.caveaudesoubliettes.fr; ✆ **01-46-34-23-09;** Métro: St-Michel)— the entertainment and drinking or the setting. An *oubliette* is a dungeon with a trapdoor at the top as its only opening, and the name is accurate. Located in the Latin Quarter, just across the river from Notre-Dame, this nightspot is housed in a genuine 12th-century prison, complete with dungeons, spine-tingling passages, and scattered skulls, where prisoners were tortured and sometimes pushed through portholes to drown in the Seine. Today patrons laugh, drink, talk, and flirt in the narrow *caveau,* or else retreat to the smoke-filled jazz lounge. There's a free jam session every night, perhaps Latin jazz or rock. At some point on Friday and Saturday nights concerts are staged and a 15€ cover is charged. It's open daily 5pm to 2am.

DANCE CLUBS The area around the Eglise St-Germain-des-Prés is full of dance clubs. **Batofar ★**, facing 11 quai François Mauriac, 13e (www.batofar.org; ✆ **01-53-14-76-59;** Métro: Quai de la Gare), sits on a converted barge that floats on the Seine, sometimes attracting hundreds of dancers, most of whom are in their 20s and 30s, gyrating to house, garage, techno, and live jazz by groups that hail from (among other places) Morocco, Senegal, and Germany. The cover ranges from 10€ to 14€. It's open Tuesday to Saturday 10pm to 6am; closed November to March.

LGBT SCENE Gay life is centered on **Les Halles** and **Le Marais,** with the greatest concentration of gay and lesbian clubs, restaurants, bars, and shops between the Hôtel de Ville and Rambuteau Métro stops. Gay dance clubs come and go so fast that even the magazines devoted to them, such as *Illico*—distributed free in the gay bars and bookstores—have a hard time keeping up. For lesbians, there is *Lesbian Magazine.* Also look for Gai Pied's *Guide Gai* and *Pariscope*'s regularly featured English-language section, "A Week of Gay Outings." Also important for both men and women is *Têtu Magazine,* sold at most newsstands.

Although **Open Café/Café Cox,** 15 rue des Archives, 4e (www.cox.fr; ✆ **01-42-72-26-18** or **01-42-72-08-00;** Métro: Hôtel de Ville), are independent, the clientele of these side-by-side gay men's bars is so interconnected, and there's such traffic between them, that we—like many other residents of this neighborhood—usually jumble them together. Both define themselves as bars rather than dance clubs, but on particularly busy nights, one couple or another might actually begin to dance. Open Sunday to Thursday 11am to 2am, Friday and Saturday to 4am.

This is the best-known lesbian bar in the Marais: **Le 3w Kafe,** 8 rue des Ecouffes, 4e (𝒞 **01-48-87-39-26**. Métro: St. Paul). The 3w means "Woman with Woman." Straight men are welcome too, if accompanied by a woman. Gay men are admitted without problem. Open Wednesday to Sunday 5pm to 2am, Friday and Saturday 5pm to 4am.

Where to Stay

Although Paris hotels are quite expensive, there is some good news. Scores of lackluster lodgings, where the wallpaper dated from the Napoleonic era, have been renovated and offer much better value in the moderate-to-inexpensive price range. The most outstanding examples are in the **7e arrondissement,** where several good-value hotels have blossomed from dives.

By now, the "season" has almost ceased to exist. Most visitors visit in July and August and because many French are on vacation, and trade fairs and conventions come to a halt, there are usually plenty of rooms, even though these months have traditionally been the peak season for European travel. In most hotels, February is just as busy as April or September because of the volume of business travelers and the increasing number of tourists who've learned to take advantage of off-season discount airfares.

Hot weather doesn't last long in Paris, so most hotels, except the deluxe ones, tend not to provide air-conditioning. To avoid the noise problem when you have to open windows, request a room in the back when making a reservation.

Some hotels offer a continental breakfast of coffee, tea, or hot chocolate; a freshly baked croissant and roll; and butter and jam or jelly. Though nowhere near as filling as a traditional English or American breakfast, it is quick to prepare—it'll be at your door moments after you request it—and can be served at almost any hour. The word "breakfast" in these entries refers to this version.

Rates quoted include service and value-added tax unless otherwise specified. Unless otherwise noted, all hotel rooms have private bathrooms.

RIGHT BANK: LES HALLES, LOUVRE & PALAIS ROYAL (1ER & 2E)
Very Expensive
Hôtel Meurice ★★★   This landmark hotel, which lies between the place de la Concorde and the Grand Louvre, facing the Tuileries Gardens, is media-hip and style-conscious. Since the 1800s, it has welcomed the royal, the rich, and even the radical. The mad genius Salvador Dalí made the Meurice his headquarters, and in 2008 that other mad genius, Philippe Starck, overhauled the hotel's public areas, bringing an exquisite contemporary touch of the surreal to the lobby and downstairs bar and restaurant. Each room is individually decorated with period pieces, fine carpets, Italian and French fabrics, marble bathrooms, and modern features. Our favorites and the least expensive are the sixth-floor rooms. Some have painted ceilings of puffy clouds and blue skies, along with canopy beds. Suites are among the most lavish in France.

228 rue de Rivoli, 75001 Paris. www.meuricehotel.com. 𝒞 **01-44-58-10-10.** Fax 01-44-58-10-15. 160 units. 790€–1,070€ double; 1,300€–1,900€ junior suite; from 2,100€ suite. AE, DC, MC, V. Parking 45€. Métro: Tuileries or Concorde. **Amenities:** 2 restaurants; bar; health club and spa; concierge; room service; babysitting. *In room:* A/C, TV/DVD player, fax, minibar, hair dryer, Wi-Fi (24€/day).

Paris Restaurants & Hotels

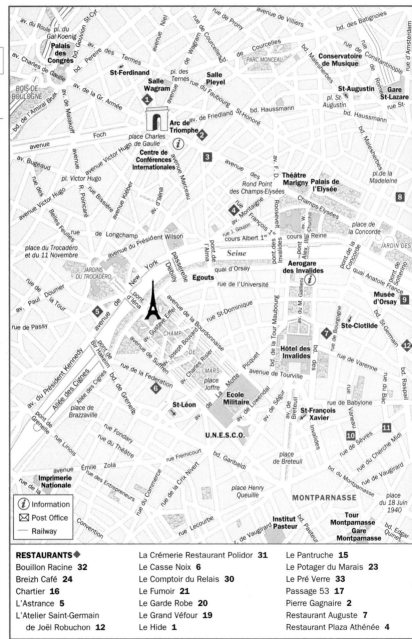

RESTAURANTS◆

Bouillon Racine **32**

Breizh Café **24**

Chartier **16**

L'Astrance **5**

L'Atelier Saint-Germain
  de Joël Robuchon **12**

La Crémerie Restaurant Polidor **31**

Le Casse Noix **6**

Le Comptoir du Relais **30**

Le Fumoir **21**

Le Garde Robe **20**

Le Grand Véfour **19**

Le Hide **1**

Le Pantruche **15**

Le Potager du Marais **23**

Le Pré Verre **33**

Passage 53 **17**

Pierre Gagnaire **2**

Restaurant Auguste **7**

Restaurant Plaza Athénée **4**

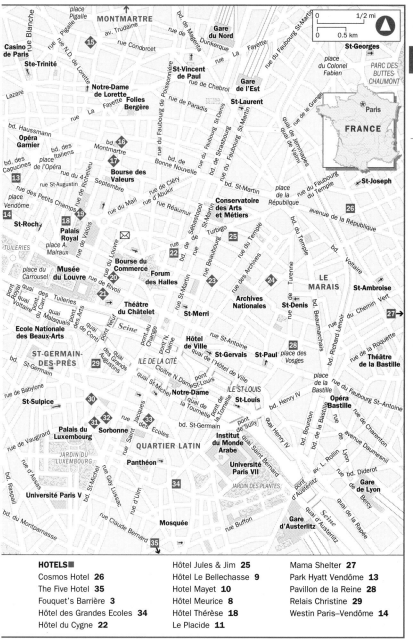

HOTELS ■

Cosmos Hotel **26**	Hôtel Jules & Jim **25**	Mama Shelter **27**
The Five Hotel **35**	Hôtel Le Bellechasse **9**	Park Hyatt Vendôme **13**
Fouquet's Barrière **3**	Hotel Mayet **10**	Pavillon de la Reine **28**
Hôtel des Grandes Ecoles **34**	Hôtel Meurice **8**	Relais Christine **29**
Hôtel du Cygne **22**	Hôtel Thérèse **18**	Westin Paris–Vendôme **14**
	Le Placide **11**	

Park Hyatt Vendôme ★★★ American interior designer Ed Tuttle took five separate Haussmann-era buildings and wove them into a seamless entity to create this citadel of 21st-century luxury living. High ceilings, colonnades, and interior courtyards speak of the buildings' former lives, but other than the facades, all is completely modern and luxurious inside. The third Hyatt in Paris, this palace enjoys the greatest and most prestigious location in "Ritz Hotel country." Graced with modern art, it is filled with elegant fabrics, huge mirrors, walk-in closets, mahogany doors, and Jim Thompson silk. Bedrooms and bathrooms are spacious and state-of-the-art, with elegant furnishings and glamorous bathrooms with "rain showers," plus separate tubs.

5 rue de la Paix, 75002 Paris. www.paris.vendome.hyatt.com. ⓒ **01-58-71-12-34** or **800/492-8804** in the U.S. and Canada. Fax 01-58-71-12-35. 168 units. 800€–910€ double; from 1,010€ suite. AE, DC, DISC, MC, V. Métro: Tuileries or Opéra. Free parking. **Amenities:** 2 restaurants; bar; health club and spa; concierge; room service; babysitting. *In room:* A/C, TV, DVD, minibar, hair dryer, CD player, Wi-Fi (19€/day).

Expensive

Westin Paris–Vendôme ★ ☺ At this hotel it's location, location, location: You're 30 seconds from the Tuileries, 3 minutes from the Place Vendôme, 5 minutes from the place de la Concorde, and 7 minutes from the Louvre. The guest rooms are elegantly decorated, comfortable, and well maintained, and they feature Westin's Signature "Heavenly Beds." Two connecting rooms can be blocked off for families, and family rates are available. Many of the units overlook an inner courtyard, but others have panoramic views over the Eiffel Tower, the Louvre, the Tuileries gardens, and the place de la Concorde.

3 rue de Castiglione, Paris 75001. www.thewestinparis.fr. ⓒ **01-44-77-11-11** or 800/454-6835 in the U.S. and Canada. Fax 01-44-77-14-60. 428 units. 350€–430€ double; from 600€ suite. AE, DC, MC, V. Métro: Tuileries. **Amenities:** 2 restaurants; bar; exercise room; spa; concierge; room service; babysitting. *In room:* A/C, TV, DVD player, minibar, hair dryer, Wi-Fi (19€/day).

Moderate

Hôtel Thérèse ★★ Close to the Louvre, Place Vendôme, and the Tuileries, this hotel combines French charm with English classicism. For example, the library and bar evoke a London club with wood-paneled walls and plush armchairs, but the lounge is adorned with Parisian art. Owner Sylvia de Lattre, who likes shades of pistachio and royal blue, trolled the flea markets for paintings and prints to personalize each bedroom. The rooms are unpretentious but filled with quality furnishings, from the soft, efficient lighting by Philippe Starck to the natural wool quilts. The hotel's public areas were redecorated in late 2011.

5–7 rue Thérèse, Paris 75001. www.hoteltherese.com. ⓒ **01-42-96-10-01.** Fax 01-42-96-15-22. 43 units. 165€–295€ double. AE, MC, V. Métro: Musée du Louvre. **Amenities:** Library/bar; room service; nonsmoking rooms. *In room:* A/C, TV, hair dryer, Wi-Fi (free).

Inexpensive

Hôtel du Cygne This centrally located hotel is within walking distance of the charming gourmand-friendly Rue Montorgueil, the Place des Victoires, the Marais, and the Louvre. In a restored 17th-century building, the hotel combines the old with touches of the new; much of the eclectic decor has been handpicked by the hotel's friendly owner, Isabelle. The staff is helpful, but there is no elevator, so be prepared to carry your luggage up the narrow, winding stairs. Avoid the rooms overlooking the street, as they can be noisy. Room 35 is the largest.

3–5 rue du Cygne, 75001 Paris. www.cygne-hotel-paris.com. ⓒ **01-42-60-14-16.** Fax 01-42-21-37-02. 18 units. 122€–132€ double; 147€ suite. MC, V. Métro: Etienne Marcel. **Amenities:** Breakfast room. *In room:* TV, hair dryer, Wi-Fi (free).

RIGHT BANK: LE MARAIS, ILE ST-LOUIS & ILE DE LA CITÉ (3E & 4E)

Expensive

Pavillon de la Reine ★★ 📖 This is a hidden gem that opens onto the most romantic square in Paris: the Place des Vosges. You enter through an arcade that opens onto a small formal garden. In days of yore the 1612 mansion was a gathering place for the likes of Racine, La Fontaine, Molière, and Madame de Sévigné. Today, the Louis XIII decor evokes the heyday of the square itself, and iron-banded Spanish antiques create a rustic aura. Each guest room is individually furnished in a historic or modern style—take your pick. Some units are duplexes with sleeping lofts above cozy salons.

28 place des Vosges, 75003 Paris. www.pavillon-de-la-reine.com. 🕻 **01-40-29-19-19.** Fax 01-40-29-19-20. 56 units. 330€–450€ double; 600€–800€ suite. AE, MC, V. Métro: Bastille. **Amenities:** Bar; concierge; room service. *In room:* A/C, TV, minibar, Wi-Fi (free).

Moderate

Hôtel Jules & Jim ★★ Proudly gay-friendly, this new boutique hotel opened in late 2011. Spread across three buildings, it's a little urban oasis arranged around two beautiful, paved courtyards. The rooms either look out at the rooftops of Paris or into the lush vertical garden in the courtyard. Guest rooms are sleek, and designed with durable materials, like glass, wood, stone, and concrete; they are soundproofed and equipped with sophisticated amenities, like luxury linens and an iPod docking station. The bar is a great place to wind down your day, with a working outdoor fireplace (in winter) and live music (in summer).

11 rue des Gravilliers, 75003 Paris. www.hoteljulesetjim.com. 🕻 **01-44-54-13-13.** Fax 01-42-78-10-01. 23 units. 180€–310€ double; 390€–550€ suite. AE, MC, V. Métro: Arts-et-Métiers. **Amenities:** Bar; concierge; room service. *In room:* AC, TV, hair dryer, iPod dock, Wi-Fi (free).

RIGHT BANK: CHAMPS-ELYSÉES & WESTERN PARIS (8E, 16E & 17E)

Very Expensive

Fouquet's Barrière ★★★ This deluxe boutique hotel on the corner of the Champs-Élysées may lack the historic cachet of the neighboring George V or Plaza Athénée, but it's a more contemporary brand of glitz and glamour. Standing alongside its namesake, the legendary restaurant, Fouquet's, it offers some of the most luxurious and spacious bedrooms in Paris, its decor dominated by ceiling-high padded headboards in shiny gold. The hotel contains such novel features as waterproof floating TV remotes in the bathtub, and a bedside button that, when pressed, will summon your butler. There's one butler to every eight guests, and the service is the best in Paris. That butler even arrives to unpack your luggage and serve you champagne.

46 av. George V, 75008 Paris. www.fouquets-barriere.com. 🕻 **01-40-69-60-00.** Fax 01-40-69-60-05. 107 units. 750€–1,300€ double; 1,100€–1,700€ junior suite; 1,700€–3,600€ suite. AE, MC, V. Métro: George V. Parking 45€. **Amenities:** 2 restaurants; 2 bars; pool (indoor); health club and spa; concierge; room service. *In room:* A/C, TV, TV/DVD, minibar, hair dryer, Wi-Fi (free).

RIGHT BANK: RÉPUBLIQUE, BASTILLE & EASTERN PARIS (11E & 12E)

Inexpensive

Cosmos Hotel 📖 This no-frills option in the heart of the animated Oberkampf neighborhood has got to be one of the best deals in town. The simply furnished rooms are clean and have fresh towels provided on a daily basis. The staff is helpful, and the hotel is also home to a little furry feline mascot. The only downside is that the hotel can be noisy on the weekends as people spill out of the busy local bars and restaurants.

35 rue Jean-Pierre Timbaud, 75011 Paris. www.cosmos-hotel-paris.com. © **01-43-57-25-88.** Fax 01-43-57-25-88. 36 units. 62€–70€ double; 78€ triple. AE, MC, V. Métro: Parmentier. *In room:* TV, hair dryer, Wi-Fi (free).

RIGHT BANK: BELLEVILLE, CANAL ST-MARTIN & NORTH-EAST PARIS (10E, 19E & 20E)
Moderate
Mama Shelter ★★ 🎿 Even though it's located off the beaten track, this Philippe Starck-designed hotel nevertheless attracts the in-crowd with its buzzing downstairs restaurant–bar space, sleek design, and high-tech features. The stylish yet simple rooms are equipped with iMac computers, offering on-demand movies, Internet access, and television programs. Plus, the low rates make the rooms great value. This is a place for the young and hip, and the in-house bar and restaurant are local hot spots.

109 rue de Bagnolet, 75020 Paris. www.mamashelter.com. © **01-43-48-48-48.** Fax 01-43-48-48-49. 170 units. 89€–209€ double. Rates include breakfast. MC, V. Free parking. Métro: Gambetta. **Amenities:** Restaurant; bar; bicycle rental; concierge; babysitting. *In room:* A/C, minibar, iMac, microwave, Wi-Fi (free).

LEFT BANK: LATIN QUARTER (5E & 13E)
Moderate
The Five Hotel ★★ 🏨 A charmer among Left Bank boutique hotels, the Five is named for the 5th arrondissement and lies in a restored 1800s town house on a U-shaped street off boulevard de Port-Royal. The funky interior design is not to everyone's taste, including a red leather paneled hall and red-painted gas fireplace. The rooms are individually designed in various colors (blood red or Halloween orange, for example), and tiny white lights evoke a planetarium. Of course, if you want a room the color of a prune, that too is available. A Chinese lacquer artist, Isabelle Emmerique, has certainly been busy here. Some rooms are small, but all the beds are exceedingly comfortable.

3 rue Flatters, Paris 75005. www.thefivehotel.com. © **01-43-31-74-21.** Fax 01-43-31-61-96. 24 units. 245€–315€ double. AE, MC, V. Métro: Bastille or Gobelins. **Amenities:** Bar; room service. *In room:* A/C, TV, hair dryer, Wi-Fi (free).

Inexpensive
Hôtel des Grandes Ecoles ★★ 🎿 Few hotels in the neighborhood offer so much low-key charm at such reasonable prices. It's composed of a trio of high-ceilinged buildings, interconnected via a sheltered courtyard, where in warm weather, singing birds provide a worthy substitute for the TVs deliberately missing from the rooms. Accommodations, as reflected by the price, range from snug, cozy doubles to more spacious chambers. Each room is comfortable, but with a lot of luggage the very smallest would be cramped. The decor is old-fashioned, with feminine touches such as flowered upholsteries and ruffles. Many have views of a garden where trellises and flower beds evoke the countryside.

75 rue de Cardinal-Lemoine, 75005 Paris. www.hotel-grandes-ecoles.com. © **01-43-26-79-23.** Fax 01-47-47-65-48. 51 units. 118€–145€ double. Extra bed 20€. MC, V. Parking 30€. Métro: Cardinal Lemoine, Jussieu, or Place Monge. RER: Port-Royal, Luxembourg. **Amenities:** Room service; babysitting. *In room:* Hair dryer, Wi-Fi (free).

LEFT BANK: ST-GERMAIN DES PRÉS & LUXEMBOURG (6E)

Expensive

Relais Christine ★★ This hotel welcomes you into a former 16th-century Augustinian cloister. From a cobblestone street, you enter a symmetrical courtyard and find an elegant reception area with sculpture and Renaissance antiques. Each room is uniquely decorated with wooden beams and Louis XIII-style furnishings; the rooms come in a range of styles and shapes. Some are among the Left Bank's largest, with extras such as mirrored closets, plush carpets, and some balconies facing the courtyard. The least attractive rooms are in the interior. Bed configurations vary, but all mattresses are on the soft side, offering comfort with quality linens.

3 rue Christine, 75006 Paris. www.relais-christine.com. ✆ **01-40-51-60-80.** Fax 01-40-51-60-81. 51 units. 300€–510€ double; 450€–930€ duplex or suite. AE, DC, MC, V. Free parking. Métro: Odéon or St-Michel. **Amenities:** Bar; exercise room; spa; concierge; room service; babysitting. *In room:* A/C, TV, TV/DVD, minibar, hair dryer, Wi-Fi (free).

Moderate

Le Placide ★★ 🛏 Converted from a former family home in the 19th century, Le Placide has the aura of a private club. This small boutique hotel—there are only two rooms per floor—lies just steps from the chic Bon Marché department store. It was designed by a member of Philippe Starck's firm, who brought a 21st-century style of luxury and comfort to the interior, featuring white Moroccan leather, lots of glass, a bit of chrome, and a crystal pedestal table. Fresh flowers adorn each room, and rose petals are placed on your bed at night. The spacious bathrooms provide natural light.

6 rue St-Placide, 75006 Paris. www.leplacidehotel.com. ✆ **01-42-84-34-60.** 11 units. 153€–530€ double. AE, MC, V. Métro: St-Placide. **Amenities:** Bar. *In room:* A/C, TV/DVD, minibar, hair dryer, CD player, MP3 docking station, Wi-Fi (free).

Inexpensive

Hotel Mayet ★ 🛏 This affordable hotel has a great location close to shopping heaven Le Bon Marché and St-Germain. The compact rooms are clean, comfortable, and contemporary, designed in a bordeaux and gray color scheme. The low-key lobby sets the scene: deep, comfortable sofas are set against a brightly painted wall with some original graffiti by Parisian artist André. There's an iMac computer in the lobby with Internet access. Service goes the extra mile.

3 rue Mayet, 75006 Paris. www.mayet.com. ✆ **01-47-83-21-35.** Fax 01-40-65-95-78. 23 units. 140€–175€ double. Rates include breakfast. AE, DC, MC, V. Métro: Duroc. **Amenities:** Bar; breakfast room. *In room:* A/C, TV, minibar, Wi-Fi (free).

LEFT BANK: EIFFEL TOWER & NEARBY (7E)

Moderate

Hôtel Le Bellechasse ★★ 🛏 This gem of a hotel, seconds on foot from the Musée d'Orsay, is still one of the city's most fanciful designer hotels. It's the creation of couturier Christian Lacroix, who let his imagination go wild. A stay here is like wandering into a psychedelic garden. Each guest room is different in a pastiche of colors with baroque overtones. One French critic called Lacroix's designs "magpie sensibility," perhaps a reference to one room where top-hatted, frock-coated Paris dandies with butterfly wings wrap around both walls and ceilings. The helpful staff is part of the fun—that and taking a bath in a fiberglass tub.

8 rue de Bellechasse, 75007 Paris. www.lebellechasse.com. ✆ **01-45-50-22-31.** Fax 01-45-51-52-36. 34 units. 160€–245€ double. MC, V. Métro: Solferino. RER: Musée d'Orsay. **Amenities:** Dining room (breakfast). *In room:* A/C, TV/DVD, minibar, hair dryer, CD player, MP3 docking station, Wi-Fi (free).

Day Trips from Paris: The Ile de France

VERSAILLES ★★★

Within 50 years, the **Château de Versailles** (www.chateauversailles.fr; ✆ **01-30-83-78-00**) was transformed from Louis XIII's hunting lodge into an extravagant palace. Begun in 1661, its construction involved 32,000 to 45,000 workmen, some of whom had to drain marshes and move forests. Louis XIV set out to build a palace that would be the envy of Europe and created a symbol of opulence often copied, yet never duplicated, the world over.

The six magnificent **Grands Appartements ★★★** are in the Louis XIV style; each bears the name of the allegorical painting on the ceiling. The best known and largest is the **Hercules Salon ★★**, with a ceiling painted by François Lemoine, depicting the Apotheosis of Hercules. In the **Mercury Salon** (with a ceiling by Jean-Baptiste Champaigne), the body of Louis XIV was put on display in 1715; his 72-year reign was one of the longest in history.

The most famous room at Versailles is the 71m-long (233-ft.) **Hall of Mirrors ★★★**. Begun by Mansart in 1678 in the Louis XIV style, it was decorated by Le Brun with 17 arched windows faced by beveled mirrors in simulated arcades.

Spread across 100 hectares (247 acres), the **Gardens of Versailles ★★★** were laid out by landscape artist André Le Nôtre. A walk across the park takes you to the pink-and-white-marble **Grand Trianon ★★**, designed by Hardouin-Mansart for Louis XIV in 1687. Traditionally it has been lodging for important guests. Gabriel, the designer of place de la Concorde in Paris, built the **Petit Trianon ★★** in 1768 for Louis XV. Louis used it for his trysts with Mme. du Barry. In time, Marie Antoinette adopted it as her favorite residence, a place to escape the rigid life at the main palace.

In 2005, a previously off-limits section of the vast palace was opened to the public for the first time by an act of the Parliament. The decision adds some 25,085 sq. m (270,000 sq. ft.) of the south wing to public access. Up to now, the area had been reserved for use by Parliament itself. Among the rooms opened up is the mammoth **Battle Gallery,** which at 119m (390 ft.) is the longest hall at Versailles. The gallery displays monumental paintings depicting all of France's great battles, ranging from the founding of the monarchy by Clovis, who reigned in the 5th and 6th centuries, through the Napoleonic wars in the early 19th century.

The château is open from April to October, Tuesday through Sunday from 9am to 6pm (5pm the rest of the year). Call or visit the website for a complete schedule of fees, which vary depending on which attractions you visit. The grounds are open daily from dawn to dusk; the individual attractions may have earlier opening and closing times.

GETTING THERE To get to Versailles, catch the **RER** line C1 to Versailles–Rive Gauche at the Gare d'Austerlitz, St-Michel, Musée d'Orsay, Invalides, Pont de l'Alma, Champ de Mars, or Javel stop, and take it to the Versailles/Rive Gauche station. The trip takes 35 to 40 minutes. Do not get off at Versailles Chantier, which will leave you on the other end of town, a long walk from the château. The round-trip fare is 5.60€; Eurailpass holders travel free on the RER but need to show the pass at the ticket kiosk to receive an RER ticket. **SNCF trains** make frequent runs from Gare St-Lazare and Gare Montparnasse in Paris to Versailles. Trains departing from Gare St-Lazare arrive at the Versailles/Rive Droite railway station; trains departing from Gare Montparnasse arrive at Versailles Chantiers station, a long walk as mentioned.

Both Versailles stations are within a 10-minute walk of the château, and we recommend the walk as a means of orienting yourself to the town, its geography, its scale,

Paris
FRANCE

and its architecture. If you can't or don't want to walk, you can take bus B, or (in midsummer) a shuttle bus marked CHATEAU from either station to the château for either a cash payment of around 2€ (drop the coins directly into the coin box near the driver) or the insertion of a valid ticket for the Paris Métro. Because of the vagaries of the bus schedules, we highly recommend the walk. Directions to the château are clearly signposted from each railway station.

If you're **driving,** exit the *périphérique* (the ring road around Paris) on N10 (av. du Général-Leclerc), which will take you to Versailles; park on place d'Armes in front of the château.

VISITOR INFORMATION   The **Office de Tourisme** is at 2 bis av. de Paris (www. versailles-tourisme.com; ℰ **01-39-24-88-88**). The office is closed Sunday and Monday.

CHARTRES ★★★

The architectural aspirations of the Middle Ages reached their highest expression in the **Cathédrale Notre-Dame de Chartres,** 16 Cloître Notre-Dame (www.monum. fr; ℰ **02-37-21-22-07**), where visitors are transfixed by the light from the **stained glass ★★★**. Covering an expanse of more than 2,500 sq. m (26,900 sq. ft.), the peerless glass is truly mystical. It was spared in both world wars because of a decision to remove it piece by piece. Most of it dates from the 12th and 13th centuries. It's difficult to single out one panel or window—depending on the position of the sun, the images change constantly; however, an exceptional one is the 12th-century *Vierge de la Belle Verrière (Virgin of the Beautiful Window)* on the south side. Of course, there are three fiery rose windows, but you couldn't miss those even if you tried.

The cathedral you see today dates principally from the 13th century, when it was rebuilt with the efforts of kings, princes, churchmen, and pilgrims from all over Europe. One of the world's greatest High Gothic cathedrals, it was the first to use flying buttresses. French sculpture in the 12th century broke into full bloom when the **Royal Portal ★★★** was added. The portal is a landmark in Romanesque art. The sculptured bodies are elongated, often formalized beyond reality, in long, flowing robes. But the faces are amazingly (for the time) lifelike, occasionally betraying Mona Lisa smiles. Admission is free; the cathedral is open daily from 8:30am to 7:30pm.

If you're fit enough, don't miss the opportunity to climb to the top of the tower. You can visit the crypt, gloomy and somber but rich with medieval history, only as part of a French-language tour. The cost is 2.70€ per person.

GETTING THERE   From Paris's Gare Montparnasse, **trains** run directly to Chartres, taking less than an hour. Tickets cost 27€ round-trip. Call ℰ **08-92-35-35-35.** If **driving,** take A10/A11 southwest from the *périphérique,* and follow signs to Le Mans and Chartres. (The Chartres exit is clearly marked.)

VISITOR INFORMATION   The **Office de Tourisme** is on place de la Cathédrale (www.chartres-tourisme.com; ℰ **02-37-18-26-26;** fax 02-37-21-51-91).

THE LOIRE VALLEY CHÂTEAUX ★★★

Bordered by vineyards, the winding Loire Valley cuts through the land of castles deep in France's heart. Medieval crusaders returning here brought news of the opulence of the East, and soon they began rethinking their surroundings. Later, word came from

Italy of an artistic flowering led by Leonardo and Michelangelo. Royalty and nobility built châteaux in this valley during the French Renaissance, and an era of pomp reigned until Henri IV moved his court to Paris, marking the Loire's decline.

The Loire is blessed with attractions, including medieval, Renaissance, and classical châteaux, Romanesque and Gothic churches, and treasures such as the Apocalypse Tapestries. There's even the castle that inspired *Sleeping Beauty.* Trains serve some towns, but the best way to see this region is by car.

Tours ★

232km (144 miles) SW of Paris; 113km (70 miles) SW of Orléans

Although it doesn't have a major château, Tours (pop. 137,000), at the junction of the Loire and Cher rivers, is known for its food and wine. Many of its buildings were bombed in World War II, and 20th-century apartment towers have taken the place of châteaux. However, the downtown core is quite charming and as Tours is on the doorstep of some of the most magnificent châteaux in France, it makes a good base or starting point from which to explore. Pilgrims en route to Santiago de Compostela in northwest Spain once stopped here to pay homage at the tomb of St-Martin, the "Apostle of Gaul," who was bishop of Tours in the 4th century. One of the most significant conflicts in European history, the 732 Battle of Tours, checked the Arab advance into Gaul. In the 15th century, French kings started setting up shop here, and Tours became the capital of France for over 100 years.

Most Loire Valley towns are rather sleepy, but Tours is where the action is, with busy streets and cafes. A quarter of the residents are students, who add a vibrant touch to a soulless commercial enclave. Allow a morning or an afternoon to see Tours.

ESSENTIALS

GETTING THERE   There are as many as 14 high-speed TGV **trains** per day departing from Paris's Gare Montparnasse and arriving at St-Pierre des Corps station, 6km (3¾ miles) east of the center of Tours, in an hour. Free *navettes*, or shuttle buses, await on arrival to take you to the center of town (the Tours Centre train station). There are also a limited number of conventional trains that depart from Gare d'Austerlitz and arrive in the center of Tours, but they take twice as long (about 2¼ hr.). One-way fares range from 18.30€ to 56€. For information, visit www.voyages-sncf.com or call © **36-35.** If you're **driving,** take highway A10 to Tours.

GETTING AROUND   It's easy to walk from one end of central Tours to the other, and many of the good hotels are near the train station. For taxi service, call **Taxi Radio** (© 02-47-20-30-40). You can rent a car at **Avis** (www.avis.fr; © **02-47-20-53-27**), located in the Tours Centre train station, or **Europcar,** at the St-Pierre des Corps station (www.europcar.fr; © **02-47-63-28-67**). You can rent a bike at **Detours de Loire,** 35 rue Charles Gilles (www.locationdevelos.com; © **02-47-61-22-23**), at a cost of 14€ per day. A deposit is required.

VISITOR INFORMATION   The **Office de Tourisme** is at 78–82 rue Bernard-Palissy (www.ligeris.com; © **02-47-70-37-37**).

EXPLORING TOURS

The heart of town is **place Jean-Jaurès.** The principal street is **rue Nationale,** running north to the Loire River. Head west along rue du Commerce and rue du Grand-Marché to Vieux Tours/Vieille Ville (old town).

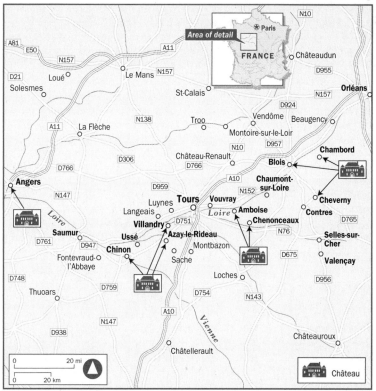

Cathédrale St-Gatien CATHEDRAL   This cathedral honors a 3rd-century evangelist and has a flamboyant Gothic facade flanked by towers with bases from the 12th century. The lanterns date from the Renaissance. The choir is from the 13th century, with new additions built in each century through the 16th. Sheltered inside is the handsome 16th-century tomb of Charles VIII and Anne de Bretagne's two children. Some of the glorious stained-glass windows are from the 13th century.

5 place de la Cathédrale. © **02-47-70-21-00.** Free admission. Daily 9am–7pm.

Musée des Beaux-Arts ART MUSEUM   This fine provincial museum in the Palais des Archevêques is worth a visit just to see its lovely rooms and gardens. There are old masters here as well, including works by Rubens, Delacroix, Rembrandt, and Boucher. The sculpture collection includes works by Houdon and Bourdelle.

18 place François Sicard. www.tours.fr/culture/musees/bxarts. © **02-47-05-68-73.** Admission 4€ adults, 2€ seniors and students, free for children 12 and under. Wed–Mon 9am–6pm. Bus: 3.

WHERE TO EAT
La Roche le Roy ★★ MODERN FRENCH   Alain Couturier, one of the hottest chefs in town, blends new and old techniques in a gabled 18th-century manor south

of the town center. Couturier's repertoire includes lobster risotto, foie gras with caramelized apples, bass with champagne cream sauce, and *matelote* (stew) of eel with Vouvray wine. His masterpiece is suprême of pigeon with "roughly textured" sauce. For dessert, try a warm orange soufflé flavored with Grand Marnier.

55 rte. St-Avertin. www.rocheleroy.com. © **02-47-27-22-00.** Reservations recommended. Main courses 25€–38€, lunch menu 34€, dinner menu 78€. AE, MC, V. Wed–Sat noon–1:30pm and 7:30–9:30pm. Closed 2 weeks in Feb and 3 weeks in Aug. From the center of town, take av. Grammont south (follow signs to St-Avertin–Vierzon).

Rive Gauche ★ TRADITIONAL FRENCH Having recently changed chefs, this gourmet restaurant now touts "responsible gastronomy," which takes into consideration both taste and environmental impact. The talented young chef, Gaëtan Evrard, uses his lively imagination and high-quality local and/or artisan products to create surprising dishes like steamed Loire mullet with crushed apples, gambas with Rioja chorizo, foie gras stuffed Olréans partridge with Japanese Dashi bouillon and Sancho pepper. Dessert includes an award-winning *nougat de Tours,* a light almond cake, served warm and topped with apricot sherbet. You can savor these delicacies in either of the two cozy dining rooms or, in warm weather, outdoors on the terrace.

23 rue du Commerce. www.tours-rivegauche.com. © **02-47-05-71-21.** Reservations required. Main courses 15€–32€; fixed-price menu 26€–69€. AE MC, V. Daily 12:30pm–2pm and 7:30–10pm.

WHERE TO STAY

Best Western Le Central Off the main boulevard, this old-fashioned hotel is within walking distance of the train station, the river, and the cathedral. Despite its central location, there is plenty of greenery here: The back of the hotel looks out on a leafy garden, and the front is set off by a lawn. The decor is classic and conservative, and blends well with the 19th-century building. Half of the guest rooms have tub/showers, the others only showers.

21 rue Berthelot, Tours 37000. www.bestwesterncentralhoteltours.com. ©**02-47-05-46-44** or **800/528-1234** in the U.S. and Canada. Fax 02-47-66-10-26. 37 units. 95€–155€ double; 195€–250€ suite. AE, DC, MC, V. Parking 10€. **Amenities:** Bar; room service; babysitting. *In room:* A/C, TV, minibar, hair dryer, free Wi-Fi.

Hôtel du Manoir On a quiet street near the train station, this 19th-century residence is a comfortable and affordable place to stay. The cheerful reception area reflects the quality of the rooms. Though small to average in size, all units have windows that let in lots of light and afford views of the neighborhood or the hotel courtyard. Most have simple furnishings.

2 rue Traversière, Tours 37000. http://hotel.manoir.tours.voila.net. © **02-47-05-37-37.** Fax 02-47-05-16-00. 20 units. 65€–75€ double. AE, MC, V. Parking 7€. *In room:* TV, hair dryer, free Wi-Fi.

Villandry ★★★

253km (157 miles) SW of Paris; 32km (20 miles) NE of Chinon; 18km (11 miles) W of Tours; 8km (5 miles) E of Azay-le-Rideau

The 16th-century-style gardens of the Renaissance **Château de Villandry ★★★** (www.chateauvillandry.com; © **02-47-50-02-09**) are celebrated throughout Touraine and amaze visitors from around the world with their beauty and faithful historic preservation.

Every square of the gardens is like a geometric mosaic. Designed on a trio of superimposed cloisters with a water garden on the highest level, they were restored by the

Spanish doctor and scientist Joachim Carvallo, great-grandfather of the present owner. The grounds contain 17km (11 miles) of boxwood sculpture, which the gardeners cut to style in only 2 weeks each September. The borders symbolize the faces of love: tender, tragic (represented by daggers), and crazy (with a labyrinth that doesn't get you anywhere). Pink tulips and dahlias suggest sweet love; red, tragic; and yellow, unfaithful. All colors signify crazy love. The vine arbors, citrus hedges, and walks keep six men busy full-time. They are also reverting the French vegetable garden to being completely organic.

A feudal castle once stood at Villandry. In 1536, Jean le Breton, François I's finance minister and former ambassador to Italy, acquired the property and built the present château with strong influences of the Italian Renaissance. The buildings form a U and are surrounded by a moat. Near the gardens is a terrace from which you can see the small village and its 12th-century church. A tearoom on-site, **La Doulce Terrasse** (www.chateauvillandry.com; ℂ **02-47-50-02-10;** closed mid-Nov to mid-Feb) serves regional cuisine, including hot dishes, with vegetables for the garden, freshly baked bread, and homemade ice cream.

Admission to the gardens, including a guided tour of the château, costs 9.50€ for adults, 5.50€ for children 8 to 18, and is free for children 7 and under. Visiting the gardens separately, without a guide, costs 6.50€ for adults and 4€ for children 8 to 18. The gardens are open daily 9am to between 5 and 7:30pm, depending on the hour of sunset; the château is open daily from 9am to between 4:30 and 6:30pm, depending on a complicated seasonal schedule. Tours are conducted in French; leaflets are available in English. Allow 1½ hours to see Villandry.

ESSENTIALS

GETTING THERE There are three daily **buses** from Tours that operate from July to October only; the trip takes about 30 minutes and costs 1.70€. For bus information, visit www.touraine-filvert.com or call ℂ **02-47-05-30-49.** Villandry has no train service. The nearest connection from Tours is at the town of Savonnières; the trip takes around 15 minutes and costs 3.20€ one-way. For information, visit www.voyages-sncf.com or call ℂ **36-35.** From Savonnières, you can walk along the Loire for 4km (2½ miles) to reach Villandry, rent a **bike** at the station, or take a **taxi.** You can also **drive,** following D7 from Tours.

VISITOR INFORMATION The **Office de Tourisme** is located in a kiosk in front of the hotel Le Cheval Rouge (see below), in the center of town (www.villandry-tourisme.com; ℂ **02-47-50-12-66**).

WHERE TO EAT & STAY

Le Cheval Rouge MODERN FRENCH The well-known dining stopover near the château extends a congenial welcome. The conservatively decorated dining room lies about 91m (298 ft.) from the banks of the Cher. Specialties include bream flavored with vanilla, scallops flambéed with whiskey, roast lamb with thyme, and veal with *pleurotes,* a type of wild mushroom. The inn also rents 41 rooms, all with free in-room Wi-Fi. A double is 47€ to 62€.

9 rue Principale, Villandry 37510. www.lecheval-rouge.com. ℂ **02-47-50-02-07.** Fax 02-47-50-08-77. Reservations recommended. Main courses 15€–18€; fixed-price menu 20€–35€. AE, DC, MC, V. Daily noon–2:30pm and 7–9pm.

Azay-le-Rideau ★★

261km (162 miles) SW of Paris; 21km (13 miles) SW of Tours

With its idyllic location and fairy tale turrets the Renaissance **Château d'Azay-le-Rideau ★★**, rue Pineau, Azay-le-Rideau 37190 (http://azay-le-rideau.monuments-nationaux.fr; ℂ **02-47-45-42-04**) instantly enchants visitors and was even deemed by neighboring writer Honoré de Balzac as "a facetted diamond set in the Indre." Its machicolated towers and blue-slate roof pierced with dormers give it a medieval air, however, its defensive fortress-like appearance is all for show. The château was actually commissioned in the early 1500s for Gilles Berthelot, François I's finance minister, and his wife, Philippa, who supervised its construction. They didn't have long to enjoy their elegant creation: In 1527, Berthelot was accused of misappropriation of funds and forced to flee, and the château reverted to the king. He didn't live here, but granted it to Antoine Raffin, one of his high-ranking soldiers. It became the property of the state in 1905.

Before you enter, circle the château and note the perfect proportions of the crowning achievement of the Renaissance in the Touraine. Check out its most fancifully ornate feature, the bay enclosing a grand stairway with a straight flight of steps.

From the second-floor Royal Chamber, look out at the gardens. This lavish bedroom housed Louis XIII when he came through in 1619. The private apartments are lined with rich tapestries dating from the 16th and 17th centuries and feature examples of rare period furniture, like the Spanish *bargueno,* a carved wooden chest that held writing materials.

The château is open daily in July and August 9:30am to 7pm, April to June and September 9:30am to 6pm, and October to March 10am to 12:30pm and 2 to 5:30pm. Admission is 8.50€ for adults, 5.50€ for ages 18 to 25, and free for children 17 and under. Allow 2 hours for a visit.

Every evening from the second week in July to the third week in August, there is a guided outdoor performance, **Spectacle Nocturne**, that features actors in period dress, animals, recorded music, and lights beaming on the exterior of the château. The show, which lasts about 1 hours, begins at 9pm and 10:15pm. Tickets are 11€ for adults, 8€ for ages 13 to 25, and 3€ for children 4 to 12; free for 4 and under.

ESSENTIALS

GETTING THERE   To reach Azay-le-Rideau, take the **train** from Tours or Chinon. From either starting point, the trip time is about 30 minutes; the one-way fare is 4.70€ from Chinon, 5.30€ from Tours. For the same fare, the SNCF railway also operates a bus between Tours and Azay; the trip takes 50 minutes. For schedules and information, visit www.voyages-sncf.com or call ℂ **36-35.** If you're **driving** from Tours, take D751 southwest to Azay-le-Rideau.

VISITOR INFORMATION   The **Office de Tourisme** is on place de L'Europe (www.ot-paysazaylerideau.com; ℂ **02-47-45-44-40**).

WHERE TO EAT & STAY

L'Aigle d'Or ★ TRADITIONAL FRENCH   This excellent restaurant is set in a century-old house. Located in the village center, the service is professional, the welcome charming, and the food the best in Azay. In a dining room accented with ceiling beams, a fireplace, and pastel colors, you can savor dishes including foie gras with pears and *blanquette* (stew) of Loire Valley whitefish prepared with local white wine.

Desserts include baked apple with rice pudding mousse, and chocolate cake with sour cherry coulis. In summer, dining extends onto an outdoor terrace.

10 av. Adélaïde-Riché. ℰ **02-47-45-24-58.** Reservations recommended. Main courses 12€–24€; fixed-price menus 27€–54€. V. Mon–Tues and Thurs–Sat noon–1:30pm and 7:30–9pm.

Le Grand Monarque The ivy that covers the exterior of this hotel—less than 150m (492 ft.) from the château—seems to protect it from the modern world. The large guest rooms are outfitted with antiques; ancient exposed beams adorn the lobby ceiling. Units in the annex aren't as well decorated but are more tranquil; those looking out on the wide courtyard are particularly quiet.

The restaurant features dishes like a brochette of crayfish with sesame sauce, suprême of *sandre* in shallot-flavored broth, and rack of Touraine pork with oyster mushrooms and tarragon. Fixed-price menus range from 29€ to 35€. During warmer months, you can dine out on the courtyard terrace.

3 place de la République, Azay-le-Rideau 37190. www.legrandmonarque.com. ℰ **02-47-45-40-08.** Fax 02-47-45-46-25. 24 units. 75€–148€ double. AE, MC, V. Parking 10€. Closed Dec to mid-Jan. Amenities: Restaurant; bar; room service; babysitting. In room: TV, hair dryer, free Wi-Fi.

Amboise ★★★

219km (136 miles) SW of Paris; 35km (22 miles) E of Tours

Amboise is on the banks of the Loire in the center of vineyards known as Touraine-Amboise. The good news: This is a real Renaissance town. The bad news: Because it is so beautiful, tour buses overrun it, especially in summer. Other than the myriad of notable royal residences, the town has also played host to Leonardo da Vinci, who spent his last years here and more recently, royal rocker Mick Jagger, lord of a nearby château.

ESSENTIALS
GETTING THERE About a dozen **trains** per day leave from both Tours and Blois. The trip from Tours takes 20 minutes and costs 5.10€ one-way; from Blois, it takes 20 minutes and costs 6.50€ one-way. Several conventional trains a day leave from Paris's Gare d'Austerlitz (trip time: about 2 hr., 15 min.), and several TGVs depart from the Gare Montparnasse, with a change to a regular train at St-Pierre-des-Corps, next to Tours (trip time: 1 hr., 30 min.). Fares from Paris to Amboise start at 23€. For information, visit www.voyages-sncf.com or call ℰ **36-35.**

If you prefer to travel by bus, **Fil Vert Buses** (www.tourainefilvert.com), which operates out of Gare Routière in Tours, just across from the railway station, runs about six to eight **buses** every day between Tours and Amboise. The one-way trip takes about 45 minutes and costs 1.70€.

If you're **driving** from Tours, take the D751, following signs to Amboise.

VISITOR INFORMATION The **Office de Tourisme** is on quai du Général-de-Gaulle (www.amboise-valdeloire.com; ℰ **02-47-57-09-28**).

EXPLORING AMBOISE
Château d'Amboise ★★ CASTLE On a rocky spur above the town, the medieval château was rebuilt in 1492 by Charles VIII, the first in France to reflect the Italian Renaissance.

You enter on a ramp that opens onto a panoramic terrace fronting the river. At one time, buildings surrounded this terrace, and fêtes took place in the enclosed courtyard. The castle fell into decline during the Revolution, and today only about a quarter of the once-sprawling edifice remains. You first come to the flamboyant Gothic **Chapelle de St-Hubert,** distinguished by its lacelike tracery and where you can visit the **tomb of Leonardo da Vinci,** who died in Amboise. Tapestries cover the walls of what's left of the château's grandly furnished rooms, which include **Logis du Roi (King's Apartment).** The vast **Salle du Conseil,** bookended by a Gothic and a Renaissance fireplace, was once the venue of the lavish fêtes designed by da Vinci. Exit via the **Tour des Minimes** (also known as the Tour des Cavaliers), noteworthy for its ramp up which horsemen could ride. The other notable tower is the Heurtault, which is broader than the Minimes, with thicker walls.

www.chateau-amboise.com ℭ **02-47-57-00-98.** Admission 10€ adults, 8.50€ students, 6.50€ ages 7–14, free for children 7 and under. Daily as follows: Jan 9am–12:30pm and 2–4:45pm; Feb 9am–12:30pm and 1:30–5pm; Mar 9am–5:30pm; Apr–June 9am–6:30pm; July–Aug 9am–7pm; Sept–Oct 9am–6pm; Nov 2–15 9am–5:30pm; Nov 16–Dec 31 9am–12:30pm and 2–4:45pm.

Château du Clos-Lucé ★ HISTORIC HOME/MUSEUM   Within 3km (1¾ miles) of the base of Amboise's château, this brick-and-stone building was constructed in the 1470s. Bought by Charles VII in 1490, it became the summer residence of the royals and also served as a retreat for Anne de Bretagne, who, according to legend, spent a lot of time praying and meditating. Later, François I installed "the great master in all forms of art and science," Leonardo himself. Da Vinci lived here for 3 years, until his death in 1519. (The paintings of Leonardo dying in François's arms are probably symbolic; the king was supposedly out of town at the time.) Today the site functions as a small museum, offering insights into Leonardo's life and a sense of the decorative arts of the era. The manor contains furniture from his era; examples of his sketches; models for his flying machines, bridges, and cannon; and even a primitive example of a machine gun.

2 rue de Clos-Lucé. www.vinci-closluce.com. ℭ **02-47-57-00-73.** Mar–Nov 15 admission 13€ adults, 8€ students and children 6–18, 35€ family ticket (2 adults, 2 children), free for children 5 and under; Nov 16–Feb admission 10€ adults, 7€ students, 6.50€ children 6–18, 28€ family ticket (2 adults, 2 children), free for children 5 and under. Jan daily 10am–6pm; Feb–June daily 9am–7pm; July–Aug daily 9am–8pm; Sept–Oct daily 9am–7pm; Nov–Dec daily 9am–6pm.

WHERE TO EAT & STAY

For fine dining, the restaurants at **Le Choiseul** and **Le Fleuray** are excellent.

Brasserie de l'Hotel de Ville ☺ FRENCH   In the town's historic core, a short walk from the château, this bustling Paris-style brasserie has a solid local reputation. Expect a noisy environment focused on rows of banquettes, hassled waiters, and steaming platters that emerge relatively quickly from the overworked kitchen. Menu items include a full range of old-fashioned cuisine that locals may remember from their childhoods, like local sausage splashed with Vouvray sparkling wine, standard grilled beefsteak with french fries, duck with honey and rosemary, as well as lighter salads and omelets.

1 and 3 rue François 1er. ℭ **02-47-57-26-30.** Reservations recommended. Main courses 7€–18€; fixed-price menu 15€–26€; children's menu 6.90€. AE, MC, V. Daily noon–2pm and 7–9:30pm.

Le Choiseul ★★★   This 18th-century mansion, nestled on the banks of the Loire River, harbors the best hotel in Amboise and serves its best cuisine. Guest rooms are luxurious; though modernized, they retain their old-world charm. The small bathrooms contain combination tub/showers. The formal dining room has a view of the

Loire and welcomes nonguests who phone ahead. The restaurant is superb; the menu features classic and regional French, utilizing the freshest ingredients. Lunch ranges from 27€ to 60€, and the dinner menu is 47€.

36 quai Charles-Guinot, Amboise 37400. www.le-choiseul.com. ✆ **02-47-30-45-45.** Fax 02-47-30-46-10. 32 units. 108€–305€ double; 292€-365€ suite. AE, DC, MC, V. **Amenities:** Restaurant; bar; outdoor pool; bicycles; room service. *In room:* A/C, TV, minibar, hair dryer, free Wi-Fi.

Le Fleuray ★★ 🏨 One of the most appealing hotels in the region is this well-maintained ivy-covered manor house, a short drive from Amboise. A 19th-century farm, it was purchased in 1991 by the Newingtons, a family of English expatriates, whose hard work restoring the site was honored with a French medal of tourism in 2011. Guest rooms have been recently renovated and evoke an elegant but not terribly formal English country house, several have private terraces. The peaceful surroundings make it an excellent base for château touring and unwinding as there's also plenty to do in the extensive grounds: Aside from a swimming pool and Jacuzzi, there is a tennis court, 9-hole golf course, and children's play area.

Don't miss the restaurant—it's one of the best in the area and is manned by a hot young chef. Items on the fixed-price menus (27€–51€) include carpaccio of monkfish drizzled with dried fruit and lemon vinaigrette, farmer's citrus chicken with young leeks and polenta, braised lamb shank with buttered berry lentils, or vegetarian-friendly wild mushroom risotto.

Route D74, Cangey 37530, near Amboise. www.lefleurayhotel.com. ✆ **02-47-56-09-25.** Fax 02-47-56-93-97. 23 units. 78€–148€ double. MC, V. Free parking. From Amboise, take the D952 on the north side of the river, following signs to Blois; 12km (7½ miles) from Amboise, turn onto D74, in the direction of Cangey. **Amenities:** Restaurant; bar; outdoor pool; golf course; tennis court; Jacuzzi; free bikes; room service; massage. *In room:* TV, hair dryer.

Blois ★

180km (112 miles) SW of Paris; 60km (37 miles) NE of Tours

The star attraction in this town of 52,000 is the **Château de Blois ★★★**, but if time remains after a visit to the château, you may want to walk around the town. It's a piece of living history, with cobblestone streets and restored white houses with slate roofs and red-brick chimneys. Blois (pronounce it "Blwah") hugs a hillside overlooking the Loire. Some of its "streets" are mere alleyways originally laid out in the Middle Ages, or lanes linked by a series of stairs. Allow 1½ hours to see Blois.

ESSENTIALS

GETTING THERE A dozen or so **trains** run from Paris's Gare d'Austerlitz every day (1 hr., 45 min.; 27€ one-way), and several others depart from the Gare Montparnasse, which involves a change in Tours (around 1 hr., 50 min.; 26.60€–62€). From Tours, trains run almost every hour (trip time: 40 min.), at a cost of 10€ one-way. For information and schedules, visit www.voyages-sncf.com or dial ✆ **36-35.** From June to September, you can take a **bus** (www.tlcinfo.net; ✆ **02-54-58-55-44**) from the Blois train station to tour châteaux in the area, including Chambord, Chaumont, Chenonceau, and Amboise. If you're **driving** from Tours, take RN152 east to Blois, which runs along the Loire; if you want to get there fast, take the A10 autoroute. If you'd like to explore the area by **bike,** check out **Traineurs de Loire,** 1 rue Chemonton (www.traineursdeloire.com; ✆ **02-54-79-36-71**). Rentals start at 6€ per hour, 13€ per day.

VISITOR INFORMATION The **Office de Tourisme** is at 23 place du Château (www.bloispaysdechambord.com; ✆ **02-54-90-41-41**).

EXPLORING BLOIS & THE CHATEAU

If you have time for **shopping,** head for the area around **rue St-Martin** and **rue du Commerce** for high-end items such as clothing, perfume, shoes, and jewelry. For a one-of-a-kind piece of jewelry, have something created by the master jeweler **Philippe Denies,** 3 rue St-Martin (www.atelierdeniesphilippe.com; ✆ **02-54-74-78-24**). If you prefer antique jewelry, stop by **Antebellum,** 12 rue St-Lubin (✆ **02-54-78-38-78**), and browse its selection of precious and semiprecious stones set in gold and silver. If you want to acquire a copy of tapestries like the ones at the nearby châteaux, you'll find a wide range at **Tapisserie Langlois,** Voûte du Château (✆ **02-54-78-04-43**). Chocoholics flock to award-winning **Max Vauché,** 50 rue du Commerce (www.maxvauche-chocolatier.com; ✆ **02-54-78-23-55**). On Saturday all day, a **food market** is on place Louis XII and place de la République, lining several blocks in the center of town at the foot of the château.

Château de Blois ★★★ CASTLE   A wound in battle earned him the name Balafré (Scarface), but he was quite a ladies' man. In fact, on the misty morning of December 23, 1588, Henri I, the duc de Guise, had just left a warm bed and the arms of one of Catherine de Médicis's ladies-in-waiting. His archrival, King Henri III, had summoned him, but when the duke arrived, only the king's minions were about. The guards approached with daggers. Wounded, the duke made for the door, where more guards awaited him. Staggering, he fell to the floor in a pool of his own blood. Only then did Henri emerge from behind the curtains. "Mon Dieu," he reputedly exclaimed, "he's taller dead than alive!" The body couldn't be shown: The duke was too popular. Quartered, it was burned in a fireplace.

The murder of the duc de Guise is only one of the events associated with the Château de Blois, begun in the 13th century by the comte de Blois. Blois reached the apex of its power in 1515, when François I moved to the château. For that reason, Blois is often called the "Versailles of the Renaissance," the second capital of France, and the "City of Kings." Blois soon became a palace of exile. Louis XIII banished his mother, Marie de Médicis, to the château, but she escaped by sliding into the moat down a mound of dirt left by the builders.

A mix of different styles, if you stand in the courtyard, you'll find that the château is like an illustrated storybook of French architecture. The Hall of the Estates-General is a beautiful 13th-century work; Louis XII built the Charles d'Orléans gallery and the Louis XII wing from 1498 to 1501; Mansart constructed the Gaston d'Orléans wing between 1635 and 1637. Most remarkable is the François I wing, a French Renaissance masterpiece, containing a spiral staircase with ornamented balustrades and the king's symbol, the salamander.

41000 Blois. www.chateaudeblois.fr. ✆ **02-54-90-33-33.** Admission 8€ (Oct–May) and 9.50€ (June–Sept) adults, 6.50€ (Oct–May) and 7€ (June–Sept) students, 4€ children 6–17, free for children 5 and under. July–Aug daily 9am–7pm; Apr–June and Sept daily 9am–6:30pm; Oct daily 9am–6pm; Nov–Mar daily 9am–12:30pm and 1:30–5:30pm.

WHERE TO EAT

Au Rendez-vous des Pêcheurs ★★ TOURAINE/SEAFOOD   This restaurant occupies a 16th-century house and former grocery a short walk from the château. Chef Christophe Cosme enjoys a reputation for quality, generous portions, and creativity. He prepares two or three meat dishes, including roasted Racan pigeon with caramelized cabbage, and seared Charolais steak with potatoes Maxime. These appear alongside a longer roster of seafood dishes, such as poached filet of local *sandre* (a freshwater fish; "zander" in English) served with citrus-flavored fennel confit, and freshwater pike stuffed with mussels.

27 rue du Foix. www.rendezvousdespecheurs.com. ✆ **02-54-74-67-48.** Reservations required. Main courses 31€–37€; fixed-price menu 30€–69€. AE, MC, V. Tues–Sat noon–2:30pm; Mon–Sat 7–10pm. Closed 1 week in Jan and the 1st 2 weeks of Aug.

L'Orangerie du Château ★★★ ☺ TOURAINE   Next to the château, one of the castle's former outbuildings holds the grandest and best restaurant in the area, with a floral-themed dining room. Faithful customers and the most discerning foodies visiting Blois delight in the filet mignon with truffles. You can also sample a freshly caught monkfish flavored with fresh thyme or autumnal venison with sweet potatoes purée and roasted figs. Everything tastes better with a Sauvignon de Touraine. Junior *gastronomes* can satisfy their palates with the special children's menu.

1 av. Jean-Laigret. www.orangerie-du-chateau-fr. ✆ **02-54-78-05-36.** Reservations required. Main courses 23€–37€; fixed-price menu 35€–79€; children's menu 14€. AE, MC, V. Thurs–Tues noon–1:30pm; Thurs–Sat and Mon–Tues 7:15–9:15pm. Closed mid-Feb to mid-Mar.

WHERE TO STAY

Some of the best rooms in town are at **Le Médicis** (see "Where to Eat," above).

Côté Loire–Auberge Ligérienne   About a 5-minute walk from Blois Castle, these B&B-like lodgings include impeccably maintained rooms decorated with an interesting mix of antique headboards, country throw rugs, and 1930s shipping posters. There is a low-key maritime theme here, which makes sense for a hotel that sits on the edge of a river that served as a major transportation link up until the 19th century. Parts of this small inn were constructed in the 12th, 15th, and 16th centuries, which explains the narrow stairways and exposed beams. One of the owners does double duty as chef: There is a tiny restaurant that features fresh, local ingredients.

2 place de la Grève, Blois 41000. www.coteloire.com. ✆ **02-54-78-07-86.** Fax 02-54-56-87-33. 8 units. 57€–89€ double. MC, V. Closed Jan. **Amenities:** Bar; restaurant. *In room:* TV, hair dryer, free Wi-Fi.

Chambord

191km (118 miles) SW of Paris; 18km (11 miles) E of Blois

The **Château de Chambord ★★★** (www.chambord.org; ✆ **02-54-50-40-00**) is the culmination of François I's two biggest obsessions: hunting and architecture. Built as a "hunting lodge," this colossal edifice is a masterpiece of architectural derring-do. Some say Leonardo da Vinci had something to do with it, and when you climb the amazing double spiral staircase, that's not too hard to believe. The staircase is superimposed upon itself so that one person may descend and a second ascend without ever meeting. While da Vinci died a few months before construction started in 1519, what emerged after 20 years was the pinnacle of the French Renaissance, the largest château in the Loire Valley. The castle's proportions are of an exquisite geometric harmony, and its fantastic arrangement of turrets and chimneys makes it one of France's most recognizable chateaux.

Construction continued for decades; François I actually stayed at the chateau for only a few weeks during hunting season, though he ensured Chambord would forever carry his legacy by imprinting his "F" emblem and symbol, the Salamander, wherever he could. After he died, his successors, none too sure what to do with the vast, unfurnished, and unfinished castle, basically abandoned it. Finally, Louis XIII gave it to his brother, who saved it from ruin; Louis XIV stayed there on several occasions and saw to restorations, but not a single monarch ever really moved in. The state acquired Chambord in 1932, and restoration work has been going on ever since.

Four monumental towers dominate Chambord's facade. The three-story keep has a spectacular terrace from which the ladies of the court used to watch the return of their men from the hunt. While many of the vast rooms are empty, several have been restored and filled with an impressive collection of period furniture and objects, giving an idea of what the castle looked like during the periods when parts of it were occupied. The château is in a park of more than 5,260 hectares (12,992 acres), featuring miles of hiking trails and bike paths, as well as picnic tables and bird-watching observation posts.

The château is open daily April to September 9am to 6pm, and October to March 9am to 5pm (until 7pm mid-July to mid-August). Admission is 9.50€ for adults and free for ages 17 and under accompanied by an adult. Allow 1½ hours to visit the château.

ESSENTIALS

GETTING THERE   It's best to **drive** to Chambord. Take D951 northeast from Blois to Saint Dyé, turning onto the rural road to Chambord. You can also rent a **bicycle** in Blois and ride the 18km (11 miles) to Chambord, or take a **tour** to Chambord from Blois in summer. From May to September, **Transports du Loir et Cher** (www.tlcinfo.net; ☏ **02-54-58-55-44**) operates a bus service to Chambord.

VISITOR INFORMATION   The **Maison de Tourisme,** on place Saint Louis (☏ **02-54-33-39-16**), is open April to October.

WHERE TO EAT & STAY

Hôtel du Grand-St-Michel   Across from the château, and originally built as a kennel for the royal hounds, this inn is the only one of any substance in the tiny village. Try for a front room overlooking the château, which is dramatically floodlit at night. Accommodations are plain but comfortable, with provincial decor. Most visitors arrive for lunch, which in summer is served on a terrace. High points from the menu include pheasant with chestnuts (in late autumn and winter), *filet mignon* with black chanterelle mushrooms and artichokes, and several local pâtés and terrines, including coarsely textured, flavorful rillettes of regional pork.

103 place St-Louis, Chambord 41250, near Bracieux. www.saintmichel-chambord.com. ☏ **02-54-20-31-31.** Fax 02-54-20-36-40. 40 units. 61€–102€ double; 85€–114€ triple. MC, V. Free parking. Restaurant: Main courses and fixed menus 19€–26€. Closed 2 weeks in Jan. **Amenities:** Restaurant; tennis court; Internet. *In room:* TV.

Cheverny

192km (119 miles) SW of Paris; 19km (12 miles) SE of Blois

The upper crust heads to the Sologne area for the hunt as if the 17th century had never ended. However, 21st-century realities—like formidable taxes—can't be entirely avoided, so the **Château de Cheverny ★★★** (www.chateau-cheverny.fr; ☏ **02-54-79-96-29**) opens its rooms to visitors.

Unlike most of the Loire châteaux, Cheverny is the residence of the original owner's descendants. The family of the vicomte de Sigalas can trace its lineage from Henri Hurault, the son of the chancellor of Henri III and Henri IV, who built the château in 1634. Designed in classic Louis XIII style, it is resolutely symmetrical, with square pavilions flanking the central pile. Its elegant lines and sumptuous furnishings provoked the Grande Mademoiselle, otherwise known as the Duchess of Montpensier, to proclaim it an "enchanted castle."

You, too, will be impressed by the antique furnishings, tapestries, and objets d'art. A 17th-century French artist, Jean Mosnier, decorated the fireplace with motifs from the legend of Adonis. The Guards' Room contains a collection of medieval armor; also on display is a Gobelin tapestry depicting the abduction of Helen of Troy. In the king's bedchamber, another Gobelin traces the trials of Ulysses. Most impressive is the stone stairway of carved fruit and flowers. To complete the regal experience, your arrival or departure from the château might be heralded by red-coated trumpeters accompanied by an enthusiastic pack of hunting hounds.

The château is open daily November to March 9:45am to 5pm, April to June and September 9:15am to 6:15pm, July and August 9:15am to 6:45pm, and October 9:45am to 5:30pm. Admission is 7.70€ for adults, 5€ for students under 25, and children 7 to 18, and free for children 6 and under. Allow 2 hours for your visit.

ESSENTIALS

GETTING THERE   Cheverny is 19km (12 miles) south of Blois, along D765. It's best reached by **car** or on a **bus tour** (Apr–Aug only) from Blois with **TLC Transports du Loir et Cher** (www.tlcinfo.net; ✆ **02-54-58-55-44**). Bus no. 4 leaves from the railway station at Blois once or twice per day; see the TLC website for the schedule. You can also take a **taxi** (✆ **02-54-78-07-65**) from the railway station at Blois.

VISITOR INFORMATION   The **Maison de Tourisme** is at 12 rue Chêne des Dames (www.bloispaysdechambord.com; ✆ **02-54-79-95-63**).

WHERE TO EAT & STAY

Les Trois Marchands TRADITIONAL FRENCH   This coaching inn, more comfortable than St-Hubert (see below), has been handed down for many generations. Jean-Jacques Bricault owns the three-story building, which has a mansard roof, a glassed-in courtyard, and sidewalk tables under umbrellas. In the tavern-style main dining room, the menu may include foie gras, lobster salad, frogs' legs, fresh asparagus in mousseline sauce, game dishes, or fish cooked in a salt crust. The inn rents 24 well-furnished, comfortable rooms with TVs for 42€ to 55€ for a double.

60 place de l'Eglise, Cour-Cheverny 41700. ✆ **02-54-79-96-44.** Fax 02-54-79-25-60. Dining room main courses 18€–47€; fixed-price menu 22€–45€. AE, DC, MC, V. Tues–Sun 7am–11pm. Closed Sun night Dec–Mar.

St-Hubert TRADITIONAL FRENCH   About 500m (1,640 ft.) from the château, this inn was built in the 1950s in the provincial style. The least expensive menu (served only at lunchtime Mon–Fri) may include terrine of wild boar with pistachios, poached ray with mustard sauce, and tarte tatin with vanilla bourbon ice cream. The most expensive menu may list sautéed scallops with red onion fondu, filet of Rossini beef with truffles, and profiteroles with ginger and chocolate sauce. The St-Hubert offers 20 conservatively decorated rooms with TVs for 57€ to 65€ for a double. Each room comes with free Wi-Fi.

122 rte. Nationale, Cour-Cheverny 41700. www.hotel-sthubert.com. ✆ **02-54-79-96-60.** Fax 02-54-79-21-17. Main courses 18€–22€; fixed-price menu 19€–39€; children's menu 12€. AE, MC, V. Daily noon–2pm and 7–9pm. Closed Sun night off-season.

Chenonceaux

224km (139 miles) SW of Paris; 26km (16 miles) E of Tours

Chenonceau is one of the most remarkable castles in France because it spans an entire river. Its impressive setting along with its intriguing history and renowned residents make it many visitors' favorite château in the whole country.

A Renaissance masterpiece, the **Château de Chenonceau ★★★** (www. chenonceau.com; ☏ **02-47-23-90-07**) is best known for the dames de Chenonceau who once occupied it. (The village, whose year-round population is less than 300, is spelled with a final *x*, but the château isn't.) Built first for Katherine Briçonnet, the château was bought in 1547 by Henri II for his mistress, Diane de Poitiers. For a time, this remarkable woman was virtually queen of France, infuriating Henri's dour wife, Catherine de Médicis. Diane's critics accused her of using magic to preserve her celebrated beauty and to keep Henri's attentions from waning. Apparently, Henri's love for Diane continued unabated, and she was in her 60s when he died in a jousting tournament in 1559.

When Henri died, Catherine became regent (her eldest son was still a child) and one of the first things she did was force Diane to return the jewelry Henri had given her and to abandon her beloved home. Catherine added her own touches, building a two-story gallery across the bridge—obviously inspired by her native Florence. The gallery, which was used for her opulent fêtes, doubled as a military hospital in World War I. It also played a crucial role in World War II, serving as the demarcation line between Nazi-occupied France and the "free" zone.

Gobelin tapestries, including one depicting a woman pouring water over the back of an angry dragon, and several important paintings by Poussin, Rubens, and Tintoretto adorn the château's walls. The chapel contains a marble *Virgin and Child* by Murillo, as well as portraits of Catherine de Médicis in black and white. There's even a portrait of the stern Catherine in the former bedroom of her rival, Diane de Poitiers. In François I's Renaissance bedchamber, the most interesting portrait is that of Diane as the huntress Diana.

The women of Chenonceau are the subject of the **Musée de Cire (Wax Museum),** located in a Renaissance-era annex a few steps from the château.

The château is open daily 9am to 8pm July and August; 9am to 7pm for the last two weeks of March; 9am to 7:30pm in June and September; October 9am to 6pm; 9am to 5pm the rest of the year. Admission is 11€ for adults and 8.50€ for students and children 7 to 17. You can purchase a combination ticket including entrance to the château and the museum for 13€ adults, 11€ children aged 7 to 17, free for 6 and under. Allow 2 hours to see this château.

ESSENTIALS

GETTING THERE About a dozen daily **trains** run from Tours to Chenonceaux (trip time: 30 min.), costing 6.30€ one-way. The train deposits you at the base of the château; from there, it's an easy walk. For information, visit www.voyages-sncf.com or call ☏ **36-35**. If you're **driving,** from the center of Tours, follow the signs to the D40 east, which will take you to the signposted turnoff for Chenonceaux.

VISITOR INFORMATION The **Syndicat d'Initiative** (tourist office), 1 rue du Dr. Bretonneau (☏ **02-47-23-94-45**), is open year-round.

WHERE TO EAT & STAY

La Roseraie and the **Auberge du Bon-Laboureur** (see below) have very good restaurants.

Auberge du Bon-Laboureur ★★ This inn, within walking distance of the château, is your best bet for a comfortable night's sleep and exceptional Loire Valley cuisine. Founded in 1786, the hotel maintains the flavor of that era, thanks to thick walls, solid masonry, and a scattering of antiques. Most guest rooms open out onto the garden, which features formally planted roses. Menu choices in the restaurant include crispy lobster with beet vinaigrette, and roasted pigeon with red cabbage celery root compote; the kitchen uses fresh produce direct from the hotel's garden. The prix-fixe menu at lunch is 30€; dinner menus run from 48€ to 85€.

6 rue du Dr. Bretonneau, Chenonceaux 37150. www.amboise.com/laboureur. ☏ **02-47-23-90-02.** Fax 02-47-23-82-01. 25 units. 125€–170€ double; 230€–280€ suite. AE, MC, V. Closed mid-Nov to mid-Dec and Jan 7–Feb 14. **Amenities:** Restaurant; bar; outdoor pool; room service. *In room:* A/C, TV, hair dryer, free Wi-Fi.

La Roseraie ★ 🌸 If charm is what you are after, you will be very happy at this friendly inn, where cheerful rooms are individually decorated with lots of period prints and old-fashioned furniture. History has left its mark: Just after World War II, Churchill, Truman, and Eleanor Roosevelt all came through; a framed letter from Mrs. Roosevelt hangs in the cozy salon. The exceptionally helpful and enthusiastic owners also welcome guests at the restaurant, which features homemade foie gras, haddock with dill, and pork medallions with mustard sauce.

7 rue du Dr. Bretonneau, Chenonceaux 37150. www.hotel-chenonceau.com. ☏ **02-47-23-90-09.** Fax 02-47-23-91-59. 18 units. 69€–135€ double. AE, DC, MC, V. Closed mid-Nov to mid-Feb. Free parking. **Amenities:** Restaurant; bar; outdoor pool; Wi-Fi in lobby and bar. *In room:* A/C, TV.

Chinon ★★

283km (175 miles) SW of Paris; 48km (30 miles) SW of Tours; 31km (19 miles) SW of Langeais

In the film *Joan of Arc,* Ingrid Bergman identified the dauphin as he tried to conceal himself among his courtiers. This took place in real life at the Château de Chinon, one of the oldest fortress-châteaux in France. Charles VII centered his government at Chinon from 1429 to 1450. In 1429, with the English besieging Orléans, the Maid of Orléans prevailed upon the dauphin to give her an army. The rest is history. The seat of French power stayed at Chinon until the end of the Hundred Years' War.

Today Chinon remains a tranquil town known mainly for its delightful red wines. After you visit the attractions, we recommend taking a walk along the Vienne River; definitely stop to taste the wine at one of Chinon's terraced cafes. Allow 3 hours to see Chinon.

ESSENTIALS

GETTING THERE The SNCF runs about seven **trains** and four **buses** every day to Chinon from Tours (trip time: 45 min. by train; 1 hr., 15 min. by bus), the one-way fare is 8.90€. For schedules and information, visit www.voyages-sncf.com or call ☏ **36-35.** Both buses and trains arrive at the train station, which lies at the edge of the very small town. If you're **driving** from Tours, take D751 southwest through Azay-le-Rideau to Chinon.

VISITOR INFORMATION The **Office de Tourisme** is at place Hofheim (www.chinon-valdeloire.com; ☏ **02-47-93-17-85**).

EXPLORING CHINON & THE CHATEAU

On the banks of the Vienne, the winding streets of Chinon are lined with many medieval turreted houses, built in the heyday of the court. The most typical street is rue Voltaire, lined with 15th- and 16th-century town houses. At no. 44, Richard the Lion-Heart died on April 6, 1199, from a wound suffered during the siege of Chalus in Limousin. The Grand Carroi, in the heart of Chinon, served as the crossroads of the Middle Ages. For the best view, drive across the river and turn right onto quai Danton. From this vantage point, you'll be able to see the castle in relation to the town and the river.

Château de Chinon ★★ CASTLE   The château, which was more or less in ruins, has undergone a massive excavation and restoration effort that started in 2003 and so far has resulted in beautifully restored ramparts, castle keep, and royal apartments, which now look more or less as they did in the good old days. After being roofless for 200 years, the apartments now sport pitched and gabled slate roofs and wood floors, and the keep is once again fortified. The restoration, while not exact (due to the state of the original building), gives the overall impression of what the castle looked like around the time of Joan of Arc's visit. The buildings are separated by a series of moats, adding to its medieval look. A new building has been constructed on the foundations of the Fort of St-George, which serves as an entrance hall and museum, featuring new archeological finds discovered during the restoration, as well as objects and interactive displays that recount the story of Joan of Arc, Charles VII, and the history of the castle.

Btw. rue St-Maurice and av. Francois Mitterrand. www.forteressechinon.fr. ✆ **02-47-93-13-45.** Admission 7€ adults, 4.50€ students, free for children 12 and under. Open daily May–Aug 9:30am–7pm; Mar, Apr, and Sept 9am–6pm; Oct–Feb 9:30am–5pm.

WHERE TO EAT

Les Années 30 FRENCH   On the oldest street in Chinon, you'll find the town's most innovative restaurant. If the charming 16th-century building doesn't entice you, the excellent-value menu certainly will. In summer, savor lobster duo with avocado and papaya salsa on the shady terrace and in winter, feast on pheasant with roasted figs or venison marinated with spiced gin with a vegetable and chestnut tart beside the cozy fireplace.

78 Rue Haute St Maurice. www.lesannees30.com. ✆ **02-47-93-37-18.** Reservations recommended. Main courses 18€–32€; fixed-price lunch menu 16€, dinner menus 27€–43€. MC, V. Thurs–Mon 12:15–2:00pm; Tues–Sat 7:30–10pm.

WHERE TO STAY

Hôtel Diderot ★ 🛄   Within a 5-minute walk of the town's historic core, this is a comfortable hotel with strands of ivy climbing romantically up its stone front. Although the foundations date from the 14th century, the building was radically altered in the 1700s; today you'll see remnants of thick wall and ceiling beams throughout the public rooms and in some of the guest rooms. Rooms are midsize to spacious, outfitted in Henry II or Napoleon III style, usually with big windows letting in maximum sunlight. One of the architectural highlights is a magnificent 15th-century fireplace in the breakfast room, where you'll enjoy as many as 52 kinds of jams and jellies as part of your morning ritual. The congenial hosts' enthusiasm for the charms of their home town is contagious.

4 rue du Buffon, Chinon 37500. www.hoteldiderot.com. ✆ **02-47-93-18-87.** Fax 02-47-93-37-10. 27 units. 55€–82€ double. AE, DC, MC, V. Parking 7€. **Amenities:** Bar. *In room:* TV, hair dryer, free Wi-Fi. Closed first 2 weeks of Dec and last week of Jan through first week of Feb.

Angers ★★★

288km (179 miles) SW of Paris; 89km (55 miles) E of Nantes

Once the capital of Anjou, Angers straddles the Maine River at the western end of the Loire Valley. Though it suffered extensive damage in World War II, it has been restored, blending provincial charm with a suggestion of sophistication. The bustling regional center is often used as a base for exploring the château district to the west. Young people, including some 30,000 college students, keep this vital city of 155,700 jumping until late at night. Allow 3 hours to see the attractions at Angers.

ESSENTIALS

GETTING THERE   High-speed **trains** make the 1½ hour trip every hour from Paris's Gare Montparnasse; the cost is 28€ to 61€ one-way. From Tours, about 10 trains per day make the 1-hour trip; a one-way ticket is 17€. The Angers train station is a convenient walk from the château. For schedules and information, visit www.voyages-sncf.com or call ✆ **36-35.** From Saumur, there are direct **bus** connections (1½ hr.); visit www.angoubus.fr or call ✆ **08-20-16-00-49** (.12€/min.) for schedules. If you're **driving** from Tours, take the A85 autoroute west and exit at Angers Centre.

VISITOR INFORMATION   The **Office de Tourisme,** 7 place Kennedy (www.angers-tourisme.com; ✆ **02-41-23-50-00**), is opposite the entrance to the château.

EXPLORING ANGERS

If you have time for shopping, wander to the pedestrian zone in the center of town. Its boutiques and small shops sell everything from clothes and shoes to jewelry and books. For regional specialties, head to **Maison du Vin de l'Anjou,** 5 bis place Kennedy (www.vinsdeloire.fr; ✆ **02-41-88-81-13**), where you can learn about the area's vineyards and buy a bottle or two for gifts or a picnic.

Château d'Angers ★★★ CASTLE   The château, dating from the 9th century, was the home of the comtes d'Anjou. The notorious Black Falcon lived here, and in time, the Plantagenets took up residence. From 1230 to 1238, the outer walls and 17 enormous towers were built, creating a fortress. King René favored the château, and during his reign, a brilliant court life flourished until he was forced to surrender to Louis XI. Louis XIV turned the château into a prison. In World War II, the Nazis used it as a munitions depot, and the Allies bombed it in 1944.

Visit the castle to see the **Apocalypse Tapestries ★★★**. They weren't always so highly regarded—they once served as a canopy to protect orange trees and were also used to cover the damaged walls of a church. Woven in Paris by Nicolas Bataille, from cartoons by Jean de Bruges, around 1375 for Louis I of Anjou, they were purchased for a nominal sum in the 19th century. The series of 77 sections, illustrating the Book of St. John, stretches 100m (328 ft.).

In 2009, the roof of the Logis Royal burned in an electrical fire and the château suffered damage (fortunately, the tapestries are housed in a separate building and were untouched). The Logis, which includes the royal apartments, is currently closed for repairs, but you can still tour the fortress, including the courtyard, ramparts, windmill tower, and 15th-century chapel, and see the tapestries. Once you've paid the entrance fee, you can take an hour-long guided tour focusing on the architecture and history of the château, or a tour devoted to the Apocolypse Tapestries. Both are available only in French; a self-guided tour with audio guides is available in English.

A Toast with the Home-Brew—Cointreau

Another libation unique to Angers is Cointreau. Two confectioner brothers set out to create a drink of "crystal-clear purity." The result was Cointreau, a twice-distilled alcohol from the peels of two types of oranges, bitter and sweet. The factory has turned out the drink since 1849. Cointreau flavors such drinks as the cosmopolitan and the sidecar. Recent marketing campaigns, including one featuring seductress Dita Von Teese, have helped modernize the brand and today some 13 million bottles of Cointreau are consumed annually.

La Carée Cointreau, 2 bd. des Bretonnières (www.cointreau.fr; © **02-41-31-50-50**), is in the suburb of St-Barthèlemy, a 10-minute drive east of the town center. If you call ahead to reserve, you can take a 1½-hour guided tour of the distillery and then visit the showroom, where you can sample and stock up on the fruity liqueur. Hours are variable; tours run on Saturdays only from October to April, and Tuesday through Saturday the rest of the year (9.80€ adult, 3.60€ children 12–17, free 12 and under).

2 promenade du Bout-du-Monde. http://angers.monuments-nationaux.fr. © **02-41-86-48-77.** Admission 8€ adults, 5€ seniors and students 18–25, free for children 17 and under. Sept–Apr daily 10am–5:30pm; May–Aug daily 9:30am–6:30pm.

WHERE TO EAT

La Salamandre ★ CLASSIC FRENCH   The salamander was the symbol of Renaissance king François I. In this formal, elegant restaurant, you'll see portraits of and references to that cunning strategist everywhere. Beneath massive sculpted ceiling beams, beside a large wooden fireplace, you'll enjoy the most impeccable service and best food in town. Shining examples include scallops with chanterelle mushrooms, lobster stew, roasted Challans region duck, and sautéed filet of beef and fresh foie gras with a reduction of red Anjou wine.

In the Hotel d'Anjou, 1 bd. du Maréchal Foch. www.restaurant-lasalamandre.fr. © **02-41-88-99-55.** Reservations recommended. Main courses 21€–38€; fixed-price menu 28€–48€. AE, DC, MC, V. Daily noon–2pm and Mon–Sat 7:30–9:30pm.

WHERE TO STAY

Best Western Hôtel d'Anjou   Beside a park, this hotel built in 1846 is the best choice for overnighting in the area. It has upscale appointments and amenities, along with a good restaurant, La Salamandre (see "Where to Eat," above). The lower rooms have higher ceilings and are more spacious.

1 bd. de Maréchal Foch, Angers 49100. www.hoteldanjou.fr. © **02-41-21-12-11** or **800/528-1234** in the U.S. and Canada. Fax 02-41-87-22-21. 53 units. 89€–193€ double. AE, DC, MC, V. Parking 8.50€. **Amenities:** Restaurant; bar. *In room:* TV, minibar, free Wi-Fi.

L'Hôtel de France   For a good night's sleep near the railway station, this comfortable 19th-century hotel is your best bet. Run by the Bouyer family since 1893, the rooms are decorated in light shades of cream and beige, nicely furnished and well maintained. Room rates go up 15€ to 25€ per night when trade shows are in town.

8 place de la Gare, Angers 49100. www.hoteldefrance-angers.com. © **02-41-88-49-42.** Fax 02-41-87-19-50. 55 units. 80€–140€ double. AE, DC, MC, V. Parking 7€. **Amenities:** Restaurant; bar; room service. *In room:* A/C, TV, minibar, hair dryer, free Wi-Fi.

PROVENCE & THE CÔTE D'AZUR

Provence has been called a bridge between the past and the present, which blend in a quiet, often melancholy way. Peter Mayle's *A Year in Provence* and its sequels have played a large role in the popularity of this sunny corner of southern France.

The Greeks and Romans filled the landscape with cities boasting baths, theaters, and arches. Romanesque fortresses and Gothic cathedrals followed. In the 19th century, the light and landscapes attracted painters such as Cézanne and van Gogh.

Provence has its own language and its own customs. The region is bounded on the north by the Dauphine, on the west by the Rhône, on the east by the Alps, and on the south by the Mediterranean. Each resort on the Riviera, known as the Côte d'Azur (Azure Coast), offers its own unique flavor and charms. This narrow strip of fabled real estate, less than 201km (125 miles) long and located between the Mediterranean and a trio of mountain ranges, has always attracted the jet set with its clear skies, blue waters, and orange groves.

A trail of modern artists captivated by the light and setting has left a rich heritage: Matisse at Vence, Cocteau at Menton and Villefranche, Picasso at Antibes and seemingly everywhere else, Léger at Biot, Renoir at Cagnes, and Bonnard at Le Cannet. The best collection is at the Foundation Maeght in St-Paul-de-Vence.

The Riviera's high season used to be winter and spring only. In recent years, July and August have become the most crowded, and reservations are imperative. The average summer temperature is 75°F (24°C); in winter it's 49°F (9°C).

The corniches of the Riviera, depicted in countless films, stretch from Nice to Menton. The Alps drop into the Mediterranean here, and roads were carved along the way. The lower road, 32km (20 miles) long, is the Corniche Inférieure. Along this road are the ports of Villefranche, Cap-Ferrat, Beaulieu, and Cap-Martin. The 31km (19-mile) Moyenne Corniche (Middle Road), built between World War I and World War II, runs from Nice to Menton, winding in and out of tunnels and through mountains. The highlight is at Eze. Napoleon built the Grande Corniche—the most panoramic—in 1806. La Turbie and Le Vistaero are the principal towns along the 32km (20-mile) stretch, which reaches more than 480m (1,575 ft.) high at Col d'Eze.

Avignon ★★★

691km (428 miles) S of Paris; 83km (51 miles) NW of Aix-en-Provence; 98km (61 miles) NW of Marseille

In the 14th century, Avignon was the capital of Christendom. What started as a temporary stay by Pope Clement V in 1309, when Rome was deemed too dangerous, became a 67-year golden age. The cultural and architectural legacy left by the six popes who served during this period makes Avignon one of Europe's most beautiful medieval destinations.

Today this walled city of some 95,000 residents is a major stop on the route from Paris to the Mediterranean. In recent years, it has become known as a cultural center, thanks to its annual international performing arts festivals and wealth of experimental theaters and art galleries. To make the most of the many galleries, museums, and the papal complex, plan to spend at least 2 days here.

ESSENTIALS

GETTING THERE   Over the summer months, you can **fly** from Paris's Beauvais Airport to **Aéroport Avignon-Caumont** (www.avignon.aeroport.fr; © **04-90-81-51-51**), 8km (5 miles) southeast of Avignon (trip time: 1 hr.). Taxis from the airport to the center cost approximately 25€. Call © **04-90-82-20-20.** However, it's nearly as quick to hop aboard one of the frequent TGV **trains** from Gare de Lyon: the ride takes 2 hours and 40 minutes and arrives at a modern station 10 minutes from town by shuttle bus. The one-way fare is between 65€ and 90€, depending on the date and time, although it can also be as cheap as 30€ if booked well in advance. Trains arrive frequently from Marseille (trip time: 80 min.; 19.40€ one-way) and Arles (trip time: 20 min.; 7€ one-way), arriving at either the TGV or Avignon's central station. Hourly trains from Aix-en-Provence (trip time: 20 min.; 29€ one-way) shuttle exclusively between the two towns' TGV stations. For rail information, call © **36-35** (www.voyages-sncf.com). The regional **bus** routes go from Avignon to Arles (trip time: 1 hr., 20 min.; 8.50€ one-way) and Aix-en Provence (trip time: 1 hr., 15 min.; 15 € one-way). The bus station at Avignon is the **Gare Routière,** 5 av. Monclar (©**04-90-82-07-35**). If you're **driving** from Paris, take A6 south to Lyon, and then A7 south to Avignon.

VISITOR INFORMATION   The **Office de Tourisme** is at 41 cours Jean-Jaurès (www.avignon-tourisme.com; © **04-32-74-32-74;** fax 04-90-82-95-03).

EXPLORING AVIGNON

Every French child knows the ditty *"Sur le pont d'Avignon, l'on y danse, l'on y danse"* ("On the bridge of Avignon, we dance, we dance"). The bridge in question, **Pont St-Bénézet** ★★ (www.palais-des-papes.com; © **04-90-27-51-16**), was constructed between 1177 and 1185. Once spanning the Rhône and connecting Avignon with Villeneuve-lèz-Avignon, it is now a ruin, with only 4 of its original 22 arches remaining (half of it fell into the river in 1669). On the third pillar is the **Chapelle St-Nicolas,** its first story in Romanesque style, the second in Gothic. The remains of the bridge are open November through February daily 9:30am to 5:45pm, first two weeks of March daily 9:30am to 6:30pm, mid-March through June and mid-September through October daily 9am to 7pm, July and first two weeks of September daily 9am to 8pm, and August daily 9am to 9pm. Admission is 4.50€ for adults, 3.50€ for seniors and students, and free for children 7 and under. Entrance to the chapel is included.

Cathédrale Notre-Dame des Doms   Near the Palais des Papes, this majestic 12th-century cathedral contains the elaborate tombs of popes Jean XXII and Benoît XII. Crowning the top is a 19th-century gilded statue of the Virgin. From the cathedral, enter the **Promenade du Rocher-des-Doms** to stroll in its garden and enjoy the view across the Rhône to Villeneuve-lez-Avignon.

Place du Palais des Papes. © **04-90-82-12-21.** Free admission. Daily 8am–6pm. Hours may vary according to religious ceremonies.

Palais des Papes ★★★   Dominating Avignon from a hilltop is one of the most famous, or notorious, palaces in the Christian world. Headquarters of a schismatic group of cardinals who came close to destroying the authority of the popes in Rome, this fortress is the city's most popular monument. Because of its massive size, you may be tempted to opt for a guided tour—but these can be monotonous. The detailed audio guide, included in the price of admission, will likely suffice.

A highlight is the Chapelle St-Jean, known for its frescoes of John the Baptist and John the Evangelist, attributed to the school of Matteo Giovanetti and painted

Provence & the Côte d'Azur

between 1345 and 1348. The **Grand Tinel (Banquet Hall)** is about 41m (134 ft.) long and 9m (30 ft.) wide; the pope's table stood on the south side. The walls of the **Pope's Bedroom,** on the first floor of the Tour des Anges, are painted with foliage, birds, and squirrels. The **Studium (Stag Room)**—the study of Clement VI—was frescoed in 1343 with hunting scenes. The **Grande Audience (Great Receiving Hall)** contains frescoes of the prophets, also attributed to Giovanetti and painted in 1352. If you have time, consider a visit to the Musée du Petit-Palais (see above), at the northern end of the Palace's square.

Place du Palais des Papes. www.palais-des-papes.com. © **04-90-27-50-00.** Admission (including audio guide) 10.50€ adults, 8.50€ seniors and students, free for children 8 and under. Mar 1–14 9am–6:30pm; March 15–June and Sept 16–Oct daily 9am–7pm; July and Sept 1–15 daily 9am–8pm; Aug 9am–9pm; Nov–Feb daily 9:30am–5:45pm; Christmas and New Year's Day 10:30am–5:45pm.

WHERE TO EAT

Christian Etienne ★★★ PROVENÇAL   The stone house containing this restaurant was built in 1180, around the same time as the Palais des Papes next door. Etienne's fixed-price menus center on featured ingredients such as duck or lobster; the pricier tasting menu relies on his imagination for unique combinations. In summer, look for the vegetable (not vegetarian) menu entirely based on ripe tomatoes, the main course a mousse of lamb, eggplant, tomatoes, and herbs. The a la carte menu includes innovative desserts such as jellied beets with green pepper coulis and lemongrass sorbet. The dining room contains early-16th-century frescoes honoring the marriage of Anne de Bretagne to the French king in 1491.

10 rue de Mons. www.christian-etienne.fr. ℂ **04-90-86-16-50.** Reservations required. Main courses 30€–50€; fixed-price lunch 31€, dinner 75€–150€. AE, DC, MC, V. Tues–Sat noon–1:15pm and 7:30–9:15pm.

La Fourchette ✦ PROVENÇAL   An upscale bistro serving innovative cuisine at a moderate price, La Fourchette is open only on weekdays. Its homey decoration (with collected items arranged on the walls) and large bay windows create a pleasant atmosphere. Among the dishes created by the sixth-generation chef: fresh sardines flavored with citrus, haddock-filled ravioli, and beef stew à l'Avignonnaise. It's popular with locals, so reservations are a must.

17 rue Racine. ℂ **04-90-85-20-93.** Main courses 19€; fixed-price menu 33€. MC, V. Mon–Fri 12:15–1:45pm and 7:15–9:45pm. Closed 3 weeks in Aug.

WHERE TO STAY

Hôtel d'Europe ★★★   This deluxe property, in operation since 1799, has welcomed luminaries from Charles Dickens to Jacqueline Kennedy. The entrance is through a shady courtyard dominated by a gurgling fountain, where dining is possible in warmer months. Antiques fill the grand hall and salons, and the guest rooms are handsomely decorated with period furnishings. Two top-floor suites offer private terraces with views of the Palais des Papes. Overall, accommodations are comfortable, with spacious, well-equipped bathrooms. The hotel's Michelin-starred restaurant, La Vieille Fontaine, specializing in traditional French and Provençal cuisine, is one of the best in Avignon.

12 place Crillon, Avignon 84000. www.heurope.com. ℂ **04-90-14-76-76.** Fax 04-90-14-76-71. 44 units. 210€–540€ double; 690€–920€ suite. AE, DC, MC, V. Parking 18€. **Amenities:** Restaurant; bar; room service; babysitting. *In room:* A/C, TV, minibar, hair dryer, free Wi-Fi.

Thames Résidences ★✦   Just a 5-minute stroll from the main train station, these pretty, Provençal-styled apartments (some with kitchenette) make an ideal base. Each one offers satellite television, a Nespresso Pixie expresso machine, DVD players, and free telephone calls abroad. North-facing apartments look out over Avignon's city walls, while apartments at the back have their own private balconies. Note that Thames Résidences shares its entrance with the Grand Hotel, although the two are separately owned and managed.

36 bd. Saint Roch, Avignon 84000. www.thames-residences.com. ℂ **04-32-70-17-01.** 9 units. 105€–161€ 2-person apartments, 131€–187€ 4-person apartments. MC, V. Free parking. *In room:* A/C, TV, hair dryer, free Wi-Fi.

St-Rémy-de-Provence ★

710km (440 miles) S of Paris; 24km (15 miles) NE of Arles; 19km (12 miles) S of Avignon; 10km (6¼ miles) N of Les Baux

Though Nostradamus, the physician and astrologer, was born here in 1503, most associate St-Rémy with Vincent van Gogh, who committed himself to a local asylum in 1889 after cutting off his left ear. *Starry Night* was painted during this period, as were many versions of *Olive Trees* and *Cypresses.*

Come to sleepy St-Rémy not only for its history and sights, but also for an authentic experience of daily Provençal life. The town springs into action on Wednesday mornings, when stalls bursting with the region's bounty, from wild-boar sausages to olives, elegant antiques to local crafts, and bolts of French country fabric, huddle between the sidewalk cafes beneath the plane trees.

ESSENTIALS

GETTING THERE A regional bus, the Cartreize, runs four to nine times daily between Avignon's Gare Routière and St-Rémy's place de la République (trip time: 45 min.; 3.10€ one-way). For bus information, see www.lepilote.com or call ✆ **08-10-00-13-26.** The St-Rémy Tourist Office also provides links to up-to-date bus schedules on their website (see below). If you're driving, head south from Avignon along D571.

VISITOR INFORMATION The **Office de Tourisme** is on place Jean-Jaurès (www.saintremy-de-provence.com; ✆ **04-90-92-05-22;** fax 04-90-92-38-52).

EXPLORING ST-RÉMY & ENVIRONS

Monastère Saint Paul de Mausole ★ This former monastery and clinic is where Vincent Van Gogh was confined from 1889 to 1890. It's now a psychiatric hospital for women. You can't see the artist's actual cell, but there is a reconstruction of his room. The Romanesque chapel and cloisters are worth a visit in their own right, as Van Gogh depicted their circular arches and beautifully carved capitals in some of his paintings. The path between the town center and the site (east of the D5 and opposite Glanum, see below) is dotted with reproductions of Van Gogh's paintings from the period he resided here.

Route des Baux-de-Provence. www.cloitresaintpaul-valetudo.com. ✆ **04-90-92-77-00.** Admission 4€ adults, 3€ students, free for children 12 and under. Apr–Oct daily 9:30am–7pm; Nov–Mar daily 10:15am–4:45pm. Closed Nov 1, Nov 11, and Christmas.

Site archéologique de Glanum ★★ A Gallo-Roman settlement thrived here during the final days of the Roman Empire. Its monuments include a **triumphal arch** from the time of Julius Caesar; garlanded with sculptured fruits and flowers, it dates from 20 B.C. and is the oldest in Provence. Another interesting feature is the baths, which, back in the day, had separate chambers for hot, warm, and cold. You can see entire streets and foundations of private residences from the 1st-century town, plus some remains from a Gallo-Greek town of the 2nd century B.C.

Route des Baux-de-Provence. http://glanum.monuments-nationaux.fr. ✆ **04-90-92-23-79.** Admission 7.50€ adults, 4.50€ students, free for European nationals 18–25 and children 18 and under. Apr–Aug daily 9:30am–6:30pm; Sept Tues–Sun 9:30am–6:30pm; Oct–Mar Tues–Sun 10am–5pm. Closed Jan 1, May 1, Nov 1, Nov 11, and Christmas. From St-Rémy, take D5 1.5km (1 mile) south, following signs to Les Antiques.

WHERE TO EAT

L'Estagnol 📷 MEDITERRANEAN Run by Corinne Meynadier and her husband chef Fabrice, L'Estagnol ("little pond" in the local dialect) sits within the light, bright environs of a former orangery glasshouse. Mediterranean cuisine focuses on top-notch local ingredients like Bouzigues oysters, and regional recipes, such as *cassoulet Languedocien.* The wine list is particularly strong on Corbières AOC offerings from the Languedoc-Roussillon region, where the Meynadiers owned a restaurant for 18 years. During summertime, dining takes place on the pretty garden terrace.

16 bd. Victor Hugo. www.restaurant-lestagnol.com. ℭ **04-90-92-05-95.** Reservations recommended. Main courses 17€–35€; fixed-price lunch 13€, dinner 34€; children's menu 11€. MC, V. Open May–Sept Tues–Sun noon–2:30pm and 7 :15–10pm; Oct–Apr Tues–Sun noon–2:30pm, Fri–Sat 7:15–10pm.

La Maison Jaune ★★ FRENCH/PROVENÇAL One of the most enduringly popular restaurants in St-Rémy is in the former residence of an 18th-century merchant. Today, in a pair of dining rooms occupying two floors, you'll appreciate cuisine prepared and served with flair. In warm weather, additional seats extend onto the terrace overlooking the Hôtel de Sade. Menu items include pigeon roasted in wine and honey; braised artichoke hearts with white wine and tomatoes; mussel soup with fennel; and roast rack of lamb served with tapenade of black olives and anchovies.

15 rue Carnot. www.lamaisonjaune.info. ℭ **04-90-92-56-14.** Reservations required. Fixed-price menu 38€–68€. MC, V. Wed–Sun noon–1:30pm; Tues–Sat 7:30–9pm. Closed Nov–Feb.

WHERE TO STAY

Hostellerie du Vallon de Valrugues ★★★ Surrounded by a park, this hotel has the best accommodations and restaurant in town. Constructed in the 1970s, it resembles an ancient Roman villa. Rooms are tastefully decorated in neoclassical style; many were recently renovated. All have huge, comfortable beds and marble bathrooms. Activities include an outdoor pool, bicycles, and the brand-new spa, La Maison d'Ennea. The restaurant's terrace is as appealing as its cuisine; its Italian-influenced dishes have earned a Michelin star (www.restaurant-marcdepassorio.fr). Fixed-price menus are 59€ to 105€. A less formal bistro is open in the afternoons.

9 Chemin Canto-Cigalo, St-Rémy-de-Provence 13210. www.vallondevalrugues.com. ℭ **04-90-92-04-40.** Fax 04-90-92-44-01. 48 units. 210€–340€ double; 270€–1,200€ suite. AE, MC, V. Free parking. Closed 3 weeks in Jan. **Amenities:** 2 restaurants; bar; outdoor pool; exercise room; spa; sauna; bikes; room service; babysitting; ping-pong table; pool table. *In room:* A/C, TV, minibar, hair dryer, free Wi-Fi.

Les Baux ★★★

Cardinal Richelieu called Les Baux "a nesting place for eagles." On a wind-swept plateau overlooking the southern Alpilles, Les Baux is a ghost of its former self, though still very dramatic. It was once the citadel of seigneurs who ruled with an iron fist and sent their armies as far as Albania. Today, the castle and ramparts are mere shells, though you can see remains of Renaissance mansions. The dry, foreboding countryside around Les Baux, which nestles in a valley surrounded by shadowy rock formations, offers its own fascination. Vertical ravines lie on either side of the town. Vineyards—officially classified as Coteaux d'Aix-en-Provence—surround Les Baux, facing the Alpilles. If you follow the signposted *route des vin,* you can motor through the vineyards in an afternoon, perhaps stopping off at growers' estates.

Now the bad news: Because of the beauty and drama of the area, Les Baux is virtually overrun with visitors; it's not unlike Mont-St-Michel in that respect.

ESSENTIALS

GETTING THERE Les Baux is best reached by car; there is no rail service. From Arles, take the express highway D570 northeast until you reach the turnoff for a secondary road (D17), which will lead you northeast to Fontvieille. From there, follow the signs east into Les Baux. By **train,** most passengers get off at Arles, then take a 35-minute local bus (2.10€ one-way). The same line runs in the opposite direction from St-Remy. For bus information, see www.lepilote.com or call ℭ **08-10-00-13-26.** You can also book 1-day coach tours through **Autocars Lieutaud** (www.excursion provence.com; ✆ **04-90-86-36-75**) in Avignon or the tourist office in Aix-en-Provence (✆ **04-42-16-11-61**; www.aixenprovencetourism.com).

VISITOR INFORMATION The **Office de Tourisme** (www.lesbauxdeprovence. com; ✆ **04-90-54-34-39**; fax 04-90-54-51-15) is at Maison du Roy, near the northern entrance to the old city.

EXPLORING LES BAUX

Les Baux is one of the most dramatic towns in Provence. You can wander through feudal ruins, called **La Ville Morte (Ghost Village) ★★★**, at the northern end of town. The **Château des Baux** (www.chateau-baux-provence.com; ✆ **04-90-54-55-56**) is carved out of the rocky mountain peak; the site of the castle covers an area at least five times that of Les Baux itself. As you stand at the ruins, you can look out over the Val d'Enfer (Valley of Hell) and even see the Mediterranean in the distance.

At the castle you can enjoy the panorama from the **Tour Sarrazin (Saracen Tower).** Admission to the castle, including the museum and access to the ruins, is 7.80€ for adults, 5.80€ for students, and free for children 17 and under. The site is open in July and August daily 9am to 7:30pm, March to June and in September and October daily 9am to 6:30pm, and November to February daily 9:30am to 5pm.

WHERE TO EAT & STAY

La Cabro d'Or ★★★ This is the lesser-known sibling of the nearby Oustau de Baumanière. You'll find some of the most comfortable accommodations in the region here, with a Michelin-starred restaurant. Set in a vast, well-manicured garden, the original building is an 18th-century farmhouse, while the dining room is situated in another building from the same period (meals are also served on the terrace). The massive ceiling beams are works of art in their own right. Guest rooms evoke authentic Provence with art and antiques; some have views over the tranquil countryside. Unlike the Oustau de Baumanière, the annexes in this hotel are not as impressive as the original buildings.

Route d'Arles, Les Baux de Provence 13520. www.lacabrodor.com. ✆ **04-90-54-33-21.** Fax 04-90-54-45-98. 26 units. 165€–390€ double; 293€–600€ suite. AE, DC, MC, V. Free parking. Closed Sun–Mon mid–Oct to Mar. **Amenities:** Restaurant; bar; outdoor pool; 2 tennis courts; spa; room service; babysitting. *In room:* A/C, TV, minibar, hair dryer, free Wi-Fi.

Arles ★★★

744km (461 miles) S of Paris; 36km (22 miles) SW of Avignon; 92km (57 miles) NW of Marseille

Often called the soul of Provence, this town on the Rhône attracts art lovers, archaeologists, and historians. To the delight of visitors, many of the vistas van Gogh painted so luminously remain. The painter left Paris for Arles in 1888, the same year he cut off part of his left ear. He painted some of his most celebrated works here, including *The Starry Night, The Bridge at Arles, Sunflowers,* and *L'Arlésienne.*

Though Arles doesn't possess as much charm as Aix-en-Provence, it's still rewarding to visit, with first-rate museums, excellent restaurants, and summer festivals. The city today isn't quite as lovely as it was, but it has enough of the antique charm of Provence to keep its appeal alive.

ESSENTIALS

GETTING THERE Trains run almost every hour between Arles and Avignon (trip time: 20 min.; 7€ one-way), Marseille (trip time: 50 min.; 14.30€), and Nîmes (trip time:

Les Taureaux

Bulls are a big part of Arlesien culture. It's not unusual to see bull steak on local menus, and *saucisson de taureau* (bull sausage) is a local specialty.

The first bullfight, or *corrida*, took place in the amphitheater in 1853. Appropriately, Arles is home to a bull-fighting school. Bulls are run through the streets during major festivals, while spectators behind metal barriers look on.

Today *corridas* are held on Easter weekend, during the Festival of Arles in July and on 1 weekend in September. The bull is killed only during the Easter *corrida*; expect a few protestors. During the others, the bull is spared. The Easter event begins at 11am, others around 5pm.

30 min.; 8€ one-way). Be sure to take local trains from city center to city center, not the TGV, which, in this case, takes more time. For rail information, go to www.voyages-sncf. com or call ✆ **36-35.** There are **buses** from Aix-en-Provence (trip time: 1 hr., 20 min.; 9.20€ one-way) and other major towns; for information, see www.lepilote.com or call ✆ **08-10-00-13-26.** If **driving,** head south along D570 from Avignon.

For bicycles, head to **Europebike Provence** (www.europbike-provence.fr; ✆ **06-38-14-49-50**), which rents bikes from 14€ per day. Pick-up is from several locations around Arles, and they deliver to certain hotels. It is possible to reserve online.

VISITOR INFORMATION The **Office de Tourisme** is on esplanade Charles-de-Gaulle (www.arlestourisme.com; ✆ **04-90-18-41-20;** fax 04-90-18-41-29).

EXPLORING ARLES

The **Place du Forum,** shaded by plane trees, stands around the old Roman forum. The Terrasse du Café le Soir, immortalized by van Gogh, is now the square's Café van Gogh. You can see two Corinthian columns and fragments from a temple at the corner of the Hôtel Nord-Pinus. Three blocks south is **Place de la République,** dominated by a 15m-tall (49-ft.) red granite obelisk.

One of the city's great classical monuments is the Roman **Théâtre Antique ★★**, rue du Cloître (✆ **04-90-49-59-05**). Augustus began the theater in the 1st century; only two Corinthian columns remain. The *Venus of Arles* (now in the Louvre in Paris) was discovered here in 1651. The theater is open May through September daily 9am to 7pm; March, April, and October daily 9am to 6pm; and November through February daily 10am to 5pm. Closed public holidays. Admission is 6.50€ for adults, 5€ for students, and free for children 18 and under. The same ticket admits you to the nearby **Amphitheater (Les Arènes) ★★**, rond-pont des Arènes (✆ **04-90-49-59-05**), also built in the 1st century. Sometimes called Le Cirque Romain, it seats almost 25,000. For a good view, climb the three towers that remain from medieval times, when the amphitheater was turned into a fortress. Hours are the same as those for the Théâtre Antique.

WHERE TO EAT & STAY

L'Hôtel Particulier ★★★ 🍴 Occupying an 18th-century pavilion, this edifice was the last of the private town houses built in the center of Arles. It may not be as grand as the Jules César, weighing in at just a fraction of the size, but its distinctive elegance has made it a formidable challenger. Behind a monumental gate, you'll encounter ancient yew trees and a courtyard with teak lounges and a limestone-built *bassin* containing a lap pool. Each bedroom is decorated individually in cool, neutral tones with Provençal antiques, elegantly draped fabrics, and designer knickknacks. Gourmet dining is available in the crisp white dining room or outside.

4 rue de la Monnaie, 13200 Arles. www.hotel-particulier.com. ✆ **04-90-52-51-40.** Fax 04-90-96-16-70. 14 units. 259€–329€ double; 299€–429€ suite. AE, MC, V. Parking 19€. **Amenities:** Restaurant; outdoor pool; small spa and hammam; room service. *In room:* A/C, TV, minibar, free Wi-Fi.

Aix-en-Provence ★★

760km (471 miles) S of Paris; 84km (52 miles) SE of Avignon; 34km (21 miles) N of Marseille; 185km (115 miles) W of Nice

One of the most surprising things about Aix is its size. Frequently guidebooks and travel programs proclaim it the very heart of Provence, evoking a sleepy town filled with flowers and fountains. Which it is—in certain quarters. But Aix is also a bustling judicial center and university town of nearly 143,000 inhabitants (the Université d'Aix dates from 1413).

Founded in 122 B.C. by Roman general Caius Sextius Calvinus, who named the town Aquae Sextiae, after himself, Aix originated as a military outpost. Its former incarnations include a civilian colony, the seat of an archbishop, and official residence of the medieval counts of Provence.

Paul Cézanne, Aix's most celebrated son, immortalized the countryside in his paintings. Just as he saw it, the Montagne Ste-Victoire looms over the town today, though a string of high-rises now interrupts the landscape.

Time marches on, but there are still plenty of decades-old, family-run shops on the narrow streets of the old town. A lazy summer lunch at one of the bourgeois cafes on the cours Mirabeau is an experience not to be missed.

ESSENTIALS

GETTING THERE **Trains** arrive daily from Marseille (trip time: 1 hr.; 8.70€ one-way), Nice (trip time: 3 hr.; 38€ one-way), and Cannes (trip time: 2 hr., 30 min.; 32.70€ one-way). High-speed TGV trains—from Paris as well as Marseille and Nice—arrive at the modern station near Vitrolles, 18km (11 miles) west of Aix. For rail information, see www.voyages-sncf.com or call ✆ **36-35.** Bus transfers to the center of Aix cost 3.60€ one-way. There are **buses** from Marseille, Avignon, and Nice; for information, see www.lepilote.com or call ✆ **08-10-00-13-26.** If you're **driving** to Aix from Avignon or other points north, take A7 south to A8 and follow the signs into town. From Marseille or other points south, take A51 north.

VISITOR INFORMATION The **Office de Tourisme** is at Les Allées Provençales, 300 av. Giuseppe Verdi (www.aixenprovencetourism.com; ✆ **04-42-16-11-61;** fax 04-42-16-11-62).

EXPLORING THE CITY

Aix's main street, **Cours Mirabeau** ★, is one of Europe's most beautiful. A double row of plane trees shades it from the Provençal sun and throws dappled daylight onto its rococo fountains. Shops and sidewalk cafes line one side; 17th- and 18th-century sandstone *hôtels particuliers* (mansions) take up the other. The street begins at the 1860 fountain **La Rotonde,** on place du Général-de-Gaulle, and is named for Honoré Gabriel Riqueti, Count of Mirabeau, the revolutionary and statesman. Boulevard Carnot and Cours Sextius circle the heart of the old quarter (Vieille Ville), which contains the pedestrian zone.

Atelier de Cézanne ★★ Cézanne was the major forerunner of cubism. This studio, surrounded by a wall and restored by American admirers, is where he worked. As the building remained locked up and virtually untouched for decades after Cézanne death in 1906, visitors are offered a unique glimpse into the artist's daily life, "his coat hanging on the wall, his easel with an unfinished picture waiting for a touch of the master's brush," as Thomas R. Parker wrote.

9 av. Paul-Cézanne (outside town). ✆ **04-42-21-06-53.** Admission 5.50€ adults, 2€ students and children 13–25, free for children 12 and under. July–Aug daily 10am–6pm, English tour at 5pm; Apr–June and Sept daily 10am–noon and 2–6pm, English tour at 5pm; Oct–Mar daily 10am–noon and 2–5pm, English tour at 4pm.

WHERE TO EAT

Le Mille Feuille ★ PROVENÇAL This small restaurant and tea shop is one of Aix's best-kept secrets. It was opened by two former staff of the l'Oustau de Baumanière in Les Baux. The talented Nicolas Monribot is a pastry chef by training and also a musician, which shows through in his melodious savory dishes such as cream of Jerusalem artichoke soup, roasted lamb with soft polenta, and monkfish with orange-flavored curry. You'll be competing with some serious local fans, particularly at dinnertime, so be sure to reserve in advance. Wine expert Sylvain Sendra offers an unusual collection of local vintages, most of them biodynamic.

8 rue Rifle-Rafle. ✆ **04-42-96-55-17.** Dinner reservations essential. Main courses 15€; fixed-price lunch 22€–27€, dinner 32€–37€. MC, V. Tues–Sat noon–2pm and Wed–Sat 7:45–10pm. Closed 3 weeks in Aug.

WHERE TO STAY

Hôtel Cézanne ★★ Colorful and chic, Aix's finest boutique hotel pays homage to Provence and the paintings of Cézanne. Conceived by one of the designers of both Villa Gallici and 28 à Aix, the Cezanne could be considered a younger, hipper cousin, with details such as mother-of-pearl-inlaid walls and elaborate tiles in some of the bathrooms. Bedrooms are spacious and filled with light; amenities include rain showers and free cold drinks in the minibar. Breakfast, served until noon, might include smoked salmon and champagne. Modern art is exhibited in the public spaces, which include a bar.

40 av. Victor Hugo, Aix-en-Provence 13100. www.hotelaix.com/cezanne. ✆ **04-42-91-11-11.** Fax 04-42-91-11-10. 55 units. 200€–250€ double; 290€–350€ junior suite; 380€ suite. AE, MC, V. Free parking, by reservation. **Amenities:** Bar; business center. *In room:* A/C, TV, minibar, hair dryer, free Wi-Fi.

Hôtel du Globe A good budget option for a city where expensive is the norm. A short walk from the Cathédrale St-Sauveur, this hotel is just on the northwest edge of Aix's old town, and around a 10-minute walk to cours Mirabeau. Rooms are basic but clean; at the press of a button, an automatic shade descends to shield them from sun or unwanted noise. Bathrooms are on the small side. Some rooms have balconies, and a rooftop terrace is open to all. The staff is especially helpful and will do everything to ensure a pleasant stay.

74 cours Sextius, Aix-en-Provence 13100. www.hotelduglobe.com. ✆ **04-42-26-03-58.** Fax 04-42-26-13-68. 46 units. 78€–90€ double; 102€–119€ triple. AE, DC, MC, V. Parking 9.80€. **Amenities:** Breakfast in room. *In room:* A/C, TV, free Wi-Fi.

St-Tropez

874km (542 miles) S of Paris; 76km (47 miles) SW of Cannes

An air of hedonism runs rampant in this sun-kissed town, but Tropezian style is blissfully understated—not in-your-face. St-Tropez attracts artists, novelists, and the film

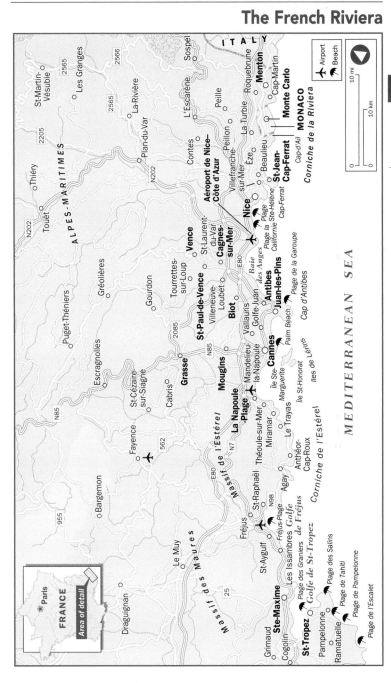

colony each summer, with a flamboyant parade of humanity trailing behind. In winter it morphs back into a boho fishing village, albeit one studded with modern art galleries and some of the best restaurants along the coast.

The Brigitte Bardot movie *And God Created Woman* put St-Tropez on the tourist map. Yet more decadent tourists, baring almost all on the peninsula's white-sand beaches, followed in her wake. In 1995, Bardot pronounced St-Tropez dead, "squatted by a lot of no-goods, drugheads, and villains." But 1997 saw her return, followed in recent years by celebrity A-listers including Keith Richards, David Beckham, Paris Hilton, Jay-Z, and Beyoncé.

ESSENTIALS

GETTING THERE The nearest rail station is in St-Raphaël, a neighboring coastal resort. **Boats** depart (www.bateauxsaintraphael.com; ✆ **04-94-95-17-46**) from its Vieux Port for St-Tropez (trip time: 50 min.) every 15 minutes in high summer, reducing to twice-daily sailings in winter. The one-way fare is 14€. Year-round, 10 to 15 Varlib **buses** per day leave from the Gare Routière in St-Raphaël (www.varlib.fr; ✆ **04-94-44-52-70**) for St-Tropez. The trip takes 1½ to 2 hours, depending on the bus and the traffic, which during midsummer is usually horrendous. A one-way ticket costs 2€. Buses and boats run directly to St-Tropez from Toulon and Hyères. Buses also run from the nearest airport, at Toulon-Hyères, 56km (35 miles) away.

If you **drive,** note that parking in St-Tropez is very difficult, especially in summer. For parking, follow the signs for **Parking des Lices** (✆ **04-94-97-34-46**), beneath place des Lices, or **Parking du Nouveau Port,** on waterfront avenue Charles de Gaulle (✆ **04-94-97-74-99**). To get here from **Cannes,** drive southwest along the coastal highway (RD98), turning east when you see signs pointing to St-Tropez.

VISITOR INFORMATION The **Office de Tourisme** is on quai Jean-Jaurès (www.ot-saint-tropez.com; ✆ **08-92-68-48-28;** fax 04-94-97-82-66).

EXPLORING ST-TROPEZ & ENVIRONS

At the foot of St-Tropez's yacht-filled port lies the bronze **Statue de Suffren,** paying tribute to Vice Admiral Pierre André de Suffren. This St-Tropez native was one of the greatest sailors of 18th-century France and fought in the Franco-American wars against the British in the 1780s.

In the old town, one of the most interesting streets is **rue de la Miséricorde.** It's lined with stone houses that hold boutiques and evokes medieval St-Tropez better than any other in town. At the corner of rue Gambetta is **Chapelle de la Miséricorde,** with a blue, green, and gold tiled roof. Towering above the town is the **Citadelle,** a fortified castle complete with drawbridges and stunning views across the Bay of St-Tropez. It's open daily from 10am to 6:30pm (until 5:30pm from October to March). Admission is 2.50€; entrance is free for those 8 and under.

Port Grimaud ★ makes an interesting outing. From St-Tropez, drive 4km (2¼ miles) west on A98 to route 98, and then 1.5km (1 mile) north to the Port Grimaud exit. If you approach the village at dusk, when it's bathed in Riviera pastels, it looks like a 16th-century hamlet. However, the vision is a mirage: Port Grimaud is the dream of its promoter, architect François Spoerry, who carved it out of marshland and dug canals. Flanking the canals, fingers of land extend from the square to the sea. The homes are Provençal style, many with Italianate window arches. Boat owners can anchor at their doorsteps, and visitors can putter around the "village" on a rented electric boat. One newspaper called the port "the most magnificent fake since Disneyland."

HITTING THE BEACH & OTHER OUTDOOR ACTIVITIES

BEACHES   The hottest Riviera beaches are at St-Tropez. The best for families are closest to the center, including **Plage de la Bouillabaisse, Plage des Graniers,** and **Plage des Salins.** More daring is the 5km (3-mile) crescent of **Plage de Pampelonne,** about 10km (6¼ miles) from St-Tropez. Here around 35 hedonistic beach clubs dot the sand. For better or worse, the cash-only **La Voile Rouge**—where champagne was sprayed over diners, who regularly proceeded to dance on the table tops—closed in late 2011. Equally decadent is **Club 55** (www.club55.fr; ✆ **04-94-55-55-55**), a former Bardot hangout, while American-run **Nikki Beach** (www.nikki beach.com; ✆ **04-94-79-82-04**) is younger and more understated, but nevertheless painfully chic. Gay-friendly **Aqua Club** (www.aqua-club-plage.fr; ✆ **04-94-79-84-35**) and bare-all **Plage de Tahiti** (www.tahiti-beach.com; ✆ **04-94-97-18-02**) are extremely welcoming. More relaxed still are **Tropicana** (✆ **04-94-79-83-96**) and **Plage des Jumeaux** (www.plagedesjumeaux.com; ✆ **04-94-55-21-80**), the latter drawing many families with young kids.

You'll need a car, bike, or scooter to get from town to Plage de Pampelonne. Parking is around 10€ for the day. More than anywhere else on the Riviera, topless bathing is the norm.

WHERE TO EAT

Auberge des Maures ★ PROVENÇAL   One of our favorite restaurants lies close to one end of the all-pedestrian rue Allard. The stone-sided building, highlighted with Provençal murals, has a rollaway roof and garden seating (both experienced during nice weather). The open kitchen affords views of the staff preparing Provençal specialties, including stuffed zucchini blossoms and *gigot d'agneau* lamb with rosemary confit, and *petits farcis* (stuffed vegetables). The Salinesi family takes pride in using seasonal, all-fresh ingredients.

4 rue du Docteur Boutin. www.aubergedesmaures.fr. ✆ **04-94-97-01-50.** Reservations recommended. Main courses 42€–60€; fixed-price menu 51€. AE, DC, MC, V. Daily 7:30pm–1am. Closed mid-Nov to Mar.

Spoon Byblos ★★ FRENCH/INTERNATIONAL   Originally launched in Paris, Spoon's Riviera incarnation draws special inspiration from Catalonian, Andalusian, and Moroccan cuisine. It also offers more than 300 wines from around the world. It's terribly fashionable, as you might expect, given its location in one of the world's hippest hotels. Diners are advised to concentrate on the imaginative cuisine rather than the self-conscious sense of chic. The restaurant opens onto a circular bar made of blue-tinted glass and polished stainless steel. Dig into shrimp and squid consommé with a hint of jasmine and orange, or pan-seared tuna. Local favorites for two people sharing include farm-reared shoulder of lamb with fennel and *socca* pancakes, and whole-roasted lobster with onion confit.

In the Hôtel Byblos, av. Paul-Signac. ✆ **04-94-56-68-20.** Reservations required. Main courses 25€–49€; fixed-price menu 86€. AE, DC, MC, V. Daily 8–11pm. Closed Nov to mid-Apr.

ENTERTAINMENT & NIGHTLIFE

On the lobby level of the Hôtel Byblos, **Les Caves du Roy,** avenue Paul-Signac (✆ **04-94-97-16-02**), is the most self-consciously chic nightclub in St-Tropez. Entrance is free, but drink prices are eye-wateringly high. Any riff-raff (or paparazzi, for that matter) are kept away from the beautiful people by owner Jean de Colmont. It's open nightly from Easter to late September from 11:30pm until dawn. **Le**

Papagayo, in the Résidence du Nouveau-Port, rue Gambetta (✆ **04-94-97-95-95**), is one of the largest nightclubs in town. The decor was inspired by the psyche-delic 1960s. Entrance is around 20€ and includes one drink, although those dining at the attached restaurant can routinely sneak in free. Adjacent to Le Papagayo is **Le VIP Room,** in the Résidence du Nouveau-Port (✆ **04-94-97-14-70**), a younger yet similarly chic version of Les Caves du Roy. Paris Hilton and Snoop Dogg have been known to drop by. Cocktails hover around the 20€ mark.

Le Pigeonnier, 13 rue de la Ponche (✆ **04-94-97-84-26**), rocks, rolls, and welcomes a mostly gay or lesbian crowd between 20 and 50. Most of the socializing revolves around the long, narrow bar, where patrons from all over Europe chatter. There's also a dance floor. **L'Esquinade,** 2 rue de Four (✆ **04-94-56-26-21**), is the habitual sweaty follow-on club.

Below the Hôtel Sube, **Café de Paris,** sur le Port (✆ **04-94-97-00-56**), is one of the most popular—and most friendly—hangouts in town. It has 1900s-style globe lights, an occasional 19th-century bronze artifact, masses of artificial flowers, and a long zinc bar. **Café Sénéquier,** sur le Port (✆ **04-94-97-00-90**), is historic, vener-able, snobbish by day, and off-puttingly stylish by night.

WHERE TO STAY

Hôtel Byblos ★★★ The builder said he created "an anti-hotel, a place like home." That's true—if your home resembles a palace in Beirut and has salons deco-rated with Phoenician gold statues from 3000 B.C. On a hill above the harbor, this complex has intimate patios and courtyards. It's filled with antiques and rare objects such as polychrome carved woodwork and marquetry floors. Every room is unique, and all have elegant beds. Unusual features might include a fireplace on a raised hearth or a bed recessed on a dais. The rooms range in size from medium to spacious, often with high ceilings and antiques or reproductions. Some units have such special features as four-posters with furry spreads or sunken whirlpool tubs. Le Hameau, a stylish annex, contains 10 duplex suites built around a small courtyard with an out-door spa. However, service can be snooty, and the crown of St Tropez's coolest hotel may pass from Byblos to the new Hotel de Paris, when the latter opens for its first full season in 2013.

Av. Paul Signac, St-Tropez 83990. www.byblos.com. ✆ **04-94-56-68-00.** Fax 04-94-56-68-01. 91 units. 395€–950€ double; from 650€ suite. AE, DC, MC, V. Parking 30€. Closed Nov–Mar. **Ameni-ties:** 2 restaurants; 1 bar; outdoor pool; exercise room; spa; sauna; concierge; room service; mas-sage; babysitting; nightclub. *In room:* A/C, TV, minibar, hair dryer, free Wi-Fi.

Hôtel Sezz ★★ ☺ This designer dream took on the mantle of St-Tropez's hip-pest hotel with the opening of 35 wow-factor suites in 2010, plus 2 stand-out villas in 2011. Accomplished French hotelier Shahé Kalaidjian has combined practical architecture (curved bedroom ceilings that draw eyes skyward) with smile-inducing additions (secluded outdoor showers with rainforest heads). The resulting atmo-sphere, no doubt aided by the vast palm-lined pool with huge concrete stepping stones, is laid back, beachy, and communal, although those craving luxurious privacy can doze in their own secret grassy garden that lies to the rear of each unit. Sunrise yoga and open-air massage are the order of the day at the Payot Spa. The restaurant Colette sprouts from inside the glass cube dining room and creeps right around the pool. Dining under the innovative eye of rising star Patrick Cuissard is a delight. Light, summery dishes are prepared with elan: think carpaccio of seabass bathed in coconut milk.

Rte Des Salins, Saint Tropez 83990. www.hotelsezz-sainttropez.com. ℂ **04-94-55-31-55.** Fax 04-94-55-31-51. 37 units. 400€–850€ double; from 1400€ suite. AE, DC, MC, V. Free parking. Closed mid-Oct to mid-Apr. Amenities: Restaurant; bar; outdoor pool; exercise room; sauna; bikes; concierge; room service; massage; babysitting; free shuttle to beach; spa. In room: A/C, TV, minibar, hair dryer, free Wi-Fi.

Cannes ★★★

905km (561 miles) S of Paris; 163km (101 miles) E of Marseille; 26km (16 miles) SW of Nice

When Coco Chanel came here and got a suntan, returning to Paris bronzed, she shocked the milk-white society ladies—who quickly began to copy her. Today the bronzed bodies, clad in nearly nonexistent swimsuits, line the beaches of this chic resort and continue the late fashion designer's example. A block back from the famed promenade de la Croisette are the boutiques, bars, and bistros that make Cannes the Riviera's capital of cool. The opening of a museum dedicated to French painter Pierre Bonnard in the suburb of Le Cannet in 2011 added a cultural string to the resort's sophisticated charms.

ESSENTIALS

GETTING THERE By **train,** Cannes is 15 minutes from Antibes, 35 minutes from Nice, and 50 minutes from Monaco. The TGV from Paris reaches Cannes in an incredibly scenic 5 hours. The one-way fare from Paris is 50€ to 100€. For rail information and schedules, visit www.voyages-sncf.com or call ℂ **36-35. Rapide Côte d'Azur,** place de l'Hôtel de Ville, Cannes (www.rca.tm.fr; ℂ **04-93-85-64-44**), provides bus service to Nice via Antibes and Cagnes-sur-Mer every 20 minutes during the day (trip time: 1½ hr.). The one-way fare is 1€.

Nice **international airport** (www.nice.aeroport.fr; ℂ **08-20-42-33-33**) is a 30-minute drive east. **Buses** pick up passengers at the airport every 30 minutes during the day (hourly at other times) and drop them at the Gare Routière, place de l'Hôtel de Ville (www.rca.tm.fr; ℂ **04-93-85-64-44**). The one-way fare is 15.60€.

By **car** from Marseille, take A51 north to Aix-en-Provence, continuing along A8 east to Cannes. From Nice, follow A8 southwest to Cannes.

VISITOR INFORMATION The **Office de Tourisme** is at 1 bd. de la Croisette (www.cannes.travel; ℂ **04-92-99-84-22;** fax 04-92-99-84-23). There is an additional office by the train station.

EXPLORING CANNES

For many visitors, Cannes might as well consist of only one street, the promenade de la Croisette—or just **La Croisette**—curving along the coast and split by islands of palms and flowers.

A port of call for cruise liners, the grand hotels, apartments, and boutiques that line the seafront are the first things that visitors arriving by ship will see. Many of the bigger hotels, some dating from the 19th century, indulge their guests with exclusive beach clubs on the sand. Above the harbor, the old town of Cannes sits on Suquet Hill, where you'll see the 14th-century **Tour de Suquet,** which the English dubbed the Lord's Tower.

Musée Bonnard ★★ The first museum in the world dedicated to the Impressionist ace Pierre Bonnard opened 3km (1¾ miles) north of Cannes in 2011. Bonnard lived nearby in the later years of his life, capturing the colors of Cannes, Antibes, and St-Tropez on canvas. This sparkling new museum may be petite, but its collection of portraits, sculptures, and sketches is set to grow over the coming years.

6 bl Sidi Carnot, Le Cannet. www.museebonnard.fr. ✆ **04-93-94-06-06.** Admission 6€ adults, 3.50€ ages 12–18, free for children 11 and under. Apr–mid Oct Tues–Sun 10am–8pm; mid Oct–Mar Tues–Sun 10am–6pm. Closed Nov.

Musée de la Castre ★ In the Château de la Castre above Cannes' old town, this large museum displays paintings of Cannes from yesteryear, plus sculpture and works of decorative art. The ethnography section includes objects from all over the world, including spears from the South Seas and Maya pottery. There's also a gallery devoted to relics of Mediterranean civilizations, from the Greeks to the Romans, from the Cypriots to the Egyptians. The best part, however, is climbing the 101 steps of the museum's viewing tower: The views across the Riviera are astounding.

Quai de l'Epi le Port. ✆ **04-93-38-55-26.** Admission 3.40€ adults, 2.20€ ages 18 to 25, free for children under 17. July–Aug daily 10am–7pm; Sept–Mar Tues–Sun 10am–1pm and 2-5pm; Apr–Jun Tues–Sun 10am–1pm and 2–6pm.

HITTING THE BEACH & OTHER OUTDOOR ACTIVITIES

BEACHES Beachgoing in Cannes has more to do with exhibitionism than actual swimming. **Plage de la Croisette** extends between the Vieux Port and the Port Canto. The beaches along this billion-dollar stretch of sand are *payante*, meaning entrance costs 15€ to 30€, but you don't need to be a guest of the Martinez or Carlton to use the beaches associated with these high-end hotels (see "Where to Stay"), and there are plenty of buzzing beach clubs dotted around, including sassy **3.14 Beach** (www.314cannes.com; ✆ **04-93-94-25-43**).

Why should you pay a fee at all? Well, it includes a full day's use of a mattress, a chaise longue (the seafront is more pebbly than sandy), and a parasol, as well as easy access to freshwater showers. The beaches have outdoor restaurants and bars (some with organic menus, others with burgers and sushi) where no one minds if you appear in your swimsuit. Every beach allows topless bathing, and you're likely to find the same forms of décolletage along the entire strip.

Looking for a free public beach without renting chaises or parasols? Head for **Plage du Midi,** sometimes called Midi Plage, just west of the Vieux Port, or **Plage Gazagnaire,** just east of the Port Canto. Here you'll find families with children and lots of caravan-type vehicles parked nearby.

BOATING Several companies around Cannes's Vieux Port rent boats of any size, with or without a crew, for a day, a week, or even longer. An outfit known for short-term rentals of small motorcraft is **Elco Marine,** 110 bd. du Midi (www.elcomarine. fr; ✆ **04-93-47-12-62**). For kayak rental and guided tours of the coastline by canoe, try **SeaFirst,** 110 bd. du Midi (www.seafirst.fr; ✆ **04-93-65-06-14**).

WHERE TO EAT

La Palme d'Or ★★★ MODERN FRENCH The ultimate dining experience in Cannes is this double-Michelin-starred restaurant, commanding panoramic sea views from the second floor of the Hotel Martinez. Top chef Christian Sinicropi has presided over the inventive cuisine for more than a decade. He routinely greets diners at their table to best assess their culinary desires before wowing them over six, seven, or eight courses. Although the food is the true star, a celebrity fan base has put this on the see-and-be-seen circuit. Menu items change with the seasons but are likely to include warm foie gras with fondue of rhubarb; or crayfish, clams, and squid marinated in peppered citrus sauce. Intriguing bites on the tasting menus may include olive-flavored marshmallows, beetroot sorbet, and bread made with squid ink. The service is worldly without being stiff.

In the Hôtel Martinez, 73 bd. de la Croisette. www.hotel-martinez.com. ℂ **04-92-98-74-14.** Reservations required. Main courses 48€–85€; fixed-price menu 95€–185€. AE, DC, MC, V. Wed–Sat 12:30–2pm and 8–10pm. Closed Jan–Feb.

ENTERTAINMENT & NIGHTLIFE

Cannes is invariably associated with easygoing permissiveness, film-making glitterati, and gambling. If the latter is your thing, Cannes has some world-class casinos loaded with high rollers, voyeurs, and everyone in between. The better established is the **Casino Croisette,** in the Palais des Festivals, Esplanade Lucien Barrière (www.lucienbarriere.com; ℂ **04-92-98-78-50**). A well-respected fixture in town since the 1950s, a collection of noisy slot machines it is most certainly not.

Its main competitor is the newer **Palm Beach Casino,** place F-D-Roosevelt, Pointe de la Croisette (ℂ **04-97-06-36-90**), on the southeast edge of La Croisette. It attracts a younger crowd with a summer-only beachside poker room, a beach club with pool, a restaurant, and a disco that runs until dawn. Both casinos maintain slots that operate daily lunchtime to 5am. Smarter dress is expected for the *les grands jeux* salons (for (blackjack, roulette, craps, poker, and chemin de fer), which open nightly 8pm to 4am. The casino also pulls in daytime visitors with tasty inexpensive lunches and Sunday brunches, both of which come with free gaming chips.

After-dark diversions continue to grow, with a strip of sundowner bars stretching along rue Félix Faure. Most are chic, some have happy-hour cocktails, and several have DJs after dinner. It's best to walk by and take your pick. Nearby is **Chokko,** 15 rue Frères Pradignac (ℂ **04-93-39-62-70**), where killer cocktails are served by haughty waiting staff. Dance floor-filling tunes get everyone on their feet after 10pm. Less showy is **Morrison's Irish Pub,** 10 rue Teisseire (ℂ **04-92-98-16-17**), which has become the meeting place for visiting yachties and the expat community. There's a live DJ on Thursday, Friday, and Saturday in the attached **Morrison's Lounge** club.

The **Bar l'Amiral,** in the Hôtel Martinez, 73 La Croisette (ℂ **04-92-98-73-00**), is where deals go down during the film festival. Directors, producers, stars, press agents, screenwriters, and wannabes crowd in here at festival time. The bow-tied barmen have won several world championship cocktail-mixing trophies. Places around the bar come complete with a nametag of the star that once propped it up, Humphrey Bogart among them.

Gay and lesbian bar **Zanzibar,** 85 rue Félix-Faure (ℂ **04-93-39-30-75**), is the oldest stop on Cannes's scene. The pace picks up at midnight and throbs until 4am. Cannes's most uplifting option is gay-friendly club **Le Nightlife,** 52 rue Jean-Jaurès (ℂ **04-93-39-20-50**). It was reoutfitted late in 2008 with white walls, a busy bar, occasional fashion shows, and lots of randomly scheduled parties that last until dawn.

WHERE TO STAY

Five Hôtel ★★ Open since summer 2011, Cannes's hippest hotel offers designer opulence that harks back to the 1920s, when international travel was a high-society preserve. Decor is light, luxurious, and laced with Art Deco. Furnishings are clearly inspired by Louis Vuitton's classic luggage sets. Rooms and suites are arranged like a Wallpaper* photo shoot. Each features hardwood rocking chairs, a Mac Mini computer, Nespresso machine, and Asprey bath products. New for 2012 is the Cinq Mondes spa and Intuitions sweet shop, created by 27-year-old World Pastry

Champion Jérôme de Oliveira. The rooftop terrace tops off the Five's inspired design. It features an infinity pool, linen-shaded sun loungers, and a cocktail bar backed up by DJs and frequent live music. The terrace is also the location of the acclaimed Sea Sens restaurant.

1 rue Notre Dame, Cannes 06400. www.five-hotel-cannes.com. ✆ **04-63-36-05-05.** No fax. 45 units. 295€–805€ double; from 595€ suite. AE, DC, MC, V. Amenities: Restaurant; bar; outdoor pool; spa; concierge; room service. In room: A/C, TV, minibar, hair dryer, free Wi-Fi.

Hôtel Martinez ★★★   When this Art Deco masterpiece was built in the 1930s, it rivaled any other lodging along the coast in sheer size. Over the years, however, it fell into disrepair. But in the '80s, the hotel and its restaurants were given a Belle Epoque makeover and returned to their former luster. The suite-laden penthouse floor has become most sought-after in town following a recent restyling. Several more suites look out over the sea from the first floor, including the Suite des Oliviers, a pleasure palace of upholstered silk bedsteads, a sauna, crystal chandeliers, and a 250-sq.-m (2,691-sq.-ft.) terrace with its own Jacuzzi. All units have full marble bathrooms, wood furnishings, and writing desks. The Martinez also possesses ZPlage (a beach club for the glitterati), plus a water-skiing school, a kids' club, a very cool bar for grown-ups, and one of the finest restaurants in the South of France (La Palme d'Or, p. 340). A new seventh-floor spa with products by L. Raphael opened in spring 2012.

73 bd. de la Croisette, Cannes 06406. www.hotel-martinez.com. ✆ **04-92-98-73-00.** Fax 04-93-39-67-82. 412 units. 690€–890€ double; from 3,300€ suite. AE, DC, MC, V. Parking 38€. **Amenities:** 3 summer restaurants; 2 winter restaurants; bar; outdoor pool; exercise room; spa; sauna; children's center; concierge; room service; babysitting; private beach. In room: A/C, TV, minibar, hair dryer, free Wi-Fi.

Antibes & Cap d'Antibes ★★

913km (566 miles) S of Paris; 21km (13 miles) SW of Nice; 11km (6¾ miles) NE of Cannes

On the other side of the Baie des Anges (Bay of Angels) from Nice is the pretty port of Antibes. The town has a quiet charm unique on the Côte d'Azur. Its harbor is filled with fishing boats and pleasure yachts, and its winding streets are packed with promenading locals and well-dressed visitors. A pedestrianized port and several car-free squares make it a family-friendly destination, too. There's also an excellent covered market located near the harbor, open every morning except Mondays.

Spiritually, Antibes is totally divorced from Cap d'Antibes, a peninsula studded with the villas of the super-rich. But the less affluent are welcome to peek at paradise, and a lovely 6km (3¾ mile) coastal path rings the headland, passing picnic and diving spots en route.

ESSENTIALS

GETTING THERE   **Trains** from Cannes arrive at the rail station, place Pierre-Semard, every 20 minutes (trip time: 15 min.); the one-way fare is 2.70€. Trains from Nice arrive at the rate of 25 per day (trip time: 20 min.); the one-way fare is 4.20€. For rail information, visit www.voyages-sncf.com or call ✆ **36-35.** The **bus** station, La Gare Routière, place Guynemer (✆ **04-89-87-72-00**), receives buses from throughout Provence. Bus fares to Nice, Cannes, Grasse, and Cagnes-sur-Mer cost 1€ one-way.

If you're **driving,** follow E1 east from Cannes and take the turnoff to the south for Antibes, which will lead to the historic core of the old city. From Nice, take E1 west until you come to the turnoff for Antibes. The Cap d'Antibes is clearly visible from most parts of the Riviera. To drive here from Antibes, follow the coastal road, boulevard Leclerc, south—you can't miss it.

VISITOR INFORMATION The **Office de Tourisme** is at 11 place du Général-de-Gaulle (www.antibesjuanlespins.com; ☏ **04-97-23-11-11;** fax 04-97-23-11-12).

EXPLORING ANTIBES & CAP D'ANTIBES

Musée Napoleonien ☺ In this stone-sided fort and tower on the Cap d'Antibes, built in stages in the 17th and 18th centuries, you'll find an interesting collection of Napoleonic memorabilia, naval models, and paintings. A toy-soldier collection depicts various uniforms, including one used by Napoleon in the Marengo campaign. A wall painting on wood shows Napoleon disembarking at Golfe-Juan on March 1, 1815, to start his 100 days' march to Paris. In contrast to Canova's Greek-god image of Napoleon, a miniature pendant by Barrault reveals the general as he really looked, with pudgy cheeks and a receding hairline. In the rear rotunda is one of the many hats worn by the emperor. You can climb to the top of the tower for a view of the coast that's worth the admission price alone.

Batterie du Graillon, bd. J.-F.-Kennedy. ☏ **04-93-61-45-32.** Admission 3€ adults; 1.50€ seniors, students, and ages 19–25; free for children 18 and under. Mid-June to mid-Sept Tues–Sat 10am–6pm; mid-Sept to mid-June Tues–Sat 10am–4:30pm.

Musée Picasso ★★ On the ramparts above the port is the Château Grimaldi, once the home of princes from the Grimaldi family, who ruled the city from 1385 to 1608. Today it houses a stunning collection of Picasso artworks. The Spanish artist came to town after the war in 1946 and lived and worked in the château at the invitation of the municipality. When he departed, he gifted all the work he'd completed to the château museum: 23 paintings, 80 ceramics, 44 drawings, 32 lithographs, 11 oils on paper, 2 sculptures, and 5 tapestries. In addition to this collection, a gallery of contemporary art exhibits works by Léger, Miró, Ernst, and Calder, among others. An expansive outdoor terrace offers views over the Cap d'Antibes, which Picasso aficionados may recognize from his paintings.

Château Grimaldi, Place du Mariejol. ☏ **04-92-90-54-20.** Admission 6€ adults, 3€ students and seniors, free for children 18 and under. Mid-June to mid-Sept Tues–Sun 10am–6pm; mid-Sept to mid-June Tues–Sun 10am–noon and 2–6pm.

WHERE TO EAT

La Taverne du Safranier PROVENÇAL Earthy and irreverent, this brasserie in a century-old building serves a changing roster of Provençal specialties. Zany art is hung up the walls of the car-free square that the restaurant occupies, making this spot a favorite of bohemian locals (who are all actually wealthy in this part of the world). It's also great for kids, as they can run around freely. Menu examples include a platter of *petits farcis* (stuffed vegetables), a mini bouillabaisse for single diners, savory fish soup, and an assortment of grilled fish (including sardines) that's served with just a dash of fresh lemon.

1 place du Safranier. www.taverne-du-safranier.fr. ☏ **04-93-34-80-50.** Reservations recommended. Main courses 18€–28€; fixed-price menu 26€–32€. MC, V. Tues–Sun noon–2pm; Tues–Sat 7–10pm. Closed mid-Nov to mid-Feb.

Restaurant de Bacon ★★★ SEAFOOD The Eden Roc restaurant at the Hôtel du Cap is more elegant, but Bacon serves the best seafood around, and has done so for over 6 decades. Surrounded by ultra-expensive residences, this restaurant on a rocky peninsula offers a panoramic coast view. Bouillabaisse aficionados claim that Bacon offers the best in France. In its deluxe version, saltwater crayfish float atop the savory brew; we prefer the simple version, where a waiter adds the finishing touches at your table. If bouillabaisse isn't your favorite, try fish soup with garlic-laden rouille sauce, fish terrine, sea bass, or John Dory, or see what's on offer on the two fixed-price menus.

Bd. de Bacon. www.restaurantdebacon.com. © **04-93-61-50-02.** Reservations required. Main courses 45€–145€; fixed-price lunch 49€–79€, dinner 79€. AE, DC, MC, V. Wed–Sun noon–2pm; Tues–Sun 8–10pm. Closed Nov–Feb.

WHERE TO STAY

Hôtel du Cap–Eden Roc ★★★   Legendary for the glamour of both its setting and its clientele, this Second Empire hotel, opened in 1870, is surrounded by a maze of manicured gardens. It's like a country estate, with spacious public rooms, marble fireplaces, paneling, chandeliers, and upholstered armchairs. Accommodation is among the most sumptuous on the Riviera. Guest rooms recently benefited from a thorough renovation, with sleek modern fittings, iPod docks, and LED screens in every room. Even though the guests snoozing by the pool—blasted out of the cliff at enormous expense—appear artfully undraped during the day, evenings are upscale, with lots of emphasis on clothing and style. The stunning Restaurant Eden Roc spills out onto a panoramic sea view terrace. The Bellini Bar is the summertime meeting place of the stars. Casual visitors normally won't even get a look in, especially during the Cannes Film Festival and Monaco Grand Prix. However, the hotel is less elitist than it once was, and even bowed to the masses by accepting credit cards a few years ago (before that it was cash only).

Bd. J.-F.-Kennedy, Cap d'Antibes 06600. www.edenroc-hotel.fr. © **04-93-61-39-01.** Fax 04-93-67-76-04. 67 units. 350€–1,250€ double; 1,130€–5,800€ suite; 5,200€–12,500€ villa. AE, DC, MC, V. Closed mid-Oct to mid-Apr. Bus: A2. **Amenities:** 2 restaurants; 2 bars; outdoor pool; exercise room; spa; room service; massage; babysitting. *In room:* A/C, TV, hair dryer, free Wi-Fi.

Le Bosquet ★ 🎁   This fabulous, family-run bed and breakfast midway along the Cap d'Antibes is as far removed from the Riviera bustle as you can get. A leafy, unkempt garden laps up against the pink-hued main villa, which is 2½ centuries old. It's here that the four boutique guest rooms are housed. All are utterly charming: The Chambre Sable has traditional *tomette* floors and antique fittings; the Chambre Galet has a large bathroom and sitting area, and is large enough for a family.

14 chemin des Sables, Cap d'Antibes 06160. www.lebosquet06.com. © **04-93-67-32-29.** 4 units. 100€–200€ double. MC, V. Free parking. Closed mid-Nov–last week Dec. **Amenities:** Bar. *In room:* A/C, TV, fridge, hair dryer, free Wi-Fi.

Nice ★★★

929km (576 miles) S of Paris; 32km (20 miles) NE of Cannes

Nice is known as the "Queen of the Riviera" and is the largest city on this fabled stretch of coast. It's also one of the most ancient, founded by the Greeks, who called it Nike (Victory). By the 19th century, Russian aristocrats and the British upper class—led by Queen Victoria herself—were flocking here. But these days, it's not as chichi as Cannes or St-Tropez. In fact, of all the major French resorts, Nice is the most down-to-earth, with an emphasis on fine dining and high culture. Indeed, it hosts more museums than any other French city outside of Paris.

It's also the best place to base yourself on the Riviera, especially if you're dependent on public transportation. You can go to San Remo, a glamorous town over the Italian border, for lunch and return to Nice by nightfall. From Nice airport, the second largest in France, you can travel by train or bus along the entire coast to resorts such as Antibes, Juan-les-Pins, and Monaco.

Because of its brilliant sunshine and liberal attitude, Nice has long attracted artists and writers, among them Dumas, Nietzsche, Flaubert, Hugo, Sand, and Stendhal. Henri Matisse, who made his home in Nice, said, "Though the light is intense, it's also soft and tender." The city averages 300 sunny days a year.

ESSENTIALS

GETTING THERE   **Trains** arrive at Gare Nice-Ville, avenue Thiers (www.voyages-sncf.com; ℭ **36-35**). From there you can take trains to Cannes for 6.10€, Monaco for 3.40€, and Antibes for 4€, with easy connections to Paris, Marseille, and anywhere else along the Mediterranean coast.

Buses to and from Monaco (no. 100), Cannes (no. 200), and all points in between serve the streets immediately around the **Gare Routière,** 5 bd. Jean-Jaurès (www.lignesdazur.com; ℭ **08-10-06-10-06**), the former main bus station, which is currently under renovation.

Transatlantic and intercontinental flights land at **Aéroport Nice–Côte d'Azur** (www.nice.aeroport.fr; ℭ **08-20-42-33-33**). From there, municipal bus nos. 98 and 99 depart at 20-minute intervals for Gare Routière (see above) and Gare Nice-Ville, respectively; the one-way fare is 4€. A **taxi** from the airport into the city center will cost between 30€ and 40€ each way. Trip time is about 20 minutes.

Ferryboats operated by **Trans-Côte d'Azur** (www.trans-cote-azur.com; ℭ **04-92-00-42-30**), on quai Lunel on Nice's port, link the city with Ile Ste-Marguerite in July and August, and St-Tropez from June to September.

VISITOR INFORMATION

TOURIST OFFICES   Nice maintains three **tourist offices.** The largest and most central is at 5 promenade des Anglais, near place Masséna (www.nicetourisme.com; ℭ **08-92-70-74-07**). Additional offices are in the arrivals hall of the Aéroport Nice–Côte d'Azur and the railway station on avenue Thiers. Any office can make a hotel reservation (but only for the night of the day you show up), for a modest fee.

GETTING AROUND

ON FOOT   Nice is very walkable, and no point of interest downtown is more than a 10-minute walk from place Massena, including the seafront Promenade, Old Town, and harbor.

BY BUS   Most local buses serve the streets around the main bus station, or **Gare Routière,** 10 av. Félix-Faure (ℭ **08-92-70-12-06**), which is currently under renovation near Place Masséna. Municipal buses charge 1€ for rides within the entire Alpes-Maritime province, even as far as Monaco or Cannes. The same ticket can also be used on Nice's tramway, which connects the Gare Routière with Gare Nice-Ville and northern Nice. Tickets can be purchased at tobacco shops or at electronic kiosks around the city.

One of the most fun ways to quickly gain an overview of Nice involves boarding a **Nice–Le Grand Tour** (www.nicelegrandtour.com; ℭ **04-92-29-17-00**) double-decker bus. Every day of the year, between 9:45am and 6:15pm, one of a flotilla of this company's buses departs from a position adjacent to the Jardins Albert I. The panoramic 90-minute tour takes in the harbor, the museums of Cimiez, the Russian church, and the promenade. Per-person rates for the experience are 20€ for adults, 18€ for students, and 5€ for children 4 to 11. Participants can get off at any of 12 stops en route and opt to reboard any other buses, which follow at roughly 40-minute intervals, after they've explored the neighborhood. Advance reservations aren't necessary, and commentary is piped through to headsets in seven different languages.

BY BIKE   A recent addition to the transport scene is **Vélo Bleu** (www.velobleu. org), a bike-sharing scheme with over 175 stations throughout the city. However, registering for the scheme on the electronic stands takes a degree of patience, so register in advance online if possible. A more human place to rent both bikes and scooters is **Holiday Bikes,** 23 rue de Belgique (www.holiday-bikes.com; ✆ 04-93-16-01-62), by Nice-Ville train station. Open Monday to Saturday 9am to 12.30pm and 2 to 6.30pm, and on Sunday 10am–noon and 4–6pm, it charges from 12€ per day for a bike, or from 30€ per day for a 50cc scooter. A valid driver's license and deposit are required.

BY TOURIST TRAIN   Another easy way to see the city is by the small **Train Touristique de Nice** (www.trainstouristiquesdenice.com; ✆ 06-08-55-08-30), which also departs from the Jardins Albert I. The 45-minute ride passes many of Nice's most-heralded sites, including place Masséna, promenade des Anglais, and quai des Etats-Unis. Departing every 30 minutes, the train operates daily 10am to 5pm (until 6pm April–May and Sept, until 7pm June–Aug). The round-trip price is 7€ for adults and 4€ for children 9 and under.

BY SEGWAY   Possibly the coolest way to get around Nice is by Segway, the two-wheeled electronic scooters. Bespoke tours are run by **Mobilboard,** 2 rue Halévy (www.mobilboard.com; ✆ 04-93-80-21-27). Children 18 and under must be accompanied by an adult. An hour-long tour of Nice costs 25€ per person.

BY ELECTRIC CAR   Another novel addition to the Nice transport scene is **Auto Bleue** (www.autobleue.org; ✆ 09-77-40-64-06). The scheme allows visitors to rent an electric Peugeot car from one of 70 vehicle stands around Nice for 50€ per day, inclusive of electricity, parking, and insurance.

EXPLORING NICE

In 1822, Nice's orange crop had an awful year. The workers faced a lean time, so the English residents employed them to build the **promenade des Anglais ★★**, today a wide boulevard fronting the bay, split by "islands" of palms and flowers and stretching for about 7km (4¼ miles) all the way to the airport. Along the beach are rows of grand cafes, the Musée Masséna, villas, and the city's most glamorous hotels.

Crossing this boulevard in the tiniest bikinis are some of the world's most attractive bronzed bodies. They're heading for the **beach.** Tough on tender feet, *le plage* is made not of sand, but of pebbles (and not small ones, either).

Rising sharply on a rock at the eastern end of the promenade is **Le Château,** where the ducs de Savoie built their castle, which was torn down in 1706. The hill has since been turned into a wonderful public park complete with a waterfall, cafes, and a giant children's play area. To reach the site and take in the view, board an elevator from the quai des Etats-Unis; the fit can walk up one of five sets of steep steps. The park is open daily from 8am to dusk. At the north end of Le Château is the famous old **graveyard** of Nice, known primarily for lavish monuments that form their own enduring art statement. It's one of the largest in France.

Continuing east from "the Rock" (the site of Le Château) you reach the **Vieux Port,** or harbor, where the restaurants are even cheaper and are filled with locals. While lingering over a drink at a sidewalk cafe, you can watch the boats depart for Corsica. The harbor was excavated between 1750 and 1830. Since then, it has gained an outer harbor, protected by two jetties, and is great for a stroll around.

The "authentic" Niçoise live in **Vieille Ville ★**, the old town, beginning at the foot of the Rock and stretching to place Masséna. Sheltered by sienna-tiled roofs, many of the Italianate facades suggest 17th-century Genoese palaces. The old town is a maze of narrow streets, teeming with local life and studded with the least expensive restaurants in Nice. Buy a Niçoise-style onion pizza (*pissaladière*) from a vendor. Many of the buildings are painted a faded Roman gold, and their banners are laundry flapping in the sea breezes.

While here, try to visit the **Marché aux Fleurs.** This flower market lies on the **cours Saleya,** the old town's principal walkway, which is filled with alfresco restaurants and cafes. A flamboyant array of carnations, violets, roses, and birds of paradise, the market operates Tuesday to Sunday 8am to 6pm in summer, and 8am until between 2 and 4pm in winter, depending on the vendors' remaining inventory and energy level. On Monday the same space is occupied by a superb antiques market, with vendors carting wares from across France and Italy.

Nice's newly pedestrianized centerpiece is **place Masséna,** with pink buildings in the 17th-century Genoese style and fountains with water jets. Stretching from the main square to the promenade is the **Jardin Albert-1er,** with an open-air terrace and a Triton Fountain. With palms and exotic flowers, it's the most relaxing oasis in town.

Founded by the Romans, who called it Cemenelum, **Cimiez** was the capital of the Maritime Alps province. Excavations have uncovered the ruins of a Roman town, and you can wander the dig sites. To reach this suburb and its attractions, take bus no. 15 or 17 from place Masséna.

Musée Matisse ★★ This museum, in a beautiful old Italian villa, honors Henri Matisse, one of the 20th century's greatest painters. He came to Nice for the light and made the city his home, living in the Hotel Beau Rivage and on the cours Saleya, and dying in Cimiez in 1954. Seeing his playful nude sketches today, you'll wonder how early critics could have denounced them as "the female animal in all her shame and horror." Most of the pieces in the museum's permanent collection were painted in Nice (you may recognize a few of the backdrops). These include *Nude in an Armchair with a Green Plant* (1937), *Nymph in the Forest* (1935–42), and the famous *Portrait of Madame Matisse* (1905). There's also an assemblage of designs he prepared as practice sketches for Matisse's final masterpiece, his *Chapel at Vence*. Also here are *The Créole Dancer* (1951), *Blue Nude IV* (1952), and around 50 dance-related sketches he did between 1930 and 1931.

In the Villa des Arènes-de-Cimiez, 164 av. des Arènes-de-Cimiez. www.musee-matisse-nice.org. ℂ **04-93-81-08-08.** Free admission. Wed–Mon 10am–6pm. Closed Tues.

HITTING THE BEACH & OTHER OUTDOOR ACTIVITIES

BEACHES Along Nice's seafront, beaches extend uninterrupted for more than 7km (4¼ miles), going from the edge of Vieux Port (the old port, or harbor) to the international airport. Tucked between the public areas are several rather chic private beaches. Many of these beach bars provide mattresses and parasols for 12€ to 20€. The coolest clubs include **Hi Beach** (www.hi-beach.net; ℂ **04-97-14-00-83**), which has a sushi bar, weights room, and swing chairs; and **Castel Plage** (www.castelplage.com; ✆ **04-93-85-22-66**), which is a celebrity hangout in summer. The most family-friendly, with its giant pile of outdoor toys, is **Opera Plage** (✆ **04-93-62-31-52**).

SCUBA DIVING   Of the many diving outfits in Nice harbor, **Nice Diving,** 14 quai des Dock (www.nicediving.com; ✆ **04-93-89-42-44**), offers bilingual instruction and *baptêmes* (dives for first-timers) around Nice and Cap Ferrat. A two-tank dive for experienced divers, equipment included, costs around 150€; an appropriate diver's certificate is required.

WHERE TO EAT

La Merenda ★★ 🎁 NIÇOISE   Because there's no phone, you have to go by this place twice—once to make a reservation and once to dine—but it's worth the effort. Forsaking his chef's crown at Le Chantecler, Dominique Le Stanc took over this tiny local bistro serving sublime cuisine. Although he was born in Alsace, the chef's heart and soul belong to the Mediterranean, the land of black truffles, wild morels, sea-bass, and asparagus. His food is a lullaby of gastronomic unity, with texture, crunch, richness, and balance. Le Stanc never knows what he's going to serve until he goes to the market. Look for specials on a chalkboard. Perhaps you'll find stuffed cabbage, fried zucchini flowers, or oxtail flavored with fresh oranges. Service is discreet and personable.

4 rue Raoul Bosio. No phone. Reservations required. Main courses 14€–29€. No credit cards. Mon–Fri noon–2pm and 7:30–10pm.

Le Chantecler ★★★ TRADITIONAL/MODERN FRENCH   This is Nice's most prestigious, most formal, and most commended restaurant. Its walls are decked with panels removed from a château in Pouilly-Fuissé, rich tapestries hang from the ceilings, and bow-tied multilingual waiters anticipate your every move. The menu is revised each week to include the most sophisticated and creative dishes in the city. Dishes may include turbot filet served with purée of broad beans, sundried tomatoes, and asparagus; flash-fried seabass served with baked red onion confit; and a melt-in-your-mouth fantasy of marbled hot chocolate drenched in almond-flavored cream sauce. Michelin-starred dining doesn't come any better value than the lunchtime set menu, which costs 65€ including wine.

In the Hôtel Negresco, 37 promenade des Anglais. ✆ **04-93-16-64-00.** Reservations required. Main courses 48€–80€; fixed-price lunch 55€–130€, dinner 90€–130€. AE, MC, V, DC. Wed–Sun 12:30–1:45pm and 7:30–10pm. Closed Jan.

Le Safari ★ PROVENÇAL/NIÇOISE   Highly recommended for its honest prices and solid cooking, this establishment has been in business for over 50 years. Diners can choose the alfresco terrace on the bustling cours Saleya from spring to autumn, or they may cozy up inside around the wood-fired oven in winter. Menu items include a pungent *bagna cauda,* which calls for diners to immerse vegetables in a sizzling brew of hot oil and anchovy paste; grilled peppers bathed in olive oil; *daube* (stew) of beef; and an omelet with *blettes* (tough but flavorful greens). The unfortunately named *merda de can* (dog poop) is gnocchi stuffed with spinach, and a lot more appetizing than it sounds. Even the pizzas and bottles of inexpensive house wine are commendable.

1 cours Saleya. www.restaurantsafari.fr. ✆ **04-93-80-18-44.** Reservations recommended. Main courses 11€–32€. AE, DC, MC, V. Daily noon–11pm.

ENTERTAINMENT & NIGHTLIFE

Nice has some of the most active nightlife along the Riviera. Evenings usually begin at a cafe. At kiosks around town you can pick up a copy of *La Semaine des Spectacles,* which outlines the week's diversions.

The major cultural center on the Riviera is the **Opéra de Nice,** 4 rue St-François-de-Paule (✆ **04-92-17-40-00**), built in 1885 by Charles Garnier, fabled architect of the Paris Opéra. It presents a full repertoire, with emphasis on serious, often large-scale operas. In one season you might see *Tosca, Les Contes de Hoffmann,* Verdi's *Macbeth,* Beethoven's *Fidelio,* and *Carmen,* as well as a *saison symphonique,* dominated by the Orchestre Philharmonique de Nice. The opera hall is also the major venue for concerts and recitals. Tickets are available (to concerts, recitals, and full-blown operas) a day or two before any performance. You can show up at the box office (Mon–Sat 10am–5:30pm; Sun 10am–6pm), or buy tickets in advance with a major credit card by phoning ✆ **04-92-17-40-47.** Tickets run from 10€ for nosebleed seats (and we mean it) to 100€ for front-and-center seats on opening night.

WHERE TO STAY

Hôtel Negresco ★★★   The Negresco, on the seafront in the heart of Nice, is one of the Riviera's superglamorous hotels. This Victorian wedding-cake hotel is named after its founder, Henry Negresco, and has hosted each era's superstars, from The Beatles to Michael Jackson. The hotel's decorators scoured Europe to gather antiques, tapestries, and art for the ritzy interior and domed central salon. Guest rooms benefitted from a modern makeover in 2011, mixing sea views with state-of-the-art wetrooms and contemporary furniture. The entire fifth floor is now dedicated to VVIPs (that's right, "very, very important persons") and has a private luncheon area and bar. Dining is among the best in town, with the Michelin-starred Chantecler and the funky brasserie-style Rotonde, which was also given a thorough makeover in 2011. Despite the changes, the staff still wear 18th-century costumes and are as fawningly polite as ever.

37 promenade des Anglais, Nice 06000. www.hotel-negresco-nice.com. ✆ **04-93-16-64-00.** Fax 04-93-88-35-68. 117 units. 240€–610€ double; from 595€ suite. AE, DC, MC, V. Free parking. **Amenities:** 2 restaurants; bar; exercise room; room service; massage; babysitting. In room: A/C, TV, minibar, hair dryer, free Wi-Fi.

La Pérouse ★★ 🏠   Once a prison, La Pérouse has been reconstructed and is now a spectacular and unique Riviera hotel. Set on a cliff, it's built right in the gardens of the ancient château hill, with a secluded swimming pool almost carved out of the rock to the rear. No hotel aside from the adjoining Hotel Suisse affords a better view over both the old city and the Baie des Anges. Inside it resembles an old Provençal home, with low ceilings, white walls, and antique furnishings. The lovely, spacious rooms are beautifully furnished, often with Provençal fabrics. Most have balconies overlooking the bay. The bathrooms are large, clad in Boticino marble, and hold tubs and showers.

11 quai Rauba-Capéu, Nice 06300. www.hotel-la-perouse.com. ✆ **04-93-62-34-63.** Fax 04-93-62-59-41. 65 units. 170€–540€ double; 630€–1,700€ suite. AE, DC, MC, V. Parking 25€. **Amenities:** Restaurant (mid-May to mid-Sept); bar; outdoor pool; exercise room; Jacuzzi; sauna; room service; babysitting. *In room:* A/C, TV, minibar, hair dryer, free Wi-Fi.

Nice Pebbles ★   We cannot recommend this apartment rental company highly enough. Nice Pebbles manages around 100 high-class properties in the city's premier zones, including the old town and harbor, and along the promenade des Anglais. All of its properties are carefully selected, presumably to minimize any complaints or hassles. Its stock is thus in excellent condition and has first-class amenities (generally iPod docks, high-definition TVs, and designer bathrooms). Sizes vary from one-bedroom properties with large terraces, to large seaview places sleeping 10 or more guests. When booked by the week, prices work out much more competitive than a hotel, especially when traveling with a family. Booking can be made online, although due to high demand, reservations are best made as far in advance as possible.

23 rue Gioffredo, Nice 06000. www.nicepebbles.com. ℂ **04-97-20-27-39.** 100 units. 90€–350€ per apartment per night. MC, V. **Amenities:** Babysitting. *In apartments:* A/C (generally in all), TV, hair dryer, free Wi-Fi.

Villa Saint-Exupéry 🗡 This former Carmelite monastery has been completely

renovated and turned into an award-winning hostel for young and old alike. It won the Best Hostel in France award in 2011. It's busy year-round with seasoned travelers on a budget, artists, musicians, families, hikers, and, of course, students on summer break. The restored and comfort-filled villa offers standard hotel rooms (some with kitchenette), as well as some dormitory accommodations at youth hostel tariffs. Echoing its past life, the former chapel preserved its stained-glass windows. There is also a bar with all drinks at 1€, free Wi-Fi, free luggage storage, free breakfast, and a barbeque area. Guests are also welcome to use a fully equipped kitchen. A new sister hostel offering the same facilities, **Villa Saint Exupéry Beach,** 6 rue Sacha Guitry (ℂ **04-93-16-13-45**), opened downtown opposite Galleries Lafayette in 2010.

22 av. Gravier, Nice 06100. www.villahostels.com. ℂ **04-93-84-42-83.** Fax 04-92-09-82-94. 60 units. 27€–40€ per person in a single or twin-bedded room; 16€–30€ per person for dormitory bed. Rates include continental breakfast. MC, V. Free parking. **Amenities:** Bar; cooking facilities; free Wi-Fi. *In room:* Kitchenettes (in some).

Monaco ★★★

939km (582 miles) S of Paris; 18km (11 miles) E of Nice

Monaco, or more precisely its capital of Monte Carlo, has for a century been a symbol of glamour. The 1956 marriage of Prince Rainier III to American actress Grace Kelly enhanced its status. Though not always happy in her role, Princess Grace won the respect and admiration of her people. The Monégasques still mourn her death in a 1982 car accident.

Monaco became the property of the Grimaldi clan as early as 1297. It has maintained something resembling independence since. In a fit of impatience, the French annexed it in 1793, but the ruling family recovered it in 1814.

ESSENTIALS

GETTING THERE Monaco has rail, bus, and highway connections from other coastal cities, especially Nice. There are no border formalities when entering Monaco from mainland France. The 19km (12-mile) **drive** from Nice takes around 30 minutes and runs along the N7 Moyenne Corniche. The pretty D6098 coast road takes a little longer. Ligne d'Azur (www.lignesdazur.com; ℂ **08-10-06-10-06**) runs a **bus** service at 15-minute intervals aboard line no. 100 from Nice to Monte Carlo. One-way bus transit from Nice costs 1€. **Trains** arrive every 30 minutes from Cannes, Nice, Menton, and Antibes. For more rail information, visit www.voyages-sncf.com or call ℂ **36-35.** Monaco's underground railway station (Gare SNCF) is on place St. Devote. A system of pedestrian tunnels, escalators, and elevators riddles the

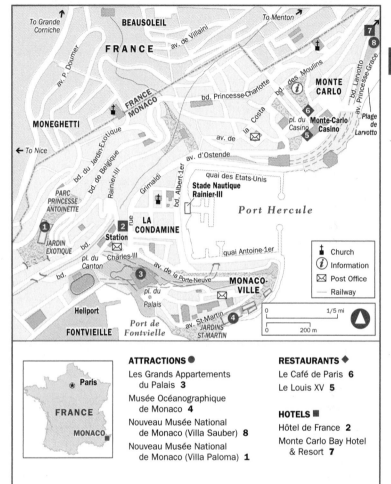

To Grande Corniche

BEAUSOLEIL

FRANCE

av. de Villaini

To Menton

7
8

av. P. Doumer

FRANCE MONACO

bd. Princesse-Charlotte

bd. des Moulins

MONTE CARLO

i

MONEGHETTI

la Costa

6

pl. du Casino

Monte-Carlo Casino

Plage de Larvotto

bd. Larvotto

av. Princesse-Grace

← To Nice

bd. du Jardin-Exotique

bd. de Belgique

Rainier-III

Grimaldi

av. de

5

av. d'Ostende

PARC PRINCESSE ANTOINETTE

quai des Etats-Unis

Stade Nautique Rainier-III

Port Hercule

1

JARDIN EXOTIQUE

2 LA CONDAMINE

Station

pl. du Canton

bd. Charles-III

quai Antoine-1er

av. de la Porte-Neuve

3

MONACO-VILLE

pl. du Palais

Heliport

Port de Fontvielle

FONTVIEILLE

av. St-Martin

JARDINS ST-MARTIN

4

✝	Church
i	Information
✉	Post Office
----	Railway

0 — 1/5 mi
0 — 200 m

Paris
★

FRANCE

MONACO ■

ATTRACTIONS ●

Les Grands Appartements du Palais **3**

Musée Océanographique de Monaco **4**

Nouveau Musée National de Monaco (Villa Sauber) **8**

Nouveau Musée National de Monaco (Villa Paloma) **1**

RESTAURANTS ◆

Le Café de Paris **6**

Le Louis XV **5**

HOTELS ■

Hôtel de France **2**

Monte Carlo Bay Hotel & Resort **7**

Principality, and such an underground walkway links the train station to Monte Carlo. If you'd rather take a **taxi** but can't find one at the station, call ℂ **08-20-20-98-98.**

VISITOR INFORMATION   The **Direction du Tourisme et des Congrés** office is at 2A bd. des Moulins (www.visitmonaco.com; ℂ **92-16-61-16**).

EXPLORING MONACO

The second-smallest state in Europe (Vatican City is the tiniest), Monaco consists of four parts. The old town, **Monaco-Ville,** on a promontory, "the Rock," 60m (197 ft.) high, is the seat of the royal palace and the government building, as well as the Oceanographic Museum. To the west, **La Condamine** is at the foot of the old town, forming its ritzy harbor and port sector. Up from the port (Monaco is steep) is **Monte Carlo,** once the playground of royalty and still the center for the wintering wealthy, the setting for the casino, and the luxurious hotels. The fourth part, **Fontvieille,** is a neat industrial suburb housing the Monaco Football club.

Monaco used to be slow in summer, but now July and August tend to be so crowded that it's hard to get a room. Dine alfresco, and you'll be passed by a motorcade of Bugattis, Lamborghinis, and Rolls Royces (regular Porches and Mercedes are considered parvenu here).

Les Grands Appartements du Palais ★   Most summer day-trippers want to see the home of Monaco's royal family, the Palais du Prince, which dominates the Principality from the Rock. A tour of the Grands Appartements allows you a glimpse of the Throne Room and some of the art, including works by Bruegel and Holbein, as well as Princess Grace's state portrait. The palace was built in the 13th century, and part dates from the Renaissance. The ideal time to arrive is 11:55am, to watch the 10-minute **Relève de la Garde (Changing of the Guard).**

Place du Palais. www.palais.mc. © **93-25-18-31.** Admission 7€ adults, 3.50€ children 8–14, free for children 7 and under. Daily Apr 10:30am–6pm; May–Sept 9:30am–6:30pm; Oct 10am–5:30pm. Closed Nov–Mar.

Musée Océanographique de Monaco ★★ ☺   Albert I, great-grandfather of the present prince, founded this museum in 1910. You'll see models of the ships aboard which he directed his scientific cruises from 1885 to 1914. Some of the exotic creatures he found on his travels were unknown before he captured them. Skeletons of specimens, including a whale that drifted ashore in 1896, are on the main floor. An exhibition devoted to the discovery of the ocean is in the physical-oceanography room on the first floor. Underwater movies are shown in the lecture room. There is also a shark lagoon and over 90 aquariums recreating tropical reefs, arctic zones, and jellyfish feeding grounds.

Av. St-Martin. www.oceano.mc. © **93-15-36-00.** Admission 13€ adults, 6.50€ children 4–18, free for children 5 and under. Apr–June and Sept daily 9:30am–7pm; July–Aug daily 9:30am–7:30pm; Oct–Mar daily 10am–6pm.

Nouveau Musée National de Monaco ★★   The Villa Sauber and the Villa Paloma, two stunning new art spaces set in palatial former homes, opened in summer 2010. Both make up the Nouveau Musée National de Monaco although they are set on the other side of the city—well, country, actually—from each other. They explore contemporary art themes by way of paintings, sculpture, and installations. The exhibitions that have been carried in so far have been magnificent, such is the pulling power of these state-backed galleries.

Villa Sauber, 17 av. Princess Grace; Villa Paloma, 56 bd. du Jardin Exotique. www.nmnm.mc. © **98-98-16-82.** Admission to both 10€ adults, admission to individual gallery 6€ adults, free entrance for visitors 26 and under. May–Sept daily 10am–7pm. Oct–Apr daily 10am–6pm.

HITTING THE BEACH & OTHER OUTDOOR ACTIVITIES

BEACHES   Just outside the border, on French soil, the **Monte-Carlo Beach Club** adjoins the Monte-Carlo Beach Hotel, 22 av. Princesse-Grace (© **98-06-54-54**). Princess Grace used to come here in flowery swimsuits, and now it's an integral part of Monaco social life. The sand is replenished at regular intervals. The entire establishment was given a chic overhaul in 2009 and now encompasses two mosaic-lined pools, a La Prairie spa, cabanas, a poolside fine dining restaurant called Le Deck, and a low-key Mediterranean restaurant with lunch buffet called La Vigie. New for 2011 was Sea Lounge, an afternoon and late evening club, which features live DJs and *nargile* hubble-bubble pipes. Beach activities include donuts, jet skis, and parachute rides. As the temperature drops in September, the beach closes for the winter. The admission charge of 45€ to 130€, depending on the season, grants you access to the changing rooms, toilets, restaurants, and bar, along with use of a mattress for sunbathing. As usual, topless bathing is common.

More low-key swimming and sunbathing is also available at **Plage du Larvotto,** off avenue Princesse-Grace. Part of this popular manmade strip of sand is public. The other part contains private beach clubs with bars, snacks, and showers, plus a kids club. A jogging track runs behind the beach.

SWIMMING   Overlooking the yacht-studded harbor, the **Stade Nautique Rainier-III,** quai Albert-1er, at La Condamine (✆ **93-30-64-83**), a pool frequented by the Monégasques, was a gift from Prince Rainier to his subjects. It's open May to October daily 9am to 6pm (until 8pm July–Aug). Admission costs 5.10€ per person. Between November and April, it's an ice-skating rink.

WHERE TO EAT

Le Café de Paris TRADITIONAL FRENCH   Its *plats du jour* are well prepared, and its location, the plaza adjacent to the casino and the Hôtel de Paris, allows a front-row view of the comings and goings of the Principality's nerve center. Despite its very public location, this recreation of old-time Monaco still attracts the stars and a sampling of Monte-Carlo old money. The menu has taken on a classic edge since late 2011 under new head chef Jean-Claude Brugel, who trained alongside several top Riviera chefs including Roger Vergé and Joël Garault. Hors d'ouevre platters include steak tartare, carpaccio of beef, and gambas fricassée. Mains are mostly very classic: Sautéed veal escalope, Provençal beef stew and, as a very un-French addition, hamburger.

Place du Casino. ✆ **98-06-76-23.** Reservations recommended. Main courses 12€–45€; fixed-price menu 35€. AE, DC, MC, V. Daily 8am–2am.

Le Louis XV ★★★ MEDITERRANEAN   In the Hôtel de Paris, the Louis XV offers one of the finest dining experiences in southern France. Superstar chef Alain Ducasse oversees the refined but not overly adorned cuisine. The restaurant's head chef, Franck Cerutti, can be seen in Nice's market at dawn purchasing local cheeses, or wandering through the corridors of the Hôtel de Paris carrying white truffles purchased from over the Italian border. Everything is light and attuned to the seasons, with intelligent, modern interpretations of Provençal and northern Italian dishes. You'll find chargrilled breast of baby pigeon with sautéed duck liver, and an ongoing specialty known as Provençal vegetables with crushed truffles. All is served under a magnificent frescoed ceiling, which also includes the portraits of Louis XV's six mistresses. Service is easily the best in the Principality. Each diner routinely uses 50 individual pieces of cutlery.

In the Hôtel de Paris, place du Casino. ✆ **98-06-88-64.** Reservations recommended. Jacket and tie recommended for men. Main courses 70€–125€; fixed-price lunch 140€, dinner 210€–280€. AE, MC, V. Thurs–Mon 12:15–1:45pm and 8–9:45pm; also June–Sept Wed 12:15–1:45pm. Closed first 2 weeks Mar.

ENTERTAINMENT & NIGHTLIFE

CASINOS   The **Casino de Monte-Carlo,** place du Casino (www.montecarlo casinos.com; © **98-06-21-21**), is one of the most famous in the world. Its creation by architect Charles Garnier (of Paris Opera house fame) in 1863 turned the tables for Monaco, turning a weary port into a world-class destination.

The casino's marble-floored **Atrium,** containing only slot machines, opens at 2pm Monday to Friday, noon on weekends. Doors for roulette and *trente et quarante* in the rococo **Salon Europe** open at the same time, or at 3pm for private players. Blackjack opens in the hallowed **Salle des Amériques** at 5pm (2pm weekends). The gambling continues until very late (or early), depending on the crowd. The casino classifies its "private rooms" as the more demure, nonelectronic areas without slots. To enter the casino, you must show a passport or other photo ID and be at least 18. After 8pm, the staff will insist that men wear jackets and neckties for entrance to the private rooms. Entrance costs 10€ to anywhere past the Atrium; 20€ to the Salons Privés. And entrance to the Les Salons Supers Privés? It's by invitation only.

No dress code or entry fee applies in the **Café de Paris Casino,** place du Casino (© **98-06-77-77**), across the square. Video gaming machines open at 10am, with roulette and blackjack tables in operation from 8pm.

MUSIC   Opéra de Monte-Carlo (www.opera.mc; © **98-06-28-28**) is headquartered in the lavish, recently renovated Belle Epoque **Salle Garnier** of the casino. The grand salon hosted the wedding reception of Prince Albert of Monaco and Charlene Wittstock in July 2011. Tickets to the operas and other events scheduled inside range from 20€ to 120€. Tickets to events within the Salle Garnier are available from a kiosk outside the Café de Paris Casino; tickets can be purchased Tuesday to Saturday from 10am to 5:30pm.

WHERE TO STAY

Hôtel de France   Not all Monégasques are rich, as a stroll along workaday rue de la Turbie will convince you. Here you'll find some of the cheapest accommodations and eateries in the high-priced Principality. This 19th-century hotel, 3 minutes from the rail station, has modest furnishings but is well kept and comfortable. It benefitted greatly from thorough renovation, which was completed in 2012. The guest rooms and bathrooms are small, and each unit has a shower.

6 rue de la Turbie, Monaco 98000. www.monte-carlo.mc/france. © **93-30-24-64.** Fax 92-16-13-34. 27 units. 85€–135€ double. MC, V. Parking nearby 7.50€ for 24 hours. **Amenities:** Bar; room service. *In room:* TV, hair dryer, Wi-Fi (free).

Monte Carlo Bay Hotel & Resort ★★★   Occupying a 4-hectare (10-acre) Mediterranean garden, this is a plush garden of Eden in the Principality. It's the most child-friendly and business-friendly of all the Monaco hotels. Vast lagoons, pools, exotic gardens, the Cinq Mondes spa, and an indoor pool covered with a monumental glass dome are linked by a network of teak footbridges. A network of five restaurants, bars, and a summer casino round out the complex. Of the beautifully furnished bedrooms, more than three-quarters of them open onto sea views. Rooms are decorated with white-oak furnishings, often sandstone floors, and soft Mediterranean pastels.

40 av. Princesse Grace, Monaco 98000. www.montecarlobay.com. © **98-06-02-00.** Fax 98-06-00-03. 334 units. 335€–920€ double; from 860€ suite. AE, DC, MC, V. Parking 30€. **Amenities:** 4 restaurants; 2 bars; 3 pools (indoor, outdoor, and children's); exercise rooms; spa; concierge; babysitting; nightclub; casino; disco. *In room:* A/C, TV, minibar, hair dryer, Wi-Fi (free in lobby, or 20€/day).

GERMANY

by Caroline Sieg

Seamlessly merging yesterday with today, Germany has solidly established itself as a delicious mix of culture, history, and modern life. Berlin has solidly established itself as Europe's coolest capital, firmly moving forward from its unique past—the former path of the Berlin Wall is now a bicycle path where Berliners push baby strollers and the city has evolved into the nightlife and art hub of the country. Restored baroque Munich, in the south, known as Germany's "secret capital," is the gateway to the Bavarian Alps and colorful alpine villages. For a taste of medieval Germany, explore the untouched towns of the Romantic Road and Ludwig II's fairytale castle of Neuschwanstein.

8

BERLIN ★★★

Ask Berliners what they love about the German capital and some will talk about the joys of post-Communist freedom, others about areas such as Kreuzberg's throbbing nightlife or Mitte's exciting young designers. Berlin can fill you with wonder, contemplating the future in the crystalline Reichstag parliament building or the high-rise Potsdamer Platz, and with horror, revisiting the past at the Jewish Museum and remnants of the Berlin Wall.

In fact, when poet Heinrich Heine arrived in Berlin in 1819, he exclaimed, "Isn't the present splendid!" Were he to arrive today, he might make the same remark. Visitors who come by plane to Berlin see a splendid panorama. Few metropolitan areas are blessed with as many lakes, woodlands, and parks—these cover one-third of the city's area.

The nostalgic, the party lover, the trendsetter, the city visitor who relishes green spaces, today's Berlin is one city, many characters—different every time you look but never looked at indifferently.

Essentials

GETTING THERE

BY PLANE At the time of writing, Berlin has two airports: Tegel Airport in the northwest and Schönefeld in the southeast. Both are due to close when the new Berlin Brandenburg International Airport (BBI) opens, but BBI has suffered a series of scheduling setbacks and the exact date when it will open is still unclear. At press time, it was due to open in March 2013 (but Berliners are not holding their breath, and neither should you). Consult your airline for the latest information.

Buses from each airport take you into the city center; Schönefeld is also connected by S-Bahn and regional train. Both airports are roughly 30 to 40 minutes from the city center by public transportation. From Tegel, hop on bus TXL, which has drop-offs across the city center. A one-way ticket costs 2.30€. A **taxi** between Tegel and the city center costs roughly 20 to 25€. From Schönefeld, take the S-Bahn or regional **train** to the city center. A slower option is to hop on **bus** X7 or 171 to Rudow, where you can connect with the U7 subway. The fare for either option is 3€ one-way. A **taxi** between Schönefeld and the city center costs roughly 25 to 30€. For information on all three airports—Tegel, Schönefeld, and BBI—visit www.berlin-airport.de or call ☎ **0180/500-01-86.**

At press time, Schönefeld and Tegel were due to close in August or September 2012. Be sure to check the Berlin airport website (www.berlin-airport.de) and consult your airline for the most up-to-date information.

BY TRAIN   Frankfurt and Hamburg, among other cities, have good rail connections to Berlin. Frankfurt to Berlin takes about 4 hours. Hamburg is 2 hours and 8 minutes away, thanks to a high-speed InterCity Express train running between the two cities nonstop. Eurailpass and GermanRail passes are valid on these services. Most arrivals from western European and western German cities terminate at the **Berlin Hauptbahnhof,** the main train station, which is well connected to public transportation. Facilities include a tourist information counter dispensing free maps and tourist brochures, open daily from 10am to 7pm. The staff can make same-day hotel reservations for 4€. Berlin has three other main train stations, the **Bahnhof Zoologischer Garten, Berlin Ostbahnhof,** and **Berlin Spandau.** For information about any railway station, visit www.bahn.de or call ☎ **01805/996633.**

BY BUS   The **ZOB Omnibusbahnhof am Funkturm,** Messedamm 6 (www.iob-berlin.de; ☎ **030/302-53-61**), is the operations center for several independent bus operators.

BY CAR   From Frankfurt, take A-66 to Bad Herzfeld, and either go east on A-4 to pick up A-9 to Berlin, or continue on A-7 to Braunschweig and east on A-2 toward Berlin. North of Nürnberg, A-9 leads to Berlin. From Leipzig, take A-14 in the direction of Halle; at the intersection of A-9, head northeast into Berlin. From Dresden, head northeast on A-13 into Berlin. Expect heavy traffic delays on *Autobahnen*, especially on weekends and sunny days when everyone is out touring.

VISITOR INFORMATION

TOURIST INFORMATION CENTER   For tourist information and hotel bookings, head for the **Berlin Tourist Information Center,** in the Europa-Center near the Memorial Church, entrance on the Budapesterstrasse side (www.visitberlin.de; ☎ **030/25-00-24**), open Monday to Saturday from 10am to 7pm and Sunday from 10am to 6pm.

CITY LAYOUT   The center of activity in the western part (Charlottenburg, Kurfürstendamm & Around) of Berlin is the 3km-long (1¼-mile) Kurfürstendamm, called the Ku'Damm by Berliners. Along this wide boulevard, you'll find the best hotels, restaurants, theaters, cafes, nightclubs, shops, and department stores. The huge Tiergarten, the city's largest park, is crossed by Strasse des 17 Juni, which leads to the famed Brandenburg Gate (Brandenburger Tor); just north is the Reichstag. On the southwestern fringe of the Tiergarten is the Zoologischer Garten (Berlin Zoo). From the Ku'damm you can take Hardenbergstrasse, crossing Bismarckstrasse and traversing Otto-Suhr-Allee, which leads to Schloss Charlottenburg, one of your major

Germany

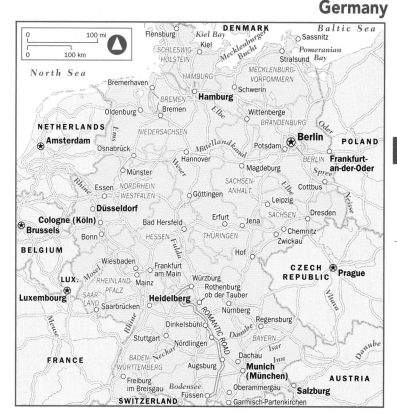

Scale: 0 – 100 mi / 0 – 100 km

Map labels: DENMARK, Baltic Sea, Flensburg, Kiel Bay, Kiel, Sassnitz, SCHLESWIG-HOLSTEIN, Mecklenburger Bucht, Pomeranian Bay, Stralsund, North Sea, MECKLENBURG-VORPOMMERN, Bremerhaven, HAMBURG, Schwerin, Hamburg, BREMEN, Bremen, Oldenburg, Elbe, Wittenberge, BRANDENBURG, Oder, NETHERLANDS, Ems, NIEDERSACHSEN, Amsterdam, Osnabrück, Mittellandkanal, Potsdam, Berlin, POLAND, Hannover, Weser, Magdeburg, BERLIN, Frankfurt-an-der-Oder, Münster, Spree, SACHSEN-ANHALT, Essen, NORDRHEIN-WESTFALEN, Göttingen, Elbe, Cottbus, Neisse, Düsseldorf, Leipzig, SACHSEN, Dresden, Cologne (Köln), Bad Hersfeld, Erfurt, Jena, Chemnitz, Brussels, Bonn, HESSEN, Fulda, THÜRINGEN, Zwickau, BELGIUM, Hof, Wiesbaden, Frankfurt am Main, CZECH REPUBLIC, Prague, LUX., Mosel, RHEINLAND-PFALZ, Mainz, Würzburg, Luxembourg, SAAR LAND, Saarbrücken, Heidelberg, Rothenburg ob der Tauber, Vltava, ROMANTIC ROAD, Nürnberg, Dinkelsbühl, Regensburg, Danube, Stuttgart, Nördlingen, BAYERN, Isar, Danube, FRANCE, BADEN-WÜRTTEMBERG, Neckar, Augsburg, Dachau, Inn, Munich (München), AUSTRIA, Freiburg im Breisgau, Bodensee, Oberammergau, Salzburg, Füssen, Garmisch-Partenkirchen, SWITZERLAND, Rhine

sightseeing goals. The Dahlem Museums are on the southwestern fringe, often reached by going along Hohenzollerndamm.

The Brandenburg Gate is the start of Berlin's most celebrated street, Unter den Linden, the cultural heart of Berlin before World War II. This also marks the beginning of **Mitte,** which extends east of the gate. The famous street runs from west to east, cutting a path through the city. It leads to **Museumsinsel (Museum Island),** where the most outstanding museums of eastern Berlin, including the Pergamon, are situated. As it courses along, Unter den Linden crosses another major Berlin artery, Friedrichstrasse. If you continue south along Friedrichstrasse, you'll reach the former location of Checkpoint Charlie, the famous border-crossing site of the Cold War days.

Unter den Linden continues east until it reaches Alexanderplatz, a large open plaza with the iconic landmark Fernsehturm (TV tower). A short walk away is the restored **Nikolaiviertel (Nikolai Quarter),** a neighborhood of bars, restaurants, and shops that evoke life in the prewar days.

GETTING AROUND
BY PUBLIC TRANSPORTATION The Berlin transport system consists of buses, trams, and U-Bahn and S-Bahn trains. The network is run by the **BVG** (www.bvg.de;

Western Berlin

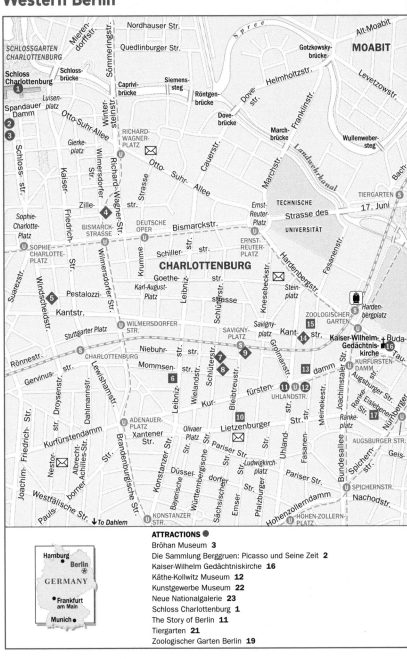

ATTRACTIONS ●
Bröhan Museum **3**
Die Sammlung Berggruen: Picasso und Seine Zeit **2**
Kaiser-Wilhelm Gedächtniskirche **16**
Käthe-Kollwitz Museum **12**
Kunstgewerbe Museum **22**
Neue Nationalgalerie **23**
Schloss Charlottenburg **1**
The Story of Berlin **11**
Tiergarten **21**
Zoologischer Garten Berlin **19**

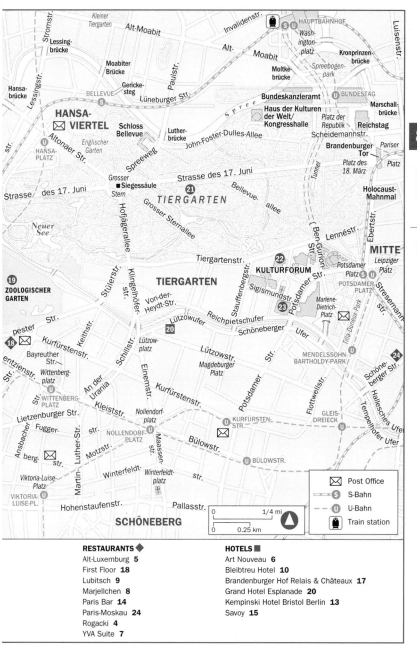

RESTAURANTS ◆
Alt-Luxemburg **5**
First Floor **18**
Lubitsch **9**
Marjellchen **8**
Paris Bar **14**
Paris-Moskau **24**
Rogacki **4**
YVA Suite **7**

HOTELS ■
Art Nouveau **6**
Bleibtreu Hotel **10**
Brandenburger Hof Relais & Châteaux **17**
Grand Hotel Esplanade **20**
Kempinski Hotel Bristol Berlin **13**
Savoy **15**

The Welcome Card

If you're going to be in Berlin for a while, you can purchase a **Welcome Card** granting holders certain discounts, especially on public transportation. A card valid for 48 hours costs 17.90€ or else 23.90€ for a 72-hour card. A 5-day card sells for 30.90€. This also includes admission into many museums, tours, and other attractions or price reductions of up to 50%. Reductions of 25% are granted at 10 of the city's theaters as well. It's valid for one adult. Several variations that include additional museums, Potsdam, and children are also available. For more information, go to www.visit berlin.de.

© 030/1-94-49), which operates an information booth outside the Bahnhof Zoo on Hardenbergplatz, open daily from 6am to 10pm. The staff will provide details about which U-Bahn (underground) or S-Bahn (elevated railway) line to take to various locations and the ticket options. You can also purchase tickets, including discount cards.

The **BVG standard ticket** (*Einzelfahrschein*) costs 2.30€ to 3€ and is valid for 2 hours of transportation in one direction, transfers included. Also available at counters and vending machines is a Day Pass ticket; the price is 6.30€ to 6.80€ and it is valid the day you purchase it until 3am the following day. On buses, only standard tickets can be purchased, and on trams tickets can be purchased from machines on the trams. Tickets should be kept until the end of the journey; otherwise, you'll be liable for a fine of 50€.

BY TAXI   Taxis are available throughout Berlin. The meter starts at 3.20€, plus 1.65€ per kilometer (⅓ mile) after that. After 7km (4⅓ miles), the fare is 1.30€ per kilometer. Visitors can flag down taxis that have a T-sign illuminated. © **21-02-02, 26-10-26,** or **44-33-22** are all reliable taxi telephone numbers.

BY CAR   Touring Berlin by car isn't recommended. Free parking places are difficult to come by. The most convenient way to get around is by public transport.

BY BICYCLE   Berlin marks biking trails along major streets, especially in the leafy neighborhoods of the former West Berlin. A bike is also ideal for exploring old East Berlin, a city still in redevelopment. One of the best companies for rentals is **Little John Bikes** (www.little-john-bikes.de), with branches in Mitte, Kreuzberg, and Schöneberg renting bikes for 10€ for one calendar day.

[FastFACTS] BERLIN

ATMs/Banks   Most **banks** are open Monday to Friday 9am to 1 or 3pm.

Business Hours   Most other **businesses** and **stores** are open Monday to Friday 9 or 10am to 6:30pm and Saturday 9am to 4pm. On *langer Samstag,* the first Saturday of the month, shops stay open until 4 or 6pm. Some stores observe late closing on Thursday, usually at 8:30pm.

Currency   Germany's currency is the European euro €.

Doctors & Hospitals   The Berlin tourist office in the Europa-Center (see "Visitor Information," above) keeps a list of English-speaking dentists and doctors in Berlin. In case of a medical emergency, call © **030/31-00-31.**

Drugstores   If you need a pharmacy (*Apotheke*) at night, go to one on any corner. There you'll find a sign in the window giving the address of the nearest drugstore open at night. A central pharmacy is **Europa-Apotheke,** Osnabrücker Strasse 4 (℡ **030/3-44-56-56;** U-Bahn: Kurfürstendamm). It's open Monday to Friday 9am to 8pm and Saturday to 6pm.

Embassies & Consulates For U.S. residents, the **American Consulate,** Clayallee 170 (U-Bahn: Oskar-Heleme-Heim), is the office that addresses most mundane passport issues and problems. Americans in need of nonemergency services can call ℡ **030/832-9233** Monday to Friday 2 to 4pm. Persons with very important business or with emergencies can call the general switchboard at ℡ **030/83050.** The **U.S. Embassy,** Pariser Platz 2 at the Brandenburg Gate (http://germany.usembassy. gov), is a "closed building," not open to anyone except for missions of major military, diplomatic, or economic concern to the U.S. Hours are Monday to Friday 8:30am to 4pm. **Canada** maintains an embassy at Leipziger Platz 17 (http:// www.canadainternational. gc.ca/germany-allemagne; ℡ **030/20-31-20;** U-Bahn: Potsdamer Platz). Hours are Monday to Friday 9 to 11am. The **British Embassy** is at Wilhelmstrasse 70–71 (http://ukingermany.fco.gov. uk; ℡ **030-20457-0;** U-Bahn: Friedrichstrasse), open Monday to Friday 9am to noon and 2 to 4pm. The embassy of **Australia** is at Wallstrasse 76–79

(www.germany.embassy.gov. au; ℡ **030/8-80-08-80;** U-Bahn: Märkisches Museum). Hours are Monday to Thursday 8:30am to 5:30pm, Friday 8:30am to 4:15pm. The embassy of **New Zealand** is at Friedrichstrasse 60 (www.nz embassy.com/germany; ℡ **030/20-62-10;** U-Bahn: Friedrichstrasse). Hours are Monday to Friday 9am to 1pm and 2 to 5:30pm. The embassy of **Ireland** is at Jägerstrasse 51 (www. embassyofireland.de; ℡ **030/22-07-20;** U-Bahn: Taubenstrasse). Hours are Monday to Friday 9:30am to 12:30pm and 2:30 to 4:45pm.

Emergencies Police ℡ **110;** dial ℡ **112** to report a fire or call an ambulance.

Internet Access If you're feeling out of touch, visit **Easy Internet Café,** Kurfürstendamm 224 (℡ **030/88-70-79-70;** U-Bahn: Kurfürstendamm, and then bus no. 109 or 129). Open 24 hours daily. Many cafes and restaurants also have free Wi-Fi for customers. Starbucks is one well-known chain that offers free Wi-Fi to customers.

Post Office You'll find yellow post offices scattered throughout Berlin, with particularly large branches positioned at Bahnhof Zoo, Hardenbergplatz (U-Bahn: Zoologischer Garten); at both Tegel and Schönefeld airports; at the main railway station (Hauptbahnhof); and in the town center at Joachimstalerstrasse 10.

With a limited number of exceptions, most post offices in Germany are open Monday to Friday from 8am to 6pm and Saturday from 8am to 1pm. None of them receives direct telephone calls from the public, but if you're interested in postal rates and procedures, go to www.deutschepost.de or call ℡ **0180/23-333** for information about postal procedures throughout Germany. Unlike the old days, German post offices no longer offer the use of pay telephones for long-distance calls, and no longer send international telegrams. (A limited number, however, offer telegram service for destinations within Germany.) When you enter a German post office, know in advance that the yellow-painted windows are for issues about the mail, and that the blue-painted windows are for issues associated with money orders and banking rituals. If you just want to buy **stamps** for mailing a letter, it's usually more convenient to buy them at any of thousands of small stores, newsstands, or tobacco shops throughout the country that stock them.

Safety Germany is a reasonably safe country in which to travel, although neo-Nazi skinheads have sometimes attacked black or Asian travelers, especially in the rural eastern part of the country. Some of the most dangerous places, especially at night, are around the large railway stations and in city parks so those are best avoided after dark.

Taxes As a member of the European Union, Germany imposes a tax on most goods and services known as the **value-added tax (VAT)** or, in German, **Mehrwertsteuer.** Nearly everything is taxed at 19%, including vital necessities such as gas or luxury items like jewelry. VAT is included in the price of restaurants and hotels. Note that goods for sale, such as cameras, also have the 19% tax already factored into the price; but the listed prices of services, such as having a mechanic fix your car, don't include VAT, so an extra 19% will be tacked on to your bill. Stores that display a TAX FREE sticker will issue you a Tax-Free Shopping Check at the time of purchase. You can then get a refund at one of the Tax-Free Shopping Service offices in the major airports and many train stations (and some of the bigger ferry terminals). Otherwise, send checks to Tax-Free Shopping Service, Mengstrasse 19, 23552 Lübeck, Germany.

Telephone The **country code** for Germany is **49;** the **city code** for Berlin is **30** for calls from outside Germany or **030** if you're calling within the country.

If you're going to make a lot of phone calls and want to avoid roaming charges, purchase a local SIM card. There are oodles of corner shops that advertise cellphones and SIM cards (look for signs that say Cell, Mobile, or SIM). Make sure your phone is unlocked in order to use a foreign SIM card. A SIM card usually costs around 10€ for the initial set-up fee. The corner shops are better for this; if you walk into a standard phone shop they will request to see a local utility bill, etc. before giving you a SIM card.

Tipping If a **restaurant** bill says Bedienung, that means a service charge has already been added, so just round up to the nearest euro. If not, add 10% to 15%. Round up to the nearest euro for taxis. **Bellhops** get 1€ per bag, as does the doorperson at your hotel, restaurant, or nightclub. **Room cleaning** staffs get small tips in Germany, as do **concierges** who perform some special favors such as obtaining hard-to-get theater or opera tickets. Tip **hairdressers** or barbers 5% to 10%.

Exploring Berlin

Berlin is a monster-sized capital, eight times the size of Paris. Plan wisely. Be sure to head up to Norman Foster's panoramic glass-domed **Reichstag** (German parliament), and join photographers for the obligatory twilight snapshot of the glowing **Brandenburg Gate.** You can spend days roaming **Tiergarten** park's lake-dotted woodlands and UNESCO-listed **Museum Island**'s galleries, where Egypt's Queen Nefertiti hides. Trace Berlin's turbulent past at the Libeskind-designed **Jewish Museum** and walk the artiest stretch of Wall at the **East Side Gallery.**

MITTE & MUSEUMSINSEL (MUSEUM ISLAND)
Mitte

Brandenburger Tor (Brandenburg Gate) ★★ ICON This triumphal arch stood for many years next to the Wall, symbolizing the divided city. Today it represents the reunited German capital. Six Doric columns hold up an entablature inspired by the Propylaea of the Parthenon at Athens. Surrounded by the famous and much-photographed Quadriga of Gottfried Schadow from 1793, the gate was designed by Carl Gotthard Langhans in 1789. Napoleon liked the original Quadriga so much he ordered them taken down and shipped to Paris, but they were returned to Berlin in 1814. In Berlin's heyday before World War II, the gate marked the grand western extremity of the "main street," Unter den Linden. In the Room of Silence, visitors still gather to meditate and reflect on Germany's past.

Pariser Platz. Free admission. Room of Silence daily 10am–6pm. S-Bahn: Unter den Linden. Bus: 100.

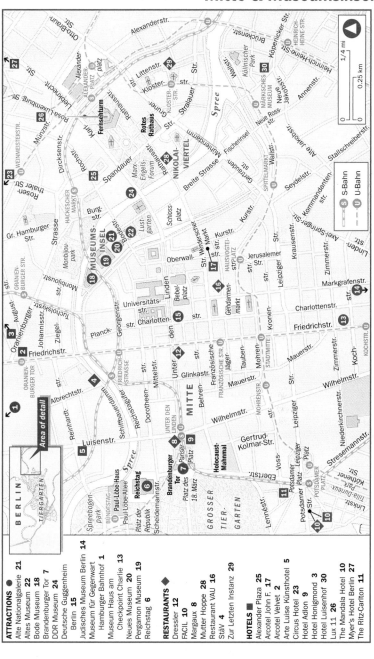

ATTRACTIONS ●
Alte Nationalgalerie **21**
Altes Museum **22**
Bode Museum **18**
Brandenburger Tor **7**
DDR Museum **24**
Deutsche Guggenheim
Berlin **15**
Judisches Museum Berlin **14**
Museum fur Gegenwart
Hamburger Bahnhof **1**
Museum Haus am
Checkpoint Charlie **13**
Neues Museum **20**
Pergamon Museum **19**
Reichstag **6**

RESTAURANTS ◆
Dressler **12**
FACIL **10**
Margaux **8**
Mutter Hoppe **28**
Restaurant VAU **16**
StäV **4**
Zur Letzten Instanz **29**

HOTELS ■
Alexander Plaza **25**
Arcotel John F. **17**
Arcotel Velvet **2**
Arte Luise Künsthotel **5**
Circus Hotel **23**
Hotel Adlon **9**
Hotel Honigmond **3**
Hotel Luisenhof **30**
Lux 11 **26**
The Mandala Hotel **10**
Myer's Hotel Berlin **27**
The Ritz-Carlton **11**

Deutsche Guggenheim Berlin ★ MUSEUM This state-of-the-art museum is devoted to organizing and presenting exhibitions of modern and contemporary art. The Guggenheim Foundation conceives, organizes, and installs several exhibitions annually, and presents exhibitions of newly commissioned works created specifically for this space by world-renowned artists. In addition to contemporary artists, exhibition subjects in the past have ranged from Picasso and Cézanne to Gerhard Richter.

Unter den Linden 13–15. www.deutsche-guggenheim.de. © **030/2020-930.** Admission 4€ adults, 3€ students and seniors, free for children 11 and under; free admission on Mon. Daily 10am–8pm. U-Bahn: Französiche Strasse.

DDR Museum MUSEUM This museum admirably sets out to showcase what daily life was like for the citizens of the now-defunct German Democratic Republic. It is interactive in that visitors are encouraged to open drawers and cupboards and touch almost everything, and descriptions are in English. What a way to experience life in the GDR firsthand. Here's your chance to drive the famous Trabi and to handle other once utilitarian, but now historic, artifacts of the Communist-held East Germany. It expanded in late 2010 to include an examination of the "bureaucratic smokescreen" in the GDR, and explores topics including the GDR state and economy, brother states, ideology, opposition, and the Stasi (the GDR Ministry for State Security).

Karl-Liebknecht-Strasse 1. www.ddr-museum.de. © **030/847123731.** Admission 6€ adults, 4€ students. Sat 10am–10pm; Sun–Fri 10am–8pm. S-Bahn or U-Bahn: Alexander-Platz.

Judisches Museum Berlin ★★ MUSEUM The Jewish Museum is the most talked-about museum in Berlin, housed in a building that is one of the most spectacular in the city. Called "the silver lightning bolt," it was designed by architect Daniel Libeskind. To some viewers, the building suggests a shattered Star of David by its building plan and the scarring in the zinc-plated facade.

Inside, the spaces are designed to make the visitor uneasy and disoriented, simulating the feeling of those who were exiled. A vast hollow cuts through the museum to mark what is gone. When the exhibits reach the rise of the Third Reich, the hall's walls, ceiling, and floor close in as the visitor proceeds. A chillingly hollow Holocaust Void, a dark, windowless chamber, evokes much that was lost.

The exhibits concentrate on three themes: Judaism and Jewish life, the devastating effects of the Holocaust, and the post-World War II rebuilding of Jewish life in Germany. The on-site Liebermanns Restaurant features world cuisine, with an emphasis on Jewish recipes—all strictly kosher.

Lindenstrasse 9–14. www.jmberlin.de. © **030/259-93-300.** Admission 5€ adults, 2.50€ students and seniors, free for children 6 and under, 10€ family ticket for 2 adults and up to 4 children. Mon 10am–10pm; Tues–Sun 10am–8pm. U-Bahn: Hallesches Tor or Kochstrasse. Bus: M29, M41, or 248.

Museum für Gegenwart Hamburger Bahnhof MUSEUM This Museum of Contemporary Art is housed in the stunning old Hamburger Bahnhof train station, the former terminus for trains from Hamburg. Today, it lives on as a premier storehouse of postwar art. Traces of its former function are still evident in the building, including the high roof designed for steam engines. The modern art on display is some of the finest in Germany and includes significant American pop art, like Andy Warhol's legendary Mao Zedong and Marilyn Monroe portraits. The museum also houses excellent collections of Cy Twombly and Anselm Kiefer. Other works on display are by Rauschenberg, Lichtenstein, and Dan Flavin. The conceptual artist Beuys is also well represented with more than 400 of his drawings.

Holocaust Memorial

Colloquially referred to as the Holocaust Memorial, Stresemannstrasse 90 (www.stiftung-denkmal.de; ℂ 030/26394336; U-Bahn: Potsdamer Platz or Bundestag. Free admission. 24 hr.), the **Memorial to the Murdered Jews of Europe** (direct translation: Stiftung Denkmal für die ermordeten Juden Europas) now occupies a vast site in the center of Berlin, just south of the Brandenburg Gate, with 2,711 matte gray stelae. The memorial was opened on May 10, 2005, 2 days after the 60th anniversary of VE Day, signaling the end of World War II in Europe.

Peter Eisenman was the architect who designed the site, filled with claustrophobic pathways through the stelae, some of which are 4.5m (15 ft.) long.

The American architect deliberately placed many of the dark gray slabs, with their knife-sharp edges, off-kilter, evoking tombstones in an unkempt graveyard. Wandering through the memorial is like getting lost in a maze. James Young, a professor at the University of Massachusetts, called it "the Venus flytrap of Holocaust memorials."

Underneath the monument, photo and text exhibits at the **Information Center** (free admission; Tues–Sun 10am–8pm Apr–Sep, 10am–7pm Oct–Mar; closed Mon) document Nazi crimes against humanity, including the stories of those who perished and survived the ghettos and concentration camps.

Invalidenstrasse 50–51. www.hamburgerbahnhof.de. ℂ **030/397-834-11.** Admission 12€ adults, 6€ students, free for children 16 and under. Tues–Fri 10am–6pm; Sat 11am–8pm; Sun 11am–6pm. U-Bahn: Hauptbahnhof.

Museum Haus am Checkpoint Charlie MUSEUM This small building houses exhibits depicting the tragic events leading up to and following the erection of the former Berlin Wall. You can see some of the instruments of escape used by East Germans. Photos document the construction of the Wall, escape tunnels, and the postwar history of both parts of Berlin from 1945 until today, including the airlift of 1948 and 1949. One of the most moving exhibits is the display on the staircase of drawings by schoolchildren who, in 1961 and 1962, were asked to depict both halves of Germany in one picture.

Friedrichstrasse 43–45. www.mauermuseum.de. ℂ **030/253-72-50.** Admission 12.50€ adults, 6.50€ children 7–18. Daily 9am–10pm. U-Bahn: Kochstrasse or Stadtmitte. Bus: 129.

Reichstag (Parliament) On the night of February 17, 1933, a fire broke out in the seat of the German parliament, the Reichstag. It was obviously set by the Nazis, but the German Communist Party was blamed. That was all the excuse Hitler's troops needed to begin mass arrests of "dissidents and enemies of the lawful government." During World War II, the Reichstag faced massive Allied bombardment. Today it's once again the home of Germany's parliament. A glass dome, designed by English architect Sir Norman Foster, now crowns the neo-Renaissance structure originally built in 1894. You can hop in a lift up to the dome, where a sweeping vista of Berlin opens before you at an observation platform. Note that there are always long lines to enter; arrive early in the morning or late at night for the shortest wait. Alternatively, book a table at the rooftop **Dachgartenrestaurant** (ℂ **226-2990**). The view is better than the food but you'll skip the queue.

Platz der Republik 1. www.bundestag.de. ✆ **030/2273-2152.** Free admission. Daily 8am–midnight (last entrance at 10pm). U-Bahn: Bundestag. Bus: 100.

Museumsinsel (Museum Island)

Alte Nationalgalerie ★ ART MUSEUM   This museum is known for its collection of 19th-century German art as well as for its French Impressionists. A feature of the museum is the world's largest collection of the works of one of the best known of all Berlin artists, Adolph von Menzel (1815–1905). Look out for his *Das Balkonzimmer (The Balcony Room)*. Other paintings include a galaxy of art representing the romantic and classical movements as well as the Biedermeier era. Allow at least an hour and a half to take in all the canvasses by everybody from Pissarro to Cézanne, from Delacroix to Degas, and from van Gogh to Monet. The collection would have been far greater than it is had not the Nazis either sold or destroyed so many early-20th-century works they viewed as "degenerate."

Bodestrasse 1–3. www.smb.spk-berlin.de. ✆ **030/2090-5577.** Admission 8€ adults, 4€ children 6–18. Tues–Sun 10am–6pm (Thurs to 10pm). S-Bahn: Hackescher Markt. Tram: 3, 4, 5, 12, 13, 15, or 53. Bus: 100, 157, or 378.

Altes Museum ★ MUSEUM   Karl Friedrich Schinkel, the city's greatest architect, designed this structure, which resembles a Greek Corinthian temple, in 1822. On its main floor is the **Antikensammlung,** or Museum of Greek and Roman Antiquities. This great collection of world-famous works of antique decorative art was inaugurated in 1960. It's rich in pottery; Greek, Etruscan, and Roman bronze statuettes and implements; ivory carvings, glassware, objects in precious stone, and jewelry of the Mediterranean region, as well as gold and silver treasures; mummy portraits from Roman Egypt; wood and stone sarcophagi; and a few marble sculptures. The collection includes some of the finest Greek vases of the black-and-red-figures style dating from the 6th century to the 4th century B.C. The best known is a large Athenian wine jar (amphora) found in Vulci, Etruria, dating from 490 B.C., which shows a satyr with a lyre and the god Hermes.

Museumsinsel am Lustgarten. www.smb.spk-berlin.de. ✆ **030/20-90-55-77.** Admission 8€ adults, 4€ children 6–18. Tues–Sun 10am–6pm (Thurs to 10pm). U-Bahn/S-Bahn: Friedrichstrasse. Bus: 100 to Lustgarten, 147, 157, or 358.

Bode Museum ★★★ MUSEUM   One of the great museums of Germany holds a vast array of museums, including the Museum of Late Ancient and Byzantine Art, the Sculpture Collection, the **Picture Gallery ★★**, the Museum of Prehistory, the Children's Gallery, and the extensive Cabinet of Coins and Medals.

The Museum of Late Ancient and Byzantine Art has displays of early Christian sarcophagi, Coptic and Byzantine sculpture, icons, and even gravestones dating from the 3rd through the 18th century. The rich Sculpture Collection exhibits magnificent pieces from ancient churches and monasteries, including a sandstone pulpit support by Anton Pilgram (1490) carved in the shape of a medieval craftsman.

The Picture Gallery is devoted in part to masterpieces from the Dutch and German schools of the 15th and 16th centuries, as well as great works by Italian, Flemish, Dutch, French, and British painters from the 14th to the 18th century.

Monbijoubrücke, Bodestrassel 1–3 Museumsinel. www.smb.spk-berlin.de. ✆ **030/2090-5577.** Admission 8€ adults, 4€ students and children 6–18. Daily 10am–6pm (Thurs to 10pm). U-Bahn: Friedrichstrasse.

Neues Museum ★★★ MUSEUM   When the doors of this museum opened in 2009, it was the first time in 70 years that all five museums on Museum Island could be visited. Severely damaged in World War II, it was left in ruins for decades. The museum contains the collections of the **Egyptian Museum ★★★** and the Papyrus Collection as well as part of the collection of the Museum of Prehistory and Early History and the Antiquities Collection.

The famous artifact of Berlin takes residence here: the bust of **Queen Nefertiti ★★★** in the North Cupola. She gazes through the Niobe Room, the Bacchus Room, and the Roman Room into the South Cupola. Here, her gaze is returned by two monumental statues that stood in the Egyptian city of Alexandra during the late Roman Empire.

The Egyptian collection ranges from the huge sphinx of Hatshepsut (1490 B.C.) to fragments of reliefs from Egyptian temples. Of special interest is the **Burial Cult Room ★★**, where coffins, mummies, and grave objects are displayed along with life-size X-ray photographs of the mummies of humans and animals.

The **Papyrus Collection ★★** displays about 25,000 documents of papyrus, ostraca, parchment, limestone, wax, and wood in eight languages.

Museumsinsel. www.neues-museum.de. ② **030/266-424-242.** Admission 10€ adults, 5€ students and children 7–18. Sun–Wed 10am–6pm; Thurs–Sat 10am–8pm. U-Bahn: Friedrichstrasse.

Pergamon Museum ★★★ MUSEUM   The Pergamon Museum houses several departments, but if you have time for only one exhibit, go to the central hall of the

---

Seeing Remnants of the Berlin Wall

Berliners won't forget the **Berlin Wall** any time soon, but the majority was torn down in the early 1990s. However, there are still a few places to see remnants of the Wall.

The **East Side Gallery** (www.eastside gallery.com; U-Bahn: Warschauerstrasse Strasse), a ¾-mile section of the Wall along the Spree River southeast of Alexanderplatz, is the longest and best-preserved section left standing. It was painted by artists in the '90s and the feel is more like an outdoor art gallery.

Just north of the center the government reconstructed a partial stretch of the Wall at Bernauer Strasse and Ackerstrasse (**Berlin Wall Memorial/Berliner Mauer Dokumentationszentrum;** www. berliner-mauer-gedenkstaette.de; ② **0467-98-66-77;** Bernauer Strasse 111. Free admission. Tues–Sun 9:30am–7pm Apr–Oct, 9:30am–6pm Nov–Mar; closed Mon. U-Bahn: Bernauer Strasse). The memorial consists of two 70m-long (230-ft.) walls that include some fragments of the original Wall (pieces not

bulldozed away or carried off by souvenir hunters). Across from the walls is a memorial building with newspaper clippings and stations where you can see photos of the area pre-1989, listen to eyewitness testimonies of what it was like when the Wall stood, and overlook the two walls from an elevated viewing platform. Part of the memorial extends on both ends of the site along the Wall's former path; informative plaques include photos of people who perished trying to flee across the Wall and details of one of the escape routes tunneled underneath the Wall. Additionally, the memorial contains the **Chapel of Reconciliation (Kapelle der Versöhnung),** a contemporary wood, round building set on the site of the former church, which was blown up in 1985 in order to widen the border strip at this spot. A 20-minute service (in German), held to remember those who perished trying to flee to the West, takes place in the church every Tuesday to Friday at 12-noon.

U-shaped building to see the **Pergamon Altar** ★★★. This Greek altar (180–160 B.C.) has a huge room all to itself. Some 27 steps lead up to the colonnade. Most fascinating is the frieze around the base, tediously pieced together over a 20-year period. Depicting the struggle of the Olympian gods against the Titans as told in Hesiod's *Theogony*, the relief is strikingly alive, with figures projecting as much as a foot from the background. This, however, is only part of the collection of Greek and Roman antiquities, housed in the north and east wings. You'll also find sculptures from many Greek and Roman cities, including a statue of a goddess holding a pomegranate (575 B.C.), found in southern Attica. If you were looking to see the famed Market Gate of Miletus, you're out of luck. This towering Roman gate, built around A.D. 120 at the entrance to the market square in the Aegean coastal city of Miletus (now Turkey), has been dismantled. Museum experts will spend 10 years restoring it, perhaps putting it on display once again in 2015. The **Near East Museum** ★, in the south wing, contains one of the largest collections anywhere of antiquities discovered in the lands of ancient Babylonia, Persia, and Assyria. Among the exhibits is the Processional Way of Babylon with the Ishtar Gate (580 B.C.).

Bodestrasse 1–3. www.smb.spk-berlin.de. ✆ **030/2090-55-77.** Admission 10€ adults, 5€ children 7–18, free the 1st Sun of the month. Daily 10am–6pm (Thurs to 10pm). U-Bahn/S-Bahn: Friedrich-strasse. Tram: 1, 2, 3, 4, 5, 13, 15, or 53.

CHARLOTTENBURG, KURFÜRSTENDAMM & AROUND
Charlottenburg

Bröhan Museum MUSEUM   This wonderful museum specializes in decorative objects of the Art Nouveau (*Jugendstil* in German) and Art Deco periods (1889–1939), with exquisite vases, glass, furniture, silver, paintings of artists belonging to the Berlin Secession, and other works of art arranged in drawing-room fashion, including an outstanding porcelain collection.

Schlossstrasse 1a. www.broehan-museum.de. ✆ **030/3269-0600.** Admission 6€ adults, 4€ students under 31, free for children under 18. Tues–Sun 10am–6pm. U-Bahn: Sophie-Charlotte-Platz. Bus: 109 or 145 to Luisenplatz/Schloss Charlottenburg.

Die Sammlung Berggruen: Picasso und Seine Zeit (The Berggruen Collection: Picasso and His Era) ★ 📷 ART MUSEUM   *At press time, this museum was closed for expansion and renovation, but due to reopen autumn 2012.* One of the most unusual private museums in Berlin has accumulated the awesome collection of respected art and antiques dealer Heinz Berggruen. A native of Berlin who fled the Nazis in 1936, he later established antiques dealerships in Paris and California before returning, with his collection, to his native home in 1996. The setting is a renovated former army barracks designed by noted architect August Stüler in 1859. Although most of the collection is devoted to Picasso, there are also works by Cézanne, Braque, Klee, and van Gogh. Some 60 or more works in all, the Picasso collection alone is worth the trip, ranging from his teenage efforts to all of his major periods.

Schlossstrasse 70. www.smb.museum. ✆ **030/2090-5577.** Admission 8€ adults, 4€ students and children. Tues–Sun 10am–6pm. U-Bahn: Richard-Wagner-Platz, followed by a 10-min. walk. Bus: 129, 145, or 210.

Kaiser-Wilhelm Gedächtniskirche (Kaiser Wilhelm Memorial Church)
CHURCH   There is no more evocative site in the western sector of Berlin to remind us of the horrors of war. The massive red-sandstone church that originally stood here was dedicated in 1895 as a memorial to Kaiser Wilhelm II. In 1945, during the

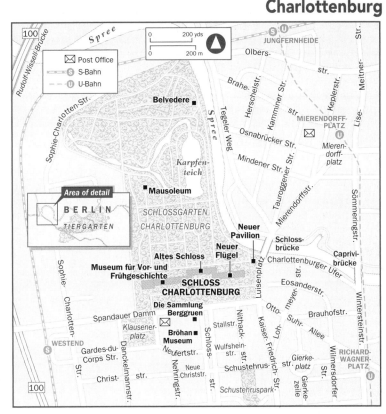

closing months of World War II, a bomb dropped by an Allied plane blasted it to pieces, leaving only a few gutted walls and the shell of the neo-Romanesque bell tower. After the war, West Berliners decided to leave the artfully evocative ruins as a reminder of the era's suffering and devastation. In 1961, directly at the base of the ruined building, they erected a small-scale modern church designed by Egon Eierman. Always irreverent, Berliners, noting the avant-garde architecture and geometric design of the new church, nicknamed it "the lipstick and powder box." Its octagonal hall is lit solely by thousands of colored glass windows set into a honeycomb framework. On its premises, you can visit a small museum with exhibitions and photographs documenting the history of the original church and the destructive ravages of war. The new church can hold up to 1,200 worshipers, and 10-minute religious services—conceived for office workers heading home—are held there every day at 1, 5:30, and 6pm. Free organ concerts take place every Saturday year-round at 6pm.

Breitscheidplatz. www.gedaechtniskirche-berlin.de. ✆ **030/2185023.** Free admission. Daily 9am–7pm. U-Bahn: Zoologischer Garten or Kurfürstendamm.

Käthe-Kollwitz Museum ★ MUSEUM   More than any other museum in Germany, this one reflects the individual sorrow of the artist whose work it contains.

Some visitors call it a personalized revolt against the agonies of war, as well as a welcome change from the commercialism of the nearby Ku'damm. Established in 1986, it was inspired by Berlin-born Käthe Kollwitz, an ardent socialist, feminist, and pacifist whose stormy social commentary led to the eventual banning of her works by the Nazis. Many Kollwitz works show the agonies of wartime separation of mother and child, inspired in part by her loss of a son in Flanders during World War I and a grandson during World War II.

Fasanenstrasse 24. www.kaethe-kollwitz.de. *℃* **030/882-52-10.** Admission 6€ adults, 3€ children 6–18 and students. Wed–Mon 11am–6pm. U-Bahn: Uhlandstrasse or Kurfürstendamm. Bus: 109, 119, 129, or 219.

Kunstgewerbe Museum (Museum of Decorative Arts) MUSEUM *At press time this museum was closed for renovation—check the website for updates on the reopening date.* When it does reopen it is an exceptional collection devoted to European applied arts from the early Middle Ages to the present, including the Renaissance, baroque, rococo, Jugendstil (German Art Nouveau), and Art Deco periods. Displayed are glassware, porcelain, silver, furniture, jewelry, and clothing. The collection of medieval goldsmiths' works is outstanding, as are the displays of Venetian glass, early Meissen and KPM porcelain, and Jugendstil vases, porcelain, furniture, and objects.

Matthäiskirchplatz. www.smb.museum. *℃* **030/266-2902.** U-Bahn/S-Bahn: Potsdamer Platz. Bus: 129 from Ku'damm to Potsdamer Brücke, also bus 142, 148, 248, 346, or 348.

Neue Nationalgalerie (New National Gallery) ★ ART MUSEUM In its modern glass-and-steel home designed by Ludwig Mies van der Rohe, the Neue Nationalgalerie contains a continually growing collection of modern European and American art. Here you'll find works of 19th-century artists, with a stellar concentration of French Impressionists. German art starts with Adolph von Menzel's paintings from about 1850. The 20th-century collection includes works by Max Beckmann, Edvard Munch, and E. L. Kirchner *(Brandenburger Tor)*, as well as a few paintings by "the usual suspects," Bacon, Picasso, Ernst, Klee, and American artists such as Barnett Newman. The museum cafe serves hot meals from 11am to 5pm.

Potsdamer Strasse 50 (just south of the Tiergarten). www.smb.museum. *℃* **030/2-66-42-30-40.** Admission 8€ adults, 4€ children 7–18. Tues–Wed 10am–6pm; Thurs 10am–10pm; Fri–Sun 10am–8pm. U-Bahn: Mendelssohn-Bartholdy-Park. S-Bahn: Potsdamer Platz.

Schloss Charlottenburg (Charlottenburg Palace) ★★ CASTLE Napoleon exaggerated a bit in comparing Schloss Charlottenburg to Versailles when he invaded Berlin in 1806, but in its heyday this palace was the most elegant residence for Prussian rulers outside the castle in Potsdam. Begun in 1695 as a summer palace for the Electress Sophie Charlotte, patron of philosophy and the arts and wife of King Frederick I (Elector Frederick III), the little residence got out of hand until it grew into the massive structure you see today. The main wing contains the apartments of Frederick I and his "philosopher queen." The **new wing,** known as the **Knobelsdorff-Flügel** and built from 1740 to 1746, shelters the apartments of Frederick the Great, which now houses a collection of paintings, many of which were either collected or commissioned by the king.

Luisenplatz. www.spsg.de. *℃* **030/320-91.** Old palace 12€ adults, 8€ children 13 and under and students; new wing 6€ adults, 5€ children 13 and under and students. Old palace Tues–Sun 10am–6pm Apr-Oct, 10am–5pm Nov–Mar, new wing Wed–Mon 10am–6pm Apr-Oct, 10am–5pm Nov–

Mar; gardens (free admission) daily 6:30am–8pm (close at 6pm Nov–Feb). U-Bahn: Richard-Wagner-Platz. Bus: 145 or 204.

The Story of Berlin MUSEUM   This multimedia extravaganza portrays 8 centuries of the city's history through photos, films, sounds, and colorful displays. Beginning with the founding of Berlin in 1237, it chronicles the plague, the Thirty Years' War, Frederick the Great's reign, military life, the Industrial Revolution and the working poor, the golden 1920s, World War II, divided Berlin during the Cold War, and the fall of the Wall. Lights flash in a media blitz as you enter the display on the fall of the Wall, making you feel like one of the first East Berliners to cross to the West. Conclude your tour on the 14th floor with a panoramic view over today's Berlin. Though the displays are a bit jarring and the historical information is too jumbled to be truly educational, the museum does leave a lasting impression. Allow at least 2 hours.

Ku'damm-Karree, Kurfürstendamm 207–208 (at the corner of Uhlandstrasse). www.story-of-berlin. de. ✆ **030/887-201-00.** Admission 10€ adults, 8€ students and seniors, 5€ children 6–13, 23€ families. Daily 10am–8pm (you must enter by 6pm). U-Bahn: Uhlandstrasse.

Tiergarten ★ PARK/GARDEN   Tiergarten, the largest green space in central Berlin, covers just under 2.5 sq. km (1 sq. mile), with more than 23km (14 miles) of meandering walkways. Late in the 19th century, partly to placate growing civic unrest, it was opened to the public, with a layout formalized by one of the leading landscape architects of the era, Peter Josef Lenné. The park was devastated during World War II, and the few trees that remained were chopped down for fuel as Berlin shuddered through the winter of 1945 and 1946. Beginning in 1955, trees were replanted and alleyways, canals, ponds, and flowerbeds rearranged in their original patterns through the cooperative efforts of many landscape architects.

The park's largest monuments include the Berlin Zoo, described below, and the **Siegessäule (Victory Column),** which perches atop a soaring red-granite pedestal from a position in the center of the wide boulevard (Strasse des 17 Juni) that neatly bisects the Tiergarten into roughly equivalent sections.

From the Bahnhof Zoo to the Brandenburger Tor. Free admission. Bus: 100, 141, or 341 to Grosser Stern.

Zoologischer Garten Berlin (Berlin Zoo) ★ ☺ ZOO   Occupying most of the southwest corner of Tiergarten is Germany's oldest and finest zoo. Founded in 1844, it's a short walk north from the Ku'damm. Until World War II, the zoo boasted thousands of animals of every imaginable species and description—many familiar to Berliners by nicknames. The tragedy of the war struck here as well, and by the end of 1945, only 91 animals remained. Since the war, the city has been rebuilding its large and unique collection; today more than 13,000 animals are housed here. The zoo has Europe's most modern birdhouse, with more than 550 species. The most valuable inhabitants here are giant pandas.

Hardenbergplatz 8. www.zoo-berlin.de. ✆ **030/25-40-10.** Zoo 13€ adults, 10€ seniors, 6.50€ children 5–15. Zoo and aquarium 20€ adults, 15€ seniors, 10€ children. Zoo Nov–Feb daily 9am–5pm; Mar daily 9am–5:30pm; Apr–Sept daily 9am–6:30pm; Oct daily 9am–6pm. Aquarium year-round daily 9am–6pm. S-Bahn/U-Bahn: Zoologischer Garten.

ORGANIZED TOURS

BUS & BOAT TOURS   **BEX Sightseeing Berlin,** Kurfürstendamm 216 (www. berlinerstadtrundfahrten.de; ✆ **030/880-41-90**), runs half a dozen tours of Berlin and its environs. Their 3-hour **"Berlin Classic Live Tour"** departs April to October daily 10am and 2pm and November to March Wednesday to Saturday at 10am.

Kebabs & Currywurst

For food on the run, try one of the dozens of *Imbisse* (permanent street food stalls) that dot the streets. The quintessential Berlin street food, *Currywurst*, is at the city's ubiquitous *Wurst* (sausage) stands. It's a simple affair: grilled pork sausage sliced up, topped with a hefty dollop of ketchup, sprinkled with curry powder and ta-da, a *Currywurst* is born. Do as the locals do and order it with *pommes* (French fries) for the true experience.

Some 200,000 Turks live in Berlin, and the food that they've introduced—*döner* (doner kebab), a pita-like bread filled with shaved chicken or veal and salad and a white, garlick and yoghurt sauce—makes a filling, cheap meal. Good sit-down Turkish restaurants are harder to find, but one of the best is **Defne,** Planufer 92 (www.defne-restaurant.de; ✆ **030/8179-71-11**), right on the canal, serving a full array of Turkish specialties. It's open daily 4pm to 1am.

Priced at 20€ per person, 10€ ages 6 to 14, the tour passes most of the important attractions using buses equipped with taped commentaries in eight languages. Among the attractions visited are the East Side Gallery, the Brandenburg Gate, and Unter den Linden. The "Sans Souci/Potsdam" tour lasts 4 hours and visits Potsdam and Sans Souci Palace, former residence of Frederick the Great. The price is 39€ per person. Departures are Tuesday, Thursday, Saturday, and Sunday at 10am; May and October, there are additional departures Friday, Saturday, and Sunday at 2:15pm.

The city's best-known boat operator is **Stern und Kreisschiffahrt,** Pushkinallee 15 (www.sternundkreis.de; ✆ **030/5363600**). The most popular of the cruises, **"Historische Stadtfahrt,"** takes you for a 1-hour ride along the banks of the Spree, the river that helped build Berlin. Departing at 30-minute intervals March to October daily between 10:30am and 6:30pm, they take in river-fronting views of the city's central core, beginning at a point in the Nikolaiviertel, close to Berlin's imposing 19th-century cathedral, on the Am Palast Ufer (U-Bahn: Nikolaiviertel).

Where to Eat

If you are craving traditional German fare, Berlin has plenty of options but the city is also home to an excellent mix of international fare, albeit with a European focus. Mitte is full of restaurants that are more hip and modern, but Charlottenburg and the Ku'damm area generally attract a more reserved and conservative crowd. Reservations are essential on weekends, especially at the higher-end options. But keep in mind that Berlin is a fairly casual city so even the fanciest of restaurants here rarely have dress codes.

MITTE
Very Expensive
FACIL ★★★ CONTINENTAL   At tremendous expense, in the infrastructure of the Mandala Hotel (p. 382), a crane lifted a vast tonnage of glass, steel, and garden supplies to the hotel's fifth-floor terrace. Don't expect a view of the city skyline, as you'll probably get something even better: a verdant oasis of Zen-like calm smack in the middle of one of Berlin's most frenetic neighborhoods. A glass roof, tightly closed for midwinter views of the falling rain and snow, opens dramatically during clement weather for a view of the moon and stars.

A medley of sophisticated menu items changes with the seasons and the inspiration of the chef, but may include such starters as lukewarm octopus with clams or gnocchi with cèpes (porcini or flap mushrooms). The freshest of fish is shipped in, fashioning the bounty into Atlantic turbot with fresh fennel and an anchovy sauce or sea bass with bouillabaisse salad. Meat and poultry dishes also use quality ingredients, and our favorites are the black feather fowl with kohlrabi and dumplings or the lobster with roasted vegetables.

In the Mandala Hotel, Potsdamer Strasse 3. www.facil.de. (✆) **030/590051234.** Reservations recommended. Main courses 40€–52€; fixed-price menus 86€–146€. AE, DC, MC, V. Mon–Fri noon–3pm and 7–11pm. Closed early–mid Jan and late July–early Aug. U-Bahn: Potsdamer Platz.

Expensive

Margaux ★★★ CONTINENTAL   Chef Michael Hoffmann will dazzle your palate with his seductive, inventive dishes and his brilliant wine cellar. Several 21st-century food magazines have named his the best gourmet restaurant in Berlin. Only a few steps from the Brandenburg Gate, the restaurant has a stunning modern interior, designed by the noted architect Johanne Nalbach. The exceptional food is made from only the highest-quality ingredients. The menu begins with starters like marinated duck liver and Breton lobster, which appears with curry and, surprisingly, watermelon. Hoffmann's star shines brightest with his fish, such as John Dory with a Mediterranean "aroma" that turned out to be anchovies, olives, tomatoes, and pepper. Frogs' legs are delectably perfumed with parsley and garlic.

Unter den Linden 78. www.margaux-berlin.de. (✆) **030/22-65-26-11.** Reservations required. Main courses 28€–49€; fixed-price dinner 110€–160€. AE, DC, MC, V. Tues–Sat 7–10:30pm. Closed late July–early Aug. U-Bahn: Friedrichstrasse.

Restaurant VAU ★★ INTERNATIONAL   This Michelin-starred restaurant is the culinary showcase of master chef Kolja Kleeberg. Choices include terrine of salmon and morels with rocket salad; aspic of suckling pig with sauerkraut; salad with marinated red mullet, mint, and almonds; crisp-fried duck with marjoram; ribs of suckling lamb with thyme-flavored polenta; and desserts such as woodruff soup with champagne-flavored ice cream. The wine list is international and well chosen.

Jägerstrasse 54–55 (near the Four Seasons Hotel and the Gendamenmarkt). www.vau-berlin.de. (✆) **030/202-9730.** Reservations recommended. Main courses 35€–40€; set-price lunches 65€–85€; set-price dinners 120€. AE, DC, MC, V. Mon–Sat noon–2:30pm and 7–10:30pm. U-Bahn: Hausvoig-teiplatz.

Moderate

Dressler CONTINENTAL   No other bistro along Unter den Linden so successfully recreates Berlin's prewar decor and style. Designed to resemble an arts-conscious bistro of the sort that might have amused and entertained tuxedo-clad clients in the 1920s, it's outfitted with leather banquettes, tile floors, mirrors, and film memorabilia from the great days of early German cinema. Waiters scurry around, carrying trays of everything from caviar to strudel, as well as three kinds of oysters and hefty portions of lobster salad. Substantial menu items include perfectly prepared turbot with champagne vinaigrette; pheasant breast with Riesling sauce; local salmon trout with white-wine sauce and braised endive; stuffed breast of veal; and calves' liver with apples.

Unter den Linden 39. www.restaurant-dressler.de. (✆) **030/204-44-22.** Reservations recommended. Main courses 14€–29€. AE, DC, MC, V. Daily 8am–1am. S-Bahn: Unter den Linden.

In general, Germans are rather candid, especially if they don't agree with something. Whereas this could appear argumentative to foreigners, in general they are merely being honest and straightforward.

As a rule, expect formality in Germany (people will greet you with Herr or Frau). And punctuality is very important here: if you have an appointment, show up on time or face disapproval.

Zur Letzten Instanz GERMAN   Reputedly, this is Berlin's oldest restaurant, dating from 1525. Zur Letzten Instanz has supposedly been frequented by everybody from Napoleon to Beethoven. Prisoners used to stop off here for one last beer before going to jail. The place is located on two floors of a baroque building just outside the crumbling brick wall that once ringed medieval Berlin. Double doors open on a series of small woodsy rooms, one with a bar and ceramic *Kachelofen* (stove). At the back, a circular staircase leads to another series of rooms, where every evening at 6pm, food and wine (no beer) are served. The menu is old-fashioned, mainly limited to good, hearty fare in the best of the Grandmother Berlin tradition of staples.

Waisenstrasse 14–16 (near the Alexanderplatz). www.zurletzteninstanz.de. ℭ **030/2425528.** Reservations recommended. Main courses 13€–22€. AE, DC, MC, V. Mon–Sat noon–1am. U-Bahn: Klosterstrasse.

Inexpensive

Mutter Hoppe GERMAN   This cozy, wood-paneled restaurant still serves the solid Teutonic cuisine favored by a quasi-legendary matriarch (Mother Hoppe) who used to churn out vast amounts of traditional cuisine to members of her extended family and entourage. Within a quartet of old-fashioned dining rooms, you'll enjoy heaping portions of such rib-sticking fare as *sauerbraten* (beef marinated in vinegar) with roasted potatoes; creamy goulash with wild mushrooms; filets of pikeperch with dill-flavored cream sauce; and braised filets of pork in mushroom-flavored cream sauce. Wine is available, but most guests opt for at least one foaming mug of beer.

Rathausstrasse 21, Nikolaiviertel. www.prostmahlzeit.de/mutterhoppe. ℭ **030/241-56-25.** Reservations recommended. Main courses 8€–27€. DC, MC, V. Daily 11:30am–11:30pm. U- and S-Bahn: Alexanderplatz.

StäV ★ 🏛 RHENISH   For years, this upscale tavern entertained the politicians and journalists whose business involved the day-to-day running of the German government from Germany's former capital of Bonn. Although its owners at first opposed the reinauguration of Berlin as the German capital, when the switch was made, they valiantly pulled out of the Rhineland and followed their clientele to new digs within a 5-minute walk of the Brandenburg Gate near the Friedrichstrasse Bahnhof. The only beer served is Kölsch, a brew more closely associated with the Rhineland than any other beer. Rhenish food items include a mass of apples, onions, and blood sausage known as *Himmel und Ärd* ("heaven and hell"); braised beef with pumpernickel and raisin sauce; and Rhineland *sauerbraten* with noodles. Other items, many influenced by the culinary traditions of Berlin, include braised liver with bacon and onions; a crisp version of Alsatian pizza known as *Flammenküche;* and a potato cake topped with apples and shredded beets or with smoked salmon and sour cream.

Schiffbauerdamm 8. ℭ **030/282-3965.** Reservations recommended. Main courses 12€–24€. AE, DC, MC, V. Daily 10am–1am. U-Bahn: Friedrichstrasse.

CHARLOTTENBURG, KURFÜRSTENDAMM & AROUND
Very Expensive
First Floor ★★ REGIONAL GERMAN/FRENCH This is the showcase restaurant within one of the most spectacular hotels (the Palace Berlin) ever built near the Tiergarten. Set one floor above street level, it features a perfectly orchestrated service and setting that revolve around the cuisine of a master chef. Winning praise are such dishes as sophisticated variations of Bresse chicken; guinea fowl stuffed with foie gras and served with a truffle vinaigrette sauce; a cassoulet of lobster and broad beans in a style vaguely influenced by the culinary precepts of southwestern France; filet of sole with champagne sauce; and a mascarpone mousse with lavender-scented honey.

In the Palace Berlin, Budapesterstrasse 42. ✆ **030/25-02-10-20.** Reservations recommended. Main courses 22€–43€; set menus 45€ at lunch only, 92€–112€ at lunch and dinner. AE, DC, MC, V. Mon–Fri noon–3pm; daily 6:30–11pm. U-Bahn: Zoologischer Garten.

Expensive
Alt-Luxemburg ★★ CONTINENTAL/FRENCH/GERMAN Alt-Luxemburg's Chef Karl Wannemacher is one of the most outstanding chefs in eastern Germany. Known for his quality and market-fresh ingredients, he prepares a seductively sensual plate. Everything shows his flawless technique, especially the stuffed veal or the saddle of venison with juniper sauce. Taste his excellent lacquered duck breast with honey sauce or saddle of lamb with stewed peppers. Alt-Luxemburg offers a finely balanced wine list, and service is both unpretentious and gracious.

Windscheidstrasse 31. www.alt-luxemburg.de. ✆ **030/323-87-30.** Reservations required. Main courses 29€–36€. Fixed-price 4-course menu 67€; fixed-price 5-course menu 73€. AE, DC, MC, V. Mon–Sat 5–11pm. U-Bahn: Sophie-Charlotte-Platz.

Paris Bar ★ FRENCH This French bistro has been a local favorite since the postwar years, when two Frenchmen established the restaurant to bring a little Parisian cheer to the dismal gray of bombed-out Berlin. The place is just as crowded with elbow-to-elbow tables as a Montmartre tourist trap, but you'll find it a genuinely pleasing little eatery. It's a true restaurant on the see-and-be-seen circuit between Savignyplatz and Gedächtniskiche. The food is invariably fresh and well prepared but not particularly innovative.

Kantstrasse 152. ✆ **030/313-80-52.** Reservations recommended. Main courses 15€–44€. AE. Daily noon–2am. U-Bahn: Uhlandstrasse.

Paris-Moskau INTERNATIONAL The grand days of the 19th century are alive and well at this restaurant in the beautiful Tiergarten area, where good dining spots are scarce. Menu items are both classic and more cutting-edge. The fresh tomato soup is excellent. Some of the dishes are mundane—the grilled filet of beef in mushroom sauce comes to mind—but other, lighter dishes with delicate seasonings are delightful, such as the grilled North Sea salmon with herbs accompanied by basil-flavored noodles. The chef should market his recipe for saffron sauce, which accompanies several dishes. You'll receive attentive service from the formally dressed staff.

Alt-Moabit 141. www.paris-moskau.de. ✆ **030/3-94-20-81.** Reservations recommended. Main courses 25€–28€; fixed-price menus 56€–85€. AE, DC, MC, V. Mon–Fri noon–3pm; daily 6–11:30pm. S-Bahn: Hauptbahnhof.

Moderate
Marjellchen ★ EAST PRUSSIAN This is the only restaurant in Berlin specializing in the cuisine of Germany's long-lost province of East Prussia, along with the

cuisines of Pomerania and Silesia. Amid a Bismarckian ambience of still lifes, vested waiters, and oil lamps, you can enjoy a savory version of red-beet soup with strips of beef, East Prussian potato soup with crabmeat and bacon, *falscher Gänsebraten* (pork spare-ribs stuffed with prunes and bread crumbs), and *mecklenburger Kümmelfleisch* (lamb with chives and onions).

Mommsenstrasse 9. www.marjellchen-berlin.de. © **030/883-26-76.** Reservations recommended. Main courses 10€–20€. DC, MC, V. Mon–Sat 5pm–midnight. Closed Dec 23–24 and 31. U-Bahn: Adenauerplatz or Uhlandstrasse. Bus: 109, 119, or 129.

YVA Suite ★ 🎁 INTERNATIONAL   There's an excellent restaurant associated with this club, a meeting place for the hip denizens of Berlin's inner sanctum of writers, artists, and cultural icons. Expect a high-ceilinged, stylish, and almost surgically minimalist decor, with walls almost entirely sheathed in slabs of volcanic lava rock, elegant table settings, well-prepared food that includes selections for both hearty and delicate appetites, and a formidable tradition of welcoming stars and starlets from Germany's world of high fashion, sports, and the arts. Menu items vary with the season and the inspiration of the chefs, but are likely to include lemon-coconut soup with chicken satay; terrine of goose liver; various forms of carpaccio; curried breast of duck with chorizo sausages; and Thai-style bouillabaisse.

Schlüterstrasse 52. © **030/88-72-55-73.** Reservations recommended. Main courses 16€–30€. AE, MC, V. Bar and full menu daily 6pm–midnight; bar and limited menu daily midnight–2am. S-Bahn: Savignyplatz.

Inexpensive

Lubitsch CONTINENTAL   Its conservative chic reputation was enhanced in 1999 when Chancellor Schröder dropped in for lunch and a photo op, causing ripples of energy to reverberate through the neighborhood. Menu items include lots of cafe drinks and steaming pots of afternoon tea, but if you drop in for a meal, look forward to platters of chicken curry salad with roasted potatoes; Berlin-style potato soup; braised chicken with salad and fresh vegetables; a roulade of suckling pig; and Nürnberger-style wursts. Expect brusque service, a black-and-white decor with Thonet-style chairs, and a somewhat arrogant environment that, despite its drawbacks, is very, very *Berliner.*

Bleibtreustrasse 47. www.restaurant-lubitsch.de. © **030/88-72-84-99.** Main courses 10€–22€; business lunch 13€. AE, DC, MC, V. Mon–Sat 10am–midnight; Sun 6pm–1am. U-Bahn: Kurfürstendamm.

Rogacki ★ GERMAN/DELI   Since 1928, this deluxe deli has been installed in a former stable. Every day it feeds some 1,500 people, many eating at stand-up tables. Separate counters contain the various food groups—more than 200 varieties of cured and fresh meats, some 150 kinds of cheese. The fish soup is perhaps the finest in Berlin. It is estimated that Rogacki makes two tons of potato salad in any given week. In the basement, workers stay busy all day filleting herring. The freshly baked breads, fresh salads, and other specialties from throughout the world make this a culinary adventure. You can

---

Cafe Society

The breakfast menu at family-owned **Café/Bistro Leysieffer,** Friedrichstrasse 68 (© **030/2064-9715;** www.leysieffer. de; U-Bahn: Stadtmitte), is one of the most elegant in town: Parma ham, smoked salmon, a fresh baguette, French butter, and—to round it off—champagne.

order smoked salmon, vegetable dishes, lobster, various pastas including spaghetti with the "fruits of the sea," even chili con carne.

Wilmersdorfer Strasse 145–146. www.rogacki.de. ☎ **030/343-8250.** Reservations required. Main courses 5€–16€. MC, V. Mon–Wed 9am–6pm; Thurs–Fri 9am–7pm; Sat 8am–4pm. U-Bahn: Sophie-Charlotte-Platz.

KREUZBERG

Hartmanns ★ GERMAN/MEDITERRANEAN   Chef Stefan Hartmann is arguably the best chef in Kreuzberg, at least among his many fans. This talented chef turns out dishes that are often inspired; many of his specialties have Mediterranean flavors. His market-fresh menu is wisely limited so that all ingredients are shopped for on the day. Among starters, we recommend, if featured, smoked duck liver terrine with mango and shiitake mushrooms or else codfish with a mussel jus, perhaps seared foie gras and caramelized apples. For a main course, he carefully crafts such delights as roast lamb with artichokes or pikeperch in a laurel jus.

Fichtestrasse 31. www.hartmanns-restaurant.de ☎ **030/61201003.** Reservations recommended. Main courses 28€; fixed-price menus 47€–74€. AE, DC, MC, V. Mon–Fri noon–2:30pm; Mon–Sat 6pm–midnight. U-Bahn: Kottbusser Tor.

PRENZLAUER BERG

Pasternak ★ 🍴 RUSSIAN   Its setting, a pink-walled dining room within a distinguished-looking 150-year-old building adjacent to a synagogue in what used to be the eastern zone, evokes nostalgia in many of its patrons. Menu items read like what the characters in a Dostoevski novel might have ordered: borscht, blinis, chicken Kiev, pork skewers with pomegranate and walnut sauce, *Taig Taschen* (Russian-style ravioli stuffed with spinach and cheese), beef stroganoff, and Russian-style hot apple tart. Expect generous portions, an evocative setting, and the kind of clients who don't necessarily remember the former Russian regime in Berlin with any particular distaste. You might get the vague suspicion that some, in fact, even miss it.

Knaackstrasse 22–24, Prenzlauer Berg. www.restaurant-pasternak.de. ☎ **030/4413399.** Reservations recommended. Main courses 12€–38€. AE, MC, V. Daily 11am–1am. U-Bahn: Senefelderplatz.

Shopping

The central shopping destinations are **Kurfürstendamm & Tauentzienstrasse** in Charlottenburg, and **Oranienburgerstrasse, Hackesche Höfe, Neue Schönhauserstrasse** and around in Mitte. Most stores are open Monday through Friday from 9 or 10am to 6 or 6:30pm. Many stores stay open late on Thursday evening, usually until about 8:30pm. Saturday hours for most stores are from 9 or 10am to 2pm.

The city's most dynamic shopping and entertainment complex is the **Potsdamer Platz Arkaden,** Alte Potsdamer Strasse 7 (www.potsdamer-platz-arkaden.de; ☎ **030/25-59-27-0**), where you'll find nearly 150 shops, cafes, and restaurants on three different levels. The square is also home to the Ritz-Carlton Berlin and a movie complex.

One of Berlin's largest indoor shopping centers, topped by the Mercedes-Benz logo, is the **Europa-Center,** Breitscheidplatz Tauentzienstrasse (www.europa-center-berlin.de; ☎ **030/264-97-940;** U-Bahn: Kurfürstendamm). It is vast but feels a tad outdated. Still, this is home to a number of restaurants and cafes, in addition to many shops offering wide-ranging merchandise.

LUXURY GOODS & FLEA MARKETS

Known popularly as KaDeWe (pronounced Kah-*Day*-Vay), **Kaufhaus des Westens,** Wittenbergplatz (www.kadewe.de; ☎ **030/21-21-0;** U-Bahn: Wittenbergplatz), is about two blocks from the Kurfürstendamm. The huge luxury store, whose name means "department store of the west," was established some 75 years ago. Displaying extravagant items, it's known mainly for its sixth-floor food department. It's been called the greatest food emporium in the world. More than 1,000 varieties of German sausages are displayed, and delicacies from all over the world are shipped in.

The vast flea market, **Berliner Trödelmarkt,** Strasse des 17 Juni (www.berliner-troedelmarkt.de; ✆ 030/26550096; S-Bahn: Tiergarten), is one of the favorite weekend shopping spots of countless second-hand-treasure-loving Berliners, who come here to find an appropriate piece of nostalgia, a battered semi-antique, or used clothing. The market is held every Saturday and Sunday 10am to 5pm.

8 Entertainment & Nightlife

Performance arts calendars are covered in *ExBerliner* (www.exberliner.com), a monthly publication in English. Berlin's best listings magazines are only in German: **Zitty** (www.zitty.de) and *Tip* (www.tip-berlin.de) keep you informed about various nightlife and cultural venues.

THE PERFORMING ARTS

The **Berliner Philharmonisches Orchester (Berlin Philharmonic)** is one of the world's premier orchestras. Its home, the **Philharmonie,** in the Kulturforum, Herbert-von-Karajan Strasse 1 (www.berliner-philharmoniker.de; ✆ 030/254-88-999; U-Bahn: Potsdamer Platz), is a significant piece of modern architecture; you can visit even if you don't attend a performance. None of the 2,218 seats is more than 30m (100 ft.) from the rostrum. The box office is open Monday to Friday 3 to 6pm and Saturday and Sunday 11am to 2pm. You can place orders by phone at ✆ 030/25-48-89-99. If you're staying in a first-class or deluxe hotel, you can usually ask the concierge to obtain seats for you. Tickets are 20€ to 85€, special concerts 40€ to 130€.

The famed **Deutsche Oper Berlin (Berlin Opera),** Bismarckstrasse 35 (www.deutscheoperberlin.de; ✆ 030/34-384-343; U-Bahn: Deutsche Oper; S-Bahn: Charlottenburg), performs in one of the world's great opera houses, built on the site of the prewar opera house in Charlottenburg. A ballet company performs once a week. Concerts, including *Lieder* evenings, are also presented on the opera stage. Tickets are 12€ to 125€.

Deutsche Staatsoper (German State Opera), Unter den Linden 7 (www.staatsoperberlin.de; ✆ 030/20-35-44-38; U-Bahn: Französische Strasse), presents some of the finest opera in the world, along with a regular repertoire of ballet and concerts. Its home was rebuilt within the walls of the original 1740s Staatsoper, destroyed in World War II. The box office generally is open Monday to Friday 11am to 7pm and Saturday and Sunday 2 to 7pm. Concert tickets are 15€ to 56€; opera tickets are 5€ to 180€. The opera closes from late June to the end of August.

Komische Oper Berlin, Behrensstrasse 55–57 (www.komische-oper-berlin.de; ✆ 030/20-26-00; U-Bahn: Französische Strasse; S-Bahn: Friedrichstrasse or Unter den Linden), lies in the middle of the city near Brandenburger Tor. Over the years, it has become one of the most innovative theater ensembles in Europe, presenting many avant-garde productions. The box office is open Monday to Saturday 11am to 7pm and Sunday 1pm until 1½ hours before the performance. Tickets are 8€ to 115€.

LIVE MUSIC

A-Trane, Bleibtreustrasse 105 (www.a-trane.de; ✆ 030/313-25-50; S-Bahn: Savignyplatz), is a small and smoky jazz house where the great names from the jazz world's

COME TO THE cabaret!

If you know how to sing "Life is a cabaret, old chum," in German no less, you may enjoy an evening in this postwar "Porcupine." Like its namesake, **Die Stachelschweine,** Tauentzienstrasse and Budapester Strasse (in the basement of the Europa-Center; www.stachelschweine-berlin.de; ✆ **030/261-47-95;** U-Bahn: Kurfürstendamm), pokes prickly fun at German, and often American, politicians. Get a ticket early, because the Berliners love this one. Shows are presented Tuesday to Friday at 8pm and Saturday at 6 and 9pm. The box office is open Tuesday to Friday 11am to 2pm and 3 to 7:30pm, and Saturday 10am to 2pm and 3 to 8:45pm. Cover is 15€ to 28€. The cabaret is closed during July.

Opened in 1893 as one of the most popular purveyors of vaudeville in Europe, the **Wintergarten,** Potsdamer Strasse 96 (www.wintergarten-berlin.de; ✆ **030/588-43-40;** U-Bahn: Kurfürstenstrasse), was operated in fits and starts throughout the war years, until it was demolished in 1944 by Allied bombers. In 1992, a modernized design reopened. Today, it's the largest and most nostalgic Berlin cabaret, laden with schmaltzy reminders of yesteryear and staffed with chorus girls; magicians from America, Britain, and countries of the former Soviet bloc; circus acrobats; political satirists; and musician/dancer combos. Shows begin at 8pm Monday to Friday, at 6 and 10pm Saturday, and at 6pm Sunday. Shows last around 2¼ hours. The box office is open Monday to Saturday 10am to 6pm and Sunday 2 to 6pm. Cover Friday and Saturday is 25€ to 65€, Sunday to Thursday 15€ to 55€, depending on the seat. The price including a two-course meal is 82€–85€. On Friday and Saturday, the price including a two-course meal is 87€–90€. The price includes your first drink.

past and present have hit the stage, from Diana Krall to Herbie Hancock. The name is a hybrid of the old Duke Ellington standard "Take the 'A' Train," with the "ane" in "trane" derived from the legendary John Coltrane's name. It's open daily at 8pm; music begins around 10pm. Closing hours vary. Mondays are free; on other days cover is 10€ to 30€, depending on who's playing.

With its Elvis paraphernalia, colored lights, and wine-red walls, **Wild at Heart,** Wienerstrasse 20 (www.wildatheartberlin.de; ✆ **030-6-11-92-31;** U-Bahn: Görlitzer Bahnhof), is dedicated to the rowdier side of rock. Hard-core punk, rock, and rockabilly bands from Germany and elsewhere are featured. It's open Monday to Friday 8pm to 3am, and Saturday and Sunday 8pm to 10am (yes, you may miss breakfast). Cover is 10€ to 15€. Gays, straights, and everybody in between show up at **SO 36,** Oranienstrasse 190 (www.so36.de; ✆ **030/61-401-308;** U-Bahn: Görlitzer Bahnhof), for wild action and frantic dancing into the wee hours. A young, vibrant Kreuzberg crowd is attracted to this joint where the scene changes nightly. On Wednesday and Sunday it's strictly gay and lesbian disco. On Friday and Saturday the parties "get really wild, man," as the bartender accurately promised. Some nights are devoted to themes such as James Bond where you can show up looking like a Cold War spy. Hours are Wednesday through Saturday from 10pm until "we feel like closing," and Sunday from 5pm to 1am. Cover ranges from 6€ to 25€, depending on the venue.

CLUBS

First opened almost 100 years ago, **Clärchens Ballhaus,** Augustrasse 24 (www.ballhaus.de; ☎ **030/282-9295;** S-Bahn: Oranienburger Strasse), has re-emerged as a landmark in old East Berlin. The legendary dance hall opened in the autumn of 1913 right before the Great War. The club thrived until the end of World War II. A hot DJ and live bands rage through the night, with occasional tango dancers or whatever, even Johann Strauss music. Gypsy street musicians are a favorite. Everybody from wild Turks out for a night on the town to elderly East Berlin couples fill the joint. Nazi officers once used the top floor as a private club. It's usually open from 7 to 11pm but not every night, so call before heading here.

Club der Visionaere, Am Flutgraben 1 (www.clubdervisionaere.de; ☎ **030/6951-8942;** U-Bahn: Schlesischestor), is a riverside bar in Kreuzberg that, on any busy night, looks like a shipwreck-party. A hip 20-something crowd rocks here until the sun rises. Outside look for the concrete watchtower across the street, one of the last surviving of those built by East German police to guard the Wall. In summer, the outdoor deck with a DJ playing house music is the site of late-night dance parties, including one that begins on Sunday and lasts until the wee hours of Monday. Cover is free to 10€. Open Monday to Friday 2pm to 4am, Saturday and Sunday until dawn.

Hypertrendy **Oxymoron,** in the courtyard at Rosenthaler Strasse 40–41 (www.oxymoron-berlin.de; ☎ **030/283-91-88-6;** S-Bahn: Hackenscher Markt), is a lot of fun on most nights. The setting is a high-ceilinged room with old-fashioned proportions and enough battered kitsch to remind you of a century-old coffeehouse in Franz-Josef's Vienna. Local wits refer to it as a Gesamtkunstwerk—a self-obsessed, self-sustaining work of art that might have been appreciated by Wagner. On Friday and Saturday after around 11pm, a slightly claustrophobic, much-used annex room—all black with ghostly flares of neon—opens as a disco, usually with a clientele that's about 75% hetero and 100% iconoclastic. The restaurant is open daily from 11am to 2am. Cover is 8€ to 15€.

Watergate Club, Falckensteinstrasse 49 (www.water-gate.de; ☎ **030/612-803-94;** U-Bahn: Schlesischestor), is one of Berlin's coolest bars along the Spree River. During the Cold War, Berlin turned its back to the river, which was divided with East Germany. But today riverfront nightlife is flourishing, none more so than at the Watergate, sprawling across two floors, with rotating DJs. In summer the floating terrace is a fantastic place to watch the sunrise. Cover is 10€, rising to 12€ on Friday and Saturday. Open Wednesday and Friday 11pm to around 4am, Saturday midnight to dawn.

Where to Stay

MITTE

Very Expensive

Hotel Adlon ★★★   Berlin's most historic hotel is a phoenix, freshly raised from the ashes of 1945. No other hotel sits as close to the Brandenburg Gate, at the top of an avenue that's reasserting its claim on the city's sense of chic. Grand and historic, and permeated with the legends of the glamour and tragedies that befell it during various eras of its life, it was originally built by legendary hotelier Lorenz Adlon in 1907, and then reopened with a well-publicized flourish in 1997. Public areas, some of them illuminated with lavishly detailed stained-glass domes, contain coffered ceilings, mosaics, inlaid paneling, and lots of Carrara marble. Rooms have state-of-the-art electronic extras and are mostly large. Those on the top floor offer the best views but are a bit cramped and lack some extras.

Unter den Linden 77, 10117 Berlin. www.hotel-adlon.de. ☎ **030/22610** or 800/426-3135 in the U.S. and Canada. Fax 030/22612222. 394 units. 240€–440€ double; from 700€ suite. AE, DC, MC, V. Parking 28€. S-Bahn: Unter den Linden. **Amenities:** 3 restaurants; bar; indoor heated pool; health club & spa; concierge; room service; babysitting. *In room:* A/C, TV, DVD player (in some), kitchenette (in some), fax (in some), minibar, hair dryer, Wi-Fi (12€/hr.).

The Ritz-Carlton ★★★   One of Berlin's most glamorous and prestigious hotels opened in January 2004 at the Potsdamer Platz. The building evokes the Art Nouveau heyday of the New York City skyscrapers constructed in the 1920s. All guest rooms are modern (with iPod docking stations) and luxurious with polished mahogany furniture, marble bathrooms (with rain showers), and room controls on the bedside table—you can turn the lights off or press the do-not-disturb indicator at the touch of a finger right from your plush bed. The hotel offers afternoon tea in the lobby lounge by an open fireplace and an indoor pool. The Curtain Club bar, modeled after a British Gentlemen's Club, features a mixologist who creates perfume-inspired cocktails and at 6pm daily a real Beefeater who opens the bar with a lively announcement. Brasserie Debrosses, the casual-but-classy French restaurant, is a welcome departure from the often-stuffy five-star hotel dining options.

Potsdamer Platz 3, 10785 Berlin. www.ritzcarlton.com. ☎ **030/33-77-77** or **800/241-3333** in the U.S. and Canada. Fax 030/777-55-55. 303 rooms. 165€–290€ double; 300€–320€ junior suite; 35€–995€ suite. AE, DC, MC, V. Parking 20€. U-Bahn: Potsdamer Platz. **Amenities:** restaurant; bar; indoor pool; exercise room; Jacuzzi; sauna; room service. *In room:* A/C, TV, minibar, hair dryer, Wi-Fi (20€/day).

Expensive

Alexander Plaza ★   A short walk from both Alexanderplatz and the historic district of Hackescher Höfe, this hotel originated in 1897 as an office building. In 1997, it was converted into one of the neighborhood's most charming and best-managed hotels. A labyrinth of hallways opens into rooms with unique floor plans. Each has parquet floors, high ceilings, and neo-Biedermeier blond-wood furniture. The executive rooms are very large. Low-end rooms are smaller and less dramatic, but still very comfortable. The staff here is among the most attentive in Berlin.

Rosenstrasse 1, 10178 Berlin. www.hotel-alexander-plaza.de. ☎ **030/24-00-10** or **800/223-5652** for reservations in the U.S. and Canada. Fax 030/24001777. 92 units. 135€–235€ double; 175€–330€ suite. AE, DC, MC, V. Parking 15€. S-Bahn: Hackescher Markt. **Amenities:** Restaurant; bar; exercise room; sauna; concierge; room service; babysitting. *In room:* A/C, TV, fax, minibar, hair dryer, Wi-Fi (13€/day).

Hotel Honigmond ★ 👔   A romantic retreat today, ideal for honeymooners, this boutique hotel in a restored building from 1899 was once a retreat for East German opposition leaders. As such, it was often closed by the dreaded Stasi. The sad history of the repression of East Germany has been wiped away without a trace. Today, guests are coddled in comfort in individually furnished rooms with ornate stucco ceilings, wood floors, and even bed linen designed by Paloma Picasso. The hotel lobby is filled with oil paintings, and a half dozen caged rabbits nibble away contentedly in the inner courtyard. In the cozy restaurant, with its wooden tables and candles, you can relish old-fashioned treats that the Kaiser enjoyed, including Königsberg Klopse and Bohemian dumplings.

Tieckstrasse 12, 10115 Berlin. www.honigmond-berlin.de. ☎ **030/2844550.** Fax 030/28445511. 44 units. 145€–235€ double. MC, V. U-Bahn: Oranienburger Tor. **Amenities:** Restaurant; bar; room service. *In room:* A/C, TV, minibar, hair dryer, Internet (free).

Lux 11 ★ 👔   In the hip central Mitte district, among fashionable art galleries and trendy media firms, this is an oasis of charm, comfort, and style. Outfitted in a chic minimalist style, its bedrooms have modern, glamorous decors. The open-to-view bathrooms are furnished in honey-colored wood and concrete. Lux 11 is the latest creation from a well-known duo, Claudio Silvestrin and his wife, Giuliana Salmaso, known for their minimalist designs. In the basement is the Aveda Spa, and adjacent to the lobby, there's a "micro" department store operated by a former buyer for Quartier 206, a posh fashion emporium in Berlin. An on-site restaurant and chill-out bar serves Italian and Asian fusion cuisine. Guests can get acquainted in the cozy cafe/lounge.

Rosa-Luxemburg-Strasse 9–13, 10178 Berlin. www.lux-eleven.com. © **030/93-62-80-0.** Fax 030/93-62-80-80. 72 units. 175€–205€ double; 255€–295€ suite. AE, DC, MC, V. Parking 18€. U-Bahn: Weinmeisterstrasse. **Amenities:** Restaurant; cafe; bar; health club; spa; sauna; room service. In room: A/C, TV, kitchenette, hair dryer, Wi-Fi (free).

The Mandala Hotel ★   Built in 1999, this 11-story establishment is one of the poshest and most elegant hotels in the pivotal Potsdamer Platz neighborhood. The hotel's exterior is sheathed in steel and warmly textured Italian brick. Each of the units inside is configured as a suite and is upholstered in discreetly plush fabrics, decorated with top-of-the-line stone, tile, or marble, and ringed with big windows that flood the postmodern interiors with sunlight. The upper levels, including the lounge, Qiu, one floor above lobby level, are spacious and opulent, in vivid contrast to the discreet and nonflamboyant scale of the reception area. One of this hotel's most charming features is its fifth-floor restaurant, **FACIL** (p. 372).

Potsdamer Strasse 3, 10785 Berlin. www.themandala.de. © **030/590050000.** Fax 030/590050500. 167 units (all suites). 170€–400€ standard suites; 1,700€–3,800€ deluxe suites. AE, DC, MC, V. Parking 20€. U-Bahn: Potsdamer Platz. **Amenities:** Restaurant; bar; exercise room; spa; bikes; concierge; room service; babysitting. In room: A/C, TV/DVD, minibar, hair dryer, Wi-Fi (10€/day).

Moderate

Arcotel Velvet ★ 👜   With its Andy Warhol-inspired decor, this hotel stands in what used to be a Cold War no-man's land. Enveloped by a vibrant artist and designer scene, the hotel lies right in the midst of some of Mitte's hippest cafes, bars, and restaurants. Its glass facade conceals a comfortably modern hotel that employs minimalist design and innovative concepts in its use of modern equipment, soft furnishings, and tasteful materials. All the beautifully designed bedrooms are stylish and inviting. The on-site restaurant, Lutter & Wegner, is run by Joe Laggner, a legendary star of Austrian innkeeping, and he serves a sublime regional cuisine. That's not all: The Velvet Bar is as hip as Lady Gaga and is a Mitte hot spot, known for its to-die-for cocktails.

Oranienburger Strasse 52, 10117 Berlin. www.arcotel.at. © **030/2787530.** Fax 030/278753800. 85 units. 110€–230€ double. AE, DC, MC, V. Parking 18€. S-Bahn: Oranienburger Strasse. **Amenities:** Restaurant; bar; bikes; room service; babysitting. In room: A/C, TV/DVD, minibar, hair dryer, CD player, Wi-Fi (20€/day).

Arte Luise Künsthotel ★ 👜   Its name translates as "home for artists." No, it's not a communal crash pad for the bohemian fringe, but a choice and select boutique hotel where a different German artist designed and individually furnished each of the guest rooms. Under historic preservation, the hotel is in a restored 1825 city palace. Clients from the arts, media, and even the political or business world are drawn to this unusual hostelry. Each room comes as a total surprise, and, of course, you're treated to some of each artist's work, which runs the gamut from pop to classicism. Some units evoke modern minimalism, whereas others are much more quirky.

Luisenstrasse 19, 10119 Berlin. www.luise-berlin.com. 🕿 **030/28448-0.** Fax 030/28448-448. 50 units, 30 with bathroom. 79€–110€ double without bathroom; 99€–210€ double with shower; 135€–240€ double with bathroom. AE, DC, MC. Parking 12€. U-Bahn: Friedrichstrasse. **Amenities:** Restaurant/bar next door. *In room:* A/C (in some), TV, Wi-Fi (free).

Hotel Luisenhof ★ One of the most desirable small hotels in Berlin's eastern district, the Luisenhof occupies a dignified 1822 house. Five floors of high-ceilinged rooms will appeal to those desiring to escape modern Berlin's sterility. Rooms range greatly in size, but each is equipped with good queen-size or twin beds. Bathrooms, though small, are beautifully appointed, with shower stalls (often with a large tub).

Köpenicker Strasse 92, 10179 Berlin. www.luisenhof.de. 🕿 **030/246-28-10.** Fax 030/246-28-160. 27 units. 119€–299€ double; 249€–399€ suite. Rates include breakfast. AE, DC, MC, V. Parking 8€. U-Bahn: Märkisches Museum. **Amenities:** Restaurant; bar; room service. *In room:* TV, minibar, hair dryer, Wi-Fi (free).

Myer's Hotel Berlin 🕯 Spared from the 1945 bombings, this classical building from the 19th century has been renovated and turned into a good-value hotel that is comfortable, well-maintained, and immaculate. Nostalgia and charm are combined with modern amenities. Guest rooms, midsize to spacious, come with a well-appointed bathroom with the latest fixtures, including tub and shower. The hotel offers several charming features, including a lobby bar with parquet flooring and chairs and tables that look as if they came from Old Havana. Drinks are also served on the garden roof terrace.

Metzer Strasse 26, 10405 Berlin. www.myershotel.de. 🕿 **030/440140.** Fax 030/44014104. 135€–195€ double; 210€–345€ suite. Rates include buffet breakfast. AE, MC, V. Free parking. U-Bahn: Senefelderplatz. Bus: 143. **Amenities:** Bar. *In room:* TV, minibar, hair dryer, Wi-Fi (15€/day).

Inexpensive

Arcotel John F. ★ This privately owned design hotel was inspired by the era of the popular U.S. president John F. Kennedy. It lies in the government quarter within view of Berlin Cathedral. Kennedy, of course, won the hearts of Berliners with his famous 1963 "Ich bin ein Berliner" speech. The increasingly rare dark zebrawood is used throughout, and the delicate lamps were based on a widely publicized dress once worn by Mrs. Kennedy. As a token to JFK, a rocking chair is found in every room. For a true "West Wing" aura, the Kennedy Room presents Oval Office window drapings, U.S. flags, American bathroom fixtures, and a light blue draped bed like the former First Lady once had. The hotel bar claims to have the largest selection of high-quality bourbons in Berlin, including the 25-year-old Bitter Truth Bourbon.

Werderscher Markt 11, 10117 Berlin. www.arcotel.at. 🕿 **030/405-0460.** Fax 030/405-046-100. 190 units. 95€–135€ double. AE, MC, V. U-Bahn: Hausvogteiplatz. **Amenities:** Restaurant; bar; room service. *In room:* A/C, TV/DVD, minibar, hair dryer, CD player, Wi-Fi (free).

Circus Hotel 🕯 This is the greenest hotel and the hippest, attracting a youth-oriented clientele intent on saving a planet in peril. Among its many features, all papers used are recycled, some 80% of the lamps are fitted with energy-saving bulbs, and all waste is separated for recycling. There's no A/C, as the owners believe it is an unnecessary burning of resources. The well-designed bedrooms have blue, tangerine, lime, or hot-pink accents, and all have dark oak floors along with vintage flea market accessories. The staff loads iPods with the best of Berlin music; there is a garden courtyard for you to unwind, and you can hire bikes or Segways. In the Fabish Restaurant, local products are featured, and you can also sip cocktails à la Sally Bowles.

8

GERMANY

Berlin

Across the street is a hostel of the same name, Weinbergsweg 1A (© 030/20003939), offering 16 simple bedrooms, costing 19€ to 25€ if shared, 28€ in a double, and 43€ in a single. In a double with bathroom, the rate is 70€ to 85€.

Rosenthalerstrasse 1, 10119 Berlin. www.circus-berlin.de. © **030/20003939.** 60 units. 80€–95€ double; 100€ junior suite; from 110€ 2-room apt.; from 160€ 3-room apt. MC, V. U-Bahn: Rosenthaler Platz. **Amenities:** Restaurant; bar; bikes. *In room:* Wi-Fi (free).

CHARLOTTENBURG, KURFÜRSTENDAMM & AROUND
Very Expensive

Brandenburger Hof Relais & Châteaux ★★★ Elegance and high class dominate at this palatial turn-of-the-20th-century structure set around a lovely Japanese courtyard garden. Rooms, perhaps too severe and minimalist for some tastes, are still among the most stylish in the city. This is authentic Bauhaus—torchiere lamps, black leather upholstery, and platform beds—plus Missoni carpets and high-thread-count sheets. French doors let in lots of light and some open to small balconies. The hotel's Michelin-starred restaurant, Die Quadriga, led by a creative Finnish chef serving new Nordic cuisine alongside German specialties, also boasts an enormous all-German wine list. Rates include access to SportClub Tiergarten (where local politicians work out) nearby; the hotel will drive you there and back. Definitely indulge in the gargantuan breakfast; several choices are served, like an English tea service, and you can sample oodles of specialties (lots of tiny portions like fruit salad infused with vanilla, plates stacked with decadent cheeses and cured seafood and meats, eggs cooked to order and homemade jams).

Eislebener Strasse 14, 10789 Berlin. www.brandenburger-hof.com. © **030/21-40-50.** Fax 030/21-40-51-00. 72 units. 265€–315€ double; from 395€ suite. AE, DC, MC, V. Parking 24€. U-Bahn: Kurfürstendamm or Augsburger Strasse. S-Bahn: Zoologischer Garten. **Amenities:** Restaurant; piano bar; room service; babysitting. *In room:* TV, minibar, hair dryer, Wi-Fi (12€/day).

Kempinski Hotel Bristol Berlin ★★★ The legendary Kempinski, or "Kempi," is matched in style only by the Grand Hotel Esplanade. Rooms range in size from medium to spacious. Furnishings are elegant and the mattresses firm. The cheapest (and smallest) rooms are called the Berlin rooms. The high-category Bristol rooms are larger and better appointed, and the finest accommodations of all are the refined Kempinski rooms. Each room has a spacious bathroom, dual basins, scales, shoehorns, and deluxe toiletries.

Kurfürstendamm 27, 10719 Berlin. www.kempinskiberlin.de. © **030/88-43-40** or 800/426-3135 in the U.S. and Canada. Fax 030/88-360-75. 301 units. 119€–270€ double; 199€–1,095€ suite. AE, DC, MC, V. Parking 18€–21€. U-Bahn: Kurfürstendamm. **Amenities:** 2 restaurants; bar; indoor pool; exercise room; sauna; room service; babysitting. *In room:* A/C, TV, minibar, hair dryer, Wi-Fi (25€/day).

Expensive

Savoy ★ If you don't demand the full-service facilities of the grander choices, this is the hotel for you. In general, rooms are a bit small but they are comfortable nonetheless, with such features as double-glazed windows and fine furnishings. Bathrooms are a decent size and maintained spotlessly. For a nightcap, try the cozy **Times Bar.**

Fasanenstrasse 9–10, 10623 Berlin. www.hotel-savoy.com. © **030/3-11-0-30** or **800/223-5652** in the U.S. and Canada. Fax 030/3-11-03-333. 125 units. 146€–277€ double; 180€–325€ suite. Children 11 and under stay free in parent's room. AE, DC, MC, V. Parking 15€. U-Bahn: Kurfürstendamm. **Amenities:** Restaurant; bar; sauna; room service; babysitting. *In room:* A/C (in some), TV, minibar, hair dryer, Internet (10€ for 5 hr.).

Moderate

Art Nouveau ★ ⅲ   On the fourth floor of an Art Nouveau apartment house, this little-known hotel is an atmospheric choice. Even the elevator is a historic gem of the upmarket and desirable neighborhood. The comfortable midsize rooms are pleasantly decorated and high ceilinged, with excellent beds and immaculate bathrooms. Rooms in the rear are more tranquil, except when the schoolyard is full of children. There's an honor bar in the lobby where guests keep track of their own drinks. A generous breakfast is the only meal served.

Leibnizstrasse 59, 10629 Berlin. www.hotelartnouveau.de. ℂ **030/3-27-74-40.** Fax 030/327-744-40. 20 units. 126€–176€ double; 176€–236€ suite. Rates include breakfast. AE, MC, V. Parking 4€. U-Bahn: Adenauerplatz. **Amenities:** Honor bar. *In room:* TV, hair dryer, Internet (free).

Bleibtreu Hotel ★   Hidden away from the bustle of Berlin, this is a trend-conscious choice. Its tiny lobby is accessible via an alleyway that leads past a garden and a big-windowed set of dining and drinking facilities. The setting is the labyrinthine premises of what was built long ago as a Jugendstil-era apartment house. Rooms are small, minimalist, and furnished in carefully chosen natural materials. Bathrooms are cramped but well designed.

Bleibtreustrasse 31, 10707 Berlin (1 block south of the Kurfürstendamm). www.bleibtreu.com. ℂ **030/88474-0.** Fax 030/88474-444. 60 units. 118€–198€ double. AE, DC, MC, V. No parking. U-Bahn: Uhlandstrasse. **Amenities:** 2 restaurants; bar; room service; steam bath. *In room:* TV, minibar, hair dryer, Wi-Fi (free).

Grand Hotel Esplanade ★★★   The Esplanade rivals the Kempinski for supremacy in Berlin. Rooms are spacious, bright, and cheerfully decorated, with sound insulation. Beds are large with quality linens and duvets. Bathrooms, which contain tub/shower combos, are among the city's most luxurious. When reserving, ask for one of the corner rooms, as they're the biggest and have the best views. Even if you don't stay here, stop in for a drink at the elegant Harry's New York Bar, or go native at the traditional German EckKneipe.

Lützowufer 15, 10785 Berlin. www.esplanadeberlin.com. ℂ **030/25-47-80** or 866/597-8341 in the U.S. and Canada. Fax 030/254-78-82-22. 386 units. 132€–144€ double; from 209€ suite. AE, DC, MC, V. Parking 23€. U-Bahn: Kurfürstenstrasse, Nollendorfplatz, or Wittenbergplatz. **Amenities:** 3 restaurants; 2 bars; indoor pool; sauna; room service; babysitting. *In room:* A/C, TV, kitchenettes (in some), minibar, hair dryer, safe, Wi-Fi (free).

KREUZBERG

Michelberger Hotel ⚘   This hotel, which opened in 2009, immediately became a hangout for hipsters. The modest bedrooms have been installed in a converted factory building. Management claims their establishment hopes to bring Berlin's vibrant lifestyle and historical patina inside its doors. Their self-described clientele consists of Austrian carpenters, Swedish models, English rock stars, Japanese businessmen, German racing-car drivers, and American dudes. The Michelberger is a cosmopolitan, yet street-savvy hangout. Many of the rooms are quite small. Management will rent a single to a budget-conscious couple at a cost of 60€ to 80€ a night, but with the understanding that the space will be very cramped.

Warschauer Strasse 39–40, 10243 Berlin. www.michelbergerhotel.com. ℂ **030/297-785-90.** Fax 030/297-785-929. 119 units. 70€–95€ double; 150€ suite. AE, DC, MC, V. U-Bahn/S-Bahn: Warschauer Strasse. **Amenities:** Restaurant (lunch); bar. *In room:* TV, Wi-Fi (free).

PRENZLAUER BERG

Ackselhaus Blue Home ★ 🖋 A majestic building from the 1800s has been restored and turned into a bastion of elegance and affordability. Although completely modernized, the hotel presents a design backdrop of the colonial era and a touch of Balinese romance. A harmonious decor prevails in the midsize to spacious bedrooms, and the supersize bathtubs beckon you to pause for a bath, pronto. The stylish breakfast cafe, Club del Mar, opens onto a tree-lined street in the Prenzlauer Berg neighborhood.

Belforter Strasse 21, 10405 Berlin. www.ackselhaus.de. ⓒ **030/44337633.** Fax 030/44312603. 35 units. 110€–170€ double; 180€–250€ studio apt. MC, V. Free parking. U-Bahn: Senefelderplatz. **Amenities:** Bar; room service. *In room:* A/C, TV, hair dryer, Wi-Fi (free).

Side Trips from Berlin: Potsdam ★★★

Of all the tours possible from Berlin, the best attraction is the baroque town of Potsdam, 24km (15 miles) southwest of Berlin on the Havel River, often called Germany's Versailles. From the beginning of the 18th century it was the residence and garrison town of the Prussian kings. World attention focused on Potsdam from July 17 to August 2, 1945, when the Potsdam Conference shaped postwar Europe.

West of the historic core lies Sans Souci Park, with its palaces and gardens. Northwest of Sans Souci are the New Garden and the Cecilienhof Palace, on the Heiliger See.

ESSENTIALS

GETTING THERE There are 29 daily connections by rail from Bahnhof Zoo (trip time: 23 min.) and Berliner Hauptbahnhof (40 min.). For rail information in Potsdam, call ⓒ **018/05-99-66-33.** Potsdam can also be reached by S-Bahn (30 min.). Car access is via the E-30 Autobahn east and west or the E-53 north and south.

VISITOR INFORMATION The organization known as **Tourist-Information der Stadt Potsdam** maintains two offices in Potsdam, one at Brandenburger-Strasse 3 and another at the Neuer Markt (both branches can be reached at www.potsdam-tourism.com; ⓒ **0331/275-58-50**). Both branches are open April to October, Monday to Friday 9am to 7pm, Saturday and Sunday 9am to 4pm; November to March, Monday to Friday 10am to 6pm, Saturday and Sunday 10am to 4pm.

EXPLORING POTSDAM

In the 18th century, Prussia's answer to Paris's Château de Versailles was clustered within the **Sans Souci Park ★★★**, whose gardens and fountains represented the finest and most elegant aspect of north Germany during the Age of Enlightenment. Covering about a square mile of terraced, statue-dotted grounds, a very short walk west of Potsdam's center, it's the destination of many locals, who stroll around its precincts, perhaps reflecting on another era of German history. You can enter from many points around the perimeter of the park, but the main entrance, and the one closest to the park's major monument, is in **Zur Historisches Mühle,** inside of which you'll find the Besucher Zentrum (Welcome Station; www.historische-muehle-potsdam.de; ⓒ **0331/96-94-200**), full of information about all palaces and sights situated in the park. Whereas you can visit the park's buildings only during the hours noted below, you can stroll within most areas of the park at any hour.

Frederick II ("the Great") chose Potsdam rather than Berlin as his permanent residence. The style of the buildings he ordered erected is called Potsdam rococo, an achievement primarily of Georg Wenzeslaus von Knobelsdorff. Knobelsdorff built

Sans Souci Palace ★★★ (www.spsg.de), with its terraces and gardens, as a summer residence for Frederick II. The palace, inaugurated in 1747, is a long one-story building crowned by a dome and flanked by round pavilions. The music salon is the supreme example of the rococo style, and the elliptical Marble Hall is the largest in the palace. As a guest of the king, Voltaire visited in 1750.

The Palace of Sans Souci is open April to October, daily 9am to 5pm; November to March, Tuesday to Sunday 9am to 4pm. You'll have to visit its interior as part of a guided, 40-minute tour that's conducted mostly in German, and which costs 8€ for adults and 5€ for children 17 and under. Entrance is free for children 5 and under.

Schloss Charlottenhof ★, south of Okonomieweg (www.spsg.de; *©* **0331/969-42-28;** tram: 1 or 4), was designed by Karl Friedrich Schinkel, the great neoclassical master, and built between 1826 and 1829. He erected the palace in the style of a villa and designed most of the furniture inside. It's open only between May and October, every Tuesday to Sunday from 10am to 5pm, and completely closed the rest of the year. Guided tours, mostly in German, depart at 30-minute intervals throughout opening hours, and are priced at 4€ for adults, 3€ for children 6 to 17, free for children 5 and under.

North of the 80-hectare (198-acre) park, the **Cecilienhof Palace ★**, Im Neuer Garten (www.spsg.de; *©* **0331/969-42-00;** tram: 92 or 95, and then bus no. 692), was built in the style of an English country house by Kaiser Wilhelm II between 1913 and 1917. The 176-room mansion became the new residence of Crown Prince Wilhelm of Hohenzollern. It was occupied as a royal residence until March 1945, when the crown prince and his family fled to the West, taking many of their possessions. Cecilienhof was the headquarters of the 1945 Potsdam Conference. It's open year-round, Tuesday through Sunday, as follows: April through October from 9am to 5pm; November through March from 9am to 4pm. Visitors can see the palace interior only as part of a guided or audio tour; adults pay 6€, and children 6 and under and students pay 5€.

MUNICH ★★★ & THE BAVARIAN ALPS ★★

Sprawling Munich, home of some 1.5 million people and such industrial giants as Siemens and BMW, is the pulsating capital and cultural center of Bavaria. One of Germany's most festive cities, Munich exudes a hearty Bavarian *Gemütlichkeit* (cheer).

Longtime resident Thomas Mann wrote, "Munich sparkles." Although the city he described was swept away by some of the most severe bombing of World War II, Munich continues to sparkle, as it introduces itself to thousands of new visitors annually.

The Munich cliché as a beer-drinking town of folkloric charm is marketed by the city itself. Despite a roaring gross national product, Munich likes to present itself as a large, agrarian village peopled by jolly beer drinkers who cling to rustic origins despite the omnipresence of symbols of the computer age, high-tech industries, a sophisticated business scene, a good deal of Hollywood-style glamour, and fairly hip night action. Bavarians themselves are a minority in Munich—more than two-thirds of the population comes from other parts of the country or from outside Germany—but everybody buys into the folkloric charm and schmaltz.

Munich

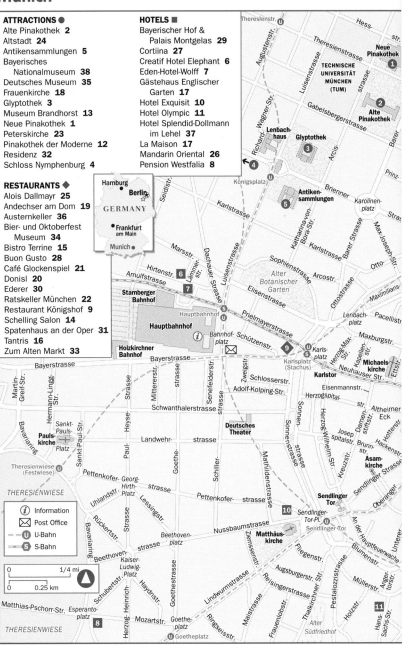

ATTRACTIONS ●
Alte Pinakothek **2**
Altstadt **24**
Antikensammlungen **5**
Bayerisches
  Nationalmuseum **38**
Deutsches Museum **35**
Frauenkirche **18**
Glyptothek **3**
Museum Brandhorst **13**
Neue Pinakothek **1**
Peterskirche **23**
Pinakothek der Moderne **12**
Residenz **32**
Schloss Nymphenburg **4**

RESTAURANTS ◆
Alois Dallmayr **25**
Andechser am Dom **19**
Austernkeller **36**
Bier- und Oktoberfest
  Museum **34**
Bistro Terrine **15**
Buon Gusto **28**
Café Glockenspiel **21**
Donisl **20**
Ederer **30**
Ratskeller München **22**
Restaurant Königshof **9**
Schelling Salon **14**
Spatenhaus an der Oper **31**
Tantris **16**
Zum Alten Markt **33**

HOTELS ■
Bayerischer Hof &
  Palais Montgelas **29**
Cortiina **27**
Creatif Hotel Elephant **6**
Eden-Hotel-Wolff **7**
Gästehaus Englischer
  Garten **17**
Hotel Exquisit **10**
Hotel Olympic **11**
Hotel Splendid-Dollmann
  im Lehel **37**
La Maison **26**
Mandarin Oriental **26**
Pension Westfalia **8**

Information
Post Office
U-Bahn
S-Bahn

0 ____ 1/4 mi
0 ____ 0.25 km

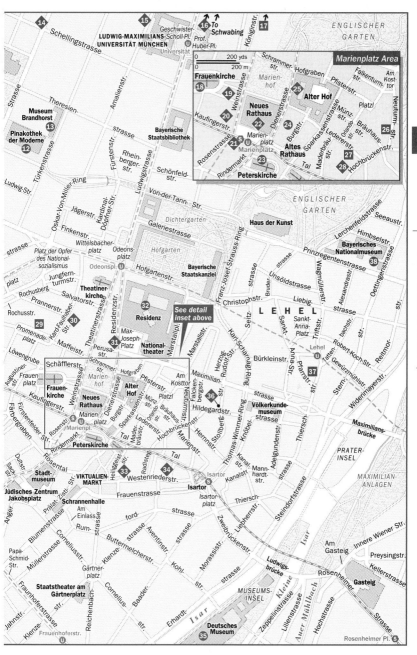

Marienplatz Area

0   200 yds
0   200 m

Essentials

GETTING THERE

BY PLANE   The **Munich International Airport** (www.munich-airport.de; ☏ **089/ 97-52-13-13**) lies 27km (17 miles) northeast of central Munich at Erdinger Moos.

S-Bahn (☏ **089/41-42-43-44**) trains connect the airport with the Hauptbahn- hof (main railroad station) in downtown Munich, with departures every 20 minutes for the 40-minute trip. The fare is 10€; Eurailpass holders ride free. A taxi into the center costs about 50€ to 60€. You can also take the Lufthansa Airport Bus, which runs directly into the heart of Munich, with just one stop in Schwabing. The trip takes 35 to 50 minutes, depending on traffic, and costs 10€ to 15€ round-trip.

BY TRAIN   Munich's main rail station, the **Hauptbahnhof,** on Bahnhofplatz, is one of Europe's largest. Near the city center, it contains a hotel, restaurants, shops, a parking garage, and banking facilities. All major German cities are connected to this station, most with service every hour. For information about long-distance trains, call ☏ **0800/150-7090.**

BY BUS   Munich is one of the biggest metropolitan areas in Europe, and as such, receives dozens of buses that congregate here from other parts of Europe. A few of them, including the bus that services central Munich from the airport, stop in the town center, at the **Zentraler BusBahnhof,** immediately adjacent (on the western end) of the city's main railway station (Hauptbahnhof München), with an entrance on the Arnulfstrasse. Note, however, that the majority of long-distance buses pulling into Munich arrive in the city's northern suburbs, at the **Fröttmanning Bus Termi- nal,** about 7km (4⅓ miles) north of the Marienplatz, beside the highway running between Munich and Nürnberg. (From central Munich, take U-Bahn line 6 for a 15-min. ride to reach it.) For information about most bus services coming into Munich from other parts of Germany and the rest of Europe, contact **Touring** at www.touring.de; ☏ **069/7903-501.**

VISITOR INFORMATION

TOURIST OFFICES   There are three tourist offices in Munich: Sendlinger Strasse 1 (☏ **089/233-03-00**), open Monday to Friday 8am to 8pm, Saturday 9am to 8pm, and Sunday 10am to 6pm; Bahnhofplatz 2, Monday to Saturday 9am to 8pm, Sunday 10am to 6pm; and Marienplatz in Neuen Rathaus, Monday to Friday 10am to 8pm, Saturday 10am to 4pm. For information, contact www.discover-munich.info; ☏ **089/233-96-500.**

WEBSITES   Updated for each year's Oktoberfest, **www.muenchen.de** from the Munich Tourist Office includes a program of events, a guide to various beer tents, and images from past festivals. Also included are descriptions of hotel packages and discount voucher packages. All things Bavarian are touched on at **www.bayern.by**, including Mad King Ludwig's castle, Oktoberfest beers, and a music raft ride down the river Isar.

CITY LAYOUT

Munich's Hauptbahnhof lies just west of the town center and opens onto Bahnhof- platz. From the square, you can take Schützenstrasse to **Karlsplatz** (nicknamed Stachus), one of the major centers of Munich. Many tramlines converge on this square. From Karlsplatz, you can continue east along the pedestrians-only Neuhäus- erstrasse and Kaufingerstrasse until you reach Marienplatz, where you'll be deep in the **Altstadt** (Old Town) of Munich.

From **Marienplatz,** the center and heart of the city, you can head north on Die-nerstrasse, which will lead you to Residenzstrasse and finally to **Max-Joseph-Platz,** a landmark square, with the National Theater and the former royal palace, the Residenz. East of this square runs **Maximilianstrasse,** the most fashionable shopping and dining street of Munich. Between Marienplatz and the National Theater is the **Platzl** quarter, where you'll want to head for nighttime diversions, as it's the seat of some of the finest (and some of the worst) restaurants in Munich, along with the landmark Hofbräuhaus, the most famous beer hall in Europe.

North of the old town is **Schwabing,** the university and former bohemian section whose main street is Leopoldstrasse. The large, sprawling municipal park grounds, the Englischer Garten, are found due east of Schwabing.

GETTING AROUND

BY PUBLIC TRANSPORTATION The city's efficient rapid-transit system is the **U-Bahn,** or Untergrundbahn, one of the most modern subway systems in Europe. The **S-Bahn** rapid-transit system, a 420km (260-mile) network of tracks, provides service to various city districts and outlying suburbs. The city is also served by a network of **trams** and **buses.** The same ticket entitles you to ride the U-Bahn, the S-Bahn, trams, and buses. For more information, call ✆ **089/233-00** or go to www.muenchen.de.

A single-journey ticket for a ride within the city's central zone—a large area that few tourists ever leave—costs 2.30€. If you go to the outermost zones of the subway system, your ride could cost as much as 9.20€. One of the best things about Munich's transit system is that you can make as many free transfers between subways, buses, and trams as you need to reach your destination.

A Money-Saving Tip

Munich's S-Bahn is covered by Eurail, so if you have a Eurailpass, there's no need to buy a separate ticket.

More economical than single-journey tickets is the *Streifenkarte,* a strip-ticket that contains 10 units, two of which are annulled for each zone of the system you travel through. A Streifenkarte costs 11.50€. Children aged 6 to 14 can purchase a *Kinderstreifenkarte* for 11.50€. With this type of ticket, you can travel in one continuous direction during any 2-hour period with unlimited transfers. You can also use it for multiple passengers (for two people to ride two zones, simply stamp four units).

An even better deal may be the *Tageskarte* (day ticket), which for 5.20€ gives you unlimited access within the central zone for a full day. Double the price for access to all of Greater Munich—an 80km (50-mile) radius. For more information, contact www.mvv-muenchen.de; ✆ **089/41-42-43-44.**

BY TAXI Cabs are relatively expensive—you'll pay 2.70€ when you get inside, plus 1.60€ to 1.90€ per kilometer (⅔ mile); add 1€ if you call for pickup. In an emergency, call ✆ **089/2161-0** or **089/194-10** for a radio-dispatched taxi.

BY CAR Driving in the city, which has an excellent public transportation system, is not advised. The streets around Marienplatz in the Altstadt are pedestrian-only. If you are interested in renting a car locally, try **Sixt,** Einsteinstrasse 106 (www.sixt.de; ✆ **1805/25-25-25**), or look under *Autovermietung* (car rental) in the Munich Yellow Pages.

ON FOOT Of course, the best way to explore Munich is by foot, as it has a vast **pedestrian zone** in the center. Many of its attractions can, in fact, be reached only by foot. Pick up a good map and set out.

BY BIKE The tourist office sells a pamphlet that outlines itineraries for touring Munich by bicycle called *Radl-Touren für unsere Gäste*, costing .40€. One of the most convenient places to rent a bike is **Radius Bikes** (www.radiustours.com; © **089/59-61-13**), at the far end of the Hauptbahnhof, near lockers opposite tracks 27 and 36. The charge is 14.50€ to 18€ for up to 4 hours, or else 17€ to 22€ from 10am to 6pm. Mountain bikes are rented for about 25% more. A deposit of 50€ is assessed; students and Eurailpass holders are granted a 10% discount. The store is open May to early October daily 10am to 6pm; it's closed November to April.

[FastFACTS] MUNICH

ATMs/Banks Most **banks** are open Monday to Friday 8:30am to 12:30pm and 1:30 to 3:30pm (many stay open until 5:30pm on Thurs).

Business Hours Most **businesses** and **stores** are open Monday to Friday 9am to 6pm and Saturday 9am to 2pm. On *langer Samstag* (first Sat of the month), stores remain open until 6pm. Many observe an 8 or 9pm closing on Thursday.

Consulates There's a **U.S.** consulate at Königinstrasse 5 (© **089/288-80;** U-Bahn: Universiäl); hours are Monday to Friday 8 to 11am. The consulate of **Canada** at Tal Strasse 29 (© **089/219-95-70;** U-Bahn: Marienplatz) is open Monday to Thursday 9am to noon and 2 to 5pm, and Friday 9am to noon and 2 to 3:30pm. The Consulate General Office for the **U.K.** at Möhlstrasse 5 (© **089/21-10-90;** U-Bahn: Prinzregentenplatz) is open Monday to Friday 8:30am to noon and 1 to 3:30pm. The governments of Australia and New Zealand do not maintain offices in Munich.

Currency See "Fast Facts: Berlin," p. 360.

Currency Exchange You can get a better rate at a bank than at your hotel. On weekends or at night, you can exchange money at the Hauptbahnhof exchange, open daily from 6am to 11:30pm.

Doctors The American, British, and Canadian consulates keep a list of recommended English-speaking physicians. For dental or medical emergencies, call **Notfallpraxis,** Elisenstrasse 3 (© **089/55-17-71;** bus: 69). It's open Monday, Tuesday, and Thursday from 7 to 11pm; Wednesday and Friday from 2 to 11pm; and Saturday, Sunday, and holidays from 8am to 11pm.

Drugstores For an international drugstore where English is spoken, go to **Bahnhof Apotheke,** Bahnhofplatz 2 (© **089/59-41-19;** U-Bahn/S-Bahn: Hauptbahnhof), open Monday to Friday from 8am to 6:30pm and Saturday from 8am to 2pm. If you need a prescription filled during off-hours, call © **089/55-76-61** for information

about what's open. The information is recorded and in German only, so you may need to ask someone from your hotel staff to assist you.

Emergencies Call the police at © **110.**

Internet Access You can send e-mails or check your messages at the **Easy Internet Café,** Bahnhofplatz 1; U-Bahn: Hauptbahnhof. It's open daily 7:30am to 11:45pm.

Post Office The most central post office is at Bahnhofplatz (U-Bahn/S-Bahn: Hauptbahnhof), opposite the main train-station exit. It's open Monday to Friday 7am to 8pm, and Saturday 9am to 4pm. You can have your mail sent here Poste Restante (general delivery), but include the postal code 80335. You'll need a passport to claim mail, and you can't call for information but have to show up in person.

Telephone The **country code** for Germany is **49.** The **city code** for Munich is **89.** Use this code when you're calling from outside Germany; if you're within Germany, use **089.**

Exploring Munich

CENTRAL MUNICH

Alte Pinakothek ★★★ ART MUSEUM   This is one of the most significant art museums in Europe. The paintings represent the greatest European artists of the 14th through the 18th century. Begun as a small court collection by the royal Wittelsbach family in the early 1500s, the collection has grown and grown. There are two floors with exhibits, but the museum is immense. Albrecht Altdorfer, landscape painter par excellence of the Danube school, is represented by no fewer than six monumental works. Albrecht Dürer's works include his greatest—and final—*Self-Portrait* (1500). Here the artist has portrayed himself with almost Christlike solemnity. Also displayed is the last great painting by the artist, his two-paneled work called *The Four Apostles* (1526).

Barer Strasse 27. www.pinakothek.de/alte-pinakothek. *©* **089/238-052-16.** Admission 7€ adults, 5€ students and seniors, free for children 15 and under, 1€ for all Sun. Tues 10am–8pm; Wed–Sun 10am–5pm; closed Mon. U-Bahn: Theresienstrasse. Tram: 27. Bus: 53.

Altstadt (Old Town) ★   Marienplatz, dedicated to the patron of the city whose statue stands on a huge column in the center of the square, is the heart of the Altstadt. On its north side is the **Neues Rathaus (New City Hall),** built in 19th-century Gothic style. Each day at 11am, and also at noon and 5pm in the summer, the Glockenspiel on the facade performs a miniature tournament, with enameled copper figures moving in and out of the archways. Because you're already at the Rathaus, you may wish to climb the 55 steps to the top of its tower (an elevator is available if you're conserving energy) for a good overall view of the city center. The **Altes Rathaus (Old City Hall),** with its plain Gothic tower, is to the right. It was reconstructed in the 15th century, after being destroyed by fire.

Marienplatz. Rathaus tower 2.50€ adults, 1.50€ students and seniors, free for children 14 and under. 10am–7pm daily May–Oct, 10am–5pm Mon–Fri Nov–Apr. U-Bahn: Marienplatz.

Antikensammlungen (Antiquities Collections) ★ MUSEUM   Ludwig I's collection of Greek vases is the centerpiece of this museum, which was celebrated by art historians as one of the greatest in the world. Meant to complement the Glyptothek, the current collection of more than 650 vases and a few other pieces of antique art is astounding, yet leaves a lot of guesswork for those unfamiliar with German, as the lack of signage and up-to-date literature on the museum is scant, especially in English. However, it makes for a pleasant Sunday stroll through the world of Greek pottery, the likes of which you're not likely to find anywhere else.

   Among its prized possessions is the oldest piece, a pre-Mycenaean "goddess from Aegina" (3000 B.C.) carved out of a mussel shell. Another highlight is Exekias's finely preserved **Dionysus Cup** (540 B.C.), with a depiction of the god of wine lounging in his vessel underneath a canopy of grape leaves.

Königsplatz 1. www.antike-am-koenigsplatz.mwn.de. *©* **089/599888-30.** Admission 3.50€ adults, 2.50€ students and seniors, free for children 15 and under. Joint ticket to the Museum of Antiquities and the Glyptothek 5.50€ students and seniors, free for children 15 and under. Tues–Sun 10am–5pm (Thurs to 8pm); closed Mon. U-Bahn: Königsplatz.

Bayerisches Nationalmuseum (Bavarian National Museum) ★★ MUSEUM   Three vast floors of sculpture, painting, folk art, ceramics, furniture, textiles, and scientific instruments demonstrate Bavaria's artistic and historical riches. Entering the museum, turn to the right and go into the first large gallery, called the **Wessobrunn Room.** Devoted to early church art from the 5th to the 13th century, this room holds some of the oldest and most valuable works. The desk case contains ancient and medieval ivories, including the so-called Munich ivory, from about A.D. 400. The **Riemenschneider Room** is devoted to the works of the great sculptor Tilman Riemenschneider (ca. 1460–1531) and his contemporaries. The second floor contains a fine collection of stained and painted glass—an art in which medieval Germany excelled—baroque ivory carvings, Meissen porcelain, and ceramics.

Prinzregentenstrasse 3. www.bayerisches-nationalmuseum.de. ⓒ **089/211-2401.** Admission 5€ adults, 4€ students, free for children 18 and under, 1€ for all Sun. Tues–Sun 10am–5pm; Thurs 10am–8pm; closed Mon. U-Bahn: Lehel. Tram: 17. Bus: 53.

Deutsches Museum (German Museum of Masterpieces of Science and Technology) ★★★ MUSEUM

On an island in the Isar River is the largest technological museum of its kind in the world. Its huge collection of priceless artifacts and historic originals includes the first electric dynamo (Siemens, 1866), the first automobile (Benz, 1886), the first diesel engine (1897), and the laboratory bench at which the atom was first split (Hahn, Strassmann, 1938). There are hundreds of buttons to push, levers to crank, and gears to turn, as well as a knowledgeable staff to answer questions and demonstrate how steam engines, pumps, or historical musical instruments work. Among the most popular displays are those on mining, with a series of model coal, salt, and iron mines, as well as the electrical power hall, with high-voltage displays that actually produce lightning. There are many other exhibits, covering the whole range of science and technology.

Museumsinsel 1. www.deutsches-museum.de. ⓒ **089/2-17-91.** Admission 8.50€ adults, 7€ seniors, 3€ children 6–15, free for children 5 and under. Daily 9am–5pm. Closed major holidays. S-Bahn: Isartor. Tram: 18. U-Bahn: Fraunhoferstrasse.

Frauenkirche (Cathedral of Our Lady) ★ CATHEDRAL

With her twin spires gracing the skyline and many emblematic images, Munich's largest church provides the best testament of the city's postwar perseverance. It's astonishing to consider that the massive Gothic church lay in ruins after the shelling of 1945, and even more remarkable that workers and architects rebuilt the 15th-century structure piece by piece. Simple and dignified, its interior also retains relics such as Hans Krumpper's ornate cenotaph of Ludwig the Bavarian (next to the rear entrance), for whom the church was built beginning in 1468.

Also in the rear is the "devil's footstep," created by the imp himself according to legend. From there, the visitor can appreciate the slender pillars masking the windows, a concept which made the devil laugh so hard and stamp his foot into the marble floor. Bavaria's last king, Ludwig III, lies in the royal crypt under the altar with many others from his lineage.

Since 1821 the Frauenkirche has been the seat of the archbishopric, which was held between 1977 and 1982 by Joseph Ratzinger, known these days as Pope Benedict XVI.

Frauenplatz 1. www.muenchner-dom.de. ⓒ **089/2900820.** Free admission. Daily 7am–7pm (Fri until 6pm). U-Bahn or S-Bahn: Marienplatz.

Glyptothek (Museum of Sculpture) ★ MUSEUM

The centerpiece of this collection is the marbles from the pediments of the temple on Aegina, a Greek island off the coast near Athens, which ranks up there with the Pergamon Altar in Berlin, the Ephesus antiquities in Vienna, and the still-disputed Acropolis marbles in the British Museum in London. No need to worry, Ludwig I got a receipt for this transaction. This is the best chance to get up close and personal with the statues that you usually have to peer up at on the real thing in Greece.

Königsplatz 3. www.antike-am-koenigsplatz.mwn.de. ⓒ **089/28-61-00.** Admission 3.50€ adults; 2.50€ students, seniors, and children. Joint ticket to the Glyptothek and the Museum of Antiquities 5.50€ adults; 3.50€ students, seniors, and children. Tues–Sun 10am–5pm; Thurs 10am–8pm; closed Mon. U-Bahn: Königsplatz.

Museum Brandhorst ★ ART MUSEUM   In the Museum Quarter, Udo and Anette Brandhorst have donated their collection of contemporary art, assembled over a lifetime, to this museum, which is unique in Munich. The building, using sustainable "green" features, is the most avant-garde in Munich. Perfectly lit, its exhibits are arranged according to the latest in 21st-century design. Paintings and sculptures range from Andy Warhol to a dozen original editions of books illustrated by Picasso—almost the whole of his *oeuvre* in this field.

The museum owns 60 works by Cy Twombly, an American artist celebrated for his calligraphic-style graffiti paintings. Damien Hirst, the British artist famous for his series of dead animals preserved in formaldehyde, has the most gruesome works on display.

Kunstareal, Theresienstrasse 35A. www.museum-brandhorst.de. ⓒ**089/238-052-286.** Admission 7€ adults, 5€ children aged 5–16, 1€ for all Sun. Tues–Sun 10am–6pm (Thurs to 8pm); closed Mon. U-Bahn: Königsplatz or Theresienstrasse. Bus: 100 or 154.

Neue Pinakothek ★★ ART MUSEUM   This gallery is a showcase of Munich's most valuable 18th- and 19th-century art, an artistic period that was hardly the Renaissance but has its artistic devotees nonetheless. Across Theresienstrasse from the Alte Pinakothek, the museum has paintings by Gainsborough, Goya, David, Manet, van Gogh, and Monet. Among the more popular German artists represented are Wilhelm Leibl and Gustav Klimt. Note particularly the genre paintings by Carl Spitzweg.

Barer Strasse 29. www.pinakothek.de/neue-pinakothek. ⓒ **089/23-80-51-95.** Admission 7€ adults, 5€ students and seniors, free for children 15 and under, 1€ for all Sun. Thurs–Mon 10am–6pm; Wed 10am–8pm; closed Tues. U-Bahn: Theresienstrasse. Tram: 27. Bus: 53.

Peterskirche (St. Peter's Church) CHURCH/OBSERVATION   Munich's oldest church (1180 A.D.) boasts gilded baroque interior murals by Johann Baptist Zimmermann, in addition to a magnificent high altar and eye-catching statues of the four church fathers (1732) by Egid Quirin Asam. Its tall steeple is worth the climb up the 296 steps in clear weather for the **panoramic view** as far as the Alps.

Rindermarkt 1. www.erzbistum-muenchen.de. ⓒ **089/260-48-28**. Free admission. Mon–Fri 9am–6pm; Sat–Sun 10am–6pm. U-Bahn/S-Bahn: Marienplatz.

Pinakothek der Moderne ★★ MUSEUM   When this equivalent of London's Tate Gallery or Paris's Pompidou opened in 2002, it was one of the world's largest museums dedicated to the visual arts of the 19th and 20th centuries. It encompasses four collections: **Staatsgalerie Moderner Kunst (State Gallery of Modern Art)** ★★★, with paintings, sculpture, photography, and video; **Die Neue Sammlung (New Collection),** which constitutes the national museum of applied art featuring design and craft work; the **Architekturmuseum der Technischen Universität (Technical University's Architectural Museum),** with architectural drawings, photographs, and models; and the **Staatliche Graphische Sammlung (State Collection of Graphics),** with its outstanding collection of prints and drawings, which can be viewed only by request.

The structure, designed by Stefan Braunfels, is a work of art itself, a veritable cathedral of light, lines, and space. Your tastes may dictate which collection to see first, but the upstairs Gallery of Modern Art is not to be missed. The paintings by Matisse, Picasso, Braque, Magritte, and Dalí alone would make an amazing gallery.

Yet, the museum possesses a wealth of excellent German Modern art, represented by Die Brücke artists like Kirchner and Schmidt-Rotluff, and the Blaue Reiter group with Kandinsky, Franz Marc, and Auguste Macke. Some of these turned up in a revealing collection of *Entartete Kunst,* or Degenerate Art, which the Nazis deemed as unworthy of their collections of "fine" art. Works by Warhol, Francis Bacon, and Joseph Beuys wrap up the tour, leaving you with just enough energy to enjoy the rest.

Barerstrasse 40. www.pinakothek.de. © **089/23805360.** Admission 10€ adults; 7€ students, seniors, and children 16 and under. Sun admission for all 1€. Tues–Sun 10am–6pm (Thurs until 8pm); closed Mon. U-Bahn: Odeonsplatz.

Residenz ★ MUSEUM/THEATER The official residence of Bavaria's rulers from 1385 to 1918, the complex is a conglomerate of various styles of art and architecture. Depending on how you approach the Residenz, you might first see a German Renaissance hall (the western facade), a Palladian palace (on the north), or a Florentine Renaissance palace (on the south facing Max-Joseph-Platz). The Residenz has been completely restored since its almost total destruction in World War II and now houses the Residenz Museum, a concert hall, the Cuvilliés Theater, and the Residenz Treasure House.

Residenzmuseum comprises the southwestern section of the palace, some 120 rooms of art and furnishings collected by centuries of Wittelsbachs. There are two guided tours, one in the morning and the other in the afternoon, or you may visit the rooms on your own.

If you have time to view only one item in the **Schatzkammer (Treasure House) ★★**, make it the 16th-century Renaissance statue of *St. George Slaying the Dragon.* The equestrian statue is made of gold, but you can barely see the precious metal for the thousands of diamonds, rubies, emeralds, sapphires, and semiprecious stones embedded in it.

From the Brunnenhof, you can visit the **Cuvilliés Theater ★**, whose rococo tiers of boxes are supported by seven bacchants. The huge box, where the family sat, is in the center. In summer, this theater is the scene of frequent concert and opera performances. Mozart's *Idomeneo* was first performed here in 1781.

Max-Joseph-Platz 3. www.residenz-muenchen.de. © **089/29-06-71.** Admission 9€ adults, 8€ students and seniors, free for children 14 and under. Ticket for either Schatzkammer or Residenzmuseum 6€ adults, 5€ seniors and students, free for children 14 and under. Fri–Wed 9am–6pm; Thurs 10am–8pm. U-Bahn: Odeonsplatz.

NYMPHENBURG

Schloss Nymphenburg ★★ CASTLE/MUSEUM In summer, the Wittelsbachs would pack up their bags and head for their country house, Schloss Nymphenburg. A more complete, more sophisticated palace than the Residenz, it was begun in 1664 in Italian villa style and went through several architectural changes before completion.

The main building's great hall, decorated in rococo colors and stuccoes with frescoes by Zimmermann (1756), was used for both banquets and concerts. Concerts are still presented here in summer. From the main building, turn left and head for the arcaded gallery connecting the northern pavilions. The first room in the arcade is the Great Gallery of Beauties. More provocative, however, is Ludwig I's Gallery of Beauties in the south pavilion (the apartments of Queen Caroline). Ludwig commissioned no fewer than 36 portraits of the most beautiful women of his day. The paintings by J. Stieler include the *Schöne Münchnerin (Lovely Munich Girl)* and a portrait of Lola

Montez, the dancer whose "friendship" with Ludwig I caused a scandal that factored into the revolution of 1848.

To the south of the palace buildings, in the rectangular block of low structures that once housed the court stables, is the **Marstallmuseum.** In the first hall, look for the glass coronation coach of Elector Karl Albrecht, built in Paris in 1740. From the same period comes the elaborate hunting sleigh of Electress Amalia, adorned with a statue of Diana, goddess of the hunt; even the sleigh's runners are decorated with shell work and hunting trophies. The coaches and sleighs of Ludwig II are displayed in the third hall.

One of Nymphenburg's greatest attractions is the **park ★**. Stretching for 200 hectares (494 acres) in front of the palace, it's divided into two sections by the canal that runs from the pool at the foot of the staircase to the cascade at the far end of the English-style gardens.

Within the park are a number of pavilions. The guided tour begins with **Amalienburg ★★**, whose plain exterior belies the rococo decoration inside. Built as a hunting lodge for Electress Amalia (in 1734), the pavilion carries the hunting theme through the first few rooms and then bursts into salons of flamboyant colors, rich carvings, and wall paintings. The most impressive room is the Hall of Mirrors, a symphony of silver ornaments on a faint blue background.

Other attractions include the **Porzellansammlung,** or Museum of Porcelain, which is above the stables of the Marstallmuseum. Some of the finest pieces of porcelain in the world, executed in the 18th century, are displayed here, along with an absolute gem—extraordinarily detailed miniature porcelain reproductions of some of the grand masterpieces in the Old Pinakothek, each commissioned by Ludwig I.

The **Botanischer Garten (Botanical Gardens) ★★** is among the most richly planted in Europe. It's worth a spring trip to Munich for garden lovers to see this great mass of vegetation burst into bloom.

Schloss Nymphenburg 1. www.schloesser-bayern.de. ⓒ **089/17-908-668.** Admission to all attractions 12€ adults, 9€ seniors, free for students and children 17 and under. Separate admission to Schloss Nymphenburg 6€ adults, 5€ seniors, free for students and children 17 and under. Admission to either Marstallmuseum, Amalienburg, or Porzellansammlung 4.50€ adults, 3.50€ seniors, free for students and children 17 and under. 9am–6pm Apr to mid-Oct, 10am–4pm mid-Oct to Mar. U-Bahn: Gern. Bus: 51. Tram: Schloss Nymphenburg.

ORGANIZED TOURS

City tours encompass aspects of both modern and medieval Munich, and depart from the main railway station aboard red-sided buses. Departures, depending on the season and the tour, occur between two and eight times a day, and tours are conducted in both German and English. Most tours don't last more than 2½ hours.

Depending on the tour, adults pay 11€ to 16€; children 13 and under are charged 6€ to 14€. Advance reservations for most city tours aren't required, and you can buy your ticket from the bus driver at the time you board. Tours leave from the square in front of the Hauptbahnhof.

To go farther afield and visit major attractions in the environs (such as Berchtesgaden or Ludwig II's castles), contact **Sightseeing Gray Line,** Schützenstrasse 9 (www.grayline.com; ⓒ **089/54907560;** U-Bahn/S-Bahn: Hauptbahnhof), open year-round Monday to Friday 9am to 6pm and Saturday 9am to 1pm. (Travel agents in Munich, as well as the concierge or reception staff at your hotel, can also book these tours.) At least a half-dozen touring options are available, ranging from a quick 1-hour overview of the city to full-day excursions to such outlying sites as Berchtesgaden, and the stunning Bavarian palaces in Oberammergau and Hohenschwangau.

Pedal pushers will want to try Mike Lasher's **Mike's Bike Tour** (www.mikesbike tours.com; ☏ **089/255-43-988**). His bike rentals for 12€ to 18€ include maps and locks, child and infant seats, and helmets at no extra charge. English and bilingual tours of central Munich run from March to November, leaving daily at 10:30am (call to confirm). The 4-hour tour is 24€.

Where to Eat

Munich, one of the few European cities with more than one Michelin-rated three-star restaurant, is the place to practice *Edelfresswelle* ("high-class gluttony"). The classic local dish, traditionally consumed before noon, is *Weisswurst,* herb-flavored white-veal sausage blanched in water. Sophisticated international cuisine is popular throughout the city, too.

For beer halls serving plenty of low-priced food, see the box "Beer Gardens, Cellars & Taverns" on p. 404.

CENTRAL MUNICH
Very Expensive
Restaurant Königshof ★★ INTERNATIONAL/FRENCH   On the top floor of a deluxe hotel, this is Munich's best shot at hotel dining. You're rewarded not only with fine cuisine, but also with a view of the city. Appetizers are sometimes pleasantly startling in their originality, as exemplified by the delicately diminutive rib and loin chops, liver, and rolled duck in a sweet-and-sour ice wine, the flavor enhanced by a pumpkin vinaigrette. Instead of the typical lasagna, you get pasta layered with morels and crayfish, a real delicacy. The city's best veal dishes are served here; veal sweetbreads rest on a bed of fresh vegetables, including beets and green beans. The wine list is one of the finest in Germany, though it may take you a good hour just to read it.

In the Hotel Königshof, Karlsplatz 25 (Am Stachus). www.koenigshof-hotel.de. ☏ **089/55-13-60.** Reservations required. Main courses 42€–49€; fixed-price menus 90€–198€. AE, DC, MC, V. Tues–Sat noon–2:30pm and 6:30–10:30pm. S-Bahn: Karlsplatz. Tram: 19, 20, or 21.

Expensive
Alois Dallmayr ★ CONTINENTAL   One of the city's most historic and famous dining spots was established in 1700 as a food shop. Today, you'll find one of the city's most prestigious delicatessens on the street level, and a rather grand restaurant upstairs, where you'll find a subtle German version of continental cuisine that owes many of its inspirations to France. The food array is rich, varied, and sophisticated, including superb herring and sausages, very fresh fish, meats, and game dishes. Partially thanks to its dual role as a delicatessen, with products imported from around the world, you'll find such rare treats as vine-ripened tomatoes flown in from Morocco, splendid papayas from Brazil, and the famous French hens, *poulets de Bresse,* believed by many gourmets to be the world's finest.

Dienerstrasse 14–15. www.dallmayr.de. ☏ **089/213-51-00.** Reservations recommended. Main courses 35€–55€; set-price menus 95€–128€. AE, MC, V. Mon–Fri 11:30am–7pm; Sat 9am–4pm. Tram: 19.

Austernkeller ★ SEAFOOD   This "oyster cellar," with the largest selection of oysters in town, from raw oysters to oysters Rockefeller, is a delight to visitors and locals. A terrific starter is the shellfish platter with fresh oysters, mussels, clams, scampi, and sea snails. Or you may begin with a richly stocked fish soup or cold hors d'oeuvres. French meat specialties are also offered, but the focus is seafood—everything from lobster Thermidor to shrimp grilled in the shell. The decor is elegant and refined, and the service is attentive.

Stollbergstrasse 11. www.austernkeller.de. ℂ **089/298787.** Reservations required. Lunch main courses 13€–15€; dinner main courses 21€–24€. AE, DC, MC, V. Mon–Fri 11:30am–2pm; daily 5–11:30pm. Closed Dec 23–26. U-Bahn: Isartor.

Ederer ★★ MODERN INTERNATIONAL   Noted as one of the poshest and immediately desirable addresses in Munich, and the culinary domain of celebrity chef Karl Ederer, this restaurant occupies an antique building with huge windows, very high ceilings, several blazing fireplaces, and an appealing collection of paintings. Inspiration for the menu items covers the gamut of cuisines from Bavaria, France, Italy, the New World, and the Pacific Rim. The menu changes with the seasons and the whim of the kitchen staff but might include such starters as marinated sweet-and-sour pumpkin served with shiitake mushrooms, parsley roots, and lukewarm chunks of octopus; and terrine of duckling foie gras with a very fresh brioche and a dollop of pumpkin jelly. Main courses might include a roasted breast of duckling with stuffing, glazed baby white cabbage, mashed potatoes, and gooseliver sauce; or pan-fried angler fish with a sauce made from olive oil, lemon grass, and thyme.

Kardinal Faulhaber Strasse 10. www.restaurant-ederer.de. ℂ**089/24-23-13-10.** Reservations recommended. Main courses 25€–38€; set-price 2-course lunch 29€; set-price 6-course dinner 150€. AE, DC, MC, V. Mon–Sat noon–2pm and 6:30–10pm. U-Bahn: Marienplatz or Odéonsplatz.

Moderate

Buon Gusto (Talamonti) ★ ITALIAN   Some of Munich's best Italian food is served here in the rustic-looking bistro, or in the more formal and more upscale-looking dining room. Menu items and prices are identical in both. Owned and managed by an extended family, the Talamontis, the restaurant emphasizes fresh ingredients, strong and savory flavors, and food items inspired by the Italian Marches and Tuscany. Stellar examples include ravioli stuffed with mushrooms and herbs, roasted lamb with potatoes, lots of scaloppine, and fresh fish that seems to taste best when served simply, with oil or butter and lemon. Especially appealing are the array of risottos whose ingredients change with the seasons. During Oktoberfest and trade fairs, the place is mobbed.

Hochbruckenstrasse 3. www.buon-gusto-talamonti.de. ℂ **089/296-383.** Reservations recommended. Main courses 12€–28€. AE, MC, V. Mon–Sat 11am–1am. Closed Dec 23–Jan 3. U-Bahn/S-Bahn: Marienplatz.

Café Glockenspiel PASTRIES/INTERNATIONAL   Overlooking Munich's central square, this fifth-floor perch offers the best view of the clockwork of the Neues Rathaus, not to mention pastries, tasty pies, and a few delectable dishes for dinner. You can select from the intimate Red Salon, a sunny courtyard-side veranda, or the cafe, which usually fills up around midday and 5pm for the Glockenspiel performance. The spinach and goat's cheese strudel with stewed eggplants makes an excellent starter or light meal, followed by jumbo shrimp and scallops in garlic butter with asparagus, baby carrots, and saffron foam. For dessert, just join the drooling patrons eyeing the fruit tortes and Viennese Sacher torte in the glass counter.

Marienplatz 28. www.cafe-glockenspiel.de. ℂ **089/264256.** Main courses 12€–24€; fixed-price menus 24€–33€. MC, V. Mon–Sat 10am–1am; Sun 10am–7pm. U-Bahn or S-Bahn: Marienplatz.

Ratskeller München BAVARIAN   Throughout Germany, you'll find *Ratskellers,* traditional cellar restaurants in Rathaus (city hall) basements, designed to serve decent and inexpensive food and wine to all citizens. Thus, a city hall restaurant should be roomy. Whether you descend from the inner courtyard or from Marienplatz, you'll find a forest of pillars and vaults that is said to hold up to 1,100 diners. The decor, with dark wood and carved chairs, resembles a sophisticated beer cellar. The coziest tables are in the semiprivate dining nooks in the rear, under the vaulted painted ceilings. In addition to the prominent regional fare, the chefs include an array of international, vegetarian, and lighter dishes not normally found on a Ratskeller menu. Hearty-tasting regional fare includes Munich white sausages with sweet mustard, and roast Bavarian duckling with mustard-seed gravy. Another regional dish much in favor with diners is the roast pork shank with potato dumplings and red cabbage.

Im Rathaus, Marienplatz 8. www.ratskeller.com. ℂ **089/2199890.** Reservations required. Main courses 13€–27€. AE, MC, V. Daily 10am–midnight. U-Bahn or S-Bahn: Marienplatz.

Spatenhaus an der Oper ★ BAVARIAN/INTERNATIONAL   One of Munich's best-known beer restaurants has wide windows overlooking the opera house on Max-Joseph-Platz. Of course, to be loyal, you should accompany your meal with the restaurant's own beer, Spaten-Franziskaner-Bier. You can sit in an intimate, semiprivate dining nook or at a big table. The Spatenhaus has old traditions, offers typical Bavarian food, and is known for generous portions and reasonable prices. If you want to know what all this fabled Bavarian gluttony is about, order the "Bavarian plate," which is loaded down with various meats, including lots of pork and sausages.

Residenzstrasse 12. www.kuffler-gastronomie.de. ℂ **089/290-70-60.** Reservations recommended. Main courses 11€–31€. AE, MC, V. Daily 9:30am–12:30pm. U-Bahn: Odeonsplatz or Marienplatz.

Inexpensive

Andechser am Dom GERMAN/BAVARIAN   This brewery outlet manages to mix class with beer hall rowdiness, and the suave clientele includes members of Bavarian high society. Not only is Andechs known for its beer, which is brewed near the Ammersee southwest of town, but owner Sepp Krätz also runs the Hippodrom tent at Oktoberfest, a so-called VIP tent. Although not the roomiest restaurant in town, the tavern and patio manage to pack all the guests in, while the leftovers trickle down to the cellar that has the feel of a secret chapel. The house specialty is the *Kloster Schmaus*, spicy sausages with dumplings, green beans, and veggie strips served piping hot in the pan itself. The *Schweinsbraten* (pork roast) features a dark beer sauce, and gluten-free and vegetarian offerings attest to their modern tastes in cuisine.

Weinstrasse 7A. www.andechser-am-dom.de. ℂ **089/298481.** Reservations recommended. Main courses 8.50€–18€. AE, DC, MC, V. Daily 10am–1am. U-Bahn or S-Bahn: Marienplatz.

Bier- und Oktoberfest Museum ★ 🏛 BAVARIAN   This authentically Bavarian locale is part museum, part party. The Augustiner Brewery operates this unique cultural and culinary combination as a nonprofit organization in a building dating back to 1327. The multi-story museum explains the beer-making process and the history of the world-famous beer bacchanalia. The ticket includes a voucher for a glass of brew and a snack including the Bavarian cheese *Obatzda* with *Leberwurst* (liver sausage). Your doctor may not like it, but to go Bavarian all the way you can spread *schmalz* (chicken fat) over your freshly baked rye bread.

After 6pm you can return for the regional Bavarian fare, starting perhaps with a beer-infused goulash and noodles and following with sausage salads or *schnitzels* and the like. Naturally, everything is washed down with the Augustiner brew.

Sterneckstrasse 2. www.museumsstueberl.de. ℂ **089/24243941.** Reservations not needed. Main courses 4€–14€. No credit cards. Museum Tues–Sat 1–5pm; beer hall Tues–Sat 6pm–midnight. U-Bahn or S-Bahn: Isartor.

Donisl ★ 🍴 BAVARIAN/INTERNATIONAL   This is one of Munich's oldest beer halls, dating from 1715. The seating capacity of this relaxed and comfortable restaurant is about 550, and in summer you can enjoy the hum and bustle of Marienplatz while dining in the garden area out front. The standard menu offers traditional Bavarian food, as well as a weekly changing specials menu. The little white sausages, Weisswürst, are a decades-long tradition here.

Weinstrasse 1. www.bayerischer-donisl.de. ℗ **089/29-62-64.** Reservations recommended. Main courses 10€–15€. AE, DC, MC, V. Daily 9am–midnight. U-Bahn/S-Bahn: Marienplatz.

Zum Alten Markt 🍴 BAVARIAN/INTERNATIONAL   Snug and cozy, Zum Alten Markt serves beautifully presented fresh cuisine. Located on a tiny square off Munich's large outdoor food market, the restaurant has a mellow charm and a welcoming host, Josef Lehner. The interior decor, with its intricately coffered wooden ceiling, came from a 400-year-old Tyrolean castle. In summer, tables are set up outside. Fish and fresh vegetables come from the nearby market. You may begin with a tasty homemade soup, such as cream of carrot or perhaps black-truffle tortellini in cream sauce with young onions and tomatoes. The chef makes a great *Tafelspitz* (boiled beef). You can also order classic dishes such as roast duck with applesauce or a savory roast suckling pig.

Am Viktualienmarkt, Dreifaltigkeitsplatz 3. www.zumaltenmarkt.de. ℗ **089/29-99-95.** Reservations recommended. Main courses 8€–20€. No credit cards. Mon–Sat noon–midnight. U-Bahn/S-Bahn: Marienplatz. Bus: 53.

SCHWABING

Bistro Terrine ★★ FRENCH   The restaurant in Schwabing looks like an Art Nouveau French bistro, and its nouvelle cuisine is based on traditional recipes as authentic and savory as anything you'd find in Lyon or Paris. There's room for up to 50 diners at a time, but because of the way the dining room is arranged, with banquettes and wood and glass dividers, it seems bigger than it actually is. During clement weather, there's additional seating on an outdoor terrace.

Menu items are innovative, and might include tartar of herring with freshly made potato chips and salad, watercress salad with sweetbreads, cream of paprika soup, an autumn fantasy of nuggets of venison served with hazelnut-flavored gnocchi in portwine sauce, pikeperch baked in herb-and-potato crust, or an alluring specialty salmon with a chanterelle-studded risotto.

Amalienstrasse 89. www.restaurant-terrine.de. ℗ **089/28-17-80.** Reservations recommended. Main courses 14€–32€; fixed-price lunch 14€–26€; fixed-price dinner 79€–89€. AE, MC, V. Tues–Fri noon–3pm; Mon–Sat 6:30pm–midnight. U-Bahn: U3 or U6 to Universität.

Schelling Salon GERMAN/BAVARIAN   Dating from 1872, this tavern is known for its Bavarian *Knödel* and billiards, and it's been a tradition since 1872, having survived World War II bombings. In days of yore, you could see everybody from Lenin to Hitler playing billiards here. On-site is a billiard museum, tracing the history of pool since the days of ancient Egypt. The waitstaff serves hearty fare washed down with mugs of beer. Start perhaps with the goulash soup or one of the freshly made salads, including a Russian salad. You face a selection of dishes from the cold or hot kitchen, featuring such courses as *Wiener Schnitzel* or sausage platters. A small selection of fish dishes is also offered.

Schellingstrasse 54. www.schelling-salon.de. ✆ **089/2720788.** Reservations not needed. Breakfast 3€–5€; main courses 4€–11€. AE, MC, V. Thurs–Mon 10am–1am. U-Bahn: Universität.

Tantris ★★★ FRENCH/INTERNATIONAL   Tantris's Hans Haas was voted the top chef in Germany in 1994, and, if anything, he has refined and sharpened his culinary technique since. Once inside, you're transported into an ultramodern atmosphere with fine service. You might begin with a terrine of smoked fish served with green cucumber sauce, and then follow with classic roast duck on mustard-seed sauce, or perhaps a delightful concoction of lobster medallions on black noodles. These dishes show a refinement and attention to detail that you find nowhere else in Munich. And just when you think you've had the perfect meal, the dessert arrives, and you're hungry again as you sample the gingerbread soufflé with chestnut sorbet.

Johann-Fichte-Strasse 7, Schwabing. www.tantris.de. ✆ **089/3-61-95-90.** Reservations required. Fixed-price 4-course lunch 115€; fixed-price dinner 165€–210€. AE, DC, MC, V. Tues–Sat noon–2pm and 6:30–1am. Closed public holidays and annual holidays in Jan and May. U-Bahn: Dietlindenstrasse.

Shopping

The most interesting shops are concentrated on Munich's pedestrians-only streets between **Karlsplatz** and **Marienplatz.**

Handmade crafts can be found on the fourth floor of Munich's major department store, **Ludwig Beck am Rathauseck,** Am Marienplatz 11 (✆ **089/236-910;** U-Bahn/S-Bahn: Marienplatz). **Wallach,** Residenzstrasse 3 (✆ **089/22-08-72;** U-Bahn/S-Bahn: Odeonsplatz), is a fine place to obtain handicrafts and folk art, both new and antique. Shop here for a memorable object to remind you of your trip. You'll find antique churns, old hand-painted wooden boxes and trays, painted porcelain clocks, and many other items.

In the grounds of Schloss Nymphenburg at Nördliches Schlossrondell 8, you'll find **Nymphenburger Porzellan-manufaktur** (✆ **089/17-91-970;** U-Bahn: Rotkreuzplatz, and then tram no. 17 toward Amalienburgstrasse; bus: 41), one of Germany's most famous porcelain makers. You can visit the exhibition and sales rooms; shipments can be arranged if you make purchases.

Entertainment & Nightlife

To find out what's happening in the Bavarian capital, go to the tourist office and buy a copy of *Monatsprogramm* (1.80€). This monthly publication contains complete information about what's going on in Munich and how to purchase tickets.

If you're looking for activity any hour of the day or night, head for **Schrannenhalle,** on the south side of the Viktualienmarkt, a former 19th-century grain depot completely restored. Today it is home to some great little shops, a bevy of bars, and every sort of restaurant, serving everything from Japanese sushi to old-fashioned Bavarian dishes. Entertainment, ranging from jazz to rock, is often provided. Locals like to drop in here before dawn to order *Weisswurst,* those Bavarian white sausages.

PERFORMING ARTS

Nowhere else in Europe, other than London and Paris, will you find so many musical and theatrical performances. And the good news is the low cost of the seats—you'll get good tickets if you're willing to pay anywhere from 10€ to 45€. Residenz (p. 396), **Altes Residenztheater (Cuvilliés Theater),** Residenzstrasse 1 (www.residenz-muenchen. de; ✆ **089/2185-19-40;** U-Bahn: Odeonsplatz), is a sightseeing attraction in its own right, and Germany's most outstanding example of a rococo tier-boxed theater. During

World War II, the interior was dismantled and stored. You can tour it Tuesday to Friday from 2 to 4pm and Sunday from 11am to 5pm. **Bavarian State Opera** and the **Bayerisches Staatsschauspiel (State Theater Company;** www.residenz-muenchen.de; ✆ **089/2185-1920)** perform smaller works here in keeping with the tiny theater's intimate character. Box office hours are Monday to Friday 10am to 6pm, plus 1 hour before performances; Saturday 10am to 1pm only. Opera tickets are 15€ to 265€; theater tickets, 15€ to 65€.

The regular season of the **Deutsches Theater,** Schwanthalerstrasse 13 (www. deutsches-theater.de; ✆ **089/552-34-444;** U-Bahn: Karlsplatz/Stachus), lasts year-round. Musicals, operettas, ballets, and international shows are performed here. During carnival season (Jan–Feb), the theater becomes a ballroom for more than 2,000 guests. Tickets are 19€ to 50€, higher for special events.

Münchner Philharmoniker, Rosenheimer Strasse 5 (www.mphil.de; ✆ **089/48-09-80;** S-Bahn: Rosenheimerplatz; tram: 18; bus: 51), the philharmonic, was founded in 1893. Its present home opened in 1985 and shelters the Richard Strauss Conservatory and the Munich Municipal Library. The orchestra performs in Philharmonic Hall. Purchase tickets Monday to Friday 9am to 6pm, Saturday 9am to 2pm, for 15€ to 65€. The Philharmonic season runs mid-September to July.

THE BAR & CAFE SCENE

Once a literary cafe, **Alter Simpl,** Türkenstrasse 57 (www.eggerlokale.de; ✆ **089/272-30-83;** U-Bahn: University), attracts a diverse crowd of locals, including young people. The real fun begins after 11pm, when the iconoclastic artistic ferment becomes more reminiscent of Berlin than Bavaria. It's open Sunday to Thursday 11am to 3am, Friday and Saturday 11am to 4am.

Schumann's Bar am Hofgarten, Odeonsplatz 6–7 (www.schumanns.de; ✆ **089/22-90-60),** is Munich's most legendary bar. It has an international fan club, lots of pizazz, a history that goes back forever, and new premises that have been the subject of many architectural reviews. Some of the staff members here consider the layout, the ample use of green marble, and the wooden paneling evocative of a church. All of that changes, however, when the drinks begin to flow and the crowd gets animated. This bar is a grand-slam rip-roaring affair that gets very crowded. There's a simple roster of menu items that changes with the season and the outside temperature. Schumann's is open Monday to Friday 5pm to 3am, Saturday and Sunday 6pm to 3am.

THE CLUB & MUSIC SCENE

You'll find some of Munich's most sophisticated entertainment at **Bayerischer Hof Night Club,** in the Hotel Bayerischer Hof, Promenadeplatz 2–6 (www.bayerischer-hof.de; ✆ **089/212-00;** tram: 19). Within one very large room is a piano bar where a musician plays melodies every night except Monday from 10am to 3am. The piano bar is free, but there's a nightclub cover charge of 5€ to 50€. Daily happy hour is from 7 to 8:30pm in the piano bar.

Jazzclub Unterfahrt, Einsteinstrasse 42 (www.unterfahrt.de; ✆ **089/448-27-94;** U-Bahn/S-Bahn: Ostbahnhof), is Munich's leading jazz club, lying near the Ostbahnhof in the Haidhausen district. The club presents live music Tuesday to Sunday 8:30pm to 1am (it opens at 8pm). Wine, small snacks, beer, and drinks are sold as well. Sunday night there's a special jam session for improvization. Cover Tuesday to Saturday is 6€ to 35€. Small, dark, and popular with blues and jazz aficionados, **Mister B's,** Herzog-Heinrichstrasse 38 (www.misterbs.de; ✆ **089/534901;** U-Bahn: Goetheplatz), hosts a slightly older, mellower crowd than the rock and dance clubs.

BEER GARDENS, cellars & TAVERNS

Regardless of the time of year, you will find Bavarians congregating somewhere to take part in one of their favorite pastimes: socializing over a beer. In winter, the countless *Bierkeller* (cellars) and *Bierstuben* (taverns) are packed to the brim with frothy-faced locals (and visitors, let's be honest). Once the sun peeks through in early spring, the benches and chairs of the *Biergärten* fill up on a daily basis throughout summer, culminating in the one last hurrah of Oktoberfest, when the waning sunlight of a Bavarian autumn sends everyone back into the cellars and halls. These beer joints are Munich institutions, with a tradition dating as far back as the foundation of the city. In a sense, these establishments are restaurants, bars, and sometimes nightlife wrapped in one, where Bavarians come to relax and just be themselves any time of the day or night. Check out some of the traditional garb for proof. Always be aware of table reservations for the *Stammgäste* (regulars), who will certainly show up at the time indicated on plaques or notes on the tables to down their daily rounds.

Although half-liter mugs are available, you might want to join the masses and order a *Mass*, or a liter. To order, ask for "ein Mass, bitte." You also might want to try the massive pretzels *(breze)*, and add *obatzda*, a Bavarian cheese spread with paprika. *Radi*, white radish slices with chives on bread, are also a popular snack.

Producing what many locals call the best beer in town, the **Augustinerbräu** operates several establishments and countless affiliates, but three are worth mention. In the heart of the city, the **Augustinerbräu Stüberl/Grossgaststätten,** Neuhauserstrasse 27 (www.augustiner-restaurant.com; ✆ 089/23183257; U-Bahn: Marienplatz), keeps getting bigger the farther back you explore the vaulted rooms; it feels like an indoor *Biergarten*, but remains classy enough for dining. The **Augustiner-Keller,** Arnulfstrasse 52 (www.augustinerkeller.de; ✆ **089/ 594393;** tram: 16 or 17), is the spacious sister-branch with the best garden, as well as medieval cellars. For the cheapest *Mass* in town (5.10€), check out the **Augustiner Bräustuben,** Landsbergerstrasse 19 (www.braeustuben.de; ✆ 089/5022569; tram: 18 or 19), installed into the former stalls right next to the brewery itself, and a short walk from the Oktoberfest grounds.

Bamberger Haus, Brunnerstrasse 2 (www.restaurant-la-villa.de; ✆ **089/ 3088966;** U-Bahn: Scheidplatz), located northwest of Schwabing at the edge of Luitpold Park, is named after a city noted for mass consumption of beer. The

It's open Tuesday to Sunday 8pm to 3am. Blues, jazz, and rhythm-and-blues combos take the stage Thursday to Saturday. Cover is 7€ to 20€.

THE LGBT SCENE

Much of Munich's gay and lesbian scene takes place in the blocks between the Viktualienmarkt and Gärtnerplatz, particularly on Hans-Sachs-Strasse.

The major gathering place for lesbians is **Inges Karotte,** Baaderstrsse 13 (www.inges-karotte.de; ✆ **089/201-0669;** U-Bahn: Frauenhofer Strasse). One patron called the clients "a female jungle," a widely diverse group of ages, professions, and interests. It's a good atmosphere for drinking and mating. Cocktails begin at 5€, and happy hour is only from 4 to 6pm. Disco music sometimes rules the night. Hours are Monday to Saturday 6pm to 1am, Sunday 4pm to 1am.

street-level restaurant, **La Terrazza,** serves Bavarian and international specialties: well-seasoned soups, grilled steak, veal, pork, and sausages. If you only want to drink, you might visit the rowdier and less expensive beer hall in the cellar. Main courses in the restaurant range from 8€ to 15€.

The **Biergarten Chinesischer Turm,** Englischer Garten 3 (www.chinaturm.de; ✆ **089/3838730;** U-Bahn: Universität), may seem gaudy and touristy until you realize most of the *Mass*-raising clientele are locals. You may find an oom-pah band puffing away in the pagoda tower. The place is open every day March to November 10am to midnight, but December to February its hours depend on the weather and the number of patrons.

Hirschgarten, Hirschgartenstrasse 1, in Nymphenburg Park, near the palace (www.hirschgarten.de; ✆ **089/17999199;** S-Bahn: Laim; tram: 17 to Romanplatz), is the largest open-air restaurant in Munich, and likely in Europe for that matter, with seating for more than 8,000 beer drinkers and merrymakers. Full meals cost 7.50€ to 18€. A 1-liter stein of Augustiner beer is 6.30€. It's open daily 9am to midnight. MasterCard and Visa are accepted.

Some might claim that the world-renowned **Hofbräuhaus am Platzl ★,** Am Platzl 9 (www.hofbraeuhaus.de; ✆ 089/221676; U-Bahn: Marienplatz), is too gaudy and touristy, but Bavarians have never shied away from kitsch. In fact, the place is so gaudy that even some locals may secretly sneak in for a *Mass* of brew and *wurst*. Waitresses in dirndls survey the scene and others in candy cane outfits distribute pretzels bigger than your head. The brass band puffs their cheeks to the beat and everybody has a good time. Be sure to check out the lockers where denizens lock up their personal mugs for next time. Rent is only 4€ per year, but the waiting list is long—longer than it takes to grow some of the curly mustaches here.

The **Waldwirtschaft Grosshesselöhe,** George-Kalb-Strasse 3 (www.waldwirtschaft.de; ✆ **089/74994030;** S-Bahn: Isartal Bahnhof; tram: 7), is a popular summertime rendezvous, located above the Isar River near the zoo with seats for some 2,000 drinkers. Recorded music ranging from Dixieland to jazz to Polish polka is played throughout the week. Entrance is free, and you bring your own food. It's open daily 11am to 11pm (they have to close early because neighborhood residents complain), with live music on Friday to Sunday nights.

Gay and neighborly, and ringed with varnished pine and a collection of teddy bears, **Teddy-Bar,** Hans-Sachs-Strasse 1 (www.teddybar.de; ✆ **089/2603359;** U-Bahn: Sendlinger Tor), is a congenial bar patronized by gay men over 30. It's relatively easy to strike up a conversation, and if you're hungry, there are platters of Bavarian and German food. It's open nightly 6pm to 4am. October to April it opens for brunch at 11am on Sunday.

Where to Stay

Most visitors will be most comfortable in central Munich, within walking distance of many of the major sights and convenient for getting to other parts of the city. It's lively but also the most expensive area to stay; then again, you'll save money on transport. Schwabing, the upmarket residential section of town full of many cafes and restaurants, is quieter and pleasant but requires 20 minutes to get into the center of the city.

CENTRAL MUNICH

Very Expensive

Bayerischer Hof & Palais Montgelas ★★★ Together, the Bayerischer Hof and the 17th-century Palais Montgelas make up the *crème de la crème* of Munich hotels. You can add your name to the litany of distinguished guests who have stayed here since it opened in 1841, including Ludwig I himself (due to a lack of bathtubs at the palace back then). Rooms range from medium to extremely spacious, and the decor from Bavarian rustic to R&B (red and beige tones) to Colonial African. The English designer Laura Ashley even designed one room. Palais Montgelas has 20 of the most upscale rooms in this complex.

Promenadeplatz 2–6, 80333 München. www.bayerischerhof.de. ℭ **089/21200.** Fax 089/2120906. 350 units. 340€–520€ double; from 1,800€ suite. AE, DC, MC, V. Parking 30€. Tram: 19. **Amenities:** 3 restaurants; 5 bars; rooftop heated pool; exercise room; spa; concierge; room service; babysitting; airport transfers (120€). *In room:* TV, minibar, hair dryer, Wi-Fi (27€/day).

Mandarin Oriental ★★★ Although one of Munich's smaller hotels, this is by no means a lightweight. Only the Hotel Vier Jahreszeiten Kempinski München and the Bayerischer Hof (see above) outclass this sophisticated and luxurious winner. Located within sight of the Frauenkirche, the stylish and elegant wedge-shaped 1880s building combines neo-Renaissance, neoclassical, and Biedermeier touches. A marble staircase sweeps upward to the very comfortable large rooms, each with specially crafted furniture or original antiques. Many have private terraces opening onto views of Munich.

Neuturmstrasse 1, 80331 München. www.mandarinoriental.com/munich. ℭ **089/290980.** Fax 089/222539. 73 units. 325€–555€ double; from 585€ suite. AE, DC, MC, V. Parking 24€. U-Bahn or S-Bahn: Marienplatz. Tram: 19. **Amenities:** 2 restaurants; bar; rooftop heated pool; exercise room; bikes; concierge; room service; babysitting. *In room:* A/C, TV/DVD, minibar, hair dryer, CD player, Wi-Fi (25€/day).

Expensive

Cortiina ★ 👜 Built in 2001 and run by the designing duo of Rudi Kull and Albert Weinzerl, the Cortiina exudes the fresh and trendy side of Munich that attracts the business crowd and young "elegentia." The chic receptionists are straight out of a Tarantino film, and the dimmed halls for soothing bleary eyes make you forget you're in a hotel. A new annex with an additional 40 rooms features a rooftop terrace and the latest furnishings including wooden swivel doors and marble bathrooms. The junior suites offer an added kitchenette for longer stays.

Ledererstrasse 8, 80331 München. www.cortiina.com. ℭ **089/2422490.** Fax 089/242249100. 75 units. 195€–380€ double; 285€–500€ suite. AE, DC, MC, V. Parking 19€. U-Bahn: Marienplatz. **Amenities:** Bar; room service; babysitting. *In room:* TV/DVD, minibar, hair dryer, MP3 docking station, Wi-Fi (free).

Moderate

Eden-Hotel-Wolff ★ This dignified hotel hides behind a modest facade across the street from the train station and the airport bus terminus. If you have an early departure and still seek a touch of luxury, you'll be glad you chose this hotel. The traditional interiors vary from room to room. Some are classic with chandeliers and dark-wood paneling; others have rustic touches like antler ornaments and white clapboard walls. Hypoallergenic units are available, with special beds and a private ventilation system. Also ask about special weekend rates, which may or may not be available.

Arnulfstrasse 4–8, 80335 München. www.ehw.de. ℭ **089/551150.** Fax 089/55115555. 210 units. 184€–325€ double; 295€–410€ suite. 1 child 6 and under stays free in parent's room. Rates include buffet breakfast. AE, DC, MC, V. Parking 17€. U-Bahn or S-Bahn: Hauptbahnhof. **Amenities:**

Restaurant; bar; exercise room; spa; concierge; room service; babysitting. *In room:* TV, minibar, hair dryer, Wi-Fi (10€/day).

Hotel Exquisit ★ ☺   This great choice benefits from a traffic-reduced street, and is a short walk from the center, Deutsches Theater, and nightlife in the Glockenbach district. The paneled lobby adjoins an inviting bar and lounge, where your night may begin. A wood-lover's dream, the interior is bedecked with bold stained mahogany wherever possible alongside salmon and hummus shades. The classically designed suites feature a separate living room, and families will enjoy the multistory maisonettes in the pitched roof. Whether your window overlooks the street or the ivy-draped courtyard, you'll sleep comfortably.

Pettenkoferstrasse 3, 80336 München. www.hotel-exquisit.com. ℂ **089/5519900.** Fax 089/55199499. 50 units. 185€–295€ double; 239€–355€ suite. Rates include buffet breakfast. AE, MC, V. Parking 15€. U-Bahn: Sendlinger Tor. **Amenities:** Restaurant; bar; sauna; room service. *In room:* TV, minibar, hair dryer, Wi-Fi (20€/day).

Hotel Olympic ★   Built as a private villa around 1900, this hotel represents one of Munich's most appealing conversions of an antique building into a hip and attractive hotel. The lobby occupies a high-ceilinged Victorian vestibule that retains many of the original details. Breakfast is served in a very large, graciously proportioned dining room, where memories of the grand bourgeoisie of the Industrial Revolution still seem to permeate the woodwork. Rooms are minimalist and all white, much more modern than the reception areas, but comfortable and well-engineered.

Hans Sachs Strasse 4, 80469 München. www.hotel-olympic.de. ℂ **089/231890.** Fax 089/23189199. 38 units. 155€–200€ double; 530€–890€ apt. Rates include buffet breakfast. AE, DC, MC, V. Parking 15€. U-Bahn: Sendlinger Tor. **Amenities:** Room service; babysitting. *In room:* TV, minibar, hair dryer, Wi-Fi (free).

Hotel Splendid-Dollmann im Lehel ★ 🏨   Check in here if you want a hotel that's up-to-date yet replete with antiques, fine paintings, quality Oriental carpets, and a sense of Munich's sometimes gracious 18th- and 19th-century past. The venue is an elegant 19th-century town house, fronted with chiseled white-stone blocks, in the upscale Lehel district. Inside, an attentive staff welcomes you into a small, boutique-style hotel fitted with a library-style bar and many of the decorative accessories of an upscale private home. Bedrooms are cozy, colorful, and well maintained, each with a different theme and reproductions of antique furniture.

Thierschstrasse 49, 80538 München. www.splendid-dollmann.de. ℂ **089/238080.** Fax 089/23808365. 37 units. 160€–250€ double; 230€–400€ suite. AE, DC, MC, V. Parking 8.50€. U-Bahn: Lehel. **Amenities:** Bar; room service. *In room:* TV, hair dryer, Wi-Fi (3€/hour).

Inexpensive

Creatif Hotel Elephant 🏅   This takes the cake for the most daring use of color in town, which helps offset the otherwise lackluster area around the main rail station. Its salmon-colored facade announces the brightness of the interior with simple but comfortably furnished rooms. There's nothing antique about the design, just clean, new materials and colors to brighten your stay.

Lämmerstrasse 6, Leopoldvorstadt, 80335 München. www.creatifelephanthotel.com. ℂ **089/555785.** Fax 089/5501746. 40 units. 68€–250€ double. AE, DC, MC, V. U-Bahn or S-Bahn: Hauptbahnhof. **Amenities:** Concierge. *In room:* TV, hair dryer, Wi-Fi (free).

Pension Westfalia ★ 🏅   Originally built in 1895, this four-story villa near Goetheplatz provides easy access to the mania on the Theresienwiese during Oktoberfest time, and overlooks the pleasant meadow and Bavaria Statue the rest of the year. Rooms are rather functional and short on extras, but they are well maintained. Parking on the street, when available, is free.

Mozartstrasse 23, 80336 München. www.pension-westfalia.de. ℂ **089/530377.** Fax 089/5439120. 19 units, 14 with bathroom. 50€–65€ per person double without bathroom; 68€–82€ per person double with bathroom. Rates include buffet breakfast. AE, MC, V. U-Bahn: Goetheplatz. Bus: 58. *In room:* TV, Wi-Fi (free).

SCHWABING

Gästehaus Englischer Garten ★★ ☺ This ivy-covered retreat provides a unique experience in Munich. As one of the few hotels bordering the Englischer Garten, this villa feels more like a private home with an expansive backyard. Roselinde Zankl keeps a tidy home and does an excellent job at making you feel welcome, which may make you want to stick around longer. The genuine antiques, comfortable beds, and Oriental rugs add to the grandmotherly appeal of the interior. Although a short walk and a few U-Bahn stops from the center, the location is ideal for a bike ride or stroll through the city's largest park, or a night out in the trendy Schwabing district.

Liebergesellstrasse 8, 80802 München-Schwabing. www.hotelenglischergarten.de. ℂ **089/ 3839410.** Fax 089/38394133. 31 units, 26 with bathroom. 75€–109€ double without bathroom; 129€–169€ double with bathroom; 110€–163€ apt. AE, DC, MC, V. Parking 9€. U-Bahn: Münchner Freiheit. **Amenities:** Bikes; babysitting. *In room:* TV, minibar, Wi-Fi (free).

La Maison ★ 🛏 If Goth-posh was ever possible, this hotel might embody it. Shades of black and white permeate the sleek furnishings of this oasis of class in the otherwise grungy neighborhood of Schwabing. The somber furnishings with black velvet touches seem to recall a lost era of pouting crooners in Parisian cabarets, which may make you want to leave your tuxedo on. The lounge sofas in the lobby feel like a cloud, and a recently opened Japanese Restaurant provides refined cuisine. Whether it's your style or not, expect all the comforts and amenities of a successfully run hotel.

Occamstrasse 24, 80802 München. www.hotel-la-maison.com. ℂ **089/33035550.** Fax 089/330355555. 31 units. 180€–220€ double. AE, MC, V. Parking 15€. U-Bahn: Münchener Freiheit. **Amenities:** Restaurant; bar; room service. *In room:* TV/DVD, minibar, hair dryer, CD player, Wi-Fi (free).

Side Trips from Munich
DACHAU CONCENTRATION CAMP MEMORIAL SITE

In 1933, what had once been a quiet little artists' community just 15km (10 miles) from Munich became a tragic symbol of the Nazi era. Shortly after Hitler became chancellor, Himmler and the SS set up the first German concentration camp in the grounds of a former ammunition factory. The list of prisoners at the camp included enemies of the Third Reich, including everyone from communists and Social Democrats to Jews, homosexuals, Gypsies, Jehovah's Witnesses, clergymen, political opponents, some trade union members, and others.

During its notorious history, between 1933 and 1945, more than 206,000 prisoners from 30 countries were imprisoned at Dachau, perhaps a lot more. Some were forced into slave labor, manufacturing Nazi armaments for the war and helping to build roads, for example. Others fell victim to SS doctors, who conducted grotesque medical experiments on them. And still others were killed after Dachau became a center for mass murder: Starvation, illness, beatings, and torture killed thousands who were not otherwise hanged, shot by firing squads, or lethally injected. At least 30,000 people were registered as dead while in Dachau between 1933 and 1945. However,

PRE-WWII—DACHAU artists' COLONY

Unknown to many, Dachau had a glorious history long before it became infamous in the annals of human cruelty. At the end of the 19th century, it was one of the leading artists' colonies of Germany, and landscape painting was virtually developed in the Dachau moorlands. Women were not yet allowed in the Munich Art Academy, but they were educated in the town's private art schools.

If you have time to spare, you can explore Dachau's historic core, including its **Schloss Dachau,** a hilltop Renaissance castle that dominates the town at Schlossplatz (℃ **08131/87923**). All that's left of a much larger palace is a wing from 1715. Stand in the east terrace for a panoramic view of Munich in the distance. The highlight is the grand Renaissance hall, with its scenes of figures from ancient mythology. Chamber concerts are staged here. The on-site brewery hosts the town's beer and music festival annually during the first 2 weeks of August. Charging 2€ for admission for adults (kids under 18 are free), the castle is open April to September Tuesday to Sunday 9am to 6pm, and October to March Tuesday to Sunday 10am to 4pm.

Many paintings from the artists who settled here in the 1800s are still in town, especially the works on display in **Gemäldegalerie,** Konrad-Adenauer-Strasse 3 (℃ **08131/567516**), open Tuesday to Friday 11am to 5pm, Saturday and Sunday 1 to 5pm, charging an admission of 4€.

there are many other thousands who were also murdered there, even if their deaths weren't officially logged.

The SS abandoned the camp on April 28, 1945, and the liberating U.S. Army moved in to take charge the following day. In all, a total of 67,000 living prisoners—all of them on the verge of death—were discovered at Dachau and its subsidiary camps.

Upon entering the camp, **KZ-Gedenkstätte Dachau,** Alte-Römerstrasse 75 (www.kz-gedenkstaette-dachau.de; ℃ **08131/669970**), you are faced by three memorial chapels—Catholic, Protestant, and Jewish—built in the early 1960s. Immediately behind the Catholic chapel is the Lagerstrasse, the main camp road lined with poplar trees, once flanked by 32 barracks, each housing 208 prisoners. Two barracks have been rebuilt to give visitors insight into the conditions the prisoners endured.

The museum is housed in the large building that once contained the kitchen, laundry, and bathrooms. Photographs and documents show the rise of the Nazi regime and the SS; other exhibits show the persecution of Jews and other prisoners. Every effort has been made to present the facts. The tour of Dachau is a truly moving experience.

You can get to the camp by taking the frequent S-Bahn train S2 from the Hauptbahnhof to Dachau (direction: Petershausen), then bus no. 726 to the camp. The camp is open Tuesday to Sunday 9am to 5pm; admission is free. The English version of a 22-minute documentary film, *The Dachau Concentration Camp,* is shown at 11:30am, 2pm, and 3:30pm. All documents are translated in the catalog, which is available at the museum entrance.

Garmisch-Partenkirchen ★★★

In spite of its urban flair, Garmisch-Partenkirchen, Germany's top alpine resort, has maintained the charm of an ancient village. Even today, you occasionally see country

SPORTS IN THE bavarian ALPS

Hitting the Slopes & Other Winter Activities   The winter **skiing** here is the best in Germany. A regular winter snowfall in January and February measures 30 to 50cm (12–20 in.), which in practical terms means about 2m (6½ ft.) of snow in the areas served by ski lifts. The great **Zugspitzplatt** snowfield can be reached in spring or autumn by a rack railway. The Zugspitze, at 2,960m (9,710 ft.) above sea level, is the tallest mountain peak in Germany. Ski slopes begin at a height of 2,650m (8,700 ft.).

The second great ski district in the Alps is **Berchtesgadener Land,** with alpine skiing centered on Jenner, Rossfeld, Götschen, and Hochschwarzeck, and consistently good snow conditions until March. Here you'll find a cross-country skiing center and many miles of tracks kept in first-class condition, natural toboggan runs, one artificial ice run for toboggan and skibob runs, artificial ice-skating, and ice-curling rinks. Call the local "Snow-Telefon" at the **Berchtesgaden Tourist Office** (www.berchtesgaden.de; ℭ **08652/9670**) for current snow conditions. And from October to February, you can huddle with a companion in the back of a **horse-drawn sled.** For a fee of 55€ to 85€ per hour, this can be arranged by calling ℭ **08652/1760.**

Hiking & Other Summer Activities   In summer, **alpine hiking** is a major attraction—climbing mountains, enjoying nature, watching animals in the forest. Hikers are able at times to observe endangered species firsthand. One of the best areas for hiking is the 1,237m (4,058-ft.) **Eckbauer** lying on the southern fringe of Partenkirchen (the tourist office at Garmisch-Partenkirchen will supply maps and details). Many visitors come to the Alps in summer just to hike through the **Berchtesgaden National Park,** bordering the Austrian province of Salzburg. The 2,466m (8,091-ft.) Watzmann Mountain, the Königssee (Germany's cleanest, clearest lake), and parts of the Jenner—the pride of Berchtesgaden's four ski areas—are within the boundaries of the national park, which has well-mapped trails cut through protected areas, leading the hiker along spectacular flora and fauna. Information about hiking in the park is provided by the **Nationale Parkhaus,** Franciscanalplatz 7, 83471 Berchtesgaden (www.nationalpark-berchtesgaden.bayern.de; ℭ **08652/64343**). It's open daily from 9am to 5pm.

From Garmisch-Partenkirchen, serious hikers can embark on full-day or, if they're more ambitious, overnight alpine

folk in traditional costumes, and you may be held up in traffic while the cattle are led from their mountain grazing grounds down through the streets of town. Garmisch is about 88km (55 miles) southwest of Munich.

ESSENTIALS
Getting There
BY TRAIN   The **Garmisch-Partenkirchen Bahnhof** lies on the major Munich–Weilheim–Garmisch–Mittenwald–Innsbruck rail line with frequent connections in all directions. Twenty trains per day arrive from Munich (trip time: 1 hr. 22 min.). For rail information and schedules, call ℭ **0800/1-50-70-90.**

BY BUS   Both long-distance and regional buses through the Bavarian Alps are provided by **RVO Regionalverkehr Oberbayern** in Garmisch-Partenkirchen (www.rvo-bus.de; ℭ **08821/948-274** for information).

treks, following clearly marked footpaths and staying in isolated mountain huts maintained by the German Alpine Association (Deutscher Alpenverein/DAV). Some huts are staffed and serve meals. For the truly remote unsupervised huts, you'll be provided with information on how to gain access and your responsibility in leaving them tidy after your visit. For information, inquire at the local tourist office or write to the **German Alpine Association,** Am Franciscanalplatz 7, 83471, Berchtesgaden (www.alpenverein. de; ℭ **08652/64343**). At the same address and phone number, you'll also be routed to staff members of a privately owned tour operator, the **Summit Club,** an outfit devoted to the organization of high-altitude expeditions throughout Europe and the world.

If you're a true outdoors person, you'll briefly savor the somewhat touristy facilities of Garmisch-Partenkirchen, and then use it as a base for exploring the rugged **Berchtesgaden National Park,** which is within an easy commute of Garmisch. You can also stay at one of the inns in Mittenwald or Oberammergau and take advantage of a wide roster of sporting diversions within the wide-open spaces. Any of the outfitters below will provide directions and linkups with their sports programs from wherever you decide to stay. Street maps of Berchtesgaden and its environs are usually available free from the **Kurdirektion** (the local tourist office) at Berchtesgaden (ℭ **08652/967-0**), and more intricately detailed maps of the surrounding alpine topography are available for a fee.

In addition to hill climbing and rock climbing, activities include **ballooning,** which, weather permitting, can be arranged through **Outdoor Club Berchtesgaden,** Am Gmundberg (www. outdoor-club; ℭ **08652/9776-0**), open Monday to Friday from 8am to 6pm. Local enthusiasts warn that ballooning is not a sport for the timid or anyone who suffers unduly in the cold: Warm thermal currents that prevail around Berchtesgaden in summer limit the sport to the cold-weather months. Consequently, the seasonal heyday for ballooning is from December to February.

Cycling and **mountain biking,** available through the rental facilities of **Para-Taxi,** Maximilianstrasse 16 (www.parataxi. de; ℭ **08652/948450**), give outdoor enthusiasts an opportunity to enjoy the outdoors and exercise their leg muscles simultaneously. It's open Monday to Friday 9am to 12:30pm and 2 to 6pm, Saturday 9am to 12:30pm.

BY CAR Access is via A-95 Autobahn from Munich; exit at Eschenlohe.

Visitor Information

For tourist information, contact the **Kurverwaltung und Verkehrsamt,** Richard-Strauss-Platz (ℭ **08821/180-700**), open Monday to Saturday 8am to 6pm, Sunday 10am to noon.

Getting Around

An unnumbered municipal bus services the town, depositing passengers at Marienplatz or the Bahnhof, from where you can walk to all central hotels. This free bus runs every 15 minutes.

EXPLORING GARMISCH-PARTENKIRCHEN

The symbol of the city's growth and modernity is the **Olympic Ice Stadium,** Spiridon-Louis-Ring (ℭ **089/30-67-21-50;** U-Bahn: 3 to Olympia-Zentrum), built for the 1936 Winter Olympics and capable of holding nearly 12,000 people. On the slopes at the edge of town is the much larger **Ski Stadium,** with two ski jumps and a slalom course. In 1936 more than 100,000 people watched the events in this stadium. Today it's still an integral part of winter life in Garmisch—the World Cup Ski Jump is held here every New Year.

Garmisch-Partenkirchen is a center for winter sports, summer hiking, and mountain climbing. In addition, the town environs offer some of the most panoramic views and colorful buildings in Bavaria. The **Philosopher's Walk** in the park surrounding the pink-and-silver 18th-century pilgrimage **Chapel of St. Anton** is a delightful spot to enjoy the views of the mountains around the low-lying town.

EXPLORING THE ALPINE ENVIRONS

One of the most beautiful of the alpine regions around Garmisch is the **Alpspitz region,** which hikers and hill climbers consider uplifting and healing for both body and soul. Here, you'll find alpine meadows, masses of seasonal wildflowers, and a rocky and primordial geology whose savage panoramas might strike you as Wagnerian. Ranging in altitude from 1,200 to 1,800m (3,900–5,900 ft.) above sea level, the Alps around Garmisch-Partenkirchen are accessible via more than 30 ski lifts and funiculars, many of which run year-round.

The most appealing and panoramic of the lot includes the Alpspitz (Osterfelderkopf) **cable car** that runs uphill from the center of Garmisch to the top of the **Osterfelderkopf** peak, at a height of 1,980m (6,500 ft.). It makes its 9-minute ascent at least every hour, year-round, from 8am to 5pm. The round-trip cost for nonskiers is 47€ adults, 32.50€ persons aged 16 to 18, and 26€ children aged 6 to 15. After admiring the view at the top, you can either return directly to Garmisch or continue your journey into the mountains via other cable cars. If you opt to continue, take the **Hochalm cable car** across the high-altitude plateaus above Garmisch. At its terminus, you'll have two options, both across clearly marked alpine trails. The 20-minute trek will take you to the uppermost station of the **Kreuzbergbahn,** which will carry you back to Garmisch. The 75-minute trek will carry you to the upper terminus of the **Hausbergbahn,** which will also carry you back to Garmisch.

Another of the many cable-car options within Garmisch involves an eastward ascent from the center of Partenkirchen to the top of the 1,780m (5,840-ft.) Wank via the Wankbahn, for a round-trip price of 18€ adults, 13€ persons aged 16 to 18, and 10.50€ children. From here, you'll get a sweeping view of the plateau upon which the twin villages of Garmisch and Partenkirchen sit. With minor exceptions, the Wankbahn is open only between mid-April and early October. But during clement weather, the top of the Wank is a favorite with the patrons of Garmisch's spa facilities because the plentiful sunshine makes it ideal for the *Liegekur* (deck-chair cure).

If you plan on pursuing any of these options, it's to your advantage to invest in a day pass, the **Classic Garmisch Pass,** with which you'll be able to ride most of the cable cars in the region (including those to the above-recommended Alpspitz, Kreuzeck, and Wank, as well as several others that fan out over the Eckbauer and the Ausberg) as many times as you like within the same day. Available at any of the town's cable-car stations, the pass costs 33€ for adults, 25.50€ for ages 16 to 18, and 18.50€ for ages 6 to 15. For information on all the cable-car schedules and itineraries within the region, call ℰ **08821/7970.**

Another option for exploring the environs of Garmisch involves an ascent to the top of the **Zugspitze,** at 2,960m (9,710 ft.) the tallest mountain in Germany, with a base set astride the Austrian frontier. Ski slopes begin at 2,650m (8,700 ft.). For a panoramic view over both the Bavarian and Tyrolean Alps, go to the summit. The first stage begins in the center of Garmisch by taking the **cog railway** to an intermediary alpine plateau (Zugspitzplatz). Trains depart hourly throughout the year from 7:39am to 2:15pm, although we recommend that you begin by 1:15pm (and preferably earlier) and not wait until the cog railway's final ascent from Garmisch. At Zugspitzplatz, you can continue uphill on the same cog railway to the debut of a high-speed, 4-minute ride aboard the Gletscherbahn cable car, the high-altitude conveyance you'll ride to the top of the Zugspitz peak. A ZugspitzCard, valid for 3 days, costs 44€ for adults or 25€ for ages 6 to 18. For more information, go to www.zugspitze.de or call ☎ **08821/720-688.**

THE ROMANTIC ROAD ★★

No area of Germany is more aptly named than the **Romantische Strasse.** Stretching 290km (180 miles) from Würzburg to Füssen in the foothills of the Bavarian Alps, it passes through untouched medieval villages and 2,000-year-old towns.

The best way to see the Romantic Road is by car, stopping whenever the mood strikes you and then driving on through vineyards and over streams until you arrive at the alpine passes in the south. Frankfurt and Munich are convenient gateways. Access is by A-7 Autobahn from north and south, or A-3 Autobahn from east and west; A-81 Autobahn has links from the southwest. You can also explore the Romantic Road by train or bus, or by organized tour.

Rothenburg ob der Tauber ★★★

This city was first mentioned in written records in 804 as Rotinbure, a settlement above (*ob*) the Tauber River that grew to be a free imperial city, reaching its apex of prosperity under a famous Burgermeister, Heinrich Toppler, in the 14th century.

The place is such a gem and so well known that its popularity is its chief disadvantage—tourist hordes march through here, especially in summer, and the concomitant souvenir peddlers hawk kitsch. Even so, if your time is limited and you can visit only one town on the Romantic Road, make it Rothenburg.

Contemporary life and industry have made an impact, and if you arrive at the railroad station, the first things you'll see are factories and office buildings. But don't be discouraged. Inside those undamaged 13th-century city walls is a completely preserved medieval town, relatively untouched by the passage of time.

ESSENTIALS
Getting There
BY TRAIN   Rothenburg lies on the Steinach–Rothenburg rail line, with frequent connections to all major German cities, including Nürnberg and Stuttgart. Daily trains arrive from Frankfurt (trip time: 3 hr.), Hamburg (5½ hr.), or Berlin (7 hr.). For information, call ☎ **0800/1-50-70-90.**

BY BUS   The bus that traverses the length of the Romantic Road is EB189 or EB189E, operated by **Deutsche Touring Frankfurt** (www.touring.de; ☎ **069/790-3521**). Two buses operate along this route every day, but only from April to October. Know in advance that although you'll see a lot of romantic color en route, travel time to Rothenburg from Frankfurt via these buses is 5 hours because of frequent stops en route. Any travel agent in Germany or abroad can book you a seat on any of these buses, each of which stops at Würzburg, Augsburg, Füssen, and Munich.

Regional bus service that's limited to towns and hamlets within the vicinity of Rothenburg and the rest of the Romantic Road is provided by **OVF Omnibus-verkehr Franken GmbH,** Kopernikusplatz 5, 90459 Nürnberg (www.ovf.de; ✆ **0911/43-90-60**).

Visitor Information

Contact **Stadt Verkehrsamt,** Marktplatz (www.rothenburg.de; ✆ **09861/404800**), open Monday to Friday 9am to 6pm, Saturday and Sunday 10am to 5pm (Nov–Mar it closes at 5pm weekdays and is shut Sundays).

EXPLORING THE MEDIEVAL TOWN

The **Rathaus (Town Hall)** ★ on the Marktplatz (✆ **09861/404-92**) and the Jako-bskirche are the outstanding attractions, along with the medieval walls. The town hall consists of two sections; the older, Gothic section dates from 1240. From the 50m (164-ft.) tower of the Gothic hall, you get an overview of the town. The belfry has quite a history—in 1501, fire destroyed part of the building, and after that the belfry became a fire watchtower. Guards had to ring the bell every quarter-hour to prove they were awake and on the job. The newer Renaissance section, built in 1572, is decorated with intricate friezes, an oriel extending the building's full height, and a large stone portico opening onto the square. The octagonal tower at the center of the side facing the square contains a grand staircase leading to the upper hall. On the main floor is the large courtroom.

Admission to the tower is 2€ adults, .50€ children under 18. The Rathaus is open Monday to Friday 8am to 5pm. The tower is open April to October, daily 9:30am to 12:30pm and 1 to 5pm; November to March, Saturday, Sunday, and holidays only, from noon to 3pm.

St. Jakobskirche (Church of St. James), Klostergasse 15 (✆ **09861/404-92**), contains the famous *Altar of the Holy Blood* ★★ (west gallery), a masterpiece of the Würzburg sculptor and woodcarver Tilman Riemenschneider (1460–1531). The Rothenburg Council commissioned the work in 1499 to provide a worthy setting for the *Reliquary of the Holy Blood.* The relic is contained in a rock-crystal capsule set in the reliquary cross in the center of the shrine, and beneath it the scene of *The Last Supper* makes an immediate impact on the viewer—Jesus is giving Judas the morsel of bread, marking him as the traitor. The altar wings show (left) the *Entry of Christ into Jerusalem* and (right) *Christ Praying in the Garden of Gethsemane.*

The vertical Gothic church has three naves. The choir, dating from 1336, is the oldest section and has fine late-Gothic painted-glass windows. To the left is the tabernacle (1390–1400), which was recognized as a "free place," a sanctuary for con-demned criminals where they could not be touched. It's open April to October, Monday to Saturday 9am to 5:30pm, Sunday 11am to 5:30pm. In December, it's open daily 10am to 5pm. In November and January to March, it's open daily 10am to noon and 2 to 4pm. Admission costs 2€ adults, and .50€ children 12 and older and students, free for kids 11 and under.

Also of interest is the **Reichsstadtmuseum** ★, Klosterhof 5 (www.reichsstadtmu-seum.rothenburg.de; ✆ **09861/939-043**). This is Rothenburg's historical collection, housed in a 13th-century Dominican nunnery with well-preserved cloisters. You'll find on display here an enormous tankard that holds 3.5 liters, whose story has echoes all over the city. In 1631, during the Thirty Years' War, the Protestant city of Rothenburg was captured by General Tilly, commander of the armies of the Catholic

The Romantic Road

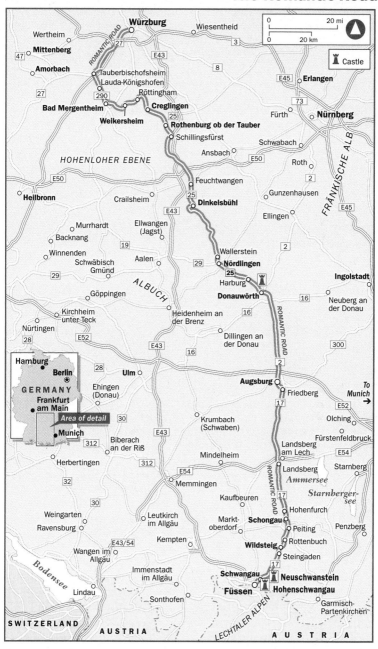

League. He promised to spare the town from destruction if one of the town burghers would drink the huge tankard full of wine in one draft. Burgermeister Nusch accepted the challenge and succeeded, and so saved Rothenburg. There's a festival every spring at Whitsuntide to celebrate this event. Among the exhibits is the 1494 *Rothenburg Passion* series, 12 pictures by Martinus Schwartz, and works by English painter Arthur Wasse (1854–1930), whose pictures managed to capture in a romantic way the many moods of the city. Admission to the museum is 4€ adults, 3.50€ students and children aged 6 to 18. The museum is open April to October daily 10am to 5pm, November to March daily 1 to 4pm.

Kriminal Museum, Burggasse 3 (www.kriminalmuseum.rothenburg.de; ✆ 09861/53-59), is the only one of its kind in Europe. The museum's four floors display 10 centuries of legal history and provide insight into the life, laws, and punishments of medieval days. You'll see chastity belts, shame masks, a shame flute for bad musicians, and a cage for bakers who baked bread too small or too light. It's open daily April to October 9:30am to 6pm; November and January to February 2 to 4pm; and December and March 10am to 4pm. Admission is 4€ adults, 2.80€ students, 2.40€ children 6 and older.

WHERE TO EAT

Baumeisterhaus ★ FRANCONIAN   Right off Marktplatz, the Baumeisterhaus is housed in an antique patrician residence, built in 1596. It has Rothenburg's most beautiful courtyard (which only guests can visit), with colorful murals, serenely draped by vines. Frankly, although the menu is good, the romantic setting is better. The food, for the most part, is rib-sticking fare beloved of Bavarians, including roast suckling pig with potato dumplings, and one of the chef's best dishes, *sauerbraten,* served with *spaetzle.*

Obere Schmiedgasse 3. www.baumeisterhaus-rothenburg.de. ✆ **09861/94-700.** Reservations required for courtyard tables. Main courses 8€–26€. AE, DC, MC, V. Wed–Mon 11am–7:30pm. Closed mid-Nov and mid-Mar.

Ratsstube FRANCONIAN   This restaurant enjoys a position right on the market square, one of the most photographed spots in Germany. It's a bustling center of activity throughout the day—a day that begins when practically every Rothenburger stops by for coffee. Inside, a true tavern atmosphere prevails with hardwood chairs and tables, vaulted ceilings, and pierced copper lanterns. Downstairs you'll find a wine bar offering live music nightly. The a la carte menu of Franconian wines and dishes includes *sauerbraten* and venison, both served with fresh vegetables and potatoes. For dessert, you can order homemade Italian ice cream and espresso. This is a longtime favorite of those who prefer typical Franconian cookery without a lot of fuss and bother.

Marktplatz 6. ✆ **09861/55-11.** Reservations recommended. Main courses 10€–20€. MC, V. Mon–Sat 9am–10pm; Sun 9am–6pm.

Reichs-Küchenmeister FRANCONIAN   The main dishes served here are the type Bavarians have loved for years, including *sauerbraten,* or pork tenderloin; white herring and broiled salmon are also available. The *lebensknodel* (liver dumpling) or goulash soup is perfect for cold days. The chef makes one of the best *Wiener schnitzels* in town. The restaurant is near St. Jakobskirche and has a typical Weinstube decor, along with a garden terrace and a *Konditorei* (cake shop). Service is warm and efficient.

In Hotel Reichs-Küchenmeister (p. 417), Kirchplatz 8. ✆ **09861/9700.** Reservations required. Main courses 8€–26€. AE, DC, MC, V. Daily 7:30am–10pm.

WHERE TO STAY

Eisenhut ★★★   The most celebrated inn on the Romantic Road, Eisenhut is also one of the finest small hotels in Germany. Four medieval patrician houses were joined to make this distinctive inn. Demand for rooms is great, and the staff appears forever overworked. No two rooms are alike—yours may contain hand-carved, monumental pieces or have a 1940s Hollywood touch with a tufted satin headboard. All are enhanced by comforters and pillows piled high on state-of-the-art German beds. Extras include bedside controls and spacious bathrooms outfitted with twin basins. The three-story galleried dining hall is one of the most distinctive in Germany, with a multitiered flagstone terrace on the Tauber.

Herrngasse 3–5, 91541 Rothenburg o.d.T. www.eisenhut-rothenburg.com. © **09861/70-50.** Fax 09861/70-545. 78 units. 100€–225€ double; 250€–350€ suite. AE, DC, MC, V. Parking 9€. Closed Jan 3–Feb 28. **Amenities:** Restaurant; piano bar; room service; Bavarian beer garden. *In room:* TV, minibar, hair dryer, Wi-Fi (14€/day).

Hotel Reichs-Küchenmeister ★   This hotel, one of Rothenburg's oldest structures, near St. Jakobskirche, is comparable with Tilman Riemenschneider. The owners take special care with the guests' comfort. Rooms are nicely furnished with painted wooden furniture. Bathrooms are a bit small, each with a shower stall. An extra 25 rooms are available in the duller annex across the street.

Kirchplatz 8, 91541 Rothenburg o.d.T. www.reichskuechenmeister.com. © **09861/9700.** Fax 09861/970-409. 45 units. 80€–135€ double; 145€–170€ suite for 2; 150€–215€ suite for 5. Rates include buffet breakfast. AE, DC, MC, V. Parking 6.50€ in garage. **Amenities:** Restaurant (see p. 416); wine bar; sauna; Internet (12€/day). *In room:* TV, minibar (in some), hair dryer.

Hotel Tilman Riemenschneider ★   This hotel's half-timbered facade rises directly above one of Rothenburg's busy historic streets. Its rear courtyard, adorned with geraniums, offers a cool and calm oasis from the heavy pedestrian traffic in front. Most rooms are medium size though a few are small. All have well-kept bathrooms.

Georgengasse 11–13, 91541 Rothenburg o.d.T. www.tilman-riemenschneider.de. © **09861/9790.** Fax 09861/29-79. 60 units. 110€–235€ double; 160€–285€ triple. Rates include buffet breakfast. AE, DC, MC, V. Parking 6€. **Amenities:** Restaurant; lounge; exercise room; sauna; room service; Wi-Fi (free). *In room:* TV, hair dryer.

Ringhotel Glocke ◆   South of the town center off Wenggasse, this hotel does not have the charm and style of the premier inns, but it's a good choice for those who want plain, simple, affordable rooms; a family atmosphere; and good food. The small rooms, though a bit institutional, are nonetheless comfortable and good value for pricey Rothenburg. Bathrooms are exceedingly small, each with a shower stall.

Am Plönlein 1, 91541 Rothenburg o.d.T. www.glocke-rothenburg.de. © **09861/95899-0.** Fax 09861/95899-22. 24 units. 909€–1208€ double. Rates include continental breakfast. AE, DC, MC, V. Parking 5€. Closed Dec 23–Jan 7. **Amenities:** Restaurant; nonsmoking rooms. *In room:* TV, Internet (free).

Romantik Hotel Markusturm ★★   This is one of the charming nuggets of Rothenburg, without the facilities and physical plant of the Eisenhut, but a winner in its own right. When this hotel was constructed in 1264, one of Rothenburg's defensive walls was incorporated into the building. Some rooms have four-poster beds. Many guests request room no. 30, a cozy attic retreat. The hotel employs one of the most helpful staff in town.

Rödergasse 1, 91541 Rothenburg o.d.T. www.markusturm.de. ℰ **09861/9-42-80.** Fax 09861/9-42-81-13. 25 units. 125€–190€ double. Rates include buffet breakfast. AE, DC, MC, V. Parking 3€–12€. **Amenities:** Restaurant; room service; babysitting. *In room:* TV, hair dryer, Internet (free).

Nördlingen ★

One of the most irresistible and perfectly preserved medieval towns along the Romantic Road, Nördlingen is still completely encircled by its well-preserved 14th- to 15th-century **city fortifications.** You can walk around the town on the covered parapet, which passes 11 towers and five fortified gates set into the walls.

Things are rather peaceful around Nördlingen today, and the city still employs sentries to sound the message *"So G'sell so"* ("All is well"), as they did in the Middle Ages. However, events around here weren't always so peaceful. The valley sits in a gigantic crater, the Ries. The Ries was once thought to be the crater of an extinct volcano; it is now known that a large meteorite was responsible. It hit the ground at more than 100,000 mph, the impact having the destructive force of 250,000 atomic bombs. Debris was hurled as far as Slovakia, and all plant and animal life within a radius of 160km (100 miles) was destroyed. This momentous event took place some 15 million years ago. Today it is the best-preserved and most scientifically researched **meteorite crater** on earth. The American Apollo 14 and 17 astronauts had their field training in the Ries in 1970.

ESSENTIALS
Getting There
BY TRAIN   Nördlingen lies on the main Nördlingen–Aalen–Stuttgart line, with frequent connections in all directions (trip time: 2 hr. from Stuttgart and Nürnberg, 1 hr. from Augsburg). Go to www.bahn.com or call ℰ **0800/1-50-70-90** for information.

BY BUS   The long-distance bus that operates along the Romantic Road includes Nördlingen; see "Rothenburg ob der Tauber," p. 413.

BY CAR   Take B-25 south from Dinkelsbühl.

Visitor Information
Contact the **Verkehrsamt,** Marktplatz 2 (www.noerdlingen.de; ℰ **09081/84-116**). The office is open Easter to October, Monday to Thursday 9am to 5pm and Friday 9am to 3:30pm. The rest of the year, hours are Monday to Thursday 9am to 6pm, Friday 9am to 4:30pm, and Saturday 9:30am to 1pm.

EXPLORING NÖRDLINGEN
At the center of the circular Altstadt within the walls is **Rübenmarkt.** If you stand in this square on market day, you'll be swept into a world of the past—the country people have preserved many traditional customs and costumes here, which, along with the ancient houses, create a living medieval city. Around the square stand a number of buildings, including the Gothic **Rathaus.** An antiquities collection is displayed in the **Stadtmuseum,** Vordere Gerbergasse 1 (www.stadtmuseum-noerdlingen.de; ℰ **09081/273-8230**), open Tuesday to Sunday 1:30 to 4:30pm; closed Mondays and November through February. Admission is 2.80€ adults and 1.75€ children 18 and under.

The 15th-century Hallenkirche, the **Church of St. George,** on the square's northern side, is the town's most interesting sight and one of its oldest buildings. Plaques and epitaphs commemorating the town's more illustrious 16th- and 17th-century residents decorate the fan-vaulted interior. Although the original Gothic altarpiece by Friedrich Herlin (1470) is now in the Reichsstadt Museum, a portion of it, depicting the Crucifixion, remains in the church. Above the high altar today stands a more elaborate baroque altarpiece. The church's most prominent feature, however, is the 90m (295-ft.) French Gothic tower, called the "Daniel." At night, the town watchman calls out from the steeple, his voice ringing through the streets. The tower is open daily April to October 9am to 8pm. Admission is 2€ adults and 1€ children under 18.

Rieskrater-Museum, Hintere Gerbergasse (www.rieskrater-museum.de; ✆ **09081/273-8220**), documents the impact of the stone meteorite that created the Ries. Examine fossils from Ries Lake deposits and learn about the fascinating evolution of this geological wonder. Hours are Tuesday through Sunday from 10am to noon and from 1:30 to 4:30pm. Admission is 3€ adults; 1.50€ students, seniors, and large groups; free for children under 18. Tours of the crater are possible through the museum.

WHERE TO EAT & STAY

Kaiserhof Hotel Sonne ★　Next to the cathedral and the Rathaus is the Sonne, an inn since 1405. Among its guests have been Frederick III, Maximilian I, Charles V, and, in more recent times, the American Apollo astronauts. Many of the midsize rooms contain hand-painted four-posters to bring out the romantic in you. Others are regular doubles or twins. Goethe may have complained of the lack of comfort he found here, but you'll fare well. Bathrooms are fresh and immaculate.

Marktplatz 3, 86720 Nördlingen. www.kaiserhof-hotel-sonne.de. ✆ **09081/50-67.** Fax 09081/23-999. 18 units. 75€–95€ double Rates include breakfast. AE, DC, MC, V. Free parking. **Amenities:** Restaurant; bar; room service; babysitting. *In room:* TV, minibar, hair dryer, Wi-Fi (free).

Meyer's Keller CONTINENTAL　The conservative, modern decor here seems a suitable setting for the restrained *neue Küche* (new kitchen) of talented chef and owner Joachim Kaiser, adroit with both rustic and refined cuisine. The menu changes according to availability of ingredients and the chef's inspiration; typical selections are likely to include roulade of sea wolf and salmon with baby spinach and wild rice, or—a perfect delight—John Dory with champagne-flavored tomato sauce. The wine list is impressive, with many bottles quite reasonably priced.

Marienhöhe 8. www.meyerskeller.de. ✆ **09081/44-93.** Reservations required. Main courses 20€–38€; fixed-price meals 95€–165€. AE, MC, V. Wed–Sun 11am–2pm; Tues–Sun 6–10pm. Local bus to Marktplatz.

NH Klösterle Nördlingen ★　This is the best place to stay in town. In 1991, this 13th-century former monastery was renovated, a new wing added, and the entire complex transformed into the town's most luxurious hotel. Rated four stars by the government, it offers elevator access and a hardworking, polite staff. Rooms have excellent furnishings, lots of electronic extras, and large bathrooms with tub/shower combos and deluxe toiletries.

Am Klösterle 1, 86720 Nördlingen. www.nh-hotels.com. ✆ **09081/81-870-80.** Fax 09081/870-8100. 97 units. 120€–180€ double; 190€ suite. Rates include breakfast. AE, DC, MC, V. Parking 8€. **Amenities:** Restaurant; bar; exercise room; sauna; room service. *In room:* TV, minibar, hair dryer, Wi-Fi (free).

EN ROUTE TO AUGSBURG

After Nördlingen, B-25 heads south to Augsburg. After a 19km (12-mile) ride you can stop to visit **Schloss Harburg** ★ (it's signposted), one of the best-preserved medieval castles in Germany. It once belonged to the Hohenstaufen emperors and contains treasures collected by the family over the centuries. It is open mid-March to

October, Tuesday to Sunday 9am to 5pm; November, Tuesday to Sunday from 10am to 4pm. Admission is 5€ adults and 3€ children under 18, including a guided tour. For information, visit www.fuerst-wallerstein.de or call ℂ **09080/96860.**

After exploring the castle, continue 11km (6¾ miles) south to the walled town of **Donauwörth** ★, where you can stop to walk through the oldest part of the town, on an island in the river, connected by a wooden bridge. Here the Danube is only a narrow, placid stream. The town's original walls overlook its second river, the Woernitz.

After a brief stopover, continue your southward trek for 48km (30 miles) to Augsburg, the largest city on the Romantic Road.

Augsburg ★★

Augsburg is near the center of the Romantic Road and the gateway to the Alps and the south. Founded 2,000 years ago by the Roman emperor Augustus, for whom it was named, it once was the richest city in Europe. Little remains from the early Roman period. However, the wealth of Renaissance art and architecture is staggering. Over the years, Augsburg has boasted an array of famous native sons, including painters Hans Holbein the Elder and Hans Holbein the Younger, and playwright Bertolt Brecht. It was here in 1518 that Martin Luther was summoned to recant his 95 theses before a papal emissary. Only 15% of the city was left standing after World War II, but there's still much here to intrigue. Today, Augsburg is an important industrial center on the Frankfurt–Salzburg Autobahn, and Bavaria's third-largest city after Munich and Nürnberg.

ESSENTIALS
Getting There
BY TRAIN About 90 Euro and InterCity trains arrive here daily from all major German cities. Go to www.bahn.com or call ℂ **0800/1-50-70-90** for information.

There are 60 trains a day from Munich (trip time: 30–50 min.), and 35 from Frankfurt (3–4½ hr.).

BY BUS Long-distance buses (lines EB190 and 190A, plus line 189) service the Romantic Road. The buses are operated by **Deutsche Touring GmbH** at Am Römerhof in Frankfurt (ℂ **069/790-350** for reservations and information).

Visitor Information
Contact **Tourist-Information,** Schiessgrabenstrasse (www.augsburg-tourismus.de; ℂ **0821/50-20-70**), Monday to Friday 9am to 6pm, Saturday at Rathausplatz from 10am to 1pm; closed Sunday.

Getting Around
The public transportation system in Augsburg consists of 4 tram and 31 bus lines covering the inner city and reaching into the suburbs. Public transportation operates daily 5am to midnight.

EXPLORING AUGSBURG
Church of St. Ulrich and St. Afra ★ CHURCH This is the most attractive church in Augsburg. It was constructed between 1476 and 1500 on the site of a Roman temple. The church stands immediately adjacent to St. Ulrich's Evangelical Lutheran Church, a tribute to the 1555 Peace of Augsburg, which recognized the two denominations, Roman Catholic and Lutheran. Many of the church's furnishings,

including the three altars representing the birth and resurrection of Christ and the baptism of the church by the Holy Spirit, are baroque. In the crypt are the tombs of the Swabian saints, Ulrich and Afra.

Ulrichplatz 19. ℰ **0821/34-55-60.** Free admission. Daily 9am–5pm. Tram: 1.

Dom St. Maria CATHEDRAL   The cathedral of Augsburg has the distinction of containing the oldest stained-glass windows in the world. Those in the south transept, dating from the 12th century, depict Old Testament prophets in a severe but colorful style. They are younger than the cathedral itself, which was begun in 944. You'll find the ruins of the original basilica in the crypt beneath the west chancel. Partially Gothicized in the 14th century, the church stands on the edge of the park, which also fronts the **Episcopal Palace,** where the basic Lutheran creed was presented at the Diet of Augsburg in 1530. The 11th-century bronze doors, leading into the three-aisle nave, are adorned with bas-reliefs of biblical and mythological characters. The cathedral's interior, restored in 1934, contains side altars with altarpieces by Hans Holbein the Elder and Christoph Amberger.

Hoher Weg. ℰ **0821/31-66-353.** Free admission. Mon–Sat 9am–5pm; Sun noon–5pm. Tram: 1.

Rathaus HISTORIC SITE   In 1805 and 1809, Napoleon visited the Rathaus, built by Elias Holl in 1620. Regrettably, it was also visited by an air raid in 1944, leaving a mere shell of the building that had once been a palatial eight-story monument to the glory of the Renaissance. Its celebrated "golden chamber" was left in shambles. Now, after costly restoration, the Rathaus is open to the public.

Am Rathausplatz 2. ℰ **0821/3249-2120.** Admission 2€ adults, 1€ children 7–14. Daily 10am–6pm. Tram: 1.

Schaezlerpalais ART MUSEUM   Facing the Hercules Fountain is the Schaezlerpalais, home to the city's art galleries. Constructed as a 60-room mansion between 1765 and 1770, it was willed to Augsburg after World War II. Most of the paintings are Renaissance and baroque. One of the most famous is Dürer's portrait of Jakob Fugger the Rich, founder of the dynasty that was once powerful enough to influence the elections of the Holy Roman emperors. Other works are by local artists Hans Burgkmair and Hans Holbein the Elder; Rubens, Veronese, and Tiepolo are also represented.

Maximilianstrasse 46. www.kunstsammlungen-museen.augsburg.de. ℰ **0821/324-4102.** Admission 8€ adults, 6€ children 10-18. Wed–Sun 10am–4pm. Tram: 1.

WHERE TO EAT

Die Ecke ★ FRENCH/SWABIAN   Dripping with atmosphere, this place seemingly dates from the Last Supper. Well, almost. At least it was founded in the year Columbus sighted the New World, and its guests have included Hans Holbein the Elder, Wolfgang Amadeus Mozart, and, in more contemporary times, Bertolt Brecht, whose sharp-tongued irreverence tended to irritate diners of more conservative political leanings. The Weinstube ambience belies the skilled cuisine of the chef, which wins us over year after year. Breast of duckling might be preceded by pâté, and the filet of sole in Riesling is deservedly a classic. Venison dishes in season are a specialty—the best in town.

Elias-Holl-Platz 2. www.restaurant-die-ecke.de. ℰ **0821/51-06-00.** Reservations required. Main courses 18€–48€; fixed-price dinner 50€–85€. AE, DC, MC, V. Daily 11am–2pm and 5:30–10pm. Tram: 2.

WHERE TO STAY

Dom Hotel Although it may not have the decorative flair of the more expensive hotels such as Drei Mohren, the low rates and an indoor pool make this one of the most appealing choices in town. The hotel is a half-timbered structure, next to Augsburg's famous cathedral, and was built in the 15th century. Rooms on most floors are medium size and nicely appointed, but the smaller attic accommodations allow you to rest under a beamed ceiling and enjoy a panoramic sweep of the rooftops of the city. Only breakfast is served, but it's a treat in a garden beside the town's medieval fortifications.

Frauentorstrasse 8, 86152 Augsburg. www.domhotel-augsburg.de. ℂ **0821/34-39-30.** Fax 0821/34-39-32-00. 52 units. 89€–135€ double; 115€–185€ suite. Rates include buffet breakfast. AE, DC, MC, V. Free street parking; 6€ garage. Tram: 2. **Amenities:** Indoor pool; sauna. *In room:* TV, minibar, hair dryer, Wi-Fi (free).

Hotel Am Rathaus ✦ Many repeat guests consider this hotel's location just behind the town hall to be its best asset. Built in a three-story contemporary format in 1986, it offers comfortable, midsize rooms but small bathrooms with well-maintained showers. The hotel serves a very generous breakfast buffet. It may be short on style but it's long on value.

Am Hinteren Perlachberg 1, 86150 Augsburg. www.hotel-am-rathaus-augsburg.de. ℂ **0821/34-64-90.** Fax 0821/346-49-99. 32 units. 105€–140€ double. Rates include breakfast. AE, DC, MC, V. Parking 9€. Tram: 1. **Amenities:** Bar. *In room:* TV, minibar, hair dryer, Wi-Fi (free).

Hotel Garni Weinberger ✦ One of the best budget accommodations in the area lies about 3km (1¾ miles) from the center along Augsburgerstrasse in the western sector. Rooms are small but well kept with good beds. The bathrooms are rather cramped with shower stalls, but housekeeping is excellent. The place is well patronized by bargain-hunting Germans.

Bismarckstrasse 55, 86391 Stadtbergen. www.cafe-weinberger.de. ℂ **0821/24-39-10.** Fax 0821/43-88-31. 31 units. From 65€ double. Rates include buffet breakfast. AE, MC, V. Closed last 2 weeks of Aug. Tram: 3. **Amenities:** Cafe. *In room:* No phone.

Steigenberger Drei Mohren ★★ This is one of the premier choices for a stopover along the Romantic Road and one of the top inns if you didn't book into the Eisenhut at Rothenburg. The original hotel, dating from 1723, was renowned in Germany before its destruction in an air raid. In 1956, it was rebuilt in a modern style. Decorators worked hard to create a decor that was both comfortable and inviting, with thick carpets, subdued lighting, and double-glazing at the windows. Rooms vary in size and appointments, however, ranging from some economy specials that are a bit small with narrow twin beds and showers (no tubs) to spacious, luxurious rooms with full shower and tub.

Maximilianstrasse 40, 86150 Augsburg. www.steigenberger.com/en/Augsburg. ℂ **0821/5-03-60.** Fax 0821/15-78-64. 105 units. 120€–200€ double; 225€–650€ suite. AE, DC, MC, V. Parking 16€. Tram: 1. **Amenities:** Restaurant; bar; golf by arrangement; sauna (in suites); room service; babysitting. *In room:* TV, minibar, hair dryer, Wi-Fi (free).

Neuschwanstein ★★★ & Hohenschwangau ★★: The Royal Castles

The 19th century saw a great classical revival in Germany, especially in Bavaria, mainly because of the enthusiasm of Bavarian kings for ancient art forms. Beginning with Ludwig I (1786–1868), who was responsible for many Greek Revival buildings in

Munich, this royal house ran the gamut of ancient architecture in just 3 short decades. It culminated in the remarkable flights of fancy of "Mad" King Ludwig II, who died under mysterious circumstances in 1886. In spite of his rather lonely life and controversial alliances, both personal and political, he was a great patron of the arts.

Although the name "Royal Castles" is limited to Hohenschwangau (built by Ludwig's father, Maximilian II) and Neuschwanstein, the extravagant king was responsible for the creation of two other magnificent castles, Linderhof (near Oberammergau) and Herrenchiemsee (on an island in Chiemsee).

In 1868, after a visit to the great castle of Wartburg, Ludwig wrote to his good friend, composer Richard Wagner: "I have the intention to rebuild the ancient castle ruins of Hohenschwangau in the true style of the ancient German knight's castle." The following year, construction began on the first of a series of fantastic edifices, a series that stopped only with Ludwig's death in 1886, only 5 days after he was deposed because of alleged insanity.

The nearest towns to the castles are **Füssen,** 3km (1¾ miles) away at the very end of the Romantic Road, and **Schwangau.**

ESSENTIALS
Getting There
BY TRAIN   There are frequent trains from Munich (trip time: 2½ hr.) and Augsburg (3 hr.) to Füssen. For information, go to www.bahn.de or call ✆ **01805/99-66-33.** Frequent buses travel to the castles.

BY BUS   Long-distance bus service into Füssen from other parts of the Romantic Road, including Würzburg, Augsburg, and Munich, is provided by the **Deutsche Touring GmbH** bus no. EB189 or EB190A. For information and reservations, go to www.deutsche-touring.com or call ✆ **069/790-268** in Frankfurt. Regional service to villages around Füssen is provided by **RVA Regionalverkehr Allgau GmbH** in Füssen (✆ **08362/939-0505).** Its most important routing, at least for visitors to Füssen, includes about 14 orange, yellow, or white-sided buses that depart every day from Füssen's railway station for the village of Hohenschwangau, site of both Hohenschwangau Palace and Neuschwanstein Palace, a 10-minute ride. The cost of a one-way ticket to the village or to either of the two palaces is 2€. For more information, contact the Füssen tourist office, or Kurverwaltung (see below).

BY CAR   Take B-17 south to Füssen; then head east from Füssen on B-17.

Visitor Information
For information about the castles and the region in general, contact the **Kurverwaltung,** Kaiser-Maximilian-Platz 1, Füssen (✆ **08362/938-50),** open in summer Monday to Friday 8:30am to 6:30pm, Saturday 9am to 2:30pm; winter hours are Monday to Friday 9am to 5pm, Saturday 10am to noon. Information is also available at the Kurverwaltung, Rathaus, Münchenerstrasse 2, Schwangau (www.schwangau. de; ✆ **08362/8-19-80).** Hours vary so call ahead.

VISITING THE ROYAL CASTLES
There are often very long lines in summer, especially in August. With 25,000 people a day visiting, the wait in peak summer months can be as long as 4 or 5 hours for a 20-minute tour. For more information on Neuschwanstein, go to **www. neuschwanstein.de** or call ✆ **08362/9-39-88-0.** For information on Hohenschwangau, visit **www.hohenschwangau.de** or call ✆ **08362/8-11-27.**

Neuschwanstein ★★★

This is the fairy-tale castle of Ludwig II. Construction went on for 17 years, until the king's death, when all work stopped, leaving a part of the interior uncompleted. Ludwig lived here on and off for about 6 months from 1884 to 1886.

The doorway off the left side of the vestibule leads to the king's apartments. The study, like most of the rooms, is decorated with wall paintings showing scenes from the Nordic legends (which inspired Wagner's operas). The theme of the study is the Tannhäuser saga, painted by J. Aigner. The curtains and chair coverings are in hand-embroidered silk, designed with the Bavarian coat of arms. From the vestibule, you enter the throne room through the doorway at the opposite end. This hall, designed in Byzantine style by J. Hofmann, was never completed. The floor, a mosaic design, depicts the animals of the world. The columns in the main hall are the deep copper red of porphyry.

The king's bedroom is the most richly carved and decorated in the entire castle—it took 4½ years to complete. Aside from the mural showing the legend of Tristan and Isolde, the walls are decorated with panels carved to look like Gothic windows. In the center is a large wooden pillar completely encircled with gilded brass sconces. The ornate bed is on a raised platform with an elaborately carved canopy.

The fourth floor of the castle is almost entirely given over to the **Singer's Hall,** the pride of Ludwig II and all of Bavaria. Modeled after the hall at Wartburg, where the legendary song contest of Tannhäuser supposedly took place, this hall is decorated with marble columns and elaborately painted designs interspersed with frescoes depicting the life of Parsifal.

The castle is open year-round, and in September, visitors have the additional treat of hearing Wagnerian concerts and other music in the Singer's Hall. *Note:* At press time, the western and northern facades of the castle were under scaffolding but due to be finished by early 2013. For information and reservations, contact the tourist office in Schwangau, **Verkehrsamt,** at the Rathaus (✆ **08362/93-85-23**). The castle, which is seen by guided tour, is open daily April to September 9am to 6pm, October to March 10am to 4pm. Admission is 12€ adults, 11€ students and seniors over 65, free for children 18 and under. Combination ticket with Hohenschwangau is 23€ adults, 21€ students and seniors over 65. For ticket information for either castle, go to www.neuschwanstein.de or call ✆ **08362/930-830.**

Reaching Neuschwanstein involves a steep 1km (⅔-mile) climb from the parking lot of Hohenschwangau Castle—about a 25-minute walk for the energetic, an eternity for anybody else. To cut down on the climb, you can take a bus to Marienbrücke, a bridge that crosses over the Pollat Gorge at a height of 93m (305 ft.). From that vantage you, like Ludwig, can stand and meditate on the glories of the castle and its panoramic surroundings. If you want to photograph the castle, don't wait until you reach the top, where you'll be too close. It costs 2€ for the bus ride up to the bridge or 1€ if you'd like to take the bus back down the hill. From the Marienbrücke Bridge it's a 10-minute walk to Neuschwanstein over a very steep footpath that is not easy to negotiate for anyone who has trouble walking up or down precipitous hills.

The most colorful way to reach Neuschwanstein is by horse-drawn carriage, costing 6€ per person for the ascent, 3€ for the descent. However, some readers have objected to the rides, complaining that too many people are crowded in.

Hohenschwangau ★★

Not as glamorous or spectacular as Neuschwanstein, the neo-Gothic Hohenschwangau Castle nevertheless has a much richer history. The original structure dates from the 12th-century knights of Schwangau. When the knights faded away, the castle began to do so, too, helped along by the Napoleonic Wars. When Ludwig II's father, Crown Prince Maximilian (later Maximilian II), saw the castle in 1832, he purchased it and 4 years later had completely restored it. Ludwig II spent the first 17 years of his life here and later received Richard Wagner in its chambers, although Wagner never visited Neuschwanstein on the hill above.

The rooms of Hohenschwangau are styled and furnished in a much heavier Gothic mode than those in Ludwig's castle and are typical of the halls of medieval knights' castles. Also unlike Neuschwanstein, this castle has a comfortable look about it, as if it actually were a home, not just a museum. The small chapel, once a reception hall, still hosts Sunday Mass. The suits of armor and the Gothic arches set the stage. Among the most attractive chambers is the **Hall of the Swan Knight,** named for the wall paintings that tell the saga of Lohengrin.

Hohenschwangau is open April 1 to September from 8am to 5:30pm daily, off-season from 9am to 3:30pm daily. Admission is 12€ adults, 11€ students and seniors over 65, free for children 18 and under. Combination ticket with Hohenschwangau is 23€ adults, 21€ students and seniors over 65. For ticket information for either castle, go to www.hohenschwangau.de or call ☏ **08362/930-830.**

WHERE TO EAT
Fischerhütte SEAFOOD In Hopfen am See, at the edge of the lake within sight of dramatic mountain scenery 5km (3 miles) northwest of Füssen, lie four old-fashioned dining rooms, plus a terrace in summer. As the name "Fisherman's Cottage" suggests, the establishment specializes in an array of international fish dishes: half an Alaskan salmon (for two); a garlicky version of French bouillabaisse; fresh alpine trout, pan-fried or with aromatic herbs in the style of Provence; North Atlantic lobster; and grilled halibut. A few meat dishes are also offered, as well as tempting desserts. The food is well prepared and top rate.

Uferstrasse 16, Hopfen am See. www.fischerhuette-hopfen.de. ☏ **08362/91-97-0.** Reservations recommended. Main courses 14€–46€. AE, DC, MC, V. Daily 10am–10:30pm.

Zum Schwanen SWABIAN/BAVARIAN This small, old-fashioned restaurant serves a conservative yet flavor-filled blend of Swabian and Bavarian specialties. Good-tasting and hearty specialties include homemade sausage, roast pork, lamb, and venison. Expect robust flavors and a crowd of cheery diners who don't believe in low-cal packaged dinners.

Brotmarkt 4, Füssen. ☏ **08362/61-74.** Reservations required. Main courses 6€–18€. MC, V. Tues–Sun 11:30am–2:30pm; Tues–Sat 5:30–9pm. Closed Nov plus 3 weeks in Mar and Sun in winter.

WHERE TO STAY
Hotel Müller Hohenschwangau As if the yellow walls, green shutters, and gabled alpine detailing of this hospitable inn weren't incentive enough, its location near the foundation of Neuschwanstein Castle makes it even more alluring. Midsize rooms are inviting and have a bit of Bavarian charm, each with a good bed. The shower-only bathrooms are spotless. Nature lovers usually enjoy hiking the short distance to nearby Hohenschwangau Castle. All rooms are nonsmoking.

Alpseestrasse 16, 87645 Hohenschwangau. www.hotel-mueller.de. ☏ **08362/8-19-90.** Fax 08362/81-99-13. 41 units. 98€–220€ double; 210€–270€ suite. Rates include buffet breakfast. AE, DC, MC, V. Free parking. Closed Jan–Feb. **Amenities:** 5 restaurants; bar; room service. *In room:* TV, minibar (in some), hair dryer, Wi-Fi (free).

Schlosshotel Lisl and Jägerhaus ★★   This graciously styled villa and its annex in a historic building across the street are among the better addresses in the area. Most rooms have a view of one or both castles. If you're assigned to the annex, never fear, as its rooms are just as fine as—or in some cases, better than—those in the main building. Some of the bathrooms are larger than some hotel rooms, and come complete with a large tub and shower. Both for charm and price, this one is a winner.

Neuschwansteinstrasse 1–3, 87645 Hohenschwangau. www.hohenschwangau.de. ✆ **08362/88-70.** Fax 08362/81-107. 47 units. 85€–115€ double; 95€–125€ suite. AE, DC, MC, V. Free parking. Closed Dec 21–26. **Amenities:** 2 restaurants; bar; Wi-Fi (lobby only). *In room:* TV, minibar.

GREECE

by Peter Kerasiotis and Sherry Marker

Today's Greece is a sophisticated, modern country going through its worst post-World War II crisis. Greece spent much of 2011 and the first months of 2012 with its head hung low as the country plunged into a severe economic depression—the result of harsh austerity measures that get harsher every 2 to 3 months. Despite the protests, strikes, and troubles that have left the country shaken, Greece remains as spectacular, beautiful, and majestic as ever. The mood may have darkened but hope for a better tomorrow, as so often in Greece, is in the air and the dazzling glories of its fabled antiquity along with 21st-century pleasures and conveniences are all around.

In addition to all that is new, the "glory that was Greece" continues to lure visitors, to attractions such as Olympia, where the games began; Delphi, with the magnificent temple of Apollo; Mycenae, where Agamemnon met his bloody death when he returned home from Troy; Epidaurus, with its astonishingly well-preserved ancient theater; and, of course, the best-known symbol of Greece: the Acropolis. But myths and monuments are only one aspect of the country's allure: Greece is also the quintessential vacationland of glorious beaches and towering mountain ranges. After sightseeing, you can laze the day away on a perfect beach—and then dance the night away in a cafe at the foot of the Acropolis or on one of the breathtakingly beautiful "isles of Greece." And no matter where you go, you can still experience the Greek *philoxenia*—the generous hospitality offered to a stranger that leaves visitors determined to return as soon as possible.

ATHENS ★★★

Athens is the city that Greeks love to hate, complaining that it's too expensive, too polluted, and too crowded. More than five million people—some 40% of Greece's population—live in Athens, its port of Piraeus, and the surrounding suburbs. This is a city in constant flux with an irresistible energy even in the midst of savage government austerity measures and an uncertain future. Battered and scarred yet resilient, Athens continues the urban renewal that began with the lead up to the 2004 Olympics, determined not to allow the country's current massive financial problems to darken its residents' souls any more than it already has. Forever the city of a thousand contradictions, Athens is one of the few ancient cities in the world where the cutting edge, the hip, and the modern coexist harmoniously with the classical, and historic.

The 3 miles of pedestrianized streets and walkways that make up Athens's Archaeological Promenade link most major archaeological sites including Hadrian's Gate, the Acropolis, the Ancient Agora, and Kerameikos cemetery. Frequent exhibits are held along the walkways, and new cafes, restaurants, and galleries have sprung up nearby. Following the lead of Psirri and Thissio—two once down-at-heel ancient neighborhoods that are now among the hippest downtown destinations—Gazi and Kerameikos have also risen from the ashes, going from gritty to urban chic. Meanwhile the city's coastline with its beaches, open-air bars/clubs, and limitless shopping and dining options remains as seductive as ever and seldom explored by most tourists.

Still, visitors momentarily overwhelmed by Athens's round-the-clock hustle and bustle (which sometimes includes motorcycles barreling along walkways) may be forgiven for sometimes wondering if Athens, even with all its recent updates and fabled glories, is the ideal holiday destination. Don't despair. You'll almost certainly develop your own love–hate relationship with this seductive and highly addictive city, snarling at the traffic, gasping in wonder at the Acropolis, fuming at the taxi driver who tries to overcharge you, and marveling at the stranger who realizes that you're lost and walks several blocks out of his way to get you where you're going.

Essentials

GETTING THERE

BY PLANE   **Athens International Airport Eleftherios Venizelos** (www.aia.gr; ℗ 210/353-0000) is located 27km (17 miles) northeast of downtown Athens at Sparta. Allow at least an hour for the journey from the airport to downtown (and vice versa). The airport has plenty to keep you busy, including a small museum with ruins found during the airport's construction, rotating art exhibits, and an Info-Point with excellent city brochures and guides, plus digital (iPads and flatscreen) tours of the city.

Line 3 of the Metro (www.amel.gr; 8€ one-way, 14€ round-trip—valid for 48 hr.; one-way fare for two people is 15€ and 20€ for three) is more convenient and faster than any other way of getting from the airport to downtown or vice versa. Metro **line 3** serves the **city center** (where you can switch to the other lines at either Monastiraki or Syntagma stations) from the airport. The trip takes roughly 40 minutes and trains run every half-hour from 6:30am to 11:30pm. From the city to the airport (leaving from Syntagma and Monastiraki), trains run from 5:50am to 10:50pm. To get to Piraeus, switch at Monastiraki station to line 1; total travel time is about 1 hour. The airport ticket is valid for all forms of public transportation for 90 minutes; if you're approaching the deadline and are still in transit, simply revalidate your ticket by having it punched again. The Metro runs from 5:30am to midnight Sunday through Thursday and until 2am on Friday and Saturday.

Airport Taxi Savvy

If you decide to take a taxi, ask an airline official or a policeman what the fare should be, and let the taxi driver know you've been told the official rate before you begin your journey. If you're taking a taxi to the airport, try to have the desk clerk at your hotel order it for you well in advance of your departure.

Greece

Tourist information, currency exchange, a post office, baggage storage (left luggage), and car rentals are available at the Arrivals level of the Main Terminal. ATMs, telephones, toilets, and luggage carts (1€) are available at the baggage-claim area. There are also several free phones from which you can call for a porter. *Note:* Porters' fees are highly negotiable.

The Athens International Airport's website (www.aia.gr) has live streaming of all flight information—departures, arrivals, times, and gates.

BY TAXI   The City of Athens has created a **flat rate** from the airport to downtown Athens (Omonia Sq. and the Plaka/Makrigianni districts). Once you are in the taxi, make sure the meter is set on the correct tariff (tariff 1 is charged 5am–midnight; tariff 2 midnight–5am). For Omonoia, the price is 32€ (tariff 1) and 42€ (tariff 2); each rate **includes all additional charges** such as tolls and luggage. If you're heading for the Plaka/Makrigianni districts (at Hadrian's Gate), the rate is daytime 35€ and nighttime 50€. Depending on traffic, the cab ride can take under 30 minutes or well over an hour—something to remember when you return to the airport. For more information check out the **Athens Taxi Info** site at **www.athenstaxi.info**. If there's a problem with the taxi driver, you may threaten to call the police (ⓒ **100**).

Athens

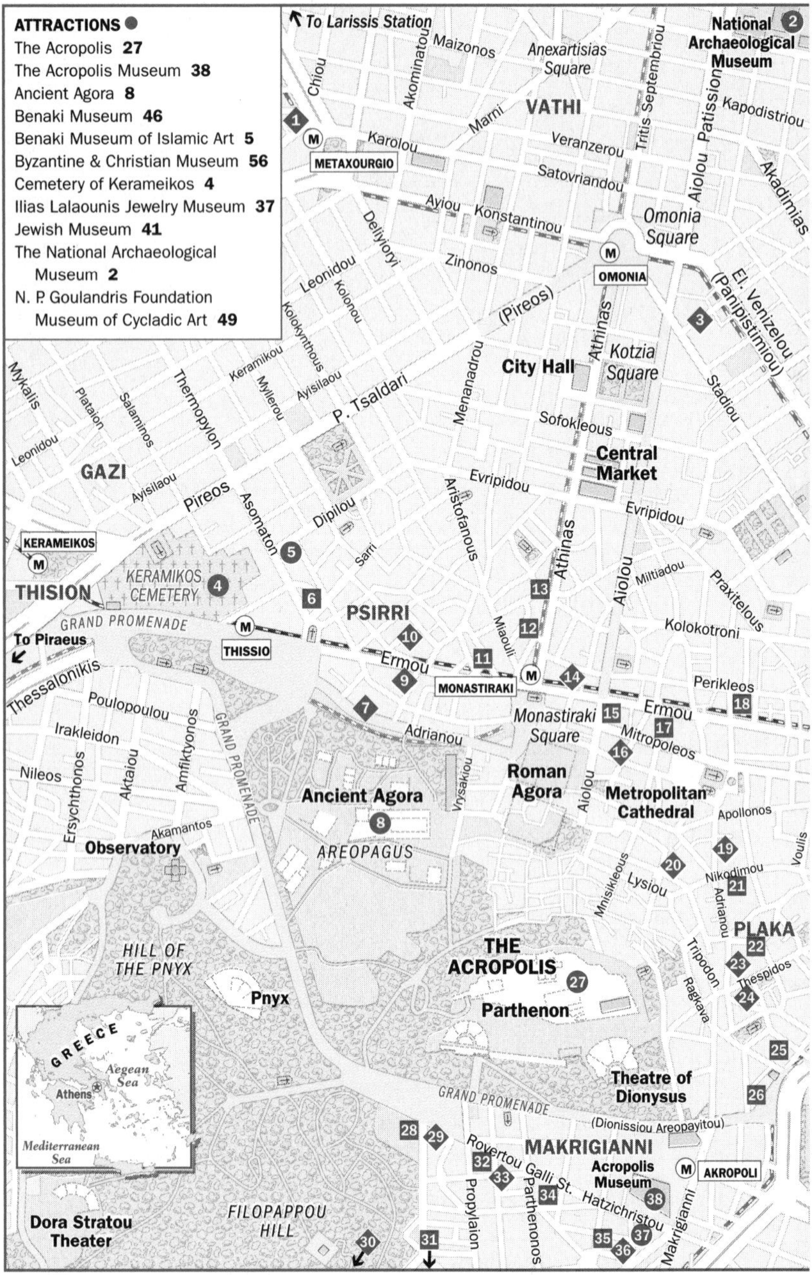

ATTRACTIONS ●
The Acropolis **27**
The Acropolis Museum **38**
Ancient Agora **8**
Benaki Museum **46**
Benaki Museum of Islamic Art **5**
Byzantine & Christian Museum **56**
Cemetery of Kerameikos **4**
Ilias Lalaounis Jewelry Museum **37**
Jewish Museum **41**
The National Archaeological
  Museum **2**
N. P. Goulandris Foundation
  Museum of Cycladic Art **49**

To Larissis Station

National Archaeological Museum **2**

VATHI

METAXOURGIO

Omonia Square

OMONIA

City Hall

Kotzia Square

Central Market

GAZI

KERAMEIKOS

THISION

KERAMIKOS CEMETERY

GRAND PROMENADE

To Piraeus

THISSIO

PSIRRI

MONASTIRAKI

Ermou

Monastiraki Square

Roman Agora

Metropolitan Cathedral

Ancient Agora

AREOPAGUS

Observatory

HILL OF THE PNYX

Pnyx

PLAKA

THE ACROPOLIS

Parthenon

Theatre of Dionysus

GRAND PROMENADE

(Dionissiou Areopayitou)

MAKRIGIANNI

Acropolis Museum

AKROPOLI

Dora Stratou Theater

FILOPAPPOU HILL

GREECE
Aegean Sea
Athens
Mediterranean Sea

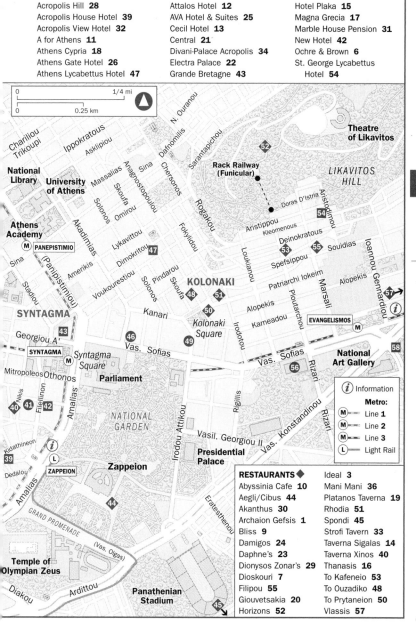

HOTELS ■
Acropolis Hill **28**
Acropolis House Hotel **39**
Acropolis View Hotel **32**
A for Athens **11**
Athens Cypria **18**
Athens Gate Hotel **26**
Athens Lycabettus Hotel **47**
Athens Studios **35**
Attalos Hotel **12**
AVA Hotel & Suites **25**
Cecil Hotel **13**
Central **21**
Divani-Palace Acropolis **34**
Electra Palace **22**
Grande Bretagne **43**
Hilton Athens **58**
Hotel Plaka **15**
Magna Grecia **17**
Marble House Pension **31**
New Hotel **42**
Ochre & Brown **6**
St. George Lycabettus
Hotel **54**

Theatre of Likavitos

Chariliou Trikoupi
Ippokratous
Asklipiou

National Library
University of Athens

Dafnomilis
N. Ouranou
Sarantapichou

Rack Railway (Funicular)

LIKAVITOS HILL

Massalias
Anagnostopoulou
Sina
Skoufa
Chersonos
Rogakou

Athens Academy

Akadimias
Solonos
Omirou
Lykavittou
Dimokritou
Fokylidou

Doras D'Istria

54

Aristippou
Kleomenous
Deinokratous

55 Souidias

(M) **PANEPISTIMIO**

Amerikis
Voukourestiou
Solonos
Pindarou
Skoura

47

48 **51**

KOLONAKI

Loukianou
Spefsippou

Patriarchi Iokeim

Marsali

Alopekis
Ioannou Gennadiou

Sina
Stadiou

SYNTAGMA

Kanari

50
49

Kolonaki Square

Irodotou
Alopekis
Karneadou

Ploutarchou

EVANGELISMOS
(M)

57
(i)

Georgiou A'
43
SYNTAGMA (M)
Syntagma Square
Mitropoleos Othonos

Vas. Sofias

Vas. Sofias

56

Rizari

National Art Gallery

58

Parliament

40 **41** **42**

Nikis
Filellinon
Amalias

NATIONAL GARDEN

Irodou Attikou

Vasil. Georgiou II

Rigillis

Vas. Konstandinou

(i) **Information**

Metro:
(M) ▭▭ Line 1
(M) ▭▭ Line 2
(M) ▭▭ Line 3
(L) ▭▭ Light Rail

Kidathineon
(i)
39
Dedalou
(L) **ZAPPEION**
Amalias

Zappeion

Presidential Palace

GRAND PROMENADE

(Vas. Olgas)

44

Eratesthenou

Temple of Olympian Zeus

Diakou
Ardittou

Panathenian Stadium

45

RESTAURANTS ◆
Abyssinia Cafe **10**
Aegli/Cibus **44**
Akanthos **30**
Archaion Gefsis **1**
Bliss **9**
Damigos **24**
Daphne's **23**
Dionysos Zonar's **29**
Dioskouri **7**
Filipou **55**
Giouvetsakia **20**
Horizons **52**
Ideal **3**
Mani Mani **36**
Platanos Taverna **19**
Rhodia **51**
Spondi **45**
Strofi Tavern **33**
Taverna Sigalas **14**
Taverna Xinos **40**
Thanasis **16**
To Kafeneio **53**
To Ouzadiko **48**
To Prytaneion **50**
Vlassis **57**

9

GREECE | Athens

431

BY SUBURBAN RAILROAD The suburban railroad (www.trainose.gr) runs to and from the Larissa station, Doukissis Plakentias, with a connection to Metro line 1 at Nerantziotissa (at the Athens Mall in Marousi near the Athens Olympic Complex) and from the airport to the port of Piraeus. Trains to the airport run from 4:30am to midnight, while the trains from the airport to the city run from 5am to 1:20am. The suburban railroad has the same pricing as the Metro; the only difference is that the return ticket is valid for a month. **This is the best option to get from the airport to the port of Piraeus.** Total travel time: 60 minutes.

Arriving in Greece

If you plan to travel by air in Greece or elsewhere in Europe, keep in mind that the luggage allowance for most flights within Greece and Europe is 20 kilos (44 lb.). This is almost certainly less than you would have been allowed if you have flown to Greece from the U.S. or Canada.

BY BUS Buses (**www.oasa.gr**) are far slower than the Metro but they run 24 hours, and can reach areas the Metro does not, such as the coast. If you want to take a bus from the airport into central Athens, be prepared for what may be a long wait and a slow journey.

Several bus lines travel to and from the airport to destinations throughout the city. All buses depart from the designated area outside the Arrivals Hall of the main terminal building (doors 4 and 5). Bus service from the airport to Syntagma Square (X95) or to Piraeus (X96) costs 5€. The X95 runs every 10 minutes from 7am–10pm and every half-hour from 10pm–7am. The X96 runs every 20 minutes from 7am–10pm and every 40 minutes from 10pm–7am.

BY CAR Athens is not an easy city to drive in, and if you're unfamiliar with the streets, it can be downright horrific and best avoided. If you still choose to drive into Athens, the efficient highway Attica Odos will get you there. Numerous exits serve the most important areas of the city.

If you plan to rent a car and head north or south, avoiding the city altogether, it's easier to do so thanks to the new **National Highway.** If you're headed for Peloponnese, simply follow the signs for Elefsina. If you're headed toward northern Greece (including the city of Thessaloniki), get off at the Lamia exit.

BY TRAIN Central Athens has two train stations, both about 1.5km (1 mile) northwest of Omonia Square. Trains from the west, including Eurail connections via Patra, arrive at the **Stathmos Peloponnissou** (Peloponnese Station; ☏ **210/513-1601**). Trains from the north arrive three blocks north of (and on the opposite side of the tracks from) the Peloponnese Station at the **Stathmos Larissis** (Larissa Station; ☏ **210/529-8837**). If you are making connections from one station to the other, allow 15 minutes for the walk. Both stations have currency-exchange offices usually open daily from 8am to 9:15pm, and luggage-storage offices charging 5€ per bag per day, open daily from 6:30am to 9:30pm.

Trains **from the south and west,** including Eurail (www.eurail.com) connections via Patras, arrive at the **Peloponnese station** (Stathmos Peloponnisou; ☏ **210/513-1601**), about a mile northwest of Omonia Square on Sidirodromeon. Trains **from the north** arrive at **Larissa station** (Stathmos Larissis; ☏ **210/529-8837**), just across the tracks from the Peloponnese station on Deligianni. The Larissa station has both an exchange office (daily 8am–9:15pm) and luggage storage (daily 6:30am–9pm).

To get to the train stations, you can take the **Metro** to Larissa (line 2), close to both stations. A taxi from the center of town should cost about 10€. The Metro runs from Omonia, Syntagma, and Koukaki to the Larissa Metro station, which is near the train stations. The most central place to catch the Metro is the stop in front of the Parliament building on Syntagma Square.

You can purchase train tickets just before your journey at the train station (running the risk that all seats may be sold); at the Omonia Square ticket office, 1 Karolou (© 210/524-0647); at 17 Filellinon, off Syntagma Square (© 210/323-6747); or from most travel agents. Information (in theory in English) on timetables is available by dialing © 145 or 147.

BY BOAT   **Piraeus,** the main harbor of Athens's main seaport, 11km (7 miles) southwest of central Athens, is a 15-minute Metro ride from Monastiraki, Omonia, and Thissio Metro stations. The subway runs from about 5am to midnight and costs 1.40€. The far slower bus no. 040 runs from Piraeus to central Athens (with a stop at Filellinon, off Syntagma Sq.) every 15 minutes between 5am and 1am and hourly from 1am to 5am for 1.20€. To get to Athens International Airport, you can take the X96 bus (5€), the Suburban Railroad (8 €), or the Metro—which will require a change at Monastiraki station to line 3 (8€).

You may prefer to take a **taxi** to avoid what can be a long hike from your boat to the bus stop or subway terminal. Be prepared for serious bargaining. The normal fare on the meter from Piraeus to Syntagma should be about 15€ to 20€, but many drivers offer a flat fare, which can be as much as 30€. Pay it if you're desperate; or walk to a nearby street, hail another taxi, and insist that the meter be turned on.

If you arrive at Piraeus by hydrofoil (Flying Dolphin), you'll probably arrive at **Zea Marina** harbor, about a dozen blocks south across the peninsula from the main harbor. Even our Greek friends admit that getting a taxi from Zea Marina into Athens can involve a wait of an hour or more—and that drivers usually drive hard (and exorbitant) bargains. To avoid both the wait and big fare, you can walk up the hill from the hydrofoil station and catch bus no. 905 for 1.20€, which connects Zea to the Piraeus Metro (subway) station, where you can complete your journey into Athens. You must buy a ticket at the small stand near the bus stop or at a newsstand before boarding the bus. **Warning:** If you arrive late at night, you may not be able to do this, as both the news and ticket stands may be closed.

>
> **The Attica Zoological Park**
>
> If you find yourself with 2 or more hours' layover at Athens International Airport, consider taking a taxi (12€) to the nearby **Attica Zoological Park ★** (www.atticapark.com) in Sparta. It's open daily from 9am to sunset. Admission is 15€ adults, 11€ children.

VISITOR INFORMATION

TOURIST OFFICES   The **Greek National Tourism Organization** (**EOT** or **GNTO**) is at 7 Tsochas St., Ambelokipi (www.visitgreece.gr; © 210/870-0000; Metro: Ambelokipi). The office is officially open Monday through Friday, 8am to 3pm, and is closed on weekends. The GNTO information desk office is at 18–20 Dionissiou Aeropagitou St. (© 210/331-0392; Mon–Fri 9am–7pm; Sat–Sun 10am–4pm; Metro: Acropolis). An information desk (© 210/345-0445) and an Info-Point (www.atedco.gr; © 210/325-3123) are also located at the airport. Two

Info-Points are in the city: In the Makrigianni district on the corner of Amalias Avenue and Dionisiou Aeropagitou Street (near the Acropolis metro station and the Acropolis Museum) and in the port of Piraeus. Both have excellent brochures and city maps, plus digital tours of the city. All Info-Points operate daily from 9am–9pm. Information about Athens, free city maps, transportation schedules, hotel lists, and booklets on the regions of Greece are available at the office in Greek, English, French, and German.

Available 24 hours a day, the **tourist police** (*☏* **210/171**) speak English as well as other languages, and will help you with problems or emergencies.

WEBSITES   Helpful sites for Greece include the Ministry of Culture information site for archaeological sites, monuments, and museums (**www.culture.gr**), and the Greek National Tourist Office site (**www.gnto.gr** or **www.visitgreece.gr**). The Parliament also has its own website, **www.parliament.gr**. Two websites with a wealth of information and daily updates are **www.athensinfoguide.com** and **www. breathtakingathens.com**. Other helpful sites include **www.athensnews.gr** (*The Athens News,* Greece's English-language newspaper); **www.eKathimerini.com** (an insert of translations from the Greek press sold with the *International Herald Tribune*); **www.dilos.com** (travel information, including discounted hotel prices); **www.gtp.gr** (information on ferry service); **www.greekislands.gr** (information on the islands); **www.greektravel.com** (a helpful site run by American Matt Barrett); and **www.ancientgreece.com** and **www.perseus.tufts.edu** (excellent sources on ancient Greece).

CITY LAYOUT

Think of central Athens as an almost perfect equilateral triangle, with its points at **Syntagma (Constitution) Square, Omonia (Harmony) Square,** and **Monastiraki (Little Monastery) Square,** near the **Acropolis.** Most Greeks consider Syntagma Square the city center, where the House of Parliament stands beside the National Gardens. Omonia and Syntagma squares are connected by the parallel **Stadiou Street** and **Panepistimiou Street,** also called **Eleftheriou Venizelou.** West from Syntagma Square, ancient **Ermou Street** and broader **Mitropoleos Street** lead slightly downhill to **Monastiraki Square.** Monastiraki is flanked by the flea market, the **Ancient Agora (Market)** below the Acropolis, and the **Plaka,** the oldest neighborhood, with a scattering of antiquities and many street names from antiquity, including its main drag, pedestrianized **Adrianou Street,** named for the emperor Hadrian. Off Pireos avenue, the increasingly chic former industrial wasteland of **Gazi** is giving the longtime posh haven of **Kolonaki,** on the slopes of Mt. Lykabettus, a run for its money as the place to see and be seen. Still low-key by day, the nighttime scene in Gazi's wall-to-wall art galleries, cafes, and restaurants makes Kolonaki seem sedate.

In general, finding your way around Athens is not too difficult, except in the Plaka, at the foot of the Acropolis. This labyrinth of narrow, winding streets can challenge even the best navigators. Don't panic: The area is small enough that you can't go far astray, and its side streets, with small houses and neighborhood churches, are so charming that you won't mind being lost. One excellent map may help: the Greek Archaeological Service's *Historical Map of Athens,* which includes the Plaka and the city center and shows the major archaeological sites. The map costs about 5€ and is sold at many bookstores, museums, ancient sites, and newspaper kiosks.

Neighborhoods in Brief

Athens is a big city that's a collection of many different neighborhoods, each with its own distinctive flair. Here are some of the neighborhoods that await you. If you have the time, why not just stroll, get lost, and be pleasantly surprised when you discover that you're on a street where almost all of the shops sell only icons or sugared almonds (an essential gift for guests at weddings and baptisms), or where there's a little park with a bench where you can sit and watch the world go by.

CENTRAL ATHENS

Commercial Center The commercial center (a bureaucratic name no one uses, and that appears on no map) lies between **Omonia, Syntagma,** and **Monastiraki** squares, and includes the **Plaka** and **Psirri** districts. The commercial center, or historic center as most Greeks call it, has been the most visibly affected area by the crisis; The large illegal migrant population and the riots have left many marble squares and sidewalks damaged. Regrettably several historic buildings have also been damaged by riot fires and/or graffiti. The Onassis Foundation has a grand plan ("Rethink Athens") to upgrade the historic center by pedestrianizing and redesigning the majority of the area including Panepistimou Ave and Omonia Square and restoring the recent damages. The ambitious project is expected to be completed in 2015.

Omonia Square Once a grand *plateia* (square), Omonia today is in its worst shape ever and attracts less desirable elements at night—so it's best avoided after 9pm. Athinas Street (or better yet, pedestrianized Aiolou—also spelled Eolou—with its charming cafes, lounges, and shops) will lead you away from the grunge and into Monastiraki. For a look at grand old Athens of the 19th century, check out **Kotzia Square** with its grand neoclassical buildings including the **Athens City Hall** designed in 1874 and the **National Bank of Greece Cultural Center.**

Athinas Street This street links Omonia and Monastiraki squares, and has Athens's **Central Market.** Here you can browse fish and meat halls, and buy vegetables and fruit from all over Greece.

Syntagma (Constitution) Square The heart of Athens—Syntagma Square is the focal point of the city's political and civic life.

This is also where you'll find the major banks, travel agencies, and several fine hotels, including the **Grande Bretagne,** the grande dame of Greek hotels. The handsome neoclassical building at the head of the square is the **Greek Parliament** building, formerly the Royal Palace where you'll see the **Changing of the Guard** in front of the **Tomb of the Unknown Soldier.** Next to the Parliament, you will find two of Athens's most beautiful parks: **The National Garden** and the **Zappeion Gardens.** Tucked away off Stadiou Street, across the street from the **National Historical Museum,** there is a cobblestone oasis known as **Karitsi Square** with some of downtown's funkiest eateries, galleries, and multipurpose cafe/bars spilling over onto Kolokotroni Street.

Plaka Right below the Acropolis, Plaka is the oldest neighborhood in the city. A maze of narrow, medieval streets twist their way through ancient sites, Byzantine churches, offbeat museums, and 19th-century homes. You may lose yourself in the labyrinthine streets in this characterful and atmospheric neighborhood. Maybe you will find the tiny village within a village of Anafiotika, a Cycladic town at the base of the Acropolis.

Monastiraki This neighborhood fringes the **Agora** and the **Roman Forum,** and the flea markets are open every day but are usually best—and most crowded—on Sunday. Many tavernas, cafes, and shops line the streets.

Psirri Between Athinas and Ermou, Psirri was once derelict and forgotten; now it's home to trendy restaurants, bars, cafes, and tavernas with live music, clubs, and galleries side by side with some still-remaining workshops and dilapidated buildings—this area comes alive in the late afternoon, even though its outer pockets remain a bit gritty.

Gazi Once an industrial wasteland, Gazi is one of the hottest after-dark destinations in the entire city. Today the old foundry's smoke-stacks are illuminated in neon red, and the streets are filled with the edgiest and hippest nightlife in the city—arts spaces, fusion restaurants, galleries, theaters, bars, cafes, and a gay "village." Here, you will find the **Technopolis center,** an arts complex for shows, festivals, exhibitions, and the small **Maria Callas Museum.** Nearby you will also find two excellent museums: the **Foundation of the Hellenic World** and the **Beanaki Annex.**

Thissio With its restored neoclassical buildings, uninterrupted Acropolis views, the temple of Hephaestos, a wonderful open-air cinema, and some of the city's best places to hang out, Thissio is the place to be. It's charming and old-fashioned, modern and happening, with hip hangouts on the ultratrendy Iraklidou Street like **Stavlos**—the former royal stables converted into an all-day cafe/bar/restaurant, near to the **Herakleidon Museum**. Be sure to check out the grand **National Observatory,** a beautiful neoclassical mansion from the late 1800s.

Kolonaki This chic neighborhood tucked beneath the slopes of **Lycabettus Mountain** has long been the favorite address of the socialites. The streets (many pedestrianized) are packed with boutiques, designer houses, art galleries, restaurants, and hip cafes. Take your time soaking up all the urban chic you can before making your way to the top of Lycabettus Mountain for an extraordinary sunset with Athens laid under your feet like a sparkling map.

Exarchia Kolonaki gradually merges to the northwest with the university area, which is spread loosely between the 19th-century university buildings (the **Neoclassical University Trilogy**) on Panepistimiou and the **Polytechnic** and near the excellent **National Archaeological Museum,** is **Exarchia.** This bohemian neighborhood is a lively area to spend a few hours in, with excellent tavernas around a buzzing square, bar-lined streets, plus the city's finest rock clubs and live music venues. If you have the time, explore **Streffi Hill,** which offers incredible views of the city

and the Acropolis all the way to the Saronic Gulf. Across busy **Leoforos Alexandras** is central Athens's largest park, **Pedion Areos.**

Koukaki & Makrigianni Koukaki is one of central Athens's most desirable neighborhoods. The district lies at the base of **Lofos Filopappou (Filopappos Hill),** also known as the Lofos Mousseon (Hill of the Muses). A number of pleasant paths lead from streets at the base of Filopappos up through its pine-clad slopes, some ending at the **Dora Stratou Theater** or the observatory. In 2013, the **Museum of Modern Art** plans to open its doors here. **Makrigianni,** the upscale neighborhood just north of Koukaki, at the southern base of the Acropolis, has a new lease of life with the arrival of the **Archaeological Promenade,** the **Acropolis Museum,** the Metro, the pedestrianization of Makrigianni Street and its close proximity to the Plaka. You will also find several smaller museums, many wonderfully restored mansions, and several good restaurants.

Pangrati & Mets Surrounding the reconstructed Athens Stadium known to the Greeks as **Kallimarmaro (Beautiful Marble),** where the first modern Olympics were held in 1896, you will find two residential areas with excellent dining and nightlife options. Mets is a taste of old Athens, full of pre-World War II houses with tiled roofs and courtyards. To the south of the stadium is **Pangrati,** a residential area with lots of restaurants (the excellent **Spondi** for starters) and many charming traditional tavernas.

The Embassy District Leoforos Vas. Sofias (Queen Sophia Blvd.) runs from Syntagma Square toward Athens's fashionable northeastern suburb of Kifissia. The Embassy District is also known as the **Museum Mile** for the excellent museums found here just downhill from Kolonaki: The **Benaki Museum,** the **Goulandris Museum of Cycladic Art,** the **Byzantine Museum,** the **National War Museum,** and the **National Gallery.**

THE NORTHEAST SUBURBS

Going north on **Leoforos Kifissias,** you will pass by **Ambelokipi** (with its many first-rate bar/restaurants such as **Vlassis, Baraonda,** and **Balthazar**), popular **Panormou Street,** and **Neo Psihiko** (with many first-rate cafes, lounges, tea houses, and restaurants), and you will find yourself in **Marousi** and **Kifissia. Marousi** is home to Santiago Calatrava's **Athens Olympics Sports Complex,** the elegant, soaring modernist complex that stole the show during the 2004 Olympics. The last stop on Metro line 1 is elegant **Kifissia.** Here you'll find 19th-century neoclassical mansions, outrageous 21st-century ones, graceful tree-lined streets, excellent shopping options, attractive parks, two outstanding museums (the **Goulandris Museum of Natural History** and the **Gaia Center**), trendy hotels, hip lounges and bars, and an open-air cinema dating back to 1919.

PIRAEUS (PIREAS)

The main port of Athens, Piraeus is where you catch a boat to the islands from the **main harbor (Mega Limani** or **Great Harbor),** or from **Zea Marina,** also called Pasalimani. **Mikrolimano (Little Harbor),** also called Turkolimano (Turkish Harbor), is a picturesque harbor featuring a bustling marina with cafes and eateries. Zea Marina also has plenty of cafes and a bustling shopping center.

THE SOUTHERN SUBURBS—COASTAL ATHENS

The coastal avenue **Leoforos Poseidon** is where Athenians love to hang out and party during the hot summer months. Pleasant beaches, boardwalks, marinas, open-air bars and clubs, along with excellent shopping and dining options make the coast irresistible. Head to the yacht marina of **Flisvos** (at tram stop Trocadero) for strolling, wining and dining by the surf (there's also a lovely open-air cinema here), or to the **Balux Café House Project** (www.baluxcafe.com) in trendy **Glyfada.** Even if you're on a tight schedule try to at least have dinner or drinks in the city's most romantic venue **Island** (www.islandclubrestaurant.gr).

GETTING AROUND

ON FOOT   Since most of what you'll want to see and do in Athens is in the city center, it's easy to do most of your sightseeing on foot. Fortunately, Athens has created pedestrian zones in sections of the **Commercial Triangle** (the area bounded by Omonia, Syntagma, and Monastiraki squares), the **Plaka,** and **Kolonaki,** making strolling, window-shopping, and sightseeing infinitely more pleasant. **Dionissiou Areopagitou,** at the southern base of the Acropolis, was also pedestrianized, with links to walkways past the Ancient Agora, Thissio, and Kerameikos. Nonetheless, visitors should keep in mind that here, as in many busy cities, a red traffic light or stop sign is no guarantee that cars will stop for pedestrians.

BY METRO   The Metro (www.amel.gr) runs from 5:30am to midnight Sunday through Thursday; on Friday and Saturday, trains run until 2am. All stations are wheelchair accessible. Stop at the Syntagma station or go to the GNTO for a system map. A single ticket costs 1.40€; a day pass costs 4€. Make sure you have your ticket punched in the machines as you enter the waiting platform and hold on to it until your final destination or you'll risk a fine. Metro and bus tickets are interchangeable, except for bus E22 that heads to the coast and costs an additional 1.60€.

Even if you do not use the Metro to get around Athens, you may want to take it from Omonia, Monastiraki, or Thissio to Piraeus to catch a boat to the islands. (Don't miss the spectacular view of the Acropolis as the subway goes aboveground by the Agora.) The harbor in Piraeus is a 5-minute walk from the Metro station. Take the footbridge from the Metro and you're there.

BY BUS & TROLLEY BUS   Although you can get almost everywhere you want in central Athens and the suburbs by bus or trolley, it can be confusing to figure out which bus to take. This is especially true now, when many bus routes change as new

Metro stations open. Even if you know which bus to take, you may have to wait a long time until the bus appears—usually stuffed with passengers. Check out the **Athens Urban Transport Organization** (www.oasa.gr; © **185**) for directions, timetables, route details, and maps.

Tickets cost 1.20€ each (or 1.40€ to be combined with the Metro, trolley, and tram for up to 90 min.) and can be bought from *periptera* (kiosks) scattered throughout the city. The tickets are sold individually or in packets of 10 and are good for rides anywhere on the system. **Be certain to validate** yours when you get on. *Tip:* Hold on to your ticket. Uniformed and plainclothes inspectors periodically check tickets and can levy a fine of 30€ to 60€ on the spot.

If you're heading out of town and take a blue A-line bus to transfer to another blue A-line bus, your ticket will still be valid for the transfer. In central Athens, minibus nos. 60 and 150 serve the commercial area free of charge. Buses headed to farther points of Attica leave from Mavromateon on the western edge of Pedion tou Areos Park, at the western end of Leoforos Alexandras.

> ### Cultured Commuting
>
> Allow extra time when you catch the Metro in central Athens: Three stations—**Syntagma Square, Monastiraki,** and **Acropolis**—handsomely display finds from the subway excavations in what amount to Athens's newest small museums. For more info, visit **www. amel.gr**.

BY TRAM Athens's tram (www.tramsa.gr) connects downtown to the city's coast. Though it may not be the fastest means of transport, it takes a scenic route once it hits the coast and is handy for those wishing to visit the city's beaches and the coastline's attractions and nightlife. The tram runs on a 24-hour schedule Friday and Saturday and 5am to midnight Sunday through Thursday; tickets are 1.20€ (1.40€ if you wish to continue your journey with the Metro, bus, or trolley bus for up to 90 min.) and must be validated at the platform or inside the tram. Trams are comfortable and air-conditioned. A ride from Syntagma Square to the current last stop in seafront Voula takes a little over an hour.

BY TAXI It's rumored that there are more than 15,000 taxis in Athens, but finding an empty one is not easy. Especially if you have travel connections to make, it's a good idea to reserve a radio taxi (see below). Fortunately, taxis are inexpensive, and most drivers are honest men trying to wrest a living by maneuvering through the city's endemic gridlock. However, some drivers, notably those working Piraeus, the airports, and popular tourist destinations, can't resist trying to overcharge obvious foreigners.

When you get into a taxi during the day and up until midnight, check the **meter.** Make sure it is **turned on** and set to 1 (the daytime rate) rather than 2 (the night rate). The meter will register 1€. The meter should be set on 2 (double fare) only between midnight and 5am *or* if you take a taxi outside the city limits; if you plan to do this, negotiate a flat rate in advance. The "1" meter rate is .32€ per kilometer. There's a surcharge of 1€ for service from a port or from a rail or bus station. Luggage costs .32€ per 10 kg (22 lb.). Taxis to and from the airport, heading downtown, have a flat rate of 35€ (5am–midnight), and 50€ (midnight–5am). Don't be surprised if the driver picks up other passengers en route; he will work out everyone's share of the fare. The minimum fare is 2.80€. These prices will almost certainly be higher by the time you visit Greece.

If you suspect that you have been overcharged, ask for help at your hotel or destination before you pay the fare.

There are about 15 **radio taxi** companies in Athens; their phone numbers change often, so check the daily listing in "Your Guide" in the *Athens News*. Some established companies include **Athina** (✆ 210/921-7942), **Express** (✆ 210/993-4812), **Parthenon** (✆ 210/532-3300), and **Piraeus** (✆ 210/418-2333). If you're trying to make travel connections or are traveling during rush hour, a radio taxi is well worth the 2.80€ surcharge. Your hotel can call for you and make sure that the driver knows where you want to go. For more information, log on to www.athenstaxi.info.

BY CAR　In Athens, a car is far more trouble than convenience. The traffic is heavy, and finding a parking place is extremely difficult. Keep in mind that if you pick up your rental car at the airport, you may pay a hefty (sometimes daily) surcharge. Picking up a car in town involves struggling through Athens's traffic to get out of town.

If you decide to rent a car in Athens, you'll find many rental agencies south of Syntagma Square and in Athens International Airport. Some of the better agencies include **Avis,** 46–48 Leoforos Amalias (www.avis.gr; ✆ 210/687-9600); **Budget Rent a Car,** 8 Leoforos Syngrou (www.budget-athens.gr; ✆ 210/898-1444); **Eurodollar Rent a Car,** 29 Leoforos Syngrou (✆ 210/922-9672 or 210/923-0548); **Hellascars,** 148 Leoforos Syngrou (✆ 210/923-5353 to -5359); **Hertz,** 12 Leoforos Syngrou (www.hertz.gr; ✆ 210/922-0102 to -0104) and 71 Leoforos Vas. Sofias (✆ 210/724-7071 or 210/722-7391); and **Thrifty Hellas Rent a Car,** 24 Leoforos Syngrou (www.thriftygreece.gr; ✆ 210/922-1211 to -1213). Prices for rentals range from 50€ to 100€ per day. *Warning:* Be sure to take full insurance and ask if the price you are quoted includes everything—taxes, drop-off fee, gasoline charges, and other fees.

[FastFACTS] ATHENS

ATMs　Automated teller machines are increasingly common at banks throughout Athens. The National Bank of Greece operates a 24-hour ATM in Syntagma Square.

Banks　Banks are generally open Monday through Thursday, 8am to 2pm and Friday 8am to 2:30pm. In summer, the exchange office at the **National Bank of Greece** in Syntagma Square (✆ 210/334-0015) is open Monday through Thursday from 3:30 to 6:30pm, Friday from 3 to 6:30pm, Saturday from 9am to 3pm, and Sunday from 9am to 1pm. Other centrally located banks include **Citibank,** in Syntagma Square (✆ 210/322-7471); **Bank of America,** 39 Panepistimiou (✆ 210/324-4975); and **Barclays Bank,** 15 Voukourestiou (✆ 210/364-4311). All banks are closed on the long list of Greek holidays. Most banks exchange currency at the rate set daily by the government. This rate is often more favorable than that offered at unofficial exchange bureaus. Still, a little comparison shopping is worthwhile. Some hotels offer better-than-official rates, though only for cash, as do some stores, usually when you are making a big purchase.

Business Hours　Even Greeks get confused by their complicated, changeable business hours. In winter, shops are generally open Monday and Wednesday from 9am to 5pm; Tuesday, Thursday, and Friday from 10am to 7pm; and Saturday from 8:30am to 3:30pm. In summer, shops are generally open Monday, Wednesday, and Saturday from 8am to 3pm; and Tuesday, Thursday, and Friday from 8am to 2pm and 5:30 to 10pm. Most stores in central Athens, though, remain open all day.

Department stores and supermarkets are open 8am to 8pm Monday to Friday and 8am to 6pm Saturday.

Dentists & Doctors

Embassies (see below) may have lists of dentists and doctors. If you need an English-speaking doctor or dentist, try **SOS Doctor** (✆ **1016** or **210/361-7089**). Some English-speaking physicians advertise in the daily *Athens News*.

Embassies & Consulates

Australia, Level 6, Thon Building, corner Kiffisias & Alexandras, Ambelokipi (www.greece.embassy. gov.au; ✆ **210/870-4000**); **Canada,** 4 Ioannou Yenadiou (www.greece.gc.ca; ✆ **210/727-3400** or **210/725-4011**); **Ireland,** 7 Vas. Konstantinou (✆ **210/723-2771**); **New Zealand,** 76 Kifissias Ave, Ambelokipi (✆ **210/692-4136**); **South Africa,** 60 Kifissias, Maroussi (✆ **210/680-6645**); **United Kingdom,** 1 Ploutarchou (www.bhcc.gr; ✆ **210/723-6211**); **United States,** 91 Leoforos Vas. Sofias (www.athens.usembassy.gov; ✆ **210/721-2951** or **210/729-4301** for emergencies). Be sure to phone ahead before you go to any embassy; most keep limited hours and are usually closed on their own holidays as well as Greek ones. For a list of all embassies, log on to www.embassyfinder.com.

Emergencies

In an emergency, dial ✆ **100** for the **police** and ✆ **171** for the **tourist police.** Dial

✆ **199** to report a **fire** and ✆ **166** for an **ambulance** and the **hospital.** Athens has a **24-hour** line for foreigners, the **Visitor Emergency Assistance** at ✆ **112** in English and French. If you need an English-speaking doctor or dentist, try **SOS Doctor** (✆ **1016** or **210/361-7089**). There are two medical hot lines for foreigners: ✆ **210/721-2951** (day) and **210/729-4301** (night) for U.S. citizens; and ✆ **210/723-6211** (day) and **210/723-7727** (night) for British citizens. The English-language *Athens News* (published Fri) lists some American- and British-trained doctors and hospitals offering emergency services. Most of the larger hotels can call a doctor for you in an emergency.

KAT, the emergency hospital in Kifissia (✆ **210/801-4411** to **4419**) and **Asklepion Voulas,** the emergency hospital in Voula (✆ **210/895-3416** to **3418**) have emergency rooms open 24 hours a day. **Evangelismos,** a centrally located hospital below the Kolonaki district on 9 Vassilis Sophias (✆ **210/722-0101**), usually has English-speaking staff on duty. If you need medical attention fast, don't waste time trying to call these hospitals: Just go. They will see you as soon as possible.

In addition, each major hospital takes its turn each day being on emergency duty. A recorded message in Greek at ✆ **210/106** tells

which hospital is open for emergency services and gives the telephone number but with severe cuts in healthcare spending, many hospitals are expected to have severely reduced staff.

Internet Access

Internet cafes, where you can check and send e-mail, have proliferated in Athens almost as fast as cellphones. Most midrange to top-end hotels have at least an "Internet corner," but for a current list of Athenian cybercafes, check out **www. breathtakingathens.com**. Also, several **Wi-Fi hot spots** can be found across the city, such as Syntagma Square, Kotzia Square, Flisvos marina, and the Thission; the airport and several cafes also offer free Wi-Fi.

Lost & Found

If you lose something on the street or on public transportation, it is probably gone for good. If you wish, contact the police's **Lost and Found,** 173 Leoforos Alexandras (✆ **210/642-1616**), open Monday through Saturday from 9am to 3pm. For losses on the Metro, there is an office in Syntagma station (www.amel.gr; ✆ **210/327-9630;** Mon–Fri 7am–7pm, Sat 8am–4pm). Lost passports and other documents may be returned by the police to the appropriate embassy, so check there as well. It's an excellent idea to travel with photocopies of your important documents, including passport, prescriptions, tickets, phone numbers, and addresses.

Luggage Storage & Lockers If you're coming back to stay, many hotels will store excess luggage while you travel. There are storage facilities at Athens International Airport, at the Metro stations in Piraeus and Monastiraki, and at the train stations.

Newspapers & Magazines The *Athens News* is published every Friday in English, with a weekend section listing events of interest; it's available at kiosks everywhere. Most central Athens newsstands also carry the *International Herald Tribune*, which has an English-language insert of highlights from the Greek daily *Kathimerini*, and *USA Today*. Local weeklies include the *Hellenic Times,* with entertainment listings, and *Athinorama* (in Greek), which has comprehensive listings of events. *Athens Best Of* (monthly) and *Now in Athens* (published every other month) have information on restaurants, shopping, museums, and galleries, and are available free in major hotels and sometimes from the National Tourism offices.

Pharmacies *Pharmakia,* identified by green crosses, are scattered throughout Athens. Hours are usually Monday through Friday, 8am to 2pm. In the evenings and on weekends, most are closed, but each posts a notice listing the location of pharmacies that are open or will open in an emergency. Newspapers such as the *Athens News* list

the pharmacies open outside regular hours.

Police In an **emergency,** dial ✆ **100.** For help dealing with a troublesome taxi driver, hotel staff, restaurant staff, or shop owner, stand your ground and call the **tourist police** at ✆ **171.**

Post Offices The main post offices in central Athens are at 100 Eolou, south of Omonia Square; and in Syntagma Square, at the corner of 60 Mitropoleos. They are open Monday to Friday 7:30am to 8pm, Saturday 7:30am to 2pm, and Sunday 9am to 1pm.

Safety Athens is among the safest capitals in Europe, and there are few reports of violent crimes. **Pickpocketing,** however, is on the rise—due to the city's high unemployment. Unfortunately, it is a good idea to be wary of gypsy children and super-friendly strangers. When in the Metro, always place your valuables in your front pockets. We advise travelers to avoid the side streets of Omonia and Piraeus at night. As always, leave your passport and valuables in a security box at the hotel. Carry a photocopy of your passport, not the original.

Taxes A VAT (value-added tax) of between 4% and 18% is added onto everything you buy. Some shops will attempt to cheat you by quoting one price and then, when you hand over your credit card, they will add on a hefty VAT charge. Be wary. In theory, if

you are not a member of a Common Market/E.U. country, you can get a refund on major purchases at the Athens airport when you leave Greece. In practice, you would have to arrive at the airport a day before your flight to get to the head of the line, do the paperwork, get a refund, and catch your flight.

Telephones Many of the city's public phones now accept only phone cards, available at the airport, newsstands, and the **Telecommunications Organization of Greece (OTE)** offices in several denominations, currently starting at 3€. Most OTE offices and **Germanos** stores (including the one in the airport) now sell cellphones and phone cards at reasonable prices; if you are in Greece for a month, you may find this a good option. Some kiosks still have metered phones; you pay what the meter records. North Americans can phone home directly by contacting **AT&T** (✆ **00/ 800-1311), MCI** (✆ **00/ 800-1211),** or **Sprint** (✆ **00/800-1411**); calls can be collect or billed to your phone charge card. For reverse (collect) calls, dial **161.** All visitors can call home (beware of hotel surcharges if you decide to call from your hotel room) by first dialing the **International Direct Dial Code, 00,** followed by the country's code (U.S.: 1, UK: 0044, Canada: 011, Ireland: 353, Australia: 61, New Zealand: 64), the area code, and then the number. You can send a telegram or fax from OTE offices. The OTE office at 15 Stadiou, near Syntagma, is open 24 hours a day. The Omonia Square OTE, at 50 Athinas, and the Victoria Square OTE, at 85 Patission, are open Monday through Friday 7am to 9pm, Saturday 9am to 3pm, and Sunday 9am to 2pm. Outside Athens, most OTEs are closed on weekends.

Tipping   Athenian restaurants include a service charge in the bill, but many visitors add a 10% tip. Most Greeks do not give a percentage tip to taxi drivers, but often round up the fare; for example, you would round up a fare of 2.80€ to 3€.

Toilets   Public restrooms are in the underground station beneath Omonia and Syntagma squares and beneath Kolonaki Square, but you'll probably prefer a hotel or restaurant restroom. (Toilet paper is often not available, so carry tissue with you. Do not flush paper down the commode; use the receptacle provided.)

Exploring Athens
THE TREASURES OF ANTIQUITY

The Acropolis ★★★ RUINS   At press time, The **Temple of Nike** was scaffold-free and reassembled, having just completed an extensive 9-year renovation; the temple's **frieze,** however, is in the Acropolis Museum. Work continues on the west side of the Parthenon and a minor section of the Propylaia. Restorations are expected to be completed—at the earliest—by 2020.

If you do climb up the Acropolis—the heights above the city—you'll realize why people seem to have lived here as long ago as 5000 B.C. The sheer sides of the Acropolis make it a superb natural defense, just the place to avoid enemies and be able to see invaders coming across the sea or the plains of Attica. And, of course, it helped that in antiquity there was a spring here, ensuring a steady supply of water.

In classical times, when Athens's population had grown to around 250,000, people lived on the slopes below the Acropolis, which had become the city's most important religious center. Athens's civic and business center, the Agora, and its cultural center, with several theaters and concert halls, bracketed the Acropolis; when you peer over the sides of the Acropolis at the houses in the Plaka and the remains of the ancient **Agora** and the **Theater of Dionysos,** you'll see the layout of the ancient city. Syntagma and Omonia squares, the heart of today's Athens, were well out of the ancient city center.

Even the Acropolis's height couldn't protect it from the Persian invasion of 480 B.C., when most of its monuments were burned and destroyed. You may notice some immense column drums built into the Acropolis's walls. When the great Athenian statesman Pericles ordered the monuments rebuilt, he had the drums from the

 Ticket Prices & Free Museum & Site Guides

Keep in mind that many discounts are valid only for Common Market citizens. The currently priced 12€ ticket that admits you to the Acropolis, Ancient Agora, Theater of Dionysos, Karameikos Cemetery, Roman Forum, Tower of the Winds, and Temple of Olympian Zeus is one of the best buys in town (most individual admissions are 4€–6€). The ticket is usually available at the Acropolis. Also, ask for the handy free information brochure available at most sites and museums.

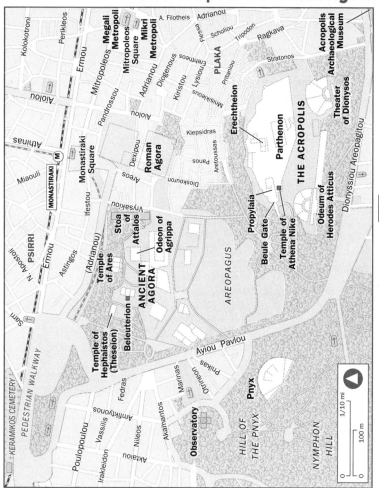

destroyed Parthenon built into the walls lest Athenians forget what had happened—and so they would remember that they had rebuilt what they had lost. Pericles's rebuilding program began about 448 B.C.; the new Parthenon was dedicated 10 years later, but works on other monuments continued for a century.

The **Parthenon ★★★**—dedicated to Athena Parthenos (the Virgin), patron goddess of Athens—was the most important religious monument, but there were shrines to many other gods and goddesses on the Acropolis's broad summit. As you climb up, you pass first through the **Beule Gate,** built by the Romans and now known by the name of the French archaeologist who discovered it in 1852. Next you'll notice the beautifully proportioned **Temple of Athena Nike (Athena of Victory) ★**, which is perched above the monumental 5th-century-B.C. entryway of **Propylaia ★**. Off to the left of the Parthenon is the **Erechtheion ★★**, which the Athenians honored as the tomb of Erechtheus, a legendary king of Athens. A hole in the ceiling and floor of the northern porch indicates the spot where Poseidon's trident struck to make a spring gush forth during his contest with Athena to be the city's chief deity. Athena countered with an olive tree; the tree planted beside the Erechtheion reminds visitors of her victory. Give yourself a little time to enjoy the delicate carving on the Erechtheion, and be sure to see the original **caryatids** (the monumental female figures who served as columns on the Erechtheion's porch) in the Acropolis Museum.

However charmed you are by these elegant little temples, you're probably still heading resolutely toward the **Parthenon,** and you may be disappointed to realize that visitors are not allowed inside, both to protect the monument and to allow any ongoing restoration work to proceed safely. If you find this frustrating, keep in mind that in antiquity only priests and honored visitors were allowed in to see the monumental 11m (36-ft.) statue of Athena designed by the great Phidias, who supervised Pericles's building program. Nothing of the huge gold-and-ivory statue remains, but there's a small Roman copy in the National Archaeological Museum—and renditions on souvenirs ranging from T-shirts to ouzo bottles.

The Parthenon's entire roof and much of the interior were blown to smithereens in 1687, when a party of Venetians attempted to take the Acropolis from the Turks. A shell fired from nearby Mouseion Hill struck the Parthenon—where the Turks were storing gunpowder and munitions—and caused appalling damage to the building and its sculptures. Most of the remaining sculptures were carted off to London by Lord Elgin in the first decade of the 19th century. Those surviving sculptures—known to much of the world as the **Elgin Marbles,** but known here as the **Parthenon Marbles**—are on display in the British Museum.

The Parthenon originally had sculpture in both its pediments, as well as a frieze running around the entire temple. Alternating **triglyphs** (panels with three incised grooves) and **metopes** (sculptured panels) made up the frieze. The message of most of this sculpture was the triumph of knowledge and civilization over the forces of darkness and barbarism. An interior frieze showed scenes from the Panathenaic Festival each August, when citizens walked in procession through the streets, bringing a new *peplos* (tunic) for the statue of Athena. Only a few fragments of any of the sculptures remain in place.

Dionyssiou Areopagitou. ✆ **210/321-0219.** Admission 12€ adults, free on Sun. This ticket, valid for 1 week, includes admission to the Acropolis, Ancient Agora, Theater of Dionysos, Karameikos Cemetery, Roman Forum, Tower of the Winds, and Temple of Olympian Zeus. The Acropolis is usually open summer daily 8am–7pm; winter daily 8:30am–3pm. Metro: Acropolis.

Ancient Agora ★★ MUSEUM/RUINS The Agora was Athens's commercial and civic center, with buildings used for a wide range of political, educational, philosophical, theatrical, and athletic purposes—which may be why what remains seems such a jumble. This is a nice place to wander and enjoy the views up toward the Acropolis, taking in the herb and flower gardens planted around the 5th-century-B.C. **Theseion (Temple of Hephaistos);** peek into the heavily restored 11th-century church of **Ayii Apostoli (Holy Apostles);** and get a sense of what an entire ancient civic building looked like from the 2nd-century-B.C. **Stoa of Attalos,** which was reconstructed in the 1950s.

The Stoa houses a museum; the top floor was reopened in 2012 after a long renovation and displays treasures that have remained, until recently, in vaults for hundreds of years. There are finds here from 5,000 years of Athenian history, including sculpture and pottery, as well as a voting machine and a child's potty seat, all with labels in English. The museum closes 15 minutes before the site. You'll want to spend at least 2 hours here.

Below the Acropolis on the edge of Monastiraki (entrance on Adrianou, near Ayiou Philippou Sq., east of Monastiraki Sq. and on Ay. Apostoli, the road leading down into Plaka from the Acropolis). www.agathe.gr. ✆ 210/321-0185. Admission (includes museum) 6€, or free with purchase of 12€ Acropolis ticket. The Agora is usually open summer daily 8am–7pm; winter daily 8:30am–3pm. Metro: Monastiraki.

Cemetery of Kerameikos ★ CEMETERY This ancient cemetery, where **Pericles** gave his famous funeral oration during the Peloponnesian War, is a short walk from the Ancient Agora and not far from the presumed site of **Plato's Academy.** There are a number of well-preserved funerary monuments and the remains of the colossal **Dipylon Gate,** the main entrance to the ancient city of Athens. In 2002, the well-preserved marble figure of a *kouros* (youth) was found in excavations here, a hint of what treasures remain to be found. For now, you can see the substantial remains of the 5th-century-B.C. fortifications known as the "Long Walls" that ran from Athens to Piraeus. The Kerameikos is seldom crowded, which makes it a pleasant spot to sit and read.

148 Ermou. ✆ 210/346-3553. Admission 4€, or free with purchase of 12€ Acropolis ticket. Summer Tues–Sun 8:30am–6pm; winter Tues–Sun 8:30am–3pm. Walk west from Monastiraki Sq. on Ermou past Thisio Metro station; cemetery is on the right. Metro: Monastiraki or Thisio.

The Top Museums

The National Archaeological Museum ★★★ MUSEUM Often listed as one of the world's finest museums, this is a huge and enormously popular museum, featuring collections of objects from the Neolithic to the Roman eras. Don't miss the stunning gold masks, cups, dishes, and jewelry unearthed from the site of Mycenae by Heinrich Schliemann in 1876; the elegant marble Cycladic figurines (ca. 2000 B.C.); and the famous marble and bronze statues. The museum's **Egyptian Art Collection** is considered one of the world's finest. The enormous collection of Greek vases on the second floor is dazzling—and daunting! The restored 3500-B.C. frescoes from the site of Akrotiri on the island of Santorini (Thira) also on view on the second floor are worth noting. You'll probably want to spend a minimum of 3 hours here—and return a few times to cover everything there is to see.

44 Patission (Patission appears as OKTOVRIOU/OCTOBER on some street signs). www.namuseum.gr; ✆ 210/821-7717. Admission 6€, or 12€ with Acropolis entrance. Mon 12:30–5pm; Tues–Fri 8am–6pm; Sat–Sun and holidays 8:30am–3pm. Sometimes open until 7pm in summer. Metro: Omonia or Viktoria.

The Acropolis Museum ★★★ MUSEUM   This 21,000-sq.-m (226,000-sq.-ft.) glass-and-concrete museum is a stunning—some would say disconcertingly so—addition to Athens. The museum was built not merely to house the more than 4,000 treasures on display (10 times more than in the previous Acropolis museum) but to make a statement: Send the Parthenon marbles (aka the Elgin Marbles) in the British Museum back to Athens!

Planning Ahead

When you plan your sightseeing, keep in mind that three top museums—the Goulandris, the Benaki, and the Byzantine and Christian—are clustered near each other on or just off Vasilissis Sofias Avenue. If three major museums in one excursion seems like a lot, remember that the Benaki and Goulandris both have excellent cafes.

The museum's first two floors display an astonishing number of artifacts, statues, sculptures, and free-standing objects that used to adorn the sacred rock. The museum's top floor is the all-important Parthenon Gallery. The glass-walled gallery is rotated 23 degrees off its axis to mirror the layout of the Parthenon, which is splendidly visible throughout the gallery. On display within the gallery is all that remains in Greece of the original Parthenon sculptures and frieze—36 of the 115 original panels, alongside stark white plaster casts of the originals that are in London. The contrast is meant to bring home all that is missing, in the hopes that someday the Parthenon marbles will be reunited. Beginning July 2012, visitors will be able to explore the basement and stroll through the remarkable findings thus far excavated—an ancient Athenian neighborhood and an early Christian settlement.

15 Dionisiou Aeropagitou. www.theacropolismuseum.gr. ⓒ **210/900-0901.** Admission 5€. Tues–Sun 8am–8pm; Fri 8am–10pm. Metro: Akropolis.

Benaki Museum ★★★ MUSEUM   This stunning private collection includes treasures from the Neolithic era to the 20th century. The folk-art collection (including magnificent costumes and icons) is superb, as are the two rooms which house pieces from 18th-century northern Greek mansions, ancient Greek bronzes, gold cups, Fayum portraits, and rare early Christian textiles. A new wing doubles the exhibition space of the original 20th-century neoclassical town house that belonged to the wealthy Benaki family. Dine with a spectacular view over Athens at the excellent rooftop cafe, which offers a buffet supper (40€) Thursday evenings, when the museum remains open until midnight.

1 Koumbari (at Leoforos Vasilissis Sofias, Kolonaki, 5 blocks east of Syntagma Sq.). www.benaki.gr. ⓒ **210/367-1000.** Admission 6€, free on Thurs. Mon, Wed, and Fri–Sat 9am–5pm; Thurs 9am–midnight; Sun 9am–3pm. Metro: Syntagma or Evangelismos.

Benaki Museum of Islamic Art ★★ MUSEUM   The world-class collection, in a 19th-century neoclassical building complex, displays Islamic art, ceramics, carpets, woodcarvings, and other objects, plus two reconstructed living rooms from the Ottoman times and a 17th-century reception room from a Cairo mansion. Objects on display date from the 14th century to the present. Labels are in Greek and English.

22 Agion Asomaton and Dipylou, Psirri. www.benaki.gr. ⓒ **210/367-1000.** Admission 5€. Tues and Thurs–Sun 9am–3pm; Wed 9am–9pm. Metro: Thissio.

Byzantine and Christian Museum ★★ MUSEUM   As its name makes clear, this museum, with two large new galleries flanking a 19th-century Florentine-style villa, is devoted to the art and history of the Byzantine era (roughly 4th–15th century A.D.). If you love icons (paintings, usually of saints, often on wood) or want to find out about them, this is the place to go. Exhibits include selections from Greece's most important collection of icons and religious art—along with sculptures, altars, mosaics, religious vestments, Bibles, and a small-scale reconstruction of an early Christian basilica. Allow at least an hour for your visit—two if a special exhibit is featured.

22 Vasilissis Sofias Ave. www.byzantinemuseum.gr. ℂ **210/723-1570** or 210/721-1027. Admission 4€. Tues–Sun 8:30am–3pm. Metro: Evangelismos.

Ilias Lalaounis Jewelry Museum ★★ MUSEUM   The 3,000 pieces on display here are so spectacular that even those who don't usually care much for jewelry will enjoy this small, sparkling museum, founded by one of Greece's most successful designers of the craft. Jewelry displayed includes pieces inspired by ancient Byzantine and Cycladic designs, as well as by flora and fauna. The museum also has frequent special exhibits, a cafe, a seductive boutique, and a small workshop. The jewelers in the shop can reproduce pieces in the museum, something to keep in mind if you want your own gold necklace inspired by insect vertebrae. Many of the exhibits here are small and detailed, so you may want to spend several hours here, with a break at the cafe.

12 Kalisperi (at Karyatidon). www.lalaounis-jewelrymuseum.gr. ℂ **210/922-1044.** Admission 4€. Mon and Thurs–Sat 9am–4pm; Wed 9am–9pm (free after 3pm); Sun 10am–4pm. Metro: Akropolis.

Jewish Museum ★★ MUSEUM   Greece's Jewish community, a strong presence throughout the country and a dominant force in Thessaloniki, was essentially obliterated in the Holocaust. Perhaps the most impressive exhibit is the handsome reconstruction of part of the interior of the Patras synagogue. Articles of daily life and religious ceremony include children's toys and special Passover china. Most exhibits have English labels. If you contact museum curator Zanet Battinou in advance of your visit, she will try to have a staff member take you through the collection.

39 Nikis (discreetly marked on the left side of Nikis as you walk away from Syntagma Sq.). www.jewishmuseum.gr. ℂ **210/322-5582.** Fax 210/323-1577. Admission 5€. Mon–Fri 9am–2:30pm; Sun 10am–2pm. Metro: Syntagma.

N. P. Goulandris Foundation Museum of Cycladic Art ★★★ MUSEUM   This handsome museum just off Vasilissis Sofias Avenue houses the largest collection of Cycladic art outside the National Archaeological Museum—and is a much more congenial, less crowded place to visit. See if you agree with those who have compared the faces of the Cycladic figurines to the works of the Italian painter Modigliani. A courtyard leads into the elegant 19th-century Stathatos Mansion, which forms part of the museum. The mansion, which is used for special exhibits, has some of its original furnishings and provides a glimpse of how wealthy Athenians lived a hundred years ago. The museum shop has a wide variety of books and reproductions. You'll want to spend at least 3 hours here, perhaps with a break in the garden cafe.

4 Neophytou Douka. www.cycladic.gr. ℂ **210/722-8321.** Admission 6€. Mon and Wed–Fri 10am–4pm; Sat 10am–3pm. Metro: Evangelismos.

GALLERIES

One of the great (usually free) pleasures of visiting Athens is browsing in its small art galleries. Occasionally a gallery will have an admission fee for a special exhibit, but usually there is no charge. This is a wonderful way to get a sense of the contemporary Greek art scene and possibly buy something to take home. A good way to find out

The Archaeological Promenade ★★★

One of the great pleasures in Athens is strolling through what's been dubbed the **Archaeological Promenade,** Europe's longest and arguably prettiest pedestrian promenade. It takes visitors past the most important of the city's ancient monuments from Hadrian's Gate past the Acropolis on Dionissiou Areopagitou to the Ancient Agora, past the Acropolis Museum through Thissio to the temple of Hephaistus, and on to Kerameikos and Gazi to the west, veering north through Monastiraki to the Plaka. Athenians use the walkways for their evening *volta* (stroll).

what's on is to pick up a free copy of the quarterlies *Art and the City* and the *Athens Contemporary Art Map.* Both are free, published in Greek and English, and usually available in hotels in galleries. Here are some galleries to keep an eye out for in central Athens. In trendy Psirri, **About Gallery,** 18 Miaouli (www.about-art.gr; ℂ 210/331-4480) hosts exhibitions by contemporary artists and has a great bookstore and **a.antonopoulou.art,** 20 Aristofanous (www.aaart.gr; ℂ 210/321-4994) is one of the most stunning art spaces in the city concentrating on Greek contemporary artists.

Just off Athinas Street, the **Epikentro Gallery,** 10 Armodiou (ℂ 210/331-2187) stages frequent exhibits in its improbable location in the Athens Central Market. The **Rebecca Camhi Gallery,** 9 Leonidou (www.rebeccacamhi.com; ℂ 210/523-3049) and **the Breeder,** 45 Iasonos (www.thebreedersystem.com; ℂ 210/331-7527) showcase some of the more interesting up-and-coming artists in solo shows, group shows, and gallery swaps. In Monastiraki, off Ermou Street, the **TAF–The Art Foundation,** 5 Normanou (www.theartfoundation.gr; ℂ 210/323-8757), in a renovated neoclassical building complex, houses art exhibitions around a lively courtyard bar where you can have a drink and browse at your leisure.

There are also frequent shows at the **Melina Mercouri Cultural Center,** Iraklidon and 66 Thessalonikis (ℂ 210/345-2150) and at the **Melina Mercouri Foundation,** 9–11 Polygnotou (www.melinamercourifoundation.org.gr; ℂ 210/331-5601) in the Plaka. Also in Plaka, the **Athens Gallery,** 14 Pandrossou St. (www.athensgallery.gr; ℂ 210/324-6942) occupies three floors in a beautiful old neoclassical home. In the fashionable Kolonaki district, **Astrolavos Art Life,** 11 Irodotou (www.astrolavos.gr; ℂ 210/722-1200) and **Medusa,** 7 Xenokratous (www.medusaartgallery.com; ℂ 210/724-4552) both feature cutting-edge contemporary Greek and international artists. A must-see here are also the **Gagosian Gallery,** 3 Merlin (www.gagosian.com; ℂ 210/364-0215) and **Zoumboulakis Gallery,** 20 Kolonaki Sq. (www.zoumboulakis.gr; ℂ 210/360-8278).

And keep in mind the **Athens Municipal Art Gallery,** 32 Mylierou and Leonidou (ℂ 210/324-3023), with its rich collection of more than 2,300 works from leading 19th- and 20th-century Greek artists.

ORGANIZED TOURS

The **City Sightseeing bus** (www.city-sightseeing.com; 18€ adults, 8€ children) is an open-top double-decker bus that begins and ends its journey at Syntagma Square. The ride through central Athens lasts 90 minutes and prerecorded commentaries are available in a wide range of languages. Tickets are valid for 24 hours and buses depart every half-hour from 7am to 6pm. Also, **Hop in Sightseeing** (www.hopin.com; ✆ **210/428-5500**) allows you to get on and off the bus tour over 2 days and even does hotel pickups.

Fantasy Travel, 19 Filelinon (www.fantasytravel.gr; ✆ **210/331-0530**) often has great deals and can come up with excellent suggestions and ideas on the spot. They offer half-day and full-day tours of the city, an Athens Segway tour (which is a fun way to get around the city), an "Athens by Night" tour for 62€ including dinner at the Mikrolimano harbor, and great packages for the islands. Also recommended are **CHAT Tours,** 4 Stadiou (www.chatours.gr; ✆ **210/323-0827**) and **Key Tours,** 4 Kalliroïs (www.keytours.gr; ✆ **210/923-3166**). To take any of these tours, you must book and pay in advance. At that time, you will be told when you will be picked up, or where you should meet the tour. **Athens Walking Tours** (www.athenswalking tours.gr; ✆ **210/884-7269**) runs a "shopping tour" and a very popular "food tour."

Each company also offers excursions from Athens. A visit to the popular **Temple of Poseidon at Sounion** costs about 60€ for a half-day trip, including swimming and a meal. A trip to **Delphi** usually costs about 110€ for a full day, and often includes stops at the Monastery of Osios Loukas and Arachova village. If you want to spend the night in Delphi (included are hotel, site, and museum admissions, as well as dinner, breakfast, and sometimes lunch), the price ranges from 50€ to 160€. Rates for excursions to the **Peloponnese,** taking in Corinth, Mycenae, and Epidaurus, are similar to those for Delphi. If your time in Greece is limited, you may find one of these day trips considerably less stressful than renting a car for the day and driving yourself.

If you want to hire a private guide, speak to the concierge at your hotel or contact the **Panhellenic Guides Federation,** 9a Apollonas (www.touristguides.gr; ✆ **210/322-9705**). Expect to pay 90€ for a 4-hour tour.

ATHENS BEACHES

Take the tram to the Glyfada stop at "Palio Dimarheio," "Paralia," or "Plateia Katraki" and walk along the coast to **Asteras Glyfada** (www.asterascomplex.com). Inside this complex is a clean and family-friendly beach (admission weekdays 6€; weekends 7.50€) with a snack bar, cafe, children's playground, and watersport options. Admission to this complex also grants you use of **Balux House** (www.baluxcafe.com), a glass-fronted beach house with a series of living rooms, a library, an indoor and outdoor playroom for children, TV sets with Xbox and PlayStation consoles, table games, a pool table, beanbags to curl up on, a restaurant, cafe and lounge area, volleyball court, and gardens. After the sun has set, the house morphs into a fun, louder, but still casual lounge-bar club.

The tram's last stop (Asklipeio Voulas) is right outside **Voula A** beach (www.thalassea.gr; admission weekdays 6€, weekends 7€). Quiet, pretty, and clean, with a water slide, ample space, and a snack bar, this beach is more for families seeking a quiet time, or anyone looking for a peaceful, inexpensive, and clean beach.

To reach **Astir Beach** (www.astir-beach.com), take the tram to Glyfada, then bus no. 114 or 116. This super-trendy beach (admission 15€ on weekdays, weekends vary) is nestled in a sheltered bay, and is clean and pleasant with many amenities including shops, a cafe, a restaurant, and sport facilities. It even has ruins—a temple to Apollo.

Take the tram to Glyfada, then bus no. 114 or 116 to reach **Attica Vouliagmeni Beach.** Set on an enormous stretch of sand on a beautiful coastline with playgrounds, tennis courts, basketball courts, all the usual beach amenities, and a beautiful coastline, this is the best-value beach for your money (admission 6€).

At **Lake Vouliagmeni** (© **210/896-2239**) you can swim in the springs, which are open year-round daily 7am–7:30pm (admission 7€, children 4 and under free). Take the tram to Glyfada, then bus no. 114. The setting is strikingly beautiful (a huge cavelike rock) where the blue-green mineral water remains the same temperature year-round (24°C/75°F) and is said to have many healing properties.

Varkiza Beach (© **210/897-2414**) is one of the fanciest beaches with pristine waters and is a lot of fun for both adults and children with beach bars, a water park, volleyball and tennis courts, and private cabanas. Though the beach gets busy during the weekends, it can be delightfully quiet weekdays. Take the tram to Glyfada, then bus no. 116, 125, or 171. Admission is 12€.

Where to Eat

Athens has an astonishing number of restaurants and tavernas (and a growing number of fast-food joints, known locally as *Fastfooddadiko*) offering everything from good, cheap Greek food in bare-bones surroundings to fine Greek, French, Asian, and other international cuisines served in elegant dining rooms, and a surprising number of neighborhood tavernas. In summer, when the heat soars, many Greeks have lunch inside and dinner outside—seldom before 10pm, although you can get served most places from 8pm.

Don't Count on Credit Cards

Much has changed in Athens, but many Athenian restaurants still do not accept credit cards.

Most restaurants have menus in Greek and English, but many don't keep their printed (or handwritten) menus up-to-date. If a menu is not in English, there's almost always someone working at the restaurant that can either translate or rattle off suggestions for you in English. That may mean you'll be offered some fairly repetitive suggestions because restaurant staff members tend to suggest what most tourists request. In Athens, that means **moussaka** (baked eggplant casserole, usually with ground meat), **souvlakia** (chunks of beef, chicken, pork, or lamb grilled on a skewer), **pastitsio** (baked pasta, usually with ground meat and béchamel sauce), or **dolmadakia** (grape leaves, stuffed usually with rice and ground meat). Although all these dishes can be delicious, all too often restaurants catering to tourists serve profoundly dull moussaka and unpleasantly chewy *souvlakia*.

Mezedes (appetizers served with bread) are one of the great delights of Greek cuisine, and often can be enjoyed in lieu of a main course. Some perennial favorites include **tzatziki** (garlic, cucumber, dill, and yogurt dip), **melitzanosalata** (eggplant dip), **skordalia** (garlic sauce), **taramosalata** (fish roe dip), **keftedes** (crispy meatballs), **kalamaria** (squid), **gigantes** (large white beans in tomato sauce), **loukanika** (little sausages), and **oktopodi** (octopus).

To find out about the wide range of excellent Greek wines, pick up a copy of Dimitri Hadjinicolaou's **The A to Z Guide of Greek Wines** (published by Oenos O Agapitos). This handy pocket-size Greek/English guide has illustrations of labels and information on vintages, and sells for about 10€.

When it comes time for dessert or a mid-afternoon infusion of sugar, Greeks usually head to a **zaharoplastion** (sweet shop). Consequently, most restaurants don't offer a wide variety of desserts. Almost all do serve fruit (stewed in winter, fresh in season), and, increasingly, many serve sweets such as **baklava** (pastry and ground

When you are at a restaurant that caters to tourists, tell your waiter you'd like to have a look at the food display case, often positioned just outside the kitchen, and then point to what you'd like to order. Many restaurants are perfectly happy to have you take a look in the kitchen itself, but it's not a good idea to do this without checking first. Not surprisingly, you'll get the best value and be able to avoid the ubiquitous favorites-for-foreigners dishes at establishments serving a predominantly Greek, rather than a transient tourist, clientele.

nuts with honey), *halva* (sesame, chopped nuts, and honey), and *kataifi* (shredded wheat with chopped nuts and lots of honey).

Greek **brandy** is a popular after-dinner drink (although—you guessed it—it's a bit sweet for non-Greek tastes), but the most popular Greek hard drink is **ouzo.** The anise-flavored liqueur is taken either straight or with water, which turns it cloudy white. You may see Greeks drinking quarter and even half-bottles of ouzo with lunch; if you do the same, you'll find out why the after-lunch siesta is so popular. There are many cafes (*ouzeri*) where ouzo, wine, and a selection of *mezedes* are served from breakfast to bedtime.

In 2009, an E.U. non-smoking law went into effect in restaurants, shops, and public buildings. The law is unlikely to have much effect on the city's countless warm-season alfresco dining and drinking establishments.

IN THE PLAKA

Some of the most charming old restaurants in Athens are in the Plaka—as are some of the worst tourist traps. Here are a few things to keep in mind when you head off for a meal. First, Plaka is a bit of a maze: If you have trouble finding a particular restaurant—and you probably will—don't ask for directions at another restaurant—you may be told the place you want is closed and urged to sit right down and eat right there.

In general, it's a good idea to avoid places with floor shows; many charge outrageous amounts (and levy surcharges not always openly stated on menus) for drinks and food. If you get burned, and the proprietor is insistent, stand your ground, phone the **tourist police** (© 171), and pay nothing before they arrive. Often the mere mention of the tourist police can miraculously cause a bill to be lowered.

Expensive

Daphne's ★★ ELEGANT GREEK   Frescoes adorn the walls of this neoclassical 1830s home, which includes a shady garden courtyard displaying bits of ancient marble found on-site. Diners from around the world sit at Daphne's tables. The courtyard makes it a real oasis in Athens, especially on hot summer nights. The food here—recommended by the *New York Times, Travel + Leisure,* and just about everyone else—gives you all the old favorites with new distinction (try the zesty eggplant salad), and combines familiar ingredients in innovative ways (delicious hot pepper and feta cheese dip). We could cheerfully eat the hors d'oeuvres all night. We have also enjoyed the *stifado* (stew) of rabbit in *mavrodaphne* (sweet-wine) sauce and the tasty prawns with toasted almonds. Live music plays unobtrusively in the background on some nights. The staff is attentive, endearing, and beyond excellent.

9

GREECE

Athens

4 Lysikratous. www.daphnesrestaurant.gr. ☎/fax **210/322-7971.** Reservations recommended. Main courses 30€–40€, with some fish priced by the kilo. AE, DC, MC, V. Daily 7pm–1am. Metro: Syntagma

Inexpensive

Damigos (The Bakaliarakia) ★★ 🍴 GREEK   This basement taverna just off Adrianou Street, with enormous wine barrels in the back room and an ancient column supporting the roof in the front room, has been serving delicious deep-fried codfish and eggplant, as well as chops and stews, since 1865. The wine comes from the family vineyards. There are few pleasures greater than sipping retsina—if you wish, you can buy a bottle to take away—while you watch the cook turn out unending meals in the absurdly small kitchen. Don't miss the delicious *skordalia* (garlic sauce), equally good with cod, eggplant, fresh tomatoes, bread—well, you get the idea.

41 Kidathineon. ☎ **210/322-5084.** Main courses 8€–12€. No credit cards. Daily 7pm to anytime from 11pm to 1am. Usually closed June–Sept. Metro: Syntagma or Akropolis.

Giouvetsakia ★ TRADITIONAL GREEK   Run by the same family since 1950, this traditional taverna at the bustling junction of Adrianou and Thespidos is perfect for people-watching in a scenic environment, while enjoying some delicious, traditional fare. Try the Giouvetsi pasta (still the house's specialty and its namesake) and be sure to leave room for the complimentary fruit dish topped with cinnamon.

144 Adrianou and Thespidos. ☎ **210/322-7033.** Main courses 6€–15€. MC, V. Daily 10am–2am. Metro: Syntagma.

Platanos Taverna ★★ TRADITIONAL GREEK   This taverna on a quiet pedestrian square has tables outdoors beneath a spreading plane tree (*platanos* means plane tree). The Platanos has been serving hearty *spitiko fageto* (home cooking) since 1932 and has managed to keep steady customers happy while enchanting visitors. If artichokes or spinach with lamb are on the menu, you're in luck: They're delicious. There's a wide choice of bottled wines from many regions of Greece, although the house wine is a good choice. Plan to come here and relax, not rush, through a meal.

4 Diogenous. ☎ **210/322-0666.** Fax 210/322-8624. Main courses 8€–20€. No credit cards. Mon–Sat noon–4:30pm and 8pm–midnight; Sun in Mar–May and Sept–Oct noon–4:30pm. Metro: Syntagma.

Taverna Xinos ★ TRADITIONAL GREEK   In summer, sit at tables in the courtyard; in winter, warm yourself by the coal-burning stove and admire the frescoes while dining on traditional Greek taverna food—often, as is traditional, served room temperature. Most evenings, tourists predominate until after 10pm, when locals begin to arrive—as they have since Xinos opened in 1935.

4 Geronta. ☎ **210/322-1065.** Main courses 8€–20€. No credit cards. Daily 8pm to any time from 11pm to 1am; sometimes closed Sun. Usually closed part of July and Aug. Metro: Syntagma.

NEAR MONASTIRAKI SQUARE
Moderate

Abyssinia Cafe ★ GREEK   This small cafe in a ramshackle building across from the entrance to the Ancient Agora sports a nicely restored interior featuring lots of gleaming dark wood and polished copper. You can sit indoors or out with a coffee, but it's tempting to snack on Cheese Abyssinia (feta scrambled with spices and garlic), mussels and rice pilaf, or *keftedes*. Everything is reasonably priced here, but it's easy to run up quite a tab, because everything is so good—especially the *mezedes*. For a quieter experience, book a table on the mezzanine with its awesome views.

QUICK BITES IN & around SYNTAGMA

In general, Syntagma Square is not known for good food, but the area has a number of places where you can grab a quick meal/snack. **Apollonion Bakery,** 10 Nikis and **Elleniki Gonia,** 10 Karayioryi Servias make sandwiches to order and sell croissants, both stuffed and plain. **Ariston** is a small chain of *zaharoplastia* (confectioners) with a branch at the corner of Karayioryi Servias and Voulis (just off Syntagma Sq.); it sells snacks as well as pastries. **Meliotos** ★★, 15 Xenofontos, (℃) **210/322-2458,** might be inside the lobby of a commercial building but the menu here is beyond exceptional and the prices are hard to beat. This is the perfect place to pick up your meal and head across the street to the National Gardens for a picnic. For the quintessentially Greek *loukoumades* (round donut-like pastries that are deep-fried, then drenched with honey, and topped with powdered sugar and cinnamon), try **Doris** ★, 30 Praxitelous, a continuation of Lekka, a few blocks from Syntagma Square. If you want something more substantial, there are also hearty stews and pasta dishes at absurdly low prices. If you're near Omonia Square when you feel the need for loukoumades or a soothing dish of rice pudding, try **Aigina** ★, 46 Panepistimiou. A short walk from Syntagma, the **Oraia Ellada (Beautiful Greece)** ★★ cafe at the Center of Hellenic Tradition, opening onto both 36 Pandrossou and 59 Mitropoleos near the flea market, has a spectacular view of the Acropolis. For the best espresso, cappuccino, Italian pastries, and brioche sandwiches in town, venture to **Alfiere Café** ★ in Kolonaki, right behind the Italian Embassy at 5 Sekeri.

Plateia Abyssinia, Monastiraki. (℃) **210/321-7047.** Appetizers and main courses 8€–30€. No credit cards. Tues–Sun 10:30am–2pm (often open evenings as well). Usually closed for a week at Christmas and Easter; sometimes closed part of Jan and Feb and mid-July to mid-Aug. Metro: Monastiraki.

Inexpensive

Bliss ★ MEDITERRANEAN/ORGANIC   Three levels in this extremely popular all-day multiuse space include a wonderful cafe/restaurant that serves delicious organic fare: teas, coffee, smoothies, sandwiches, salads, and Greek taverna main courses; beginning with their first-rate breakfast. There's also yoga and alternative therapy rooms, a New Age bookstore, and gift shop.

24A Romvis St., Monastiraki. www.purebliss.gr. (℃) **210/325-0360.** Appetizers and main courses 5€–15€. MC, V. Daily 7am–2am. Metro: Monastiraki/Thissio.

Dioskouri ★ GREEK MEZEDES   On busy Adrianou, ideal for its Acropolis, Agora and Temple of Hephaestus views, not to mention the countless passers-by, Dioskouri has been serving tasty *mezedes* at affordable prices for many years, becoming a favorite for locals and tourists alike. Highlights are the seafood dishes and meat *mezedes*.

37 Adrianou, Monastiraki. (℃) **210/325-3333.** Appetizers 5€–15€. No credit cards. Daily 11am–1am. Metro: Monastiraki/Thissio.

Taverna Sigalas ★ GREEK   This longtime Plaka taverna, housed in a vintage 1879 commercial building with a newer outdoor pavilion, boasts that it has been run by the same family for a century, and is open 365 days a year. Huge old retsina kegs stand piled against the back walls; dozens of black-and-white photos of Greek movie stars are everywhere. After 8pm, Greek Muzak plays. At all hours, both locals and tourists dine on large portions of stews, moussaka, grilled meatballs, baked tomatoes, and gyros, paired with the house red and white retsinas.

2 Plateia Monastiraki. ℂ **210/321-3036.** Main courses 8€–19€. No credit cards. Daily 7am–2am. Metro: Monastiraki.

Thanasis ★ 🍴 GREEK/SOUVLAKI   Just across from the Monastiraki Metro station, Thanasis serves terrific *souvlaki* and pita—and exceptionally good French fries—to take out, or eat at its outdoor and indoor tables. On weekends, it often takes the strength and determination of an Olympic athlete to get through the door and place an order here but it's worth the effort: This is both a great budget choice and an ideal place to take in the local scene.

69 Mitropoleos. ℂ **210/324-4705.** Main courses 6€–15€. No credit cards. Daily 9am–2am. Metro: Monastiraki.

NEAR SYNTAGMA SQUARE

Aegli/Cibus ★★ INTERNATIONAL   A wonderful bistro, along with an open-air cinema, a hip and highly recommended outdoor bar/club, and a fine restaurant. Popular with chic Athenian families who head here to enjoy the cool of the Zappeion Gardens, and the frequently changing menu. Some of the specialties include foie gras, oysters, tenderloin with ginger and coffee sauce, profiteroles, fresh sorbets, strawberry soup, and delicious yogurt crème brûlée.

Zappeion Gardens (adjacent to the National Gardens fronting Vas. Amalias Blvd.). www.aegli zappiou.gr. ℂ **210/336-9363.** Reservations recommended. Main courses 35€–55€. AE, DC, MC, V. Daily 10am–midnight. Sometimes closed in Aug. Metro: Syntagma.

IN KOLONAKI
Expensive

Horizons ★★ MEDITERRANEAN   For a table with a view, you can't do better than this. It sits on the top of Lycabettus Hill, with the city laid under your feet like a sparkling map. The Mediterranean menu is highly recommended. Start with the lobster salad gradine with Gorgonzola cheese and grilled vegetables, or the fried salmon with wasabi—all exceptional. The grilled shrimp, pasta risotto, and smoked pork tenderloin and lamb shank that follow as mains are all top-notch but it is the view that always steals the show. Arrive for sunset and enjoy.

Lycabettus Hill. www.orizonteslycabettus.gr. ℂ **210/722-7065.** Reservations recommended. Main courses 40€–60€. AE, MC, V. Daily 1pm–1am. Taxi or walk to the top of Lycabettus to Ploutarchou St. to take the funicular (6€ with return), or walk up from Dexamini Sq.

Moderate

Filipou ★ TRADITIONAL GREEK   This longtime Athenian favorite almost never disappoints. The traditional dishes such as stuffed cabbage, stuffed vine leaves, vegetable stews, and fresh salads are consistently good. In the heart of Kolonaki, this is a place to go when you want quality home cooking in the company of the Greeks and resident expatriates who prize the food.

19 Xenokratous. ℂ **210/721-6390.** Main courses 8€–20€. No credit cards. Mon–Fri 8:30pm–midnight; Sat lunch. Metro: Evangelismos.

Rhodia ★ TRADITIONAL GREEK   This respected taverna is located in a handsome old Kolonaki house. In good weather, tables are set up in its small garden—although the interior, with its tiled floor and old prints, is equally charming. The

Rhodia is a favorite of visiting archaeologists from the nearby British and American Schools of Classical Studies, as well as of Kolonaki residents. The octopus in mustard sauce is terrific, as are the veal and *dolmades* (stuffed grape leaves) in egg-lemon sauce. The house wine is excellent, as is the *halva*, which manages to be both creamy and crunchy.

44 Aristipou. ☏ **210/722-9883.** Main courses 8€–18€. No credit cards. Mon–Sat 8pm–2am. Metro: Evangelismos.

To Kafeneio ★★ GREEK/INTERNATIONAL This is hardly a typical *kafeneio* (coffeeshop/cafe). Two can easily run up a tab of 60€ for lunch or dinner, but you can also just snack here. If you have something light, like the leeks in crème fraîche or onion pie, washed down with draft beer or the house wine, you can finish with profiteroles and not put too big a dent in your budget.

26 Loukianou. ☏ **210/722-9056.** Reservations recommended. Main courses 12€–25€. MC, V. Mon–Sat 11am–midnight or later. Closed most of Aug. Metro: Evangelismos.

To Ouzadiko ★★ GREEK/MEZEDES This lively ouzo bar in the rather grim Lermos Shopping Center offers at least 40 kinds of ouzo and as many mezedes, including fluffy *keftedes* that make all others taste leaden. To Ouzadiko is very popular with Athenians young and old (maybe too popular—service can be slow).

25–29 Karneadou (in the Lemos International Shopping Center), Kolonaki. ☏ **210/729-5484.** Reservations recommended. Most *mezedes* and main courses 10€–20€. No credit cards. Tues–Sat 1pm–12:30am. Closed Aug. Metro: Evangelismos.

To Prytaneion ★ GREEK/INTERNATIONAL The trendy decor here features stone walls, decorated with movie posters and illuminated by baby spotlights. Waiters serve customers tempting plates of some of Athens's most expensive and eclectic mezedes, including beef carpaccio, smoked salmon, bruschetta, and shrimp in fresh cream, as well as grilled veggies and that international favorite, the hamburger.

7 Milioni. www.prytaneion.gr. ☏ **210/364-3353.** Reservations recommended. Main courses 20€–35€. DC, MC, V. Daily 10am–1:30am. Metro: Syntagma.

AROUND OMONIA SQUARE & THE NATIONAL ARCHAEOLOGICAL MUSEUM

Archaion Gefsis (Ancient Flavors) ★ GREEK More than a little on the kitsch side (columns, torches, and waitresses in togas), this is your one chance to dine like the ancients did. With recipes from ancient Greece (recorded by the poet Archestratos), offerings include cuttlefish in ink with pine nuts, wild-boar cutlets, goat leg with mashed vegetables, and pork with prunes and thyme, among other such delicious fare. Just remember: You may use a spoon and a knife, but no fork—ancient Greeks did not use them. Popular with tourists, this place also draws curious locals, foodies, and those in search of something truly different.

22 Kodratou, Plateia Karaiskaki, Metaxourgeio. www.arxaion.gr. ☏ **210/523-9661.** Main courses 20€–33€. MC, V. Mon–Sat 8pm–1am. Metro: Metaxourgeio.

Ideal ★ GREEK TRADITIONAL The oldest restaurant in the heart of Athens, today's Ideal has an Art Deco decor and lots of old favorites, from egg-lemon soup to stuffed peppers; from pork with celery to lamb with spinach. Ideal often attracts business people, and the service is usually brisk, especially at lunchtime. Not the place for a quiet rendezvous, but definitely the place for decent, hearty Greek cooking.

46 Panepistimiou. ☏ **210/330-3000.** Reservations recommended. Main courses 10€–20€. AE, DC, MC, V. Mon–Sat noon–midnight. Metro: Omonia.

RISING stars IN THE PSIRRI, THISSIO & GAZI DISTRICTS

It's hard to keep up with all the bar/restaurants opening in the increasingly fashionable Psirri, Thissio, and Gazi districts. Here are some highlights.

The oldest taverna in Psirri remains the best: **Taverna Tou Psiri ★★**, 12 Eshylou (© **210/321-4923**) is where you'll find delicious traditional taverna fare (try the lamb chops), good house wine, live music, moderate prices, and a pleasant outdoor garden. **Oineas ★★**, 9 Aisopou (© **210/321-5614**) attracts an early crowd of tourists and locals all night long, all of whom enjoy the wide range of *mezedes* (try the fried feta in light honey). If you want to watch a movie while you eat on a summer night, head for **Kouzina Cine-Psyrri,** 40 Sarri (© **210/321-5534**), which maintains Athens's long tradition of outdoor cinemas. Many of Psirri's galleries stay open late, which means that you can eat and browse—or browse and eat as you please.

In Thissio, there's a terrific cluster of restaurants. **Kuzina ★★**, 9 Adrianou

(www.kuzina.gr; © **210/324-0133**) combines awesome views of the Temple of Hephaestus, the Agora, and the Acropolis from its roof garden; great contemporary Greek cuisine (such as delicious dumplings with feta cheese and pomegranate syrup); and a cutting-edge art gallery. At **Filistron ★★**, 23 Apostolou Pavlou (www.filistron.com; © **210/346-7554**), a short walk away, you'll still have views of the Acropolis and agora from the rooftop terrace along with a wide range of reasonably priced *mezedes*. **To Steki Tou Ilia ★**, 7 Thessalonikis (© **210/342-2407**) is an outstanding grill house (excellent lamb chops) and **Chez Lucien ★**, 32 Troon (© **210/346-4236**) is a French bistro with a small menu and a symposium-like atmosphere. Nearby the very moderately priced taverna **O Santorinios ★★** (The Man from Santorini), 8 Doreion (© **210//345-1629**) serves traditional cuisine from the island of Santorirni in an old Athenian home with a small garden. Their famous *tomatokeftedes* (tomato rissoles) and red

NEAR THE ACROPOLIS (KOUKAKI & MAKRIGIANNI)

Dionysos Zonar's ★ CONTEMPORARY/TRADITIONAL GREEK   In a picturesque location by Fillipapous Hill with Acropolis views, this all-day restaurant has great traditional fare (including an excellent moussaka), as well as contemporary choices, including risotto with cheese, salmon, hearty salads, and good meat selections, including a stroganoff. But it is the made-on-site baklava (prepared on request, so it'll be a half-hour but well worth the wait) that will prove the highlight of any meal here.

43 Robertou Galli St, Makrigianni. www.dionysoszonars.gr. © **210/923-1936.** Main courses 25€– 100€. DC, MC, V. Daily 12pm–1am. Metro: Akropolis.

Mani Mani ★★ CONTEMPORARY/REGIONAL GREEK   Delicious and moderately priced, Mani Mani's menu is based on traditional dishes from Mani in the south of the Peloponnese. The rooster *bardouniotikos* (rooster stewed with feta) is exceptional, as is the lamb shank, and the homemade pasta (*hilopites*). Appetizers include *siglino* (cured pork that is first salted, then smoked, and finally boiled) and grilled sausages. The salads are recommendable, and the service is a delight.

10 Falirou, Makrigianni. www.manimani.com.gr. © **210/921-8180.** Main courses 9.50€–17€. DC, MC, V. Tues–Sat 8pm–1am; Sun 2–5pm. Metro: Akropolis.

snapper paired with a fine wine from the island are simply out of this world (open only in the evening). From Thissio towards Kerameikos, be sure to visit **Meson El Mirador** ★, 88 Agisilaou at Salaminas (www.el-mirador.gr; ✆ **210/342-0007**), a Mexican restaurant right off the ancient cemetery, with a beautiful roof terrace and Acropolis views. New arrival and winner of the 2012 Michelin star, **Funky Gourmet** ★, 13 Paramythias and Salaminos (www.funkygourmet.com; ✆ **210/524-2727**) is housed in a lovingly restored neoclassical house, and serves an exceptional lobster with pasta.

In neighboring **Gazi,** head for **Mamacas** ★★, 41 Persefonis (www.mamacas. gr; ✆ **210/346-4984**), an upmarket taverna that was one of the first of the new wave of restaurants here, is still one of the best; the spicy meatballs (*keftedakia*) take standard restaurant fare to a new and exuberant level. Directly across the street, you will find **Dirty Ginger** ★, 46 Triptopolemou and Persefonis (www.dirtyginger.gr; ✆ **210/342-3809**),

a party restaurant with tasty Mediterranean cuisine that is the perfect place to eat, drink, and linger to watch and participate in the highly infectious nightly party.

If it's seafood you crave, Gazi won't disappoint either. Michelin-star winner **Varoulko** ★★★, 80 Piraios (www. varoulko.gr; ✆ **210/522-8400**) is considered by many to be the finest seafood restaurant in the entire city, and is well-placed on a gorgeous roof terrace overlooking the Acropolis. The menu features smoked eel, artichokes with fish roe, crayfish with sundried tomatoes, and outstanding seabass and monkfish. Be warned, however, the restaurant is on the expensive side (60€ minimum per person) and reservations are essential. For moderately priced seafood, **Sardelles** ★, 15 Persefonis (www. sardelles.gr; ✆ **210/347-8050**) serves up tasty mixed seafood *mezedes*. Gazi also has many affordable tavernas, our favorite these days being **Gazohori** ★ (Gazi Village), 2 Dekeloen, ✆ **210/342-4044.**

Strofi Tavern ★ TRADITIONAL GREEK The Strofi serves standard Greek taverna fare (the *mezedes* and lamb and goat dishes are especially good here), and offers a terrific view of the Acropolis. Strofi is popular with the after-theater crowd that pours out of the nearby Herodes Atticus Theater during the Athens Festival.

25 Rovertou Galli, Makriyianni. ✆ **210/921-4130.** Reservations recommended. Main courses 8€–25€. DC, MC, V. Mon–Sat 8pm–2am. Metro: Akropolis. Located 2 blocks south of Acropolis.

ELSEWHERE IN THE CITY

Akanthus ★★ GREEK/MODERN TAVERNA Akanthus has a picturesque location inside the Asteras Glyfada beach complex. Begin with the *ouzokatastasi* (the ouzo situation) *mezedes* dish—a delightful combo of shrimp, smoked salmon, black caviar, and grilled octopus. Main menu items such as the veal filet and large shrimps are also delicious. Come for the scenery, the food, and the sunset over the sea, and stay on for the beach party.

58 Leoforos Poseidonas, Asteras Glyfada. www.asterascomplex.com. ✆ **210/968-0800.** Main courses 25€–30€. MC, V. May–Oct daily 8pm–1am. Tram to Plateia Glyfadas, then 5-min. walk along Leof. Poseidonos.

Spondi ★★★ INTERNATIONAL *Athinorama*, the weekly review of the Athenian scene, has chosen Spondi several years running as the best place in town. The menu covers many light dishes—the fresh fish, especially the salmon, is superb—as well as dishes that you will find either delightful or a bit cloying (roast pork with myzithra cheese and a fig-and-yogurt sauce). The setting, a handsome 19th-century town house with a courtyard, is lovely; the wine list, extensive; the service, excellent; and the desserts, divine. Spondi won its first Michelin star in 2002 and a second in 2008. It is considered by many to be the best restaurant in Greece.

5 Pyrronos, Pangrati. www.spondi.gr. 𝄞 **210/752-0658.** Reservations recommended. Main courses 45€–130€. AE, DC, MC, V. Daily 8pm–midnight. Closed Sun in Aug. Pyrronos runs btw. Empedokleous and Dikearchou, behind the Old Olympic Stadium.

Vlassis ★★★ TRADITIONAL GREEK Greeks call this kind of food *paradisiako* (traditional), but paradisiacal is just as good a description. The reasonably priced menu is fit for the gods: delicious fluffy vegetable croquettes, a unique eggplant salad, and hauntingly tender lamb in egg-lemon sauce.

15 Meandrou, Ilissia. 𝄞 **210/725-6635.** Reservations recommended. Main courses 15€–30€. MC, V. Mon–Sat 1pm–midnight; Sun noon–5pm Closed much of June–Sept. Metro: Megaro Mousikis. Once you exit the Metro, cross the avenue and head down (adjacent the hospital) toward Michalacopoulou St. Meandrou is 1 block before. Across the street from the Crowne Plaza hotel.

Shopping

You're in luck shopping in Athens, because almost everything you'll probably want to buy can be found in the central city, bounded by Omonia, Syntagma, and Monastiraki squares. This is where you'll find most of the shops frequented by Athenians, including a number of large **department stores.**

Monastiraki has its famous **flea market,** which is especially lively on Sundays. Although it has a vast amount of tacky stuff for sale here, it also has some real finds, including retro clothes and old copper. Many Athenians furnishing new homes head here to try to pick up old treasures.

The **Plaka** has pretty much cornered the market on souvenir shops, with enough T-shirts, reproductions of antiquities (including rude playing cards, drink coasters, and more), fishermen's sweaters (increasingly made in the Far East), and jewelry (often not real gold) to circle the globe.

In the Plaka–Monastiraki area, several shops worth seeking out amid the endlessly repetitive souvenir shops include **Stavros Melissinos,** the Poet-Sandalmaker of Athens, relocated after 50 years on Pandrossou to his new location at 2 Agias Theklas (www.melissinos-poet.com; 𝄞 **210/321-9247**), where his son is now in charge; **Iphanta,** the weaving workshop, 6 Selleu (𝄞 **210/322-3628**); **Emanuel Masmanidis' Gold Rose Jewelry Shop,** 85 Pandrossou (𝄞 **210/321-5662**); the **Center of Hellenic Tradition,** 59 Mitropoleos and 36 Pandrossou (𝄞 **210/321-3023**), which sells arts and crafts; and the **National Welfare Organization,** 6 Ipatias and Apollonos, Plaka (𝄞 **210/321-8272**), where a portion of the proceeds from everything sold (including handsome woven and embroidered carpets) goes to the National Welfare Organization, which encourages traditional crafts.

Kolonaki, on the slopes of Mount Likavitos, is boutique heaven—but it's a better place to window-shop than to buy, as much of what you see is imported and heavily taxed. If you're here during the January or August sales, you may find some bargains. If not, it's still a lot of fun to work your way up pedestrian Voukourestiou, along Tsakalof and Anagnostopoulou, before collapsing at a cafe on one of the pedestrian shopping streets (Milioni is a good choice) in Kolonaki Square. If you want to make a small, traditional purchase, have a look at the "worry beads" at **Kombologadiko,** 6 Koumbari (© **210/362-4267**), or check out charms that ward off the evil eye at **To Fylakto Mou,** 20 Solonos (© **210/364-7610**).

Pedestrianized Ermou Street is the longtime main shopping drag in the city with more stores than you will have time to visit, but if you want to do all your shopping in one take and not walk around outdoors, check out some of the 300 shops on the eight floors of the **Attica** department store in the CityLink Building at 9 Panepistimiou (www.atticadps.gr; © **210/180-2500**). If you're not in the mood to shop, you'll still be wowed by the window displays. Athens's largest malls, **The Mall Athens** (www.themallathens.gr) and the **MacArthurGlen Athens Designer Outlet mall** (www.mcarthurglenathens.gr) are also two excellent options.

Entertainment & Nightlife

Greeks enjoy their nightlife so much that they take an afternoon nap to rest up for it. The evening often begins with a leisurely *volta* (stroll); you'll see it in most neighborhoods, including the Plaka and Kolonaki Square. Most Greeks don't think about having dinner until at least 10pm. Around midnight the party may move on to a club for the start of an evening of music and dancing. Feel free to try places on your own, although you may feel like the odd man out because Greeks seldom go anywhere alone.

Ask the concierge or desk clerk at your hotel for nightlife recommendations. The listings in the weekly *Athinorama* (Greek) or in publications such as the English-language *Athens News,* the *Kathimerini* insert in the *Herald Tribune,* and hotel handouts such as *Best of Athens* and *Welcome to Athens* can also be very helpful.

Wherever you go, you're likely to face a cover charge of at least 10€. Thereafter, each drink will probably cost between 10€ and 15€ but in most places the cover charge includes a drink. Many clubs plop a bottle on your table and then they try very hard to charge you at least 100€ whether you drink it or not so it's best to linger by the bar.

FESTIVALS

New festivals spring up every year in Athens and throughout Greece. You may want to check with the Greek National Tourist Office (www.visitgreece.gr) to see what's new at your destination. Additional information on the festivals below is available at www.greekfestival.gr, www.breathtakingathens.com, and www.greektourism.com.

Hellenic Festival ★★★ Early June through September, the Hellenic Festival (also known as the **Athens** or **Greek Festival**) features famous Greek and foreign artists from Elton John to Placido Domingo performing on the slopes of the Acropolis. You may catch an opera, concert, drama, or ballet here—and see the Acropolis illuminated over your shoulder at the same time. Schedules and advance tickets are usually available at the **Hellenic Festival Office,** 39 Panepistimiou (www.greekfestival.gr; © **210/928-2900**). If available, tickets (15€–50€) can be purchased at the Odeion of Herodes Atticus (© **210/323-2771** or **210/323-5582**) several hours before the performance. Shows usually begin at 9pm.

Epidaurus Festival ★★★ From late June to late August, performances of ancient Greek tragedies and comedies (usually given in modern Greek translations) take place at Epidaurus, in Greece's most beautiful ancient theater. You can purchase bus service along with your ticket (about 2 hr. each way). Contact the **Greek**

National Tourism Organization, the **Hellenic Festival Office** (see above), or the **Rex Theater** box office (℃ **210/330-1881**) on Panepistimiou just outside Spiromilios Arcade. You can sometimes get tickets at **Epidaurus** (℃ **27530/22-006**) just before a performance.

PERFORMING ARTS

The acoustically impressive **Megaron Mousikis Concert Hall ★★★**, 89 Leoforos Vas. Sofias (www.megaron.gr; ℃ **210/729-0391**) hosts a classical music program that includes everything from solo performances to operas. Ticket prices run from 5€ to more than 100€. The Megaron has a limited summer season but is in full swing the rest of the year. The **Greek National Opera** performs at **Olympia Theater,** 59 Akadimias at Mavromihali (www.nationalopera.gr; ℃ **210/361-2461**). The summer months are usually off-season. **Pallas Theater,** 5 Voukourestiou (www.ticketshop.gr; ℃ **210/321-310**) hosts jazz and rock concerts, as well as some classical performances. The **Onassis Cultural Center,** 107–109 Syngrou Ave. (www.sgt.gr; ℃ **210/178-0000**) holds events, theater, visual art, and music performances. Since 1953, **Dora Stratou Folk Dance Theater ★** has been giving performances of traditional Greek folk dances on Filopappos Hill (May–October). You can buy tickets at the box office, 8 Scholio or online (www.grdance.org; ℃ **210/924-4395**). Prices range from 15€ to 25€. Tickets are also available at the theater before the performances.

BARS & CLUBS

Athens nightlife has a reputation for getting started after the rest of Europe has already gone to bed, but the city also has many all-day hangout places too. Here are a few highlights from the city's most popular districts.

Akrotiri Club Restaurant, Leof Vas Georgiou B5, Agios Kosmas (www.akrotiri lounge.gr; ℃ **210/985-9147**) is a massive, beautiful, and stylish open-air club next to the beach. Cover, including a drink, costs 10€ to 15€. **Athens Sports Bar,** 3a Veikou, Makrigianni (www.athenssportsbar.com; ℃ **210/923-5811**) is just that, with snacks, projection screens, karaoke, and theme nights; happy hour is nightly 7–8pm. **Balthazar,** 27 Tsoha and Soutsou, Ambelokipi (www.balthazar.gr; ℃ **210/644-1215**) is an absolutely beautiful bar in an old mansion's lantern-lit courtyard. There is always something cool going on at **Bios,** 84 Pireos (www.bios.gr; ℃ **210/342-5335**), an art-space/cafe/bar/club, from avant-garde performances to exhibitions and foreign art film showings. **Booze Coopertiva,** 57 Koloktroni (www.boozecoopertiva. com; ℃ **210/324-0944**) is an all-day hangout cafe with art exhibitions, screenings, and performances, and lively bar at night. **Brettos Bar,** 41 Kydathineon, Plaka (www. brettosplaka.com; ℃ **210/323-2110**), with its backlit wall of bottles, has been an Athenian landmark for over a century. **Cantina Social,** 6–8 Leokoreiou (℃ **210/ 325-1668**) is a funky bar directly across the "Ochre & Brown" boutique hotel, set inside an old arcade. Expect inexpensive drinks, a courtyard, and a friendly crowd. **Chandelier,** 4 Benizelou, Plaka (www.chandelier.gr; ℃ **210/631-6330**) is a cozy and laid-back lounge in a neoclassical building. The oldest bar in Gazi, **Gazaki,** 31 Triptopolemou (℃ **210/346-0901**) remains one of the best. The non-pretentious, mixed crowd makes this a sure bet for any night of the week and the roof terrace is another plus. **K44,** 33 Leof. Konstantinoupoleos (www.k44.gr; ℃ **210/342-6804**) is a multilevel warehouse that is a popular cafe/bar with live music performances on the bottom floor, and art exhibitions upstairs. **Tiki Athens,** 15 Falirou, Makrigianni (www.tikiathens.com; ✆ **210/923-6908**) is a fun and funky bar with '50s exotic decor and Asian-inspired cuisine. **Magaze,** 33 Eolou (www.magaze.gr; ✆ **210/324-3740**) is an all-day cafe and laid-back evening bar with a mixed and friendly crowd on pedestrian Eolou. **Mai Tai,** 18 Ploutarhou, Kolonaki (www.mai-tai.gr; ✆ **210/725-83062**) is open all day serving a tasty menu, good drinks, and gathering an attractive 30-plus crowd. **Seven Jokers,** 7 Voulis (✆ **210/321-9225**) is a quiet cafe during the day, intimate bar in the early evening, and insanely busy after-hours bar with a serious crush on the Rolling Stones. **Six D.O.G.S.,** 6–8 Avramiotou (www.sixdogs. gr; ✆ **210/321-0510**) is a daytime cafe and gallery space, with live music performances and energetic bar in the evenings. **TAF–The Art Foundation,** 5 Normanou (www.theartfoundation.gr; ✆ **210/323-8757**), set in a neoclassical building complex from the 19th century, houses a series of galleries surrounded by a lively courtyard bar. **Villa Mercedes,** Andronikou and 11 Jafferi (www.mercedes-club.gr; ✆ **210/342-3606**) is an impressive nightclub with many rooms and an internal courtyard (plus a restaurant) that's always hopping (cover is 10€–15€).

LIVE MUSIC CLUBS

Walk the streets of the Plaka on any night and you'll find lots of tavernas offering pseudo-traditional live music (usually at clip-joint prices) and a few offering the real thing. Don't bother to phone ahead to these places—the phone is almost never answered. **Taverna Mostrou,** 22 Mnissikleos (✆ **210/324-2441**) is one of the largest, oldest, and best known for traditional Greek music and dancing. Shows begin about 11pm and usually last to 2am. The cover charge (from about 30€) includes a fixed-price supper; a la carte fare is available but expensive. Nearby, **Palia Taverna Kritikou,** 24 Mnissikleos (✆ **210/322-2809**) is a lively open-air taverna with music and dancing.

Those interested in authentic *rembetika* (music of the urban poor and dispossessed) should consult their hotel receptionist or the current issue of *Athenscope* or *Athinorama* (in Greek) to find out which clubs are featuring the best performers. One of the more central places for *rembetika* is **Stoa Athanaton,** 19 Sofokleous, in the Central Meat Market (✆ **210/321-4362**), which has been serving good grub and live music since 1930. Open from between 3 and 7:30pm to after 11pm. It's closed Sunday. Open Wednesday through Monday, **Frangosyriani,** 57 Arachovis, Exarchia (✆ **210/360-0693**) specializes in the music of *rembetika* legend Markos Vamvakaris. The legendary Maryo I Thessaloniki (Maryo from Thessaloniki), described as the Bessie Smith of Greece, sometimes sings *rembetika* at **Perivoli t'Ouranou,** 19 Lysikratous (✆ **210/323-5517** or **210/322-2048**), in Plaka.

A number of clubs and cafes specialize in jazz, but also offer everything from Indian sitar music to rock and punk. The popular—and well thought of—**Half Note Jazz Club,** 17 Trivonianou, Mets (www.halfnote.gr; ✆ **210/921-3310**) schedules performers who play everything from medieval music to jazz; set times vary from 8 to 11pm and later (cover is 30€ with one drink). In Gazi, at the **Art House,** 46 Konstantinoupoleos (www.art-house-athens.gr; ✆ **210/461-1535**), you can often hear jazz from 11pm. **Jazz n' Jazz,** 4 Deinokratous (✆ **210/725-8362;** Tues–Sat 8pm–3am), a small, cozy, and charming jazz museum/bar in Kolonaki, is a great place to take in the vibe and listen to their extensive jazz collection. If you're visiting in late May, check out the **European Jazz Festival** at **Technopolis,** 100 Pireos (www. technopolis.gr; ✆ **210/346-0981**).

THE LBGT SCENE

You will not find a shortage of gay bars, cafes, and clubs in Athens, and while some of them can be found in Monastiraki, Makrigianni, and Exarchia, the real scene is at Gazi. The weekly publications *Athinorama* and *Time Out* often list gay bars, discos, and special events in the nightlife section. You can also look for the Greek publication **Deon Magazine** (www.deon.gr; ✆ **210/953-6479**) or surf the Web at www.gaygreece.gr, www.greekgayguide.eu, www.gayathens.gr, or www.lesbian.gr.

Keep in mind that **Athens Pride** (www.athenspride.eu) takes place the first weekend in June.

Blue Train, 84 Konstantinoupoleos, Gazi (www.bluetrain.gr; ✆ **210/346-0677**) is right by the railway tracks on the edge of Gazi. The friendly scene here is a great place to begin the evening, preferably at an outside table, where you can watch the trains and the boys go by, except on Fridays when the night belongs to the girls. **Eighth Sin,** 141 Megalou Alexandrou (www.8thsin.gr; ✆ **210/347-7048**) is a beautiful bar with a sexy crowd and excellent cocktails based on, you got it, the seven deadly sins, plus an eighth one: the delicious and potent namesake's signature cocktail. **Mayo,** 33 Persefonis, Gazi (✆ **210/342-3066**), a quiet bar with an inner courtyard and a rooftop terrace with a killer view, is an excellent place to begin your evening. **My Bar,** 6 Kakourgiodikiou, Monastiraki (www.mybar.gr; ✆ **210/486-2161**) is a more intimate, less rowdy bar than its Gazi counterparts but just as energetic. **Noiz,** 41 Evmolpidon and Konstantinoupoleos, Gazi (www.noizclub.gr; ✆ **210/342-477**) is the most popular lesbian bar/club in town. **Sodade,** 10 Triptopolemou, Gazi (✆ **210/346-8657**) was the first gay bar to open in Gazi, and has grown to become an institution. **S'Cape,** Iera Odos and 139 Meg. Alexandrou, Gazi (www.s-cape-club.blogspot.com; ✆ **210/345-2751**) is a large club with army bunks, military-style motif, and attracts an enthusiastic crowd. **Rooster,** 4 Agia Irini Sq., Monastiraki (✆ **210/322-4410**), by the Roman Forum, is a cafe/bar during the daytime that packs in an attractive crowd into the night.

SPECTATOR SPORTS

The Greeks are devoted to soccer and basketball, and love to bet on sports. All sports events are listed in the Greek press and sometimes in the English-language daily *Athens News.* The concierge or desk clerk at your hotel should know what's on. The best known soccer teams are the fierce rivals **Olympiakos** (Piraeus) and **Panathanaikos** (Athens). Greece's Euro Cup Victory in 2004 brought the entire nation first to its feet and then to a halt for weeklong celebrations.

The Greek national **basketball** team endeared itself to the nation when it won the European Championship by defeating Russia in 1987. The championships take place in July or August at different venues in Europe. You may also be able to catch a game between Greek teams in Athens.

If you're in Greece when major international soccer or basketball events take place, you probably will be able to see them on Greek television or CNN. Many games take place at the **Athens Olympic Sports Complex** (www.oaka.com.gr; ✆ **210-683-4777**).

Where to Stay

The Monastiraki and Plaka districts remain as popular as ever with tourists, with many new hotels popping up especially in the Monastiraki area. Syntagma Square, Kolonaki, and the Museum Mile also remain popular but since the arrival of the

Acropolis Museum, Makrigianni (and Koukaki) have become extremely popular with visitors.

Tip: With the economic crisis still unresolved, it remains to be seen if the country will adopt its own currency, which will certainly mean significantly lower prices. Until then, however, protests and strikes remain a common occurrence, prompting many hotel owners to lower their rates; good deals can be found either by a reputable local travel agency or online. Always ask for the discount usually given for stays of more than three nights and be sure to ask if the rates vary on different days of the week. Weekend hotel rates are sometimes cheaper in Athens, but usually *more* expensive outside of Athens (especially in the islands). Winter rate reductions are common in many small Athenian hotels, while some well-known large downtown Athenian hotels offer reductions in August, when savvy travelers tend to avoid the heat. If you have found a hotel deal online make sure to contact the hotel with the information to make sure the offer is legit. *Warning:* Whenever you go and wherever you stay, be sure to bring along a printout of your hotel reservation.

IN PLAKA
Expensive
AVA Hotel & Suites ★★   With its excellent location, clean and spacious grounds, and a personable and helpful staff, the AVA has stolen our hearts. This smoke-free hotel is actually 46 self-contained apartments all equipped with kitchenettes. The executive apartments and suites are preferable not only because they are spacious enough for four guests (perfect for a family) but because they have a living room and a large balcony with Acropolis views. The standard rooms are fine too, spacious for a couple of guests, with modern furnishings, polished wood floors, but they only have a sitting room (not a separate living room) and their balconies are smaller.

9-11 Lysikratous, 10558 Athens. www.avahotel.gr. ℂ **210/325-9000.** Fax 210/325-9001. 46 units. 180€ double. 400€ executive apt./suite. Rates include breakfast buffet. AE, DC, MC, V. Metro: Acropolis. **Amenities:** Concierge; room service. *In room:* A/C, TV, kitchenette, minibar, hair dryer, Wi-Fi (free).

Electra Palace ★★   The Electra, a few blocks southwest of Syntagma Square on a quiet side street, is a modern and stylish hotel. The rooms on the fifth, sixth, and seventh floors are smaller than those on lower floors, but a top-floor room is where you want to be, both for the view of the Acropolis and to escape traffic noise. (Ask for a top-floor unit when you make your reservation. Your request will be honored "subject to availability"). Guest rooms here are pleasant and decorated in soft pastels and the rooftop pool is a great touch. The hotel restaurant (the Electra Roof Garden) is one of the best in town, with a view as sublime as the food.

18–20 Nikodimou, Plaka, 10557 Athens. www.electrahotels.gr. ℂ **210/337-0000.** Fax 210/324-1875. 106 units. 180€ double; 190€ triple. Rates include breakfast buffet. AE, DC, MC, V. Parking 12€/day. Metro: Syntagma. About 2 blocks down on the left as you walk along Ermou with Syntagma Sq. behind you. **Amenities:** Restaurant; bar; rooftop pool; indoor pool; gym; spa. *In room:* A/C, pay TV, minibar, hair dryer, Wi-Fi (free).

Moderate
Central ★★   This stylish hotel welcomes guests with a marble lobby, while rooms are comfortable with modern decor and high ceilings, attractive sea grass or wooden floors, marble bathrooms, and excellent soundproofing. Family and interconnecting rooms are also available and the large wood roof-deck has superb Acropolis views and a hot tub.

21 Apollonos, 10557 Athens. www.centralhotel.gr. © **210/323-4357.** 84 units. 100€–160€ double. AE, DC, MC, V. Private parking. Metro: Syntagma. **Amenities:** Bar; hot tub; non-smoking rooms. *In room:* A/C, TV, hair dryer, Internet (free).

Hotel Plaka ★★   This hotel is popular with Greeks, who prefer its modern conveniences to the old-fashioned charms of most other hotels in the area. It has a terrific location just off Syntagma Square. Most guest rooms have balconies; those on the fifth and sixth floors in the rear, where it's quieter, have views of the Plaka and the Acropolis (also visible from the roof-garden snack bar).

7 Mitropoleos and Kapnikareas, 10556 Athens. www.plakahotel.gr. © **210/322-2096.** Fax 210/322-2412. 67 units, 38 with shower only. 135€ double; 145€ triple. Rates include breakfast. AE, MC, V. Follow Mitropoleos out of Syntagma Sq. past cathedral and turn left onto Kapnikareas. **Amenities:** Bar. *In room:* A/C, TV, minibar, hair dryer, Wi-Fi (free).

Magna Grecia ★★   Inside a beautiful 19th-century neoclassical building in a hard-to-beat location (right on Mitropoleos Sq.), this is easily one of the best hotels in the Plaka. You'll find high ceilings, French doors, and hardwood floors. All front rooms have sweeping Acropolis views, and there is a pleasant and relaxing rooftop eatery, the Acropolis View Restaurant, that has become one of the most well-regarded restaurants in the city.

54 Mitropoleos, 10563 Plaka. www.magnagreciahotel.com. © **210/324-0314.** Fax 210/324-0317. 12 units. 120€–145€ double; 180€ triple. AE, DC, MC, V. **Amenities:** Cafe/bar; room service. *In room:* A/C, TV/DVD, hair dryer, CD/MP3 player, Internet (free).

Inexpensive

Acropolis House Hotel ★   This small hotel in a handsomely restored 150-year-old villa retains many of its original architectural details. It offers a central location—just off Kidathineon in the heart of the Plaka, a 5-minute walk from Syntagma Square—and the charm of being on a quiet pedestrian side street. Room nos. 401 and 402 offer the best views, and can be requested (but not guaranteed) when making a reservation. A recent (2012) restoration has added new wood floors, polished the beautiful murals on display, and added double-glazed windows and new bathrooms.

6–8 Kodrou, 10558 Athens. www.acropolishouse.gr. © **210/322-2344.** Fax 210/324-4143. 19 units, 15 with bathroom. 70€ double without bathroom, 80€ with bathroom; 104€ triple. 10€ surcharge for A/C. Rates include continental breakfast. V. Walk 2 blocks out of Syntagma Sq. on Mitropoleos and turn left on Voulis, which becomes Kodrou. *In room:* A/C, TV, Internet (free).

NEAR MONASTIRAKI SQUARE

A for Athens ★ 🛅   This funky, hip, and modern arrival in Monastiraki has 35 rooms (apartments) with some of the best views in the city. The "Wide View" rooms (for one to three guests) all have windows facing bustling Monastiraki Square, the Plaka, and the Acropolis, and are spacious with modern decor, hardwood floors, and double-glazed windows while the "Comfy" rooms (for up to four guests) are just as pleasant inside, but face the backstreets of Psiri. The top floor cafe has some of the best city vistas around and has become a new favorite nighttime spot, particularly at sunset and after dark.

20 Miaouli St, 10552 Athens. www.aforathens.com. © **210/324-4244.** 35 units. 95€–150€ double. AE, MC, D, V. Metro: Monastiraki. **Amenities:** bar. *In room:* A/C, TV, fridge, minibar, hair dryer.

Attalos Hotel ★ 🔌   The six-story Attalos is well situated for visitors wanting to take in the daytime street life of the nearby Central Market and the downtown district's exuberant nighttime scene. Half of the plain yet perfectly adequate rooms have balconies, 12 with Acropolis views. The roof garden also offers fine views of the city. The Attalos (whose staff is very helpful) often gives Frommer's readers a 10% discount.

29 Athinas, 10554 Athens. www.attalos.gr. ✆ **210/391-2801.** Fax 210/324-3124. 80 units. 94€ double; 110€ triple; 134€ quad. AE, MC, V. Metro: Monastiraki. Exit from the Athinas St. exit and head 1 block north. **Amenities:** Luggage storage; non-smoking rooms; Internet (free). *In room:* A/C, TV, hair dryer.

Cecil Hotel ★   The Cecil offers reasonably priced rooms in a beautifully restored neoclassical town house with great architectural details—the rooms might be small but they all have polished wood floors, high ceilings, and are soundproof. Full breakfast is served and there's also a welcoming roof garden restaurant.

39 Athinas, 10554 Athens. www.cecil.gr. ✆ **210/321-7079.** Fax 210/321-8005. 36 units. 80€–90€ double; 115€ triple; 160€ suite. AE, MC, V. Metro: Monastiraki. **Amenities:** Restaurant/cafe; bar; Wi-Fi (free). *In room:* A/C, TV.

PSIRRI

Ochre & Brown ★★   This trendy, small boutique hotel in the heart of Psirri has found its niche for fashion-conscious and experienced travelers looking for style, highly personalized service, high-tech amenities, and a chic urban experience. Some rooms have Thissio views, but the finest room is the junior suite where you can see the Acropolis from its terrace. Rooms have stylish furnishings, large work desks, Wi-Fi access, and marble bathrooms with glass-enclosed showers. The hotel's lounge/ bar and restaurant have become one of the city's favorite haunts.

7 Leokoriou, 10554 Athens. www.ochreandbrown.com. ✆ **210/331-2950.** Fax 210/331-2942. 17 units. 120€–192€ double; 208€ junior suite. AE, MC, V. Metro: Monastiraki/Thissio. **Amenities:** Restaurant; lounge bar. *In room:* A/C, TV, Wi-Fi (free).

ON & AROUND SYNTAGMA SQUARE

Athens Cypria ★★ 🛏   In a convenient location on a (usually) quiet street, the Cypria overlooks the Acropolis from unit nos. 603 to 607. With bright white halls and rooms, cheerful floral bedspreads and curtains, and freshly tiled bathrooms with new fixtures, the Cypria is a welcome addition to the city's moderately priced hotels. The breakfast buffet offers hot and cold dishes from 7 to 10am. Be warned, the hotel can be infuriatingly slow in responding to faxed reservation requests.

5 Diomias, 10562 Athens. www.athenscypria.com. ✆ **210/323-8034.** Fax 210/324-8792. 115 units. 117€ double; 143€ triple. Reductions possible off-season. Rates include buffet breakfast. AE, MC, V. Take Karayioryi Servias out of Syntagma Sq.; Diomias is on the left, after Lekka. **Amenities:** Bar; snack bar; luggage storage. *In room:* A/C, TV, minibar, hair dryer, Internet (free).

Grande Bretagne ★★★   The Grande Bretagne, one of Athens's most distinguished 19th-century buildings, is back after a 2-year renovation. The changes preserved the Beaux Arts lobby, made dingy rooms grand once more, and added indoor and outdoor swimming pools. From Winston Churchill to Sting, the guests who stay here expect the highest level of attention. The Grande Bretagne prides itself on its service; you are unlikely to be disappointed. Ask for a room with a balcony overlooking Syntagma Square, the Parliament building, and the Acropolis.

Syntagma Sq., 10564 Athens. www.grandebretagne.gr. ✆ **210/333-0000.** Fax 210/333-0160. 328 units (one room for those w/limited mobility). 277€–285€ double. AE, DC, MC, V. Metro: Syntagma. **Amenities:** 2 restaurants; 2 bars; 2 pools (indoors and outdoors); health club and spa w/Jacuzzi; concierge; room service; non-smoking rooms; free airport pickup. *In room:* A/C, TV, minibar, hair dryer, Wi-Fi (5€/hr.).

New Hotel ★   The "Yes" (Young Enthusiastic Seductive) hotel chain, responsible for some of the city's finest and trendiest hotels (Semiramis, Periscope, 21) has done it again and this time right off Syntagma Square, on the site of the former Olympic Palace Hotel. Designed by award-winning Brazilian architects Fernando and Humberto Campana, this super-trendy hotel—think jagged mirrors, nice-size rooms, contemporary furnishings from recycled materials, original art pieces throughout, and balconies with side-street views—is a sophisticated newcomer. Guests receive a 10% discount at the well-regarded Zouboulakis Art Gallery.

16 Fillelinon St., 10557 Athens. www.yeshotels.gr. ℂ **210/628-4565.** Fax 210/628-4640. 79 units. 127€–200€ double; **Amenities:** Restaurant; bar; exercise room; luggage storage. *In room:* A/C, TV, minibar, hair dryer, Wi-Fi (free).

IN KOLONAKI

Athens Lycabettus Hotel ★   This stylish boutique hotel is on Valeoritou, a pedestrian street filled with trendy cafes, bars, restaurants, and lounges for the fashion-conscious crowd. Apart from its ideal location, the hotel has made a name for itself for its outstanding service. Rooms, though on the small side, are pleasant and bright with contemporary furnishings and marble bathrooms. The hotel also has a popular bar/cafe restaurant.

6 Valeoritou and Voukourestiou St., 10671 Athens. www.athenslycabettus.gr. ℂ **210/360-0600.** 25 units. 100€–120€ double; 160€–200€ suite. Metro: Syntagma. **Amenities:** Restaurant/bar; Wi-Fi (free). *In room:* A/C, TV, minibar, hair dryer.

St. George Lycabettus Hotel ★★   As yet, the distinctive, classy St. George does not attract many tour groups, which contributes to its tranquil, sophisticated tone. The rooftop pool is a real plus, as is the excellently redesigned rooftop restaurant, Le Grand Balcon, much favored by wealthy Greeks for private events. Floors have differing decorative motifs, from Baroque to modern Italian. Most rooms look toward pine-clad Mount Likavitos; some have views of the Acropolis. Others overlook a small park or have interior views. This impeccable boutique hotel is steps from chic restaurants, cafes, lounges, and shops. Check out the Frame lounge in the hotel lobby after dark; this ultra-hip lounge/bar is one of the hottest Athenian destinations.

2 Kleomenous, 10675 Athens. www.sglycabettus.gr. ℂ **210/729-0711.** Fax 210/721-0439. 154 units. 140€–170€ double; 280€ suite. Continental breakfast 20€. AE, DC, MC, V. Parking 14€/day. From Kolonaki Sq., take Patriarchou Ioachim to Loukianou and follow Loukianou uphill to Kleomenous. Turn left on Kleomenous; the hotel overlooks Dexamini Park. **Amenities:** 2 restaurants; 2 bars; outdoor pool; exercise room; spa; room service; non-smoking rooms; rooms for those w/ limited mobility. *In room:* A/C, TV, minibar, hair dryer, Wi-Fi (free).

IN THE EMBASSY DISTRICT

Hilton Athens ★★★   The guest rooms at this Hilton (looking toward either the hills outside Athens or the Acropolis) have large marble bathrooms and are decorated in the generic but comfortable international Hilton style, with some Greek touches. The Plaza Executive floor of rooms and suites offers a separate business center and a higher level of service. Small shops, a salon, and cafes and restaurants surround the glitzy glass-and-marble lobby. The Milos restaurant has superb seafood and the rooftop Galaxy bar has amazing views of just about everything there is to see for miles around (including drop-dead-elegant Athenians).

46 Leoforos Vas. Sofias, 11528 Athens. www.hiltonathens.gr. ℂ **210/728-1000** or 800/445-8667 in the U.S. Fax 210/728-1111. 527 units. 179€–339€ single/double; 274€ triple. AE, DC, MC, V. Parking 27€/day. Metro: Evangelismos. **Amenities:** 4 restaurants; 3 bars; 2 pools (outdoor and indoor);

health club and spa w/Jacuzzi; room service; babysitting; non-smoking rooms/floors; rooms for those w/limited mobility; free airport pickup. *In room:* A/C, TV, minibar, hair dryer, Wi-Fi (5€/hr.).

NEAR THE ACROPOLIS (MAKRIGIANNI & KOUKAKI DISTRICTS)

Expensive

Athens Gate Hotel ★   This small boutique accommodation is stylish, elegant, and close to the sights and the Metro. The seven-floor hotel has 99 rooms; the front rooms on the busy Leof. Syngrou have Temple of Olympian Zeus views; you'll find a partial view of the Acropolis from the lower-floor back rooms (which are also quieter); the rooms on the seventh floor have spectacular Acropolis and city views. The rooms are comfortable and spacious with polished wood floors, modern furnishings, comfortable beds, and good-size bathrooms. The top floor restaurant with its spellbinding views is also a major plus.

10 Syngrou Ave., Makrigianni, 11742 Athens. www.athensgate.gr. (C) **210/923-8302.** Fax 210/237-4993. 99 units. 130€–185€ double; 195€ triple. Rates include breakfast buffet. AE, DC, MC, V. Metro: Akropolis. **Amenities:** Restaurant; 2 bars/cafe; room service; non-smoking rooms, Wi-Fi (free). *In room:* A/C, TV, minibar, hair dryer.

Divani-Palace Acropolis ★★   Just three blocks south of the Acropolis, in a quiet residential neighborhood, this place does a brisk tour business but also welcomes independent travelers. The plain guest rooms are large and comfortable, and some of the large bathrooms even have two washbasins. The cavernous marble-and-glass lobby contains copies of classical sculpture; a section of Athens's 5th-century-B.C. defensive wall is preserved behind glass in the basement by the gift shop. The breakfast buffet is extensive, the hotel's two restaurants offer reasonable fare (particularly the summer-only rooftop Acropolis Secret Roof Garden), and the outdoor pool is a nice touch.

19–25 Parthenonos, Makrigianni, 11742 Athens. www.divaniacropolis.gr. (C) **210/922-2945.** Fax 210/921-4993. 253 units. 110€–180€ double; 300€ suite. Rates include breakfast buffet. AE, DC, MC, V. Metro: Akropolis. **Amenities:** 2 restaurants; 2 bars; outdoor pool; room service; non-smoking rooms. *In room:* A/C, TV, minibar, hair dryer, Internet (free).

Moderate

Acropolis Hill ★   This boutique hotel, near the Filopappos Hill (Hill of the Muses), is pretty, spacious, clean, and in a quiet location. Here you'll find tasteful rooms with modern furnishings and polished wood floors, marble bathrooms, and many of the rooms on the top floor have balconies commanding Acropolis views. There's also a nice rooftop restaurant/bar and a small outdoor pool. It's up a rather steep hill, if that makes a difference to you.

7 Mouson, Filopappou, 11742 Athens. www.acropolishill.gr. (C) **210/923-5151.** Fax 210/924-7350. 36 units. 130€ double; 150€ triple. Rates include breakfast buffet. AE, DC, MC, V. Metro: Syngrou-Fix. From Syngrou-Fix station, ascend Drakou St. for a few blocks to Mouson St. and turn left. **Amenities:** 2 restaurants; 2 bars; outdoor pool; room service; non-smoking rooms. *In room:* A/C, TV, minibar, hair dryer, Wi-Fi (free).

Acropolis View Hotel ★   This well-maintained hotel is on a residential side street off Rovertou Galli, not far from the Herodes Atticus theater. The quiet neighborhood, at the base of Filopappos Hill (a pleasant area to explore) is a 10- to 15-minute walk from the heart of the Plaka. Many of the cozy but appealing guest rooms are freshly painted each year. All units have balconies. Some, like no. 405, overlook

Filopappos Hill, while others, like no. 407, face the Acropolis. A big draw is the roof-top garden with awesome Acropolis views.

Rovertou Galli and 10 Webster, 11742 Athens. www.acropolisview.gr. ℂ **210/921-7303.** Fax 210/923-0705. 32 units. 125€ double. Rates include buffet breakfast. Substantial reductions Nov–Mar. AE, MC, V. Metro: Akropolis. On Dionissiou Areopagitou, head west past Herodes Atticus theater to Rovertou Galli. Webster (Gouemster on some maps) is the little street intersecting Rovertou Galli btw. Propilion and Garabaldi. **Amenities:** Bar. *In room:* A/C, TV, minibar.

Inexpensive

Athens Studios 📛 Located on Veikou street, down the Makrigianni pedestrian block from the Acropolis Metro station between a laundromat and the fun and affordable Athens Sports Bar, the studio apartments come with either two or four beds (some with six), and are bright, modern, and spacious, each with a kitchenette and balcony. The higher-floor apartments have larger balconies and better views but all in all, this is a wonderful hostel in a great location with a warm homey feel to it that won't break the bank.

3a Veikou, Makigianni, 11742 Athens. www.athensstudios.gr. ℂ **210/923-5811.** 15 units. 60€–65€ double; 50€ quad. AE, MC, V. Metro: Akropolis. *In room:* A/C, TV, Internet (free).

Marble House Pension ★ Named for its marble facade, which is usually covered with bougainvillea, this small hotel, whose front rooms have balconies overlooking quiet Zinni Street, is famous among budget travelers (including many teachers) for its friendly staff. Over the last several years, the pension has been remodeled and redecorated, gaining new bathrooms and guest-room furniture (including small fridges). Two units have kitchenettes. If you're spending more than a few days in Athens, this is a homey base.

35 A. Zinni, Koukaki, 11741 Athens. www.marblehouse.gr. ℂ **210/923-4058.** Fax 210/922-6461. 16 units, 12 with bathroom, two rooms for those w/limited mobility. 45€ double without bathroom, 49€ with bathroom. 9€ supplement for A/C. Monthly rates available off-season. No credit cards. Metro: Syngrou-Fix. *In room:* A/C (9 units), TV, minibar.

THE COAST

Good beaches, excellent restaurants, and open-air clubs and bars, as well as excellent shops, make the coast very appealing during the summer and are a good choice if you don't have time to make it to the islands. You can get into downtown Athens by the hotel shuttles, bus, tram, or taxi.

Very Expensive

Astir Palace Resort ★★ We're talking serious creature comfort here—as well as every activity from windsurfing to private Pilates instruction! Tranquil and beautiful, with incredible sea vistas and private pine-clad grounds, the Astir Palace is a series of secluded bungalows and three hotels with their own private beaches on 30 hectares (74 acres). Seven well-regarded restaurants, including Matsuhisa Athens and 2012 Michelin star winner Galazia Hytra, are on-site.

40 Apollonos, 16671 Vouliagmeni. www.astir-palace.com. ℂ **210/890-2000.** Fax 210/896-2582. 526 units. Arion: 380€–460€ double. Westin: 340€–410€ double. AE, DC, MC, V. Free parking. Tram to Glyfada, then either taxi or bus 114. **Amenities:** 7 restaurants; 7 bars; 3 outdoor pools; 3 tennis courts w/floodlighting; health club; spa. *In room:* A/C, TV, Wi-Fi (free).

Divani Apollon Palace & Spa ★★ In a prime location on Kavouri beach with towering palm trees, picturesque gardens, and two large swimming pools, this is as close to a secluded island experience as you are likely to get in any large city. With sea views from every room, large balconies, and green marble bathrooms, this is perhaps the most romantic of Athens's hotels. Complementing the romantic ambience is the well-regarded on-site seafood restaurant, Mythos tis Thalassas (Legend of the Sea), with seafront tables.

10 Agiou Nikolaou and Iliou, 16671 Vouliagmeni. www.divaniapollon.gr. © **210/891-1100.** Fax 210/965-8010. 286 units. 220€ double; 340€ executive double; 1,600€ suite. AE, DC, MC, V. Free parking. Tram to Glyfada, then either taxi or bus 114. **Amenities:** 3 restaurants; bar; 2 pools; tennis court w/floodlighting; health club; spa; free shuttle bus to Glyfada and/or Syntagma Sq. *In room:* A/C, TV, Wi-Fi (free).

THE NORTHERN PELOPONNESE & DELPHI ★★★

With the obvious exception of the Acropolis in Athens, Greece's most famous and beautiful ancient sites are clustered around the Gulf of Corinth, whose deep blue waters separate the mainland from southern Greece, called the Peloponnese. On the mainland north of the Gulf, the sanctuary of Apollo's famous oracle at Delphi clings to mountain slopes; across the Gulf in the Peloponnese are Agamemnon's palace at Mycenae, the Mycenaean fortress of Tiryns, a beautifully restored (and still used) ancient stadium at Nemea, the steep-sided 4th-century-B.C. theater of Epidaurus, and Olympia, the birthplace of the Olympic Games. Some say that Delphi is the most spectacular ancient site in Greece; others give the laurels to Olympia. You decide—perhaps while relaxing at a taverna on a lane in Nafplion, or on a beach after a day's sightseeing.

The Northern Peloponnese & the Classical Sites ★★★

One of the delights of visiting the northern Peloponnese during the summer high season (July–Aug) is that it's relatively uncrowded when many of the Cycladic islands

---

 Driving Tips

The multi-lane National Road along the coast from Athens to Corinth (89km/55 miles), and from Corinth on to Olympia (222km/120 miles) is almost always very heavily utilized by both kamikaze car drivers and lumbering long-distance trucks and buses. Most drivers scorn the use of directional signals and seem to try to change lanes as often as possible, forcing other drivers to test their swerving and braking skills. The easiest way to take in Delphi after visiting the North Peloponnese is to head from Olympia to Rio, just north of Patras (90km/55 miles), and take the Rio-Antirio Bridge (13€–24€ 1-day round-trip ticket; www.gefyra.gr) across the Gulf. With a 2,252m (7,388-ft.) fully suspended continuous deck and 40km (25 miles) of cables, this is the longest cable-stayed bridge in the world, built to withstand both earthquakes and bombs. From the north shore of the Gulf, a road runs all the way to Delphi, 177km (110 miles) west of Athens. Try to allow at least 4 days (spending 2 nights at Nafplion and 1 night each at Olympia and Delphi) for your visit to the Northern Peloponnese and Delphi. If you're driving your own car, keep in mind that the **Greek Automobile Association** (ELPA; Athens Tower, 2–4 Mossogion, Athens 115 27; © **210/778-1614**) has a reciprocity arrangement with many foreign auto clubs. The ELPA emergency number is © **104-00.** Remember that only Portugal has more traffic fatalities each year than Greece, so buckle up and be careful out there!

in the Aegean are sagging under the weight of tourists. That doesn't mean you'll have famous spots like Mycenae, Epidaurus, and Olympia to yourself if you arrive at high noon in August. If you arrive just as sites open or just before they close, you may have an hour under the pine trees at Olympia or Epidaurus virtually alone, and be able to stand in Mycenae's Treasury of Atreus with swallows as your only companions.

Even the most avid tourists do not live by culture alone, and it's good to know that one of the great delights of spending time in the northern Peloponnese is whiling away a few quiet hours watching shepherds minding their flocks and fishermen mending their nets. And be sure to allow yourself time to enjoy Nafplion, with its stepped streets, flowery courtyards, handsome neoclassical buildings, shops, and cafes—and the best ice cream in the Peloponnese. If all this sounds too tame for you, check out these websites: **www.trekking.gr** offers hiking and whitewater rafting tours, **www.eumelia.com** runs retreats and seminars on topics from alternative medicine to the Argentine tango on an organic farm deep in the Peloponnese near Sparta, and **www.limnisa.com** offers writing seminars and silent meditation retreats for up to 10 guests by the sea near Methana, not far from Epidauros. If you want to get really close to nature, you can stay in a tent in Limnisa's garden—and get a considerable discount on the usual room rate. If you want to stay in a seaside hotel while visiting the ancient sites, check out the Kalamaki Beach Hotel (p. 473).

CORINTH ★★

Today, as in antiquity, the cities of Corinth and Patras are the two major gateways to the Peloponnese. Patras was relatively unimportant in antiquity, but Corinth dominated trade in Greece for much of the 8th and 7th centuries B.C., when it exported its pottery around the Mediterranean and brought back goods to sell at home. Corinth experienced another burst of prominence and wealth under the Romans in the 2nd century A.D. As you enter the Peloponnese, you'll want to leave the main highway (look for the turnoff for the Canal Tourist Area) to take a look at the Corinth Canal and visit ancient Corinth before heading deeper into the northern Peloponnese. If you are driving, keep an eye out for signs for Archaia Korinthos/Ancient Corinth. Try not to be misled by signs into the modern town of Corinth, which has no antiquities and, as far as I have ever discovered, no accurate signs showing the way to Ancient Corinth.

Essentials

GETTING THERE   There are several **trains** a day from Athens's Stathmos Peloponnisou (train station for the Peloponnese) to the Corinth train station off Demokratias (✆ **27410/22-522** or **27410/22-523**). These trains are almost invariably late,

Changes to Opening Hours

Let's get the bad news over with first: At press time, many sites and museums were open only from 8am–3pm due to the economic crisis in Greece. In addition, many of the galleries in some museums are closed due to the shortage of guards. Many small sites have been closed altogether. If the situation improves, perhaps the usual summer hours (8am–7pm) will be reinstated. Now, the good news for travelers at least: Some museums have lowered their entrance fees from 3€ or 4€ to 2€. Many hotels plan to lower their prices if tourism to Greece, which has fallen steadily since 2009, does not increase.

THE CORINTH canal

The new highway rushes you over the Corinth Canal very quickly, and unless you're vigilant you can miss the turnoff to the **Canal Tourist Area.** Before the new road was completed in 1997, almost everyone stopped here for a coffee, a *souvlaki*, and a look at the ships squeezing through the narrow canal that separates the Peloponnese from the mainland. Since then, the traffic hurtles past, and the cafes, restaurants, and shops here are hurting badly. There's a small post office at the canal, along with a kiosk with postcards and English-language newspapers; most of the large *souvlaki* places have clean toilet facilities (but tough souvlaki). **Warning:** Be sure to lock your car door. This is a popular spot for thieves who prey on unwary tourists.

The French engineers who built the Corinth Canal between 1881 and 1893 blasted through 87m (285 ft.) of sheer rock to make this 6km-long (3¾-mile), 27m-wide (89-ft.) passageway. The canal utterly revolutionized shipping in the Mediterranean; vessels that previously had spent days making their way around Cape Matapan, at the southern tip of the Peloponnese, could dart through the canal in hours. Although it took modern technology to build the canal, the Roman emperors Caligula and Nero had tried, and failed, to dig a canal with slave labor. Nero was obsessed with the project, going so far as to lift the first shovelful of earth with a dainty golden trowel. That done, he headed back to Rome and left the real work to the 6,000 Jewish slaves he had brought in from Judea.

often taking 4 hours or more. For information on schedules and fares, call ✆ **210/529-8735** or **210/513-1601,** or go to www.ose.gr. Greece's economic crisis has slowed plans for the Athens suburban rail service (Proastiakos) to extend its service from Athens International Airport as far as Corinth and Patras. Check for updates at www.proastiakos.gr.

There are at least 15 **buses** a day, taking 2 to 2½ hours, from the Stathmos Leoforia Peloponnisou (bus station for the Peloponnese) in Athens, 100 Kifissou (www.ktel.org; ✆ **210/512-4910** or **210/512-9233**), to Corinth, where you can catch a bus for the short (15–20 min.) trip to Archaia Korinthos. For general information on Athens–Peloponnese schedules and fares, try www.ktel.org or ✆ **210/512-4910.** *Warning:* Telephones in bus stations are not always answered. Buses from Athens to Corinth sometimes terminate at the canal; from there, another bus will run into Corinth itself. From Corinth, you can continue to Ancient Corinth.

Confusingly, at present buses for destinations in the Peloponnese leave Corinth from one of two badly signposted stations: one at the corner of Kolokotroni and Koilatsou (✆ **27410/24-444**) and the other at the corner of Ethnikis Konstantinou and Aratou (✆ **27410/24-403**). For most destinations in the Peloponnese beyond Tripolis, you'll need to change at Tripolis.

By car, the National Highway runs from Athens to Corinth. Once you get out of central Athens, it takes about 1½ hours for the journey to the canal. The highway, which has been widened over the past decade, still contains some nasty three-lane stretches. The highway now sweeps over the Corinth Canal; if you want to stop here, look for the signs indicating the **Canal Tourist Area.** Shortly after the canal, you'll see signs for Corinth (the modern town and ancient site), Isthmia (site of the Isthmian Games), Epidauros (ancient theater), and the port of Patras.

VISITOR INFORMATION The official **Greek Ministry of Culture** website for information on museums and monuments in Greece is www.odysseus.culture.gr. Unfortunately, the site is seldom up-to-date. Increasingly, if you Google any of the major *nomes* (provinces), towns, and cities in Greece, you'll discover its official website, often with an English translation. Nafplion's website, however, is one of the best (www.nafplion.gr).

Some travel agencies attempt to present their websites as official government-sponsored information sites. Websites for the bus, train, and ferry lines are often out-of-date and inaccurate; telephones for the bus, train, and ferry lines often are not answered. The most up-to-date transportation information is often available at travel agents, or at bus and train stations, and at ticket agents in port towns.

Exploring Corinth

To reach Ancient Corinth, follow the signs after the Corinth Canal for Ancient Corinth or Old Corinth (the small modern village with the large ancient site). It's about a 20-minute bus ride from the train or bus station, or 10 minutes by taxi.

Acrocorinth ★★ 📷 CASTLE It's hard to say what's more impressive here: The massive fortifications or the spectacular view across the plain of Corinth to the Gulf and beyond into central Greece. A winding dirt road runs from the site of Ancient Corinth to the summit of this rugged limestone sugar loaf mountain topped by centuries of fortifications. A superb natural acropolis, Acrocorinth was fortified first by the Greeks and later by just about everyone who came here: The Romans, Byzantines, Franks, Venetians, and Turks. Extensive remains of the centuries of walls, turrets, and towers can be seen, including some repaired and used in World War II. A small cafe just outside the main gate is sometimes open. The steep shadeless walk up takes at least an hour so bring bottled water. Round-trip cab fare is around 25€, with a 30-minute wait on the summit; a cab only going up, if you can find a willing driver, is about 15€.

Old Corinth. ✆ **27410/31-966.** Admission 3€. Usually open daily 8:30am–7pm; winter daily 9am–3pm.

Ancient Corinth ★★ RUINS The site of Ancient Corinth is dominated by its spectacular 6th-century-B.C. **Temple of Apollo.** If you can, find a perch near the temple and look out over the sprawling site, which would have stretched from the temple to the sea. Much of what you are looking at is the extensive remains of the enormous **Roman Agora** (forum or marketplace). Razed and destroyed when the Romans conquered Greece in 146 B.C., Corinth was refounded by Julius Caesar in 44 B.C. and rapidly began a period of wealth and prosperity. When Saint Paul visited here in 52 A.D., he supported himself as a tent maker and delivered tirades against the worldly ways of the Corinthians.

By the 2nd century A.D., Corinth was much larger and more powerful than Athens, but during the next hundred years, a series of barbarian invasions and attacks undermined the city's prosperity. Historians concluded that Corinth lapsed into a long stagnant period as a provincial backwater with a glorious past. New evidence has turned up to make historians question that conclusion: Beginning in 1995, excavations unearthed finds ranging from an extensive Roman villa of the 4th century A.D. to imported English china of the 19th century A.D.—important evidence that Corinth's prosperity lasted a very long time, indeed.

Ancient Corinth's main drag, the 12m-wide (39-ft.) marble-paved road that ran from the port of Lechaion into the heart of the marketplace, is clearly visible from the temple. Along the road, and throughout the Agora, are the foundations of hundreds of the small shops that once stocked everything from spices imported from Asia Minor to jugs of wine made from Corinth's excellent grapes.

Two spots in the Agora are especially famous—the **Fountain of Peirene** and the **Bema.** The fountain honors the maternal devotion of Peirene, a woman who wept so hard when her son died that she dissolved into the spring that still flows here. In the 2nd century A.D., the famous Roman traveler, philhellene, benefactor, and compulsive monument builder Herodes Atticus is thought to have encased the modest Greek fountain in an elaborate two-story building with arches, arcades, and a 5-sq.-m (54-sq.-ft.) courtyard. Later benefactors further elaborated the fountain. As for the Bema (public platform), this was where Paul had to plead his case when the Corinthians, irritated by his constant criticisms, hauled him in front of the Roman governor Gallo in 52 A.D.

Old Corinth. ✆ **27410/31-207.** Admission to archaeological site and museum 6€. Summer daily 8am–8pm; winter daily 8am–3pm.

Archaeological Museum ★ MUSEUM As you'd expect, this museum just inside the site entrance has a particularly fine collection of the famous Corinthian pottery, which is often decorated with charming red-and-black figures of birds and animals. There are also a number of statues of Roman worthies and several mosaics, including one in which Pan is shown piping away to an appreciative clutch of cows. The museum courtyard is a shady spot in which to sit and read up on the ancient site, which has virtually no shade; the toilets are just off the courtyard. When you visit, be sure to see the handsome sculpture and vases stolen from the museum in 1990, which were discovered hidden in a fish-processing factory in Miami, Florida, in 1998; and officially handed back to Greece in 2001.

Insider Tip: The Archaeological Museum has an extensive collection of finds from the Shrine of Asclepius; because many of these are graphic representations of intimate body parts, they are kept in a room that is usually locked. If you look solemn and express a scholarly interest, you may be able to persuade a guard to unlock the room.

Ancient Corinth, in the town of Old Corinth. ✆ **27410/31-207.** Admission 6€. Summer daily 8am–7pm; winter daily 8am–3pm; sometimes closed Mon until noon.

Where to Stay & Eat

Marinos Rooms (✆ **27410/31-209**), with a great location only a 5-minute walk from the excavations, has 22 *very* simple rooms (around 50€) and a restaurant with excellent home cooking (hearty lunch or dinner from around 15 €). In summer, you should book well ahead, as this place is usually taken over by visiting archaeologists. The grandly named **Splendid** (no phone) restaurant across from the site and the **Ancient Corinth** on the main square serve decent lunch and dinner (simple stews, chops, and salads) for around 15€. If you are heading on to Nafplion, you will be able to get excellent accommodations and food there.

Insider Tip: If you don't like moving from hotel to hotel, Nafplion (see below) is a great base for visiting Corinth, Mycenae and Tiryns, Nemea, and Epicauros. But if you want to be by the sea, try the 80-unit **Kalamaki Beach Hotel** (www.kalamaki beachhotel; ✆ **27410/37-653**), about 10 miles from Corinth, near Ancient Isthmia. The large rooms have balconies (doubles with breakfast and lunch or dinner from 100€), the two pools (one for children) are great when the sea is rough, the buffet-style restaurant is efficient and satisfactory, and the garden is lovely.

NAFPLION ★★★

Nafplion is far and away the most charming town in the Peloponnese, with stepped streets overhung with balconies dripping with bougainvillea, handsome neoclassical buildings, and enticing shops, restaurants, cafes, and, for that matter, several fine museums—and even a miniature castle (the Bourtzi) on a small island in the harbor. A good deal of Nafplion's appeal comes from the fact that for several years after the Greek War of Independence (1821–28), this was the country's first capital. Although the palace of Greece's young King Otto—a mail-order monarch from Bavaria—burned down in the 19th century, an impressive number of handsome neoclassical civic buildings and private houses have survived, as has a scattering of Turkish fountains and several mosques. You could spend several pleasant days here simply enjoying wandering the streets of this port town itself, but you'll probably want to use Nafplion as your home base for day trips to the ancient sites at Mycenae, Nemea, Tiryns, and Epidaurus, and—if you didn't see it on the way here—Corinth. Keep in mind that *lots* of Greeks come here year-round on weekends, so if you're visiting Nafplion on a weekend, reserve your hotel well in advance.

Essentials

GETTING THERE There are at least a dozen **buses** a day to Nafplion from the Stathmos Leoforia Peloponnisou (bus station for the Peloponnese) in Athens, 100 Kifissou (www.ktel.org; © 210/512-4910). The trip is a slow one (about 4 hr.) because the bus usually goes into both Corinth and Argos before reaching the Nafplion station on Syngrou Street (by Plateia Kapodistrias; © 27520/28-555). For general information on Athens–Peloponnese schedules and fares try www.ktel.org (© 210/512-4910 or -9233).

By car, from Athens, follow signs for Epidaurus and head south to the Corinth Canal. Take the Corinth–Tripolis national road to the Argos exit and follow signs into Argos and then for Nafplion. You'll almost certainly get lost at least once in Argos, which has an abysmal system of directional signs. Allow 3 hours for the drive from Athens to Nafplion, considerably more if you stop at Corinth, Nema, or Mycenae (all clearly signposted) en route. When you reach Nafplion, try to park in the freelot by the harbor and be sure to lock your car and put any valuables out of sight in the trunk. There's also some on-street parking available.

VISITOR INFORMATION The **Municipal Tourist Office** is at 25 Martiou (© 27520/24-444), diagonally across from the bus station. It's usually open Monday through Friday from 9am to 1pm and 5 to 8pm (but is often mysteriously closed during work hours). Ask for the useful brochure *Nafplion Day and Night.* The website www.mafplion.gr is helpful—when functioning. Information and tickets for special events, such as the concerts in the June **Nafplion Music Festival,** are sometimes available from the Town Hall (Demarkeion) in the old high-school building on Iatrou Square (www.nafplionfestival.gr; © 27520/23-33).

There are a number of travel agencies in Nafplion, such as **Staikos Travel,** by the harbor (© 27520/27-950); **Yiannopoulos Travel,** on Plateia Syntagma (© 27520/28-054); and **Nafplion Car Hire,** 51 Bouboulinas St. (© 27570/24-160), the local Avis car hire agent.

On Nafplion's main square, Plateia Syntagma, the **Odyssey bookshop** (© 27520/23-430) has maps, guides, newspapers, magazines, with a wide range of books in English. If you want to read a delightful guide to Nafplion, see if there are any copies of Timothy Gregory's *Nafplion* (Lycabettus Press); although published in 1980, it offers a superb insight to the city's history and monuments.

Take a Dip, a Sail, or a Train Ride

The best place to swim is at Arvanitia Beach beneath the Palamidi. Unfortunately, winter storms early in 2012 did extensive damage to the beach, changing facilities and walkways beneath the Palamidi at Arvanita Beach. If you want to see if the beach and its facilities have been repaired, with the Bourtzi on your right, you can easily walk there in about 5 minutes by heading south along the quay past the harbor-side cafes. If you'd rather be out on the sea looking back at the shore, contact Captain Aris, whose sailing ship is usually moored near where the shuttle runs to the Bourtzi. Captain Aris (✆ **69443/53-200**) gives day sails, complete with instruction and lunch and opportunities for swimming and snorkeling, from about 80€ per person. The Captain speaks fluent English and gets high praise for his patience from his novice sailors. You can also take a day trip down the coast to **Monembassia** on the Alkyonis (run by Pegasus Cruises), which sometimes departs from Nafplion, sometimes from nearby Tolon. Information available at www.pegasus-cruises.gr or on harbor-side posters. Don't like the water? Hop on the miniature train that leaves from the harbor-side parking lot every hour or so, and gives a 45-minute tour of the city (4€).

Exploring Nafplion

Nafplion is a stroller's delight, and one of the great pleasures here is simply walking through the parks, up and down the stepped side streets, and along the harbor. Don't make the mistake of stopping your harbor-side stroll when you come to the last of the large seaside cafes on the quay. If you continue, you can watch fishing boats at the pier and explore several cliff-side chapels. Nafplion is so small that you can't get seriously lost, so have fun exploring. Here are some suggestions on how to see Nafplion's impressive fortresses and museums after you've had your initial stroll.

Acronafplia & the Palamidi ★★ CASTLE   The Acronafplia and the Palamidi dominate Nafplion's skyline and, as usual with fortresses, are most impressive when seen from afar. There have been fortifications on these summits since prehistoric times, but most of what stands today was built by the Venetians, when they controlled Nafplion for much of the 15th through the 17th centuries. It's a very stiff climb to either fortress, and you may prefer to take a taxi up (around 8€) and walk back down. If you do walk up to **Acronafplia,** follow signs in the lower town to the **Church of Saint Spyridon,** one of whose walls has the mark left by one of the bullets that killed Ianni Kapodistria, the first governor of modern Greece.

From Saint Spyridon, follow the signs farther uphill to the **Catholic Church of the Metamorphosis.** This church is as good a symbol as any for Nafplion's vexed history. Built by the Venetians, it was converted into a mosque by the Turks and then reconsecrated as a church after the War of Independence. Inside, an ornamental doorway has an inscription listing philhellenes who died for Greece, including nephews of Lord Byron and George Washington. As you continue to climb to Acronafplia, keep an eye out for several carvings of the **winged lion** that was the symbol of Mark, the patron saint of Venice. The Nafplia Palace Hotel (p. 479) now sprawls across the top of the summit (archaeologists still shudder that the hotel was allowed to be built here) and enjoys superb views across the sea to the Parnon mountain range.

More than 800 steps wind their way up 220m (722 ft.) to the summit of the **Palamidi ★**; I'm glad I once did this climb, and equally glad now usually to drive up.

The Venetians spent 3 years fortifying the Palamidi, only to have it conquered the following year after completion in 1715 by the Turks. Enter the fortress the way the Turkish attackers did, through the main gate to the east. Once inside, you can trace the course of the massive wall that encircled the entire summit and wander through the considerable remains of the five fortresses that failed to stop the raid. If you're in Nafplion during the June **Music Festival,** find out if any evening concerts are being held at the Palamidi, which is open in summer, Monday through Friday from 8am to 7pm, and Saturday and Sunday from 8am to 3pm; in winter, daily from 8am to 3pm. Admission is 3€.

The Bourtzi ★★ CASTLE   Everyone's favorite fortress—and perhaps the only one to evoke squeals of "how cute" from tourists—the miniature **Bourtzi Fortress** was built by Venetians in the 15th century to guard the entrance to Nafplion's harbor. Since then, it's had a checkered career, serving as a home for retired executioners in the 19th century and as a hotel in the 20th century. Small boats ply back and forth between the dock and the Bourtzi (from 6€ round-trip); usually, you can stay as long as you wish, explore, and return with the same or a different boat. Take something to drink and a snack with you, as the small cafe here is often closed; toilet facilities are rudimentary.

Nafplion's Museums

Nafplion's museums are within easy walking distance of one another; all have explanatory labels in English and Greek.

Nafplion Archaeological Museum ★ MUSEUM   This museum reopened in 2010 after 5 years of renovations. Large, bright rooms have replaced dusty display cases and exhibits have been themed to demonstrate life in the area from Neolithic to Christian times. An excellent video (with English text) shows and explains the sites where most objects were found. The collection includes pottery, jewelry, and some quite terrifying Mycenaean terracotta idols, as well as a handsome bronze suit of armor. The museum is in one of the best-looking buildings in town, the handsome 18th-century Venetian arsenal that dominates Plateia Syntagma. The thick walls make this a deliciously cool place to visit on even the hottest day.

Plateia Syntagma (Constitution Sq.) ℂ **27520/27-502.** Admission 2€. Tues–Sun 9am–3pm.

National Gallery-Alexandros Soutzos Museum MUSEUM   The National Gallery in Athens has begun an ambitious scheme to open branches throughout Greece. Nafplion's branch in a former neoclassical 19th-century town house facing Kolokotronis Park has a permanent exhibit of paintings showing scenes from the Greek War of Independence, including both handsome young warriors lounging by classical remains and wounded veterans begging alms. There are frequently changing temporary exhibits, sometimes featuring local artists, and a small shop.

23 Sidiras Merarhias St. ℂ **27520/21-915.** Admission 3€; free Mon. Mon and Thurs 10am–3pm; Wed and Fri 10am–3pm and 5–8pm; Sat 10am–2pm.

Peloponnesian Folklore Foundation (Folk Art Museum) ★★★ MUSEUM Almost as soon as it opened in 1981, this small museum occupying three floors of an 18th-century house won the European Museum of the Year Award. In 2005, the museum installed a new permanent exhibition focusing on urban Greece, particularly Nafplion in the 19th and 20th centuries. Dioramas show elegant town-house parlors stuffed with marble-topped furniture, Persian carpets, and ornate silver and china bibelots, and elegantly dressed matrons. Keep an eye out for the exhibit added in

2012 on Kalliopi Papalexopoulou, every inch a society matron, but also a fierce opponent of the monarchy in Greece's fight for democracy 150 years earlier. Her role in forcing King Otto to flee Greece in 1862 was honored when the warship *Hellas* conveyed her in triumph to Athens, where she was honored with a rapturous reception. The museum also often has special exhibitions by contemporary artists in a ground-floor gallery near the small shop.

1 V. Alexandros. www.pli.gr. 🕐 **27520/28-947.** Admission 4€. Museum Wed–Mon 9am–3pm; shop most days 9am–2pm and 6–9pm. Closed Feb.

Where to Eat

Nafplion is so popular with Greek visitors that a number of the restaurants in and just off Nafplion's central Syntagma Square are not the tourist traps that you might expect. Furthermore, you'll see plenty of Greeks at the big harbor-side cafes on Akti Miaoulis; wealthy Athenians think nothing of driving to Nafplion for Sunday lunch and a stroll.

Moderate

Hellas Restaurant ★ ☺ GREEK   Children who normally squirm in restaurants will enjoy the Hellas: Between courses, they can join the other kids kicking soccer balls and racing up and down Plateia Syntagma. Shady awnings make this a cool spot to eat outdoors and locals tend to congregate in the indoor dining room year-round. Forget about seafood or haute cuisine and stick to the simple dishes: the *dolmades* (made with vine leaves in summer, cabbage in winter) in egg-lemon sauce are usually on the menu, as well as bean soup in winter, or stuffed tomatoes and peppers over summer. Just about everyone in town passes through Plateia Syntagma, so this is a great spot to watch the world go by.

Plateia Syntagma. 🕐 **27520/27-278.** Main courses 7€–12€. AE, MC, V. Daily 9am–midnight.

Karamanlis ★ 🍴 GREEK   This simple harbor-front taverna, several blocks east of the main cluster of cafes, tends to get fewer tourists than most of the places in town. It serves up grills and several kinds of meatballs (*keftedes, sousoutakia,* and *yiouvarlakia*). If you like the food here, you'll probably also enjoy **Arapakos, Kanares Taverna,** and **Hundalos Taverna,** also on Bouboulinas. If you order fish, unless money is no object, be sure to ask the price.

1 Bouboulinas. 🕐 **27520/27-668.** Main courses 8€–15€; fresh fish priced by the kilo. AE, MC, V. Usually daily 11am–midnight.

Ta Phanaria ★ GREEK   A shaded table under the enormous scarlet bougainvillea makes for one of the prettiest places in the center of town for lunch or dinner. Ta Phanaria usually has several inventive vegetable dishes on the menu in addition to regulars such as moussaka. The stews and chops here are also good and in winter, hearty bean dishes are usually available.

13 Staikopoulou. 🕐 **27520/27-141.** Main courses 7€–15€. MC, V. Daily about noon–midnight.

Taverna Old Mansion (Paleo Archontiko) ★★ GREEK   There is something very appealing about spending a cozy evening here, enjoying the good food and lively local scene. In summer, tables spill out along Siokou Street. The menu offers consistently good traditional Greek *spitiko* (home) cooking: Stews, chops, and usually several vegetarian choices. When live music is featured in the evening, tables are at a premium. If you like the food here, you'll probably also enjoy the grills at the pleasantly simple **Taverna Byzantino,** 15 Alexandrou (🕐 **27520/21-631**) and the charming

Omorfo Tavernaki, Kotsonopoulou & Queen Olga (www.omorfotavernaki.gr; ✆ 27520/25944).

7 Siokou. ✆ **27520/22-449.** Main courses 8€–15€. MC, V. Daily 7pm–midnight; summer weekends noon–4pm.

Inexpensive

Antica Gelateria di Roma ★★★★ CAFÉ/DESSERT   This is where I head first when I get to Nafplion and where I stop last before I leave, to enjoy the best ice cream and ices in the Peloponnese—perhaps in Greece! You can have anything from a banana split to a tiny cup with just a taste. Still hungry? Have a panini with mozzarella, prosciutto, and fresh tomatoes. You can finish off with espresso and learn about soccer, a passion of the *gelateria*'s genial Italian owner.

3 Pharmakopoulou and Komninou. ✆ **27520/23-520.** Sweets and sandwiches 2.50€–12€. No credit cards. Daily 10am–midnight.

Sokaki ★ BAR/CAFÉ   In the morning, tourists tuck into the full American breakfast here, while locals toy with tiny cups of Greek coffee. In the evening, people come to lounge and people-watch, and sometimes to drink cocktails.

8 Ethniki Antistaseos. ✆ **27520/26-032.** Drinks and snacks 5€–15€. No credit cards. Daily 8am–8pm; summer daily 8am–midnight.

Shopping

As you might expect of a town that has so many Greek repeat-visitors, Nafplion has some terrific shops. For a wide range of handsome handcrafted jewelry, try **Preludio,** 2 Vas. Konstantinou (✆ **27520/25-277**), just off Plateia Syntagma a few steps from the Hellas Restaurant. Staikopoulou Street, 1 block uphill from Plateia Syntagma, is window-shopping territory. The **Komboloi Museum,** 25 Staikopoulou (✆/fax **27520/ 21-618**; www.komboloi.gr) is on the second floor of a shop selling *kombolo*—the round "worry beads" that many Greek men twirl. The beads sell for anything from a few to many thousand euros; museum admission is 2€. A few doors along, **Nafplio tou Nafpliou,** 56A Staikopoulou (no phone) sells icons showing virtually every saint in the Greek Orthodox church. Over on Siokou Street, **Konstantine Beselmes,** 7 Ath. Siokou (✆ **27520/25-842**) offers magical paintings of village scenes, sailing ships, and idyllic landscapes. Although new, the paintings are done on weathered boards to give them a vintage look. Nearby, **Agynthes,** 10 Siokou (✆ **27520/21-704**) has hand-loomed fabrics, some fashioned into throws, bags, and scarves.

Greek wine can be sourced at the **Wine Shop,** 5 Amalias (✆/fax **27520/24-446**). **Nektar and Ambrosia,** 6 Pharmakopoulou (✆ **27520/43-001**) is one of several new shops selling delicious herbs and organic honey products, including scented soaps.

Where to Stay

Due to its year-round popularity, hotel reservations are usually strongly advised. Before the Greek economic crisis set in, every room in town was often taken on summer and holiday weekends. If the crisis continues, you may find that many of these hotels lower their high-season prices and offer discounts for non-weekend bookings. A number of hotels require that you guarantee your reservation with a credit card—but only accept cash payment. Be sure to bring a print copy with you confirming your reservation, and double-check to make sure that the hotel will accept payment by credit card.

In addition to the hotels below, here are a few others to consider. Nafplion's 172-room **Amalia** (www.amalia.gr; ✆ **27520/24-400**) is the place to stay if you don't mind being a mile or two out of Nafplion itself and want to relax in a big swimming pool. Like all Amalia Hotels, this one has extensive gardens; large, comfortable rooms; large bathrooms; efficient, attentive service—and lots of tour groups and wedding parties. The Amalia is still spruced up after a total renovation in 2008. Doubles start from 120€. If you feel like a serious splurge, check out the 42-unit **Amphitryon** (www.amphitryon.gr; © **27520/70-700**), transformed from its down-at-heel days into a five-star member of the Leading Small Hotels of the World, the Amphitryon has drop-dead-gorgeous flower arrangements, enormous bathrooms with hydrojet showers, pool privileges up the hill at the Nafplia Palace Hotel, and promises "romantic moments in an ambience of privileged scenery." Doubles start at 250€. If you prefer the ambience of the pleasant residential neighborhood around Ayios Spiridon church, try the 21-unit **Pension Acronafplia** (www.pensionacronafplia.gr; © **27570/24-581**). The pension occupies four thoughtfully restored town houses whose very congenial accommodations range from simple (small room, no private bathroom) to quite elegant (large room, private bathroom, and balcony with harbor view). Doubles range in price from 50€ to 150€.

Very Expensive

Nafplia Palace Hotel (formerly Xenia Palace Hotel) ♨

Atop Acronafplia, the Nafplia Palace has the best view in town, not only of Nafplion itself, but across the bay to the mountains of the Peloponnese. Complete renovations in 1999 and 2005 substantially modernized and upgraded the old Xenia Palace. Though it is true that the bungalow villas are glamorous, with bathrooms the size of battleships, and gimmicks such as "remote-controlled bed mattresses," the service throughout the hotel remains lax, the room decor bland, the lobby sterile, and the food ranges from tedious to pretentious. In short, I find this a seriously overrated hotel—with a view to die for.

Acronafplia, 21000 Nafplion. www.nafplionhotels.gr. © **27520/28-981** or 27522/89-815. Fax 27520/28-783. 105 units, including 54 bungalows. From 300€ double; from 600€ bungalow. Significant off-season reductions possible. Rates include breakfast. AE, DC, MC, V. **Amenities:** 2 restaurants; 2 snack bars; 2 outdoor pools. *In room:* A/C, TV, DVD, minibar, Wi-Fi (free).

Moderate

Byron Hotel ★★

This little hotel has a quiet, breezy location overlooking the Church of Agiou Spiridona, a short but steep hike from the main square. Sitting rooms and guest rooms contain nice bits of Victoriana, as well as modern conveniences. The cheapest rooms are quite small with no view; usually, for another 15€, you can get a view of Nafplion—and more space. One of the first of the "boutique" hotels in Nafplion, the Byron maintains a devoted following.

2 Platonos, Plateia Agiou Spiridona, 211 00 Nafplion. www.byronhotel.gr. © **27520/22-351.** 17 units. 50€–110€. AE, MC, V. **Amenities:** Breakfast room. *In room:* A/C, TV, minibar, hair dryer, Wi-Fi (free).

Hotel Ilion ★

You'll have to decide whether you find the decor in this boutique hotel in a restored 19th-century town house engaging or overwhelming. Virtually every ceiling is painted (often with cupids), and wall frescoes with scenes from Greek mythology alternate with borders of fruit and flowers. Windows and beds alike are draped with hangings. A friend who spent a happy week here reported that the service was top-notch, the neighborhood was quiet, and the breakfasts were delicious.

4 Efthimiopoulou and 6 Kapodistriou sts., 211 00 Nafplion. www.ilionhotel.gr. © **27520/25-114.** Fax 27520/24-497. 15 units. 90€–125€ double; 140€–200€ suite. Breakfast 10€. No credit cards. **Amenities:** Bar/breakfast room. *In room:* A/C, TV, minibar, Wi-Fi.

Hotel Leto ★ ✦   Your effort in climbing up to the Leto, perched under Acronafplia, is rewarded with fine views over Nafplion. Guest units are simply furnished, with decent-size bathrooms; ask for a room with a balcony. The staff here has been praised as very helpful.

28 Zigomala, 211 00 Nafplion .www.leto-hotel.gr. ✆ **27520/28-098.** Fax 27520/29-588. 15 units. 7€–95€ double. No credit cards. *In room:* A/C, TV, minibar.

Hotel Nafsimedon ★   Another boutique hotel, this one is in a handsome mid-19th-century neoclassical house with a small garden with palm trees overlooking relatively quiet Kolokotronis Park. The guest rooms, many done in shades of apricot and peach, have handsome chandeliers, marble-topped tables, old paintings—and good-sized bathrooms and beds with firm mattresses. When the Nafsimedon is full, rooms are sometimes available at its younger sister hotel, the **Ippoliti** (www.ippoliti. gr), also a boutique hotel in a restored 19th-century town house at 9 Ilia Miniati and Aristidou just off the harbor (some rooms have harbor views) with a small outdoor pool (doubles 100€–150€).

Nafsimedon, 9 Sidiras Merarhias (on Kolokotronis Park), 211 00 Nafplion. www.nafsimedon.gr. ✆ **27520/25-060.** Fax 27520/26-913. 13 units. 90€–120€ double. AE, MC, V. **Amenities:** Bar/ breakfast room. *In room:* A/C, TV.

King Othon I and II ★★   Now, Nafplion has two small hotels that contend for the honor of the most breathtaking curved staircase in the Peloponnese, long-time favorite the "old" Othon I and the new Othon II, which opened in 2002. Both Otho hotels have high ceilings (some with frescoes), wood floors, and period furniture, including marble-topped tables. The new Othon is more expensive, because every guest room offers attractive views. Each hotel has a garden, a real plus for breakfast or a quiet hour's reading. Both sometimes close in winter.

King Otho I: 4 Farmakapoulou, 21100 Nafplion. www.kingothon.gr. ✆ **27520/27-585.** 12 units. 90€. double. Rates include continental breakfast. AE, MC, V. **Amenities:** Breakfast room. *In room:* A/C, TV, minibar.

Inexpensive

Omorfi Poli Pension ★★   What a pleasant place! This small pension/hotel above the charming cafe by the same name (Greek for "beautiful city") has gone all out. The restoration of the building gives guests the sense that they are staying in a Nafplion home—but with privacy; when business is not brisk, you can sometimes get a suite at a double-room price. The beds are comfortable, the prints (many by Greek artists) on the pastel walls are engaging, the ceilings are high and the windows are large, and the shared parlor is quietly elegant. Families will like the rooms with fridges and sleeping lofts for children as well as the breakfasts with freshly baked bread. Groups planning a long stay may want to inquire about the Omorphi Poli's rental apartment, which sleeps up to eight guests.

5 Sofroni, 211 00 Nafplion. www.omorfipoli-pension.com. ✆ **27520/21-565.** 9 units, all with shower only. 65€ double; 120€ family suite (for up to 5 persons). AE, MC, V.

Side Trips to Tiryns & Nemea

It's easy, and a lot of fun, to take in the spectacular Mycenaean palace of Tiryns and Nemea's endearing small ancient sanctuary, with its picturesque temple, restored stadium, and user-friendly museum on a day trip. Nemea is in the midst of excellent vineyards, many of which have tours and wine tastings, which are perhaps best done after, and not before, visiting the site and museum. After seeing Nemea and Tiryns, you can head back to Nafplion for a swim, dinner, and more ice cream at the Antica Gelateria di Roma (p. 478).

Tiryns ★★   Tiryns is 5km (3 miles) outside Nafplion on the Argos road. If anything can outdo Mycenae's fortifications, it's Tiryns: From the moment you look up at these monumental dark stone walls, you'll understand why Homer called the **citadel,** which may have been Mycenae's port, "well walled." Tiryns stands on a rocky outcrop 27m (89 ft.) high and about 302m (990 ft.) long, girdled by the massive walls that so impressed Homer—but that didn't keep Tiryns from being destroyed around 1200 B.C. Later Greeks thought that only the giants known as Cyclopes could have hefted the 14-ton red limestone blocks into place for the walls that archaeologists still call "Cyclopean." Even today, Tiryns's walls stand more than 9m (30 ft.) high; originally—and almost unimaginably—they were twice as tall and as much as 17m (56 ft.) thick. The citadel is crowned by the palace, whose **megaron** (great hall) has a well-preserved circular hearth and the base of a throne. This room would have been gaily decorated with frescoes (the surviving frescoes are now in the National Archaeological Museum in Athens).

The site is officially open Monday through Sunday, from 8am to 3pm (☏ **27520/ 22-657**); it is sometimes open later in summer. Admission is 4€. Visitors without cars can reach Tiryns from Nafplion by taxi (expect to pay about 30€ for the round-trip and an hour or so wait while you visit the site) or by the frequent (about every half-hour) Nafplion–Argos–Nafplion bus (about 2€; tell the driver you want to get off at Tiryns).

Nemea ★★   Nemea is 30 km (19 miles) from Nafplion; take the Nafplion–Argos road to the link road to the National Road toward Athens; Ancient Nemea is signposted on the link road. (The modern village of Nemea is beyond the site; if you reach the village, you've missed the turn for the site.) Nemea is a gem of a site, with a restored stadium, a temple with standing columns, the remains of a Roman bath and an early Christian church, and the most appealing and helpful small museum in the Peloponnese, with cases full of handsome ancient coins and gold jewelry from nearby Mycenaean tombs. The most famous Panhellenic Games were held every 4 years at Olympia and Delphi, but there were also games every 2 years at Isthmia, near Corinth, and at Nemea, tucked into a gentle valley in the eastern foothills of the Arcadian Mountains, from about 573 B.C. to 100 B.C. Around 100 B.C., Nemea's powerful neighbor Argos moved the festival from Nemea to Argos itself, putting an end to the games here. But, thanks to the Society for the Revival of the Nemean Games, games have been held here every 4 years since 1996, with the next ones planned for 2016. Contestants run barefoot, as in antiquity, but wear short tunics rather than running naked—a considerable relief to me when I ran here! If you want to know more about the Nemean Games, contact the Society for the Revival of the Nemean Games (www.nemeangames.org).

Nemea is famous for its wines, especially its red wines, some known as the "blood of Heracles." Signs along local roads indicate wine routes. On the road between Ancient and New Nemea, several vineyards, including **Palivos** (www.palivos.gr), offer tours and tastings of the excellent local wines most days in summer and a number of local vineyards give tours (check out www.greekproducts.com/nemea). If you get hungry, you can get a bite at the **Nemeios Dias** (☏ **27450/24-244**), a welcome cafe/restaurant signposted SNAK BAR/SOUVENIR near Ancient Nemea, usually open from 10am to mid-afternoon.

Visiting the Mycenae

If at all possible, visit Mycenae early in the morning (to avoid the mid-morning and midday tour groups) or during the hour or two before closing (when crowds thin out). Wear a hat and sturdy shoes. There's no shade at the site (except in the cistern and the beehive tombs), and the rocks are very slippery. Bring a flashlight if you plan to explore the cistern. And, if you are staying here at full moon, be sure to see Mycenae's walls gleaming in the moonlight.

The site and museum are open Tuesday through Friday from 8:30am to 3pm, sometimes also weekends and until 7pm in summer (© **27460/22-739**). Joint admission to site, stadium, and museum is 8€.

Mycenae ★★★   Virtually every visitor to the Peloponnese comes to Mycenae, which can make for bumper-to-bumper tour buses on the narrow roads to the citadel and wall-to-wall tourists inside the citadel itself. Why do they all come here? As the English philhellene Robert Liddell once wrote: "Mycenae is one of the most ancient and fabulous places in Europe. I think it should be visited first for the fable, next for the lovely landscape, and thirdly for the excavations."

First, the fable: Greek legend and the poet Homer tell us that King Agamemnon of Mycenae was the most powerful leader in Greece at the time of the Trojan War. In about 1250 B.C., Homer says, Agamemnon led the Greeks from Mycenae to Troy, where they fought for 10 years to reclaim fair Helen—who had eloped with the Trojan prince Paris. Helen just happened to be the wife of Agamemnon's brother Menelaus, so family honor was at stake, and the first of many wars between Greece and Turkey erupted. Centuries later, in 1874, the German archaeologist Heinrich Schliemann, who found and excavated Troy, began to dig at Mycenae, searching for evidence of Agamemnon's kingdom. Did Schliemann's excavations here prove that what Homer wrote was based on an actual event, not myth and legend? Scholars are suspicious, although most admit that Mycenae could be rebuilt from Homer's descriptions of its palace.

Essentials

GETTING THERE   **Buses** run frequently from Athens's **Stathmos Leoforia Peloponnisou**, 100 Kifissou (www.ktel.org; © **210/512-4910** or **210/512-9233**) to Corinth, Argos, and Nafplion. Allow 3 to 4 hours for the initial journey, plus an hour for the connecting bus trip to Mycenae.

By car, from Corinth, take the new national highway toll road to the Nemea exit, where a link road leads you to the old Corinth–Argos highway, which has a clearly marked turnoff for Mycenae. If you prefer, you can take the old Corinth–Argos road to the village of Mycenae turnoff. This takes longer and you may get stuck behind a bus or truck, but you will have a better sense of the countryside than on the elevated highway. Either way, Mycenae is about 90km (56 miles) south of Corinth. From Nafplion, take the road out of town toward Argos. When you reach the Corinth–Argos highway, turn right and then, after about 16km (10 miles), turn right again at the sign for Mycenae. When you return from Mycenae to Nafplion, follow the signs for Nafplion—and expect to dodge speeding tour buses.

Exploring Ancient Mycenae

Archaeological Museum of Mycenae ★★ MUSEUM   The museum on the slopes below the citadel focuses on the story of the excavations at the site, and of Mycenaean civilization in general. Unfortunately, because the museum's galleries are quite small, both the displays and the labels (in Greek and English) are hard to see when the museum is crowded, which it often is. The so-called **Cult Center** has striking pottery snakes and wide-eyed terracotta figures although it is not certain whether the figurines represent the deities who were worshiped, or the mortals who worshiped them. Throughout the museum, exhibits are labeled in Greek and English, and there are toilet facilities, and an excellent shop.

💲 **27510/76-585.** Admission 8€, including admission to Treasury of Atreus and site; guidebook 5€. Summer daily 8am–7pm; winter shorter hours.

The Citadel & the Treasury of Atreus ★★★ RUINS   As you walk uphill to Mycenae you begin to get an idea of why people settled here as long ago as 5000 B.C. Mycenae straddles a low bluff between two protecting mountains and is a superb natural citadel overlooking one of the richest plains in Greece. By the time of the classical era, almost all memory of the Mycenaeans had been lost, and Greeks speculated that places like Mycenae and Tiryns had been built by the Cyclopes. Only such enormous giants, people reasoned, could have moved the huge rocks used to build the ancient citadels' defense walls.

You enter Mycenae through just such a wall, passing under the massive **Lion Gate,** which originally stood to symbolize Mycenae's strength. The door itself (missing, like the lions' heads) was probably made of wood and covered with bronze for additional protection; cuttings for the doorjambs and pivots are clearly visible in the lintel. The round tower to the right of here would have housed soldiers ready to shoot arrows at attackers who tried to storm the citadel.

One of the most famous spots at Mycenae is immediately ahead of the Lion Gate—the so-called **Grave Circle A,** where Schliemann found the gold jewelry now on display at the National Archaeological Museum in Athens. When archaeologist Heinrich Schliemann opened the tombs and found some 14 kilograms of gold here, including several solid-gold face masks, he concluded he had found the grave of Agamemnon himself. However, recent scholars have concluded that Schliemann was wrong, and that the kings buried here died long before Agamemnon was born.

From the grave circle, head uphill past the low remains of a number of houses. Mycenae was not merely a palace, but a small village, with administrative buildings and homes on the slopes below the palace. The **palace** had reception rooms, bedrooms, a throne room, and a large *megaron* (ceremonial hall). You can see the imprint of the four columns that held up the roof in the *megaron*, as well as the outline of a circular altar on the floor.

If you're not claustrophobic, head to the northeast corner of the citadel and climb down the flight of stairs to have a look at Mycenae's enormous **cistern.** (You may find someone selling candles, but it's a good idea to bring your own flashlight.) Along with Mycenae's great walls, this cistern, which held a water supply channeled from a spring 450m (1,476 ft.) away, helped make the citadel impregnable for several centuries.

There's one more thing to see before you leave Mycenae. The massive tomb known as the **Treasury of Atreus** is the largest of the *tholos* tombs (circular marble structures) found here. You'll see signs for the tombs on your right as you head down the modern road away from Mycenae. The Treasury of Atreus may have been built around 1300 b.c. at about the same time as the Lion Gate, in the last century of Mycenae's real greatness. The enormous tomb, with its 118-ton lintel, is 13m (43 ft.) high and 14m (46 ft.) wide. To build it, workers first cut the 35m (115-ft.) passageway into the hill and faced it with stone blocks. Then the tholos chamber itself was built, by placing slightly overlapping courses of stone one on top of the other until a capstone could close the final course. As you look up toward the ceiling of the tomb, you'll see why these are called "beehive tombs." Once your eyes get accustomed to the poor light, you can make out the nails that once held hundreds of bronze rosettes in place in the ceiling. This tomb was robbed even in antiquity, so we'll never know exactly what it contained, although the contents of Grave Circle A give an idea of what riches must have been here. If this was the family vault of Atreus, it's entirely possible that Agamemnon himself was buried here.

There's a good deal of up-and-down walking here, much on slippery terrain; give yourself at least 3 hours to absorb this magnificent and mysterious site.

© **27510/76-585.** Admission 8€ including Treasury of Atreus and museum. Summer daily 8am–7pm; winter daily 8am–3pm.

Where to Stay & Eat

Most of the restaurants around Mycenae serve set-price meals to tour groups. If you eat at one of the big impersonal roadside restaurants, you're likely to be served a bland, lukewarm "European-style" meal of overcooked roast veal, underripe tomatoes, and brutally overcooked vegetables. You'll have better luck at the smaller restaurants at the hotels listed below.

La Belle Helene ★   The real reason to stay here is to add your name to that of Schliemann and other luminaries in the guest book. The rooms are *very* simple, bathrooms are shared. If you ever backpacked, this is the sort of place you'll remember. Because of Schlieman, this remains one of the most famous small hotels in Greece, and its spacious restaurant does a brisk business with tour groups.

Mycenae, 212 00 Argolis. © **27510/76-225.** Fax 27510/76-179. 8 units. 50€–65€ double, sometimes lower off-season. All rooms use a separate bathroom. Rates include breakfast. DC, V. **Amenities:** Restaurant.

La Petite Planete ★★   A 15-minute walk from the site of Mycenae, this would be a nice place to stay even without its small swimming pool, which is irresistible after a hot day's trek around Mycenae. We've usually found it quieter here than at La Belle Helene, whose helpful owners take pride both in the comforts of the hotel and the reliability of the home cooking in its restaurant. There are fine views over the plain of Argos to the hills beyond (from the front rooms). If you are here at full moon, you're in luck: Mycenae by moonlight is very grand.

Mycenae, 212 00 Argolis. www.petite-planet.gr. © **27510/76-240.** 30 units. 55€–70€ double. AE, V. Often closed Jan–Feb. **Amenities:** Restaurant; bar; outdoor freshwater pool. *In room:* A/C, TV.

EPIDAURUS ★★★

The Theater of Epidaurus is one of the most impressive sights in all Greece, in one of the most famous places in ancient Greece. Pilgrims once came to the shrine of Asclepios here as they go today to the shrine of the Virgin on the Cycladic island of Tinos: some to give thanks for good health, others in hopes of finding cures for ailments. At Epidaurus, visitors could "take the waters" at any one of a number of healing springs, or take in a performance in the theater, just as you can today. Probably

Performances at the Ancient Theater

Performances at the **ancient theater** are usually given Saturday and Sunday at around 9pm June through September. Many productions are staged by the **National Theater of Greece,** some by foreign companies. Classical Greek drama is usually performed in modern Greek; programs are available with summaries of the plots. A big hit in recent years was the Royal Shakespeare Company's production of "Richard the Third," with Kevin Spacey in the lead role. Ticket prices range from 20€ to 50€. For further information, contact the **Hellenic Festival Box Office,** 39 Panepistimiou, Athens (www.greekfestival.gr; ℰ **210/928-2900**), the **Rex Theater** box office (ℰ **210/330-1881**) on Panepistimiou just outside Spiromilios Arcade, or the **Epidaurus Festival Box Office** (ℰ **27530/22-006**). It's also possible to buy tickets at most of Nafplion's travel agencies and at the theater itself, starting at 5pm on the day of a performance.

built in the 4th century, the theater seats some 14,000 spectators and is astonishingly well preserved.

Warning: The village of Palea Epidaurus, a beach resort 10km (6¼ miles) from Epidaurus, is confusingly sometimes signposted ANCIENT EPIDAURUS; the theater and sanctuary are usually signposted ANCIENT THEATER.

To confuse things further, Palea Epidaurus has its own small theater and festival. If you want a swim, Palea Epidaurus is the nearest beach—but it is often quite crowded.

Essentials

GETTING THERE   Two **buses** a day run from the **Stathmos Leoforia Peloponnisou,** 100 Kifissou, Athens (www.ktel.org; ℰ **210/512-4910** or **210/512-9233**) The trip takes about 3 hours. There are three buses a day to Epidaurus from the Nafplion bus station, off Plateia Kapodistrias (ℰ **27520/28-555**), with extra buses when there are performances at the Theater of Epidaurus. The trip takes about an hour. *Warning:* Telephones in bus stations are not always answered.

Epidaurus is 63km (39 miles) south of Corinth and 32km (20 miles) east of Nafplion. If you're **driving** from Athens or Corinth, turn left at the sign for Epidaurus immediately after the Corinth Canal and take the coast road to the Theatro (ancient theater), not to Nea Epidaurus or Palaia Epidaurus. From Nafplion, follow the signs for Epidaurus. If you drive to Epidaurus from Nafplion for a performance, be alert; the road will be clogged with road-hogging tour buses.

Exploring Ancient Epidauros

Excavation Museum MUSEUM   If you are pressed for time, skip this dusty museum near the site's entrance. There's an extensive collection of architectural fragments from the sanctuary, including lovely acanthus flowers from the mysterious *tholos.* Also on view are an impressive number of votive offerings from pilgrims: The terracotta body parts show precisely what part of the anatomy was cured. The display of surgical implements will send you away grateful that you didn't have to go under the knife here, although hundreds of inscriptions record the gratitude of satisfied patients. Alas, the labels (Greek and English) are scanty, the lighting is poor, and museum staff disinterested in visitors' questions.

ℰ **27530/23-009.** Admission (including theater) 6€. Summer Mon–Fri 8am–7pm, Sat & Sun 8am–3pm; winter daily 8am–3pm.

Sanctuary of Aesclepios ★ RUINS   It's pleasant to wander through the shady sanctuary, but it's not easy to decipher the scant remains; more signs to identify the monuments would be a great help. What you're looking at are the extensive scattered remnants of ancient hotels and hostels, several large bathhouses, civic buildings, a stadium and gymnasium, and several temples and shrines. One monument stands out: The round *tholos*, which you'll pass about halfway into the sanctuary. The famous 4th-century-B.C. architect Polykleitos, who built similar round buildings at Olympia and Delphi, was the designer. If you wonder why the inner foundations of the *tholos* are so convoluted and labyrinthine, you're in good company—scholars aren't sure what went on here; some suspect that Asclepios's healing serpents lived in the labyrinth.

Tip: Although the Sanctuary is shady, the theater is not and it can be very hot under the summer sun at the Theater of Epidaurus. Keep an eye out for the several benches almost hidden under the pine trees outside the theater near the stage. This is an especially welcome spot to sit after sprinting—or huffing and puffing—to the top of the theater. You can sit in the shade, and enjoy a great view—and watch others toiling up to the topmost seats. If you're a theater buff, be sure to take in the **Epidaurus Festival Museum,** near the entrance to the site, with its displays of props, costumes, programs, and memorabilia from past performances.

The Theater ★★ RUINS   If you found the remains of the ancient sanctuary a bit of a letdown, don't worry—the **Theater of Epidaurus** is one of the most impressive sights in Greece. Probably built in the 4th century B.C., possibly by Polykleitos, the architect of the *tholos,* the theater seats some 14,000 spectators. Unlike so many ancient buildings, and almost everything at the Sanctuary of Asclepios, the theater was not pillaged for building blocks in antiquity. As a result, it's astonishingly well preserved, and restorations have been minimal and tactful. It's always a magical moment when a performance begins, as the sun sinks behind the orchestra and the first actor steps onto the stage.

If you climb to the top of the theater, you can look down over the seats, divided into a lower section with 34 rows and an upper section with 21 rows. The upper seats were added when the original theater was enlarged in the 2nd century B.C. The acoustics are famous; you'll almost certainly see someone demonstrating that a whisper can be heard all the way from the orchestra to the topmost row of seats. Just as the stadium at Olympia brings out the sprinter in many visitors, the theater at Epidaurus tempts many to step center stage and recite poetry, or burst into song.

© **27530/23-009.** Admission (including site & museum) 6€. Summer Mon–Fri 8am–7pm, Sat & Sun 8am–3pm; winter daily 8am–3pm.

 Musical July Festival

If you are in Epidaurus in July, check out the **Musical July Festival** at the **Little Theater** of Ancient Epidaurus, 7km (4½ miles) from Epidaurus. Performances in the past have ranged from chamber music to flamenco. Information on ticket prices and chartered bus and excursion-boat transportation from Athens is usually available by June from the **Athens Concert Hall (Megaron Mousikis),** 1 Kokkali and Vas. Sophias (www.megaron.gr; © **210/728-2000**), or the **Municipality of Palea Epidaurus** (© **27530/41-250**).

Galerie Orphee, Antonios Kosmopoulos's shop on the main street in Ancient Olympia (© **26240/23-555**), has a wide selection of books, an extensive range of CDs of Greek music, plus frequent displays of contemporary art. What a pleasant contrast to Olympia's other shops, which have all too many T-shirts, museum reproductions, and machine-made rugs and embroideries sold as "genuine handmade crafts." That said, keep an eye out for any shops also on the main drag selling attractively presented honey, olive oil, and other local products. I'm not giving shop names as, in this economic climate, these shops tend, alas, to open and close unpredictably.

Where to Stay & Eat

You'll almost certainly want to stay in Nafplion when you visit Epidaurus. The small hotels closer to Epidaurus are usually booked by large tour groups well in advance of theater performances and are not sufficiently charming to recommend if you visit here when there is not a performance.

As for food, the best place to eat is the **Leonidas** (© **27530/22-115**), on the main Epidaurus access road. This small restaurant with a garden is usually open for lunch and dinner year-round, has consistently good food, and attracts a post-theater crowd that often includes actors. Unusually for most Greek restaurants, this one serves desserts—often rich and gooey! Lunch or dinner from 15€.

OLYMPIA ★★★

Olympia is the most beautiful major site in the Peloponnese. Unlike visits to so many ancient sites, where, clutching a guide book, you try to turn scant remains into once handsome buildings, you don't have to try to figure out what's what at Olympia. Here, in clear view, are the considerable remains of two temples and the stadium where the first Olympic races were run in 776 B.C. On even the hottest summer day, there's welcome shade, and places to sit and simply enjoy the moment and the monuments. Both the site museums—the Archaeological Museum and the Museum of the Olympic Games in Antiquity—are terrific. It's wonderful to have more than just 1 day here, especially if your hotel back in the village has a swimming pool. The ancient site is a 15-minute walk south of the modern village. Except for early in the morning, parking near the site is virtually non-existent; you'll probably have to park in town and walk—with care: The road teems with tour buses, and the walk is less than relaxing.

The straggling modern village of Olympia (confusingly known as Ancient Olympia) is bisected by its one main street, Leoforos Kondili. The town has about 20 hotels and restaurants and the usual assortment of tourist shops.

Essentials

GETTING THERE   Several **trains** a day run from Athens to Pirgos, where you change to the train for Olympia. Information on schedules and fares is available from the **Stathmos Peloponnisou** (railroad station for the Peloponnese) in Athens (www.ose.gr; © **210/513-1601**).

There are three **buses** a day to Olympia from the Stathmos Leoforia Peloponnisou (bus station for the Peloponnese) in Athens, 100 Kifissou (www.ktel.org; © **210/512-4910** or **210/512-9233**). There are also frequent buses from Patras to Pirgos, with connecting service to Olympia. In Patras, KTEL buses leave from the intersection of Zaimi and Othonos (© **2610/273-694**).

Olympia, 320km (199 miles) from Athens, can easily be a good 5-hour **drive,** whether you take the coast road that links Athens to Corinth, Patras, and Olympia or head inland to Tripolis and Olympia on the Corinth–Tripolis road. Heavy traffic in Patras, 207km (128 miles) south of Athens, means that the drive from Patras to Olympia can easily take 2 hours.

VISITOR INFORMATION   The tourist information office is on the way to the ancient site near the south end of Leoforos Kondili, the main street (© **26240/22-262**). It's officially open daily, from 9am to 10pm in the summer and from 11am to 6pm in the winter. That said, on a number of occasions when I have been in Olympia out of high season, the office had an open sign in its window, but was closed.

Exploring Olympia

The Ancient Site ★★★ RUINS   Olympia's setting is magical—pine trees shade the little valley, dominated by the conical Hill of Kronos that lies between the Alphios and Kladeos rivers. Recent excavations have concentrated on Roman Olympia, especially in the southern area of the site. Although considerable progress has been made, neither the main entrance nor the route of the ceremonial way during Roman times is yet known. The handsome temples and the famous stadium are not what you see first as you enter the site. Immediately to the left are the unimpressive low walls of the **Roman baths** where athletes and spectators could enjoy a hot or cold plunge in the waters; some recently restored mosaics are on view. The considerably more impressive slender columns on your right mark the **gymnasium** and **palestra,** where athletes practiced their foot racing and boxing skills. The enormous gymnasium had one roofed track where athletes could practice in bad weather. Also on the right are the fairly meager remains of a number of structures, including a swimming pool and the large square **Leonidaion,** which served as a hotel for visiting dignitaries until a Roman governor decided it would do nicely as his private villa.

The religious sanctuary is dominated by two shrines: The good-sized **Temple of Hera** and the massive **Temple of Zeus.** The Temple of Hera, with its three standing columns, is the older of the two, built around 600 B.C. If you look closely, you'll see that the temple's column capitals and drums are not uniform. That's because this temple was originally built with wooden columns, and as each column decayed, it was replaced; inevitably, each new column had slight variations. The Hermes of Praxiteles was found here, buried under the mud that covered Olympia for so long, due to repeated flooding. The Temple of Zeus, which once had a veritable thicket of 34 stocky Doric columns, was built around 456 B.C. The entire temple—so austere and gray today—was anything but plain in antiquity. Gold, red, and blue paint was everywhere, and inside the temple stood an enormous gold-and-ivory statue of Zeus seated on an ivory-and-ebony throne. The statue was so ornate that it was considered one of the Seven Wonders of the Ancient World—and so large that people joked that if the Zeus stood up, his head would go through the temple's roof. In fact, the antiquarian Philo of Byzantium suggested that Zeus had created elephants simply so that the sculptor Phidias would have the ivory to make his statue.

Not only do we know that Phidias made the 13m (43-ft.) statue, but we know where he made it, thanks to a cup with his name inscribed on it that was found in a well-preserved workshop with terracotta molds used in making the great statue of Zeus. As so often in antiquity, the building (signposted just west of the Zeus Temple) has had several incarnations, including being used for the foundations of a Christian church. You can see his cup in the Archaeological Museum. Between the Temples of Zeus and Hera are the remains of a substantial round building that Philip of Macedon, never modest, built here to pat himself on the back after conquering Greece in 338 b.c.

Beyond the temples of Zeus and Hera, built up against the Hill of Kronos, are the curved remains of a once-elegant **Roman fountain** and the foundations of 11 treasuries where Greek cities stored votive offerings and money. In front of the treasuries are the low bases of a series of bronze statues of Zeus dedicated not by victorious athletes but by those caught cheating in the stadium. The statues would have been the last thing competitors saw before they entered the stadium.

©/fax **26240/22-529.** Admission to site and museum 9€. Summer Mon–Fri 8:30am–7pm, Sat–Sun 8:30am–3pm; winter Mon–Fri 8am–5pm, Sat–Sun 8:30am–3pm.

Archaeological Museum ★★★ MUSEUM The museum's collection makes clear Olympia's astonishing wealth and importance in antiquity: Every victorious city and almost every victorious athlete is dedicated a bronze or marble statue here, creating what was in effect one of the first outdoor museums of sculpture. Nothing but the best was good enough for Olympia, and many of these superb works of art are on view (with labels in Greek, German, and English). Most of the exhibits are displayed in rooms to the right and left of the main entrance and follow an essentially chronological sequence, from severe Neolithic vases to baroque Roman imperial statues, neither of which will probably tempt you from heading straight ahead to see the museum's superstars. Still, don't miss the superb bronze heads of snarling griffins or the painted terracotta statue of a resolute Zeus abducting the youthful Ganymede.

The monumental **sculpture from the Temple of Zeus** is probably the finest surviving example of archaic Greek sculpture. The sculpture from the west pediment shows the battle of the Lapiths and Centaurs raging around the magisterial figure of Apollo, the god of reason. On the east pediment, Zeus oversees the chariot race between Oinomaos, the king of Pisa, and Pelops, the legendary figure who wooed and won Oinomaos's daughter by the unsporting expedient of loosening his opponent's chariot pins. Pelops not only won his bride but had the entire region named after him: The Peloponnese (Pelops's island). At either end of the room, sculptured metopes show scenes from the Labors of Hercules, including the one he performed at Olympia: Cleansing the foul stables of King Augeus by diverting the Alfios River.

Just beyond the sculpture from the Temple of Zeus is the 5th-century-b.c. **Winged Victory,** created by the artist Paionios, and the 4th-century-b.c. figure of Hermes and the infant Dionysos, known as the ***Hermes of Praxiteles.***

Directly across the street from the Ancient Site (see below). ©/fax **26240/22-529.** Admission to site and museum 9€. Summer Mon–Fri 8:30am–7pm, Sat–Sun 8:30am–3pm; winter Mon–Fri 8am–5pm, Sat–Sun 8:30am–3pm.

Museum of the History of the Olympic Games in Antiquity ★★ MUSEUM The museum, which opened in 2004 in time for the Athens Olympics, occupies the handsome neoclassical building that served as the site's original archaeological museum. The path to the museum is steep; it is sometimes possible to get permission to drive up and drop off passengers by the museum's entrance. The superb collection includes chariot wheels, musical instruments, statues of athletes, all manner of athletic gear, and bronze dedications to Zeus. There are, alas, 76 fewer bronzes on display here as a result of a daring early-morning robbery in February of

2012. Each of the 12 galleries has a theme, including "The Beginning of the Games," "Zeus and His Cults," "The Events," and Games at other ancient sites (Nemea, Isthmia, Delphi). A number of photos and drawings highlight the religious sanctuary.

© **26240/22-529.** Free admission (but a fee is planned). Summer Mon noon–7pm, Tues–Sun 8am–7pm; winter, usually closes by 5pm.

Tip: If you follow the modern Olympic games, you'll enjoy the small **Museum of the Olympic Games,** signposted in the village of Ancient Olympia; admission 2€; open Monday to Saturday from 8am to 3:30pm, Sunday and holidays 9am to 2:30pm.

Where to Stay & Eat

There are lots of restaurants in Olympia, but only a handful of good ones. Some of the best food in town is served at the **Hotel Europa** and the **Hotel Pelops** (see below). On the main drag, **Tessera Epochi (Four Seasons), Zeus,** and the **Aegean** stand out from the many places that tend to have indifferent food and service. **Taverna Ambrosia,** by the railroad station, does a brisk business with tour groups, but also treats independent travelers well. Local cafes and bakeries are a good place to stop for a snack. If the excellent **Kladeos Taverna,** also near the train station, has reopened, it would be well worth visiting.

Olympia has more than 20 hotels, which means you can almost always find a room, although if you arrive without a reservation in July or August, you might not get your first choice. In the winter, many hotels are closed. If you're here in winter, check to see if the hotel you choose has functioning central heating.

Hotel Europa ★★★ The Europa is the best hotel in town—possibly the best in the Peloponnese. Part of the Best Western chain (but managed by a very helpful local family), it's a few minutes' drive just out of town on a hill overlooking both the modern village and the ancient site. Most units overlook the large pool and garden, and several have views of a bit of the ancient site. The rooms are large, with extra-firm mattresses and sliding glass doors opening onto generously sized balconies. The two very

A BREAK ON THE way TO DELPHI

If you approach Delphi by car along the northern shore of the Gulf of Corinth, you might want to take a lunch-and-swim break at the miniature port of **Galaxidi** (35km/22 miles southwest of Delphi). One thing to remember: on summer weekends, when Galaxidi's cobblestoned streets, boutiques, cafes, and restaurants are thronged with excursion-loving Athenians, it can be standing room only. In the 19th and 20th centuries, Galaxidi was a center of shipbuilding, and its harbor is flanked with the very good-looking stone homes of 19th-century ship captains and seafarers, many of which have been transformed into restaurants, cafes, and small hotels. **Tassos** (© **22650/41-291**) and

Omilos (© **22640/42-111**) both have fresh fish. If you just want a snack, try the *amagdalopasta* (an almond sweet somewhere between a candy and a cookie). Almost every Greek island makes its own version of this confection, but some connoisseurs think Galaxidi does it best. Athenian friends of mine especially praise those on sale at **Mina** (© **22650/41-1117**), just off the waterfront. If you're tempted to stay the night, the eight-unit **Hotel Ganimede** (www.ganimede.gr; © **22650/41-328**) is set in a charming 19th-century sea captain's house with a garden, and wonderful breakfasts with homemade jams and freshly baked bread. Doubles start at 70€.

professional restaurants include a taverna in the garden, which serves tasty grills and stews; the indoor breakfast buffet is extensive.

27065 Ancient Olympia, Peloponnese. www.hoteleuropa.gr. *©* **26240/22-650** or 800/528-1234 in the U.S. Fax 26240/23-166. 80 units. 70€–110€ double. Rates include breakfast. AE, DC, MC, V. **Amenities:** Restaurant; bar; outdoor pool. *In room:* A/C, fridge, minibar, hair dryer, Wi-Fi (free).

Hotel Pelops ★★★ 🦴 If you've heard how helpful Aussie expat Susanna Spiliopoulou and her family are, believe every word! Susanna, husband Theo, and the family make this one of the most welcoming hotels in Greece. Rooms are of a decent size, cheerful, and very comfy, unlike all too many Greek hotels. Check out their website to learn about their 3- and 4-day cooking, writing, and painting classes, usually offered off-season. Guests here can use the dishy pool at the Hotel Europa but the real bonus of staying here is leaving the all-too-often anonymous world of hotels and entering a welcoming haven, in the center of town, but on a blissfully quiet street.

2 Varela, 270 65 Ancient Olympia. www.hotelpelops.gr. *©* **26240/22-543.** 25 units. 70€ double. MC, V. **Amenities:** Breakfast room. *In room:* A/C, TV, Wi-Fi (free).

Delphi ★★★

The ancient Greeks believed that Delphi was the center of the world—and why not? Even more than Olympia, Delphi has it all: a long and glorious history as the scene of Apollo's famous oracle and the Pythian games; a gravity-defying cliff-side location with the remains of treasuries, small temples, a stadium, and a theater; the massive temple of Apollo and a view over a plain of gnarled olive trees to the Gulf of Corinth. Look up and you see the cliffs and crags of Parnassus; look down and there's Greece's most beautiful plain of olive trees, stretching as far as the eye can see toward the town of Itea on the Gulf of Corinth. The museum is excellent, and its star is the famous bronze statue of the wide-eyed charioteer who raced his horses to victory in Delphi's stadium.

Many tour companies offer day trips to Delphi, stopping at the Byzantine monastery of Osios Loukas (see "Organized Tours," earlier in this chapter). In the summer, tour groups clog Delphi's few streets by day, but many head to their next stop for the night, which means that hotel rooms are usually available—although often all the cheap rooms are gone by mid-morning. In the winter, thousands of Greeks head here each weekend, not for the archaeological site, but for the excellent skiing on Mount Parnassus. Getting a room in the nearby once-sleepy hamlet of Arachova is virtually impossible without a reservation on winter weekends, and Delphi itself is often full.

Every summer (usually in June), the European Cultural Center of Delphi (www.eccd.eu) sponsors the **Festival of Delphi,** with performances of ancient Greek drama and distinctly non-classical rock music, hip-hop, synthpop, and other electronica. Tickets and schedules are usually available at the Center's Athens office at 9 Frynihou, Plaka (*©* **210/331-2798**), and at the Center's Delphi office (*©* **22650/82-731**). *Budget travelers take note:* Tickets are sometimes substantially discounted or even free close to performance time.

ESSENTIALS
Getting There
BY BUS There are usually five buses daily to Delphi from the Athens bus station at 260 Liossion (www.ktel.org; *©* **210/831-7096** or **210/831-7179** in Athens, or **22650/82-317** in Delphi).

The Delphi Tram

If you want to tour today's Delphi as well as the ancient sanctuaries, check out the free train that leaves from the Hotel Vouzas and gives 30-minute rides around the village of Delphi daily in the summer. Information on the train is available from the tourist information office (see "Visitor Information," above).

BY CAR Take the Athens–Corinth National Highway 74km (46 miles) west of Athens to the Thebes turnoff and continue 40km (25 miles) west to Levadia. If you want to stop at the monastery of Osios Loukas, take the Distomo turnoff for 9km (5⅔ miles). At the fork in the road in the village of Distomo, bear left, lest you follow a dead-end, but scenic, road to the sea. Return to Distomo and continue via Arachova for 26km (16 miles) to Delphi or via the seaside town of Itea for 64km (40 miles) to Delphi. The approach from Itea on a steeply climbing road with views back to the sea is well worth the time if you aren't in a hurry—and don't mind hairpin bends. As always near important sites in Greece, be prepared to encounter a tour bus at any turn in the road.

Visitor Information

The tourist information office (the former **Greek National Tourism Organization [GNTO]** office; ☏ **22650/82-900**) on the main street (Frederikis) is usually open from 8am to 3pm (sometimes later in summer)—and sometimes mysteriously closed. The website www.visitdelphi.gr is useful.

Getting Around

The village of Delphi, with its two main one-way parallel streets connected by stepped side streets, is small enough that most visitors find it easiest to abandon their cars and explore on foot. If you have to drive to the site rather than make the 5- to 10-minute walk from town, be sure to set off early to get one of the few parking places. Whether you walk or drive, keep an eye out for the enormous tour buses that barrel down the center of the road—and for the poorly marked one-way streets in the village.

EXPLORING DELPHI

If possible, begin your visit when the site and museum open in the morning (both are also sometimes relatively uncrowded in the hour before closing). If you begin your visit at the museum, you'll arrive at the site already familiar with many of the works of art that once decorated the sanctuary. As with Olympia, it's easy to spend a whole day here. Unlike Olympia, the main site at Delphi—built on a slope of Mt. Parnassus—involves a great deal of climbing with almost no shade. When you explore the site, you will follow the route that most visitors took in antiquity: first climbing up to the Sanctuary of Apollo, then walking down past the Castalian Spring, before climbing down the steep hill to the Sanctuary of Athena Pronaia.

Archaeological Museum ★★★ MUSEUM   Each of the museum's rooms has a specific focus: sculpture from the elegant Siphnian treasury in one room, finds from the Temple of Apollo in two rooms, discoveries from the Roman period (including the Parian marble statue of the epicene youth Antinous, the beloved of the emperor Hadrian) in another. Keep an eye out for the impressively large 4th-century-B.C. marble egg, a symbol of Delphi's position as the center of the world. According to legend, when Zeus wanted to determine the earth's center, he released two eagles from Mount Olympus. When the eagles met over Delphi, Zeus had his answer. (You still can see eagles in the sky above Delphi—but as often as not, the large birds circling overhead are the less distinguished Egyptian vultures.)

The star of the museum is the "must-see" 5th-century-B.C. **Charioteer of Delphi,** a larger-than-life bronze figure that was part of a group that originally included a four-horse chariot. It's an irresistible statue; the handsome youth's delicate eyelashes shade wide enamel and stone eyes, and realistic veins stand out in his hands and feet.

Although the charioteer is the star of the collection, he's in good company. Delphi was chockablock with superb works of art given by wealthy patrons, such as King Croesus of Lydia, who contributed the massive **silver bull** that's on display. Many of the finest exhibits are quite small, such as the elegant bronzes in the museum's last room, including one that shows Odysseus clinging to the belly of a ram. According to Homer, this is how the wily hero escaped from the cave of the ferocious (but nearsighted) monster Cyclops.

ⓒ **22650/82-312.** Admission 9€ including site; museum only, 6€. Summer Mon 11am–7pm, Tues–Fri 8am–7pm, Sat–Sun and holidays 8am–3pm; winter daily 8:30am–3pm. (Be sure to check these hours when you arrive in Delphi, as they can change without warning.)

Sanctuary of Apollo, Castalian Spring & Sanctuary of Athena Pronaia ★★★ RUINS You pass the museum to reach the Sanctuary of Apollo and then continue on to the Castalian Spring, before heading down to the Sanctuary of Athena Pronaia. As you enter the **Sanctuary of Apollo,** you'll be on the marble **Sacred Way,** following the route that visitors to Delphi have taken for thousands of years. The Sacred Way twists uphill past the remains of Roman *stoas* (covered walkways lined by shops and offices) and a number of **Greek treasuries,** including the Siphnian and Athenian treasuries, whose sculpture is in the museum. The Athenian treasury is easy to spot, as it's the only one that has been restored. Take a close look at the Athenian treasury's walls: You'll see not only beautiful drywall masonry, but countless inscriptions. The ancient Greeks were never shy about using the walls of their buildings as bulletin boards. Alas, so many contemporary visitors have added their own names to the ancient inscriptions that the Greek Archaeological Service no longer allows visitors inside the massive 4th-century-B.C. **Temple of Apollo,** which was built here after several earlier temples were destroyed, usually by earthquakes.

From the temple, it's a fairly steep uphill climb to the remarkably well-preserved 4th-century-B.C. theater and the stadium, extensively remodeled by the Romans. In antiquity, contests in the Pythian festivals took place in both venues.

Keep your ticket as you leave the Sanctuary of Apollo and begin the 10-minute walk along the Arachova–Delphi road to the Sanctuary of Athena (also called the Marmaria, which refers to all the marble found here). En route, you'll pass the famous **Castalian Spring,** where Apollo planted the laurel from which later victory crowns were fashioned. Above are the rose-colored cliffs known as the ***Phaedriades*** (the Bright Ones), famous for the way they reflect the sun's rays. Drinking from the Castalian Spring has inspired legions of poets; however, the spring has been off-limits for some years, awaiting the repeatedly-delayed repairs to the Roman fountain facade.

A path descends from the main road to the **Sanctuary of Athena Pronaia,** goddess of wisdom, who shared the honors at Delphi with Apollo. The remains here are quite fragmentary, except for the large 4th-century-B.C. gymnasium, and you might choose simply to wander about and enjoy the site without trying too hard to figure out what's what. The round 4th-century-B.C. *tholos* with its three graceful standing Doric columns is easy to spot—but no one knows why the building was constructed, why it was so lavishly decorated, or what went on inside.

✆ **22650/82-313.** Admission including museum 9€; site only, 6€. Summer Mon–Fri 7:30am–6:30pm, Sat–Sun and holidays 8:30am–3pm; winter usually daily 8:30am–3pm. (Be sure to check these hours when you arrive in Delphi, as they can change without warning.)

Where to Stay & Eat

You won't starve in Delphi, but restaurants here can sometimes be overwhelmed by tour groups; so if you are here anytime but winter, and have a car, you may prefer to head to the village of Arachova, 10km (6 miles) to the north; try the venerable **Taverna Basssaryiris,** the **Kaplanis**—or almost any other place (including long-time favorites, **Fterolakka** or **Agnadi**) here. No phones to call at any of these, but when you get there and find them, just sit, relax, and enjoy.

In Delphi, I strongly recommend the **Epikouros** restaurant (*✆* **22650/83-250**), at 33 Pavlou and Frederikis, owned and managed by the same helpful Kourelis family that runs the excellent Hotel Acropolis and Hotel Parnassos. This is a great place to make an entire meal of *mezedes* (appetizers). The astonishingly wide and varied menu includes tasty vegetable fritters, the delicious local formaella cheese, lamb with fresh tomato sauce, and, in season, wild boar. The Epikouros also easily has the best view in town from a restaurant; entrees run from 8€ to 18€. **Taverna Skala,** also on Pavlou and Frederikis (*✆* **22650/82-762**); **Taverna Vakchos,** 31 Apollonos (*✆* **22650/83-186**); and **Taverna Lekaria,** 33 Apollonos (*✆* **22650/82-776**) are reliable for simple taverna fare.

There's no shortage of hotels or restaurants in Delphi, and you can usually get a room even in July and August. Still, if you want a room in a specific price category or with a view, it's best to make a reservation. Finally, in summer (but not in winter when the skiers take over this hamlet), consider staying in nearby **Arachova** (10km/6 miles away), where the hotels include the appealing **Paradisiakos Xenonas Maria** (www.mariarooms.com; *✆* **22670/31-803**) and **Generalis Guesthouse** (www.generalis.gr; *✆* **22670/31-529**). Wherever you stay, be sure to check whether your hotel has good heating if you visit in the winter.

In addition to the following options in Delphi, consider these three recently renovated hotels: The **Delphi Palace,** just out of the village, with pool and gardens; the **King Iniohos,** on one of the quiet upper streets; and the **Pythia Art Hotel,** on the non-view side of the main street, are jointly managed and share a reservations number and website (www.delphi-hotels.com; *✆* **22650/82-151**).

Hotel Acropole ★★★ One street below Delphi's main street, the 42-room Acropole has one of the quietest locations and best views in town over private houses, gardens, and the olive groves that stretch beneath Delphi to the sea. The Acropole stays open year-round and is owned and managed by the helpful and charming

---

A Room with a View

If you want a room with a view, be sure to ask for a room with a balcony that faces the Gulf of Corinth. You may not always see the water, but from your balcony you will almost always see the magnificent valley of olive trees that leads down to the Gulf—and avoid the traffic noise of the main street.

Kourelis family. If the Acropole is full, the staff can usually find you a room at one of their other Delphi hotels, both on the main street: the slightly more modest and less expensive **Parnassos** (www.delphi.com.gr; *C* **22650/83-675**) and the very appealing **Fedriades** (www.fedriades.com; *C* **22650/82-370**).

13 Filellinon St., 330 54 Delphi. www.delphi.com.gr. *C* **22650-82-675.** 42 units. From 60€ double. Rates include breakfast. AE, MC, V. **Amenities:** Breakfast room; lounge w/fireplace. *In room:* A/C, TV, fridge, Wi-Fi (free).

Hotel Varonos ★★★ 🖋 This small hotel has to be the best buy in town, with Delphi's famous views over the olive plain from most rooms. Some 20 years ago, I once arrived here with an ailing gardenia plant, and the entire family pitched in to make sure it was well taken care of. In those days, the hotel was very simple, almost austere, but over the years, this has become one of the coziest and most comfortable small hotels in Greece. The guest rooms are very comfortable (terrific mattresses), painted in soothing pastels, and the lobby is anything but austere, with lots of plants and a fire when it's chilly. Check out the family-owned shop next door with local honey, herbs, preserves, and other goodies.

25 Vasileos Pavlou, 330 54 Delphi. www.hotel-varonas.gr. *C*/fax **22650/82-345.** 12 units, 11 with shower (1 with tub/shower). From 50€ double. Rates include breakfast. MC, V. **Amenities:** Breakfast room; lounge w/fireplace. *In room:* A/C, TV, fridge, Wi-Fi (free).

THE CYCLADES

When most people think of the "Isles of Greece," they're thinking of the Cyclades, the rugged (even barren) chain of Aegean islands whose villages of dazzling white houses look from a distance like so many sugar cubes. The Cyclades got their name from the ancient Greek word meaning "to circle," or surround, because the island chain encircles the sacred island of Delos. Today, especially in the summer, it's the visitors who circle these islands, taking advantage of the swift island boats and hydrofoils that link them. Visitors come to see the white villages, the blue-domed chapels, and the fiery sunsets over the cobalt blue sea. They also come to relax in chic boutique hotels, eat in varied and inventive restaurants, and enjoy an ouzo—or a chocolate martini—in some of the best bars and cafes in Greece. In summer, only the fearless would come here without a hotel reservation! *Tip:* On many of these islands, the capital town has the name of the island itself. It's also sometimes called "Hora," or "Chora," a term meaning "the place" that's commonly used for the most important regional town.

Mykonos, with its maze of twisting lanes paved with stone and lined with blue-domed churches and white sugar-cube houses, was the first of the islands to become popular in the 1960s. Although the Beautiful People may have moved on, Mykonos remains a "must see"—hence, expensive—island for virtually every visitor to Greece. The crescent of **Santorini (Thira),** with its black-sand beaches and blood-red cliffs, is all that remains of the island that was blown apart in antiquity by a volcano that still steams and hisses today; in 2012, the volcano did enough hissing and steaming to make it into all Greek and many foreign newspapers. Santorini's exceptional physical beauty, dazzling relics, and elegant restaurants and boutiques make it contend with Mykonos for the title of the most popular Cycladic island. Both Santorini and Mykonos draw so many day-trippers from summer cruise ships that the islands almost sink under the weight of tourists. **Tinos,** whose hills are dotted with elaborate dovecotes, is the most important destination in all Greece for religious pilgrims, yet it remains one of the least commercialized islands of the Cyclades—and a joy to visit for that reason. Remember, however, that all these islands are seriously crowded between June and September. Unless tourism to Greece takes a more severe nose-dive, you should prepare to be grateful for a tiny room with no view if you show up without a hotel reservation on summer weekends.

Tip: You can access a useful website for each of the Cyclades by entering "www. greeka.com/cyclades" and the name of the island (for example, www.greeka.com/cyclades/santorini).

Essentials

GETTING TO THE CYCLADES

BY AIR   **Olympic Air** (www.olympicair.com; ✆ **210/966-6666** or **210/936-9111**), the former Olympic Airlines, offers daily flights between Athens and the Santorini airport at Monolithos (which also receives European charters). There are connections with Mykonos five times per week, service three or four times per week to and from Rhodes, and service two or three times per week to and from Iraklion, Crete. **Aegean Airlines** (www.aegeanair.com; ✆ **210/998-2888,** or **210/998-8300** in Athens) has an office at the airports in Santorini (✆ **22860/28405**) and Mykonos (✆ **22890/28-720**).

BY SEA   The best websites to check for ferry information are www.ferries.gr, www.gtp.gr, and www.openseas.gr. Boat schedules are also available from the Athens **GNTO** (www.gnto.gr; ✆ **210/870-0000**), the **Piraeus Port Authority** (✆ **210/451-1311, 210/451-1440,** or **-1441**), and the Rafina Port Police (✆ **22940/22-300**); phones not always answered. **Ferries** leave daily from Athens's main port of Piraeus and from Rafina, the port east of Athens. The speedy **Seajet** (✆ **210/414-1250**) catamaran service also departs from Rafina and zips between Andros, Syros, Tinos, Mykonos, Paros, Naxos, and Santorini. Tickets can be purchased online from individual ferry companies or at the many harbor-side ticket offices.

Piraeus, the port of Athens, is easily reached in less than half an hour by Metro. It can take an hour for the 27km (17-mile) bus ride from Athens to Rafina (the most convenient port for Mykonos and Tinos), but you save about an hour of sailing time and usually about 20% on the fare. Buses for Rafina leave every 30 minutes from 6am to 10pm from 29 Mavromateon (✆ **210/821-0872**), near Areos Park north of the National Archaeological Museum (indicated on most city maps).

GETTING AROUND

In order to travel from island to island, it is often necessary to double-back to Piraeus or Rafina and head out again. Islands with good inter-island connections include Mykonos, Santorini, Tinos, Syros, and Paros. Service diminishes suddenly at the end of the season (October). Changes in the line that serves an island can occur with little—or no—advance warning. To further complicate matters, a line will often authorize only one agent to sell tickets or limit the number of tickets available to an agency, giving other agents little incentive to tout its service. (For specifics, see "Getting There," under "Essentials," for each island.)

For information on cruises, contact the **Greek National Tourist Organization** (www.visitgreece.gr; ✆ **212/421-5777** in New York, **020/7734-5997** in London, or **210/331-0437** or **210/870-0000** in Athens) or the **Greek Island Cruise Center** (www.gicc.net; ✆ **800/341-3030** in the U.S.). **Sea Cloud Cruises** (www.seacloud.com; ✆ **888/732-2568** in the U.S.) uses a four-masted private yacht that takes up to 60 passengers on Aegean cruises.

The Cyclades

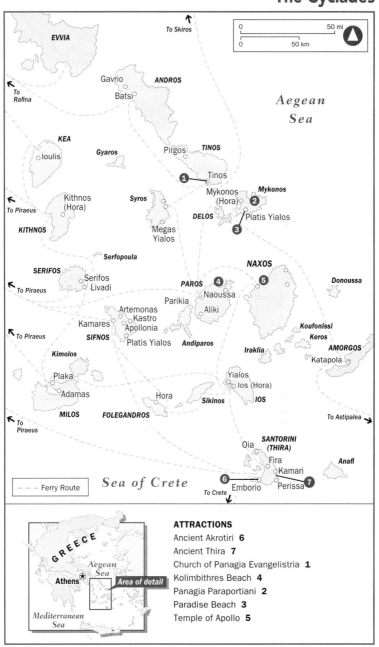

ATTRACTIONS

Ancient Akrotiri **6**

Ancient Thira **7**

Church of Panagia Evangelistria **1**

Kolimbithres Beach **4**

Panagia Paraportiani **2**

Paradise Beach **3**

Temple of Apollo **5**

The winds frequently complicate sea travel on the Aegean. For this reason, plan to arrive back in Athens from the islands **at least** 24 hours before you have to make any critical air or sea connections. In July the strong winds known as the *meltemi* usually kick up, often playing havoc with boat schedules. The larger ferries still run, but if you're prone to seasickness, take precautions. In the winter the *vorias* (strong north winds) frequently make sea travel impossible for days at a time. This is still one of the best ways to travel and enjoy Greece—but, perhaps, as we say in Greece: *siga, siga* (slowly, slowly)—with all the more time to enjoy the moment.

Mykonos ★★★

What makes this small (about 16km/10-mile long), arid island so popular? At least initially, it was the exceptionally handsome Cycladic architecture—and the fact that many on the poor island were more than eager to rent their houses to visitors. First came the jet-setters, artists, and expatriates (including a number of sophisticated gay visitors), as well as the mainland Greeks who opened many of the chic shops and restaurants—all followed by a curious mixture of jet-set wannabes and backpackers. Now, with cruise ships lined up in the harbor all summer and as many as 10 flights each day from Athens, it's easier to say who *doesn't* come to Mykonos than who does. That's why it's very important not to arrive here without reservations in July and August (when it can feel as if every one of the island's million annual visitors is here), unless you enjoy sleeping outdoors—and don't mind being moved from your sleeping spot by the police.

ESSENTIALS

GETTING THERE   Mykonos is served by **Olympic Air** (www.olympicair.com), the former Olympic Airlines, and **Aegean Airlines** (www.aegeanair.com). Although there may be as many as 10 flights from Athens to Mykonos a day in summer, it's not easy to get a last-minute seat, so book well in advance.

Mykonos now has two ports: the old port in Mykonos town, and the new port north of Mykonos town at Tourlos. Check before you travel to find out which port your **boat** will use; the best websites to check for ferry information are www.ferries.gr, www.gtp.gr, and www.openseas.gr. From Piraeus, the **Blue Star Ithaki** has departures once daily at 7:30am. The **Pegasus** has two weekly departures during summer at 7:30pm (Mon and Sat). The *High Speed* has two departures daily, at 7:15am and 4:45pm, and the *Marina* has three departures weekly at 11:50pm on Tuesday, and 5pm Thursday and Saturday. From Rafina, the *Super Ferry* has one departure at 8am daily; the *Super Jet 2* has two departures daily at 7:40am and 4pm. The *Aqua Jewel* has one departure daily at 5pm, while the *Penelope* leaves at 7:35pm daily. **High Speed** boats, lines **2** and **3,** have daily afternoon departures at 7:30pm and 4:30pm, respectively. Schedules can be checked with the **port police** (✆ **22890/22-218**). There are daily ferry connections between Mykonos and Andros, Paros, Syros, and Tinos; five to seven trips a week to Ios; four a week to Iraklio, Crete; several a week to Kos and Rhodes; and two a week to Ikaria, Samos, Skiathos, Skyros, and Thessaloniki. **Hellas Flying Dolphins** offers service from Piraeus (www.dolphins.gr;

© **210/419-9100** or **210/419-9000**) in summer. From the port of Lavrio, the *Fly Cat 3* has an 11:15am departure daily to Mykonos.

On Mykonos, your best bet for getting up-to-date lists of sailings is to check at individual agencies. Or you can check with the **port authority,** by National Bank (© **22890/22-218**); **tourist police,** at the north end of the harbor (© **22890/22-482**); or **tourist office,** also on the harbor (© **22890/23-990; fax 22890/22-229**).

Warning: Check each travel agency's current schedule, because most ferry tickets are not interchangeable. Reputable agencies on the main square in Mykonos (Hora) town include **Sunspots Travel** (© **22890/24-196;** fax 22890/23-790); **Delia Travel** (© **22890/22-490;** fax 22890/24-440); **Sea & Sky Travel** (© **22890/22-853;** fax 22890/24-753); and **Veronis Agency** (© **22890/22-687;** fax 22890/23-763).

VISITOR INFORMATION **Mykonos Accommodations Center,** Enoplon Dhinameon and Malamatenias (www.mykonos-accommodation.com; © **22890/23-160**) not only helps visitors find somewhere to stay but also functions as a tourist information center. **Windmills Travel ★** (www.windmillstravel.com; © **22890/23-877**) has an office at Fabrica Square where you can get general information, book accommodations, arrange excursions, and rent a car or moped. The free *Mykonos Summertime* magazine, available in cafes, shops, and hotels throughout the island, is helpful.

GETTING AROUND One of Hora's greatest assets is the government decree that made the town an architectural landmark and prohibited motorized traffic on its streets. If you don't arrive with your donkey or bicycle, you can walk around town. Many of the town's large hotels ring the busy peripheral road, and a good bus system serves much of the rest of the island.

Mykonos has one of the best **bus** systems in the Greek islands; the buses run frequently and on schedule. Depending on your destination, a ticket costs about .50€ to 4€. There are two bus stations in Hora: one near the Archaeological Museum and one near the Olympic Air office (follow the blue signs). At the tourist office, find out from which station the bus you want leaves, or look for schedules in hotels. Bus information in English is sometimes available from the **KTEL** office (© **22890/23-360**).

By boat, caiques to beaches including Super Paradise, Agrari, and Elia depart from Platis Yialos every morning, weather permitting; there is also service from Ornos in high season (July–Aug) only. Caique service is highly seasonal, with almost continuous service in high season but nothing running October through May. Excursion

---

 Finding an Address

Although some shops hand out maps of Mykonos town, you'll probably do better finding restaurants, hotels, and attractions by asking people to point you in the right direction—and saying *efcharisto* (thank you) when they do. Don't panic at how to pronounce *efcharisto;* think of it as a name and say "F. Harry Stowe." Most streets do not have their names posted. Also, maps leave off lots of small, twisting streets— and Mykonos has almost nothing but small, twisting streets. The map published by **Stamatis Bozinakis,** sold at most kiosks for 2€, is quite decent. The useful **Mykonos Sky Map** is free at some hotels and shops.

boats to Delos depart Tuesday through Sunday between 8:30am and 1pm, from the west side of the harbor near the tourist office. (For more information, see a travel agent; guided tours are available.)

Rental cars are available from about 50€ per day, including insurance, in high season; most agencies are near one of the two bus stops in town. **Windmills Travel** (see "Visitor Information," above) can arrange a car rental for you and get good prices. The largest concentration of **moped** shops is just beyond the south bus station. Expect to pay about 15€ to 30€ per day, depending on the moped's engine size. Greek law now requires wearing a helmet; not all agents supply the helmet. Take great care when driving: Many drivers here are new to the island and unfamiliar with the roads.

Warning: If you park in town or in a no-parking area, the police may remove your license plates. You—not the rental office—will have to find the police station and pay a steep fine to get them back.

There are two types of taxis in Mykonos: standard **car taxis** for destinations outside town, and tiny, cart-towing **scooters** that buzz through the narrow streets of Hora. The latter are seen primarily at the port, where they wait to bring new arrivals to their lodgings in town—a good idea, as most in-town hotels are a challenge to find. Getting a car taxi in Hora is easy: Walk to Taxi (Mavro) Square, near the statue, and join the line. A notice board gives rates for various destinations. You can also call **Mykonos Radio Taxi** (© 22890/22-400).

TOWN LAYOUT Legend has it that the streets of Mykonos town—which locals call Hora—were designed to confuse pirates, so your own confusion is understandable. The main square south across the harbor beyond the small town beach and a cluster of buildings is called **Taxi Square,** although it's officially named Plateia Manto Mavroyenous, after a local heroine. Here you'll find several travel agents, kiosks, snack bars, and, of course, the town's taxi stand.

The main street, **Matogianni,** leads south off Taxi Square behind the church; it's narrow, but you can hardly miss the bars, boutiques, and restaurants. Several "blocks" along it you'll find a "major" cross street, **Kaloyera,** and by turning right, you'll find several of the hotels and restaurants we recommend. If you get lost—and you will—remember that in Mykonos that's part of the fun.

EXPLORING THE ISLAND
HORA (Mykonos Town)

Ask anybody who has visited the Greek islands and they will tell you that apart from the beaches, nothing compares to an early evening stroll in the islands' towns. The light of the late hour, the pleasant buzz, the narrow streets filled with locals and tourists alike, and the romantic ambience in the air as you stroll along can lead you to anything from a modern restaurant, a pleasant taverna, a fortress, or an ancient, unassuming site.

Despite its commercialism and seething crowds in high season, Hora is still the quintessential Cycladic town and is not to be missed.

As is often the case in the Cyclades, the island's main town and surrounding villages are its greatest attraction. Here, the best way to see the town is to venture inland from the port and just wander. Browse the shop window displays, go inside an art gallery, or an old church that may be open. Try to remember to make haste slowly, and enjoy the unexpected sights you'll see when you (inevitably) get lost in Hora's maze of narrow passageways. It may help to keep in mind that the town is bounded on two

Hitting the Beach

Activity on the beaches is highly seasonal, and all the information offered here pertains only to the months of June through September. The prevailing winds on Mykonos (and throughout the Cyclades) blow from the north, which is why the southern beaches are the most protected and calm. The exception to this rule is a southern wind that occurs periodically during the summer, making the northern beaches more desirable for sunning and swimming. In Mykonos town, this southern wind is heralded by particularly hot temperatures and perfect calm in the harbor. On such days, those in the know will avoid Paradise, Super Paradise, and Elia, heading instead to the northern beaches of Ayios Sostis and Panormos—or simply choose another activity for the day.

sides by the bay, and on the other two by the busy vehicular District Road, and that all paths funnel eventually into one of the main squares: **Plateia Mantos Mavroyenous,** on the port (called **Taxi Square** because it's the main taxi stand); **Plateia Tria Pigadia;** and **Plateia Laka,** near the south bus station.

As you wander, you'll see Hora's small **Venetian Kastro** (fortress) and the island's most famous church, the **Panagia Paraportiani (Our Lady of the Postern Gate),** a thickly whitewashed asymmetrical edifice made up of four small chapels. Beyond the Panagia Paraportiani is the Alefkandra quarter, better known as **Little Venice ★★**, for its cluster of homes built overhanging the sea. This is the place to have that martini or margarita in one of the cheek-by-jowl edgy bars with drop-dead sunset views. Another place for sunset views and sundowners: the famous **Tria Pigadia (Three Wells) ★★**. Local legend says that if a virgin drinks from all three she is sure to find a husband; it's probably not a good idea to test this hypothesis by drinking the brackish well water. After you visit the Tria Pigadia, you may want to take in the famous **windmills** of **Kato Myli** and enjoy the views back toward Little Venice and out to sea.

Mykonos has a clutch of (largely neglected) small museums; visit almost any one and you may have it to yourself—and learn a lot about the island. Many of the museums keep somewhat irregular hours, but if one is closed, another is open nearby. The **Nautical Museum of the Aegean** (℃ 22890/22-700), across from the park on Enoplon Dinameon Street, has just what you'd expect, including some handsome ship models; usually open daily from 10:30am to 1pm and 7 to 9pm; admission is 3€. Also on Enoplon Dinameon Street, **Lena's House** (℃ 22890/22-591) recreates the home of a middle-class 19th-century Mykonos family; usually open daily Easter through October; free admission. The **Museum of Folklore** (℃ 22890/25-591), in a 19th-century sea captain's mansion near the quay, has examples of local crafts and furnishings and a recreated 19th-century island kitchen; usually open Monday through Saturday from 4 to 8pm; admission is free. The **Archaeological Museum** (℃ 22890/22-325), near the harbor, has finds from Delos; it's open Monday and Wednesday through Saturday from 9am to 3:30pm, Sunday and holidays from 10am to 3pm. Admission is 3€; free on Sunday. And, as you wander from museum to museum, be sure to enjoy Mykonos's many shops and art galleries (see "Shopping," below).

9

GREECE

The Cyclades

501

Beaches

If you've come to Mykonos to find a secluded beach, you have made a serious mistake! People come to Mykonos to see and be seen, whether in their best togs at cafes or naked on nudist beaches. If you want to hit the "in" beaches, take a little time to ask around, because beaches change character and go in and out of favor quickly. Then catch the bus or a caique to the beach of your choice. If you want a quick swim, the closest beach to Hora is **Megali Ammos** (Big Sand), about a 10-minute walk south of town, and usually very crowded.

With all the south-coast beaches, keep in mind that most people begin to arrive in the early afternoon, and you can avoid the worst of the crowds by going in the morning. By late afternoon and evening—and then until dawn—there's often more dancing than swimming going on at the south coast beaches. **Psarou** has gone from being a family beach to being perhaps one of the most sophisticated of them all (for visiting Athenians mostly). **Ornos** is now popular with families; it's about 2.5km (1½ miles) south of town and has a fine-sand beach in a sheltered bay, with extensive hotel development along the shore. Buses to Ornos run hourly from the south station between 8am and 11pm.

Plati Yialos is another favorite. It's served by a bus that runs every 15 minutes from 8am to 8pm, and then every 30 minutes until midnight during the summer. If Plati Yialos is too crowded, you can catch a caique there for the more distant beaches of Paradise, Super Paradise, Agrari, and Elia. **Paradise,** the island's most famous nude beach, is popular with the gay crowd despite the wall-to-wall umbrellas.

Paradise is never a quiet experience but it is the premier party beach of the island and shows no signs of stopping. I'm not giving phone numbers for these places because the phones are never answered. The **Tropicana Beach Bar** and the **Sunrise Bar** are both havens for the party crowd long after the sun has set. On top of the hill, the popular and internationally known **Cavo Paradiso Club** is a large, open-air nightclub with rotating international DJs and doors that do not open until after 2am. In fact, the "cool crowd" begins to arrive only after 5am. On the beach, **Paradise Club** is the club destination from 6pm to midnight and then reopens again from 2 to 6am. One beach party on Paradise you shouldn't miss is the Full Moon Party, once a month. The only other party that compares to it is the Closing Party every September that has become an island institution. As in most of the island, the water here is breathtakingly beautiful, but hardly anybody comes to Paradise for the sea.

Elia, a 45-minute caique ride from Plati Yialos, is one of the island's best and largest beaches, attracting many nudists, and gays. The next major beach, **Kalo Livadi** (Good Pasture), a beautiful spot in an idyllic farming valley, is accessible by a scramble over the peninsula east from Elia and by bus from the north station in the summer. This is about as quiet a beach as you will find on Mykonos.

The last resort area on the southern coast accessible by bus from the north station is at **Kalafati,** a fishing village that was once the port for the ancient citadel of Mykonos. It's now dominated by the large Aphrodite Beach Hotel complex. Several miles farther east, accessible by a fairly good road from Kalafati, is **Lia,** which has fine sand, clear water, bamboo windbreaks, and a small taverna.

On the north coast, **Panormos** and **Ayios Sostis** are popular, and usually less crowded than beaches to the south. The north wind can be fierce, which is making this an increasingly popular place for wind surfers. At press time, rental chairs and umbrellas were not widely available at these beaches, but there are several small tavernas.

DIVING

Mykonos is known throughout the Aegean for diving. Scuba diving on many islands is prohibited to protect undersea archaeological treasures from plunder. The best month is September, when the water temperature is typically 75°F (24°C) and visibility is 30m (98 ft.). Certified divers can rent equipment and participate in guided dives; first-time divers can rent snorkeling gear or take an introductory beach dive. The best-established dive center is **Mykonos Diving Centre,** at Paradise beach (©/fax **22890/24-808**), which offers 5-day PADI certification courses in English from about 500€, including equipment. **Psarou Diving Center** in Mykonos town (© **22890/24-808**) has also been around for a long time. As always, before you sign up for lessons, be sure that all instructors are PADI certified. The **Union of Diving Centers** in Athens (© **210/411-8909**) usually has up-to-date information. In general, certified divers can join guided dives from 50€ per dive; beginners can take a 2-hour class and beach dive from 60€. There's a nearby wreck at a depth of 20 to 35m (65–114 ft.); wreck dives run from 60€.

Tip: Beaches to avoid on Mykonos because of pollution, noise, and crowds include Tourlos and Korfos Bay.

WHERE TO EAT

Nothing on Mykonos is cheap. The most expensive hotels have their own restaurants, most of which are seriously pricey. Also be careful of restaurants that do not show you a menu, but just recommend dishes and wines—it's easy to run up a big bill.

Very Expensive

Matsuhisha Mykonos ★★ JAPANESE   Nobu Matsuhisha has extended his sushi empire to this, his only open-air restaurant in the most happening hotel in town, the Belvedere. Right by the hotel's pool, with views of the sea and town, try the exceptional Japanese cuisine with Latin influences. Prices are very steep but the top-quality ingredients and sushi are flown in daily from Japan. Begin with a Sakepirnha, the famous Brazilian cocktail made with sake instead of cachaca, and then continue to pick your way through the chef's choice tasting menu. If Matsuhisha is booked up, try the excellent Greek food at the Belvedere's other top-notch restaurant, **Club Belvedere.**

At the Belvedere Hotel, Hora. www.matsuhisamykonos.com. © **22890/25-122.** Reservations essential July–Sept. Main courses 70€–85€. AE, DC, MC, V. Daily 8pm–1am.

Expensive

Uno con Carme ARGENTINE   Starting to have daydreams about a tender, juicy, steak? In addition to its excellent selection of meats (the T-bones are amazing), this place also has generously proportioned fresh salads, an excellent wine selection, and Art Deco ambience to spare. There's also a good bar, for a post-dinner cocktail.

Panachra, Hora. © **22890/24-020.** Main courses 30€–60€. AE, DC, MC, V. Daily 8pm–1am.

Moderate

Chez Marinas ★ GREEK   Formerly known as Maria's Garden, this is another longtime favorite, with a lovely, lantern- and candlelit garden full of bougainvillea and cacti, often animated by live music and fits of dancing. The vegetable dishes are always fresh and tasty, the lamb succulent, and the seafood enticing. In short, this is a place where ambience and cuisine come together to make a very successful restaurant. There's often a good-value set menu for around 25€.

27 Kaloyera, Hora. © **22890/27-565.** Reservations recommended July–Aug. Main courses 15€–30€. DC, V. Daily 7pm–1am.

Interni ★★ ASIAN FUSION With its avant-garde decor and fusion cuisine, Interni is one of the island's most fashionable restaurants. A happening bar scene is popular with affluent young Athenians, but the main attraction is the cuisine. Try the marinated salmon and stir-fried seafood noodles, and you'll understand what the fuss is about.

Hora, Matoyanni. www.interni.gr. © **22890/26-333.** Main courses 18€–40€. DC, V. Daily 8pm–2am.

Mamakas Mykonos ★★ GREEK/MODERN This is a branch of the Mamakas that opened its second location in the down-at-the-heels area of Gazi in Athens in 1998 and helped transform the area from gritty to chic, and managed to start a new trend, traditional taverna fare with modern twists. This is where it all started, right by the Taxi Square, inside a lovely house built in 1845. You can dine in the courtyard (the terracotta planters were a gift from the Princess of Malta to the present owner's grandmother) or indoors. The meals are just as delicious and reasonably priced as ever. Check out the trays of cooked dishes (*magirefta*) and a range of dependable and delicious grills and appetizers—the spicy meatballs (*keftedakia*) are a must!

Hora, Mykonos. © **22890/26-120.** Main courses 15€–30€. AE, MC, V. Daily 8pm–1:30am.

Philippi ★ GREEK/CONTINENTAL Philippi's quiet garden is one of Mykonos's most low-key and romantic places to eat. Old Greek favorites share space on the menu with French dishes and an impressive wine list. What this restaurant provides in abundance is atmosphere, and that's what has made it a perennial favorite.

Just off Matogianni and Kaloyera behind the eponymous hotel, Hora. © **22890/22-294.** Reservations recommended July–Aug. Main courses 10€–25€. AE, MC, V. Daily 7pm–1am.

Sea Satin Market ★★ GREEK/SEAFOOD Location, location, location: Below the famous windmills, beyond the small beach adjacent to Little Venice, the *paralia* (coastline) ends in a rocky headland facing the open sea. This is the remarkable

---

Eating on the Island

You don't want to trek back to Hora for a bite when you're out sunning or exploring, so here are some tips on where to eat when you are out on the island: On Psarou Beach, **N'Ammos** (© **22890/22-440**), with its casual elegance, varied menu (lobster-pumpkin risotto for example), and beachfront setting, is one of the island's finest restaurants; entrees start at 25€. At Ayios Sostis Beach, **Kiki's Taverna** is reminiscent of the days when visitors fell in love with the small, simple, family-owned Greek tavernas (no phone, no sign, no electricity) where perfect grills and salads were served in a shady garden; entrees start at 12€. At Fokos Beach, the **Fokos** (© **22890/23-205**) combines the best of old and new: Fresh caught local fish and farm fresh meat is garnished with fresh veggies flown in from the owners' garden on Crete; entrees start at 12€.

location of one of Hora's most charming restaurants. Set apart from the clamor of the town, it's one of the quietest spots in the area. On a still night just after sunset, the atmosphere is all you could hope for on a Greek island. At the front of the restaurant, the kitchen activity is on view along with the day's catch sizzling on the grill. You can make a modest meal on *mezedes* here, or let it rip with grilled bon filet.

Near the Mitropolis Cathedral, Hora. ✆ **22890/24-676.** Main courses 30€–45€. No credit cards. Daily 6:30pm–12:30am.

Inexpensive

Antonini's ★ 🗡 GREEK   Antonini's is one of the oldest of Mykonos's restaurants. It serves consistently decent stews, chops, and *mezedes*. Locals eat here, although in summer they tend to leave the place to tourists.

Plateia Manto, Hora. ✆ **22890/22-319.** Main courses 9€–18€. No credit cards. Summer daily noon–3pm and 7pm–1am. Usually closed Nov–Mar.

Camares Café ★ 🗡 GREEK   Cheap, decent food, open 24 hours, this place on Taxi Square has been around a long time, serving up grills (lamb chops usually reliable) and salads. If you like Antoni's and Camares, you'll probably also like another long-time favorite, **Kounelas** (no phone) on the harbor, with grills and fresh fish. Dinner for two at either place—if you go easy on the fish—comes to around 50€.

Mavrogenous (Taxi Square). ✆ **22890/28-570.** Main courses 8€–18€; fish and lamb chops priced by the kilo. No credit cards. Open 24 hr.

SHOPPING

If you can dodge the overpriced souvenirs, clothing, and jewelry aimed at cruise ship day-trippers, there is some excellent shopping to be had in Mykonos. **Soho-Soho,** 81 Matoyanni (✆ **22890/26-760**) is by far the best-known clothing store on the island; pictures of its famous clientele (Tom Hanks, Sarah Jessica Parker, and so forth) carrying the store's bags have been in gossip publications around the world. Mykonos is also well known for its house-designed sandals in many colors and styles; perhaps no better selection can be found in the entire island than at **Eccentric by Design,** 11 Fiorou Zouganelis St. (✆ **22890/28-499**), where you can buy sandals encrusted with Swarovski crystals. For more traditional sandals, check out **Kostas Rabias** on Matogianni Street (✆ **22890/22-010**). The finest jewelry shop on the island remains **LALAoUNIS ★,** 14 Polykandrioti (✆ **22890/22-444**), associated with the famous LALAoUNIS museum and shops in Athens. It has superb reproductions of ancient and Byzantine jewelry as well as original designs. If you can't afford LALAoUNIS, you might check out one of the island's oldest jewelry shops, the **Gold Store,** right on the waterfront (✆ **22890/22-397**). **Delos Dolphins,** Matoyanni at Enoplon Dimameon (✆ **22890/22-765**) specializes in copies of museum pieces; **Vildiridis,** 12 Matoyianni (✆ **22890/23-245**) also has jewelry based on ancient designs. Also be sure to check out **Karkalis,** 17 Matoyanni (www.gold.gr; ✆ **22890/24-022**), the newest arrival in town, with striking original and contemporary designs. If you want to see some serious works of art, try the **Scala Gallery,** 48 Matoyianni (www.scalagallery.gr; ✆ **22890/23-407**), which represents a wide range of contemporary Greek artists and frequently holds exhibitions. Nearby on Panahrandou is **Scala II Gallery** (✆ **22890/26-993**), where the overflow from the Scala Gallery is sold at reduced prices. In addition, manager Dimitris Roussounelos of Scala Gallery manages a number of studios and apartments in Hora, so you might find lodgings as well as art at Scala! Luxury fashion boutique **Scoop NYC** (www.scoopnyc.com; ℃ **22890/25-122**) opened its first European location in the Belvedere Hotel. Its exquisite jewelry line by native Mykonian designer Ileana Makri sets this store apart from its New York counterpart.

Mykonos was once world famous for its vegetable-dyed hand-loomed weavings, especially those of the legendary Kuria Vienoula. Today, **Nikoletta** (℃ **22890/27-503**) is one of the few shops where you can still see the island's traditional loomed goods. Eleni Kontiza's tiny shop **Hand Made** (℃ **22890/27-512**), on a lane between Plateia Tria Pigadia and Plateia Laka, has a good selection of hand-woven scarves, rugs, and tablecloths from around Greece.

The best bookstore on Mykonos is **To Vivlio** ★ (℃ **22890/27-737**), on Zouganeli, one street over from Matoyianni. It carries a good selection of books in English, including many works of Greek writers in translation, plus some art and architecture books and a few travel guides.

There's sweets, preserves, herbs, and spices at **Skaropoulos** (℃ **22890/24-983**), 1.5km (1 mile) out of Hora on the road to Ano Mera, featuring the Mykonian specialties of Nikos and Frantzeska Koukas. Nikos's grandfather started making confections here in 1921, winning prizes and earning a personal commendation from Winston Churchill. Try their famed *amygdalota* (an almond sweet) or the almond cookies (Churchill's favorite). You can also find Skaropoulos sweets at **Pantopoleion,** 24 Kaloyerou (℃ **22890/22-078**), along with Greek organic foods and natural cosmetics; the shop is in a beautifully restored 300-year-old Mykonian house. And, when the time comes to leave Mykonos, try to find space in your suitcase for a box of the melt-in-your-mouth almond biscuits from **Efthemios,** 4 Florou Zouganeli (℃ **22890/22-281**), just off the harbor front, where biscuits have been made since the 1950s.

ENTERTAINMENT & NIGHTLIFE

Mykonos has the liveliest, most abundant (and expensive), and most chameleon-like day and nightlife—especially gay nightlife—in the Aegean. New places open and shut here every season. I'm not giving phone numbers for these bars and clubs—the official phones simply are not answered at these places, where staff carry and use private cellphones. How much are you going to spend for one drink at a chic spot on Mykonos? As much as 10€—and after that, the sky really is the limit! By the way, don't think that you have to wait until after dark to party: There are plenty of virtually all-day beach parties here, especially at Psarrou, Paradise, and Super Paradise beaches. At Super Paradise, two loud bar/clubs on opposite sides of the beach cater to gay and mixed crowds, respectively. At Paradise Beach's **Paradise Club,** all-day partying becomes all night around the gigantic swimming pool in the middle of the club, which steals the show with its nightly fireworks.

Back in town, things are less wild and more sophisticated around sunset—when it's often standing room only in Little Venice. For over quarter of a century, **Caprice** has been the island's Little Venice sunset institution, with chairs lined along its narrow porch overlooking the windmills and the sea. Other Little Venice hot spots include **Kastro,** near the Paraportiani Church; **Montparnasse,** cozy with classical music by day, and a popular gay piano bar by night; **Veranda,** in an old mansion overlooking the water; and **Galeraki,** with its wide variety of exotic cocktails (and customers)—the in-house art gallery gives this popular spot its name, "Little Gallery."

The Mykonos scene really gets going well after dinner—some of these places are at their liveliest just before dawn. Right at the entrance of town from the old harbor, the Athenian hot spot Spanish restaurant/bar/club **El Pecado (the Sin)** moves to

Mykonos in the summer and is famous for its sangria and the rum-based drinks combined with the Latin beats. Right on busy Matoyanni Street, in one of the finest people-watching locations, the **Aroma** bar opens all hours, as does **Astra. Uno,** a tiny bar also on Matoyanni, is a popular destination for Athenians. Also on Matoyanni, **Pierro's** is extremely popular with gay visitors and rocks all night long to American and European music; drag shows are not uncommon. Adjacent **Icarus** is best known for its terrace and late-night drag shows. During the early-evening hours, both bars are so popular that sometimes just walking by is difficult. In Taxi Square, another popular gay club, **Ramrod,** has a terrace with a view over the harbor and live drag shows after midnight.

The **Anchor** plays blues, jazz, and classic rock for its 30-something clients, as do **Argo, Stavros Irish Bar, Celebrities Bar,** and **Scandinavian Bar-Disco.** They draw customers from Ireland, Scandinavia, and quite possibly as far away as Antarctica. If you'd like to sample Greek music and dancing, try **Thalami,** a small club underneath the town hall. For a more intense Greek night out, head to **Guzel**—at Gialos, by the waterfront and near the Taxi Square—the place to experience a super-trendy hangout populated mostly by trendy Athenians with Greek and international hits that drive the crowd into a frenzy, with people dancing on the tables.

If having a quiet evening and catching a movie is more your speed, head for **Cinemanto** (✆ **22890/27-190**), which shows films nightly around 9pm. Many films are American; most Greek films have English subtitles. If, on the other hand, you want to see the sunrise, Paradise Beach parties all night—and all day, for that matter. The **Yacht Club** in Mykonos town, despite its sedate name, goes all night, and is a popular place to find someone to end the night with.

WHERE TO STAY

In summer, reserve a room 1 to 3 months in advance (or more), if possible. Ferry arrivals are often met by a throng of people hawking rooms, some in small hotels, others in private homes. If you don't have a hotel reservation, one of these rooms may be very welcome. Keep in mind that Mykonos is an easier, more pleasant place to visit in the late spring or early fall. Off-season hotel rates are sometimes half the quoted high-season rate. Also note that many small hotels, restaurants, and shops close in winter, especially if business is slow. *Tip:* If the decline in tourism in Greece continues, many of these hotels may have special offers, even in high season.

Hora
Very Expensive
Belvedere Hotel ★★   The all-white oasis of the Belvedere, in part occupying a handsomely restored 1850s town house, has stunning views over the town and harbor, only a few minutes' walk away. Rooms are distinctively furnished, in one of eight understated to over-the-top styles. Stay here if you want many of the creature comforts of Mykonos's beach resorts but prefer to be within walking distance of Hora. The ultrachic poolside scene buzzes all night and day, in part due to Nobu Matsuhisa's only open-air restaurant, the impeccable and beyond-chic **Matsuhisa Mykonos** (p. 503). Also on site are the excellent Greek restaurant **Club Belvedere** and the **CBar Lounge**—ideal for its sunset views.

Hora, 84600 Mykonos. www.belvederehotel.com. ✆ **22890/25-122.** Fax 22890/25-126. 48 units. 230€–460€ double; 650€ suite. Rates include buffet breakfast. DC, MC, V. **Amenities:** 2 restaurants; bar/lounge; outdoor pool; exercise room; Jacuzzi; sauna. *In room:* A/C, TV, minibar, hair dryer, Wi-Fi (free).

Cavo Tagoo ★★   This exceptional hotel set into a cliff with spectacular views over Mykonos town is hard to resist—if money is no object. Hora's harbor is only a 15-minute walk away, although you may find it hard to budge from Cavo Tagoo's sybaritic pleasures: Saltwater and freshwater pools, bars and a good restaurant are right here. The hotel's island-style architecture has won awards, and its gleaming marble floors, nicely crafted wooden furniture, queen and kingsize beds, and local-style weavings are a genuine pleasure. Elegantly minimalist with spacious bathrooms, and large balconies with stunning sea vistas, Cavo Tagoo offers spacious double rooms which they refer to as "unique sanctuaries," suites with private pools, a Spa Center, and fresh and saltwater pools.

Hora, 846 00 Mykonos. www.cavotagoo.gr. (© **22890/23-692** to **-695**. 69 units. 225€–420€ double. Rates include buffet breakfast. AE, DC, MC, V. Closed Nov–Mar. **Amenities:** Restaurant; bar; fresh and saltwater pools; exercise room; sauna. *In room:* A/C, TV, minibar, hair dryer, Wi-Fi (free).

Mykonos Theoxenia ★★   When the Mykonos Theoxenia reopened its doors in 2004 after an extensive makeover, it quickly became the talk of the town once again as it was in the '60s. With its stone-clad walls and orange and turquoise fabrics, the mood is already set before you venture beyond the reception. In the 52 rooms and suites, funky '60s-inspired furniture and loud colors dominate the decor with spacious bathrooms (stuffed with luxuries) enclosed in glass walls. The location, right by the windmills and impossibly romantic Little Venice, could not be any more ideal. A wonderful pool and restaurant are the perfect finishing touches. When you arrive at the hotel you will be treated to a welcoming drink, a fruit basket, and bottle of wine.

Kato Mili, Hora, 84600 Mykonos. www.mykonostheoxenia.com. (© **22890/22-230.** 52 units. 282€–420€ single/double, depending on balcony and view; 625€ junior suite; 830€ 2-bedroom suite. AE, DC, MC, V. Free parking. **Amenities:** Restaurant; bar; outdoor pool. *In room:* A/C, TV, hair dryer, Wi-Fi (free).

Expensive

Andronikos Hotel ★★   Beautiful, elegant, and right in town, this impeccably designed hotel offers spacious verandas or terraces with vistas of the sea and the town, a good restaurant, and spa, at affordable (for Mykonos) prices.

Hora 86400, Mykonos. www.andronikoshotel.com. (© **22890/24-231.** Fax 22890/24-691. 53 units. 180€–290€ double; 310€–380€ suite. AE, DC, MC, V. **Amenities:** Restaurant; bar; outdoor pool; exercise room; spa; gallery. *In room:* A/C, TV/DVD, hair dryer, minibar, Jacuzzi (in some rooms), Wi-Fi (free).

Elysium ★★   The smartest gay-friendly hotel on the island is located on a steep hillside right in the old town; a walk down the steep hill will have you back in town in 3 minutes. Gardens, a pool, great views, a gym, a sauna, and a very relaxed atmosphere keep guests returning again and again.

Mykonos Old Town, 846 00 Mykonos. www.elysiumhotel.com. (© **22890/23-952.** 42 units. 180€ double. AE, DC, MC, V. **Amenities:** Bar/cafe; outdoor pool; exercise room; spa; sauna. *In room:* A/C, TV, hair dryer, Wi-Fi (free).

Moderate

Matina Hotel ★ *✦*   The Matina has the one thing you don't expect to find in Mykonos: A central location on a blissfully quiet residential street, just steps from the hustle and bustle. Many rooms have balconies overlooking the large garden, with its geraniums, hibiscus, and palm trees. If you want to avoid Mykonos's isolated hotels and enjoy the comings and goings in a Hora neighborhood, this may be just the place for you. Some rooms are a bit on the small side, but all rooms are modern, cheerful, and comfortable.

3 Fournakion, Hora, 846 00 Mykonos. www.hotelmatina-mykonos.com. ✆ **22890/22-387.** Fax 22890/24-501. 19 units. 60€–100€ double. AE, MC, V. Closed Nov–Mar. **Amenities:** Breakfast room; garden. *In room:* AC, TV, hair dryer, Wi-Fi (free).

Inexpensive
Apollon Hotel ◢ No-nonsense, no-frills hotels in Mykonos are hard to find. Rooms here are basic yet comfortable and well kept. The price seals the deal.

Hora, 84600 Mykonos. ✆ **22890/22-223.** Fax 22890/2437. 10 units. 50€–65€ single or double with shower. No credit cards. *In room:* A/C, TV.

Philippi Hotel ★ ◢ Each room in this homey little hotel in the heart of Mykonos town is different, so you might want to have a look at several before choosing yours. The owner tends the garden that often provides flowers for her son's restaurant, the Philippi (see p. 504), which is steps away.

25 Kaloyera, Hora, 846 00 Mykonos. www.philippihotel.com. ✆ **22890/22-294.** Fax 22890/24-680. 13 units. 90€ double. No credit cards. **Amenities:** Restaurant. *In room:* A/C, TV, minibar, Wi-Fi (free).

Around the Island
If you'd rather stay at a beach and commute into Hora, you've got lots of choices. There's a good bus service from most beaches into town; many hotels have their own shuttle service, and taxis are always available.

There are private studios and simple pensions at Paradise and Super Paradise beaches; but rooms are almost impossible to get, and prices more than double in July and August. Contact the **Mykonos Accommodations Center** (✆ **22890/23-160**)—or, for Super Paradise, **GATS Travel** (✆ **22890/22-404**)—for information on the properties they represent. The tavernas at each beach may also have suggestions.

At Kalafati
Aphrodite Hotel The sprawling Aphrodite Hotel has a large pool, two restaurants, and 150 rooms. It's good value in May, June, and October, when a double costs from 100€. This place is popular with tour groups and Greek families. Mykonos is a popular wedding destination and the Aphrodite has two wedding chapels.

Kalafi, 84600 Mykonos. www.aphrodite-mykonos.com. ✆ **22890/71-367.** 150 units. 100€–150€ double. AE, DC, MC. **Amenities:** 2 restaurants; bar; outdoor pool; tennis; spa. *In room:* A/C, TV, Wi-Fi (free).

At Ornos Bay
Families traveling with children will find staying at one of the Ornos Bay hotels especially appealing. The beach is excellent and slopes into shallow, calm water. Furthermore, this is not one of Mykonos's all-night party beaches. If your hotel does not have watersports facilities, several of the local tavernas have surfboards and pedal boats to rent, as well as umbrellas. One minus: The beach is close to the airport, so you will hear planes come and go.

Kivotos Club Hotel ★★ This is a small, superb luxury hotel about 3km (1¾ miles) outside Mykonos town. Most of the 45 individually decorated units overlook the Bay of Ormos, but if you don't want to walk that far for a swim, head for the saltwater or freshwater pool, the Jacuzzi and sauna, or the pool with an underwater sound system piping in music! Kivotos is small enough to be intimate and tranquil; the service (including frozen towels for poolside guests on hot days) gets raves from guests. If you're ever tempted to leave, the hotel minibus will whisk you into town, but there are several restaurants on-site. The hotel even has its own yacht, a traditional sailing ship, at the ready for spur-of-the-moment sails.

Ornos Bay, 846 00 Mykonos. www.kivotosclubhotel.gr. ✆ **22890/25-795.** 45 units. 290€–390€ double; 650€–1,000€ suites. DC, MC, V. **Amenities:** Restaurant; bar; 2 outdoor pools; tennis; spa; Jacuzzi. *In room:* A/C, TV, Wi-Fi (free).

Santa Marina ☺ Santa Marina sprawls across 8 landscaped hectares (20 acres) overlooking the bay. From a distance, it looks like a residential development—or the sort of hotel one more often finds in the Caribbean. Like Kivotos, it has pools and spa facilities and its own restaurant; what it lacks is Kivotos's elegant intimacy. Lots of Greek families stay here, so if you are traveling with kids that may be a big plus.

Ormos Bay, 84600 Mykonos. www.starwoodhotels.com. ✆ **22890/23-200.** 100 units. 395€–600€ double; 625€–2,400€ suites and villas. AE, DC, MC, V. **Amenities:** 2 restaurants; 4 bars; 2 outdoor pools; tennis; spa; water sports. *In room:* A/C, TV, Wi-Fi (free).

Hotel Yiannaki ★ ✦ This place is characteristic of many small hotels in the Cyclades, in that its architecture is a larger version of a typical small Cycladic house, with white walls and blue shutters—but suddenly three stories tall, with most rooms with balconies. The hotel is about 200m (656 ft.) away from the beach and has its own pool and restaurant. The nicest units have sea views and balconies. In pricey Mykonos, the Yiannaki is a good deal.

Ormos Beach, 84600 Mykonos. www.yiannaki.gr. ✆ **22890/23-393.** 42 units. 75€–150€ double. DC, MC, V. **Amenities:** Restaurant; bar; outdoor pool; sauna. *In room:* A/C, TV, minibar.

At Plati Yialos
Petassos Beach Resort & Spa ★ Like most Mykonos beach hotels, the Petassos has good-sized rooms and all the usual creature comforts. Each room has a balcony overlooking the relatively secluded beach, which is less than 36m (132 ft.) away. The hotel has a good-sized pool, sun deck, Jacuzzi, gym, and sauna. It offers free round-trip transportation to and from the harbor or airport, safety-deposit boxes, and laundry service.

Plati Yialos, 84600 Mykonos. www.petasos.gr. ✆ **22890/23-737.** 82 units. 150€–300€ double. AE, DC, MC, V. **Amenities:** Restaurant; bar; exercise room; outdoor pool, sauna. *In room:* A/C, TV, Wi-Fi (free).

AT AYIOS IOANNIS
Mykonos Grand ★★ This 107-room luxury resort a few kilometers out of Hora is grand, indeed, and has its own beach and many amenities—pools, tennis, squash, Jacuzzis, and a spa. In short, this is a very comfy and stylish place and it may be the only hotel on Mykonos that includes a skipping rope as well as a hair dryer, slippers, and robe in each guest room. The ambiance here is usually quiet, at least for Mykonos, and elegant.

Ayios Ioannis, 846 00 Mykonos. www.mykonosgrand.gr. ✆ **22890/25-555.** 100 units. 250€ double. AE, DC, MC, V. **Amenities:** Restaurants; bar; cafe; 2 outdoor pools; tennis; squash; exercise room; spa; Jacuzzi. *In room:* A/C, TV, Wi-Fi (free).

AT AYIOS STEPHANOS
This popular resort, about 4km (2½ miles) north of Hora, has a number of hotels. Most close from November to March. Here's the best of the bunch.

Grace Mykonos ★★ This boutique hotel offers rooms ranging from standard to VIP suites, all with sleek minimalistic design, some with Jacuzzi or plunge pool. Decor, food, privacy, and the new spa, with sauna and massage, all get high marks—as do the prices, which are less steep than at some of Mykonos's other luxury hotels. It's also only a 5-minute walk into town.

Ayios Stefanos, 846 00 Mykonos. www.mykonosgrace.com. © **22890/26-690.** 38 units. 230€–330€ double; 320€–420€ junior suite. **Amenities:** Restaurant; bar; outdoor pool; spa; sauna. *In room:* A/C, TV, Jacuzzi (in some), Wi-Fi (free).

AT PSARROU BEACH

Grecotel Mykonos Blu ★★ This is another of the island's serious luxury hotels with award-winning Cyclades-inspired architecture. Like Cavo Tagoo and Kivotos, this place is popular with wealthy Greeks, honeymooners, and jet-setters. The private beach, infinity seawater pool, and in-house **Poets of the Aegean** restaurant allow guests to be as lazy as they wish, although there is a fitness club and spa (chocolate symphony facial anyone?). Many villas have private plunge pools. The service here is praised as attentive and unobtrusive. Be sure to ask about special packages, which can be excellent value.

Psarrou Beach, 846 00 Mykonos. www.grecotel.gr. © **22890/27-900.** fax 22890/27-783. 111 units, 250€–450€ doubles; 550€ villas. **Amenities:** Restaurants; 3 bars; outdoor pool; exercise room; spa. *In room:* A/C, TV, minibar, Wi-Fi (free).

A SIDE TRIP TO THE ISLAND OF DELOS ★★★

There is as much to see at **Delos** as at Olympia and Delphi, and there is absolutely no shade on this blindingly white marble island covered with shining marble monuments. Just 3km (1¾ miles) from Mykonos, little Delos was considered by the ancient Greeks to be one of the holiest of sanctuaries, the fixed point around which the other Cycladic islands circled. It was Poseidon who anchored Delos to make a sanctuary for Leto, impregnated by Zeus and pursued by Zeus's aggrieved wife Hera. Here, on Delos, Leto gave birth to Apollo and his sister Artemis; thereafter, Delos was sacred to both gods, although Apollo's sanctuary was the more important. For much of antiquity, people were not allowed to die or be born on this sacred island, but were bundled off to the nearby islet of Rinia.

Delos was not exclusively a religious sanctuary: For much of its history, the island was a thriving commercial port, especially under the Romans in the 3rd and 2nd centuries B.C. As many as 10,000 slaves a day were sold here on some days; the island's prosperity went into a steep decline after Mithridates of Pontus, an Asia Minor monarch at war with Rome, attacked Delos in 88 B.C., slaughtered its 20,000 inhabitants, and sailed home with as much booty as his ships could carry.

 Carpe Diem

Heavy seas can suddenly prevent boats docking at Delos. Follow the advice of the Roman poet Horace and *carpe diem* (seize the day). If you want to visit Delos, come here as soon as possible; if you decide to save your visit here for your last day in the area, rough seas may keep you stranded on Mykonos.

The easiest way to get to Delos is by caique from Mykonos; in summer, there are sometimes excursion boats here from Tinos and Paros. Try not to have a late night before you come here and catch the first boat of the day (usually around 8:30am). As the day goes on, the heat and crowds can be overwhelming. On summer afternoons, when cruise ships disgorge their passengers, Delos can make the

Acropolis look shady and deserted. Sturdy shoes are a good idea, as are hats, bottled water, munchies, and most importantly sunscreen. There is a cafe near the museum, but the prices are high, the quality is poor, and the service is even worse.

GETTING THERE   From Mykonos, organized guided and unguided excursions leave about four times a day (starting about 8:30am), Tuesday through Sunday at the harbor's west end. Every travel agency in town advertises its Delos excursions (some with guides). Individual caique owners also have signs stating their prices and schedules. The trip takes about 30 minutes and costs about 10€ round-trip; as long as you return with the boat that brought you, you can (space available) decide which return trip you want to take when you've had enough. The last boat for Mykonos usually leaves by 4pm. The site is **closed** on Mondays.

Exploring the Site

Joint entrance to the site and museum costs 6€, unless this was included in the price of your excursion. Signs throughout the site are in Greek and French (the French have excavated here since the late 19th century).

The remains at Delos are scattered and not easy to decipher, but when you come ashore, you can head right toward the theater and residential area or left to the more public area of ancient Delos, the agora, the famous **Avenue of the Lions ★**, and the museum. If your time is limited, head left, toward the **Agora,** with scattered remains of the central market and civic area on ancient Delos. The Agora mainly dates from the Roman period when Delos was more important as a port than as a religious sanctuary. To reach the earlier religious sanctuary, take the **Sacred Way** north from the agora toward the Sanctuary of Apollo. As at Delphi and Olympia, the sanctuary here on Delos would have been chockablock with temples, altars, statues, and votive offerings. You can see some of what remains in the **museum,** which has finds from the various excavations on the island. Beside the museum, the remains of the **Sanctuary of Dionysos** are usually identifiable by the crowd snapping shots of the display of marble phalluses, many on tall plinths.

North of the museum and the adjacent Tourist Pavilion is the **Sacred Lake,** where swans credited with powers of uttering oracles once swam. The lake is now little more than a dusty indentation most of the year, surrounded by a low wall. Beyond it is the famous **Avenue of the Lions ★**, made of Naxian marble and erected in the 7th century B.C. There were originally at least nine lions. One was taken away to Venice in the 17th century and now stands before the arsenal there. The whereabouts of the others lost in antiquity remain a mystery; five were carted off to the museum for restoration some years ago and replaced by replicas. Beyond the lake to the northeast is the large square courtyard of the gymnasium and the long narrow stadium, where the athletic competitions of the Delian Games were held.

If you stroll back along the Sacred Way to the harbor, you can head next to the **Maritime quarter,** a residential area with the remains of houses from the Hellenistic and Roman eras, when the island reached its peak in wealth and prestige. Several houses and magnificent villas contain brilliant **mosaics ★**, including Dionysos riding a panther in the **House of the Masks,** and a similar depiction in the **House of Dionysos.** Farther to the south is the massive **Theater,** which seated 5,500 people and was the site of choral competitions during the Delian Festivals, an event held every 4 years that included athletic competitions in addition to musical contests. If you visit here in spring, the wildflowers are especially beautiful, and the chorus of frogs that live in and around the ancient cisterns near the theater will be at its peak.

If you want to take in a great view of the site—and of the Cyclades—take the stepped path up **Mount Kinthos ★**, the highest point (112m/370 ft.) on the island. On many days, nearby Mykonos, Siros to the west, Tinos to the north, and Naxos and Paros to the south are easy to spot. On your way down, keep an eye out for the **Grotto of Hercules,** a small temple built into a natural crevice in the mountainside—the roof is formed of massive granite slabs held up by their own enormous weight.

Santorini (Thira) ★★★

Santorini is one of the most spectacular islands in the world. Many Greeks joke, somewhat begrudgingly, that there are foreigners who know where Santorini is—but are confused about where Greece is. If you arrive by sea, you won't confuse Santorini with any of the other Cyclades when you look up at the 335m (1,100-ft.) high, black, gray, and red cliffs that enclose Santorini's enormous harbor. The caldera (crater) formed when a volcano blew out the island's center sometime between 1600 and 1500 B.C. To this day, some scholars speculate that this destruction gave birth to the myth of the lost continent of Atlantis.

What may confuse you as you arrive here is that the island is known both as Santorini and as Thira—and its capital Fira is known both as Thira and as Hora. And be sure to check the name of the port you arrive and depart from, while large ships to Santorini (pop. 7,000) dock at the port of Athinios, many small ships dock at Skala.

If you disembark at Skala, your first choice will be to decide whether you want to ride the funicular (5€), or a donkey (5€) to the island's capital, Fira. If you arrive on a large ship, you'll be spared this choice, as you'll dock at the new harbor at Athinios and grab a bus (2€) or cab (about 9€) into Fira. Once there, you may decide to reward yourself with a glass of the island's rosé wine before you explore the shops and restaurants, swim at the black volcanic beach of Kamari, or visit the dazzling site of Minoan Akrotiri, an Aegean Pompeii destroyed when the volcano erupted around 1600 B.C. In 2011, the volcano began to show some unwelcome activity, but—thus far—there's been nothing to worry about.

Tip: The best advice we can offer is to avoid visiting here during the months of July and August. Santorini disappears under the weight of tourists during peak season, and crowds make strolling the streets of Fira and Oia next to impossible.

The real wonder is that Santorini exceeds all glossy picture-postcard expectations. Like an enormous crescent moon, Santorini encloses the pure blue waters of its caldera, the core of its usually dormant volcano. Its two principal towns, **Fira** and **Oia** (also transliterated as **Ia**), perch at the summit of the caldera; as you approach by ship, bending back as far as possible to look as far up the cliffs as possible, white-washed houses look like a dusting of new snow along the rim of the cliffs. Up close, you'll find that both Oia and Fira have more hotels, shops (particularly jewelry shops), restaurants, and discos than private homes.

Akrotiri is Santorini's principal archaeological wonder: a town destroyed by the volcano eruption here, but miraculously preserved under layers of ash and lava. The site's protective roof collapsed in 2005 and the site was closed for repair work until April of 2012. If Akrotiri is again closed, don't despair: If it weren't that Akrotiri steals its thunder, the site of **Ancient Thira** would be the island's must-see destination. Spectacularly situated atop a high promontory, overlooking a black lava beach, the remains of this Greek, Roman, and Byzantine city sprawl over acres of rugged terrain. Ancient Thira is reached after a vertiginous hike or drive up (and up) to the acropolis itself.

Arid Santorini isn't known for the profusion of its agricultural products, but the rocky island soil has long produced a plentiful grape harvest, and the local wines are among the finest in Greece. Be sure to visit one of the island **wineries** for a tasting. And keep an eye out for the tasty, tiny unique Santorini tomatoes and white eggplants—and the unusually large and zesty capers. Most important, allow yourself time to see at least one sunset over the caldera; the best and least crowded views are often from the footpath between Fira and Oia.

Tip: Some accommodations rates can be marked down by as much as 50% if you come off-season. Virtually all accommodations are marked up by at least as much for desperate arrivals without reservations in July and August. Only a catastrophic decline in global tourism would produce lower prices here in high summer.

ESSENTIALS

GETTING THERE   **Olympic Air** (www.olympicair.com; © **210/926-9111**), the former Olympic Airlines, offers daily flights between Athens and the Santorini airport Monolithos (© **22860/31-525**), which also receives European charters. There are frequent connections with Mykonos and Rhodes, and service two or three times per week to and from Iraklion, Crete. **Aegean Airlines** (www.aegeanair.com; © **210/998-2888**), with an office at the Monolithos airport (© **22860/28-500**), also has several flights daily between Athens and Santorini. A bus to Fira (4€) meets most flights; the schedule is posted at the bus stop, beside the airport entrance. A taxi to Fira costs about 12€.

The best websites to check for **ferry** information are www.ferries.gr, www.gtp.gr, and **www.openseas.gr**. The ferry service runs to and from Piraeus at least twice daily; the trip takes 9 to 10 hours by car ferry on the Piraeus–Paros–Naxos–Ios–Santorini route, or 4 hours by catamaran if you go via Piraeus–Paros–Santorini. **Excursion boats** go to and from Iraklion, Crete, almost daily. All boats are notoriously late or early; your travel or ticket agent will give you an estimate of times involved in your journey. High-speed **hydrofoils** connect Santorini with Ios, Paros, Mykonos, and Iraklio, Crete, almost daily in the high season and three times weekly in the low season, if the winds aren't too strong. Information on all schedules is available from the Athens **GNTO** (www.gnto.gr; © **210/870-0000**), the **Piraeus Port Authority** (© **210/451-1311** or **1440** or **1441**), or the **Santorini Port Authority** (© **22860/22-239**).

VISITOR INFORMATION   Nomikos Travel (www.nomikosvillas.gr; © **22860/23-660**), **Bellonias Tours** (© **22860/22-469**), and Pelican Travel (www.pelican.gr; © **22860/22-220**) are well established on the island. Nomikos and Bellonias offer bus tours of the island, boat excursions around the caldera, and submarine tours beneath the caldera. Expect to pay about 40€ to join a bus tour to Akrotiri or Ancient Thira, about the same for a day-trip boat excursion to the caldera islands, and about twice that for the submarine excursion.

GETTING AROUND   Santorini has an efficient **bus** service. The island's central bus station is just south of the main square in Fira. Schedules and prices are posted on the wall of the office above it; most routes are serviced every half-hour from 7am to 11pm in the summer, less frequently in the off-season.

The travel agents listed above can help you rent a **car.** You might find that a local company such as **Zeus** (© **22860/24-013**) offers better prices than the big names, although the quality might be a bit lower. Be sure to take full insurance. Of the better-known agencies, try **Budget,** at the airport (© **22860/33-290**), or in Fira a block below the small square that the bus station is on (© **22860/22-900**); a small car should cost about 60€ a day, with unlimited mileage.

Warning: Something to keep in mind if you rent a car. If you park in town or in a no-parking area, the police may remove your license plates and you, not the car-rental office, will have to find the police station and pay a steep fine to get them back. There's a free parking lot—often full—on the port's north side.

By moped: Many roads on the island are narrow and winding; add local drivers who take the roads at high speed, and visiting drivers who aren't sure where they're going, and you'll understand the island's high accident rate. If you're determined to use two-wheeled transportation, expect to pay about 25€ per day, less during off-season. Greek law now requires wearing a helmet; not all agents supply the helmet.

The **taxi** station in Fira is just south of the main square. In high season, book ahead by phone (© **22860/22-555** or **22860/23-951**) if you want a taxi for an excursion; be sure that you agree on the price before you set out. For most point-to-point trips (Fira to Oia, for example), the prices are fixed. If you call for a taxi outside Fira, you'll be charged a pickup fee of at least 2€; also, you're required to pay the driver's fare from Fira to your pickup point. Bus service shuts down at midnight, so book a taxi in advance if you'll need it late at night.

EXPLORING SANTORINI

Ancient Akrotiri ★★ RUINS   It's not easy to get an idea how people lived in Ancient Athens, or Olympia, or almost any ancient city. Walk into Akrotiri and you walk down actual streets, flanked with homes, some with pots and tools still lying where their owners left them before abandoning the town. Since excavations began at Akrotiri in 1967, this site has presented the world with an intimate look at life from the 5th millennium B.C. until Akrotiri's destruction in the 17th century B.C. From roughly 3000 B.C. until its destruction, Akrotiri may have been a Minoan colony, perhaps one of Minoan Crete's many trading outposts in the Aegean. For this reason, Akrotiri is sometimes nicknamed the "Minoan Pompeii." Many scholars think that the powerful volcanic explosion destroyed the Minoan civilization, not just on Santorini, but across the Aegean as far away as Crete. Unlike Pompeii, where people and animals were buried in the volcano's lava and ash, Akrotiri's residents seem to have had enough warning of the volcano to flee the island—although whether they escaped the smothering clouds of ash is unknown.

You enter Akrotiri along the ancient town's main street, on either side of which are houses, shops, and warehouses. *Pithoi* (large earthen jars) found here contained traces of olive oil, fish, and onion. In order to get the best sense of the scale and urban nature of this town, you should go to the triangular plaza, near the exit, where you'll see two-story buildings and a spacious gathering place—Akrotiri's "plateia" (town square). Keep in mind as you explore the extensive remains that archaeologists think that less than 5% of Akrotiri has been excavated. A few reproductions on some of the excavated buildings give a sense of the magnificent wall paintings that decorated homes and public buildings here. The best frescoes were taken to the National Archaeological Museum in Athens, although Santorini continues to agitate for their return. For now, you can see some originals in the Museum of Prehistoric Thera (see p. 517) and a splendid recreation of many frescoes in the Thera Foundation in Fira (see p. 517). As you leave the site, you may notice a cluster of flowers beside one of the ancient walls. This marks the burial spot of Akrotiri's excavator, Professor S. Marinatos, who died in a fall at Akrotiri in 1974. Allow at least an hour to fully explore.

Akrotiri. © **22860/81-366.** Admission 6€. Tues–Sun 8:30am–3pm.

How Akrotiri Was Rediscovered

In 1860, Santorini workers quarrying blocks of volcanic ash—for use in building the Suez Canal—discovered ancient remains here. The quarry was relocated and, some 100 years later, the excavation of Akrotiri began. Who knows what unnoticed treasures may have been walled into the canal if the workers had not been alert.

Ancient Thira ★★ RUINS A high rocky headland **Mesa Vouna** separates two popular beaches (Kamari and Perissa), and at its peak stand the ruins of ancient Thira. Walk up here and you'll be absolutely baffled why anyone decided to live on this steep windswept cliff-top. It's an incredible site, where cliffs drop precipitously to the sea on three sides and there are 360-degree views of Santorini and neighboring islands. This group of ruins is not easy to take in because of the many different periods on view—Roman baths jostle for space beside the remains of Byzantine walls and Hellenistic shops. One main street runs the length of the site, passing first through two agoras. The arc of the theater embraces the town of Kamari, Fira beyond, and the open Aegean. Greeks lived here as early as the 9th century B.C., though most buildings are from much later and date from the Hellenistic era (4th century B.C.). You may not decipher everything, but do take in the view from the large **Terrace of the Festivals.** This is where naked lads danced to honor Apollo—and titillated, some of the graffiti on rocks and walls makes clear, many spectators.

You can reach Ancient Thira by bus, car, or taxi or, if you wish, on foot, passing on the way a cave that holds the island's only spring (see "Walking," under "Outdoor Pursuits," below). Excursion buses for the site of Thira leave from Fira and from the beach at Kamari. Allow yourself at least 5 hours to view the site if you walk up and down; if you come and go by transport, allow an hour for the trip and at least an hour at the site.

Kamari. ✆ **22860/31-366.** Admission 4€. Tues–Sun 8am–2:30pm; site sometimes open later in summer.

The Caldera and The Caldera Islets ★★

If you don't come to Santorini by sea, a sunset trip around the caldera or a daytime trip out to the caldera islets is a great way to get a sense of just how little remains of the original island of Santorini. Most travel agents sell tickets out to the islets (trips from around 50€); check out www.santorini.com/sailing and www.santoriniyachting. com and www.santoriniyacht.com for some popular excursions.

Thirassia is a small, inhabited island west across the caldera from Santorini; a cliff-top village of the same name faces the caldera, and is a quiet(er) retreat from Santorini's summer crowds. You can reach the village from the caldera side only by a long flight of steep steps. Full-day **boat excursions** departing daily from the port of Fira (accessible by cable car, donkey, or on foot) make brief stops at Thirassia, just long enough for you to have a quick lunch in the village; the cost of the excursion—which includes Nea Kameni, Palea Kameni, and Ia—is about 50€ per person; check out www.santoriniyachting.com and www.santoriniyacht.com for some options. Another option is local caiques, which make the trip in summer from Armeni, the port of Oia; ask for information at your hotel or at one of the Fira travel agents (see "Visitor Information," earlier).

9

GREECE | The Cyclades

516

The two smoldering dark islands in the middle of the caldera are **Palea Kameni (Old Burnt),** the smaller and more distant one, which appeared in 157 A.D.; and **Nea Kameni (New Burnt),** which began to appear sometime in the early 18th century. The day excursion to Thirassia (a far more enjoyable destination) often includes these two (unfortunately often litter-strewn) volcanic isles.

If you'd rather explore the caldera underwater, check out the hour-long submarine excursions to the submerged crater; **Santorini Yacht** (www.santoriniyacht.com/submarine) is one of a number of companies offering trips from around 65€.

Fira ★★

If you're staying overnight on Santorini, take advantage of the fact that almost all the day-trippers from cruise ships leave in the late afternoon. That means the best time to explore Fira is after the cruise ships sail and before they return mid-morning. If you've visited other Greek islands, you'll immediately realize that Fira is no great shakes as a Cycladic village. The town's architecture was never particularly interesting and now shops, bars, restaurants, and hotels have virtually smothered the town that was. Don't despair: there are plenty of lovely villages out on the island.

As you stroll, you may be surprised to discover that Fira has a Roman Catholic cathedral and convent in addition to the predictable Greek Orthodox cathedral, a legacy from the days when the Venetians controlled much of the Aegean. The name Santorini, in fact, is a Latinate corruption of the Greek for "Saint Irene." The **Megaron Gyzi Museum** (*C* 22860/22-244; admission 3€; Mon–Sat 10:30am–1pm and 5–8pm, Sun 10:30am–4:30pm), by the cathedral, has church and local memorabilia, including some before-and-after photographs of the island at the time of the devastating earthquake of 1956. The small **Archaeological Museum** (*C* 22860/22-217; admission 3€; Tues–Sun 8:30am–3pm) has both Minoan and classical finds. You might find it almost deserted, as most visitors head directly for Thira's shops. Before you do the same (see "Shopping," below), stop at the **Thera Foundation ★★** (*C* 22860/230-16; admission 4€; Tues–Sun 8:30am–3pm), near the cable car station en route to Firostephani, to have a look at the spectacular reproductions and recreations of the frescoes from Akrotiri. The **Museum of Prehistoric Thera**

SANTORINI'S beaches

They may not be the best in the Cyclades, but the volcanic black and red sand here is unique in these isles—and gets very hot, very fast. **Kamari,** a little over halfway down the east coast, has the largest beach on the island. It's also the most developed, lined with hotels, restaurants, shops, and clubs. The natural setting is excellent, at the foot of cliffs rising precipitously toward Ancient Thira, but the black-pebbled beach becomes unpleasantly crowded in July and August. The **Volcano Diving Center** (www.scubagreece.com; *C* **22860/33-177**), at Kamari, offers guided snorkel swims for around 25€ and scuba lessons from around 60€. **Perissa,** to the south, is another increasingly crowded beach resort, albeit one with beautiful black sand. **Red beach** (Paralia Kokkini), at the end of the road to Ancient Akrotiri, gets its name from its small red volcanic pebbles; it is—but for how long?—usually much less crowded than Kamari and Perissa. All three beaches have accommodations, cafes, and tavernas.

(℗ 22860/232-17; admission 3€; Tues–Sun 8:30am–3pm) near the bus station has a small, but excellent, collection of finds (mainly from ancient Akrotiri).

THE WHITE VILLAGES

Oia (also spelled "Ia"), at the north end of the Caldera, receives most visitors' votes as the most beautiful village on the island. Oia made an amazing comeback from the 1956 earthquake which left it a virtual ghost town for decades. Several fine 19th-century mansions survived and have been restored, including the elegant Restaurant-Bar 1800 and the Naval Museum (see below). Much of the reconstruction continues the ancient Santorini tradition of excavating dwellings from the cliff's face, and some of the island's most beautiful examples can be found here. The village has basically two streets: one with traffic, and the much more pleasant inland pedestrian lane, paved with marble and lined with an ever-increasing number of jewelry shops, tavernas, and bars.

The **Naval Museum ★** (℗ 22860/71-156) is a great introduction to Oia, where, until the advent of tourism, most young men found themselves working at sea and sending money home to their families. The museum, in a restored neoclassical mansion, was almost completely destroyed during the 1956 earthquake. Workers meticulously rebuilt the mansion using photographs of the original structure. The museum's collection includes ship models, figureheads, naval equipment, and fascinating old photographs. Its official hours are Wednesday through Monday from 12:30 to 4pm and 5 to 8:30pm, although this varies considerably. Admission is 3€.

The battlements of the ruined **kastro** (fortress), at the western end of town, are the best place to catch the famous Oia sunset. Keep in mind that many cruise ships disgorge busloads of passengers who come here just to catch the sunset; unless you are here on a rainy February day, you may prefer to find a more secluded spot (see "Imerovigli," below). Below the castle, a long flight of steps leads to the pebble beach at **Ammoudi,** which is okay for swimming and sunning, and has some excellent fish tavernas (see "Where to Eat," later in this chapter). To the west is the more spacious, sandy **Koloumbos Beach.** To the southeast, below Oia is the fishing port of **Armeni,** where ferries sometimes dock and you can catch an excursion boat around the caldera.

Vineyards

Boutari (www.boutari.gr; ℗ **22860/81-011**) is the island's largest winery, and Greece's best-known wine exporter. A variety of tours are offered at their winery in **Megalochiri** on the road to Akrotiri, from a simple tasting of three wines (6€) to the "Libation to Santorini," with four wines, nibbles, and a multimedia show. This is a pleasant way to spend an hour or so (but never on Sunday, when the winery, like most on Santorini, is closed). If you want to sample other local wines, stop by the underground **Volcan Wine Museum** (www.volcanwines.gr; ℗ **22860/31-322**), just outside Fira, on the mail road to Kamari. The museum, which occupies subterranean caves and tunnels, has an audio tour and reconstructions of the winemaking process; admission is 6€. Volcan's once-a-week **Greek Night,** featuring dinner and belly dancers, is popular with large tour groups. For information on a number of winery tours on Santorini, check out www.santonet.gr/wineries.

WALKING tours

If it's not too hot, there are many walks you can enjoy on Santorini. Below are three: One takes you from Fira to Oia to watch Santorini's famous sunset, another takes in a castle and a lovely village, both also spectacular at sunset (Imerovigli & Skaros), and the third (the most rigorous) takes you from Kamari to Ancient Thira. Be sure to wear stout shoes, a good hat and sunscreen, and take some water. You'll probably want to take the bus or a taxi back to your starting point.

Fira to Oia ★★ The path from **Fira** to **Oia** (10km/6 miles) follows the edge of the caldera, passes several churches, and climbs two substantial hills along the way. Beginning at Fira, take the pedestrian path on the caldera rim, climbing past the **Catholic Cathedral** to the villages of **Firostephani** and **Imerovigli.** In Imerovigli, signs on the path point the way to Oia; you'll be okay so long as you continue north, eventually reaching a dirt path along the caldera rim that parallels the vehicular road. The trail leaves the vicinity of the road with each of the next two ascents, returning to the road in the valleys. The descent into Oia eventually leads to the main pedestrian street in town. Allow yourself at least 2 hours. If you end up at Oia around sunset, you'll feel that every minute of the walk was worth it.

Imerovigli & Skaros ★★ In Imerovigli, a rocky promontory jutting into the sea is known as **Skaros.** From medieval times until the early 1800s, this small spot was home to the island's administrative offices. There is little to be seen of the Skaros castle now; it probably collapsed during a 19th-century earthquake. Skaros's view

of the caldera is especially nice at sunset. Getting out on the promontory takes just enough effort that it is usually a tranquil haven from the crowds and bustle of the adjacent towns. The trail (signposted) descends steeply to the isthmus connecting Skaros with the mainland. The path wraps around the promontory, after a mile, reaching a small chapel with a panoramic view of the caldera. On the way, note the cliffs of glassy black volcanic rock, beautifully reflecting the brilliant sunlight. People used this rock to decorate many of the older buildings in Santorini. Allow an hour or two for this excursion.

Kamari to Ancient Thira ★ The trail from Kamari to the site of ancient Thira is steep but manageable. It passes the beautiful site of Santorini's only freshwater spring, which you will wish to drink dry. To reach the trail head from Kamari, take the road (in the direction of ancient Thira) past the Kamari beach parking, and turn right into the driveway of the hotel opposite Hotel Annetta, to the right of a minimarket. The trail begins behind the hotel. Climbing quickly by means of sharp switchbacks, the trail soon reaches a small chapel with a terrace and olive trees at the mouth of a cave. You can walk into the cave, which echoes with purling water, a surprising and miraculous sound in this arid place. Continuing upward, the trail rejoins the car road after a few more switchbacks, about 300m (984 ft.) from ancient Thira. The full ascent from Kamari takes a good hour if you are in better shape than I am; I took two hours, with plenty of stops en route to enjoy the views (and catch my breath).

9

GREECE

The Cyclades

Oia's considerable charms have made it the island's most visited village. All the more reason to head for **Pirgos,** an equally enticing village perched on a steep hill just above the island's port at Athinios. It overlooks the district of **Megalochori,** with the island's best vineyards. Pirgos is a maze of narrow pathways, steps, chapels, and squares—and, for several years now, home to the island's best restaurant, **Selene** (p. 521). Until the mid-19th century, this hamlet hidden away behind the port was the island's capital. Near the summit of the village is the crumbling Venetian kastro, with sweeping views over the island. There is less tourism in Pirgos than in most island villages, and the central square, just off the main road, has just about all the village's shops and cafes. If you want a break, try the **Café Kastelli,** with tasty snacks, *glyka tou koutalou* (spoon sweets of preserved fruits), and fine views. If you want a sweet-and-sour treat, try the preserved *nerangi* (bitter orange).

Tip: As you travel around Santorini, watch for the troglodytic **cave houses** hollowed into the island's solidified volcanic ash. Some of these dwellings are still modest homes, others conceal mini-mansions with Jacuzzis. Another thing to look for as you explore the island: In many fields, you'll see what look like large brown circles of intertwined sticks neatly placed on the ground. What you're looking at is a vineyard. Santorinians twist the grape vines into sturdy wreaths that encircle the grapes and protect them from the island's fierce winds.

WHERE TO EAT
In Fira

Koukoumavlos ★★ INTERNATIONAL   The terrace at Koukoumavlos enjoys the famous caldera view, but unlike most caldera restaurants where a spectacular view compensates for mediocre food, here the view is a distraction from the inventive, even idiosyncratic, menu. One example: crayfish in white chocolate sauce, with ginger, lime, anchovy caviar, and green apple carpaccio. In short, you are likely to be either titillated or terrified by the combination of ingredients in most dishes. In either case, you are likely to be knocked over by the prices (salads at around 20€). Despite the pretentions of the cuisine, the staff is helpful and attentive.

Below the Hotel Atlantis, facing the caldera. www.koukoumavlos.eu. ℭ **22860/23-807.** Reservations recommended for dinner. Main courses 20€–50€. AE, MC, V. Daily noon–3pm and 7:30pm–midnight.

Sphinx Restaurant ★ INTERNATIONAL   Antiques, sculpture, and ceramics by local artists fill this restored mansion and large terrace with views of the caldera and the port at Skala Fira. The homemade pasta is tasty, the seafood fresh (and inventive—grouper with seashells and white wine, anyone?). If you like the Sphinx, you'll probably also like **Lithos** (www.lithossantorini.com; ℭ **22860/24-421**), offering reasonably priced, good food and a great caldera view.

Odos Mitropoleos (near the Panagia Ypapantis Church). www.sphinx.gr. ℭ **22860/23-823.** Reservations recommended. Main courses 20€–35€; fish priced by the kilo. AE, DC, MC, V. Daily 11am–3pm and 7pm–1am.

Taverna Nikolas ★ 🍴 GREEK   This is another one of the few restaurants in Fira where locals queue up alongside throngs of travelers for a table—high praise for a place that has been here forever. There aren't any surprises; you'll get traditional Greek dishes prepared very well. The lamb with greens in egg-lemon sauce is particularly praised. The dining room is always busy, so arrive early or plan to wait. We've had one or two reports that this place is not delighted when tourists show up dressed for the beach, so keep this in mind if you plan to eat here.

Just up from the main square in Fira. No phone. Main courses 12€–18€. No credit cards. Daily noon–midnight.

Around the Island

Restaurant-Bar 1800 ★★ CONTINENTAL   For many years recognized as the best place in Oia for a formal dinner, the 1800 has a devoted following among visitors and locals. Many items are Greek dishes with a difference, such as the tender lamb chops with green applesauce and the cheese pie filled not just with feta, but with five cheeses. The restaurant, housed in a splendidly restored neoclassical captain's mansion, has undeniable romantic charm whether you eat indoors or on the rooftop terrace.

Odos Nikolaos Nomikos, Oia. www.oia-1800.com. (✆ **22860/71-485.** Main courses 15€–30€. AE, DC, MC, V. Daily 8pm–midnight.

Selene ★★★ 📷 GREEK   If you eat only one meal on Santorini, it should be eaten here. This is the best restaurant on Santorini—and one of the best in Greece. Selene was in Fira from 1986 to 2010, when it moved to Pyrgos to continue to delight guests with what owner George Haziyannakis calls the "creative nature of Greek cuisine." The appetizers, often including a sea urchin salad on artichokes and fluffy fava balls with caper sauce, are famous. Main dishes include *brodero* (seafood stew) and baked mackerel with caper leaves and tomato wrapped in a crêpe of fava beans. If you prefer something a little more casual, and less expensive, you can have an equally satisfying meal at Selene's bistro/café/patisserie/wine bar.

Pyrgos. www.selene.gr. (✆ **22860/22-249.** Fax 22860/24-395. Reservations recommended. Main courses restaurant 17€–30€; bistro main courses from 12€. MC, V. Restaurant open Apr to Oct 30 daily 7–11:30pm; bistro open early Mar to Oct 30 daily noon–11pm.

SHOPPING

Fira and **Oia** (Ia) have an astonishing number of jewelry shops, but keep in mind that many prices on Santorini are higher than in Athens. Fira's best-known jeweler, with lovely reproductions of ancient baubles, is **Kostas Antoniou** (✆ 22860/22-633), on Ayiou Ioannou, near the cable-car station. **Porphyra** (✆ 22860/22-981), in the Fabrica Shopping Center, near the cathedral, also has impressive work. The **Bead Shop** (✆ 22860/25-176), by the Archaeological Museum, sells beads, mostly carved from island lava. Generally, the farther away from the caldera you go, the higher the prices and the less certain the quality. In **Firostephani,** which is virtually a suburb of Fira, **Cava Sigalas Argiris** (✆ 22860/22-802) stocks all the local **wines,** including their own. Also for sale are locally grown and **prepared foods,** often served as *mezedes: fava,* a spread made with chickpeas; *tomatahia,* small pickled tomatoes; and *kapari* (capers).

The main street in Oia, facing the caldera, has many interesting stores, several with prints showing local scenes, in addition to the inevitable souvenir shops. The **Loulaki** (✆ 22860/71-856) has a variety of handmade and painted ceramics, some antiques, some reproductions, and a very pleasant ambiance. **Replica** (✆ 22860/71-916) is a source of contemporary statuary and pottery as well as museum replicas; it will ship purchases to your home at post office rates. Farther south on the main street is **Nakis** (✆ 22860/71-813), which specializes in amber jewelry and, not surprisingly, has a collection of insects in amber. And, if you're running low on reading material by the time you get to Santorini, head to Oia's **Atlantis Books** (www.atlantisbooks.org; ✆ 22860/72-346). You'll find everything from guidebooks and detective novels for the beach to poetry and philosophy. Oia's main drag is very crowded at sunset time, but much quieter than Fira the rest of the day.

ENTERTAINMENT & NIGHTLIFE

Fira offers all-night partying; as always on the islands, places that are hot one season are gone the next. I'm not listing phone numbers here because phones simply are not answered. If you want to kick off your evening with a drink on the caldera while watching the spectacular sunset, **Franco's, Tropical,** and **Palaia Kameni** are still the most famous and best places for this magic hour; be prepared to pay 15€ and up for a drink. Franco's often has great live music, sometimes including classical favorites. If you are willing to forgo the caldera view, you'll find almost too many spots to sample along the main drag and around the main square, including the inevitable Irish pub, **Murphy's. Kirathira Bar** plays jazz at a level that permits conversation, and the nearby **Art Café** offers muted music.

Discos come and go, and you need only follow your ears to find them. **Koo Club** is the biggest, whereas **Enigma** is thronged most nights. **Tithora** is popular with a young, heavy-drinking crowd. There's usually no cover, but the cheapest drinks at most places are at least 15€.

Out on the island, in **Oia, Zorba's** is a popular cliff-side pub. The fine restaurant/bar **1800** (see above) is a quiet and sophisticated place to stop for a drink—and certainly for a meal. Thus far, Oia is keeping the sort of loud discos and all-night rowdy bars that have proliferated in Fira at bay. On the other hand, **Kamari Beach** has lots of disco bars, including **Disco Dom, Mango's, Yellow Donkey,** and **Valentino's,** all popular with youngish tour groupers. At virtually all of these places, be prepared to pay 15€ and way up for one drink.

WHERE TO STAY

Santorini is always packed in July and August—and increasingly crowded virtually year-round. If you plan a summer visit, make a reservation at least 2 months in advance. If you arrive without a reservation, try not to accept rooms offered (sight unseen) at the port—many are located in villages quite a distance from what you've come here to see. If you come between April and mid-June or in September or October, when the island is less crowded and far more pleasant, the rates can be less than the high-season rates we quote. Keep in mind that during the off-season many of the hotels, restaurants, shops, and bars here close. Most of the hotels recommended below don't have air-conditioning, but with cool breezes blowing through, you won't need it; if you take a room here in the winter, make sure that it offers working central heat or a serviceable room heater. *Note:* Unless you're going to be participating in Fira's energetic nightlife, you may want to consider avoiding the hubbub by staying in one of the villages out on the island. We do suggest several hotels in Fira that are usually quiet.

 Santorini Swings

The height of the tourist season is also the height of the music season in Santorini: If you are here in July, you may want to take in the annual **Santorini Jazz Festival** (www.jazzfestival.gr), which has been bringing several dozen international jazz bands and artists here every summer since 1997. Many performances are on Kamari beach. In Fira in September, the **Santorini International Music Festival** (www.santorinimusicfestival.com), founded in 1978, features 2 weeks of mostly classical music.

In addition to the choices below, we get good reports on the long-popular and usually quiet 25-room **Hotel Atlantis** (www.atlantishotel.gr; *C* **22860/22-232**), where guests can spend the sunset hours with a bottle of wine on the balcony overlooking the caldera; doubles from 205€–315€. The eight-unit **Enigma Apartments** (www.enigmahotel.com; *C* **22860/24-024;** studios from 200€ a night) has elegantly simple furnishings and spectacular views of the caldera and its sunsets.

For a more modest place in Fira, consider **Loizos Apartments** (www.loizos.gr; *C* **22860/24-046**), with 12 units, many with balconies, steps from that caldera view. The owners describe the Loizos's style as "minimal design and simple lines," but I'd only agree if they added "stylishly comfortable" to their description. Studios at Loizos cost from 65€ a night.

In & Around Fira

Aigialos ★★   In a quiet caldera location, occupying 16 restored 18th- and 19th-century town houses, the Aigialos proclaims its intention to be a "Luxury Traditional Settlement." The oxymoron aside—rather few traditional settlements here or elsewhere have a counter swim exercise swimming pool with Jacuzzi —this is a nifty place. As the price goes up, you get more space (two bathrooms, not just one) and more privacy (your own, not a shared terrace or your own balcony). There's an extensive breakfast buffet and a highly praised in-house, guests-only restaurant.

Fira, 847 00 Santorini. www.aigialos.gr. *C* **22860/25-191.** 16 units. 300€–400€ house; 600€–1,000€ mansion. Rates include breakfast. AE, DC, MC, V. Closed Nov–Mar. **Amenities:** Restaurant, bar; outdoor pool; room service. *In room:* A/C, TV/DVD, fridge, CD player, Wi-Fi (free).

Hotel Aressana ★★   This hotel compensates for its lack of caldera view with a large swimming pool and an excellent location, tucked away behind the Orthodox cathedral, in a relatively quiet location. Most rooms have balconies or terraces; many have the high barrel-vaulted ceilings typical of this island. Unusual in Greece are the non-smoking rooms. The breakfast room opens onto the pool terrace, as do most of the guest rooms; the elaborate buffet breakfast includes numerous Santorinian specialties. The Aressana also maintains seven nearby apartments facing the caldera, starting at 250€, which includes use of the hotel pool.

Fira, 847 00 Santorini. *C* **22860/23-900.** Fax 22860/23-902. www.aressana.gr. 50 units. 250€–300€ double. Rates include full breakfast. AE, DC, MC, V. Closed mid-Nov to Feb. **Amenities:** Snack bar; bar; freshwater outdoor pool; room service. *In room:* A/C, TV, minibar, Wi-Fi (free).

Hotel Keti ★★ *♦*   This simple hotel offers one of the best bargains on the caldera. Most of the (smallish) rooms have traditional vaulted ceilings and white walls and coverlets, and open onto a shared terrace overlooking the caldera. The bathrooms, at the back of the rooms, are carved into the cliff face. One drawback if you have trouble walking: It's a steep 5- to 10-minute walk from the Keti's quiet cliff-side location to Fira itself.

Fira, 847 00 Santorini. www.hotelketi.gr. *C* **22860/22-324.** 7 units. 95€–100€ double; 150€ suite. No credit cards. Closed Nov to mid-Mar. **Amenities:** Bar. *In room:* A/C, TV, fridge, safe.

Pension George ★ *♦*   If you like the idea of being near, but not actually in, Fira, the Pension George—a 15- to 20-minute walk away—may be the place for you. With simple wood furnishings, attractive and reasonably priced rooms, and helpful owners, the Pension offers excellent value for budget travelers. To save even more money, opt for a room without a balcony. George and Helen Halaris will help you arrange car and boat rentals. They also have the very reasonably priced five-unit Karterados Beach Apartments at Karterados Beach. Every unit has a kitchenette and the hotel has an outdoor pool for those who don't always want to make the 100m (328-ft.) walk to the beach (doubles from 60€–75€).

P.O. Box 324, Karterados, 847 00 Santorini. www.pensiongeorge.com. © **22860/22-351.** 25 units. 50€–90€ double. Inquire about apts that sleep 2–5. No credit cards. **Amenities:** Breakfast on request; free transportation to airport or harbor. *In room:* A/C, TV (in some), fridge.

Around the Island

ASTRA Suites ★★★   Perched on a cliff side, with spectacular views, this is one of the nicest places to stay in all of Greece. There are other places nearby which also have pools with envious views, but manager George Karayiannis is a large part of what makes Astra so special: He is always at the ready to arrange car rentals, recommend a beach or restaurant—or even help you plan your wedding and honeymoon here. The Astra Apartments look like a tiny, whitewashed village (with an elegant pool) set in the village of Imerovigli, which is still much less crowded than Fira or Oia. Nothing is flashy here; everything from the compact studios to the expansive pool suites is just right. There are spa services (massage, sauna, and Jacuzzi) and a Greek-Mediterranean full-service restaurant that emphasizes local cuisine.

Imerovigli, 847 00 Santorini. www.astrasuites.com. © **22860/23-641.** Fax 22860/24-765. 16 apts, 12 suites. 220€–300€ studio; 620€–820€ pool suite. MC, V. **Amenities:** Restaurant; bar; outdoor pool; spa; Jacuzzi; sauna. *In room:* A/C, TV/DVD, kitchenette, CD player, Wi-Fi (free).

Katikies ★★   If you find a more spectacular pool anywhere on the island, let us know: The larger of the two outdoor pools runs virtually to the side of the caldera so that you can paddle around and enjoy an endless view. (There's also a smaller pool intended for the use of guests staying in suites.) The hotel's island-style architecture incorporates twists and turns, secluded patios, beamed ceilings, and antiques. If the people in the next room like to sing in the shower, you might hear them—but most people who stay here treasure the tranquility.

Oia, 847 02 Santorini. www.katikieshotelssantorini.com. © **22860/71-401.** Fax 22860/71-129. 22 units. 350€–420€ double; 400€–1000€ pool side or caldera view suites. Rates include breakfast. MC, V. **Amenities:** 4 restaurants; bar; 2 outdoor infinity pools; health club; spa; 2 Jacuzzis. *In room:* A/C, TV, minibar, hair dryer, Wi-Fi (free).

Zannos Melathron ★★   Relatively uncrowded Pyrgos sits inland between Megalohori and Kamari. This 12-room boutique hotel, on one of the highest points on the island, occupies an 18th-century and a 19th-century building. The rooms mix antiques with modern pieces, and the island views from here are lovely. If you want nightlife, this is not the place for you; if you want a peaceful retreat and near-perfect service, this may be just the spot. If you want a cigar bar, look no further. If the Zannos Melathron is too expensive for you, check out Donna's House, a much cheaper and very charming small hotel in a handsome renovated mansion in the center of Pyrgos (www.donnashouse.gr; © **22860/31-873;** doubles from 55€ in high season).

Pyrgos, 847 00 Santorini. www.zannos.gr. © **22860/28-220.** 12 units. 200€–450€ double; 550€–900€ suite. MC, V (credit card required to make reservation, but cash usually expected for payment). **Amenities:** Restaurant; bar; outdoor pool; room service; airport pickup. *In room:* A/C, TV, minibar, Wi-Fi (free).

Tinos ★★★

Unlike Santorini and Mykonos—where foreigners often outnumber locals—**Tinos** is one Cycladic island where you are likely to hear more Greek spoken in shops and restaurants than German or French. Tinos is the most important destination in Greece for Greek religious pilgrims, yet it remains one of the least commercialized islands of the Cyclades. That makes Tinos a real joy to visit—as do its lovely villages, uncrowded beaches, green hills crossed by stone walls and dotted with the elaborate *peristerionades* (**dovecotes**) for which the island is famous, and good restaurants that serve the thousands of pilgrims who come here year-round to visit the **Panayia Evanyelistria** ("Our Lady of Good Tidings"), sometimes called the "Lourdes of Greece."

From well out to sea, the Panayia Evanyelistria—illuminated at night—is visible atop a hill overlooking Tinos town, which the inhabitants call "Hora." Like many of the Cyclades, Tinos had a Venetian occupation, and a number of fine, old mansions (locally known as *pallada,* the name also used for the harbor front), still stand on the side-streets off the harbor. **Megalocharis** is the long, steep street that leads from the harbor to the red-carpeted steps that are the final approach to the cathedral; some devout pilgrims make the entire journey on their knees. Running uphill parallel to Megalocharis, pedestrianized **Evangelistria** is a market street, as well as a pilgrimage route, with many shops selling candles and icons. Evangelistra also has several jewelry and handicraft shops, one or two cafes, sweet shops, and several old-fashioned dry-goods stores.

It's important to remember that Tinos *is* a pilgrimage place: It is considered disrespectful to wear shorts, mini skirts, halters, or sleeveless shirts in the precincts of the Evanyelistria (or any other church, for that matter). And taking snapshots of the pilgrims, especially those approaching the shrine on hands and knees, is not appreciated.

The inland villages of Tinos are some of the most beautiful in the Cyclades. Many of the most picturesque are nestled into the slopes of **Exobourgo,** the rocky pinnacle visible from the port, connected by a network of walking paths that make this island a hiker's paradise. In these villages and dotting the countryside, you'll see the elaborately carved marble lintels, doorjambs, and fan windows on village houses, and ornately decorated medieval dovecotes. The island's beaches may not be the best in the Cyclades, but they are plentiful and uncrowded throughout the summer. All this may change if an airport is built here—all the more reason to visit Tinos now.

 When *Not* to Visit Tinos

Don't even think about arriving on Tinos without a reservation around **August 15,** when thousands of pilgrims travel here to celebrate the Feast of the Assumption of the Virgin. **March 25** (Feast of the Annunciation) is the second-most-important feast day here.

Pilgrims also come here on **July 23** (the anniversary of St. Pelagia's vision of the icon) and **January 30** (the anniversary of the finding of the icon). In addition, it's not a good idea to show up here without a reservation on a weekend, when many Greek tours and families visit.

ESSENTIALS

GETTING THERE The best websites to check for ferry information are www. ferries.gr, www.gtp.gr, and www.openseas.gr. Several ferries travel to Tinos daily from Piraeus (5 hr.). Catamaran (1½ hr.) and ferry services (4 hr.) are available daily in summer from Rafina. Check schedules at the Athens **GNTO** (✆ **210/870-0000**); **Piraeus Port Authority** (✆ **210/459-3223** or **210/422-6000;** phone seldom answered); or **Rafina Port Authority** (✆ **22940/22-300**).

Several times a day, boats connect Tinos with nearby Mykonos and Siros (20–50 min.; there's usually daily service to Santorini, Paros, and Naxos in summer). Tinos has more winter connections than most Cycladic isles due to its religious tourism.

Be sure to find out from which pier your ship will depart—and be prepared for last-minute changes. Most ferries, and the small catamarans (Seajet, Flying Cat, and Jet One), dock at the old pier in the town center; some use the new pier to the north, on the side of town in the direction of Kionia. **Tinos Port Authority** (not guaranteed to be helpful) can be reached at ✆ **22830/22-348.**

VISITOR INFORMATION For information on accommodations, car rentals, island tours, and Tinos in general, contact **Windmills Travel ★★** (www.windmills travel.com; ✆ **22830/23-398;** fax 22830/23-327). They have unparalleled knowledge of Tinos and its neighboring islands and offer a friendly service.

GETTING AROUND The bus station (✆ **22830/22-440**) is beside the Catholic church on the harbor, above the pier where the large island boats dock. Schedules are usually posted on the door or available at the desk in the bus station. There are frequent daily buses to most island villages. The local bus company also offers a tour of the island for 15€, which usually departs from the Tinos town station daily from late June to late September at 10am; it returns to Tinos town around 5pm, after stopping at a number of villages and for lunch (not included in price), and a swim at Panormos. It is an excellent way to get an initial sense of the island. If you speak Greek, or feel adventurous, do this tour on your own simply by hopping on and off a variety of local buses.

Vidalis Car Hire on the harbor at 2 Trion Hierarchon, where taxis congregate (www.vidalis-rentacar.gr; ✆ **22830/15-670**), has a wide range of vehicles. Expect to pay from 40€ per day for a car, half that for a moped; prices lower off-season.

Taxis can be found on Trion Ierarchon, which runs uphill from the harbor by the Palamaris supermarket and the Hotel Tinion.

EXPLORING THE ISLAND

If it's a clear day, one of your first sights of Tinos from the ferry will be the odd mountain with a bare summit that looks bizarrely like a twisted fist. This is **Exobourgo,** a mountain eminence (565m/1,864 ft.) crowned by the remains of a Venetian kastro (castle) about 15km (9 miles) outside Hora. Sheer rock walls surround the fortress on three sides; the only path to the summit starts behind a Catholic church at the base of the rock, on the road between Mesi and Koumaros. As you make the ascent (allow a good 15 minutes for the steep walk), you'll pass several lines of fortification—the entire hill is riddled with walls and hollowed with chambers. The fortress itself has long been in ruins—and was never as imposing as, for example, the massive Venetian fortress at Nafplion in the Peloponnese. The Turks defeated the Venetians here in 1714 and drove them from the island.

In Tinos town, it's easy to fall into the habit of strolling along the harbor and taking one of the two main streets to go up to the Cathedral. Don't! Tinos town's side-streets

A SWIM, A snack, AN ANCIENT SITE

If you're staying in Tinos town, the easiest place to take a dip is the beach at **Kionia,** about 3km (2 miles) west of Hora. Just across from the pebble-and-sand strand where you'll swim are the island's only excavated antiquities, the modest remains of the **Temple of Poseidon** and one of his many conquests, Amphitrite, a semi-divine sea nymph (Tues–Sun 8:30am–3pm; admission 3€). When sheep or the custodians have trimmed the vegetation at the site, you can make out the foundations of the 4th-century-B.C. temple, and a large altar and long stoa, both built in the 1st century B.C. As usual with a site where Romans lived, there are the remains of a bath. Finds from the site are on display at the Tinos town **Archaeological Museum** on Megalocharis St. (Tues–Sun 8:30am–3pm; admission 3€). When you head back to town from Kionia, you can have a drink and a snack at the Mistral or Tsambia taverna, both on the main road near the site. Depending on your mood, you can do this excursion on foot, by public bus, or taxi. If on foot, keep to the side of the road and don't expect the trucks and motorcycles to cut you much slack.

have any number of handsome houses, small churches, and flowery nooks and crannies. Wander around, and let yourself get lost in the marble lanes bordered by whitewashed houses with blue shutters and red geraniums. If you get *really* lost, just keep heading downhill, and you'll end up at the harbor.

Most people who come to Tinos head promptly to the **Church of Panagia Evangelistria (Our Lady of Good Tidings) ★★★**. The church and its museums are usually open from about 7am to 5pm in winter, later in summer. In 1822, a local nun, Pelagia, had a vision that a miraculous icon of the Virgin Mary would be found here; it was, and the church was erected to house the icon, which the faithful believe was painted by Saint Luke. The church is made of gleaming marble from Paros and Tinos, with handsome black-and-white pebble mosaics in the exterior courtyard. Inside, hundreds of gold and silver hanging lamps illuminate the icon, which is almost entirely hidden by the votive offerings of gold, silver, diamonds, and other precious jewels, dedicated by the faithful. Even those who do not make a lavish gift customarily make a small offering and light a candle. Beneath the church is the crypt with the **chapel of the Zoodochos Pigi,** where the icon was found, and several smaller chapels; the crypt is often crowded with Greek parents and children in white, waiting to be baptized with water from the font, or to fill vials with holy water from the spring.

Note: To enter the church, you will need to dress suitably, which means no shorts, or sleeveless tops for men, and women should wear longer dresses or skirts and blouses with sleeves. Please remember that it's not appropriate to explore the church during a service, which usually take place in the early morning and in early evening; a full schedule is sometimes posted on the main door of the cathedral.

Within the high walls that surround the church are various **museums and galleries,** each of which is worth a quick visit. The gallery of 14th- through 19th-century religious art displays icons and church garments and vessels; the gallery of Tinian artists is just that; the picture gallery has the private collection of a local collector of Greek paintings of the 19th and 20th centuries; the sculpture museum has works by former and current island sculptors, many of whom studied with the help of the cathedral charitable foundation. A small admission fee is sometimes charged at these collections, which keep irregular hours.

Aetofolia and Volax

If you're interested in island crafts and good food, head for the villages of **Aetofolia** and **Volax,** north of Tinos town. The **Museum of Traditional Pottery** (no phone or website at present; admission 2€; open Apr–Sept Tues–Sun 10am–4pm) opened in 2009 in **Aetofolia,** one of the smallest and most charming Tinian villages. There are labels throughout in Greek and English and the museum guide speaks excellent English. The museum showcases pottery made—or found—not only on Tinos, but on the neighboring island of Sifnos, as well as other Cyclades. The displays are delightful as is the traditional 19th-century island house that is now the museum, with its kitchen filled with locally made pottery. Don't miss the little pottery barbecue, called a "foufou" from the sound made when cooks blow on the coals!

After touring the **pottery** museum's well-stocked kitchen, you may be thinking of food, so head for the village of **Volax,** which is known for it's locally hand-weaved baskets of all sizes and shapes. Just as you come into Volax, you'll see the tall trees that shade the family-run **Taverna Volax** (☎ **22830/41-021**). Don't miss the local *loukanika* (sausages), best washed down with some Tinian wine. As you walk around the village, you may be startled to notice a **stone amphitheater,** which the villagers built about 20 years ago from the massive round boulders that are found here. Call **Windmills Travel** (☎ **22830/23-398**) for details of theater performances (most occur during August).

Convent of Kechrovouniou & Surrounding Villages

Almost all pilgrims who come to Tinos head for this convent, once the home of Pelagia, the nun whose vision revealed the location of the island's famous icon. This means that if you are driving, you should be prepared to encounter tour buses as you drive up the increasingly narrow road to the convent. The convent is usually closed from 1 to 4pm; if you arrive then, while you wait, you can visit the very small deer park and a chapel with an impressive array of the skulls of deceased nuns and monks. When you leave the convent, take in the hamlets of **Dio Horia, Arnados,** and **Triandaros,** all on the slopes below. Arnados has a number of *stegasti,* tunnel-like streets formed by the overhanging second-floor rooms of village houses; Dio Hora has an attractive village fountain, and Triandaros has several restaurants.

On your way back to Tinos town, perhaps stop at **Loutra,** which also has a number of *stegasti;* building a room out over the street below was a clever way for Tinians to have as much house as possible on a small amount of land.

 Affordable & Portable Tinian Folk Art

In a small hardware shop across from Pirgos's two museums, **Nikolaos Panorios ★★★** (☎ **22830/32-263;** usually open from 9am to 1pm) makes and sells whimsical tin funnels, boxes, spoon holders, and dustpans, as well as dovecotes, windmills, and sailing ships. Each item is made of tin salvaged from containers like those that hold olive oil; each one is different, some with scenes of Pallas Athena, others with friezes of sunflowers, olive gatherers, or fruit and vegetables. Prices start from 20€.

Tinos is not best known for its beaches, but you'll find a decent sand beach 3km (1¾ miles) west of Tinos town at **Kionia,** and a better one 2km (1¼ miles) east of town at busy **Ayios Fokas.** From Tinos, there's bus service on the south beach road (usually four times a day) to the resort of **Porto,** 8km (5 miles) to the east. Porto offers several long stretches of uncrowded sand, a few hotel complexes, and numerous tavernas, several at or near the beach. The beach at **Ayios Ioannis,** facing the town of Porto, is okay, but you'd be better off walking west across the small headland to a longer, less populous beach, extending from this headland to the church or Ayios Sostis at its western extremity; you can also get there by driving or taking the bus to Ayios Sostis. **Kolimbithres** has two good sand beaches on the north side of the island, easily accessed by car, although protection from the *meltemi* winds can be a problem—the smaller, in a small rocky cove has beach umbrellas, showers, and two tavernas. The high winds are making Kolimbrithes an increasingly popular destination for wind surfers. If you're a surfer, check out www.tinossurflessons.com. Just beyond Pirgos, the beach at **Panormou** is in the throes of development as a holiday resort. Finally, a series of hairpin roads, some unpaved, leads down—and we mean "way down"—to beaches at **Ayiou Petrou, Kalivia,** and **Giannaki,** west of Tinos town.

Most visitors to Tinos think that **Pirgos ★★**, at the western end of the island, is its most beautiful village. You can spend a good part of a day here, and at the nearby beach of Panormos. Pirgos has an enchanting small plateia with trees, a marble fountain, several cafes, and a couple of (overpriced) tavernas, usually open for lunch and dinner in summer, less regularly off-season. Renowned for its school of fine arts, Pirgos is a center for marble sculpting, and many of the finest sculptors of Greece have trained here. In 2008, the superb **Museum of Marble Crafts ★★★** (✆ **22830/31-290;** admission 3€; open summer Wed to Mon 10am to 6pm, off-season 10am to 5pm) opened on a hill above the village, accessed by a narrow road. The museum takes visitors into the lives of the sculptors and artisans of Tinos, with the help of photos and films. Displays include examples of the more than 100 kinds of Greek marble, glorious fanlight windows, doorway ornaments, and grave monuments—and a selection of the tools used to make them. There's also a cafe and small shop. Nearby, the **Dellatos Marble Sculpture School** (www.tinosmarble.com; ✆ **22830/23-164**) organizes workshops for would-be marble workers.

The **Museum of Yiannoulis Chalepas** and the **Museum of Panormian Artists** occupy adjacent houses, and give visitors a chance not only to see sculpture by local artists, but also to step into an island house. The museums are located near the bus station, on the main lane leading into the village; both are open Tuesday through Sunday from 11am to 1:30pm and 5:30 to 6:30pm (admission 2€).

WHERE TO EAT

As in many other Greek coastal towns, it's a good idea to avoid most harbor-front joints, where the food is generally inferior and service rushed. That said, if you just want a pizza or a sweet (priced at 10€ and up), head to **Mesklies** (✆ **22830/22-151**) on the harbor. For the best coffee—and a full pot of it for only 2 €—try **Le**

Caffe (no phone), also on the harbor. Le Caffe also has the best *loukoumades* (like doughnuts but drenched in honey, sprinkled with cinnamon, and if you wish, topped with ice cream).

Palaia Pallada ★★ 🍴 GREEK Palaia Pallada serves up consistently well-pre-pared food—at reasonable prices. There are few ruffles and flourishes here, but the dishes (grills, stews, salads) in this family-run place are excellent, as is the local wine. You can eat indoors or outside in the lane, or at tables by the old bakery, where you can spy on Tinos's elegant youths plying their cellphones at a cluster of nearby cafes.

Kontoyioryi, Paralia, Hora. Off the harbor, in the lane btw. the old and new harbors. 📞 **22830/23-516.** Main courses 7€–15€. No credit cards. Daily noon–midnight.

To Koutouki tis Eleni ★ GREEK Known in town simply as Koutouki, this excellent small taverna off Evangelistra Street doesn't usually have a menu. What it does have is simple meals using basic ingredients that remind you how satisfying Greek food can be. Local cheese and wine, fresh fish and meats, delicious vegetables—these are the staples that come together so well in this taverna, which demonstrates that you don't have to pay a fortune to experience good traditional home-cooking.

Paralia, Hora. 📞 **22830/24-857.** Main courses 7€–15€. No credit cards. Daily noon–midnight.

SHOPPING IN TINOS TOWN

Two favorite shops in town are on Megalocharis, the main traffic road that leads up to the Cathedral. **Enosis,** a few steps up from the harbor, is the shop of the local agricultural cooperative, where pungent capers, creamy cheeses, olive oil, and the fiery local *tsiporo* liqueur are on sale (📞 **22830/21-184**). If you like capers, stock up on a vacuum pack or two. Continue to 34 Megalocharis and you'll find **Nostos** (📞 **22830/22-208**). Everything here—the ceramics, wood work, jewelry, weav-ings—is handmade. The owner, Litsa Malliari Toufekli, is a painter and many of her scenes of Tinos, created on old wood panels, are on view.

Pedestrianized **Evangelistria Street** parallels Megalocharis Street. Shops and stalls lining Evangelistria Street sell icons, incense, candles, medallions, *tamata* (tin, silver, and gold votives), snowglobes containing religious scenes, and even toy kittens that roll over and mew. Two fine jewelry shops stand side by side on Evangelistria: **Artemis,** 18 Evangelistria (📞 **22830/23-781**) and **Harris Prassas Ostria-Tinos,** 20 Evangelistria (📞 **22830/23-893;** fax 22830/24-568). Both have contemporary, Byzantine, and classical styles; silverwork; and religious objects, including reproduc-tions of the miraculous icon. Near the top of the street, on the left, in a neoclassical building, the small **Evangelismos Biotechni Shop,** the outlet of a local weaving school (📞 **22830/22-894**), sells reasonably priced table and bed linens, embroi-dered aprons, and rugs. You'll also see plenty of shops selling a delicious local nougat, as well as *loukoumia* (Turkish delight) from Siros.

ENTERTAINMENT & NIGHTLIFE

There's less nightlife on Tinos than on many islands; as always on the islands, places that are hot one season are often gone the next. I'm not listing phone numbers here because phones are simply not answered. Two sweets shops, **Epilekto** and **Meskiles** (fantastic *loukoumades* with ice cream), both on the waterfront, stay open late. At the end of town near the largest quay, there is a clutch of bars with music, TV, and some-times dancing, including **Koursaros, Kaktos, Volto,** and **Syvilla,** and, on the road toward Kiona, **Paradise.** If you want a late-night (or early-morning) coffee, try **Monopolio** on the harbor front; instead of a cup, this place brings you a pot of French filtered coffee.

WHERE TO STAY

In addition to the following hotels, check out the good-value **Asteria** (✆ **22830/22-830**), perched above the harbor where the big boats dock. The Asteria was remodeled in 2010 and now its guest rooms and bathrooms fit the cliché "simple but comfortable;" most rooms have a balcony, and corner rooms have large balconies (doubles from 55€–75€).

Oceanis Hotel ★ This 10-year-old hotel is on the harbor but not where the boats dock, so it is quieter than other lodgings by the port. The balconies, with views of Siros in the distance, are a real plus. The hotel is often taken over by Greek groups visiting the island's religious shrines. As an independent traveler, you may feel a bit odd-man-out. The rooms are simply furnished, with good-sized bathrooms. The Oceanis stays open all year and has reliable heat in the winter.

Akti G. Drossou, Hora, 842 00 Tinos. ✆ **22830/22-452.** Fax 22830/25-402. 47 units. From 90€ double. No credit cards. From the old harbor, walk south (right) along the paralia until you come to the Oceanis, whose large sign is clearly visible from the harbor. **Amenities:** Restaurant; bar. *In room:* A/C, TV.

Tinos Beach Hotel ★★ ☺ Despite a somewhat impersonal character, this is the best choice for a beachfront hotel. The decent-sized rooms all have balconies, most with views of the sea and pool. The suites are especially pleasant—large sitting rooms open onto poolside balconies. The pool is the longest on the island, and there's a separate children's pool as well. If you want to be on Tinos, near Tinos town but on the beach, this is the place to be.

Kionia, 842 00 Tinos. www.tinosbeach.gr. ✆ **22830/22-626** or 22830/22-627. Fax 22830/23-153. 180 units. 80€–120€ double. Rates include breakfast. Children 7 and under stay free in parent's room. AE, DC, MC, V. Closed Nov–Mar. 4km (2½ miles) west of Tinos town on the coast road. **Amenities:** Restaurant; bar; saltwater pool; children's pool; tennis courts; watersports. *In room:* A/C, TV, fridge, Wi-Fi (free).

9

GREECE | The Cyclades

HUNGARY

by Ryan James

Having joined the European Union in 2004, the tourism infrastructure in Hungary has developed at a furious pace. Poised between East and West, both geographically and culturally, the country is at the center of the region's rebirth.

BUDAPEST

Budapest has a glorious history, having once rivaled its neighboring Vienna under the Austro-Hungarian monarchy. The city's rich past has been on an economic rollercoaster since, but don't let this fool you. The Budapest of today, regardless of economic woes, buzzes with culture that rivals most European capitals. A vibrant young generation working side by side with the old guard has made the cultural scene top notch. While the political elite continue to argue about the past and infringe on the rights of the populace, the youth are concentrating on the future. They're becoming multilingual and creating new art photography exhibitions, film festivals, and fashion shows. The scene they're developing is vibrant and fun—if a bit secretive and cliquish. While it might take some time to enter into their world, it's a pleasurable journey in the end.

Essentials
GETTING THERE
BY PLANE   Budapest is served by **Ferenc Liszt International Airport** (sometimes still known by its former name, Ferihegy) **Terminal 2,** located in the XVII district in southeastern Pest. Terminal 1 recently closed while Terminal 2 (which has a **Terminal 2A** and a **Terminal 2B**) serves both traditional and budget airlines. Between Terminals 2A and 2B is the new Sky Court, where you'll find five levels of shops, restaurants, as well as security check-in. With Hungary's entry into the Schengen zone, Terminal 2A is used exclusively for flights to Schengen countries, so you will pass through security, but not Passport Control. All other flights depart from 2B where there is Passport Control. There are several main information numbers: For airport information, call ✆ **1/296-9696;** and for general information, call ✆ **1/296-7000.** For ease of language, use the airport's English-version website at **www.bud.hu/english** for flight information.

   The airport exclusively contracts with **Főtaxi** services (✆ **1/222-2222**). Fares are fixed rates per cab, not per person, and adhere to pre-destined zones within the city. Fares run from zones 1 to 4 and cost from 3,800 Ft to 6,500 Ft. These taxis are also metered, so if the fare is less than the zone rate, you pay the reduced fare. By law, all taxis must give you a paper receipt for your fare, but many don't unless you request it.

Hungary

Airport Shuttle (www.airportshuttle.hu; (✆ 1/296-8555) is a public service owned and operated by the Budapest Airport Authority. There is a clearly visible kiosk for the shuttle in each terminal. A round-trip ticket is less expensive than two one-way tickets. A round-trip fare for one person is 5,500 Ft and one-way is 3,200 Ft. For two or more traveling together, there is a discount: for two, a one-way trip is 4,790 Ft and 8,790 Ft for a round-trip. The fares are the same for both airports. To arrange your return to the airport from where you are staying, call the number above between 24 hours and 12 hours in advance from 6am to 10pm, but be warned that you may have to wait on hold for some time. Or use their online booking system—it is easy and efficient.

There are also two public transportation options with the trip taking about 1 hour total on either. Two **buses** leave the airport for the metro. From **Ferenc Liszt 2,** you will take **bus no. 200E** to the last stop, Kőbánya-Kispest. From there, the Blue metro line runs to the Inner City of Pest. The metro's last run is at 11:15pm. The cost is two transit tickets, which is 640 Ft for both; tickets can be bought from the automated vending machine at the airport bus stop (coins only and not recommended), the Budapestinfo Point office, or from any newsstand in the airport. From **Ferenc Liszt 1,** take **bus no. 93 or 200E** to the same metro stop as above.

Trains stop at Ferenc Liszt 1 only and go to Nyugati train station. After using the highway overpass, stand on the tracks and wait for the train. Take note that there is no station at the airport, just a siding where the train stops. You must buy the 300 Ft ticket for a one-way journey at the airport. Purchasing a ticket on the train could result in a hefty fine. There are more than 30 trains daily. If you arrive at Ferenc Liszt 2, take bus no. **200E** to Ferenc Liszt 1 in order to catch the train. Plans to extend the train tracks to the second airport have remained in limbo for years.

BY TRAIN Trains arrive regularly from Vienna, Bratislava, and other European cities either as a destination or as a train passing through for somewhere else. It will depend on where your journey began as to which of the three stations you arrive at: **Déli pu,**

Budapest

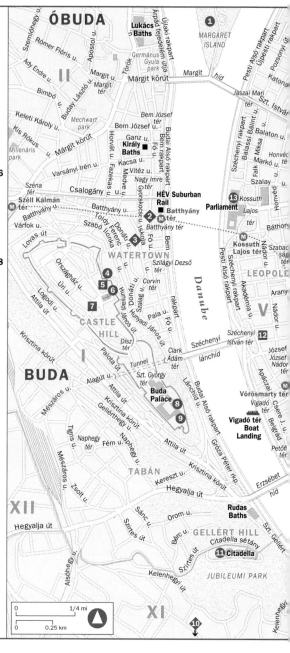

10

Budapest

HUNGARY

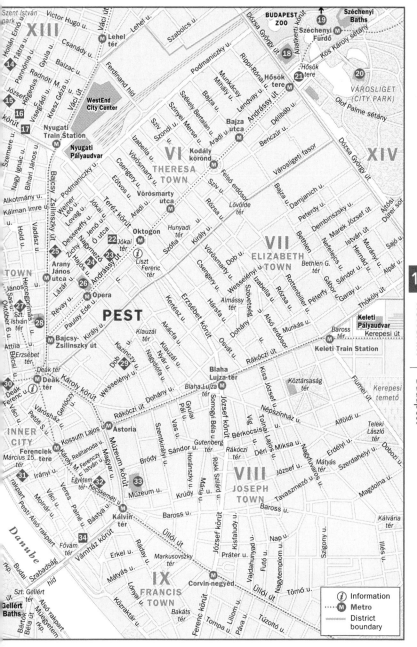

Keleti pu, or **Nyugati pu.** Inspectors will want to see your ticket when you're leaving a train as well as boarding it so don't toss your tickets until you leave the station. Never take a taxi from a train station; you will be taken for a ride in multiple ways. For more information about Budapest train stations, see "Getting Around," below.

VISITOR INFORMATION

Tourism offices can assist you with finding appropriate accommodations, restaurants, and tickets to events. **Budapestinfo Points** (www.budapestinfo.hu; ✆ 1/438-8080 or 06/80-630-800) were formerly called TourInform so you may still find the old signs. At the time of writing, due to funding issues, it has not been determined which of these two names will be the official and lasting name for the Budapest offices in the future. Offices are found at each of the Ferenc Liszt Airport terminals. The hours for Terminals 1 and 2A are 8am to 10pm; for Terminal 2B the hours are 10am to 8pm. In the city, you will find them at V. Sütő u. 2; open daily from 8am to 8pm. You'll also find a branch office at Andrássy út 47 at Liszt Ferenc tér, open daily from noon to 8pm.

For general country information and a variety of pamphlets and maps before you leave home, contact the government-sponsored tourism authority **Magyar Turizmus Rt** (www.gotohungary.com; ✆ 1/695-1221), which also has offices throughout the world. The **Hungarian National Tourist Office** in New York is at 450 7th Ave., NY 10123 (✆ 212/695-1221); in London you'll find it at 46 Eaton Place, London SW1X 8AL (www.gotohungary.co.uk; ✆ 020/7823-1055).

Other sites with information including news, shopping, entertainment, and current venues for music, dance, and theatrical events for visitors and English-speaking locals are *Funzine* (www.funzine.hu), published every 2 weeks, and *Where* magazine, published monthly, both free at Budapestinfo Points and many restaurants and hotels. *Time Out,* found in many major cities, is free from the Budapestinfo Points or 495 Ft at newsstands. The *Budapest Times* (www.budapesttimes.hu), both in print at newsstands and online, has news articles with an entertainment section. The Budapestinfo Point office puts out a monthly brochure called *Budapest Panorama* listing all of the scheduled events during the month.

CITY LAYOUT

The city of Budapest came into being in 1873, making it relatively young in its present form. It is the result of a union of three separate cities: **Buda, Pest,** and **Óbuda** (literally meaning Old Buda) consisting of 23 self-governing municipal districts. Budapest is divided by the **River Danube (Duna)** with Pest, almost completely flat, on the eastern shore, making up almost two-thirds of the city. On the western bank is Buda and, farther yet, Óbuda, which has the hilly areas, these areas being much older settlements. If you look at a map of the city, you will see that the districts are numbered in a spiral pattern for the most part with districts I, II, and III on the Buda side and then IV starts the Pest side until XI, which again is the Buda side.

Neighborhoods in Brief

BUDA

Castle District (Várnegyed). This district is the city's most beautiful and historic dating back to the 13th century, with some settlements here even earlier. This is **district I,** which is a small district that encompasses the plateau where the grand Royal Palace and grounds fill the southern end above the surrounding neighborhoods and the Danube below. The Castle District is defined by its medieval walls. The northern end is home to small winding streets, with old homes, St.

Matthias Church, the Fisherman's Bastion, and the Hilton Hotel.

Watertown (Víziváros). A long, narrow neighborhood wedged between the Castle District and the Danube makes up **district II.** Víziváros is historically a quarter where fishermen and artisans reside. Built on the steep slope of Castle Hill, it has narrow alleys and stairs instead of roads in many places. Its main street, Fő utca, runs the north–south length of the Víziváros, parallel to and a block away from the river. It is a high-rent district for residents and tourists.

Rose Hill (Rózsadomb). This is part of Buda Hills and still part of district II, closest to the city center and one of the city's most fashionable and luxurious residential neighborhoods.

Buda Hills. The Buda Hills are numerous remote neighborhoods that feel as if they're nowhere near, let alone within, a capital city. By and large, the hills are considered a classy place to live. Neighborhoods are generally known by the name of the hill on which they stand. Unless you like to walk neighborhoods, there is nothing more for the traveler in this part of the city.

ÓBUDA

Óbuda makes up **district III** and is mostly residential now, though its long Danube coastline was a favorite spot for workers' resorts under the old regime. Most facilities have been privatized, so a large number of hotels are found here. Transportation for the traveler into Pest would be cumbersome, so we do not recommend staying out here. The extensive Roman ruins of Aquincum and the beautifully preserved old-town main square are Óbuda's chief claims to fame.

PEST

Inner City (Belváros). The historic center of Pest, the Belváros, literally meaning "city center" is the area inside the Inner Ring, bound by the Danube to the west. Making up part of **district V**, it has many of Pest's historic buildings in this area. In addition, a number of the city's showcase luxury hotels and most of its best-known shopping streets are here.

Leopold Town (Lipótváros). The continuation of district V is just north of the Belváros, making Lipótváros a part of central Pest. Development began here at the end of the 18th century, and the neighborhood soon emerged as a center of Pest business and government. Parliament, plus a number of government ministries, courthouses, banks, and the former stock exchange are all found here. Before the war, this was considered a neighborhood of the "high bourgeoisie."

Theresa Town (Terézváros). The character of Terézváros, **district VI,** is defined by Andrássy út, the great boulevard running the length of the neighborhood from Heroes' Square through Oktogon and down into the Inner City. This grand street has been regaining its reputation of elegance: Andrássy út is once again the "best address" in town, especially since the upper part is now a UNESCO World Heritage site. The Teréz körút section of the Outer Ring cuts through Terézváros; Oktogon is its major square. The area around Nagymező utca is the city's small theater district.

Elizabeth Town (Erzsébetváros). This is **district VII.** Directly to the southeast of Terézváros, Erzsébetváros is the historic Jewish neighborhood of Pest. During the German occupation from 1944 to 1945, this district was where the ghettos were established for the Jewish people. This district is still the center of Budapest's Jewish life. Although it had been exceedingly run-down due to the war, in the last couple of years it has become gentrified and is considered one of the up-and-coming districts to invest in.

Joseph Town (Józsefváros). One of the largest central Pest neighborhoods is **district VIII.** Józsefváros is to the southeast of Erzsébetváros. It has had a reputation of being a less-than-desirable district of Pest, but there are some places in this district worth your time and energy. It should not be dismissed across the board. It is working hard at gentrifying.

GETTING AROUND

Budapest has an extensive, efficient, and inexpensive public transportation system, but locals without global experiences disagree. There are currently three **metro** lines in operation (see "By Metro" below) but the existing system is not without its glitches, due to the construction of a fourth metro line that has turned into a never-ending construction project. There have been interruptions throughout parts of the city at various points in time, and this is likely to continue until 2014 or beyond. The current system, although bankrupt, is efficient enough. However, when buses replace a tram or metro route that has been disrupted by construction, it can be confusing.

The biggest drawback to the system is that metro and tram routes shut down for the night at around 11:10 to 11:45pm, depending on the line. One exception is the **number 6 tram** that services the outer ring road as it is now operating 24 hours with longer waiting times between trams from 11pm to 5am. Inspectors ride each car to check tickets and maintain appropriate behavior. Increased **night bus** service to overcome some of these problems has been dramatic, but it is still not perfect, with some long waits at dark and lonely bus stops.

Castle Hill can be reached in only three ways by public transportation and all of these modes of transportation are quite crowded in the high seasons. Crowded public transport is the place where you're most likely to be targeted by Budapest's few, but professional, pickpockets. Keep your hand on your wallet or purse and you will be fine.

FARES Transport passes provide unlimited transportation on all forms of public transportation (metro, bus, tram, trolleybus—an electric bus evident by the connection to wires above—some portions of the HÉV railway lines, and cogwheel railway) within Budapest city limits. If you are using individual tickets (*vonaljegy*), which cost 320 Ft apiece (children 5 and under and E.U. citizens 65 and over travel free), you are required to validate the tickets as soon as you board the transport. Each time you change lines, you have to validate a new ticket.

You can buy **single tickets** at metro ticket windows, newspaper kiosks, and the occasional tobacco shop. There are also automated machines in most stations and at major transportation hubs. You can also buy a 10-ticket pack (*tizes csomag*) for 2,800 Ft. Buying a transport **pass** is the best option, which does not require validation. They are available for 1 day (*napijegy*) for 1,550 Ft and are good for 24 hours from the day and time marked. The other pass options are 72 hours (*turistajegy*) for 3,850 Ft, 7 days for 4,600 Ft, or, for longer stays, 14 days (*kéthétibérlet*) for 6,500 Ft. The 7- and 14-day passes need to be signed. If your plans are even longer, there is a 30-consecutive-day pass (*30 napos bérlet*) at 9,800 Ft, which requires a photo. If you are going to be here for 4 to 5 days, the 7-day (*hetijegy*) pass is still a saving over individual tickets.

While the standard ticket is valid on the metro, there are other types of optional single-ride metro tickets introduced years ago, making ticket buying a bit more complicated. A metro section ticket (*metrószakaszjegy*), at 260 Ft, is valid for a single metro trip stopping at three stations or fewer. A metro transfer ticket (*metróátszállójegy*), at 490 Ft, allows you to transfer from one metro line to another on the same ticket, without any limit to the number of stations that the train stops at during your journey.

The **fines** for not having a validated ticket or pass are 10,000 Ft if paid on the spot or 16,000 Ft if paid later; this does not include the embarrassment of getting caught. An inspector has the right to ask for your passport (legally, you are required to carry it at all times) or ID and to call a police officer if the need arises.

BY METRO   The system is clean and efficient, with old Russian trains from the 1980s running every 3 to 5 minutes on weekdays and 6 to 8 minutes on weekends, from about 4:30am to about 11:10pm. The three lines are known by colors: Yellow, Red, and Blue. Officially, they have numbers as well (1, 2, and 3, respectively), which is what you will see on maps. All lines converge at **Deák tér,** the only point where any lines meet. This is the only place where you can change lines without the need to validate a new ticket.

BY BUS   With almost 175 different bus (*busz*) lines in greater Budapest, many parts of the city, most notably the Buda Hills, are best accessed by bus. With the exception of night buses, most lines are in service from about 4:30am to about 11:45pm. Some bus lines run far less frequently (or not at all) on weekends, while others run far more frequently (or only) on weekends.

Each time you change buses, you need a new ticket to validate. Black-numbered local buses constitute the majority of the city's lines. Buses with red numbers are express buses that follow the same routes as local buses with the same number, skipping minor stops along the way. If the red number on the bus is followed by an *E* (there are 30 routes with an *E*), the bus makes very few stops between terminals and is best avoided unless you are certain your stop is included on the route.

BY TRAM   You'll find Budapest's 32 bright-yellow tram lines (*villamos*) very useful, particularly **nos. 4 and 6,** which travel along the Outer Ring (Nagykörút). Tram 6 now runs 24 hours. After 11pm, the wait is about 8 minutes between trams. **Tram no. 2,** which travels along the Danube on the Pest side between Margit híd and Boráros tér, provides an incredible view of the Buda Hills, including the Castle District, and is as good as any sightseeing tour on a bus. This route is best at night when the castle is lit on the Buda side and Parliament is spot lit on the Pest side.

You need to self-validate tickets onboard. As with buses, tickets are valid for one ride, not for the line itself. When a tram line is closed for maintenance, replacement buses are assigned the tram route. They go by the same number as the tram, with a *V* (for *villamos*) preceding the number.

BY TROLLEYBUS   These are the electric buses; all of the 15 trolleybus lines are in Pest. Of particular interest to train travelers is **no. 73,** the fastest route between Keleti Station and within a block of Nyugati Station. The estimated travel time is 9 minutes. All information in "By Bus" above regarding ticket validation and stops also applies to trolleybuses.

BY COGWHEEL RAILWAY & FUNICULAR   Budapest's **cogwheel railway** (*fogaskerekű*) runs from Városmajor, across the street from the Hotel Budapest on

Szilágyi Erzsébet fasor in Buda, to Széchenyi-hegy, one terminus of the Children's Railway (Gyermek Vasút) and site of Hotel Panoráma in 20 minutes. The cogwheel railway runs from 5am to 11pm, and normal transportation tickets are used.

The **cable car** or **funicular** (*sikló*) connects Buda's Clark Ádám tér, at the head of the Széchenyi Chain Bridge, with Dísz tér, just outside the Buda Castle. The funicular is one of only two forms of public transportation serving the Castle District (buses no. 16 and 16A are the other possibilities). An extremely steep and short ride, but with a fun view, though hot on sunny days, the funicular runs at frequent intervals from 7:30am to 10pm (closed on the second Monday of the month). Tickets cost 840 Ft to go up, and 1,450 Ft for a round-trip for adults, while children (5–14) get a break at 520 Ft up and 940 Ft round-trip. After public protest, the funicular now goes slower, as riders wanted to enjoy the scenery longer. The ride is less than 2 minutes long.

BY TAXI Budapest taxis fall into two general categories: legitimately legal and otherwise. All legal taxis must have a yellow license plate and a yellow taxi sign on the roof. The fare to be paid at the destination consists of three basic parts: the base fee; the kilometer fare, based on the distance traveled; and the waiting tariff, which is used if the taxi has had to stop or fails to move in traffic at a rate slower than 15km/h (9 mph). Calling for a taxi is less expensive than getting one on the street, but if you cannot call, use only the following companies where their names are clearly displayed on the side. Make sure the driver starts the meter once you are in the taxi. By law, they must provide a written receipt. If you have a problem, write down the name of the driver from his license, his taxi number, and the company name and report it to the **Budapestinfo Point** at ✆ **06/80-630-800.** Generally, none of these companies hang out at the railroad stations, so you are going to get an illegal taxi regardless of any of the drivers' protests. Do not take a taxi from the train or bus stations unless you get someone to call one of the following recommended companies.

The best is **City Taxi** (✆ **1/211-1111**). Other reliable fleets include **Volántaxi** (✆ **1/466-6666**), **Rádió Taxi** (✆ **1/377-7777**), Tele5 (✆ **1/355-5555**), 6×6 (✆ **1/266-6666**), and **Budataxi** (✆ **1/233-3333**). You will seldom, if ever, wait more than 5 minutes for a fleet taxi unless you're in a remote neighborhood.

[FastFACTS] BUDAPEST

ATMs/Banks There is no shortage of ATMs in Budapest, although there may be fewer in smaller towns and cities. ATMs operate with a four-figure PIN code. Not all establishments take credit cards, such as American Express, so check before you enter. **Banks** in general are open Monday to Friday from 8am to 4pm. Some banks open a half-hour later on some days, but stay open an hour later that day too.

Business Hours Most **stores** are open Monday to Friday from 10am to 6pm and Saturday from 10am to 2pm with a few closing earlier at 1pm. The majority of stores are closed on Sunday, except those in central tourist areas or malls. On weekdays, food stores open early, at around 6 or 7am, and close around 6 or 7pm. Convenience stores, called "nonstops," are open 24 hours and just about every neighborhood has one.

Currency The basic unit of currency in Hungary is the **forint (Ft).**

Doctors & Hospitals Recommended centers include **First Med Center,** I. Hattyu u. 14, 5th floor (www. firstmedcenters.com; ✆ **1/224-9090**) and **Rózsakert Medical Center** (www. medical-center.hu; ✆ **1/392-0505**), located in the Rózsakert Shopping Center, II. Gábor Áron u. 74–78/a.

Embassies & Consulates The **Australian**

Embassy is at XII. Királyhágó tér 8–9 (www.hungary. embassy.gov.au; ☎ **1/457-9777**). The **Canadian Embassy** is at II. Ganz u. 12–14 (www.canada international.gc.ca/hungary-hongrie/; ☎ **1/392-3360**). The **Republic of Ireland Embassy** is at V. Szabadság tér 7 (www.embassyof ireland.hu; ☎ **1/301-4960**); the **U.K. Embassy** is at V. Harmincad u. 6 (http://ukin hungary.fco.gov.uk/en/; ☎ **1/266-2888**); and the **U.S. Embassy** is at V. Szabadság tér 12 (http:// hungary.usembassy.gov/; ☎ **1/475-4400**). For **New Zealand** citizens, the U.K. embassy can handle matters as there is no dedicated embassy.

Emergencies The general emergency number in Europe is ☎ **112.** Dial ☎ **104** for an ambulance, ☎ **105** for the fire department, ☎ **107** for the police, and ☎ **188** for car breakdown service. ☎ **1/438-8080** is a 24-hour hotline in English for reporting crime.

Internet Access Most hotels now provide free Wi-Fi access. Outside of hotels, you will find dozens of places where one drink will allow you to stay as long as you want to trawl the Web. Look for Wi-Fi signs on windows, doors, and standing signs outside doors of cafes, restaurants, and bookstores.

Mail & Postage The postal system is not the most efficient or honest, so take great care with sending or receiving packages. Even letters mailed "Registered with a Return Receipt Requested"

card have not made it to their destination without issues. Most post offices are open Monday through Friday from 8am to 4pm; however, with the current state of the economy, many have shortened or will be shortening their hours even further on an office-by-office situation. Sending postcards priority mail to anywhere in Europe is 260 Ft, while anywhere else in the world is 300 Ft. Mailing a priority mail letter under 20 grams to anywhere in Europe is 260 Ft, but the rest of the world are all 300 Ft. If you opt for non-priority mail, you will save a measly 30 Ft, not worth the lack of assurance that it may arrive. **Note:** For packages, there is a high percentage of mailings that never arrive at their destination, so I would avoid it at any cost. The exception being if a store will ship your purchases for you; using their service, you generally are safe. FedEx or UPS are prohibitively expensive for even sending a document. For example, sending a letter to the U.S. can cost over 5,500 Ft.

Police Dial ☎ **107** or for general emergency dial ☎ **112.**

Smoking Budapest has introduced fines for smoking at any transportation stop or in any underground area leading to a metro. Fines are up to 50,000 Ft. As of April 2012, smoking in any public building is prohibited. Any eating or drinking establishment that allows smoking is subject to a fine as well as the person smoking. Multiple fines will

be a reason for the city to close down a business.

Taxes Hungary has a value-added tax (VAT) on everything, but the rate depends on the service or product. Hotel VAT is now 18% and VAT on goods in shops is 27%. When you are shopping, the VAT is included in the posted price. However, some stores will break it down showing a "netto" and "brutto" price. You want to pay attention to the brutto, as this is what you will pay at the register.

Telephones The country code for Hungary is **36.** All telephone numbers in this chapter are listed with the city code/telephone number. The area code for Budapest is **1.** Many convenience stores, kiosks, and Internet cafes sell **prepaid calling cards** in denominations up to 5,000 Ft; for international visitors these can be the least expensive way to call home. Many public pay phones are not properly serviced, but most require the use of a specific pay phone calling card also available as above.

Tipping In hotels, tip **bellhops** at least 500 Ft per bag (750–1,000 Ft if you have a lot of luggage) and tip the **chamber staff** 500 Ft per day (more if you've left a disaster area for him or her to clean up). Tip the **valet-parking attendant** 500 Ft every time you get your car. In restaurants, bars, and nightclubs, tip **service staff** and **bartenders** 10% to 15% of the check, and tip **valet-parking attendants** 500 Ft per vehicle. Tip **cabdrivers** 10% of the fare.

Exploring Budapest

Historic Budapest is smaller than people realize when they first arrive. Because this is an ideal walking city, many attractions listed in this chapter are easily reached on foot from the city center; if you would rather save some time, public transport will get you there too at very reasonable rates. For this reason, the Budapest Card is an unnecessary purchase: you would need to rush from place to place and spend a great deal of time on transportation for it to be any saving at all.

BUDA

Budapesti Történeti Múzeum (Budapest History Museum) ★ MUSEUM
This museum, also referred to as the Castle Museum, tucked in the courtyard behind the palace is easily overlooked. As you approach, there are no lavish signs advertising it either. If you're interested in the history of this great city, as well as the whole Carpathian basin from medieval times, you will love this museum.

What you shouldn't miss is the third-floor exhibit where you'll find historic maps of battle plans and weapons used in the liberation from the Turkish occupation. At the back of the main floor, the statue area has an outstanding collection of Roman and medieval-era pieces. The highlight is the lowest level; it is actually part of the old palace and hidden at the back there is a chapel.

I. In Buda Palace, Wing E., on Castle Hill. www.btm.hu. © **1/487-8854.** Admission 1,500 Ft adults, 750 Ft students and seniors. Photo 800 Ft; video 1,600 Ft. Audio-guided tours 1,200 Ft. Mar 1–Oct 31 Tues–Sun 10am–6pm; Nov 1–Feb 28 Tues–Sun 10am–4pm. Bus: 16A from Széll Kálmán tér or 16 from Deák tér to Castle Hill. Funicular: From Clark Ádám tér to Castle Hill.

Gellért Hegy (Gellért Hill) ★★★ LANDMARK   Towering 229m (750 ft.) above the Danube, Gellért Hill offers the city's best panorama on a clear day (bus: 27 from Móricz Zsigmond körtér to Búsuló Juhász-Citadella). It's named for the Italian bishop Gellért, who assisted Hungary's first Christian king, Stephen I, in converting the Magyars to Catholicism. Gellért became a martyr when, according to legend, outraged vengeful pagans converted through the force and violent nature of Stephen's proselytism rolled Gellért in a nail-studded barrel to his death from the side of the hill. An enormous statue now stands on the hill to celebrate his memory. On top of Gellért Hill you'll find the **Liberation Monument,** built in 1947 to commemorate the Red Army's liberation of Budapest from Nazi occupation. Also atop the hill is the **Citadella,** built by the Austrians shortly after they crushed the Hungarian uprising from 1848 to 1849. Views of the city from both vistas are excellent, but the Citadella is spectacular. Don't bother paying the extra to traipse up to the upper part of the Citadella; the view is not that much better.

Halászbástya (Fisherman's Bastion) ★★★ LANDMARK   The neo-Romanesque Fisherman's Bastion behind Matthias Church and the Hilton Hotel has a spectacular panorama of the river and Pest beyond it. Built at the turn of the 20th century, it was included as part of the refurbishing of the church area. Local legend states that this stretch of medieval parapets was a protected area by the fishermen's guild, but the area was once a fish-market area, so either could be true. The local city council imposed a fee of 450 Ft to pass through the turnstile allowing you to climb to the top lookout points. If you happen to be in the area after 9pm in summer, it is no longer manned and you can pass the turnstile for free. In winter, the turnstile disappears completely, so there is no charge. Either way, the short climb is well worth the advantageous views.

Admission 450 Ft to enter the towers, free to explore the lower levels.

Mátyás Templom (Matthias Church) ★★★ CHURCH   Founded by King Béla IV in the 13th century, this church is officially named the Church of Our Lady and is a symbol of Buda's Castle District. It is popularly referred to as Matthias Church after the 15th-century king Matthias Corvinus, who added a royal oratory and was twice married here. It is a church not to be missed, especially now the renovations have finally been completed. Head upstairs to the museum; often overlooked by travelers who do not realize it is there, it has an interesting history of the royal crown and a wonderful view of the church. Check the website for the concert calendar.

I. Szentháromság tér 2. www.matyas-templom.hu. ℭ **1/355-5657.** Admission 1,000 Ft adults, 700 Ft students. Photos free. Mon–Fri 9am–5pm; Sat 9am–1:00pm, but depends on weddings; Sun 1–5pm. Metro: Széll Kálmán tér, then bus 16A; or Deák tér, then bus 16. Funicular: From Clark Ádám tér to Castle Hill.

Nemzeti Galéria (Hungarian National Gallery) ★★ MUSEUM   With a collection of more than 10,000 art objects, this museum is not for the culturally faint of heart. Permanent exhibitions include medieval and Renaissance lapidariums, Gothic woodcarvings, Gothic winged altars, Renaissance and baroque art, and the Hungarian celebrities Mihály Munkácsy, László Paál, Károly Ferenczy, and Pál Szinyei Merse. In the heat of summer, it can be brutally hot.

I. In Buda Palace, Wings B, C, and D, on Castle Hill. www.mng.hu. ℭ **1/375-5567.** Admission to permanent collection 1,200 Ft adults, 600 Ft students and seniors; temporary exhibits vary. Dome or Crypt 600 Ft. Photo 500 Ft; video 1,000 Ft. Tues–Sun 10am–6pm. Bus: 16A from Széll Kálmán tér or 16 from Deák tér to Castle Hill. Funicular: From Clark Ádám tér to Castle Hill.

PEST

Hősök tere (Heroes' Square) ★★★ ☺ SQUARE   If you want a dramatic experience, come up from the Yellow metro station at Hősök tere from the city center at night. When Hősök tere is lit it is majestic in its splendor, not to say that it isn't impressive during the day too. Located at the end of the grand World Heritage boulevard, Andrássy út, the square is the entryway into the best-known park in the city, Városliget (City Park).

Two of Budapest's major museums, the Szépművészeti Múzeum (Museum of Fine Arts) and the Exhibition Hall, flank Heroes' Square.

Free admission. Metro: Hősök tere (Yellow line).

Magyar Állami Operaház (Hungarian State Opera House) ★★★ OPERA HOUSE   Built in a neo-Renaissance style, this is the most beautiful building of this style on Andrassy út. The architect was Miklós Ybl, the most successful and prolific architect of his time. He created what many agree is one of the most beautiful opera houses in Europe. It was completed in 1884. It is Budapest's and Hungary's most celebrated performance hall; the Opera House boasts a fantastically ornate interior featuring frescoes by two of the best-known Hungarian artists of the day, Bertalan Székely and Károly Lotz.

VI. Andrássy út 22. www.opera.hu. ℭ **1/332-8197.** Tour 2,900 Ft adults, 1,900 Ft students with international ID. Photo 500 Ft; video (with small camera) 500 Ft. Tours daily 3 and 4pm, except when it interferes with a rehearsal; check the website. Metro: Opera (Yellow line).

Margit-sziget (Margaret Island) ★★★ PARK/GARDEN   Margaret Island has an interesting royalty-related history going back to King Béla. He vowed that if he were successful in the Mongol invasion from 1242 to 1244, his daughter Margaret would be brought up as a nun. Well he was successful, so when she was 10, she was brought to the island to live a life of pious chastity. On the island, you can walk around what is left of the Dominican Convent, where you'll find signs mentioning St. Margaret's, a 13th-century Franciscan church. The island was once called Rabbit Island since it seemed to be infested with them. No bunny was able to leave without a bridge connecting the island to shore at the time. The island has been open to the public since 1908, but visitors were charged a fee, double on Sunday. It was not until 1945 that it was declared free for all. The long, narrow island is a leisurely escape from the hectic city. This is a relaxing place to bike ride or sunbathe.

Free admission. Tram: 4 or 6.

Nemzeti Múzeum (Hungarian National Museum) ★★ MUSEUM

Founded in 1802 thanks to the numismatic, book, and document collections of Count Ferenc Szénchényi, this enormous neoclassical structure was finished in 1846. It was here that the poet Sándor Petőfi and others of like mind are said to have roused the emotions of the people of Pest to revolt against the Habsburgs on March 15, 1848. The permanent exhibit holds more than one million pieces of Hungarian historical artifacts, including the main attraction, a replica of the so-called crown of King St. Stephen.

VIII. Múzeum krt. 14. www.mnm.hu. (✆) **1/327-7749.** Admission for permanent exhibits 1,100 Ft, 550 Ft children and seniors; temporary exhibits vary. Free admission Mar 15, Aug 20, and Oct 23. Photo 2,000 Ft; video 4,000 Ft. Tues–Sun 10am–6pm. Metro: Kálvin tér (Blue line).

Parlament ★★★ GOVT. BUILDING

Budapest's great Parliament, the second largest in Europe after London, is an eclectic design mixing the predominant Gothic revival style with a neo-Renaissance dome. Construction began in 1884, 16 years after Westminster, and was completed in 1902. Standing proudly on the Danube bank, visible from almost any riverside point, it has from the outset been one of Budapest's greatest symbols, though until 1989 a democratically elected government had convened here only once (just after World War II, before the Communist takeover). As you walk up the imposing staircase, you are led under the dome along a 16-sided hallway with 16 statues of rulers. In the center floor under the dome is a glass case with the legendary jeweled crown and scepter of King St. Stephen. Historical records have shown that the crown is of two parts and from two different eras, neither from King St. Stephen's time, but Hungarians want to believe it was Stephen's. Regardless, it is one of the oldest royal crowns in history.

V. Kossuth tér. Tourist.office@parliament.hu. (✆) **1/441-4415.** Admission (by guided tour only) 50-min. tour in English 2,640 Ft adults, 1,320 Ft students, but rates will be increasing and have not been publicized yet. Hungarians and E.U. passport holders with passport will now have to pay admission, but at a reduced amount also undetermined at the time of writing. Photo free. Tickets available at gate X for individuals; prebooking for large groups mandatory by e-mail or phone; (✆) **1/441-4904** or 1/441-4415. English-language tours year-round daily 10am, noon, and 2pm when tickets are available. Ticket office hours Mon–Fri 8am–6pm; Sat 8am–4pm; Sun 8am–2pm. Closed to tours when Parliament is in session, usually Mon and Thurs. Recently it has often happened that tours have been reserved for tour company groups only, where the cost is significantly higher. Metro: Kossuth tér (Red line). Tram: 2 or 2A Szalay u.

Szent István Bazilika (St. Stephen's Church) ★★★ CHURCH

The country's largest church, this basilica took more than 50 years to build (the 1868 collapse of the dome caused significant delay) and was finally completed in 1906, which explains the differences in architectural designs. As you wander into the church and to the left in the back chapel, you can view St. Stephen's mummified ruling right hand or you can wait until August 20, his feast day, and see it free when it is reverently paraded around the city. To get the box to light up to actually see it, you will have to spring for 100 Ft or just wait for someone else to drop their coin in.

V. Szent István tér 33. www.basilica.hu. *1/311-0839.* Church free admission, but 200 Ft donation suggested; treasury 400 Ft; panorama tower 500 Ft, 400 Ft students and seniors. Photos free. Tour 1,600 Ft adults, 1,200 Ft students and seniors. Church Mon–Fri 9am–5pm, Sat 9am–1pm, Sun 1–5pm. Services at 8:30am, 10am (high mass), noon, 6pm; treasury daily 9am–5pm; Szent Jobb Chapel Mon–Sat 9am–5pm, Sun 1–5pm; panorama tower daily 10am–6pm. Metro: Arany János u. (Blue line) or Bajcsy-Zsilinszky út (Yellow line).

Szépművészeti Múzeum (Museum of Fine Arts) ★★★ MUSEUM During the 1896 millennial celebration of the Magyars' settling and forming a nation in 896, plans were proposed for the Museum of Fine Arts. Ten years later in the presence of Franz Josef, the king and emperor of Austria and Hungary, the Museum of Fine Arts was opened at the left side of Heroes' Square. This was the last great monument to be built during the most prosperous period of Hungary's history. Designed in the Beaux Arts style, the museum is the main repository of foreign art in Hungary and it houses one of central Europe's major collections of such works. The overall collection consists of more than 3,000 paintings, 10,000 drawings, and 100,000 prints. Trained docents offer a 1-hour guided tour, in English, free of charge with general admission. They are offered Tuesday through Friday at 11am and 2pm and Saturday at 11am.

XIV. Hősök tere. www.szepmuveszeti.hu. *1/469-7100.* Admission 1,800 Ft, 900 Ft children and seniors for permanent collection; varying temporary exhibits are available. Photography permitted only in the permanent collection. Photos ticket 300 Ft allowed in permanent exhibits only; video 1,500 Ft. Tues–Sun 10am–6pm (every 2nd Thurs on odd weeks until 10pm). Metro: Hősök tere (Yellow line).

Városliget (City Park) ★★ PARK/GARDEN City Park sits behind Heroes' Square and is just as popular as Margaret Island for lazy walks, picnics in the grass, and the many attractions located in and around the park. The **Vajdahunyad Castle,** located by the lake, is magical when lit at night. The lake is used for small boat rides in the summer. Near the lake, an area is flooded to provide a frozen surface for **ice-skating** in winter. The park also embraces **Állatkerti körút (Animal Garden Boulevard),** where a zoo, a circus, and an amusement park are all found. You will also find Széchenyi Baths (p. 547) on one outer rim of the park. The nearby **Petőfi Csarnok** is the venue for a variety of popular cultural events, concerts, and a week-end flea market scheduled for Sat–Sun 7am–2pm, but actually held erratically.

Metro: Széchenyi fürdő or Hősök tere (Yellow line).

Vidám Park (Amusement Park) ★★ ☺ AMUSEMENT PARK This is a must if you're traveling with kids or are a child at heart. Some rides in particular aren't to be missed. The 100-year-old **Merry-Go-Round** (*Körhinta*), constructed almost entirely of wood, has been restored to its original grandeur, though it still creaks mightily as it spins. The riders must actively pump to keep the horses rocking, which is a sight in itself, and authentic Würlitzer music plays. The **Roller Coaster,** operating since 1926, has a wooden frame and is listed as a historic monument. You rush over nine waves before finishing the ride. The **Ikarus** will tickle your senses with its 30m (98-ft.) height and 30km/h (18-mph) speed making for a titillating 3-minute ride.

XIV. Állatkerti krt. 14–16. www.vidampark.hu. *1/343-9810.* Admission 4,700 Ft adults, 3,300 Ft children 90–140cm (35–55 in.) tall. Admission includes most rides with the wristband provided, but a few others and arcade games have extra fees. Oct weekends noon–6pm; Mar–Apr weekends only noon–6pm; May–Aug daily 10am–8pm, Sept weekdays 11am–6pm, weekends 10am–8pm. Variable special nights open until 1:30am. Metro: Széchenyi fürdő.

10

HUNGARY | Budapest

ORGANIZED TOURS

What distinguishes the **Budapest Sightseeing Hop-on Hop-off Bus Tour** (www. programcentrum.hu/en; ✆ 1/317-7767) from the others, besides costing an extra 500 Ft to 1,000 Ft, is that you get many extras, including two Danube riverboat rides. The boat tickets are good until the end of the year in which you buy your bus ticket, so don't feel obliged to cruise the same night of your bus tour. The added bonus is a discount booklet for different specials within the city; amongst others, there is a free bowl of Gulyás soup and a beer. The office is located at the Meridien Hotel, Program Centrum Travel Agency, I. Erzsébet tér 9–11. The first and earliest starting point is directly across the street.

Where to Eat

Étterem is the most common Hungarian word for restaurant and is applied to everything from cafeteria-style eateries to first-class restaurants. A *vendéglő*, an inn or guesthouse, is a smaller, more intimate restaurant, often with a Hungarian folk motif; a *csárda* is a countryside *vendéglő* (often built on major motorways and frequently found around Lake Balaton and other holiday areas). An *önkiszolgáló* indicates a self-service cafeteria. *Büfés* (snack counters) are not to be confused with buffets in English. They are found all over the city, including transportation hubs. A *cukrászda* is a bakery for pastries and a coffee, while a *kávéház* is a coffeehouse that generally has a limited selection of pastries. Traditionally, many coffeehouses are places to sit for hours to meet with friends, read a book, or just people-watch. Today, some establishments use the word *kávéház* in their name, but really are restaurants providing full meals.

The U.S. Embassy provides a list of restaurants that engage in unethical business practices, such as excessive billing, using physical intimidation to compel payment of excessive bills, and assaulting customers for non-payment of excessive bills. Check the U.S. Embassy website for updated information: visit http://hungary.usembassy.gov/tourist_advisory.html.

THE INNER CITY & CENTRAL PEST
Expensive

Dió ★★★ 🏛 MODERN HUNGARIAN   Recreating Hungarian folk art with oversize carved dark wooden panels on the walls interspersed with etched glass mirrors, the dining room has a cozy hearth-like warmth. Service is beyond reproach, but the food is a competitive shining star. Splurge by having the starter of three pieces of pumpkin and spinach pie. It is heavenly. Continue with the duck breast served with

---

A Cave Tour

You can tour the Pál-völgyi–Mátyás-hegyi cave system with **Barlangaszat** ★★★ (www.caving.hu; ✆ 06/20-928-4969 [cellphone]). All the necessary equipment is provided with the tour: protective clothing, helmet, and headlamp. A changing room is available at the cave entrance. Crawling, scrambling, and hunkering down will be done many times during the tour, but no previous experience in caving is needed. The minimum age is 6 years, but there is no upper age limit. It is not recommended for those who are claustrophobic or unable to squeeze through tight places.

BATHING IN history: BUDAPEST'S THERMAL BATHS

Thermal baths were popularized by the Turks, who started building them in 1565. Budapest and other parts of Hungary are built over hot springs, making this a natural way of acquiring the mineral-rich waters for bathing.

The city of Budapest owns all of the thermals. They can drive a sane person crazy with the spontaneous changes they make without a warning or publicizing the information. The **Spas Budapest** website (www.spasbudapest.com) is often a year out of date. Sometimes various baths offer a refund system where you get some change back if you leave within specified time limits, but other times they discontinue it so no refund is forthcoming. When you are at the cashier, ask what the rate and rules happen to be. You are given a plastic bracelet with a chip on it for entry and exit through the turnstiles; keep it safe. You will need it to exit and could be fined if you lose it.

- **Király Baths ★★**, I. Fő u. 84 (℃ **1/202-3688**; metro: Batthyány tér, Red line), are some of the oldest baths in Hungary, dating from around 1563. The domed roof allows sunlight to filter through, giving the water a special glow. There is no longer a time restriction, so you can stay all day, though you're required to head to the lockers a half-hour before closing time. Bathing suits are required for both sexes, and take a towel with you for sure. The rules change here often. Currently, it is unisex every day. This may change to segregated men and women days again depending on the economics of the situation.

- **Rudas Baths ★★**, I. Döbrentei tér 9 (℃ **1/356-1322**; bus: 7), near the Erzsébet Bridge in Buda, are the second oldest of Budapest's classic Turkish baths, built in the 16th century. The centerpiece is an octagonal pool under a domed roof with some stained-glass windows. On weekdays, these baths are for men only every day but Tuesday, when they're for women only. Open for mixed use on weekends.

- **Széchenyi Baths ★★★**, XIV. Állatkerti út 11–14 (℃ **1/340-4505**; metro: Széchenyi fürdő, Yellow line), are located in City Park, and are the most popular. From the outside, you'd never believe their enormity. Any tourist photo of older gentlemen playing chess on floating chess boards while half immersed in water is a photo of this bath.

sweet-potato soufflé with fig and thyme mousse or choose the Mangalitsa pork chops stuffed with goat cheese and chandelle mushrooms accompanied by a potato cake.

V. Sas u. 4. www.diorestaurant.com. ℃ **1/328-0360**. Reservations recommended. Main courses 3,490 Ft–5,880 Ft. AE, MC, V. Daily noon–midnight. Metro: Bajcsy-Zsilinszky út (Blue line) or Deák Ferenc tér (all lines).

Mátyás Pince ★★★ 📷 TRADITIONAL HUNGARIAN   Art, history, or music buffs will love this restaurant established in 1904, named for King Mátyás; the myths and legends of his reign grace the walls in magnificent style. The frescoes and stained glass decorating the dining areas were registered as national monuments in 1973.

Music is provided by the Sándor Déki Lakatos Gypsy music dynasty every night 7pm until closing, creating an all-around romantic experience. Sample the cold blackberry soup, rich in creamy fruit flavor, and follow with King Mátyás's favorite menu of sirloin of beef on a spit, leg of duck, goose liver wrapped in bacon, roast sausage, onion potatoes, steamed cabbage, and *letcho* (green pepper stew). The menu is extensive and the combination of an excellent meal and entertainment makes for an enjoyable evening out. Some visitors have complained it is too tourist-oriented, but Hungarians love it, returning as often as their wallets will allow.

V. Március 15 tér 7–8. www.eng.matyaspince.eu/. (f) **1/266-8008.** Main courses 2,890 Ft–9,000 Ft. AE, MC, V. Daily 11am–midnight. Metro: Ferenciek tere (Blue line).

Moderate

Alföldi Kisvendéglő ★★ HUNGARIAN   Alföldi is named after Hungary's flat plain region and is paneled with horizontal brown wood-strip walls with assorted old plates above, creating a cozy country feel. The dining room offers wooden booths or tables with traditional country hand-embroidered tablecloths and place mats in folk designs. Each table has a basket of spicy homemade *pogácsas* (a type of biscuit), and you will be charged for each one eaten, but it's worth the nominal charge. The buttered veal scallops were ultra tender with a light buttery sauce that was used for the potatoes and rice that came with it. The pork medallions were also splendid, served in a down-home country manner.

V. Kecskeméti u. 4. www.alfoldivendeglo.hu/eng. (f) **1/267-0224.** Reservations recommended. Main courses 1,790 Ft–5,140 Ft. MC, V. Daily 11am–11pm. Metro: Astoria (Red line) or tram 47 or 49 to Kálvin tér.

Blue Tomato Pub ★★★ HUNGARIAN   Don't let the "Pub" in the name fool you; this is a serious place for treating your taste buds to tasty morsels. Try the corn soup with bacon and almond slivers as a starter—thick, creamy, and with chunks of bacon and lots of almonds. Continue the meal with layered chicken breast with sliced potatoes, tomato, onion, bacon of course, and a creamy cheese Dijon sauce served in an earthenware dish. Or opt for chicken breast with green mascarpone sauce with forest mushrooms.

XIII. Pannónia u. 5–7. www.bluetomato.hu. (f) **1/339-8099.** Reservations recommended. Main courses 1,590 Ft–3,900 Ft. MC, V. Sun–Tues noon–midnight; Wed–Thurs noon–2am; Fri–Sat noon–4am. Tram: 4 or 6, Jászai Mari tér.

Café Eklektika ★★★ 🍴 INTERNATIONAL   With tables and booths, a mellow mood is created by the soothing vocals with a cabaret feel serenading in the background, the monthly changing artwork on the walls, and the dependably excellent service. Menus (and hours) change continually depending on tourism and may include chicken breast stuffed with spinach served with a potato pie layered with cheese, or gnocchi with mozzarella balls and olives. Outside seating is available in good weather, but inside you will be treated to unlimited Wi-Fi, for the price of a coffee.

V. Nagymező 30. www.eklektika.hu. (f) **1/266-1226.** Reservations recommended. Main courses 1,490 Ft–3,290 Ft; pizza 1,390 Ft–1,890 Ft. MC, V. Daily noon–midnight. Metro: Opera (Yellow line).

Firkász ★★★ MODERN HUNGARIAN   The name means scribbler in English, referring to journalists who scribble their notes. The decor matches the name. Walls are covered with old newspapers from the early 20th century, accented with old typewriters; clocks; shadow boxes of old pens, erasers, and pencil sharpeners; and other memorabilia of yesteryear. Menu options include duck steak in bolete mushroom sauce served with pan fried potatoes with onions, and Mangalica pork with pickles. A piano player plays from 7pm to midnight. This is one of the few restaurants of its class to add a 15% service charge to all tabs.

XIII. Tátra u. 18. www.firkasz-etterem.hu. ⓒ **1/450-1118.** Reservations recommended. Main courses 3,390 Ft–5,200 Ft. MC, V. Daily noon–11pm. Tram: 4 or 6, Jászai Mari tér.

Hard Rock Café ★★★ 📷 AMERICAN   Once you walk through the gift shop, you will be seated in either the downstairs or upstairs restaurants. A mobile of over life-sized Plexiglas guitars hangs from the ceiling along the spiral staircase. Like all Hard Rocks, the walls are covered with memorabilia. Choose burgers and salads such as S.O.B. burger, Hickory BBQ Bacon Cheeseburger, or Cobb Salad. The food, atmosphere, and service all match those of any Hard Rock Café, so fans won't be disappointed.

V. Deák Ferenc u. 3–5. www.hardrock.com/budapest. ⓒ **1/302-4086.** Reservations recommended. Main courses 2,500 Ft–4,800 Ft. MC, V. Sun–Thurs noon–1am; Fri–Sat noon–2am. Metro: Arany János (Blue line). Bus: 70 or 78 to Bajcsy-Zsilinszky út.

Marquis de Salade ★★ 📷 EASTERN EUROPEAN/RUSSIAN   This has been a favorite for many years and is still going strong. The entrance is at street level, but the restaurant is downstairs in a cavelike atmosphere, decorated with Asian rugs on the walls and ceiling. Popular starters include the Marquis's salads, which is a sampler platter of six different salads. Along with the bread, this constitutes a diversely sumptuous meal, but make room for main courses such as lamb shank with sweet red peppers.

VI. Hajós u. 43. www.marquisdesalade.hu. ⓒ **1/302-4086.** Reservations recommended. Main courses 2,600 Ft–3,900 Ft. No credit cards. Daily noon–1am. Metro: Arany János (Blue line). Bus: 70 or 78 to Bajcsy-Zsilinszky út.

Inexpensive

Főzelékfalo Ételbar ★★ 🍴 HUNGARIAN   This tiny restaurant is so popular with Hungarians there is a line out the door at lunchtime. *Főzelék,* a cross between a soup and a stew, though it is puréed, is a national dish and treasure, so if you have not tried it, you have not officially been to Hungary. You can also get chicken in a variety of forms. The roasted and stuffed breast is particularly juicy and delicious. Inside there are only bar tables and stools, but if the weather is good, the sidewalk will be packed with tables. Take it to go if you have to. The blend comes in a number of varieties, but green pea and potato are the most popular. If you want something heartier, they sell fried chicken too.

VI. Nagymező 18. No phone. Reservations not accepted. Main courses 399 Ft–920 Ft; salads 220 Ft per 10 dkg. No credit cards. Mon–Fri 9am–10pm; Sat 10am–9pm; Sun 11am–6pm. Metro: Opera (Yellow line).

Kőleves Vendéglő (Stone Soup) ★★★ 🍴 MODERN HUNGARIAN   If you know the story of *Stone Soup,* the playfulness of this establishment will charm you with light fixtures made of inverted wine glasses or cheese graters, the pieces of contemporary art that grace the walls, and the soup bowls adorning the bar. But the real delight comes with the food, made from preservative-free ingredients. The menu changes often, but some top dishes include a thick and tangy corn soup with chilies. A recurring offering is chicken with Roquefort dressing, which is delightful. Some dishes are a la carte with a suggested side dish that is extra, at 360 Ft to 400 Ft, but others are complete meals.

VII. Kazinczy u. 35. www.koleves.com. ⓒ **1/322-1011.** Reservations recommended. Main courses 2,250 Ft–3,560 Ft. AE, MC, V. Daily noon–midnight. Close to Dohány Synagogue on the corner of Kazinczy u. and Dob u.

CENTRAL BUDA

Expensive

Hemingway ★★★ 📷 MODERN HUNGARIAN   You will feel as though you are escaping the city when visiting this restaurant next to a small lake with plenty of trees. Inside you'll feel like you have joined Hemingway in one of his favorite Spanish getaways. The piano and bass duo adds to the relaxing Casablanca atmosphere with the Latin music. It may seem contradictory that the cuisine is Hungarian, but the fusion of food and atmosphere blend once you take your first bite. The menu is constantly being revised, which is what makes this establishment great. They always have some dish with the indigenous Hungarian fares; the famous Mangalica pork and the most expensive menu item, the rare Hungarian Gray beef. In fine weather, reserve a table outside on the terrace overlooking the water.

XI. Kosztolányi D. tér 2, Feneketlen tó. www.hemingway-etterem.hu. ☎ **1/381-0522.** Reservations recommended. Main courses 2,980 Ft–8,900 Ft. AE, DC, MC, V. Mon–Sat noon–midnight, Sun noon–4pm. Bus: 7 toward Buda from Ferenciek tér to Feneketlen tó, a small "lake." Tram: 19 or 49 to Kosztolányi Dezső tér.

Moderate

Angelika Kaveház és Étterem ★★ MODERN HUNGARIAN   Angelika is housed in a historic building next to St. Anne's Church. Better known as a place for drinks and pastries on a summer's day, the multilevel terrace has perfect views of Parliament across the Danube. Inside you will find extra-large rooms where smokers and nonsmokers are truly segregated. The menu has expanded over time: pork chops with cheese and beer sauce served with mashed potatoes and Roquefort salad or pork with barbecue sauce are appealing. The vegetable soufflés served with it are a pleasant change of pace for a vegetable side dish.

I. Batthyány tér 7. www.angelikacafe.hu. ☎ **1/225–1653.** Main courses 1,950 Ft–3,990 Ft. MC, V. Apr– Oct daily 9am–midnight, Nov–Mar 9am–11pm. Metro: Batthyány tér (Red line).

Inexpensive

Eden ★★ 🍴 VEGETARIAN   This historic building houses the first and only vegan restaurant in Buda. All ingredients are natural and fresh without any coloring, additives, or preservatives. After making your selection from the limited offerings, you have the choice of sitting in the charming country-cozy dining room or in the atrium

---

Coffeehouses: Historic & Traditional

As part of the Austro-Hungarian Empire, Budapest (just as in Vienna) developed a coffeehouse culture where people of like minds met to discuss politics, literature, or music. Each coffeehouse has its own story as to which literary movement or political circles favored their establishment. Of the old classics, we prefer **Centrál Kávéház**, V. Károlyi Mihály u. 9 (www.centralkavehaz.hu; (☎ **1/266-2110**), in the Inner City; **Művész Kávéház**, VI. Andrássy út 29

(www.muveszkavehaz.hu; ☎ **1/345-3544**), diagonally across Andrássy út from the Opera House; and **Rétesvar**, I. Balta köz 4 (no phone), in Castle Hill.

For a more modern take on coffee culture, find a spot at **Aztek Choxolat Café**, V. Karoly korut 22 or Semmelweiss u. 19 (☎ **1/266-7113**); **Café Noé**, VII. Wesselényi u. 13 (www.torta.hu; ☎ **1/787-3842**); or **Fröhlich Kóser Cukrászda**, VII. Dob u. 22 (☎ **1/267-2851**), all in Pest.

garden. The food is quite tasty, and the selection of 12 juices freshly squeezed from fruit or vegetables will quench anyone's thirst. When you order, take note that the price for salad is by weight and the drinks are by volume.

I. Iskola utca 31, Batthyány tér. www.edenivegan.hu. ☏ **06/70-414-2736** (cellphone only). 590 Ft–990 Ft. No credit cards. Sun–Fri 10am–7pm. Metro: Batthyány (Red line).

Shopping
MAIN SHOPPING STREETS
The hub of the tourist-packed capital is the first pedestrian shopping street in Budapest, **Váci utca.** It runs from the stately Vörösmarty tér in the center of Pest, across Kossuth Lajos utca, all the way to Vámház körút. The street is now largely occupied by Euro-fashion chain stores that flood every major city with their European-style prices. There are an overwhelming number of folklore/souvenir shops, which might be good for window-shopping, but unless we have recommended them below, you may be paying more than you should for that souvenir. This area is home to many cafes and bars, but, like Castle Hill, is notorious for tourist traps. Another popular shopping area for travelers is the **Castle District** in Buda, with its abundance of overpriced folk-art boutiques and art galleries.

The **Központi Vásárcsarnok (Central Market Hall),** IX. Vámház krt. 1–3 (☏ **1/336-3300;** metro: Kálvin tér on Blue line; tram: 47 or 49), is the largest and most spectacular market hall. Located on the Inner Ring (Kiskörút), just on the Pest side of the Szabadság Bridge, it was impeccably reconstructed in 1995. This bright, three-level market hall is a pleasure to visit. Fresh produce, meat, and cheese vendors dominate the space. Keep your eyes open for inexpensive saffron and dried mushrooms. We have had French guests who found truffles for less than 10€. The mezzanine level features folk-art booths, coffee and drink bars, and fast-food booths. The basement level houses fishmongers, pickled goods, along with a large grocery store. Open Monday 6am to 5pm, Tuesday through Friday 6am to 6pm, and Saturday 6am to 3pm.

BEST BUYS
FOLKLORE
Check out the second floor of the Central Market (see above) for a wide selection of popular handcrafted Hungarian gifts. Antiques shops, running along **Falk Miksa utca** in downtown Budapest, feature a broad selection of vintage furniture, ceramics, carpets, jewelry, and accessories, but over the years it has become more expensive with less bargaining going on for tourists. One shop that has a wide selection and helpful staff is **Folkart Craftman's House** (☏ **1/318-5143**) on the side street, V. Régiposta u. 12, right off of Váci utca, and open Monday to Friday 10am to 6pm, weekends 10am to 3pm. An outstanding private shop on Váci utca is **Vali Folklór,** in the courtyard of V. Váci u. 23 (☏ **1/337-6301**), open Monday to Saturday 11am to 7pm and Sunday 12:30 to 7pm.

Ethnic Hungarians from Transylvania come to Budapest with bags full of handmade craftwork, selling their goods to Hungarians and tourists alike. Their prices are generally quite reasonable, and bargaining is customary. Keep your eyes open for these vendors—they are unmistakable in their characteristic black boots and dark-red skirts, with red or white kerchiefs tied around their heads.

FOOD
Hungarian salami is world famous. Connoisseurs generally agree that Pick Salami, produced in the southeastern city of Szeged, is the best brand. Herz Salami,

produced locally in Budapest, is also a very popular product (though not as popular as Pick). You should be aware that a number of people have reported difficulty in clearing U.S. Customs with salami in checked luggage; take it home at your own risk. Another typical Hungarian food product is chestnut paste *(gesztenye pu[um]ré)*, available in a tin or block wrapped in foil; it's used primarily as a pastry filling but can also top desserts and ice cream. Paprika paste *(pirosarany)* is another product that's tough to find outside Hungary. It usually comes in a bright-red tube. Three types are available: hot *(csípős)*, deli-style *(csemege)*, and sweet *(édes)*. Powdered paprika also comes in the same three varieties as the paste. In the great market, you will find the powdered version in little decorated cloth bags, making it ready for gift giving. All of these items can generally be purchased at grocery stores *(élelmiszer)*, delicatessens *(csemege)*, and usually any convenience store.

PORCELAIN

Another popular Hungarian item is porcelain, particularly from the country's two best-known producers, Herend and Zsolnay. Although both brands are available in the West, you'll find a better selection, but not lower prices, in Hungary. **Ajka Crystal,** V. József Attila u. 7 (✆ **1/317-8133**), is Hungary's renowned crystal producer from the Lake Balaton region. The **Herend Shop**s are located at V. József nádor tér 11 (www.herend.hu; ✆ **1/317-2622**), VI. Andrássy út 16 (✆ **1/374-0006**), and I. Szentháromság u. 5 (✆ **1/225-1051**). An alternative to the classic Herend porcelain is **Herend Village Pottery,** II. Bem rakpart 37 (www.herendimajolika.hu; ✆ **1/356-7899**), which is not associated with the Herend porcelain company. The *majolika* (village pottery) is a hand-painted folklore-inspired way of making pottery.

WINE

The sweet white Tokaji Aszú, Tokaji Eszenzia, and Tokaji Szamorodni, and the mouth-tingling Egri Bikavér, Villányi Cuveé, Szekszárdi Bikavér, and Kékfrankos are the most representative of Hungarian wines. Stop at **In Vino Veritas,** VII. Dohány u. 58–62 (www.borkereskedes.hu; ✆ **1/413-0002**). Sophisticated, classy, and welcoming with excellent customer service, this wine shop is a cut above the others. **Pántlika Borház,** V. Király Pál u. 10 (✆ **1/328-0115**), carries a vast selection of Hungarian wines, and the owner's knowledge of them is equally impressive.

Locals say that good palinka (a traditional form of brandy) should warm the stomach and not burn the throat. Visit the **A Magyar Pálinka Háza (House of Hungarian Pálinka),** VIII. Rákcozi u. 17 (www.magyarpalinkahaza.hu; ✆ **1/338-4219**), for an initiation. Remember purchases to take home will have to be packed in your checked luggage; you will not be able to carry them on board.

Entertainment and Nightlife

For the most up-to-date information, go to **www.jegymester.hu** and click on the English link. This site includes information for the opera house as well as the major theaters in the city. A complete schedule of mainstream performing arts is found in the free bimonthly *Koncert Kalendárium,* available at any of the Budapestinfo Points, or you can check it online at **www.muzsika.net/koncertkalendarium**.

The **Cultur-Comfort Központi Jegyiroda (Cultur-Comfort Ticket Office),** VI. Paulay Ede u. 46 (www.cultur-comfort.hu; ✆ **1/322-0000**), is open Monday to Friday 10am to 6pm. They sell tickets to just about everything, from theater and operettas to sports events and rock concerts.

THE PERFORMING ARTS

The **Budapesti Operettszínház (Budapest Operetta Theatre),** VI. Nagymező u. 17 (www.operettszinhaz.hu; ℂ 1/312-4866), is a highlight among Art Nouveau-style buildings. The off season is mid-July to mid-August. The box office is open Monday to Friday 10am to 7pm and Saturday 1 to 7pm. Take the Metro to Opera or Oktogon (Yellow line). The season at the landmark **Magyar Állami Operaház (Hungarian State Opera House;** p. 543) runs from mid-September to mid-June. Summer visitors can take in approximately eight performances (both opera and ballet) during the Summer **Operafest** in July or August. The box office is open weekdays from 11am until the beginning of the performance, or to 5pm when there is no performance, and Sunday from 10am to 1pm and 4pm until the beginning of the performance. Take the Yellow line metro to Opera.

The main concert hall of the **Palace of Arts ★★,** IX. Komor Marcell u. 1 (www.mupa.hu; ℂ 1/555-3001), is the finest contemporary classical music venue in Budapest; it now hosts concerts from celebrated orchestras from around the world. To get there, take tram no. 2 from downtown toward the Lágymányos Bridge.

FOLK-DANCE

Authentic folk-music workshops are held at least once a week at several locations around the city. The leading Hungarian folk band is **Muzsikás,** the name given to musicians playing traditional folk music in Hungarian villages. They have toured the U.S., playing to great acclaim, so may not always be available at a Budapest *táncház* (dance house). Every Thursday (Sept–May only) from 8pm to midnight for 700 Ft, there's music at the **Marczibányi tér Művelődési Ház (Marczibányi Square Cultural House),** II. Marczibányi tér 5/a (ℂ 1/212-2820). Take the Red line metro to Széll Kálmán tér. Also try the **Fővárosi Művelődési Ház (Municipal Cultural House),** at XI. Fehérvári út 47 (ℂ 1/203-3868). At the **Kalamajka Dance House,** Belvárosi Ifjúsági Művelődési Ház, V. Molnár u. 9 (ℂ 1/371-5928), reachable by M3 Ferenciek tere, is the biggest weekend dance, with dancing and instruction on the second floor, while jam sessions and serious palinka drinking take place on the fourth. The Kalamajka band is led by Béla Halmos, who started the dance-house movement in the 1970s. Usually, traditional villagers give guest performances. Open Saturday from 8pm to 1am for 700 Ft; you can dance until you drop.

An important heritage-preserving center, the **Almássy téri Művelődési Központ (Almássy Square Culture Center),** VII. Almássy tér 6 (ℂ 1/352-1572), hosts folk dances to the music of the electric Greeks Sirtos in the main hall from 6 to 10pm. Before you venture off to find it, call first as the building has been under renovation and a reopening date was still unconfirmed at the time of writing. When it was open, the upstairs was a bit crazier with the small fanatic band of Magyar dancers who twirl to the Kalotaszeg sounds of the Berkó Band until midnight. A short walk from Blaha Lujza tér (Blue line or tram no. 4 or 6) gets you to this folk center. Entrance fees vary from 700 Ft to 1,500 Ft. In the City Park is **Petőfi Csarnok,** XIV. Zichy Mihály út 14 (www.pecsa.hu; ℂ 1/363-3730), an old-style no-frills hall whose stages are used for some of the best folk performances in the city.

DANCE CLUBS

Budapest has a cyclical hot club scene depending on the economic state of affairs, what is offered at any given time is apt to change. If you dare, try **Piaf,** VI. Nagymező u. 25 (ℂ 1/322-0700; where you have to ring a bell and then get approval from the bouncer before you can get in. This is the bar to go to when all others are yelling "Last call." It is open until 6am.

Meeting Hungarian guys or young fashionable ladies is not a problem at the huge and hedonistic **E-Klub,** X. Népligeti u. 2 (www.e-klub.hu; ℂ 1/263-1614). Touted as the biggest and most famous of the university pubs, **School Club Közgáz,** IX. Fővám tér 8 (ℂ 1/215-4359), is packed solid during weekends.

LIVE MUSIC

The **A38 Boat ★★**, XI. Pázmány Péter sétány (www.a38.hu; ℂ 1/464-3940), is a former Ukrainian stone-carrying ship anchored at the Buda-side foot of the Petőfi Bridge. On the lower deck, you can get your fill of the city's best range of jazz, world, electronic, hip-hop, and rock music bands.

For the best jazz and blues in Hungary, head to **Old Man's Music Pub ★★**, V. Akácfa u. 13 (www.oldmans.hu; ℂ 1/322-7645), where Hobo and his blues band are regulars. See the list of current entertainment posted inside the door. At the back of **Spinoza Étterem ★★**, VII. Dob u. 15 (www.spinozahaz.hu; ℂ 1/413-7488), a small restaurant, is a small cabaret offering nightly music performances ranging from Klezmer to classical.

PUBS & CAFE BARS

Café Aloe, VI. Zichy Jenő u. 37 (ℂ 1/269-4536), is a sizzling, comfortable cellar that offers powerful, yet remarkably cheap drinks prepared by attentive bar staff. For a lounge, cafe, restaurant, and bar all rolled into one, head to **Szilvuplé,** VI. Ó u. 33 (www.szilvuple.hu; ℂ 20/992−5115 [cellphone]). Talented DJs set the tone with rock and indie music; it also features karaoke nights and dance lessons, including Salsa, during the week. For a cultural experience, you cannot pass up **Szimpla Kert ★★**, VII. Kertész u. 48 (www.szimpla.hu; ℂ 1/321-9119), a beer garden and alternative culture Mecca to spin your head. Located in an abandoned apartment courtyard, Szimpla Kert mixes junkyard aesthetics with such modernisms as Wi-Fi, a daytime cafe, and evenings of live music and indie film screenings. Try the honey beer from the bar on the inner left side.

THE LGBT SCENE

Gay bars open and close in the blink of an eye. For reliable and up-to-date information, visit **www.gayguide.net** or subscribe to the free **Yahoo Gay Budapest Information** group by sending an e-mail to gaybudapestinfo-subscribe@yahoogroups.com. Unless noted, all of these bars have a minimum consumption fee or entrance charge. **Action Bar,** V. Magyar u. 42 (www.action.gay.hu; ℂ 1/266-9148), has been a long-time survivor and perennial favorite of gay men. It attracts men of all ages, but older men will feel comfortable. There are weekend strip shows that are not to be missed. **CoXx,** VII. Dohány u. 38 (www.coxx.hu; ℂ 1/344-4884), is another bar that has been around for years. It has a dance floor, backrooms, and hosts theme parties. **AlterEgo,** VI. Dessewffy u. 33 (www.alteregoclub.hu; ℂ 06/70-345-4302 [cellphone]), is a hip jumping club for the younger set, but older folks of both genders are welcome too for their different events. The two following venues do not have entrance fees. **Habrolo Bisztro,** V. Belvaros Szep u. 1/b (www.habrolo.hu; ℂ 1/950-6644), is a small gay bar where locals hang out, so you can practice your Hungarian skills. **Mystery Bar,** V. Nagysándor József u. 3 (ℂ 1/312-1436), was the first gay bar in the city (it changes from the Mystery Bar to Le Café M repeatedly, but it is currently the Mystery Bar). It is a very tiny, but friendly place that draws a large foreign clientele, making it a great place to meet new people.

Where to Stay

Lodging rates in Budapest have risen considerably, becoming more comparable to other European capitals, but deals can be had if you are a savvy Internet bargain hunter. Compare rates with the hotel's own website and try e-mailing the hotel directly.

The majority of hotels and pensions in Budapest list prices in euros (€), so the rates listed in this chapter are as the hotel designates. Listing rates in euros is not just intended as a means of transition to the E.U. currency (Hungary is not expected to join the euro zone until 2015 at the earliest and most likely much later), it is also a hedge against forint inflation. All hotels charge a whopping 18% value-added tax (VAT). Most build the tax into their rates, while a few tack it on top. When booking a room, ask whether the VAT is included in the quoted price. Unless otherwise indicated, prices in this chapter include the VAT.

THE INNER CITY & CENTRAL PEST

City Ring Hotel ★★★   This hotel is only a block away from Nyugati train station. Situated on the ring road, you have easy access to transportation, shopping, and restaurants. The rooms are a bit overwhelmed by the modern furniture, giving them a crowded feeling, but if you are out all day touring, they are more than adequate, impeccably clean, and the beds are comfy. One caution is that the shower is on the small side, which may pose a challenge for larger people. Free Wi-Fi is available only in some rooms.

XIII. Szent István krt. 22. www.cityhotel.hu. ✆ **1/340-5450.** Fax 1/340-4884. 39 units. 50€–262€ double. Rates include full breakfast. AE, MC, V. Public parking nearby. Metro: Nyugati (Blue line) or tram 4 or 6. **Amenities:** Nonsmoking rooms. *In room:* A/C, TV, fridge, hair dryer (on request), Wi-Fi (free; in some).

Four Seasons Hotel Gresham Palace ★★★   This Art Nouveau building, one of the most elegant and majestic properties in the city, stands as one of the finest in the world. With the Chain Bridge directly opposite the front doors, it has a picture-perfect view of the Buda Castle, making this the most picturesque location of any hotel in the city. As is Four Seasons tradition, guests are pampered in every way possible. While all rooms are beautifully decorated with mahogany furniture, the most expensive suites are equipped with bedroom sets made of mother-of-pearl and some have fireplaces. Every bathroom is fitted with Italian and Spanish marble with deep-soak bathtubs. No detail in design has been overlooked, and each room has been recreated in its original glory.

V. Széchenyi István tér 5–6. www.fourseasons.com/budapest. ✆ **1/268-6000** or 800/819-5053 in North America. Fax 1/268-5000. 179 units. 250€–790€ double; 1,000€–5,000€ suite. Rates do not include VAT or tourist tax. Children stay free in parent's room. Breakfast 8,900 Ft. AE, DC, MC, V. Parking 9,800 Ft. Metro: Deák tér (all lines). **Amenities:** Restaurant; bar; pool (luxurious heated indoor); exercise room; sauna; concierge; room service; smoke-free rooms. *In room:* A/C, TV, fax machine (on request), minibar, hair dryer, Internet (for a fee).

Hotel Zara ★★   Located on a small side street off Váci utca, the pedestrian shopping street, this hotel, opened in 2006, is just two short blocks from the great market, a convenient location for shoppers. The decor is a beautifully executed mix of eclectic styles with Murano glass light coverings to Thai designs for the carpeting and drapery, created by Hungarian craftsman. Rooms seem small at 18 sq. m (194 sq. ft.), as most of them sport a queen-size bed, a rarity in less than a five-star hotel, but are roomy enough to be comfortable. The furniture style is Asian modern with a soft pink and chocolate brown theme, while the bathrooms are tiled in browns and beiges, with showers only. Each corridor has only five rooms for an intimate feeling with designated smoking and nonsmoking floors. Excellent staff adds to the stay here.

V. Só u. 6. www.boutiquehotelbudapest.com. ✆ 1/577-0700. Fax 1/577-0710. 74 units. 69€–199€ double. Rates include breakfast and city tax. Children 6 and under stay free in parent's room. AE, MC, V. Parking 18€. Metro: Kálvin tér (Blue line). **Amenities:** Restaurant; bar; room service; Wi-Fi in public areas. *In room:* A/C, TV, minibar, Internet.

Medosz ★ This hotel, formerly a trade-union hotel for agricultural workers, retains its Communist utilitarian appearance with tread-worn carpeting and ugly halls. The rooms are simple, on the smallish side, and clean, but you can't beat the location. Jókai tér is less than a block from the bustling Oktogon and across from Liszt Ferenc tér with a dozen restaurants. Because of this, it can be noisy at night with the many restaurants and clubs in the area. Courtyard-view rooms are subject to neighbor noise, but are not nearly as bad as the front of the hotel. The hotel remains good value given its location. A reader in the past reported their bed had springs popping from the mattress; so perhaps check out the mattress immediately upon checking in and ask for a room change if needed. The entire hotel is nonsmoking.

VI. Jókai tér 9. www.medoszhotel.hu. ✆ 1/374-3001. Fax 1/332-4316. 68 units. 59€–69€ double; 69€–79€ triple; 99€ quad. Extra bed 10€ per night. Rates include breakfast and all taxes. MC, V. Metered on-street parking; indoor garage nearby. Metro: Oktogon (Yellow line). *In room:* A/C some rooms, TV, phone.

NH Hotel ★★★ Built from the ground up in 2003 directly behind the Vigszinház Theater, this hotel has taken a modern, minimalist approach, oozing a warm welcome. The use of a variety of textiles in the room decor spanning shades of browns and tans with rich dark wood adds a cozy warmth to the spacious rooms. Add the mottled brown-and-tan marble used in the bathrooms, and the feeling of quiet elegance is carried throughout. Sleep-inducing beds bring it all together for a perfect night's sleep. Although the exercise room on the eighth floor is limited, it contains the most modern exercise equipment, separate changing rooms for women and men, a solarium (for a fee), and a relaxation room with beautiful lounge chairs. It's eco-friendly to boot.

XIII. Vigszinház u. 3. www.nh-hotels.com. ✆ 1/814-0000. Fax 1/814-0100. 160 units. 79€–196€ double. Rates include VAT. Breakfast 17€ included with some rates. AE, DC, MC, V. Secured parking 16€. Metro: Nyugati (Blue line) or tram 4 or 6. **Amenities:** Restaurant; bar; exercise room; room service. *In room:* A/C, TV, minibar, hair dryer, Wi-Fi (free).

THE CASTLE DISTRICT

Burg Hotel ★★★ An overlooked treasure on Castle Hill, this hotel sits on a corner directly across from St. Matthias Church. The multilingual staff is as friendly as they are talented with languages. The rooms are spacious and beautifully decorated in muted greens, rose, and beige with modern comfortable furniture from their last remodel in 2007. The corner room is extra large, but any room would be comfortable. The blue-tiled bathrooms are simple, but sizable. All rooms have a view of Trinity Square. Breakfast is served in a large room with windows overlooking the square. There is no lift, but it is only three floors above the ground-floor entrance.

I. Szentháromság tér 7–8. www.burghotelbudapest.com. ✆ 1/212-0269. Fax 1/212-3970. 26 units. High season 99€–115€ double; extra bed 15€. Rates include breakfast and city tax. Children 13 and under stay free in parent's room. AE, MC, V. Parking free. Bus: 16A from Széll Kálmán tér or 16 from Deák tér. **Amenities:** Bar. *In room:* A/C, TV, minibar, hair dryer, Wi-Fi (free).

Hilton Budapest ★★★ This Hilton has the most enviable piece of real estate in Budapest, sitting right next door to St. Matthias Church with part of the

Fisherman's Bastion behind it. The hotel's award-winning design incorporates both the ruins of a 13th-century Dominican church (the church tower is alongside the hotel) and the baroque facade of a 17th-century Jesuit college, which makes up the hotel's main entrance. The hotel was renovated in 2007; the rooms are now a uniform rose, green, and beige color scheme. The corner suites are beautifully decorated with separate sitting areas, a dining area, and a bedroom with oversize windows for a spectacular view of the Bastion and Danube. The elegant Baroque Room is three levels and has a fully equipped kitchen. There are a limited number of smoking rooms.

I. Hess András tér 1–3. www.hilton.com. ℃ **1/889-6600.** Fax 1/889-6644. 322 units. 90€–230€ double. Rates do not include VAT or city tax. 1 child per adult stays free in parent's room. Breakfast included, but extra guests 28€ each. AE, DC, MC, V. Parking 25€. Bus: 16A from Széll Kálmán tér or 16 from Deák tér. **Amenities:** Restaurant; bar; exercise room; concierge; room service; babysitting. *In room:* A/C, TV, minibar, hair dryer, Wi-Fi (for a fee in standard room).

HOSTELS

Not all hotel alternatives are created equal and should not be considered for young party people only. There are alternatives out there and some of these have been listed here. There is intense competition in Budapest between youth hostel companies and various privately run hostels as there are more than 85 hostels in the city and more are being added continually. Some are here today and gone tomorrow, so be careful if you are required to make a deposit.

BudaBaB, VII. Akácfa u. 18. (www.budabab.com; ℃ 1/267-5240), is a B&B, not a hostel, centrally situated at the edge of the historic Jewish ghetto, owned by the author of this chapter. They are native English speakers with over 10 years of Budapest living. They also have a self-catering apartment available during summer months and long term the rest of the year.

Loft Hostel, V. Veres Palne u. 19 IV/6 bell 44 (www.lofthostel.hu; ℃ 1/328-0916), is on the top floor of a building with dormer loft-type ceilings. The young owners want to provide more for less, but they also want to keep their lease, so this is not a late-night party place. The owners have a band so they know the music scene.

Mellow Mood Ltd operates a hotel and hostel accommodations office for their own properties at Keleti Station (℃ 1/343-0748), near the Baross Restaurant. The office gives the impression that it is a tourist information office, but it is not. Opening times are daily May 1 to October 31, 7am to 7pm. From November 1 to April 30 they are open Thursday to Tuesday, 7am to 5pm. Mellow Mood's **Marco Polo Hostel,** VII. Nyár u. 6 (www.marcopolohostel.com; (℃ 1/413-2555), is in a central location that is good for hopping on a bus or catching the metro. The rooms have clean and attractive linen. There is a 24-hour club adjoining the hostel, so if noise will disrupt a good night's sleep ask for a room on an upper floor and at the back. Staff seems to have less than adequate language skills. For other hostels, check out the website **www.hostelworld.com** for other offerings in the city.

THE DANUBE BEND

The small but historic towns along the snaking Bend, in particular, Szentendre, Visegrád, and Esztergom, are easy day trips from Budapest as they're all within a half-hour to 2 hours from the city. The natural beauty of the area, where forested hills loom over the river, makes it a welcome haven for those weary of the city. Travelers may want to make a long weekend out of a visit to the Bend, but they can each easily be done in a half-day or full-day trip.

Essentials

GETTING TO THE DANUBE BEND

By Boat

From May to September, Tuesday to Sunday, a boat leaves Budapest at 10:30am for the town of Szentendre. The returning boat back to Szentendre leaves at 6pm. A leisurely boat ride through the countryside is one of the highlights of a boat excursion, especially in autumn. All boats depart from Budapest's Vigadó tér boat landing, which is located in Pest between Erzsébet Bridge and Szabadság Bridge, stopping to pick up passengers 5 minutes later at Buda's Batthyány tér landing, which is also a Red line metro stop, before it continues up the river.

Schedules and towns served are complicated and change sometimes due to the weather and water levels of the river, so contact **Mahart,** the state shipping company, at the Vigadó tér landing (www.mahartpassnave.hu, click on the British flag; ✆ 1/318-1704), for information. You can also get Mahart information from Tourinform in Szentendre or Budapestinfo Points in Budapest.

One-way prices by riverboat are 1,490 Ft to Vác, 1,790 Ft to Visegrád, and 1,990 Ft to Esztergom. Trips to Szentendre cost 2,390 Ft round-trip. Children 2 and under ride free, children 2–14 receive a 50% discount, and E.U. retirees receive a 25% discount as do students with the ISIC card.

The approximate travel time by boat from Budapest is 1½ hours to Szentendre, 3 hours to Visegrád, and 4¾ hours hours to Esztergom. If time is tight, consider the train or bus (both of which are considerably cheaper, though less scenic).

By Train

TO SZENTENDRE The **HÉV** suburban railroad connects Budapest's Batthyány tér Station with Szentendre. On the Pest side, you can catch the HÉV from the Margit Híd, Budai Híd Fő stop on tram no. 4 or 6. Trains leave daily, year-round, every 10–12 minutes from 4am to 11:30pm. The one-way fare is 620 Ft. If you have a valid Budapest public transportation pass, the supplemental ticket is 310 Ft each way. Generally, the trip is 45 minutes, but there is occasional ongoing work on the tracks, causing passengers to be transferred free of charge to a bus for the rest of the journey.

TO VISEGRÁD There's no direct train service to Visegrád. Instead, you can take one of 28 daily trains departing from Nyugati Station for Nagymaros–Visegrád (trip time: 40 min.–1 hr.). From Nagymaros, take a ferry across the river to Visegrád. The ferry dock (**RÉV;** ✆ 26/398-344) is a 5-minute walk from the train station. A ferry leaves every hour throughout the day. The train ticket to Nagymaros costs 1,120 Ft; the ferryboat ticket to Visegrád costs 280 Ft.

TO ESZTERGOM One train every hour makes the direct run daily between Budapest's Nyugati Station and Esztergom (trip time: 1½ hr.); InterCity trains are not available on this route. Train tickets cost 1,120 Ft each way.

By Bus

For all bus information, call **Volán Bus** (✆ 1/382-0888). Approximately 16 buses travel the same route to Szentendre, Visegrád, and Esztergom, departing from Budapest's **Árpád híd bus station;** at the Blue line metro station of the same name. Some are only on specific days of the week, while others are daily. Buses charge by mileage ranges. Depending on the bus, the number of stops, and the day of the week, it can be a pleasant or excruciatingly long ride. The one-way fare to Szentendre is 475 Ft; the trip takes about 45 minutes. The fare to Visegrád is 750 Ft, and the trip takes

The Danube Bend

HUNGARY

anywhere from 1¼ to 3 hours. To Esztergom, take the bus that travels via a town called Dorog; it costs 1,050 Ft and takes from 1¼ hours to 2 hours depending on the day of the week or bus selected. Keep in mind, of course, that all travel by bus is subject to traffic delays, especially during rush hour.

Szentendre

Szentendre (pronounced *Sen*-ten-dreh, St. Andrew), 21km (13 miles) north of Budapest, has been populated since the Stone Age by Illyrians, the Celtic Eraviscus tribe, Romans, Lombards, Avars, and, naturally, Hungarians. Serbians settled here in the 17th century, embellishing the town with their unique characteristics. Szentendre counts half a dozen Serbian churches among its rich collection of historic buildings.

Since the turn of the 20th century, Szentendre has been home to an artists' colony, where today about 100 artists live and work, referred to as "The City of Artists." The town is an extremely popular destination, with buses pouring tourists into the streets for a few rushed hours of exploring. This is sometimes a turnoff for those bussed in as they see a limited amount of the town. Other visitors are turned off by the sudden tsunami of people, but the town really is a treasure. To appreciate its rich flavor, we recommend you look beyond the touristy shops and wander the streets looking at the architecture, the galleries, and the churches, if only from the outside. There is much to hold your attention beyond the shopkeepers trying to lure you into their stores.

ESSENTIALS

VISITOR INFORMATION   One of Szentendre's information offices, **Tourinform,** is and will be again at Dumtsa Jenő u. 22 (© **26/317-965**). However, it is undergoing renovations and is currently located at Duna Korzó 8. You may need to check both places if you want maps of Szentendre (and the region), as well as concert and exhibition schedules. The office can also provide hotel information. It is open April through August, Monday to Friday from 9am to 5:30pm, weekends 10am to 5:30pm. In September to November it is open Monday to Friday from 9:30am to 4:30pm, weekends 10am to 4pm. December through March, the hours are the same as autumn, but they open half an hour later weekdays. Check the first location by following the flow of pedestrian traffic into town on Kossuth Lajos utca. The temporary location is along the river. If you arrive by boat, you may find the **Ibusz** office sooner, located on the corner of Bogdányi út and Gőzhajó utca (© **26/310-181**). This office is open April to October, Monday through Friday from 10am to 6pm and weekends 10am to 3pm. From November to March, it's open weekdays only, 10am to 5pm. Like all things in this town, these offices and the sights that follow march to their own beat, not always keeping with scheduled times on websites or even outside their doors.

EXPLORING SZENTENDRE

The tiny **Blagovestenska Church ★** at Fő tér 4 dates from 1752 and was built on the site of a wooden church from the Serbian migration of 1690. It's open from Tuesday to Sunday, 10am to 5pm; admission is 300 Ft. The **Margit Kovács Museum ★★**, Vastagh György u. 1 (© **26/310-244**), features the work of Hungary's best-known ceramic artist, Margit Kovács. It's open from Tuesday to Sunday, 10am to 6pm. Admission is 1,000 Ft. The **Szabó Marzipan Museum ★★**, Dumsta Jeno u. 12 (© **26/311-931**), is the most widely known museum in this village. Who could pass up the chance to see the 1.5m-long (5-ft.) Hungarian Parliament made entirely in marzipan? The museum is open May to September daily from 9am to 7pm, and October to April daily 10am to 6pm. Admission is 450 Ft.

SHOPPING

Blue Land Folklor ★★★, Alkotmány u. 8 (© **26/313-610**), carries decorated eggs from 38 regions of Hungary, including some from the ethnic Hungarian areas prior to the Trianon Treaty's loss of land. From March 15 to January 10, they are open

---

 BEST LÁNGOS ever

If you get a snack attack, you will find the best *lángos* in Hungary here in Szentendre at **Álom Lángos ★★★** at Fő tér 8 (© **06/20-970-7827** [cellphone]), an unassuming little stand. Sometimes the long waiting lines attest to this fact, since most will be Hungarians in the know. *Lángos* is the Hungarian version of fried dough with toppings. In Fő tér,

there are yellow signs near an alley with LÁNGOS written on them. Halfway up the very narrow alley is a gate for the small shed. This alone is worth a trip to Szentendre. The stand is open only April through November Tuesday through Saturday 10am to 6pm, and a *lángos* will cost you 350 Ft to 550 Ft.

daily from 10am to 6pm. The rest of January through February, hours are at the whim of the owner.

If you want to find a unique shop while in Hungary, come to **Handpets ★★★**, Dumsta Jeno u. 15 (© **30/954–2584** [cellphone only]). Handpets are the most creative hand puppets. Designed by Kati Szili, they are handmade in high-quality material and are sure to delight children of all ages. This is the only shop where the entire collection is available, although limited designs and poor imitations are sold elsewhere. The shop has no outdoor signage, so if they are closed, you will pass without realizing. Hours are hit and miss.

WHERE TO STAY

We're not sure why anyone would want to stay in Szentendre as it is an easy and short ride from Budapest. However, if you are the exception to the rule, try **Róz Panzió ★**, located at Pannónia utca 6/b (www.hotelrozszentendre.hu; © **26/311-737;** fax 26/310-979), it has 10 units and a garden overlooking the Danube where you can eat breakfast when weather permits. Rooms are 50€ for a double; breakfast is included.

WHERE TO EAT

Aranysárkány Vendéglő (Golden Dragon Inn) ★, Alkotmány u. 1/a (www. aranysarkany.hu; © **26/301-479**), located just east of Fő tér on Hunyadi utca, is always filled to capacity. The crowd includes a large percentage of Hungarians, definitely a good sign in a heavily visited town like Szentendre. You can choose from such enticing offerings as alpine lamb, roast leg of goose, Székely-style stuffed cabbage (the Székely are a Hungarian ethnic group native to Transylvania), spinach cream, and venison steak. Vegetarians can order the vegetable plate, a respectable presentation of grilled and steamed vegetables in season. If you walk directly south from Fő tér, you'll find **Régimódi ★★**, Futó u. 3 (© **26/311-105**). An elegant restaurant in a former private home, Régimódi is furnished with antique Hungarian carpets and chandeliers. The menu offers a wide range of Hungarian specialties, with an emphasis on game dishes. There are also numerous salad options, with specials each day on the board. Whatever you choose, the portions are hearty. The only drawback is that it does get crowded with tour groups.

Visegrád

Halfway between Szentendre and Esztergom, Visegrád (pronounced *Vee*-sheh-grod) is a sparsely populated, sleepy riverside village, which makes its history all the more fascinating and hard to believe. The Romans built a fort here, which was still standing when Slovak settlers gave the town its present name in the 9th or 10th century. It means "High Castle." After the Mongol invasion (1241–42), construction began on both the present ruined hilltop citadel and the former riverside palace. Eventually, Visegrád boasted one of the finest royal palaces ever built in Hungary.

ESSENTIALS

GETTING THERE & GETTING AROUND   See "Getting to the Danube Bend," above. **Visegrád Tours,** RÉV u. 15 (www.visegrad.org; © **26/398-160**), is located across the road from the RÉV ferryboat landing. It is open daily year-round, 8am to 5:30pm. The liveliest time is summer, when there are historical recreations, but other times of the year are fine for a sedate vacation experience.

EXPLORING VISEGRÁD

Once covering much of the area where the boat landing and Fő utca (Main St.) are now found are the excavated remnants and restoration of parts of the **King Matthias Museum ★★**, at Fő u. 23 (www.visegradmuzeum.hu; ℂ **26/597-010**). The tower of the lower castle, known as **Solomon's Tower,** was built in the 13th century. Entrance to the palace is 1,100 Ft and 700 Ft for the tower. Both are open Tuesday to Sunday from 9am to 5pm, but the tower is closed from October 1 to April 30. The buried ruins of the palace, having achieved a near-mythical status, were not discovered until the 21st century.

The **Fellegvár (Cloud Castle) ★★★** (www.parkerdo.hu/visegradi_var; ℂ **26/398-101**), a mountaintop citadel above Visegrád, affords one of the finest views you'll find over the Danube. Admission to the citadel is 1,700 Ft. It is open daily from 9:00am to 5:00pm from March 15 to April 30 and the month of October; it stays open one hour later May 1 to September 30; all November and January 2 to March 14 9:00am to 4:00pm; closed December. The "**City Bus,**" a van taxi that awaits passengers outside Visegrád Tours, takes people up the steep hill for a steep fare of 2,500 Ft apiece or 4,000 Ft for a round-trip, but to get the round-trip fare, you must stay at the top a maximum of 30 minutes; otherwise, it is again 2,500 Ft for the ride down. Note that it is not a casual walk to the citadel; consider it a day hike and pack accordingly with bottled water.

WHERE TO STAY

Good accommodations can be found at **Honti Panzió and Hotel,** Fő utca 66 (www.ohm.hotelhonti.hu; ℂ **26/398-120**). Double rooms cost 14,000 Ft in the Panzio and 16,000 Ft in the hotel, both with multinight packages. Hotel rooms are a bit larger than the Panzio rooms. All rates include breakfast and VAT, but not the 300 Ft tax per person per night; parking is provided.

WHERE TO EAT

Set on a hilltop featuring one of the finest views of the Danube bend, **Nagyvillám Vadászcsárda (Big Lightning Hunter's Inn),** Fekete-hegy (www.nagyvillam.hu; ℂ **26/398-070**), infuses a leafy, countryside dinner with an elegant and warm atmosphere. Although vegetarians may struggle with a menu overwhelmingly consisting of meat and game, it is nevertheless an extensive menu combining Mediterranean influences with Hungarian recipes using 12 varieties of wild forest mushroom. It's open Monday to Friday 11am to 4pm, weekends 11am to 6pm.

Esztergom

Formerly a Roman settlement, **Esztergom** (pronounced *Ess*-tair-gome) was the seat of the Hungarian kingdom for 300 years. Hungary's first king, István I (Stephen I), renamed from Vajk by German priests, received the crown from the pope in A.D. 1000. He converted Hungary to Catholicism, and Esztergom became the country's center of the early church. Although its glory days are long gone due to invasions from the Mongols and later the Turks, it was rebuilt in the 18th and 19th centuries. This quiet town remains the seat of the archbishop primate, known as the "Hungarian Rome."

From Esztergom west all the way to the Austrian border, the Danube marks the border between Hungary and Slovakia, with an international ferry crossing at Esztergom. There's little to entice anyone to stay overnight here with Budapest so close, so make this a day trip and return to Budapest at the end of the day.

ESSENTIALS

GETTING THERE & GETTING AROUND   See "Getting to the Danube Bend," above. The **train** station is on the outskirts of town, while the tourist information center is in the city center. The primary reason to take the trip here is the cathedral, but you will have to take a **taxi** or **walk** because all public transportation in the town of Esztergom ended as of July 2011 (although it is always worth checking to see if it has restarted again). Take heart, the walk from the station will only take you about 30 minutes at a healthy pace, longer if you want to stroll leisurely along the river path part of the way. The only buses you may see are those going to the hypermarkets.

EXPLORING ESZTERGOM

Esztergom Cathedral ★★ ☺   This massive, neoclassical cathedral on Szent István tér on Castle Hill, is the largest church in Hungary. In good weather, it is a 3.5km (2-mile) walk The cathedral is Esztergom's most popular attraction and one of Hungary's most impressive buildings. Built in the last century, it was to replace the original cathedral ruined during the Turkish occupation. The blue and red marble coloring in the church and chapel is striking, and it claims the world's largest altarpiece painted on one continuous piece of canvas. The crypt, built in old Egyptian style with a magnificent statue of an angel, is also the last resting place of bishops. The cathedral **treasury (*kincstár*)** ★ contains a dazzling array of ecclesiastical jewels and gold works. If you brave the ascent of the cupola, you're rewarded with unparalleled views of Esztergom and the surrounding Hungarian and Slovakian countryside. There is a warning for the cupola that if you're agoraphobic, you should not risk it. Actually, it should be if you're claustrophobic, as the staircase and walking areas are extremely narrow. If you happen to be in town during the first week of August, don't miss out on one of the classical guitar concerts performed in the cathedral; the acoustics are said to be sublime. The concerts are part of Esztergom's annual **International Guitar Festival** ★★.

Szent István tér. www.bazilika-esztergom.hu. ℂ **33/411-895.** Cathedral admission free; treasury 800 Ft adults, 350 Ft children; cupola 600 Ft; crypt 200 Ft. Cathedral end-Mar–end-Oct daily 8am–6pm, Nov–end-Mar daily 8am–4pm; treasury and crypt Mar–Oct daily 9am–4:30pm, Nov–Jan Tues–Fri 11am–3:30pm & Sat–Sun 10am–3:30pm; cupola Apr–Oct daily 9:30am–5pm, closed Feb & most Mar.

WHERE TO EAT

Creative specialties abound at **Padlizsán Étterem** ★★★, Pazmány Peter u. 21 (www.padlizsanetterem.hu; ℂ **33/311-212**), a homey restaurant behind the basilica. In warm weather, enjoy the view of the basilica above the hill. We particularly like their pork dishes, but fellow diners appreciated the pikeperch choices.

For a few other cafes and snack stops you can try the limited selections on the main square, **Széchenyi tér.**

11 IRELAND

by Christi Daugherty & Jack Jewers

Which Ireland do you want to visit? The traditional "Auld Country" of thatched cottages, craggy seascapes, and pubs where the craic is good and the Guinness flows as freely as the music? Or do you imagine the modern, urban country of trendy bistros, sushi bars, and modern-art galleries? These days, both await you with open arms.

Old Ireland is still there to some extent, and the country remains a land of breathtaking beauty. But today's Ireland is fiercely aware of its modernity and sophistication, despite the economic crash that has made the "Celtic Tiger" glory days of the 1990s and 2000s a somewhat bitter memory. After the mid-1990s, some "old Ireland" disappeared, replaced by designer shops, stomped by an army of Manolo Blahniks, and hidden behind a new forest of overpriced suburban McMansions.

Meanwhile, in Northern Ireland—the six counties that still remain part of the United Kingdom—the peace agreement has continued to hold. This is despite some shaky moments and tough tests, including the occasional flare-up of violence in Derry or Belfast. The fact that all sides remain committed to peace is enough to give you hope that the dangerous old days of the Troubles really are long gone.

All of this adds up to one thing: whether you're rushing to see old Ireland before it disappears, or getting to know the trendy modern country that is still, in some ways, searching for a new identity, go now. Ireland may not be as rich as it was, nor even as happy. But one thing's for certain: these sure are interesting times for this fascinating, infuriating, beguiling, and intoxicating old country.

DUBLIN

"Seedy elegance" aptly described much, if not most, of Dublin until the mid-1990s, when the city's transformation from endearingly frumpy to cutting-edge cool began. Today's Dublin is a trendy place, where expensive restaurants and nightspots sprout up (and, in these tough times, disappear) with startling speed. It is the emotional and political center of the country.

Essentials
GETTING THERE
BY PLANE **Dublin International Airport** (www.dublinairport.com; ✆ **01/814-1111**) is 11km (6¾ miles) north of the city center. A **Travel**

Information Desk in the Arrivals Concourse provides information on public bus and rail services throughout the country.

An excellent airport-to-city shuttle bus service called **AirCoach** (www.aircoach.ie; ✆ 01/844-7118) operates 24 hours a day (every 10 min. during the day, 20 min. at night, and hourly after midnight). Its buses run direct from the airport to Dublin's city center and south side, stopping at O'Connell Street, St. Stephen's Green, Fitzwilliam Square, Merrion Square, Ballsbridge, and Donnybrook—that is, all the key hotel and business districts. The fare is €7 one-way or €12 round-trip (children 11 and under €2 one-way, €4 round-trip); buy your ticket from the driver. Although AirCoach is slightly more expensive than other bus services (see below), it makes fewer intermediary stops, so it is faster (the journey to the city center takes about 45 min.), and it brings you right into the hotel districts.

If you need to connect with the Irish bus or rail service, the **Airlink Express Coach** (www.dublinbus.ie; ✆ 01/844-4265) provides express coach services from the airport into central Dublin and beyond. The destination may be shown in English or Gaelic on the timetable. Route 747 goes to the city's central bus station, **Busáras,** on Store Street, and on to **O'Connell Street** (*Sráid Uí Chonaill*) and **Heuston** railway station (*Stáisiún Iarnród Heuston*). Service runs daily from 6am to 11:30pm

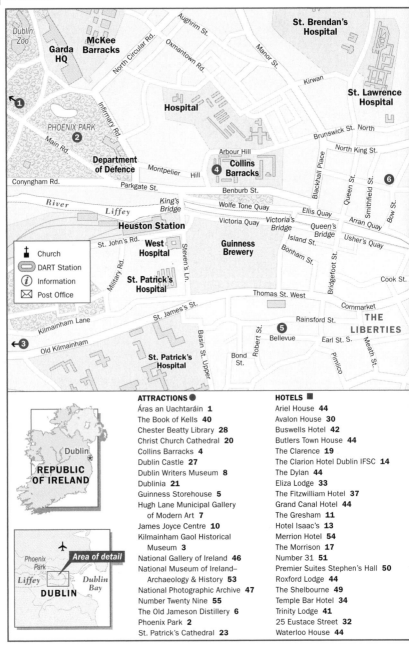

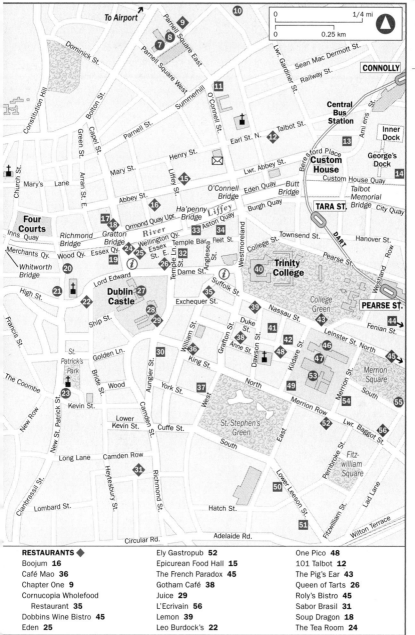

(Sun 7am–11:30pm), with departures every 15 to 20 minutes. One-way fare is €6 for adults and €3 for children 11 and under.

Finally, **Dublin Bus** (www.dublinbus.ie; ✆ 01/836-6111) runs connections between the airport and the city center from 6am to 11:30pm. The one-way trip takes about 30 minutes, and the fare is €6. Nos. 16a, 41, 41b, and 748 all serve the city center from Dublin Airport. Consult the Travel Information Desk in the Arrivals Concourse to figure out which bus will bring you closest to your hotel.

For speed and ease—especially if you have a lot of luggage—a **taxi** is the best way to get directly to your hotel or guesthouse. Depending on your destination in Dublin, fares average between €20 and €30. Surcharges include €.50 for each additional passenger and for each piece of luggage. Depending on traffic, a cab should take between 20 and 45 minutes to get into the city center. A 10% tip is standard. Taxis are lined up at a first-come, first-served taxi stand outside the arrivals terminal.

Major international and local car-rental companies operate desks at Dublin Airport.

BY FERRY   Passenger and car ferries from Britain arrive at the **Dublin Ferryport** (✆ 01/855-2222), on the eastern end of the North Docks, and at **Dún Laoghaire Ferryport** (✆ 01/842-8864). Call **Irish Ferries** (www.irishferries.co.uk; ✆ 0818/300-400), **P&O Irish Sea** (www.poirishsea.com; ✆ 01/407-3434), or **Stena Line** (www.stenaline.com; ✆ 01/204-7700) for bookings and information. There is a bus and taxi service from both ports.

BY TRAIN   **Irish Rail** (www.irishrail.ie; ✆ 01/850-366222), also called Iarnród Éireann, operates a daily train service to Dublin from Belfast, Northern Ireland, and all major cities in the Irish Republic, including Cork, Galway, Limerick, Killarney, Sligo, Wexford, and Waterford. Trains from the south, west, and southwest arrive at **Heuston Station,** Kingsbridge, off St. John's Road; from the north and northwest at **Connolly Station,** Amiens Street; and from the southeast at **Pearse Station,** Westland Row, Tara Street.

BY BUS   Bus Éireann (www.buseireann.ie; ✆ 01/836-6111) operates daily express coach and local bus service from all major cities and towns in Ireland into Dublin's central bus station, **Busáras,** Store Street.

BY CAR   If you are arriving by car from other parts of Ireland or on a car ferry from Britain, all main roads lead into the heart of Dublin and are well signposted to An Lar (City Centre). To bypass the city center, the East Link (toll bridge €2) and West Link are signposted, and M50 circuits the city on three sides. See also "Getting Around, By Car" below.

VISITOR INFORMATION

Dublin Tourism (www.visitdublin.com; ✆ 1850/230-330) operates walk-in visitor centers in Dublin that are open every day except Christmas. The principal center is on Suffolk Street, Dublin 2, open from June to August Monday to Saturday from 9am to 6:30pm, Sunday and bank holidays 9am to 5:30pm, and the rest of the year Monday to Saturday 9am to 5:30pm, Sunday and bank holidays 10:30am to 3pm. The Suffolk Street office has a currency exchange counter, a car-rental counter, an accommodations-reservations service, bus and rail information desks, a gift shop, and a cafe.

The other centers are on **Upper O'Connell Street,** Dublin 1; the arrivals hall of **Dublin Airport;** and the ferry terminal at **Dún Laoghaire Harbor** (all telephone inquiries should be directed to the number listed above). Opening times are generally Monday to Saturday 9am–5pm.

For information on Ireland outside of Dublin, contact **Bord Fáilte** (www.discover ireland.com; ✆ **1850/230-330** in Ireland).

At any of these centers you can pick up the free *Tourism News. In Dublin,* a biweekly arts-and-entertainment magazine selling for €3, is available at most newsstands, or online at www.indublin.ie.

CITY LAYOUT

The city is neatly divided down the middle by the curves of the River Liffey, which empties into the sea at the city's farthest edge. To the north and south, the city center is encircled by canals: The **Royal Canal** arcs across the north and the **Grand Canal** through the south. Traditionally, the area south of the river has been Dublin's buzzing, prosperous hub. It still holds most of the best hotels, restaurants, shops, and sights, but the **Northside** has undergone something of a renaissance in the last few years, with a slew of hip new bars and trendy hotels. Both north and south, Dublin is compact and easily walked in an hour. In fact, a 45-minute walk from the bucolic peace of St. Stephen's Green, up Grafton Street, and across the Liffey to the top of O'Connell Street offers a good overview of the city's prosperous present and troubled past.

The most interesting suburban towns tend to be along Dublin Bay—these include (heading north along the bay) Drumcondra, Glasnevin, Howth, Clontarf, and Malahide; and (heading south along the bay) Ballsbridge, Blackrock, Dún Laoghaire, Dalkey, Killiney, Rathgar, and Rathmines.

GETTING AROUND

BY BUS **Dublin Bus** (www.dublinbus.ie; ✆ **01/873-4222**) operates a fleet of green double-deckers and single-deckers, and minibuses (the latter charmingly called "imps"). Most originate on or near O'Connell Street, Abbey Street, and Eden Quay on the Northside, and at Aston Quay, College Street, and Fleet Street on the south side. Bus stops, which resemble big blue or green lollipops, are located every two or three blocks on main thoroughfares. To tell where the bus is going, look at the destination street and bus number above its front window; those heading for the city center indicate that with an odd mix of Gaelic and Latin: VIA AN LAR.

Bus services run daily throughout the city, starting at 6am (later on Sunday—usually about 9am), with the last bus at around 11:30pm. On Thursday, Friday, and Saturday nights, the **Nitelink** service runs from the city center to the suburbs from midnight to 3am. Buses operate every 10 to 15 minutes for most runs; schedules are posted on revolving notice boards at bus stops.

Inner-city fares are based on distances traveled. The minimum fare is €1.40; the maximum fare for journeys in the city center is €2.65, rising to €4.10 if you go as far as the outer suburbs. The Nitelink fare is a flat €5. Buy your tickets from the driver as you enter the bus; exact change is required, so have some change available.

Following a spate of robberies of bus drivers in Dublin a few years ago, all buses in the capital now operate a 24-hour "Autofare" scheme. This means that fares must be paid with coins directly into a fare box next to the driver's cab, after which a ticket is issued. Notes are not accepted and no change is given. If you have to pay more than the cost of the ticket, the driver will issue you a refund ticket, which must be presented along with your travel ticket at the Dublin Bus office on Upper O'Connell Street to claim a refund for the difference. Inevitably this is rarely worth the effort, so be sure to have plenty of change handy if you're going to travel by bus, or buy a **bus pass.** Discounted 1-day, 3-day, and 5-day "rambler" passes are available in advance. The 1-day bus-only pass costs €6; the 3-day pass costs €13.50; and the

Leap Cards

Introduced in 2012, the excellent Leap Card is an electronic payment system for public transport, similar to London's Oyster or New York's MetroCard. You pay a refundable deposit of €3 for a card, which you then top up with a pre-payment of between €5 and €125. This gives you significantly reduced fares on all Dublin public transport, automatically deducted when you swipe the card against a reader. You can buy them at hundreds of shops around the city, including Dublin Airport (look for the Leap Card logo of a jolly jumping frog), or online at www.leapcard.ie.

5-day pass goes for €20. Another option worth considering is the **freedom ticket.** Specially designed for tourists, it works like a standard 3-day bus pass, but also includes unlimited travel on the Airlink, Nitelink, and Dublin City Tour buses. The cost is €28 adults, €12 children 13 and under.

BY DART   While Dublin has no subway in the strict sense, there is an electric rapid-transit train, known as the **DART** (Dublin Area Rapid Transit; www.dart.ie; *©* **01/703-3592**). It travels mostly at ground level or on elevated tracks, linking the city-center stations at **Connolly Station, Tara Street,** and **Pearse Street** with suburbs and seaside communities as far as Malahide to the north and Greystones to the south. Services operate roughly every 10 to 20 minutes Monday to Saturday from around 6am to midnight and Sunday from 9:30am to 11pm. Typical adult fares cost around €1.60 for a single journey; combination rail and bus tickets, valid all day within the "short hop" zone of the city center, start from €9 adults. One-day, 3-day, and 10-trip passes, as well as student and family tickets, are available at reduced rates from ticket windows in stations. There are plans to extend the system into a proper subway, but this is unlikely to start until at least 2016.

BY TRAM   A relative newcomer to Dublin's public transportation network, the sleek light-rail tram system known as **LUAS** (www.luas.ie; *©* **01/800-300-604**) opened in 2004. With trams traveling at a maximum speed of 70kmph (45 mph) and departing every 5 minutes in peak hours, LUAS has been popular enough to make at least a small impact on Dublin's appalling traffic congestion. Services run from 5:30am (6:30am Sat) to 12:30pm Monday to Saturday, and 7am to 11:30pm on Sundays. The lines link the city center at **Connolly Station** and **St. Stephen's Green** with the suburbs of Tallaght in the southwest and Dundrum and Sandyford to the south. For visitors, one of the handiest reasons to use the LUAS is to get between Connolly and Heuston stations. The one-way fare within the city center is €1.70 adults, €1 children. One-day and multiple-day passes are also available.

ON FOOT   Marvelously compact, Dublin is ideal for walking, as long as you remember to look right and then left (and in the direction opposite your instincts if you're from the U.S. or Canada) before crossing the street. Pedestrians have the right of way at specially marked, zebra-striped crossings (there are usually two flashing lights at these intersections). For some walking-tour suggestions, see "Seeing the Sights," later in this chapter.

BY TAXI   It's very difficult to hail a taxi on the street; instead, they line up at taxi stands (called "ranks") outside major hotels, at bus and train stations, and on prime thoroughfares such as Upper O'Connell Street, College Green, and the Northside of St. Stephen's Green.

You can also phone for a taxi. Some of the companies that operate a 24-hour radio-call service are **Co-Op** (✆ 01/677-7777), **Trinity** (✆ 01/708-2222), and **VIP/ ACE Taxis** (✆ 01/478-3333). If you need a wake-up call, VIP offers that service, along with especially courteous dependability.

Taxi rates are fixed by law and posted in each vehicle. The following are typical travel costs in the city center: The starting fare for the first kilometer (⅔ mile) is €4.10 by day and €4.45 at night. For the next 14km (8⅔ miles) the fare is €1.03 per kilometer by day, €1.35 by night, rising to a maximum of €1.77 per kilometer thereafter, day and night. You may instead be charged an equivalent price per minute (which runs a minimum €.36 during the day, up to a maximum of €.63 at night). It costs an extra €2 if you order a cab by phone, with €1 extra per passenger. *Be warned:* At some hotels, staff members will tack on as much as €5 for calling you a cab, although this practice violates city taxi regulations. Ask before you request a taxi whether you'll be charged.

BY CAR   Unless you plan to do a lot of driving from Dublin to neighboring counties, it's not practical or affordable to rent a car. If you must drive in Dublin, remember to keep to the *left-hand side of the road,* and don't drive in bus lanes. The most reliable and safest places to park are at surface parking lots or in multistory **car parks** in central locations, such as Kildare Street, Lower Abbey Street, Marlborough Street, and St. Stephen's Green West, although these can be expensive. The speed limit in the city is 50kmph (31 mph), although the last time anybody ever reached it was probably around 1955. Seat belts must be worn at all times by both drivers and passengers.

BY BIKE   The steady flow of Dublin traffic rushing down one-way streets may be a little intimidating for most cyclists, but there are many opportunities for more relaxed pedaling in residential areas and suburbs, along the seafront, and around Phoenix Park. The Dublin Tourism office can supply you with bicycle touring information and suggested routes. Bicycle rental averages around €20 per day, €75 per week, with a €70 deposit. In the center, bicycles can be rented from **Cycleways,** 185 Parnell St., Dublin 1 (www.cycleways.com; ✆ 01/873-4748).

[FastFACTS] DUBLIN

ATMs/Banks   Nearly all banks are open Monday to Friday 10am to 4pm (sometimes 5pm Thurs) and have ATMs that accept Cirrus network cards as well as MasterCard and Visa. Convenient locations include the Bank of Ireland, at 2 College Green, Dublin 2, and 88 Camden St., Dublin 2; and the Allied Irish Bank (AIB), at 100 Grafton St., Dublin 2, and 37 O'Connell St., Dublin 1.

Business Hours Museums and sights are generally open 10am to 5pm Tuesday to Saturday, and 2 to 5pm Sunday. **Shops** generally open 9am to 6pm Monday to Saturday, with late opening on Thursday. In the city center most department stores and many shops are open noon to 6pm on Sunday.

Currency   The official currency of Ireland is the **euro** (€).

Currency Exchange Currency-exchange services, signposted as BUREAU DE CHANGE, are in most Dublin banks and at many branches of the Irish post office system, known as **An Post.** A bureau de change operates daily during flight arrival and departure times at Dublin airport; a foreign-currency note-exchanger machine is also available on a 24-hour basis in the main arrivals hall. Some hotels and travel agencies offer bureau de change services, although the best rate of exchange is usually with your bank card at an ATM.

Doctors If you need to see a physician, most hotels and guesthouses will contact a house doctor for you. The **American Embassy** (see "Embassies & Consulates," below) can provide a list of doctors in the city and you should contact them first. Otherwise, you can try the **Dame Street Medical Center,** 16 Dame St. (ℂ **01/679-0754**), or the **Suffolk Street Surgery,** 107 Grafton St. (ℂ **01/679-8181**).

Drugstores Centrally located drugstores, known locally as pharmacies or chemists, include **City Pharmacy,** 14 Dame St., Dublin 2 (ℂ **01/670-4523**) and branches of **Boots,** 20 Henry St. (ℂ **01/873-0209**), also at the Jervis Shopping Centre, Jervis St. (ℂ **01/878-0200**) and 12 Grafton St. (ℂ **01/677-3000**).

Embassies & Consulates The **American Embassy** is at 42 Elgin Rd., Ballsbridge, Dublin 4 (http://dublin.usembassy.gov/; ℂ **01/668-8777**); the **Canadian Embassy** at 7–8 Wilton Terrace, 3rd Floor, Dublin 2 (http://www.canadainternational.gc.ca/ireland-irlande/; ℂ **01/234-4000**); the **British Embassy** at 29 Merrion Rd., Dublin 2 (http://britishembassyinireland.fco.gov.uk/en/; ℂ **01/205-3700**); and the **Australian Embassy** at 7th Floor, Fitzwilton House, Wilton Terrace, Dublin 2 (www.ireland.

embassy.gov.au; ℂ **01/664-5300**). In addition, there is an **American Consulate** at 120 Malone Road, Belfast BT9 5HR (http://belfast.usconsulate.gov/; ℂ **028/9038-6100**).

Emergencies For police, fire, or other emergencies, dial ℂ **999** or ℂ **112.**

Hospitals For emergency care, two of the most modern are **St. Vincent's University Hospital,** Elm Park (www.stvincents.ie; ℂ **01/221-4000**), on the south side of the city, and **Beaumont Hospital,** Beaumont (www.beaumont.ie; ℂ **01/809-3000**), on the Northside.

Internet Access Internet access is everywhere in Dublin; look for signs in cafes, pubs, shopping malls, hotels, and hostels. Like all of Dublin's public libraries, the **Central Library,** in the ILAC Centre, off Henry Street, Dublin 1 (ℂ **01/873-4333**), has a bank of PCs with free Internet access. Centrally located Internet cafes include the **Central Internet Cafe**, 6 Grafton St. (ℂ 01/677-8298) and **Global Internet Café,** 8 Lower O'Connell St. (ℂ **01/878-0295**). A half-hour online averages €4. Most hotels now have Wi-Fi, although it's not always free (especially in the larger places).

Post Office The Irish post office is best known by its Gaelic name, **An Post.** The **General Post Office (GPO)** is located on O'Connell Street, Dublin 1 (www.anpost.ie;

ℂ **01/705-7000**). Hours are Monday to Saturday 8:30am to 6pm. Branch offices, identified by the sign OIFIG AN POST/POST OFFICE, are generally open Monday to Saturday, 9am to 5pm.

Taxes Sales tax is called VAT (value-added tax) and is often already included in the price quoted to you or shown on price tags. VAT rates vary—for hotels, restaurants, and car rentals, it's 13.5% (temporarily reduced to 9% until the end of 2013); for souvenirs and gifts, it's 21%. If you're not a citizen of an E.U. country, you're entitled to have this money refunded. You can get your money back through **Global Blue** (www.global-blue.com), the world's largest private company offering VAT refunds. If a shop isn't part of the Global Refund network, get a full receipt at the time of purchase that shows the shop's name, address, and VAT paid. When you're ready to depart Ireland, go to the Customs office at the airport or ferry port and have your receipts stamped; then send the stamped receipts back to the store where you made your purchase, which will then mail you a VAT refund check.

Telephone The **country code** for the Republic of Ireland is **353.** The **city code** for Dublin is **01.** If you're calling from outside Ireland, drop the initial 0 (zero) from the city code. Thus, to call Dublin from the United States, you would dial ℂ **011-353-1,** followed by the seven-digit local number; from the U.K. dial **00-353-1.** For direct-dial calls to the United States, dial the international access code (**00** from Ireland), and then the U.S. country code **(1),** followed by area code and number. To place a collect call to the United States from Ireland, dial ℭ **1-800/550-000** for USA Direct service. The toll-free international access codes are **AT&T,** ℭ **1-800-550-000; Sprint,** ℭ **1-800-552-001;** and **MCI,** ℭ **1-800-551-001.**

You can rent a cellphone for €70 per week plus call charges from **Rentaphone Ireland** (www.cell-phone-ireland.com; ℭ **087/683-4563**). They have a pick-up point at Dublin Airport. However, prepaid "burner" phones (called

"pay-as-you-go" in Ireland) are usually the cheapest option. Several of the big phone store chains, including **O2** and **Vodafone,** have branches at Dublin Airport; alternatively, try the **Carphone Warehouse** at 30 Grafton St., Dublin 2 (www.carphonewarehouse.ie; ℭ **185/042-4800**). The supermarket chain **Tesco** sells phones for €20, with calls to the U.S. at ¢2 per minute (bought in €10 bundles). You can also call or text other people with Tesco phones for free. There are several branches in Dublin, including Fleet St., Temple Bar, Dublin 2 (ℭ **189/092-8523**), and Jervis St., Dublin 1 (ℭ **189/092-8472**). The Irish toll-free number for **directory assistance** is ℭ **11811.**

Tipping Some hotels and guesthouses add a service charge to the bill, usually 12.5% to 15%, although some smaller places add only 10% or nothing at all. If you feel the service charge is sufficient, there is no need for more gratuities. If, however, staff members have provided exceptional service, by all means tip them extra. For taxi drivers, tip as you would at home, 10% to 15%. For restaurants, the policy is usually printed on the menu—either a gratuity of 10% to 15% is automatically added to your bill or it's left up to you (always ask if you are in doubt). As a rule, bartenders do not expect a tip, except when table service is provided.

Exploring Dublin

Áras an Uachtaráin (The Irish President's House) ★ GOVERNMENT BUILDING Áras an Uachtaráin (Irish for "House of the President") was once the Viceregal Lodge, the summer retreat of the British viceroy, whose main digs were in Dublin Castle. From what were never humble beginnings, the original 1751 country house has been expanded several times, gradually accumulating more splendor. Sadly, you see only a bit of it. The house is open to the public only on Saturdays, and then only for guided tours. A bus brings you from Phoenix Park Visitor Centre to the house, and the main focus of the 1-hour guided tour is the state reception rooms. Only 525 tickets are given out each Saturday morning on a first-come, first-served basis. No backpacks, strollers, cameras, or cellphones are allowed.

In Phoenix Park, Dublin 8. www.president.ie. ℭ **01/677-0095.** Free admission. Summer Sat 10am–5pm; winter 10:15am–3:30pm. Closed Dec 24–26. Same-day tickets issued at Phoenix Park Visitor Centre (see below). Bus: 10, 37, or 39.

The Book of Kells 👜 MUSEUM   This extraordinary hand-drawn manuscript of the four gospels, dating from the year 800, is one of Ireland's jewels, and with elaborate scripting and colorful illumination, it is undeniably magnificent. It is displayed, along with another early Christian manuscript, at Trinity College's Old Library. Unfortunately, the need to protect the books for future generations means that there's little for you to see. The volumes are very small and displayed inside a wooden cabinet shielded by bulletproof glass. So all you really see here are the backs of a lot of tourists leaning over a small table trying to get a peek at two pages of the ancient books. It's quite anticlimactic, but the Library's Long Room goes some way toward making up for that, at least for bibliophiles. The grand, chained library holds many rare works on Irish history and has frequently changing displays of rare works. Still, it's hard to say that it's all worth the large admission fee. For a cheaper and more fulfilling alternative, try the Chester Beatty Library (below).

College Green, Dublin 2. www.tcd.ie. © **01/608-2320.** Admission to Book of Kells €9 adults, €8 seniors and students, €18 families, free for children 11 and under. Combination tickets for the Library and Dublin Experience also available. Mon–Sat 9:30am–5pm; Sun 9:30am–4:30pm (opens at noon Oct–Apr). Bus: Any cross-city bus marked AN LAR.

Chester Beatty Library ★★★ 🏛 MUSEUM   Sir Alfred Chester Beatty was an American of Irish heritage who made a fortune in the mining industry and collected rare manuscripts. In 1956, he bequeathed his extensive collection to Ireland, and this fascinating museum inside the grounds of Dublin Castle was the ultimate result of his largesse. The breathtaking array of early illuminated gospels and religious manuscripts outshines the Book of Kells, and there are endless surprises here: ancient editions of the Bible and other religious books, beautiful copies of the Koran, and endless icons from Western, Middle Eastern, and Far Eastern cultures. This is one of the best museums in Ireland, and it's free.

Clock Tower Bldg., Dublin Castle, Dublin 2. www.cbl.ie. © **01/407-0750.** Free admission. Tues–Fri 10am–5pm (Mon–Fri May–Sept); Sat 11am–5pm; Sun 1–5pm. Tours €3 adults, €2 seniors and students. Wed 1pm, Sun 3 and 4pm. DART: Sandymount. Bus: 5, 6, 6A, 7A, 8, 10, 46, 46A, 46B, or 64.

Christ Church Cathedral ★ CATHEDRAL   This magnificent cathedral is difficult to appreciate fully if you walk up the street that runs in front of it, as it is actually below street level. It was designed to be seen from the river, so walk to it from the river side in order to appreciate its size and the way it dominates the neighborhood. It dates from 1038, when Sitric, Danish king of Dublin, built the first wooden Christ Church here. In 1171, the original foundation was extended into a cruciform and rebuilt in stone by the Norman warrior Strongbow (who some believe is buried here, though historians aren't convinced). However, the present structure dates mainly from 1871 to 1878, when a huge restoration took place that is controversial to this day, as much of the old detail was destroyed in the process. Still, magnificent stonework and graceful pointed arches survive. The best way to get a glimpse of what the original building must have been like is to visit the crypt, which is original to the 12th-century structure. There's a macabre mystery associated with the southeast chapel. Until recently it contained the preserved heart of St. Laurence O'Toole, but the relic was stolen in 2012. Police were baffled, as the theft was meticulously planned, but no other valuables were taken.

Christ Church Place, Dublin 8. © **01/677-8099.** Adults €6, students and children 14 and under €4. June–Aug Mon–Sat 9:30am–7pm, Sun 12:30–2:30pm and 4:30–6pm; Apr–May and Sept–Oct Mon–Sat 9:30am–6pm, Sun 12:30–2pm; Nov–Mar Mon–Sat 9:30am–5pm. Last entry 45 min before closing. Closed Dec 26. Bus: 21A, 50, 50A, 78, 78A, or 78B.

Collins Barracks ★ MUSEUM   Collins Barracks is a splendidly restored, early-18th-century military building, converted to display the vast decorative arts collection of the National Museum of Ireland. There's a huge display of Irish silver and furniture; a magnificent collection of rare 19th-century art from Tibet, China, and Japan; and an exhibition devoted to the work of the influential Irish designer and architect Eileen Gray (1878–1976). Collins Barracks is also a prime site for touring exhibitions, so check out the website to see what's on.

Benburb St., Dublin 7. www.museum.ie. ℂ **01/677-7444.** Free admission. Tues–Sat 10am–5pm; Sun 2–5pm. Bus: 34, 70, or 80.

Dublin Castle CASTLE/GOVERNMENT BUILDING   This 13th-century structure was the center of British power in Ireland for more than 7 centuries, until the new Irish government took it over in 1922. You can walk the grounds for free, although this is largely municipal office space now and is disappointingly dominated by parking lots. Still, it's worth a wander. To see the inside you have to join a tour, although they're reasonably priced; highlights include the 13th-century Record Tower; the State Apartments, once the residence of English viceroys; and the Chapel Royal, a 19th-century Gothic building with particularly fine plaster decoration and carved-oak gallery fronts and fittings. If they're open, check out the Undercroft, an excavated site on the grounds where an early Viking fortress stood, and the Treasury, built in the early 18th century. There are also a vaguely interesting on-site craft shop, heritage center, and restaurant.

Palace St. (off Dame St.), Dublin 2. www.heritageireland.ie/en/Dublin/DublinCastle. ℂ **01/645-8813.** Guided tours €4.50 adults, €3.50 seniors and students, €2 children 11 and under. Mon–Sat 10am–4:45pm; Sun and holidays noon–4:45pm. Guided tours every 20–25 min. Bus: 50, 50A, 54, 56A, 77, 77A, or 77B.

Dublinia ☺ MUSEUM   This museum aims to teach the little ones about the Viking and medieval history of Dublin through a series of interactive exhibits. With visual effects, background sounds (some on an annoying loop seem to follow you around repeating the same phrase over and over, until you can still hear it in your sleep weeks, even years later), and aromas ostensibly from that time. It's designed to stimulate, but will probably bore anybody over the age of 14. Still, you and the kids can dress up in medieval garb, be chained up as a Viking slave, and put yourselves in the town stocks. This seems to be one of those museums largely directed at kids on school field trips. If you plan to visit Dublinia and Christ Church Cathedral on the same day, keep hold of your ticket to claim reduced-price admission.

St. Michael's Hill, Christ Church, Dublin 8. www.dublinia.ie. ℂ **01/679-4611.** Adults €7.50, students €6.50, seniors €6.50, children 15 and under €5, families €23. Daily Mar–May & Aug–Sept 10am–5pm; Jun & Jul 9:30am–5pm; Oct–Feb 10am–4:30pm. Closed Dec 23–26 and Mar 17. Bus: 50, 78A, or 123.

Dublin Writers Museum ★★ 📷 MUSEUM   This excellent little museum represents the best of what literary galleries can be, and lovers of Irish literature will find it hard to tear themselves away. The attraction is more than just seeing Joyce's typewriter or reading early playbills for the Abbey Theatre when Yeats helped to run it. The draw also comes from long letters from Brendan Behan to friends, talking about parties he was invited to with the Marx Brothers in Los Angeles after he hit the big time, and scrawled notes from Behan, Joyce, and Beckett about work, life, and love. This museum opens a window and lets light shine on Ireland's rich literary heritage, and it is wonderful to walk in that glow.

18–19 Parnell Sq. N., Dublin 1. www.writersmuseum.com. ℂ **01/872-2077.** Adults €7.50, children 15 and under €4.70, family €18. Mon–Sat 10am–5pm, Sun (and Tues–Sat, late Dec.) 11am–5pm. Last admission 45 min. before closing. DART: Connolly Station. Bus: 11, 13, 16, 16A, 22, or 22A.

Guinness Storehouse ★ FACTORY TOUR/MUSEUM   Founded in 1759, the Guinness Brewery produces the distinctive dark stout known the world over. The tour takes in the whole place, starting in a converted 19th-century hops store, which

NATIVE behavior: THE ART OF POURING GUINNESS

No trip to Ireland is complete without sampling the national beverage, whether you call it Guinness or simply "the black stuff." Despite its thick-as-pitch color, don't be afraid of it; Guinness isn't a heavy beer, only 11 calories per ounce or about 150 calories per pint, about the same as domestic beer. Draft Guinness is actually lower in alcohol than Coors Light. To the Irish, it's a classic "session beer," one with low alcohol and a great taste that can be enjoyed without leaving you feeling bloated. There are plenty of hops thrown in to give it a robust taste, and the Irish will vouch for the old advertising slogan "Guinness is good for you."

Yet the Guinness ritual doesn't begin in the drinking; it starts in the pouring. And pouring the perfect pint is, as any respectable Irish barman will tell you, an art form known as the "two-shot pour." Watch as he quickly fills the pint glass three-quarters of the way with swirling stout, and then sets the glass on the counter for about a minute and a half so that the gas can break out. It's the 75% nitrogen to 25% carbon dioxide mix that builds the famous Guinness head. Next, the barman tops up the pint, and serves it while a sepia-colored storm brews inside. Patience, patience: No sipping until the pint has settled into a distinct line between the black stout and the honey-colored head. Classically, the head should stand "proud," just slightly above the rim of the glass and quite thick and moussey. And with a "Cheers!" or *"Slainte!"* (pronounced *slahn*-chuh, Irish for "To your health!") you're finally ready to enjoy your pint.

contains the World of Guinness Exhibition, then moves on to the Gilroy Gallery, dedicated to the famous design work of John Gilroy. Last but not least, stop in at the breathtaking Gravity Bar, where you can sample a glass of the famous brew in the glass-enclosed bar 61m (200 ft.) above the ground.

St. James's Gate, Dublin 8. www.guinness-storehouse.com. ℰ **01/408-4800.** Adults €15, seniors and students €11, children 6–12 €5, families €33. Daily 9:30am–5pm. Guided tours every half-hour. Bus: 51B, 78A, or 123.

Hugh Lane Municipal Gallery of Modern Art ★ ART MUSEUM   This small art gallery punches above its weight with a strong collection of Impressionist works, including pieces by Edgar Degas and Édouard Manet, sculptures by Auguste Rodin, a marvelous collection of stained glass by Dubliner Harry Clarke, and numerous works by modern Irish artists. One room contains the maddeningly cluttered studio of the Irish painter Francis Bacon, which the gallery purchased from London, moved to Dublin piece by piece, and then reconstructed here behind glass. They moved everything—right down to the dust. It's an excellent, compact art museum, and a great place to spend an afternoon.

Parnell Sq. N., Dublin 1. www.hughlane.ie. ℰ **01/222-5550.** Free admission. Tues–Thurs 10am–6pm; Fri–Sat 10am–5pm; Sun 11am–5pm. DART: Connolly or Tara stations. Bus: 3, 10, 11, 13, 16, or 19.

James Joyce Centre MUSEUM   Near Parnell Square and the Dublin Writers Museum, the Joyce Centre is in a restored 1784 Georgian town house, once the home of Denis J. Maginni, a dancing instructor who appears briefly in *Ulysses*. There are pros and cons to this place—there's not much in the way of real memorabilia related to Joyce, save for a writing table Joyce used in Paris when he was working on

Finnegan's Wake, although there are early copies of his work. Overall, it's best to come here if an interesting speaker is scheduled. True Joyce fans, of course, will be in heaven. Call about James Joyce walking tours.

35 N. Great George's St., Dublin 1. www.jamesjoyce.ie. ℂ **01/878-8547.** Adults €5; seniors, students, and children 9 and under €4. Separate fees for walking tours and events. Tues–Sat 10am–5pm, Sun noon–5pm. Closed Dec 21–Jan 3, Mar 17, and Good Friday. DART: Connolly. Bus: 3, 10, 11, 11A, 13, 16, 16A, 19, 19A, 22, or 22A.

Kilmainham Gaol Historical Museum ★★★ MUSEUM

For anyone interested in Ireland's struggle for independence from British rule, this is a key sight. Within these walls, Irish rebels became political prisoners from 1796 until 1924. The leaders of the 1916 Easter Uprising were all executed here, along with many others. The country's first *Taoiseach* (prime minister), Eamon de Valera, was the gaol's final prisoner. To walk along these corridors, through the grim exercise yard, or into the walled compound is a moving experience that lingers in your memory.

Kilmainham, Dublin 8. www.heritageireland.ie. ℂ **01/453-5984.** Guided tour: adults €6, seniors €4, students and children 15 and under €2, families €14. Apr–Sept daily 9:30am–6pm; Oct–Mar Mon–Sat 9:30am–5:30pm (last admission 4pm), Sun 10am–6pm. Last admission 1 hr. before closing. Bus: 51B, 78A, or 79.

The Old Jameson Distillery MUSEUM

This museum illustrates the history of Irish whiskey, known in Irish as *uisce beatha* (the water of life). Learn as much as you can from the film, whiskey-making exhibitions, and right-in-front-of-your-eyes demonstrations. At the conclusion of the tour, you can sip a little of the firewater and see what you think. A couple of lucky people on each tour are selected to sample different Irish, Scotch, and American whiskeys.

Bow St., Smithfield Village, Dublin 7. www.whiskeytours.ie. ℂ **01/807-2355.** Adults €13.50; seniors €9.60; students €10.60; children 17 and under €7.70; families €29. Daily 9:30am–6pm (last tour at 5pm). Closed Good Friday and Christmas holidays. Bus: 67, 67A, 68, 69, 79, or 90.

National Gallery of Ireland ★ ART MUSEUM

This museum houses Ireland's national art collection, as well as a collection of European art spanning the 14th to the 20th century. Every major European school of painting is represented, including selections by Italian Renaissance artists (notably Caravaggio's *The Taking of Christ*), French Impressionists, and Dutch 17th-century masters. The highlight of the Irish collection is the room dedicated to the mesmerizing works of Jack B. Yeats, brother of the poet W. B. Yeats. All public areas are wheelchair accessible. The museum has a shop and an excellent self-service cafe.

Merrion Sq. W., Dublin 2. www.nationalgallery.ie. ℂ **01/661-5133.** Free admission. Mon–Sat 9:30am–5:30pm (Thurs until 8:30pm); Sun noon–5:30pm. Free guided tours (meet in the Shaw Room) Sat 2pm; Sun 1 and 2pm. DART: Pearse. Bus: 5, 6, 7, 7A, 8, 10, 44, 47, 47B, 48A, or 62.

National Museum of Ireland–Archaeology and History ★★ MUSEUM

Four museums comprise the National Museum of Ireland—the **Collins Barracks** on Benburb St. (see p. 574); the **Natural History Museum** on Merrion St.; the **Country Life Museum** in County Mayo; and this, our runaway favorite, the **Archaeology & History Museum.** Many of the country's greatest archaeological treasures are here, including a breathtaking array of ancient Irish gold jewelry and artifacts discovered during the excavations of the early Dublin settlements. There are also important Christian relics here, including the Tara Brooch, the Ardagh Chalice, and the Cross of Cong.

Kildare St., Dublin 2. www.museum.ie. © **01/677-7444.** Free admission. Tues–Sat 10am–5pm; Sun 2–5pm. Closed Dec 25 and Good Friday. DART: Pearse. Bus: 7, 7A, 8, 10, 11, or 13.

National Photographic Archive MUSEUM   Until recently this archive used to house the National Library's 300,000-strong photo collection. Now that has been reabsorbed into the main library, but this building is still used for photographic exhibitions—and a very fine space it is too. Photos are rotated out regularly, so there's always something new to see. There is also a small gift shop.

Meeting House Sq., Temple Bar, Dublin 2. www.nli.ie. © **01/603-0374.** Free admission. Mon–Sat 10am–5pm; Sun noon–5pm. DART: Tara St. Bus: 21A, 46A, 46B, 51B, 51C, 68, 69, or 86.

Number Twenty Nine 🏠 ☺ MUSEUM   This little museum in a typical town house on one of the fashionable Georgian streets on Dublin's south side recreates the lifestyle of a middle-class family from 1790 to 1820. The exhibition is designed to be authentic all the way from the artifacts and artwork of the time to the carpets, curtains, plasterwork, and bell pulls. Tables are set with period dishes and the nursery is filled with toys from the time. It's both educational and particularly beautiful.

29 Lower Fitzwilliam St., Dublin 2. www.esb.ie/numbertwentynine. © **01/702-6165.** Tours: adults €6, seniors and students €3, children 15 and under free. Tues–Sat 10am–5pm; Sun noon–5pm. Closed 2 weeks at Christmas. DART: Pearse. Bus: 7, 8, 10, or 45.

Phoenix Park PARK/GARDEN   The vast green expanses of Phoenix Park are Dublin's playground, and it's easy to see why. This is a well-designed, user-friendly park crisscrossed by a network of roads and quiet pedestrian walkways that make its 704 hectares (1,740 acres) easily accessible. It's a gorgeous place to spend a restful afternoon, but there's plenty to do here should you feel active. The homes of the Irish president, **Áras an Uachtaráin** (p. 573), and the U.S. ambassador are both in the park. Livestock graze peacefully on pasturelands, deer roam the forested areas, and horses romp on polo fields. The Phoenix Park Visitor Centre has background information on the park's history, for the particularly curious. The cafe/restaurant is open 10am to 5pm weekdays, 10am to 6pm weekends. Free car parking is adjacent to the center. The park is 3km (1¾ miles) west of the city center on the north bank of the River Liffey.

The **Dublin Zoo** (www.dublinzoo.ie; © **01/677-1425**), also located in the park, provides a naturally landscaped habitat for more than 235 species of wild animals and tropical birds. Highlights for youngsters include the Children's Pets' Corner and a train ride around the zoo. There are playgrounds interspersed throughout the zoo, as well as several restaurants, coffee shops, and gift shops.

Phoenix Park: Dublin 8. www.heritageireland.ie. © **01/677-0095.** Free admission. Mid-Mar–Oct daily 10am–5:45pm; Nov–mid-Mar Wed–Sun 10am–5:45pm. Zoo: www.dublinzoo.ie. © **1800/924-848.** Adults €15, special needs adults €8.70, seniors €12, students €12.50, special needs children €5.50, children 3–16 €10.50, children 2 & under free. Daily Mar–Sept 9:30am–6pm; Oct 9:30am–5:30pm; Nov–Jan 9:30am–4pm; Feb 9:30am–5pm. Last admission 1hr. before closing Bus: 10, 25, or 26.

St. Patrick's Cathedral ★ CATHEDRAL   This is the largest church in Ireland, and one of the best-loved churches in the world. The present cathedral dates from 1190, but because of a fire and 14th-century rebuilding, not much of the original foundation remains. It is mainly early English in style, with a square medieval tower that houses the largest ringing peal bells in Ireland, with an 18th-century spire. The 90m-long (295-ft.) interior allows for sweeping perspectives of soaring vaulted ceilings and the vast nave. Consecrated by its namesake, it acts as a memorial to Irish war dead (represented in banners and flags throughout the building, some literally rotting away on their poles), and holds a memorial to the Irish soldiers who died fighting in the two world wars (although Ireland was neutral in World War II, at least 50,000 Irish volunteers died fighting with the British army in that war). St. Patrick's is closely associated with the writer **Jonathan Swift,** who was dean here from 1713 to 1745, and he is buried here alongside his longtime partner, Stella. St. Patrick's is the national cathedral of the Church of Ireland.

21–50 Patrick's Close, Patrick St., Dublin 8. www.stpatrickscathedral.ie. ℂ **01/475-4817.** Adults €5.50, seniors, students, and children 15 and under €4.70, families €15. Year-round Mon–Fri 9am–5pm; Nov–Feb Sat 9am–5pm, Sun 9–10:30am and 12:30–2:30pm; Mar–Oct Sat 9am–6pm, Sun 9–10:30am, 12:30–2:30pm, and 4:30–6pm. Closed except for services Dec 24–26. Bus: 65, 65B, 50, 50A, 54, 54A, 56A, or 77.

ORGANIZED TOURS

BUS TOURS   The city bus company, **Dublin Bus** (www.dublinbus.ie; ℂ **01/873-4222**) operates several tours of Dublin (see below), all of which depart from the Dublin Bus office at 59 Upper O'Connell St., Dublin 1. You can buy your ticket from the bus driver or book in advance at the Dublin Bus office or at the Dublin Tourism ticket desk on Suffolk Street.

The 75-minute guided **Dublin City Tour** operates on a hop-on, hop-off basis, connecting 10 major points of interest, including museums, art galleries, churches and cathedrals, libraries, and historic sites. Rates are €18 for adults, €14 seniors and students, €6 for children 15 and under. Tours operate daily from 9:30am to 6:30pm, every 10 to 15 minutes.

The 2¼-hour **Dublin Ghost Bus** is a spooky evening tour run by Dublin Bus, departing Monday to Thursday at 8pm, Friday and Saturday at 8 and 9:30pm. The tour addresses Dublin's history of felons, fiends, and phantoms. You'll see haunted houses, learn of Dracula's Dublin origins, and even get a crash course in body snatching. The fare is €28 (no children aged 13 and under allowed).

The 3-hour **North Coast and Castle Tour** departs daily at noon, traveling up the north coast to Malahide and Howth. Fares are €20 for adults, €14 for children 14 and under. The tour includes free admission to Malahide Castle.

The 3¾-hour **South Coast and Gardens Tour** departs daily at 10:30am, traveling south through the seaside town of Dún Laoghaire, through the upscale "Irish Riviera" villages of Dalkey and Killiney, and farther south to visit the vast Powerscourt Estate. Fares are €24 for adults, €12 for children 14 and under.

Gray Line (www.irishcitytours.com; ℂ **01/605-7705**) operates its own hop-on, hop-off city tour, covering all the same major sights as Dublin Bus's "Dublin City Tour." The first tours leave at 9:30am from outside the Dublin Tourism office at 14 Upper O'Connell St., and run every 10 to 15 minutes thereafter. The last departures are at 6pm in summer, 4:30pm in winter. You can also join the tour at any of a number of pickup points along the route and buy your ticket from the driver. Gray Line's Dublin city tour costs €18 for adults and €16 for seniors and students. Two kids can travel free with every adult. Gray Line also offers a range of full-day excursions from Dublin to such nearby sights as Glendalough, Newgrange, and Powerscourt. Adult fares for their other tours range from about €20 to €40.

WALKING TOURS   Small and compact, Dublin was made for walking. If you prefer to set off on your own, the **Dublin Tourism** office, St. Andrew's Church, Suffolk Street, Dublin 2, has maps for four tourist trails signposted throughout the city: Old City, Georgian Heritage, Cultural Heritage, and the "Rock 'n Stroll" music tour. However, if you'd like more guidance, historical background, or just some company, consider one of the following.

A walk with **Historical Walking Tours of Dublin** (www.historicalinsights.ie; ℂ **01/878-0227**) is like a 2-hour primer on Dublin's historic landmarks, from medieval walls and Viking remains around Wood Quay, to the architectural splendors of Georgian Dublin, to highlights of Irish history. Guides are historians, and participants are encouraged to ask questions. Tours assemble just inside the front gate of Trinity College daily at 11am and 3pm from May to September; daily at 11am in April and October; Friday to Sunday at 11am from November to March. No reservations are needed. Costs are €12 adults, €10 seniors and students, free for children 13 and under.

If you prefer an evening tour, there's the **Literary Pub Crawl** (ℂ **01/670-5602;** www.dublinpubcrawl.com), a winner of the "Living Dublin Award." The tour follows in the footsteps of Joyce, Behan, Beckett, Shaw, Kavanagh, and other Irish literary greats to local pubs, with actors providing humorous performances and commentary between stops. Throughout the night, there is a Literary Quiz with prizes for the winners. Tours happen every night at 7:30pm from April to October, and Thursday to Sunday at 7:30pm from November to March. Meet upstairs at the Drake Pub, 9 Duke Street, Dublin 2. The tour costs €12 adults, €10 students. No children allowed, for obvious reasons.

HORSE-DRAWN CARRIAGE TOURS   If you don't mind being conspicuous, you can tour Dublin in style in a handsomely outfitted horse-drawn carriage while your driver points out the sights. To arrange a ride, consult with one of the drivers stationed with carriages on the Grafton Street side of St. Stephen's Green. Rides range from a short swing around the Green to an extensive half-hour Georgian tour or an hour-long Old City tour. Rides are available on a first-come, first-served basis from April to October (weather permitting) and cost anywhere from €20 to €60 for one to four passengers, depending on the duration of the ride.

LAND & WATER TOURS   The immensely popular **Viking Splash Tour** (www. vikingsplash.ie; ℂ **01/707-6000**) is an unusual way for kids to see Dublin. Aboard a reconditioned American World War II amphibious landing craft, or "duck," this tour starts on land (from Bull Alley St. beside St. Patrick's Cathedral) and eventually splashes into the Grand Canal. Passengers wear horned Viking helmets (a reference to the original settlers of the Dublin area) and are encouraged to issue war cries at appropriate moments. One of the ducks even has bullet holes as evidence of its military service. Tours depart roughly on the half-hour every day 9:30am to 5pm and last an hour and 15 minutes. It costs €20 for adults, €10 for children 12 and under, €15 for teenagers (13 to 17), €18 seniors and students, and €60 for a family of five.

Where to Eat

HISTORIC OLD CITY & TEMPLE BAR/TRINITY COLLEGE AREA
Expensive

Eden ★★ INTERNATIONAL/MEDITERRANEAN   This is one of Temple Bar's hippest restaurants, a cool minimalist space with an open-plan kitchen overlooking Meeting House Square. The food is influenced by the global village, with a special penchant for Mediterranean flavors and local meats and seafood, so Castletownbere scallops may be served with a side of pasta with tomato dressing and chive beurre blanc, or filet of wild Irish venison alongside an *osso bucco*, rooster mash, and braised red cabbage.

Meeting House Sq. (entrance on Sycamore St.), Dublin 2. www.edenrestaurant.ie. ℂ **01/670-5372.** Main courses €20; fixed-price lunch 3 courses €25. AE, DC, MC, V. Daily 12:30–3pm; Mon–Sat 6–10:30pm; Sun 6–10pm. Bus: 51B, 51C, 68, 69, or 79.

The Pig's Ear ★★ MODERN IRISH   Head chef Stephen McAllister (of the superb One Pico) is something of a TV celebrity in these parts, although most customers are too cool to turn their heads if he puts in an appearance. The menu is an imaginative modern interpretation of traditional Irish cuisine; classics such as shepherd's pie are offset by the occasional dish out of left field, such as carrot soup with grapefruit and tarragon. The staff is lovely, the view of Trinity College from the upstairs dining room is handsome, and prices aren't too steep for a trendy joint.

4–5 Nassau St., Dublin 2. www.thepigsear.ie. ℭ **01/670-3865.** Reservations required. Main courses €17–€27; fixed-price early-bird menus €18–€28. AE, DC, MC, V. Mon–Sat 12:30–3pm and 5:30–10pm. DART: Pearse. Bus: 7, 8, 10, 11, or 46A.

The Tea Room ★★★ INTERNATIONAL   This ultrasmart restaurant, ensconced in the U2-owned Clarence hotel, is guaranteed to deliver one of your most memorable meals in Ireland. This gorgeous room's soaring yet understated lines are the perfect backdrop for the complex but controlled cooking that takes form in dishes like filet of John Dory with wild mushroom and razor clams, or red leg partridge with juniper flavored jus. The fixed-price "market menu," offering more straightforward fare, is exceptional value at €25 for three courses—although not available past 7:30pm on Thursday to Saturday nights.

The Clarence, 6–8 Wellington Quay, Dublin 2. www.theclarence.ie. ℭ **01/407-0800.** Reservations required. Main courses €13–€29; set lunches & dinners €20–€25 (3 courses). AE, MC, V. Mon–Fri 12:30–2pm; daily 6:30–9:45pm. Bus: 51B, 51C, 68, 69, or 79.

Inexpensive

Juice ★ VEGETARIAN   The best thing about Juice is that if nobody told you it was a vegetarian restaurant, you'd probably never notice, so interesting is the menu and so tasty is the food. The look of the place is lovely, with soaring 9m (30-ft.) ceilings softened by suspended sailcloth and muted lighting. Brunch is classic here, with pancakes, huevos rancheros, and French toast topped with fresh fruit or organic maple syrup. The rest of the day, you can sample the homemade dips—hummus, baba ghanouj, tapenade, roasted carrot pâté—with crudités and pita-bread strips. True to its name, there are about 30 kinds of juices and smoothies on offer.

Castle House, 73–83 S. Great Georges St., Dublin 2. www.juicerestaurant.ie. ℭ **01/475-7856.** Reservations recommended Fri–Sat. Main courses €12–€16, early-bird menu €15 (3 courses). AE, MC, V. Daily 11am–11pm. Bus: 50, 54, 56, or 77.

Leo Burdock's FISH AND CHIPS   Established in 1913, this quintessential Irish take-away shop across from Christ Church Cathedral is a cherished Dublin institution. Cabinet ministers, university students, and Hollywood stars alike (Tom Cruise and Liam Neeson are both fans) can be found at the counter waiting for fish bought fresh that morning and good Irish potatoes, both cooked in "drippings" (none of that modern cooking oil!). There's no seating, but you can sit on a nearby bench or stroll down to the park at St. Patrick's Cathedral.

2 Werburgh St., Dublin 8. www.leoburdocks.com. ℭ **01/454-0306.** Main courses €6–€8. No credit cards. Mon–Sat noon–midnight; Sun 4pm–midnight. Bus: 21A, 50, 50A, 78, 78A, or 78B.

Queen of Tarts ★★ ☺ CAFE   This tiny tearoom is one of our favorite places to blow the diet on decadent cakes and cookies, with a pot of tea on the side to make it all legal. Delicious, hearty breakfasts and light lunches are also served. Inch your way to one of the few tables (it's usually packed) and give in to temptation.

4 Cork Hill, Dame St. www.queenoftarts.ie. ℭ **01/633-4681.** Items €2–€5. No credit cards. Mon–Fri 8am–7pm; Sat 9am–7pm; Sun 10am–6pm. Bus: Any city-center bus.

ST. STEPHEN'S GREEN/GRAFTON STREET AREA
Very Expensive
One Pico ★★★ MODERN EUROPEAN   About a 5-minute walk from Stephen's Green, on a wee lane off Dawson Street, this is a sophisticated, grown-up, classy place, with excellent service and fantastic food. The food is a mixture of European influences in a menu that changes daily. If you're lucky, you might find the sea bream with saffron potato or the roast duck with sweet potato fondant. For dessert, a caramelized lemon tart is the end to a near-perfect meal. The fixed-price dinner menu is excellent value for those who want to treat themselves without breaking the bank, although you must be finished by 8:45pm.

5–6 Molesworth Place, Schoolhouse Lane, Dublin 2. www.onepico.com. © **01/676-0300.** Reservations required. Fixed-price menu lunch €20–€35, dinner €25–€39; dinner main courses €28–€35. AE, DC, MC, V. Mon–Sat 12:30–2:30pm and 6–11pm; Sun 6–8pm. DART: Pearse. Bus: 10, 11A, 11B, 13, or 20B.

Moderate
Café Mao ★ ASIAN   This is where to go when you feel like some Asian cooking with an exhilarating attitude. The exposed kitchen lines one entire wall, and the rest of the space is wide open—great for people-watching. The menu reads like a Best of Asia list: Thai fish cakes, *nasi goreng*, five spice chicken, salmon ramen. Everything is delicious—you can't go wrong. There are also branches in the Pavilion in Dún Laoghaire (© **01/214-8090**), and in Civic Square, Dundrum, Dublin 16 (© **01/296/2802**).

2 Chatham Row, Dublin 2. www.cafemao.com. © **01/670-4899.** Reservations recommended. Main courses €11–€17. AE, MC, V. Mon–Wed noon–10:30pm; Thurs noon–11pm; Fri–Sat noon–11:30pm; Sun noon–10pm. DART: Pearse. Bus: 10, 11A, 11B, 13, or 20B.

Inexpensive
Cornucopia Wholefood Restaurant ★★ 🍴 VEGETARIAN   This little cafe just off Grafton Street is one of the best vegetarian restaurants in the city, and also serves wholesome meals for people on various restricted diets (vegan, nondairy, low sodium, low fat). Soups are particularly good here, as are the salads and hot dishes such as roast squash and fennel with olive polenta and romescu sauce. This place is a delicious healthy alternative.

19 Wicklow St., Dublin 2. www.cornucopia.ie. © **01/677-7583.** Main courses €10–€13. MC, V. Mon–Sat 8:30am–8pm; Sun noon–7pm. Bus: Any city-center bus.

Lemon 🍴 ☺ PANCAKES   The kids are bound to drag you to this one with its bright orange interior and fresh crepes with a dazzling array of fillings. Go sensible and have a savory filling for breakfast (mushrooms and eggs) or dive into chocolate and banana. In addition to pancakes there are waffles served with fruit, ice cream, and most things naughty, and there's good coffee as well.

60 Dawson St. www.lemonco.com. © **01/672-8898.** Crepes €3.50–€10. No credit cards. Breakfast to early evening daily. DART: Pearse. Bus: 10, 11A, 11B, 13, or 20B.

FITZWILLIAM/MERRION SQUARE AREA
Very Expensive
L'Ecrivain ★★ FRENCH   This is one of Dublin's truly exceptional restaurants, from start to finish. The atmosphere is relaxed, welcoming, and unpretentious, and chef Derry Clarke's food is extraordinary. Most dishes consist of Irish ingredients, prepared without dense sauces. You might find, on the constantly changing menu, seared wild Irish venison loin with caramelized pear, or seared Bere Island scallops

with lobster strudel. Dinner prices are terrifying (and regularly raised), but the fixed-price lunch menus allow a chance to try the food here for slightly less.

109 Lower Baggot St., Dublin 2. www.lecrivain.com. ℂ **01/661-1919.** Reservations required. Fixed-price 3-course lunch €25; fixed-price dinners €55 2 courses, €65 3 courses; tasting menu €90. AE, DC, MC, V. Mon–Fri 12:30–2pm; Mon–Sat 6:30–10:30pm. Bus: 10.

Expensive

Dobbins Wine Bistro ★ BISTRO   Almost hidden in a lane between Upper and Lower Mount streets, this hip, friendly bistro is a haven for inventive Continental cuisine. The menu changes often, but it usually includes such items as duckling with orange and port sauce; or steamed paupiette of black sole with salmon, crab, and prawn filling; and sirloin of beef with mustard butter.

15 Stephen's Lane (off Upper Mount St.), Dublin 2. ℂ **01/661-9536.** Reservations recommended. Dinner main courses €19–€29. AE, DC, MC, V. Mon–Fri 12:30–2:30pm; Tues–Sat 7:30–10:30pm. DART: Pearse. Bus: 5, 7A, 8, 46, or 84.

Moderate

Gotham Café INTERNATIONAL   This busy cafe with magazine-covered walls and a small covered terrace always has a funky vibe. The menu is like an edible geography lesson, from Thai curry with chili jam, to burgers (American style, or Moroccan lamb if you prefer), steaks and pasta. The pizzas are what most people come for, however, with a similarly eclectic range of unusual and imaginative toppings that will offend purists (hummus! Peking duck!) but are always fresh and crisp.

8 S. Anne St., Dublin 2. www.gothamcafe.ie. ℂ **01/679-5266.** Fixed-price 2 course menu €15; main courses €11–€19. AE, MC, V. Mon & Tues 11am–10pm; Wed–Sat 11am–11pm; Sun 11:30am–10pm. Bus: 7, 7A, 8, 10, 11, or 13.

Ely Gastropub ★ MODERN IRISH   Tough times often make a food culture reassess its roots, and this stylish gastropub embraces traditional Irish cuisine, before knocking it down, giving it a shake, and serving it to you with a glass of artisan beer. Dishes such as Burren rib eye and rare-breed pork bangers and mash are complemented by equally *nouveau-trad* sides such as sprouts with bacon and fresh Guinness bread. Or you could just have a burger and a pint.

22 Ely Place (off Merrion Row), Dublin 2. www.elywinebar.ie. ℂ **01/633-9986.** Dinner main courses €14–€28. AE, DC, MC, V. Mon–Thurs noon–11:30pm; Fri & Sat noon–12:30am; Sun noon–11pm. Bus: 1, 2, 3, 50, 56A, and 77A.

O'CONNELL STREET AREA
Very Expensive

Chapter One ★★ MODERN IRISH   One of the city's most atmospheric restaurants, this remarkable eatery fills the vaulted basement space of the **Dublin Writers Museum.** Artfully lighted and tastefully decorated, it's a romantic location, although all that loveliness does not come cheap. Meals are prepared with local, organic ingredients, all cleverly used in remarkable dishes like the ravioli with Irish goat cheese and warm asparagus, and the Irish beef with shallot gratin.

18–19 Parnell Sq., Dublin 2. www.chapteronerestaurant.com. ℂ **01/873-2266.** Reservations recommended. Fixed-price lunches, 2 courses €30, 3 courses €38; fixed-price 3-course dinner menu €65. AE, DC, MC, V. Tues–Fri 12:30–2:30pm and 6–11pm; Sat 6–11pm. Bus: 27A, 31A, 31B, 32A, 32B, 42B, 42C, 43, or 44A.

Moderate

101 Talbot ★ INTERNATIONAL   This modest eatery above a shop may be unassuming, but don't be fooled—it's actually a bright beacon of good cooking on the

Northside. The menu features light, healthy food, with a strong emphasis on vegetarian dishes. Dishes change regularly, but mains might include linguine with homemade pork sausage, pan-fried sea trout with capers and cherry tomatoes, or a classic chargrilled Irish steak with mushroom and brandy sauce. The dining room is casually funky, with contemporary Irish art, big windows, and newspapers scattered about, if you should want one. The staff is endlessly friendly, making it a pleasure to visit.

101 Talbot St. (at Talbot Lane near Marlborough St.), Dublin 1. www.101talbot.ie. ✆ **01/874-5011.** Reservations recommended. 2-course early-bird menu €22; dinner main courses €15–€22. AE, MC, V. Tues–Sat 5–11pm. DART: Connolly. Bus: 27A, 31A, 31B, 32A, 32B, 42B, 42C, 43, or 44A.

Inexpensive

Boojum ☺ MEXICAN   The classic tacos, burritos, and fajitas here are good, fast, and cheap. This is an order-at-the-bar, stay-or-go kind of place, popular with a younger crowd. Ideal for a cheap and cheerful dinner, or lunch on the move.

Millennium Walkway, Dublin 1. www.boojummex.com. ✆ **01/872-9499.** All items €6–€7. No credit cards. Mon–Sat 12–9pm; Sun 1–6pm. LUAS: Jervis. Bus: 39B or 69X.

Epicurean Food Hall INTERNATIONAL   This wonderful food hall houses a wide variety of artisan produce, delicious local Irish meats, and regional specialties. Favorites include **Bagelrush,** for its bagels, soups, and salads; **Moonstar Café,** for Turkish food; **Ramos,** for Greek delicacies; **Leo Burdock's,** for traditional fish and chips; and **Layden's Fine Wines,** which sells wine by the bottle or glass. There is some seating in the hall, but this place gets jammed during lunchtime midweek.

Middle Abbey St. and Liffey St. No phone. All items around €4–€15. No credit cards. Mon–Sat 10am–6pm. Bus: 70 or 80.

Soup Dragon LIGHT FARE   This place is tiny, with fewer than a dozen stools alongside a bar, but it's big on drama: blue walls, black and red mirrors, orange slices and spice sticks flowing out of giant jugs. The menu changes daily, but usually features a few traditional choices (potato and leek, carrot and coriander) as well as the more exotic (Thai green chicken curry, for example). They also serve salads, bagels, sandwiches, and wraps. Breakfast is pretty good here too, with a nice balance of the healthy (banana bread, muesli, oatmeal/"porridge") and the hearty (such as the "dragon breakfast" with eggs and bacon, which will keep you going for hours).

168 Capel St., Dublin 1. www.soupdragon.com. ✆ **01/872-3277.** Breakfast €2–€7.50; soup €5.50–€13; other lunch items €4–€7. MC, V. Mon–Fri 8am–5pm; Sat 10–4pm. Bus: 70 or 80.

BALLSBRIDGE/EMBASSY ROW AREA
Expensive

Roly's Bistro IRISH/INTERNATIONAL   This two-story, shop-front restaurant is a local institution, beloved for providing the kind of reliably good, tummy-warming food you never get tired of: roasted breast of chicken with orzo pasta and wild mushrooms or braised shank of lamb with root vegetable purée and rosemary jus, to name just two. The bright and airy main dining room can be noisy when the house is full, but there's also an enclave of booths for those who prefer a quiet tête-à-tête.

7 Ballsbridge Terrace, Dublin 4. www.rolysbistro.ie. ✆ **01/668-2611.** Reservations required. Main courses €20–€30; early-bird dinners €24 2 courses, €26.50 3 courses; fixed-price dinner menus € 30 2 courses, €35.50 3 courses; fixed-price 3-course lunch €22.50 Mon–Fri. AE, DC, MC, V. Daily noon–3pm and 6–9:45pm. DART: Lansdowne Rd. Station. Bus: 5, 6, 7, 8, 18, or 45.

Sabor Brasil ★★★ BRAZILIAN   Tucked away in the 'burbs south of St. Stephen's Green (take a taxi—it's hard to find and the neighborhood's not great), Sabor

Brasil is an oasis of Celtic-inflected Latin charm. Outstanding South American food is served in the teeny-tiny dining room (don't even think of coming without a reservation). Typical dishes include *Tutu de Feijão*—locally sourced pork flavored with garlic, lime, and rock salt, served with authentic Brazilian sides. It's so friendly and romantic that you'll almost forget the wallet-busting price. The only snag is that they don't take cards, but that may change in the near future.

50 Pleasant St., Dublin 8. www.saborbrazil.ie. ℂ **01/475-0304.** Main courses €37–€42. No credit cards. Tues–Sun 6–11pm. Bus: 65 or 65X. Suburban rail to Harcourt St.

Moderate
The French Paradox ★★★ ✦ BISTRO/WINE BAR   This is a darling little bistro and wine bar that endears itself to everyone. The wine's the thing here, so relax with a bottle of Bordeaux or Côte du Rhône and nibbles from the menu. There's a lovely cheese plate and superb Iberico hams from Spain, or, if you prefer, the small dining menu offers bistro favorites such as gravlax and blinis.

53 Shelbourne Rd., Dublin 4. www.thefrenchparadox.com. ℂ **01/660-4068.** Reservations recommended. Main courses €10–€19; platters €14–€25. AE, MC, V. Mon–Fri noon–3pm and 6pm–midnight; Sat 3pm–midnight. DART: Lansdowne Rd. Bus: 5, 6, 7, 8, or 18.

Shopping

In recent years, Dublin has surprised everyone by becoming a great shopping town. You'll find few bargains, but for your money you will get excellent craftsmanship in the form of hand-woven wool blankets and clothes in a vivid array of colors, big-name Irish crafts, and chic clothes from the seemingly limitless line of Dublin designers.

While the hub of mainstream shopping south of the Liffey is **Grafton Street,** crowned by the city's most fashionable department store, Brown Thomas (known as BT), and the jeweler Weirs, there's much better shopping on the smaller streets radiating from Grafton, like **Duke, Dawson, Nassau,** and **Wicklow.** On these streets proliferate the smaller, interesting shops that specialize in books, handicrafts, jewelry, gifts, and clothing. For clothes, look out for tiny **Cow Lane,** off Lord Edward Street—it is popular with those in the know for its excellent clothing boutiques selling the works of local designers.

Generally, Dublin shops are open from 9am to 6pm Monday to Saturday, and Thursday until 9pm. Many of the larger shops have Sunday hours from noon to 6pm.

Major department stores include, on the Northside, **Arnotts,** 12 Henry St., Dublin 1 (www.arnotts.ie; ℂ **01/805-0400**), and the marvelously traditional **Clerys ★,** 18–27 Lower O'Connell St., Dublin 1 (www.clerys.com; ℂ **01/878-6000**); and, on the south side, **Brown Thomas ★★,** 15–20 Grafton St., Dublin 2 (www.brownthomas. com; ℂ **01/605-6666**).

Dublin also has several clusters of shops in **multistory malls** or ground-level **arcades,** ideal for indoor shopping on rainy days. On the Northside, these include the **ILAC Centre,** off Henry Street, Dublin 1, and the **Jervis Shopping Centre,** off Henry Street, Dublin 1. On the south side, there's the **Royal Hibernian Way,** 49–50 Dawson St., Dublin 2; **St. Stephen's Green Centre,** at the top of Grafton Street, Dublin 2; and the **Powerscourt Townhouse Centre ★★,** 59 William St. S., Dublin 2.

BOOKS   This city of literary legends has quite a few good bookstores. The granddaddy of them all is **Hodges Figgis ★,** 57 Dawson St., Dublin 2 (ℂ **01/677-4754**), an enormous place (mentioned in *Ulysses*) in which you could happily lose an afternoon browsing; for rare secondhand books and first editions, **Cathac Books,** 10

Duke St., Dublin 2 (© **01/671-8676**), is much beloved of serious bibliophiles; and the small but perfectly formed **Noble & Beggerman** ★ at the Hugh Lane Gallery, Parnell Square North, Dublin 1 (www.nobleandbeggarmanbooks.com; © **01/633-3568**), is packed full of books on Irish art, architecture, and design. Finally, if all this inspires you to put pen to paper yourself, check out the lovely selection of stylish writing gear, arty cards, and notepaper at the **Pen Corner** ★, 12 College Green, Dublin 2 (© **01/679-3641**), which has been supplying pens and paper to the literati since 1927.

CRAFTS & GIFTS   A wonderland of color fills **Avoca Handweavers** ★★★, 11–13 Suffolk St., Dublin 2 (www.avoca.ie; © **01/677-4215**), which offers soft, intricately woven fabrics, blankets, throws, light woolen sweaters, children's clothes, and toys, all in a delightful shopping environment spread over three floors near Trinity College. All the fabrics are woven using traditional methods in the Vale of Avoca in the Wicklow Mountains. The top-floor **cafe** is a great place for lunch. In a restored 18th-century town house, **Powerscourt Townhouse Centre** ★★, 59 S. William St., Dublin 2 (www.powerscourtcentre.com; © **01/671-7000**), has more than 60 boutiques, as well as craft shops, art galleries, snack bars, wine bars, and restaurants. If you want to take home an antique but can't usually afford the price tag, check out the **Drawing Room** ★, 29 Westbury Mall, Dublin 2 (© **01/677-2083**). This unique place specializes in antique gifts, knickknacks, and furniture, all beautifully crafted, highly individual—and completely fake (they're reproductions).

FASHION   **Alias Tom** ★, Duke House, Duke Street (© **01/671-5443**), is one of Dublin's best small men's designer shops. The emphasis is on Italian (Gucci, Prada, Armani) labels, but the range covers chic designers from the rest of Europe and America. **Claire Garvey** ★, 6 Cow's Lane (www.clairegarvey.com; © **01/671-7287**), is a Dublin native with a talent for creating romantic, dramatic, and feminine clothing with Celtic flair. A favorite designer of Irish divas Enya and Sinead O'Connor, Garvey transforms hand-dyed velvet and silk into sumptuous garments that beg to be worn on special occasions. Her one-of-a-kind bijou handbags are a sublime fashion accessory. **Jenny Vander** ★★, 50 Drury Street, South Great Georges Street, Dublin 2 (© **01/677-0406**), is where local actresses and models come to find extraordinary and stylish antique clothing. There are plenty of jeweled frocks, vintage day wear, and stunning costume jewelry filling the clothing racks and display cases. For something a little funkier (not to mention easier on the wallet) try **Om Diva** ★★ (39 Capel Street, Dublin 1; © **01/679-1211**). It's a lovely, friendly store that sells a mixture of vintage and designer gear at thoroughly reasonable prices. Head to the basement for the most eclectic selection, or upstairs for jewelry and accessories sold direct by the designers themselves.

KNITWEAR   **Avoca,** mentioned above, is an excellent option for delicate knits. **Dublin Woollen Mills,** 41 Lower Ormond Quay (www.woollenmills.ie; © **01/828-0301**), is on the north side of the River Liffey next to the Ha'penny Bridge, a leading source of Aran hand-knit sweaters as well as vests, hats, jackets, and tweeds.

Entertainment & Nightlife

Nightlife in Dublin is a mixed bag of traditional old pubs, where the likes of Joyce and Behan once imbibed and where traditional Irish music is often reeling away, and cool modern bars, where the repetitive rhythms of techno now fill the air and the crowd knows more about Prada than the Pogues. There's little in the way of crossover, although there are a couple of quieter bars and a few with a rock music angle. Aside from the eternal elderly pubs, things change rapidly on the nightlife scene, so pick up a copy of *In Dublin* and the *Event Guide* at local cafes and shops for listings on the latest club scene.

The award-winning website of the ***Irish Times*** (**www.ireland.com**) offers a "what's on" daily guide to cinema, theater, music, and whatever else you're up for. The **Dublin Events Guide,** at www.dublinevents.com, also provides a comprehensive listing of the week's entertainment possibilities.

Advance bookings for most large concerts, plays, and so forth can be made through **Ticketmaster Ireland** (www.ticketmaster.ie; ✆ **081/871-9300**), with ticket centers in most HMV stores, as well as at the Dublin Tourism Centre, Suffolk Street, Dublin 2.

THE PERFORMING ARTS

National Concert Hall, Earlsfort Terrace, Dublin 2 (www.nch.ie; ✆ **01/417-0000**), is home to the National Symphony Orchestra and Concert Orchestra, and is host to an array of international orchestras and performing artists. In addition to classical music, there are Broadway-style musicals, opera, jazz, and recitals. The box office is open Monday to Saturday from 10am to 6pm, and on Sundays from two hours before performances. Tickets range from about €10 to €50.

The **O2,** East Link Bridge, North Wall Quay (12–16 Andrews Lane, Dublin 2; www.theo2.ie; ✆ **01/819-8888**), is one of Dublin's most high-profile music venues. Major international acts and other high-profile events play here. All ticket sales are handled by **Ticketmaster** (✆ 081/871-9300).

For more than 90 years, the **Abbey Theatre,** Lower Abbey Street, Dublin 1 (www. abbeytheatre.ie; ✆ **01/878-7222**), has been the national theater of Ireland. The Abbey's artistic reputation within Ireland has risen and fallen over the years and is at present reasonably strong. The box office is open Monday through Saturday from 10:30am to 7pm; performances begin at 8 or 8:15pm. Tickets range from about €15 to €40.

Less well known than the Abbey, but just as distinguished, is the **Gate Theatre,** 1 Cavendish Row, Dublin 1 (www.gate-theatre.ie; ✆ **01/874-4045**). This recently restored 370-seat theater was founded in 1928 by Irish actors Hilton Edwards and Michael MacLiammoir to provide a venue for a broad range of plays. That policy prevails today, with a program that includes a blend of modern works and the classics. Tickets run from about €15 to €40.

THE PUB SCENE

Pubs for Conversation & Atmosphere

The brass-filled and lantern-lit **Brazen Head ★★,** 20 Lower Bridge St. (www. brazenhead.com; ✆ **01/679-5186**), has atmosphere in spades. It's a tad touristy, which isn't surprising when you consider that it's the city's oldest pub—licensed in 1661 and occupying the site of an earlier tavern dating from 1198. On the south bank of the River Liffey, it's at the end of a cobblestone courtyard and was once the meeting place of Irish freedom fighters such as Robert Emmet and Wolfe Tone.

The competition is stiff, but **Doheny and Nesbitt ★★★,** 5 Lower Baggot St. (www.dohenyandnesbitts.com; ✆ **01/676-2945**), may well be the best-looking traditional pub in town. The Victorian bar houses two fine old "snugs"—small rooms behind the main bar where women could have a drink out of sight of the men in the olden days.

Converted from an old Victorian bank, the **Bank on College Green ★,** 20 College Green (www.bankoncollegegreen.com; ✆ **01/677-0677**), is a beautiful old building with mosaic floors and carved stonework—all meticulously restored. Its dead-central location makes it an ideal stop on the sightseeing trail for a pint and some above-average bar food.

Referred to as a "moral pub" by James Joyce in *Ulysses*, **Davy Byrnes** ★★, 21 Duke St., just off Grafton Street (www.davybyrnes.com; ✆ 01/677-5217), has drawn poets, writers, and lovers of literature ever since. Davy Byrnes first opened the doors in 1873; he presided here for more than 50 years and visitors today can still see his likeness on one of the turn-of-the-20th-century murals hanging over the bar. Joyce was also a regular at **Mulligan's** ★★, 8 Poolbeg Street (www.mulligans.ie; ✆ 01/677-5582), where his characters in *Dubliners* drank hot whiskeys. Today it's better known for the quality of its Guinness and is a slice of heaven for those who appreciate a smooth pint, ornate dusty mirrors, and mahogany snugs.

The Library Bar ★★, at the Central Hotel on Exchequer Street (✆ 01/679-7302), is the antithesis to the trendiness of the city's fashion-conscious Temple Bar district. Sink into your leather armchair, immersed in hush and surrounded by groaning bookshelves and wooden floorboards. Tucked into a busy commercial street, the **Long Hall** ★★★, 51 S. Great George's St. (✆ 01/475-1590), is one of the city's most photographed pubs, with a beautiful Victorian decor of filigree-edged mirrors and polished dark woods. The hand-carved bar is said to be the longest counter in the city. More gorgeous Victoriana is to be found at **J. W. Ryan** ★★, 28 Parkgate St. (✆ 01/677-6097), on the north side of the Liffey near Phoenix Park. The pub is like a time capsule, featuring a pressed-tin ceiling and domed skylight, etched glass, brass lamp holders, and a handsome mahogany bar.

Pubs with Traditional & Folk Music

Overlooking the Ha'penny Bridge, **The Grand Social,** 35 Lower Liffey Street (www.thegrandsocial.ie; ✆ 01/874-0090), is an artfully bohemian, three-floored pub that hosts gigs ranging from traditional to rock, ska, jazz, indie, and alternative, plus pretty much everything in between. The downstairs bar serves a good range of European beers and one of the best Irish stews in town.

Revolutions were plotted in the brass-filled, lantern-lit **Brazen Head** ★★, 20 Lower Bridge Street (www.brazenhead.com; ✆ 01/679-5186). The pub was first licensed in 1661, which makes it one of the oldest pubs in Ireland. Nestled on the south bank of the Liffey, it is at the end of a cobblestone courtyard and was once the meeting place of rebels Robert Emmet and Wolfe Tone. Traditional music sessions start at 9:30pm nightly.

In the heart of Temple Bar and named for one of Ireland's literary greats, **Oliver St. John Gogarty** ★, 57–58 Fleet St. (www.gogartys.ie; ✆ 01/671-1822), has an inviting old-world atmosphere, with shelves of empty bottles, stacks of dusty books, a horseshoe-shaped bar, and old barrels for seats. There are traditional music sessions upstairs from Monday to Friday 2:30pm to 2am, and in the Library Bar from Sunday to Thursday from 10pm until 12:30am. The management warns that spontaneous music sessions can break out at any time in the bar downstairs—and frequently do.

THE CLUB & MUSIC SCENE

The club and music scene in Dublin is confoundingly complex and changeable. Jazz, blues, folk, country, traditional, rock, and comedy move from venue to venue, night by night. The first rule is to get the very latest listings and see what's on and where. Dozens of clubs and pubs all over town feature rock, folk, jazz, and traditional Irish music. This includes the so-called "late-night pubs"—pubs with an exemption allowing them to remain open past the usual closing time, mandated by law (11pm in winter, 11:30pm in summer). Check *In Dublin* magazine or the *Event Guide* (see above) for club schedules. One of the most popular rock clubs is **Whelan's,** 25 Wexford St., Dublin 2 (www.whelanslive.com; ✆ **01/478-0766**). Another old favorite, named Irish Music Venue of the Year in 2008 and 2009, is **Vicar Street,** 58 Thomas Street, Dublin 8 (www.vicarstreet.ie; ✆ **01/775-5800**). They also host big-name stand-up comedy acts.

Dance clubs include **Lillie's Bordello** ★★, Adam Court, Dublin 2 (www.lillies bordello.ie; ✆ **01/679-9204**), with its well-deserved reputation for posers and boy-band celebrities, and a callous door policy. More friendly is **Rí-Rá** ★★, 11 S. Great George's St., Dublin 2 (www.rira.ie; ✆ **01/671-1220**), which is both trendy and laid-back. **Howl at the Moon** ★ (8 Lower Mount Street, Dublin 2; www.howlat themoon.ie; ✆ **01/634-5460**), is popular with fashionable 30-somethings who like the fact that the emphasis here is off dance and firmly on socializing.

The city's largest gay bar is **The George** ★★, 89 S. Great George's St., Dublin 2 (www.thegeorge.ie; ✆ **01/478-2983**), a two-story venue where both the decor and the clientele tend toward camp. It's open daily from 12:30pm to 2:30am; check listings for theme nights, which start around 10pm—including cabaret on Wednesdays and karaoke on Saturdays.

Where to Stay

HISTORIC OLD CITY & TEMPLE BAR/TRINITY COLLEGE AREA

Very Expensive

The Clarence ★★★   This has been the most famous hotel in Dublin since 1992, when U2's Bono and the Edge bought it. For some, knowing that a hotel is owned by rock stars might actually be a strike against the place, but don't be put off—this is one of the most sophisticated hotels in the city. The mid-19th-century, Regency-style building was beautifully renovated, keeping the best of its antique charm, but adding layers of contemporary elegance. Rooms are designed with lush fabrics in neutral tones of oatmeal and chocolate, light Shaker-style oak furniture, and exceptionally comfortable, firm king-size beds. Suites and deluxe rooms have balconies, some with views over the Liffey. The elegant **Tea Room** restaurant (p. 581) is one of the best in town for con-temporary Irish cuisine. The **Octagon Bar** has a good buzz, and the **Study,** which has the feel of an old-style gentlemen's club, is a relaxing place to read the papers and sip a glass of wine.

A Parking Note

The majority of Dublin hotels do not offer parking; if you have a car, you'll have to find (and pay for) street parking. In this section, we've provided parking information only for the few hotels that do offer parking arrangements or discounts for guests.

6–8 Wellington Quay, Dublin 2. www.the clarence.ie. ✆ **01/407-0800.** 47 units. €170–€250 double. Full Irish breakfast €19. AE, DC, MC, V. Valet parking €25. Bus: 51B, 51C, 68, 69, or 79. **Amenities:** Restaurant; bar; exercise room; spa; concierge; room service; babysitting; nonsmoking rooms. *In room:* A/C, TV/DVD, minibar, hair dryer, Wi-Fi (free).

Moderate

Buswells Hotel ★   The spacious, slightly masculine rooms at this traditional hotel are spread throughout three Georgian buildings—which can make finding your room a challenge after a few pints of Guinness. But it's worth the wandering. It has a unique style and ambience, in part because the location near the Irish government buildings makes the bar a hotbed of political intrigue.

23–25 Molesworth St., Dublin 2. www.buswells.ie. ✆ **01/614-6500.** Fax 01/676-2090. 69 units. €90–€165 double. AE, DC, MC, V. Free parking nearby. DART: Pearse. Bus: 10, 11, 13, or 46A. **Amenities:** Restaurant; bar; exercise room; concierge; room service; babysitting; nonsmoking rooms. *In room:* TV, hair dryer, Wi-Fi (free).

Eliza Lodge ★   This hotel lies right beside the Liffey and embodies all the exuberance and zest of Temple Bar. Guest rooms are simple and attractive, done up in neutral creams and blond woods, with big floor-to-ceiling windows—the better to take in the riverside vistas. At the top end, executive rooms have Jacuzzi tubs and bay windows looking out over the quay. But a better-value splurge are the smaller penthouse doubles that have balconies overlooking the river. Road noise here is a problem for some light sleepers.

23–24 Wellington Quay, Dublin 2. www.elizalodge.com. ✆ **01/671-8044.** Fax 01/671-8362. 18 units. €80–€160 double. AE, MC, V. Bus: 51B, 51C, 68, 69, or 79. **Amenities:** Restaurant; bar; Wi-Fi (free); nonsmoking rooms. *In room:* A/C, TV, hair dryer.

Temple Bar Hotel   This five-story hotel was developed from a former bank building, and great care was taken to preserve the brick facade and Victorian mansard roof. Guest rooms are quite plain, if comfortable. The orthopedic beds are firm, although the smallish rooms are a bit cramped. **Buskers** and **Alchemy,** the hotel's nightclubs, are very popular and *very* loud. Bear that in mind before you book—if you're looking for peace and quiet, this is probably not the place for you, at least on the weekend. Midweek, rooms are quieter and often cheaper.

> ### 📎 Room-Booking Savvy
>
> Very good deals are available in the off-season for those who book a month or more in advance. Discounts of 70% are not unusual in the winter and early spring, even at five-star hotels.

Fleet St., Temple Bar, Dublin 2. www.templebarhotel.com. ✆ **01/677-3333** or **800/44-UTELL (448-8355)** in the U.S. 129 units. €120–€180 double. Rates include full Irish breakfast. AE, MC, V. DART: Tara St. Bus: 78A or 78B. **Amenities:** Restaurant; 2 bars; concierge; room service; babysitting. *In room:* TV, hair dryer, Wi-Fi (free).

Self-Catering
25 Eustace Street   This wonderfully restored Georgian town house, dating from 1720, has an enviable location in the heart of Temple Bar. It is a showcase property for the Irish Landmark Trust (ILT), whose mission is to rescue neglected historic buildings and restore them. The three-story house has been faithfully restored, with a superb timber-paneled staircase, fireplaces in every room, mahogany furniture, and brass beds. There's a huge drawing room with a baby grand piano, full dining room, equipped galley kitchen, and three bedrooms. There are two bathrooms, one with a cast-iron claw-foot tub placed dead center. Bookshelves have been thoughtfully stocked with classics by Irish novelists. As with all ILT properties, there is no TV, phone, or Internet. All this, and Temple Bar at your doorstep. Some readers have reported that the house is a little too close for comfort to Temple Bar's party scene and the noise can be a bit much on weekends.

25 Eustace St., Dublin 2. Contact the Irish Landmark Trust. www.irishlandmark.com. ✆ **01/670-4733.** 1 apt. €900 for 3 nights, rising to €2,100 per week during peak months. AE, MC, V. Bus: Any marked AN LAR. **Amenities:** Full kitchen.

ST. STEPHEN'S GREEN/GRAFTON STREET AREA
Very Expensive

The Fitzwilliam Hotel ★★★ Take an unbeatable location with sweeping views over the Green, add a Michelin-starred restaurant, throw in contemporary design by Terence Conran, and you have a hit on your hands. Conran has a knack for easygoing sophistication, and in the Fitzwilliam he uses clean lines and only a few neutral colors (white, beige, gray) throughout the public rooms and guest rooms. Rooms are simply done in neutral tones with stripped-down furniture. **Thornton's,** the hotel restaurant, is very good.

109 St. Stephen's Green, Dublin 2. www.fitzwilliamhoteldublin.com. ✆ **01/478-7000.** Fax 01/478-7878. 130 units. €165–€270 double. Breakfast €15. AE, DC, MC, V. DART: Pearse. Bus: 10, 11A, 11B, 13, or 20B. **Amenities:** 2 restaurants; bar; concierge; room service; babysitting; nonsmoking rooms. *In room:* A/C, TV, minibar, hair dryer, CD/MP3 player, Wi-Fi (free).

The Shelbourne ★★★ One of the city's true grande dame hotels, the Shelbourne has been a Dublin landmark since 1824. The hotel has played a significant role in Irish history—the Irish constitution was drafted here in 1922, in room no. 112. Now owned by the Marriott chain, the rooms are decorated in grand, traditional style, with soft yellows and pinks, and the hotel claims to have "Ireland's most luxurious beds," with 300-thread-count Egyptian cotton linens wrapped around feather mattresses. Rooms also have international power sockets, so your hair straightener shouldn't explode. The bars, restaurant, and lobby are still warmed by fireplaces and lighted by Waterford chandeliers, and the **Lord Mayor's Lounge** is still ideal for afternoon tea. Each evening guests are greeted with freshly made nibbles (fish cakes one day, brownies the next). The hotel even offers an in-house **genealogy butler,** who can help guests with Irish backgrounds explore their family histories.

27 St. Stephen's Green, Dublin 2. www.theshelbourne.ie. ✆ **01/663-4500** or 888/236-2427 in the U.S. Fax 01/661-6006. 265 units. €220–€310 double. Breakfast €20–€26. AE, DC, MC, V. Limited free parking. DART: Pearse. Bus: 10, 11A, 11B, 13, or 20B. **Amenities:** 2 restaurants; 2 bars; exercise room; concierge; room service; babysitting. *In room:* A/C, TV, minibar, hair dryer, Wi-Fi (€9/hr.).

Expensive

Number 31 A discreet plaque outside an elegant locked gate on a tiny side street is your only clue that what lies beyond is an award-winning guesthouse. It's actually two converted buildings—one a grand Georgian town house, the other a more modern coach house. In the main house, rooms are large and simply but classily decorated, while in the coach house rooms are elegant; some have their own patios. Handmade beds are enveloped in natural linens. Note that there's no restaurant, no bar, no room service, and no air-conditioning. Breakfast here is some consolation—cooked to order for you, with organic, seasonal ingredients, and choices ranging from mushroom frittatas to fresh-baked cranberry bread.

31 Leeson Close, Lower Leeson St., Dublin 2. www.number31.ie. ✆ **01/676-5011.** Fax 01/676-2929. 21 units. €150–€220 double. Rates include breakfast. AE, MC, V. Free parking. Bus: 11, 11A, 11B, 13, 13A, or 13B. **Amenities:** Lounge. *In room:* TV, hair dryer, Wi-Fi (free).

Moderate

Premier Suites Stephen's Hall This all-suite hotel offers a bit of value for families, visitors who plan an extended stay, or folks who want to entertain or do their own cooking. The building recently underwent a full renovation, which renewed each suite in tasteful modern style. Each apartment contains a sitting room, dining area, fully equipped kitchenette, tiled bathroom, and bedroom. On the website there's a link that allows you to pre-order groceries and have them delivered on the day you arrive. If you're not there, the reception staff will also unpack them for you. How suite is that?

14–17 Lower Leeson St. Dublin 2. www.premiersuitesdublin.com. ✆ **01/638-1111.** 30 units. €100–€175 double. Rates include breakfast. AE, MC, V. DART: Pearse. Bus: 11, 11A, 11B, 13, 13A, or 13B. **Amenities:** Concierge; nonsmoking floor. *In room:* TV, radio, Wi-Fi (free).

Trinity Lodge   In an enormous Georgian town house, the Trinity is a classy option a few blocks off Grafton Street. The gray stone building dates to 1785, and its 10 large guest rooms are brightly decorated in keeping with that period, some with paintings by the respected Irish artist Graham Knuttel. The breakfast room downstairs is warmly designed in country-house style. There's a second building across the street where six large rooms have a more contemporary edge. These buildings are protected historical structures, so there's no elevator access to their four levels.

12 S. Frederick St., Dublin 2. www.trinitylodge.com. ✆ **01/679-5044.** 16 units. €100–€160 double. Rates include breakfast. MC, V. Bus: All An Lar (cross-city) buses. **Amenities:** Restaurant; bar; room service; nonsmoking rooms. *In room:* A/C (some), TV, Wi-Fi (free).

Inexpensive
Avalon House ✦   This warm and friendly hostel in a beautiful old red-brick building is well known among those who travel to Dublin on a budget. Its pine floors, high ceilings, and open fireplace make it a pleasant place in which to relax, and its cafe is a popular hangout for international travelers. Most beds are in dorms of varying sizes, with a few single and twin-bedded rooms available, too. There's no curfew, but passes must be shown on entry after 9pm. It's not exactly the Clarence, but it has all you really need—clean, cheerful rooms in a safe location at a cheap price.

55 Aungier St., Dublin 2. www.avalon-house.ie. ✆ **01/475-0001.** Fax 01/475-0303. 12 units. €30 per person double with private bathroom. Includes light continental breakfast. AE, MC, V. Bus: 16, 16A, 19, 22, or 155. No curfew but passes must be shown on entry after 9pm. **Amenities:** Cafe; Wi-Fi (free); nonsmoking rooms.

FITZWILLIAM/MERRION SQUARE AREA
Very Expensive
Merrion Hotel ★   This hotel offers gorgeous Georgian luxury, created from elegant town houses—including the Duke of Wellington's birthplace. The impressive contemporary art on the walls is part of one of the country's largest private collections. Service is discreetly omnipresent, and the spacious rooms have the finest linen, antiques, and high sash windows. Pamper yourself in the **Tethra Spa.** Stretch your credit card's limit at the Michelin-starred **Restaurant Patrick Guilbaud** or save a few pennies at the somewhat cheaper and more atmospheric **Cellar** restaurant. If your budget won't cover a room here, take afternoon tea in the drawing room in front of the open fire. You could get used to this.

Upper Merrion St., Dublin 2. www.merrionhotel.com. ✆ **01/603-0600.** Fax 01/603-0700. 143 units. €230–€495 double. Breakfast €24–€29. AE, DC, MC, V. Parking €20 per night. DART: Pearse. Bus: 10, 13, or 13A. **Amenities:** 2 restaurants; 2 bars; indoor pool; health club & spa; concierge; room service; babysitting. *In room:* A/C, TV/DVD, minibar, hair dryer, Wi-Fi (free).

O'CONNELL STREET AREA
Expensive
The Morrison ★★   This is really an oversize boutique hotel, with an ideal location just across the Liffey from Temple Bar. Fashion fans will surely have no trouble

pegging the design as the work of design star John Rocha, who is responsible for everything from the crushed velvet bed throws in blood red to the Waterford crystal vases. Rocha uses a palette of neutral colors—cream, chocolate, and black—to achieve a kind of warm minimalism in the guest rooms, which have stereos, Egyptian-cotton linens, and cool Portuguese limestone in the bathrooms. The stylish atrium-style restaurant, **Halo,** is a favorite with celebrities.

Lower Ormond Quay, Dublin 1. www.morrisonhotel.ie. ✆ **01/887-2400.** Fax 01/874-4031. 138 units. €106–€270 double. AE, DC, MC, V. DART: Connolly. Bus: 70 or 80. **Amenities:** 2 restaurants; 2 bars; concierge; room service; babysitting. In room: A/C, minibar, hair dryer, CD/MP3 player, Internet (free).

Moderate

The Clarion Hotel Dublin IFSC ★ All smooth straight lines and extra touches, this relaxing, modern hotel is a good option for business travelers. The comfortable rooms are softened by Egyptian-cotton bedding, and filled with the latest electronic gadgets, including PlayStation units. The stylish bar and restaurant are workaday but useful. This hotel's best offering is arguably its state-of-the-art health club, with its gorgeous low-lit pool that urges you to exercise. Happily, the sauna, steam room, and whirlpool require no physical exertion at all. Rooms at the front have a gorgeous view of the Liffey and Dublin skyline. *Tip:* It can be significantly cheaper to get a room-only rate here and grab breakfast somewhere else; good alternatives can be found nearby.

International Financial Services Centre, Dublin 1. www.clarionhotelifsc.com. ✆ **01/433-8800.** Fax 01/433-8811. 163 units. €120–€175 double. AE, DC, MC, V. Parking €12. Dart: Connolly. Bus: All An Lar (cross-city) buses. **Amenities:** Restaurant; bar; indoor pool; health club; spa; concierge; room service; babysitting; nonsmoking rooms. *In room:* A/C, TV/DVD, minibar, hair dryer, Wi-Fi (free).

The Gresham ★★ Along with the Shelbourne, this is one of Dublin's two most historic hotels, and it has welcomed visitors for 200 years. With a row of flags out front and its grand, up-lighted facade, this hotel stands out, and the vast lobby is one of the best places in the city to have a cup of tea or a cocktail in elegant but relaxed surroundings. Rooms are generally small, but coolly decorated in neutral tones, with big, firm beds and huge windows. It has a friendly, modern bar, and a handy, slightly old-fashioned restaurant serving European cuisine. *Tip:* Take no notice of the (enormous) rack rates listed on the website. If you book far enough in advance, it's often possible to get a room for under €100.

23 Upper O'Connell St., Dublin 1. www.gresham-hotels.com. ✆ **01/878-6881.** Fax 01/878-7175. 288 units. €110–€144 double. Rates include breakfast. AE, DC, MC, V. Parking €15 per night. Bus: 11 or 13. **Amenities:** Restaurant; 2 bars; concierge; room service; babysitting; nonsmoking rooms. *In room:* A/C, TV, fridge, hair dryer, Wi-Fi (free).

Hotel Isaac's This friendly guesthouse has basic, clean, and comfortable bedrooms, with polished pine furniture and big screen TVs—and, by Irish standards, it's cheap. Rooms in the "Georgian Wing" are a little fancier, but they cost more. On the downside, the super-central location can get noisy on weekends and all extras are at an additional cost—right down to air conditioning or a DVD player in your room.

Store St, Dublin 1. www.isaacs.ie. ✆ **01/813-4700.** 54 units. €73–€160 double. Rates include breakfast. MC, V. DART: Lansdowne Rd. All cross-city buses. **Amenities:** Restaurant; cafe/bar; exercise room. *In room:* A/C (extra fee), TV, Wi-Fi (free).

BALLSBRIDGE/EMBASSY ROW AREA

Situated south of the Grand Canal, this elegant part of town is known for its embassies, and leafy, tree-lined streets. If you're in Dublin for a conference at the RDS show grounds or a match at the Lansdowne Rugby Ground, this area is ideal. The downside is that it's a good 20- to 30-minute walk to the town center.

Very Expensive

The Dylan ★   This absurdly trendy hotel puts its cards on the table the moment you walk in the door—here, only two things matter: the size of your bank account, and how good you look. Chanel bag? Prada skirt? Some €500 shoes? Welcome to your new home! It's hallmarked by vivid colors: bright carpets and curtains, Murano glass chandeliers, studded leather wallpaper, and lime-green sofas. Guest rooms are quite small, and the decor is disco chic, albeit with Frette linens and 7th Heaven beds. Service here is excellent, but beauty's in the eye of the beholder, so this very hip, very adult hotel is certainly not for everyone. Families in particular might find its party-hearty atmosphere (it has a signature cocktail—vanilla vodka with crème de banana—as well as a thumping club soundtrack) a bit off-putting. But 20-somethings line up to spend the night.

Eastmoreland Place, Ballsbridge, Dublin 4. www.dylan.ie. ℂ **01/660-3000.** Fax 01/660-3005. 44 units. €200–€425 double. Rates include full breakfast. AE, MC, V. Bus: 10, 46A, 46B, 63, or 84. **Amenities:** Restaurant; bar; lounge; concierge; room service; nightclub; nonsmoking rooms. *In room:* TV/MP3, minibar, hair dryer, Wi-Fi (free).

Expensive

Butlers Town House ★★ ◆   This beautifully restored Victorian town house feels like a gracious family home. The atmosphere is elegant, but comfortable; rooms are richly furnished with four-poster or half-tester beds, draped in luxurious fabrics in rich colors. The gem here is the Glendalough Room, with a lovely bay window and small library; it requires booking well in advance. Free tea and coffee are offered all day, and breakfast and afternoon tea are served in the atrium dining room.

44 Lansdowne Rd., Ballsbridge, Dublin 4. www.butlers-hotel.com. ℂ **01/667-4022.** Fax 01/667-3960. 20 units. €240 double. Rates include full breakfast. AE, DC, MC, V. Secure free parking. Closed Dec 23–Jan 10. DART: Lansdowne Rd. Bus: 7, 7A, 8, or 45. **Amenities:** Breakfast room; room service; babysitting. *In room:* A/C, TV, hair dryer, Wi-Fi (free).

Moderate

Ariel House ★★   This charming, friendly little Victorian guesthouse is dwarfed by the glinting enormity of the Aviva Stadium, just down the street. Guestrooms are clean and uncluttered, with tasteful heritage color schemes and king-size beds. The junior suite has chandeliers and a four-poster. Breakfasts are outstanding and afternoon tea can be taken in the drawing room, where there's also an honesty bar.

50–54 Lansdowne Rd., Dublin 4. www.ariel-house.net. ℂ **01/668-5512.** 37 units. €89–€150 double. AE, MC, V. DART: Lansdowne Rd. Bus: 7, 7A, 8, or 45. **Amenities:** Honesty bar; concierge; free parking. *In room:* A/C, TV, hair dryer, Wi-Fi (free).

Grand Canal Hotel ★ ◆   Popular with business travelers, this place is a short walk from the center, next to the Grand Canal and DART coastal train, and a stone's throw from the colossal, ultramodern Aviva Stadium. The comfortable rooms are spacious and quiet, with extras such as Wi-Fi throughout and ice machines on every floor (a rarity in European hotels). Balcony rooms boast amazing views.

Grand Canal St. Upper, Ballsbridge, Dublin 4. www.grandcanalhotel.com. ℂ **01/646-1000.** 142 units. €80–€164 double. AE, DC, MC, V. DART: Grand Canal. **Amenities:** Restaurant; bar; room service; nonsmoking rooms. *In room:* TV, hair dryer, Wi-Fi (free).

Roxford Lodge ★ ◆   This lovely little hotel is slightly outside central Dublin (Grafton Street is a 25-min. walk), but about as good as it gets anywhere in the city for the price. Rooms are simple and elegant, with little flourishes that incorporate elements of the original Victorian building, such as corniced ceilings and bay windows. Most bedrooms have their own whirlpool bathtubs and saunas, which sacrifices a little space but raises the luxury quotient. Service is personable and breakfasts are delicious. Guests can help themselves to free coffee all day in the lounge.

46 Northumberland Rd., Ballsbridge, Dublin 4. www.roxfordlodge.ie. ✆ **01/668-8572.** Fax 01/668-8158. €82–€224 double. Rates include breakfast. AE, MC, V. Bus: 11 or 13. **Amenities:** Lounge. *In room:* TV/CD, hair dryer, Wi-Fi (free).

Waterloo House ★ This classy guesthouse is charming in an old-world kind of way, with an elegant, high-ceilinged drawing room where you can linger over the morning papers or a good book. Guest rooms are large (some have two double beds), and most have fluffy white comforters and walls in lemony yellow. The varied breakfast menu offers more than the usual Irish fried eggs and bacon (French toast, waffles, croissants, for example). A quiet, peaceful alternative.

8–10 Waterloo Rd., Ballsbridge, Dublin 4. www.waterloohouse.ie. ✆ **01/660-1888.** 17 units. €80–€200 double. Rates include full breakfast. MC, V. Free parking. Closed Christmas week. DART: Lansdowne Rd. Bus: 5, 7, or 8. **Amenities:** Breakfast room. *In room:* TV, hair dryer, Wi-Fi (free).

KERRY & THE DINGLE PENINSULA

With its softly rolling green fields; long, sweeping seascapes; and vibrant little towns, it's easy to see why so many visitors make a beeline for County Kerry. Charming villages like colorful Kenmare, and bustling historic towns like Killarney, seem as familiar as the Irish folk songs written about them. Craggy mountain ranges punctuated by peaceful green valleys are just what you hope for when you come to Ireland.

Kerry's tremendous popularity has been great for local businesses, but during the summer it can mean that the spectacular rural scenery fairly bursts at the seams with millions of tourists. In July and August, tour buses struggle to share narrow mountain roads with local traffic, and at the best vantage points, the view is often blocked by two or three of the behemoths.

Luckily, it's still easy to escape the crowds. If you're driving along a busy road and the crowds are getting to you, simply turn off onto a small country lane and you'll find yourself virtually alone and in the peaceful Irish wilderness within seconds. In the high season in Kerry, taking the road less traveled can be the best way to go.

ESSENTIALS
Getting to County Kerry
BY TRAIN Irish Rail (www.irishrail.ie; ✆ 1850/366-222) operates daily train service from Dublin, Limerick, Cork, and Galway to the **Killarney Railway Station** (✆ 064/663-1067) on Railway Road, off East Avenue Road.

BY BUS Bus Éireann (www.buseireann.ie; ✆ 01/836-6111) operates daily express coach and local bus services to Killarney from Dublin and other parts of Ireland. The bus depot (✆ 064/663-0011) is adjacent to the train station at Railway Road, off East Avenue Road. Once you're there, there's also limited daily service from Killarney to Caherciveen, Waterville, Kenmare, and other towns on the Ring of Kerry. Some private, Killarney-based companies offer daily sightseeing tours of the Ring of Kerry by bus.

BY CAR   Roads leading into Kerry include N6 from Dublin, N21 and N23 from Limerick, and N22 from Cork. The best way to do the Ring of Kerry (comprising the N70 and N71) is by car.

Killarney Town

Perhaps the busiest tourist hub in rural Ireland, Killarney's sidewalks are spacious enough in the winter, but in the summertime, they're packed, as the streets become one giant tour-bus traffic jam and horse-and-buggy drivers risk life and limb to push their way through. The locals are well practiced at dispensing a professional brand of Irish charm, even as they hike up the hotel and restaurant prices to capitalize on the hordes descending from the buses. It all feels a bit cynical, with a few too many cheesy gift shops for its own good. (There are actually road signs on the Ring of Kerry that say LEPRECHAUN CROSSING.) It's a bit much for some people, but luckily, it's easy enough to resist Killarney's gravitational pull and spend your time exploring the quieter countryside around it. You can always sneak into town from time to time for dinner or a night out in the pub with lots of people from your home nation.

Although Killarney is pleasant enough, the real attraction is the valley in which it nestles—a verdant landscape of lakes and mountains. Exploring its glories is certainly easy—just walk (or drive) from the town parking lot toward the cathedral and turn left. In a matter of minutes, you'll forget all that Killarney stress amid the quiet rural splendor of the 65-sq.-km (25-sq.-mile) **Killarney National Park.** Here the ground is a soft carpet of moss and the air is fragrant with wildflowers.

ESSENTIALS

GETTING AROUND   Killarney Town is so small and compact that there is no local bus service; the best way to get around is on foot. For a quick and easy tour, follow the signposted **Tourist Trail** for the highlights of the main streets. It takes less than 2 hours to complete. A booklet outlining the sights along the trail is available at the tourist office.

Taxicabs line up at the stand on **College Square** (✆ 064/663-1331). You can also phone for a taxi from **Killarney Cabs** (✆ 064/663-7444), **Kerry Autocabs** (✆ 1890/230-230), or **Euro Cabs** (✆ 064/663-7676.

There are a couple of large public parking lots near the town center, where parking costs €1 per hour. It's a good idea to leave your car in one of these unless you're heading out to Killarney National Park on the Muckross and Kenmare road (N71).

If you need to rent a car in Killarney, contact **Budget,** c/o International Hotel, Kenmare Place (✆ 064/663-4341), and at Kerry Airport (www.budget.ie; ✆ 066/976-3199). Alternatively, **Avis** also has a branch at Kerry Airport (www.avis.ie; ✆ 01/605-7500) and **Hertz** has branches at Cork Airport (www.hertz.ie; ✆ 021/496-5849) and Shannon Airport (www.hertz.ie; ✆ 061/471-369).

Horse-drawn **buggies,** called "jarveys," line up at Kenmare Place in Killarney Town. They offer rides to Killarney National Park sites and other scenic areas. Depending on the time and distance, prices range from around €15 to upwards of €50 per ride (up to four people).

VISITOR INFORMATION   The **Killarney Tourist Office,** Áras Fáilte, is at the town center on Beech Road (✆ 064/663-1633). It's open October to May Monday to Saturday 9:15am to 5:15pm; June and September daily 9am to 6pm; July and August daily 9am to 8pm. During low season, the office occasionally closes for lunch from 1 to 2pm. It offers many helpful booklets and maps.

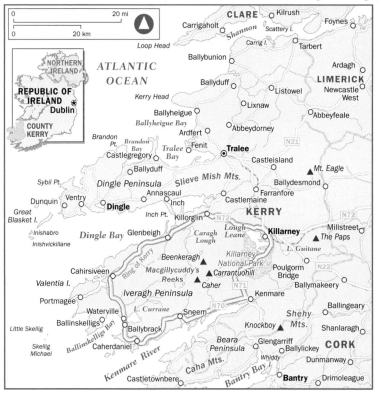

Useful local publications include ***Where: Killarney,*** a quarterly magazine distributed free at hotels and guesthouses. It is packed with current information on tours, activities, events, and entertainment.

Killarney National Park ★★★

This is Killarney's centerpiece: a 10,000-hectare (25,000-acre) area of natural beauty. For many, the main attractions are the park's three lakes. The largest of these, the **Lower Lake,** is sometimes called Lough Leane or Lough Lein ("the lake of learning"). It's more than 6km (3¾ miles) long and is dotted with 30 small islands. Nearby is the Middle Lake or **Muckross Lake,** and the smallest of the three, the **Upper Lake.** The most noteworthy of Killarney's islands, **Innisfallen,** is on the Lower Lake; if you can hire a boat and row yourself out (they're sometimes available for rent from Ross Castle, but we've found that often there's nobody around to actually rent you the boat), you'll find what's left of the monastery **St. Fallen,** which was founded in the 7th century and flourished for 1,000 years.

The park also contains a large variety of wildlife, including a rare herd of red deer.

You can't drive through the park (parking lots are available, however, if you want to drive *to* it), so touring is best done by foot, bicycle, or horse-drawn jaunting car. The park offers four signposted walking and nature trails along the lakeshore. Access to the park is available from several points along the Kenmare road (N71), with the main entrance being at Muckross House. Admission is free, and the park is open year-round during daylight hours.

VIEWS & VISTAS   The journey through the **Gap of Dunloe ★★** is gorgeous. The winding and rocky mountain pass sits amid rocky mountains and cool lakes about 10km (6¼ miles) west of Killarney. The route through the gap passes a kaleidoscope of sharp cliffs, meandering streams, and deep valleys. The route through the gap ends at Upper Lake. Horse fanciers may want to take one of the excursions offered by **Corcoran's Tours,** 8 College St. (www.corcorantours.com; *(C)* **064/663-6666**), or **Dero's Tours,** 22 Main St. (www.derostours.com; *(C)* **064/663-1251**).

The little hillside opposite Aghadoe Heights hotel (see below), on the Tralee Road (off N22), is a spectacular **viewing point** over the lakes and town. In the churchyard adjacent are the evocative ruins of a stone church and round tower dating from 1027.

Muckross House and Gardens ★★   This rambling ivy-covered Victorian mansion was built for a wealthy landowner in 1843 and donated to the state in the 1930s. It is now a museum of sorts, of life in the county, showcasing locally made furniture, prints, art, and needlework, although it mixes them with non-Irish items like Oriental screens, Chippendale chairs, and Turkish carpets. The gardens are lovely, and you can wander to the on-site restaurant and workshops, where local artisans demonstrate bookbinding, weaving, and pottery.

The ruin of the 15th-century **Muckross Abbey,** founded about 1448 and burned by Cromwell's troops in 1652, is also near the house. The abbey's central feature is a vaulted cloister around a courtyard that contains a huge yew tree, said to be as old as the abbey itself. W. M. Thackeray once called it "the prettiest little bijou of a ruined abbey ever seen."

Kenmare rd. (N71), Killarney, County Kerry. www.muckross-house.ie. *(C)* **064/667-0144.** Admission to house only, €7 adults, €5.50 seniors, €3 students and children 18 and under, €17.50 families. Joint ticket with Muckross Traditional Farms (below) €12 adults, €10 seniors, €6 students and children, €32 families. Daily 9am–5:30pm (9am–7pm July–Aug). Last admission 1 hr. before closing.

Muckross Traditional Farms ★ ☺   Not far from the Muckross House estate, these farms are designed to demonstrate what traditional farm life was like in previous centuries in County Kerry. It's cleverly done—the farmhouses and barns are so authentically detailed that you feel as if you've dropped in on real farms. Work really does go on here, so farmhands work the fields, while the blacksmith, carpenter, and wheelwright ply their trades. Women draw water from the wells and cook meals in historically accurate kitchens. Children get a kick out of the animals, and it's interesting enough to keep adults from getting bored as well.

Kenmare rd. (N71), Killarney, County Kerry. www.muckross-house.ie. *(C)* **064/663-1440.** Admission €7.50 adults, €6 seniors, €4 students and children 18 and under, €22 families. Joint ticket with Muckross House and Gardens (above) €12 adults, €10 seniors, €6 students and children, €32 families. Mar 17–Apr and Oct weekends 1–6pm; May daily 1–6pm; June–Sept daily 10am–6pm; also bank holidays 1–6pm.

Ross Castle   This 15th-century restored fortress sits on the edge of the Lower Lake, 3km (1¾ miles) outside Killarney Town. Built by the O'Donoghue chieftains, this castle distinguished itself in 1652 as the last stronghold in Munster to surrender to Cromwell's forces. All that remains today is a tower house, surrounded by a fortified bawn (enclosure) with rounded turrets. The tower has been furnished in the style of the late 16th and early 17th centuries. While you can wander the grounds at will, you can see inside the castle only on a guided tour, and these tend to be a bit tedious, as the guides seem to scrounge around a bit for facts interesting enough to justify the ticket price. In good weather, the best way to reach it is via a lakeside walk (it's 3km/1¾ miles from Killarney to the castle). From the castle, you can take a boat tour of the lake, although these are not for those allergic to touristy things.

Ross Rd., off Kenmare rd. (N71), Killarney, County Kerry. ℂ **064/663-5851.** Admission €6 adults, €4 seniors, €2 students and children, €14 family. Mar and Oct daily 9:30am–5:45pm; Apr–Sept daily 9am–5:45pm. Last admission 45 min. before closing. Closed Nov–Mar.

ORGANIZED TOURS

BUS TOURS   **Dero's Tours,** 22 Main St. (www.derostours.com; ℂ **064/663-1251**), offers a 3-hour tour showing off Killarney's lakes from the best vantage points, including Aghadoe, the Gap of Dunloe, Ross Castle, Muckross House, and the Torc Waterfall. The tour is offered May through September daily at 10:30am, returning at about 4pm, but schedules vary, so check in advance. In addition they run various coach/boat/pony-and-trap packages around the Ring of Kerry, the Gap of Dunloe, and Dingle and the Slea Head Peninsula. Prices range from €30 to €50, with discounts for online booking.

   Bus Eireann, Bus Depot, Railway Road, off East Avenue Road (www.buseireann. ie; ℂ **064/663-4777**), and **Corcoran's Tours,** 8 College St. (www.corcorantours. com; ℂ **064/663-6666**), also offer tours around the Ring and to Dingle.

   Gap of Dunloe Tours, 7 High St., Killarney (www.gapofdunloetours.com; ℂ **064/663-0200**), takes you on a tour through the spectacularly scenic countryside above Killarney. You then walk the 7 miles to Kate Kearney's Cottage (or go by jaunting car for an extra €20, or pony for €30—cash only), and take a boat ride on the Killarney Lakes. The cost is €30.

JAUNTING-CAR TOURS   Enter the park as most visitors do, at Muckross House, and you're unlikely to go 5 minutes before a chirpy man in a flat cap offers to take you around on his jaunting car. These quaint horse-driven buggies are one of the main features of the landscape here and, cycling aside, they're the best way to cover ground in the park, as cars are not allowed. Jaunting-car rates are set and carefully monitored by the Killarney Urban District Council. Current rates (per person, based on four people to a jaunting cart) run roughly from €15 to upwards of €50, depending on how far you go. Destinations include Ross Castle, Muckross House and Gardens, Torc Waterfall, Muckross Abbey, Dinis Island, and Kate Kearney's Cottage, gateway to the Gap of Dunloe. You can hire a buggy at the park near Muckross House, or to arrange a tour in advance, contact **Tangney Tours,** 10B Muckross Close, Killarney (www. killarneyjauntingcars.com; ℂ **064/663-3358**). *Tip:* If you plan a long ride, spare your bottom and take a cushion. One hour clopping along on those hard wooden benches and you really know how bumpy the paths are.

BOAT TOURS   There is nothing quite like seeing the sights from a boat on the Lakes of Killarney. Two companies operate regular boating excursions, with full commentary. MV *Pride of the Lakes* **Tours** (www.killarneylaketours.ie; ℂ **064/663-2638**) sails daily in an enclosed boat from the pier at Ross Castle from April to October at 11am and 12:30, 2:30, 4, and 5:15pm. The trip lasts just over an hour, and reservations are suggested. MV *Lily of Killarney* **Tours** (www.killarneyjauntingcars.com; ℂ **064/663-3358**) sails from April to October daily at 10:30am, noon, and 1:45, 3:15, and 4:30pm. The cost for either tour is €12 adults, €6 children 11 and under.

OUTDOOR ACTIVITIES

BICYCLING   Killarney National Park, with its many lakeside and forest pathways, trails, and byways, is a paradise for bikers. Various vehicles are available for rent, from 21-speed touring bikes and mountain bikes to tandems. Rental charges average around €15 per day, €80 per week. Bicycles can be rented from **David O'Sullivan's Cycles,** Bishop Lane, New Street (www.killarneyrentabike.com; ✆ **064/663-1282**). Most shops are open year-round daily 9am to 6pm, until 8 or 9pm in the summer.

FISHING   Fishing for salmon and brown trout in Killarney's unpolluted lakes and rivers is a big attraction. Brown trout fishing is free on the lakes, but a permit is necessary for the rivers Flesk and Laune. A trout permit costs around €8 to €15 per day.

Salmon fishing anywhere in Ireland requires a license; the cost is around €36 per day, €50 for 21 days. Some rivers also require a salmon permit, which costs €10 to €15 per day. Permits and licenses can be obtained at the Fishery Office at the **Knockreer Estate Office,** New Street (✆ **064/663-1246**).

For fishing tackle, bait, rod rental, and other fishing gear, as well as permits and licenses, try **O'Neill's,** 6 Plunkett St. (✆ **064/663-1970**). The shop also arranges rentals of boats and *ghillies* (fishing guides) for around €80 per day on the Killarney Lakes, leaving from Ross Castle.

GOLF   Visitors are always welcome at the twin 18-hole championship courses of the **Killarney Golf & Fishing Club,** Killorglin Road, Fossa (www.killarney-golf. com; ✆ **064/663-1034**), 5km (3 miles) west of the town center. Widely praised as one of the most scenic golf settings in the world, these courses are surrounded by lake and mountain vistas. Greens fees are €30 to €90, depending on the course, and don't go up at weekends.

HORSEBACK RIDING   Many trails in the Killarney area are suitable for horseback riding. Hiring a horse costs about €25 per hour at **Killarney Riding Stables,** N72, Ballydowney (www.killarney-riding-stables.com; ✆ **064/663-1686**). Lessons and weeklong trail rides can also be arranged.

WALKING   There are four signposted nature trails in the **Killarney National Park.** The **Mossy Woods Nature Trail** starts near Muckross House, by Muckross Lake, and rambles 2.4km (1.5 miles) through yew woods along low cliffs. **Old Boat House Nature Trail** begins at the 19th-century boathouse below Muckross Gardens and leads half a mile around a small peninsula by Muckross Lake. **Arthur Young's Walk** (4.8km/3 miles) starts on the road to Dinis, traverses natural yew woods, and then follows a 200-year-old road on the Muckross Peninsula. The **Blue Pool Nature Trail** (2.4km/1.5 miles) goes from Muckross village through woodlands and past a small lake known as the Blue Pool. In addition, the **Cloghereen Nature Trail** is a small section of the Blue Pool trail that's designed to be fully accessible to blind visitors. A guide rope leads you along the route, which is lined by plants identified by scent and touch. An audio guide can be obtained from Muckross House in addition to leaflets and maps for the other four trails.

WHERE TO EAT

Bricín ★ TRADITIONAL IRISH   Seafood dishes and old-time Kerry *boxty* (a traditional dish of potato pancakes filled with chicken, seafood, curried lamb, or vegetables) are the trademarks of this relaxed restaurant above a craft-and-book shop. Don't be put off by the fact that you enter through the shop—the building dates from the

1830s, and the dining room has a pleasant rustic feel, with wood-paneled walls, turf fireplaces, and wood floors. The seafood is excellent and the service is charming.

26 High St., Killarney, County Kerry. www.bricin.com. © **064/663-4902.** Reservations recommended for dinner. Fixed-price dinners €19–€35; dinner main courses €19–€26. AE, DC, MC, V. Apr–Oct Tues–Sat 5:30–9pm.

Gaby's Seafood Restaurant ★★ SEAFOOD   The walls at Gaby's are filled with commendations and awards, which could be a bit tacky if the food weren't so good. Gaby's is known for its succulent lobster, served grilled or in a house sauce of cream, cognac, and spices. Other choices include turbot with glazed pastry, black sole meunière, and a giant Kerry shellfish platter—a veritable feast of prawns, scallops, mussels, lobster, and oysters.

27 High St., Killarney, County Kerry. www.gabysireland.com. © **064/663-2519.** Reservations recommended. Main courses €25–€48. AE, DC, MC, V. Mon–Sat 6–10pm. Closed late Feb to mid-Mar and Christmas week.

Treyvaud's ★ IRISH   When this place opened a couple of years back, it immediately became one of the most popular lunch spots in town. Owned by two Irish brothers, it offers a clever mix of traditional Irish favorites for lunch (stews, steak pie, and sandwiches). For dinner, steaks and roast guinea fowl sit alongside more adventurous fare, including pan-fried ostrich and kangaroo skewers. It all works, and the crowds keep coming.

62 High St., Killarney, County Kerry. www.treyvaudsrestaurant.com. © **064/663-3062.** Reservations recommended. Dinner main courses €17–€30. MC, V. Tues–Sat noon–10:30pm.

SHOPPING

Shopping hours are normally Monday through Saturday from 9am to 6pm, but from May to September or October most shops stay open to 9 or 10pm. Although there are more souvenir and crafts shops in Killarney than you can shake a shillelagh at, here are a few of the best.

   Christy's Irish Stores, 10 Main St., at the corner of Plunkett Street in the center of town (www.christysirishstores.com; © **064/663-3222**), carries an array of reasonably priced wares ranging from cheesy leprechaun souvenirs to genuinely attractive hand-knit or hand-loomed sweaters, crystal, china, and pottery. **Quill's Woolen Market,** 1 High St. (© **064/663-2277**), is one of the best shops in town for hand-knit sweaters of all kinds, as well as tweeds, mohair, and sheepskins.

   The **Mucros Craft Centre ★,** in the grounds of Muckross House (www.muckross-house.ie; © **064-663-1440**), is a studio and shop carrying on many County Kerry craft traditions; it features an on-premises weaver's workshop as well as a working pottery. There is also a wide selection of quality crafts from all over Ireland, and a sky-lit cafeteria overlooking the walled garden area. In town, **Serendipity ★,** 15 College St. (© **064/663-1056**), offers a wide range of unusual crafts from local artisans, such as hand-thrown pottery from the likes of Nicholas Mosse and Stephen Pearce, Jerpoint glass, and handcrafted jewelry.

WHERE TO STAY

Aghadoe Heights Hotel & Spa ★★   A few miles outside of town, and with spectacular views of the lake, Aghadoe Heights is a jarringly modern structure sitting rudely by an ancient ruined church, but inside it's a five-star oasis of luxury. Rooms are spacious and calming in neutral tones, with big, orthopedic beds. Many rooms have breathtaking views of the lake and surrounding hills through floor-to-ceiling, wall-to-wall windows. Nothing is impossible here, with 24-hour room service and the excellent **spa** available at the push of a button. Guests can book a relaxing hour in the steam rooms and saunas for €25. Breakfast is silver service, and the in-house **restaurant** specializes in modern Irish cuisine.

Lakes of Killarney, Killarney, County Kerry. www.aghadoeheights.com. ℂ **064/663-1345.** Fax 064/663-1345. 74 units. €190–€270 double. Rates include full breakfast. MC, V. Free parking. **Amenities:** Restaurant; bar; indoor pool; exercise room; full-service spa. *In room:* TV/DVD, minibar, hair dryer, Wi-Fi (free).

Fairview House ★ ☺ Somewhere between boutique hotel and upmarket guesthouse, Fairview House is an airy, modern kind of place in the center of town. Rooms are spacious and comfortable, with polished wood floors, subtle cream and red colors, and enormous beds. There are also good-sized family rooms as well as wheelchair-accessible rooms. The restaurant earns good reviews, as its head chef came from the Cooperage, one of Killarney's best restaurants before it closed a couple of years ago.

College St., Killarney. www.fairviewkillarney.com. ℂ **064/663-4164.** 29 units. €90–€150 double. MC, V. **Amenities:** Restaurant; room service. *In room:* TV, hair dryer, Wi-Fi (free).

Randles Court ★ A former rectory dating from the early 20th century, this attractive yellow, gabled four-story house sits just outside Killarney Town on the road to Muckross House. With marble floors and chandeliers, and warmed by open fireplaces, the lounges and lobby are quite elegant. Rooms have traditional decor, including heavy armoires, antique desks, and vanities, and are tastefully decorated in bright colors.

Muckross rd. (N71), Killarney, County Kerry. www.randlescourt.com. ℂ **064/663-5333** or 800/4-CHOICE (424-6423) in the U.S. Fax 064/663-5206. 55 units. €110–€170 double. Rates include service charge and full breakfast. AE, DC, MC, V. Free parking. **Amenities:** Restaurant; bar; indoor pool; exercise room; room service; babysitting. *In room:* TV.

Iveragh Peninsula/The Ring of Kerry

The Iveragh Peninsula is nearly 1,820 sq. km (700 sq. miles) of wild splendor, which you'll notice once you get off the tourist strip. Admittedly, almost everyone who gets this far feels compelled to "do" the Ring of Kerry; so, once it's done, why not take an unplanned turn, get truly lost, and let serendipity lead you to the unexpected and the unspoiled?

ESSENTIALS
Getting There
BY BUS Bus Eireann (ℂ 064/663-0011) provides limited daily service from Killarney to Caherciveen, Waterville, Kenmare, and other towns on the Ring of Kerry.

BY CAR This is by far the best way to get around the Ring. For the most part, the route follows N70.

Visitor Information
Stop in at the **Killarney Tourist Office,** Aras Fáilte, at the Town Centre Car Park, Beech Road, Killarney (www.killarney.ie; ℂ 064/663-1633), before you explore the area. For hours, see "Visitor Information," under "Killarney Town," earlier in this chapter. The **Kenmare Tourist Office,** Market Square, Kenmare (www.kenmare.ie; ℂ 064/664-1233), is open daily Easter through September 9:15am to 5:30pm, with extended hours in July and August. The rest of the year (Oct–Easter), it's open Monday to Saturday.

EXPLORING THE RING OF KERRY

Although it's possible to circle the peninsula in as little as 4 hours, the only way to get a feel for the area and the people is to leave the main road, and get out of your car to explore some of the inland and coastal towns. The ring is not short of good hotels and B&Bs, but most visitors choose to base themselves in **Killarney ★** for the convenience of having plentiful restaurants and shops. We prefer the gentler charms of **Kenmare ★★★**. Originally called *Neidin* (pronounced Nay-*deen*, meaning "little nest" in Irish), Kenmare is indeed a little nest of verdant foliage and colorful buildings nestled between the River Roughty and Kenmare Bay.

From Kenmare to busy **Killarney**, the Ring road takes you through a scenic mountain stretch known as **Moll's Gap.** Killarney is best known for its glorious surroundings, in particular the spectacular landscapes of **Killarney National Park** (see "Killarney Town," earlier in this chapter).

Departing Killarney, follow the signs for **Killorglin ★★**, a smallish town that lights up in mid-August when it has a traditional horse, sheep, and cattle fair. Continue on the N70, and glimpses of Dingle Bay will soon appear on your right. **Carrantuohill**, at 1,041m (3,414 ft.) Ireland's tallest mountain, is to your left, and bleak views of open bog land constantly come into view.

Glenbeigh ★★ is next on the Ring, and it's a sweet little seafront town with streets lined with palm trees and a sandy beach. **Portmagee ★★** is another lovely seaside town, connected by a bridge to **Valentia Island,** which houses the informative Skellig Heritage Centre.

The most memorable and magical site to visit on the Iveragh Peninsula is **Skellig Michael ★★★**, a rocky pinnacle towering over the sea, where medieval monks built their monastery in ascetic isolation. The crossing to the island can be rough, so you'll want to visit on a clear and calm day, if possible (the boat doesn't run in very bad weather). Seabirds nest here in abundance, and more than 20,000 pairs of gannets inhabit neighboring **Little Skellig** during the summer nesting season.

Continuing on the N70, the next point of interest is **Derrynane**, at **Caherdaniel. Derrynane** is the former seat of the O'Connell clan and erstwhile home to Daniel O'Connell ("the Liberator" who freed Irish Catholics from the last of the English Penal Laws in the 19th century). Watch for signs to **Staigue Fort ★★**, about 3km (1¾ miles) off the main road. The well-preserved ancient circular fort is constructed of rough stones without mortar of any kind. The walls are 4m (13 ft.) thick at the base, and the diameter is about 27m (89 ft.). Experts think it dates from around 1000 B.C.

Sneem, the next village on the circuit, is a charming little place, where houses are painted in vibrant shades. The colors—blue, pink, yellow, and orange—burst out on a rainy day, like a little ray of sunshine.

WHERE TO EAT

The Blue Bull TRADITIONAL IRISH   The village of Sneem is so small that if you blink, you miss it. Yet it has several good pubs, and this one serves excellent food. There are three small rooms, each with an open fireplace, plus a sky-lit conservatory in the back. Traditional Irish fare, like smoked salmon and Irish stew, shares the menu with such dishes as salmon stuffed with spinach and Valencia scallops in brandy—all served to a backdrop of traditional Irish music on most nights.

South Sq., Ring of Kerry rd. (N70), Sneem, County Kerry. ℂ **064/664-5382.** Reservations recommended. Main courses €10–€26. AE, MC, V. Bar food year-round daily 11am–8pm. Restaurant Mar–Oct daily 6–10pm.

Lime Tree ★★ MODERN IRISH   Innovative cuisine is the focus at this Kenmare restaurant in an 1821 landmark renovated schoolhouse next to the Park Hotel. Paintings by local artists line the stone walls in the atmospheric dining room. The menu offers modern interpretations of classic Irish dishes and European cuisine; typical mains could include filet of beef with colcannon, sautéed onions and peppercorn jus, or hummus and blue cheese with orzo salad and beet salsa. Typical desserts include homemade praline ice cream and warm crepes with butterscotch sauce.

Shelbourne Rd., Kenmare, County Kerry. www.limetreerestaurant.com. © **064/664-1225.** Reservations recommended. Main courses €18–€28. MC, V. Apr–Nov daily 6:30–10pm.

Prego ★ 🏅 ITALIAN   When you're craving a break from all that heavy Irish food, head here for fresh, tasty Italian cuisine. The pasta is all homemade, and served with a light touch on the sauce. Salads are big and crisp, and the thin-crust pizzas are all made from scratch to order. All the classics are here and are well made.

Henry St., Kenmare, County Kerry. © **064/664-2350.** All items €7–€16. MC, V. Daily 9am–10:30pm.

Purple Heather ★ IRISH   This lovely little eatery is *the* place to lunch in Kenmare. The food consists of tearoom classics with a gourmet twist—wild smoked salmon or prawn salad; smoked trout pâté; vegetarian omelets; Irish cheese platters; and fresh, homemade soups.

Henry St., Kenmare, County Kerry. © **064/41016.** All items €7–€18. No credit cards. Mon–Sat 11am–5:30pm. Closed Sun and bank holidays.

SHOPPING

At **De Barra Jewellery,** Main Street (© **064/664-1867**), talented jeweler Shane de Barra makes lovely freshwater pearl concoctions in silver and gold, and his restrained touch on gold rings and bangles marks this place as special. **Quills Woollen Market,** Main Street (© **064/664-1078**), is good for chunky, Aran hand-knits, traditional Donegal tweed, delicate Irish linen, and Celtic jewelry. **Avoca Handweavers at Moll's Gap,** N71 (www.avoca.ie; © **064/663-4720**), is a branch of the famous tweed makers of County Wicklow. This outlet is set on a high mountain pass between Killarney and Kenmare. The wares range from colorful hand-woven capes, jackets, throws, and knitwear to pottery and jewelry. It also has a great gourmet cafe.

WHERE TO STAY

The Park Hotel ★★★ 🎁   Ensconced in a palm-tree-lined garden beside Kenmare Bay, this imposing 19th-century building is a grand, luxury hotel. In the high-ceilinged sitting rooms, fires crackle in the open fireplaces and original oil paintings decorate the walls. Guest rooms have exquisite Georgian and Victorian furnishings, and some have four-posters, all with firm mattresses, rich fabrics, and peaceful waterfront or mountain views. The hotel restaurant is acclaimed for its modern Irish cuisine. The hotel spa, **Sámas,** is famed in Ireland for its creative use of the gorgeous, bucolic setting.

Kenmare, County Kerry. www.parkkenmare.com. © **064/664-1200** or 800/323-5463 in the U.S. Fax 064/664-1402. 46 units. €350–€470 double. AE, DC, MC, V. Closed Nov 30–Dec 22 and Jan 4–Feb 12. **Amenities:** Restaurant; bar; 18-hole golf course; tennis court; spa; concierge; room service; babysitting; nonsmoking rooms. *In room:* TV/DVD, minibar, hair dryer, CD player, Wi-Fi (free).

Sheen Falls Lodge ★★★   Originally the 18th-century home of the earl of Kerry, this salubrious resort sits beside a natural waterfall amid vast, sprawling grounds. Reception staff addresses guests by name, the bar feels like a drawing room, and the 1,000-volume library, with its green leather sofas and floor-to-ceiling bookshelves, resembles an old-fashioned gentlemen's club. Guest rooms are spacious, decorated in rich, contemporary style; each overlooks the falls (stunning when floodlit at night) or the bay. There are self-catering cottages and villas available for those with deep pockets and a desire for privacy.

Kenmare, County Kerry. www.sheenfallslodge.ie. © **064/664-1600** or 800/537-8483 in the U.S. Fax 064/664-1386. 66 units. €435–€575 double. Full breakfast €17–€24. AE, DC, MC, V. Closed Jan 2–Feb 1. **Amenities:** 2 restaurants; bar; indoor pool; tennis court; exercise room; spa; Jacuzzi; concierge; room service. *In room:* A/C, TV/VCR, minibar, hair dryer, Wi-Fi (free).

Shelburne Lodge ★★   This Georgian farmhouse has been transformed into one of the most original, stylish, and comfortable B&Bs in Killowen. Every room has polished wood parquet floors, quality antique furnishings, contemporary art, and a luxurious but homey feel. The guest rooms are all large and gorgeously appointed, and breakfasts are virtually decadent.

Killowen, Cork Rd., Kenmare, County Kerry. www.shelburnelodge.com. © **064/664-1013.** Fax 064/664-2067. 9 units. €100–€160 double. Rates include service charge and full breakfast. MC, V. Closed Dec to mid-Mar. **Amenities:** Tennis court. *In room:* TV, Wi-Fi (free).

The Dingle Peninsula

Like the Iveragh Peninsula, Dingle has a spectacularly scenic peripheral road, and a substantial tourist trade has blossomed along it. But as soon as you veer off the main roads, you'll discover extraordinary desolate beauty, seemingly worlds away from the tour buses. Dingle Town itself is smaller and less congested than Killarney, and the Dingle Peninsula is an ideal drive or bicycling tour.

Don't miss **Slea Head,** at the southwestern extremity of the peninsula, with its pristine beaches, great walks, and fascinating archaeological remains. The little village of **Dunquin,** which sits between Slea Head and Clogher Head, is home to the **Blasket Centre** (© **066/915–6444**), which has an excellent exhibition on the literary heritage of the Blasket Islands. It's open April to October, daily from 10am to 6pm. Admission costs €4.

Dating from the Bronze Age, **Dunbeg Fort** sits on a stunning promontory, just south of Slea Head. The circular ruins are no more than a few feet high, but it's worth the €3 admission fee for the view alone. From Slea Head, the Dingle Way continues east to Dingle Town (24km/15 miles) or north along the coast toward Ballyferriter.

Just offshore from Dunquin are the seven **Blasket Islands;** a ferry (www.blasketislands.ie; © **086/335-3805**) connects Great Blasket with the mainland when the weather permits. Ferries depart from Duquin Harbour and take about 20 minutes. Alternatively, you can take a 3-hour cruise around the islands with one of their **Eco-Marine Tours** (www.marinetours.ie), which leave from Ventry Harbour in Ventry, 7km (4.3 miles) east of Dunquin. The islands were abandoned by the last permanent residents in 1953 and now are inhabited only by a few summer visitors who share the place with the seals and seabirds. A magnificent 13km (8-mile) **walk** goes to the west end of Great Blasket and back, passing sea cliffs and ivory beaches; you can stop along the way at the only cafe on the island.

Dingle Town (An Daingean)

Dingle (*An Daingean*) is a charming, brightly colored little town at the foot of steep hills and on the edge of a gorgeous stretch of coast. There's not much to do here, but it has plenty of hotels and restaurants and makes a good base for exploring the region.

EXPLORING DINGLE TOWN

Despite the big-sounding name, **Dingle's Oceanworld Aquarium,** Dingle Harbour (www.dingle-oceanworld.ie; ℂ **066/915-2111**), is a nicely designed (if small) aquarium featuring a tunnel you can walk through with the fish swimming above and around you. Tickets are €13 adults, €7.50 children 15 and under, and €38 families. It's open daily from 10am to 5pm.

Forget Flipper. In Dingle, the name to know is Fungie. Every day, **Fungie the Dolphin Tours ★★,** The Pier, Dingle (ℂ **066/915-2626**), ferries visitors out into the nearby waters to see the famous village mascot. Trips cost €16 for adults and €8 for children 11 and under. They last about 1 hour and depart regularly, roughly every 2 hours in the off-season and as frequently as every half-hour in high season. Fungie swims up to the boat, and the boatmen stay out long enough for ample sightings (you get a refund if he doesn't show). Wonderful though this tour can be, however, we do wonder how much longer Fungie will be drawing in the crowds, given that he's been at it for 25 years—and nobody quite knows how old he is, so best to call ahead before you raise the hopes of dolphin-loving youngsters.

ENJOYING THE GREAT OUTDOORS

BEACHES   The Dingle Peninsula is known for its dramatic beaches. The best known is **Inch Strand ★,** a 5km-long (3-mile) sandy stretch.

Kilmurray Bay at Minard ★★ is a Lilliputian dream come to life, as in the shadow of Minard Castle, giant sausage-shaped sandstone boulders form a beach unlike anything you've ever seen. Nearby, **Trabeg Beach ★★** features exquisite wave-sculptured maroon sandstone statues, sheer rock cliffs, and sea caves lined with veins of crystalline quartz.

Castlegregory ★ *(Caislean an Ghriare)* is a seaside village with two wide, sandy beaches. It's known for its good diving waters, and scuba divers and watersports fans flock to the place in summer. It's a bit bustling for isolationists, who are better off heading to tiny **Cloghane** *(An Clochán)* on the southern edge of Brandon Bay. With a population of 270 and a lovely beach, it's got much to offer.

BICYCLING   Mountain bikes can be rented at **Foxy John Moriarty,** Main Street, Dingle (ℂ **066/915-1316**). Foxy John's has the added advantage of also being a pub, although you might want to save your pints until after your ride. Alternatively, the staff at the **Mountain Man Outdoor Shop,** Strand Street, Dingle (www.themountain manshop.com; ℂ **066/915-2400**), can handle the arrangements for you. The cost is normally around €15 per day, or €60 per week.

DIVING   On the North Dingle Peninsula, **Harbour House,** Scraggane Pier, Castlegregory, County Kerry (www.waterworld.ie; ℂ **066/713-9292**), is a diving center that offers packages including diving, room, and board at good rates. Classes for beginners are available.

SAILING   The **Dingle Sailing Centre,** the Marina, Dingle (www.saildingle.com; ℂ **066/915-6426**), offers an array of courses taught by experienced, certified instructors. Summer courses run from about €130 to €200.

SEA ANGLING   For sea-angling packages and day trips, contact Nick O'Connor at **Angler's Rest,** Ventry (ℂ **066/915-9947**), or Seán O'Conchúir (ℂ **066/915-5429**), representing the **Kerry Angling Association.**

WALKING   The **Dingle Way** circles the peninsula, covering 153km (95 miles) of gorgeous mountain and coastal landscape. The most rugged section is along Brandon

Head, where the trail passes between Mount Brandon and the ocean; the views are tremendous, but the walk is long (about 24km/15 miles or 9 hr.) and strenuous, and should be attempted only when the sky is clear. For more information, look for *The Dingle Way Map Guide,* available in local tourist offices and shops.

WHERE TO EAT

An Cafe Liteartha CAFE/TEAROOM   "The Literary Cafe" is a self-service cafe in an excellent bookstore. This is heaven for those interested in Irish history, literature, maps, and scones. The cafe sells fresh soups, sandwiches, salads, seafood, and scones and cakes. It's ideal for a quiet lunch or snack.

Dykegate St., Dingle, County Kerry. *Ⓒ* **066/915-2204.** All items €3–€6. No credit cards. Mon–Sat 9am–6pm (later in summer).

The Chart House ★★ MODERN IRISH   Book ahead at this popular restaurant with an inviting bistro atmosphere, lots of polished pine and warm, rose-colored walls. The cooking here is an ambitious blend of Irish dishes and outside influences. Main courses might include steak filet with black pudding mash, or pork with brandied apples. With unusual food and excellent service, it has carved out quite a reputation.

The Mall, Dingle, County Kerry. www.charthousedingle.com. *Ⓒ* **066/915-2255.** Reservations required. Fixed-price 2-course menu €32.50; main courses €18–€27. MC, V. Wed–Mon 6:30–10pm. Closed Jan 8–Feb 12.

Doyle's Seafood Bar ★★ SEAFOOD   This is a great, laid-back place to enjoy fresh local seafood. You can start with a plate of local oysters, and then move on to a perfectly prepared salmon Nicoise, or shellfish fricassee. The early-bird menu (served until 7:30pm) is excellent value, and more than just the disappointing selection one often finds with such deals.

4 John St., Dingle, County Kerry. www.doylesofdingle.ie. *Ⓒ* **066/915-2674**. Fixed-price early-bird menus, 2 courses €23, 3 courses €28; dinner main courses €23–€30. MC, V. Mon–Sat 5–9:30pm.

Lord Bakers SEAFOOD/PUB GRUB   The ages-old decor in this pub restaurant combines a stone fireplace and cozy alcoves with a more modern, sunlit conservatory and a few Art Deco touches. The menu offers standard bar food, but juices it up with things like crab claws in garlic butter, Kerry oysters, seafood Mornay, and steaks. Dinner specialties are more elegant, including sole stuffed with smoked salmon and spinach in cheese sauce, lobster, and rack of lamb.

Main St., Dingle, County Kerry. www.lordbakers.ie. *Ⓒ* **066/915-1277.** Reservations recommended for dinner. Bar food €10–€16; dinner main courses €16–€30. AE, MC, V. Fri–Wed 12:30–2pm and 6–9:30pm.

WHERE TO STAY

Dingle Skellig Hotel ☺   This three-story hotel has an idyllic location next to Dingle Bay on the eastern edge of town. The look of the place is all polished pine and contemporary touches. Most guest rooms are done in neutral colors with floral touches, although some have slightly lurid color combinations. Many have gorgeous views. This is a family hotel in the classic sense—in the summer, there's a kids club with organized day and evening fun.

Annascaul Rd., Dingle, County Kerry. www.dingleskellig.com. *Ⓒ* **066/915-1144.** Fax 066/915-1501. 111 units. €130–€228 double. Rates include full breakfast. AE, MC, V. Free parking. Closed Jan–Feb Mon–Thurs (open weekends). **Amenities:** Restaurant; bar; lounge; indoor pool; exercise room; spa; Jacuzzi; steam room; children's playroom; room service. *In room:* TV, hair dryer, Wi-Fi (free).

Greenmount House ★★   This modern bungalow on a hill above Dingle isn't much to look at from the outside, but don't be fooled. Inside it's a stylish place, with lush colors and clever design. Each of the spacious guest rooms has its own sitting area and large bathroom—some are split-level, a few have balconies, and some have sea views. Breakfasts, ranging from smoked salmon omelets to ham-and-pineapple toasted sandwiches, have won awards for owners Mary and John Curran.

John St., Dingle, County Kerry. www.greenmount-house.com. ✆ **066/915-1414.** 12 units. €100–€150 double. Rates include full breakfast. MC, V. Closed Dec 20–26. **Amenities:** Nonsmoking rooms. *In room:* TV, Wi-Fi (free).

Galway City

For many travelers to Ireland, Galway is the farthest edge of their journey. It's just far enough from the madding crowds (3-hr. drive from Dublin) without pushing the limits of some people's comfort. If you've come this far, you've seen the land that drew the ancient settlers to Connemara and seduced the early Christian monks with its isolation. In fact, some went even farther—monastic remains have been found on 17 islands off the Galway coast.

These days, this region is bustling and affluent, its villages are brightly painted, and property prices are soaring. Galway City, the heart of the county, has an affluent, artsy population of 70,000, and is one of Ireland's most appealing cities. It is a busy worka-day town, but it also has a lively art and music scene that has made it the unofficial arts capital of the country. The excellent Galway Arts Festival, held every summer, is an accessible, buzzing culture fest.

Essentials

GETTING THERE

BY TRAIN   **Irish Rail** trains from Dublin and other points arrive daily at **Ceannt Station** (www.irishrail.ie; ✆ 091/561444), off Eyre Square, Galway.

BY BUS   Buses from all parts of Ireland arrive daily at **Bus Éireann Travel Centre,** Ceannt Station, Galway (www.buseireann.ie; ✆ 091/562000).

BY CAR   As the gateway to west Ireland, Galway is the terminus for many national roads. They lead in from all parts of Ireland, including N84 and N17 from the north, N63 and N6 from the east, and N67 and N18 from the south.

VISITOR INFORMATION

For information about Galway and the surrounding areas, contact or visit **Galway Discover Ireland Centre (Aras Fáilte),** Foster Street (www.irelandwest.ie; ✆ 091/537700). Hours are May to September daily 9am to 5:45pm; October to April Monday to Saturday 9am to 5:45pm. For further detailed information on events and news in Galway, consult www.galway.net.

GETTING AROUND

Galway has an excellent local bus service. Buses run from the **Bus Éireann Travel Centre** (✆ 091/562000) or Eyre Square to various suburbs, including Salthill and the Galway Bay coastline. The fare starts at around €1.70.

There are taxi stands at Eyre Square and all the major hotels in the city. If you need to call a cab, try **Abbey Cabs** (✆ 091/533333), **Big-O Taxis** (✆ 091/585858), or **Galway Taxis** (✆ 091/561111).

A town of medieval arches, alleyways, and cobblestone lanes, Galway is best explored on foot (wear comfortable shoes). To see the highlights, follow the signposts on the Tourist Trail of Old Galway. A handy booklet, available at the tourist office and at most bookshops, provides historical and architectural details. If you must bring your car into the center of town, park it and then walk. There is free parking in front of Galway Cathedral, but most street parking uses a pay-to-park system. It costs upward of €2 per hour. Multistory parking garages average €2.60 per hour or €22 per day (though the **Harbour Hotel** on New Dock Road offers a day rate of €8).

Exploring Galway City

Tucked between the Atlantic and the navy blue waters of Lough Corrib, Galway was founded by fishermen. Local legend has it that Christopher Columbus attended Mass at Galway's **St. Nicholas Collegiate Church ★★** in 1477, before one of several attempts to circumnavigate the globe. Originally built in 1320, the church has been enlarged, rebuilt, and embellished over the years.

In the center of town, on Shop Street, is **Lynch's Castle,** dating from 1490 and renovated in the 19th century. It's the oldest Irish medieval town house used daily for commercial purposes (it's now a branch of the Allied Irish Bank). The stern exterior is watched over by a handful of amusing gargoyles.

In the 16th and 17th centuries, Galway was wealthy and cosmopolitan, with particularly strong trade links to Spain. Close to the city docks, you can still see the area where Spanish merchants unloaded cargo from their galleons. The **Spanish Arch** was one of four arches built in 1594, and the **Spanish Parade** is a small open square.

The hub of the city is a pedestrian park at **Eyre Square** (pronounced *Air Square*), officially called the **John F. Kennedy Park** in commemoration of his visit here in June 1963, a few months before his assassination. From here, it's a minute's walk to the **medieval quarter ★** with its festive, Left Bank atmosphere.

Galway Irish Crystal Heritage Centre ★★   Visitors to this distinctive crystal manufacturer can watch the craftsmen at work—blowing, shaping, and hand-cutting glassware—and then shop for the perfect pieces to take back home. Glassmaking demonstrations are continuous on weekdays. The shop and restaurant are open daily.

East of the city on the main Dublin road (N6), Merlin Park, Galway, County Galway. www.galway crystal.ie. **℘091/757311.** Free admission. Mon–Fri 9am–5:30pm; Sat 10am–5:30pm; Sun 11am–5pm.

Nora Barnacle House ★   Just across from the St. Nicholas church clock tower, this restored 19th-century terrace house was once the home of Nora Barnacle, who later would become the wife of **James Joyce.** It contains letters, photographs, and other exhibits on the lives of the Joyces and their connections with Galway.

Bowling Green. **℘ 091/564743.** Admission €2.50 adults, €2 seniors, students and children 6–12. Daily 10am–1pm and 2–5pm.

ORGANIZED TOURS

BOAT TOURS   The *Corrib Princess* (www.corribprincess.ie; **℘ 091/592447**) is a 157-passenger, two-deck boat that cruises along the River Corrib, with commentary on points of interest. The trip lasts 90 minutes, passing castles, historical sites, and wildlife. There is a full bar and snack service. You can buy tickets at the dock or in the tourist office; fares are €15 adults, €13 seniors and students, €35 families (up to 3 children; extra children 15 and under €7 each).

OUTDOOR ACTIVITIES

BICYCLING   To rent a bike, contact **Richard Walsh Cycles,** Headford Road, Woodquay (**℘ 091/565710**).

FISHING Set beside the River Corrib, Galway City and nearby Connemara are popular fishing centers for salmon and sea trout. For the latest information on requirements for licenses and local permits, check with the **Inland Fisheries Ireland–Galway,** Weir Lodge, Earl's Island, Galway (www.fishinginireland.info; ✆ **091/563118**). For gear and equipment, try **Duffys Fishing,** 5 Mainguard St. (✆ **091/562367**), **Freeney Sport Shop,** 19 High St. (✆ **091/568794**), or **Great Outdoors Sports Centre,** Eglinton Street (✆ **091/562869**).

GOLF Less than 3km (1¾ miles) west of the city is the 18-hole, par-69 seaside course at **Galway Golf Club,** Blackrock, Galway (www.galwaygolf.com; ✆ **091/522033**). Greens fees are €25.

HORSEBACK RIDING Riding enthusiasts head to **Aille Cross Equestrian Centre,** Aille Cross, Loughrea, County Galway (www.aille-cross.com; ✆ **091/841216**), about 32km (20 miles) east of Galway City. For about €25 to €40 an hour, you can ride through nearby farmlands, woodlands, forest trails, and along beaches.

Where to Eat

Ard Bia at Nimmo's ★★ WINE BAR/SEAFOOD This is one of Galway's trendy tables—and with good reason. The menu changes according to season and tends to feature seafood during the summer and game in the winter. Typical dishes include Atlantic brill with saffron, or roast breast of free-range duck with almond couscous. Desserts could be burned honey and blood orange panna cotta, or chocolate mousse. The atmosphere is bohemian and romantic—just make sure you book.

Long Walk, Spanish Arch. www.nimmos.ie. ✆ **091/561114.** Reservations recommended. Main courses €16–€25. MC, V. Daily 7–10pm.

Busker Browne's ★ CAFE/BAR A modern cafe in a medieval building, Busker Browne's is a favorite of locals and travelers for its funky decor—mixing ancient stonework with modern art—and for its big breakfasts, hamburgers, sandwiches, fresh stews, and pasta. It's one of just a few Galway eateries that stays open late.

Upper Cross St. www.buskerbrownes.com. ✆ **091/563377.** Main courses €10–€19. MC, V. Mon–Sat 10:30am–11:30pm; Sun 12:30–11:30pm.

Kirwan's Lane ★★ CONTINENTAL Chef-owner Michael O'Grady's stylish, inviting restaurant is widely acclaimed, and for good reason. The dining room is rustic chic, with pine furnishings and brightly painted walls. It's particularly good value at lunchtime, when the constantly changing menu might include a starter of Irish brie crostini and marinated salmon roulade. The dinner menu features dishes with fresh local produce and seafood, all beautifully presented.

Kirwan's Lane. www.kirwanslane.com. ✆ **091/568266.** Reservations recommended. Main courses €18–€28. AE, MC, V. Daily 12:30–2:30pm and 6–10:30pm. Closed Sun Sept–June.

The Malt House ★★ MODERN IRISH This long-established place on High Street has developed something of a new lease of life since new owners came in a few years ago. The dining room is bright and spacious, with chic contemporary art. The food is upmarket Irish bistro dishes with an international twist, and an emphasis on locally sourced, seasonal ingredients—seabass with parsley mash and lemon caramel, or chargrilled beef filet with cheddar, onion, and potato soufflé. Lunch strikes a more traditional note (fish and chips, chicken breast with mashed potatoes, BLT salad), and it's decidedly cheaper too.

High St. www.themalthouse.ie. ✆ **091/567866.** Reservations recommended. Early-bird menus, 2 courses €24, 3 courses €29; main courses €19–€28. AE, MC, V. Mon–Sat 12:30–3pm and 6–10:30pm.

11

IRELAND

Kerry & the Dingle Peninsula

McDonagh's FISH AND CHIPS/SEAFOOD   For superfresh seafood, straight off the boat, this is one of Galway's best choices. The place is divided into three parts: a traditional "chipper" for fish and chips, a smart restaurant in the back, and a fish market where you can buy raw seafood. The McDonaghs, fishmongers for more than four generations, buy direct from local fishermen every day, and it shows; crowds line up every night to get in. The menu includes salmon, trout, lemon or black sole, turbot, and silver hake, all cooked to order. In the back restaurant, you can crack your own prawns' tails and crab claws in the shell, or tackle a whole lobster.

22 Quay St. www.mcdonaghs.net. ✆ **091/565809.** Reservations not accepted. Main courses €13–€20 (seafood platter €24); fish and chips about €9. AE, MC, V. Restaurant daily 5–10pm; fish and chips takeout Mon–Sat noon–11pm, Sun 4–10pm.

Shopping

Some of Galway's best shopping is in tiny malls of small shops clustered in historic buildings, such as the **Cornstore ★★** on Middle Street, the **Grainstore** on Lower Abbeygate Street, and the **Bridge Mills,** a 430-year-old mill building beside the River Corrib. **Eyre Square Centre,** the downtown area's largest shopping mall, with 50 shops, incorporates a section of Galway's medieval town wall into its complex.

Mac Eocagain/Galway Woollen Market at 21 High St. (✆ **091/562696**) is an excellent resource if you're shopping for traditional Aran hand-knits and colorful hand-loomed sweaters and capes. Each item has two prices, one including value-added tax (VAT) and one tax-free for non-European Union (E.U.) residents.

P. Powell and Sons at the Four Corners, Williamsgate St. (✆ **091/562295**) is a family-run shop with a large supply of traditional Irish music, instruments, and recordings.

Also on Williamsgate Street, **Fallers of Galway ★** (www.fallers.com; ✆ **091/561226**) is a prime source of Claddagh rings. Another option is nearby **Hartmann & Son Ltd. ★** (✆ **091/562063**), a traditional Galway jeweler.

For handicrafts, visit **Design Concourse ★★** on Kirwan's Lane (✆ **091/566927**), which is filled with the work of dozens of talented Irish craftspeople.

Where to Stay

The G ★ 🎁   This trendy place was designed by the hat designer Philip Treacy and it shows. Wonderfully over-the-top, it looks like the errant love child of *My Fair Lady* and *Beyond the Valley of the Dolls*. There are psychedelic touches (the Pink Salon is the color of Pepto-Bismol) and a clear love of disco chic (the otherwise subtle taupe-and-white grand salon has masses of huge glass baubles hanging overhead). Rooms are calmer, in soothing white with touches of coffee and cream, and luxuriant beds. Bathrooms are sensational, and many have showers built for two. The **ESPA spa** is oh-so-sophisticated, and it's all very Manhattan. It's about a 15-minute walk from central Galway. There is no place trendier on the Ireland's west coast.

Wellpark, Galway, County Galway. www.ghotel.ie. ✆ **091/865200.** Fax 091/865203. 101 units. €160–€280 double. Rates include full breakfast. AE, MC, V. **Amenities:** Restaurant; bar; spa; nonsmoking rooms. *In room:* TV, DVD/CD player, hair dryer, Wi-Fi (free).

Glenlo Abbey Hotel ★★   About 3km (1¾ miles) outside of Galway on the main Clifden road, this secluded, sprawling stone hotel overlooks Lough Corrib in a sylvan setting, surrounded by a 9-hole golf course. Dating from 1740, the building has retained its grandeur in the public areas, with hand-carved wood furnishings, ornate plasterwork, and an extensive collection of Irish art and antiques. The guest rooms, which have lovely views of Lough Corrib and the countryside, are luxuriously decorated with traditional furnishings.

Bushy Park, Galway, County Galway. www.glenlo.com. ℂ **091/526666.** Fax 091/527800. 46 units. €225–€340 double. Rates include full Irish breakfast. AE, MC, V. Free parking. **Amenities:** 2 restaurants; 2 bars; 9-hole golf course; concierge; room service. *In room:* TV, hair dryer, Wi-Fi (free).

The House Hotel ★★   This four-story stone building, in Galway's historic area next to the Spanish Arch, was formerly a warehouse, and is now a boutique loft hotel. From its low-key lobby with polished oak floors, columns, and big windows, to its subtle, contemporary rooms, it's a comfortable, modern alternative. Rooms are divided into categories like "comfy," "classy," and "swanky," and they pretty much do what it says on the label. The swanky rooms are definitely, well, the swankiest. But all have comfortable beds, soft linens, lots of sunlight, high ceilings, and a refreshing urban feel.

Lower Merchant's Rd., Galway, County Galway. www.thehousehotel.ie. ℂ **091/538900.** Fax 091/568262. 45 units. €130–€230 double. AE, DC, MC, V. **Amenities:** Restaurant; bar. *In room:* TV, minibar, hair dryer, Wi-Fi (free).

ITALY

by Eleonora Baldwin, John Moretti,
Stephen Keeling, Donald Strachan

taly is a feast for the senses and the intellect. Any mention of Italy calls up visions of Pompeii, the Renaissance, and Italy's rich treasury of art and architecture. But some of the country's best experiences can involve the simple act of living in the Italian style, eating the regional cuisines, and enjoying the countryside.

ROME ★★★

Rome is a city of images and sounds, all vivid and all unforgettable. You can see one of the most striking images at dawn—ideally from Gianicolo (Janiculum Hill)—when the Roman skyline, with its bell towers and cupolas, gradually comes into focus. As the sun rises, the Roman symphony begins. First come the peals of church bells calling the faithful to Mass. Then the streets fill with cars, taxis, tour buses, and Vespas, the drivers gunning their engines and blaring their horns. Next the sidewalks are overrun with office workers, chattering as they rush off to their desks, but not before ducking into a cafe for their first cappuccino. Shop owners loudly throw up the metal grilles protecting their stores; the fruit-and-vegetable stands are crowded with Romans out to buy the day's supply of fresh produce, haggling over prices and caviling over quality.

Around 10am, the visitors—you included, with your guidebook in hand—take to the streets, battling the crowds and traffic as they wend from Renaissance palaces and baroque buildings to ancient ruins like the Colosseum and the Forum. After you've spent a long day in the sun, marveling at the sights you've seen millions of times in photos and movies, you can pause to experience the charm of Rome at dusk.

Find a cafe at summer twilight, and watch the shades of pink and rose turn to gold and copper as night falls. That's when a new Rome awakens. The cafes and restaurants grow more animated, especially if you've found one in an ancient piazza or along a narrow alley deep in Trastevere. After dinner, you can stroll by the lighted fountains and monuments (the Trevi Fountain and the Colosseum look magical at night) or through Piazza Navona and have a gelato.

Essentials

GETTING THERE

BY PLANE Chances are, you'll arrive at Rome's **Leonardo da Vinci International Airport** (www.adr.it; ℭ **06-65951**), popularly known as **Fiumicino,** 30km (19 miles) from the city center. (If you're flying by charter, you might land at Ciampino Airport, discussed below.) There is a tourist information office at the airport's Terminal B, International arrival, open daily 9am to 6:30pm.

A *cambio* (money exchange) operates daily 7:30am to 11pm, offering surprisingly good rates.

There's a **train station** in the airport. To get into the city, follow the signs marked TRENI for the 30-minute shuttle to Rome's main station, **Stazione Termini.** The shuttle (the Leonardo Express) runs from 5:52am to 11:36pm for 14€ one-way. On the way, you'll pass a machine dispensing tickets, or you can buy them in person near the tracks if you don't have small bills on you. When you arrive at Termini, get out of the train quickly and grab a baggage cart. (It's a long schlep from the track to the exit or to the other train connections, and baggage carts can be scarce.)

A **taxi** from da Vinci airport to the city costs 40€ and up for the 1-hour trip, depending on traffic. The expense might be worth it if you have a lot of luggage. Call ✆ **06-6645, 06-3570,** or **06-4994** for information. Note that the flat rate of 40€ is applicable from the airport to central Rome and vice versa, but only if your central Rome location is inside the Aurelian Walls (most hotels are). Otherwise, standard metered rates apply, which can be 75€ higher.

If you arrive on a charter flight at **Ciampino Airport** (www.adr.it; ✆ **06-65951**), you can take a Terravision bus (✆ **06-4880086**) to Stazione Termini. Trip time is about 45 minutes and costs 4€. A **taxi** from here to Rome costs 30€, a flat rate that applies as long as you're going to a destination within the old Aurelian Walls. Otherwise, you'll pay the metered fare, but the trip is shorter (about 40 min.).

BY TRAIN OR BUS   Trains and buses (including trains from the airport) arrive in the center of old Rome at the silver **Stazione Termini,** Piazza dei Cinquecento (✆ **06-478411**). This is the train, bus, and subway transportation hub for all Rome, and it is surrounded by many hotels (especially cheaper ones).

If you're taking the **Metropolitana** (subway), follow the illuminated red-and-white M signs. To catch a bus, go straight through the outer hall and enter the sprawling bus lot of **Piazza dei Cinquecento.** You'll also find **taxis** there.

The station is filled with services. At a branch of the Intesasanpaolo bank (at tracks 1 and 24), you can exchange money. **Informazioni Ferroviarie** (in the outer hall) dispenses information on rail travel to other parts of Italy. There are also a **tourist information booth,** baggage services, newsstands, and snack bars.

BY CAR   From the north, the main access route is the **Autostrada del Sole (A1).** Called "Motorway of the Sun," the highway links Milan with Naples via Bologna, Florence, and Rome. At 754km (469 miles), it is the longest Italian autostrada and is the "spinal cord" of Italy's road network. All the autostrade join with the **Grande Raccordo Anulare,** a ring road encircling Rome, channeling traffic into the congested city. Long before you reach this road, you should study a map carefully to see what part of Rome you plan to enter and mark your route accordingly. Route markings along the ring road tend to be confusing.

Warning: Return your rental car immediately, or at least get yourself to a hotel, park your car, and leave it there until you leave Rome. Don't even think about driving in Rome—the traffic is just too nightmarish.

VISITOR INFORMATION

TOURIST OFFICE   Information is available at **Azienda Provinciale di Turismo** (APT; www.aptprovroma.it; ✆ **06-421381**), Via XX Settembre 26. The headquarters is open Monday to Friday 9am to 1pm. On Monday and Thursday it also is open 2 to 4pm.

Italy

FRANCE ALPS SWITZERLAND
Courmayeur
VALLE Aosta Lake Maggiore Merano TRENTINO– ALPS AUSTRIA
D'AOSTA Novara ALTO ADIGE
Turin Como LOMBARDY Bolzano Cortina d'Ampezzo
Vercelli Bergamo Trent Belluno
Asti Brescia Lake Vicenza FRIULI–VENEZIA
PIEDMONT Milan Garda VENETO Udine GIULIA
Cremona Verona Treviso
Cuneo Parma Mantua Padua Venice SLOVENIA
Savona Genoa Ferrara Trieste
LIGURIA Modena Gulf of
San Remo Gulf of Rapallo EMILIA– Venice
Genoa La Spezia ROMAGNA Ravenna CROATIA
Lucca Bologna
Ligurian Pisa SAN Rimini
Sea Florence MARINO BOSNIA
Livorno Pesaro
TUSCANY Gubbio Ancona
Elba Siena
Corsica Perugia MARCHES
(France) Orvieto Assisi
Viterbo UMBRIA
Spoleto
Civitavecchia Terni Teramo
ROME L'Aquila Pescara
VATICAN CITY Chieti
LAZIO ABRUZZI
Campobasso
Caserta MOLISE
Gulf of Benevento Foggia
Gaeta Naples Mt. Vesuvius APULIA
Ischia Pompeii Bari
Sorrento
Capri Amalfi Salerno
Paestum Potenza Brindisi
CAMPANIA BASILICATA
Tyrrhenian Taranto Lecce
Sea Gulf of
Taranto
Cosenza CALABRIA
Aeolian Islands Catanzaro
Trapani
Marsala Palermo
Selinunte Messina
Enna Reggio di
Agrigento Taormina Calabria Ionian
Mt. Etna Sea
SICILY Catania
Ragusa Syracuse
MEDITERRANEAN SEA

Ólbia
Sassari
Nuoro
SARDINIA
Cagliari

0 100 mi
0 100 km

More helpful, and stocking maps and brochures, are the offices maintained by the **Comune di Roma** at various sites around the city. They're staffed daily from 9:30am to 7pm, except the one at Termini (daily 8am–8:30pm). Here are the addresses of others in Stazione Termini: at Piazza Pia near the Castel Sant'Angelo; on Via Nazionale 183, near the Palazzo delle Esposizioni; on Piazza Sonnino, in Trastevere; on Piazza Cinque Lune, near Piazza Navona; and on Via dell'Olmata, near Piazza Santa Maria Maggiore. All phone calls for Comune di Roma are directed through a centralized number: ✆ **06-060608** (www.060608.it). Call daily 9am to 9pm.

Enjoy Rome, Via Marghera 8A (www.enjoyrome.com; ✆ **06-4451843**), was begun by an English-speaking couple, Fulvia and Pierluigi. They dispense information about almost everything in Rome and are far more pleasant and organized than the Board of Tourism. They'll also help you find a hotel room, with no service charge (in anything from a hostel to a three-star hotel). Hours are Monday to Friday 8:30am to 5pm, and Saturday 8:30am to 2pm.

CITY LAYOUT

Arm yourself with a detailed street map, not the general overview handed out free at tourist offices. Most hotels hand out a pretty good version at their front desks.

The bulk of ancient, Renaissance, and baroque Rome (as well as the train station) lies on the east side of the **Tiber River (Fiume Tevere),** which meanders through town. However, several important landmarks are on the other side: **St. Peter's Basilica** and the **Vatican,** the **Castel Sant'Angelo,** and the colorful **Trastevere** neighborhood.

The city's various quarters are linked by large boulevards (large, at least, in some places) that have mostly been laid out since the late 19th century. Starting from the **Vittorio Emanuele Monument,** a controversial pile of snow-white Brescian marble that's often compared to a wedding cake, there's a street running practically due north to **Piazza del Popolo** and the city wall. This is **Via del Corso,** one of the main streets of Rome—noisy, congested, crowded with buses and shoppers, and called simply "Il Corso." To its left (west) lie the Pantheon, Piazza Navona, Campo de' Fiori, and the Tiber. To its right (east) you'll find the Spanish Steps, the Trevi Fountain, the Borghese Gardens, and Via Veneto.

Back at the Vittorio Emanuele Monument, the major artery going west (and ultimately across the Tiber to St. Peter's) is **Corso Vittorio Emanuele.** Behind you to your right, heading toward the Colosseum, is **Via dei Fori Imperiali,** laid out in the 1930s by Mussolini to show off the ruins of the Imperial Forums he had excavated, which line it on either side. Yet another central conduit is **Via Nazionale,** running from **Piazza Venezia** (just in front of the Vittorio Emanuele Monument) east to **Piazza della Repubblica** (near Stazione Termini). The final lap of Via Nazionale is called **Via Quattro Novembre.**

GETTING AROUND

Rome is excellent for walking, with sites of interest often clustered together. Much of the inner core is traffic free, so you'll need to walk whether you like it or not. However, in many parts of the city it's hazardous and uncomfortable because of the crowds, heavy traffic, and narrow sidewalks.

BY SUBWAY   The **Metropolitana,** or **Metro** for short, is the fastest means of transportation, operating 5:30am to 11:30pm Sunday to Thursday, and until 1:30am on Friday and Saturday. A big red ᴍ indicates the entrance to the subway.

Tickets are 1€ and are available from *tabacchi* (tobacco shops), many newsstands, and vending machines at all stations. Some stations have managers, but they won't give change. Booklets of tickets are available at *tabacchi* and in some terminals. You can also buy a **tourist pass** on either a daily or a weekly basis (see "By Bus & Tram," below).

Building a subway system for Rome hasn't been easy, because every time workers start digging they discover an old temple or other archaeological treasure and heavy earth moving has to cease for a while.

BY BUS & TRAM   Roman buses and trams are operated by an organization known as **ATAC** (Agenzia del Trasporto Autoferrotranviario del Comune di Roma; www.atacmobile.it; ✆ **06-57003**), Piazzale degli Archivi 40, in the Eur suburb of Rome.

For 1€ you can ride to most parts of Rome, although it can be slow going in all that traffic, and the buses are often very crowded. Your ticket is valid for 75 minutes, and you can get on many buses and trams during that time by using the same ticket (as well as one run on the Metro). You can buy tickets in *tabacchi* or bus terminals. You must have your ticket before boarding, because there are no ticket-issuing machines on the vehicles.

At Stazione Termini, you can buy a special **tourist pass,** which costs 4€ for a day or 16€ for a week. This pass allows you to ride on the ATAC network without bothering to buy individual tickets. The tourist pass is also valid on the subway—but never ride the trains when the Romans are going to or from work, or you'll be smashed flatter than fettuccine. On the first bus you board, you place your ticket in a small machine, which prints the day and hour you boarded, and then you withdraw it. You do the same on the last bus you take during the valid period of the ticket. One-day and weekly tickets are also available at *tabacchi,* many newsstands, and at vending machines at all stations.

Buses and trams stop at areas marked FERMATA. At most of these, a yellow sign will display the numbers of the buses that stop there and a list of all the stops in order along each bus's route so that you can easily search out your destination. In general, they're in service daily from 5am to midnight. After that and until dawn, you can ride on special night buses (they have an N in front of their bus number), which run only on main routes. It's best to take a taxi in the wee hours—if you can find one.

At the **bus information booth** at Piazza dei Cinquecento, in front of the Stazione Termini, you can purchase a directory with maps of the routes.

Although routes change often, a few old reliable routes have remained valid for years, such as **no. 75** from Stazione Termini to the Colosseum, **H** from Stazione Termini to Trastevere, and **no. 40** from Stazione Termini to the Vatican. But if you're going somewhere and are dependent on the bus, be sure to carefully check where the bus stop is and exactly which bus goes there—don't assume that it'll be the same bus the next day.

BY TAXI   If you're accustomed to hopping a cab in New York or London, then do so in Rome. But don't count on hailing a taxi on the street or even getting one at a stand. If you're going out, have your hotel call one. At a restaurant, ask the waiter or cashier to dial for you. If you want to phone for yourself, try one of these numbers: ✆ **06-6645, 06-3570,** or **06-4994.**

The meter begins at 2.80€ for the first 3km (1¾ miles) and then rises .92€ per kilometer. The first suitcase is free. Every additional piece of luggage costs 1€. There's another 5.80€ supplement from 10pm to 7am. Avoid paying your fare with large bills; invariably, taxi drivers claim that they don't have change, hoping for a bigger tip (stick to your guns and give only about 15%).

BY CAR All roads might lead to Rome, but you don't want to drive once you get here. Because the reception desks of most Roman hotels have at least one English-speaking person, call ahead to find out the best route into Rome from wherever you're starting out. You're usually allowed to park in front of the hotel long enough to unload your luggage. You'll want to get rid of your rental car as soon as possible, or park in a garage.

You might want to rent a car to explore the countryside around Rome or drive to another city. You'll save the most money if you reserve before leaving home. But if you want to book a car here, know that **Hertz** is at Via Giovanni Giolitti 34 (www.hertz. com; ☎ **06-4740389**; Metro: Termini) and **Avis** is at Stazione Termini (www.avis. com; ☎ **06-4814373**; Metro: Termini). **Maggiore,** an Italian company, has an office at Stazione Termini (www.maggiore.it; ☎ **06-4880049**; Metro: Termini). There are also branches of the major rental agencies at the airport.

BY BIKE Other than walking, the best way to get through the medieval alleys and small piazzas of Rome is perched on the seat of a bicycle. The heart of ancient Rome is riddled with bicycle lanes to get you through the murderous traffic. The most convenient place to rent bikes is **Bici & Baci,** Via del Viminale 5 (www.bicibaci.com; ☎ **06-4828443**), lying 2 blocks west of Stazione Termini, the main rail station. Prices start at 4€ per hour or 11€ per day.

[Fast FACTS] ROME

American Express The Rome offices are at Piazza di Spagna 38 (☎ **06-67641;** Metro: Spagna). The travel service is open Monday to Friday 9am to 5:30pm. Hours for the financial and mail services are Monday to Friday 9am to 5pm. The tour desk is open during the same hours as those for travel services and also Saturday from 9am to 12:30pm (May–Oct).

Business Hours In general, **banks** are open Monday to Friday 8:30am to 1:30pm and 3 to 4pm. Some banks keep afternoon hours from 2:45 to 3:45pm. Regular business hours are generally Monday to Friday 9am (sometimes 9:30) to 1pm, and 3:30 (sometimes 4) to 7 or 7:30pm. The *riposo* (midafternoon closing) is often observed in Rome, Naples, and most

southern cities. Most shops are closed, except for certain tourist-oriented stores that are now permitted to remain open on Sunday during the high season.

Currency Italy uses the **euro** (€).

Currency Exchange There are exchange offices throughout the city. They're also at all major rail and air terminals, including Stazione Termini, where the cambio beside the rail information booth is open daily 8am to 8pm. At some exchange offices, you'll have to pay commissions, often 1½%. Likewise, banks often charge commissions.

Dentists For dental work, go to **American Dental Arts Rome,** Via del Governo Vecchio 73 (www. adadentistsrome.com; ☎ **06-6832613**) bus: 41, 44,

or 46B), which uses all the latest technology, including laser dental techniques. There is also a 24-hour **G. Eastman Dental Hospital** at Viale Regina Elena 287B (☎ **06-844831;** Metro: Policlinico).

Doctors Call the U.S. Embassy at ☎ **06-46741** for a list of doctors who speak English. All big hospitals have a 24-hour first-aid service (go to the emergency room, *pronto soccorso*). You'll find English-speaking doctors at the privately run **Salvator Mundi International Hospital,** Viale delle Mura Gianicolensi 67 (☎ **06-588961;** bus: 75). For medical assistance, the **International Medical Center** is on 24-hour duty at Via Firenze 47 (www.imc84. com; ☎ **06-4882371;** Metro: Piazza Repubblica). You could also contact the **Rome American Hospital,** Via Emilio

Longoni 69 (www.rah.it; ☎ 06-22551), with English-speaking doctors on duty 24 hours. A more personalized service is provided 24 hours by **MEDI-CALL**, Studio Medico, Via Cremera 8 (www.medi-call.it; ☎ 06-8840113; bus: 86). It can arrange for a qualified doctor to make a house call at your hotel or anywhere in Rome. In most cases, the doctor will be a general practitioner who can refer you to a specialist if needed. Fees begin at around 100€ per visit and can go higher if a specialist or specialized treatments are necessary.

Drugstores A reliable pharmacy is **Farmacia Internazionale,** Piazza Barberini 49 (☎ 06-4825456; Metro: Barberini), open day and night. Most pharmacies are open from 8:30am to 1pm and 4 to 7:30pm. In general, pharmacies follow a rotation system, so several are always open on Sunday.

Embassies & Consulates The embassy of the **United States** is at Via Vittorio Veneto 121 (http://rome.usembassy.gov; ☎ 06-46741). The embassy of **Canada** is at Via Salaria 243 (www.canada.it; ☎ 06-85444-2911). The embassy

of the **United Kingdom** is at Via XX Settembre 80 (http://ukinitaly.fco.gov.uk/en; ☎ 06-42200001). The embassy of **Australia** is at Via Antonio Bosio 5 (www.italy.embassy.gov.au; ☎ 06-852-721). The embassy of **New Zealand** is at Via Zara 28 (www.nzembassy.com/Italy; ☎ 06-4417171).

Emergencies To call the police, dial **113;** for an ambulance, **118;** for a fire emergency, **115.**

Internet Access You can log onto the Web in central Rome at **Internet Train,** Via dei Marrucini 12 (www.internetcafe.it; ☎ 06-4454953; bus: 3, 71, or 492). It is open Monday to Friday 9:30am to 1am, Saturday 10am to 1am, and Sunday 2pm to midnight. A 30-minute visit costs 1.50€.

Mail It's easiest to buy stamps and mail letters and postcards at your hotel's front desk. Stamps (francobolli) can also be bought at tabacchi. You can buy special stamps at the **Vatican City Post Office,** adjacent to the information office in St. Peter's Square; it's open Monday to Friday 8:30am to 7pm and Saturday 8:30am to 6pm. Letters mailed from Vatican

City often arrive far more quickly than mail sent from Rome for the same cost.

Safety Pickpocketing is the most common problem. Men should keep their wallets in their front pocket or inside jacket pocket. Purse snatching is also commonplace, with young men on Vespas who ride past you and grab your purse. To avoid trouble, stay away from the curb and keep your purse on the wall side of your body, and place the strap across your chest. Don't lay anything valuable on tables or chairs, where it can be grabbed. Gypsy children have long been a particular menace, although the problem isn't as severe as in years past. If they completely surround you, you'll often literally have to fight them off. They might approach you with pieces of cardboard hiding their stealing hands. Just keep repeating a firm no!

Telephone The **country code** for Italy is **39.** The **city code** for Rome is **06;** use this code when calling from anywhere outside or inside Italy—you must add it within Rome itself (you must include the 0, even when calling from abroad).

Exploring the Eternal City

Rome's ancient monuments, whether time-blackened or gleaming white in the wake of a recent restoration, are a constant reminder that Rome was one of the greatest centers of Western civilization. In the heyday of the Empire, all roads led to Rome, with good reason. It was one of the first cosmopolitan cities, importing slaves, gladiators, great art, and even citizens from the far corners of the world. Despite its carnage and corruption, Rome left a legacy of law, a heritage of great art, architecture, and engineering, and an uncanny lesson in how to conquer enemies by absorbing their cultures.

Rome Attractions

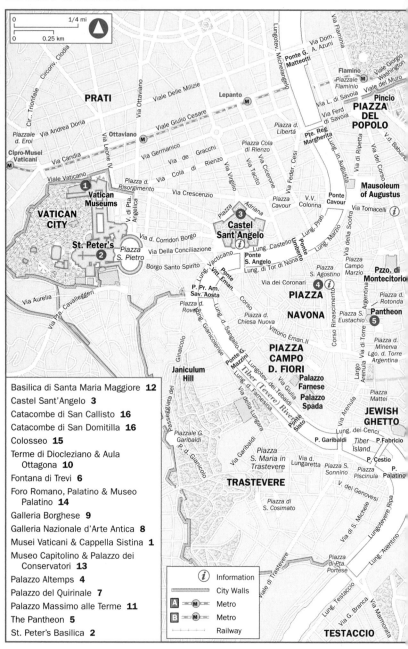

Basilica di Santa Maria Maggiore **12**

Castel Sant'Angelo **3**

Catacombe di San Callisto **16**

Catacombe di San Domitilla **16**

Colosseo **15**

Terme di Diocleziano & Aula Ottagona **10**

Fontana di Trevi **6**

Foro Romano, Palatino & Museo Palatino **14**

Galleria Borghese **9**

Galleria Nazionale d'Arte Antica **8**

Musei Vaticani & Cappella Sistina **1**

Museo Capitolino & Palazzo dei Conservatori **13**

Palazzo Altemps **4**

Palazzo del Quirinale **7**

Palazzo Massimo alle Terme **11**

The Pantheon **5**

St. Peter's Basilica **2**

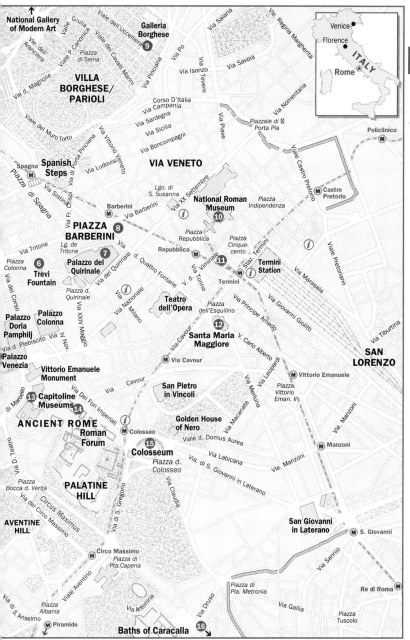

National Gallery
of Modern Art

Galleria
Borghese
9

Piazza
di Siena

**VILLA
BORGHESE/
PARIOLI**

Corso D'Italia
Via Campania
Via Sardegna
Via Sicilia
Via Boncompagni

Piazzale di ⊠
Porta Pia

Policlinico
M

Spagna
M
**Spanish
Steps**
Piazza
di Spagna

VIA VENETO

Lgo. di
S. Susanna
Via XX Settembre

Barberini
M
Via Barberini

**National Roman
Museum**
10
i

Piazza
Indipendenza

Castro
Pretorio

**PIAZZA
BARBERINI**
8

Piazza
Repubblica

Piazza
Cinque-
cento
i

Lg. de
Tritone

**Palazzo del
Quirinale**
7

Repubblica
M

**Termini
Station**
i

Piazza
Colonna
6
**Trevi
Fountain**

Via Viminale
11
i

Via Torino

Termini

Piazza d.
Quirinale
i

**Teatro
dell'Opera**

Piazza
dell'Esquilino

**Palazzo
Doria
Pamphilj**

**Palazzo
Colonna**

12
**Santa Maria
Maggiore**

**SAN
LORENZO**

**Palazzo
Venezia**

M Via Cavour

Vittorio Emanuele
M

**Vittorio Emanuele
Monument**

**San Pietro
in Vincoli**

Piazza
Vittorio
Eman. II

13 **Capitoline
Museums**
14

**Golden House
of Nero**
Viale d. Domus Aurea

M Manzoni

ANCIENT ROME
**Roman
Forum**
i
M Colosseo

15
Colosseum
Piazza d.
Colosseo

Via Labicana

Piazza
Bocca d. Verità

**PALATINE
HILL**

**AVENTINE
HILL**

**San Giovanni
in Laterano**
M S. Giovanni

Circo Massimo
Piazza di
Pta.Capena

Re di Roma
M

Piazza
Albania
M Piramide

Piazza di
Pla. Metronia

Piazza
Tuscolo

Baths of Caracalla
16

Venice ●
Florence ●

ITALY

● Rome ✳

But ancient Rome is only part of the spectacle. The Vatican has had a tremendous influence on making the city a tourism center. Although Vatican architects stripped down much of the city's glory, looting ancient ruins for their precious marble, they created great Renaissance treasures and even occasionally incorporated the old into the new—as Michelangelo did when turning the Baths of Diocletian into a church. And in the years that followed, Bernini adorned the city with the wonders of the baroque, especially his glorious fountains.

ST. PETER'S & THE VATICAN

St. Peter's Basilica ★★★ CHURCH   In ancient times, the Circus of Nero, where St. Peter is said to have been crucified, was slightly to the left of where the basilica is now located. Peter was allegedly buried here in A.D. 64 near the site of his execution, and in 324 Constantine commissioned a basilica to be built over Peter's tomb. That structure stood for more than 1,000 years, until it verged on collapse. The present basilica, mostly completed in the 1500s and 1600s, is predominantly High Renaissance and baroque. Inside, the massive scale is almost too much to absorb, showcasing some of Italy's greatest artists: Bramante, Raphael, Michelangelo, and Maderno. In a church of such grandeur—overwhelming in its detail of gilt, marble, and mosaic—you can't expect much subtlety. It's meant to be overpowering.

In the nave on the right (the first chapel) stands one of the Vatican's greatest treasures: Michelangelo's exquisite *Pietà* **★★★**, created while the master was still in his 20s but clearly showing his genius for capturing the human form. (The sculpture has been kept behind reinforced glass since a madman's act of vandalism in the 1970s.) Much farther on, in the right wing of the transept near the Chapel of St. Michael, rests Canova's neoclassical **sculpture of Pope Clement XIII ★★**. The truly devout stop to kiss the feet of the 13th-century **bronze of St. Peter ★**, attributed to Arnolfo di Cambio (at the far reaches of the nave, against a corner pillar on the right). Under Michelangelo's dome is the celebrated twisty-columned **baldacchino ★★** (1524), by Bernini, resting over the papal altar.

In addition, you can visit the **treasury ★**, which is filled with jewel-studded chalices, reliquaries, and copes. The sacristy contains a **Historical Museum (Museo Storico) ★** displaying Vatican treasures, including the large 1400s bronze tomb of Pope Sixtus V by Antonio Pollaiuolo and several antique chalices.

You can head downstairs to the **Vatican grottoes ★★**, with their tombs of the popes, both ancient and modern (Pope John XXIII got the most adulation until the recent interment of Pope John Paul II). Behind a wall of glass is what's assumed to be the tomb of St. Peter himself.

To go even farther down, to the **Necropolis Vaticana ★★**, the area around St. Peter's tomb, you must send a fax or e-mail 3 weeks beforehand, or apply in advance in person at the Ufficio Scavi (*C*/fax **06-69873017;** e-mail: scavi@fsp.va), through the arch to the left of the stairs up the basilica. You specify your name, the number in your party, your language, and dates you'd like to visit. When you apply at the Ufficio Scavi by fax or e-mail you also need to specify how you would like to be contacted (by e-mail, fax, or postal address). For details, check **www.vatican.va**. Children 14 and under are not admitted to the Necropolis Vaticana.

After you leave the grottoes, you'll find yourself in a courtyard and ticket line for the grandest sight: the climb to **Michelangelo's dome ★★★**, about 114m (375 ft.) high. You can walk up all the steps or take the elevator as far as it goes. The elevator saves you 171 steps, and you'll *still* have 320 to go after getting off. After you've made it to the top, you'll have an astounding view over the rooftops of Rome and even the Vatican Gardens and papal apartments—a photo op, if ever there was one.

Piazza San Pietro. ✆ **06-69881662.** Basilica (including grottoes) free admission. Guided tour of excavations around St. Peter's tomb 12€; children 14 and younger are not admitted. Stairs to the dome 5€; elevator to the dome 7€; sacristy (with Historical Museum) free. Basilica (including the sacristy and treasury) daily 9am–6pm. Grottoes daily 8am–5pm. Dome Oct–Mar daily 7am–6:30pm; Apr–Sept daily 7am–7pm. Bus: 49. Metro: Cipro, Ottaviano/San Pietro, then a long stroll.

Musei Vaticani (Vatican Museums) & Cappella Sistina (Sistine Chapel) ★★★ ART MUSEUM/ICON

The Vatican Museums boast one of the world's greatest art collections. They're a gigantic repository of treasures from antiquity and the Renaissance, housed in a labyrinthine series of lavishly adorned palaces, apartments, and galleries leading you to the real gem: the Sistine Chapel. The Vatican Museums occupy a part of the papal palaces built from the 1200s on. From the former papal private apartments, the museums were created over a period of time to display the vast treasure trove of art acquired by the Vatican.

You'll climb a magnificent spiral ramp to get to the ticket windows. After you're admitted, you can choose your route through the museum from **four color-coded itineraries** (A, B, C, D) according to the time you have (1½–5 hr.) and your interests. You determine your choice by consulting panels on the wall and then following the letter/color of your choice. All four itineraries culminate in the **Sistine Chapel.**

Michelangelo labored for 4 years (1508–12) over this epic project, which was so physically taxing that it permanently damaged his eyesight. He painted nine panels, taken from the pages of Genesis, and surrounded them with prophets and sibyls. The most notable panels detail the expulsion of Adam and Eve from the Garden of Eden and the creation of man; you'll recognize the image of God's outstretched hand as it imbues Adam with spirit. (You might want to bring along binoculars so you can see the details.)

Vatican City, Viale Vaticano (a long walk around the Vatican walls from St. Peter's Sq.). www.vatican. va. ✆ **06-69884676.** Admission 15€ adults, 8€ children 6–13, free for children 5 and under. Mon–Sat 9am–4pm. Closed Jan 1 and 6, Feb 11, Mar 19, Easter, May 1, June 29, Aug 14–15, Nov 1, and Dec 8 and 25–26. Reservations for guided tours 31€ per person through Vatican website. Metro: Cipro–Musei Vaticani.

THE FORUM, THE COLOSSEUM & THE HIGHLIGHTS OF ANCIENT ROME

Foro Romano (Roman Forum), Palatino (Palatine Hill), and Museo Palatino (Palatine Museum) ★★★ MUSEUM/RUINS

Traversed by the **Via Sacra** (Sacred Way) ★, the main thoroughfare of ancient Rome, the Forum was built in the marshy land between the Palatine and Capitoline hills, and flourished as the center of Roman life in the days of the Republic, before it gradually lost prestige to the Imperial Forums.

You'll see only ruins and fragments, an arch or two, and lots of overturned boulders, but with some imagination you can feel the rush of history here.

You can spend at least a morning wandering through the ruins of the Forum. If you're content with just looking, you can do so at your leisure. But if you want the stones to have some meaning, buy a detailed plan at the gate (the temples are hard to locate otherwise).

Turn right at the bottom of the entrance slope to walk west along the old Via Sacra toward the arch. Just before it on your right is the large brick **Curia ★★**, the main seat of the Roman Senate, built by Julius Caesar. Pop inside to see the 3rd-century marble inlay floor.

The triumphal **Arch of Septimius Severus ★★** (A.D. 203) displays time-bitten reliefs of the emperor's victories in what are today Iran and Iraq. Nearby, the much-photographed trio of fluted columns with Corinthian capitals supporting a bit of architrave form the corner of the **Temple of Vespasian and Titus ★★** (emperors were routinely turned into gods upon dying).

Start heading to your left toward the eight Ionic columns marking the front of the **Temple of Saturn ★★** (rebuilt in 42 B.C.), which housed the first treasury of republican Rome. Turn left to start heading back east, past the worn steps and stumps of brick pillars outlining the enormous **Basilica Julia ★★**, built by Julius Caesar. Past it are the three Corinthian columns of the **Temple of the Dioscuri ★★★**, dedicated to the Gemini twins, Castor and Pollux. Forming one of the most celebrated sights of the Roman Forum, a trio of columns supports an architrave fragment. The founding of this temple dates from the 5th century B.C.

Beyond the bit of curving wall that marks the site of the little round **Temple of Vesta** (rebuilt several times after fires started by the sacred flame within), you'll find the partially reconstructed **House of the Vestal Virgins ★★** (3rd–4th centuries A.D.) against the south side of the grounds. This was the home of the consecrated young women who tended the sacred flame in the Temple of Vesta. Vestals were girls chosen from patrician families to serve a 30-year-long priesthood. During their tenure, they were among Rome's most venerated citizens, with unique powers such as the ability to pardon condemned criminals.

The path dovetails back to join Via Sacra at the entrance. Turn right and then left to enter the massive brick remains and coffered ceilings of the 4th-century **Basilica of Constantine and Maxentius ★★**. These were Rome's public law courts.

Return to the path and continue toward the Colosseum. Veer right to the second great surviving triumphal arch, the **Arch of Titus ★★** (A.D. 81); the war that this arch glorifies ended with the expulsion of Jews from the colonized Judea, signaling the beginning of the Jewish Diaspora throughout Europe. From here you can enter and climb the **Palatine Hill ★** (with the same hours as the Forum; the same ticket will get you into both the Forum and Palatine Hill).

The **Palatine Museum (Museo Palatino) ★** displays a good collection of Roman sculpture from the digs in the Palatine villas. In summer you can take guided tours in English daily at 11am, 11:45am, and 4:15pm for 4€; call in winter to see if they're still available. The same ticket that you buy for the Palatine Hill and the Palatine Museum includes the visit to the Colosseum.

Via della Salara Vecchia 5/6. ℰ **06-39967700.** Forum and Palatine Hill admission 12€. Oct 30–Dec and Jan 2–Feb 15 daily 8:30am–4:30pm; Feb 16–Mar 15 daily 8:30am–5pm; Mar 16–24 daily 8:30am–5:30pm; Mar 25–Aug daily 8:30am–7:15pm; Sept daily 8:30am–7pm; Oct 1–29 daily 8:30am–6:30pm. Last admission 1 hr. before closing. Guided tours are given daily at 11am, lasting 1 hr., costing 4€. Closed holidays. Metro: Colosseo. Bus: 75 or 84.

Colosseo (Colosseum) ★★★ RUINS   Now a mere shell, the Colosseum still remains the greatest architectural legacy from ancient Rome. Vespasian ordered the construction of the elliptical bowl, called the Amphitheatrum Flavium, in A.D. 72; it was inaugurated by Titus in A.D. 80 with a bloody combat, lasting many weeks, between gladiators and wild beasts. At its peak, under the cruel Domitian, the Colosseum could seat 50,000. The Vestal Virgins from the temple screamed for blood, as exotic animals were shipped in from the far corners of the Empire to satisfy jaded

The Colosseum, the Forum & Ancient Rome Attractions

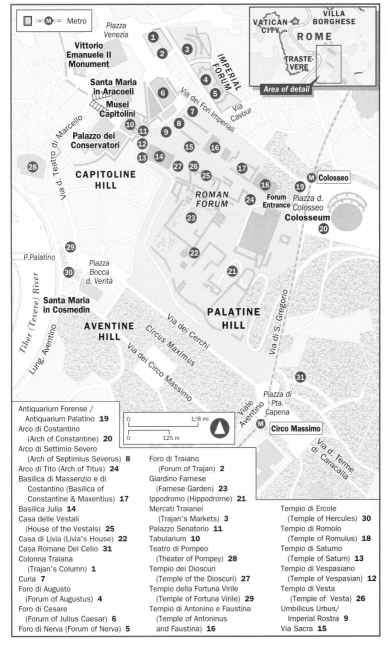

Antiquarium Forense /
  Antiquarium Palatino **19**
Arco di Costantino
  (Arch of Constantine) **20**
Arco di Settimio Severo
  (Arch of Septimius Severus) **8**
Arco di Tito (Arch of Titus) **24**
Basilica di Massenzio e di
  Costantino (Basilica of
  Constantine & Maxentius) **17**
Basilica Julia **14**
Casa delle Vestali
  (House of the Vestals) **25**
Casa di Livia (Livia's House) **22**
Casa Romane Del Celio **31**
Colonna Traiana
  (Trajan's Column) **1**
Curia **7**
Foro di Augusto
  (Forum of Augustus) **4**
Foro di Cesare
  (Forum of Julius Caesar) **6**
Foro di Nerva (Forum of Nerva) **5**

Foro di Traiano
  (Forum of Trajan) **2**
Giardino Farnese
  (Farnese Garden) **23**
Ippodromo (Hippodrome) **21**
Mercati Traianei
  (Trajan's Markets) **3**
Palazzo Senatorio **11**
Tabularium **10**
Teatro di Pompeo
  (Theater of Pompey) **28**
Tempio dei Dioscuri
  (Temple of the Dioscuri) **27**
Tempio della Fortuna Virile
  (Temple of Fortuna Virile) **29**
Tempio di Antonino e Faustina
  (Temple of Antoninus
  and Faustina) **16**

Tempio di Ercole
  (Temple of Hercules) **30**
Tempio di Romolo
  (Temple of Romulus) **18**
Tempio di Saturno
  (Temple of Saturn) **13**
Tempio di Vespasiano
  (Temple of Vespasian) **12**
Tempio di Vesta
  (Temple of Vesta) **26**
Umbilicus Urbus/
  Imperial Rostra **9**
Via Sacra **15**

tastes (lion vs. bear, two humans vs. hippopotamus). Not-so-mock naval battles were staged (the canopied Colosseum could be flooded), and the defeated combatants might have their lives spared if they put up a good fight. Many historians now believe that one of the most enduring legends about the Colosseum—that Christians were fed to the lions—is unfounded.

The same ticket that you buy for the Colosseum includes the visit to the Palatine Hill and the Palatine Museum.

Piazzale del Colosseo, Via dei Fori Imperiali. *C* **06-39967700.** Admission 12€ all levels. Nov–Feb 15 daily 8:30am–4:30pm; Feb 16–Mar 15 daily 8:30am–5pm; Mar 16–27 daily 8:30am–5:30pm; Mar 28–Aug daily 8:30am–7:15pm; Sept daily 9am–7pm; Oct daily 8:30am–7pm. Guided tours in English year-round daily at 10:15, 11:15am, 12:30, 3, 4:15, and 5:15pm. Tours 4€. Admission to Colosseo includes visit to Palatine Hill.

Museo Capitolino (Capitoline Museum) and Palazzo dei Conservatori ★★

ART MUSEUM/SQUARE   Of Rome's seven hills, the Capitoline (Campidoglio) is the most sacred: its origins stretch from antiquity; an Etruscan temple to Jupiter once stood on this spot. The approach is dramatic as you climb the long, sloping steps by Michelangelo. At the top is a perfectly proportioned square, **Piazza del Campidoglio ★★**, also laid out by the Florentine artist. Michelangelo positioned the bronze equestrian statue of Marcus Aurelius in the center, but it has now been moved inside for protection from pollution (a copy is on the pedestal).

One side of the piazza is open; the others are bounded by the **Senatorium (Town Council),** the statuary-filled **Palace of the Conservatori (Curators),** and the **Capitoline Museum.** These museums house some of the greatest pieces of classical sculpture in the world.

The **Capitoline Museum,** built in the 17th century, was based on an architectural sketch by Michelangelo. In the first room is *The Dying Gaul ★★*, a work of majestic skill that's a copy of a Greek original dating from the 3rd century B.C. In a special gallery all on her own is the *Capitoline Venus ★★*, who demurely covers herself.

The **equestrian statue of Marcus Aurelius ★★**, whose years in the piazza made it a victim of pollution, has been restored and is now kept in the museum for protection. This is the only such equestrian statue to have survived from ancient Rome, mainly because it was thought for centuries that the statue was that of Constantine the Great, and papal Rome respected the memory of the first Christian emperor.

Palace of the Conservatori ★★ ART MUSEUM

Across the way, this building was also based on a Michelangelo architectural plan and is rich in classical sculpture and paintings. One of the most notable bronzes, a Greek work of incomparable beauty dating from the 1st century B.C., is *Lo Spinario ★★★* (a little boy picking a thorn from his foot). In addition, you'll find *Capitoline Wolf (Lupa Capitolina) ★★★*, a rare Etruscan bronze that may date from the 5th century B.C. (Romulus and Remus, the legendary twins who were suckled by the wolf, were added at a later date.) The palace also contains a Pinacoteca (Picture Gallery)—featuring works by Caravaggio, Rubens, and Titian.

Piazza del Campidoglio 1. www.museicapitolini.org. *C* **060608.** Admission 8.50€. Tues–Sun 9am–9pm. Bus: 44, 81, 95, 160, 170, 715, or 780.

Castel Sant'Angelo ★ CASTLE

This overpowering castle on the Tiber was built in the 2nd century as a tomb for Emperor Hadrian; it continued as an imperial mausoleum until the time of Caracalla. If it looks like a fortress, it should—that was its function in the Middle Ages. It was built over the Roman walls and linked to the

Vatican by an underground passage that was used by the fleeing Pope Clement VII, who escaped from unwanted visitors such as Charles V during his 1527 sack of the city. In the 14th century, it became a papal residence, enjoying various connections with Boniface IX, Nicholas V, and Julius II, patron of Michelangelo and Raphael.

But its legend rests largely on its link with Pope Alexander VI, whose mistress bore him two children (those darlings of debauchery, Cesare and Lucrezia Borgia). Even those on a rushed visit might want to budget time for a stopover here because it's a most intriguing sight, an imposing fortress that has seen more blood, treachery, and turmoil than any other left in Rome. An audio guide is available to help you understand what you're seeing.

Lungotevere Castello 50. www.castelsantangelo.com. ☎ **06-6819111.** Admission 8.50€. Tues–Sun 9am–7pm. Bus: 23, 40, 34, 46, 49, 62, 64, 87, 280, 492, or 926, 982, 990. Metro: Cipro or Ottaviano, then a long stroll.

The Pantheon ★★★ ICON Of all ancient Rome's great buildings, only the Pantheon ("All the Gods") remains intact. It was built in 27 B.C. by Marcus Agrippa and was reconstructed by Hadrian in the early 2nd century A.D. This remarkable building, 43m (142 ft.) wide and 43m (142 ft.) high (a perfect sphere resting in a cylinder) and once ringed with white marble statues of Roman gods in its niches, is among the architectural wonders of the world because of its dome and its concept of space. Hadrian himself is credited with the basic plan, an architectural design that was unique for the time. The once-gilded dome is merely show. A real dome, a perfect, massive hemisphere of cast concrete, is supported by a solid ring wall. Before the 20th century, the dome was the biggest pile of concrete ever constructed. The ribbed dome outside is a series of almost weightless cantilevered bricks. Animals were sacrificed and burned in the center, and the smoke escaped through the only means of light, the oculus, an opening at the top 5.5m (18 ft.) in diameter.

Michelangelo came here to study the dome before designing the cupola of St. Peter's (whose dome is .5m/1½ ft. smaller than the Pantheon's).

Piazza della Rotonda. ☎ **06-68300230.** Free admission. Mon–Sat 8:30am–7:30pm; Sun 9am–1pm. Bus: 30, 40, 62, 64, 81, or 492 to Largo di Torre Argentina.

THE APPIAN WAY & THE CATACOMBS

Of all the roads that led to Rome, **Via Appia Antica** (built in 312 B.C.) was the most famous. It eventually stretched all the way from Rome to the seaport of Brindisi, through which trade with the colonies in Greece and the East was funneled. Along the Appian Way the patrician Romans built great monuments, while early Christians buried their dead in the catacombs beneath. Of the catacombs open to the public, those of St. Callixtus and St. Domitilla are best.

Catacombe di San Callisto (Catacombs of St. Callixtus) ★★ CATA-COMB "The most venerable and most renowned of Rome," said Pope John XXIII of these funerary tunnels. The founder of Christian archaeology, Giovanni Battista de Rossi (1822–94), called them "catacombs par excellence." These catacombs are often packed with tour-bus groups, and they have perhaps the cheesiest tour, but the tunnels are simply phenomenal. They're the first cemetery of the Christian community of Rome, burial place of 16 popes in the 3rd century. They bear the name of St. Callixtus, the deacon whom Pope St. Zephyrinus put in charge of them and who was later elected pope (A.D. 217–22) in his own right. The complex is a network of galleries stretching for nearly 19km (12 miles), structured in five levels and reaching a depth of about 20m (65 ft.). There are many sepulchral chambers and almost half a million tombs of early Christians. Paintings, sculptures, and epigraphs (with symbols such as the fish, anchor, and dove) provide invaluable material for the study of the life and customs of the ancient Christians and the story of their persecutions.

Via Appia Antica 110–126. www.catacombe.roma.it. ℂ **06-5130151.** Admission 8€ adults, 5€ children 6–15, free for children 5 and under. Thurs–Tues 9am–noon and 2–5pm. Bus: 118.

Catacombe di San Domitilla (Catacombs of St. Domitilla) ★★★ CATACOMB   This oldest of the catacombs is the hands-down winner for most enjoyable catacombs experience. Groups are small, most guides are genuinely entertaining and personable, and, depending on the mood of the group and your guide, the visit may last anywhere from 20 minutes to over an hour. You enter through a sunken 4th-century church. There are fewer "sights" than in the other catacombs—although the 2nd-century fresco of the *Last Supper* is impressive—but some of the guides actually hand you a few bones out of a tomb niche. (Incidentally, this is the only catacomb where you'll still see bones; the rest have emptied their tombs to rebury the remains in ossuaries on the inaccessible lower levels.)

Via d. Sette Chiese 280. www.domitilla.info. ℂ **06-5110342.** Admission 8€ adults, 5€ children 6–14. Wed–Mon 9am–noon and 2–5pm. Closed Jan.

MORE ATTRACTIONS

Basilica di Santa Maria Maggiore ★ CHURCH   This great church, one of Rome's four major basilicas, was built by Pope Liberius in A.D. 358 and rebuilt by Pope Sixtus III from 432 to 440. Its 14th-century **campanile** is the city's loftiest. Much doctored in the 18th century, the church's facade isn't an accurate reflection of the treasures inside. The basilica is noted for the 5th-century Roman mosaics in its nave, and for its coffered ceiling, said to have been gilded with gold brought from the New World. In the 16th century, Domenico Fontana built a now-restored "Sistine Chapel." In the following century, Flaminio Ponzo designed the **Pauline (Borghese) Chapel** in the baroque style. The church also contains the **tomb of Bernini,** Italy's most important baroque sculptor/architect.

Piazza di Santa Maria Maggiore. ℂ**06-69886800.** Free admission. Daily 7am–7pm. Metro: Termini.

Fontana di Trevi (Trevi Fountain) ★★ MONUMENT   As you elbow your way through the summertime crowds around the Trevi Fountain, you'll find it hard to believe that this little piazza was nearly always deserted before the 1954 film *Three Coins in the Fountain* brought renewed interest to this lovely spot.

Supplied by water from the Acqua Vergine aqueduct and a triumph of the baroque style, it was based on the design of Nicola Salvi (who's said to have died of illness contracted during his supervision of the project) and was completed in 1762. The design centers on the triumphant figure of Neptunus Rex, standing on a shell chariot drawn by winged steeds and led by a pair of tritons. Two allegorical figures in the side niches represent good health and fertility.

Piazza di Trevi. Metro: Barberini.

Galleria Borghese ★★★ ART MUSEUM   This legendary art gallery includes such masterpieces as Bernini's *Apollo* and *Daphne,* Titian's *Sacred and Profane Love,* Raphael's *Deposition,* and Caravaggio's *Jerome.* The collection began with the gallery's founder, Scipione Borghese, who, by the time of his death in 1633, had accumulated some of the greatest art of all time, even managing to acquire Bernini's early sculptures. Some paintings were spirited out of Vatican museums and even confiscated when their rightful owners were hauled off to prison until they became "reasonable" about turning over their art.

Important information: There is a limit to the number of people allowed into the museum, so reservations are essential. Call ✆ **06-32810** (Mon–Fri 9am–6pm; Sat 9am–1pm). The number is often busy, so you can also make reservations by going online at www.ticketeria.it. If you'll be in Rome for a few days, try stopping by in person on your first day to reserve tickets for a later day. Better yet, before you leave home, contact **Select Italy** (www.selectitaly.com; ✆ **800/877-1755**).

Piazzale del Museo Borghese 5 (off Via Pinciana). www.galleriaborghese.it. ✆ **06-32810.** Admission 8.50€. Tues–Sun 9am–7pm. Bus: 5, 19, 52, 116, 204, 490, or 910.

Galleria Nazionale d'Arte Antica (National Gallery of Ancient Art) ★★

ART MUSEUM   Palazzo Barberini, right off Piazza Barberini, is one of the most magnificent baroque palaces in Rome. It was begun by Carlo Maderno in 1627 and completed in 1633 by Bernini, whose lavishly decorated rococo apartments, the **Gallery of Decorative Art (Galleria d'Arte Decorativa),** are on view. This gallery is part of the **National Gallery of Ancient Art.**

On the first floor is a splendid array of paintings from the 13th to the 16th centuries, most notably *Mother and Child,* by Simone Martini, and works by Filippo Lippi, Andrea Solario, and Francesco Francia. Il Sodoma has some brilliant pictures here, including the *Rape of the Sabines* and the *Marriage of St. Catherine.* One of the best known is Raphael's *La Fornarina,* the baker's daughter who was his mistress and who posed for his Madonna portraits. Titian is represented by his *Venus and Adonis.* Also here are Tintorettos and El Grecos. Many visitors come just to see the magnificent Caravaggios, including *Narcissus.*

Via delle Quattro Fontane 13. http://galleriabarberini.beniculturali.it. ✆ **06-4824184.** Admission 5€. Tues–Sun 8:30am–6:30pm. Metro: Barberini.

Palazzo del Quirinale ★★ PALACE

Until the end of World War II, this palace was the home of the king of Italy; before the crown resided here, it was the residence of the pope. Despite its Renaissance origins (nearly every important architect in Italy worked on some aspect of its sprawling premises), this *palazzo* is rich in associations with ancient emperors and deities. The colossal statues of the Dioscuri Castor and Pollux, which now form part of the fountain in the piazza, were found in the nearby great Baths of Constantine; in 1793, Pius VI had the ancient Egyptian obelisk moved here from the Mausoleum of Augustus. The sweeping view of Rome from the piazza, which crowns the highest of the seven ancient hills of Rome, is itself worth the trip. This palace houses the president of the republic.

Piazza del Quirinale. www.quirinale.it. ✆ **06-46991.** Admission 5€. Sun 8:30am–noon. Closed late June to early Sept. Metro: Barberini.

MUSEO NAZIONALE ROMANO

This museum is divided into four sections: Palazzo Massimo alle Terme; the Terme di Diocleziano (Diocletian Baths); the annex Octagonal Hall; and Palazzo Altemps.

Palazzo Altemps ★ ART MUSEUM

This branch of the National Roman Museum is housed in a 15th-century palace that was restored and opened to the public in 1997. It is home to the fabled Ludovisi Collection of Greek and Roman sculpture. Among the masterpieces of the Roman Renaissance, you'll find the *Ares Ludovisi,* a Roman copy of the original dated 330 B.C. and restored by Bernini during the 17th century. In the Sala delle Storie di Mosè is *Ludovisi's Throne,* representing the birth of Venus. The Sala delle Feste (the Celebrations' Hall) is dominated by a sarcophagus depicting the Romans fighting against the Ostrogoth barbarians; this masterpiece, carved from a single block, dates back to the 2nd century A.D. and nowadays is called *Grande Ludovisi (Great Ludovisi)*.

Piazza San Apollinare 46, near the Piazza Navona. ℂ **06-39967700.** Admission 10€. Tues–Sun 9am–7:45pm. Last admission 1 hr. before closing. Bus: 70, 81, 87, or 116.

Palazzo Massimo alle Terme ★ ART MUSEUM   If you'd like to go wandering in a virtual garden of classical statues, head for this *palazzo*, built from 1883 to 1887 and opened as a museum in 1998. Much of the art here, including the frescoes, stuccoes, and mosaics, was discovered in excavations in the 1800s but has never been put on display before.

Works include an altar from Ostia Antica, the ancient port of Rome, plus a statue of a wounded Niobid from 440 B.C. that is a masterwork of expression and character. Upstairs, stand in awe at all the traditional art from the 1st century B.C. to the Imperial Age. The most celebrated mosaic is of the *Four Charioteers*. In the basement are a rare numismatic collection and an extensive collection of Roman jewelry.

Largo di Villa Peretti. ℂ **06-39967700.** Admission 7€. Tues–Sun 9am–7:45pm. Last admission 1 hr. before closing. Admission includes entrance to Terme di Diocleziano (see above). Metro: Termini.

Diocletian Baths (Terme di Diocleziano) and the Octagonal Hall (Aula Ottagona) ★ MUSEUM   Near Piazza dei Cinquecento, which fronts the rail station, this museum occupies part of the 3rd-century-A.D. Diocletian Baths and part of a convent that may have been designed by Michelangelo. The Diocletian Baths were the biggest thermal baths in the world. Nowadays they host a marvelous collection of funereal artworks, such as sarcophagi, and decorations dating from the Aurelian period.

The **Octagonal Hall** occupies the southwest corner of the central building of the Diocletian Baths. Here you can see the *Lyceum Apollo,* a copy of the 2nd-century-A.D. work inspired by the Prassitele. Also worthy of a note is the *Aphrodite of Cyrene,* a copy dating from the second half of the 2nd century A.D. and discovered in Cyrene, Libya.

Viale E. di Nicola 79. ℂ **06-39967700.** Admission 7€. Tues–Sun 9am–7:45pm. Last admission 1 hr. before closing. Metro: Termini.

ORGANIZED TOURS

Because of the sheer number of sights to see, some first-time visitors like to start out with an organized tour. While few things can really be covered in any depth on these overview tours, they're sometimes useful for getting your bearings.

One of the leading tour operators is **American Express,** Piazza di Spagna 38 (ℂ **06-67641;** Metro: Piazza di Spagna). One popular tour is a 4-hour orientation to Rome and the Vatican, which departs most mornings at 9:30am or afternoons at 2:20pm and costs 75€ per person. Another 4-hour tour, which focuses on the Rome of antiquity (including visits to the Colosseum, the Roman Forum, the ruins of the Imperial Palace, and St. Peter in Chains), costs 75€. From April to October, a popular excursion outside Rome is a 5-hour bus tour to Tivoli, where tours are conducted of the Villa d'Este and its spectacular gardens and the ruins of the Villa Adriana, all for 65€ per person. The American Express Travel Office is open Monday to Friday 9am to 5:30pm and Saturday 9am to 12:30pm.

Context Rome, Via Santa Maria Maggiore 145 (www.contexttravel.com; ℂ **800/ 691-6036**), is a collaboration of scholars. Guides offer small-group tours, including visits to monuments, museums, and historic piazzas, as well as culinary walks and meals in neighborhood *trattorie*. Custom-designed tours are also available. Prices of the regular tours begin at 30€. There is also a special kids' program, including treasure hunts and other experiences that feature visits to museums of appeal to the younger set.

Where to Eat

Rome remains one of the world's great capitals for dining, with even more diversity today than ever. Most of its *trattorie* haven't changed their menus in a quarter of a century (except to raise the prices, of course), but there's an increasing number of chic, upscale spots with chefs willing to experiment, as well as a growing handful of Chinese, Indian, and other ethnic spots for those days when you just can't face another plate of pasta. The great thing about Rome is that you don't have to spend a fortune to eat really well.

NEAR STAZIONE TERMINI

Agata e Romeo ★★ NEW ROMAN   One of the most charming places near the Vittorio Emanuele Monument is this striking duplex restaurant done up in turn-of-the-20th-century Liberty style. You'll enjoy the creative cuisine of Romeo Caraccio (who manages the dining room) and his wife, Agata Parisella (who prepares her own version of sophisticated Roman food). The pasta specialty is *paccheri all'amatriciana* (large macaroni tubes with pancetta and a savory tomato sauce topped with pecorino cheese). The chef is equally adept at fish or meat dishes, including braised beef cheeks laid on chestnut purée or swordfish rolls scented with orange and fennel cream. The starters are a feast for the eye and palate, especially wild salmon with sour cream, chives, and salmon eggs, or else scallops wrapped in a crispy pancetta with leek sauce. The most luscious dessert is Agata's *millefoglie*, puff pastry stuffed with almonds. The wine cellar offers a wide choice of international and domestic wines.

Via Carlo Alberto 45. www.agataeromeo.it. **℃ 06-4466115.** Reservations recommended. All pastas 30€; meat and fish 45€; fixed-price menus 110€–130€. AE, DC, MC, V. Mon–Fri 12:30–2:30pm and 8–10:30pm. Closed Aug 8–30. Metro: Vittorio Emanuele.

Monte Arci ROMAN/SARDINIAN   On a cobblestone street near Piazza Indipendenza, this restaurant is set behind a sienna-colored facade. It features Sardinian specialties such as *nialoreddus* (a regional form of *gnocchetti*); pasta with clams, lobster, or the musky-earthy notes of porcini mushrooms; and lamb sausage flavored with herbs and pecorino cheese. The best pasta dish we've sampled is *paglia e fieno al Monte Arci* (homemade pasta with pancetta, spinach, cream, and Parmesan). It's all home cooking; hearty but not that creative.

Via Castelfirdardo 33. **℃ 06-4941347.** Reservations recommended. Main courses 10€–18€. AE, MC, V. Mon–Fri 12:30–3pm; Mon–Sat 7–11:30pm. Closed Aug. Metro: Stazione Termini or Repubblica.

NEAR VIA VENETO & PIAZZA BARBERINI

Colline Emiliane ★★ 🕑 EMILIANA-ROMAGNOLA   Serving the *classica cucina Bolognese*, Colline Emiliane is a small, family-run place—the owner is the cook and his wife makes the pasta (about the best you'll find in Rome). The house specialty is an inspired *tortellini alla panna* (with cream sauce and truffles), but the less-expensive pastas, including *maccheroni al funghetto* (with mushrooms) and *tagliatelle alla Bolognese* (in meat sauce), are excellent, too. As an opener, we suggest *culatello di Zibello,* a delicacy from a small town near Parma that's known for having the world's finest prosciutto. Main courses include *braciola di maiale* (boneless rolled pork cutlets stuffed with ham and cheese, breaded, and sautéed) and an impressive *giambonnetto* (roast veal Emilian style with roast potatoes).

Via degli Avignonesi 22 (off Piazza Barberini). ☎ **06-4817538.** Reservations highly recommended. Main courses 12€–22€. MC, V. Tues–Sun 12:45–2:45pm; Tues–Sat 7:45–10:45pm. Closed Aug. Metro: Barberini.

Tuna ★ SEAFOOD   This seafood emporium in the center of Rome, overlooking the Via Veneto, is dedicated to serving some of the freshest fish in the capital. Not only is the fish fresh, but the chef also requires it to be of optimal quality. From crayfish to sea truffles, from oysters to sea urchins, the fish is turned into platters of delight with perfect seasonings and preparation. Start with the midget mussels or the octopus salad, or else calamari and artichoke tempura. For a main course, the catch of the day is in general the best choice, or else you may order sliced seabass with chives and fresh thyme.

Via Veneto 11. www.tunaroma.it. ☎ **06-42016531.** Reservations required. Main courses 15€–30€. AE, MC, V. Tues–Sun 12:30–3pm and 7:30pm–midnight. Closed 2 weeks in Aug. Metro: Barberini.

NEAR ANCIENT ROME

Crab ★ SEAFOOD   For Rome, this is an unusual name. Launched at the dawn of the 21st century, this trattoria is ideal after a visit to the nearby Basilica of San Giovanni. As you enter, you are greeted with a display of freshly harvested crustaceans and mollusks, which are what you can expect to headline the menu. The signature dish is king crab legs (hardly from the Mediterranean). Fish is shipped in "from everywhere," including oysters from France, lobster from the Mediterranean and the Atlantic, and some catches from the Adriatic. The antipasti is practically a meal in itself, including a savory sauté of mussels and clams, an octopus salad, and scallops gratin, which might be followed by a succulent lobster ravioli in *salsa vergine* (a lobster-based sauce). You can also order fresh sea urchins. For dessert, we recommend an arrangement of sliced tropical fruit that evokes the campy hat worn by Carmen Miranda in all those late-night movies. Most of the main courses, except for some very expensive shellfish and lobster platters, are closer to the lower end of the price scale.

Via Capo d'Africa 2. ☎ **06-77203636.** Reservations required. Main courses 22€–45€. AE, DC, MC, V. Mon 7:45–11:30pm; Tues–Sat 1–3:30pm and 8–11:30pm. Closed Aug. Metro: Colosseo. Tram: 3.

Hostaria Nerone ★ ROMAN/ITALIAN   Built atop the ruins of the Golden House of Nero, this trattoria is run by the energetic de Santis family, which cooks, serves, and handles the crowds of hungry locals and visitors. Opened in 1929 at the edge of Colle Oppio Park, it contains two compact dining rooms and a flowering shrub-lined terrace that offers a view over the Colosseum and the Bath of Trajan. The copious antipasti buffet offers the bounty of Italy's fields and seas. The pastas include savory spaghetti with clams and our favorite, *pasta e fagioli* (with beans). There are also grilled crayfish and swordfish, and Italian sausages with polenta. Roman-style tripe is a favorite, but maybe you'll skip it for the *osso buco* (veal shank) with mashed potatoes and seasonal mushrooms. The list of some of the best Italian wines is reasonably priced.

Via Terme di Tito 96. ☎ **06-4817952.** Reservations recommended. Main courses 12€–15€. AE, DC, MC, V. Mon–Sat noon–3pm and 7–11pm. Metro: Colosseo. Bus: 75, 85, 87, 117, or 175.

NEAR CAMPO DE' FIORI & THE JEWISH GHETTO

Camponeschi ★ SEAFOOD/ROMAN   The fish dishes served here are legendary, and so is the front-row view of the Piazza Farnese. The restaurant is elegance itself, with a two-to-one staff/diner ratio. The cuisine is creative, refined, and prepared with only the freshest of ingredients, with a superb wine list. The chefs work hard to make their reputation anew every night, and they succeed admirably with such dishes as lobster with black truffles and raspberry vinegar for an appetizer, or foie gras with port and sultana. We love their generous use of truffles, particularly in a masterpiece of a dish, *tagliolini* soufflé flavored with white truffles. Among the more succulent pastas is one made with a roe deer sauce. If the pope ever dined here, he would assuredly bestow papal blessings on such main courses as the rack of venison marinated with blueberries or a heavenly partridge in a brandy sauce with fresh mushrooms.

Piazza Farnese 50. www.ristorantecamponeschi.it. ℂ **06-6874927.** Reservations required. Main courses 20€–40€. MC, V. Mon–Sat 8pm–midnight. Closed 2 weeks in Aug. Metro: Piazza Argentina.

Trattoria Der Pallaro ★★ 🎁 ROMAN   The cheerful woman in white who emerges with clouds of steam from the bustling kitchen is owner Paola Fazi, who runs two dining rooms where value-conscious Romans go for good food at bargain prices. (She also claims—though others dispute it—that Julius Caesar was assassinated on this site.) The fixed-price menu is the only choice and has made the place famous. Ms. Fazi prepares everything with love, as if she were feeding her extended family. As you sit down, your antipasto, the first of eight courses, appears. Then comes the pasta of the day, followed by such main dishes as roast veal with broad beans and home-made potato chips, or roast pork cutlets, tender and flavorful. For your final courses, you're served mozzarella, cake with custard, and fruit in season.

Largo del Pallaro 15. www.trattoriaderpallaro.com. ℂ **06-68801488.** Reservations recommended. Fixed-price menu 25€. No credit cards. Tues–Sun noon–3:30pm and 7pm–12:30am. Closed Aug 12–25. Bus: 40, 46, 60, 62, or 64.

NEAR PIAZZA NAVONA & THE PANTHEON

Armando al Pantheon ★ ROMAN   In business for half a century, this incred-ibly inviting oasis lies near the Pantheon and off one of the most trafficked squares in historic Rome. The aura is romantic and classic, with paintings adorning the walls. Claudio and Fabrizio invite you into their little joint for a special dinner. If you want the tried and true, there are plenty of traditional recipes. But if you want fancier fare such as duck with prunes, you'll find that, too. The most delightful dish is *tagliolini al tartufo,* a bowl of steaming hot pasta topped with rich black truffles uprooted in Umbria. Less grand is the spaghetti with fresh mushrooms and saffron. Spelt balls come in a truffle sauce, and guinea fowl is cooked in dark beer and served with fat porcini mushrooms.

Salita dei Crescenzi 31. www.armandoalpantheon.it. ℂ **06/68803034.** Reservations recom-mended. Main courses 10€–24€. AE, DC, MC, V. Mon–Fri 12:30–3pm and 7–11pm; Sat 12:30–3pm.

Il Convivio Troiani ★ ROMAN/INTERNATIONAL   This is one of the most acclaimed restaurants in Rome, and one of the few to be granted a coveted Michelin star. Its 16th-century building is a classic setting in pristine white with accents of wood. The Troiani brothers turn out an inspired cuisine based on the best and fresh-est ingredients at the market. Their menu is seasonally adjusted to take advantage of what's good during any month. Start with a tantalizing fish and shellfish soup with green tomatoes and sweet peppers, and follow with such pastas as homemade lasagna with red prawns, coconut milk, pine nuts, artichokes, and mozzarella. More imagina-tive is the homemade duck ravioli in a red chicory sauce. A main dish might be oxtail served with spicy "smashed" potatoes and black truffles.

Vicolo dei Soldati 31. www.ilconviviotroiani.com. ℂ **06-6869432.** Reservations required. All main courses 28€–44€; fixed-price menu 98€. AE, DC, MC, V. Mon–Sat 8–11pm. Bus: C3, 30, 70, or 81. Metro: Piazza di Spagna.

NEAR PIAZZA DEL POPOLO & THE SPANISH STEPS

Brunello Ristorante ★★ ITALIAN   This chicly modern bar, lounge, and restaurant is helping bring back the Via Veneto as an elegant rendezvous place. The days of *la dolce vita* live on here. Your martini will arrive with a few drops of Chanel No. 5 rubbed along its glass stalk. Earthy tones such as brown dominate among the wall coverings and the upholstered seating in autumnal shades, along with gilt sculptures. The menu is impressively innovative, with fresh ingredients that explode in your mouth. The chef likes to experiment. Starters might include black fried king prawns, shrimp, and artichokes in a creamy sweet pepper sauce, or else crispy radicchio pie with cream cheese. Among the more tempting mains are vodka- and-honey-marinated salmon with a sea terrine and citrus petals or else turbot *escalopes* with fresh herbs and vanilla-scented fennel. The wine cellar boasts 500 labels, with wines from every region of Italy.

In the Regina Hotel Baglioni, Via Vittorio Veneto 70/A. www.brunellorestaurant.com. © **06-48902867**. Reservations recommended. Main courses 21€–34€; fixed-price 3-course lunch menu 37€. AE, DC, MC, V. Restaurant Mon–Sat noon–3pm and 7:30–11pm. Lounge Mon–Sat 6pm–1am. Metro: Piazza di Spagna.

Café Romano ★ INTERNATIONAL   On the most exclusive "fashion street" of Rome, this stylish venue is neither restaurant nor brasserie. Annexed to the landmark Hotel d'Inghilterra, the cafe can serve you throughout the day, beginning with a late breakfast or concluding with a post-theater dinner well after midnight. Two salons are divided by an arch resting on two columns under a barrel-vaulted ceiling with padded settees. The atmosphere is cosmopolitan, with an eclectic, well-chosen menu. You can taste dishes from around the world: from moussaka to fish couscous, from the Lebanese *mezze* (appetizers) to Chicago rib-eye steak, from the Thai-like green chicken curry to the Japanese-inspired salmon teriyaki. Flavors are beautifully blended in such starters as smoked goose breast with candied peaches or beef tartare with thyme-flavored mushrooms. Among the more appealing mains are homemade fusilli pasta with wild mushrooms, smoked bacon, and Parmesan, or sautéed roast tuna served with sweet peppers, olives, and capers. Everything is served on fine bone china with silver cutlery and crystal glassware.

In the Hotel d'Inghilterra, Via Borgognona 4. www.royaldemeure.com. © **06-69981500**. Main courses 18€–35€. AE, DC, MC, V. Daily noon–midnight. Metro: Piazza di Spagna.

Otello alla Concordia ☺ ROMAN   On a side street amid the glamorous boutiques near the northern edge of the Spanish Steps, this is one of Rome's most reliable restaurants. A stone corridor from the street leads into the dignified Palazzo Povero. Choose a table in the arbor-covered courtyard or the cramped but convivial dining rooms. Displays of Italian bounty decorate the interior, where you're likely to rub elbows with the shopkeepers from the fashion district. The *spaghetti alle vongole veraci* (with clams) is excellent, as are Roman-style saltimbocca (veal with ham), *abbacchio arrosto* (roast lamb), eggplant parmigiana, a selection of grilled or sautéed fish dishes (including swordfish), and several preparations of veal.

Via della Croce 81. www.otello-alla-concordia.it. © **06-6791178**. Reservations recommended. Main courses 8€–20€. AE, DC, MC, V. Mon–Sat 12:30–3pm and 7:30–11pm. Closed 2 weeks in Jan. Metro: Piazza di Spagna.

NEAR VATICAN CITY

Siciliainbocca ★ 🔆 SICILIAN   The best Sicilian restaurant in Rome lies close to the Vatican, ideal for a lunch when visiting either St. Peter's or the papal museums. Natives of Sicily own and operate this place, and their specialties taste virtually the same as those encountered in Sicily itself. The menu features a large variety of delectable smoked fish, including salmon, swordfish, and tuna. The homemade pastas here are the best Sicilian versions in town, especially the classic *maccheroni alla Norma,* with ricotta, a savory tomato sauce, and sautéed eggplant. You might also opt for such dishes as linguine with sautéed scampi and cherry tomatoes, or a typical Palermitan pasta with sardines, wild fennel, and pine nuts. Other good-tasting and typical dishes include swordfish with capers, olives, tomatoes, and Parmesan cheese.

Via E. Faà di Bruno 26. www.siciliainboccaweb.com. ℰ **06-37358400.** Main courses 15€–25€. AE, DC, MC, V. Mon–Sat 1:30–3pm and 8–11:30pm. Closed 3 weeks in Aug. Metro: Ottaviano San Pietro.

IN TRASTEVERE

Antico Arco ★ 🏛 ITALIAN   Named after one of the gates of early medieval Rome (Arco di San Pancrazio), which rises nearby, Antico Arco is on Janiculum Hill not far from Trastevere and the American Academy. It's a hip restaurant with a young, stylish clientele. Carefully crafted dishes with fresh ingredients include ravioli stuffed with beans in a seafood soup or green homemade *tagliolini* with red mullet and a saffron sauce. Other palate-pleasing dishes include crispy suckling pig in a sweet-and-sour sauce, with fennel and a citrus soufflé, or else crunchy shrimp with artichoke purée and an anise sauce. A white chocolate tiramisu is a heavenly concoction.

Piazzale Aurelio 7. www.anticoarco.it. ℰ **06-5815274.** Reservations recommended. Main courses 15€–32€; fixed-price menu 75€. AE, DC, MC, V. Daily 7pm–midnight. Bus: 115 or 870.

Glass ★★ 🏛 ROMAN   When this chic restaurant and wine bar opened, management claimed it was an "attempt to give Trastevere back to the Romans." Pretend you're a native and you should have a good time here on one of its two floors. Theatrical lighting and lots of glass (including the floors) give the place a modernist aura, rather rare for the district. Glass doubles as a wine bar. The cuisine is both innovative and traditional. Some of our favorite dishes are gnocchi with pancetta, chanterelle mushrooms, and almonds; and risotto with almond milk, zucchini flowers, and king crab. Other innovative dishes are a filet of tuna under a coffee-flavored crust and pistachio-crusted scallops, fresh pork belly, and baby asparagus. One dessert is about as good as it gets: a caramelized banana tart with strawberry gelatin and peanut-butter ice cream.

Vicolo del Cinque 58. www.glass-restaurant.it. ℰ **06-58335903.** Reservations recommended. Main courses 18€–26€; fixed-price menus 60€–75€. AE, DC, MC, V. Restaurant daily 8–11:30pm. Wine bar daily 8pm–2am. Bus: 23 or 125.

VILLA BORGHESE

Casina Valadier ★ ROMAN   Once one of the hottest dining tickets in Rome, this chic restaurant closed its doors seemingly forever. But once again, the glitterati of Rome are flocking here for the to-die-for cocktails, the superb cuisine, and the panoramic views of Rome itself. In the heart of Villa Borghese, the terrace of the restaurant is the most evocative in the city. Placed on the site of the ancient Collis Hortulorum, the highest point of the Pincio district, the original building dates from 1816 and was the creation of the famous architect Giuseppe Valadier. In its heyday, this restaurant was the most fashionable place in Rome, attracting people such as King Farouk of Egypt and Gandhi.

The best of the menu is a regionally based repertoire of savory dishes with imaginative, intelligent associations of flavors. Diners take delight in jazzed-up Roman classics such as rigatoni with bacon, onions, peppers, and pecorino, or a cherry- and sesame-encrusted pork filet. Start, perhaps, with a duck-breast carpaccio or a warm ricotta cheese round with an olive and pistachio pesto. For dessert, dare you try the fried zucchini flowers stuffed with rice and served with cinnamon ice cream?

Villa Borghese, Piazza Bucarest. www.casinavaladier.it. ✆ **06-69922090.** Reservations required. Main courses 15€–35€. AE, DC, MC, V. Daily 1–3pm and 8–11pm. Bus: 53.

IN TESTACCIO

Checchino dal 1887 ★ ROMAN   During the 1800s, a wine shop flourished here, selling drinks to the butchers working in the nearby slaughterhouses. In 1887, the ancestors of the restaurant's present owners began serving food, too. Slaughterhouse workers in those days were paid part of their meager salaries with the *quinto quarto* (fifth quarter) of each day's slaughter (the tail, feet, intestines, and other parts not for the squeamish). Following centuries of Roman tradition, Ferminia, the wine shop's cook, transformed these products into the tripe and oxtail dishes that form an integral part of the menu. Many Italian diners come here to relish the *rigatoni con pajata* (pasta with small intestines), *coda alla vaccinara* (oxtail stew), *fagioli e cotiche* (beans with intestinal fat), and other examples of *la cucina povera* (food of the poor). In winter, a succulent wild boar with dried prunes and red wine is served. Safer and possibly more appetizing is the array of salads, soups, pastas, steaks, cutlets, grills, and ice creams. The English-speaking staff is helpful, tactfully proposing alternatives if you're not ready for Roman soul food.

Via di Monte Testaccio 30. www.checchino-dal-1887.com. ✆ **06-5743816.** Reservations recommended. Main courses 10€–25€; fixed-price menu 46€–63€. AE, MC, V. Tues–Sat 12:30–3pm and 8pm–midnight (June–Sept closed Sun–Mon). Closed Aug and 1 week in Dec (dates vary). Metro: Piramide. Bus: 75 from Termini Station.

IN PARIOLI

Al Ceppo ★★ ROMAN   Because the place is somewhat hidden (only 2 blocks from the Villa Borghese, near Piazza Ungheria), you're likely to rub elbows with more Romans than tourists. It's a longtime favorite, and the cuisine is as good as ever. "The Log" features an open wood-stoked fireplace on which the chef roasts lamb chops, liver, and bacon to perfection. The beefsteak, which comes from Tuscany, is succulent. Other dishes that we continue to delight in are *tagliatelle* with porcini mushrooms and roast sausage, cod ravioli with sautéed shrimp, braised beef with lemon meatballs, and baked scampi with cherry tomatoes and green olives.

Via Panama 2. www.ristorantealceppo.it. ✆ **06-8419696.** Reservations recommended. Main courses 17€–30€. AE, DC, MC, V. Tues–Sun 12:30–3pm and 8–11pm. Closed last 2 weeks of Aug. Bus: 52 or 910.

Shopping

The posh shopping streets **Via Borgognona** and **Via Condotti** begin near Piazza di Spagna, and both the rents and the merchandise are chic and ultraexpensive. **Via Frattina** runs parallel to Via Condotti, its more famous sibling. Not attempting the stratospheric image or prices of Via Condotti or Via Borgognona, **Via del Corso** boasts styles aimed at younger consumers. Some gems are scattered amid the shops selling jeans and sporting equipment. The most interesting are nearest the cafes of Piazza del Popolo.

Beginning at the top of the Spanish Steps, **Via Sistina** runs to Piazza Barberini. The shops are small, stylish, and based on the tastes of their owners. The pedestrian traffic is less dense than on other major streets. Most shoppers reach **Via Francesco Crispi** by following Via Sistina 1 long block from the top of the Spanish Steps. Near the intersection of these streets are several shops well suited for unusual and less expensive gifts. **Via Veneto** is filled these days with expensive hotels and cafes and an array of relatively expensive stores selling shoes, gloves, and leather goods.

Traffic-clogged **Via Nazionale** begins at Piazza della Repubblica and runs down almost to the 19th-century monuments of Piazza Venezia. You'll find an abundance of leather stores (more reasonable in price than those in many other parts of Rome) and a welcome handful of stylish boutiques.

Entertainment & Nightlife

When the sun goes down, Rome's palaces, ruins, fountains, and monuments are bathed in a theatrical white light. Few evening occupations are quite as pleasurable as a stroll past the solemn pillars of old temples or the cascading torrents of Renaissance fountains glowing under the blue–black sky.

Even if you don't speak Italian, you can generally follow the listings of special events and evening entertainment featured in *La Repubblica,* a leading Italian newspaper. *Wanted in Rome* has listings of jazz, rock, and such and gives an interesting look at expatriate Rome. And *Un Ospite a Roma,* available free from the concierge desks of top hotels, is full of details on what's happening. Check **InRome Now.com** online for monthly updates of current cultural events.

During the peak of summer, usually in August, all nightclub proprietors seem to lock their doors and head for the seashore, where they operate alternate clubs. Some close at different times each year, so it's hard to keep up to date. Always have your hotel check to see if a club is operating before you make a trek to it. (Dance clubs, in particular, open and close with freewheeling abandon.)

THE PERFORMING ARTS

If you're in the capital for the opera season, usually from late December to June, you might want to attend the historic **Teatro dell'Opera,** Piazza Beniamino Gigli 1, off Via Nazionale (www.operaroma.it; ✆ **06-481601;** Metro: Repubblica). Nothing is presented in July and August; in summer, the venue usually switches elsewhere. Call ahead or ask your concierge before you go. Tickets are 11€ to 130€.

LIVE-MUSIC CLUBS

At **Alexanderplatz,** Via Ostia 9 (www.alexanderplatz.it; ✆ 06-58335781; Metro: Ottaviano), you can hear jazz Monday through Saturday from 9pm to 2am, with live music beginning at 10pm. The good restaurant here serves everything from *gnocchi alla romana* to Japanese fare. There's no cover; instead you pay a 1-month membership fee of 10€.

Big Mama, Vicolo San Francesco a Ripa 18 (www.bigmama.it; ✆ **06-5812551;** Metro: Piramide; bus: H or 780), is a hangout for jazz and blues musicians where you're likely to meet the up-and-coming stars of tomorrow, and sometimes even the big names. For big acts, the cover is 12€ to 30€, plus 14€ for a seasonal membership fee.

Fonclea, Via Crescenzio 82A (www.fonclea.it; ✆ **06-6896302;** bus: 49, 492, or 982), offers live music every night: Dixieland, rock, and R&B. This is basically a cellar jazz place and crowded pub that attracts folks from all walks of Roman life. The music starts at 7pm and usually lasts until 2am. There's also a restaurant featuring grilled meats, salads, and crepes. A meal starts at 20€; but if you want dinner, it's best to reserve a table.

Arciliuto, Piazza Monte Vecchio 5 (www.arciliuto.it; ✆ **06-6879419;** bus: 46, 62, or 64), is a romantic candlelit spot that was reputedly once the studio of Raphael.

Monday through Saturday from 10pm to 1:30am, you can enjoy a music-salon ambience, with a pianist, guitarist, and violinist. The presentation also includes live Neapolitan songs, new Italian madrigals, and even current hits from Broadway or London's West End. This place is hard to find, but it's within walking distance of Piazza Navona. There is no cover, but there's a one-drink minimum with beverages starting at 10€. It's closed from July 15 to September 5.

NIGHTCLUBS & DANCE CLUBS

In a high-tech, futuristic setting, **Boheme,** Via Velletri 13–19 (www.boeme.it; ✆ 06-8412212; bus: 63, 86, or 92), provides two dance floors with a house and pop soundtrack. It's open Friday to Sunday 11pm to 3:30am. Admission is 10€. It is closed in July and August.

Piper, Via Tagliamento 9 (www.piperclub.it; ✆ 06-8555398; bus: 63), opened in 1965 in a former cinema and became the first modern disco of its kind in Italy. Today it lures with fashion shows, screenings, some of the hottest parties in town, and various gigs, drawing a casual and mixed-age crowd. The kind of music you'll hear depends on the night. It's open Tuesday to Sunday 11pm to 5am, charging a cover of 20€ to 26€, including one drink.

Gilda, Via Mario de' Fiori 97 (www.midra.it; ✆ 06-6797396; Metro: Piazza di Spagna), is an adventurous nightclub/disco/restaurant that attracts a post-35 set, most often couples. Expect first-class shows, and disco music played between the live acts. The disco (midnight–4am) presents music of the 1960s plus more current tunes. The attractive piano bar, Swing, features Italian and Latin music. The cover ranges from 15€ to 30€ and includes the first drink. It's closed on Monday.

Don't be put off by the facade of **Locanda Atlantide,** Via dei Lucani 22B (www.locandatlantide.it; ✆ 06-44704540; Metro: Porta Maggiore; bus: 71). This former warehouse in San Lorenzo is the setting of a nightclub, bar, concert hall, and theater. Every day there's something different—perhaps jazz on Tuesday, a play on Wednesday, or a concert on Thursday, giving way to dance-club action on Friday and Saturday with DJ music. The cover ranges from 3€ to 15€, depending on the evening; hours are Tuesday to Sunday from 8pm to 2am. It's closed June 15 to September 15.

Where to Stay

All the hotels listed serve breakfast (often a buffet with coffee, fruit, rolls, and cheese), but it's not always included in the rate, so check the listing carefully.

Nearly all hotels are heated in the cooler months, but not all are air-conditioned in summer, which can be vitally important during a stifling July or August. The deluxe and first-class ones are, but after that it's a tossup. Be sure to check the listing carefully before you book a stay in the dog days of summer!

NEAR STAZIONE TERMINI

Despite a handful of pricey choices, this area is most notable for its concentration of cheap hotels. It's not the most picturesque location and parts of the neighborhood are still transitional, but it's certainly convenient in terms of transportation and easy access to many of Rome's top sights.

Exedra ★★   This neoclassical palace overlooking the Piazza della Repubblica at the rail terminal also fronts the Baths of Diocletian and Michelangelo's Basilica degli Angeli. The Exedra is a study in modern elegance combined with the romance of the past. It's luxury living on a grand scale, from the spacious standard double rooms to a variety of suites. Our favorite rooms are the top-floor accommodations in the Clementino Wing, each with bare brick walls and the original ceiling beams. Rooms feature such decorative notes as printed leather headboards and whorled silk wall coverings. You can take morning coffee on the rooftop garden terrace overlooking the Fountain of the Naiads. The spa is linked to the rooftop swimming pool by a glass elevator.

Piazza della Repubblica 47, 00187 Roma. www.exedra-roma.boscolohotels.com. © **06-489381.** Fax 06-48938000. 240 units. 260€–700€ double; from 506€ junior suite; from 1,100€ suite. AE, DC, MC, V. Parking 35€. Metro: Repubblica. **Amenities:** 3 restaurants; 2 bars; rooftop pool; spa; room service; babysitting; Wi-Fi (20€ per 24 hr.). *In room:* A/C, TV, minibar, hair dryer.

Royal Court ★ 👔   This winner lies in a restored Liberty-style palace a short walk from the Termini. The hotel evokes a tranquil, elegantly decorated private town house. Some of the superior rooms offer Jacuzzis in their bathrooms, but all units feature well-maintained-and-designed bathrooms with tub/shower combinations. The superior rooms also come with small balconies opening onto cityscapes. Even the standard doubles are comfortable; but if you're willing to pay the price, you can stay in the deluxe doubles, which are like junior suites in most Rome hotels. Some of the bedrooms are large enough to sleep three or four guests comfortably.

Via Marghera 51, 00185 Roma. www.morganaroyalcourt.com. © **06-44340364.** Fax 06-4469121. 24 units. 130€–250€ double. Rates include buffet breakfast. AE, DC, MC, V. Parking 25€. Metro: Termini. **Amenities:** Bar; room service; babysitting; airport transfers (55€). *In room:* A/C, TV, minibar, hair dryer, Wi-Fi (10€ per 24 hr.).

Yes Hotel 🗝   We'd definitely say yes to this hotel, which lies only 100m (328 ft.) from Stazione Termini. Opened in 2007, it was quickly discovered by frugally minded travelers who want a good bed and comfortable surroundings for the night. It's a two-story hotel housed in a restored 19th-century building with simple, well-chosen furnishings resting on tiled floors. There is a sleek, modern look to both the bedrooms and public areas, and the staff is helpful but not effusive.

Via Magenta 15, 00185 Roma. www.yeshotelrome.com. © **06-44363836.** Fax 06-44363829. 29 units. 95€–220€ double. DC, MC, V. Parking 17€. Metro: Termini. **Amenities:** Bar; room service; babysitting. *In room:* A/C, TV, hair dryer, Wi-Fi (5€ per 24 hr.).

NEAR VIA VENETO & PIAZZA BARBERINI

If you stay in this area, you definitely won't be on the wrong side of the tracks. Unlike the area near the dreary rail station, this is a beautiful and upscale commercial neighborhood, near some of Rome's best shopping.

Hotel Eden ★★★   It's not as grand architecturally as the Westin Excelsior, nor does it have the views of the Hassler, and it's certainly not a summer resort like the Hilton. But the Eden is Rome's top choice for discerning travelers who like grand comfort but without all the ostentation.

For several generations after its 1889 opening, this hotel, about a 10-minute walk east of the Spanish Steps, reigned over one of the world's most stylish shopping neighborhoods. Recent guests have included Pierce Brosnan, Tom Cruise, Emma Thompson, and Nicole Kidman. The Eden's hilltop position guarantees a panoramic city view from most guest rooms; all are spacious and elegantly appointed with a decor harking back to the late 19th century, plus marble-sheathed bathrooms. Try to get one of the front rooms with a balcony boasting views over Rome.

Via Ludovisi 49, 00187 Roma. www.edenroma.com. © **06-478121.** Fax 06-4821584. 121 units. 328€–840€ double; from 1,340€ suite. AE, DC, DISC, MC, V. Parking 60€. Metro: Piazza Barberini. **Amenities:** Restaurant; bar; exercise room; sauna; room service; babysitting; airport transfers (85€). *In room:* A/C, TV/DVD, minibar, hair dryer, CD player, Wi-Fi (19€ per 24 hr.).

Rome Hotels

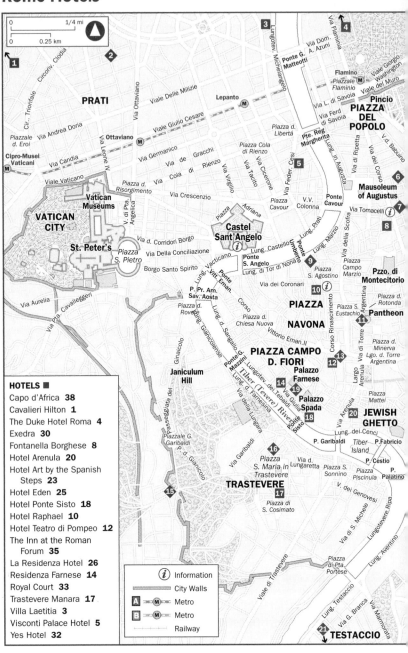

PRATI

Viale Delle Milizie

Lepanto

Viale Giulio Cesare

Ottaviano

Via Germanico

Via de Gracchi

Via Cola di Rienzo

Via Crescenzio

Cipro-Musei Vaticani

Viale Vaticano

Piazza d. Risorgimento

Vatican Museums

VATICAN CITY

St. Peter's

Piazza S. Pietro

Borgo Santo Spirito

Via della Conciliazione

Castel Sant'Angelo

Via d. Corridori Borgo

Ponte S. Angelo

Flamino

PIAZZA DEL POPOLO

Pincio

Mausoleum of Augustus

PIAZZA NAVONA

Piazza Cavour

Piazza Campo Marzio

Pzzo. di Montecitorio

PIAZZA CAMPO D. FIORI

Pantheon

Palazzo Farnese

Palazzo Spada

JEWISH GHETTO

Janiculum Hill

Tiber (Tevere) River

TRASTEVERE

Piazza S. Maria in Trastevere

Piazza di S. Cosimato

Tiber Island

TESTACCIO

HOTELS

Capo d'Africa **38**
Cavalieri Hilton **1**
The Duke Hotel Roma **4**
Exedra **30**
Fontanella Borghese **8**
Hotel Arenula **20**
Hotel Art by the Spanish Steps **23**
Hotel Eden **25**
Hotel Ponte Sisto **18**
Hotel Raphael **10**
Hotel Teatro di Pompeo **12**
The Inn at the Roman Forum **35**
La Residenza Hotel **26**
Residenza Farnese **14**
Royal Court **33**
Trastevere Manara **17**
Villa Laetitia **3**
Visconti Palace Hotel **5**
Yes Hotel **32**

Information
City Walls
Metro
Metro
Railway

National Gallery of Modern Art

Galleria Borghese

Venice

Florence

ITALY

Rome

Policlinico

VILLA BORGHESE/ PARIOLI

Via dell'Uccelliera

Viale Giulia

Piazza di Siena

Viale P. Canonica

Viale dei Cavalli Marini

Via dell' Arancera

Vle. delle Magnolie

Via d. Magnolie

Viale del Muro Torto

Viale del Muro Torto

Via Pinciana

Corso D'Italia

Via Campania

Via Sardegna

Via Sicilia

Via Boncompagni

Via Vittorio Veneto

Via Ludovisi

Spagna

Spanish Steps

Piazza di Spagna

Via Sistina

Via d.

Via di Crispi

Via Fr. Crispi

Barberini

PIAZZA BARBERINI

Via Barberini

Lgo. de Tritone

Via Tritone

Via del Corso

Via del Tritone

Via Due Macelli

Piazza Colonna

Trevi Fountain

Palazzo del Quirinale

Piazza d. Quirinale

Palazzo Doria Pamphilj

Palazzo Colonna

Via d.-Plebiscito

Via IV Nov.

Palazzo Venezia

Vittorio Emanuele Monument

Capitoline Museums

ANCIENT ROME

Roman Forum

Piazza Bocca d. Verità

PALATINE HILL

Circus Maximus

AVENTINE HILL

Via di S. Anselmo

Piazza Albania

Piramide

Baths of Caracalla

Via Salaria

Vle. Regina Margherita

Via Po

Via Isonzo

Via Tevere

Via Savoia

Via Nomentana

Piazzale di Porta Pia

Via Piave

Via Castro Pretorio

Castro Pretorio

Lgo. di S. Susanna

VIA VENETO

Via XX Settembre

National Roman Museum

Piazza Indipendenza

Via Nazionale

Piazza Repubblica

Piazza Cinquecento

Staz. Termini

Termini Station

Via Marasala

Viale Pretoriano

SAN LORENZO

Repubblica

Via del Quirinale

d. Quattro Fontane

Via Viminale

Termini

Via Principe Amedeo

Via Giovanni Giolitti

Via Tiburtina

Via Nazionale

Via Milano

Teatro dell'Opera

Piazza dell'Esquilino

Santa Maria Maggiore

Via Cavour

V. Carlo Alberto

Via Cavour

Vittorio Emanuele

Piazza Vittorio Eman. II

Via Merulana

Via Leopardi

San Giovanni in Laterano

San Pietro in Vincoli

Golden House of Nero

Colosseo

Colosseum

Piazza d. Colosseo

Viale d. Domus Aurea

Via Labicana

Via di S. Giovanni in Laterano

Via Claudia

Piazza di Pla. Metronia

Via Druso

Via Gallia

Via Antonina

Via Aventino

Viale del Circo Massimo

Via di S. Gregorio

Circo Massimo

Piazza di Pta.Capena

Via D. Teatro

Via di Marcello

Via Dei Fori Imperiali

La Residencia Hotel ★★ In a superb but congested location, this little hotel successfully combines intimacy and elegance. A bit old-fashioned and homey, the converted villa has an ivy-covered courtyard and a series of public rooms with Empire divans, oil portraits, and rattan chairs. Terraces are scattered throughout. The guest rooms are generally spacious, containing bentwood chairs and built-in furniture, including beds. The dozen or so junior suites boast balconies. The bathrooms have robes, and rooms even come equipped with ice machines.

Via Emilia 22–24, 00187 Roma. www.hotel-la-residenza.com. © **06-4880789.** Fax 06-485721. 29 units. 160€–280€ double; 230€–380€ suite. Rates include buffet breakfast. AE, MC, V. Parking (limited) 20€. Metro: Piazza Barberini. **Amenities:** Bar; room service; babysitting. *In room:* A/C, TV, minibar, hair dryer.

NEAR ANCIENT ROME

Capo d'Africa ★ 🎁 Installed in a beautiful 19th-century building and boasting a strong colonial look, this hotel lies in the heart of Imperial Rome between the Forum and the Domus Aurea in the Celio district of Rome, a few steps from the Colosseum. Endowed with a "contemporary classic" look, it attracts visitors with its sophisticated interior design, works of art, high-tech facilities, and impeccable service. Best of all is a splendid rooftop terrace with a panoramic view over some of the dusty ruins of the world's most famous monuments. Rooms are midsize and furnished with good taste; they are spread across three floors.

Via Capo d'Africa 54, 00184 Roma. www.hotelcapodafrica.com. © **06-772801.** Fax 06-77280801. 65 units. 380€–400€ double; 480€–540€ suite. Rates include buffet breakfast. AE, DC, MC, V. Parking 45€. Metro: Colosseo. **Amenities:** Restaurant; bar; exercise room; room service; babysitting. *In room:* A/C, TV, minibar, hair dryer.

Hotel Arenula ★ 🌶 At last a hotel has opened in Rome's old Jewish ghetto, and it's a winner and quite affordable. It takes its name from Via Arenula, that timeworn street linking Largo Argentina to Ponte Garibaldi and the Trastevere area. The restored building is from the 19th century, and the Patta family turned it into this undiscovered and comfortable inn. Close at hand are such attractions as the Pantheon, the Colosseum, and the Piazza Navona. Rooms are furnished in a tasteful, traditional way. They are most inviting and comfortable, with pale-wood pieces and immaculate bathrooms. There's no elevator, so be prepared to climb some stairs.

Via Santa Maria de Calderari 47, 00186 Roma. www.hotelarenula.com. © **06-6879454.** Fax 06-6896188. 50 units. 100€–133€ double. Rates include buffet breakfast. AE, DC, MC, V. Metro: Colosseo. Bus: 40. **Amenities:** Room service. *In room:* A/C, TV, hair dryer.

The Inn at the Roman Forum ★ 🎁 This is one of the secret discoveries of Rome, with the Roman Forum itself as a neighbor. A restored 15th-century building dripping with antiquity, the inn even has a small section of Trajan's Marketplace on-site. You enter the front doorway like a resident Roman, greeting your host in the living room. Sleek, classically styled bedrooms are spread across three upper floors, opening onto views of the heart of Rome. Three back bedrooms open onto a walled-in garden complete with fig and palm trees. The most elegant and expensive double has a private patio with a designer bathroom.

Via degli Ibernesi 30, 00185 Roma. www.theinnattheromanforum.com. © **06-69190970.** Fax 06-45438802. 12 units. 210€–960€ double; from 1,040€ suite. Rates include buffet breakfast. AE, DC, MC, V. Parking 30€. Bus: 64 or 117. **Amenities:** Bar; room service; babysitting; airport transfers (55€). *In room:* A/C, TV/DVD, minibar, hair dryer, MP3 docking station, Wi-Fi (10€ per day).

NEAR CAMPO DE' FIORI

Hotel Teatro di Pompeo ★★ 🛍 Built atop the ruins of the Theater of Pompey, this small charmer lies near the spot where Julius Caesar met his end on the Ides of March. Intimate and refined, it's on a quiet piazza near the Palazzo Farnese and Campo de' Fiori. The rooms are decorated in an old-fashioned Italian style with hand-painted tiles, and the beamed ceilings date from the days of Michelangelo. The guest rooms range from small to medium in size, each with a tidy but cramped bathroom.

Largo del Pallaro 8, 00186 Roma. www.hotelteatrodipompeo.it. ⓒ**06-68300170.** Fax 06-68805531. 13 units, shower only. 180€–210€ double; 240€–270€ triple. Rates include buffet breakfast. AE, DC, MC, V. Bus: 46, 62, or 64. **Amenities:** Bar; room service; babysitting; Wi-Fi (3€ per hour, in lobby). *In room:* A/C, TV, minibar, hair dryer.

Residenza Farnese ★ 🌿 Among the boutique hotels springing up around Campo de' Fiori, the new Farnese in a 15th-century mansion emerges near the top. Opt for one of the front rooms overlooking Palazzo Farnese, with Michelangelo's Renaissance cornice bathed in sunlight. Bedrooms are fresh and modernized, ranging in size from small to spacious, each with a freshly restored private bathroom with a shower. The location in the heart of ancient Rome puts you within walking distance of many of the major sights, particularly the Roman Forum or even St. Peter's.

Via del Mascherone 59, 00186 Roma. www.residenzafarneseroma.it. ⓒ 06-68210980. Fax 06-80321049. 31 units. 145€–300€ double; 230€–500€ junior suite. Rates include buffet breakfast. MC, V. Bus: 64. **Amenities:** Bar; room service. *In room:* A/C, TV, minibar, hair dryer, Wi-Fi (free).

NEAR PIAZZA NAVONA & THE PANTHEON

Hotel Raphael ★★ With a glorious location adjacent to Piazza Navona, the Raphael is within easy walking distance of many sights. The ivy-covered facade invites you to enter the lobby, which is decorated with antiques that rival the cache in local museums (there's even a Picasso ceramics collection). The guest rooms (some quite small) were refurbished with a Florentine touch. Some of the suites have private terraces. The deluxe rooms, the executive units, and the junior suites were conceived by Richard Meier, the famous architect who has designed buildings all over the world. Each of them is lined with oak and equipped in a modern high-tech style that includes a digital sound system. We love its rooftop restaurant with views of all of the city's prominent landmarks.

Largo Febo 2, 00186 Roma. www.raphaelhotel.com. ⓒ **06-682831.** Fax 06-6878993. 50 units. 272€–600€ double; 442€–900€ suite. AE, DC, MC, V. Parking 40€. Bus: 70, 81, 87, or 115. **Amenities:** Restaurant; bar; exercise room; sauna; room service; babysitting; Wi-Fi (free, in lobby). *In room:* A/C, TV/DVD, minibar, hair dryer.

NEAR PIAZZA DEL POPOLO & THE SPANISH STEPS

Fontanella Borghese ★ 🛍 Close to the Spanish Steps in the exact heart of Rome, this hotel surprisingly remains relatively undiscovered. Much renovated and improved, it has been installed on the third and fourth floors of a palace dating from the end of the 18th century. The building once belonged to the princes of the Borghese family, and the little hotel looks out onto the Borghese Palace. It lies within walking distance of the Trevi Fountain, the Pantheon, and the Piazza Navona. The location is also close to Piazza Augusto and the Ara Pacis. In the midsize bedrooms, plain wooden furniture rests on parquet floors, and everything is in a classical tradition comfortably modernized for today's travelers. Half of the bathrooms come with tubs, the rest with showers. The staff of the front desk is one of the most helpful in central Rome.

Largo Fontanella Borghese 84, 00186 Roma. www.fontanellaborghese.com. ☎ **06-68809504.** Fax 06-6861295. 29 units, half with shower only. 160€–230€ double; 230€–280€ triple. AE, DC, MC, V. Nearby parking 25€. Metro: Piazza di Spagna. **Amenities:** Room service. *In room:* A/C, TV, minibar, hair dryer.

Hotel Art by the Spanish Steps ★★ 🛎

This discovery lies near the Spanish Steps on "the street of artists," as Via Margutta is called. A former college has been turned into a hotel in a modern, minimalist style. Of particular interest is the Hall. The lobby, once a chapel, sits under a frescoed vaulted ceiling, where works of contemporary artists abound. The corridors of the four floors housing the rooms are decorated in blue, orange, yellow, and green. Forming a border for the corridors are stretches of milky glass with verses from poets such as Federico García Lorca. High-tech furnishings and bright colors adorn the bedrooms, which make good use of wood and Florentine leather. The rooms also feature glass, metal, and mosaic tiles that pick up the colors of the corridor.

Via Margutta 56, 00187 Roma. www.hotelartrome.com. ☎ **06-328711.** Fax 06-36003995. 46 units. 250€–350€ double; from 500€ suite. AE, DC, MC, V. Parking 25€. Metro: Piazza di Spagna. **Amenities:** Bar; exercise room; sauna; bikes; room service; babysitting. *In room:* A/C, TV, minibar.

NEAR VATICAN CITY

Villa Laetitia ★★★

Anna Fendi, of the fashion dynasty, has opened this stylish and superchic haven of elegance along the Tiber. With its private gardens, this Art Nouveau mansion lies between the Piazza del Popolo and the Prati quarter. The bedrooms are virtual works of art and are decorated with antique tiles gathered by Fendi on her world travels along with other objets d'art. For the smart, trendy, and well-heeled traveler, this is a choice address. Many of the rooms contain well-equipped kitchenettes. Accommodations are like small studios with terraces or gardens. Each rental unit has a different design and personality. Artists and designers in particular are attracted to this intimate, personalized hotel.

Lungotevere delle Armi 22–23, 00195 Roma. www.villalaetitia.com. ☎ **06-3226776.** Fax 06-3232720. 15 units. 190€–220€ double; 270€–350€ suite. AE, DC, MC, V. Metro: Lepanto. **Amenities:** Bar; spa; room service; babysitting; airport transfers (55€); Wi-Fi (free, in lobby). *In room:* A/C, TV/DVD, minibar, hair dryer.

Visconti Palace Hotel ★★

Completely restructured and redesigned, this palatial hotel is graced with one of the most avant-garde contemporary designs in town. Stunningly modern, it uses color perhaps with more sophistication than any other hotel. The location is idyllic, lying in the Prati district between Piazza di Spagna and St. Peter's. The rooms and corridors are decorated with modern art, the bathrooms are in marble, and there are many floor-to-ceiling windows and private terraces. Taste and an understated elegance prevail in this bright, welcoming, and functional atmosphere.

Via Federico Cesi 37, 00193 Roma. www.viscontipalace.com. ☎ **06-3684.** Fax 06-3200551. 242 units. 350€–380€ double; 450€ junior suite; 650€ suite. AE, DC, MC, V. Parking 35€. Metro: Ottaviano. Bus: 30, 70, or 913. **Amenities:** Bar; exercise room; room service; Wi-Fi (7€ per hour). *In room:* A/C, TV, minibar, hair dryer.

IN TRASTEVERE

Hotel Ponte Sisto ★ 🛎

This hotel is imbued with a bright, fresh look that contrasts with some of the timeworn buildings surrounding it. Windows look out on the core of Renaissance and baroque Rome. This 18th-century structure has been totally renovated with class and elegance. If you can live in the small bedrooms (the singles are really cramped), you'll enjoy this choice address with its cherrywood furnishings. Try for one of the upper-floor rooms for a better view; some come with their own terrace.

Via dei Pettinari 64, 00186 Roma. www.hotelpontesisto.it. *(C)* **06-6863100.** Fax 06-68301712. 103 units. 200€–320€ double; 450€–550€ suite. Rates include buffet breakfast. AE, DC, MC, V. Parking 26€. Tram: 8. **Amenities:** Airport transfers (55€); room service. *In room:* A/C, TV, minibar, hair dryer.

Trastevere Manara ★ ✦ This little gem has fresh, bright bedrooms with immaculate tiles. All of the bathrooms, which also have been renovated and contain showers, are small. The price is hard to beat for those who want to stay in one of the most atmospheric sections of Rome. Most of the rooms open onto the lively Piazza San Cosimato, and all of them have comfortable, albeit functional, furnishings. Breakfast is the only meal served, but many good restaurants lie just minutes away.

Via L. Manara 24a–25, 00153 Roma. www.hoteltrastevere.net. *(C)* **06-5814713.** Fax 06-5881016. 18 units. 103€–105€ double. Rates include buffet breakfast. AE, DC, MC, V. Bus: H. Tram: 8. **Amenities:** Airport transfers 52€. *In room:* A/C, TV, hair dryer.

IN PARIOLI

The Duke Hotel Roma ★★ This boutique hotel has burst into a renewed life, as celebrities are once again staying here. The Duke is nestled between the parks of Villa Borghese and Villa Glori. A free limo service links the hotel to the Via Veneto. The elegant bedrooms and superior suites are distributed across six floors, with many opening onto private balconies. All the accommodations are different in size and shape. The interior design combines a classical Italian bourgeois style with the warmth of an English gentleman's club.

Via Archimede 69, 00197 Roma. www.thedukehotel.com. *(C)* **800/223-5652** in the U.S. and Canada, or 06-367221. Fax 06-36004104. 78 units. 410€–515€ double; 920€–1,385€ suite. Rates include buffet breakfast. AE, DC, MC, V. Parking 25€. Metro: Piazza Euclide. **Amenities:** Restaurant; bar; room service; airport transfers (65€). *In room:* A/C, TV, minibar, hair dryer, Wi-Fi (6.50€ per hour).

IN MONTE MARIO

Cavalieri Hilton ★★ ☺ If you want resort-style accommodations and don't mind staying a 15-minute drive from the center of Rome (the hotel offers a frequent, free shuttle service), consider the Hilton. With its pools and array of facilities, Cavalieri Hilton overlooks Rome and the Alban Hills from atop Monte Mario. It's set among 6 hectares (15 acres) of trees, flowering shrubs, and stonework. The guest rooms and suites, many with panoramic views, are contemporary and stylish. Soft furnishings in pastels are paired with Italian furniture in warm-toned woods, including beds with deluxe linen. Each unit has a spacious balcony.

Via Cadlolo 101, 00136 Roma. www.romecavalieri.com. *(C)* **800/445-8667** in the U.S. and Canada, or 06-35091. Fax 06-35092241. 372 units. 310€–800€ double; from 650€ suite. AE, DC, DISC, MC, V. Parking 30€. **Amenities:** 2 restaurants; 3 bars; 2 pools (including 1 heated indoor pool); 2 outdoor tennis courts (lit); exercise room; spa; concierge; room service; babysitting; airport transfers (90€–380€). *In room:* A/C, TV/DVD, minibar, hair dryer, CD player (in suites), Wi-Fi (12€ per hour).

Side Trips from Rome

TIVOLI

Tivoli, known as Tibur to the ancient Romans, is 32km (20 miles) east of Rome on Via Tiburtina, about an hour's drive with traffic. If you don't have a car, take Metro Line B to the end of the line, the Rebibbia station. After exiting the station, board a Cotral bus for the trip the rest of the way to Tivoli. Cotral buses to Tivoli depart from

EXPLORING THE VILLAS

While the **Villa d'Este** ★★, a dank Renaissance structure with second-rate paintings, is not that noteworthy, its **spectacular gardens**—designed by Pirro Ligorio—dim the luster of Versailles. Visitors descend the cypress-studded slope to the bottom; on the way you're rewarded with everything from lilies to gargoyles spouting water, torrential streams, and waterfalls. The loveliest fountain is the **Fontana dell Ovato** (Ovato Fountain), by Ligorio. But nearby is the most spectacular achievement: the **Fontana dell'Organo Idraulico (Fountain of the Hydraulic Organ),** dazzling with its water jets in front of a baroque chapel, with four maidens who look tipsy. The best walk is along the promenade, with 100 spraying fountains. The garden is worth hours of exploration, but it's a lot of walking, with some steep climbs. Admission is 8€. The villa is open Tuesday to Sunday from 8:30am to 1 hour before sunset.

The Villa d'Este dazzles with artificial glamour, but the **Villa Gregoriana** relies more on nature. The gardens were built by Pope Gregory XVI in the 19th century. At one point on the circuitous walk carved along a slope, you can stand and look out onto the most panoramic waterfall (Aniene) at Tivoli. The trek to the bottom on the banks of the Anio is studded with grottoes and balconies that open onto the chasm. Admission is 5€. It's open April 1 to October 15 Tuesday to Sunday 10am to 6:30pm; March and October 16 to November 30, Tuesday to Saturday 10am to 2:30pm, and Sunday 10am to 4pm.

Of all the Roman emperors dedicated to *la dolce vita,* the globe-trotting Hadrian spent the last 3 years of his life in the grandest style. Less than 6km (3¾ miles) from Tivoli, he built one of the greatest estates ever erected—**Villa Adriana (Hadrian's Villa) ★★★**, Via di Villa Adriana (www.villa-adriana.net; ✆ **0774-530203**)—and he filled acre after acre with some of the architectural wonders he'd seen on his many travels. Hadrian directed the staggering feat of building much more than a villa: It was a self-contained world for a vast royal entourage and the hundreds of servants and guards they required to protect them, feed them, bathe them, and satisfy their libidos. Hadrian erected theaters, baths, temples, fountains, gardens, and canals bordered with statuary throughout his estate. He filled the palaces and temples with sculptures, some of which now rest in the museums of Rome. For a glimpse of what the villa used to be like, see the plastic reconstruction at the entrance.

OSTIA ANTICA'S RUINS ★★

Ostia Antica is one of the area's major attractions, particularly interesting to those who can't make it to Pompeii. If you want to see both ancient and modern Rome, grab your swimsuit, towel, and sunblock and take the Metro Line B from Stazione Termini to the Magliana stop. Change here for the Lido train to Ostia Antica, about 26km (16 miles) from Rome. Departures are about every half-hour, and the trip takes only 20 minutes. The Metro lets you off across the highway that connects Rome with the coast. It's just a short walk to the excavations.

Ostia, at the mouth of the Tiber, was the port of ancient Rome, serving as the gateway for all the riches from the far corners of the Empire. It was founded in the 4th century B.C. and became a major port and naval base primarily under two later emperors, Claudius and Trajan.

A prosperous city developed, full of temples, baths, theaters, and patrician homes. Ostia flourished for about 8 centuries before it began to wither away. Gradually it

12

Rome

ITALY

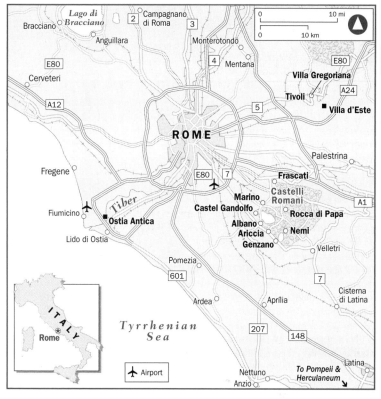

became little more than a malaria bed, a buried ghost city that faded into history. A papal-sponsored commission launched a series of digs in the 19th century; however, the major work of unearthing was carried out under Mussolini's orders from 1938 to 1942 (the work had to stop because of the war). The city is only partially dug out today, but it's believed that all the chief monuments have been uncovered. There are quite a few visible ruins unearthed, so this is no dusty field like the Circus Maximus.

These principal monuments are clearly labeled. The most important spot is **Piazzale delle Corporazioni,** an early version of Wall Street. Near the theater, this square contained nearly 75 corporations, the nature of their businesses identified by the patterns of preserved mosaics. Greek dramas were performed at the **ancient theater,** built in the early days of the Empire. The classics are still aired here in summer (check with the tourist office for specific listings), but the theater as it looks today is the result of much rebuilding. Every town the size of Ostia had a forum, and during the excavations a number of pillars of the ancient **Ostia Forum** were uncovered. At one end is a 2nd-century-B.C. temple honoring a trio of gods, Minerva, Jupiter, and Juno (little more than the basic foundation remains). The ruins of **Capitolium and Forum** remain; this was once the largest temple in Ostia, dating from the 2nd century A.D. There are perfect picnic spots beside fallen columns or near old temple walls.

Via dei Romagnoli 717. www.ostiaantica.net. (© **06-56352830.** Admission 6.50€. Nov–Feb Tues–Sun 8:30am–4pm; Mar Tues–Sun 8:30am–5pm; Apr–Oct Tues–Sun 8:30am–6pm. Metro: Ostia Antica Line Roma–Ostia–Lido.

FLORENCE ★★

Botticelli, Michelangelo, and Leonardo da Vinci all left their mark on Florence, the cradle of the Renaissance and Tuscany's alfresco museum. With Brunelleschi's dome as a backdrop, follow the River Arno to the Uffizi Gallery and soak in centuries of great painting. Wander across the Ponte Vecchio, taking in the tangle of Oltrarno's medieval streets. Then sample seasonal Tuscan cooking in a Left Bank trattoria. You've discovered the art of fine living in this masterpiece of a city.

Essentials

GETTING THERE

BY PLANE Several European airlines service Florence's **Amerigo Vespucci Airport** (www.aeroporto.firenze.it; (© **055-306-1300** for the switchboard; **055-306-1700** or **055-306-1702** for flight info), also called **Peretola,** just 5km (3 miles) northwest of town. The half-hourly **SITA-ATAF "Vola in bus"** to and from downtown's bus station at Via Santa Caterina 15r (© **800-424-500**), beside the train station, costs 5€ one-way or 8€ round-trip. There's also a less frequent service operated by **Terravision** (www.terravision.eu; (© **050-26-080**). Metered **taxis** line up outside the airport's arrival terminal and charge a flat, official rate of 20€ to the city center (22€ on holidays, 23€ after 10pm).

The closest major international airport with direct flights to North America is Pisa's **Galileo Galilei** Airport (www.pisa-airport.com; (© **050-849-300**), 97km (60 miles) west of Florence. Two to three **trains** per hour leave the airport for Florence, most requiring a change at Pisa Centrale (60–90 min.; 5.80€). Alternatively, 10 daily buses operated by **Terravision** (www.terravision.eu; (© **050-26-080**) connect downtown Florence directly with Pisa Airport in 70 minutes. One-way ticket prices are 10€ adults, 4€ children ages 5 to 12; round-trip fares are 16€ and 8€, respectively.

BY TRAIN Florence is Tuscany's rail hub, with regular connections to all Italy's major cities. To get here from Rome, take high-speed Frecciarossa or Frecciargento trains (40 daily; 1½ hr.; make sure it's going to Santa Maria Novella station, not Campo di Marte; reserve tickets ahead). There are high-speed and intercity trains to Milan (at least hourly; 1¾–3 hr.) via Bologna (37 min.–1 hr.). There's also a daily night-train sleeper service from Paris Bercy, operated by **Thello** (www.thello.com).

Most Florence-bound trains roll into **Stazione Santa Maria Novella,** Piazza della Stazione (www.trenitalia.it), which you'll see abbreviated as **S.M.N.**

BY CAR The **A1 autostrada** runs north from Rome past Arezzo to Florence and continues to Bologna. The **A11** connects Florence with Lucca, and **unnumbered superhighways** run to Siena (the *SI-FI raccordo*) and Pisa (the so-called *FI-PI-LI*).

Driving to Florence is easy; the problems begin once you arrive. Almost all cars are banned from the historic center—only residents or merchants with special permits are allowed into this camera-patrolled *zona a trafico limitato* (the "ZTL").

Your best bet for overnight or longer-term parking is one of the city-run garages. The best deal if you're staying the night (better than many hotels' garage rates) is at the **Parterre parking lot** under Piazza Libertà, at Via Madonna delle Tosse 9 (**☎ 055-550-1994**). It's open round the clock, costing 2€ per hour, or 20€ for 24 hours; it's 65€ for up to a week's parking. There's voluminous information on Florence's parking options at **www.firenzeparcheggi.it**.

Don't park your car overnight on the streets in Florence without local knowledge; if you're towed and ticketed, it will set you back substantially—and the headaches to retrieve your car are beyond description.

VISITOR INFORMATION

TOURIST OFFICES The most convenient tourist office is at Via Cavour 1r (www.firenzeturismo.it; **☎ 055-290-832**), about 3 blocks north of the Duomo. The office is open Monday through Saturday from 8:30am to 6:30pm.

The train station's nearest tourist office (**☎ 055-212-245**) is opposite the terminus at Piazza della Stazione 4. The office is usually open Monday through Saturday from 8:30am to 7pm (sometimes to 2pm in winter) and Sunday 8:30am to 2pm. This office often gets crowded; unless you're really lost, press on to the Via Cavour office, above.

CITY LAYOUT

Florence is a smallish city, sitting on the Arno River and petering out to olive-planted hills rather quickly to the north and south but extending farther west and, to a lesser extent, east along the Arno valley with suburbs and light industry. It has a compact center best negotiated on foot. No two major sights are more than a 20- or 25-minute walk apart, and most of the hotels and restaurants in this chapter are in the relatively small *centro storico* (**historic center**), a compact tangle of medieval streets and *piazze* (squares) where visitors spend most of their time. The bulk of Florence, including most of the tourist sights, lies north of the river, with the **Oltrarno,** an old artisans' working-class neighborhood, hemmed in between the Arno and the hills on the south side. The tourist offices hand out two versions of a Florence *pianta* (city plan) free: Ask for the one *con un stradario* (with a street index), which shows all the roads and is better for navigation.

GETTING AROUND

BY FOOT Florence is a **walking** city. You can take a leisurely stroll between the two top sights, the Duomo and the Uffizi, in less than 5 minutes. The hike from the most northerly sights, San Marco with its Fra' Angelico frescoes and the Accademia with Michelangelo's *David,* to the most southerly, the Pitti Palace across the Arno, should take no more than 30 minutes. From Santa Maria Novella across town to Santa Croce is an easy 20- to 30-minute walk.

BY BUS You'll rarely need to use Florence's efficient **ATAF bus system** (www.ataf.net; **☎ 800/424-500** in Italy) since the city is so compact. Bus tickets cost 1.20€ and are good for 90 minutes. A four-pack (*biglietto multiplo*) is 4.70€, a 24-hour pass 5€, a 3-day pass 12€, and a 7-day pass 18€. Tickets are sold at *tabacchi* (tobacconists), bars, and most newsstands. *Note:* Once on board, validate your ticket in the box near the rear door to avoid a steep fine.

BY TAXI Taxis aren't cheap, and with the city so small and the one-way system forcing drivers to take convoluted routes, they aren't an economical way to get about town. The standard rate is .90€ per kilometer (slightly more than a half-mile), with a whopping minimum fare of 3.30€ to start the meter (that rises to 5.30€ on Sun; 6.60€ 10pm–6am), plus 1€ per bag. There's a taxi stand outside the train station; otherwise, call **Radio Taxi** at **☎ 055-4242** or **055-4390.** For the latest taxi information, see **www.socota.it**.

Florence

ATTRACTIONS ●
Battistero **32**
Campanile di Giotto **31**
Duomo **30**
Galleria degli Uffizi **41**
Galleria dell'Accademia **27**
Museo Nazionale del Bargello **42**
Palazzo Pitti & Giardino
    di Boboli **1**
Piazzale Michelangiolo **47**
Ponte Vecchio **7**
Santa Croce **45**
Santa Maria Novella **16**
Santo Spirito **2**

RESTAURANTS ◆
Cantinetta Antinori **13**
Cantinetta dei Verrazzano **38**
Cibrèo **36**
Da Benvenuto **43**
Il Latini **11**
Il Santo Bevitore **5**
Il Vegetariano **23**
Kome **44**
Le Mossacce **37**
L'Osteria di Giovanni **12**
Mario **24**
Nerbone **22**
Olio e Convivium **3**
Ora d'Aria **40**
Trattoria Cibrèo **35**

HOTELS ■
Abaco **14**
Alessandra **9**
Burchianti **15**
Calzaiuoli **39**
Casa Howard **17**
Casci **26**
Davanzati **10**
Four Seasons Florence **29**
Hermitage **8**
Hotel Home Florence **46**
Il Guelfo Bianco **25**
Mario's **20**
Merlini **21**
Monna Lisa **33**
Montebello Splendid **18**
Morandi alla Crocetta **28**
Nuova Italia **19**
Palazzo Galletti **34**
Palazzo Magnani Feroni **4**
UNA Vittoria **6**

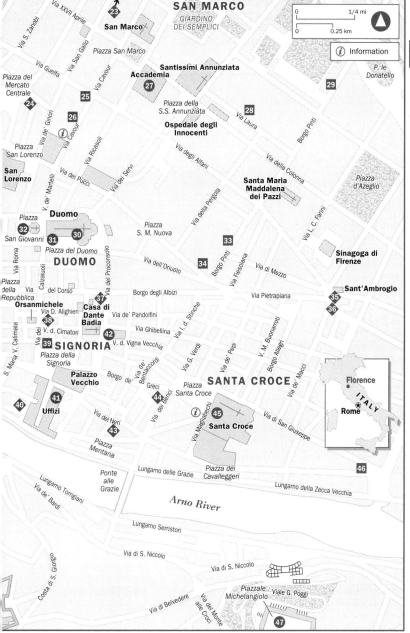

BY BICYCLE & MOTOR SCOOTER Many of the bike-rental shops in town are located just north of Piazza San Marco, such as **Alinari,** Via San Zanobi 38r (www. alinarirental.com; ☏ **055-280-500**), which rents bikes (2.50€ per hour; 12€ per day) and mountain bikes (3€ per hour; 18€ per day). It also rents 50cc and 100cc scooters (10€ or 15€ per hour; 30€ or 55€ per day). Another renter with similar prices is **Florence by Bike,** Via San Zanobi 120–122r (www.florencebybike.it; ☏ **055-488-992**).

BY CAR Trying to drive in the *centro storico* is a frustrating, useless exercise; and, moreover, unauthorized traffic is not allowed past signs marked ZTL. On top of that, 2012 will likely see the introduction of a city charge (1€ per day or thereabouts) even to drive into the center to park.

[FastFACTS] FLORENCE

Business Hours Hours mainly follow the Italian norm (see p. 618, Fast Facts: Rome). In Florence, however, many of the larger and more central shops stay open through the midday *riposo* or nap (note the sign *orario nonstop*).

Doctors There's a walk-in Tourist Medical Service, Via Lorenzo il Magnifico 59, north of the city center between the Fortezza del Basso and Piazza della Libertà (☏ **055-475-411**), open Monday to Friday 11am to noon and 5 to 6pm, Saturday 11am to noon only; take bus no. 8 or 20 to Viale Lavagnini, or bus no. 12 to Via Poliziano.

Hospitals The most central hospital is Santa Maria Nuova, a block northeast of the Duomo on Piazza Santa Maria Nuova (☏ **055-27-581**), open 24 hours. For a free translator to help you describe your symptoms, explain the doctor's instructions, and aid in medical issues in general, call the volunteers at the Associazione Volontari Ospedalieri (AVO; www.federavo.it;

☏ **055-234-4567**) Monday, Wednesday, and Friday from 4 to 6pm and Tuesday and Thursday from 10am to noon.

Internet Access Most hotels in the city center now offer wireless Internet, for free or a small fee. Otherwise, head to the chain Internet Train (www.internettrain. it), with six locations in Florence, including their very first shop at Via dell'Oriuolo 40r, a few blocks from the Duomo (☏ **055-263-8968**); Via Guelfa 54r, near the train station (☏ **055-214-794**); Borgo San Jacopo 30r, in the Oltrarno (☏ **055-265-7935**); and Via de' Benci 36r (no phone).

Pharmacies There are 24-hour pharmacies (also open Sun and state holidays) in Stazione Santa Maria Novella (☏ **055-216-761**; ring the bell between 1 and 4am); at Piazza San Giovanni 20r, just behind the Baptistery at the corner of Borgo San Lorenzo (☏ **055-211-343**); and at Via dei Calzaiuoli 7r, just off Piazza della Signoria (☏ **055-289-490**). On holidays and at night, look for

the sign in any pharmacy window telling you which ones are open.

Police To report lost property or passport problems, call the questura (urban police headquarters) at ☏ **055-49-771**. Note: It is illegal to knowingly buy fake goods anywhere in the city (and, yes, a "Rolex" watch at 20€ counts as knowingly). You may be served a hefty on-the-spot fine if caught.

Post Offices Florence's main post office (☏ **055-273-6481**) is at Via Pellicceria 3, off the southwest corner of Piazza della Repubblica. It is open Monday through Saturday from 8:15am to 7pm.

Safety As in any city, plenty of pickpockets are out to ruin your vacation, and in Florence you'll find light-fingered youngsters (especially around the train station), but otherwise you're safe. Do steer clear of the Cascine Park after dark, when it becomes somewhat seedy and you may run the risk of being mugged.

Exploring Florence

ON PIAZZA DEL DUOMO

The cathedral square is filled with tourists and caricature artists during the day, strolling crowds in the early evening, and knots of students strumming guitars on the Duomo's steps at night. Though it's always crowded, the piazza's vivacity and the glittering facades of the cathedral and the Baptistery doors keep it an eternal Florentine sight. The square's closure to traffic in 2009 has made it a more welcoming space than ever for strolling.

Battistero (Baptistery) ★★★ RELIGIOUS SITE In choosing a date to mark the beginning of the Renaissance, art historians often seize on 1401, the year Florence's powerful wool merchants' guild held a contest to decide who would receive the commission to design the **North Doors ★★** of the Baptistery to match the Gothic **South Doors,** cast 65 years earlier by Andrea Pisano. The era's foremost Tuscan sculptors each cast a bas-relief bronze panel depicting his own vision of the *Sacrifice of Isaac.* Twenty-two-year-old Lorenzo Ghiberti, competing against the likes of Donatello, Jacopo della Quercia, and Filippo Brunelleschi, won. He spent the next 21 years casting 28 bronze panels and building his doors.

The result so impressed the merchants' guild—not to mention the public and Ghiberti's fellow artists—they asked him in 1425 to do the **East Doors ★★★**, facing the Duomo, this time giving him the artistic freedom to realize his Renaissance ambitions. Twenty-seven years later, just before his death, Ghiberti finished 10 dramatic lifelike Old Testament scenes in gilded bronze, each a masterpiece of Renaissance sculpture and some of the finest examples of low-relief perspective in Italian art. The panels now mounted here are excellent copies; the originals are in the Museo dell'Opera del Duomo (see below). Years later, Michelangelo was standing before these doors and someone asked his opinion. His response sums up Ghiberti's accomplishment as no art historian could: "They are so beautiful that they would grace the entrance to Paradise." They've been called the Gates of Paradise ever since.

The interior is ringed with columns pilfered from ancient Roman buildings and is a spectacle of mosaics above and below. The floor was inlaid in 1209, and the ceiling was covered between 1225 and the early 1300s with glittering **mosaics ★★**. Most were crafted by Venetian or Byzantine-style workshops, which worked off designs drawn by the era's best artists. Coppo di Marcovaldo drew sketches for the over 7.8m-high (26-ft.), ape-toed *Christ in Judgment* and the *Last Judgment* that fills over a third of the ceiling.

Piazza San Giovanni. www.operaduomo.firenze.it. ℂ **055-230-2885.** Admission 4€. Mon–Sat 12:15–7pm; Sun and 1st Sat of month 8:30am–2pm. Bus: C2, 14, 23, or 71.

Campanile di Giotto (Giotto's Bell Tower) ★★ HISTORIC SITE In 1334, Giotto started the cathedral bell tower but completed only the first two levels before his death in 1337. He was out of his league with the engineering aspects of architecture, and the tower was saved from falling by Andrea Pisano, who doubled the thickness of the walls. Andrea, a master sculptor of the Pisan Gothic school, also changed the design to add statue niches—he even carved a few of the statues himself—before quitting the project in 1348. Francesco Talenti finished the job between 1350 and 1359.

You can climb the 414 steps to the top of the tower. What makes this 84m-high (276-ft.) **view ★★** memorable are great views of the Baptistery as you ascend and the best close-up shot in the entire city of Brunelleschi's dome.

Piazza del Duomo. www.operaduomo.firenze.it. © **055-230-2885.** Admission 6€. Daily 8:30am–6:50pm. Bus: C2, 14, 23, or 71.

Duomo (Cattedrale di Santa Maria del Fiore) ★★ CATHEDRAL   The Duomo's most distinctive feature is its enormous **dome,** which dominates the skyline and is a symbol of Florence itself. The raising of this dome, the largest in the world in its time, was no mean architectural feat, tackled admirably by Filippo Brunelleschi between 1420 and 1436. You can climb up between the two shells of the cupola for one of the classic panoramas across the city (not recommended for claustrophobes or anyone lacking a head for heights). At the base of the dome, just above the drum, Baccio d'Agnolo began adding a balcony in 1507. One of the eight sides was finished by 1515, when someone asked Michelangelo—whose artistic opinion was by this time taken as cardinal law—what he thought of it. The master reportedly scoffed, "It looks like a cricket cage." Work was halted, and to this day the other seven sides remain rough brick.

Piazza del Duomo. www.operaduomo.firenze.it © **055-230-2885.** Admission to church free; Santa Reparata excavations 3€; cupola 8€. Church Mon–Wed and Fri 10am–5pm; Thurs 10am–4:30pm (July–Sept till 5pm, May and Oct till 3:30pm); Sat 10am–4:45pm; Sun 1:30–4:45pm. Free tours every 40 min. daily; times vary. Cupola Mon–Fri 8:30am–7pm; Sat 8:30am–5:40pm. Bus: C1, C2, 14, 23, or 71.

AROUND PIAZZA DELLA SIGNORIA & SANTA TRÍNITA

Galleria degli Uffizi (Uffizi Gallery) ★★★ ART MUSEUM   The Uffizi is one of the world's great museums, and the single best introduction to Renaissance painting, with works by Giotto, Masaccio, Paolo Uccello, Sandro Botticelli, Leonardo da Vinci, Perugino, Michelangelo, Raphael Sanzio, Titian, Caravaggio … and the list goes on.

The walls separating **Rooms 10 to 14** were knocked down in the 20th century to accommodate the resurgent popularity of Sandro Filipepi—better known by his nickname, Botticelli ("little barrels"). Fourteen of his paintings line the walls, along with works by his pupil (and son of his former teacher) Filippino Lippi, and by Domenico Ghirlandaio, Michelangelo's first artistic master. In the *Birth of Venus* ★★, the love goddess is born of the sea on a half shell, blown to shore by the Zephyrs.

Primavera: Allegory of Spring ★★ is harder to evaluate, since contemporary research indicates it may not actually be an allegory of spring influenced by the humanist poetry of Poliziano but rather a celebration of Venus, who stands in the center, surrounded by various complicated references to Virtues through mythological characters.

Room 15 boasts Leonardo da Vinci's *Annunciation* ★★★, which the young artist painted in 1472 or 1475 while still in the workshop of his master, Andrea del Verrocchio. The *Adoration of the Magi* ★★, on which Leonardo didn't get much beyond the sketching stage, shows how he could retain powerful compositions even when creating a fantasy landscape.

Room 26 is devoted largely to High Renaissance darling Raphael. His *Madonna of the Goldfinch* ★ (1505) was painted in a Leonardesque style for a friend's wedding, and is more vivid than ever after a 2009 restoration. Also here are important portraits, including *Pope Leo X with Cardinals Giulio de' Medici and Luigi de' Rossi* ★★ and *Pope Julius II,* as well as a famous *Self-Portrait.*

Room 28 honors the great Venetian Titian, of whose works you'll see include a warm full-bodied *Flora* ★★ and a poetic, somewhat suggestive *Venus of Urbino* ★ languishing on her bed.

Reserving Tickets for the Uffizi & Other Museums

Bypass the hours-long line at the Uffizi by reserving a ticket and an entry time in advance by calling **Firenze Musei** at ℰ **055-294-883** (Mon–Fri 8:30am–6:30pm; Sat until 12:30pm) or visiting **www.firenzemusei.it** (you may need to have patience with their website, however). You can also reserve for the Accademia Gallery (another interminable line, to see *David*), as well as the Galleria Palatina in the Pitti Palace, the Bargello, and several others. There is a 3€ fee (4€ for the Uffizi or Accademia, where a reservation is very strongly advised); you can pay by credit card.

Pay your respects to Dutch master Rembrandt in **Room 44,** where he immortalized himself in two *Self-Portraits,* one done as a youth and the other as an old man. If you need to pause for breath, prices at the Uffizi's terrace **cafe** are no worse than in the piazza below. It's a nice spot to catch a new angle on the Palazzo Vecchio's facade.

Downstairs is a space used to house temporary exhibitions that, at their best, provide some added context to the permanent collection, but at worst are just a way to slap a few more euros onto your entrance fee. However, it's certainly worth visiting the space devoted to Caravaggio and the Caravaggeschi (painters who followed his style). Caravaggio was the baroque master of chiaroscuro—painting with extreme harsh light and deep shadows. The Uffizi preserves his painting of the severed head of *Medusa,* a *Sacrifice of Isaac,* and his famous *Bacchus* ★. The Caravaggeschi included Artemisia Gentileschi, the only female painter to make a name for herself in the early baroque. Artemisia was the victim in a sensational rape trial: It evidently affected her professional life; the violent *Judith Slaying Holofernes* ★ is featured here, in all its gruesome detail.

Piazzale degli Uffizi 6 (off Piazza della Signoria). www.uffizi.firenze.it. ℰ **055-238-8651.** (Reserve tickets at www.firenzemusei.it or ℰ 055-294-883.) Admission 6.50€ (10€–11€ with compulsory temporary exhibition). Tues–Sat 8:15am–6:50pm; also same hours 1st, 3rd, and 5th Sun of month. Ticket window closes 45 min. before museum. Bus: C1 or C2.

Museo Nazionale del Bargello (Bargello Museum) ★★ MUSEUM

Inside this 1255 Gothic *palazzo* is Florence's premier sculpture museum, with works by Michelangelo, the della Robbias, and Donatello.

In the *palazzo*'s old **armory** are 16th-century works, including some of Michelangelo's earliest sculptures. Carved by a 22-year-old Michelangelo while he was visiting Rome, *Bacchus* ★ (1497) was obviously inspired by the classical antiquities he studied there but is also imbued with his own irrepressible Renaissance realism—here is a (young) God of Wine who's actually drunk, reeling back on unsteady knees and holding the cup aloft with a distinctly tipsy wobble. The *palazzo*'s inner **courtyard**—one of the few medieval *cortile* in Florence to survive in more or less its original shape—is studded with the coats of arms of past *podestà* (mayors) and other notables.

Via del Proconsolo 4. ℰ **055-238-8606.** Admission 4€. Daily 8:15am–1:50pm. Closed 2nd and 4th Mon and 1st, 3rd, and 5th Sun of each month. Bus: C1 or C2.

Ponte Vecchio (Old Bridge) ★ ARCHITECTURE

The oldest and most famous bridge across the Arno. The characteristic overhanging shops have lined the bridge since at least the 12th century. In the 16th century, it was home to butchers until Cosimo I moved into the Palazzo Pitti across the river. He couldn't stand the stench as he crossed the bridge from on high in the Corridoio Vasariano every day, so he evicted the meat cutters and moved in the classier gold- and silversmiths, tradesmen who occupy it to this day.

Via Por Santa Maria/Via Guicciardini. Bus: C3 or D.

AROUND SAN LORENZO & THE MERCATO CENTRALE

The church of San Lorenzo is practically lost behind the leather stalls and souvenir carts of Florence's vast **San Lorenzo street market.** In fact, the hawking of wares and bustle of commerce characterize all the streets of this neighborhood, centered on both the church and the nearby **Mercato Centrale food market.** This is a colorful scene, but one of the most pickpocket-happy in the city, so be wary. *Note:* You are liable for a fine if you knowingly buy counterfeit goods in the city.

ON OR NEAR PIAZZA SANTA MARIA NOVELLA

Piazza Santa Maria Novella boasts patches of grass and a central fountain. The two squat obelisks, resting on the backs of Giambologna tortoises, once served as the turning posts for the "chariot" races held here from the 16th to the mid-19th centuries. Once a depressed and down-at-heel part of the center, the area now hosts some of Florence's most fashionable hotels.

Santa Maria Novella ★★ CHURCH   Of all Florence's major churches, the home of the Dominicans is the only one with an original **facade** ★ that matches its era of greatest importance. Inside, on the left wall, is **Masaccio's *Trinità*** ★★★ (ca. 1428), the first painting ever to use perfect linear mathematical perspective. Florentine citizens and artists flooded in to see the fresco when it was unveiled, many remarking in awe that it seemed to punch a hole back into space, creating a chapel out of a flat wall. The **transept** is filled with spectacularly frescoed chapels. The **sanctuary** ★ behind the main altar was frescoed after 1485 by Domenico Ghirlandaio with the help of his assistants and apprentices, probably including a young Michelangelo.

The **Cappella Gondi** to the left of the high altar contains a *Crucifix* carved by Brunelleschi.

Piazza Santa Maria Novella. ℂ **055-219-257.** Admission 3.50€. Mon–Thurs 9am–5:30pm; Fri 11am–5:30pm; Sat 9am–5pm; Sun noon–5pm. Bus: C2, 6, 11, 22, 36, or 37.

NEAR SAN MARCO & SANTISSIMA ANNUNZIATA

Galleria dell'Accademia ★★ ART MUSEUM   The first long hall here is devoted to Michelangelo and, although you pass his *Slaves,* most visitors are immediately drawn down to the far end, a tribune dominated by the most famous sculpture in the world: **Michelangelo's *David*** ★★★. A hot young sculptor fresh from his success with a *Pietà* in Rome (p. 622), Michelangelo took on in 1501 a huge slab of marble that had been lying around the Duomo's work yards so long it earned a nickname, Il Gigante (the Giant). It was with a twist of humor that Michelangelo, only 29 years old, finished in 1504 a Goliath-size David for his city.

There was originally a spot reserved for it high on the left flank of the Duomo, but Florence's republican government soon wheeled it down to stand on Piazza della Signoria in front of the Palazzo Vecchio to symbolize the defeated tyranny of the Medici, who had been ousted a decade before (but would return with a vengeance). The sculpture was moved to the Accademia in 1873 and replaced with a copy.

The hall leading up to *David* is lined with perhaps Michelangelo's most fascinating works, the four famous *nonfiniti* (unfinished) **Slaves,** or **Prisoners** ★★★. Like no others, these statues symbolize Michelangelo's theory that sculpture is an "art that takes away superfluous material." The great master saw a true sculpture as something that was inherent in the stone, and all it needed was a skilled chisel to free it from the extraneous rock.

Nearby, in a similar mode, is a statue of **St. Matthew** ★★ (1504–08), which Michelangelo began carving as part of a series of Apostles he was at one point going to complete for the Duomo. (The *Pietà* at the end of the corridor on the right is by one of Michelangelo's students, not by the master as was once thought.)

Off this hall of *Slaves* is the first wing of the painting gallery, which includes a panel, possibly from a wedding chest, known as the ***Cassone Adimari*** ★, painted by Lo Scheggia in the 1440s. It shows the happy couple's promenade to the Duomo, with the green-and-white marbles of the Baptistery prominent in the background. Other rooms house a fine collection of pre-Renaissance panels dating to the 1200s and 1300s.

Via Ricasoli 60. www.polomuseale.firenze.it. ✆ **055-238-8609.** (Reserve tickets at www.firenze musei.it or ✆ 055-294-883; booking fee 4€). Admission 6.50€; 11€ with temporary exhibition. Tues–Sun 8:15am–6:50pm. Last admission 30 min. before close. Bus: C1, 6, 7, 11, 14, 23, 31, or 32.

AROUND PIAZZA SANTA CROCE

Piazza Santa Croce is pretty much like any grand Florentine square—a nice bit of open space ringed with souvenir and leather shops and thronged with tourists. Its unique feature (aside from the one time a year it's covered with dirt and violent, Renaissance-style soccer is played on it) is **Palazzo Antellesi** on the south side. This well-preserved, 16th-century patrician house is owned by a contessa who rents out her apartments.

Santa Croce ★★ CHURCH   The center of the Florentine Franciscan universe was begun in 1294 by Gothic master Arnolfo di Cambio in order to rival the church of Santa Maria Novella being raised by the Dominicans across the city. The church wasn't consecrated until 1442, and even then it remained faceless until the neo-Gothic **facade** was added in 1857. It's a vast complex that demands 2 hours of your time, at least, to see properly.

The Gothic **interior** is vast, and populated with the tombs of rich and famous Florentines. Starting from the main door, immediately on the right is the first tomb of note, a mad Vasari contraption containing the bones of the most venerated Renaissance master, **Michelangelo Buonarroti,** who died of a fever in Rome in 1564 at the ripe age of 89. The pope wanted him buried in the Eternal City, but Florentines managed to sneak his body back to Florence. Close to Michelangelo's monument is a pompous 19th-century cenotaph to Florentine **Dante Alighieri,** one of history's great poets, whose *Divine Comedy* codified the Italian language. Elsewhere, seek out monuments to philosopher **Niccolò Machiavelli, Gioacchino Rossini** (1792–1868), composer of the *Barber of Seville,* architect **Lorenzo Ghiberti,** and **Galileo Galilei** (1564–1642).

Piazza Santa Croce. www.santacroceopera.it. ✆ **055-246-6105.** Admission 5€ adults, 3€ ages 11–17; combined ticket with Casa Buonarroti 8€. Mon–Sat 9:30am–5pm; Sun 1–5pm. Bus: C1, 3, or 23.

THE OLTRARNO, SAN NICCOLÒ & SAN FREDIANO
Palazzo Pitti & Giardino di Boboli (Pitti Palace & Boboli Garden) ★★
ART MUSEUM/PARK/GARDENS   Although the original, much smaller Pitti Palace was a Renaissance affair probably designed by Filippo Brunelleschi, that *palazzo* is completely hidden by the enormous Mannerist mass we see today, designed largely by Bartolomeo Ammanati. Inside is Florence's most extensive set of museums,

including the Galleria Palatina, a huge painting gallery second in scope only to the Uffizi, with works by Raphael, Titian, and Rubens.

The painting gallery—the main, and for many visitors, most interesting of the Pitti museums—is off Ammannati's **interior courtyard ★** of gold-tinged rusticated rock grafted onto the three classical orders. The ticket office is outside the main gate, on the far right as you face it from the piazza.

The statue-filled park behind the Pitti Palace is one of the earliest and finest Renaissance gardens, laid out mostly between 1549 and 1656 with box hedges in geometric patterns, groves of ilex, dozens of statues, and rows of cypress. Just above the entrance through the courtyard of the Palazzo Pitti is an oblong **amphitheater** modeled on Roman circuses, with a **granite basin** from Rome's Baths of Caracalla and an **Egyptian obelisk** of Ramses II. Around the park, don't miss the rococo **Kaffehaus,** with bar service in summer, and, near the high point, the **Giardino del Cavaliere ★**, the Boboli's prettiest hidden corner—a tiny walled garden of box hedges with private views over the hills of Florence's outskirts. Toward the south end of the park is the **Isolotto ★**, a dreamy island marooned in a pond full of huge goldfish, with Giambologna's *L'Oceano* composition at its center.

Piazza de' Pitti. **Galleria Palatina and Apartamenti Reali:** ✆ **055-238-8614;** reserve tickets at www.firenzemusei.it or ✆ 055-294-883. Admission (with Galleria d'Arte Moderna) 8.50€; 13€ with temporary exhibition. Tues–Sun 8:15am–6:50pm. **Galleria d'Arte Moderna:** ✆ **055-238-8616.** Admission (with Galleria Palatina) 8.50€. Tues–Sun 8:15am–6:50pm. **Museo degli Argenti and Galleria del Costume:** ✆ **055-238-8709.** Admission (with Giardino di Boboli) 7€; 9€ with temporary exhibition. Nov–Feb daily 8:15am–4:30pm; Mar and Oct daily 8:15am–5:30pm; Apr–May and Sept daily 8:15am–6:30pm; June–Aug daily 8:15am–6:50pm. Closed 1st and last Mon of month. **Giardino di Boboli:** ✆ **055-238-8791.** Admission (with Museo degli Argenti) 7€. Nov–Feb daily 8:15am–4:30pm; Mar and Oct daily 8:15am–5:30pm; Apr–May and Sept daily 8:15am–6:30pm; June–Aug daily 8:15am–7:30pm. Closed 1st and last Mon of month. Cumulative ticket for everything, valid 3 days, 12€. E.U. citizens ages 18 and under or 65 and over enter free. Bus: C3, D, 11, 36, or 37.

Piazzale Michelangiolo SQUARE   This panoramic piazza is a required stop for every tour bus. The balustraded terrace was laid out in 1885 to give a sweeping **vista ★★** of the entire city, spread out in the valley below and backed by the green hills of Fiesole beyond. The bronze replica of *David* here points right at his original home, outside the Palazzo Vecchio.

Viale Michelangelo. Bus: 12 or 13.

Santo Spirito ★ CHURCH   One of Filippo Brunelleschi's masterpieces of architecture, this 15th-century church doesn't look like much from the outside (no true facade was ever built), but the **interior ★** is a marvelous High Renaissance space—an expansive landscape of proportion and mathematics worked out in classic Brunelleschi style, with coffered vaulting, tall columns, and the stacked perspective of arched arcading. Good late-Renaissance and baroque paintings are scattered throughout, but the best stuff lies up in the transepts and in the east end, surrounding the extravagant **baroque altar** with a ciborium inlaid in *pietre dure* around 1607.

The famed **piazza** outside is one of the focal points of the Oltrarno, shaded by trees and lined with trendy cafes that see some bar action in the evenings.

Piazza Santo Spirito. ✆ **055-210-030.** Free admission. Mon–Tues and Thurs–Sat 10am–12:30pm and 4–5:30pm; Sun 4–5:30pm. Bus: C3, D, 11, 36, or 37.

ORGANIZED TOURS

If you want to get under the surface of the city, **Context Travel ★** (www.context travel.com; ✆ **800-691-6036** in the U.S. or **06-976-25-204** in Italy), offers insightful tours led by academics and other experts in their field in a variety of specialties, from the gastronomic to the archaeological. Tours are limited to six people and cost between 40€ and 75€ per person. **CAF Tours,** Via Roma 4 (www.caftours. com; ☏ **055-283-200**), offers two half-day bus tours of the town (47€), including visits to the Uffizi, the Accademia, and Piazzale Michelangiolo, as well as several walking tours and cooking classes from 25€ to 80€. **ArtViva** (www.italy.artviva.com; ☏ **055-264-5033**) has a huge array of walking tours and museum guides for every budget, starting at 25€.

Where to Eat

Florence is awash with restaurants, though many in the most touristy areas (around the Duomo and Piazza della Signoria) are of low quality, charge high prices, or both. We'll point out the few that are worth a visit. The highest concentrations of excellent *ristoranti* and *trattorie* are around Santa Croce and across the river in the Oltrarno. Bear in mind that menus at restaurants in Tuscany can change weekly or even (at the best places) daily.

NEAR THE DUOMO

Cantinetta dei Verrazzano ★ WINE BAR   Owned by the Castello di Verrazzano, one of Chianti's best-known wine-producing estates, this wood-paneled *cantinetta* with a full-service bar/*pasticceria* and seating area helped spawn a revival of stylish wine bars as convenient spots for fast-food breaks. It promises a delicious self-service lunch or snack of focaccia, plain or studded with rosemary, onions, or olives; buy it hot by the slice or as *farcite* (sandwiches filled with prosciutto, arugula, cheese, or tuna). Platters of Tuscan cold cuts and aged cheeses are also available.

Via dei Tavolini 18r (off Via dei Calzaiuoli). www.verrazzano.com. ☏ **055-268-590.** Tasting plates 4.50€–8€; glass of wine 4€–8€. AE, DC, MC, V. Mon–Sat 8am–9pm. Bus: C1 or C2.

Le Mossacce ★ 🍴 FLORENTINE   Delicious, cheap, abundant, fast home cooking: This tiny *osteria,* filled with lunching businesspeople, farmers in from the hills, locals who've been coming since 1942, and a few knowledgeable tourists, is authentic to the bone. The waiters hate breaking out the printed menu, preferring to rattle off a list of Florentine faves like *ribollita, crespelle,* and *lasagne al forno.* Unlike in many cheap joints catering to locals, the *secondi* are pretty good. You could try the *spezzatino* (goulashy veal stew) or a well-cooked, reasonably priced *bistecca alla fiorentina,* but I put my money on the excellent *involtini* (thin slices of beef wrapped tightly around a bread stuffing and artichoke hearts, then cooked to juiciness in tomato sauce).

Via del Proconsolo 55r (a block south of the Duomo). www.trattorialemossacce.it. ☏**055-294-361.** Reservations recommended for dinner. Main courses 9€–11€. AE, MC, V. Mon–Fri noon–2:30pm and 7–9:30pm. Bus: C1 or C2.

NEAR PIAZZA DELLA SIGNORIA

Da Benvenuto ★ ☺ 🍴 TUSCAN/ITALIAN   This is a no-nonsense trattoria, simple and good, a neighborhood hangout that somehow found its way into many a guidebook over the years. Yet it continues to serve good helpings of tasty Florentine home cooking to travelers and locals seated together in two brightly lit rooms. This is often our first stop on any trip to Florence, where we usually order ravioli or *gnocchi*—both served in tomato sauce—and follow with a *scaloppa di vitello al vino bianco* (veal escalope cooked in white wine).

Via della Mosca 16r (at the corner of Via dei Neri). ☏**055-214-833.** Main courses 6€–18€. AE, MC, V. Daily 12:30–3pm and 7–10:30pm. Bus: C1, 3, 13, 23, or 71.

Ora d'Aria ★★★ CONTEMPORARY TUSCAN   Marco Stabile is a celebrated young Tuscan chef at the very height of his creative powers, and the 2010 relocation of his signature restaurant right into the heart of the *centro storico* has only seen his fame grow. Seasonality and a modern interpretation of Tuscan food traditions are the overarching themes of his cooking. You'll need to book ahead (and save up) to enjoy the delights of *gnocchetti di patate con pomodorini confit e guancia affumicata* (gnocchi with confit tomatoes and smoked pig's cheek) or *maialino con sottobosco, aglio e lavanda* (piglet with berries, garlic, and lavender).

Via dei Georgofili 11r (off Via Lambertesca). www.oradariaristorante.com. ℂ **055-200-1699.** Main courses 32€–34€. AE, MC, V. Tues–Sat 12:30–2:30pm; Mon–Sat 7:30–10:30pm. Closed Aug. Bus: C1 or C2.

NEAR SAN LORENZO & THE MERCATO CENTRALE

Mario ★ 🍴 FLORENTINE   This is down-and-dirty Florentine lunchtime at its best, a trattoria so basic the little stools don't have backs and a communal spirit so entrenched the waitresses will scold you if you try to take a table all to yourself. Since 1953, their stock in trade has been feeding market workers, and you can watch the kitchen through the glass as they whip out a wipe-board menu of simple dishes at lightning speed. Hearty *primi* include *tortelli di patate al ragù* (ravioli stuffed with potato in meat *ragù*), *minestra di farro e riso* (emmer-and-rice soup), and *penne al pomodoro* (pasta quills in fresh tomato sauce). The *secondi* are basic but good; try the *coniglio arrosto* (roast rabbit) or go straight for the *fiorentina* steak, often priced to be the best deal in town.

Via Rosina 2r (north corner of Piazza Mercato Centrale). www.trattoria-mario.com. ℂ **055-218-550.** Reservations not accepted. Main courses 7.50€–11€. No credit cards. Mon–Sat noon–3:30pm. Closed Aug. Bus: C1.

Nerbone ★ 📷 FLORENTINE   Nerbone has been stuffing stall owners and market patrons with excellent Florentine *cucina povera* (poor people's food) since the Mercato Centrale opened in 1874. You can try *trippa alla fiorentina, pappa al pomodoro,* or a plate piled with boiled potatoes and a single fat sausage. But the mainstay here is a *panino con bollito,* a boiled beef sandwich that's *bagnato* (dipped in the meat juices). Eat standing with the crowd of old men at the side counter, sipping glasses of wine or beer, or arrive early to fight for one of the few tables.

In the Mercato Centrale, entrance on Via dell'Ariento, stand no. 292. ℂ **055-219-949.** All dishes 4€–7€. No credit cards. Mon–Sat 7am–2pm. Bus: C1.

NEAR PIAZZA SANTA TRINITA

Cantinetta Antinori TUSCAN   The Antinori *marchesi* started their wine empire 26 generations ago, and, taking their cue from an ancient vintner tradition, installed a wine bar in their 15th-century *palazzo* 30 years ago. Most ingredients come fresh from the Antinori farms, as does all the fine wine. Start with the *fettuccine all'anatra* (noodles in duck sauce) and round out the meal with the mighty *gran pezzo* (a thick slab of oven-roasted Chianina beef). If you choose this worthy splurge as a *secondo,* skip the first course and instead follow your steak with *formaggi misti,* which may include pecorino made fresh that morning. Their *cantucci* (Pratese biscotti) come from Tuscany's premier producer.

Palazzo Antinori, Piazza Antinori 3 (at the top of Via Tornabuoni). www.cantinetta-antinori.com. ℂ **055-292-234.** Reservations recommended. Main courses 24€–30€. AE, DC, MC, V. Mon–Fri noon–2:30pm and 7–10:30pm. Closed Aug and Dec 24–Jan 6. Bus: C1, 6, 11, 22, 36, 37, or 68.

L'Osteria di Giovanni ★★ TUSCAN   Giovanni Latini comes from one of Florence's best-known culinary clans, whose eponymous eatery on Via del Palchetti is a household name in Florence, but he and his daughters Caterina and Chiara have made quite a name for themselves in the same neighborhood. Their *osteria* features a sophisticated but social atmosphere, with well-dressed Italians and tourists sharing either the quiet front room or the more communal back room. If they are in season, you may be offered some fresh, garden-raised fava beans with pecorino, followed by sautéed squid with asparagus and cherry tomatoes. Don't miss the *involtini di vitello con pecorino fresco, melanzane e funghi* (sliced veal wrapped around fresh pecorino, eggplant, and mushrooms). Save room for chocolate mousse.

Via del Moro 22 (near the Ponte alla Carraia). www.osteriadigiovanni.com. ✆ **055-284-897.** Reservations recommended. Main courses 19€–26€. AE, MC, V. Tues–Sat noon–2:30pm and 7–11pm; Mon 7–11pm. Closed Aug. Bus: C3, 6, 11, 36, 37, or 68.

NEAR SANTA MARIA NOVELLA

Il Latini ★ ☺ FLORENTINE   Arrive here at 7:30pm to join the crowd massed at the door, for even with a reservation you'll have to wait as they skillfully fit parties together at the communal tables. In fact, sharing a common meal with complete strangers is part of the fun here. Under hundreds of hanging prosciutto ham hocks, the waiters try their hardest to keep a menu away from you and suggest something themselves. This usually kicks off with *ribollita* and *pappa al pomodoro* or *penne strascicate* (in a *ragù* mixed with cream). If everyone agrees on the *arrosto misto,* you can get a table-filling platter heaped high with assorted roast meats. Finish off with a round of *cantucci con vin santo* for all the adults.

Via del Palchetti 6r (off Via della Vigna Nuova). www.illatini.com. ✆ **055-210-916.** Reservations strongly recommended. Main courses 14€–22€. AE, DC, MC, V. Tues–Sun 12:30–2:30pm and 7:30–10:30pm. Closed 15 days in Aug and Dec 24–Jan 6. Bus: 1, 6, 36, 37, or 68.

NEAR SAN MARCO & SANTISSIMA ANNUNZIATA

If you're staying north of San Marco and don't fancy the walk into the center, locals swear by **Da Tito ★**, Via San Gallo 112r (www.trattoriadatito.it; ✆ **055-472-475**), where you'll find traditional Florentine cooking, fresh pasta handmade daily, and a friendly welcome. It's popular, so book ahead. San Marco is also the place to head for *schiacciata alla fiorentina,* sweetish olive-oil flatbread loaded with savory toppings. You'll find the best in the city at **Pugi ★**, Piazza San Marco 9b (www.focacceria-pugi.it; ✆ **055-280-981**), open 7:45am (8:30am Sat) to 8pm Monday to Saturday, but closed most of August.

Il Vegetariano VEGETARIAN   Come early to one of Florence's best vegetarian restaurants and use your coat to save a spot at one of the communal wood tables before heading to the back to get your food. The self-service menu changes constantly but uses only fresh produce in such dishes as risotto with yellow squash and black cabbage; a quichelike *pizza rustica* of ricotta, olives, tomatoes, and mushrooms; and a plate with *farro* (emmer) and a hot salad of spinach, onions, sprouts, and bean-curd chunks sautéed in soy sauce. There's a nice patio in back.

Via delle Ruote 30r (off Via Santa Reparata). www.il-vegetariano.it. ✆ **055-475-030.** Reservations not accepted. Main courses 7.50€–9€. No credit cards. Tues–Fri 12:30–3:30pm; Tues–Sun 7:30pm–midnight. Closed 3 weeks in Aug and Dec 24–Jan 2. Bus: C1 or anything to San Marco.

NEAR SANTA CROCE

Cibrèo ★★ TUSCAN   There's no pasta and no grilled meat—can this be Tuscany? Rest assured that while Fabio Picchi's culinary creations are a bit out of the ordinary, most are based on antique recipes. Picchi's fan-cooled main restaurant room, full of intellectual babble, is where the elegance is in the substance of the food and the service, not in surface appearances. Waiters pull up a chair to explain the list of daily specials, and those garlands of hot peppers hanging in the kitchen window are a hint at the chef's favorite spice. All the food is spectacular, and dishes change regularly, but if they're available try the yellow pepper soup drizzled with olive oil; the soufflé of potatoes and ricotta spiced and served with pecorino shavings and *ragù;* or the roasted duck stuffed with minced beef, raisins, and *pinoli.*

Via Andrea del Verrocchio 8r (next to Sant'Ambrogio Market). www.edizioniteatrodelsalecibreo firenze.it. ℂ **055-234-1100.** Reservations required. Main courses 36€. AE, DC, MC, V. Tues–Sat 1–2:30pm and 7:30–11:15pm. Closed July 26–Sept 6. Bus: C2, C3, 14, or 71.

Kome ★ 🎎 JAPANESE/SUSHI There's something refreshingly cosmopolitan about perching in a *kaiten,* grazing on *hosomaki* made by a skilled Japanese chef right in front of you. Florence's best sushi joint gets the formula about right: nigiri with octopus, cuttlefish, prawn, or tuna are light and fresh straight from the conveyor. An excellent mixed tempura of seasonal vegetables, prawn, and anchovy is the best among five or six hot dishes cooked to order. Keep track of your total as you eat, however: The check soon mounts up, especially if you wash it all down with a Kirin or two. They also offer delivery via **www.thefood.it.**

Via de' Benci 41r. ℂ **055-200-8009.** Reservations not accepted. Sushi 3.50€–8€. AE, MC, V. Mon–Sat noon–3pm; daily 7–11pm. Bus: C3 or 23.

Trattoria Cibrèo ★★ 🍴 FLORENTINE This is the casual trattoria of cele-brated chef-owner Fabio Picchi; its limited menu comes from the same creative kitchen that put on the map his premier and more than twice as expensive *ristorante* next door. Picchi takes his inspiration from traditional Tuscan recipes, and the first thing you'll note is the absence of pasta. After you taste the velvety *passata di peperoni gialli* (yellow bell-pepper soup), you won't care much. The stuffed roast rabbit demands the same admiration.

Via de' Macci 122r. ℂ **055-234-1100.** Main courses 14€. AE, DC, MC, V. Tues–Sat 1–2:30pm and 7–11:15pm. Closed July 26–Sept 6. Bus: C2, C3, 14, or 71.

IN THE OLTRARNO & SAN FREDIANO

Dining right in the deli is hot in foodie Tuscany right now, and you'll find Florence's best spots south of the Arno. As well as **Olio e Convivium,** below, we love **Zeb** ★★, Via San Miniato 2r (www.zebgastronomia.com; ℂ **055-234-2864**), where an all-chalkboard menu features creative dishes such as ravioli stuffed with pear and pecorino cheese in a pear sauce. It's all about the ingredients in all their dishes, which range 8€ to 15€. Zeb serves lunch Thursday through Tuesday and dinner Thursday to Saturday.

Il Santo Bevitore ★★ CONTEMPORARY ITALIAN Encapsulating all that's best about the new generation of Florentine eateries, this restaurant-enoteca (wine cellar) takes the best of Tuscan tradition and sprinkles it with some contemporary fairy dust. A buzzing, candlelit interior is the setting for clever combinations pre-sented with style—and a smile. Best of the antipasti are the tasting platters, including cured meats sliced right at the bar and an *assaggio di sott'olio* (a trio of preserved vegetables in olive oil). Pastas skew to the unusual, pulling in influences from across Italy, such as in the *tortelloni* filled with *cavolo nero* cabbage and pancetta served with a pecorino cream sauce. Seasonal mains might include a tartare of Chianina beef or roast *baccalà* (salt cod) with late-harvest radicchio. The wine list is similarly intriguing. Lunch is a daily menu only.

Via Santo Spirito 66r (corner of Piazza N. Sauro). www.ilsantobevitore.com. ℂ **055-211-264.** Reservations highly recommended. Main courses 8.50€–25€. MC, V. Mon–Sat 12:30–3pm; daily 7–11pm. Closed 10 days in Aug. Bus: C3, D, 6, 11, 36, 37, or 68.

Olio e Convivium ★★ CONTEMPORARY ITALIAN   This slightly fussy, but nevertheless thoroughly satisfying little restaurant is set in tiled surrounds inside one of the Oltrarno's best delicatessens. Its menu eschews the style and content of "typical Florence." You can choose one of their creative, skillfully presented pasta combinations like *tagliolini con capesante, carciofi e calamari* (thin pasta with scallops, artichokes, and squid), or order one of their "gastronomy tasting plates," built straight from the deli counter. The wines-by-the-glass list is short, creative, and a little pricey; the soft classical music soundtrack makes for a refined atmosphere.

Via Santo Spirito 6. www.conviviumfirenze.it. ℂ **055-265-8198.** Main courses 14€–28€. MC, V. Mon–Sat noon–2:30pm; Tues–Sat 7–10:30pm. Closed 3 weeks in Aug. Bus: C3, D, 6, 11, 36, 37, or 68.

IN THE HILLS

Le Cave di Maiano ★ TUSCAN   This converted farmhouse is the countryside trattoria of choice for Florentines wishing to escape the city heat on a summer Sunday afternoon. You can enjoy warm-weather lunches on the tree-shaded stone terrace with a bucolic view. In cooler weather, you can dine inside rustic rooms with paintings scattered haphazardly on the walls. The *antipasto caldo* of varied *crostini* and fried polenta is a good way to kick off a meal, followed by a *misto della casa* that gives you a sampling of *primi*. This may include *penne strascicate* (stubby pasta in cream sauce and tomato *ragù*) or *riso allo spazzacamino* (rice with beans and black cabbage). The best *secondo* is the *pollastro al mattone* (chicken roasted under a brick with pepper) or the *lombatina di vitello alla griglia* (grilled veal chop).

Via Cave di Maiano 16 (in Maiano, halfway btw. Florence and Fiesole east of the main road). www. trattoriacavedimaiano.it. ℂ **055-59-133.** Reservations recommended. Main courses 10€–18€. AE, DC, MC, V. Daily 12:30–3pm and 7:30pm–midnight. Bus: 7 (get off at Villa San Michele, then turn around and take the road branching to the left of the winding one your bus took; continue on about 1.2km/¾ mile up this side road, past the Pensione Bencistà); a taxi is a better idea.

Shopping

The cream of the crop of Florentine shopping lines both sides of elegant **Via de' Tornabuoni,** with an extension along **Via della Vigna Nuova** and other surrounding streets. Here you'll find big names like Gucci, Armani, and Ferragamo ensconced in old palaces or modern minimalist boutiques.

On the other end of the shopping spectrum is the haggling and general fun of the colorful and noisy **San Lorenzo street market.** Antiques gather dust by the truckload along **Via Maggio** and other Oltrarno streets. Another main corridor of stores somewhat less glitzy than those on Via de' Tornabuoni begins at **Via Cerretani** and runs down **Via Roma** through the Piazza della Repubblica area; it keeps going down **Via Por Santa Maria,** across the **Ponte Vecchio** with its gold jewelry, and up **Via Guicciardini** on the other side. Store-laden side tributaries off this main stretch include **Via della Terme, Borgo Santissimi Apostoli,** and **Borgo San Jacopo** (which becomes **Via Santo Spirito** as it heads west). Over in the east of the center, **Borgo degli Albizi** has seen a flourishing of one-off stores, with an emphasis on young, independent fashions.

General Florentine **shopping hours** are Monday through Saturday from 9:30am to noon or 1pm and 3 or 3:30 to 7:30pm, although increasingly, many shops are staying open on Sunday and through that midafternoon *riposo* or nap (especially the larger stores and those around tourist sights).

Entertainment & Nightlife

Florence has bundles of excellent, mostly free, listings publications. At the tourist offices, pick up the free monthly *Informacittà* (www.informacitta.net), which is strong on theater and other arts events, as well as markets. Younger and hipper, pocket-size monthly *Zero* (http://firenze.zero.eu) is hot on the latest eating, drinking, and nightlife. It's available free from trendy cafe-bars, shops, and usually the tourist office, too.

THE PERFORMING ARTS

One of Italy's busiest stages, Florence's contemporary **Teatro Comunale,** Corso Italia 12 (www.maggiofiorentino.com; ✆ **055-277-9350**), offers everything from symphonies to ballet to plays, opera, and concerts.

The **Teatro Verdi,** Via Ghibellina 99r (www.teatroverdionline.it; ✆ **055-212-320**), is Florence's opera and ballet house, with the nice ritual of staging Sunday-afternoon shows during the January-through-April season. The **Orchestra della Toscana** (www.orchestradellatoscana.it) plays classical concerts here November through May, and occasionally plays cheap Saturday afternoon shows aimed at children.

The biggest national and international touring companies stop in Florence's major playhouse, the **Teatro della Pergola,** Via della Pergola 12 (www.teatrodellapergola.com; ✆ **055-226-4353**). La Pergola is the city's chief purveyor of classical and classic plays from the Greeks and Shakespeare through Pirandello, Samuel Beckett, and Italian modern playwrights. Performances are professional and of high quality—and, of course, in Italian.

Many concerts and recitals staged in major halls and private spaces are sponsored by the **Amici della Musica** (www.amicimusica.fi.it; ✆ **055-607-440**), so check their website to see what "hidden" concert might be on while you're here.

LIVE-MUSIC CLUBS

Florence's best jazz venue is the aptly named **Jazz Club,** Via Nuova de' Caccini 3 (www.jazzclubfirenze.com; ✆ **055-247-9700**). You need to join, online or at the venue, which costs 8€ for the year and entitles you to free entry to all concerts. It's closed Sunday, Monday, and all summer. New kid on the block is **Volume ★**, Piazza Santo Spirito 5r (www.volume.fi.it; ✆ **055-2381-460**), which opened in 2010; it's an artsy cafe-cum-creperie-cum-*gelateria* by day, with contemporary art hanging on the walls. When night falls, Left Bank revelers stop in for cocktails (around 6€), followed by live acoustic music 4 or 5 nights a week (Thurs night is a blues jam).

Any guide to nightclubbing should come with a health warning: What's hot (and what's not) can change from month to month. If you're clubbing at the cutting edge, we suggest you consult the listings magazines recommended above, or check the websites for **Zero** (http://firenze.zero.eu) and **Firenze Spettacolo** (www.firenze spettacolo.it).

It's not exactly cutting edge, but the most centrally located nightclub is **Yab,** Via Sassetti 5r (www.yab.it; ✆ **055-215-160**), just behind the post office on Piazza della Repubblica. This dance club for 20-somethings is a perennial favorite, an archetypal 1980s disco complete with velvet rope, bouncers, and an eclectic, upbeat music policy.

Much more fashionable is **Dolce Vita,** Piazza del Carmine (www.dolcevita florence.com; ✆ **055-284-595**), still going strong after 3 decades leading Florence's nightlife scene, and these days attracting clued-up 30-somethings who have grown up with the city's iconic DJ bar.

CAFES

Café Rivoire ★, Piazza della Signoria 4R (www.rivoire.it; ✆ **055-214-412**), offers a classy and amusing old-world ambience with a direct view of the statues on one of our favorite squares in the world. There's a selection of small sandwiches, omelets, and ice creams, and the cafe is noted for its hot chocolate.

At the refined, wood-paneled, stucco-ceilinged, and very expensive 1733 cafe **Gilli,** Via Roma 1r (www.gilli.it; ✆ **055-213-896**), tourists gather to sit with the ghosts of Italy's Risorgimento, when the cafe became a meeting place of the heroes and thinkers of the unification movement from the 1850s to the 1870s. The red-jacketed waiters at **Giubbe Rosse,** Piazza della Repubblica 13–14r (www.giubberosse.it; ✆ **055-212-280**), must have been popular during the 19th-century glory days of Garibaldi's redshirt soldiers. This was once a meeting place of the Futurists, but today it, too, is mainly a tourists' cafe with ridiculous prices.

BARS & PUBS

Via dei Benci ★, which runs south from Piazza Santa Croce toward the Arno, is the *centro storico*'s cool-bar central, and a great place to kick off a night with *aperitivo* hour. (Wander in from around 7pm, buy a drink, and help yourself to any of the food laid out buffet style.) **Moyo,** at no. 23r (www.moyo.it; ✆ **055-247-9738**), does some of the best *aperitivo* in Florence. **Oibò,** up the road at Borgo de' Greci 1A (corner of Via dei Benci; www.oibo.net; ✆ **055-263-8611**), is also popular with fashionable 20- and 30-somethings. They mix a decent cocktail and after 10pm DJs spin house and dance sounds.

At **Sei Divino ★,** Borgo Ognissanti 42r (✆ **055-217-791**), you'll find artisan beers, Tuscan wines by the glass, and some interesting cocktails, as well as *aperitivo* plates piled high from 7pm every night. **Caffe Sant'Ambrogio,** Piazza Sant'Ambrogio 7 (www.caffesantambrogio.it; ✆ **055-247-7277**), is a funky cafe-bar by day and a popular wine bar after dark. South of the river, neighbors **Zoe,** Via dei Renai 13 (✆ **055-243-111**), and **Negroni** (at no. 17r; ✆ **055-243-647**) are buzzing on a weekend, pumping out music and fashionable chatter until late.

If it's a pub you're seeking, try **Kikuya,** Via dei Benci 43r (www.kikuyapub.it; ✆ **055-234-4879**), where you'll find draft ales and soccer on the screens.

Where to Stay

In the past few years, thanks to growing competition, the recent financial crises, and unfavorable euro–dollar and euro–pound exchange rates, the trusty forces of supply and demand have brought hotel prices in Florence down for the first time in memory, but it is still difficult to find a high-season double you'd want to stay in for much less than 100€. In addition, some of the price drops have been added back in taxes: Since July 2011, Florence's city government levies an extra 1€ per person per night per government-rated hotel star, for the first 5 nights of any stay. The tax is payable on arrival.

NEAR THE DUOMO

The city's best located, quality B&B, **La Dimora degli Angeli ★,** Via Brunelleschi 4 (www.ladimoradegliangeli.it; ✆ **055-288-478**), has six rooms that combine contemporary and 19th-century styling in midsize units ideally suited to a romantic getaway. Doubles range 110€ to 155€ including breakfast.

Abaco ★   Owner Bruno continues to please his guests with a clean, efficient little hotel in a prime location, albeit short on creature comforts. The Abaco has inherited a few nice touches from its 15th-century *palazzo*, including high wood ceilings, stone floors (some parquet), and even a carved *pietra serena* fireplace. Each room is themed after a Renaissance artist, with framed reproductions of the painter's works; this hotel is more beatnik, less Bulgari, and has been done up with quirky antique-style pieces such as gilded frame mirrors and rich half-testers over the beds. It's at a busy intersection, but the double-paned windows help. Those who are not okay with lugging suitcases up stairs should look elsewhere.

Via dei Banchi 1 (off Via de' Panzani), 50123 Firenze. www.abaco-hotel.it. ✆ **055-238-1919.** Fax 055-282-289. 7 units. 45€–75€ double without bathroom; 60€–90€ double with bathroom; extra 20€ per person to make a triple or quad. Rates include breakfast. AE, MC, V. Garage parking 24€. Bus: C2, 6, 14, 22, 36, or 37. **Amenities:** Bar; concierge. *In room:* A/C, TV, hair dryer, Wi-Fi (free).

Burchianti ★★ 🛏   In 2002, rising rents forced the kindly owner of this venerable inn (established in the 19th century) to move up the block into the *piano nobile* of a neighboring 15th-century *palazzo*. She definitely traded up. Incredible frescoes dating from the 17th century and later decorate virtually every ceiling. This little gem fills up quickly, so be sure to book well in advance.

Via del Giglio 8 (off Via Panzani), 50123 Firenze. www.hotelburchianti.it. ✆ **055-212-796.** Fax 055-272-9727. 12 units. 100€–130€ double; 115€–155€ triple; 140€–170€ junior suite. Rates include breakfast. AE, DC, MC, V. Garage parking 25€. Bus: C2, 6, 14, 22, 36, or 37. **Amenities:** Concierge. *In room:* A/C, TV, minibar, hair dryer, Wi-Fi (free).

Calzaiuoli ★   As central as you can get, the Calzaiuoli offers comfortable, well-appointed rooms on the main strolling drag halfway between the Uffizi and the Duomo. The halls' rich runners lead up a *pietra serena* staircase to the midsize and largish rooms decorated with painted friezes and framed etchings. The firm beds rest on patterned carpets; the bathrooms range from huge to cramped, but all have fluffy towels (and a few have Jacuzzis). The rooms overlook the street, with its pedestrian carnival and some of the associated noise, or out the back—either over the rooftops to the Bargello and Badia towers or up to the Duomo's cupola.

Via Calzaiuoli 6 (near Orsanmichele), 50122 Firenze. www.calzaiuoli.it. ✆ **055-212-456.** Fax 055-268-310. 53 units. 120€–490€ double. Rates include breakfast. AE, DC, MC, V. Valet garage parking 26€. Bus: C2. **Amenities:** Bar; concierge; babysitting. *In room:* A/C, TV, minibar, hair dryer, Wi-Fi (free).

NEAR PIAZZA DELLA SIGNORIA

The best B&B close to this bustling civic heart of the city is aptly named **In Piazza della Signoria** ★, Via dei Magazzini 2, 50122 Firenze (www.inpiazzadellasignoria. com; ✆ **055-239-9546**). The 10 refined rooms, named after famous Florentines through the ages and embellished in the *residenza d'epoca* style with antique furnishings, cost between 160€ and 220€ without a view; it's an extra 30€ to 40€ per night for one of the best views in Florence.

Hermitage ★   This ever-popular hotel is located right at the foot of the Ponte Vecchio. The rooms are of moderate size, occasionally a bit dark, but they're full of 17th- to 19th-century antiques and boast double-glazed windows to cut down on noise. Rooms have either wood floors or thick rugs, and superior room bathrooms have Jacuzzis; those that don't face the Ponte Vecchio are on side alleys and quieter. Their famous roof terrace is covered in bright flowers that frame postcard views of the Arno, Duomo, and Palazzo Vecchio. The charming breakfast room full of picture windows gets the full effect of the morning sun. The owners and staff excel in doing the little things that help make your vacation go smoothly—but prices are a bit inflated.

Vicolo Marzio 1/Piazza del Pesce (to the left of the Ponte Vecchio as you're facing it), 50122 Firenze. www.hermitagehotel.com. ☏ **055-287-216.** Fax 055-212-208. 28 units. 120€–220€ double; 160€–250€ triple. Rates include breakfast. AE, MC, V. Valet garage parking 25€. Bus: C1, 3, 12, 13, or 23. **Amenities:** Bar; concierge; babysitting; Wi-Fi (2€ per hour). In room: A/C, TV, hair dryer.

NEAR SAN LORENZO & THE MERCATO CENTRALE

Casci ★ ☺ ✦   This clean hotel in a 15th-century *palazzo* is run by the Lombardis, one of Florence's most accommodating families. It's patronized by a host of regulars who know good value when they find it. The frescoed bar room was, from 1851 to 1855, part of an apartment inhabited by Gioachino Rossini, composer of the *Barber of Seville* and *William Tell Overture*. The rooms ramble on toward the back forever, overlooking the gardens and Florentine rooftops, and are mouse-quiet except for the birdsong. Ask for a double with a bath and shower, as those units are the most recently updated. A few family suites in back sleep four to five. The central location means some rooms (with double-paned windows) overlook busy Via Cavour, so if you're seeking quiet ask for a room facing the inner courtyard.

Via Cavour 13 (btw. Via dei Ginori and Via Guelfa), 50129 Firenze. www.hotelcasci.com. ☏ **055-211-686.** Fax 055-239-6461. 25 units. 80€–150€ double; 100€–190€ triple; 120€–230€ quad. Rates include buffet breakfast. 10% discount for cash payment; check website for offers, including 1 free museum ticket per guest Nov–Feb. AE, DC, MC, V. Garage parking 15€–23€. Bus: C1, 14, or 23. Closed 2 weeks in Dec and 3 weeks in Jan. **Amenities:** Bar; concierge; babysitting. In room: A/C, TV/DVD, fridge, hair dryer, DVD library, Wi-Fi (free).

Il Guelfo Bianco ★★   Once you enter this refined hotel you'll forget it's on busy Via Cavour. Its windows are triple-paned, blocking out nearly all traffic noise, and many rooms overlook quiet courtyards and gardens out back. The interior successfully combines modern comforts with antique details. Some rooms have retained such 17th-century features as frescoed or painted wood ceilings, carved wooden doorways, and the occasional parquet floor—deluxe rooms 101, 118, 228, and 338 have a separate seating area. The friendly staff is full of advice.

Via Cavour 29 (near the corner of Via Guelfa), 50129 Firenze. www.ilguelfobianco.it. ☏ **055-288-330.** Fax 055-295-203. 40 units. 99€–250€ double; 133€–300€ triple. Rates include breakfast. AE, DC, MC, V. Valet garage parking 26€–32€. Bus: C1, 14, or 23. **Amenities:** Restaurant; bar; concierge; room service; babysitting. In room: A/C, TV, minibar, hair dryer, Wi-Fi (free).

NEAR PIAZZA SANTA TRÍNITA

Alessandra ★ ✦   This old-fashioned *pensione* in a 1507 *palazzo* just off the river charges little for its simple comfort and kind hospitality. The rooms differ greatly in size and style, and while they won't win any awards from *Architectural Digest*, there are a few antique pieces and parquet floors to add to the charm. The bathrooms are outfitted with fluffy white towels, and the shared bathrooms are ample, clean, and numerous enough that you won't have to wait in line in the morning.

Borgo SS. Apostoli 17 (btw. Via dei Tornabuoni and Via Por Santa Maria), 50123 Firenze. www.hotelalessandra.com. ☏ **055-283-438.** Fax 055-210-619. 27 units, 20 with private bathroom. 110€ double without bathroom; 150€–175€ double with bathroom; 150€ triple without bathroom; 195€ triple with bathroom; 160€ quad without bathroom; 215€ quad with bathroom. Rates include buffet breakfast. AE, MC, V. Valet garage parking 22€–27€. Bus: 6, 11, 36, 37, or 68. **Amenities:** Bar; concierge. In room: A/C, TV, minibar (in some), hair dryer, Wi-Fi (free).

Davanzati ★★ ☺ 🗲 A dizzying array of recently renovated rooms, each equipped to a high specification, plus a great location at an unbeatable value make this one of our favorite moderately priced hotels in the *centro storico.* No two units in the sympathetically converted 15th-century *palazzo* are the same: Your best bet is to tell the friendly staff your party size and requirements, and let them advise. Our personal favorite is no. 100, in light wood with cream fabrics and multiple split levels that have private sleeping areas, ideal if you're traveling with kids (who will also like the laptop and PlayStation that are standard in every room).

Via Porta Rossa 5 (on Piazza Davanzati), 50123 Firenze. www.hoteldavanzati.it. ℰ **055-286-666.** Fax 055-265-8252. 21 units. 120€–188€ double; 150€–312€ superior sleeping up to 4; 190€–352€ suite. Rates include breakfast. Valet garage parking 26€. AE, MC, V. Bus: C2, 6, 11, 22, 36, 37, or 68. **Amenities:** Bar; concierge; babysitting. *In room:* A/C, TV, minibar, hair dryer, Wi-Fi (free).

NEAR SANTA MARIA NOVELLA

Casa Howard ★★ 🗲 Quirky, midsize, individual rooms in this *palazzo* turned chic, contemporary guesthouse come with stylized themes: If you're the intellectual type, you'll enjoy the Library Room, which is filled with wall-to-wall reading. Our other favorite rooms include the Fireplace Room, with two picture windows. The three different rooms that comprise the Oriental Room are filled with objects collected by the owners in Asia, including a gigantic lacquer red shower. The Black and White Room lives up to its name, right down to a zebra armchair, and the small, cozy Hidden Room is dressed in sensual red. *Note:* The surroundings are plush and refined, and the welcome is friendly, but this is *not* a hotel. If you require hotel-type services to enjoy a stay, look elsewhere.

Via della Scala 18, 50123 Firenze. www.casahoward.com. ℰ **0669-924-555.** Fax 0667-94-644. 13 units. 120€–240€ double. Rates include breakfast. AE, MC, V. Bus: 11, 36, 37, or 68. **Amenities:** Concierge. *In room:* A/C, TV, minibar, hair dryer, Wi-Fi (free), no phone.

Montebello Splendid ★★ For charm and grace—as well as realistically priced luxury—this boutique hotel just west of the center is a hit. Enter a splendid garden in front of this restored palace, with a columned Tuscan-style *loggia,* and be ushered into a regal palace with Italian marble, stuccowork, and luminous niches. Each of the midsize to spacious bedrooms is individually decorated and soundproof—with a lavish use of parquet, marble, soft carpeting, and elegant fabrics—and deluxe beds and first-class bathrooms are clad in marble and equipped with hydromassages, among other features.

Via Garibaldi 14, 50123 Firenze. www.montebellosplendid.com. ℰ **055-27471.** Fax 055-2747700. 60 units. 199€–369€ double. AE, DC, MC, V. Parking 30€. Bus: C2, C3, or D. **Amenities:** Restaurant; bar; gym and spa; concierge; room service. *In room:* A/C, TV, hair dryer, Wi-Fi (free).

BETWEEN SANTA MARIA NOVELLA & THE MERCATO CENTRALE

Mario's ★★ In a traditional Old Florence atmosphere, the Masieri and Benelli families run a first-rate ship. Your room might have a wrought-iron headboard and massive reproduction antique armoire, and look out onto a peaceful garden. The beamed ceilings in the common areas date from the 17th century, although the building became a hotel only in 1872. The only major drawback is its location—it's a bit far from the Duomo nerve center. Hefty discounts during off-season months "desplurge" this lovely choice.

Via Faenza 89 (1st floor; near Via Cennini), 50123 Firenze. www.hotelmarios.com. ℰ **055-216-801.** Fax 055-212-039. 16 units. 80€–150€ double; 110€–185€ triple. Rates include breakfast. AE, DC, MC, V. Bus: 1, 2, 12, 13, 28, 29, 30, 35, 57, or 70. **Amenities:** Bar; concierge; babysitting. *In room:* A/C, TV/DVD, hair dryer, Wi-Fi (free).

Merlini ★ Run by the Sicilian Gabriella family, this cozy third-floor walk-up renovated in 2010 is a notch above your average budget place, the best in a building full of tiny *pensioni*. The optional breakfast is served on a sunny glassed-in terrace decorated in the 1960s with frescoes by talented American art students and overlooking a leafy large courtyard. Room nos. 1, 4 (with a balcony), 6 through 8, and 11 all have views of the domes topping the Duomo and the Medici Chapels across the city's terra-cotta roofscape.

Via Faenza 56 (3rd floor), 50123 Firenze. www.hotelmerlini.it. ℂ **055-212-848.** 10 units. 50€–80€ double without bathroom; 50€–100€ double with bathroom. Garage parking 20€. AE, DC, MC, V. Bus: 1, 2, 12, 13, 28, 29, 30, 35, 57, or 70. **Amenities:** Bar. *In room:* A/C, TV, hair dryer, Wi-Fi (free), no phone.

Nuova Italia A Frommer's fairy tale: With her trusty Arthur Frommer's *Europe on $5 a Day* in hand, the fair Eileen left the kingdom of Canada on a journey to faraway Florence. At her hotel, Eileen met Luciano, her baggage boy in shining armor. They fell in love, got married, bought a castle (er, hotel) of their own called the Nuova Italia, and their clients live happily ever after … The rooms are medium to small, and a little characterless, but the attention to detail and impeccable service makes the Nuova Italia stand out. Every room has triple-paned windows, though some morning rumble from the San Lorenzo market still gets through. The family's love of art is manifested in framed posters and paintings, and staff here really puts itself out for guests, recommending restaurants, shops, and day trips.

Via Faenza 26 (off Via Nazionale), 50123 Firenze. www.hotel-nuovaitalia.com. ℂ **055-287-508.** Fax 055-210-941. 20 units. 54€–139€ double; 74€–149€ triple. Rates include breakfast. AE, MC, V. Garage parking 24€. Bus: 1, 2, 12, 13, 28, 29, 30, 35, 57, or 70. **Amenities:** Bar; concierge. *In room:* A/C, TV, hair dryer, Wi-Fi (free).

NEAR SAN MARCO & SANTISSIMA ANNUNZIATA

Four Seasons Florence ★★★ If the Medici should miraculously return to Florence, surely the clan would move in here. Installed in the overhauled historic Palazzo della Gherardesca and a former convent, this spa hotel offers spectacular frescoes, museum-worthy sculptures, and Florentine artisanal works, with its oldest wing dating from the 1440s. Its grounds are on one of the largest private gardens in the city. Damask draperies, regal appointments in all the bedrooms, fabric-trimmed walls, ceramic floors, an elegant spa, rich marble bathrooms, and luxurious beds and furnishings are just some of the features that make this perhaps the finest Four Seasons in Europe.

Borgo Pinti 99, 50121 Firenze. www.fourseasons.com/florence. ℂ **055-2626-250.** Fax 055-2626-500. 116 units. 550€–850€ double. AE, DC, MC, V. Free valet parking. Bus: 8 or 70. **Amenities:** 4 restaurants; 2 bars; outdoor pool; spa; gym; concierge; room service. *In room:* TV/DVD, fax (on request), fridge (on request), hair dryer, CD player, MP3 docking station, Wi-Fi (free).

Morandi alla Crocetta ★ This subtly elegant hotel belongs to a different era, when travelers stayed in private homes filled with family heirlooms and well-kept antiques. Although the setting is indeed historic (it was a 1511 Dominican nuns' convent), many of the old-fashioned effects, such as the wood-beam ceilings, 1500s artwork, and antique furnishings, are the result of a redecoration. It has all been done in good taste, however, and there are still plenty of echoes of the original structure, from exposed brick arches to one room's 16th-century fresco fragments.

Via Laura 50 (a block east of Piazza Santissima Annunziata), 50121 Firenze. www.hotelmorandi.it. ℂ **055-234-4747.** Fax 055-248-0954. 10 units. 100€–150€ double; 150€–180€ triple. Rates include breakfast. AE, DC, MC, V. Garage parking 20€. Bus: 6, 14, 23, 31, 32, or 71. **Amenities:** Bar; concierge; babysitting. *In room:* A/C, TV, minibar, hair dryer, Wi-Fi (8€ per day; free in low season).

NEAR SANTA CROCE

Hotel Home Florence ★★ Minimalist chic meets dazzling bright-white (like an ultrafashionable ski resort) at this 2009 addition to Florence's crop of design hotels. A harmonious colonial villa on the eastern fringe of the *centro storico* was transformed in 2009 into the ultimate city bolt-hole for anyone seeking sleek design at a reasonably sensible price. Rooms are kitted out to a top contemporary spec: All-white home wares and furnishings are by the Cyrus Company (which owns the hotel); there are Nespresso machines and iPods in all the rooms and a free bar (alcoholic drinks extra) throughout. If money is no object, the suite has a terrace that surveys the city skyline, and there's an unforgettable rooftop Jacuzzi rentable by the night (250€) with a 360-degree panorama of Florence.

Piazza Piave 3, 50122 Firenze. www.hhflorence.it. ✆ **055-243-668.** Fax 055-200-9852. 38 units. 150€–300€ double; 300€–450€ suite. Rates include breakfast. AE, DC, MC, V. Garage parking 30€. Bus: 8, 12, 13, 14, 23, 31, 32, 33, 70, or 71. **Amenities:** Bar; gym; Jacuzzi; bikes; concierge; room service; babysitting; airport transfer (free). *In room:* A/C, TV, minibar (free), hair dryer, Wi-Fi (free).

Monna Lisa ★★ There's a certain old-world elegance, reminiscent of an English country manor, to the richly decorated common rooms and the gravel-strewn garden of this 14th-century *palazzo*. Among the potted plants and framed oils, the hotel has Giambologna's original rough competition piece for the *Rape of the Sabines*, along with many pieces by neoclassical sculptor Giovanni Duprè, whose family's descendants own the hotel. They try their best to keep the entire place looking like a private home, and many rooms have the original painted wood ceilings, as well as antique furniture and richly textured wallpaper and fabrics, although the Jacuzzi tubs in superior units are very much 21st-century additions. Outbuildings known as La Scudera and La Limonaia overlook a peaceful garden.

Borgo Pinti 27, 50121 Firenze. www.monnalisa.it. ✆ **055-247-9751.** Fax 055-247-9755. 45 units. 139€–289€ double. Rates include buffet breakfast. AE, DC, MC, V. Garage parking 20€. Bus: C1, C2, 14, 23, or 71. **Amenities:** Bar; exercise room; concierge; babysitting. *In room:* A/C, TV, minibar, hair dryer, Wi-Fi (5€ per 30 min.).

Palazzo Galletti ★★ Palazzo living doesn't come much more refined than in the restored 18th-century surrounds of this *residenza d'epoca* B&B. Elegant rooms are arranged around a tranquil atrium, and named after the planets (which themselves are named after Roman gods). Doubles are on the big side for Florence, with tall ceilings, but if you can stretch to a suite such as Giove or Cerere, you'll have a memorable stay surrounded by original 18th-century frescoes restored by the owners. Breakfast is served in a vaulted former kitchen that predates the *palazzo*—it originally belonged to a building that stood here in the 1500s.

Via Sant'Egidio 12, 50122 Firenze. www.palazzogalletti.it. ✆ **055-390-5750.** Fax 055-390-5752. 11 units. 100€–160€ double; 170€–240€ suite. Rates include breakfast. MC, V. Bus: C1, C2, 14, 23, or 71. **Amenities:** Concierge. *In room:* A/C, TV, hair dryer, Internet (free).

A Soothing Central Spa

If you can't stretch to one of Florence's upscale spa hotels, book a session at **Soulspace,** Via Sant'Egidio 12 (www.soulspace.it; ✆ **055-200-1794**). This calm, contemporary spot has a heated pool and hammam (Turkish bath), and a range of modern spa treatments for women and men including aromatherapy massages. Day spa packages cost from 50€ upward.

IN THE OLTRARNO & SAN FREDIANO

Palazzo Magnani Feroni ★★   A luxurious Renaissance palace from the 16th century, and a 5-minute walk from the Ponte Vecchio, this place has been converted from a nobleman's residence to boutique accommodations with a dozen suites in six grades. Painstaking attention has been paid to the restoration and conversion of each one, and the palace houses extensive period furnishings and packs bags of character. The suites themselves combine luxury and charm with modern conveniences. At dusk each evening you can enjoy a drink on a panoramic terrace watching the sun set over Florence's rooftops.

Borgo San Frediano 5, 50124 Firenze. www.palazzomagnaniferoni.com. ✆ **055-239-9544.** Fax 055-260-8908. 12 units. 180€–490€ suite. Rates include breakfast. Parking 42€. Bus: C3, D, 6, 11, 36, 37, or 68. **Amenities:** Bar; exercise room; concierge; room service. *In room:* A/C, TV/DVD, minibar, CD player, Wi-Fi (free).

UNA Vittoria ★★   Is this a boutique hotel or a disco? Either way, this outpost of the small Italian chain UNA is in a class of its own when it comes to contemporary styling at an affordable price. The second you step into the floor-to-ceiling mosaic in the reception area, you realize this is no ordinary Florentine inn. Midsize rooms are bold and contemporary (quite unchainlike), and all come equipped with modern amenities like 32-inch plasma TVs. A rolling program of renovations ensures interiors never grow tired. Executive rooms come with supersexy all-in-one rainfall shower/tub combos.

Via Pisana 59 (at Piazza Pier Vettori), 50143 Firenze. www.unahotels.it. ✆ **055-22-771.** Fax 055-22-772. 84 units. 109€–306€ double. Rates include breakfast. MC, V. Garage parking 20€. Bus: 6. **Amenities:** Restaurant; bar; bikes; concierge. *In room:* TV, hair dryer, Wi-Fi (free).

A Side Trip to Fiesole

Fiesole, once an Etruscan settlement, is a virtual suburb of Florence and its most popular outing. Florentines often head for these hills when it's just too hot in the city. Bus no. 7, from the station or down the right flank of San Marco, on Via La Pira, will take you here in 25 minutes and give you a breathtaking view along the way. You'll pass fountains, statuary, and gardens strung out over the hills like a scrambled jigsaw puzzle.

In Fiesole you won't find anything as dazzling as the Renaissance treasures of Florence; the town's charms are more subtle. Fortunately, all major sights branch out within walking distance of the main square, **Piazza Mino da Fiesole,** beginning with the **Cattedrale di San Romolo (Duomo).** At first this cathedral might seem austere, with its concrete-gray Corinthian columns and Romanesque arches. But it has its own beauty. Dating from A.D. 1000, it was much altered during the Renaissance, and in the Salutati Chapel are important sculptural works by Mino da Fiesole. It's open daily in the spring and summer from 8am to noon and 3 to 6pm, and in autumn through winter from 2 to 5pm.

The hardest task you'll have in Fiesole is to take the steep goat-climb up to the **Convent of San Francesco,** Via San Francesco 13 (✆ **055-59-175**). You can visit the Gothic-style Franciscan church, built in the first years of the 1400s and consecrated in 1516. Inside are many paintings by well-known Florentine artists. Open daily 9am to noon and 3 to 5pm, sometimes later in summer.

The ecclesiastical **Museo Bandini (Bandini Museum),** Via Dupré 1 (✆ **055-59-118**), belongs to the Fiesole Cathedral Chapter, established in 1913. The main entrance floor has terra-cotta works, as well as art by Michelangelo and Pisano. On the top floors are paintings by the best Giotto students, reflecting ecclesiastical and worldly themes, most of them the work of Tuscan artists of the 14th century.

Not far from the main square, Fiesole's **archaeological area** is romantically over-grown with grasses, amid which sit sections of column, broken friezes, and other remnants of architectural elements. Beyond the **Roman Theater** to the right, recognizable by its three rebuilt arches, are the remains of the 1st-century-A.D. **baths.** At the other end of the park from the baths are the floor and steps of a 1st-century-B.C. **Roman Temple** built on top of a 4th-century-B.C. Etruscan one. To the left are some oblong **Lombard tombs** from the 7th century A.D., when this was a necropolis.

Fiesole's two museums and its Teatro Romano archaeological site keep the same hours and use a single admission ticket, costing 10€ adults, 6€ students age 7 to 25 and seniors 65 and over, and free for children 6 and under. A family ticket costs 20€. They are all open April through September daily from 10am to 7pm, March and October daily from 10am to 6pm, and in winter Wednesday through Monday from 10am to 2pm. For more information, visit www.museidifiesole.it or call 📞 **055-596-1293.**

HIGHLIGHTS OF THE TUSCAN & UMBRIAN COUNTRYSIDE

The Tuscan landscapes look just like Renaissance paintings, with rolling plains of grass, cypress trees, and olive groves; ancient walled hill towns; and those fabled Chianti vineyards. **Tuscany** was where the Etruscans first appeared in Italy. The Romans followed, absorbing and conquering them. By the 11th century, the region had evolved into a collection of independent city-states, such as Florence and Siena, each trying to dominate the others. Many of the cities reached the apogee of their economic and political power in the 13th century. The Renaissance reached its apex in Florence, but was slow to come to Siena, which remains a gem of Gothic glory.

Tuscany might be known for its Renaissance artists, but the small region of **Umbria,** at the heart of the Italian peninsula, is associated mainly with saints. Christendom's most beloved saints were born here, including St. Francis of Assisi, founder of the Franciscans. Also born here were St. Valentine, a 3rd-century bishop of Terni, and St. Clare, founder of the Order of Poor Clares.

However, Umbrian painters also contributed to the glory of the Renaissance. Il Perugino, whose lyrical works you can see in the National Gallery of Umbria in Perugia, is one such example.

Umbria's countryside, also the subject of countless paintings, remains as lovely as ever today: You'll pass through a hilly terrain dotted with chestnut trees, interspersed with fertile plains of olive groves and vineyards.

Pisa ★★

Nothing says Pisa more than its Leaning Tower, keystone of the Romanesque Campo dei Miracoli, but this city of ancient architectural wonders also has a young and upbeat feel. Native son Galileo may be long gone but students still come here to study at the prestigious university where he taught, and to enjoy the city's vibrancy. It is probably Tuscany's liveliest city when night falls: Locals and students while away their evenings in the bars and nightclubs around Piazza Garibaldi, and along Borgo Stretto and the banks of the Arno.

ESSENTIALS

GETTING THERE   There are around 20 direct **trains** daily from **Rome** (2¼–4 hr.). From **Florence,** 50 daily trains make the trip (60–90 min.). **Lucca** offers over 25

runs here every day (25–35 min.). On the Lucca line, day-trippers should get off at **San Rossore station,** a few blocks west of Piazza del Duomo and the Leaning Tower. All other trains—and eventually the Lucca one—pull into **Pisa Centrale** station. From here, bus no. 4 or the **LAM Rossa** bus will take you close to Piazza del Duomo.

There's a Florence–Pisa fast **highway** (the so-called FI.PI.LI) along the Arno valley. Take the SS12 or SS12r from Lucca. For details on parking locations and charges, see **www.pisamo.it**.

Tuscany's main international **airport, Galileo Galilei** (www.pisa-airport.com), is just 3km (2 miles) south of the center. Trains zip you from the airport to Centrale station in 5 minutes; the LAM Rossa bus departs every 9 minutes for Centrale station and then the Campo. A metered taxi ride will cost 10€ to 15€ (drivers accept credit cards).

VISITOR INFORMATION   The main **tourist office** is at Piazza Vittorio Emanuele II 16, Pisa (www.pisaunicaterra.it; ✆ **050-42-291;** Mon–Sat 9am–7pm, Sun 9am–4pm). There's also a desk inside the arrivals hall at the airport (✆ **055-502-518;** daily 9:30am–11:30pm).

EXPLORING THE CITY

On a grassy lawn wedged into the northwest corner of the city walls, medieval Pisans created one of the most dramatic squares in the world. Dubbed the **Campo dei Miracoli (Field of Miracles) ★★★**, Piazza del Duomo contains an array of elegant buildings that heralded the Pisan-Romanesque style.

Admission charges for the monuments and museums of the Campo are tied together in a complicated way. The Cattedrale alone costs 2€ (though it's free Nov–Feb). Any other single sight is 5€; any two sites cost 6€. To access everything except the Leaning Tower costs 8€ between November and February and 10€ the rest of the year. Children 9 and under enter free. For more information, visit their website at **www.opapisa.it**. Admission to the Leaning Tower is separate (see below).

Battistero (Baptistery) ★★ CHURCH   Italy's biggest baptistery (104m/341 ft. in circumference) was begun in 1153 by Diotisalvi, who gave it its lower Romanesque drum. Nicola and Giovanni Pisano "Gothicized" the upper part from 1277 to 1297 and Cellino di Nese capped it with a Gothic dome in the 1300s.

The **pulpit ★★** by Nicola Pisano (1255–60) is perhaps his masterpiece and the prototype for a series he and his son Giovanni carried out over the years (the last is in Pisa's Duomo; the other two are in Pistoia and Siena). The other main attraction of the baptistery is its renowned **acoustics.**

Piazza del Duomo. www.opapisa.it. ✆ **050-835-011.** For prices, see above. Apr–Sept daily 8am–8pm; Mar daily 9am–6pm; Oct daily 9am–7pm; Nov and Feb daily 9am–5pm; Dec–Jan daily 9:30am–4:30pm. Bus: E, 4, LAM Rossa.

Il Duomo ★★ CATHEDRAL   Buscheto, the architect who laid the cathedral's first stone in 1063, kicked off a new era in art by building what was to become the model for the Pisan-Romanesque style. All the key elements are here on the **facade,** designed and built by Buscheto's successor, Rainaldo: alternating light and dark banding, rounded blind arches with Moorish-inspired lozenges at the top and colored marble inlay designs, and Lombard-style open galleries of tiny mismatched columns stacked to make the facade much higher than the church roof.

The **main door** is one of three cast by students of Giambologna after a 1595 fire destroyed the originals. On the back of the right transept, across from the bell tower, is a 2008 cast of the bronze **Door of San Ranieri ★★★**; the only original door survives in the Museo dell'Opera (see below) and was cast by Bonnano Pisano in 1180 while he was working on the bell tower.

On the north side of the nave is Giovanni Pisano's masterpiece **pulpit ★★** (1302–11)—it's the last of the famed Pisano pulpits and, along with the one in Pistoia, the greatest. Hanging low near the pulpit is a large **bronze lamp** that, according to legend, a bored Galileo was staring at one day during Mass, watching it sway gently back and forth, when his law of pendulum motion suddenly hit him.

Piazza del Duomo. www.opapisa.it. ✆ **050-835-011.** For prices, see above. Apr–Sept Mon–Sat 10am–8pm, Sun 1–8pm; Mar Mon–Sat 10am–5:30pm, Sun 1–5:30pm; Oct Mon–Sat 10am–6:30pm, Sun 1–6:30pm; Nov–Feb Mon–Sat 10am–12:45pm and 2–4:30pm, Sun 2–4:30pm. Bus: E, 4, LAM Rossa.

Leaning Tower of Pisa (Campanile) ★★★ ☺ ICON   The problem with Pisa's Torre Pendente—and the bane of local engineers for 8 centuries—is that you can't stack that much heavy marble on shifting subsoil and keep it all upright. It was started in 1173 by Guglielmo and Bonnano Pisano, who also cast the Duomo's original doors. They reached the third level in 1185 when they noticed a lean, at that point about 3.8cm (1½ in.). Work stopped and wasn't resumed until 1275 under Giovanni di Simone. He tried to correct the tilt by curving the structure back toward the perpendicular, giving the tower its slight banana shape. In 1284, work stopped yet again. In 1360, Tommaso di Andrea da Pontedera capped it off at about 51m (167 ft.) with a vaguely Gothic belfry.

Excavations around the base in the early 19th century caused the tower to start falling faster than ever (about 1mm/.04 in. a year), and by 1990 the lean was about 4.6m (15 ft.), so Pisa's mayor closed the tower. Stabilization work continued until December 2001 when, righted to its lean of 1838 (when it was a mere 4m/13 ft. off), the tower reopened. Now the number of visitors is controlled via 30-minute slots—and a massive admission charge.

Piazza del Duomo. www.opapisa.it. ✆ **050-835-011.** Admission 15€, or 17€ if you reserve a timed slot (essential in peak periods). Apr–Sept daily 8:30am–8pm (sometimes until 10:30pm June–Aug); Mar daily 9am–5:30pm; Oct daily 9am–7pm; Nov and Feb daily 9:30am–5pm; Dec–Jan daily 10am–4:30pm. Children 7 and under not permitted. Bus: E, 4, LAM Rossa.

Museo dell'Opera del Duomo (Duomo Museum) ★★ ART MUSEUM   The old Chapter-House-cum-convent has been transformed into a storehouse for sculptures, paintings, and other works from the ecclesiastical buildings on Piazza del Duomo. Room 2 is the home of the cathedral's last remaining 12th-century original portal, the **Door of San Ranieri** ★★★. Elsewhere, seek out the Islamic 11th-century bronze **griffin** ★, war booty from the Crusades, which long decorated the Duomo's cupola before it was replaced by a copy.

Piazza Arcivescovado 6. www.opapisa.it. ✆ **050-835-011.** For prices, see above. Same hours as Baptistery; see above. Bus: E, 4, LAM Rossa.

WHERE TO STAY & EAT

La Mescita ★ PISAN/WINE BAR   The marketplace location and simple decor of this popular spot belie its reputation for skillful cooking. The menu changes each month, but often includes the delicious likes of a *sformatino di melanzane* (eggplant soufflé in tomato sauce), to be followed perhaps by *ravioli di ceci con salsa di gamberetti e pomodoro fresco* (ravioli stuffed with a garbanzo bean pâté and served in shrimp-and-tomato sauce) or *strozzapreti al trevisano e Gorgonzola* (pasta curlicues in a cheesy sauce topped with shredded bitter radicchio). Because the place operates as an *enoteca* after hours, the wine list is long and detailed.

Via Cavalca 2 (just off the market square). www.osterialamescitapisa.it. ✆ **050-957-019.** Reservations recommended. Main courses 15€. AE, DC, MC, V. Tues–Sun 7:45–11pm; Sat–Sun 1–2:30pm. Closed 20 days in Aug. Bus: 4, E, Lam Rossa, or LAM Verde.

Novecento ★   This immaculately converted colonial villa set around a courtyard garden is Pisa's best affordable boutique hotel. Rooms are small, certainly—none has a bath, for example, nor are there family-size units—but decor is refreshingly contemporary, with muted colors, the occasional flash of exuberance, and not an antique armoire in sight. The most peaceful and most comfortable of the rooms is the Garden Room, a self-contained unit with a small "antechamber" standing alone amid the lush subtropical greenery.

Via Roma 37, 56100 Pisa. www.hotelnovecento.pisa.it. ✆ **050-500-323.** Fax 050-220-9163. 14 units. 80€–120€ double; 90€–170€ Garden Room. Rates include breakfast. AE, MC, V. Parking on street (10€ per day). Bus: E or 4. **Amenities:** Concierge; babysitting. *In room:* A/C, TV, minibar, hair dryer, Wi-Fi (free).

San Gimignano ★★★

In its medieval heyday, **San Gimignano** had as many as 72 towers. Today, 13 towers remain. The city's fortress-like severity is softened by the subtlety of its harmonious squares. Many of its palaces and churches are enhanced by Renaissance frescoes. Stay overnight, if you can, so that you can enjoy the late afternoon or early evening and get a sense of the town without the crowds.

ESSENTIALS

GETTING THERE The approximately 30 daily **trains** on the line between **Siena** (trip time: 25–40 min.) and Empoli, where you can connect from **Florence** (1 hr.), stop at Poggibonsi. From **Poggibonsi,** over 30 buses make the 25-minute run to San Gimignano Monday through Saturday, but only six buses run on Sunday.

SITA (www.sitabus.it; ✆ **055-47-821**) and TRA-IN (www.trainspa.it; ✆ **0577-204-111**) codeshare hourly (at least, fewer on Sun) **buses** for most of the day from both **Florence** (50 min.) and **Siena** (45 min.) to Poggibonsi, many of which meet right up with the connection to San Gimignano (a further 20–25 min.). From **Siena** there are also 10 direct buses (1¼ hr.) Monday through Saturday.

Arriving by **car,** take the Poggibonsi Nord exit off the **Florence–Siena** highway or the SS2. San Gimignano is 12km (7½ miles) from Poggibonsi.

VISITOR INFORMATION The **tourist office** is at Piazza Duomo 1 (www.sangimignano.com; ✆ **0577-940-008**). It's open daily March through October from 9am to 1pm and 3 to 7pm, and November through February from 9am to 1pm and 2 to 6pm.

EXPLORING SAN GIMIGNANO

Anchoring the town, at the top of Via San Giovanni, are its two interlocking triangular *piazze:* **Piazza della Cisterna ★★**, centered on a 1237 well, and **Piazza del Duomo,** flanked by the city's main church and civic palace. The town also has some fascinating outdoor frescoes that you can view for free. The archway to the left of the Collegiata's facade leads to a pretty brick courtyard called Piazza Pecori. On the right, under brick vaulting, is a fresco of the *Annunciation* painted in 1482 by either Domenico Ghirlandaio or his brother-in-law and pupil Sebastiano Mainardi. The door to the right of the tourist office leads into a courtyard of the Palazzo del Comune, where Taddeo di Bartolo's 14th-century *Madonna and Child* is flanked by two works on the theme of justice by Sodoma, including his near-monochrome *St. Ivo.*

Duomo Collegiata o Basilica di Santa Maria Assunta ★ CHURCH The main church in town—it no longer has a bishop, so it's no longer officially a *duomo* (cathedral)—was started in the 11th century and took its present form in the 15th century. It's not much from the outside, but the interior is smothered in 14th-century frescoes, making it one of Tuscany's most densely decorated churches.

The right wall was frescoed from 1333 to 1341—most likely by Lippo Memmi—with three levels of **New Testament scenes** (22 in all) on the life and Passion of Christ along with a magnificent *Crucifixion.* In 1367, Bartolo di Fredi frescoed the left wall with 26 scenes out of the **Old Testament,** and Taddeo di Bartolo provided the gruesome **Last Judgment** frescoes around the main door in 1410.

In 1468, Giuliano da Maiano built the **Cappella di Santa Fina ★★** off the right aisle, and his brother Benedetto carved the relief panels for the altar. Florentine Renaissance master Domenico Ghirlandaio decorated the tiny chapel's walls with some of his finest, airiest works: In 1475 he frescoed two scenes summing up the life of Santa Fina, a local girl who, though never officially canonized, is one of San Gimignano's patron saints. Little Fina, who was very devout and wracked with guilt for having committed the sin of accepting an orange from a boy, fell down ill on a board one day and didn't move for 5 years, praying the entire time. Eventually, St. Gregory appeared to her and foretold her death, whereupon the board on which she lay miraculously produced flowers. The town still celebrates their child saint every year on March 12.

Piazza del Duomo. ✆ **0577-940-316.** Admission 3.50€ adults, 1.50€ ages 6–18. Nov–Mar Mon–Sat 10am–4:40pm, Sun 12:30–4:40pm; Apr–Oct Mon–Fri 10am–7:10pm, Sat 10am–5:10pm, Sun 12:30–7:10pm. Closed 1st Sun in Aug, Mar 12, Nov 16–30, and Jan 16–31.

Museo Civico (Civic Museum) ★ ART MUSEUM   In the late 13th century, the city government moved from the Palazzo del Podestà, across from the Collegiata, to the brand-new **Palazzo del Comune** (or del Popolo). You can climb its **Torre Grossa (Big Tower)** ★★, finished in 1311, for one of the best tower-top views of the cityscape and rolling countryside in Tuscany.

The small museum was built around a large fresco in the Sala del Consiglio of the *Maestà* ★★ (1317) by the Sienese Lippo Memmi. Up the stairs is the **Pinacoteca (Civic Painting Gallery),** but before entering it, duck through the door to the Camera del Podestà to see perhaps San Gimignano's most famous **frescoes** ★. Painted in the 14th century by Memmo di Filippuccio, they narrate a rather racy story of courtship and love in quite a departure from the usual religious themes of the era.

The first major work in a painting gallery that's especially strong on pre-Renaissance works is a Coppo di Marcovaldo Crucifix, immediately on the right, surrounded by Passion scenes, one of the masterpieces of 13th-century Tuscan art. Benozzo Gozzoli's *Madonna and Child with Saints* (1466) has an almost surreal *Pietà* with a delicate landscape running the length of the predella. A 25-year-old Filippino Lippi painted the matching tondi of the *Annunciation* in 1482, and the huge early-16th-century *Madonna in Glory with Sts. Gregory and Benedict,* with its wild Umbrian landscape, is a late work by Pinturicchio.

Two works in the rooms to the right tell the stories of the city's most popular patron saints. Lorenzo di Niccolò Gerini did a passable job in 1402 on the *Tabernacle of Santa Fina,* built to house the teen saint's head and painted with scenes of the four most important miracles of her brief life. In the late 14th century, Taddeo di Bartolo painted the *Life of St. Gimignano* as an altarpiece for the Collegiata; the saint himself sits in the middle, holding in his lap the town he was constantly invoked to protect.

Piazza del Duomo. ✆ **0577-990-312.** Admission 5€ adults, 4€ ages 6–18 and 65 and over. Apr–Sept daily 9:30am–7pm; Oct–Mar daily 10am–5:30pm.

WHERE TO STAY & EAT

Chiribiri ☺ ✦ ITALIAN   This cramped, eight-table trattoria in a tiny cellar at the southern tip of town is an oasis of value among some distinctly overpriced competition. The food is straight-up Italian classics with a Tuscan twist: lasagna or spaghetti with a choice of sauces to start; beef in chianti, *cinghiale in umido* (wild boar stew), and *osso buco* are among the well-executed mains. Handily for families, it's also open all day, so kids can eat when they want.

Piazzetta della Madonna 1. ✆ **0577-941-948.** Reservations recommended. Main courses 8€–12€. No credit cards. Daily 11am–11pm.

Dorandò ★★ TUSCAN   Dorandò is an elegant splurge tucked away just off Piazza Duomo, where the stone-walled rooms, alabaster platters, and knowledgeable waiters create a backdrop for San Gimignano's best fine dining. The chef attempts to keep the oldest traditions of Sangimignanese cooking alive—many of the recipes purport to be medieval, some even Etruscan, in origin—while balancing Slow Food philosophy with hearty home-cooking quality. The menu varies with the season and market, but if the excellent *cibrèo* (chicken livers and giblets scented with ginger and lemon) is offered, by all means order it. Desserts are excellent, too.

Vicolo dell'Oro 2. www.ristorantedorando.it. ✆ **0577-941-862.** Reservations highly recommended. Main courses 20€–24€; tasting menu 50€. AE, MC, V. Tues–Sun noon–2:30pm and 7–9:30pm (daily Easter–Sept). Closed Dec 10–Jan 31.

L'Antico Pozzo ★ L'Antico Pozzo is the choicest inn within the walls, a 15th-century *palazzo* converted to a hotel in 1990 with careful attention to preserving the structural antiquity without sacrificing convenience. Over the building's colorful history it has hosted Dante, the Inquisition trials, a religious community, and an 18th-century salon. Accommodations vary in size and decor, but none is small, and the large junior suites have wood ceilings and spumante waiting for you. "Superior" doubles have 17th-century ceiling frescoes and the smaller "standard" rooms on the third floor have wood floors and a view of the Rocca and a few towers.

Via San Matteo 87, 53037 San Gimignano. www.anticopozzo.com. ✆ **0577-942-014.** Fax 0577-942-117. 18 units. 110€–140€ double; 165€–180€ superior double. Rates include breakfast. DC, MC, V. Garage parking 20€. Closed for 20 days Jan–Feb. **Amenities:** Bar; bikes; concierge; babysitting; nonsmoking rooms. *In room:* A/C, TV, minibar, hair dryer, Wi-Fi (1 hr. daily free).

Leon Bianco ★ Typical of a 500-year-old building turned hotel, the rooms here can't seem to agree on a style or decor scheme, but most retain some element from the 14th-century *palazzo*—a painted wood-beam ceiling here, an old stone wall in a bathroom there, or a brick barrel vault filling one room. Accommodations overlook the pretty well of the tower-lined piazza out front or across rooftops to the countryside. (A few, however, overlook the partially glassed-in courtyard of the lobby.) "Superior" rooms are larger and come with minibars.

Piazza della Cisterna, 53037 San Gimignano. www.leonbianco.com. ✆ **0577-941-294.** Fax 0577-942-123. 26 units. 85€–118€ standard double; 115€–138€ superior double. Rates include breakfast. AE, DC, MC, V. Closed Nov 10 until just before Christmas and Jan 10 to early Feb. **Amenities:** Bar; exercise room; Jacuzzi; room service. *In room:* A/C, TV, minibar, hair dryer, Wi-Fi (free).

Siena ★★★

Siena is a medieval city of brick. Viewed from the summit of the Palazzo Pubblico's tower, its sea of roof tiles blends into a landscape of steep, twisting stone alleys. This cityscape hides dozens of Gothic palaces and pastry shops galore, unseen neighborhood rivalries, and painted altarpieces of unsurpassed elegance.

ESSENTIALS

GETTING THERE The bus is often more convenient than the train, because Siena's **rail** station is outside town. Some 19 trains daily connect Siena with **Florence** (usually 90 min.), via Empoli. Siena's **train station** is at Piazza Rosselli, about 3km (1¾ miles) north of town. Take the no. 9 or 10 bus to Piazza Gramsci in Terza di Camollia or a taxi.

Buses are faster and let you off right in town: **TRA-IN** and **SITA** (www.sitabus.it) codeshare express (*corse rapide;* around 25 daily; 75 min.) and slower buses (*corse ordinarie;* 14 daily; 95 min.) from **Florence**'s main bus station to Siena's Piazza Gramsci. Siena is also connected with **San Gimignano** (at least hourly Mon–Sat;

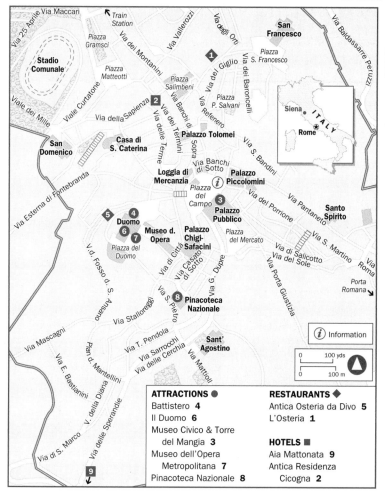

Via Maccari
Via 25 Aprile
Train Station
Via Valerozzi
Via degli Orti
Via Baldassarre Peruzzi

Piazza Gramsci

Stadio Comunale

Piazza Matteotti

Via dei Montanini

San Francesco

Piazza S. Francesco

Via del Giglio

Via dei Baroncelli

Piazza Salimbeni

Piazza P. Salvani

Via Curtatone

Viale dei Mille

Viale dei Mille

Via della Sapienza

Via dei Termini

Via Banchi di Sopra

Via Refenero

Palazzo Tolomei

Via S. Bandini

Siena · ITALY

Rome

San Domenico

Casa di S. Caterina

Via delle Terme

Via Banchi di Sotto

Via Esterna di Fontebranda

Loggia di Mercanzia

Palazzo Piccolomini

Piazza del Campo

Palazzo Pubblico

Via del Porrione

Via Pantaneto

Santo Spirito

Duomo

Museo d. Opera

Palazzo Chigi-Safacini

Piazza del Mercato

Via di Salicotto

Via del Sole

Via S. Martino

Via Roma

Piazza del Duomo

V. d. Fosso d. S. Ansano

Via di Città

Via Casato di Sotto

Via G. Dupre

Via di Porta Giustizia

Porta Romana

Pinacoteca Nazionale

Via Stalloreggi

Via S. Pietro

Information

0   100 yds
0   100 m

Via Mascagni

Via E. Bastianini

Pian di Mantellini

V. della Diana

Via delle Sperandie

Via di S. Marco

Via T. Pendola

Via Sarrocchi

Via delle Cerchia

Via Mattioli

Sant' Agostino

9

ATTRACTIONS ●	RESTAURANTS ◆
Battistero **4**	Antica Osteria da Divo **5**
Il Duomo **6**	L'Osteria **1**
Museo Civico & Torre	
del Mangia **3**	**HOTELS** ■
Museo dell'Opera	Aia Mattonata **9**
Metropolitana **7**	Antica Residenza
Pinacoteca Nazionale **8**	Cicogna **2**

10 direct, rest change in Poggibonsi; 65–80 min. not including layover), **Perugia** (two to four daily; 90 min.), **Arezzo** (eight daily; 90 min.), and **Rome**'s Tiburtina station (five to nine daily; 3 hr.).

There's a fast **road** direct from **Florence** (it has no route number; follow the green signs toward Siena), or take the more scenic route, down the Chiantigiana SS222. From **Rome** get off the A1 north at the Val di Chiana exit and follow the SS326 west for 50km (31 miles). From **Pisa** take the highway toward Florence and exit onto the SS429 south just before Empoli (100km/62 miles total). The easiest way into the center is from the Siena Ovest highway exit.

Siena **parking** (www.sienaparcheggi.com; ℂ **0577-228-711**) is now coordinated, and lots charge between .50€ and 1.60€ per hour (most at the top end of that scale).

Luckily, many hotels have a discount deal with the nearest lot; around 15€ per day is standard. All lots are well signposted, with locations just inside city gates.

VISITOR INFORMATION   The **tourist office,** where you can get a useless free map or pay .50€ for a useful one, is at Piazza del Campo 56, 53100 Siena (www. terresiena.it; ☏ **0577-280-551**). It's open daily 9am to 7pm.

EXPLORING SIENA

Start in the heart of Siena, the shell-shaped **Piazza del Campo ★★★**, described by Montaigne as "the finest of any city in the world." Pause to enjoy the **Fonte Gaia,** which locals sometimes call the Fountain of Joy. The square is truly stunning, designed like a sloping scallop shell; you'll want to linger in one of the cafes along its edge.

Battistero (Baptistery) ★   The Duomo's baptistery was built between 1355 and 1382 beneath the cathedral's choir and supports a Gothic facade left unfinished by Domenico di Agostino. The upper walls and vaulted ceilings inside were **frescoed by Vecchietta** and his school in the late 1440s (look for the alligator) but "touched up" in the 19th century. What you're principally here to see, though, is the **baptismal font ★★** (1417–30). The frames are basically Gothic, but the gilded brass panels were cast by the foremost Sienese and Florentine sculptors of the early Renaissance, including Jacopo della Quercia, Lorenzo Ghiberti, and Donatello, whose *Feast of Herod* is a masterful early study of precise perspective and profound depth.

Piazza San Giovanni (down the stairs around the rear right flank of the Duomo). ☏ **0577-283-048.** Admission on cumulative ticket, or 3€. Mid-June to mid-Sept daily 9:30am–8pm; mid-Sept to Oct and Mar to mid-June daily 9:30am–7pm; Nov–Feb daily 10am–5pm.

Il Duomo ★★★ CATHEDRAL   Siena's cathedral is a rich treasure house of Tuscan art. Despite being an overwhelmingly Gothic building, the Duomo has one eye-popping Romanesque holdover: its 1313 **campanile** with its black-and-white banding. The Duomo was built from around 1215 to 1263, involving Gothic master Nicola Pisano as architect at some point. His son, Giovanni, drew up the plans for the lower half of the **facade,** begun in 1285. Giovanni Pisano, along with his studio, also carved many of the statues adorning it (most of the originals are now in the Museo dell'Opera Metropolitana; see below).

By 1339, having defeated Florence 80 years earlier, Siena was its rival's equal. It began its most ambitious project yet: to turn the already huge Duomo into merely the transept of a new cathedral, one that would dwarf St. Peter's in Rome and trumpet Siena's political power, spiritual devotion, and artistic prowess. The city started the new nave off the Duomo's right transept but completed only the fabric of the walls when the Black Death hit in 1348, decimating the population and halting building plans forever. The **half-finished walls** remain—a monument to Siena's ambition and one-time wealth.

You could wander inside for hours, just staring at the **flooring ★★★**, a mosaic of 59 etched and inlaid marble panels (1372–1547). At the entry to the left transept is Nicola Pisano's masterpiece **pulpit ★★** (1265–68). The elegantly Gothic panels depict the life of Christ in crowded, detailed turmoil, divided by figures in flowing robes.

Umbrian master Pinturicchio is the star in the **Libreria Piccolomini ★★★**, built in 1485 by Cardinal Francesco Piccolomini (later Pope Pius III—for all of 18 days before he died in office) to house the library of his famous uncle, Pope Pius II. Pinturicchio and his assistants covered the ceiling and walls with 10 giant frescoes (1507) displaying rich colors and a fascination with mathematically precise, but somewhat cold, architectural space.

Piazza del Duomo. ☏ **0577-283-048.** Admission on cumulative ticket, or 3€, except when floor uncovered 6€. Mar–May and Sept–Oct Mon–Sat 10:30am–7:30pm, Sun 1:30–5:30pm; Nov–Feb Mon–Sat 10:30am–6:30pm, Sun 1:30–5:30pm; June–Aug Mon–Sat 10:30am–8pm, Sun 1:30–6pm.

Museo Civico (Civic Museum) & Torre del Mangia ★★★ ART MUSEUM

There are a number of wonderful frescoed rooms here, but the museum's pride comes with the masterpieces of Sienese painting giants Simone Martini and Ambrogio Lorenzetti. The **Sala del Mappamondo**—named after a now lost Ambrogio Lorenzetti painting of the world—contains two of Simone Martini's greatest works. On the left is his masterpiece, a *Maestà* ★★★. Incredibly, this was his very first painting, finished in 1315 (he went over it again in 1321). It's the next generation's answer to Duccio's groundbreaking work on the same theme painted just 4 years earlier and now in the Museo dell'Opera Metropolitana (see below).

The adjacent **Sala della Pace** was where the Council of Nine met, and to keep them mindful of how well they needed to govern, the city commissioned Ambrogio Lorenzetti (1338) to fresco the walls with the single most important piece of secular art to survive from medieval Europe, the *Allegory of Good and Bad Government and Their Effects on the Town and Countryside* ★★★. Good government is represented by a bearded old man surrounded by virtues. A prosperous 14th-century Siena is pictured here—recognizable by its towers, battlemented houses, and the Duomo squeezed into the corner. The *Bad Government* frescoes are, perhaps appropriately, in a high state of ruin. Monstrous Tyranny reigns with the help of such henchmen as Cruelty, Fraud, and the creaturelike Deceit. Unfortunately, in the aftermath of the Black Death of 1348, *Bad Government* pretty much came to pass.

Accessible from the courtyard of the Palazzo Pubblico is the slender 100m-tall (328-ft.) brick **Torre del Mangia** ★ (1338–48), crowned with a Lippo Memmi-designed cresting in white travertine. If you fancy climbing 503 steps and aren't particularly claustrophobic, the tower is a great place to check out the unforgettable view across Siena's cityscape and the rolling countryside beyond.

Palazzo Pubblico, Piazza del Campo. ☏ **0577-292-226.** Admission on cumulative ticket with Torre del Mangia 13€; or 7.50€ adults with reservation, 8€ adults without reservation; 4€ students and seniors 65 and over with reservation, 3.50€ students and seniors without reservation; free for ages 11 and under. Nov–Mar 15 daily 10am–6pm; Mar 16–Oct daily 10am–7pm. Bus: A (pink), B.

Museo dell'Opera Metropolitana (Duomo Museum) ★★ MUSEUM

Housed in the walled-up right aisle of the Duomo's abortive new nave, Siena's outstanding Duomo museum contains all the works removed from the facade for conservation as well as disused altarpieces, including Duccio's masterpiece. It also offers one of the city's best views. A highlight is Duccio's restored 30 sq. m (323 sq. ft.) **stained glass window** ★★ made in the late 1280s for the window above the cathedral's apse. Nine panels depict the Virgin Mary, Siena's four patron saints, and the four Biblical Evangelists.

Upstairs is the museum's (indeed, the city's) masterpiece, **Duccio's** *Maestà* ★★★. It's impossible to overstate the importance of this double-sided altarpiece: Not only did it virtually found the Sienese school of painting, but it has also been considered one of the most important medieval paintings in Europe since the day it was unveiled.

Piazza del Duomo 8. www.operaduomo.siena.it. ☏ **0577-283-048.** Admission on cumulative ticket, or 6€. Mid-June to mid-Sept daily 9:30am–8pm; mid-Sept to Oct and Mar to mid-June daily 9:30am–7pm; Nov–Feb daily 10am–5pm.

Pinacoteca Nazionale (National Picture Gallery) ★★ ART MUSEUM
Siena's painting gallery houses the most representative collection of the Sienese
school of art. It wouldn't be fair to label it a museum of second-rate paintings by first-
rate artists, but the supreme masterpieces of Siena do lie elsewhere. It's laid out more
or less chronologically starting on the second floor, though the museum is constantly
rearranging (especially the last bits).

Rooms 3 and 4 have works by the first great Sienese master, Duccio, including an
early masterpiece showing Cimabue's influence, the tiny 1285 *Madonna dei Frances-
cani* (in poor condition, it's kept under glass). Rooms 5 to 8 pay homage to the three
great early-14th-century painters, Simone Martini and the brothers Pietro and
Ambrogio Lorenzetti. Of Martini, be sure to look at the four charming narrative panels from the *Altar of Beato Agostino Novello.* The best Lorenzetti works are in the
small side rooms off Room 7, including a *Madonna Enthroned* and a *Madonna of the
Carmelites* by Pietro; also look for Ambrogio's tiny landscapes in Room 12, an expres-
sive but much deteriorated *Crucifixion,* and his last dated work, a 1343 *Annunciation.* On the first floor, look for Domenico Beccafumi's huge **cartoons** ★★, from
which many of the panels in the Duomo floor were made.

Via San Pietro 29. ☎ **0577-286-143**. Admission 4€. Sun–Mon 9am–1pm; Tues–Sat 8:15am–7:15pm.

WHERE TO STAY & EAT
Aia Mattonata ★★ 🏠 This tiny, tranquil boutique inn, crafted from an old
stone farmhouse, is enveloped by the gently rolling Tuscan hills just a 10-minute ride
from central Siena. Both the midsize guest rooms and the classy common areas
(where you'll find an honesty snack bar) remain true to their Tuscan roots, but have
an added touch of rustic refinement. Two rooms have romantic *baldacchino* (canopy)
beds, but the smallest (not by much) shares with the garden a sublime view toward
the Torre del Mangia and Siena's ochre rooftops.

Strada del Ceraiolo 1, 53100 Siena. www.aiamattonata.it. ☎ **0577-592-677.** Fax 0577-392-073. 6
units. 155€–240€ double. Rates include breakfast. AE, MC, V. Free parking. Closed Nov–Feb. Bus:
31. From Siena Ovest junction, head toward Roccastrada, then after 1km/½ mile follow SS46 left
toward Casciano di Murlo; after 2km/1¼ miles Strada del Ceraiolo is on left. No children 11 and
under. **Amenities:** Bar; outdoor pool; exercise room; small spa; bikes (free); concierge; room service; nonsmoking rooms. *In room:* A/C, TV, hair dryer, Wi-Fi (free).

Antica Osteria da Divo ★★ CONTEMPORARY SIENESE This former trattoria has thrived since it went midscale and greatly improved its menu to offer excellent
innovative dishes rooted in Sienese traditions in a classy, but not frosty, atmosphere.
The main dining room is a crazy medieval mélange of stone, brick, wood supports, and
naked rock, while the rooms in back and in the basement are actually Etruscan tombs
carved from the tufa. *Pici al ragout di lepre* (thick hand-rolled pasta in hare *ragù*) and
gnocchetti di patate con erbe cipollina e pecorino di fossa (gnocchi with chives swimming
in melted pecorino cheese) are palate-pleasing *primi.* For the main course, they ascribe
to the growing school of Italian cooking wherein a side dish is included with each *secondo* (making a meal here less costly than the prices below would suggest).

Via Franciosa 25–29 (2 streets down from the left flank of the Duomo). www.osteriadadivo.it.
☎ **0577-284-381.** Reservations recommended. Main courses 20€–24€. MC, V. Wed–Mon noon–
2:30pm and 7–10:30pm. Closed 2 weeks Jan–Feb. Bus: A (green, yellow).

Antica Residenza Cicogna ★★ 🛢 This friendly, family-run B&B has established itself as one of the most desirable pads in the center of town—and you'll need

to book ahead in peak season to secure one of the handful of rooms. Units are compact, but the place is dripping with character, and its location (a 5-min. walk from the Campo) could hardly be better. Among the neat doubles, all of which come with textured wallpaper and carefully matched fabrics, our favorite is "Liberty," which comes with slightly more space (including room for an extra bed if necessary) and a *baldacchino* (canopy) bed.

Via dei Termini 67, 53100 Siena. www.anticaresidenzacicogna.com. $ **0577-285-613.** 7 units. 80€–100€ double; 110€–150€ suite. Rates include buffet breakfast. MC, V. Garage parking 18€. **Amenities:** Nonsmoking rooms. *In room:* A/C, TV, hair dryer, Wi-Fi (free).

L'Osteria ★★ TUSCAN/GRILL   The mission at this boisterous grill is straightforward: to turn out tasty cooking using local ingredients whenever possible. The menu is short and focused, emphasizing simple, ingredient-led dishes. The dishes from the grill are the stars of the menu with flavor packed into seared beef, wild boar, *bistecca di vitello* (veal steak), and (our favorite) a succulent *tagliata* of the local Cinta Senese breed of pig. Pair any of the above with a simple side of *patate fritte* (fries) or garbanzo beans dressed with olive oil and you have yourself a Tuscan taste sensation.

Via de' Rossi 79–81. $ **0577-287-592.** Reservations highly recommended. Main courses 7.50€–18€. AE, MC, V. Mon–Sat 12:30–2:30pm and 7:30–10:30pm.

Assisi ★★★

Arrive early in the morning, before the first tour buses, and you'll soon see that Assisi is a special place—the rising sun behind Monte Subasio, often shrouded in mist, cuts massive silhouettes behind this medieval city of miracles. A peculiar blend of romance, architecture, and devotion make it the quintessential Umbrian hill town—the absolutely essential stop on any Umbrian tour.

ESSENTIALS

GETTING THERE   From **Perugia,** there are about 20 **trains** daily (25–30 min.). From **Florence** (2–3 hr.), there are trains every 2 hours or so, though some require a transfer at Terontola. The station is in the modern valley town of Santa Maria degli Angeli, about 5km (3 miles) from Assisi, with bus connections to Assisi every 20 minutes (1€), or you can take a **taxi** for about 15€ to 20€.

By **car,** Assisi is 18km (11 miles) east of Perugia, off the SS75bis. Driving the center's steep streets is forbidden for tourists. The best strategy is to **park** in Piazza Matteotti (1.15€ per hour), keep walking west, and finish at the basilica; it's all downhill.

Eight Umbria Mobilità **buses** (www.umbriamobilita.it; $ **800/512-141**) run seven times daily (Mon–Fri) between **Perugia** and Assisi's Piazza Matteotti (50 min.; 3.20€; 4€ if you pay on the bus). They also run about five buses from **Gubbio** (1¼ hr.). **SULGA** (www.sulga.it; $ **075-500-9641**) runs two buses daily from **Rome's** Tiburtina station, taking about 3 hours, and one daily trip from Piazza Adua in **Florence,** which takes about 2½ hours.

VISITOR INFORMATION   The **tourist office** (www.comune.assisi.pg.it; $ **075-812-534**) is in the Palazzo S. Nicola on Piazza del Comune, 06081 Assisi. It's open summer daily from 8am to 6:30pm, winter Monday through Saturday from 8am to 2pm and 3 to 6pm, Sunday from 9am to 1pm. The private websites **www.assisi online.com** and **www.assisiweb.com** also have good info.

EXPLORING ASSISI

The main square in town is **Piazza del Comune.** The medieval edition of what may have been the old Roman forum is most famous for the six gleaming white Corinthian columns and tympanum of the **Tempio di Minerva,** a 1st-century-B.C. Roman temple the Assisians sensibly recycled into the church of **Santa Maria sopra Minerva** (daily 6:45am–8pm; free), with a thoroughly uninteresting baroque interior.

Basilica di San Francesco (St. Francis) ★★★ ICON   Although Assisi's basilica is first and foremost a site of Christian pilgrimage, it's also a masterpiece of medieval architecture and the home of some exuberant medieval art. The almost simultaneous construction of huge Lower (1228) and Upper (1230) churches in contrasting Romanesque and Gothic styles had no peer or precedent. Franciscan Brother Elias, the probable architect, built the basilica to house Francis's recently sanctified bones. Today it still moves the devout to tears and art lovers to fits of near-religious ecstasy.

Piazza San Francesco. www.sanfrancescoassisi.org. (𝘊 **075-819001.** Free admission. Daily 8:30am–6:30pm.

Basilica di Santa Chiara ★ CHURCH   The vast interior of this 1260, early Gothic church is dark and perennially crowded with people filing down into the neo-Gothic crypt to see the original stone **tomb of St. Clare.** Born to a local minor noble family in 1193, Chiara (anglicized to Clare) was a friend of Francis who followed the mystic's example against her parents' wishes. In 1211, she abandoned her parental household and ran off to meet Francis, who clothed her in sackcloth after his own fashion and hacked off her hair, signaling Clare's renunciation of earthly goods and the beginning of her quest for spiritual enlightenment. She soon gathered a large enough female following at San Damiano that Francis urged her to set up a convent there, and she became abbess. (The order she founded, the Poor Clares, didn't move into town until after her death.)

Off the right wall of the church built to house her tomb is the **Oratorio del Cro-cifisso,** preserving the venerated 12th-century crucifix that spoke to St. Francis at San Damiano and set him on his holy path.

Piazza Santa Chiara. (𝘊 **075-812-282.** Free admission. Daily 6:30am–noon and 2–7pm (6pm in winter).

Foro Romano ★ RUINS   Assisi's secular highlight is a little underwhelming for non-history buffs, but the remnants of this Roman Forum can still hold some magic. An entrance room (the old crypt of San Nicolò Church) houses inscribed tablets and headless statues, but the main passage leading off from here preserves a tiny piece of 2nd-century-B.C. Asisium—a slice of the old forum some 3.9m (13 ft.) below 21st-century Piazza del Comune.

Via Portica 2 (on the edge of Piazza del Comune). (𝘊 **075-815-5077.** Admission 4€ adults; 2.50€ students, children 8–17, and seniors 65 and over; free for children 7 and under; joint ticket with Rocca Maggiore and Pinacoteca Comunale 8€ and 5€. June–Aug daily 10am–1pm and 2:30–7pm; Mar–May and Sept–Oct daily 10am–1pm and 2:30–6pm; Nov–Feb daily 10:30am–1pm and 2–5pm.

WHERE TO STAY & EAT

La Fortezza ★★ 🍴 UMBRIAN   This is one of Assisi's great hidden treasures. Since 1960, the Chiocchetti family has offered refined *ristorante* service and inspired cuisine at trattoria prices, and all just a few steps above the main piazza. The *cannelloni all'Assisiana* are scrumptious (fresh pasta sheets wrapped around a veal *ragù*, all baked under parmigiana), as is the *gnocchi alla Fortezza* (homemade gnocchi tossed with a garden of chopped vegetables: tomatoes, mushrooms, zucchini, peas, onions,

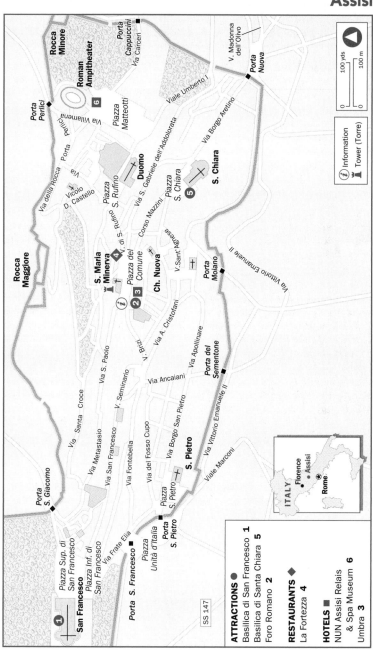

12

i Information
Ⓘ Tower (Torre)

Rocca
Minore

Roman
Ampitheater

Porta
Cappuccini

Via Carceri

V. Madonna
dell'Olivo

Porta
Nuova

Porta
Perlici

Via Villamena

Perlici
Porta

Piazza
Matteotti

Viale Umberto I

Via Borgo Aretino

Rocca
Maggiore

Via della Rocca
Porta

Porta

Via

Vicolo
D. Castello

Piazza
S. Rufino

Duomo

Via S. Gabriele dell'Addolorata

S. Chiara

Piazza
S. Chiara

S. Maria
Minerva

V. di S. Ruffino

Piazza del
Comune

Corso Mazzini

Ch. Nuova

V. Sant'Agn.

Porta
Moiano

Via Vittorio Emanuele II

Via S. Paolo

V. Brizi

Via A. Cristofani

Via Apollinare

Porta del
Sementone

Via S. Croce

V. Seminario

Via Ancaiani

Via Metastasio

Via San Francesco

Via Fontebella

Via del Fosso Cupo

Via Borgo San Pietro

S. Pietro

Via Vittorio Emanuele II

Viale Marconi

Piazza
S. Pietro

Porta
S. Pietro

Porta S. Francesco

Porta
S. Giacomo

Piazza Sup. di
San Francesco

Piazza Inf. di
San Francesco

Via Frate Elia

Piazza
Unità d'Italia

Porta
S. Pietro

San Francesco

SS 147

ⓛ

100 yds
100 m
0
0

ITALY

Florence

● Assisi

Rome

ATTRACTIONS ●
Basilica di San Francesco **1**
Basilica di Santa Chiara **5**
Foro Romano **2**

RESTAURANTS ◆
La Fortezza **4**

HOTELS ■
NUN Assisi Relais
& Spa Museum **6**
Umbra **3**

and more). For a *secondo,* try the *coniglio in salsa di mele* (rabbit in a sort of curry of white wine, saffron, and apples) or marinated wild boar in sweet and sour sauce.

Vicolo della Fortezza/Piazza del Comune (up the stairs near the Via San Rufino end). www.lafortezza hotel.com. ✆ **075-812-993.** Reservations recommended. Main courses 10€–13€. MC, V. Fri–Wed 12:30–2:30pm and 7:30–9:30pm. Closed Feb and 1 week in July.

NUN Assisi Relais & Spa Museum ★★   This slick boutique hotel offers an elegant blend of medieval Italy and contemporary style, with rooms decked out in crisp white designer furniture. The renovated building once formed part of St. Catherine's 13th-century nunnery, with original vaulted ceilings and frescoes sprinkled throughout the rooms. The "museum" is actually a posh spa set atmospherically among Roman foundations. The breakfast buffets are delicious minibanquets. Note that some rooms have problems receiving reliable Wi-Fi.

Eremo delle Carceri 1A, 06081 Assisi. www.nunassisi.com. ✆ **075-815-5150.** Fax 075-816-580. 8 units. 260€ double. Rate includes breakfast. AE, DC, MC, V. Garage parking 25€ per day. **Amenities:** Restaurant; bar; indoor pool; spa (free); concierge; room service. *In room:* A/C, TV, minibar, Wi-Fi (free).

> ### Dress Appropriately
>
> San Francesco and Santa Chiara, like many other churches throughout Italy, have a strict **dress code:** Entrance to the basilica is *forbidden* to those wearing shorts or miniskirts or showing bare shoulders. You also must remain silent and cannot take photographs in the Upper Church of San Francesco.

Umbra ★★   Antiques buffs will feel right at home in the collection of 13th-century houses from which the Umbra was converted, thanks to agreeable old furniture like 19th-century dressers, 18th-century desks, and 17th-century armoires. Many rooms have views over the rooftops and valley, some have balconies, and the hotel is graced with little hidden panoramic terraces. Ask to see the basement kitchen and laundry rooms, where the town's Roman walls make up part of the foundations.

Via Delgli Archi 6 (off the west end of Piazza del Comune), 06081 Assisi. www.hotelumbra.it. ✆ **075-812-240.** Fax 075-813-653. 24 units. 110€ standard double; 125€ superior double. Rates include breakfast. AE, DC, MC, V. Garage parking 10€ per day. Closed mid-Jan to Easter. **Amenities:** Restaurant; bar; bikes; concierge; room service; babysitting. *In room:* A/C, TV, minibar, hair dryer, Wi-Fi (free).

VENICE ★★★

Few cities in the world are one of a kind, and in that tight fraternity several stand out, perhaps none more than Venice, formerly the Most Serene Republic of Venice. To see for the first time this most improbable cityscape of canals, bridges, gondolas, and stone palaces that seem to float on water is to experience one of life's great pleasures. To see it a second, third, and fourth time is to appreciate Venice's greatness. Tucked away in Italy's northeastern corner at the upper reaches of the Adriatic Sea, it is hard to imagine how Venice parlayed its position into becoming a great maritime power. But then again, this city is full of surprises—from the grandeur of Piazza San Marco, to the splendid solitude of Cannaregio's canal-side quays and Rialto's vibrant fish market.

Essentials
GETTING THERE

The arrival scene at unattractive **Piazzale Roma** is filled with nervous expectation; even the most veteran traveler can become confused. Whether arriving by train, bus, car, or airport limo, everyone walks to the nearby docks (less than a 5-min. walk) to select a method of transport to his or her hotel. The cheapest way is by *vaporetto* (water bus); the more expensive is by gondola or motor launch (see the "Getting Around" section, below).

BY PLANE   You can fly into Venice from North America via Rome or Milan with **Alitalia** or a number of other airlines, or by connecting through a major European city with European carriers.

Flights land at the **Aeroporto Marco Polo,** 7km (4¼ miles) north of the city on the mainland (www.veniceairport.it; ☏ **041-260-9260**). The **ATVO airport shuttle bus** (www.atvo.it; ☏ **0421-594-671**) connects with Piazzale Roma not far from Venice's Santa Lucia train station (and the closest point to Venice's attractions accessible by car or bus). Buses leave for/from the airport about every 30 minutes, cost 5€, and make the trip in about 20 minutes. The less expensive local public **ACTV bus no. 5** (☏ **041-2424**) costs 2€, takes 30 to 45 minutes, and runs between two and four times an hour depending on the time of day. Buy tickets for either at the newsstand just inside the terminal from the signposted bus stop. With either bus, you'll have to walk to or from the final stop at Piazzale Roma to the nearby ***vaporetto*** stop for the final connection to your hotel.

A **land taxi** from the airport to the Piazzale Roma (where you get the *vaporetto*) will run to about 40€. The most fashionable and traditional way to arrive in Piazza San Marco is by sea. For 15€, 13€ if you buy online, the **Cooperative San Marco/ Alilaguna** (www.alilaguna.it; ☏ **041-240-1701**) operates a large *motoscafo* (shuttle boat) service from the airport with stops at Murano and the Lido before arriving after about 1 hour and 15 minutes in Piazza San Marco. This *Linea Blu* (the blue line) runs almost every 30 minutes from about 6am to midnight. The *Linea Arancio* (orange line) has the same frequency, costs the same, and takes the same amount of time to arrive at San Marco, but gets there through the Grand Canal (Canal Grande), which is much more spectacular and offers the possibility of getting off at one of the stops along the Grand Canal.

A **private water taxi** (20–30 min. to/from the airport) is convenient but costly—there is a fixed 100€ fee to arrive in the city, for up to four passengers with one bag each (10€ more for each extra person up to a maximum of 12). Try the **Corsorzio Motoscafi Venezia** (www.motoscafivenezia.it; ☏ **041-522-2303**) or **Venezia Taxi** (www.veneziataxi.it; ☏ **041-723-112**).

BY TRAIN   Trains from Rome (3¾ hr.), Milan (2½ hr.), Florence (2 hr.), and all over Europe arrive at the **Stazione Venezia Santa Lucia.** To get there, all must pass through (though not necessarily stop at) a station marked Venezia-Mestre. Don't be confused: Mestre is a charmless industrial city that's the last stop on the mainland. Occasionally trains end in Mestre, in which case you have to catch one of the frequent 10-minute shuttles connecting with Venice; it's inconvenient, so when you book your ticket, confirm that the final destination is Venezia Santa Lucia.

BY CAR   The only wheels you'll see in Venice are those attached to luggage. Venice is a city of canals and narrow alleys. **No cars are allowed;** or more to the point, no cars could drive through the narrow streets and over the footbridges—even the police, fire department, and ambulance services use boats. Arriving in Venice by car is problematic and expensive—and downright exasperating if it's high season and the parking facilities are full (they often are).

Venice

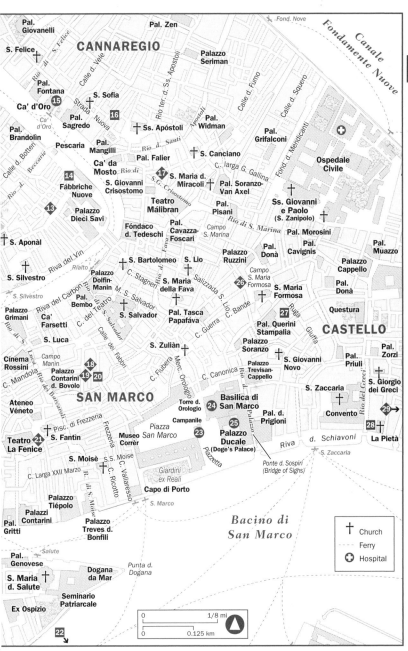

Pal. Giovanelli

S. Felice

CANNAREGIO

Pal. Zen

Palazzo Seriman

Canale Fondamente Nuove

Fond. Nove

Pal. Fontana

Ca' d'Oro ⑮

S. Sofia

⑯

Pal. Sagredo

Ss. Apóstoli

Pal. Widman

Pal. Grifalconi

Ospedale Civile

Pal. Brandolin

Pescaria

Pal. Mangilli

Pal. Falier

S. Canciano

Ca' da Mosto

⑰ S. Maria d. Miracoli

Pal. Soranzo-Van Axel

Ss. Giovanni e Paolo (S. Zanipolo)

⑭ Fábbriche Nuove

S. Giovanni Crisostomo

Pal. Pisani

⑬ Palazzo Dieci Savi

Fóndaco d. Tedeschi

Teatro Málibran

Pal. Cavazza-Foscari

Campo S. Marina

Rio di S. Marina

Pal. Donà

Pal. Morosini

Pal. Muazzo

S. Aponàl

Riva del Vin

S. Bartolomeo

Palazzo Ruzzini

Pal. Cavignis

Palazzo Cappello

S. Silvestro

Rialto

S. Lio

Campo S. Maria Formosa

Pal. Donà

S. Silvestro

Palazzo Dolfin-Manin

S. Maria della Fava

⑳ S. Maria Formosa

Questura

Palazzo Grimani

Pal. Bembo

Pal. Tasca Papafáva

Ruga Giuffa

CASTELLO

Ca' Farsetti

S. Salvador

Pal. Querini Stampalia

Pal. Zorzi

S. Luca

S. Zulián

Palazzo Soranzo

Cinema Rossini

Campo Manin

⑱

Palazzo Trevisan-Cappello

S. Giovanni Novo

Pal. Priuli

Palazzo Contarini d. Bovolo

⑲ ⑳

S. Zaccaria

S. Giorgio dei Greci

Ateneo Véneto

SAN MARCO

Torre d. Orologio

Basilica di S. Marco

⑳

Convento

㉙

Teatro La Fenice

㉑ S. Fantin

Pisc. di Frezzeria

Campanile

㉓

Piazza San Marco

㉔

Pal. d. Prigioni

㉘

La Pietà

Museo Corrèr

Palazzo Ducale (Doge's Place)

S. Moisè

Giardini ex Reali

Riva d. Schiavoni

C. Larga XXII Marzo

Ponte d. Sospiri (Bridge of Sighs)

S. Zaccaria

Capo di Porto

Palazzo Tiépolo

S. Marco

Palazzi Contarini

Palazzo Treves d. Bonfili

Pal. Gritti

Bacio di San Marco

† Church

--- Ferry

✚ Hospital

Pal. Genovese

S. Maria d. Salute

Salute

Dogana da Mar

Punta d. Dogana

Seminario Patriarcale

Ex Ospizio

㉒

0   1/8 mi

0   0.125 km

689

VISITOR INFORMATION

TOURIST OFFICE   The main office is on Fondamenta San Lorenzo, 5 minutes from Piazza San Marco (www.turismovenezia.it; ℂ **041-529-8711;** *vaporetto:* San Zaccaria). It's open daily from 10am to 6pm.

CITY LAYOUT

Keep in mind as you wander seemingly hopelessly among the *calli* (streets) and *campi* (squares) that the city wasn't built to make sense to those on foot but rather to those plying its canals. No matter how good your map and sense of direction, time after time you'll get lost. Just view it as an opportunity to stumble across Venice's most intriguing corners and vignettes.

Venice lies 4km (2½ miles) from terra firma, connected to the mainland burg of Mestre by the Ponte della Libertà, which leads to Piazzale Roma. Snaking through the city like an inverted S is the **Grand Canal,** the wide main artery of aquatic Venice.

The city is divided into six *sestieri* ("sixths," or districts or wards): **Cannaregio, Castello, San Marco, San Polo, Santa Croce,** and **Dorsoduro.** In addition to the six *sestieri* that cluster around the Grand Canal there are a host of other islands in the Venice lagoon. Opposite Piazza San Marco and Dorsoduro is **La Giudecca,** a tranquil, mostly residential and working-class place that is administratively part of Dorsoduro and offers great views of Piazza San Marco.

The **Lido di Venezia** is the city's sandy beach; it's a popular summer destination and holds a concentration of seasonal hotels. **San Michele,** located just off of the Cannaregio and Castello *sestieri,* is the cemetery island where such celebrities as Stravinsky and Diaghilev are buried.

Murano, Burano, and **Torcello** are popular destinations northeast of the city and easily accessible by *vaporetto.* Since the 13th century, Murano has exported its glass products worldwide; it's an interesting trip, but if your scope is a glass chandelier or something similar, you can do just as well in "downtown" Venice's myriad glass stores. Fishing village Burano is dotted with colorful houses and is famous for its lace, an art now practiced by very few island women. Torcello is the most remote and least populated. The 40-minute boat ride is worthwhile for history and art buffs, who'll be awestruck by the Byzantine mosaics of the cathedral (some of Europe's finest outside Ravenna). The cathedral's foundation dates to the 7th century, making this the oldest Venetian monument in existence.

The industrial city of **Mestre,** on the mainland, is the gateway to Venice, and while it holds no reason for exploration, in a pinch its host of inexpensive hotels is worth consideration when Venice's are full.

GETTING AROUND

Aside from on boats, the only way to explore Venice is by walking—and by getting lost repeatedly. You'll navigate many twisting streets whose names change constantly and don't appear on any map, and streets that may very well simply end in a blind alley or spill abruptly into a canal. You'll also cross dozens of footbridges. Treat getting bewilderingly lost in Venice as part of the fun, and budget more time than you'd think necessary to get wherever you're going.

BY BOAT   The various *sestieri* are linked by a comprehensive *vaporetto* system of about a dozen lines operated by the **Azienda del Consorzio Trasporti Veneziano (ACTV),** Calle Fuseri 1810, near the northwest corner of Piazza San Marco (www. actv.it; ℂ **041-528-7886**). Transit maps are available at the tourist office and most ACTV stations. It's easier to get around on foot, as the *vaporetti* principally serve the

Grand Canal, the outskirts, and the outer islands. The crisscross network of small canals is the province of delivery vessels, gondolas, and private boats.

A ticket valid for 1 hour of travel on a *vaporetto* is a steep 6.50€, while the 24-hour ticket is 18€. Most lines run every 10 to 15 minutes from 7am to midnight, and then hourly until morning. Most *vaporetto* docks (the only place you can buy tickets) have timetables posted.

Just three bridges spanned the Grand Canal until 2008, when a fourth was added connecting the train station with Piazzale Roma. To fill in the gaps, *traghetti* skiffs (oversize gondolas rowed by two standing *gondolieri*) cross the Grand Canal at eight intermediate points. You'll find a station at the end of any street named Calle del Traghetto on your map and indicated by a yellow sign with the black gondola symbol. The fare is .50€, which you hand to the gondolier when boarding.

BY WATER TAXI *Taxi acquei* (water taxis) charge high prices and aren't for visitors watching their euros. The meter starts at a hefty 15€ and clicks at 2€ per minute. Each bag over 50cm long (20 in.) costs 3€, plus there's a 10€ supplement for service from 10pm to 7am and a 10€ surcharge on Sundays and holidays (these last two charges, however, can't be applied simultaneously). If they have to come and get you, tack on another 8€. Those rates cover up to two people; if any more squeeze in, it's another 1.50€ per extra passenger (maximum 20 people).

BY GONDOLA If you come all the way to Venice and don't indulge in a gondola ride you might still be kicking yourself long after you have returned home. Yes, it's touristy; and yes, it's expensive; but only those with a heart of stone will be unmoved by the quintessential Venetian experience.

[FastFACTS] VENICE

Business Hours Standard hours for shops are Monday to Saturday 9am to 12:30pm and 3 to 7:30pm. In winter, shops are closed on Monday morning, while in summer it's usually Saturday afternoon. In Venice, just about everything is closed on Sunday, though tourist shops in the tourist spots such as the San Marco area are permitted to stay open during high season.

Consulates The **U.K. Consulate** in Venice is on the mainland in Mestre, at Piazzale Donatori di Sangue 2 (🕿 **041-505-5990**); it's open Monday to Friday 10am to 1pm. The **U.S., Australia, Canada,** and New Zealand have embassies in Rome.

Crime Be aware of petty crime like pickpocketing on the crowded *vaporetti*, particularly the tourist routes, where passengers are more intent on the passing scenery than on watching their bags. Venice's deserted back streets are virtually crime free, though occasional tales of theft have circulated. Generally speaking, Venice is one of Italy's safest cities.

Emergencies The best number to call in Italy with a **general emergency** is 🕿 **112;** this connects you to the military-trained **Carabinieri** who will transfer your call as needed. For the **police,** dial 🕿 **113;** for a medical emergency and to call an **ambulance,** the number is 🕿 **118;** for the **fire department,** call 🕿 **115.** All are free calls.

Hospitals The **Ospedale Civile Santi Giovanni e Paolo** (🕿 **041-529-4111**), on Campo Santi Giovanni e Paolo, has English-speaking staff and provides emergency service 24 hours a day (*vaporetto:* San Toma).

Internet **Sala Giochi SS Apostoli** (🕿 **041-099-3684**), which is open daily 9:30am to 11pm, is in Campo SS Apostoli, right at the base of the bridge that leads toward Rialto and San

Marco. It costs 3€ for 30 minutes and 5€ for an hour, though from 9:30 to 10:30am and 6 to 7pm you can surf for free, if you buy a drink. You can also pay for Wi-Fi access (1.50€ for half an hour and 2.50€ for an hour) and there are phones for making cheap international calls.

Luggage Storage
The *deposito bagagli* in the train station (☏ **041-785-531**) is located to the left of the station as you disembark from your train and

head toward the exit. It's open daily from 6am to 11:50pm and charges 4€ for each bag for the first 5 hours, and then .60€ for each additional hour through the 12th hour. Then it's .20€ an hour.

Pharmacies Venice's pharmacies take turns staying open all night. To find out which one is on call in your area, ask at your hotel or check the rotational duty signs posted outside all pharmacies.

Post Office Venice's **Posta Centrale** is at San Marco 5554, 30124 Venezia, on the San Marco side of the Rialto Bridge at Rialto Fontego dei Tedeschi (☏ **041-271-7111** or **041-528-5813;** *vaporetto:* Rialto). This office sells *francobolli* (stamps) at Window 12 Monday to Saturday 8:30am to 6:30pm (for parcels, 8:10am–1:30pm).

Telephones The area code for Venice is ☏ **041.**

Exploring Venice

Venice appears to have been created specifically to entertain its legions of callers. Ever since the body of St. Mark was smuggled out of Alexandria and entombed in the basilica, the city has been host to a never-ending stream of visitors—famous, infamous, and otherwise. Venice has perpetually captured the imagination of poets and artists. Wordsworth, Byron, and Shelley addressed poems to the city, and it has been written about or used as a setting by many contemporary writers.

Venice is notorious for changing and extending the opening hours of its museums and, to a lesser degree, its churches. Before you begin your exploration of Venice's sights, ask at the tourist office for the season's list of museum and church hours. During the peak months, you can enjoy extended museum hours—some places stay open until 7 or even 10pm. Unfortunately, these hours are not released until approximately Easter of every year. Even then, little is done to publicize the information, so you'll have to do your own research.

THE CANAL GRANDE (GRAND CANAL) ★★★

A leisurely cruise along the "Canalazzo" from Piazza San Marco to the Ferrovia (train station), or the reverse, is one of Venice's (and life's) must-do experiences. Hop on the **no. 1 *vaporetto*** in the late afternoon (try to get one of the coveted outdoor seats in the prow), when the weather-worn colors of the former homes of Venice's merchant elite are warmed by the soft light and reflected in the canal's rippling waters, and the busy traffic of delivery boats, *vaporetti,* and gondolas that fills the city's main thoroughfare has eased somewhat. The sheer number and opulence of the 200-odd *palazzi,* churches, and imposing Republican buildings dating from the 14th to the 18th centuries is enough to make any boat-going visitor's head swim. Many of the largest canal-side buildings are now converted into imposing international banks, government or university buildings, art galleries, and consulates. The *vaporetto*'s Ferrovia (train station) stop is the obvious place to start or conclude a Grand Canal tour (the other being Piazza San Marco), though if you go one stop farther up the canal away from San Marco to Piazzale Roma you get to pass under the Ponte della Costituzione.

THE BASILICA, DOGE'S PALACE & CAMPANILE

Piazza San Marco was the heart of Venice in the heyday of its glory as a seafaring republic. If you have only 1 day for Venice, you need not leave the square: Some of the city's major attractions, such as St. Mark's Basilica and the Doge's Palace, are centered here or nearby.

Thanks to Napoleon, the square was unified architecturally. The emperor added the Fabbrica Nuova facing the basilica, thus bridging the Old and New Procuratie on either side. Flanked with medieval-looking palaces, Sansovino's Library, elegant shops, and colonnades, the square is now finished—unlike Piazza della Signoria in Florence.

If Piazza San Marco is Europe's drawing room, then the piazza's satellite, **Piazzetta San Marco ★**, is Europe's antechamber. Hedged in by the Doge's Palace, Sansovino's Library, and a side of St. Mark's, the tiny square faces the Grand Canal. Two tall granite columns grace the square. A winged lion, representing St. Mark, surmounts one. A statue of a man taming a dragon, supposedly the dethroned patron saint Theodore, tops the other. Both columns came from the East in the 12th century.

Basilica di San Marco (St. Mark's Basilica) ★★★ CATHEDRAL Venice for centuries was Europe's principal gateway between the East and the West, so not surprisingly the architectural style for the sumptuous Byzantine Basilica di San Marco, replete with five mosquelike bulbed domes, was borrowed from Constantinople. Through the centuries (the original church was consecrated in the 9th century though much of what you see was constructed in the 11th century), wealthy Venetian merchants and politicians alike vied with one another in donating gifts to expand and embellish this church, the saint's final resting place and, with the adjacent Palazzo Ducale, a symbol of Venetian wealth and power. Exotic and mysterious, it is unlike any other Roman Catholic church.

For a closer look at many of the most remarkable ceiling mosaics and a better view of the Oriental carpetlike patterns of the pavement mosaics, pay the admission to go upstairs to the **Galleria** (the entrance to this and the Museo Marciano is in the atrium at the principal entrance); this was originally the women's gallery, or *matroneum*. It is also the only way to access the outside Loggia dei Cavalli.

A visit to the outdoor **Loggia dei Cavalli** is an unexpected highlight, providing a panoramic view of the piazza and what Napoleon called "the most beautiful salon in the world" upon his arrival in Venice in 1797. The 500-year-old **Torre dell'Orologio (Clock Tower)** stands to your right; to your left is the **Campanile (Bell Tower)** and, beyond, the glistening waters of the open lagoon and Palladio's **Chiesa di San Giorgio** on its own island. It is any amateur photographer's dream.

The church's greatest treasure is the magnificent 10th-century altarpiece known as the **Pala d'Oro (Golden Altarpiece),** a Gothic masterpiece encrusted with close to 2,000 precious gems and 255 enameled panels. Also worth a visit is the **Tesoro (Treasury),** with a collection of the crusaders' plunder from Constantinople and other icons and relics amassed by the church over the years. Much of the Venetian booty has been incorporated into the interior and exterior of the basilica in the form of marble, columns, capitals, and statuary.

In July and August (with much less certainty the rest of the year), church-affiliated volunteers give free tours Monday to Saturday, leaving four or five times daily (not all tours are in English), beginning at 10:30am; groups gather in the atrium, where you'll find posters with schedules.

San Marco, Piazza San Marco. www.basilicasanmarco.it. ☎ **041-522-5697.** Basilica, free admission; Museo Marciano (St. Mark's Museum, also called La Galleria, includes Loggia dei Cavalli) 4€, Pala d'Oro 2€, Tesoro (Treasury) 3€. Basilica, Tesoro, and Pala d'Oro summer Mon–Sat 9:45am–5pm, Sun 2–4pm; winter closes an hour earlier. Museo Marciano summer daily 9:45am–4:45pm. *Vaporetto:* San Marco.

Campanile di San Marco ★★★ ICON

An elevator will whisk you to the top of this 97m (318-ft.) bell tower where you get a breathtaking view of St. Mark's cupolas. It is the highest structure in the city, offering a pigeon's-eye view that includes the lagoon, its neighboring islands, and the red rooftops and church domes and bell towers of Venice—and, oddly, not a single canal. On a clear day, you may even see the outline of the distant snowcapped Dolomite Mountains.

San Marco, Piazza San Marco. ☎ **041-522-4064.** Admission 8€. Easter to June daily 9am–5pm; July–Sept daily 9am–9pm; Oct daily 9am–7pm; Nov–Easter daily 9:30am–3:45pm. *Vaporetto:* San Marco.

Palazzo Ducale & Ponte dei Sospiri (Ducal Palace & Bridge of Sighs) ★★★

PALACE   The pink-and-white marble Gothic–Renaissance Palazzo Ducale, residence and government center of the doges who ruled Venice for more than 1,000 years, stands between the Basilica di San Marco and St. Mark's Basin. A symbol of prosperity and power, it was destroyed by a succession of fires and was built and rebuilt in 1340 and 1424 in its present form. Forever being expanded, it slowly grew to be one of Italy's greatest civic structures. A 15th-century **Porta della Carta (Paper Gate),** the entrance adjacent to the basilica where the doges' official proclamations and decrees were posted, opens onto a splendid inner courtyard with a double row of Renaissance arches.

Ahead you'll see Jacopo Sansovino's enormous **Scala dei Giganti (Stairway of the Giants),** scene of the doges' lavish inaugurations and never used by mere mortals, which leads to the wood-paneled courts and elaborate meeting rooms of the interior. The walls and ceilings of the principal rooms were richly decorated by the Venetian masters, including Veronese, Titian, Carpaccio, and Tintoretto, to illustrate the history of the puissant Venetian Republic while at the same time impressing visiting diplomats and emissaries from the far-flung corners of the maritime republic with the uncontested prosperity and power it had attained.

One of the main sights to visit is the **Sala del Maggior Consiglio (Great Council Hall).** This enormous space is animated by Tintoretto's huge *Paradiso* at the far end of the hall above the doge's seat (the painter was in his 70s when he undertook the project with the help of his son). Measuring 7×23m (23×75 ft.), it is said to be the world's largest oil painting; together with Veronese's gorgeous *Il Trionfo di Venezia (The Triumph of Venice)* in the oval panel on the ceiling, it affirms the power emanating from the council sessions held here. Tintoretto also did the portraits of the 76 doges encircling the top of this chamber; note that the picture of the Doge Marin Falier, who was convicted of treason and beheaded in 1355, has been blacked out—Venice has never forgiven him.

Exit the Great Council Hall via the tiny doorway on the opposite side of Tintoretto's *Paradiso* to find the enclosed **Ponte dei Sospiri (Bridge of Sighs),** which connects the Ducal Palace with the grim **Palazzo delle Prigioni (Prisons).** The bridge took its current name only in the 19th century, when visiting northern European poets romantically envisioned the prisoners' final breath of resignation upon

VENICE discounts

The **Museum Pass** grants one admission to all the city-run museums over a 6-month period. That includes the museums of St. Mark's Square—Palazzo Ducale, Museo Correr, Museo Archeologico Nazionale, and the Biblioteca Nazionale Marciana—as well as the Museo di Palazzo Mocenigo (Costume Museum), the Ca' Rezzonico, the Ca' Pesaro, the Museo del Vetro (Glass Museum) on Murano, and the Museo del Merletto (Lace Museum) on Burano. The Museum Pass is available at any of the participating museums and costs 18€ for adults and 12€ for students under 29. There is also a **San Marco Museum Pass** that lets you into the museums of St. Mark's plus one of the other museums. It costs 14€ and 8€ for students.

The **Venice Card** is the Museum Pass on steroids, with a juiced-up price to match: 40€ and 30€ for those 6 to 29. It includes, among other things and in addition to everything the Museum Pass offers, discounts on temporary exhibits, more museums and (no kidding) two entrances to the municipal public toilets. You can pick one up at any of the Hellovenezia (www.hellovenezia.com) offices around town (there's one in the train station as well as at the Rialto and Santa Zaccaria *vaporetto* stops) or at the tourist information offices.

Venice, so delicate it cannot handle the hordes of visitors it receives every year, has been toying with the idea of charging admission to get into the very city itself. Slightly calmer heads seem to have prevailed, though, and instead we have **Venice Connected** (www.venice connected.it), which started in 2009 and gives discounts if you buy tickets through the website before arriving. You can get tickets for everything from transportation to museums, but you must do it for a particular day that is at least 4 days in the future. In return, the city gets, at least in theory, a better idea of how many people will be in town on a given day.

Also, for tourists between the ages of 14 and 29, there is the **Rolling Venice** card, which is something akin to the Venice Connected discounts for students. It's valid until the end of the year in which you buy it, costs just 4€, and entitles the bearer to significant (20%–30%) discounts at participating restaurants, and a similar discount on *traghetto* tickets. Holders of the Rolling Venice card also get discounts in museums, stores, language courses, hotels, and bars across the city (it comes with a thick booklet listing everywhere that you're entitled to get discounts). The card can be acquired at the same places as the Venice Card (see above).

viewing the outside world one last time before being locked in their fetid cells awaiting the quick justice of the Council of Ten.

San Marco, Piazza San Marco. (C) **041-271-5911.** Admission only on San Marco cumulative ticket (see "Venice Discounts," below). Daily 8:30am–7pm (Nov–Mar until 5pm). *Vaporetto:* San Marco.

DORSODURO
Collezione Peggy Guggenheim (Peggy Guggenheim Collection) ★★★
MUSEUM   The eccentric and eclectic American expatriate Peggy Guggenheim assembled this compilation of painting and sculpture, considered to be one of the most comprehensive and important collections of modern art in the world. She did an excellent job of it, with particular strengths in cubism, European abstraction,

surrealism, and abstract expressionism since about 1910. Max Ernst was one of her early favorites (she even married him), as was Jackson Pollock.

Among the major works here are Magritte's *Empire of Light,* Picasso's *La Baignade,* Kandinsky's *Landscape with Church (with Red Spot),* and Pollock's *Alchemy.* The museum, one of Venice's most-visited attractions, is also home to Ernst's disturbing *The Antipope* and *Attirement of the Bride,* Giacometti's unique figures, Brancusi's fluid sculptures, and numerous works by Braque, Dalí, Léger, Mondrian, Chagall, and Miró.

Dorsoduro 701 (on Calle San Cristoforo). www.guggenheim-venice.it. ⓒ **041-240-5411.** Admission 12€ adults, 10€ 65 and over and those who present a train ticket to Venice on one of Italy's fast trains (Frecciarossa, Frecciargento, or Frecciabianca) dated no more than 3 days previous, 7€ students 26 and under and children ages 10–18. Wed–Mon 10am–6pm. *Vaporetto:* Accademia (walk around left side of Accademia, take 1st left, and walk straight ahead following signs—you'll cross a canal and then walk alongside another, until turning left to the museum).

Galleria dell'Accademia (Academy Gallery) ★★★ ART MUSEUM   The glory that was Venice lives on in the Accademia, the definitive treasure house of Venetian painting and one of Europe's great museums. Exhibited chronologically from the 13th through the 18th centuries, the collection features no one hallmark masterpiece; rather, this is an outstanding and comprehensive showcase of works by all the great master painters of Venice, the largest such collection in the world.

It includes Paolo and Lorenzo Veneziano from the 14th century; Gentile and Giovanni Bellini (and Giovanni's brother-in-law Andrea Mantegna from Padua) and Vittore Carpaccio from the 15th century; Giorgione (whose *Tempest* is one of the gallery's most famous highlights), Tintoretto, Veronese (see his *Feast in the House of Levi* here), and Titian from the 16th century; and, from the 17th and 18th centuries, Canaletto, Piazzetta, Longhi, and Tiepolo, among others.

Most of all, the works open a window to the Venice of 500 years ago. Indeed, the canvases reveal how little Venice has changed over the centuries. Housed in a deconsecrated church and its adjoining *scuola,* the church's confraternity hall, it is Venice's principal picture gallery, and one of the most important in Italy. Because of fire regulations, admission is limited, and lines can be daunting (check for extended evening hours in peak months), but put up with the wait and don't miss it.

Dorsoduro, at foot of Accademia Bridge. www.gallerieaccademia.org. ⓒ **041-520-0345.** Admission 6.50€ adults, 3.25€ EU citizens 19–25 and free for EU citizens 18 and under, free for children 12 and under. Paying 1€ more a ticket, you can reserve tickets by phone or online, thereby saving yourself from potential lines. Daily 8:15am–7:15pm (Mon until 2pm). *Vaporetto:* Accademia.

CANNAREGIO

Ca' d'Oro (Galleria Giorgio Franchetti) ★★ ARCHITECTURE/MUSEUM   The 15th-century Ca' d'Oro is one of the best preserved and most impressive of the hundreds of *palazzi* lining the Grand Canal. After the Palazzo Ducale, it's the city's finest example of Venetian Gothic architecture. Its name, the Golden Palace, refers to the gilt-covered facade that faded long ago and is now pink and white. Inside, the beam ceilings and ornate trappings provide a backdrop for the collection of former owner Baron Franchetti, who bequeathed his home and artworks to the city during World War I.

The core collection, expanded over the years, now includes sculptures, furniture, 16th-century Flemish tapestries, an impressive collection of bronzes (12th–16th centuries), and a gallery whose most important canvases are Andrea Mantegna's *San*

Sebastiano and Titian's *Venus at the Mirror,* as well as lesser paintings by Tintoretto, Carpaccio, Van Dyck, Giorgione, and Jan Steen.

Cannaregio btw. 3931 and 3932 (on Calle Ca' d'Oro north of Rialto Bridge). www.cadoro.org. ✆ **041-520-0345.** Admission 6.50€, 6€ for ages 6–14 and students 30 and under. Mon 8:15am–2pm; Tues–Sun 8:15am–7:15pm. *Vaporetto:* Ca' d'Oro.

Where to Eat

Eating cheaply in Venice is not easy, though it's by no means impossible. So plan well and don't rely on the serendipity that may serve you in other cities. Bear in mind that, compared with Rome and other points south, Venice is a city of early meals: you should be seated by 7:30 to 8:30pm. Most kitchens close at 10 or 10:30pm, even though the restaurant may stay open until 11:30pm or midnight.

IN SAN MARCO

Antico Martini ★★ INTERNATIONAL/VENETIAN One of Venice's top restaurants started out in 1720 as a cafe, and the Baldi family, since 1921, has retained its airy, clubby atmosphere, especially at the outdoor tables in summertime. Venetian specialties such as *risotto di frutti di mare* and *fegato alla Veneziana* are prepared perfectly here, but the food, reputation, and location across from the opera house all come at a stiff price. If you want to dine as if you were at a classic Italian wedding, then try the tasting menu, which comes with both a fish and meat *secondo* broken up by a lemon sorbet. The price of the tasting menu might not even seem that expensive when you consider you probably won't have to dine for the next 24 hours.

Campo San Fantin (on the square occupied by La Fenice opera house). www.anticomartini.com. ✆ **041-522-4121.** Reservations required. Main courses 25€–45€; fixed-price tasting menu 115€. AE, DC, MC, V. Daily noon–midnight. *Vaporetto:* Santa Maria del Giglio (walk straight up from the *vaporetto* stop and turn right out of the *campo*, cross the bridge, follow the street that goes to the left and then the right before opening onto the broad Calle Larga XXII Marzo; turn left up Calle delle Veste into Campo San Fantin).

Rosticceria San Bartolomeo ★ ☺ DELI/ITALIAN With long hours and a central location, this refurbished old-timer is Venice's most popular *rosticceria*, so the continuous turnover guarantees fresh food. With a dozen pasta dishes and as many fish, seafood, and meat entrees, this place can satisfy most any culinary desire. Because the ready-made food is displayed under a glass counter, you (and the kids) will know exactly what you're ordering, and that is sure to help avoid long, little faces. There's no *coperto* (cover charge) if you take your meal standing up or seated at the stools in the aroma-filled ground-floor eating area. If you prefer to linger, head to the dining hall upstairs, though it costs more and, frankly, for the money you can do much better elsewhere than this institutional setting.

San Marco 5424 (on Calle della Bissa). ✆ **041-522-3569.** Main courses 10€–18€. Prices are about 20%–30% higher upstairs, and there is a discount if you order to take away. AE, MC, V. Daily 9:30am–10pm (Mon until 3:30pm). *Vaporetto:* Rialto (with bridge at your back on San Marco side of canal, walk straight ahead to Campo San Bartolomeo; take underpass slightly to your left marked SOTTOPORTEGO DELLA BISSA; you'll come across the *rosticceria* at 1st corner on your right; look for GISLON [its old name] above the entrance).

Trattoria da Fiore ★★ TRATTORIA/VENETIAN Don't confuse this laid-back trattoria with the expensive Osteria da Fiore near the Frari church. Start with the house specialty, the *pennette alla Fiore* for two (with olive oil, garlic, and seven in-season vegetables), and you may be happy to call it a night. Or try the *frittura mista,* over a dozen varieties of fresh fish and seafood. The Bar Fiore next door is a great place to snack or make a light lunch out of *cicchetti* (Wed–Mon 10:30am–10:30pm).

San Marco 3461 (on Calle delle Botteghe, off Campo Santo Stefano). ✆ **041-523-5310.** Reservations recommended. Main courses 14€–25€. AE, MC, V. Wed–Mon noon–3pm and 7–10pm. Closed 2 weeks in Jan and 2 weeks in Aug. *Vaporetto:* Accademia (cross bridge to San Marco side and walk straight ahead to Campo Santo Stefano; as you are about to exit the *campo* at northern end, take a left at Bar/Gelateria Paolin onto Calle delle Botteghe; also close to Sant'Angelo *vaporetto* stop).

IN CASTELLO

Al Covo ★★★ SEAFOOD/VENETIAN For years, this lovely restaurant has been deservedly popular with American food writers, putting it on the shortlist of every food-loving American tourist. There are nights when you hear nothing but English spoken here. But this slightly unpleasant fact has never compromised the dining at this warm and welcoming spot, where the preparation of superfresh fish and a wide selection of moderately priced wines is as commendable today—perhaps more so—as it was in its days of pre-trendiness. Much of the tourist-friendly atmosphere can be credited to Diane Rankin, the co-owner and dessert whiz who hails from Texas. She will eagerly talk you through a wondrous fish-studded menu. Her husband, Cesare Benelli, is known for his infallible talent in the kitchen. Together they share an admirable dedication to their charming gem of a restaurant—the quality of an evening here is tough to top in this town.

Castello 3968 (Campiello della Pescheria, east of Chiesa della Pietà in the Arsenale neighborhood). www.ristorantealcovo.com. ✆ **041-522-3812.** Reservations required. Main courses 28€–36€; menu with choice of any combination of 1 *primo,* 1 *secondo,* and 1 dessert 54€. MC, V. Fri–Tues 12:45–2pm and 7:30–11pm (closed Mon and Tues at lunch). Closed usually 1 week in Jan and 1 week in Aug. *Vaporetto:* Arsenale (walk a short way back in the direction of Piazza San Marco, crossing over the 1st bridge and taking the 2nd right onto Calle della Pescheria; otherwise, it is an enjoyable 20-min. stroll along the waterfront Riva degli Schiavoni from Piazza San Marco, past the Chiesa della Pietà; take the 3rd left after the Hotel Metropole).

Osteria alle Testiere ★★ ITALIAN/VENETIAN The limited seating for just 24 savvy (and lucky) patrons at butcher paper-covered tables, the relaxed young staff, and the upbeat tavernlike atmosphere belie the seriousness of this informal *osteria.* This is a guaranteed choice if you are a foodie curious to experience the increasingly interesting Venetian culinary scene without going broke. Start with the carefully chosen wine list; any of the 90 labels can be ordered by the half-bottle. The delicious homemade *gnocchetti ai calamaretti* (with baby squid) makes a frequent appearance, as does the traditional specialty *scampi alla busara,* in a "secret" recipe some of whose identifiable ingredients include tomato, cinnamon, and a dash of hot pepper. Cheese is not a fundamental part of Venetian cuisine, but Alle Testiere has an exceptional cheese platter.

Castello 5801 (on Calle del Mondo Novo off Salizada San Lio). www.osterialletestiere.it. ✆ **041-522-7220.** Reservations required for each of 2 seatings. Main courses 25€, and many types of fish sold by weight. MC, V. Mon–Sat 2 seatings at 7 and 9:15pm. *Vaporetto:* Equidistant from either the Rialto or San Marco stops. Find the store-lined Salizada San Lio (west of the Campo Santa Maria Formosa), and from there ask for the Calle del Mondo Novo).

IN CANNAREGIO

Ai Tre Spiedi ★★ ☺ VENETIAN Once upon a time, Venetians brought their visiting friends here to make a *bella figura* (good impression) without breaking the bank, and then swore them to secrecy. Well, the secret is out, and the prices have surely crept up, roughly coinciding with a change in ownership in 2006. Still, it is a very pleasant setting and the meal is just as appetizing as ever in this small, casually elegant trattoria with great, fresh fish. (When a restaurant is filled exclusively with French tourists, you know the cuisine can't be bad.) Try the traditional *bisato in umido con polenta* (braised eel), or, for a less daring but excellent choice, you can't go wrong with the grilled *orata* (John Dory). This is going to be one of the most reasonable choices for an authentic Venetian dinner of fresh fish; careful ordering needn't mean much of a splurge, either.

Cannaregio 5906 (on Salizada San Cazian). ℭ **041-520-8035.** Reservations not accepted. Main courses 11€–20€. AE, MC, V. Tues–Sat noon–3pm and 7–10pm; Sun 7–10pm. Closed July 20–Aug 10. *Vaporetto:* Rialto (on San Marco side of bridge, walk straight ahead to Campo San Bartolomeo and take a left, passing a post office, Coin department store, and the San Crisostomo church; cross 1st bridge after church, turn right at shoe store onto Salizada San Cazian).

Osteria L'Orto dei Mori ★★ VENETIAN   In this wonderful corner of Venice where the tourists thin out to the point that you can almost forget you are in a sort of Disneyland, you can sample a cuisine that perfectly blends Sicily and Venice while sitting at a table in a splendid, intimate *campo*. The simple, modern decor almost seems a gambit by the two owners, one Venetian and one Sicilian, to get you to concentrate on the food. For those in need of a break from pasta and rice, there are the scrumptious crepe filled with scampi, radicchio, and ricotta held together by a thin piece of bacon. The turbot cooked in foil is moist and light, a good thing as you must save space for dessert; the ricotta-and-pear mousse mixed with a hint of red wine will have you calculating if you can manage another meal here before you go back to the mainland.

Cannaregio 3386 (Fondamenta dei Mori at Campo dei Mori). www.osteriaortodeimori.com. ℭ **041-524-3677.** Reservations recommended. Main courses 18€–23€. AE, MC, V. Wed–Mon 12:30–3:30pm and 7–midnight (July–Aug closed for lunch Mon–Fri). *Vaporetto:* Madonna dell'Orto (from the *vaporetto* launch, walk through the *campo* to the canal and turn right; take the 1st bridge to your left, walk down the street and turn left at the canal onto Fondamenta dei Mori; go straight until you hit Campo dei Mori).

IN SAN POLO

Cantina do Mori ★★★ ✦ WINE BAR   Since 1462, this has been the local watering hole of choice in the market area; legend even pegs Casanova as a habitué. *Tramezzini* (sandwiches; the roast pork with radicchio is incredible) and *cicchetti* (side dishes) take center stage here at what is one of the best of the few remaining old-time *bacari*. For the *ombra*, you've got an embarrassment of choice. Venetians stop in to snack and socialize before and after meals, but if you don't mind standing (there are no tables), this is the perfect choice for a light lunch. Though the *cicchetti* are cheap at about 1.50€ a pop, you are going to need quite a few to fill up, so beware that the cost can add up quickly. The best value are the small, 1€ *tramezzini*; four of these plus two *cicchetti* and a glass of wine will leave you satisfied and only about 12€ will be missing from your wallet as you head out the door.

San Polo 429 (entrances on Calle Galiazza and Calle Do Mori). ℭ **041-522-5401.** *Tramezzini* and *cicchetti* 1€–1.50€ per piece. No credit cards. Mon–Sat 8:30am–8pm (Wed until 2pm; June–Aug closed daily 2–4:30pm). *Vaporetto:* Rialto (cross Rialto Bridge to San Polo side, walk to end of market stalls, turn left on Ruga Vecchia San Giovanni and then immediately right, and look for small wooden cantina sign on right).

Da Sandro ★ ☺ ITALIAN/PIZZERIA   Sandro offers dozens of varieties of pizza (his specialty), as well as a full trattoria menu of simple pastas and entrees that will appeal to the kids if they can't stomach another pizza (as unlikely as that is). If you're looking for a 15€ pizza-and-beer meal where you can sit outside, this is a reliably good spot on the main drag linking the Rialto to Campo San Polo. Although Italians consider it sacrilegious, you won't raise any eyebrows if you order a pasta and pizza and pass on the meat or fish: This city has seen it all. There's communal seating at a few wooden picnic tables placed outdoors, with just a handful of small tables stuffed into the two dining rooms—which, unusually, are on opposite sides of the street. You can also get a takeaway pizza and have it in nearby Campo San Polo.

San Polo 1473 (Campiello dei Meloni). © **041-523-4894.** Reservations not necessary. Main courses 11€–22€. AE, MC, V. Sat–Thurs 11:30am–11:30pm. *Vaporetto:* San Silvestro (with your back to Grand Canal, walk straight to store-lined Ruga Vecchia San Giovanni and take a left; head toward Campo San Polo until you come on Campiello dei Meloni).

IN SANTA CROCE

Al Bacco Felice ★★ 🍴 ITALIAN   This is the place in town if you are looking for great Italian standbys like *spaghetti alla carbonara* or *spaghetti all'amatriciana.* While not incredible, the food is very good, and you'll be hard pressed to find a better price-to-quality ratio in town. There is also fresh fish, including a mixed grill; and for those in need of a pizza, you won't be disappointed by the more than 50 choices. While Al Bacco Felice is just steps from the train station and Piazzale Roma, in this wonderfully quiet corner of town you will feel miles from the hustle and bustle.

Santa Croce 197E (on Corte dei Amai). © **041-528-7794.** Main courses 8€–20€. MC, V. Daily noon–3:30pm and 6:15–11pm. *Vaporetto:* Piazzale Roma (you can walk here in 10 min. from the train station; otherwise, from the Piazzale Roma *vaporetto* stop keep the Grand Canal on your left and head toward the train station, passing a park on your right; cross the small canal at the end of the park and immediately turn right onto Fondamenta Tolentini; when you get to Campo Tolentini turn left onto Corte dei Amai).

IN DORSODURO

Osteria Enoteca Ai Artisti ★★ VENETIAN   Adding a touch of Trentino and Naples to traditional Venetian cuisine, Chef Francesca, who shops herself for the raw materials that end up on your plate, turns out memorable dishes that are always fresh and never disappoint. The *tagliatelle* with zucchini flowers and small prawns reaches near perfection, as do most of the fish dishes, including the grilled seabass and the John Dory with tomatoes and pine nuts. In nice weather, ask for a seat outside on the lovely canal that's a 5-minute walk from the Accademia bridge.

Dorsoduro 1169A (on Fondamenta della Toletta). www.enotecaartisti.com. © **041-523-8944.** Reservations recommended. Main courses 19€–22€. AE, DC, MC, V. Mon–Sat noon–4pm and 7–10pm. *Vaporetto:* Accademia (walk to right around Accademia and take a right onto Calle Gambara; when this street ends at small Rio di San Trovaso, turn left onto Fondamenta Priuli; take the 1st bridge over the canal and onto a road that will quickly lead into Fondamenta della Toletta).

Trattoria ai Cugnai ★★ 🍴 VENETIAN   The unassuming storefront of this longtime favorite does little to announce that herein lies some of the neighborhood's best dining. The owners serve classic *cucina veneziana,* like the reliably good *spaghetti alle vongole veraci* (with clams) or *fegato alla veneziana* (liver). The homemade gnocchi and lasagna would meet most any Italian grandmother's approval (you won't go wrong with any of the menu's *fatta in casa* choices of daily homemade specialties, either). Equidistant from the Accademia and the Guggenheim, Ai Cugnai is the perfect place to recharge after an art overload.

Dorsoduro 857 (on Calle Nuova Sant'Agnese). © **041-528-9238.** Reservations not necessary. Main courses 14€–20€. AE, MC, V. Tues–Sun 12:30–3pm and 7–10:30pm. *Vaporetto:* Accademia (head east of bridge and Accademia in direction of Guggenheim Collection; restaurant will be on your right, off the straight street connecting the 2 museums).

Shopping

A mix of low-end trinket stores and middle-market-to-upscale boutiques line the narrow zigzagging **Mercerie** running north between Piazza San Marco and the Rialto Bridge. More expensive clothing and gift boutiques make for great window-shopping on **Calle Larga XXII Marzo,** the wide street that begins west of Piazza San Marco and wends its way to the expansive Campo Santo Stefano near the Accademia. The narrow **Frezzaria,** just west of Piazza San Marco and running north–south, offers a grab bag of bars, souvenir shops, and tiny clothing stores.

Venice is uniquely famous for local crafts that have been produced here for centuries and are hard to get elsewhere: the **glassware** from Murano, the **delicate lace** from Burano, and the *cartapesta* **(papier-mâché) Carnevale masks** you'll find in endless *botteghe* (shops), where you can watch artisans paint amid their wares.

Entertainment & Nightlife

Visit one of the tourist information centers for current English-language schedules of the month's special events. The monthly *Ospite di Venezia* is distributed free or online at **www.unospitedivenezia.it** and is extremely helpful but usually available only in the more expensive hotels. If you're looking for serious nocturnal action, you're in the wrong town. Your best bet is to sit in the moonlit Piazza San Marco and listen to the cafes' outdoor orchestras, with the illuminated basilica before you—the perfect opera set.

For just plain hanging out at most any time of day, popular spots that serve as meeting points include **Campo San Bartolomeo,** at the foot of the Rialto Bridge (though it is a zoo here in high season), and nearby **Campo San Luca.** In less busy times you'll see Venetians of all ages milling about engaged in animated conversation, particularly from 5pm until dinnertime. In late-night hours, for low prices and low pretension, the absolute best place to go is **Campo Santa Margherita,** a huge open *campo* about halfway between the train station and the Accademia bridge.

THE PERFORMING ARTS

Venice has a long and rich tradition of classical music, and there's always a concert going on somewhere. Several churches regularly host classical music concerts (with an emphasis on the baroque) by local and international artists. This was, after all, the home of Vivaldi. One of the more popular spots to hear the music of Vivaldi and his contemporaries is **Chiesa Santa Maria della Pietà** (www.vivaldichurch.it), between Campo Santo Stefano and the Accademia bridge. Concerts are held on weekends at 8:30pm; check the website for specific dates and tickets.

Teatro La Fenice ★★★ (San Marco 1965, on Campo San Fantin; www.teatro lafenice.it; ✆ **041-2424** or **041-786-511**) went up in flames in January 1996. Carpenters and artisans rebuilt the theater, which originally opened in 1836, according to archival designs, and in December 2003 La Fenice (which appropriately means "the Phoenix") arose from the ashes as Ricardo Muti conducted the Orchestra and Chorus of La Fenice in an inaugural concert in a completely renovated hall. Its performances now follow a regular schedule.

CAFES

For tourists and locals alike, Venetian nightlife mainly centers on the many cafe/bars in one of the world's most remarkable *piazze:* Piazza San Marco. It is also the most expensive and touristed place to linger over a Campari or anything else for that matter, but it's a splurge that should not be dismissed too readily. For those on a particularly tight budget, you can hang out near the cafes and listen to the sometimes quite surprisingly good live classical music (you won't be alone).

The nostalgic 18th-century **Caffè Florian ★★** (San Marco 56A–59A; ℂ **041-241-7286;** closed Wed in winter), on the south side of the piazza, is the most famous and most theatrical inside. Have a Bellini (prosecco and fresh peach nectar) at the bar for half what you'd pay at a table; alfresco seating is even more expensive when the band plays, but it's worth every cent. On the opposite side of the square at San Marco 133–134 is the old-world **Caffè Lavena** (ℂ **041-522-4070;** closed Tues in winter), and at no. 120 is **Caffè Quadri ★** (www.caffequadri.it; ℂ **041-522-2105;** closed Mon in winter), the first to introduce coffee to Venice, with a restaurant upstairs that sports Piazza San Marco views. At all spots, a cappuccino, tea, or Coca-Cola at a table will set you back about 8€. But no one will rush you, and if the sun is warm and the orchestras are playing, there's no more beautiful public open-air salon in the world.

Around the corner (no. 11) and in front of the pink-and-white marble Palazzo Ducale is the best deal, **Caffè Chioggia ★★★** (ℂ **041-528-5011;** closed Sun). Come here at midnight and watch the Moors strike the hour atop the Clock Tower from your outside table, while the quartet or pianist plays everything from quality jazz to pop.

If the weather is chilly or inclement, dress up and stroll into the landmark lobby of the Danieli hotel and **Bar Dandolo** (Castello 4196 on Riva degli Schiavoni, east of Piazza San Marco; ℂ **041-522-6480**). A pianist plays from 7 to 9pm and from 10pm to 12:30am. Drinks are far more expensive; ask for the price list before ordering.

BARS & DANCE CLUBS

Although Venice boasts an old and prominent university, dance clubs barely enjoy their 15 minutes of popularity before changing hands or closing down (some are open only in the summer months). Young Venetians tend to go to the Lido or mainland Mestre. Evenings are better spent lingering over a late dinner, having a pint in a *birrerie,* or nursing a glass of prosecco in one of Piazza San Marco's or Campo Santa Margherita's overpriced outdoor cafes. (***Note:*** Most bars are open Mon–Sat 8pm–midnight.)

The **Devil's Forest Pub ★**, San Marco 5185, on Calle Stagneri (www.devilsforest. com; ℂ **041-520-0623**), offers the outsider an authentic chance to take in the convivial atmosphere and find out where Venetians hang out—despite the fact that the atmosphere is more British than Italian. It's popular for lunch with the neighborhood merchants and shop owners, and ideal for relaxed socializing over a beer and a host of games like backgammon, chess, and Trivial Pursuit. It is open daily 10am to 1am.

The party spills well out from the plate-glass windows of **Bar Torino,** San Marco 459 (Campo San Luca; ℂ **041-522-3914**), a bar that has brought this square to life after dark with live jazz many nights, unusual beer from Lapland, and good panini. It's open Tuesday to Sunday 7am to 2am.

In 1931, famed restaurateur and hotelier Giuseppe Cipriani opened **Harry's Bar ★★** right at the San Marco–Vallaresso *vaporetto* stop, San Marco 1323 (Calle Vallaresso; ℂ **041-528-5777**). This has been a preferred retreat for everyone from Hemingway—when he didn't want a Bloody Mary, he mixed his own drink: 15 parts gin, 1 part dry vermouth—to Woody Allen. Harry's is most famous for inventing the Bellini, a mix of champagne and peach purée. Prices—for both drinks and the fancy cuisine—are rather extravagant.

Where to Stay

Few cities boast as long a high season as that of Venice, beginning with the Easter period. May, June, and September are the best months weather-wise and, therefore, the most crowded. July and August are hot (few of the one- and two-star hotels offer air-conditioning; when they do it usually costs extra). Like everything else, hotels are more expensive here than in any other Italian city, with no apparent upgrade in amenities.

IN SAN MARCO

Hotel Gritti Palace ★★★   Although there are arguably more chichi hotels along the *bacino* off St. Mark's Square, if you're going for luxury status and the classiest hotel on the Grand Canal, the Gritti has been *it* for decades. It was the 16th-century palace of Doge Andrea Gritti, whose portrait graces one of the antiques-filled lounges, and everyone who is anyone has stayed here over the centuries, from international royalty to captains of industry, literary giants, and rock stars. Rooms have inlaid antique furnishings, gilt mirrors, ornate built-in dressers hand-painted in 18th-century Venetian style, tented curtains over the tall windows, and real box-spring beds set into curtained nooks. Many rooms have connecting doors so that families can share. Three of the suites on the *piano nobile* overlook the Grand Canal from small stone balconies; three more suites overlook the *campo*. Three junior suites open onto a side canal, with walk-in closets and one-and-a-half bathrooms.

San Marco 2467 (Campo del Traghetto/Campo Santa Maria del Giglio), 30124 Venezia. www.hotelgrittipalacevenice.com. ✆ **041-794-611.** Fax 041-520-0942. 90 units. 950€ double deluxe; 1,295€ double with Grand Canal view; 2,300€ junior suite; 2,950€ suite with *campo* (square) view; 4,500€ presidential suite with canal view. AE, DC, MC, V. *Vaporetto:* Santa Maria del Giglio (the hotel is right there). **Amenities:** Restaurant; bar; concierge; room service; babysitting; nonsmoking rooms; Wi-Fi. *In room:* A/C, TV w/pay movies, VCR (in suites), fax (in suites), minibar, hair dryer.

Hotel Locanda Fiorita ★★ 🌡   This pretty little hotel is located in a red *palazzo* that retains the flair of its renovation in 18th-century Venetian style. The wisteria vine partially covering the facade is at its glorious best in May and June, but the Fiorita is appealing year-round, as much for its simply furnished rooms boasting new bathrooms as for its location on a *campiello* off the grand Campo Santo Stefano. Rooms 1 and 10 have little terraces beneath the wisteria pergola and overlook the *campiello*; they can't be guaranteed on reserving, so ask when you arrive. Right next door is **Bloom B&B** (www.bloom-venice.com; ✆ **340-149-8872**), the Fiorita's more modern and more expensive (250€ double) annex.

San Marco 3457a (on Campiello Novo), 30124 Venezia. www.locandafiorita.com. ✆ **041-523-4754.** Fax 041-522-8043. 10 units. 170€ double. Rates include continental breakfast. AE, DC, MC, V. *Vaporetto:* Sant'Angelo (walk to the tall brick building, and turn right around its side; cross a small bridge as you turn left down Calle del Pestrin; a bit farther down on your right is a small square 8 stairs above street level; hotel is in the *campiello*). **Amenities:** Concierge; room service; babysitting; nonsmoking rooms. *In room:* A/C, TV, hair dryer, Wi-Fi.

IN CASTELLO

Hotel Al Piave ★★ 🌡   The Puppin family's tasteful hotel is a steal: This level of attention, coupled with the sophisticated *buon gusto* in decor and spirit, is rare in this price category. You'll find orthopedic mattresses under ribbon candy-print or floral spreads, immaculate white-lace curtains, stained-glass windows, new bathrooms, and even (in a few rooms) tiny terraces. The family suites—with two bedrooms, minibars, and shared bathrooms—are particularly good deals, as are the small but stylishly rustic apartments with kitchenettes and washing machines (in the two smaller ones). Reserve far in advance.

Castello 4838–40 (on Ruga Giuffa), 30122 Venezia. www.hotelalpiave.com. ✆ **041-528-5174.** Fax 041-523-8512. 13 units. 125€–180€ double; 145€–235€ superior double; 190€–300€ family suite for 3; 260€–390€ family suite for 4 or 5. Rates include continental breakfast. AE, DC, MC, V. Closed Jan 7 to Carnevale. *Vaporetto:* Rialto (head southeast to the Campo Santa Maria Formosa, which is equidistant from Piazza San Marco and the Rialto Bridge; Ruga Giuffa is the road leaving the southeast corner of the *campo*). **Amenities:** Concierge; babysitting; nonsmoking rooms; Wi-Fi. *In room:* A/C, TV, fridge (family suite), minibar, hair dryer.

Hotel Metropole ★★ Vivaldi lived here from 1704 to 1738, when it was the chapter house of the La Pietà church next door, and he was its violin and concert master. The owner has tried to outfit his hotel as a Victorian-style home, packed with quirky collections of curios (fans, purses, bottle openers, crucifixes, cigarette cases), and its public salons are tucked with cozy bars and sitting niches. Accommodations vary widely in true Romantic style; you may find such details as Murano glass lamps and chandeliers, inlaid wood furnishings, and Romantic-era watercolors and prints. Rooms overlook the Bacino San Marco, the side canal where water taxis pull up, or the courtyard housing the lovely garden restaurant enlivened by nightly keyboard music. You get free car parking if you let them know you need it before 8pm the day you arrive.

Castello 4149 (Riva degli Schiavoni), 30122 Venezia. www.hotelmetropole.com. ✆ **041-520-5044.** Fax 041-522-3679. 67 units. 225–500€ double; 338–750€ junior suite; 383–1,150€ suite. Buffet breakfast 20€ (sometimes included). AE, DC, MC, V. *Vaporetto:* San Zaccaria (walk right along Riva degli Schiavoni over 2 footbridges; the hotel is next to La Pietà church). **Amenities:** Venetian/Italian restaurant; bar; concierge; room service; babysitting; nonsmoking rooms. *In room:* A/C, TV, minibar, hair dryer, Wi-Fi.

IN CANNAREGIO

Giardino dei Melograni ★★★ 🏠 In a building once used as a rest home for Venice's elderly Jews, the city's Jewish community offers you simple, spotless accommodations, a welcoming staff, and a perfect setting right on Campo del Ghetto Nuovo. Rooms in this nonsmoking, kosher building, where gentiles are just as warmly greeted as Jews, face either the *campo,* where you can watch the kids play in the afternoon, or a pleasant canal. The kosher breakfast is served in a room overlooking the *campo* and there is a private tree-shaded courtyard that invites relaxation; or if you are not the relaxing type and have to catch up on e-mail, the free Wi-Fi reaches out here. **Note:** For religious reasons, payment cannot be made on Saturday, so if that is your checkout day, be sure to settle accounts early.

Cannaregio 4587 (Campo del Ghetto Nuovo), 30131 Venezia. www.pardesrimonim.net. ✆/fax **041-822-6131.** 14 units. 120€–140€ standard double; 180€–210€ larger rooms that sleep 4. Rates include kosher breakfast. AE, MC, V. *Vaporetto:* Guglie or San Marcuola (from either of the 2 *vaporetto* stops, or if walking from the train station, locate the Ponte delle Guglie; walking away from the Grand Canal along the Fondamenta di Cannaregio, take the 2nd right at the corner where the Gam Gam restaurant is located; this is the entrance to the Calle del Ghetto Vecchio that leads to the Campo del Ghetto Nuovo). **Amenities:** Wi-Fi (free). *In room:* A/C, TV, minibar, hair dryer (on request).

Hotel Bernardi-Semenzato ★★★ 😊 🔥 Don't be misled by the weatherworn exterior of this *palazzo;* inside, there are exposed hand-hewn ceiling beams, air-conditioned rooms outfitted with antique-style headboard/spread sets, and bright modern bathrooms. The enthusiastic, young English-speaking owners, Maria Teresa and Leonardo Pepoli, offer three-star style at one-star rates. The *dépendance* (annex),

3 blocks away, offers you the chance to feel as if you've rented an aristocratic apartment, with parquet floors and Murano chandeliers—room no. 5 is on a corner with a beam ceiling and fireplace, no. 6 (a family-perfect two-room suite) looks out on the confluence of two canals, and no. 2 overlooks the lovely garden of a *palazzo* next door. The Pepolis also opened yet another annex nearby consisting of just four rooms, all done in Venetian style, including one large family suite (two guest rooms, one of which can sleep four, with a common bathroom).

Cannaregio 4366 (on Calle de l'Oca), 30121 Venezia. www.hotelbernardi.com. ✆ **041-522-7257.** Fax 041-522-2424. Hotel 18 units, 11 with private bathroom. Main annex 7 units (www.locandaleo. it). New annex 6 units. *Frommer's* readers take 8% off these official rates: 75€ double with shared bathroom; 110€ double with private bathroom; 95€ triple with shared bathroom; 125€ triple with private bathroom; 110€ quad with shared bathroom; 155€ quad with private bathroom. Rates include breakfast. AE, DC, MC, V. *Vaporetto:* Ca' d'Oro (walk straight ahead to Strada Nova, turn right toward Campo SS. Apostoli; in the *campo,* turn to your left and take the 1st side street on your left, which is Calle de l'Oca). **Amenities:** Concierge; room service; babysitting (on request); Wi-Fi. *In room:* A/C, TV, hair dryer.

Hotel San Geremia ★★ 🛅 If this gem of a two-star hotel had an elevator and was in San Marco, it would cost twice as much and still be worth it. Consider yourself lucky to get one of the tastefully renovated rooms—ideally, one of the seven overlooking the *campo* (better yet, one of three top-floor rooms with small terraces). The rooms have blond-wood paneling with built-in headboards and closets, or whitewashed walls with deep-green or burnished rattan headboards and matching chairs. The small bathrooms offer hair dryers and heated towel racks, and rooms with shared bathrooms have been renovated. Everything is overseen by an English-speaking staff and the owner/manager Claudio, who'll give you helpful tips and free passes to the casino.

Cannaregio 290A (on Campo San Geremia), 30121 Venezia. www.hotelsangeremia.com. ✆ **041-716-245.** Fax 041-524-2342. 20 units, 14 with private bathroom. 60€–75€ double with shared bathroom; 80€–100€ double with private bathroom. Rates do not include breakfast. AE, DC, MC, V. Closed the week of Christmas. *Vaporetto:* Ferrovia (exit the train station, turn left onto Lista di Spagna, and continue for a few minutes to Campo San Geremia). **Amenities:** Concierge; room service; babysitting. *In room:* TV, hair dryer, Wi-Fi.

IN SAN POLO

Ca' Angeli ★★★ ☺ 🛅 Brothers Giorgio and Matteo Wulten, from Dutch stock that came to Venice many generations ago, run this little gem right on the Grand Canal with a care and tenderness that is hard to find in Venice. The doubles are reasonably sized and most allow plenty of light to shine in on the paisley bedspreads and curtains. The bathrooms are modern, but everything else in this nonsmoking hotel is antique. Room 5 is the smallest double, but it more than makes up for it with a phenomenal terrace. Room 1, the junior suite, is the only one with a view of the Grand Canal, but everybody else can enjoy the view at breakfast while eating organic products in a wonderfully cheerful room with red carpets, chairs, and curtains that will get your day off in splendid fashion. The apartment sleeps five and is ideal for a family.

San Polo 1434 (on Calle del Traghetto della Madoneta), 30125 Venezia. www.caangeli.it. ✆ **041-523-2480.** Fax 041-241-7077. 7 units. 85€–195€ double; 95€–245€ small double with big terrace; 195€–395€ junior suite with Grand Canal view; 215€–395€ apartment for up to 5. Rates include buffet breakfast with certified organic products. MC, V. *Vaporetto:* San Silvestro (leaving the stop at your back go straight ahead to Campo Sant'Aponal; take the middle left, Calle di Mezzo, and follow it for a few minutes to Calle de Forno [if you end up in Campo San Polo you have gone too far], which turns into Calle del Traghetto della Madoneta; the building is at the end on your right). *In room:* A/C, TV, minibar, hair dryer, Wi-Fi.

Pensione Guerrato ★★★ ☺ 🍴 The Guerrato is as reliable and clean a budget hotel as you're likely to find at these rates. Brothers-in-law Roberto and Piero own this former *pensione* in a 13th-century convent and manage to keep it almost always booked (mostly with Americans). The firm mattresses, good modern bathrooms, and flea-market finds (hand-carved antique or Deco headboards and armoires) show their determination to run a top-notch budget hotel in pricey Venice. The Guerrato is in the Rialto's heart, so think of 7am noise before requesting a room overlooking the marketplace (with a peek down the block to the Grand Canal and Ca' d'Oro). Piero and Roberto have also renovated the building's top floor (great views; no elevator, 70 steps) to create five more rooms—with air-conditioning (for which you will pay 10€).

San Polo 240A (on Calle Drio or Dietro la Scimia, near the Rialto Market), 30125 Venezia. www. pensioneguerrato.it. ℂ **041-522-7131.** Fax 041-528-5927. 20 units. 95€ double with shared bathroom; 140€ double with private bathroom; 120€ triple with shared bathroom; 155€ triple with private bathroom; 185€ quad with private bathroom. Pay in cash, get 10% off. Rates include buffet breakfast. AE, MC, V. Closed Dec 22–26 and Jan 8–early Feb. *Vaporetto:* Rialto (from the north side of the Ponte Rialto, walk straight ahead through the stalls and market vendors until the corner with the UniCredit Banca; go 1 more short block and turn right; the hotel is halfway down the narrow street). **Amenities:** Concierge; babysitting; nonsmoking rooms; Wi-Fi. *In room:* A/C (top floor only), hair dryer.

IN SANTA CROCE

Hotel Ai Due Fanali ★★ 🎒 Ai Due Fanali's 16th-century altar-turned-reception-desk is an immediate clue to this hotel's impeccable taste and pursuit of aesthetic perfection. In a quiet square that's a 10-minute walk from the train station, Signora Marina Stae and her daughter Stefania have turned a part of the 14th-century *scuola* of the San Simeon Profeta church into this lovely hotel. Guest rooms boast headboards painted by local artisans, high-quality bed linens, chrome and gold bathroom fixtures, and good, fluffy towels. Breakfast is served on a panoramic terrace. Prices drop considerably from November 8 through March 30 with the exception of Christmas week and Carnevale. Ask about the four classy waterfront apartments with views (and kitchenettes), near Vivaldi's Church (La Pietà) east of Piazza San Marco, which sleep four to five people.

Santa Croce 946 (Campo San Simeon Profeta), 30125 Venezia. www.aiduefanali.com. ℂ **041-718-490.** Fax 041-718-344. 20 units. 95€–230€ double; 185€–380€ apt (minimum 3-day stay). Rates include breakfast, though not at apts. AE, MC, V. Closed most of Jan. *Vaporetto:* Ferrovia (cross the bridge over the Grand Canal; once you are to the other side of the canal, continue straight taking the 2nd left, which will have you cross a bridge before coming to Campo San Simeon Profeta). **Amenities** (at hotel only): Bar; concierge; room service. *In room:* A/C, TV, minibar, hair dryer, Wi-Fi.

IN DORSODURO

Pensione Accademia ★★ The outdoor landscaping (a flowering patio on the small Rio San Trovaso and a grassy formal rose garden behind) and interior details (original pavement, wood-beam and decoratively painted ceilings) of this *pensione* create the impression that you're a guest in an aristocratic Venetian home from another era. The 17th-century villa is fitted with period antiques in first-floor "superior" rooms, and the atmosphere is decidedly old-fashioned and elegant (Katharine Hepburn's character lived here in the 1955 classic *Summertime*). Formally and appropriately called the Villa Maravege (Villa of Wonders), it was built as a patrician villa in the 1600s and used as the Russian consulate until the 1930s. The best rooms overlook the breakfast garden, which is snuggled into the confluence of two canals. In good weather, breakfast is served in the front garden.

Dorsoduro 1058 (Fondamenta Bollani, west of the Accademia Bridge), 30123 Venezia. www.pensioneaccademia.it. ℂ **041-521-0188.** Fax 041-523-9152. 27 units. 135€–260€ double; 170€–320€ superior double; 200€–350€ junior suite. Rates include buffet breakfast. AE, DC, MC, V. *Vaporetto:* Accademia (step off the *vaporetto* and turn right down Calle Gambara, which doglegs 1st left and then right; it becomes Calle Corfu, which ends at a side canal; walk left for a few meters to cross over the bridge, and then head to the right back up toward the Grand Canal and the hotel). **Amenities:** Bar; concierge; babysitting; room service; Wi-Fi. *In room:* A/C, TV, minibar, hair dryer.

ON GIUDECCA

You don't stay on Giudecca—the only one of Venice's main islands you must access by boat—for the atmosphere, the sights, or the hotel scene (though it does host the official IYH Hostel, an utterly average hostel that's terribly inconvenient, especially with its curfew). You come for the Cipriani.

Hotel Cipriani ★★★ Long regarded as Venice's top hotel, the elegant Cipriani is set into a string of Renaissance-era buildings on 1.2 hectares (3 acres) at the tip of Giudecca. Although by staying here you give up a central location and easy access to central Venice's sights, shops, and restaurants (it's a 10-min. boat ride to Piazza San Marco), that's the whole point. The hotel was opened in 1959 by Giuseppe Cipriani, who founded Harry's Bar and Torcello's Locanda Cipriani, and was such a good buddy to Ernest Hemingway that he appeared in one of the master's novels (*Across the River and into the Trees*). Room decor varies greatly, from full-bore 18th-century Venetian to discreetly contemporary, but all are among Venice's most stylish accommodations. The 15th-century Palazzo Vendramin annex, connected via a garden, is for guests who desire more privacy (not unusual, given their celebrity guest list) and a private butler.

Giudecca 10, 30133 Venezia. www.hotelcipriani.com. ℂ **041-520-7744.** Fax 041-520-3930. 95 units. 930€ double with garden view; 1,100€ double with lagoon view; 1,350€ double with lagoon view and balcony; 2,150€ junior suite with lagoon view and balcony; 2,840€ suite with lagoon view. Rates include American breakfast. AE, DC, MC, V. Closed Nov 2–Apr 11. *Vaporetto:* Zitelle. **Amenities:** 3 restaurants; 3 bars; outdoor pool; golf course; indoor tennis courts; exercise room; spa; sauna; concierge; room service; babysitting. *In room:* A/C, TV/VCR (free movies), fax (on request), kitchenette (only in junior suites and suites of the Palazzo Vendramin), minibar, hair dryer, Wi-Fi.

ON THE LIDO

The Lido offers an entirely different Venice experience. The city is relatively close at hand, but you're really here to stay at an Italian beach resort and day-trip into the city for sightseeing. Although there are a few lower-end, moderately priced hotels here, they are entirely beside the point of the Lido and its jet-set reputation.

If you are looking for a more reasonable option—and one that's open year-round—check out the **Hotel Belvedere,** Piazzale Santa Maria Elisabetta 4 (www.belvedere-venezia.com; ℂ **041-526-0115;** fax 041-526-1486). It's right across from the *vaporetto* stop, has been in the same family for nearly 150 years, and sports a pretty good restaurant and a free beach cabana. It charges 80€ to 319€ for a double.

Hotel Excelsior ★★★ The Excelsior is the first place most celebs phone for film festival or Biennale accommodations. The hotel was the first successful attempt to turn the grassy wilds between the Lido's fishing villages into a bathing resort. Its core was built a century ago in a faux-Moorish style, with horseshoe arches peeking out all over; lots of huge, ornate salons and banquet halls; and a fountain-studded Arabian-style garden. As a purpose-built hotel, the rooms were cut quite large, with nice big bathrooms. Standard rooms keep the Moorish look going, with latticework doors, richly patterned wall fabrics, flamboyant bentwood headboards, and tented ceilings. Even if you don't have a sea view from your balcony, you might overlook the gorgeous garden or the private boat launch. A modern bar spills onto a large terrace overlooking the beach.

Lungarno Marconi 41, 30126 Venezia Lido. www.hotelexcelsiorvenezia.com. ℂ **041-526-0201.** Fax 041-526-7276. 197 units. 920€ double; 1,020€ double with sea or lagoon view; 2,100€ junior suite; 3,500€ sea-view suite. Rates include buffet breakfast. AE, DC, MC, V. Closed mid-Oct to mid-Mar. *Vaporetto:* Lido, then bus A. **Amenities:** 3 restaurants; 2 bars; outdoor pool; outdoor lighted tennis courts; exercise room; watersports equipment/rentals; bikes; children's program; concierge; executive-level rooms; room service; babysitting; special rates at nearby golf course; courtesy boat from airport; nonsmoking rooms. *In room:* A/C, TV w/pay movies, minibar, hair dryer, Wi-Fi.

Exploring Venice's Islands

Venice shares its lagoon with three other principal islands: Murano, Burano, and Torcello. Guided tours of the three are operated by a dozen agencies with docks on Riva degli Schiavoni/Piazzetta San Marco (all interchangeable). The 3- and 4-hour tours run 20€ to 35€, usually include a visit to a Murano glass factory (you can easily do that on your own, with less of a hard sell), and leave daily around 9:30am and 2:30pm (times change; check in advance).

You can also visit the islands on your own conveniently and easily using the *vaporetti*. Line nos. 5, 13, 18, 41, 42, A, B, and LN make the journey to Murano from Fondamente Nove (on the north side of Castello), and line LN continues on to Burano from where there is a boat that makes the short trip to Torcello. The islands are small and easy to navigate, but check the schedule for the next island-to-island departure (usually hourly) and your return so that you don't spend most of your day waiting for connections.

MURANO ★★

The island of **Murano** has long been famous throughout the world for the products of its glass factories, but there's little here in variety or prices that you won't find in Venice. A visit to the **Museo del Vetro (Museum of Glass),** Fondamenta Giustinian 8 (ℂ **041-739-586**), will put the island's centuries-old legacy into perspective and is recommended for those considering major buys. Hours are Thursday to Tuesday 10am to 6pm (Nov–Mar to 5pm), and admission is 6€ for adults and 3.50€ children 6 to 14 and students 30 and under, or free with the cumulative Museum Pass (see "Venice Discounts," on p. 695).

Dozens of *fornaci* (kilns) offer free shows of mouth-blown glassmaking almost invariably hitched to a hard-sell tour of the factory outlet. These retail showrooms of delicate glassware can be enlightening or boring, depending on your frame of mind. Almost all the places will ship their goods, but that often doubles the price.

Murano also has two worthy churches: **San Pietro Martire ★**, with its altarpieces by Tintoretto, Veronese, and Giovanni Bellini, and the ancient **Santa Maria e Donato ★**, with an intricate Byzantine exterior apse and a 6th-century pulpit and columns inside resting on a fantastic 12th-century inlaid floor.

BURANO ★★★

Lace is the claim to fame of tiny, colorful **Burano,** a craft kept alive for centuries by the wives of fishermen waiting for their husbands to return from sea. It's worth a trip if you have time to stroll the back streets of the island, whose canals are lined with the brightly colored simple homes of the Buranesi fishermen. The local government continues its attempt to keep its centuries-old lace legacy alive with subsidized classes.

Visit the **Museo del Merletto (Museum of Lace Making),** Piazza Galuppi (ℰ **041-730-034**), to understand why something so exquisite should not be left to fade into extinction. It's open Tuesday to Sunday 10am to 6pm (Nov–Mar to 5pm), and admission is 5€ adults and 3.50€ children 6 to 14 and students 29 and under, or free with the cumulative Museum Pass (see "Venice Discounts," on p. 695).

TORCELLO ★★

Nearby **Torcello** is perhaps the most charming of the islands. It boasts the oldest Venetian monument, the **Cattedrale di Torcello (Santa Maria Assunta) ★★★**, whose foundation dates from the 7th century (ℰ **041-270-2464**). It's famous for its outstanding 11th- to 12-century Byzantine mosaics—a *Madonna and Child* in the apse and *Last Judgment* on the west wall—rivaling those of Ravenna's and St. Mark's basilicas. The cathedral is open daily 10:30am to 6pm (Nov–Feb to 5pm), and admission is 5€. You can climb the bell tower for a panorama for 3€. Also of interest is the adjacent **11th-century church** dedicated to St. Fosca and a **small archaeological museum;** the church's hours are the same as the cathedral's, and the museum is open Tuesday to Sunday 10am to 5:30pm (Nov–Feb to 5pm). Museum admission is 3€. A combined ticket for all three sights is 8€.

Peaceful Torcello is uninhabited except for a handful of families and is a favorite picnic spot (you'll have to bring the food from Venice—there are no stores on the island; there is a bar/trattoria and one rather expensive restaurant, the Cipriani, of Hemingway fame, which is worth a splurge). Once the tour groups have left, it offers a very special moment of solitude and escape when St. Mark's bottleneck becomes oppressive.

THE LIDO & ITS BEACHES

Although a convenient 15-minute *vaporetto* ride away from San Marco, Venice's **Lido beaches** are not much to write home about. For bathing and sun-worshipping there are much nicer beaches nearby—in Jesolo, to the north, for example.

There are two beach areas at the Lido. **Bucintoro** is at the opposite end of Gran Viale Santa Maria Elisabetta (referred to as the Gran Viale) from the *vaporetto* station Santa Elisabetta. It's a 10-minute stroll; walk straight ahead along Gran Viale to reach the beach. **San Nicolò,** about 1.5km (1 mile) away, can be reached by bus B. You'll have to pay 1€ per person (standard procedure at Italy's beaches) for use of the cabins and umbrella rental. Alternatively, you can patronize the more crowded and noisier **public beach,** Zona A at the end of Gran Viale. Keep in mind that if you stay at any of the hotels on the Lido, most of them have some kind of agreement with the different *bagni* (beach establishments).

A number of bike-rental places along the Gran Viale rent bicycles for 5€ to 10€ an hour. *Vaporetto* line nos. 1, 2, 51, 52, and LN cross the lagoon to the Lido from the San Zaccaria–Danieli stop near San Marco.

THE NETHERLANDS

by George McDonald

13

L ike an Atlantis in reverse, Holland has emerged from the sea. Much of the country was once underwater. As the centuries rolled past, the land was recovered and stitched together through a combination of Dutch ingenuity and hard work. The result: a green-and-silver Mondrian of a country, with nearly half its land and two-thirds of its 16 million people located below sea level.

Amsterdam, the capital of the Netherlands, is as much a fixture on any well-conceived European tour as London, Paris, and Rome. From Amsterdam you can make easy day trips to historic Haarlem and the old IJssel-meer lakeside villages of Volendam and Marken. In addition, make time for ultra-contemporary Rotterdam; Delft, an ancient seat of Dutch royalty, hometown of Dutch master Vermeer, and famous for its blue-and-white porcelain; and for Leiden, known for its associations with the Pilgrim Fathers.

AMSTERDAM

Easygoing and prosperous, Amsterdam is the natural focus of a visit to the Netherlands. The graceful waterways, bridges, and canal-houses in the Dutch capital recall Holland's 17th-century *Gouden Eeuw* (Golden Age) as the head of a vast trading network and colonial empire, a time when wealthy merchants constructed gabled residences along the city's laid-out canals.

A delicious irony is that some of those placid old structures now host brothels, smoke shops, and extravagant nightlife. The city's inhabitants, heirs to a live-and-let-live attitude (based on pragmatism as much as a long history of tolerance), aim to control what they cannot effectively outlaw. They permit licensed prostitution in the Rosse Buurt (Red-Light District) and the sale of hashish and marijuana in designated "coffeeshops." Tolerance may have been a long-term tradition, but in recent years both the coffeeshops and the red-light haunts have been under pressure as the city works to improve its quality of life and reduce the perceived negative values in its portfolio.

Small entrepreneurs have revitalized old neighborhoods like the Jordaan, turning distinctive houses into offbeat stores and bustling cafes and restaurants. Meantime, the city government and entrepreneurs both

big and small have been redeveloping the old harbor waterfront along the IJ (pronounced *Aye*) waterway in a shiny, modern style that's a long way from the spirit of Old Amsterdam.

Between dips into Amsterdam's artistic and historical treasures, be sure to take time out to absorb the freewheeling spirit of Europe's most vibrant city.

Essentials

GETTING THERE

BY PLANE   The efficient, single-terminal **Amsterdam Airport Schiphol** (www. schiphol.nl; *⑦* **0900/0141** from inside Holland, or **31-20/794-0800** from outside Holland), is 13km (8 miles) southwest of the city center. You can get questions answered and make last-minute hotel reservations at the **Holland Tourist Information** desk in Arrivals Hall 2, open daily from 7am to 10pm.

From Schiphol Station, a floor below Schiphol Plaza, **trains** connect the airport with Amsterdam's Centraal Station. Frequency ranges from six trains an hour at peak times to one an hour at night. The one-way fare is 3.80€ in second class and 6.50€ in first class, and the ride takes 15 to 20 minutes.

Amsterdam

13

Amsterdam

THE NETHERLANDS

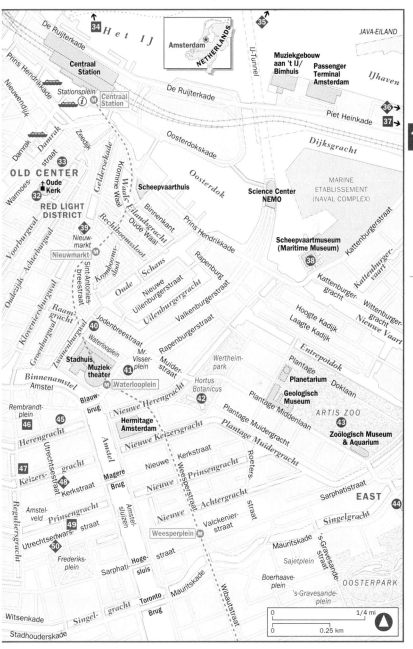

The **Connexxion Schiphol Hotel Shuttle** (www.airporthotelshuttle.nl; ⊘ **038/339-4741**) runs daily every 10 to 30 minutes from 6am to 9pm, between the airport and about 100 Amsterdam hotels. Buy tickets from the Connexxion desk inside Schiphol Plaza or onboard from the driver. The fare is 16€ one-way and 26€ round-trip; 8€ and 13€, respectively, for children ages 4 to 14; and free for children 3 and under. It takes only 15 minutes to the Hilton from the airport, but almost an hour to the NH Barbizon Palace.

You find **taxi** stands in front of Schiphol Plaza. All taxis from the airport are metered. Expect to pay around 35€ to the city center.

BY TRAIN   Whether you arrive by high-speed international train from Brussels, Paris, or Frankfurt, by ordinary international train, or by a train from elsewhere in the Netherlands, you'll likely find yourself deposited at **Amsterdam Centraal Station.** For information on trains (and other public transportation) in the Netherlands, go to www.9292.nl; or call ⊘ **0900/9292** for trains in Holland and ⊘ **0900/9296** for international trains.

The station, an 1889 Dutch neo-Renaissance architectural monument, is more or less of a confusing construction site. A new Metro station, to be the hub of the Noord–Zuid (North–South) line, due to enter service in 2017, is being dug out and fitted out at the front; a new main entrance for the rail station and all-around improved passenger facilities are being tackled at the same time; and the waterfront zone at the rear is being completely revamped.

When you emerge at the front of the station, you will find a taxi stand; a bunch of stops for trams (streetcars) and buses; the entrance to the Metro station; and docks for tour boats, the Canal Bus, the Museum Boat, and the Water Taxi. At the rear of the station are the new **CS IJsei** bus station and docks for the ferryboats that shuttle passengers across the city's fast-developing waterfront.

BY BUS   Buses from London, Paris, Brussels, and other cities, operated by **Eurolines** (www.eurolines.com; ⊘ **020/560-8788**), arrive at the bus station adjoining Amstel rail station (Metro: Amstel) in the south of the city.

BY CAR   Major European expressways to Amsterdam are E19 north from Brussels (2 hr. 20 min.) and from Paris (5 hr. 20 min.), and E30 west from Berlin (7 hr.). After you arrive in Amsterdam, do yourself a favor: Leave the car at a parking garage.

VISITOR INFORMATION

Tourist Office   The office of **Amsterdam Tourist Board/VVV Amsterdam** (www.iamsterdam.com; ⊘ **020/201-8800**) at Stationsplein 10 in front of Centraal Station, is open Monday to Saturday from 9am to 6pm (July–mid-Sept to 7pm), and Sunday from 9am to 5pm.

CITY LAYOUT

When you step out of Centraal Station's main entrance, you're facing south toward the center. From here the **Old City** is laid out along five concentric semicircular canals: **Singel, Herengracht, Keizersgracht, Prinsengracht,** and **Singelgracht** (*gracht* means "canal"). Along this necklace of manmade waterways, wealthy 17th-century merchants constructed their elegant homes, most of which are still standing. Within these canals are many smaller canals and connecting streets, radiating from the center.

Damrak, a heavily touristic street, leads from Centraal Station to the **Dam,** once the location of the original dam on the Amstel River that gave the city its name and now a large open square on which stands the Royal Palace. To the left is the (in) famous **Red-Light District,** where government-licensed prostitutes sit in their windows, waiting for customers. A block to the right of Damrak is **Nieuwendijk** (which becomes **Kalverstraat** when it crosses the Dam), a pedestrianized shopping street. If you follow Kalverstraat to the end, you'll be at **Muntplein** (*plein* means "square"), identified by the old Munttoren (Mint Tower). Cross Singel and continue in the same direction to reach **Rembrandtplein,** one of the main nightlife areas. Beyond Rembrandtplein, **Waterlooplein** hosts the Muziektheater and a great flea market.

At the heart of another important nightlife zone is **Leidseplein,** on Singelgracht. Leidseplein is at the end of Leidsestraat, a pedestrians-only shopping street (but watch out for the trams). **Museumplein**—where you find Amsterdam's three most famous museums: the Rijksmuseum, Van Gogh Museum, and Stedelijk Museum—is a short walk along Singelgracht from Leidseplein.

The **Jordaan,** an old neighborhood now speckled with inexpensive restaurants, unusual stores, and small galleries, lies between Prinsengracht, Brouwersgracht, Singelgracht, and Rozengracht. Turn right off Damrak at any point between Centraal Station and the Dam, and when you cross Prinsengracht, you're in the Jordaan.

Back at Centraal Station, at the rear and on both sides of the station, Amsterdam's **Waterfront** along the IJ channel has been opening up steadily in recent years and will continue to do so in future. New residential, business, cultural, nightlife, and entertainment assets have been developed, all of them marked either by the latest thing in modern architecture, or by old harbor installations that have been refurbished and put to new uses. Ferries, fast trams, and buses get you around these far-flung districts.

Neighborhoods in Brief

The **Centrum (Center)** This is the core area around the Dam and Centraal Station, and through the neighborhood known as De Wallen (the Walls), and is the oldest part of the city. It includes the Red Light District and is home to attractions such as the **Royal Palace,** the **Amsterdam Historical Museum, Madame Tussauds,** and canalboat piers. Centered on Centraal Station and stretching east and west along both banks of the IJ channel known as *Het IJ,* the fast-redeveloping **Waterfront** area includes the artificial islands, warehouses, and other installations of Amsterdam's old harbor (the new harbor is situated west of the city). Across the water from Centraal Station is **Amsterdam-Noord** (Amsterdam North).

The **Canal Belt, (known as the Grachtengordel in Dutch)** A semicircular "necklace" of man-made waterways—Herengracht, Keizersgracht, and Prinsengracht—this area was built around the old heart of town during the

17th century. It also takes in the 16th-century Singel canal. The city's most happening nightlife squares, **Leidseplein** and **Rembrandtplein,** intersect with the Canal Belt.

The **Jordaan** A nest of tightly packed streets and canals west of the Center, the Jordaan is filled with artists, students, and professionals, served by trendy eateries and a growing number of upscale boutiques and restaurants.

Museum District & Vondelpark Gracious and residential, the Museum District and Vondelpark area surrounds the three major museums: the **Rijksmuseum,** the **Van Gogh Museum,** and the **Stedelijk Museum,** which accounts for its Dutch name: *Museumbuurt.* There's also the **Concertgebouw** (a superb concert hall), many restaurants, Amsterdam's most elegant shopping streets (Pieter Cornelisz Hooftstraat and Van Baerlestraat), and the city's best-known park, Vondelpark itself.

GETTING AROUND

BY TRAM, BUS & METRO   Looking at a map of Amsterdam, you might think the city is too large to explore by foot. This isn't true: It's possible to see almost every important sight in the Old City on a 4-hour walk.

Public transportation begins around 6am; regular service ends around midnight. After that, there are infrequent night buses. Riding the blue–gray **trams** (streetcars) is the most convenient means of getting around; they're fast, cheap, and fun, and provide a great view of the sights. Out of 16 tram routes in the city, 10 begin and end at Centraal Station (and another one passes through). An extensive **bus** network complements the trams and reaches many points the trams don't cover.

The city's four **Metro** (subway) lines—50, 51, 53, and 54—don't serve most areas you'll likely want to visit. They're used mainly to get people to and from the suburbs, but from Centraal Station you can use Metro trains to reach both Nieuwmarkt and Waterlooplein in the central zone.

Maps showing the city's transit network are posted at most tram/bus shelters and all Metro stations. A free transit map is available from tourist information offices and from the **GVB Amsterdam Tickets & Info** office (www.gvb.nl; © **0900/9292**) on Stationsplein in front of Centraal Station. You can buy transit cards from this office, from sales points and ticket machines at Metro and train stations, and from some bus and tram drivers and conductors.

Most public transportation in the Netherlands uses an electronic card called the **OV-chipkaart** in place of old-style tickets. Three main types of OV-chipkaart are available: a reloadable "personal" card that can be used only by its pictured owner, who must have a Dutch mailing address; a reloadable "anonymous" card that can be used by anyone; and non-reloadable "throwaway" cards. The personal and anonymous cards, both valid for 5 years, cost 7.50€ and can be loaded and reloaded with up to 150€. Throwaway cards cost 2.70€ for one ride. A better bet for short-term visitors may be a 1-day or multiday card: 24 hours (7.50€), 48 hours (12€), 72 hours (16€), 96 hours (21€), 120 hours (25€), 144 hours (29€), 168 hours (31€). Reduced-rate cards are available for seniors and children. Electronic readers automatically deduct the correct fare; just hold your card up against the reader at both the start and the end of the ride.

Keep in mind that inspectors, sometimes undercover, may demand to see your card at any time. If you haven't paid the proper fare, you'll be fined 38€ on the spot plus the fare for the ride.

BY BIKE   Follow the Dutch example and pedal. A bike is one of the best ways of getting around in this flat city where too many cars clog the narrow streets. Sunday, when the city is quiet, is a good day to pedal through the parks and to practice riding on cobblestones and dealing with trams before venturing into a rush-hour fracas.

Warning: Watch out for unpredictable car drivers and tourists who are unused to dealing with bicycles en masse and always lock your bike and its front wheel to something fixed and solid—theft is common.

Rental rates typically begin around 12€ a day or 50€ a week, for a basic "city bike," and go up from there for a fancier pair of wheels; add 50% for theft insurance; a deposit of 50€ is generally required. You can rent bikes from Centraal Station when you arrive, and from many rental stores, all of which have similar rates. **MacBike** (www.macbike.nl; © **020/620-0985**) rents a range of bikes, including tandems and six-speed touring bikes; it has a branch at Centraal Station, Stationsplein 5 (tram: 1, 2, 4, 5, 9, 13, 16, 17, 24, 25, or 26); Waterlooplein 199 (tram: 4, 9, or 14), close to the Muziektheater; Weteringschans 2 (tram: 1, 2, 5, 7, or 10), at Leidseplein; and at Marnixstraat 220 (tram: 10, 13, 14, or 17), in the Jordaan. **Damstraat Rent-a-Bike** is at Damstraat 20–22 (www.rentabike.nl; ✆ **020/625-5029;** tram: 4, 9, 14, 16, 24, or 25), close to the Dam.

BY TAXI You can hail a cab from the street, or get one in front of any major hotel, and at Centraal Station, the Dam, Leidseplein, Rembrandtplein, and other strategically located taxi stands sprinkled around town. To phone for a cab from **Taxicentrale Amsterdam,** call ✆ **020/777-7777;** or reserve online at www.tca-amsterdam. nl. Taxis are metered. For up to four passengers, the fare, which includes a service charge, is 2.65€ from when the meter starts, and runs up at 1.95€ a kilometer (3.15€ a mile).

BY BOAT The **Museum Line** (www.lovers.nl; ✆ **020/530-5412**) operates tour boats near virtually all Amsterdam's museums and attractions. The boats leave from in front of Centraal Station every 30 to 45 minutes daily from 10am to 5pm. Tickets are available from the Lovers Canal Cruises counter near the dock. A day ticket is 16€ for adults, 8€ for children ages 4 to 12, and free for children 3 and under. Combination tickets are available that allow reduced admission to museums and attractions on the route.

The **Canal Bus** (www.canal.nl; ✆ **020/623-9886**) boats operate daily from 10am to around 6:30pm on three fixed routes—Green, Red, and Blue—that connect important museums and shopping and entertainment districts, with two buses an hour at peak times. A same-day ticket, including reduced admission to some museums and attractions, is 22€ for adults and 11€ for children ages 4 to 12, and free for children 3 and under; 24-hour and 48-hour tickets are available, for 24€ and 34€, respectively, for adults, and 12€ and 17€ for children.

BY CAR Don't drive in Amsterdam. The city is a jumble of one-way streets, narrow bridges, and trams and cyclists darting every which way. Tough measures are in place to make driving as difficult as possible. No-parking zones are rigorously enforced and the limited parking spaces are expensive.

Outside the city, driving is a different story and you may want to rent a car for an excursion outside Amsterdam. All the top international firms have desks at Schiphol Airport and one or more rental locations in the city: **Avis** (www.avis.nl; ✆ **088/284-7000); Budget** (www.budget.nl; ✆ **088/284-7500); Europcar** (www.europcar.nl; ✆ **0900/0540);** and **Hertz** (www.hertz.nl; ✆ **020/201-3512).** Rates begin at around 60€ a day for a no-frills, subcompact auto with a stick shift and unlimited mileage.

BY FOOT Walking is the best way to appreciate the city's relaxed rhythm. Be sure to wear comfortable walking shoes, as those charming cobbles get under your soles and on your nerves after a time; leave thin-soled shoes and boots at home.

[FastFACTS] AMSTERDAM

ATMs/Banks Some centrally located bank branches with **automated teller machines (ATMs)** are **ABN AMRO,** Dam 2 (tram: 4, 9, 14, 16, 24, or 25), Singel 548 (tram: 4, 9, 14, 16, 24, or 25), and Leidseplein 29 (tram: 1, 2, or 5); and **Rabobank,** Nieuwmarkt 20 (Metro: Nieuwmarkt).

Business Hours Banks are open Monday to Friday from 9am to 4 or 5pm, and some to 7pm on Thursday. Regular **shopping** hours are Monday from 10 or 11am to 6pm; Tuesday, Wednesday, and Friday from 9am to 6pm; Thursday from 9am to 9pm; and Saturday from

9am to 5pm. Some **stores** are open Sunday from noon to 5pm.

Currency The Netherlands currency is the **euro** (€). The best options for changing money are banks and the fair-dealing currency-exchange chain **GWK Travelex** (✆ **0900/0566**), which has multiple offices in the city, including those at Centraal Station; Damrak 1–5 (tram: 4, 9, 14, 16, 24, 25, or 26); and Leidseplein 31A (tram: 1, 2, 5, 7, or 10).

Dentists For urgent dental care, call the **Central Doctors Service** (✆ **020/ 592-3434**).

Doctors & Hospitals For urgent medical care, call the **Central Doctors Service** (✆ **020/592-3434**). Two hospitals with emergency services are **Onze-Lieve-Vrouwe Gasthuis,** Oosterpark 9 (www.olvg.nl; ✆ **020/599-9111;** tram: 3, 7, or 10), in Amsterdam Oost; and the giant **Academisch Medisch Centrum (AMC),** Meibergdreef 9 (www.amc.nl; ✆ **020/566-9111;** Metro: Holendrecht), in Amsterdam-Zuidoost.

Embassies & Consulates In Amsterdam, the **U.S. Consulate** is at Museumplein 19 (http:// amsterdam.usconsulate.gov; ✆ **020/575-5309;** tram: 3, 5, 12, or 16). The **U.K. Consulate** is at Koningslaan 44 (www.britain.nl; ✆ **020/676-4343;** tram: 2).

Embassies are in The Hague (Den Haag). The embassy of the **United States** is at Lange Voorhout

102 (http://thehague.us embassy.gov; ✆ **070/310-2209**). The embassy of **Canada** is at Sophialaan 7 (www.canada.nl; ✆ **070/311-1600**). The embassy of the **United Kingdom** is at Lange Voorhout 10 (www.britain.nl; ✆ **070/427-0427**). The embassy of **Ireland** is at Scheveningseweg 112 (www.irishembassy.nl; ✆ **070/363-0993**). The embassy of **Australia** is at Carnegielaan 4 (www. netherlands.embassy.gov. au; ✆ **070/310-8200**). The embassy of **New Zealand** is at Eisenhowerlaan 77N (www.nzembassy.com/ netherlands; ✆ **070/346-9324**).

Emergencies For police (*politie*) assistance, an ambulance (*ziekenwagen*), or the fire department (*brandweer*), call ✆ **112.**

Internet Access Many hotels, coffeehouses (note that this doesn't mean pot-selling "coffeeshops"), and other businesses offer Internet access, either Wi-Fi or with online computers.

Mail & Postage The office of **PostNL** at Singel 250, at the corner of Raadhuisstraat (✆ **076/527-2727;** tram: 13, 14, or 17), is open Monday to Friday 8am to 6:30pm and Saturday 9 to 5pm. Standard postage for a postcard or an ordinary letter up to 50 grams (1¾ oz.) to the U.K., Ireland, and other European countries is .85€ and 1.70€, respectively; to the U.S., Canada, Australia, New Zealand, and the rest of the world, it's .95€ and 1.90€.

Newspapers & Magazines The main British and Irish daily newspapers, and the *International Herald Tribune, Wall Street Journal Europe, USA Today, Time, Newsweek, U.S. News & World Report, Business Week, Fortune, The Economist,* and more are available at the **American Book Center** and **Waterstone's** (see "Shopping," later in this chapter. Newsstands at Schiphol Airport and Centraal Station stock a wide range of international publications.

Pharmacies For both prescription and nonprescription medicines, go to an *apotheek* (pharmacy). Regular pharmacy hours are Monday to Saturday 9am to 5:30pm. Try **Dam Apotheek,** Damstraat 2 (✆ **020/ 624-4331;** tram: 4, 9, 14, 16, 24, or 25). All pharmacies post locations of nearby all-night and Sunday pharmacies on the door.

Safety Random violent crime is not common in Amsterdam, though it does happen. Nonviolent crimes like pickpocketing and theft from cars are common; tourists in particular are targets. Muggings are rarer, but you still need to watch out in some places and circumstances, like strolling through the Red-Light District or along a deserted canalside at night.

Telephone The **country code** for the Netherlands is **31.** The **city code** for Amsterdam is **20;** use this code when you're calling from outside the Netherlands. If you're within the Netherlands but not in Amsterdam, use **020.** If you're calling within Amsterdam, simply leave off the code and dial only the regular seven-digit phone number. You can purchase SIM cards from any mobile phone store. Prices start out at 5€ (or maybe even free), plus the amount of credit you choose to purchase.

Exploring Amsterdam

Amsterdam has an almost bewildering embarrassment of riches. There are 160 canals to cruise, with a combined length of 76km (47 miles), spanned by 1,281 bridges; hundreds of narrow streets to wander; almost 8,000 historic buildings to see in the city center; more than 40 museums of all types to visit; diamond cutters and craftspeople to watch as they practice generations-old skills. The list is as long as every visitor's individual interests—and then some.

THE CENTER

Just steps from busy shopping streets, the **Begijnhof ★**, at Spui (www.begijnhof amsterdam.nl; tram: 1, 2, or 5), is the city's most tranquil spot. Hidden behind a plain facade is a 14th-century courtyard with a central garden ringed with restored almshouses formerly occupied by *begijns,* pious laywomen of the order of the Beguines. Most of the tiny 17th- and 18th-century buildings house elderly widows, and you should respect their privacy. In the southwest corner of the cloister, at no. 34, stands **Het Houten Huys,** one of Amsterdam's pair of surviving timber houses, built around 1425. The complex includes a clandestine Roman Catholic church and the former Beguine church from 1419, donated by the city's Protestant rulers to Scottish Presbyterian exiles in 1607, and now misnamed slightly as the Engelse Kerk (English Church). You may visit the Begijnhof daily from 9am to 5pm. Admission is free.

Amsterdam Museum ★★ MUSEUM Set in a huge 17th-century former orphanage, now housing exhibits covering nearly 700 years of the city's history, this fascinating museum gives you a better understanding of everything you'll see as you explore the city. Gallery by gallery, century by century, you learn how a fishing village became a major world trading center. The main focus is on the city's 17th-century Golden Age, a period when Amsterdam was the richest city in the world, and some of the most interesting exhibits are of the trades that made it rich. You can also view many famous paintings by Dutch masters. Next to the museum is the **Schuttersgalerij (Civic Guard Gallery),** a narrow chamber bedecked with 17th-century group portraits of militiamen. The hours are the same as for the museum, and admission is free.

Kalverstraat 92 and Sint-Luciënsteeg 27 (next to the Begijnhof). www.amsterdammuseum.nl. 📞 **020/523-1822.** Admission 10€ adults, 7.50€ students, 5€ children 5–18, free for children 4 and under. Daily 10am–5pm. Closed Jan 1, Apr 30, and Dec 25. Tram: 1, 2, 4, 5, 9, 14, 16, 24, or 25 to Spui.

 Passport to Amsterdam

One of the best discounts in town is the **I amsterdam City Card,** available at VVV tourist offices for 40€ for 1 day, 50€ for 2 days, and 60€ for 3 days. It affords free or discounted admission to around 40 museums and attractions (including the Rijksmuseum, Rembrandthuis, and Oude Kerk), a free canal cruise, and discounts on selected restaurants and stores. A free 1-, 2-, or 3-day public transportation card is included.

Koninklijk Paleis PALACE The 17th-century neoclassical Royal Palace was Amsterdam's town hall for 153 years. It was first used as a palace during Napoleon's rule in the early 19th century, when from 1806 to 1810 the French emperor's brother Louis Bonaparte was king of the Netherlands. You can visit its high-ceilinged Citizens' Hall, Burgomasters' Chambers, and Council Room, as well as the Vierschaar, a marble tribunal where in the 17th century death sentences were pronounced. Although this is the monarch's official palace, Queen Beatrix rarely uses it for more than occasional receptions or official ceremonies.

Dam. www.paleisamsterdam.nl. ✆ **020/620-4060.** Admission 7.50€ adults, 6.50€ seniors and students, 3.75€ children 5–18, free for children 4 and under. Generally July–Aug Tues–Sun 11am–5pm; Sept–June Tues–Sun noon–5pm (open days and hours vary; check details on website before going). Closed during periods of royal residence and state receptions. Tram: 1, 2, 4, 5, 9, 13, 14, 16, 17, 24, or 25 to the Dam.

Nieuwe Kerk CHURCH This church across from the Royal Palace is the "New Church" in name only. Construction on this late-Gothic structure began about 1400, but much of the interior, including the organ, dates from the 17th century. Since 1815, all Dutch kings and queens have been crowned here. Today the church is used primarily as a cultural center where special art exhibits are held. Regular performances on the church's huge organ are held in summer.

Dam (next to the Royal Palace). www.nieuwekerk.nl. ✆ **020/638-6909.** Admission varies with different events; free when there's no exhibit. Daily 10am–6pm (Thurs to 10pm during exhibits). Tram: 1, 2, 4, 5, 9, 13, 14, 16, 17, 24, or 25 to the Dam.

Ons' Lieve Heer op Solder MUSEUM Just after the Protestant Reformation, Amsterdam's Roman Catholics fell into disfavor. Forced to worship in secret, they devised ingenious ways of gathering for Sunday services. In an otherwise ordinary-looking 17th-century canal-house in the middle of the Red-Light District is "Our Lord in the Attic," the most amazing of these clandestine churches. Built in the 1660s by a wealthy Catholic merchant, the three houses making up this museum were designed specifically to house a church. Today they're furnished much as they would have been in the 18th century. Nothing prepares you for the minicathedral you come upon when you climb the last flight of stairs into the attic. A large baroque altar, religious statuary, pews to seat 150, and an 18th-century organ complete this miniature church.

Oudezijds Voorburgwal 40 (near the Oude Kerk). www.opsolder.nl. ✆ **020/624-6604.** Admission 8€ adults, 4€ students and children 6–18, free for children 5 and under. Mon–Sat 10am–5pm; Sun and holidays 1–5pm. Closed Jan 1 and Apr 30. Tram: 1, 2, 4, 5, 9, 13, 16, 17, 24, 25, or 26 to Centraal Station.

Oude Kerk ★ CHURCH The Gothic Old Church from the 13th century is the city's oldest. It stands in the middle of the Red-Light District, surrounded by old almshouses turned into prostitutes' rooms. Inside are monumental tombs, including that of Rembrandt's wife, Saskia van Uylenburg, and handsome stained-glass windows. The organ, built in 1724, is played regularly in summer; many connoisseurs believe it has the best tone of any organ in the world. You can climb the 70m (230-ft.) tower for an excellent view of old Amsterdam.

Oudekerksplein 23 (at Oudezijds Voorburgwal). www.oudekerk.nl. ✆ **020/625-8284.** Admission: Church 8€ adults; 6€ seniors, students, and children 5–13; free for children 4 and under; tower 7€. Mon–Sat 10:30am–5:30pm; Sun 1–5:30pm. Closed Apr 30; tower Apr–Sept Thurs–Fri 1–5pm; tours every 30 min. Metro: Nieuwmarkt.

Ferry Tale

Free ferries across the IJ waterway connect the city center with Amsterdam-Noord (North). The short crossings for foot passengers and bikes on two of these ferries—the *Buiksloterwegveer* and the *IJpleinveer*—make ideal mini-cruises for the cash-strapped and provide a good view of the harbor. Ferries depart from the Waterplein-West dock behind Centraal Station on De Ruyterkade every 10 to 15 minutes round-the-clock to Buiksloterweg, and from around 6:30am to midnight to IJplein.

THE WATERFRONT

Amsterdam's waterfront along the narrow ship channel known as Het IJ hosts the city's biggest redevelopment project, touted as "a new life on the water." In the **Oosterdok (Eastern Harbor),** Java-Eiland, KNSM-Eiland, and other artificial islands have been cleared of most of their warehouses and other harbor installations. Modern housing and infrastructure take their place. A visit here is a good way to see how Amsterdam sees its future, away from its Golden Age heart.

A fast-tram service (line 26) connects Centraal Station with the Oosterdok. Among its stops are ones for the Muziekgebouw aan 't IJ and Bimhuis concert halls, the Passenger Terminal Amsterdam cruise-liner dock, and the Eastern Islands' new residential, shopping, and entertainment zones. The service goes out as far as the new IJburg suburb, constructed on an artificial island in the IJsselmeer's southern reaches.

In recent years, some of the redevelopment focus has switched to the **Westerdok (Western Harbor),** west of Centraal Station.

Scheepvaartmuseum (Maritime Museum) ★★ MUSEUM   A bonanza for anyone who loves the sea, this museum is housed in the recently refurbished former arsenal of the Amsterdam Admiralty dating from 1656 and appropriately overlooks the busy harbor. Around the inner courtyard are 25 rooms with exhibits: ship models, charts, instruments, maps, prints, and paintings—a chronicle of Holland's abiding ties to the sea through commerce, fishing, yachting, navigational development, and war. Old maps include a 15th-century Ptolemaic atlas and a sumptuously bound edition of the *Great Atlas* by Jan Blaeu, master cartographer of Holland's Golden Age.

A full-size replica of the **Dutch East India Company's *Amsterdam,*** which in 1749 foundered off Hastings on her maiden voyage to the fabled Spice Islands (Indonesia), is moored at the museum's wharf. Other ships include a steam icebreaker, a motor lifeboat, and a herring lugger. You can reach this museum by taking a 20-minute walk from Centraal Station along the historical waterfront, the Nautisch Kwartier (Nautical Quarter).

Kattenburgerplein 1 (in the Eastern Dock). www.scheepvaartmuseum.nl. ℗ **020/523-2222.** Admission 15€ adults; 7.50€ seniors, students, and children 5–17; free for children 4 and under. Daily 9am–5pm. Closed Jan 1, April 30, and Dec 25. Bus: 22, 42, or 43 to Kattenburgerplein.

THE CANAL BELT

Anne Frankhuis ★★ HISTORIC SITE   A teenage Jewish girl, Anne Frank wrote her famous diary here while she and seven other Jewish refugees hid from the Nazis in a secret annex at the back of this large canal-house. Anne, the youngest Frank daughter, had been given a diary for her 13th birthday in 1942. With the eyes of a child and the writing skills of a girl who hoped one day to be a writer, she chronicled the almost silent life in hiding of the *onderduikers* ("divers," or hiders) and her personal growth as a young woman. Anne achieved her dream of being a famous writer: *The Diary of Anne Frank* (also titled *The Diary of a Young Girl*) has been translated into more than 60 languages.

The cramped, gloomy hiding place kept them safe for more than 2 years until they were betrayed in August 1944. Anne died of typhus in March 1945 at Bergen-Belsen; six of the others also died in concentration camps. Although the rooms contain no furniture and are as bare as they were when Anne's father, Otto, the only survivor, returned, the exhibits, including a year-by-year chronology of Anne's life, fill in the missing details. This lack of distraction allows you to project yourself into Anne's claustrophobic, fear-filled world.

Prinsengracht 263–267 (at Westermarkt). www.annefrank.org. (✆) **020/556-7100** or 020/556-7105 for recorded information. Admission 9€ adults, 4.50€ children 10–17, free for children 9 and under. Mid-Mar–June and 1st 2 weeks of Sept Sun–Fri 9am–9pm, Sat 9am–10pm; July–Aug daily 9am–10pm; mid-Sept–mid-Mar daily 9am–7pm; variations are listed on the website. Closed Yom Kippur. Tram: 13, 14, or 17 to Westermarkt.

Museum Van Loon MUSEUM   This magnificent patrician house from 1672 was owned by the van Loon family from 1884 to 1945. On its walls hang more than 80 family portraits, including those of Willem van Loon, one of the founders of the Dutch United East India Company; Nicolaas Ruychaver, who liberated Amsterdam from the Spanish in 1578; and another Willem van Loon, who became mayor in 1686. A marble staircase with an ornately curlicued brass balustrade leads up through the house, connecting restored period rooms that are filled with richly decorated paneling, stuccowork, mirrors, fireplaces, furnishings, porcelain, chandeliers, rugs, and more. In the garden are carefully tended hedges and a coach house modeled on a Greek temple.

Keizersgracht 672 (near Vijzelstraat). www.museumvanloon.nl. (✆) **020/624-5255.** Admission 8€ adults, 6€ students, 4€ children 6–18, free for children 5 and under. Wed–Mon 11am–5pm. Closed Jan 1, Apr 30, and Dec 25. Tram: 16, 24, or 25 to Keizersgracht.

Museum Willet-Holthuysen MUSEUM   For a glimpse of what life was like for Amsterdam's wealthy merchants during the 18th and 19th centuries, pay a visit to this elegant canal-house museum. Each room is furnished much as it would have been 200 years ago. In addition, there's an extensive collection of ceramics, china, glass, and silver. Of particular interest are the large old kitchen and the formal garden in back.

Herengracht 605 (at the Amstel). www.willetholthuysen.nl. (✆) **020/523-1822.** Admission 8€ adults, 6€ students, 4€ children 6–18, free for children 5 and under. Mon–Fri 10am–5pm; Sat–Sun and holidays 11am–5pm. Closed Jan 1, Apr 30, and Dec 25. Tram: 4, 9, or 14 to Rembrandtplein.

Gay Remembrance

The **Homomonument** at Westermarkt (tram: 13, 14, or 17), a sculpture group of three pink granite triangles near the Anne Frankhuis, is dedicated to the memory of gays and lesbians killed during World War II, or as a result of oppression and persecution because of their sexuality. People also visit to remember those who have died of AIDS.

Westerkerk ★ CHURCH   Built between 1620 and 1630, the Western Church is a masterpiece of Dutch Renaissance style. At the top of the 84m (276-ft.) tower—the highest, most beautiful tower in Amsterdam—is a giant replica of the imperial crown of Maximilian of Austria. Somewhere in this church (no one knows where) is Rembrandt's grave. During summer, regular organ concerts are played on a 300-year-old instrument. You can climb the tower or go by elevator to the top for a great view.

Westermarkt. www.westerkerk.nl. ✆ **020/624-7766.** Free admission to the church; tower 6€. Church Mon–Sat 11am–3pm; tower Apr–Oct Mon–Sat 10am–6pm (to 8pm July–Aug); tours every 30 min. Tram: 13, 14, or 17 to Westermarkt.

AROUND REMBRANDTPLEIN

Joods Historisch Museum ★ MUSEUM   Housed in the four restored 17th- and 18th-century synagogues of the Ashkenazi Synagogue complex, the Jewish Historical Museum tells the intertwining stories of Jewish identity, religion, culture, and history of the Jewish Dutch community. Inside are objects, photographs, artworks, and interactive displays. Jewish religious artifacts are a major focus. An exhibit covers the persecution of Jews in the Netherlands and throughout Europe under Hitler. The synagogues stand at the heart of a neighborhood that was the Jewish quarter for 300 years until the Nazi occupation during World War II emptied the city of its Jewish population. The oldest of the four, built in 1670, is the oldest public synagogue in western Europe; the newest dates from 1752.

Nieuwe Amstelstraat 1 (at Waterlooplein). www.jhm.nl. ✆ **020/531-0380.** Admission 12€ adults, 6€ students and children 13–17, 3€ children 6–12, free for children 5 and under. Daily 11am–5pm. Closed Jewish New Year and following day, and Yom Kippur. Metro: Waterlooplein. Tram: 9 or 14 to Waterlooplein.

Museum Het Rembrandthuis ★★ MUSEUM   When Rembrandt moved into this three-story house in 1639, he was already a well-established wealthy artist. However, the cost of buying and furnishing the house led to his financial downfall in 1656. The museum houses a nearly complete collection of Rembrandt's etchings, and the artist's printing press. Of the 300 prints he made, 250 are here, with around half hanging on the walls at any one time. Rembrandt's prints show amazing detail, and you can see his use of shadow and light for dramatic effect. Wizened patriarchs, emaciated beggars, children at play, Rembrandt himself in numerous self-portraits, and Dutch landscapes are the subjects you'll long remember after a visit here. Temporary exhibits are mounted in an adjacent house that belonged to Rembrandt's wife, Saskia.

Jodenbreestraat 4 (at Waterlooplein). www.rembrandthuis.nl. ✆ **020/520-0400.** Admission 10€ adults, 7€ students, 3€ children 6–17, free for children 5 and under. Daily 10am–5pm. Closed Jan 1, Apr 30, and Dec 25. Metro: Waterlooplein. Tram: 9 or 14 to Waterlooplein.

THE JORDAAN

Few traditional sights clutter the old Jordaan district that lies just west of the Canal Belt's northern reaches, yet 800 of its buildings are protected monuments. But the area does provide an authentic taste of Old Amsterdam. The neighborhood of tightly packed houses and narrow streets and canals was built in the 17th century for craftsmen, tradesmen, and artists. Its name may have come from the French *jardin* (garden), from Protestant French Huguenot refugees who settled here in the late 17th century. Indeed, many streets and canals are named for flowers, trees, and plants. Some of today's streets used to be canals until they were filled in during the 19th century. The neighborhood's modest nature persists even though renewal and gentrification have brought in an influx of offbeat boutiques, quirky stores, cutting-edge art galleries, and trendy restaurants.

THE MUSEUM DISTRICT

When the sun shines in Amsterdam, people head for the parks. The most popular and conveniently located of Amsterdam's 30 parks is the 49-hectare (121-acre) **Vondelpark ★★** (tram: 1, 2, 3, 5, 7, 10, or 12), home to skateboarding, Frisbee flipping, in-line skating, model-boat sailing, soccer, softball, basketball, open-air concerts and theater, smooching in the undergrowth, parties, picnics, crafts stalls, topless sunbathing—you name it. Its lakes, ponds, and streams are surrounded by meadows, trees, and colorful flowers. Vondelpark lies generally southwest of Leidseplein and has entrances all around; the most popular is adjacent to Leidseplein, on Stadhouderskade. This park, open daily from 8am to sunset, is extremely popular in summer with young people from all over the world; admission is free.

Rijksmuseum ★★★ MUSEUM Most of this museum at Museumplein is closed for renovations until a date in 2013 that at the time of writing this guide had not been announced. The majority of the collection will be "invisible" to visitors until then. However, key paintings and other stellar works from the magnificent 17th-century Dutch Golden Age collections can be viewed in the museum's Philips Wing, under the head *The Masterpieces.* The Rijksmuseum contains the world's largest collection of paintings by the Dutch masters, including the most famous of all: *The Shooting Company of Captain Frans Banning Cocq and Lieutenant Willem van Ruytenburch* (1642), better known as *The Night Watch,* by Rembrandt. In the scene it depicts, gaily uniformed city militiamen are checking their weapons and accouterments. Works by Jacob van Ruisdael, Maarten van Heemskerck, Frans Hals, Paulus Potter, Jan Steen, Jan Vermeer, Pieter de Hooch, Gerard ter Borch, and Gerard Dou also are displayed. The impressive range includes individual portraits, guild paintings, landscapes, seascapes, domestic scenes, medieval religious subjects, allegories, and the nearly photographic Dutch still lifes.

Jan Luijkenstraat 1 (at Museumplein). www.rijksmuseum.nl. ℂ **020/647-7000.** Admission 14€ adults, free for children 18 and under. Daily 9am–6pm. Closed Jan 1. Tram: 2 or 5 to Hobbemastraat.

Stedelijk Museum ★ ART MUSEUM This is the place to see works by such Dutch painters as Karel Appel, Willem de Kooning, and Piet Mondrian, alongside works by the French artists Chagall, Cézanne, Picasso, Renoir, Monet, and Manet and by the Americans Calder, Oldenburg, Rosenquist, and Warhol. The Stedelijk centers its collection on the De Stijl, Cobra, post-Cobra, Nouveau Réalisme, pop art, color-field painting, zero, minimalist, and conceptual schools of modern art. **Note:** Amsterdam's modern-art Municipal Museum was closed for renovation and expansion at the time of writing, and reopened on September 23, 2012. New opening times and admission charges are at www.stedelijk.nl/en/visit-us/hours-and-admission.

Museumplein 10 (at Paulus Potterstraat). www.stedelijk.nl. ℂ **020/573-2911.** Admission 9€ adults; 4.50€ seniors, students, and children 7–16; free for children 6 and under. Daily 10am–6pm. Closed Jan 1. Tram: 2, 3, 5, 12, 16, or 24 to Museumplein.

Van Gogh Museum ★★★ ART MUSEUM Anyone who has responded to van Gogh's vibrant colors and vivid landscapes should be moved when walking through the rooms of this rather stark contemporary building. The museum displays, in chronological order, more than 200 van Gogh paintings. As you move through the rooms, the canvases reflect the artist's changing environment and much of his inner life, so that gradually van Gogh himself becomes almost a tangible presence standing at your elbow. By the time you reach the vaguely threatening painting of a flock of black crows rising from a waving cornfield, you can almost feel the artist's mounting inner pain.

In addition to the paintings, nearly 600 drawings by van Gogh are on display in the museum's new wing, a free-standing, multistory, half-oval structure designed by the Japanese architect Kisho Kurokawa. It's constructed in a bold combination of titanium and gray–brown stone, and is connected to the main building by a subterranean walkway. **Note:** Lines at the museum can be very long, especially in summer. Try going on a weekday morning. Allow 2 to 4 hours to get around. Be advised also that the museum is closed for renovations from the end of September 2012 until the end of April 2013; during this period, some of the collection will exhibited at the **Hermitage Amsterdam Museum** (www.hermitage.nl; © 020/530-8755).

Paulus Potterstraat 7 (at Museumplein). www.vangoghmuseum.nl. © **020/570-5200.** Admission 14€ adults, free for children 17 and under. Sat–Thurs 10am–6pm; Fri 10am–10pm. Closed Jan 1; and Sept 29, 2011 to Apr 25, 2013. Tram: 2, 3, 5, 12, 16, or 24 to Museumplein.

AMSTERDAM SOUTH

To enjoy nature on the city's doorstep, head out to the **Amsterdamse Bos** (bus: 170 or 172 from outside Centraal Station to the main entrance on Amstelveenseweg), a large park in the Amstelveen southern suburb. At the entrance on Amstelveenseweg, stop by the **Bezoekerscentrum,** Bosbaanweg 5 (www.amsterdamsebos.nl; © 020/545-6100), the park's visitor center, where you can trace the park's history, learn about its wildlife, and pick up a plan of the park. The center is open Tuesday to Sunday (except Dec 25–26) from noon to 5pm, and admission is free. Across the way is a **bicycle rental** shop (www.amsterdamsebosfietsverhuur.nl; © 020/644-5473) where bikes are available April to September, Tuesday to Sunday, for from 10€ a day.

Follow the path to a long stretch of water called the **Bosbaan,** a 2km (1¼-mile) competition-rowing course. Beyond the course's western end is a big pond, the **Grote Vijver,** where you can rent boats, and the **Openluchttheater,** which often has open-air theater performances on summer evenings. The Amsterdamse Bos is open 24 hours; admission is free.

Heineken Experience BREWERY The experience unfolds inside the former Heineken brewing facilities, which date from 1867 to 1988. You "meet" Dr. Elion, the 19th-century chemist who isolated the renowned Heineken "A" yeast, which gives the beer its taste. In one amusing attraction, you stand on a moving floor, facing a large video screen, and get to see and feel what it's like to be a Heineken beer bottle—one of a half-million every hour—careening on a conveyor belt through a modern Heineken bottling plant. Best of all, in another touchy-feely presentation, you "sit" aboard an old brewery dray-wagon, "pulled" by a pair of big Shire horses on the video screen in front of you, that shakes, rattles, and rolls on a minitour of Amsterdam. The admission is steep, though, even if you do get two "free" glasses of Heineken beer.

Stadhouderskade 78 (at Ferdinand Bolstraat). www.heinekenexperience.com. © **020/523-9222.** Admission 17€ adults; 13€ children 8–15; free for children 7 and under (children 17 and under must be accompanied by an adult). June–Aug daily 10:30am–9pm (last admission 7pm); Sept–May daily 11am–7:30pm (last admission 5:30pm). Closed Jan 1, Apr 30, and Dec 25. Tram: 16, 24, or 25 to Stadhouderskade.

AMSTERDAM EAST

Hortus Botanicus ★ GARDEN   Established in 1682, Amsterdam's Botanical Garden is a medley of color and scent, containing 250,000 flowers and 115,000 plants and trees from 8,000 different varieties. It owes its origins to the treasure trove of tropical plants the Dutch found in their colonies of Indonesia, Suriname, and the Antilles, and its popularity to the Dutch love affair with flowers. Among highlights are the **Semicircle,** which reconstructs part of the original design from 1682; the **Mexico–California Desert House; Palm House,** with one of the world's oldest palm trees; and the **Tri-Climate House,** which displays tropical, subtropical, and desert plants.

Plantage Middenlaan 2A (close to Artis Zoo). www.dehortus.nl. ✆ **020/625-9021.** Admission 7.50€ adults, 3.50€ seniors and children 5–14, free for children 4 and under. Daily 10am–5pm. Closed Jan 1 and Dec 25. Tram: 9 or 14 to Plantage Middenlaan.

Tropenmuseum ★ ☺ MUSEUM   Founded in the 19th century as a monument to the nation's colonial empire, in particular the Dutch East Indies, today's Indonesia. Today, the Tropical Museum focuses on contemporary culture and problems in tropical areas. On the three floors surrounding the spacious main hall are numerous life-size tableaux depicting life in tropical countries. There are displays of beautiful handicrafts and antiquities from these regions, but the main focus is the life of the people today. There are hovels from the ghettos of Calcutta and Bombay, and mud-walled houses from the villages of rural India. Bamboo huts from Indonesia and crowded little stores no bigger than closets show you how people live in such areas as Southeast Asia, Latin America, and Africa. Sound effects play over hidden speakers.

Linnaeusstraat 2 (at Mauritskade). www.tropenmuseum.nl. ✆ **020/568-8200.** Admission (Quick, Basic, or In-Depth) 10€, 12€, or 16€ adults; 6€, 8€, or 10€ students and children 4–12; free for children 3 and under. Tues–Sun (and Mon during holidays and school vacations, except summer vacation) 10am–5pm (to 3pm Dec 5, 24, and 31). Closed Jan 1, Apr 30, May 5, and Dec 25. Tram: 9, 10, or 14 to Alexanderplein.

ORGANIZED TOURS

Although you could see most of Amsterdam's important sights in one long walking tour, it's best to break the city into shorter walks. Luckily, the **VVV Amsterdam** tourist office has done that. For 1€ to 3€, buy a brochure outlining one of five walking tours: among them the City Center, Golden Age Amsterdam, and the Jordaan.

A **canal-boat cruise** ★ is the best way to view the old houses and warehouses. If you have to choose from a walking tour, a bus tour, or a boat tour, definitely take a boat. This is a city built on the shipping trade, so it's only fitting you should see it from the water, just as the Golden Age merchants saw their city. There are several canal-boat jetties, all of which have signs stating the time of the next tour. The greatest concentration of canal-boat operators is along Damrak and Rokin from Centraal Station; another cluster is on Singelgracht, near Leidseplein. Most tours last 1 hour and are around 10€–13€ for adults, 5€–7€ for children ages 4 to 12, and free for children 3 and under (prices vary a bit from company to company). Because the tours are all basically the same, simply pick the one that's most convenient for you. Some cruises include snacks and drinks, with floating candlelit dinners extra.

Mike's Bike Tours, Kerkstraat 123 (www.mikesbiketoursamsterdam.com; ✆ **020/622-7970**), offers tours of 2½–3 hours around the canals in town, and a ride outside the city to see windmills, a cheese farm, and a clog factory. The cost is 19€ for adults and 16€ for seniors and students; there's a reduction of 5€ if you bring your own bike. March to November, meet daily at 4pm near the reflecting pool behind the

Rijksmuseum (tram: 2 or 5); December to February, you need to book in advance (minimum three people).

You can take a self-guided, self-powered tour on a **water bike.** These small pedal boats (also known as *pedalos*) for two to four are available from three docks of **Canal Bike** (www.canal.nl; ✆ 020/626-5574) at Leidseplein near the Rijksmuseum (tram: 1, 2, 5, 7, or 10), at Westerkerk (tram: 13, 14, or 17), and on Keizersgracht near Leidsestraat (tram: 1, 2, or 5). Canal bikes can be rented daily from 10am to 6pm in spring and autumn (to 9:30pm in summer). The hourly rate per water bike begins at 8€ a head for one or two people and 7€ a head for three or four. There's a 20€ refundable deposit. You can pick up a water bike at one dock and drop it off at another.

A 24-hour pass on the **Hop-On Hop-Off** tour bus costs 17€ for adults. A basic 2½-hour **bus tour** of the city is around 22€. Children aged 4 to 13 are charged half price, and children aged 3 and under ride free. Tour companies include **Keytours,** Paulus Potterstraat 8 (www.keytours.nl; ✆ 020/305-5333); and **Lindbergh,** Damrak 26 (www.lindbergh.nl; ✆ 020/622-2766).

ESPECIALLY FOR KIDS

Artis ★★ ☺ ZOO   If you're at a loss for what to do with the kids, Artis is a safe bet. Established in 1838, the oldest zoo in the Netherlands houses 6,000 animals from 1,400 species. Of course, you'll find the usual tigers, lions, giraffes, wolves, leopards, elephants, camels, monkeys, penguins, and peacocks no self-respecting zoo can do without. Yet Artis has much more, for no extra charge, like the excellent **Planetarium** (closed Mon morning) and a **Geological and Zoological Museum.** The refurbished **Aquarium,** built in 1882, is superbly presented, particularly the sections on the Amazon River, coral reefs, and Amsterdam's own canals with their fish populations and burden of wrecked cars, rusted bikes, and other urban detritus. In the children's **farm** kids can stroke and help tend to the needs of resident Dutch species. You can rest and have a snack or lunch at restaurant **Flamingoserre.**

Plantage Kerklaan 38–40 (at Plantage Middenlaan). www.artis.nl. ✆ **020/523-3400.** Admission 19€ adults, 18€ seniors, 16€ children 3–9, free for children 2 and under. Apr–Oct daily 9am–6pm (Sat June–Aug to sunset); Nov–Mar daily 9am–5pm. Tram: 9 or 14 to Plantage Kerklaan.

Where to Eat

As a trading and gateway city with a multiethnic population, Amsterdam has absorbed culinary influences from far and wide. You find dozens of ethnic eateries serving everything from Algerian to Vietnamese food—still waiting for W, X, Y, and Z! Indonesian food is extremely popular, notably the *rijsttafel* (see "Spice of Life," below). Many of these ethnic places serve hearty and delicious meals at very reasonable prices. And you'll find plenty of traditional Dutch restaurants.

Considering that you'll find great restaurants just about everywhere in Amsterdam, the main dining zones just about mirror those for lodgings, but not totally. The **Centrum (Center)** district is replete with eating options, and the neighboring **Waterfront** along Het IJ has places that offer harbor views.

More waterways dining is to be found along the romantic 16th- and 17th-century **Grachtengordel (Canal Belt),** interrupted by a pair of brash hotspots, the squares **Leidseplein** and **Rembrandtplein.** The trendy **Jordaan** neighborhood makes up with a notable dining roster for what it lacks in hotels.

Heading south from the city center, the **Museum District and Vondelpark** area and adjoining **Amsterdam-Zuid (South)** extend the eating possibilities out toward the city's edge.

Spice of Life

You haven't really eaten in Amsterdam until you've had an **Indonesian *rijsttafel*.** This traditional "rice table" banquet consists of as many as 20 succulent and spicy foods served in tiny bowls. Pick and choose from among the bowls and add your choice to the pile of rice on your plate. It's almost impossible to eat all the food set on your table, but give it a shot since it's a true taste of multicultural Amsterdam. For an abbreviated version served on one plate, try *nasi rames*. At lunch, the standard Indonesian fare is *nasi goreng* (fried rice with meat and vegetables) or *bami goreng* (fried noodles prepared in the same way).

THE CENTER
Expensive
De Silveren Spiegel ★★ MODERN DUTCH   The menu at "The Silver Mirror," one of the oldest and best known restaurants in Amsterdam, offers traditional seafood and meat dishes with a modern twist, such as baked sole filets with wild spinach, and trilogy of lamb with ratatouille. Just as in the old days, though, the lamb from Texel is still Holland's finest. Be sure to try the Zaanse mustard. The two houses that form the premises were built in 1614 for a wealthy soap maker, Laurens Jansz Spieghel. It's typical Old Dutch inside, with a bar downstairs and dining rooms where bedrooms used to be.

Kattengat 4–6 (off Singel). www.desilverenspiegel.com. ✆ **020/624-6589.** Main courses 30€–31€; set menus 40€–53€. AE, MC, V. Mon–Sat 5:30–10:30pm. Tram: 1, 2, 5, 13, or 17 to Martelaarsgracht.

D'Vijff Vlieghen ★ MODERN DUTCH   Touristy? Yes, but the "Five Flies" is one of Amsterdam's most famous restaurants, and the food is authentic stick-to-the-ribs Dutch fare. The chef is passionate about an updated form of Dutch cuisine he calls "the new Dutch kitchen." If you're feeling adventurous, try the wild boar with sweet chestnuts and a sauce made with *jenever* (liquor flavored with juniper berries). The restaurant is a kind of Dutch theme park, within five canal-houses decorated with artifacts from Holland's Golden Age. Don't miss the four original Rembrandt etchings in the Rembrandt Room and the collection of handmade glass in the Glass Room.

Spuistraat 294–302 (at Spui; entrance at Vliegendesteeg 1). www.vijffvlieghen.nl. ✆ **020/530-4060.** Reservations recommended on weekends. Main courses 26€–29€; seasonal menu 26€–53€. AE, DC, MC, V. Daily 6–10pm. Tram: 1, 2, or 5 to Spui.

Moderate
Haesje Claes TRADITIONAL DUTCH   If you're yearning for a cozy Old Dutch environment and hearty Dutch food at moderate prices, this is the place to go. It's inviting and intimate, with lots of nooks and crannies and with brocaded benches and traditional Dutch hanging lamps. The menu covers a lot of ground, ranging from canapés to caviar, but you'll likely be happiest with such Dutch stalwarts as *tournedos* (tenderloin/filet steak), *hutspot* (stew), *stampot* (mashed potatoes and cabbage), or various fish stews, including those with IJsselmeer *paling* (eel).

Spuistraat 273–275 (at Spui). www.haesjeclaes.nl. ✆ **020/624-9998.** Main courses 16€–26€; set menu 28€. AE, DC, MC, V. Daily noon–10pm. Tram: 1, 2, or 5 to Spui.

In de Waag ★ CONTINENTAL   The castle-like 14th-century Sint-Antoniespoort Gate in the city walls, later a public weigh house, holds one of Amsterdam's most stylish cafe-restaurants, in an area that's becoming hipper by the day. It's indelibly romantic, with its long banquet-style tables lit by hundreds of candles in the evening. The breast of Barbary duck with sesame-cracker and sherry dressing is pretty good, as is the vegetarian Kashmir bread with braised vegetables and coriander-yogurt sauce.

Nieuwmarkt 4. www.indewaag.nl. © **020/422-7772.** Main courses 18€–28€. AE, DC, MC, V. Daily 10am–1am. Metro: Nieuwmarkt.

Kantjil & de Tijger ★ INDONESIAN   Unlike Indonesian restaurants that wear their ethnic origins on their sleeve, the "Antelope and the Tiger" is modern and cool. Two bestsellers here are *nasi goreng Kantjil* (fried rice with pork kabobs, stewed beef, pickled cucumbers, and mixed vegetables) and the 20-item *rijsttafel* for two. Other choices are stewed chicken in soy sauce, tofu omelet, shrimp with coconut dressing, Indonesian pumpkin, and mixed steamed vegetables with peanut-butter sauce. Finish with cinnamon layer cake or a coffee with ginger liqueur and whipped cream.

Spuistraat 291–293 (beside Spui). www.kantjil.nl. © **020/620-0994.** Reservations recommended on weekends. Main courses 11€–16€; *rijsttafel* 40€–50€ for two people. AE, DC, MC, V. Daily 4:30–11pm. Tram: 1, 2, or 5 to Spui.

THE WATERFRONT
Expensive
Fifteen Amsterdam ★★ CONTINENTAL   British celeb-chef Jamie Oliver has brought his unique restaurant concept from London to the old Brazilië building in the harbor redevelopment zone east of Centraal Station. His Amsterdam hotspot has drop-dead gorgeous staff, who serve-up dishes like a salad of the day with figs, prosciutto, Gorgonzola, and toasted almonds on field greens; seafood risotto; and pan-fried calves' liver with balsamic figs. Though Oliver rarely presides in person, his signature breezy yet professional approach permeates both the service and the fusiony Mediterranean cuisine, in a setting that artfully combines graffiti, sheet metal, and white table linens. You can dine outdoors on a waterside terrace.

Pakhuis Amsterdam, Jollemanhof 9 (at Oostelijke Handelskade). www.fifteen.nl. © **020/509-5015.** Main courses 18€–23€. AE, DC, MC, V. Mon–Sat noon to 3pm and 5:30pm–1am, Sun 5:30pm–1am. Tram: 25 or 26 to Passenger Terminal Amsterdam.

Moderate
Pont 13 ★ 🍴 CONTINENTAL   A floating restaurant might suggest an image of a luxury yacht or a retired old windjammer. Sorry to sink any such hopes, but this is an Amsterdam harbor ferry that was laid up in 1995. Still, the conversion has been done with loving care. Whether you dine outside on the deck in good weather or in the glassed-in interior, there's enough of the romance of the sea to go around. Plus you have great views of the fast-redeveloping Western Harbor. The menu's concise, with just a few seafood and meat dishes and a single vegetarian option, and the cooking is as commendable as the service is bright and friendly.

Haparandadam 50 (at Danzigerkade). www.pont13.nl. © **020/770-2722.** Main courses 19€–23€. AE, MC, V. Daily noon–11pm. Bus: 22 or 48 to Oostzaanstraat, then walk north on Archangelweg and east on Haparandaweg, for a total of 1km (⅔ mile).

Wilhelmina-Dok ★★ CONTINENTAL   Across the IJ waterway from Centraal Station, this great waterfront eatery more than justifies a short, free ferryboat ride followed by a 5-minute walk. Plain wood, candlelit tables, wood floors, and oak cabinets give the interior an old-fashioned maritime look, and large windows serve up views across the narrow, boat-speckled channel. The menu favors plain cooking and organic products. Tables on the outdoor terrace are sheltered from the wind in a glass-walled enclosure.

Nordwal 1 (at IJplein). www.wilhelmina-dok.nl. © **020/632-3701.** Reservations recommended on weekends. Main courses 18€–21€; set menu 28€. AE, DC, MC, V. Daily 11am–midnight. Ferry: IJveer (IJ ferry) from Waterplein-West behind Centraal Station to the dock at IJplein; then walk east along the dike-top path.

THE CANAL BELT
Moderate
De Belhamel ★★ 🎁 CONTINENTAL   Classical music complements Art Nouveau in a graceful setting overlooking the Herengracht and Brouwersgracht canals. The menu changes seasonally, and game is a specialty. You can expect such menu dishes as puffed pastries layered with salmon, shellfish, crayfish tails, and chervil beurre blanc to start; and beef tenderloin in Madeira sauce with zucchini rösti and puffed garlic for a main course. Vegetarian dishes are also available.

Brouwersgracht 60 (at Herengracht). www.belhamel.nl. © **020/622-1095.** Main courses 22€–27€; set menus 35€–45€. AE, MC, V. Sun–Thurs noon–4pm and 6–10pm; Fri–Sat noon–4pm and 6–10:30pm. Tram: 1, 2, 5, 13, or 17 to Martelaarsgracht.

Tempo Doeloe ★★ INDONESIAN   For authentic Indonesian cuisine, from Java, Sumatra, and Bali—which doesn't leave out much—this place is hard to beat. Though its local reputation goes up and down with the tide, it's invariably busy. You dine in a batik ambience that's Indonesian but restrained, and a long way short of being kitsch. The attractive decor and the fine china are unexpected pluses. For a variety of small tastes, try one of the three *rijsttafel* options, which include the 15-plate vegetarian *rijsttafel sayoeran* and the sumptuous 25-plate *rijsttafel istemewa.*

Utrechtsestraat 75 (btw. Prinsengracht and Keizersgracht). www.tempodoeloerestaurant.nl. © **020/625-6718.** Reservations required. Main courses 15€–26€; *rijsttafel* 28€–36€; set menu 27€–45€. AE, DC, MC, V. Mon–Sat 6–11:30pm. Tram: 4 to Keizersgracht.

Inexpensive
Bolhoed ★ VEGETARIAN   Forget the dull, tofu-and-brown-rice image of vegetarian dining. Bolhoed adds a touch of spice to its health food formula with its Latin style, world music background, candlelight in the evenings, and fine views of the canal. Service is zestful and friendly. Try the *ragout croissant* (pastry filled with leeks, tofu, seaweed, and curry sauce) or *zarzuela* (tomato-based fish stew). If you want to go whole-hog, so to speak, and eat vegan, most dishes can be so prepared on request, and in any case most are made with organically grown produce. For outdoors dining in summer, there are a few canalside tables.

Prinsengracht 60–62 (near Noordermarkt). © **020/626-1803.** Main courses 14€–18€; set menus 14€–19€. No credit cards. Sun–Fri noon–11pm; Sat 11am–11pm. Tram: 13, 14, or 17 to Westermarkt.

De Prins ★★ 🍴 MODERN DUTCH/CONTINENTAL   In a 17th-century canal-house, this companionable brown cafe/restaurant opposite the Anne Frankhuis serves the kind of food you'd expect from a much more expensive place. The clientele is loyal, so the relatively few tables fill up quickly. It's a quiet neighborhood restaurant, nothing fancy or trendy, but quite appealing, with the bar on a slightly lower level than the restaurant and a sidewalk terrace for drinks in summer.

Prinsengracht 124 (at Egelantiersgracht). www.deprins.nl. © **020/624-9382.** Main courses 11€–17€; set menu 12€. AE, DC, MC, V. Daily 10am–1 or 2am (kitchen to 10pm). Tram: 13, 14, or 17 to Westermarkt.

Golden Temple ★ VEGETARIAN   In its fourth decade of tickling meat-shunning palates, this is still one of the best vegetarian (and vegan) options in town. If anything, it's a tad too hallowed, an effect enhanced by a minimalist absence of decorative flourishes. The menu livens things up, however, with an unlikely roster of Indian, Middle Eastern, and Italian dishes, and the multiple-choice platters are a good way to go.

Utrechtsestraat 126 (close to Frederiksplein). www.restaurantgoldentemple.com. © **020/626-8560.** Main courses 14€–16€; mixed platter 16€. MC, V. Daily 5–10pm. Tram: 4 to Prinsengracht.

AROUND LEIDSEPLEIN

Café Americain ★ INTERNATIONAL   In her pre-espionage days, Mata Hari held her wedding reception in this national monument of Dutch Art Nouveau architecture. Since its 1900 opening, it has been a haven for Dutch and international artists, writers, dancers, and actors. Leaded windows, newspaper-littered reading tables, bargello-patterned velvet upholstery, frosted-glass chandeliers from the 1920s, and tall, carved columns are all part of the dusky sit-and-chat setting. Menu dishes include monkfish, perch, rack of Irish lamb, and rosé breast of duck with creamed potatoes. Jazz lovers can dine to good music at a Sunday jazz brunch.

In the Eden Amsterdam American Hotel, Leidsekade 97 (at Leidseplein). www.edenamsterdam americanhotel.com. © **020/556-3010.** Main courses 16€–23€. AE, DC, MC, V. Mon–Fri 6:30am–11:30pm; Sat 7am–11:30pm. Tram: 1, 2, 5, 7, or 10 to Leidseplein.

THE JORDAAN

Bordewijk ★★ FRENCH/FUSION   This pleasantly located restaurant is often regarded as one of the best in the city. The decor is tasteful, with potted plants offsetting the severity of the white walls and metallic black tables. Service is relaxed yet attentive, and on mild summer evenings you can't beat dining alfresco on the canalside terrace. But the real treat is the food. An innovative chef accents French standards with Mediterranean and Asian flourishes to create an elegant fusion of flavors.

Noordermarkt 7 (at Prinsengracht). www.bordewijk.nl. © **020/624-3899.** Main courses 24€–29€; set menus 39€–72€. AE, MC, V. Tues–Sat 6:30–10:30pm. Tram: 1, 2, 5, 13, or 17 to Martelaarsgracht.

Toscanini ★ SOUTH ITALIAN   This restaurant has a warm, welcoming ambience and excellent southern Italian food. At least that's the point of emphasis, but most regional Italian dishes, with the notable exception of pizza, are available. Popular with the artists and bohemians who inhabit the neighborhood, Toscanini has unembellished country-style decor and an open kitchen. Cooking is home-style and there's a long-as-your-arm list of Italian wines. Service is congenial and chatty but can be slow, though that doesn't deter loyal regulars.

Lindengracht 75 (off Brouwersgracht). www.toscanini.nu. © **020/623-2813.** Main courses 17€–23€; fixed-price menu 48€. AE, MC, V. Mon–Sat 6–10:30pm. Tram: 3 to Nieuwe Willemsstraat.

Shopping

Strolling Amsterdam's streets, you could get the impression the city is one giant outdoor mall. Everywhere you look are stores ranging in price and variety from the Jordaan's used-clothing stores and bookstores to Pieter Cornelisz Hooftstraat's designer boutiques. Alas, most stores have little in the way of bargains. However, many typically Dutch souvenirs and gift items might appeal to you and can be real bargains if you shop around.

Best buys in Amsterdam include special items produced by the Dutch to perfection, or produced to perfection in the past and that now retail as antiques. Look out for brand-name Delftware (or even plain everyday delftware), pewter, crystal, and old-fashioned clocks. Then there are commodities in which they have significantly cornered a market, like diamonds. If cost is an important consideration, remember the Dutch also produce inexpensive specialties such as cheese, flower bulbs, and chocolate.

For jewelry, trendy clothing, and athletic gear, try the department stores and specialized stores around the Dam. On the long, pedestrianized Nieuwendijk-Kalverstraat shopping street and on Leidsestraat, you find inexpensive clothing and souvenir stores. For designer boutiques and upscale fashion and accessories, shop on Pieter Cornelisz Hooftstraat and Van Baerlestraat. Pricey antiques and art dealers congregate on Nieuwe Spiegelstraat. For fashion boutiques and funky little specialty stores, or a good browse through a flea market or secondhand store, roam the streets of the Jordaan. The Red-Light District specializes in stores selling erotic clothing, sex aids and accessories, and pornographic books and magazines.

MARKETS

Buying flowers at the **Bloemenmarkt (Flower Market) ★★**, on a row of barges permanently moored along Singel between Muntplein and Leidsestraat (tram: 1, 2, 4, 5, 9, 14, 16, 24, or 25), is an Amsterdam ritual. The market is open Monday to Saturday 9am to 5:30pm, and Sunday from 11am to 5:30pm.

You can still find a few antiques and near-antiques at the **Waterlooplein flea market** (tram: 9 or 14), on the square around the Muziektheater, but most of what's for sale these days is used and cheap clothing. It's open Monday to Saturday from 10am to 5pm. The open-air **Albert Cuyp market,** Albert Cuypstraat (www.albert cuypmarkt.com; tram: 4, 16, 24, or 25), open Monday to Saturday 9am to 5pm, has more cheap clothing, plus fresh fish and flowers, Asian vegetables, textiles, electronics, cosmetics, and more. There's also a **flea market** on Noordermarkt in the Jordaan (tram: 1, 2, 5, 13, or 17) on Monday morning 8am until midday, and a market for **organic food** on Saturday from 10am to 4pm.

Spread through several old warehouses along the Jordaan canals, **Kunst & Antiekcentrum de Looier,** Elandsgracht 109 (*©* **020/624-9038;** tram: 7, 10, or 17), is a big art and antiques market. Individual dealers rent booths and corners to show their best wares in antique jewelry, prints, and engravings.

 Healthy Bulbs Make Light Work

You might think the bulbs you choose are nobody's blooming business, but Customs in the U.S., Canada, and some other countries won't let you bring them home if they don't have a clean bill of health known as a "phytosanitary certificate." You can spend a lot of money on bulbs, so make sure the ones you buy are health-certified and approved for export. You can take certified bulbs with you, or ship them yourself, or (at some stores) have them shipped for you.

SHOPPING HIGHLIGHTS

The city's top department store, with the best selection of goods and a great cafe, is **de Bijenkorf,** Dam 1 (www.bijenkorf.nl; ℂ 0800/0818). You can find almost everything there is to buy in Amsterdam at **Magna Plaza ★**, Nieuwezijds Voorburgwal 182 (www.magnaplaza.nl; ℂ 020/570-3570), a splendid three-story mall in the old main post office building, behind the Dam.

For brand-name hand-painted pottery, head to opulent **Jorrit Heinen ★★**, Muntplein 12, at the medieval Munttoren (www.jorritheinen.com; ℂ 020/623-2271), and Prinsengracht 440, off Leidsestraat (ℂ 020/627-8299). Also recommendable is cluttered **Galleria d'Arte Rinascimento,** Prinsengracht 170 (www.delft-art-gallery.com; ℂ 020/622-7509).

Diamond showrooms offering free individual and small-group tours of their diamond-cutting and -polishing facilities include **Gassan Dam Square,** Rokin 1–5 (www.gassandamsquare.nl; ℂ 020/624-5787), just off the Dam; **Coster Diamonds,** Paulus Potterstraat 2–8 (www.costerdiamonds.com; ℂ 020/305-5555), across from the Rijksmuseum; and **Choices by DL,** Nieuwe Uilenburgerstraat 173–175 (www.choicesbydl.nl; ℂ 020/622-5333), behind Waterlooplein.

A fine antiquarian since 1878, **Mathieu Hart,** Rokin 122 (www.hartantiques.com; ℂ 020/623-1658), at Spui, stocks color etchings of Dutch cities alongside rare old prints, 18th-century Delftware, and grandfather clocks. Jewelry and antique silver establishment **Premsela & Hamburger ★**, Rokin 98 (www.premsela.com; ℂ 020/627-5454), at Spui, purveyors to the Dutch royal court, opened in 1823.

For English-language books and magazines, the choice is large. Try the centrally located **American Book Center,** Spui 12 (www.abc.nl; ℂ 020/625-5537), or the nearby branch of British chain **Waterstone's,** Kalverstraat 152 (www.waterstones.com; ℂ 020/638-3821).

Entertainment & Nightlife

Nightlife in the city centers on Leidseplein and Rembrandtplein, and you'll find dozens of bars, nightclubs, cafes, dance clubs, and movie theaters around these two squares.

To reserve and purchase tickets for almost every venue in the city, stop by or contact the **Amsterdams Uitburo-Ticketshop,** Leidseplein 26, on the corner of Marnixstraat (www.amsterdamsuitburo.nl; ℂ 020/795-9950; tram: 1, 2, 5, 7, or 10), open Monday to Friday from 10am to 7pm, Saturday from 10am to 6pm, and Sunday from noon to 6pm. Their free monthly magazine, *De Uitkrant,* has a thorough listing of events in Dutch (which should not be too hard for English speakers to follow) and is available from this office and from VVV offices, performance venues, and clubs.

PERFORMING ARTS

The renowned **Royal Concertgebouw Orchestra** is based at the **Concertgebouw ★★**, Concertgebouwplein 2–6 (www.concertgebouw.nl; ℂ 0900/671-8345, or 31-20/671-8345 from outside Holland; tram: 2, 3, 5, 12, 16, or 24), which has some of the best acoustics of any hall in the world. Performances take place almost every night in the building's two halls. There are free half-hour rehearsal concerts on Wednesdays at 12:30pm. The box office is open daily from 10am to 7pm (to 8:15pm for same-day tickets), with tickets from 17€ to 100€.

A spectacular piece of modern architecture, the **Muziekgebouw aan 't IJ ★**, Piet Heinkade 1 (www.muziekgebouw.nl; © **020/788-2000;** tram: 25 or 26), on the IJ waterfront just east of Centraal Station, is the city's home for avant-garde and experimental music. You can look for concerts of modern, old, jazz, electronic, and non-Western music, along with small-scale musical theater, opera, and dance. The box office is open Monday to Saturday from noon to 7pm; tickets are 10€ to 65€.

The **Netherlands Opera** and the **National Ballet** both perform regularly at the modern **Muziektheater ★★★**, Waterlooplein (www.muziektheater.nl; © **020/625-5455;** tram: 9 or 14); and the innovative **Netherlands Dance Theater** company from The Hague is a frequent visitor. The box office is open Monday to Saturday from 10am to 8pm, and Sunday and holidays from 11:30am to 6pm, with tickets from 10€ to 110€.

Boom Chicago Theater ★, Leidsepleintheater, Leidseplein 12 (www.boom chicago.nl; © **020/423-0101;** tram: 1, 2, 5, 7, or 10), puts on great improvisational comedy, and Dutch audiences have no problem with the English-language sketches. You can have dinner and a drink while enjoying the show at a candlelit table. It's open daily in summer, closed Sunday in winter. Dinner/theater packages 30€–100€ per person; and tickets without dinner go from around 20€.

LIVE MUSIC CLUBS

A shiny metal box with windows that's an extension of the Muziekgebouw aan 't IJ (see above), on the waterfront east of Centraal Station, is home to the **Bimhuis ★**, Piet Heinkade 3 (www.bimhuis.nl; © **020/788-2188;** tram: 25 or 26), the city's premier jazz, blues, and improvisational club. Top local and international musicians are regularly featured.

A regular crowd frequents the small, intimate **Jazz Café Alto,** Korte Leidsedwarsstraat 115 (www.jazz-café-alto.nl; © **020/626-3249;** tram: 7, 10, or 17), for nightly performances by both regular and guest combos. Check out also the funky **Bourbon Street ★★**, Leidsekruisstraat 6–8 (www.bourbonstreet.nl; © **020/623-3440;** tram: 1, 2, 5, 7, or 10), for late-night blues and rock. Both bars are near Leidseplein.

BARS & CLUBS

There are countless bars—or cafes, as they're called here—in the city, many around **Leidseplein** and **Rembrandtplein.** They usually open at noon and stay open all day. The most popular drink is draft Pilsener served in small glasses with two fingers of head on top. Also popular is *jenever* (Dutch gin) available in *jonge* (young) and *oude* (old) varieties; oude is stronger, more refined in taste, and higher in alcoholic content.

BROWN CAFES   Particularly old and traditional bars often earn the appellation of ***bruine kroeg*** (brown cafe), a name said to have been derived as much from the preponderance of wood furnishings as from the browning of the walls from years of dense tobacco smoke. Some have been around since Rembrandt's time. At these warm and friendly cafes you can sit and sip a glass of beer or a mixed drink; at some you can even get a cheap meal.

Papeneiland, Prinsengracht 2, at the corner of Brouwersgracht (© **020/624-1989;** tram: 1, 2, 5, 13, or 17), is Amsterdam's oldest cafe: Since 1600 or thereabouts, folks have been dropping by for shots of jenever and glasses of beer. Originally a tasting house where people could try liqueurs distilled and aged on the premises,

De Drie Fleschjes, Gravenstraat 18, between the Nieuwe Kerk and Nieuwendijk (✆ **020/624-8443;** tram: 1, 2, 4, 5, 9, 13, 14, 16, 17, 24, or 25), has been in business for more than 300 years. It's popular with businesspeople and journalists, who stop by to sample the wide variety of jenevers.

The dark walls, low ceilings, and old wooden furniture at **Hoppe,** Spui 18–20 (✆ **020/420-4420;** tram: 1, 2, or 5), one of Amsterdam's oldest and most popular brown cafes, have literally remained unchanged since the cafe opened in 1670. It has become a tourist attraction, but locals love it too, often stopping for a drink on their way home. There's usually standing room only and the crowds overflow onto the sidewalk.

MODERN CAFES Amid subdued lighting, dark wood surfaces, and red tones, fancy **Bubbles & Wines ★**, Nes 37 (✆ **020/422-3318;** tram: 4, 9, 14, 16, 24, or 25), a few minutes' walk from the Dam, serves an extensive roster of champagne and wine labels, along with light snacks. **Café Schiller ★**, Rembrandtplein 26 (✆ **020/ 624-9846;** tram: 4, 9, or 14), which has a bright, glassed-in terrace on the square and a finely carved Art Deco interior, is popular with artists and writers.

Soft chairs, long banquettes, and chandeliers draw a hip, youthful crowd to **Café Kale de Grote ★★**, Marie-Heinekenplein 33 (✆ **020/670-4661;** tram: 16 or 24), in the Pijp district, to sip mojitos and other cocktails, graze on plates of tempura, and dance to DJs on Friday and Saturday nights.

DANCE CLUBS

Popular clubs include **Tonight ★★**, at the Hotel Arena, Gravesandestraat 51 (www. hotelarena.nl; ✆ **020/850-2400;** tram: 7 or 10); **Escape ★**, Rembrandtplein 11 (www.escape.nl; ✆ **020/622-1111;** tram: 4, 9, or 14); **Odeon,** Singel 460 (www. odeontheater.nl; ✆ **020/521-8555;** tram: 1, 2, or 5); **Paradiso,** Weteringschans 6–8 (www.paradiso.nl; ✆ **020/626-4521;** tram: 1, 2, 5, 7, or 10); and **Melkweg ★**, Lijnbaansgracht 234A (www.melkweg.nl; ✆ **020/531-8181;** tram: 1, 2, 5, 7, or 10).

THE LGBT SCENE

Amsterdam bills itself as the gay capital of Europe, proud of its open and generally tolerant attitude toward homosexuality. To find out more about the LGBT scenes, stop by **COC,** Rozenstraat 14 (www.cocamsterdam.nl; ✆ **020/626-3087;** tram: 13, 14, or 17), 2 blocks off Westerkerk. You can also call the **Gay and Lesbian Switchboard** at ✆ **020/623-6565,** open daily from 10am to 10pm. *Gay News,* a monthly newspaper in English, is available free in gay establishments throughout Amsterdam.

Some of the more popular spots for men are **Club FUXXX,** Warmoesstraat 96 (www.clubfuxxx.com; ✆ **020/624-3807;** tram: 4, 9, 14, 16, 24, or 25), a heavy-duty dance club; and **Amstel Fifty Four,** Amstel 54 (www.amstelfiftyfour.nl; ✆ **020/623- 4254;** tram: 4, 9, or 14), a late-night bar.

Vivelavie, Amstelstraat 7 (www.vivelavie.net; ✆ **020/624-0114;** tram: 4, 9, or 14), on the edge of Rembrandtplein, is the city's only lesbian bar; this convivial little corner spot on Rembrandtplein hosts periodic parties. **Saarein,** Elandsstraat 119 (✆ **020/623-4901;** tram: 7, 10, or 17), near Leidseplein, is a mixed-gender bar/cafe that has a large lesbian following.

COFFEESHOPS

Amsterdam is a mecca for the marijuana smoker and seems likely to remain that way. Visitors often get confused about "smoking" coffeeshops and how they differ from "nonsmoking" ones. Well, to begin with, "smoking" and "nonsmoking" don't refer to cigarettes—they refer to cannabis. "Smoking" coffeeshops not only sell cannabis, most commonly in the form of hashish, but also provide somewhere patrons can sit and smoke it all day if they so choose. Generally, these smoking coffeeshops are the only places in Amsterdam called "coffeeshops"—regular cafes are called *cafes* or *eetcafes*.

You are allowed to buy only 5 grams (⅕ oz.) of soft drugs at a time for personal use, but you're allowed to be in possession of 30 grams (1 oz.) for personal use.

Coffeeshops are not allowed to sell alcohol, so they sell coffee, tea, and fruit juices. You won't be able to get any food, so don't expect to grab a quick bite. You're even allowed to smoke your own stuff in the coffee shop, as long as you buy a drink.

Some notable coffeeshops: **The Rookies,** Korte Leidsedwarsstraat 145 (www.rookies.nl; ✆ **020/428-3125;** tram: 1, 2, 5, 7, or 10); **Sheeba,** Warmoesstraat 73 (no phone; Metro: Centraal Station); and the brash **Bulldog,** Leidseplein 17 (www.thebulldog.com; ✆ **020/624-8248;** tram: 1, 2, 5, 7, or 10). Two places with more of a neighborhood atmosphere (even if a thick one) are relaxed, clean smoking **Kadinsky,** Rosmarijnsteeg 9 (✆ **020/624-7023;** tram: 1, 2, or 5), at Spuistraat; and friendly **Paradox,** Eerste Bloemdwarsstraat 2 (www.paradoxcoffeeshop.com; ✆ **020/623-5639;** tram: 13, 14, or 17), off Bloemgracht, in the Jordaan.

Where to Stay

There are good reasons to lodge in the busy **Centrum (Center)** district around the Dam and Centraal Station, and a few reasons not to. If it's tranquility you seek, a zone filled with traffic, noise, and social whirl is generally not the ideal place to find it. That said, there are some quiet side streets. Stretching east and west of Centraal Station along the channel known as Het IJ, the redeveloped **Waterfront** has dining and entertainment venues aplenty, and a few noteworthy hotels.

It would be a shame to visit this canal-threaded city without staying in a canal-view hotel, particularly since those lodgings are usually in 300-year-old buildings. So to really experience Amsterdam, splurge a bit, even if it's only for a night or two, to stay at a hotel along the **Grachtengordel (Canal Belt),** the semicircular, multistrand "necklace" of man-made 16th- and 17th-century waterways: Singel, Herengracht, Keizersgracht, and Prinsengracht. **Leidseplein** and **Rembrandtplein,** the most happening nightlife squares and their immediate surroundings, intersect with the Canal Belt. There are plenty of good hotels in these frenetically busy areas, which won't suit those who don't like crowds and bustle. Just off the Canal Belt, the **Jordaan** is a trendy neighborhood that just doesn't have many lodging options.

The gracious **Museum District and Vondelpark** area around the city's three premier museums—Rijksmuseum, Van Gogh Museum, Stedelijk Museum—hosts small, value-oriented hotels. Although Amsterdam is not so big, the adjoining **Amsterdam-Zuid (South)** district is just about far enough away from the action to be not quite convenient for the city center.

Should you arrive without a reservation, consult the **VVV Amsterdam tourist office** (www.iamsterdam.nl; ✆ **020/201-8800**); see "Visitor Information," earlier in this chapter.

THE CENTER

Hotel de l'Europe ★★★
Change has come to this grande dame of Amsterdam hotels, which dates from 1896 and occupies a stretch of prime waterfront where the

Amstel River flows into the city's canal net. While it keeps the airs and graces of a dignified, *fin de siècle* style behind its pastel-red and white façade, the hotel has implemented major renovations and upgrades to all guest rooms. And this is in addition to a new, exclusive annex, the Dutch Masters Wing, containing 23 suites that are the last word in contemporary luxury. Try for a room with a balcony overlooking the river. The **Bord'Eau** is among the toniest restaurants in town.

Nieuwe Doelenstraat 2–14 (facing Muntplein), 1012 CP Amsterdam. www.leurope.nl. ✆ **020/531-1777.** Fax 020/531-1778. 111 units. 429€–617€ double; from 655€ suite; add 5% city tax. AE, DC, MC, V. Valet and self-parking 58€. Tram: 4, 9, 14, 16, 24, or 25 to De Munt. **Amenities:** 2 restaurants; 2 bars; small heated indoor pool; health club; spa; sauna; concierge; room service; babysitting. *In room:* A/C, TV, minibar, hair dryer, MP3 docking station, Wi-Fi (free).

Sint Nicolaas ★ 🗡 Named after Amsterdam's patron saint, this hotel is conveniently near Centraal Station, in a prominent corner building at the apex of two converging streets. Heavy tram, bus, and car traffic passing by outside is the downside to this location. New owners have upgraded the interior to near-boutique status, affording a level of comfort that's rarely achieved by Amsterdam hotels in this price range. Each room has a different character; the regular ones emphasize classic comforts, warm colors, prints, and exposed wood beams; the deluxe doubles are all cool blacks, grays, and whites.

Spuistraat 1A (at Nieuwendijk), 1012 SP Amsterdam. www.hotelnicolaas.nl. ✆ **020/626-1384.** Fax 020/623-0979. 27 units. 100€–295€ double. Rates include continental breakfast. AE, MC, V. Limited street parking. Tram: 1, 2, 5, 13, or 17 to Martelaarsgracht. **Amenities:** Lounge; bar. *In room:* TV, hair dryer, Wi-Fi (free).

THE WATERFONT

Amstel Botel ☺ Where better to experience a city on the water than on a boat? The Botel, moored permanently to a dock on the IJ waterway northwest of Centraal Station, is popular largely because of that extra thrill added by sleeping on the water—its modest (for Amsterdam) rates don't hurt either. This retired inland waterways cruise boat has cabins on four decks that are connected by an elevator. The bright, modern rooms are no-nonsense but comfortable, the showers small. Be sure to ask for a slightly more expensive room with a view on the water, to avoid the uninspiring quay.

NDSM-Werf 3 (Amsterdam-Noord), 1033 RG Amsterdam. www.amstelbotel.com. ✆ **020/521-0350.** Fax 020/639-1952. 175 units. 87€–105€ double. AE, DC, MC, V. Limited free parking on quay. Boat: NDSM ferry from Centraal Station. **Amenities:** Bar; bikes. *In room:* TV, Wi-Fi (free).

Lloyd Hotel ★ Located at the redeveloped old steamship docks east of Centraal Station, the Lloyd was originally a hotel for emigrants when it opened in 1921. It was thoroughly renovated and reopened in 2004 as a hotel. Just about every room has a different shape, style, and modern decor, which accounts for the unusually large range of room rates. The most expensive rooms are the largest and have a view on the water, or a specially designed interior (or both). In its self-appointed "Cultural Ambassador" role, the hotel hosts a program of events, live performances, and exhibits.

Oostelijke Handelskade 34, 1019 BN Amsterdam (at IJhaven). www.lloydhotel.com. ✆ **020/561-3636.** Fax 020/561-3600. 117 units, 106 with ensuite bathroom. 150€–250€ double with bathroom; 95€ double without bathroom. AE, DC, MC, V. Parking 23€. Tram: 10 or 26 to Rietlandpark. **Amenities:** Restaurant; bar; bikes; room service; babysitting. *In room:* TV, Wi-Fi (free).

THE CANAL BELT

Expensive

Ambassade ★★ 🎒 Perhaps more than any other hotel in Amsterdam, this one, spread over ten 17th- and 18th-century canal-houses on the Herengracht and Singel canals, recreates the feeling of living in an elegant canal-house. The pastel-toned rooms are individually styled, their size and shape varying according to the character of the individual houses. Anyone who lodges here is sure to enjoy the view each morning over breakfast in the bi-level, chandeliered breakfast room, or each evening in the adjoining parlor, with its Persian rugs and a stately grandfather clock.

Herengracht 341 (near Spui), 1016 AZ Amsterdam. www.ambassade-hotel.nl. ℂ **020/555-0222.** Fax 020/555-0277. 58 units. 195€–275€ double; 325€–375€ suite. AE, DC, MC, V. Limited street parking. Tram: 1, 2, or 5 to Spui. **Amenities:** Lounge; bikes; room service; babysitting; access to nearby spa. *In room:* TV, hair dryer, Wi-Fi (free).

Estheréa ★★★ If you like to stay at elegant, not-too-big hotels, you'll be pleased by the Estheréa. It's been owned by the same family since its beginnings and, like so many hotels in Amsterdam, was constructed anew within the walls of a group of neighboring 17th-century canal-houses. The wood bedsteads and dresser-desks bring warmth to renovated and upgraded rooms. The room sizes vary considerably according to their location in the canal-houses.

Singel 303–309 (near Spui), 1012 WJ Amsterdam. www.estherea.nl. ℂ **800/223-9868** in the U.S. and Canada, or 020/624-5146. Fax 020/623-9001. 92 units. 220€–410€ double. AE, DC, MC, V. Parking 55€. Tram: 1, 2, or 5 to Spui. **Amenities:** Bar; lounge; babysitting. *In room:* TV, minibar, hair dryer, Wi-Fi (free).

Moderate

Amsterdam Wiechmann ★ It takes only a moment to feel at home in the antiques-adorned Wiechmann, a classic, comfortable, casual kind of place. Besides, the location is one of the best you'll find in this or any price range. Most of the rooms are standard, with good-size twin or double beds, and some have big bay windows. Furnishings are modern, and Oriental rugs grace many of the floors in public spaces. The higher-priced doubles have a view of the Prinsengracht canal. There's no elevator.

Prinsengracht 328–332 (at Looiersgracht), 1016 HX Amsterdam. www.hotelwiechmann.nl. ℂ **020/626-3321.** Fax 020/626-8962. 37 units. 125€–170€ double. Rates include continental breakfast. MC, V. Limited street parking. Tram: 1, 2, or 5 to Prinsengracht. **Amenities:** Lounge. *In room:* TV, Wi-Fi (free).

Dikker & Thijs Fenice Where Prinsengracht intersects lively Leidsestraat is this small, homey hotel, a business that started out here 1921, and whose smart but cozy character emanates from the marble-rich lobby and stylish facade. Upstairs, spacious and tasteful rooms cluster in groups of two or four around small lobbies, which makes this feel more like an apartment building than a hotel. There are often flowers in the rooms, a subtle but elegantly modern Art Deco decor, and double-glazed windows to eliminate the noise rising up from Leidsestraat. Rooms at the front have a super view of classy Prinsengracht.

Prinsengracht 444 (at Leidsestraat), 1017 KE Amsterdam. www.dtfh.nl. ℂ **020/620-1212.** Fax 020/625-8986. 42 units. 115€–275€ double; add 5% city tax. AE, DC, MC, V. Limited street parking. Tram: 1, 2, or 5 to Prinsengracht. **Amenities:** Restaurant; bar; lounge; concierge; room service. *In room:* TV, minibar, hair dryer, Wi-Fi (2.50€/hr. or 10€/day).

A Canal-House Warning

Be prepared to climb hard-to-navigate stairways if you want to save money on lodging in Amsterdam by staying in a canal-house. Narrow and as steep as ladders, these stairways were designed to conserve space in the narrow houses along the canals. If you have difficulty climbing stairs, ask for a room on a lower floor.

Inexpensive

Prinsenhof A modernized canal-house near the Amstel River, this hotel offers rooms with beamed ceilings and basic yet reasonably comfortable beds. Front rooms look out onto the Prinsengracht, where colorful houseboats are moored. Breakfast is served in an attractive blue-and-white decorated dining room. There's no elevator, but a pulley hauls your luggage up and down the stairs.

Prinsengracht 810 (at Utrechtsestraat), 1017 JL Amsterdam. www.hotelprinsenhof.com. ☎ **020/623-1772.** Fax 020/638-3368. 11 units, 6 with bathroom. 89€ double with bathroom; 69€ double without bathroom (5% charge). Rates include continental breakfast. AE, MC, V. Limited street parking. Tram: 4 to Prinsengracht. *In room:* No phone.

AROUND LEIDSEPLEIN

Eden Amsterdam American ★★★ A fanciful, castle-like mix of Venetian Gothic and Art Nouveau, the American has been both a prominent landmark and a popular meeting place for Amsterdammers since 1900. While the exterior must always remain a protected architectural treasure of turrets, arches, and balconies, the interior (except that of the cafe, which also is protected) is modern and chic. Rooms are subdued, refined, and superbly furnished. Some have a view on Singelgracht; others overlook kaleidoscopic Leidseplein. The Art Deco **Café Americain** (p. 731) is among Amsterdam's most elegant eateries.

Leidsekade 97 (at Leidseplein), 1017 PN Amsterdam. www.edenamsterdamamericanhotel.com. ☎ **020/556-3000.** Fax 020/556-3001. 175 units. 170€–290€ double; from 315€ suite. AE, DC, MC, V. No parking. Tram: 1, 2, 5, 7, or 10 to Leidseplein. **Amenities:** Restaurant; bar; exercise room; sauna; concierge; room service. *In room:* A/C, TV, minibar, hair dryer, Wi-Fi (free).

AROUND REMBRANDTPLEIN

NH Schiller Hotel ★ An Amsterdam gem from 1912, fully restored, this hotel boasts a blend of Art Nouveau and Art Deco in its public spaces, a theme that is reflected in the tasteful furnishings in the rooms. Its sculpted facade, wrought-iron balconies, and stained-glass windows stand out on the often brash Rembrandtplein. **Brasserie Schiller** is a gracious, oak-paneled dining room, and **Café Schiller** is one of Amsterdam's few permanent sidewalk cafes.

Rembrandtplein 26–36, 1017 CV Amsterdam. www.nh-hotels.com. ☎ **020/554-0700.** Fax 020/624-0098. 92 units. 140€–205€ double; from 250€ suite; add 5% city tax. AE, DC, MC, V. Limited street parking. Tram: 4, 9, or 14 to Rembrandtplein. **Amenities:** Restaurant, 2 bars; room service; babysitting. *In room:* TV, minibar, hair dryer, Wi-Fi (free).

Seven Bridges ★★ One of Amsterdam's canal-house gems, not far from Rembrandtplein, gets its name from its view of seven arched bridges. There are antique furnishings, handmade Italian drapes, hand-painted tiles and wood-tiled floors, and

Impressionist art posters. The biggest room, on the first landing, can accommodate up to four and has a huge bathroom with marble floor and double sinks. Attic rooms have exposed wood beams, and there are big, bright basement rooms decorated almost entirely in white. There's no elevator and no breakfast room; continental breakfast is served in the room for an extra charge of 12.50€.

Reguliersgracht 31 (at Keizersgracht), 1017 LK Amsterdam. www.sevenbridgeshotel.nl. © **020/623-1329.** Fax 020/624-7652. 11 units. 135€–240€ double. AE, MC, V. Limited street parking. Tram: 4 to Keizersgracht. *In room:* TV, hair dryer, Wi-Fi (free).

THE JORDAAN

Acacia ★ Not on one of the major canals, but facing a small canal just a block away from Prinsengracht, the Acacia is run by a friendly couple who are justifiably proud of their welcoming and well-kept hotel. All rooms are simple, clean, and comfortable; the large front corner rooms are shaped like pie slices, and have windows on three sides. All rooms have been outfitted with new beds, writing tables, and chairs. There's no elevator.

Lindengracht 251 (at Lijnbaansgracht), 1015 KH Amsterdam. www.hotelacacia.nl. © **020/622-1460.** Fax 020/638-0748. 14 units. 80€–95€ double. Rates include continental breakfast. MC, V (5% charge). Limited street parking. Tram: 3 or 10 to Marnixplein. *In room:* TV, Wi-Fi (free).

THE MUSEUM DISTRICT

Museumzicht ★ This hotel, in a town house that dates from 1890 across from the Rijksmuseum's rear, is ideal for museumgoers on a budget. The breakfast room, which has numerous stained-glass windows, commands an excellent view of the museum. Proprietor Robin de Jong has filled guest rooms with eclectic furniture that spans from the 1930s (think English wicker) to the present day. Note that there's no elevator and the staircase up to reception is quite steep.

Jan Luijkenstraat 22 (facing the Rijksmuseum), 1071 CN Amsterdam. www.hotelmuseumzicht.nl. © **020/671-2954.** Fax 020/671-3597. 14 units, 3 with bathroom. 115€ double with bathroom; 55€–85€ double without bathroom. Rates include continental breakfast. AE, MC, V (2% charge). Limited street parking. Tram: 2 or 5 to Hobbemastraat. **Amenities:** Lounge; room service (coffee and tea); Wi-Fi (free). *In room:* No phone.

Sandton Hotel De Filosoof ★ On a quiet street of brick houses near Vondelpark, this extraordinary, elegant hotel might be the very place if you fancy yourself as something of a philosopher. Each room is dedicated to a mental maestro or an important cultural figure—Aristotle, Plato, Goethe, Wittgenstein, Nietzsche, Marx, and Einstein are among those who get a look-in—or it is based on motifs like Eros, the Renaissance, and astrology. You can even consult your private bookshelf of philosophical works or join in a weekly philosophy debate. The rooms in an annex across the street are larger; some open onto a terrace.

Anna van den Vondelstraat 6 (off Overtoom, at Vondelpark), 1054 GZ Amsterdam. www.sandton. eu. © **020/683-3013.** Fax 020/685-3750. 38 units. 140€–200€ double; from 250€ suite. AE, MC, V. Limited street parking. Tram: 1 to Jan Pieter Heijestraat. **Amenities:** Lounge. *In room:* TV, hair dryer, Wi-Fi (free).

AMSTERDAM SOUTH

Bicycle Hotel Amsterdam ★ The proprietors of this establishment hit on an interesting idea: They cater to visitors who wish to explore Amsterdam on bikes and can help guests plan biking routes around the city. You can rent bikes for 7.50€ daily, no deposit, and stable your trusty steed indoors. The rooms have plain but comfortable modern furnishings; some have kitchenettes and small balconies, and there are large rooms for families. There's no elevator.

Van Ostadestraat 123 (off Ferdinand Bolstraat), 1072 SV Amsterdam. www.bicyclehotel.com. © **020/679-3452.** Fax 020/671-5213. 16 units, 8 with bathroom. 60€–120€ double with bathroom; 40€–85€ double without bathroom. Rates include continental breakfast. AE, MC, V (4% charge). Parking 25€. Tram: 3, 12, or 25 to Ceintuurbaan-Ferdinand Bolstraat. **Amenities:** Lounge; bikes; Wi-Fi (free). *In room:* TV.

SIDE TRIPS FROM AMSTERDAM

If Amsterdam is your only stop in the Netherlands, try to make at least one excursion into the countryside. Dikes, windmills, and some of Holland's quaintest villages await you just beyond the city limits.

Haarlem ★★

Just 18km (11 miles) west of Amsterdam, Haarlem is a graceful town of winding canals and medieval neighborhoods that also has several fine museums. The best time to visit is Saturday, for the market on the Grote Markt, or in tulip season (Mar to mid-May), when the city explodes with flowers.

ESSENTIALS
GETTING THERE   Haarlem is 15 minutes from Amsterdam by **train,** and two or three depart every hour from Centraal Station. A round-trip ticket is 13€ in first class and 7.60€ in second class. The historic center is a 5- to 10-minute walk from Haarlem's graceful 1908 Art Nouveau train station, which is decorated with painted tiles and has a fine station restaurant.

There are frequent **buses** from outside Amsterdam Centraal Station. By **car,** take N200/A200 west.

VISITOR INFORMATION   VVV Haarlem, Verwulft 11, 2011 GJ Haarlem (www. haarlemmarketing.nl; © **0900/616-1600**), at Grote Houtstraat. The office is open April to September Monday to Friday from 9:30am to 6pm, Saturday from 9:30am to 5pm, and *Koopzondag*/Shopping Sunday (one or two days per month) from noon to 4pm; October to March Monday from 1 to 5:30pm, Tuesday to Friday from 9:30am to 5:30pm, and Saturday from 10am to 5pm.

EXPLORING HAARLEM
Haarlem is where Frans Hals, Jacob van Ruysdael, and Pieter Saenredam were living and painting their famous portraits, landscapes, and church interiors while Rembrandt was living and working in Amsterdam.

Handel and Mozart made special visits just to play the magnificent organ of **Sint-Bavokerk (St. Bavo's Church),** also known as the **Grote Kerk ★**, Oude Groenmarkt 23 (www.bavo.nl; © **023/553-2040**). Look for the tombstone of painter Frans Hals (ca. 1580–1666) and for a cannonball that has been embedded in the church's wall ever since it flew through a window during the 1572–73 Spanish siege of Haarlem. And, of course, don't miss seeing the famous **Christian Müller Organ** (1738). It has 5,068 pipes and is nearly 30m (98 ft.) tall. Mozart played the organ in 1766 when he was just 10 years old. St. Bavo's is open June to September Monday to Saturday from 10am to 5pm, and Sunday from 10am to 7pm; October to May Monday to Saturday from 10am to 4pm. Admission is 2€ for adults, 1.25€ for children aged 12 to 16, and free for children 11 and under.

From St. Bavo's, it's a short walk to the **Frans Halsmuseum ★★**, Groot Heiligland 62 (www.franshalsmuseum.com; ℂ **023/511-5775**), where the galleries are set within the halls and furnished chambers of a former pensioners' home, and famous paintings by the masters of the Haarlem school hang in settings that look like the 17th-century homes they were intended to adorn. The museum is open Tuesday to Saturday from 11am to 5pm, Sunday and holidays from noon to 5pm. It's closed January 1 and December 25. Admission is 13€ for adults ages 25 and over, 7.50€ for those ages 19 to 24, and free for under-18s.

The oldest and perhaps the most unusual museum in the Netherlands, the **Teylers Museum,** Spaarne 16 (www.teylersmuseum.nl; ℂ **023/531-9010**), contains a curious collection. There are drawings by Michelangelo, Raphael, and Rembrandt; fossils, minerals, and skeletons; instruments of physics; and an odd assortment of inventions, including a 19th-century radarscope. The museum is open Tuesday to Saturday from 10am to 5pm, and Sunday and holidays from noon to 5pm. Admission is 10€ for adults, 2€ for children ages 6 to 17, and free for children 5 and under.

An ideal way to tour the city is by **canal-boat cruise,** operated by **Post Verkade Cruises** (www.postverkadecruises.nl; ℂ **023/535-7723**), from their Spaarne River dock at Gravenstenenbrug. Cruises run from April to October at 10:30am, noon, 1:30, 3, and 4:30pm (during some months the first and last tours are on request only), and are 11€ for adults, 5.50€ for children aged 3 to 10, and free for children 2 and under.

WHERE TO EAT

Jacobus Pieck ★ DUTCH/INTERNATIONAL   This popular cafe-restaurant has a lovely shaded terrace in the garden for fine-weather days; inside, it's bustling and stylish. Outside or in, you get excellent food for reasonable prices and friendly, efficient service. Lunchtime features generous sandwiches and burgers, and salads that are particularly good. Main dinner courses range from pastas and Middle Eastern or Asian dishes to wholesome Dutch standards.

Warmoesstraat 18 (off Oude Groenmarkt). www.jacobuspieck.nl. ℂ **023/532-6144.** Main courses 13€–18€; *dagschotel* (daily special) 13€. AE, MC, V. Mon 11am–4pm; Tues–Sat 11am–4pm and 5:30–10pm.

Volendam & Marken

Volendam and Marken have long been combined on bus-tour itineraries from Amsterdam as a kind of "packaged Holland and costumes to go." Nonetheless, it's possible to have a delightful day in the bracing air of these two communities on the IJsselmeer lake, where a few residents (fewer with each passing year) may be seen going about their daily business in traditional dress.

There are separate, hourly **buses** from Amsterdam to Volendam and Marken from the **CS IJsei** bus station at the rear of Centraal Station. The round-trip fare to Volendam is 7.30€, and to Marken 8.45€; the ride takes 30 minutes to Volendam and 40 minutes to Marken.

Geared to tourism, **Volendam,** 18km (11 miles) northeast of Amsterdam, has souvenir stores, boutiques, and restaurants. Its boat-filled harbor, tiny streets, and traditional houses have an undeniable charm. If you want a snapshot of yourself surrounded by fishermen wearing little caps and balloon-legged pants, Volendammers will gladly pose. They understand that the traditional costume is worth preserving, as is the economy of a small town that lost most of its fishing industry when the Zuiderzee enclosure dam cut it off from the North Sea. You can visit attractions like the fish auction, a diamond cutter, a clog maker, and a house with a room entirely wallpapered in cigar bands.

A causeway now connects the one-time island of **Marken** ★, 16km (10 miles) northeast of Amsterdam, with the mainland, but it remains as insular as ever. Quieter than Volendam, with a village of green-painted houses on stilts around a tiny harbor, it also feels more rural. Clusters of farmhouses dot the *polders* (the reclaimed land from the sea that makes up a quarter of the Netherlands), and a candy-striped lighthouse stands on the IJsselmeer shore.

Marken does not gush over tourists, but it will feed and water them, and let them wander around its pretty streets. Some villagers wear traditional costume, as much to preserve the custom as to appease the tourists who arrive daily. The **Marker Museum,** Kerkbuurt 44–47 (www.markermuseum.nl; ✆ **0299/601-904**), is a typical house museum open from April to October, Monday to Saturday 10am to 5pm (11am–4pm in Oct) and Sunday from noon to 4pm. Admission is 2.50€ for adults, 1.25€ for children aged 5 to 12, and free for children 4 and under.

ROTTERDAM ★★★

Rotterdam is Holland's most futuristic city, centuries removed from Amsterdam in both appearance and personality. Here, instead of the usual Dutch web of little streets, alleyways, and winding canals, there's an abundance of fascinating modern architecture, spacious and elegant malls, and one of the world's busiest ocean harbors. This bustling metropolis is fascinating to see, particularly when you consider the city was a living monument to Holland's Golden Age until it was bombed to rubble during World War II. Traces of Old Rotterdam survive most vividly in only two areas: Delfshaven (Delft Harbor) and Oude Haven (Old Harbor).

At the war's end, rather than try to recreate the old, Rotterdammers looked on their misfortune as an opportunity and relished the chance to create an efficient, workable modern city.

Essentials

GETTING THERE   There's a frequent **train** service to Rotterdam Centraal Station from Amsterdam, with between two and six trains departing each hour round the clock. On **NS Hispeed** *Fyra* trains, the ride takes 40 minutes; on ordinary **Inter-City** trains, it takes 70 to 80 minutes. The one-way fare from Amsterdam is 14€ in second class and 23€ in first class.

By **car** from Amsterdam, take A4/E19 and then A13/E19.

VISITOR INFORMATION   **Rotterdam.info,** Coolsingel 195–197 (www.rotterdam. info; ✆ **010/271-0120;** fax 010/271-0128), close to the junction with Westblaak, is open Monday to Friday from 10am to 7pm, Saturday from 9:30am to 6pm, and Sunday from 10am to 5pm. The **VVV Rotterdam Info Cafe** in the Grand Café-Restaurant Engels, Stationsplein 45 (Weena entrance), is open Monday to Saturday from 9am to 5:30pm and Sunday from 10am to 5pm.

GETTING AROUND   Rotterdam's sprawling size and large gaps between genuine points of interest make it a city to be explored on foot one area at a time, making use of the extensive **RET** (www.ret.nl; ✆ **0900/500-6010**) public transportation network of bus, tram, and Metro (which runs on north–south and east–west axes). Pick up a map of public transportation routes at the VVV tourist office.

You can get around the city's extensive waterfront using waterbuses operated by **RET Fast Ferry** (see above for RET contact information) and **Watertaxi Rotterdam** (www.watertaxirotterdam.nl; ℂ **010/403-0303**).

Taxi stands are sprinkled throughout the city. For a pick-up, turn to **Rotterdamse Taxi Centrale** (www.rtcnv.nl; ℂ **010/462-6060**).

Exploring Rotterdam

Not all of Rotterdam is brand new. Take the Metro to the tiny harbor area known as **Delfshaven (Delft Harbor),** a neighborhood the German bombers missed, and from where the Puritans known as Pilgrims embarked on the first leg of their trip to Massachusetts. This is a pleasant place to spend an afternoon. Wander into the 15th-century **Pelgrimvaderskerk (Pilgrim Fathers Church)** ★, Aelbrechtskolk 20 (www.pelgrimvaderskerk.nl; ℂ **010/477-4156**), in which the Pilgrims prayed before departure, and where they are remembered in special services every Thanksgiving Day. The church is open irregularly; admission is free. Then, peek into antiques stores and galleries.

Euromast and Space Adventure ★★ ☺ ENTERTAINMENT COMPLEX This slender tower, 188m (617 ft.) tall, is indisputably the best vantage point for spectacular views of the city and the harbor. A superfast elevator brings you up to the viewing platform. On a clear day you can see for 30km (19 miles) from the Euroscoop platform. More than that, though, the tower contains interesting exhibits, a restaurant 100m (328 ft.) above the harbor park, and an exciting Space Cabin ride.

Parkhaven 20 (at Het Park). www.euromast.nl. ℂ **010/436-4811.** Admission 9.25€ adults, 8.25€ seniors, 5.90€ children 4–11, free for children 3 and under. Apr–Sept daily 9:30am–1pm; Oct–Mar daily 10am–11pm. Tram: 8 to Euromast/Erasmus MC.

Maritiem Museum Rotterdam ★ ☺ MUSEUM Dedicated entirely to the history of Rotterdam Harbor, this marvelous museum consists of two sections: the main building and *De Buffel,* a beautifully restored warship from 1868. Constantly changing exhibits give you new insight into the close relationship between the Dutch and the sea. In the museum harbor basin, some 20 vessels dating from 1850 to 1950 are moored.

Leuvehaven 1 (at the harbor). www.maritiemmuseum.nl. ℂ **010/413-2680.** Admission 7.50€ adults, 4€ children 4–16, free for children 3 and under. Tues–Sat 10am–5pm (also Mon July–Aug and school vacations); Sun and holidays 11am–5pm. Closed Jan 1, Apr 30, and Dec 25. Metro: Beurs, Churchillplein.

Museum Boijmans Van Beuningen ★★★ ART MUSEUM Art lovers will enjoy this collection of works by 16th- and 17th-century Dutch and Flemish artists, such as Rubens, Hals, Rembrandt, and Steen. They share wall space with an international contingent that includes Salvador Dalí and Man Ray, Titian and Tintoretto, Degas and Daumier. Other galleries hold international modern art, sculpture, porcelain, silver, glass, and Delftware, and regular exhibits of prints and drawings. After viewing the collections you can stroll through the tree-shaded sculpture garden and adjacent Museumpark.

Museumpark 18–20 (at Westersingel). www.boijmans.nl. ℂ **010/441-9400.** Admission 12.50€ adults, 6.25€ students, free for children 18 and under and for all Wed. Tues–Sun (also Easter Mon and Pentecost Mon) 11am–5pm. Closed Jan 1, Apr 30, and Dec 25. Metro: Eendrachtsplein.

Witte de With, Center for Contemporary Art ★ ART MUSEUM Despite being located in a somewhat staid-looking building in the center of town, the city's museum of modern art keeps its changing exhibits program at the cutting edge of modern trends in art and photography, both Dutch and international.

Witte de Withstraat 50 (at Boomgaardsstraat). www.wdw.nl. ✆ **010/411-0144.** Admission 5€ adults; 2.50€ seniors, students, children 12–18; free for children 11 and under. Tues–Sun 11am– 6pm. Metro: Eendrachtsplein.

ORGANIZED TOURS

An essential part of the Rotterdam experience is taking a **Spido Harbor Tour ★★** (www.spido.nl; ✆ **010/275-9988**). You board a boat with two tiers of indoor seating and open decks, and then feel dwarfed by the hulking oil tankers and container ships that glide into their berths along the miles of docks. The vast **Europoort** (pronounced the same as "port" in English) was created when its several harbors were opened directly to the sea, 32km (20 miles) away, by the dredging of a deepwater channel that accommodates even the largest oil tankers. From April to September, departures from a dock below the Erasmus Bridge are every 30 to 45 minutes from 9:30am to 5pm; October to March, departures are limited to two to four times a day. The basic tour, offered year-round, is a 75-minute sail along the city's waterfront; between April and September, it's possible to take an extended (2¼-hour) trip daily at 10am and 12:30pm. On a limited schedule in July and August, you can make all-day excursions along Europoort's full length and to the Delta Works sluices. Tours start at 10.50€ for adults, 6.50€ for children aged 4 to 11, and free for children 3 and under.

ESPECIALLY FOR KIDS

Diergaarde Blijdorp ★★ ☺ ZOO Rotterdam Zoo inhabits a large enclosed plaza in the city's northern Blijdorp district, containing elephants, crocodiles, reptiles, amphibians, and tropical plants and birds. An Asian section houses Javanese monkeys, a bat cave, and exotic birds. The **Oceanium** presents a submarine world inhabited by sharks, jellyfish, and other creatures of the deep brought here from around the world.

Blijdorplaan 8 (at Abraham van Stolkweg). www.rotterdamzoo.nl. ✆ **0900/1857.** Admission 21€ adults, 16.50€ children 3–9, free for children 2 and under. Apr–Sept daily 9am–6pm; Oct–Mar daily 9am–5pm. Bus: 32 to Abraham van Stolkweg.

Where to Eat

Café-Brasserie Dudok ★★ DUTCH/CONTINENTAL Named after the Dutch modernist architect Willem Marinus Dudok, who designed the building, this stylish light-filled, modern cafe in the heart of town serves up snacks and continental meals over two floors. It's a popular meeting place for breakfast, lunch, and afternoon coffee, and is renowned for its apple pie.

Meent 88 (off Coolsingel). www.dudok.nl. ✆ **010/433-3102.** Main courses 15€–21€. AE, DC, MC, V. Mon–Thurs 8am–midnight; Fri 8am–10pm; Sat 9am–9:30pm; Sun 10am–9:30pm. Metro: Stadhuis.

Dewi Sri ★ INDONESIAN Soberly decorated Dewi Sri has been making culinary magic since 1977, in a merchant's house dating from 1880 along the Nieuwe Maas. There are plenty of individual choices for those who know their way around an Indonesian menu, while for newcomers the 14-dish Sumatra rijsttafel affords a wide-ranging insight into traditional Indonesian cuisine.

Westerkade 20 (at Het Park). www.dewisri.nl. ✆ **010/436-0263.** Main courses 8€–12€; *rijsttafel* 25€. AE, DC, MC, V. Mon–Fri noon–2:30pm and 5:30–10:30pm; Sat–Sun 5–10:30pm. Tram: 7 to Westplein.

In den Rustwat ★★★ FRENCH   You'd swear you're in the country at the "Rest Some," but then, back in the 16th century, this thatched farmhouse-style restaurant used to be an inn. Patron/cuisinier Marcel van Zomeren has transformed it into one of the city's top establishments. Using only the freshest organic ingredients, he keeps himself and his staff inspired by constantly adapting the menu to seasonal produce. A salad of Bresse pigeon breast with poached quail's eggs and ravioli of pigeon and goose liver is an example of a starter, which might be followed by crisp sautéed sea-bass filet on a bed of warm tomatoes and young vegetables.

Honingerdijk 96 (next to Arboretum Trompenburg). www.idrw.nl. ☏ **010/413-4110.** Reservations recommended on weekends. Main courses 25€–28€; Set lunch 33€; set dinner menus 43€–58€. AE, DC, MC, V. Tues–Fri noon–3pm and 6–10pm; Sat 6–10pm. Tram: 21 to Woudestein.

Where to Stay

Bazar ★★   On a busy street near the main museums, the main floor of this place oozes with the atmosphere of *1,001 Nights*—golden pillars, frilly textiles, open-worked shutters, Persian rugs, stained-glass lamps, and brass fittings. By way of the-matic variation, there's an African floor and a South American floor. The rooms follow these cues in both design and spirit, making for a distinctive experience, so long as you feel comfortable in whichever ambience you're given. If not, ask to change. Higher-priced rooms have balconies. The ground-floor international cafe-restaurant doubles as hotel reception.

Witte de Withstraat 16 (at William Boothlaan), 3012 BP Rotterdam. www.hotelbazar.nl. ☏ **010/206-5151.** Fax 010/206-5159. 27 units. 80€–125€ double. Rates include Middle Eastern breakfast. AE, DC, MC, V. Limited street parking. Tram: 7 or 20 to Museumpark. **Amenities:** Restaurant; bar. *In room:* TV, minibar, hair dryer, Wi-Fi (8€/day).

Bienvenue   This small, budget hotel is one of the best in its price range and is within easy walking range (400m/440 yds.) of the city's main train station. The bright guest rooms are plain but clean, and have comfortable beds, showers (two bathrooms have tubs), and include a few three- and four-person rooms. There's a tree-shaded canal in front of the hotel, and rooms at the back open onto the terrace. Steep stairs and lack of an elevator might be a problem for some people.

Spoorsingel 24B (2 blocks north of Centraal Station), 3033 GL Rotterdam. www.hotelbienvenue.nl. ☏ **010/466-9394.** Fax 010/467-7475. 10 units, 7 with bathroom. 78€ double with bathroom; 66€ double without bathroom. Rates include buffet breakfast. AE, DC, MC, V. Limited street parking. Metro: Centraal Station. *In room:* TV, Wi-Fi (free).

New York ★★   This building, one of Europe's first skyscrapers, was constructed at the beginning of the 20th century to house the headquarters of the Holland–America shipping line, which sailed to New York. Many of the city's emigrants passed through these portals with their trunks. In the bright guest rooms, which encompass a surprising range of styles, furnishings combine the old and the new; some rooms have stunning balcony views. The downstairs cafe-restaurant has a great view over the river and docklands.

Koninginnenhoofd 1 (at Cruise Terminal Rotterdam), 3072 AD Rotterdam. www.hotelnewyork.nl. ☏ **010/439-0500.** Fax 010/484-2701. 72 units. 99€–260€ double. AE, DC, MC, V. Limited street parking. Metro: Wilhelminaplein. **Amenities:** Cafe-restaurant; room service. *In room:* TV, minibar, Wi-Fi (free).

DELFT ★

Yes, Delft, 54km (34 miles) southwest of Amsterdam, is the town of the famous blue-and-white porcelain. And, yes, you can visit the factory. But don't let delftware be your only reason to visit. Not only is this one of the prettiest small cities in the Netherlands, with linden trees bending over gracious canals, Delft is also important as a cradle of the Dutch Republic and the traditional burial place of the royal family. Plus, it was the birthplace, and inspiration, of the 17th century master of light and subtle emotion, painter Jan Vermeer.

Essentials

GETTING THERE   There are several **trains** an hour from Amsterdam's Centraal Station to Delft Station, which is southwest of the center of town. The ride takes about 1 hour and is 40€ round-trip in first class and 23€ in second. By **car,** take A4/E19 and then A13/E19 past Den Haag (The Hague) and watch for the Delft exit coming up.

VISITOR INFORMATION   **Tourist Information Point Delft,** Hippolytusbuurt 4, 2611 HN Delft (www.delft.nl; *C* **015/215-4051**), is in the center of town. The office is open April to September, Sunday and Monday from 10am to 6pm, Tuesday to Friday from 9am to 6pm, and Saturday from 10am to 5pm; October to March, Sunday from 11am to 4pm, and Tuesday to Saturday from 10am to 4pm.

Exploring Delft

Vermeer's house is long gone from Delft, as are his paintings. Instead, visit the **Oude Kerk ★**, Heilige Geestkerkhof, where he's buried. You might want to visit also the **Nieuwe Kerk ★★**, on Markt, where Prince William of Orange and other members of the House of Oranje-Nassau are buried, and to climb its tower, which is 109m (358 ft.) high. Both churches (www.oudeennieuwekerkdelft.nl) are open mid-March to October, Monday through Saturday from 9am to 6pm; November to mid-March, Monday to Friday from 11am to 4pm, and Saturday from 10am to 5pm. Combined admission is 3.50€ for adults, 2€ for students and children 12–18, 1.50€ for children ages 6 to 11, and free for children 5 and under; separate admission to the Nieuwe Kerk tower is 3.50€ for adults, 2€ for students and children 12–18, 1.50€ for children ages 6 to 11, and free for children 5 and under.

The **Museum Het Prinsenhof ★**, Sint-Agathaplein 1 (www.prinsenhof-delft.nl; *C* **015/260-2358**), on the nearby Oude Delft canal, is where William I of Orange (William the Silent) lived and had his headquarters in the years during which he helped found the Dutch Republic. It's where he was assassinated in 1584, and you can still see the musket-ball holes in the stairwell. Today the Prinsenhof is a museum of paintings, tapestries, silverware, and pottery. It's open Tuesday to Sunday from 11am to 5pm. Admission is 7.50€ for adults, 4€ for students and children ages 12 to 18, and free for children 11 and under.

To watch a demonstration of the traditional art of making and hand-painting delftware, visit the factory and showroom of **Koninklijke Porceleyne Fles (Royal Delft) ★**, Rotterdamseweg 196 (www.royaldelft.com; *C* **015/251-2030;** bus: 63, 121, or 129 to Jaffalaan), founded in 1653. It's open April to October, daily from 9am to 5pm; November to March, Monday to Saturday from 9am to 5pm. Admission is 12€ and free for children 11 and under.

Where to Eat

Spijshuis de Dis ★ DUTCH   Fine Dutch cooking that's traditional at heart but given a modern accent is served up at this atmospheric old restaurant. Among the top dishes are *bakke pot*—a stew made from beef, chicken, and rabbit; V.O.C. mussels (named after the Dutch initials for the East India Company), prepared with garlic, ginger, and curry; and asparagus when in season (May–June). Don't miss the home-made mushroom soup.

Beestenmarkt 36 (2 blocks from Markt). www.spijshuisdedis.com. ✆ **015/213-1782.** Main courses 16€–25€. AE, DC, MC, V. Tues–Sat 5–10pm.

Stadsherberg De Mol TRADITIONAL DUTCH   Food is served here in the medieval manner—in wooden bowls from which you eat with your hands. Set menus include a starter (such as pâté in puff pastry), soup, a variety of meats (such as chicken, lamb, ham, and rabbit), salad, and baked potato. Prices are moderate and quantities copious; and there is fun, too, with live music and dancing on some evenings.

Molslaan 104 (off Beestenmarkt). www.stadsherbergdemol.nl. ✆ **015/212-1343.** Main courses 12€–18€. MC, V. Tues–Sun 6–11pm.

LEIDEN ★★

Students of U.S. history may know that the Pilgrim Fathers lived in this town, 36km (22 miles) southwest of Amsterdam, for 11 years before sailing for North America on the *Mayflower*. Leiden's proudest moment came in 1574, when it was the only Dutch town to withstand a full-blown siege by the Spanish invaders. This was the birthplace of the Dutch tulip trade, and of the painters Rembrandt and Jan Steen, and it is the home of the oldest university in the Netherlands. Finally, with 14 museums, covering subjects ranging from antiquities, natural history, and anatomy to clay pipes and coins, Leiden seems justified in calling itself Museum Stad (Museum City).

Essentials

GETTING THERE   There are several trains an hour from Amsterdam Centraal Station to Leiden Centraal Station, which is northwest of the town center (about a 10-min. walk). The ride takes around 35 minutes and is 28€ round-trip in first class and 16€ in second. If you go by car, take A4/E19 in the direction of The Hague and watch for the Leiden exit.

VISITOR INFORMATION   **Visitor Center Leiden,** Stationsweg 41, 2312 AT, Leiden (www.leiden.nl; ✆ **071/516-6000**), is situated outside the rail station. The office is open Monday to Friday from 8am to 6pm, Saturday from 10am to 4pm, and Sunday from 11am to 3pm.

Exploring Leiden

Among the spectacular antiquities housed at the **Rijksmuseum van Oud-heden ★★**, Rapenburg 28 (www.rmo.nl; ✆ **071/516-3163**), is the 1st-century-A.D. **Temple of Taffeh** presented by the Egyptian government as a gift to the Dutch nation for its assistance in saving monuments prior to the construction of the Aswan High Dam. The museum is open Tuesday to Sunday from 10am to 5pm (also Mon during school vacations). Admission is 9€ for adults, 7.50€ for seniors and students, 5.50€ for children ages 13 to 17, free for children 12 and under, and 25€ for families.

Also noteworthy is the University of Leiden's **Hortus Botanicus (Botanical Gardens),** Rapenburg 73 (www.hortus.leidenuniv.nl; ℂ **071/527-7249**), from 1587. In 1592, botanist Carolus Clusius brought the first-ever tulip bulbs to Holland and planted them here, but he never got to see them flower because they were stolen by rivals. The gardens are open April through October, daily from 10am to 6pm; November through March, Tuesday to Sunday from 10am to 4pm. Admission is 6€ for adults, 2€ for students, 3€ for children ages 4 to 12, and free for children 3 and under.

Visit the **Museum de Lakenhal ★**, Oude Singel 28–32 (www.lakenhal.nl; ℂ **071/516-5360**), to view works by local heroes Rembrandt and Jan Steen, and others, plus period rooms from the 17th to the 19th centuries, and a copper stew pot said to have been retrieved by a boy who crawled through a chink in the city wall just minutes after the lifting of the Spanish siege. He found this very pot full of boiling stew in the enemy's camp and brought it back to feed the starving inhabitants. The museum is open Tuesday to Friday from 10am to 5pm, and weekends and holidays from noon to 5pm. Admission is 7.50€ for adults, 4.50€ for seniors, and free for children 17 and under.

LEIDEN & THE PILGRIM FATHERS

To touch base with the Pilgrims, pick up the VVV tourist office's brochure *A Pilgrimage Through Leiden: A Walk in the Footsteps of the Pilgrim Fathers.* The walk starts at the **Lodewijkskerk,** which was used as a meeting place by the cloth guild, of which William Bradford, who later became governor of New Plymouth, was a member. The walk takes you past the house on William Brewstersteeg where William Brewster's Pilgrim Press published the religious views that angered the Church of England. Plaques at **Sint-Pieterskerk** (in a small square off Kloksteeg) memorialize the Pilgrims, in particular Rev. Jon Robinson, who was forced to stay behind because of illness and is buried in this church.

At the **Leiden American Pilgrim Museum ★**, Beschuitsteeg 9 (www.rootsweb. ancestry.com ℂ **071/512-2413**), you can hear a recorded commentary on the Pilgrims and see photocopies of documents relating to their 11-year residence in Leiden. The museum is open Wednesday to Saturday from 1 to 5pm. Admission is 3€ and free for children 5 and under.

Where to Eat

Annie's DUTCH/CONTINENTAL   This lively water-level restaurant has vaulted cellars that are a favorite eating spot for both students and locals, who spill out onto the canalside terrace in fine weather. When the canals are frozen, the view is enchanting, as skaters practice their turns. The dinner menu is simple but wholesome, and during the day you can snack on sandwiches and tapas.

Hoogstraat 1A (at Oude Rijn). www.annies.nu. ℂ **071/512-5737.** Main courses 14€–28€. MC, V. Daily 11am–1am.

Stadscafé van der Werff ★ CONTINENTAL   This relaxed cafe-restaurant in a grand 1930s villa on the edge of the old town is popular with the town's students and ordinary citizens alike. Diners enjoy dishes like a basic Indonesian satay or their surf-and-turf *kalfsbiefstukje met gebakken gambas en een kreeftensaus* (beefsteak with fried prawns in a lobster sauce).

Steenstraat 2 (at Kiekpad). www.stadscafevanderwerff.nl. ℂ **071/513-0335.** Main courses 15€–22€. AE, DC, MC, V. Daily 9am–10pm (cafe to 1am).

NORWAY

by Roger Norum

T he "Land of the Midnight Sun" offers a truly unique and unforgettable experience in an environment like no other on planet Earth. To the ancients, Norway was a mythical land—a place of unspeakable perils known as "Ultima Thule," feared for the strange, barbaric, and fabulous creatures that inhabited it. Today, Norway is definitively a land of tradition, as exemplified by its rustic stave churches, folk dances, strong ties to nature, and quirky social sensibilities. But it is also an extremely modern nation, a technologically advanced welfare state with cradle-to-grave care that provides pensions, health and unemployment insurance, and rehabilitation assistance. The system is financed by citizens' contributions, making Norway one of the most heavily taxed nations on Earth.

14

In terms of its natural draws, however, this is one of the world's last great natural frontiers—a place of astonishing beauty, with steep and jagged fjords, salmon-rich rivers, glaciers, mountains, and sprawling meadows. Norwegians view these scrub-covered islands, snow-crested peaks and glacier-born fjords as strong symbols of wilderness culture. During the summer, the midnight sun shines late and warm; in the colder months, the shimmering northern lights beckon.

OSLO

After World War II, Oslo grew to 450 sq. km (174 sq. miles), making it one of the 10 largest capitals in the world in sheer area, yet not in urban buildup. The city is one of the most heavily forested on Earth, and fewer than half a million Norwegians live and work here. One of the oldest Scandinavian capital cities, founded in the mid-11th century, Oslo has never been a mainstream tourist site. But the city is culturally rich with many diversions—enough to fill at least 3 or 4 busy days. It's also the center for many easy excursions along the Oslofjord or to towns and villages in its environs.

In recent years Oslo has grown from what even the Scandinavians viewed as a Nordic backwater to one of Europe's happening cities. Restaurants, nightclubs, cafes, shopping complexes, and other venues keep on opening. A kind of Nordic *joie de vivre* permeates the city; the only drawback is that all this fun is going to cost you—Oslo ranks as one of the world's most expensive cities.

Essentials

GETTING THERE

BY PLANE **Oslo International Airport** is in Gardemoen (✆ **06400** or **91-50-64-00**), about 50km (31 miles) east of downtown Oslo, a 45-minute drive from the center. All domestic and international flights coming into Oslo arrive through this much-upgraded airport, including aircraft belonging to SAS, British Airways, Norwegian, and Ryanair. Two smaller airports, **Torp** (www.torp.no; ✆ **33-42-70-00**) and **Rygge** (www.ryg.no; ✆ **69-23-00-00**), both south of Oslo city center, serve various budget European airlines.

A high-speed railway service, **Flytoget** (www.flytoget.no; ✆ **81-50-07-77**), runs between Gardemoen and Oslo's main railway station, taking 19 minutes and departing approximately every 10 minutes, priced at NOK140 per person each way. There are also local trains to both Rygge and Torp airports. A regular bus service operates

Oslo

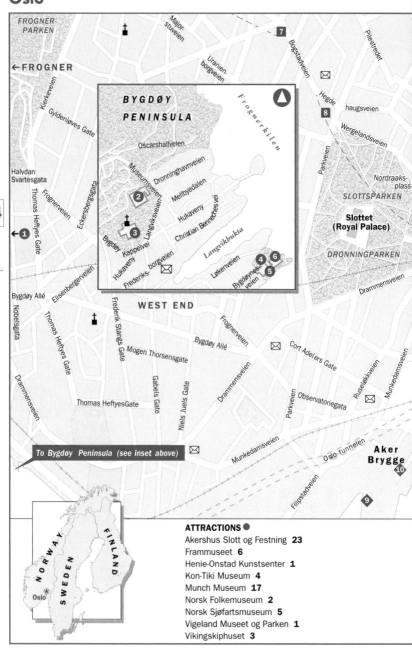

14

NORWAY | Oslo

←1

ATTRACTIONS ●

Akershus Slott og Festning **23**
Frammuseet **6**
Henie-Onstad Kunstsenter **1**
Kon-Tiki Museum **4**
Munch Museum **17**
Norsk Folkemuseum **2**
Norsk Sjøfartsmuseum **5**
Vigeland Museet og Parken **1**
Vikingskiphuset **3**

To Bygdøy Peninsula (see inset above)

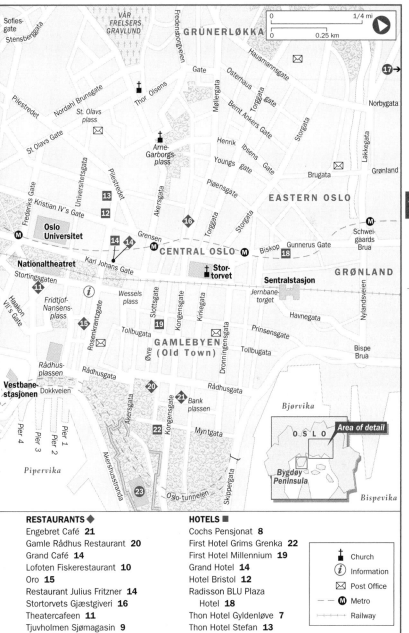

RESTAURANTS ◆
Engebret Café **21**
Gamle Rådhus Restaurant **20**
Grand Café **14**
Lofoten Fiskerestaurant **10**
Oro **15**
Restaurant Julius Fritzner **14**
Stortorvets Gjæstgiveri **16**
Theatercafeen **11**
Tjuvholmen Sjømagasin **9**

HOTELS ■
Cochs Pensjonat **8**
First Hotel Grims Grenka **22**
First Hotel Millennium **19**
Grand Hotel **14**
Hotel Bristol **12**
Radisson BLU Plaza
  Hotel **18**
Thon Hotel Gyldenløve **7**
Thon Hotel Stefan **13**

✝	Church
ⓘ	Information
✉	Post Office
– – Ⓜ	Metro
┼┼┼┼	Railway

from all three airports into downtown Oslo. The bus service for Gardemoen costs NOK120 per person and is maintained by **SAS** (www.flybussen.no; ☎ **81-50-01-76**), and will take you to the Central Railway station and to most of the SAS hotels within Oslo. For Rygge, contact **Rygge Expressen** (www.rygge-ekspressen.no); the ticket price is NOK130. For Torp, contact **Torp Expressen** (www.torpekspressen.no); the ticket price is NOK190. **Taxis** cost a minimum of NOK700 for up to four passengers plus luggage to Gardemoen; both other airports will cost significantly more. If you need a "maxi-taxi," a minivan that's suitable for between 5 and 15 passengers plus luggage, you'll be charged a minimum NOK900.

BY TRAIN   The first high-speed train between Oslo and Stockholm operated by Swedish Railways, **SJ** (www.sj.se), has reduced travel time to 4 hours and 50 minutes between these two Scandinavian capitals. There are two to three trains daily in each direction. Trains from the Continent, Sweden, and Denmark arrive at **Oslo Sentralstasjon (Central Station),** Jernbanetorget 1 (www.nsb.no; ☎ **81-50-08-88** for train information), at the beginning of Karl Johans Gate, in the center of the city. The station is open daily from 4:30am to 1am. From here, trains leave for Bergen, Stavanger, Trondheim, Bodø, and all other rail links in Norway. You can also take trams to all major parts of Oslo. Lockers and a luggage office are available at the station if needed.

BY CAR   If you're driving from mainland Europe, the fastest way to reach Oslo is to take the **Stena Line** (www.stenaline.com) car ferry from Frederikshavn, Denmark. From Frederikshavn, car ferries run to several towns near Oslo and to Gothenburg, Sweden. You can also take a car ferry from Copenhagen to several points in western Sweden, or from Helsingør, Denmark, to Helsingborg, Sweden. Highway E6 runs the length of Sweden's western coast from Malmö through Helsingborg and Gothenburg, right up to Oslo. If you're driving from Stockholm to Oslo, take the E3 west to Örebro, where it connects with the E18 to Oslo. Once you near the outskirts of Oslo from any direction, follow the signs into the *sentrum* (center).

BY FERRY   Ferries from Europe arrive at **Oslo port,** a 15-minute walk (or a short taxi ride) from the center. From Denmark, Scandinavia's link with the Continent, ferries depart for Oslo from Copenhagen (DFDS Seaways; www.dfds.com), Kiel (Color Line; www.colorline.com), and Frederikshavn (see By Car above) in Denmark. The daily Color Line (www.colorline.com) summer crossing from Strømstad, Sweden, to Sandefjord, Norway, takes 2½ hours; from Sandefjord, it's an easy drive or train ride north to Oslo.

VISITOR INFORMATION

You can pick up free maps and brochures, and book hotel accommodation, sightseeing tickets, and guide services at the **Tourist Information office,** at Fridtjof Nansens Plass 5 near City Hall. The office is open June to August daily 9am to 7pm, April to May and September Monday to Saturday 9am to 5pm, and October to March Monday to Friday 9am to 4pm. There is an additional information office at **Oslo Sentralstasjon (Central railway station),** Jernbanetorget 1, which is open daily from May to September 8am to 8pm and October to April daily 8am to 6pm. The centralized phone number for all the tourist offices in Oslo is ☎ **81-53-05-55.** For information online, try the Norwegian Tourist Board (**www.visitnorway.com**) or Visit Oslo (**www.visitoslo.com**). The **Oslo–Official City App** is a free app that you can download for Apple and Android. It can be used when data roaming is switched off and provides information about restaurants, attractions, and events.

CITY LAYOUT

Oslo is at the mouth of the 95km (59-mile) Oslofjord. Opening onto the harbor is **Rådhusplassen** (City Hall Square), dominated by the modern City Hall, a major attraction. Guided bus tours leave from this square, and fjord cruises depart from the pier facing the municipal building. Out on a promontory to the east is the **Akershus Castle. Oslo** is made for walking and, except for excursions to the museum-loaded Bygdøy Peninsula and Holmenkollen, most attractions can be covered on foot.

NEIGHBORHOODS IN BRIEF

Oslo consists mainly of **central Oslo,** with Oslo Central railway station to the east of the city center and the Royal Palace to the west. Karl Johans Gate, the principal street, connects these two points. Most Oslo hotels and restaurants are here, as are almost 50 museums and galleries—enough to fill plenty of rainy days. The best of the lot include Akershus Castle, the Historical Museum, and the National Gallery.

The **Old Town** (or Gamlebyen) lies south of the Parliament building (the Stortinget) and Karl Johans Gate. This area has some of the city's old-fashioned restaurants, along with the Norwegian Resistance Museum and the Old Town Hall.

Aker Brygge is one of Oslo's newest neighborhoods, an excellent place for dining and diversions, but with few hotels. It's the best place for long walks to take in the harbor life.

The main attractions in **Eastern Oslo** are the Botanisk Hage (Botanical Garden), the Zoological Museum, and the Edvard Munch Museum in Tøyen—little more is worth seeing.

Farther west—6km (3¾ miles) by car, but better reached by car ferry—is the **Bygdøy Peninsula.** Here you'll find such attractions as the Norwegian Folk Museum, the Viking ships, the polar ship *Fram,* and the *Kon-Tiki* Museum. Break up your sightseeing venture with a meal here, but plan to stay elsewhere.

Lying behind Oslo Central railway station is the **Grønland district,** where many Oslovians go for ethnic dining and great nightlife. There is little of sightseeing interest here.

Lying in east Oslo is **Grünerløkka,** which most of its inhabitants refer to affectionately as "Løkka." This once-run-down sector of Oslo traditionally was known as the workers' district. Today many professional Oslovians are moving in to restore apartments, and the district is the site of several fashionable cafes and restaurants.

Nearly all visitors want to see **Holmenkollen,** a wooded range of hills northwest of the city rising to about 226m (741 ft.). You can reach it in 35 minutes by electric train from the city center.

GETTING AROUND

The **Oslo Pass** (www.visitoslo.com) can help you become acquainted with the city. It includes travel on public transportation, admission to museums and other top sights, discounts on sightseeing buses and boats, a rebate on your car rental, and special treats in restaurants. You can purchase the card at hotels and tourist information offices; from travel agents; and in the branches of Sparebanken Oslo Akershus. Adults pay NOK270 for a 1-day card, NOK395 for 2 days, and NOK495 for 3 days. Children's cards cost NOK120, NOK145, and NOK190, respectively.

BY BUS, TRAM & SUBWAY Jernbanetorget is Oslo's major **bus and tram** terminal station. Most buses and trams passing through the heart of town stop at Wessels Plass, next to the Parliament, or at Stortorvet, the main marketplace. Many also stop at the National Theater or University Square on Karl Johans Gate. At a subway stop near the National Theater, you can catch an **electric train** to the Holmenkollen ski jump.

The **subway (T-banen)** has four branch lines to the east. The Western Suburban subway route (including Holmenkollen) has four lines to the residential sections and recreation grounds west and north of the city. Subways and trains leave from near the National Theater on Karl Johans Gate.

For schedule and fare information, call **Trafikanten** (© 81-50-01-76; www.trafikanten.no). Automated machines on board buses and trams stamp and validate tickets. Bus drivers sell single-trip tickets for NOK50; children travel for half-fare, though you can save nearly 50% if you buy these ahead of time at various ticket machines at bus stops (tram tickets, however, must be bought at the machines in tram stations as they are not sold on board). There are also 24-hour (NOK74) and 7-day (NOK220) unlimited passes. If you are caught traveling without a valid ticket, the fine is NOK900.

BY CAR Driving is not a practical way to get around Oslo because parking is limited. The efficient public transportation network, even to isolated areas, makes a car unnecessary.

BY TAXI Hiring a taxi is very expensive in Oslo. Tariffs start at NOK46 (flagfall) for a taxi hailed in the street or at NOK50 if you book one in advance. The approximate fare from Oslo International Airport to the center of Oslo tends to be a minimum of NOK600. In addition to regular fares, there are pricey surcharges between 5 and 10pm; these increase even further between 10pm and 6am. If you need a taxi, call **Oslo Taxis** © 23-23-23-23, available 24 hours a day; reserve at least an hour in advance.

Taxis can be hailed on the street, provided they're more than 91m (298 ft.) from a taxi rank. When a cab is available, its roof light goes on. The most difficult time to hail a taxi is Monday to Friday 8:30 to 10am and 3 to 5pm, and Saturday 8:30 to 10am.

BY FERRY Beginning in mid-April, ferries depart for Bygdøy from pier 3 in front of the Rådhuset. For schedules, call **Båtservice** (© 23-35-68-90). If you're visiting the museums in Bygdøy, the ferry or bus is a good choice because parking there is limited. Other ferries leave for various parts of the Oslofjord. Inquire at the **tourist information office,** Fridtjof Nansens Plass 5 (© 81-53-05-55).

BY BIKE City bikes (**Oslo Bysykkel**) are available from a large number of bike stations around Oslo. You need an electronic card costing NOK90 to use the bikes, and these cards can be purchased at the Tourist Information office at Oslo Central Station or behind City Hall. Visit www.oslobysykkel.no or call © 81-50-02-50 for more information; bikes are rented April to November daily 6am to midnight.

[FastFACTS] OSLO

ATM/Banks Most **banks** are open Monday to Friday 8:30am to 3:30pm (Thurs to 5pm). ATMs are widely available around the country; check with your own bank to find out charges.

Business Hours Most **businesses** are open Monday to Friday 9am to 4pm. **Stores** are generally open Monday to Friday 9am to 5pm (many stay open later on Thurs to 6 or 7pm) and Saturday 9am to 1 or 2pm.

Currency You'll pay your way in Norway with Norwegian kroner or crowns, which are universally abbreviated NOK. There are

100 øre in 1 krone. The exchange rate used in this chapter is US$1 = NOK6 (or NOK1 = approximately 16.6¢). Note that Norway is not a member of the European Union.

Currency Exchange

Banks will exchange most foreign currencies or cash traveler's checks. Bring your passport for identification. If the banks are closed, try the ATMs at the Oslo Central railway station. Alternatively, go to **Forex,** Oslo Central station, Jernbanetorget 1 (*✆* **22-17-60-80**), open Monday to Friday 8am to 8pm and Saturday 9am to 5pm.

Doctors/Hospitals

Some larger hotels have arrangements with doctors in case a guest becomes ill, or you can try the 24-hour **Legevaktsentralen (Emergencies),** Storgata 40 (*✆* **22-93-22-93**). A privately funded alternative is **Oslo Akutten,** Nedre Vollgate 8 (*✆* **22-00-81-60**), located two blocks from the Stortinget (Parliament building). For more routine medical assistance, you can contact the biggest hospital in Oslo, **Ullevål,** Kirkeveien 166 (*✆* **02770** or **22-11-80-80**). To consult a private doctor (nearly all of whom speak English), check the telephone directory or ask at your hotel for a recommendation.

Embassies & Consulates

In case you lose your passport or have some other emergency, contact your embassy in Oslo. The **United States** embassy is at Henrik Ibsensgate 48, N-0244 Oslo (norway.us embassy.gov; *✆* **21-30-85-40**); **United Kingdom**, Thomas Heftyesgate 8, N-0244 Oslo (ukinnorway. fco.gov.uk; *✆* **23-13-27-00**); and **Canada**, Wergelands- veien 7, N-0244 Oslo (www. canadainternational.gc.ca; *✆* **22-99-53-00**). The **Irish Embassy** is at Haakon VII's gate 1, N-0244 Oslo (www. embassyofireland.no; *✆* **22-01-72-00**). The de facto **Australian Embassy** is the honorary consul of the Australian Consulate, Strandveien 20, N-1324 Lysaker (*✆* **67-58-48-48**). For **New Zealand**, contact the consulate at Strandveien 50, N-1366 Lysaker (*✆* **67-11-00-30**). In addition, there is a British consulate in Bergen at Carl Øvre Ole Bulls Plass 1 (*✆* **55-36-78-10**).

Emergencies

Dial the Oslo **Police** at *✆* **112;** report a **fire** at *✆* **110;** call an **ambulance** at *✆* **113.**

Internet Access

You can log on for free at the Rådhuset (City Hall) on Råd- husplassen (*✆* **23-46-16-00**).

Mail/Postage

The **Oslo General Post Office** is at Dronningensgatan 15 (*✆* **23-14-90-00** for information). Enter at the corner of Prinsensgate. It's open Monday to Friday 8am to 5pm and Saturday 9am to 2pm; it's closed Sunday and public holidays. You can arrange for mail to be sent to the main post office c/o General Delivery. The address is Poste Restante, P.O. Box 1181-Sentrum, Dronningensgatan 15, N-0101 Oslo, Norway. You must show your passport to collect it.

Pharmacies Jernbane- torvets Apotek, Jernbane- torget 4A (*✆* **22-41-24-82**) is open 24 hours.

Safety Of the four Scandinavian capitals, Oslo is widely considered the safest. However, it is still a major city, so don't be lulled into a false sense of security. Be careful, and make sure your wallet, purse or bag is hidden or secured to you.

Telephones The country code for Norway is **47,** and the city code for Oslo is **22** (in some rare cases, **23**). For operator assistance in English, dial *✆* **115.** Local SIM cards for your mobile phone can be purchased at many tobacconists and mobile phone shops in all cities and most towns. You'll generally pay around NOK200 for a local phone number and half an hour of calling credit.

Tipping Hotels add a 10% to 15% service charge to your bill, which is sufficient unless someone has performed a special service. Most bellhops get at least NOK10 per suitcase. Nearly all restaurants add a service charge of up to 15% to your bill. Barbers and hairdressers usually aren't tipped, but toilet attendants and hatcheck people expect at least NOK3. Don't tip theater ushers. Taxi drivers don't expect tips unless they handle heavy luggage.

Exploring Oslo

CENTRAL OSLO

Akershus Slott og Festning (Akershus Castle & Fortress) CASTLE It has withstood fierce battles, drawn-out sieges, and a few fires, and changed shape architecturally since King Haakon V ordered it built in 1299, when Oslo was named capital of Norway. A fortress, or *festning*, with thick earth-and-stone walls surrounds the castle, with protruding bastions designed to resist artillery bombardment. The moats and reinforced ramparts were added in the mid-1700s. For several centuries it was not only a fortress, but also the abode of the rulers of Norway. Now the government uses it for state occasions. From the well-manicured lawns there are **panoramic views** ★ of Oslo and the Oslofjorden.

Festnings-Plassen. www.forsvarsbygg.no/festningene/Festningene/Akershus-festning (Norwegian only). ✆ **23-09-39-17.** Admission NOK40 adults, NOK20 children, free 6 and under; family NOK100; seniors and students NOK30. June–Aug Mon–Sat 10am–4pm, Sunday 12:30–5pm; Sept–May Sat–Sun noon–5pm. English tours: Mid-June–Aug daily 11am, 1, 2, and 4pm. May–mid-June and mid-Aug–end-Aug Sat and Sun 3pm; mid-June–end June Sat and Sun 1 and 4pm. Tram: 10 or 12.

BYGDØY PENINSULA

Frammuseet (Polar Ship Fram) MUSEUM A long walk from the Viking ship museum (see below), the Frammuseet contains the sturdy polar exploration ship *Fram*, which Fridtjof Nansen sailed across the Arctic (1893–96). The vessel was later used by Norwegian explorer **Roald Amundsen,** the first man to reach the South Pole (1911).

Bygdøynesveien 36. www.fram.museum.no. ✆ **23-28-29-50.** Admission NOK60 adults, NOK25 children 7–15, NOK120 family ticket. June–Aug daily 9am–6pm; Sept and May daily 9am–5:45pm; Nov–Feb daily 10am–3pm. Ferry: From Pier 3 facing the Rådhuset (summer only). Bus: 30 from the Nationaltheatret.

Kon-Tiki Museum MUSEUM *Kon-Tiki* is the world-famed balsa-log raft in which the young Norwegian scientist **Thor Heyerdahl** and his five comrades sailed for 7,000km (4,350 miles) in 1947—all the way from Callao, Peru, to Raroia, Polynesia. Besides the raft, there are exhibits from Heyerdahl's subsequent visit to Easter Island, including an Easter Island family cave, with a collection of sacred lava figurines.

Bygdøynesveien 36. www.kon-tiki.no. ✆ **23-08-67-67.** Admission NOK60 adults, NOK25 children 5–16. Apr–May and Sept daily 10am–5pm; June–Aug daily 9:30am–5:30pm; Oct and Mar daily 10:30am–4pm; Nov–Feb 10:30am–3:30pm. Ferry: From Pier 3 facing the Rådhuset (summer only). Bus: 30 from the Nationaltheatret.

Norsk Folkemuseum ★★ MUSEUM Buildings from all over Norway have been transported and reassembled on 14 hectares (35 acres) on the Bygdøy Peninsula. The 140 reconstructions at this open-air folk museum include a number of medieval buildings, such as the Raulandstua, one of the oldest wooden dwellings still standing in Norway, and a stave church from about 1200. Rural buildings are grouped together by region of origin, while the urban houses have been laid out in the form of an old town.

Museumsveien 10. www.norskfolke.museum.no. ✆ **22-12-37-00.** Admission NOK75–NOK100 children 6–16, free for children 5 and under, NOK150–NOK200 family ticket. Jan to mid-May and mid-Sept to Dec Mon–Fri 11am–3pm, Sat–Sun 11am–4pm; mid-May to mid-Sept daily 10am–6pm. Ferry: from Pier 3 facing the Rådhuset (summer only). Bus: 30 from the National Theater.

Norsk Sjøfartsmuseum (Norwegian Maritime Museum) MUSEUM Containing a complete ship's deck with helm and chart house, and a three-deck-high section of the passenger steamer *Sandnaes,* the museum chronicles the maritime history and culture of Norway. The fully restored polar vessel *Gjoa,* used by Roald Amundsen in his search for America's Northwest Passage, is also on display. The three-masted 1916 schooner *Svanen (Swan)* now belongs to the museum and is used as a training vessel.

Bygdøynesveien 37. www.norsk-sjøfartsmuseum.no. ℂ **24-11-41-50.** Admission to museum and boat hall NOK60 adults, free for children. Mid-May–Aug daily 10am–6pm; Sept–mid-May Mon–Wed and Fri–Sun 10am–4pm; Thurs 10am–6pm. Ferry: From Pier 3 facing the Rådhuset (summer only). Bus: 30 from the Nationaltheatret.

Vikingskiphuset (Viking Ship Museum) ★★★ MUSEUM Three Viking burial vessels that were excavated on the shores of the Oslofjord and preserved in clay are displayed here. The most spectacular is the 9th-century dragon ship *Oseberg* ★, discovered near Norway's oldest town. This 20m (66-ft.) vessel features a wealth of ornaments and is the burial chamber of a Viking queen and her slave. Look for the *Oseberg* animal-head post, the elegantly carved sleigh used by Viking royalty, and the *Oseberg* four-wheeled cart. The *Gokstad* find is an outstanding example of Viking vessels because it's so well preserved. The smaller *Tune* ship has never been restored.

Huk Aveny 35, Bygdøy. www.khm.uio.no. ℂ **22-85-19-00.** Admission NOK60 adults, NOK30 children 7–16. Oct–Apr daily 10am–4pm; May–Sept daily 9am–6pm. Ferry: from Pier 3 facing the Rådhuset (summer only). Bus: 30 from the Nationaltheatret.

WESTERN OSLO

Vigeland Museet og Parken (Museum and Park) ★★ MUSEUM/PARK More than 200 sculptures in granite, bronze, and iron by Norway's greatest sculptor, Gustav Vigeland, are displayed inside the Vigeland Museum as well as throughout the nearby 80-hectare (198-acre) Frogner Park in western Oslo. *Sinnataggen (The Angry Boy)* is the most photographed statue in the park, but the really celebrated work is the 16m (52-ft.) *Monoliten* (monolith), composed of 121 figures of colossal size—all carved into a single piece of stone. Also look out for his four granite columns, symbolizing the fight between humanity and evil (a dragon, the embodiment of evil, embraces a woman).

Frogner Park, Nobelsgate 32. www.vigeland.museum.no. ℂ **22-49-37-00.** Free admission to park. Museum NOK50 adults, NOK25 children 7–16 and seniors. Park daily 24 hr. Museum Oct–Mar. June–Aug Tues–Sun 10am–5pm; off-season Tues–Sun noon–4pm. T-banen: 12 or 15 to Majorstuen.Bus: 20 or 45.

EASTERN OSLO

Munch Museum MUSEUM Devoted exclusively to the works of Edvard Munch (1863–1944), Scandinavia's leading painter, this exhibit (Munch's gift to the city) traces his work from early realism to his latter-day expressionism. The collection comprises 1,100 paintings, some 4,500 drawings, around 18,000 prints, numerous graphic plates, six sculptures, and important documentary material. Munch's *The Scream,* one of the world's most reproduced paintings, along with the artist's *Madonna,* were stolen in August 2004 in a daring daylight robbery (prompting a major security overhaul). The two paintings were recovered in good condition in 2006, so visitors can once again gaze upon these masterpieces.

Tøyengata 53. www.munch.museum.no. ℂ **23-49-35-00.** Admission NOK95 adults, children 15 and under free. June–Aug daily 10am–6pm; Sept–May Tues–Fri 10am–4pm, Sat–Sun 11am–5pm. T-banen: Tøyen. Bus: 60.

14

NORWAY | Oslo

FARTHER AFIELD

Henie-Onstad Kunstsenter (Henie-Onstad Art Center) ★★ ART MUSEUM   Norway's largest collection of modern art is worth the trip to the museum's beautiful setting beside Oslofjord, 11km (6¾ miles) west of Oslo. It was inaugurated in 1968 to house a gift of some 300 works of art from Sonja Henie, former figure skating champion and movie star, and her husband, shipping tycoon Niels Onstad. Henie's bequest, beefed up by later additions, virtually spans modern art in the 20th century, from Cubism with Braque to Surrealism with Ernst. In fact, the collection is so vast that it frequently has to be rotated. Visitors are often drawn to the CoBrA Group, with works by its founder, Asger Jorn, and by Karel Appel. You can head downstairs to Henie's trophy room to see her three Olympic gold medals—she was the star at the 1936 skating competition—and 10 world championship prizes. Henie garnered 600 trophies and medals, all of which are on display.

Besides the permanent collection, plays, concerts, films, and special exhibits take place. An open-air theater-in-the-round is used in the summer for folklore programs, jazz concerts, and song recitals. A top-notch, partly self-service restaurant, the Piruetten, is also on the premises. Plan to spend about 2 hours here.

Høkvikodden, Sonja Henlesvie 31. www.hok.no. ✆ **67-80-48-80.** Admission NOK80 adults, NOK30 children 6–16, free for children 6 and under. Free for all Wed. Tues–Fri 11am–7pm; Sat–Sun 11am–5pm. Bus: 151, 161, 252, or 261.

ORGANIZED TOURS

H. M. Kristiansens Automobilbyrå, Hegdehaugsveien 4 (www.hmk.no; ✆ **23-15-73-00**), has been showing visitors around Oslo for more than a century. Both of their bus tours are offered daily year-round. The 4-hour "**Oslo Highlights**" tour is offered at 10:15am. It costs NOK320 for adults, NOK160 for children. The 2-hour "**Oslo Panorama**" tour costs NOK215 for adults and NOK105 for children. It departs at 10:15am. The starting point is in front of the Nationaltheatret. Arrive 15 minutes before departure; tours are conducted in English by trained guides.

Where to Eat

Norwegians are as fond of *smørbrød* (smorgasbord) as the Danes (you'll see it offered everywhere for lunch). Basically, this is an open-faced sandwich that can be stacked with virtually anything, including ham with a peach slice resting on top or perhaps a mound of dill-flavored shrimp.

VERY EXPENSIVE

Oro ★★★ CONTINENTAL/MEDITERRANEAN   Among the top five choices for food in the city is this very stylish Michelin-star winner run by chef Mads Larsson. The three-faceted establishment includes a European gourmet restaurant, a separate section called Oro Bar & Grill, and a boutique-style deli (Mon–Fri 11:30am–3pm) for enthusiasts who want to haul some of its raw ingredients back home. The restaurant is a curvaceous, slick-looking testimonial to stainless steel and warm-toned hardwoods. Choose one of the fixed-price menus, although be warned that each of them will be prepared only for every member of the table at the same time. One option includes a five-course vegetarian menu at NOK545. Representative dishes, each one delectable, include pasta with truffle, codfish with spinach and hazelnut, deer with mushroom and foie gras, and pigeon with cabbage and bacon.

Tordenskiolds 6A (entrance on Kjeld Stubs Gate). www.ororestaurant.no. © **23-01-02-40.** Reservations required. Fixed-price menus: NOK545–NOK995 for 5 courses. AE, DC, MC, V. Mon–Sat 11am–3pm and 5–10pm. T-banen: Stortinget.

Restaurant Julius Fritzner ★★ NORWEGIAN/CONTINENTAL   Dining at the Grand Hotel has long been a marker of tradition—when Roald Amundsen returned to Oslo after his successful expedition to the South Pole in 1912, a banquet here honored him. Opened in 1995 to rave reviews, thanks in part to a battalion of impeccably trained waiters who maintain their humor and personal touch despite the sophisticated setting, this spot is now one of the best and most impressive restaurants in Oslo. The dishes here, all made with the finest Scandinavian ingredients, change with the season and the chef's inspiration. Some of the best dishes are orange and pepper-crusted trout with a parsley purée, and smoked rabbit with forest mushrooms and parsnips. Desserts, which are occasionally theatrical, include a terrine of chocolate with a compote of peaches and sorbet flavored with basil and cinnamon.

In the Grand Hotel, Karl Johans Gate 31. www.grand.no. © **23-21-20-00.** Reservations recommended. Main courses NOK295–NOK395; 5 courses including wine pairings and aperitif NOK1,490. AE, DC, MC, V. Mon–Sat 5–10:30pm. Closed June 21–Aug 11. T-banen: Stortinget.

EXPENSIVE

Gamle Rådhus Restaurant ★ NORWEGIAN   Set in Oslo's former Town Hall (1641), this is strictly for nostalgia buffs. You'll dine within a network of manorial-inspired rooms with dark wooden panels and Flemish, 16th-century-style wooden chairs. In the spacious dining room, a full array of open-faced sandwiches is served on weekdays only. A la carte dinner selections can be made from a varied menu that includes fresh fish, game, and Norwegian specialties. If you want to sample a dish that Ibsen might have enjoyed, check out the house specialty (and acquired taste), *lutefisk*—but hold your nose. This traditional Scandinavian dish is eaten just before Christmas and is made from dried fish that has been soaked in lye and then poached in broth. More to your liking might be smoked salmon (cured right on the premises), pikeperch from nearby streams sautéed in a lime sauce, or Norwegian lamb coated with herbs and baked with a glaze.

Nedre Slottsgate 1. www.gamleraadhus.no. © **22-42-01-07.** Reservations recommended. Main courses NOK210–NOK345. AE, DC, MC, V. Mon–Fri 11:30am–3pm and 4–10pm; Sat 1–3pm and 4–10pm; Kroen Bar Mon–Sat 4pm–midnight. Closed last 3 weeks in July. Bus: 27, 29, 30, 41, or 61.

Lofoten Fiskerestaurant ★★ SEAFOOD   This is the Aker Brygge district's most appealing—and best—seafood restaurant. Opening onto the waterfront, the interior sports nautical accessories that evoke life on an upscale yacht. In good weather, tables are set up on an outdoor terrace lined with flowering plants. Menu items change according to the available catch, with few choices for meat-eaters. The fish is served in generous portions, and is always very fresh. Look for culinary inspirations from Italy and France, and an ample use of such Mediterranean flavors as pesto. Old-guard diners don't find their tried-and-true dishes on the menu but are introduced to Norwegian fish enriched with various sauces and accompaniments, including baked halibut with garlic cream. Other temptations include seabass baked with spices, filet of beef with rosemary jus and pimientos, and baked salmon with horseradish butter.

Stranden 75. www.lofoten-fiskerestaurant.no. © **22-83-08-08.** Reservations recommended. Main courses NOK140–NOK265 lunch; NOK185–NOK325 dinner. AE, DC, MC, V. Mon–Sat 11am–11pm; Sun noon–10pm. Bus: 27.

14

NORWAY | Oslo

Theatercafeen ★ INTERNATIONAL   If you like to eat and drink in opulence, head to the last of the grand Viennese cafes in northern Europe for your fix. This long-standing favorite was founded a century ago to rival the Grand Café. With soft lighting, antique bronzes, cut-glass lighting fixtures, and Art Nouveau mirrors, it's the type of place that encourages lingering, and it attracts present-day *boulevardiers* and businesspeople. The entire establishment was renovated in 2010, adding a private dining room for 38 guests, as well as a new smaller eatery and bar. Menu items are well prepared and traditional, and are adjusted accordingly to get the best flavors out of each season. That might mean butter-roasted turbot with toasted bacon, chives, and boiled potatoes; or breast of duck with spinach and Madeira sauce.

In the Hotel Continental, Stortingsgaten 24. www.hotel-continental.no. ℂ **22-82-40-50.** Reservations recommended. Main courses NOK235–NOK295; open-faced sandwiches NOK130 at lunch. AE, DC, MC, V. Mon–Sat 11am–11pm; Sun 3–10pm. T-banen: Stortinget.

MODERATE

Grand Café ★★ NORWEGIAN   Over the decades, this 1874 cafe has served as the living and dining room for the elite of Christiania (an old name for Oslo). The country's greatest artists have dined here with foreign diplomats, kings, and explorers. While it's not as chic as it once was, a night here is a true Norwegian experience. A large mural on one wall depicts Ibsen and Edvard Munch, along with other, less famous, former patrons. The atmosphere and tradition here are sometimes more compelling than the cuisine, but if you like solid, honest flavors, this is the place to eat. The menu relies on Norwegian country traditions (how many places still serve elk stew?). Representative dishes include chicken with green asparagus, sun-dried tomatoes, and a basil cream pasta; or herb-marinated monkfish with beans, rice pilaf, and a demi-glace of figs.

In the Grand Hotel, Karl Johans Gate 31. www.grand.no. ℂ **23-21-20-00.** Reservations recommended. Main courses NOK165–NOK320. AE, DC, MC, V. Mon–Fri 11am–11pm; Sat noon–11pm; Sun 1–10pm. T-banen: Stortinget.

Stortorvets Gjæstgiveri ★ NORWEGIAN   Many legends surround this nostalgic dining room. It is the oldest restaurant in Oslo, composed of a trio of wood-framed buildings, the most antique of which dates from the 1700s. The inn's upstairs bedchambers with their wood-burning stoves are virtually unchanged since their original construction, although they're now used as private dining rooms. This restaurant changes radically throughout the day: Expect a cafe near the entrance; an old-fashioned, charming, and usually packed restaurant in back; and outside dining in good weather. Menu items are traditional, well prepared, and flavorful, and include steamed mussels in white wine and garlic; poached salmon in a creamy butter sauce with horseradish; or pan-fried trout served with asparagus in Parma ham, mushrooms, and mussel sauce. A specialty is roast reindeer in a port sauce spiked with wild berries.

Grensen 1. www.stortorvet.no. ℂ **23-35-63-60.** Reservations recommended. Small platters and snacks NOK98–NOK145; main courses NOK179–NOK349. AE, DC, MC, V. Cafe and restaurant Mon–Sat 11am–10:30pm. Tram: 12 or 17.

Tjuvholmen Sjømagasin ★★ SEAFOOD   Recently opened on a stretch of reclaimed land at the far end of Aker Brygge, this chic, silvery seafood restaurant is run by Bjørn Tore Furset, the local wunderkind restaurateur whose empire includes city eateries Havsmak, Ekeberg, and Argent. His philosophy is all about fresh, locally sourced ingredients. The heralded restaurant seats up to 300 diners—from well-heeled locals to in-the-know tourists—in a sprawling dining room that offers panoramic views of Oslofjord harbor. You can pick your catch right out of the casks that greet you as you walk in, then hand them to the team of chefs manning the open kitchen, and watch them cook your food. Or try a dish from the seafood bar, where things are a bit more informal. The restaurant serves excellent grilled lobster (Norwegian- or American-caught), Varanger king crab, and charcoal-grilled Hordaland trout.

Tjuvholmen Allé 14. www.sjomagasinet.no. © **23-89-77-77.** Main courses NOK270–NOK395; 3-course fixed-price menu NOK465; 5-course fixed-price menu NOK595. Mon–Sat 11am–midnight. Bus: 27.

INEXPENSIVE

Engebret Café NORWEGIAN   Regrettably, it's no longer possible to sit, eat, and drink the night away with Henrik Ibsen, Edvard Grieg, and Bjørnstjerne Bjørnson, former patrons of this cafe. A favorite since 1857, this restaurant sits directly north of Akershus Castle in two buildings that have been joined together to form this establishment. The facade of the buildings has been preserved as an architectural landmark. It has an old-fashioned atmosphere and good food, served in a former bohemian literati haunt. During lunch, a tempting selection of open-faced sandwiches is available. The evening menu is more elaborate; you might begin with a terrine of game with blackberry port-wine sauce, or Engebret's always reliable fish soup. Main dishes include a truly savory dish, red wild boar with whortleberry sauce. Or you can try Norwegian reindeer, salmon Christiania, or Engebret's big fish pot. For dessert, try the cloudberry parfait.

Bankplassen 1. www.engebret-cafe.no.© **22-82-25-25.** Reservations recommended. Main courses NOK235–NOK345; 3-course lunch menu NOK275. AE, DC, MC, V. Mon–Fri 11:30am–11pm. Bus: 27, 29, or 30.

Shopping

The best place for shopping in Oslo is easily the main pedestrian thoroughfare of **Karl Johans Gate,** where you'll find dozens of boutiques selling traditional Norwegian sweaters, Viking and Nordic souvenirs, books, and more. City shopping hours tend to be Monday through Friday from 10am to 5pm (late openings Thursdays evenings until 7pm) and Saturday from 10am to 2pm. Supermarkets are generally open later—until 8pm during the week and 6pm on Saturdays.

Near the marketplace and the Oslo Domkirche (cathedral), **Den Norske Husfliden,** Møllergata 4 (www.dennorskehusfliden.no; © 22-42-10-75; T-banen: Stortinget; tram: 17)—or Husfliden, as it's called—is the display and retail center for the Norwegian Association of Home Arts and Crafts, founded in 1891 with two floors displaying the finest of Norwegian design in ceramics, glassware, furniture, and woodworking. You can also purchase souvenirs, gifts, textiles, rugs, knotted Rya rugs, embroidery, wrought iron, and fabrics by the yard. Goods can be shipped worldwide.

Norway's largest department store, **Steen & Strøm,** Kongensgate 23 (www.steenstrom.no; © **22-00-40-01;** T-banen: Stortinget), is a treasure house with hundreds of Nordic items spread through 58 individual departments. Look for hand-knit sweaters and caps, hand-painted wooden dishes reflecting traditional Norwegian art, and pewter dinner plates made from old molds. **Heimen Husflid,** Rosenkrantzgate 8 (© **23-21-42-00;** T-banen: Nationaltheatret), about a block from Karl Johans Gate, carries traditional Norwegian handicrafts and apparel,

Norway imposes a 20% value-added tax (VAT) on most goods and services, which is figured into your final bill. If you buy goods in any store bearing the TAX-FREE sign, you're entitled to a cash refund of 12 to 19% on purchases costing over NOK315. Ask the shop assistant for a tax-free shopping check. You may not use the articles purchased before leaving Norway, and they must be taken out of the country within 3 months of purchase. Complete the information requested on the back of the check you're given at the store; at your point of departure, report to an area marked by the TAX-FREE sign, not at Customs. Your refund check will be exchanged there in kroner for the amount due you. Refunds are available at airports, ferry and cruise-ship terminals, borders, and train stations.

including antique, reproduction, and original regional and national folk costumes (*bunads*) from many different counties of Norway. Some 5,000 handcrafted sweaters are in stock at **Oslo Sweater Shop,** Gunnerus Gate 3 (www.oslosweatershop.com; ✆ **22-42-42-25;** Bus: 30, 31, or 41). You can tell the origin of a Norwegian sweater by its pattern and design, but with the growth in machine-made sweaters and the increased sophistication of Norwegian knitwear, the distinction is becoming blurred. Sweaters start at around NOK1,000, rising to several thousands of kroner. Other items include necklaces, pewterware, souvenirs, and Norway-inspired trinkets.

The downtown boutique of **Pur Norsk,** Theresesgate 14 (www.purnorsk.no; ✆ **22-46-40-45;** tram: 18 or 19 to Stensgaten) is now the best place in the country to get your Nordic design fix. They sell innovative Norwegian-designed housewares, including tumblers, wine glasses, kitchenware, and furniture items—little of which you're likely to have encountered before.

Entertainment & Nightlife

To find out what's happening when you're visiting, pick up **What's On in Oslo,** which details concerts and theaters and other useful information.

Theater, ballet, and opera tickets are sold at various box offices and also at **Billett-sentralen,** Karl Johans Gate 35 (www.billettservice.no; ✆ **81-53-31-33;** T-banen: Stortinget)—although this service costs quite a bit more than your typical box office. Tickets to sports and cultural events can now be purchased easily and more cheaply via computer linkup at any post office in the city; so when you buy a stamp, you can also buy a voucher for a ticket to the ballet, theater, or hockey game.

PERFORMING ARTS

At long last Oslo has an opera house worthy of itself set smack on the Oslofjord waterfront. The **Operahuset ★★★** (www.operaen.no; ✆ **21-42-21-21**), a graceful Italian marble building which resembles a glacier slipping its way into the fjord, won the 2009 Mies van der Rohe award for contemporary architecture. Sheathed in white marble, the cultural complex consists of two companies—the **National Opera** and the **National Ballet.** Tickets, costing on average NOK180 to NOK450 for most performances, are sold at the box office Monday to Friday 10am to 8pm and Saturday from 11am to 6pm. You can walk over the pedestrian bridge to Bjørvika from the Central Station in Oslo.

The **National Theater,** Johanne Dybwads Plass 1 (www.nationaltheatret.no; *C* **81-50-08-11;** T-banen: Nationaltheatret), may be of interest to drama lovers who want to hear Ibsen and Bjørnson in the original. Avant-garde productions go on up at the **Amfiscenen,** in the same building. There are no performances in July and August. Guest companies often perform plays in English. Tickets range from NOK150 to NOK400 adults and NOK85 to NOK170 students and seniors.

Two blocks from the National Theater, **Oslo Konserthus,** Munkedamsveien 14 (www.oslokonserthus.no; *C* **23-11-31-11;** T-banen: Stortinget), is the home of the widely acclaimed **Oslo Philharmonic.** Performances are given from autumn to spring, on Thursday and Friday. Guest companies from around the world often appear on other nights. The hall is closed from June 20 to mid-August, except for occasional performances by folkloric groups. Tickets run from NOK200 to NOK850.

Norwegian Folk Museum, Museumsveien 10, Bygdøy (www.norskfolke museum.no; *C* **22-12-37-00**), often presents folk dance performances by its own ensemble on summer Sunday afternoons at the museum's open-air theater. Admission to the museum includes admission to the dance performance: NOK70 to NOK120 adults, NOK50 to NOK85 students and seniors, NOK30 children.

THE CLUB & MUSIC SCENE

Smuget, Rosenkrantzgate 22 (www.smuget.no; *C* **22-42-52-62;** T-banen: Nationaltheatret), is the most talked-about nightlife hot spot in the city, and has the longest lines (especially on weekends) to prove it. It's in a 19th-century building in the back of the City Hall and has a restaurant, an active dance floor, and a stage where live bands perform. It's open Monday to Saturday from 7pm to 4am; the cover ranges from NOK75 to NOK100.

Herr Nilsen ★, C.J. Hambros Place 5 (www.herrnilsen.no; *C* **22-33-54-05;** T-banen: Stortinget), is one of the most congenial spots in Oslo and it hosts some of the top jazz artists in Europe—and America, too. Overlooking the courthouse square, it's the perfect place to while away a snowy evening. The Dixieland music played here evokes New Orleans. Open Monday to Saturday 2pm to 3am, Sunday 3pm to 3am. The cover is NOK150. **Muddy Waters,** Grensen 13 (www.muddywaters.no; *C* **22-40-33-70**), features live music almost nightly in its cavernous cellar pulsating to high-volume bands (often from the U.S.). The club also has what may be the longest bar in Norway. The cover ranges from NOK100 to NOK252, while beer costs NOK55. Open daily 2pm to 3am.

Native Behavior

Although Norwegians love their beer, note that buying a round is virtually unheard of in a Norwegian pub. In this independent country, both men and women pay for their own libations. During the week, never ask someone you meet "out for a drink." He or she will think you're a drunk. On Friday or Saturday night, it's different. Anything goes. Beer taverns are wild and riotous, and few patrons are satisfied with a mere 10 beers.

Where to Stay

VERY EXPENSIVE

First Hotel Grims Grenka ★   This elegant boutique hotel, in which the lobby has a seven-story glassed-in atrium with Oriental carpets, columns, and a fireplace, has a personalized feel and excellent, professional staff. This is one of the few hotels anywhere where the regular rooms are preferable to the oddly laid-out, curiously spartan suites. Each of the suites is thematically decorated, based on the life of a famous Scandinavian, such as opera and ballet personalities Kirsten Flagstad, Ingrid Bjoner, and Indra Lorentzen. Rooms and suites are accessed via a labyrinthine pathway of stairs and angled hallways.

Kongensgate 5, N-0153 Oslo. www.grimsgrenka.no. ✆ **23-10-72-00.** Fax: 23-10-72-10. 45 units. NOK1,495–NOK2,195 double; from NOK2,495–NOK2,995 suite. Rates include breakfast. AE, DC, MC, V. Parking NOK100–NOK170 per night. T-banen: Stortinget. **Amenities:** Fitness room; wellness center; outdoor Jacuzzi on roof terrace; sauna; nightclub. *In room:* A/C, TV, kitchenette, minibar, Wi-Fi (free).

Grand Hotel ★★★ ☺   This is one of the country's best known and most beloved hotels—Norway's most famous guests still stay here—and it maintains a great classical character throughout. Tradition and style reign supreme, as they did when the Grand opened its doors in 1874 in a Louis XVI revival-style building imbued with Art Nouveau touches. Constant modernization has not managed to erase the original character of the hotel, which stands on the wide boulevard leading to the Royal Palace. In fact, the stone-walled hotel with its mansard gables and copper tower is now one of the most distinctive landmarks of Oslo. Guest rooms are in the 19th-century core or in one of the tasteful modern additions—both styles contain plush facilities and electronic extras. An eight-story extension contains larger, brighter doubles. Children enjoy the indoor heated pool, and the staff keeps a list of activities of interest to families.

Karl Johans Gate 31, N-0159 Oslo. www.grand.no. ✆ **23-21-20-00.** Fax: 23-21-21-00. 292 units. NOK1,495–NOK2,400 double; from NOK9,000–NOK25,000 suite. Rates include buffet breakfast. AE, DC, MC, V. Parking NOK330. T-banen: Stortinget. **Amenities:** 3 restaurants; 2 bars; indoor heated pool; fitness center; health club; sauna; room service; babysitting; nightclub. *In room:* A/C, TV, minibar, hair dryer, Wi-Fi (free).

EXPENSIVE

Hotel Bristol ★★★   Imbued with character, this 1920s-era hotel features lavish public areas that still evoke the Moorish-inspired Art Deco heyday in which they were built. Rivalling the city's other great historic properties, the Grand and the

---

Prices

Oslo's hotels tend to be of a very high standard, and you'll rarely have a problem with cleanliness or efficiency. Buffet breakfasts are often extremely abundant in fresh meats, fruits, and breads, and are almost always included in the room rate. Furthermore, weekends at city hotels tend to be cheaper since many properties are aimed at business travelers. On the down side, hotel rooms, while midsize, are often very boring in terms of decor, with bland IKEA-esque furnishings and bathrooms. Prices for anything worth staying in will tend to exceed NOK1,000 (and often NOK1,200) for a double, though there are definitely exceptions to this rule.

Continental, the Bristol consistently emerges as the hippest and the most accessible. Set in the commercial core of Oslo, one block north of Karl Johans Gate, the Bristol is warm, rich with tradition, and comfortable. It also isn't as formal as either the Grand or the Continental, attracting the media, arts, and showbiz communities, with a sense of playfulness and fun that's unmatched by either of its rivals. Bedrooms are comfortable and dignified, but not as plush or as intensely "decorated" as the rooms in either of its grander competitors. The Bristol Grill restaurant and piano bar add to a sense of elegant yet unpretentious conviviality.

Kristian IV's Gate 7, N-0164 Oslo 1. www.thonhotels.com/bristol. ℂ **22-82-60-00.** Fax: 22-82-60-01. 252 units. NOK2,650–NOK3,200 double; year-round daily NOK8,000 suite. Rates include breakfast buffet. AE, DC, MC, V. Parking NOK300. Tram: 10, 11, 17, or 18. **Amenities:** 2 restaurants; 2 bars; small exercise room and fitness center; spa and Turkish bath; room service; nightclub/dance bar. *In room:* A/C, TV, minibar, hair dryer, Wi-Fi (free).

MODERATE

First Hotel Millennium ★★ ☺ The Millennium is one of Oslo's "personality" hotels, known for its cozy atmosphere, character, and excellent views. In 1998, the owners took over a 1930s office building, successfully transforming it into this comfortable refuge. Rising nine floors behind a pale pink facade, the hotel is noted for a stylish kind of minimalism. Rooms range from standard to superior, and most are very spacious, with many Art Deco touches. On the top floor are a dozen accommodations with their own large balconies opening onto cityscape views. Family rooms are also very spacious, with a separate bedroom and living area. All bedrooms feature hardwood flooring.

Tollbugate 25, N-0157 Oslo. www.firsthotels.com/millennium. ℂ **21-02-28-00.** Fax: 21-02-28-30. 112 units. NOK850–NOK1,695 double. AE, DC, MC, V. No on-site parking. T-banen: Stortinget. **Amenities:** Restaurant; bar; room service; babysitting. *In room:* TV, minibar, hair dryer, Wi-Fi (free).

Radisson BLU Plaza Hotel ★ If for no other reason, check in here for the panoramic views of the city and the Oslofjord. With an exterior sheathed in blue-tinted glass and a needle-nosed summit that soars high above everything else in Oslo, this is the tallest building in Norway, and the largest hotel in northern Europe. The hotel struggles to permeate its vast, impersonal interior with a sense of intimacy and individuality. Guests do a lot of high-velocity elevator riding and stay in fairly predictable but comfy rooms high above the city's commercial core, almost immediately next to the city's bus and railway stations. The high-altitude views are sublime, and the comfortable, well-decorated rooms have flair and original works of art. The bar on the 34th floor has a panoramic view and is the perfect place to watch the sunset over the city.

Sonja Henies Plass 3, N-0134 Oslo. www.radissonblu.com/plazahotel-oslo. ℂ **22-05-80-00.** Fax: 22-05-80-10. 673 units. NOK995–NOK2,095 double; from NOK3,900 suite. Rates include breakfast. AE, DC, MC, V. Parking NOK300. T-banen: Jernbanetorget. **Amenities:** 2 restaurants; bar; indoor pool; sauna; room service. *In room:* A/C, TV, minibar, hair dryer, Wi-Fi (free).

Thon Hotel Gyldenløve ★ The roomy digs at the "Golden Lion" are done up in modern Nordic style, light and airy with Scandinavian pastel tones. Lying just a 10-minute walk from the Royal Palace, it stands on a tree-lined street in the West End, a highly desirable neighborhood. In its latest reincarnation as part of the ever-growing Thon chain, it has become one of the city's most desirable addresses.

Bogstadveien 20, N-0355 Oslo. www.thonhotels.com/gyldenlove. ℂ **23-33-23-00.** Fax: 23-33-23-03. 164 units. NOK995–NOK1,795 double. Rates include breakfast. AE, DC, MC, V. Parking NOK150. Tram: 11, 19. **Amenities:** Breakfast room. *In room:* TV, minibar, hair dryer, Wi-Fi (free).

Thon Hotel Stefan ✦ Set in an excellent central location, the color-coordinated guest rooms in this mid-brow spot are traditional in style and well furnished and maintained. There are bigger and better hotels in Oslo, but very few that offer comparable comfort at such affordable rates. From May until September 1, weekend rates are granted only to those who make reservations less than 48 hours before arrival.

Rosenkrantzgate 1, N-0159 Oslo 1. www.thonhotels.com/stefan. ℂ **23-31-55-00.** Fax: 23-31-55-55. 150 units. NOK1,195–NOK1,995. Rates include buffet breakfast. AE, DC, MC, V. Parking NOK180. Tram: 10, 11, 17, or 18. **Amenities:** Coffeeshop/bar. *In room:* A/C, TV, minibar, hair dryer, Wi-Fi (free).

INEXPENSIVE

Cochs Pensjonat ✦ The most famous and most enduring boardinghouse in Oslo, built in 1927, features an ornate facade curving around a bend in a boulevard that banks the northern edge of the Royal Palace. This is a comfortable but simple lodging whose newer rooms are high ceilinged, spartan but pleasant, and outfitted with birchwood furniture. If possible, book one of the rooms looking out onto Slottsparken from the "Royal Rooms," which were created in 1996 when a large apartment was incorporated into the guesthouse. Expect very few, if any, amenities and services at this hotel—rooms are without telephones. Breakfast is served at KafeCaffé, Parkveien 21.

Parkveien 25, N-0350 Oslo. www.cochspensjonat.no. ℂ **23-33-24-00.** Fax: 23-33-24-10. 88 units. Rooms w/private bathroom and kitchenette NOK780 double, NOK990 triple, NOK1,120 quad; rooms w/shared bathroom and no kitchenette NOK680 double, NOK870 triple, NOK1,060 quad. MC, V. No on-site parking. Tram: 11 or 12. *In room:* TV, kitchenette (in some), no phone.

Side Trips from Oslo

The best day excursion from Oslo includes a visit to Fredrikstad and Tønsberg, which gives you a chance to explore the scenic highlights of the Oslofjord. A trip to Fredrikstad, in Østfold on the east bank of the Oslofjord, can easily be combined in 1 day with a visit to the port of Tønsberg on the west bank, by crossing over on the ferry from Moss to Horten and then heading south.

FREDRIKSTAD ★

In recent years Fredrikstad, 95km (59 miles) south of Oslo, has become a major tourist center, thanks to its old town (Gamlebyen) and 17th-century fortress. Across the river to the west is a modern industrial section, and although a bridge links the two sections, the best way to reach Gamlebyen is by **ferry,** which costs NOK10. The departure point is about four blocks from the Fredrikstad railroad station—simply follow the crowd out the main door of the station, make an obvious left turn, and continue down to the shore of the river. It's also possible to travel between the two areas by **bus** no. 360 or 362, although most pedestrians opt for the ferry.

Essentials

GETTING THERE To reach Fredrikstad **by car** take E-6 south from Oslo toward Moss. Continue past Moss until you reach the junction of Route 110, which is signposted south of Fredrikstad. About six **buses** per day depart for the town from the Central Station in Oslo. **Trains** from Oslo's Central Station depart from Fredrikstad about every 2 hours during the day (trip time: 30 min.).

VISITOR INFORMATION The **Fredrikstad Turistkontor** is Torvgaten 59 (www.opplevfredrikstad.com; ✆ **69-30-46-00**). It's open June 10 to September 4 Monday to Friday 9am to 5pm, Saturday to Sunday 11am to 4pm. The rest of the year, it's open Monday to Friday from 9am to 4:30pm. You can also rent **bikes** here.

Exploring Fredrikstad

Fredrikstad was founded in 1567 as a marketplace at the mouth of the River Glomma. **Gamlebyen** (the **Old Town**) ★ became a fortress in 1663 and continued in that role until 1903, boasting some 200 guns in its heyday. It still serves as a military camp and is the best-preserved fortress town in Scandinavia, but the moats and embankments make for an evocative walk.

The main guardroom and the old prison contain part of the **Fredrikstad Museum,** Tøihusgata 41 (www.ostfoldmuseene.no; ✆ **69-11-56-50**). At the southwestern end of Gamblebyen is a section of the museum in a former guardhouse from 1731 (it was militarily active until 2002). Inside are a model of the old town and a collection of artifacts, both civilian and military, collected by city fathers over a span of 300 years. It's open Tuesday to Friday from noon to 3:30pm, Saturday and Sunday 11am–4pm; closed October to April. Admission is NOK50 for adults and NOK20 for children.

Outside the gates of Gamlebyen is **Kongsten Fort,** on what was first called Gallows Hill, an execution site. When Fredrikstad Fortress was built, it was provisionally fortified in 1677, becoming known as Svenskeskremme (Swede Scarer). Present-day Kongsten Fort, with its 20 cannons, underground chambers, passages, and countermines, eventually replaced it.

Gamlebyen has always attracted **craftspeople** and artisans, many of whom create their products in the old town's historic houses and barns. Many of these glass blowers, ceramic artists, and silversmiths choose not to display or sell their products at their studios, preferring instead to leave the sales aspect to local shops.

TØNSBERG ★

Bordering the western bank of the Oslofjord, Tønsberg, 100km (62 miles) south of Oslo, is Norway's oldest town. It's divided into a historic area, filled with old clapboard-sided houses, and the commercial center, where the marketplace is located.

Essentials

GETTING THERE You can drive back north from Fredrikstad to the town of Moss, where you can take the **car ferry** (http://basto-fosen.no) to Horten. Once at Horten, signs will point the way south for the short drive to Tønsberg. **Trains** depart for Tønsberg from Oslo's main railway station at intervals of between 60 and 90 minutes from 6am to 11:30pm every day, requiring a travel time of about 90 minutes and a fare of NOK201 each way.

VISITOR INFORMATION Tønsberg Turistkontor (**Tourist Centre**) is at Storgaten 38, N-3126 Tønsberg (www.visittonsberg.com; ✆ **48-06-33-33**). It's open Monday to Friday 9am to 4pm. You can rent **bikes** from NOK60 per half day. A little tourist kiosk on the island of **Tjøme** provides information in July daily from 11am to 5pm.

Exploring Tønsberg

Tønsberg was founded a year before King Harald Fairhair united parts of the country in 872, and this Viking town became a royal coronation site. Svend Foyn, who invented modern whaling and seal hunting, was born here.

Tønsberg was also a Hanseatic town during the Middle Ages, and some houses, such as those in **Fjerdingen** and **Nordbyen,** have been charmingly restored in typical Hanseatic style.

Slottsfjellet, a huge hill fortress near the train station, is loftily touted as "the Acropolis of Norway." In its heyday, these 13th-century ruins blossomed as the largest medieval fortifications in Norway, attracting the victorious Swedes across the border who came to destroy it in 1503. It has only some meager ruins today, and most people visit for the view from the 1888 lookout tower, **Slottsfjelltårnet** (✆ **33-31-18-72**), rising 17m (56 ft.) tall. It's open May 15 to June 25 Monday to Friday from 10am to 3pm, June 26 to August 20 daily from 11am to 6pm, and the rest of the year Sunday from noon to 4pm. Admission is NOK40 for adults and NOK20 for children.

In the **Vestfold County Museum (Vestfold Fylkemuseum)** ★, Frammannsveien 30 (www.vfm.no (Norwegian only); ✆ **33-31-29-19**), you'll find many Viking and whaling treasures, including the huge skeleton of a blue whale and a real Viking ship, the *Klastad* from Tjolling, built around A.D. 800. Admission is NOK60 adults, NOK40 children. It's open June to August Monday to Friday 11am to 5pm and weekends noon to 5pm, and from September to May Wednesday to Sunday from 11am to 4pm.

Haugar cemetery, at Møllebakken, is right in the town center, with the Viking graves of King Harald's sons, Olav and Sigrød.

BERGEN & THE FJORDS

In western Norway the landscape takes on an awesome beauty, with iridescent glaciers; deep fjords that slash into rugged, snowcapped mountains; roaring waterfalls; and secluded valleys that lie at the end of corkscrew-twisting roads. From Bergen, the most beautiful fjords to visit are the **Hardanger** (best at blossom time, May and early June) to the south; the **Sogne,** Norway's longest fjord, immediately to the north; and the **Nordfjord,** north of that. A popular excursion on the Nordfjord takes visitors from Loen to Olden along rivers and lakes to the Brixdal Glacier.

If you have time, on the Hardangerfjord stop over at one of the fjord resorts, such as Ulvik or Lofthus. The Folgefonn Glacier, Norway's second-largest ice field, which spans more than 250 sq. km (100 sq. miles), can be seen from many vantage points.

Bergen, with its many sightseeing attractions, good hotels and restaurants, and excellent boat, rail, and coach connections, is the best center for touring the fjord district. This ancient city looms large in Viking sagas. Until the 14th century, it was the seat of the medieval kingdom of Norway. The Hanseatic merchants established a major trading post here, holding sway until the 18th century.

Bergen: Gateway to the Fjords
ESSENTIALS
Getting There
BY PLANE   Flights to and from larger cities such as Copenhagen and London land at the **Bergen airport** in Flesland, 19km (12 miles) south of the city. Dozens of direct or non-stop flights go to just about every medium-size city in Norway with such airlines as **SAS** (www.sas.no; ✆ **91-50-54-00**), **Widerøe** (www.wideroe.no; ✆ **81-00-12-00**), and **Norwegian** (www.norwegian.no; ✆ **81-52-18-15**). Frequent **airport bus** services connect the airport to the Radisson BLU Royal Hotel and the city bus station. Departures are every 15 minutes Monday to Friday and every 30 minutes

Oslo to Bergen & Along the Fjords

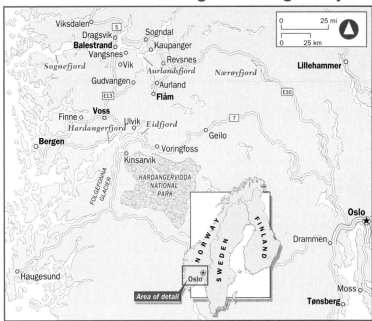

Saturday and Sunday. The one-way fare is NOK90. Taxis are readily available at the airport, or call ☎ **33-30-11-11.** A ride to the city center costs NOK450 to NOK500.

BY TRAIN   Trains arrive from Oslo and stations en route. For information, visit www.nsb.no or call ☎ **81-50-08-88.** Travel time from Oslo to Bergen is roughly 8½ hours. The Jernbanestasjonen (railway station) is at Strømgaten 1.

BY BUS   Nor-way Express buses (www.nor-way.no) travel to Bergen from Oslo, Trondheim, Ålesund, and the Nordfjord area. The trip from Oslo takes 11 hours.

BY CAR   A toll is charged on all vehicles driven into the city center Monday to Friday 6am to 10pm. A single ticket costs NOK20; a book of 20 tickets is NOK300.

The trip from Oslo to Bergen is a mountainous drive filled with dramatic scenery. Because mountains split the country, there's no direct road. The southern route, E76, takes you through mountain passes until the junction with Route 47; then you head north to Kinsarvik and make the ferry crossing to E16 leading to Bergen. Fjords and snowcapped peaks line the way, and you can photograph waterfalls, fjord villages, and ancient stave churches. Visitors with a lot of time may spend 2 or 3 days driving from Oslo to Bergen, but it's quickest to take the northern route following E16 west. In 2001 the world's longest road tunnel opened—the longest tunnel is the Gothard railway tunnel in Switzerland, due for completion in 2017, which is over double the length of the 40km (25-mile) Laerdal Tunnel. It begins 300km (186 miles) northwest of Oslo and goes as deep as 1,470m (4,820 ft.) beneath one of Norway's most scenic mountain areas. It takes 20 minutes to go through the tunnel.

Visitor Information

The Bergen **tourist office,** Vågsallmenningen 1 (www.visitbergen.com; ℂ **55-55-20-00**), provides information, maps, and brochures about Bergen and the rest of the region and can also help you find a place to stay, exchange foreign currency, and cash traveler's checks when banks are closed. You can also buy tickets for city sightseeing or for tours of the fjords. It's open daily June to August 8:30am to 10pm, May and September 9am to 8pm, and Monday to Saturday October to April 9am to 5pm.

The Bergen Card

The **Bergen Card** entitles you to free bus transportation and free entrance to most museums throughout Bergen, plus discounts on car rentals, parking, and some cultural and leisure activities. You can buy it at the tourist office (see above). A 24-hour card costs NOK190 for adults and NOK75 for children 3 to 15; a 48-hour card is NOK250 for adults and NOK100 for children 3 to 15. Children under 3 are free.

SPECIAL EVENTS The annual **Bergen Festival,** generally held the last 2 weeks in May, features performances by regional, national, and international orchestras, dance ensembles, and theater groups. The complete festival schedule is usually available by February of each year. For festival and ticket information, contact the **Bergen Festival Office** (www.fib.no; ℂ **55-21-06-30**).

Getting Around

BY BUS The **Bystasjonen (Central Bus Station),** Strømgaten 8 (ℂ **55-31-44-30**), is the terminal for all buses serving the Bergen and the Hardanger area, as well as the airport bus. Bergen is serviced by a network of buses; if you didn't purchase the Bergen Card (see above), the average fare within the city is NOK25.

BY TAXI Sightseeing by taxi costs about NOK600 for the first hour and then NOK400 per hour after that (ℂ **55-99-70-10**). A ride from the airport to the city center shouldn't cost more than NOK400.

EXPLORING BERGEN

In addition to the sights below, take a stroll around **Bryggen (the Quay)** ★★★. This row of Hanseatic timbered houses, rebuilt along the waterfront after the fire of 1702, is what remains of medieval Bergen. The northern half burned to the ground as recently as 1955. Bryggen is on UNESCO's World Heritage List as one of the world's most significant cultural and historical recreations of a medieval settlement. It's a center for arts and crafts, where painters, weavers, and craftspeople have their workshops.

Bergen Art Museum ★★ In the center of the city, this vastly expanded art museum—one of the largest in Scandinavia—displays an impressive array of Norwegian and international artists. Overlooking Lille Lungegard Lake, the museum after massive rebuilding is now displaying its extensive collection of art for the first time, including such renowned artists as Edvard Munch, Miró, and Picasso. Norwegian art from the 18th century to 1915 is also exhibited. The Steneresen collection offers one of Europe's finest assemblages of the work of Paul Klee.

Rasmus Meyers Allé 3–9. www.kunstmuseene.no. ℂ **55-56-80-00.** Combined ticket to all 3 galleries NOK60 adults, NOK40 students. Mid-May–mid-Sept daily 9am–7pm; mid-Sept–mid-May daily 11am–7pm. Bus: 1, 5, or 9.

Det Hanseatiske Museum ★   In one of the best-preserved wooden buildings at Bryggen, this museum illustrates Bergen's commercial life on the wharf centuries ago. German merchants, representatives of the Hanseatic League centered in Lübeck, lived in these medieval houses built in long rows up from the harbor. The museum is furnished with authentic articles dating from 1704.

Finnegårdsgaten 1A, Bryggen. www.museumvest.no. ℂ **55-54-46-90.** Admission May–Sept NOK50; Oct–Apr NOK30; year-round free for children 14 and under. June–Aug daily 9am–5pm; Sept–May Tues–Sat 11am–2pm. Bus: 20, 21, 22, 23, or 24.

Fløibanen   A short walk from the Fish Market (p. 775) is the station where the funicular heads up to Fløien (Mount Floyen), the most famous of Bergen's seven hills. The nearly century-old funicular was recently upgraded with new cable cars to haul visitors to the 320m (1,050-ft.) summit. Two modern carriages featuring glass ceilings and panoramic windows carry visitors to the top to take in the spectacular vista. Once there, you can take one of several paths that provide easy walks through lovely wooded terrain with views of lakes and mountains in the distance. In summer, you can order lunch at the restaurant here, which is open daily and includes a souvenir shop.

Vetrlidsalm 23A. www.floibanen.com. ℂ **55-33-68-00.** Round-trip NOK70, NOK35 children 4–15. April–Aug Mon–Fri 7:30am–midnight, Sat 8am–midnight, Sun 9am–midnight; Sept–Mar Mon–Thurs 7:30am–11pm, Fri 7:30am–11:30pm, Sat 8am–11:30pm, Sun 9am–11pm.

Gamle Bergen ★   This museum offers a rare look at small-town life during the 18th and 19th centuries, with various antique dwellings and shops, a bakery, and even the town's local barber and dentist. Comprising houses from the 18th and 19th centuries set in a park, this "Old Town" is complete with streets, an open square, and narrow alleyways. Some of the interiors are exceptional, including a merchant's living room in the typical style of the 1870s—padded sofas, heavy curtains, potted plants—a perfect setting for Ibsen's *A Doll's House.*

Elsesro & Sandviken. www.bymuseet.no. ℂ **55-39-43-00.** Admission NOK50, free for children 15 and under and students. Houses mid-May to Aug only, guided tours daily on the hour 10am–5pm. Park and restaurant daily noon–5pm. Bus: 20, 23, or 24 from city center (every 10 min.).

Troldhaugen ★★★   This can be the most romantic setting in Norway if you arrive as Edvard Grieg's music is drifting up from a summer concert in the 200-seat Troldsalen, a concert hall on the grounds. This Victorian house, in beautiful rural surroundings on Lake Nordås, was Grieg's summer villa and the site where he composed many of his famous works. The house still contains his furniture, paintings, and other mementos. His Steinway grand piano is frequently used at concerts given here during the annual Bergen International Festival (p. 772), and at Troldhaugen's summer concerts. Grieg and his wife, Nina, are buried in a cliffside grotto on the estate.

Troldhaugveien 65, Hop. www.kunstmuseene.no. ℂ **55-92-29-92.** Admission NOK60 adults, free for children 15 and under. May–Sept daily 9am–6pm; Oct–Apr 10am–4pm. Bus 20, 23, 24, or 50. Take the bus south toward Nesttun, get off at the Hopsbraoen exit, turn right and follow a well-marked path to Troldhaugen (15-min. walk).

WHERE TO EAT

Bryggeloftet & Stuene ★ NORWEGIAN   Charming and well managed, this is the best-established restaurant along the harborfront, a two-level affair originally built in 1910 as a warehouse. The street-level dining room (known as the Stuene) has low-beamed ceilings, carved banquettes, 19th-century murals of old Bergen, and dozens of clipper-ship models. The Bryggeloftet, upstairs, showcases high ceilings, wood paneling, and a venue that's a bit more formal and less animated. Come to this traditional place if you're seeking authentic Norwegian flavors. Dinner in either section might include filet of wolffish, peppered steak, or grilled reindeer filet with a creamy wild-game sauce. Several different preparations of salmon and herring are featured, along with roast pork with Norwegian sour cabbage and various preparations of reindeer, grouse, and elk, depending on the season. Between September and February, the menu offers *lutefisk,* an old-fashioned and strong-flavored Norwegian delicacy that is not for the weak-stomached.

Bryggen 11–13. www.bryggeloftet.no. © **55-30-20-70.** Reservations recommended. Main courses NOK220–NOK360; lunch *smørbrød* NOK110–NOK140. AE, DC, MC, V. Mon–Sat 11am–11:30pm; Sun 1–11:30pm. Bus: 1, 5, or 9.

Hanne På Høyden ★ NORWEGIAN   A short walk up from the UNESCO-listed harbor is one of Norway's most outstanding restaurants. This newly renovated, rustic chic spot is run by award-winning chef Hanne Frosta, who spends her time coming up with organic, exclusively Norwegian-sourced meals. Crowned Norway's Kitchen Chef of the Year in 2006, Hanne has since become one of Norway's most outspoken advocates of the use of local products and of the Slow Food movement, which stresses the importance of food traditions passed down through generations. Try her pumpkin soup with birch oil and apple-glazed red onions (NOK110), followed by entrecote of deer—from nearby Odd Ohnstad farm—with gravy served alongside baked root vegetables and wild mushrooms (NOK325). For dessert, go for her seasonal berries and fruit compote with gooseberry sorbet (NOK120). Eating here, you may well rethink your stereotypes of Scandinavian cuisine.

Fosswinckelsgate 18. www.spisestedet.no. © **55-32-34-32.** Main courses from NOK230. AE, DC, MC, V. Mon–Tues 11:30am–6pm; Wed–Sat 11:30am–10pm. Bus: 2, 3, or 4.

Smauet Mat & Vinhus ★ CONTINENTAL   The romantic, cozy atmosphere and high-quality food continues to lure visitors here. Tempting smells and lots of energy emanate from the open kitchen of this candle-studded restaurant whose decor emulates the style of a 19th-century Norwegian farmhouse. In a place so authentically Norwegian, you wouldn't expect a cuisine this Continental. Subtly intermingled flavors emerge in the monkfish with nut crust and chorizo francese, or the guinea fowl with chanterelles, celery purée, and red whortleberries. Other standouts include ox tenderloin with Jerusalem artichoke, red onion, mushrooms, and red wine sauce; and, as a starter, pan-fried scallops with cabbage and leek purée, pomegranate, and grapefruit. This 1870 house lies just a few steps from the Ole Bulls Plass.

Vaskerelvsmauet 1–3. www.smauet.no. © **90-29-99-00.** Reservations recommended, especially on weekends. Main courses NOK225–NOK275; 3-course menu NOK495; 6-course menu NOK645. AE, DC, MC, V. Sun–Thurs 5–10pm; Fri–Sat 5–11pm. Closed Christmas to New Year. Bus: 2, 3, or 4.

To Kokker ★ FRENCH/NORWEGIAN   To Kokker ("Two Cooks"—in this case, Norway-born partners Daniel Olsen and Grete Halland) is a favorite with celebrities ranging from Britain's Prince Andrew to a bevy of French starlets. Savvy local foodies increasingly gravitate here for the chef's well-considered juxtaposition of flavors and textures. Menu items include such time-tested favorites as foie gras with the traditional accompaniments; goose liver terrine with balsamico syrup; filet of venison with chanterelle sauce; and herb-fried monkfish served with mushroom sauce. The 1703 building is adjacent to the oldest piers and wharves in Bergen. The classic dining room, one floor above street level, has a warmly tinted decor of deep red and soft orange, old paintings, and a solidly reliable staff.

Enhjørninggården 3. www.tokokker.no. *©* **55-30-69-55.** Reservations required. Main courses NOK295–NOK340; 5-course menu NOK675. AE, DC, MC, V. Mon–Sat 5–10pm. Bus: 1, 5, or 9.

SHOPPING

Bargain hunters head to the **Fisketorget (Fish Market) ★★**. Many local handicrafts from the western fjord district, including rugs and handmade tablecloths, are displayed here. This is one of the few places in Norway where bargaining is welcomed. The market keeps no set hours, but it is best visited June to August daily from 7am to 7pm, and September to May Monday to Saturday from 7am to 4pm. Take bus no. 1, 5, or 9.

You'll find the widest selection of national handicrafts in and around **Bryggen Brukskunst,** the restored Old Town near the wharf, where many craftspeople have taken over old houses and ply ancient Norwegian trades. Crafts boutiques often display Bergen souvenirs, many based on designs 300 to 1,500 years old; be sure to check out Juhls' Silvergallery for jewelry. Attractive items here are likely to include sheepskin-lined booties and exquisitely styled hand-woven wool dresses. The leading outlet for glassware and ceramics, **Hjertholm,** Torgallmenningen 8 (*©* **55-31-70-27;** www.hjertholm.no), purchases much of its merchandise directly from the studios of Norwegian and other Scandinavian artisans who turn out quality goods not only in glass and ceramics, but also in pewter, brass, wood, and textiles.

ENTERTAINMENT & NIGHTLIFE

The modern, 1,500-seat **Grieghallen (Grieg Hall),** Edvard Grieg Plass 1 (www. grieghallen.no; *©* **55-21-61-00**), is Bergen's monumental showcase for music, drama, and a host of other cultural events. The **Bergen Symphony Orchestra,** founded in 1765, performs here from August to May on Thursday at 7:30pm and Saturday at 12:30pm.

Norway's oldest theater performs from September to June at **Den National Scene,** Engen 1 (www.dns.no; *©* **55-54-97-00**). Its repertoire consists of classical Norwegian and international drama and contemporary plays, as well as visiting productions of opera and ballet in conjunction with the annual Bergen Festival. Performances are held from Monday to Saturday.

From early June to mid-August, the **Bergen Folklore dancing troupe** (*©* **55-55-20-00**) arranges a 1-hour folklore program at the Bryggens Museum on Tuesday at 9pm. Tickets cost NOK100 and are sold at the tourist information center or at the door.

The most-frequented pub in the city center, **Kontoret Pub,** Ole Bulls Plass 8–10 (*©* **55-36-31-33**), lies adjacent to the Hotel Norge next to the Dickens restaurant/pub. Drinkers can wander freely between the two places, since they're connected. In the Kontoret you can order the same food served at Dickens, though most people seem to come here to drink. The local brew is called Hansa, a half-liter of which costs NOK60. It's open Sunday to Thursday 4pm to 12:30am, Friday and Saturday 4pm to 2am.

WHERE TO STAY

Augustin Hotel ★ 👜 With one of the best locations in Bergen—in the harbor-front shopping district—and front rooms with harbor views, this spot wins in the moderately priced category. The oldest family-run hotel in town was constructed in 1909 in Art Nouveau style, but it more than doubled its size by adding a new wing in

1995, with modern rooms equipped with larger showers and tubs designed by award-winning Bergen architect Aud Hunskår (somewhat less up-to-date and desirable rooms remain in the old section). The hotel is decorated with art, much of it by well-known contemporary Norwegian artists. The Altona Tavern, once the haunt of Bergen artists and concertmasters in the 17th century, has been creatively integrated into the hotel. The on-site Brasserie No. 22 has some of the best shellfish and meat grills in the city.

C. Sundts Gate 22–24, N-5004 Bergen. www.augustin.no. © **55-30-40-00.** Fax 55-30-40-10. 109 units. NOK1,150–NOK2,050 double. AE, DC, MC, V. Parking NOK100. Bus: 2 or 4. **Amenities:** Restaurant; bar; rooms for those with limited mobility. *In room:* A/C, TV, minibar, hair dryer.

First Hotel Marin ★★ ☺ This hotel in a brown-brick building is imbued with a strong maritime theme as befits its location at the Bryggen waterfront, with several of its bedrooms opening onto views of the harbor and the famous Fish Market. This is one of the better first-class hotels in the city, rising seven floors in a streamlined format on a steep hillside. Standard doubles are available, but if you're willing to pay more, you'll get a superior double with more space and upgraded amenities. Each room is tastefully furnished in Nordic modern style with spic-and-span tiled bathrooms. Families often book one of the suites (the Princess Room or the Pirate Room) that come with a separate bedroom with a large double bed and a living room.

Rosenkrantzgaten 8, N-5003 Bergen. www.firsthotels.com. © **53-05-15-00.** 152 units. NOK964–NOK1,945 double; NOK2,295–NOK3,295 suite. AE, DC, MC, V. Free parking. Bus: 1, 5, or 9. **Amenities:** 2 restaurants; bar; fitness center; Jacuzzi; sauna; Turkish bath; room service. *In room:* TV, minibar, hair dryer (in some); Wi-Fi.

Steens Hotel ★ ♨ Among the more established B&Bs, the Steens is the best Bergen has to offer. This is a stylish 1890 house that has been successfully converted to receive guests. Owned and operated by the same family since 1950, Steens offers great accommodations at reasonable prices. The bedrooms are moderate in size and comfortable, and the bathrooms, though small, are well maintained. The best rooms are in front and open onto a park; each unit comes with a neatly maintained private bathroom equipped with a shower. Thoughtful, personal touches include hot coffee served throughout the day in public rooms that evoke a historic aura. The B&B is within a short walk of the bus or rail station.

22 Parkveien, N-5007 Bergen. www.steenshotel.no. © **55-30-88-88.** Fax 55-30-88-89. 18 units. NOK1,340 double. Extra bed NOK250. Rates include Norwegian breakfast. AE, MC, V. Free parking. Bus: 1 or 5. **Amenities:** Breakfast room; lounge. *In room:* TV.

Exploring the Fjords

Norway's fjords can be explored from both Oslo and Bergen by ship and car or by a scenic train ride. Here are the details.

BY CAR FROM BERGEN

Bergen is the best departure point for trips to the fjords: To the south lies the famous **Hardangerfjord ★★** and to the north the **Sognefjord ★★★**, cutting 180km (112 miles) inland. We've outlined a driving tour of the fjords, starting in Bergen and heading east on Route 7 to Ulvik, a distance of 150km (93 miles).

Ulvik

Ulvik is that rarity: an unspoiled resort. It lies like a fist at the end of an arm of the Hardangerfjord that's surrounded in summer by misty peaks and fruit farms. The village's 1858 church is attractively decorated in the style of the region. It's open June through August, daily from 9am to 5pm, and presents concerts.

From Ulvik, you can explore the **Eidfjord** district, which is the northern tip of the Hardangerfjord, home to some 1,000 people and a paradise for hikers. Anglers are attracted to the area because of its mountain trout.

The district contains nearly one-quarter of **Hardangervidda National Park ★**, which is on Europe's largest high-mountain plateau. It's home to 20,000 wild reindeer. Well-marked hiking trails connect a series of 15 tourist huts.

Several canyons, including the renowned **Måbø Valley,** lead down from the plateau to the fjords. Here, you'll see the famous 170m (558-ft.) **Voringfoss ★** waterfall. The **Valurefoss** in **Hjømo Valley** has a free fall of almost 245m (800 ft.).

Part of the 1,000-year-old road across Norway, traversing the Måbø Valley, has been restored for hardy hikers.

EN ROUTE TO VOSS From Ulvik, take Hwy 20 to Route 13. Follow Route 13 to Voss, 40km (25 miles) west of Ulvik and 100km (62 miles) east of Bergen.

Voss

Set on the main road between east and west Norway, there are few better pit stops than Voss. A heavily folkloric site situated between two fjords, Voss is a famous year-round resort and the birthplace of the American football hero Knute Rockne. Even if trolls no longer strike fear in the hearts of farm children, revelers dressed as trolls still appear in costumed folklore programs to spice things up a bit for visitors.

Voss is a natural base for exploring the two largest fjords in Norway, the Sognefjord to the north and the Hardangerfjord to the south. In and around Voss are glaciers, mountains, fjords, waterfalls, orchards, rivers, and lakes.

The **Voss Tourist Information Center** is at Evangervegen on the lakeside opposite the train station (www.visitvoss.no; ✆ **56-51-94-90**). It's open June to August Monday to Friday 8am to 7pm, Saturday 9am to 7pm, Sunday noon to 7pm; September to May Monday to Friday 8:30am to 3:30pm. A ride on the **Hangursbanen cable car** (✆ **47-00-47-00**) will be a memorable part of your visit. It offers panoramic views of Voss and its environs. The mountaintop restaurant serves refreshments and meals. The hardy take the cable car up and then spend the rest of the afternoon strolling down the mountain, which is our personal favorite of all the walks possible in the area (visit the tourist board's website for a great description of the walk). A round-trip ride costs NOK100 for adults, NOK60 for children 7 to 15, and is free for children 6 and under. Entrance to the cable car is on a hillside, a 10-minute walk north of the town center. It's open from early June to early September, daily, 10am to 5pm. Built in 1277, the **Vangskyrkja,** Vangsgata 3 (✆ **56-52-38-80**), with a timbered tower, contains a striking Renaissance pulpit, a stone altar and triptych, fine woodcarvings, and a painted ceiling. It's a 5-minute walk east of the railroad station. We recommend that you call in advance to reserve an English-speaking guide. Admission is free. The church is open only June to August Monday to Saturday 10am to 4pm, Saturday 10am to 2pm, Sunday 2 to 4pm.

Voss Folkemuseum, Mølster (www.vossfolkemuseum.no; ✆ **56-51-15-11**), is a collection of authentically furnished houses that shows what early farm life was like. Lying just north of Voss on a hillside overlooking the town, the museum consists of more than a dozen farmhouses and other buildings, ranging in age from the 1500s to around 1870. Admission is NOK60 for adults and free for children. It's open mid-May to August, daily from 10am to 5pm; and from September to mid-May, Monday to Friday 10am to 3pm, Sunday noon to 3pm.

A little west of Voss in Finne, **Finnesloftet** (℗ 56-51-16-75) is one of Norway's oldest timbered houses, dating from the mid-13th century. It's a 15-minute walk west of the railway station. Admission is NOK50 for adults and NOK20 for children. It's open June 15 to August 15, Tuesday to Sunday from 11am to 4pm.

Balestrand

Long known for its arts and crafts, Balestrand lies on the northern rim of the Sognefjord, at the junction of the Vetlefjord, the Esefjord, and the Fjaerlandsfjord. Kaiser Wilhelm II, a frequent visitor, presented the district with two statues of old Norse heroes, King Bele and Fridtjof the Bold, which stand in the town center.

You can explore by setting out in nearly any direction, on scenic country lanes with little traffic, or a wide choice of marked trails and upland farm tracks. There's good sea fishing, as well as lake and river trout fishing. Fishing tackle, rowboats, and bicycles can all be rented in the area. A touring map may be purchased at the **tourist office** (www.visitbalestrand.no; ℗ 57-69-16-17) in the town center. It is open from June to August Monday to Saturday 8am to 6pm and 10am to 5:30pm on Sunday; May and September daily 10am to 1pm and 3 to 5:30pm; October to April Monday to Saturday 9am to 4pm.

EN ROUTE TO FLÅM From Balestrand, follow Route 55 east along the Sognefjord, crossing the fjord via ferry at Dragsvik and by bridge at Sogndal. At Sogndal, drive east to Kaupanger, where you'll cross the Ardalsfjord by ferry, south to Revsnes. In Revsnes, pick up Route 11 heading southeast. Drive east until you connect with a secondary road heading southwest through Kvigno and Aurland. When you arrive in Aurland, take Route 601 southwest to the town of Flåm, 95km (59 miles) southeast of Balestrand and 165km (103 miles) east of Bergen.

Flåm ★

Flåm (pronounced *Flawm*) lies on the Aurlandsfjord, a tip of the more famous Sognefjord. In the village you can visit the old church dating from 1667, with painted walls done in typical Norwegian country style.

Flåm is an excellent starting point for excursions by car or boat to other well-known centers on the Sognefjord, Europe's longest and deepest fjord. Worth exploring are two of the wildest and most beautiful fingers of the Sognefjord: Nærøyfjord and Aurlandsfjord. Ask at the **tourist office** (www.alr.no; ℗ 91-35-16-72), near the railroad station and open May to September daily 8:30am to 8:30pm, about a cruise from Flåm, from which you can experience the dramatic scenery of both of these fjords. From Flåm by boat, you can disembark in either Gudvangen or Aurland and continue the tour by coach. Alternatively, you can return to Flåm by train.

The tourist office rents bicycles for NOK50 per hour or NOK250 per day, and also provides a map detailing a number of easy walks in the Flåm district.

BY SHIP/TOUR FROM BERGEN

There are several ways to visit Sognefjord, Norway's longest fjord, from Bergen. One way is to cross the fjord on an express steamer that travels from Bergen to **Gudvangen.** From Gudvangen, passengers go to Myrdal, and from Myrdal a train runs back to Bergen. You can go by boat, bus, and then train for NOK1,150 round-trip. Details about this and other tours are available from **Bergen Visitor Information** in Bergen (www.visitbergen.com; ℗ 55-55-20-00).

If you have more than a day to see the fjords in the environs of Bergen, you can take the grandest fjord cruise in the world, a **coastal steamer** going to the North Cape and beyond. The coastal steamers are elegantly appointed ships that cruise the western coast of Norway from Bergen to Kirkenes, carrying passengers and cargo to 34 ports along the Norwegian coast. Eleven ships in all make the journey year-round. The ships sail through Norway's more obscure fjords, providing panoramic scenery and numerous opportunities for adventure. Along the way, sightseeing excursions to the surrounding mountains and glaciers are offered, as well as sails on smaller vessels through some of the more obscure fjords.

One of the chief operators of these coastal cruisers is **Hurtigruten** (www. hurtigruten.com; ✆ **81 00 30 30**). Tours may be booked heading north from Bergen or south from Kirkenes. The 12-day northbound Classic Round Voyage includes meals, taxes, and port charges.

PORTUGAL

by Darwin Porter & Danforth Prince

Portugal, positioned at what was once thought to be the edge of the Earth, has long been a seafaring nation. At the dawn of the Age of Exploration, mariners believed that two-headed, fork-tongued monsters as big as houses lurked across the Sea of Darkness, waiting to chew up a caravel (a 15th-century Portuguese sailing ship) and gulp its debris down their fire-lined throats.

There's a general feeling of optimism in Portugal; in spite of a world economic downturn, the Portuguese have high hopes for the new century. Lisbon's sidewalks are as crowded in the evening as Madrid's. Young Portuguese are much better tuned in to Europe than their parents were. The younger generation is as well versed in the electronic music coming out of London and Los Angeles as in fado repertoires, and more taken with French and Spanish films than with Portuguese lyric poetry. Still, as Portugal advances with determination deeper into the 21st century, its people retain pride in their historic culture.

15

LISBON & ENVIRONS

Lisbon, Europe's smallest capital, has blossomed into a cosmopolitan city. Sections along Avenida da Liberdade, the main street of Lisbon, at times evoke thoughts of Paris. As in Paris, sidewalk portrait painters will sketch your likeness, and artisans will offer you jewelry claiming that it's gold (when you both know it isn't). Handicrafts, from embroidery to leather work, are peddled right on the streets as they are in New York.

Lisbon is growing and evolving, and the city is considerably more sophisticated than it once was, no doubt due in part to Portugal's joining the European Union (E.U.). The smallest capital of Europe is no longer a backwater at the far corner of Iberia. Some 1.8 million people now live in Lisbon, and many of its citizens, having drifted in from the far corners of the world, don't even speak Portuguese.

Consider an off-season visit, especially in April, May, and October, when the city enjoys glorious weather. The city isn't overrun with visitors then, and you can wander about and take in its attractions without being trampled or broiled during the hot, humid weather of July and August.

Essentials
GETTING THERE
BY PLANE Foreign and domestic flights land at Lisbon's **Aeroporto de Lisboa** (www.ana-aeroportos.pt; ✆ **21/841-35-00**), about 6.5km

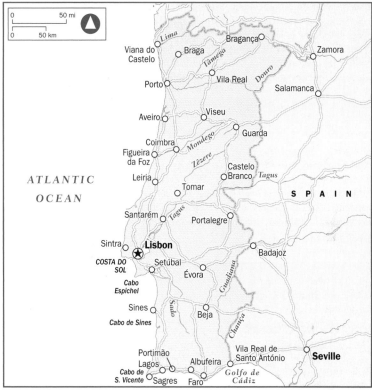

(4 miles) from the heart of the city. For ticket sales, flight reservations, and information about the city and the country, you can get in touch with the Lisboa personnel of **TAP Air Portugal,** Aeroporto de Lisboa (www.tap-airportugal.pt; ✆ **70/720-57-00** for reservations).

An **AERO-BUS** runs between the airport and the Cais do Sodré train station every 20 minutes from 7:45am to 8:15pm. The fare is 3.50€. It makes 10 intermediate stops, including Praça dos Restauradores and Praça do Comércio. There's no charge for luggage.

Taxi passengers line up in front of the airport, or you can call **Rádio Táxi** at ✆ **21/811-90-00.** The average taxi fare from the airport to central Lisbon is 12€. Each piece of luggage is 1.60€ extra.

BY TRAIN Most international rail passengers from Madrid and Paris arrive at **Lisboa–Santa Apolónia,** Avenida Infante Dom Henrique, the major terminal. It's by the Tagus near the Alfama district. Two daily trains make the 10-hour run from Madrid to Lisbon. Rail lines from northern and eastern Portugal also arrive at this station.

Connected to the Metro system, the newer and modern **Lisboa–Oriente** is the hub for some long-distance and suburban trains, including to such destinations as Porto, Sintra, the Beiras, Minho, and the Douro.

For trains to Sintra, go to the **Estação do Rossio,** between Praça dos Restauradores and Praça de Dom Pedro IV.

For Cascais and Estoril on the Costa do Sol, head to the **Estação do Cais do Sodré,** just beyond the south end of Rua Alecrim, east of Praça do Comércio. For Tunes on the Algarve, head to **Lisboa–Entrecampos**. Finally, you can catch a ferry at **Sul e Sueste,** next to the Praça do Comércio. It runs across the Tagus to the suburb of Barreiro; at the station there, **Estação do Barreiro,** you can catch a train for the Algarve and Alentejo. For all rail information regarding any of the terminals above, see www.cp.pt or call ✆ **80/820-82-08** between 7am and 11pm daily.

BY BUS   Buses from all over Portugal, including the Algarve, arrive at the **Rodoviária da Sete Rios** (www.rede-expressos.pt; ✆ **21/358-14-72**). If your hotel is in Estoril or Cascais, you can take bus no. 1, which goes on to the Cais do Sodré. At least six buses a day leave for Lagos, a gateway to the Algarve, and nine buses head north every day to Porto. There are 14 daily buses to Coimbra, the university city to the north. The one-way fare from Lagos to Lisbon is 20€.

BY CAR   International motorists must arrive through Spain, the only nation connected to Portugal by road. You'll have to cross Spanish border points, which usually pose no great difficulty. The roads are moderately well maintained. From Madrid, if you head west, the main road (N620) from Tordesillas goes southwest by way of Salamanca and Ciudad Rodrigo and reaches the Portuguese frontier at Fuentes de Onoro. Most of the country's 15 border crossings are open daily from 7am to midnight.

VISITOR INFORMATION

The main **tourist office** in Lisbon is at the Palácio da Foz, Praça dos Restauradores (www.visitportugal.com; ✆ **21/120-50-50**), at the Baixa end of Avenida da Liberdade. Open daily from 9am to 8pm (Metro: Restauradores), it sells the **Lisbon Card,** which provides free city transportation and entrance fees to museums and other attractions, plus discounts on admission to events. For adults, a 1-day pass costs 17€, a 2-day pass costs 29€, and a 3-day pass costs 35€. Children 5 to 11 pay 10€ for a 1-day pass, 15€ for a 2-day pass, and 18€ for a 3-day pass. Another tourist office is located across from the general post office in Lisbon on Rua do Arsenal 15, 1100-038 Lisbon (www.visitlisboa.com; ✆ **21/031-27-00**). This tourist office is open daily from 9am to 7pm.

CITY LAYOUT

MAIN STREETS & SQUARES   Lisbon is the westernmost capital of continental Europe. According to legend, it spreads across seven hills, like Rome, but that statement has long been outdated—Lisbon now sprawls across more hills than that. Most of the city lies on the north bank of the Tagus.

No one ever claimed that getting around Lisbon was a breeze. Streets rise and fall across the hills, at times dwindling into mere alleyways.

Lisbon is best approached through its gateway, **Praça do Comércio (Commerce Square),** bordering the Tagus. It's one of the most perfectly planned squares in Europe, rivaled only by the Piazza dell'Unità d'Italia in Trieste, Italy. Before the 1755 earthquake, Praça do Comércio was known as **Terreiro do Paço,** the Palace Grounds, because the king and his court lived in now-destroyed buildings on that

Lisbon

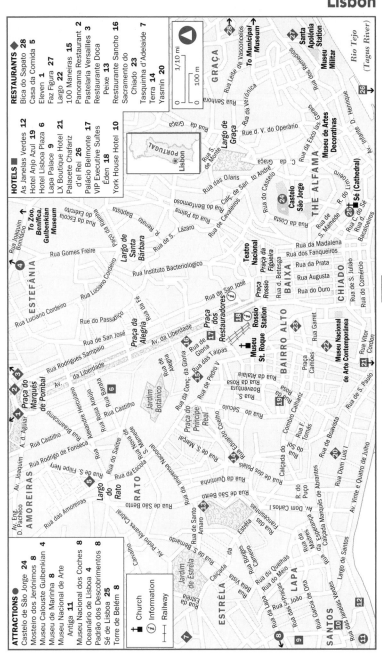

ATTRACTIONS ●
Castelo de São Jorge **24**
Mosteiro dos Jerónimos **8**
Museu Calouste Gulbenkian **4**
Museu de Marinha **8**
Museu Nacional de Arte Antiga **11**
Museu Nacional dos Coches **8**
Oceanário de Lisboa **4**
Padrão dos Descobrimentos **8**
Sé de Lisboa **25**
Torre de Belém **8**

➕ Church
ⓘ Information
┝━┥ Railway

HOTELS ■
As Janelas Verdes **12**
Hotel Anjo Azul **19**
Hotel Lisboa Plaza **6**
Lapa Palace **9**
LX Boutique Hotel **21**
Palacete Chafariz d'el Rei **26**
Palácio Belmonte **17**
VIP Executive Suites Éden **18**
York House Hotel **10**

RESTAURANTS ◆
Bica do Sapato **28**
Casa da Comida **5**
Eleven **1**
Faz Figura **27**
Largo **22**
100 Maneiras **15**
Panorama Restaurant **2**
Pastelaria Versailles **3**
Restaurante Doca Peixe **13**
Restaurante Sancho **16**
Sacramento do Chiado **23**
Tasquinha d'Adelaide **7**
Terra **14**
Yasmin **20**

PORTUGAL | Lisbon & Environs

15

783

site. To confuse matters further, English-speaking residents often refer to it as Black Horse Square because of its statue (actually a bronze–green color) of José I.

Heading north from Black Horse or Commerce Square, you enter the hustle and bustle of **Praça de Dom Pedro IV,** popularly known as the **Rossio.** Opening onto the Rossio is the Teatro Nacional de Dona Maria II, a free-standing building whose facade has been preserved. From 1967 to 1970, workers gutted the interior to rebuild it completely. If you arrive by train, you'll enter the Estação do Rossio, whose exuberant Manueline architecture is worth seeing.

Separating the Rossio from Avenida da Liberdade is **Praça dos Restauradores,** named in honor of the Restoration, when the Portuguese chose their own king and freed themselves of 60 years of Spanish rule. An obelisk commemorates the event.

Lisbon's main avenue is **Avenida da Liberdade (Avenue of Liberty).** The handsomely laid-out street dates from 1880. Avenida da Liberdade is like a 1.5km-long (1-mile) park, with shade trees, gardens, and center walks for the promenading crowds. Flanking it are fine shops, the headquarters of many major airlines, travel agents, coffeehouses with sidewalk tables, and hotels. The comparable street in Paris is the Champs-Elysées; in Rome, it's Via Vittorio Veneto.

FINDING AN ADDRESS   Finding an address in the old quarters of Lisbon is difficult because street numbering at times follows no predictable pattern. When trying to locate an address, always ask for the nearest cross street before setting out. Addresses consist of a street name followed by a number. Sometimes the floor of the building is given as well. For example, Av. Casal Ribeiro 18 3 means that the building is at number 18 and the address is on the third floor.

Neighborhoods in Brief

Baixa   The business district of Lisbon, Baixa contains much Pombaline-style architecture. (The term refers to the prime minister who rebuilt Lisbon following the earthquake.) Running south, the main street of Baixa separates Praça do Comércio from the Rossio. A triumphal arch leads from the square to Rua Augusta, lined with many clothing stores. The two most important streets of Baixa are **Rua da Prata** (Street of Silver) and **Rua Áurea,** formerly called Rua do Oro (Street of Gold). Silversmiths and goldsmiths are located on these streets.

Chiado   If you head west from Baixa, you'll enter this shopping district. From its perch on a hill, it's traversed by **Rua Garrett,** named for the noted romantic writer João Batista de Almeida Garrett (1799–1854). Many of the finest shops in the city are here. One coffeehouse in particular, **A Brasileira,** has been a traditional gathering spot for the Portuguese literati.

Bairro Alto   Continuing your ascent, you'll arrive at the Bairro Alto (Upper City). This sector, reached by trolley car, occupies one of the legendary seven hills of Lisbon. Many of its buildings were left fairly intact by the 1755 earthquake. Containing much of the charm and color of the Alfama, it's the location of some of the finest fado (meaning "fate" and describing a type of music) clubs in Lisbon, as well as excellent restaurants and bars. There are also antiques shops. Regrettably, many of the side streets at night are peopled with drug dealers and addicts, so be duly warned.

Santos   This waterfront district is one of the emerging new neighborhoods of Lisbon, attracting artists, designers, architects, and other creative people. Big development plans are underway to add a vast array of studios, restaurants, bars, design outlets, and galleries. The area still has many 19th-century warehouses with wrought-iron balconies that are being recycled for 21st-century use. The neighborhood of **Bairro Alto** lies next door, and locals go there for their nightlife, but Santos is beginning to develop its own after-dark diversions.

The Alfama   East of Praça do Comércio lies the city's oldest district, the Alfama. Saved only in part from the devastation of the 1755 earthquake, the Alfama was the Moorish section of the capital. Nowadays it's home in some parts to stevedores, fishermen, and *varinas* (fishwives). Overlooking the Alfama is **Castelo São Jorge,** or St. George's Castle, a Visigothic fortification that was later used by the Romans. On the way to the Alfama, on Rua dos Bacalhoeiros, stands another landmark, the **Casa dos Bicos (House of the Pointed Stones),** an early-16th-century town house whose facade is studded with diamond-shape stones. Be careful of muggers in parts of the Alfama at night.

Belém   In the west, on the coastal road to Estoril, the suburb of Belém contains some of the finest monuments in Portugal, several built during the Age of Discovery, near the point where the caravels set out to conquer new worlds. (At Belém, the Tagus reaches the sea.) At one time, before the earthquake, Belém was an aristocratic sector filled with elegant town houses.

Two of the country's principal attractions stand here: the **Mosteiro dos Jerónimos,** a Manueline structure erected in the 16th century, and the **Museu Nacional dos Coches,** the National Coach Museum, the finest of its kind in the world. Belém is Lisbon's land of museums—it also contains the Museu de Arte Popular and the Museu de Marinha.

Cacilhas   On the south side of the Tagus, where puce-colored smoke billows from factory stacks, is the left-bank settlement of Cacilhas. Inhabited mainly by the working class, it's often visited by right-bank residents who come here for the seafood restaurants. You can reach here by way of a bridge or a ferryboat from Praça do Comércio.

The most dramatic way to cross the Tagus is on the **Ponte do 25 de Abril.** Completed in 1966, the bridge helped open Portugal south of the Tagus. The bridge is 2.2km (1⅓ miles) long and its towers are 190m (623 ft.) high. The longest suspension bridge in Europe (it stretches for 16km/10 miles), **Ponte Vasco da Gama,** also spans the Tagus here. Standing guard on the left bank is a monumental statue of Jesus with arms outstretched.

GETTING AROUND

TRANSPORT PASSES   CARRIS (www.carris.pt; ☏ 21/361-30-00) operates the network of funiculars, trains, subways, and buses in Lisbon. The company sells a *bilhete de assinatura turístico* (tourist ticket). A 1-day pass goes for 3.80€. Passes are sold in CARRIS booths, open from 8am to 8pm daily, in most Metro stations and network train stations. You must show a passport to buy a pass.

METRO   Lisbon's Metro stations are designated by large M signs. A single ticket costs .90€; a day pass is 4€. One of the most popular trips—and likely to be jampacked on *corrida* (bullfight) days—is from Avenida da República to Campo Pequeno, the brick building away from the center of the city. The service runs daily from 6:30am to 1am. For more information, see www.metrolisboa.pt or call ☏ 21/350-01-15.

Surprisingly, riding the Lisbon Metro is like visiting an impressive art collection. Paintings, glazed tiles, and sculptures make for an underground museum. You'll see interesting collections of contemporary art, including some works by famous Portuguese artists such as Maria Keil and Maria Helena Vieira da Silva. Stations that display some of the finest art include Cais do Sodré, Baixa/Chiado, Campo Grande, and Marquês de Pombal.

BUS & TRAM   Lisbon's buses and trams are among the cheapest in Europe. The *eléctricos* (trolley cars or trams) make the steep run up to the Bairro Alto. The double-decker buses come from London and look as if they need Big Ben in the background to complete the picture. If you're trying to stand on the platform at the back of a jammed bus, you'll need both hands free to hold on.

The basic fare on a bus or *eléctrico* is 1.45€ if you buy the ticket from the driver (www.carris.pt; ✆ **21/361-30-00**). The transportation system within the city limits is divided into zones ranging from one to five. The fare depends on how many zones you traverse. Buses and *eléctricos* run daily from 6am to 1am.

At the foot of the Santa Justa Elevator, on Rua Áurea, there's a stand with schedules pinpointing the zigzagging tram and bus routes. Your hotel concierge should have information.

The antediluvian *eléctricos,* much like San Francisco's cable cars, have become a major tourist attraction. Beginning in 1903, the *eléctricos* replaced horse-drawn trams. The most interesting ride for sightseers is on *eléctrico* **no. 28,** which takes you on a fascinating trip through the most history-rich part of Lisbon.

ELECTRIC TRAIN A smooth-running, modern electric train system connects Lisbon to all the towns and villages along the Portuguese Riviera. There's only one class of seat, and the rides are cheap and generally comfortable. You can board the train at the waterfront Cais do Sodré Station in Lisbon and head up the coast all the way to Cascais.

The electric train does not run to Sintra. For Sintra, you must go to the Estação do Rossio station, opening onto Praça de Dom Pedro IV, or the Rossio, where frequent connections can be made. The one-way fare from Lisbon to Cascais, Estoril, or Sintra is 2€ to 5€ per person (www.carris.pt; ✆ **21/261-30-00**).

FUNICULARS Lisbon has a trio of funiculars: the **Glória,** which goes from Praça dos Restauradores to Rua São Pedro de Alcântara; the **Bica,** from the Calçada do Combro to Rua da Boavista; and the **Lavra,** from the eastern side of Avenida da Liberdade to Campo Mártires da Pátria. A one-way ticket on any of these costs 1.45€ (www.carris.pt; ✆ **21/261-30-00**).

FERRY Long before the bridges across the Tagus were built, reliable ferryboats chugged across the river, connecting the left bank with the right. They still do, and have been rebuilt and remotorized so they're no longer noisy. Many Portuguese who live on the bank opposite Lisbon take the ferry to avoid the heavy bridge traffic during rush hour.

Most boats leave from **Cais de Alfândega** (Praça do Comércio) and **Cais do Sodré,** heading for Cacilhas. The trip is worth it for the scenic views alone. Arrivals are at the Estação do Barreiro, where trains leave about every 30 minutes for the Costa Azul and the Algarve. Ferries depart Lisbon throughout the day about every 15 to 20 minutes; trip time across the Tagus is 15 minutes. The cost of the continuing

Up, Up & Away

For a splendid rooftop view of Lisbon, take the **Santa Justa elevator,** on Rua de Santa Justa. The ornate concoction was built by a Portuguese engineer, Raul Mesnier de Ponsard, born to French immigrants in Porto in 1849. The elevator goes from Rua Áurea, in the center of the shopping district near Rossio Square, to the panoramic viewing platform. It operates daily from 9am to 9pm. A ticket costs 1.45€, and children under 4 ride free (✆ **21/361-30-00;** www.carris.pt). Metro: Rossio.

train ticket includes the ferry. The separate ferry fare from the center of Lisbon to Cacilhas is 1€ (www.transtejo.pt; ☎ **80/820-30-50**).

BY TAXI   Taxis in Lisbon tend to be inexpensive and are a popular means of transport for all but the most economy-minded tourists. They usually are diesel-engine Mercedes and can be hailed on the street or at designated stands. The basic fare is 2.50€ for the first 153m (502 ft.), .20€ for each extra 162m (531 ft.), plus 20% from 10pm to 6am. The law allows drivers to tack on another 50% to your bill if your luggage weighs more than 30kg (66 lbs). Portuguese tip about 20% of the modest fare. For a **Rádio Táxi**, www.retalis.pt or call ☎ **21/811-90-00.**

BY CAR   In congested Lisbon, driving is extremely difficult and potentially dangerous—the city has an alarmingly high accident rate. It always feels like rush hour in Lisbon. (Theoretically, rush hours are Mon–Fri 8–10am, 1–2pm, and 4–6pm.) Parking is seemingly impossible. Wait to rent a car until you're making excursions from the capital. If you drive into Lisbon from another town or city, call ahead and ask at your hotel for the nearest garage or other place to park. Leave your vehicle there until you're ready to depart.

Car-rental kiosks at the airport and in the city center include **Avis,** Av. Praia da Vitória 12C (www.avis.com; ☎ **21/351-45-60**); **Hertz,** Rua Castilho 72 (www.hertz.com; ☎ **21/381-24-30**); and **Budget,** Rua Castillo 167B (www.budget.com; ☎ **21/386-05-16**).

[Fast FACTS] LISBON

ATMs/Banks   ATMs offer the best exchange rates. They pepper the streets of the central Baixa district and are also found less frequently in other parts of the city. **Banks** generally are open Monday to Friday 8:30am to 3pm.

Business Hours   **Shops** are open, in general, Monday to Friday 9am to 1pm and 3 to 7pm, and Saturday 9am to 1pm.

Currency   Portugal uses the **euro** (€).

Doctors   See "Hospitals," below.

Drugstores Farmácia Valmor, Av. Visconde Valmor 60B (☎ **21/781-97-43**), is centrally located and well stocked.

Embassies   The embassy of the **United States,** on Avenida das Forças Armadas (Sete Rios), 1600 Lisboa (http://portugal.usembassy.gov; ☎ **21/727-33-00**), is open Monday to Friday 8am to 12:30pm and 1:30 to 5pm. The embassy of **Canada,** Av. da Liberdade 200, EDIT Victoria 4th Floor, 1269 Lisboa (www.canadainternational.gc.ca/portugal; ☎ **21/316-46-00**), is open Monday to Friday 9am to noon and 2 to 4pm (to 1pm Fri July–Aug). The embassy of the **United Kingdom,** Rua São Bernardo 33, 1249 Lisboa (http://ukinportugal.fco.gov.uk/en; ☎ **21/392-40-00**), is open Monday to Thursday 9:30 to 11:30am and 3 to 4:30pm, Friday 9am to 12:30pm. The embassy of the **Republic of Ireland,** Rua de Imprensa à Estrela 1, 1200 Lisboa (www.embassyofireland.pt; ☎ **21/392-94-40**), is open Monday to Friday 9:30am to 12:30pm and 2:30 to 4:30pm. The embassy of **Australia,** Av. de Liberdade 200, 1250 Lisboa (www.portugal.embassy.gov.au; ☎ **21/310-15-00**), is open Monday to Friday 9 to 11:30am and 3 to 4:30pm. **New Zealanders** should go to the British Embassy.

Emergencies   To call the police or an ambulance, telephone ☎ **112.**

Hospitals   In case of a medical emergency, ask at your hotel or call your embassy and ask the staff there to recommend an English-speaking physician. Or try the **British Hospital,** Rua Saraiva de Carvalho 49 (☎ **21/394-31-00**), where the telephone operator, staff, and doctors speak English.

Internet Access You can check your e-mail at **Cyber.bica,** Duques de Bragança 7 (www.cyberbica.com; ✆ **21/322-50-04**), in the Chiado district (Metro: Baixa-Chiado). It's open Monday to Friday 11am to midnight.

Mail While in Portugal, you can have your mail directed to your hotel (or hotels), to the American Express representative, or to Poste Restante (General Delivery) in Lisbon. You must present your passport to pick up mail. The main post office, **Correio Geral,** in Lisbon is at Praça do Restauradores, 1100 Lisboa (✆ **21/323-89-71**). It's open Monday to Friday 8am to 10pm, and Saturday and Sunday 9am to 6pm.

Police Call ✆ **112.**

Safety Lisbon used to be one of the safest capitals of Europe, but that hasn't been true for a long time. It's now quite dangerous to walk around at night. Many travelers report being held up at knifepoint. Some bandits operate in pairs or in trios. Not only do they take your money but they demand your ATM code. One of the robbers holds a victim captive while another withdraws money. (If the number proves to be fake, the robber might return and harm the victim.) During the day, pickpockets galore prey on tourists, aiming for wallets, purses, and cameras. Congested areas are particularly hazardous. Avoid walking at night, especially if you're alone.

Taxes Lisbon imposes no city taxes. However, the national value-added tax (VAT) applies to purchases and services.

Telephone You can make a local call in Lisbon in one of the many telephone booths. For most long-distance telephone calls, particularly transatlantic calls, go to the central post office (see "Mail," above). Give an assistant the number, and he or she will make the call for you, billing you at the end. Some phones are equipped for using calling cards, including American Express and Visa. You can also purchase phone cards. Lisbon's city code is ✆ 01.

Tipping Hotels add a service charge (known as *servio*), which is divided among the staff, but individual tipping is also the rule. Tip 1€ to the **bellhop** for running an errand, 1€ to the **doorman** who hails you a cab, 1€ to the **porter** for each piece of luggage carried, and 1.50€ to the **chambermaid.** Figure on tipping about 20% of your **taxi** fare for short runs. For longer treks, 15% is adequate.

Exploring Lisbon

Many visitors use Lisbon as a base for exploring nearby sites, but they often neglect the cultural gems tucked away in the Portuguese capital. One reason Lisbon gets overlooked is that visitors don't budget enough time for it. You need at least 5 days to do justice to the city and its environs. In addition, even Lisbon's principal attractions remain relatively unknown, a blessing for travelers tired of fighting their way to overrun sights elsewhere in Europe.

This chapter guides you to the unknown treasures of the capital. If your time is limited, explore the **National Coach Museum,** the **Jerónimos Monastery,** and the **Alfama** and the **Castle of St. George.**

Castelo de São Jorge ★★ Locals speak of Saint George's Castle as the cradle of their city, and it might have been where the Portuguese capital began. Its occupation is believed to have predated the Romans—the hilltop was used as a fortress to guard the Tagus and its settlement below. Beginning in the 5th century A.D., the site was a Visigothic fortification; it fell to the Saracens in the early 8th century. Many of the existing walls were erected during the centuries of Moorish domination. The

Moors held power until 1147, the year Afonso Henríques chased them out and extended his kingdom south. Even before Lisbon became the capital of the newly emerging nation, the site was used as a royal palace.

For the finest **view ★★** of the Tagus and the Alfama, walk the esplanades and climb the ramparts of the old castle. The castle's name commemorates an Anglo-Portuguese pact dating from as early as 1371. (George is the patron saint of England.) Portugal and England have been traditional allies, although their relationship was strained in 1961, when India, a member of the Commonwealth of Nations, seized the Portuguese overseas territories of Goa, Diu, and Damão.

Huddling close to the protection of the moated castle is a sector that appears almost medieval. At the entrance, visitors pause at the Castle Belvedere. The Portuguese refer to this spot as their "ancient window." It overlooks the Alfama, the mountains of Monsanto and Sintra, Ponte do 25 de Abril, Praça do Comércio, and the tile roofs of the Portuguese capital. In the square stands a heroic statue—sword in one hand, shield in the other—of the first king, Afonso Henríques.

Rua da Costa do Castelo. www.castelodesaojorge.pt. ℂ **21/880-06-20.** Admission 7€ adults, free for children under 10. Mar–Oct daily 9am–9pm; Nov–Feb daily 9am–6pm. Bus: 37. Tram: 12 or 28.

Mosteiro dos Jerónimos ★★ In an expansive mood, Manuel I, the Fortunate, ordered this monastery built to commemorate Vasco da Gama's voyage to India and to give thanks to the Virgin Mary for its success. Manueline, the style of architecture that bears the king's name, combines Flamboyant Gothic and Moorish influences with elements of the nascent Renaissance. Prince Henry the Navigator originally built a small chapel dedicated to St. Mary on this spot. Today this former chapel is the Gothic and Renaissance **Igreja de Santa Maria ★★**, marked by a statue of Henry. The church is known for its deeply carved stonework depicting such scenes as the life of St. Jerome. The church's interior is rich in beautiful stonework, particularly evocative in its **network vaulting ★** over the nave and aisles.

The west door of the church leads to the **Cloisters ★★★**, which represent the apex of Manueline art. The stone sculpture here is fantastically intricate. The two-story cloisters have groined vaulting on their ground level. The recessed upper floor is not as exuberant but is more delicate and lacelike in character. The monastery was founded in 1502, partially financed by the spice trade that grew following the discovery of the route to India. The 1755 earthquake damaged but didn't destroy the monastery. It has undergone extensive restoration, some of it ill-conceived.

The church encloses a trio of naves noted for their fragile-looking pillars. Some of the ceilings, like those in the monks' refectory, have a ribbed barrel vault. The "palm tree" in the sacristy is also exceptional.

Many of the greatest figures in Portuguese history are said to be entombed at the monastery; the most famous is Vasco da Gama. The Portuguese also maintain that Luís Vaz de Camões, author of the epic *Os Lusíadas* (The Lusiads), in which he glorified the triumphs of his compatriots, is buried here. Both tombs rest on the backs of lions. Camões's epic poetry is said to have inspired a young Portuguese king, Sebastião, to dreams of glory. The foolish king—devoutly, even fanatically, religious—was killed at Alcácer-Kibir, Morocco, in a 1578 crusade against the Muslims. Those refusing to believe that the king was dead formed a cult known as Sebastianism; it rose to minor influence, and four men tried to assert their claim to the Portuguese throne. Each maintained steadfastly, even to death, that he was King Sebastião. Sebastião's remains were reputedly entombed in a 16th-century marble shrine built in the

The Famous Custard Cream Tarts of Belém

While you're in Belém visiting the Mosteiro dos Jerónimos, drop in at **Pasteis de Belém,** Rua de Belém 84 (*℃* **21/363-74-23**), to sample the best custard cream tart you are likely to taste in your life. They come with a slightly burnt crust on top and a flaky edge, over which cinnamon is sprinkled. You can devour them on the spot or take them away with you in nicely packaged tubes.

When the monasteries were closed in 1834, the clergy had to eat so they started selling these sweet pastries. They were so tasty, they attracted visitors from Lisbon who savored them. Over the years, the recipe for these pastries has been passed on to the master confectioners who handcraft them in "a secret room." The recipe has come down unchanged. The pastry shop is open daily from 8am to 11pm.

Mannerist style. The romantic poet Herculano (1800–54) is also buried at Jerónimos, as is the famed poet Fernando Pessoa.

Praça do Império. www.mosteirojeronimos.pt. *℃* **21/362-00-34.** Admission: Church free; cloisters 7€ adults, free for those under 14. Those over 65 pay 3.50€. May–Sept Tues–Sun 10am–6pm; Oct–Apr Tues–Sun 10am–5pm.

Museu Calouste Gulbenkian ★★★ Opened in 1969, this museum, part of the Fundação Calouste Gulbenkian, houses what one critic called one of the world's finest private art collections. It belonged to the Armenian oil tycoon Calouste Gulbenkian, who died in 1955. The modern, multimillion-dollar center is in a former private estate that belonged to the count of Vilalva.

The collection covers Egyptian, Greek, and Roman antiquities; a remarkable assemblage of Islamic art, including ceramics and textiles from Turkey and Persia; Syrian glass, books, bindings, and miniatures; and Chinese vases, Japanese prints, and lacquerware. The European displays include **medieval illuminated manuscripts and ivories ★**, 15th- to 19th-century paintings and sculpture, Renaissance tapestries and medals, important collections of 18th-century French decorative works, French Impressionist paintings, René Lalique jewelry, and glassware.

In a move requiring great skill in negotiation, Gulbenkian managed to buy art from the Hermitage in St. Petersburg. Among his most notable acquisitions are two Rembrandts: *Portrait of an Old Man* and *Alexander the Great.* Two other well-known paintings are *Portrait of Hélène Fourment,* by Peter Paul Rubens, and *Portrait of Madame Claude Monet,* by Pierre-Auguste Renoir. In addition, we suggest that you seek out Mary Cassatt's *The Stocking.* The French sculptor Jean-Antoine Houdon is represented by a statue of Diana. Silver made by François-Thomas Germain, once used by Catherine the Great, is also here, as is one piece by Thomas Germain, the father.

As a cultural center, the Gulbenkian Foundation sponsors plays, films, ballets, and concerts, as well as a rotating exhibition of works by leading modern Portuguese and foreign artists.

Av. de Berna 45. www.museu.gulbenkian.pt. *℃* **21/782-30-00.** Admission 4€; free for seniors 65 and over, students, and teachers; free for all Sun. Tues–Sun 10am–5:45pm. Metro: Sebastião or Praça de Espanha. Bus: 16, 26, 31, 41, 46, or 56.

Museu de Marinha (Maritime Museum) ★★ The Maritime Museum, one of the best in Europe, evokes the glory that characterized Portugal's domination of the high seas. Appropriately, it's installed in the west wing of the Mosteiro dos Jerónimos. These royal galleys recreate an age of opulence that never shied away from excess. Dragons' heads drip with gilt; sea monsters coil with abandon. Assembling a large crew was no problem for kings and queens in those days. Queen Maria I ordered a magnificent galley built for the 1785 marriage of her son and successor, Crown Prince João, to the Spanish Princess Carlota Joaquina Bourbon. Eighty dummy oarsmen, elaborately attired in scarlet-and-mustard-colored waistcoats, represent the crew.

The museum contains hundreds of models of 15th- to 19th-century sailing ships, 20th-century warships, merchant marine vessels, fishing boats, river craft, and pleasure boats. In a section devoted to the East is a pearl-inlaid replica of a dragon boat used in maritime and fluvial corteges. A full range of Portuguese naval uniforms is on display, from one worn at a Mozambique military outpost in 1896 to a uniform worn as recently as 1961. In a special room is a model of the queen's stateroom on the royal yacht of Carlos I, the Bragança king who was assassinated at Praça do Comércio in 1908. It was on this craft that his son, Manuel II; his wife; and the queen mother, Amélia, escaped to Gibraltar following the collapse of the Portuguese monarchy in 1910. The Maritime Museum also honors some early Portuguese aviators.

Praça do Império. http://museu.marinha.pt. ℂ **21/362-00-19.** Admission 4€ adults, 2€ students and children ages 6–17, free for seniors 65 and over and children under 5. May–Sept Tues–Sun 10am–6pm; Oct–Apr Tues–Sun 10am–5pm; closed holidays.

Museu Nacional de Arte Antiga ★★★ The National Museum of Ancient Art houses the country's greatest collection of paintings. It occupies two connected buildings—a 17th-century palace and an added edifice that was built on the site of the old Carmelite Convent of Santo Alberto. The convent's chapel was preserved and is a good example of the integration of ornamental arts, with gilded carved wood, glazed tiles, and sculpture of the 17th and 18th centuries.

The museum has many notable paintings, including the **polyptych** ★★★ from St. Vincent's monastery attributed to Nuno Gonçalves between 1460 and 1470. There are 60 portraits of leading figures of Portuguese history. Other outstanding works are Hieronymus Bosch's triptych *The Temptation of St. Anthony* ★★★, Hans Memling's *Mother and Child*, Albrecht Dürer's *St. Jerome,* and paintings by Velázquez, Poussin, and Courbet. Especially noteworthy is the *12 Apostles,* by Zurbarán. Paintings from the 15th through the 19th centuries trace the development of Portuguese art.

The museum also exhibits a remarkable collection of gold- and silversmiths' works, both Portuguese and foreign. Among these is a cross from Alcobaça and the monstrance of Belém, constructed with the first gold brought from India by Vasco da Gama. Another exceptional example is the 18th-century French silver tableware ordered by José I. Diverse objects from Benin, India, Persia, China, and Japan were culled from the proceeds of Portuguese expansion overseas. Two excellent pairs of **screens** ★★ depict the Portuguese relationship with Japan in the 17th century. Flemish tapestries, a rich assemblage of church vestments, Italian polychrome ceramics, and sculptures are also on display.

Rua das Janelas Verdes 95. www.mnarteantiga-ipmuseus.pt. ℂ **21/391-28-00.** Admission 5€ adults, free for students and children under 14. Tues 2–6pm; Wed–Sun 10am–6pm. Tram: 15 or 18. Bus: 27, 49, 51, or 60.

Museu Nacional dos Coches (National Coach Museum) ★★ The most visited attraction in Lisbon, the National Coach Museum is the finest of its type in the world. Founded by Amélia, wife of Carlos I, it's housed in a former 18th-century riding academy connected to the Belém Royal Palace. The coaches stand in a former horse ring; most date from the 17th to the 19th centuries. Drawing the most interest is a trio of opulently gilded baroque carriages used by the Portuguese ambassador to the Vatican at the time of Pope Clement XI (1716). Also on display is a 17th-century coach in which the Spanish Habsburg king, Phillip II, journeyed from Madrid to Lisbon to see his new possession.

Praça de Afonso de Albuquerque. http://en.museudoscoches.pt. *℺* **21/361-08-50.** Admission 5€, 2.50€ ages 14–25, free for children under 14. Tues–Sun 10am–6pm; closed holidays. Bus: 28, 714, 727, 729, or 751.

Oceanário de Lisboa ★★ This world-class aquarium is the most enduring and impressive achievement of EXPO '98. Marketed as the second-biggest aquarium in the world (the largest is in Osaka, Japan), it's in a stone-and-glass building whose centerpiece is a 5-million-liter (1.3-million-gal.) holding tank. Its waters consist of four distinct ecosystems that replicate the Atlantic, Pacific, Indian, and Antarctic oceans. Each is supplemented with aboveground portions on which birds, amphibians, and reptiles flourish. Look for otters in the Pacific waters, penguins in the Antarctic section, trees and flowers that might remind you of Polynesia in the Indian Ocean division, and puffins, terns, and seagulls in the Atlantic subdivision. Don't underestimate the national pride associated with this huge facility: Most Portuguese view it as a latter-day reminder of their former mastery of the seas.

Esplanada d. Carlos I. www.oceanario.pt. *℺* **21/891-70-02.** Admission 12€ adults, 6€ students and children under 13. Summer daily 10am–8pm; winter daily 10am–7pm. Metro: Estação do Oriente. Pedestrians should turn right after leaving the metro station and go along Av. Dom João II where you'll see a signpost directing you left and to the water for the attraction itself.

Padrão dos Descobrimentos ★ Like the prow of a caravel from the Age of Discovery, the Monument to the Discoveries stands on the Tagus, looking ready to strike out across the Sea of Darkness. Notable explorers, chiefly Vasco da Gama, are immortalized in stone along the ramps.

At the point where the two ramps meet is a representation of Henry the Navigator, whose genius opened up new worlds. The memorial was unveiled in 1960, and one of the stone figures is that of a kneeling Philippa of Lancaster, Henry's English mother. Other figures in the frieze symbolize the crusaders (represented by a man holding a flag with a cross), navigators, monks, cartographers, and cosmographers. At the top of the prow is the coat of arms of Portugal at the time of Manuel the Fortunate. On the floor in front of the memorial lies a map of the world in multicolored marble, with the dates of the discoveries set in metal.

Praça da Boa Esperança, Av. de Brasília. www.padraodescobrimentos.egeac.pt. *℺* **21/303-19-50.** Admission 2.50€. May–Sept Tues–Sun 10am–7pm; Oct–Apr Tues–Sun 10am–6pm.

Sé de Lisboa ★ Even official tourist brochures admit that this cathedral is not very rich. Characterized by twin towers flanking its entrance, it represents an architectural wedding of Romanesque and Gothic style. The facade is severe enough to resemble a medieval fortress. At one point, the Saracens reportedly used the site of the present Sé as a mosque. When the city was captured early in the 12th century by Christian crusaders, led by Portugal's first king, Afonso Henríques, the structure was rebuilt. The Sé then became the first church in Lisbon. The earthquakes of 1344 and 1755 damaged the structure.

Beyond the rough exterior are many treasures, including the font where St. Anthony of Padua is said to have been christened in 1195. A notable feature is the 14th-century Gothic chapel of Bartolomeu Joanes. Other items of interest are a crib by Machado de Castro (the 18th-century Portuguese sculptor responsible for the equestrian statue on Praça do Comércio), the 14th-century sarcophagus of Lopo Fernandes Pacheco, and the original nave and aisles.

A visit to the sacristy and cloister requires a guide. The cloister, built in the 14th century by King Dinis, is of ogival construction, with garlands, a **Romanesque wrought-iron grill ★**, and tombs with inscription stones. In the sacristy are marbles, relics, valuable images, and pieces of ecclesiastical treasure from the 15th and 16th centuries. In the morning, the stained-glass reflections on the floor evoke a Monet painting.

Largo da Sé. www.patriarcado-lisboa.pt. ✆ **21/886-67-52.** Admission: Cathedral free; cloister 2.50€. Daily 9am–7pm; holidays 9am–5pm. Tram: 28 (Graça). Bus: 37.

Torre de Belém ★★ The quadrangular Tower of Belém is a monument to Portugal's Age of Discovery. Erected between 1515 and 1520, the Manueline-style tower is Portugal's classic landmark and often serves as a symbol of the country. A monument to Portugal's great military and naval past, the tower stands on or near the spot where the caravels once set out across the sea.

Its architect, Francisco de Arruda, blended Gothic and Moorish elements, using such architectural details as twisting ropes carved of stone. The coat of arms of Manuel I rests above the loggia, and balconies grace three sides of the monument. Along the balustrade of the loggias, stone crosses represent the Portuguese crusaders.

The richness of the facade fades once you cross the drawbridge and enter the Renaissance-style doorway. Gothic severity reigns. A few antiques can be seen, including a 16th-century throne graced with finials and an inset paneled with pierced Gothic tracery. If you scale the steps leading to the ramparts, you'll be rewarded with a panorama of boats along the Tagus and pastel-washed, tile-roofed old villas in the hills beyond.

Facing the Tower of Belém is a monument commemorating the first Portuguese to cross the Atlantic by airplane (not nonstop). The date was March 30, 1922, and the flight took pilot Gago Coutinho and navigator Sacadura Cabral from Lisbon to Rio de Janeiro.

At the center of Praça do Império at Belém is the **Fonte Luminosa** (the Luminous Fountain). The patterns of the water jets, estimated at more than 70 original designs, make an evening show lasting nearly an hour.

Praça do Império, Av. de Brasília. www.mosteirojeronimos.pt. ✆ **21/362-00-34.** Admission 5€ adults, 2€ ages 15–25 years, free for children under 14 and for seniors 65 and over; free for all Sun until 2pm. Oct–Apr Tues–Sun 10am–5pm; May–Sept Tues–Sun 10am–6pm.

ORGANIZED TOURS

The best tours of Lisbon are offered by **Lisboasightseeing,** Rua Pascoal de Melo 3 (www.lisboasightseeing.com; ✆ **96/708-65-36**). The half-day tour of Lisbon, costing 34€, is the most popular, taking in the highlights of the Alfama and visiting the major monuments, including Jerónimos Monastery and other attractions of Belém. It even goes over the bridge spanning the Tagus, for a panoramic view. Both morning and afternoon tours leave daily throughout the year.

The most recommended tour of the environs of Lisbon is a daily full-day tour costing 82€ and taking in all the highlights, concentrating on Sintra, Cascais, and Estoril. There's also a full-day (and jampacked) tour offered daily of the highlights north of Lisbon—Fátima, Batalha, Nazaré, and Óbidos. This tour costs 86€. Many other tours are offered that might be more suited for your desires—check with the agency for the current agenda.

If you want a more personalized tour, check out the offerings of **Inside Lisbon Tours,** Av. Forças Armadas 95 (www.insidelisbon.com; ✆ **96/841-26-12**). Patrons are transported around in small vans and then taken on different walking tours through the most colorful and historical zones of Lisbon. A popular summer addition is a twice-weekly pub crawl. The tours are given in English and enough free time is provided to explore each district in some depth. Only eight people at a time are taken on a tour. The labyrinths of the Alfama are the most desirable and intriguing of the tours.

Where to Eat

CENTER

Very Expensive

Casa da Comida ★★★ FRENCH/TRADITIONAL PORTUGUESE Local gourmets tout Casa da Comida as offering some of the finest food in Lisbon. The dining room is handsomely decorated, the bar is done in the French Empire style, and there's a charming walled garden. Specialties include lobster with vegetables, roast kid with herbs, a medley of shellfish, and *faisão à convento de Alcântara* (stewed pheasant marinated in port wine for a day). The cellar contains an excellent selection of wines. The food is often more imaginative here than at some of the other top-rated choices. The chef is extraordinarily attentive to the quality of his ingredients, and the menu never fails to deliver some delightful surprises.

Travessa de Amoreiras 1 (close to Jardim de Las Amoreiras). www.casadacomida.pt. ✆ **21/388-53-76.** Reservations required. Main courses 32€–45€; menu degustation 40€; fixed-price menu 35€. AE, DC, MC, V. Tues–Fri 1–4pm; Mon–Sat 8–11pm. Metro: Rato.

Eleven ★★★ MEDITERRANEAN/MODERN PORTUGUESE Housed in an avant-garde building, Eleven is the only restaurant in Lisbon to win the coveted Michelin star. Filled with contemporary art, it opens onto a panoramic view across Lisbon, including the port. The restaurant is named for 11 friends who banded together because of their love of good food and their desire to see a world-class restaurant open in Lisbon. The location is just above Parque Eduardo VII, next to the Amália Rodrigues Gardens. You will wax poetic after feasting here on chef Joachim Koerper's specialties, each based on market-fresh ingredients in harmony with the seasons. He uses locally grown, fresh, and natural produce, creating a luminous, elegant, and innovative cuisine. Starters include a foie gras terrine with banana chutney or scallops carpaccio with black truffles, followed by such fish selections as seabass with beetroot or roasted lobster with butter beans. Meat main courses range from Challans duck with stuffed baby pumpkin to lamb in a lemon crust with a chestnut parfait.

Rua Marquês de Fronteira. www.restauranteleven.com. ✆ **21/386-22-11.** Reservations required. Main courses 35€–55€; tasting menu 79€. MC, V. Mon–Sat 12:30–3pm and 7:30–11pm. Metro: Parque.

Expensive

100 Maneiras ★★★ INTERNATIONAL   Bosnian-born chef Ljubomir Stanisic is hailed by the local press as one of the most creative culinary artists in Lisbon, and we concur. The name of the restaurant translates as "100 ways of preparation." It's tucked away in a little section of the Chiado and may be hard to find. The setting is intimate, the welcome warm. Arguably, the chef offers the best tasting menu in town, nine wonderful courses, and you can also order a matching wine-tasting menu as well. Stanisic puts together lovely impromptu menus bursting with freshness and originality. There are many artful touches—your pieces of cod arrive at table hanging from clothespins. All the ingredients are fresh from the city's Ribeira market and the chef is constantly changing the menu. You might encounter a Brazilian rump steak, tender to the fork and full of flavor. He also does a great Brazilian *feijoada* or bean stew. Not unexpectedly, there are Serbian dishes on the menu, but for the most part he explores the kitchens of the world for his inspiration.

Rua do Teixeira 35. www.restaurante100maneiras.com. ℂ **21/099-04-75.** Reservations required. Tasting menu 75€; 18€–28€. AE, DC, MC, V. Mon–Fri noon–2pm; Mon–Sat 7pm–2am. Metro: Baixa-Chiado.

Panorama Restaurant ★★ INTERNATIONAL/PORTUGUESE   For a restaurant and bar with a view, consider this spot in the 25-story Sheraton Lisboa Hotel & Spa. It's a celestial setting at night as you survey the twinkling lights of Lisbon. Dull, international hotel cuisine is eschewed in favor of sublime taste sensations created with market-fresh ingredients. The chef is always creating some new dish to tantalize diners, perhaps a salad of dried fruits and fresh papaya sprinkled with sheep's milk cheese. His filet of cod is served in a savory ragout of fresh clams. Some of his dessert concoctions are pure poetry, especially the Belgian chocolate fondant with ginger ice cream.

Rua Latino Coelho 1. www.sheratonlisboa.com. ℂ **21/312-00-00.** Reservations required. Fixed-price menus 30€–39€. AE, DC, MC, V. Daily 12:30–3pm and 7:30–11:30pm. Bus: 1, 36, 44, or 45.

Moderate

Restaurante Doca Peixe ★★ SEAFOOD   This restaurant, whose Portuguese name means "Fish Dock," stands virtually under the Ponte do 25 de Abril. The best views of the Tagus are from the tables upstairs. The fresh fish served here is among the best quality offered in the markets of Lisbon. Every variety of fish and shellfish seems to be swimming in the small aquarium at the entrance. If you don't want your fish chargrilled, you can order it cooked in salt or baked. Codfish is a specialty, appearing cooked with clams and flavored with fresh coriander (cilantro), or you can order the grilled platter of shellfish, a true delight. For carnivores, succulent sirloin steaks are among several winning choices.

Doca de Santo Amaro, Armazém 14. www.docapeixe.com. ℂ **21/397-35-65.** Reservations recommended. Main courses 17€–39€. AE, MC, V. Tues–Sun noon–3pm and 9:30pm–1am. Bus: 15 or 38.

Inexpensive

Pastelaria Versailles ★ CAFE/PASTRIES   This is the most famous teahouse in Lisbon, and it has been declared part of the "national patrimony." Some patrons reputedly have been coming here since it opened in 1932. In older days, the specialty was *licungo,* the famed black tea of Mozambique; you can still order it, but nowadays many drinkers enjoy English brands. (The Portuguese claim that they introduced the custom of tea-drinking to the English court after Catherine of Bragança married

Charles II in 1662.) The decor is rich, with chandeliers, gilt mirrors, stained-glass windows, tall stucco ceilings, and black-and-white marble floors. You can also order milkshakes, mineral water, and fresh orange juice, along with beer and liquor. The wide variety of snacks includes codfish balls and toasted ham-and-cheese sandwiches. A limited array of platters of simple but wholesome Portuguese fare is on offer, too.

Av. da República 15A. www.pastelariaversailles.com. © **21/354-63-40.** Sandwiches 3€; pastries 1€; plats du jour 9.50€–22€. AE, MC, V. Daily 7:30am–10pm. Metro: Saldanha.

Restaurante Sancho INTERNATIONAL/PORTUGUESE   Sancho is a cozy rustic-style restaurant with classic Iberian decor—beamed ceiling, fireplace, leather-and-wood chairs, and stucco walls. In summer, it has air-conditioning. Fish gratinée soup is a classic way to begin. Shellfish, always expensive, is the specialty. Main dishes are likely to include the chef's special hake or pan-broiled Portuguese steak. If your palate is fireproof, order *churrasco de cabrito ao piri-piri* (goat with pepper sauce). For dessert, sample the crêpes suzette or perhaps chocolate mousse. This is a longtime (since 1962) local favorite, and the recipes never change. As a waiter explained, "As long as we can keep the dining room full every night, why change?"

Travessa da Glória 14 (just off Av. da Liberdade, near Praça dos Restauradores). www.restaurante sancho.com.pt. © **21/346-97-80.** Reservations recommended. Main courses 14€–26€. AE, DC, MC, V. Mon–Fri noon–3pm and 7pm–midnight; Sat 7pm–midnight. Metro: Avenida or Restauradores.

BAIRRO ALTO & CHIADO
Expensive

Largo ★★ MEDITERRANEAN   Formerly of the celebrated Buddha Bar in Paris, chef Miguel Castro e Silva has brought his creative specialties to the Chiado. The setting itself is elegant, with a main floor plus a mezzanine, all in a medley of architectural styles, including stone arches and pillars, mixed with a sleek contemporary design in such colors as lettuce green or fuchsia. The main restaurant was converted from the old Convent of the Cloisters of the Church of the Martyrs. The cooking is original and highly personalized with market-fresh ingredients. Vigorous flavors appear in perfectly balanced dishes. Try such fish dishes as grilled seabass in an orange fennel sauce, or sautéed squid with shrimp in a beurre blanc sauce. Filet steak appears with a sautéed foie gras in a wine sauce, or else you can sample a delightful duck magret with a truffled risotto. Starters might include a cold almond and fennel cream soup or else smoked codfish in a pine nut vinaigrette.

Rua Serpa Pinto 10A. www.largo.pt. © **21/347-72-25.** Reservations required. Main courses 25€–30€. AE, DC, MC, V. Mon–Fri 12:30–3pm; Sat 7:30pm–midnight. Metro: Baixa/Chiado.

Tasquinha d'Adelaide ★ 💼 REGIONAL PORTUGUESE   At the western edge of the Bairro Alto, about 2 blocks northeast of the Alcântara subway station and 2 blocks west of the Basilica da Estrela, this small restaurant is cramped and convivial. It's known for the culinary specialties of Trás-os-Montes, a rugged province in northeast Portugal, and for its homey, unpretentious warmth. Robust specialties include *alheiras fritas com arroz de grelos* (tripe with collard greens and rice) and *lulas grelhadas* (grilled squid served in a black clay casserole). To finish, try Dona Adelaide's *charcade de ovos* (a secret recipe made with egg yolks). Although we like this hearty cooking, the flavors might be too pungent for some palates.

Rua do Patrocínio 70–74. © **21/396-22-39.** Reservations recommended. Main courses 16€–30€. AE, DC, MC, V. Mon–Sat 12:30–4pm and 8pm–2am. Metro: Rato. Tram: 25, 28, or 30. Bus: 9, 15, or 28.

Moderate

Sacramento do Chiado ★ 🎁 INTERNATIONAL/PORTUGUESE   This place has emerged as the virtual symbol of the new and trendy Chiado district. If you opt for a meal here, get ready for access to a labyrinth of inner chambers loaded with intriguingly carved arts and crafts, some of them from Indonesia, and much of them, based on this place's self-definition as an "emporium," for sale. Beginning around 8pm, you're likely to find a hip mixture of Brazilian and Portuguese night owls scattered throughout the various bars and dining areas associated with this place. Steak tartare, tenderloin steak, pork tenderloin with prunes, stuffed breast of chicken with ratatouille, and de-boned filet of cod "Sacramento," with potatoes and garlic, are each well prepared and flavorful.

Calçada do Sacramento 44. www.sacramentodochiado.com. ⓒ **21/342-05-72.** Main courses 9€–32€. AE, DC, MC, V. Tues–Sat noon–3pm; Sun 7:30pm–midnight. Metro: Chiado.

Inexpensive

Terra VEGETARIAN   Vegetarians do not have to forego tasty treats in Lisbon—even nonvegetarians are likely to be enthralled with the rich flavors served by the Mediterranean kitchen here. In a restored 18th-century house with a private garden, you can enjoy their daily changing buffet. Regularly featured is an array of curries, tempura dishes, burritos, and kebabs. The chef claims that for his salads he finds inspirations on all the continents of the world, including classics such as a Greek salad or a Waldorf salad. Some of the combinations are unexpected and delicious. Desserts range from a delectable chocolate brownie to a rice pudding based on a medieval recipe. There is also a classic tiramisu. The restaurant also serves the first kosher wines to be produced in Portugal in 500 years.

Rua da Palmeira 15. www.restauranteterra.pt. ⓒ **70/710-81-08.** Reservations recommended Sat–Sun. Buffet 20€. AE, DC, MC, V. Tues–Sun 12:30–3pm and 7:30–10:30pm. Metro: Avenida.

GRAÇA DISTRICT
Moderate

Faz Figura ★ INTERNATIONAL/PORTUGUESE   This is one of the best and most attractively decorated dining rooms in Lisbon—decked out in 19th-century style with pretty antique tiles and wall prints of city scenes—and the service is faultless. When reserving a table, ask to be seated on the veranda, overlooking the Tagus. You can stop for a before-dinner drink in the "international cocktail bar." The cuisine, including such specialties as *feijoada de marisco* (shellfish stew) and *cataplana* (a cooking pot) of fish and seafood, is generally very flavorful and occasionally spicy.

Rua do Paraíso 15B. www.fazfigura.com. ⓒ **21/886-89-81.** Reservations recommended. Main courses 16€–32€. AE, DC, MC, V. Mon–Fri 12:30–3pm and 7:30–11pm; Sat 7:30–11pm. Bus: 12, 39, or 46.

SANTA APOLÓNIA
Moderate

Bica do Sapato ★★ 🎁 MODERN PORTUGUESE   This hip restaurant has a retro-minimalist decor that's calculated to attract what a local commentator described as "the scene-savvy, design-obsessed jet set." Actor John Malkovich, along with four other partners (the most visible of whom is restaurant pro Fernando Fernandes), transformed what had once functioned as a boat factory into a three-part restaurant that packs in enthusiastic scene-setters virtually every night. A sushi bar is set one floor above ground level, and a "cafeteria" shares its space on street level with the establishment's gastronomic citadel, the restaurant, which is the place we heartily recommend above the other two. Its decor evokes the waiting lounge at a 1960s international airport, but the food takes brilliant liberties with traditional Portuguese cuisine. Stellar examples include seafood broth with grilled red prawns and Asian vegetables; codfish salad in olive oil, served with chickpea ice cream; and veal knuckle browned in olive oil, with garlic, sautéed potatoes, and bay leaves.

Av. Infante Dom Henrique, Armazém (Warehouse) 8, Cais da Pedra à Bica do Sapato. www. bicadosapato.com. *©* **21/881-03-20.** Reservations recommended. Main courses and platters 21€–32€ in restaurant; 9€–20€ in cafeteria; 6€–50€ in sushi bar. AE, MC, V. Restaurant Tues–Sun 12:30–2:30pm and 8–11:30pm, Mon 8–11:30pm; cafeteria Tues–Sun 12–3:30pm and 7:30pm–1am, Mon 5pm–1am; sushi bar Mon–Sat 7:30pm–1am. Bus: 9, 35, 39, 46, 59, 104, or 105.

IN THE SANTOS DISTRICT
Inexpensive

Yasmin ★ 🎁 PORTUGUESE   The waterfront Santos quarter of Lisbon was once where only shady characters went at night. But it is emerging as a splashy new venue after dark. Once a dreary industrial area, it's fast becoming a favorite haunt for dining and drinking, and it also has a number of museums. A crowd of up-and-coming young professionals have adopted Yasmin as their favorite place. With a contemporary decor that is often called "sexy," you can dine while sitting in a Saarinen chair fashionably placed on a polished concrete floor. Surprising tastes and combinations greet you. Ever had a mango–tomato–avocado–honey vinaigrette? It's served with grilled cheeses from the Azores. For your main course, opt for the cod confit with garlic-laced sautéed spinach or perhaps loin of deer with grilled shiitake mushrooms and a corn foam. The kitchen shuts down at 12:20am, but the club stays open later.

Rua da Moeda 1A. www.yasmin-lx.com. *©* **21/393-00-74.** Reservations required. Main courses 13€–21€. Tues–Sat noon–3pm and 7:30pm–2am. AE, MC, V. Metro: Cais do Sodré.

Shopping

Portuguese handicrafts often exhibit exotic influences, in large part because of the artisans' versatility and their skill in absorbing other styles. Portugal's vast history as a seafaring nation also surely has something to do with it. The best place to see their work is in Lisbon, where shopkeepers and their buyers hunt out unusual items from all over Portugal, including the Madeira Islands and the Azores.

Shops operate all over the city, but **Baixa,** in downtown Lisbon, is the major area for browsing. **Rua Áurea** (Street of Gold, the location of the major jewelry shops), **Rua da Prata** (Street of Silver), and **Rua Augusta** are Lisbon's three principal shopping streets. The Baixa shopping district lies between the Rossio and the river Tagus.

Rua Garrett, in the Chiado, is where you'll find many of the more upmarket shops. A major fire in 1988 destroyed many shops, but new ones have arisen.

Antiques lovers gravitate to Rua Dom Pedro V in the Bairro Alto. Other streets with antiques stores include Rua da Misericórdia, Rua de São Pedro de Alcântara, Rua da Escola Politécnica, and Rua do Alecrim. Along both sides of the narrow Rua de São José in the Graça District are treasure troves of shops packed with antiques from all over the world. Antiques dealers from the United States come here to survey the wares. You'll find ornate spool and carved beds, high-back chairs, tables, wardrobes with ornate carvings, brass plaques, copper pans, silver candelabra, crystal sconces, chandeliers, and a wide selection of wooden figures, silver boxes, porcelain plates, and bowls. Don't, however, count on getting spectacular bargains.

At the **Feira da Ladra,** an **open-air flea market,** vendors peddle their wares on Tuesday and Saturday; haggling is expected. Portable stalls and dropcloth displays are lined up in Campo de Santa Clara behind the Igreja São Vicente. Take bus no. 12 from the Santa Apolónia station.

Pottery is one of the best buys in Portugal, and pottery covered with brightly colored roosters from Barcelos is legendary, as is the ubiquitous blue-and-white pottery made in Coimbra. From Caldas da Rainha come yellow-and-green dishes in the shapes of vegetables, fruit, and animals. Vila Real is known for its black pottery, polychrome pieces come from Aceiro, and the red-clay pots from the Alentejo region are based on designs that go back to the Etruscans.

SHOPPING CENTERS

Centro Vasco da Gama   This modern shopping mall is hailed as the finest in Portugal, with 164 shops, 36 restaurants, a 10-screen movie theater, a health club, and a playground. Along with Portuguese-made products, you'll also find a lot of designer labels in clothing, including Vuitton and Hugo Boss selling at cheaper prices than you might find in other western European capitals. The shops keep hours that benefit almost all customers: They're open daily 10am to midnight. Av. Dom João II within Parque das Nações. www.centrovascodagama.pt. ©**21/893-06-00.** Metro: Estação Oriente.

Entertainment & Nightlife

If you have only 1 night in Lisbon, spend it at a **fado** club. The nostalgic sounds of fado, Portuguese "songs of sorrow," are at their best in Lisbon—the capital attracts the greatest *fadistas* (fado singers) in the world (see the box "Fado: The Music of Longing," below). Fado is high art in Portugal, so don't plan to carry on a private conversation during a show—it's bad form. Most of the authentic fado clubs are clustered in the Bairro Alto and in the Alfama, between St. George's Castle and the docks. You can "fado hop" between the two quarters.

For more information about nighttime attractions, go to the tourist office (see "Visitor Information," earlier in this chapter), which maintains a list of events. Another helpful source is the **Agência de Bilhetes para Espectáculos Públicos,** in Praça dos Restauradores (© 21/347-58-24). It's open daily from 9am to 9:30pm; go in person instead of trying to call. The agency sells tickets to most theaters and cinemas.

Also check out copies of ***What's On in Lisbon***, available at most newsstands; *Sete,* a weekly magazine with entertainment listings; or the free monthly guides *Agenda Cultural* and *LISBOaem.* Your hotel concierge is a good bet for information, too, because one of his or her duties is reserving seats.

"The party" in Lisbon begins late. Many bars don't even open until 10 or 11pm, and very few savvy young Portuguese would set foot in a club before 1am. The Bairro Alto, with some 150 restaurants and bars, is the most happening place after dark.

THE PERFORMING ARTS

Centro Cultural de Belém ★★   This center is a major venue for the presentation of concerts by various international orchestras and classical recitals, even performances by top jazz artists and other visiting musicians. Some of the best dance programs in Portugal are also presented here, along with top-of-the-line theatrical productions. You can check the local newspapers upon your arrival in Lisbon to see if a featured presentation interests you. Praça do Império. www.ccb.pt. © **21/361-24-44.** Tram: 15.

FADO: THE music OF LONGING

The *saudade* (Portuguese for "longing" or "nostalgia") that infuses the country's literature is most evident in fado. The traditional songs express Portugal's sad, romantic mood. The traditional performers are women *(fadistas)*, often accompanied by a guitar and a viola.

Experiencing the nostalgic sounds of fado is essential to comprehending the Portuguese soul. Fado is Portugal's most vivid art form; no visit to the country is complete without at least 1 night spent in a local tavern listening to this traditional folk music.

A rough translation of *fado* is "fate," from the Latin *fatum* (prophecy). Fado songs usually tell of unrequited love, jealousy, or a longing for days gone by. The music, as is often said, evokes a "life commanded by the Oracle, which nothing can change."

Fado became famous in the 19th century when Maria Severa, the beautiful daughter of a Gypsy, took Lisbon by storm. She sang her way into the hearts of the people of Lisbon—especially the count of Vimioso, an outstanding bullfighter. Present-day *fadistas* wear a black-fringed shawl in her memory.

The most famous 20th-century exponent of fado was Amália Rodriguez, who was introduced to American audiences in the 1950s at the New York club La Vie en Rose. Born into a simple Lisbon family, she was discovered while walking barefoot and selling flowers on the Lisbon docks near the Alfama. For many, she is the most famous Portuguese figure since Vasco da Gama. Swathed in black, sparing of gestures and excess ornamentation, Rodriguez almost single-handedly executed the transformation of fado into an international form of poetic expression.

Museu Calouste Gulbenkian ★ From October to June, concerts, recitals, and occasionally ballet performances take place here; sometimes there are also jazz concerts. Ticket prices vary according to the performance. Av. de Berna 45. www.museu. gulbenkian.pt. ✆ **21/782-30-00.** Metro: Sebastião. Bus: 16, 56, 718, or 726.

Teatro Nacional de São Carlos ★★ This 18th-century theater attracts opera and ballet aficionados from all over Europe, and top companies from around the world perform here. The season begins in mid-September and extends through July. There are no special discounts. Rua Serpa Pinto 9. www.saocarlos.pt.✆ **21/325-30-45.** Tickets 10€–100€. Box office Mon–Fri 1–7pm, Sat–Sun and holidays from 1pm to 30 min. after the show begins. Tram: 28, 58, 100, or 204 (night service). Bus: 58. Metro: Baixa-Chiado.

BARS

Bar Procópio ★ 👔 A longtime favorite of journalists, politicians, and foreign actors, the once-innovative Procópio has become a tried-and-true staple among Lisbon's watering holes. Guests sit on tufted red velvet, surrounded by stained and painted glass and ornate brass hardware. Mixed drinks cost 7€ and up; beer costs 3€ and up. Procópio might easily become your favorite bar, if you can find it. It lies just off Rua de João Penha, which is off the landmark Praça das Amoreiras. Open Monday to Friday 6pm to 3am, Saturday 9pm to 3am. Alto de São Francisco 21. www.barprocopio. com. ✆ **21/385-28-51.** Closed Aug 11–Sept 8. Metro: Rato. Bus: 9.

CINCO Lounge ★★ This is the hottest, chicest bar in all of Lisbon. Lying above the Bairro Alto section, it features an array of dazzling cocktails—some 100 in all—using only the most expensive of liquors and the freshest of fruits. Age is not a factor here, providing you're of drinking age. The waiter will exchange your drink for one you prefer, if you don't like the first choice. That is, if you order anything but The Black Amex, which costs 235€. It's a crystallized brown sugar cube dissolved in Hennessy VS Cognac and Cuvée du Centenaire Grand Marnier, spiked with Dom Perignon. The setting is elegant, with floor-to-ceiling windows, glass-topped tables, and the most flattering lighting in Lisbon. It's open daily from 5pm to 2am. Rua Ruben A. Leitão 17A. www.cincolounge.com. © **21/342-40-33.** Metro: Rato.

Restô do Chapitô ★ 🍴 Hidden away deep in the heart of the Alfama, right below the castle, is one of the drinking (or dining) secrets of Lisbon. The weathered building that contains it has been used, during its turbulent history, as a 17th-century prison and later as a state-sponsored school for the training of circus performers. The view is one of the most panoramic in the Alfama. You can drop in for a coffee or return later, taking a candlelit table to enjoy a limited but choice menu, ranging from succulent and large steaks to a vast array of tapas, often stuffed calamari or even roasted green chili peppers, and lots more. Open Tuesday to Friday 7:30pm to 2am and Saturday and Sunday from 10am to 2am. Rua Costa do Castelo 7, São Cristóvão. www.chapito.org. © **21/886-73-34.** Tram: 28.

FADO CLUBS

Adega Machado ★★ This spot has been open since 1937, but has passed the test of time—it's still one of the country's favorite fado clubs. Alternating with such modern-day *fadistas* as the critically acclaimed Marina Rosa are folk dancers whirling, clapping, and singing native songs in colorful costumes. Dinner is a la carte, and the cuisine is mostly Portuguese, with a number of regional dishes. Expect to spend 25€ to 35€ for a complete meal. The dinner hour starts at 8pm, music begins at 9:15pm, and the doors don't close until 3am. It's open Tuesday through Sunday. Rua do Norte 91. www.adegamachado.web.pt. © **21/322-46-40.** Cover (including 2 drinks) 16€. Bus: 58 or 100.

Museu do Fado ★ Some of the most outstanding *fadistas*, both male and female, perform most nights at this restaurant attached to the municipal **Museu do Fado.** If you're exploring the Alfama during the day, you can drop in for a visit to the museum, which pays homage to Portugal's most distinctive musical style, fado music. The museum is entirely devoted to the world of urban song in Lisbon, tracing the origins and history of fado through photographs, sheet music, musical instruments, phonograms, collections of periodicals, costumes, trophies, and medals. The museum is open Tuesday to Sunday 10am to 6pm, charging 4€ for admission. Adjoining the museum is a restaurant serving regional food Tuesday to Sunday 7pm to 2am. Meals cost from 30€. Largo do Chafariz de Dentro 1. www.museudofado.pt. © **21/882-34-70.** Bus: 28, 735, 745, 759, or 790.

DANCE CLUBS & JAZZ

Cabaret Maxime ★ An old cabaret bar, a meeting place for spies in World War II, has reopened. Through its long history, it's been a brothel, a former strip club, a gay disco, and even a luxury cabaret, drawing such clients as the King of Spain. Today it's been turned into a concert venue and a first-rate bar. You can visit to enjoy the music and the exotic cocktails. Open Thursday 10pm to 2am, and Friday and Saturday from 10pm to 4am. Praça da Alegria 58. © **21/346-70-90.** Metro: Avenida.

Onda Jazz ★   The best jazz in Lisbon, often featuring artists from Africa, is presented here in this Alfama dive. The area is surrounded by fado bars, but the sounds coming from here are distinctly different. In addition to the wide array of jazz rhythms, the bar often features Latin and Asian jazz. The cover can vary, but it's usually around 10€. Open Tuesday, Thursday, and Sunday 8pm to 2am; Friday and Saturday 8pm to 3am. Arco de Jesus 7. www.ondajazz.com. © **21/888-32-42.** Tram: 28.

Silk ★★   If we had a date for a night in Lisbon with Madonna, we'd take her to this hot spot, all black and fuchsia, with a sexy sultriness. What you see going on in its deep plush couches would bring a blush to aging party boy Jack Nicholson. The visit here would be worthy if just for the incredible vista from the floor-to-ceiling windows. You can also perch on a candlelit outdoor deck on the sixth floor. The DJ spins the tunes as chic young things sip Moët & Chandon, or whatever. The club lies on the upper two floors of **Espaço Chiado** with a fantastic 270-degree view of Lisbon. Open Tuesday to Saturday 10pm to 4am. Rua da Misericórdia 14. www.silk-club.com. © **21/780-34-70.** Metro: Baixa-Chiado.

THE LGBT SCENE

Bar 106   A short walk from the also-recommended Finalmente, this is a popular bar, rendezvous point, and watering hole for gay men, most of whom arrive here after around 10pm. Expect a simple, restrained decor, a busy bar area, and enough space to allow subgroups and cliques of like-minded friends to form quickly and easily. It's open nightly from 9pm until 2am. Rua de São Marçal 106. www.bar106.com. © **21/342-73-73.** Tram: 28. Bus: 100.

Finalmente Club   This is the dance club that many gay men in Lisbon end up at after an evening of drinking and talking in other bars around the Bairro Alto. There's a hardworking, hard-drinking bar area; a crowded dance floor; lots of bodies of all shapes and sizes; and a small stage upon which drag shows allow local *artistes* to strut their stuff and emulate—among others—Carmen look-alikes from Seville. A stringent security system requires that you ring a bell before an attendant will let you in. It's open daily from 1am to between 3 and 6am, depending on business. Rua da Palmeira 38. www.finalmenteclub.com. © **21/347-99-23.** Cover 14€, includes 1st drink. Bus: 100.

Where to Stay

CENTER
Very Expensive

Lapa Palace ★★★ ☺   In a palace built in 1870 for the count of Valença, this government-rated five-star hotel, purchased by Orient Express in 1998, is the most talked-about accommodation in Lisbon and the city's premier address. In 1910, the de Valença family sold the villa and its enormous gardens to a wealthy, untitled family that retained it until 1988. Its lushly manicured gardens lie close to the Tagus, south of the city center. All but about 20 of the rooms are in a modern six-story wing. The spacious guest rooms in both sections contain amply proportioned marble surfaces, reproductions of French and English furniture, and a classic design inspired by a late-18th-century model. The marble bathrooms are among the city's most elegant, often adorned with bas-reliefs. Each unit opens onto a balcony. The older rooms have more charm and grace; many of the newer ones open onto panoramic vistas of Lisbon. The public areas have multicolored ceiling frescoes and richly patterned marble floors.

Rua do Pau da Bandeira 4, 1249-021 Lisboa. www.lapapalace.com. © **21/394-94-94.** Fax 21/395-06-65. 109 units. 370€–675€ double; from 1,300€ suite. Rates include buffet breakfast. AE, DC, MC,

V. Free parking. Bus: 13 or 27. **Amenities:** 2 restaurants; bar; 2 pools (1 heated indoors); exercise room; spa; children's center; concierge; room service; babysitting; Wi-Fi (15€ per 24 hr., in lobby). *In room:* A/C, TV, minibar, hair dryer.

Expensive
Hotel Lisboa Plaza ★★
Hotel Lisboa Plaza, in the heart of the city, is a charmer of a boutique hotel. A family-owned and -operated government-rated four-star hotel, it has many appealing Art Nouveau touches, including the facade. The hotel was built in 1953 and has been frequently overhauled and modernized since. A well-known Portuguese designer, Graça Viterbo, decorated it in contemporary classic style. The midsize guest rooms—with well-stocked marble bathrooms and double-glazed windows—are well styled and comfortable. Try for a unit in the rear, looking out over the botanical gardens.

Travessa do Salitre 7, Av. da Liberdade, 1269-066 Lisboa. www.heritage.pt. © **21/321-82-18.** Fax 21/347-16-30. 106 units. 99€–385€ double; 270€–625€ suite. Children under 12 stay free in parent's room. AE, DC, MC, V. Parking nearby 10€. Metro: Avenida. Bus: 1, 2, 36, or 44. **Amenities:** Restaurant; bar; exercise room; concierge; room service; babysitting. *In room:* A/C, TV/DVD, minibar, hair dryer, CD player, Wi-Fi (free).

Moderate
As Janelas Verdes ★★ 🏛
Although York House Hotel (see below) is still the most atmospheric—and certainly the most famous in its category—in Lisbon, this hotel is giving it serious competition and is almost its equal. In fact, it used to be an annex to York House Hotel but broke away and is becoming known as a historic hotel in its own right. Located near the Museum of Ancient Art, it was the former house of the Portuguese novelist Eça de Queirós. Though it's modern, its traditional past has been respected. Rooms are luxurious with comfortable furniture, style, and abundant closet space. The red lounge evokes turn-of-the-20th-century Lisbon. Other special features include a small but beautiful garden and two honor bars as well as a top-floor library and terrace.

Rua das Janelas Verdes 47, 1200-690 Lisboa. www.asjanelasverdes.com. © **21/396-81-43.** Fax 21/396-81-44. 29 units. 135€–295€ double; 225€–380€ triple. Parking 10€. AE, DC, MC, V. Bus: 27, 40, 49, or 60. **Amenities:** Bar; concierge; room service; babysitting. *In room:* A/C, TV/DVD, hair dryer, CD player, Wi-Fi (free).

York House Hotel ★★
Once a 17th-century convent, this boutique hotel is outside the center of traffic-filled Lisbon, and so attracts those who desire peace and tranquillity. It has long been known to the English and to diplomats, artists, writers, poets, and professors. Book well in advance. Near the National Art Gallery, it sits high on a hillside overlooking the Tagus and is surrounded by a garden. A distinguished Lisbon designer selected the tasteful furnishings. About five of the rooms here are outfitted with antiques and early-20th-century bric-a-brac; the others are contemporary in their styling. The public rooms boast inlaid chests, coats of armor, carved ecclesiastical figures, and ornate ceramics. The former monks' dining hall has deep-set windows, large niches for antiques, and—best of all—French–Portuguese cuisine.

Rua das Janelas Verdes 32, 1200-691 Lisboa. www.yorkhouselisboa.com. © **21/396-24-35.** Fax 21/397-27-93. 32 units. 60€–300€ double. AE, DC, MC, V. Parking nearby 10€. Bus: 27, 40, 49, 54, or 60. **Amenities:** Restaurant; bar; concierge; room service; babysitting. *In room:* A/C, TV, hair dryer, Wi-Fi (free).

Inexpensive

LX Boutique Hotel ★ 📠 Launched in 2010, this quirky hotel is outside the center of Lisbon, convenient to Belém and the beaches of Costa do Sol. Its motto is "five floors, five themes—one Lisbon." That means that each floor is dedicated to a particular aspect of the city, including one that covers the Tejo (Tagus) River with nautical artifacts and (naturally) has river views. Another floor is devoted to one of Lisbon's greatest poets, Fernando Pessoa (1888–1935); and yet another, "The Fado Floor," is filled with drawings and musical instruments evoking the sound of fado. Bedrooms are well furnished but tend to be small. The most desirable accommodation is the Xplendid Suite, with a retracting glass roof. The on-site restaurant specializes in sushi, and you can relax over a glass of port wine in the stylish bar.

Rua do Alecrim 12, Cais do Sodré, 1200-017 Lisboa. www.lxboutiquehotel.com. ✆ **21/347-43-94.** Fax 21/347-31-82. 45 units. 100€–145€ double; from 300€ suite. AE, DC, MC, V. Metro: Cais do Sodré. **Amenities:** Restaurant; bar; concierge; room service. *In room:* A/C, TV, fridge, Wi-Fi (free).

VIP Executive Suítes Éden ★ ☺ One of the most unusual conversions in central Lisbon, this hotel occupies the site of the former Eden Theater, a landmark Art Deco building whose enviable location puts its occupants close to the center of virtually everything. At least some of its clients are in town for business, making use of each unit's kitchenette during company-sponsored stays of a month or more. Since its opening, however, units have suffered a bit and in some cases might benefit from a decorative overhaul. But if you don't mind their need of some updating, you might find the place appropriate because of its location, its panoramic rooftop terrace and swimming pool (whose views extend out over the core of antique Lisbon but whose opening hours seem to change with the whim of the staff), and a sense that its developers made good use of the site's original Art Deco design and framework.

Praça dos Restauradores 24, 1250-187 Lisboa. www.edenaparthotelvip.com. ✆ **21/321-66-00.** Fax 21/321-66-66. 134 units. 62€–97€ studio; 88€–144€ apartment. AE, DC, MC, V. Parking not available at the hotel. Metro: Restauradores. Bus: 2, 11, 32, 36, 44, 45, or 91. **Amenities:** Bar; outdoor pool; babysitting. *In room:* A/C, TV, kitchen, hair dryer, Wi-Fi (3€ per hour).

ALFAMA

Expensive

Palacete Chafariz d'el Rei ★★★ 📠 This is the true insider's special address in Lisbon, a restored Brazilian Art Nouveau mansion on the edge of the ancient district of the Alfama. Returning to his native Lisbon after striking it rich in Brazil, João Antonio Santos erected this stunning mansion with stained glass windows. Over the past decades, the micro hotel fell into disrepair, until lovingly restored by a Spaniard and his Portuguese partner. Today everyone from Barcelona architects to English filmmakers to Berlin fashionistas occupy the lavish suites, which come with a Brazilian butler. The stunning suites open onto views of the Tagus and the Alfama. Elaborate moldings and antiques are found throughout, especially in the ground-floor public rooms. Our favorite is the Suite Amaya, which is spacious, glamorous, and even sensual with vintage decorations. There's even embroidery work on the ceiling. A special delight is the private terrace garden filled with the aroma of flowering plants.

Chafariz del Rei 6, 1100-140 Lisboa. www.chafarizdelrei.com. ✆ **91/897-33-76.** 6 units. 180€–360€. AE, MC, V. Tram: 28. **Amenities:** Breakfast room. *In room:* A/C, TV, minibar, hair dryer, Wi-Fi (free).

Palácio Belmonte ★★★ 📠 Deep in the heart of the Alfama lies this romantic hideaway found outside the walls of Castelo de São Jorge. When the hotel was launched at the dawn of the millennium, *Condé Nast Traveler* called it one of the "21 coolest hotels in the world." Each accommodation is a luxuriously furnished suite named after a towering figure in Portuguese arts and letters, including, for example, Gil Vicente. The inn is imbued with antique art, Portuguese tiles, antiques, and works of art, and it has a 4,000-tome library. Its special feature is a swimming pool lined in black marble. Our favorite is the Fernão Magalhães Suite, named after the maritime explorer who circumnavigated the globe for the first time. It lies in the western Muslim tower and has a luxe marble bathroom.

Páteo Dom Fradique 14, 1100-624 Lisboa. www.palaciobelmonte.com. (℡ **21/881-66-00.** Fax 21/881-66-09. 11 suites. 600€–1,200€. AE, MC, V. Free parking. Tram: 28. **Amenities:** Bar; outdoor pool; room service. *In room:* A/C, TV, minibar, hair dryer, Wi-Fi (free).

IN THE BAIRRO ALTO
Inexpensive
Hotel Anjo Azul (Blue Angel) 🏩 This is the only hotel in Lisbon that markets itself to a gay clientele, although heterosexual clients also check in and are welcome. Set on a narrow street in the Bairro Alto, a short walk from such well-recommended gay or mixed bars as Portas Largas and Frágil, it occupies a narrow, much-renovated 18th-century town house that retains many of its original blue-and-white tiles. Don't expect luxury or even an elevator—just clean but small and exceptionally simple rooms, and a thoughtful and helpful staff well versed in the advantages of the surrounding neighborhood. No meals of any kind are served and there's no bar on site, but the attractive, international, and worldly clientele, many of whom return for second and third visits, don't really seem to mind.

Rua Luz Soriano 75, 1200-246 Lisboa. www.anjoazul.com. (℡/fax **21/347-80-69.** 20 units, 7 with private bathroom. 40€–50€ double without bathroom; 50€–85€ double with bathroom. AE, MC, V. No parking available at the hotel. Metro: Baixa Chiado. Tram: 28. *In room:* TV/DVD, hair dryer.

The Portuguese Riviera: Excursions Along the Costa do Sol

Lured by Guincho (near the westernmost point in continental Europe), the Boca do Inferno (Mouth of Hell), and Lord Byron's "glorious Eden" at Sintra, many travelers spend much of their time in the area around Lisbon. You could spend a day drinking in the wonders of the library at the monastery-palace of Mafra (Portugal's El Escorial), dining in the pretty pink rococo palace at Queluz, or enjoying seafood at the Atlantic beach resort of Ericeira.

However, the main draw in the area is the Costa do Sol. The string of beach resorts, including Estoril and Cascais, forms the Portuguese Riviera on the northern bank of the mouth of the Tagus. If you arrive in Lisbon when the sun is shining and the air is balmy, consider heading straight for the shore. Estoril is so near to Lisbon that darting in and out of the capital to see the sights or visit the fado clubs is easy. An inexpensive electric train leaves from the Cais do Sodré station in Lisbon frequently throughout the day and evening; its run ends in Cascais.

ESTORIL ★
The first stop is 24km (15 miles) west of Lisbon. This once-chic resort has long basked in its reputation as a playground for monarchs. **Parque Estoril,** in the center of town, is a well-manicured landscape. At night, when it's floodlit, you can stroll amid the subtropical vegetation. The palm trees studding the grounds have prompted many to call it "a corner of Africa." At the top of the park sits the **casino,** which offers gambling, international floor shows, dancing, and movies.

Across the railroad tracks is the **beach,** where some of the most fashionable people in Europe sun themselves on peppermint-striped canvas chairs along the Praia Estoril Tamariz. The beach is sandy, unlike the pebbly strand at Nice. Although it is a lovely stretch of sand, we don't recommend going into the water, which is almost too polluted for swimming. You can enjoy the sands and the beach scene, but for actual swimming, head to one of the many hotel pools in the area.

CASCAIS ★

Just 6km (3¾ miles) west of Estoril and 61km (38 miles) west of Lisbon, Cascais was a tiny fishing village that attracted artists and writers to its little cottages. To say Cascais is growing would be an understatement: It's exploding! Apartment houses, new hotels, and the finest restaurants along the Costa do Sol draw a never-ending stream of visitors every year.

However, the life of the simple fisher folk goes on. Auctions, called *lotas,* of the latest catch still take place on the main square. In the small harbor, rainbow-colored fishing boats share space with pleasure craft owned by an international set that flocks to Cascais from early spring to autumn.

The most popular excursion outside Cascais is to **Boca do Inferno (Mouth of Hell) ★**. Thundering waves sweep in with such power that they've carved a wide hole resembling a mouth, or *boca,* into the cliffs. However, if you should arrive when the sea is calm, you'll wonder why it's called a cauldron. The Mouth of Hell can be a wind-swept roar if you don't stumble over too many souvenir hawkers.

QUELUZ ★★

From the Estação do Rossio in Lisbon, take the Sintra line to Queluz. Departures during the day are every 15 minutes. The trip takes 30 minutes. There are two train stations in town. Get off at Queluz-Massamá, as it is closer to the palace. A one-way ticket costs 1.50€. Call ⓒ **808/208-208** for schedules. At Queluz, take bus no. 101 or 103, both of which run in front of the palace, or turn left and follow the signs for less than 1km (⅔ mile) to the **Palácio Nacional de Queluz ★★**, Largo do Palácio, 2745-191 Queluz (www.pnqueluz.imc-ip.pt; ⓒ **21/434-38-60**), a brilliant example of the rococo in Portugal. Pedro III ordered its construction in 1747, and the work dragged on until 1787. What you'll see today is not what the palace was like in the 18th century; during the French invasions, almost all of its belongings were transported to Brazil with the royal family. A 1934 fire destroyed a great deal of Queluz, but tasteful and sensitive reconstruction restored the lighthearted aura of the 18th century. Inside you can wander through the queen's dressing room, lined with painted panels depicting a children's romp; the Don Quixote Chamber (Dom Pedro was born here and returned from Brazil to die in the same bed); the Music Room, complete with a French *grande pianoforte* and an 18th-century English harpsichord; and the mirrored throne room adorned with crystal chandeliers. The palace is open Wednesday to Monday 9am to 5pm. It's closed on holidays. Admission is 7€, free for children under 14.

SINTRA ★★★

Sintra, 29km (18 miles) northwest of Lisbon, is a 45-minute ride from the Estação do Rossio at the Rossio in Lisbon. Lord Byron called it "glorious Eden," and so it remains. Visitors flock here not only to absorb the town's beauty and scenic setting, but also to visit the two major sights of Pena and Sintra Palaces. Sintra is a 45-minute ride from the Estação do Rossio at the Rossio in Lisbon. A train leaves every 10 to

20 minutes. The round-trip fare is 3.80€. For information, call ✆ **808/208-208.** From the train station in the heart of Sintra, bus no. 434 goes up to Castelo dos Mouros and on to Pena Palace, costing 4.50€ round-trip. A schedule is posted at the tourist information booth in the train station.

Palácio Nacional da Pena ★★   Pena perches above Sintra on a plateau about 450m (1,476 ft.) above sea level. Part of the fun of visiting the castle is the ride up the verdant, winding road through the Parque das Merendas.

The inspiration behind this castle in the sky was Ferdinand of Saxe-Coburg-Gotha, the husband of Maria II. Ferdinand called on a fellow German, Baron Eschwege, to help him build his fantasy. You can see a sculpture of the baron if you look out from the Pena toward a huge rock across the way. The palace's last royal occupant was Queen Amélia. One morning in 1910, she clearly saw that the monarchy in Portugal was ending. Having lost her husband and her soldier-son to an assassin 2 years before, she was determined not to lose her second son, Manuel II. Gathering her most precious possessions, she fled to Mafra, where her son waited. She did not see the Pena palace again until 1945, when she returned to Portugal under much more favorable conditions. Pena has remained much as Amélia left it, making it a rare record of European royal life in the halcyon days preceding World War I.

Pena Park was designed and planted for more than 4 years, beginning in 1846. Ferdinand was the force behind the landscaping. He built one of the most spectacular parks in Portugal, known for the scope of its shrub and tree life. Admission to the park is included in the price of a ticket for entrance to the palace. A little carriage service inside the gate of the palace will take you up the steep hill to the palace for 2€ each way.

Estrada de Pena. www.parquesdesintra.pt. ✆ **21/910-53-40.** Admission 9€, 7€ children 6–17, 9€ seniors, free for children 5 and under. Oct 16–Mar Tues–Sun 10am–6pm; Apr–Oct 15 Tues–Sun 10am–6:30pm.

Palácio Nacional de Sintra ★★★   A royal palace until 1910, the Sintra National Palace was last inhabited by Queen Maria Pia, the Italian grandmother of Manuel II, the last king of Portugal. Much of the palace was constructed in the days of the first Manuel, the Fortunate. Long before the arrival of the crusaders under Afonso Henríques, this was a summer palace of Moorish sultans. The original palace was torn down in 1863, and Moorish-style architecture was incorporated into latter-day versions.

The structure is now a conglomeration of styles, with Gothic and Manueline predominant. The glazed earthenware tiles lining many of the chambers are among the most beautiful in Portugal, but some of the chambers stand out for other reasons. The Swan Room was a favorite of João I, one of the founding kings of Portugal, father of Henry the Navigator and husband of Philippa of Lancaster. The Room of the Sirens or Mermaids is one of the most elegant in the palace. The Heraldic or Stag Room holds coats of arms of aristocratic Portuguese families and hunting scenes. Tile-fronted stoves are in the Old Kitchen, where feasts were held in bygone days.

The palace is also rich in paintings and Iberian and Flemish tapestries, but perhaps it's simply worth a visit for its good views: In most of the rooms, wide windows look out onto attractive views of the Sintra mountain range.

As you approach the palace, you can buy a ticket at the kiosk on your left. The palace opens onto the central town square. Outside, two conical chimney towers form the most distinctive landmark on the Sintra skyline. The walk from the train station at Sintra to the national palace takes about 10 minutes. After leaving the station, take a left and follow the road.

Largo da Rainha Dona Amélia. http://pnsintra.imc-ip.pt. © **21/910-68-40.** Admission 7€ adults, 5€ ages 15–25, free for children under 14; free admission on Sun and some holidays. Thurs–Tues 9:30am–5:30pm; closed Wed.

THE ALGARVE

The maritime province of the Algarve, often called the Garden of Portugal, is the southwesternmost part of Europe. Its coastline stretches 160km (99 miles) from Henry the Navigator's Cape St. Vincent to the border town of Vila Real de Santo António, fronting once-hostile Spain. The varied coastline contains sluggish estuaries, sheltered lagoons, low-lying areas where clucking marsh hens nest, long sandy spits, and promontories jutting out into the white-capped aquamarine foam.

Called Al-Gharb by the Moors, the land south of the *serras* (mountains) of Monchique and Caldeirão remains a spectacular anomaly that seems more like a transplanted section of the North African coastline. The countryside abounds in vegetation: almonds, lemons, oranges, carobs, pomegranates, and figs.

Even though most of the towns and villages of the Algarve are more than 240km (149 miles) from Lisbon, the great 1755 earthquake shook this area. Entire communities were wiped out; however, many Moorish and even Roman ruins remain. In the fret-cut chimneys, mosquelike cupolas, and cubist houses, a distinct Oriental flavor prevails. Phoenicians, Greeks, Romans, Visigoths, Moors, and Christians all touched this land.

Much of the historic flavor is gone forever, however, swallowed by a sea of dreary high-rise apartment blocks surrounding most towns. Years ago, Portuguese officials, looking in horror at what happened to Spain's Costa del Sol, promised more limited and controlled development so that they wouldn't make "Spain's mistake." That promise, in our opinion, has not been kept.

Many former fishing villages—now summer resorts—dot the Algarvian coast: Carvoeiro, Albufeira, Olhão, Portimão. The sea is the source of life, as it always has been. The village marketplaces sell esparto mats, copper, pottery, and almond and fig sweets, sometimes shaped like birds and fish.

Lagos and Faro make logical home bases, with ample lodging choices, railroad and air connections with Lisbon, and an easy driving range to all the likely destinations along the coast.

Lagos ★

34km (21 miles) E of Sagres; 69km (43 miles) W of Faro; 264km (164 miles) S of Lisbon; 13km (8 miles) W of Portimão.

An ancient port city (one historian traced its origins to the Carthaginians, 3 centuries before the birth of Christ), Lagos was well known by the sailors of Admiral Nelson's fleet. From Liverpool to Manchester to Plymouth, the sailors spoke wistfully of the beautiful green-eyed, olive-skinned women of the Algarve. Eagerly they sailed into port, looking forward to carousing and drinking.

Actually, not that much has changed since Nelson's day. Few go to Lagos wanting to know its history; rather, the mission is to drink deeply of the pleasures of table and beach. In winter, the almond blossoms match the whitecaps on the water, and the

The Algarve

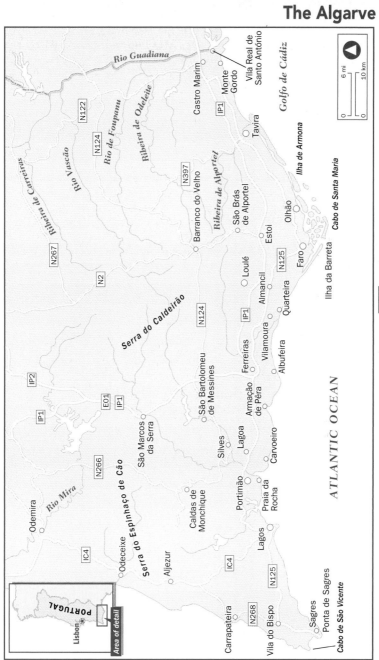

weather is often warm enough for sunbathing. In town, a flea market sprawls through the narrow streets.

Less than 2km (1¼ miles) down the coast, the hustle and bustle of market day is forgotten as the rocky headland of the **Ponta da Piedade (Point of Piety)** ★★ appears. This spot is the most beautiful on the entire coast. Amid the colorful cliffs and secret grottoes carved by the waves are the most flamboyant examples of Manueline architecture.

Much of Lagos was razed in the 1755 earthquake, and it lost its position as the capital of the Algarve. Today only the ruins of its fortifications remain. However, traces of the old linger on the back streets.

ESSENTIALS
Getting There
BY FERRY & TRAIN   From Lisbon (Lisboa Entrecampos station), take an Algarve-bound train to the junction at Tunes, where a change of trains will take you south all the way to Lagos. Five trains a day arrive from Lisbon. The trip takes 2½ hours and costs at least 22€ one-way. For more information and schedules, call ✆ 80/820-82-08.

BY BUS   Six buses a day make the run between Lisbon and Lagos. The trip takes 4 hours and costs 19€ each way. Call ✆ 28/989-97-60 for schedules.

BY CAR   If you're coming from Lisbon, after leaving Sines, take Route 120 southeast toward Lagos and follow the signs into the city. From Sagres, take N268 northeast to the junction with N125, which will lead you east to Lagos.

Visitor Information
The **Lagos Tourist Office,** Praça Gil Eanes, Lagos (www.visitalgarve.pt; ✆ 28/276-30-31), is open daily 9:30am to 1pm and 2 to 5:30pm.

EXPLORING LAGOS
Antigo Mercado de Escravos   The Old Customs House stands as a painful reminder of the Age of Exploration. The arcaded slave market, the only one of its kind in Europe, looks peaceful today, but under its four Romanesque arches, captives were once sold to the highest bidders. The house opens onto the tranquil main square dominated by a statue of Henry the Navigator.

Praça do Infante Dom Henríques. Free admission. Daily 24 hr.

Igreja de Santo António ★   The 18th-century Church of St. Anthony sits just off the waterfront. The altar is decorated with some of Portugal's most notable baroque **gilt carvings** ★, created with gold imported from Brazil. Begun in the 17th century, they were damaged in the earthquake but subsequently restored. What you see today represents the work of many artisans—each, at times, apparently pursuing a different theme.

Rua General Alberto Carlos Silveira. ✆ **28/276-23-01.** Admission 2€ adults, 1€ students and seniors 65 and older, free for children under 12. Tues–Sun 9:30am–12:30pm and 2–5pm.

Museu Municipal Dr. José Formosinho   The Municipal Museum contains replicas of the fret-cut chimneys of the Algarve, three-dimensional cork carvings, 16th-century vestments, ceramics, 17th-century embroidery, ecclesiastical sculpture, a painting gallery, weapons, minerals, and a numismatic collection. There's also a believe-it-or-not section displaying, among other things, an eight-legged calf. In the archaeological wing are Neolithic artifacts, Roman mosaics found at Boca do Rio near

Budens, fragments of statuary and columns, and other remains of antiquity from excavations along the Algarve.

Rua General Alberto Carlos Silveira. ✆ **28/276-23-01.** Admission 3.50€ adults; 2.50€ children 12–14. Tues–Sun 9:30am–12:30pm and 2–5pm. Closed holidays.

HITTING THE BEACH & OTHER OUTDOOR ACTIVITIES

BEACHES Some of the best beaches—including **Praia de Dona Ana,** the most appealing—are near Lagos, south of the city. Follow signs to the Hotel Golfinho. If you go all the way to the southernmost point, **Ponta da Piedade,** you'll pass some pretty cove beaches set against a backdrop of rock formations. Steps are sometimes carved into the cliffs to make for easier access. Although it's crowded in summer, another good white-sand beach is at the 2.5km-long (1½-mile) **Meia Praia** (Half Beach), across the river from the center of town.

GOLF **Palmares Golf,** Meia Praia, 8600 Lagos (www.palmaresgolf.com; ✆ **28/ 279-05-00**), is not a particularly prestigious or championship-level course—it's "medium" in both difficulty and desirability. Frank Pennink designed it in 1975 on land with many differences in altitude. Some fairways require driving a ball across railroad tracks, over small ravines, or around palm groves. Its landscaping suggests North Africa, partly because of its hundreds of palms and almond trees. The view from the 17th green is exceptionally dramatic. Par is 71. Greens fees are 63€ to 95€, depending on the season. The course lies on the eastern outskirts of Lagos, less than 1km (⅔ mile) from the center. To reach it from the heart of town, follow signs toward Meia Praia.

WHERE TO EAT

Restaurante D. Sebastião ★ REGIONAL PORTUGUESE This rustically decorated tavern on the main pedestrian street is one of the finest dining choices in Lagos. Portuguese-owned and -operated, it offers a varied menu of local specialties. Options include lip-smacking pork chops with figs, succulent shellfish dishes like clams and shrimp cooked with savory spices, and grills. Live lobsters are kept on the premises. One of the best selections of Portuguese vintage wines in town accompanies the filling, tasty meals. In summer, outdoor dining is available.

Rua do 25 de Abril 20–22. www.restaurantedonsebastiao.com. ✆ **28/278-04-80.** Reservations recommended. Main courses 9€–25€. AE, MC, V. Daily noon–10pm. Closed Dec 24–26 and Dec 31–Jan 2.

ENTERTAINMENT & NIGHTLIFE

You'll find hints of big-city life in Lagos and a devoted cadre of night owls. On Rua Cândido dos Reis are lots of hot spots, including **Inside Out Bar,** Rua Cândido dos Reis 119 (no phone), with a fun staff and the largest *carte* of drinks in town. It usually stays open until 4am. Equally popular is the **Red Eye,** Rua Cândido dos Reis 63 (no phone), attracting a lot of Londoners and Aussies as well, who pile in here for the inexpensive drinks and the rock music. It's said to be the best place to find a partner for the night. It stays open until 2am.

WHERE TO STAY

Casa da Moura ★ 📖 The "House of Moors" was built originally in 1892 for a rich Lagos family. It has been brought completely up to date with a pool and a rooftop terrace overlooking the Atlantic Ocean. Lying inside the ramparts, a 5-minute walk from the center, the Casa imported much of its raw materials from Morocco. The manor house is filled with wood-lined ceilings, stone and wooden floors, and wide corridors. For rent are two attractively furnished studios and six apartments. All accommodations have a different decoration and color scheme. Breakfast is served on an open-air terrace.

Rua Cardeal Neto 10, 8600-645. www.casadamoura.com. ℰ **28/277-07-30.** Fax 28/278-05-89. 8 units. 49€–149€. AE, MC, V. Free parking. **Amenities:** Outdoor pool. *In room:* A/C, TV, kitchenette, hair dryer, Wi-Fi (free).

Sagres ★★: "The End of the World"

280km (174 miles) S of Lisbon; 34km (21 miles) W of Lagos; 114km (71 miles) W of Faro.

At the extreme southwestern corner of Europe—once called *o fim do mundo* (the end of the world)—Sagres is a rocky escarpment jutting into the Atlantic Ocean. From here, Henry the Navigator, the Infante of Sagres, launched Portugal and the rest of Europe on the seas of exploration. Here he established his school of navigation, where Magellan, Diaz, Cabral, and Vasco da Gama apprenticed. A virtual ascetic, Henry brought together the best navigators, cartographers, geographers, scholars, sailors, and builders; infused them with his rigorous devotion; and methodically set Portuguese caravels upon the Sea of Darkness.

ESSENTIALS
Getting There
BY FERRY & TRAIN   From Lisbon, take an Algarve-bound train to the junction at Tunes, where a change of trains will take you south all the way to Lagos. The rest of the distance is by bus (see below). For information and schedules, see www.cp.pt or call ℰ **80/820-82-08.** From Lagos, buses go to Sagres.

BY BUS   Ten **EVA buses** (www.eva-bus.com; ℰ **28/989-97-60**) in Lagos run hourly from Lagos to Sagres each day. The trip time is 1 hour, and a one-way ticket costs 3.60€.

BY CAR   From Lagos, drive west on Route 125 to Vila do Bispo, and then head south along Route 268 to Sagres.

EXPLORING SAGRES

Both the cape and Sagres offer a view of the sunset. In the ancient world, the cape was the last explored point, although in time the Phoenicians pushed beyond it. Many mariners thought that when the sun sank beyond the cape, it plunged over the edge of the world.

Today, at the reconstructed site of Henry's windswept fortress on Europe's Land's End (named after the narrowing westernmost tip of Cornwall, England), you can see a huge stone compass dial. Henry supposedly used the Venta de Rosa in his naval studies at Sagres. Housed in the **Fortaleza de Sagres,** Ponta de Sagres, is a small museum of minor interest that documents some of the area's history. It's open May to September daily 9:30am to 8pm, October to April 9:30am to 5:30pm. Admission is 3€ for adults, 1.50€ for ages 15 to 25, and free for children 14 and under. At a simple chapel, restored in 1960, sailors are said to have prayed for help before setting out into uncharted waters. The chapel is closed to the public.

About 5km (3 miles) away is the promontory of **Cabo de São Vicente ★★**. It got its name because, according to legend, the body of St. Vincent arrived mysteriously here on a boat guided by ravens. (Others claim that the body of the patron saint, murdered at Valencia, Spain, washed up on Lisbon's shore.) A lighthouse, the second most powerful in Europe, beams illumination 100km (62 miles) across the ocean. To reach the cape, you can take a bus Monday through Friday only leaving from Rua Comandante Matoso near the tourist office. Trip time is 10 minutes, and departures are at 11:15am and 2:25pm; a one-way ticket costs 2€.

HITTING THE BEACH & OTHER OUTDOOR ACTIVITIES

BEACHES　　Many beaches fringe the peninsula; some attract nude bathers. Mareta, at the bottom of the road leading from the center of town toward the water, is the best and most popular. East of town is Tonel, also a good sandy beach. The beaches west of town, Praia da Baleeira and Praia do Martinhal, are better for windsurfing than for swimming.

FISHING　　Fishing is worthwhile (and legal) between October and January, although you should be warned in advance that quantities of fish seem to have diminished in recent years. You can walk down to almost any beach and hire a local fisherman to take you out for a half-day, and just about every large-scale hotel along the Algarve will arrange a fishing trip for you. Most fishing excursions are configured as half-day events, priced, with equipment included, at around 40€ per adult per half-day excursion.

WHERE TO EAT

Restaurante Vila Velha ★★ INTERNATIONAL　　In a rustic setting in a villa, this first-class restaurant with its covered terrace in summer is elegant. It's air-conditioned in summer, but in winter a cozy fire awaits you. Pleasure will explode on your palate as you sample such great dishes as stuffed quail in wine sauce; prawn curry; small pork filets with mango sauce; hake filets with scallops and hollandaise sauce; or tagliatelle with prawns and monkfish. Desserts are sumptuous, especially the homemade walnut ice cream with flambé bananas and a chocolate sauce. Prepare yourself for one of your finest gastronomic evenings on the Algarve if you eat here.

Rua Patrão António Faustino. ✆ **28/262-47-88.** www.vilavelha-sagres.com. Reservations required. Main courses 28€–38€. MC, V. Tues–Sun 6:30–10pm (until 10:30pm July 15–Sept 15).

ENTERTAINMENT & NIGHTLIFE

The best of the many nightspots in the town's historic core include the **Bar Dromedário,** Rua Comandante Matos (www.dromedariosagres.com; ✆ **28/262-42-19**), and the **A Rosa dos Ventos (Pink Wind) Bar,** Praça da República (www.rosadosventos.info; ✆ **28/262-44-80**). Folks from all over Europe talk, relax, and drink beer, wine, or sangria.

WHERE TO STAY

Pousada do Infante ★★　　Pousada do Infante, the best address in Sagres, seems like a monastery built by ascetic monks who wanted to commune with nature. You'll be charmed by the rugged beauty of the rocky cliffs, the pounding surf, and the sense of the ocean's infinity. Built in 1960, the glistening white government-owned tourist inn spreads along the edge of a cliff that projects rather daringly over the sea. It boasts a long colonnade of arches with an extended stone terrace set with garden furniture, plus a second floor of accommodations with private balconies. Each midsize guest room is furnished with traditional pieces. Room nos. 1 to 12 are the most desirable.

The public rooms are generously proportioned, gleaming with marble and decorated with fine tapestries depicting the exploits of Henry the Navigator. Large velvet couches flank the fireplace.

Ponta da Atalaia, 8650-385 Sagres. www.pousadas.pt. ✆ **28/262-02-40.** Fax 28/262-42-25. 39 units. 92€–240€ double; 115€–300€ suite. Rates include buffet breakfast. AE, DC, MC, V. Free parking. **Amenities:** Restaurant; bar; outdoor freshwater pool; outdoor tennis court (lit); room service; babysitting. *In room:* A/C, TV, minibar, hair dryer, Wi-Fi (in some; 12€ per 24 hr.).

Praia da Rocha

En route to Praia da Rocha, off N125 between Lagos and Portimão, 18km (11 miles) away, you'll find several good beaches and rocky coves, particularly at Praia dos Três Irmãos and Alvor. But the most popular seaside resort on the Algarve is the creamy yellow beach of Praia da Rocha. At the outbreak of World War II there were only two small hotels on the Red Coast, but nowadays Praia da Rocha is booming. At the end of the mussel-encrusted cliff, where the Arcade flows into the sea, lie the ruins of the **Fortress of Santa Catarina.** The location offers views of Portimão's satellite, Ferragudo, and of the bay.

ESSENTIALS

GETTING THERE To reach Praia da Rocha from Portimão, you can catch a bus for the 2.5km (1½-mile) trip south. Service is frequent. Algarve buses aren't numbered but are marked by their final destination, such as PRAIA DA ROCHA.

VISITOR INFORMATION At Praia da Rocha, the **Tourist Office** (www.visit algarve.pt; ✆ **28/247-07-32**) is on Avenida Zeca Alfonso and is open daily 9:30am to 1pm and 2 to 5:30pm (closes in summer at 7pm).

WHERE TO EAT

Restaurante Titanic ★★★ INTERNATIONAL   Replete with gilt and crystal, the 100-seat air-conditioned Titanic is the most elegant restaurant in town. Its open kitchen serves the best food in Praia da Rocha, including shellfish and flambé dishes. Despite the name, it's not on—or in, thank goodness—the water, but in a modern residential complex. You can dine very well here on such appealing dishes as the fish of the day, pork filet with mushrooms, prawns *a la plancha* (grilled on a plank of wood), Chinese fondue, or excellent sole Algarve. Service is among the best in town.

In the Edifício Colúmbia, Rua Eng. Francisco Bivar. www.titanic.com.pt. ✆ **28/242-23-71.** Reservations recommended, especially in summer. Main courses 12€–32€. AE, DC, MC, V. Daily 7pm–midnight. Closed Nov 27–Dec 27.

WHERE TO STAY

Hotel Algarve Casino ★★★ The leading hotel in this area is strictly for those who love glitter and glamour and don't object to the prices. With a vast staff at your beck and call, you'll be well provided for in this elongated block of rooms poised securely on the top ledge of a cliff. The midsize to spacious guest rooms have white walls, colored ceilings, intricate tile floors, mirrored entryways, indirect lighting, balconies with garden furniture, and bathrooms with separate tub/shower combinations. Many are vaguely Moorish in design, and many have terraces opening onto the sea. The Yachting, Oriental, Presidential, and Miradouro suites are decorative tours de force.

Av. Tomás Cabreira, Praia da Rocha, 8500-802 Portimão. www.solverde.pt. ✆ **28/240-20-00.** Fax 28/240-20-99. 208 units. 78€–248€ double; 121€–452€ suite. Rates include buffet breakfast. AE, DC, MC, V. Parking 12€. **Amenities:** 2 restaurants; 2 bars; 2 seawater pools (1 heated indoor); 2 outdoor tennis courts (lit); exercise room; Jacuzzi; sauna; limited watersports equipment/rentals; children's center; room service; babysitting. *In room:* A/C, TV, minibar, hair dryer, free Wi-Fi (in some).

Praia dos Três Irmãos & Alvor ★★

Although **Praia dos Três Irmãos** is one of Portugal's more expensive areas, you may want to visit its beach, 5km (3 miles) southwest of Portimão. From Portimão's center, you can take one of the public buses; they run frequently throughout the day. The bus is marked PRAIA DOS TRÊS IRMÃOS. Departures are from the main bus terminal in Portimão, at Largo do Duque (✆ **28/241-81-20**).

Praia dos Três Irmãos has 15km (9⅓ miles) of burnished golden sand, interrupted only by an occasional crag riddled with arched passageways. This beach has been discovered by skin divers who explore its undersea grottoes and caves.

Nearby is the whitewashed fishing village of **Alvor,** where Portuguese and Moorish arts and traditions have mingled since the Arab occupation ended. Alvor was a favorite coastal haunt of João II, and now summer hordes descend on the long strip of sandy beach. It's not the best in the area, but at least you'll have plenty of space.

GOLFING

Penina (www.lemeridienpenina.com; ✆ **28/242-02-00**) is 5km (3 miles) west of the center of Portimão, farther west than many of the other great golf courses. Completed in 1966, it was one of the first courses in the Algarve and the universally acknowledged masterpiece of the British designer Sir Henry Cotton. It replaced a network of marshy rice paddies on level terrain that critics said was unsuited for anything except wetlands. The solution involved planting groves of eucalyptus (350,000 trees in all), which grew quickly in the muddy soil. Eventually they dried it out enough for the designer to bulldoze dozens of water traps and a labyrinth of fairways and greens. The course wraps around a luxury hotel (Le Méridien Penina Golf & Resort). You can play the main championship course (18 holes, par 73), and two 9-hole satellite courses, Academy and Resort. Greens fees for the 18-hole course are 50€ to 120€; for either of the 9-hole courses, they're 33€ to 65€. To reach it from the center of Portimão, follow signs to Lagos, turning off at the signpost for Le Méridien Penina Golf & Resort.

WHERE TO EAT

Restaurante Búzio ★ INTERNATIONAL   Restaurante Búzio stands at the end of a road encircling a resort development dotted with private condos and exotic shrubbery. In summer, so many cars line the narrow road that you'll probably need to park near the resort's entrance and then walk downhill to the restaurant. Dinner is served in a room whose blue curtains reflect the shimmering ocean at the bottom of the cliffs. Your meal might include excellent fish soup, refreshing gazpacho, or *carré de borrego Serra de Estrela* (gratinée of roast rack of lamb with garlic, butter, and mustard). Other good choices are Italian pasta dishes, boiled or grilled fish of the day, flavorful pepper steak, and lamb kabobs with saffron-flavored rice. The restaurant maintains an extensive wine cellar.

Aldeamento da Prainha, Praia dos Três Irmãos. www.restaurantebuzio.com. ✆ **28/245-87-72.** Reservations recommended. Main courses 10€–30€; fixed-price menus at 30€–54€. AE, DC, MC, V. Daily 7–10:30pm. Closed Dec 15–Jan 7.

WHERE TO STAY

Pestana Alvor Praia ★★★   This citadel of hedonism, built in 1968 and constantly renewed, has more *joie de vivre* than any other hotel on the Algarve. Its location, good-size guest rooms, decor, service, and food are ideal. "You'll feel as if you're loved the moment you walk in the door," one guest of the hotel told us. Poised regally on a landscaped crest, many of the guest and public rooms face the ocean, the gardens, and the free-form Olympic-size pool. Gentle walks and an elevator lead down the palisade to the sandy beach and the rugged rocks that rise out of the water.

Accommodations vary from a cowhide-decorated room evoking Arizona's Valley of the Sun to typical Portuguese-style rooms with rustic furnishings. Most contain oversize beds, plenty of storage space, long desk-and-chest combinations, and well-designed bathrooms. All rooms have balconies and most have sea views.

Praia dos Três Irmãos, Alvor, 8501-904 Portimão. www.pestana.com. © **28/240-09-00.** Fax 28/240-09-75. 195 units. 82€–300€ double; 140€–460€ suite. Rates include buffet breakfast. AE, DC, MC, V. Free parking. **Amenities:** 2 restaurants; 2 bars; 3 saltwater pools (1 heated indoor); 7 outdoor tennis courts (lit); health club; sauna; bikes; room service; babysitting; Wi-Fi (18€ per 24 hr., in lobby). In room: A/C, TV, minibar, hair dryer.

Albufeira ★

37km (23 miles) W of Faro; 325km (202 miles) SE of Lisbon.

This cliffside town, formerly a fishing village, is the St. Tropez of the Algarve. The lazy life, sunshine, and beaches make it a haven for young people and artists, although the old-timers still regard the invasion that began in the late 1960s with some ambivalence. That development turned Albufeira into the largest resort in the region. Some residents open the doors of their cottages to those seeking a place to stay. Travelers with less money often sleep in tents.

ESSENTIALS
Getting There
BY TRAIN   Trains run between Albufeira and Faro (see "Faro," later), which has good connections to Lisbon. For schedule information, call © **80/820-82-08.** The train station lies 6.5km (4 miles) from the town's center. Buses from the station to the resort run every 30 minutes; the fare is 3.50€ one-way.

BY BUS   Buses run between Albufeira and Faro every hour. Trip time is 1 hour, and a one-way ticket costs 4.50€. Twenty-three buses per day make the 1-hour trip from Portimão to Albufeira. It costs 4.30€ one-way. For information and schedules, call © **28/989-97-60.**

BY CAR   From east or west, take the main coastal route, N125. Albufeira also lies near the point where the express highway from the north, N264, feeds into the Algarve. The town is well signposted in all directions. Take Route 595 to reach Albufeira and the water.

Visitor Information
The **Tourist Information Office** is at Rua do 5 de Outubro (www.visitalgarve.com; © **28/958-52-79**). From July to September, hours are daily from 9:30am to 7pm; October to June, they're from 10am to 5:30pm.

EXPLORING ALBUFEIRA
With steep streets and villas staggered up and down the hillside, Albufeira resembles a North African seaside community. The big, bustling resort town rises above a sickle-shape beach that shines in the bright sunlight. A rocky, grottoed bluff separates the strip used by sunbathers from the working beach, where brightly painted fishing boats are drawn up on the sand. Access to the beach is through a tunneled rock passageway.

After walking Albufeira's often hot but intriguing streets, you can escape and cool off at **Zoomarine,** N125, Guia (www.zoomarine.pt; © **28/956-03-00**), 6.5km

(4 miles) northwest. It's a popular water park, with rides, swimming pools, gardens, and even sea lion and dolphin shows. Opening hours are March 1 to June 19 and September 3 to October 31 Tuesday to Sunday 10am to 6pm, June 20 to September 2 Tuesday to Sunday 10am to 7:30pm. Admission is 25€ for adults and 16€ for children 10 and under.

HITTING THE BEACH & OTHER OUTDOOR ACTIVITIES

BEACHES   Some of the best beaches—but also the most crowded—are near Albufeira. They include Falésia, Olhos d'Água, and Praia da Oura. Albufeira, originally discovered by the British, is now the busiest resort on the Algarve. To avoid the crowds on Albufeira's main beaches, head west for 4km (2½ miles) on a local road to São Rafael and Praia da Galé. You might also go east to the beach at Olhos d'Água.

GOLF   Many pros consider the extremely well maintained **Pine Cliffs** course, Praia da Falésia 644, 8200 Albufeira (www.pinecliffs.com; ✆ 28/950-01-00), relaxing but not boring. It has only 9 holes scattered over a relatively compact area. Opened in 1990, its fairways meander beside copper-colored cliffs that drop 75m (246 ft.) down to a sandy beach. Par is 33. The greens fees are 39€ to 49€ for Sheraton Algarve Hotel guests and 45€ to 59€ for nonguests. The course lies 6.5km (4 miles) west of Vilamoura and less than 5km (3 miles) east of Albufeira. To reach it from Albufeira, follow signs to the hamlet of Olhos d'Água, where more signs direct you to the Sheraton Algarve Hotel and Pine Cliffs.

WHERE TO EAT

Restaurante A Ruína ★ PORTUGUESE   This restaurant sits opposite the fish market, overlooking the main beach. From the arcaded dining room, with its long candlelit wooden tables, you can watch the fishers mending their nets. Another cave-like room has more tables and a bar. The decor is unpretentious, and the reasonably priced seafood is fresh. A bowl of flavorful soup will get you going; then it's on to one of the fish specialties, such as grilled fresh tuna. The fish stew, *caldeirada,* is the chef's specialty and our favorite dish. Typical desserts are custard and mousse.

Cais Herculano, Albufeira. www.restaurante-ruina.com. ✆ **28/951-20-94.** Reservations recommended. Main courses 15€–30€. AE, DC, MC, V. Daily 12:30–3pm and 7–11pm.

ENTERTAINMENT & NIGHTLIFE

You can have a lot of fun in this hard-drinking, fun-in-the-sun town, discovering your own favorite tucked-away bar. To get rolling, you might begin at the **Falan Bar,** Rua São Gonçalo de Lagos (no phone), or the nearby **Fastnet Bar,** Rua Cândido dos Reis 10 (✆ **28/958-91-16**), where no one will object if you jump to your feet and begin to dance. A few storefronts away is the **Classic Bar,** Rua Cândido dos Reis 8 (✆ **28/951-20-75**), a folksy, comfortably battered place that's almost completely devoid of pretension. The bars are usually open until 3 or 4am, depending on business.

WHERE TO STAY

Hotel Vila Galé Cerro Alagoa ★★ ☺   A sort of South Seas ambience predominates at this fine resort. Most guests hail from northern Europe, and they find this a relaxing environment in which to soak up the sun. A large, sprawling property, it lies near the sandy beach of Albufeira and is also within an easy commute of several other Algarvian beaches, both east and west. Each room has a balcony; comfortable, durable furnishings; and tiled bathrooms. You can also dine in style here; the chefs are fond of presenting theme evenings, and the restaurants offer a great variety of cuisines. Nonguests often drop in here to patronize the Dog & Duck Pub, a British-style bar featuring live music and karaoke.

Rua do Município, 8200-916 Albufeira. www.vilagale.pt. © **28/958-31-00.** Fax 28/958-31-99. 310 units. 65€–214€ double; 85€–130€ junior suite. Rates include buffet breakfast. AE, DC, MC, V. Parking 8€. **Amenities:** Restaurant; 2 bars; 2 freshwater pools (1 heated indoor); exercise room; Jacuzzi; sauna; bikes; children's center; room service. *In room:* A/C, TV, minibar, Wi-Fi (5€ per hour).

Vale do Lobo ★ & Quinta do Lago

Almancil is a small market town of little tourist interest, but it's a center for two of the most exclusive tourist developments along the Algarve. **Vale do Lobo** lies 6.5km (4 miles) southeast of Almancil, and **Quinta do Lago** is less than 10km (6¼ miles) southeast of town.

The name *Vale do Lobo* (Valley of the Wolf) suggests a forlorn spot, but in reality the vale is the site of a golf course designed by Sir Henry Cotton, the British champion. It's west of Faro, about a 20-minute drive from Faro airport. Some holes are by the sea, which results in many an anxious moment as shots hook out over the water. The property includes a 9-hole course, a 9-hole par-3 course, a putting green, and a driving range. The tennis center is among the best in Europe.

Quinta do Lago, one of the most elegant "tourist estates" on the Algarve, also has superb facilities. The pine-covered beachfront property has been a favored retreat of movie stars and European presidents. The resort's 27 superb holes of golf are also a potent lure. This is true luxury—at quite a price.

GOLFING

One of the most deceptive golf courses on the Algarve, **Pinheiros Altos,** Quinta do Lago, 8135 Almancil (www.pinheirosaltos.com; © **28/935-99-00**), has contours that even professionals say are far more difficult than they appear at first glance. American architect Ronald Fream designed the 100 hectares (247 acres), which abut the wetland refuge of the Rio Formosa National Park. Umbrella pines and dozens of small lakes dot the course. Par is 72. Greens fees are 45€ to 60€ for 9 holes and 90€ to 120€ for 18 holes. Pinheiros Altos lies about 5km (3 miles) south of Almancil. From Almancil, follow the signs to Quinta do Lago and Pinheiros Altos.

The namesake course of the massive development, **Quinta do Lago,** Quinta do Lago, 8135 Almancil (www.quintadolagogolf.com; © **28/939-07-00**), consists of two 18-hole golf courses, Quinta do Lago and Rio Formosa. Together they cover more than 240 hectares (593 acres) of sandy terrain that abuts the Rio Formosa Wildlife Sanctuary. Very few long drives here are over open water; instead, the fairways undulate through cork forests and groves of pine trees, sometimes with abrupt changes in elevation. Greens fees are 139€ to 178€ depending on the season. The courses are 6km (3¾ miles) south of Almancil. From Almancil, follow signs to Quinta do Lago.

Of the four golf courses at the massive Quinta do Lago development, the par-72 **San Lorenzo (São Lourenço)** course, Quinta do Lago, Almancil, 8100 Loulé (www.sanlorenzogolfcourse.com; © **28/939-65-22**), is the most interesting and challenging. San Lorenzo opened in 1988 at the edge of the grassy wetlands of the Rio Formosa Nature Reserve. American golf designers William (Rocky) Roquemore and Joe Lee created it. The most panoramic hole is the 6th; the most frustrating is the 8th. Many long drives, especially those aimed at the 17th and 18th holes, soar over a saltwater lagoon. Greens fees are 85€ for 9 holes and 165€ for 18 holes. From Almancil, drive 8km (5 miles) south, following signs to Quinta do Lago.

The **Vale do Lobo** course, Vale do Lobo, 8135 Almancil (www.valedolobo.com; ✆ 28/935-34-65), technically isn't part of the Quinta do Lago complex. Because it was established in 1968, before any of its nearby competitors, it played an important role in launching southern Portugal's image as a golfer's mecca. Designed by the late British golfer Sir Henry Cotton, it contains four distinct 9-hole segments. All four include runs that stretch over rocks and arid hills, often within view of olive and almond groves, the Atlantic, and the high-rise hotels of nearby Vilamoura and Quarteira. Some long shots require driving golf balls over two ravines, where variable winds and bunkers that have been called "ravenous" make things particularly difficult. Greens fees, depending on the day of the week and other factors, range from 83€ to 155€ for 18 holes. From Almancil, drive 4km (2½ miles) south of town, following signs to Vale do Lobo.

WHERE TO EAT

Restaurante Amadeus ★★★ INTERNATIONAL   One of the very few restaurants in Portugal to be granted a coveted Michelin star, Amadeus is known for its innovative cuisine and outstanding cellar. As you might expect, the menu strikes rich, full chords and seemingly avoids all pitfalls. If the weather's fine (and it usually is), you can dine outside, enjoying the seductive cuisine in a modern setting. You are likely to have one of your finest Algarvian dining experiences here as you sample such sublime dishes as ravioli with wild broccoli, wild white seabass with stewed fennel, filet of John Dory flavored with Spanish manzanilla olives, or a paprika risotto with wild octopus. The desserts are among the finest along the coast; you might opt for an orange crème brûlée with a carob tree tartlet or else prickly pears with a white chocolate sorbet.

Escanxinas, Estrada Almancil-Quarteira. www.amadeus.hm. ✆ **28/939-91-34.** Reservations required. Fixed-price menus 69€, 79€, and 98€. AE, DC, MC, V. Wed–Mon 6:30–11pm.

WHERE TO STAY

Dona Filipa Hotel ★★★ ☺   This deluxe golf hotel is a citadel of ostentatious living. The grounds are impressive, embracing 180 hectares (445 acres) of rugged coastline with steep cliffs, inlets, and sandy bays. The hotel's exterior is comparatively uninspired, but the interior features such lavish touches as green silk banquettes, gold-painted palms holding up the ceiling, marble fireplaces, Portuguese ceramic lamps, and old prints over baroque-style love seats. The midsize to spacious guest rooms are handsomely decorated with antiques, rustic accessories, and handmade rugs. Most have balconies and twin beds.

Vale do Lobo, 8135-901 Almancil. www.donafilipahotel.com. ✆ **28/935-72-23.** Fax 28/935-72-01. 154 units. 189€–290€ double; 315€–510€ junior suite; 450€–665€ deluxe suite. Rates include buffet breakfast. AE, MC, V. Free parking. **Amenities:** 2 restaurants; bar; outdoor heated pool; 3 outdoor tennis courts (lit); spa; bikes; children's center; concierge; room service; babysitting; Wi-Fi (3€ per hour, in lobby). *In room:* A/C, TV, minibar, hair dryer.

Hotel Quinta do Lago ★★★   A pocket of the high life since 1986, Hotel Quinta do Lago is a sprawling 800-hectare (1,977-acre) estate that contains some private plots beside the Ria Formosa estuary. Its riding center and 27-hole golf course are among the best in Europe. The estate's contemporary Mediterranean-style buildings rise three to six floors. The luxurious guest rooms overlook a saltwater lake and feature modern comforts. Decorated with thick carpeting, pastel fabrics, contemporary art, and light-wood furniture, the rooms are generally spacious, with tile or marble bathrooms and balconies that open onto views of the estuary.

Quinta do Lago, 8135-024 Almancil. www.quintadolagohotel.com. © **28/935-03-50** or © 800/223-6800 in the U.S. Fax 28/939-63-93. 141 units. 213€–569€ double; 569€–2,650€ suite. Rates include buffet breakfast. AE, DC, MC, V. Free parking. **Amenities:** 2 restaurants; bar; 2 freshwater heated pools (1 indoor); 2 outdoor tennis courts (lit); exercise room; spa; bikes; children's center; room service; babysitting. *In room:* A/C, TV, minibar, hair dryer, Wi-Fi (7€ per 24 hr.).

Faro ★

258km (160 miles) SE of Setúbal; 309km (192 miles) SE of Lisbon.

Once loved by the Romans and later by the Moors, Faro is the provincial capital of the Algarve. In this bustling little city of some 30,000 permanent residents, you can sit at a cafe, sample the wine, and watch yesterday and today collide as old men leading donkeys brush past German backpackers in shorts. Faro is a hodgepodge of life and activity: It has been rumbled, sacked, and "quaked" by everybody from Mother Nature to the Earl of Essex (Elizabeth I's favorite).

Many visitors use Faro only as an arrival point, rushing through en route to a beach resort. Those who stick around will enjoy the local charm and color, exemplified by the tranquil fishing harbor. A great deal of antique charm is gone, thanks to the Earl of Essex, who sacked the town in 1596, and the 1755 earthquake. Remnants of medieval walls and some historic buildings stand in the Cidade Velha, or Old Town, which can be entered through the Arco da Vila, a gate from the 18th century.

ESSENTIALS

Getting There

BY PLANE Jet service makes it possible to reach Faro from Lisbon in 30 minutes. For flight information, call the **Faro airport** (© **28/980-08-00**). To get from the airport to the rail station, take one of the **EVA Buses** (www.eva-bus.com; © **28/989-97-60**). EVA runs 20 buses per day from the airport to the railway station, from 7:10am to 9:15pm, costing 1.70€.

BY TRAIN Trains arrive from Lisbon five times a day. The trip takes 4¾ hours and costs 20€. The train station is at Largo da Estação (© **80/820-82-08**). This is the most strategic railway junction in the south of Portugal, thanks to its position astride lines that connect it to the north–south lines leading from Lisbon.

BY BUS There are five buses per day from Lisbon to Faro. The journey takes 3½ hours. The bus station is on Av. da República 5 (www.eva-bus.com; © **28/989-97-60**); a one-way ticket costs 19€.

BY CAR From the west, Route 125 runs into Faro and beyond. From the Spanish border, pick up N125 west.

Visitor Information

The **tourist office** is at Rua da Misericórdia 8–11 (© **28/980-36-04**) or at the airport (© **28/981-85-82**). It's open daily 9:30am to 5:30pm September to May, and 9:30am to 7pm June to August.

EXPLORING FARO

The most bizarre attraction in Faro is the **Capela dos Ossos (Chapel of Bones).** Enter through a courtyard from the rear of the **Igreja de Nossa Senhora do Monte do Carmo do Faro,** Largo do Carmo (© **28/982-44-90**). Erected in the 19th century, the chapel is completely lined with human skulls (an estimated 1,245) and bones. It's open daily 10am to 2pm and 3 to 5:30pm. Entrance is free to the church and 1€ to the chapel.

The church, built in 1713, contains a gilded baroque altar. Its facade is also baroque, with a bell tower rising from each side. Topping the belfries are gilded, mosquelike cupolas connected by a balustraded railing. The upper-level windows are latticed and framed with gold; statues stand in niches on either side of the main portal.

Other religious monuments include the old **Sé** (cathedral), on Largo da Sé (© **28/ 989-83-00**). Built in the Gothic and Renaissance styles, it stands on a site originally occupied by a mosque. Although the cathedral has a Gothic tower, it's better known for its tiles, which date from the 17th and 18th centuries. The highlight is the Capela do Rosário, on the right. It contains the oldest and most beautiful tiles, along with sculptures of two Nubians bearing lamps and a red chinoiserie organ. Admission is free. The beautiful cloisters are the most idyllic spot in Faro. The cathedral is open daily from 10am to 5:30pm. Admission is 2€.

Igreja de São Francisco, Largo de São Francisco (© **28/987-08-70**), is the other church of note. Its facade doesn't even begin to hint at the baroque richness inside. Panels of glazed earthenware tiles in milk-white and Dutch blue depict the life of the patron saint, St. Francis. One chapel is richly gilded. Hours are Monday through Friday from 8 to 9:30am and 5:30 to 7pm (but in the sleepy Algarve, you might sometimes find it closed).

If it's a rainy day, two minor museums might hold some interest. The municipal museum, or **Museu Municipal de Faro,** Largo Dom, Afonso III 14 (© **28/989- 74-19**), is in a former 16th-century convent, the Convento de Nossa Senhora da Assunção. Even if you aren't particularly interested in the exhibits, the two-story cloister is worth a visit. Many artifacts dating from the Roman settlement of the area are on display. Some of the Roman statues are from excavations at Milreu. The museum is open Monday to Saturday 10am to 6pm. Admission is 2€ for adults, 1€ for those 13 to 26 years old, and free to those 12 and under.

The dockside **Museu Marítimo,** Rua Comunidade Lusíada (© **28/989-49-90**), displays models of local fishing craft and of the boats that carried Vasco da Gama and his men to India in 1497. There are replicas of a boat the Portuguese used to sail up the Congo River in 1492 and of a vessel that bested the entire Turkish navy in 1717. It's open Monday to Friday 9am to noon and 2:30 to 4:30pm. Admission is 2€.

WHERE TO EAT

Adega Nortenha ✦ PORTUGUESE   It's hardly a deluxe choice, but if you gravitate to simple yet well-prepared regional food, this little restaurant does the job. It's also one of the best value spots in town, which is probably why locals swear by it. Fresh tuna steak is a delicious choice, as is the roast lamb, which is herb flavored and perfumed with garlic. The service is friendly and efficient, and the restaurant is done up in typical Algarvian style—there's even a balcony that's great for people-watching on the street below.

Praça Ferreira de Almeida 25. © **28/982-27-09.** Main courses 7€–13€. AE, DC, MC, V. Daily noon– 3pm and 7–10:30pm.

ENTERTAINMENT & NIGHTLIFE

What Bourbon Street is to New Orleans, **Rua do Prior** is to Faro. In the heart of town, adjacent to the Faro Hotel, it's chockablock with dozens of night cafes, pubs (English and otherwise), and dance clubs that rock from around 10:30pm until dawn. Head to this street anytime after noon for insights into the hard-drinking, hard-driving nature of this hot southern town. Our favorite watering hole along this street is **CheSsenta Bar,** Rua do Prior 34 (http://chessentabar.blogspot.co.uk; ℭ **91/874-58-37**), where the crowd is in their 20s and 30s, and downs one beer after another at 1.50€ a mug. It's open daily 9pm to 4am. Karaoke on Wednesday and Friday often rules the night at **O Conselheiro,** in the center of Rua Conselheiro Bívar (no phone). The best recorded music in town is played here by a DJ, and sometimes the bar converts to a dance floor. It, too, is open daily 10pm to 4am, and charges the same for beer.

WHERE TO STAY

Hotel Residencial S. Algarve ★ Faro's best hotel deal opened in 1999, but in 2006 it added a modern annex that greatly increased its room count. The inn was created from an 1880s private dwelling that once belonged to a rich seafarer. When the present owner took over the premises, the building had deteriorated to the point that it had to be demolished. The reconstruction, however, honored the original architectural style. Some of the original hand-painted tiles have been preserved in glass cabinets in the foyer. Only a short walk from the historic core of Faro, the inn is most inviting. All the midsize to spacious bedrooms are well furnished and comfortable, with up-to-date amenities and bathrooms that rival those of many a first-class hotel.

Rua Infante Dom Henrique 62, 8000-363 Faro. www.residencialalgarve.com. ℭ **28/989-57-00.** Fax 28/989-57-03. 40 units. 45€–80€ double; 60€–95€ triple. Rates include continental breakfast. AE, DC, MC, V. Parking 5€. **Amenities:** Bar; babysitting; Wi-Fi (free, in lobby). *In room:* A/C, TV, minibar, hair dryer.

DAY TRIP FROM FARO

TAVIRA A gem 31km (19 miles) east of Faro, Tavira is approached through green fields studded with almond and carob trees. Sometimes called the Venice of the Algarve, Tavira lies on the banks of the Ségua and Gilão rivers, which meet under a seven-arched Roman bridge. In the town square, palms and pepper trees rustle under the cool arches of the arcade. In spite of modern encroachments, Tavira is festive looking. Floridly decorated chimneys top many of the houses, some of which are graced with emerald-green tiles and wrought-iron balconies capped by finials. Fretwork adorns many doorways. The liveliest action centers are the fruit and vegetable market on the river esplanade.

The **Tavira Tourist Office** is on Rua da Galeria 9 (ℭ **28/132-25-11**). Tavira has frequent bus connections with Faro throughout the day. It's open June to September daily 9:30am to 7pm; and October to May Monday to Friday 9:30am to 1pm and 2 to 5:30pm.

Climb the stepped street off Rua da Liberdade, and you can explore the battlemented walls of a castle once known to the Moors. From here you'll have the best view of the town's church spires; across the river delta, you can see the ocean. The castle is open daily from 9am to 5pm. Admission is free.

A tuna-fishing center, Tavira is cut off from the sea by an elongated spit of sand. The **Ilha de Tavira** begins west of Cacela and runs all the way past the fishing village of Fuzeta. On this sandbar, accessible by motorboat, are two beaches: the Praia de Tavira and the Praia de Fuzeta. Some people prefer the beach at the tiny village of Santa Luzia, about 3km (1¾ miles) from the heart of town.

If you're here for lunch, try the **Restaurante Imperial,** Rua José Pires Padinha 22 (✆ **28/132-23-06**). A small, air-conditioned place off the main square, it serves regional food, including shellfish, shellfish rice, garlic-flavored pork, roast chicken, fresh tuna, and other Portuguese dishes, accompanied by vegetables and good local wines. A favorite meal is pork and clams with french fries, topped off with a rich egg-and-almond dessert. Meals cost 8€ to 22€ or more, including wine. Food is served daily from noon to 3:30pm and 7 to 11pm. American Express, MasterCard, and Visa are accepted.

SCOTLAND

by Lesley Anne Rose

Scotland delivers on every expectation of a deeply romantic land filled with misty lochs, fields of heather, and moody mountain ranges, while its thoroughly modern cities are welcoming cultural hubs. Whether you're seeking out your ancestral roots, driving the Malt Whisky Trail, celebrating Hogmanay in Edinburgh, or teeing off on the oldest golf course in the world, you'll experience a nation that champions its history, loves to share its present, and believes in its future.

EDINBURGH & ENVIRONS

Edinburgh is the second most-visited city in Britain after London and has been Scotland's capital since the 15th century. A designated World Heritage Site and home to the world's largest arts festival, this dramatic city is famous for its split personality. On the city's south side the dark, narrow, cobbled streets of its medieval Old Town close in over a vast plug of volcanic rock crowned with the brooding Edinburgh Castle and sealed with the Palace of Holyroodhouse. To the north, Edinburgh's New Town spreads out into a vista of neoclassical town planning framed by the Firth of Forth and dotted with an array of parks, gardens, and leafy public squares.

Essentials

GETTING THERE

BY PLANE Edinburgh is an hour's flying time from London, 633km (393 miles) south. Edinburgh Airport (www.edinburghairport.com; © 0844/481-8989) is 12km (7½ miles) west of the city center, receiving flights from within the British Isles, the rest of Europe, New York (Newark), and Orlando (summer only). Double-decker Airlink buses make the round trip from the airport to Edinburgh city center every 10 minutes, letting you on and off at Haymarket or Waverley train stations. The fare is £3.50 one-way or £6 round-trip, and the ride takes about 25 minutes. For more information visit www.flybybus.com or call © 0131/555-6363. There is a busy taxi rank at the airport and a ride into the city center costs around £25, depending on traffic.

BY TRAIN Edinburgh has two train stations—Haymarket in the West End, which receives trains that travel up the west coast of England before terminating at Waverley, the city's main station in the city center at the east end of Princes Street. The **East Coast** trains that link London's King's Cross with Waverley station are fast and efficient and include a

buffet bar. Trains depart London every hour or so, taking about 4½ hours and costing £115 to £200 return. Considerable savings can be made if you book in advance and commit to traveling on specific trains; see www.eastcoast.co.uk for details or ✆ **08457/225-111. Scotrail** (www.scotrail.co.uk; ✆ **0845/601-5929**) operates the Caledonian Sleeper service—overnight trains with sleeper berths. Single fares cost around £94. There is a taxi rank in Waverley station and Edinburgh's bus station (see below) is only a short walk away.

BY BUS   The least expensive way to travel between London and Edinburgh is by bus, but it's a 9½ hour journey. **MegaBus** (www.megabus.com; ✆ **0871/266-3333**) is the cheapest option, with single fares costing from £14, **National Express** (www. nationalexpress.com; ✆ **08717/818-178**) also runs a regular service and singles cost anywhere between £17 and £68. Coaches depart from London's Victoria Coach Station, delivering you to Edinburgh's **St. Andrews Square Bus Station,** St. Andrews Square.

BY CAR   Edinburgh is 74km (46 miles) east of Glasgow and 169km (105 miles) north of Newcastle-upon-Tyne, in England. No express motorway links Edinburgh with London. The M1 from London takes you part of the way north; it then becomes

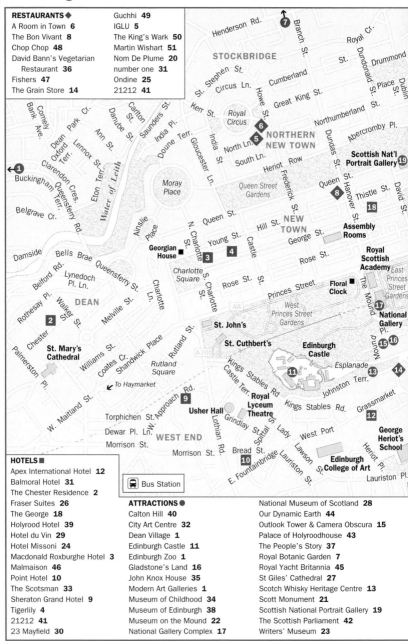

RESTAURANTS◆
A Room in Town **6**
The Bon Vivant **8**
Chop Chop **48**
David Bann's Vegetarian
    Restaurant **36**
Fishers **47**
The Grain Store **14**
Guchhi **49**
IGLU **5**
The King's Wark **50**
Martin Wishart **51**
Nom De Plume **20**
number one **31**
Ondine **25**
21212 **41**

HOTELS■
Apex International Hotel **12**
Balmoral Hotel **31**
The Chester Residence **2**
Fraser Suites **26**
The George **18**
Holyrood Hotel **39**
Hotel du Vin **29**
Hotel Missoni **24**
Macdonald Roxburghe Hotel **3**
Malmaison **46**
Point Hotel **10**
The Scotsman **33**
Sheraton Grand Hotel **9**
Tigerlily **4**
21212 **41**
23 Mayfield **30**

Bus Station

ATTRACTIONS●
Calton Hill **40**
City Art Centre **32**
Dean Village **1**
Edinburgh Castle **11**
Edinburgh Zoo **1**
Gladstone's Land **16**
John Knox House **35**
Modern Art Galleries **1**
Museum of Childhood **34**
Museum of Edinburgh **38**
Museum on the Mound **22**
National Gallery Complex **17**

National Museum of Scotland **28**
Our Dynamic Earth **44**
Outlook Tower & Camera Obscura **15**
Palace of Holyroodhouse **43**
The People's Story **37**
Royal Botanic Garden **7**
Royal Yacht Britannia **45**
St Giles' Cathedral **27**
Scotch Whisky Heritage Centre **13**
Scott Monument **21**
Scottish National Portrait Gallery **19**
The Scottish Parliament **42**
Writers' Museum **23**

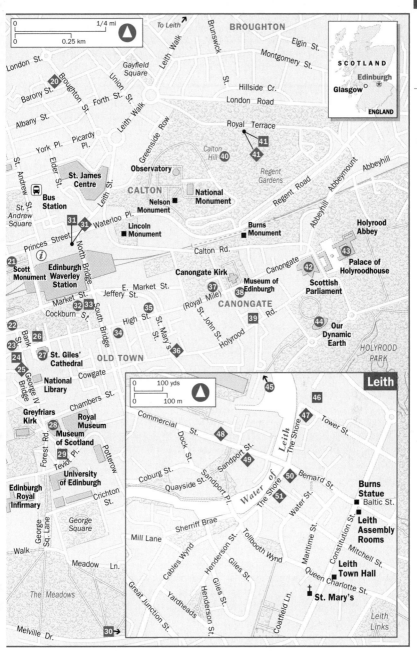

the A1—otherwise known as the "Great North Road"—and leads drivers along the coast to enter Edinburgh from the east. Allow 8 hours or more if you're driving from London. A city by-pass, the A720, circles Edinburgh and routes from all other directions meet this road, making it easy to enter the city from whichever point suits you. The M8 links Edinburgh with Glasgow and connects with the city on the west side of the by-pass, while the M90/A90 travels down from the north over the Forth Road Bridge.

VISITOR INFORMATION

TOURIST OFFICE   Edinburgh's main **Tourist Information Office** is located in Princes Street Mall, which is adjacent to Waverley train station and the Balmoral Hotel (www.edinburgh.org; ℭ **0845/225-5121**). Here you can gather information; staff can also help book a place to stay and sightseeing tickets. The office is open from 9am Monday through Saturday and 10am on Sunday until between 5pm in winter and 7 or 8pm in summer. There's also an information desk at Edinburgh Airport (ℭ **0870/040-0007**).

WEBSITES   The official site of **Visit Scotland** (www.visitscotland.com; ℭ **0845/859-1006**) is an excellent source for events, accommodation, things to do, outdoor activities, and travel information. The site of the regional tourist board for **Edinburgh and the Lothians** (www.edinburgh.org) is packed with information about the city and surroundings, including sections on history and culture, ideas for itineraries, and a detailed section on food and drink.

CITY LAYOUT

The center of Edinburgh is divided between its Old and New Towns. The renowned **Royal Mile** forms the spine of **Old Town,** leading downhill from Edinburgh Castle to the Palace of Holyroodhouse. A labyrinth of ancient wynds (narrow pathways between buildings), closes, and steep stone stairways spread out on either side of the Royal Mile, and on the south side of the castle Old Town opens out into the **Grassmarket**—a wide medieval street where the city's convicted criminals were once hung until dead on the dreaded gallows. Today cafes, pubs, and shops line this historic thoroughfare, spilling out onto its pavements in summer.

To the north of Old Town, joined by the high vaulted North Bridge, lies Edinburgh's **New Town.** Still hailed as a masterpiece of city planning, its wide neoclassical streets, squares, crescents, and gardens were created between 1765 and 1850 in response to the cramped, claustrophobic, dark Old Town.

New Town is flanked by **Princes Street,** whose shop-lined north side gazes across the wide expanse of Princes Street Gardens to Old Town. North of, and running parallel to, Princes Street is New Town's second great street, **George Street,** which begins at Charlotte Square and extends east to St. Andrews Square and is lined with upmarket shops and restaurants. Directly north of George Street lies New Town's third main thoroughfare **Queen Street,** which opens out onto Queen Street Gardens and is a main traffic route through the city. Nestled between Princes Street and George Street is **Rose Stree**t—a narrow pedestrianized lane lined with pubs, shops, and restaurants. And the equally narrow **Thistle Street** between George Street and Queen Street is a secret haven of boutique shopping and fine dining.

GETTING AROUND

ON FOOT   **Walking** is the best way to explore Edinburgh, particularly Old Town, with its narrow lanes, wynds, and closes. Many of the city's attractions are located within a small area along or around the Royal Mile, Princes Street, or one of the major streets in New Town. All of which are easy, and often quicker, to reach by foot.

BY BUS   Edinburgh's bus system is operated by **Lothian Buses** (www.lothian buses.com; ✆ **0131/555-6363**), whose frequent, inexpensive service covers every corner of the city. The fare for a single journey of any distance is £1.40 for adults, 70p for children aged 5 to 15, and free for children under 4. A **Day Saver Ticket** allows 1 day of unlimited travel on city buses at a cost of £3.50 for adults and £2 for children. A network of night buses runs throughout the night and a one-way fare on any of these services is £3. Exact change is required to purchase any ticket. Route maps and timetables can be downloaded from Lothian Buses' website or call into one of their travel shops on either Waverley Bridge or Hanover Street for more information. Both offices are open Monday to Friday 9am to 6pm, Saturday 10am to 6pm, and the Waverley Bridge Travel shop also opens on Sunday 10am to 5.15pm.

BY TAXI   You can hail a taxi or pick one up at any of Edinburgh's numerous taxi stands. Meters begin at £2 and increase £2 every 1km (⅔ mile). Taxi ranks are at Hanover Street, North St. Andrews Street, Waverley Station, Haymarket Station, Lothian Road, and Lauriston Place. Fares are displayed in the front of the taxi, including extra charges for night drivers or destinations outside the city limits. You can also call a taxi. Try **City Cabs** (www.citycabs.co.uk; ✆ **0131/228-1211**) or **Central Radio Taxis** (✆ **0131/229-2468**).

BY CAR   Edinburgh's public transport is so good there's little point in hiring a car. Also, driving around the city can be tricky as the traffic system takes some working out and parking is expensive and difficult to find. Metered parking is available (exact change required), but some zones are only for permit holders; vehicles with no permit are towed away and Edinburgh's traffic wardens are notoriously active in handing out tickets. Major car parks (parking lots) are at Castle Terrace, convenient for Edinburgh Castle, Lothian Road, and the West End; St. John Hill, convenient for the Royal Mile and St. James Centre (entrance from York Place), close to the east end of Princes Street.

Most of the major car rental companies have offices both at Edinburgh airport and in the city center. Options include **Enterprise** (www.enterprise.co.uk; ✆ **0800/800-227**) and **Hertz** (www.hertz.co.uk; ✆ **0843/309-3026**).

BY BICYCLE   Edinburgh is relatively tolerant toward cyclists, but the city's many cobbled roads both in New and Old Towns make for difficult terrain on two wheels. Also, Edinburgh is constructed around a series of hills, so don't expect a flat ride. There's a network of cycle paths round the city, especially on the north side, and athletic types wanting to explore areas beyond the city center will find cycling a good option. Cycle hire companies include **Leith Cycles'** Abbeyhill branch on Cadzow Place (www.leithcycleco.com; ✆ **0131/652-1760**), rentals start at £17 for a full day and include a helmet, lock, map, and puncture repair kit. Children's bikes, trailers, and tagalongs can also be hired.

BY TRAM   Edinburgh is in the process of installing a tram system. The proposed route will run from Edinburgh airport to York Place via Haymarket and Waverley train stations and the bus station in St. Andrew's Square. At the time of writing the tram system is still under construction. Updates are available at www.edinburghtrams.com.

Business Hours In Edinburgh, banks are usually open Monday to Friday 9am to 5pm, some also open on Saturdays 10am to 3pm. Shops are generally open Monday to Saturday 10am to 6pm; on Thursday, some stores stay open to 8pm.

Currency The basic unit of currency is the **pound sterling** (£), which is divided into 100 **pence** (p). The exchange rate at press time is £1 = $1.58. Note that though the United Kingdom is part of the E.U., it does not plan to switch to the euro.

Currency Exchange There are currency exchanges at Edinburgh airport and Waverley train station.

Dentists & Doctors For a dental emergency, go to the Chalmers Dental Centre, 3 Chalmers Street (② **0131/536-4800**), open Monday to Thursday 9am to 4.45pm, Friday 9am to 4.15pm. In a medical emergency, you can seek help from the 24-hour Accident

and Emergency Department at the Edinburgh Royal Infirmary, 51 Little France Crescent, Old Dalkeith Rd. (www.nhslothian.scot.nhs.uk; ② **0131/536-1000**).

Embassies & Consulates The consulate of the **United States** is at 3 Regent Terrace (http://edinburgh.usconsulate.gov; ② **0131/556-8315**), open Monday to Friday 1pm–5.30pm. Appointments required. All the other embassies are in London (see Chapter #).

Emergencies Call ② **999** in an emergency to summon the police, an ambulance, or firefighters.

Hospital See "Dentists & Doctors" above.

Internet Access The **Internet Café** (www.edininternetcafe.com; ② **0131/226-5400**) on West Bow in the heart of Old Town supplies Internet access on a ticket basis with tickets starting at £1.

Pharmacies There are no 24-hour pharmacies (also called chemists) in Edinburgh. The major one is

Boots, 101–103 Princes Street (www.boots.com; ② **0131/225-8331**), open Monday to Saturday 8am to 7pm (Thursday to 8pm), Saturday 8am to 6pm, and Sunday 10am to 6pm.

Post Office There are many post offices dotted throughout the city; a central option is located inside the **St. James's Centre** on Leith Street. Open Monday to Saturday 9am to 5.30pm. For postal information and customer service, call ② **0845/722-3344.**

Telephones The United Kingdom's **country code** is **44.** The city code for **Edinburgh** is **0131.** If you're calling from inside the United Kingdom but outside the city code area, dial the complete area code; if you're calling from outside the United Kingdom, drop the zero. If you're calling from inside the code area, dial just the seven-digit number.

Tipping In most restaurants service charge is not included. The standard tip is 15%. Taxi drivers also expect a 10% to 15% tip.

Exploring Edinburgh
ALONG THE ROYAL MILE ★★★

The **Royal Mile** stretches from Edinburgh Castle to the Palace of Holyroodhouse. **Holyrood Park** opens out at the east end of the Royal Mile and the crowning glory of this dramatic landscape is **Arthur's Seat ★★★**, a 250m-high (820-ft.) peak which rewards all who climb it a breathtaking panorama over Edinburgh and beyond. Most of the attractions in Old Town are located on or just off the Royal Mile.

Edinburgh Castle ★★★ CASTLE   Few places in Scotland are filled with as much history, legend, and lore as Edinburgh Castle, which is in fact a complex of buildings spread over the summit of an ancient plug of volcanic rock. Evidence suggests its settlement dates back at least 3,000 years. After centuries of invasions, demolitions, and upheavals, the buildings that stand today are a result of the castle's role as a military garrison and include the **National War Museum of Scotland.** Visitors can view the Royal Palace home and the bedchamber where Mary, Queen of Scots, gave birth to James VI of Scotland (later James I of England). Other highlights include the **Honors of Scotland** (Scottish Crown Jewels) and the **Stone of Destiny** upon which generations of Scottish and English monarchs have been inaugurated. Take time to seek out **Mons Meg,** a 15th-century cannon weighing more than 5 tons which stands guard on the castle battlements, and enjoy unbeatable views over the city and beyond.

Castlehill. www.edinburghcastle.gov.uk. ✆ **0131/225-9846.** Admission £14.50 adults, £11.60 seniors, £8.60 children 5–15. Apr–Sept daily 9:30am–6pm; Oct–Mar daily 9:30am–5pm.

Gladstone's Land ★ HISTORIC SITE   This 17th-century merchant's house is one of the few surviving examples of a typical Old Town tenement and provides a tangible flavor of the living conditions for those with money at this time. A reconstructed shop displays replicas of goods from the period, but the best part is an upstairs apartment, which is decorated in keeping with its original style and filled with period furnishings and a glorious painted ceiling dating back to 1620.

477B Lawnmarket. www.nts.org.uk. ✆ **0844/493-2120.** Admission £6 adults, £5 seniors and children. Apr–June and Sept–Oct daily 10am–5pm; July–Aug daily 10am–6.30pm.

John Knox House HISTORIC HOME   This distinctive, medieval building was the final home of hard-line Protestant reformer John Knox. Even if you're not interested in Knox, this late-15th-century house is well worth a visit as its three floors are a showcase of medieval craftsmanship, including a frescoed ceiling in **The Oak Room.** Today Knox's house is joined with the **Scottish Storytelling Centre,** an award-winning modern build which seamlessly integrates with the adjacent 15th-century house.

43–45 High St. www.scottishstorytellingcentre.co.uk. ✆ **0131/556-9579.** Admission £4.25 adults, £3.75 seniors, £1 children over 7, under 7s free. Mon–Sat 10am–6pm; July–Aug also Sun noon–6pm.

Museum of Childhood ☺ MUSEUM   This small but fascinating museum devoted solely to the history of childhood takes visitors on a journey through the toys and games that children have grown up with from the 18th to 21st centuries. Exhibits include pedal cars, magnificent dolls houses, and toy soldiers, as well as books and clothes. Hands-on areas keep young children occupied while parents take a walk down memory lane.

Public transport along the Royal Mile

No buses run the length of the Royal Mile and some attractions, especially those at the top end towards Edinburgh Castle, cannot be reached via public transport. However, many bus routes serve the roads that cross over the Royal Mile and most attractions are a short walk from one of these intersections.

Bus routes along George IV Bridge include nos. 23, 27, 41, 42, 45, and 67. Buses that travel along both North and South Bridges include nos. 3, 5, 7, 8, 14, 29, 31, 37, and 47. And bus no. 35 travels up Cannongate at the east end of the Royal Mile as far as South Bridge.

42 High St. www.edinburghmuseums.org.uk. ✆ **0131/529-4142.** Free admission. Mon–Sat 10am–5pm; Sun noon–5pm.

Museum of Edinburgh MUSEUM   Housed in Huntly House, a fine example of a restored 16th-century mansion, this warren-like museum is dedicated to the history of Edinburgh and features faithfully crafted reproductions of rooms inspired by the city's traditional industries, including glassmaking and pottery. Original plans for New Town are also on display along with the National Covenant, a petition for religious freedom created in 1638.

142 Canongate. www.edinburghmuseums.org.uk. ✆ **0131/529-4143.** Free admission. Mon–Sat 10am—5pm; Aug also open Sun noon–5pm.

Outlook Tower & Camera Obscura ☺ OBSERVATION POINT   Housed in the top chamber of this white Victorian outlook tower is an 1853 periscope which throws a revolving image of Edinburgh's streets and buildings onto a circular table. Visitors are invited to interact with these images while guides share stories of the city's landmarks and history. Additional attractions include a **Magic Gallery** crammed with optical illusions and the Electric Room complete with a giant plasma sphere.

Castlehill. www.camera-obscura.co.uk. ✆ **0131/226-3709.** Admission £10.95 adults, £8.95 seniors and students, £7.95 children 5–15. Daily July-Aug 9.30am–8.30pm; Sept–Oct and Apr–June 9.30am–7pm, Nov–Mar 10am–6pm.

Palace of Holyroodhouse ★★ ROYAL BUILDING   Built by James IV in the 16th century, the Palace of Holyroodhouse is the Queen's official residence in Scotland. This magnificent baroque building sits adjacent to a ruined 12th-century Augustinian abbey. The palace has been altered by various monarchs and highlights include the **Royal Apartments** and the chambers where Mary, Queen of Scots, lived. Some of the rich tapestries, paneling, massive fireplaces, and antiques from the 1700s are still in place. The **Great Gallery** is lined with portraits of Scottish monarchs by Dutch artist Jacob De Wet, who was commissioned by Charles II in the 17th century to create a series of paintings of the royal figures who pre-dated him. The **Queen's Gallery** stands in front of the palace and displays a changing program of exhibitions of art work from the Royal Collection.

Canongate. www.royalcollection.org.uk. ✆ **0131/556-5100.** Admission £10.75 adults, £9.80 seniors and students, £6.50 children 5–16, £28.60 families. Joint Palace and Queen's Gallery ticket £15.10 adults, £13.75 seniors and students, £8.55 children 5–16, £39.50 families. Apr–Oct daily 9.30am–6pm; Nov–Mar 9.30am–4:30pm.

The People's Story HISTORIC SITE   Housed in Canongate Tolbooth (built in 1591 as a place to collect taxes and serve as a local jail), The People's Story celebrates the social history of Edinburgh residents from the late 18th century to the present day. There's no sniff of royalty here; instead the stories of ordinary folk, how they worked, how they played, the hardships they endured, and the rights they fought for are thoughtfully presented.

163 Canongate. www.edinburghmuseums.org.uk. ✆ **0131/529-4057.** Free admission. Mon–Sat 10am–5pm. Sundays in August noon–5pm.

Scotch Whisky Heritage Centre MUSEUM   Visitors to this entertaining and informative attraction are taken on a whisky barrel ride dedicated to the making of Scotland's favorite tipple before being taught how to sample a wee dram of choice. You're then invited to view the world's largest whisky collection before the tour

Edinburgh folklore is rich with tales of an underground city. It's long been rumored that a network of secret tunnels spreads out from Edinburgh Castle, one of which leads under the Royal Mile to the Palace of Holyroodhouse. However, more grounded in the real world are stories of bricked-over streets. In the late 18th and early 19th centuries as the fortunes of Old Town declined, anyone with the funds to do so fled its cramped unhygienic closes for the wide open streets of the blossoming New Town. Most of the dilapidated housing around the Royal Mile was demolished; and in the case of streets such as Mary King's Close, the lower levels were simply built over and tales of underground streets with resident ghosts passed into urban legend.

In the late 1990s, the old street-level sections of Mary King's Close were rediscovered and today form one of Edinburgh's spookiest tourist attractions. Located beneath the City Chambers, **The Real Mary King's Close** (www.real marykingsclose.com; ✆ **08702/430-160**) is accessed via Warriston's Close off the Royal Mile and transports visitors back to the 17th century. Expect to be led through a hidden and haunted underground warren of old houses where people once lived and worked for centuries.

Learn about Mary King herself and the last man to leave her close, whose ghost is believed to still occupy his old house. This attraction is open November to March Sunday to Thursday 10am to 5pm and Friday and Saturday 10am to 9pm, and April to October daily 10am to 9pm. Admission is £11.50 for adults and £6 for children aged 5 to 15.

Dubbed as the most haunted place in Britain, the layers of vaults that lie beneath **South Bridge** are no place for the fainthearted. When the bridge was built in the late 18th century, a complex of vaults was built into its enormous arches. Some of these dark spaces were used for storage while various tradesmen occupied others, but the damp drove them out and the city's poor, destitute, and often criminally inclined moved in, transforming the complex into a slum which was soon closed down. Today **Mercat Tours** (www.mercattours.com; ✆ **0131/225-5445**) takes visitors deep into these forgotten vaults via a series of tours, some of which focus on the history of these hidden spaces, others introduce those who dare to descend to the many ghosts who call this place home. Tours run on various days at set times and tickets start at £5 for adults and £4 for children.

concludes in a whisky bar where long views of Edinburgh complement the many malts available to sample.

354 Castlehill www.scotchwhiskyexperience.co.uk. ✆ **0131/220-0441.** Admission £12.50 adults; £9.50 seniors and students; £6.50 children 6–17; £30 families. Open daily Sept–May 10am–6pm; June–Aug daily 10am–7pm.

The Scottish Parliament ★★ ARCHITECTURE   This bold and controversial modern building stands opposite, and in contrast to, the Palace of Holyroodhouse at the east end of the Royal Mile. Love it or loathe it, the building embodies a strong statement of Scotland's past, present, and future. Designed by the late Spanish architect Enric Miralles, who died before his vision was completed, this unique building cost a cool $893 million and the first debate finally took place in its chambers in 2004. The facade is amazing enough in itself, but to truly understand the philosophy

Edinburgh Pass

If you're planning to visit a number of Edinburgh attractions the Edinburgh Pass (www.edinburghpass.com) could save you money. This pass allows the holder entry to over 30 attractions in and around the city and prices range from £29 adults and £18 children for 1 day to £49 adults and £30 children for 3 days.

behind the architecture, a guided tour is a must. You can also visit the debating chamber, shop, café, and exhibitions without a tour guide.

Canongate. www.scottish.parliament.uk. ✆ **0131/348-5200.** Free admission. Open April–Sept Mon–Fri 10am– 5.30pm, Sat 11am–5.30pm; Oct–March 10am–4pm, Sat 11am–5.30pm. Free guided tours can be arranged through a website booking form.

St Giles' Cathedral ★★ CATHE-DRAL Also known as the High Kirk of Edinburgh, St Giles' is one of the most important churches in Scotland and a key architectural landmark along the Royal Mile. The oldest parts date back to 1124, but following a fire in 1385 many sections have since been rebuilt. The brooding stone exterior features a distinctive crowned spire and one of the outstanding features of the large vaulted interior is the **Thistle Chapel.** Built in 1911 and dedicated to the Knights of the Thistle, Scotland's order of chivalry, this intricate space houses beautiful stalls and detailed heraldic stained-glass windows.

High St. www.stgilescathedral.org.uk. ✆ **0131/225-9442.** Free admission (£3 donation suggested). May–Sept Mon–Fri 9am–7pm, Sat 9am–5pm, Sun 1–5pm; Oct–April Mon–Sat 9am–5pm, Sun 1–5pm.

Writers' Museum MUSEUM This 1622 house is a treasure trove of portraits, relics, and manuscripts relating to three of Scotland's greatest men of letters; Robert Burns, Sir Walter Scott, and Robert Louis Stevenson. Collections include Burns' writing, Sir Walter Scott's pipe and chess set, and a number of Stevenson's early editions.

In Lady Stair's House, off Lawnmarket. www.edinburghmuseums.org.uk. ✆ **0131/529-4901.** Free admission. Mon–Sat 10am–5pm; Aug also Sun noon–5pm.

OTHER OLD TOWN ATTRACTIONS

City Art Centre GALLERY Spread out over six floors of an imposing former warehouse behind Waverley station, the City Art Centre hosts a changing program of exhibitions that showcase paintings, drawings, photographs, sculpture, and installations from subjects as broad as Highland art to human anatomy, alongside new work from local and international artists.

2 Market St. www.edinburghmuseums.org.uk. ✆ **0131/529-3993.** Admission charges vary with each exhibition. Mon –Sat 10am–5pm, Sun noon–5pm. Bus: 36.

Museum on the Mound MUSEUM This is one of Edinburgh's newest museums and is dedicated to the subject of money. Detailed displays bring visitors face to face with a million pounds and Scotland's oldest banknote, and bring to life the history of the Bank of Scotland, the rise of building societies, and much more. The Mound, on which the museum stands, is a manmade structure and a glass display shows just what this city center hill is made of.

The Mound. www.museumonthemound.com. ✆ **0131/243-5464.** Free admission. Tues–Fri 10am–5pm, Sat and Sun 1–5pm. Bus: 23, 27, 41, 41, 45, or 67.

National Museum of Scotland ★★★ MUSEUM Consisting of two distinctive buildings, one dating back to 1866 and a second modern build which opened in 1998, this national treasure house is the place to delve deep into Scotland's rich history from its geological origins to the present day. The multitude of objects that tell

GREYFRIARS KIRK & bobby

A short detour along George IV Bridge from the Royal Mile leads to Greyfriars Kirk (www.greyfriarskirk.com), an old Edinburgh church built in 1620 whose 17th-century churchyard, crammed with gravestones and mausoleums, is a favorite stop for local ghost tours. It is also where many signed the National Covenant in 1638 in commitment to Scottish Presbyterian. The most famous graves here are those of John Gray, a member of the Edinburgh City Police and night watchman who died in 1858, and his faithful dog Bobby who guarded his owner's grave for 14 years until he too passed away in 1867. A statue of the loyal Bobby stands close to the main entrance of Greyfriars Kirkyard and a number of books and films retelling the story of this faithful hound have since been created. This remarkable dog was awarded Freedom of the City status and his collar and bowl are now on display in the Museum of Edinburgh (p. 832).

the story of Scotland include Bonnie Prince Charlie's traveling canteen and The Maiden beheading machine which sliced 150 Scottish heads off between 1564 and 1710. The museum also turns a curatorial and often interactive eye to many other world cultures, as well as science and nature. Following a major transformation, the Victorian section of the museum reopened in 2011 and contains 16 new exhibition galleries, making this the largest museum in the U.K. outside of London. New exhibits include a stunning 18m (59-ft.) high **Window on the World** which contains around 1,000 items from the national collection.

Chambers St. www.nms.ac.uk. ℂ **0300/123-6789.** Free admission. Daily 10am–5pm. Bus: 35.

NEW TOWN

New Town is Edinburgh's main shopping area and there are limited attractions to see in this region of the city. Many major bus routes run along Princes Street, location of most New Town attractions; others are a short walk away.

National Gallery Complex ★★★ GALLERY   Located in the center of Princes Street Gardens, this imposing complex is made up of three connected buildings dedicated to displaying Scotland's national collection of fine art from the early Renaissance to the end of the 19th century. The main building is the National Gallery itself, whose wide galleries house the main collection and contain masterpieces from around the world from artists such as Raphael, Rubens, Van Gogh, and Cézanne, as well as a collection dedicated to the history of Scottish painting. The Royal Scottish Academy Building displays a program of temporary world-class exhibitions and is joined with the National Gallery via the Weston Link, which contains a cafe and IT gallery.

The Mound. www.nationalgalleries.org. ℂ **0131/624-6200.** Free admission; charge for some temporary exhibitions. Fri–Wed 10am–5pm; Thurs 10am–7pm. Bus: Any of the many buses that travel along Princes Street, including nos. 10, 11, 16, or 22.

Scott Monument ★ MONUMENT   Completed in the mid-19th century, the Gothic-inspired Scott Monument rises over 60m (220 ft.) on the east end of Princes Street. A large statue of Sir Walter Scott sits beneath an elaborate spire which visitors can climb to enjoy spectacular views of the city.

Princes St. www.edinburghmuseums.org.uk. ℂ **0131/529-4068.** Admission £3. Apr–Sept Mon–Sat 9am–7pm, Sun 10am–6pm; Oct–Mar Mon–Sat 9am–4pm, Sun 10am–6pm. Bus: Any of the many buses that travel along Princes Street, including nos. 10, 11, 16, or 22.

Scottish National Portrait Gallery ★★ GALLERY   Housed in a grand red sandstone neo-Gothic building, the Scottish National Portrait Gallery was the first of its kind in the world and is filled with images, from paintings to photographs, of famous and not so famous Scots. The gallery has undergone a large-scale restoration aimed at restoring and revealing more of this glorious building, including a detailed frieze of famous Scots in chronological order. Around 850 works are on display in themed exhibitions, which range from the historical to the contemporary.

1 Queen St. www.nationalgalleries.org. ⓒ **0131/624-6200.** Free admission, charge for some temporary exhibits. Fri–Wed 10am–5pm; Thurs 10am–7pm. Bus: 11, 16, 22, or 25.

OUTLYING ATTRACTIONS

Dean Village ★ HISTORIC SITE   Beautiful Dean Village is one of the city's most photographed sights. Dating from the 12th century, this former grain-milling center occupies a valley about 30m (100 ft.) below the rest of Edinburgh on the edge of the Water of Leith. It's a few minutes from the West End, at the end of Bells Brae off Queensferry Street and you can enjoy a celebrated view by looking downstream, under the high arches of Dean Bridge (1833), designed by Telford. The village's old buildings have been restored and converted into apartments and houses. You don't come here for any one particular site, but to stroll around, people-watch, and enjoy the village. Bus: 19, 36, 37, 41,or 47.

Modern Art Galleries ★★ GALLERY   The two galleries that make up the Modern Art Galleries—the Gallery of Modern Art and Dean Gallery—house Scotland's finest collection of modern and contemporary art. The **Modern Art Gallery** sits in 4.8 hectares (12 acres) of landscaped grounds which feature sculptures by Henry Moore and Barbara Hepworth. The gallery itself contains a large collection of international postwar work from artists including Francis Bacon, Andy Warhol, and Damien Hirst, and work from the early 20th century, such as cubist paintings and pieces by Matisse and Picasso. Across the road the **Dean Gallery** displays a wide collection of Dada and Surrealism, including work by Salvador Dalí, Max Ernst, Joan Miró, and Edinburgh-born sculptor Sir Eduardo Paolozzi, who gave an extensive body of his private collection to the National Galleries of Scotland, including prints, drawings, plaster maquettes, and molds. This gallery also hosts a number of temporary exhibitions and both are a 15-minute walk from the west end of Princes Street.

75 Belford Rd. www.nationalgalleries.org. ⓒ **0131/624-6200.** Free admission; charge for some temporary exhibitions. Daily 10am–5pm. Bus: 13.

Royal Yacht Britannia ★ HISTORIC SITE   Launched on April 16, 1953, this 125m (410-ft.) luxury yacht sailed more than a million miles before she was decommissioned on December 11, 1997, and laid to rest at the port of Leith, 3km (1¼ miles) from the center of Edinburgh. Once aboard, you're guided around all five levels by an audio tour and can walk the decks where Prince Charles and Princess Diana strolled on their honeymoon. A visit also includes a trip to the Royal Apartments, engine room, and captain's cabin.

Ocean Terminal, Leith. www.royalyachtbritannia.co.uk. ⓒ **0131/555-5566.** Admission £11.75 adults, £10 seniors and students, £7.50 children aged 5–17, under-5s free. Daily Nov–Mar 10am–3.30pm; April, May, June and Oct 9.30am–4pm; July–Sept 9.30am–4.30pm. Bus: 11, 22, 34, 35, or 36.

ORGANIZED TOURS

If your time in Edinburgh is limited an organized tour can provide a quick introduction to the city's main sights. One of the most popular ways to tour is via an **open-top bus.**

These trips run daily throughout the year and depart from Waverley Bridge every 15 minutes in summer and every 30 minutes in winter from 9:35am. You can hop on and off stops along the way and the last tour of the day departs just after 4pm. A number of different tours are on offer, including City Sightseeing, Edinburgh World Heritage, and a Majestic Tour, which concentrates on the city's royal attractions. Commentaries are available in a number of languages and tickets cost £12 for adults, £11 for seniors and students, and £5 for children aged 5 to 15. For more information see www.edinburghtour.com or call ✆ **0131/220-0779** or just turn up at Waverley Bridge.

Mercat Tours (www.mercattours.com; ✆ **0131/225-5445**) runs the city's only five-star walking tours. All of Mercat's trained guides hold history degrees and their many tours are as entertaining as they are informative. Choose from tours such as "Secrets of the Royal Mile" and the ever popular "Ghosts and Ghouls," all of which run daily throughout the year and meet outside the Mercat Cross by St Giles' Cathedral on the Royal Mile. Tickets start at £9 for adults and £5 for children aged 5–15 and can be bought on the day at the start of a tour or booked in advance at Tourist Information (see p. 828), Mercat's office on Blair Street, online, or by phone. Mercat also run regular tours in Spanish. For details of Mercat's underground tours see "Edinburgh Underground" box on p. 833.

Those seeking to tap into Edinburgh's prodigious literary history by walking the city's streets can do so via **Edinburgh Literary Tours** (www.edinburghbooklovers tour.com). This company leads a daytime Edinburgh Book Lovers' tour (£10 full price/£8 concessions) and an evening Lost World Literary Pub Crawl (£8 full price/£7 concessions). Book through the website.

One of the more unusual ways to see the city is via a rickshaw. **B-spokes** (www.b-spokes.com; ✆ **0131/656-6499**) operate a selection of rickshaw tours, including a Photography Tour that takes you to the best views Edinburgh has to offer and a **Kids' Tour,** which is full of tales of wizards and ghosts, or you can create a tour of your own. Rates start at £25 per person and waterproof screens and blankets are provided if needs be. These rickshaws also operate as **Pedicabs** at night. They can be hailed in the same way as a regular taxi and operate throughout the city center.

Many other tour companies offer an ever-increasing range of ways to navigate Edinburgh and learn about its past, literary heritage, and many ghosts. Details can be picked up at Tourist Information (see p. 828).

OUTDOOR ACTIVITIES

Calton Hill ★★★ MONUMENT   Rising 106m (350 ft.) off Regent Road, Carlton Hill and its assortment of monuments have helped Edinburgh earn the sobriquet "Athens of the North." Construction began on the large **Scottish Monument,** which dominates the summit in 1826, and although this ambitious structure was intended to replicate the Parthenon, funds dried up and the building was never completed. Other completed buildings include the 32m (106-ft.) high **Nelson Monument** (www.edinburghmuseums.org.uk; ✆ **0131/556-2716**), which contains relics of the man himself and is crowned by a large time ball that enables vessels on the Firth of Forth to accurately set their chronometers. Modeled after the Tower of the Winds in Athens, the **Dugald Stewart Monument** is one of the best vantage points in Edinburgh and a choice spot from which to be buffeted by panoramic views of the city as they spread out below.

Carlton Hill can be entered via Waterloo Place and Royal Terrace. Entrance is free except for the Nelson Monument, which costs £3 to enter and is open Oct–Mar Mon–Sat 10am–3pm, April–Sept Mon–Sat 10am–7pm, Sun noon–5pm.

Royal Botanic Garden ★★ GARDEN   One of the grandest outdoor spaces in Britain, the "Botanics," as these gardens are affectionately known, cover over 28 landscaped hectares (70 acres) 1 mile north of Princes Street. The gardens date back to the late 17th century when they were used for medical studies and now form an exquisite tranquil haven loved by visitors and residents alike. The many areas to stroll through include a Chinese Garden, a Scottish Heath Garden, and a glorious Victorian Temperate **Palm House.** The stunning visitor center by the western entrance features plenty of child-friendly displays, a very popular cafe, and a changing program of exhibitions.

Inverleith Row. www.rbge.org.uk. ℂ **0131/552-7171.** Free admission to gardens; Glasshouse £4.50 adults, £3.50 seniors, £1 children aged 9 and under. Daily Feb and Oct daily 10am–5pm; Nov–Jan 10am–4pm; Mar–Sept daily 10am–6pm. Bus: 8, 17, 23, or 27.

ESPECIALLY FOR KIDS

Edinburgh Zoo ★★ ☺ ZOO   Scotland's largest animal collection is located on the western edges of the city and spreads over 32 hectares (79 acres) of hillside parkland with unrivaled views towards the Pentland Hills. The zoo is home to over 1,000 animals, including many endangered species, and best-loved creatures include the sun bears, Sumatran tigers, koala bears, and Malayan tapirs. A recent addition is the **Bungo Trail,** a state-of-the-art chimpanzee facility that allows visitors close-up viewings and opportunities to learn about their links with humans. The zoo also boasts a large penguin population who leave their enclosure every day at 2.15pm to take a stroll. However, the stars of the show are giant pandas, Tian Tian and Yang Guang, who arrived from China in late 2011. Panda viewing is included in the admission price but is time limited. Prebooking is highly recommended.

134 Corstorphine Rd. www.edinburghzoo.org.uk. ℂ **0131/334-9171**. Admission £15.50 adults, £13 seniors and students, £11 children 3–14, £47.70 family ticket. Apr–Sept daily 9am–6pm; Oct and Mar daily 9am–5pm; Nov–Feb daily 9am–4:30pm. Parking £4. Bus: 12, 26, or 31 from Princes St.

Our Dynamic Earth ★ ☺ THEME PARK   This family-friendly attraction leads visitors on an entertaining journey through the physical Earth and natural diversity from the Big Bang to a tropical rainforest where skies darken at 15-minute intervals and torrents of rain cascade onto the recreated landscape. En route you'll be transported to different terrains via a 4D experience, encounter a simulated volcano and a real (if small) iceberg. A multitude of opportunities to interact and learn are provided along the way. A visit also includes a show in the Future Dome digital **planetarium.**

THE water OF LEITH

The Water of Leith (www.waterofleith. org.uk) is a small river that meanders a course through the center of Edinburgh before meeting the Firth of Forth at The Shore in Leith. A 19km (12-mile) long signposted walk leads from the visitor center in Balerno to Leith and en route passes landmarks such as Murrayfield Stadium, the Modern Art Galleries, Dean Village, Stockbridge, and the Royal Botanic Garden. You can join the walkway at any point and enjoy a tranquil, scenic escape from the hustle and bustle of the city streets. This is a recommended diversion for bird watchers and maps can be picked up at the visitor center or downloaded from the website.

Holyrood Rd. www.dynamicearth.co.uk. ℂ **0131/550-7800.** Admission £11.50 adults, £9.75 seniors, £7.50 children 3–15, free for children 2 and under. Nov–Mar Wed–Sun 10am–5.30pm; Apr–June and Sept–Oct daily 10am–5.30pm; Jul–Aug daily 10am–6pm. Bus: 35 or 36.

Where to Eat

Edinburgh's eating out scene has changed dramatically over the past few years and the choice, style, and types of cuisine on offer are more diverse than ever before. A host of new vibrant eateries have sprung up all over the city, perfectly complementing Edinburgh's long-standing top tables. Many establishments specialize in Scottish cuisine and local seafood, but visitors can also expect to choose from dishes celebrating food from all over the world. Leith has rapidly established itself as the best region in the city for eating out. In New Town, George Street is the place to be seen dining out, but the parallel Thistle Street is lined with many of Edinburgh's more intimate dining experiences. While in Old Town some of the city's most established restaurants still pack a considerable culinary punch.

NEW TOWN
Expensive
number one ★★ SCOTTISH/CONTINENTAL   This intimate, crimson and gold-colored enclave is the Balmoral Hotel's premier restaurant and a longtime holder of a Michelin star. Renowned for its Scottish-and-French-influenced cuisine presented in a traditional setting, number one is a haven of innovative dining which makes full use of the finest local ingredients and seasonal produce. Starters could include Isle of Skye scallops with pig cheek and black pudding, for a main course you might savor Barbary duck with chervil root, lentil, duck heart, sage, and hazelnuts, all of which could be rounded off with bitter chocolate and orange soufflé. Vegetarian options are always available.

In the Balmoral Hotel, 1 Princes St. www.restaurantnumberone.com. ℂ **0131/557-6727.** Reservations recommended. Set menu £64 for 3 courses; tasting menu £70. AE, DC, MC, V. Daily 6:30–10pm. Nearest bus stops are located on North Bridge and Princes St, both of which are served by many routes.

21212 ★★★ MODERN FRENCH   One of Edinburgh's top restaurants, 21212 serves outstanding Michelin-starred cuisine with style and more than a little flair. The plush dining room is infused with an intimate luxury through which the passion for fine food of top chef Paul Kitching and his partner Katie O'Brien shine through. The best feature is the surprisingly calm open kitchen (ask for table one for a front-row view) where an array of chefs conjure up truly memorable and well thought through, slow-cooked cuisine. Each course is a delight and could include Highland roe deer and young vegetable ragout or pink ginger trout. The accompanying wine list is equally impressive, and expect touches of humor and excellent customer service.

3 Royal Terrace. www.21212restaurant.co.uk. ℂ **0845/222-1212.** Reservations recommended. Lunch from £28 for 3 courses, Dinner £68 for 5 courses. AE, MC, V, DC. Daily noon–3pm and 5.30–10pm. Nearest bus stop Leith Walk, which is served by many bus routes.

Moderate
A Room in Town ★★ SCOTTISH   Deliberately downbeat, this eatery is characterized by stripped-back wooden floors, loud art work, excellent food, and a lively atmosphere. Expect melt-in-the-mouth Scottish food such as Orkney herring and Stornoway black pudding on the daily changing lunch menu or spiced lamb cutlets

with steamed jasmine rice and a sticky hot dipping sauce for dinner. All of which can all be rounded off with a selection of Scottish and Irish cheeses.

18 Howe St. www.aroomin.co.uk. ✆ **0131/225-8204.** Main courses (dinner only) £11–£23. Set lunch £9 for 1 course, £13 for 2 courses. AE, MC, V. Daily noon–3pm and 5.30–10pm. Bus: 24.

IGLU ★ SCOTTISH   Tucked away off a main New Town street, IGLU is a down to earth, friendly, simple in a rustic kind of way restaurant that champions wild, organic, and local produce. Menus include dishes such as Borders boar burger, steak and Black Isle porter pie, and mackerel tartar all creatively prepared and accompanied by a strong wine list.

2b Jamaica St. www.theiglu.com. ✆ **0131/476-5333.** Main courses (dinner only) £11–£20. Set lunch £12 for 2 courses. AE, MC, V. Tues–Sat 6–10pm, Fri and Sat noon–3pm, Sun 11am–8pm. Bus: 24.

Inexpensive

Nom De Plume ★★ CONTINENTAL   Set high up on Broughton Street, this bistro is the kind of place you'll pop in for a quick coffee and end up staying for hours. Stripped wooden pine table and floors, blend with comfy sofas, bookshelves, soft jazz, and the aroma of good food, all of which makes for one of the friendliest, most relaxed, and least pretentious of New Town's many dining options. The long menu features filling, freshly made food such as hearty stews, fish pies, and hot chili and nachos.

60 Broughton St. ✆ **0131/478-1372**. Main courses £7–£13. MC, V. Mon–Sat 11am–10.30pm, Sun noon–10.30pm. Bus: 8.

The Bon Vivant ★★ CONTINENTAL   Discreet and intimate yet rustic around the edges, The Bon Vivant is a warm, inviting, candlelit haven of good food and fine wine. The relatively small menu changes daily and represents exceptional value for money. All main courses hover around the £9–£10 mark and options may include wild garlic, artichoke, and basil risotto, or braised lamb shank, but it's the before and afters that make this place stand out. Starter bites could include broccoli and sun-dried tomato quiche or duck liver pâté and after bites includes such treats as winter berry pancakes or rhubarb tart.

55 Thistle St. www.bonvivantedinburgh.co.uk. ✆ **0131/225-3275.** Main courses £8–£10. AE, MC, V. Daily noon–10pm. Bus: 24, 28, 45.

OLD TOWN
Moderate

Ondine ★★ SEAFOOD   One of Edinburgh's most heralded new restaurants, Ondine butts up against Hotel Missoni (p. 847) and serves seafood with flair in an elegant, contemporary setting. At the heart of the restaurant is the Crustacean Bar where oysters from all over Britain can be "shucked." Dishes such as Eyemouth brown crab with butternut squash risotto sit alongside British favorites like haddock and chips. A small selection of meat dishes such as sirloin served on the bone complement a menu which prides itself on championing sustainably sourced ingredients.

2 George IV Bridge. www.ondinerestaurant.co.uk. ✆ **0131/226-1888.** Lunch and pre-theater £17 for 2 courses, £20 for 3 courses, dinner mains £15–£25. MC, V. Daily noon–3pm and 5.30–10pm. Bus: 23, 27, 41, 42, 45, or 67.

The Grain Store ★★ SCOTTISH   A local favorite serving some of the best food based on regional produce. From field and stream comes an array of market-fresh ingredients, including game birds in the autumn, forest-fresh mushrooms, lamb from the Borders, Scottish salmon from the rivers, Angus beef, and Perthshire venison. Starters are complemented with a choice of homemade breads baked every morning. You can round off the night with a choice of melt-in-the-mouth homemade desserts such as white chocolate parfait all created by the in-house pastry chef. Decor is rustic, with exposed stonework and polished wooden floors.

30 Victoria St. www.grainstore-restaurant.co.uk. ℭ **0131/225-7635.** Main courses (dinner only) £18–£28. Set lunch £12.50 for 2 courses, £15 for 3 courses. AE, MC, V. Mon–Thurs noon–2pm and 6–10pm, Fri noon–2pm and 6–10pm, Sat noon–3pm and 6–11pm, Sun noon–3pm and 6–10pm.

Inexpensive

David Bann's Vegetarian Restaurant ★ ◢ VEGETARIAN   Hailed as Edinburgh's best vegetarian restaurant, the food is so good here that even carnivores come to savor the well-flavored dishes whipped up with market-fresh ingredients, often shipped in that day from the fertile fields of Scotland. The atmosphere exudes a relaxed ambience all encased in a warm and minimalist decor. The man himself— chef Bann—roams the world for inspiration for his meat-free recipes, and dishes can include rice pancake with spicy potato, cauliflower, chick pea, and cashew; or ginger and tomato jasmine rice with home-smoked tofu. Leave room for dessert so you can round off the night with the likes of hot pear and passion fruit tart. The weekend brunch served every Saturday and Sunday until 5pm is a steal at £6.50.

56–58 St Mary's St. www.davidbann.com. ℭ **0131/556-5888.** Main courses £9–£13. AE, MC, V. Sun–Thurs 12–10pm; Fri noon–10.30pm, Sat 11am–10:30pm, Sun 11am–10pm. Bus: 36.

LEITH
Expensive

Martin Wishart ★★★ MODERN FRENCH   For many this is one of the finest restaurants in Scotland. The owner-chef Martin Wishart is a long time holder of a Michelin star and strives to bring the best of French cuisine to this historic area of Leith. With white walls, modern art, and minimalist decor, the restaurant's interior is epitomized by simple, refined style. Many dishes, such as lemon sole fillets with cockles and squid, are simply prepared to allow the natural flavors to shine through. Others, such as Wagyu beef blade and oxtail pastilla, display a touch of daring. Martin Wishart has also recently opened his second Edinburgh restaurant, **The Honours,** on North Castle Street in the heart of New Town (www.thehonours.co.uk; ℭ **0131/ 220-2513**).

54 The Shore, Leith. www.martin-wishart.co.uk. ℭ **0131/553-3557.** Reservations required. Set menu £65, 6-course tasting menu £70, *Du Jour* lunch available Tues–Fri £29. MC, V. Tues–Fri noon– 2pm and 7–10pm. Sat noon–1.30pm and 7–10pm. Bus: 22, 35, or 36.

Moderate

Fishers ★★ INTERNATIONAL/SEAFOOD   This long-standing restaurant is renowned for its outstanding seafood both in terms of selection and quality. Fishers sits at the end of Leith's old harbor and a suitably nautical aura prevails with fishnets, pictures of the sea, and various marine memorabilia spilling out over the restaurant walls. Sample some of Scotland's best fish, such as halibut from Shetland or Anstruther lobster. A vegetarian menu and some meat choices, including slow-roasted pork, are also available. A sister restaurant—Fishers in the City—can be found on Thistle Street in New Town and is no less impressive.

1 The Shore. www.fishersbistros.co.uk. ℭ **0131/554-5666.** Main courses £12–£25. AE, MC, V. Mon–Sat noon–4pm and 5–10pm; Sun noon–4pm and 5–10:30pm. Bus: 22, 35, or 36.

Inexpensive

Chop Chop ★ CHINESE   Endorsed by Gordon Ramsey's *F-Word,* Chop Chop's award-winning northern Chinese cuisine keeps locals coming back again and again to tuck into an impressive range of meat and fish dishes and its famous *Jiao Zi* (boiled dumplings) and *Guo Tie* (fried dumplings)—small parcels of wheat flour pastry stuffed with all manner of ingredients, such as pork and green pepper and beef and chili, all served with the ingredients for you to create your own accompanying sauce. Set meals and banquets are also served in informal, minimalist surroundings looking out over a cobbled, landscaped section of the old port. The original Haymarket branch can be found at 248 Morrison St. (✆ **0131/221-1155**).

76 Commercial Quay. www.chop-chop.co.uk. ✆ **0131/553-1818.** Main courses £8–£11. Mon–Thurs 6–10pm, Fri 6–10.30pm, Sat noon–2pm and 5–10.30pm, Sun 12.30–2.30pm and 5–10pm. Bus: 22, 35, or 36.

Guchhi ★★ 🎯 INDIAN/SEAFOOD   A relative new comer on Leith's culinary scene, Guchhi takes the freshest of Scottish seafood and serves it up Indian style. The owners and head chefs Vishart Das and Sachin Dhanola trained in restaurants in Goa and seafood restaurants throughout the U.K. before finally creating Guchhi, where they celebrate the food and flavors they know so well. Choose from tandoori smoked mackerel and oven-baked scallops in Bombay duck sauce, or Indian tapas.

9–10 Commercial St. www.guchhi.com. ✆ **0131/555-5604.** Main courses £10–£24. AE, MC, V. Daily noon–11pm. Bus: 22, 35, or 36.

The King's Wark ★★ SCOTTISH/SEAFOOD   This centuries-old building stands on one of the oldest spots in Leith, and entices people in with crackling open fires—and outstanding, reasonably priced food. Expect simple and inventive dishes such as seabass laced with wild mushrooms, grilled salt and pepper sardines with shrimp butter, alongside the inevitable haggis. All of which can be washed down with a good selection of Scottish beers.

36 The Shore. www.thekingswark.co.uk. ✆ **0131/554-9260.** Main courses £9–£17. MC, V. Mon–Sat noon–3pm and 6–10pm, Sun 11am–3pm and 6pm–10pm.

Shopping

In New Town, **Princes Street,** the main shopping area, is lined with big-name chain stores. At the east end sits **Jenners** (www.houseoffraser.co.uk), Edinburgh's much-loved department store which has been trading since 1838. Head a block north to George Street for more exclusive stores, crowned at its east end off St. Andrews Square with a large branch of **Harvey Nichols** and a cluster of chic shops along Multrees Walk. In Old Town, the **Royal Mile** is dedicated to tourists and soaked with tartan-focused gift shops; however, there are many unusual stores to be discovered along **Cockburn Street** and **Victoria Street.** The **Grassmarket** is the place to shop for vintage clothes. Bargain hunters should take

---

West End Village

The West End Village (www.westend village.org) sits on the far western edges of New Town to the north of Shandwick Place. It is a small, picturesque, and little discovered by visitors patch of Edinburgh dedicated to the finer things in life. An impressive cluster of independent, upmarket clothes, accessories, and home furnishing stores line these small Georgian streets, all interspersed with a selection of fine cafes, pubs, and restaurants.

time to explore the many thrift stores in Stockbridge and food lovers will delight in the weekly **farmers' market** (www.edinburghfarmersmarket.co.uk) that gathers on Castle Terrace every Saturday morning.

Geoffrey (Tailor) Kiltmakers & Weavers ★ at 57–59 High St. (www.geoffrey kilts.co.uk; ✆ **0131/557-0256**) is the most famous kiltmaker in Edinburgh and past customers have included Sean Connery, Charlton Heston, and Mel Gibson. Traditional ladies' and gentlemen's kilts are hand sewn and made to measure. An accompanying array of accessories such as sporrans, kilt pins, Celtic patterned buckles, and brochures can also be purchased. **Bagpipes Galore,** 82 Canongate (www.bagpipe. co.uk; ✆ **0131/556-4073**), is the place to pick up a set of traditional bagpipes. Prices start at £250 and go all the way up to over £1,000. For antique prints and old maps of Scotland head to **The Royal Mile Gallery,** 272 Canongate (www.royal milegallery.com; ✆ **0131/558-1702**), and **Royal Mile Whiskies,** 379 High St. (www.royalmilewhiskies.com; ✆ **0131/225-3383**), stock an extensive range of whiskies from all over Scotland, as well as a fine selection of the ever-increasing number of Scottish gins.

Entertainment & Nightlife

For detailed up-to-date information on all entertainment options pick up a copy of *The List,* £3.50, which is published every 4 weeks, or check listings online at www. list.co.uk.

THEATER

Edinburgh has many theaters. At the mainstream end of the market options include the **Edinburgh Playhouse**, 18–22 Greenside Place (www.edinburghplayhouse.org. uk; ✆ **0844/847-1660**), the city's largest theater whose program focuses on large-scale touring musicals, comedy, and dance; and the **Festival Theatre**, 13–29 Nicolson St., and **King's Theatre**, 2 Leven St. They are both managed by the same company and tickets for their wide repertoire of classical entertainment, including ballet, opera, and West End productions, can be booked by phone or online (www. fctt.org.uk; ✆ **0131/529-6000**). The resident company of **Royal Lyceum Theatre,** Grindlay St. (www.lyceum.org.uk; ✆ **0131/248-4848**), produces a strong program of work from major and establishing playwrights. While the **Traverse Theatre,** Cambridge St. (www.traverse.co.uk; ✆ **0131/228-1404**), is funded to present new work by contemporary Scottish writers and the **Scottish Story Telling Centre,** 43 High St. (www.scottishstorytellingcentre.co.uk; ✆ **0131/556-9579**), presents a regular program of storytelling and music events in its small performance space.

BALLET, OPERA & CLASSICAL MUSIC

Performances by the **Scottish Ballet** and the **Scottish Opera** can be enjoyed at the **Edinburgh Playhouse** (see above). The **Scottish Chamber Orchestra** performs at the **Queen's Hall,** Clerk St. (www.thequeenshall.net; ✆ **0131/668-2019**). Edinburgh's other major music venue is the **Usher Hall,** Lothian Rd. (www.usher hall.co.uk; ✆ **0131/228-1155**), which presents mainly classical concerts but also some jazz and rock and pop.

FOLK MUSIC & CEILIDHS

Folk music is performed in a number of pubs around the city such as **Sandy Bells** (✆ **0131/2252-751**), 25 Forrest Road. Some hotels regularly feature traditional Scottish music in the evenings, including **King James Hotel,** 107 Leith St. (www.

EDINBURGH'S WORLD-famous FESTIVALS

August is the jewel in the crown of Edinburgh's year, and throughout this month the city is transformed by a clutch of world-class festivals celebrating theater, music, opera, dance, comedy, street theater, literature, art, politics, and diversity to name but a few. This can be a confusing time, as many people think there is just one festival taking place when in fact there are many, and navigating your way through the increasing number of brochures and websites promoting the literally thousands of events that take place during this period can be mind boggling for the first-time visitor.

The festival that started it all is the **Edinburgh International Festival** (www.eif.co.uk; ☎ **0131/473-2000**) which has been running since 1947 and brings internationally renowned performers from across the world of theater, opera, music, and dance to the city's prominent venues. You can get information from the festival's offices and box office at **The Hub,** an old church on Castle Hill at the junction between the Royal Mile and Johnston Terrace which is open daily year round.

The **Edinburgh Festival Fringe** (www.edfringe.com; ☎ **0131/226-0026**) commonly known as "the Fringe," was created alongside the International Festival in 1947 as an opportunity for anybody—professional or amateur—to put on a show wherever they can find an empty stage or street corner. The Fringe has grown to become the biggest arts festival in the world and is an outpouring of creativity from around the world, encompassing street performers, comedy, offbeat theater, late-night cabaret, and much more. The Fringe's box office and shop is located on 180 High St. (the Royal Mile).

One of the most exciting August spectacles is the **Royal Edinburgh Military Tattoo** (www.edintattoo.co.uk; ☎ **0131/225-1188**), which takes place over 3 weeks every night except Sundays on the floodlit esplanade in front of Edinburgh Castle. First performed in 1950, the Tattoo features the precision marching of the Massed Band of Her Majesty's Royal Marines and other regiments from around the world, along with Highland dancing, motorcycle displays, the heart-stirring massed pipes and drums bands, all concluding by the poignant spectacle of the Lone Piper playing high up on the castle ramparts. The Tattoo Office and Shop is at 32 Market Street behind Waverley station.

The other major festivals that take place during August include the **Edinburgh International Book Festival** (www.edbookfest.co.uk; ☎ **0845/373-5888**), the **Edinburgh Art Festival** (www.edinburghartfestival.com; ☎ **0131/226-6558**), and the **Edinburgh Comedy Festival** (www.edcomfest.com).

thistle.com; ☎ **0871/376-9016**), whose **Jamie's Scottish Evening** is presented daily at 7pm from April to October and includes dinner and a show. Also look out for information on the **Scots Music Group** (www.scotsmusic.org; ☎ **0131/555-7668**) who organize regular ceilidhs in the city.

PUBS & BARS

The historic **Café Royal,** 19 W. Register St. (www.caferoyal.org.uk; ☎ **0131/556-4124**), opened the doors of its present location in 1863 and is one of Edinburgh's most famous bars. All the opulent trappings of the Victorian era are still in place and the Café Royal is also renowned for its opulent oyster bar.

The Bow Bar, 80 West Bow, Victoria St. (℅ **0131/226-7667**), is a long-established bar in the heart of Old Town and a firm favorite with locals. Choose from a selection of real ales that are still drawn through tall founts and a suburb selection of single-malt whiskies from virtually every corner of Scotland.

For anyone wanting to glean a sense of fine old Edinburgh pubs, the **Kenilworth,** 152–154 Rose St. (℅ **0131/226-1773**), is a must. This glorious old establishment is characterized by an old-fashioned central bar and shines with wood and brass and cozy nooks. While **The Queens Arms,** 49 Fredrick St. (www.queensarmsedinburgh. com; ℅ **0131/225-1045**), is a relatively new pub that has all the feel of an establishment that's been around for a long time. There's a good mix of tradition and gleaming new, and drinks include a fine selection of wines, whiskies (including a Japanese whisky), ales, and cocktails.

Where to Stay

Edinburgh boasts a dizzying choice of accommodation from iconic opulent hotels to a plethora of inexpensive hostels and seemingly limitless guesthouses. At the luxury end of the market bold new boutique hotels rub shoulders with more traditional, long-established options. The majority of Edinburgh's hotels are gathered in New Town and within easy walking distance of the city's main attractions and nightlife. Old Town is popular with hostelling students but is also home to some of Edinburgh's more unusual luxury hotels. Many of the city's guesthouses and B&Bs are to be found south of Old Town around Edinburgh University and to the west of New Town around Haymarket train station. All vary in quality and cost, and many are within walking distance of the city center.

NEW TOWN
Very Expensive
Balmoral Hotel ★★★ When this legendary hotel opened in 1902 it was the grandest in northern Britain and today it remains top of the luxury options for those seeking a traditional Scottish experience. The Balmoral commands the east end of Princes Street and is famous for its soaring clock tower, one of Edinburgh's landmarks. The sophisticated rooms and suites are influenced by Scottish heritage and incorporate generous-size marble-finished bathrooms. Dining options include the opulent **number one** (see p. 839) and the more convivial brasserie **Hadrian's.** Piano-accompanied afternoon tea is served in the **Palm Court,** which in the

---

FESTIVAL accommodation

Throughout August and early September when Edinburgh's festivals (see box p. 844) are in full swing, demand and rates for accommodation in the city both increase dramatically. If you're planning to stay in Edinburgh at this time it pays to shop around and book well in advance. Many visitors choose to rent an apartment during the festival period as it often makes economic sense and a large number of festival lets are available to choose from. Companies dealing with festival rentals include: **Edinburgh Festival Rentals** (www.edinburghfestival rentals.com; ℅ **0131/221-1646**), **Festival Flats** (www.festivalflat.net; ℅ **01620/810-620**), and **The Festival Partnership** (http://edinburghfestival.net; ℅ **0131/478-1294**).

evenings is a choice spot for a glass of chilled champagne. The exclusive **Balmoral Spa** is one of Scotland's best urban spas.

1 Princes St., EH2 2EQ. www.thebalmoralhotel.com. ✆ **0131/556-2414.** Fax 0131/557-3747. 188 units. £165–£514 double; from £395 suite. AE, DC, MC, V. Valet parking £25 per overnight. **Amenities:** 2 restaurants; 2 bars; indoor pool; health club; spa; concierge; room service. *In room:* A/C, TV, hairdryer, Wi-Fi (£15 per day).

The Chester Residence ★★★ ☺

Tucked away in a quiet corner of the West End, the Chester Residence is a collection of well-appointed suites spread over four immaculate Georgian town houses and offers an appealing combination of an apartment of your own, alongside all the services you'd expect of a five-star hotel. These award-winning suites all come with well-equipped kitchens and sitting rooms and are fully decked out with modern technology. Mews suites also have their own private gardens, while the roof-top penthouses claim magnificent views. The main reception area includes a swish bar and the many services that can be arranged for guests include in-room dining and spa treatments.

9 Rothesay Place, EH3 7SL. www.chester-residence.com. ✆ **0131/226-2075.** Fax 0131/226-2191. 23 units. £155–£1,100 suite. AE, MC, V. Parking £25 for 24 hours. **Amenities:** Bar; concierge; room service; babysitting. *In room:* TV/DVD, kitchens, hairdryer, iPod docking station, Wi-Fi (free).

The George ★★

The George commands a prime and prominent spot near St. Andrew Square and is a cocoon of elegant luxury in the heart of an area busy with shops and restaurants. Designed by famed architect Robert Adam, The George opened in 1755, was transformed into a hotel in 1972, and has recently emerged from a £20-million restoration looking better than ever. Public areas ooze all the style and gentility of a country house, while the various-size bedrooms, which have undergone frequent refurbishments, have a distinctly more modern feel—the best units are those with views and the quietest are those at the back of the hotel. The **Tempus** restaurant and bar epitomizes New Town at its most chic.

19–21 George St., EH2 2PB. www.principal-hayley.com. ✆ **0131/225-1251.** Fax 0131/226-5644. 249 units. £110–£365 double; £210–£500 suite. AE, DC, MC, V. **Amenities:** Restaurant; bar; concierge; babysitting. *In room:* A/C, TV, minibar, hairdryer, Wi-Fi (free).

Sheraton Grand Hotel ★★

A six-story modern hotel and oasis of glamour in the heart of Edinburgh's West End. Set back from the busy Lothian Road at the far end of Festival Square, this sumptuous hotel welcomes guests into soaring public rooms, while the guest rooms and suites exude comfort, style, and mood lighting. The castle-view rooms on the top three floors are the best. A roof-top hydro pool is the star of the hotel's leisure facilities and dining options include **One Square** and **One Spa Café.**

1 Festival Sq., EH3 9SR. www.sheraton.com. ✆ **0131/229-9131.** Fax 0131/228-4510. 269 units. £145–£275 double; £285–£500 suite. AE, DC, MC, V. **Amenities:** 2 restaurants; 2 bars; 2 pools (indoor/outdoor); health club and spa; concierge; room service; babysitting. *In room:* A/C, TV, minibar, hairdryer, Wi-Fi (£10).

21212 ★★★

Occupying a prime elevated spot on Edinburgh's Royal Terrace, this elegantly restored listed town house offers four sumptuously large bedrooms each of which is a haven of intimate luxury. The individually designed rooms include lounge areas, bathrooms designed to relax in, and uninterrupted views. Memorable breakfasts are served in a cozy "pod" overlooked by a large Caravaggio mural, and with views out over the Firth of Forth. Modern French cuisine is served in the Michelin-starred restaurant (see p. 839).

3 Royal Terrace, EH7 5AB. www.21212restaurant.co.uk. © **0845/222-1212.** 4 units. £175–£325. AE, DC, MC, V. Offsite car parking £1.20 per hour. **Amenities:** Restaurant. *In room:* TV, hairdryer, radio, iPod docking station, Wi-Fi (free).

Expensive

Macdonald Roxburghe Hotel ★   Overlooking the large, neoclassical, tree-lined Charlotte Square, the Roxburghe oozes understated tradition and is well placed for the shops along Princes and George Streets, Edinburgh's theaters, and Old Town. Recent refurbishment has remained faithful to the hotel's Georgian architecture and modern luxuries blend seamlessly with a period feel in the guestrooms. The largest rooms are in the original building and maintain original features such as imposing fireplaces. The **Melrose** restaurant overlooks Charlotte Square and sources many ingredients from Scottish suppliers.

38 Charlotte St., EH2 4HQ. www.macdonaldhotels.co.uk. © **0844/879-9063.** Fax 0131/240-5555. 198 units. £106–£300 double; £209–£450 suites. AE, DC, MC, V. **Amenities:** Restaurant; bar; indoor pool; exercise room; spa; concierge; room service. *In room:* TV, minibar, hairdryer, Wi-Fi (£10 per day).

Tigerlily ★★   One of the coolest Edinburgh hotels, Tigerlily has swiftly built a reputation as the best boutique hotel in town. Lavish comfort, contemporary fabrics, polished wooden floors, and bold colors epitomize the spacious rooms and suites, which are all topped off with modern facilities such as flat-screen TVs and pre-loaded iPods. Suites come complete with modern fireplaces and en-suite wet rooms with extra large baths. The on-site restaurant and bar is extremely popular and contemporary Scottish food alongside a menu of cocktails is served in a maze of individually decorated areas all exuding a different atmosphere and style.

125 George St., EH2 4JN. www.tigerlilyedinburgh.co.uk. © **0131/225-5005.** 33 units. £135–£220 double; £280–£435 suites. AE, MC, V. **Amenities:** Restaurant; bar; room service. *In room:* TV/DVD, hairdryer, iPod docking station, DVD library, Wi-Fi (free).

OLD TOWN
Very Expensive

Hotel Missoni ★★★   Hugging a prime Old Town spot at the corner of George IV Bridge and the Royal Mile, this hotel is the epitome of style, having been developed in collaboration with the renowned Missoni fashion dynasty in Italy. With its distinctive yet minimalist design, Missoni blends fashion with function, form with design, and is one of the most exclusive places to stay in Edinburgh. This cool and contemporary hotel is spread over six floors and many of the fabulously chic bedrooms and suites open onto the panoramic views of the city and come complete with designer bathrooms. Missoni's **Cucina** restaurant is a feast of light, geometric design, specialty Italian food, and fine wine.

1 George IV Bridge, EH1 1AD. www.hotelmissoni.com. © **0131/220-6666.** Fax 0131/226-6660. 136 units. £90–£350 double; £400–£1,000 suite. AE, MC, V. **Amenities:** Restaurant; bar; exercise room; concierge; room service. *In room:* A/C, TV, coffee machine, minibar, hairdryer, iPod docking station, Wi-Fi (free).

The Scotsman ★★★   Standing proud on North Bridge, The Scotsman is one of Edinburgh's most iconic luxury hotels. Traditional styling and cutting-edge design are harmoniously wed in the spacious bedrooms, all of which, with names like Editor or

Publisher's Suite, remain faithful to the building's history. They include state-of-the-art bathrooms and The Scotsman's lower levels house a well-equipped modern gym which occupies the space where printing presses once steamed out the latest news.

20 N. Bridge, EH1 1DF. www.thescotsmanhotel.co.uk. ☏ **0131/556-5565.** Fax 0131/652-3652. 68 units. £100–£490 double; £265–bp]550 suite. AE, DC, MC, V. **Amenities:** Restaurant; bar; indoor pool; gym; spa room service; babysitting. *In room:* TV/DVD, minibar, hairdryer, Wi-Fi (free).

Expensive

Fraser Suites ★★   One of the plethora of new and luxurious accommodations that have sprung up in Edinburgh over recent years, Fraser Suites is a complex of boutique rooms and suites that offers visitors space, style, and location, location, location. All rooms have the added advantage of kitchenettes with fridges and microwaves and larger rooms contain full-blown kitchen and dining areas, while super-size suites come with stunning views and walk-in wardrobes.

12–26 St Giles St., EH1 1PT. http://edinburgh.frasershospitality.com. ☏ **0131/221-7200.** Fax 0131/221-7201. 75 units. £90–£176 double; £206–£311 suite. AE, MC, V. **Amenities:** Restaurant; bar; exercise room; concierge; room service. *In room:* TV, kitchenette, hairdryer, iPod docking station, Wi-Fi (free).

Hotel du Vin ★★   This enticing boutique hotel, occupying the site of a former lunatic asylum, is conveniently close to the heart of all the action during festival time. Richly styled rooms are embellished with added elements such as monsoon showers and luxurious Egyptian cotton sheets. Eating and drinking facilities are top rate and include the French-style **Bistro du Vin** and outdoor terrace seating in summer. There's even a cigar shack, a whisky "snug" (cozy bar), and a tasting room where you can sample wine from some of the world's finest vineyards.

11 Bristo Place, EH1 1EZ. www.hotelduvin.com. ☏ **0131/247-4900.** Fax 0131/247-4901. 47 units. £100–£320 double; £210–£445 suite. AE, MC, V. **Amenities:** Restaurant; bar; room service. *In room:* A/C, TV/DVD, hairdryer, Wi-Fi (free).

Holyrood Hotel ★★   Holyrood is an impressive and exceedingly stylish, modern hotel in the shadow of the Palace of Holyroodhouse. Bedrooms come with marble en-suite bathrooms, while suites with their extra space are a good choice for families. Excellent dining and leisure facilities include a piano lounge, spa, and health club. This end of the Royal Mile has spruced itself up dramatically over recent years and the arrival of the Scottish Parliament and Our Dynamic Earth has attracted new restaurants and cafes to the area.

81 Holyrood Rd., EH8 8AU. www.macdonaldhotels.co.uk/holyrood. ☏ **0131/550-4500.** Fax 0131/550-4545. 156 units. £75–£270 double; suites from £200. AE, MC, V. **Amenities:** Restaurant; bar; pool (indoor); health club w/sauna; room service. *In room:* A/C, TV, hairdryer, Wi-Fi (£9 per hr.).

Moderate

Apex International Hotel ★ ☺   A modern European-styled hotel on the edge of Grassmarket, the Apex is an appealing combination of central location, mod cons, and good facilities. Rooms at the front have wide views over the hustle of Grassmarket and Edinburgh Castle and larger rooms come with added extras such as a fridge and bathrobes. **Yu Time,** the Japanese-influenced leisure facilities, include a sleek stainless steel ozone pool and tropicarium, and the roof-top **Heights** restaurant is a spectacular spot to indulge in some fine Scottish cuisine. A second Apex is situated practically next door and other hotels in this small chain are also located on Waterloo

Place in New Town and on Haymarket Terrace close to the train station. Children can stay and eat for free as long as they are sharing a room with two adults.

31–35 Grassmarket, EH1 2HS. www.apexhotels.co.uk. © **0845/365-0000.** Fax 0871/221-1353. 169 units. £80–£230 double. AE, DC, MC, V. **Amenities:** Restaurant; bar; pool (indoor); exercise room; spa; room service. *In room:* TV, hairdryer, Wi-Fi (free).

Point Hotel   This modern hotel, in the shadow of Edinburgh Castle, is a surprising moderate option in the heart of the city. The minimalist decor emphasizes color and innovation and the bedrooms are spacious and attractively furnished (premium units are more comfortable and roomier than standard units). The hotel's bistro-style restaurant serves international cuisine with a focus on Scottish seafood and meats and the **Monbooddo** bar is a relaxing spot for a cocktail.

34 Bread St., EH3 9AF. www.pointhoteledinburgh.co.uk. © **0131/221-5555.** Fax 0131/221-9929. 139 units. £80–£160 double. AE, DC, MC, V. **Amenities:** Restaurant; bar; room service. *In room:* TV, hairdryer, Wi-Fi (£15 per day).

SOUTH OF OLD TOWN

23 Mayfield ★★ ☺ 👔   23 Mayfield combines comfort with tradition and first class service with award-winning breakfasts. Bedrooms are decorated in a Tudor style; the highlights are the Jacobean Rooms complete with four-poster beds. Modern luxuries include music systems with surround sound, mood lighting, rain-drop showers, and Scottish sea kelp toiletries and the top-floor family room features a Nintendo Wii and telescope for peering into the night sky. In the evening guests can relax into deep couches in the book-lined drawing room. The owners can also organize bike hire, complete with packed lunches and backpacks.

23 Mayfield Gardens, EH7 2BX. www.23mayfield.co.uk. © **0131/667-5806.** Fax 0131/667-6833. 9 units. £50–£80 per person per night. MC, V. **Amenities:** Breakfast room. *In room:* TV, hairdryer, music system, Wi-Fi (free).

LEITH

Malmaison ★★   This stylish boutique hotel perched on the edge of Leith's old harbor is a good choice for those wanting a slice of luxury outside the bustle of the city center, plus an array of fine dining options on the doorstep. Like all buildings in Leith, Malmaison has history. This baronial-style Victorian building complete with a stately stone clock tower served as a seamen's mission before being converted to a swish hotel in the mid-90s. Malmaison is hip and unpretentious, boasting a minimalist decor and low-key elegance. Rooms are individually designed and well equipped and suites come complete with tartan roll top baths and views over the Firth of Forth. The facilities include a **Brasserie,** a cafe and wine bar favored by locals, and state-of-the-art gym.

1 Tower Place, Leith, EH6 7DB. www.malmaison.com. © **0131/468-5000.** Fax 0131/468-5002. 100 units. £70–£285 double; £200–£370suite. AE, DC, MC, V. Free parking. Bus: 16 or 35. **Amenities:** Restaurant; bar; health club. *In room:* TV, hairdryer, minibar, CD player/music library, Wi-Fi (free).

Side Trips from Edinburgh

STIRLING

Standing on the main east–west route across Scotland, Stirling is an ancient settlement and is often described as "the brooch which clasps the Highlands and Lowlands together." Its central location ensured Stirling's strategic importance for anyone wanting to rule Scotland and the city's history is bloody and turbulent—freedom fighter William Wallace won a decisive victory over England here in 1297. Find out more about this Scottish national hero, known to many through Mel Gibson's film *Braveheart,* at the **National Wallace Monument** (www.nationalwallacemonument.com; ℂ **01786/472-140**) which stands on Abbey Craig, 2½ km (1½ miles) north of Stirling. Exhibits include Wallace's mighty sword. The monument opens daily November to March 10.30am to 4pm, April to June and September to October 10am to 5pm and July and August 10am to 6pm. Admission is £8.25 for adults, £5.25 for children.

Any visit to Stirling should concentrate on its Old Town, the city's ancient center, which straddles a steep rocky outcrop and is crowned with the imposing **Stirling Castle,** Upper Castle Hill ★★ (www.stirlingcastle.gov.uk; ℂ **01786/450-000**). One of Scotland's most imposing and impregnable historical sites, Stirling Castle dates from the Middle Ages and commands sweeping views over the surrounding countryside. The castle was an important seat for Scotland's late medieval monarchs and home of Mary, Queen of Scots, for the early years of her life. The 16th-century **Royal Palace** ★★ forms the castle's centerpiece and remains one of the finest examples of Renaissance architecture in Britain. The castle opens daily April to September 9.30am to 6pm and October to March 9.30am to 5pm. Admission is £13 for adults and £6.50 for children. Other historical highlights in the Old Town include **Old Town Jail** (www.oldtownjail.com; ℂ **01786/450-050**), where the harsh squalor of 19th-century justice is revealed in all its grim glory, and the **Church of the Holy Rude** ★ (http://holyrude.org; ℂ **01786/475-275**), which was founded in the 12th century and hosted James VI of Scotland's (later James I of England's) coronation in 1567. However, to get a real feel for Stirling's past and present, stroll along the **Back Walk,** which leads along the 16th-century **city walls** from the castle, past an old watchtower and down into the modern town center.

GETTING THERE Stirling is 60km (37 miles) northwest of Edinburgh and less than an hour's drive away along the M9. Frequent direct trains run between Edinburgh and Stirling. The journey takes 50 minutes and a day return ticket costs £13.30 adults, £9 children.

NORTH BERWICK

This royal burgh dating from the 14th century is an upmarket holiday resort on the edge of the Firth of Forth, 39km (24 miles) east of Edinburgh and the place where city residents head when the sun shines. Visitors are drawn here for the golf and wide, open beaches with views of **Bass Rock**—a steep-sided plug of volcanic rock just offshore that once served a prison and today is the breeding ground of about 10,000 gannets. The gannets return from Africa in the spring, usually around April, to nest here until fall. You can discover more about these birds and others along this coastline at the **Scottish Seabird Centre** ★ ☺ (www.seabird.org; ℂ **01620/890-202**), which sits at the center of North Berwick's harbor. Here you can also spy on dolphins and seals in the surrounding waters and take a boat trip to Bass Rock. The center opens daily year round from 10am to 6pm in the summer and between 4pm and 5.30pm in winter. Admission costs £8 for adults and £5 for children aged 4–15. Boat trips to Bass Rock run from March to October and cost extra.

GETTING THERE North Berwick is a 30-minute drive from Edinburgh along the A198. Direct trains run between the two destinations roughly every 30 minutes. The journey takes half an hour and a day return ticket costs £7 adults, £3.50 children.

GLASGOW ★★

Glasgow is just 75km (47 miles) west of Edinburgh, but the contrast between the two cities is striking. Scotland's largest city (Britain's third-largest), and home to much of its population, Glasgow's origins are far older than Edinburgh's. The city began life as a medieval ecclesiastical center in the area that is now Glasgow's East End. Sprawling ever larger around the banks of the River Clyde as city merchants grew rich on transatlantic trade in tobacco, then cotton in the 18th and 19th centuries, Glasgow was once famous for its formidable ship-building industry. Fueled by this success, the city's planners at this time designed on a grand scale and many hail Glasgow as "the greatest surviving example of a Victorian city." From the embers of an industrial past that shaped the British Empire, the ever resourceful Glasgow forged a new identity in the latter years of the 20th century and now stands proud as one of Europe's most vibrant cultural capitals.

Essentials

GETTING THERE

BY PLANE **Glasgow Airport** is at Abbotsinch (www.glasgowairport.com; ℂ **0870/ 040-0008**), 16km (10 miles) west of the city via the M8 and receives flights from London Heathrow and Gatwick and various other U.K. airports, plus a number of U.S. destinations. **First** (www.firstgroup.com; ℂ **0141/423-6600**) operates service 500, a shuttle bus between the airport and Glasgow city center. This 24-hour service runs up to every 10 minutes; the ride takes 25 minutes and costs £5 adult, £3 children for a single fare, or £7.50 adults, £5.50 children, return fare.

Glasgow's second airport, **Prestwick** (www.glasgowprestwick.com; ℂ **0871/223-0700**), receives flights from destinations across Europe and stands on the Ayrshire coast 53km (33 miles) southwest of the city center. This airport is connected with Glasgow by **ScotRail** trains from Central Station (www.scotrail.co.uk; ℂ **0845/601-5929**) and the X77 **Stagecoach** bus (www.stagecoachbus.com; ℂ **01292/613-500**) from Buchanan Street bus station.

BY TRAIN Glasgow's main train station is **Central Station** on Gordon Street. **Virgin Trains** (www.virgintrains.co.uk; ℂ **08719/744-222**) operates a regular service between London Euston and Glasgow Central. The journey time is approximately 4½ hours and an advance single costs between £65 and £150. You can also travel from London King's Cross on some **East Coast** (www.eastcoast.co.uk; ℂ **08457/225-111**) trains via Edinburgh. The journey is an hour longer and a single fare is between £40 and £135. **Scotrail** (www.scotrail.co.uk: ℂ **0845/601-5929**) operates the Caledonian Sleeper service to London, with single fares costing around £94. Central Station also serves southern Scotland. Glasgow's **Queen Street Station** stands on the north side of George Square and serves the north and east of Scotland, with trains arriving from and departing to Edinburgh every 15 minutes throughout the day until 11.30pm. The journey between the two cities takes 50 minutes and a return fare costs £12 off peak or £21 to travel in peak hours, which are before 9.15am and between 4.30 and 6.30pm. You can also travel to Highland destinations from this station as well as Aberdeen and Stirling.

BY BUS **Buchanan Street Bus Station** is just north of Queen Street Station on Killermont Street. **National Express** (www.nationalexpress.com; ℂ **08717/818-178**) operates a regular service from London's Victoria coach station. Coaches take

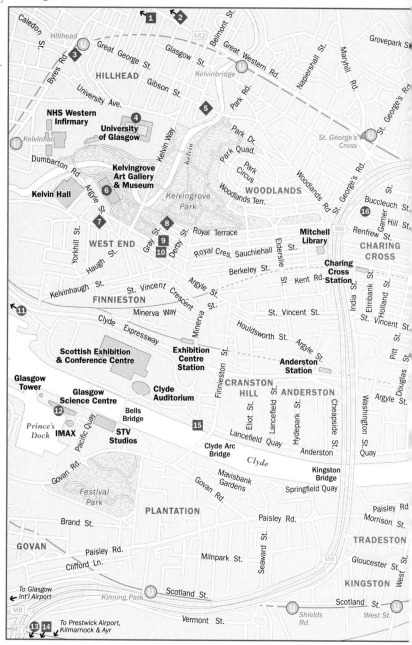

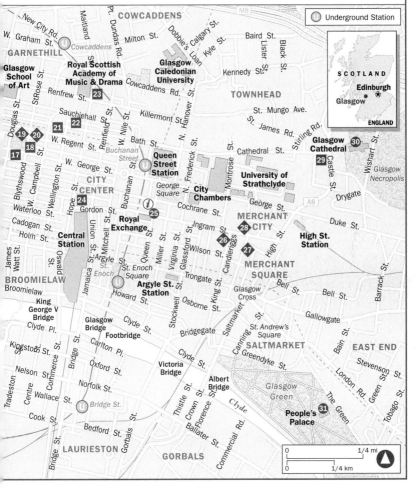

between 8½ and 11 hours to reach Glasgow, depending on the number of stops and a single fare is between £15 and £70. **Megabus** (www.megabus.com; ✆ **0871-266-3333**) also operates a coach service between London Victoria and Buchanan Street. The journey takes between 8 and 10 hours and single fares are from £16. **Scottish Citylink** (www.citylink.co.uk; ✆ **08705/505-050**) operates a frequent bus service between Glasgow and Edinburgh, a return ticket costs £10, the journey time is around 1 hour 20 minutes but can be much longer in rush hour.

BY CAR   Glasgow is 75km (47 miles) west of Edinburgh, 348km (216 miles) north of Manchester, and 651km (404 miles) north of London. From England, Glasgow is reached by via the M74, which becomes the A74 as it leads into the city center. From Edinburgh the M8 joins the two cities and travels directly through the heart of Glasgow. Other major routes into the city are the A77 from Prestwick and Ayr, which becomes the M77 as it leads into the city, and the A8 from the west, which becomes the M8 around the port of Glasgow. The A82 leads from the northwest (the Highlands) on the north bank of the Clyde, and from the northeast the M80 joins the M8 east of the city center.

VISITOR INFORMATION

TOURIST OFFICE   The **Greater Glasgow and Clyde Valley Tourist Board,** 11 George Sq. (www.seeglasgow.com; ✆ **0141/204-4400**), is open October through May, Monday to Saturday 9am to 6pm; June through September, Monday to Saturday 9am to 7pm; and also Sundays during April to September, from 10am to 6pm. There is also a Tourist Information desk at Glasgow airport.

CITY LAYOUT

It's hard to identify the center of Glasgow, as the city's focus has shifted west over the centuries from its medieval heart—an area that is now located in the northeast corner of the city. High Street runs south from this ancient area and links it with Glasgow's East End, one of the poorer areas of the city. From the East End, the area west of High Street marks Glasgow's growth away from its medieval roots. From High Street, Ingram Street leads through Merchant City into the monumental heart of modern Glasgow around George Square, which, along with the area west up until the M8 and south to the banks of the River Clyde, is considered to be the center of the modern city.

Glasgow's Victorian **West End** spreads out past the M8 and is easily reachable from the city center via public transport—both buses and subway. Although the River Clyde has played a formative role in Glasgow's development, until recent years there have been few reasons for visitors to seek it out, let alone cross over to its south side. Redevelopment has altered this with modern attractions such as the **Glasgow Science Centre** directly south of the West End drawing tourists to this area. Further south still at around 5km (3 miles) southwest of the city center is the heavily wooded **Pollok Country Park,** home to the **Burrell Collection Gallery.** Both of these areas are well connected with the city center by public transport.

Neighborhoods in Brief

Medieval Glasgow Also referred to as Old Glasgow, this is where St. Mungo arrived in A.D. 543 and built his church in what's now the northeastern part of the city. At the top of High Street stands the **Cathedral of St. Kentigern** and the **Necropolis,** one of Britain's largest Victorian cemeteries. You enter the **Necropolis** by crossing the Bridge of Sighs, styled after the famous bridge of the same name in Venice. Old Glasgow's major terminal is High Street Station. South of the cathedral, **Glasgow Green,** opening onto the River Clyde, has been a public park since 1662. This East End of Glasgow has many interesting attractions that are fine to explore in daylight hours, but this is not a region to walk through alone at night.

Along the River Clyde It was once said that "The Clyde made Glasgow; Glasgow made the Clyde." Although the city is no longer dependent on the river, you can still enjoy a stroll along the **Clyde Walkway ★**, which stretches from King Albert Bridge, at the western end of Glasgow Green, for 3km (1¾ miles) downstream to Stobcross, now the site of the **Scottish Exhibition and Conference Centre.** This is one of the city's grandest walks; on these waters, Glasgow once shipped its manufactured goods around the world.

The Merchant City Glasgow spread west of High Street in the 18th century, largely because of profits made from sugar, cotton, and tobacco in trade with the Americas. The Merchant City extends from Trongate and Argyle Street in the south to George Street in the north. Its major terminal is Queen Street Station and it boasts some of

Britain's most **elegant Georgian and Victorian buildings,** as well as **Greek Revival churches.** Tobacco barons once occupied much of the area, but their buildings have been recycled for other uses.

Glasgow Center Continuing its western progression, the city center of Glasgow is dominated by George Square and Central Station. This is the major shopping district, including such venues as Buchanan Galleries. Also here are many of Glasgow's major theaters and other entertainment venues, as well as Buchanan Street Bus Station.

The West End Beyond the M8 lies the West End home to the University of Glasgow and several major galleries and museums, most of which gather around **Kelvingrove Park.** The West End mixes culture, art, and parks, and is dominated by university students. Also in the West are the city's **Botanic Gardens.**

The South Side The area south of the River Clyde to the west of the center is growing in popularity thanks to new attractions such as the Glasgow Science Center and old-time favorites including the Burrell Collection.

GETTING AROUND

The best way to explore the center of Glasgow is on foot. Its grid system makes getting around a logical process, but there are in places some punishingly steep streets to navigate. That said, most of the city's attractions are outside of the center and to see those you need to rely on public transport.

BY BUS Glasgow is serviced by **First** buses (www.firstgroup.com; ℂ **0141/423-6600**). Services run frequently throughout the day, but are greatly curtailed after 11pm. Schedules can be picked up at **Buchanan Street Bus Station** on Killermont Street or downloaded from the Glasgow section of First's website. Single fares cost £1.85 and exact change is required. Alternatively, day passes cost £4.50 for adults and £2 for children.

BY UNDERGROUND Called the "Clockwork Orange" (from the vivid orange of the trains), Glasgow's subway is a fast and efficient way for traveling around the city. The circular route contains 15 stops and trains run every 5–12 minutes, including on Sunday. The service operates Monday to Saturday 6:30am to 11.30pm and Sunday 10am to 6pm. Tickets can be bought at any subway station and the fare for a single journey is £1.20 adults, 60p children, or a day **Discovery Ticket** costs £3.50. Full information on public transport can be obtained at the information desk at Buchanan bus station or the **Travel Centre** at St. Enoch Square subway station (www.spt.co.uk/subway; ℂ **0141/333-3708**) which is open Monday to Saturday 8:30am to 5:30pm.

BY TAXI   Taxis in Glasgow are excellent. You can hail them on the street or call **Glasgow Taxis** (www.glasgowtaxis.co.uk; ✆ **0141/429-7070**). Fares are displayed on a meter next to the driver. Most taxi trips within the city cost £5 to £9. The taxi meter starts at £2 and increases by 25p every 261m (856 ft.). A £2 surcharge is imposed midnight to 6am.

BY CAR   Driving around Glasgow is a tricky business, even for locals. You're better off with public transport. The city is a warren of one-way streets, and parking is expensive and difficult to find. Metered parking is available; exact change is required. And you must watch out for zealous traffic wardens issuing tickets. Some zones are marked PERMIT HOLDERS ONLY—your vehicle will be towed if you have no permit. A yellow line along the curb indicates no parking. Multistory car parks (parking lots), open 24-hours a day, are found at Anderston Cross, Cambridge, George, Mitchell, Oswald, and Waterloo streets.

   If you want to rent a car to explore the countryside, it's best to do so before leaving home. But if you want to rent a car locally, most companies will accept your American or Canadian driver's license. All the major rental agencies are represented at Glasgow airport. In addition, **Enterprise** has a branch on Oswald Street (www.enterprise. co.uk; ✆ **0141/221-2124**), which is close to Central Station, and further west there is a branch of **Avis** at 70 Lancefield St. (www.avis.co.uk; ✆ **0844/581-0147**).

BY BICYCLE   Parts of Glasgow are fine for biking, and you might want to rent a bike to explore the surrounding countryside. Bikes can be hired at **Gear of Glasgow**, 19 Gibson Street in the West End (http://gearbikes.com; ✆ **0141/339-1179**). Rates range from £10 for a half day, £15 for a full day, to £60 for a week and a driver's license or passport must be left as a deposit. Bikes come with a lock and panniers can be hired for an extra £5 and car racks for £5–£20. The store opens daily 10am to 6pm and Sunday noon until 5pm.

[Fast FACTS] GLASGOW

Business Hours   Most **offices** and **banks** are open Monday to Friday 9am to 5pm; some banks also open on Saturday until lunchtime. **Shops** are generally open Monday to Saturday 10am to 6pm. On Thursday, stores remain open until 8pm, many also open on Sunday 11am to around 5pm.

Currency Exchange
Most city-center banks operate a *bureau de change*, and nearly all will cash traveler's checks if you have the proper ID. There are also currency exchanges at Glasgow Airport and Central Station.

Dentists   If you have a dental emergency it can be treated at the **Glasgow Dental Hospital & School,** 378 Sauchiehall St. (www. gla.ac.uk/schools/dental; ✆ **0141/232-6323**). It is not a walk-in facility and appointments need to be made by telephone first. Hours are Monday to Friday 8.30am to 5.15pm. Out of hours, call **NHS 24** ✆ **08454/242-424**.

Doctors & Hospitals
Glasgow's major hospital is the **Royal Infirmary,** 82–86 Castle St. (✆ **0141/211-4000**). This and the Western

Infirmary, on Dumbarton Road (✆ 0141/211-2000), both have Accident & Emergency Departments. For medical advice at any time call **NHS 24** ✆ **08454/242-424.**

Emergencies   Call ✆ **999** in an emergency to summon the police, an ambulance, or firefighters.

Internet Access   You can get online at the **iCafe** on Great Western Road (www.icafe.uk.com; ✆ **0141/572-0788**). Wi-Fi is free with the purchase of food or coffee; otherwise free Internet access is available at the Mitchell Library on North Street.

Pharmacies There are branches of Boots (www. boots.com) in most of the main shopping malls and at 200 Sauchiehall St. (© **0141/ 332-1925**), open Monday to Wednesday, Friday and Saturday 8am to 7pm, Thursday 8am to 8pm, and Sunday 10.30am to 5.30pm.

Post Office The main branch is at 47 St. Vincent St. (© **0845/722-3344**). It's open Monday to Saturday 9.30am to 5.30pm.

Exploring Glasgow

Glasgow's attractions are scattered all around the city. In order to make the most efficient use of time it's useful to think of the city in terms of its different districts and what each has to offer.

CITY CENTER & MERCHANT CITY

Gallery of Modern Art ★★ GALLERY Housed in an elaborate neoclassical building that was built in 1778 as a town house for one of Glasgow's notoriously wealthy tobacco lords, this thoroughly modern gallery makes full use of its elegant interior to showcase the work of the U.K.'s top contemporary artists. Its permanent collection includes pieces by major modern Scots artists such as Douglas Gordon and Ken Currie.

Royal Exchange Sq. www.glasgowlife.org.uk. © **0141/287-3005.** Free admission. Mon–Wed and Sat 10am–5pm, Thurs 10am–8pm, Fri and Sun 11am–5pm. Subway: Buchanan Street or St Enoch.

Tenement House HISTORIC HOME For an insight into Glasgow's working class who lived in the city's many tenements in the early part of the 20th century, head to this authentic 19th-century property. Tenements are small apartments and this one was occupied for 50 years from 1911 by a Miss Agnes Toward. Miss Toward did little to alter her tiny home and kept many household items such as wartime leaflets that most people threw away. Her diligence and unwillingness to alter her surroundings now allows visitors the opportunity to step back in time at this fascinating property.

145 Buccleuch St. www.nts.org.uk. © **0844/493-2197.** Admission £6 adults, £5 seniors and children, £15.50 families. Mar–Oct 1–5pm. Subway: Cowcaddens.

THE EAST END & MEDIEVAL GLASGOW

Glasgow Cathedral ★★★ CATHEDRAL One of Glasgow's most memorable buildings, this early medieval Gothic-style structure dates back to the 12th century and is mainland Scotland's only complete medieval cathedral. Once a place of pilgrimage, before 16th-century zeal purged it of all monuments of idolatry, Glasgow's cathedral is dedicated to St. Mungo (also known as St. Kentigern), whose tomb lies in the **Laigh Kirk** (lower church), a vaulted crypt said to be the finest in Europe. Other highlights include the nave, which dates from the 1400s and is crowned by an open timber roof, and a fine collection of modern stained glass that throws stunning dashes of light across the dark interior.

Cathedral Square, Castle St. www.glasgowcathedral.org.uk. © **0141/552-6891.** Free admission. Apr–Sept Mon–Sat 9:30am–6pm, Sun 1–5.30pm; Oct–Mar Mon–Sat 9:30am–4pm, Sun 1–4pm. Subway: Buchanan Street. Bus: 11, 12, 36, 38, 42, 51, or 56.

CHARLES rennie MACKINTOSH (1868–1928)

The internationally celebrated artist, architect, and designer Charles Rennie Mackintosh was born in Glasgow in 1868. Mackintosh believed that architects and designers should be allowed more artistic freedom and many of his most important buildings can be found in and around the city. The place to start any Mackintosh tour is the **Glasgow School of Art** (www.gsa.ac.uk; ✆ **0141/ 353-4526**) on Renfrew Street, where Mackintosh studied before designing the magnificent building the school is housed in today. Regular tours of the building depart daily and cost £8.75 for adults, £7 for seniors, and £4 for under-18s.

Two very different Mackintosh-designed buildings can be found in the Southside. **House for an Art Lover** (www.houseforanartlover.co.uk; ✆ **0141/353-4770**) in Bellahouston Park on Dumbreck Road was built from designs by Macintosh entered into a competition whose remit was to design "a grand house in a thoroughly modern style." Although admired, his plans did not win and this house wasn't built until after Mackintosh's death. The house opens daily 10am to 4pm, although it sometimes closes for private functions; so call ahead before visiting. Admission costs £4.50 for adults, £3 for seniors and children over 10, under-10s free. Also on the Southside, **Scotland Street School Museum** (www.glasgowlife.org.uk; ✆ **0141/287-0513**) on Scotland Street is

a Mackintosh-designed building that was a school until 1979 and now serves as a museum, which recreates Glasgow school life over the last century and is open Tuesday to Thursday and Saturday 10am to 5pm and Friday and Sunday 11am to 5pm. Admission is free.

There are two further stops on any Mackintosh tour of the city in the West End, most notably **Mackintosh House,** the artist's old Glasgow home adjacent to the **Hunterian Art Gallery** (see p. 859), and the **Kelvingrove Art Gallery & Museum** (see p. 859) which displays samples of Mackintosh's work.

To conclude a tour head back to the city center and take tea at the famed **Willow Tea Rooms** (www.willowtea rooms.co.uk; ✆ **0141/332-0521**) at 217 Sauchiehall Street. When they opened in 1904, the tearooms were a sensation thanks to its Mackintosh design, which has since been restored to its original glory.

A one-day **Macintosh Trail Ticket** is the cheapest way to view all these and Glasgow's other Macintosh properties. Tickets cost £16 per person and include admission to all attractions plus subway or bus travel between them. Tickets can be bought in person at the Tourist Information Centre on George Square (see p. 854), at any of the participating venues, or in advance via the Charles Rennie Mackintosh Society website www.crm society.com.

People's Palace MUSEUM   Housed in a rich sandstone building opposite the grand 19th-century Doulton Fountain, the People's Palace tells the story of both the city of Glasgow and its residents from 1750 to the end of the 20th century. Glimpses into how Glaswegians lived, worked, and played are brought to life via photographs, films, old artifacts, and new interactive computer displays. Most memorable is the adjoining **Winter Gardens,** a large, delicate glasshouse filled with exotic plants and a buzzing cafe.

Glasgow Green. www.glasgowlife.org.uk. ✆ **0141/276-1625.** Free admission. Tues–Thurs and Sat 10am–5pm; Fri and Sun 11am–5pm. Bus: 16, 18, 40, 61, 62, or 263.

THE WEST END

Hunterian Museum & Art Gallery ★★ GALLERY This attraction is divided into two parts. Its museum, which opened in 1807, sits on one side of University Avenue and displays many fascinating items from the private collections of its early benefactor William Hunter, including dinosaur fossils and Viking plunder. Across the avenue is the art gallery, which exhibits 17th- and 18th-century paintings (Rembrandt to Rubens) and 19th- and 20th-century Scottish work and includes **The Macintosh House,** which was once the architect's own home and today contains the Mackintosh Collection, the largest single holding of his work.

University of Glasgow, University Avenue. www.hunterian.gla.ac.uk. ℂ **0141/330-5431** or 0141/330-4221. Free admission to the gallery and museum; admission to Mackintosh House is £3 adults, £2 seniors and children. Mon–Sat 9:30am–5pm. The university is 3km (1¾ miles) west of the city center and the nearest subway station is Hillhead. Subway: Hillhead. Bus: 44.

Kelvingrove Art Gallery & Museum ★★ MUSEUM/GALLERY Hailed as one of Glasgow's landmark attractions, Kelvingrove is one of the U.K.'s most visited museums outside of London. Its 22 themed galleries display around 8,000 objects from its internationally significant collections. Exhibits include sections covering ancient Egypt, 300-million-year-old marine-life fossils, and one of the world's greatest collections of arms and armor. The galleries also contain a superb collection from Dutch and Italian Old Masters, and Scottish painting is well represented from the 17th century to the present. Expect plenty of interactive exhibits to keep young visitors engaged.

Argyle St. www.glasgowlife.org.uk. ℂ **0141/276-9599.** Free admission. Mon–Thurs and Sat 10am–5pm; Fri and Sun 11am–5pm. The Kelvingrove is 3km (1¾ miles) west of the city center and the nearest subway station is Kelvinhall. Subway: Kelvinhall. Bus: 9, 16, 23, 42, or 62.

CLYDESIDE

Glasgow Science Centre ★★★ ☺ PLANETARIUM This modern family-friendly attraction showcases Glasgow's contribution to science and technology over the past, present, and future. The main part of this attraction is its Science Mall, which spreads over three floors and features imaginative and fun interactive exhibits, as well as a changing program of exhibitions. For an extra £2.50 you can tag a **Planetarium** show onto a visit. This site also features an **IMAX cinema** which charges a separate admission of £10 for adults or £8 seniors and children.

50 Pacific Quay. www.gsc.org.uk. ℂ **0141/540-5000.** Admission £10 adults, £8 students and seniors. Daily 10am–5pm. Hours are restricted in the winter, so check in advance. Bus: 23, 24, 89, or 90.

Riverside Museum ★★ MUSEUM Housed in a striking new building on the banks of the Clyde, Glasgow's latest museum displays over 3,000 objects showcasing transport and travel. It incorporates the city's old transport museum and much more besides, and memorable exhibits include a South African locomotive as well as old trams and vintage cars. The last remaining Clyde-built tall ship in the U.K., the SV *Glenlee* (www.thetallship.com; ℂ **0141/222-2513**), is moored beside the museum and its gleaming decks, which include the old captain's cabin, can be explored for an admission fee of £5 adults, £3 children.

100 Pointhouse Place. www.glasgowlife.org.uk. ℂ **0141/287-2720.** Free admission. Mon–Thurs and Sat 10am to 5pm, Fri and Sun 11am to 5pm. Bus: 100.

SOUTHSIDE

The Burrell Collection ★★★ GALLERY/MUSEUM   This museum houses the mind-boggling treasures left to Glasgow by Sir William Burrell, a wealthy ship owner who had a lifelong passion for art. Burrell started collecting art when he was 14, and his passion continued until he died aged 96 in 1958. His tastes were eclectic and here you can see a vast aggregation of furniture, textiles, ceramics, stained glass, silver, art objects, and pictures in the dining room, hall, and drawing room, which were reconstructed from Sir William's home, Hutton Castle at Berwick-upon-Tweed.

Pollok Country Park, 2060 Pollokshaws Rd. www.glasgowlife.org.uk. © **0141/287-2550.** Free admission. Mon–Thurs and Sat 10am–5pm, Fri and Sun 11am–5pm. Pollok Country Park is 5km (3 miles) south of the city center. Bus: 45, 48, or 57.

ORGANIZED TOURS

City Sightseeing Glasgow (www.citysightseeingglasgow.co.uk; © **0141/204-0444**) operates frequent open-top bus tours around the city throughout the year. A complete tour takes about 1¼ hours, but you're free to hop off and on at any of the 15 stops along the way and a ticket is valid for 2 days. Buses depart from stop number one at George Square from 9.30am until 4.30pm and run every 15 minutes from April to October and every 30 minutes from November to March. Tickets can be bought from the driver and cost £11 for adults and £5 for children 5 to 15, or £25 for families.

Where to Eat

Merchant City has developed into a strong focal point for dining out. Here streets such as Candleriggs and Royal Exchange Square are lined with choices of bars, cafes, and restaurants. In the West End, Bryes Road, particularly at the south end near Dumbarton Road and north end close to the Great Western Road, is awash with an array of restaurants serving every kind of cuisine imaginable. Some higher-end restaurants close on Sundays and from 2:30pm until their pre-theater menus kick in around 5.30pm the rest of the week. Reservations are recommended at all the restaurants listed below, especially at weekends.

CITY CENTER

Brian Maule at Chardon d'Or ★★★ FRENCH/SCOTTISH   Ayr-born Brian Maule is one of Scotland's finest chefs. After a stint as head chef of Le Gavroche, one of London's best restaurants, he brought his culinary skill and finesse back to his native turf. Maule's cuisine is prepared with passion, commitment, and the best Scottish produce and each dish is a creation of his own original style. The menu changes every few days and starters include such delights as pan-fried scallops with spaetzel and prawn, and squid ink lasagna, while light full-flavored, inventive main courses feature the likes of roast lamb filet with aubergine caviar. Leave room for sumptuous desserts, which could include homemade ice cream or tarte tatin of apple, or simply round off the night with a selection of French and Scottish cheeses. There is also an excellent vegetarian menu.

176 W. Regent St. www.brianmaule.com. © **0141/248-3801.** Main courses (dinner only) £22–£28. Lunch and pre-theater set menu £17.50 for 2 courses, £20.50 for 3 courses. AE, MC, V. Mon–Fri noon–2.30pm and 5–10pm, Sat noon–11pm. Subway: Cowcaddens. Bus: 16, 57, 42, or 44.

Two Fat Ladies City Centre ★ MODERN SCOTTISH/SEAFOOD   This intimate charmer of a restaurant, like the other three restaurants in this small chain, is known for exceptional customer service and suburb seafood. The first Two Fat Ladies restaurant sits at 88 Dumbarton Road in the West End—two fat ladies is the nickname for the number 88 in bingo and there is no connection to the "Two Fat Ladies" of TV Food Network fame. This city-center branch is popular with business folk at lunchtime, but the ambience changes after dark and gains a more romantic feel. Seafood takes pride of place on the menu, but there are some meat dishes on offer such as filet of Scotch beef with bourguignon sauce.

118a Blythswood St. www.twofatladiesrestaurant.com. ℭ **0141/847-0088.** Main courses (dinner only) £19–£25. Lunch and pre-theater set menu £16 for 2 courses; £18 for 3 courses. MC, V. Mon–Sat noon–3pm and 5:30–10:30pm, Sun 1pm–9pm. Subway: Cowcaddens. Bus: 16, 57, 42, or 44.

MERCHANT CITY

Cafe Gandolfi ☺ SCOTTISH/FRENCH   This cafe is many people's favorite in the city. Resembling a Victorian pub, it boasts rustic wooden floors, benches, and stools and if you don't fill up on breakfast dishes like eggs Hebridean with Stornoway black pudding, then head straight for the main menu, which caters very well for vegetarians and also includes meat dishes such as meatloaf served with sweet potato mash. The amiable atmosphere and willingness to create smaller portions for children make this a good family choice. **Bar Gandolfi** occupies the attic space above the cafe and is a stylish spot to sample some of the many wines on offer, while farther along Albion Street, **Gandolfi Fish** is the newest addition to this chain and specializes in serving sustainably sourced Scottish seafood.

64 Albion St. www.cafegandolfi.com. ℭ **0141/552-6813.** Main courses £7.50–£16. MC, V. Mon–Sat 8am–11.30pm, Sun 9am–11.30pm. Subway: St Enoch. Bus: 16, 19, 39, 40, 61, or 62.

City Merchant SCOTTISH   This cozy restaurant offers friendly service and a strong menu of Scottish flavors. Food is fresh, well prepared, and reasonably priced. Seafood choices come from both coastal waters and river and you can expect to choose from Shetland salmon and west-coast shellfish. Meats are similarly sourced across Scotland; sample a starter of Highland game terrine followed by a pan-seared loin of venison. Top off a Scottish-themed dinner with a traditional *clootie* dumpling, made with flour, spices, and dried fruit and served with custard.

97–99 Candleriggs. www.citymerchant.co.uk. ℭ **0141/553-1577.** Main courses (dinner only) £18–£28. Lunch and pre-theater set menu £12.50 for 2 courses; £16 for 3 courses. AE, DC, MC, V. Mon–Sat noon–10.30pm; Sun 4.30–9.30pm. Subway: St Enoch. Bus: 31, 61, 62, 40, or 43.

Ingram Wynd ★ SCOTTISH/CONTINENTAL   A surprisingly refreshing slice of Victorian-style dining in the midst of Merchant City's many trendy restaurants, Ingram Wynd serves mainly traditional Scottish dishes in equally traditional surroundings. Polished wood, leather, and gold-framed mirrors are overlooked by a stuffed stag's head which graces the walls and watches diners linger over haggis-stuffed mushrooms or filet of Scottish salmon, all rounded off with mixed berry shortcake stack. Take time to peruse the local memorabilia adorning the walls, which include old maps and photographs.

58 Ingram St. www.ingramwynd.co.uk. ℭ **0141/553/2470.** Main courses (dinner only) £13–£19; set lunch £11 for 2 courses, £14 for 3 courses. AE, MC, V. Mon–Fri noon–2.30pm and 5pm until late, Sat and Sun noon until late. Bus: 31.

WEST END
Expensive
Ubiquitous Chip ★ SCOTTISH   An old timer of Glasgow's eating out scene— this restaurant opened its doors in 1971—Ubiquitous Chip has championed Scottish produce for over 40 years and still creates inventive dishes with flair and passion. Like

the ambience, the decor is unpretentious and appealingly rustic, characterized by rough-textured stone walls and a glass-covered courtyard with reams of climbing vines and a fish pond. Set menus and cheaper dishes served in the brasserie area include roast Ayrshire chicken breast, lobster fresh from Troon, and Loch Eil mussels, while the main restaurant menus feature mains such as roast Perthshire pigeon breast and Scotch Aberdeen Angus filet.

12 Ashton Lane, off Byres Rd. www.ubiquitouschip.co.uk. © **0141/334-5007.** Main courses (brasserie) £9–£23; set lunch and pre-theater menu £16 for 2 courses, £30 for 3 courses; set dinner £35 for 2 courses, £40 for 3 courses. AE, DC, MC, V. Mon–Sat noon–2:30pm and 5:30–11pm, Sun 12.30–3pm and 5pm–11pm. Subway: Hillhead. Bus: 8, 89, or 90.

Moderate

Cail Bruich ★ SCOTTISH   The award-winning Cail Bruich is a small family-run restaurant close to Glasgow's Botanical Gardens that's swiftly established a strong reputation for refined seasonal Scottish cuisine. Seasonal and fresh prevail on the relatively short but imaginative menu, all served in classical, sophisticated surroundings. Start the evening with melt-in-mouth Loch Duart oak-smoked salmon, before choosing from the likes of North Sea monkfish or Perthshire venison. A selection of British and French cheeses is served on fresh walnut bread, and desserts of glazed lemon tart or Comice pear tatin will leave a final zing in your mouth.

725 Great Western Rd. www.cailbruich.co.uk. © **0141/334-6265.** Main courses (dinner only) £17–£29; set lunch and pre-theater menu £15 for 2 courses, £18 for 3 courses. MC, V. Tues–Sat noon–2.30pm and 5.30–9.30pm; Sun 12.30–3pm and 5.30–10pm. Subway: Kelvinbridge. Bus: 3, 8, 10, 20, or 40.

No. Sixteen ★ MODERN SCOTTISH/INTERNATIONAL   The restaurant itself may be small but the reputation and quality of the cuisine served here since 1991 is massive. Old Scottish and European recipes are turned on their heads with innovative dishes such as slow-cooked pork belly with celeriac puree, or Vietnamese fish broth with scallops. Prices are surprisingly reasonable for the quality of the cuisine—innovative desserts like lavender panna cotta or poached rhubarb jelly with sherry sponge are a steal at under £7 and one of the many reasons this place is consistently busy.

16 Byres Rd. www.number16.co.uk. © **0141/339-2544.** Main courses (dinner only) £16–£18; set lunch and pre-theater menu £11 for 2 courses, £14 for 3 courses. MC, V. Mon–Sat noon–2:30pm and 5:30–10pm; Sun 12:30–2:30pm and 5:30–9pm. Subway: Kelvinhall. Bus: 8, 89, or 90.

Stravaigin ★★ SCOTTISH/INTERNATIONAL   Stravaigin is old Scots for "to wander," and under the philosophy of "think global eat local" this longtime Glasgow favorite eatery creates memorable cuisine inspired by trips across the globe. Although ideas are sourced globally, ingredients are very much sourced locally and the finest regional Scottish produce is used to create Turkish steamed sea bream or Carolina braised Ramsay's pork belly. Another branch, Stravaigin 2, is situated on Ruthven Lane.

28 Gibson St. www.stravaigin.com. © **0141/334-2665.** Main courses (dinner only) £10–£23; Set lunch £12 for 2 courses, £15 for 3 courses. AE, DC, MC, V. Mon–Sun 11am–11pm. Subway: Kelvinbrudge. Bus: 11 or 44.

Inexpensive

Mother India's Cafe ★ INDIAN   This ambient, laid-back eatery opposite the Kelvingrove art gallery is a gem of fine Indian cuisine and efficient service. The tapas-style menu enables diners to try many different dishes from staples of vegetable, chicken, and fish pakoras, to more unusual house specialties, including butter chicken topped with almonds and lamb cooked in a rich pepper sauce. If casual dining and the chance to mix and match small portions sounds appealing this local favorite won't let you down.

1355 Argyle St. www.motherindiascafeglasgow.co.uk. © **0141/339-9145.** Tapas £3–£5. MC, V. Mon–Thurs noon–10.30pm, Fri and Sat noon–11pm, Sun noon–10pm. Subway: Kelvinhall. Bus: 9, 16, 23, 42, or 62.

Shopping

Most of Glasgow's shopping focuses around its **Style Mile** (www.glasgowstylemile. com), whose southern edge stretches east from Central Station along Argyle Street and into Merchant City and northwards along Sauchiehall Street and Buchanan Galleries shopping mall. In addition to the Buchanan Galleries, which includes an enormous branch of the John Lewis department store, there are two other large indoor shopping complexes in this region.

The third and newest shopping complex is the **St. Enoch Shopping Centre** on St. Enoch Square off Argyle Street to the east of Central Station. Here visitors can spend all day shopping under the biggest glass roof in Europe.

More upmarket shopping lies on the east side of the Style Mile at **Merchant City.** Here, the main designer thoroughfare is **Ingram Street,** where many grand buildings built by Glasgow's merchants in the 18th and 19th centuries now house exclusive clothing stores. Highlights in this area include the **Italian Centre,** a small complex in a courtyard, off Ingram Street, nicknamed "mini Milan," whose exclusive stores are honey pots for designer label shoppers.

Outside of the Style Mile, the West End is the place to potter around more independent, quirkier shops, most of which are located along or close to Bryes Road and Great Western Road. This is also a good spot for vintage clothes shopping, arts and crafts, and specialty food shops. **De Courcy's Arcade** on Cresswell Lane, off Bryes Road, is a veritable heaven for vintage clothes shoppers.

Entertainment & Nightlife

Glasgow is one of the most culturally vibrant cities in the U.K. Its year-round program of theater, music, dance, and film is second to none and all complemented by an excellent clubbing scene, which some claim is the best in Scotland.

THEATER

Glasgow has an enviable selection of theaters. At the mainstream end of the market, the **King's Theatre,** 297 Bath St. (www.ambassadortickets.com; © **0844/871-7648**), offers a wide range of plays, musicals, and comedies; and the **Theatre Royal,** 282 Hope St. (www.ambassadortickets.com; © **0844/871-7647**), is resplendent with Victorian Italian Renaissance plasterwork and glittering chandeliers and hosts touring productions by national theater companies from across the U.K. One of Glasgow's best-loved theaters is the **Citizens Theatre,** 119 Gorbals St. (www.citz. co.uk; © **0141/429-0022**). Fondly known as "the Citz," this glorious Victorian theater favors both emerging and established playwrights.

The **Tron Theatre,** 63 Trongate (www.tron.co.uk; © **0141/552-4267**), occupies the site of the former Tron Church; it was transformed into a small theater in the 1980s and presents contemporary drama. On the Southside, the **Tramway,** 25 Albert Drive (www.tramway.org; © **0845/330-3501**), specializes in a vibrant mix of contemporary theater and dance in an auditorium that once served as one of the city's tram sheds. In the West End, **Òran Mór,** Bryes Rd. (www.oran-mor.co.uk; ✆ **0141/ 357-6200**), which means "great melody of life," is known for music, comedy, and theater.

BALLET, OPERA & CLASSICAL MUSIC

The **Theatre Royal** (see above) hosts performances by **Scottish Opera** (www. scottishopera.org.uk; ✆ **0141/248-4567**), while the **Scottish Ballet** (www.scottish ballet.co.uk; ✆ **0141/331-2931**) also performs here (see above). The **Glasgow Royal Concert Hall**, 2 Sauchiehall Street, is home to the **Royal Scottish National Orchestra** (www.rsno.org.uk; ✆ **0141/226-3868**), while **City Halls,** Candleriggs, is home to the **Scottish Chamber Orchestra** (www.sco.org.uk; ✆ **0131/557- 6800**). These two venues are run by **Glasgow Concert Halls** and tickets and information can be obtained from www.glasgowconcerthalls.com; ✆ **0141/353-8000.**

THE CLUB & MUSIC SCENE

Barrowland, 244 Gallowgate (www.glasgow-barrowland.com; ✆ **0141/552-4601**), is one of Europe's top small venues. Its 1,900-capacity hall is known for its excellent acoustics and has played host to many top acts and continues to draw big names. It's also a good place to catch Glasgow's emerging talent on the music scene. Gig tickets (from £11 to £26) must be booked well in advance. **King Tut's Wah-Wah Hut** 272A St. Vincent St. (www.kingtuts.co.uk; ✆ **0141/221-5279**), borrowed its name from a New York venture and is one of Glasgow's longest standing leading concert venues. Numerous top-name bands played here before they hit the big time and King Tut's continues to promote a mix of new and established bands. Tickets cost £5 to £18. **Nice 'n' Sleazy,** 421 Sauchiehall St. (www.nicensleazy.com; ✆ **0141/333-0900**), is one of Glasgow's most unpretentious, down-to-earth clubs. It's intimate and friendly and boasts reasonable entry charges (from £3), except on nights when more well-known bands are playing. If you don't mind rough around the edges in terms of decor, **The 13th Note,** 50–60 King St. (www.13thnote.co.uk; ✆ **0141/553-1638**), is a recommended place to catch local gigs. Indie, rock, punk, new wave, and experimental bands all play here over the course of a week. Entry is free to £5. Although many know **Òran Mór,** top of Byres Rd. (www.oran-mor.co.uk; ✆ **0141/357-6200**), for its theater, music events here are just as good. Regular **Club O** nights are laid-back affairs and focus on alternative music on Thursdays and pop, R 'n' B, and electro on Friday and Saturday (entry free to £6).

FAVORITE PUBS

The amiably battered **Bon Accord,** 153 North St. (www.bonaccordweb.co.uk; ✆ **0141/248-4427**), is a longtime favorite and one of the finest places in the city to enjoy a pint of real ale. Whisky lovers will also find a large selection of malts from across Scotland and live music and quiz nights ensure a lively atmosphere. Open Monday to Saturday noon to midnight, Sunday noon to 11pm with food served daily 12.30 to 8pm. **WEST** (www.westbeer.com; ✆ **0141/550-0135**), a brewery-cum-bar, occupies the former wool-winding room of Glasgow's iconic Templeton Carpet Factory which lies in the East End of Glasgow Green near the People's Palace. Today the beer that's brewed here is amongst the finest in Scotland and is created in accordance with the Reinheitsgebot (known as the German Purity Law) that ensures no artificial additives make their way into the beers. The range of brews includes refreshing lagers and full-flavored wheat beers, all of which can be sampled in the grand beer hall which looks down onto the brewhouse below. Open Sunday to Thursday 11am to 11pm, Friday and Saturday 11am to midnight.

Fans of whisky will travel a long way to sample a wee dram at **The Pot Still,** 154 Hope St. (www.thepotstill.co.uk; *☎* **0141/333-0980**), a fabulous old city-center pub which sells an incredible 483 whiskies. The bar itself has all the feel of a good mellow whisky and knowledgeable owners will advise on the malt that's right for you. Open Monday to Thursday noon to 11pm, Friday and Saturday noon to midnight.

Where to Stay

Most places to stay in Glasgow are to be found in the city center or West End, although visitors will find a few options on the east side of the city. In the center, large hotels and big chains dominate, both of which target business and vacationing travelers. In the West End a string of guest houses and smaller hotels cluster around the Sauchiehall Street and Kelvingrove Park area. All vary in quality, style, and price and most come with family-size rooms; however, many don't have elevators due to the age and era of the buildings. It's a good idea to reserve in advance for high season (late July and August) and New Year, and take time seeking out discount package deals.

CITY CENTER AND MERCHANT CITY
Very Expensive

Blythswood Square ★★★   Blythswood occupies the old Royal Scottish Automobile Club (RSAC) in the center of the city, a building dating from 1823, which the hoteliers restored to its former glory. Deluxe hotel rooms and state-of-the-art bathrooms are elegant, supremely comfortable, and the epitome of good taste, while public areas maintain many of the building's original features, including wood paneling, grand staircases, marble floors, and flourishes of Art Deco. The restaurant occupies the RSAC's former ballroom and is grand in both dimensions and cuisine and the famous **Rally Bar,** named after the Monte Carlo Rally, which once started from Blythswood Square, is well known for its sublime cocktails.

11 Blythswood Square, G2 4AD. www.townhousecompany.com. *☎* **0141/208-2458.** 88 units. £110–£285 double; suites from £400. AE, DC, MC, V. **Amenities:** Restaurant; bar; 2 indoor pools; spa; health club; concierge; room service. *In room:* A/C, TV/DVD, minibar, hairdryer, CD player, Wi-Fi (free).

Expensive

Baby ABode Hotel   This appealingly restored Edwardian charmer is one of central Glasgow's most-loved hotels. The public spaces celebrate the building's civic history and feature a grand staircase, listed wallpaper, and, best of all, an old-fashioned original cage lift. All the rooms have high ceilings and are very spacious; some have the added appeal of original stained glass. Rates are dependent on the size and style of the rooms which are ranked in four categories—"comfortable," "desirable," "enviable," and the truly fab "fabulous."

129 Bath St., G2 2SY. www.abodehotels.co.uk. *☎* **0141/221-6789.** Fax 0141/221-6777. 59 units. £75–£165 double. AE, DC, MC, V. **Amenities:** Restaurant; bar; room service. *In room:* TV/DVD, minibar, hairdryer, Wi-Fi (free).

Grand Central Hotel ★★   Few restored hotels have created so much buzz and generated so much recognition so quickly. Once Glasgow's most prestigious hotel, this historic property is joined with the city's Central Station and its restoration remains faithful to all the romance of the bygone age of travel it was originally created to serve. Archive images of past guests including Frank Sinatra and Roy Rogers line walls and the stunning Champagne Bar overlooks the station concourse where JF Kennedy made his first public speech aged 17. Other past claims to fame include being the site from which John Logie Baird transmitted the world's first long-distance television pictures in 1927. History aside, guests can expect first-class customer service, bedrooms, and suites epitomized by contemporary style and comfort, sweeping public areas, and fine dining at the swish **Tempus** restaurant.

99 Gordon St., G1 3SF. www.principal-hayley.com. ✆ **0141/240-3700.** Fax 0141/240-3701. 186 units. £80–£165 double. AE, MC, V. **Amenities:** Restaurant; bar; concierge; room service. *In room:* TV, hairdryer, Wi-Fi.

Malmaison ★★   The Malmaison chain has transformed this former Greek Orthodox church built in the 1830s into one of Glasgow's hippest hotels. Behind the suitably imposing exterior few original details remain, as the contemporary interior oozes the ultramodern. Bedrooms vary in size from smallish to average, but are chic and appointed with such extras as specially commissioned art and top-of-the-line toiletries, while suites range from one-bedroom deluxe affairs to the deeply luxurious Big Yin. A popular brasserie lies in a vaulted basement or guests can relax in the former crypt—now a sleek modern bar.

278 W. George St., G2 4LL. www.malmaison.com. ✆ **0141/572-1000.** Fax 0141/572-1002. 72 units. £100–£160 doubles; £170–£320 suites. AE, DC, MC, V. **Amenities:** Restaurant; bar; health club; room service; Wi-Fi in public areas. *In room:* A/C, TV, hairdryer, CD player, Wi-Fi (free).

Moderate

Marks Hotel ☺   Easily identifiable by its stepped, angular glass frontage, this contemporary hotel is a decent, affordable central option. Floor-to-ceiling windows are the winning feature in some rooms and city views get better and longer the higher the floor. In addition to standard and executive choices, spacious family rooms are also available. Bold design extends to the hotel's informal One Ten bar and grill, where the menu is a mix of traditional Scottish and international cuisine.

110 Bath St., G2 2EN. www.markshotels.com. ✆ **0141/353-0800.** Fax 0141/353-0900. 103 units. £60–£140 double. AE, MC, V. **Amenities:** Restaurant; bar; room service. *In room:* TV, A/C, hairdryer, Wi-Fi (free).

Inexpensive

Citizen M ★   A relative newcomer on Glasgow's ever-diversifying accommodation scene, Citizen M is big, bold, trendy, and a rare bargain. This large, very square hotel sits bang in the middle of town and its 198 rooms spread out over eight floors. Rooms are small in size but big in functional luxury. The beds are large and super comfortable, but it's features such as touch-screen controllable blinds, temperature, and mood lighting, as well as rainfall showers in the bathrooms, that make this place stand out. **Canteen M,** the on-site grab-and-go restaurant stocks the likes of sandwiches and sushi. Reservations can only be made online, not via telephone.

60 Renfrew St., G2 3BW. www.citizenmglasgow.com. ✆ **0141/404-9485.** No fax. 198 units. £60–£100 double. AE, MC, V. **Amenities:** Restaurant; bar; room service. *In room:* TV, hairdryer, Wi-Fi (free).

WEST END

Alamo Guest House ★★ 🗡   This large Victorian hotel is tucked away in a quiet cul-de-sac on the edge of Kelvingrove Park and is very convenient for all West End attractions and restaurants. Classically decorated rooms come in various shapes and sizes, the largest boasts a king-size Louis XV bed and luxury bath, plus two large bay windows overlooking the park. Smaller doubles still feature period furniture but are not all en-suite. Breakfasts are served in a park-facing dining room and those wanting a night in can choose from an enormous film collection.

46 Gray St., G3 7SE. www.alamoguesthouse.com. ✆ **0141/339-2395.** No fax. 12 units. £50–£105 double. MC, V. *In room:* TV/DVD player, hairdryer, Wi-Fi (free).

Argyll Hotel ☺   Small but friendly, this traditional hotel housed in a Georgian building is well placed for the art galleries and museums around Glasgow University and West End restaurants. The modernized guest rooms are basic, clean, and comfortable and the breakfasts are superb. The Scottish-themed **Sutherlands** restaurant is also open for evening meals and often hosts events, including live music, whisky tasting, and murder mystery nights. Family rooms available.

973 Sauchiehall St., G3 7TQ. www.argyllhotelglasgow.co.uk. ✆ **0141/337-3313.** Fax 0141/337-3283. 38 units. £60–£160 double. AE, MC, V. **Amenities:** Restaurant; bar; room service. *In room:* TV, hairdryer, Wi-Fi (free).

Hotel du Vin ★★ ☺   Despite stiff competition from a sprinkle of new luxury accommodation choices in the city center, this glamorous and tranquil hotel continues to very definitely hold its own. Set back behind a line of trees at the exclusive One Devonshire Gardens, Hotel du Vin spreads out over three Victorian properties each now even more elegant than in their heyday. The rooms and suites are furnished in period style and feature lots of luxurious accessories, including drench showers. Despite the antiques, Hotel du Vin is more than happy to cater to children by providing toys, cots, and highchairs. There are also interconnecting bedrooms and the restaurant can prepare meals for smaller appetites.

1 Devonshire Gardens, G12 0UX. www.hotelduvin.com. ✆ **0141/339-2001.** Fax 0141/337-1663. 49 units. £110–£300 double; £350–£500 suite. AE, DC, MC, V. Free parking. **Amenities:** 2 restaurants; bar; exercise room; room service. *In room:* TV/DVD, minibar, hairdryer, CD player, Wi-Fi (free).

EAST END

Cathedral House Hotel ⚑   The panoramic views of Glasgow cathedral and the Necropolis are reason enough to stay at this well-run, affordable hotel. The building itself is a restored Glaswegian baronial-style house dating back to the 1800s and stands on a tree-lined square adjacent to the cathedral. It's a small but choice hotel that's packed with atmosphere and history and within walking distance of the city center. All of the comfortable bedrooms are individually designed in an attractive minimalist style. This simple style extends into the restaurant and bar where a reasonably priced menu of bar food is supported by a choice of draft ales and short cocktail menu.

29–32 Cathedral Sq., G4 0XA. http://cathedralhousehotel.org. ✆ **0141/552-3515.** Fax 0141/552-2444. 7 units. £90 double. MC, V. Free parking. **Amenities:** Restaurant; bar; room service. *In room:* TV, hairdryer.

CLYDESIDE

Hilton Garden Inn   Breathe in wide views of the Clyde and the scent of maritime Glasgow at this ultramodern riverside hotel, formally called Mint. This is the accommodation of choice for anyone preferring the contemporary over the traditional, as clean, functional design and new technology shine throughout. Each of the spacious guestrooms features an iMac multimedia entertainment system and super-fast free Wi-Fi; many also have long views of the river. This hotel is more central than you might think with the city center around 2½ km (1½ miles) east and the West End a short walk north. The on-site cafe and restaurant offer al fresco dining on the banks of the Clyde in summer.

Finnieston Quay, G3 8HN. www.hilton.com. ✆ **0141/240-1002.** Fax 0141/248-2754. 164 units. £75–£130 double. AE, MC, V. Free parking. **Amenities:** Restaurant; bar; room service. *In room:* iMac, hairdryer, Wi-Fi (free).

SOUTHSIDE

Sherbrooke Castle Hotel ★★   If staying in the city center is not a priority, this splendid Scottish baronial hotel set deep inside landscaped gardens is an excellent way to get away from it all. Traditional touches and modern efficiencies are the hallmarks of this architectural delight, built in 1896 as the private residence of a rich contractor. During World War II, the building was used by the Royal Navy, but was converted into a hotel after the war. Bedrooms are the epitome of luxury and comfort and a large romantic suite occupies the castle's "Sleeping Beauty" tower. Local produce is a mainstay of the carefully crafted Scottish and international dishes served at the on-site restaurant.

11 Sherbrooke Ave., Pollokshields G41 4PG. www.sherbrooke.co.uk. © **0141/427-4227.** Fax 0141/427-5685. 25 units. £80 double; £175–£225 suite. AE, DC, MC, V. **Amenities:** Restaurant; bar; room service. *In room:* TV, hairdryer, Wi-Fi (free).

TAYSIDE & GRAMPIAN

Tayside and Grampian, two history-rich regions in northeast Scotland, offer a vast array of sightseeing within relatively small areas. The two regions share the North Sea coast between the Firth of Tay in the south and the Firth of Moray farther north—the Highland Line separates the Lowlands in the south from the Highlands in the north. The Grampians, the highest mountain range in Scotland, are to the west of this line.

Carved out of the old counties of Perth and Angus, **Tayside** is named for its major river, the 190km (118-mile) Tay. The region is easy to explore, and its tributaries and dozens of lochs and Highland streams are among the best salmon and trout waters in Europe. One of the loveliest regions of Scotland, Tayside is filled with heather-clad Highland hills, long blue lochs, and miles of walking trails. Tayside provided the backdrop for many of Sir Walter Scott's novels, including *The Fair Maid of Perth, Waverley,* and *The Abbot.* Its golf courses are world famous, especially the trio of 18-hole courses at Gleneagles.

The **Grampian** region has Braemar, site of the most famous of the Highland gatherings. The Queen herself comes here to holiday at Balmoral Castle, her private residence, a tradition dating back to the days of Queen Victoria. Scotland's northeast is whisky country, and as you travel through its scenic roads you'll pass heather-covered moorland, lochs, and woodland glens. The city of Aberdeen stands on the northern coastline and is bordered by fine sandy beaches, old fishing harbors, and beach resorts.

Crieff

The market town of Crieff sits at the edge of the Perthshire Highlands, 29km (18 miles) west of Perth along the A85 and 96km (60 miles) northwest of Edinburgh. This small burgh boasts excellent golf and fishing and makes a pleasant stopover. Crieff was the seat of the court of the earls of Strathearn until 1747, and the gallows in its marketplace was once used to execute Highland cattle rustlers.

You can take a "day trail" into **Strathearn,** the valley of the River Earn, the very center of Scotland. Here, Highland mountains meet gentle Lowland slopes, and moorland mingles with rich green pastures. North of Crieff, the road to Aberfeldy passes through the narrow pass of the **Sma' Glen,** a famous spot of beauty, with hills rising on either side to 600m (1,970 ft.).

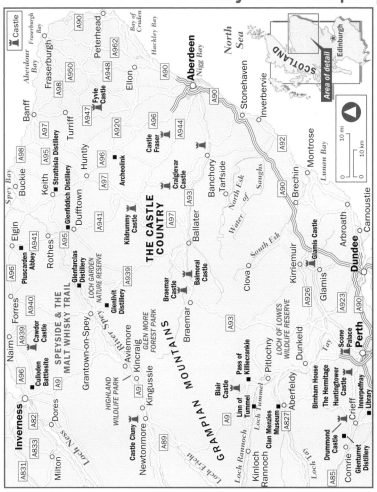

ESSENTIALS

GETTING THERE   An hourly bus service to Crieff runs during the day from Perth bus station. For information and schedules, contact **Stagecoach** (www.stagecoach bus.com, ✆ **01738/629-339**).

There's no direct **train** service. The nearest rail stations are at Gleneagles, 14km (8⅔ miles) away, and at Perth, 29km (18 miles) away. For information and schedules check the National Rail website www.nationalrail.co.uk or ✆ **08457/484-950**.

VISITOR INFORMATION   The year-round **tourist information office** is in the Town Hall on High Street (✆ **01764/652-578**). It's open October to April, daily 10am to 4pm; April to June and September to October, Monday through Saturday

9.30am to 5pm and Sunday 10am to 2pm; and July and August, Monday through Saturday 9.30am to 6.30pm and Saturday 10am to 4pm.

EXPLORING CRIEFF

Drummond Castle Gardens ★ GARDEN   The gardens of Drummond Castle, first laid out in the early 17th century by John Drummond, second earl of Perth, are among the finest formal gardens in Europe. There's a panoramic view from the upper terrace, overlooking an example of an early Victorian parterre in the form of St. Andrew's Cross. The multifaceted sundial by John Mylne, master mason to Charles I, has been the centerpiece since 1630. The castle itself is not open to the public.

Grimsthorpe, Crieff. www.drummondcastlegardens.co.uk. ✆ **01764/681-433.** Admission £5 adults, £4 seniors, £2 children. May–Oct daily 1–6pm. Closed Nov–Apr. Take A822 for 5km (3 miles) south of Crieff.

Glenturret Distillery Ltd DISTILLERY   This distillery is Scotland's oldest and was established in 1775 on the banks of the River Turret. Visitors can see the milling of malt, mashing, fermentation, distillation, and cask filling at the Famous Grouse Experience, followed by the offer to taste a couple of malts. A visit includes a 20-minute film and a wander around a small museum devoted to the implements of the whisky trade. Dedicated connoisseurs can opt for more expensive tours with more opportunities to taste.

The Hosh, off the A85, Glenturret. www.thefamousgrouse.com. ✆ **01764/656-565.** Guided tours from £7.50, children under 12 free. March–Dec daily 9am–6pm; Jan–Feb daily 10am–4.30pm. Take A85 toward Comrie; 1.2km (¾ mile) from Crieff, turn right at the crossroads; the distillery is .5km (⅓ mile) up the road.

Innerpeffray Library ★★ LIBRARY   One of Perthshire's hidden gems, this extraordinary library was founded around 1680 by local landowner Lord Madertie, who donated his precious collection of leather-bound books to provide a book lending service to the local population. The library moved to this purpose-built home in 1760, which sits next to an old chapel—also worth a visit—and the librarian is always willing to provide a guided tour through the fascinating collection of volumes on an array of subjects.

Just off the B8062, near Crieff, PH7 3RF. www.innerpeffraylibrary.co.uk. ✆ **01764/652-819.** Admission £5 adults, under 15s free. Mar–Oct Wed–Sun 10am–12.45pm and 2pm–4.45pm; Nov–Feb visits by appointment only. Take the B8062 southeast from Crieff in the direction of Auchterarder and look out for Historic Scotland signs about 5 miles from Crieff; the library is situated a few minutes' drive down a lane on your right.

Dundee & Glamis Castle ★★

The old seaport of Dundee is Scotland's fourth largest city and spreads out along the north shore of the Firth of Tay. Dundee became the leading home port for ships from the 1860s until World War I. Long known for its jute and flax operations, Dundee is also famous for fruitcakes, marmalades, and jams.

Spanning the Firth of Tay is the **Tay Railway Bridge,** opened in 1888. Constructed over the tidal estuary, the bridge is some 3km (1¼ miles) long, one of the longest in Europe. There's also a road bridge 2km (1¼ miles) long, with four traffic lanes and a walkway in the center.

Although there are few attractions in the city itself, Dundee has a fast growing cultural scene with work starting on a Victoria & Albert Museum, which will become an international center for design, in 2013. The city serves as a base for visiting the medieval town of St Andrew's on the south side of the Firth of Tay and Glamis Castle.

ESSENTIALS
GETTING THERE **ScotRail** (www.scotrail.co.uk; ℂ **08457/484-950**) offers frequent train services to Dundee from Edinburgh, Glasgow, Perth, and Aberdeen. One-way fares to Dundee from Edinburgh £23, from Glasgow £25, from Perth £6, and from Aberdeen £24.

CityLink **buses** offer a frequent service from Edinburgh and Glasgow. For bookings and information see www.citylink.co.uk or ℂ **0871/266-3333.**

If you're **driving,** the fastest way to reach Dundee is via the A90, which leads east from the M90 and A9 at Perth.

VISITOR INFORMATION The **tourist information office** is at Discovery Point, Discovery Quay (www.angusanddundee.co.uk; ℂ **01382/527-527**). Open April to September, Monday through Saturday 10am to 6pm, Sunday 10am to 4pm; October to March, Monday to Saturday 9am to 5pm.

EXPLORING DUNDEE
For a panoramic view of Dundee, the Tay bridges across to Fife, and mountains to the north, go to **Dundee Law,** a 175m (574-ft.) hill just north of the city. The hill is an ancient volcanic plug.

Broughty Castle CASTLE   This 15th-century estuary fort lies about 6km (3¾ miles) east of the city center on the seafront, at Broughty Ferry, a little fishing hamlet and once the terminus for ferries crossing the Firth of Tay before the bridges were built. Besieged by the English in the 16th century, and attacked by Cromwell's army under General Monk in the 17th century, the castle was restored as part of Britain's coastal defenses in 1861. The museum features displays on local history, arms and armor, and Dundee's history as a whaling port. The observation area at the top of the castle provides fine views of the Tay estuary and northeast Fife.

Castle Green, Broughty Ferry. www.dundeecity.gov.uk/broughtycastle. ℂ **01382/436-916.** Free admission. Apr–Sept Mon–Sat 10am–4pm, Sun 12:30–4pm; Oct–Mar Tues–Sat 10am–4pm, Sun 12:30–4pm. Bus: 75 or 76.

HM Frigate Unicorn ★ ☺ HISTORIC SITE   This 46-gun wooden ship of war commissioned in 1824 by the Royal Navy is the oldest British-built ship afloat. The Unicorn has been fully restored and visitors can explore all four decks: the quarterdeck with 32-lb. carronades; the gun deck with its battery of 18-lb. cannons and the captain's quarters; the berth deck with officers' cabins and crews' hammocks, and the lower deck and hold. Displays portraying life in the navy and the ship's history make this a rewarding visit.

Victoria Dock. www.frigateunicorn.org. ℂ **01382/200-900.** Admission £5.25 adults, £4.25 seniors and children, £11–£14 families. April–Oct daily 10am–5pm; Nov–Mar Wed–Fri noon–4pm, Sat–Sun 10am–4pm. Bus: 6, 23, or 78.

WHERE TO STAY & EAT
Jahangir Tandoori INDIAN   Built around an indoor fishpond in a dining room draped with the soft folds of an embroidered tent, this is the best Indian restaurant in Dundee. Meals are prepared with fresh ingredients and cover the gamut of recipes

from both north and south India. Tandoori specials are also on offer as well as a good selection of vegetarian dishes, alongside a choice of steaks and fajitas.

1 Sessions St. (at the corner of Hawk Hill). www.jahangirdundee.com. ✆ **01382/202-022.** Reservations recommended. Main courses £10–£18. AE, MC, V. Daily 5pm to midnight.

The Landmark ★ ☺   Located on the western outskirts of Dundee this restored Victorian mansion is a good choice for families and those wanting a taste of luxury away from the city center. The grounds include a nature trail and children's adventure playground, while inside the swish leisure facilities feature a gym, pool, and Jacuzzi. The onsite **Garden Room** restaurant transforms fresh local produce into first-class Scottish cuisine and stylish bedrooms come with all contemporary comforts.

Kingsway West, Invergowrie, DD2 5JT. www.thelandmarkdundee.co.uk. ✆ **01382/641-122.** Fax 01382/631-201. 95 units. £80–£115 double. AE, MC, V. Free parking. Signposted on the Dundee Kingsway, on the western outskirts of Dundee. **Amenities:** Restaurant; bar; indoor pool; health club; spa; room service; babysitting; Wi-Fi (free). *In room:* TV, minibar, hair dryer.

A DAY TRIP TO GLAMIS

The little village of Glamis (pronounced *Glams*) grew up around **Glamis Castle** ★★, Castle Office (www.glamis-castle.co.uk; ✆ **01307/840393**). For 6 centuries it has been connected to members of the British Royal Family. The late Queen Mother was brought up here; and Princess Margaret was born here, making her the first royal princess born in Scotland in 3 centuries. The current owner is the Queen's great-nephew. The castle contains Duncan's Hall, which the Victorians claimed was where Macbeth murdered King Duncan, but in Shakespeare's play the murder takes place at Macbeth's castle, Cawdor, near Inverness. Shakespeare was also wrong in naming

---

PLAYING THE WORLD'S oldest GOLF COURSE

At **St. Andrew's,** 21km (13 miles) southeast of Dundee and 80km (50 miles) northeast of Edinburgh, the rules of golf in Britain and the world were codified and arbitrated. Golf was played for the first time in the 1400s, probably on the site of St. Andrew's Old Course, and enjoyed there by Mary, Queen of Scots, in 1567.

St Andrews Links is made up of six public courses, including the fabled 6,721-yard par-72 (ladies 6,032-yard par-76) **Old Course;** established in 1552, it's the oldest golf course in the world. All courses are maintained by the **St Andrews Link Trust** (www.standrews. org.uk; ✆ **01334/466-666**), and around 42,000 rounds of golf are played on the Old Course each year. Applications to play (minimum two golfers) must be submitted by phone (see above) or in person before 2pm. Applications are

entered into a ballot and results are published on the website (see above), and at various places on the Links, by 4pm. Single golfers can chance their luck by arriving at the starter as early as possible on the day they wish to play to see if they can join the first available two- or three-ball. A current handicap certificate and proof of identity are required for all golfers. Greens fees are £70 to £155 for the Old Course.

Encircling St. Andrews Links is the world's most prestigious golf club, the **Royal and Ancient** (www.randa.org; ✆ **01334/460-000**), founded in St. Andrews in 1754 by a group of noblemen, professors, and landowners; it remains more or less rigidly closed as a private-membership men's club and governs the rules of golf everywhere except the U.S.

Macbeth Thane of Glamis; Glamis wasn't made a thaneship—a sphere of influence in medieval Scotland—until years after the action in the play took place.

The present Glamis Castle dates from the early 15th century, but there are records of a hunting lodge having been here in the 11th century. It has been in the possession of the Lyon family since 1372, and it contains some fine plaster ceilings, furniture, and paintings.

The castle is open to the public, with access to the Royal Apartments and many other rooms, as well as the fine gardens, from April to October daily 10am to 6pm (last admission 4.30pm); and November and December daily 11am to 4.30pm (last admission 3.30pm). Admission to the castle and grounds is £9.75 adults, £7.25 children, £28 families and admission to the grounds only costs £5.75 adults, £3.25 children, £16.50 families. Buses run between Dundee and Glamis; the journey time is approximately 35 minutes. *Note:* Buses don't stop in front of the castle, which lies 1km (⅔ mile) from the bus stop.

Where to Eat

Strathmore Arms CONTINENTAL/SCOTTISH   Try this cozy place near the castle for one of the best lunches in the area. The menu offers a wide and varied choice and makes good use of local ingredients. You might begin with soup of the day and move onto traditional mains such as lamb shank or fish and chips. Be warned, the portions are generous.

The Square, Glamis. http://strathmorearmsglamis.com. (C) **01307/840-248.** Reservations recommended. Main courses £9–£21. AE, MC, V. Daily noon–2pm and 6.30–9pm.

Braemar

In the heart of some of Grampian's most beautiful scenery is Braemar, known for its romantic castle. It's also a good center for exploring the area which includes Balmoral Castle (see "Ballater & Balmoral Castle," below) and is home to the most famous of Highland Gatherings. This Highland village is set against a massive backdrop of hills, covered with heather in summer, where Clunie Water joins the River Dee. The massive **Cairn Toul** towers over Braemar, reaching a height of 1,293m (4,242 ft.).

ESSENTIALS

GETTING THERE   Take the **train** to Aberdeen, and then continue the rest of the way by bus. For information and schedules, check with National Rail (www.national rail.co.uk; (C) **08457/484-950**).

Buses run six times a day from Aberdeen to Braemar (trip time: 2 hr.). One-way fare is £10. The bus and train stations in Aberdeen are next to each other on Guild Street. For information and schedules, check with **Stagecoach** (www.stagecoach bus.com; (C) **01224/597-590**).

To reach Braemar from Dundee **by car,** return west towards Perth and then head north along A93, following the signs into Braemar. The 113km (70-mile) drive takes between 70 and 90 minutes.

VISITOR INFORMATION   The **Braemar Tourist Office** is in The Mews, Mar Road ((C) **01339/741-600**). In June, hours are daily 9.30am to 5pm; July and August, daily 9.30am to 6pm; and in September, daily 10am to 5pm. In the off-season, hours are Monday to Saturday 10am to 1pm and 2 to 5pm, Sunday noon to 5pm.

SPECIAL EVENTS   The spectacular **Royal Highland Gathering** (www.braemar gathering.org; (C) **01339/741-098**) takes place annually in late August or early September in the Princess Royal and Duke of Fife Memorial Park. The Queen herself often attends the gathering. It's thought these ancient games were originated by King Malcolm Canmore, a chieftain who ruled much of Scotland at the time of the Norman conquest of England. He selected his hardiest warriors from all the clans for a "keen and fair contest."

Braemar is overrun with visitors during the gathering—anyone thinking of attending would be wise to book tickets well in advance via the website and reserve accommodation in the area no later than early April.

EXPLORING BRAEMAR

You might spot members of the Royal Family at **Crathie Church,** 14km (8⅔ miles) east of Braemar on A93 (www.braemarandcrathieparish.org.uk; ✆ **01339/742-208**), where they attend Sunday services when in residence. Services are at 11:30am; otherwise, the church is open to view April to October, Monday to Saturday 9:30am to 5:30pm and on Sunday 2 to 5:30pm.

Nature lovers may want to drive to the **Linn of Dee,** 10km (6¼ miles) west of Braemar, a narrow chasm on the River Dee and local beauty spot. Other nature sites include Glen Muick, Loch Muick, and Lochnagar. A **Scottish Wildlife Trust Visitor Centre,** reached by a minor road, is located in this Highland glen, off the South Deeside Road. An access road joins B976 at a point 26km (16 miles) east of Braemar. Pick up a map at the tourist office (see above).

Braemar Castle ★ CASTLE   This romantic 17th-century castle was built by John Erskine the Earl of Mar as a lavish, fortified hunting lodge. Braemar has been the seat of the Chiefs of Clan Farquharson since the mid-18th century and its history and fortunes, like many Scottish castles, are intertwined with Union of the Crowns and the Jacobite revolutions. Following their purchase of nearby Balmoral Castle, Queen Victoria and Prince Albert were known to take tea with the Farquharsons in the drawing room at Braemar; however, the castle's recent history has been marred by the need for renovation and conservation. Let none of that put you off, as Braemar oozes architectural grace, scenic charm, and historical interest. Highlights include barrel-vaulted ceilings, an underground prison, and a remarkable star-shaped defensive curtain wall.

On the Aberdeen–Ballater–Perth Rd. (A93). www.braemarcastle.co.uk. ✆ **01337/41600.** Admission £6 adults; £5 seniors; £3 children; £14 families. April–Oct Sat–Sun 11am–4pm; also Wed July–Aug. Closed Nov–March. Take A93 .8km (½ mile) northeast of Braemar.

GOLFING

Braemar Golf Club, at Braemar (www.braemargolfclub.co.uk; ✆ **01339/741-618**), is the highest golf course in the country. The second-hole green is 380m (1,247 ft.) above sea level—this is the trickiest hole on the course. Pro golf commentator Peter Alliss has deemed it "the hardest par 4 in all of Scotland." Set on a plateau, the hole is bordered on the right by the River Clunie and lined on the left by rough. Greens fees are £25 for 18 holes and £30 for a day ticket. Trolleys and clubs can be hired. The course is open only April to October daily (call in advance as hours can vary).

WHERE TO STAY & EAT

Braemar Lodge Hotel ☺   Popular with skiers who frequent the nearby Glenshee slopes, Braemar Lodge is set amongst beautiful and extensive grounds at the head of Glen Clunie near the cottage where Robert Louis Stevenson wrote *Treasure*

Island. Bedrooms vary in shape and size, but each is comfortable and well equipped. On cold evenings, you're greeted by log fires and the on-site restaurant serves hearty food year round. Three log cabins have been built on the grounds; all come fully equipped with modern conveniences and sleep up to six people.

6 Glenshee Rd., Braemar AB35 5YQ. www.braemarlodge.co.uk. ©/fax **01339/741-627.** 7 units. £90–£100 double; £490–£665 weekly cabin rental. MC, V. Free parking. Closed Nov. Situated a 2-min. walk south from the bus station. **Amenities:** Restaurant; bar. *In room:* TV, hair dryer.

Invercauld Arms Thistle Hotel   This grand Victorian hotel dates back to the 18th century and is a good base from which to enjoy the surrounding countryside— hill walking, fishing, and, in winter, skiing are all close by. On cool evenings a roaring log fire burns in the lounge and the hotel's restaurant serves decent Scottish fare. The rooms are comfortable, if rather ordinary, and come in a range of sizes.

Invercauld Rd., Braemar AB35 5YR. www.shearings.com. © **01339/741-605.** Fax 01339/741-428. 68 units. £79–£119 double. AE, DC, MC, V. Free parking. **Amenities:** Restaurant; bar. *In room:* TV, hair dryer.

Ballater & Balmoral Castle ★★

Located on the banks of the River Dee and surrounded by the Grampian Mountains, Ballater is mainly a resort for visitors wishing to explore the natural surroundings and nearby Balmoral Castle, the Scottish home of the Royal Family. The town still centers on its Station Square, where the Windsors used to be photographed as they arrived to spend holidays. The railway is now closed.

ESSENTIALS

GETTING THERE   From Aberdeen train station you can catch a connecting bus. For information and schedules, check with **National Rail** (www.nationalrail.co.uk; © **08457/484-950**).

   Buses run hourly from Aberdeen to Ballater. The bus and train stations in Aberdeen are next to each other on Guild Street. For information and schedules check with **Stagecoach** (www.stagecoachbus.com; © **01224/597-590**). Buses 201 and 202 run between Braemar and Ballater, taking 30 minutes.

   If you're **driving** from Braemar, head east along the A93.

VISITOR INFORMATION   The **Tourist Information Centre** is at Station Square (© **01339/755-306**). July and August, hours are daily 10am to 1pm and 2 to 6pm; September, October, May, and June Monday to Saturday 10am to 1pm and 2 to 5pm, Sunday 1 to 5pm. Closed November to April.

THE CASTLE

Balmoral Castle ★★ CASTLE   "This dear paradise" is how Queen Victoria described Balmoral Castle, rebuilt in the Scottish baronial style by her "beloved" Albert and completed in 1855. Today Balmoral, 13km (8 miles) west of Ballater, is still a private residence of the British sovereign. Its principal feature is a 30m (100-ft.) tower. Of the actual castle, only the ballroom is open to the public; it houses an exhibit of pictures, porcelain, and other works of art. There is also an exhibition in the outside Carriage Hall. In the grounds are many memorials to the Royal Family, along with gardens, country walks, souvenir shops, and a refreshment room.

Balmoral, Ballater. www.balmoralcastle.com. © **01339/742-534.** Admission £9 adults, £8 students and seniors, £5 children 5–16, free for children 4 and under; £25 families. Apr–July daily 10am– 5pm. Closed Aug–Mar. Crathie bus from Aberdeen to the Crathie station; Balmoral Castle is signposted from there (a short walk).

WHERE TO STAY & EAT

Darroch Learg Hotel ★   Built in 1888 as an elegant country home, this hotel stands in 2 hectares (5 acres) of lush woodlands opening onto views of the Dee Valley and the Grampian Mountains and is imbued with a relaxing charm. The individually decorated bedrooms are divided between the main house and Oakhall, a baronial mansion on the same grounds. Some rooms have four-poster beds and private terraces; however, the hotels best feature is its restaurant, which claims sweeping views over the River Dee and serves award-winning Scottish cuisine, accompanied by a superb wine menu (three course a la carte dinner £43).

Darroch Learg, Braemar Rd. (on A93 at the west end of Ballater), Ballater AB35 5UX. www.
darrochlearg.co.uk. *ⓒ* **01339/755-443.** Fax 01339/755-252. 17 units. £140–£250 double. AE, DC,
MC, V. Free parking. Closed Christmas and last 3 weeks in Jan. **Amenities:** Restaurant; room
service. *In room:* TV, hair dryer.

Green Inn ★★ SCOTTISH/FRENCH   Situated in the heart of town, this award-winning family-run restaurant was once a temperance hotel, and is now one of the finest places to eat in the region. The menu features a combination of traditional Scottish dishes and French flair with an emphasis on seasonal local produce. The menu features dishes such as terrine of guinea fowl, slow-braised Aberdeen Angus beef, wild seabass, and bittersweet chocolate cakes for dessert. The Green Inn also offers two simply furnished double rooms for £80 for bed and breakfast.

9 Victoria Rd., Ballater. www.green-inn.com. *ⓒ*/fax **01339/755-701.** Reservations required. Fixed-
price menu £35 for 2 courses, £39 for 3 courses. AE, DC, MC, V. Mar–Oct daily 7–9pm; Nov–Feb
Tues–Sat 7–9pm.

Oaks Restaurant BRITISH   The Oaks is located within a century-old mansion that was originally built by the "marmalade kings" of Britain, the Keiller family, and is now owned by Hilton Hotels. This is the more formal of the restaurants in this resort complex which includes hotel rooms, timeshare villas, and access to a nearby golf course. Some tables claim views of the Dee Valley and menus include fresh Scottish seafood and local game as well as vegetarian options.

In the Hilton Craigendarroch Hotel, Braemar Rd. www.hilton.co.uk/craigendarroch. *ⓒ* **01339/755-
858.** Reservations strongly recommended. Set dinner £40 for 4 courses. AE, DC, MC, V. Thurs–Sun
6:30–9pm.

Aberdeen

Standing proud on the edge of the North Sea, the port city of Aberdeen is Scotland's third largest city. Home to an esteemed university and a clutch of cultural attractions, Aberdeen is nicknamed "the granite city" as many of its buildings feature locally quarried gray granite. There's plenty to keep visitors occupied for a day or two, including the best shopping in northeast Scotland, and the city makes a good base from which to explore inland castles and a stunning coastline.

ESSENTIALS
Getting There
BY PLANE   Aberdeen's airport (www.aberdeenairport.com; *ⓒ* **0844/481-6666**) is located 11km (6¾ miles) northwest of the city center and is served by a number of airlines, including British Airways, British Midland, easyJet, and KLM. A regular bus service connects the airport with Aberdeen bus station.

BY TRAIN   Frequent train services to Aberdeen run from Edinburgh, Glasgow, Dundee, and Perth. One-way fares to Aberdeen from Edinburgh cost £23, from

Glasgow £45, from Dundee £16, and from Perth £14. For schedules and information, check **National Rail** (www.nationalrail.co.uk; ✆ **08457/484-950**).

BY BUS **City Link** (www.citylink.co.uk; ✆ **0871/266-3333**) runs regular connecting services between Aberdeen and Scotland's other major cities. For bus schedules in Aberdeen, check **Stagecoach** (www.stagecoachbus.com; ✆ **01224/212-266**).

BY CAR The main route into town is the A90, which leads along the coast north from Dundee. Alternatively, the A93 is a direct route from Perth via the Cairngorms National Park, and the A96 leads into town from the north. Aberdeen is 203km (126 miles) from Edinburgh and 234km (145 miles) from Glasgow.

Visitor Information
TOURIST OFFICE The **Aberdeen Tourist Information Centre** is at 23 Union St. (www.aberdeen-grampian.com; ✆ **01224/288-828**). In July and August, it's open Monday to Friday 9am to 7pm, Saturday 9am to 5pm, and Sunday 10am to 4pm. All other months it's open Monday to Friday 9am to 5pm and Saturday 10am to 2pm.

EXPLORING ABERDEEN
Start your exploration of Aberdeen away from the city center and head 1.6km (1 mile) north to the cobbled streets of **Old Aberdeen,** home to the **University of Aberdeen** (bus no. 20 runs every 15 minutes from the city center). Here you can wander around the old **King's College** with its ancient chapel (from around 1500), the **Cathedral of St. Machar,** one of Scotland's most important and where legend claims William Wallace's left arm is buried in a wall, and the exquisite **Cruickshank Botanic Garden.**

Back in the city center, Aberdeen focuses around Union Street to the north of the city's docks, which are always busy with deep-sea trawlers and ferries. Delve into the city's seafaring history at the **Aberdeen Maritime Museum** (www.aagm.co.uk; ✆ **01224/337-700**) on Shiprow, whose enormous windows open onto stunning views of the harbor. The museum is free to enter and is open Tuesday to Saturday 10am to 5pm and Sunday noon to 3pm.

North of Union Street on Broad Street stands **Marischal College,** the world's second biggest granite structure, and tucked away opposite the college on Guestrow is the historically fascinating **Provost Skene's House** (www.aagm.co.uk; ✆ **01224/641-086**). Dating from 1545, the house showcases period rooms from across the centuries, but best of all is the 17th-century **Painted Gallery.** The house is free to enter and open Monday to Saturday 10am to 5pm.

Aberdeen Art Gallery Housed in an airy late-19th-century neoclassical building, the gallery showcases one of the U.K.'s most important art collections. Highlights of the permanent collection include portraits by Raeburn, Hogarth, and Reynolds, as well as acclaimed 20th-century works by Paul Nash and Francis Bacon, all complemented by a changing program of special exhibitions and events.

Schoolhill. www.aagm.co.uk. ✆ **01224/523-700.** Free admission. Tues–Sat 10am–5pm, Sun 2–5pm.

WHERE TO STAY & EAT
Marcliffe Hotel & Spa ★★ Located in the westerns outskirts of Aberdeen, the Marcliffe is an appealing combination of luxury, comfort, and fine dining. The Victorian house is surrounded by 4½ hectares (11 acres) of wooded landscaped gardens, while inside the public areas are a feast of antique furniture and contemporary style.

All rooms and suites are individually decorated and feature added extras such as fresh fruit. Dine in the elegant **Conservatory Restaurant** which champions Scottish fare and an extensive wine list, or relax after a busy day's sightseeing in the on-site spa.

N. Deeside Rd., Aberdeen AB1 9YA. www.marcliffe.com. ⓒ **01224/861-000.** Fax 01224/868-860. 42 units. £155–£249 double; £279–bp]349 suite. AE, DC, MC, V. Free parking. Located on Deeside Rd., out of Aberdeen (well signposted). **Amenities:** Restaurant; bar; spa; room service. *In room:* TV, minibar, hair dryer, Wi-Fi (free).

Silver Darling ★ FRENCH/SEAFOOD   Occupying a prime harborfront spot in Aberdeen's former custom house, Silver Darling is the local nickname of a herring. A longtime favorite of Aberdeen's eating out scene, this acclaimed restaurant is known for serving an array of local seafood with French flair. Pick from the likes of seared king scallops with leek and onion fondue or steamed filet of halibut topped with a brioche and cheese crust. Panoramic views of Aberdeen harbor are as mouthwatering as the food.

Porca Quay, North Quay. http://thesilverdarling.co.uk. ⓒ **01224/576-229.** Reservations recommended. Main courses: lunch, £10–£16; dinner, £18–£20. AE, DC, MC, V. Mon–Fri noon–1.45pm and 6.30–9.30pm, Sat 6.30–9.30pm and Sun noon–2.30pm.

Speyside & the Malt Whisky Trail ★

Much of the Speyside region covered in this section is in the Moray district, on the southern shore of the Moray Firth, a large inlet cutting into the northeastern coast of Scotland. The district stretches in a triangular shape south from the coast to the wild heart of the Cairngorm Mountains near Aviemore. It's a land steeped in history, as its many castles, battle sites, and ancient monuments testify. It's also a good place to fish and, of course, play golf. Golfers can purchase a 5-day ticket from tourist information centers that will allow you to play at more than 11 courses in the area.

One of the best of these courses is **Boat of Garten,** Speyside (www.boatgolf.com; ⓒ **01479/831-282**). Relatively difficult, the almost 5,500m (6,000-yd.) course is dotted with many bunkers and wooded areas. April to October greens fees are £39 per round, £51 per day Monday to Friday and hours are from 9:30am to 11pm. Saturday greens fees are £44 per round, £56 per day, and hours are from 10am to 4pm. In winter, call to see if the course is open. Pull-carts can be rented for £3 and clubs can be rented for £20. Dress reasonably; blue jeans aren't acceptable.

The valley of the second-largest river in Scotland, the Spey, lies north and south of Aviemore and is a land of great natural beauty. The Spey is born in the Highlands above Loch Laggan, which lies 64km (40 miles) south of Inverness. Little more than a creek at its inception, it gains in force, fed by the many "burns" that drain water from the surrounding hills. One of Scotland's great rivers for salmon fishing, it runs between the towering Cairngorms in the east and the **Monadhliath Mountains** in the west. Its major center is **Grantown-on-Spey.**

The primary tourist attraction in the area is the **Malt Whisky Trail,** 113km (70 miles) long, running through the glens of Speyside. Here distilleries, many of which can be visited, are known for their production of *uisge beatha,* or "water of life." "Whisky" is its more familiar name.

Half the malt distilleries in Scotland lie along the River Spey and its tributaries. Peat smoke and Highland water are used to turn out single-malt (unblended) whisky. The five malt distilleries in the area are **Glenlivet, Glenfiddich, Glenfarclas, Strathisla,** and **Tamdhu.** Allow about an hour for each visit.

SPOTTING nessie

Sir Peter Scott's *Nessitera rhombopteryx*, one of the world's greatest mysteries, continues to elude her pursuers. The Loch Ness Monster or "Nessie," as she's more familiarly known, has captured the imagination of the world, drawing thousands each year to Loch Ness. All types of high-tech underwater contraptions have gone after the Loch Ness monster, but no one can find her despite numerous sightings, some of which have been captured on film. Dr. Robert Rines and his associates at the Academy of Applied Science in Massachusetts maintain an all-year watch with sonar-triggered cameras and strobe lights suspended from a raft in Urquhart Bay. However, many locals aren't keen on her being found as a local prophesy claims it will be the end of Inverness if she is.

The loch itself is 39km (24 miles) long, 1.6km (1 mile) wide, and some 239m (751 ft.) deep. In summer, you can take boat cruises across it from both Fort Augustus and Inverness. If you're driving take the A82 between Fort Augustus and Inverness, which threads along the western banks of the loch and leads through the bucolic hamlet of Drumnadrochit. Here you can drop into the **Loch Ness Exhibition Centre** (www.lochness.com; ☎ **01456/450-573**) and catch up on the full history of Nessie as well as take a trip onto the loch via a sonar research boat. Nearby, the romantic ruins of the **Urquhart Castle** (www.historic-scotland.gov. uk; ☎ **01456/450-551**) stand on a promontory overlooking the loch, offering superb views of the water and Great Glen. Alternatively you can trace the eastern shoreline of Loch Ness via the B862, a quieter, more rural route.

The best way to reach Speyside from Aberdeen is to take A96 northwest, signposted ELGIN. If you're traveling north on the A9 road from Perth and Pitlochry, your first stop might be Dalwhinnie, which has the highest whisky distillery in the world at 575m (1,886 ft.). It's not in the Spey Valley but is at the northeastern end of Loch Ericht, with fine views of lochs and forests.

KEITH

Keith, 18km (11 miles) northwest of Huntly, grew up because of its strategic location, where the main road and rail routes between Inverness and Aberdeen cross the River Isla. It has an ancient history, but owes its present look to the town planning of the late 18th and early 19th centuries. Today it's a major stopover along the Malt Whisky Trail.

The oldest operating distillery in the Scottish Highlands, the **Strathisla Distillery,** on Seafield Avenue (☎ **01542/783-044**), was established in 1786. From April to October, hours are Monday to Saturday 9:30am to 5pm, Sunday noon to 5pm. Admission is £6 for adults, free for children age 8 to 18; children age 7 and under are not admitted. The entrance cost includes a £3 voucher redeemable in the distillery shop against a 70cl bottle of whisky.

DUFFTOWN

James Duff, the fourth earl of Fife, founded this town in 1817. The four main streets of town converge at the clock tower, which is also the **Tourist Information Centre** (☎ **01340/820-501**), open from April to October, Monday to Saturday 10am to 1pm and 2pm to 5pm.

A center of the whisky-distilling industry, Dufftown is surrounded by seven malt distilleries. The family-owned **Glenfiddich Distillery** is on the A941, 1km (⅔ mile) north (www.glenfiddich.com; ☏ **01340/820-373**). It's open daily 9.30am to 4.30pm. Guides in kilts show you around the plant and explain the process of distilling. A film of the history of distilling is also shown. At the end of the tour, you're given a dram of malt whisky to sample. There's also a souvenir shop.

Other sights include **Balvenie Castle,** along the A941 (www.historic-scotland. gov.uk; ☏ **01340/820-121**), the ruins of a moated 14th-century stronghold that lie on the south side of the Glenfiddich Distillery. During her northern campaign against the Earl of Huntly, Mary, Queen of Scots, spent 2 nights here. It's open from April to September daily 9:30am to 6:30pm. Admission is £4 for adults, £3.20 for seniors, and £2.40 for children.

Mortlach Parish Church in Dufftown is one of the oldest places of Christian worship in the country. It's reputed to have been founded in 566 by St. Moluag. A Pictish cross stands in the graveyard. The present church was reconstructed in 1931 and incorporates portions of an older building.

Where to Eat

A Taste of Speyside ★ SCOTTISH   True to its name, this restaurant just off the main square avidly promotes Speyside cuisine as well as the products of Speyside's 46 distilleries. Try the platter, which includes a slice of smoked salmon, venison, and trout, pâté flavored with malt whisky, locally made cheese, salads, and homemade oat cakes. Hearty soups are made daily and served with homemade bread. There's also a choice of meat pies, including venison with red wine and herbs, or rabbit. For dessert, try homemade fruit dumpling with whisky.

10 Balvenie St. http://atasteofspeyside.com. ☏ **01340/820-860.** Reservations recommended for dinner. Main courses £18–£24; set lunch £13; set dinner £24. AE, MC, V. Tues–Sat noon–2pm and 6–9pm, Sun 6–9pm.

GLENLIVET

From Grantown-on-Spey head east along the A95, drive to the junction with the B9008; go south and you won't miss the **Glenlivet Distillery.** The location of the **Glenlivet Reception Centre** (www.theglenlivet.com; ☏ **01340/821-720**) is 16km (10 miles) north of the nearest town, Tomintoul. Near the River Livet, a Spey tributary, this distillery is one of the most famous in Scotland. It's open April to October, Monday to Saturday from 9.30am to 4pm, and Sunday from noon to 4pm. Admission is free.

Back on the A95, you can visit the **Glenfarclas Distillery** at Ballindalloch (www. glenfarclas.co.uk; ☏ **01807/500-209**), one of the few malt whisky distilleries that's still independent of the giants. Founded in 1836, Glenfarclas is managed by the sixth generation of the Grant family. A 90-minute tour of the distillery costs £5 per person and visits are possible October to March Monday to Friday 10am to 4pm; April to September Monday to Friday 10am to 5pm, plus Saturdays from 10am to 4pm from July to September.

SPAIN

by Patricia Harris & David Lyon

We agree with the sentiment apocryphally attributed to Ernest Hemingway: "If you visit only one foreign country in your lifetime, make it Spain." Nowhere else is quite as rich, or quite as demanding. When you go to Spain, you must surrender to Spain. You must accept the rhythms of daily life—so unlike the rest of Europe—and think nothing of going to dinner after 10pm and then closing down the flamenco bar after the 3am final set.

There is a Spain for every taste. The country stretches from long, sandy beaches on three coasts to mountain ranges that rise into the clouds. The small towns and villages of every region will beguile you, just as the hip modern European metropolises of Barcelona and Madrid will make your pulse race. The Moorish legacy of Andalucía will have you in its thrall. With architecture that ranges from Roman aqueducts to Moorish palaces to Gaudí's phantasmagorical basilica to Frank O. Gehry's armored fish of the Guggenheim Bilbao Museum, and art that progresses from cave paintings to Picasso, Spain will dazzle your eyes. Its classical music and flamenco will dazzle your ears. And everywhere you go, its great chefs will dazzle your taste buds.

MADRID ★★★

Madrid was conceived, planned, and built when Spain was at the peak of its power, and the city became the solid and dignified seat of a great empire stretching around the world. Monumental Madrid glitters almost as much as Paris, Rome, or London—and it parties more than any other city in Europe. Although it lacks the spectacular Romanesque and Gothic monuments of older Spanish cities, Madrid never fails to charm with its grandeur.

Madrid sits at the highest altitude of any European capital, and its climate is blisteringly hot in summer but often quite cold in winter. Traffic roars down wide boulevards that stretch from the narrow streets of the city's 17th-century core to the modern late-20th-century suburbs.

Don't come to Madrid expecting a city that looks classically Iberian. True, many of the older buildings in the historic core look as Spanish as those you might encounter in rural towns across the plains of La Mancha. However, a great number of the monuments and palaces mirror the architecture of France—an oddity that reflects the link between the royal families of Spain and France.

Most striking is how the city has blossomed since Franco's demise. During the 1980s, Madrid was the epicenter of La Movida ("the Movement"), a creative burst of expression in the arts and pop culture after decades of puritanical and fascistic repression. Today, despite competition from Barcelona, Sevilla, and Bilbao, Madrid still reigns as the country's artistic and creative center.

More world-class art is on view in the central neighborhood around the stellar Museo del Prado than within virtually any concentrated area in the world. You can see Caravaggios and Rembrandts at the Thyssen-Bornemisza; Goyas, Zurbaráns, and Velázquezes at the Prado itself; and Dalís and Mirós—not to mention Picasso's wrenching *Guernica*—at the Reina Sofía.

Madrid seems forever *en obras*—that is, under construction—but the new structures rising throughout the city tend to reflect cutting-edge design, likely as not by Spanish designers. Still, some of the best of Old Madrid remains: the opulence of the Palacio Real, the bustle of El Rastro's flea market, and the sultry fever of late-night flamenco. And visitors still find rest and relaxation in the verdant oasis of Parque del Retiro, just a stone's throw from the Prado.

Essentials

GETTING THERE

BY PLANE Madrid's international airport, **Barajas** (airport code: MAD), lies 15km (9⅓ miles) east of the city center and has two terminals—one for international traffic, the other for domestic—that are connected by a moving sidewalk and light rail. For Barajas Airport information, call ✆ **90-240-47-04,** or check www.aena.es.

Air-conditioned airport **buses** can take you from the arrivals terminal to the Atocha train station. The fare is 2€; buses leave every 10 to 15 minutes, either to or from the airport. By **taxi,** expect to pay 25€ and up, plus surcharges, for the trip to the airport and for baggage handling. If you take an unmetered limousine, make sure you negotiate the price in advance. A **subway** connecting Barajas Airport and central Madrid provides additional ground transportation options; however, the ride involves a transfer: Take line 8 to Nuevos Ministerios and switch to line 4; the one-way trip costs 3€.

BY TRAIN Madrid has two major railway stations: **Atocha** (Glorieta Carlos V; Metro: Atocha RENFE), for trains to and from Lisbon, Toledo, Andalucía, and Extremadura; and **Chamartín** (in the northern suburbs at Augustín de Foxá; Metro: Chamartín), for trains to and from Barcelona, Asturias, Cantabria, Castilla y León, the Basque Country, Aragón, Catalunya, Levante (Valencia), Murcia, and the French frontier. For information about connections from any of these stations, call **RENFE (Spanish Railways)** at ✆ **90-232-03-20** (daily 5am–11:50pm).

For tickets, go to RENFE's main office at Alcalá 44 (www.renfe.es; ✆ **90-232-03-20;** Metro: Banco de España). The office is open Monday to Friday 9:30am to 11:30pm.

BY BUS Madrid has at least 14 major bus terminals, including **Estación Sur de Autobuses,** Calle Méndez Álvaro 83 (www.estaciondeautobuses.com; ✆ **91-468-42-00;** Metro: Méndez Álvaro). Most buses pass through this large station.

BY CAR The following are the major highways into Madrid, with driving distances to the city: Route NI from Irún, 507km (315 miles); NII from Barcelona, 626km (389 miles); NIII from Valencia, 349km (217 miles); NIV from Cádiz, 625km (388 miles); NV from Badajoz, 409km (254 miles); and NVI from Galicia, 602km (374 miles).

VISITOR INFORMATION

TOURIST OFFICE   The most convenient **tourist office** is located on Plaza Mayor 27 (Salón de Columnas de la Casa de la Panadería) (www.esmadrid.com; ✆ **91-588-16-36;** Metro: Sól or Ópera); it's open daily from 9:30am to 8:30pm. Ask for a street map of the next town on your itinerary, especially if you're driving. The staff here can give you a list of hotels and *hostales*.

CITY LAYOUT   Every new arrival must find the **Gran Vía,** which cuts a winding pathway across the city, beginning at **Plaza de España,** where you'll find one of Europe's tallest skyscrapers, the Edificio España. This avenue is home to a large concentration of shops, hotels, restaurants, and movie houses in the city, with **Calle de Serrano** a close runner-up.

South of the Gran Vía lies **Puerta del Sol,** the starting point for all road distances within Spain and the central crossroads of the public transit system. The bustling square is the interstice between the oldest quarters of Madrid and the commercial heart of the city. **Calle de Alcalá** begins here at Sol and runs for 4km (2½ miles).

Plaza Mayor lies at the heart of Old Madrid and is an attraction in itself, with its mix of French and Georgian architecture. Pedestrians pass beneath the arches of the huge square onto the narrow streets of the district known as La Latina, where you can find intriguing restaurants and *tascas* serving bountiful tapas and drinks. The colonnaded ground level of the plaza is filled with shops, many of which sell souvenir trinkets.

Madrid

RESTAURANTS ◆
Asiana **18**
Astrid y Gastón **19**
Café de Oriente **8**
Café Restaurante El Espejo **24**
Casa Lucio **15**
Casa Salvador **26**
Dassa Bassa **32**
El Brillante **52**
El Cosaco **14**
El Mentidero de la Villa **25**
El Schotis **16**
Iroco **23**
La Biotika **45**
La Gamella **33**
La Gastroteca de Santiago **10**
La Manduca de Azagra **17**
La Terraza del Casino **31**
Mosaiq **17**
Pan de Lujo **23**
Sobrino de Botín **13**
Tocororo **41**
Viavélez **17**
Viridiana **35**

HOTELS ■
AC Palacio del Retiro **34**
Casa de Madrid **3**
Chic & Basic Colors **50**
De Las Letras **28**
Hesperia Madrid **21**
Hostal Cervantes **43**
Hostal la Macarena **12**
Hostal Residencia Don Diego **21**
Hotel Adler **22**
Hotel Catalonia Gran Vía **29**
Hotel Inglés **39**
Hotel Moderno **7**
Hotel Mora **46**
Hotel Ópera **2**
Hotel Preciados **4**
Hotel Urban **38**
HUSA Hotel Paseo del Arte **49**
Laura **6**
ME Madrid **42**
NH Nacional **48**
Oscar **27**
Rafaelhoteles Orense **21**
The Ritz **36**

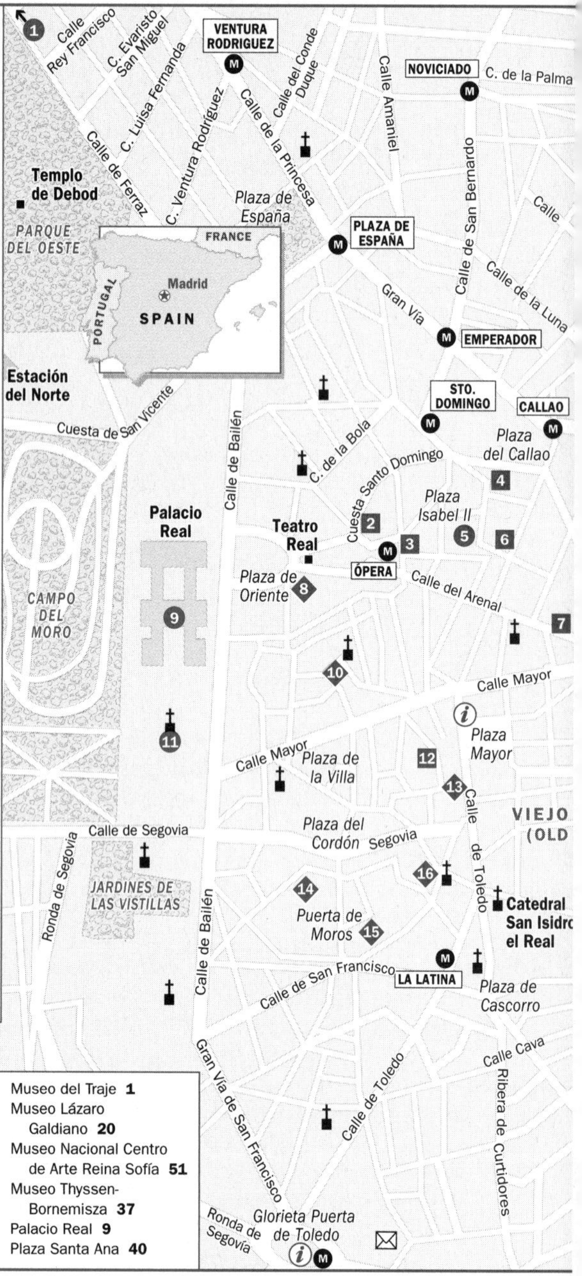

Calle Rey Francisco
C. Evaristo San Miguel
C. Luisa Fernanda
VENTURA RODRIGUEZ
Calle del Conde Duque
Calle Amaniel
NOVICIADO
C. de la Palma
Calle de Ferraz
C. Ventura Rodríguez
Calle de la Princesa
Templo de Debod
Plaza de España
Calle de San Bernardo
PARQUE DEL OESTE
FRANCE
PORTUGAL
Madrid
SPAIN
PLAZA DE ESPAÑA
Calle de la Luna
Gran Vía
EMPERADOR
Estación del Norte
Cuesta de San Vicente
STO. DOMINGO
CALLAO
Plaza del Callao
C. de la Bola
Cuesta Santo Domingo
Calle de Bailén
Plaza Isabel II
Palacio Real
Teatro Real
ÓPERA
Plaza de Oriente
Calle del Arenal
CAMPO DEL MORO
Calle Mayor
Plaza Mayor
Plaza de la Villa
VIEJO (OLD
Calle de Segovia
Plaza del Cordón
Calle de Toledo
Ronda de Segovia
JARDINES DE LAS VISTILLAS
Catedral San Isidro el Real
Puerta de Moros
Calle de San Francisco
LA LATINA
Plaza de Cascorro
Calle Cava
Gran Vía de San Francisco
Ribera de Curtidores
Glorieta Puerta de Toledo
Ronda de Segovia

ATTRACTIONS ●
CaixaForum **47**
Catedral de la Almudena **11**
Monasterio de las Descalzas Reales **5**
Museo de la Real Academia de Bellas Artes de San Fernando **30**
Museo del Prado **44**
Museo del Traje **1**
Museo Lázaro Galdiano **20**
Museo Nacional Centro de Arte Reina Sofía **51**
Museo Thyssen-Bornemisza **37**
Palacio Real **9**
Plaza Santa Ana **40**

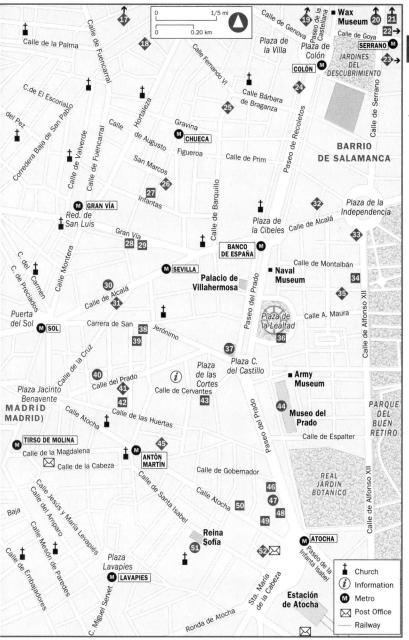

Calle de la Palma

Calle de Fuencarral

C. de El Escorial

del Pez

Corredera Baja de San Pablo

Calle de Valverde

Calle de Fuencarral

Calle

Hortaleza

Calle Fernando VI

Calle de Genova

Calle de la Castellana

Plaza de la Villa

Plaza de Colón

■ Wax Museum

Calle de Goya

SERRANO Ⓜ

JARDINES DEL DESCUBRIMIENTO

COLÓN Ⓜ

Calle Bárbara de Braganza

Gravina

CHUECA Ⓜ

de Augusto

Figueroa

San Marcos

Calle de Prim

Paseo de Recoletos

BARRIO DE SALAMANCA

Calle de Serrano

Infantas

GRAN VÍA Ⓜ

Red. de San Luis

Gran Vía

Calle de Barquillo

Plaza de la Cibeles   Calle de Alcalá

Plaza de la Independencia

C. del Carmen

C. de Preciados

Calle Montera

BANCO DE ESPAÑA Ⓜ

Calle de Montalbán

SEVILLA Ⓜ

Palacio de Villahermosa

■ Naval Museum

Calle de Alfonso XII

Puerta del Sol

SOL Ⓜ

Calle de Alcalá

Carrera de San

Jerónimo

Paseo del Prado

Plaza de la Lealtad

Calle A. Maura

Plaza C. del Castillo

Calle de la Cruz

Calle del Prado

Ⓘ

Plaza de las Cortes

Calle de Cervantes

■ Army Museum

PARQUE DEL BUEN RETIRO

Plaza Jacinto Benavente

MADRID MADRID)

Calle Atocha

Calle de las Huertas

Museo del Prado

Calle de Espalter

TIRSO DE MOLINA

Calle de la Magdalena

✉ Calle de la Cabeza

ANTÓN MARTÍN Ⓜ

Calle de Santa Isabel

Calle de Gobernador

Calle Atocha

REAL JARDIN BOTANICO

Calle de Alfonso XII

Calle Jesús y María Levapiés

Calle del Amparo

Baja

Calle Mesón de Paredes

Calle de Embajadores

Reina Sofía

Plaza Lavapiés

LAVAPIES Ⓜ

ATOCHA Ⓜ

Paseo de la Infanta Isabel

Sta. María de la Cabeza

Estación de Atocha

Ronda de Atocha

C. Miguel Servet

✝	Church
Ⓘ	Information
Ⓜ	Metro
✉	Post Office
---	Railway

0   1/5 mi

0   0.20 km

The area immediately south of Plaza Mayor—known as *barrios bajos*—is a colorful district of medieval cobblestone streets lined with 16th- and 17th-century architecture. Exit Plaza Mayor through the **Arco de Cuchilleros** to Cava Baja, a street packed with markets, restaurants, and taverns.

Gran Vía ends at Calle de Alcalá, and at this juncture lies the grand **Plaza de la Cibeles,** with its fountain to Cybele, "the mother of the gods," and the main post office (known as "the cathedral of post offices"). From Cibeles, the wide **Paseo de Recoletos** begins a short run north to Plaza de Colón. From this latter square rolls the serpentine central artery of Madrid: **Paseo de la Castellana,** flanked by expensive shops, apartment buildings, luxury hotels, and foreign embassies.

Heading south from Cibeles is **Paseo del Prado,** where you'll find Spain's major attraction, the Museo del Prado, as well as the Jardín Botánico (Botanical Garden). The *paseo* leads to the Atocha railway station. To the west of the garden lies **Parque del Retiro,** a magnificent park once reserved for royalty, with a restaurant, a rose garden, and two lakes.

The Neighborhoods in Brief

Madrid can be divided into three principal districts—Old Madrid, which holds the most tourist interest; Ensanche, the new district, often with the best shops and hotels; and the periphery, of less interest to visitors.

Puerta del Sol and Las Letras　The old city radiated from Puerta del Sol even before Habsburg kings made Madrid the capital. The hub of public transport, Sol, connects ancient and modern Madrid. Heading south and uphill from Sol is the barrio called Las Letras, because it has attracted writers for centuries. Lope de Vega, Cervantes, and even Lorca lived and worked here. It includes the Plaza Santa Ana, one of the city's best spots for tapas and nightlife.

Plaza Mayor and La Latina　This is the heart of the district most visitors come to see, especially after dark. Sometimes called the "Madrid of the Asturias," it is better known as La Latina. From Plaza Mayor, the Arco de Cuchileros leads to Cava de San Miguel, Cava Alta, and Cava Baja, all full of taverns and bars. La Latina continues downhill west to the Manzanares River. Also in this area, Muslim Madrid is centered on the Palacio de Oriente and Las Vistillas. What is now Plaza de la Paja was actually the heart of the city and its main marketplace during the medieval period. In 1617, Plaza Mayor became the hub of Madrid, and it remains a center of evening tourist activity.

Ópera and Palacio Real　Adjacent to Plaza Mayor and La Latina, this section of Madrid revolves around the Teatro Real, the Plaza de Oriente, and the Palacio Real with its parks and gardens. It forms a buffer zone, of sorts, between Puerta del Sol and Plaza Mayor, and the uphill, modern district around Gran Vía.

Gran Vía and Plaza de España Gran Vía was constructed in the early 20th century to be Madrid's main street. It is flanked by cinemas, department stores, and bank and corporate headquarters. It begins at Plaza de España, with its bronze figures of Don Quixote and his faithful squire, Sancho Panza.

Chueca This revitalized district north of the Gran Vía includes the main streets of Hortaleza, Infantas, Barquillo, and San Lucas. It is the center of gay nightlife, with dozens of clubs, some superb restaurants, and some of the city's hippest shopping.

Argüelles and Moncloa The university area is bounded by the streets of Pintor Rosales, Cea Bermúdez, Bravo Murillo, San Bernardo, and Conde Duque. Students haunt its famous alehouses.

Salamanca, Retiro, and Chamberí Ever since Madrid's city walls came down in the 1860s, the district of Salamanca to the north has been the fashionable address. Calle de Serrano cuts through this neighborhood and is lined with stores and boutiques. The street is also home to the U.S. Embassy. The adjacent leafy streets near Parque del Retiro and Chamberí (west of the Paseos) are often lumped with Salamanca because they are also upscale enclaves.

Art District and Paseos Not a real city district, the Paseos form Madrid's north–south axis, and the street name changes along the way. As it approaches Atocha station, the district is suddenly thick with museums and park amenities. The Museo del Prado and some of the city's more expensive hotels are found here. Many restaurants and other hotels are located along its side streets. In summer, the large medians of the Paseos become open-air terraces filled with animated crowds.

GETTING AROUND

The tourist office (see above) provides a street map that includes a schematic of the public transit system. The bus and expanding Metro networks are efficient and extensive, and taxis are abundant. Because traffic is nearly always heavy, though, plan to cover distances under 10 blocks by walking.

BY METRO (SUBWAY) The Metro system is quite easy to learn and use. The fare is 1.50€ for a one-way trip, and the central converging point is the Puerta del Sol. The Metro operates from 6am to 2am (try to avoid rush hours). For information, call ✆ **90-244-44-03** (www.metromadrid.es). A 10-trip Metrobus ticket, good on buses and Metro, costs 9.30€.

BY BUS A bus network also services the city and suburbs, with routes clearly shown at each stop on a schematic diagram. Buses are fast and efficient because they travel in special lanes. Both red and blue buses charge 1.50€ per ride. For 9.30€ you can purchase a 10-trip *bonos* ticket (but without transfers) for Madrid's bus system. The ticket is sold at **Empresa Municipal de Transportes,** Calle Cerro de Plata 4 (www.emtmadrid.es; ✆ **91-406-88-00** or **90-250-78-50**), where you can buy a guide to the bus routes. The office is open Monday to Friday from 8am to 2pm.

BY TAXI Cab fares are pretty reasonable. When you flag down a taxi, the meter should register 2.10€ 6am to 9pm or 2.20€ 9pm to 6am; for every kilometer thereafter, the fare increases between 1€ and 1.20€. A supplement is charged for trips to the railway station or the bullring. The ride to Barajas Airport carries a 5.50€ surcharge, and there is a 2.95€ supplement from railway stations and to or from Juan Carlos I Trade Fair. In addition, a 1.20€ supplement is charged on Sundays and holidays. It's customary to tip at least 10% of the fare.

BY CAR Driving in congested Madrid always feels like rush hour, although theoretically rush hours are 8 to 10am, 1 to 2pm, and 4 to 6pm Monday to Saturday. Parking is next to impossible except in expensive garages. About the only time you can drive around Madrid with a minimum of hassle is in August, when thousands of Madrileños have taken their cars and headed for Spain's vacation oases. Save your car rentals for excursions from the capital. If you drive into Madrid from another city, ask at your hotel for the nearest garage or parking possibility and leave your vehicle there until you're ready to leave.

In addition to its office at Barajas Airport (www.avis.es; ☏ **90-220-01-62**), **Avis** has a main city office at Gran Vía 60 (☏ **91-548-42-04**).

[Fast FACTS] MADRID

Business Hours Banks are open Monday to Friday 9:30am to 2pm and Saturday 9:30am to 1pm. Major stores are open Monday to Saturday from 9:30am to 8pm; smaller establishments, however, often take a siesta, doing business 9:30am to 1:30pm and 4:30 to 8pm. Hours can vary from store to store.

Currency Exchange The currency exchange at Chamartín railway station (Metro: Chamartín) is open 24 hours and gives the best rates. If you exchange money at a bank, ask about the commission charged. Many banks in Spain still charge a 1% to 3% commission with a minimum charge of 3€. However, branches of **Banco Santander Central Hispano** charge no commission. Branches of **El Corte Inglés,** the department store chain, offer exchange facilities with varying rates. You get the worst rates at street kiosks such as Chequepoint, Exact Change, and Cambios-Uno. Although they're handy and charge no commission, their rates are very low. Naturally, American

Express offices offer the best rates on their own checks. ATMs are plentiful in Madrid.

Dentists & Doctors For an English-speaking dentist, contact the **U.S. Embassy,** Calle de Serrano 75 (http://spanish.madrid. usembassy.gov; ☏ **91-587-22-40**), which maintains a list of dentists who offer their services to Americans abroad. For dental services, you can also consult **Unidad Médica Anglo-Americana,** Conde de Arandá 1 (www. unidadmedica.com; ☏ **91-435-18-23**). Office hours are Monday to Friday from 9am to 8pm and Saturday 10am to 1pm. For an English-speaking doctor, contact the **U.S. Embassy,** Calle de Serrano 75 (http:// spanish.madrid.usembassy. gov; ☏ **91-587-22-40**).

Emergencies A centralized number for fire, police, and ambulance services is ☏ **112.**

Hospitals & Clinics **Unidad Médica Anglo-Americana,** Conde de Arandá 1 (www.unidad medica.com; ☏ **91-435-18-23;** Metro: Retiro), is not a

hospital but a private outpatient clinic offering specialized services. This is not an emergency clinic, although someone on the staff is always available. Unidad Medica Anglo-Americana is open Monday to Friday 9am to 8pm and Saturday 10am to 1pm. In a medical emergency, call ☏ **112** for an ambulance.

Internet Access Internet cafes have sprung up all over the city. Ask at your hotel for the location nearest to where you are staying.

Pharmacies For a late-night pharmacy, look in the daily newspaper under *Farmacias de Guardia* to learn which drugstores are open after 8pm. Another way to find one is to go to any pharmacy, which, even if closed, always posts a list of nearby pharmacies that are open late that day. Madrid has hundreds of pharmacies; one of the most central is **Farmacia de la Paloma,** Calle de Toledo 46 (☏ **91-365-34-58;** Metro: Puerta del Sol or La Latina).

Post Office Madrid's central post office is in the

Palacio de Comunicaciones at Plaza de la Cibeles (ℂ **91-523-06-94**). Hours are Monday to Friday 8:30am to 9:30pm and Saturday 8:30am to 2pm.

Safety As in every crowded city around the world, purse snatching is common. Criminals often work in pairs, grabbing purses from pedestrians, cyclists, and even cars. A popular scam involves one robber smearing the back of the victim's clothing, perhaps with mustard, ice cream, or something worse. An accomplice then pretends to help clean up the mess, all the while picking the victim's pockets.

Telephones The country code for Spain is **34** and the city code for Madrid is **91**.

Exploring Madrid

The main sightseeing attractions of Madrid tend to cluster by dynasty. The Palacio Royal, the religious sights, and the Plaza Mayor lie in the part of Madrid built by the Habsburgs—that is, near Sol and Ópera Metro stops. The once-residential neighborhood uphill from Puerta del Sol dates from the same era, and contains the attractions of the Barrio de las Letras.

The Bourbon dynasty attractions include all the major art museums, which lie within a few blocks of the Atocha Metro stop. Note that the Paseo del Arte pass (about 15€) provides discounted admission to the big three: the Prado, the Reina Sofía, and the Thyssen-Bornemisza. Almost all the museums in this book have free admission for at least a few hours each week. If you are in town long enough to take advantage of these times, you might want to plan sightseeing accordingly. Typically, many museums are closed Mondays, and most are closed December 24 and 25, December 31, January 1, January 6, May 1, May 15, and November 9.

PUERTA DEL SOL & LAS LETRAS

Museo de la Real Academia de Bellas Artes de San Fernando (Fine Arts Museum) ART MUSEUM An easy stroll from Puerta del Sol, the Fine Arts Museum is located in the restored and remodeled 17th-century baroque palace of Juan de Goyeneche. The collection—more than 1,500 paintings and 570 sculptures, ranging from the 16th century to the present—was started in 1752 during the reign of Fernando VI (1746–59), and organized by Goya himself. It emphasizes works by Spanish, Flemish, and Italian artists. You can see masterpieces by El Greco, Rubens, Velázquez, Zurbarán, Ribera, Cano, Coello, Murillo, Goya, and Sorolla.

Alcalá 13. http://rabasf.insde.es. ℂ **91-524-08-64.** Admission 5€ adults, 2.50€ students, free for children 17 and under; free for all visitors Wed. Tues–Sat 9am–3pm; Sun 9am–2:30pm. Metro: Sol or Sevilla. Bus: 3, 5, 15, 20, 51, 52, 53, or 150.

Plaza Santa Ana ★ SQUARE Sooner or later you will have a drink on Plaza Santa Ana, and you'll probably wonder what took you so long. The neighborhood has been Madrid's theater district for roughly the last 400 years, as open-air theaters on the spot produced the plays of Lope de Vega (who lived nearby) and other satirists. The **Teatro Español** was erected here in the mid-19th century, and made Plaza Santa Ana as hip then as it is now. Because it made the area an entertainment district, dozens of bars and cafes popped up. They still represent one of the city's top tapas scenes. The theater continues to anchor the east side of the square and presents performances of dance, orchestral, and chamber music, as well as live theater.

Teatro Español, Príncipe 25. www.teatroespanol.es. ℂ **91-360-14-84.** Metro: Antón Martín or Tirso de Molina. Bus: 6, 9, 10, 14, 26, 27, 32, 34, 37, 45, or 57.

ÓPERA & PALACIO REAL

Catedral de la Almudena CATHEDRAL   Political conflicts, wars, and a simple lack of money led to incredible delays in the building of Madrid's cathedral. Construction began in 1883, but it took 110 years for this cathedral to officially open. It's named after the Virgen de la Almudena, whose icon was found during the Reconquest on this site (which, incidentally, housed Madrid's first Muslim mosque). Originally planned in the neo-Gothic style, it was subsequently changed to neoclassical by the architect Fernando Chueca. The "pop art" stained-glass windows and multicolored ceiling, along with the grand Grezing organ, graced the wedding of Prince Felipe to newscaster Doña Letizia in May 2004, the first royal wedding in nearly a century.

Calle Bailén 10.*(C)* **91-542-22-00.** Free admission. Summer daily 10am–1pm and 6–8pm; off season daily 9am–9pm. Metro: Ópera.

Monasterio de las Descalzas Reales ★★ CONVENT   In the mid-16th century, aristocratic women—either disappointed in love or wanting to be the "bride of Christ"—stole away to this convent to take the veil. Each brought a dowry, making this one of the richest convents in the land. By the mid-20th century, the convent sheltered mostly poor women. True, it still contained a priceless collection of art treasures, but the sisters were forbidden to auction anything, so they were literally starving. The state intervened, and the Pope granted special dispensation to open the convent as a museum. Today, the public can look behind the walls of what was once a mysterious edifice on one of the most beautiful squares in Old Madrid.

In the reliquary are the noblewomen's dowries, one of which is said to contain bits of wood from the True Cross; another, bones of San Sebastían. The most valuable painting is Titian's *Caesar's Money.* The Flemish Hall shelters other fine works, including paintings by Hans de Beken and Bruegel the Elder. All the tapestries were based on Rubens's cartoons, displaying his chubby matrons. Be warned that the tours are not in English, but there is much to see even if you don't speak Spanish. Allot 1 hour for a visit here.

Plaza de las Descalzas Reales s/n. www.patrimonionacional.es.*(C)* **91-454-88-00.** Admission 7€ adults, 4€ children 5–16, free for children 4 and under. Tues–Sat 10am–2pm and 4–6:30pm; Sun 10am–3pm. Metro: Ópera. Bus: 3, 25, 39, or 148. From Plaza del Callao, off Gran Vía, walk down Postigo de San Martín to Plaza de las Descalzas Reales; the convent is on the left.

Palacio Real (Palacio Royal) ★★ PALACE   This huge palace was begun in 1738 on the site of the Madrid Alcázar, which burned to the ground in 1734. Some of its 2,000 rooms—which that "enlightened despot" Charles III called home—are open to the public; others are still used for state business. The palace was last used as a royal residence in 1931, before King Alfonso XIII and his wife, Victoria Eugénie, fled Spain.

Highlights of a visit include the Reception Room, State Apartments, Armory, and Royal Pharmacy. The **Reception Room** and **State Apartments** should get priority here if you're rushed. They include a rococo room with a diamond-studded clock; a porcelain salon; the Royal Chapel; the Banquet Room, where receptions for heads of state are still held; and the sumptuous Throne Room.

Tip: If your visit falls on the first Wednesday of the month, look for the changing-of-the-guard ceremony, which occurs at noon and is free to the public.

Plaza de Oriente, Calle de Bailén 2. www.patrimonionacional.es.*(C)* **91-454-88-00.** Admission 10€ adults, 5€ students and children 16 and under. Oct–Mar daily 10am–6pm; Apr–Sept daily 10am–8pm. Metro: Ópera or Plaza de España. Bus: 3, 25, 39, or 148.

SALAMANCA, RETIRO & CHAMBERÍ

Museo Lázaro Galdiano ★ 🏛ART MUSEUM   This house of art is a showplace for the holdings of Don José Lázaro Galdiano (1862–1947), a Gilded Age banker, writer, and collector known as "the Renaissance man of Madrid." He collected art by some of the greatest Spanish masters, including El Greco, Velázquez, Zurbarán, Ribera, Murillo, and Valdés-Leal. The Prado has its masterpieces, but the lesser works of these artists are worth viewing, too. One section is devoted to works by the English portrait and landscape artists Reynolds, Gainsborough, and Constable. Italian artists are represented by Tiepolo and Guardi, among others.

Calle de Serrano 122. www.flg.es. ⓒ**91-561-6084.** Admission 6€ adults, 3€ students and seniors, free for children 12 and under; free for all Mon and Wed–Sat 3:30–4:30pm, Sun 2–3pm. Mon and Wed–Sat 10am–4:30pm; Sun 10am–3pm. Metro: Rubén Darío. Bus: 9, 12, 16, 19, 27, 45, or 51.

ARGÜELLES & MONCLOA

Museo del Traje 🏛 MUSEUM   There is a real poignancy about some of the displays at this "costume" museum that traces the evolution of Spanish style. Because fabrics are so perishable, few examples of Spanish clothing before the 18th century survive. The exhibits, which cover around 1800 to the present, are set up in a maze inside a cavernous dark room, with each display lit brightly enough to see, but not brightly enough to further damage the fabrics. The path recapitulates the history of Spanish costume from folkloric peasant clothes through the rustling silks and stiff corsets of the 19th century to brilliant modern designers like Balenciaga. It is a lesson in the nexus of fashion and history.

Av. Jean de Herrera 2. http://museodeltraje.mcu.es. ⓒ **91-550-47-00.** Admission 3€, free for children 17 and under; free for all visitors Sat 2:30–7pm and all day Sun. Tues–Sat 9:30am–7pm; Sun and holidays 10am–3pm. Metro: Moncola. Bus: 46, 82, 83, 132, or 133.

ART DISTRICT & PASEOS

CaixaForum ★ 🏛 🍴 ART MUSEUM   Madrid's so-called triangle of great art—the Prado, the Thyssen-Bornemisza, and Reina Sofía—has become a quartet. Swiss architects Pierre de Meuron and Jacques Herzog, who transformed a factory into the Tate Modern in London, have taken a 1901 power station in Madrid and created an art complex. The museum, with both its permanent collection and its ever-changing exhibitions, showcases some of the most avant-garde art in Iberia.

The new museum is also home to film screenings and free concerts. The permanent collection includes stunning, often daring paintings from the foundation's permanent archives, including works by such artists as Cindy Sherman, Anselm Kiefer, Sigmar Polke, Carlos Armorales, Roni Horn, and Ferrán García Sevilla.

Paseo del Prado 36. ⓒ**91-330-73-00.** Free admission. Daily 10am–8pm. Metro: Atocha or Banco de España.

Museo del Prado ★★★ ART MUSEUM   With more than 7,000 paintings, the Prado is one of the most important repositories of art in the world. It began as a royal collection and was enhanced by the Habsburgs, especially Charles V, and later by the Bourbons. For paintings of the Spanish school, the Prado has no equal.

El Greco (ca. 1541–1614) was born in Crete, and although he spent most of his life working in Toledo, the Prado considered him a "foreign" artist and did not begin collecting his work until the 20th century. Given the late start, the museum managed to acquire some striking canvases, and you can see a parade of the Greek's saints, Madonnas, and Holy Families—even a ghostly *John the Baptist*.

You'll find a splendid array of works by the incomparable Diego Velázquez (1599–1660). The museum's most famous painting, in fact, is his *Las Meninas (The Maids of Honor),* a triumph in its use of light effects and perspective.

Francisco de Goya (1746–1828) ranks along with Velázquez and El Greco in the trio of great Spanish artists. Hanging here are his unflattering portraits of his patron, Charles IV, and his family, as well as the *Clothed Maja* and the *Naked Maja.* You can see the much-reproduced *Third of May* (1808), plus a series of Goya sketches (some of which, depicting the decay of 18th-century Spain, brought the Inquisition down on the artist) and his expressionistic "black paintings."

If time allows, check out some of the museum's other major collections which include Italian works by Raphael, Botticelli, Mantegna, Andrea del Sarto, Fra Angelico, and Correggio. The Prado also has an outstanding collection of the work of Hieronymus Bosch (ca. 1450–1516), the Flemish genius. *The Garden of Earthly Delights,* the best-known work of "El Bosco," is here. You'll also see his *Seven Deadly Sins* and his triptych *The Hay Wagon. The Triumph of Death* is by another Flemish painter, Pieter Bruegel the Elder (ca. 1525–69), who carried on Bosch's ghoulish vision.

After a massive expansion, there are now several new galleries, a restaurant, a lecture hall, and a gift shop. The highlight of the new building is a bright, airy room containing the reassembled cloister of the adjacent San Jéronimo church. Give yourself at least 3 hours here; you could spend a week.

Paseo del Prado. www.museoprado.es.© **91-330-28-00.** Admission 12€ adults, 6€ EU seniors, free for students and children 17 and under, and free for all visitors on Tues–Sat 6–8pm, Sun 5–8pm. Tues–Sun 9am–8pm; holidays 9am–2pm. Call for info on guided tours. Closed Jan 1, Good Friday, May 1, and Dec 25. Metro: Atocha or Banco de España. Bus: 9, 10, 14, 19, 27, 34, 37, or 45.

Museo Nacional Centro de Arte Reina Sofía ★★ ♦ ART MUSEUM   What the Prado is to traditional art, this museum is to modern art: the greatest repository of 20th- to 21st-century works in Spain. Set within the echoing, futuristically renovated walls of the former General Hospital, originally built between 1776 and 1781, the museum is a sprawling, high-ceilinged showplace. Once designated "the ugliest building in Spain" by Catalan architect Oriol Bohigas, the Reina Sofía's design hangs in limbo somewhere between the 18th and the 21st centuries.

Special emphasis is paid to the great artists of 20th-century Spain: Juan Gris, Salvador Dalí, Joan Miró, and Pablo Picasso. What many critics consider Picasso's masterpiece, **Guernica,** now rests at this museum after a long and troubled history of traveling.

After a 90€-million expansion (2004–09), the museum now better accommodates its ever-increasing collection of contemporary art. With its latest space, Reina Sofía enters the world-class rank of modern museums, rivaling the Centre Pompidou in Paris. The new complex is devoted to more than just paintings and includes a 450-seat auditorium for concerts and a 350,000-volume reference library. A third building contains two mammoth galleries for large-scale exhibitions. Allot about 1½ hours here.

Santa Isabel 52. www.museoreinasofia.es.© **91-774-10-00.** Admission 6€ adults, free for students and children 17 and under, free for all Mon–Fri 7–9pm, Sat 2:30–9pm, and Sun. Mon and Wed–Sat 10am–9pm; Sun 10am–2:30pm. Metro: Atocha. Bus: 6, 10, 14, 19, 26, 27, 32, 34, 36, or 37.

Museo Thyssen-Bornemisza ★★ ART MUSEUM   The Thyssen is a curious assemblage of wonderful art through the ages, all from one of the great private collections of the 20th century. Rooms are arranged numerically, so that by following the order of the rooms (nos. 1–48, spread out over three floors) a logical sequence of

European painting can be traced from the 13th to the 20th centuries. The nucleus of the collection consists of 700 world-class paintings. They include works by, among others, El Greco, Velázquez, Dürer, Rembrandt, Watteau, Canaletto, Caravaggio, Hals, Memling, and Goya.

Unusual among the world's great art collections because of its eclecticism, the Thyssen group also contains 19th- and 20th-century paintings by many of the notable French Impressionists. It houses as well works by Picasso, Sargent, Kirchner, Nolde, and Kandinsky—artists who had never been well represented in Spanish museums. In addition to European paintings, major American works can be viewed here, including paintings by Thomas Cole, Winslow Homer, Jackson Pollock, Mark Rothko, Edward Hopper, Robert Rauschenberg, Stuart Davis, and Roy Lichtenstein. Plan to spend about 2 hours here.

Palacio de Villahermosa, Paseo del Prado 8. www.museothyssen.org. ℂ **91-369-01-51.** Admission 8€ adults, 5.50€ students and seniors, free for children 11 and under. Tues–Sun 10am–7pm. Metro: Banco de España. Bus: 1, 2, 5, 9, 10, 14, 15, 20, 27, 34, 45, 51, 52, 53, 74, 146, or 150.

ORGANIZED TOURS

The city of Madrid offers a series of walking tours with professional multilingual guides. Most tours cost less than 5€ and depart from the **Discover Madrid** headquarters at the Plaza Mayor Tourist Center, Plaza Mayor 27. The office can also give information about hiring a private tour guide.

Many of the city's hotel concierges and all of the city's travel agents will book anyone who asks for a guided tour of Madrid or its environs with one of Spain's largest tour operators, **Pullmantur,** Plaza de Oriente 8 (www.pullmantur.es; ℂ **90-208-55-12**). Regardless of destination and trip duration, virtually every tour departs from the Pullmantur terminal at that address.

OUTDOOR ACTIVITIES

The former hunting grounds of **Casa de Campo** cover miles of parkland lying south of the Palacio Royal across the Manzanares River. A lake contained within Casa de Campo is usually filled with rowers. You can have drinks and light refreshments by the water or go swimming in a city-run pool. Children will love both the zoo and the Parque de Atracciones. Open daily 8am–9pm; Metro: Batán or Lago.

To meet Madrileños at their most relaxed, plan to spend a Sunday among the families enjoying **Parque del Retiro.** Originally a royal playground for the Spanish monarchs and their guests, the park covers 140 hectares (346 acres), but most of the main attractions are located adjacent to the central pathway. Join families rowing in rental rowboats on the small lake and watch the children with bags of potato chips entranced by the puppet shows on the grass. Open summer daily 7am to midnight; winter daily 7am–10pm. Metro: Retiro.

Across Calle de Alfonso XII, at the southwest corner of Parque del Retiro, is the charming **Real Jardín Botánico** (www.rjb.csic.es. ℂ **91-420-30-17;** Metro: Atocha). Founded in the 18th century, the gardens contain more than 104 species of trees and 3,000 types of plants. Open summer daily 10am–9pm; winter daily 10am–6pm; admission 2.50€ adults, 1.25€ students.

Where to Eat

Virtually every regional Spanish cuisine and culinary trend is represented in Madrid's vibrant dining scene. Prices at the fancy tourist restaurants reach the same heights as New York, London, or Paris, but the city also has many affordable taverns and family restaurants.

PUERTA DEL SOL & LAS LETRAS
Very Expensive
La Terraza del Casino ★★★ SPANISH/INTERNATIONAL   Ferrán Adrià, the innovative master of cuisine, created all the dishes on the menu here and flies in regularly to see that his cooks are following his orders. His restaurant in Madrid occupies the top floor of the Casino, a historic building and a former gentlemen's club with a history going back to 1910. But the grand dons of those days didn't dine as well as you can today. The exquisite food, prepared with fresh seasonal ingredients, reinterprets traditional Spanish dishes. An example is *raya* (skate) in oil and saffron with parsley purée and nuts on a bed of finely diced fries. More traditional dishes are the succulent *merluza a la gallega* (Galician hake) and the *crema de la fabada asturiana* (creamed Asturian bean soup) served with *menestra* (mixed vegetables) al dente.

Alcalá 15. www.casinodemadrid.es. ✆ **91-532-12-75.** Main courses 30€–40€. AE, DC, MC, V. Mon–Fri 1:30–4pm; Mon–Sat 9–11:45pm. Closed Aug. Metro: Sevilla or Puerta del Sol.

Moderate
Tocororo 🍴 CUBAN   This is Madrid's finest Cuban restaurant. The nostalgia is evident in the pictures of Old Havana. Expect typical Caribbean dishes, such as *ropa vieja* (shredded meat served with black beans and rice) and lobster enchiladas. If you prefer a simpler repast, try a selection of *empanadas y tamales* (fried potato pastries and plantain dough filled with onions and ground meat). Special house cocktails include mojitos (rum, mint, and a hint of sugar) and daiquiris. Winter brings live Cuban music.

Calle del Prado 3 (at the corner of Echegaray). www.el-tocororo.com. ✆ **91-369-40-00.** Reservations required Thurs–Sat. Main courses 15€–22€; *menú del día* 10€. AE, DC, MC, V. Tues–Sun 1–4pm and 8pm–midnight. Closed last 2 weeks Feb and last 2 weeks Sept. Metro: Sevilla.

Inexpensive
El Brillante 🍴 SPANISH   Practically in the shadow of the Reina Sofía, El Brillante offers some of the best cheap eats in the entire city. Knowledgeable Madrileños flock here for great sandwiches on fresh rolls. The specialty of the house is the fried calamari sandwich, but choices range from sliced pork with cheese or peppers to anchovies with tomatoes. *Mini-bocadillos* are 2.50€ to 2.75€; 25cm (10-inch) *super bocatas* are 4€ to 5.60€. Whatever you order, you'll probably have to eat it standing at one of the stainless steel bars, as chairs at the tables are hard to find.

Atocha 122. ✆ **91-468-05-48.** Sandwiches 3€–7€. Daily 6:30am–midnight or later. Cash only. Metro: Atocha.

La Biotika 🍴 VEGETARIAN   Vegetarianism is anathema in Spanish cuisine, but this spot gives vegans and vegetarians a place to get their fix of seitan and tofu. On the east side of Plaza Santa Ana, it is intimate and charming. The best starters are the homemade soups, which are made fresh daily, or the large, crisp salads. The bread is also made fresh every day. A specialty is the "meatball without meat"—made with vegetables and rolled into a sphere. Sautéed tofu with zucchini or other veggies is always available.

Amor de Dios 3. www.labiotika.es. ✆ **91-429-07-80.** *Menú del día* 11€. MC, V. Mon–Sat 10am–11:30pm; Sun 10am–3pm. Metro: Antón Martín.

PLAZA MAYOR & LA LATINA
Expensive
El Schotis ★ SPANISH   If you've come to Madrid because it is one of the hubs of international culinary creativity, you're in the wrong place. But even the most

adventurous eater would do well to sample the traditional dishes that serve as a springboard for the *nueva cocina*. Specialties of the house include roast baby lamb, grilled steaks and veal chops, shrimp with garlic, and fried hake in green sauce. El Schotis was established in 1962 on one of Madrid's oldest and most historic streets. A series of large and pleasingly old-fashioned dining rooms is the setting for an animated crowd of Madrileños and foreign visitors. There's a bar near the entrance for tapas and before- or after-dinner drinks.

Cava Baja 11. © **91-365-32-30.** Reservations recommended. Main courses 22€–30€. AE, DC, MC, V. Mon–Sat 1–4pm and 8:30pm–midnight; Sun 1–4pm. Closed Aug 15–Sept 7. Metro: Sol or La Latina.

Moderate

Casa Lucio ★ CASTILIAN   Set on a historic street whose edges once marked the perimeter of Old Madrid, this venerable *tasca* with all the requisite antique accessories actually opened in 1974. Dozens of cured hams hang from hand-hewn beams above the well-oiled bar. Some surprisingly well-known public figures (even the king, on occasion) favor Casa Lucio for its classics of the Castilian grill. The retro menu features Jabugo ham with broad beans, shrimp in garlic sauce, hake with green sauce, several types of roasted lamb, and a thick steak served sizzling hot on a heated platter (called *churrasco de la casa*).

Cava Baja 35. www.casalucio.es. © **91-365-32-52.** Reservations required. Main courses 16€–28€. AE, DC, MC, V. Sun–Fri 1–4pm and 9–11:30pm; Sat 9–11:30pm. Closed Aug. Metro: La Latina.

Sobrino de Botín ★ SPANISH   Ernest Hemingway made this restaurant famous: In the final pages of his novel *The Sun Also Rises,* Jake invites Brett to Botín for the Segovian specialty of roast suckling pig, washed down with Rioja Alta. The menu is still the same. As you enter, you step back to 1725, the year the restaurant was founded. You'll see an open kitchen with a charcoal hearth, hanging copper pots, an 18th-century tile oven for roasting the suckling pig, and a big pot of soup whose aroma wafts across the tables. The two house specialties are roast suckling pig and roast Segovian lamb, and they are the main reason to dine here. If some in your party demur, you might try the fish-based "quarter-of-an-hour" soup, the baked Cantabrian hake, or the grilled filet mignon with potatoes. The dessert list features strawberries (in season) with whipped cream. You can accompany your meal with Valdepeñas or Aragón wine, although most guests order sangria.

Calle de Cuchilleros 17. www.botin.es. © **91-366-42-17.** Reservations recommended. Main courses 14€–29€; fixed-price menu 42€. AE, DC, MC, V. Daily 1–4pm and 8pm–midnight. Metro: La Latina, Ópera, Sol, or Tirso de Molina.

Inexpensive

El Cosaco ♦ RUSSIAN   One of the few Russian restaurants in Madrid sits adjacent to one of the most charming and evocative squares in town. Inside, you'll find dining rooms outfitted with paintings and artifacts from the former Soviet Union. Menu items seem to taste best when preceded with something from a long list of vodkas, many from small-scale distilleries you might not immediately recognize. Items include rich and savory cold-weather dishes that seem a bit at odds with the sweltering heat of Madrid, but they can be satisfying alternatives to the all-Spanish restaurants in the same neighborhood. Examples include beef stroganoff; quenelles of pike or perch with fresh dill; and thin-sliced smoked salmon or sturgeon artfully arranged with capers, chopped onions, and chopped hard-boiled eggs. The red or the white version of borscht makes a worthy starter. Blinis, stuffed with caviar or paprika-laced beef, are always excellent.

Plaza de la Paja 2. www.restauranteelcosaco.com.© **91-365-35-48.** Reservations recommended. Main courses 9€–18€; menú del día 13€. MC, V. Daily 9pm–midnight. Metro: La Latina.

ÓPERA & PALACIO REAL

Café de Oriente SPANISH/FRENCH   With its view of the Palacio Real, Plaza de Oriente is probably the swankest spot in Madrid for outdoor dining, and the Café de Oriente is the fanciest place on the plaza. The complex has two upscale indoor restaurants serving elegant if fussy food, but the prices are as haute as the cuisine. On the other hand, the outdoor cafe is elegant in its own way and far more affordable. Sandwiches are dainty and little tarts (like chicken with asparagus) are light but delectable. It's also a great spot for the ice-cream treat known as a copa princessa: scoops of vanilla and peach ice cream drenched in peach sauce.

Plaza de Oriente 2.© **91-541-39-74.** Cafe plates 6€–18€; dining room main dishes from 35€. Cafe daily 10am–1am; dining rooms daily 1:30–4pm and 9pm–midnight. Metro: Ópera.

La Gastroteca de Santiago ★ 🏛 SPANISH   This small space, with room for only 18 foodies, is one of the special favorites of in-the-know Madrileños, who guard its address somewhat zealously. It's typical of trendy restaurants rising through Madrid offering haute cuisine at good-value prices. The menu is authentic and regional and changes frequently based on the best market conditions every week. Here you dine on well-prepared, robust fare, including terrine of pig tail, blood sausage, garlic-laden snails, and lobster or confit of goat with broad beans and mint.

Plaza Santiago 1. www.lagastrotecadesantiago.es.© **91-548-07-07.** Reservations required. Main courses 26€–31€; sampler menu 60€. AE, MC, V. Tues–Sat 1:30–4pm and 8:30pm–midnight; Sun 1:30–4pm. Metro: Ópera.

CHUECA

Asiana ★★ 🏛 FRENCH/ASIAN   This is one of Madrid's most romantic and perhaps excessive dining experiences. After ringing the bell, you'll be shown to one of seven candlelit tables in a cellar space filled with gilt Buddhas and Ming vases. Walk-ins are not accepted, and a major credit card is needed to reserve a table at what is the most private public restaurant in town. The 16-course menu changes monthly, and combines Asian aesthetic with French culinary technique. Two of the best dishes are ravioli stuffed with fish and potato mousse, and melon gazpacho with lobster. Fresh and tender squid is shipped in from Galicia and mated with porcini petals and a macadamia oil aioli.

Travesia de San Mateo 4. www.asianadeco.com.© **91-310-09-65.** Reservations required. Tasting menu 105€. AE, DC, MC, V. Daily 10:30am–2:30pm and 5–8:30pm. Closed Aug. Metro: Alonso Martínez.

Casa Salvador SPANISH/ANDALUCÍAN   This is a robust, macho enclave of Madrid. The owner of this bustling restaurant configured it as a minimuseum to his hobby and passion, the Spanish art of bullfighting. Inside, near a bar that stocks an impressive collection of sherries and whiskeys, you'll find the memorabilia of years of bull watching, including photographs of great matadors beginning in the 1920s, and agrarian artifacts used in the raising and development of fighting bulls. The menu is as robust as the decor, featuring macho-size platters of oxtail in red-wine sauce; different preparations of hake (one of which is baked delectably in a salt crust); stuffed pepper, fried calamari, and shrimp entrees; and, for dessert, the local version of *arroz con leche.*

Calle Barbieri 12. © **91-521-45-24.** Reservations recommended. Main courses 10€–28€. AE, DC, MC, V. Mon–Sat 1:30–4pm and 9–11:30pm. Closed 2 weeks July–Aug. Metro: Chueca.

SALAMANCA, RETIRO & CHAMBERÍ
Very Expensive

La Manduca de Azagra ★★ SPANISH/NAVARRESE   A table here at night is one of the most sought after in Madrid. Fashionistas show up, blending in with French sophisticates, bourgeois Madrileños, and young gay professionals. Fortunately, the cuisine lives up to the hype, playing games with the traditions of a steakhouse by emphasizing outstanding raw dishes (crudos and tartars, mostly) with just enough modern cooked plates to justify calling itself a brasserie. Some great versions of the classics are available, such as fried asparagus and fresh artichokes. To get an idea of the kitchen's artistry, try the smoked layered potatoes and foie gras. The menu emphasizes the fresh market, and service is polite and efficient. Wine choices reflect some of the rising districts, with superb whites from Galicia and daunting Navarra reds.

Sagasta 14. www.lamanducadeazagra.com. © **91-591-01-12.** Reservations required. Main courses 32€–45€. AE, DC, MC, V. Mon–Sat 1:30–4pm and 9pm–midnight. Closed Aug. Metro: Alonso Martínez.

Expensive

Dassa Bassa ★★ SPANISH/INTERNATIONAL   Right across from Puerta de Alcalá, this hot dining ticket run by a chef who is a TV personality in his own right attracts celebrities, models, fashionistas, and VIPs at large—which means that getting a table can be difficult. The place is expensive but suitable for an extravagant night out on the town. The chef is Darío Barrio, and his wife, Itziar, is the maître d'. Barrio trained with "the master," fabled chef Ferran Adrià, hailed as Spain's greatest. Rather than being a slavish imitator, though, Barrio forges ahead with his own style—exemplified by the mashed potato and truffle. You might enjoy a chilled almond soup poured around ginger ale gelée, or else dried codfish and trout eggs.

Villalar 7. www.dassabassa.com. © **91-576-73-97.** Reservations required. Main courses 25€–30€; fixed-price menus 25€–80€. AE, MC, V. Tues–Sat 1:30–4pm and 9–11:30pm. Closed Aug 1–21. Metro: Retiro.

Pan de Lujo ★★ MEDITERRANEAN/ASIAN   Artful and elegant, with a battery of lights that is almost breathtaking, this big-windowed restaurant near Parque del Retiro has earned rave reviews for its interior design and its cuisine. Alberto Chicote, one of the city's most famous chefs, mixes Asian and Mediterranean ideas in ways that have pleased late-night Madrileños. Some of Spain's finest regional produce goes into the imaginative, creative dishes served here. One notable entree is poached red snapper with crisp baby vegetables. Some areas of the floor in the restaurant are lit from beneath, creating the illusion that diners and staff are bathed in patterns of light that subtly change throughout the course of a meal.

Calle Jorge Juan 20. www.pandelujo.es. © **91-436-11-00.** Reservations required. Main courses 19€–42€. AE, DC, MC, V. Daily 1:30–4pm and 9pm–midnight. Metro: Serrano or Retiro.

Moderate

Iroco ★ FUSION   Named for a tree native to the continent of Africa, this welcoming restaurant in the Salamanca district has walls with botanical prints. It offers one of Madrid's prettiest outdoor eating spaces in its little central courtyard. When making a reservation (if it's a fair day), ask for a garden table in the rear. The fusion cuisine, with a lot of inspiration from Asia, is elaborately prepared and beautifully presented. Main dishes are best accompanied by fine wines from Rioja or Ribera del Duero. For appetizers, sample the white fish salad drizzled with a Jerez (sherry) vinaigrette, or try the prawn-stuffed rolls. The vegetable tempuras are so good here that even a carnivore might be tempted. Eggplant (aubergine) lasagna, studded with fresh mushrooms, rests under a layer of creamy mozzarella. Hake comes in an asparagus sauce. And fresh fish is flown in daily from Galicia.

Calle Velásquez 18. www.grupovips.com. ℂ **91-431-73-81.** Reservations required. Main courses 14€–25€; fixed-price lunch menu 25€. AE, MC, V. Daily 1:30–4pm and 8:30pm–midnight. Metro: Goya.

Viavélez ★★★ SPANISH A brilliant chef, Paco Ron, started out in a modest place in a small fishing village in northern Asturias. Soon gourmets heard of him and were beating a path to his door. Even Michelin discovered him there, awarding him a star. Here in Madrid, you can discover his savory cuisine, perhaps beginning with his clam-laden potato stew that is about the best you are likely to taste in the capital. Even mayonnaise here tastes wonderful since it's homemade and laced with fresh herbs. A specialty is a salpicón of lobster that is flavored with a tangy jolt of pepper.

Av. General Perón 10. www.restauranteviavelez.com. ℂ **91-579-95-39.** Reservations required. Main courses 20€–31€. AE, DC, MC, V. Tues–Sat 2–4pm and 9pm–midnight; Sun 2–4pm. Closed 3 weeks in Aug. Metro: Santiago Bernabeu.

Inexpensive

Mosaiq ★ 🌶 ARABIAN This trio of colorfully and elegantly decorated dining rooms with low tables and such touches as Moroccan pillows and hassocks has become a darling of the city. Taking some literary liberty, the chef calls his kitchen "a thousand and one delights." The cuisine is well prepared and authentically North African/Middle Eastern. For a casual introduction, order some hummus along with brochettes of shrimp and lamb kofta redolent of cardamom. The chicken tagine with preserved lemon and green olives is a special temptation, as is the tuna steak with fresh herbs. For dessert, a variety of Arabic pastries are prepared fresh daily.

Calle Caracas 21. www.mosaiqrestaurante.com. ℂ **91-308-44-46.** Reservations required. Main courses 10€–19€; *menú degustación* 25€. AE, DC, MC, V. Daily 1:30–3:30pm and 9pm–midnight. Metro: Rubén Darío.

GRAN VÍA & PLAZA DE ESPAÑA

El Mentidero de la Villa ★ MEDITERRANEAN The Mentidero ("Gossip Shop," in English) is a truly multicultural synthesis, combining contemporary Spanish cuisine with a broader Mediterranean palate and a Japanese sensibility in the presentation. The technique, however, remains classical—no foams, no liquid nitrogen, no spherification. Run by Borja Anabitarte and José Ynglada, the kitchen plays with such adventuresome combinations as fried duck liver with caramelized eggplant; lasagna with mushrooms and duck liver; noisettes of veal with tarragon; filet steak with a sauce of mustard and brown sugar; and medallions of venison with purée of chestnut and celery.

Almagro, 20. www.mentiderodelavilla.es. ℂ **91-308-12-85.** Reservations required. Main courses 16€–25€; fixed-price menus 60€–75€. AE, DC, MC, V. Mon–Fri 1:30–4:30pm and 9pm–midnight; Sat 9pm–midnight. Closed Aug. Metro: Alonso Martínez.

ART DISTRICT & PASEOS

Astrid y Gastón ★ PERUVIAN   This restaurant is a posh import from Peru, a country whose cuisine is currently one of the hottest in the world. Here chefs tempt Madrileños with a range of ceviches from the country that originated the dish. In a rainbow of tastes and flavors, ceviche is made with such delicacies as hake cheeks or clams flavored with cilantro, curry, and fresh lime. An authentic Peruvian dish—though not for every taste—is corn crepes topped with suckling-pig skin and a chili-and-honey marmalade. Service is first rate, and the wine list is fairly priced.

13 Paseo de la Castellana. www.astridygastonmadrid.com. ✆ **91-702-62-62.** Reservations required. Main courses 24€–32€. MC, V. Mon–Sat 1:30–3:30pm and 8:30–11:30pm. Metro: Gregorio Marañón.

Viridiana ★★ INTERNATIONAL   Viridiana—named after the 1961 Luis Buñuel film classic—is known for the creative imagination of its chef Abraham García. Menu specialties are contemporary adaptations of traditional recipes, and they change frequently according to availability of ingredients. Examples of the singular cooking include sauté of filet of beef with fresh porcini mushrooms; roast pigeon with pearl barley, chestnuts, and black chanterelles; and honey-glazed roast lamb with saffron couscous. The food is sublime, and the ambience invites you to relax as you enjoy dishes that dazzle the eye, notably venison and rabbit arranged on a plate with fresh greens to evoke an autumnal scene in a forest.

Juan de Mena 14. www.restauranteviridiana.com. ✆**91-523-44-78.** Reservations recommended. Main courses 30€–37€. AE, DC, MC, V. Mon–Sat 1:30–4pm and 8:30pm–midnight. Closed Easter week. Metro: Banco de España.

Moderate

Café Restaurante El Espejo ★ INTERNATIONAL   To read the menu here is to wipe away the last century of culinary innovation. But if classic Continental cuisine as it was intended by Auguste Escoffier is your thing, you have come to the right place. The food belongs to the same era as the perfectly crafted Art Nouveau decor. Upon entering, you'll find yourself in a charming cafe/bar, where many visitors linger before heading toward the spacious dining room. If the weather is good, you can sit at one of the outdoor tables and be served by uniformed waiters who carry food across the busy street to a green area flanked by trees. The tables inside have charming views of the tile maidens with vines and flowers entwined in their hair. Some good dishes that are part of the regular repertoire include lasagna with prawns and fresh vegetables; baked hake with a cream sauce and shellfish; and sirloin steaks grilled far too long for American tastes, but pleasing to Europeans. Try profiteroles with cream and chocolate sauce for dessert.

Paseo de Recoletos 31. www.restauranteelespejo.com. ✆ **91-308-23-47.** Reservations required. Main courses 18€–22€; fixed-price menus 30€. AE, DC, MC, V. Daily 1–4pm and 9pm–midnight. Metro: Colón. Bus: 5, 27, 45, or 150.

La Gamella ★★ INTERNATIONAL   With its Spanish market food and emulation of the grand New York restaurants of the 20th century, La Gamella is a vibrant alternative to the prestigious Horcher just across the street. This restaurant occupies the 19th-century building where the Spanish philosopher Ortega y Gasset was born. The russet-colored, high-ceilinged design invites customers to relax. The founder has prepared his delicate and light-textured specialties for Madrid's most talked-about artists and merchants, many of whom he knows and greets personally between sessions in his kitchen.

Start, perhaps, with cream of lentil soup with porcini mushrooms, and go on to such temptations as ravioli filled with pumpkin and almonds with a creamy herb sauce, or pan-seared fresh codfish in a mushroom sauce. Another specialty is baby squid stuffed with caramelized onions and served with black pasta.

Alfonso XII, no. 4. www.lagamella.com.📞 **91-532-45-09.** Reservations required. Main courses 17€–26€; fixed-price menu 25€; *menú degustación* 36€. AE, DC, MC, V. Mon–Fri 1:30–4pm and 9pm–midnight; Sat 9pm–midnight. Closed 4 days around Easter. Metro: Retiro. Bus: 19.

Shopping

THE MAIN SHOPPING AREAS

The sheer diversity of Madrid's shops is staggering. One of the greatest concentrations of stores lies immediately north of **Puerta del Sol,** along the pedestrian streets of Calle del Carmen and Calle Preciados.

Conceived, designed, and built in the 1910s and 1920s as a showcase for the city's best shops, hotels, and restaurants, the **Gran Vía** has since been eclipsed by other shopping districts, although fragments of its Art Nouveau and Art Deco glamour still survive. The book and music shops along here are among the best in the city, as are the outlets for fashion, shoes, jewelry, and handicrafts from all regions of Spain.

The **Salamanca** district is the quintessential upscale shopping neighborhood. Here, you'll find exclusive furniture, fur, fashion, and jewelry stores, plus rug and art galleries.

El Rastro is the biggest flea market in Spain, drawing collectors, dealers, buyers, and hopefuls from throughout Madrid and its suburbs. The makeshift stalls are at their most frenetic on Sunday morning.

SOME NOTEWORTHY SHOPS

El Corte Inglés ★★, Preciados 3 (www.elcorteingles.es; 📞 **91-379-80-00;** Metro: Puerta del Sol), is Spain's number-one department store chain. The store sells Spanish handicrafts along with glamorous fashion articles, such as Pierre Balmain designs, often at lower prices than you'll find in most European capitals.

For unique craft items, **El Arco de los Cuchilleros Artesania de Hoy,** Plaza Mayor 9 (basement; 📞 **91-365-26-80;** Metro: Puerta del Sol or Opera), may be a mouthful of a name to remember, but it has an unparalleled array of pottery, leather, textiles, glassware, and jewelry produced by individual artisans throughout Spain. It's open daily 11am to 9pm, even during siesta.

Just outside the walls of Plaza Mayor, **Mercado de San Miguel ★★**, Plaza de San Miguel (www.mercadodesanmiguel.es; 📞 **91-542-49-39;** Metro: Opéra), has been updated for 21st-century shoppers, with more than three dozen vendors sheltered under the gigantic wood-and-iron roof. With its dazzling display of foodstuff, you can go "grazing" here for an offbeat luncheon stopover.

Since 1846, **Loewe ★★★**, Gran Via 8 (www.loewe.com; 📞 **91-522-68-15;** Metro: Banco de España or Gran Via), has been Spain's most elegant leather store. Its designers keep abreast of changing tastes and styles, but the inventory retains a timeless chic. The store sells luggage, handbags, and jackets for men and women (in leather or suede). In addition to the Gran Vía location, two other branches carry much the same merchandise; they are located at Serrano 26 (📞 **91-577-60-56**) and at Serrano 34 (📞 **91-426-35-88**).

Entertainment & Nightlife

Madrid abounds with dance halls, *tascas*, cafes, theaters, movie houses, and nightclubs. Because dinner is served late in Spain, nightlife doesn't really get underway until after 11pm, and it generally lasts until at least 3am—Madrileños are so fond of prowling at night that they are known around Spain as *gatos* (cats). If you arrive at 9:30pm at a club, you'll have the place all to yourself, assuming it's even open yet.

In summer, Madrid becomes a virtually free festival because the city sponsors a series of plays, concerts, and films. Pick up a copy of the *Guía del Ocio* (available at most newsstands, in Spanish) for listings of these events. This guide provides information about occasional discounts for commercial events, such as the concerts that are given in Madrid's parks.

Although flamenco was born in Andalucía, Madrid has been central to the art form's revival since the early 1980s. Flamenco is alive and well in small clubs, peñas, and bars, usually in late-night shows that you will also find in *Ocio*. Avoid the pricy early-evening flamenco *tablaos* designed as tourist spectacle. Nightclubs also tend to be expensive, but since Madrid is preeminently a city of song and dance, you can often be entertained at very little cost—in fact, the price of a glass of wine or beer if you sit at a bar with live entertainment.

THE PERFORMING ARTS

Madrid has a number of theaters, opera companies, and dance companies. To discover where and when specific cultural events are being performed, pick up a copy of *Guía del Ocio* at any city newsstand.

Tickets to dramatic and musical events usually range in price from 6€ to 200€ and can be purchased from the box office. In the event your choice is sold out, you may be able to get tickets (with a reasonable markup) at **Localidades Galicia,** Plaza del Carmen 1 (www.bullfightticketsmadrid.com; ℂ **91-531-91-31;** Metro: Sol). This agency also markets tickets to bullfights and sporting events. It is open Tuesday through Saturday 9:30am to 1:30pm and from 4:30 to 7pm, and Sunday 10am to 1pm. In May, it's open daily 9am to 8pm.

You might also get discounts up to 50% on performance-day tickets through **Taquilla Ultimo Minuto,** Plaza del Carmen 1 (www.taquillaultimominuto.com). It is open Wednesday, Thursday, and Sunday from 5 to 8pm, and Friday and Saturday 5 to 10pm.

CLASSICAL MUSIC

Teatro Real, Plaza Isabel II (www.teatro-real.es; ℂ **91-516-06-60;** Metro: Opera), is one of the world's finest stage and acoustic settings for opera. Today, the building is home to the Compañía del Teatro Real and the Teatro de la Opera, and is the major venue for classical music and opera. Tickets are 8€ to 294€.

Auditorio Nacional de Música, Príncipe de Vergara 146 (www.auditorionacional. mcu.es; ℂ **91-337-01-39;** Metro: Cruz del Rayo), is the ultramodern home of both the **National Orchestra of Spain,** which pays particular attention to the music of Spanish composers, and the **National Chorus of Spain.** Just north of Madrid's Salamanca district, the concert hall ranks as a major addition to the classical music circuit in Europe. Tickets are 8€ to 125€.

FLAMENCO

At Madrid's flamenco tablaos, doors usually open at 9 or 9:30pm, and the show starts at about 10:45pm and ends at 12:30am or even later. To save money, go after dinner, when the still-hefty admission at least includes a drink. The later performances are usually better anyway, after the tour groups leave and the performers are warmed up. These stages feature large troupes with several dancers, two or three guitarists, and one or two singers, all in costume. Among the established tablaos are **Las Tablas ★**, Plaza de España 9 (www.lastablasmadrid.com; ☎ **91-542-05-20;** Metro: Plaza de España); Corral de la Morería, Morería 17 (www.corraldelamoreria.com; ☎ **91-365-84-46;** Metro: La Latina or Opera); and **Café de Chinitas ★**, Torija 7 (☎ **91-547-15-02;** Metro: Santo Domingo).

For a flamenco club that doesn't cater primarily to tourists, try **Casa Patas ★**, Cañizares 10 (www.casapatas.com; ☎ **91-369-04-96;** Metro: Antón Martín). This club is one of the best places to see "true" flamenco, as opposed to the more touristy version presented at Corral de la Morería (see below). It is also a bar and restaurant, with space reserved in the rear for flamenco. Shows are presented at 10:30pm Monday to Thursday, with two shows at 9pm and midnight on Friday and Saturday, and more frequent shows during Madrid's major fiesta month of May. The best flamenco in Madrid is found here. Proof of the pudding is that flamenco singers and dancers often hang out here after hours. Tapas—priced at 4€ to 18€—are available at the bar. Open Monday to Saturday from 8pm to 2:30am.

LIVE MUSIC
Off Plaza de Santa Ana, **Café Central ★**, Plaza del Angel 10 (www.cafecentral madrid.com; Metro ☎ **91-369-41-43;** Metro: Antón Martín), is *the* place for live jazz. Performances are usually at 10pm and midnight. While jazz is the main course, the cafe also hosts folk and blues. It's open daily 1:30pm to 2 or 3am, with a cover that varies from 7€ to 15€.

Not far from the Central is **Café Jazz Populart ★**, Calle Huertas 22 (www.populart.es; ☎ **91-429-84-07;** Metro: Antón Martín), a showcase for American blues, Latin salsa, and Caribbean reggae as well as many varieties of jazz. The large space allows for a little elbowroom, and the atmosphere is laid-back. Admission is often free, but the drink prices tend to jump sharply when music is playing. Open Monday to Thursday 6pm to 2:30am, Friday and Saturday 6pm to 3:30am; the music usually starts around 11pm.

With dozens of small tables and a huge bar in its dark and smoky interior, **Clamores ★**, Albuquerque 14 (www.salaclamores.com; ☎ **91-445-79-38;** Metro: Bilbao), is the largest and one of the most popular jazz clubs in Madrid. It has thrived because of the noted American and Spanish jazz bands that appear here. Clamores is open daily from 7pm to 3am or so, but jazz is presented only from Tuesday to Saturday. From Tuesday to Thursday, performances are at 11pm and 1am; Saturday they're at 11:30pm and 1:30am. There are no live performances Sunday or Monday. Cover from Tuesday to Saturday is 7€ to 27€, depending on the act.

DANCE CLUBS
The most multicultural, multifarious, and multimusical disco in Madrid is **Kapital,** Atocha 125 (www.grupo-kapital.com; ☎ **91-420-29-06;** Metro: Atocha). Set within what was originally a theater, it contains seven different levels, each sporting at least one bar and an ambience that's often radically different from that of the previous floor. Voyeurs of every age have a great time at Kapital because there's a lot to watch in the mixed crowd that pursues whatever form of sexuality seems appropriate at the moment. Open Thursday to Sunday midnight to 6am. Second drinks from 10€ each. **Pachá,** Barceló 11 (www.pacha-madrid.com; ☎ **91-447-01-28;** Metro: Tribunal),

is a late-night club, attracting the 20- to 40-year-old age group to a setting that in the 1930s was a movie theater. By the 1980s it had become a "dance cathedral." Loud music and hard drinking rule the night. Cover ranges from 15€ to 20€, including the first drink.

PUBS & BARS

Bar Cock, Reina 16 (www.barcock.com; ℂ **91-532-28-26;** Metro: Gran Vía), a dark, cavernous room on a narrow street parallel to Gran Vía, is another old-timer, where Madrid's artistic and showbiz elite routinely assault their livers. It was given renewed cachet by the presence of internationally known film director Pedro Almodóvar. Open Sunday to Thursday 7pm to 3am, and Friday and Saturday 7pm to 4am.

Del Diego, Reina 12 (ℂ **91-522-75-44;** Metro: Gran Vía), is the pleasant spot to chill out with a dry martini or a margarita. Don't expect contemporary drinks; Del Diego is a family-owned operation that caters to an older, sedate clientele. The bar is open Monday to Saturday from 7pm to 3:30am (closed Aug).

In the much-recommended Hotel Urban (see below), the **Glass Bar** (ℂ **91-787-77-70;** Metro: Sevilla) is the hottest rendezvous spot in Madrid. The *très* cosmopolitan bar and cocktail lounge does the town's best mojitos. Open daily 11am to 3am.

THE LGBT SCENE

Black and White, Libertad 34 (www.discoblack-white.net; ℂ **91-531-11-41;** Metro: Chueca), remains the major gay bar of Madrid, but draws a mixed crowd on weekends. There's a disco in the basement. Open Monday to Thursday 10pm to 5am, Friday to Saturday 10pm to 6am.

Cruising, Perez Galdos 5 (ℂ **91-524-51-43;** Metro: Chueca or Gran Via), is one of the landmark gay bars of Madrid. There are virtually no women inside, but count on meeting a hustler looking for a tourist john. It doesn't get crowded or lively until late at night. Open daily from 8pm to 3:30am.

Where to Stay

The economic straits facing Spain over the last few years have proven to be a boon for travelers, as day-to-day hotel prices in Madrid have declined, even though the official national ratings book permits them to charge far more. More than 50,000 rooms blanket the city, from grand bedchambers fit for princes and rock stars to serviceable but sparse bedrooms in some neighborhood *hostales* and *pensiones* (technically, more boardinghouses than hotels).

PUERTA DEL SOL & LAS LETRAS

Expensive

Hotel Urban ★★ With a postage-stamp swimming pool open to the sky, a moonlit restaurant, and a spectacular patio, Urban is the latest in city chic. The lobby evokes an office-building atrium, but its grace notes are the towering sculptures from Papua, New Guinea, that are found along one wall. Rooms are luxurious and modern with dark-wood furnishings and lots of dark leather. Soundproof windows block off traffic noise. At night, elegant Madrileños flood the sleek **Restaurante Europa Deco** to savor its Mediterranean fusion cuisine. Just below the lobby is a Museum of Egyptian Art with sculptures from the heyday of the pharaohs.

Carrera de San Jerónimo, 28014 Madrid. www.derbyhotels.com/Urban-Hotel-Madrid. ℂ **91-787-77-70.** Fax 91-787-77-99. 96 units. 190€–470€ double; 275€–645€ junior suite; from 305€ suite. AE, DC, MC, V. Parking 30€. Metro: Sevilla. **Amenities:** Restaurant; bar; outdoor heated pool; exercise room; airport transfers (90€). *In room:* A/C, TV, minibar, Wi-Fi (20€ per 24 hr.).

ME Madrid ★ This landmark hotel began as private palace in 1923, and its ornate stone facade is protected by National Heritage (a governmental organization). History ends when you walk in the door, as the interior design is self-consciously hip. Most of the contemporary, well-maintained, and comfortable bedrooms are small to midsize, although some are spacious. You can stay in a standard double, a self-contained studio, or a suite (among the most glamorous in Madrid). Ernest Hemingway preferred to lodge in the Tower Suite, but Papa wouldn't recognize the old Reina Victoria in its iPad makeover.

Plaza de Santa Ana 14, 28012 Madrid. www.memadrid.com. ℂ **91-701-60-00.** Fax 91-522-03-07. 191 units. 199€–260€ standard double; 354€–415€ studio; from 510€ suite. AE, DC, MC, V. No parking. Metro: Tirso de Molina or Sol. **Amenities:** Restaurant; 2 bars; exercise room; concierge; room service; babysitting. *In room:* A/C, TV/DVD, minibar, hair dryer, MP3 docking station, Wi-Fi (free).

Moderate

Hotel Inglés ★ You'll find this little hotel (where Virginia Woolf used to stay) on a central street lined with *tascas*. Behind the redbrick facade is a modern, impersonal hotel with contemporary, well-maintained rooms. The lobby is air-conditioned, but guest rooms are not; those who open their windows at night are likely to hear noise from the enclosed courtyard, so light sleepers beware. Units come in a variety of shapes, most of them small; some in the back are quite dark.

Calle Echegaray 8, 28014 Madrid. www.hotel-ingles.net. ℂ **91-429-65-51.** Fax 91-420-24-23. 58 units. 125€ double; 135€ suite. AE, DC, MC, V. Parking 15€. Metro: Sol or Sevilla. **Amenities:** Bar; concierge. *In room:* TV, hair dryer.

Hotel Moderno ★★ 🦪 The building dates from 1857 and the hotel opened in 1939 as part of the rebuilding of Puerta del Sol after the destruction of the Civil War. It's been in the family ever since; they love the place and it shows. As with all older buildings, it has some quirks. Rooms are small because the original support beams limit expansions, but ask for a room on floors five to seven, which are about 10% larger. They are also quieter. Marble and tile bathrooms are especially nice, and 17 doubles have outdoor patios. Exterior rooms look out on the pedestrian street of Arenal or on the main entrance to El Corte Inglés. One especially nice touch we haven't found elsewhere: The sheets and towels smell very fresh because the hotel does its own laundry and dries them in the sun on the roof.

Arenal 2, 28014 Madrid. www.hotel-moderno.com. ℂ **91-531-09-00.** 97 rooms. 80€–125€ double; 90€–120€ triple. Metro: Sol. **Amenities:** Bar, concierge. *In room:* A/C, TV, hair dryer, Wi-Fi (free).

Inexpensive

Chic & Basic Colors ★ 🦪 A short walk from the Atocha station, the chic and basic philosophy here is no frills and no ostentation, but exquisite taste and a fun ambience. The six-floor *hostal* attracts a gay clientele, although many straights check in, too. The hotel is divided into zones—"be yourself," where you can let your hair down; "help yourself," with free coffee and munchies; and "love yourself," where you'll find a sun terrace, chaise longues, and a shower to freshen up. Guests can adjust the intensity of light in their bedrooms to fit their moods. A "wake-up kit" is left at your modern bedroom door with a "tasty morsel" to launch your day.

Calle Atocha 113, 28012 Madrid. www.chicandbasic.com. ℂ **91-369-28-95.** Fax 91-420-08-40. 10 units. 60€–110€ double. AE, DC, MC, V. Free parking. Metro: Tirso de Molina. Amenities: Restaurant; bar; cafeteria; room service. In room: A/C, TV, hair dryer, Wi-Fi (free).

Hostal Cervantes 🦪 One of Madrid's most pleasant family-run hotels, the Cervantes is much appreciated by our readers, and has been for years. You'll take a tiny bird-cage-style elevator to the immaculately maintained second floor of this stone-and-brick building. Each guest room contains a comfortable bed and spartan furniture. No breakfast is served, but the owners, the Alfonsos, will direct you to a nearby cafe. The establishment is convenient to the Prado, Parque del Retiro, and the older sections of Madrid.

Cervantes 34, 28014 Madrid. www.hostal-cervantes.com. ☎ **91-429-83-65.** Fax 91-429-27-45. 20 units. 50€–70€ double; 70€–80€ apt. MC, V. Metro: Antón Martín. *In room:* Ceiling fan, TV, hair dryer, Wi-Fi (free).

PLAZA MAYOR & LA LATINA

Hostal la Macarena ★ 🥄   Known for its reasonable prices and praised by readers for its warm hospitality, this unpretentious hotel is run by the Ricardo González family. A 19th-century facade with Belle Epoque designs stands in ornate contrast to the chiseled simplicity of the ancient buildings facing it. The location is one of the hotel's assets: it's on a street (a noisy one) immediately behind Plaza Mayor, near one of the best clusters of *tascas* in Madrid. Guest rooms, ranging from small to medium, are all well kept, with modest furnishings and comfortable beds. Windows facing the street have double panes.

Cava de San Miguel 8, 28005 Madrid. www.silserranos.com. ☎ **91-365-92-21.** Fax 91-364-27-57. 20 units. 59€–69€ double; 84€–90€ triple. MC, V. Parking nearby 25€. Metro: Sol, Ópera, or La Latina. **Amenities:** Bar. *In room:* TV, hair dryer.

ÓPERA & PALACIO REAL

Expensive

Casa de Madrid ★★   This small boutique hotel cum B&B—one of Madrid's most elegant—stands across the street from the Royal Opera. Home of the Friends of Madrid Club, it occupies the second floor of an 18th-century mansion. Each bedroom is exquisitely decorated with antiques, including Persian rugs, and each of the accommodations has a different theme. The simplest chamber is called the Japan room (a tight double). Among the most elegant units are the Leaves of April, the Syria Mediterranean Room, the Royal India Room, and the Lavender Blue Room; the grandest is the Damascus Suite. Surely you'll agree that breakfast always tastes better when served on silver trays. The house is filled with valuable objets d'art.

Calle Arrieta 2, 28013 Madrid. www.casademadrid.com. ☎ **91-559-57-91.** Fax 91-540-11-00. 7 units. 99€–285€ double; 793€ suite. Rates include continental breakfast. AE, MC, V. Nearby parking 18€. Metro: Ópera. Amenities: Airport transfers (55€; free with 3 or more nights). In room: A/C, TV, minibar, Wi-Fi (free).

Moderate

Hotel Ópera ★   The boxy exterior hides the fact that, once you're in the door, this lovely boutique hotel near the Teatro Real and Palacio Real is a real find. Try for one of the upper-level rooms with outdoor terraces, glassed-in Jacuzzi tubs, and skylights. The biggest problem with the Hotel Ópera is that between the nice room and room service (along with massage services), you may never get out to see Madrid.

Cuesta de Santo Domingo 2, 28103, Madrid. www.hotelopera.com. ☎ **91-541-28-00.** 79 rooms. 100€–170€ double. Metro: Ópera. Amenities: Restaurant; bar; gym; sauna; concierge; room service; massage; babysitting; personal shopper. In room: A/C, TV, hair dryer, Wi-Fi (free).

Hotel Preciados ★ ☺   One of Madrid's most centrally located hotels was created from a historic 1881 structure. The original facade, entryway, grand staircase, and other architectural details have been retained, but everything else has been reconstructed from scratch for modern comfort. The five-floor hotel, which opened in 2001, is close to such landmarks as the Palacio Royal, the opera house, and Puerta del Sol (the very center of Madrid). Children are especially welcome here; special facilities for them such as extra beds can be added to the standard rooms. There's even a kids' menu in the restaurant. Guest rooms are midsize to spacious.

Preciados 37, 28013 Madrid. www.preciadoshotel.com. ⓒ **91-454-44-00.** Fax 91-454-44-01. 73 units. 126€–180€ double; 190€–250€ suite. MC, V. Parking 25€. Metro: Sol or Santo Domingo/Callao. Amenities: Restaurant; bar; concierge; room service; babysitting; airport transfers (70€); Internet (free, in lobby). In room: A/C, TV, minibar, hair dryer, Wi-Fi (free).

Inexpensive

Laura ★   The interior designer for this Room Mate hotel managed to cram a spacious lobby and avant-garde decoration into a narrow, triangular building. Some guests have likened Laura to a modern hotel in New York, and the location is one of the best in town, a 2-minute walk from the heart of Plaza Mayor or a 4-minute walk from the Puerta del Sol (the Times Square of Madrid). Bedrooms are loftlike or else duplexes, each unit beautifully decorated and comfortable, even elegantly furnished, if your tastes are minimalist. We are impressed with the hotel's room amenities and the fact that the maid leaves a fresh apple on the nightstand. Each of the rooms also comes with a minikitchen.

Travesia de Trujillos 3, 28013 Madrid. www.room-matehotels.com. ⓒ **91-701-16-70.** Fax 91-521-76-55. 36 units. 80€–102€ double; 104€–120€ suite. Rates include breakfast until noon. AE, DC, MC, V. Parking 22€. Metro: Sol. **Amenities:** Concierge; babysitting. In room: A/C, TV/DVD, kitchenette, minibar, hair dryer, Wi-Fi (free).

CHUECA

Oscar ★   In many ways this is the most modern and stylish of the Room Mate chain hotels sweeping across trendy Madrid. It was the personal statement of Tomás Alía, the famous interior designer, who transformed a bland box into an interior sculptural puzzle. A haven for "fun" furniture, the hotel decorates some of its rooms with erotic wallpaper, others with very futuristic decor, perhaps resembling the inside of a lava lamp. The neighborhood is gay friendly and the hotel design makes no assumptions about who is sleeping with whom. A wide variety of rooms are offered, from standard to executive doubles, even junior or regular suites. Some units have a balcony opening onto the bustling Plaza Vázquez de Mella.

Plaza Vázquez de Mella 12, 28004 Madrid. www.room-matehotels.com. ⓒ **91-701-11-73.** Fax 91-521-87-18. 75 units. 103€–138€ double; 153€–163€ junior suite. Rates include breakfast until noon. AE, DC, MC, V. Parking 28€. Metro: Sol. **Amenities:** Concierge; babysitting. In room: A/C, TV, minibar, hair dryer, Wi-Fi (free).

SALAMANCA, RETIRO & CHAMBERÍ
Very Expensive

Hotel Adler ★★   At the intersection of Velázquez and Goya streets, this is one of the most elegant places to stay in Madrid. You're housed in grand comfort at a location nicknamed "the golden triangle of art" (near the Prado, Reina Sofía, and the Thyssen-Bornemisza collection). The exclusive shops of Serrano are also near at hand. The classic building has been carefully restored and offers gracious comfort in a setting that evokes the 1880s but includes decidedly modern touches. The guest rooms provide ultimate comfort with luxe furnishings and totally modernized bathrooms.

Calle Velázquez 33, 28001 Madrid. www.adlermadrid.com. ⓒ**91-426-32-20** or **866/376-7831** in the U.S. and Canada. Fax 91-426-32-21. 45 units. 250€–495€ double; from 690€ junior suite. AE, DC, MC, V. Parking 30€. Metro: Velázquez. **Amenities:** Restaurant; bar; bikes; concierge; room service; babysitting; airport transfers (105€). In room: A/C, TV/DVD, minibar, hair dryer, Wi-Fi (12€ per 24 hr.).

Expensive

Hesperia Madrid ★★★   A member of the "Leading Hotels of the World," the Hesperia is a citadel of grace, comfort, and stylishly minimalist charm. Small Japanese gardens are located throughout the building, and there are many Asian influences in the decor, along with the most modern fixtures—exemplified by the chic bathrooms and bed linens. Suites are among the most luxurious in Madrid (some come with their own butler). Even those not staying here often visit to sample the cuisine of Santceloni.

Paseo de la Castellana 57, 28046 Madrid. www.hesperia-madrid.com. ✆ **91-210-88-00.** Fax 91-210-88-89. 170 units. 145€–350€ double; from 450€ suite. AE, MC, V. Parking 30€. Metro: Gregorio Marañón. **Amenities:** Restaurant; bar; access to health club; sauna; concierge; room service; babysitting. *In room:* A/C, TV, minibar, hair dryer, Wi-Fi (free).

Moderate

Rafaelhoteles Orense ★   At first glance, you might mistake this silver-and-glass tower for one of the many upscale condominium complexes surrounding it on all sides. Stylish and streamlined, with a design inaugurated in the late 1980s, it offers reproduction Oriental carpets and conservatively contemporary furniture that's comfortable, tasteful, and upscale. Accommodations, equipped along the lines of a private apartment, are appropriate for a stay of up to several weeks.

Pedro Teixeira 5, 28020 Madrid. www.rafaelhoteles.com. ✆ **91-597-15-68.** Fax 91-597-12-95. 140 units. 118€–157€ double; from 173€ suite. AE, DC, MC, V. Parking 20€. Metro: Santiago Bernabeu. **Amenities:** Restaurant; bar; room service; Wi-Fi (free, in lobby). *In room:* A/C, TV, minibar, hair dryer.

Inexpensive

Hostal Residencia Don Diego   On the fifth floor of an elevator building, Don Diego is in a residential/commercial neighborhood that's relatively convenient to many of the city monuments. The vestibule contains an elegant winding staircase with a balustrade supported by iron griffin heads. The hotel is warm and inviting, filled with leather couches and attractively angular but comfortable furniture. Guest rooms are small but comfortable for the price. The staff is very service oriented and keeps the place humming efficiently.

Calle de Velázquez 45, 28001 Madrid. www.hostaldondiego.com. ✆ **91-435-07-60.** Fax 91-431-42-63. 58 units. 60€–85€ double; 75€–127€ triple. AE, DC, MC, V. Parking 28€. Metro: Velázquez. **Amenities:** Bar. *In room:* A/C, TV, hair dryer, Wi-Fi (free).

GRAN VÍA & PLAZA DE ESPAÑA

De Las Letras ★ ▮▮   This hotel with its youthful vibe was inspired by literature. A member of the Barcelona-based Anima Hotels chain, it stands in the heart of the Gran Vía, the erstwhile main street of Madrid. Inscriptions by notable Spanish writers adorn walls in the public areas, with stone carvings and original hand-painted tiles. The wood-and-iron elevator remains from the original 1917 building. The contemporary bedrooms are painted in vivid colors such as ocher or burgundy, and most units have wooden floors with high ceilings. Bathrooms are the latest in modern design, and each suite opens onto a terrace with a whirlpool.

Gran Vía 11, 28013 Madrid. www.hoteldelasletras.com. ✆ **91-523-79-80.** Fax 91-523-79-81. 103 units. 133€–174€ double; 210€–300€ suite. AE, DC, MC, V. No parking. Metro: Sevilla or Gran Vía. **Amenities:** Restaurant; bar; exercise room; spa; room service. *In room:* A/C, TV, minibar, hair dryer, Wi-Fi (free).

Hotel Catalonia Gran Vía ★   In the heart of Madrid, this hotel is located in a beautifully restored turn-of-the-20th-century building that's a modernist landmark. It was constructed in 1898 by Emilio Salas y Cortés, one of the teachers of the great Barcelona architect Gaudí. Some of Madrid's most important attractions are within an easy walk, including the Prado, Thyssen-Bornemisza Museum, and Plaza Mayor with its rustic taverns. The guest rooms come in different sizes, each comfortably furnished and beautifully maintained. You may want to sample the Catalan cuisine in the on-site restaurant, **Pedrera** (especially if Barcelona is not on your itinerary).

Gran Vía 9, 28013 Madrid. www.hoteles-catalonia.es. © **91-531-22-22.** Fax 91-531-54-69. 185 units. 80€–205€ double; from 117€ suite. AE, DC, MC, V. Nearby parking 30€. Metro: Gran Vía. **Amenities:** Restaurant; bar; exercise room; Jacuzzi; sauna; room service; babysitting. *In room:* A/C, TV, minibar, hair dryer, Wi-Fi (free).

ART DISTRICT & PASEOS
Very Expensive
The Ritz ★★★   With soaring ceilings and graceful columns, the Ritz offers all the luxury and pampering you'd expect from a grand hotel. Although the building has been thoroughly modernized, great effort was expended to retain its Belle Epoque character and architectural details. No other Madrid hotel, except the Westin Palace (see below), has a more storied past. The Ritz was built in 1908 by King Alfonso XIII with the aid of César Ritz. It looks onto the circular Plaza de la Lealtad in the center of town, facing the Prado, the Palacio de Villahermosa, and the Stock Exchange, and is near 120-hectare (297-acre) Parque del Retiro. Its facade has been designated a historic monument. The glory days of 1910 live on in the units with their roomy closets, antique furnishings, and hand-woven carpets.

Plaza de la Lealtad 5, 28014 Madrid. www.ritz.es. ©**91-701-67-67** or 800/237-1236 in the U.S. and Canada. Fax 91-701-67-76. 167 units. 260€–455€ double; from 551€ junior suite; from 1,454€ suite. AE, DC, MC, V. Parking 35€. Metro: Atocha or Banco de España. **Amenities:** Restaurant; bar; exercise room; spa; sauna; concierge; room service; airport transfers (120€). *In room:* A/C, TV, minibar, hair dryer, Wi-Fi (free).

Expensive
AC Palacio del Retiro ★★   Perhaps the best-located hotel in Madrid, this well-run oasis across from the Parque del Retiro sits close to the cultural triangle formed by the Thyssen-Bornemisza, Prado, and Reina Sofía museums. The restored building dates from the early 20th century and is a protected National Heritage monument. Its interior has been completely restored to modern tastes. Much of its elegant past can be seen in the stained-glass windows from Paris, the ceramics handmade in Talavera, the marble floors, and the Grecian columns. The midsize bedrooms are stylish and comfortable, with state-of-the-art bathrooms. Most bedrooms open onto panoramic views of Retiro Park.

Alfonso XII 14, 28014 Madrid. www.ac-hotels.com. © **91-523-74-60.** Fax 91-523-74-61. 51 units. 265€–290€ double; from 570€ suite. AE, DC, MC, V. Nearby parking 30€. Metro: Banco de España. **Amenities:** Restaurant; bar; exercise room; spa; concierge; room service; babysitting; airport transfers (114€–121€). *In room:* A/C, TV, minibar, hair dryer, Wi-Fi (free).

Moderate
HUSA Hotel Paseo del Arte ★   Timing is everything with this contemporary international style hotel. If it's hosting a conference, rooms are overpriced. If not, they are a steal. The Paseo del Arte is a good business hotel and it's also across a small plaza from the Reina Sofía and just down the street a short walk from the flamenco joint Casa Patas. (There's a chocolatería on the way, if you're walking home late.)

Bargain with them to include breakfast, as the buffet is one of Madrid's best. A handful of suites with terraces are some of the nicest rooms in the city.

Atocha 123, 28014, Madrid. www.husa.es.© **91-298-48-00.** 260 rooms. 90€–160€ double. Metro: Atocha. Nearby parking 30€. Metro: Banco de España. **Amenities:** Restaurant; bar; exercise room; spa; concierge; room service; babysitting. *In room:* A/C, TV, minibar, hair dryer, Wi-Fi (free).

NH Nacional ★   This stately hotel was built around 1900 to house the hundreds of passengers flooding into Madrid through the nearby Atocha railway station. In 1997, a well-respected nationwide chain, NH Hotels, ripped out much of the building's dowdy interior, reconstructing the public areas and guest rooms with a smooth, seamless decor that takes maximum advantage of the building's tall ceilings and large spaces. Guest rooms feature modern designer decor (including avant-garde art), giving the units a welcoming ambience. Today, the Nacional is a destination for dozens of corporate conventions.

Paseo del Prado 48, 28014 Madrid. www.nh-hotels.com.© **91-429-66-29.** Fax 91-369-15-64. 214 units. 105€–145€ double; 145€–168€ suite. AE, DC, MC, V. Parking 28€. Metro: Atocha. **Amenities:** Restaurant; bar; concierge; room service; babysitting. *In room:* A/C, TV, minibar, hair dryer, Wi-Fi (17€ per 24 hr.).

Inexpensive

Hotel Mora   This hotel can be recommended for location alone—it's across from Paseo del Prado and the Botanical Gardens. It is a fine and decent choice, especially if you want to make several visits to the Prado. The reception is bright and airy, with *trompe l'oeil* marble columns and carpets. Most of the guest rooms range from midsize to spacious, and each is comfortably and tastefully furnished, though far from lavish. Opt for a guest room opening onto the street, as these have the best views of the gardens and the magnificent Prado itself. Double-glazed windows keep down some of the noise level.

Paseo del Prado 32, 28014 Madrid. www.hotelmora.com.© **91-420-15-69.** Fax 91-420-05-64. 62 units. 84€ double; 102€ triple. AE, DC, MC, V. Nearby parking 21€. Metro: Atocha. **Amenities:** Restaurant; bar. *In room:* A/C, TV, Wi-Fi (free).

DAY TRIPS FROM MADRID

Toledo ★★★

If you have only 1 day for an excursion outside Madrid, go to Toledo—69km (43 miles). The hilltop Old City is a national landmark and its appearance has hardly changed since it inspired El Greco in the 16th century. The close, narrow streets—barely wide enough to let a man and his donkey pass—offer cool, welcome shade in the summer and a shield from winter winds.

Surrounded on three sides by a bend in the Tagus River, Toledo overlooks the arid plains of La Mancha from a high bluff—a natural fortress in the center of the Iberian Peninsula.

ESSENTIALS

GETTING THERE   RENFE trains run here frequently every day. Those departing Madrid's Atocha railway station for Toledo run daily from 6:50am to 9:50pm; those leaving Toledo for Madrid run daily from 6:50am to 9:30pm. Traveling time is approximately 35 minutes on an *alta velocidad* (high-speed) train. The fare one-way is 11€. For train information in Madrid, call © **90-232-03-20,** or visit www.renfe.es.

From Madrid, it's also feasible to take the **bus** instead of the train. The main service is provided by **Alsa** (www.alsa.es; ☏ **90-242-22-42**). They depart daily, from Madrid's Estación de Plaza Elíptica, Avenida Vía Lusitana, between 6:30am and 11pm at 15- to 30-minute intervals. Travel time is 50 minutes to 1¼ hours, and a one-way transit costs 4.80€ and can be purchased only at the station.

VISITOR INFORMATION   The **tourist information office,** Plaza del Consistorio 1 (www.toledo-turismo.com; ☏ **92-525-40-30**), is open daily 10am to 6pm.

EXPLORING TOLEDO

Although ranked among the greatest of Gothic structures, the **cathedral** (www.catedralprimada.es; ☏ **92-522-22-41**), actually reflects a variety of styles because of the more than 2½ centuries that passed during its construction, from 1226 to 1493. Among its art treasures, the *transparente* stands out—a wall of marble and florid baroque alabaster sculpture overlooked for years because of the cathedral's poor lighting. The sculptor Narcisco Tomé cut a hole in the ceiling, much to the consternation of Toledans, and now light touches the high-rising angels, a *Last Supper* in alabaster, and a Virgin in ascension. The Treasure Room has a 225kg (496-lb.) 15th-century gilded monstrance (receptacle of the Host)—allegedly made with gold brought back from the New World by Columbus—that's still carried through the streets of Toledo during the feast of Corpus Christi. Admission to the cathedral is free; admission to the Treasure Room is 7€. Both are open Monday to Saturday 10:30am to 6pm and Sunday 2 to 6pm.

The **Alcázar,** Cuesta de Carlos V, near Plaza de Zocodover (☏ **92-523-88-00**), at the eastern edge of the old city, dominates the Toledo skyline. It became world famous at the beginning of the Spanish Civil War, when it underwent a 70-day siege that almost destroyed it. Today it has been rebuilt and houses the permanent collections of the **Museo del Ejército (Military Museum)** with such exhibits as a plastic model showing the fortress after the Civil War, electronic equipment used during the siege, and photographs taken during the height of the battle. A walking tour gives a realistic simulation of the siege. An outstanding array of exhibits from military history is on display, including El Cid's original sword. Admission is 5€ for adults and free for under-18s. There's free entry for all visitors on Sunday. It's open October through May Tuesday to Sunday 10am to 7pm, with closing extended to 9pm during June to September.

Queen Isabel had a hand in arranging the construction of the 16th-century building housing the **Museo-Hospital Santa Cruz,** Calle Miguel de Cervantes 3 (☏ **92-522-10-36**), with its impressive Plateresque facade. The paintings within are mostly from the 16th century and 17th century, with yet another by El Greco, *The Assumption of the Virgin,* his last known work. Admission is free. Hours are Monday to Saturday 10am to 6:30pm and Sunday 10am to 2pm.

San Lorenzo de El Escorial Palace ★★

The second-most-important excursion from Madrid is a 55km (34-mile) trip to the Royal Monastery in the village of San Lorenzo de El Escorial. Felipe II commissioned Juan Bautista de Toledo and his assistant, Juan de Herrera, to build this gloomy Xanadu in the Sierra de Guadarrama, northwest of Madrid. Its purported intent was to commemorate an important victory over the French in Flanders, but the likely real reason was that the ascetic Felipe was unnerved by the stress of overseeing an empire bridging four continents and this retreat insulated him from the intrigues of the

Madrid court. He ruled his troubled empire from the rooms here for the last 14 years of his life, and it was from here that he ordered his doomed "Invincible Armada" to set sail.

ESSENTIALS

GETTING THERE   More than two dozen *cercanía* **commuter trains** depart daily from Madrid's Atocha, Nuevos Ministerios, Chamartín, and Recoletos railway stations. For schedules and information, call ☎ 90-232-03-20, or visit www.renfe.es. A one-way fare costs 4.50€, and trip time is a little more than 1 hour.

Empresa Herranz, Calle Del Rey 27, in El Escorial (☎ 91-890-19-15), runs some 50 **buses** per day back and forth between Madrid and El Escorial. Trip time is an hour, and the one-way fare is 6€.

If you're driving, follow the N-VI highway (marked on some maps as A-6) from the northwest perimeter of Madrid toward Lugo, A Coruña, and San Lorenzo de El Escorial. After about a half-hour, fork left onto the C-505 heading toward San Lorenzo de El Escorial. Driving time from Madrid is about an hour.

VISITOR INFORMATION   The **tourist information office,** Calle Grimaldi 4 (www.sanlorenzoturismo.org; ☎ 91-890-53-13), is open Tuesday to Saturday 10am to 2pm and 3 to 6pm, and Sunday 10am to 2pm.

EXPLORING THE MONASTERY

The huge monastery/palace/mausoleum that is the **Real Monasterio de San Lorenzo de El Escorial ★★★**, Calle Juan de Borbón s/n (www.patrimonionacional.es; ☎ 91-890-59-03), is typically praised for its massive, brooding simplicity. That impression is allayed inside, as the wealth of sumptuous detail, the hundreds of rooms, and the 24km (15 miles) of corridors are revealed. The **Royal Library** houses a priceless collection of 60,000 volumes—one of the most significant in the world. The galleries and royal apartments contain canvases by El Greco, Titian, Ribera, Tintoretto, Rubens, and Velázquez, among others. During April to September, El Escorial is open Tuesday to Sunday 10am to 6pm (to 5pm in winter). An all-inclusive ticket is 10€ adults and 5€ seniors and students.

Segovia ★★★

Less commercial than Toledo, Segovia, 87km (54 miles) northwest of Madrid, typifies the glory of Old Castile. Wherever you look, you'll see reminders of a golden era—whether it's the spectacular Alcázar or the well-preserved Roman aqueduct. Segovia lies on the slope of the Guadarrama Mountains, where the Eresma and Clamores rivers converge. Isabel was proclaimed queen of Castile here in 1474.

ESSENTIALS

GETTING THERE   Seventeen **trains** leave Madrid every day. Five take 90 minutes to reach Segovia, but the others arrive in less than a half-hour. Once in Segovia, board bus no. 3, departing every quarter-hour for the Plaza Mayor. The five slow commuter trains that leave from Chamartín first travel through Atocha station, making it closer to some travelers' hotels. A one-way rail fare on the slow train costs 6€, while the high-speed train from Atocha costs 10€ to 13€.

Buses arrive and depart from **Estacionamiento Municipal de Autobuses,** Paseo de Ezequiel González 10 (☎ 92-142-77-06), near the corner of Avenida Fernández Ladreda and the steeply sloping Paseo Conde de Sepúlveda. There are 20 to 35 buses a day to and from Madrid (which depart from Paseo de la Florida 11;

Metro: Norte), and about 4 a day traveling between Ávila and Segovia. One-way tickets from Madrid cost 8€.

If you're driving, take the N-VI (on some maps it's known as the A-6), in the direction of A Coruña, northwest from Madrid, toward León and Lugo. At the junction with Rte. 110 (signposted SEGOVIA), turn northeast (AP-61 or N-603).

VISITOR INFORMATION The **tourist information office,** Plaza Mayor 10 (www.turismodesegovia.com; ✆ **92-146-03-34**), is open Monday to Saturday 9am to 2pm and 5 to 8pm.

EXPLORING SEGOVIA

The town is quite walkable. Its narrow medieval streets suffer less from the ravages of mass tourism (except on weekends and holidays) than other destinations in Madrid's orbit and reveal much about what life must have been like here 500 years ago.

Located here is what might be the most recognizable structure in Spain—an intact **Roman Aqueduct ★★**, Plaza de Azoguejo. A spectacular engineering feat even if it were contemplated today, the double-tiered Roman aqueduct cuts across the city to the snow-fed waters of the nearby mountains. Almost 730m (2,400 ft.) long and nearly 30m (98 ft.) at its highest point at the east end of town, it contains more than 160 arches fashioned of stone cut so precisely that no mortar was needed in the construction. Probably completed in the 2nd century A.D. (although some sources date it as many as 3 centuries earlier), it has survived war and partial dismantling by the Moors.

Constructed between 1515 and 1558, the **Cabildo Catedral de Segovia ★★**, Plaza de la Catedral, Marqués del Arco (✆ **92-146-22-05**), was the last Gothic cathedral built in Spain. Fronting the Plaza Mayor, it stands on the spot where Isabel I was proclaimed queen of Castile. It contains numerous treasures, such as a chapel created by the flamboyant Churriguera, elaborately carved choir stalls, and 16th- and 17th-century paintings. The attached 15th-century **cloister** houses a museum. To reach the cathedral, walk west along Calle de Cervantes, which becomes Calle Bravo. Admission is 3€ for adults, free for children under 13. It's open April to October daily 9am to 6:30pm, November to March daily 9:30am to 5:30pm.

Continue west on Calle de Daolz, where the prow of the old town rears above the confluence of the Clamores and Eresma rivers. **El Alcázar,** Plaza de la Reina Victoria Eugenia (www.alcazardesegovia.com; ✆ **92-146-07-59**), a fortified castle almost as familiar a symbol of Castilla (Castile) as the aqueduct, occupies this dramatic location. Though it satisfies our "castles in Spain" fantasies, at least from the outside, note that it's essentially a late-19th-century replica of the medieval fortress that stood here before a devastating fire in 1862. Admission is 4.50€ adults; 3€ seniors, students, and children; and free for children 5 and under. It's open April through September daily 10am to 7pm; October, Sunday to Thursday 10am–6pm, Friday to Saturday 10am to 7pm; November through March daily 10am–6pm.

BARCELONA ★★★

Blessed with rich and fertile soil, an excellent harbor, and a hardworking population, Barcelona has always prospered. When Madrid was still a dusty fortress village on the Manzanares, Barcelona was already a powerful, diverse capital, influenced by the Mediterranean empires that conquered it. Carthage, Rome, and Charlemagne-era France overran Catalunya, and each left an indelible mark on the region's identity.

The Catalan people have clung fiercely to their unique culture and language, both of which Franco systematically tried to eradicate. But Catalunya has endured, becoming a semiautonomous region of Spain (with Catalan its official language). And Barcelona, the region's economic, political, and intellectual capital, has truly come into its own. The city's most powerful monuments open a window onto its history: the intricately carved edifices of the medieval Gothic Quarter; the curvilinear *modernisme* (Catalan Art Nouveau) architecture that blossomed alongside Gaudí's Gothic reinterpretation expressed in Sagrada Família; and the seminal works of Picasso and Miró, in museums that mark Barcelona as a crucial incubator for 20th-century art. Parks, restaurants, nightlife (Barcelona is a *big* bar town), and shopping possibilities, plus nearby wineries, ensure that you'll be entertained round the clock. Barcelona is set for serious sightseeing; you'll need plenty of time to take it all in—as much time as it takes to see Madrid, if not more.

Essentials

GETTING THERE

BY PLANE Most travelers to Barcelona fly to Madrid and change planes there, although there are direct flights to Barcelona on American Airlines. The Barcelona airport, **El Prat de Llobregat,** 08820 Prat de Llobregat (www.aena.es; ✆ **90-240-47-04**), is 12km (7½ miles) southwest of the city.

The route to the center of town is carefully signposted. A train runs between the airport and Barcelona's Estació Central de Barcelona-Sants every day from 5:40am (the first airport departure) to 11:10pm (from Sants) or 11:40pm (the last city departure). The 20-minute trip costs 3.65€. If your hotel is near Plaça de España, you might opt for an **Aerobús** (www.aerobusbcn.com; ✆ **93-415-60-20**). It runs daily every 10 minutes between 6:10am and 1am from the airport, and till 12:30am from the Plaça de Catalunya. The fare is 5.05€ single trip, 8.75€ round-trip. A taxi from the airport into central Barcelona costs 20€ to 27€.

BY TRAIN A train with sleeper cars called the **Trenhotel** provides rail service between Paris and Barcelona in 12 hours. For many other routes from the rest of Europe, you change trains at Port Bou, on the France–Spain border. Most trains issue seat and sleeper reservations. Trains arrive at the **Estació de França,** Avenida Marqués de L'Argentera (Metro: Barceloneta, L3), from points throughout Spain as well as from international cities. High-speed trains now link Madrid with Barcelona, with some 25 daily connections. The fast nonstop services between Spain's two leading cities take 2 hours and 38 minutes, with those stopping en route taking 45 minutes longer. From Sevilla one train makes the 12½-hour trip to Barcelona. There are also two AVE trains per day from Sevilla to Barcelona, taking 5½ hours.

RENFE also has a terminal at **Estació Central de Barcelona-Sants,** Plaça de Països Catalanes (Metro: Sants-Estació). For general RENFE information, log on to www.renfe.es or call ✆ **90-232-03-20.**

BY BUS Bus travel to Barcelona is possible, but not popular—it's pretty slow. Barcelona's Estació del Nord is the arrival and departure point for **Alsa** (www.alsa.es; ✆ **90-242-22-42**) buses to and from southern France and Italy. Alsa also operates 27 buses per day to and from Madrid (trip time: 8½ hr.). A one-way ticket from Madrid costs 28€ to 61€.

Linebús (www.linebus.com; ✆ **90-233-55-33**) offers six trips a week to and from Paris. **Eurolines Viagens,** Carrer Viriato (www.eurolines.es; ✆ **93-490-40-00**),

Barcelona

ATTRACTIONS ●

Casa Batlló **18**
Catedral de Barcelona **28**
Fundació Joan Miró **2**
L'Aquarium de Barcelona **36**
La Pedrera **11**
La Sagrada Família **13**
Museu Barbier-Mueller d'Art
　Precolombí **32**
Museu d'Art Contemporani
　de Barcelona **23**
Museu Nacional d'Art de
　Catalunya **1**

RESTAURANTS ◆

ABaC **31**
Alkimia **12**
Café de L'Academia **30**
Cal Pep **33**
Can Costa **39**
Can Ravell **16**
Comerç 24 **27**
Dos Cielos **14**
Els Quatre Gats **26**
Gaig **20**
Gorría **15**
Hisop **3**
La Dentellière **34**
Moo **10**
Restaurant Hofmann **5**
Tapaç 24 **22**

HOTELS ■

Casa Fuster **7**
Claris **17**
Cram **19**
Duquesa de Cardona **35**
Eurostars Grand Marina Hotel **37**
Gallery Hotel **8**
H1898 **25**
Hostal Gat Xino **24**
Hotel 54 **38**
Hotel Arts **41**
Hotel Astoria **6**
Hotel Murmuri **9**
Neri **29**
Pullman Barcelona Skipper **40**
Soho Hotel **21**
Wilson Boutique Hotel **4**

Plaça de
Francesc Macià

Travessara de Gràcia

Carrer de Buenos Aires

Carrer de Londres

Carrer de Paris

Via Augusta

Gran de Gràcia

Avinguda Diagonal

Travessara de Gràcia

Av. de Sant Antoni Maria Claret

Carrer de la Industria

Carrer de Còrsega

Diagonal

EIXAMPLE

ℹ️ Information
Ⓜ️ Metro Station

Carrer de Provença

Carrer de Rosselló

Carrer Enric Granados

Carrer de Balmes

Rambla de Catalunya

Passeig de Gràcia

Carrer de Pau Claris

Carrer de Roger de Flor

Avinguda Diagonal

Plaça de la
Sagrada
Família

Carrer de Mallorca

Carrer de València

Passeig
de Gràcia

Carrer del Consell de Cent

Carrer de R. de Llúria

Carrer d'Aragó

Carrer de R. de Llúria

Carrer del Bruc

Carrer de Girona

Carrer de Bailén

Passeig de Sant Joan

Carrer de Napols

Carrer de Sicília

Carrer de Comte Borrell

Carrer del Comte d'Urgell

Carrer de Villarroel

Carrer de Casanova

Carrer de Muntaner

Carrer d'Aribau

Carrer de la Diputació

Plaça de la
Universitat

Gran Vía de les Corts Catalanes

Plaça de
Tetuan

Carrer de Sardenya

Urgell

Universitat

Ronda Universitat

Plaça
Catalunya

Carrer de Pelai

Catalunya

Ronda Sant Pau

Ronda de Sant Antoni

Plaça
Urquinaona

Carrer de Casp

Carrer d'Ausias Marc

RAVAL

Av. Portal de l'Angel

Urquinaona

Ronda de Sant Pere

Carrer d'Ali Bei

St. Antoni

Carrer de Hospital

La Rambla

Palau de la
Música Catalana

Arc de Carrer de Ribes
Triomf

Paral.lel

Carrer de Sant Pau

Gran Teatre
del Liceu

Catedral de
Barcelona ✝

BARRI
GÒTIC

Liceu

C. de

Ferran C. de la Princesa

Jaume I

Passeig de Lluis Companys

Passeig de Picasso

Passeig del Comerç

Paral.lel

Carrer Nou de la Rambla

Avda. de les Drassanes

La Rambla

LA RIBERA

PARC DE LA
CIUTADELLA

Carrer de Wellington

Drassanes

Carrer Ample

Passeig de Pujades

Plaça Portal
de la Pau

Passeig de Colom

Moll de la Fusta

Pg. Isabel II

Barceloneta

PARC
ZOOLOGIC

Avinguda d'Icaria

Vila
Olímpica →

Ciutadella-
Vila Olimpica

Moll d'Espanya

Port
Vell

BARCELONETA

Passeig Marítim

3 · 4 · 5 · 6 · 7 · 8 · 10 · 11 · 12 · 13 · 14 · 15 · 16 · 17 · 18 · 19 · 20 · 21 · 22 · 23 · 24 · 25 · 26 · 27 · 28 · 29 · 30 · 31 · 32 · 33 · 34 · 35 · 36 · 37 · 38 · 39 · 40 · 41

operates seven buses a week to and from Frankfurt and another five per week to and from Marseille.

BY CAR From **France** (the usual European road approach to Barcelona), the major access route is at the eastern end of the **Pyrenees.** You have a choice of the express highway (E-15) or the more scenic coastal road. If you take the coastal road in July and August, you will often encounter bumper-to-bumper traffic. You can also approach Barcelona via **Toulouse.** Cross the border into Spain at **Puigcerdà** (where there are frontier stations), near the Principality of Andorra. From there, take the N-152 to Barcelona.

From **Madrid,** take the N-2 to Zaragoza and then the A-2 to El Vendrell, followed by the A-7 freeway to Barcelona. From the **Costa Blanca** or **Costa del Sol,** follow the E-15 north from Valencia along the eastern Mediterranean coast.

VISITOR INFORMATION

TOURIST OFFICE A conveniently located tourist office is the **Oficina de Informació de Turisme de Barcelona,** Plaça de Catalunya 17-S (www.barcelona turisme.com; ☎ **93-285-38-34**). The office is open daily 9am to 9pm.

CITY LAYOUT

Plaça de Catalunya (**Plaza de Cataluña** in Castilian Spanish) is the city's heart; the world-famous **Les Rambles** (**Las Ramblas,** in Spanish) are its arteries. Les Rambles begin at the Plaça Portal de la Pau, with its 49m-high (161-ft.) monument to Columbus, and stretch north to the Plaça de Catalunya. Along this wide promenade you'll find bookshops and newsstands, stalls selling birds and flowers, and benches or cafe tables where you can sit and watch the passing parade.

West of Les Rambles is **Raval,** a sector of the Ciutat Vella (Old City) also sometimes known as **Barri Xinés** (**Barrio Chino** or **Chinese Quarter**). Once a haven of prostitution and drugs, it was spruced up by the city and is the principal immigrant quarter where many Eastern Europeans, Pakistanis, and Indonesians live.

Off Les Rambles lies **Plaça Reial (Plaza Real),** the most harmoniously proportioned square in Barcelona. Come here on Sunday morning to see the stamp and coin collectors peddle their wares.

The major wide boulevards of Barcelona are the **Avinguda (Avenida) Diagonal** and **Passeig (Paseo) de Colom,** as well as the elegant shopping street, **Passeig de Gràcia.**

A short walk from Les Rambles brings you to the **Passeig del Moll de la Fusta,** a waterfront promenade developed in the 1990s. It's home to some of the best (but hardly cheapest) restaurants in Barcelona. If you can't afford the prices, come here at least for a drink in the open air and a view of the harbor.

To the east is the old port **La Barceloneta,** which dates from the 18th century. This strip of land between the port and the sea has traditionally been a good place for seafood. **Barri Gòtic** (**Barrio Gótico** or **Gothic Quarter**) is east of Les Rambles. This is the site of the city's oldest buildings, including the cathedral.

North of Plaça de Catalunya, **l'Eixample** unfolds. An area of wide boulevards, it contains two major roads that lead out of Barcelona: Avinguda Diagonal and Gran Vía de les Corts Catalanes. Another major neighborhood, working-class **Gràcia,** is north of l'Eixample.

Montjuïc, one of the city's mountains, begins at Plaça d'Espanya, a traffic rotary, beyond which are Barcelona's famous fountains. Montjuïc was the setting for the principal events of the 1992 Summer Olympic Games. The other mountain is **Tibidabo,** in the northwest, which boasts great views of the city and the Mediterranean. It has an amusement park.

GETTING AROUND

To save money on public transportation, buy a card that's good for 10 trips. **Tarjeta T-10,** for 9.25€, is good for the Metro and the bus. Passes *(abonos temporales)* are available at **Transports Metropolitans de Barcelona,** Plaça de la Universitat. It's open Monday to Friday 8am to 8pm (www.tmb.net; ✆ **93-138-70-74**).

The sightseeing **Bus Turistic** passes by 24 of the most popular sights. You can get on or off the bus as you please, and the price covers the Tibidabo funicular and the Montjuïc cable car and funicular. Tickets, which can be purchased on the bus or at the tourist office at Plaça de Catalunya, cost 24€ for 1 day, 31€ for 2 days; for children, it's 14€ for 1 day and 18€ for 2 days.

BY METRO (SUBWAY) Barcelona's Metro system consists of six main lines; it crisscrosses the city more frequently and with greater efficiency than the bus network. Two commuter trains run between the city and the suburbs. The service operates Sunday to Thursday from 5am to midnight and Friday and Saturday from 5am to 2am. The one-way fare is 2€. Each Metro station entrance is marked with a red diamond. The major station for all subway lines is **Plaça de Catalunya.**

BY BUS Some 190 bus lines traverse the city and, not surprisingly, you don't want to ride them at rush hour. The driver issues a ticket as you board at the front. Most buses operate daily from 5:30am to 10pm; some night buses go along the principal arteries from 11pm to 4am. Buses are color coded—red ones cut through the city center during the day and yellow ones operate at night. The one-way fare is 2€.

BY TAXI Each yellow-and-black taxi bears the letters SP *(Servicio Público)* on its front and rear. A lit green light on the roof and a LIBRE sign in the window indicate the taxi is free to pick up passengers. The basic rate begins at 2€. For a taxi, contact **Ràdio Taxi** (www.radiotaxi033.com; ✆ **93-303-30-33**).

BY CAR Driving in congested Barcelona is frustrating and potentially dangerous. It's also unlikely you'd ever find a parking place. Try other means of getting around. Save car rentals for excursions and moving on.

All three of the major U.S.-based car-rental firms are represented in Barcelona, both at the airport and (except for Budget) downtown. **Avis,** Calle Corcega 293–295 (www.avis.es; ✆ **90-211-02-75**), is open Monday to Friday 8am to 9pm, Saturday 8am to 8pm, and Sunday 8am to 1pm.

BY FUNICULAR & TELEFERIC At some point in your journey, you may want to visit Tibidabo or Montjuïc (or both). A train called **Tramvía Blau (Blue Streetcar)** goes from Plaça Kennedy to the bottom of the funicular to Tibidabo. It operates every 15 to 20 minutes when it's running. From mid-April to September service is daily 10am to 8pm. In the off season it usually operates only Saturday and Sunday 10am to 6pm. The fare is 3€ one-way, 4.70€ round-trip. During the week, buses run from the Plaça Kennedy to the bottom of the funicular from approximately 10am to 6pm daily. The bus costs 2€ one-way.

At the end of the run, you can go the rest of the way by funicular to the top, at 503m (1,650 ft.), for a stunning panoramic view of Barcelona. The funicular operates only when the Fun Fair at Tibidabo is open. Opening times vary according to the time of year and the weather conditions. As a rule, the funicular starts operating 20 minutes before the Fun Fair opens and then every half-hour. During peak visiting hours, it runs every 15 minutes. The cost is 2€ one-way, 3€ round-trip.

The **Tibibus** (ⓒ **93-211-79-42**) goes from the Plaça de Catalunya (in the city center) to Tibidabo from June 24 to September 15 on Saturday and Sunday. It runs every 30 minutes from 11am to 6:30pm and sometimes 8:30pm, depending on when the park closes. The one-way fare is 2.50€. To reach Montjuïc, the site of the 1992 Olympics, take the **Montjuïc funicular** (ⓒ **93-318-70-74**). It links with subway lines 2 and 3 at Paral·lel. In fall and winter, the funicular runs Monday to Friday 7:30am to 8pm and Saturday and Sunday noon to 7pm; in spring and summer, it runs Monday to Friday 7:30am to 10pm, Saturday and Sunday 9am to 10pm.

[FastFACTS] BARCELONA

Consulates The **U.S. Consulate,** Reina Elisenda 23 (ⓒ **93-280-22-27;** train: Reina Elisenda), is open Monday to Friday 9am to 1pm. The **Canadian Consulate,** Plaça de Catalunya 9 (ⓒ **93-412-72-36;** Metro: Plaça de Catalunya), is open Monday to Friday 9am to 12:30pm. The **U.K. Consulate,** Av. Diagonal 477 (ⓒ **93-366-62-00;** Metro: Hospital Clínic), is open Monday to Friday 8:30am to 1:30pm. The **Australian Consulate** is at Av. Diagonal 458, 3rd floor (ⓒ **93-490-90-13;** Metro: Diagonal), and is open Monday to Friday 10am to noon.

Currency Exchange Most banks exchange currency Monday to Friday 8:30am to 2pm and often again in the afternoon. A major *oficina de cambio* (exchange office) is at the Estació Central de Barcelona-Sants, the principal rail station. It's open Monday to Saturday 8:30am to 10pm, and Sunday 8:30am to 2pm and 4:30 to

10pm. Exchange offices at Barcelona's airport are open daily 6:30am to 11pm.

Dentists For dental needs, contact **Clínica Dental Barcelona,** Passeig de Gràcia 97 (ⓒ **93-487-83-29;** Metro: Diagonal), open daily 9am to midnight.

Emergencies To report a fire, call ⓒ **080;** to call an ambulance, ⓒ **061;** to call the police, ⓒ **091.**

Hospitals Barcelona has many hospitals and clinics, including **Clínic Barcelona** (www.hospitalclinic.org; ⓒ **93-227-54-00**) and **Hospital de la Santa Creu i Sant Pau,** at the intersection of Carrer Cartagena and Carrer Sant Antoni María Claret (ⓒ **93-291-90-00;** Metro: Hospital de Sant Pau).

Internet Access Internet cafes are found throughout Barcelona. Charging only 2€ per hour, **Cybercafe Coffee & Bit,** Carrer de Fluvià 40 (ⓒ **93-266-45-64;** Metro: Selva de Mar), is open daily 9am to 1am.

Pharmacies The most centrally located one is **Farmacia Montserrat,** La Rambla 118 (ⓒ **93-302-43-45;** Metro: Liceu). It's open daily 9am to 8pm. Pharmacies take turns staying open late at night. Those that aren't open post the names and addresses of pharmacies in the area that are.

Post Office The main post office is at Plaça d'Antoni López (www.correos.es; ⓒ **93-486-80-50;** Metro: Jaume I). It's open Monday to Friday 8:30am to 9:30pm and Saturday 8:30am to 2pm for sending letters and telegrams.

Safety Be particularly careful with cameras, purses, and wallets, all favorite targets of thieves and pickpockets in Barcelona, particularly on the world-famous Les Rambles. The southern part of the boulevard, near the waterfront, is the most dangerous section, especially at night. Proceed with caution.

Exploring Barcelona

Spain's second-largest city is also its most cosmopolitan. Barcelona is more European and internationalist than Madrid. The city is filled with landmark buildings and world-class museums, including Antoni Gaudí's Sagrada Família, Museu Picasso, the Gothic cathedral, and La Rambla, the famous tree-lined promenade cutting through the heart of the old city from Plaça de Catalunya to the harbor.

BARRI GÒTIC

One of Barcelona's greatest attractions is not a single sight but an entire neighborhood, the **Barri Gòtic (Gothic Quarter)** ★★. This is the old aristocratic quarter, parts of which have survived from the Middle Ages. Spend at least 2 or 3 hours exploring its narrow streets and squares, which continue to form a vibrant, lively neighborhood.

Catedral de Barcelona ★★ CATHEDRAL   Barcelona's cathedral is a celebrated example of Catalan Gothic architecture. Construction began at the end of the 13th century and was nearly completed in the mid-15th century (although the west facade dates from the 19th century). The three naves, cleaned and illuminated, have splendid Gothic details. With its large bell towers, blending of medieval and Renaissance styles, beautiful **cloister** ★, high altar, side chapels, handsomely sculptured choir, and Gothic arches, this ranks among Spain's most impressive cathedrals. Vaulted galleries in the cloister, enhanced by forged iron grilles, surround a garden of magnolias, medlars, and palm trees. The cloister, illuminated on Saturday and during fiestas, also contains a museum of medieval art. You can take an elevator to the roof (Mon–Sat 10:30am–12:15pm and 5:15–7pm), where you'll have a wonderful view of Gothic Barcelona. At noon on Sunday, you can watch the *sardana*, a Catalan folk dance, performed in front of the cathedral.

Plaça de la Seu s/n. www.catedralbcn.org. 📞 **93-315-15-54.** Admission to cathedral free; museum 2€; global ticket to museum, choir, rooftop terraces, and towers 5€. Cathedral daily 8am–12:45pm and 5:15–7:30pm; cloister museum daily 10am–12:30pm and 5:15–7pm. Metro: Jaume I.

BARRI DE LA RIBERA

Museu Barbier-Mueller d'Art Precolombí ★ MUSEUM   Inaugurated by Queen Sofía in 1997, this is one of the most important collections of pre-Columbian art in the world. Housed in the restored medieval Palacio Nadal, the collection contains almost 6,000 pieces of tribal and ancient art from Mesoamerica, Central America, the Andes, and the Amazon Basin. Josef Mueller (1887–1977) acquired the first pieces by 1908. Pre-Columbian cultures created religious, funerary, and ornamental objects of great stylistic variety with relatively simple means. Stone sculpture and ceramic objects are especially outstanding.

Carrer de Montcada 12–14. www.barbier-mueller.ch. 📞 **93-310-45-16.** Admission 3.50€ adults, 1.70€ students, free for children 15 and under; free to all 1st Sun of the month. Tues–Fri 11am–7pm; Sat–Sun 11am–8pm. Metro: Jaume I. Bus: 14, 17, 19, 39, 40, 45, or 51. Tourist bus: Ruta Sur (Azul).

EL RAVAL

Museu d'Art Contemporani de Barcelona ★ ART MUSEUM   A soaring white edifice in the once-shabby but rebounding Raval district, the Museum of Contemporary Art is to Barcelona what the Pompidou Center is to Paris. Designed by the American architect Richard Meier, the building itself is a work of art, manipulating sunlight to offer brilliant, natural interior lighting. On display in the 6,875 sq. m

(74,000 sq. ft.) of exhibit space is the work of modern luminaries Tàpies, Klee, Miró, and many others. The museum has a library, bookshop, and cafeteria.

Plaça dels Angels 1. www.macba.es. © **93-412-08-10.** Admission 8€ adults, 6.50€ students, free for children 14 and under and seniors 65 and over. Late June to late Sept Mon and Wed–Fri 11am–8pm; Sat 10am–8pm, Sun 10am–3pm; late Sept to late June Mon and Wed–Fri 11am–7:30pm, Sat 10am–8pm, Sun 10am–3pm. Metro: Plaça de Catalunya.

L'EIXAMPLE

Casa Batlló ★★ HISTORIC HOME Next door to the Casa Amatller, Casa Batlló was designed by Gaudí in 1905. Using sensuous curves in iron and stone, the architect gave the facade a lavish baroque exuberance. The balconies have been compared to "sculpted waves." The upper part of the facade evokes animal forms, and delicate tiles spread across the design. The downstairs building is the headquarters of an insurance company. Many tourists walk inside for a view of Gaudí's interior, which is basically as he designed it. *Note:* This is a place of business, so be discreet. The paid cultural visit takes you on an audio tour of the mezzanine where the Batlló family lived, the central light and air shaft, the attic, and the rooftop with its amazing chimneys. The visit also includes the hall and main staircase.

Passeig de Gràcia 43. www.casabatllo.es. © **93-216-03-06.** Admission 18€ adults; 15€ children 5–16, students, and Catalunya residents; free for children 7 and under. Daily 9am–8pm. Metro: Passeig de Gràcia.

La Pedrera (Casa Milà) ★★★ HISTORIC HOME When locals first took a gander at this architectural masterpiece by Antoni Gaudí, they ridiculed it, nicknaming it "the Quarry" because of its fortresslike appearance. Today, a more sympathetic generation views it as one of the most outstanding examples of *modernista* architecture. Constructed between 1906 and 1912, the building was declared a World Heritage site by UNESCO in 1984. Currently, the structure houses the office of Fundació Caixa Catalunya, but guests are allowed to wander about the patios and the **Espai Gaudí** (loft and roof). Visitors may also go inside the **Pedrera Apartment,** allowing them to see how an apartment might have looked at the turn of the 20th century.

Provença 261–265. www.catalunyacaixa.com/obrasocial. © **93-484-59-00.** Admission 15€ adults, 11€ seniors and students, free for children 13 and under. Nov–Feb daily 9am–6:30pm; Mar–Oct daily 9am–8pm. Metro: Diagonal.

La Sagrada Família ★★★ CHURCH If you have time to see only one Catalan landmark, make it this one. Gaudí's unfinished masterpiece is one of the country's more idiosyncratic creations. Begun in 1882 and incomplete at the architect's death in 1926, this incredible basilica—the Church of the Holy Family—is a bizarre wonder. The languid, amorphous structure embodies the essence of Gaudí's style, which some have described as "Art Nouveau run wild." Admission includes a 20-minute video presentation. Work continues on the structure, with a completion date projected for 2025. Plan to spend an hour or more here.

Entrance from Carrer de Sardenya or Carrer de la Marina. www.sagradafamilia.org. © **93-207-30-31.** Admission 13€ adults, 11€ under 18 or retired; elevator to the top (about 60m/200 ft.) 3€; guide or audio guide additional 4€. Oct–Mar daily 9am–6pm; Apr–Sept daily 9am–8pm. Closed Christmas Day, Dec 26, New Year's Day, and Jan 6. Metro: Sagrada Família.

MONTJUÏC

In the southern part of the city, the mountain park of **Montjuïc** ★ has splashing fountains, gardens, outdoor restaurants, and museums, making for quite an outing. There are many walks and vantage points from which to view the Barcelona skyline.

To reach the park, take the Montjuïc **funicular** (𝄞 **93-318-70-74**), which links with subway lines 2 and 3 at Paral·lel. In fall and winter, the funicular runs Monday to Friday 7:30am to 8pm, and Saturday and Sunday noon to 7pm; in spring and summer, it runs Monday to Friday 7:30am to 10pm, Saturday and Sunday 9am to 10pm. The round-trip fare is 9€.

Fundació Joan Miró ★★ ART MUSEUM   Born in 1893, Joan Miró was one of Spain's greatest artists, known for his whimsical abstract forms and brilliant colors. Some 10,000 works by the Catalan surrealist, including paintings, graphics, and sculptures, are collected here. The building has been greatly expanded in recent years, following the design of Miró's close friend Catalan architect Josep Lluís Sert. An exhibition in a modern wing charts Miró's artistic evolution from his first drawings at the age of 8 to his final works. The museum frequently mounts temporary exhibitions of contemporary art. Allow at least 1 hour.

Plaça de Neptú, Parc de Montjuïc. http://fundaciomiro-bcn.org. 𝄞 **93-443-94-70.** Admission 10€ adults, 8€ students, free for children 14 and under. July–Sept Tues–Wed and Fri–Sat 10am–8pm, Thurs 10am–9:30pm, Sun 10am–2:30pm; Oct–June Tues–Wed and Fri–Sat 10am–7pm, Thurs 10am–9:30pm, Sun 10am–2:30pm. Bus: 50 (at Plaça d'Espanya) or 55.

Museu Nacional d'Art de Catalunya ★★★ ART MUSEUM   This museum, which underwent massive renovations, is the major depository of Catalan art, both antique and modern. More than 100 pieces, including sculptures, icons, and frescoes, are on display. The highlight is the collection of murals from various Romanesque churches. The frescoes and murals are displayed in apses much like those in the churches in which they were found. They're in sequential order, giving the viewer a tour of Romanesque art from its primitive beginnings to the more advanced late Romanesque and early Gothic eras.

Palau Nacional, Parc de Montjuïc. www.mnac.es. 𝄞 **93-622-03-76.** Admission 10€ adults, 7€ ages 15–20, free for children 16 and under and seniors 65 and older. Tues–Sat 10am–7pm; Sun 10am–2:30pm. Metro: Espanya (line 1 or 3).

THE WATERFRONT & BARCELONETA

L'Aquarium de Barcelona ★★ ☺ AQUARIUM   One of the most impressive testimonials to sea life anywhere opened in 1996 in Barcelona's Port Vell, a 10-minute walk from the bottom of Les Rambles. Among the largest aquariums in Europe, it contains 21 glass tanks positioned along either side of a wide, curving corridor. Each tank depicts a different marine habitat, with emphasis on everything from multicolored fish and corals to seagoing worms to sharks. The highlight is a huge "oceanarium" representative of the Mediterranean as a self-sustaining ecosystem. You view it from the inside of a glass-roofed, glass-sided tunnel that runs along its entire length, making fish, eels, and sharks appear to swim around you.

Port Vell. www.aquariumbcn.com. 𝄞 **93-221-74-74.** Admission 18€ adults, 15€ ages 60 and older, 13€ children 4–12 and students, free for children 3 and under. July–Aug Mon–Fri 9:30am–9pm, Sat–Sun 9:30am–11pm; June and Sept Mon–Fri 9:30am–9pm, Sat–Sun 9:30am–9:30pm; Oct–May daily 9:30am–9pm. Metro: Drassanes or Barceloneta. Bus: 14, 17, 19, 36, 38, 40, or 45.

ORGANIZED TOURS

Pullmantur, Gran Vía de les Corts Catalanes 645 (www.pullmantur.es; 𝄞 **902-09-55-12;** Metro: Plaça de Catalunya), offers a number of tours and excursions with English-speaking guides. For a preview of the city, you can take a morning tour. They depart from the company's terminal at 9:45am; tickets cost 44€. An afternoon tour leaves at 3:30pm and visits some of the most outstanding architecture in l'Eixample, including Gaudí's La Sagrada Família. The tour includes Park Güell and a stop at the Picasso Museum. The cost is 43€.

Pullmantur also offers several excursions outside Barcelona. The daily tour of the monastery of Montserrat includes a visit to the Royal Basilica to view the famous sculpture of the Black Virgin. This tour, which costs 53€, departs at 9:30am and returns at 2:30pm to the company's terminal. A full-day Girona-Figueres tour includes a visit to Girona's cathedral and its Jewish Quarter, plus a trip to the Dalí museum. This excursion, which costs 153€, leaves Barcelona at 8:30am and returns at approximately 6:30pm (June–Sept Tues and Thurs). Call ahead—a minimum number of participants is required.

Another company that offers tours of Barcelona and the surrounding countryside is **Juliá Travel,** Ronda Universitat 5 (www.juliatravel.com; ℂ **93-317-64-54**).

OUTDOOR ACTIVITIES

Parc Güell, a fanciful park on the northern edge of Barcelona's inner core, is much more than green space. Begun by Antoni Gaudí as an upper-crust real-estate venture for his wealthy patron, Count Eusebi Güell, it was never completed. Only two houses were constructed, but Gaudí's whimsical creativity, seen in soaring columns that impersonate trees and splendid winding benches of broken mosaics, is on abundant display. The city took over the property in 1926 and turned it into a public park. Open May through September daily 9am to 9pm; October through April daily 9am to 7pm. Metro: Lesseps.

Parc de la Ciutadella (ℂ **93-225-67-80;** Metro: Ciutadella) occupies the former site of a detested 18th-century citadel, some remnants of which remain. Today lakes, gardens, and promenades fill most of the park, which also holds a **zoo.** Gaudí contributed to the monumental fountain in the park when he was a student; the lampposts are also his. Open March daily 10am to 6pm; April daily 10am to 7pm; May through August daily 10am to 8pm; September daily 10am to 6pm; October through February daily 10am to 5pm.

Another attraction, **Tibidabo Mountain ★**, offers the best panoramic view of Barcelona. A funicular takes you up 488m (1,600 ft.) to the summit. A retro amusement park—with Ferris wheels and airplanes that spin over Barcelona—has been there since the '30s.

Where to Eat

If money is no object, you'll find some of the grandest culinary experiences in Europe here. Diverse Catalan cuisine reaches its pinnacle in Barcelona, but you don't get just Catalan fare—the city is rich in the cuisines of all the major regions of Spain, including Castilla and Andalucía. Because of Barcelona's proximity to France, many of the finer restaurants serve French or French-inspired dishes. At the other end of the spectrum, finding an affordable restaurant in Barcelona is easier than finding an inexpensive hotel. There are many budget restaurants in and around the **Carrer de Montcada.**

CIUTAT VELLA (BARRI GÒTIC, EL RAVAL & LA RIBERA)
Very Expensive

ABaC ★★ CONTEMPORARY SPANISH   One of the leading chefs of Barcelona, Jordi Cruz follows his own culinary path, creating a *cuisine d'auteur* based on his imagination and a certain level of wizardry with the techniques of molecular cuisine.

This means a menu of dishes you've had nowhere else. Cruz's savory cooking, a balance of flavor and harmonious combinations, charms most palates. Perhaps sometimes he doesn't quite hit the mark, but no one faults his creativity. Tempting dishes might include smoked salmon with cauliflower purée served under a smoke-filled bell jar, or a small glass of mushroom bisque with a hazelnut foam accompanied by an airy mushroom-truffle focaccio.

Carrer del Rec 7989. www.abacbarcelona.com. © **93-319-66-00.** Reservations required. Main courses 30€–55€; tasting menus 125€–145€. Mon 8:30–10:30pm; Tues–Sat 1:30–3:30pm and 8:30–10:30pm. Metro: Barceloneta or Jaume I.

Expensive

Restaurant Hofmann ★ CATALAN/FRENCH   This restaurant is famous in part because its German/Catalan chef-owner Mey Hofmann cuts a wide public swath. Trained as a jewelry designer, she turned her talents to cooking, catering, and teaching cooking. Her menu changes roughly six times a year with the season and cuts across borders with both Catalan and Gascogne dishes—all given a modern touch. You might start with her traditional warm sardine tart, or opt for a modern interpretation of stuffed mushrooms (false cepes stuffed with caramelized pumpkin and mascarpone). The fish changes nightly, but one of her signature preparations is grilled fish with thin slices of bacon, market vegetables, and a red-wine sauce. Desserts come from Hofmann's French-style pastry shop.

Granada del Penedes 14. www.hofmann-bcn.com. © **93-218-71-65.** Reservations recommended. Main courses 20€–35€; 4-course fixed-price lunch menu 45€, 4-course fixed-price dinner Tues–Wed 55€. AE, DC, MC, V. Mon–Fri 1:30–3:15pm and 9–11:15pm. Metro: Diagonale.

Moderate

Comerç 24 ★★ 🍴 CONTEMPORARY CATALAN   View a dining visit here as an opportunity to experience the culinary vision of a rare artist. The chef and owner is Carles Abellan, a Ferran Adrià protege who has given his imaginative, distinctive interpretation to all the longtime favorite dishes of Catalunya. Abellan uses fresh seasonal ingredients, balanced sauces, and bold but never outrageous combinations; more to the point, he believes in split-second timing. Perhaps you'll sample his fresh salmon "perfumed" with vanilla and served with yogurt. Other vibrant, earthy dishes include a veal entrecote with wasabi sauce or ravioli with cuttlefish and fresh morels. The dining room's avant-garde, minimalist design provides a soothing, neutral backdrop to the culinary pyrotechnics.

Carrer Comerç 24, La Ribera. www.projectes24.com. © **93-319-21-02.** Reservations required. Main courses 16€–40€; tasting menus 72€–95€. MC, V. Tues–Sat 1:30–3:30pm and 8:30–11:30pm. Closed 10 days in Dec. Metro: Arco de Triompho or Estación de Francia.

Els Quatre Gats 🍴 SPANISH   This has been a Barcelona legend since 1897. "The Four Cats" (in Catalan slang, "just a few people") was a favorite of Picasso, Rusiñol, and other artists, who once hung their works on its walls. On a narrow cobblestone street in the Barri Gòtic near the cathedral, the *fin de siècle* cafe has been the setting for piano concerts by Isaac Albéniz and Ernie Granados, and for murals by Ramón Casas. It was a base for members of the *modernisme* movement and figured in the city's intellectual and bohemian life. Today the restored bar remains a popular meeting place for Catalans, as well as a must-visit spot for Picasso fans. (One of his first jobs was designing the original menu.) The fixed-price meal is one of the better bargains in town, considering the locale. The unpretentious Spanish cooking here is simple market cuisine that adds seasonal specials to a cuisine otherwise based on the larder. For starters, you might try the onion soup au gratin with egg and Parmesan cheese. The kitchen also does a great job with the classic *alcachofas y jamón* (artichokes and bits of ham and sausage), as well as roasted salt cod with a garlicky mayonnaise. The seabass stuffed with red peppers and served with a garlic vinaigrette is also very good.

Montsió 3. www.4gats.com.🕐 **93-302-41-40.** Reservations required Sat–Sun. Main courses 12€–28€. AE, DC, MC, V. Daily 10am–2am. Metro: Plaça de Catalunya.

Inexpensive
Café de L'Academia ★ 🍴 CATALAN/MEDITERRANEAN
In the center of the Barri Gòtic, a short walk from Plaça Sant Jaume, this 15-table (20–25 in summer) restaurant looks expensive but is really one of the most affordable (and one of the best) in the medieval city. The building dates from the 15th century, but the restaurant was founded in 1987. Chef-owner Jordí Casteldi is a proponent of market cuisine. Try such delights as *lassanye de butifarra i ceps* (lasagna with Catalan sausage and porcini), *bacalla gratinado i musselina de carofes* (salt cod gratiné with an artichoke mousse), or *terrina d'berengueras amb formatge de cabra* (terrine of eggplant with goat cheese).

Carrer Lledó 1 (Barri Gòtic), Plaça Sant Just.🕐 **93-319-82-53.** Reservations required. Main courses 10€–18€; fixed-price menu (lunch only) 16€. AE, MC, V. Mon–Fri 1:30–4pm and 8:30pm–1am. Closed last 2 weeks of Aug. Metro: Jaume I.

Tapaç 24 ★★ TAPAS
If you sometimes prefer to make an entire meal of small plates, this chef-driven tapas bistro is one of the best bets in Barcelona. First-rate produce, such as purple-tinged artichokes, is transformed into tantalizing treats. You can stop in for breakfast, lunch, or dinner at this nonstop kitchen where the tapas of the day are always changing. If they are available, try the cod omelet with white beans and guindilla peppers, the truffled grilled-cheese sandwich of mozzarella and Iberian ham, or perhaps the silvery spread of anchovies on slices of Requesón cheese. A good lunch dish is a plate of french fries glued together with just-barely-set duck eggs.

Carrer de la Disputació 269. www.tapas24.net.🕐 **93-488-09-77.** Reservations not required. Tapas 4€–15€. MC, V. Mon–Sat 9am–midnight. Metro: Tetuan.

L'EIXAMPLE
Very Expensive
Gaig ★★★ CONTEMPORARY CATALAN
Media darling Carles Gaig earned his fame by reinventing the Catalan cuisine of his family restaurant in the same way that Juan Marí Arzak (one of his models) helped create the New Basque cuisine at his family restaurant in San Sebastian. This 16-table haute restaurant, moved to l'Eixample in 2004, is Gaig's gastronomic venue, and he is widely acclaimed for serving the finest Catalan cuisine of his generation. He keeps the dishes deceptively simple, making a tomato soup with mussels, cockles, and razor clams in an intensely reduced seafood broth, or serving veal sweetbreads with tiny whole potatoes and a mustard sauce. One of his great seasonal specialties is aromatic Bomba rice from the Ebro delta with plump pigeon and porcini mushrooms. His famed canneloni with black truffle announces the arrival of fall. Gaig shops personally every morning at La Boquería. Few dishes last long on the menu, as he is a restless inventor.

Aragó 214. www.restaurantgaig.com. 🕐 **93-429-10-17.** Reservations required. Main courses 24€–42€; tasting menus 77€–96€. AE, DC, MC, V. Mon–Sat 1:30–3:30pm and 9–11pm; Sun 9–11pm. Metro: Passeig de Gràcia.

Expensive

Can Ravell ★ 👜 SPANISH/CATALAN   Founded in 1929 by Ignasy Ravell and now run by his son Josep, Can Ravell began as a delicatessen for Barcelona's carriage trade and somehow survived the Franco years by catering to discerning Catalans. Many shoppers know its delights, but fewer realize that there's a gourmet restaurant above the shop. You reach it by going through a catering kitchen and climbing a spiral staircase. Chef Jesus Benavente adjusts his menu to take advantage of the best in the market during any given season, choosing just four dishes for each course daily from his vast repertoire. In the spring you might find roast lamb with pearl onions, pigs' trotters stuffed with shrimp, and veal steak accompanied by a torchon of foie gras. At all seasons you can get the *salmorejo* (a thicker cousin of gazpacho) topped with lobster and a poached egg.

Aragó 313. www.ravell.com. 📞 **93-457-51-14.** Reservations required. Main courses 13€–32€. AE, DC, MC, V. Tues–Wed 10am–9pm; Thurs–Sat 10am–11pm; Sun 10am–4pm. Metro: Gerona.

Moo ★★★ MEDITERRANEAN   Style and substance meet in this design-centric enclave of sublime food, where steel and slate dead-end into a glassed-in bamboo garden at the chic Hotel Omm. The famed Roca brothers' creativity in the kitchen approaches a kind of culinary genius night after night. The lobster with licorice curry (you read that right) is a celestial dish, playing the unctuous meat off the aromatic anise and ginger. Baby goat is slow-cooked in a rosemary-honey glaze and served on a "cloud" of goat's milk foam. None of the three brothers is on premises during meal service, but the kitchen is under the guidance of their accomplished lieutenant Felip Llufriu.

In the Hotel Omm, Rosselló 265. www.hotelomm.es. 📞 **93-445-40-00.** Reservations required. Main courses 21€–27€; fixed-price menus 55€–100€ plus wines. AE, DC, MC, V. Mon–Sat 1:30–4pm and 8:30–11pm. Metro: Diagonal.

Moderate

Alkimia ★★ 👜 CATALAN   If the idea of a "fried egg" as an appetizer sounds a bit dull, try it here in l'Eixample, where chef Jordi Vilà stretches the fundamental boundaries of Catalan cuisine. Begin with that fried egg, which just happens to be a ring of cauliflower cream studded with candied lemon and caramelized onion. The "yolk" is a scoop of unsweetened egg-yolk ice cream with a dollop of Sevruga caviar. Vilà is a deconstructivist who breaks down traditional recipes into components and reinterprets them in creative ways. The rice in the fried egg dish is creamed and ringed with black squid ink. Some of his other imaginative delights could include red mullet in garlic oil with a yogurt and cucumber–apple chutney, monkfish with cauliflower purée and black-olive jam, and glazed veal shank with seasonal mushrooms.

Calle Industria 79. www.alkimia.cat. 📞 **93-207-61-15.** Reservations required. Main dishes 11€–20€; fixed-price menus 38€–84€. DC, MC, V. Mon–Fri 1:30–3:30pm and 8:30–10:30pm. Closed 3 weeks in Aug. Metro: Sagrada Família.

Hisop ★★ 👜 CATALAN/INTERNATIONAL   On the northern tier of l'Eixample, Oriol Ivern and Guillem Pla are in the vanguard of gifted chefs revolutionizing Spanish—and European—cuisine. The decor is hip, stylish, minimalist, and dominated by a sleek red-and-black gloss. Their philosophy is to take the recipes of the past and give them an entirely contemporary interpretation. Their signature dish is a rosy pigeon breast served with pear purée and tomato confit. The pigeon comes with different peppers (ranging from Jamaican to Szechuan) and different salts (ranging from red to *fleur de sel*). You more or less get to season to taste. Duck liver comes with the unusual accompaniments of beets and mangoes. Fresh scallops are tossed with pumpkin flowers, and John Dory appears on your platter with truffles.

Pasaje Marimon 9. www.hisop.com. © **93-241-32-33.** Reservations required. Main courses 21€–25€. AE, DC, MC, V. Mon–Fri 1:30–3:30pm and 9–11pm; Sat 9–11pm. Closed 1 week in Aug. Metro: Hospital Clínic.

Inexpensive
La Dentellière ★ 🎁 MEDITERRANEAN   Evelyne Ramelot, the French writer who owns this charming little bistro, has modeled it after some of the welcoming boites of provincial France. After an aperitif at the sophisticated cocktail bar, you can order from an imaginative menu that might include a lasagna of strips of salt cod, peppers, and tomato sauce; or a delectable carpaccio of filet of beef with pistachios, lemon juice, vinaigrette, and Parmesan cheese. Like many good bargain dining spots, the menu also features a lot of pastas and rice dishes. Unlike most others, it also offers three fondues: a classic, a blue-cheese version, and a goat-cheese version.

Ample 165. www.ladentellierebcn.com. © **93-319-68-21.** Reservations recommended. Main courses 9€–16€; fixed-price dinner 17€. MC, V. Daily 7:30pm–midnight. Metro: Diagonal or Jaume I.

NORTE DIAGONAL
Very Expensive
Dos Cielos ★★★ MEDITERRANEAN   This gourmet citadel of chefs Sergio and Javier Torres sits high above Barcelona on the 24th floor of the Hotel Meliá. What you find here is rich, elegant Mediterranean cuisine. The selection of starters, both hot and cold, is as celestial as the lofty setting, including foie gras ravioli, blue lobster flavored with citrus, and summer truffles with spinach and mushrooms. For a main, select one of their creamy rice dishes, such as one with pigeon and black olives, or fish and meat selections, including grilled wild turbot or suckling kid shoulder. One particularly intensely flavored specialty is wild hare, a confit of tender meat beneath an inky reduction sauce enriched with rabbit blood.

In the Hotel Meliá, Diagonal Pere IV. www.doscielos.com. © **93-3672070.** Reservations recommended Fri–Sat. Main courses 27€–45€; tasting menu 120€. AE, DC, MC, V. Tues–Thurs 1–4pm and 8–11pm; Fri–Sat 1–4pm and 8–11:30pm.

Expensive
Gorría ★ 🎁 BASQUE/NAVARRESE   If you're a devotee of the cookery of both Navarra and the coastal Basque Country in northern Spain, then head for this quite wonderful restaurant lying only 200m (656 ft.) from La Sagrada Família and just 50m (164 ft.) from Plaza de Toros (the bullring). No dish is finer than the herb-flavored baby lamb baked in a wood-fired oven. The classic Basque dish, hake, comes in a garlic-laced green-herb sauce with fresh mussels and perfectly cooked asparagus on the side. The grilled turbot is fresh and straightforward, perfection itself with its flavoring of garlic, virgin olive oil, and a dash of vinegar. Braised pork also emerges from the wood-fired oven.

Diputación 421, Eixample. www.restaurantegorria.com. © **93-245-11-64.** Reservations recommended. Main courses 14€–33€. AE, DC, MC, V. Mon 11am–3:30pm; Tues–Sat 1–3:30pm and 9–11:30pm. Closed Easter and Aug. Metro: Monumental.

MOLL DE LA FUSTA & LA BARCELONETA
Expensive
Can Costa ★ SEAFOOD   This is one of the oldest seafood restaurants in this seafaring town. Established in the late 1920s, it has two busy dining rooms, a practiced

staff, and an outdoor terrace, although a warehouse blocks the view of the harbor. Fresh seafood prepared according to traditional recipes rules the menu. It includes the best baby squid in town—sautéed in a flash so that it has a nearly grilled flavor, almost never overcooked or rubbery. A long-standing chef's specialty is *fideuà de peix*, a relative of the classic Valencian shellfish paella, with noodles instead of rice. The kitchen also makes a "black" version colored and flavored with squid ink. Other temptations on the menu include grilled lobster with lemon sauce, baked monkfish, and grilled king prawns. Desserts are made fresh daily.

Passeig Don Joan de Borbò 70. www.cancosta.com. (℃ **93-221-59-03.** Reservations recommended. Main courses 12€–32€. MC, V. Daily 12:30–4pm; Thurs–Tues 8–11:30pm. Metro: Barceloneta.

Moderate

Cal Pep ★★ CATALAN   One of the most celebrated casual dining spots in Barcelona, Cal Pep lies on a postage-stamp square close to the Picasso Museum. There's actually a real Pep, and he's a great host, going around to make sure that everybody is one happy family. A selection of perfectly cooked dishes—all a little big to be called tapas and too small to be *raciones*—emerges from the kitchen in the back. They are, nonetheless, meant for sharing. Try the fried artichokes or the mixed medley of seafood that includes small sardines. Tiny clams come swimming in a well-seasoned broth given extra spice by a sprinkling of hot peppers. A delectable tuna dish comes with a sesame sauce, and fresh salmon is flavored with basil.

Plaça des les Olles 8. www.calpep.com. (℃ **93-310-79-61.** Reservations for groups of 4–20 only. Main courses 14€–28€. AE, MC, V. Mon 8–11:30pm; Tues–Fri 1–4pm and 8–11:30pm; Sat 1–4pm. Closed Aug. Metro: Barceloneta or Jaume I.

Shopping

If you're a window-shopper, stroll along the **Passeig de Gràcia** from the Avinguda Diagonal to the Plaça de Catalunya. Along the way, you'll see some of the most elegant and expensive shops in Barcelona, plus an assortment of splendid turn-of-the-20th-century buildings and cafes, many with outdoor tables. Another prime spot is **La Rambla de Catalunya** (upper end of Les Rambles).

Yet another shopping destination is the **Mercat de la Boqueria** ★★★, Rambla 91 (no phone), near Carrer del Carme. Here you'll see a wide array of straw bags and regional products, along with artfully displayed food sold to home cooks and restaurants alike: fruits, vegetables, breads, cheeses, meats, and fish. Vendors sell their wares Monday to Saturday 8am to 8pm. Similarly, in La Ribera, the **Mercat de Santa Caterina,** Av. Francesc Cambó 16 (www.mercatsantacaterina.net), has a somewhat smaller selection of food vendors (only 21 butchers, for example, and only 17 fishmongers). Hours at Santa Caterina are somewhat briefer, ending at 2pm on Mondays, and at 2:30pm on Tuesdays, Wednesdays, and Saturdays.

In the **Old Quarter,** not far from Plaça de Catalunya, the principal shopping streets are all five of Les Rambles, plus Carrer del Pi, Carrer de la Palla, and Avinguda Portal de l'Angel, to cite some major thoroughfares. Moving north in **l'Eixample,** you'll walk through Passeig de Catalunya, Passeig de Gràcia, and Ramble de Catalunya. Even farther north, **Avinguda Diagonal** is a major shopping boulevard. Other prominent shopping streets include Bori i Fontesta, Vía Augusta, Carrer Muntaner, Travessera de Gràcia, and Carrer de Balmes.

In general, shopping hours are Monday to Saturday 9am to 8pm. Smaller shops may close from 1:30 to 4pm.

THE BEST BUYS

El Corte Inglés ★ is Spain's most prominent department store. Its main Barcelona emporium is at Plaça de Catalunya 14 (www.elcorteingles.es; © **93-306-38-00;** Metro: Plaça de Catalunya). It stays open through the siesta period and has a full-size supermarket in the basement and a cafeteria/restaurant on the ninth floor. Corte Inglés has other Barcelona locations: Av. Diagonal 617–619 (© **93-366-71-00;** Metro: María Cristina) and Av. Diagonal 471 (© **93-493-48-00;** Metro: Hospital Clínic).

For designer housewares and the best in Spanish contemporary furnishings, a good bet is **Vinçón ★★**, Passeig de Gràcia 96 (www.vincon.com; © **93-215-60-50;** Metro: Diagonal), housed in the former home of artist Ramón Casas. Various high-end shops on the Passeig de Gràcia and Avinguda Diagonal showcase men's and women's fashions. You'll find cutting-edge boutiques (and few tourists) on **Carrer Verdí** in the Gràcia neighborhood, from the Plaça Revolució stretching about 6 blocks north and onto side streets. Pick up a shopping map from any of the Verdi boutiques.

In the city of Miró, Tàpies, and Picasso, art is a major business. There are dozens of galleries, especially in the Barri Gòtic and around the Picasso Museum. In business since 1840, **Sala Parés ★★**, Petritxol 5 (www.salapares.com; © **93-318-70-08;** Metro: Plaça de Catalunya), displays paintings in a two-story amphitheater; exhibitions change about once a month. At **Art Picasso,** Tapinería 10 (© **93-268-32-40;** Metro: Jaume I), you can purchase good lithographic reproductions of the works of not only Picasso, but also Miró and Dalí.

For antiques, drop by **El Bulevard des Antiquarius ★★**, Passeig de Gràcia 55–57 (www.bulevarddelsantiquaris.com; © **93-215-44-99;** Metro: Passeig de Gràcia). This 70-unit complex, just off the city's most aristocratic avenues, has a huge collection of art and antiques assembled in a series of boutiques.

Seeking out small specialty shops is a particular treat. A number of shops offer authentic ceramics from various regions of the country that are known for their pottery. One worthwhile stop is **Itaca,** Carrer Ferrán 26 (© **93-301-30-44;** Metro: Liceu).

La Manual Alpargatera, Carrer Avinyó (www.lamanual.net; © **93-301-01-72;** Metro: Jaume I), is the best shop for the handmade espadrilles seen on dancers of the sardana. It offers many styles and also sells hats and folk art.

Entertainment & Nightlife

Barcelona comes alive at night with a staggering array of diversions. There is something to interest almost everyone and to fit most pocketbooks. The **funicular ride** to Tibidabo and the illuminated **fountains** of Montjuïc are especially popular, and fashionable **clubs** operate in nearly every major district of the city. For families, the **amusement parks** are the busiest venues.

Your best source of local information is a little magazine called *Guía del Ocio,* which previews "La Semana de Barcelona" ("This Week in Barcelona"). It's in Spanish, but most of its listings should be comprehensible to those who don't speak Spanish. Almost every news kiosk along Les Rambles carries the publication.

THE PERFORMING ARTS

The **Gran Teatre del Liceu ★★★**, La Rambla 51–54 (www.liceubarcelona.com; © **93-485-99-13;** Metro: Liceu), is the traditional home to opera and ballet. It suffered a devastating fire in 1994 but has reopened after extensive renovations. The result is glorious, especially considering that only the walls were left standing after the fire. The decision was made to replicate the neobaroque interior, with lashings of gilt, intricate carvings, and swaths of brocade and velvet. The theater presents 8 to 12 operas every season and strives to make them accessible to a wide audience.

A magnificent *modernista* concert hall, the **Palau de la Música Catalana ★★★**, Sant Francese de Paulo 2 (www.palaumusica.org; ✆ **93-295-72-00;** Metro: Urquinaona), is the work of Catalán architect Lluís Domènech i Montaner, a rival of Antoni Gaudí. Its distinctive facade is a tour de force of brick, mosaic, and glass. Concerts and leading recitals take place here. The box office is open Monday to Saturday 10am to 9pm and Sunday 1 hour before concerts.

LIVE-MUSIC CLUBS

The most popular jazz club, **Jamboree ★★**, Plaça Reial 17 (www.masimas.com; ✆ **93-319-17-89;** Metro: Liceu), is on a raucously diverse plaza off the lower Rambla. The cover charge can be anywhere from 10€ to 13€, depending on who's playing; you descend to a vaulted brick cellar filled with young to middle-aged natives and visitors. Arrive around 9:30pm and you'll probably get in free and might also catch the rehearsal.

A popular old-timer is the **Harlem Jazz Club ★**, Comtessa de Sobradiel 8 (www.harlemjazzclub.es; ✆ **93-310-07-55**), with live jazz nightly in all its permutations—flamenco fusion, Brazilian salsa, Afro-Caribbean, blues.

For the best Latino and jazz on weekends, head for **Luz de Gas,** Carrer de Muntaner 246 (www.luzdegas.com; ✆ **93-209-77-11;** Metro: Diagonal), which has cabaret on other nights. The lower two levels open onto a stage floor and stage. Call to see what the lineup is on any given night—jazz, pop, soul, rhythm and blues, whatever. Open daily from 11pm until 4 or 5am. Cover 15€ includes one drink.

Flamenco is best seen in Sevilla or Madrid, but if you aren't getting to those cities on your trip, **El Tablao de Carmen ★**, Poble Espanyol de Montjuïc (www.tablaodecarmen.com; ✆ **93-325-68-95**), is the best place in Barcelona to see the passionate dance and music of Andalucía. Admission is 69€ to 94€ for dinner and the first show, or 35€ for the first show and a drink. Dinner begins at 9pm; the first show is at 7:30pm.

DANCE CLUBS

La Paloma, Tigre 27 (✆ **93-301-68-97;** Metro: Universitat), is a retreat for those with a sense of nostalgia—remember the fox trot? The mambo? Live orchestras provide the music in this old-time dance hall, the most famous in Barcelona. Cover is 8€.

Mojito Club, Carrrer Rossellón 217 (www.mojitobcn.com; ✆ **93-237-65-28;** Metro: Diagonal), rocks with a Latin beat, as its name suggests. An international crowd keeps the place festive; cover is 10€.

Sala Razzmatazz, Carrer Pamplona 88 (www.salarazzmatazz.com; ✆ **93-320-82-00;** Metro: Bogatell), lies in a converted warehouse, five clubs in one. Each club within the club presents its own music. One entrance fee, ranging from 13€ to 30€, includes admission to each club.

BARS & PUBS

Established in 1933, **Cocktail Bar Boadas,** Tallers 1 (✆ **93-318-88-26;** Metro: Placa de Catalunya), lies near the top of Las Ramblas. The bar stocks a wide range of Caribbean rums, Russian vodkas, and English gins. It opens daily at noon and closes at 2am Sunday to Thursday and 3am Friday and Saturday.

Facing a rustic-looking square, a former fish store has been cleverly converted into **El Born,** Passeig del Born 26. (© **93-319-53-33;** Metro: Jaume I or Barceloneta). The music varies from Louis Armstrong to classic rock and roll. Opening hours are Sunday to Thursday 6pm to 2am, Friday and Saturday 6pm to 3am.

A young and stylish crowd can be seen crossing Plaça Reial, with its Gaudí lamp-posts, heading for this old cafe to sample its drinks, succulent pastas, savory tapas, and panini. Forsaking Barcelona's fabled modernism, **Schilling,** Carrer Ferran 23 (www.cafeschilling.com; © **93-317-67-87;** Metro: Liceu), revels in another era, with its iron columns, marble tables, and wall of wine bottles. It's open Monday to Thursday from 10am to 2:30am, Friday and Saturday from 10am to 3am, and Sunday from noon to 2am.

THE LGBT SCENE

Metro, Sepúlveda 185 (www.metrodiscobcn.com; © **93-323-52-27;** Metro: Universitat), still reigns as one of the most popular gay discos, attracting everyone from startlingly thin male models to beefy macho men. There are two dance floors playing everything from Spanish pop to contemporary house. Cover is 15€.

Where to Stay

Barcelona may be one of the most expensive cities in Spain, but prices at Barcelona's first-class and deluxe hotels are completely in line with those in other major European cities—and they even look reasonable compared with prices in Paris and London.

Safety is an important factor when choosing a hotel. Some of the least expensive hotels are not in good locations. A popular area for budget-conscious travelers is the **Barri Gòtic (Gothic Quarter),** in the heart of town. You'll live and eat less expensively here than in any other part of Barcelona, but you should be careful when returning to your hotel late at night.

More modern, but more expensive, hotels can be found north of the Barri Gòtic in **l'Eixample,** centered on the Metro stops Plaça de Catalunya and Universitat. Many buildings are in the *modernisme* style, from the first 2 decades of the 20th century— and sometimes the elevators and plumbing are of the same vintage. L'Eixample is a desirable and safe neighborhood, especially along its wide boulevards. Noise is the only problem you might encounter.

Farther north, above the Avinguda Diagonal, you'll enter the **Gràcia** area, where you can enjoy distinctively Catalan neighborhood life. The main attractions are a bit distant from here but can be reached easily by public transportation.

CIUTAT VELLA (BARRI GÒTIC, EL RAVAL & LA RIBERA)

The Ciutat Vella (Old City) forms the monumental center of Barcelona, taking in Les Rambles, Plaça de Sant Jaume, Vía Laietana, Passeig Nacional, and Passeig de Colom. It contains some of the city's best hotel bargains. Most of the glamorous, and more expensive, hotels are here.

Very Expensive

H1898 ★★ H1898's location is on the most bustling stretch of Les Rambles, but the elegant rooms inside, evoking a colonial yacht club, are soundproof. The owners recreated the opulence of Spain in the 1800s but with 21st-century conveniences. The hotel takes its name from the year Spain lost the Philippines to the United States; the impressive building was converted from the former headquarters of the Philippines Tobacco Company. The rooftop terrace and lap pool are certainly a decadent spot for lounging. The hotel offers five levels of rooms, ranging from Classic to the most spacious, known as Privilege. If money is no object, book one of three dramatic colonial suites with a Jacuzzi, a swimming pool, and a private garden opening onto Les Rambles.

La Rambla 109 (entrance on Pinto Fortuny), 08002 Barcelona. www.hotel1898.com. ☎ **93-552-95-52.** Fax 93-552-95-50. 169 units. 255€–385€ double; 1,228€–1,460€ colonial suite. AE, DC, MC, V. Free parking. Metro: Plaça de Catalunya. **Amenities:** Restaurant; bar; 2 heated pools (1 indoor); exercise room; spa; concierge. *In room:* A/C, TV, minibar, hair dryer, MP3 docking station, Wi-Fi (free).

Hotel Murmuri ★★　In the heart of Barcelona, this small hotel is a hip address in a city already blessed with plenty of urban hotel chic. It has all the elements for today's modern traveler, right down to the efficient black-clad staff, a chic Asian restaurant, and even a cocktail bar often filled with young beauties from South America. In the midsize to spacious bedrooms, you can adjust the lighting to fit your mood. Guest rooms have tasteful furnishings in neutral tones and twin or queen-size beds overlooking a pedestrian street. Soundproof double-glazed windows protect you from the traffic noises.

La Rambla de Catalunya 104, 08008 Barcelona. www.murmuri.com. ☎ **93-550-06-00.** 7 units. 139€–338€ double; 379€–478€ suite. AE, MC, V. Parking 24€. Metro: Diagonal. **Amenities:** Restaurant; bar; concierge; room service. *In room:* A/C, TV, hair dryer, MP3 docking station, Wi-Fi (17€ per 24 hr.).

Expensive

Neri ★★　In the heart of the Barri Gòtic, this boutique hotel was created by joining a medieval palace and a stone building that had been destroyed during the Civil War and then rebuilt in 1958. Today's stunning facade overlooks Plaça Sant Felip Neri, one of the most evocative old squares of Barcelona. An avant-garde design has been woven into ancient structures—for example, a 12th-century stone wall separates the restaurant area from the lounge bar. Interior designer Cristina Gabás said she wanted to create a unique ambience in the bedrooms—"to play with the limits without falling into vulgarity." She succeeded admirably, using wood and stone enlivened with artwork seemingly inspired by Mark Rothko. The roof terrace, for drinks and breakfast, is ideal in summer. The aromatic Mediterranean cuisine served at the on-site restaurant is another compelling reason to stay here.

Sant Severe 5, Barri Gòtic, 08002 Barcelona. www.hotelneri.com. ☎ **93-304-06-55.** Fax. 93-304-03-37. 22 units. 180€–270€ double; from 215€ suite. AE, DC, MC, V. Public parking nearby 25€. Metro: Liceu or Jaume I. **Amenities:** Restaurant; cafe/bar; babysitting. *In room:* A/C, TV/DVD, minibar, hair dryer, CD player, Wi-Fi (free).

Moderate

Duquesa de Cardona ★★　A marvelous example of a recycled antique building, this structure dating from the 16th century has been given a new lease on life as an elegant boutique hotel. The palace was mainly constructed in the 1800s, though many stylings smack of Art Deco. Located at the maritime promenade, Moll de la Fusta, the hotel's backdrop is the historic Barri Gòtic. From its rooms you can enjoy a panoramic view of Montjuïc, as well as the Christopher Columbus monument and the Olympic Port. Ideal for honeymooners, many of the midsize bedrooms have a romantic feel, as well as sleek, contemporary bathrooms. Pay a few extra euros for the harborfront rooms, as the rear units are cramped. The public lounges are stylish, and the Mediterranean restaurant, with its original marble tiles, looks chic and serves good food.

Passeig Colom 12, 08002 Barcelona. www.hduquesadecardona.com. ☏ **93-268-90-90.** Fax 93-268-29-31. 40 units. 87€–195€ double; 210€–350€ junior suite. AE, DC, MC, V. Parking 30€. Metro: Jaume I or Drassanes. **Amenities:** Restaurant; concierge; room service; babysitting. *In room:* A/C, TV, minibar, hair dryer, Wi-Fi (free).

Soho Hotel ★★   Innovative and minimalist, this nugget of a boutique hotel was the creation of some of Europe's best designers and architects, notably the award-winning Barcelona-born Alfredo Arribas. Interior design touches were also added by Franc Aleu, who reproduces various parts of the human body on the walls. Look for other such designer frills as globelike Verner Panton lamps. The beds offer super comfort, as do the natty glassed-in bathrooms; the best rooms are on the seventh floor, complete with wood-decked terraces. Rooms on the lower level can be noisy because of heavy Gran Vía traffic. On an August day, the cool rooftop plunge pool is idyllic.

Gran Vía 543. www.hotelsohobarcelona.com. ☏ **93-552-96-10.** Fax 93-552-96-11. 51 units. 65€–168€ double. AE, DC, MC, V. Parking 25€. Metro: Plaça de Catalunya. **Amenities:** Bar; outdoor heated pool. *In room:* A/C, TV, minibar, hair dryer, Wi-Fi (free).

Inexpensive

Hostal Gat Xino ★ ⚑   This budget hotel is part of a pioneering chain that gives face-lifts to hostels, turning them into comfortable oases that rent at affordable prices. "Gat" is Catalan for cat, incidentally. One of the chic color schemes involves acid apple greens combined with black trim, and the overall look is modern and inviting. There's a roof terrace, for siestas in the sun and for the daily Mediterranean-style buffet at lunchtime. The Gat is just a 2-minute walk from Les Rambles.

Calle Hospital 149–155, 08001 Barcelona. www.gatrooms.com. ☏ **93-324-88-33.** Fax 93-324-88-34. 35 units. 57€–91€ double; 67€–120€ suite. AE, DC, MC, V. Parking 25€. Metro: Liceu. **Amenities:** Bikes. *In room:* A/C, TV, Wi-Fi (6.50€ per hr.).

L'EIXAMPLE
Very Expensive

Claris ★★   This postmodern lodging at the north end of town is a posh, grand luxe property that incorporates vast quantities of teak, marble, steel, and glass behind the facade of a landmark 19th-century building (Verdruna Palace). Opened in 1992 to make a big splash in time for the Olympics, the seven-story structure has a swimming pool and garden on its roof and a museum of Egyptian antiquities from the owner's private collection on the second floor. The blue–violet guest rooms contain state-of-the-art electronic accessories as well as unusual art objects—Turkish kilims, English antiques, Hindu sculptures, Egyptian stone carvings, and engravings. The spacious, soundproof rooms are among the most opulent in town, with wood marquetry and paneling, custom furnishings, and some of the city's most sumptuous beds.

Carrer de Pau Claris 150, 08009 Barcelona. www.hotelclaris.com. ☏ **93-487-62-62** or 800/888-4747 in the U.S. Fax 93-215-79-70. 120 units. 135€–525€ double; 245€–3,150€ suite. AE, DC, MC, V. Parking 25€. Metro: Passeig de Gràcia. **Amenities:** 2 restaurants; 2 bars; outdoor heated pool; exercise room; sauna; bikes; concierge; room service; babysitting. *In room:* A/C, TV, minibar, hair dryer, Wi-Fi (17€ per 24 hr.).

Expensive

Casa Fuster ★★ ⬚   One of the city's grandest *modernisme* buildings, a former private home designed by Lluís Domenech i Montaner for the Fuster family, has been turned into one of Barcelona's finest addresses, thanks to an $80-million investment. When it was first built in 1908, the use of high-quality marble made Casa Fuster the most expensive residence in the city. Today it is a five-star deluxe hotel. The glory days of the Belle Epoque live again in the palette of magenta, mauve, and taupe. Many of the beautifully furnished bedrooms contain private balconies that open onto Passeig de Gràcia. The **Café Vienés,** once a meeting place for literati, now serves as a posh late-hours jazz club.

Passeig de Gràcia 132, 08008 Barcelona. www.hotelcasafuster.com. © **93-255-30-00.** Fax 93-255-30-02. 96 units. 173€–270€ double; 270€–322€ junior suite; from 648€ suite. AE, DC, MC, V. Parking 33€. Metro: Diagonal. **Amenities:** Restaurant; bar; outdoor heated pool; exercise room; Jacuzzi; sauna; concierge; room service; babysitting; airport transfers (99€); Wi-Fi (free, in lobby). *In room:* A/C, TV, minibar, hair dryer.

Moderate

Cram ★ 🛎 Clearly the name of this hotel means something else in Catalan, as the hotel itself has nothing of the crassness implied by the name in English. Guests tend to be a hip crowd in their 30s and 40s who enjoy the bravado of textured red-leather walls, glossy black surfaces, and contoured furniture such as Eames chairs. The hotel opened in 2005 in a restored, architecturally beautiful 19th-century building. The architects kept the facade but turned the interior into a modern palace of convenience and comfort. The bedrooms have mirrored walls, amber-wood floors, and sophisticated color schemes such as mustard yellow and saffron. The location is good, too, right in the center of Barcelona, just 4 blocks from the Passeig de Gràcia and an easy walk from Les Rambles. To the delight of both guests and nonguests, restaurant **Gaig** has taken up residence here as well.

Aribau 54, 08011 Barcelona. www.hotelcram.com. © **93-216-77-00.** Fax 93-216-77-07. 67 units. 116€–268€ double; 200€–422€ executive and privilege units; 280€–515€ suite. Rates include buffet breakfast. AE, MC, V. Parking 15€. Metro: Universitat. **Amenities:** Restaurant; bar; outdoor pool; spa; bikes; concierge; room service. *In room:* A/C, TV/DVD, hair dryer, movie library, Wi-Fi (free).

Inexpensive

Hotel Astoria ★ 🌶 Excellent value, the Astoria is near the upper part of Les Rambles and Diagonal. Built in 1952, it has an Art Deco facade that makes it appear older than it is. The high ceilings, geometric designs, and brass-studded detail in the public rooms could be Moorish or Andalucían. Modernist sculpture fills the lounge where guests meet each other over coffee. The comfortable, midsize guest rooms are soundproof and contain slick louvered closets and glistening white paint.

París 203, 08036 Barcelona. www.derbyhotels.es. © **93-209-83-11.** Fax 93-202-30-08. 114 units. 70€–140€ double; 170€–265€ suite. AE, DC, MC, V. Nearby parking 25€. Metro: Diagonal. **Amenities:** Restaurant; bar; outdoor pool; exercise room; sauna; room service. *In room:* A/C, TV, minibar, hair dryer, Wi-Fi (16€ per 24 hr.).

NORTE DIAGONAL

Gallery Hotel ★ 🛎 This is a winning, modern choice lying between the Passeig de Gràcia and La Rambla de Catalunya. The name, Gallery, comes from its location close to a district of major art galleries. The stylishly decorated hotel lies in the upper district of l'Eixample, just below Diagonal. Guest rooms are midsize for the most part and tastefully furnished. The on-site restaurant is known for its savory Mediterranean cuisine.

Calle Rosello 249, 08008 Barcelona. www.galleryhotel.com. © **93-415-99-11.** Fax 93-415-91-84. 115 units. 139€–193€ double; 200€–406€ suite. AE, DC, MC, V. Parking 25€. Metro: Diagonal. **Amenities:** Restaurant; bar; exercise room; sauna; room service; babysitting. *In room:* A/C, TV, fax, minibar, hair dryer, Wi-Fi (free).

Wilson Boutique Hotel This well-run hotel stands in an architecturally rich neighborhood. The small lobby isn't indicative of the rest of the building; the second floor opens into a large, sunny lounge. The guest rooms are well kept, generally spacious, and furnished in a modern minimalist style with parquet floors.

Av. Diagonal 568, 08021 Barcelona. www.wilsonbcn.com. ✆ **93-209-25-11.** Fax 93-200-83-70. 53 units. 65€–130€ double; 95€–175€ suite. AE, DC, MC, V. Parking 25€. Metro: Diagonal. **Amenities:** Bar. *In room:* A/C, TV, minibar, hair dryer, Wi-Fi (free).

MOLL DE BARCELONA

Eurostars Grand Marina Hotel ★★ Evoking New York's iconic Guggenheim Museum with its circular, upside-down wedding cake design, the Grand Marina stands next to Barcelona's World Trade Center. Standing at the end of a long pier that juts into the Barcelona harbor, its windows have panoramic views of the harbor and the cityscape. The Barri Gòtic is about a 20-minute walk away, although most guests take a taxi. The eight-floor hotel offers spacious, well-furnished guest rooms, with private terraces in some units. Elegant decoration, soothing colors, and luxurious woods and fabrics characterize the hotel. Guest rooms feature high-tech audiovisual equipment and top-notch bathrooms.

Moll de Barcelona s/n, 08039 Barcelona. www.grandmarinahotel.com. ✆ **93-603-90-00.** Fax 93-603-90-90. 278 units. 130€–280€ double; 271€–373€ junior suite; from 346€ suite. AE, DC, MC, V. Parking 25€. Metro: Drassanes. **Amenities:** Restaurant; bar; small outdoor heated pool; exercise room; Jacuzzi; sauna; concierge; room service; babysitting. *In room:* A/C, TV, minibar, hair dryer, Wi-Fi (free).

Hotel 54 ★ In the increasingly fashionable former fishermen's village of La Barceloneta, this boutique hotel occupies the former home of the Association of Fishermen—giving it panoramic views of the harbor and skyline. It stands in front of Port Vell, close to Playa San Sebastián and within an easy walk of Les Rambles. Elegantly modern following a major renovation, the hotel has such decorative touches as LED mood lighting (bedrooms have a lighting system allowing you to "personalize" your choice of color) and green-glass sinks in the bathrooms.

Passeig Joan de Borbó 54, 08003 Barcelona. www.hotel54barceloneta.com. ✆ **93-225-00-54.** Fax 93-225-00-80. 28 units. 51€–140€ double. MC, V. Nearby parking 20€. Metro: Barceloneta. **Amenities:** Bar; room service. *In room:* A/C, TV, minibar, hair dryer, Wi-Fi (free).

VILA OLÍMPICA

Hotel Arts ★★★ This hotel occupies 33 floors of one of the tallest buildings in Spain, and one of Barcelona's few skyscrapers. (The upper floors of the 44-floor postmodern tower contain private condominiums of some of the country's most gossiped-about aristocrats and financiers.) The spacious, well-equipped guest rooms have built-in furnishings, generous desk space, and large, sumptuous beds. Clad in pink marble, the deluxe bathrooms come with fluffy robes, dual basins, and phones. Views take in the skyline and the Mediterranean, and the hotel possesses the city's only beachfront pool.

Carrer de la Marina 19–21, 08005 Barcelona. www.ritzcarlton.com. ✆ **93-221-10-00** or 800/241-3333 in the U.S. Fax 93-221-10-70. 483 units. 250€–404€ double; 475€–7,000€ suite. AE, DC, MC, V. Parking 38€. Metro: Ciutadella–Vila Olímpica. **Amenities:** 5 restaurants; 2 bars; outdoor heated pool; exercise room; spa; children's programs; concierge; room service. *In room:* A/C, TV/DVD, minibar, hair dryer, Wi-Fi (free).

Pullman Barcelona Skipper ★ Lying only 50m (164 ft.) from the beach, this hotel is imbued with a stylish contemporary design, opening onto a view of a private interior garden. It stands next to the Arts Hotel at Port Olímpic. There are many luxurious touches and a lot of high-tech gadgets. Upon request, your bathtub can be filled with flower petals or salts. Showers are equipped with rain heads, the rooms are soundproof, the beds are draped in Egyptian cotton, and entire floors are reserved for nonsmokers. The executive junior suites are decorated in the style of modern yacht cabins, with a conceptual Japanese minimalism, evoking the spaciousness of a New York City loft.

Litoral 10, 08005 Barcelona. www.pullman-barcelona-skipper.com. ℂ **93-221-65-65.** Fax 93-221-36-00. 154 units. 220€–305€ double; from 680€ executive junior suite; from 919€ suite. AE, DC, MC, V. Parking 26€. Metro: Ciutadella-Vila Olímpica. **Amenities:** 2 restaurants; 3 bars; 2 pools (outdoor); health club and spa; bikes; concierge; room service; babysitting; airport transfers (116€); Wi-Fi (free, in lobby). *In room:* A/C, TV, TV/DVD player, minibar, hair dryer, CD player.

DAY TRIPS FROM BARCELONA

Sitges ★

Sitges (40km/25 miles south of Barcelona) is one of the most popular resorts of southern Europe, the brightest spot on the Costa Daurada. It's especially crowded in summer, mostly with affluent, young northern Europeans, many of them gay. For years, the resort was filled with the prosperous Barcelona middle class, but the staid days of bankers and factory owners are long gone. Sitges today can be as youthful (and raucous) as Benidorm and Torremolinos farther south on the coast.

Sitges has long been known as a city of culture, thanks in part to resident artist, playwright, and bohemian mystic Santiago Rusiñol. The 19th-century *modernisme* (*modernista* in Castilian) movement took hold early in Sitges, and the town remained the scene of artistic encounters and demonstrations long after the movement waned. Sitges continued as a resort of artists, attracting such giants as Salvador Dalí and poet Federico García Lorca. The Spanish Civil War (1936–39) erased what has come to be called the golden age of Sitges. Although other artists and writers arrived in the decades to follow, none had the fame or the impact of those who had gone before.

ESSENTIALS

GETTING THERE   **RENFE** (www.renfe.es) runs trains from Barcelona-Sants to Sitges; the 30-minute trip costs 3.50€. Call ℂ **90-232-03-20** in Barcelona for information about schedules. Four trains leave Barcelona per hour.

Sitges is a 45-minute drive from Barcelona along the C-246, a coastal road. An express highway, the A-7, opened in 1991. The coastal road is more scenic, but it can be extremely slow on weekends because of the heavy traffic, as all of Barcelona seemingly heads for the beaches.

VISITOR INFORMATION   The **tourist office** is at Plaza Eduard Maristany 2 (www.sitgestur.cat; ℂ **93-894-42-51**). Year-round hours are Monday to Friday 9am to 2pm and 4 to 6:30pm, Saturday 10am to 2pm and 4 to 7pm, and Sunday 10am to 2pm.

EXPLORING SITGES

The **beaches** attract most visitors. They have showers and changing facilities, and kiosks rent such items as motorboats and floating air cushions. Beaches on the eastern end and those inside the town center are the most peaceful, including **Aiguadoiç** and **Els Balomins. Playa San Sebastián, Fragata Beach,** and **"Beach of the Boats"** (under the church and next to the yacht club) are the area's family beaches.

Most young people go to the **Playa de la Ribera,** in the west. The main gay beach is the **Playa del Mort.**

Beaches aside, Sitges has a couple of good museums. **Museu Cau Ferrat,** Fonollar 8 (www.mnac.es; ☎ **93-894-03-64**), is the legacy of wealthy Catalán painter Santiago Rusinyol, a leading light of Belle Epoque Barcelona. His 19th-century house, fashioned of two 16th-century fishermen's homes, contains not only a collection of his works, but also several pieces by Picasso and El Greco, much ornate wrought iron (a Catalán specialty), folk art, and archaeological finds.

Next door is **Museu Maricel de Mar,** Carrer del Fonallar (☎ **93-894-03-64**), the legacy of Dr. Pérez Rosales, whose impressive accumulation of furniture, porcelain, and tapestries draws largely from the medieval, Renaissance, and baroque periods. Both museums are open mid-June through September Tuesday to Saturday 9:30am to 2pm and 4–7pm, Sunday 10am to 3pm; October through to early June Tuesday to Saturday 9:30am to 2pm and 3:30 to 6:30pm, Sunday 10am to 3pm. Admission is 3.50€ adults, 2€ seniors and students, free for children 5 and under.

Montserrat ★

The vast **Montserrat Monastery** complex (www.abadiamontserrat.net), 52km (32 miles) northwest of Barcelona, contains a basilica with a venerated Black Virgin, an art museum, hotels, restaurants, and an excess of souvenir shops and food stalls. One of the most important pilgrimage spots in Spain, it's a good place to avoid on weekends.

ESSENTIALS

GETTING THERE   The best and most exciting way to get to Montserrat is via the Catalunyan railway, **Ferrocarrils de la Generalitat de Catalunya** (Manresa line), with 12 trains a day leaving from the Plaça d'Espanya in Barcelona. The central office is at Plaça de Catalunya 1 (www.fgc.es; ☎ **93-237-71-56**). The train connects with an aerial cableway (Aeri de Montserrat), which is included in the fare of 18€ round-trip.

To drive to Montserrat, take the N-2 southwest of Barcelona toward Tarragona, turning west at the junction with the N-11. The signposts and exit to Montserrat will be on your right. From the main road, it's 15km (9⅓ miles) up to the monastery through eerie rock formations and dramatic scenery. Many people prefer to park below and take the funicular to the monastery. The 9-minute **funicular ride** to the 1,236m-high (4,055-ft.) peak, Sant Joan, makes for a panoramic trip. The funicular operates about every 20 minutes daily from 10:10am to 5:45pm in low season and to 7pm in summer. The cost is 8.50€ round-trip.

VISITOR INFORMATION   The **tourist office,** at Plaça de la Creu (www.montserrat visita.com; ☎ **93-877-77-01**), is open daily from 9am to 5:30pm.

EXPLORING MONTSERRAT

One of the monastery's noted attractions is the 50-member **Escolanía ★★**, one of the oldest and most renowned boys' choirs in Europe, dating from the 13th century. At 1pm daily you can hear them singing "Salve Regina" and the "Virolai" (hymn of Montserrat) in the **basilica ★★★**. The basilica is open daily from 8 to 10:30am and noon to 6:30pm. Admission is free. To view **La Moreneta (The Black Virgin),** the 12th-century polychrome carving of the Virgin and Child around which this entire complex was erected, enter the church through a side door to the right. The meter-high carving is mounted in a silver altar in a chapel high above the main altar. You will be in a long line of people who parade past the statue, which is behind bulletproof acrylic. There is a cutout so the faithful may kiss her extended hand.

At the Plaça de Santa María you can also visit the **Museu de Montserrat** ((C) **93-877-77-77**), known for its ecclesiastical paintings, including works by Caravaggio and El Greco. Modern Spanish and Catalan artists are also represented; you'll want to see Picasso's early *El Viejo Pescador* (1895). Works by Dalí and such French Impressionists as Monet, Sisley, and Degas are shown. The collection of ancient artifacts is quite interesting; make sure to look for the crocodile mummy, which is at least 2,000 years old. The museum has no active acquisition program—all the art comes from gifts of the faithful. The museum is open Monday to Friday from 10am to 5:45pm, charging 6.50€ adults, 5.50€ seniors, and 3.50€ for students and children 17 and under; it's free for kids 5 and under.

You can also make an excursion to **Santa Cova (Holy Grotto),** the alleged site of the discovery of La Moreneta. The grotto dates from the 17th century and was built in the shape of a cross. You go halfway by funicular, but must complete the trip on foot. The grotto is open daily from 10am to 1pm and 4 to 7pm. The funicular operates April through October every 20 minutes daily from 10am to 5:45pm, and November through March daily from 11am to 4:45pm. Note that it closes between 1 and 2pm. The round-trip fare is 3.50€.

ANDALUCÍA & THE COSTA DEL SOL

Much of what the world imagines as Spain is, in fact, Andalucía. It was the cradle of flamenco, the stomping grounds of the amorous Don Juan, and the tragic setting for *Carmen.* It is the region where bulls are bred and matadors are more famous than rock stars. Nothing in Andalucía is done halfway. The flowers are brighter, the food more spiced, and the music both more melancholy and more joyful.

Although Andalucía is often a stand-in for Spain in the popular imagination, it was, in fact, the last stronghold of the Moors, who held al-Andalus for more than 7 centuries. Consequently, Andalucía shines with all the medieval Muslim glories of Europe: the world-famous Mezquita (mosque) of Córdoba, the Alhambra palace of Granada, and (in their own way as Christian–Muslim hybrids) Sevilla's imposing Alcázar and looming Gothic cathedral.

Go to the Costa del Sol for beach resorts, the bar scene, and water sports; visit Andalucía for its architectural wonders, signature cuisine and music, and its sheer beauty.

Sevilla ★★★

Orange trees, *señoritas* wearing hand-woven *mantillas,* lovesick matadors, flower-filled patios, and black-clad *flamencos* come to life in Sevilla. From its tapas bars to its flamenco patios and bullfights, this southern city epitomizes the traditions of Andalucía. And it evokes images of romance, with iconic figures ranging from Don Juan to Carmen. (Opera lovers flock to see *Don Giovanni, Carmen,* and even *The Barber of Sevilla.*) But you may just want to wander through its tangled streets flanked by palaces and monuments created with proceeds from the wealth of the New World.

Andalucía & the Costa del Sol

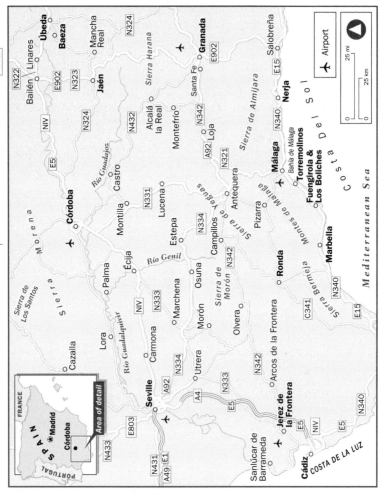

Sevilla

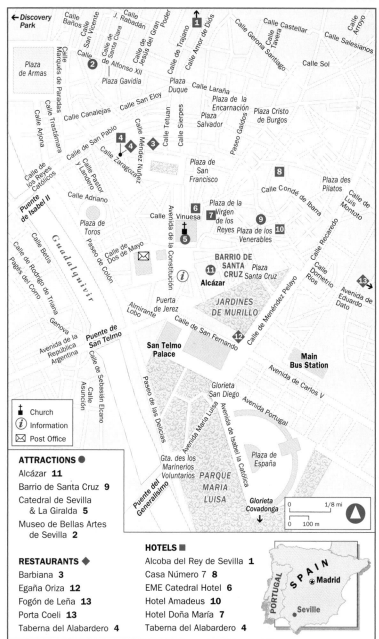

Map labels:

← Discovery Park

Plaza de Armas

Calle Baños · Calle San Vicente · J. Calle Rabadán · Calle de Santa Clara · Calle de Jesús del Gran Poder · Calle de Trajano · Calle Amor de Diós

Calle Gerona · Calle Santiago · Calle Castellar · Calle Tavera · Calle Arroyo · Calle Salesianos

Calle Sol

Calle Marqués de Paradas

Calle de Alfonso XII

Plaza Gavidia

Plaza Duque · Calle Laraña · Plaza de la Encarnación · Plaza Cristo de Burgos

Calle Canalejas · Calle San Eloy · Plaza Salvador

Calle Trastámara

Calle Arjona

Calle de los Reyes Católicos

Calle de San Pablo · Calle Tetuan · Calle Sierpes · Paseo Galdos

Calle Méndez Nuñez · Calle Zaragoza · Calle Pastor y Landero · Calle Adriano

Puente de Isabel II

Plaza de San Francisco

Plaza des Pilatos · Calle de Luis Montoto

Calle Condé de Ibarra

Guadalquivir

Plaza de Toros

Paseo de Colón · Calle de Dos de Mayo

Plaza de la Virgen de los Reyes · Plaza de los Venerables

Calle Vinuesa

Avenida de la Constitución

Calle Betis · Calle de Rodrigo de Triana · Pagés del Corro

Calle Recaredo · Calle Domerio Rios · Avenida de Eduardo Dato

BARRIO DE SANTA CRUZ · Plaza Santa Cruz

Alcázar

Puerta de Jerez · Almirante Lobo

JARDINES DE MURILLO

Calle de Menéndez Pelayo

Genova · Avenida de la República Argentina

Puente de San Telmo

Calle de Sebastián Elcano · Calle Asunción

San Telmo Palace

Calle de San Fernando

Main Bus Station

Avenida de Carlos V

Glorieta San Diego · Avenida Portugal

Paseo de las Delicias

Gta. des los Marinerios Voluntarios

Avenida María Luisa · Avenida de Isabel la Católica

PARQUE MARIA LUISA

Plaza de España

Puente del Generalísimo

Glorieta Covadonga ↓

0 — 1/8 mi
0 — 100 m

Legend:

† Church
ⓘ Information
⊠ Post Office

ATTRACTIONS ●

Alcázar **11**

Barrio de Santa Cruz **9**

Catedral de Sevilla & La Giralda **5**

Museo de Bellas Artes de Sevilla **2**

RESTAURANTS ◆

Barbiana **3**

Egaña Oriza **12**

Fogón de Leña **13**

Porta Coeli **13**

Taberna del Alabardero **4**

HOTELS ■

Alcoba del Rey de Sevilla **1**

Casa Número 7 **8**

EME Catedral Hotel **6**

Hotel Amadeus **10**

Hotel Doña María **7**

Taberna del Alabardero **4**

PORTUGAL · SPAIN · ● Madrid · ● Seville

ESSENTIALS

GETTING THERE   Sevilla's **Aeropuerto San Pablo,** Calle Almirante Lobo (www. aena.es; ✆ **90-240-47-04**), is served by **Iberia** (www.iberia.com; ✆ **90-240-05-00**), which flies several times a day between Madrid (and elsewhere via Madrid) and Sevilla. The airport lies about 9.6km (6 miles) from the center of the city, along the highway leading to Carmona. A bus run by **Transportes Urbanos de Sevilla** (✆ **90-245-99-54**) meets all incoming flights and transports you into the center of Sevilla for 2.50€.

Train service into Sevilla is centralized into the **Estación Santa Justa,** Av. Kansas City s/n (www.renfe.es; ✆ **90-242-22-42** for information and reservations). The high-speed AVE train has reduced travel time from Madrid to Sevilla to 2½ hours. The train makes 20 trips daily, with a stop in Córdoba, and costs 84€. A total of 37 trains a day connect Sevilla and Córdoba; the AVE train takes 45 minutes and costs 17€ to 33€. (A regional train that takes an extra half-hour goes a few times a day for 11€.) Eleven trains a day run to Málaga, taking 3 hours; there are also four trains per day to Granada (3 hr.).

Sevilla is 549km (341 miles) southwest of Madrid and 217km (135 miles) northwest of Málaga. Several major highways converge on Sevilla, connecting it with the rest of Spain and Portugal. During periods of heavy holiday traffic, the N-V (E-90) from Madrid through Extremadura—which, at Mérida, connects with the southbound N-630 (E-803)—is usually less congested than the N-IV (E-5) through eastern Andalucía. Sevilla is easy to drive to, but extremely difficult to drive around (or to park in).

VISITOR INFORMATION   The tourist office, **Oficina de Información del Turismo,** at Av. de la Constitución 21B (www.andalucia.org; ✆ **95-478-20-35**), is open Monday to Friday 9am to 7:30pm, Saturday 9:30am to 7:30pm, and Sunday 9:30am to 3pm.

GETTING AROUND   Don't even consider driving around Sevilla. If you give up a parking space you will never find another. Fortunately, the city is eminently walkable. If you need to get from one end to another in a hurry, hop on an inexpensive bus (1.50€) instead of paying 10€ for a taxi. A good alternative for covering a lot of ground quickly is the municipal bicycle rental program, **SEVICI,** which provides access to bikes for a small subscription charge plus an even smaller hourly fee. The snazzy red bikes are parked in 250 areas all over the city, each with a kiosk where you can subscribe by credit card as well as pick up or deposit bikes. A 1-week membership is 5€, and time fees range from .50€ to 1€ per hour (www.sevici.es; ✆ **90-201-10-32**).

EXPLORING SEVILLA

Alcázar ★★★ PALACE   The complex of palaces and fortifications dates from the Almohad dynasty rule of Sevilla but was almost entirely rebuilt after the Reconquest of Sevilla in 1248. The older, more austere building is the **Palacio Gótico,** built by Alfonso X ("the Wise") in the 13th century. Carlos V modified the Great Hall and the Sala de Fiestas to celebrate his 1526 wedding to his Habsburg cousin (an unfortunate union that triggered the genetic problems of the dynasty). The far more beautiful and much larger **Palacio Mudéjar** was built in the 14th century by Pedro I ("the Cruel"), quite possibly employing some of the same artisans who worked on the Alhambra in Granada. It is a tour de force of carved plaster and stone, delicate calligraphic friezes, carved wooden ceilings, and splendid decorative tiles. It is the oldest European royal residence still in use: King Juan Carlos and Queen Sofía stay here when they're in town. The well-kept **gardens,** filled with beautiful flowers, shrubbery, and fruit trees, are alone worth the visit. Plan to spend about 1½ hours here.

Plaza del Triunfo s/n. www.patronato-alcazarsevilla.es. ℂ **95-450-23-23.** Admission 7.50€. Oct–Mar daily 9:30am–5pm; Apr–Sept daily 9:30am–7pm.

Barrio de Santa Cruz ★★ HISTORIC SITE   What was once a ghetto for Spanish Jews—who were forcibly expelled from Spain in 1492—is today one of Sevilla's most colorful districts. Near the old walls of the Alcázar, winding medieval streets with names like Vida (Life) and Muerte (Death) open onto pocket-size plazas. Part of the quintessential experience of visiting Sevilla is getting lost in the Barrio de Santa Cruz, only to stumble into a plaza where a waiter will offer you a seat and a drink. Flower-filled balconies with draping bougainvillea and potted geraniums jut over this labyrinth, shading you from the ferocious Andalucían summer sun. Feel free to look through numerous wrought-iron gates into patios filled with fountains and plants. In the evening it's common to see Sevillanos sitting in the patios sipping wine under the glow of lanterns.

To enter the Barrio de Santa Cruz, turn right after leaving the Patio de Banderas exit of the Alcázar. Turn right again at Plaza de la Alianza, going down Calle Rodrigo Caro to Plaza de Doña Elvira.

Catedral de Sevilla and La Giralda ★★ CATHEDRAL   The largest Gothic building in the world and the third-largest church in Europe, after St. Peter's in Rome and St. Paul's in London, the Catedral de Sevilla was designed by builders with a stated goal—that "those who come after us will take us for madmen." Construction began in the late 1400s on the site of an ancient mosque and took centuries to complete. The tomb of Columbus is held by four carved pallbearers.

Works of art abound here, many of them architectural, such as the 15th-century stained-glass windows, the iron screens (*rejas*) closing off the chapels, the elaborate 15th-century choir stalls, and the Gothic reredos above the main altar. The treasury has works by Goya, Murillo, and Zurbarán, as well as a display of skulls. After touring the dark interior, you emerge into the sunlight of the Patio de Naranjas (Patio of the Orange Trees), with its fresh citrus scents and chirping birds.

La Giralda, the bell tower of the cathedral, is the city's most emblematic monument. Erected as a minaret in the 12th century, it has seen later additions, such as 16th-century bells. If you elect to walk up, you'll have a dazzling view of Sevilla. Entrance is through the cathedral. Allot about 1½ hours here.

Av. de la Constitución s/n. www.catedraldesevilla.es. ℂ **95-421-49-71.** Cathedral and tower 8€ adults, 3€ students 25 and under, free for children 14 and under. Sept–June Mon–Sat 11am–5:30pm, Sun 2:30–6:30pm; July–Aug Mon–Sat 9:30am–4:30pm, Sun 2:30–6:30pm.

Museo de Bellas Artes de Sevilla ★★ ART MUSEUM   This lovely old convent off Calle de Alfonso XII houses a collection of Spanish paintings second only to the Prado in Madrid. A whole gallery is devoted to two paintings by El Greco, and the devoutly religious, if somewhat saccharine, paintings of Sevilla-born Bartolomé Esteban Murillo fill room after room. The 19th-century galleries upstairs have sunnier images of carnal cigar rollers, society ladies, and swells making the evening *paseo*. An hour gives you enough time to see it all, but you might want to linger in the beautiful tiled central courtyard.

Plaza del Museo 9. www.museosdeandalucia.es. ℂ **95-478-65-00.** Admission 1.50€. Tues–Sat 9am–8:30pm; Sun 9am–2:30pm.

Where to Eat

VERY EXPENSIVE

Egaña Oriza ★★★ BASQUE/SPANISH   Sevilla's most stylish restaurant is within the conservatory of a restored mansion adjacent to the Murillo Gardens. Its reputation stems in large part from a game-heavy menu in a region otherwise devoted to seafood. Specialties depend on the season but might include ostrich carpaccio, gazpacho with prawns, steak with foie gras in grape sauce, casserole of wild boar with cherries and raisins, duck *quenelles* in a potato nest with apple purée, and woodcock flamed in Spanish brandy. The view from the dining room encompasses a garden and a wall that formed part of the fortifications of Muslim Sevilla.

San Fernando 41. www.restauranteoriza.com. ⓒ **95-422-72-54.** Reservations required. Main courses 14€–28€; fixed-price menus 18€–30€. AE, DC, MC, V. Mon–Sat 1:30–3:30pm and 8:30–11:30pm. Closed Aug. Bus: 21 or 23.

EXPENSIVE

Taberna del Alabardero ★★ ANDALUCÍAN   One of Sevilla's most prestigious restaurants occupies a 19th-century town house 3 blocks from the cathedral. Nearly every politician and diplomat who visits Sevilla dines here because the restaurant grew out of a priest's mission to save and train street youth in what is now a hotel school. They certainly left their tough pasts behind: Amid a collection of European antiques and oil paintings, you'll dine in any of two main rooms or three private ones, and perhaps precede your meal with a drink or tapas on the flowering patio. There's a garden in back with additional tables. Consider starting with a veal carpaccio or ham soup with a truffle croquette before moving on to Basque crab crêpes in white-wine sauce, or grilled wild boar chops with a savory dark oloroso sherry sauce and lentils.

Calle Zaragoza 20. www.tabernadelalabardero.es. ⓒ **95-450-27-21.** Reservations recommended. Main courses 19€–32€. AE, DC, MC, V. Daily 1:30–4:30pm and 8:30pm–midnight. Closed Aug. Bus: 21, 25, 30, or 43.

MODERATE

Barbiana ★★ ANDALUCÍAN/SEAFOOD   Close to the Plaza Nueva in the heart of Sevilla, this superb seafood restaurant gets fresh fish daily from the Huelva coast and the Bay of Cádiz, and every few days from the Galician coast. In classic Andalucían fashion, you enter through a tapas bar to get to the cluster of rustically decorated dining rooms in the back. The trick here is not to consume so much wine and tapas in the front that you are too stuffed to enjoy the main courses. If you visit for lunch, you can try the chef's specialty, seafood with rice (not available in the evening). Some of the best items on the menu are *ortiguilla,* a sea anemone quick-fried in oil, and the *tortillitas de camarones,* chickpea fritters with bits of chopped shrimp and fresh scallions. If you're going to order shellfish—the specialty here, since it comes from the Bay of Cádiz—get it grilled (*a la plancha*).

Calle Albareda 11. www.restaurantebarbiana.com. ⓒ **95-422-44-02.** Reservations recommended. Main courses 14€–24€. AE, DC, MC, V. Mon–Sat noon–5pm and 8pm–midnight. Bus: 21, 25, 30, or 40.

Porta Coeli ★★ MEDITERRANEAN   With one of Sevilla's most sophisticated decors, Porta Coeli offers some of the city's best hotel dining. Even if you're not a hotel guest, consider reserving one of 15 tables set against a backdrop of tapestry-hung walls. The flavor combinations are contemporary, and rely on fresh ingredients.

The menu boasts a wide variety of dishes, featuring duck with fried white beans and ham. Another savory offering is *ensalada de bacalao con tomate* (salt cod salad with tomatoes) and *arroz marinero con bogavante* (rice with crayfish). The locals rave about the *corazón de solomillo al foie con zetas al vino* (beef heart with liver and mushroom in red-wine sauce). For dessert, nothing beats the luscious napoleon with fresh fruit.

In the Hesperia Sevilla, Eduardo Dato 49. www.hesperia.es. ℂ **95-454-83-00.** Reservations recommended. Main courses 16€–34€. AE, DC, MC, V. Mon–Sat 1:30–4pm and 9pm–midnight. Closed Aug. Bus: 23.

INEXPENSIVE

Fogón de Leña ★ ✦ ANDALUCÍAN   With a folksy name like "wood stove," you'd expect a certain rustic quality in this landmark dining room near the Old City, and Fogón de Leña doesn't disappoint. The main door to the old building is intricately carved, and the roof is covered with traditional red-clay tiles. The food follows the decor: rustic and lusty. Savor such dishes as *chuletón de buey* (ox steak) or *carne con chimichurri* (steak with chopped parsley and garlic dressing in virgin olive oil). Desserts are made daily and include traditional puddings and tasty tarts, often with fresh fruit.

Santo Domingo de la Calzada 13. www.elfogon.com. ℂ **95-453-17-10.** Reservations required. Main courses 12€–25€; fixed-price menu 22€. AE, DC, MC, V. Daily 1–4:30pm and 8:30pm–midnight. Closed last 2 weeks in Aug. Bus: 24, 27, or 32.

Shopping

Sevilla's major shopping street is the pedestrianized **Calle Sierpes,** which runs from Plaza Magdalena Campaña to the top of Plaza San Francisco. For handmade ceramics, you should also prowl **Calle Alfareria** across the Isabel II bridge from the old town. On Sunday mornings, once the Saturday-night drunks have been cleared away, a huge flea market is held on the **Alameda de Hercules** plaza in the Macarena neighborhood. Close to Sevilla's town hall, **Ceramics Martian,** Sierpes 74 (ℂ **95-421-34-13**), sells a wide array of painted tiles and ceramics, all made in or near Sevilla. Many pieces reproduce traditional patterns of Andalucía.

Past the north end of Sierpes, over to the left, is the local branch of the preeminent national department store, **El Corte Inglés,** Plaza del Duque de la Victoria 10 (ℂ **95-459-70-00**).

Entertainment & Nightlife

In the 1990s, Sevilla finally got its own opera house, **Teatro de la Maestranza,** Paseo de Colón 22 (www.teatromaestranza.com; ℂ **95/422-33-44**), which quickly became a premier venue for world-class operatic performances.

A showcase for Spanish folk song and dance, **El Patio Sevillano,** Paseo de Cristóbal Colón 11 (www.elpatiosevillano.com; ℂ **95-421-41-20**), presents the most widely varied flamenco program in town. The presentation includes a wide variety of Andalucían flamenco and songs, as well as classical pieces by such composers as de Falla, Albéniz, Granados, and Chueca. Two shows, at 7 and 9:30pm, are presented nightly. The cover of 37€ includes your first drink.

Consider a visit to **Los Gallos Tablao Flamenco,** Plaza de Santa Cruz 11 (www.tablaolosgallos.com; ℂ **95-421-69-81**), a reputable nightclub where male and female performers stamp, clap, and exude rigidly controlled Iberian passion on a small stage in front of appreciative observers. A cover charge of 30€ includes the first drink.

Where to Stay

During Holy Week and the Feria de Sevilla, hotels often double, even triple, their rates. Price increases are often not announced until the last minute. If you're going to be in Sevilla at these times, arrive with an ironclad reservation and an agreement about the price before checking in.

VERY EXPENSIVE

EME Catedral Hotel ★★   Slowly but surely, the EME hotel group captured the cluster of fourteen 18th- and 19th-century town houses facing La Giralda and has converted them into a futuristic design concept hotel, while keeping a handful of Andalucían architectural details intact on the facade. The location is just about ideal for Sevilla, but the sparely postmodern rooms are not to everyone's taste, and those that overlook the cathedral can be noisy. The suites and two superior doubles open onto private terraces with whirlpool baths. Shaded courtyards and a panoramic rooftop pool terrace provide additional glamour, but most of the public space is taken over with dining and drinking facilities. The best of the restaurants is superchef Martin Berasategui's **Santo,** which serves contemporary Mediterranean cuisine.

Calle de los Alemanes 27, 41004 Sevilla. www.emecatedralhotel.com. ✆ **95-456-00-00.** 60 units. 150€–470€ double; 600€–950€ suite. AE, DC, MC, V. No parking. Bus: C5. **Amenities:** 4 restaurants; 2 bars; pool (outdoor); exercise room; spa; concierge; room service; airport transfers (60€). *In room:* A/C, TV, minibar, hair dryer, Wi-Fi (free).

EXPENSIVE

Casa Número 7 ★★ 🎁   This is as close as you can get to staying in an elegant private home in Sevilla. Next to the Santa Cruz barrio, the little inn is in a beautiful, sensitively restored 19th-century mansion where you live in style, with a butler to serve you breakfast. Small in size, Casa Número 7 is big on style and grace notes, recapturing the aura of old Sevilla. The building envelops an old atrium and is filled with such touches as family photographs, Oriental area rugs, a marble fireplace, and floral-print love seats. Rooms are individually decorated in vintage Sevillano style, with impeccable taste and an eye to comfort.

Vírgenes 7, 41004 Sevilla. www.casanumero7.com. ✆ **95-422-15-81.** Fax 95-421-45-27. 6 units. 177€–275€ double. Rates include buffet breakfast. MC, V. Parking nearby 15€. Bus: 10, 15, 24, or 32. **Amenities:** Bar. *In room:* A/C, hair dryer, Wi-Fi (free).

MODERATE

Alcoba del Rey de Sevilla ★ 🎁   This small boutique hotel, in a building dating from the 13th century, is inspired by the Sevilla of al-Andalus. Located adjacent to the Basilica de Macarena, the building incorporates some of the same kind of handcrafted materials as were used 8 centuries ago. Rooms open onto a central Andalucían patio. Each midsize bedroom not only features an exotic name—Princess Zaida or Rumaykiyya, for example—but also has a distinctive decor that might include horseshoe arches, silk fabrics, carved headboards, king-size beds with canopy, and the scent of cedar furnishings. The stuccoed bathrooms are a special feature with much use made of marble. Guests can buy everything they see in the hotel, even the beds and furnishings.

Calle Bécquer, 41009 Sevilla. www.alcobadelrey.com. ✆ **95-491-58-00.** Fax 95-491-56-75. 15 units. 98€–173€ double; 150€–278€ suites. Rates include buffet breakfast. AE, DC, MC, V. Parking 16€. Bus: C1, C2, or 32. **Amenities:** Concierge; room service. *In room:* A/C, TV, hair dryer, Wi-Fi (free).

Hotel Doña María ★ ☺ Highlights here include the Iberian antiques in the stone lobby and upper hallways and a location a few steps from the cathedral, which allows for dramatic views from the rooftop terrace. An ornate neoclassical entryway is offset with a pure white facade and iron balconies, which hint at the building's origin in the 1840s as a private villa. Amid the flowering plants on the upper floor you'll find garden-style lattices and antique wrought-iron railings. Room sizes range from small to large enough for the entire family, and some have four-poster beds, while others have a handful of antique reproductions. Light sleepers might find the noise of the church bells jarring. There are a garden courtyard and a rooftop pool.

Don Remondo 19, 41004 Sevilla. www.hdmaria.com. ℰ **95-422-49-90.** Fax 95-421-95-46. 64 units. 97€–183€ double. AE, DC, MC, V. Parking 20€. Bus: C1, C2, or C4. **Amenities:** 2 bars; outdoor pool; room service. *In room:* A/C, TV, minibar, hair dryer, Wi-Fi (free).

Taberna del Alabardero ★★ 🏠 This tavern now houses one of the most charming places to stay in the city. Close to the bullring and a 5-minute walk from the cathedral, this restored 19th-century mansion has a spectacular central patio and a romantic atmosphere. The units on the third floor have balconies overlooking street scenes as well as whirlpool tubs. All the rooms are spacious and comfortable, each individually decorated in a specific regional style.

Zaragoza 20, 41001 Sevilla. www.tabernadelalabardero.es. ℰ **95-450-27-21.** Fax 95-456-36-66. 7 units. 90€–150€ double; 100€–190€ junior suite. Rates include continental breakfast. AE, DC, MC, V. Parking 15€. Bus: 21, 25, 30, or 43. **Amenities:** Restaurant; bar; room service; babysitting. *In room:* A/C, TV/DVD, minibar, hair dryer, Wi-Fi (free).

INEXPENSIVE

Hotel Amadeus ★ 🏠 In the Santa Cruz district, this family-run small hotel honors Mozart with a musical theme throughout. Instruments line some of the walls, and there are pianos in some rooms. An 18th-century manor house was totally renovated and adapted to receive today's guests, although the Sevillano style was left intact. María Guerrero and her helpful daughters are the gracious hosts. Designer bedrooms are midsize to spacious, created with your comfort in mind. Breakfast is served on the roof terrace, opening onto views of Giralda Tower in the distance.

Calle Farnesio 6, Barrio de Santa Cruz, 41004 Sevilla. www.hotelamadeussevilla.com. ℰ **95-450-14-43.** Fax 95-450-00-19. 14 units. 77€–160€ double; 180€–200€ junior suite. AE, DC, MC, V. Nearby parking 16€. Bus: C3, C4, 1, or 21. **Amenities:** Babysitting. *In room:* A/C, TV, minibar, hair dryer, Wi-Fi (free).

Córdoba ★★★

Ten centuries ago, Córdoba was among the world's great cities. The capital of Muslim Spain, it was Europe's largest city and a cultural and intellectual center where scholars from around the known world came to rediscover classics that had been lost in Europe's Dark Ages and puzzle over the Arabic mathematics of algebra. It flourished with public baths, mosques, a great library, and palaces. Once Córdoba fell into Christian hands, the city was looted for its artistic treasures and much of its architecture was dismantled. Yet Córdoba persevered, retaining enough traces of its former glory to rival Sevilla and Granada.

Today this provincial capital is known chiefly for its mosque, but it abounds with other artistic and architectural riches, especially its lovely homes. The old Arab and Jewish quarters—the Judería—are famous for their narrow streets lined with whitewashed houses boasting flower-filled patios and balconies. It's perfectly acceptable to walk along, gazing into the courtyards.

A visit to Andalucía can easily begin in Córdoba, 418km (260 miles) southwest of Madrid.

ESSENTIALS

GETTING THERE The train is the most convenient and most popular means of transport to Córdoba, because the city is a rail junction for routes to the rest of Andalucía and is on the vital rail link between Madrid and Sevilla. The most used line is the **AVE high-speed train** racing between Madrid and Córdoba or between Córdoba and Sevilla. In the Spain of today, train travel between Sevilla and Córdoba has been cut to just 25 minutes. Amazingly, the AVE train ride between Madrid in the north and Córdoba in the south takes just 1½ hours.

There are between 22 and 31 trains per day arriving from Madrid, costing 68€ for a one-way ticket. A one-way ticket between Córdoba and Sevilla on the AVE sells for 33€, but the slower train (80 min.) costs only 11€ and runs six times a day. If you're on the Costa del Sol and want to visit Córdoba, you can take one of the 10 to 12 trains per day from Málaga. Depending on the train, the trip takes 2 to 3 hours and costs from 21€ to 38€ for a one-way ticket. For rail information, call ✆ **90-242-22-42**; for AVE schedules or information call ✆ **90-242-22-42.** The RENFE advance-ticket office in Córdoba is at Ronda de los Tejares 10 (www.renfe.es; ✆ **95-747-58-84**). To reach the heart of the city from the station, head south on Avenida de Cervantes or Avenida del Gran Capitán.

Getting to this old Moorish city by **bus** is easier than ever now that **Alsa** (www.alsa.es; ✆ **95-740-40-40**) has taken over many smaller companies and improved service. Buses now arrive at the city's new bus station, behind the train depot on Glorieta de las Tres Culturas. The most popular routes are between Córdoba and Sevilla, with seven buses per day. The trip takes 2 hours and costs 12€ for a one-way ticket. Another popular run is between Granada and Córdoba, where eight to nine buses per day make the 3-hour run, costing 13€ for a one-way ticket.

VISITOR INFORMATION   The **tourist office,** Calle Torrijos 10 (www.andalucia.org; ✆ **95-735-51-79**), is open Monday to Friday 9am to 7:30pm and Saturday and Sunday 9:30am to 3pm.

EXPLORING CÓRDOBA

Alcázar de los Reyes Cristianos ★ ☺ PALACE   Commissioned in 1328 by Alfonso XI, the Alcázar of the Christian Kings is a fine example of military architecture. Fernando and Isabel governed Spain from this fortress on the river as they prepared to reconquer Granada, the last Moorish stronghold in Spain. Columbus journeyed here to fill Isabel's ears with his plans for discovery.

Two blocks southwest of the Mezquita, this quadrangular building is notable for powerful walls and a trio of towers—the Tower of the Lions, the Tower of Allegiance, and the Tower of the River. The Tower of the Lions contains intricately decorated ogival ceilings that are the most notable example of Gothic architecture in Andalucía. The beautiful gardens and Arabic baths (a holdover from an earlier Moorish fortress) are celebrated attractions. The **Patio Morisco** is another lovely spot, its paved courtyard decorated with the arms of León and Castilla.

Caballerizas Reales. ✆ **95-742-01-51**. Admission 4€ adults (2€ for gardens), 2€ for students (1€ for gardens), free for children 14 and under with parent. Tues–Sat 10am–2pm and 4:30–6:30pm; Sun 9:30am–2:30pm. Gardens illuminated July–Sept 10pm–midnight. Bus: 3 or 12.

Mezquita Catedral de Córdoba ★★★ MOSQUE From the 8th to 11th centuries, the Mezquita was the crowning architectural achievement of western Islam. It's a fantastic forest of arches painted with alternating red and white stripes—a realization in stone of a billowing desert tent. A Roman Catholic cathedral interrupts the vistas, as it sits awkwardly in the middle of the mosque as an enduring symbol of Christian hubris. The 16th-century cathedral may have been architectural sacrilege, but it does have an intricately carved ceiling and baroque choir stalls. One of the interesting features of the mosque is the **mihrab**, a domed shrine of Byzantine mosaics that once housed the Qu'ran. After exploring the interior, stroll through the **Patio de los Naranjos** (Courtyard of the Orange Trees), which has a beautiful fountain where worshippers performed their ablutions before prayer and tourists rest their weary feet. The hardy can climb a 16th-century tower to catch a panoramic view of Córdoba and its environs.

Calles Torrijos and Cardenal Herrero s/n (south of the train station, just north of the Roman bridge). www.mezquitadecordoba.org. ✆ **95-822-52-45**. Admission 8€ adults, 4€ children 13 and under. Mon–Sat 8:30am–6pm; Sun 8:30–10:15am and 2–6pm. Bus: 3.

Museo de Bellas Artes de Córdoba ART MUSEUM A charming regional art museum with six exhibition halls arranged on three levels, this museum focuses on Córdoban painting from the 14th through the 20th centuries. Among the strongest holdings are the often macabre works of mannerist painter Juan de Valdés-Leal, including his famous *Virgin of the Silversmiths*. The father–son pair of romantic 19th-century painters, Rafael Romero Barro and Rafael Romero de Torres, are well represented with images of matadors, bullfights, and other folkloric subjects. The 20th-century hall is dominated by the sculptor Mateo Inurria Lainosa, a profound naturalist who dealt largely in religious iconography.

Plaza del Potro 1. www.museosdeandalucia.es. ✆ **95-735-55-50**. Admission 1.50€. Tues 2:30–8:30pm; Wed–Sat 9am–8:30pm; Sun 9am–2:30pm. Bus: 3 or 7.

WHERE TO EAT

Córdoban cuisine probably draws more extensively on Arabic and North African cooking than anywhere else in Spain. Not only does it liberally mix sweet flavors into savory dishes, you'll find a lot of dried fruits and nuts and such spices as cumin, turmeric, and cinnamon. Lamb and kid are usually the meats of choice, although many menus feature beef, a side effect of the local bull-breeding industry.

Expensive

Bodegas Campos ★ SPANISH/ANDALUCÍAN You'll eat one of your best meals in Córdoba at this local favorite, located on a narrow cobblestone street in a residential neighborhood 10 minutes from the Mezquita. The front of the restaurant has one of Córdoba's hippest and most crowded tapas bars. It's filled with attractive singles—some more interested in the scene than the food. Bodegas Campos has a welcoming rustic atmosphere and has been going strong since 1908 as both a wine cellar (bodega) and a tavern. Typical fare would include a salad of salt cod and thinly sliced oranges on lettuce dressed only with olive oil and salt, or tiny fried fish served with thick Andalucían *salmorejo* sauce (a tomato-bread purée). Other specialties include roasted partridge with vegetables in a vinegar sauce and a casserole of braised Iberian pig's cheek.

Calle de los Lineros 32. www.bodegascampos.com. ✆ **95-749-75-00**. Reservations recommended. Main courses 17€–28€. DC, MC, V. Mon–Sat 11am–midnight; Sun 11am–5pm. Closed Dec 25 and 31. Bus: 1, 3, 4, or 7.

La Almudaina ★★ ANDALUCÍAN/CONTINENTAL   The owners of this historic restaurant near the Alcázar deserve as much credit for their renovations of a decrepit 15th-century palace as they do for the excellent cuisine produced in their bustling kitchen. Set into the ancient city walls at the gate closest to the Alcázar, La Almudaina is serene and lovely. You can dine in one of the lace-curtained salons or on a glass-roofed central courtyard. The menu has two tracks, so to speak: Many of the dishes are almost medieval in their origins, like the Cordoban version of *salmorejo* (a thick cold soup made with bread, tomato, fresh garlic, Iberian ham, and olive oil) or the white gazpacho redolent of garlic and ground almonds. The other track is Continental classic—Escoffier with a Spanish accent. If you're visiting during the late fall when black truffles are available, try the pork tenderloin in truffle sauce. One of the favorite desserts is Córdoban quince pastry prepared according to a 19th-century recipe.

Plaza Campos de los Santos Mártires 1. www.restaurantealmudaina.com. ✆ **95-747-43-42.** Reservations required. Set menus 12€–75€; main courses 18€–35€. AE, DC, MC, V. Mon–Sat noon–4pm and 8:30pm–midnight; Sun 12:30–4pm. Closed Sun July 15–Sept 1. Bus: 3 or 16.

Moderate

El Caballo Rojo ★★ SPANISH   Within walking distance of the Mezquita in the Old Town, this restaurant is one of the most popular in Andalucía, and—with the exception of La Almudaina (see above)—the best in Córdoba. The place has a noise level no other restaurant here matches, but the skilled waiters manage to cope with all demands. Stop in the restaurant's popular bar for a predinner drink, and then take the iron-railed stairs to the upper dining room, where a typical meal might include gazpacho, a main dish of chicken, and then ice cream (often homemade pistachio) and sangria. The Red Head serves the classic Córdoban version of gazpacho, a dish that predates the introduction of tomatoes and peppers from the New World. Here the almond-milk broth is thickened with bread, and it enrobes pieces of apple cut into small dice. The chef also offers Sephardic and Mozarabic specialties, such as monkfish in a tagine of pine nuts, currants, carrots, and cream.

Cardinal Herrero 28, Plaza de la Hoguera. www.elcaballorojo.com. ✆ **95-747-53-75.** Reservations required. Main courses 14€–26€; fixed-price menu 26€. AE, DC, MC, V. Daily 1–4:30pm and 8pm–midnight. Bus: 2.

Taberna Casa Pepe de la Judería ★ CORDOVAN   Around the corner from the mosque, this taberna is often dismissed as a tourist trap, yet it serves good, authentic Andalucían fare with a strong emphasis on simple grilled meats. Several small rooms decorated with flamboyant tiles and filled with heavy wooden furniture are spread over three floors. From May to October, tables are placed on the rooftop where chicken, pork, and cuts of beef are grilled over charcoal and an Andalucían guitarist entertains. Traditional starters here would include crisply fried red mullet, pickled anchovies, or either the Córdoban white gazpacho or the Sevillan tomato gazpacho. Roasted fish dishes (especially yellowfin tuna) are often prepared in a North African style with raisins and pine nuts, while the slow-roasted leg of lamb is smothered in sweet peppers, onion, garlic, and rosemary.

Calle Romero 1. www.casapepejuderia.com. ✆ **95-720-07-44.** Reservations recommended. Main courses 9€–15€; fixed-price menu 23€ (Mon–Fri). AE, MC, V. Sun–Thurs 1–4:30pm and 8:30–11:30pm; Fri–Sat 1–4pm and 8:30pm–midnight. Bus: 3.

Inexpensive

Café Siena 🍴 SPANISH   The layout of Córdoba makes it far too easy to get enmeshed in the medieval neighborhood around the Mezquita, and not venture anywhere else. This big, angular, and *moderno* cafe is the most appealing of those that ring the centerpiece of Córdoba's 19th- and early-20th-century commercial core, the Plaza de las Tendillas. In nice weather, most diners and drinkers opt for an outdoor table on the square. As day turns to evening, the clientele morphs from shoppers and local office workers to night owls. The food is fairly standard, a litany of the country's favorite dishes, but you can't go wrong with a *tortilla española* (potato omelet) or a *plato combinado* that includes a salty little beef or pork steak, with or without the extra fried eggs.

Plaza de las Tendillas s/n. ℂ **95-747-30-05.** Reservations recommended Fri–Sat. Main courses 8€–16€; *menú del día* 14€; tapas 3€–9€. AE, DC, MC, V. Mon–Sat 9am–2am. Bus: 1, 3, 4, or 7.

SHOPPING

You might want to seek out the following shop, especially if you're interested in Córdoban handicrafts: **Artesanía Andaluza,** Tomás Conde 3 (no phone), features a vast array of handicrafts, especially filigreed silver from the mines of Sierra Morena, and some excellently crafted embossed leather, a holdover from the Muslim heyday. The shop is open Monday to Saturday 9am to 5pm.

Córdoba has a branch of Spain's major department store, **El Corte Inglés,** at Ronda de los Tejares 30 (www.elcorteingles.es; ℂ **95-722-28-81**), in the new city. Some of the staff speak English. It's open Monday to Saturday 10am to 9pm.

Arte Zoco, Calle de los Judíos s/n (ℂ **95-729-05-75**), is the largest association of craftspeople in Córdoba. Established in the Judería in the mid-1980s, the site has stalls where about a dozen artisans sell their leather, wood, silver, crystal, terra cotta, and iron wares. About a half-dozen of them maintain their studios on the premises, so you can visit and check out their techniques and tools. The shop is open Monday to Friday 9:30am to 8pm and Saturday and Sunday 9:30am to 2pm.

Alejandro and Carlos López Obrero run **Taller Meryan,** Calleja de Las Flores 2 (www.meryancor.com; ℂ **95-747-59-02**), on one of the most colorful streets in the city. In this 250-year-old building you can see artisans plying their crafts. Although most items must be custom-ordered, some ready-made pieces are for sale, including cigarette boxes, jewel cases, attaché cases, book and folio covers, and ottoman covers. Hours are Monday to Friday 9am to 8pm and Saturday 9am to 2pm.

WHERE TO STAY

El Conquistador Hotel ★   Built centuries ago as a private villa, this hotel—one of the most attractive in town—has been tastefully renovated. It sits opposite an unused rear entrance to the Mezquita and has triple rows of stone-trimmed windows and ornate iron balustrades. The quality and comfort of the rooms—each with a black-and-white marble floor and a private bathroom—make the hotel a favorite with seasoned travelers, but the European-size rooms make it not as good a choice for travelers with lots of luggage.

Magistral González Francés 15, 14003 Córdoba. www.hotelconquistadorcordoba.com. ℂ **95-748-11-02.** Fax 95-747-46-77. 132 units. 70€–176€ double; from 99€ junior suite. AE, DC, MC, V. Parking 15€. Bus: 3 or 16. **Amenities:** Restaurant; bar; babysitting; room service. *In room:* A/C, TV, hair dryer, minibar, Wi-Fi (free).

Los Omeyas ★   If you want to stay in the very heart of Córdoba, you can't find a better location than this hotel nestled in the Jewish Quarter. Although in no way grand, rooms are comfortable, tasteful, and have modern bathrooms. Those on the top floor offer a panoramic view of the ancient tower of the mosque, which is literally around the corner.

Calle Encarnación 17, 14003 Córdoba. www.hotel-losomeyas.com. *℃* **95-749-22-67.** Fax 95-749-16-59. 33 units. 57€–80€ double; 72€–95€ triple; 87€–110€ quad. AE, DC, MC, V. Parking 15€. Bus: 3 or 16. **Amenities:** Bar. *In room:* A/C, TV, Wi-Fi (free).

Granada ★★★

Granada, 415km (258 miles) south of Madrid, is 670m (2,200 ft.) above sea level. The last stronghold of Moorish Spain, it was finally captured in 1492 by the Catholic monarchs Ferdinand and Isabella. Granada is best known for the castle complex of the **Alhambra ★★★** (www.alhambra-patronato.es), one of the world's grandest and most elegant monuments, ranking up there with the Acropolis and the Taj Mahal. Author/diplomat Washington Irving lived in a former royal apartment on the grounds before he wrote his *Tales of the Alhambra.*

But Granada itself has much more to offer. The winding, hilly streets of the formerly Jewish Albayzín quarter and the gracious plazas of the 19th-century city below come together into a supremely civilized city, one that rewards wandering.

ESSENTIALS

GETTING THERE **Iberia** (www.iberia.com; *℃* **90-240-05-00**) flies to Granada from Madrid four times daily. **Vueling** (www.vueling.com; *℃* **80-720-01-00** from within Spain) has three direct flights a day from Barcelona to Granada. Granada's **Federico García Lorca Airport** *(aeropuerto nacional)* is 16km (10 miles) west of the center of town on Carretera Málaga; call *℃* **90-240-47-04** for information. A bus route links the airport with the center of Granada. The one-way fare is 3€. The bus runs daily 5:30am to 8pm. Trip time is 45 minutes.

The **train** station is **Estación de RENFE de Granada,** Av. Andaluces s/n (www.renfe.es; *℃* **90-232-03-20**). Granada is well linked with the most important Spanish cities, especially those of Andalucía. Four trains per day arrive from Sevilla, taking 4 to 5 hours, depending on the train, and costing 25€ for a one-way ticket. From Madrid, two daily trains arrive in Granada, taking 4½ hours and costing 68€.

Granada is served by far more **buses** than trains. It has links to virtually all the major towns and cities in Andalucía, and even to Madrid. The main bus terminal is **Estación de Autobuses de Granada,** Carretera de Jaén s/n (*℃* **95-818-54-80**). One of the most heavily used bus routes is the one between Sevilla and Granada. Ten buses run per day, costing 19€ for a one-way ticket. The trip is 3 hours. You can also reach Granada in 3 hours on one of nine daily buses from Córdoba; cost is 14€ for a one-way ticket. For bus information, contact **Alsa** (www.alsa.es; *℃* **95-818-54-80**).

Granada is connected by superhighway to Madrid, Málaga, and Sevilla. Many sightseers prefer to make the drive from Madrid to Granada in 2 days, rather than 1.

VISITOR INFORMATION The **Patronato Provincial de Turismo de Granada,** Plaza de Mariana Pineda 10 (www.turgranada.es; *℃* **95-824-71-46**), is open Monday to Friday 9am to 8pm, Saturday 10am to 7pm, and Sunday 10am to 3pm.

EXPLORING GRANADA

Alhambra ★★★ PALACE A fortress-palace of grand ambition, built over centuries for the governing caliphs during the long Moorish occupation, the Alhambra was a royal city surrounded by walls. The heart of the Alhambra, the **Palacios Nazaríes (Nasrid Palaces),** is a series of three connected palaces. Here, sultans and emirs conducted state business, concocted conspiracies, raised their families, and were entertained by their harems.

The first structure you'll enter is the **Casa Real,** built between 1335 and 1410. Signs direct visitors through rooms with reliefs of Arabic script and floral motifs carved in the plaster walls. This pathway leads into one of the Alhambra's most-photographed spaces, the **Patio de Comares (Court of the Myrtles),** a long, flat band of water bordered by rows of sculptured myrtle. At one end is the splendid **Salón de Embajadores (Hall of the Ambassadors),** one of the palace's loveliest rooms, with a high vaulted ceiling of carved cedar and walls of lustrous tiles and carved script. Exiting, you soon arrive in the **Patio de los Leones (Court of Lions),** named after its fountain, a basin resting on the haunches of 12 stylized stone lions standing in a circle. This was the heart of the palace, the most private section. Opening onto the court are the Hall of the Two Sisters, where the "favorite" of the moment was kept, and the Gossip Room, a factory of intrigue. In the dancing room in the Hall of Kings, entertainment was provided nightly to amuse the sultan's party. You can see the room where Washington Irving lived (in the chambers of Carlos V).

Carlos V may have been horrified when he saw the cathedral placed in the middle of the great mosque at Córdoba, but he's responsible for his own architectural meddling here, building a ponderous Renaissance palace in the middle of the Alhambra. Today, it houses the **Museo de la Bellas Artes en la Alhambra** (✆ **95-822-14-49**), a site devoted to painting and sculpture from the 16th to the 19th centuries; and the **Museo de la Alhambra** (✆ **95-822-75-27**), which focuses on the region's traditions of Hispanic-Muslim art and architecture. Both museums are open Monday to Saturday 9am to 2pm.

Palacio de Carlos V. www.alhambra-patronato.es. ✆ **90-244-12-21.** Comprehensive ticket, including Alhambra and Generalife (see below), 13€; Museo Bellas Artes 2€; Museo de la Alhambra free; garden visits 7€; illuminated visits 13€. Oct 15–Mar 14 daily 8:30am–6pm, floodlit visits Fri–Sat 8–9:30pm; Mar 15–Oct 14 daily 8:30am–8pm, floodlit visits Fri–Sat 10–11:30pm. Bus: 30 or 32.

Catedral & Capilla Real ★ CATHEDRAL   This Renaissance–baroque cathedral, with its spectacular altar, is one of the country's architectural highlights, acclaimed for its beautiful facade and gold-and-white decor. It was begun in 1521 and completed in 1714. Behind the cathedral (entered separately) is the Flamboyant Gothic **Capilla Real (Royal Chapel),** where the remains of Isabel and Fernando lie. It was their wish to be buried in recaptured Granada, not their home regions of Castile or Aragón. The coffins are remarkably tiny—a reminder of how short they must have been. Accenting the tombs is a wrought-iron grill masterpiece. In much larger tombs are the remains of their daughter, Joanna the Mad, and her husband, Philip the Handsome. The Capilla Real abuts the cathedral's eastern edge.

Plaza de la Lonja, Gran Vía de Colón 5. www.capillarealgranada.com. ✆ **95-822-29-59.** Cathedral 3.50€; chapel 3.50€. Daily 10:30am–1:30pm and 3:30–6:30pm (4–8pm in summer). Bus: 6, 9, or 11.

Generalife ★ PALACE   The sultans used to spend their summers in this palace (pronounced, roughly, Hay-nay-rahl-*ee*-fay) with their wives, consorts, and extended families. Built in the 13th century to overlook the Alhambra, the Generalife's glory is in its gardens and courtyards. Don't expect an Alhambra in miniature: There are no major buildings—the Generalife is a place of fragrances and fountains, a retreat even from the splendors of the Alhambra.

Alhambra, Cerro de Sol. For tickets and hours, see the Alhambra, above.

WHERE TO STAY & EAT

Casa Morisca ★★ 🛏   This little charmer is tucked away in a house from the late 15th century in the historic lower district of Albayzín at the foot of the Alhambra. In the patio you can still see the remains of a Moorish pool and galleries supported by pilasters and columns. The interior was kept and restored, although the facade was given a 17th-century overlay. Bedrooms are individually decorated in a Moorish decorator style with all modern comforts. Parking is available on the street out front but must be arranged ahead to get a permit to drive up Carrera del Darro.

Cuesta de la Victoria 9, 18010 Granada. www.hotelcasamorisca.com. ✆ **95-822-11-00.** Fax 95-821-57-96. 14 units. 86€–160€ double; 155€–215€ suite. AE, DC, MC, V. Free parking. Bus: 31 or 32. **Amenities:** Room service. *In room:* A/C, TV, hair dryer, minibar, Wi-Fi (free).

El Claustro ★★ ANDALUCÍAN   Also serving New Andalucían cooking, this stylish and soothing restaurant is set within what was originally built in 1540 as a cloister for nuns. Chef-owner Juan Andrés R. Morilla, who represented Spain in the 2011 Bocuse D'Or international cooking competition, has created a menu that is savory, well conceived, and imaginative, and includes such starters as a salad of marinated rabbit, a casserole of red lentils with razor-shell clams, and a Granada-style salad of salt cod with oranges. Main courses change several times a year. You can enjoy Dublin prawns with artichoke salad, black rice with large prawns, filet of sole with a confit of carrots, and a succulent roast suckling pig.

In the AC Hotel Palacio Santa Paula, Gran Vía de Colón 31, 18001 Granada. www.restaurante elclaustro.com. ✆ **95-880-57-40.** Reservations recommended. Main courses 16€–26€; *menú degustación* 60€–100€. AE, DC, MC, V. Daily 1:30–4pm and 8:30–11pm. Bus: 3, 6, 9, or 11.

Restaurante Sevilla SPANISH   Attracting a mixed crowd of all ages, the Sevilla is definitely *típico,* but with an upbeat elegance. The place was discovered by García Lorca, a patron in the 1930s, and composer Manuel de Falla, and it still has ancient photos on the wall of all the Hollywood types who used to come here in the Franco years. Among the most popular menu items are Andalucían veal with fresh vegetables, topped off by flan, plus crusty homemade bread and the wine of Valdepeñas. To a change of pace, try *sopa virule,* made with pine nuts and chicken breast, followed by *cordero a la pastoril* (lamb with herbs and paprika). The best dessert is bananas flambé. You can dine inside, which is pleasantly decorated, or on the terrace. The restaurant is opposite the Royal Chapel, near the Plaza Isabel Católica.

Calle Oficios 12. www.restaurantesevilla.es. ✆ **95-822-12-23.** Reservations recommended. Main courses 12€–26€; *menú degustación* 36€. AE, DC, MC, V. Tues–Sat 1–4:30pm and 8–11:30pm. Bus: 32 or 39.

ALBAYZÍN ★

This old Arab quarter (also spelled "Albaicín") occupies one of the two main hills of Granada, but it doesn't belong to the city of 19th-century buildings and wide boulevards beneath it. The district once flourished as the residential section of the Moors, even after the city's reconquest, but it fell into decline when the Christians eventually drove the Moors out. A labyrinth of steep, crooked streets, it escaped the fate of much of Granada, which was torn down in the name of progress. Fortunately, it has been preserved, as have its plazas, whitewashed houses, villas, and the decaying remnants of the old city gate. Here and there, you can catch a glimpse of a private patio filled with fountains and plants—these are home to a traditional and graceful way of life that flourishes today. Car traffic is allowed only 6 hours a day, so walk or take bus no. 31 from the Plaza Nueva deep into the quarter. Many bars and restaurants cluster around the Plaza Larga. You can always get out by walking down-hill until you hit the Gran Vía or the river.

Bus: 31 or 32.

THE GYPSY CAVES OF SACROMONTE

Hundreds of Gypsies once lived on the "Holy Mountain" on the outskirts of Granada above the Albayzín. The mountain was named for the Christians martyred here and for its long-ago role as a pilgrimage site. Many of the caves were heavily damaged by rain in 1962, forcing most occupants to seek shelter elsewhere. Nearly all the Gypsies remaining are in one way or another involved with tourism. (Some don't even live here they commute from modern apartments in the city.)

A visit to the caves is almost always included as part of the morning and (more frequently) afternoon city tours offered every day by such companies as **Grana Visión** (www.granavision.com; ✆ **90-233-00-02**).

You can also walk uphill by yourself, although we advise a bus or taxi after dark. The best way to see some of the caves and to actually learn something about Gypsy Granada is to visit the **Museo Cuevas del Sacromonte ★**, Barranco de los Negros (www.sacromontegranada.com; ✆ **95-821-51-20**). This interpretation center is a great source of Roma (Gypsy) pride. Several caves are shown as lodgings, while others are set up as studios for traditional weaving, pottery, basketry, and metalwork. The museum is open April to October Tuesday to Sunday 10am to 2pm and 5 to 9pm, and November to March Tuesday to Sunday 10am to 2pm and 4 to 7pm. Admission is 5€. The best way to get here is via Bus 34.

In the evenings, many caves become performance venues for the Granada Gypsy flamenco style known as zambra. Performances demonstrate varying degrees of authenticity and artistry, but one of the best spectaculars is presented at **Venta El Gallo**, Barranco Los Negros 5 (www.ventaelgallo.com; ✆ **95-822-84-76**). A zambra performance has three stages, corresponding to the three parts of a Gypsy wedding. It is an atmospheric evening that you will not soon forget, but expect a certain amount of flim-flam, ostentatious showmanship, and attempts to sell you overpriced drinks. Make your reservation for the show without dinner (unless you feel you have to sit in front), but do pay the extra charge for transportation via minibus because city buses stop running at 11pm, when the musicians and dancers will just be hitting their stride. Admission is 22€, with an additional 6€ for transportation. Dinner and show are 52€.

SHOPPING

Alcaicería, once the Moorish silk market, is next to the cathedral in the lower city. The narrow streets of this rebuilt village of shops are filled with vendors selling the arts and crafts of Granada province. For the souvenir hunter, the Alcaicería offers a good assortment of tiles, castanets, and wire figures of Don Quixote chasing wind-mills. Lots of Spanish jewelry can be found here. For the window-shopper in particu-lar, it makes a pleasant stroll. A more interesting shopping experience is found in the souk of the alleyways of **Calderería Vieja** and **Calderería Nueva,** where wall hangings, pillows, silk tassels, and silver teapots abound. The area is a low-key version of what you'd find in North Africa, and a certain amount of bargaining is not only permitted but also virtually expected.

Handicrafts stores virtually line the main shopping arteries, especially those cen-tered on Puerta Real, including Gran Vía de Colón, Reyes Católicos, and Angel Ganivet. For the best selection of antiques stores, mainly selling furnishings of Anda-lucía, browse the shops along Cuesta de Elvira.

Málaga

Málaga is a bustling commercial and residential center whose economy doesn't depend exclusively on tourism. Its chief attraction is the mild off-season climate—summer can be sticky. Málaga's most famous native son is Pablo Picasso, born in 1881 at Plaza de la Merced, in the center of the city.

ESSENTIALS

GETTING THERE   Some airlines (including British Airways from London) offer nonstop flights to Málaga. **Iberia** has a frequent service. Flights can be booked through Iberia's reservations line (www.iberia.com; ℂ **90-240-05-00**).

Five to nine **trains** a day arrive in Málaga from Madrid (trip time: 2½ hr.). Three trains a day connect Sevilla and Málaga (trip time: 3 hr.). For ticket prices and rail information in Málaga, contact RENFE (www.renfe.es; ℂ **90-232-03-20**).

Buses from all over Spain arrive at the terminal on the Paseo de los Tilos, behind the RENFE offices. Buses run to all the major Spanish cities, including eight buses per day from Madrid (trip time: 7 hr.), five per day from Córdoba (trip time: 3 hr.), and 10 per day from Sevilla (trip time: 3 hr.). Call ℂ **90-242-22-42** in Málaga for bus information.

From resorts in the west (such as Torremolinos and Marbella), you can drive east along the N-340/E-15 to Málaga. If you're in the east at the end of the Costa del Sol (Almería), take the N-340/E-15 west to Málaga, with a stopover at Nerja.

VISITOR INFORMATION   The **tourist office,** at Plaza de la Marina 11 (www.malagaturismo.com; ℂ **95-192-62-20**), is open Monday to Friday 9am to 7pm and Saturday and Sunday 10am to 7pm.

EXPLORING MÁLAGA

The remains of the Moorish **Alcazaba ★**, Plaza de la Aduana, Alcazabilla (ℂ **95-212-20-20**; bus: 4, 18, 19, 24, or 135), are within easy distance of the city center, off Paseo del Parque (plenty of signs point the way up the hill). The fortress was erected in the 10th or 11th century, though there have been later additions and reconstructions. Fernando and Isabel stayed here when they reconquered the city. The Alcazaba has extensive gardens and houses a small archaeological museum, with artifacts from cultures ranging from Greek to Phoenician to Carthaginian. Admission is 5€; it's open Tuesday to Sunday from 8:30am to 8pm.

The 16th-century Renaissance **cathedral,** Plaza Obispo (ℂ **95-221-59-17**; bus: 14, 18, 19, or 24), in Málaga's center, was built on the site of a great mosque. It suffered damage during the Civil War, but it remains vast and impressive, reflecting changing styles of interior architecture. Its most notable attributes are its richly ornamented choir stalls by Ortiz, Mena, and Michael. Admission is 3.50€. It's open Monday to Friday 10am to 6pm and Saturday 10am to 5pm.

In the Old Quarter, **Museo Picasso Málaga ★★★**, San Augustin 8 (www.museopicassomalaga.org; ℂ **95-212-76-00**), displays some of his most important works. Many of the artworks are virtual family heirlooms, including paintings depicting one of the artist's wives, such as *Olga Kokhlova with Mantilla,* or one of his lovers, *Jacqueline Seated.* Basically this is the art Picasso gave to his family or else the art he wanted to keep for himself—in all, more than 200 paintings, drawings, sculpture, ceramics, and graphics. Some other notable works on display—many of them never on public view before—include *Bust of a Woman with Arms Crossed Behind Her Head, Woman in an Armchair,* and *The Eyes of the Artist.* There is also a memorable painting of Picasso's son, done in 1923. A combined ticket for the permanent collection and exhibitions costs 8€; half price for seniors, students, and children 11 to 16; free for kids 10 and under. Hours are Tuesday to Thursday and Sunday 10am to 8pm, Friday and Saturday 10am to 9pm.

WHERE TO STAY & EAT

José Carlos García Restaurante ★★ SPANISH   Long known as the Café de Paris, Málaga's best restaurant moved in 2011 to the city's newest shopping center, Muelle Uno, in the port area. Chef José Carlos García interned with both the Basque master Martin Berasategui and the Catalan genius Joan Roca, and he brings their sense of playful invention to the flavors of the Andalucían coast. In the winter season, the chef might fill *crêpes gratins* with precious baby eels. He takes the classic salt cod salad and reinvents it as a cream of cod, citrus fruits, and black olives, for example, or turns simple fried crayfish into a nest of fried noodles around the prawn ceremonially placed at the shoreline of sea lettuce foam. Look for his raspberry cannelloni dressed with a little vinegar and stuffed with drained yogurt and fresh berries. In addition to the a la carte menu, García offers a tasting menu and a market menu composed exclusively of that day's finds.

Muelle Uno. www.rcafedeparis.com. ℰ **95-222-50-43.** Reservations required. Main courses 18€–28€; fixed-price menus 43€–130€. AE, DC, MC, V. Tues–Sat 1:30–3:30pm and 8:30–11pm. Closed July 1–15. Bus: 251.

Parador de Málaga Gibralfaro ★★   Restored in 1994, this is one of Spain's oldest, most tradition-heavy *paradores*. It enjoys a scenic location high on a plateau near an old fortified castle. Overlooking the city and the Mediterranean, it has views of the bullring, mountains, and beaches. Rooms have private entrances, living room areas, and wide glass doors opening onto private sun terraces. The **restaurant,** notable for its views, serves Spanish cuisine.

Castillo de Gibralfaro s/n, 29016 Málaga. www.parador.es. ℰ **95-222-19-02.** Fax 95-222-19-04. 38 units. 155€–185€ double. AE, DC, MC, V. Take the coastal road, Paseo de Reding, which becomes Av. de Pries, and then Paseo de Sancha. Turn left onto Camino Nuevo and follow the small signs. Free parking. **Amenities:** Restaurant; bar; outdoor pool; room service. *In room:* A/C, TV, minibar, hair dryer, Wi-Fi (free).

Marbella

Though packed with visitors, ranking just behind Torremolinos in numbers, Marbella is still the most exclusive resort along the Costa del Sol—with such bastions of posh as the Hotel Puente Romano. Despite the hordes, Marbella persists as a large, busy, but still mostly pleasant town at the foot of the Sierra Blanca, 80km (50 miles) east of Gibraltar and 76km (47 miles) east of Algeciras, or 60km (37 miles) south of Madrid.

ESSENTIALS

GETTING THERE   The main **bus** link is between Málaga and Marbella, with the **Portillo** (www.ctsa-portillo.com; ℰ **90-214-31-44**) running 14 buses a day. The trip takes 1 hour and 25 minutes and costs 5.15€ one-way. Madrid and Barcelona each have three daily buses to Marbella. The bus station is located on the outskirts of Marbella on Avenida Trapiche, a 5-minute ride from the center of town.

If you're driving, Marbella is the first major resort as you head east on the N-340/E-15 from Algeciras.

VISITOR INFORMATION The **tourist office,** Glorieta de la Fontanilla s/n (www.marbella.es; ☎ **95-277-14-42**), is open Monday to Friday 9:30am to 9pm and Saturday 10am to 2pm. Another tourist office with the same hours is on the Plaza de los Naranjos (☎ **95-277-46-93**).

EXPLORING MARBELLA

Traces of the recent and distant past are found in Marbella's palatial town hall, its medieval ruins, and fragments of its Moorish walls. The most attractive area is the **Old Quarter,** with its narrow cobblestone streets and clustered houses, centering around Plaza de los Naranjos, which is planted with palms, trumpet vines, and orange trees. Seek out the Plaza de la Iglesia and the streets around it, with a church on one side and a rampart of an old fortress on the other.

The biggest attractions in Marbella are **El Fuerte** and **La Fontanilla,** the two main beaches. There are other, more secluded beaches, but you'll need your own transportation to get to them.

ENTERTAINMENT & NIGHTLIFE

There's more international wealth hanging out in the watering holes of Marbella, and a wider choice of glam (or pseudo-glam) discos, than virtually anywhere else in the south of Spain. Foremost among these is **Olivia Valere** on Carretera Istan, N-340 Km 0.8 (www.oliviavalere.com; ☎ **95-282-88-61**); it's open every night from midnight to 7am and charges a cover of 30€. A fashionable place to rendezvous at night, **La Notte,** Camino de la Cruz s/n (☎ **95-277-76-25**), stands next to the swank La Meridiana restaurant. Decorated in a style intended to evoke Morocco, La Notte offers a terrace and an elegant atmosphere with rich decoration. Live music and shows are presented here during its nightly hours from 12:30 to 4am.

If you're in the heart of historic Marbella, enjoy a night in the bodegas and taverns of the Old Town. Conveniently located adjacent to one of the town's widest thoroughfares is **Bodega La Venensia,** Plaza de los Olivos s/n (www.bodegaslavenencia.com; ☎ **95-277-99-63**). Its wide choice of sherries, wines, and tapas draws lots of chattering patrons. **Vinacoteca La Cartuja,** Plaza Joaquín Gómez Agüera 2 (☎ **95-277-52-03**), is dedicated to offering as many Spanish wines as possible. Drinking here provides the opportunity to compare vintages from the surrounding region.

Although hardly authentic, Marbella's best flamenco is offered at **Tablao Flamenco Ana María,** Av. Severo Ochoa 24 (☎ **95-277-56-46**). It's a good start for foreign visitors who speak limited Spanish. The long, often-crowded bar area sells tapas, wine, sherry, and a selection of more international libations. This is late-night entertainment—the doors don't open until 11:30pm, and the crowd really gets going between midnight and 3am. Cover (which includes one drink) is 25€.

Seven kilometers (4⅓ miles) west of Marbella, near Puerto Banús, **Casino Marbella** (www.casinomarbella.com; ☎ **95-281-40-00**) is on the lobby level of the Bajo Hotel Andalucía Plaza resort complex at Urbanización Nueva. Unlike the region's competing casino, at the Hotel Torrequebrada, the Marbella does not offer cabaret or nightclub shows.

WHERE TO STAY & EAT

Casa de la Era ★ 🛏🍴 ANDALUCÍAN   This little discovery outside Marbella is in a rustic house, very much in the style of an old hacienda with internal patios decorated with plants, trees, and flowers. Wooden furniture only adds to the old-fashioned look, as do hanging hams and ceramics used for decoration. In addition, the restaurant offers a beautiful terrace. On a full night the place is a whirl of color and activity. The charming waiters rather proudly bring out the chef's specialties.

Some of the best of the chef's specialties include noodles with anglerfish and baby clams, as well as baby goat from the mountains above Málaga. Codfish is a savory dish here when cooked in a spicy fresh tomato sauce. Other good dishes include free-range chicken stewed with Montilla wine and fresh garlic, as well as rabbit pan-cooked with fresh thyme and served with almond sauce.

Finca El Chorraero, Carretera de Ojén Km 0.5. www.casadelaera.com. ✆ **95-277-06-25.** Reservations recommended. Main courses 13€–25€. AE, DC, MC, V. Sept–June Mon–Sat 1–4pm and 8–11pm; July–Aug daily 8–11pm.

Gran Meliá Don Pepe ★★ Located on the beach a short stroll from the town center, this chain-run hotel is one of Marbella's best resorts, offering taste, elegance, and grand comfort. The hotel is known for its spacious, beautiful rooms opening onto views of the Mediterranean, as well as for its tropical gardens and fine dining. Most of the guest rooms have a terrace or balcony with a sea view. At night, the hotel features shows and live music—often including flamenco. Guests get free entrance to the Casino de Marbella.

José Meliá, 29600 Marbella. www.gran-melia-don-pepe.com. ✆ **95-277-03-00.** Fax 95-277-99-54. 201 units. 164€–480€ double; from 380€ suite. AE, DC, MC, V. Parking 20€. **Amenities:** 4 restaurants; 2 bars; 3 pools (1 heated indoor); 2 outdoor tennis courts (lit); small health club; Jacuzzi; sauna; bikes; room service; babysitting; Wi-Fi (4€ per hr. in lobby). In room: A/C, TV, kitchenette (in some), minibar, hair dryer.

The Town House ★★ 🎁 Deep in the heart of the Old Quarter, this former private home has been tastefully converted into the town's most romantic-looking boutique hotel. Of all the hotels in Marbella, this one comes the closest to evoking life in a private town house from yesterday, yet it has been completely modernized with today's comforts. The day begins with morning coffee on the roof terrace and comes to an end with a cold drink, perhaps a cocktail, on that same terrace as the sun sets. The house lies some 300m (984 ft.) from the boardwalk along the beach (which extends all the way to Puerto Banús, incidentally). The midsize bedrooms were designed with exquisite care, with antique objects combined with contemporary design. Some of the objects you might admire, such as candleholders or pictures, can be purchased.

Plaza Tetuán, Calle Alderete 7, 29600 Marbella. www.townhouse.nu. ✆/fax **95-290-17-91.** 9 units. 125€–145€ double. MC, V. **Amenities:** Bar; room service. In room: A/C, TV.

Torremolinos

This Mediterranean beach resort is the most famous in Spain. It's known as a melting pot for international visitors, mostly Europeans and Americans. Many relax here after a whirlwind tour of Europe—the living is easy, the people are fun, and there are no historical monuments to visit. A sleepy fishing village until the 1950s, Torremolinos has been engulfed in cement-walled resort hotels, and that overconstruction makes "Torrie" one of Europe's vacation bargains.

ESSENTIALS

GETTING THERE The nearby Málaga airport serves Torremolinos, and frequent **trains** also run from the terminal at Málaga. For train information, call ✆ **90-232-03-20** or log on to www.renfe.es. **Buses** run frequently between Málaga and Torremolinos; call ✆ **90-214-31-44** for schedules.

If you're driving, take the N-340/E-15 west from Málaga or the N-340/E-15 east from Marbella.

VISITOR INFORMATION   The tourist **information office** is at Plaza Independencia (✆ **95-237-42-31**). It's open daily 8am to 3pm (in winter Mon–Fri 9:30am–2:30pm).

ENTERTAINMENT & NIGHTLIFE

Torremolinos has more nightlife than any other spot along the Costa del Sol. The earliest action is always at the bars, which stay lively most of the night, serving drinks and tapas until at least 3am. Sometimes it seems that in Torremolinos there are more bars than people, so you shouldn't have trouble finding one you like. Note that some bars are open during the day as well.

La Bodega, San Miguel 40 (✆ **95-238-73-37**), relies on its colorful clientele and the quality of its tapas to draw customers, who seem to rank this place above the dozens of other *tascas* in this popular tourist zone. Many guests come here for lunch or dinner, making a satisfying meal from the plentiful bar food. You'll be lucky if you find space at one of the small tables, but once you begin to order—platters of fried squid, pungent tuna, grilled shrimp, tiny brochettes of sole—you might not be able to stop. Most tapas cost 2€. A beer costs 1.50€, a hard drink at least 3.50€ to 4€. La Bodega is open daily from noon to 5pm and 7:30pm to midnight.

Ready to dance off all those tapas? **El Palladium,** Palma de Mallorca (✆ **95-238-42-89**), a well-designed nightclub in the town center, is one of the most convivial in Torremolinos. Strobes, spotlights, and a loud sound system set the scene. There's even a swimming pool. Expect to pay 3.50€ or more for a drink; cover is 15€, including one drink after 11pm. The club is open from 11pm to 6am in summer months only.

For unabashed tourist flamenco, try **Taberna Flamenca Pepe López,** Plaza de la Gamba Alegre (www.tabernaflamencapepelopez.com; ✆ **95-238-12-84**), in the center of Torremolinos. In an old house (at least old in the Torremolinos sense), this is a tavern-style joint with darkened-wood furnishings. Many of the artists come from the bars of Sevilla and Granada, and they perform Monday through Saturday at 10pm April to October. The frequency of shows is substantially reduced during the cooler months, and performances are confined mainly to the weekends—call to confirm first. A 27€ cover includes your first drink and the show.

Gay men and women from throughout northern Europe are almost always in residence in Torremolinos; if you want to meet some of them, consider having a drink or two at **Abadía,** La Nogalera 521 (no phone), open daily 6pm to dawn.

One of the Costa del Sol's major casinos, **Casino Torrequebrada,** Avenida del Sol, Benalmádena-Costa (www.casinotorrequebrada.net; ✆ **95-257-73-00**), is on the lobby level of the Hotel Torrequebrada. It has tables devoted to blackjack, chemin de fer, punto y banco, and two kinds of roulette. The casino is open daily from 8pm to 5am. The nightclub offers a flamenco show year-round at 10:30pm Tuesday to Saturday; in midsummer, there might be more glitz and more frequent shows (ask when you get there, or call). Nightclub acts begin at 10:30pm (Las Vegas revue) and 11:30pm (Spanish revue). The restaurant is open nightly from 9:30pm to midnight. Casino admission is 3€. Bring your passport to be admitted.

WHERE TO STAY & EAT

Casa Juan ★ SEAFOOD   In a modern-looking building in La Carihuela, this 170-seat seafood restaurant is about 1.6km (1 mile) west of Torremolinos's center and a stone's throw from the water. Menu items include selections from a lavish display of fish and shellfish prominently positioned near the entrance. You might try *mariscada de mariscos* (shellfish), a fried platter of mixed fish, cod, kebabs of meat or fish, or paella. Of special note is *lubina a la sal*—seabass roasted in a casing of coarse salt, broken open at your table and deboned in front of you.

Calle San Gines 18–20. www.losmellizos.net/casajuan. © **95-237-35-12.** Reservations recommended. Main courses 12€–45€. AE, DC, MC, V. Daily 12:30–4:30pm and 7:30–11:30pm. Closed Dec.

El Figón de Montemar ★ ASTURIAN/ANDALUCÍAN One of the more

unusual restaurants in the area, Figón de Montemar lies near the beach, and like so many others it's decorated with glass, tiles, and assorted nautical paraphernalia, but its food is equal parts Andalucían and Asturian. Menus are based on what was good and fresh at the market that day, including the daily seafood catch. Small-boat fishermen also bring in their catch of red mullet, whiting, and other small fish as the day goes on. The kitchen seasons mountain lamb with garlic and spices, roasts it to perfection, and serves the dish with mint sauce. *Merluza* (hake) is oven roasted with fresh herbs, and fresh codfish is prepared in a delightful red sauce. The Asturian bean-and-pork specialty, *fabada,* is available as a special on Wednesdays, and the traditional Easter week feast dish of salt cod and garbanzos is served on Fridays.

Av. Espada 101. www.elfigondemontemar.com. © **95-237-26-88.** Reservations recommended. Main courses 14€–24€. AE, DC, MC, V. Daily 1–4pm and 8pm–midnight.

Roc Lago Rojo ★ 🎁 In the heart of the fishing village of La Carihuela, Roc Lago

Rojo is one of the nicer places to stay in Torrie. It's only 45m (148 ft.) from the beach and has its own gardens and sunbathing terraces. Built in the 1970s and renovated in 2006, it offers tastefully decorated studio-style rooms, all of which have terraces with views. In the late evening, there is disco dancing. Note that all rooms are furnished with either two or three twin-style beds.

Miami 5, 29620 Torremolinos. www.roc-hotels.com. © **95-238-76-66.** Fax 95-238-08-91. 144 units. 50€–155€ double. Rates include buffet breakfast. AE, DC, MC, V. Parking 15€. **Amenities:** Restaurant; bar; outdoor freshwater pool; babysitting; Wi-Fi (4€ per hr. in lobby). *In room:* A/C, TV.

SWEDEN

by Mary Anne Evans

Although it was founded 7 centuries ago, Stockholm didn't become Sweden's capital until the mid-17th century. Today it's the capital of a modern welfare state with a strong focus on leisure activities and access to nature only a few minutes away.

Stockholm is the most regal, elegant, and intriguing city in Scandinavia with a long history as a trading and commercial city. It's an important north European capital, presiding over a country the size of California without the massive population of that state.

Because of Sweden's neutrality in World War II, it was spared from aerial bombardment, so much of what you see today is genuinely old, especially the historical heart, Gamla Stan (Old Town). In contrast, Stockholm is one of the world's leading exponents of modern architecture. Stockholm is also one of the world's most environmentally friendly cities.

STOCKHOLM & ENVIRONS

Stockholm is built on 14 islands in Lake Mälaren, marking the beginning of an archipelago of 24,000 islands, skerries, and islets that stretches all the way to the Baltic Sea. It's a city of bridges and islands, towers and steeples, cobblestone squares and broad boulevards, Renaissance splendor and modern steel-and-glass buildings. The medieval walls of Gamla Stan (Old Town) no longer stand, but the winding streets have been preserved. You can even go fishing in downtown waterways, thanks to a long-ago decree from Queen Christina, and the crystal clear waters that surround Stockholm.

Once an ethnically homogeneous society, Stockholm has experienced a vast wave of immigration over many years. More than 10% of Sweden's residents are immigrants or children of immigrant parents, with many coming from other Scandinavian countries. Because of Sweden's strong stance on human rights, the country has become a major destination for political and social refugees from Africa, the Middle East, and the former Eastern bloc countries as well.

An important aspect of Stockholm today is a genuine interest in cultural activities. Over the past quarter of a century, attendance at live concerts has grown, book sales are up, and more and more people are visiting museums.

Essentials

GETTING THERE

BY PLANE You'll arrive at **Stockholm Arlanda Airport** (www.swedavia.com/arlanda; ✆ **08/797-60-00**) about 42km (26 miles) north of Stockholm on the E-4 highway. **SAS** (www.flysas.com; ✆ **800/221-2350**) is the most common carrier.

The fastest way to go from the airport to the Central Station in Stockholm is on the **Arlanda Express** (www.arlandaexpress.com) train, which takes only 20 minutes and is covered by the Eurail pass. Trains run every 15 minutes daily from 5am to midnight (six times an hour during rush hour Mon–Fri). If you don't have a rail pass, the cost of a one-way ticket is 280SEK for adults and 130SEK for seniors and students (kids 8 and under ride free). For more information, call ✆ **0771/720 200**. The **Flygbussarna bus** (www.flygbussarna.se; ✆ **08/588-22-828**), from outside the terminal building, goes to the City Terminal, Klarabergsviadukten, in the city center every 10 to 15 minutes (trip time: 45 min.) for 99SEK. A taxi to or from the airport should be a fixed price from 450SEK to around 550SEK. ***Travelers beware:*** Smaller taxi companies may charge up to 700SEK for the same ride. Be sure to ask in advance what the price is to your destination. **Flygtaxi** (www.flygtaxi.se; ✆ **08/120-92-000**) is a large, reputable company with a fixed-price policy of 520SEK for the transfer.

BY TRAIN   The high-speed train between Stockholm and Oslo has reduced travel time to 5 hours and 40 minutes between these two once remotely linked Scandinavian capitals. Depending on the day, there are two to three trains daily in each direction. Trains arrive at Stockholm's **Centralstationen (Central Station)** on Centralplan, in the city center (www.sj.se; ✆ **08/410-62-600**). There you can make connections to Stockholm's subway, the T-bana. Follow the TUNNELBANA sign.

BY BUS   Buses arrive at the **Cityterminales** at Klarabergsviadukten 72. From here you can catch the T-bana (subway) to your Stockholm destination. For information in the Stockholm area, call ✆ **08/762-59-97.** Ticket office hours are Sunday to Friday 9am to 6pm and Saturday 9am to 4pm.

BY CAR   Getting into Stockholm by car is relatively easy because the major national expressway from the south, E-4, joins with the national express highway, E-18, coming in from the west and leads right into the heart of the city. Stay on the highway until you see the turnoff for Central Stockholm or Centrum.

VISITOR INFORMATION

TOURIST OFFICES   The **Tourist Centre** is at Vasagatan 14 (opposite Central Station) Norrmalm (www.visitstockholm.com; ✆ **08/508-28-508**). It's open January to April and mid-September to December Monday to Friday 9am to 6pm, Saturday 10am to 5pm, and Sunday 10am to 4pm. Closed December 24 and 25, and January 1. May to mid-September Monday to Friday 9am to 7pm, Saturday 9am to 4pm, Sunday 10am to 4pm. Maps and other free materials are available.

Kulturhuset, Sergels Torg 3 (www.kulturhuset.stockholm.se; ✆ **08/508-314-00**), distributes information about cultural activities and organizations throughout Sweden and Europe. The largest organization of its kind in Sweden, it was built in 1974 by the city of Stockholm as a showcase for Swedish and international art and theater. There are no permanent exhibits; display spaces hold a changing array of paintings, sculpture, photographs, and live performance groups. Inside are cafes, a library (with newspapers in several languages), a reading room, and a collection of recordings. It's open Monday to Friday 9am to 7pm and Saturday and Sunday 11am to 5pm.

WEBSITES   Go to the **Scandinavian Tourism Board** website at **www.go scandinavia.com** for general information on Sweden, maps, sightseeing information, ferry schedules, and other advice. Other useful sites are **www.visitstockholm. com**, for updated events listings and advice on dining, lodging, and museums, and **www.visitsweden.com**, which covers the whole of Sweden.

CITY LAYOUT

North of the Old Town (Gamla Stan), the main areas and major streets lie in Norrmalm. Here you'll find **Kungsgatan** (the main shopping street), **Birger Jarlsgatan,** and **Strandvägen** (leading to Djurgården—home of many of the city's top sights). **Stureplan,** at the junction of the major avenues Kungsgatan and Birger Jarlsgatan, is the city's commercial hub.

The Stockholm Card

Stockholmskortet (Stockholm Card) is a discount card that allows unlimited travel by bus (except airport buses), subway, and local trains throughout the city and county of Stockholm. It includes admission to 80 attractions, and discounts on sightseeing bus tours with Stockholm Panorama and Open Top Tour, and some boat trips. You can also benefit from free bicycle sightseeing in English (summer only) and a free guidebook.

You can buy the card at many places in the city, including the Tourist Centre at Vasagatan 14, Hotellcentrallen in the Central Station, tourist information desks in many hotels, City Hall (summer only), the Kaknäs TV tower, SL-Center Sergels Torg (subway entrance level), and Pressbyrån newsstands. The cards are stamped with the date and time of the first use. A 24-hour card costs 450SEK for adults, 215SEK for children 7 to 17. A 2-day adult card is 625SEK (child 255SEK); a 3-day card is 750SEK (child 285SEK), and a 5-day card is 950SEK (child 315SEK). The card is a bargain if you plan to make a lot of use of it, running around all over the city, with an action-filled agenda.

About four blocks west of the Stureplan rises **Hötorget City,** a landmark of modern urban planning. Its main traffic-free artery is **Sergelgatan,** a three-block shoppers' promenade leading to the modern sculptures in the center of **Sergels Torg.** South of Stureplan, at **Gustav Adolfs Torg,** are the Royal Dramatic Theater and the Royal Opera House. A block east of the flaming torches of the Royal Opera House, the verdant north–south stretch of **Kungsträdgården,** part avenue, part public park, serves as a popular gathering place and as a resting perch for shoppers. Three blocks southeast, on a promontory, lie the landmark Grand Hotel and the National Museum.

Kungsholmen, King's Island, is across a narrow canal from the rest of the city, a short walk west of the Central Station. It's visited chiefly by those wanting to tour Stockholm's elegant Stadshuset (City Hall). South of the island where **Gamla Stan (Old Town)** is located—and separated from it by a narrow but much-navigated stretch of water—is **Södermalm,** the southern district of Stockholm, now famous worldwide as the main area in Stieg Larsson's Millennium trilogy. Originally the working class area of Stockholm, today has seen a change in its fortunes, with its cutting-edge boutiques, bars, and clubs making it Stockholm's liveliest residential sections.

To the east of Gamla Stan, on a large and forested island completely surrounded by the complicated waterways of Stockholm, is **Djurgården (Deer Park).** The rustically unpopulated summer pleasure ground of Stockholm, it's the site of many of the city's most popular attractions: the open-air museums of Skansen, the *Vasa* man-of-war, Gröna Lund's Tivoli, the Waldemarsudde estate of the "painting prince" Eugen, and the Nordic Museum.

GETTING AROUND

ON FOOT Walking is the best way to get to know the city. In any case, you have to explore Gamla Stan on foot, as cars are banned from many of the streets. Djurgården and Skeppsholmen are other popular haunts for strolling.

BY PUBLIC TRANSPORTATION You can travel throughout Stockholm county by bus, local train, subway (T-bana), and tram, going from Singö in the north to

Nynäshamn in the south. The routes are divided into zones, and one ticket is valid for all types of public transportation in the same zone within 1 hour of being stamped.

REGULAR FARES   The basic fare for public transportation (subway, tram, street-car, or bus) is 25SEK. Purchase a ticket for a tram or streetcar at the tollbooth before getting to the subway platform. You cannot pay the driver on buses. To travel in most of Stockholm, all the way to the borders of the inner city, requires two tickets. The maximum ride, to the outermost suburbs, requires five tickets. You can transfer free (or double back and return to your starting point) within 1 hour of your departure.

SPECIAL DISCOUNT TICKETS   Your best transportation bet is a **travelcard.** A 1-day card costs 115SEK for adults (child 7 to 17 costs 70SEK; kids 6 and under travel free with an adult) and is valid for 24 hours of unlimited travel by T-bana (subway), bus, and commuter train within Stockholm. It also includes passage on the ferry to Djurgården. Most visitors will probably prefer the 3-day card for 230SEK, valid for 72 hours in Stockholm and the adjacent county. The 3-day card is also valid for admission to the Kaknäs tower and to Gröna Lund Tivoli, and a 50% discount to the Skansen museum. Tickets are available at tourist information offices, in subway stations, and from most news vendors. Call ✆ **08/689-10-00** for more information.

You can also opt for the **Stockholm Card;** see the box above for full details.

BY T-BANA (SUBWAY)   Subway entrances are marked with a blue T on a white background. Tickets are bought on the concourse before you get down to the platform. For information about schedules, routes, and fares, phone ✆ **08/600-10-00.**

BY BUS   Where the subway line ends, the bus begins. If the subway doesn't reach an area, a bus will. Many visitors ride the bus to Djurgården (although you can walk), where the T-bana doesn't go. If you're staying long enough to warrant it, you can buy the *SL Stockholmskartan* booklet for 100SEK at the Tourist Centre at Sweden House, Hamngatan 27, off Kungsträdgården (✆ **08/789-24-95** for a list of bus routes).

BY FERRY   Ferries from Skeppsbron on Gamla Stan (near the bridge to Söder-malm) and Skeppsholmen can take you to Djurgården if you don't want to walk or go by bus. They leave every 20 minutes Monday to Saturday and about every 15 minutes on Sunday from 9am to 6pm. The fare is 40SEK for adults, 25SEK for seniors and children 7 to 12, and free for children 6 and under.

BY TAXI   Taxi fares in Stockholm are very expensive and vary with different taxi companies. You can hail those that display the sign LEDIG, or you can request one by phone. **Taxi Stockholm** (www.taxistockholm.se; ✆ **08/728-27-00**) is a large, reputable company.

BY CAR   In general, you can park in marked spaces Monday through Friday from 8am to 6pm, but these spaces are hard to come by. Consider leaving your car in a parking garage—there are several in the city center and on the outskirts—and using public transportation. Parking exceptions or rules for specific areas are indicated on signs in the area. At Djurgården, parking is always prohibited, and from April to mid-September it's closed to traffic Friday to Sunday.

Avis (www.avis.se; ✆ **08/79799-70**) and **Hertz** (www.hertz.se; ✆ **08/797-99-00**) maintain offices at Arlanda Airport. Hertz's downtown office is at Vasagatan 26 (✆ **08/454-62-50**); Avis's central office is at Vasagatan 10B (✆ **010/49-48-050**). Rentals at both organizations are usually cheaper if you reserve them by phone or Internet before leaving home.

[Fast FACTS] STOCKHOLM

Currency You'll pay your way in Sweden with Swedish krone (singular, krona), or crowns, which is universally abbreviated SEK. These are divided into 100 øre. The exchange rate used throughout this chapter was $1 = 7SEK. Note that although Sweden is a member of the E.U., in 2002 it opted not to adopt the euro as its national currency.

Doctors For 24-hour emergency medical care, check with **Medical Care Information** (www.1177.se; ☎ **1177**). There's also a private clinic, **City Akuten,** Apelbergsgatan 48, 1st Floor (www.cityakuten.se; ☎ **08/412-29-60**).

Drugstores One central 24-hour pharmacy is **C. W. Scheele,** Klarabergsgatan 64 (☎**0771/450-450**; T-bana: Centralen).

Embassies & Consulates The embassy of the **United States** is at Dag Hammarskjölds Väg 31, 115 89 Stockholm (www.sweden.usembassy.gov; ☎ **08/783-53-00**; T-bana: Östermalmstorg); the embassy of the **United Kingdom** (http://ukinsweden.fco.gov.uk/en; ☎ **08/671-30-00**) is at Skarpogatan 6–8 (mailing address: P.O. Box 27819, 115 93 Stockholm); Bus 69; the embassy of **Canada** is at Klarabergsgatan 23, 6th floor, 103 23 Stockholm (www.canadaemb.se; ☎ **08/453-30-00**; T-bana: Centralen); the embassy of

Ireland (www.embassyofireland.se; ☎ **08/545-04-040**; T-bana: Östermalmstorg) is at Hovslagargatan 5 (mailing address: P.O. Box 10326, 100 55 Stockholm); the embassy of **Australia** (www.sweden.embassy.gov.au; ☎ **08/613-29-00**; T-bana: Hötorget) is at Klarabergsviadukten 63, 8th Floor); the embassy of **South Africa** is at Flemingatan 20, 112 26 Stockholm (www.southafrica.se; ☎ **08/24-39-50**; T-bana: Östermalmstorg); and the General Consulate of **New Zealand** is at Nybrogatan 11, 3rd Floor, 114 39 Stockholm (www.nzembassy.com/Sweden; ☎ **08-459-69-40**; T-bana: Östermalmstorg). Call for opening hours.

Emergencies Call ☎ **112** for the police, ambulance service, or the fire department.

Internet Most hotels and hostels offer free Wi-Fi in your room and also have a computer you can use. Many 7-Elevens, newsstands, and grocery stores have Internet access. **Sidewalk Express** (www.sidewalkexpress.se) has many terminals throughout the city, including at City terminalen, T-bana: Terminalen.

Post Office The main post office is at Central Station, Vasagatan, Norrmalm (☎ **08/781-24-25**), open Monday to Friday 9am to 6pm and Saturday 9am to noon.

Taxes Sweden imposes a "value-added tax," called *moms,* on most goods and services. Visitors from North America can beat the tax, however, by shopping in stores with the yellow-and-blue tax-free shopping sign. There are more than 15,000 of these stores in Sweden. To get a refund, your total purchase must cost a minimum of 200SEK. Tax refunds range from 14% to 18%, depending on the amount purchased. Moms begins at 12% on food items, but is 25% for most goods and services. The tax is part of the purchase price, but ask for a tax-refund voucher before you leave the store. When you leave Sweden, take the voucher to a tax-free Customs desk at the airport or train station you're leaving from. They will give you your moms refund (minus a small service charge) before you travel. Two requirements: You cannot use your purchase in Sweden (it should be sealed in its original packaging) and it must be taken out of the country within 1 month from purchase. For more information, go to www.global refund.com.

Telephone The **country code** for Sweden is **46.** The **city code** for Stockholm is **8;** use this code when you're calling from outside Sweden. If you're within Sweden but not in Stockholm, use **08.** If you're calling within Stockholm, simply leave off the code and dial the regular phone number.

Instructions in English are posted in **public phone boxes,** which can be found on street corners. Very few phones in Sweden are coin-operated; most require the purchase of a phone card (called a **Telekort**). You can obtain phone cards at most newspaper stands and tobacco shops.

You can make international calls from the **Tele-Center Office** on the Central Station's ground floor (© **08/789-24-56**), open daily from 8am to 9pm, except major holidays. Long-distance rates are posted.

For directory listings or other information for Stockholm or other parts of Sweden only, dial © **118118;** for other parts of Europe, dial © **118119.**

Tipping Hotels include a 15% service charge in your bill. Restaurants do not add on a service charge; so add 10% to the bill. Taxi drivers are entitled to 8% of the fare, and cloakroom attendants usually get 20SEK.

Exploring Stockholm

Everything from the *Vasa* Ship Museum to the changing of the guard at the Royal Palace to the Gröna Lund Tivoli amusement park will keep you intrigued. Even just window-shopping for well-designed Swedish crafts can be a great way to spend an afternoon.

ON GAMLA STAN & NEIGHBORING ISLANDS

Kungliga Slottet (Royal Palace) & Museum ★★ PALACE/MUSEUM Severely dignified, even cold looking on the outside, this palace has a lavish interior designed in the Italian baroque style. Kungliga Slottet is one of the few official residences of a European monarch that's regularly open to the public. Although the Swedish king and queen prefer to live at Drottningholm, this massive 608-room showcase, built between 1691 and 1754, remains their official address. The most popular rooms are the **State Apartments** ★★ and the **Bernadotte Apartments** ★★, with magnificent baroque ceiling frescoes and fine tapestries. In the building's cellar, the **Stattkammaren (Treasury)** ★★ is the repository for Sweden's crown jewels. Most intriguing to any student of war and warfare is the **Livrustkammaren (Royal Armory),** whose entrance is on the castle's rear side, at Slottsbacken 3. Gustavus III's collection of sculpture from the days of the Roman Empire in the **Antikmuseum (Museum of Antiquities)** is startling with its depictions of Tiberius, Caligula, Nero, and others.

Kungliga Husgerådskammaren, Gamla Stan. www.kungahuset.se. © **08/402-61-30.** Royal Apartments 150SEK adults, 50SEK seniors and students, free for children 6 and under. Free with Stockholm Card. Mid-May–mid-Sep daily 10am–5pm; mid-Sep–mid-May Tues–Sun noon–6pm; closed during government receptions. T-bana: Gamla Stan. Bus: 2, 3, 43, 53, 55, 71 or 76.

Riddarholm Church ★ CHURCH The second-oldest church in Stockholm is on the tiny island of Riddarholmen, next to Gamla Stan. Founded in the 13th century as Greyfriars abbey, it's the place where nearly all the royal heads of state are buried, apart from Queen Christina, who is buried in Rome, and Gustav VI, who is buried at Haga. It's a wonderful mix of chapels and tombs, burial vaults, and coats of arms. There are three principal royal chapels, including one, the Bernadotte wing, that belongs to the present ruling family.

Birger Jarls Torg, Riddarholmen. © **08/402-61-30.** Admission 40SEK adults, 20SEK students and children 7–18 years, free for children 6 and under. May 15–Sept 16 daily 10am–5pm. T-bana: Gamla Stan.

Although not as common as it once was, partaking in a Swedish smörgåsbord is the most typical of Swedish culinary delights. Some restaurants and hotels still stage this lavish banquet. The secret of surviving it is to go gracefully to the table that's groaning with heaping platters of food and not overload your plate. You can always return for more of the likes of *gravad lax* (thinly sliced salmon cured in dill) or Swedish meatballs.

And when you've had too much smörgåsbord or other Swedish food delicacies, and joined in too many toasts fueled by the lethal aquavit, you can also always do as the Swedes do and retire to the nearest sauna to revitalize yourself for yet more revelry in the evening to come.

CITY CENTER

Historiska Museet (Museum of National Antiquities) ★★ ☺ MUSEUM

If you're interested in Swedish history, especially the Viking era, here you'll find the nation's finest repository of relics left by those legendary conquerors who once terrorized Europe. Many relics have been unearthed from ancient burial sites, all displayed as human stories with a question-and-answer approach, models, and interactive displays. The collection of artifacts ranges from prehistoric to medieval times, including Viking stone inscriptions and 10th-century coins, silver and gold jewelry, large ornate charms, elaborate bracelet designs found nowhere else in the world, and a unique neck collar from Färjestaden.

Narvavägen 13–17. www.historiska.se. ℭ **08/519-556-00.** Adult 80SEK, seniors and students 60SEK, child under 18 years free, Fri 1–5pm free. Free with Stockholm Card. May–Aug daily 10am–5pm; Sept–Apr Tues–Sun daily 11am–5pm (to 8pm on Wed). T-bana: Karlaplan or Östermalmstorg. Bus: 44, 56, 69, or 76.

Moderna Museet (Museum of Modern Art) ★★ ART MUSEUM

This important museum, one of Europe's best, focuses on contemporary works by Swedish and international artists, including kinetic sculptures. Highlights are a small, impressive collection of Cubist art by Picasso, Braque, and Léger; Matisse's *Apollo* decoupage; the famous *Enigma of William Tell*, by Salvador Dalí; and works by Brancusi, Max Ernst, Giacometti, and Arp, among others. It's linked to the Arkitekturmuseet (Architecture Museum), which is worth a visit to see models of many well-known European buildings. There's a good restaurant looking over the sea.

Klarabergsviadukten 61, Skeppsholmen. www.modernamuseet.se. ℭ **08/519-552-82.** Admission 100SEK adults, free for ages 18 and under; combined with the Arkitekturmuseet 140SEK. Free with Stockholm Card. Tues 10am–8pm; Wed–Sun 10am–6pm. T-bana: Kungsträdgården. Bus: 65.

Nationalmuseum (National Museum of Art) ★★ ART MUSEUM

At the tip of a peninsula, a short walk from the Royal Opera House and the Grand Hotel, is Sweden's state treasure house of paintings and sculpture, one of the oldest museums in the world. The first floor is devoted to applied arts and displays silverware, handicrafts, porcelain, and furnishings, some from the royal castles, from 1500 to 1740. The 20th-century section shows the evolution of modern design and Sweden's part in the European movement. The second floor houses an important painting collection with works from the Middle Ages to the 20th century by artists from Rubens to

Stockholm

SWEDEN | Stockholm & Environs

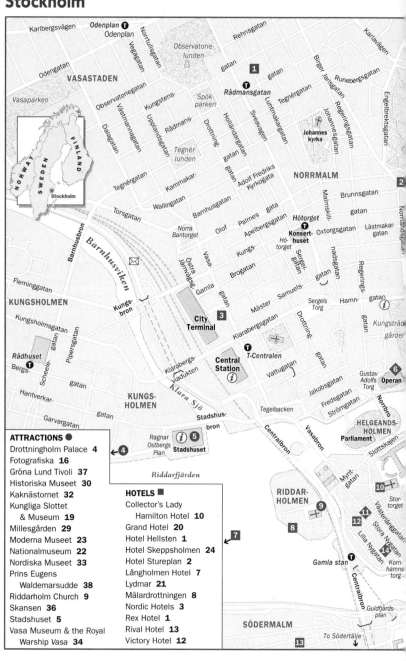

ATTRACTIONS ●
Drottningholm Palace **4**
Fotografiska **16**
Gröna Lund Tivoli **37**
Historiska Museet **30**
Kaknästornet **32**
Kungliga Slottet
  & Museum **19**
Millesgården **29**
Moderna Museet **23**
Nationalmuseum **22**
Nordiska Museet **33**
Prins Eugens
  Waldemarsudde **38**
Riddarholm Church **9**
Skansen **36**
Stadshuset **5**
Vasa Museum & the Royal
  Warship *Vasa* **34**

HOTELS ■
Collector's Lady
  Hamilton Hotel **10**
Grand Hotel **20**
Hotel Hellsten **1**
Hotel Skeppsholmen **24**
Hotel Stureplan **2**
Långholmen Hotel **7**
Lydmar **21**
Mälardrottningen **8**
Nordic Hotels **3**
Rex Hotel **1**
Rival Hotel **13**
Victory Hotel **12**

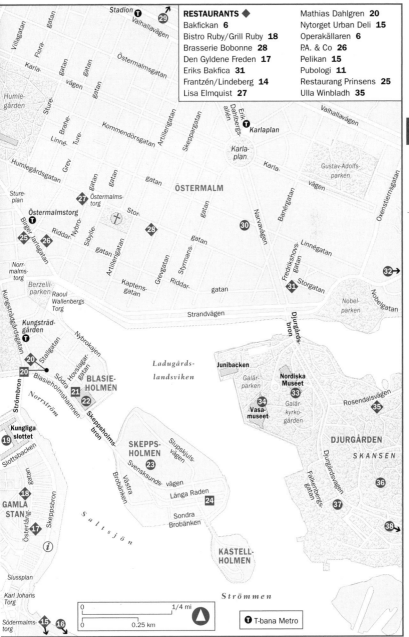

RESTAURANTS ◆

Bakfickan **6**
Bistro Ruby/Grill Ruby **18**
Brasserie Bobonne **28**
Den Gyldene Freden **17**
Eriks Bakfica **31**
Frantzén/Lindeberg **14**
Lisa Elmquist **27**

Mathias Dahlgren **20**
Nytorget Urban Deli **15**
Operakällaren **6**
P.A. & Co **26**
Pelikan **15**
Pubologi **11**
Restaurang Prinsens **25**
Ulla Winbladh **35**

Stadion

Karlaplan

Karla-plan

ÖSTERMALM

Östermalms-torg

Östermalmstorg

Gustav-Adolfs-parken

Sture-plan

Norr-malms-torg

Berzelii-parken

Raoul Wallenbergs Torg

Strandvägen

Nobel-parken

Kungsträd-gården

Ladugårds-landsviken

Junibacken

Galär-parken

Nordiska Museet

BLASIE-HOLMEN

Rosendalsvägen

Norrström

Vasa-museet

Galär-kyrko-gården

Kungliga slottet

SKEPPS-HOLMEN

DJURGÅRDEN

SKANSEN

GAMLA STAN

Slupskjuls-vägen

Svensksunds-vägen

Västra Brobänken

Länga Raden

Sondra Brobänken

KASTELL-HOLMEN

Slussplan

Karl Johans Torg

Södermalms-torg

Strömmen

Saltsjön

| 0 | | 1/4 mi |
| 0 | 0.25 km | |

🚇 T-bana Metro

18

Gauguin, plus a good Swedish section. The most important room in the gallery has one whole wall devoted to Rembrandt, and features his *Portrait of an Old Man, Portrait of an Old Woman,* and *Kitchen Maid.* The museum is closed for total refurbishment from February 2013 for a year. The collections will travel around Sweden and some will be displayed at the Royal Swedish Academy of Fine Arts (Fredsgatan 12; www.konstakademien.se; ℂ08/23-29-25).

Södra Blasieholmshamnen. www.nationalmuseum.se. ℂ **08/519-544-10.** Admission 100SEK adults, 80SEK students and seniors, free for ages 19 and under. Additional fees for special exhibitions. Free with Stockholm Card. Jun–Aug Tues 11am–8pm, Wed–Sun 11am–5pm; Sept–May Tues, Thurs 11am–8pm, Wed, Fri–Sun 11am–5pm. T-bana: Kungsträdgården. Bus: 2, 55, 62, 65, or 76.

Stadshuset (Stockholm City Hall) ★ GOVERNMENT BUILDING   Built in the Swedish "National Romantic Style," the Stockholm City Hall, on the island of Kungsholmen, is one of Europe's finest examples of modern architecture. Designed by Ragnar Ostberg, the red-brick structure is dominated by a lofty square tower, topped by three gilt crowns and the national coat of arms. The **Nobel Prize** banquet is held annually in the Blue Hall, its walls covered in around 18 million pieces of gold and colored mosaics made of special glass. The impressive southern gallery contains murals by Prins Eugens, the painter prince. You can only visit with a guided tour. In summer you can visit the tower for panoramic views over Stockholm.

Hantverksgatan 1. www.stockholm.se/cityhall. ℂ **08/508-290-58.** Admission Jan–Mar, Nov–Dec 60SEK adults, 50SEK students and seniors, 20SEK children 12–17, free for children 11 and under; Apr–Oct. 90SEK adults, 70SEK students and seniors, 40SEK children 12–17, free for children 11 and under; Tower May-Sept 40SEK. Free with Stockholm Card. City Hall tours daily on the hour 10am–4pm. T-bana: T- Centralen or Rådhuset. Bus: 3 or 62.

DJURGÅRDEN

Gröna Lund Tivoli ☺ AMUSEMENT PARK   For those who like Coney Island-type thrills, this is a good adventure park. Unlike its Copenhagen namesake, this is an amusement park, not a fantasyland. You'll find everything here from bumper cars to the Tunnel of Love to the Hall of Mirrors. The Blue Train takes you on a classic horror trip.

Lilla Allmänna Gränd 9. www.gronalund.com. ℂ **08/587-501-00.** Admission 95SEK; free for children 6 and under. All-day ride pass 299SEK. Late Apr to Sept daily noon–midnight (hours subject to weekly variation; check first). Bus: 44, 47. Tram: 7. Djurgården ferry from Nybroplan.

 CHANGING THE royal GUARD

It may not have the pomp of a similar show in London, but **Changing the Royal Guard** (*Vaktavlosning*) in Stockholm at least provides a photo op. In summer you can watch the parade of the military guard daily. In winter it takes place less frequently; on days when there's no parade, you can still see the changing of the guard. For information on the time of the march, ask at the Tourist Center. The event takes place at 12:15pm Monday to Saturday, 1:15pm Sunday from May to August; April, September, and October, Wednesday and Saturday 12:15pm, Sunday 1:15pm; November to March, Wednesday and Saturday noon, Sunday 1pm, in front of the Royal Palace.

Kaknästornet (Kaknäs Television Tower) 📷 OBSERVATION TOWER   Situated in the northern district of Djurgården, the tallest constructed structure in Scandinavia—a radio and television tower—stands 155m (509 ft.) high. Two elevators take visitors to an observation platform, where you can see everything from the cobblestone streets of Gamla Stan (Old Town) to the city's modern concrete-and-glass structures and the archipelago beyond. There's a very good restaurant and a cafe (free elevator ride to the top with table booking).

Mörkakroken. www.kaknastornet.se. 🕐 **08/667-21-05.** Elevator fee 45SEK adults, 20SEK children 7–15, free for children 6 and under. Mon–Sat 10am–9pm; Sun 10am–6pm. Closed Jan 1 and Dec 24–25. Bus: 69.

Nordiska Museet (Nordic Museum) ★★ MUSEUM   This museum houses an impressive collection of implements, costumes, and furnishings of Swedish life from the 1500s to the present, placing modern design within a historical context. The highlights are the period costumes ranging from matching garters and ties for men to purple flowerpot hats from the 1890s, and the small room settings. The museum gives you a very real insight into Swedish life, including nomadic Lappish customs.

Djurgårdsvägen 6–16. www.nordiskamuseet.se. 🕐 **08/519-546-00.** Admission 90SEK adults, free for ages 18 and under. Free with Stockholm Card. Daily 10am–5pm. Bus: 44 or 47.

Prins Eugens Waldemarsudde ★ ART MUSEUM   This once-royal residence is today an art museum and a memorial to one of the most famous royal artists in recent history, Prins Eugens (1865–1947). The youngest of King Oscar II's four children, he is credited with making innovative contributions to the techniques of Swedish landscape paintings, specializing in depictions of his favorite regions in central Sweden. Among his most visible works in the city are the murals on the inner walls of the Stadshuset. There's a charming restaurant and cafe, which is useful as this is at the eastern end of Djurgården and relatively remote.

Prins Eugens Väg 6. www.waldemarsudde.se. 🕐 **08/545-837-00.** Admission 100SEK adults, 80SEK seniors and students, free for ages 18 and under. Tues–Sun 11am–5pm (to 8pm Thurs). Tram: 7. Bus: 47.

Skansen ★★★ MUSEUM/ZOO   Often called "Old Sweden in a Nutshell," this 35-hectare (86-acre) open-air museum and zoological park contains more than 150 dwellings, most from the 18th and 19th centuries. You start in a complete town quarter, going into the old workshops and seeing how the early book publishers, silversmiths, and pharmacists worked. Handicrafts (glass-blowing, for example) are demonstrated here, along with peasant crafts like weaving and churning. Then walk through the park, past the old buildings brought here from all over Sweden, a windmill and manor houses, farm houses, and a temperance hall. You can also see wild animals from elk to bears and rare breeds. At the **Children's Zoo,** open May to September, children can ride on the ponies. There's a large stage and Skansen is famous for folk dancing and open-air concerts and Christmas festivities.

Djurgården 49–51. www.skansen.se. 🕐 **08/442-80-00.** Depending on time of day, day of the week, and season, admission is 70SEK–150SEK adults, 30SEK–60SEK children 6–15, free for children 5 and under. Free with Stockholm Card. Nov–mid-Mar weekdays 10am–3pm, Sat, Sun 10am–4pm; mid-March–end Apr 10am–4pm, May–June 1 10am–7pm; June 22–end Aug 10am–10pm, Sep 10am–6pm; Oct 10am–4pm. Bus: 47 from central Stockholm. Ferry from Slussen.

Vasa Museum & the Royal Warship Vasa ★★★ ☺ MUSEUM   This 17th-century man-of-war is the number one attraction in Scandinavia—and for good reason. Housed in a museum specially constructed for it at Djurgården near Skansen, the *Vasa* is the world's oldest identified and complete ship. In 1628, on its maiden voyage and in front of horrified onlookers, the ship capsized and sank to the bottom of the sea. When it was salvaged in 1961, more than 4,000 coins, carpenters' tools, and other items of archaeological interest were found onboard. Some 97% of the ship's 700 original sculptures were retrieved; and now carefully restored and preserved, they're back for all to see. The museum is stunning. Walking into the darkened space, the ship looms above you. Films and special exhibits surround the ship on several floors. You look into the glorious fated vessel and wonder about the lives of the crew, hundreds of years ago.

Galärvarvsvägen. www.vasamuseet.se. ✆ **08/519-548-00.** Admission 110SEK adults, 80SEK seniors and students, free for children 17 and under. Free with Stockholm Card. June–Aug daily 8:30am–6pm; Sept–May Wed 10am–8pm, Thurs–Tues 10am–5pm. Closed Jan 1 and Dec 23–25. Bus: 44, 47, or 69. Ferry from Slussen year-round, from Nybroplan in summer only.

SÖDERMALM

Fotografiska ★★   ART MUSEUM   This contemporary photography gallery in a former red-brick warehouse on the waterfront is Stockholm's latest attraction. It has six to seven major exhibitions each year featuring the world's top photographers, such as Steve Schapiro, whose stills from *The Godfather* are legendary, and André Kertész. Both historically important and contemporary photographers are exhibited and there are also subject-based exhibitions on figures like August Strindberg. Video installations complete the programs. There's an excellent cafe looking over the water, and a good bookshop.

Stadsgårdshamnen 22. www.fotograriska.eu. ✆ **08/509-005-00.** Adult 110SEK, seniors and students 80SEK, child under 12 years free. Daily 10am–9pm. Closed Midsummer's Eve and Dec 24. T-bana: Slussen then short walk.

JUST OUTSIDE STOCKHOLM

Drottningholm Palace ★★★ PALACE   Designed by the royal architect Nicodemus Tessin the Elder (1615–81) and inspired by Versailles, Drottningholm is a delightful palace built on an island in Lake Mälaren about 11km (6¾ miles) from the center of Stockholm. Today it's a UNESCO World Heritage site. The palace, loaded with courtly art and furnishings, sits amid fountains and parks, and functions as one of the royal family's official residences. It's also their favorite. Set in spacious grounds, the palace has State Rooms as well as more intimate, private apartments and rooms. The most pleasant way to reach the palace is by boat, slipping past marshes and inlets, hidden houses, and boatyards.

In the grounds is one of the most perfectly preserved 18th-century theaters in the world, **Drottningholm Court Theater** (www.dtm.se; ✆ **08/759-04-06**). The theater can be visited only as part of a guided tour, which focuses on the original sets and stage mechanisms. Between June and August, the theater puts on a summer festival of some 30 performances, devoted almost exclusively to 18th-century opera. See p. 979 for details.

Ekerö, Drottningholm. ✆ **08/402-62-80.** Palace 100SEK adults, 50SEK students and ages 7 to 18, free for children 6 and under; in summer inc the Chinese Pavilion. Adult 145SEK, students and children 7 to 18 years 50SEK, free for children under 7 years. Free with Stockholm Card. Theater

Stieg Larsson's Millennium Tour

Since the book, the TV series, and the films opened the world's eyes to a Sweden that was unexpectedly violent and antisocial, the streets of Södermalm are full of earnest Stieg Larsson fans walking the streets and looking at the buildings where Mikael Blomkvist and Lisbeth Salander and a host of odd characters played out their particular drama. You can book a guided tour at the Stadsmuseum, Slussen (www.stadsmuseum.stockholm. se; ☎ **08/508-31-600**), or at the Stockholm Tourist Centre (see p. 962). The walk starts at Bellmansgtan 1 and takes about 2 hours. English tours run on Saturdays and some Wednesdays all year round (more frequent in summer) and cost 140SEK. Or buy the Millennium map (40SEK) at the Stockholm Tourist Center and do the walk by yourself.

guided tour 90SEK adults, 70SEK students, free for children under 16 years. Palace Dec 31 to mid-Mar daily noon–3.30pm (closed 2nd week in Jan); Mar–Apr Fri–Sun 11am–3.30pm; May–Aug daily 10am–4.30pm; Sept daily 11am–3.30pm; Nov–end 1st week of Dec Sat, Sun noon–3.30pm. Closed Mid–end Dec. Out of season check the website for extra openings/closings. Theater guided tours May–Aug daily 11am–4:30pm; Sept daily noon–3pm. T-bana: Brommaplan, and then bus 301 or 323 to Drottningholm; or from Stockholm center 177 or 178. Ferry from the dock near City Hall, call ☎ **08/587-140-00**.

Millesgården ★★ MUSEUM/PARK Don't miss Carl Milles's former villa and sculpture garden beside the sea on the island of Lidingö, just northeast of Stockholm. Milles (1875–1955) studied under Rodin and became Sweden's most famous sculptor. Millesgården is a beautiful site with stunning views and the museum is fascinating. Many of his best-known works are displayed in the gardens, plus works of other artists.

Carl Milles Väg 2, Lidingö. www.millesgarden.se. ☎ **08/446-75-90**. Admission 100SEK adults, 80SEK seniors and students, free for ages 19 and under. Free with Stockholm Card. May–Sept daily 11am–5pm; Oct–Apr Tues–Sun 11am–5pm. T-bana: Ropsten, and then bus to Torsviks Torg or train to Norsvik.

ORGANIZED TOURS

The quickest and most convenient way to see the highlights of Stockholm is to take one of the bus tours that leave from Karl XII Torg, near the Kungsträdgården. **City Sightseeing** (www.city-sightseeing.com; ☎ **08/587-140-20**) operates a 24-hour Hop-on, Hop-off Sightseeing Tour of the city, including the Nybro Ferry. The tour costs 220SEK for adults, 50SEK for ages 6 to 11, and free for kids 5 and under. The bus takes you to the highlights of Stockholm, and you can get off, see what you want, and then continue on the next bus.

Stockholm Sightseeing, Skeppsbron 22 (www.stromma.se; ☎ **08/120-040-00**), offers a variety of tours, mostly in the summer. "Under the Bridges" takes 2 hours and goes through two locks and two bodies of water. Departures are from Strömkajen (near the Grand Hotel), daily from Apr to November. The cost is 210SEK (children 6–11 105SEK, under 5s free). The 1-hour "Royal Canal Tour" costs 160SEK and leaves daily 10:30am to 3:30pm year-round from the shady canal of Djurgården. The company also operates dinner cruises, cruises out to the Archipelago, and other Stockholm boat tours.

Where to Eat

CITY CENTER

If you're into gourmet and ethnic foods, stop at **Hötorgshallen** (www.hotorgshallen.
se; T-bana: Hötorget), an indoor market with 32 stores and cafes. Food specialties
from all over the world are sold here, including delectable lamb, bitter orange marmalade, fresh shellfish, rare jams (some from Nordic climes), cheeses, and all kinds
of meats. The market dates from the 13th century, although the present building is
more recent. It's an ideal place to grab something to eat and take in the cultural dif-
fusion of Sweden.

The better known **Östermalms Saluhall** is gourmet Sweden at its best. A very
good selection of delicatessen foods from reindeer smoked and marinated in a dozen
different ways to fish and seafood, vegetables, cheeses, and more make this one of
the most tempting places and great for those looking for a picnic.

Eating in Stockholm is expensive, with alcohol startlingly so. However, most restaurants, including the priciest, serve a daily lunch which is always extremely good
value. So it's worth checking those out. Also, breakfast at the hotels is very good value,
with a large selection of sweet and savory possibilities.

Very Expensive

Mathias Dahlgren ★★★ SWEDISH/INTERNATIONAL   At this exclusive
restaurant, two different dining experiences complement each other: the *Matsalen*
("Dining Room") and *Matbaren* ("Food Bar"). Mathias Dahlgren leads the list of Sweden's top chefs. He is known for his surprising combinations of taste, his contrasting
textures, and his highly evolved sauces. Changing seasonally, a spring menu might
include sashimi in cucumber, ginger, horseradish, soy, and herbs; and leek, oysters,
and clams with mussel cappuccino and the flavors of the sea. Main courses might be
a simple, but perfectly executed seared filet of turbot with potatoes, onions, and
herbs; or fried veal sweetbreads with white asparagus and morels. There's also a top
vegetarian menu (with some fish included). The main Matsalen is small, intimate and
very chic. Guests pass through a sea-blue bar on their way to the Matbaren (Food
Bar), a modern bistro with contemporary dishes, all produced with imagination and
using fresh local ingredients, such as baked cauliflower creme with truffle, Gruyere,
and hazelnuts; fried lemon sole with new potatoes, raw vegetables, lemon, mayonnaise, and dill and a wildly popular dessert of oven-baked wild chocolate from
Colombia.

In the Grand Hotel, Södra Blasieholmshamnen 8. www.mdghs.com. ✆ **08/679-35-84.** Reservations required. *Matsalen* menu 1,650SEK; *Matbaren* mains 130SEK–285SEK. AE, DC, MC, V. *Matsalen* Tues–Sat 7pm–midnight; *Matbaren* Mon–Fri noon–2pm, Mon–Sat 6pm–midnight. T-bana:
Kungsträdgården.

Operakällaren (The Opera House) ★★★ FRENCH/SWEDISH   Opposite
the Royal Palace, this famous and unashamedly luxurious restaurant is so elegant it
takes you straight to a banquet at the royal court, which the restaurant also caters for.
The cooking is classic French with a Swedish twist in the remarkable fresh and different flavors. Dishes like seared scallops with onion salad and a potato and leek
cream come in a mussel foam. Then try the likes of spring lamb with leek terrine in
a wild garlic and nettle foam. Swedish ingredients like salmon and game, including
grouse from the northern forests, are prepared in various ways. And as you'd expect,
everything is beautifully presented and served.

Operahuset, Kungsträdgården. www.operakallaren.se. ✆ **08/676-58-01** or **08/676-58-00.** Reservations required. Main courses 300SEK–495SEK; 4-course fixed-price menu 1,100SEK; 9-course menu dégustation 1,400SEK, with wine 2,900SEK. AE, DC, MC, V. Tues–Sat 6pm–midnight. Closed July. T-bana: Kungsträdgården.

Moderate

Bakfickan ★ 🏛 SWEDISH   Tucked away behind the Operakällaren, the "Hip Pocket" is a chic place to eat for a moderate price. It shares a kitchen with its glamorous neighbor Operakällaren (see above), but is more laid-back and casual and concentrates on Swedish traditional cooking. Locals come here for classics like crayfish toast; prawn salad; salmon with dill creamed potatoes; and that staple of Swedish cooking, meatballs with potato puree and lingonberry preserve. Seasonal reindeer and elk appear, and in summer order rich ice cream with a sauce of arctic cloudberries. You can eat in the main part or join the locals at the horseshoe-shaped bar.

Jakobs Torg 12. www.operakallaren.se. ✆ **08/676-58-09.** Reservations not accepted. Main courses 160SEK–290SEK. AE, DC, MC, V. Mon–Fri 11:30am–11pm. Sat noon–10pm. T-bana: Kungsträdgården.

Brasserie Bobonne ★ 🏛 BRASSERIE   A local feel to this small friendly restaurant with daily dishes chalked up on a board and an open kitchen makes this a winner. The French brasserie theme carries through with dishes like warm goat's cheese or snails to start, followed by boeuf bourguignon or calf's liver with peppers and beetroot. Sorbets, soufflés, or crème brulée finish off an excellent meal that would not be out of place in Paris.

Storgatan 12. www.bobonne.se. ✆ **08/660-03-18.** Reservations recommended. Main courses 185SEK–295SEK; menu 498SEK. AE, MC, V. Mon–Sat 5–11pm. T-bana: Östermalmstorg.

Eriks Bakfica 🦐 SWEDISH   Of the three "Eriks" restaurants in Stockholm, this small, relatively inexpensive branch offers particularly good value. Established in 1979, it features a handful of Swedish dishes from the tradition of husmanskost (wholesome home cooking). Longtime classic favorites include a starter of seafood toast with shrimps, lobster, scallop, and lemon; and reindeer steak with caulifower, artichoke puree, herb sauce, and hash brown potatoes for a main dish. Fish is particularly varied; the shellfish platter groans with piscatorial goodies. You might also try Eriks's famous cheeseburger with the special secret sauce, but you have to ask for it—you won't find it on the menu.

Storgatan 12. www.eriks.se ✆ **08/660-03-18.** Reservations recommended. Main courses 195SEK–295SEK. Set menu 495SEK. AE, DC, MC, V. Mon–Fri 11:30am–2.30pm and 5pm–1am; Sat 4pm–1am. Bus: 47.

Lisa Elmquist ★ ☺ SEAFOOD   Under the soaring roof of the main hall, amid the food stalls of Stockholm's tantalizing produce market (the **Östermalms Saluhall**), you'll find this likable cafe and oyster bar. Because of its good food, this is the most popular choice for Stockholm families visiting the market. It's owned by one of the city's largest fish distributors, so its menu varies with the catch. Some patrons come here just for shrimp with bread and butter. Typical dishes include fish soup, salmon cutlets, and sautéed filet of lemon sole. This is an authentic "taste of Sweden," done exceedingly well.

Östermalms Saluhall, Nybrogatan 31. www.lisaelmqvist.se. ✆ **08/553-404-10.** Reservations recommended. Main courses 248SEK–320SEK. AE, DC, MC, V. Mon–Thurs 9.30am–6pm; Fri 9.30am–7pm, Sat 9.30am–4pm. T-bana: Östermalmstorg.

P.A.& Co ★ ☺ BISTRO   The small neighborhood restaurant always seems full of groups of friends and families, a popular choice as much for the atmosphere as for the good-value classics. Go here for dishes like veal burgers with potatoes and lingonberry sauce, pastas, and sausages, all chalked up on boards. A meal here is filling and, for Stockholm, inexpensive.

Riddargatan 8. www.paco.se. ℂ **08/611-08-45.** Main courses 155SEK–250SEK. AE, DC, MC, V. Daily 5pm–midnight. T-bana Östermalmstorg.

Restaurang Prinsens ★ SWEDISH   A 2-minute walk from Stureplan, this artists' haunt is increasingly popular with foreign visitors. It looks like a typical brasserie with wood-paneled walls covered in pictures of some of the famous and contented customers it's been serving since 1897. The fresh, flavorful cuisine is Swedish-based food prepared in a conservative French style. Order the likes of gaspacho with scallop and basil sorbet, bouillabaisse, and traditional Swedish dishes such as veal with homemade lingonberry preserves, sautéed fjord salmon, and roulades of beef. For dessert, try the homemade vanilla ice cream. Later in the evening, the restaurant becomes something of a drinking club and there's an outside terrace for the summer.

Mäster Samuelsgatan 4. www.restaurangenprinsen.eu. ℂ **08/611-13-31.** www.restaurangprinsen. com. Reservations recommended. Main courses 199SEK–369SEK. Set menu 495SEK. AE, DC, MC, V. Mon–Fri 11:30am–11:30pm; Sat, Sun 1–11pm. T-bana: Östermalmstorg.

GAMLA STAN (OLD TOWN)
Very Expensive
Frantzén/Lindeberg ★★★ FRENCH/AMERICAN   The most talked-about restaurant in Sweden is not for the faint-hearted and is something of a foodies' haven. The young owners describe the restaurant as a stage for their creativity and you're in for an extraordinary and unusual performance. Using Swedish ingredients where possible, including vegetables from their own kitchen garden, you hand yourself over to the chefs. Dishes like oysters with frozen apple, cream, and juniper; reindeer tartar paired with caviar; and scallops with truffle are presented. You never quite know what to expect as the menu is changed daily according to the market. It's expensive, but another example of top Nordic cooking that is definitely different from the French style.

Lilla Nygatan 21. www.frantzen-lindeberg.com. ℂ **08/20-85-80.** Reservations necessary. Set menu 1,900SEK. AE, DC, MC, V. Tues–Sat 7pm–11pm. T-bana: Gamla Stan.

Expensive
Bistro Ruby/Grill Ruby ★★ FRENCH/AMERICAN   Two restaurants side by side that epitomize Paris/Texas. Bistro Ruby is classic French, where caviar comes with blinis, fried moules with aioli, and venison with root vegetable gratin. Grill Ruby goes more American mainstream from crab cakes with lime aioli to great steaks and hamburgers from the chargrill. You can eat at the bar in both places, or take a table in the wooden-floored main restaurants.

Österlånggatan 14. www.grillruby.com. Bistro Ruby ℂ **08/20-57-76.** Main courses 189SEK–395SEK. Mon–Sat 5pm–midnight, Grill Ruby ℂ **08/20-60-15.** Main courses 199SEK–499SEK. Mon–Fri 5pm–midnight; Sat, Sun noon–midnight. AE, DC, MC, V. T-bana: Gamla Stan.

Den Gyldene Freden ★ SWEDISH   'Golden Peace,' said to be Stockholm's oldest tavern, opened in 1722. The Swedish Academy owns the building, and members frequent the place every Thursday night. The cozy dining rooms on three floors are named after former patrons who were Swedish historical figures. Popular today with a mix of artists, lawyers, and poets, it's known for traditional Swedish cooking with a modern interpretation. Expect fresh Baltic fish and game from the forests. A selection of herrings prepared in different ways is a favorite appetizer, as are dishes like pork terrine, and foie gras. Main courses run from a simple fried lemon sole to veal and wild garlic sausage with veal tongue, green peas, and caper sauce. Desserts are equally imaginative with a hazelnut savarin with elderflower sorbet, meringue, raspberry cream, and berries providing a fitting climax to an excellent meal.

Österlånggatan 51. www.gyldenefreden.se. (℃) **08/24-97-60.** Reservations recommended. Main courses 195SEK–385SEK. Menus 405SEK–645SEK. AE, DC, MC, V. Mon–Thurs 11:30am–2:30pm and 5–10pm; Fri 11.30am–2.30pm and 5–10pm; Sat 1–11pm. T-bana: Gamla Stan.

Pubologi ★★ ⚑ 🏠 GASTROPUB   Under the ownership of the Collectors Hotel group, this is Sweden's answer to the British gastropub/wine bar. Sit on high barstool chairs at a long communal table running down the middle, or at tables along the side of the long narrow room. Plates come as half courses, so you can mix and match excellent charcuterie platters with beef tartar with oyster juice and salad, or order a classic hamburger. Cheeses are from Philippe Olivier in France. The meal is then priced according to the number of plates you order. The "Todo" menu consists of 10 courses of everything and dessert, all of which you can share. Good wine list, buzzing atmosphere, great fun.

Stora Nygatan 20. www.pubologi.se. (℃) **08/506-400-86.** One plate 175SEK, 2 plates 330SEK, 3 plates 480SEK, 10-course "Todo" menu 795SEK. AE, DC, MC, V. Mon–Sat 5.30–11.30pm. Closed July. T-bana: Gamla Stan.

DJURGÅRDEN
Expensive
Ulla Winbladh ★ SWEDISH   Since it opened in 1994, this romantic, old-fashioned restaurant has been a favorite with Stockholm's restaurant aficionados. It's in a white stone structure, built as part of Stockholm's International Exposition of 1897. There's a large dining room decorated with works by Swedish artists, and a summer-only outdoor terrace decorated with flowering plants. The menu focuses on conservative Swedish cuisine, all impeccably prepared. Perhaps order marinated salmon with mustard sauce or seafood cocktail of scallops, lobster, and shrimp with avocado cream. Fish selections continue with mains of seabass or steamed cod. Meat dishes are equally well prepared; try apple-smoked pork belly with apple and parsley salad, or spring lamb with sweetbreads and Swedish goat cheese.

Rosendalsvägen 8. www.ullawinbladh.se. (℃) **08/534-89-701.** Reservations required. Main courses 185SEK–325SEK. AE, DC, MC, V. Mon 11:30am–10pm; Tues–Fri 11:30am–11pm; Sat 12:30–11pm; Sun 12:30–10pm. Bus: 47 or 69.

SÖDERMALM
Moderate
Nytorget Urban Deli ★ SWEDISH   This buzzing deli, food hall, bakery, and very trendy restaurant/bar reinforces Södermalm's reputation as the place to be in the Swedish capital. With a New York feel to it, Stockholm's urbanites dine off charcuterie, oysters, salads, seafood, and excellent steaks. Weekend brunches set the seal on this smart, popular joint.

Nytorget 4. www.urbandeli.org. (℃) **08/599-091-80.** Main courses 190SEK–365SEK. AE, VC, V. Sun–Tues 8am–11pm, Wed–Thurs 8am–midnight, Fri, Sat 8am–1am. Bus 2.

Inexpensive

Pelikan SWEDISH   This old-stager caters for everybody, from locals after a beer to artists, musicians, and tourists. There's a bar, a smart restaurant, and the best place to eat—an echoing wood-paneled large room with walls painted with animal and plant paintings in a vaguely Art Deco style. Service is brisk and friendly; food is a run through the Swedish classics. Pickled herrings and cheese or asparagus soup with roe and sour cream to start; salmon with dill creamed potatoes, meatballs with a cream sauce and lingonberries; boiled knuckle of pork with mash and mustard are all dishes most Swedes grew up with. Fun, unpretentious, noisy and good value.

Blekingegatan 40. www.pelikan.se. ☎ **08/556-090-90.** Main courses 168SEK–252SEK. AE, MC, V. Mon–Thurs 4pm–midnight, Fri, Sat 1pm–1am, Sun 1pm–midnight. T-bana: Skanstull.

Shopping

A whopping 25% goods tax makes shopping in Sweden expensive, and you can buy most items at home for less money. On the positive side, Swedish stores usually stock items of the highest quality. Swedish glass is world famous; wooden items are outstanding, and many people love the functional furniture in blond pine or birch. Other items to look for include children's playsuits, silver necklaces, reindeer gloves, hand-woven neckties and skirts, sweaters and mittens in Nordic patterns, clogs, and colorful handicrafts from the provinces. The most famous souvenir is the Dala horse from Dalarna.

For details on **tax rebates** on local goods, go to the "Fast Facts: Stockholm" section, earlier in this chapter.

For gift shopping and window-shopping, explore the boutiques, art galleries, and jewelry stores along the streets of **Gamla Stan** (especially **Västerlånggatan**). For alternative fashion and cutting-edge boutiques, go to **Södermalm's Götgatan** in the area known as SoFo (south of Folkingagatan). Attractive shops and galleries can also be found along **Hornsgats-Puckeln** (Hornsgatan-Hunchback, a reference to the shape of the street). Other good browsing streets are around **Stureplan,** and **Hamngatan, Birger Jarlsgatan, Biblioteksgatan,** and **Kungsgatan,** all in **Norrmalm.**

In the center of Stockholm, the largest department store in Sweden is **Åhléns City,** Klarabergsgatan 50 (www.ahlens.se; ☎ **08/676-60-00;** T-bana: T-Centralen), with a gift shop, a restaurant, and a famous food department. Also seek out the fine collection of home textiles and Orrefors and Kosta crystal ware. **Nordiska Kompaniet (NK),** Hamngatan 18–20 (www.nk.se; ☎ **08/762-80-00;** T-bana: Kungsträdgården), is the best high-quality department store. Most of the big names in Swedish glass are displayed at NK, plus high fashion. Swedish handcrafted items are in the basement.

Entertainment & Nightlife

Pick up the free monthly magazine **What's On Stockholm,** distributed at the Tourist Center in Vasagatan (see "Visitor Information," earlier in this chapter), to see what's on.

THE PERFORMING ARTS

All the major opera, theater, and concert seasons begin in autumn, except for special summer festival performances. Most of the major opera and theatrical performances are funded by the state, which often means reasonable ticket prices.

Founded by Gustavus III in 1766, the **Drottningholm Court Theater,** Drottningholm (www.dtm.se; ✆ **08/759-04-06;** T-bana: Brommaplan, then bus no. 301 or 323; boat from the City Hall in Stockholm), is on an island in Lake Mälaren, 11km (6¾ miles) from Stockholm. It stages operas and ballets with full 18th-century regalia, period costumes, and wigs, and using original machinery and 30 or more complete theater sets. Seating only 450, this is one of the most unusual entertainment experiences in Sweden. The season is from May to September. Most performances begin at 8pm and last 2½ to 4 hours. Many performances sell out far in advance to season-ticket holders. For tickets to the evening performances, which range in cost from 274SEK to 895SEK, book at the Stockholm Tourist Centre, online at www.ticnet.se, or call ✆ **+46 77-170-70-70** (from Europe). See p. 962.

Filharmonikerna I Konserthuset (Concert Hall), Hötorget 8 (www.konserthuset.se; ✆ **08/50-66-77-88;** T-bana: Hötorget), home of the **Royal Stockholm Philharmonic Orchestra,** is the principal place to hear classical music in Sweden. (The Nobel Prizes are also awarded here.) Box-office hours are Monday to Friday 11am to 6pm, Saturday 11am to 3pm. Tickets are 70SEK to 350SEK.

Founded in 1773 by Gustavus III (who was later assassinated here at a masked ball), the **Operahuset (Royal Opera House),** Gustav Adolfs Torg (www.operan.se; ✆ **08/24-82-40;** T-bana: Kungsträdgården), is the home of the Royal Swedish Opera and the Royal Swedish Ballet. Performances in the glorious building dating from 1898 are usually Monday to Saturday at 7:30pm (closed mid-June to Aug). The box office is open Monday to Friday 10am to 6pm (until 7:30pm on performance nights) and Saturday noon to 3pm. Tickets cost from 60SEK to 790SEK; ask about the 10%-to-30% senior and student discounts.

BARS & PUBS

Cadierbaren (Cadier Bar), Södra Blasieholmshamnen 8 (www.grandhotel.se; ✆ **08/679-35-85;** T-bana: Kungsträdgården), is one of the most sophisticated places in Stockholm. From the bar in the Grand Hotel—one of the most famous hotels in Europe—you'll have a view of the harbor and the Royal Palace. Light meals—open-faced sandwiches and smoked salmon—are served all day in the extension overlooking the waterfront. Cocktails cost around 150SEK to 160SEK. It's open Monday to Friday 7am to 2am, Saturday 8am to 2am, and Sundays 8am to 1am.

Guldbaren, Norrmalmstorg 2–4 (www.nobishotel.se; ✆ **08/614-10-00;** T-bana: T-Centralen), has become one of Stockholm's great after-work meeting places. It glitters with its gold decoration and gets very crowded, so take your drinks into the soaring atrium inside the hotel or chill out on the terrace. Cocktails are around 150SEK. It's open Monday to Thursday and Sunday 5pm to 1am, Friday and Saturday 4pm to midnight.

Kvarnen, Tjarhovsgatan 4 in Södermalm (www.kvarnen.com; ✆ **08/643-03-80;** T-bana: Medborgarplatsen), was pretty well known before it appeared in Stieg Larsson's Millennium trilogy (the girls' band Evil Fingers plays here, watched by Lisbeth Salander). It's crowded, noisy, and great fun. DJs spin the music most nights. Entrance for shows only is around 130SEK. Beers from 65SEK.

CLUBS & LIVE MUSIC

Café Opera, Operahuset, Kungsträdgården (www.cafeopera.se; ✆ **08/676-58-07;** T-bana: Kungsträdgården)—Swedish Beaux Arts at its best—functions as a brasserie-style restaurant during dinner hours and is one of the most popular nightclubs in Stockholm late at night. Near the entrance of the cafe a stairway leads to one of the

Opera House's most beautiful corners, the clublike Operabaren (Opera Bar). Cover is 220SEK. Café Opera is open Wednesday to Sunday 10pm to 3am.

Sturecompagniet in Östermalm at Sturegatan 4 (www.sturecompagniet.se; ✆ **08/545-076-10;** T-bana: Östermalmstorg), is the chicest of venues. It's difficult to get into unless you're dressed right. Go early; there's less competition. Expect the young and trendy aged between 23 and 30 in any of the various bars and dance floors. It's open Tuesday to Saturday 10pm to 3am. Cover is 120SEK.

Small, cozy, and internationally well known, **Fasching,** Kungsgatan 63, Norrmalm (www.fasching.se; ✆ **08/534-829-60;** T-bana: T-Centralen), is one of the most visible of the jazz clubs of Stockholm, with top artists appearing from North America, Europe, and around the world. Cramped to the point of claustrophobia, you're very close to the performers. After the end of most live acts, there's likely to be dancing to salsa, soul, and perhaps R&B. The club is usually open Monday to Saturday from 8pm to at least midnight. Cover costs vary from 60SEK to 170SEK (if there is a big star, the price can reach 400SEK).

Engelen, Kornhamnstorg 59, Gamla Stan (www.engelen.se; ✆ **08/50-55-60-90;** T-bana: Gamla Stan), is a restaurant, pub, and nightclub. Eat some of the best steaks in town in the restaurant, open Sunday to Thursday 5 to 11:30pm, Friday and Saturday 5pm to 1:30am (main courses 151SEK to 220SEK). Live performances, usually soul, funk, and rock by Swedish groups, take over the pub daily from 8:30pm to midnight. The pub is open daily from 4pm to 3am. Club Kolingen is a dance club nightly from 10pm to about 3am. It charges the same food and drink prices as the pub, and you must be 23 or over to enter. Cover runs from 70SEK to 100SEK after 8pm.

Pet Sounds Bar, Skånegatan 80 (www.petsoundsbar.se; ✆ **08/643-82-25;** T-bana: Medborgarplatsesn), started out life in the eponymous rock store opposite. There's a good restaurant (main courses from 210SEK to 240SEK), a bar and the cellar where guest DJs pound out the music. There are also club nights. Open Tuesday to Sunday 5pm to 1am. Charges for the music vary.

THE LGBT SCENE

Looking for a nonconfrontational bar peopled with regular guys who happen to be gay? Consider a round or two at **Sidetrack,** Wollmar Yxkullsgatan 7 (www.sidetrack. nu; ✆ **08/641-16-88;** T-bana: Mariatorget). Small and committed to shunning trendiness, it's named after the founder's favorite gay bar in Chicago. It's open Wednesday to Saturday night from 6pm to 1am. Other nights are fine, too—Sidetrack is something like a Swedish version of a bar and lounge at the local bowling alley where everyone happens to be into same-sex encounters.

Many gays and lesbians gather at **Torget,** Mälartorget 13 (✆ **08/20-55-60;** T-bana: Gamla Stan), a cozy, Victorian-era cafe and bar in the Old City (Gamla Stan) that's open for food every afternoon and for drinks around 5pm until around midnight. Sunday nights are famous all over Europe at **Patricia,** Stadsgårdskajen 152 (www.patricia.se; ✆ **08/743-05-70;** T-bana: Slussen). The boat was built in Middlesbrough, England, in 1938 and became the British royals' private yacht. Today it has a restaurant, live music, and DJs. It's open Wednesday and Thursday 5pm to midnight, Friday and Saturday 6pm to 5am, and Sunday 6pm to 3am.

For an online version of the online gay and lesbian magazine *QX,* which is available in hard copy in newsstands, go to www.qx.se.

Where to Stay

By the standards of many North American cities, hotels in Stockholm are very expensive. If the prices make you want to cancel your trip, read on. Dozens of hotels offer reduced rates on weekends all year and daily from around mid-June to mid-August. For further information, inquire at a travel agency or the tourist office (see "Visitor Information," above). In the summer, it's best to make reservations in advance just to be on the safe side.

Most medium-priced hotels are in Norrmalm or Vasastaden, north of the Old Town, and many of the least expensive lodgings are near the Central Station. There are comparably priced inexpensive accommodations within 10 to 20 minutes of the city, easily reached by subway, streetcar, or bus. We'll suggest a few hotels in the Old Town, but they're limited and more expensive.

Note: In most cases a service charge ranging from 10% to 15% is included in the bill, plus the inevitable 25% moms value added tax. Unless otherwise indicated, all our recommended accommodations come with a private bathroom.

Very Expensive

Grand Hotel ★★★ Opposite the Royal Palace over the water, this hotel—a bastion of elite hospitality since 1874 and a member of Leading Hotels of the World—is the finest in Sweden. The style is classic with a touch of King Gustav in the spacious guest rooms, traditional furniture, sparkling chandeliers, and comfortably large sofas and chairs. The public rooms are just as grand, with plasterwork ceilings and wooden paneling. Matthias Dahlgren offers gourmet cooking in his restaurant Matsalen and more casual bistro dishes at Matbaren (see p. 974). The hotel's Verandah restaurant has a great view and an all-year-round smorgasbord, while the elegant Cadier bar makes a great meeting place. The priciest rooms overlook the water. The hotel's ballroom is an exact copy of Louis XIV's Hall of Mirrors at Versailles. The Nordic Spa is just as chic.

Södra Blasieholmshamnen 8, 103 27 Stockholm. www.grandhotel.se. ℰ **08/679-35-60** or **800/745-8883** in the U.S. and Canada. Fax 08/679-35-61. 368 units. 3,900SEK–15,00SEK double. AE, DC, MC, V. Parking 495SEK. T-bana: Kungsträdgården. Bus: 46, 55, 62, or 76. **Amenities:** 2 restaurants; bar; exercise room; spa; concierge; room service; babysitting. *In room:* A/C (in some), minibar, hair dryer, Wi-Fi (free).

Expensive

Lydmar ★★★ Stockholm's latest boutique hotel has become the most fashionable place to stay in the capital. Located by the National Museum and looking over to the Royal Palace, it's relaxed and welcoming with no signs outside to give it away. You walk into a light-filled entrance with dramatic photographs on the walls that change regularly. Bedrooms all have a different decor and vary in size. The restaurant resembles a library with a booklined wall on one side and views over the water on the other. Feeling more like a grand town house than a hotel, it's decorated with objects scattered throughout and great flower arrangements. It's become a favorite meeting place for fashionable young locals, particularly with its open-air first-floor terrace. The whole place is chic, comfortable and self-assured and is run by a young, knowledgeable, and helpful staff.

Södra Blasieholmshamnen 2, 103–24 Stockholm. www.lydmar.com. ℰ **08/22-31-60.** Fax 08/223-170. 46 units. 3,200SEK–12,500SEK double. Rates include breakfast. AE, DC, MC, V. Parking 220SEK. Bus: 46 or 53. **Amenities:** Restaurant; bar; concierge; room service; babysitting. *In room:* TV, A/C, minibar, Wi-Fi (free).

Nordic Hotels ★★ 🛍 Two hotels side by side, **Nordic Sea** and **Nordic Light** have always been cutting edge. According to *Elle UK* magazine, Nordic Light is "The World's Sexiest Hotel." You're given a choice of a room of "watery calm" in the 367-room Nordic Sea, all of which were renovated in 2011, or different lighting systems in the "Mood" bedrooms in the 175-room Nordic Light. Each hotel has its own individual design. Nordic Sea turns to the ocean for its inspiration and features a huge aquarium. Nordic Light is filled with sun-shaped projections that guarantee a bright light even on the darkest winter days. The suggestive light patterns projecting from the walls recreate the ever-changing patterns of the lights of the north. These hotels are not just about gimmicks—they offer real comfort. Nordic Light guest rooms have the best sound insulation in town. Wood, steel, and glass create both clublike and maritime auras in Nordic Sea rooms.

Vasaplan 4 and 7, 101 37 Stockholm. www.nordicseahotel.se. ℂ**08/505-630-00** or **800/337-4685** in the U.S. Fax 08/50-56-30-40. 367 units in Nordic Sea, 1,080SEK–2,820SEK double; 175 units in Nordic Light (www.nordiclighthotel.se/en) 2,600SEK–3,750SEK double. AE, DC, MC, V. T-bana: Centralen. **Amenities:** Restaurant; 2 bars; babysitting; exercise room; spa; sauna; steam bath; concierge; room service; Wi-Fi (120SEK per day). *In room:* TV, minibar, hair dryer.

Moderate

Hotel Hellsten ★★ 🛍 The Hellsten was the first of the four Stockholm hotels owned and run by Per Hellsten, and it's full of individual touches that make it stand out from its fellows. You enter the late-19th-century building down a dark passageway into the reception, lounge, and bar, decorated with colonial artifacts and photographs from Per Hellsten's Africa days. The striking decor continues in the bedrooms, which sport strong colors, wooden floors, rich fabrics, and dramatic four-poster beds. Some have delightful ceramic stoves. It all makes you feel as if you're in a Strindberg production. Bathrooms, by contrast, are chic and modern. Located on a quiet residential street, this well-kept secret provides a delightful stay.

Luntmakargatan 68, 113 51 Stockholm. www.hellsten.se. ℂ **08/661-86-00.** Fax 08/661-86-01. 78 units. 1,290SEK–2,690SEK double. Rates include breakfast. AE, DC, MC, V. T-bana: Rådmansgatan. **Amenities:** Breakfast room; bar; exercise room, sauna. *In room:* TV, hair dryer, Wi-Fi (free).

Hotel Skeppsholmen ★★★ 🛍 ☺ Two long, three-storey historic buildings, originally built for the navy in 1699, have been converted into this charming hotel. Rooms are relatively small but have been cleverly designed to feel larger. They are decorated in a simple, very chic Scandinavian style, with stripped wood floors, natural fabrics, and modern furniture; bathrooms are equally stylish and well thought out and come with beautiful stone basins. Generous windows give a fantastic view over the water to Södermalm. Located on the tiny island of Skeppsholmen, this is the most rural of Stockholm's hotels, but just a stone's throw from the Museum of Modern Art. Adding to the away-from-it-all feeling is the ferry that plies between Södermalm and Djurgården. The restaurant serves modern Scandinavian food and the terrace fills up in summer with people relaxing over a drink.

Gröna Gången 1. www.hotelskeppsholmen.se. ℂ **08/407-23-00.** Fax 08/407-23-99. 81 units. 1,595SEK–2,595SEK double. Rates include breakfast. AE, DC, MC, V. Parking 250SEK per night. Bus: 65. **Amenities:** Restaurant; bar; sauna. *In room:* TV, A/C, hair dryer, Wi-Fi (free).

Hotel Stureplan ★ Just north of Stureplan shopping mall and a whole collection of good restaurants, this is a boutique hotel with two different styles. Housed in a 19th-century building, large, high-ceilinged rooms in the main hotel are elegant with comfortable furniture and crisp linen. One floor has a delightful living room and library. The modern rooms on the Penthouse floor have fitted carpets and loft windows. There's no spa, but you get reduced entry to the Art Nouveau Sturebadet nearby.

Birger Jarlsgatan 24, 102 16 Stockholm. www.hotelstureplan.se. ℂ **08/440-66-00.** Fax 08/440-66-11. 101 units. 1,375SEK–5,100SEK double. Rates include breakfast. AE, DC, MC, V. Parking 360SEK. T-bana: Östermalmstorg. **Amenities:** Restaurant; bar; concierge; room service. *In room:* A/C (some rooms), TV, minibar, hair dryer, Wi-Fi (free).

Rex Hotel ⚓ The sister of Hotel Hellsten opposite, the 1866 building has been converted into a hotel with all the delightful touches that the owner Per Hellsten adds to each of his hotels. Rooms have old pine floors and simple decorations in bold colors. There's also a smaller, budget hotel in the basement: **Rex Petit,** with 20 cabin-style rooms from 495SEK to 1,295SEK. You take breakfast in the brick-walled dining room of the main Rex Hotel above.

Luntmakargatan 73, 113 51 Stockholm. www.rexhotel.se. ℂ **08/16-00-40.** Fax 08/661-86-01. 78 units. 1,290SEK–2,690SEK. Rates include breakfast. AE, DC, MC, V. **Amenities**: Breakfast room; bar; concierge; room service. *In room:* TV, hair dryer, Wi-Fi (free).

GAMLA STAN (OLD TOWN)

Collector's Lady Hamilton Hotel ★ 📇 Three connected buildings on a quiet street surrounded by antiques shops and restaurants make up this delightful hotel in a great location. Odd objects and antiques are scattered among the well-furnished guest rooms, most of which have beamed ceilings. The beds (queen-size or double) are of high quality. Top-floor rooms have skylights and memorable views over the Old Town. You'll get a sense of the 1470 origins of this hotel in the luxurious sauna, which incorporates the stone-rimmed well that formerly supplied the building's water. The hotel is particularly welcoming for single women, who get special lady kits in their rooms.

Storkyrkobrinken 5, 111 28 Stockholm. www.ladyhamiltonhotel.se. ℂ **08/506-401-00.** Fax 08/506-401-10. 34 units. 1,690SEK–3,690SEK double. Rates include breakfast. AE, DC, MC, V. Parking 395SEK. T-bana: Gamla Stan. Bus: 48. **Amenities:** Restautant; room service; sauna. *In room:* TV, hair dryer, Wi-Fi (120SEK per day; 1st 6 hr. free).

Mälardrottningen ★ 📇 During its heyday, this famous boat was the subject of gossip columns everywhere. Built in 1924 by millionaire C. K. G. Billings, it was the largest (72m/236 ft.) motor yacht in the world, and was later acquired by the Woolworth heiress, Barbara Hutton. The below-deck space originally contained only seven suites. The yacht was converted into a hotel in the early 1980s, and was permanently moored beside a satellite island of Stockholm's Old Town. The cabins are small, of course, and most have bunk-style twin beds. But it's near everything in the Old Town and will appeal to the nautical minded.

Riddarholmen, 111 28 Stockholm. www.malardrottningen.se. ℂ **08/545-187-80.** Fax 08/24-36-76. 60 units. 1,125SEK–2,000SEK double. Rates include breakfast. AE, DC, MC, V. Parking 220SEK per 24 hr. T-bana: Gamla Stan. **Amenities:** Restaurant; bar; sauna. *In room:* TV, hair dryer, Wi-Fi (free).

Victory Hotel ★★ A small but stylish hotel, the Victory has warm, inviting rooms, each named after a prominent sea captain. Decorated with exposed wood, antiques, and 19th-century memorabilia, beds are comfortable and bathrooms well equipped. The hotel rests on the foundations of a 1382 fortified tower. In the 1700s the building's owners buried a massive silver treasure under the basement floor—you can see it in the Stockholm City Museum. From the stairs you'll see one of Sweden's largest collections of 18th-century nautical needlepoint, much of it created by sailors during their long voyages. There's a gay-friendly bar and a welcome outside summer terrace.

Lilla Nygatan 3–5, 111 28 Stockholm. www.victory-hotel.se. ⓒ **08/506-400-00.** Fax 08/506-400-10. 45 units. 1,790SEK–3,690SEK double; 2,390SEK–4,890SEK suite. Rates include breakfast. AE, DC, MC, V. Parking 395SEK. T-bana: Gamla Stan. Bus: 48. **Amenities:** Restaurant; bar; plunge pool; room service. *In room:* TV, minibar, hair dryer, Wi-Fi (free).

LÅNGHOLMEN

Långholmen Hotel In 1724 this was a state penitentiary for women charged with "loose living." The last prisoner was released in 1972, and today it's a newly restored and reasonably priced hotel on the peaceful island of Långholmen. The rooms were created from around 200 cells into cramped but serviceable rooms. Eighty-nine of the rooms are rented only to solo travelers, making this one of the best hotels in Stockholm for single visitors. There's also, appropriately, a museum of Sweden's prison history and a good restaurant. Instead of a prison induction area, you get the hotel's reception area. There's outside seating and peace and quiet as well.

Längholm, 102 72 Stockholm. ⓒ **08/720-85-00.** Fax 08/720-85-75. www.langholmen.com. 102 units. Sun–Thurs 1,650SEK single, 2,020SEK double; Fri–Sat 1,110SEK single, 1,590SEK double. Extra bed 250SEK per person. Rates include breakfast. AE, DC, MC, V. T-bana: Hornstul. Bus: 4, 40, or 66. **Amenities:** Restaurant; bar. *In room:* TV, hair dryer, Wi-Fi (free).

SÖDERMALM

Rival Hotel ★★ 📷 Stockholm's first boutique hotel is a hip charmer, and it's also home to a stylish restaurant, bar, and bistro, and even a cinema, cocktail lounge, cafe with an outside terrace, and bakery. Brightly colored, the Art Deco designs and film theme combine well. The hotel's owner, Benny Anderson of ABBA fame, wanted to recreate the aura of the Aston Hotel, which opened on this site in the 1930s. There's a variety of bedroom sizes and some have a French-style balcony. Movie scenes decorate the walls in each room.

Mariatorget 3, 118 91 Stockholm. www.rival.se. ⓒ **08/545-78900.** Fax 08/545-78924. 99 units. Sun–Thurs 2,595SEK–3,455SEK double; Fri–Sat 1,595SEK–2,495SEK double. AE, DC, MC, V. T-bana: Mariatorget. **Amenities:** 2 restaurants; cafe; bar. *In room:* A/C, TV/DVD, minibar, hair dryer, Wi-Fi (free).

DAY TRIPS FROM STOCKHOLM

Uppsala ★★

The major university city of Sweden, Uppsala, 68km (42 miles) northwest of Stockholm, is the most popular destination for day-trippers from Stockholm, and for good reason. Uppsala has not only a great university, but also a celebrated 15th-century cathedral. Even in the time of the Vikings, this was a religious center, the scene of animal and human sacrifices in honor of the old Norse gods. And it was once the center of royalty as well: Queen Christina occasionally held court here. The church is still the seat of the Swedish archbishop, and the first Swedish university was founded here in 1477.

ESSENTIALS

GETTING THERE The **train** from Stockholm's Central Station to Uppsala's Central Station takes about 40 minutes. Trains, which run 24 hours, leave about every 15 minutes during peak daylight hours. The cost is from 78SEK. More information is on www.sj.se. Some visitors spend the day in Uppsala and return to Stockholm on the commuter train in the late afternoon. Eurail pass holders ride free. **Boats** sail between Uppsala and Skokloster in summer. For details, check with the tourist office in any of the towns or with the two companies that run the service: www.mslinnea.se and www.mskungcarlgustaf.se.

VISITOR INFORMATION The **Tourist Information Office** is at Fyristorg 8 (www.destinationuppsala.se/en; ℂ **018/727-48-00**), open Monday to Friday 10am to 6pm and Saturday from 10am to 3pm.

EXPLORING UPPSALA

Many of Uppsala's main attractions lie along the waterfront. Dominating the skyline is **Uppsala Slott** (www.uppsalaslot.se; ℂ **018/727-2485**), originally built by Gustav Vasa, then rebuilt in 1757. Guided tours take you around the decorated state hall, and you also see a superb collection of art from Uppsala University from the 13th to 19th centuries. End June to September, guided tours are Tuesday to Sunday, in English, 1pm and 3pm. Audio guides are also available. Admission is adult 80SEK; child 7 to 18 years 15SEK. At the end of Drottninggatan is the **Carolina Rediviva (University Library)** ★ (www.ub.uu.se; ℂ **018/471-39-18;** bus: 6, 7, 9, 18, 20, or 22) with its more than five million volumes and 40,000 manuscripts, among them many rare works from the Middle Ages. Highlights include the *Codex Argentus* (Silver Bible), translated into the old Gothic language in the middle of the 3rd century and copied in about A.D. 520, the only book extant in the old Gothic script. Admission is free. The library's exhibition room is open Monday to Friday 9am to 8pm and Saturday 10am to 5pm.

Linnaeus Garden & Museum, Svartbäcksgatan 27 (ℂ **018/471-28-38** for the museum or **018/471-25-76** for the garden; walk straight from the rail station to Kungsgatan and proceed for about 10 min. to Svartbäcksgatan), is the former home of Swedish botanist Carl von Linné, also known as Carolus Linnaeus, who developed a classification system for the world's plants and flowers. He also restored Uppsala University's botanical garden, which resembles a miniature baroque garden following his detailed sketches and descriptions. Admission to the museum and garden is 60SEK adults, free for ages 16 and under. Open May to September, Tuesday to Sunday 11am to 5pm. The gardens are open from May to September daily from 9am to 9pm.

The largest cathedral in Scandinavia at nearly 120m (395 ft.) tall, the twin-spired Gothic **Uppsala Domkyrka** ★, Domkyrkoplan 5 (www.uppsaladomkyrka.se; ℂ **018/18-71-53;** bus: 1 or 2) was founded in the 13th century. Severely damaged in 1702 in a disastrous fire in Uppsala, it was restored near the turn of the 20th century. Look out for the tombs of Gustavus Vasa in the crypt, Linnaeus, and philosopher–theologian Emanuel Swedenborg. The remains of St. Erik, patron saint of Sweden, are entombed in a silver shrine. The treasury has Gustav Vasa's sword and medieval textiles. Admission to the cathedral is free; museum admission is 40SEK adults, free for children 15 and under. Open daily 8am to 6pm. The gift shop and Treasury are open May to September Monday to Saturday 10am to 5pm and Sunday 12:30 to 5pm; October to April Monday to Saturday from 10am to 4pm and Sunday 12:30 to 4pm.

There's a lively nightlife centered around the students' quarter in the streets behind the university, near St Olofsgata. The "Nations" houses host parties and events that are technically only for locals, but international students with an international student card will be able to get in too. Otherwise, many of the *krog* (pub) restaurants in central Uppsala provide entertainment. **O'Connor's,** at Stora Torget 1 (www.oconnorsuppsala.se; ℂ **018/14-40-10**), is a great Irish pub with live entertainment open to 1am or 3am.

18

SWEDEN | Day Trips from Stockholm

Skokloster Castle ★★

Skoklosters Slott (www.skoklossersslott.se; ✆ **08/402-30-60**) is a splendid 17th-century castle and one of the most interesting baroque museums in Europe. It's on the shores of Lake Mälaren, 64km (40 miles) west of Stockholm and 40km (25 miles) south of Uppsala. Original interiors aside, the castle is noted for its rich collections of paintings, furniture, applied art, tapestries, arms, and books, as well as its beautiful park. Wander at your own pace through the castle and grounds, or take a guided tour in English. Admission is 70SEK, free for ages 18 and under. Free with the Stockholm Card. Guided tours in English of 1 hour take place May to mid-June and September Saturday and Sunday 12.30 and 2.15pm, mid-June to August daily and hourly from 12.30pm to 3.30pm, and cost 40SEK. Open May to mid-June and September Saturday and Sunday noon to 4pm; mid-June to August daily 11am to 5pm. Closed October to April.

ESSENTIALS
GETTING THERE From Stockholm Central Station take either the commuter **train** or the regional train to Bålsta, which is 19km (12 miles) from the castle. Trains take either 27 minutes (regional train) or 40 minutes (commuter train) and go between two and four times per hour. Costs are 75SEK to 90SEK on regional trains and 90SEK to 100SEK on commuter trains. At the village train station, walk 3 minutes to the nearby bus station and take UL **bus** 311 directly to Skokloster. Or call for a **taxi** from a direct telephone line that's prominently positioned just outside the railway station. The whole journey takes around 1 hour 20 minutes. Or make a whole day trip by taking the boat with the stromma from Stockholm. From June 20 to mid-August, boats depart from Stadshusbron in Stockholm. The return price is 340SEK and the whole trip plus seeing the castle takes 8½ hours. More information from www.stromma.se.

Gripsholm Castle ★★

On an island in Lake Mälaren, **Gripsholm Slottsfervaltning** (Gripsholm Castle) (www.kungahuset.se; ✆ **0159/101-94**)—the fortress built by Gustavus Vasa in the late 1530s—is one of the best-preserved castles in Sweden. It lies near **Mariefred,** an idyllic small town known for its vintage narrow-gauge railroad.

Even though Gripsholm was last occupied by royalty (Charles XV) in 1864, it's still a royal castle. Its outstanding features include a large collection of portrait paintings depicting obscure branches of the Swedish monarchy, its brooding architecture, and its 18th-century theater built for the amusement of the 18th-century actor-king Gustavus III. It's open mid-May to mid-September daily 10am to 4pm; mid-September to November Saturday and Sunday noon to 3pm; January 5–8, April 6–9, and May 1–14 noon to 3pm. Admission is 100SEK for adults, 50SEK for children 7 to 18, and free for ages 6 and under. You can wander at will or take a guided tour in English, which lasts 45 minutes and takes place mid-May to mid-September daily at 3pm and first 2 weeks of May and last 2 weeks of September Saturday and Sunday at 1pm. You cannot prebook the tour and the price is included in the entrance fee. The castle is closed from October to April.

ESSENTIALS

GETTING THERE   Gripsholm Castle is 70km (42 miles) southwest of Stockholm. By **train,** take the train from Stockholm Central Station in the direction of Eskilstuna to **Läggesta.** Trains leave each hour and take between 38 and 40 minutes. A one-way ticket is 110SEK to 120SEK. For information, see www.sj.se or ✆ **771-75-75-75.** From Läggesta station take the bus to Mariefred. Buses leave regularly and take 7 minutes. Tickets are 26SEK. Or call a taxi with the Strängnäs company ✆ **0152/186-00.** By **car** from Stockholm, follow E4 south to Södertälje then E20 to Strängnäs and Mariefred. **Boats** leave from mid-May to September from Stockholm's City Hall Quay to Klara Mälarstrand Pier. The castle is a 10-minute walk from the center of Mariefred. You could also try taking the steam train from Läggesta to Gripsholm Castle which runs at weekends in May and first part of June, daily in July and first half of August, and then weekends to the end of September. Fares run from 80SEK return. For information, see www.oslj.nu or ✆ **159-210-00.**

SWITZERLAND

by Darwin Porter & Danforth Prince

S witzerland evokes images of towering peaks, mountain lakes, lofty pastures, and alpine villages, but it also offers a rich cultural life, with many fine museums, theaters, and world-renowned orchestras, in cities such as sophisticated Geneva and perfectly preserved medieval Bern.

19

GENEVA

Geneva dazzles from first glance. It sits in a prime Rhône Valley position at the southwestern corner of Lac Léman (Lake Geneva), within view of the pinnacle of Mont Blanc. As you stroll through its cobbled Old Town, the pristine parks, and promenades, you notice the cosmopolitan atmosphere is palpable. That's no surprise—more than 200 international organizations are based here, including the European headquarters of the United Nations. The city's strong French influence shows itself everywhere: in mansard roofs, iron balconies, sidewalk cafes, and French signs.

Essentials

GETTING THERE

BY PLANE Geneva-Cointrin Airport (www.gva.ch; ✆ 022/717-71-11), although busy, is quite compact and easily negotiated. **Swiss International Air Lines** (www.swiss.com; ✆ 877/359-7947 in the U.S.) serves Geneva more frequently than any other airline and offers the best local connections, connecting Geneva with Lugano, Zurich, and Bern, plus flying in from several European capitals. Other international airlines flying into Geneva include **Air France** (www.airfrance.com; ✆ 800/237-2747 in the U.S.), with 10 flights daily from Paris, and **British Airways** (www.britishairways.com; ✆ 800/247-9297 in the U.S.; ✆ 0844/493-0787 in the U.K.), with eight daily flights from London. **easyJet** (www.easyjet.com) also operates out of Geneva to various airports in Europe, including four daily flights to London Gatwick and flights to other U.K. airports.

If you're flying with Swiss, you can arrange for your luggage to be sent on to your hotel (via the Swiss Rail system) with the **Fly Rail Baggage** (http://www.sbb.ch/en/station-services/services/baggage/fly-rail-baggage.html) service. You check your luggage in at your airport of departure and it will be sent on to the Swiss station of your choice. This allows you to travel to your destination luggage free and stop at destinations along the way. Some hotels will arrange a pick-up service for you if you can provide them on arrival with your ticket.

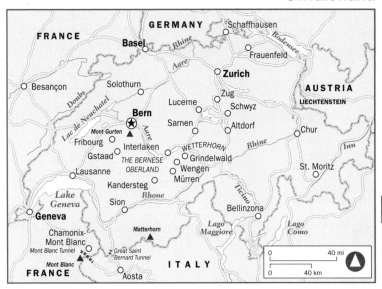

To get into the center of Geneva, there's a train station linked to the air terminal with trains leaving about every 8 to 20 minutes from 5:25am to 12:25am for the 7-minute trip; the one-way fare is 13SFR in first class and 10SFR in second class. A taxi into town will cost between 30SFR and 40SFR, or you can take bus no. 10 for 12SFR.

BY TRAIN   Switzerland's train system is one of the most efficient in Europe. If you're planning on spending time in the country, it is worth investing in a **Swiss Pass** (available from Rail Europe, www.raileurope.com). Geneva's CFF (Chemins de Fer Fédéraux) train station in the city center is **Gare Cornavin,** Place Cornavin (www.sbb.ch; ✆ **0900/300-300** for ticket information). Luggage can be stored and lockers rented (✆ **0900/022-021**). A small tourist office branch is at the train station.

BY CAR   From Lausanne, head southwest on N1 to the very end of southwestern Switzerland.

BY LAKE STEAMER   There are frequent daily arrivals by lake steamer year-round from Montreux, Vevey, Lausanne (you can use your Eurail pass for the trip), and Evian in France. If you're staying in the Left Bank (Old Town), get off at the Jardin Anglais stop in Geneva; Mont Blanc and Pâquis are the two Right Bank stops. For more information about the **Compagnie Générale de Navigation sur le lac Léman,** visit www.cgn.ch or call ✆ **0848/811-848.**

VISITOR INFORMATION

Geneva's tourist office, the **Office du Tourisme de Genève,** is located at 18, rue du Mont-Blanc (www.geneve-tourisme.ch; ✆ **022/909-70-00**), and is open daily year-round from 9am to 6pm. The staff provides information about the city, can arrange hotel reservations both in Geneva and throughout Switzerland, and also refer

Geneva

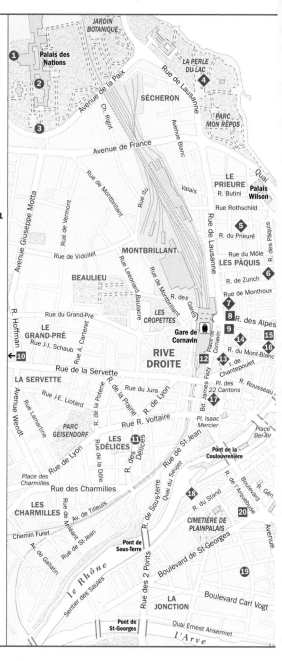

Lake Geneva

FRONTENEX

Quai Cologny

Rampe de Cologny

Route de Vandoeuvres

Plateau de Frontenex

Quai Gustave Ador

PARC DES
EAUX-VIVES

29

PARC
LA GRANGE

Avenue W. Favre

Chemin Frank Thomas

Av. Rosemont

MONTCHOISY

Rue des Eaux-Vives

Rue de Montchoisy

Vollandes

Route de Frontenex

Woodrow Wilson

R. Jacquet

Rue Plantamour

Quai du Mont-Blanc

21

22
23

24

Rade de
Genève

Quai Gustave Ador

Rue du 31 Décembre

R. de la Mîarie

Route de Chêne

Ch. de la Petite Boissière

Av. de l'Amandolier

Promenade Martin

25

Pont du-
Mont-Blanc

ILE
ROUSSEAU

Pont des
Bergues

JARDIN
ANGLAIS

Quai Général Guisan

Av. Pictet de Rochemont

Rue Agasse

RIVE
GAUCHE

Rue du Rhône

26
27
28

R. de Rive

27

rd.-pt
de Rive

Rue de la Terassière

R. Lachenal

Route de Malagnou

Chemin Rieu

RUES BASSES

les Rues Basses

R. la Fontaine

VIELLE VILLE
(OLD TOWN)

32

34
33
31

Grand Rue

R. de l'Hôtel de Ville

la Corraterie

Place
Neuve

Dufour

Favon

R. de la Croix Rouge

Promenade
des Bastions

Université

R. de Candolle

Rue St. Léger

Rue Hodler

Bd. Jacques Dalcroze

Boulevard Helvétique

30

Ch. Galland

Pl. Em.
Guyenot

l'Athenée

Cours ses Bastions

Place Ed.
Claparède

Philosophes

Bd. des Tranchées

Rue de l'Athénée

Avenue Peschier

FLORISSANT

Route de Florissant

Avenue Bertrand

PARC
A. BERTRAND

Avenue Louis Aubert

PLAINE DE
PLAINPALAIS

Rd.-pt. de
Plainpalais

du Mail

35

A. Henri Dunant

Rue A. Lombard

Bd. de la Cluse

Boulevard du Pont d'Arve

R. Prevost-Martin

R. de Carouge

LA CLUSE

Avenue de Champel

CHAMPEL

Avenue de Miremont

Av. Calas

36

🏠 Train Station

0   1/5 mi
0   0.20 km

you to other establishments specializing in car and motorcycle rentals and excursion bookings. They can also give you details about audio-guided visits to the Old Town for 10SFR. This tour covers more than two dozen highlights in the Old Town, and comes complete with MP3 player and map. Its estimated duration is 2½ hours. A 50SFR deposit is collected prior to your receipt of an MP3 player.

You can also download an official Switzerland Tourism free Geneva City Guide app for iPhone.

CITY LAYOUT

Geneva is a perfect city to explore on foot. It's divided by the end of Lake Geneva (Lac Léman) and the Rhône River into two sections: the Right Bank and the Left Bank.

RIVE GAUCHE (LEFT, OR SOUTH BANK) This compact and colorful area is the oldest section of the city. Here you'll find the **Vieille Ville (Old Town),** some major shopping streets, the famous Flower Clock, the university, and several important museums.

Grand-Rue is the well-preserved main street of Old Town. It's flanked by many houses dating from the 15th and 18th centuries. The street winds uphill from the Ponts de l'Ile; at Place Bel-Air it becomes Rue de la Cité, then Grand-Rue, and finally Rue de l'Hôtel-de-Ville. (Rousseau was born in a simple house at 40, Grand-Rue.) Eventually it reaches **Place du Bourg-de-Four**—one of the most historic squares of Geneva. South of this street is **Promenade des Bastions,** a greenbelt area overlooking the Arve River, with a monument to the Reformation. Directly to the west, in the northern corner of Promenade des Bastions, is **Place Neuve,** which is the finest square in Geneva.

From Place Neuve, you can take Rue de la Corraterie, which was once surrounded by the city wall, to the Rhône and the **Ponts de l'Ile** (island bridges). On this bridge is the **Tour-de-l'Ile,** what's left of the 13th-century bishops' castle.

On the shore of Lake Geneva is the **Jardin Anglais (English Garden)** with its Flower Clock and, farther out, the **Parc La Grange** and the nearby **Parc des Eaux-Vives.**

RIVE DROITE (RIGHT, OR NORTH BANK) You can cross to the other side of the Rhône on any of several bridges, including Pont du Mont-Blanc, Pont de la Machine, Pont des Bergues, and Ponts de l'Ile. The Right Bank is home to Gare Cornavin, the major international organizations, and several attractive parks.

Place St-Gervais is in the St-Gervais district; this has been the area for jewelers and watchmakers since the 18th century.

Along the northern shore of Lake Geneva is **Quai du Président-Wilson,** named for the U.S. president who helped found the League of Nations.

The Right Bank is surrounded by parks, from the tree-shaded promenades along the Rhône to the **Parc de la Perle du Lac, Parc Barton,** and, on the city outskirts, **Parc Mon-Repos.**

Neighborhoods in Brief

RUES BASSES

Rues Basses (translated either as "low streets" or figuratively as "lower town") is found between Old Town and the south bank of the Rhône. It's the major commercial and shopping district of Geneva. Its major street is Rue du Rhône, although Rue de la Confédération and Rue du Marché are also important arteries.

VIEILLE VILLE (OLD TOWN)

At an altitude of 398m (1,305 ft.), the Old Town is the most history-rich section of Geneva. This is **Left Bank** Geneva, with its narrow streets, flower-bedecked fountains, and architectural blends of Gothic, Renaissance, and 18th-century features. The twin towers of the Cathedral of St. Pierre dominate the Old Town, whose geographical and spiritual center is Place du Bourg-de-Four.

THE PROMENADES

These streets almost constitute a "neighborhood" in themselves. This section of quais along both Lake Geneva and the Rhône is best experienced by walking. One of the most scenic walks is from the Parc des Eaux-Vives on the Left Bank to the Parc de Mon-Repos on the Right Bank. Along the way is a clear view of Geneva's most famous and visible monument, the **Jet d'Eau.** Set a few inches above the surface of the lake, this fountain spurts a plume of shimmering water that rises to heights, depending on the wind on the day it's being measured, of between 140m (459 ft.) and 145m (476 ft.) tall. Except for a 2-week maintenance regime conducted every midwinter, Jet d'Eau operates year-round, except when winds blow hard down from the Alps, during which period it's shut off to avoid drenching the passersby on the nearby quais.

PAQUIS

One of Geneva's most animated and colorful districts, **Les Pâquis** offers a view of a workaday world that's far removed from the luxurious consumerism and (some say) indolence of better-heeled neighborhoods closer to the lake. Les Pâquis is a sector of bistros, nightclubs, ateliers, hipster boutiques, and banks.

Its main thoroughfare, the Rue des Pâquis, runs parallel to the Rue de Berne. To reach it, head north along Quai des Bergues, which leads into Quai du Mont-Blanc. On your left, at the intersection of Quai du Mont-Blanc and Gare Routière, stands the **Brunswick Monument,** the tomb of Charles II of Brunswick, who died in Geneva in 1873. One of the most infamous events in the history of the area was the assassination of Empress Elisabeth of Austria, in 1898, at the landing stage facing the duke of Brunswick's mausoleum. In 1873, construction began on the **Hôtel National** (Palais Wilson); from 1925 to 1936 this housed the first secretariat of the League of Nations.

CAROUGE

Carouge, a suburb of Geneva, is a historic European town. It dates from the 18th century, when it was built by the king of Sardinia to rival Geneva. Architects from Turin supplied the Piedmontese charm.

Switzerland considers Carouge a national landmark because of its architecture. It can be reached from Geneva by tram no. 12 or 13 from the center. Begin your exploration in the Market Square, with its old fountain, plane trees, and markets. A Roman stone was embedded in the Church of the Holy Cross. As you walk around, you'll pass the court of the count of Veyrier's palace, dating from 1783; place du Temple, with a fountain from 1857; and a Louis XVI carved door at 18, rue St-Victor.

Getting Around

Walking, of course, is the cheapest, most practical form of transportation in Geneva. It's also the most advantageous from a tourist's point of view. Tree-shaded promenades line the edges of the lake, and you can browse many chic shops walking at a moderate pace along streets that include Rue du Rhône.

BY PUBLIC TRANSPORTATION Most of Geneva's public tram and bus lines begin at the central Place Cornavin in front of the main rail station. Local buses and trams operate daily from 5am to midnight, and you can purchase a ticket from a vending machine before you board, paying the exact fare (it will not give you any change back). Instructions are given in English. **Transport Publics Genevois** (www.tpg.ch (in French only); ℅ **0900/022-021**), next to the tourist office in Gare Cornavin, offers free maps of local bus routings. Trips that stay within zone 10, enveloping most of Geneva, cost 3.50SFR, and unlimited use of all zones for 1 day costs adults 10.60SFR and children 7.60SFR.

Guests who have proof that they are booked into a hotel, B&B, or hostel are granted free rides on public transportation. Ask at your hotel for a public transportation ticket.

BY TAXI   The meter on whatever cab you take in Geneva will automatically begin calculating your fare at 7SFR, and then add between 3SFR and 3.50SFR for every kilometer you travel, depending on the time of day or night. The fare from the airport to the center of town ranges from 30SFR to 40SFR. No tipping is required, but extra baggage may cost 1.50SFR. To call for a **taxi,** contact **TaxiPhone** at www.taxi-phone. ch or call ℅ **022/331-41-33.**

BY CAR   Driving is not recommended; parking is difficult and the many one-way streets make navigation complicated. However, should you wish to rent a car and tour Lake Geneva, you'll find many car-rental companies represented in the arrivals hall of the airport and in the center of the city. If you absolutely insist on driving a car, and if your hotel doesn't offer parking facilities and valet parking, the best bet for parking within the city limits tends to be within any of the many underground parking garages, whose presence is indicated with large blue-and-white signs designated with a letter "P." Rates for underground parking average between 1.50SFR and 2SFR per hour.

BY BIKE   Touring the city by bicycle isn't particularly practical because of the steep cobblestone streets, speeding cars, and general congestion. However, you might want to consider renting a bike for touring the countryside around Geneva. The major rental outlet is at the baggage desk at **Gare Cornavin** (℅ **022/791-02-50**), where city bikes cost 33SFR per day. Another major outlet, charging from 24SFR to 34SFR per day, depending on the degree of sophistication of the bicycle, is **Genève Roule,** 17, Place Montbrillant (www.geneveroule.ch; ℅ **022/740-13-43**).

[Fast FACTS] GENEVA

ATMs/Banks   Most banks are open Monday to Friday 8:30am to 4:30pm (until 5:30pm Wed).

Business Hours   Most offices are open Monday to Friday 8:30am to 5:30pm, although this can vary. It's always best to call first.

Consulates   If you lose your passport or have other business with your home government, go to your nation's consulate: **Australia,**

2, chemin des Fins (www. geneva.mission.gov.au; ℅ **022/799-91-00**); **Canada,** 5, av. de L'Ariana (www.international.gc.ca/ genev/services/; ℅ **022/ 919-92-00**); **New Zealand,** 2, chemin des Fins (http:// www.nzembassy.com/ switzerland; ℅ **022/929-03- 50**); the **United Kingdom,** 58, av. Louis Casaï, Cointrin (http://ukmissiongeneva.fco. gov.uk; ℅ **022/918-24-00**); **United States,** 7, rue

Versonnex (http://bern. usembassy.gov; ℅ **022/ 840-51-60**).

Currency & Currency Exchange   The unit of currency is the Swiss franc (SFR). In a city devoted to banking and the exchange of international currencies, you'll find dozens of places to exchange money in Geneva. Two of the most visible outlets, however, are run by **UBS-SA.** You'll find a branch at the **Gare**

Cornavin, 12, place Cornavin (℡ **022/375-33-47**), that's open Monday to Friday from 8am to 6pm and a branch at the **Cointrin Airport** (℡ **022/306-14-88**) that's open Monday to Friday from 8:30am to 4:30pm. They also have "money-automats"—insert notes or bills into the machine and you receive an equivalent amount of Swiss francs.

Doctors & Hospitals If you become ill and want to consult a doctor, including one who will travel to your hotel, call ℡ **022/322-20-20;** or arrange an appointment with an English-speaking doctor at the **Hôpital Cantonal,** 22, rue Micheli-du-Crest (℡ **022/372-33-11**). A prime choice for medical aid is the **Geneva University Hospital,** 24, rue Micheli-du-Crest (www.hug-ge.ch; ℡ **022/372-33-11**). Most physicians speak English and German.

Drugstores Each night a different set of four drugstores stays open either till 9 or 11pm. Call ℡ **144** or **111** to find out which drugstore will be open. One of the world's biggest drugstores,

Pharmacie Principale, in Confédération-Centre, 8, rue de la Confédération (℡ **022/318-66-60**), sells everything from medicine to clothing, perfumes, optical equipment, cameras, and photo supplies. It's open daily 9am to 9pm.

Emergencies In an emergency, dial ℡ **117** for the police, ℡ **144** for an ambulance, or ℡ **118** to report a fire.

Mail & Postage There's a limited **Office de Poste** at Gare Cornavin, 16, rue des Gares (℡ **0848/888-888**), open Monday to Friday from 6am to 10:45pm, Saturday from 6am to 8pm, and Sunday from noon to 8pm. A better bet is the city's main post office, **Bureau de Poste Montbrillant,** Rue des Gares (℡ **022/739-23-58**), which offers a full range of telephone, telegraph, and mail-related services Monday to Friday from 8am to 10:45pm, Saturday 8am to 10pm, and Sunday noon to 8pm.

Police In an emergency, call ℡ **117.** For nonemergency matters, call ℡ **022/327-41-11.**

Safety Geneva is one of the safest cities in the world, but that doesn't mean you shouldn't take the usual precautions when traveling anywhere. Protect your valuables. Car thefts have been on the rise. High-class prostitutes and confidence swindlers proliferate in Geneva to prey on the well-heeled.

Taxes There is no special city tax, other than the 7.6% value-added tax (VAT) attached to most goods and services throughout Switzerland.

Tipping Most restaurants and hotels, even taxis, add a service charge of between 10% and 15% to your bill, so, strictly speaking, no further tipping is necessary. Tipping rituals have evolved recently within Geneva to reflect practices within neighboring France; so, today, many diners leave a few coins—we established guidelines of around 2SFR extra for each member of a dining party, merely as a sign of respect for your waitstaff, but only if the service was adequate.

Exploring Geneva

In addition to the sites listed below, Geneva's other top attractions—all premier sights—are the **Jet d'Eau,** the famous fountain that has virtually become the city's symbol; the **Flower Clock,** in the Jardin Anglais, with 6,500 flowers (it was the world's first when it was inaugurated in the 1950s; today, it's less of a showstopper); and **Old Town,** the oldest part of the city.

After wandering through the district with no particular fixed itinerary, visitors may tour Lake Geneva on a lake steamer. Steamers leave from Quai du Mont-Blanc.

Cathédrale de St. Pierre ★ CATHEDRAL The Old Town, or Vieille Ville, on the Left Bank, is dominated by the cathedral which was built in the 12th and 13th centuries and partially reconstructed in the 15th century. Recent excavations have disclosed that a Christian sanctuary was here as early as A.D. 400. In 1536 the people of Geneva gathered in the cloister of St. Pierre's and voted to make the cathedral Protestant. The church, which has been heavily renovated over the years, has a modern organ with 6,000 pipes. Sunday service is held in the cathedral at 10am, and an hour of organ music is presented on Saturday at 6pm from June to September. The northern **tower** was reconstructed at the end of the 19th century, with a metal steeple erected between the two stone towers. If you don't mind the 145 steps, you can climb to the top of the north tower for a panoramic view of the city, its lake, the Alps, and the Jura Mountains.

To enter the St. Pierre archaeological site, called **Site Archéologique de Saint-Pierre,** go through the entrance in Cour Saint-Pierre, at the right-hand corner of the cathedral steps. The underground passageway extends under the present cathedral and the High Gothic (early-15th-century) **Chapelle des Macchabées,** which adjoins the southwestern corner of the church. The chapel was restored during World War II, after having been used as a storage room following the Reformation. Excavations of the chapel have revealed baptisteries, a crypt, the foundations of several cathedrals, the bishop's palace, 4th-century mosaics, sculptures, and geological strata.

Cour Saint-Pierre, www.saintpierre-geneve.ch. ℭ **022/319-71-90.** June–Sept daily 9:30am–6:30pm; March–May and Oct daily 9am–noon and 2–6pm; Nov–Feb daily 10am–5:30pm. Free admission (donations are welcome); tower admission 4SFR. Archaeological site: June–Sept daily 11am–5pm, Oct–May Tues–Sun 2–5pm. Admission 8SFR adults, 4SFR for students and seniors. Bus: 2, 7, 12, or 36.

Institut et Musée Voltaire MUSEUM   This house is where Voltaire lived from 1755 to 1760 and from time to time after that up to 1765; he wrote part of *Candide* here. The museum displays furniture, manuscripts, letters, and portraits, as well as a terra-cotta model of the famous seated Voltaire by Houdon.

25, rue des Délices. www.ville-ge.ch. ℭ **022/418-95-60.** Free admission. Mon–Fri 2–5pm. Bus: 6, 7, 11, 26, or 27.

Maison Tavel ★ MUSEUM   Constructed in 1303 and partially rebuilt after a fire in 1334, this is the city's oldest house. The building underwent several transformations over the centuries before opening as a museum in 1986. The front wall is typical 17th century, with gray paint, white joints, and stone sculpted heads. The house contains a courtyard with a staircase, a 13th-century cellar, and a back garden. The museum exhibits historical collections from Geneva dating from the Middle Ages to the mid-19th century. The Magnin relief in the attic is outstanding, as is the copper-and-zinc model of Geneva in 1850, which is accompanied by a light-and-recorded commentary. Objects of daily use are displayed in the old living quarters.

6, rue du Puits Saint-Pierre. www.ville-ge.ch. ℭ **022/418-37-00.** Free admission to permanent collection, 3SFR temporary expositions. Tues–Sun 10am–6pm. Bus: 3, 5, or 17.

Musée Ariana ★★ MUSEUM   Located to the west of the Palais des Nations, this Italian Renaissance building was constructed by Gustave Revilliod, the 19th-century Genevese patron who began the collection. Today, it's one of the top porcelain, glass, and pottery museums in Europe. You'll see Sèvres, Delft faience, and Meissen porcelain, as well as pieces from Japan and China.

10, av. de la Paix. www.ville-ge.ch. ℭ **022/418-54-50.** Free admission to the permanent collection; temporary exhibitions 5SFR adults, 3SFR students; free for children 17 and under. Tues–Sun 10am–6pm. Bus: 8 or F.

Musée d'Art et Contemporain (MAMCO) ★ MUSEUM   Some 20 years in the making, Geneva's first modern art museum opened in 1994 in a former factory building, and immediately evoked comparisons to some of the excellent collections of modern art in Paris. This prestigious showcase displays a vast collection of European and American art covering the last 4 decades. Out of some 1,000 works of art owned by the museum, only 300 are permanently on display. This space is packed with all the big names—Frankenthaler, Stella, Segal, and others. Some 150 sq. m (1,600 sq. ft.) of space is set aside for exhibitions that change three times a year.

10, rue des Vieux-Grenadiers. www.mamco.ch. © **022/320-61-22.** Admission 8SFR adults, 6SFR students, free for children 17 and under. Tues–Fri noon–6pm; Sat–Sun 11am–6pm. Bus: 1 or 32.

Musée d'Art et d'Histoire ★★ MUSEUM   At Geneva's most important museum, displays include prehistoric relics, Greek vases, medieval stained glass, 12th-century armor, Swiss timepieces, Flemish and Italian paintings, and Switzerland's largest collection of Egyptian art. The Etruscan pottery and medieval furniture are both impressive. A 1444 altarpiece by Konrad Witz depicts the "miraculous" draft of fishes. Many galleries also contain works by such artists as Rodin, Renoir, Hodler, Vallotton, Le Corbusier, Picasso, Chagall, Corot, Monet, and Pissarro. There's a well-managed restaurant on the premises.

2, rue Charles-Galland (btw. Bd. Jacques-Dalcroze and Bd. Helvétique). www.centre.ch. © **022/ 418-26-00.** Free admission. 5SFR temporary exhibitions adults, 2SFR for children. Tues–Sun 10am–6pm. Bus: 1, 3, 5, 8, or 17.

Musée International de la Croix-Rouge et du Croissant-Rouge (International Red Cross and Red Crescent Museum) ★ MUSEUM   Here you can experience the legendary past of the Red Cross in the city where it started; it's across from the visitors' entrance to the European headquarters of the United Nations. The dramatic story from 1863 to the present is revealed through displays of rare documents and photographs, films, multiscreen slide shows, and cycloramas. You're taken from the battlefields of Europe to the plains of Africa to see the Red Cross in action. When Henry Dunant founded the Red Cross in Geneva in 1863, he needed a recognizable symbol to suggest neutrality. The Swiss flag (a white cross on a red field), with the colors reversed, ended up providing the perfect symbol for one of the world's greatest humanitarian movements.

17, av. de la Paix. www.micr.org. © **022/748-95-25.** Admission 10SFR adults; 5SFR students, seniors, and children 12–16; free for children 11 and under. Wed–Mon 10am–5pm. Bus: 8, F, V, or Z.

Palais des Nations ★★ MUSEUM   The former home of the defunct League of Nations is the present headquarters of the **United Nations** in Europe, lying 1.6km (1 mile) north of Mont Blanc Bridge. The complex of buildings is the second largest in Europe after Versailles. Tours, conducted in English, last about an hour. They depart from the visitors' entrance opposite the Red Cross building. To join the tour, you'll need to show your passport. The highlights of the tour include the Assembly Hall, with a balcony made entirely of marble and lofty bays looking out over the Court of Honor. You are shown the Council Chamber, the home of the Conference on Disarmament with its allegorical murals by José Maria Sert, an artist from Catalonia. The **Philatelic Museum** offers collections of stamps relating to the League of Nations, along with a wide selection of philatelic publications from around the world, and the League of Nations Museum documents the history of the precursor to the United Nations.

Parc de l'Ariana, 14, av. de la Paix. www.unog.ch. ✆ **022/917-48-96.** Admission 12SFR adults, 10SFR students, 7SFR children 6–17. July–Aug daily 10am–5pm; Apr–June and Sept–Oct daily 10:30am–noon and 2:30–4pm; Nov–Mar Mon–Fri 10:30am–noon and 2:30–4pm. Bus: 5, 8, 11, 14, 18, F, V, or Z.

Patek Philippe Museum MUSEUM   Watch lovers flock here from all over the world to see one of the best collections of timepieces in existence. Positioned close to the larger and more visible MAMCO Museum of Modern Art, the Patek Philippe Museum contains two collections that are permanently on display here—the Antiques Collection (also known as the Archives Collection) and the Patek Philippe Collection (founded in 1839, the Patek Philippe company is one of the most venerated watchmakers in the world).

7, rue de Vieux Grenadiers. www.patekmuseum.com. ✆ **022/807-09-10.** Admission 10SFR adults, 7SFR students and seniors, free for children 17 and under. Tues–Fri 2–6pm; Sat 10am–6pm. Bus: 1 or 4. Tram: 12 or 13.

ORGANIZED TOURS

A 2-hour City Tour, on foot and by bus, is operated daily all year by **Key Tours S.A.,** 7, rue des Alpes, Square du Mont-Blanc (www.keytours.ch; ✆ 022/731-41-40). The tour starts from the Gare Routière, the bus station at Place Dorcière, near the Key Tours office. In the Old Town, you can take a walk down to the Bastions Park and the Reformation Wall. After a tour through the International Center, where you'll be shown the headquarters of the International Red Cross, the bus returns to its starting place. Adults pay 23SFR and children 4 to 12 accompanied by an adult are charged 12SFR, while children 3 and under go free. From November to March, the tour is offered only once a day at 1:30pm; but from April to October, two tours leave daily at 10:30am and 1:30pm.

The cold, clear waters of Lac Léman have attracted visitors for many generations. If you're interested in cruising on these waters (which never freeze, even in winter), at least two companies offer worthwhile tours. Regardless of which you select, you'll enjoy sweeping waterside views of the ringing hills, bucolic calm, and some of the most famous vineyards in Switzerland, many of which seem to roll down to the historic waters. Because of bad weather and low visibility in winter, cruises only run between April and late October, and in some cases, only between May and September.

The smaller company of the two, **Mouettes Genevoises Navigation,** 8, quai du Mont-Blanc (www.swissboat.com; ✆ 022/732-47-47), specializes in small-scale boats carrying only about 100 passengers at a time. Each features some kind of pre-recorded commentary, in French and English, throughout. An easy promenade that features the landscapes and bird life along the uppermost regions of the River Rhône draining the lake is the company's 2¾-hour **Tour du Rhône (Rhône River Tour).** The trip originates at Quai des Moulins, adjacent to Geneva's Pont de l'Ile, and travels downstream for about 14km (9 miles) to the Barrage de Verbois (Verbois Dam) and back. From April to October, departures are Wednesday, Saturday, and Sunday at 2:15pm. It costs 25SFR for adults and 18SFR for children 4 to 12; it's free for children 3 and under.

Mouettes Genevoises Navigation's largest competitor, **CGN (Compagnie Générale de Navigation),** Quai du Mont-Blanc (www.cgn.ch; ✆ 0848/811-848), offers roughly equivalent tours, in this case between May and September, that last an hour, departing six to seven times a day (depending on the season) from the company's piers along Quai du Mont-Blanc. Known as **Les Belles Rives Genevoises,** the tours cost 16SFR for adults and 9SFR for children 6 to 16; children 5 and under ride free.

Although its hour-long cruises are popular, CGN devotes most of its time, energy, and money to hauling boatloads of commuters and sightseers between the ports that line the perimeter of the lake. They're conducted aboard larger craft. None includes guided commentary. In most cases, CGN vessels depart from the piers beside Quai du Mont-Blanc. The most comprehensive ride requires a full day: the **Tour du Grand Lac.** It departs every morning at 9am, pulls for very brief interludes into about half a dozen ports en route, and returns to Geneva that night at 8:45pm. A 2-hour stopover in Montreux and a leisurely lunch onboard are included as part of the experience. The round-trip circuit costs 67SFR for adults and 34SFR for ages 6 to 25; it's free for children 5 and under. A more recommendable, and more practical, tour is **Le Tour du Petit Lac ★,** which incorporates only the lower portion of the lake, including stops at Nyon (in Switzerland) and the picturesque medieval village of Yvoire (in France), and lasts for about half a day. It departs from Quai du Mont-Blanc every afternoon at 3pm. The round-trip cost is from 27SFR.

CGN also offers a tour that combines a lake cruise and a visit to the Château de Chillon with a return by train back to Geneva. Between June and September, a boat leaves from the Mont Blanc pier daily at 9:15am, arriving in Chillon at 2:15pm. During July and August, an additional boat departs from the Jardin Anglais pier at 10:30am, arriving in Chillon around 3:50pm. The cost for the full round-trip excursion is 54SFR in second class and 73SFR in first class. For more information on all of the CGN tours, visit www.cgn.ch or call ℂ **0848/811-848.**

OUTDOOR ACTIVITIES

Like most cities in health-conscious Switzerland, Geneva has many sports facilities. However, locals often pursue activities outside the city.

The big spectator event of the year, the world's most important **lake regatta** is known as the **Bol d'Or** and takes place sometime in June (the Swiss National Tourist Office abroad will provide exact dates), attracting approximately 600 sailboats and more than 3,500 competitors. The lake is virtually covered with white sails. It takes 7 hours for the luckiest to sail from one end to the other—and more than 24 hours for the unluckiest.

BIKING   Cyclists consider the Geneva countryside a paradise. What could be better than a ride through forest, vineyard, and cornfield? The most passionate bikers climb Bernex's hill or cross the border into France (bring a passport). See "Getting Around," earlier in this chapter, for details about renting a bike.

GOLF   The best course is **Golf Club de Genève,** 7, rte. de la Capite at Cologny (ℂ **022/707-48-00**), which is an 18-hole course open March to December, Tuesday to Friday 8am to noon and 2 to 6pm. Greens fees are 150SFR for 18 holes.

JOGGING   In addition to the many trails that have been laid out in the parks, you can also jog along the quais and the lakeshore beaches. The best places for jogging are Parc Bertrand, Parc des Eaux-Vives, and Parc Mon-Repos.

SAILING   This is the most popular sport in Geneva. In the summer, you'll find kiosks offering sailboats for rent all along the quays.

SKIING   In winter, the people of Geneva flock to the resorts of the Haute Savoie in France, notably Chamonix and Megève. Each resort is about an hour's drive from Geneva. The smaller, lesser known French resort of **Flaine** is even closer to Geneva.

19

SWITZERLAND

Geneva

In Switzerland itself, the place nearest Geneva where there's good skiing is the Glacier of Les Diablerets or the resort of Champéry.

SWIMMING   In summer, swimmers usually head for the beaches along the lake. The most popular of these is **Geneva Beach (Genève Plage),** Port Noir (www.geneve-plage.ch; ✆ **022/736-24-82**), where you can swim mid-May to mid-September 10am to 8pm for 7SFR.

TENNIS   Tennis somehow seems more invigorating in the sunshine and sometimes-brisk mountain air near the French Alps. An option for tennis in Geneva is the courts at **Tennis Club de Genève,** Parc des Eaux-Vives (www.tc-geneve.ch; ✆ **022/735-53-50**).

Where to Eat

Geneva is one of the gastronomic centers of Europe, with an unmistakable French influence. Genevans today take their dining seriously, and practice fine eating with consummate flair and style.

Naturally, Geneva serves all the typically Swiss dishes, such as filets of perch from Lake Geneva and fricassee of pork. In season, many of its restaurants offer cardoon, which is similar to an artichoke and is usually served gratiné. By all means, try the Genevese sausage *longeole*. *Omble chevalier* comes from the waters of Lac Léman and is like a grayling, although some compare it to salmon.

Cheese is also a staple on the Genevese table, including such Swiss varieties as *tomme* and Gruyère, plus, in season, *vacherin* from the Joux Valley. Naturally, everything will taste better with the Perlan (white wine) and gamay (red wine) from Geneva's own vineyards.

THE RIGHT BANK
Very Expensive
Le Chat-Botté ★★★ FRENCH   This grand restaurant is in one of the fanciest hotels in Geneva. Suitably decorated with tapestries, sculpture, and rich upholstery, with a polite and correct staff, it serves some of the best food in the city. There are some critics who consider it among the best restaurants of Europe. If the weather is right, you can dine on the flower-bedecked terrace, overlooking the Jet d'Eau. The cuisine, although inspired by French classics, is definitely contemporary. Typical starters include delectable zucchini flowers stuffed with vegetables and essence of tomato; and lobster salad with eggplant "caviar," olive oil, and fresh herbs. Some of the most enticing items on the menu include carpaccio with black olives and Parmesan cheese, poached wing of skate in a herb-flavored sauce, and oven-roasted Sisteron lamb with stuffed vegetables. The chef's best-known dish is a delicate filet of perch from Lake Geneva, which is sautéed until it's golden.

In the Hôtel Beau-Rivage, 13, quai du Mont-Blanc. www.beau-rivage.ch/uk/le-chat-botte.php. ✆ **022/716-69-20.** Reservations required. Main courses 45SFR–90SFR; fixed-price menus 140SFR–220SFR. AE, DC, MC, V. Mon–Fri noon–2pm and Mon–Sat 7–9:45pm. Bus: 1.

Windows ★ CONTINENTAL   Flooded with sunlight from large panoramic windows, and permeated with an undeniably upscale but discreet and rather clubby sense of old-fashioned exclusivity, it attracts a clientele of French-Swiss politicians, film industry personnel, writers, and the merely rich. Menu items change with the seasons, but are likely to include orange-marinated chicken cutlets with a yogurt-flavored avocado sauce and bulgur wheat; zucchini flowers stuffed with eggplant "caviar" and Provençal herbs; asparagus and Roquefort soup; roasted omble chevalier, a whitefish from the nearby lake, served with a reduction of carrot juice and a passion-fruit-flavored butter sauce; and pan-fried veal cutlets served with a demi-glacé of veal drippings and green asparagus. And if you happen to be walking along the quais between 3 and 5pm, consider dropping into this place for high tea (30SFR per person), which includes finger sandwiches and pastries.

In the Hôtel d'Angleterre, 17, quai du Mont-Blanc. www.dangleterrehotel.com/dining. ✆ **022/906-55-14.** Reservations recommended. Main courses 51SFR–74SFR; fixed-price lunch 51SFR, dinner 79SFR–190SFR. AE, DC, MC, V. Daily noon–2pm and 7–10:30pm. Bus: 1.

EXPENSIVE

Brasserie ★ MEDITERRANEAN   In the Parc des Eaux-Vives, this is the less formal and more affordable of the restaurants in this mansion that dates back to the 18th century. In this more modern brasserie section, a light and varied cuisine is offered, as you sit on a large summer terrace overlooking the lake. The chefs cook with energy and verve, and use pure, authentic ingredients to concoct memorable meals. Begin with such starters as a Maine lobster in a ravioli of cauliflower semolina, or else pan-fried duck foie gras with confit of apple and a beet chutney. All pastas are handmade, including tagliatelle carbonara.

Both the fish and meat courses are sublime, in flavors ranging from slow-cooked pig's cheek with a perfume of orange peel and creamy polenta to salmon in lemon butter with shellfish-studded black rice. Desserts are luscious and creative, including a caramel tartlet with caramelized popcorn.

In the more formal restaurant, **Parc des Eaux-Vives** (same phone as below), meals can run up to 230SFR or beyond.

82, quai Gustave. www.parcdeseauxvives.ch. ✆ **022/849-75-75.** Reservations required. Main courses 24SFR–53SFR. AE, DC, MC, V. Daily noon–2pm and 7–10pm. Bus: 1.

Chez Jacky ★ 🍴 SWISS   This provincial bistro should be better known, although it already attracts everyone from grandmothers to young skiers en route to Verbier. It's the domain of Jacky Gruber, an exceptional chef from the Valais. There's subtlety in Monsieur Gruber's cooking that suggests the influence of his mentor, Frédy Giradet, hailed as Switzerland's greatest chef before his recent retirement. The chef tirelessly seeks the most select produce for his imaginative and innovative dishes, and he continues to dazzle his regular clients year after year, winning new converts as well. You may begin with Chinese cabbage and mussels and continue with filet of turbot roasted with thyme, or perhaps beautifully prepared pink duck on a bed of spinach with a confit of onions. Be prepared to wait for each course, though.

9–11, rue Jacques-Necker. www.chezjacky.ch. ✆ **022/732-86-80.** Reservations recommended. Main courses 44SFR–47SFR; dinner menus 70SFR–96SFR. AE, DC, MC, V. Mon–Fri 11:30am–2pm and 7–10pm. Closed 1st week of Jan and mid-July to mid-Aug. Bus: 5, 10, or 44.

La Perle du Lac ★ SWISS   Situated in a single-story pavilion owned by the city, this is the only restaurant in Geneva that's not separated from the waters of the lake by a stream of traffic. It's set beneath the venerable trees of Mon-Repos Park, not far from the United Nations complex. Although the candlelit interior is lovely, you may want to reserve a table on the outdoor terrace in warm weather. A talented French chef prepares a marvelous mousseline of sweetbreads and mushrooms. Other specialties, each delectable, include line-caught grilled seabass with fresh fennel and olive oil, and braised strips of fera (freshwater lake fish) flavored with saffron. Ravioli appears in an unusual version stuffed with fresh watercress. The real allure here involves competent, but not necessarily inspired, cuisine and a location and lakeside setting that more than compensates.

128, rue de Lausanne. www.laperledulac.ch. ✆ **022/909-10-20.** Reservations required. Main courses 35SFR–65SFR; fixed-price menu 88SFR–130SFR. AE, DC, MC, V. Tues–Sun noon–2pm and 7–10pm. Closed mid-Dec to mid-Jan. Bus: 4 or 44.

MODERATE
Wine & Beef STEAK   With its convivial bar and terraces, this contemporary bistro has won its acclaim by serving a single dish—Swiss beef rib-eye steak with a copyrighted sauce, along with crispy french fries and a fresh garden salad. The entrecote emerges piping hot from a sizzling grill, where it's been cooked to your specifications. Still hungry? You can order a cheese plate, which is served with quince jelly. Desserts are extra, in the 12SFR to 15SFR range, and they are luscious creations, ranging from the tiramisu to the crème brûlée. A wisely chosen wine list complements the menu, with such selections as smooth tasting merlots or pinot noirs. Wine can be served by the glass. The decor is über-chic with displays of vintage wine bottles, artistic ceramic plates, and blowups of photographs.

3, rue Ami-Levrier. www.wine-and-beef.com. ✆ **022/732-53-45.** Reservations recommended. Main course 39SFR. AE, DC, MC, V. Daily noon–3pm and 7pm–midnight. Bus: 1.

INEXPENSIVE
Jeck's Place ★ THAI/SINGAPOREAN   Near the Gare Cornavin, this place is a delight. It's like taking a culinary trip to Southeast Asia, with stopovers in such places as China, Malaysia, Thailand, and India. Escaping from the traffic outside, you enter a warm and friendly enclave, where Jeck Tan of Singapore will greet you. The cuisine of Asian specialties provides temptation with every order, and the trays of delicacies are brought out by waitresses in sarongs. The specials of the day will be seasoned with delicate blends of spices, notably lemon grass and curry, but also chili and galaga (from the ginger family). It's not the dull beef sauté, for example, but a medley of delight in a sauce flavored with cloves, curry, cinnamon, coconut milk, and lemon grass. You can make a meal of the appetizers alone, including homemade steamed dumplings stuffed with a blend of pork and vegetables flavored with coriander. The house specialty is Jeck's chicken in green curry.

14, rue de Neuchâtel. www.jecksplace.ch. ✆ **022/731-33-03.** Reservations recommended. Main courses 24SFR–33SFR; special lunch platter 14SFR. AE, DC, MC, V. Mon–Fri 11:30am–2pm; daily 6:30–10:30pm. Bus: 4, 5, or 9.

ON THE LEFT BANK
Moderate
Auberge du Savièse ★★ 👔   This is the best place in Geneva for authentic fondues. The fondue is made with a combination of Gruyère, Emmental, and Vacherin cheese, along with white wine and kirsch. In an old-fashioned and very traditional atmosphere, this bistro in the Pâquis district perpetuates with a passion for Swiss culinary traditions. The recipes of these good-tasting dishes seem to have been passed on from generation to generation. If you're not into fondue, try the raclette, or other delectable Swiss specialties like beef steak with homemade butter or grilled veal sausages with *rösti* (potatoes grated and fried). Finish, perhaps, with homemade apple pie with vanilla ice cream.

20, rue de Pâquis. www.aubergedesaviese.ch. ✆ **022/732-83-30.** Reservations required. Main courses 19SFR–40SFR. MC, V. Daily noon–2:30pm and Mon–Fri 6:30pm–midnight. Bus: 1.

Brasserie de l'Hôtel de Ville ★ SWISS   This is one of the most deliberately archaic-looking restaurants in Geneva, with a reputation that dates from 1764 and a clientele that prefers that absolutely nothing changes in either its old-fashioned decor or its choice of dishes. In spite of its look, it's rather hip and popular with the Genevans. Be aware that this place doesn't have a lot of patience with diners who aren't familiar with dining rituals as practiced in an upscale brasserie, and the staff can be brusque. Nonetheless, we recommend it as we would a time capsule to another era. The menu is more sophisticated and better than ever. Try the filets of freshwater lake perch meunière. Sometimes the prized fish of Lake Geneva, omble chevalier, is also served in a butter sauce. One old-fashioned dish remains on the menu: *Longeole du val d'Arve* (traditional Geneva-style sausages flavored with cumin). You can also order such delights as rack of lamb flavored with herbs of Provence.

39, Grand-Rue. www.hdvglozu.ch. ⓒ **022/311-70-30.** Reservations recommended. Main courses 27SFR–45SFR; fixed-price menu 47SFR–67SFR. AE, DC, MC, V. Daily 11:30am–11:30pm. Bus: 36.

Café du Centre SWISS/CONTINENTAL   This cafe is usually hysterically busy, and permeated with a kind of brusque anonymity. But despite its drawbacks, this remains very much an Old Geneva institution, established in 1871. Despite the thousands of cups of coffee and glasses of beer served here, it's more akin to a restaurant that serves drinks than a cafe that offers food. During clement weather, most of the business takes place outdoors on a terrace opening onto the square, while the rest of the year, business moves inside into a pair of street-level rooms whose nostalgic decor may remind you of an old-fashioned brasserie in Lyon. A thick, multilingual menu offers food items such as excellent versions of fresh fish as well as *Wiener schnitzel*, a savory version of onglet of beef, and pepper steak.

5, place du Molard. www.cafeducentre.ch. ⓒ **022/311-85-86.** Reservations recommended. Main courses 27SFR–48SFR; fixed-price *assiette du jour* 19SFR at lunch Mon–Fri only. AE, DC, MC, V. Mon 6am–midnight; Tues–Sat 9am–1am; Sun 9am–midnight. Tram: 12.

Café Metropole SWISS   Convenient and cozy, this brasserie-style restaurant and cafe attracts a young crowd for its cocktails, wine list, and good, market-fresh food. Dishes tend to be light and flavorful. You might begin with the fish soup with rouille or else a niçoise salad, perhaps one of the pâtés. Fish dishes are well prepared, especially sole from the Atlantic or red tuna. Seabass from Mediterranean waters is another specialty, as is Swiss beef. Even the hamburger on the menu is special here: it comes with truffles. For dessert, try a slice of melon from Cavaillon, France. Gourmets claim they are the best in Europe.

6, rue du Prince. www.cafe-metropole.ch. ⓒ**022/310-06-70.** Main courses 19SFR–45SFR. AE, MC, V. Daily 10am–11pm. Bus: 12.

La Broche SWISS/FRENCH/MIDDLE EASTERN   This restaurant turns out some of the best rotisserie platters in Geneva, especially that baby farmhouse Swiss chicken roasted on a spit. The chefs also specialize in lamb from the Limousin region of France, and this succulent meat is also roasted on a spit. Many dishes have a Middle Eastern tone, and tabbouleh (an Arabic salad with bulgur wheat, parsley, mint, tomato, scallions, cucumbers, and other herbs is served with some courses). Main dishes are likely to include filet of half-cooked tuna in a sesame crust with ginger sauce, or else pan-fried prawns with herb butter.

36, rue du Strand. www.restaurantlabroche.ch. ⓒ **022/321-22-60.** Reservations recommended. Main courses 24SFR–45SFR; express menu 28SFR. AE, MC, V. Mon–Fri noon–2pm; Mon–Sat 7–10:30pm. Bus: 12.

La Favola ★ TUSCAN/ITALIAN   It's the best Italian restaurant in Geneva, and its most devoted habitués hail it as the best restaurant in Geneva—period. Set a few steps from the Cathédrale de St. Pierre, it contains only two cramped dining rooms. The menu is small but choice, varying with the availability of ingredients and the seasons. Look for such delightful dishes as carpaccio of beef; *vitello tonnato* (paper-thin veal with a tuna sauce); lobster salad; potato salad with cèpe mushrooms; such pastas as fresh ravioli with either eggplant or bolet mushrooms; and a luscious version of tortellini stuffed with ricotta, meat juices, red wine, and herbs. Meat and fish vary daily.

15, rue Calvin. www.lafavola.com. ☎ **022/311-74-37.** Reservations required. Main courses 34SFR–55SFR. AE, MC, V. Mon–Fri noon–2pm, 7-10pm and Sat 7–10pm. Closed 2 weeks in July–Aug and 1 week at Christmas. Tram: 12.

Restaurant de la Cigogne ★★ CONTINENTAL   This is one of the most appealing and best-staffed restaurants on Geneva's Left Bank. Classified as a member of the prestigious Relais & Châteaux group, it's housed within an opulently paneled ground-floor room of the also-recommended hotel (p. 1,010). Cosseted, discreetly elegant, and cozy, with impeccable service, it offers a full bar, a spectacular wine list, and well-groomed cuisine. At lunch, the venue is a bit more businesslike and rapid, segueing into a more relaxed and leisurely venue at dinner. Menu items reflect whatever ingredients are in season at the time of your arrival, but are likely to include a superb ravioli of shrimp with a brunoise (finely diced) of vegetables and a mousseline sauce; turbot prepared *façon grand-mère*; and a delectable *cordon bleu* of veal stuffed with foie gras and truffles, served with a galette of polenta with Parmesan and asparagus.

In the Hôtel de la Cigogne, 17, place Longemalle. www.cigogne.ch. ☎ **022/818-40-40.** Reservations recommended. Main courses 43SFR–52SFR; fixed-price menus 65SFR–175SFR. AE, DC, MC, V. Mon–Sat noon–2pm and daily 7–10pm. Bus: 6 or 9.

Restaurant Edelweiss ☺ SWISS   This is the most famous folkloric alpine-style restaurant in Geneva. It's set within the cellar of the also-recommended Hôtel Edelweiss, an establishment that carries the alpine chalet theme into its bedrooms, and its restaurant is the most artfully rustic within its neighborhood. Tables are lined up cozily under a high ceiling that showcases the flagstone columns, the fluegelhorns, the cowbells, and the live folkloric bands that oompah throughout the dinner hour. Rib-sticking menu items include six kinds of fondues, raclettes, roasted lamb chops with herbs, Zurich-style sliced veal in cream sauce, and several kinds of fish. If you have children, this may be a particularly worthy choice because of the folkloric distractions that add to the experience of dining here.

In the Hôtel Edelweiss, 2, place de la Navigation. ☎ **022/544-51-51.** Reservations recommended. Main courses 22SFR–43SFR; fixed-price menus 46SFR–75SFR. AE, DC, MC, V. Daily 7–11pm. Bus: 1.

Inexpensive

Chez Ma Cousine 🍴 FRENCH/SWISS   This is one of the least pretentious, and least expensive, sit-down restaurants in Geneva. What you'll find is an amiable venue of spartan-looking wooden tables and chairs, and a kitchen whose interior is open. The very limited menu lists the kind of food that French-speaking residents of Switzerland might have been nurtured on during their respective childhoods. A free salad accompanies most main courses, and the only option for potatoes is "Provençal-style." Platters include several variations of grilled chicken, the house specialty; at least two meal-sized salads of Indian-style (with curry) and Thai-style (with soy, coconut, and spicy tomato sauce) chicken; and roasted and sliced pork with a brown sauce, salad, and Provençal potatoes.

Although this branch in the Rue Lissignol is the most popular, there's a second branch of Chez Ma Cousine across the river in the Old Town with the same prices and longer hours (daily 11am–11:30pm). You'll find it at 6, place du Bourg-de-Four (ℂ 022/310-96-96).

5, rue Lissignol. ℂ **022/731-98-98.** Reservations not necessary. Main courses 15SFR–17SFR. MC, V. Mon–Fri 11:30am–2:30pm and 6:30–11:30pm. Bus: 1.

Nologo ★ MEDITERRANEAN/ITALIAN   Surrounded by a gaggle of less creative restaurants, this is the most sophisticated, most upscale, and most "design-conscious" restaurant in the burgeoning Pâquis district, a bustling and irreverent working-class neighborhood immediately downhill from the railway station. It features the kind of high-style black and stainless steel decor you might have expected in Milan and some of the most sophisticated and creative food in the neighborhood. Examples include veal cutlets with pesto-mint sauce, served with rosemary-roasted potatoes; seabass with ratatouille and caponata; beefsteak with rocket and exotic mushrooms; and wide-noodle pappardelle with fresh tuna, roasted eggplant, fresh tomatoes, and mint.

11, rue de Fribourg. www.nologo.ch. ℂ **022/901-0333.** Reservations recommended Fri–Sat nights. Main courses 20SFR–40SFR. AE, DC, MC, V. Mon–Fri noon–2:30pm; Mon–Sat 7–10:30pm. Bus: 1.

CAROUGE

Café des Negociants ★ CONTINENTAL   This is our favorite restaurant in Carouge. There's seating on the pavement outside, as well as within two separate dining rooms, each accented with portraits of great writers from France's 19th-century literary legacy. Menu items include cream of asparagus soup; rillettes of trout and salmon in puff pastry; carpaccio of tuna with strawberries and ginger; roasted filet of seabass with tomatoes and herbs; and a minirack of lamb with a mustard-flavored merlot sauce. Be warned in advance that despite its genuine ability to welcome its patrons, the staff has absolutely no sense of humor for anyone asking for food outside of the below-noted dining hours.

29, rue de la Filature (at the corner of rue St-Victor), in Carouge. www.negociants.ch. ℂ **022/300-31-30.** Reservations recommended. Main courses 37SFR–58SFR; fixed-price lunch 29SFR, dinner 64SFR. AE, DC, MC, V. Mon–Fri 9am–10:30pm. Tram: 12 or 13 from Geneva.

L'Olivier de Provence ★ ▮▮ FRENCH   Set in Carouge, this Provençal restaurant offers some of the best dining on Geneva's perimeter. Though open throughout the year, it's especially popular in warm weather, when patrons can dine on its tree-shaded terrace. The savory dishes include flambéed versions of *loup de mer* (seabass), ragout of scampi, entrecotes, *soupe de poisson,* and fresh salmon with sorrel. In autumn the restaurant is especially known for its game dishes, such as pheasant, rabbit, pigeon, and venison. A platter of guinea fowl appears in two different versions, both a supreme and a chartreuse of guinea with thighs, each served with fresh morels. In all, this is a good, bourgeois restaurant if you don't mind the slight excursion south of the city.

13, rue Jacques-Dalphin, Carouge. www.olivierdeprovence.ch. ℂ **022/342-04-50.** Reservations required. Main courses 37SFR–56SFR; fixed-price menus 19SFR–48SFR. AE, V. Mon–Fri noon–2pm; Mon–Sat 7–10:15pm. Tram: 12.

Shopping

From boutiques to department stores, Geneva is a shopper's dream come true. The city, of course, is known for its watches and jewelry, but it's also a good place to buy embroidered blouses, music boxes from the Jura region, cuckoo clocks from German Switzerland, cigars from Havana (not allowed into the U.S.), chocolate, Swiss Army knives, and many other items.

Be sure to avoid purchasing a Swiss watch in one of the souvenir stores. If jewelers are legitimate, they'll display a symbol of the Geneva Association of Watchmakers and Jewelers.

A shopping spree may begin at **Place du Molard,** once the harbor of Geneva before the water receded. Merchants from all over Europe used to bring their wares to trade fairs here in the days before merchants migrated to the richer markets in Lyon.

If you walk along **Rue du Rhône** and are put off by the prices, go one block south to **Rue du Marché,** which in various sections becomes **Rue de la Croix-d'Or** and **Rue de Rive,** and is sometimes referred to by locals as "la rue du Tram" because of the many trolleys that run along its length.

Shopping in Carouge is more whimsical and lighthearted than what you're likely to find in *haute Genève,* and often with garments or objects that aren't easily duplicated anywhere else. Here's a selection of some of the most intriguing—all of them centered within a relatively small area of less than three square blocks.

Store hours vary in Geneva. Most stores are open Monday to Friday 8am to 6:30pm and Saturday from 8am to 5pm.

CHOCOLATES

Confiserie Rohr   The aroma from this chocolate store practically pulls you in off the street. Among other specialties, you'll find chocolate-covered truffles, "gold" bars with hazelnuts, and *poubelles au chocolat* (chocolate "garbage pails"). Another store is at 42, rue du Rhône. www.chocolats-rohr.ch. 3 place du Molard. ✆ **022/311-63-03.**

CLOTHING

Anne-Claude Virchaux ★★   She's a one-woman show, a locally born *artiste* who designs and weaves her own textiles before cutting them into the kind of artfully "bohemian" garment that women as far away as California would fight to own. Perennially attractive colors include pumpkin, persimmon, wheat, and several heavenly shades of ocher and blue. Garments, each completely original and one-of-a-kind, cost from 500SFR to 1,600SFR each. Anne-Claude herself is usually on-site, usually with a tape measure thrown around her neck that her fans view as a combination fashion accessory and badge of honor. 13, rue St-Joseph, in Carouge. ✆ **022/342-35-26.**

DEPARTMENT STORES

Bon Genie   Located on Place du Molard, this department store sells mostly high-fashion women's clothing. Its storefront windows display art objects from local museums alongside designer clothes. There's also a limited selection of men's clothing, as well as furniture, cosmetics, and perfumes. 34, rue du Marché. www.bongenie-grieder.ch. ✆ **022/818-11-11.**

Globus   This is one of the largest department stores in Geneva, with many boutique-style departments that flourish inside and a self-image that's firmly patterned after the upscale Galeries Lafayette in Paris. Expect glamour, lots of upbeat cheerfulness, and departments devoted separately to travel bureaus, an agency selling theater tickets, a hairdresser, newspaper kiosks, and a bistro and sandwich shop/cafe. 48, rue du Rhône. www.globus.ch. ℭ **022/319-50-50.**

JEWELRY/WATCHES

Bucherer ★ Located opposite the Mont Blanc Bridge, this chrome-and-crystal store sells deluxe watches and diamonds. The store offers such name brands as Rolex, Piaget, Ebel, Baume & Mercier, Omega, Tissot, Rado, and Swatch. You'll also find a large selection of cuckoo clocks, music boxes, embroideries, and souvenirs, as well as porcelain pill boxes and other gift items. 45, rue du Rhône. www.bucherer.com. ℭ **022/319-62-66.**

TOBACCO

Davidoff ★ This is the most famous tobacco store in the world, with the best cigars you'll find in Europe. This is the place where the Davidoff retail empire all began. For many years, this was the business headquarters of Zino and Marthe Davidoff, Russian émigrés who arrived in Switzerland in 1911. 2, rue de Rive. www.davidoff. com. ℭ **022/310-90-41.**

Entertainment & Nightlife

Geneva has a more diverse and varied nightlife than any other city in Switzerland. Some of the activities are centered around **Place du Bourg-de-Four.**

For a listing of nightlife and cultural activities, free copies of the bilingual monthly *Genève Le Guide* (www.le-guide.ch) are distributed at hotel desks and tourist information centers.

THE PERFORMING ARTS

Geneva has always attracted the culturally sophisticated, including Byron, Jean-Baptiste Camille Corot, Victor Hugo, Balzac, George Sand, and Franz Liszt. Ernst Ansermet founded Geneva's great **Orchestre de la Suisse Romande,** whose frequent concerts entertain music lovers at **Victoria Hall,** 14, rue du Général-Dufour. (www.osr.ch; ℭ **022/807-00-00**). For opera there's the 1,500-seat **Grand Théâtre,** Place Neuve (www.geneveopera.ch; ℭ **022/418-31-30**), which welcomes Béjart, the Bolshoi, and other ballet companies, in addition to having a company of its own.

The **Bâtiment des Forces Motrices (Le BFM)** 2, place des Volontaires (www. bfm.ch; ℭ **022/322-12-20**), stages an ongoing series of theater and musical concerts that are among the most controversial and iconoclastic in town. It was originally inaugurated in 1886 as a hydroelectric and pumping station and is now a venue for classical and rock concerts, theater pieces, fashion *defiles*, and political rallies.

THE CLUB & MUSIC SCENE

There is a lack of decent clubs in Geneva, so it's also worth keeping an eye out for "parties" set up in various venues.

Au Chat Noir 👔 In the suburb of Carouge, this is a venue for funk, rock, salsa, jazz, and some good old New Orleans blues. There are many similar bars on the same street. It's crowded on weekends but the club will take reservations. Live music is presented nightly at 9pm (10pm Fri–Sat). After a few drinks, you begin to fear that the car suspended from the ceiling might fall on you. It's open Tuesday to Thursday from 6pm to 4am, Friday 6pm to 5am, Saturday 9pm to 5am, and Sunday 8pm to 4am. 13, rue Vautier, Carouge. www.chatnoir.ch. ℭ **022/307-10-40.** Cover 16SFR–22SFR.

Javaclub ★   Night-owling VIPs have made this dance club their favorite rendez-vous, which is going strong as most of Geneva sleeps. The atmosphere is chic and sophisticated in the extreme, the clientele urban and glamorous. The latest music is played in this spacious setting. The club is hailed in the local press as a venue for "nocturne genevoise." Open Tuesday to Saturday 11pm to 5am. In the Grand Hotel Kempinski, 19 quai du Mont-Blanc, Les Pâquis. www.javaclub.ch. ℂ **022/908-90-98.** Cover 60SFR.

THE BAR SCENE
Most bars in Geneva close at 1:30 or 2am.

Arthur's Rive Gauche ★   Left Bank sophistication and a chic atmosphere draw a clientele to this bar and restaurant opening onto the banks of the Rhône River. The interior is a study in elegance and charm. You can visit to eat or drink, sampling such dishes as filet of beef with ravioli stuffed with wok-sautéed fresh vegetables or marinated raw sea bream with guacamole and a bloody mary granité. The wine list is one of the best in the neighborhood. Open Monday to Friday 7:30am to 2am, Saturday noon to 2am. 7–9 rue du Rhône. www.arthurs.ch. ℂ **022/810-32-60.**

Le Bar des Bergues ★★★   In what's probably the most consistently expensive hotel in Geneva, the suave and silky bar staff at the Hôtel des Bergues (p. 1009) is ready, willing, and able to welcome you into the inner sanctums of this elegant and very upscale wood-paneled bar. If you're not actually living at the hotel at the time of your appearance, you won't be alone: At least half the clients of this bar aren't residents of the hotel. Entrance is free. Whiskey-sodas begin at around 16SFR. In the Four Seasons Grand Hôtel des Bergues, 33, quai des Bergues. ℂ **022/908-70-00.**

The Leopard Room ★   Outfitted with the antique trunks and Grand Tour accessories that Lord Byron might have hauled with him on his poetic and revolutionary peregrinations around 19th-century Europe, it's a bit less overwhelming than the glossier and more in-the-news Le Bar des Bergues. Woodsy and a bit like a library, it's in the cellar level of the Hôtel d'Angleterre. Live music from a piano begins every night except Sunday at 7pm. Tapas and sashimi cost from 15SFR to 32SFR per portion. It's open every night from 5:30pm to 1am, and if you get hungry after too many drinks, the hotel dining room, Windows (p. 1000), is immediately upstairs. In the Hôtel d'Angleterre, 17, quai du Mont-Blanc. ℂ **022/906-55-55.**

Little Buddha Geneva   This restaurant, lounge, and bar is the latest entry in the Rive Gauche sweepstakes for a hot, new, trendy address in an elegant setting. As the inspiration for their cocktails, the bartenders have roamed the world for their inspiration—try the vodka-laced Mango Spicy from Thailand or a real rum-laced mojito from Cuba, once the favorite libation of Ernest Hemingway. As a special feature, it offers an array of such snacks as sushi, sashimi, freshly made salads, and *soups exotiques*. There is also a selection of some of the best tapas in town. Open Monday to Saturday 6pm to 2am. Place Neuve, 10 rue J.-Fr. Bartholoni. www.littlebuddhageneva.com (in French only). ℂ **022/307-10-00.**

Mr. Pickwick Pub 🍺   This pub serves simple, English-style meals, but most patrons come here to drink. The paneled rooms are filled in the evening with a young crowd, who enjoy the dim lighting and American music. The place gets very crowded and can be fun. Irish coffee is a specialty, but most visitors order beer. Because so many United Nations employees hang out here, this pub is sometimes called the "Tower of Babble." Open daily from 10am to 2am. 80, rue de Lausanne (corner of Rue Rothschild). www.mrpickwick.ch. ℂ **022/731-67-97.**

Scandale Many 20- and 30-somethings seem to congregate here, a site vaguely akin to a warehouse, which includes dining, drinking, and dancing facilities that seem to rock virtually every night it's open. Furnishings include artfully battered, hand-me-down sofas, an elongated bar, and a blend of house and electro-jazz music that keeps everybody hopping. This gay-friendly place is open every Tuesday to Saturday from 10am to 2am, with a DJ whose music begins in the cellar-level dance bar at 11pm. If you get hungry, a somewhat lackluster, mostly black-and-stainless-steel restaurant charges from 11SFR to 27SFR for pastas and pizzas. Two large plasma screens broadcast everything from sporting events to punk-rock concerts. 24, rue de Lausanne. ✆ **022/731-83-73.** www.lescandale.ch.

THE LGBT SCENE

Geneva's gay switchboard is **Dialogai,** 11–13, rue de la Navigation (✆ **022/906-40-40;** www.dialogai.org). It provides multilingual information and advice to anyone who calls. On the basement level are a library, a cafe and bar, and meeting rooms for Wednesday-night dinners and Sunday-morning brunches. The organization publishes a free list of the gay bars in Geneva and French-speaking Switzerland.

Where to Stay

A truly world-class city, Geneva has plenty of hotels, most of which are clustered around the railway terminal or stretched along the lakefront. But be warned—Geneva hosts a number of international conferences and conventions, so many of its hotels are booked months in advance. And while it does incorporate dozens of expensive hotels in all different architectural styles (from the antique to the supermodern), it doesn't have very many intimate, family-run inns.

Very Expensive

Four Seasons Hôtel des Bergues ★★★ This elegant, four-story hotel—designated a historic monument by the Swiss—once catered to the monarchs of Europe. It is now the most ostentatiously elegant hotel in Geneva.

Stratospherically expensive, with an armada of uniformed, polite staff members, the Four Seasons is a favorite with the haute international business community, diplomats, and members of European society. Grandly memorable from its centrally located position at the edge of the Rhône, the hotel also hosted many meetings of the League of Nations.

The hotel's public rooms are among the most lavish in Switzerland. The bedrooms have Directoire and Louis Philippe furnishings. Accommodations ranked "superior" on the Bel Etage floor are the finest choices here, although all units are beautifully appointed. Lake-view rooms are more expensive.

33, quai des Bergues, CH-1211 Genève. www.hoteldesbergues.com. ✆ **022/908-70-00.** Fax 022/908-74-00. 103 units. 810SFR–1,040SFR double; from 1,750SFR suite. AE, DC, MC, V. Parking 40SFR. Bus: 1. **Amenities:** Restaurant; bar; indoor pool (mid-2013); exercise room; spa; children's programs; concierge; room service; babysitting; airport transfers (110SFR). *In room:* A/C, TV/DVD, minibar, hair dryer, CD player, Wi-Fi (30SFR/24 hr.).

Hôtel Beau-Rivage ★★★ This grand old landmark 1865 hotel receives our highest recommendation for its traditional Victorian charm and impeccable service. The most tragic event in its history was the assassination of Empress Elisabeth ("Sissi") of Austria, who was stabbed on the nearby quays in 1898 by the anarchist Luigi Lucheni, and then carried back to her lodgings in the Beau-Rivage to die a few hours later. To this day, history buffs rent the pale-blue Empress Suite.

Its most striking feature is the open, five-story lobby. The hotel also became the first in Europe to install elevators. The rooms are individually furnished and frequently redecorated. All front rooms have views of the lake. Accommodations are categorized by size, with "romantic" rooms being more spacious and "classical" rooms being medium in size. Some of the romantic units contain ceiling frescoes teeming with cherubs and mythical heroes.

13, quai du Mont-Blanc, CH-1201 Genève. www.beau-rivage.ch. © **022/716-66-66.** Fax 022/716-60-60. 94 units. 800SFR–1,400SFR double; from 1,600SFR suite. AE, DC, MC, V. Parking 40SFR. Bus: 1. **Amenities:** 2 restaurants; bar; exercise room; concierge; room service; babysitting. *In room:* A/C, TV/DVD, fax, minibar, hair dryer, CD player, Wi-Fi (free).

Expensive

Hôtel de la Cigogne ★★★   Personalized and charming, this is our favorite Left Bank hotel, a chic, glamorous retreat for the discerning. This deluxe hotel was rebuilt after years of dilapidation and turned into an offbeat Relais & Châteaux that showcases designer and decorator talent. Combined with an adjoining building, the old hotel and its mate have the renovated facades of the original 18th- and 19th-century structures. With three sheltered courtyards overlooking a flowering plaza, this is one of the most tranquil hotels in Geneva. The bedrooms contain handmade mattresses, luxurious bathrooms, and bed linens embroidered with the hotel's coat of arms. Each bedroom is furnished differently, ranging from 1930s movie-mogul style to the "baron and baroness at their country place." Some units have working fireplaces.

17, place Longemalle, CH-1204 Genève. www.cigogne.ch. © **022/818-40-40.** Fax 022/818-40-50. 52 units. 520SFR–665SFR double; 950SFR–1,150SFR suite. Rates include continental breakfast. AE, DC, MC, V. Parking 27SFR. Bus: 12. **Amenities:** Restaurant; room service; babysitting. *In room:* A/C, TV, minibar, hair dryer, Wi-Fi (free).

Les Armures ★★★   Surpassed only by La Cigogne, this is one of the most elegant and prestigious hotels on Geneva's Left Bank. Positioned a few steps from both the cathedral and the medieval Maison Tavel, it lacks the late-19th-century grandeur of its five-star competitors across the river. Instead, you'll find a labyrinth of narrow corridors, and architectural gems that include beamed (and sometimes frescoed) ceilings and carefully preserved remnants of the building's 17th-century origins. Each unit is different from its neighbors, usually with exposed brick or stone, and each alternates modern plumbing with richly detailed tile work in its bathrooms. The ambience here is cozy and well upholstered, with an ostentation that's subtle and based for the most part on the building's sense of quirky, antique charm.

1, rue du Puits Saint-Pierre, CH-1204 Genève. www.hotel-les-armures.ch. © **022/310-91-72.** Fax 022/310-98-46. 32 units. 695SFR–720SFR double; 855SFR–995SFR suite. Rates include buffet breakfast. AE, DC, MC, V. Parking 35SFR. Bus: 12. **Amenities:** Restaurant; bar; concierge; room service; babysitting. *In room:* A/C, TV/DVD, minibar, hair dryer, Wi-Fi (free).

Moderate

Cornavin ★   Standing close to the main railway station, this central hotel dazzles you as you enter. The lobby contains "the biggest clock in the world," according to Guinness Records, rising nine floors. You can take in this timepiece as you ride in the glass-walled elevator to the top floor, where the magnificent glassed-in breakfast hall opens onto panoramic views of Geneva. The midsize bedrooms are imbued with a contemporary design and such special features as soundproof windows. The hotel rents more than a dozen triple bedrooms along with half a dozen interconnecting doubles, these accommodations usually rented to families.

Gare de Cornavin, CH-1201 Genève. www.fhotels.ch. ✆ **022/716-12-12.** 164 units. 200SFR–426SFR double; 320SFR–460SFR suite. AE, MC, V. Bus: 10. **Amenities:** Bar; concierge; room service. *In room:* A/C, TV, hair dryer, Wi-Fi (free).

Hôtel International & Terminus ☺   This hotel lies across the street from the main entrance of Geneva's railway station and has been directed by three generations of the Cottier family. Originally built in 1900, it has been radically upgraded, with pairs of smaller rooms reconfigured into larger units especially good for families. Rated three stars by the local tourist board, the hotel offers exceedingly good value. The small to spacious bedrooms are fitted with first-rate furnishings and the maintenance level is high. Bathrooms seem to have been added as an afterthought in areas not designed for them, and are a bit cramped with shower stalls. The restaurant, La Veranda, serves some of the most reasonable meals in Geneva, and keeps the pizza ovens cauldron hot.

20, rue des Alpes, CH-1201 Genève. www.international-terminus.ch. ✆ **022/906-97-77.** Fax 022/906-97-78. 60 units. 170SFR–290SFR double. Rates include buffet breakfast. AE, DC, MC, V. Bus: 10. **Amenities:** Restaurant. *In room:* TV, minibar, hair dryer, Wi-Fi (free).

Hôtel Tiffany ★ ✍   This little charming five-story Belle Epoque boutique hotel lies on a Left Bank street 3 blocks south of the river and about a 12-minute stroll from the center and the lake. Although it can hardly match the style and glamour of the lakeside palaces, it's attractive in its own modest way, featuring touches like stained glass, Art Nouveau bed frames, leather-clad armchairs, and a summertime sidewalk cafe. In its category, it offers some of the most reasonable prices in Geneva, especially considering its style. Bedrooms are midsize with lots of extras, including soundproofing and spacious bathrooms. We prefer the rooms in the "attic," with their beams, rooftop vistas, and sloping walls.

20, rue de l'Arquebuse, CH-1204 Genève. www.hotel-tiffany.ch. ✆ **022/708-16-16.** Fax 022/708-16-17. 46 units. 230SFR–460SFR double; from 600SFR suite. AE, DC, MC, V. Parking nearby 34SFR. Bus: 12. **Amenities:** Restaurant; bar; exercise room; room service. *In room:* A/C, TV, DVD and CD player (in suites), minibar, hair dryer, Wi-Fi (free).

Inexpensive

EastWest ★★ ▮▮   This small town house is a bastion of charm, comfort, and grace. It is a tranquil oasis between the main train station and the lake. The intimate, cozy atmosphere creates the aura of a private home. The contemporary decor blends elements of the Western world with the East, with such features as a wall of free-flowing water framed with plants. The elegant and functional bedrooms have dark wooden furniture, parquet flooring, tasteful fabrics, and such extras as espresso machines and deluxe bathrobes. Unusual accommodations include two junior suites on the top floor overlooking the rooftops of Geneva, and a duplex with stairs leading up to a luxurious bedroom. The library offers a selection of books, magazines, and DVDs. A delightful jewel is the on-site restaurant with its southern French cuisine, opening onto a small terrace.

6, rue des Pâquis, Les Pâquis, CH-1201 Genève. www.eastwesthotel.ch. ✆ **022/708-17-17.** 41 units. 308SFR–387SFR double; 526SFR junior suite; 791SFR–853SFR duplex. AE, DC, MC, V. Bus: 1. **Amenities:** Restaurant; bar; exercise room; room service. *In room:* A/C, TV, DVD player, hair dryer, Wi-Fi (free).

Hôtel Bernina   Set directly across from Gare Cornavin, this is an old-fashioned but worthy family-run hotel with a reputation for fair prices and relatively comfortable accommodations. Just don't expect luxury; there's a Sputnik-era severity to the lobby, with furniture resembling that in an airport waiting lounge, and a blasé, not particularly responsive staff. Rooms are high-ceilinged and sunny, albeit somewhat battered, but they're clean, filled with angular modern furniture, and soundproof against the noise of the traffic outside. The restaurant congestion of the railway station is just across the square.

22, place Cornavin, CH-1211 Genève. www.bernina-geneve.ch. ℂ **022/908-49-50.** Fax 022/908-49-51. 80 units. 160SFR–250SFR double. Rates include buffet breakfast. AE, DC, MC, V. Bus: 10. **Amenities:** Room service. *In room:* TV, Wi-Fi (free).

Tor 💣   Finding an economical place to stay in high-priced Geneva is a daunting challenge, but Tor is a fine possibility, taking over three stories of a classical building across from the English Church between the main rail station and Lake Geneva. Bedrooms, often small, are clean, comfortable, and furnished in a convenient but simple way with modern pieces. Things are a bit minimalist here, but high ceilings and big windows in some rooms add more grace notes. There's no air-conditioning, but in Geneva you often don't need it for most of the year. A wide range of accommodations include "Easy," the smallest units with a shower and sink (toilet down the hall). The quietest rooms, called "Compact," are in the rear overlooking a courtyard and have full plumbing. "Standard" and "Family" accommodations have full facilities, and family rooms sleep four guests. Breakfast, included in the price, is brought to your room since there is no restaurant.

Ville Rive Droite, CH-1201 Genève. www.torhotel.com. ℂ **022/909-88-20.** 26 units. 80SFR–140SFR double without toilet; 90SFR–160SFR compact and standard double; 130SFR–210SFR family unit. AE, MC, V. Bus: 10. *In room:* TV (in some), phone (in some), Wi-Fi (in some, free).

Easy Excursions from Geneva

There are many attractions in the region around Geneva.

MONT SALEVE ★

The limestone ridge of Mont Salève (House Mountain) is 6.4km (4 miles) south of Geneva, in France. Its peak is at 1,200m (3,936 ft.), but you'll need a passport to get near it. If you have a car, you can take a road that goes up the mountain, which is popular with rock climbers. **Bus no. 8** will take you to Veyrier-Douane, on the French border, where there's a passport and Customs control. A 6-minute **cable-car** (www.telepheriquedusaleve.com) ride will take you to a height of 1,125m (3,690 ft.) on Mont Salève. From there, you'll have a **panoramic sweep ★** of the Valley of the Arve, with Geneva and Mont Blanc in the background. A return costs adults 10.80SFR, students (17–25) 7.60SFR; children aged 3 to 16 6SFR.

LAUSANNE ★★

66km (41 miles) NE of Geneva; 214km (133 miles) SW of Zurich.

Lausanne, whose 140,000 inhabitants make it the second-largest city on Lake Geneva and the fifth largest in Switzerland, is built on three hills overlooking the lake. The upper and lower towns are connected by a small metro (subway).

Lausanne has been inhabited since the Stone Age (it was the ancient Roman town of Lousanna). In 1803, the canton of Vaud, of which Lausanne is the capital, became the 19th to join the Swiss Confederation.

Lausanne flourished particularly in the Age of Enlightenment, when it was associated with Rousseau and Voltaire, two of the leading writers in the 18th century. Even today the city is cited by many French-speaking Swiss as the place they would most like to live because of its low-key elegance and sense of grace. Regrettably, it's no longer a center of the intellectual or artistic elite. Voltaire and the likes have given way to water-skiers, swimmers, and "Sunday sailors," most of whom have never heard of Rousseau, much less read him. Even so, Lausanne retains an aesthetic charm and a cultural tradition—today it's the headquarters of the International Olympic Committee.

Essentials

GETTING THERE   The **train** from Geneva leaves for Lausanne every 20 minutes and the trip takes between 30 and 45 minutes, depending on the individual train. Visit www.sbb.ch or call ✆ **0900/300-300** for train schedules.

In addition, between late May and late September, a lake steamer cruises several times a day in both directions between Geneva and Lausanne. Sailing time from Geneva is about 3½ hours. Round-trip transit from Geneva costs 91SFR in first class and 67SFR in second class, with 50% discounts for children 16 and under. For information, contact the **Compagnie Générale de Navigation (CGN),** 17, av. de Rhodanie (www.cgn.ch; ✆ **0848/811-848**).

If you're **driving,** Lausanne is connected by freeway (N1) to Geneva. The Great Saint Bernard tunnel is 113km (70 miles) to the southeast, reached along E2, which becomes E21 during your final approach. The speed limit on most of the highways leading into Lausanne, and throughout the rest of Switzerland as well, is 120kmph (75 mph).

VISITOR INFORMATION   There are two branches of the **Office du Tourisme et des Congrès** in Lausanne. The larger of the two faces the lakefront in Ouchy, at 2, av. de Rhodanie (www.lausanne-tourisme.ch; ✆ **021/613-73-21** or **021/613-73-73**). Hours are Monday to Friday 8am to 5pm, Saturday and Sunday 9am to 5pm. The tourist office in the railway station (✆ **021/321-77-66**) is open daily, year-round, 9am to 7pm.

CITY LAYOUT   Lausanne is spread out along the shore of Lake Geneva, surrounded by suburbs. There are two sections in particular that attract the most visitors—the Upper Town (**Haute Ville**) and the once-industrial neighborhood of **Flon,** which collectively comprise the oldest parts of the city, and the Lower Town (**Basse Ville**) and its lake-fronting district of **Ouchy;** the two sections are connected by a small subway (metro). The metro features 14 separate stations, incorporating Lausanne with many of its outlying suburbs. This is the only underground (metro) in Switzerland.

Lausanne's Upper Town still evokes the Middle Ages—a night watchman calls out the hours from 10pm to 2am from atop the cathedral's belfry. A visit to the Haute Ville takes about 2 hours and is best done on foot. In fact, walking through the old town of Lausanne is one of its major attractions. It's easy to get lost—and that's part of the fun. This area is north of the station; you can reach it by proceeding uphill along Rue du Petit-Chêne. The focal point of the Upper Town, and the shopping and business heart of Lausanne, is **Place Saint-François.** While vehicles are permitted south of the church, the historic area to the north of the church is a pedestrian-only zone; it has more than 2km (1¼ miles) of streets, including **Rue de Bourg,** northeast of the church, the best street for shopping. Rue de Bourg leads to the large, bustling Rue Caroline, which winds north to **Pont des Bessières,** one of the three bridges erected at the turn of the 20th century to connect the three hills on which Lausanne was built.

From the bridge, you'll see the Haute Ville on your right, with the 13th-century **Cathedral of Lausanne** ★★, opening onto Place de la Cathédrale (ℂ **021/316-71-61**; free admission to cathedral, tower 2SFR; Apr–Sept Mon–Fri 7am–7pm, Sat 8am–7pm, Sun 2–7pm; Oct–Mar Mon–Fri 7:30am–6pm, Sat 8:30am–5pm, Sun 2–5:30pm. Visits not permitted Sun morning during services; Bus: 7 or 16); it is the focal point of the Upper Town and one of the finest medieval churches in Switzerland.

From the square, Rue du Cité-de-Vant goes north to the 14th-century Château Saint-Maire, on Place du Château—once the home of bishops and now containing the offices of the canton administration. From here, Avenue de l'Université leads to **Place de la Riponne,** at the edge of which sits the Italianate **Palais de Rumine,** built in 1906. It contains several museums, a university founded in 1537, and the university and cantonal library with some 700,000 volumes. It is also the site of Lausanne's biweekly food and produce **markets** (Wed and Sat May–Oct 8am–1pm). From Place de la Riponne, Rue Pierre-Viret leads to the **Escaliers du Marché,** a covered stairway dating back to the Middle Ages. You can also take Rue Madeleine from the Place de la Riponne, continuing south to Place de la Palud. On the side of Place de la Palud is the 17th-century **Hôtel de Ville (town hall).**

South of Place de la Palud is Rue du Pont, which turns into Rue Saint-François (after crossing Rue Centrale). Nearby, **Place du Flon,** with its cafes and bars, is a favorite evening hangout and you can also catch the subway to Ouchy.

Ouchy is the lakeside resort and bustling port of Lausanne. Its tree-shaded quays have flower gardens that are nearly half a mile long. The small harbor contains a 700-boat marina, and the Savoy Alps are visible on the opposite shore. The **Château d'Ouchy** is now a hotel and restaurant. The Allies, Greece, and Turkey signed a peace treaty here in 1923. The 13th-century keep is still standing. In the **Hôtel d'Angleterre,** formerly the Auberge de l'Ancre, is a plaque commemorating the stay of Lord Byron, who wrote *The Prisoner of Chillon* here. In the **Beau-Rivage,** the Treaty of Lausanne was ratified in 1923; it settled the final reparations disputes after World War I.

Olympic Museum Seeing that the Comité International Olympique has been installed in Lausanne since 1915, the city decided in 1993 to open a museum recalling the history of the games since ancient Greece. The largest information center for the Olympic movement in the world, it's a tribute to the union of sport, art, and culture, with a coin and stamp collection, an Olympic Study Center, a library, an information center, and a video library recalling some of the games' most historic moments. There's even a scattering of artifacts commemorating the sporting triumphs of South America's Aztec empire. Advanced audiovisual, computer, and robotic technology allows visitors to share in the great feats and the emotions of the athletes. An Olympic flame burns alongside a column that lists the venues where the games have been held.

1, quai d'Ouchy. www.olympic.org. ℂ **021/621-65-11.** Admission 15SFR adults; 10SFR seniors, students, and children 6–16; free for children 5 and under; 35SFR family ticket. Apr–Oct daily 9am–6pm (till 8pm Thurs); Nov–Mar Tues–Sun 9am–6pm. Closed Jan 1 and Dec 25. Take bus 8 from the center of Lausanne or the metro from the rail station to Ouchy, then walk for 15 min. with the lake on your right, passing the Beau-Rivage Palace hotel en route.

MONTREUX ★★

3km (2 miles) E of Vevey; 24km (15 miles) E of Lausanne; 100km (62 miles) E of Geneva.

The chief resort of the Swiss Riviera, Montreux rises in the shape of an amphitheater from the shores of Lac Léman. An Edwardian town with a distinct French accent.

TO FRANCE BY lake STEAMER

Evian-les-Bains in France lies on one of the southern shores of Lake Geneva and is the leading spa resort in eastern France, its lakeside promenade fashionable since the 19th century. Bottled Evian is, of course, one of the great French table waters.

Lake steamers to Evian from Lausanne are operated by **CGN (Compagnie Générale de Navigation;** www.cgn.ch; © **0848/811-848**). They depart every hour in summer (mid-May to mid-Sept), and about three times per day in the dead of winter. Transit takes only 35 minutes each way. Once you get to Evian, you can wander on your own, as there are no guided tours available. Round-trip cost of passage from Lausanne to Evian is 31SFR in second class or 42SFR in first class.

Known for its balmy climate, it sports a profusion of Mediterranean vegetation, which grows lushly in the town's many lakeside parks. The mountains at the town's back protect it from the winds of winter, allowing fruit trees, cypresses, magnolias, bay trees, almonds, and even palms to flourish.

Essentials

GETTING THERE   Montreux not only lies on the famous *Orient Express* line linking Paris to Milan, but it's also connected to the link between Geneva and the Simplon Tunnel. Dozens of trains stop at Montreux every day headed in both directions. The most famous is the ***Train Panoramique,*** a big-windowed train with a transparent roof that links Montreux to Interlaken. For bookings, contact **Golden Pass,** Gare de Montreux (www.goldenpass.ch; © **41840/245-245**). For more Swiss **rail information,** visit www.sbb.ch or dial © **0900/300-300.**

If you're **driving,** Montreux sits in the middle of a network of superhighways linking Germany, France, and Italy with Switzerland. The divider of the traffic coming from Germany via Bern is just outside Montreux. From that vantage point, you can go either east or west across Switzerland.

In addition, Montreux is one of the stops on the east–west steamer route between Villeneuve and Geneva. Travel by **lake steamer** from Lausanne is about 1 hour, or about 3 hours from Geneva. Most boats depart between May and September, with limited service throughout the rest of the year. For information and bookings, contact **CGN (Compagnie Générale de Navigation)** (www.cgn.ch; © **0848/811-848**).

VISITOR INFORMATION   The **Montreux Convention & Tourist Information Office,** Rue du Theater (www.montreux.ch/tourism; © **021/962-84-84**), is opposite the boat-landing pier. Throughout the year, it's open daily from 9am to 6pm.

Exploring Montreux

Explore the old houses and crooked streets of Old Montreux. Later, stroll along the quay-side promenade by the lake. Along the quayside at the Place du Marché, music lovers look out for the statue of **Freddie Mercury,** a copy of the image used on the cover of Queen's album, Made in Heaven, which was recorded in Montreux.

The most impressive castle in Switzerland, the **Château of Chillon ★★** (www. chillon.ch; © **021/966-89-10**) is on the lake 3.2km (2 miles) south of Montreux. To reach it, you can ride trolley bus no. 1 for 3SFR each way. But for many, the most enthralling way to reach Chillon from Montreux is to walk along the scenery-studded

MONTREUX jazz FESTIVAL

One of the biggest musical bashes in Europe occurs at the internationally known **Montreux Jazz Festival** (www.montreuxjazz.com; ☎ **021/966-44-44**). Beginning the first week of July and running for 2 weeks, everyone from Bob Dylan to Buddy Guy is likely to show up for the music and festivities. Ticket prices are high. You pay from 65SFR to 300SFR for each individual ticket. The tourist office in Montreux provides advance information and even sells tickets. Tickets for many events, especially the top ones, often sell out early. If you show up and can't get a ticket, you can still enjoy Jazz Off, some 500 hours of admission-free open-air concerts, often staged by new or wannabe talent throughout the city. The tourist office keeps a schedule, but much of the fun is spontaneous.

3km (2-mile) lake path; it's the grandest promenade you can take in Montreux. Most of the castle dates from the 13th century, but its oldest section is thought to be 1,000 years old. The castle was built by Peter II of Savoy and is one of the best preserved, and most frequently photographed, medieval castles of Europe. So-called sorcerers were tried and tortured here. The most famous prisoner, François Bonivard, was described by Byron in *The Prisoner of Chillon*. Bonivard was the prior of St. Victori in Geneva, and when he supported Geneva's independence in 1532, the Catholic duke of Savoy chained him in the dungeon until 1536, when he was released by the Bernese.

The château is open April to September daily from 9am to 7pm, March and October daily from 9:30am to 6pm, and November to February daily from 10am to 5pm. It's closed Christmas and New Year. Admission costs 12SFR for adults and 6SFR for children 6 to 16.

Rochers-de-Naye ★★★ at 2,042m (6,698 ft.) is one of the most popular tours along Lake Geneva. From Montreux, a cogwheel train takes visitors up to Rochers-de-Naye in less than an hour. The train ascends the slopes over Lac Léman, passing **Glion,** a little resort on a rocky crag almost suspended between lake and mountains. You come to **Caux** at 1,097m (3,598 ft.), lying on a natural balcony overhanging the blue bowl of the lake. Finally, the peak of Rochers-de-Naye raises high in the Vaudois Alps. In the distance, you can see the Savoy Alps, including Mont Blanc and the Jura Alps. At the end is an **alpine flower garden,** the loftiest in Europe. The train departs from the railway station of Montreux every hour during the day, beginning at 7:30am, with the last departure between 5:30 and 7pm, depending on the season. The travel time to Caux is 20 minutes. The round-trip fare between Montreux and Rochers-de-Naye is 59SFR. Holders of Swiss Rail passes or Eurail passes pay half-price. Call ☎ **021/989-81-90** or see www.myswitzerland.com for more information.

Villeneuve, the little port town at the end of the lake, is where Lord Byron wrote *The Prisoner of Chillon* in 1816. Mahatma Gandhi visited Romain Rolland when the French novelist and pacifist lived here. The town and its surrounding countryside have been painted by many artists, including Oskar Kokoschka, who once lived here. Villeneuve is a 25-minute walk from the Château of Chillon, which is visible from virtually every point in the village.

ZURICH

Self-confident and prosperous, Zurich is the blueprint of Swiss perfection, with its banking muscle, alpine backdrop, and love of good living. Blessed with pure air, dazzling Lake Zurich and a walkable Altstadt district full of fine boutiques and restaurants, it's little wonder the locals look so pleased. But where is the urban edge? You need only delve into Dada at Cabaret Voltaire, enjoy a literary pint at the James Joyce Pub, or buy a funky Freitag bag to realize that, behind its super-slick facade, Zurich inspires and innovates.

Essentials

GETTING THERE

BY PLANE   **Kloten Airport** (www.zurich-airport.com; ✆ **0900/300-313**), the international airport of Zurich, is the biggest airport in Switzerland and the most popular gateway to the country; in fact, it's among the 10 busiest airports in Europe. The airport is approximately 11km (7 miles) north of the city center, and the trip by taxi costs between 55SFR and 60SFR. A far better and cheaper option is to take the Swiss Federal Railways train service. You'll arrive in less than 15 minutes at the **Zurich Hauptbahnhof,** the main railway station in the center of the city. Zurich is a fairly compact city—from the train station, you can walk or hop on a tram or bus to most Zurich hotels in less than 30 minutes. The train ticket from the airport to the main railway station costs 6.40SFR in second class and 10.60SFR in first class. A 24-hour version of the same ticket costs 24SFR in second class and 40SFR in first class. The train runs every 15 to 20 minutes between 5:02am and 12:41am. You can also take bus no. 768 (Zurich Airport–Seebach), but you'll have to change to tram no. 14 to get to the center of the city.

BY TRAIN   Several trains bound for Switzerland leave from the Gare de l'Est in **Paris.** Two nonstop trains leave from Paris to Zurich daily, taking 6 hours. There are also good links between Austria and Switzerland, with trains arriving from **Salzburg** in 6 hours or **Vienna** in 9 hours. The best connection from Italy is via **Milan** (4½ hr.). Trains to Zurich run every hour from **Geneva** (a 3-hr. journey) and from **Basel** (1¼ hr.). From **Munich,** high-speed express trains depart for Zurich frequently. All trains arrive at the **Zurich Hauptbahnhof** (www.sbb.ch; ✆ **0900/300-300**). The station also has left-luggage lockers and shower facilities.

BY BUS   Zurich's bus routes function only as feeder lines from outlying suburbs, which lie off the train lines, into the vicinity of the city's rail station.

BY CAR   From Basel, take N3 east, and from Geneva, take N1 northeast, going via Bern, where you'll connect with E4 and E17 heading east into Zurich.

BY BOAT   The **Zurichsee-Schifffahrtsgesellschaft,** Mythenquai 333 (www.zsg. ch; ✆ **044/487-13-33**), offers a regularly scheduled service on modern passenger ships as well as old steamers plying both sides of Lake Zurich. The service is operated year-round, going from Zurich as far as Rapperswil.

VISITOR INFORMATION

The **Zurich Tourist Office,** Bahnhofplatz 15 (www.zuerich.com; ✆ **044/215-40-00**), is in the main railway station. It's open November to April, Monday to Saturday from 8:30am to 7pm and Sunday 9am to 6pm; May to October, hours are Monday to Saturday 8am to 8:30pm and Sunday 8:30am to 6:30pm.

Zurich

Kraftstrasse
Bergstrasse
Forsterstrasse
Knäubühlstrasse
Kleinjoggstrasse
Riesbergstrasse
Hadlaubstrasse
Toblerstrasse
Gladbachstrasse
Voltastrasse
Gloriastrasse
Zürichbergstrasse
Attenhoferstrasse
Hofstrasse
Dolderstrasse
Doloderstrasse
Ilgenstrasse
Asylstrasse
Gemeindestrasse
Pestalozzistrasse
Plattenstrasse
Freiestrasse
Hottingerstrasse
Zeltweg
Bahnhof Stadelhofen
Hochstrasse
Bolleystrasse
Spöndlistrasse
Culmannstrasse
Universitätstrasse
Vogelsangstrasse
Schmelzbergstrasse
Rämistrasse
Gloriastrasse
Federal Institute of Technology (ETHZ)
Künstlergasse
Heim-
OBERDORF
Oberdorfstrasse
Stapferstrasse
Sonneggstrasse
Clausiusstrasse
Leonhardstrasse
Hirschengraben
Seilergraben
Münstg.
Spiegelgasse
Münstergasse
Turnerstrasse
Weinbergstrasse
Sumatrastrasse
Stampfenbachstrasse
Central
Polybahn
Niederdorfstr.
Mühleg.
Brun-gasse
NIEDERDORF
Grossmünster-platz
Münster-Br.
Beckenhof str.
Nordstrasse
Neumühlequai
Limmat River
PLATZSPITZ
Walcher-
Bahnhof-Br.
Bahnhofquai
Mühlesteg (Ped bridge)
Limmatquai
Rud. Brun-Br.
Rathaus-Br.
Storchengasse
Münster-Br.
Limmat River
Stadthausquai
Fraumünsterstr.
Zoll-Br.
Hauptbahnhof (Main Train Station)
Bahnhof-platz
Beaten-platz
Bahnhofstrasse
Oetenbachgasse
Fortunag.
Rennweg
Bahnhofstrasse
Talstrasse
Post-Br.
Linthescherg.
St. Peterstr.
Parade-platz
Bärengasse
Bärengasse
Sihlquai
Ausstellungsstrasse
Limmatstrasse
Heinrichstrasse
Josefstrasse
Neugasse
Zollstrasse
Häfnerstrasse
Löwenstrasse
Uraniastrasse
Talackerstrasse
Pelikanstrasse
Bahnhofstrasse
Bastei-platz
Langstrasse
Lagerstrasse
Kasernenstrasse
Militärstrasse
Sihl River
Gessner Allee
Zeughausstrasse
Müllerstrasse
Stauffacher-platz
Selnaustrasse
Brandschenkstrasse
Gartenstrasse
Freigutstr.
Bleicherweg
LEFT BANK
Teilstrasse
Kanonengasse
Bäckerstrasse
Sihlstr.
Stauffbr.
Badenerstrasse
Zweierstrasse
Ankerstrasse
Werdstrasse
Morgartenstrasse
Birmensdorferstrasse
Schimmelstr.
Dienerstrasse
Hohlstrasse
Kernstrasse
Langstrasse
Stauffacherstrasse
Sihltalstrasse
Stauffacherquai

1/5 mi
0.20 km

Train Station

Beatengasse

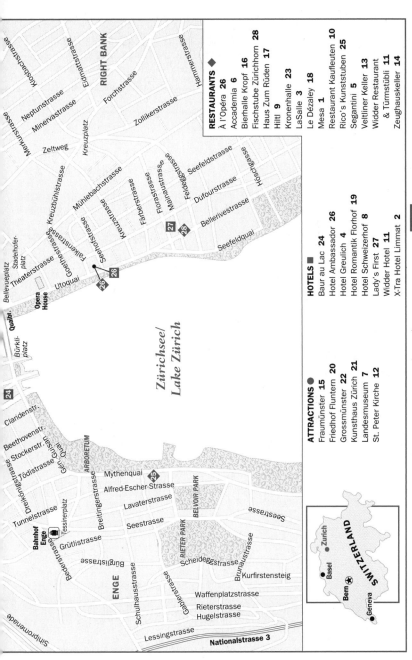

RESTAURANTS ◆

À l'Opéra **26**
Accademia **6**
Bierhalle Kropf **16**
Fischstube Zürichhorn **28**
Haus Zum Rüden **17**
Hiltl **9**
Kronenhalle **23**
LaSalle **3**
Le Dézaley **18**
Mesa **1**
Restaurant Kaufleuten **10**
Rico's Kunststuben **25**
Segantini **5**
Veltliner Keller **13**
Widder Restaurant
& Türmstübli **11**
Zeughauskeller **14**

HOTELS ■

Baur au Lac **24**
Hotel Ambassador **26**
Hotel Greulich **4**
Hotel Romantik Florhof **19**
Hotel Schweizerhof **8**
Lady's First **27**
Widder Hotel **11**
X-Tra Hotel Limmat **2**

ATTRACTIONS ●

Fraumünster **15**
Friedhof Fluntern **20**
Grossmünster **22**
Kunsthaus Zürich **21**
Landesmuseum **7**
St. Peter Kirche **12**

*Zürichsee/
Lake Zürich*

SWITZERLAND

You can also download an official Switzerland Tourism free Zurich City Guide app for iPhones.

CITY LAYOUT

Zurich lies situated on both shores of the Limmat River, which flows from the northern end of Lake Zurich. The Sihl River, a tributary of the Limmat, also flows through the city, and quays line the riverbanks and the lake. The city spreads across a ravine in the eastern hills between the wooded slopes of the Zürichberg and Kääferberg hills into the Glatt River Valley.

The hamlet that became Zurich began at the **Lindenhof,** which is where you, too, may begin your orientation to the city. This square is the architectural center of historic Zurich.

Below this square runs **Bahnhofstrasse,** one of the most elegant and expensive shopping streets in the world. It begins in the north, at the Hauptbahnhof (the railway station), opening onto Bahnhofplatz, and runs south to the lake. It crosses **Paradeplatz,** a converging point for trams and the modern center of the city. From Paradeplatz continue east, passing Fraumünster church and crossing Münsterbrücke to reach the right bank of the river. Here, the narrow streets of the **Limmatquai** are the second-best place in the city to shop. Running parallel to Limmatquai is **Niederdorfstrasse,** in the so-called red-light district of Zurich.

Old Town, or **Altstadt,** was developed during the early medieval period and is focused on Lindenhof, Fraumünster, Grossmünster, and St. Peter's. It expanded to **Weinplatz,** the oldest market square, and **Strehlgasse.** By the 11th century, the city developed on the right bank with such centers as **Kirchgasse** and **Neumarkt.**

Neighborhoods in Brief

Zurich is divided by the Limmat River into two general areas:

WEST OR LEFT BANK

This district is dominated by Bahnhofplatz, center of rail connections, and Bahnhofstrasse, which is the main commercial and banking thoroughfare. This is the Zurich world of high finance and elegant shops. The venerable Fraumünster church, on Fraumünsterstrasse, dominates the west bank. Included within the west bank, but somewhat removed from its sense of high-flying prosperity, is the increasingly visible, increasingly gentrified, warehouse-cum-*artmeisters* district of Zurich West.

EAST OR RIGHT BANK

Opposite Fraumünster, on the other side of the river, rises Grossmünster church, on Grossmünsterplatz; its two Gothic towers are an east-bank landmark. The historic guildhalls of Zurich, such as the Zunfthaus zur Saffran, rise on the east bank of the river. So, too, does the Rathaus, the city's town hall, completed in 1698. On the east bank you can explore the eastern part of Altstadt, strolling along Neumarkt, one of the best preserved of the old streets. The area beyond is Niederdorf, the center of the city's hot spots.

ZURICH WEST

Change is in the air, as Züri-West or Zurich West, growing into a chic area, is often compared to New York's SoHo district, with clubs, restaurants and chic hotels in converted industrial buildings. In a sector of the city becoming rapidly gentrified, Züri-West lies only a 10-minute taxi ride from the heart of Zurich. Sightseers head for the 19th-century red-brick **Löwenbräu Brewery** at 270 Limmatstrasse (𝄽 **044/272-15-15**) which has been turned into an art center housing a trio of museums.

GETTING AROUND

BY PUBLIC TRANSPORTATION The public transport system of Zurich is operated by ZVV, or **Zurich Public Transport** (www.vbz.ch; ℂ **0848/988-988**). The modern and extensive network of trams and buses (there is no subway) runs daily from 5:30am to 12:30am. You should have to wait no longer than 6 minutes during rush hours. Most trams and buses connect at the Zurich Hauptbahnhof, in the heart of the city.

You can buy tickets from automatic vending machines located at every stop. You must have a ticket before you get on a vehicle; if you're caught without one, you'll pay a fine of 80SFR. The fare is 4.10SFR for a trip of 1 hour. Visitors can get the most for their money by buying a *Tageskarte* (1-day ticket), which costs 8.20SFR and allows you to travel on all city buses and trams for 24 hours.

BY TAXI Taxis are very expensive. The budget-conscious will want to use them only as a last resort. Your hotel will usually be glad to call a taxi for you, but if you're making the call yourself, call **Taxi 444** (www.taxi444.ch; ℂ **044/444-44-44**). The basic charge before you even get into the vehicle is 6SFR, plus 3.80SFR for each kilometer you travel.

BY CAR We don't recommend attempting to see Zurich by car—the city is way too congested, and parking is too scarce and too expensive. Save the car for exploring the environs.

BY BIKE Biking is a good way to get around Zurich, especially in the outlying areas. Bicycles can be rented at the baggage counter of the railway station, the **Hauptbahnhof** (ℂ **051/222-29-04**), for 33SFR per day or 25SFR for a half-day for a city bike. Hours are daily from 7am to 7:30pm.

ON FOOT Zurich and its quays are ideal for walking, and many of the places of interest, such as the sights of Altstadt on both sides of the Limmat, are conveniently grouped together.

[Fast FACTS] ZURICH

ATMs/Banks Banks are generally open Monday to Wednesday and on Friday from 8:15am to 4:30pm, and on Thursday from 8:15am to 6pm. A convenient bank is **Crédit Suisse** at Paradeplatz 8 (ℂ **044/333-99-11**), open Monday to Friday 8am to 7pm. There are ATMs all over the city.

Consulates If you lose your passport or have another emergency, go to the **U.S. Consulate,** Dufourstrasse 101 (ℂ **043/499-29-60**). The British, Canadians,

and Australians should contact their respective embassies in Bern.

Currency Exchange Most banks and travel agencies will exchange money for you. There's also an exchange office of **Credit Suisse** at the Zurich Hauptbahnhof, the main railway station, open daily from 6:30am to 11:30pm, at Minervastrasse 117.

Doctors & Hospitals Contact the **Zurich Universitätsspital (University Hospital),** Rämistrasse 100 (ℂ **044/255-11-11**).

Drugstores For 24-hour service, **Bellevue Apotheke,** at Theaterstrasse 14 (ℂ www.bellevue-apotheke. com; **044/266-62-22**), lies off Bellevueplatz.

Emergencies Call the **police** at ℂ **117**. For **first aid,** phone ℂ **114;** for the **City Ambulance Service,** dial ℂ **144**. For a fire, dial ℂ **118**. Zurich's Bahnhof (main railway station) contains a limited roster of medical and dental facilities which, if they can't treat an ailment effectively themselves, will at least direct you to larger medical facilities that can.

Internet Access Head for an Internet cafe such as **Telefon-Corner,** Kanzleistrasse 57 (www.telefon corner.ch; ℂ **044/297-20-80**), open Monday to Thursday 9am to midnight, Friday and Saturday 9am to 2am, and Sunday 10am to 11pm.

Police See "Emergencies," above.

Post Office The main post office is the **Sihlpost,** Kasernenstrasse 95–97 (ℂ **0848/88-88-88**), across the Sihl River from Löwenstrasse; an emergency-service window is open from 6:30am to 10pm daily. Most post offices—listed under "Post" in the phone directory—are open Monday to Friday 7:30am to 6:30pm and on Saturday from 6:30 to 11am.

Safety Zurich is one of the safest cities in Europe, both during the day and at night. The most potentially dangerous place is Niederdorf, the red-light district in Altstadt.

Taxes An 8% VAT (value-added tax) is added to hotel and restaurant bills. There are no other special taxes.

Exploring Zurich

Zurich has a rich history and many reminders of its past. There are 20 museums, nearly 100 galleries, and 24 archives (including one devoted to Thomas Mann). The historic buildings, religious monuments, and quays are worth discovering, as are the well-preserved homes of rich burghers, lovely parks, and gardens. Even if you don't have time to visit all those museums and galleries, a walk along the quays of Zurich shouldn't be missed.

The **quays of Zurich ★★**, with their promenades, are among the city's most popular attractions. They're made for walking. The most famous is **Limmatquai,** in the center of Zurich. It begins at the Bahnhof Bridge and extends east to the Rathaus (town hall) and beyond. Many of the quays have lovely gardens. **Uto Quai** is the major promenade along Zurichsee (Lake Zurich), running from Badeanstalt Uto Quai (a swimming site) to Bellevueplatz and Quaibrücke. The site (a wooden sun deck with changing rooms, floating on pontoons above the water) is open daily from 8am to 7pm mid-May to mid-September. Most adults head there afternoons from noon until 7 or 8pm. Entrance costs 3.50SFR for children under 12, 5SFR for students, and 7SFR for adults. For more info, click on www.badi-info.ch/utoquai.html.

If you stroll as far as **Mythenquai,** you'll be following the lake along its western shore and out into the countryside.

Fraumünster This church, with its slender, blue spire, is on the left bank overlooking the former pig market, Münsterhof. Münsterhof is one of the historic old squares of Zurich and is well worth a visit. The present church dates from the 13th and 14th centuries, but the crypt of the old abbey church is preserved in the undercroft.

The chief attractions of Fraumünster are five **stained-glass windows ★**—each with its own color theme—designed by Marc Chagall in 1970. They are best seen in bright morning light. The Fraumünster is also celebrated for its elaborate organ. The basilica has three aisles; the nave is in the Gothic style.

Fraumünsterstrasse. www.fraumuenster.ch. ℂ **044/211-41-00.** Free admission. May–Sept Mon–Sat 9am–noon, daily 2–6pm; Oct and Mar–Apr Mon–Sat 10am–noon, daily 2–5pm; Nov–Feb Mon–Sat 10am–noon, daily 2–4pm. Tram: 4 to City Hall.

Friedhof Fluntern (Fluntern Cemetery) James Joyce, the author of *Ulysses,* lived in Zurich from 1915 to 1919, at Universitätsstrasse 38. In 1941 he returned to

Zurich from Paris, only a month before his death. Near his tomb is a statue depicting the great Irish writer sitting cross-legged with a book in his hand. The grave of Johanna Spyri (1827–1901), who wrote the famous story *Heidi,* is in the Central Cemetery.

Zürichberg district. Free admission. May–Aug daily 7am–8pm; Mar–Apr and Sept–Oct daily 7am–7pm; Nov–Feb daily 8am–5pm. Tram: 6 to zoo.

Grossmünster   This Romanesque and Gothic cathedral was, according to legend, founded by Charlemagne, whose horse bowed down on the spot marking the graves of three early Christian martyrs. The cathedral has two three-story towers and is situated on a terrace above Limmatquai, on the right bank. In the crypt is a weather-beaten, 15th-century statue of Charlemagne, a copy of which crowns the south tower.

The cathedral is dedicated to the patron saints of Zurich: Felix, Regula, and Exuperantius. In the 3rd century, the three martyrs attempted to convert the citizens of Turicum (the original name for Zurich) to Christianity. The governor, according to legend, had them plunged into boiling oil and forced them to drink molten lead. The trio refused to renounce their faith and were beheaded. Miraculously, they still had enough energy to pick up their heads and climb to the top of a hill (the present site of the cathedral), where they dug their own graves and then interred themselves. The seal of Zurich honors these saints, depicting them carrying their heads under their arms. The remains of the saints are said to rest in one of the chapels of the *Münster* (cathedral).

The cathedral was once the parish church of Huldrych Zwingli, one of the great leaders of the Reformation. He urged priests to take wives (he himself had married) and attacked the "worship of images" and the Roman Catholic sacrament of Mass. In 1531 Zwingli was killed in a religious war at Kappel. The hangman quartered his body and soldiers burned the pieces with dung. The site of his execution is marked with an inscription: "They may kill the body but not the soul." In accordance with Zwingli's beliefs, Zurich's Grossmünster is austere, stripped of the heavy ornamentation you'll find in the cathedrals of Italy. The view from the towers is impressive.

Grossmünsterplatz. www.grossmuenster.ch. ✆ **044/252-59-49.** Free admission to cathedral; towers 4SFR. Cathedral Mar 15–Oct daily 10am–6pm; Nov–Mar 14 daily 10am–5pm. Towers (weather permitting) Mar–Oct daily 10am–5pm; Nov–Feb Sat–Sun 10am–5pm. Tram: 4.

Kunsthaus Zürich (Fine Arts Museum) ★★   One of the most important art museums in Europe, the Kunsthaus Zürich is devoted mainly to the 19th and 20th centuries, although the range of paintings and sculpture reaches back to antiquity. The museum was founded in Victorian times and was overhauled in 1976. Today it's one of the most modern and sophisticated museums in the world, both in its lighting and its display of art.

 An Open Sesame & Bargain Pass

The **ZurichCARD** offers a 50% reduction on public transportation, free visits to 43 museums, reduced prices at the zoo, and a welcome drink at more than two dozen restaurants. The pass is widely available, sold at such outlets as the Zurich Main Rail Station, the airport, and at certain hotels. It costs 20SFR for 24 hours or 40SFR for 72 hours. See www.zuerich.com/en/visitor/information/zuerich-card.html for more information.

The collection of modern art includes works by all the greats—Bonnard, Braque, Chagall, Lipschitz, Marini, Mondrian, Picasso, and Rouault. The gallery owns the largest collection of works by the Norwegian artist Edvard Munch outside of Oslo. Two old masters, Rubens and Rembrandt, are also represented. To brighten a rainy day, come see the pictures by Cézanne, Degas, Monet, Toulouse-Lautrec, and Utrillo.

Heimplatz 1. www.kunsthaus.ch. © **044/253-84-84.** Admission 18SFR adults, 12SFR seniors and students, free for children 16 and under. Tues 10am–6pm; Wed–Fri 10am–8pm; Sat–Sun 10am– 6pm. Tram: 3 (marked KLUSPLATZ).

Landesmuseum (Swiss National Museum) ★★★ This museum offers an epic survey of the culture and history of the Swiss people. Its collection, housed in a feudal-looking, 19th-century building behind the Zurich Hauptbahnhof, contains works of religious art, including 16th-century stained glass from the Tanikon Convent and frescoes from the church of Mustair. Some of the Carolingian art dates from the 9th century. The altarpieces are carved, painted, and gilded.

The prehistoric section is also exceptional. Some of the artifacts are from the 4th millennium B.C. There's a large display of Roman clothing, medieval silverware, 14th-century drinking bowls, and 17th-century china, as well as painted furniture, costumes, and dollhouses of various periods. A display of weapons and armor shows the methods of Swiss warfare from 800 to 1800. There's also an exhibit tracing Swiss clock making from the 16th to the 18th centuries.

Museumstrasse 2. www.nationalmuseum.ch. © **044/218-65-11.** Admission 10SFR, 8SFR students and seniors. Tues–Sun 10am–5pm (until 7pm Thurs). Tram: 4, 6, 7, 11, 13, or 14.

St. Peter Kirche (St. Peter's Church) Built in the 13th century, St. Peter's— on the left bank south of Lindenhof—is the oldest church in Zurich. It has the largest clock face in Europe: 9m (30 ft.) in diameter; the minute hand alone is almost 4m (13 ft.) long. Inside, the choir is Romanesque, but the three-aisle nave is baroque.

St. Peterhofstatt 1. www.st-peter-zh.ch. © **044/211-25-88.** Free admission. Mon–Fri 8am–6pm; Sat 10am–4pm; Sun noon–5pm.

ORGANIZED TOURS

BOAT TOURS At some point during your stay in Switzerland's largest city, you'll want to take a **lake steamer** for a tour around Lake Zurich. Walk to Bahnhofstrasse's lower end and buy a ticket at the pier for any of the dozen or so boats that ply the waters from late May to late September. The boats are more or less the same, so it doesn't matter which one you take. Most of the steamers contain simple restaurant facilities, and all have two or three levels of decks and lots of windows for wide-angle views of the Swiss mountains and shoreline. During peak season, boats depart at approximately 30-minute intervals. The most distant itinerary from Zurich is to **Rapperswil,** a historic town near the lake's southeastern end. A full-length, **round-trip tour** of the lake from Zurich to Rapperswil will require 2 hours each way, plus whatever time you opt to explore towns en route. This trip is the highlight of the boat tours offered, and if you can spare the time, you'll find it a rewarding way to see the area in and around Zurich. Many visitors opt for shorter boat rides encompassing only the northern third of the lake; those trips take about 90 minutes total.

The full-length tour of the lake costs 27SFR in second class and 42SFR in first class. The shorter boat ride on the northern third of the lake costs 9SFR.

For more information on all the boats mentioned above, contact the **Zürichsee Schifffahrtsgesellschaft** online at www.zsg.ch or by calling © **044/487-13-33.**

WALKING TOURS   One of the most appealing walking tours in Zurich is a 2-hour guided stroll through the Old Town. If you're interested in participating, meet in the main hall of Zurich's railway station, at the Tourist Service office (www.zuerich.com; © 044/215-40-00). The cost of the tour is 20SFR for adults, 10SFR for children 6 to 16, and free for children 5 and under. From April to October, tours in German and English are operated Monday to Friday at 3pm, and on Saturday and Sunday at 11am. The walking tours are also operated from November to March on Wednesday and Sunday at 11am and Saturday at 11am and 3pm.

OUTDOOR ACTIVITIES

Zurichers are not big on spectator sports—they like to get out and participate. Many of the larger hotels have added swimming pools and tennis courts or handball and racquetball facilities. Some also have fitness centers.

HIKING   Zurich has seven Vita-Parcours, or fitness trails. Someone at the Zurich Tourist Office, Bahnhofplatz 15 (© 044/215-40-00), will map these trails for you.

JOGGING   The nearest woodland jogging route is on the **Allmend Fluntern,** which is a wide-open public park, crisscrossed with jogging paths, on the northeastern outskirts of Zurich, near the zoo. To get here from the center, take tram no. 6. Joggers are also seen frequently along the quays and elsewhere in the city.

SWIMMING   You can go swimming in Lake Zurich, which has an average summer temperature of 68°F (20°C). The finest beach is the **Tiefenbrunnen.** To get to Tiefenbrunnen (which is also popular with the gay crowd), take tram no. 4 from central Zurich (Bahnhofplatz) to Tiefenbrunnen Bahnhof, a ride of about 15 minutes. The **public pool** at Sihlstrasse 71 also has a sauna with its indoor swimming facilities.

Where to Eat

Zurich restaurants feature a selection of both international and Swiss specialties. The local favorite is *rösti.* You should also try *Züri-Gschnätzlets* (shredded veal cooked with mushrooms in a cream sauce laced with white wine) and *Kutteln nach Zürcherart* (tripe with mushrooms, white wine, and caraway seed). Another classic dish is *Leberspiesschen* (liver cubes skewered with bacon and sage and served with potatoes and beans).

Among local wines, the white Riesling Sylvaner is outstanding and great with fish. The light Clevner wines, always chilled, are made from blue Burgundy grapes that grow around the lake.

THE LEFT BANK
Expensive

Accademia ★★ ITALIAN   The finest and most elegant Italian restaurant in Zurich, Accademia is much appreciated at lunchtime by bankers and businesspeople, who use it to entertain their clients. In an Art Deco setting scattered with a collection of oil paintings, a uniformed staff politely serves Italian regional dishes, ranging from Venetian to Neapolitan. Some of the tastiest specialties include baked veal chop with mozzarella; braised veal cheeks in a Barolo wine sauce; and baked and delicately seasoned seabass. Specialties, when in season, may include various game dishes, including pheasant, venison, wild boar, and partridge. Offerings here rarely disappoint.

Rotwandstrasse 48. www.accademiadelgusto.ch. ☎ **044/241-62-43.** Reservations recommended, especially in summer. Main courses 38SFR–58SFR. AE, DC, MC, V. Mon–Fri noon–3pm and 6:30–10pm; Mar–Oct also Sat 6:30–10pm. Tram: 2, 3, 5, 8, or 13.

Veltliner Keller ★ SWISS/ITALIAN/FRENCH If endurance and longevity are hallmarks of a good restaurant, this dining room would emerge near the top. Veltliner Keller has been a restaurant since 1551; before that it was a wine cellar. Located next to St. Peter's Church in Old Town, it has an ancient interior of carved mountain pine wood called *arve* (grown only in Switzerland). The chef prepares familiar Swiss specialties, and does so exceedingly well, including *züri-gschnätzlets,* the classic chopped-veal dish of Zurich. Several Italian dishes are also featured, including veal piccata and *osso buco.* A lot of the seafood is grilled or poached, including salmon. Ingredients change with the season, but you can always count on the house's signature dish, a Veltliner pot—baked macaroni with meat and beef liver cooked in a casserole.

Schlüsselgasse 8. www.veltlinerkeller.ch. ☎ **044/225-40-40.** Reservations recommended. Main courses 42SFR–50SFR. AE, DC, MC, V. Mon–Fri 11:30am–2pm and 6:30–9:30pm. Closed mid-July to mid-Aug. Tram: 4, 6, 7, 11, or 13.

Widder Restaurant & Türmstübli ★ INTERNATIONAL When this restaurant opened in the mid-1990s, many of its clients came as an excuse to view the iconoclastic architecture of the hotel that contained it (p. 1034). But since then, these twin dining rooms have taken on a life of their own, and are now sought out as independent eateries in their own right. Although the Widder Restaurant is outfitted in a rustic, folksy style, and the Türmstübli is angular, minimalist, and devoid of most alpine reminders, the same menu is served in both. Look for a clientele from Zurich's financial community, along with a scattering of wealthy bohemians. Menu items include filet of pikeperch with mustard seeds in a tarragon sauce; grilled turbot in a chili-laced chive butter; a sumptuous breast of Barbary duckling in an orange-flavored crust served with a pumpkin-and-lettuce-based piccata sauce and galettes of sweet corn; a delectable scampi with morel-stuffed ravioli in a pepper-flavored butter sauce; and a particularly delicious gratin of salmon-trout with cucumber sauce, dill weed, and new potatoes.

In the Widder Hotel, Rennweg 7. www.widderhotel.ch. ☎ **044/224-25-26.** Reservations recommended. Main courses 32SFR–68SFR; fixed-price 3-course dinner menu 95SFR, 5-course dinner menu 145SFR. AE, DC, MC, V. Daily 11:30am–2pm and 6:30–11pm. Tram: 6, 7, 11, or 13.

Inexpensive
Bierhalle Kropf ★ ☺ SWISS/BAVARIAN/AUSTRIAN Everyone in Zurich goes to "Der Kropf" for its old-fashioned ambience and generous portions at reasonable prices. The restaurant is in one of the oldest burgher houses in town, a few steps from Paradeplatz. Its dining room has stained-glass windows, polished paneling, chandeliers, and plaster columns. On the walls hang stag horns and painted hunting scenes. You get authentic and well-prepared dishes here. Almost no one, including visiting personalities, local political figures, and finicky children, leaves disappointed. Bring along a healthy appetite. Specialties include roast pork knuckle or boneless smoked rib of pork with sauerkraut. The chefs also prepare a sirloin of lamb roasted pink and served with potato croquettes.

In Gassen 16. www.zumkropf.ch. ☎ **044/221-18-05.** Reservations recommended. Main courses 24SFR–45SFR. AE, MC, V. Mon–Sat 11:30am–11:30pm. Closed Easter, Dec 25, and Aug 1. Tram: 4, 6, 7, 11, or 13.

19

SWITZERLAND | Zurich

Hiltl VEGETARIAN/INDIAN   Founded in 1898, this bright, inviting place is Zurich's leading vegetarian restaurant. Its main attraction is a large salad bar, containing more than 40 different types of freshly prepared vegetables. House creations include vegetable paella, mushroom stroganoff, and curry colonial. There's a vast choice of fruit juices, teas, draft beer, and wines priced by the glass. The restaurant is also known for its vegetarian Indian specialties.

Sihlstrasse 28. www.hiltl.ch. © **044/227-70-00.** Reservations recommended. Main courses 24SFR–36SFR. AE, MC, V. Mon–Sat 7am–11pm; Sun 11am–11pm. Tram: 6, 7, 11, or 13.

Restaurant Kaufleuten ★ 🎁 INTERNATIONAL   Despite its location in the heart of one of Europe's most gilt-edged neighborhoods, a few steps from the Bahnhofstrasse, there's something artfully disheveled and happy-go-lucky about this restaurant. You'll find a deliberately mismatched collection of tables and chairs. The menu is just as eclectic, with offerings derived from virtually everywhere. These include favorites from Thailand (including *tom kha kai,* made of chicken, coconut, and fiery spices), Japan (sushi, sashimi, and miso soup), and Austria (Wiener schnitzel). Also available are tender steaks and several kinds of saltwater and freshwater fish, including salmon, sole, and seabass. The setting is pleasant, and the place is a fine cost-conscious alternative to more formal spots nearby. The site contains a worn, heavily trafficked bar area that's open daily from 9am till whenever the restaurant closes, and a nightclub that's separately recommended (p. 1032).

Pelikanstrasse 18. www.kaufleuten.com. © **044/225-33-33.** Reservations recommended. Main courses 28SFR–58SFR. AE, DC, MC, V. Mon–Fri 11:30am–2pm; daily 7pm–1am (till 2am Fri–Sat). Tram: 2, 5, 9, or 13.

Zeughauskeller ★ SWISS   This mammoth restaurant, dating from 1487, was once an arsenal; its vast dining room now seats 200. Large wooden chandeliers hang from cast-iron chains, and the walls are decorated with medieval halberds and illustrations of ancient Zurich noblemen. Generous portions of traditional and tasty Swiss dishes are served with steins of local beer. Owners Kurt Andreae and Willy Hammer say that patrons consume some 30 tons of potato salad a year. Hurlimann draft beer is poured from 1,000-liter barrels. Specialties, and excellent ones at that, include pan-fried sausages made of lean pork with various spices and herbs; and a tender veal escalope with *rösti.* For 88SFR, you can order a meter-long sausage—enough to feed four hungry people. Service is quick and efficient.

Bahnhofstrasse 28a (near Paradeplatz). www.zeughauskeller.ch. © **044/211-26-90.** Reservations recommended. Main courses 13SFR–34SFR. AE, MC, V. Daily 11:30am–11pm. Tram: 2, 6, 7, 8, 9, 11, or 13.

THE RIGHT BANK
Very Expensive

Haus Zum Rüden ★★ SWISS/FRENCH   The Gothic room in this historic guild house dating from 1295 contains one of the best restaurants in the city. It's especially popular with foreign visitors, even though they often get a somewhat stuffy greeting from the staff. The spacious yet intimate dining room has a hardwood ceiling and stone walls decorated with medieval halberds and stag horns. The chef specializes in *cuisine du marché* (market-fresh cuisine). For a stunning opening, try the cream of lobster soup with diced mango and scampi, followed by such mains as grilled filet of turbot on leaf spinach or sautéed filet of pikeperch with lentils and a celery truffle butter.

Limmatquai 42. www.hauszumrueden.ch. © **044/261-95-66.** Reservations required. Main courses 48SFR–76SFR; fixed-price menu 138SFR. AE, DC, MC, V. Mon–Fri noon–2pm and 6:30–9:30pm. Tram: 4 or 15.

Mesa ★★★ INTERNATIONAL This is one of the grandest restaurants of Zurich, and one of the few in the country to receive a coveted Michelin star. Marcus G. Lindner, one of the most talented chefs of Switzerland, knows about balanced sauces and split-second timing, and we urge you to sample some of his intensely flavored dishes. His vibrant cuisine is as modern as tomorrow and highly innovative, and the menu changes every day—when you show up, expect to be surprised. Take delight in such dishes as mussels in a white-wine sauce, or else the marinated lamb cutlets with a saffron, mint, and herb sauce. Desserts are memorable, including a yogurt mousse with strawberry-and-basil ice cream. The chef aims to please and, indeed, he rarely disappoints.

Weinbergstrasse 75. www.mesa-restaurant.ch. © **043/321-75-75.** Reservations required. Main courses 52SFR–79SFR. AE, DC, MC, V. Tues–Fri 11:45am–3pm; Tues–Sat 6:45pm–midnight. Tram: 7 or 15.

Expensive

À l'Opéra ★★ 🛏 CONTINENTAL In 2007, a rising young artist, Tatiana Tiziana, slap-dashed, in fewer than 10 hysterical days, a sprawling series of neo-baroque *trompe l'oeil* murals onto this restaurant's ceiling. Since then, diners invariably look upward, between courses, at the world's most amusing take on Michelangelo's Sistine Chapel. Fish is particularly well prepared here within a culinary palette that changes monthly. Menus might focus heavily on, among others, fresh asparagus, fresh peaches, exotic mushrooms, and even ripe olives from Spain, Italy, or North Africa. Service is impeccable and laced with genuine sensitivity on the part of the staff. The best specialties include Irish salmon with potato pancakes; veal escalope with cranberries; and Black Tiger king prawns cooked in coconut milk.

In the Hotel Ambassador, Falkenstrasse 6. © **044/258-98-98.** Reservations recommended. Main courses 38SFR–58SFR; fixed-price menus 68SFR for 3 courses, 82SFR for 4 courses. AE, DC, MC, V. Daily 11:30am–2pm and 5:30–11:30pm. Tram: 4.

Kronenhalle ★ SWISS/FRENCH This is one of Zurich's most famous restaurants, and it also serves some of the best cuisine. The restaurant is in a five-story, gray Biedermeier building with gold crowns above the six windows on the first floor. The decor includes original paintings by Klee, Chagall, Matisse, Miró, Kandinsky, Braque, Bonnard, and Picasso. Each was acquired, inexpensively, by the restaurant's early-20th-century founder and reigning matriarch. Regional specialties are served on a trolley and include smoked pork with lentils and *bollito misto* (boiled beef, chicken, sausage, and tongue). For a main dish, try shredded calves' liver with *rösti* or filet of sole baked with olives and tomatoes. You may also enjoy *bündnerfleisch*—thinly sliced, smoked, dried beef. This is one of the most outstanding and consistently reliable restaurants in Zurich. In the Kronenhalle Bar the specialty is the Ladykiller.

Rämistrasse 4. www.kronenhalle.com. © **044/262-99-00.** Reservations required. Main courses 28SFR–65SFR. AE, DC, MC, V. Daily noon–midnight. Closed Dec 24. Tram: 2, 4, 5, 6, 11, or 15.

Moderate

Fischstube Zürichhorn ☺ SWISS/SEAFOOD Ideal on a summer evening, this seafood restaurant with outdoor tables is built on pilings over the lake. The scenery, service, and cuisine make it a worthy choice if the weather is balmy. We recommend the lake trout, filet of Dover sole Champs-Elysées, grilled lobster with curry butter, and lake fish sautéed in butter and served with market-fresh vegetables. The cuisine here has a sprightly, original taste, flavored with a dash of this or a dab of that. The chefs rely on the sound principles of simplicity and accurate timing in all their dishes, and the servings are generous. Kids delight at sitting outside overlooking the lake and even like the vegetables cooked here since they're so fresh and delectably prepared.

Bellerivestrasse 160. www.fischstube.ch. ℂ **044/422-25-20.** Reservations required. Main courses 28SFR–62SFR. AE, MC, V. Daily 11:30am–6pm and 6–10:30pm. Closed late Sept to Easter. Tram: 2 or 4.

Le Dézaley ★ 🎁 SWISS/FRENCH Named after a remote corner of the Vaud region of French-speaking Switzerland, this restaurant celebrates the food and traditions of the countryside north of Lake Geneva. Many of the regular clients speak French as they dine on an array of fondues (cheese, chinoise, and bourguignon) or other dishes such as minced liver, veal kidneys with *rösti*, pork sausages flavored with leeks, and shredded veal Zurich style. The chefs are more obsessed with flavor than novelty, and they certainly succeed. Many wines from the Dézaley region, some rather rare, are offered. The large, wood-paneled dining room is set in a pair of interconnected houses originally built during the late 13th century. In summer, you can dine in a little garden out back.

Römergasse 7–9. www.le-dezaley.ch. ℂ **044/251-61-29.** Reservations recommended. Main courses 22SFR–40SFR; fondues 25SFR–43SFR. AE, DC, MC, V. Mon–Sat 11:30am–2pm and 6pm–midnight. Tram: 4 or 15.

Segantini ★ 🎁 ORGANIC CONTINENTAL One of the city's most stylish and offbeat restaurants occupies a small but high-ceilinged dining room near Helvetiaplatz. You'll find a roster of glass mosaics, enormous bouquets of artfully arranged flowers, and elaborate table settings. The list of food options here is limited but choice, often with no more than four appetizers, four main courses, and four desserts offered for consumption on any given evening. All ingredients are organic and seasonal, listed on an oft-changing handwritten menu, and "spun" into a frequently changing array of dishes likely to include elaborate salads; a "trio" of soups served within three espresso cups (they are likely to include potato leek soup, creamy redbeet soup, and a carrot-with-orange soup); homemade ravioli stuffed with ricotta and strips of organic salmon; succulent pastas; roasted filet of lamb served with olives and roasted potatoes; and stroganoff of beef.

Ankerstrasse 120. ℂ **044/241-07-00.** Reservations recommended. Main courses 29SFR–50SFR. AE, DC, MC, V. Tues–Fri 11:30am–2pm and 6pm–midnight; Sat 6pm–midnight. Bus: 31.

SOUTH OF THE CENTER

Rico's Kunststuben ★★★ CONTINENTAL Arguably this is the best restaurant in Switzerland. Relentlessly elegant, but with a staff that's more hip and alert than you may expect, it lies 10km (6 miles) south of Zurich in the hamlet of Küsnacht, near Rapperswil, within a house whose date of construction (1873) is marked above a wood-burning stove in the dining room.

Most of the year, the restaurant accommodates only 45 diners, but in summer an outdoor terrace ringed with shrubs and flowers adds another 40 seats. You can enjoy such inventive dishes as a "cigar" of foie gras with black truffles and sauterne aspic, roasted duck with honey-lemon sauce, lobster with a purée of celery, lobster-studded potato salad with a leek-based cream sauce, stuffed squid with a confit of fennel, and young hen stuffed with shrimp. Dessert may include a gratin of wild strawberries and cannelloni stuffed with almond paste. You'll find almost anything you order irresistible within a setting that some of the most seasoned and jaded diners in the world have found utterly charming.

Seestrasse 160, Küsnacht. www.kunststuben.com. © **044/910-07-15.** Reservations required. Main courses 58SFR–85SFR; fixed-price menus 78SFR–135SFR. AE, DC, MC, V. Tues–Sat noon–2pm and 7pm–midnight. Closed 2 weeks in Feb and 2 weeks in Aug. Take a taxi or the train from Zurich's Hauptbahnhof to Küsnacht, then walk for 5 min.

ZURICH WEST

LaSalle ★ INTERNATIONAL   One of the most hip and sought-after restaurants in Zurich today is housed within a severe-looking factory built during the 19th century to manufacture boats and lake cruisers. Today, it's the centerpiece of an urban renewal known as Zurich West. The restaurant is enclosed within an enormous but delicate-looking high-tech box of steel beams and Plexiglas, all of it suspended from the building's ceiling and redbrick walls. Centered within the area's core is a massive Murano chandelier. Menu items seem deceptively simple when listed on the stark-white menu, and except for an occasional gaff, are incredibly flavor-filled and artful upon delivery. Examples include *vitello tonnato* (filets of veal with Italian-style tuna sauce); homemade terrine; thinly sliced veal liver Provençal; filets of pikeperch with spinach and coconut milk; cannelloni with ricotta, spinach, and a truffle-flavored cream sauce; and a vegetarian version of tortilla with guacamole and sour cream. There are also daily variations of fish, vegetarian dishes, and raviolis of the day.

Schiffbaustrasse 4. www.lasalle-restaurant.ch. © **044/258-70-71.** Reservations necessary. Main courses 28SFR–55SFR. AE, DC, MC, V. Mon–Fri 11:30am–2pm and 5–11pm; Sat–Sun 5:30–10:45pm. Closed Sun July–Aug. Tram: 4 or 13.

Shopping

In the heart of Zurich is a square kilometer (about ⅓ sq. mile) of shopping, including the exclusive stores along **Bahnhofstrasse.** Your shopping adventure might begin more modestly at the top of the street, at Bahnhofplatz. Below this vast transportation hub is a complex of shops known as **ShopVille.** ShopVille is open from 8am to 8pm every day except Christmas. Most shops are open Monday to Friday from 8am to 6:30pm and on Saturday from 8am to 4pm.

Some of the larger stores stay open until 9pm on Thursday, and other shops are closed on Monday morning.

ART

Löwenbräu   Massively built of red brick around 1900 as a brewery by the you-know-who company, its fortresslike interior was radically transformed a few years ago into one of the biggest art exhibition spaces in town—an ugly, industrial-looking mixed-use showplace for both publicly funded museums and privately owned art galleries where artworks are for sale. Of the six or seven private art galleries inside, one of the most impressive is **Daros Exhibitions** (www.daros.ch; © **044/447-70-00**), whose works are about as cutting edge as they come. Also on-site, and funded by a chain of local grocery stores, is the **Migros Museum for Contemporary Art** (www.migrosmuseum.ch; © **044/277-20-50**). *Tip:* Avoid the place on Monday, when virtually everything is closed. Limmatstrasse 268, in Zurich-West.

BAGS & KNAPSACKS

Freitag Shop Zurich   This shop achieved fame and notoriety throughout Switzerland, thanks to a physical plant that's composed of 17 seagoing containers piled to a height of 26m (85 ft.). In Zurich, it ranks as a tall building. Inside, you'll find the entire line of backpacks, wallets, bike saddlebags, dopp kits, wallets, and duffel bags for which Freitag, within counterculture fashion accessories for the young and the restless, is famous. Many of the goods are crafted from colorful scraps of canvas, and some have been singled out by Manhattan's Museum of Modern Art for the integrity and originality of their designs. Geroldstrasse 17, in Zurich West. www.freitag.ch. ℂ **043/366-95-20.**

DEPARTMENT STORES

Jelmoli Department Store ★   This Zurich institution has everything a large department store should have, from cookware to clothing. Founded more than 150 years ago by the Ticino-born entrepreneur Johann Peter Jelmoli, the store is a legend in the Zurich business community. Seidengasse 1. www.jelmoli.ch. ℂ **044/220-44-11.**

FASHION

Thema Selection   This site functions as a purveyor of stylish women's clothing, much of it designed in-house by a local personality known as Thema. If you enter for a look at the evening wear and sportswear, you'll invariably notice an elaborate Jugendstil ceiling fresco that has been in place since its beginning. The clothes are breezy, comfortable, and hip, conveying a wide spectrum of various degrees of formality. Spiegelgasse 16. www.themaselection.ch. ℂ **044/261-78-42.**

Tran Hin Phu ★★   For modern fashion with a certain sensuality and understatement, head here. The shop is named for its Vietnamese fashion designer, who specializes in graphic print silk blouses and silk jersey, cotton, and linen dresses in a neutral palette. The designs are fashionable, soft, and feminine. All of the clothing is manufactured in Switzerland in limited editions. Tran Hin Phu is hailed as one of the most promising of young Swiss designers, having achieved a certain fame in 2001 when he won the Swiss Textiles Awards. Birmendorferstrasse 32. www.tranhinphu.com. ℂ **043/317-97-17.**

FOOD & DRINK

Distillerie zur Schnapsboutique   Oversized, balloon-shaped glass decanters nestle side by side in this small and aromatic shop. Each is filled to the brim with various vintages of schnapps from local distillers. A staff member will advise you of what you're seeing (and smelling) here. Before your liqueur of choice is decanted, you'll have to select, and pay for, a container. The contents of your decanter, depending on the vintage and its age, begin at around 30SFR and can go up to 10 times that amount. This is liquor as it was sold several generations ago, within a venue that we were told is now unique within Switzerland. Napfgasse 3. ℂ **044/262-32-27.**

Sprüngli ★★★   In a country famous for its chocolates, Sprüngli is the most famous chocolatier. The inventory of virtually everything dark and "meltable in your mouth" is featured at this temple to chocolate. A variety of pastries and chocolates are sold on the ground floor. Adjacent to the store, you'll find a coffeeshop (many old-time Zurichers journey across town for a cup of hot chocolate here), a small restaurant with a limited menu, and a room exclusively for mailing your high-caloric gifts to friends and family abroad. Additional outlets of Sprüngli are located at Bahnhofstrasse 67, Löwenplatz, Stadelhoferplatz, and, to tempt last-minute buyers, the Zurich International Airport. Paradeplatz. www.spruengli.ch. ✆ **044/224-47-11.**

JEWELRY & WATCHES

Beyer ★   If you have your heart set on buying a timepiece in Zurich, try this well-established store midway between the train station and the lake. Besides carrying just about every famous brand of watch made in Switzerland—Rolex, Corum, Cartier, and Patke Philippe—it also has a museum in the basement, containing timepieces from as early as 1400 B.C. Exhibitions include all kinds of water clocks, sundials, and hourglasses. Bahnhofstrasse 31. www.beyer-ch.com. ✆ **044/344-63-63.**

Bucherer   A longtime name in the Swiss watch industry, this store also carries an impressive collection of jewelry. Some of the most famous names in watchmaking are represented in their latest offerings, including Chopard, Rado, and Rolex. www.bucherer.com. Bahnhofstrasse 50. ✆ **044/211-26-35.**

Entertainment & Nightlife

The city's nightlife is becoming less conservative, but don't expect it to be too wild. Most of the nightspots in Zurich close down early, so you should begin early. Concerts, theater, opera, and ballet all flourish here.

For more information, pick up a copy of "*City Guide*" free at the tourist office.

THE PERFORMING ARTS

The Zurich Opera is the most outstanding local company, performing at the **Opernhaus ★**, Falkenstrasse 1 (www.opernhaus.ch; ✆ **044/268-66-66**). The Zurich Tonhalle Orchestra, performing at **Tonhalle ★** Claridenstrasse 5 (www.tonhalle.ch; ✆ **044/206-34-34**), also enjoys an international reputation. This concert hall facing Bürkliplatz is the biggest and most famous concert hall in Zurich, with 1,500 seats in the big hall and 700 seats in the small hall. Brahms opened Tonhalle Gesellschaft in 1895 with a presentation of "Song of Triumph."

THE CLUB & MUSIC SCENE

Bierhalle Wolf   With 160 seats, this is the best-known beer hall in Zurich, drawing people of all ages and all walks of life. It features "evergreen music" in a sometimes rowdy but safe environment. Folk music is played by an oompah band in regional garb whose instruments include a tuba, accordion, saxophone, clarinet, and bass. The large beer hall is decorated with pennants and flags of different cantons. Beer is available in tankards costing 7SFR and up. Live music is presented every day from 4 to 6:30pm and from 8:30pm to midnight, and every Sunday morning from 10am to noon. During the breaks, slides of alpine scenery are shown. You can also dine on hearty fare, with main courses starting at 14SFR. Open daily from 11am to 2am. Limmatquai 132. www.bierhalle-wolf.ch. ✆ **044/251-01-30.** Cover 4SFR–5SFR.

Kaufleuten   This club attracts a wide cross-section of Zurich society, partly because of the central location and partly because of the comfortably battered, old-fashioned interior whose mismatched tables and chairs imply a certain unstructured comfort. Inside are four different bar areas with mostly house and garage music playing. The Restaurant Kaufleuten (p. 1027) is separately recommended. Open daily 11pm to 2am (till 4am Fri–Sat). Pelikanstrasse 18. www.kaufleuten.com. ✆ **044/225-33-22.** Cover 15SFR–30SFR, depending on the night of the week.

Moods in Schiffbau ★★   This venue in Zurich West is touted as the best jazz club in Europe, hosting some of the finest bands from either Europe or America. It is ranked up there with Ronnie Scott's in London or New Morning in Paris. The location is in Schiffbau, an arts complex housed in a converted old shipyard. Jazz reigns here, but on certain nights funk, soul, blues, and electro music rule the night.

When concerts are featured, they are staged Monday to Saturday at 8:30pm, Sunday at 7pm. Schiffbaustrasse 6. www.moods.ch. ✆ **414/427-680-00.** Entrance fee depends on the group appearing.

THE BAR SCENE

James Joyce Pub   The furnishings and paneling of this pub were acquired in the early 1970s by the Union Bank of Switzerland, when Jury's, an 18th-century hotel in Dublin, was demolished. The Union Bank reassembled the bar (with slightly more comfortable banquettes) near Bahnhofstrasse to entertain business clients and named it after famous Dubliner James Joyce, who had described its decor in certain passages of *Ulysses.* The blackboard menu lists the daily specials (*Plattes*). In December, Irish stew is traditionally served. Other fare includes fish and chips, hamburgers, and fried chicken legs. Open Monday to Friday 11am to 12:30am, and on Saturday from 11:30am to 6pm. Pelikanstrasse 8. www.jamesjoyce.ch. ✆ **044/221-18-28.**

Wings ★   This is the most unusual bar in Zurich, with memorabilia gathered in the wake of the bankruptcy of Swissair in 2001 (a cataclysm that shocked and deeply wounded, it's been said, the national psyche of Switzerland). A small group of pilots and flight attendants saved what they defined as the "essence" of the Swissair spirit, airline seats removed from the first-class cabins of Boeing 747s and MD-11s formerly associated with the airline.

Drinks cost 16SFR each, and include cocktails with names like Sex on the Wings, Jet Lag, Turbulence, and Grounding. Don't overlook the viability of this place as a lunch or dinner stopover, since rib-sticking platters, priced at 20SFR to 26SFR, are served Monday to Friday noon to 2pm and 5 to 10pm. Bar hours are Monday to Thursday noon to midnight, Friday and Saturday noon to 2am, and Sunday 2 to 10pm. Limmatquai 54. www.wings-lounge.ch. ✆ **043/268-40-55.**

THE LGBT SCENE

Barfüsser   A few years ago, in the rush to "gentrify" the place, this Zurich institution was scrubbed squeaky-clean, a sushi bar was installed, a yuppy-style cocktail menu was made available, and everyone began looking like metrosexual wannabes. Despite the controversial cleanup, which hasn't been universally well received, Barfüsser proudly lays claim to being the oldest continuously operated gay bar in Europe, with occasional (but increasingly rare) sightings of a clientele that has patronized the place since its establishment in 1956. Most show up after 8pm, and it's especially popular on weekends. The sushi bar serves continuously throughout the day until 11pm. It's open Monday to Wednesday from 11am to 1am, Thursday 11am to 2am, Friday and Saturday 11am to 3am, and Sunday 3pm to 1am. Spitalgasse 14. www.barfuesser.ch. ✆ 044/251-40-64.

Club Aaah!   Set on the third floor of the same building as the all-gay hotel recommended previously, but with which it is not associated (the Hotel Goldenes Schwert), this is a techno-rock dance club with a bar; a minimalist, vaguely industrial-looking decor; and an animated, rather sweaty dark room in back. There's a cover charge of

25SFR per person that's imposed only on Friday and Saturday nights. Otherwise, entrance is free, and beers cost around 10SFR each. Open daily 9:30pm to 2am. For more gay action, refer to the Pigalle Bar a t the same address, in the Hotel Goldenes Schwert. Marktgasse 14. www.aaah.ch. ☏ **044/253-20-60.**

Where to Stay
VERY EXPENSIVE

Baur au Lac ★★★ One of the world's great hotels, owned by the same family since it opened in 1844, Baur au Lac is ideally located at the end of Bahnhofstrasse, right next to the Schanzengraben Canal. The three-story stone building is surrounded by a private park that's filled with red geraniums in summer. In grandeur, style, service, and amenities, it's superior to its nearest competitor, the Widder. The dining facilities are among the finest in Zurich.

In rooms where Richard Wagner and Franz Liszt once entertained at the piano, guests today are treated to Jugendstil glass, tapestries, antiques, marble floors, and Oriental carpets. All bedrooms and suites are luxuriously and uniquely furnished. Suites have the best antiques, but regular rooms may have an Empire piece, a style from one of the Louis periods, or modern furnishings. Try for a room with a lake view.

Talstrasse 1, CH-8022 Zurich. www.bauraulac.ch. ☏ **044/220-50-20.** Fax 044/220-50-44. 130 units. 870SFR double; from 1,800SFR suite. AE, DC, MC, V. Parking 45SFR. Tram: 4. **Amenities:** 3 restaurants; bar; exercise room; concierge; room service airport transfers (150SFR). *In room:* A/C, TV/DVD, minibar, hair dryer (in some), MP3 docking station (in some), Wi-Fi (free).

Hotel Schweizerhof ★★ Located in one of the city's busiest areas, the landmark Schweizerhof is accessible from anywhere in town by tram. This is a grand old station hotel in turn-of-the-20th-century tradition, although major renovations have kept it in step with the times. When stacked up against the Baur au Lac, Widder, and Savoy, it would definitely be number four, although the Schweizerhof is far superior to the average station hotel in a European capital. The stone building has gables, turrets, and columns and is decorated with flags. Inside, the public rooms are pleasant and unpretentious. The ideal rooms are the semicircular corner units. In spite of its central location, rooms are generally quiet because of the triple glazing on the windows. Most units are roomy and filled with many thoughtful extras, including spongy carpeting, alarm clocks, fruit baskets, and deluxe toiletries.

Bahnhofplatz 7, CH-8023 Zurich. www.hotelschweizerhof.com. ☏ **044/218-88-88.** Fax 044/218-81-81. 115 units. 560SFR–770SFR double; 790SFR junior suite; 1,240SFR suite. Rates include buffet breakfast. AE, DC, MC, V. Parking 30SFR. Tram: 3 or 4. **Amenities:** 2 restaurants; bar; concierge; room service; babysitting. *In room:* A/C, TV, minibar, hair dryer, Wi-Fi (free).

Widder Hotel ★★★ This is Zurich's most up-to-date deluxe hotel, rivaled in the neighborhood only by the superior Baur au Lac, but ahead of the Savoy in overall tranquillity and comfort. In the early 1990s, the Union Bank of Switzerland managed to acquire 10 individual, interconnected buildings—some associated with the city's medieval butchers' guild—clustered around a central courtyard in the capital's historic core. The buildings were then combined into this sophisticated international hotel. During the renovations, great care was taken to retain the original stone walls, murals, frescoes, and ceilings. The result is a unique hotel where every room is different—sometimes radically so—from its neighbors, and where the color scheme (pastel beige, pink, blue, or yellow) reflects the color of the exterior of whichever of the 10 buildings you happen to be in. Interior furnishings range from the metallic, minimalist, and very modern to the traditional.

Rennweg 7, CH-8001 Zurich. www.widderhotel.ch. ℂ **044/224-25-26.** Fax 044/224-24-24. 49 units. 635SFR–935SFR double; 1,120SFR–1,970SFR suite. Rates include buffet breakfast. AE, DC, MC, V. Parking 40SFR. Tram: 6, 7, or 11. **Amenities:** Restaurant; bar; exercise room; concierge; room service; babysitting; airport transfers (150SFR). *In room:* TV, fax, minibar, hair dryer (in some), Wi-Fi (10SFR per day).

Expensive

Hotel Ambassador ★★ One of our favorite hotels in Zurich is a small-scale gem with a lot of charm and pizzazz. It was originally built late in the 19th century as the "Falkenschloss," a then-private villa whose distinguished Beaux Arts facade complements the opera house immediately across the street, near the important tramway junction at Bellevue Platz. After the turn of the millennium, its interior was radically upgraded into the modernized baroque decor you see today. Bedrooms are high ceilinged, with supremely comfortable beds (each adjusts, hospital style, to whatever angle and configuration you want), and generally spacious. A well-trained staff attends to your comfort, providing the services that a traveling business representative may need. The on-site restaurant, **À l'Opéra** (p. 1028), is one of the best restaurants in Zurich, but more reasonably priced than you might expect.

Falkenstrasse 6, CH-8008 Zurich. www.ambassadorhotel.ch. ℂ **044/258-98-98.** Fax 044/258-98-00. 45 units. 295SFR–490SFR double; 480SFR–640SFR suite. AE, DC, MC, V. Parking 34SFR. Tram: 4. **Amenities:** Restaurant; bar; concierge; room service. *In room:* A/C, TV, minibar, hair dryer, Wi-Fi (free).

Hotel Romantik Florhof ★ ✦ This is the most charming and tranquil of the little boutique hotels of Zurich, located on the eastern edge of the Old Town. Originally built in the 15th century as a merchant's home, these premises became a hotel during the 1920s. The Florhof represents top value in Zurich, and is known as a gracious and well-managed hotel with a loyal clientele. Although the public rooms retain much of their antique glamour (including a noteworthy blue-and-white Kachelofen often used long ago for heating), many of the bedrooms are modern and functional. The single units are a bit small, but most doubles are of decent size and are nicely outfitted with plasterwork on the ceilings, exceedingly comfortable beds, stone-topped nightstands, and generous bathrooms.

Florhofgasse 4, CH-8001 Zurich. www.florhof.ch. ℂ **044/250-26-26.** Fax 044/250-26-27. 35 units. 370SFR–430SFR double; 540SFR–670SFR junior suite. Rates include continental breakfast. AE, DC, MC, V. Parking 17SFR. Tram: 3. **Amenities:** Restaurant; room service. *In room:* TV, minibar, hair dryer, Wi-Fi (free).

Lady's First ★ ▮▮ The first hotel of its type in Switzerland, this is a boutique hotel with its top floor, rooftop terrace, and its spa facilities available only to women. It's installed in an elegant town house from the 1880s, which lies close to the core of town and Lake Zurich. Bedrooms come in various shapes and sizes, and each is furnished in a sleekly modern and tasteful way, with well-maintained bathrooms with tub or shower. The best rooms open onto a small balcony with a view of the lake. Along with chic furnishings, rooms have parquet floors and high ceilings. Grace notes include a fireplace in the lounge and a summer rose garden.

Mainaustrasse 24, CH-8008 Zurich. www.ladysfirst.ch. ℂ **044/380-80-10.** Fax 044/380-80-20. 28 units. 290SFR–395SFR double. Rates include buffet breakfast. AE, DC, MC, V. Parking nearby 35SFR. Tram: 2 or 4. **Amenities:** Spa. *In room:* TV, minibar, hair dryer, Wi-Fi (free).

Moderate

Hotel Greulich ★★   This is an oasis in the center of the city. A commercial building from the 1970s, it has been redesigned into this strikingly modern building, creating one of the best small boutique hotels of Zurich. The interior is elegant, the monochrome guest rooms designed by the Swiss painter Jean Plaff. The bedrooms are small to midsize, each in an all-white minimalist design. A glass screen separates the bathroom from the sleeping area, and a raised sitting area is another feature. The central courtyard is planted with birch trees, the Swiss answer to a Japanese Zen garden. Its Slow Food restaurant specializes in innovative dishes.

Herman-Greulich-Strasse 56, CH-8004 Zurich. www.greulich.ch. ✆ **043/242-42-43.** 18 units. 213SFR–290SFR. AE, DC, MC, V. Tram: 8. **Amenities:** Restaurant; bar; room service. *In room:* A/C, TV, hair dryer, Wi-Fi (free).

Inexpensive

X-Tra Hotel Limmat ★ 🎁   The Limmat is one of the most durable of the cost-conscious hotels of downtown Zurich. The hotel occupies part of a four-story building erected in 1935 in the Bauhaus style as a convention center, and whose boxy-looking facade is today protected as a historic monument. You can expect more here than just a place to stay: Its management, in place since 1997, is one of the largest organizers of rock-'n'-roll concerts in Switzerland, often staging their acts in the cavernous restaurant and nightclub that occupies the ground floor. Consequently, members of the bands that play here are often in residence, a policy that adds to the cachet of the place for counterculture rock-'n'-roll enthusiasts across Switzerland. (Hotel guests receive a 15SFR discount off their admission to the nightclub.) Accommodations are streamlined, partially paneled, and outfitted in a style reminiscent of Danish modern.

In the Limmathaus, Limmatstrasse 118, CH-8005 Zurich. www.x-tra.ch. ✆ **044/448-15-00.** Fax 044/448-15-01. 43 units. 186SFR–205SFR double; 224SFR–230SFR triple. Rates include buffet breakfast. Parking 20SFR per night. AE, DC, MC, V. Tram: 4 or 13 to Limmatplatz. **Amenities:** Restaurant; bar; discounted admission at a nearby health club. *In room:* TV, minibar, Wi-Fi (30SFR per day).

Index

See also Accommodations index, below.

General Index

A

AAA, 11
Abadía (Torremolinos), 958
Abbey Ales (Bath), 268
Abbey Theatre (Dublin), 587
Aberdeen (Scotland), 876–878
Aberdeen Art Gallery, 877
Aberdeen Maritime Museum, 877
About Gallery (Athens), 448
Academy Gallery
    Florence, 656–657
    Venice, 696
Accommodations, tips on, 19–21
Accor, 20
Acrocorinth, 472
Acronafplia (Nafplion), 475
Acropolis (Athens), 442–444
Acropolis Museum (Athens), 446
Action Bar (Budapest), 554
Adega Machado (Lisbon), 801
Aer Lingus, 4
Aeroporto Marco Polo (Venice), 687
Aetofolia (Tinos), 528
Aferry.co.uk, 6
Agência de Bilhetes para Espectáculos Públicos (Lisbon), 799
AghaRTA Jazz Centrum (Prague), 152
Agora
    Athens, 442, 444–445
    Delos, 512
Agritourism, 21
Agynthes (Nafplion), 478
Åhléns City (Stockholm), 978
Aille Cross Equestrian Centre (Ireland), 610
Air Berlin, 4
Air Canada, 4
Air France, 4
Air One, 12
Airport Sheraton Hotel (Brussels), 109
Air travel, 1, 4–5, 11–12
    Aberdeen, 876
    Amsterdam, 711, 714
    Athens, 428–429
    Barcelona, 913
    Bergen, 770–771
    Berlin, 355–356
    Brussels, 91–92
    Budapest, 532–533
    Copenhagen, 176
    the Cyclades, 496, 498

Dublin, 564–565, 568
Edinburgh, 824
Faro, 820
Florence, 648
Geneva, 988–989
Glasgow, 851
Granada, 950
Innsbruck, 77
Lisbon, 780–781
London, 199–200
Madrid, 882
Munich, 390
Nice, 345
Oslo, 751, 754
Paris, 270–272
Pisa, 673
Prague, 131, 134
Rome, 613
Salzburg, 59–60
Sevilla, 940
Stockholm, 961–962
Venice, 687
Vienna, 31–32
Zurich, 1017
Aix-en-Provence, 333–334
Ajka Crystal (Budapest), 552
Akershus Slott og Festning (Akershus Castle & Fortress; Oslo), 758
Akrotiri (Santorini), 513
Akrotiri, Ancient (Santorini), 515
Akrotiri Club Restaurant (Athens), 460
A la Mort Subite (Brussels), 108
Albayzín (Granada), 952–953
Albert Cuyp market (Amsterdam), 732
Albertina (Vienna), 41
Albert Memorial (London), 212
Albufeira (Portugal), 816–818
Alcaicería (Granada), 953
Alcazaba (Málaga), 954
Alcázar
    Segovia, 912
    Sevilla, 940–941
    Toledo, 910
Alcázar de los Reyes Cristianos (Córdoba), 946
Alexanderplatz (Rome), 637
The Alfama (Lisbon), 785
Alfi's Goldener Spiegel (Vienna), 55
The Algarve (Portugal), 808–823
Alhambra (Granada), 950–951
Alias Tom (Dublin), 586
Alice's Shop (Oxford), 247
A l'Imaige de Nostre-Dame (Brussels), 108
Alitalia, 4
Allatkerti körút (Animal Garden Boulevard; Budapest), 545
All Saints' Day (Spain), 19
Almássy téri Muvelodési Központ (Almássy Square Culture Center; Budapest), 553

Alpine Flower Garden Kitzbühel, 88–89
Alpspitz region, 412
Alte Nationalgalerie (Berlin), 366
Alte Pinakothek (Munich), 393
AlterEgo (Budapest), 554
Alter Simpl (Munich), 403
Altes Museum (Berlin), 366
Altes Rathaus (Old City Hall; Munich), 393
Altes Residenztheater (Munich), 396, 402–403
Altstadt (Old Town)
    Innsbruck, 78
    Munich, 393
    Salzburg, 59, 60, 63–68
        restaurants, 68–72
Alvor (Portugal), 815
Alžbetiny Lázne-Lázne V (Karlovy Vary), 165
Amalienborg Palace (Copenhagen), 184
Amalienburg (Munich), 397
Amboise, 313–315
American Airlines, 4
American Airlines Vacations, 23
American Book Center (Amsterdam), 733
American Express, Rome, 618, 630
Amesbury Hill (near Salisbury), 260
Amfiscenen (Oslo), 765
Amici della Musica (Florence), 664
Ammoudi (Oia), 518
Amphitheater (Les Arènes; Arles), 332
Amstel Fifty Four (Amsterdam), 735
Amsterdam, 710–741
    accommodations, 736–741
    ATMs and banks, 717
    business hours, 717–718
    currency and currency exchange, 718
    doctors and dentists, 718
    embassies and consulates, 718
    emergencies, 718
    entertainment and nightlife, 733–736
    exploring, 719–727
    getting around, 716
    getting there, 711, 714
    hospitals, 718
    Internet access, 718
    layout, 714–715
    mail and postage, 718
    neighborhoods, 715
    newspapers and magazines, 718
    organized tours, 726–727
    pharmacies, 718
    restaurants, 727–731

Accommodations